Cases
and Materials
on Corporations

ASPEN PUBLISHERS

Cases
and Materials
on Corporations

SEVENTH EDITION

Jesse H. Choper
University of California at Berkeley

John C. Coffee, Jr.
Columbia University

Ronald J. Gilson
*Columbia University and
Stanford University*

Wolters Kluwer
Law & Business

AUSTIN   BOSTON   CHICAGO   NEW YORK   THE NETHERLANDS

Aspen Publishers
Attn: Permissions Department
76 Ninth Avenue, 7th Floor
New York, NY 10011-5201

To contact Customer Care, e-mail customer.care@aspenpublishers.com, call 1-800-234-1660, fax 1-800-901-9075, or mail correspondence to:

Aspen Publishers
Attn: Order Department
PO Box 990
Frederick, MD 21705

Printed in the United States of America

1 2 3 4 5 6 7 8 9 0

ISBN 978-0-7355-7034-4

Library of Congress Cataloging-in-Publication Data

Choper, Jesse H.
    Cases and materials on corporations / Jesse H. Choper, John
C. Coffee, Jr., Ronald J. Gilson. — 7th ed.
        p. cm.
    Includes index.
    ISBN 978-0-7355-7034-4 (casebound : alk. paper)
    1. Corporation law — United States — Cases. I. Coffee, John C.,
1944- II. Gilson, Ronald J., 1946- III. Title.

KF1414.F694 2008
346. 73′ 066 — dc22

2008007609

About Wolters Kluwer Law & Business

Wolters Kluwer Law & Business is a leading provider of research information and workflow solutions in key specialty areas. The strengths of the individual brands of Aspen Publishers, CCH, Kluwer Law International and Loislaw are aligned within Wolters Kluwer Law & Business to provide comprehensive, in-depth solutions and expert-authored content for the legal, professional and education markets.

CCH was founded in 1913 and has served more than four generations of business professionals and their clients. The CCH products in the Wolters Kluwer Law & Business group are highly regarded electronic and print resources for legal, securities, antitrust and trade regulation, government contracting, banking, pension, payroll, employment and labor, and healthcare reimbursement and compliance professionals.

Aspen Publishers is a leading information provider for attorneys, business professionals and law students. Written by preeminent authorities, Aspen products offer analytical and practical information in a range of specialty practice areas from securities law and intellectual property to mergers and acquisitions and pension/ benefits. Aspen's trusted legal education resources provide professors and students with high-quality, up-to-date and effective resources for successful instruction and study in all areas of the law.

Kluwer Law International supplies the global business community with comprehensive English-language international legal information. Legal practitioners, corporate counsel and business executives around the world rely on the Kluwer Law International journals, loose-leafs, books and electronic products for authoritative information in many areas of international legal practice.

Loislaw is a premier provider of digitized legal content to small law firm practitioners of various specializations. Loislaw provides attorneys with the ability to quickly and efficiently find the necessary legal information they need, when and where they need it, by facilitating access to primary law as well as state-specific law, records, forms and treatises.

Wolters Kluwer Law & Business, a unit of Wolters Kluwer, is headquartered in New York and Riverwoods, Illinois. Wolters Kluwer is a leading multinational publisher and information services company.

SUMMARY OF CONTENTS

Contents   ix
Preface   xxv
Acknowledgments   xxvii

I. INTRODUCTION   1

II. BASIC NORMS AND DUTIES FOR MANAGEMENT OF CORPORATIONS   55

III. AN INTRODUCTION TO CORPORATE FINANCE   177

IV. FORMING THE CORPORATION   233

V. CORPORATE DISCLOSURE AND SECURITIES FRAUD   299

VI. VOTING AND CORPORATE CONTROL   541

VII. *BUSINESS ORGANIZATION FOR THE SMALLER ENTERPRISE: PARTNERSHIPS, CLOSE CORPORATIONS, LIMITED LIABILITY COMPANIES, AND OTHER NON-CORPORATE FORMS*   **703**

VIII. *SHAREHOLDERS' SUITS*   **825**

IX. *CORPORATE ACQUISITIONS, TAKEOVERS, AND CONTROL TRANSACTIONS*   **937**

Table of Cases   *1149*
Table of Statutes   *1167*
Index   *1181*

CONTENTS

Preface   *xxv*
Acknowledgments   *xxvii*

I. *INTRODUCTION*   **1**

A. The Legal Character of the Corporation: Factors Influencing
    Choice of the Corporate Form   1
B. An Overview of This Casebook   3
C. A Scorecard of the Players: Public Corporations, Managers,
    Directors, and Shareholders   4
    1. A Corporate Census   4
    2. The Individual Participants   5
D. History and Evolution of the Business Corporation   17
    1. The Early American Experience   18
                Lawrence Friedman, A History of
                    American Law   18
    2. Nineteenth-Century Efforts to Control the Corporation   22
                Lawrence Friedman, A History of
                    American Law   22
    3. Twentieth-Century Developments   25
        a. The "Race to the Bottom" Thesis   25
        b. The Rise of Managerial Capitalism   27
E. Economic Analysis of the Corporation   29
    1. The Nature of the Firm and the Rise of the M-Form
        Corporation   29
    2. Managerial Discretion: The Debate over the Berle-Means
        Thesis   30
    3. The Agency Cost Model   32

F. The Social Responsibility of the Corporation   34
    1. To Whom Do Fiduciary Duties Run?   34
            E. Merrick Dodd, For Whom Are Corporate
                Managers Trustees?   35
            Milton Friedman, The Social Responsibility of
                Business Is to Increase Its Profits   36
            American Law Institute, Principles of Corporate
                Governance — Objective and Conduct of the
                Corporation   37
    2. The Rise of Corporate Constituency Statutes   40
            New York Business Corporation Law — Duty
                of Directors   41
            Connecticut Business Corporation Law — Board
                of Directors   42
    3. Objections to Constituency Statutes   42
            American Bar Association Committee on Corporate
                Laws, Report: Other Constituencies Statutes:
                Potential for Confusion   43
    4. The Case for Constituency Statutes   45
    5. The Judicial Development of Non-Shareholder
        Fiduciary Duties   46
G. The Global Perspective   48

II. BASIC NORMS AND DUTIES FOR MANAGEMENT OF CORPORATIONS

                                                                    55

A. Transaction of Corporate Business   55
    1. Introduction   55
            Revised Model Business Corporation Act — Duties
                of Board of Directors   56
    2. Directors   57
        a. Formalities Required   57
                Revised Model Business Corporation Act — Meetings 57
        b. Effect of Failure to Follow Requirements   58
    3. Officers   59
        a. Authority   59
                Menard, Inc. v. Dage-MTI, Inc.   59
        b. Ultra Vires Doctrine   67
                Real Estate Capital Corp. v. Thunder Corp.   68
                Ohio General Corporation Law — Authority of
                    Corporation   72
                Revised Model Business Corporation Act — Ultra
                    Vires   72
B. Managers' Responsibilities and Compensation   73
    1. Introduction   73

2. Disinterested Conduct: Duty of Care 73
    Shlensky v. Wrigley 75
    Miller v. American Telephone & Telegraph Co. 78
    Francis v. United Jersey Bank 82
    Smith v. Van Gorkom 84
    *In re Walt Disney Co. Derivative
      Litigation* 88
    In re Caremark Int'l, Inc. Derivative Litigation 97
    Stone v. Ritter 99
    *American Law Institute, Principles of Corporate
      Governance — Duty of Care; Business
      Judgment Rule* 103
    Joy v. North 106
3. Transactions in Which Directors, Officers, and
  Shareholders Have a Personal Interest: Duty of Loyalty 110
  a. Contracts with Interested Directors 111
    *Cookies Food Products, Inc. v. Lakes Warehouse
      Distributing, Inc.* 112
    *New York Business Corporation Law — Interested
      Directors* 119
    *California General Corporation Law —
      Contracts in Which Director Has Financial
      Interest* 120
    *American Law Institute, Principles of Corporate
      Governance — Transactions with the
      Corporation* 120
  b. Special Problems of Parent-Subsidiary 128
    Case v. New York Central R.R. 128
    Sinclair Oil Corp. v. Levien 131
  c. Compensation of Managers 136
    i. Salaries, Bonuses, Pensions 137
      Adams v. Smith 138
      Osborne v. Locke Steel Chain Co. 139
      Mlinarcik v. E.E. Wehrung Parking, Inc. 142
    ii. Stock Options 148
      *New Mexico Business Corporation Act — Stock
        Options* 150
      Eliasberg v. Standard Oil Co. 150
      Beard v. Elster 154
  d. Corporate Opportunities and Competition with the
    Corporation 161
    Irving Trust Co. v. Deutsch 161
    Rapistan Corp. v. Michaels 167
    Burg v. Horn 170
    Alexander & Alexander of N.Y., Inc. v. Fritzen 172
    *American Law Institute, Principles of Corporate
      Governance — Taking of Corporate
      Opportunities* 174

III. *AN INTRODUCTION TO CORPORATE FINANCE*   **177**

A. Valuation: How Are Financial Assets Valued?   179
  1. Valuation Under Certainty: Present Value and the Time Value of Money   179
       William A. Klein & John C. Coffee Jr., Business Organization and Finance   179
  2. Valuation Under Uncertainty: Risk and Diversification   183
       a. Expected Value   184
       b. Risk   184
       c. Diversification   187
       d. The Capital Asset Pricing Model   189
  3. The Efficient Capital Market Hypothesis   192
       Kamin v. American Express Company   198
B. Capital Structure: Does the Ownership Structure of a Corporation Affect Its Value?   199
  1. A Survey of Financial Assets   200
       a. Common Stock   200
       b. Debt   201
       c. Preferred Stock   202
       d. Warrants   202
       e. Hybrid Financial Assets   203
  2. Why Capital Structure Should Not Affect the Value of the Corporation: The Miller-Modigliani Irrelevance Proposition   204
  3. Why Capital Structure May Affect Firm Value   206
       a. Taxes   206
       b. The Information Content of Capital Structure   207
       c. The Disciplinary Effect of Debt   208
       d. Bankruptcy Costs   210
C. Opportunism Among the Holders of Financial Claims: Option Pricing   211
  1. The Basic Structure of Put and Call Options   212
  2. The Determinants of Option Value   213
       a. Current Value of the Underlying Asset   214
       b. The Exercise Price   214
       c. The Time Value of Money   214
       d. Variability in the Value of the Underlying Asset   214
       e. Time Remaining Until Expiration   216
  3. Modes of Opportunistic Behavior Among Holders of Financial Assets   216
       a. Increasing the Riskiness of the Corporation's Investments   216
       b. Increasing the Firm's Leverage by Withdrawing Funds   218
       c. Increasing the Value of the Option by Extending Its Term   219

D. Protection Against Intracorporate Opportunism 219
   1. Weak Protection: The Statutory Legal Capital Structure 220
   2. Fraudulent Conveyance Law 224
   3. Contractual Protection: Bond Covenants 225
      a. Investment Activity Covenants 225
      b. Capital Structure Covenants 226
      c. Dividend and Stock Repurchase Covenants 226
   4. Fiduciary Duty and the Covenant of Good Faith and
      Fair Dealing 228
         Credit Lyonnais Bank Nederland, N.V. v.
            Pathe Communications Corp. 230

IV. *FORMING THE CORPORATION* **233**

A. Selection of State of Incorporation 233
B. Compliance with State Requirements 238
   1. Preparation of Documents 238
         Delaware General Corporation Law — How
            Corporation Formed 238
   2. Meeting Statutory Formalities 240
   3. "Domestication" of Foreign Corporations 241
C. Defective Incorporation 241
         Thompson & Green Machinery Co. v. Music
            City Lumber Co. 243
         Don Swann Sales Corp. v. Echols 246
         Delaware General Corporation Law — Defective
            Organization as a Defense 248
         Revised Model Business Corporation Act —
            Liability for Preincorporation Transactions 248
         Sulphur Export Corp. v. Carribean Clipper
            Lines, Inc. 249
         Ohio General Corporation Law — Liability for
            Nonpayment of Stated Capital 250
D. Disregarding the Corporate Entity 251
         Perpetual Real Estate Services, Inc. v.
            Michaelson Properties, Inc. 253
         Kinney Shoe Corp. v. Polan 256
         Texas Business Corporation Act — Liability
            of Shareholders 261
         Walkovsky v. Carlton 261
         Fletcher v. Atex, Inc. 266
         Bartle v. Home Owners Cooperative 275
         Stone v. Eacho 277
E. Pre-Formation Transactions 281
   1. Liability of the Corporation for Debts of Its Predecessor 281
         Tift v. Forage King Industries, Inc. 282
         J. F. Anderson Lumber Co. v. Myers 285
         Kulka v. Nemirovsky 287

2. Promoters' Contracts — 288
   a. Introduction — 288
   b. Liability of the Corporation — 290
      Kridelbaugh v. Aldrehn Theatres Co. — 290
   c. Liability of the Promoters — 292
      Sherwood & Roberts–Oregon, Inc. v. Alexander — 292
      How & Associates, Inc. v. Boss — 294
      Stewart Realty Co. v. Keller — 296

V. CORPORATE DISCLOSURE AND SECURITIES FRAUD — *299*

A. Introduction — 299
B. The Disclosure System — 300
  1. The Securities Act of 1933 — 301
  2. The Securities Exchange Act of 1934 — 302
  3. "Blue Sky" Regulation — 304
  4. Disclosure Requirements of Self-Regulatory Organizations — 305
      New York Stock Exchange Listed Company Manual — 306
  5. When Does the Disclosure Obligation Arise? — 307
      Financial Industrial Fund, Inc. v. McDonnell Douglas Corp. — 308
      Basic, Inc. v. Levinson — 312
      Backman v. Polaroid Corp. — 318
      In re Time Warner Securities Litigation — 322
  6. Reforming the Disclosure System: The Sarbanes-Oxley Act of 2002 — 326
    a. The Public Company Accounting Oversight Board — 327
    b. Auditor Independence — 329
    c. Corporate Governance — 330
    d. Improved Financial Disclosures — 332
    e. SEC Authority over Attorneys — 333
    f. What Remains? — 333
C. Civil Liability — 334
  1. Common Law Remedies — 335
  2. Blue Sky Statutes — 336
  3. The Fiduciary Duty of Disclosure — 336
      Malone v. Brincat — 336
  4. Federal Law: Express Actions — 342
      Securities Act of 1933, Section 11 — 342
      Securities Act of 1933, Section 12 — 343
  5. Federal Law: Implied Civil Liabilities — 344
    a. The Origin of Rule 10b-5 — 344
      Securities Exchange Act of 1934, Section10 — 344
      Rule 10b-5 — 345

b. The Rationale and Scope of Implied Liabilities 345
    J. I. Case Co. v. Borak 346
    Piper v. Chris-Craft Industries, Inc. 349
    Touche Ross & Co. v. Redington 351
    Herman & MacLean v. Huddleston 352
c. The Elements of a Cause of Action Under Rule 10b-5 353
  i. Standing Under Rule 10b-5: Limiting the
    Plaintiff Class 353
    Blue Chip Stamps v. Manor Dug Stores 353
    SEC v. Zanford 366
    *Wharf (Holdings) Ltd. V. United Int'l
      Holdings, Inc.* 367
    Small v. Fritz Cos. 368
    Merrill Lynch, Pierce, Fenner & Smith v. Dabit 368
  ii. Materiality 369
    SEC v. Texas Gulf Sulphur Co. 369
    TSC Industries, Inc. v. Northway, Inc. 372
    Virginia Bankshares, Inc. v. Sandberg 374
    *In re Donald Trump Casino Securities
      Litigation* 378
    *Private Securities Litigation Reform Act
      of 1995* 381
  iii. Causation 382
    Affiliated Ute Citizens v. United States 382
    Basic, Inc. v. Levinson 384
    Dura Pharmaceuticals, Inc. v. Michael Broudo 391
  iv. Scienter 396
    Ernst & Ernst v. Hochfelder 396
    Aaron v. SEC 403
    Tellabs, Inc. v. Makor Issues & Rights, Ltd. 404
  v. Damages 412
    Mitchell v. Texas Gulf Sulphur Co. 412
  vi. Statute of Limitations Applicable to Rule 10b-5 422
  vii. Contribution 422
d. The Policy Dilemma Surrounding Securities Class
  Actions 423
    The Empirical Evidence: A Complex Thicket 424
e. The Response of the Private Securities Litigation
  Reform Act of 1995 426
f. The Impact of the 1995 Act 428
g. Transactions Not Covered by the Rule 429
  i. Corporate Mismanagement 429
    *Superintendent of Insurance v. Bankers Life &
      Casualty Co.* 429
    Santa Fe Industries, Inc. v. Green 432
    Goldberg v. Meridor 437
  ii. Aiding and Abetting 440
    *Central Bank of Denver v. First Interstate
      Bank of Denver* 440

D. Insider Trading 446
   1. Rule 10b-5 and Insider Trading 446
     a. The Rationale and Scope of the Prohibition ... 446
       In the Matter of Cady, Roberts & Co. 446
     b. The Harms from Insider Trading 449
       i. Corporate Harm 449
       ii. Allocational Efficiency and the Injury of
         Delayed Disclosure 450
       iii. Investor Injury 450
     c. The "Benefits" of Insider Trading 452
     d. The Enforceability of the Prohibition 453
       Dirks v. SEC 454
     e. Selective Disclosure and Regulation FD 466
       Regulation FD, Section 100 467
     f. Misappropriation Theory 470
       United States v. O'Hagan 470
       Rule 10b5-1 486
     g. Insider Trading and the Remote Tippee 488
       United States v. Chestman 488
       Rule 10b5-2 497
     h. Causation and Damages in Insider
       Trading Cases 497
       Securities Exchange Act of 1934, Section 20A .. 498
       Elkind v. Liggett & Myers, Inc. 499
       Insider Trading Sanctions Act of 1984 502
   2. Section 16(b) and "Short Swing" Profits 505
       Securities Exchange Act of 1934, Section 16 . 505
     a. Who Is Covered? 506
       Merrill Lynch, Pierce, Fenner & Smith, Inc. v.
         Livingston 506
       CBI Industries, Inc. v. Horton 508
       Reliance Electric Co. v. Emerson Electric Co. . 511
       Foremost-McKesson, Inc. v. Provident
         Securities Co. 514
       Chemical Fund, Inc. v. Xerox Corp. 517
       Smolowe v. Delendo 518
     b. The Definition of "Purchase or Sale" 520
       Kern County Land Co. v. Occidental Petroleum
         Corp. 520
   3. Common Law Liability to the Corporation 529
       Diamond v. Oreamuno 529
       Freeman v. Decio 534
       Walton v. Morgan Stanley & Co. 539

VI. *VOTING AND CORPORATE CONTROL*   **541**

A. Overview: Voting and "Shareholder Democracy" 541
B. The Substantive Law of Shareholder Voting 548

1. Who Votes?   549
   *Delaware General Corporation Law — Classes
      and Series of Stock*   549
   *Delaware General Corporation Law — Voting,
      Inspection, and Other Rights of Debenture
       Holders*   549
   Frank Easterbrook & Daniel Fischel, Voting
      in Corporate Law   550
2. What Vote Is Required?   551
3. When Should a Shareholder Vote Be Required?   553
   a. A Shareholder Power of Initiative?   554
   b. Timing   555
      Hilton Hotels Corp. v. ITT Corp.   555
   c. Evasions of the Voting Requirement   557
      Hilton Hotels Corporation v. ITT Corp.   558
4. What Voting Power Should a Share Carry? Rule 19c-4
   and the "One Share, One Vote" Controversy   566
   a. The New York Stock Exchange's Policy   566
      *Voting Rights Listing Standards — Proposed
       Disenfranchisement Rule*   569
   b. SEC Response and Judicial Reaction   571
   c. State Law Limitations   572
      Lacos Land Co. v. Arden Group, Inc.   572
5. Vote Buying   577
   New York Business Corporation Law — Proxies   577
   Schreiber v. Carney   578

C. Voting Procedures   584
   1. Record Dates   584
   2. Proxies   585
   3. "Street Name" Ownership   587
   4. Inspector of Elections   589
   5. Stockholder Consents   590
      *Delaware General Corporation Law — Consent
       in Lieu of Meeting*   590
      Datapoint Corp. v. Plaza Securities Co.   591
D. Proxy Contest Expenses   595
      Rosenfeld v. Fairchild Engine & Airplane Corp.   595
E. Special Voting Systems: Cumulative, Class, and
   Supermajority Voting   598
   1. Cumulative Voting   598
   a. Evasions   599
   b. Cumulative Voting and the Removal of Directors   600
   c. Pros and Cons of Cumulative Voting   600
   d. Cumulative Voting in Practice   601
   2. Class Voting   602
      *New York Business Corporation Law — Class
       Voting on Amendment*   602
   a. Is Coercion Still Possible?   603
   b. Ambiguities   604
   c. Mergers   604

3. Supermajority Voting 604
    Revised Model Business Corporation Act —
      Greater Quorum or Voting Requirements 604
F. Removal and Vacancies 605
1. Directors 605
    Delaware General Corporation Law — Board of
      Directors 606
2. Filling Board Vacancies 608
    New York Business Corporation Law — Newly
      Created Directorships and Vacancies 608
3. Removal of Officers 609
    New York Business Corporation Law —
      Removal of Officers 609
G. Judicial Supervision of Election Contests 610
    Schnell v. Chris-Craft Industries, Inc. 610
    Stroud v. Grace 612
    MM Companies, Inc. v. Liquid Audio, Inc. 619
    Mercier v. Inter-Tel, Inc. 630
H. Shareholders' Right of Inspection 632
    Delaware General Corporation Law —
      Stockholder's Right of Inspection 633
    Seinfeld v. Verizon Communications, Inc. 634
I. Federal Law 644
    Securities Exchange Act of 1934, Section 14 644
1. Solicitations to Which Rules Apply 647
    Securities Exchange Act Release No. 34-31326 647
2. Reform of the Nomination and Election Process 657
3. Information Required to Be Furnished 659
    a. Executive Compensation 660
    b. Annual Report 660
    c. Soliciting Materials and Preliminary Review 661
4. Requirements as to Proxy 661
    Rule 14a-4 — Requirements as to Proxy 661
5. Mailing Communications for Security Holders 665
6. Shareholder Proposals 667
    Medical Committee for Human Rights v. SEC 667
    Roosevelt v. E.I. DuPont de Nemours & Co. 676
    Securities Exchange Act Release No. 34-40018 677
    American Federation of State, County &
      Municipal Employees, Employees Pension
      Plan v. American International Group, Inc. 681
7. Antifraud Liability 689
    Rule 14a-9 — False or Misleading Statements 689
    GAF Corp. v. Heyman 691
    Gould v. American-Hawaiian S.S. Co. 692
    Adams v. Standard Knitting Mills, Inc. 693
8. Causation 694
    Mills v. Electric Auto-Lite Co. 694
    Virginia Bankshares, Inc. v. Sandberg 697

VII. BUSINESS ORGANIZATION FOR THE SMALLER ENTERPRISE: PARTNERSHIPS, CLOSE CORPORATIONS, LIMITED LIABILITY COMPANIES, AND OTHER NON-CORPORATE FORMS 703

A. Introduction 703
B. Partnerships 705
  1. The Nature of Partnership: Aggregate or Entity? 706
     Fairway Development v. Title Ins. Co. of Minnesota 707
  2. Formation 708
     Vohland v. Sweet 708
  3. Powers of Partners 712
  4. Liabilities of Partners 713
  5. Partnership Governance 714
  6. Fiduciary Duties 715
     Meinhard v. Salmon 715
     Revised Uniform Partnership Act — General Standards of Partner's Conduct 719
     Revised Uniform Partnership Act — Nonwaivable Provisions 720
  7. Partnership Dissolution 722
C. Close Corporations 722
  1. Restrictions on Transfer of Shares 726
     Allen v. Biltmore Tissue Corp. 727
     Delaware General Corporation Law — Restriction on Transfer of Securities 731
  2. Special Agreements Allocating Authority 734
    a. Shareholder Agreements Respecting Election of Directors 735
     Revised Model Business Corporation Act — Greater Quorum or Voting Requirements 737
     Ringling v. Ringling Bros.-Barnum & Bailey Combined Shows, Inc. 737
    b. Voting Trusts 744
     Abercrombie v. Davies 745
     Delaware General Corporation Law — Voting Trusts 749
    c. Agreements Respecting Actions of Directors 751
     McQuade v. Stoneham 751
     New York Business Corporation Law — Greater Requirement as to Quorum and Vote of Directors 755
     Clark v. Dodge 756
     New York Business Corporation Law — Control of Directors 759
     Maryland General Corporation Law — Unanimous Stockholders' Agreement 760

d. Agreements Implied by Majority's Fiduciary
Duty 761
Wilkes v. Springside Nursing Home, Inc. 761
Zidell v. Zidell, Inc. 768
e. Directors' Delegation of Management
Authority 770
Pioneer Specialties, Inc. v. Nelson 771
3. Resolution of Disputes and Deadlocks 773
a. Arbitration 774
b. Receivers, Provisional Directors, or Custodians 775
*Delaware General Corporation Law —
Appointment of Custodian or Receiver* 775
Giuricich v. Emtrol Corp. 777
c. Dissolution and Oppression 780
Nelkin v. H.J.R. Realty Corp. 781
Meiselman v. Meiselman 785
D. Limited Partnerships 796
1. Formation 798
2. Control and Liability 798
*Revised Uniform Limited Partnership
Act — Safe Harbor* 799
3. Fiduciary Duty 800
a. Contractual Amendment of the General
Partner's Fiduciary Duty 800
*Gotham Partners, L.P. v.
Hallwood Realty Partners, L.P.* 800
b. Who Owes the Fiduciary Duty? 809
E. Limited Liability Companies 810
1. Tax Advantages 810
2. Organization, Structure, and Terminology 811
*Westec v. Lanham and Preferred Income
Investors, LLC* 812
3. What Is a Limited Liability Company? 817
a. Piercing the Veil of an LLC 818
Bastan v. RJM & Associates, LLC 818
b. The Scope of Fiduciary Duties 820
c. Miscellaneous Categorization Problems 821
F. Limited Liability Partnerships 822
*Delaware Revised Uniform Limited
Partnership Act — Partner's Liability* 822
G. Entity Rationalization and the Proliferation of
Organizational Forms 823

VIII. *SHAREHOLDERS' SUITS* 825

A. Introduction 825
*Federal Rules of Civil Procedure 23.1 —
Derivative Actions* 828

B. Exhaustion of Internal Remedies   829
    1. Demand on Directors   829
            Marx v. Akers   829
            Kamen v. Kemper Financial Services, Inc.   838
    2. The Board's Authority to Terminate the Suit   838
            Levine v. Smith   839
            Galef v. Alexander   842
            In re PSE & G Shareholder Litigation   844
            Zapata Corp. v. Maldonado   845
            Joy v. North   850
            Alford v. Shaw   853
            *Revised Model Business Corporation
                Act — Dismissal*   858
            *American Law Institute, Principles of
                Corporate Governance — Dismissal of a
                Derivative Action*   859
    3. Demand on Shareholders   862
            Mayer v. Adams   862
            Smith v. Dunlap   868
            Rogers v. American Can Co.   868
C. Qualifications of Plaintiff Shareholder   870
            California General Corporation Law   871
            *American Law Institute, Principles of
                Corporate Governance — Standing to
                Maintain a Derivative Action*   873
            Courtland Manor, Inc. v. Leeds   874
            Goldie v. Yaker   878
D. Security for Expenses   881
            Donner Management Co. v. Schaffer   881
            *New Jersey Business Corporation Act —
                Actions by Shareholders*   885
E. Defending Against Derivative Suits   887
    1. Conflicting Interests of Defendants   887
            Otis & Co. v. Pennsylvania R.R.   887
    2. Conflicting Interests of Defendants' Counsel   890
            Cannon v. U.S. Acoustics Corp.   890
            Hausman v. Buckley   894
            Seifert v. Dumatic Industries, Inc.   895
F. Dismissal, Discontinuance, and Settlement   896
            *New York Business Corporation Law —
                Shareholders' Derivative Action*   896
            Alleghany Corp. v. Kirby   897
G. Characterization of the Suit   899
    1. Derivative or Direct   899
            Grimes v. Donald   900
    2. Special Circumstances in Derivative Suits   905
            Barth v. Barth   905
            Landstrom v. Shaver   907
            Kirk v. First Nat'l Bank   909

H.	Reimbursement of Plaintiff's Expenses	910
	In re Wachovia Shareholders Litigation	*910*
	Mills v. Electric Auto-Lite Co.	*913*
	American Law Institute, Principles of Corporate Governance	*917*
I.	Indemnification of Defendants	919
	Waltuch v. Conticommodity Services, Inc.	*921*
	Baker v. Health Management Systems, Inc.	*927*
	Ridder v. CityFed Financial Corp.	*931*

IX. *CORPORATE ACQUISITIONS, TAKEOVERS, AND CONTROL TRANSACTIONS* — *937*

A.	Introduction	937
	1. Transactional Techniques: Allocation of Decision Authority for Control Transactions	939
	2. Types of Control Transactions and Their Regulation	942
	3. Public Policy and Corporate Control Transactions: The Stakeholder Debate	944
B.	Hostile Transactions	945
	1. The Early Doctrine	945
	Cheff v. Mathes	*945*
	2. The Demand for and Supply of Defensive Tactics	949
	a. Charter and Bylaw Provisions	950
	b. Poison Pill Plans	951
	c. The Effect on Shareholder Wealth	954
	3. The Adoption and Early Development of Proportionality Review	955
	Unocal Corp. v. Mesa Petroleum Co.	*955*
	4. The *Time-Warner* Case: Chancery and Supreme Court Opinions	964
	Paramount Communications, Inc. v. Time Incorporated (Del. Ch.)	*964*
	Paramount Communications, Inc. v. Time Incorporated (Del.)	*976*
	Unitrin, Inc. v. American General Corp.	*979*
C.	Friendly Transactions	992
	Revlon, Inc. v. MacAndrews & Forbes Holdings, Inc.	*993*
	1. *Revlon's* Substantive Obligations	998
	a. Information Requirement	998
	b. Structuring the Transaction	999
	Mills Acquisition Co. v. Macmillan, Inc.	*1000*
	2. What Triggers *Revlon*?	1003
	Paramount Communications, Inc. v. Time Inc. (Del. Ch.)	*1003*
	Paramount Communications, Inc. v. Time Inc. (Del.)	*1006*

   3. Strategic Alliances: Paramount Tries Again   1009
      Paramount Communications, Inc. v. QVC
        Network, Inc.   1009
   4. *Revlon* Review in Practice   1023
      In re Toys "R" Us, Inc., Shareholder Litigation   1023
   5. What Is the Standard of When *Revlon* Is Not Triggered?   1030
      Ace Limited v. Capital Re Corp.   1030
      Omnicare, Inc. v. NCS Healthcare, Inc.   1034
D. Sale of Control at a Premium   1050
      Perlman v. Feldmann   1051
      Mendel v. Carroll   1055
      In re Digex Shareholders Litigation   1069
E. Federal Regulation of Takeovers   1076
   1. Regulation of the Bidder   1076
     a. An Overview of the Williams Act   1076
       Securities Exchange Act of 1934, Sections 13(d),
        14(d), 14(e)   1076
     b. What Is a Tender Offer?   1082
     c. Disclosure   1084
   2. Regulation of the Target   1086
     a. Mandatory Disclosure: Schedule 14D-9   1086
     b. Disclosure of Negotiations in Tender Offers   1087
     c. Issuer Repurchases   1088
F. Freeze-out Mergers   1088
   1. Introduction: The History of the Conflict   1089
   2. The Current Framework: Entire Fairness   1091
      Weinberger v. UOP, Inc.   1091
   3. Fair Price   1101
   4. Fair Dealing   1102
      Kahn v. Lynch Communication Systems, Inc.   1102
   5. Using a Tender Offer to Avoid Entire Fairness   1113
      In re Pure Resources, Inc. Shareholders
       Litigation   1115
G. State Takeover Regulation   1127
      Delaware General Corporation Law — Business
       Combinations with Interested Stockholders   1130
      CTS Corp. v. Dynamics Corp. of America   1132
H. Public Policy and Corporate Control Transactions: The
Stakeholder Debate   1143

Table of Cases   *1149*
Table of Statutes   *1169*
Index   *1181*

PREFACE

This edition represents a complete revision of its predecessor, including a thorough updating of the cases and statutes. The major development of the past decade was the crisis for corporate law posed by the Enron, WorldCom, and Tyco scandals and the response of the Sarbanes-Oxley Act. In the four years since the last edition, we have seen the continued growth of alternative organizational forms and the movement in Delaware toward treating these entities as creatures of contract. Significant judicial attention in respect to directors' duty of care has been given to their obligation to act in "good faith." In the takeover area, the courts' focus has shifted to the standards governing the conduct of negotiated transactions. All these matters have been given extensive coverage throughout the materials.

The impact on corporate law provided by "law and economics" continues to be given extensive coverage: in Chapter I (which focuses on agency costs), in Chapter III (which provides students with the background in finance required in a sophisticated business law practice and includes valuation of the firm, the Miller-Modigliani Irrelevance Proposition, and the efficient capital market hypothesis (ECMH)), in Chapter V (which treats securities disclosure and the "fraud on the market" doctrine), in Chapter VI (which covers collective action problems as they bear on shareholder voting), and in Chapter IX (which takes note of the financial economics literature on takeovers and defensive tactics).

The book continues to introduce students early to those areas of corporation law that experience indicates are most interesting to many — particularly issues concerning the social role of corporations, which we have sought to emphasize throughout, and the responsibilities imposed by federal law on corporate insiders and others.

This edition continues to stress the importance of corporate legislation by abundant inclusion of relevant state and federal statutes, often accompanied by problems that require student analysis. Text notes, analyses by commentators, and problems and queries are interspersed within the case and statutory materials in an effort not only to inform students of existing doctrine, but to stimulate their critical examination of it. Thus, we have sought to produce a teaching tool rather than a reference book or treatise.

This casebook has long given close attention to securities regulation as, in effect, a federal lever by which to influence corporate governance. Recently, the Supreme Court has also turned its attention to the area of securities class actions, and its concerns have been expressed in four recent decisions since 2005: Dura Pharmaceuticals v. Broudo; Tellabs, Inc. v. Makor Issues & Rights, Ltd.; Merrill Lynch, Pierce, Fenner & Smith, Inc. v. Dabit; and, most recently, Stoneridge Investment Partners LLC v. Scientific-Atlanta, Inc. — all of which are noted in this edition.

To go through the entire volume in class at a reasonable pace would probably require more hours than are customarily allotted to a basic course in corporations or business associations. But it is neither possible nor necessary to cover, in a single course, an entire field of law such as corporations, and each instructor necessarily develops his or her own selection of topics. We have sought to include a range of topics, amply developed, sufficient to enable instructors to treat those areas that they prefer in some depth. We have also sought to present the topics in such an order that, in schools not limited to a single course in corporation law, a group of chapters can be used for an adequate basic course, and the remainder for an advanced course.

To indicate the growth of statutory law, the date of enactment or that of the most recent significant revision has been appended to each quoted statute. Footnotes reproduced in cases and quoted materials appear with their original numbers; footnotes of the editors are numbered consecutively in each chapter and do not contain the designation "ED." unless the omission would be confusing.

Although the book contains a great many separate statutory provisions, it does not include the entire text of any single state corporation law, nor are the federal statutes and all rules thereunder reprinted in full; all of these are available elsewhere at relatively modest cost.

We are pleased to acknowledge our indebtedness to co-authors of earlier editions of this book. We also wish to express appreciation for the able research assistance of Jenna Levine, Stefan Paulovic, Shellka Arora and Priyanka Mehta, and to Wanda Castillo and Jeffrey Kent for valuable technical and secretarial aid.

Jesse H. Choper
John C. Coffee, Jr.
Ronald J. Gilson

March 2008

ACKNOWLEDGMENTS

We appreciate the permission of the following publishers, authors, and periodicals to reprint excerpts from their publications:

Derek C. Bok, Reflections on the Distinctive Character of American Labor Laws, 84 Harvard Law Review 1394 (1971). Copyright © 1971 by the Harvard Law Review Association. Reprinted by permission of the Harvard Law Review Association and Derek C. Bok, Cambridge, Mass.

George W. Brooks, The Strengths and Weaknesses of Compulsory Unionism, 11 New York University Review of Law and Social Change 32 (1982-1983). Reprinted by permission of the New York University Review of Law and Social Change. New York, N.Y.

Archibald Cox, Labor Decisions of the Supreme Court at the October Term, 1957, 44 Virginia Law Review 1051 (1958). Reprinted by permission of The Virginia Law Review Association, Charlottesville, Va., and Fred B. Rothman & Company, Littleton, Colo.

Kenneth Dau-Schmidt, Bargaining Analysis of American Labor Law and the Search for Bargaining Equity and Industrial Peace, 91 Michigan Law Review 419 (1992). Copyright © 1992. Reprinted by permission of the Michigan Law Review Association, Ann Arbor, Mich., and Kenneth Dau-Schmidt.

Ronald B. Ehrenberg & Robert S. Smith, Modern Labor Economics (3d ed. 1988). Copyright © 1988 by Scott, Foresman and Company. Reprinted by permission of Pearson Education, Inc.

Samuel Estreicher, Collective Bargaining or "Collective Begging"?: Reflections on Antistrikebreaker Legislation, 93 Michigan Law Review 577 (1994). Reprinted by permission of The Michigan Law Review Association, Ann Arbor, Mich.

Samuel Estreicher, Deregulating Union Democracy, 21 Journal of Labor Research 247 (2000), reprinted in The Internal Governance and Organizational Effectiveness of Labor Unions, ch. 17 (Estreicher et al. eds., 2001). Reprinted by permission of the Journal of Labor Research. George Mason University, Fairfax, Va.

Samuel Estreicher, Policy Oscillation at the Labor Board, 37 Administrative Law Review 176 (1985). Reprinted by permission of the American Bar Association, Chicago, Ill.

Samuel Estreicher, Win-Win Labor Law Reform, 10 The Labor Lawyer 674 (1994). Reprinted by permission of the American Bar Association, Chicago, Ill.

William Forbath, Law and the Shaping of the American Labor Movement. Cambridge, Mass.: Harvard University Press. Copyright © 1989 by the Harvard Law Review Association. Copyright © 1991 by the President and Fellows of Harvard College. Reprinted by permission of Harvard University Press.

Mayer G. Freed et al., Unions, Fairness, and the Conundrums of Collective Choice, 56 Southern California Law Review 461 (1983). Reprinted with the permission of the Southern California Law Review, Los Angeles, Cal.

Richard B. Freeman, Is Declining Unionization of the U.S. Good, Bad, or Irrelevant? in Unions and Economic Competitiveness (Lawrence Mishel & Paula Voos eds., 1992). Reprinted by permission of M.E. Sharpe, Inc., Armonk, N.Y.

Michael C. Harper, The Consumer's Emerging Right to Boycott: *NAACP v. Claiborne Hardware* and Its Implications for American Labor Law, 93 Yale Law Journal 409 (1984). Reprinted by permission of The Yale Law Journal Company, New Haven, Conn. and Fred B. Rothman & Company, Littleton, Colo.

Michael C. Harper, Leveling the Road from *Borg Warner* to *First National Maintenance:* The Scope of Mandatory Bargaining, 68 Virginia Law Review 1447 (1982). Reprinted by permission of The Virginia Law Review Association, Charlottesville, Va. and Fred B. Rothman & Company, Littleton, Colo.

Michael C. Harper, Limiting Section 301 Preemption: Three Cheers for the Trilogy, Only One for *Lingle* and *Lueck,* 66 Chicago-Kent Law Review 685 (1990). Copyright © 1992. Reprinted by special permission of the Chicago-Kent College of Law, Illinois Institute of Technology.

Michael C. Harper, Union Waiver of Employee Rights, 4 Industrial Relations Law Journal 335 (1981). Copyright © 1981 by Industrial Relations Law Journal. Reprinted by permission.

Michael C. Harper & Ira Lupu, Fair Representation as Equal Protection, 98 Harvard Law Review 1212 (1985). Copyright © 1985 by the Harvard Law Review Association, Cambridge, Mass. Reprinted by permission.

Bruce Kaufman & Jorge Martinez-Vasquez, Monopoly, Efficient Contract and Median Voter Models of Union Wage Determination: A Critical Comparison, 11 Journal of Labor Research 401 (1990). Reprinted by permission of the Journal of Labor Research, George Mason University, Fairfax, Va.

Douglas L. Leslie, Right to Control: A Study in Secondary Boycotts and Labor Antitrust, 89 Harvard Law Review 904 (1976). Copyright © 1976 by the Harvard Law Review Association, Cambridge, Mass. Reprinted by permission.

Howard Lesnick, The Gravamen of the Secondary Boycott. Article originally appeared at 62 Columbia Law Review 1363 (1962). Reprinted by permission of the author, Professor Howard Lesnick at the University of Pennsylvania Law School, Philadelphia, Pa.

Mancur Olson, The Logic of Collective Action: Public Goods and the Theory of Groups. Cambridge, Mass.: Harvard University Press. Copyright © 1965 and 1971 by the President and Fellows of Harvard College. Reprinted by permission of Harvard University Press.

Albert Rees, The Economics of Trade Unions (2d ed. 1977). Copyright © 1977 by The University of Chicago Press. Reprinted by permission of The University of Chicago Press.

Paul C. Weiler, Governing the Workplace: The Future of Labor and Employment Law. Cambridge, Mass.: Harvard University Press. Copyright © 1990 by the President and Fellows of Harvard College. Reprinted by permission of Harvard University Press.

Paul C. Weiler, Promises to Keep: Securing Workers' Rights to Self-Organization Under the NLRA, 96 Harvard Law Review 1769 (1983). Copyright © 1983 by the Harvard Law Review Association. Reprinted by permission of the Harvard Law Review Association, Cambridge, Mass. and Professor Paul Weiler at the Harvard Law School, Cambridge, Mass.

Cases
and Materials
on Corporations

I INTRODUCTION

A. THE LEGAL CHARACTER OF THE CORPORATION: FACTORS INFLUENCING CHOICE OF THE CORPORATE FORM

The number of corporations in the United States is vastly dwarfed by the number of other business organizations, particularly sole proprietorships.[1] Yet corporations account for the great majority of total business revenues (roughly 84 percent in 2007)[2] and are the form of business organization chosen by the vast majority of firms once the scale of the business enterprise reaches a significant level.[3]

Why is this? Generally, four distinct factors motivate the owners of a business to conduct it as a corporation: (1) limited liability of shareholders, (2) perpetual existence of the corporation, (3) easy transferability of ownership interests, and (4) centralized management. In addition, a fifth factor — tax considerations — may also loom large, depending on the tax laws then in effect and the plans and tax position of the firm's owners. Historically, these factors not only distinguish the corporation from other business entities,[4] such as the partnership, but they also

---

1. The most recent data projects that, as of 2007, there will be approximately 6 million corporations, 1.24 million partnerships, 22.2 million proprietorships, and 1.81 million limited liability companies in the United States. See http://www.bizstats.com/businesses.htm.

2. This is down slightly from prior years, when corporations have accounted for over 90 percent of business receipts. See U.S. Census Bureau, 2007 Statistical Abstract, at Table 724.

3. For businesses having gross receipts of more than $1 million per year, corporations accounted for nearly 87 percent of all such receipts. See U.S. Census Bureau, 2007 Statistical Abstract, at Table 725.

4. Some newer forms of business organizations — such as the limited liability company and the limited liability partnership — combine limited liability and certain other "corporate-like" features

1

provide a roadmap of much of the substantive content of corporate law and the recurring problems that arise within corporations. Thus, at the outset, a brief overview of these factors is useful.

"Limited liability" essentially means that investors risk only their purchase price paid for their shares and have no additional liability.[5] For most investors, this may be the most important factor leading them to incorporate, because it insulates the shareholders' personal assets from corporate debts. Also, limited liability allows corporate creditors to disregard the claims of the owners' personal creditors. In contrast, a general partner of a partnership faces unlimited personal liability for the firm's debts. Still, the advantages of limited liability can be exaggerated, both because there are substitutes for it (insurance for tort debts or the use of the limited partnership form, which also allows limited partners to avoid liability for more than their capital contribution), and because "financial" creditors are likely to demand personal guarantees from the principal owners when they lend to the firm. In this light, limited liability chiefly shelters the principal shareholders from tort creditors and "trade" creditors (i.e., suppliers of goods or services to the firm, who typically do not demand guarantees because they expect payment within a short period on a relatively small indebtedness).

The significance of the second factor — perpetual existence — stems from the greater certainty it affords both creditors and other investors, particularly in circumstances where they must commit capital to the business for a prolonged or indeterminate period. In an individual proprietorship or partnership, the death, withdrawal, or insolvency of the proprietor or of any partner (assuming there is no specific contrary provision in the partnership agreement) terminates the business organization. But the legal status of the corporation is unaffected by the death, withdrawal, or insolvency of a shareholder, and under its charter the corporation typically enjoys perpetual existence. The legal stability of the corporation may be an important factor in a financial institution's willingness to extend credit to the enterprise without requiring individual endorsements or other forms of personal guarantees.

The third major advantage of incorporation results from the use of transferable securities to represent the shareholder's interest in the common business enterprise. The general norm in the case of corporations is that these shares are freely tradable, similar for most purposes to negotiable instruments. Free transferability makes possible secondary markets — such as the stock exchanges — in which investors can trade ownership interests on a regular, continuing, and impersonal basis. Secondary securities markets give investors greater liquidity and make it easier for corporations to raise capital. In contrast, partnership interests are ordinarily not transferable without the consent of all the other partners, and the sale of an interest in an unincorporated business usually involves at least a bill of sale or some other lengthy and non-negotiable instrument.

The final factor motivating use of the corporate form — centralized management — refers to the critical fact that the investors in a corporation delegate most of the authority to run the business enterprise to agents that they elect — namely,

---

with a nontaxable status. In particular, the limited liability company is coming into greater use and is examined in Chapter VII.

5. The principal exceptions to this rule of limited liability are covered in Chapter IV.D; in these instances, courts will "pierce the corporate veil" and hold shareholders personally liable for corporate debts when they sense that there has been a misuse of the corporate form.

the corporation's board of directors. These agents are unique because they cannot be instructed by the shareholders to take any specific course of action and can generally be removed only for cause pending the next election of directors. In this sense, the position of directors resembles that of elected officials in a democracy, who are expected to use their own discretion and are not bound by the day-to-day preferences of the electorate. In contrast, unless the partnership agreement provides otherwise, each partner in a partnership has an equal right to manage the business and bind the firm and other partners regarding partnership property and affairs. In short, authority in a partnership tends to be shared, not centralized, whereas in a corporation, the corporation's board of directors, not its shareholders, holds the authority to exercise corporate powers and direct the business and affairs of the enterprise. This is a default rule that can be modified by special provisions in the corporation's certificate of incorporation, but courts have been generally reluctant, in the absence of a clear charter provision, to permit shareholders to exercise powers normally belonging to the board.

B. *AN OVERVIEW OF THIS CASEBOOK*

The four defining characteristics of a corporation discussed above — limited liability, perpetual existence, free transferability, and centralized management — supply a roadmap for much of this casebook. Limited liability is subject to potential abuse (such as when it is used to defraud creditors), and as a result there are important exceptions to its availability, which are considered in Chapter IV. Perpetual existence implies that the corporation is typically a long-term venture for which it is difficult to draft a complete contract in advance that covers all contingencies and that fully specifies all the rights and relationships among the parties. In such a long-term contractual relationship, a greater need exists for a governance structure that can resolve disputes fairly and in accordance with the parties' likely expectations. Chapter II focuses on this role of the board of directors in corporate operations. Similarly, because a system of centralized management delegates great discretion from the firm's owners to its managers, issues arise as to how those agents employ that discretion. Conflicts of interest between managers and shareholders are as inevitable as death and taxes, and a recurrent concern of the law has been how to minimize and monitor these conflicts. One such means has been to view corporate directors and officers as subject to certain fiduciary duties that require that they use their discretion in the shareholders' interests. Considerable debate has surrounded the question of how strict these duties should be. Chapter II examines the trends and divisions in the substantial body of case law on this issue.

Another means of controlling managerial discretion is through shareholder voting rights. Chapter VI looks at the system of corporate democracy by which shareholders elect corporate directors and vote on certain other fundamental matters. A recurring theme throughout this casebook will be the adequacy and relative efficiency of these techniques for holding corporate officials accountable to their shareholders. In this light, Chapter VIII surveys the legal remedies available to the shareholder through which fiduciary duties may be enforced.

Finally, free transferability of shares encouraged the development of impersonal trading markets for corporate securities, which in turn increased the possibility of fraud (or at least unfair informational advantages). Since the 1930s, federal law has prescribed disclosure standards applicable to the securities markets, and these standards represent another important restraint on managerial discretion. Chapter V assesses the law at both the federal and state levels applicable to the corporation's disclosure obligations, securities fraud, and insider trading. Chapter IX examines the unique forms of corporate control transactions that such secondary markets make possible. These transactions, which include takeovers and hostile tender offers, represent the newest and potentially most important means of holding managers accountable to investor preferences.

The key point on which to focus at the outset is the nature of the agency relationships within the large public corporation. Because detailed contracts cannot be written between the shareholders and the corporation's managers to cover every contingency, substantial authority must be delegated to the corporation's managers. This broad delegation of authority to managerial agents plus the existence of inevitable conflicts of interest between the corporation's shareholders and its managers create problems of accountability with which American corporate law has struggled since the appearance of the private corporation in the early nineteenth century. The master problem of American corporate law is how to control management discretion and prevent opportunistic behavior — without chilling the efficiency and entrepreneurial style of the corporate form through excessively formalistic and confining restraints. Necessarily, this problem involves trade-offs: some controls may be too costly because they will inhibit socially desirable risk-taking. From this perspective, most of the succeeding chapters deal at bottom with alternative control devices: monitoring controls in the form of the board of directors; legal controls, as represented by the common law's derivative suit and the federal securities laws; market controls through takeovers and other corporate control transactions; and voting controls through the proxy system. Ultimately, the overriding policy question is what mix of these controls works best in achieving accountability at the lowest cost.

The remainder of this chapter focuses, first, on the political and legal debates that have attended the attempts of American law to grapple with the special status and character of the corporation; second, on the economists' perspective on this central issue of corporate accountability; and third, on the unavoidable question of corporate social responsibility — namely, to whom should the corporation and its agents be responsible?

C. A SCORECARD OF THE PLAYERS: PUBLIC CORPORATIONS, MANAGERS, DIRECTORS, AND SHAREHOLDERS

1. A CORPORATE CENSUS

Corporations can be large or small. Only a few firms fall into the category of the "large publicly held corporation." As of 2006 the New York Stock Exchange (NYSE) and its affiliate NYSE Arca were home to some 2,764 issuers (which number includes both operating companies and various forms of mutual funds); another 3,200 companies were listed on Nasdaq, the electronic securities exchange; and roughly 600 companies traded on the American Stock Exchange — for a total of roughly 6,500 corporations that are publicly traded in active securities markets (of an overall total noted earlier of 6 million corporations).[6] While the listing requirements for these markets differ (with the NYSE requiring a larger market capitalization and trading volume[7]), the minimum breakpoint for eligibility in a public trading market is a public market capitalization (the market value of all outstanding shares held by public shareholders — i.e., not insiders) in excess of $15 million.[8] Even at this level, companies tend not to have the requisite liquidity to support trading (or to interest dealers and market professionals in trading their stocks), and it is probably not until the $60 million level (which is the NYSE's floor for listing initial public offerings) that real liquidity exists.

Thus, the vast majority of corporations will have too few shareholders to support secondary trading on stock exchanges. While these corporations may still own significant assets, they are closely held or "private firms," and investments in them tend to be highly illiquid. The special rules governing these firms are covered in Chapter VII, along with the considerations applicable to the choice of corporate versus other business forms.

2. THE INDIVIDUAL PARTICIPANTS

Corporations require three necessary participants: managers, directors, and shareholders. Although one person may occupy all of these positions and a corporation can be organized and staffed by a single person, it is useful to understand who typically occupies these roles.

Managers. The day-to-day management of the American public corporation is entrusted to officers[9] who are appointed, and can be removed at any time, by the board of directors. The authority of the principal corporate officers is detailed in the corporation's bylaws, as supplemented from time to time by specific board

6. Listings on both the NYSE and Nasdaq have recently declined and vary significantly from year to year. For current listings, see www.nyse.com and www.nasdaq.com. For the overall total of 6 million corporations, see footnote 1 supra. There are also several smaller regional exchanges, which trade smaller regional companies, but inclusion of the stocks uniquely traded on these exchanges would not materially change the above estimate.

7. To list its stock on the NYSE, a domestic company must satisfy one of several alternative tests. In terms of shareholders, a listed firm must either have (a) at least 400 U.S. holders of "round lots" (i.e., a minimum of 100 shares) and 1.1 million shares in the hands of the public, or (b) a minimum of 2,200 shareholders plus an average monthly trading volume of 100,000 shares. In addition, a NYSE-listed firm must have either a market capitalization of at least $100 million for the shares in the hands of public shareholders (i.e., shareholders other than members of management or directors) or a market capitalization of at least $60 million in public hands in the case of initial public offerings and spin-offs. Finally, an issuer must satisfy one of several alternative earnings or valuation tests, with the earnings test requiring, for example, that the firm have earned at least $10 million in total over the last three years. See NYSE Listed Company Manual at 102.01 (2007).

8. The $15 million figure is the minimum market capitalization requirement for the Nasdaq Capital Market, which is the lowest tier of the three-tiered Nasdaq system. Alternatively, a firm can list in this lowest tier of Nasdaq if it has stockholders' equity of at least $4 million, a market capitalization of at least $5 million, and net income (for either its most recent fiscal year or two of the last three fiscal years) of at least $750,000.

9. Many corporation statutes provide that there be at least four officers of the corporation: president, vice president, treasurer, and secretary. Typically, one person can hold multiple offices, except that these statutes sometimes require the roles of president and secretary to be separated. In contrast, New York permits a sole shareholder to hold all corporate offices. See, e.g., N.Y. Bus. Corp. Law §715 (1997).

resolutions. At the top of the managerial hierarchy is the chief executive officer (CEO), who in most cases will also serve as chairman of the board. This is in marked contrast to the European and English pattern, under which a nonexecutive outside director always serves as chairman to ensure that the chief executive not be able to dominate the board or control its agenda. Some U.S. corporations are separating the roles of chief executive and board chairman, but they are still a small minority.

Beneath the chief executive officer will typically be a chief financial officer (CFO) and a chief operating officer (COO). They too are likely to serve on the board of directors, but generally no more than two or three corporate officers serve on the board (although others may attend board meetings to advise the board on particular matters).

The executives of a publicly held corporation rarely own sufficient stock in their firm to have a controlling influence through stock ownership. Their control over the firm and their tenure in office depends on their satisfying the board. This in turn is likely to depend on the firm's profitability and share price relative to other firms in its industry. More independent boards, increased institutional investor activism, global competition, and deregulation have all combined to shorten CEO tenure in office and to increase the frequency of CEO turnover.[10] A 2006 survey found that the average tenure of a CEO at the world's 500 largest companies (in terms of revenues) had decreased to only 6½ years.[11] Seemingly, if the firm lags its peers in its industry, the CEO's job is increasingly at risk.

As the CEO's tenure has become riskier, the CEO's income has soared. The compensation paid to chief executives is a combination of annual salary, incentive awards, stock options and other forms of equity compensation, and perquisites. In 2005 the average compensation package for a chief executive of a large public corporation was $11.3 million.[12] Only 10 percent of this compensation comes in the form of salary, with stock options accounting for 26 percent, restricted stock amounting to 22 percent, and annual bonuses accounting for another 23 percent.[13] Depending on how one values stock options and restricted stock compensation, at least five CEOs received total compensation in excess of $174 million in 2006.

Perhaps the most striking statistic about executive compensation is its rate of increase. Professors Lucian Bebchuk and Jesse Fried estimate that average real (i.e., inflation-adjusted) pay of chief executive officers of firms in the Standard & Poor's 500 (the S&P 500 is a leading market index) more than quadrupled between 1992

10. See, e.g., Rick Geddes & Hrishikesh D. Vinod, CEO Tenure, Board Composition and Regulation, 21 J. Reg. Econ. 217 (2002); Rick Geddes & Hrishikesh D. Vinod, CEO Age and Outside Directors: A Hazard Analysis, 12 Rev. Indus. Org. 767 (1997).

11. This data is from Weber Shandwick's Global 500 CEO Departures study, which also found some 74 CEO departures from these 500 firms in 2006. See http://www.weberandshandwick.com. For an earlier, similar study finding a seven-year average CEO tenure, see Denis B. K. Lyons, CEO Casualties: A Battlefield Report, Directors & Boards (June 1999) at 43.

12. See Eric Dash, Executive Pay: A Special Report: Off to the Races Again, Leaving Many Behind, N.Y. Times, April 9, 2006, at p. 3-1 (reporting survey by Pearl Meyer & Partners, an executive compensation consultant). For the CEOs of the United States' 500 largest companies, average compensation was even higher: $15.2 million in 2006. See Scott DeCarlo, Executive Pay: Big Paychecks, Forbes, May 3, 2007. In 2006 the highest-paid CEO of a U.S. company was Steve Jobs of Apple Computer, who received a nominal $1 salary but realized $647 million from vested restricted stock.

13. See Pearl Meyer & Partners, Behind the Numbers: New York Times 2006 CEO Pay Survey at 7. Forbes's survey places the gain from exercised stock options at 48 percent of total CEO compensation. See DeCarlo, supra note 12.

and 2000.[14] Increases in option-based compensation were responsible for most of this increase and jumped ninefold over this period.[15]

Behind the shift from cash-based compensation to equity compensation lie a variety of factors: (1) the desire of institutional investors to use stock options to make senior management more sensitive to the market and less bureaucratic and resistant to change; (2) the impact of the tax laws, which deny the corporation a tax deduction for very high cash compensation to a senior executive but do not similarly penalize stock options;[16] and (3) the sense of many boards that executives who create significant stock price gains for shareholders deserve to share in those gains through the award of generous stock options. At the same time, however, the very high level of compensation that stock options create has elicited criticism on a variety of grounds. Some are concerned that the new levels of executive compensation create disparities as great as 500 to 1 between the compensation of the chief executive and that of the average employee.[17]

Commentators have seen a connection between the increased use of stock options and the sudden epidemic of accounting irregularity cases that arose in 2001 to 2002, producing notorious examples such as Enron and WorldCom.[18] That is, stock options can create a rational, but perverse, incentive for corporate executives to maximize short-term earnings in order to create a temporary stock price spike, even if this earnings growth is not sustainable or is illusory, because the executives (unlike most shareholders) can bail out at the top of the market. For example, if a chief executive holds options covering two million shares and if the company's stock trades at a 30-to-1 price/earnings ratio (which was not at all uncommon in the late 1990s), then by using aggressive or dubious accounting practices that increase earnings per share by merely $1, the chief executive can realize a $60 million gain in the value of his or her stock ownership. From this perspective, the seeming breakdown in American corporate governance in the late 1990s may have occurred in substantial part because market changes relating to executive compensation outpaced developments in corporate governance. For further discussion of executive compensation, see pages 145-148 infra.

Directors. Corporate law delegates the corporation's power and authority to its board of directors, who in turn delegate much of this authority to the chief executive officer and other senior managers pursuant to the corporation's bylaws and board resolutions. In every state, there is a statutory provision

---

14. See Lucian Bebchuk & Jesse Fried, Pay Without Performance: The Unfulfilled Promise of Executive Compensation 1 (2004).

15. Id.

16. See Internal Revenue Code §162(m) (providing that, in a publicly held corporation, tax deductions for annual compensation are capped in the case of the CEO and the next four highest-paid officers at $1 million each). This provision does not apply to certain performance-based compensation, and hence performance-based bonuses have become more prevalent.

17. There have been a number of estimates of this ratio. For the 500-to-1 estimate (as of 2003), see Bebchuk & Fried, supra note 14, at 1. For another estimate, of 400 to 1, see Editorial, Atonement in the Boardroom, N.Y. Times, Sept. 21, 2002, p. A-14 (noting comments by the president of the Federal Reserve Bank of New York that chief executives' compensation had risen to 400 times the compensation of the average employee, up from 42 times in 1980). A more recent study, based on 2005 data, by the Economic Policy Institute places the ratio of the average CEO's earnings to that of the average worker at 262 to 1. See Lawrence Mishel, CEO-to-Worker Pay Imbalance Grows, Economic Snapshots, available at http://www.epinet.org. (June 21, 2006).

18. John C. Coffee, Jr., Understanding Enron: "It's About the Gatekeepers, Stupid," 57 Bus. Law. 1043 (2002) (arguing that the fundamental force destabilizing American corporate governance in the 1990s was the shift to equity-based compensation without accompanying controls).

paralleling the following language in the American Bar Association's Revised Model Business Corporation Act (RMBCA, 3d ed.): "All corporate powers shall be exercised by or under authority of, and the business and affairs of the corporation managed by or under the direction of, its board of directors. . . ."[19]

Who are these directors? In a small, closely held or family business, the directors will probably be the corporation's principal shareholders (many of whom will probably be employee-managers as well). In large publicly held corporations, however, a substantial majority of the board will be composed of "outside" directors having no employment or consulting relationship with the corporation (and usually holding in the aggregate only a small percentage of the firm's shares). This trend toward majority independent boards is accelerating, along with a concomitant trend for boards to become smaller and to have fewer insider or "affiliated" members. For example, a 2006 study of the boards at the companies included in the S&P 500 found that 81 percent of directors qualified as independent.[20] Today, the typical large public corporation has a board of roughly ten directors, only two of which on average are "insiders."[21]

Along with the trend toward fewer inside directors is a concomitant trend toward smaller board size. In 2006 the size of the average board of a corporation included in the S&P 500 index was 10.7; in 1992 it was 15.[22] The rationale underlying both these trends is that a smaller board with fewer inside directors is less likely to be dominated by the CEO and hence can better protect shareholder interests.

Of course, an "outside" director should not be automatically equated with an "independent" director; other economic or personal relationships may exist. For example, the director may be associated with a law or investment banking firm that provides services for the corporation. Although the number of such "interested" outside directors appears to be in decline,[23] one recent study finds 11 percent of all directors as falling into the intermediate category of "affiliated directors" — that is, directors who are not insiders but have some economic relationship with the firm, such as that of a consultant, attorney, or investment banker.[24] This shift over time toward an independent majority and the declining presence of "affiliated" directors is well illustrated in Figure 1.1, prepared by Professor Jeffrey Gordon.[25]

---

19. RMBCA §8.01(b) (2002).

20. See Spencer Stuart, 2006 Board Index: The Changing Profile of Directors (2006).

21. For such a finding, see Korn/Ferry International, 32nd Board of Directors Study (2006) at 36.

22. See Spencer Stuart, 2006 Board Index at 10.

23. To illustrate this trend, it is noteworthy that a 1979 SEC study found that 35 percent of directors in its sample were directly employed by the corporation, and another 29 percent had economic relationships with the corporation that necessitated disclosure in the corporation's proxy statement (for a total of 64 percent). See SEC Staff Report, Corporate Accountability 432-436, 591-597, and Table 2 (1979). By 1983 this percentage was beginning to decline, and a study in that year found that 61 percent of the directors on the boards surveyed were "independent of the senior management of the corporation." See Heidrick and Struggles, The Changing Board 3 (1983).

24. See Jeffrey Gordon, The Rise of Independent Directors in the United States, 1950-2005: Of Shareholder Value and Stock Market Prices, 59 Stan. L. Rev. 1465, 1565 (2007); see also Biao Xie, Wallace Davidson III & Peter J. DaDalt, Earnings Management and Corporate Governance: The Roles of the Board and the Audit Committee, 9 J. Corp. Fin. 295, 303 (2003).

25. See Gordon, supra note 24, at 1474.

Figure 1.1
BOARD COMPOSITION, 1950-2005

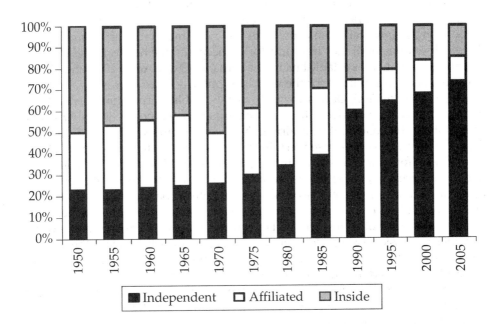

Who today serves on the board of a publicly held corporation? The simple answer is primarily chief executives and chief financial officers of other corporations,[26] with a smattering of university presidents, foundation executives, former public officials, academics, and others to add diversity. In the case of the largest public corporations, an effort has typically been made within the last decade to add women and minority representatives, but the corporate board is far from a microcosm of American society generally and still remains populated primarily by white male business executives.[27]

How hard must directors work? A 2005 survey by a leading consulting firm finds that the majority of the directors at Fortune 1000 companies spend at least 16 hours per month on board matters (or approximately 192 hours a year) — up from 159 hours in 2004.[28] This time commitment seems likely only to increase over the foreseeable future. Board compensation has risen commensurately. Typically, directors receive an annual retainer fee, a per-meeting fee, and — increasingly — stock grants or options. Looking at the 200 largest U.S. industrial corporations, an executive compensation firm estimated in 2006 that board compensation has

---

26. One study found that 63 percent of outside directors in its sample were chief executives of other corporations. See Jay W. Lorsch & Elizabeth MacIver, Pawns or Potentates: The Reality of America's Corporate Boards 18 (1989).

27. The pace of social change in the boardroom has been slow but noticeable. As of 2005, one survey found that 84 percent of Fortune 1000 corporations had at least one woman on the board, 47 percent had at least one African American, 19 percent had at least one Latino, and 10 percent had at least one Asian. See Korn/Ferry International, 32nd Annual Board of Directors Study (2006) at 37. For an earlier study, see Jeremy Bacon, Membership and Organization of Corporate Boards 10-22 (1990) (finding that 41 percent of the public corporations in this 1990 survey had at least one female director; 24.4 percent had at least one black director; and 5 percent had at least one nonblack minority director).

28. See Korn/Ferry International, 32nd Annual Board of Directors Study (2006) at 53-54.

recently grown at a rate exceeding 10 percent per year, with the median total remuneration package for the individual director slightly exceeding $200,000.[29] Of this amount, 42 percent was paid in cash and the balance in stock.

Currently, the character and operation of the American corporate board are undergoing a significant transition, with the most important changes relating to (1) the development of the "lead director" concept; (2) the new role and duties of the audit committee, as established by the Sarbanes-Oxley Act of 2002; and (3) new independence requirement for the boards of publicly listed firms:

1. *The "lead director."* Only a minority of U.S. public corporations separate the positions of chief executive officer and chairman of the board. But a functional substitute to the nonexecutive chairman has begun to appear: the "lead director." Use of at least a procedure based on this concept was mandated in 2002 by the NYSE and Nasdaq for their U.S. listed companies. Typically, the lead director (sometimes called the "presiding director") is an independent outside director elected by the board to chair an annual review of the chief executive's performance.[30] This procedure contemplates one or more meetings at which the board, in the absence of the chief executive and other insiders, will review the chief executive's performance and consider succession issues. Proponents of this system believe that other outside directors who have concerns about the chief executive's performance will contact the lead director and treat him as the natural leader of any board effort to restrain or remove the CEO. Corporations can implement this concept in a variety of ways, ranging from strong to weak. Some appoint one senior director as the lead director for a term; others rotate the position among the chairs of various board committees, thereby avoiding the institution of any permanent lead director. The NYSE requires only that the outside directors meet by themselves to review the chief executive's performance and does not require that the board elect a lead director. Nonetheless, a recent survey finds that 80 percent of the corporations in the Fortune 1000 have adopted the use of a lead director as of 2005.[31]

2. *The enhanced role of the audit committee.* Boards of directors typically operate through committees. Of particular importance is the audit committee; the board of every large publicly held corporation has such a committee, whose role is to maintain oversight over the company's accounting and financial reporting processes. This obligation involves the audit committee both in supervising internal control functions, which are designed to protect the corporation from diversion or misappropriation of its assets, and in guarding the integrity of the company's financial statements. Increasingly, audit committees have also assumed responsibility for the corporation's compliance with legal and regulatory obligations. Beyond simply monitoring the independence and performance of the company's outside and internal auditors, the audit committee must review the company's financial disclosures, meet with the auditors, and ask probing questions of both management and the auditors. In particular, the committee is expected to understand and

29. See Pearl Meyer & Partners, 2006 Director Compensation Report: Study of the Top 200 Corporations (2006) at 3-4.

30. The lead director position was originated by the General Motors board in 1992 after it discharged its chief executive following a long and difficult internal process. Under GM guidelines, the independent directors meet without management's presence at least three times a year to evaluate the CEO. The lead director also sets the board's agenda on these issues. For an overview of the concept, see Gordon, supra note 24, at 1494-1495.

31. See Korn/Ferry International, 32nd Annual Board of Directors Study (2006) at 54. In addition, a study by the Business Roundtable found that, as of 2006, 91 percent of its member firms had either a lead director or an independent chairman. See Gordon, supra note 24, at 1495.

evaluate the company's critical accounting policies, analyze its major financial risks and its policies for managing those risks, and assess the quality of the company's disclosures to the market. Not surprisingly, an incipient trend to pay audit committee members more than other directors is discernible.

A basic rationale underlying the audit committee is that, if the corporation's management were to employ overly aggressive or otherwise inappropriate accounting policies, the corporation's auditors could quietly report this to the audit committee, which is staffed exclusively (at least in theory) by independent directors. By design, the audit committee is a back channel or safety valve by which the auditors can report their concerns to the independent directors without directly confronting the company's management. For this reason, the NYSE in the late 1970s required all its listed companies to maintain an audit committee composed solely of directors independent of management.[32]

Still, the flurry of accounting irregularity cases that arose from 2000 to 2002 showed that the board was often not aware of how risky or aggressive its management's financial reporting policies were. As a result, a principal goal of the Sarbanes-Oxley Act,[33] which Congress passed by overwhelming margins in 2002, was to enhance the authority of the audit committee and rewire the internal circuitry of reporting within the corporation to ensure that any doubts or concerns held by the auditors reached the audit committee. To this end, the Sarbanes-Oxley Act specifies federal independence standards for audit committee members,[34] mandates that the audit committee "be directly responsible for the appointment, compensation, and oversight of the work" of the independent auditor, and specifies that such audit firm "shall report directly to the audit committee."[35] Control over the auditor's compensation was assigned to the audit committee because Congress feared that otherwise management could "bribe" the auditor with high fees and lucrative consulting work into acquiescing in risky or dubious accounting policies. Congress also prohibited the auditors of publicly held firms from performing certain defined consulting activities for their audit client — again to preserve the auditor's independence. Effectively, Congress's mandates regarding the audit committee override state corporation law (for listed firms) and transfer authority from the board and the shareholders to the audit committee. Further, the Act grants the audit committee the authority to hire independent counsel and other advisers, whose fees must be paid by the corporation.[36] In addition, the Act expands the role of the audit committee from simply supervising accounting and financial reporting to a broader watchdog role under which it must establish procedures for the receipt and evaluation of anonymous submissions by employees of concerns regarding "questionable accounting or auditing matters."[37]

---

32. For the current audit committee rule, see NYSE Listed Company Manual §303A.00 (2004).

33. Sarbanes-Oxley Act of 2002, Pub. L. No. 107-204, 116 Stat. 745.

34. The statutory requirements are contained in §301 of the Sarbanes-Oxley Act (codified as §10A(m) of the Securities Exchange Act of 1934) but have been implemented by SEC rules that are now set forth in Rule 10A-3 under the Securities Exchange Act of 1934. In addition, the exchanges have adopted their own requirements. See NYSE Listed Company Manual §§303A.02, 303A.06, and 303A.7 (2007). Rule 10A-3 precludes the audit committee member from receiving "directly or indirectly any consulting, advisory, or other compensatory fee from the issuer or any subsidiary thereof," other than a fee for service as a director or committee member.

35. See §301 of Sarbanes-Oxley Act of 2002 (codified as §10A(m)(2) of the Securities Exchange Act of 1934).

36. See §301 (codified as §10A(m)(5)-(6) of the Securities Exchange Act).

37. Id. (codified as §10A(m)(4) of the Securities Exchange Act).

3. *New independence requirements.* In the wake of Enron and related scandals, the SEC asked the NYSE and Nasdaq in 2002 to review their corporate governance listing standards. After much study and debate, the two exchanges agreed on new and closely similar listing standards, which include the following principal new standards:[38]

a. *Listed companies must have a majority of independent directors.* While a majority independent board was already the norm prior to Sarbanes-Oxley, a significant percentage of listed companies did not comply. Now, a public company that is listed on a major exchange must have a majority independent board.[39]

b. *Listed companies must have a nominating committee and a compensation committee composed exclusively of independent directors.* The nominating committee must both recommend to the entire board the director nominees for the next annual meeting of shareholders and specify written criteria for the selection of directors and the regular evaluation of the board and management.[40] The compensation committee reviews the compensation of the corporation's executives and recommends to the full board the terms of incentive compensation and equity-based stock plans.[41]

c. *The definition of "independent director" has been tightened.* In particular, the new definition adopted by the NYSE excludes any person having a material relationship with the company (including an officer or shareholder of another company that does business with it), as well as former employees who are within three years of their departure or retirement from the company. Stock ownership, even of a significant amount, was not, however, seen as a material relationship that made the director less than independent, but rather was regarded as a factor that naturally motivated the director to be more vigilant. Each board of a listed company is expected to develop its own categorical standards for determining director independence and to disclose in the corporation's annual proxy statement its basis for determining that a particular relationship was not material.

An assessment. How important are these new changes? More generally, what benefits have resulted from the emergence of a more active and independent board over the last two decades? Here, there is controversy. Some believe that the new emphasis on the independence level of the board does not respond in a relevant fashion to the accountability problems demonstrated by Enron, WorldCom, and other recent scandals, because the boards of these companies actually met even the new, enhanced independence requirements. In general, a number of studies have focused on the effect of board composition on firm performance, but they have taken very different approaches. One group of studies has examined discrete board tasks and functions (such as replacing the CEO or responding to a takeover bid), while a second group has sought to relate board composition to overall company performance — that is, does an independent board improve the "bottom line"?[42]

---

38. In the case of the NYSE, the new standards are codified in §303A of the Exchange's Listed Company Manual.

39. For the NYSE's rule, see NYSE Listed Company Manual, §303A.01. The NYSE's definition of "independence" is set forth in NYSE Listed Company Manual, §303A.02 and requires the board to "affirmatively determine that the director has no material relationship with the listed company."

40. See NYSE Listed Company Manual, §303A.04 ("Nominating/Corporate Governance Committee").

41. See NYSE Listed Company Manual, §303A.05 ("Compensation Committee").

42. For an overview of the evidence on the effect of board composition on corporate performance, see Gordon, supra note 24, at 1500-1509. For an earlier and more skeptical assessment of whether independent boards improve corporate performance, see Sanjai Bhagat & Bernard Black, The Uncertain Relationship Between Board Composition and Firm Performance, 54 Bus. Law. 921 (1999) (finding little

The first group of studies has produced clearer results. An independent board does seem better at resisting financial fraud and probably replaces a poorly performing CEO more quickly.[43] Independent boards may be less likely to over-pay in making an acquisition and may be less likely to resist a lucrative hostile offer for the company, but the evidence here is in dispute.[44] However, the second group of studies found little evidence to link board composition to superior company performance.[45] That is, a corporation whose board is 80 percent independent does not seem to outperform or show greater profitability than a corporation whose board is only 60 percent independent. In general, these empirical studies have not been able to find any significant relationship between the percentage of independent directors and company performance.

How should these inconsistent findings be interpreted? They could suggest that outside directors do better at certain discrete tasks (e.g., monitoring conflicts, replacing an inferior CEO, restricting defensive takeover tactics) than at improving the firm's competitive strategy or overall efficiency. Alternatively, these findings could mean that even outside directors are not sufficiently independent to have a strong impact on the firm's management (given that the firm's management typically selects, or at least approves the nomination of, outside directors). Finally, some skeptics doubt that independence really matters that much at all, in part because outside directors are usually chosen by the chief executive officer and have little incentive, time, or ability to resist the CEO.[46]

Some critics of the current system argue that the only truly independent directors are professional ones — that is, persons who would serve full-time as directors of no more than a few corporations.[47] A cadre of such director candidates, they argue, could be identified and recruited by institutional shareholders and would be primarily loyal to them, rather than to management. This proposal remains controversial because some fear that full-time directors would be a rival to the CEO, and others fear that directors would primarily be loyal to the particular constituency of shareholders that nominated them. As a result, little movement in this direction is discernible.

Finally, why do outside directors serve? Most surveys find that the financial rewards are of only secondary significance and that directors are primarily motivated by the hope that they will learn from service on a "quality" board or because of the honor in being selected.[48] Against these nonpecuniary rewards, outside directors must weigh the risk of liability (from derivative and securities litigation often based on negligence theories) and the time demands. The policy issue,

---

correlation between board independence and firm performance and even some signs of a negative correlation).

43. See Gordon, supra note 24, at 1501-1505; Michael Weisbach, Outside Directors and CEO Turnover, 20 J. Fin. Econ. 431 (1988); Jerold B. Warner, Ross L. Watts & Karen H. Wruck, Stock Prices and Top Management Changes, 20 J. Fin. Econ. 461 (1988). For an overview, see Sanjai Bhagat & Bernard Black, The Non-Correlation Between Board Independence and Long-Term Firm Performance, 27 J. Corp. L. 231 (2002).

44. See Gordon, supra note 24, at 1502-1503; Bhagat and Black, supra note 42, at 930.

45. See Bhagat & Black, supra footnote 42; see also Benjamin Hermalin & Michael Weisbach, The Effect of Board Composition and Direct Incentives on Firm Performance, 20 Fin. Mgmt. 101, 102 (1991).

46. For a classic critique of independent directors as an illusory reform, see Victor Brudney, The Independent Director — Heavenly City or Potemkin Village, 95 Harv. L. Rev. 597 (1982).

47. For such a proposal, see Ronald Gilson & Reinier Kraakman, Reinventing the Outside Director: An Agenda for Institutional Investors, 43 Stan. L. Rev. 863 (1991).

48. Lorsch & MacIver, supra footnote 26, at 26.

discussed further in Chapter VIII, is obvious: If one believes outside directors are the key to corporate accountability, exposure to liability may chill their willingness to serve. Conversely, if one is skeptical about the capacity or motivations of outside directors, the threat of liability may be necessary to maintain their loyalty and vigilance.

Shareholders. Two basic features characterize the share ownership of U.S. public corporations: First, ownership is dispersed, with relatively few publicly held corporations having a controlling shareholder or an identifiable control group. Second, roughly 50 percent of the stock in U.S. public corporations, and a much higher percentage of the largest corporations (often 70 percent or over in the case of Fortune 500 firms) is held by institutional investors, chiefly pension funds and mutual funds.

These two features partially cancel each other out. That is, dispersed ownership means that in most U.S. corporations there is not a single shareholder owning 10 percent of the stock (and in many companies not even 5 percent). As a result, collective action by shareholders to resist a management plan or proposal, or to elect a new board that will replace the incumbent management, may be difficult and certainly is costly. But the rise of institutional investors over recent decades has increased shareholder concentration considerably. From owning only 7.2 percent of all equities in 1950, institutional investors have increased their share to hold at least 50 percent of all outstanding U.S. equities as of 2002.[49] Other surveys place the level of U.S. institutional holdings in U.S. corporate equities as high as 61 percent.[50] Although a typical institution will not hold more than 5 percent of any corporation's stock, the top five institutional owners today collectively hold around 20 percent, and the top 25 institutional investors could easily own a majority, implying that the coordination costs associated with shareholder activism have declined and that shareholders may as a result be more able than in the past to resist management. Yet while shareholder activism has clearly increased over the last decade, not all institutional investors support or participate in such efforts. Rather, as discussed next, different types of institutional investors have characteristically different approaches and attitudes toward shareholder activism.

---

49. See New York Stock Exchange Fact Book (2007) (showing 49.8 percent as of 2002), available at http://www.nysedata.com. No more recent census of institutional holdings has been done by the NYSE since 2002.

50. See The Conference Board, Press Release: U.S. Institutional Investors Continue to Boost Ownership of U.S. Corporations, Jan. 22, 2007 (results as of 2005). Much depends on the nature of the sample being surveyed. The percentage goes up as the sample focuses on larger firms, reflecting the tendency of institutions to invest only in large-capitalization stocks that offer high liquidity. In a sample including all the firms in the S&P 500 Index, the S&P Midcap Index, and the S&P Smallcap Index, the average aggregate institutional ownership was 53.1 percent of the shares outstanding, and the average holdings of the top five institutional investors in a firm was 22 percent of the outstanding shares. See Jay C. Hartzell & Laura T. Starks, Institutional Investors and Executive Compensation (Sept. 2002), AFA 2003 Washington, DC, Meeting at 7 (available at SSRN: http://ssrn.com/abstract=236592). But in a sample of just the S&P 100 index, the percentage was higher. See Anthony Saunders, Marcia Millon, Alan J. Marcus & Hassan Tehranian, The Impact of Institutional Ownership on Corporate Operating Performance, NYU Stern Finance Working Paper No. 03-033 (Nov. 2003) (available at SSRN: http://ssrn.com/abstract=468800) (finding 59.3 percent of the shares of firms in the S&P 100 to be owned by institutions, and the average holdings of the top five institutional investors in a firm to be 20.1 percent of the outstanding shares).

Who are the principal institutional investors? Table 1.1, based on Federal Reserve data from 2007,[51] shows the current percentage breakdown of stock ownership by investor category.

Table 1.1

Category		Percentage
Mutual funds (including exchange-traded funds)		28.4
Pension funds		
Private funds	12.8	
Public funds	10.1	
Total		22.9
Insurance companies		8.0
Bank-managed trusts and estates		0.3
Total institutional ownership		59.6
Individual ownership		25.9
State and local governments		0.5
Foreign ownership		14.1
Total		100

Curiously, the two leading institutional investors — mutual funds and pension funds — have long displayed very different attitudes toward involvement in corporate governance and shareholder activism. While pension funds have sometimes run proxy fights, often submit shareholder proposals for votes at the corporation's annual meeting of shareholders, and regularly organize securities class actions as lead plaintiffs, mutual funds seldom, if ever, engage in any of these activities. Why? Several reasons can be cited to explain their differing behavior. First, mutual funds are active traders, often turning over their portfolios multiple times a year, while pension funds tend to follow a longer-term "buy and hold" philosophy (and many pension funds are to some degree "indexed" — meaning that they hold a constant cross-section of the market, rather than trying to outperform the market). Because involvement in corporate governance is likely to pay off only over the longer term, mutual funds may see little benefit from such activities to the extent that they are short-term holders. Second, mutual funds operate in very competitive markets and find it difficult to pass on the costs of corporate governance activities to their clients. Third, investor passivity may be the product of conflicts of interest. Because the investment advisers that organize and run many mutual funds often wish to market other advisory services to corporations, they do not wish to acquire a reputation as "activist" shareholders and thereby irritate potential clients. In contrast, pension funds tend to have fewer business relationships with the corporations in which they invest and so may be less deterred from participating in shareholder activism. Finally, the most prominent participants in shareholder activism have been public pension funds (e.g., state and municipal retirement funds), whose actions may be based on political rather than economic criteria, because they ultimately report to politically accountable

---

51. See Federal Reserve Statistical Release, Flow of Funds Accounts of the United States, First Quarter 2007, Table L 213 Corporate Equities.

state officials. Some critics fear the greater activism of public pension funds because they believe it is not grounded on truly economic criteria.[52]

Traditionally, institutional investors have not sought to participate in the "control" of public corporations and have been reluctant to nominate their officers or employees to positions as directors. In large part, this is because a basic control/liquidity trade-off complicates institutional investor participation in corporate governance: The more institutions become involved in governance and hold large equity stakes, the more they may be forced to sacrifice their liquidity.[53] There is, however, one dramatic exception to this generalization about the limited interest of institutional investors in corporate governance: hedge funds. Hedge funds are essentially unregulated mutual funds; that is, they are a pooled investment fund, typically organized as a limited partnership, that holds securities and possibly other assets for its owners and is managed by a professional investment adviser, but they are not subject to the special federal securities law (the Investment Company Act of 1940)[54] that regulates mutual funds.[55] The basis for their exemption is that hedge funds may not market or sell interests in themselves to the general investing public and must either (a) have 100 or fewer beneficial owners,[56] or (b) sell their securities only to high-net-worth individuals.[57] Because of this exemption, hedge funds are not subject to the legal rules that require mutual funds to diversify their investments broadly, restrict mutual funds from holding significant amounts of illiquid securities or borrowing heavily, and limit the fees that mutual funds' professional investment managers can charge their funds. As a result, hedge funds frequently do not diversify their investments and instead hold large equity stakes in their portfolio companies (typically up to 10 percent). They are motivated to make large and risky investments by the fact that their advisers are typically compensated based on a performance fee equal to a portion of the profits (often 20 percent) that the fund makes. Thus, they accept high risk in exchange for a high return.

Unlike mutual funds, hedge funds have been activist investors, taking large equity positions in companies and sometimes seeking to elect their candidates to the portfolio corporation's board or to force the hedge fund's investment plans and strategies (for example, a merger) upon the company. Because they hold large stakes in their portfolio companies, they will receive a much larger payoff from such involvement in corporate governance than a mutual fund, which

52. See Roberta Romano, Public Pension Fund Activism in Corporate Governance Reconsidered, 93 Colum. L. Rev. 795 (1993).

53. See John Coffee, Liquidity Versus Control: The Institutional Investor as Corporate Monitor, 91 Colum. L. Rev. 1277 (1991). For example, if institutions place their own employees on the board of a company in which they are shareholders, they may come into possession of material nonpublic information and thus be restricted from trading by the laws against insider trading. Or they may become subject to §16(b) of the Securities Exchange Act of 1934, which precludes such persons from making "short-swing" trading profits (both of these restrictions are discussed infra in Chapter V). The barrier here is that many institutional investors value their ability to sell immediately more than they value any right to a greater voice in corporate decisionmaking.

54. 15 U.S.C. §80a-1 et seq.

55. For a recent case explaining the difficulties in precisely defining the term "hedge fund" and the multiple possible definitions, see Goldstein v. SEC, 451 F.3d 873, 874-875 (D.C. Cir. 2006). For an excellent overview of the new role of hedge funds in corporate governance, see Marcel Kahan & Edward B. Rock, Hedge Funds in Corporate Governance and Corporate Control, 155 U. Pa. L. Rev. 1021 (2007).

56. See §3(c)(1) of the Investment Company Act of 1940, 15 U.S.C. §80a-3(c)(1).

57. See §3(c)(7) of the Investment Company Act of 1940, 15 U.S.C. §80a-3(c)(7) (requiring that these "qualified" purchasers own at least $5 million in investments).

typically holds a much smaller stake because of the diversification requirements to which it is subject. The tactics of hedge funds have been controversial and are discussed further in Chapter IV. The immediate point is simply that the behavior of institutional investors differs (and dramatically so). Whether they become actively involved in corporate governance depends on the expected payoff they perceive from that involvement.

Although Table 1.1 shows that individual shareholders own only approximately 26 percent of the shares in U.S. public corporations, the level of participation by individuals in the equity markets is higher in the United States than in any other country. As of 2005, slightly over 91 million U.S. citizens owned stocks (either directly, through ownership of mutual funds, or through employer-sponsored retirement plans),[58] and hence a decline in stock market levels may have political consequences in the United States that it does not have elsewhere. Although many individual shareholders are wealthy and have large portfolios, the American middle class has increasingly invested its retirement income in equity securities, largely through mutual funds. This extensive participation by the middle class in the stock market in the United States, which is not paralleled in Europe or elsewhere, explains why issues of market fairness find their way onto the national political agenda in the United States (and may also explain why the Sarbanes-Oxley Act of 2002 passed both houses of Congress by overwhelming majorities).

D. HISTORY AND EVOLUTION OF THE BUSINESS CORPORATION

Between the eighteenth and early twentieth centuries, corporate law in the United States moved from a variety of public law used to regulate legislatively chartered quasi-public entities formed for a public purpose (such as organizations formed to build canals or turnpikes or to establish banks) to an almost entirely private body of law, available to all and much more enabling than mandatory. This transition never, however, reached the point where corporate law lost all its mandatory features and became simply a model form contract. Indeed, one feature of corporate law has remained constant: only the state can create a corporation and confer limited liability on its shareholders.

At the time of the American Revolution, the established English doctrine was that only the king in Parliament could create a corporation.[59] Such royal charters had been important because they often bestowed a de facto monopoly on the recipient and also enabled their recipients to undertake the range of public functions performed by the early trading companies, such as setting up local governments and conducting negotiations with the indigenous peoples of a colonial territory. English law had sought to constrain the use of the corporate form in order to preserve the political authority of the Crown to grant charters. But private business organizations, established as joint ventures or partnerships, were still regularly formed to conduct overseas trading operations, and by the

58. See Investment Company Institute and Securities Industry Association, Equity Ownership in America, 2005, at 44.
59. For the best overview of the early development of American corporate law, see J. Willard Hurst, The Legitimacy of the Business Corporation in the Law of the United States, 1780-1970 (1970).

mid-eighteenth century judicial decisions had begun to protect their right to compete with chartered corporations.

Then, in the early eighteenth century, a famous financial panic — the "South Sea Bubble"[60] — colored the English view of the corporation, associating it with a speculative mania in which shares in worthless or overvalued firms were traded at steadily escalating prices until the inevitable collapse of the financial markets resulted in scarce credit and business failures throughout the economy. As a consequence, the Bubble Act, passed by Parliament in 1719, barred unchartered joint stock companies from selling their securities to the public, in the hope of restricting market trading to those more stable companies chartered by the Crown.[61] To evade this statute, promoters developed a functional substitute: the trust was converted to a device for holding business assets for the benefit of investors, thus forming a substitute for the corporation, one whose beneficial interests could be traded. Although the beneficiaries of this device enjoyed limited liability as a practical matter, the trustee did not. Whether this device really overcame the Bubble Act's prohibition on unincorporated business entities assuming corporate powers was never really tested, but it did link the development of corporate law with basic concepts of trust law, such as that of fiduciary duty.

1. THE EARLY AMERICAN EXPERIENCE

The foregoing reasons for skepticism about the corporate form had less relevance in the American context, although they did establish the starting point for American lawmaking after the Revolution. At the beginning of the nineteenth century, the American political context furnished independent reasons for hostility to the corporate form. Basically, the Jeffersonians were reluctant to encourage industrialization because they feared the consequences of large amounts of capital being assembled in any private enterprise; thus, they saw liberalized access to the corporate form as part of the Federalists' political program, to which they were generally hostile. In consequence, use of the corporate form was subjected to a host of restrictions, and the corporation was often regarded as a quasi-public entity.

Lawrence Friedman, A History of American Law
188-192, 194-198 (2d ed. 1985)

Corporations were uncommon before 1800. And few of those which existed were business corporations. Almost all of the colonial corporations were churches, charities, or cities or boroughs. New York City was a chartered corporation. In all of the 18th century, charters were issued to only 335 businesses. Only seven of

---

60. For a history of this period, see Carswell, The South Sea Bubble (1960); Cowles, The Great Swindle: The Story of the South Sea Bubble (1960).

61. The Bubble Act, 1719, 6 Geo. 1, ch. 18, §§18-29, was largely repealed in 1825. Many believe it had little effect and did not restrict speculative syndications. Still, the corporate form acquired such a stigma in the eyes of British investors that it was used only sparingly, for a limited number of quasi-public businesses, such as canals, turnpikes, insurance companies, and banks. Yet, truly speculative syndications continued to be offered to investors through the trust or deed-of-settlement device and joint stock associations, even though they lacked complete limited liability. See A. B. DuBois, The English Business Company After the Bubble Act of 1720-1800 (1983).

these were during the colonial period; 181 were issued between 1796 and 1800. Banks, insurance companies, water companies, and companies organized to build or run canals, turnpikes, and bridges made up the overwhelming majority of these early corporations. . . .

Until about the middle of the [nineteenth] century, the corporation was by no means the dominant form of business organization. Most commercial enterprises were partnerships. They consisted of two or three partners, often related by blood or marriage. The partnership was "used by all types of business, from the small country storekeepers to the great merchant bankers." But as the economy developed, entrepreneurs made more and more use of the corporation, especially for transport ventures. The corporate form was a more efficient way to structure and finance their ventures. The special charter system was clumsy and cumbersome. It was a waste of the legislature's time as well — or would have been, if in fact each charter was carefully scrutinized, and its clauses cut to order for the particular case. In fact, except for projects of special importance, charters became stylized, standardized, matters of rote. They were finally replaced, as we shall see, by general incorporation laws.

Early charters had many features which, from the standpoint of 20th-century corporation law, appear odd or idiosyncratic. Eternal life was not the rule. In the early 19th century, charter terms of five, twenty, or thirty years' duration were quite common. In New Jersey, every manufacturing company (except one) had a limited term of life before 1823; perpetual duration remained rare before the Civil War. In Maryland, a general law of 1839 limited corporate life (for mining or manufacturing companies) to a maximum of thirty years. Early charters often departed from the principle of one vote for each share of stock. It was not the rule in Maryland, for example, until after 1819. In New Hampshire, under the charter of the Souhegan Nail and Cotton Factory (1812), each of the fifty shares of capital stock was entitled to a vote, but no member was entitled to more than ten votes; no matter how many shares he owned. . . .

But the main line of development was clear. Gradually, these variations were leveled out, and the practice moved in the direction of a kind of common law of corporations, whose basic contours were set by business custom and the needs of entrepreneurs. Between 1800 and 1850, the essential nature of the corporation changed. No longer was the business corporation a unique, *ad hoc* creation, vesting exclusive control over a public asset or natural resource in one group of favorites or investors. Rather, it was becoming a general form for organizing a business, legally open to all, and with few real restrictions on entry, duration, and management. Business practice led the way. The living law on proxy voting, general and special meetings, inspection of books, and the transfer of stock, gradually created demands (which were granted) for standard clauses in corporate charters; and ultimately these norms were embodied in the statute and case law of corporations. . . .

[Reaction to the rise of the business corporation was often hostile during the nineteenth century, and the wellspring of this hostility was the Jeffersonian fear of private power. Professor Friedman explains the position of the anticorporate movement during this era and the gradual shift to free incorporation]:

This typical American fear was the source from which the system of checks and balances grew. It was a fear of unbridled power — the power of large landholders and dynastic wealth, and, most notably, the power of government. An influential segment of the public was willing to try many techniques to prevent concentration of authority and to offset the corrosive effect of money and power. The triumph of the corporation as a form of business association was therefore neither painless nor noiseless. The corporation was an object of great controversy in the first half of the 19th century. Partly because of the historic meaning and role of corporations, people in 1800 identified corporations with franchised monopolies. Corporations were creatures of the state, endowed with breath for the sole purpose of holding franchise or privilege, that is, some power or right that no one else could lay claim to. Most corporations were transportation monopolies, banks, insurance companies — aggregations of "capital," representing the "few" against the "many." . . .

The word "soulless" constantly recurs in debates over corporations. Everyone knew that corporations were really run by human beings. Yet the metaphor was not entirely pointless. Corporations did not die, and had no ultimate limit to their size. There were no natural bounds to their life or to their greed. Corporations, it was feared, could concentrate the worst urges of whole groups of men; the economic power of a corporation would not be tempered by the mentality of any one person, or by considerations of family or morality. People hated and distrusted corporations, the way some fear computers today, which are also soulless, also capable of joining the wit, skill, and malevolence of many minds.

In theory, the special charter system was a strong mode of corporate control. But the demand for charters was too great. By the 1840s and 1850s, it would have swamped the legislatures, if the process had not become so routine. Even so, state session laws bulged with special charters. Valuable time was spent in the drudgery of issuing, amending, and extending hundreds of charters. In the rush, there was little time to supervise those charters which perhaps needed supervision. Since even a radical routinization was not the answer, the legislatures took the next logical step, delegation: that is, the passage of general acts. The legislature could save itself time; could make effective law for all corporations, in one carefully considered law; and could turn the corporate form into a freely available right, rather than a privilege of the few.

Even in the late 18th century a few general laws were passed, which applied to churches, academies, and library societies. A New York law of 1811, "relative to incorporations for Manufacturing purposes," is usually credited as the first general law for *business* corporations. . . .

Other corporation acts picked up the New York plan. These laws were general in the sense that they applied to all corporations in a particular field — manufacturing, banking, or insurance. Typically, too, the laws did not provide an exclusive method of starting a corporation. They left the door open for private charters, if the incorporators preferred. In fact, the early general laws were not particularly effective. When they imposed rules of any bite at all, the business community ignored them and took the private-charter route. At most, entrepreneurs would incorporate temporarily under the general law, until they could extract a private charter from the legislature. To put teeth into the general laws, the New York constitution of 1846 took a somewhat more drastic step. It restricted special charters to "cases where in the judgment of the Legislature, the objects of the corporation cannot be attained under general laws." As it turned out, the legislature was quite accommodating in making such judgments. At the close of the period, then, the special charter was still dominant. But the handwriting was on the wall. The Louisiana constitution of 1845, a bellwether in many ways, contained a much stronger clause: "Corporations shall not be created in this State by special laws except for political or municipal purposes." ...

The movement against corporations could never muster the strength or consensus to strangle them, as opposed to snapping at their heels. Yet no issue was more persistent, perhaps, in the period between 1815 and 1850, than the issue of public control over corporations. In the famous case of Dartmouth College v. Woodward (1819),[61] the United States Supreme Court faced the issue squarely. By the terms of the federal Constitution, no state could impair the obligation of a contract. But what was a "contract"? In *Dartmouth College,* the court decided that a corporate charter was "a contract made on a valuable consideration," a "contract for the security and disposition of property." Consequently, no legislature could change the terms of any charter which a previous legislature had granted; to do so would "impair" the charter.

Dartmouth College was no business corporation; but the court, and the newspaper-reading public, well understood that the decision went beyond any question of the charters of colleges. News of the decision evoked a great howl of protest. Many contemporaries (and their intellectual descendants) felt that the *Dartmouth College* case was a blow to popular sovereignty; it took away from "the people and their elected representatives" a "large part of the control over social and economic affairs." That was one way of looking at the case. The court and its defenders saw it differently. The purpose of the decision was to secure property interests, and to protect ownership and management rights from shifting, temporary winds of public opinion. A climate of legal stability promoted economic growth, while doing simple justice.

Dartmouth College had a far less sweeping effect on the law of corporations than one might have guessed. In the actual decision, Joseph Story wrote a concurrence, which, perhaps offhandedly, suggested a simple way to avoid the impact of the rule. If the legislature, Story said, really wanted to alter corporate charters, it ought to reserve the right to do so when it issued them. If it did, then the right to alter the charter would, legally speaking, be part of the "contract" between the state and the corporation; and when the legislature passed a law changing the terms of the charter, that would be no "impairment." In later years, charters normally contained a standard clause (put in at the insistence of legislatures) reserving to the state the right to alter, amend, and repeal. This right was also a common feature of general incorporation laws. Finally, the right was inserted in state constitutions. The New York constitution of 1846 provided that "all general laws and special acts" about corporations "may be altered from time to time or repealed" (art. 8, sec. 1). ...

At first, the courts treated corporate powers rather gingerly. They adhered to the "general and well settled principle, that a corporation had no other powers than such as are specifically granted; or, such as are necessary for the purpose of carrying into effect the powers expressly granted." This "principle" followed logically from the concept of a corporation as an occasion for aggregating capital toward a single venture or purpose — a bridge, a factory, a bank. Chief Justice Roger Taney built on this concept in the famous case of the *Charles River Bridge* (1837).[63] This case stood for the proposition that charters were to be strictly construed; it was best

---

61. 17 U.S. [4 Wheat] 518.
63. Proprietors of the Charles River Bridge v. Proprietors of the Warren Bridge, 11 Pet. 420 (1837). On the background and meaning of the case, see Stanley I. Kutler, Privilege and Creative Destruction: The *Charles River Bridge* Case (1971).

to keep the powers of corporations, like those of government itself, within narrow boundaries.

2. NINETEENTH-CENTURY EFFORTS TO CONTROL THE CORPORATION

The *Dartmouth College* and *Charles River Bridge* cases involved the controversial political question of the degree of freedom that private corporations should have from legislative control (the Federalists won a partial victory under Marshall in *Dartmouth College* but suffered a temporary setback in *Charles River Bridge* when Taney, a Jackson appointee, read corporate powers very narrowly). A related concern during this period, however, united Federalist and Jeffersonian judges: the status of creditors. If creditors advanced money or goods to the corporation and the shareholders then withdrew their capital, creditors seemed to be left without legal recourse. Although the law on fraudulent conveyances could easily have been stretched to deal with this abuse, a distinctly American solution was instead devised that, although lacking any clear precedent in English law, responded directly to this perceived attempt to exploit creditors by those who hid behind the "soulless" corporation.

Lawrence Friedman, A History of American Law
199, 513 (2d ed. 1985)

Law had to be devised to govern the relationship of officers, directors, shareholders, and creditors. Some of this law was hammered out in the cases. Joseph Story, for example, is credited with inventing the so-called trust-fund doctrine. It stemmed from Wood v. Drummer (1824).[65] Stockholders of the Hallowell and Augusta Bank, of Maine, which was winding up its corporate existence, declared dividends amounting to seventy-five percent of the capital stock of $200,000. The bank thus became a hollow shell, especially since not all of the capital stock had actually been paid in. The plaintiffs held bank notes that became worthless. Story held that it was wrong for the stockholders to distribute the capital to themselves in such a way as to defraud the bank's creditors, that is, the holders of the bank notes. The capital stock of banks was "to be deemed a pledge or trust fund for the payment of the debts contracted by the bank." Creditors could "follow" the funds "into the hands of any persons, who are not innocent purchasers," and recover it from them. This gave the plaintiffs a right to recover from the stockholders, who had lined their pockets with the money from the bank. Later cases repeated the rule, and extended it to analogous situations.

In effect, Wood v. Drummer held that at least a portion of the capital contributed to a corporation by its shareholders was irrevocably committed and could not be withdrawn to the prejudice of creditors. From this "trust fund" concept, our

---

65. Mason C. C. Rpts. 308, Fed. Cas. No. 17,944 (1824).

contemporary law on dividends and watered stock (discussed in Chapter III.D) eventually developed. The "trust fund" doctrine acquired special prominence toward the end of the nineteenth century when the famous robber barons of that era (Jay Gould, Jim Fisk, Commodore Cornelius Vanderbilt) recurrently sought to exchange overvalued or worthless property in return for shares of a solvent corporation that they controlled (typically, a railroad) in order to dilute the interests of the other shareholders. Such stock was called "watered stock," after the practice of feeding salt to cattle in order to make them thirsty enough to consume large quantities of water and thereby increase their weight just before they were sold by the pound. Professor Friedman discusses the uncertain response of American courts and legislatures to these recurrent frauds and their first attempts to establish rules and remedies for the protection of investors:

Lawrence Friedman, A History of American Law
513-516 (2d ed. 1985)

In the 1860s and 1870s, men like Vanderbilt, Jay Gould, and Jim Fisk fought tawdry battles over the stock market, the economy, the corpses of railroad corporations. The investing public was unmercifully fleeced. . . .

The pillaging of the Erie Railroad by the robber barons, in the late 1860s, was a classic case of financial mismanagement and public corruption. The story was coldly recounted by Charles Francis Adams in his essay "A Chapter of Erie." Adams was alarmed at what was happening — not to one railroad alone, or to the stock market, but to all of America. . . . Modern society has "created a class of artificial beings who bid fair soon to be the master of their creator"; they were "establishing despotisms which no spasmodic popular effort will be able to shake off. Everywhere . . . they illustrate the truth of the old maxim of the common law, that corporations have no souls." . . .

The law of corporations, as such, is less concerned with the economic power of corporations than with their everyday behavior. The two are of course connected. The developing law had one general goal: to fashion doctrine which would produce honest dealings between the corporation, its managers and promoters, on the one hand, and investors, stockholders and creditors, on the other; but to do so in a way that would not interfere with business efficiency. The corporation should have a free hand in the business world, and rugged honesty in internal affairs. As we have seen, the courts had begun to develop a tool kit of doctrines, even before the Civil War. There was great concern, for example, with watered stock. This was stock granted to insiders, in exchange for fictitious values — stock that the promoters or subscribers then threw on the market. Investors were cheated by watered stock, because they thought they were buying shares with a solid basis in assets or cash. The New York corporation law of 1848 — on "corporations for manufacturing, mining, mechanical or chemical purposes" — declared: "Nothing but money shall be considered as payment of any part of the capital stock"; this was amended, however, in 1853, to allow a company to issue stock in exchange for "mines, manufactories, and other property necessary for . . . business." Rules of the New York type were widely adopted, later on, in other states. There were also constitutional provisions. The Illinois constitution of 1870 stated that "no railroad corporation shall issue any stock or bonds, except for money, labor or property actually received and applied to the purposes for which such corporation was created." Also outlawed were "all stock dividends, and other fictitious increase of capital stocks or indebtedness" (Const. Ill. 1870, art. XII, sec. 13).

Under laws such as these, the grossest frauds, and most clearly watered stock, were obviously illegal. There remained gray areas of doubt. If a promoter exchanged his land, or a coal mine, or a building, for $100,000 in stock, how could one tell if the promoter had transferred full value? The only *safe* rule was to require all subscriptions in cash. Yet New York found this rule unduly restrictive. Courts tended to approve transactions of promoters so long as they were done in "good faith." The concept of par value of stock, once quite meaningful, lost its significance. As shares changed hands in the open market, it meant very little that the shares bore values of $100 or $1,000 on their face. Stock was worth what it would fetch from a buyer. Par meant nothing at all to a going concern. Values were fixed by the speculating and investing public. Corporate capital, then, was not a fixed fund of assets; and par did not represent an irreducible core of truth and wealth, like the gold reserves of a bank.

In this period, the courts wrestled with problems of control of corporate management, in occasional lawsuits brought by stockholders or others who felt victimized. At first, there were serious procedural barriers. Technically, it was the corporation itself which had the right to sue officers who cheated the corporation. But precisely these officers controlled the corporation; the men who were milking the company were the last to want to sue. The *stockholders' suit* was a class action, brought on behalf of a stockholder plaintiff and all others in his position. The device was foreshadowed as early as the 1830s, but the Supreme Court gave it a further push in Dodge v. Woolsey, decided in 1856.[6] The dereliction of duty charged in *Dodge* was not one of the grand postwar piracies. It was a technical error — paying a tax, which the stockholder claimed was unconstitutional. In Morgan v. Skiddy (1875),[7] a New York case, the defendants, directors of the "Central Mining Company of Colorado," had dangled in front of the gullible public glittering prospects of endless money from "the celebrated 'Bates lode.'" In this case, a stockholder's suit was used as a weapon against plain corporate fraud.

To what standard of conduct should officers and directors be held? Case law looked to the concept of *fiduciary duty.* Officers and directors were trustees for the corporation. This meant that they could not engage in self-dealing; they could not buy from or sell to the company; they were strictly accountable for any profits they made in transactions with the company. The law of fiduciary duties was an austere body of doctrine. Courts of chancery had applied it to trustees who managed funds for widows and orphans. Now it was applied, in essence, to promoters, officers and directors. The phrase "a sacred trust" has moral overtones; but the courts borrowed trust law less for its morality than as a ready-made set of propositions that seemed to fit the problem before them.

In retrospect, many of the nineteenth-century attempts to regulate the corporation appear to have proven unsuccessful. The original legislative strategy

6. 59 U.S. 331 (1856).
7. 62 N.Y. 319 (1875).

of granting only special charters with narrowly described purposes proved unworkable because it overburdened the legislature, invited bribery and influence peddling, and disadvantaged smaller businesses that could not afford to lobby the legislature. It was universally abandoned by the end of the nineteenth century. Similarly, the attempt to deny the corporation any implied powers and to enforce rigidly the *ultra vires* doctrine under which acts of corporate managers not expressly authorized by the shareholders were deemed void, proved infeasible and created serious traps for the unwary. By the end of the nineteenth century, this doctrine also was fading, as courts began to recognize that corporate officers enjoyed implied powers. Finally, although the "trust fund" doctrine continued to require that some portion of the equity capital contributed by shareholders constitute an irrevocable trust fund for protection of creditors, promoters were able to trivialize this protection by employing various devices, such as the use of "no par" or "low par" common stock. No jurisdiction has retained the once common requirements that restricted the consideration for which shares could be issued to cash or tangible property (although some specific forms of consideration — such as notes — remain prohibited in most states). These seemingly archaic legal doctrines probably should be understood today as social experiments that either failed or worked only for their era.

3. TWENTIETH-CENTURY DEVELOPMENTS

The end of the nineteenth century saw state corporation statutes in rapid transition from an explicitly regulatory body of law to a largely enabling one. In 1888 New Jersey enacted a largely enabling statute that gave corporations incorporated under it broad powers, but included none of the traditional restrictions on size, duration, or scope of powers. In response, over 1,336 corporations incorporated in New Jersey in just the first seven months of 1899.[62] Delaware copied the New Jersey statute in 1899. Initially, this had little impact, but in 1913, when New Jersey, under the leadership of Governor Woodrow Wilson and embarrassed by its success at "chartermongering," enacted a "reform" statute that restricted corporate powers, Delaware suddenly won by default. Attracting incorporations by firms that were physically based elsewhere meant more to Delaware than to virtually any other state, because Delaware's corporate franchise taxes constitute a significant proportion of the state's aggregate tax revenues, whereas the same revenues would be trivial to a New York or California. Possibly for this reason in part, Delaware has long been the domicile of most of the Fortune 500 companies and over half of the NYSE-listed companies.

a. The "Race to the Bottom" Thesis

The apparent competition among states for incorporations produced predictable criticism. In his dissent in Liggett v. Lee, 288 U.S. 517, 557-560 (1933), Justice Brandeis articulated what became the standard "liberal" view — that the competition among

---

62. See Lawrence Friedman, A History of American Law 523-524 (2d ed. 1985); see also, Edward Q. Keasbey, New Jersey and the Great Corporations, 13 Harv. L. Rev. 198, 201 (1899).

the states for corporate franchise tax revenues had produced a "race to the bottom" that effectively ended the possibility of substantive state regulation of corporate behavior:

> The removal by the leading industrial states of the limitations upon the size and powers of business corporations appears to have been due, not to their conviction that maintenance of the restrictions was undesirable in itself, but to the conviction that it was futile to insist upon them; because local restriction would be circumvented by foreign incorporation. Indeed, local restriction seemed worse than futile. Lesser states, eager for the revenue derived from the traffic in charters, had removed safeguards from their own incorporation laws. Companies were early formed to provide charters for corporations in states where the cost was lowest and the laws least restrictive. The states joined in advertising their wares. The race was not one of diligence, but of laxity . . . and the great industrial states yielded in order not to lose wholly the prospect of the revenue and control incident to domestic incorporation.

Whether this competition has been injurious has long been debated by scholars. The original "race to the bottom" critique was answered in time by "race to the top" scholars who rejected Brandeis's view and argued that competition among the states was desirable and produced efficient changes that eliminated anachronistic elements of state corporation statutes without harming investors or shareholders.[63] The most recent scholarship on this question now doubts that there has been any serious competition for corporate charters for decades and questions whether competition is likely to produce greater efficiency or benefits for investors.[64] While this debate is certain to continue, the underlying question involves the degree to which managers make the decision to reincorporate outside their "home" jurisdiction in order to further their own interests versus those of the shareholders. Skeptics believe that managers tend to reincorporate in the jurisdiction that will most protect them from takeovers and control contests and thus that competition encourages the spread of state anti-takeover legislation.

The seeming existence of this competition for charters shifted the attention of reformers from the state to the federal level. Proposals for a federal incorporation statute have periodically appeared throughout the twentieth century, beginning in 1901 when President Theodore Roosevelt included a proposal for federal chartering of large corporations in his first message to Congress. But at no time has the idea of federal chartering received much support. Instead, at periodic intervals, Congress had responded to special crises by enacting laws regulating particular aspects of corporate behavior, such as the federal securities laws in the 1930s; the Williams Act in the late 1960s, which regulates takeovers; and the Foreign Corrupt Practices Act in the 1970s, which regulates overseas bribery and domestic political

63. For the view that interjurisdictional competition for corporate charters has led to a race not to the bottom but to the top, because it increased shareholder choice and minimized constraints that interfered with shareholder wealth maximization, see Ralph Winter, Government and the Corporation (1978); Daniel Fischel, The "Race to the Bottom" Revisited: Reflections on Recent Developments in Delaware's Corporation Law, 76 Nw. U. L. Rev. 913 (1982). Cf. Henry Butler, Nineteenth Century Jurisdictional Competition in the Granting of Corporate Privileges, 14 J. Legal Stud. 129 (1985).

64. For leading recent contributions to this continuing debate, see Marcel Kahan & Ehud Kamar, The Myth of Competition in Corporate Law, 55 Stan. L. Rev. 675 (2002) (arguing that no other state has sought to compete with Delaware for incorporations in modern times), and Lucian Bebchuk, Alma Cohen & Allen Ferrell, Does the Evidence Favor State Competition in Corporate Law?, 90 Cal. L. Rev. 1775 (2002) (state competition provides undesirable incentives for jurisdictions to prefer managerial interests over shareholder interests). See generally Chapter IV.A.

practices. The New York Stock Exchange has also at times standardized minimum practices for large corporations, such as by mandating an independent audit committee in 1975. Most recently, the Sarbanes-Oxley Act of 2002 continued this trend by prohibiting public corporations from engaging in a number of specific practices, while still leaving incorporation legislation to the states. In effect, federal corporate law standards have been enacted on a piecemeal basis, usually in response to crises and usually regulating only large public corporations. But clearly, corporate behavior is today regulated at both the state and federal levels.

b. The Rise of Managerial Capitalism

Just as important as the changes in state corporation law during this period were those occurring within the corporation itself. At the beginning of the twentieth century, many entrepreneurs were still skeptical of the corporate form. For example, Andrew Carnegie ran the Carnegie Steel Company as a limited partnership, largely in order to avoid sharing control with other investors. Other entrepreneurs found that the corporate form denied them needed flexibility because, for example, of legal restrictions on the ability of one corporation to own shares in another. Thus, John D. Rockefeller assembled his Standard Oil monopoly by using a trust device to hold the shares of the various constituent corporations. In general, the corporation at the end of the nineteenth century was a single-purpose entity that engaged in only one industry and was controlled by a single owner or a closely knit group who had founded the business.

During the late nineteenth to early twentieth centuries, three critical transitions ushered in the era of the modern public corporation: (1) the rise of the professional manager; (2) a major trend toward vertical integration, as corporations began to acquire their sources of supply and their retail distributors; and (3) the appearance of the multi-unit firm — the precursor of the modern conglomerate — that operated a variety of businesses in increasingly decentralized fashion.[65] Historians generally agree that this evolution began with technological advances that vastly increased the complexity of the administrative tasks that had to be coordinated within the firm. In particular, the large railroad and telegraph companies that appeared at the end of the nineteenth century required sustained internal coordination to regulate the volume of traffic and maintain an expensive infrastructure. Vertical integration was pursued because it gave the firm greater security by assuring it access to sources of supply that its competitors might otherwise cut off; retail distributors were similarly acquired as a defensive strategy to protect the firm against being frozen out of major markets if competitors acquired the principal retail outlets in that market.

With vertical integration, however, the scope of the decisions made by the managers within a single firm significantly expanded. Consequently, managerial

---

65. For a revealing account, from an organizational perspective, of the appearance of the multi-divisional corporation, see Neil Fligstein, The Spread of the Multidivisional Form Among Large Firms, 1919-1979, 50 Am. Soc. Rev. 377 (1985). As of the 1920s, only two American corporations (General Motors and Dupont) had reorganized themselves along multidivisional lines, but by 1979 Professor Fligstein finds that 85 percent of the largest industrial firms had adopted this more decentralized form of organization.

hierarchies arose; multiple levels of middle management became common, and managers began to specialize along functional lines (sales, finance, production, etc.). As specialization increased, the individual manager began to look less like a general merchant and more like a true professional.

The significance of this transition from family control to control by professional managers (who owned only a small percentage of the corporation's stock) was not immediately appreciated. Then, in the most famous book on corporate law written in the twentieth century, The Modern Corporation and Private Property (1932), Professors Adolf Berle Jr. and Gardiner Means argued that the dispersion of share ownership among many small owners, coupled with the ability possessed by a new class of professional managers to finance corporate projects from internally generated earnings, had given rise to a "separation of ownership and control" that left shareholders relatively powerless. Because (1) shareholders lacked effective power to control or oust management (at least without incurring costs prohibitive for most shareholders) and (2) managers did not need to resort to capital markets as long as earnings could be retained for internal expansion, Berle and Means argued that it was more accurate to describe the modern corporation as one in which managers hired owners, rather than the reverse. That is, managers negotiated for equity capital from shareholders just as they purchased other factors of production from suppliers.

Much later, in the 1950s, Professor Berle concluded that the separation of ownership from control was a desirable transition because it freed managers from any obligation to represent only shareholders and instead allowed them to act as quasi-public servants and balance the interests of all who were affected by the large corporation.[66] However, for most observers the principal implication of the Berle-Means thesis was that the new corporate manager held a substantially unaccountable discretion that could potentially be exercised in a self-interested fashion. Although the Berle-Means thesis has long been contested by economists and others who believe that market forces effectively constrain managerial discretion, their analysis shaped the subsequent debate and significantly influenced much of the federal securities legislation passed later in the 1930s. In particular, Berle and Means argued that managers dominated the election of directors through their control of the proxy machinery.[67] Although they believed this domination was inevitable and that proposals for shareholder democracy were therefore flawed, Congress responded to their critique by enacting provisions in the Securities Exchange Act of 1934 that attempted to restore greater shareholder control over the election process.[68] Still, the greater significance of the Berle-Means thesis may lie not in the specific reforms that their work encouraged, but in its broader diagnosis that significant governance problems are inherent in the structure of the modern public corporation because professional managers tend to be beyond effective shareholder control.

---

66. See Adolf Berle, Power Without Property 2-8 (1959); Adolf Berle, The Twentieth Century Capitalist Revolution (1955). See also Joseph L. Weiner, The Berle-Dodd Dialogue on the Concept of the Corporation, 64 Colum. L. Rev. 1458 (1964).

67. Adolf Berle & Gardiner Means, The Modern Corporation and Private Property 71-82, 129-131 (rev. ed. 1967). Proxies are discussed in Chapter VI.C.2.

68. This topic is discussed in Chapter VI.

E. *ECONOMIC ANALYSIS OF THE CORPORATION*

Economic analysis illuminates many fundamental issues of corporate law, including, in particular, the asserted consequences of the separation of ownership and control. Although there is considerable disagreement among economists on many of these issues, they share a common perspective that sees the corporation not as a monolithic entity but as a collection of participants — managers, investors, creditors, etc. — each pursuing its own self-interest. Economists then examine (and disagree over) the degree to which each participant is restrained by market or other forces from exploiting the others. This section considers economic analysis of the corporation as it bears on three topics already briefly noted: (1) the evolution in internal corporate structure, (2) the debate over the Berle-Means thesis, and (3) the role of the corporate charter as the contractual basis for the firm, particularly in view of the competition among states for corporate franchise taxes.

1. THE NATURE OF THE FIRM AND THE RISE OF THE M-FORM CORPORATION

A corporation is simply a legal mode of organizing a firm — an alternative to a partnership or an unincorporated association. But what is a firm? In classical economic theory, the firm is essentially seen as a method for coordinating production decisions that is an alternative to exchange transactions in the market. In theory, an entrepreneur could produce goods either by (1) hiring employees and telling them what to produce and how (in which event a "firm" arises and decisions are said to be made by "fiat") or (2) making agreements with independent contractors (i.e., a resort to the market and the price mechanism). Simple observation tells us that most goods are produced by a combination of methods. Every firm faces this "make or buy" decision. For example, General Motors is a large organization whose employees are typically hired on a long-term basis; it does not negotiate in the market for each product or service it needs, but rather produces them internally, thus relying on administrative supervision instead of price competition. Yet at the same time, General Motors does buy some components in the market — for example, steel and tires. What determines when a firm will internalize the production of goods and services rather than purchasing them in the market? In a seminal article, the economist Ronald Coase answered that relative transaction costs set the limit on firm size; that is, firms expand in size and scope of operations so long as the costs of internalizing production within the firm are below those of carrying out the same transaction in the market.[69] In theory, the firm is a means of economizing on transaction costs by relying on internal coordination. Over time, the relative costs of firms and markets might change, or even reverse themselves, and, if so, the scope of operations internalized within the firm should grow or shrink in response.

Some economists rely on this transaction cost explanation to account for why corporations evolved in this century from single-product firms into the multi-unit firm (and eventually into the modern conglomerate firm that owns unrelated

---

69. Ronald Coase, The Nature of the Firm, 4 Economica 386 (1937).

businesses). In particular, Professor Oliver Williamson has argued that the modern multidivisional firm evolved because its superior monitoring ability allows it to reduce transaction costs below those of smaller firms that manage only a single line of business.[70] His interpretation meshes closely with the finding of business historians, such as Alfred Chandler. In this view, the senior management of the modern M-form firm ("M" for "multidivisional") in effect supervises a portfolio of diverse companies and, through internal capital budgeting, can rapidly shift internally generated funds from one division that has a static or declining future to another that has higher growth prospects. In contrast, if each division were separately incorporated, internally generated earnings might be inefficiently retained within each firm, instead of being transferred to more productive uses. To the extent that the multi-unit firm more swiftly allocates internal funds toward higher-valued uses, it may outperform the capital market's efficiency at resource allocation. One reason for the relative superiority of the firm over the market may lie in the superior information possessed by the management of the M-form firm in comparison to the ordinary investor in the market. Alternatively, the M-form firm may be more efficient in replacing inferior operating managements at the divisional level than would stockholders if that same division were incorporated as an independent entity.

In Williamson's view, the rise of the M-form firm has greatly mitigated the problem of managerial discretion noted by Berle and Means.[71] Because operating management is monitored by senior management that focuses essentially on strategic planning and capital budgeting (but otherwise permits operating management at the division level to function relatively autonomously), the potential for lower-level managers either to shirk or engage in unfair self-dealing has been sharply reduced in scope. However, those less confident about the modern conglomerate's efficiency argue that this new administrative layer has a built-in bias toward expansion and will lead managers to pursue policies that maximize corporate growth at the expense of shareholder profit.

2. MANAGERIAL DISCRETION: THE DEBATE OVER THE BERLE-MEANS THESIS

Probably no issue relating to the role or legitimacy of the business corporation has engendered the same sustained controversy among economists as the Berle-Means thesis, which posits that the diffusion in shareholder ownership has resulted in a separation of ownership and control under which corporate managers can pursue their own interests largely unconstrained by shareholder opposition. Although most publicly held firms are characterized by a dispersed ownership that may prevent shareholders from coordinating their actions effectively,[72] many

70. Oliver Williamson, Corporate Control and Business Behavior (1970); Oliver Williamson, Markets and Hierarchies (1975); Oliver Williamson, The Modern Corporation: Origins, Evolution and Attributes, 19 J. Econ. Literature 1537 (1981).

71. Oliver Williamson, Organization Form, Residual Claimants, and Corporate Control, 26 J. Law & Econ. 351, 366 (1983).

72. Many doubt, however, that broad shareholder dispersion characterizes all or even most publicly held corporations. Professor Melvin Eisenberg argues that in a large number of corporations there remains a definable ownership group that could effectively monitor management if they were given greater opportunity by law to voice their consent (or opposition) to fundamental corporate decisions. The Structure of the Corporation: A Legal Analysis 42-68 (1976). See also Edward Herman, Corporate Control, Corporate Power (1981) (also contending that a significant percentage of large corporations are

economists respond to this assertion of shareholder impotence by arguing either that (1) market forces are still adequate to constrain management from overreaching shareholders, or that (2) the self-interest of managers is so closely aligned with that of shareholders, because of their common interest in maximizing the price of the firm's shares, as to make overreaching unlikely.

Others who believe that a considerable divergence remains between the interests of managers and those of shareholders have advanced a "behavioral" model of the firm. The manager within the large organization, it is argued, faces considerable insecurity.[73] The firm may be acquired (either through a hostile takeover or a friendly merger); as a result, the manager's position may be eliminated or given to a rival in a reorganization; or the manager may simply not be promoted within the firm. Since the 1960s, this school of economists has argued that corporate managers tend to act not to maximize profits, but to maximize firm size — to increase the opportunities for promotion, to obtain increased salary and perquisites thought to be associated with greater size, and to achieve greater security against the prospect of a hostile takeover.[74]

Underlying this view is the premise that corporate managers seek less to profit-maximize than to "profit satisfice" — a term meaning that managers seek the level of satisfactory profits sufficient to ensure interference-free operation of the firm.[75] Once managers achieve sufficient profits to protect against shareholder or creditor revolt, their inclination, it is argued, is to apply remaining internally generated funds toward expenditures, such as growth-maximizing acquisitions or enlarged staffs, that benefit them without being as visible as direct compensation.[76]

Attempts to develop empirical evidence to support or refute the Berle-Means thesis have produced mixed results. Some studies have reported that the level of executive compensation is higher in management-controlled firms than in shareholder-controlled firms,[77] that the level of earnings retention and the size of the corporate staff also tend to be higher in management-controlled firms,[78] and that owner-controlled firms earn higher net income in proportion to their net worth.[79]

---

controlled by a cohesive shareholder group); Harold Demsetz, The Structure of Ownership and the Theory of the Firms, 26 J.L. & Econ. 375 (1983).

73. See Victor Thompson, Modern Organization 24 (1961) ("[T]he modern organization is a prolific generator of anxiety and insecurity.").

74. The leading proponents of this behavioral model of the firm include William Baumol, Business, Value and Growth (rev. ed. 1967); Robin Marris, The Economic Theory of "Managerial" Capitalism (1964); Oliver Williamson, Managerial Discretion and Business Behavior, 53 Am. Econ. Rev. 1032 (1963). More recently, neoclassical economists, most notably Professor Michael Jensen, have also concluded that public corporations are characterized by a tendency to grow to excessive size, and to hoard earnings and often reinvest them in unprofitable expansion rather than pay them out as dividends. Agency Costs of Free Cash Flow, Corporate Finance, and Takeovers, 76 Am. Econ. Rev. 323 (1986). This inefficient growth is a primary motivation, he theorizes, for "bust-up takeovers," in which the target is liquidated.

75. The term "profit satisfice" was coined by Herbert Simon, a Nobel laureate in economics. Simon argues that decisionmakers act in a world of "bounded rationality" where constraints on time and information deny them the ability to search for the optimal solution to any problem; instead, they seek the first adequate solution and accept it. A Behavioral Model of Rational Choice, 69 Q.J. Econ. 99 (1955).

76. Such a conclusion has been reported not only by theorists, but also by business school empiricists who have conducted in-depth research into the behavior of specific corporations. See Donaldson, Managing Corporate Wealth: The Operation of a Comprehensive Financial Goals System (1984) (study of 12 mature industrial firms between 1969 and 1978 finding that the primary managerial motivation was to protect managerial autonomy by expanding firm size and financial resources).

77. William McEachern, Managerial Control and Performance (1975).

78. Williamson, footnotes 70 and 71, supra.

79. For a critical review of these studies, see Louis De Alessi, Private Property and Dispersion of Ownership in Large Corporations, 28 J. Fin. 839 (1973).

This evidence may suggest that a controlling shareholder can monitor management and reduce unnecessary expenses more effectively than can widely dispersed small shareholders.

3. THE AGENCY COST MODEL

Although many economists dispute the Berle-Means thesis that shareholders lack the capacity to control management, all recognize that potential conflicts exist between managers and shareholders. When managers hold little equity in the firm and shareholders are broadly dispersed, corporate assets may be used to benefit managers rather than shareholders. This diversion may occur either overtly, through self-dealing transactions and the consumption of executive perquisites, or more subtly through the pursuit of non-value-maximizing objectives, such as empire building and a tendency to reinvest the firm's earnings rather than pay dividends. Still, economists argue that this conflict between shareholders can be mitigated and managerial interests can be aligned with those of the shareholders through incentive compensation devices, such as stock options, which give managers an equity interest in the corporations.[80] As management ownership increases, managers bear a larger share of the costs of deviating from a corporate policy of value maximization; thus, managerial and shareholder interests tend to converge as managerial ownership of the firm rises.

This theory, that managerial ownership can curb both the problems noted by Berle and Means and the tendency noted by the managerialist critics for corporations to "profit satisfice," has been most fully articulated by Professors Jensen and Meckling, who have developed a general theoretical framework within which to assess the effect of the separation of ownership from control, including its impact on the financial structure of the firm.[81] They begin by defining the relationship between shareholders and management as an agency relationship: shareholders are principals who delegate broad discretion to managers, their agents. The principals control their agents, they argue, through three basic techniques: (1) establishing appropriate equity incentives, such as stock options; (2) "monitoring" controls (i.e., mechanisms by which the principals hire professional supervisors, such as independent auditing firms or outside directors, to evaluate their agents' performance); and (3) "bonding"

---

80. See Miron Stano, Executive Ownership Interests and Corporate Performance, 42 S. Econ. J. 272 (1975); Kevin Murphy, Corporate Performance and Managerial Remuneration: An Empirical Analysis, 7 J. Acct. & Econ. 11 (1985). Critics of this view respond, however, that the value of stock options is chiefly determined by general stock market levels and movements, not by "firm-specific" factors, and hence stock options are a crude device for aligning managerial and shareholder interests. See Note, The Executive Compensation Contract: Creating Incentives to Reduce Agency Costs, 37 Stan. L. Rev. 1147 (1985) (arguing that stock options should reward managers only for the net stock price gain by which their firm outperforms its competitors). Managerial ownership is not, however, an unmitigated good, because at some point concentrated managerial ownership permits entrenchment by management and effectively nullifies both shareholder voting rights and the threat of a takeover. Hence, there may be some optimal level of managerial ownership at which managers have a significant stake in, but not effective control of, the firm. This speculation may help explain the popularity of leveraged buyouts, in which managers receive a significant equity stake but large institutional investors obtain voting control, See Randall Morck, Andrei Schleifer & Robert Vishny, Management Ownership and Market Valuation: An Empirical Analysis, 20 J. Fin. Econ. 293 (1988).

81. Michael Jensen & William Meckling, Theory of the Firm: Managerial Behavior, Agency Costs and Ownership Structure, 3 J. Fin. Econ. 395 (1976). The Jensen and Meckling thesis has spawned a considerable body of literature in its wake. For an overview, see Symposium on the Distribution of Power Among Corporate Managers, Shareholders and Directors, 20 J. Fin. & Econ. 3 (1988).

devices (a term that refers to techniques by which agents implicitly guarantee their own performance, such as by volunteering to base their salary on the firm's profit performance).

Nonetheless, because monitoring, bonding, and incentive compensation devices are costly, principals must decide the optimal level of expenditures for these purposes. Plainly, shareholders would not wish to spend $100 to guard against a nonrecurring loss of $50. Rather, shareholders will recognize, Jensen and Meckling argue, that a certain degree of managerial misbehavior is inevitable and must be accepted as not worth the cost of prevention. Accordingly, they define the term "agency costs" to mean the sum of the dollar equivalent of (a) this residual misbehavior whose prevention would be too costly, (b) the monitoring expenses incurred by shareholders, and (c) the bonding expenses. In this light, the modern debate between the intellectual descendants of Berle and Means and the neoclassical economic viewpoint (as typified by Jensen and Meckling) is over whether stricter legal rules or public regulation can further reduce agency costs. Those dubious about regulation would argue that these costs have already been minimized and that further regulatory efforts would only raise them.

The capital structure of a firm may also affect its level of agency costs. When managers borrow, there are different agency costs applicable to the creditor-borrower relationship. Because both creditors and shareholders will need to monitor management, the financial structure of the firm — that is, the relative proportion of debt and equity — will be significantly influenced (according to the Jensen and Meckling model) by any difference between the agency costs that these two classes must incur. If creditors have lower agency costs than shareholders, the firm's capital structure (other things being equal[82]) will have a higher percentage of debt than if the opposite were true. Yet the relative monitoring costs reverse as the firm becomes more highly leveraged — i.e., as the proportion of debt to equity grows — because the equity owners of a firm financed 99 percent by debt would have great incentive to undertake high-risk investments.[83] Accordingly, Jensen and Meckling view the financial structure of the firm as reflecting that balance of debt and equity that minimizes aggregate agency costs.

One implication of their model is more controversial. They view agency costs as being borne by the entrepreneurs who founded the firm, because, to the extent they cannot convince potential shareholders that managerial misbehavior will be minimized, purchasers will pay less for their shares. That is, when securities are sold to the public by the entrepreneurial group that organized the firm, the purchasing investors will assume that the firm's organizers will act in their own self-interest, and thus they will discount the value of the firm's shares accordingly. In turn, this means that because these promoters bear the costs of their own potential misbehavior, they have an incentive to minimize these costs by installing whatever

82. Of course, other factors, such as the deductibility of interest payments for tax purposes, the risk of bankruptcy, and the desire of managers to diversify their investments, will also affect the debt/equity ratio.

83. In a highly leveraged firm, there is an incentive for shareholders to accept high-risk investments because the gain, if realized, goes primarily to the shareholders as the residual claimants (who receive all earnings that remain after payment of the fixed-interest claims of creditors), while any loss would fall primarily on the creditors (to the extent that the loss exceeded the amount of equity that the shareholders had contributed). In effect, under such a leveraged capital structure, shareholders receive all the upside gain, while creditors bear most of the downside risk. Hence, economic theory concludes that, under these circumstances, shareholders will want the firm to undertake riskier projects than they would if the firm had a less leveraged capital structure.

monitoring and bonding controls will allow them to receive a higher price for their shares. The key and controversial assertion here is that the original entrepreneurial group fully bears these agency costs. If so, the separation of ownership and control arguably lacks significant implications for shareholders' welfare.

Those who are skeptical of Jensen and Meckling's assertion that the incidence of agency costs falls exclusively on the original entrepreneurs doubt that shareholders have sufficient information to discount adequately the shares of those corporations whose managements are most likely to abuse their position as agents for the shareholders. Also, although strong incentives exist for the original promoters to assure investors of their reliability, these incentives weaken once the firm's capital has been raised. At some point, a later management team may find it in their interest to renege on the original promoters' promises and to behave opportunistically (e.g., by overcompensating themselves or engaging in unfair self-dealing transactions with their firm). Even if this potential for a midstream increase in agency costs is foreseeable, the discount that the original investors subtract from their purchase price for their shares may be too small, given the delay and the time value of money, to motivate the original promoters to prevent such delayed overreaching.

In addition, because shareholders cannot estimate accurately the degree to which management may misbehave in the future and can seldom judge whether the monitoring controls in place are adequate to minimize the potential for future loss, they face uncertainty and may instead make a judgment about the average agency costs applicable either to public corporations as a whole or to a specific industry. The more uncertainty shareholders face, the less they will pay for their shares. In this light, if the price that rational shareholders pay for their shares is based on the average risk of managerial opportunism, allocational inefficiency results, because both firms with "good" managers and those with "bad" managers will be similarly discounted in the stock market by an average agency cost factor.[84] The result may be that good firms will have too high a cost of capital and bad firms too low a cost.

To summarize: The contemporary debate in this area is between, on the one hand, those who advocate corporate law reforms in the belief that increased regulatory controls or institutional reforms (such as mandatory disclosure or rules requiring the use of independent directors) will reduce agency costs, and those, on the other hand, who reject such reforms on the grounds that agency costs have already been minimized as a result of voluntarily adopted monitoring controls and the incentive effects created by existing management compensation systems.

F. *THE SOCIAL RESPONSIBILITY OF THE CORPORATION*

1. TO WHOM DO FIDUCIARY DUTIES RUN?

A long-standing debate in American corporate law centers on to whom the directors' fiduciary responsibility runs. The traditional assumption of American corporate law has been that managers and directors owe a fiduciary duty only to their shareholders. Thus, in Dodge v. Ford Motor Co.,[85] the Michigan Supreme Court

---

84. For the classic statement of this form of economic analysis, see George Akerlof, The Market for Lemons: Quality Uncertainty and the Market Mechanism, 84 Q.J. Econ. 488 (1970).
85. 204 Mich. 459, 170 N.W. 668 (Mich. 1919).

sternly lectured Henry Ford when he had refused to pay dividends to his shareholders on the apparent grounds that they had already received sufficient profit:
"A business corporation is organized and carried on primarily for the profit of
the stockholders. The powers of the directors are to be employed for that end.
The discretion of directors is to be exercised in the choice of means to attain that
end, and does not extend to a change in the end itself, to the reduction of profits, or
to the nondistribution of profits among stockholders in order to devote them to
other purposes."[86]

But 13 years later, in a famous debate with Columbia Professor Adolf Berle,
Harvard Professor E. Merrick Dodd argued that corporate powers were held in
trust for the entire community. Compare Dodd, For Whom Are Corporate Managers Trustees?, 45 Harv. L. Rev. 1145 (1932), with Berle, For Whom Corporate
Managers Are Trustees: A Note, 45 Harv. L. Rev. 1365 (1932). Dodd's view had
become the consensus position by mid-century, probably in part because professional managers welcomed the idea that they were not wholly responsible to
shareholders and could balance the interests of other constituencies against
shareholder interests. But with the birth of the "law and economics" movement
in the 1960s, a sharp dissent was heard from economists and others who argued
that this view converted managers into unelected civil servants. The following
excerpts give the flavor of this continuing debate.

E. Merrick Dodd, For Whom Are Corporate Managers Trustees?
45 Harv. L. Rev 1145, 1153-1157, 1162-1163 (1932)

If we may believe what some of our business leaders and students of business
tell us, there is in fact a growing feeling not only that business has responsibilities
to the community but that our corporate managers who control business should
voluntarily and without waiting for legal compulsion manage it in such a way
as to fulfill those responsibilities. . . .

The view that those who manage our business corporations should concern
themselves with the interests of employees, consumers, and the general public,
as well as of the stockholders, is thus advanced today by persons whose position in
the business world is such as to give them great power of influencing both business
opinion and public opinion generally. Little or no attempt seems to have been
made, however, to consider how far such an attitude on the part of corporate
managers is compatible with the legal duties which they owe the stockholder-
owners as the elected representatives of the latter.

. . . If the social responsibility of business means merely a more enlightened
view as to the ultimate advantage of the stockholder-owners, then obviously corporate managers may accept such social responsibility without any departure
from the traditional view that their function is to seek to obtain the maximum
amount of profits for their stockholders.

And yet one need not be unduly credulous to feel that there is more to this
talk of social responsibility on the part of corporation managers than merely a
more intelligent appreciation of what tends to the ultimate benefit of their
stockholders. Modern large-scale industry has given to the managers of our

---

86. Henry Ford had openly announced his view that "a sharing [of the profit] with the public,
by reducing the price of the output of the company, ought to be undertaken." Id.

principal corporations enormous power over the welfare of wage earners and consumers, particularly the former. Power over the lives of others tends to create on the part of those most worthy to exercise it a sense of responsibility. The managers, who along with the subordinate employees are part of the group which is contributing to the success of the enterprise by day-to-day efforts, may easily come to feel as strong a community of interest with their fellow workers as with a group of investors whose only connection with the enterprise is that they or their predecessors in title invested money in it, perhaps in the rather remote past. . . .

If we recognize that the attitude of law and public opinion toward business is changing, we may then properly modify our ideas as to the nature of such a business institution as the corporation and hence as to the considerations which may properly influence the conduct of those who direct its activities.

Milton Friedman, The Social Responsibility of Business Is to Increase Its Profits
The New York Times, Sept. 13, 1970 (Magazine at 33)

In a free-enterprise, private-property system, a corporate executive is an employee of the owners of the business. He has direct responsibility to his employers. That responsibility is to conduct the business in accordance with their desires, which generally will be to make as much money as possible while conforming to the basic rules of the society, both those embodied in law and those embodied in ethical custom. . . .

What does it mean to say that the corporate executive has a "social responsibility" in his capacity as businessman? If this statement is not pure rhetoric, it must mean that he is to act in some way that is not in the interest of his employers. For example, that he is to refrain from increasing the price of the product in order to contribute to the social objective of preventing inflation, even though a price increase would be in the best interests of the corporation. Or that he is to make expenditures on reducing pollution beyond the amount that is in the best interests of the corporation or that is required by law in order to contribute to the social objective of improving the environment. Or that, at the expense of corporate profits, he is to hire "hard-core" unemployed instead of better-qualified available workmen to contribute to the social objective of reducing poverty.

In each of these cases, the corporate executive would be spending someone else's money for a general social interest. Insofar as his actions in accord with his "social responsibility" reduce returns to stockholders, he is spending their money. Insofar as his actions raise the price to customers, he is spending the customers' money. Insofar as his actions lower the wages of some employees, he is spending their money.

The stockholders or the customers or the employees could separately spend their own money on the particular action if they wished to do so. The executive is exercising a distinct "social responsibility," rather than serving as an agent of the stockholders or the customers or the employees, only if he spends the money in a different way than they would have spent it.

But if he does this, he is in effect imposing taxes, on the one hand, and deciding how the tax proceeds shall be spent, on the other.

This process raises political questions on two levels: principle and consequences. On the level of political principle, the imposition of taxes and the expenditure of tax proceeds are governmental functions. We have established elaborate constitutional, parliamentary and judicial provisions to control these functions, to assure that taxes are imposed so far as possible in accordance with the preferences and desires of the public. . . .

The whole justification for permitting the corporate executive to be selected by the stockholders is that the executive is an agent serving the interests of his principal. This justification disappears when the corporate executive imposes taxes and spends the proceeds for "social" purposes. He becomes in effect a public employee, a civil servant, even though he remains in name an employee of a private enterprise. On grounds of political principle, it is intolerable that such civil servants — insofar as their actions in the name of social responsibility are real and not just window-dressing — should be selected as they are now. If they are to be civil servants, then they must be selected through a political process. If they are to impose taxes and make expenditures to foster "social" objectives, then political machinery must be set up to guide the assessment of taxes and to determine through a political process the objectives to be served. . . .

On the grounds of consequences, can the corporate executive in fact discharge his alleged "social responsibilities"? On the one hand, suppose he could get away with spending the stockholders' or customers' or employees' money. How is he to know how to spend it? He is told that he must contribute to fighting inflation. How is he to know what action of his will contribute to that end? He is presumably an expert in running his company — in producing a product or selling it or financing it. But nothing about his selection makes him an expert on inflation. Will his holding down the price of his product reduce inflationary pressure? Or, by leaving more spending power in the hands of his customers, simply divert it elsewhere? Or, by forcing him to produce less because of the lower price, will it simply contribute to shortages? Even if he could answer these questions, how much cost is he justified in imposing on his stockholders, customers, and employees for this social purpose? What is his appropriate share and what is the appropriate share of others? . . .

American Law Institute, Principles of Corporate Governance (1994)

Sec. 2.01. *The objective and conduct of the corporation.* (a) . . . [A] corporation should have as its objective the conduct of business activities with a view to enhancing corporate profit and shareholder gain.

(b) Even if corporate profit and shareholder gain are not thereby enhanced, the corporation, in the conduct of its business:

(1) Is obliged, to the same extent as a natural person, to act within the boundaries set by law;

(2) May take into account ethical considerations that are reasonably regarded as appropriate to the responsible conduct of business; and

(3) May devote a reasonable amount of resources to public welfare, humanitarian, educational, and philanthropic purposes.

1. *ALI's middle course.* Under the ALI Principles of Corporate Governance, a Restatement-like effort to codify the common law of fiduciary duties, a corporation must always obey the law and may make "reasonable" charitable contributions even if there is no direct benefit to the corporation. Under the second clause of §2.01(b) above, ethical considerations are only permissive. The corporation may or may not take into account "ethical considerations that are reasonably regarded as appropriate to the responsible conduct of business." Suppose a corporation with annual earnings in the $15 million range has a plant that is losing $4 million a year with no realistic hope of improvement. Deciding to sell the plant, the corporation receives only one bid — from a developer who will close down the plant and lay off all its employees. Can the corporation reject this bid because of the impact on employees? In an illustration using these facts, the ALI concludes that declining the bid "cannot be justified under §2.01(b)(2) because a corporation is not ethically obligated to continue indefinitely losing large amounts of money, equal to more than one fourth of the corporation's earnings, for the purpose of keeping workers employed." 1 ALI, Principles of Corporate Governance 68 (1994). The humanitarian justification under §2.01(b)(3) is also inapplicable, it finds, because the cost of declining the bid is excessive in relation to the corporation's earnings.

The corporate obligation to obey the law has also been the source of debate and controversy. Suppose the management of a bus or trucking company instructs its drivers to drive five miles per hour above the speed limit and the corporation will pay for any resulting fines. Is this decision consistent with management's fiduciary responsibility to obey the law, even if the board concludes (after due deliberation and investigation) that such a practice will result in net savings (after fines and other legal costs) of $500,000 annually? Some economists have argued that the criminal law is only a pricing system and thus those willing to pay the fine can do the crime. On exactly these facts, however, the ALI Principles state that the corporate decisionmakers would be breaching their duty to the corporation. See §2.01, at 62. *Query:* What would be the damages on these facts?

2. *Charitable contributions.* Every state corporation statute authorizes the firm to make charitable contributions. The most common statutory format grants the corporation the "power to make donations for the public welfare or for charitable, scientific or educational purposes."[87] Almost as common is a second format under which the corporation statute first authorizes contributions "furthering the business and affairs of the corporation" and then also authorizes philanthropic donations for charitable, scientific, or educational purposes.[88] Finally, another group of states — including California, New York, and New Jersey — have gone further and enacted statutes authorizing charitable contributions "regardless of specific corporate benefit."[89]

Judicial decisions on the propriety of charitable contributions have been rare, but the modern decisions have uniformly sustained such donations and suggested that the 10 percent ceiling on the deductibility of charitable contributions in §170(b)(2)

87. See Faith Stevelman Kahn, Pandora's Box: Managerial Discretion and the Problem of Corporate Philanthropy, 44 UCLA L. Rev. 579, 602-603 (1997). Delaware follows this format. See Del. Gen. Corp. Law §122(9) (2007).
88. Id. See, e.g., Fla. Bus. Corp. Act §§607.0302(12), (14) (2007); Va. Stock Corp. Act §§13.1627(A)(12), (13) (2007); Wis. Bus. Corp. Law §§180.0302(13), (15) (2006).
89. Id. at 603. See, e.g., Cal. Gen. Corp. Law §207(e) (2007); N.J. Bus. Corp. Act §14A.3-4 (2007); N.Y. Bus. Corp. Law §202(12) (2007). New Jersey (and some other states) also require board of directors approval of charitable contributions.

of the Internal Revenue Code provides a "helpful guide" for determining their reasonableness.[90] Because corporate annual charitable contributions have averaged between 1 and 2 percent of pretax corporate profits,[91] this "guide" implies that few corporations will be subject to attack under such a "reasonableness" test. One area where potential liability may still exist, however, involves the problem of the "pet charity" — i.e., contributions motivated by the personal interests of a chief executive or director, rather than the strategic interests of the firm or a general philanthropic policy.[92]

However settled the law today may be, the rationale for corporate charitable contributions remains debatable. For example, what is the justification for a corporation that does not deal directly with the public (and so needs little institutional advertising) funding the cost of a public television program or a documentary unrelated to its business or concerns? Some argue that the corporation should instead pay a dividend and let those shareholders who wish to make individual contributions do so.[93]

One possible answer to this argument focuses on the interests of shareholders in collective giving. Charities and similar eleemosynary institutions provide public goods that many in society benefit from and that few can be excluded from consuming (even if they do not contribute). Inevitably, such institutions face a "free rider" problem: Those who do not contribute can still watch the TV documentary, attend the museum, or listen to the subsidized concert. Also, many may not contribute because they feel their individual contribution will make little difference in the charity's overall budget and they may resent the fact that others who are similarly situated probably will not contribute. The standard answer to free rider problems is to find a mechanism that taxes the free rider. Charitable contributions by large corporations (AT&T, IBM, GM) having a million or more shareholders may be a partial answer to this problem. In effect, all shareholders are taxed proportionately. Moreover, there are tax advantages to the corporation's making the payment instead of paying a dividend (as the amount of the dividend would be taxable income both to the corporation and to the shareholders receiving it). Finally, a large corporation may be better able than individual shareholders to negotiate with the charity about how its contribution will be used, thus introducing some monitoring controls over the charity's behavior.

3. *Problems of externalities.* Virtually everyone recognizes that corporate profit maximization can sometimes inflict a greater harm on society than the gain it

90. See Kahn v. Sullivan, 594 A.2d 48, 61 (Del. 1991) (the test to be applied in examining the merits of a claim that a charitable contribution amounted to corporate waste "is that of reasonableness, a test in which the provisions of the Internal Revenue Code pertaining to charitable gifts by corporations furnish a helpful guide"). See also Theodora Holding Corp. v. Henderson, 257 A.2d 398 (Del. Ch. 1969). Perhaps the best-known and most influential case in this field is A. P. Smith Mfg. Co. v. Barlow, 98 A.2d 581 (N.J. 1953), which rejected the need for any corporate benefit or nexus requirement.

91. See Giving USA Foundation, Giving USA 2007: The Annual Report on Philanthropy for the Year 2006. In 2006 corporate donations to charitable purposes came to $12.3 billion.

92. See Jayne W. Barnard, Corporate Philanthropy, Executives' Pet Charities and the Agency Problem, 41 N.Y.L. Sch. L. Rev. 1147 (1997) (discussing numerous examples and concluding that the primary remedy should be greater board activism and a more detailed board policy toward charitable contributions).

93. For the provocative recent suggestion that shareholders should choose the recipients of corporate charity, see Victor Brudney & Allen Ferrell, Corporate Charitable Giving, 69 U. Chi. L. Rev. 1191 (2002). For a rebuttal, see Richard W. Painter, Corporate Speech and Citizenship: Commentary on Brudney and Ferrell, 69 U. Chi. L. Rev. 1219 (2002).

creates for shareholders. Pollution is an obvious example. Hard-boiled proponents of profit maximization argue that it is up to society to establish penalties and incentives that make such behavior truly contrary to the corporation's interests. Proponents of a broader definition of corporate social responsibility respond that external regulation of the corporation will always prove imperfect. See Elliott Weiss, Social Regulation of Business Activity: Reforming the Corporate Governance System to Resolve an Institutional Impasse, 28 UCLA L. Rev. 343 (1981). Thus, they argue for an activist approach and would tolerate substantial inroads into the norm of profit maximization. The ALI Principles take an intermediate position, tolerating (but never requiring) deviations that are "reasonably regarded as appropriate to the responsible conduct of business." This approach, which uses a societal consensus standard, can also be justified on the ground that the market expects such behavior (whatever the formal legal standard). Hence, there is little uncertainty created in the capital markets.

A similar perspective begins from the starting point that most shareholders own a portfolio of securities, not just stock in one company. Thus, even their narrow economic self-interest is broader than the fate of a single company and arguably is more closely linked with preserving a healthy, efficient capitalist system.

For an introduction to the extended literature on the topic of corporate social responsibility, see Melvin Eisenberg, Corporate Conduct That Does Not Maximize Shareholder Gain: Legal Conduct, Ethical Conduct, the Penumbra Effect, Reciprocity, the Prisoner's Dilemma, Sheep's Clothing, Social Conduct and Disclosure, 28 Stetson L. Rev. 1 (1998); David Engle, An Approach to Corporate Social Responsibility, 32 Stan. L. Rev. 1 (1979); Edward Epstein, Societal, Managerial and Legal Perspectives on Corporate Social Responsibility — Product and Process, 30 Hastings L.J. 1287 (1979); Phillip Blumberg, Corporate Responsibility in a Changing Society (1972).

2. THE RISE OF CORPORATE CONSTITUENCY STATUTES

Since the early 1980s, the majority of the states have enacted statutes instructing directors that they either may or must take into account the interests of constituencies other than shareholders in exercising their powers.[94] Most of these statutes are merely discretionary, permitting but not requiring directors to consider the interests of employees, creditors, local communities, or other constituencies. A few statutes (including Connecticut's statute quoted below) appear to go further and mandate that directors must consider non-shareholder interests. Many of these statutes apply only to corporate control transactions (mergers, tender offers, buyouts, etc.). Others are generally applicable. Either way, it is clear that the driving force behind the adoption of these statutes was the heightened threat of hostile takeovers, which increased in frequency and scale during the 1980s. In response, managements of potential target companies sought state legislation

---

94. These states include Arizona, Connecticut, Florida, Georgia, Hawaii, Idaho, Illinois, Indiana, Iowa, Kentucky, Louisiana, Maine, Massachusetts, Minnesota, Mississippi, Missouri, New Jersey, New Mexico, New York, Ohio, Oregon, Pennsylvania, Rhode Island, South Dakota, Tennessee, Virginia, Wisconsin, and Wyoming. For good overviews, see Eric Orts, Beyond Shareholders: Interpreting Corporate Constituency Statutes, 61 Geo. Wash. L. Rev. 14 (1992); and Jonathan D. Springer, Corporate Constituency Statutes: Hollow Hopes and False Fears, 1999 Ann. Surv. Am. L. 85 (1999).

that would expand their discretion to consider employee, creditor, and other interests in justifying resistance to a hostile tender offer for their company's shares. Constituency statutes were also a response to the 1986 decision of the Delaware Supreme Court in Revlon, Inc. v. MacAndrews & Forbes Holdings, Inc. (page 993 infra), which seemed to require directors to consider only the interests of shareholders once a sale of the company had become "inevitable."

Although the passage of constituency statutes in a majority of the states is certainly a significant development, it is also noteworthy that a significant number of the states (including Delaware) have not enacted such legislation (and Nebraska repealed its constituency statute in 1995). Even where enacted, it is often unclear what the impact will be on the preexisting common law on directors' duties. Set forth below are two constituency statutes illustrating some of the possible variations.

New York Business Corporation Law (1992)

Sec. 717. *Duty of directors.* . . . (b) In taking action, including, without limitation, action which may involve or relate to a change or potential change in the control of the corporation, a director shall be entitled to consider, without limitation, (1) both the long-term and the short-term interests of the corporation and its shareholders, and (2) the effects that the corporation's actions may have in the short-term or in the long-term upon any of the following:

(i) the prospects for potential growth, development, productivity and profitability of the corporation;

(ii) the corporation's current employees;

(iii) the corporation's retired employees and other beneficiaries receiving or entitled to receive retirement, welfare or similar benefits from or pursuant to any plan sponsored, or agreement entered into, by the corporation;

(iv) the corporation's customers and creditors; and

(v) the ability of the corporation to provide, as a going concern, goods, services, employment opportunities and employment benefits and otherwise to contribute to the communities in which it does business.

Nothing in this paragraph shall create any duties owed by any director to any person or entity to consider or afford any particular weight to any of the foregoing or abrogate any duty of the directors, either statutory or recognized by common law or court decisions.

For purposes of this paragraph, "control" shall mean the possession, directly or indirectly, of the power to direct or cause the direction of the management and policies of the corporation, whether through the ownership of voting stock, by contract, or otherwise.

New York's statute makes it clear that non-shareholder groups have no standing to sue the directors if their interests have not been adequately taken into account. Is this a conceptually defensible compromise? Or does the lack of any enforcement mechanism suggest that the real purpose and effect of the statute are simply to protect target managements? Alternatively, what would be the consequence if these groups were given standing to sue?

Connecticut Business Corporation Law (1997)

Sec. 33-756. *Board of directors.* . . . (d) . . . [A] director of a corporation which . . . [is publicly held] . . . shall consider, in determining what he reasonably believes to be in the best interests of the corporation, (1) the long-term as well as the short-term interests of the corporation, (2) the interests of the shareholders, long-term as well as short-term, including the possibility that those interests may be best served by the continued independence of the corporation, (3) the interests of the corporation's employees, customers, creditors and suppliers, and (4) community and societal considerations including those of any community in which any office or other facility of the corporation is located. A director may also in his discretion consider any other factors he reasonably considers appropriate in determining what he reasonably believes to be in the best interests of the corporation.

Although the Connecticut statute states that a "director . . . shall consider" the interests of other non-shareholder constituencies, is it really a mandate? May creditors bring an action under this statute if a Connecticut corporation becomes insolvent after undertaking a risky business project? May employees claim that insufficient attention was given to their interests in the wake of layoffs? Are directors exposed to an excessive risk of litigation if they must be legally responsible to groups with typically conflicting interests?

3. OBJECTIONS TO CONSTITUENCY STATUTES

The appearance of constituency statutes has alarmed many commentators, including the Corporate Laws Committee of the American Bar Association. Typically four arguments have been raised against such statutes.

(1) Fiduciary duties should run only to the shareholders because they, as the firm's residual claimants who receive what is left over after creditors and other fixed-interest claimants are paid, have the greatest incentive to maximize corporate value and thus to realize economic efficiency. In contrast, creditors have a more risk-averse attitude toward corporate decisionmaking because of the more limited payoff to which they are entitled. Hence, it is argued, if fiduciary duties are owed to creditors, the directors will be made responsible to a group that will predictably oppose efficient risk taking.

(2) Corporate directors should not be asked to serve "too many masters." Serving principals with conflicting interests may expose the agent to excessive liability. Conversely, if directors are made responsible to all groups having an economic interest in the corporation, they may become effectively responsible to none.

(3) Constituency statutes convert directors into "unelected civil servants," with a responsibility for determining the public interest. Arguably, they lack the training, experience, diversity, and, perhaps, sensitivity to play this role effectively.

(4) Groups other than shareholders can negotiate contractual protections (and thus do not need fiduciary protections), but shareholders face severe contracting problems because of their need to protect their more amorphous residual right to

everything that is left over; thus, they uniquely need a fiduciary duty running only to them.[95]

American Bar Association Committee on Corporate Laws, Report: Other Constituencies Statutes: Potential for Confusion
45 Bus. Law. 2253 (1990)

. . . [C]onstituency statutes have typically been adopted as one measure, among others, designed to assist directors in forestalling unwanted takeovers. However, they address a question that is of much broader significance in corporate law and to society in general: whose interests should a corporation serve? The issues posed by this question are:

(1) whether the corporation has some responsibility to employees, communities, and the others enumerated in other constituency statutes;

(2) if so, how these thus far legally unenforceable responsibilities (except when they are created by contract, e.g., employment agreements, or specific statute, e.g., laws imposing environmental obligations) are to be meshed with the legally enforceable obligations of directors to shareholders; and

(3) whether the board of directors should have the power or the duty to prefer the interests of those constituencies over the interests of shareholders in some circumstances. . . .

Historical Background. A recurring debate concerning corporations and their role in American life has centered on the persons to whom corporations owe a duty and have accountability, and whose interests the management and directors of a corporation may or must serve. In the early 1930s, Professor E. Merrick Dodd of Harvard Law School and Professor Adolf A. Berle of Columbia Law School engaged in a classic debate on this subject in the pages of the Harvard Law Review. Dodd asserted that public opinion increasingly viewed the corporation as an "economic institution which has a social service as well as a profit-making function."[96]

Professor Berle took strong exception to this viewpoint. While sympathizing with the idealism of Professor Dodd and suggesting that the law might be moving in the direction of recognizing the claims of groups other than shareholders, he repudiated the notion that the management of corporations should have responsibilities beyond the interests of the shareholders. He concluded: "Unchecked by present legal balances, a social-economic absolutism of corporate administrators, even if benevolent, might be unsafe; and in any case it hardly affords the soundest base on which to construct the economic commonwealth which industrialism seems to require."[97]

This view has prevailed to the present. With few exceptions, courts have consistently avowed the legal primacy of shareholder interests when management and directors make decisions. This conventional wisdom has not, of course, prevented courts from permitting on various grounds the limited use of corporate

---

95. These arguments are incisively made (and criticized) in Jonathan Macey, An Economic Analysis of the Various Rationales for Making Shareholders the Exclusive Beneficiaries of Corporate Fiduciary Duties, 21 Stetson L. Rev. 23 (1991).

96. Dodd, For Whom Are Corporate Managers Trustees?, 45 Harv. L. Rev. 1145, 1148 (1932).

97. Berle, For Whom Corporate Managers Are Trustees: A Note, 45 Harv. L. Rev. 1365, 1372 (1932). . . .

resources for eleemosynary and other non-profit oriented purposes; usually the conceptual justification has been the long-range interest of the corporation (and therefore the shareholders). . . .

The issue then becomes whether state corporation laws, and, in particular, a broadening of the interests that directors may consider, constitute an efficient and desirable way to provide protections for non-shareholder groups. The Committee has concluded that permitting — much less requiring — directors to consider these interests without relating such consideration in an appropriate fashion to shareholder welfare (as the Delaware courts have done) would conflict with directors' responsibility to shareholders and could undermine the effectiveness of the system that has made the corporation an efficient device for the creation of jobs and wealth.

The Committee believes that the better interpretation of these statutes, and one that avoids such consequences, is that they confirm what the common law has been: directors may take into account the interests of other constituencies but only as and to the extent that the directors are acting in the best interests, long as well as short term, of the shareholders and the corporation. While the Delaware courts have related the consideration directors may give other constituencies to the interests of shareholders by stating there must be "rationally related benefits to shareholders," it may well be that other courts may choose other words with which to express the nexus.

While legislatures may not have intended it, adding other constituencies provisions to state corporation laws may have ramifications that go far beyond a simple enumeration of the other interests directors may recognize in discharging their duties. Directors might have a duty to oppose a transaction with whatever means are available because it would have a demonstrably adverse impact upon one or more of the constituencies (e.g., the acquirer plans to move the headquarters from the small town in which the company had been rooted for decades resulting in community disruption and loss of jobs). Or directors might be called upon to decide how much of the premium over market price being paid in an acceptable transaction should be allocated among the various constituencies (e.g., how much should accrue to communities in which plants might be closed; how much should be allocated to the terminated hourly employees; and how much should be allocated to a supplier who might lose his market).

The confusion of directors in trying to comply with such statutes, if interpreted to require directors to balance the interests of various constituencies without according primacy to shareholder interests, would be profoundly troubling. Even under existing law, particularly where directors must act quickly, it is often difficult for directors acting in good faith to divine what is in the best interests of shareholders and the corporation. If directors are required to consider other interests as well, the decision-making process will become a balancing act or search for compromise. When directors must not only decide what their duty of loyalty mandates, but also to whom their duty of loyalty runs (and in what proportions), poorer decisions can be expected.

If directors have, or may have, recognized legal duties to other constituencies, perhaps a new class or classes of plaintiffs will have access to the courts to redress perceived breaches of those duties or to challenge directors' failures to take various competing interests into account. An interpretation of these statutes to the effect that directors owe enforceable duties to constituencies other than shareholders would signal a major shift in the premises underlying traditional corporation law and might deter suitable candidates from undertaking board responsibilities.

Furthermore, an articulation of a director's duties that extended them to other constituencies without primacy being accorded shareholder interests would diminish the ability of shareholders to monitor appropriately the conduct of directors. Dean Robert C. Clark has said, "[a] single objective goal like profit maximization is more easily monitored than a multiple, vaguely defined goal like the fair and reasonable accommodation of all affected interests. . . . Assuming shareholders have some control mechanisms, better monitoring means that corporate managers will be kept more accountable. They are more likely do to what they are supposed to do and do it efficiently. . . ."[98]

Conclusion. In conclusion, the Committee believes that other constituencies statutes are not an appropriate way to regulate corporate relationships or to respond to unwanted takeovers and that an expansive interpretation of the other constituencies statutes cast in the permissive mode is both unnecessary and unwise. Those statutes that merely empower directors to consider the interests of other constituencies are best taken as a legislative affirmation of what courts would be expected to hold, in the absence of a statute. . . .

4. THE CASE FOR CONSTITUENCY STATUTES

Although the ABA position paper argues that constituency statutes should be given a very thin reading that does not significantly change the prior common law, some scholars (although probably a minority) believe that constituency statutes represent a major, desirable, and overdue transition in the focus of corporate law. Professor Lawrence Mitchell argues that these statutes shift the focus of corporate law from shareholder wealth maximization to social wealth maximization.[96] Professor Mitchell doubts that shareholders necessarily deserve a priority in the directors' consideration, because, in his judgment, the cost of business decisions to communities, workers, and note holders often outweighs the gains to the shareholders. Constituency statutes allow directors to focus more broadly on the overall impact of corporate action without exposing themselves to additional liability. Accountability to none will not be the result, he argues, because directors will still, as a practical matter, give greater attention to shareholder interests because of their voting power. Directors, however, will become more open about their concerns for the interests of other constituency groups.

Similarly, Professor Marleen O'Connor has argued that other constituencies should have standing to enforce their rights under these statutes and would read them "as a foundation for judicial intervention to ameliorate the impact corporate restructuring, plant closings and layoffs have on employees."[97] *Query:* If a

98. Robert C. Clark, Corporate Law 20 (1986).
96. See Lawrence Mitchell, A Theoretical and Practical Framework for Enforcing Corporate Constituency Statutes, 70 Tex. L. Rev. 579 (1992).
97. See Marleen O'Connor, Restructuring the Corporation's Nexus of Contracts: Recognizing a Fiduciary Duty to Protect Displaced Workers, 69 N.C. L. Rev. 1189, 1190 (1991). For similar arguments, see Timothy L. Fort, Corporate Constituency Statutes: A Dialectical Interpretation, 15 J.L. & Com. 257, 292 (1995) ("Stakeholder/corporate constituency analysis asks the right question of what duties corporations owe to non-shareholder constituencies. As creatures obtaining social benefits in the form of limited liability and other corporate features, corporations have duties to members of society.").

corporate constituency statute makes directors less responsive to the interests of shareholders and reduces the economic return on the shareholders' investment in the corporation, should this be seen as a "taking," for which shareholders are entitled to just compensation under the Fifth Amendment?[98] Or can such a change in legal standards be justified under the "reserved power" clause that the *Dartmouth College* case, page 21 supra, caused states to insert into their corporation statutes?

Whatever the theoretical arguments about their merit, the actual impact of constituency statutes has been modest to date in the judgment of virtually all commentators. Relatively few cases have litigated their meaning, and even fewer have sought to apply them outside the context of takeover defenses.[99]

5. THE JUDICIAL DEVELOPMENT OF NON-SHAREHOLDER FIDUCIARY DUTIES

Although the Delaware legislature has not adopted a constituency statute, the Delaware courts have recently debated whether under some limited circumstances directors may have to consider creditor interests on at least an equal footing with those of shareholders. This issue of the creditor's right to the director's fiduciary duty has also been litigated in other jurisdictions over the last decade.[100] These cases are an extension of the "trust fund" doctrine that originated in Wood v. Drummer, page 22 supra, and under them a fiduciary duty extending to creditors arises at some point when the corporation nears insolvency.

Many of these cases have involved egregious facts in which the dominant shareholder simply distributes the firm's assets to itself on the eve of insolvency; in these cases, the creditors are simply suing for recovery of the fraudulently converted assets. However, in a well-known recent decision, Credit Lyonnais Bank Nederland, N.V. v. Pathe Communications Corporation,[101] the issue was the level of business risk that a nearly insolvent firm should be permitted to accept. The 98 percent shareholder of a nearly insolvent corporation (MGM, the movie studio) alleged that the firm's management and its chief creditor had injured the shareholder by refusing to allow the company to undertake a high-risk strategy that the shareholder favored. In whose interests did the corporation's officers have to manage the firm, the creditors or the shareholders? In *Credit Lyonnais*, Chancellor Allen explained that the directors had behaved properly in rejecting the

---

98. For an affirmative answer to this question, see Lynda J. Oswald, Shareholders v. Stakeholders: Evaluating Corporate Constituency Statutes Under the Takings Clause, 24 J. Corp. L. 1 (1998).

99. In Basswood Partners v. NSS Bancorp, Inc., 1998 Conn. Super LEXIS 317 (Feb. 6, 1998), a minority shareholder in NSS Bancorp sought access to that corporation's shareholders list in order to communicate with other shareholders regarding the company's poor financial record. Defendant NSS claimed that it need not grant access to the shareholder list and invoked Connecticut's above-quoted constituency statute to justify its refusal, because it sensed a hostile bid might be forthcoming. Nonetheless, the court held for plaintiff Basswood Partners, finding that "the obligations imposed on a director by [the Connecticut constituency statute] do not restrict the rights of a shareholder under [state laws granting shareholder access to corporate books and records]." Id. at *7. Virtually every other reported decision citing these statutes has involved a clear takeover defense. See, e.g., Baron v. Strawbridge, 646 F. Supp. 690 (E.D. Pa. 1986); Amanda Acquisition Corp. v. Universal Foods Corp., 708 F. Supp. 984 (E.D. Wis. 1989), *aff'd on other grounds*, 877 F.2d 496 (7th Cir. 1989).

100. See, e.g., Clarkson Co. Ltd. v. Shaheen, 660 F.2d 506 (2d Cir. 1981); Federal Deposit Insurance Corp. v. Sea Pines Co., 692 F.2d 973 (4th Cir. 1982).

101. 1991 Del. Ch. LEXIS 215, 1991 W.L. 277613 (Del. Ch. 1991).

riskier (but legal) course of action favored by the shareholders, holding that "[a]t least where a corporation is operating in the vicinity of insolvency, a board of directors is not merely the agent of the residual risk bearer, but owes a duty to the corporate enterprise." Then, in a much discussed footnote, Allen analyzed the potentially perverse incentives of shareholders to accept extreme risk as the company nears insolvency (this example is set forth and analyzed in Chapter III infra at pages 230-232).

The basic idea underlying Chancellor Allen's analysis is that shareholders who have nothing to lose will take high-risk gambles with the firm's assets that may be economically inefficient. In such a context, shareholders could rationally decide to accept a negative net present value investment, because most of the risk will fall on creditors. Thus, they might expend the corporation's last $1 million on an investment that had a total expected value of only $500,000, because it included a 1 percent chance of a payoff of $10 million (which would keep the firm solvent and preserve their investment). Although the *Credit Lyonnais* decision actually shielded directors from liability, its seeming implication was that investment decisions appropriate for a solvent firm could constitute a breach of the directors' duties once the firm entered the vaguely defined "vicinity of insolvency."

The *Credit Lyonnais* decision (and the increased rate of corporate insolvencies after the highly leveraged financing of the 1980s) produced an outpouring of academic writing, which divided sharply over both the feasibility and desirability of Chancellor Allen's view that the board might owe a "duty to the corporate enterprise" once the firm entered into the "vicinity of insolvency."[102] One later Delaware decision seemingly imposed such a duty to creditors, based on the familiar trust fund concept, once the firm became insolvent. In Geyer v. Ingersoll Publications Co.,[103] the narrow issue was when this duty to creditors arose — as of the moment of insolvency or later, when bankruptcy ensued? Defendants claimed that a duty owed directly to creditors arose only once a petition in bankruptcy was filed. No other bright lines were available, they argued, to "give directors a clear and objective indication as to when their duties to creditors arise." Refusing to limit the legal definition of insolvency in this way, Vice Chancellor Chandler found that the duty to creditors arose as of the actual moment of insolvency. Policy reasons, he said, inclined him to this result:

> . . . [T]here are other policy concerns which suggest that I interpret the insolvency exception to arise when insolvency exists in fact. That is, it is efficient and fair to cause the insolvency exception to arise at the moment of insolvency in fact rather than waiting for the institution of statutory proceedings. See Credit Lyonnais Nederland, N.V. v. Pathe Communications Corp. . . . The existence of the fiduciary duties at the moment of insolvency rather than the institution of statutory proceedings prevents creditors from having to prophesy when directors are entering into transactions that would render the entity insolvent and improperly prejudice creditors' interests.

---

102. Compare Rutherford Campbell Jr. & Christopher W. Frost, Managers' Fiduciary Duties in Financially Distressed Corporations: Chaos in Delaware (and Elsewhere), 32 J. Corp. L. 491 (2007); Laura Lin, Shift of Fiduciary Duty upon Corporate Insolvency: Proper Scope of Directors' Duty to Creditors, 46 Vand. L. Rev. 1485 (1993); Lynn LoPucki & William Witford, Corporate Governance in the Bankruptcy Reorganization of Large, Publicly Held Companies, 141 U. Pa. L. Rev. 669 (1993), with C. Robert Morris, Directors' Duties in Nearly Insolvent Corporations: A Comment on Credit Lyonnais, 19 J. Corp. L. 61 (1993).

103. 621 A.2d 784 (Del. Ch. 1992).

In 2007 the Delaware Supreme Court pulled back from the "zone of insolvency." In North American Catholic Educational Programming Foundation, Inc. v. Gheewalla,[104] the Court was faced with a creditor who had sued the directors of a corporation that had obtained financing from it at a time when the distressed corporation was in the "zone of insolvency." The plaintiff claimed that the directors, who were agents of a major investment banking firm, knew that their corporation was near insolvency and thus were unwilling to cause their investment bank to advance further funds to it. Accepting that the corporation was within this hard-to-define "zone of insolvency," the Delaware Supreme Court ruled, first, that creditors could not assert a direct claim for breach of fiduciary duty against corporate directors, and, second, that they also could not bring a derivative action on these facts. It said, "When a solvent corporation is navigating in the zone of insolvency, the focus for Delaware directors does not change: directors must continue to discharge their fiduciary duties to the corporation and its shareholders by exercising their business judgment in the best interests of the corporation for the benefit of its shareholder owners."[105]

Basically, the Court reached the judgment that creditors should rely on privately negotiated agreements in their debt contract. Even if the corporation later became insolvent, it added, a direct action could not be brought by creditors. However, the Delaware Supreme Court did find that "[w]hen a corporation is *insolvent*, however, its creditors take the place of the shareholders as the residual beneficiaries of any increase in value. Consequently, the creditors of an *insolvent* corporation have standing to maintain derivative claims against directors on behalf of the corporation for breaches of fiduciary duties."[106]

Although this decision cut back on *Credit Lyonnais*'s seeming broad rule, should directors feel comfortable based on it when operating near insolvency? Remember that the definition of insolvency involves a murky attempt to measure assets and liabilities on a seemingly daily basis, and once a corporation goes over the insolvency line, the directors' fiduciary duties are owed to creditors.

Other jurisdictions have also divided over this issue of when a fiduciary duty to creditors arises. In In re Mortgage America Corp., 714 F.2d 1266, 1271 (5th Cir. 1983), such a duty was said to arise when the corporation could "no longer be considered a true going concern" — a point arguably well after insolvency in the usual sense. But see Saracco Tank & Welding Co. v. Platz, 65 Cal. App. 2d 306, 150 P.2d 918 (1944) (duty arises as of moment of insolvency). No other jurisdiction, however, seems to have used the "zone of insolvency" test.

G. *THE GLOBAL PERSPECTIVE*

The key features in American corporate governance — fragmented share ownership, a resulting separation of ownership and control, and the substantial reliance on independent directors as monitoring agents — are not necessarily standard in other developed economies. Nor are other corporate systems necessarily evolving

---

104. 2007 Del. LEXIS 227 (2007).
105. Id. at *25.
106. Id. at *26.

in the direction of the United States. Indeed, both Japan and Germany provide striking contrasts. Among the leading differences there are the following.

1. *Concentrated ownership and bank-centered monitoring systems.* Concentrated ownership remains very much the norm in Europe. For example, more than 50 percent of the publicly traded, nonfinancial corporations in Austria, Belgium, Germany, and Italy have a single control block that holds a majority of the voting rights in the company. This contrasts with the United States and the United Kingdom, where only about 3 percent of the publicly traded companies have such single control blocks.[107] Often, control over the voting rights results from the use of a "dual class" capitalization, under which the corporation has two (or more) classes of stock, one of which has greater voting rights than the other. Other techniques are also used to maintain control, including pyramid holding structures under which a parent corporation owns 51 percent of a subsidiary, which in turn owns 51 percent of another subsidiary (and so on), so that only a small amount of equity can control the large company at the base of this pyramid.

Finally, in some European countries, the principal lending bank often holds voting control. In Germany, for example the banks' voting power comes both from direct ownership of stock and, more important, from serving as a custodian for individual shareholders. German banks act as brokers for their clients; individual investors deposit their stock with the bank, which exercises voting power over these custodial shares. Generally, no single German bank controls an industrial firm, but the three German universal banks can usually dominate the vote for shareholder-elected directors on the corporation's supervisory board. In addition, bank nominees usually serve on the supervisory board. As a result, an underperforming CEO of a large German corporation may face a virtually permanent coalition of two or three banks that are in a position to replace the CEO, while an American CEO will face a more impersonal market characterized by high shareholder turnover and thus be less able to form a coalition of institutional investors quickly. Thus, although European companies do not face the same takeover threat that U.S. and U.K. companies do, European commentators have argued that bank-centered control could provide more active monitoring of corporate management than institutional investors furnish in the United States or the United Kingdom. More recent scholarship has, however, cast doubt on this theory of active bank monitoring.[108] An alternative possibility is that banks may use their position on the board to extract private benefits for themselves as creditors.

The level of shareholder concentration in Japan is nearly as high as in Germany, but has a novel twist: extensive cross-ownership characterizes the Japanese

---

107. For these statistics, see Marco Becht & Colin Mayer, "The Control of Corporate Europe" in The Control of Corporate Europe (Fabrizio Barca & Marco Becht eds., 2002). They similarly report that in more than 50 percent of the nonfinancial, listed companies in the Netherlands, France, Spain, and Sweden, a single control block holds 43.5 percent, 20 percent, 34.5 percent, and 34.9 percent of the voting rights, respectively. See also Luca Enriques and Paolo Volpin, Corporate Governance Reforms in Continental Europe, 21 J. Econ. Persp. 117, 119 (Winter 2007) (setting forth ownership concentration data by country); Mark Roe, Some Differences in Corporate Structure in Germany, Japan, and the United States, 102 Yale L.J. 1927, 1938 (1993).

108. Empirical research finds only limited evidence that German banks do in fact monitor German managements more actively than American or British institutional investors monitor the managements of their companies. For a skeptical assessment, see Jeremy Edwards & Klaus Fisher, Banks, Finance, and Investment in Germany (1994). For the latest research, finding that bank-influenced firms neither have lower finance costs nor are more profitable, see Robert S. Chirinko & Julie Ann Elston, Finance, Control and Profitability: The Influence of German Banks, 59 J. Econ. Behav. & Org. 69 (2006).

corporate governance system.[109] Large Japanese firms usually are members of a *keiretsu*, a grouping of corporations and financial institutions that own some of each other's stock. No single firm is likely to own more than 5 percent of another member firm's stock, but the aggregate ownership by all keiretsu members in any member firm's stock is likely to total around 50 percent. At the center of this network is a main bank, which provides loans and credit to the industrial firms in the keiretsu and typically owns 5 percent of the stock in each major firm in the group as well. These industrial firms in turn own stock in the main bank. Although this cross-ownership structure makes each member of the keiretsu effectively takeover-proof, the relationship between keiretsu members involves much more than protection from corporate control fights. Keiretsu members are typically the largest customers for, and suppliers of goods and services to, each other. If a keiretsu member needs to buy insurance, electronics, or raw steel, it will likely look to other member firms first. The main bank serves not only as the primary lender, but also as a virtual guarantor to other creditors that a keiretsu member will not become bankrupt. In part because of this responsibility, the main bank effectively acts as a delegated monitor that supervises the performance of management at each member firm, on behalf of both the keiretsu and other creditors. Sometimes it will supply management assistance to a troubled firm, lending its employees as temporary officers.

Theorists have suggested that the Japanese form of industrial organization is more than a system of monitoring, but also serves to support production and exchange among interlocked customers and suppliers.[110] That is, the cross-ownership helps to align the interests of customer and supplier, because each has less of an incentive to overreach the other when it owns a substantial equity stake in the other (and is in turn partially owned by the other). Such cross-ownership may also facilitate joint long-term planning and integration of operations.

2. *Financial intermediaries.* Why hasn't a similar system of concentrated ownership evolved in the United States? One major reason involves the difference in scale of financial institutions in these developed industrial economies compared with those in the United States. At the close of the twentieth century, the three largest German banks had assets equal to 36 percent of Germany's gross national product (GNP), while the three largest U.S. banks had assets equal to only 7 percent of American GNP. Even in absolute numbers, the difference is extraordinary. The tenth largest Japanese bank then held greater assets than the largest American bank.[111] Why? Many believe that U.S. banking regulation combined with the federal structure of U.S. government has fragmented financial intermediaries in the United States. Historically, national banks in the United States were confined to a single location, and the McFadden Act of 1927 liberalized this restriction only to the extent of allowing branches of national banks to cross state lines with the permission of each host state.[112] Until its repeal in late 1999, the Glass-Steagall Act precluded banks from entering the securities business (thereby ensuring that they will be smaller than their European and Japanese competitors).[113] Similarly, the Bank Holding Company Act used to prohibit banks from owning through affiliates more than 5 percent of a

---

109. See Ronald Gilson & Mark Roe, Understanding the Japanese Keiretsu: Overlaps Between Corporate Governance and Industrial Organization, 102 Yale L.J. 871 (1993).
110. See Gilson & Roe, footnote 109 supra.
111. See Roe, footnote 107 supra, at 1946-1947.
112. See McFadden Act, 44 Stat. 1224 (1927), codified, as amended, as 12 U.S.C. §36 (1997).
113. Act of June 16, 1933, ch. 89, 48 Stat. 162, codified in various sections of 12 U.S.C.

non-bank's voting stock.[114] In the wake of these legislative revisions, a new level of financial concentration appears to be emerging in the United States.

These restrictions were not accidental. There is a long tradition in American political life, dating back to Thomas Jefferson and Andrew Jackson, that has distrusted powerful financial institutions (banks in particular). Preventing the growth of national banks was a popular theme during the Progressive Era, when the perceived power of J. P. Morgan and Wall Street was a rallying cry for populist sentiment in rural and small-town America.

Although it seems likely that political restrictions constrained American financial institutions from assuming the monitoring role that they perform in some other developed economies, it does not necessarily follow that bank-centered systems of corporate governance are more efficient. Commercial banks as dominant shareholders have obvious conflicts of interest. When they possess voting power, they may use it not simply to promote efficiency, but to exact above-market interest rates on their loans to the corporation or other special preferences. The extent of such practices has long been debated in Germany and Japan. Also, with the growth of international financial markets, there is evidence that the linkage between corporations and their "universal" banks in Germany and their main banks in Japan is breaking down (as corporations find they can obtain cheaper financing elsewhere). Nor can it be assumed that, in the absence of regulation, American financial institutions would become concentrated block holders in American corporations. British banks, for example, play a relatively passive role in British corporate governance, even though they are not restricted as to stock ownership.[115] The desire for liquidity and the need for portfolio diversification would probably restrain most institutional investors from holding large blocks above 10 percent, even in the absence of more restrictive regulation. Finally, if the proof of a corporate governance system's success is the relative productivity and profitability of its national economy, the United States has not lagged behind either Japan or Germany over the long run.[116] Each of these alternative governance systems may in fact work comparatively well in the context of its own national environment, historical evolution, and cultural tradition.

The sharp disparity between the characteristic structure of share ownership in the Anglo-American common law environment (i.e., highly dispersed with relatively weak financial intermediaries) and that in the European civil law environment (i.e., concentrated ownership with strong block holders) has produced two rival interpretations. First, beginning in the early 1990s, legal commentators hypothesized that the relatively small scale of financial intermediaries in the United States was the product of political constraints on the U.S. marketplace, which grew out of a U.S. populist tradition of strong skepticism toward concentrated financial power.[117] Because financial intermediaries were forced into a

---

114. This prohibition was formerly contained in 12 U.S.C. §1843(a)(1) (1988).

115. See Bernard Black & John Coffee, Hail Britannia: Institutional Investor Behavior Under Limited Regulation, 92 Mich. L. Rev. 1997 (1994) (finding that British institutional investors play a more active role than those in the United States, but are still constrained by the need for stock market liquidity from holding concentrated blocks).

116. Roberta Romano, A Cautionary Note on Drawing Lessons From Comparative Corporate Law, 102 Yale L.J. 2021 (1993).

117. See Mark J. Roe, Strong Managers, Weak Owners: The Political Roots of American Corporate Finance (1994); John Pound, The Rise of the Political Model of Corporate Governance and Corporate Control, 68 N.Y.U. L. Rev. 1003 (1993).

relatively passive role by these constraints, corporate managers, it was argued, were strengthened and given inefficiently broad discretionary powers. More recently, a rival interpretation has been offered by economists who view dispersed share ownership as the product of common law legal systems, which provide significantly stronger legal protections for minority shareholders than do civil law systems.[118] In this view, dispersed ownership is the consequence not of political constraints on the marketplace, but of more protective legal systems that encourage investors to become minority owners. Absent such protections, investors might be willing to invest only if they could participate in the controlling group (or buy at an extreme discount to reflect their status as minority investors). Neither view necessarily contradicts the other, and a scholarly synthesis may be emerging.

3. *Board structure and co-determination.* Several European countries (most notably Germany and the Netherlands) have a two-tier board structure under which a "supervisory board," composed wholly of nonemployees, supervises a "management board," composed wholly of managers.[119] The powers of the supervisory board are generally more limited than those of the U.S. board of directors; in some special defined circumstances, however, this board does not make management or business decisions, but it appoints and removes the members of the management board.

More important, many European countries require that there be employee representatives on the supervisory board.[120] Germany, for example, requires the election of at least one-third of the supervisory board's members by employees. Another pattern is exemplified by the Netherlands, where the supervisory board appoints its own successors, but labor representatives can object to and appeal the choice of the employee representatives or any perceived imbalance. Although banks in Germany may appoint representatives to the supervisory board, these directors will have to negotiate with the mandatory employee representatives there. The balance of power may thus sometimes be retained by management,[121] and the outcome is probably more uncertain than in the case of U.S. "corporate constituency" statutes discussed earlier. Interestingly, labor unions do not necessarily support these co-determination provisions, as they often fear that employee representatives specially elected or appointed to the board may constitute a challenge to the power of union officers.[122]

A continuing controversy has surrounded the claimed justifications for co-determination, with critics claiming that labor has other mechanisms (most

---

118. Andrei Shleifer & Robert Vishny, A Survey of Corporate Governance, 52 J. Fin. 737 (1997); Rafael La Porta, Florencio Lopez-de-Silanes, Andrei Shleifer & Robert Vishny, Legal Determinants of External Finance, 52 J. Fin. 1131 (1997); John Coffee, The Future as History: The Prospects for Global Convergence in Corporate Governance and Its Implications, 93 Nw. U. L. Rev. 641 (1999).

119. For discussions of this structure, see Terence Blackburn, The Societas Europea: The Evolving European Corporation Statute, 61 Fordham L. Rev. 695 (1993); Alfred Conard, The European Alternative to Uniformity in Corporation Laws, 89 Mich. L. Rev. 2150 (1991).

120. See Klaus Hopt, New Ways in Corporate Governance: European Experiments with Labor Representation on Corporate Boards, 82 Mich. L. Rev. 1338 (1984); Detlev Vagts, Reforming the "Modern" Corporation: Perspectives from the German, 80 Harv. L. Rev. 23 (1966). For a recent overview of the literature, see Klaus J. Hopt, Hideki Kanda, Mark J. Roe, Eddy Wymeersch & Stefan Prigge, Comparative Corporate Governance: The State of the Art and Emerging Research (Oxford 1998).

121. Under the German system, one seat on the supervisory board is guaranteed to an executive of the corporation. Hopt, footnote 120 supra, at 1351.

122. Conard, footnote 119 supra, at 2185; Hopt, footnote 120 supra, at 1350-1351.

notably collective bargaining) to make its voice adequately heard. Procedurally, observers report that labor representation on the board often results in "factiona-lizing" the board — the use of separate, prior meetings by each faction, adjourn-ments, and group bargaining. Decisions regarding foreign investments, cutbacks, or plant shutdowns can escape veto by the labor representatives only if their social impact is minimized. For example, before Volkswagen could open a subsidiary in the United States, the final decision was delayed for two years, and consent was given only in part and subject to the condition that there would be no layoffs in Germany for a defined period.[123]

---

123. See Hopt, footnote 120 supra, at 1355.

II BASIC NORMS AND DUTIES FOR MANAGEMENT OF CORPORATIONS

A. TRANSACTION OF CORPORATE BUSINESS

1. INTRODUCTION

The dynamics of corporate management regarding the allocation of authority within the corporate structure have been briefly described in Chapter I. By common practice (and by statute in almost all states) management of the regular business affairs of the corporation is ordinarily vested in the board of directors, the members of which are elected by the shareholders. The officers of most corporations are in turn appointed by the directors, although statutes in some states permit direct election by the shareholders.

Fundamental corporate changes (such as alteration of the capital structure, amendment of the articles of incorporation, merger, or dissolution) require approval by the shareholders, usually on recommendation by the directors. Besides their power to elect directors, the shareholders may in some situations remove them. Shareholders have the power to adopt and amend the bylaws but often delegate this power to the directors. In other areas, the shareholders generally have very little direct power over the regular affairs of the corporation. Shareholder resolutions, dealing with matters other than bylaws and fundamental changes, have no legally operative effect and may be completely disregarded by the directors, who are under a positive duty to use their own best judgment as to corporate actions. The shareholders' ability to call the officers and directors to account through the mechanism of the derivative suit is an important but indirect means of exercising power over corporate affairs.

The board of directors may (and often does) delegate much of its authority to an executive committee or to the officers. An executive committee, acting under proper authorization, may perform all but the most extraordinary board functions. The corporate officers have power to operate the day-to-day business and may be authorized by the board to perform general management functions.

Revised Model Business Corporation Act (2000)

Sec. 8.01. *Requirement for and duties of board of directors.* (a) Except as provided in section 7.32, each corporation must have a board of directors.

(b) All corporate powers shall be exercised by or under the authority of the board of directors of the corporation, and the business and affairs of the corporation shall be managed by or under the direction, and subject to the oversight, of its board of directors, subject to any limitation set forth in the articles of incorporation or in an agreement authorized under section 7.32.[1]

Sec. 8.02. *Qualifications of directors.* The articles of incorporation or bylaws may prescribe qualifications for directors. A director need not be a resident of this state or a shareholder of the corporation unless the articles of incorporation or bylaws so prescribe.

Sec. 8.03. *Number and election of directors.* (a) A board of directors must consist of one or more individuals, with the number specified in or fixed in accordance with the articles of incorporation or bylaws.

(b) The number of directors may be increased or decreased from time to time by amendment to, or in the manner provided in, the articles of incorporation or the bylaws.

(c) Directors are elected at the first annual shareholders' meeting and at each annual meeting thereafter unless their terms are staggered under section 8.06.

Sec. 8.40. *Officers.* (a) A corporation has the officers described in its bylaws or appointed by the board of directors in accordance with the bylaws.

(b) The board of directors may elect individuals to fill one or more offices of the corporation. An officer may appoint one or more officers if authorized by the bylaws or the board of directors.

(c) The bylaws or the board of directors shall assign to one of the officers responsibility for preparing minutes of the directors' and shareholders' meetings and for maintaining and authenticating the records of the corporation required to be kept under sections 16.01(a) and 16.01(e).

(d) The same individual may simultaneously hold more than one office in a corporation.[2]

---

1. Section 7.32 authorizes shareholder agreements that dispense with the board of directors or limit its authority to manage the corporation. For further consideration of such provisions, see page 759 infra. — ED.

2. The statutes of many jurisdictions require specific officers, such as a president, one or more vice presidents, a treasurer, and a secretary. Some jurisdictions permit election of certain officers by the shareholders, or forbid the combining of certain offices in one person. — ED.

Sec. 8.41. *Functions of officers.* Each officer has the authority and shall perform the duties set forth in the bylaws or, to the extent consistent with the bylaws, the functions prescribed by the board of directors or by direction of an officer authorized by the board of directors to prescribe the functions of the other officers.

2. DIRECTORS

a. Formalities Required

It was generally expected that the directors' responsibility for the corporation's management was to be discharged by action taken at formal meetings with a quorum present in person. But many exceptions developed in practice and were recognized by the courts.[3] Most states now have statutes permitting action by directors without a meeting under specified conditions.

Revised Model Business Corporation Act (2001)

Sec. 8.20. *Meetings.* (a) The board of directors may hold regular or special meetings in or out of this state.

(b) Unless the articles of incorporation or bylaws provide otherwise, the board of directors may permit any or all directors to participate in a regular or special meeting by, or conduct the meeting through the use of, any means of communication by which all directors participating may simultaneously hear each other during the meeting. A director participating in a meeting by this means is deemed to be present in person at the meeting.

Sec. 8.21. *Action without meeting.* (a) Except to the extent that the articles of incorporation or bylaws require that action by the board of directors be taken at a meeting, action required or permitted by this Act to be taken by the board of directors may be taken without a meeting if each director signs a consent describing the action to be taken and delivers it to the corporation.

(b) Action taken under this section is the act of the board of directors when one or more consents signed by all the directors are delivered to the corporation. The consent may specify the time at which the action taken thereunder is to be effective. A director's consent may be withdrawn by a revocation signed by the director and delivered to the corporation prior to delivery to the corporation of unrevoked written consents signed by all the directors.

(c) A consent signed under this section has the effect of action taken at a meeting of the board of directors and may be described as such in any document.

Most states have relaxed the formalities of board meetings by permitting participation through conference telephone. Notice requirements, as provided by statute, articles, or bylaws, are still significant. They may be less stringent for regular meetings than for special meetings. Notice may easily be waived, by

---

3. Henry W. Ballantine, Corporations 125 (rev. ed. 1946).

attendance at the meeting without protest and by written waiver before the meeting. Statutes increasingly permit written waivers even after the meeting, further eroding the notion of group consultation. At common law, a majority of directors was required for a quorum; some statutes now permit a lesser number if authorized by the articles or bylaws. In a corporation that has only one director, what formalities should the director observe?

b. Effect of Failure to Follow Requirements

Action taken without following the prescribed formalities may be subject to challenge.

A was unable to pay money owed to a corporation. He talked with two of the three directors, and they agreed to settle the corporation's claim. In a suit against *A* to collect the debt brought by the corporation's trustee in bankruptcy, held for the trustee. Hurley v. Ornsteen, 311 Mass. 477, 42 N.E.2d 273 (1942).

All of the shares of the corporation were owned by its five directors, who never met because of dissension among them. They separately agreed to hire *B* as general manager. In a suit by *B* against the corporation for his salary, held for *B*. Gerard v. Empire Square Realty Co., 195 App. Div. 244, 187 N.Y.S. 306 (1921).

C, the sole shareholder, pledged his shares to *D*. *C* then sold all of the corporation's property, giving a deed executed by all the directors acting separately. In suit by *D* to cancel the deed, held for *D*. Baldwin v. Canfield, 26 Minn. 43, 1 N.W. 261 (1879).

Through action taken at special board meetings, held without proper notice, the corporation incurred debts beyond its capital stock, contrary to statute. In a suit by creditors against the directors to collect on statutory liability, held for the creditors. Colcord v. Granzow, 137 Okla. 194, 278 P. 654 (1928).

Four of seven directors attended a meeting, held without notice, and voted to declare a dividend. The declaration was recorded on the books of the corporation. The dividend was paid, but all of the directors took their dividends in the form of promissory notes. Subsequently, a regular board meeting was held. In a suit by *E*, a director, to collect on his note, held for *E*. Meyers v. El Tejon Oil & Refining Co., 29 Cal. 2d 184, 174 P.2d 1 (1946).

A referee in bankruptcy refused to accept, as evidence of authorization of the execution of notes and security agreements, minutes for a meeting that had not taken place. The minutes were prepared subsequent to the signing of the notes and agreements and were signed by all the shareholders, officers, and directors of the corporation at a "later" meeting. The court vacated the ruling of the referee. In re Kirchoff Frozen Foods, Inc., 375 F. Supp. 156 (D. Ariz. 1972).[4]

Are these cases consistent with one another? What policies are being served by their results?

---

4. See also Forbes v. Goldenhersh, 899 P.2d 246 (Colo. App. 1994); Remillong v. Schneider, 185 N.W.2d 493 (N.D. 1971); Phillips Petroleum Co. v. Rock Creek Mining Co., 449 F.2d 664 (9th Cir. 1971); Somers v. AAA Temporary Services, Inc., 5 Ill. App. 3d 931, 284 N.E.2d 462 (1972).

3. OFFICERS

a. Authority

Menard, Inc. v. Dage-MTI, Inc.
726 N.E.2d 1206 (Ind. 2000)

SULLIVAN, J.: [Sterling, the president of Dage (a closely held corporation), contracted to sell Menard 30 acres of Dage's property despite the fact that Dage's board of directors had specifically provided that Sterling must first get its approval of the offer. Menard sued for specific performance and damages. The courts below held] that Sterling did not have the express or apparent authority to bind the corporation in this land transaction. Menard, Inc. v. Dage-MTI, Inc., 698 N.E.2d 1227 (Ind. Ct. App. 1998). . . .

Two main classifications of authority are generally recognized: "actual authority" and "apparent authority." Actual authority [which may be "express" or "implied"] is created "by written or spoken words or other conduct of the principal which, reasonably interpreted, causes the agent to believe that the principal desires him so to act on the principal's account." . . . [S]ee Restatement (Second) of Agency §§7, 33 (1958). Apparent authority refers to a third party's reasonable belief that the principal has authorized the acts of its agent . . . it arises from the principal's indirect or direct manifestations to a third party and not from the representations or acts of the agent. . . .

On occasion, Indiana has taken an expansive view of apparent authority, including within the discussion the concept of "inherent agency power." See Koval v. Simon Telelect, Inc., 693 N.E.2d 1299, 1301 (Ind. 1998). . . .

"Inherent agency power is a term used . . . to indicate the power of an agent which is derived *not* from authority, apparent authority or estoppel, but solely from the agency relation and exists for the protection of persons harmed by or dealing with a servant or other agent." Koval, 693 N.E.2d at 1304 (omission in original) (emphasis added) (Ind. 1998) (quoting Restatement (Second) of Agency §8A (1958)).[5] This " 'status based' . . . [form of] vicarious liability rests upon certain important social and commercial policies," primarily that the "business enterprise should bear the burden of the losses created by the mistakes or overzealousness of its agents [because such liability] stimulates the watchfulness of the employer in selecting and supervising the agents." . . . And while "representations of the principal to the third party are central for defining apparent authority," the concept of inherent authority differs and "originates from the customary authority of a person in the particular type of agency relationship so that no representations beyond the fact of the existence of the agency need be shown." Cange v. Stotler & Co., 826 F.2d 581, 591 (7th Cir. 1987) (citing Restatement (Second) of Agency §161 cmt. b (1958)) (stating that the "plaintiff need not prove any actions on [defendant's] part besides its allowing [an employee] to act as its agent for handling

---

5. Restatement (Third) of Agency §201 cmt. b (2005) states: "The term 'inherent agency power' used in Restatement Second, Agency, and defined therein by §8A, is not used in this Restatement. . . . Other doctrines stated in this Restatement encompass the justifications underpinning §8A, including the importance of interpretation by the agent in the agent's relationship with the principal, as well as the doctrines of apparent authority, estoppel, and restitution." — ED.

plaintiff's account because the trier of fact could find [the employee's] statements within his inherent authority").

In *Cange,* the Seventh Circuit explained this concept's genesis: "Judge Learned Hand articulated this concept of inherent agency power when he upheld a jury verdict for plaintiff based on a contract the jury found to be an unconditional engagement for a singing tour despite the principal's instructions to its agent to engage the singer only for such recitals as he could later persuade record dealers to book her for, instructions which were not told to plaintiff. Kidd v. Thomas A. Edison, Inc., 239 F. 405 (S.D.N.Y.), *aff'd,* 242 F. 923 (2d Cir. 1917). He reasoned that the scope of an agency must be measured 'not alone by the words in which it is created, but by the whole setting in which those words are used, including the customary powers of such agents' and thus the contract was enforceable because 'the customary implication would seem to have been that [the agent's] authority was without limitation of the kind here imposed.' Id. 239 F. at 406. The principal benefits from the existence of inherent authority because '[t]he very purpose of delegated authority is to avoid constant recourse by third persons to the principal, which would be a corollary of denying the agent any latitude beyond his exact instructions.' Id. 239 F. at 408; see Restatement (Second) of Agency §§8A comment a, 161 comment a (1958)."[6] *Cange,* 826 F.2d at 590-91 (alterations in original).

We find the concept of inherent authority — rather than actual or apparent authority — controls our analysis in this case. Menard did not negotiate and ultimately contract with a lower-tiered employee or a prototypical "general" or "special" agent, with respect to whom actual or apparent authority might be at issue. Menard dealt with the president of the corporation, whom "[t]he law recognizes . . . [as one of] the officers [who] are the means, the hands and the head, by which corporations normally act." . . .

Our determination that the inherent agency concept controls our analysis does not end the injury, however. The Restatement (Second) of Agency §161 provides that an agent's inherent authority "subjects his principal to liability for acts done on his account which [(1)] usually accompany or are incidental to transactions which the agent is authorized to conduct if, although they are forbidden by the principal, [(2)] the other party reasonably believes that the agent is authorized to do them and [(3)] has no notice that he is not so authorized." . . .

Distilled to its basics, we find that Sterling had inherent authority here if: (1) first, Sterling acted within the usual and ordinary scope of his authority as president; (2) second, Menard reasonably believed that Sterling was authorized to contract for the sale and purchase of Dage real estate; and (3) third, Menard had no notice that Sterling was not authorized to sell the 30-acre parcel without Board approval. See also *Koval,* 693 N.E.2d at 1304 n.7 (quoting Restatement (Second) of Agency §161). . . .

As to whether Sterling acted within the usual and ordinary scope of his authority as president, the trial court found that Sterling, a director and substantial shareholder of Dage, had served as Dage's president from its inception; had managed the affairs of Dage for an extended period of time with little or no Board

---

6. "[I]f it be the law that persons dealing with the president of a corporation about matters of business clearly within the powers of the corporation to transact must deal at arm's length, and demand that the president exhibit his credentials before entering into contracts with him, it seems to us that not only the corporation, but also those dealing with corporations, will be seriously hampered." Moyse Real Estate Co. v. First National Bank, 110 Miss. 620, 70 So. 821 (1916). — ED.

oversight; and had purchased real estate for Dage without Board approval. However, the trial court reached the conclusion that "[t]he record persuasively demonstrates that the land transaction in question was an extraordinary transaction" for Dage, which manufactures electronic video products. Thus, the court concluded that "Sterling was not performing an act that was appropriate in the ordinary course of Dage's business." . . .

The Restatement looks at the agent's office or station in the company to gauge the scope of the agent's authority, whereas our analysis in *Koval* looked to the purpose and scope of the business in which the general agent (i.e., attorney) was employed. We find the Restatement, which is focused "solely [on] the agency relation," is more appropriate in the current situation involving corporate officers, who are "natural persons who hold and administer the offices of the corporation." . . .[7]

Given that the trial court found that Sterling, as president of the company since its inception, had managed its affairs for an extended period of time with little or no Board oversight and, in particular, had purchased real estate for Dage in the past without Board approval, we conclude that Sterling's actions at issue here were acts that "usually accompany or are incidental to transactions which [he was] authorized to conduct." Restatement (Second) of Agency §161.

Next, we must determine whether Menard reasonably believed that Sterling was authorized to contract for the sale and purchase of Dage real estate. While Sterling's *apparent authority* to bind Dage was "vitiated" by Menard's knowledge that the sale of Dage real estate required Board approval, see *Menard, Inc.*, 698 N.E.2d at 1232, this information did not defeat Sterling's *inherent authority* as Dage president to bind the corporation in a "setting" where he was the sole negotiator, see *Cange*, 826 F.2d at 591.

Because the inherent agency theory "originates from the customary authority of a person in the particular type of agency relationship," id., we look to the *agent's indirect or direct manifestations* to determine whether Menard could have "reasonably believe[d]" that Sterling was authorized to contract for the sale and purchase of Dage real estate. *Koval*, 693 N.E.2d at 1304 n.7.[8] And considering that the "agent" in this case is a general officer of the corporation (as opposed to an "appointed general agent" or "company general manager"), we find that Menard "should not be required to scrutinize too carefully the mandates of [this] permanent . . . agent[] . . . who [did] no more than what is usually done by a corporate president." Restatement (Second) of Agency §161 cmt. a. . . .[7]

---

7. Under a standard "apparent authority" analysis, we agree with the trial court and Court of Appeals that the land transaction in question was an extraordinary transaction. See, e.g., Tedesco v. Gentry Dev. Inc., 521 So. 2d 717, 724 (La. Ct. App. 1988) (declining to enforce a sales contract for land signed by the president of a corporation and concluding "that the doctrine of apparent authority is inappropriate in the realm of sales and mortgages of real estate" where the president only had the actual authority "to initially list the property," and he had not obtained approval from the board of directors to sell the corporation's "immovable property"), aff'd, 540 So. 2d 960 (La. 1989). . . .

[See also Bresnahan v. Lighthouse Mission, Inc., 230 Ga. App., 389, 496 S.E.2d 351 (1998) (president had no apparent authority to sell a piece of corporation's real estate because this "did not involve matters within the scope of Lighthouse's ordinary business"). — ED.]

8. This inquiry is in contradistinction to the test for apparent authority, which looks to the *principal's indirect or direct manifestations* to determine whether the third party could have reasonably believed that the principal had authorized the acts of its agent.

7. Should the third party's "reasonable belief" be affected by the fact that the agent appears to be acting in his own interest rather than the principal's? See Schmidt v. Farm Credit Services, 977 F.2d 511 (10th Cir. 1992) (when bank knew that corporation's president, who gave mortgage on corporation's property to bank, planned to cause corporation to lend proceeds to himself so that he could satisfy

We find it reasonable that Menard did not question the corporate president's statement that he had "authority from his Board of Directors to proceed" with the land transaction. . . . We believed this especially to be the case where (1) Sterling himself was a member of the Board; (2) the agreement contained an express representation that "[t]he persons signing this Agreement on behalf of the Seller are duly authorized to do so and their signatures bind the Seller in accordance with the terms of this Agreement"; and (3) Menard was aware that Dage's corporate counsel, Patrick Donoghue, was involved in the review of the terms of the agreement. . . .

It is true, as the Court of Appeals noted, that Menard was advised early in the transaction that Sterling had to go to the Board to obtain approval. *Menard*, 698 N.E.2d at 1232. This knowledge would have vitiated the apparent authority of a lower-tiered employee or a prototypical general or special agent. But we do not find it sufficient notice that Sterling, an officer with inherent authority, was not authorized to bind Dage at the closing. . . .

In *Koval*, this Court said: "if one of two innocent parties must suffer due to a betrayal of trust — either the principal or the third party — the loss should fall on the party who is most at fault. Because the principal puts the agent in a position of trust, the principal should bear the loss."

That maxim has particular resonance here. The record fails to reveal a single affirmative act that Dage took to inform Menard of Sterling's limited authority with respect to the 30-acre parcel, and the Board did not notify Menard that Sterling had acted without its authority until 104 days after it learned of Sterling's action. By this time, Sterling had taken additional steps to close the transaction. Dage's failure to act should not now form the basis of relief, penalizing Menard and depriving it of its bargain. . . .

We . . . vacate the opinion of the Court of Appeals. . . .

Shepard, C.J., dissenting. . . .

A board of directors authorizes the president to sell some real estate but requires that the sale be submitted to the board for approval or disapproval. The president understands that he must submit any sale to the board. He tells the potential buyer that he must submit it. The buyer knows that its offer must be submitted to the board after the president signs the sales agreement. The agreement is in fact submitted to the board and disapproved. Our Court holds that the agreement is binding anyway. . . .

While I agree with the general legal principles laid out by the majority, those principles seem undercut by the resolution of this case.

---

1. *President/chief executive officer.* At a time when the title "president" indicated only the person who presides at meetings, the chief executive officer (CEO) was called the "general manager." When those functions were combined in the same person, customarily only the title of president was used; an understanding

---

personal debts, bank had duty to inquire further as to president's authority). See also Mohr v. State Bank of Stanley, 241 Kan. 42, 734 P.2d 1071 (1987) (one of corporation's two 50 percent shareholders, who had authority to endorse and deposit checks payable to corporation in its bank account, had no authority to deposit such checks in his personal account, and thus bank was liable to corporation for the proceeds). — Ed.

developed that the president is the chief executive officer. In some companies the president did not preside; some other director (often a recently retired president) did. The president, then, was the chief executive officer, and the presiding officer was the chairman of the board. History then repeated itself. Today, when the functions of president and chairman are united in the same person, the chief executive officer has the "chairman" title. In those situations, the persons second in command are often given the title of president, though they have neither of the traditional roles that title implies. As a result, there are conflicting precedents concerning the meaning of "president." Many cases can be understood as based on different unstated premises concerning the office of general manager. The older decisions deny the president much power. More recent ones consider "president" to mean chief executive officer. The courts have not yet been troubled by the new use of the title to refer to "the second in command," a person who neither presides nor is chief.[8]

2. *Treasurer.* Kraft, treasurer of Anaconda Co., executed a guarantee of Robin International's debt to GOF, Ltd., apparently as a personal favor to Robin's chief executive. When Robin became insolvent, GOF sued Anaconda for the $300,000 balance. GOF agreed Kraft had no actual authority to make the guarantee but claimed he had apparent authority. The court held for Anaconda:

> The general rule in New York is that "[o]ne who deals with an agent does so at his peril, and must make the necessary effort to discover the actual scope of his authority." . . . [Apparent authority] is invoked when the principal's own misleading conduct is responsible for the agent's ability to mislead. . . .
>
> GOF relies on several aspects of Anaconda's conduct in arguing that Anaconda conferred apparent authority on Kraft for the transactions in which he engaged with GOF. Anaconda placed Kraft in a high and visible corporate position, with broad powers over financial affairs. It gave Kraft Anaconda stationery displaying his corporate titles, an office in the company's executive suite, business cards, access to the corporate seal, and put his picture in its annual report. Anaconda officers and publications announced to the financial community that Kraft was the individual at Anaconda with whom to discuss the company's "financial needs." Plaintiff argues that "Anaconda held Kraft out as having the full range of authority and responsibility for Anaconda's financial matters," and characterizes Kraft as Anaconda's "emissary to the financial community." Specifically, Anaconda adopted and made available to Kraft Article 9 of Anaconda's bylaws, conferring upon Kraft, as Treasurer, authority "to sign checks, notes, drafts, bills of exchange and other evidences of indebtedness. . . ." Kraft showed this bylaw, as well as his picture in Anaconda's annual report, to Haggiag [GOF's chief executive] at their initial meeting. By these actions, plaintiff contends, Anaconda gave such convincing evidence of Kraft's authority to sign guarantees that several sophisticated banks extended some $34 million in credit to [Robin and its associated companies], at Kraft's request, through transactions similar to GOF's with Robin. . . .
>
> GOF's arguments would have force in a situation that fell within the range of transactions in which companies like Anaconda normally engage. But the transaction involved in this case is extraordinary, and should have alerted Haggiag to the danger

---

8. To avoid ambiguity in companies with both a chairman and a president, it has become the custom to add the phrase "and chief executive officer" to the title of the person in command. This easily identifies the president who is in charge but does not preside. But in companies where the chairman gets the "chief executive officer" title, the president's ego needs protection. The phrase "chief operating officer" has been coined to describe the person who is not really chief.

of fraud. Because the circumstances surrounding the transaction were such as to put Haggiag on notice of the need to inquire further into Kraft's power and good faith, Anaconda cannot be bound. See . . . Lee v. Jenkins Bros., 268 F.2d 357, 365 (2d Cir. 1959). . . .

The existence of apparent authority depends in part upon "who the contracting third party is." Lee v. Jenkins Bros., supra, 268 F.2d at 370. GOF is not a bank, or otherwise the type of company with whom Anaconda needed to deal swiftly and regularly in its financial affairs. It had no relationship with Anaconda before the transaction concerning Robin. It had neither the need nor the capacity to seek or compete for Anaconda's financial business by extending services or courtesies without the investigation normally made. . . .

More important, the nature of the specific transaction — a guarantee by Anaconda of the debt of an unrelated corporation — was extraordinary and thus sufficient to require inquiry by GOF before it relied on Kraft's purported authority. . . . GOF has no basis for arguing that Article 9 of Anaconda's bylaws conferred or reasonably appeared to confer authority on Kraft to sign a guarantee, let alone one to a third, unrelated company. The bylaw implicitly but clearly refutes the notion that Kraft had authority to sign guarantees. The language conferring power on him to sign evidence of indebtedness occurs in a context that pertains entirely to Anaconda's direct borrowing activities. It reads: "The Treasurer or Assistant Treasurer shall have the custody of all the funds and securities of the Company, and shall have power on behalf of the Company to sign checks, notes, drafts, bills of exchange and other *evidences of indebtedness*, to borrow money for the current needs of the business of the Company and assign and deliver for money so borrowed stocks and securities and warehouse receipts or other documents representing metals in store or transit and to make short-term investments of surplus funds of the Company and shall perform such other duties as may be assigned to him from time to time by the Board of Directors, the Chairman of the Board, the Vice Chairman of the Board or the President." (Emphasis added.) . . . A guarantee is not, however, an "evidence of indebtedness"; it is an agreement collateral to the debt itself. . . . The general rule is that "[e]xpress authority to execute or indorse commercial paper in the principal's name . . . does not include authority to draw or indorse negotiable paper for the benefit . . . of any other person; *authority to sign accommodation paper or as security for a third person must be specifically given*." . . .

Had Kraft purported to borrow money for Anaconda, or in a credible manner for Anaconda's benefit, he could have bound Anaconda even if he in fact intended and managed to steal the money involved. Had Anaconda itself done anything to suggest it had an interest in Robin or in the transactions at issue, a stronger case for apparent authority would be presented. But in this case, Anaconda was neither directly nor indirectly involved in the transaction between GOF and Robin, and GOF has not pointed to any actions by Anaconda suggesting involvement. . . . Kraft made no presentation about any connection between Robin and Anaconda, and even if he had, he could not thereby have supplied any more of a basis for apparent authority than he did by his assertions to Haggiag that he had the power to execute the guarantee. . . . Haggiag's negligence, not Anaconda's, precipitated the loss.

General Overseas Films, Ltd. v. Robin Int'l, Inc., 542 F. Supp. 684 (S.D.N.Y. 1982).

3. *Secretary.* (a) The person responsible for the minutes of all corporate proceedings is usually called "secretary." In American Union Financial Corp. v. University National Bank, 44 Ill. App. 3d 566, 358 N.E.2d 646 (1976), Mr. Hartley was president and his wife was secretary of two corporations, American and Prophecy. Several stockholders and directors were common to both corporations, but not all.

When Prophecy borrowed $10,000 from the bank, the bank required security. Mr. and Mrs. Hartley pledged American's savings account to secure the loan to Prophecy. Mrs. Hartley gave the bank a copy of a resolution by the American board of directors that authorized any two American officers to pledge corporate accounts to banks. She affixed the corporate seal to the copy and added her certification that it was an accurate extract from the corporate minutes. In fact, the board had not adopted such a resolution. When Prophecy defaulted on the loan, American's new management claimed the pledge was unauthorized. A judgment in American's favor was reversed.

The court relied on In re Drive-In Development Corp., 371 F.2d 215 (7th Cir. 1966), a factually similar case.

> [In that case, the] court held that the corporation was estopped to deny the manager's authority to sign the guaranty in the absence of actual or constructive knowledge on the part of the bank that the representation of authority was untrue. The court noted that it was within the authority of the secretary to certify such a resolution, and that representations made by a corporate agent in the course of a transaction which are within the scope of his authority are binding on the corporation. The court also stated: "Furthermore, the realities of modern corporate business practices do not contemplate that those who deal with officers or agents acting for a corporation should be required to go behind the representations of those who have authority to speak for the corporation and who verify the authority of those who presume to act for the corporation." . . . [T]he purported resolution certified by American's secretary was one of the indicia of Hartley's apparent authority to pledge American's funds. The Bank was under no obligation to go behind the representation of the secretary as to Hartley's authority.[9]

(b) *Questions.* Mr. Hartley appears to be a classic case of an agent who has no actual authority. His apparent authority arises solely from a representation by his principal to the bank. But why is Mrs. Hartley's action binding on the bank? Does she have "authority" to tell this lie? What representation binding on the corporation gave her that authority? Or is this simply an "inherent power" (one of the "powers of position") of her office? In contracting with a corporation, what risks can be avoided by demanding of the secretary a certified copy of the board resolution authorizing the transaction? See Keystone Leasing v. People's Protective Life Insurance Co., 514 F. Supp. 841 (E.D.N.Y. 1981) (purported resolution specifically authorizing guarantee dated earlier than the corporation could have heard of the transaction).

4. *Special rules for close corporations?*

> The legal standards for both implied authority and apparent authority leave substantial room for judicial flexibility. The factual differences in the patterns of operation of closely held and publicly held corporations lead to wide disparities in the powers the courts actually recognize in corporate officers. The courts have held officers in a close corporation to possess powers to bind the corporation under circumstances which would make a similar holding questionable in a publicly held corporation. . . .
>
> Most of these holdings can be reconciled with traditional doctrine by viewing the officer in question as a general manager of the company and as having a general

---

9. *Query:* What result if the person purporting to be the secretary is really only a clerk in the secretary's office who gives a false extract of the minutes reporting the authorization and another false extract reporting his appointment as secretary, both extracts bearing a false certification and the corporate seal? — ED.

manager's broad inherent powers, or by applying principles of apparent authority or acquiescence by the directors or shareholders. Yet, another principle may also be at work, a principle which courts themselves have seldom articulated. In a close corporation, ownership and management usually coalesce, and the participants often conduct their enterprise internally much as if it were a partnership. Aware of this, courts naturally are inclined to recognize in shareholder-officers of a close corporation the powers possessed by partners in a firm under the general rule of partnership law that each partner is an agent of the firm within the scope of its business and that each partner has power to bind the firm by acts apparently carried on to further the firm's usual business.

2 F. Hodge O'Neal & Robert B. Thompson, O'Neal & Thompson's Close Corporations and LLC's §8.05 (3d ed. 2006).

5. *The close corporation: deadlock.* Sterling Industries, Inc. v. Ball Bearing Pen Corp., 298 N.Y. 483, 84 N.E.2d 790 (1949), involved two groups sharing control. At a directors' meeting the president moved that the corporation institute a breach of contract action against a business that was represented by one of the two groups on the board. After a tie vote the president ruled that his motion had failed; he subsequently instituted action on behalf of the corporation. Held: the president may not institute such an action. "One side should not be entitled to maintain an action in the name and at the expense of the corporation simply because the president happens to be allied with its interests." The court found no emergency, no facts alleged "to indicate that a crisis is at hand or that immediate or vital injury threatens plaintiff." Suppose a finding of emergency had been possible. See Management Technologies, Inc. v. Morris, 961 F. Supp. 640 (S.D.N.Y. 1997) (CEO of corporation faced with imminent threat to its existence has authority to put two major subsidiaries into bankruptcy when board is deadlocked if CEO can prove that opposing directors breached their duty of loyalty to company).

In West View Hills, Inc. v. Lizau Realty Corp., 6 N.Y.2d 344, 189 N.Y.S.2d 863, 160 N.E.2d 622 (1959), the court permitted a suit instituted by the president (one of three directors and a one-third shareholder) in the name of the corporation against the other two directors (who owned the remaining two-thirds of the shares) for improperly paying out corporate funds. The court held that "absent a provision in the by-laws or action by the board of directors prohibiting the president from defending and instituting suit in the name of and in behalf of the corporation, he must be deemed, in the discharge of his duties, to have presumptive authority to so act." *Sterling Industries* was distinguished on the ground that there the president's authority was "terminated when . . . the board . . . refused to sanction it." Accord, TJI Realty, Inc. v. Harris, 672 N.Y.S.2d 386 (App. Div. 1998); see also Community Collaborative of Bridgeport, Inc. v. Ganim, 241 Conn. 546, 698 A.2d 245 (1997).

See also Rothman & Schneider, Inc. v. Beckerman, 2 N.Y.2d 493, 161 N.Y.S.2d 118, 141 N.E.2d 610 (1957) (owner of half the shares with half of the seats on the board who was secretary-treasurer and actively managing the corporation's business has implied authority to bring suit for the corporation against son-in-law of other half-owner, who was president and had half of the seats on the board; *Sterling Industries* distinguished as involving a suit against "insiders" where board had affirmatively refused authority); Fanchon & Marco, Inc. v. Paramount Pictures, Inc., 202 F.2d 731 (2d Cir. 1953) (facts similar to *Sterling Industries* but no rejection of authority by the board; under Delaware law, president has no implied authority to institute suit for corporation); Anmaco, Inc. v. Bohlken, 13 Cal. App. 4th 891, 16 Cal. Rptr. 2d 675

(1993) (president has no implied authority to bring suit on behalf of corporation against co-director and equal shareholder, especially when defendant was also CEO). What result in the above cases if the president owned no shares and was not financially associated with either of the deadlocked factions? If the suit was against a third party not associated with either of the deadlocked factions?

b. Ultra Vires Doctrine

The term "ultra vires" is employed in a variety of senses. Literally translated, the expression refers to a transaction "beyond the powers" of the corporation that appears to be a party to the transaction; and the alleged ultra vires (or beyond the powers) nature of the transaction is usually based on the contention that the applicable statutes or the articles of incorporation of the corporation do not indicate "authority" on its part to enter into the transaction in question.

In the early development of corporate law, it was contended that a corporation, being an artificial person created by the state, could do (had the "capacity" to do) only those acts that it was formed to do. This doctrine, based principally on fear of the increasing economic power of corporations, led to the view that, not having been created for the purpose of committing crimes or torts, a corporation as such could not be subjected to criminal or tort liability. This reasoning long ago lost support.

The preceding section considered situations in which corporate officers allegedly acted beyond their real or apparent authority. Is such action ultra vires of the corporation despite the fact that the officer could have been properly authorized to enter into the transaction in question? For a modern case dealing with the authority of corporate officers in ultra vires terms, see Fidelity & Deposit Co. v. McClure Quarries, Inc. 376 F. Supp. 293 (S.D. Ill. 1974). If a corporation enters into a contract that violates a statute or public policy, is the transaction ultra vires? Or is it unenforceable simply because it is illegal or contrary to public policy whether entered into by a corporation, partnership, or individual? For a case involving corporate activity that was contrary to statute, discussed in ultra vires terms, see Nelson v. Dakota Bankers Trust Co., 132 N.W.2d 903 (N.D. 1964).

Until the 1960s, articles of incorporation had to specify the corporation's purposes. Purpose clauses were drafted very broadly as an attempt to avoid the ultra vires doctrine. In 1967 Delaware expressly authorized the broadest of all-purpose clauses: "to engage in any lawful act or activity for which corporations may be organized under the General Corporation Law of Delaware." All jurisdictions have adopted similar provisions, although many expressly prohibit certain purposes, such as banking, because those businesses must be incorporated under special statutes. RMBCA §3.01(a) (1984) eliminates the need for a purposes clause entirely: "Every corporation incorporated under this Act has the purpose of engaging in any lawful business unless a more limited purpose is set forth in the articles of incorporation."

Corporations must have powers to carry out their purposes. A corporation that is to own and manage an apartment house must be able to purchase land and probably will have to mortgage it. Purpose clauses often included a multitude of powers to further protect against the ultra vires doctrine.[10] All corporation statutes

---

10. See the purpose clause of the Thunder Corporation in the main case that follows. Its actual business was to own and operate apartment houses.

list a number of powers that all corporations may exercise: to sue and be sued, purchase real property, make contracts, make donations for charitable purposes, pay pensions, etc. This list is usually supplemented by permission to exercise other powers necessary or convenient to carry on the company's affairs.[11] These developments have greatly diminished the opportunity to invoke the ultra vires concept.

Real Estate Capital Corp. v. Thunder Corp.
31 Ohio Misc. 169, 287 N.E.2d 838 (1972)

CALHOUN, J.: . . . Since its incorporation on the 16th day of May, 1966, Thunder Corp. has had only two shareholders: Cohen, who has always owned 80% of the outstanding stock; and Berman, who has always owned 20% of the outstanding stock. . . .

On March 14, 1967, Thunder Corp. issued what purports to be a valid second mortgage on its property to R.E.C.C. and Weissman, in the principal amount of $105,000.00, but the $105,000.00 was not paid to Thunder Corp., rather it was paid to Winthrop Homes, Inc. (now named Amber Builders, Inc.). There was not, and is not now, any relationship between Thunder Corp. and Winthrop Homes, Inc.,

---

11. The powers section of the RMBCA provides:

Sec. 3.02. *General powers.* Unless its articles of incorporation provide otherwise, every corporation . . . has the same powers as an individual to do all things necessary or convenient to carry out its business and affairs, including without limitation power:
   (1) to sue and be sued, complain and defend in its corporate name;
   (2) to have a corporate seal, which may be altered at will, and to use it, or a facsimile of it, by impressing or affixing it or in any other manner reproducing it;
   (3) to make and amend bylaws, not inconsistent with its articles of incorporation or with the laws of this state, for managing the business and regulating the affairs of the corporation;
   (4) to purchase, receive, lease, or otherwise acquire, and own, hold, improve, use, and otherwise deal with, real or personal property, or any legal or equitable interest in property, wherever located;
   (5) to sell, convey, mortgage, pledge, lease, exchange, and otherwise dispose of all or any part of its property;
   (6) to purchase, receive, subscribe for, or otherwise acquire; own, hold, vote, use, sell, mortgage, lend, pledge, or otherwise dispose of; and deal in and with shares or other interests in, or obligations of, any other entity;
   (7) to make contracts and guarantees, incur liabilities, borrow money, issue its notes, bonds, and other obligations (which may be convertible into or include the option to purchase other securities of the corporation), and secure any of its obligations by mortgage or pledge of any of its property, franchises, or income;
   (8) to lend money, invest and reinvest its funds, and receive and hold real and personal property as security for repayment;
   (9) to be a promoter, partner, member, associate, or manager of any partnership, joint venture, trust, or other entity;
   (10) to conduct its business, locate offices, and exercise the powers granted by this Act within or without this state;
   (11) to elect directors and appoint officers, employees, and agents of the corporation, define their duties, fix their compensation, and lend them money and credit;
   (12) to pay pensions and establish pension plans, pension trusts, profit sharing plans, share bonus plans, share option plans, and benefit or incentive plans for any or all of its current or former directors, officers, employees, and agents;
   (13) to make donations for the public welfare or for charitable, scientific, or educational purposes;
   (14) to transact any lawful business that will aid governmental policy;
   (15) to make payments or donations, or do any other act, not inconsistent with law, that furthers the business and affairs of the corporation.

other than the fact that Cohen, who performed all of these transactions, was the sole shareholder of Winthrop Homes. . . . There is no . . . evidence that R.E.C.C. or Weissman had been told that there was any consideration passing to Thunder Corp. for its mortgage and assignment of rents and leases. And, although Cohen signed the mortgage as a corporate officer, Berman as a 20% shareholder objects to the mortgage of corporate property. . . .

On May 23, 1969, R.E.C.C. and Weissman filed this action as plaintiffs to foreclose on the mortgage and to appoint a receiver. . . .

As a general proposition of law, corporate officers and agents may deal only within their authority, but when a corporation allows it to appear that the officer or agent has the authority to perform certain business or to engage in certain transactions, the corporation is bound by those acts of the agent even though he in fact lacks such authority. However, a corporation has only that authority which is granted to it by the Ohio Revised Code, and acts of the agent which are outside the authority granted to it by the Ohio Statutes cannot be performed even though such acts may be within the authority granted to the agent by the corporation.

R.C. 1701.13 grants Ohio Corporations their ability to function, and the pertinent portion of that section reads as follows:

> (F) In carrying out the purposes stated in its articles and subject to limitations prescribed by law or in its articles, a corporation may: . . .
>
> (6) Borrow money, and issue, sell, and pledge its notes, bonds, and other evidences of indebtedness, and secure any of its obligations by mortgage, pledge, or deed of trust of all or any of its property, and guarantee or secure obligations of any person;

Here then is the authority for the corporation to guarantee or secure the obligation of another person, provided the guarantee is made, or the security given, in carrying out the purposes of the corporation and subject to the limitations prescribed by law.

The purpose clause of Thunder Corp. reads as follows:

> Third. The purposes for which it is formed are:
>
> To purchase, lease, take or otherwise acquire and own, use, hold, sell, exchange, lease, mortgage, work, improve, develop, subdivide, cultivate and otherwise handle and dispose of real estate, real property and any interest or right therein and to contract for and engage the services of other parties for the purpose of carrying on the same.
>
> To make, enter upon, and carry out contracts for constructing, building, altering, improving, repairing, decorating, maintaining, furnishing and fitting up buildings, structures and improvements of every description, and for fabricating and manufacturing sections and component parts of the same, to advance money to and enter into agreements of all kinds with builders, contractors, property owners and others for said purpose.
>
> To purchase, lease, take or otherwise acquire and to own, hold, sell, convey, exchange, hire, pledge, lease, mortgage or otherwise deal and dispose of all kinds of personal property, chattels real, choses in action, notes, bonds, stocks, mortgages and securities including stock issued by this corporation.
>
> To purchase or otherwise acquire all or any part of the business, good will, rights, property and assets and to assume all or any part of the liabilities of any corporation, association or individual engaged in any business in which any corporation

organized under the laws of the state of Ohio is entitled to engage, and to acquire the stock of any corporation engaged in such business, to enter into joint ventures with others to engage in such business and to enter into partnership agreements and become a member of any partnership to engage in such business.

To carry on any other lawful business and to do any and everything necessary, suitable, convenient or proper for the accomplishment of any of the purposes or the attainment of any or all of the objects hereinbefore enumerated or incidental to the powers herein named or for the enhancement of the value of the property of the corporation or which shall at any time appear conducive thereto or expedient; to have all the rights, powers and privileges now or hereafter conferred by the laws of the state of Ohio or under any act amendatory thereof, supplemental thereto or substituted therefor.

The foregoing clauses shall be construed both as purposes and powers and it is hereby expressly provided that the enumeration herein of specific purposes and powers shall not be held to limit or restrict in any manner the general powers of the corporation.

At the hearing of this matter some questions were asked about what happened to the $105,000.00 loan, and from that testimony and evidence and the depositions, there is some inference that part of those funds may have been used to repay obligations of Thunder Corp.; but such evidence, if it can be called evidence, is purely speculative in nature and not of probative value. Therefore, the court must conclude that the evidence does not establish that Thunder Corp. received any benefit from the $105,000.00 loan.

Thus, having found that there is no consideration for the mortgage it becomes exceedingly difficult for this court to conceive how the mortgage could further the corporate purpose. Further the record is clear that the $105,000.00 was paid directly for the benefit of Winthrop Homes, Inc., by R.E.C.C. and Weissman, and neither R.E.C.C. nor Weissman produced any evidence that the mortgage and rent assignment was anything more than a gratuitous guarantee.

The validity of gratuitous guarantees and gifts by corporations was passed upon by the Ohio Supreme Court in MacQueen v. The Dollar Savings Bank Co., 133 Ohio St. 579, 15 N.E.2d 529: ". . . (2) The voluntary transfer of property by a corporation to secure the individual indebtedness of one of its officers is binding upon the corporation if all its stockholders assent thereto; but such transfer is subject to the rights of creditors prejudiced thereby. . . ."

The evidence in this case is clear that Berman, a 20 percent shareholder, objects to the mortgage given to the plaintiffs and to the assignment of rents and leases, and following the *MacQueen* case, the mortgage given to the plaintiffs by Thunder Corp., as well as the assignment of rents and leases, would be valid as between the corporation and the creditor only if they secured the approval of all stockholders.

Therefore, it is the finding of this court that the mortgage and the assignment of rents and leases given to R.E.C.C. and Weissman by Thunder Corp. are invalid. . . .

---

1. *Corporate powers.* In the *MacQueen* case, the court stated: "The consent of the stockholders, of itself, does not confer corporate power, but does make the pledge good. . . ." If so, what is the relevance of whether there was corporate power to make the pledge?

2. *Benefit to the corporation.* In Rio Refrigeration Co. v. Thermal Supply of Harlingen, Inc., 368 S.W.2d 128 (Tex. 1963), defendant corporation purchased the assets of a competing business and assumed all its accounts payable, including plaintiff's account for goods furnished. Held: defense of ultra vires without merit:

> Here the contract [under which defendant assumed the accounts payable] was of direct and material benefit to [defendant], in that it eliminated a competitor and purchased parts, supplies and equipment used in [defendant's] business. The law is well settled that in all grants of corporate powers there exist not only the powers expressly granted, but also such implied powers as are necessary or reasonably appropriate to the exercise of those powers expressly granted. . . . In any event, [defendant] is estopped to assert the defense of ultra vires in that it had operated under and attained the benefits of the contract.

3. *Common law concept of ultra vires.* At common law, ultra vires contracts were void and unenforceable, but a party who could not enforce the contract might be able to recover in quasi-contract. Herbert v. Sullivan, 123 F.2d 477 (1st Cir. 1941) (lender unable to recover in a suit on an ultra vires promissory note). After a contract had been fully executed on both sides, it could not be attacked on grounds of ultra vires. Problems often arose in determining whether the contracts were wholly or partially executed; e.g., if a corporation borrows money and executes a mortgage, is the transaction wholly or partially executed? What is the state of execution of the mortgage and assignment in the *Thunder Corp.* case? See Norman D. Lattin, Corporations 226 (2d ed. 1971).

The rule was established that either party had the complete defense of ultra vires if the contract was wholly executory. "It is arguable that the rule that executory ultra vires contracts are not enforceable operates to discourage the making of ultra vires contracts. . . . [A]pplication of the rule works injustice in those instances where the fact of ultra vires is not present to the consciousness of either party at the time of contracting, but is later used by one of them as a defense of last resort. In the latter instances, the ethical position of the parties is no worse than when the contract has been partially or fully performed." Robert S. Stevens, Corporations 313-314 (2d ed. 1949). Should a party be "aware that a contemplated contract will be ultra vires" because the corporation's articles are a matter of public record?

Nonassenting shareholders have generally been held able to enjoin corporate action found to be ultra vires, unless the shareholder is barred by laches. Of what relevance is the manner in which the other party to the contract will be affected?

Courts have permitted a shareholder (in a derivative action on the corporation's behalf) to sue the directors or officers responsible for the ultra vires transaction for any losses resulting therefrom. Should there be liability if the directors or officers reasonably believed that their action was not ultra vires? Should the directors of a corporation entering into an ultra vires contract be liable to the other contracting party? See Lurie v. Arizona Fertilizer & Chemical Co., 101 Ariz. 482, 421 P.2d 330 (1966).

The state has been held to have the power to rescind the corporation's charter in a quo warranto proceeding because of its ultra vires activity or to secure an injunction against threatened ultra vires action. Should the state be permitted to do either if the corporate action was contrary neither to any statute nor to public policy (other than a statute providing that a corporation may act only pursuant to the purposes contained in its charter)?

The majority of American jurisdictions hold that, by unanimous action, the shareholders may authorize or ratify an ultra vires act. Should unanimity be required? Compare Nelson v. Web Water Dev. Ass'n, Inc., 507 N.W.2d 691 (S.D. 1993) (employment contract was binding on corporation even though bylaws denied board authority to enter into such contracts; since articles of incorporation permitted board to amend bylaws, board's entering contract operated to amend bylaws).

4. *Legislation.* Every state has enacted legislation to eliminate most of the defenses that might otherwise be asserted by a plea of ultra vires, or to abolish the doctrine of constructive notice in relation to the contents of a corporation's articles of incorporation, and the companion doctrine of limited corporate capacity. See generally Willburt D. Ham, Ultra Vires Contracts Under Modern Corporate Legislation, 46 Ky. L.J. 215 (1958).

Ohio General Corporation Law (1994)

Sec. 1701.13. *Authority of corporation.* . . . (H) No lack of, or limitation upon, the authority of a corporation shall be asserted in any action except (1) by the state in an action by it against the corporation, (2) by or on behalf of the corporation against a director, an officer, or any shareholder as such, (3) by a shareholder as such or by or on behalf of the holders of shares of any class against the corporation, a director, an officer, or any shareholder as such, or (4) in an action involving an alleged overissue of shares. This division shall apply to any action brought in this state upon any contract made in this state by a foreign corporation.

Question: Why was this provision not applied (or even referred to) in the *Thunder Corp.* case? It was at the time a subdivision of the same section of the Ohio General Corporation Law that was applied by the court with respect to "the authority for the corporation to guarantee or secure the obligation of another person" (page 69 supra).

Revised Model Business Corporation Act (1984)

Sec. 3.04. *Ultra vires.* (a) Except as provided in subsection (b), the validity of corporate action may not be challenged on the ground that the corporation lacks or lacked power to act.

(b) A corporation's power to act may be challenged:

(1) in a proceeding by a shareholder against the corporation to enjoin the act;[12]

(2) in a proceeding by the corporation, directly, derivatively, or through a receiver, trustee, or other legal representative, against an incumbent or former director, officer, employee, or agent of the corporation; or

---

12. Since state statutes authorize corporations to engage only in "lawful" business, should a shareholder be able to enjoin illegal corporate conduct even if it has increased corporate profits? See Kent Greenfield, Ultra Vires Lives! A Stakeholder Analysis of Corporate Illegality (With Notes on How Corporate Law Could Reinforce International Law Norms), 87 Va. L. Rev. 1279 (2001); for further consideration, see pages 78-82 infra — ED.

(3) in a proceeding by the Attorney General under section 14.30.

(c) In a shareholder's proceeding under subsection (b)(1) to enjoin an unauthorized corporate act, the court may enjoin or set aside the act, if equitable and if all affected persons are parties to the proceeding, and may award damages for loss (other than anticipated profits) suffered by the corporation or another party because of enjoining the unauthorized act.

B. MANAGERS' RESPONSIBILITIES AND COMPENSATION

1. INTRODUCTION

In general, corporate managers — directors, officers (and, usually, controlling shareholders as well[13]) — may be held responsible for breach of duty to three classes of persons: creditors of the corporation, shareholders of the corporation, and the corporate entity itself.[14] Liabilities of corporate managers to creditors, which usually arise after the corporation has become insolvent, are discussed mainly in subsequent chapters; the most common instances involve directors improperly declaring dividends or distributing other corporate assets to shareholders (Chapter III). Liabilities of corporate managers to shareholders are also considered principally in chapters that follow; these include their responsibility under federal (and state) statutes for misstatements and omissions in connection with the corporation's sale of securities, their duty when they personally trade the corporation's shares (Chapter V), and their obligation when they sell a controlling interest in the corporation (Chapter IX). The primary concern of this section is the third broad category of liability: corporate managers' breach of duty to the corporation itself.

2. DISINTERESTED CONDUCT: DUTY OF CARE

Most suits by the corporation (or by shareholders in a derivative suit on its behalf) against corporate managers allege that they have breached their obligation to the enterprise by engaging in self-dealing. Other sections in this chapter will consider

---

13. See, e.g., Perlman v. Feldmann, page 1051 infra, and cases discussed in footnote 18, page 1061 infra.

14. Significant potential liabilities for corporate managers also exist for violation of various federal and state regulatory statutes (in addition to the federal securities acts). See generally Robert B. Thompson, Unpacking Limited Liability: Direct and Vicarious Liability of Corporate Participants for Torts of the Enterprise, 47 Vand. L. Rev. 1, 25-29 (1994). For liabilities pertaining to the Internal Revenue Code, see 13 Mertens Law Fed. Income Taxation, §47 A.25 (2007); on civil antitrust liabilities, see 1 William Knepper & Dan Bailey, Liability of Corporate Officers and Directors, §6-9 (7th ed. 2006); on criminal antitrust liabilities, see id. at §8-12; and on environmental laws, see id. at §10. See also Annot., 11 A.L.R. Fed. 606 (2006) (liability of national bank directors for excessive loans under National Banking Act); Baystate Alternate Staffing, Inc. v. Herman, 163 F.3d 668 (1st Cir. 1998) (liability for violation of Fair Labor Standards Act); SBA v. Echevarria, 864 F. Supp. 1254 (S.D. Fla. 1994) (liability for violation of Small Business Investment Act); Knepper & Bailey at §7-2(a) (liability for violations of Civil Rights Act); id. at §8-6(d) (criminal liability under OSHA); id. at §8-6(e) (criminal liability under state laws for injuries to employers).

The high-profile Sarbanes-Oxley Act of 2002 adopted a new criminal statute that requires chief executive officers and chief financial officers to certify that any financial statement filed with the SEC under Securities Exchange Act §13(a) or 15(d) "fully complies with the requirements" of those sections and that "information contained in the periodic report fairly presents, in all material respects, the financial condition and results of operations of the issuer." 18 U.S.C. §1350. For full discussion of Sarbanes-Oxley, see pages 10-11 supra and pages 326-334 infra.

various contexts in which such charges of conflict of interest arise. The materials in this section concern conduct of directors or officers — often labeled as "misman-agement," "waste," "negligence," "lack of business judgment," "lack of reasonable diligence," or some similar descriptive term — that has allegedly caused loss to the corporation but seemingly with no benefit to the defendants themselves.

As the cases and statutes set forth below indicate, the legal standard governing the conduct of corporate directors and officers in these situations has been articu-lated in a variety of ways. While judicial language occasionally appears to be self-contradicting,[15] it appears that "in most states, in a given case, the same legal result would be reached under each of these formulations."[16]

Prior to the 1980s, most decisions holding defendants liable for not fulfilling their responsibilities in this area involved the directors of banks or other financial institu-tions, the most common misconduct being failure properly to oversee and supervise the actions of the institutions' operating officers.[17] Apart from banks and investment companies, it was said in the late 1960s that "the search for cases in which directors of industrial corporations have been held liable in derivative suits for negligence uncomplicated by self-dealing is a search for a very small number of needles in a very large haystack."[18] As indicated by several subsequent decisions in this section, however, the number of these holdings seems to have grown somewhat.

Although courts may not often find corporate managers responsible *to the cor-poration* for "negligence uncomplicated by self-dealing," materials in other chap-ters reveal decisions under provisions of the federal securities acts that do hold

---

15. E.g., "It was . . . [defendant's] duty as president of the corporation to exercise such care, skill and diligence in transacting the corporate business as might be expected in his own affairs. He cannot be charged with the consequences of mismanagement unless it was so gross as to amount to fraud." Keck Enterprises, Inc. v. Braunschweiger, 108 F. Supp. 925 (S.D. Cal. 1952). Compare the reasoning in footnote 19 on page 77 infra.

16. 1 ALI, Principles of Corporate Governance 145 (1994).

17. See, e.g., Neese v. Brown, 218 Tenn. 686, 405 S.W.2d 577 (1964); Atherton v. Anderson, 99 F.2d 883 (6th Cir. 1938); compare Briggs v. Spaulding, 141 U.S. 132 (1891). See also Hun v. Cary, 82 N.Y. 65 (1880) (bank directors held negligent for erecting new building at time of financial stress). For a modern decision involving a mutual fund, see Lutz v. Boas, 39 Del. Ch. 585, 171 A.2d 381 (1961). For develop-ment of the bank director liability cases' special protection for depositors and shareholders from high-risk loan decisions, and discussion of its present inadequacies, see Patricia A. McCoy, A Political Economy of the Business Judgment Rule in Banking: Implications for Corporate Law, 47 Case W. Res. L. Rev. 1 (1996).

18. Joseph W. Bishop Jr., Sitting Ducks and Decoy Ducks: New Trends in Indemnification of Cor-porate Directors and Officers, 77 Yale L.J. 1078, 1099 (1968). See also Lynn A. Stout, On the Proper Motives for Corporate Directors (Or, Why You Don't Want to Invite Homo Economicus to Join Your Board), 28 Del. J. Corp. L. 1, 7 (2003) (a director "is more likely to be attacked by killer bees than she is to have ever pay damages for the breach of the duty of care"). Compare Norwood P. Beveridge, The Corporate Director's Duty of Care: Riddles Wisely Expounded, 24 Suffolk U. L. Rev. 923, 947-948 (1990) ("[T]here are actually many . . . [nonbanking] cases upholding a complaint of duty of care violation," citing about 40 cases); Robinson v. Watts Detective Agency, 685 F.2d 729 (1st Cir. 1982) (negligent transfer of corporation's assets for inadequate consideration); Lussier v. Mau-Van Development, Inc., 4 Haw. Ct. App. 356, 667 P.2d 804 (1983) (same); In re Tower Air, Inc., 416 F.3d 229 (3d Cir. 2005) ("passivity in the face of negative maintenance reports" about commercial aircraft). Consider John C. Coffee Jr., Litigation and Corporate Governance: An Essay on Steering Between Scylla and Charybdis, 52 Geo. Wash. L. Rev. 789, 796 (1984): "Bishop's thesis . . . ignores the central facts that cases are most often resolved by settlement, not judicial decision, and that defendants have a particularly strong incentive to settle derivative actions because, unlike a settlement, an adjudication adverse to them will typically deprive them of eligibility for indemnification. As a result, it is likely that cases favorable to the plaintiff tend to be settled, whereas those in which the defendant has the relative advantage tend to be dismissed at a pretrial stage, often in recorded decisions. . . . [T]hus, judicial dicta about the scope of the duty has some real world effect." See also James J. Hanks Jr., Recent State Legislation on D&O Liability Limitation, 43 Bus. Law. 1207, 1208 (1988) (describing settlements in "mismanagement" suits in the mid-1980s of $25 million, $32.5 million, and $110 million).

directors, officers, and controlling shareholders liable to *individual shareholders* for negligence or failure to exercise due diligence in connection with misstatements or omissions. See, e.g., Gould v. American Hawaiian S.S. Co., page 692 infra (Sec. 14 of the Securities Exchange Act of 1934 — managers' solicitation of proxies); Escott v. BarChris Construction Corp., 283 F. Supp. 643 (S.D.N.Y. 1968) (Sec. 11 of Securities Act of 1933 — corporation's registration statement for distribution of its securities).

Shlensky v. Wrigley
95 Ill. App. 2d 173, 237 N.E.2d 776 (1968)

SULLIVAN, J.: This is an appeal from a dismissal of plaintiff's amended complaint. . . . Plaintiff sought damages and an order that defendants cause the installation of lights in Wrigley Field and the scheduling of night baseball games.

Plaintiff is a minority stockholder of defendant corporation, Chicago National League Ball Club (Inc.), a Delaware corporation . . . [that] owns and operates the major league professional baseball team known as the Chicago Cubs. . . . The individual defendants are directors of the Cubs and have served for varying periods of years. Defendant Philip K. Wrigley is also president of the corporation and owner of approximately 80% of the stock therein.

Plaintiff alleges that since night baseball was first played in 1935 nineteen of the twenty major league teams have scheduled night games . . . [and] that every member of the major leagues, other than the Cubs, scheduled substantially all of its home games in 1966 at night, exclusive of opening days, Saturdays, Sundays, holidays and days prohibited by league rules. Allegedly this has been done for the specific purpose of maximizing attendance and thereby maximizing revenue and income.

The Cubs, in the years 1961-65, sustained operating losses from its direct baseball operations. Plaintiff attributes those losses to inadequate attendance at Cubs' home games. He concludes that if the directors continue to refuse to install lights at Wrigley Field and schedule night baseball games, the Cubs will continue to sustain comparable losses and its financial condition will continue to deteriorate.

Plaintiff alleges that, except for the year 1963, attendance at Cubs' home games has been substantially below that at their road games, many of which were played at night.

Plaintiff compares attendance at Cubs' games with that of the Chicago White Sox, an American League club, whose weekday games were generally played at night. The weekend attendance figures for the two teams were similar; however, the White Sox weeknight games drew many more patrons than did the Cubs' weekday games. . . .

Plaintiff further alleges that defendant Wrigley has refused to install lights, not because of interest in the welfare of the corporation but because of his personal opinions "that baseball is a 'daytime sport' and that the installation of lights and night baseball games will have a deteriorating effect upon the surrounding neighborhood." It is alleged that he has admitted that he is not interested in whether the Cubs would benefit financially from such action because of his concern for the neighborhood, and that he would be willing for the team to play night games if a new stadium were built in Chicago.

Plaintiff alleges that the other defendant directors, with full knowledge of the foregoing matters, have acquiesced in the policy laid down by Wrigley. . . . It is charged that the directors are acting for a reason or reasons contrary and wholly unrelated to the business interests of the corporation, that such arbitrary and capricious acts constitute mismanagement and waste of corporate assets, and that the directors have been negligent in failing to exercise reasonable care and prudence in the management of the corporate affairs.

The question on appeal is whether plaintiff's amended complaint states a cause of action. It is plaintiff's position that fraud, illegality and conflict of interest are not the only bases for a stockholder's derivative action against the directors. Contra-riwise, defendants argue that the courts will not step in and interfere with honest business judgment of the directors unless there is a showing of fraud, illegality or conflict of interest.

The cases in this area are numerous and each differs from the others on a factual basis. However, the courts have pronounced certain ground rules which appear in all cases and which are then applied to the given factual situation. The court in Wheeler v. Pullman Iron and Steel Company, 143 Ill. 197, 207, 32 N.E. 420, 423, said: ". . . Everyone purchasing or subscribing for stock in a corporation impliedly agrees that he will be bound by the acts and proceedings done or sanctioned by a majority of the shareholders, or by the agents of the corporation duly chosen by such majority, within the scope of the powers conferred by the charter, and courts of equity will not undertake to control the policy or business methods of a corporation, although it may be seen that a wiser policy might be adopted and the business more successful if other methods were pursued. The majority of shares of its stock, or the agents by the holders thereof lawfully chosen, must be permitted to control the business of the corporation in their discretion, when not in violation of its charter or some public law, or corruptly and fraudulently subversive of the rights and interests of the corporation or of a shareholder."

The standards set in Delaware are also clearly stated in the cases. In Davis v. Louisville Gas & Electric Co., 16 Del. Ch. 157, 142 A. 654, a minority shareholder sought to have the directors enjoined from amending the certificate of incorporation. The court said on page 659: ". . . The response which courts make to such applications is that it is not their function to resolve for corporations questions of policy and business management. The directors are chosen to pass upon such questions and their judgment *unless shown to be tainted with fraud* is accepted as final. The judgment of the directors of corporations enjoys the benefit of a presumption that it was formed in good faith and was designed to promote the best interests of the corporation they serve." (Emphasis supplied.) . . .

Plaintiff argues that the allegations of his amended complaint are sufficient to set forth a cause of action under the principles set out in Dodge v. Ford Motor Co. [discussed at page 34 supra and footnote 60 on page 209 infra]. In that case plaintiff, owner of about 10% of the outstanding stock, brought against the directors seeking payment of additional dividends and the enjoining of further business expansion. In ruling on the request for dividends the court indicated that the motives of Ford in keeping so much money in the corporation for expansion and security were to benefit the public generally and spread the profits out by means of more jobs, etc. The court felt that these were not only far from related to the good of the stockholders, but amounted to a change in the ends of the corporation and that this was not a purpose contemplated or allowed by the corporate charter. . . .

Plaintiff in the instant case argues that the directors are acting for reasons unrelated to the financial interest and welfare of the Cubs. However, we are not satisfied that the motives assigned to Philip K. Wrigley, and through him to the other directors, are contrary to the best interests of the corporation and the stockholders. For example, it appears to us that the effect on the surrounding neighborhood might well be considered by a director who was considering the patrons who would or would not attend the games if the park were in a poor neighborhood. Furthermore, the long run interest of the corporation in its property value at Wrigley Field might demand all efforts to keep the neighborhood from deteriorating. By these thoughts we do not mean to say that we have decided that the decision of the directors was a correct one. That is beyond our jurisdiction and ability. We are merely saying that the decision is one properly before directors and the motives alleged in the amended complaint showed no fraud, illegality or conflict of interest in their making of that decision.

While all the courts do not insist that one or more of the three elements must be present for a stockholder's derivative action to lie, nevertheless we feel that unless the conduct of the defendants at least borders on one of the elements, the courts should not interfere.[19] The trial court in the instant case acted properly in dismissing plaintiff's amended complaint.

We feel that plaintiff's amended complaint was also defective in failing to allege damage to the corporation. . . .

There is no allegation that the night games played by the other nineteen teams enhanced their financial position or that the profits, if any, of those teams were directly related to the number of night games scheduled. There is an allegation that the installation of lights and scheduling of night games in Wrigley Field would have resulted in large amounts of additional revenues and incomes from increased attendance and related sources of income. Further, the cost of installation of lights, funds for which are allegedly readily available by financing, would be more than offset and recaptured by increased revenues. However, no allegation is made that there will be a net benefit to the corporation from such action, considering all increased costs.

Plaintiff claims that the losses of defendant corporation are due to poor attendance at home games. However, it appears from the amended complaint, taken as a whole, that factors other than attendance affect the net earnings or losses. For example, in 1962, attendance at home and road games decreased appreciably as compared with 1961, and yet the loss from direct baseball operation and of the whole corporation was considerably less.

The record shows that plaintiff did not feel he could allege that the increased revenues would be sufficient to cure the corporate deficit. The only cost plaintiff was at all concerned with was that of installation of lights. No mention was made of operation and maintenance of the lights or other possible increases in operating costs of night games and we cannot speculate as to what other factors might influence the increase or decrease of profits if the Cubs were to play night home games. . . .

---

19. Compare Neese v. Brown, footnote 17 supra: "It is generally held that the liability of the directors and other officers of a corporation is not limited to willful breaches of trust or excessive power but also extends to negligence." See also Rapoport v. Schneider, 28 N.Y.2d 396, 278 N.E.2d 642, 328 N.Y.S.2d 431 (1972) ("a director may be held accountable for the waste of corporate assets whether intentional or negligent without limitation to transactions from which he benefits"). Accord, Stamp v. Batastini, 263 Ill. App. 3d 1010, 636 N.E.2d 616 (1993). — ED.

Finally, we do not agree with plaintiff's contention that failure to follow the example of the other major league clubs in scheduling night games constituted negligence. Plaintiff made no allegation that these teams' night schedules were profitable or that the purpose for which night baseball had been undertaken was fulfilled. Furthermore, it cannot be said that directors, even those of corporations that are losing money, must follow the lead of the other corporations in the field. Directors are elected for their business capabilities and judgment and the courts cannot require them to forego their judgment because of the decisions of directors of other companies. Courts may not decide these questions in the absence of a clear showing of dereliction of duty on the part of the specific directors and mere failure to "follow the crowd" is not such a dereliction. . . .

Affirmed.

Profit maximization. How do the materials on pages 34-46 supra — particularly ALI, Principles of Corporate Governance §2.01 and state "constituency" statutes — bear on the *Wrigley* case?

Miller v. American Telephone & Telegraph Co.
507 F.2d 759 (3rd Cir. 1974)

SEITZ, C.J.: Plaintiffs, stockholders in American Telephone and Telegraph Company ("AT&T"), brought a stockholders' derivative action in the Eastern District of Pennsylvania against AT&T and all but one of its directors. The suit centered upon the failure of AT&T to collect an outstanding debt of some $1.5 million owed to the company by the Democratic National Committee ("DNC") for communications services provided by AT&T during the 1968 Democratic national convention. . . . The failure to collect was alleged to have involved a breach of the defendant directors' duty to exercise diligence in handling the affairs of the corporation . . . and to have amounted to AT&T's making a "contribution" to the DNC in violation of a federal prohibition on corporate campaign spending, 18 U.S.C. §610 (1970).

Plaintiffs sought permanent relief in the form of an injunction requiring AT&T to collect the debt, an injunction against providing further services to the DNC until the debt was paid in full, and a surcharge for the benefit of the corporation against the defendant directors in the amount of the debt plus interest from the due date. . . .

The pertinent law on the question of the defendant directors' fiduciary duties in this diversity action is that of New York, the state of AT&T's incorporation. . . . The sound business judgment rule, the basis of the district court's dismissal of plaintiffs' complaint, expresses the unanimous decision of American courts to eschew intervention in corporate decision-making if the judgment of directors and officers is uninfluenced by personal considerations and is exercised in good faith. . . . Where, however, the decision not to collect a debt owed the corporation is itself alleged to have been an illegal act, different rules apply. When New York law regarding such acts by directors is considered in conjunction with the underlying purposes of the particular statute involved here, we are convinced that the business judgment rule cannot insulate the defendant directors from liability if they did in fact breach 18 U.S.C. §610, as plaintiffs have charged.

Roth v. Robertson, 64 Misc. 343, 118 N.Y.S. 351 (Sup. Ct. 1909), illustrates the proposition that even though committed to benefit the corporation, illegal acts may amount to a breach of fiduciary duty in New York. In *Roth*, the managing director of an amusement park company had allegedly used corporate funds to purchase the silence of persons who threatened to complain about unlawful Sunday operation of the park. Recovery from the defendant director was sustained on the ground that the money was an illegal payment: ". . . To hold any other rule would be establishing a dangerous precedent, tacitly countenancing the wasting of corporate funds for purposes of corrupting public morals." The plaintiffs' complaint in the instant case alleges a similar "waste" of $1.5 million through an illegal campaign contribution.

Abrams v. Allen, 297 N.Y. 52, 74 N.E.2d 305 (1947), reflects an affirmation by the New York Court of Appeals of the principle of *Roth* that directors must be restrained from engaging in activities which are against public policy. In *Abrams* the court held that a cause of action was stated by an allegation in a derivative complaint that the directors of Remington Rand, Inc., had relocated corporate plants and curtailed production solely for the purpose of intimidating and punishing employees for their involvement in a labor dispute. The Court of Appeals acknowledged that, "depending on the circumstances," proof of the allegations in the complaint might sustain recovery, inter alia, under the rule that directors are liable for corporate loss caused by the commission of an "unlawful or immoral act." In support of its holding, the court noted that the closing of factories for the purpose alleged was opposed to the public policy of the state and nation as embodied in the New York Labor Law and the National Labor Relations Act.

The alleged violation of the federal prohibition against corporate political contributions not only involves the corporation in criminal activity but similarly contravenes a policy of Congress clearly enunciated in 18 U.S.C. §610.[4] That statute and its predecessor reflect congressional efforts: (1) to destroy the influence of corporations over elections through financial contributions and (2) to check the practice of using corporate funds to benefit political parties without the consent of the stockholders.

The fact that shareholders are within the class for whose protection the statute was enacted gives force to the argument that the alleged breach of that statute should give rise to a cause of action in those shareholders to force the return to the corporation of illegally contributed funds. Since political contributions by corporations can be checked and shareholder control over the political use of general corporate funds effectuated only if directors are restrained from causing the corporation to violate the statute, such a violation seems a particularly appropriate basis for finding breach of the defendant directors' fiduciary duty to the corporation. Under such circumstances, the directors cannot be insulated from liability on the ground that the contribution was made in the exercise of sound business judgment.

Since plaintiffs have alleged actual damage to the corporation from the transaction in the form of the loss of a $1.5 million increment to AT&T's treasury,[5] we

---

4. We note that prior to June 1, 1974, corporate political contributions made "directly or indirectly" violated New York law. Law of July 20, 1965, ch. 1031, §43, [1965] N.Y. Laws 1783 (repealed 1974). . . .

5. Under New York law, allegation of breach even of a federal statute is apparently insufficient to state a cause of action unless the breach caused independent damage to the corporation. See Diamond v. Davis, 263 App. Div. 68, 31 N.Y.S.2d (1st Dept. 1941); Borden v. Cohen, 231 N.Y.S.2d 902 (Sup. Ct. 1962). But see Runcie v. Bankers Trust Co., 6 N.Y.S.2d 623 (Sup. Ct. 1938).

conclude that the complaint does state a claim upon which relief can be granted sufficient to withstand a motion to dismiss.

. . . At the appropriate time, plaintiffs will be required to produce evidence sufficient to establish three distinct elements comprising a violation of 18 U.S.C. §610: that AT&T (1) made a contribution of money or anything of value to the DNC (2) in connection with a federal election (3) for the purpose of influencing the outcome of that election. . . . Proof of non-collection of a debt owed by the DNC will be insufficient to establish the statutory violation upon which the defendants' breach of fiduciary duty is predicated; plaintiffs must shoulder the burden of proving an impermissible motivation underlying the alleged inaction. In the absence of direct proof of a partisan purpose on the part of the defendants, plaintiffs may produce evidence sufficient to justify the inference that the only discernible reason for the failure to pursue the debtor was a desire to assist the Democratic Party in achieving success in a federal election. At a minimum, plaintiffs must establish that legitimate business justifications did not underlie the alleged inaction of the defendant directors. The possibility of the existence of such reasonable business motives illustrates the need for proof of more than mere non-collection even of the debt of a political party in order to establish a breach of 18 U.S.C. §610. . . .

The order of the district court will be reversed and the case remanded for further proceedings consistent with this opinion.[20]

---

1. *"Legitimate business justifications."* (a) What result in the *Miller* case if AT&T defended its inaction on the ground that to press collection of the debt might deter large organizations from installing as much communications equipment at their conventions as they might otherwise? That to press collection might create an unfavorable political climate for AT&T in its dealings with government? What result in the *Roth* case if the manager defended the bribery on the ground that the corporation profited greatly from Sunday operation? What result in the *Abrams* case if the directors defended their conduct on the ground that the immediate cost of discouraging unions would benefit the corporation financially in the future? To what extent would these defenses preclude a finding of "independent damage to the corporation"?[21]

(b) *Foreign bribes.* In the mid 1970s, it was disclosed that a large number of American corporations doing business abroad had used corporate funds to bribe various foreign government officials, in violation of the laws of the foreign countries, in order to obtain favorable business treatment. The Foreign Corrupt Practices Act, 15 U.S.C. §§78dd-1, 78dd-2 (1977), made it unlawful. Should

---

20. In Cort v. Ash, 422 U.S. 66 (1975), a shareholder of Bethlehem Steel Corp. brought a derivative suit in federal court seeking damages for the corporation against the Bethlehem directors for expending corporate funds contrary to 18 U.S.C. §610. The Court held that a *federal* private cause of action could *not* be implied for violation of the statute and the plaintiff was relegated to whatever remedies existed at state law (referring to the *Miller* case). The Court expressed no view as to the result under the 1974 amendments to the statute. — ED.

21. For support of a "fiduciary duty to comply with the law even when compliance requires sacrificing profits," see Einer Elhauge, Sacrificing Corporate Profits in the Public Interest, 80 N.Y.U. L. Rev. 733, 761-762 (2005): "This fiduciary duty counters the incentive to engage in excessive illegality otherwise created by accountability to shareholders who lack incentives to fully consider social and moral sanctions" and serves "to replicate the social and moral norms about legal compliance that apply to noncorporate actors."

corporate managers who direct or approve such payments be liable to the corporation for the amounts expended? If failure to pay bribes would endanger the success of the corporation's foreign business and place it at a serious competitive disadvantage with foreign companies that are not restricted by the laws of their countries from engaging in such conduct, should a corporation's president who abides by the Foreign Corrupt Practices Act be liable to the corporation for the resulting business losses?

2. *Public policy—moral and practical considerations.* How does ALI §2.01(b)(1), page 37 supra, bear on the above questions?

> It is sometimes maintained that whether a corporation should adhere to a given legal rule may properly depend on a kind of cost-benefit analysis, in which probable corporate gains are weighed against either probable social costs, measured by the dollar liability imposed for engaging in such conduct, or probable corporate losses, measured by potential dollar liability discounted for likelihood of detection.[22] Section 2.01 does not adopt this position.[23] . . . Cost-benefit analysis may have a place in the state's determination whether a given type of conduct should be deemed legally wrongful. Once that determination has been made, however, the resulting legal rule normally represents a community decision that the conduct is wrongful as such, so that cost-benefit analysis whether to obey the rule is out of place.

1 ALI, Principles of Corporate Governance 60 (1994).

For the view that the analogy between the "efficient breach of contract theory" (upon which the cost-benefit analysis rests) and the breaching of a regulatory law is seriously flawed, see Williams, footnote 22 supra, at 1325, 1332-1333:

> Even the most ardent advocates of the theory of efficient breach of contract recognize that actual compensation is required, or the goal of the theory (efficiency) will not be well-served. . . . The same cannot be said about breach of public law: Affected individuals may not know of their rights or that their rights have been infringed upon; or there may be strong disincentives to insisting on one's rights based on the nature of the relationship (for example, employer/employee or landlord/tenant); or public enforcement agencies may not know of law violations, since violators will have

22. See Richard Posner, The Economic Analysis of Law 5, 118-120 (4th ed. 1992); Frank H. Easterbrook & Daniel R. Fischel, The Economic Structure of Corporate Law 35-39 (1991); compare Robert Cooter, Prices and Sanctions, 84 Colum. L. Rev. 1523 (1984). "Inherent in this view of law is the legal voluntarism claim: that particularly with respect to regulatory law [that which is 'malum prohibitum' rather than 'malum in se'], a person can either conform to the law or violate it while accepting the known consequences, and that either choice is an acceptable means for an individual or corporation to fulfill its obligations as a citizen. . . . [Further,] since people and corporations will, and possibly should, make decisions about compliance with law based on a 'rational actor's' calculations of costs and benefits, their expectations about the likely outcome of violating the law or investing a certain amount in compliance ought to be recognized as settled expectations upon which they may legitimately rely." Cynthia A. Williams, Corporate Compliance with the Law in the Era of Efficiency, 76 N.C. L. Rev. 1265, 1287 (1998). For consideration of whether "the shareholders would prefer, ex ante, that this strict rule of profit maximization apply for all possible corporate purposes and activities, or whether they would prefer a rule of profit maximization for legal activities and a different rule for illegal activities," see Greenfield, footnote 12 supra, at 1330-1344. — ED.

23. Compare ALI §7.18(c), dealing with recovery for damages against corporate fiduciaries for breach of duty: "The court may permit a defendant to offset against such liability any gains to the corporation that the defendant can establish arose out of the same transaction and whose recognition in this manner is not contrary to public policy." See also ALI §7.19, Note 3(b), page 108 infra, permitting a shareholder-approved provision in the articles of incorporation to limit damages against fiduciaries for illegality except that which is "knowing and culpable." In contrast, RMBCA §2.02(b)(4) bars such a limitation on damages for any "intentional violation of criminal law." — ED.

every incentive to hide their conduct; or compensation (paying the penalties) may not occur for many reasons unrelated to the underlying conduct, such as the difficulty and expense of enforcing one's rights in court, relative to the amount of money at issue. . . . [Further, since] the harm caused by breach of contract is primarily economic, it can often be fully compensated by monetary damages. . . . [But in] the realm of public law [such as those concerned with "industrial practices . . . [that threaten] human and environmental health and safety"], specific performance of statutory obligations is always far superior to having putative defendants paying penalties when the harm to be avoided is not primarily economic. Even in those instances in which the harm to be avoided by a particular statute is purely economic, statutory compliance will usually be preferable.

The *Francis* and *Van Gorkom* cases, which follow, were the two most prominent decisions in the early 1980s that imposed liability on directors for breach of the duty of care.

Inactive (or "figurehead," "dummy," or "accommodation") directors. (a) (i) In Francis v. United Jersey Bank, 87 N.J. 15, 432 A.2d 814 (1981), the trustees in bankruptcy of a reinsurance broker firm sued the estate of Mrs. Pritchard — who, with her two sons, were the firm's directors, officers and shareholders — for losses due to the sons' siphoning over $12,000,000 from funds held by the firm in trust and recording these as "shareholder loans" on the firm's financial statements which were part of a "woefully inadequate and highly dangerous bookkeeping system." The court held that Mrs. Pritchard "was liable in negligence for the losses caused by the wrongdoing" of her sons:

> Mrs. Pritchard was not active in the business of Pritchard & Baird and knew virtually nothing of its corporate affairs. She briefly visited the corporate offices in Morristown on only one occasion, and she never read or obtained the annual financial statements. She was unfamiliar with the rudiments of reinsurance and made no effort to assure that the policies and practices of the corporation, particularly pertaining to the withdrawal of funds, complied with industry custom or relevant law. Although her husband had warned her that Charles, Jr. would "take the shirt off my back," Mrs. Pritchard did not pay any attention to her duties as a director or to the affairs of the corporation. . . .
>
> After her husband died in December 1973, Mrs. Pritchard became incapacitated and was bedridden for a six-month period. She became listless at this time and started to drink rather heavily. Her physical condition deteriorated, and in 1978 she died. . . .
>
> Directors are under a continuing obligation to keep informed about the activities of the corporation. Otherwise, they may not be able to participate in the overall management of corporate affairs. . . . Directors may not shut their eyes to corporate misconduct and then claim that because they did not see the misconduct, they did not have a duty to look.[24] The sentinel asleep at his post contributes nothing to the enterprise he is charged to protect. . . .
>
> Directorial management does not require a detailed inspection of day-to-day activities, but rather a general monitoring of corporate affairs and policies. . . . Regular attendance does not mean that directors must attend every meeting, but that directors should attend meetings as a matter of practice. A director of a publicly held corporation might be expected to attend regular monthly meetings, but a director of a small, family corporation might be asked to attend only an annual meeting. . . .

---

24. Accord, FDIC v. Bierman, 2 F.3d 1424 (7th Cir. 1993). — Ed

While directors are not required to audit corporate books, they should maintain familiarity with the financial status of the corporation by a regular review of financial statements. . . . In some circumstances, directors may be charged with assuring that bookkeeping methods conform to industry custom and usage. Lippitt v. Ashley, 89 Conn. 451, 464, 94 A. 995, 1000 (Sup. Ct. 1915). The extent of review, as well as the nature and frequency of financial statements, depends not only on the customs of the industry, but also on the nature of the corporation and the business in which it is engaged. . . . Adequate financial review normally would be more informal in a private corporation than in a publicly held corporation.

. . . [F]ulfillment of the duty of a director may call for more than mere objection and resignation. . . . Sometimes the duty of a director may require more than consulting with outside counsel. A director may have a duty to take reasonable means to prevent illegal conduct by co-directors; in any appropriate case, this may include threat of suit.

(ii) Would Mrs. Pritchard have been liable if she had resigned as a director prior to 1970, thus leaving Pritchard & Baird with only two directors (as permitted by New Jersey law)? If not, why should the result in the *Francis* case be different? Geygan v. Queen City Grain Co., 71 Ohio App. 3d 185, 593 N.E.2d 328 (1991), and Senn v. Northwest Underwriters, Inc., 875 P.2d 637 (Wash. App. 1994), follow the *Francis* case with respect to a wife-director whose husband ran the company. See also ATR-Kim Eng Financial Corp v. Araneta, 2006 WL 3783520 (Del. Ch. 2006), which imposed liability on two directors who were "stooges" of Araneta, the controlling shareholder; one was the head of Araneta's domestic operations and the other, Araneta's niece, was CFO of his international enterprise. They "allowed Araneta to do whatever he wanted, without any examination of whether his conduct benefited the . . . [corporation] and all of its stockholders, rather than simply Araneta personally."

(b) *Proximate cause.* In the *Francis* case, the court, relying on a classic decision by Judge Learned Hand in Barnes v. Andrews, 298 F. 614 (S.D.N.Y. 1924), reasoned that

the negligence of Mrs. Pritchard does not result in liability unless . . . the defendant's act or omission was a necessary antecedent of the loss, i.e., that if the defendant had observed his or her duty of care, the loss would not have occurred. . . . Further, the plaintiff has the burden of establishing the amount of the loss or damages caused by the negligence of the defendant. . . .

Usually a director can absolve himself from liability by informing the other directors of the impropriety and voting for a proper course of action. Dyson, The Director's Liability for Negligence, 40 Ind. L.J. 341, 365 (1965). . . . In many, if not most, instances an objecting director whose dissent is noted in accordance with N.J.S.A. 14A:6-13 would be absolved after attempting to persuade fellow directors to follow a different course of action.

Compare Cede & Co. v. Technicolor, Inc., 634 A. 2d 345 (Del., 1993), holding that "the tort principles of *Barnes* have no place in a business judgment rule standard of review analysis"; breach of "the duty of care rebuts the presumption that the directors have acted in the best interests of the shareholders, and requires the directors to prove that the transaction was entirely fair." For the view that "by allowing . . . [conflict of interest] standards to seep into its articulation of the duty of care obligation to be informed, the court seriously undermined the business judgment rule," see Jay P. Moran, Business Judgment Rule or Relic?: *Cede v.*

Technicolor and the Continuing Metamorphosis of Director Duty of Care, 45 Emory L.J. 339 (1996).[25]

RMBCA §8.31(b)(1) (1998) provides that the party seeking to hold the director liable for money damages shall have the burden of establishing "harm to the corporation" that was "proximately caused by the director's challenged conduct." See also ALI §4.01(d), page 104 infra. See also William T. Allen, Jack B. Jacobs & Leo E. Strine Jr., Function over Form: A Reassessment of Standards of Review in Delaware Corporation Law, 26 Del. J. Corp. L. 859, 892 (2001): "No discernible reason has been advanced for relieving the plaintiff from the burden of proving that the directors' grossly negligent acts caused quantifiable harm."

Duty of an "informed" business judgment. (a) In Smith v. Van Gorkom, 488 A. 2d 858 (Del. 1985), the board of Trans Union Corp., whose share price (which ranged between 29$^1/_2$ and 38$^1/_4$ during the current year) had been depressed because of its inability to take advantage of certain tax benefits, unanimously approved a $55-per-share offer for a cash-out merger into a company controlled by Pritzker, a well-known takeover specialist.

In August 1980 Van Gorkom, Trans Union's longtime chairman and CEO, who was near retirement age, first discussed at a senior management meeting "the sale of Trans Union to a company with a large amount of taxable income." On September 5, at another such meeting, Van Gorkom stated to Chelberg, the company's president and a director, "that he would be willing to take $55" for his shares. Van Gorkom then met with Pritzker, a social acquaintance, and presented a specific plan by which Pritzker could finance a $55-per-share purchase of Trans Union. In less than a week, Pritzker agreed on several conditions, including that (1) for ninety days, Trans Union could receive, but not actively solicit, competing offers during a "market test" and (2) the Trans Union board would act on the merger proposal within three days. At a special meeting of about two hours called for the following day, September 20, the board accepted. The court, 3-2, held that "in the specific context of a proposed merger," the board "did not reach an informed business judgment":

> Without any documents before them concerning the proposed transaction, the members of the Board were required to rely entirely upon Van Gorkom's 20-minute oral presentation of the proposal. No written summary of the terms of the merger was presented; the directors were given no documentation to support the adequacy of $55 price per share for sale of the Company; and the Board had before it nothing more than Van Gorkom's statement of his understanding of the substance of an agreement which he admittedly had never read, nor which any member of the Board had ever seen. . . .
>
> A substantial premium may provide one reason to recommend a merger, but in the absence of other sound valuation information, the fact of a premium alone does not provide an adequate basis upon which to assess the fairness of an offering price. Here, the judgment reached as to the adequacy of the premium was based on a comparison between the historically depressed Trans Union market price and the amount of the Pritzker offer. . . .

25. Is it significant that *Technicolor* involved a challenge to director approval of a merger, which, under Delaware law, often triggers the "entire fairness" standard of judicial review, in contrast to the business judgment rule's minimal standard? See Emerald Partners v. Berlin, 787 A.2d 85 (Del. 2001) (discussing such differences in connection with a merger transaction and the burden of proof regarding a corporate charter provision that eliminated director liability for breach of the duty of care — considered further in Note 4, page 109 infra).

The parties do not dispute that a publicly-traded stock price is solely a measure of the value of a minority position and, thus, market price represents only the value of a single share. Nevertheless, on September 20, the Board assessed the adequacy of the premium over market, offered by Pritzker, solely by comparing it with Trans Union's current and historical stock price. . . . [19] . . .

This brings us to the post–September 20 "market test" upon which the defendants ultimately rely to confirm the reasonableness of their September 20 decision to accept the Pritzker proposal. In this connection, the directors present a two-part argument: (a) that by making a "market test" of Pritzker's $55 per share offer a condition of their September 20 decision to accept his offer, they cannot be found to have acted impulsively or in an uninformed manner on September 20; and (b) that the adequacy of the $17 premium for sale of the Company was conclusively established over the following 90 to 120 days by the most reliable evidence available — the marketplace. Thus, the defendants impliedly contend that the "market test" eliminated the need for the Board to perform any other form of fairness test either on September 20, or thereafter.

Again, the facts of record do not support the defendants' argument. There is no evidence: (a) that the Merger Agreement was effectively amended [on September 20] to give the Board freedom to put Trans Union up for auction sale to the highest bidder; or (b) that a public auction was in fact permitted to occur. . . .

The directors' unfounded reliance on both the premium and the market test as the basis for accepting the Pritzker proposal undermines the defendants' remaining contention that the Board's collective experience and sophistication was a sufficient basis for finding that it reached its September 20 decision with informed, reasonable deliberation.[21] . . .

The October 10 amendments to the Merger Agreement did authorize Trans Union to solicit competing offers, but . . . Trans Union could accept from a third party a better offer only if it were incorporated in a definitive agreement between the parties, and not conditioned on financing or on any other contingency. . . .

[Although the investment firm of Salomon Brothers was retained to search for offers and contacted 150 corporations, a proposal by the investment firm of Kohlberg, Kravis, Roberts & Co. ("KKR")] was the first and only offer received subsequent to the Pritzker Merger Agreement. The offer resulted primarily from the efforts of Romans [Trans Union's CFO] and other senior officers to propose an alternative to Pritzker's acquisition of Trans Union. In late September, Romans' group contacted KKR about the possibility of a leveraged buy-out by all members of Management, except Van Gorkom. . . .

---

19. As of September 20 the directors did not know: that Van Gorkom had arrived at the $55 figure alone, and subjectively, as the figure to be used by Controller Peterson in creating a feasible structure for a leveraged buy-out by a prospective purchaser; that Van Gorkom had not sought advice, information or assistance from either inside or outside Trans Union directors as to the value of the Company as an entity or the fair price per share for 100% of its stock; that Van Gorkom had not consulted with the Company's investment bankers or other financial analysts; that Van Gorkom had not consulted with or confided in any officer or director of the Company except Chelberg; and that Van Gorkom had deliberately chosen to ignore the advice and opinion of the members of his Senior Management group regarding the adequacy of the $55 price.

21. Trans Union's five "inside" directors had backgrounds in law and accounting, 116 years of collective employment by the Company and 68 years of combined experience on its Board. Trans Union's five "outside" directors included four chief executives of major corporations and an economist who was a former dean of a major school of business and chancellor of a university. The "outside" directors had 78 years of combined experience as chief executive officers of major corporations and 50 years of cumulative experience as directors of Trans Union. Thus, defendants argue that the Board was eminently qualified to reach an informed judgment on the proposed "sale" of Trans Union notwithstanding their lack of any advance notice of the proposal, the shortness of their deliberation, and their determination not to consult with their investment banker or to obtain a fairness opinion.

. . . On December 2, Kravis [of KKR] and Romans hand-delivered to Van Gorkom a formal letter-offer to purchase all of Trans Union's assets and to assume all of its liabilities for an aggregate cash consideration equivalent to $60 per share. The offer was contingent upon completing equity and bank financing of $650 million, which Kravis represented as 80% complete. . . . Kravis stated that they were willing to enter into a "definitive agreement" under terms and conditions "substantially the same" as those contained in Trans Union's agreement with Pritzker. The offer was addressed to Trans Union's Board of Directors and a meeting with the Board, scheduled for that afternoon, was requested.

Van Gorkom's reaction to the KKR proposal was completely negative; he did not view the offer as being firm because of its financing condition. It was pointed out, to no avail, that Pritzker's offer had not only been similarly conditioned, but accepted on an expedited basis. Van Gorkom refused Kravis' request that Trans Union issue a press release announcing KKR's offer, on the ground that it might chill any other offer.[27] Romans and Kravis left with the understanding that their proposal would be presented to Trans Union's Board that afternoon.

Within a matter of hours and shortly before the scheduled Board meeting, Kravis withdrew his letter-offer. . . . At the Board meeting later that afternoon, Van Gorkom did not inform the directors of the KKR proposal because he considered it "dead."

. . . [P]laintiffs have not claimed, nor did the Trial Court decide, that $55 was a grossly inadequate price per share for sale of the Company. That being so, the presumption that a board's judgment as to adequacy of price represents an honest exercise of business judgment (absent proof that the sale price was grossly inadequate) is irrelevant to the threshold question of whether an informed judgment was reached.

One dissenting judge wrote that

the first and most important error made is the majority's assessment of the directors' knowledge of the affairs of Trans Union and their combined ability to act in this situation under the protection of the business judgment rule. . . .

Directors of this caliber [footnote 21 of excerpt supra] are not ordinarily taken in by a "fast shuffle." I submit they were not taken into this multi-million dollar corporate transaction without being fully informed and aware of the state of the art as it pertained to the entire corporate panorama of Trans Union. True, even directors such as these, with their business acumen, interest and expertise, can go astray. I do not believe that to be the case here. These men knew Trans Union like the back of their hands and were more than well qualified to make on the spot informed business judgments concerning the affairs of Trans Union including a 100% sale of the corporation. Lest we forget, the corporate world of then and now operates on what is so aptly referred to as the "fast track." These men were at the time an integral part of that world, all professional business men, not intellectual figureheads.

. . . Moreover, at the July, 1980 Board meeting the directors had reviewed Trans Union's newly prepared five-year forecast, and at the August, 1980 meeting Van Gorkom presented the results of a comprehensive study of Trans Union made by The Boston Consulting Group. This study was prepared over an 18 month period and consisted of a detailed analysis of all Trans Union subsidiaries, including competitiveness, profitability, cash throw-off, cash consumption, technical competence and future prospects for contribution to Trans Union's combined net income.

---

27. This was inconsistent with Van Gorkom's espousal of the September 22 press release following Trans Union's acceptance of Pritzker's proposal. Van Gorkom had then justified a press release as encouraging rather than chilling later offers.

At the September 20 meeting Van Gorkom reviewed all aspects of the proposed transaction and repeated the explanation of the Pritzker offer he had earlier given to senior management. Having heard Van Gorkom's explanation of the Pritzkers' offer, . . . the directors discussed the matter . . . [and] the proposed merger was approved.[26]

(b) In Citron v. Fairchild Camera & Instrumental Corp., 569 A.2d 53 (Del. 1989), noted in 1991 B.Y.U. L. Rev. 1377, the board of directors (eight of ten members being outsiders) accepted a "white knight's" tender offer imposed under a three-hour deadline. The court held this "was protected by the business judgment rule":

The standard for determining "whether a business judgment reached by a board of directors was an informed one" is gross negligence. *Van Gorkom* at 873.[27] In our case law since *Van Gorkom*, our due care examination has focused on a board's decision-making process. We look for evidence as to whether a board has acted in a deliberate and knowledgeable way in identifying and exploring alternatives. Within the context of this analysis, we . . . recognize that a board will receive substantial information from third-party sources. As we have noted on various occasions, however, in change of control situations, sole reliance on hired experts and management can "taint[] the design and execution of the transaction." Mills Acquisition Co. v. Macmillan, Inc., Del. Sup., 559 A.2d 1261, 1281 (1988). Thus, we look particularly for evidence of a board's active and direct role in the sale process.

. . . The Fairchild board . . . had been considering the possibility that the company would be sold for two years prior to receipt of Gould's unsolicited first proposal. The board, also in contrast with the Trans Union board, received investment advice from four leading investment banking firms, commissioned financial evaluations by three of them, shopped the company to roughly 75 potential buyers, and discussed the sale of the company at three separate board meetings over the course of three weeks. . . . The imposition of artificial time limits on the decision-making process of a board of directors may compromise the integrity of that deliberative process. See *Van Gorkom.* However, whether the constraints are self-imposed or attributable to bargaining tactics of an adversary seeking a final resolution to a belabored process must be considered. Boards that have failed to exercise due care are frequently boards

---

26. For the view that the *Van Gorkom* case "is not, at bottom, a business judgment case," but rather a "takeover case . . . [whose] function is to regulate a target's response to certain types of takeover bids, namely 'rush' offers with short time fuses," see Jonathan R. Macey & Geoffrey P. Miller, *Trans Union Reconsidered,* 98 Yale L.J. 127 (1988).

In the final analysis, the issue facing the directors in *Trans Union* was whether to accept the deal proposed and negotiated by Van Gorkom, the most knowledgeable member of the board with strong incentives to get the best deal possible, or attempt to get a better deal when doing so entailed spending additional amounts on information and risking winding up with nothing. This is the classic type of decision in which corporate law has long recognized that the directors, in light of their superior information and incentive to maximize the value of the firm, are better able to assess this trade-off than individual shareholders, plaintiffs' attorneys, or courts.

Daniel R. Fischel, The Business Judgment Rule and the *Trans Union* Case, 40 Bus. Law. 1437, 1447, 1453 (1995). — ED.

27. "Delaware corporate cases have adopted a gross negligence standard that requires a plaintiff to demonstrate a degree of culpability on the part of the directors that is akin to the recklessness standard employed in other contexts . . . a definition of gross negligence that is even more difficult for a plaintiff to establish than the gross negligence standard normally applied in American tort or criminal cases." William T. Allen, Jack B. Jacobs & Leo E. Strine Jr., Realigning the Standard of Review of Director Due Care with Delaware Public Policy: A Critique of *Van Gorkom* and Its Progeny as a Standard of Review Problem, 96 Nw. U. L. Rev. 449, 453 (2002). Contra, Brane v. Roth, 590 N.E.2d 587 (Ind. App. 1992) ("ordinary negligence"). — ED.

that have been rushed. We conclude that the time constraints placed on the Fairchild board were not of the board's making and did not compromise its deliberative process under *Van Gorkom*.[28]

In re Walt Disney Co. Derivative Litigation
906 A.2d 27 (2006)

JACOBS, J.: In August 1995, Michael Ovitz ("Ovitz") and The Walt Disney Company ("Disney" or the "Company") entered into an employment agreement ["OEA"] [that had been extensively negotiated by Michael Eisner, Disney's Chairman and CEO, and approved by the compensation committee] under which Ovitz would serve as President of Disney for five years. In December 1996, only fourteen months after he commenced employment, ["it had become clear that Ovitz was 'a poor fit with his fellow executives.' By then the Disney directors were discussing that the disconnect between Ovitz and the Company was likely irreparable and that Ovitz would have to be terminated."] Ovitz was terminated without cause ["No Fault Termination" or "NFT"], resulting in a severance payout to Ovitz valued at approximately $130 million.

In January 1997, several Disney shareholders [challenged this in] derivative actions in the Court of Chancery, on behalf of Disney, against Ovitz and the directors of Disney who served at the time of the events complained of (the "Disney defendants"). The . . . Chancellor . . . [held] that "the director defendants did not breach their fiduciary duties or commit waste." . . .

III. *The Claims Against Ovitz.* . . . [The court ruled that (1) Ovitz had no fiduciary relationship with Disney at the time he negotiated the OEA, and that (2) Ovitz did not breach any] fiduciary duty, including his duty of loyalty, by receiving the NFT payment upon his termination as President of Disney. . . . As the trial court found, "Ovitz did not 'engage' in a transaction with the corporation — rather, the corporation imposed an unwanted transaction upon him." . . .

IV. *The Claims Against the Disney Defendants.* . . . [A]ppellants' core argument in the trial court was that the Disney defendants' approval of the OEA and election of Ovitz as President were not entitled to business judgment rule protection, because those actions were either grossly negligent or not performed in good faith. . . .

1. *The Due Care Determinations.* . . . Our law presumes that "in making a business decision the directors of a corporation acted on an informed basis, in good faith, and in the honest belief that the action taken was in the best interests of the company."[61] Those presumptions can be rebutted if the plaintiff shows that the

---

28. For a later decision finding "that the defendant directors were grossly negligent in failing to reach an informed decision when they approved the agreement of merger, and to have thereby breached their duty of care," see the *Technicolor* case, Note — supra. In this same litigation, however, the court ultimately concluded that the directors had shown that the merger was "entirely fair" and were accordingly not liable for damages. Cinerama, Inc. v. Technicolor, Inc., 663 A.2d 1156, 1179 (Del. 1995). For the view that the *Technicolor* ruling will render the decision in *Van Gorkom* "largely irrelevant": "directors will only be held liable for damages" in such cases "where the directors have failed [*both*] to exercise procedural oversight of the challenged transaction *and* allow a self-interested director to manipulate the approval process," see Note, Refining Director Liability in Duty of Care Cases, 61 Mo. L. Rev. 663 (1996). — ED.

61. Aronson v. Lewis, 473 A.2d 805, 812 (Del. 1984). [For the view that although describing the business judgment rule as "presumption" is "a confusing misnomer," it does "establish special evidentiary and pleading standards," see R. Franklin Balotti & James J. Hanks Jr., Rejudging the Business Judgment Rule, 48 Bus. Law. 1337 (1993). — ED.]

directors breached their fiduciary duty of care or of loyalty or acted in bad faith. If that is shown, the burden then shifts to the director defendants to demonstrate that the challenged act or transaction was entirely fair to the corporation and its shareholders.[62]

Because no duty of loyalty claim was asserted against the Disney defendants, the only way to rebut the business judgment rule presumptions would be to show that the Disney defendants had either breached their duty of care or had not acted in good faith. At trial, the plaintiff-appellants attempted to establish both grounds, but the Chancellor determined that the plaintiffs had failed to prove either. . . .

The appellants . . . challenge the Court of Chancery's determination that the full Disney board was not required to consider and approve the OEA, because the Company's governing instruments allocated that decision to the compensation committee. This challenge . . . cannot survive scrutiny.

As the Chancellor found, under the Company's governing documents the board of directors was responsible for selecting the corporation's officers, but under the compensation committee charter, the committee was responsible for establishing and approving the salaries, together with benefits and stock options, of the Company's CEO and President. The compensation committee also had the charter-imposed duty to "approve employment contracts, or contracts at will" for "all corporate officers who are members of the Board of Directors regardless of salary." That is exactly what occurred here. The full board ultimately selected Ovitz as President, and the compensation committee considered and ultimately approved the OEA, which embodied the terms of Ovitz's employment, including his compensation.

The Delaware General Corporation Law (DGCL) expressly empowers a board of directors to appoint committees and to delegate to them a broad range of responsibilities,[69] which may include setting executive compensation. Nothing in the DGCL mandates that the entire board must make those decisions. . . .

The appellants next challenge the Chancellor's determination that although the compensation committee's decision-making process fell far short of corporate governance "best practices," the committee members breached no duty of care in considering and approving the NFT terms of the OEA. . . .

In our view, a helpful approach is to compare what actually happened here to what would have occurred had the committee followed a "best practices" (or "best case") scenario, from a process standpoint. In a "best case" scenario, all committee members would have received, before or at the committee's first meeting on September 26, 1995, a spreadsheet or similar document prepared by (or with the assistance of) a compensation expert (in this case, Graef Crystal). Making different, alternative assumptions, the spreadsheet would disclose the amounts that Ovitz could receive under the OEA in each circumstance that might foreseeably arise. One variable in that matrix of possibilities would be the cost to Disney of a non-fault termination for each of the five years of the initial term of the OEA. The contents of the spreadsheet would be explained to the committee members, either

---

62. Emerald Partners v. Berlin, 787 A.2d 85, 91 (Del. 2001); Brehm v. Eisner, 746 A.2d 244, 264 n.66 (Del. 2000) ("Thus, directors' decisions will be respected by courts unless the directors are interested or lack independence relative to the decision, do not act in good faith, act in a manner that cannot be attributed to a rational business purpose or reach their decision by a grossly negligent process that includes the failure to consider all material facts reasonably available.").

69. 8 Del. C. §141(c).

by the expert who prepared it or by a fellow committee member similarly knowledgeable about the subject. That spreadsheet, which ultimately would become an exhibit to the minutes of the compensation committee meeting, would form the basis of the committee's deliberations and decision.

Had that scenario been followed, there would be no dispute (and no basis for litigation) over what information was furnished to the committee members or when it was furnished. Regrettably, the committee's informational and decision-making process used here was not so tidy. . . .

The Disney compensation committee met twice: on September 26 and October 16, 1995. The minutes of the September 26 meeting reflect that the committee approved the terms of the OEA (at that time embodied in the form of a letter agreement), except for the option grants, which were not approved until October 16 — after the Disney stock incentive plan had been amended to provide for those options. At the September 26 meeting, the compensation committee considered a "term sheet" which, in summarizing the material terms of the OEA, relevantly disclosed that in the event of a non-fault termination, Ovitz would receive: (i) the present value of his salary ($1 million per year) for the balance of the contract term, (ii) the present value of his annual bonus payments (computed at $7.5 million) for the balance of the contract term, (iii) a $10 million termination fee, and (iv) the acceleration of his options for 3 million shares, which would become immediately exercisable at market price.

Thus, the compensation committee knew that in the event of an NFT, Ovitz's severance payment alone could be in the range of $40 million cash,[77] plus the value of the accelerated options. Because the actual payout to Ovitz was approximately $130 million, of which roughly $38.5 million was cash, the value of the options at the time of the NFT payout would have been about $91.5 million. Thus, the issue may be framed as whether the compensation committee members knew, at the time they approved the OEA, that the value of the option component of the severance package could reach the $92 million order of magnitude if they terminated Ovitz without cause after one year. The evidentiary record shows that the committee members were so informed.

On this question the documentation is far less than what best practices would have dictated. There is no exhibit to the minutes that discloses, in a single document, the estimated value of the accelerated options in the event of an NFT termination after one year. The information imparted to the committee members on that subject is, however, supported by other evidence, most notably the trial testimony of various witnesses about spreadsheets that were prepared for the compensation committee meetings. The compensation committee members derived their information about the potential magnitude of an NFT payout from two sources. The first was the value of the "benchmark" options previously granted to Eisner and Wells [Disney's deceased president and chief operating officer] and the valuations by Watson ["a member of Disney's compensation committee and a past Disney board chairman who had helped structure Wells' and Eisner's compensation packages"] of the proposed Ovitz options. Ovitz's options were set at 75% of parity with the options previously granted to Eisner and to Frank Wells. Because the compensation committee had established those earlier benchmark

---

77. . . . The actual cash payment to Ovitz was $38.5 million, which, it would appear, reflects the then-present value of the $34 million of salaries and bonuses.

option grants to Eisner and Wells and were aware of their value, a simple mathematical calculation would have informed them of the potential value range of Ovitz's options. Also, in August and September 1995, Watson and Russell [a Disney director and chairman of the compensation committee] met with Graef Crystal to determine (among other things) the value of the potential Ovitz options, assuming different scenarios. Crystal valued the options under the Black-Scholes method,[29] while Watson used a different valuation metric. Watson recorded his calculations and the resulting values on a set of spreadsheets that reflected what option profits Ovitz might receive, based upon a range of different assumptions about stock market price increases. Those spreadsheets were shared with, and explained to, the committee members at the September meeting.

The committee's second source of information was the amount of "downside protection" that Ovitz was demanding. Ovitz ["who was regarded as one of the most powerful figures in Hollywood"] required financial protection from the risk of leaving a very lucrative and secure position at [Creative Artists Agency ("CAA"), the premier talent agency whose business model had reshaped the entire industry], of which he was a controlling partner, to join a publicly held corporation to which Ovitz was a stranger, and that had a very different culture and an environment which prevented him from completely controlling his destiny. The committee members knew that by leaving CAA and coming to Disney, Ovitz would be sacrificing "booked" CAA commissions of $150 to $200 million — an amount that Ovitz demanded as protection against the risk that his employment relationship with Disney might not work out. Ovitz wanted at least $50 million of that compensation to take the form of an "up-front" signing bonus. Had the $50 million bonus been paid, the size of the option grant would have been lower. Because it was contrary to Disney policy, the compensation committee rejected the up-front signing bonus demand, and elected instead to compensate Ovitz at the "back end," by awarding him options that would be phased in over the five-year term of the OEA. . . .

The OEA was specifically structured to compensate Ovitz for walking away from $150 million to $200 million of anticipated commissions from CAA over the five-year OEA contract term. This meant that if Ovitz was terminated without cause, the earlier in the contract term the termination occurred the larger the severance amount would be to replace the lost commissions. Indeed, because Ovitz was terminated after only one year, the total amount of his severance payment (about $130 million) closely approximated the lower end of the range of Ovitz's forfeited commissions ($150 million), less the compensation Ovitz received during his first and only year as Disney's President. . . .

Exposing the lack of merit in appellants' core due care claim enables us to address more cogently (and expeditiously) the appellants' fragmented subsidiary arguments. First, the appellants argue that not all members of the compensation committee reviewed the then-existing draft of the OEA. The Chancellor properly found that that was not required, because in this case the compensation committee was informed of the substance of the OEA.[79]

---

29. The court's footnote 8 stated: "The Black-Scholes method is a formula for option valuation that is widely used and accepted in the industry and by regulators." — ED.

79. As the Court found, "the compensation committee was provided with a term sheet of the key terms of the OEA and a presentation was made by Russell (assisted by Watson), who had personal knowledge of the relevant information by virtue of his negotiations with Ovitz and discussions with Crystal."

Second, appellants point out that the minutes of the September 26 compensation committee meeting recite no discussion of the grounds for which Ovitz could receive a non-fault termination. But the term sheet did include a description of the consequences of a not-for-cause termination, and the Chancellor found that although "no one on the committee recalled any discussion concerning the meaning of gross negligence or malfeasance," those terms "were not foreign to the board of directors, as the language was standard, and could be found, for example, in Eisner's [and] Wells' . . . employment contracts."

. . . [A]ppellants stress that Crystal did not make a report in person to the compensation committee at its September 26 meeting. Although that is true, it is undisputed that Crystal was available by phone if the committee members had questions that could not be answered by those who were present. Moreover, Russell and Watson related the substance of Crystal's analysis and information to the committee. . . . Nor did the Chancellor find merit to the appellants' related argument that two committee members, Poitier and Lozano, were not entitled to rely upon the work performed by Russell, Watson and Crystal in August and September 1995, without having first seen all of the written materials generated during that process or having participated in the discussions held during that time. . . .

The Chancellor correctly applied Section 141(e) in upholding the reliance of Lozano and Poitier upon the information that Crystal, Russell and Watson furnished to them. To accept the appellants' narrow reading of that statute would eviscerate its purpose, which is to protect directors who rely in good faith upon information presented to them from various sources, including "any other person as to matters the member reasonably believes are within such person's professional or expert competence and who has been selected with reasonable care by and on behalf of the corporation." [83]

Finally, the appellants contend that Poitier and Lozano did not review the spreadsheets generated by Watson at the September 26 meeting. The short answer is that even if Poitier and Lozano did not review the spreadsheets themselves, Russell and Watson adequately informed them of the spreadsheets' contents. . . . [84]

For these reasons, we uphold the Chancellor's determination that the compensation committee members did not breach their fiduciary duty of care in approving the OEA. . . .

The appellants' final claim in this category is that the Court of Chancery erroneously held that the remaining members of the old Disney board had not breached their duty of care in electing Ovitz as President of Disney. . . .

The Chancellor found and the record shows the following: well in advance of the September 26, 1995 board meeting the directors were fully aware that the Company needed — especially in light of Wells' death and Eisner's medical problems — to hire a "number two" executive and potential successor to Eisner. There had been many discussions about that need and about potential candidates who could fill that role even before Eisner decided to try to recruit Ovitz. Before the

---

83. 8 Del. C. §141(e).

84. The appellants underscore that neither Poitier nor Lozano could recall in their respective testimony, whether they had actually received or reviewed Watson's spreadsheets. The Court of Chancery, however, attributed that lack of recollection to the length of time that had passed since the meeting and credited Watson's testimony that he had shared his spreadsheets with the committee. We will not disturb that credibility determination. . . .

September 26 board meeting Eisner had individually discussed with each director the possibility of hiring Ovitz, and Ovitz's background and qualifications. The directors thus knew of Ovitz's skills, reputation and experience, all of which they believed would be highly valuable to the Company. The directors also knew that to accept a position at Disney, Ovitz would have to walk away from a very successful business—a reality that would lead a reasonable person to believe that Ovitz would likely succeed in similar pursuits elsewhere in the industry. The directors also knew of the public's highly positive reaction to the Ovitz announcement, and that Eisner and senior management had supported the Ovitz hiring. Indeed, Eisner, who had long desired to bring Ovitz within the Disney fold, consistently vouched for Ovitz's qualifications and told the directors that he could work well with Ovitz.

The board was also informed of the key terms of the OEA (including Ovitz's salary, bonus and options). Russell reported this information to them at the September 26, 1995 executive session, which was attended by Eisner and all non-executive directors. Russell also reported on the compensation committee meeting that had immediately preceded the executive session. And, both Russell and Watson responded to questions from the board. Relying upon the compensation committee's approval of the OEA[89] and the other information furnished to them, the Disney directors, after further deliberating, unanimously elected Ovitz as President. . . .

2. The Good Faith Determinations. . . . This case . . . is one in which the duty to act in good faith has played a prominent role, yet to date is not a well-developed area of our corporate fiduciary law. . . . [A]s a matter of simple logic, at least three different categories of fiduciary behavior are candidates for the "bad faith" pejorative label.

The first category involves so-called "subjective bad faith," that is, fiduciary conduct motivated by an actual intent to do harm. That such conduct constitutes classic, quintessential bad faith is a proposition so well accepted in the liturgy of fiduciary law that it borders on axiomatic. We need not dwell further on this category, because no such conduct is claimed to have occurred, or did occur, in this case.

The second category of conduct, which is at the opposite end of the spectrum, involves lack of due care—that is, fiduciary action taken solely by reason of gross negligence and without any malevolent intent. In this case, appellants assert claims of gross negligence to establish breaches not only of director due care but also of the directors' duty to act in good faith. Although the Chancellor found, and we agree, that the appellants failed to establish gross negligence, to afford guidance we address the issue of whether gross negligence (including a failure to inform one's self of available material facts), without more, can also constitute bad faith. The answer is clearly no.

From a broad philosophical standpoint, that question is more complex than would appear, if only because (as the Chancellor and others have observed) "issues of good faith are (to a certain degree) inseparably and necessarily intertwined with the duties of care and loyalty." But, in the pragmatic,

---

89. Contrary to the appellants' assertion (made with no citation of authority), the remaining board members were entitled to rely upon the compensation committee's approval of the OEA, and upon Russell's report of the discussions that occurred at the compensation committee meeting, when considering whether to elect Ovitz as President of Disney. 8 Del. C. §141(e).

conduct-regulating legal realm which calls for more precise conceptual line drawing, the answer is that grossly negligent conduct, without more, does not and cannot constitute a breach of the fiduciary duty to act in good faith. The conduct that is the subject of due care may overlap with the conduct that comes within the rubric of good faith in a psychological sense,[104] but from a legal standpoint those duties are and must remain quite distinct. Both our legislative history and our common law jurisprudence distinguish sharply between the duties to exercise due care and to act in good faith, and highly significant consequences flow from that distinction.

The Delaware General Assembly has addressed the distinction between bad faith and a failure to exercise due care (i.e., gross negligence) in two separate contexts. The first is Section 102(b)(7) of the DGCL, which authorizes Delaware corporations, by a provision in the certificate of incorporation, to exculpate their directors from monetary damage liability for a breach of the duty of care. That exculpatory provision affords significant protection to directors of Delaware corporations. The statute carves out several exceptions, however, including most relevantly, "for acts or omissions not in good faith. . . ." Thus, a corporation can exculpate its directors from monetary liability for a breach of the duty of care, but not for conduct that is not in good faith. To adopt a definition of bad faith that would cause a violation of the duty of care automatically to become an act or omission "not in good faith," would eviscerate the protections accorded to directors by the General Assembly's adoption of Section 102(b)(7).

A second legislative recognition of the distinction between fiduciary conduct that is grossly negligent and conduct that is not in good faith, is Delaware's indemnification statute, found at 8 Del. C. §145 . . . [which authorizes corporations to compensate directors and officers who have "acted in good faith and in a manner the person reasonably believed to be in or not opposed to the best interests of the corporation" for costs incurred in their corporate activities.] Thus, under Delaware statutory law a director or officer of a corporation can be indemnified for liability (and litigation expenses) incurred by reason of a violation of the duty of care, but not for a violation of the duty to act in good faith.[30]

That leaves the third category [which] . . . the Chancellor's definition of bad faith — intentional dereliction of duty, a conscious disregard for one's responsibilities — is intended to capture. The question is whether such misconduct is properly treated as a nonexculpable, nonindemnifiable violation of the fiduciary duty to act in good faith. In our view it must be, for at least two reasons.

First, the universe of fiduciary misconduct is not limited to either disloyalty in the classic sense (i.e., preferring the adverse self-interest of the fiduciary or of a related person to the interest of the corporation) or gross negligence. Cases have arisen where corporate directors have no conflicting self-interest in a decision, yet engage in misconduct that is more culpable than simple inattention or failure to be

---

104. An example of such overlap might be the hypothetical case where a director, because of subjective hostility to the corporation on whose board he serves, fails to inform himself of, or to devote sufficient attention to, the matters on which he is making decisions as a fiduciary. In such a case, two states of mind coexist in the same person: subjective bad intent (which would lead to a finding of bad faith) and gross negligence (which would lead to a finding of a breach of the duty of care). Although the coexistence of both states of mind may make them indistinguishable from a psychological standpoint, the fiduciary duties that they cause the director to violate — care and good faith — are legally separate and distinct.

30. For a fuller treatment, see Chapter VIII.I. — ED.

informed of all facts material to the decision. To protect the interests of the corporation and its shareholders, fiduciary conduct of this kind, which does not involve disloyalty (as traditionally defined) but is qualitatively more culpable than gross negligence, should be proscribed. A vehicle is needed to address such violations doctrinally, and that doctrinal vehicle is the duty to act in good faith. The Chancellor implicitly so recognized in his Opinion, where he identified different examples of bad faith as follows:

> . . . A failure to act in good faith may be shown, for instance, where the fiduciary intentionally acts with a purpose other than that of advancing the best interests of the corporation, where the fiduciary acts with the intent to violate applicable positive law, or where the fiduciary intentionally fails to act in the face of a known duty to act, demonstrating a conscious disregard for his duties. There may be other examples of bad faith yet to be proven or alleged, but these three are the most salient. . . .

Second, the legislature has also recognized this intermediate category of fiduciary misconduct, which ranks between conduct involving subjective bad faith and gross negligence. Section 102(b)(7)(ii) of the DGCL expressly denies money damage exculpation for "acts or omissions not in good faith or which involve intentional misconduct or a knowing violation of law." By its very terms that provision distinguishes between "intentional misconduct" and a "knowing violation of law" (both examples of subjective bad faith) on the one hand, and "acts . . . not in good faith," on the other. Because the statute exculpates directors only for conduct amounting to gross negligence, the statutory denial of exculpation for "acts . . . not in good faith" must encompass the intermediate category of misconduct captured by the Chancellor's definition of bad faith. . . . [31]

Having sustained the Chancellor's finding that the Disney directors acted in good faith when approving the OEA and electing Ovitz as President, we next address the claims arising out of the decision to pay Ovitz the amount called for by the NFT provisions of the OEA . . . Article Tenth of the Company's certificate of incorporation in effect at the termination plainly states that: "The officers of the Corporation shall be chosen in such a manner, shall hold their offices for such terms and shall carry out such duties as are determined solely by the Board of Directors, subject to the right of the Board of Directors to remove any officer or officers at any time with or without cause." Article IV of Disney's bylaws provided that the Board Chairman/CEO "shall, subject to the provisions of the Bylaws and the control of the Board of Directors, have general and active management, direction, and supervision over the business of the Corporation and over its officers. . . ." . . .

31. For the "importance of clarifying the difference between the presence of subjective bad faith and the absence of good faith," as illustrated by the "difference between a conscious failure to act and improperly motivated action," see Sarah H. Duggin & Stephen M. Goldman, Restoring Trust in Corporate Directors: The Disney Standard and the "New" Good Faith, 56 Am. U. L. Rev. 211, 252, 255 (2006). Must (should) such conduct be "deliberately indifferent, egregious, or outrageous"? See Hillary A. Sale, Delaware's Good Faith, 89 Cornell L. Rev. 456 (2004). What about "recklessness"? See Matthew R. Berry, Note, Does Delaware's Section 102(b)(7) Protect Reckless Directors from Personal Liability?, 79 Wash. L. Rev. 1125 (2004). For the view that "good faith" imposes an "obligation of candor" on managers not "to make intentionally or recklessly false or misleading statements in their managerial capacity" or "to intentionally or recklessly fail to inform other managers or corporate organs (including the body of shareholders) of [material] information," see Melvin A. Eisenberg, The Duty of Good Faith in Corporate Law, 31 Del. J. Corp. L. 1, 38-39 (2006) (suggesting that this may explain the *Van Gorkom* decision because of his "withholding important information from the board," id. at 48). — ED.

The issue is whether the Chancellor's interpretation of these instruments, as giving the board and the Chairman/CEO concurrent power to terminate a lesser officer, is legally permissible. . . . [B]ecause Disney's governing instruments do not vest the removal power exclusively in the board, nor do they expressly give the Board Chairman/CEO a concurrent power to remove officers . . . [the] corporate governing instruments are ambiguous, [and] our case law . . . [indicates] the court must look to extrinsic evidence to determine which of the reasonable readings the parties intended.

Here, the extrinsic evidence clearly supports the conclusion that the board and Eisner understood that Eisner, as Board Chairman/CEO, had concurrent power with the board to terminate Ovitz as President. In that regard, the Chancellor credited the testimony of new board members that Eisner, as Chairman and CEO, was empowered to terminate Ovitz without board approval or intervention; and also Litvack's testimony that during his tenure as general counsel, many Company officers were terminated and the board never once took action in connection with their terminations. ["Although the board did not meet to vote on the termination, the Chancellor found that most, if not all, of the Disney directors trusted Eisner's and Litvack's conclusion that there was no cause to terminate Ovitz, and that Ovitz should be terminated without cause even though that involved making the costly NFT payment."]

As the Chancellor correctly held, the . . . only role delegated to the compensation committee was "to establish and approve compensation for Eisner, Ovitz and other applicable Company executives and high paid employees." The committee's September 26, 1995 approval of Ovitz's compensation arrangements "included approval for the termination provisions of the OEA, obviating any need to meet and approve the payment of the NFT upon Ovitz's termination."[124] . . .

It is undisputed that Litvack and Eisner (based on Litvack's advice) both concluded that if Ovitz was to be terminated, it could only be without cause, because no basis existed to terminate Ovitz for cause. The appellants argued in the Court of Chancery that the business judgment presumptions do not protect that conclusion, because by permitting Ovitz to be terminated without cause, Litvack and Eisner acted in bad faith and without exercising due care. . . .

After considering the OEA and Ovitz's conduct, Litvack concluded, and advised Eisner, that Disney had no basis to terminate Ovitz for cause and that Disney should comply with its contractual obligations. Even though Litvack personally did not want to grant a NFT to Ovitz, [he "did in fact make a concerted effort to determine if Ovitz could be terminated for cause, and"] concluded that for Disney to assert falsely that there was cause would be both unethical and harmful to

---

124. Id. To support their argument that the compensation committee's approval of the Ovitz termination was required, appellants point to a provision of the Option Plan giving the compensation committee "the sole power to make determinations regarding the termination of any participant's employment," including "the cause[s] therefore and the consequences thereof." That provision, however, is expressly limited by the language "or as otherwise may be provided by the [Compensation] Committee." Here, the compensation committee approved the OEA, which contained its own termination provisions and standards. Section 11 of the OEA provided that "the Company" shall determine if cause exists for a termination. The OEA does not purport to delegate any authority to the compensation committee to make such a determination. The Chancellor recognized that although the foregoing reasoning might not be dispositive, the limiting language of the Option Plan was "sufficiently ambiguous — as to whether action by the compensation committee is required in all terminations . . . of employees who possess options — to, in my opinion, absolve . . . the compensation committee for not acting with respect to Ovitz's termination."

Disney's reputation. As to Litvack, the Court of Chancery held: "I do not intend to imply by these conclusions that Litvack was an infallible source of legal knowledge. Nevertheless, Litvack's less astute moments as a legal counsel do not impugn his good faith or preparedness in reaching his conclusions with respect to whether Ovitz could have been terminated for cause. . . ."

With respect to Eisner, the Chancellor found that faced with a situation where he was unable to work well with Ovitz, who required close and constant supervision, Eisner had three options: 1) keep Ovitz as President and continue trying to make things work; 2) keep Ovitz at Disney, but in a role other than as President; or 3) terminate Ovitz. The first option was unacceptable, and the second would have entitled Ovitz to the NFT, or at the very least would have resulted in a costly lawsuit to determine whether Ovitz was so entitled. After an unsuccessful effort to "trade" Ovitz to Sony, [where "Ovitz had a good, longstanding relationship with many Sony senior executives,"] that left only the third option, which was to terminate Ovitz and pay the NFT. The Chancellor found ["that] . . . Eisner was not personally interested in the transaction in any way that would make him incapable of exercising business judgment, and I conclude that the plaintiffs have not demonstrated by a preponderance of the evidence that Eisner breached his fiduciary duties or acted in bad faith in connection with Ovitz's termination and receipt of the NFT."

These determinations rest squarely on factual findings that, in turn, are based upon the Chancellor's assessment of the credibility of Eisner and other witnesses. Even though the Chancellor found much to criticize in Eisner's "imperial CEO" style of governance, nothing has been shown to overturn the factual basis for the Court's conclusion that, in the end, Eisner's conduct satisfied the standards required of him as a fiduciary.[133]

V. *The Waste Claim.* The appellants' final claim is that even if the approval of the OEA was protected by the business judgment rule presumptions, the payment of the severance amount to Ovitz constituted waste. This claim is rooted in the doctrine that a plaintiff who fails to rebut the business judgment rule presumptions is not entitled to any remedy unless the transaction constitutes waste. . . . [This issue is discussed at page 141 infra.]

For the reasons stated above, the judgment of the Court of Chancery is affirmed.

In re Caremark Int'l, Inc. Derivative Litigation, 698 A.2d 959 (Del. Ch. 1996), involving directors' "duty to appropriately monitor and supervise the enterprise," (discussed in Stone v. Ritter, page 99 infra), included an important view by Chancellor Allen on the duty of care:

> Director liability for a breach of the duty to exercise appropriate attention may, in theory, arise in two distinct contexts. First, such liability may be said to follow *from a*

---

133. Although the appellants continue to argue as fact that Eisner allowed Ovitz to receive an NFT as an act of friendship, the Chancellor found that Eisner did not want Ovitz to receive that payment. ["Ovitz asked for several concessions, all of which Eisner ultimately rejected. Eisner told Ovitz that all he would receive was what he had contracted for in the OEA."] ("Despite the paucity of evidence, it is clear to the Court that both Eisner and Litvack wanted to fire Ovitz for cause to avoid the costly NFT payment, and perhaps out of personal motivations."). Appellants offer no tenable basis to overturn that finding.

board decision that results in a loss because that decision was ill advised or "negligent." Second, liability to the corporation for a loss may be said to arise from an *unconsidered failure of the board to act* in circumstances in which due attention would, arguably, have prevented the loss. . . . The first class of cases will typically be subject to review under the director-protective business judgment rule, assuming the decision made was the product of *a process* that was either deliberately considered in good faith or was otherwise rational. See Aronson v. Lewis, Del. Supr., 473 A.2d 805 (1984); Gagliardi v. TriFoods Int'l, Inc., Del. Ch., 683 A.2d 1049 (1996).[32] What should be understood, but may not widely be understood by courts or commentators who are not often required to face such questions, is that compliance with a director's duty of care can never appropriately be judicially determined by reference to *the content of the board decision* that leads to a corporate loss, apart from consideration of the good faith or rationality of the process employed. That is, whether a judge or jury considering the matter after the fact, believes a decision substantively wrong, or degrees of wrong extending through "stupid" to "egregious" or "irrational," provides no ground for director liability, so long as the court determines that the process employed was either rational or employed in *a good faith* effort to advance corporate interests.[33] To employ a different rule—one that permitted an "objective" evaluation of the decision—would expose directors to substantive second guessing by ill-equipped judges or juries, which would, in the long-run, be injurious to investor interests.[34] Thus, the business judgment rule is process oriented and informed by a deep respect for all *good faith* board decisions.[35]

32. In Brehm v. Eisner, 746 A.2d 244, 264 & n.6 (Del. 2000), the court amplified this point: "Due care in the decisionmaking context is *process* due care only. Irrationality is the outer limit of the business judgment rule. Irrationality may be the functional equivalent of the waste test or it may tend to show that the decision is not made in good faith, which is a key ingredient of the business judgment rule." —Ed.

33. In the *Gagliardi* case, supra, Chancellor Allen acknowledged that "there is a theoretical exception to this general statement that holds that some decisions may be so 'egregious' that liability for losses they cause may follow even in the absence of proof of conflict of interest or improper motivation. The exception, however, has resulted in no awards of money judgments against corporate officers or directors in this jurisdiction and, to my knowledge only the dubious holding in this Court of Gimbel v. Signal Companies, Inc. (Del. Ch.), 316 A.2d 599 aff'd (Del. Supr.), 316 A.2d 619 (1974), seems to grant equitable relief in the absence of a claimed conflict or improper motivation."

For a recent decision granting a preliminary injunction under such circumstances, see Levco Alternative Fund Ltd. v. Reader's Digest Ass'n, Inc., 803 A.2d 468 (Del. 2002). See also Parnes v. Bally Entertainment Corp., 722 A.2d 1243 (Del. 1999), refusing to dismiss a complaint for damages against an independent board for approving a merger that allegedly involved side payments by the acquiror to the corporation's CEO, who controlled the merger negotiations, in order to obtain his needed consent; the court found the board's action "so far beyond the bounds of reasonable judgment that it seems essentially inexplicable on any ground other than bad faith."

In respect to other jurisdictions, compare materials in footnote 18 supra. —Ed.

34. See also Casey v. Woodruff, 49 N.Y.S.2d 625 (N.Y. Sup. Ct. 1944):

The question is frequently asked, how does the operation of the so-called "business judgment rule" tie in with the concept of negligence? There is no conflict between the two. When the courts say that they will not interfere in matters of business judgment, it is presupposed that judgment—reasonable diligence—has in fact been exercised. A director cannot close his eyes to what is going on about him in the conduct of the business of the corporation and have it said that he is exercising business judgment. Courts have properly decided to give directors a wide latitude in the management of the affairs of a corporation provided always that judgment is reasonably exercised by them. —Ed.

35. Compare R. Franklin Balotti, Charles M. Elson & J. Travis Laster, Equity Ownership and the Duty of Care: Convergence, Revolution, or Evolution? 55 Bus. Law. 661, 664 (2000):

[T]here is no necessary or sufficient connection between procedural landmarks such as the information the board received, the number of meetings held, and the receipt of advice from attorneys, investment bankers, or other outside consultants, and the substantive quality of the decision ultimately reached. Perhaps more importantly, because procedural landmarks are easily mapped by attorneys who advise boards of directors, an adequate record can be crafted to justify a board's decision without regard to the merits of the action actually taken. The result is a

Indeed, one wonders on what moral basis might shareholders attack a *good faith* business decision of a director as unreasonable or irrational. Where a director *in fact exercises a good faith effort to be informed and to exercise appropriate judgment,* he or she should be deemed to satisfy fully the duty of attention. If the shareholders thought themselves entitled to some other quality of judgment than such a director produces in the good faith exercise of the powers of office, then the shareholders should have elected other directors.

Stone v. Ritter
911 A.2d 362 (2006)

HOLLAND, J.: This is an appeal from a final judgment of the Court of Chancery dismissing a derivative complaint against fifteen present and former directors of AmSouth Bancorporation ("AmSouth"). . . .

The Court of Chancery characterized the allegations in the derivative complaint as a "classic *Caremark* claim," a claim that derives its name from In re Caremark. . . . AmSouth is a Delaware corporation with its principal executive offices in Birmingham, Alabama. During the relevant period, AmSouth's wholly-owned subsidiary, AmSouth Bank, operated about 600 commercial banking branches in six states throughout the southeastern United States and employed more than 11,600 people.

In 2004, AmSouth and AmSouth Bank paid $40 million in fines and $10 million in civil penalties to resolve government and regulatory investigations pertaining principally to the failure by bank employees to file "Suspicious Activity Reports" ("SARs"), as required by the federal Bank Secrecy Act ("BSA") and various anti-money-laundering ("AML") regulations. . . .

The government investigations arose originally from an unlawful "Ponzi" scheme operated by Louis D. Hamric, II and Victor G. Nance. In August 2000, Hamric, then a licensed attorney, and Nance, then a registered investment advisor with Mutual of New York, contacted an AmSouth branch bank in Tennessee to arrange for custodial trust accounts to be created for "investors" in a "business venture." That venture (Hamric and Nance represented) involved the construction of medical clinics overseas. In reality, Nance had convinced more than forty of his clients to invest in promissory notes bearing high rates of return, by misrepresenting the nature and the risk of that investment. Relying on similar misrepresentations by Hamric and Nance, the AmSouth branch employees in Tennessee agreed to provide custodial accounts for the investors and to distribute monthly interest payments to each account upon receipt of a check from Hamric and instructions from Nance.

The Hamric-Nance scheme was discovered in March 2002, when the investors did not receive their monthly interest payments. . . . On November 17, 2003, the USAO [U.S. Attorney's Office] advised AmSouth that it was the subject of a criminal investigation. On October 12, 2004, AmSouth and the USAO entered into a Deferred Prosecution Agreement ("DPA") in which AmSouth agreed [to the $40 million fine]. . . . In neither the Statement of Facts nor anywhere else did the USAO ascribe any blame to the Board or to any individual director.

---

system that potentially elevates form over substance and risks insulating poor decision making from challenge.

Query: May (should) an incomplete and rushed deliberative process ever satisfy the business judgment rule? — ED.

On October 12, 2004, the Federal Reserve and the Alabama Banking Department concurrently issued a Cease and Desist Order against AmSouth, requiring it, for the first time, to improve its BSA/AML program. That Cease and Desist Order required AmSouth to (among other things) engage an independent consultant "to conduct a comprehensive review of the Bank's AML Compliance program and make recommendations, as appropriate, for new policies and procedures to be implemented by the Bank." KPMG Forensic Services ("KPMG") performed the role of independent consultant and issued its report on December 10, 2004 (the "KPMG Report").

Also on October 12, 2004, FinCEN and the Federal Reserve jointly assessed a $10 million civil penalty against AmSouth for operating an inadequate anti-money-laundering program. . . . Among FinCEN's specific determinations were its conclusions that "AmSouth's [AML compliance] program lacked adequate board and management oversight," and that "reporting to management for the purposes of monitoring and oversight of compliance activities was materially deficient." AmSouth neither admitted nor denied FinCEN's determinations in this or any other forum.

. . . The standard for assessing a director's potential personal liability for failing to act in good faith in discharging his or her oversight responsibilities has evolved beginning with our decision in Graham v. Allis-Chalmers Manufacturing Company,[15] through the Court of Chancery's *Caremark* decision to our most recent decision in *Disney*. . . .

Graham was a derivative action brought against the directors of Allis-Chalmers for failure to prevent violations of federal antitrust laws by Allis-Chalmers employees. There was no claim that the Allis-Chalmers directors knew of the employees' conduct that resulted in the corporation's liability. Rather, the plaintiffs claimed that the Allis-Chalmers directors should have known of the illegal conduct by the corporation's employees. In *Graham*, this Court held that *"absent cause for suspicion* there is no duty upon the directors to install and operate a corporate system of espionage to ferret out wrongdoing which they have no reason to suspect exists."

In *Caremark*, the Court of Chancery reassessed the applicability of our holding in *Graham* when called upon to approve a settlement of a derivative lawsuit brought against the directors of Caremark International, Inc. The plaintiffs claimed that the Caremark directors should have known that certain officers and employees of Caremark were involved in violations of the federal Anti-Referral Payments Law. That law prohibits health care providers from paying any form of remuneration to induce the referral of Medicare or Medicaid patients. The plaintiffs claimed that the Caremark directors breached their fiduciary duty for having "allowed a situation to develop and continue which exposed the corporation to enormous legal liability and that in so doing they violated a duty to be active monitors of corporate performance."

In evaluating whether to approve the proposed settlement agreement in *Caremark*, the Court of Chancery . . . opined it would be a "mistake" to interpret this Court's decision in *Graham* to mean that: "corporate boards may satisfy their obligation to be reasonably informed concerning the corporation, without assuring themselves that information and reporting systems exist in the organization that

---

15. Graham v. Allis-Chalmers Mfg. Co., 188 A.2d 125 (Del. 1963).

are reasonably designed to provide to senior management and to the board itself timely, accurate information sufficient to allow management and the board, each within its scope, to reach informed judgments concerning both the corporation's compliance with law and its business performance."

To the contrary, the *Caremark* Court stated, "it is important that the board exercise a good faith judgment that the corporation's information and reporting system is in concept and design adequate to assure the board that appropriate information will come to its attention in a timely manner as a matter of ordinary operations, so that it may satisfy its responsibility."[36] The *Caremark* Court recognized, however, that "the duty to act in good faith to be informed cannot be thought to require directors to possess detailed information about all aspects of the operation of the enterprise." The Court of Chancery then formulated the following standard for assessing the liability of directors where the directors are unaware of employee misconduct that results in the corporation being held liable: "Generally where a claim of directorial liability for corporate loss is predicated upon ignorance of liability creating activities within the corporation, as in *Graham* or in this case, . . . only a sustained or systematic failure of the board to exercise oversight—such as an utter failure to attempt to assure a reasonable information and reporting system exists—will establish the lack of good faith that is a necessary condition to liability."[37] . . .

As evidenced by the language quoted above, the *Caremark* standard for so-called "oversight" liability draws heavily upon the concept of director failure to act in good faith. That is consistent with the definition(s) of bad faith recently approved by this Court in its recent *Disney* decision. . . . The phraseology used in *Caremark* and that we employ here—describing the lack of good faith as a "necessary condition to liability"—is deliberate. The purpose of that formulation is to communicate that a failure to act in good faith is not conduct that results, ipso facto, in the direct imposition of fiduciary liability.[29] The failure to act in good faith may

---

36. "No case has ever held that directors have a common-law fiduciary duty either to establish or to maintain compliance programs. In fact, the leading case holdings are diametrically the opposite [citing *Graham*]." Charles Hansen, A Guide to the American Law Institute Corporate Governance Project 33 (1995).

Compare Corporate Director's Guidebook—adopted by the ABA Committee on Corporate Laws of the Section of Corporation, Banking and Business Law—33 Bus. Law. 1591, 1610 (1978): "The corporate director should be concerned that the corporation has programs looking toward compliance with applicable laws and regulations, both foreign and domestic, that it circulates (as appropriate) policy statements to this effect to its employees, and that it maintains procedures for monitoring such compliance."

See also Deborah A. DeMott, Organizational Incentives to Care about the Law, 60 Law & Contemp. Probs. 39, 45, 62 (1997): "As an organization, the corporation defines rewards and penalties; by doing so it creates incentives for agents to act in ways that promise rewards conferred by the organization. These incentives can be so strong that they mute the message otherwise conveyed by the organization's instructions to its agents. . . . Questions of good faith aside, whether a system is adequate should reflect an assessment by directors of the risks created by the corporation's own incentive system."—Ed.

37. For recent decisions sustaining allegations that this had occurred, see In re Abbott Laboratories Derivative Shareholders, Litigation, 325 F.3d 795 (7th Cir. 2003); McCall v. Scott, 239 F.3d 808 (6th Cir. 2001). *Query*: Does this duty include monitoring and seeking to prevent self-dealing transactions by fellow directors? See Canadian Commercial Workers Industry Pension Plan v. Alden, 2006 WL 456786 (Del. Ch).

"This consideration is presumably not applicable to the corporation's officers, or to officers who also serve as directors; nothing in the court's opinion addresses either the duties to monitor assumed by officers or the liability threshold applicable to officers." DeMott, footnote 36 supra, at 60.—Ed.

29. 29 That issue, whether a violation of the duty to act in good faith is a basis for the direct imposition of liability, was expressly left open in *Disney*. 906 A.2d at 67 n.112. We address that issue here.

result in liability because the requirement to act in good faith "is a subsidiary element[,]" i.e., a condition, "of the fundamental duty of loyalty."[30] It follows that because a showing of bad faith conduct, in the sense described in *Disney* and *Caremark*, is essential to establish director oversight liability, the fiduciary duty violated by that conduct is the duty of loyalty.

This view of a failure to act in good faith results in two additional doctrinal consequences. First, although good faith may be described colloquially as part of a "triad" of fiduciary duties that includes the duties of care and loyalty, the obligation to act in good faith does not establish an independent fiduciary duty that stands on the same footing as the duties of care and loyalty. Only the latter two duties, where violated, may directly result in liability, whereas a failure to act in good faith may do so, but indirectly. The second doctrinal consequence is that the fiduciary duty of loyalty is not limited to cases involving a financial or other cognizable fiduciary conflict of interest. It also encompasses cases where the fiduciary fails to act in good faith. As the Court of Chancery aptly put it in *Guttman*, "[a] director cannot act loyally towards the corporation unless she acts in the good faith belief that her actions are in the corporation's best interest."

We hold that *Caremark* articulates the necessary conditions predicate for director oversight liability: (a) the directors utterly failed to implement any reporting or information system or controls; or (b) having implemented such a system or controls, consciously failed to monitor or oversee its operations thus disabling themselves from being informed of risks or problems requiring their attention. In either case, imposition of liability requires a showing that the directors knew that they were not discharging their fiduciary obligations. Where directors fail to act in the face of a known duty to act, thereby demonstrating a conscious disregard for their responsibilities, they breach their duty of loyalty by failing to discharge that fiduciary obligation in good faith.

. . . The KPMG Report reflects that AmSouth's Board dedicated considerable resources to the BSA/AML compliance program and put into place numerous procedures and systems to attempt to ensure compliance. According to KPMG, the program's various components exhibited between a low and high degree of compliance with applicable laws and regulations.

The KPMG Report describes the numerous AmSouth employees, departments and committees established by the Board to oversee AmSouth's compliance with the BSA and . . . reflects that the directors not only discharged their oversight responsibility to establish an information and reporting system, but also proved that the system was designed to permit the directors to periodically monitor AmSouth's compliance with BSA and AML regulations. For example, as KPMG noted in 2004, AmSouth's designated BSA Officer "has made annual high-level presentations to the Board of Directors in each of the last five years." Further, the Board's Audit and Community Responsibility Committee (the "Audit Committee") oversaw AmSouth's BSA/AML compliance program on a quarterly basis. . . .

The KPMG Report shows that AmSouth's Board at various times enacted written policies and procedures designed to ensure compliance with the BSA and AML regulations. For example, the Board adopted an amended bank-wide "BSA/AML Policy" on July 17, 2003—four months before AmSouth became aware that it was

---

30. Guttman v. Huang, 823 A.2d 492, 506 n.34 (Del .Ch. 2003). [Compare the "location" of the good faith requirement in Brehm v. Eisner, footnote 32, page 98 supra.—ED.]

the target of a government investigation . . . [that] directs all AmSouth employees to immediately report suspicious transactions or activity to the BSA/AML Compliance Department or Corporate Security.

. . . Delaware courts have recognized that "[m]ost of the decisions that a corporation, acting through its human agents, makes are, of course, not the subject of director attention." Consequently, a claim that directors are subject to personal liability for employee failures is "possibly the most difficult theory in corporation law upon which a plaintiff might hope to win a judgment."

. . . KPMG's findings reflect that . . . [a]lthough there ultimately may have been failures by employees to report deficiencies to the Board, there is no basis for an oversight claim seeking to hold the directors personally liable for such failures by the employees. . . .

The judgment of the Court of Chancery is affirmed.

American Law Institute, Principles of Corporate Governance (1994)

Sec. 4.01. *Duty of care of directors and officers; the business judgment rule.* (a) A director or officer has a duty to the corporation to perform the director's or officer's functions in good faith, in a manner that he or she reasonably believes to be in the best interests of the corporation, and with the care that an ordinarily prudent person would reasonably be expected to exercise in a like position and under similar circumstances.[38] This Subsection (a) is subject to the provisions of Subsection (c) (the business judgment rule) where applicable.

---

38. An amendment to RMBCA §§8.30(a) and (b) (1998) is similar, but omits the "care that an ordinarily prudent person . . ." part of the sentence. The Official Comment to §830(b) states:

> The phrase "ordinarily prudent person" constitutes a basic frame of reference grounded in the field of tort law and . . . suggesting that negligence is the proper determinant for measuring deficient (and thus actionable) conduct, has caused confusion and misunderstanding. Accordingly, the phrase "ordinarily prudent person" has been removed from the Model Act's standard of care and in its place "a person in a like position" has been substituted. The standard is not what care a particular director might believe appropriate in the circumstances but what a person — in a like position and acting under similar circumstances — would reasonably believe to be appropriate. Thus, the degree of care that directors should employ, under subsection (b), involves an objective standard.

For the view that "application of the business judgment rule to officer conduct is not firmly established in case law" and "should not be extended to corporate officers in the same broad manner in which it is applied to directors," see Lyman P. Q. Johnson, Corporate Officers and the Business Judgment Rule, 60 Bus. Law. 439, 440-441, 460 (2005): "Officers work for the company full time, possess extensive knowledge and skill concerning company affairs, have access to considerably more and better information than directors, enjoy high company and social status, and exercise great influence over the lives of many people — both inside and outside the corporation. They should be held to the same standard of care as are all other persons who serve as agents of companies — a duty of ordinary care." See also Lyman P. Q. Johnson & David Millon, Recalling Why Corporate Officers are Fiduciaries, 46 Wm. & Mary L. Rev. 1597 (2005) (corporate officers are "agents" and their fiduciary duties "are more demanding than those of directors"). Contra, Lawrence A. Hamermesh & A. Gilchrist Sparks III, A Reply to Professor Johnson, 60 Bus. Law. 865 (2005).

In Willard v. Moneta Bldg. Supply, Inc., 515 S.E. 2d 277 (Va. 1999), the court explained that because of this omission of the "ordinarily prudent person" phrase, "in Virginia, a director's discharge of duties is not measured by what a reasonable person would do in similar circumstances or by the rationality of the ultimate decision. Instead, a director must act in accordance with his/her good faith business judgment of what is in the best interests of the corporation."

RMBCA §8.30 applies only to directors, not officers. — ED.

(1) The duty in Subsection (a) includes the obligation to make, or cause to be made, an inquiry when, but only when, the circumstances would alert a reasonable director or officer to the need therefor. The extent of such inquiry shall be such as the director or officer reasonably believes to be necessary.[39]

(2) In performing any of his or her functions (including oversight functions), a director or officer is entitled to rely on materials and persons in accordance with §§4.02 and 4.03 (reliance on directors, officers, employees, experts, other persons, and committees of the board).[40]

(b) Except as otherwise provided by statute or by a standard of the corporation and subject to the board's ultimate responsibility for oversight, in performing its functions (including oversight functions), the board may delegate, formally or informally by course of conduct, any function (including the function of identifying matters requiring the attention of the board) to committees of the board or to directors, officers, employees, experts, or other persons; a director may rely on such committees and persons in fulfilling the duty under this Section with respect to any delegated function if the reliance is in accordance with §§4.02 and 4.03.

(c) A director or officer who makes a business judgment in good faith fulfills the duty under this Section if the director or officer:

(1) is not interested in the subject of the business judgment;

(2) is informed with respect to the subject of the business judgment to the extent the director or officer reasonably believes to be appropriate under the circumstances; and

(3) rationally believes that the business judgment is in the best interests of the corporation.[41]

(d) A person challenging the conduct of a director or officer under this Section has the burden of proving a breach of the duty of care, including the inapplicability of the provisions as to the fulfillment of duty under Subsection (b) or (c), and, in a damage action, the burden of proving that the breach was the legal cause of damage suffered by the corporation.

---

39. Although only a handful of states have statutes with an "inquiry" provision, see, e.g., Cal. Gen. Corp. Law §309(a) (1987), it "is generally recognized in the case law." 1 ALI Principles of Corporate Governance 161 (1994). — ED.

40. See footnote 43 infra. — ED.

41. Although "there are no statutory formulations of the business judgment rule, . . . §4.01(c) is believed to be consistent with present law as it would be interpreted in most jurisdictions today, and each of the rule's basic elements (§4.01(c)(1)-(3)) is supported by substantial precedential authority." Id. at 173. Compare the charge of William J. Carney, Section 4.01 of the American Law Institute's Corporate Governance Project: Restatement or Misstatement?, 66 Wash. U. L.Q. 239 (1988), that, in a slightly earlier version of §4.01, "the reporters have managed to patch together a complex pattern of subtle changes that . . . [bear no] meaningful relationship to the decision rule applied in the courts, except in a limited group of cases involving financial institutions."

RMBCA §831(a)(2), although much more detailed, is similar to ALI §4.01(c), but it omits all reference to "business judgment" terminology.

Note that ALI §4.01(a) defines the normative "duty" of directors and officers differently than §4.01(c) describes when that duty is breached so as to result in liability. Do §§(a) and (c) seek to achieve an appropriate balance between "the need to preserve the board of directors' decision-making discretion and the need to hold the board accountable for its decisions," which is "the central problem for business judgment rule jurisprudence"? Stephen M. Bainbridge, The Business Judgment Rule as Abstention Doctrine, 57 Vand. L. Rev. 83, 84, 128 (2004). Does §4.01(a) state a standard of *conduct* (how managers should act) and §4.01(c) a rule of *liability* (when a court will award damages)? See generally Melvin A. Eisenberg, The Divergence of Standards of Conduct and Standards of Review in Corporate Law, 52 Ford. L. Rev. 437 (1993). RMBCA §8.31 ("Standards of Liability for Directors") makes clear that a breach of §8.30 ("Standards of Conduct for Directors") is not sufficient to impose "money damages." *Query:* Which section governs an action for injunction? — ED.

Sec. 4.02. *Reliance on directors, officers, employees, experts, and other persons.*[42] In performing his duty and functions, a director or officer who acts in good faith, and reasonably believes that his reliance is warranted, is entitled to rely on information, opinions, reports, statements (including financial statements and other financial data), and decisions, judgments, or performance (including decisions, judgments, or performance within the scope of §4.01(b)), in each case prepared, presented, made, or performed by:

(a) One or more directors, officers, or employees of the corporation, or of a business organization under joint control or common control, whom the director or officer reasonably believes merit confidence; or

(b) Legal counsel, public accountants, engineers, or other persons whom the director or officer reasonably believes merit confidence.[43]

---

1. *Varying types of directors.* To what extent, if any, does (should) the standard of care in §4.01 depend on the fact that the director is (a) a full-time manager of the corporation in charge of (i) sales or (ii) finances; (b) a member of the executive committee; (c) a banker whose usual contribution at board meetings is to advise on financial matters; (d) a person without general business experience who is added to the board to express the interests of (i) employees, (ii) consumers, (iii) the environment, (iv) minority groups, or (v) the public in general? The Official Comment to RMBCA §8.30(a) — whose language is similar to the first paragraph of §4.01(a) — states:

> The combined phrase "in a like position . . . under similar circumstances" is intended to recognize that (a) the nature and extent of responsibilities will vary, depending upon such factors as the size, complexity, urgency, and location of activities carried on by the particular corporation, (b) decisions must be made on the basis of the information known to the directors without the benefit of hindsight, and (c) the special background, qualifications, and management responsibilities of a particular director may be relevant in evaluating that director's compliance with the standard of care. Even though the combined phrase is intended to take into account the special background, qualifications and management responsibilities of a particular director, it does not excuse a director lacking business experience or particular expertise from exercising the basic director attributes of common sense, practical wisdom, and informed judgment.[44]

2. *"Rationality," business judgments, and the interests of investors.*

> The phrase "rationally believes" [in §4.01(c)(3)] is intended to permit a significantly wider range of discretion than the term "reasonable," and to give a director or officer a safe harbor from liability for business judgments that might arguably fall outside

---

42. Section 4.03 similarly authorizes reliance on "a duly authorized committee of the board upon which the director does not serve." — ED.

43. Sections 4.02 and 4.03 are similar to RMBCA §§8.30(d)-(f) and in general are "believed to be consistent with the law as it would be interpreted in most jurisdictions today." ALI Principles, footnote 39 supra, at 189. Section 4.03 "provides broader protection than present law" by covering officers as well as directors and, like RMBCA §8.30(d), by permitting reliance on a wider variety of persons with special expertise. Id. — ED.

44. For extensive discussion of various considerations for outside directors, see Bernard Black, Brian Cheffins & Michael Klausner, Outside Director Liability, 58 Stan. L. Rev. 1055 (2006). — ED.

the term "reasonable" but are not so removed from the realm of reason when made that liability should be incurred. . . . On the other hand, courts that have articulated only a "good faith" test may, depending on the court's meaning, provide too much legal insulation for directors and officers. . . . There is no reason to insulate an objectively irrational business decision — one so removed from the realm of reason that it should not be sustained — solely on the basis that it was made in subjective good faith.

1 ALI, Principles of Corporate Governance 142, 181 (1994).

Compare Bayless Manning, The Business Judgment Rule in Overview, 45 Ohio St. L.J. 615, 622 (1984):

> Proponents of the idea that directors must demonstrate a "rational business purpose" before they may invoke the business judgment rule argue that they are merely seeking to exclude deranged, "off-the-wall," or "wildly irresponsible" actions by the board of directors, actions for which the directors ought to be held liable. . . . Many inventions, industrial innovations, and discoveries, whether ultimately successful or unsuccessful, have been considered "off-the-wall" when first proposed. For that matter, history records dozens of rationally conceived and exquisitely planned corporate projects that proved to be thundering disasters. From a social standpoint, innovations and risk-taking are exactly what boards of directors of most companies (excluding, of course, special categories of financial corporate fiduciaries) should be encouraged to pursue. Precisely because many of the innovative projects proposed by the board will inevitably fail, the business judgment rule is most needed to protect directors from liability.[45]

In Joy v. North, supra, the court cautioned against director "liability for unsuccessful business decisions":

> First, shareholders to a very real degree voluntarily undertake the risk of bad business judgment. Investors need not buy stock, for investment markets offer an array of opportunities less vulnerable to mistakes in judgment by corporate officers. Nor need investors buy stock in particular corporations. In the exercise of what is genuinely a free choice, the quality of a firm's management is often decisive and information is available from professional advisors. Since shareholders can and do select among investments partly on the basis of management, the business judgment rule merely recognizes a certain voluntariness in undertaking the risk of bad business decisions.[46]
>
> Second, courts recognize that after-the-fact litigation is a most imperfect device to evaluate corporate business decisions. The circumstances surrounding a corporate decision are not easily reconstructed in a courtroom years later, since business

---

45. [T]he concern that liability for ordinary negligence will deter directors from taking worthwhile risks sounds remarkably like the lament of doctors who complain that the threat of malpractice suits has forced them to engage in "defensive medicine" with the result of unnecessary increased costs and the avoidance of worthwhile but more risky medical treatments. Similar laments can be heard coming from lawyers and other professionals faced with liability for negligence. The concern about director liability and risk taking may well be valid. It is questionable, however, whether this problem is unique to directors.

Franklin A. Gevurtz, Corporation Law 292 (2000). — ED.

46. In most cases, liability for negligence operates to shift the loss from a single human victim and spread it, by means of insurance and doctrines such as respondeat superior, across a larger, more diversified group. At least in the case of larger, publicly held corporations, directors' liability has just the opposite effect. Absent liability, the loss is spread across the portfolios of the pension funds, mutual funds, and other institutional and individual investors who hold the corporation's stock.

Kenneth B. Davis Jr., Once More, the Business Judgment Rule, 2000 Wis. L. Rev. 573, 575. — ED.

imperatives often call for quick decisions, inevitably based on less than perfect information. The entrepreneur's function is to encounter risks and to confront uncertainty, and a reasoned decision at the time made may seem a wild hunch viewed years later against a background of perfect knowledge.[47]

Third, because potential profit often corresponds to the potential risk, it is very much in the interest of shareholders that the law not create incentives for overly cautious corporate decisions. Some opportunities offer great profits at the risk of very substantial losses, while the alternatives offer less risk of loss but also less potential profit. Shareholders can reduce the volatility of risk by diversifying their holdings. In the case of the diversified shareholder, the seemingly more risky alternatives may well be the best choice since great losses in some stocks will over time be offset by even greater gains in others.[6] Given mutual funds and similar forms of diversified investment, courts need not bend over backwards to give special protection to shareholders who refuse to reduce the volatility of risk by not diversifying. A rule which penalizes the choice of seemingly riskier alternatives thus may not be in the interest of shareholders generally.

3. *Limiting damages.* (a) For development of the view that "directors' liability for negligence — designed to punish directors and compensate injured investors —

---

47. "[C]ourts routinely second guess other types of professionals, such as psychiatrists, architects or accountants, even though the courts have no more expertise in such fields than in entrepreneurial risk-taking. Merely pointing to the courts' lack of business acumen fails to articulate the crucial differences between corporate managers and other professionals and the rationale for the business judgment rule." Terry A. O'Neill, Self-Interest and Concern for Others in the Owner-Managed Firm: A Suggested Approach to Dissolution and Fiduciary Obligation in Close Corporations, 22 Seton Hall L. Rev. 646, 682 (1992).

"The reason that we allow judges and juries to pass judgment on the professional actions of, say, a neurosurgeon is not that we assume that they have the personal expertise to make an informed assessment . . . [but rather] that there exists a generally accepted body of principles and procedures dictating how a reasonable neurosurgeon should respond in a variety of situations." Davis, footnote 45 supra at 581. — ED.

6. Consider the choice between two investments in an example adapted from Klein, Business Organization and Finance 147-149 (1980):

Investment A

Estimated Probability of Outcome	Outcome Profit or Loss	Value
.4	+15	6.0
.4	+1	.4
.2	−13	−2.6
1.0		3.8

Investment B

Estimated Probability of Outcome	Outcome Profit or Loss	Value
.4	+6	2.4
.4	+2	.8
.2	+1	.2
1.0		3.4

Although *A* is clearly "worth" more than *B*, it is riskier because it is more volatile. Diversification lessens the volatility by allowing investors to invest in 20 or 200 *A*'s, which will tend to guarantee a total result near the value. Shareholders are thus better off with the various firms selecting *A* over *B*, although after the fact they will complain in each case of the 2.6 loss. If the courts did not abide by the business judgment rule, they might well penalize the choice of *A* in each such case and thereby unknowingly injure shareholders generally by creating incentives for management always to choose *B*.

presently functions with pathetic inefficiency and sometimes not at all"; that this "is probably caused by indemnification and insurance, which are supplied at the expense of the same people, or some of the same people, who are supposed to be benefited"; and that "since aggregate net benefits are slight in relation to [litigation and administration] costs, investors as a whole are more harmed than helped," see Alfred F. Conard, A Behavioral Analysis of Directors' Liability for Negligence, 1972 Duke L.J. 895. Conard suggests that "if liability is to work efficiently, a scaling down of the limits of liability must be initiated simultaneously with elimination of indemnification and insurance" and that "the measure of damages should be related to directors' compensation, rather than to corporations' or investors' losses."[48]

(b) ALI, Principles of Corporate Governance §7.19 (1994) provides that, unless the director or officer has engaged in "knowing and culpable" illegality, recklessness, or other egregious conduct, damages for violations of §4.01 may be limited (by a shareholder-approved charter provision) either generally or to "an amount not less than such person's annual compensation from the corporation."[49] The Reporter offers a number of policy considerations for a ceiling on liability: (1) unlimited damages may be "excessive in relation to the nature of the defendant's culpability and the economic benefits expected from serving the corporation"; (2) it would "reduce the pressures on directors to act in an unduly risk-averse manner" or to decline to serve; (3) it may "reduce the cost of insurance (often borne by the corporation)"; (4) "it is likely that the duty of care will be implemented by courts more evenly and appropriately when the potential penalties that may result are not perceived as Draconian." 2 id. at 241.

Similarly, see the court's view in the *Gagliardi* case, footnote 33, page 98 supra:

> Corporate directors of public companies typically have a very small proportionate ownership interest in their corporations and little or no incentive compensation. Thus, they enjoy (as residual owners) only a very small proportion of any "upside" gains earned by the corporation on risky investment projects. If, however, corporate directors were to be found liable for a corporate loss from a risky project on the ground that the investment was too risky (foolishly risky! stupidly risky! egregiously risky! — you supply the adverb), their liability would be joint and several for the whole loss (with I suppose a right of contribution). Given the scale of operation of modern public

---

48. For discussion of whether this system of indemnification and insurance *may* be justified because "shareholder litigation can be cost effective in view of the indeterminacy that characterizes corporate law," see Ehud Kamar, Shareholder Litigation Under Indeterminate Corporate Law, 66 U. Chi. L. Rev. 887 (1999):

> American corporate law relies heavily on open-ended legal standards that grant courts wide discretion in resolving corporate disputes. . . . The absence of clear legal rules is costly. First, . . . [s]ome corporate fiduciaries may overestimate the legal constraints and forgo efficient transactions, while others may underestimate the very same constraints and carry out inefficient transactions. Second, legal indeterminacy creates liability risk, which risk-averse fiduciaries are in a poor position to bear. Exposing corporate fiduciaries to this risk makes their services more costly and less productive to shareholders.

Issues concerning whether and under what circumstances the corporation may (1) indemnify its managers for liabilities incurred in the course of their duties or (2) purchase insurance for them against such liabilities are discussed in Chapter VIII.I infra.

49. Va. Stock Corp. Act §692.1 (1988) imposes a maximum liability of $100,000 or compensation during the preceding 12 months.

corporations, this stupefying disjunction between risk and reward for corporate directors threatens undesirable effects.[50]

4. *Abolishing liability.* In addition to Del. §102(b)(7) (1993) (described in the *Stone* case), which had been enacted in response to the *Van Gorkom* decision,[51] some states have directly modified the standard of liability; e.g., Ohio Gen. Corp. Law §59(D) (1999) provides that unless the articles specifically state otherwise, "a director shall be liable in damages for any action that the director takes or fails to take as a director only if it is proved by clear and convincing evidence that the director's action or failure to act involved an act or omission undertaken with deliberate intent to cause injury to the corporation or undertaken with reckless disregard for the best interests of the corporation."[52] See also Va. Stock Corp. Act §690(A) (1985), which defines a director's duty of care strictly in terms of "good faith business judgment of the best interests of the corporation."[53]

For the view that "very little of any value would be lost by outright abolition of the legal duty of care and its accompanying threat of a lawsuit," see Kenneth E. Scott, Corporation Law and the American Law Institute Corporate Governance

50. To what extent would this be remedied by "a rebuttable presumption that directors acted with due care where the directors also are substantial stockholders"? Balotti, Elson & Laster, footnote 35, page 998 supra at 662: "Five empirical studies provide support for a link between substantial equity ownership and heightened care in director decision making." Id. at 672. For further consideration of this idea, see the last paragraph of Note 2, pages 146-147 infra.

51. Within two years of Del. §102(b)(7), more than 40 states had adopted some form of legislation designed to reduce the risk of directors' personal liability for damages, and almost all presently have some type of provision directed to this end.

Cal. Corp. Code §204(a)(10) (1987) is similar, but also excludes acts or omissions that "show a reckless disregard for the director's duty . . . [when] the director was aware, or should have been aware, . . . of a risk of serious injury" or that "constitute an unexcused pattern of inattention." In addition, in contrast to a few states that extend the liability limitation to officers as well as directors, Cal. §204(a)(10) specifically prohibits eliminating or limiting the liability "of an officer, notwithstanding that the officer is also a director or that his or her actions, if negligent or improper, have been ratified by the directors."

A recent study of 200 corporations of varying size, in jurisdictions allowing these types of provisions, showed that virtually all had adopted them. Laurence A. Hamermesh, Why I Do Not Teach *Van Gorkom*, 34 Ga. L. Rev. 477 (2000).

> Shareholders approving a limited liability provision must believe that the reduction in future insurance premiums is worth foregoing the possibility of recovering against negligent directors. In fact, directors are seldom found negligent because of the incentives to settle and the high standard of proof plaintiffs must meet in duty of care litigation. . . . The financial recovery in the typical shareholder suit involving the duty of care is considerably smaller than that of other shareholder suits, and the litigation-induced organizational changes are, at best, minor. This suggests that limited liability statutes will benefit shareholders without substantial sacrifice, as the premiums paid for the eliminated litigation primarily go toward defense costs.

Roberta Romano, Corporate Governance in the Aftermath of the Insurance Crisis, 39 Emory L.J. 1155, 1167-1173 (1990).

A recent study found only about a dozen instances between 1980 and 2005 in which directors made out-of-pocket payments for breaches of the duty of care (including the defendants in *Van Gorkom* and the Enron and WorldCom scandals). Black, Cheffins & Klausner, footnote 44 supra, at 1063-1064.

52. Ind. Bus. Corp. Law §23-1-35-1(e) (1989) is similar. Wis. Bus. Corp. Law §180.0828 (2001) is also similar, but excludes "recklessness" as a basis for liability. Only Ohio, however, has the "clear and convincing evidence" standard.

Apart from the standard of proof, to what extent do the standards of director conduct in these statutes differ from Del. §102(b)(7)? See McCall v. Scott, 250 F.3d 997, amending 239 F.3d 808 (6th Cir. 2001).

53. But compare Lyman Johnson, Misunderstanding Director Duties: The Strange Case of Virginia, 56 Wash. & Lee L. Rev. 1127 (1999) ("Section 690 only partially encompasses the director duty of care"; "judicially created duties . . . outside the statute . . . [include the] duty to monitor corporate affairs and to exercise responsible supervisory oversight").

Project, 35 Stan. L. Rev. 927, 935-937 (1983): "[O]ther pressures and incentives bear on management's performance—competition in the product and capital markets, the managerial labor market, and executive incentive compensation arrangements. And, even without any threat of negligence liability, the board members, to protect their own reputation as directors, managers, or professionals and to maximize the value of their own stock holdings or those they represent, have reason to monitor and, if necessary, oust top management."[54] Compare James D. Cox, and Thomas L. Hazen, Corporations 182 (2d ed. 2003):

> One weakness of substituting a market-based approach for a duty of care standard, as advised by Professor Scott, is that most prosecutions for violations of the duty of care concern not systematic but one-time decisions. One-shot instances of inattention or ineptitude are unlikely to expose the directors or officers to a corrective shift in control because a single mistake, save one of monumental and lasting consequences, is unlikely to produce a sufficient decline in the firm's market value to attract interest in removing management. Also, the discipline of the market is lacking where the mistake occurs as part of the firm's dissolution, in which case there is no opportunity for a change in control to occur.

See also Renee M. Jones, Law, Norms and the Breakdown of the Board: Promoting Accountability in Corporate Governance, 92 Iowa L. Rev. 105, 157-158 (2006):

> Because neither markets nor social norms can induce ideal conduct from corporate directors, a credible accountability mechanism is necessary to provide an external check on managerial overreaching. . . . Reducing the weight of prospective liability might encourage judges to impose liability more often. Linking directors' personal contributions to settlements to their ability to pay could also reduce the perceived unfairness of the existing liability scheme. If director liability provisions were more widely perceived as fair (by directors and society in general), directors would be more likely to heed the values commended to them by courts and commentators.

Accord, Lisa M. Fairfax, Spare the Rod, Spoil the Director? Revitalizing Directors' Fiduciary Duty Through Legal Liability, 42 Hous. L. Rev. 393 (2005).

3. TRANSACTIONS IN WHICH DIRECTORS, OFFICERS, AND SHAREHOLDERS HAVE A PERSONAL INTEREST: DUTY OF LOYALTY

Numerous types of transactions between the corporation and its managers or shareholders (or with other business enterprises in which they are participants), as well as many other corporate activities, present problems of conflict of interest.

---

54. Compare James D. Cox, Compensation, Deterrence, and the Market as Boundaries for Derivative Suit Procedures, 52 Geo. Wash. L. Rev. 745, 761 (1984): "No dynamic market exists for managers of small privately held corporations. Therefore, for the great bulk of American corporations, market-based solutions are not available, making private litigation a necessity."

For the view that "the level of directorial care is largely driven by social norms . . . [i.e.,] the belief-system of the business community concerning the nature of the obligations associated with the directorial role . . . rather than by the threat of liability or the prospect of gain," see Melvin A. Eisenberg, Corporate Law and Social Norms, 99 Colum. L. Rev. 1253, 1265, 1269 (1999). See also Lynn A. Stout, In Praise of Procedure: An Economic and Behavioral Defense of *Smith v. Gorkom* and the Business Judgment Rule, 96 Nw. U. L. Rev. 675 (2002).

Various instances will be discussed at appropriate points in subsequent chapters that deal with the particular substantive topics in which the conflict of interest arises — e.g., use of corporate funds by management in proxy contests (Chapter VI); corporate sale of shares to, or purchase of shares from, managers or shareholders (Chapter V); corporate actions to defeat a takeover attempt (such as the purchase of the bidder's shares), allegedly to avoid loss of control by incumbents (Chapter IX); corporate dissolution, allegedly to accommodate the personal needs of those in control (Chapter IX); corporate merger or consolidation with, or sale of all its assets to, those in control (Chapter IX).

This section concerns the legal obligations of directors, officers, and shareholders principally with respect to three subjects: conventional business dealings between them (or another business in which they have an interest) and the corporation, their compensation for services to the corporation, and their ability to take advantage of opportunities in which the corporation may have an interest. The so-called fiduciary obligation imposed on them is substantially similar to the standard of conduct required in other conflict-of-interest situations.[55] In addition to the special "procedural" problems presented by a conflict of interest, the materials that follow also deal with the "substantive" corporation law doctrines that relate to the subjects under consideration.

a. Contracts with Interested Directors

The strict Anglo-American common law rule, surviving in many jurisdictions into the twentieth century, was that a corporate contract with one or more of its directors — or with another corporation or business enterprise in which one or more of the directors was associated as a manager, shareholder, or partner — was voidable by the corporation irrespective of fairness. Apart from the rule's virtue of avoiding any prolonged uncertainty as to the enforceability of such contracts, courts — analogizing directors to trustees who were forbidden to transact personal business with the trust — reasoned that a corporation was entitled to the unbiased judgment of all its directors and that it was impossible to determine the influence of interested directors over their fellow board members even though they declined to participate in discussing and voting on the transaction. But as corporations grew in size, the benefits of having outside directors with wider experience and connections with other banking and industrial enterprises and the advantages of being able

---

55. The classic formulation of the obligation of corporate "fiduciaries" — although stated in a case involving a joint enterprise rather than a corporation — is that of Justice (then Judge) Cardozo:

> Many forms of conduct permissible in a workaday world for those acting at arm's length, are forbidden to those bound by fiduciary ties. A trustee is held to something stricter than the morals of the market place. Not honesty alone, but the punctilio of an honor the most sensitive, is then the standard of behavior. As to this there has developed a tradition that is unbending and inveterate. Uncompromising rigidity has been the attitude of courts of equity when petitioned to undermine the rule of undivided loyalty by the "disintegrating erosion" of particular exceptions. . . . Only thus has the level of conduct for fiduciaries been kept at a level higher than that trodden by the crowd.

Meinhard v. Salmon, 249 N.Y. 458, 164 N.E. 545 (1928). "But," as Justice Frankfurter observed, "to say that a man is a fiduciary only begins analysis; it gives direction to further inquiry. To whom is he a fiduciary? What obligations does he owe as a fiduciary? In what respects has he failed to discharge these obligations? And what are the consequences of his deviation from duty?" SEC v. Chenery Corp., 318 U.S. 80, 85-86 (1943).

to engage in business dealings with directors led to some relaxation of this inflexible rule. Most courts began to hold that transactions with interested directors (or involving corporations with "interlocking directorates") were not voidable by the corporation if (1) the interested director was not necessary for a quorum, (2) the transaction was approved by a majority of the disinterested directors, *and* (3) the transaction was neither fraudulent nor unfair to the corporation (the burden of showing fairness usually being placed on the party seeking to uphold the transaction). Under both of these earlier approaches, however, the rule was that voidable transactions could be validated by full disclosure to and ratification by a majority of the shareholders—at least in the absence of fraud or unfairness. Further, it was held that shareholders who had an interest adverse to the corporation in the voidable transaction with directors were not disqualified from voting on the shareholder ratification.[56]

By mid-twentieth century, the rule became further liberalized: "it could be said with some assurance that the general rule was that no transaction of a corporation with any or all of its directors was automatically voidable at the suit of a shareholder, whether there was a disinterested majority of the board or not; but that the courts would review such a contract and subject it to rigid and careful scrutiny, and would invalidate the contract if it was found to be unfair to the corporation."[57]

Cookies Food Products, Inc. v. Lakes Warehouse Distributing, Inc.
430 N.W.2d 447 (Iowa 1988)

NEUMAN, J.: This is a shareholders' derivative suit brought by the minority shareholders of a closely held Iowa corporation specializing in barbecue sauce, Cookies Food Products, Inc. (Cookies). The target of the lawsuit is the majority shareholder, Duane "Speed" Herrig and two of his family-owned corporations, Lakes Warehouse Distributing, Inc. (Lakes) and Speed's Automotive Co., Inc. (Speed's). Plaintiffs alleged that Herrig, by acquiring control of Cookies and executing self-dealing contracts, breached his fiduciary duty to the company. . . .

L. D. Cook of Storm Lake, Iowa, founded Cookies in 1975 to produce and distribute his original barbecue sauce. Searching for a plant site in a community that would provide financial backing, Cook met with business leaders in seventeen Iowa communities, outlining his plans to build a growth-oriented company. He selected Wall Lake, Iowa, persuading thirty-five members of that community, including Herrig and the plaintiffs, to purchase Cookies stock. All of the investors hoped Cookies would improve the local job market and tax base. The record reveals that it has done just that.

Early sales of the product, however, were dismal. After the first year's operation, Cookies was in dire financial straits. At that time, Herrig was one of thirty-five shareholders and held only two hundred shares. He was also the owner of an auto parts business, Speed's Automotive, and Lakes Warehouse Distributing, Inc., a company that distributed auto parts from Speed's. Cookies' board of directors approached Herrig with the idea of distributing the company's products. It

---

56. For detailed discussion and citations, see Henry W. Ballantine, Corporations 167-184 (rev. ed. 1946); Harold Marsh Jr., Are Directors Trustees?, 22 Bus. Law. 35 (1966). For a different view of the early common law rule, see Norwood P. Beveridge Jr., Interested Director Contracts at Common Law: Validation Under the Doctrine of Constructive Fraud, 33 Loy. L.A. L. Rev. 39 (1999).

57. Marsh, footnote 56 supra, at 43.

authorized Herrig to purchase Cookies' sauce for twenty percent under wholesale price, which he could then resell at full wholesale price. Under this arrangement, Herrig began to market and distribute the sauce to his auto parts customers and to grocery outlets from Lakes' trucks as they traversed the regular delivery routes for Speed's Automotive.

In May 1977, Cookies formalized this arrangement by executing an exclusive distribution agreement with Lakes. Pursuant to this agreement, Cookies was responsible only for preparing the product; Lakes, for its part, assumed all costs of warehousing, marketing, sales, delivery, promotion, and advertising. Cookies retained the right to fix the sales price of its products and agreed to pay Lakes thirty percent of its gross sales for these services.

Cookies' sales have soared under the exclusive distributorship contract with Lakes. Gross sales in 1976, the year prior to the agreement, totaled only $20,000, less than half of Cookies' expenses that year. In 1977, however, sales jumped fivefold, then doubled in 1978, and have continued to show phenomenal growth every year thereafter. By 1985, when this suit was commenced, annual sales reached $2,400,000.

As sales increased, Cookies' board of directors amended and extended the original distributorship agreement. In 1979, the board amended the original agreement to give Lakes an additional two percent of gross sales to cover freight costs for the ever-expanding market for Cookies' sauce. In 1980, the board extended the amended agreement through 1984 to allow Herrig to make long-term advertising commitments. Recognizing the role that Herrig's personal strengths played in the success of their joint endeavor, the board also amended the agreement that year to allow Cookies to cancel the agreement with Lakes if Herrig died or disposed of the corporation's stock.

In 1981, L. D. Cook, the majority shareholder up to this time, decided to sell his interest in Cookies. He first offered the directors an opportunity to buy his stock, but the board declined to purchase any of his 8,100 shares. Herrig then offered Cook and all other shareholders $10 per share for their stock, which was twice the original price. Because of the overwhelming response to these offers, Herrig had purchased enough Cookies stock by January 1982 to become the majority shareholder. His investment of $140,000 represented fifty-three percent of the 28,700 outstanding shares. Other shareholders had invested a total of $67,500 for the remaining forty-seven percent.

Shortly after Herrig acquired majority control he replaced four of the five members of the Cookies' board with members he selected. This restructuring of authority, following on the heels of an unsuccessful attempt by certain stockholders to prevent Herrig from acquiring majority status, solidified a division of opinion within the shareholder ranks. Subsequent changes made in the corporation under Herrig's leadership formed the basis for this lawsuit.

First, under Herrig's leadership, Cookies' board has extended the term of the exclusive distributorship agreement with Lakes and expanded the scope of services for which it compensates Herrig and his companies. In April 1982, when a sales increase of twenty-five percent over the previous year required Cookies to seek additional short-term storage for the peak summer season, the board accepted Herrig's proposal to compensate Lakes at the "going rate" for use of its nearby storage facilities. The board decided to use Lakes' storage facilities because building and staffing its own facilities would have been more expensive.

Later, in July 1982, the new board approved an extension of the exclusive distributorship agreement. Notably, this agreement was identical to the 1980 extension that the former board had approved while four of the plaintiffs in this action were directors.

Second, Herrig moved from his role as director and distributor to take on an additional role in product development. This created a dispute over a royalty Herrig began to receive. Herrig's role in product development began in 1982 when Cookies diversified its product line to include taco sauce. Herrig developed the recipe. . . . In August 1982, Cookies' board approved a royalty fee to be paid to Herrig for this taco sauce recipe. This royalty plan was similar to royalties the board paid to L. D. Cook for the barbecue sauce recipe. That plan gives Cook three percent of the gross sales of barbecue sauce; Herrig receives a flat rate per case. Although Herrig's rate is equivalent to a sales percentage slightly higher than what Cook receives, it yields greater profit to Cookies because this new product line is cheaper to produce.

Third, since 1982 Cookies' board has twice approved additional compensation for Herrig. In January 1983, the board authorized payment of a $1,000 per month "consultant fee" in lieu of salary, because accelerated sales required Herrig to spend extra time managing the company. Averaging eighty-hour work weeks, Herrig devoted approximately fifteen percent of his time to Cookies and eighty percent to Lakes business. In August 1983, the board authorized another increase in Herrig's compensation. Further, at the suggestion of a Cookies director who also served as an accountant for Cookies, Lakes, and Speed's, the Cookies board amended the exclusive distributorship agreement to allow Lakes an additional two percent of gross sales as a promotion allowance to expand the market for Cookies products outside of Iowa. As a direct result of this action, by 1986 Cookies regularly shipped products to several states throughout the country.

As we have previously noted, however, Cookies' growth and success has not pleased all its shareholders. The discontent is motivated by two factors that have effectively precluded shareholders from sharing in Cookies' financial success: the fact that Cookies is a closely held corporation, and the fact that it has not paid dividends. Because Cookies' stock is not publicly traded, shareholders have no ready access to buyers for their stock at current values that reflect the company's success. Without dividends, the shareholders have no ready method of realizing a return on their investment in the company. This is not to say that Cookies has improperly refused to pay dividends. The evidence reveals that Cookies would have violated the terms of its loan with the Small Business Administration had it declared dividends before repaying that debt. That SBA loan was not repaid until the month before the plaintiffs filed this action. . . .

Having heard the evidence presented on these claims at trial, the district court filed a lengthy ruling that reflected careful attention to the testimony of the twenty-two witnesses and myriad of exhibits admitted. The court concluded that Herrig had breached no duties owed to Cookies. . . .

II. *Fiduciary Duties.* Herrig, as an officer and director of Cookies, owes a fiduciary duty to the company and its shareholders. . . . Herrig concedes that Iowa law imposed the same fiduciary responsibilities based on his status as majority stockholder. See Des Moines Bank & Trust Co. v. George M. Bechtel & Co., 243 Iowa 1007, 1082-1083, 51 N.W.2d 174, 217 (1952) (hereinafter Bechtel); see also 12B W. Fletcher, Cyclopedia on the Law of Private Corporations §5810, at 149 (1986). Conversely, before acquiring majority control in February 1982, Herrig owed no fiduciary duty to Cookies or plaintiffs. See Fletcher §5713, at 13 (stockholders not active in management of corporation owe duties radically different from director, and vote at shareholder's meetings merely for own benefit). Therefore, Herrig's conduct is subject to scrutiny only from the time he began to exercise control of Cookies.

... [A]ppellants claim that Herrig violated his duty of loyalty to Cookies. That duty derives from "the prohibition against self-dealing that inheres in the fiduciary relationship." *Norlin*, 744 F.2d at 264. ... As we noted in *Bechtel*: "Corporate directors and officers may under proper circumstances transact business with the corporation including the purchase or sale of property, but it must be done in the strictest good faith and with full disclosure of the facts to, and the consent of, all concerned. And the burden is upon them to establish their good faith, honesty and fairness. Such transactions are scanned by the courts with skepticism and the closest scrutiny, and may be nullified on slight grounds. It is the policy of the courts to put such fiduciaries beyond the reach of temptation and the enticement of illicit profit." 243 Iowa 1007, 1081, 51 N.W.2d 174, 216 (1952). We have repeatedly applied this standard, including the burden of proof and level of scrutiny, when a corporate director engages in self-dealing with another corporation for which he or she also serves as a director. See Holden v. Construction Mach. Co., 202 N.W.2d 348, 356-357 (Iowa 1972).

Against this common law backdrop, the legislature enacted section 496A.34, quoted here in pertinent part, that establishes three sets of circumstances under which a director may engage in self-dealing without clearly violating the duty of loyalty:

> No contract or other transaction between a corporation and one or more of its directors or any other corporation, firm, association or entity in which one or more of its directors are directors or officers or are financially interested, shall be either void or voidable because of such relationship or interest ... if any of the following occur:
>
> 1. The fact of such relationship or interest is disclosed or known to the board of directors or committee which authorizes, approves, or ratifies the contract or transaction ... without counting the votes ... of such interested director.
> 2. The fact of such relationship or interest is disclosed or known to the shareholders entitled to vote [on the transaction] and they authorize ... such contract or transaction by vote or written consent.
> 3. The contract or transaction is fair and reasonable to the corporation.

Some commentators have supported the view that satisfaction of any one of the foregoing statutory alternatives, in and of itself, would prove that a director has fully met the duty of loyalty. See Hansell, Austin & Wilcox, Director Liability Under Iowa Law — Duties and Protections, 13 J. Corp. L. 369, 382. We are obliged, however, to interpret statutes in conformity with the common law wherever statutory language does not directly negate it. See Hardwick v. Bublitz, 253 Iowa 49, 59, 111 N.W.2d 309, 314 (1961); Iowa Code §4.2 (1987). Because the common law and section 496A.34 require directors to show "good faith, honesty, and fairness" in self-dealing, we are persuaded that satisfaction of any one of these three alternatives under the statute would merely preclude us from rendering the transaction void or voidable outright solely on the basis "of such [director's] relationship or interest." Iowa Code §496A.34; see *Bechtel*, 243 Iowa at 1081-1082, 51

N.W.2d at 216. To the contrary, we are convinced that the legislature did not intend by this statute to enable a court, in a shareholder's derivative suit, to rubber stamp any transaction to which a board of directors or the shareholders of a corporation have consented. Such an interpretation would invite those who stand to gain from such transactions to engage in improprieties to obtain consent. We thus require directors who engage in self-dealing to establish the additional element that they have acted in good faith, honesty, and fairness. Holi-Rest, Inc. v. Treloar, 217 N.W.2d 517, 525 (Iowa 1974).[58]

III. *Burden of Proof.* . . . [P]laintiffs first made out a prima facie showing that Herrig had engaged in self-dealing with Cookies. Defendants then presented witnesses and exhibits to prove that Herrig's actions in these challenged transactions were done in good faith and with honesty and fairness toward Cookies. The plaintiffs countered with rebuttal testimony and exhibits. The mere fact that the district court credited Herrig and his evidence instead of accepting plaintiffs' contrary proof does not establish that the court improperly allocated the burden of proof. The assignment of error is without merit.

IV. *Standard of Law.* . . . We agree with appellants' contention that corporate profitability should not be the sole criterion by which to test the fairness and reasonableness of Herrig's fees. . . . [H]owever, we cannot agree with appellants' assertion that Herrig's services were either unfairly priced or inconsistent with Cookies corporate interest.

There can be no serious dispute that the four agreements in issue — for exclusive distributorship, taco sauce royalty, warehousing, and consulting fees — have all benefitted Cookies, as demonstrated by its financial success. Even if we assume Cookies could have procured similar services from other vendors at lower costs, we are not convinced that Herrig's fees were therefore unreasonable or exorbitant. Like the district court, we are not persuaded by appellants' expert testimony that Cookies' sales and profits would have been the same under agreements with other vendors. As Cookies' board noted prior to Herrig's takeover, he was the driving force in the corporation's success. Even plaintiffs' expert acknowledged that Herrig has done the work of at least five people — production supervisor, advertising specialist, warehouseman, broker, and salesman. While eschewing the lack of internal control, for accounting purposes, that such centralized authority may produce, the expert conceded that Herrig may in fact be underpaid for all he has accomplished. We believe the board properly considered this source of

58. Accord, Remillard Brick Co. v. Remillard-Dandini Co., 109 Cal. App. 2d 405, 241 P.2d 66 (1952) (despite fulfillment of statute's disclosure and ratification requirements to shareholders, which were similar to Iowa's, "transactions that are unfair and unreasonable to the corporation may be avoided"); Fliegler v. Lawrence, 361 A.2d 218 (Del. 1976) (shareholder approval pursuant to Del. §144(a)(2) "merely removes an 'interested director' cloud . . . and provides against invalidation of an agreement 'solely' because such a director or officer is involved. Nothing in the statute sanctions unfairness to [the corporation] or removes the transaction from judicial scrutiny"). Contra, Benihana of Tokyo, Inc. v. Benihana, Inc., 906 A.2d 114 (Del. 2006) ("after approval by disinterested directors, courts review the interested transactions under the business judgment rule"). For the view that the *Remillard* and *Fliegler* decisions turned on the fact that the shareholder approval was achieved by the votes of interested shareholders, see James D. Cox & Thomas L. Hazen, Corporations 214-215 (2d ed. 2003). In support, see Marciano v. Nakash, 535 A.2d 400 (Del. 1987) ("approval by fully informed disinterested directors under section 144(a)(1), or disinterested stockholders under section 144(a)(2), permits invocation of the business judgment rule and limits judicial review to issues of gift or waste with the burden of proof upon the party attacking the transaction") (dictum). Accord, Oberly v. Kirby, 592 A.2d 445, 465-468 (Del. 1991) (dictum). — Ed.

Cookies' success when it entered these transactions, as did the district court when it reviewed them. . . .

V. *Denial of Equitable Relief.* The appellants also claim that Herrig committed equitable fraud . . . [by] failure to disclose certain information to directors and shareholders. . . .

While both Iowa's statutes and case law impose a duty of disclosure on interested directors who engage in self-dealing, neither has delineated what information must be disclosed, or to whom. . . . While these cases strongly encourage directors to make the fullest possible disclosure of pertinent facts to persons responsible for making informed decisions, they also suggest the court must look to the particular facts of each case to determine whether a director has violated the duty of disclosure.

Examining Herrig's conduct under this duty of disclosure, we find no support for plaintiffs' assertion that Herrig owed the minority shareholders a duty to disclose any information before the board executed the exclusive distributorship, royalty, warehousing, or consultant fee agreements. These actions comprise management activity, and our statutes place the duty of managing the affairs of the corporation on the board of directors, not the shareholders. See Iowa Code §496A.34 (1987). . . .

With regard to the board of directors, the record before us aptly demonstrates that all members of Cookies' board were well aware of Herrig's dual ownership in Lakes and Speed's. We are unaware of any authority supporting plaintiffs' contention that Herrig was obligated to disclose to Cookies' board or shareholders the extent of his profits resulting from these distribution and warehousing agreements; nevertheless, the exclusive distribution agreement with Lakes authorized the board to ascertain that information had it so desired. Appellants cannot reasonably claim that Herrig owed Cookies a duty to render such services at no profit to himself or his companies. Having found that the compensation he received from these agreements was fair and reasonable, we are convinced that Herrig furnished sufficient pertinent information to Cookies' board to enable it to make prudent decisions concerning the contracts.

Nor does Herrig's status as an "inside director" of Cookies alter our determination that he disclosed adequate information about his self-dealing. An inside director is one who also serves as an officer of the corporation and is involved in the daily management of the company. Because of the inside director's experience with company affairs, directors not so intimately involved in running the company are entitled to rely on the inside director's recommendations and opinions when making their own decisions. See *Rowen*, 282 N.W.2d at 652-653. Although our review of the record indicates that Herrig was somewhat reluctant to answer all the minority shareholders' questions concerning the board's decisions, he did not withhold any crucial information from the directors that caused the company to make unnecessarily expensive commitments in reliance on his silence, and thus has not committed equitable fraud. . . .

. . . As the [district] court wisely reasoned, "[t]he very complaint of the Plaintiffs, that Herrig is too deeply involved in the total operation of the Cookies plant, is the reason for the success of this company. That some budgetary cuts might be made, some salaried positions filled by other persons, some additional papers could be filed when products are taken to the Speed's warehouse, are all possibilities that Herrig and the board of directors of Cookies might consider. However, these things are all conjecture and speculation. The reality here is that the Cookies company is profitable. In a time of economic disaster to many businesses and individuals in Iowa, this company is a shining example of success. The shareholders' investments have multiplied more than fourfold, jobs have been created in Wall Lake, more cash flows in and out of that community annually, and the consumers of Iowa are provided with a good product at a fair price. For this Court to tinker with such a successful venture, and especially to punish Herrig for this success, would be . . . inequitable. . . ."

We concur in the trial court's assessment of the evidence presented and affirm its dismissal of plaintiffs' claims.

SCHULTZ, J. (dissenting): My quarrel with the majority opinion is not with its interpretation of the law, but with its application of the law to the facts. . . . Herrig gained control of the corporation by buying a majority of the stock. His first act was to replace all of the board of directors except one, an employee of the company. From that time on, he engaged in a course of self-dealing and refused to cooperate or comply with the requests of the minority stockholders. . . . It was Herrig's burden to demonstrate that all of his self-dealing transactions were fair to the company.

Much of Herrig's evidence concerned the tremendous success of the company. I believe that the trial court and the majority opinion have been so enthralled by the success of the company that they have failed to examine whether these matters of self-dealing were fair to the stockholders. While much credit is due to Herrig for the success of the company, this does not mean that these transactions were fair to the company.

I believe that Herrig failed on his burden of proof by what he did not show. He did not produce evidence of the local going rate for distribution contracts or storage fees outside of a very limited amount of self-serving testimony. He simply did not show the fair market value of his services or expense for freight, advertising and storage cost. He did not show that his taco sauce royalty was fair. This was his burden. He cannot succeed on it by merely showing the success of the company.

. . . The appellants have put forth convincing testimony that Herrig has been grossly over compensated for his services based on their fair market value. Appellant's expert witness, a CPA, performed an analysis to show what the company would have earned if it had hired a $65,000 a year executive officer, paid a marketing supervisor and an advertising agency a commission of five percent of the sales each, built a new warehouse and hired a warehouseman. It was compared with what the company actually did make under Herrig's management. The analysis basically shows what the operating cost of this company should be on the open market when hiring out the work to experts. In 1985 alone, the company's income would have doubled what it actually made were these changes made. The evidence clearly shows that the fair market value of those services is considerably less than what Herrig actually has been paid.

Similarly, appellant's food broker expert witness testified that for $110,865, what the CPA analysis stated was the fair market value for brokerage services, his company would have provided all of the services that Herrig had performed. The company actually paid $730,637 for the services, a difference of $620,000 in one year.

. . . Herrig is not entitled to skim off the majority of the profits through self-dealing transactions unless they are fair to the minority stockholders. At trial, he failed to prove how his charges were in line with what the company could have gotten on the open market. Because I cannot ignore this inequity to the company and its shareholders, I must respectfully dissent.

---

1. *Statutes.* Nearly all states have statutory provisions governing contracts with interested directors. Although Iowa's statute has since been changed, see Iowa Bus. Corp. Act §490.831 (2003), the provision in the *Cookies* case represents a fairly standard approach. The following illustrate significant variations:

New York Business Corporation Law (1998)

Sec. 713. *Interested directors.* (a) No contract or other transaction between a corporation and one or more of its directors, or between a corporation and any other corporation, firm, association or other entity in which one or more of its directors are directors or officers, or have a substantial financial interest, shall be either void or voidable for this reason alone or by reason alone that such director or directors are present at the meeting of the board, or of a committee thereof, which approves such contract or transaction, or that his or their votes are counted for such purpose:

(1) If the material facts as to such director's interest in such contract or transaction and as to any such common directorship, officership or financial interest are disclosed in good faith or known to the board or committee, and the board or committee approves such contract or transaction by a vote sufficient for such purpose without counting the vote of such interested director or, if the votes of the disinterested directors are insufficient to constitute an act of the board . . . by unanimous vote of the disinterested directors; or

(2) If the material facts as to such director's interest in such contract or transaction and as to any such common directorship, officership or financial interest are disclosed in good faith or known to the shareholders entitled to vote thereon, and such contract or transaction is approved by vote of such shareholders.[59]

(b) If a contract or other transaction between a corporation and one or more of its directors, or between a corporation and any other corporation, firm, association or other entity in which one or more of its directors are directors or officers, or have a substantial financial interest, is not approved in accordance with paragraph (a), the corporation may avoid the contract or transaction unless the party or parties thereto shall establish affirmatively that the contract or transaction was fair and reasonable as to the corporation at the time it was approved by the board, a committee or the shareholders.

(c) Common or interested directors may be counted in determining the presence of a quorum at a meeting of the board or of a committee which approves such contract or transaction.[60]

---

59. With respect to paragraphs (1) and (2), less than one-quarter of the states require only that the "fact" of the director's "relationship or interest is disclosed or known." See, e.g., N.J. Bus Corp. Act §6-8 (1988). See also the Iowa provision in the *Cookies* case. — ED.

60. A few states do not permit an interested director to vote or count toward a quorum. See, e.g., Minn. Bus. Corp. Act §302A.255 (2000). — ED.

(d) The certificate of incorporation may contain additional restrictions on contracts or transactions between a corporation and its directors and may provide that contracts or transactions in violation of such restrictions shall be void or voidable by the corporation. . . .

California General Corporation Law (1976)

Sec. 310. *Contracts in which director has material financial interest; validity.* (a) No contract or other transaction between a corporation and one or more of its directors, or between a corporation and any corporation, firm or association in which one or more of its directors has a material financial interest, is either void or voidable because such director or directors or such other corporation, firm or association are parties or because such director or directors are present at the meeting of the board or a committee thereof which authorizes, approves or ratifies the contract or transaction, if

(1) The material facts as to the transaction and as to such director's interest are fully disclosed or known to the shareholders and such contract or transaction is approved by the shareholders in good faith, with the shares owned by the interested director or directors not being entitled to vote thereon,[61] or

(2) The material facts as to the transaction and as to such director's interest are fully disclosed or known to the board or committee, and the board or committee authorizes, approves or ratifies the contract or transaction in good faith by a vote sufficient without counting the vote of the interested director or directors and the contract or transaction is just and reasonable as to the corporation at the time it is authorized, approved or ratified, or

(3) As to contracts or transactions not approved as provided in paragraph (1) or (2) of this subdivision, the person asserting the validity of the contract or transaction sustains the burden of proving that the contract or transaction was just and reasonable as to the corporation at the time it was authorized, approved or ratified. . . .

(c) Interested or common directors may be counted in determining the presence of a quorum at a meeting of the board or a committee thereof which authorizes, approves or ratifies a contract or transaction.

American Law Institute, Principles of Corporate Governance (1994)

Sec. 5.02. *Transactions with the corporation.* (a) *General rule.* A director or senior executive[62] who enters into a transaction with the corporation (other than a

61. Several states expressly permit the votes of interested directors to be counted in a shareholder ratification. See, e.g., Ind. Bus. Corp. Law §23-1-35-2(d) (1987); Or. Bus. Corp. Act §60.361(4) (1987).

Query: Is this different from N.Y. §713(a)(2)? Does New York exclude "shares owned by the interested director," or does "shareholders entitled to vote thereon" refer to the fact that "the corporation might have outstanding classes of shares which lack voting rights under the company's articles (such as non-voting preferred)"? Gevurtz, footnote 45 supra at 342. — ED.

62. Most "interested director" statutes apply only to transactions with directors, assuming that nondirector officers or employees of the corporation are dealt with by the law of agency governing the loyalty of agent to principal. Some, however, cover a "contract or transaction between a corporation and one or more of its directors or *officers*," Del. Gen. Corp. Law §144 (1998). ALI Principles §1.33 defines the term "senior executive" as "(a) the chief executive, operating, financial, legal, and accounting

transaction involving the payment of compensation) fulfills the duty of fair dealing with respect to the transaction if:

(1) Disclosure concerning the conflict of interest and the transaction[63] is made to the corporate decisionmaker who authorizes in advance or ratifies the transaction; and

(2) Either:

(A) The transaction is fair to the corporation when entered into;

(B) The transaction is authorized in advance, following disclosure concerning the conflict of interest and the transaction, by disinterested directors, or in the case of a senior executive who is not a director by a disinterested superior, who could reasonably have concluded that the transaction was fair to the corporation at the time of such authorization;[64]

(C) The transaction is ratified, following such disclosure, by disinterested directors who could reasonably have concluded that the transaction was fair to the corporation at the time it was entered into, provided (i) a corporate decision maker who is not interested in the transaction acted for the corporation in the transaction and could reasonably have concluded that the transaction was fair to the corporation; (ii) the interested director or senior executive made disclosure to such decisionmaker pursuant to Subsection (a)(1) to the extent he or she then knew of the material facts; (iii) the interested director or senior executive did not act unreasonably in failing to seek advance authorization of the transaction by disinterested directors or a disinterested superior; and (iv) the failure to obtain advance authorization of the

---

officers of a corporation; (b) to the extent not encompassed by the foregoing, the chairman of the board of directors (unless the chairman neither performs a policymaking function other than as a director nor receives a material amount of compensation in excess of director's fees), president, treasurer, and secretary, and a vice-president or vice-chairman who is in charge of a principal business unit, division, or function (such as sales, administration, or finance) or performs a major policymaking function for the corporation." — Ed.

63. Section 1.14(b) defines *disclosure* as "the material facts," and §1.25 defines a fact as *material* "if there is a substantial likelihood that a reasonable person would consider it important under the circumstances in determining the person's course of action." For discussion of complexities in applying this standard, see Lewis v. Vogelstein, 699 A.2d 327 (Del. Ch. 1997) (shareholders ratifying stock option plan for directors need not be told the present value of the compensation afforded by options). Compare Teachers' Retirement System of Louisiana v. Aidinoff, 900 A.2d 654 (Del. Ch. 2006) ("board majority must have acted in an informed manner"). — Ed.

64. In 1989 Subchapter F, "Directors' Conflicting Interest Transactions," was added to RMBCA and amended in 2005. It has been adopted by nearly one-third of the states. "[S]ubchapter F made explicit, as many other statutory provisions did not, that if a director's conflict-of-interest transaction, as defined, was properly approved by disinterested (or 'qualified') directors or shareholders, the transaction was thereby insulated from judicial review for fairness. . . ." 2 Mod. Bus. Corp. Act Ann. 8-371 (3d. ed. 2005). But compare 1 ALI, Principles of Corporate Governance 244 (1994):

Although the black letter text of new section 8.61, if read literally, could preclude judicial review of directors' conflicting interest transactions that are approved by disinterested directors, the commentary to section 8.60 makes clear that the directors' actions must comply with the good faith and due care criteria for director actions prescribed in section 8.30(a) of the Model Act. Furthermore, an important passage of the commentary provides that terms of a transaction that are "manifestly unfavorable" to the corporation could constitute relevant probative evidence that the directors' action was not in good faith and therefore did not comply with section 8.30. In the view of the Reporters, the "manifestly unfavorable" test of Subchapter F is comparable to the test of section 5.02(a)(2)(B).

— Ed.

transaction by disinterested directors or a disinterested superior did not adversely affect the interests of the corporation in a significant way;[65] or

(D) The transaction is authorized in advance or ratified, following such disclosure, by disinterested shareholders, and does not constitute a waste of corporate assets at the time of the shareholder action.

(b) *Burden of proof.* A party who challenges a transaction between a director or senior executive and the corporation has the burden of proof, except that if such party establishes that none of Subsections (a)(2)(B), (a)(2)(C), or (a)(2)(D) is satisfied, the director or senior executive has the burden of proving that the transaction was fair to the corporation.

(c) *Ratification of disclosure or nondisclosure.* The disclosure requirements of §5.02(a)(1) will be deemed to be satisfied if at any time (but no later than a reasonable time after suit is filed challenging the transaction) the transaction is ratified, following such disclosure, by the directors, the shareholders, or the corporate decisionmaker who initially approved the transaction or the decisionmaker's successor.[66]

---

2. *Statutory alternatives for judicial review of interested director transactions.* Which of the three basic criteria for review — (1) director approval, (2) shareholder approval, or (3) fairness — was found to be satisfied in *Cookies*? Did Herrig make disclosure to "disinterested directors"? Were there *any* disinterested directors?

(a) *"Procedural" vs. "substantive" fairness.* (i) If there had been (a sufficient number of) disinterested directors in *Cookies*, should their approval after adequate disclosure end the issue of duty of loyalty? Or should Herrig have to "establish the additional element that he acted in good faith, honesty, and fairness"?

(ii) If a director discloses his interest in a proposed transaction with the corporation to an independent board of directors and then fully withdraws from participating in the transaction on behalf of the corporation, should his obligation be any greater than that of an outsider with respect to the "fairness" of the transaction?

> [I]t is difficult if not impossible to utilize a legal definition of disinterestedness in corporate law that corresponds with factual disinterestedness. A factually disinterested director would be one who had no significant relationship of any kind

---

65. Charles Hansen, John F. Johnston & Frederick H. Alexander, The Role of Disinterested Directors in "Conflict" Transactions: The ALI Corporate Governance Project and Existing Law, 45 Bus. Law. 2083, 2098 (1990), complain that there is no case "in which a court has held that ratification of a transaction by disinterested directors will not have the same effect as would prior approval. Further, the distinction seems unsupportable even on policy grounds. The Reporters appear to be concerned that the corporation will have little or no leverage after the transaction has gone forward. However, if the directors refuse to ratify, they will be in a position to disavow the transaction or, if they prefer, to renegotiate new terms." Compare Marlene A. O'Connor, How Should We Talk About Fiduciary Duty? Directors' Conflict-of-Interest Transactions and the ALI's Principles of Corporate Governance, 61 Geo. Wash. L. Rev. 954, 961 (1993): "[S]ection 5.02 takes the view that ratification presents the transaction to the board at a time when it becomes awkward to scrutinize a colleague's transaction with the corporation; the independent directors must choose between approving the transaction or exposing their colleague to litigation." For further discussion of the "structural bias" of corporate directors, see pages 848, 851 (footnote 45), 855-855 (footnote 48) infra. — Ed.

66. For consideration of different statutory approaches, see Michael P. Dooley, Two Models of Corporate Governance, 47 Bus. Law. 461, 486-495 (1992). — Ed.

with either the subject matter of the self-interested transaction, or the director or senior executive who is engaged in the transaction, that would be likely to affect his judgment. . . . [T]he law must require a fairness review of self-interested transactions even if they have been approved by "disinterested" directors, because directors who are "disinterested" under the corporate-law definition may not be disinterested in fact.

Melvin A. Eisenberg, Self-Interested Transactions in Corporate Law, 13 J. Corp. L. 997, 1002-1003 (1988). See also Mitchell, supra, at 482: "When the transacting party is . . . a corporate fiduciary, she has positional and informational advantages over third parties that may cause the corporation to prefer to do business with her or give her insights into corporate weaknesses. This position may give her bargaining advantages with the corporation over other competitors."

(iii) What result if interested directors (a) make full disclosure to the remaining board members of all relevant facts, of their participation in the proposed transaction, and of their belief that they will reap a substantial profit from it, but (b) then engage in "hard bargaining," with the result that the contract approved by the board is extremely disadvantageous to the corporation? See Globe Woolen Co. v. Utica Gas & Electric Co., 224 N.Y. 483, 121 N.E. 378 (1918) (Cardozo, J.), involving a contract between two corporations, having officers in common (the same person being the dominant figure on both boards), that was found to be very oppressive to the corporation in which this person had a minimal financial interest: "We hold that the constant duty rests on a trustee to seek no harsh advantage to the detriment of his trust, but rather to protest and renounce if through the blindness of those who treat with him he gains what is unfair. And because there is evidence that in the making of these contracts, that duty was ignored, the power of equity was fittingly exercised to bring them to an end." What result if the interested directors' profit on the transaction (and the "unfairness" to the corporation) come about because of factors unforeseen and unforeseeable at the time? See Spethmann v. Anderson, 171 S.W.3d 680 (Tex. Ct. App. 2005) (officer's enforcement of buy-sell agreement with corporation to corporation's serious disadvantage); Stortrax.com, Inc. v. Gurland, 915 A.2d 991 (Md. 2007) (no breach of fiduciary duty for director "to use the same means accorded any other creditor to collect his debt").

(b) *Fairness without disclosure.* Under ALI Principles §5.02, "if appropriate disclosure has not been made," the transaction may "be set aside even if it falls within the range of fairness, unless the transaction has been ratified after the defective disclosure or nondisclosure was cured." 1 ALI, Principles of Corporate Governance 211 (1994). The Official Comment to RMBCA §8.61(b) states that "unfair dealing arises out of the director's failure to disclose . . . and the court should offer the corporation its option as to whether to rescind the transaction on grounds of 'unfairness' even if it appears that the terms were 'fair' by market standards and the corporation profited from it." Accord, State ex rel. Hayes Oyster Co. v. Keypoint Oyster Co., 64 Wash. 2d 388, 391 P.2d 979 (1964) ("nondisclosure by an interested director or officer is, in itself, unfair"). "In many contracts fairness is a range, rather than a point, and disclosure of a material fact might have induced the corporation to bargain the price down lower in the range. Furthermore, the terms of a self-interested contract might be 'fair' in the sense that they correspond to the market terms for the relevant subject-matter, but the corporation might have refused to make the contract if disclosure had been made of a material fact that would have shown that entering into the contract was not in the corporation's interest." Melvin A. Eisenberg, The Divergence of Standards of Conduct and Standards of Review in Corporate Law, 62 Fordham L. Rev. 437, 450 (1993).

If "appropriate disclosure has not been made" but the corporation still realizes a large profit on the transaction, albeit not as large as the interested director's profit, may the corporation rescind?

3. *Scope of required disclosure.* What is (should be) the standard for determining what information must be disclosed? Whether the interested director "withheld any crucial information that caused the company to make unnecessarily expensive commitments in reliance on his silence"? Should Herrig have been "obligated to disclose the extent of his profits resulting from" the challenged agreements? "Knowing that a director or senior executive has an interest in an exchange transaction doesn't necessarily put the corporation on guard. When persons are in a relation of trust and confidence, they do not go on guard simply because they are dealing in an exchange context. If *A* sells his used car to his sister, she assumes that he will be forthcoming about the car in a way a stranger would not, even though she knows he has an interest in the transaction. The same is true of dealings between a director or senior executive and his colleagues.

"Furthermore, . . . [t]he director or senior executive knows, or at least is in a position to know, every material fact the corporation knows about the transaction. In order to level the playing field, the corporation should know every material fact that the director or senior executive knows." Eisenberg, Note 2(a)(ii) supra, at 1000.

4. *Fairness.* What is (should be) the standard for determining what is "fair," "just," or "reasonable"? Does fairness to the corporation mean (a) the very best deal obtainable, (b) a transaction that a disinterested board, exercising reasonable business judgment, could (would) have entered into, (c) a contract not so flagrantly one-sided as to come close to appearing dishonest? Or is none of these formulations satisfactory? Of what relevance is the amount of profit realized by the interested director? How was fairness defined in *Cookies*?

"It has long been settled that a 'fair' price is any price in that broad range which an unrelated party might have been willing to pay or willing to accept, as the case may be, for the property, following a normal arm's-length business negotiation, in the light of the knowledge that would have been reasonably acquired in the course of such negotiations, any result within that range being 'fair.' " 2 RMBCA Ann. 8-401 (3d ed. 2000/01/02). Similarly, "the [ALI] Commentary makes clear that fairness is to be judged within a range of reasonableness, rather than a point of reasonableness, so that a transaction involving a payment by the corporation may be fair even though it is consummated at the high end of the range." Marshall L. Small, Conflicts of Interest and the ALI Corporate Governance Project — A Reporter's Perspective, 48 Bus. Law. 1377, 1383 (1993).

For the view "that the fairness test provides a very weak procedural check, and virtually no substantive check, on fiduciary self-dealing," see Lawrence E. Mitchell, Fairness and Trust in Corporate Law, 1993 Duke L.J. 425. See also Robert C. Clark, Corporate Law 188 (1986), contending that "it is doubtful" whether the claimed advantages for permitting interested director transactions "*generally* exceed the disvalue stemming from the fact that unfairness may occur and go undetected or uncorrected" and that "[m]any of the major opportunities for realizing self-dealing [benefits for society] could be exploited in a legal system that (1) basically adopted a flatly prohibitory rule against basic self-dealing but (2) provided for administrative approval, through class exemptions and specific variances, of transactions that meet appropriate standards of justification."

For the view that current judicial and statutory developments (including ALI Principles §5.02) have "evolved so that conflicted transactions undertaken with procedural correctness are now treated with a deference that approaches the deference accorded to unconflicted transactions a century ago," see Park McGinty, The Twilight of Fiduciary Duties: On the Need for Shareholder Self-Help in an Age of Formalistic Proceduralism, 46 Emory L.J. 163, 205 (1997): "[C]ourts today employ a number of gating presumptions that create initial judicial suspicion toward conflicted management action but that allow management to follow formal sterilization procedures or to satisfy certain increasingly easy threshold questions, and thereby shift the presumptions back onto plaintiffs. Where legal advice [of the board's lawyers] has been effective, courts are increasingly unwilling to overturn procedurally proper board action." Id.[67] "The social cost of thus relaxing traditional fiduciary proscriptions is said to be minimal because stockholders expect it in public corporations; and, with liquid markets for their stock, stockholders are said to be able to diversify the risk of 'improper' managerial self-aggrandizing conduct and thus to make such conduct less costly to them." Victor Brudney, Contract and Fiduciary Duty in Corporate Law, 38 B.C. L. Rev. 595, 616 (1997).

5. *Intermediate review.*

> Care review [i.e., the business judgment rule] rarely (if ever) will reveal that management or a reliant board was irrational or grossly uninformed. And loyalty review [i.e., the fairness standard] rarely applies because the management of the modern public corporation seldom engages in classic self-dealing. . . . Neither regime accounts for the possibility of . . . corporate decision making [that] is motivated by a combination of conflicting interests and legitimate corporate purposes [in such matters as] executive compensation . . . and corporate actions taken in the control context (such as takeover defenses). . . . [A]n intermediate approach is appropriate . . . [causing] a judge (and perhaps a jury) to ask how an independent board . . . [that is] free of management influence . . . would have acted and how much deference is appropriate. . . .

Alan R. Palmiter, Reshaping the Corporate Fiduciary Model: A Director's Duty of Independence, 67 Tex. L. Rev. 1351 (1989).

6. *Burden of proof.* (a) Several statutes, in addition to New York §713(b) and Cal. §310(a)(3), explicitly impose the burden of proof as to fairness on the party defending the validity of the transaction. See, e.g., S.C. Bus. Corp. Act §33-8-310 (1990). Some cases have also so interpreted statutes similar to Iowa's. See Lynch v. Patterson, 701 P.2d 1126 (Wyo. 1985) (clear and convincing evidence standard); Noe v. Roussel, 310 So. 2d 806 (La. 1975). In the absence of a statutory provision, most

---

67. "[C]orporate law runs the risk of damaging shareholders by too assiduously 'protecting' them. . . . Shareholder votes, for example, are costly. If they cost more than the amount of managerial . . . [unfairness] that they prevent, they harm, rather than protect shareholders; and shareholders will be better off if they rely on formalistically disinterested approval by independent directors." Id. at 239.

For the view that there has been both a legislative and a judicial trend toward the dilution of fiduciary standards in light of the advent of majority "outside" boards, see Ahmed Bulbulia & Arthur R. Pinto, Statutory Responses to Interested Director Transactions: A Watering Down of Fiduciary Standards, 53 Notre Dame Law. 201 (1977); Douglas M. Branson, Countertrends in Corporation Law: Model Business Corporation Act Revisions, British Company Law Reform, and Principles of Corporate Governance and Structure, 68 Minn. L. Rev. 53 (1983).

courts similarly assign the burden of establishing fairness to the interested parties. See, e.g., Pepper v. Litton, 308 U.S. 295 (1939). Contra, Durfee v. Durfee & Canning, Inc., 323 Mass. 187, 80 N.E.2d 522 (1948) (the "Massachusetts rule").

(b) Where should the burden of proof lie? Of what significance, if any, should it be that:

(i) There was no disinterested director majority or that the contracting interested director dominated the corporation's board? See Shlensky v. South Parkway Bldg. Corp., 19 Ill. 2d 268, 166 N.E.2d 793 (1960) ("under these circumstances the defendant directors had the burden under Illinois law to establish the fairness and reasonableness of the various transactions").

(ii) The contracting director dealt with a clearly independent board? Compare Puma v. Marriott, 283 A.2d 693 (Del. Ch. 1971) with Ong Hing v. Arizona Harness Raceway, Inc., 10 Ariz. App. 380, 459 P.2d 107 (1969).

(iii) The relief sought is rescission rather than damages?

(c) As a practical matter, how important is the factor of burden of proof on the issue of fairness? Is the issue one that is likely to produce many instances where the evidence appears to the trier of fact to be in equilibrium, thus "reinforcing the frequently observed fact that the outcome of fairness analysis is dependent on whom the burden of proving fairness or unfairness is placed"? Lawrence E. Mitchell, Fairness and Trust in Corporate Law, 1993 Duke L.J. 425, 465. Or is the issue one in which the judge or jury will usually, if not always, perceive the answer one way or the other? What were the dynamics in the *Cookies* case? See Heise v. Earnshaw Publications, Inc., 130 F. Supp. 38 (D. Mass. 1955) (alternative amounts of damages depending on who had burden of proof).[68]

7. *"Conflicting interest."* What should be the standard for defining a "conflict"? ALI Principles §1.23(a) provides: "A director or officer is 'interested' in a transaction or conduct if . . . (2) The director or officer has a business, financial, or familial relationship with a party to the transaction or conduct, and that relationship would reasonably be expected to affect the director's or officer's judgment with respect to the transaction or conduct in a manner adverse to the corporation. . . ."[69] RMBCA §§8.31(a)(2)(iii) and 8.60 are similar. Do these

---

68. See Charles M. Yablon, On the Allocation of Burdens of Proof in Corporate Law: An Essay on Fairness and Fuzzy Sets, 13 Cardozo L. Rev. 497 (1991): "Fairness . . . is treated by the courts not as a distinct property which either does or does not characterize the transaction, but rather as a 'fuzzy' property which may characterize a transaction to various degrees. . . . [R]ecent work that has been done on the logic of propositions involving such fuzzy properties (so called 'fuzzy set theory') can illuminate the role of the allocations of burdens of proof in this area of corporate law."

69. In the absence of such a statutory provision, many courts have treated corporate dealings with the spouses, children, siblings, grandchildren — and even the friends of directors — as being "interested director" transactions. See Johnson v. Radio Station WOW, Inc., 144 Neb. 406, 13 N.W.2d 556 (1944). See generally Marsh, footnote 56 supra, at 70-71. See also Sarner v. Fox Hill, Inc., 151 Conn. 437, 199 A.2d 6 (1964) (defendant-director's attorney, who was also a director, was "interested" for purpose of approving contract between corporation and defendant). But see Rocket Mining Corp. v. Gill, 25 Utah 2d 434, 483 P.2d 897 (1971) (directors who were brother, wife, and father of a party to contract with corporation were not "interested" for purposes of approving contract); Geitman v. Mullins, 643 S.E.2d 435 (N.C. Ct. App. 2007) (similar); McRedmond v. Estate of Marianelli, 46 S.W.3d 730 (Tenn. Ct. App. 2000) (director, who voted to approve defendant's contract with the corporation, was a close personal friend of defendant's father, and never voted against father during their 30 years together on the board, was held not "interested"); Cinerama, Inc. v. Technicolor, Inc., 663 A.2d 1156, 1174 (Del. 1995) (director voting for takeover of corporation, who hoped for an improved job with bidder, was not "interested"). Is a corporation's outside legal counsel, who is also a director, "interested" in a transaction between the corporation and its chief executive officer (who hires the corporation's counsel)? Compare Maldonado v. Flynn, 597 F.2d 789 (2d Cir. 1979), with Gries Sports Enterprises, Inc. v. Cleveland Browns Football

definitions bar a director "from voting on a transaction which significantly benefits a religious institution to whose creed he is deeply devoted and that guides his life"? Changes in the Model Business Corporation Act — Amendments Pertaining to Director's Conflicting Interest Transactions, 43 Bus. Law. 691, 694 (1988). Should they?

8. *Remedies.* (a) Most decisions permit either rescission or damages for improper interested director transactions. See, e.g., State ex rel. Hayes Oyster Co. v. Keypoint Oyster Co., 64 Wash. 2d 388, 391, P.2d 979 (1964); Shlensky v. South Parkway Bldg. Corp., 19 Ill. 2d 268, 166 N.E.2d 793 (1960). But see New York Trust Co. v. American Realty Co., 244 N.Y. 209, 155 N.E. 102 (1926), holding that — unlike the situation of directors who sell to the corporation property that they hold as trustees for it — if a director sells to the corporation at a profit property that the director "might have retained for himself or sold to a stranger," then the "corporation may not repudiate" the contract "and at the same time retain its benefits. If the contract with the director was valid the corporation must pay the agreed price; if invalid the corporation must rescind or repudiate the contract in its entirety." Cf. Bliss Petroleum Co. v. McNally, 254 Mich. 569, 237 N.W. 53 (1931) ("when directors sell their own property to a corporation, through their own action or influence as officers, or without disclosing their interest, and the corporation does not repudiate the purchase and rescind, the directors are liable not upon the theory of secret profits, but for fraud or excessive price, and the measure of damages is the difference between the price paid by the corporation and the fair value of the property").

(b) *Problem.* The boards of two corporations with a majority of interlocking directors (who own roughly the same proportionate interest in each of the corporations) cause these corporations to enter into a contract that is subsequently determined to be unfair to one of the corporations. Minority shareholders of the "injured" corporation seek to (1) rescind the contract and (2) obtain damages for the corporation against the interlocking directors for the corporation's losses on the contract. What result? See Kaufman v. Wolfson, 153 F. Supp. 253 (S.D.N.Y. 1957): "The courts of New York have applied to suits for rescission a standard different from that applied to suits to hold a director individually liable. Chelrob, Inc. v. Barrett, 293 N.Y. 442, 57 N.E.2d 825. . . . [T]o hold the interlocking directors personally liable . . . plaintiffs must show that the directors acted in bad faith . . . or at least reaped a personal profit. . . ."

9. *Authorizing provisions.* Of what significance, if any, is the existence in the corporation's articles or bylaws of a provision specifically permitting corporate contracts with interested directors or with other corporations having common directors? Permitting such directors to be counted for a quorum? To be present for and participate in the consideration of such contracts? To have their vote counted in approving such contracts?

Co., 26 Ohio St. 3d 15, 496 N.E.2d 959 (1986). Are a corporation's controlling directors, who own a majority of the corporation's shares, "interested" in a sale of all the corporation's assets for a price that leaves nothing for the shareholders after the corporation's debt to the controlling shareholders is paid? See Huang v. Lanxide Thermo-Composites, Inc., 144 Ohio App. 3d 289, 760 N.E.2d 14 (2001) (no).

For a recent discussion of the "independence" of each of the 12 directors in the *Walt Disney* case, see In re Walt Disney Co. Derivative Litigation, 731 A.2d 342, 356-361 (Del. Ch. 1998); see also Orman v. Cullman, 794 A.2d 5, 26-31 (Del. Ch. 2002).

The issue of defining "interested" is considered again in connection with shareholder derivative suits, pages 838-862 (especially pages 854-858) infra.

Should such provisions immunize the contracts from judicial scrutiny for fraud or unfairness? Should they affect the allocation of the burden of proof? Should their impact be different in a suit to avoid the contract rather than to impose personal liability on the interested directors? For the view that "the cases, when closely read, do not give management much comfort," see Robert C. Clark, Corporate Law 176 (1986).

10. *Problem.* Corporation, with three equal shareholders — X, Y, and Z — who are its directors, has a charter provision granting the corporation a first option to purchase the shares of any shareholder who wishes to sell. X proposes to sell his shares. At the board meeting, Y moves that the corporation exercise its option and votes yes; Z votes no; X abstains. The motion having failed, X sells his shares to Z. Y seeks to invalidate the sale. What result? Compare Lash v. Lash Furniture Co., 130 Vt. 517, 296 A.2d 207 (1972), with Boss v. Boss, 98 R.I. 146, 200 A.2d 231 (1964), and Kentucky Pkg. Store v. Checani, 331 Mass. 125, 117 N.E.2d 139 (1954).

11. *Shareholder ratification.* The significance and ramifications of this factor in respect to interested director transactions will be explored in note 2, page 158 infra.

b. Special Problems of Parent-Subsidiary

Case v. New York Central R.R.
15 N.Y.2d 150, 204 N.E.2d 643, 256 N.Y.S.2d 607 (1965)

BERGAN, J.: Plaintiffs are minority stockholders of Mahoning Coal Railroad Company, an Ohio corporation, which owns railroad lines in Ohio and leases lines in Pennsylvania. Mahoning does not operate the lines, but rents them to New York Central Railroad Company, which pays it a rental of about 40% of the gross revenues from traffic on those lines.

Central pays all expenses of operating and maintaining Mahoning's lines, including taxes on the property, except Federal income taxes. . . . Thus Mahoning has no operating expenses and is bound to make a profit as long as Central is its lessee, whether or not that operation is profitable to Central.

In August, 1955 Central and 34 of its subsidiaries entered into an agreement . . . [which] sought in a systematic and regular way to take advantage in future years of an amendment to the Internal Revenue Code of 1954 which authorized filing of consolidated returns where there was 80% of stock ownership of one corporation by another. . . .

For many years Central owned a majority of Mahoning's common stock. In 1955-1956 it owned about 74%. In 1956 Central referred to Mahoning's board of directors a proposal that Mahoning agree to include itself in the tax allocation agreement, if Central acquired the necessary 80% of stock ownership; this was assented to by the board . . . composed entirely of Central officers or employees, with one exception. The approval of the agreement was unanimous. The contract was consistent with Federal tax laws and the arrangement had the approval of Federal tax officers.

The result of Mahoning's joining in the allocation agreement for the tax years 1957 to 1960 was that by utilizing Central's losses in those years Mahoning was relieved of payment of $3,825,717.43 in income taxes which it would have paid on filing separate returns. Under the formula provided in the agreement Central received from Mahoning $3,556,992.15 and Mahoning retained the difference of $268,725.28 between this amount and the tax it would have paid on separate returns.

This action is by minority stockholders of Mahoning to rescind the agreement and to compel an accounting for the entire amount by which Central benefited from the arrangement during the three tax years at issue, on the ground that Central, in control of Mahoning's board of directors, acted in a fiduciary capacity and, in the words of respondent's submission to this court, "a fiduciary parent corporation cannot retain the benefits of an unfair agreement."

The decisive issue in the case, then, is whether this was an agreement unfair to Mahoning. The court at Special and Trial Term after a careful examination of the problem at a trial determined that it was not unfair; a majority at the Appellate Division ruled that it was unfair. . . .

As to past events the agreement is, by the decision of the Appellate Division, completely avoided and Mahoning has been placed in a position of having to pay no income tax on its income during the years in question; and Central, in the position of having to repay to Mahoning a substantial part (about 93%) of the income taxes Mahoning would have paid had it filed separate returns. This results in the rather unusual status of tax advantage where, instead of paying income taxes, Mahoning gets money in hand substantially equivalent of what it would have paid had it paid.

As to the future operation of the agreement, the Appellate Division left the question open as to what would be a fair allocation, but it observed that "a total appropriation of the savings by Central is not fair." . . .

A basic ground for judicial interference with corporate decisions on complaint of minority interests is an advantage obtained by the dominant group to the disadvantage of the corporation or its minority owners. This, of course, in the way of doing, can take many forms and follow greatly diversified directions, but the reflex of gain by the use of corporate power against loss to the corporation itself is a common denominator of the decided cases.

Thus, illustratively, in the recent decision in Ripley v. International Rys. of Cent. America, 8 N.Y.2d 430, 209 N.Y.S.2d 289, 171 N.E.2d 443 [1960], the fruit company which was in a position to exert practical control over a railway used its power to obtain freight rates at once to its advantage and the disadvantage of the railway and its minority stockholders; and this misuse of power was the basis on which judicial relief was granted.

In Kavanaugh v. Kavanaugh Knitting Co., 226 N.Y. 185, 123 N.E. 148, in which minority stockholders sought to enjoin the dissolution of a corporation, Collin, J., construed the complaint as pleading (p. 197, 123 N.E. p. 152) "the inference that the directors conceived and progressed the scheme of dissolving the corporation, irrespective of the welfare or advantage of the corporation and of any cause or reason related to its condition or future, through the desire and determination to take from the corporation and to secure to themselves the corporate business freed from interference or participation on the part of the plaintiff." This is a statement in quite classic terms of the kind of misuse of corporate power which will invite judicial interposition. . . .

An example of one of the kinds of unfair dealing which will justify relief is illustrated in Globe Woolen Co. v. Utica Gas & Elec. Co., 224 N.Y. 483, 121 N.E. 378, where a director of a utility having large interests in plaintiff manufacturing company participated in the approval by the utility of a special contract for electric power and a comparative cost guarantee to the manufacturing company grossly unfair to the utility, with a special knowledge of the danger to the utility in making such a contract with his company. . . .

The arrangement made by Central had greater advantage to itself than to Mahoning. But there was no loss or disadvantage to Mahoning. The basic complaint of Mahoning's minority is that they should have gotten a larger share of the benefits of Central's tax losses than the agreement gave them. Plaintiffs do not spell out what would be the right amount.

. . . It is true enough that in the years under scrutiny Central gained very large proportionate advantages in relation to Mahoning's advantage. But the agreement must be looked at with the knowledge which those who entered into it had when it was executed; and even the Appellate Division majority felt itself unable to say what would be a fair proportion of the distribution of Central's tax loss looking forward from the date of judgment.[70]

Had the agreement not been signed at all, Mahoning would have paid the Government in taxes $268,725.28 more than it paid Central on being relieved of all tax liability. It gained this much; Central gained much more; but the pattern of managerial disloyalty to a corporation by which the stronger side takes what the weaker side loses is entirely absent from this record.

Moreover, Central could not have taken advantage of the consolidated return provisions of the Federal statute unless it were suffering substantial losses and the stockholders of Mahoning had a vital interest in Central's continued ability to pay the rent and operate the lines owned and leased by Mahoning. If that ability failed the entire profit basis of Mahoning's business might have fallen in jeopardy.

Thus, without loss to itself, and, indeed, at the equivalent of a fairly substantial rebate of its tax obligation, Mahoning was able to help a lessee suffering losses whose solvency was vital to Mahoning's interests. The argument of plaintiffs that Central got too large a share is not on this record a demonstration of such unfairness as to warrant judicial intervention.

Besides this, the loss shown by Central was under some rather flexible circumstances an asset to Central. It could have been carried forward for seven years (Internal Revenue Code [1954], §172, subd. [b], par. [1], c1. [C]) and there is nothing about the financial history of Central to suggest that it was clear in 1957 when the

---

70. The dissenters in the Appellate Division further argued:

> Even if this were an arm's length transaction, it would be extremely difficult, if not impossible, to determine what would be fair. Here both corporations have an asset or, more accurately, are in a situation where by joint action they can benefit, but neither can benefit without the other. And further, neither could get the same or even remotely similar benefits by the participation of any third party. So there is no possibility that the terms to be agreed upon would be ascertained by what someone else would offer in a competitive situation. Traditionally, what is fair is what these two parties would agree on. But actually in such a situation the terms of agreement would depend almost entirely on the bargaining ability and the personal characteristics of the parties. Such factors defy the making of an estimate of the result that would be reached. Both parties to this suit recognize this. A great part of the energy expended by counsel was in an effort to show that the burden of proving fairness or unfairness was on the other side, and each having established (at least to his own satisfaction) that it was on his adversary, each relied on the fact that it was impossible for the other to make the proof. When the factor is added that this agreement could not be made by disinterested parties, it must be the rule that anything short of gross and palpable overreaching does not warrant court interference.

19 App. Div. 2d 383, 390, 243 N.Y.S.2d 620, 627 (1963). — Ed.

agreement was made by Mahoning that Central itself could not have believed it would have carried forward and utilized the loss in future years. . . .

The order of the Appellate Division should be reversed. . . . [71]

Problem. Corporation *P* has taxable income and Corporation *S* (80 percent of whose shares are owned by *P*) has tax losses. Minority shareholders of *S* challenge *P*'s retention of all tax savings from *P*'s filing a consolidated return. What result? Of what significance, if any, is the fact that *S* has always operated at a loss with virtually no prospect of profits in the foreseeable future? See Meyerson v. El Paso Natural Gas Co., 246 A.2d 789 (Del. Ch. 1967).

Sinclair Oil Corp. v. Levien
280 A.2d 717 (Del. 1971)

WOLCOTT, C.J.: This is an appeal by the defendant, Sinclair Oil Corporation (hereafter Sinclair), from an order of the Court of Chancery, 261 A.2d 911, in a derivative action requiring Sinclair to account for damages sustained by its subsidiary, Sinclair Venezuelan Oil Company (hereafter Sinven). . . .

Sinclair, operating primarily as a holding company, is in the business of exploring for oil and of producing and marketing crude oil and oil products. At all times relevant to this litigation, it owned about 97% of Sinven's stock. The plaintiff owns about 3000 of 120,000 publicly held shares of Sinven. . . .

Sinclair nominates all members of Sinven's board of directors . . . [who, almost without exception, have been] officers, directors, or employees of corporations in the Sinclair complex. By reason of Sinclair's domination, it is clear that Sinclair owed Sinven a fiduciary duty. Getty Oil Company v. Skelly Oil Co., 267 A.2d 883 (Del. Supr. 1970). . . . Sinclair concedes this.

The Chancellor held that because of Sinclair's fiduciary duty and its control over Sinven, its relationship with Sinven must meet the test of intrinsic fairness. The standard of intrinsic fairness involves both a high degree of fairness and a shift in the burden of proof. Under this standard the burden is on Sinclair to prove, subject to careful judicial scrutiny, that its transactions with Sinven were objectively fair. . . .

Sinclair argues that the transactions between it and Sinven should be tested, not by the test of intrinsic fairness with the accompanying shift of the burden of proof, but by the business judgment rule under which a court will not interfere with the judgment of a board of directors unless there is a showing of gross and palpable overreaching. Meyerson v. El Paso Natural Gas Co., 246 A.2d 789 (Del. Ch. 1967). . . .

We think, however, that Sinclair's argument in this respect is misconceived. When the situation involves a parent and a subsidiary, with the parent controlling the transaction and fixing the terms, the test of intrinsic fairness, with its resulting shifting of the burden of proof, is applied. Sterling v. Mayflower Hotel Corp.

---

71. Contra, Smith v. Tele-Communication, Inc., 734 Cal. App. 3d 338, 184 Cal. Rptr. 571 (1982); Alliegro v. Pan American Bank, 136 So. 2d 656 (Fla. Ct. App. 1962). For comment on the *Case* decision, see 74 Yale L.J. 338 (1964); 77 Harv. L. Rev. 1142 (1964); 49 Cornell L.Q. 520 (1964); 112 U. Pa. L. Rev, 1185 (1964). See generally John A.C. Hetherington, Defining the Scope of Controlling Shareholders' Fiduciary Responsibilities, 22 Wake Forest L. Rev. 9, 33-37 (1987); Bruce A. McGovern, Fiduciary Duties, Consolidated Returns, and Fairness, 81 Neb. L. Rev. 170, 244-259, 277-282 (2002).—ED.

[33 Del. Ch. 293, 93 A.2d 107].[72] . . . The basic situation for the application of the rule is the one in which the parent has received a benefit to the exclusion and at the expense of the subsidiary.[73]

Recently, this court dealt with the question of fairness in parent-subsidiary dealings in Getty Oil Co. v. Skelly Oil Co., supra. In that case, both parent and subsidiary were in the business of refining and marketing crude oil and crude oil products. The Oil Import Board ruled that the subsidiary, because it was controlled by the parent, was no longer entitled to a separate allocation of imported crude oil. The subsidiary then contended that it had a right to share the quota of crude oil allotted to the parent. We ruled that the business judgment standard should be applied to determine this contention. Although the subsidiary suffered a loss through the administration of the oil import quotas, the parent gained nothing. The parent's quota was derived solely from its own past use. The past use of the subsidiary did not cause an increase in the parent's quota. Nor did the parent usurp a quota of the subsidiary. Since the parent received nothing from the subsidiary to the exclusion of the minority stockholders of the subsidiary, there was no self-dealing. Therefore, the business judgment standard was properly applied.

A parent does indeed owe a fiduciary duty to its subsidiary when there are parent-subsidiary dealings. However, this alone will not evoke the intrinsic fairness standard. This standard will be applied only when the fiduciary duty is accompanied by self-dealing—the situation when a parent is on both sides of a transaction with its subsidiary. Self-dealing occurs when the parent, by virtue of its domination of the subsidiary, causes the subsidiary to act in such a way that the parent receives something from the subsidiary to the exclusion of, and detriment to, the minority stockholders of the subsidiary.

We turn now to the facts. The plaintiff argues that, from 1960 through 1966, Sinclair caused Sinven to pay out such excessive dividends that the industrial development of Sinven was effectively prevented, and it became in reality a corporation in dissolution.

From 1960 through 1966, Sinven paid out $108,000,000 in dividends ($38,000,000 in excess of Sinven's earnings during the same period). The Chancellor held that Sinclair caused these dividends to be paid during a period when it had a need for large amounts of cash. Although the dividends paid exceeded earnings, the plaintiff concedes that the payments were made in compliance with 8 Del. C. §170, authorizing payment of dividends out of surplus or net profits. However, the plaintiff attacks these dividends on the ground that they resulted from an improper motive—Sinclair's need for cash. The Chancellor, applying the intrinsic fairness standard, held that Sinclair did not sustain its burden of proving that these dividends were intrinsically fair to the minority stockholders of Sinven.[74] . . .

---

72. See also T. Rowe Price Recovery Fund, L.P. v. Rubin, 770 A.2d 536 (Del. Ch. 2000) ("the Delaware Supreme Court held in Kahn v. Lynch Communication Systems, Inc., [669 A.2d 79 (1995)] that the entire fairness standard applied to the review of a transaction (in that case a merger) negotiated between a controlling stockholder and the controlled corporation, notwithstanding approval of the transaction by a special committee of disinterested directors of the controlled corporation"). Accord, In re LNR Property Corp. Shareholders Litigation, 896 A.2d 169, 176 (Del. Ch. 2005).—ED.

73. For application of the intrinsic fairness rule to a merger of the subsidiary into the parent, see page 1102 infra.—ED.

74. The Chancellor said:

[T]he overwhelming inferences from the record are, and I so find as facts, that (a) the dividend payments coincided with Sinclair's substantial needs for large amounts of cash . . . and

Sinclair contends that it is improper to apply the intrinsic fairness standard to dividend payments even when the board which voted for the dividends is completely dominated. In support of this contention, Sinclair relies heavily on American District Telegraph Co. [ADT] v. Grinnell Corp., (N.Y. Sup. Ct. 1969) aff'd, 33 A.D.2d 769, 306 N.Y.S.2d 209 (1969). Plaintiffs were minority stockholders of ADT, a subsidiary of Grinnell. The plaintiffs alleged that Grinnell, realizing that it would soon have to sell its ADT stock because of a pending antitrust action, caused ADT to pay excessive dividends. Because the dividend payments conformed with applicable statutory law, and the plaintiffs could not prove an abuse of discretion, the court ruled that the complaint did not state a cause of action. Other decisions seem to support Sinclair's contention. In Metropolitan Casualty Ins. Co. v. First State Bank of Temple, 54 S.W.2d 358 (Tex. Civ. App. 1932), rev'd on other grounds, 79 S.W.2d 835 (Sup. Ct. 1935), the court held that a majority of interested directors does not void a declaration of dividends because all directors, by necessity, are interested in and benefited by a dividend declaration. . . .

We do not accept the argument that the intrinsic fairness test can never be applied to a dividend declaration by a dominated board, although a dividend declaration by a dominated board will not inevitably demand the application of the intrinsic fairness standard. . . . If such a dividend is in essence self-dealing by the parent, then the intrinsic fairness standard is the proper standard. For example, suppose a parent dominates a subsidiary and its board of directors. The subsidiary has outstanding two classes of stock, X and Y. Class X is owned by the parent and Class Y is owned by minority stockholders of the subsidiary. If the subsidiary, at the direction of the parent, declares a dividend on its Class X stock only, this might well be self-dealing by the parent. It would be receiving something from the subsidiary to the exclusion of and detrimental to its minority stockholders. This self-dealing, coupled with the parent's fiduciary duty, would make intrinsic fairness the proper standard by which to evaluate the dividend payments.

Consequently it must be determined whether the dividend payments by Sinven were, in essence, self-dealing by Sinclair. The dividends resulted in great sums of money being transferred from Sinven to Sinclair. However, a proportionate share of this money was received by the minority shareholders of Sinven. Sinclair received nothing from Sinven to the exclusion of its minority stockholders. As such, these dividends were not self-dealing. We hold therefore that the Chancellor erred in applying the intrinsic fairness test as to these dividend payments. The business judgment standard should have been applied.

We conclude that the facts demonstrate that the dividend payments complied with the business judgment standard. . . . The motives for causing the declaration of dividends are immaterial unless the plaintiff can show that the dividend payments resulted from improper motives and amounted to waste. The plaintiff

---

(b) Sinclair's need for cash was the dominant factor in the decision to pay the dividends. . . . There is indeed little to show that [Sinven's] corporate needs were weighed in the process. Dividends were first paid only when Sinclair could receive them tax-free, and thereafter the amounts were irregular because they were almost a function of Sinclair's need for cash For example: in 1963 [Sinven] paid $28,000,000 against earnings of $10,590,000, and in that year Sinclair borrowed $150,000,000. And the irregular payment schedule was substantially inconsistent with Sinclair's own announced and conservative approach (up to 50% of earnings) to dividends.

261 A.2d 920. — ED.

contends only that the dividend payments drained Sinven of cash to such an extent that it was prevented from expanding.

The plaintiff proved no business opportunities which came to Sinven independently and which Sinclair either took to itself or denied to Sinven. As a matter of fact, with two minor exceptions which resulted in losses, all of Sinven's operations have been conducted in Venezuela, and Sinclair had a policy of exploiting its oil properties located in different countries by subsidiaries located in the particular countries.

From 1960 to 1966 Sinclair purchased or developed oil fields in Alaska, Canada, Paraguay, and other places around the world. The plaintiff contends that these were all opportunities which could have been taken by Sinven. The Chancellor concluded that Sinclair had not proved that its denial of expansion opportunities to Sinven was intrinsically fair. He based this conclusion on the following findings of fact. Sinclair made no real effort to expand Sinven. The excessive dividends paid by Sinven resulted in so great a cash drain as to effectively deny to Sinven any ability to expand. During this same period Sinclair actively pursued a company-wide policy of developing through its subsidiaries new sources of revenue, but Sinven was not permitted to participate and was confined in its activities to Venezuela.

However, the plaintiff could point to no opportunities which came to Sinven. Therefore, Sinclair usurped no business opportunity belonging to Sinven. Since Sinclair received nothing from Sinven to the exclusion of and detriment to Sinven's minority stockholders, there was no self-dealing. Therefore, business judgment is the proper standard by which to evaluate Sinclair's expansion policies. . . .

Even if Sinclair was wrong in developing these opportunities as it did, the question arises, with which subsidiaries should these opportunities have been shared? No evidence indicates a unique need or ability of Sinven to develop these opportunities. The decision of which subsidiaries would be used to implement Sinclair's expansion policy was one of business judgment with which a court will not interfere absent a showing of gross and palpable overreaching. . . . No such showing has been made here.

Next, Sinclair argues that the Chancellor committed error when he held it liable to Sinven for breach of contract.

In 1961 Sinclair created Sinclair International Oil Company (hereafter International), a wholly-owned subsidiary used for the purpose of coordinating all of Sinclair's foreign operations. All crude purchases by Sinclair were made thereafter through International.

On September 28, 1961, Sinclair caused Sinven to contract with International whereby Sinven agreed to sell all of its crude oil and refined products to International at specified prices. The contract provided for minimum and maximum quantities and prices. The plaintiff contends that Sinclair caused this contract to be breached in two respects. Although the contract called for payment on receipt, International's payments lagged as much as 30 days after receipt. Also, the contract required International to purchase at least a fixed minimum amount of crude and refined products from Sinven. International did not comply with this requirement.

Clearly, Sinclair's act of contracting with its dominated subsidiary was self-dealing. Under the contract Sinclair received the products produced by Sinven, and of course the minority shareholders of Sinven were not able to share in the receipt of these products. If the contract was breached, then Sinclair received these products to the detriment of Sinven's minority shareholders. We agree with the Chancellor's finding that the contract was breached by Sinclair, both as to the time of payments and the amounts purchased.

Although a parent need not bind itself by a contract with its dominated subsidiary, Sinclair chose to operate in this manner. As Sinclair has received the benefits of this contract, so must it comply with the contractual duties.

Under the intrinsic fairness standard, Sinclair must prove that its causing Sinven not to enforce the contract was intrinsically fair to the minority shareholders of Sinven. Sinclair has failed to meet this burden. Late payments were clearly breaches for which Sinven should have sought and received adequate damages. As to the quantities purchased, Sinclair argues that it purchased all the products produced by Sinven. This, however, does not satisfy the standard of intrinsic fairness. Sinclair has failed to prove that Sinven could not possibly have produced or someway have obtained the contract minimums. As such, Sinclair must account on this claim. . . .

[Reversed in part and affirmed in part.][75]

---

1. *Problem.* Corporation *P*'s only profitable asset is its interest in *S* (85 percent of whose voting shares, but a much smaller percentage of its total shares, are owned by *P*). Minority shareholders of *S* challenge *P*'s refusal to consider a sale of *S* (which would result in a substantial gain to all of *S*'s shareholders), thus inducing the potential buyer to purchase *P* instead (which produces a gain to *P*'s shareholders, but no significant benefit for *S*'s shareholders). What result? See In re Digex Inc. Shareholders Litigation, 789 A.2d 1176, further development, 2002 WL 749 184 (Del. Ch. 2000).

2. *Statutes.* Noting that "in contrast to widely adopted 'safe harbor' statutes that apply to transactions between directors and their corporations, very little legislation has been enacted [including RMBCA Subchapter F] to govern transactions between a controlling shareholder and the corporation," 1 ALI, Principles of Corporate Governance 326 (1994), ALI Principles §5.10 requires that such transactions be "fair to the corporation when entered into," unless "authorized in advance or ratified by disinterested shareholders" as in ALI Principles §5.02(a)(2)(D). Disclosure is not required under ALI Principles §5.10 because "the controlling shareholder will usually be dealing with its own officers and employees, and the requirement of such disclosure seems an unnecessary formality, particularly because the controlling shareholder will have the burden of proving fairness if the transaction is challenged unless the transaction is approved by disinterested directors or shareholders in the manner specified in §5.10." Id. at 327. Further, since parent corporations are often "engaged in regular and ongoing business relations with a partly owned subsidiary that may involve hundreds or even

---

75. For later decisions finding that plaintiff had established "self-dealing on the part of a dominant fiduciary . . . in order for the intrinsic fairness rule to be successfully invoked," see Trans World Airlines, Inc. v. Summa Corp., 374 A.2d 5 (Del. Ch. 1977) (parent delayed subsidiary's acquisition of jet aircraft in order to obtain tax benefits for itself); Schreiber v. Bryan, 396 A.2d 512 (Del. Ch. 1978) (parent took for itself corporate opportunity in which subsidiary had an interest). Compare In the Matter of Reading Co., 711 F.2d 509 (3d Cir. 1983) (intrinsic fairness rule inapplicable). — Ed.

thousands of individual transactions each year," id. at 329, ALI Principles §5.10(c) provides that "in the case of a transaction between a controlling shareholder and the corporation that was in the ordinary course of the corporation's business, a party who challenges the transaction has the burden of coming forward with evidence that the transaction was unfair."

c. Compensation of Managers

A classic illustration of a conflict of interest is frequently presented when a corporation undertakes to compensate its directors or officers for their services. This is particularly true in close corporations because the shareholders invariably dominate the board of directors and usually constitute the corporation's principal managers, often depending on payment from the corporation as their major source of income. Although independent directors (whose definition excludes persons who are full-time executives of the company) constitute a majority of the board (and all of the compensation committee) of most public corporations (see pages 8-13 supra), there is substantial debate over the role of "managerial power" in respect to executive compensation.[76] "The financial and nonfinancial benefits of holding a board seat give directors a strong interest in keeping their positions"; "candidates placed on the company's slate by the board have been virtually assured of being reelected"; "CEOs have had considerable and sometimes decisive influence over the nomination process"; thus, "taking care not to upset the compensation apple cart may well remain the best bet" for being on the board.[77] Therefore, corporate actions involving compensation of managers are often concerned with the application of legal principles just explored in the preceding section.[78]

In addition to further consideration of problems of conflict of interest, this section will examine the substantive corporation law doctrines that govern

76. This is also known as "management capture." See Charles M. Elson, Executive Compensation — A Board-Based Solution, 34 B.C. L. Rev. 937 (1993).

77. Lucian Bebchuck & Jesse Fried, Pay Without Performance 25-26 (2004). For disagreement, see Iman Anabtawi, Explaining Pay Without Performance: The Tournament Alternative, 54 Emory L.J. 1557, 1577-1584 (2005); Mark J. Loewenstein, The Conundrum of Executive Compensation, 35 Wake Forest L. Rev. 1, 14-18 (2000). Bebchuck and Fried contend further that, unlike the "optimal" situation of "arms length contracting," managerial power, bolstered by outside compensation consultants who are also usually beholden to management, results in "higher compensation through arrangements that have substantially decoupled pay from performance." Although "an arrangement that is perceived as 'outrageous' might reduce shareholders' willingness to support incumbents in proxy contests or takeover bids," "numerous compensation practices, such as postretirement perks and consulting arrangements, deferred compensation, pension plans, and executive loans" have been used to "camouflage" the excesses. Id. at 4-6. For general concurrence with the Bebchuck and Fried reasoning, see William W. Bratton, The Academic Tournament over Executive Compensation, 93 Cal. L. Rev 1557 (2005); Michael B. Dorff, Does One Hand Wash the Other? Testing the Managerial Power and Optimal Contracting Theories of Executive Compensation 30 J. Corp. L. 255 (2005); Stephen M. Bainbridge, Executive Compensation: Who Decides? 83 Texas L. Rev. 1615 (2005). For "some counter-arguments," see John E. Core, Wayne R. Guay & Randall S. Thomas, Is U.S. CEO Compensation Inefficient Pay Without Performance?, 103 Mich. L. Rev. 1042 (2005).

78. These transactions, however, also implicate other important areas of law, probably the most consequential and complex being federal taxation. The intricacies of the Internal Revenue Code, and the federal Employment Retirement Income Security Act (ERISA), under which both public and close corporations seek to devise compensation arrangements that minimize the tax liability of both the corporation and the recipient managers, are beyond the scope of this course. But their impact on the corporation's decisions as to compensation of executives must not be overlooked.

compensation of directors and officers. To focus attention on this latter set of issues, the first subsection — "Salaries, Bonuses, Pensions" — will deal mainly with instances in which the corporation's action was taken by a seemingly disinterested board of directors. The subsection that follows, "Stock Options," involves not only application of these substantive law principles to this particular form of compensation, but also issues raised by interested director transactions — principally the matter of shareholder ratification.

i. Salaries, Bonuses, Pensions

The traditional rule was that directors served without compensation, their rewards coming in the enhanced value of their shares resulting from the corporation's success; in performing their usual and ordinary duties, directors had no right to compensation unless authorized by statute, the corporation's charter or bylaws, a shareholder vote, or (some courts held) an express agreement prior to affording the services. This traditional rule applied even when directors undertook managerial tasks as corporate officers. At least in some jurisdictions, however, officers, who were not directors, and director-officers who performed tasks clearly outside their usual and ordinary duties could recover on a theory of implied contract (when it was well understood by the proper corporate officials as well as the claimant that the services were to be paid for) or on a theory of quantum meruit (when the corporation accepted the benefits of the services).[79] The usual rules making interested director transactions voidable[80] applied as well to the matter of compensation; beyond that, the board was held in some cases to be without power to set the compensation of directors in the absence of some form of shareholder authorization.[81]

As the number of directors with no significant share ownership in the corporation grew, corporations increasingly provided directors with meaningful compensation, well beyond "a nominal honorarium, say, $50 or $100, per meeting, the modern counterpart of the traditional $20 gold piece."[82] This has been especially true in large corporations, the 2005 Conference Board Survey of Directors' Compensation showing that the median compensation for outside directors (not including stock components) was $ 59,150 in manufacturing, $57,000 in services, and $48,000 in financial companies.[83] And statutes in most states, like RMBCA §8.11, presently stipulate that "unless the articles of incorporation or bylaws provide otherwise, the board of directors may fix the compensation of directors."

The cases that follow consider the limits of the corporation's power to provide salaries, bonuses, and pensions to directors, officers, and related individuals.

---

79. See Cox & Hazen, page 110 supra, at §11.1.

80. See page 111 supra; Lofland v. Cahall, 13 Del. Ch. 384, 118 A. 1 (1922); Binz v. St. Louis Hide & Tallow Co., 378 S.W.2d 228 (Mo. Ct. App. 1964) (when each director abstains from voting on his own compensation but votes for that of other directors, there is conflict of interest, and burden of showing reasonableness is on directors).

81. See Henry W. Ballantine, Corporations §74 (rev. ed. 1946).

82. Harry G. Henn & John R. Alexander, Corporations 665 (3d ed. 1983).

83. In addition, many corporations afford further benefits to directors, including retirement plans, medical coverage, golden parachutes, and especially stock options. See footnote 106, page 149 infra. When stock components are included, the amounts are $91,250, $81,875, and $64,500, respectively.

Adams v. Smith
275 Ala. 142, 153 So. 2d 221 (1963)

COLEMAN, J.: [In 1957, the board of directors of Alabama Dry Dock & Shipbuilding Co. resolved that $55,000 be paid in 24 monthly installments to the widow of the corporation's just-deceased president and $9,750 to the widow of its deceased comptroller. A minority shareholder — who "does not charge the directors with intentional wrongdoing or that they have received any personal benefit from the payments to the widows," but who avers that "the corporation had no contract" with either the deceased officers or with the widows "or with any other person, for the payment of any sums" to them — sued on behalf of the corporation "for personal judgment against the directors and the widows for the full amount paid to the widows; [and] for injunction against further payments."]

Complainant's right to relief is founded on the proposition that the payment of the corporation's money to the widows, without consideration, is illegal and not within the power of a mere majority of the stockholders over the objection of a single stockholder. As we hereinafter undertake to show, we are of opinion that complainant's contention is correct, unless there is in the charter of the corporation a provision which confers on the majority the power to give away the corporation's money without consideration. . . . Appellants have devoted many pages of brief and citation of more than fifty cases to establish the propositions that the alleged payments to the widows are authorized under the so-called "Business Judgment Rule," and that the alleged payments may be made lawfully by the directors under their power to manage the internal affairs of the corporation without interference by the courts, or, that if the directors could not do so, then the majority of the stockholders could ratify the alleged acts of the directors, who would not be liable after such ratification. We will respond to these contentions.

The directors say in brief that they "do not question the existence or validity of this rule" that "neither the Board of Directors nor the majority stockholders can give away corporate property." . . .

The appellants argue, however, that directors or majority stockholders have power to make bonus or retirement payments to officers and employees of the corporation, and their widows or dependents, because such payments can be and are for the benefit and furtherance of the business of the corporation. We are not disposed to contest the proposition that, in a proper case and under proper procedure, corporations can make bonus and pension payments. That, however, is not the case averred in the bill. The averment is that the payment to the widow was without valid consideration and that the corporation had no contract for the payment of the alleged sums.

. . . [I]n Moore v. Keystone Macaroni Mfg. Co., 370 Pa. 172, 87 A.2d 295, 29 A.L.R.2d 1256, a minority stockholder sought to enjoin payments by corporation to the widow of a former officer of the corporation and for restitution of payments theretofore made. . . .

The Supreme Court of Pennsylvania, in affirming the decree appealed from, said:

> To further support their argument, appellants point to the modern trend in favor of pensions and of permitting corporations to make charitable gifts, and to take other actions which the board of directors are convinced will be for the best interests of the corporation even though no immediate or direct quid pro quo results therefrom. It

will be noted, of course, that the payments to Mrs. Guerrisi were not and did not purport to be a pension, nor did they constitute a gift or contribution to a charity or to a community chest as specifically authorized by the amendment to the Pennsylvania Business Corporation Law. . . .

Moreover, we cannot overlook the fact that to approve the action of this board of directors would result in opening wide the door to a dissipation of the assets of a corporation and to fraud; and it is still the law of Pennsylvania that it is ultra vires and illegal for a corporation (unless authorized by statute) to give away, dissipate, waste or divert the corporate assets even though the objective be worthy. This general principle is widely recognized. In Fletcher Cyclopedia of Corporations, Permanent Edition, Vol. 6-a, paragraph 2939, pages 667, 668, the law is thus stated: ". . . It seems to be the rule that a private corporation has no power voluntarily to pay to a former officer or employee a sum of money for past services, which it is under no legal duty to pay, and which would not constitute a legal consideration for a promise to pay." In Rogers v. Hill, 289 U.S. 582, 591, the Court, after upholding the legality of reasonable bonus payments, said: "'If a bonus payment has no relation to the value of services for which it is given, it is in reality a gift in part, and the majority stockholders have no power to give away corporate property against the protest of the minority.'" Compare also Hornsby v. Lohmeyer, 364, Pa. 271, 275, 72 A.2d 294, 298, where this Court after sustaining the payment of reasonable bonuses and pointing out that a court is not ordinarily warranted in substituting its own judgment as to the proper compensation of officers for the judgment of the directors, said: ". . . It is also true that directors may not vote to themselves or to the officers of the corporation compensation which is excessive, unreasonable and out of proportion to the value of the services rendered, and, if any such payments are made, the court, upon protest of a minority shareholder, may examine into their propriety and reduce them if found to be exorbitant." . . .

We do not agree with appellant that Chambers v. Beaver-Advance Corporation, 392 Pa. 481, 140 A.2d 808, modified or overruled *Moore*. In *Chambers*, the court approved the payment of fair and *reasonable* bonuses for the current or prior calendar or fiscal year if such bonuses were approved by the majority stockholders. That was not the *Moore* case and is not the instant case.

In the case at bar, we hold that the bill has equity, and that the court did not err in overruling the grounds of demurrer which challenge the equity of the bill. . . .

In Osborne v. Locke Steel Chain Co., 153 Conn. 527, 218 A.2d 526 (1966), six of the company's directors voted, at their own initiative, to give the seventh (Osborne) — who was retiring after 49 years with the company, including as president for 17 years and as chairman for 3 years — $15,000 a year for the remainder of his life. He agreed to be available for consultation and not to compete in any of the areas where the company does business. The court reversed dismissal of plaintiff's suit to recover on the contract:

> The defendant [corporation] has claimed that the agreement was motivated by a desire to compensate the plaintiff during his retirement years for his past services to the company. Judging from certain language in the preamble to the agreement referring to the company's custom of paying pensions to its retired personnel, this was undoubtedly true in part. . . . It is well established, however, that if two considerations are given for a promise, only one of which is legally sufficient, the promise is nonetheless enforceable. . . .

While it was found by the trial court that some of the directors were longtime friends of the plaintiff, that he had hired one director in 1937 who later became president of the company when the plaintiff retired, and that the directors had had a long intimate business association with the plaintiff, nowhere in the finding did the trial court find or conclude that the transaction was the result of bad faith, dishonesty or unfairness. From a review of the subordinate facts, it is clear that the plaintiff's experience was a potentially valuable asset to the defendant, or to any other company engaged in a similar business, and that the annual payments to be made to the plaintiff were in a reasonable amount. The burden of showing that the agreement was fair was thus met by the plaintiff.

---

1. *Compensation for past services and the requirement of consideration.* The traditional rule — applied to pensions in the *Adams* case and found satisfied in the *Osborne* case — was that "as to bonuses, which are merely gratuitous payments, and as to similar retroactive increases of salary, it is Hornbook law that, except where there has been an express or implied understanding that they may be granted if conditions warrant, there is not consideration for them . . . ." Hurt v. Cotton States Fertilizer Co., 159 F.2d 52 (5th Cir. 1947).[84]

Should the validity of executive compensation granted by a disinterested board of directors depend on the corporation's receiving *sufficient* consideration? *Adequate* consideration? See Note, Corporate Bonus and Pension Plans: A "Legitimate Business Purpose" Test, 48 Minn. L. Rev. 947 (1964). What result if a disinterested board, knowing that the corporation is to be liquidated shortly, grants a retiring executive a lifetime pension? See Fogelson v. American Woolen Co., 170 F.2d 660 (2d Cir. 1948) (facts held to raise justifiable issue of "spoliation or waste"). (The problem of consideration is discussed further in the "Stock Option" cases in the subsection that follows.)

2. *Excessive compensation as gratuity, gift, or waste.* (a) In Rogers v. Hill, 289 U.S. 582 (1933) — referred to in the *Adams* case — the shareholders of American Tobacco Co., in 1912, adopted a bylaw providing for an annual bonus to the president of 2.5 percent of "net profits" and of 1.5 percent to each of the five vice presidents. As the company thrived, the amounts paid increased markedly — the president receiving a bonus of $840,000 in 1930 in addition to his $168,000 salary and "special cash credits" of $270,000, plus stock options at $87 per share below market value.[85] The Court — stating the famous "give away" precept quoted in the *Adams* case — held that although "when adopted the by-law was valid," the minority shareholder's allegations "that the measure of compensation fixed by it is not now equitable or fair . . . are sufficient to require that the district

---

84. Accord, Dowdle v. Texas American Oil Corp., 503 S.W.2d 647 (Tex. Civ. App. 1973). Contra, Zupnick v. Goizueta, 698 A.2d 384 (Del. Ch. 1997) (bonus for Coca-Cola's CEO upheld because "reasonable, disinterested directors could have concluded . . . that Goizueta's past services were . . . ["unusual in character and extraordinary"] and that the resulting benefit to the corporation was . . . ["great" and "remarkable"]). See also Cox & Hazen, page 110 supra, at 225: "In recent years, with respect to payments based on past services, there has been a significant retreat from formalistic attitudes and movement toward a rule of reasonableness. In some states statutes expressly grant authority to provide bonuses and retroactive pension plans."

85. These were also the subject of litigation in Rogers v. Guaranty Trust Co., 288 U.S. 123 (1933). See generally Note, Judicial Action on the American Tobacco Bonus Plan, 7 U. Cin. L. Rev. 412 (1933); Comment, Profit-Sharing for Executives and Employees — The American Tobacco Company, A Case in Point, 42 Yale L.J. 419 (1933).

court, upon a consideration of all the relevant facts brought forward by the parties, determine whether and to what extent payments to the individual defendants under the bylaw constitute misuse and waste of the money of the corporation."[86]

(b) *Problem.* Directors of Mutual Fund contract with Investment Adviser to manage Fund for ten years, the compensation to be 0.5 percent of Fund's net assets, which were $130 million in the first year. Fund grows progressively larger, so that its assets are $590 million in the eighth year. Plaintiff minority shareholder, seeking cancellation on the ground that the amount paid bears no reasonable relation to the value of the services rendered, alleges that the larger a fund grows, the cheaper it is to manage per dollar of assets and that the compensation arrangement has caused Adviser to increase the size of Fund. Adviser replies that two-thirds of all mutual fund managers have similar compensation arrangements. What result? See Saxe v. Brady, 40 Del. Ch. 474, 184 A.2d 602 (Ch. 1962): "A court is confronted with inherent difficulties in determining whether payments for services are 'reasonable' or 'excessive.' The value of services is obviously a matter of judgment on the part of the person who must pay for them. Thus, courts are often shielded by presumptions which wisely cause them to defer to decisions of directors or stockholders."

(c) In the *Walt Disney* case, page 88 supra, the court addressed the issue of "waste" as follows:

> To recover on a claim of corporate waste, the plaintiffs must shoulder the burden of proving that the exchange was so "one sided that no business person of ordinary, sound judgment could conclude that the corporation has received adequate consideration."[135] A claim of waste will arise only in the rare, "unconscionable case where directors irrationally squander or give away corporate assets."[136]
>
> ... [A]t the time the NFT amounts were paid, Disney was contractually obligated to pay them. The payment of a contractually obligated amount cannot constitute waste, unless the contractual obligation is itself wasteful. Accordingly, the proper focus of a waste analysis must be whether the amounts required to be paid in the event of an NFT were wasteful *ex ante*.
>
> Appellants claim that the NFT provisions of the OEA were wasteful because they incentivized Ovitz to perform poorly in order to obtain payment of the NFT provisions. ... In essence, appellants claim that the NFT provisions of the OEA created an irrational incentive for Ovitz to get himself fired.[139]

That claim does not come close to satisfying the high hurdle required to establish waste. The approval of the NFT provisions in the OEA had a rational business purpose: to induce Ovitz to leave CAA, at what would otherwise be a considerable cost to him, in order to join Disney. The Chancellor found that the evidence does not support any notion that the OEA irrationally incentivized Ovitz to get himself fired.

---

86. The case was subsequently settled. For further developments, see Rogers v. Hill, 34 F. Supp. 358 (S.D.N.Y. 1940); Heller v. Boylan, 29 N.Y.S.2d 653 (S. Ct. 1941).

N.C. Bus. Corp. Act §16(3) (1973) provided: "No bylaw authorizing compensation of officers measured by the amount of a corporation's income or volume of business shall be valid after five years from its adoption unless renewed by the vote of the holders of a majority of the outstanding shares regardless of limitation on voting rights." This section was deleted when the North Carolina statute was revised in 1990.

135. Brehm [v. Eisner], 746 A.2d at 263.

136. [Brehm v. Eisner, 746 A.2d at 263.]

139. The appellants also claim, because the Disney defendants had a rational basis to fire Ovitz for cause, the NFT payment to Ovitz constituted an unnecessary gift of corporate assets to Eisner's friend. Because we affirm the Court of Chancery's legal determination that no cause existed to terminate Ovitz, that claim lacks merit on its face.

Ovitz had no control over whether or not he would be fired, either with or without cause. To suggest that at the time he entered into the OEA Ovitz would engineer an early departure at the cost of his extraordinary reputation in the entertainment industry and his historical friendship with Eisner, is not only fanciful but also without proof in the record. Indeed, the Chancellor found that it was "patently unreasonable to assume that Ovitz intended to perform just poorly enough to be fired quickly, but not so poorly that he could be terminated for cause."

Mlinarcik v. E.E. Wehrung Parking, Inc.
86 Ohio App. 3d 134, 620 N.E.2d 181 (1993)

HARPER, J.: Appellant, Shirley Mlinarcik, appeals from the judgment of the Cuyahoga County Court of Common Pleas in favor of appellees, E.E. Wehrung Parking, Inc., Robert Wehrung and Marilyn Wehrung. . . .

Edgar Wehrung created E.E. Wehrung Parking, Inc. ("E.E.") in 1948. Shirley and Robert are the only children of Edgar. E.E. is the holder of a lease on a parking garage located on East 13th Street in Cleveland, Ohio. E.E.'s sole operation is the subleasing of the garage to another company for annual sum of $41,600. E.E. has a total of one hundred fifty shares of stock outstanding. One hundred and eleven of the shares are owned by Robert, nine and one-half are owned by Marilyn, twenty-eight and one-half are owned by Shirley, while the remaining one share is owned by Esther Pell. Marilyn is Robert's wife.

After the death of Edgar, Robert took over the management of the corporation while Marilyn and Shirley were placed on the board of directors and paid directors' fees. Robert paid salaries to his wife and himself.

Marilyn received $3,900 from 1967 until 1982 when her salary increased to $7,200 a year. Marilyn is employed as a secretary by the corporation. She works for a total of about thirty to thirty-five hours a year.

Robert, as the president of the corporation, is paid $10,800 a year in salaries. He has received this amount from 1982 through 1990. Robert's job consists of a once-a-month visit to the garage. He prepares the monthly payroll checks, which consists of one check for himself and one for his wife; prepares and deposits a payroll tax check each month; writes other miscellaneous checks; and goes to the post office once each year to mail shareholders reports.

Harvey Rosen, who testified as an expert witness for Shirley, stated that the value of services performed by Robert and Marilyn was between $567 and $2,000 per year. The first figure is based on the services they performed and the amount of time necessary to perform those services. The second figure is based on how much it would cost to hire a management company to perform the services undertaken by Robert and Marilyn.

Shirley testified that she received director's fees as a director of the corporation. She further testified that no shareholders' or directors' meetings were ever called. She did not know that Robert and Marilyn were being compensated for their services. She did not know what she was supposed to do as a director and never asked. . . .

Appellant argues in her first assignment of error that the trial court erred by holding that the compensation paid to appellees was not excessive. Appellant argues that compensation received by appellees did not bear a reasonable relationship to the value of the services rendered. R.C. 1701.60(A)(3) provides:

"(3) The directors, by the affirmative vote of a majority of those in office, and irrespective of any financial or personal interest of any of them, shall have authority to establish reasonable compensation, that may include pension disability, and death benefits, for services to the corporation by directors and officers, or to delegate such authority to one or more officers or directors."[87]

. . . The record shows that appellees have managed the corporation since 1966. From 1967 until 1982 they had a combined annual salary of $5,700. The record shows that Robert's annual salary before 1982 was less than what his father received as compensation before his death.

In 1982 their annual salary increased to a combined total of $18,000, where it remained until the lawsuit. While the record reveals that there is a substantial increase in appellees' annual compensation, without evidence affirmatively showing the unreasonableness of the compensation we cannot substitute our judgment for that of the trial court or corporate managers. The testimony of appellant's witness, though valuable, was insufficient to compel the conclusion that appellees' compensation was unreasonable. Appellant's expert witness did not present any evidence comparing appellees' compensation to that of similar owners in the local market. Appellant's expert witness centered his testimony on the value of appellees' time if they were working for another company, but they were not working for another company. A better comparison could have been what other owners pay themselves in the local market for similar job performance. Furthermore, the expert used a standard of compensation that would be appropriate if the services performed by appellees were done by a management company. The problem with this comparison is that in almost every situation one can find that, compared to what a corporation pays its top executives, a management company can perform the same duties and more for a considerably lesser amount. The mere fact that a management company can be paid less for the same type of services in and of itself is insufficient to render the compensation unreasonable. The expert also did not factor into his evaluation the impact fringe benefits would have on the compensation received by appellees since R.C. 1701.60(A)(3) speaks of compensation which includes fringe benefits. By this we mean that there is no expert testimony as to whether the compensation would still be considered unreasonable taking into account that appellants were not provided any fringe benefits. . . .

Appellant argues that the burden of proving reasonableness of the compensation rests with appellees. In support of her argument, appellant cites Soulas [v. Troy Donut University, Inc., 9 Ohio App. 3d 339, 460 N.E.2d 310 (1983)], as controlling. We disagree. As already stated, each case must be considered separately on its merits. The burden of proving excess compensation in *Soulas* by the noncomplaining parties was due to the facts and circumstances of that case. In *Soulas*, the directors held a meeting in which the minority director was not invited and those present extremely raised their salary. In the instant case, the compensation in question was begun in 1982 and has remained the same. Appellant has been receiving dividends and annual reports since 1982 and has actual notice or by due diligence should have had a notice of the compensation but did not challenge it until September 1989. We see no reason to apply an exception and upset the general rule that the burden of proof rests on the party challenging the cause. . . .

The record of appellees' services to the corporation is documented. The record also reveals that Edgar, the founder and the majority shareholder before Robert

---

87. A few other states have similar provisions. See, e.g., Ill. Bus. Corp. Act §8.05(c) (1994). Compare Valeant Pharmaceuticals Int'l v. Jerney, 921 A.2d 732 (Del. Ch. 2007): "Self-interested compensation decisions made without independent protections are subject to the same entire fairness review as any other interested transaction." — Ed.

took over the corporation, and Esther, who worked as the secretary for the corporation, received compensation for their services.

Accordingly, appellant's first assignment of error is overruled. . . .

---

1. *Close corporations — contrary decisions.* (a) In Crowley v. Communications for Hospitals, Inc., 30 Mass. App. Ct. 751, 573 N.E.2d 996 (1991), the trial judge found

> that during the years 1978 through 1982, Dwyer was paid, in salary and bonuses, $385,475 and that the reasonable value of those services was $131,500, yielding an excess of $253,975. Wagner, who, because of failing health, did not perform any services of value to the company after 1978, nevertheless received $368,992 thereafter. As for Dwyer's three sons, the judge found that from 1978 through 1986, William M. received $325,862 and was overcompensated by $65,000; during the same period, John received $238,456 and was overcompensated by $57,580; during the years 1979 and 1980, Richard was paid $50,234 and was overcompensated by $14,925.

Affirmed:

> There is manifest unfairness to the excluded, non-consenting minority interests for the majority, year after year, to appropriate to themselves substantially all of the net income of the enterprise, and such an operational policy, which deprives the company, and therefore its stockholders, of all opportunities for growth in net worth, serves no legitimate business purpose. . . . [W]e know of no decision . . . establishing hereditary entitlements to compensation without the consent of independent directors and a majority of the disinterested stockholders.

(b) In Ruetz v. Topping, 453 S.W.2d 624 (Mo. Ct. App. 1970), in holding that interested directors of a close corporation did not satisfy their burden "to justify the compensation they had received, and to show the reasonableness thereof"[88] — despite the fact that "an expert witness called by defendants, . . . a certified public accountant, experienced in preparing and reviewing corporate income tax returns, in answer to a hypothetical question, expressed the opinion that salaries of $26,000 per year paid by the company . . . were reasonable"[89] — the court observed:

---

88. See also Bachelder v. Brentwood Lanes, Inc., 369 Mich. 155, 119 N.W.2d 630 (1963) (salary of $350 per week to majority shareholder for operating bowling alley was excessive and he must repay $125 per week); Hirsch v. Cahn Elec. Co., 694 So. 2d 636 (La. Ct. App. 1997) ("disparity between the operating losses and the overall compensation" justified trial court ruling that corporation's two salaried director-officers return $200,000 of their salaries and bonuses of $312,000 for 1991 and 1992). Compare Fincher v. Clairborne Butane Co., 349 So. 2d 1014 (La. Ct. App. 1977) (salaries of $1,250 and $1,000 per month to sons of president and majority shareholder upheld: "amount of compensation . . . judged by . . . comparative reasonableness as against the duties and responsibilities being performed"; no discussion of burden of proof).

89. See also Security-First Nat'l Bank v. Lutz, 322 F.2d 348 (9th Cir. 1963), in which "two disinterested witnesses, expert in the field of executive compensation, testified" that the salary paid was reasonable. In reversing the trial judge's ruling to the contrary, the court observed: "Expert testimony, including testimony as to the reasonable value of services rendered, is not conclusive upon the trier of fact, even though unimpeached and uncontradicted, since the trier may apply his own experience or knowledge in determining how far to follow the expressed opinion. However, this is subject to the general rule that the trier may not act arbitrarily in disregarding uncontradicted and entirely probable testimony of witnesses whose qualifications and judgment have not been discredited."

[T]he question of what is reasonable compensation, especially at the executive level, has received attention from both the text writers and the courts. Fletcher, in his Cyclopedia Corporations, Vol. 5, Section 2133, p. 577, quotes from a New York case that: "To come within the rule of reason the compensation must be in proportion to the executive's ability, services and time devoted to the company, difficulties involved, responsibilities assumed, success achieved, amounts under jurisdiction, corporate earnings, profits and prosperity, increase in volume or quality of business or both, and all other relevant facts and circumstances."

Section 162(a)(1) of the Internal Revenue Code, 1954, allows a corporation to deduct as an ordinary and necessary expense in carrying on a business "a reasonable allowance for salaries or other compensation for personal services actually rendered," and that provision has proven to be a more prolific source of litigation as to what was or was not reasonable compensation. In that area, also, no set formula has been devised, and . . . various factors to be considered are mentioned: the employee's qualifications; the nature, extent and scope of the employee's work; the size and complexities of the business; a comparison of salaries paid with the gross income and the net income; the prevailing general economic conditions; a comparison of salaries with distribution to stockholders; the prevailing rates of compensation for comparable positions in comparable concerns; the salary policy of the taxpayer as to all employees; and in the case of small corporations with a limited number of officers the amount of compensation paid to the particular employee in previous years.[90]

2. *Public corporations.* Since the early 1990s, extensive attention has been directed to the greatly increased amount of compensation (largely driven by bonuses and stock options) paid to the executives of America's largest corporations, particularly as compared to managers of companies in Europe and Japan. By 2003, CEO compensation had increased from 140 times to 500 times that of average workers.[91] Moreover, some empirical studies suggest that "wide disparities in corporate pay scales can adversely affect firm value . . . [by] negative effects on the efforts and productivity of lower paid members of the firm."[92]

Responses have been forthcoming at the federal legislative and administrative levels. In 1998 the Securities and Exchange Commission revised its rules on

90. For a decision involving testimony by "compensation experts" respecting "compensation packages" by companies of "comparable size" in the instant corporation's "industry," see Hall v. Staha, 314 Ark. 71, 858 S.W.2d 672 (1993) (finding that president and sales manager, who controlled a closely held pharmaceutical company, "received excessive compensation of $556,172.75 and $714, 772.75 respectively during the October 1, 1987–December 31, 1990, period"). — ED.

91. Bebchuck & Fried, footnote 77 supra, at 1. In 2002 total compensation for CEOs increased to a median of $3,022,505. Wall St. J., Executive Pay (a Special Report), (April 14, 2003). In 2006 total compensation of the top 20 highest-paid CEOs of publicly held U.S. companies ranged from $71,660,000 to $24,802,000 — averaging $36,402,000. Institute for Policy Studies, Executive Excess 2007 26 (2007). In 2003 total compensation paid to the top five executives in all public companies in the prior three years equaled 10 percent of those companies' earnings. Gretchen Morgenson, Behind Every Underachiever, An Overpaid Board?, N.Y. Times (Jan. 22, 2006), 3-1. For a study showing that "despite misperceptions to the contrary, executive pay has not increased significantly as a percentage of corporate income . . . between 1980 and 2000," see Richard A. Booth, Executive Compensation, Corporate Governance, and the Partner-Manager, 2006 Ill. L. Rev. 269, 279-280.

92. Randall S. Thomas, Should Directors Reduce Executive Pay?, 54 Hastings L.J. 437, 438, 454 (2003). Another study concludes that "highly paid CEOs are more skilled than their industry counterparts when firms are small, especially when there is a large shareholder," but that "pay is negatively related to skill in firms . . . especially when there is no large shareholder to monitor management or the firm is large." Lewis A. Kornhauser, Vinay B. Nair & Robert Daines, The Good, the Bad and the Lucky: CEO Pay and Skill (New York University Law and Economics Working Paper No. 9, Jan. 1, 2005), http://lsr.nellco.org/nyu/lewp/papers/9. For a fairly detailed review of a number of recent studies on this correlation, as well as other aspects of the compensation debate, which concludes that "executives are not overpaid," see Loewenstein, footnote 77 supra.

shareholder proposals, seemingly permitting their use in respect to executive compensation, and generally allowing precatory proposals. See pages 677-680 infra. In addition, the SEC greatly expanded corporate disclosure requirements pertinent to executive pay.[93] In 1993 Congress forbade business expense deductions from the federal income tax for executive compensation in excess of $1 million unless tied to performance goals determined by a compensation committee of all independent directors, I.R.C. §162(m).[94] And the Sarbanes-Oxley Act of 2002 added a new §13K to the Securities Exchange Act of 1934, which forbids public corporations from directly or indirectly extending credit or making, renewing, or arranging a "personal loan" (with a few exceptions) to any director or executive officer.

The judicial record, however, is quite different. As indicated in Note 1 supra, courts have not been unsympathetic to excessive compensation claims in close corporations, perhaps because the cases usually involve self-dealing by the majority and the absence of any realistic alternative for the minority, who can neither vote the majority out nor sell their shares in a market. (For full discussion of the problems of minority shareholders in close corporations, see page 780 infra.) By contrast, cases involving large public corporations usually involve a compensation plan approved by either disinterested directors or shareholders, and complainants may (theoretically) seek to change the board or (more realistically) sell out. Thus, as evidenced in the *Walt Disney* case, it continues to be true that "courts have modified certain compensation plans on technicalities and invalidated others after finding no benefit accrued to the corporation . . . [but], as yet, no court has found in any case involving a large publicly held corporation that pay was so unreasonably high that its excess, by itself, constituted waste." Linda J. Barris, The Overcompensation Problem: A Collective Approach to Controlling Executive Pay, 68 Ind. L.J. 59, 84 (1992).[95]

In the mid-1990s, a report of the National Association of Corporate Directors Blue Ribbon Commission on Director Compensation recommended that directors be paid "solely in the form of equity and cash — with equity representing a substantial portion of the total up to 100 percent," urging corporations to "dismantle existing benefit programs and avoid creating new ones."[96] In support, see Elson, footnote 76 supra, at 943-944: "[I]f a director's self-interest is aligned with the equity-holders, as opposed to management, then the compensation problem, and maybe even the whole issue of management capture, might be

93. See page 660 infra.

94. For the view that the SEC and IRC efforts are "unlikely to limit compensation, and . . . may fuel the increase," see Loewenstein, footnote 77 supra at 22-25.

95. For discussion of the difficulties in judging the reasonableness of executive compensation in large corporations, see Detlev F. Vagts, Challenges to Executive Compensation: For the Market or the Courts?, 8 J. Corp. L. 231 (1983) ("self restraint must be the central factor" but "courts need to understand that while judgments on the excessiveness of compensation are not easy to make, they are usually not impossible"). Compare Note, The Executive Compensation Contract: Creating Incentives to Reduce Agency Costs, 37 Stan. L. Rev. 1147, 1169-1170 (1985), suggesting a measure that "contrasts the ratio of change in the corporation's market value to the ratio of change in the average value of an index of several companies that are in the same industry or face certain similar circumstances as the corporation." See also Alfred Rappaport, New Thinking on How to Link Executive Pay with Performance, Harv. Bus. Rev. 91 (March-April 1999), for a discussion of various types of peer group (or competitor) indexes.

96. "[G]enerous benefit programs may actually create incentives for directors to oppose actions that could benefit shareholders, if such actions would mean challenging management. This is especially true when a term of service is required before the benefits vest." Report, supra at 17 (1995).

solved. . . . Additionally, directors' term lengths must be significantly expanded both to ensure that their equity positions (or potential positions) will reach the levels necessary to influence their decision-making and to mitigate the chilling effect of a management threat not to renominate that frequent elections create."[97] As the following subsection on "Stock Options" notes, this urging in retrospect to equity-based remuneration has been heeded. But the fact that it has been the major component of the large rewards earned by many top corporate executives continues to make the topic a subject of substantial controversy. For further discussion, see pages 6-7 supra.

3. *Remedies.* If a disinterested board contracts with an executive officer for compensation that is subsequently held to be excessive, should the directors be held liable to the corporation for the excess already paid? Should the recipient officer? Cf. Beard v. Elster, page 154 infra; In re John Rich Enterprises, Inc., 481 F.2d 211 (10th Cir. 1973). Should the court enjoin further excess payments for the life of the contract? On what legal theories may affirmative answers to the above queries be grounded? For the view that courts should look to "well-established but dormant principles" that impose a fiduciary duty on the officer recipient "not to accept unreasonable compensation, *even though* the board of directors might not itself be liable for approving," see Douglas C. Michael, The Corporate Officer's Duty as a Tonic for the Anemic Law of Executive Compensation, 17 J. Corp. L. 785 (1992). The court in the *Walt Disney* case held that Ovitz had no fiduciary duties in respect to his compensation agreement before he "assumed the duties of the Disney presidency." 906 A.2d at 48-51.

4. *"Golden parachutes."* Stimulated by the great increase in corporate takeovers beginning in the 1980s (see page 942 infra), a "golden parachute" provides an executive with an annuity or cash payment (and, often, immediate vesting of stock options and pension benefits) if control of the corporation changes ("single-trigger" parachutes) or if the executive's responsibilities are decreased following a change of control ("double-trigger" parachutes).[98] Proponents of golden parachutes contend that these agreements help recruit and retain key employees: Those who fear that their corporation is a likely takeover target are less likely to seek other employment if they are assured a financial cushion following a takeover. Proponents also urge that golden parachutes reduce the incentive of executives who fear being displaced in a hostile takeover from engaging in defensive tactics that may be harmful to the corporation (so-called agency costs).[99] Critics respond that the desire

---

97. For further development, see Charles M. Elson, The Duty of Care, Compensation, and Stock Ownership, 63 U. Cin. L. Rev. 649 (1995) (several empirical studies have found "that companies with boards composed of outside directors with significant shareholdings tend to be considered better managed and to outperform those companies without such equity-holding boards"); Sanjai Bhagat, Dennis C. Carey & Charles M. Elson, Director Ownership, Corporate Performance, and Management Performance, 54 Bus. Law. 885 (1999) (study showing direct relationship between dollar value of outside directors' equity ownership and company's overall performance). See also footnote 50, page 109 supra.

98. See generally 2 Robert H. Winter, Mark H. Stumpf & Gerard L. Hawkins, Shark Repellants and Golden Parachutes: A Handbook for the Practitioner (1985 & Supp. 1989).

99. See generally Albert Choi, Golden Parachute as a Compensation-Shifting Mechanism, 20 J.L. Econ. & Org. 170 (2004); Comment, Golden Parachutes: Ripcords or Ripoffs?, 20 J. Marshall L. Rev. 237 (1986); Note, Golden Parachutes and the Business Judgment Rule: Toward a Proper Standard of Review, 94 Yale L.J. 909 (1985).

for power that motivates executives to resist a hostile takeover may not be overcome by money payments.[100] Others contend that an overly generous golden parachute may actually cause an executive to welcome, or even initiate, a takeover that is not in the best interests of the corporation.[101] Finally, it is urged that since the threat of a takeover induces managers to perform optimally, insuring against takeovers will reduce this market discipline on executive performance.[102]

In International Ins. Co. v. Johns, 874 F.2d 1447 (11th Cir. 1989), upholding a golden parachute plan and discussing the relevant cases and law review commentary in detail, the court reasoned that, under Florida law, the business judgment rule ordinarily governs the board's adoption of a golden parachute plan.[103] But "if the board intended the parachutes to be a defense to a takeover," then the rule of Unocal Corp. v. Mesa Petroleum Co., page 955 infra, must be satisfied: The directors have the burden of showing a good faith belief that the tender offer posed a threat of loss of key employees and that the measures adopted were reasonable in relation to the threat; the court invalidated some elements of the compensation plan adopted by the directors because the board was unable to establish that they were reasonable.[104]

ii. Stock Options

A stock option is a right to purchase a corporation's shares within a designated period of time (say, five years) at a set price (say, $10 per share, which is the fair market value at the date the option is granted). When the option price is less than the market value at the time the option is granted, the immediate financial benefit to the holder of the option is obvious. But when the option price is set at or above the then-market price (as in the example), the advantage to holders of the option comes about only if the market price increases during the option period (say, to $20 per share), thus enabling them to buy the shares at a price below current value.

Corporations grant stock options to executives and other employees primarily to attract and retain them, and to encourage their performance by giving them an ownership stake in the enterprise, thus aligning their interests with those of the shareholders. But the origins of the extensive use of stock options may be traced to a 1950 amendment of the Internal Revenue Code that provided extremely favorable tax treatment for stock options. Although subsequent I.R.C. provisions

---

100. David J. McLaughlin, The Myth of the Golden Parachute, Mergers & Acquisitions 47 (Summer 1982).

101. John C. Coffee Jr., Regulating the Market for Corporate Control: A Critical Assessment of the Tender Offer's Role in Corporate Governance, 84 Colum. L. Rev. 1145, 1237 (1984).

102. Note, Golden Parachute Agreements: Cushioning Executive Bailouts in the Wake of a Tender Offer, 57 St. John's L. Rev. 516, 541-544 (1983).

103. Accord, Campbell v. Potash Corp. of Saskatchewan, Inc., 238 F.3d 792, 799-801 (6th Cir. 2001) (applying Delaware law).

104. In 1984, Congress sought to limit the size of golden parachutes by prohibiting an income tax deduction for excess parachute payments—defined as compensation, contingent on a change in control, that exceeds three times the employee's average income over the preceding five years (I.R.C. §280G)—and imposing a special 20 percent excise tax on the recipient of such payments (I.R.C. §4999). Further, the SEC requires corporations to disclose golden parachute agreements in their annual reports and proxy statements (17 C.F.R. §229.402(g)(2) (2003)).

reduced the attractiveness of stock options,[105] their use continues to be widespread.[106]

Generally — and without noting certain details and exceptions — to be eligible for present favorable tax treatment under I.R.C. §422A, an "incentive stock option" plan must provide that (a) the shareholders approve; (b) the options be granted within ten years of the plan's adoption; (c) the recipient exercise the option within ten years of its being granted and while still employed by the corporation (or within three months thereafter); (d) the options not be transferred by the recipient other than by death; (e) the recipient not own more than 10 percent of the corporation's shares after the grant;[107] (f) the option price not be less than fair market value at the time of the grant; and (g) the recipient hold the shares obtained for at least two years after the option is granted and at least one year after it is exercised.

Apart from the intricacies of federal taxation, stock options present problems in several areas of corporation law in addition to those explored in the materials that follow — e.g., whether they are subject to registration under state blue sky laws and the Securities Act of 1933 and, if so, whether they fall within "private offering" exemptions; whether their exercise and the subsequent sale of the shares obtained comes within the "insider trading" restriction of §16(b) of the Securities Exchange Act of 1934; whether a misrepresentation or nondisclosure by a recipient at the

---

105. A long-standing accounting rule, adding to the attractiveness of management of stock options, held that corporations were not required to deduct any amount as an expense (and thus were not required to reduce net income) for stock options whose exercise price was not below the market price on the date the option was issued. This was changed in 2005 by the Financial Accounting Standards Board. Generally accepted accounting principles (GAAP) now provide that the "fair value" of stock options be recognized as an expense. FASB Statement No. 123.

106. Between 1981 and 1996, the percentage of companies with stock option plans increased from 68 percent to 95 percent for manufacturing companies and from 43 percent to 98 percent for retail companies. Similar increases were found in other industries surveyed. Charles M. Peck & Henry M. Silvert, Total Top Executive Compensation in 1996, at 10 (Conference Board 1998). Perhaps more significantly, recent studies indicate that "outside directors' . . . [compensations] pale in comparison to the amount of potential gain they stand to reap on stock options or grants," Richard H. Wagner & Catherine G. Wagner, Recent Developments in Executive, Director, and Employee Stock Compensation Plans: New Concerns for Corporate Directors, 3 Stan. J.L. Bus. & Fin. 5, 6-7 (1997); and "60% of CEO compensation today is in stock options . . . and 70% in all is stock-based among our 200 largest corporations," Roundtable, What's Wrong with Executive Compensation, Harv. Bus. Rev. 68, 72 (Jan. 2003) (Pearl Meyer). See also Kevin J. Murphy, Explaining Executive Compensation: Managerial Power versus the Perceived Cost of Stock Options, 69 U. Chi. L. Rev. 847 (2002) (stock options increased from 27 percent to 51 percent of total compensation in 1990s); Booth, footnote 90 supra, at 281 ("as of 2001, CEOs of the 200 largest U.S. companies took about ninety percent of their pay in some form of equity and most of that in options"). For the view that the shift to stock options was a significant underlying cause of the Enron and related corporate scandals, see pages 6-7 supra. For the view that stock options are "particularly expensive" for the corporate employer and that "deferred cash compensation . . . ordinarily gives the employee better benefits after tax," see Calvin H. Johnson, Stock Compensation: The Most Expensive Way to Pay Future Cash, 52 SMU L. Rev. 423 (1999). For criticism of several features of stock options as being unrelated to managers' performance, see Bebchuck & Fried, footnote 77 supra, at 141-142, who contend that "indexed" options — which compare the corporation's record against the average of companies in the same industry — would result in a significantly improved system. See also Mark A. Clawson & Thomas C. Klein, Indexed Stock Options: A Proposal for Compensation Commensurate with Performance, 3 Stan. J.L. Bus. & Fin. 31, 32 (1997). In defense of stock options, see Richard A. Booth, The Other Side of the Management Compensation Controversy, 22 Sec. Reg. L.J. 22 (1994).

107. Note that this provision — as well as others — greatly reduces the availability of "incentive stock option" plans for close corporations, where, it has been urged, their incentive feature is most needed. See generally Clark C. Havighurst, The Continuing Inutility of Employee Stock Options in Closely Held Businesses, 18 U. Fla. L. Rev, 251 (1965); V. Henry Rothschild, The New Stock Option: Problems of the Smaller Company, 33 Fordham L. Rev. 393 (1965).

time of grant or exercise creates liability under Rule 10b-5;[108] and whether they may be issued consistent with the preemptive rights of other shareholders.[109]

Most states have statutory provisions specifically dealing with stock options. The following, based on the prior version of the Model Act, is representative.

New Mexico Business Corporation Act (2001)

Sec. 53-11-20. *Stock rights and options.* Subject to any provisions in respect thereof set forth in its articles of incorporation, a corporation may create and issue . . . rights or options entitling the holders thereof to purchase from the corporation shares of any class or classes. Such rights or options shall be evidenced in the manner approved by the board of directors and, subject to the provisions of the articles of incorporation, shall set forth the terms upon which, the time or times within which and the price or prices at which such shares may be purchased from the corporation upon the exercise of any such right or option. In the absence of fraud in the transaction, the judgment of the board of directors as to the adequacy of the consideration received for such rights or options shall be conclusive.[110]

Eliasberg v. Standard Oil Co.
23 N.J. Super. 431, 92 A.2d 862 (1952), *aff'd*, 12 N.J. 467, 97 A.2d 437 (1953)

FREUND, J.: This action involves the legal validity of so-called restricted stock options granted as incentive to executives of the defendant Standard Oil Company, a New Jersey corporation, pursuant to a plan recommended by the unanimous vote of the board of directors. . . .

The stockholders adopted the plan by a vote of 47,830,696 shares, which represents over 78% of the total outstanding issue of 60,571,000 shares, but which was actually over 97% of the stock represented at the meeting. Stockholders owning 1,200,000 shares, or less than 2% of the total outstanding issue, voted against the plan, and stockholders owning about 13,000,000 shares, or slightly more than 20% of the shares, failed to vote. It is clear, therefore, that even if we make the unwarranted assumption that those who neglected to vote were in opposition to the plan, it would still have had the approval of the great majority of the stockholders.

---

108. See generally Joseph J. Ziino, Registration of Stock Option Plans Under the Securities Act of 1933, 58 Marq. L. Rev. 27 (1975); Melvin Katz & Robert T. Lang, Section 16(b) and "Extraordinary" Transactions: Corporate Reorganizations and Stock Options, 49 Notre Dame Law. 705 (1974).

109. RMBCA §6.30(b)(3)(ii) (1984) (options not subject to preemptive rights). Compare Dickson v. Smith, 18 F. Supp. 2d 559 (D. Md. 1998) (preemptive rights violated).

110. Some state statutes require shareholder authorization, as did the earlier version of the Model Act, but most, following RMBCA §6.24, do not, e.g., Del. Gen. Corp. Law §157 (2004). However, the rules of national securities exchanges require that listed corporations obtain shareholder approval for most stock option plans. N.Y. Stock Exch. Listed Co. Manual §303A.08. Although the federal proxy rules do not require that stock option plans be submitted for shareholder approval, proxy statements sent in connection with the annual election of directors must include information about management remuneration (Sched. 14A, Item 8), and under Securities Exchange Act §13(b) the corporation must report annually to the SEC details concerning the granting and exercise of stock options (Form 10-K). Furthermore, if a corporation subject to the federal proxy rules does seek shareholder approval of stock options—as mandated by either state law, stock exchange provisions, or I.R.C. §422A—then the rules do require that detailed disclosure as to the plan be made (Sched. 14A, item 10).—ED.

The plaintiff is the owner of 20 shares of the over 60,000,000 outstanding. Although this is a class suit, he has not been joined by any other stockholder. . . .

To obtain for its own executives the benefits of section 130A of the Revenue Code, the plan under consideration was formulated and subsequently adopted. It provides that options to purchase stock of the company may be granted to any or all of the directors and to such other executives as are designated by the board of directors. All of the directors are fulltime officers or employees of the company. The plan is in substance as follows: The board may grant options in its discretion subject to the limitations that no more than 600,000 shares amounting to less than 1% of the company's outstanding stock may be sold pursuant to such options. No more than one-third of such shares may be sold to directors. Options granted in any one year to all directors shall not exceed 60,000 shares. Options granted to any one director shall not exceed 8,000 shares in any one year and not more than 24,000 during the term of the plan. Each option is to be exercisable only after one year of continued employment immediately following the date the option is granted. The option price per share is to be determined by the board of directors, but not less than 95% of fair market value on the date the option is granted.[111] The options may be granted from time to time in the discretion of the board, but (1) all options expire December 31, 1961, unless the board fixes an earlier date; (2) in case of death of an optionee, the option shall be exercisable by his personal representatives, heirs or legatees within a year after date of death, and (3) in other cases of termination of employment, the option is exercisable only within three months of termination. No option is assignable, except as provided in case of death. All shares purchased by the exercise of options are to be acquired for investment purposes. . . .

Pursuant to the plan, on June 29, 1951 the board of directors granted options to 80 executives for a total of 163,800 shares exercisable at $57.06 per share. For the purpose of satisfying these options the company purchased 129,700 shares of its own stock at an average price of $67.136 per share. Among the optionees for a total of 55,760 shares, or about one-third of the grant, are all the directors who formulated the plan, with the exception of Frank W. Abrams, chairman of the board, who received no options. The defendant indicates that the average attained age of the executives who received options was 51 years and the average length of employment by the defendant or its affiliates was 25 years. . . .

A plan may be valid insofar as it concerns optionees other than the directors and invalid with respect to interested directors. The burden of the proof required in a proceeding wherein the validity of a plan or the execution of it is involved varies in each case and depends upon whether or not the plan had stockholder approval. Insofar as beneficiaries other than interested directors are concerned, the burden of proving illegality or invalidity would be upon the challenger. . . .

Where there is no stockholders' approval of a contract or proposal in which a director has a personal interest, the burden is upon the director to completely justify the transaction. When stockholders have notice of the director's interest and authorize the directors to enter into a contract, the agreement will be unassailable in the absence of actual fraud or want of power in the corporation. . . .

---

111. This "95% of fair market value" was permissible under the 1950 I.R.C. provision. — ED.

Here, the company, prior to the meeting, submitted to the stockholders the complete text of the plan and a proxy statement which specified that the stock options were to be of the type provided for under section 130A of the Internal Revenue Code. The plaintiff concedes that there has been technical disclosure, but contends that this was inadequate and not in compliance with the rule demanding full and fair disclosure. He argues that neither the text of the plan nor the proxy statement revealed to the stockholders the taxwise effect of the execution of the plan, that is, that any profit realized by the optionees upon acquisition of the stock at a figure less than market value would not be taxable at ordinary federal income tax rates, but at the lower capital gains rate, but the corporation might not deduct any difference between its cost and lower sale price as a taxable loss against federal income or excess profits taxes. . . . In effect, the plaintiff argues that it is the duty of a director who submits to the stockholder a full text of a proposal to accompany it with an analysis of the beneficial and detrimental aspects of the proposal. Undoubtedly, such data would be valuable material for a stockholder to receive, for I venture the opinion that a great number of stockholders do not comprehend the full impact of the reports and statements they receive from corporations. I am aware that many a stockholder relegates to the wastebasket the literature he receives from corporations upon whose dividends he depends for income. I know of no legal authority, nor does the plaintiff submit any, which imposes upon a director the duty to explain or interpret the tax effects of a proposal the full terms of which are submitted to the stockholder. I believe it to be the obligation of the stockholder who receives the complete text of a proposal which may be involved or technical, to make inquiry — either from independent sources or from the corporation or the directors. In the latter instance, it would be the duty of the company or the directors to inform or advise the stockholder. A stockholder is chargeable with knowledge he could have acquired. . . .

In this case it is most significant that no stockholder who voted approval has testified that he was misled, or that had he known the results which the plaintiff presents he would not have voted approval. The plaintiff was his only witness and he was not misled because he voted against the plan.

Before being distributed to the stockholders the proxy statement was submitted to the Securities and Exchange Commission in accordance with the Securities Exchange Act of 1934. The officials made certain suggestions which were incorporated in the proxy statement. Section 26 of the act precludes the construction that such examination by the Commission implies accuracy and truthfulness of the statements in a proxy . . . [but it] is a fact to be considered in conjunction with all other facts in the case and without according to the examination by the Commission any element of approval.

The plaintiff urges that the plan in fact is a device to grant the directors and other executives additional compensation for their services without any increase in their duties or responsibilities or change in status; and, hence, the options were without consideration and constituted an ultra vires gift of corporate property. No contract of employment was entered into between any executive and the company at the time of the issuance of the options, and there was no evidence of any change in the terms or conditions of any existing contract of employment with any executive. . . . The plaintiff points out that the director-optionees testified that prior to the issuance of the options they were rendering their full services and best efforts on behalf of the company, and that they had not agreed to perform any additional duty or assume any further obligation. . . .

The defendant contends that the purpose of the stock plan was incentive to induce executives to remain with the company.[112] However, there was no convincing evidence that any executive-director of the company contemplated leaving the service of the defendant because of inadequacy of compensation, or that the directors were confronted with a real threat that the executives were considering separation from the company unless some incentive plan was adopted. If this were so, I believe that long term contracts of employment would have been requested by the company and required as consideration for the options.

Subordinating technical to intrinsic consideration, it is my impression and belief from the evidence that the real purpose of the plan was to give executives additional compensation subject to the most favorable tax rates . . . [but] it is not invalid and the issuance of options thereunder is not illegal, under the facts of the case.

. . . The notice and proxy statement to the stockholders presented the plan in full and these are sufficiently detailed to inform them of the proposal to issue options to directors and other executives for continuing in the employ of the company without requiring them to perform any additional duties or to assume new responsibilities. . . .

Stock options may be adopted as a form of compensation for continuance in employment. . . .

In the instant case, options cannot be exercised by the optionees until after one year of service, and the granting and exercise of future options depends upon continuance of service. Such plans have invariably been upheld. . . .

Because of the stockholders' ratification, the court will look into the transaction only far enough to see whether . . . the value of the services bears a reasonable relationship to the amounts to be paid under the plan; whether the value to the company of the benefits which it would receive from any optionee was so much less than the value of the options granted to him that no person of ordinary business judgment could be expected to entertain the view that the consideration furnished was a fair exchange for the options conferred. Is the compensation to be realized from the options so large and disproportionate to the services to be rendered as to amount to spoliation or waste of corporation assets? The plaintiff has not offered any proof whatsoever upon or from which the court can make any determination of the value of the services of the company's executives or that the compensation to be paid them, including any profit that might be realized from the exercise of the options, is disproportionate to the value of the services. There was no evidence of the compensation paid to executives of competitors or other corporations as large as or comparatively as large as the defendant, so that the court could have a basis for evaluation.

The defendant's witnesses testified to the importance and value of the executives' services and the need for retaining them, at adequate salaries and benefits, in order that they should not be attracted to other companies. I am not unmindful of the interest of the defendant's witnesses, but after making due allowance therefore, there is no evidence before me which would warrant the substitution of my estimate of the value of the services for the judgment of the directors, approved by the overwhelming majority of the stockholders. . . .

---

112. N.Y. Bus. Corp. Law §505(d) (1997) provides that shares may be optioned "as an incentive to service or continued service with the corporation." — ED.

The plaintiff argues that . . . the burden of proving that the stockholders were fully and fairly informed is upon the directors, before the plaintiff can be required to prove the unfairness of the basic transaction. He urges that since the plan submitted to the stockholders for approval did not separate the proposal to issue options to directors from the proposal to issue options to other employees, but the two were fused together, therefore, the stockholders did not have an opportunity to signify their disapproval of the plan insofar as it applied to interested directors. The plaintiff further contends that while the plan indicated that the directors might participate, it omitted the names of the directors who were to participate and the extent of their participation.

I conclude, however, that the stockholders were furnished with the full terms of the proposed plan; that they were advised of the interest of the directors in the proposal, even though the names were omitted; and also of the terms upon which the options were to be issued and exercised.[113] Therefore, in view of the stockholders' approval and ratification, it was the duty of the plaintiff to prove unfairness of the basic transaction, and he failed to sustain this burden.

. . . [I]t is not to be inferred . . . that I regard the ratification by the stockholders as approval of all future options which might be granted by the directors. While the plan itself has been declared valid, the future execution of it must conform to legal standards within the framework of the plan. . . .

Beard v. Elster
39 Del. Ch. 153, 160 A.2d 731 (S. Ct. 1960)

WOLCOTT, J.: [In 1950, the directors of American Airlines, Inc. recommended, and the shareholders approved, a restricted stock option plan for employees covering 250,000 shares — exercisable in whole or in part for five years providing the optionee was still employed by the corporation. Options were issued to 289 employees.] . . .

The Board of Directors of sixteen members approving the option plan and submitting the same to the stockholders for approval was a completely disinterested Board with the exception of two members who ultimately received grants for options under the plan. After the approval of the plan a committee of disinterested Directors was formed for the purpose of granting the options to eligible employees. . . .

This lawsuit . . . sought the cancellation of the option plans and the options issued thereunder as invalid gifts of corporate assets. . . .

One hundred and eighty-nine optionees appeared . . . and moved for summary judgment. . . .

From the affidavits the following general factual background may be drawn. Some time in the spring of 1950 American's employees were informed of American's expectation of putting into effect an option plan for key employees. Thereafter, options were in fact granted to and exercised by these defendants. In order to

---

113. For cases finding inadequate disclosure to shareholders, thus nullifying a purported ratification, see Sample v. Morgan, 914 A.2d 647 (Del. Ch. 2007); Colorado Mgt. Corp. v. American Founders Life Ins. Co., 145 Colo. 413, 359 P.2d 665 (1961); Rivoli Theatre Co. v. Allison, 396 Pa. 343, 152 A.2d 449 (1959); Berkwitz v. Humphrey, 163 F. Supp. 78 (N.D. Ohio 1958). For criticism of this aspect of the *Eliasberg* decision, see Robert C. Clark, Corporate Law 214-215 (1986). — ED.

take up the options about 150 of the defendants borrowed money. Following the exercise of the options by the individuals substantial sums of money traceable to the acquisition of the optioned stock have gone into a variety of things, including education bills, living expenses, purchases of homes, cars and other things. It is alleged that these expenditures would not have been made except in reliance upon the optioned stock. Finally, the affidavits assert that the grant and exercise of the options induced the defendants to remain in the employ of American. . . .

The Vice-Chancellor held upon the authority of Kerbs v. California Eastern Airways, 33 Del. Ch. 69, 90 A.2d 632, 34 A.L.R.2d 839, that the options involved were invalidly granted, being lacking in consideration to the corporation. . . . Plaintiffs argue that the options constitute gifts of corporate assets by reason of the rule of the *Kerbs* case and Gottlieb v. Heyden Chemical Corp., 33 Del. Ch. 82, 90 A.2d 660. . . .

The *Kerbs* case involved the validity of a stock option plan. The plan provided that options granted pursuant to it could be exercised at any time within a period of five years from the date of issuance, but not later than six months after the termination of the employment of the optionee. In addition, each option could be exercised at any proper time for either the full number of shares subject to the option or any part thereof.

The option plan involved was adopted by a Board of Directors of eight, of whom five were ultimate beneficiaries under the plan. Thereafter, the plan was submitted to a stockholders meeting for approval and received the affirmative vote of a majority of outstanding shares.

The plan thus outlined was held invalid by reason of the fact that it was initially approved by an interested Board of Directors and, while it subsequently received the approval of a majority of the outstanding stock, nevertheless, did not within itself contain conditions insuring the ultimate receipt by the corporation of the contemplated benefit of the plan, viz., the retention of the services of the optionees.

We held that any option plan must contain consideration passing to the corporation, which could take variable forms, such as the retention of services of a valued employee, or the gaining of services of a new employee. We further held that the plan, itself, or the surrounding circumstances, must be such as to insure that this consideration will in all reasonable probability be received by the corporation.

For lack of a better word we described the resultant benefit from a stock option plan to the corporation as consideration passing to the corporation. It now appears, however, that the choice of this word was possibly ill-advised since it is regarded, apparently, by some as a measurable quid pro quo. . . . It, of course, by the very nature of things, cannot be that. It is incapable of measurement except in terms of business judgment that the plan will spur employees on to greater efforts which in the long run will benefit the corporation. However nebulous it may be, there must be some reasonable assurance in the plan, or the circumstances of the particular case, which can reasonably be expected to make the corporation receive the contemplated benefit. . . .

In the *Gottlieb* case we had before us a stock option plan also approved and adopted by an interested Board of Directors. This plan provided that an optionee could exercise his option only so long as he remained an employee of the corporation. This plan, too, was submitted for approval to a stockholders meeting, receiving the approval of a majority of the corporation's stock.

In the proceedings in the Court of Chancery prior to appeal to this court, the . . . parties thereupon stipulated that the Board of Directors believed at the time the plan was adopted that the interests of the corporation would be advanced by putting the plan into effect. Upon the filing of this stipulation, the Chancellor thereupon entered judgment in favor of the corporation. . . .

We held the plan to be defective on the ground that the unsupported belief of an interested Board of Directors could not supply lack of proof of the contemplated benefit to the corporation. We, accordingly, remanded the case for trial. . . . In the *Gottlieb* case it appeared that the sole optionees under the plan were also members of the Board of Directors of which they were a majority. It thus followed, we held, that the sound business judgment rule had no application and that, accordingly, there was a "necessity for the directors to prove that the bargain had in fact been at least as favorable to the corporation as they would have required if the deal had been made with strangers."

Implicit in the ruling is, of course, that a different situation would have presented itself had the Board of Directors been in fact disinterested. It follows that in such cases the sound business judgment rule might well have come to the aid of the proponents of the plan.

In the *Gottlieb* case there was present, of course, the element of stockholder ratification of the plan. However, this factor, it was held, did not operate to invoke the sound business judgment rule in favor of that ratification by a majority of the stock, for the reason that the possible indifference, or sympathy with the Directors, of a majority of the stockholders would not supply the necessary element of good faith exercise of business judgment by Directors in dealing with the corporate assets. The interested nature of the Directors' action therefore required the courts to examine the facts when a minority stockholder attacked the proposed corporate action. It was for the purpose of making such an examination that the remand was ordered upon the issue of the relationship of value between the options and the contemplated benefit to the corporation.

. . . One ground urged for reargument was that the first opinion had destroyed any distinction between cases where Directors vote themselves stock options without stockholder ratification and cases where stockholder ratification is obtained. In the second opinion we pointed out, as we . . . again held the law on the subject to be in the case of Directors voting themselves stock options and later obtaining stockholder ratification of their act, that the duty of the court to examine the facts consisted solely in sufficient examination to determine whether the terms of the option plan were so unequal as to amount to waste, or whether the question was so close factually as to fall within the realm of the exercise of sound business judgment. . . . If the question of value, which was the issue to be determined on remand, fell under the developed facts into a field in which reasonable men, fully informed, could well differ in opinion, then the sound business judgment rule required the court to approve the plan.

. . . *Kerbs* and *Gottlieb* lay down a fundamental rule governing all stock option plans, however adopted. At the risk of repetition, we again restate it. All stock option plans must be tested against the requirement that they contain conditions, or that surrounding circumstances are such, that the corporation may reasonably expect to receive the contemplated benefit from the grant of the options.[114]

---

114. Accord, Pinnacle Consultants, Ltd. v. Leucadia National Corp., 101 F.3d 900, 905 (2d Cir. 1996) (New York law). — Ed.

Furthermore, there must be a reasonable relationship between the value of the benefits passing to the corporation and the value of the options granted.

Thus, in the *Kerbs* case, the fact that the Directors who voted in favor of the plan were permitted by the plan to leave the company's employ and, yet, have the right to exercise their options for six months thereafter impaled the plan upon the prong of failure to provide reasonable safeguards that the corporation would receive the contemplated benefit, i.e., the retention of the services of the optionee.

The option plan in the *Gottlieb* case fell upon the second prong that there had been no independent appraisal of the value of the services to be retained by means of the options and the value of the options granted. It was this lack, i.e., independent appraisal, that the remand in that case was designed to supply.

What, then, is the result in the case at bar? The option plan now before us was adopted initially by an admittedly independent and disinterested Board of Directors. The plan subsequently received stockholder ratification. The options granted pursuant to the plan could be exercised by the optionee only while in the employ of the corporation, subject to two unimportant exceptions.

There are other circumstances surrounding the adoption of the plan itself which are bound to be considered. It thus appears that, compared with corporations of like size, the comparable salaries of this corporation's employees are below average. It further appears that the proposal to adopt a stock option plan was made known to the corporation's employees prior to its actual adoption and that this knowledge acted as an inducement to those employees to remain in the corporation's service.

Of prime importance is the fact that the adoption of the plan by the Directors was an exercise of independent business judgment that the plan would be of benefit to the corporation and would result in the retention of the services of valued employees. If it be objected that this is but surmise concerning the Directors' reasons, that objection is answered by the action of the Board at its regular meeting of September 16, 1953. At that meeting the Board fully reviewed and considered the benefits received and to be received by the corporation from the plan and reaffirmed its decision with respect thereto.

Furthermore, it is certainly not without significance that of the employees of the defendant corporation granted options, who in turn exercised their option rights, the great majority have remained in the company's employ. This is, of course, hindsight . . . [but] it vindicates the business judgment of the Directors who adopted the plan as insuring the corporation the benefit of the continuation of the services of the optionees. If plaintiffs object, it must be remembered that the plaintiffs were in control of this action which had dragged on past the option expiration date.

We think the fact that a disinterested Board of Directors reached this decision by the exercise of its business judgment is entitled to the utmost consideration by the courts in passing upon the results of that decision. . . .

For the foregoing reasons, the order of the Vice-Chancellor is reversed. . . .

---

1. *Reasonableness of compensation.* What result in any of these cases if the market price of the corporation's shares increases tenfold within a short time of the grant

of the stock options? In Lieberman v. Becker, 38 Del. Ch. 540, 155 A.2d 596 (Super. Ct. 1959) — involving a shareholder-approved "phantom stock" plan under which designated officers and employees are granted "units" that are credited with any market appreciation in the corporation's stock — it was urged

> that market value of common stock is too speculative an element to form a reasonable basis for determining executive compensation. . . . Plaintiff points to a variety of factors which determine the market price of common stock, including interest rate on money, corporate earnings, the business cycle, commodity prices, the psychology of the buying public, labor relations, and others, and thus argues that the employee's services do not necessarily have any direct relation to the . . . market price of the securities of the corporation for which he works.

The court, observing that the units were awarded by "a committee of five directors, themselves ineligible to participate in the plan," rejected the argument: "[W]hether or not a corporation should embark upon such a method of compensating its employees is to be decided by the board of directors in exercise of their business judgment." Contra, Berkwitz v. Humphrey, 163 F. Supp. 78 (N.D. Ohio 1958).[115]

2. *Shareholder ratification of interested director transactions.* (a) *Ambiguity in the "law."* In Lewis v. Vogelstein, 699 A.2d 327 (Del. Ch. 1997), the court stated:

> What is the effect under Delaware corporation law of shareholder ratification of an interested transaction? . . . Four possible effects of shareholder ratification appear logically available: First, one might conclude that an effective shareholder ratification acts as a complete defense to any charge of breach of duty. Second, one might conclude that the effect of such ratification is to shift the substantive test on judicial review of the act from one of fairness that would otherwise be obtained (because the transaction is an interested one) to one of waste. Third, one might conclude that the ratification shifts the burden of proof of unfairness to plaintiff, but leaves that shareholder-protective test in place. Fourth, one might conclude (perhaps because of great respect for the collective action disabilities that attend shareholder action in public corporations) that shareholder ratification offers no assurance of assent of a character that deserves judicial recognition. Thus, under this approach, ratification on full information would be afforded no effect. Excepting the fourth of these effects, there are cases in this jurisdiction that reflect each of these approaches to the effect of shareholder voting to approve a transaction.[10]

Does the *Beard* case adopt *any* of the four possible effects?

(b) *"Waste."* Does "the waste exception, which is a vestige of a long-gone era of corporation law, ha[ve] no present-day utility"? William T. Allen, Jack B. Jacobs & Leo E. Strine Jr., Function over Form: A Reassessment of Standards of Review in Delaware Corporation Law, 26 Del. J. Corp. L. 859, 891 (2000): "A judicial determination that a transaction affirmed by informed, disinterested stockholders

---

115. Accord, Pogostin v. Rice, 480 A.2d 619 (Del. 1984) (abnormally large credits to unit accounts because, during the period that credits were calculated, stock prices were driven up by a tender offer and then returned to normal after board rejected the tender offer).

10. See, e.g., In re Wheelabrator Technologies, Inc., Shareholders Litig., Del. Ch., 663 A.2d 1194 (1995) (effect one: effective ratification eliminates any claim for breach of duty of care but only breach of care); Michelson v. Duncan, Del. Supr., 407 A.2d 211, 224 (1979) (effect two: effective ratification of director interested transaction triggers waste standard); Citron v. E.I. DuPont de Nemours & Co., Del. Ch., 584 A.2d 490, 500-02 (1990), quoted with approval in Kahn v. Lynch Communication Systems, Inc., [page 1102 infra] (effect three: effective ratification shifts burden of fairness to plaintiff).

constituted waste would amount to a conclusion that the corporate electorate had acted bizarrely. Unsurprisingly, no Delaware case of which we are aware has ever held that a properly ratified transaction constituted waste." See also Note 2(c), page 141 supra.

(c) *Public corporations.* What effect *should* be given to shareholder ratification? "Public shareholders who vote to approve or ratify conflicted transactions are normally hampered by collective action problems[116] and can be swayed by the information, prominently displayed in management's public materials, that reputed investment bankers have issued formal valuation opinions describing management's preferred course of action as fair or beneficial to shareholders." McGinty, Note 4, page 125 supra, at 219. How does the greatly increased percentage of equity owned by institutional investors rather than individuals — 64 percent of the top one hundred U.S. corporations and 69 percent of the top one thousand, as of 2005 — affect this situation?[117] "Historical problems associated with collective action by a widely dispersed group of shareholders [have] been somewhat ameliorated by the increase of these institutional investors. The new tension between liquidity (exit) and control (voice) is now favoring control since 'exit' for institutional shareholders has become more difficult." Note, footnote 116supra, at 1018-1019. Compare Brudney, Note 4, page 125 supra, at 613 n.42:

> [I]nstitutional investors, particularly mutual funds, often do not have a large enough or continuous enough interest in any particular portfolio company to justify the costs of engagement in specifying or monitoring the loyalty terms of their investment. . . . Moreover, notwithstanding recent changes in the proxy rules, the willingness and power of institutional investors to collaborate in order to overcome collective action difficulties are problematic. See Bernard S. Black & John C. Coffee, Jr., Hail Britannia? Institutional Investor Behavior Under Limited Regulation, 92 Mich. L. Rev. 1997, 2055-77 (1994). But cf. Dean Strickland et al., A Requiem for the USA — Is Small Shareholder Monitoring Effective?, 40 J. Fin. Econ. 319 (1996).

But see Wagner & Wagner, footnote 106, page 149 supra, at 10: "Where once there was an assumption that any plan presented by management and directors for approval would receive no more than a token 3% to 5% disapproval, the 1995 and 1996 proxy seasons saw significantly stronger shareholder resistance to these plans, as votes against stock options plans in the range of 20-40% became more commonplace." In 2006

> investor disapproval of traditional stock plans returned to historical levels after a marked increase in 2005. In 2006, three of approximately 357 stock-plan proposals voted on by shareholders (or 0.8 percent) failed to gain shareholder approval. By contrast, 17 of 383 plan proposals (4.4 percent) voted on at study companies failed to pass in 2005. However, opposition in 2006 was more in line with that evidenced in prior years, including: 2004 when seven of 412 proposals (1.1 percent) failed to carry; and 2003, when four of 326 proposals (1.1 percent) failed to pass. . . . The 357

116. "There are generally three categories of collective action problems: free-rider problems, communication and coordination problems, and rational apathy problems. The essence of these problems is that while it would be best for all shareholders to contribute to a collective good, such as disciplining management or voting against a self-interested proposal, if the cost of participating to a shareholder is greater than the perceived benefit, that shareholder will refrain from contributing." Note, Interested Director Transactions and the Equivocal Effects of Shareholder Ratification, 21 Del. J. Corp. L. 981, 1018 n.208 (1996).

117. The Conference Board, 2007 Institutional Investment Report 35.

proposals voted on in 2006 were opposed by just 22.1 percent of votes cast, on average. This is a reversal of the trend in 2005, when average opposition to such proposals rose to 25.5 percent from 24.6 percent the prior year.

Institutional Shareholders Services, Stock Plan Dilution 6, 19 (2007).[118]

(d) *Problem.* Close Corp. has ten shareholders — *X, Y,* and *Z* being the largest, each owning 20 percent of the shares, and constituting the corporation's directors and managing officers. The board unanimously votes salaries for *X, Y,* and *Z* that appear subsequently in excess of compensation for comparable executives. The board notifies the shareholders of the fact that it has voted its members the designated salaries. The shareholders approve in the following alternative ways — *X, Y,* and *Z* voting their shares in favor:

(1) 95 percent in favor, 5 percent opposed

(2) 82 percent in favor, 18 percent opposed

(3) 70 percent in favor, 30 percent opposed

In each instance, an opposing minority shareholder sues to invalidate the salaries. What result under the three statutes set forth at pages 119-122 supra?[119] Under the Iowa statute in the *Cookies* case? Under the Ohio statute in the *E.E. Wehrung* case? In light of the discussion in the *Eliasberg* and *Beard* cases? What should be the result?[120]

What result if the corporation's charter provided that "any contract of the corporation ratified by a shareholder majority shall be as valid as though ratified by all shareholders"? See Frankel v. Donovan, 35 Del. Ch. 433, 120 A.2d 311 (Ch. 1956).

(e) *Burden of proof.* If fairness or reasonableness or "waste" or some other such issue is (or should be) a proper subject of judicial inquiry in any of the above instances, where — under the above statutes or otherwise — does (or should) the burden of proof lie? In addition to cases cited in footnote 10, page 158 supra, see Cohen v. Ayers, 596 F.2d 733 (7th Cir. 1979) (under New York law, ratification by majority of disinterested shareholders shifts burden of proof to plaintiff); Michelson v. Duncan, 407 A.2d 211 (Del. 1979) (reaffirming the rule of the *Gottlieb* case that independent shareholder ratification shifts the burden of proof to plaintiff, but "where waste of corporate assets is alleged, the court, notwithstanding independent stockholder ratification, must examine the facts";

---

118. "Dilution, measured in terms of total company dilution or of individual plan dilution, emerges consistently as a critical factor in how shareholders vote on stock option plans." Randall S. Thomas & Kenneth J. Martin, The Determinants of Shareholder Voting on Stock Option Plans, 35 Wake Forest L. Rev. 31, 47, 73 (2000).

119. If X, Y, and Z are disqualified from voting on the shareholder ratification, what is to prevent the minority shareholders from refusing to approve anything but unreasonably low salaries? See John A. C. Hetherington, Minority's Duty of Loyalty in Close Corporations, 1972 Duke L.J. 921. For a brief discussion of the "fiduciary obligation" owed by individual shareholders who join to form a prevailing majority, see Stringer v. Car Data Systems, Inc., 821 P.2d 418 (Or. App. 1991) (32 shareholders were able to outvote the other 4 by vote of 57-43 percent on particular issue involved).

120. For cases refusing to inquire into the fairness or reasonableness of transactions approved by interested shareholder votes, see Kirwan v. Parkway Distillery, Inc., 285 Ky. 605, 148 S.W.2d 720 (1941); cases cited in Note 10, page 128 supra. Cf. Stevens v. Richardson, 755 P.2d 389 (Alaska 1988) ("plaintiff can still prevail by proving substantial unfairness"). Compare Woodstock Enterprises, Inc. v. International Moorings & Marine, Inc., 524 So. 2d 1313 (La. Ct. App. 1988) (statute authorizing approval "in good faith" by "shareholders entitled to vote thereon" contemplates approval by "disinterested" shareholders). See generally Earl Sneed, The Stockholder May Vote as He Pleases: Theory and Fact, 22 U. Pitt. L. Rev. 23 (1960).

The matter of the fiduciary obligation of *shareholders* in voting on corporate transactions is further considered at page 1009 infra.

"claims of gift or waste of corporate assets are seldom subject to disposition by summary judgment"); Pappas v. Moss, 393 F.2d 865 (3rd Cir. 1968) (burden of proof remains on interested defendants where they were majority shareholders "even though a substantial majority of the shares held by independent minority stockholders were voted in favor of ratification"); Harbor Finance Partners v. Huizenga, 751 A.2d 879 (Del. Ch. 1999) (minority shareholder has burden of proof to show "unfairness" when shareholder ratification is by a "controlling or majority stockholder vote, even one expressly conditioned by a 'majority of the minority' "); Sarner v. Fox Hill, Inc., 151 Conn. 437, 199 A.2d 6 (1964) (burden of proof remains on interested defendant when he was only shareholder voting to ratify); Fliegler v. Lawrence, 361 A.2d 218 (Del. 1976) (burden of proof remains on interested defendants when they cast majority of shares to ratify); Oberhelman v. Barnes Investment Corp., 690 P.2d 1343 (Kan. 1984) (same); Krukemeier v. Kru-kemeier Mach. & Tool Co., 551 N.E.2d 885 (Ind. App. 1990) (minority shareholder has burden of proof to show that compensation set by majority shareholders for themselves is "unjust, oppressive, or fraudulent").

Should the effect of a disinterested shareholder ratification be any different from the effect of approval or ratification by a disinterested board? How do the statutes respond to this question?

(f) Closely related questions concerning shareholder ratification are explored in Chapter VIII.B.3.

d. Corporate Opportunities and Competition with the Corporation

The materials in this subsection deal with the often interrelated problems presented when corporate managers (1) take for themselves a business opportunity that allegedly belonged to the corporation and would have enabled the corporation to expand its profitable activities or decrease its financial burdens, or (2) engage in a business (which may or may not be claimed to have been a corporate opportunity) that in some way competes with the corporation. The first case, Irving Trust Co. v. Deutsch (and the notes that follow it), involves the question of whether managers may avail themselves of business opportunities that concededly belong to the corporation but that, for some reason, the corporation is unable to obtain. The remaining materials on corporate opportunity concern the issue of whether a particular business opportunity constitutes a *corporate* opportunity as an initial matter (or whether, on the other hand, it belonged to the director or officer from the outset).

Irving Trust Co. v. Deutsch
73 F.2d 121 (2d Cir. 1934)

SWAN, J.: . . . The plaintiff is the trustee in bankruptcy of a Delaware corporation, . . . Acoustic Products Company. . . . It was chartered in 1927 to deal in phonographs, radios, and similar apparatus. In March, 1928, it was essential for Acoustic to acquire rights to manufacture under basic patents in the radio art, and it was believed that such rights might be acquired through the De Forest Radio Company, which was then in receivership in the Chancery Court of

New Jersey. The defendant Bell was employed by Acoustic to negotiate with the defendants Reynolds and W. R. Reynolds & Co., who were in control of the De Forest situation by reason of a contract under which they expected to purchase 600,000 shares of stock at 50 cents per share, lift the receivership, and reorganize the De Forest Company. Although Bell's negotiations did not produce an arrangement of the sort originally contemplated by Acoustic, he did succeed with the assistance of the defendant Biddle, in obtaining from Reynolds & Co. an offer of a one-third participation in the purchase of the 600,000 shares of De Forest stock; that is, 200,000 shares for $100,000 cash. The offer was directed to Messrs. Biddle and Bell, and provided:

"Your signatures on a signed copy hereof will constitute an agreement between us which will be subject to the approval of your board of directors not later than April 9th, 1928."

It also provided that, if the stock was taken, Acoustic's nominees should hold four of the nine places on the De Forest Company's directorate and that Acoustic should have the right to enter into a contract, subject to the approval of the De Forest board of directors, "to handle the managing, operating, and selling of the De Forest products." This offer was presented to a meeting of the board of directors of Acoustic on April 3, 1928, and a resolution was passed instructing its president, the defendant Deutsch, to endeavor to obtain sufficient funds to enable Acoustic to carry out its obligations in the event of its final acceptance of the offer. On April 9th, at an adjourned meeting of the board, Mr. Deutsch reported his inability to procure the necessary funds for Acoustic, and announced that "several individuals were desirous of accepting said proposition on their own behalf" and were willing to make arrangements so as to extend to Acoustic the benefits contemplated by the acquisition of the stock. Thereupon a resolution was adopted approving Mr. Biddle's acceptance on behalf of Acoustic and directing the proper officers to notify its acceptance to Reynolds & Co. On April 10th, Mr. Deutsch telegraphed Mr. Biddle of this action, with the explanation that it was understood by the directors that, if Acoustic could not finance the purchase when time for payment came, the directors would individually acquire the stock. Partial payment for the 200,000 shares was made on April 24th by the personal checks of Biddle, Deutsch, and Hammond, for which Reynolds & Co. gave a receipt to Acoustic. The balance was paid on May 25, 1928, at which time it was explained to Reynolds that the stock was being purchased by individuals since Acoustic was without available funds. He acquiesced and caused the stock certificates to be issued to Messrs. Bell, Biddle, Deutsch, Hammond, Stein, and White. For convenience these gentlemen are referred to as the Biddle syndicate. . . . An active market for De Forest shares was created on the Curb Exchange, and the defendants made large profits in selling their shares. The bill of complaint seeks to hold the defendants jointly and severally to account for such profits. Jurisdiction of the District Court is founded on diverse citizenship.

The theory of the suit is that a fiduciary may make no profit for himself out of a violation of duty to his *cestui*, even though he risk his own funds in the venture, and that anyone who assists in the fiduciary's dereliction is likewise liable to account for the profit so made. . . . Concretely the argument is that members of the Biddle syndicate, three of whom, Messrs. Biddle, Deutsch, and Hammond, were directors and one, Mr. Bell, its agent in procuring the contract, appropriated to themselves Acoustic's rights under its contract with Reynolds & Co. for 200,000 shares of De Forest stock, when as fiduciaries they were obligated to preserve those rights for Acoustic and were forbidden to take a position where personal interest would conflict with the interest of their principal. The other defendants are claimed to have assisted in their dereliction. In answer to this argument, the defendants do not deny the principle, but dispute its applicability to the facts. . . .

The main defense asserted is that Acoustic by reason of its financial straits had neither the funds nor the credit to make the purchase and that the directors honestly believed that by buying the stock for themselves they could give Acoustic the advantage of access to the De Forest patents, while at the same time taking a stock speculation for their own benefit. In support of the proposition that the prohibition against corporate officers acting on their own behalf is removed if the corporation is itself financially unable to enter into the transaction, the appellees cite Hannerty v. Standard Theater Co., 109 Mo. 297, 19 S.W. 82. . . . The plaintiff cites Wing v. Dillingham, 239 F. 54 (C.C.A 5) as repudiating the above proposition. In Wing v. Dillingham a director of a corporation completed payments on timber land which the corporation had an option to purchase but was unable to pay for; the director taking title to the land and giving the corporation an option to acquire it by repaying his advances within six months. Long after the six months, and without repayment of the advances, the corporation's receiver was held entitled to avoid the transaction and require the director to account. The facts in the case at bar are even stronger against the defendant directors since here the directors absolutely bound Acoustic by contract to make the payments to Reynolds & Co., and thus subjected it to the risk of an action for damages for nonperformance, without committing themselves to it to relieve it of this obligation if necessary when time for payment should arrive. The defendants' argument, contrary to Wing v. Dillingham, that the equitable rule that fiduciaries should not be permitted to assume a position in which their individual interests might be in conflict with those of the corporation can have no application where the corporation is unable to undertake the venture, is not convincing. If directors are permitted to justify their conduct on such a theory, there will be a temptation to refrain from exerting their strongest efforts on behalf of the corporation since, if it does not meet the obligations, an opportunity of profit will be open to them personally. . . . Indeed, in the present suit it is at least open to question whether a stronger effort might not have been made on the part of the management to procure for Acoustic the necessary funds or credit. Thus it appears that Deutsch owed Acoustic $125,000 on his note due February 2, 1928, and secured by collateral. No effort was made to collect it or to realize on the collateral. The directors contend that they took no action because Deutsch thought he had a defense to his note; but the validity of such defense, as well as whether the possibility of resorting to this asset was actually considered, is very doubtful. After April 9th no efforts appear to have been made to raise for Acoustic the $100,000 required for the De Forest stock. Moreover, Acoustic did have substantial banking accommodations on June 6th, and, if these had been made available a few weeks earlier, it would have been able to perform its contract with Reynolds & Co. While these facts raise some question whether Acoustic actually lacked the funds or credit necessary for carrying out its contract, we do not feel justified in reversing the District Court's finding that it did. Nevertheless, they tend to show the wisdom of a rigid rule forbidding directors of a solvent corporation to take over for their own profit a corporate contract on the plea of the corporation's financial inability to perform. If the directors are uncertain whether the corporation can make the necessary outlays, they need not embark it upon the venture; if they do, they may not substitute themselves for the corporation any place along the line and divert possible benefits into their own pockets.[121] . . .

The defendant Bell was Acoustic's agent in the original negotiations with Reynolds, and it is urged by the plaintiff that as such agent he was a fiduciary precluded from making profits out of the subject-matter of his agency. On his behalf it is contended that his agency was ended when he delivered to Acoustic the written offer of Reynolds & Co. and that his participation in the Biddle syndicate was not by virtue of his former agency relationship nor because of any information he had obtained as Acoustic's agent; that he stands like any stranger to whom the syndicate might have offered a participation. But, even if the fact of his agency be disregarded, we think there is an applicable principle which requires him to account, namely, that one who knowingly joins a fiduciary in an enterprise where the personal interest of the latter is or may be antagonistic to his trust becomes jointly and severally liable with him for the profits of the enterprise.[122] . . . Bell says that on April 7th or 9th he agreed with Mr. Deutsch that, if the latter was not successful in raising the purchase money for the stock from his own associates, he would join him to the extent of $25,000. This agreement, made at a time when the offer was still open for acceptance by the corporation, brings Bell within the principle above enunciated.

The defendant Stein was an employee of Acoustic, holding the position of chief engineer at the time he became a member of the Biddle syndicate. A mere employee of a corporation does not ordinarily occupy a position of trust or confidence toward his employer unless he is also an agent in respect to the matter under consideration. . . . Stein had no part, as did the directors, in binding the corporation to the contract to purchase the stock; nor can he be held on the principle applied to the defendant Bell. Shortly after the April 9th meeting Mr. Deutsch told him that the directors had decided that Acoustic did not have the funds to purchase the stock and that Deutsch, Biddle, Hammond, and others were to purchase it on their own account. Early in May Stein was informed that one of the participants, Mr. Dows, had withdrawn and he was asked to take stock thus made available. He consented because it might assist Acoustic to get access to the De Forest patents. So far as appears, Stein did not see the minutes of the April 9th meeting, and may well have understood from his conversation with Deutsch that the company had rejected Reynolds & Co.'s offer, and that the individuals had then made an independent contract with Reynolds & Co. He is not shown to have had affirmative knowledge that the directors with whom he joined were pursuing a course which would make their personal interests antagonistic to those of Acoustic. . . .

. . . The plaintiff also argues that Reynolds & Co. knowingly participated with the directors of Acoustic in the breach of their fiduciary duty. However, Reynolds & Co. had the right to sell to whomever it could, and, on being informed that Acoustic was not able to perform, it was justified on that information in making the sale to the syndicate. No right of Acoustic was violated in so doing, as Acoustic

---

121. Accord, Regal (Hastings), Ltd. v. Gulliver 1 All E.R. 378 (House of Lords 1942) ("without the assent of the shareholders," fiduciaries must account for such profits even though there is no "proof of mala fides"). — ED.

122. Accord, Higgins v. Shenango Pottery Co., 279 F.2d 46 (3d Cir. 1960); compare Aero Drapery of Ky., Inc. v. Engdahl, 507 S.W.2d 166 (Ky. Ct. App. 1974). — ED.

could demand the stock only on fulfilling its own obligation. Reynolds & Co. was not obliged to prejudice this opportunity to dispose of the stock nor to investigate scrupulously the intracorporate affairs of Acoustic. Since it received no benefit from the transaction aside from completing the sale of the stock and there is no proof that it acted in a conspiracy to deprive Acoustic of a valuable asset, it cannot be held to an accounting. . . .

For the foregoing reasons, the decree of dismissal is reversed as against Bell, Biddle, Deutsch and Hammond; as to the other defendants, it is affirmed.

---

1. *Financial inability.* (a) What result in the *Irving Trust* case if there were no question that "Acoustic actually lacked the funds or credit necessary for carrying out its contract"?[123] In what way, if any, would your answer be affected by the fact that the patents themselves, rather than merely access to them, were "essential" to Acoustic?

(b) Can there ever be instances in which a corporation cannot itself finance a seemingly profitable business opportunity? See Cox & Perry, Inc. v. Perry, 334 So. 2d 867 (Ala. 1976). Suppose that the directors of a corporation themselves construct and lease a plant to the corporation because "the corporation did not have the liquid funds available for the purpose of erecting a new plant" and, although the corporation "might have borrowed the money," the directors "were opposed to going into debt," since in their judgment the corporation "had weathered the depression largely because they had kept clear of bank loans and mortgages"? See Gauger v. Hintz, 262 Wis. 333, 55 N.W.2d 426 (1953).[124]

---

123. Most courts "afford the corporate fiduciary the opportunity to prove, as an affirmative defense, that the corporation lacked the financial ability to pursue the opportunity." Ostrowski v. Avery, 243 Conn. 355, 703 A.2d 117 (1997); Venturetek, L.P. v. Rand Publishing Co., 39 A.D. 3d 317, 833 N.Y.S.2d 93 (2007) ("it is clear that . . . Rand did not possess the financial capacity to purchase any of the four properties . . . [and under] Delaware law, a fiduciary may 'take a business opportunity for himself . . . if it is established that [the corporation] is not in a position to take it' "). See, e.g., Ellzey v. Fyr-Pruf, Inc., 376 So. 2d 1328 (Miss. 1979):

> We think *Irving Trust* too extreme. . . . On the other hand, we agree that a complainant's case should not be deemed deficient by reason of the corporation's financial inability if the fiduciary is unable to rebut complainant's evidence that such inability resulted either from the fiduciary's failure to pay a debt owing to the corporation or from his failure to exert his best efforts to prevent or cure the inability.
>
> A corporation may be insolvent in the balance sheet sense, temporarily insolvent in the equity sense, solvent but unable to obtain credit for lack of liquidity, etc. The degrees of "inability" are of utmost importance in business opportunity cases, because it may be that investors would look more favorably upon even a fledgling corporation if its fiduciaries had developed the business opportunity as one belonging to the corporation, rather than diverted their attentions and efforts to personal gains divorced from the welfare of the corporation to which their allegiance was wedded as a matter of law.

But cf. Graham v. Mimms, 111 Ill. App. 3d 751, 444 N.E.2d 549 (1982) (if fiduciary uses corporation's assets to develop an opportunity, it is a corporate opportunity despite corporation's financial incapacity to take advantage of it).

124. Defenses similar to the company's alleged financial inability to take the corporate opportunity include (a) the unwillingness of the third party to deal with the corporation, see Energy Resources Corp. v. Porter, 14 Mass. App. 296, 438 N.E.2d 391 (1982) (no defense unless third party's refusal to deal is first disclosed to the corporation); and (b) the corporation's legal incapacity to acquire the opportunity, see Kerrigan v. Unity Savings Ass'n, 58 Ill. 2d 20, 317 N.E.2d 39 (1974) (same analysis re disclosure).

2. *Assumption of corporation's contract.* (a) In the *Irving Trust* case, of what significance was the fact that "directors of a solvent corporation [took] over for their own
profit a corporate contract on the plea of the corporation's financial inability to
perform"?

(b) *Problem.* Director (D) of manufacturing corporation (C) learns in the course of
his duties that materials being purchased by C can be produced at a price lower than
C is paying. D forms his own business to produce these materials and profitably sells
them to C at a price lower than it had been paying. C sues D for the profits. D
contends that all of C's available space had been utilized for manufacturing, that
C had been behind in filling orders, and that for C to have produced materials would
have resulted in even further delays. What result under the *Irving Trust* case? What
should be the result? See Robinson v. Brier, 412 Pa. 255, 194 A.2d 204 (1963).

(c) *Problem.* Corporation C's supplier (S) offers C's director (D) a finder's fee if D
helps S to acquire C. When another company threatens a takeover of C, C hires an
investment banking firm to find more desirable buyers, but none can be found. D
then urges that C contact S, and S ultimately acquires C. Is D entitled to the finder's
fee? See Geller v. Allied-Lyons PLC, 42 Mass. App. Ct. 120, 674 N.E.2d 1334 (1997).

3. *Disclosure.* In the *Irving Trust* case, of what significance should it be that — as
found by the district court, 2 F. Supp. 971, 986 (S.D.N.Y. 1932) — "plaintiff cannot
successfully contend that there was not a full disclosure of the whole situation, of
which it now complains, at the April 9th meeting of the Acoustic board," at which
six directors were present, four of whom neither participating nor ever planning to
participate in the Biddle syndicate? Given this disclosure, what result under the
rationale of the *Regal* case? See Klinicki v. Lundgren, 296 Or. 662, 695 P.2d 906
(1985) (declining to follow the "rigid rule" of the *Irving Trust* case and adopting the
position of ALI, Principles of Corporate Governance, page 174 infra, that a director
may take a corporate opportunity that is disclosed to and rejected by a disinterested board); see also Lussier v. Mau-Van Development, Inc., 4 Hawaii Ct. App.
356, P.2d 804 (1983) ("there is no corporate opportunity if (1) the corporation is
financially unable to undertake it and (2) before a director or officer seizes such
opportunity for himself, he discloses the opportunity to the shareholders and
obtains their consent to the acquisition of the opportunity and such action is not
detrimental to corporate creditors").

4. *Shareholders' opportunity.* Even assuming that the corporation's inability to act
may permit directors personally to take an opportunity, should they be able to
do so without first offering it to the other shareholders pro rata? See Young v.
Columbia Oil Co., 110 W. Va. 364, 158 S.E. 678 (1931).

5. *Creditors' rights.* If the persons who are both the directors and shareholders of a
close corporation cause the corporation to reject a corporate opportunity and then
take it for themselves, may the corporation's creditors recover the profits for the
corporation if it subsequently becomes insolvent? Of what significance is the corporation's financial condition at the time that it rejects the opportunity? See In re
Safety Int'l, Inc., 775 F.2d 660 (5th Cir. 1985).

6. *Remedies.* (a) In addition to an accounting for profits, a remedy often granted
for appropriation of a corporate opportunity is the imposition of a constructive
trust — a device created by equity that obligates a person who wrongfully holds
property to transfer it to another.

(b) What should have been the amount of damages in the *Irving Trust* case if the
defendants had sold the shares that they were held to have wrongfully acquired at

a price lower than they might have obtained if they had sold at an earlier (or later) date? See Marcus v. Otis, 168 F.2d 649 (2d Cir. 1948). What should have been the amount of damages if the defendants, after selling the shares at a profit, had used the funds to make another, yet more profitable investment? Compare Winger v. Chicago City Bank & Trust Co., 394 Ill. 94, 67 N.E.2d 265 (1946) with Equity Corp. v. Groves, 294 N.Y. 8, 60 N.E.2d 19 (1945).

Rapistan Corp. v. Michaels
203 Mich. App. 301, 511 N.W.2d 918 (1994)

PER CURIAM: . . . In January 1987, Lear Siegler Holdings, a Delaware corporation, acquired Lear Siegler and its subsidiaries, which included Rapistan. Rapistan, also a Delaware corporation, is one of the nation's largest manufacturers and sellers of materials-handling conveyor equipment and systems. Rapistan's marketing focus is the warehouse-distribution market. At the time of the acquisition of Rapistan by Lear Siegler Holdings, Michaels, Tilton, and O'Neill were part of the management team at Rapistan. Specifically, Michaels was the president and chief executive officer of Rapistan. He also became a shareholder in Lear Siegler Holdings. Tilton served as the vice president of finance for Rapistan. O'Neill served as the vice president of marketing and sales. Michaels, Tilton, and O'Neill resigned their positions at Rapistan on September 6, 1988. The following day, the three former Rapistan executives signed employment agreements with Alvey Holdings, Inc., a corporation created by Raebarn, Inc., a merchant bank that arranges leveraged buyouts on its own behalf and on behalf of other investors, for the purpose of acquiring Alvey, Inc., a manufacturer of both conveyors and palletizers. A palletizer is a machine that stacks a uniform package into layers on a pallet for further conveyance or distribution. Approximately two-thirds of Alvey's business is the manufacture and sale of conveyors. The remaining one-third of Alvey's business is the manufacture and sale of palletizers. A palletizer has no application in the warehouse-distribution sector of the conveyor market. Instead, a palletizer is used in the industrial sector of the market, in such industries as food, beverage, and paper manufacturing. Raebarn and its investors acquired Alvey on August 26, 1988. At the time of trial, Michaels served as the president, chief executive officer, and chairman of the board of Alvey and Alvey Holdings. Tilton served as the chief financial officer of Alvey. O'Neill served as the senior vice president of sales and marketing at Alvey.

. . . Lear Siegler Holdings and Rapistan filed a complaint against Michaels, Tilton, O'Neill . . . [alleging] that the former Rapistan executives breached their fiduciary duties owed to Rapistan, misappropriated a Rapistan corporate opportunity, and misappropriated and misused confidential Rapistan information. . . .

The trial court . . . found that Michaels, Tilton, and O'Neill learned that Alvey was for sale in their capacities as individuals, not in their capacities as Rapistan managers, that the acquisition of Alvey was not essential to Rapistan, that there was no credible evidence that Rapistan had an expectation in Alvey, that Michaels, Tilton, and O'Neill had not embarked sufficient Rapistan corporate assets on the Alvey venture to require the intervention of equity to estop the executives from denying that Alvey was a Rapistan corporate opportunity, and that Lear Siegler Holdings and Rapistan had no cause of action against defendants. . . .

The seminal Delaware case regarding the doctrine of corporate opportunity is Guth [v. Loft, Inc., 23 Del. Ch. 255, 5 A.2d 503 (1939)]. The general principles of the corporate opportunity doctrine announced in *Guth* have since been referred to as the *Guth* Rule and the *Guth* Corollary. The *Guth* Rule provides: "[I]f there is presented to a corporate officer or a director a business opportunity which the corporation is financially able to undertake, is, from its nature, in the line of the corporation's business and is of practical advantage to it, is one in which the corporation has an interest or a reasonable expectancy, and, by embracing the opportunity, the self-interest of the officer or director will be brought into conflict with that of his corporation, the law will not permit him to seize the opportunity for himself." [23 Del. Ch. at 272-273, 5 A.2d 503.] On the other hand, the *Guth* Corollary provides: "It is true that when a business opportunity comes to a corporate officer or director in his individual capacity rather than in his official capacity, and the opportunity is one which, because of the nature of the enterprise, is not essential to his corporation, and is one in which it has no interest or expectancy, the officer or director is entitled to treat the opportunity as his own, and the corporation has no interest in it if, of course, the officer or director has not wrongfully embarked the corporation's resources therein." [23 Del. Ch. at 271, 5 A.2d 503.] See also Johnston v. Greene, 35 Del. Ch. 479, 485-486, 121 A.2d 919 (1956).

. . . First, a court, when determining whether a business opportunity is a corporate opportunity, must ascertain whether the opportunity was presented to a corporate officer in the officer's individual or representative capacity. Second, after determining the manner in which the opportunity was presented, the court must determine the nature of the opportunity. Third, the nature of the opportunity is analyzed differently, depending on whether the opportunity is presented to a corporate official in the official's individual or corporate representative capacity. *Guth*, supra 23 Del. Ch. at 271-280, 5 A.2d 503. Accordingly, we cannot say that the trial court committed legal error when it concluded that Delaware law required it to consider the capacity of the corporate officer at the time of the presentation of the opportunity as a factor in determining whether a corporate opportunity existed and when it concluded that Delaware law required it to view the nature of the opportunity in light of the capacity of the corporate officer when the opportunity was received.

We also . . . reject plaintiffs' assertion that the trial court erred as a matter of law when it failed to consider whether the acquisition of Alvey was desirable to Rapistan and when the court failed to recognize that its factual findings established the desirability of Alvey's acquisition by Rapistan. The *Guth* Corollary contains no requirement that the trial court examine the desirability of the opportunity. *Guth*, supra 23 Del. Ch. at 271, 5 A.2d 503.

We also reject the assertion that the trial court erred as a matter of law when it found that the opportunity to acquire Alvey was not "essential" to Rapistan. After reviewing the record evidence and the trial court's findings, we conclude that, although plaintiffs are correct in their belief that the business of Alvey was related to the business of Rapistan, the acquisition of Alvey was not so indispensably necessary to the conduct of the business of Rapistan that the deprivation of the acquisition threatened the viability of Rapistan. *Johnston*, supra 35 Del. Ch. at 485-486, 121 A.2d 919; Alexander & Alexander of New York, Inc. v. Fritzen, 147 A.D.2d 241, 248, 542 N.Y.S.2d 530 (1989); Black's Law Dictionary (5th ed.), p. 490.

We further reject the assertion that the trial court erred as a matter of law when it failed to recognize that its factual findings demonstrated that Rapistan had an expectation or interest in the acquisition of Alvey. We cannot conclude, after reviewing the trial court's findings, that those findings establish that Rapistan had any urgent or practical need to acquire Alvey, *Guth*, supra 23 Del. Ch. at 279, 5 A.2d 503, or that the acquisition of Alvey fit into an established corporate policy or into the particular business focus of Rapistan, *Equity Corp.*, supra 43 Del. Ch. at 164, 221 A.2d 494. See also *Alexander*, supra 147 A.D.2d at 247-248, 542 N.Y.S.2d 530.

We reject plaintiffs' assertion that the trial court substituted its judgment with regard to how important the Alvey acquisition would have been to Rapistan, thereby effectively adopting the claim of Michaels, Tilton, and O'Neill that Rapistan would not have been interested in the opportunity to acquire Alvey had they brought the opportunity to the attention of Rapistan and Lear Siegler Holdings. While it may be true that the best method for determining whether an opportunity is a corporate opportunity is to allow the corporation to decide at the time the opportunity is fully disclosed, see 3 Fletcher, Cyclopedia Corporations §861.1, p. 288, it does not follow from this truth that all a corporation claiming that an opportunity was usurped need do to establish the claim is assert that, had an opportunity been disclosed, it would have seized the opportunity.[125] Where a claim is raised that a corporate opportunity has been usurped, the claim is one for the trial court to resolve by reasonable inferences drawn from objective facts. . . .

Even though a business opportunity may not constitute a corporate opportunity under the conventional tests employed in determining whether a corporate opportunity exists, a corporate representative will be estopped nevertheless from denying that the business opportunity was a corporate opportunity if the representative wrongfully embarked the corporation's assets in the development or acquisition of the business opportunity. *Guth*, supra 23 Del. Ch. at 271, 5 A.2d 503. *Equity Corp.*, supra 43 Del. Ch. at 164, 221 A.2d 494; 3 Fletcher, Cyclopedia Corporations §861.1, p. 287. . . . The rationale behind this equitable rule was explained in greater detail in Graham v. Mimms, 111 Ill. App. 3d 751, 763-764, 67 Ill. Dec. 313, 444 N.E.2d 549 (1982), as follows:

> Nevertheless, the "core principle" of the corporate opportunity doctrine is that a corporation's fiduciary will not be permitted to usurp a business opportunity which was developed through the use of corporate assets. (Brudney and Clark, 94 Harv. L. Rev. 997, 1006 (1981).) "The principle rests on the same considerations that forbid appropriations of the assets themselves, but adds the remedy of tracing the misappropriated assets into their product — a conventional remedy in the law of trusts." (94 Harv. L. Rev. 997, 1007.) Therefore, when a corporation's fiduciary uses corporate assets to develop a business opportunity, the fiduciary is estopped from denying that the resulting opportunity belongs to the corporation whose assets were misappropriated, even if it was not feasible for the corporation to pursue the opportunity or it had no expectancy in the project. . . .

---

125. Accord, Broz v. Cellular Information Systems, Inc., 673 A.2d 148 (Del. 1996) ("although presenting the opportunity to the board creates a kind of 'safe harbor' for the director, which removes the specter of a post hoc judicial determination that the director or officer has improperly usurped a corporate opportunity . . . [i]t is not the law of Delaware that presentation to the board is a necessary prerequisite to a finding that a corporate opportunity has not been usurped"); Ostrowski v. Avery, footnote 123 supra (same under Connecticut law). — ED.

Generally speaking, estoppel is applied more consistently when "hard" assets, such as cash, facilities, and contracts, are used rather than when "soft" assets, such as good will, working time, and corporate information, are used. Id. at 1007. The use of hard assets is often dispositive of the usurpation-of-opportunity issue. Id. at 1007-1008. However, "the concept 'corporate asset' and its relationship to the opportunity being diverted become less clear when what is involved is the time of an executive or information about a new project discovered by an officer during, but not strictly within, the course of his employment." Id. at 1008-1009.

Our review of the record evidence leads us to the conclusion that Rapistan funds, facilities, personnel, and compensated time, in minimal amounts, were used by Michaels, Tilton, and O'Neill to further Raebarn's attempt to acquire Alvey once the opportunity was presented to Raebarn. However, we observe that the estoppel doctrine is based on equity. Fletcher, §861.1, p. 287. Further, the doctrine "operates somewhat unpredictably in practice" when the concept of corporate asset and its relationship to the opportunity being diverted become less clear. Brudney & Clark, supra at 1008-1009. Generally, it appears that estoppel applies where there has been a significant use of corporate assets by a fiduciary and where there is a direct and substantial nexus or causal connection between the assets embarked and the creation, pursuit, and acquisition of the business opportunity. See, e.g., *Graham*, supra 111 Ill. App. 3d at 763-764, 67 Ill. Dec. 313, 444 N.E.2d 549; Goodhue Farmers' Warehouse Co. v. Davis, 81 Minn. 210, 83 N.W. 531 (1900). Cf. *Guth*, supra. In the present case, the amount of assets embarked were minimal, especially in light of the $29.5 million cost of acquiring Alvey. Moreover, we find that the record evidence fails to demonstrate a direct and substantial nexus or causal connection between use of Rapistan assets and the creation, development, and acquisition of the Alvey opportunity. Lastly, the record evidence fails to establish that confidential or proprietary information was used by the former Rapistan executives. . . .

Affirmed.

Burg v. Horn
380 F.2d 897 (2d Cir. 1967)

LUMBARD, C.J.: . . . Darand [Realty Corp.] was incorporated in September 1953 with a capital of $5500, subscribed equally by the three stockholders, Mrs. Burg and George and Max Horn, all of whom became directors, and immediately purchased a low-rent building in Brooklyn. The Horns, who were engaged in the produce business and had already acquired three similar buildings in Brooklyn through wholly-owned corporations, urged the Burgs, who were close friends then also residing in Brooklyn, to get "get their feet wet" in real estate, and the result was the formation of Darand. The Burgs testified that they expected the Horns to offer any low-rent properties they found in Brooklyn to Darand, but that there was no discussion or agreement to that effect. The Horns carried on the active management of Darand's properties, and the plaintiff's husband, Louis Burg, an accountant who became an attorney in 1957, handled its accounting and tax planning. The stockholders generally drew equal amounts from Darand at the end of each taxable year, and then immediately repaid them to "loan accounts," from which they could draw when they desired.

Darand sold its first property and acquired another in 1956, and purchased two more buildings in 1959. From 1953 to 1963, nine similar properties were purchased by the Horns, individually or through wholly-owned corporations. One, purchased by Max Horn in 1954 and sold in 1955, was partly paid for by loans of $600 from Darand and $2000 from Louis Burg. Two others, acquired in 1955 by a corporation wholly owned by the Horns, were paid for in part by a loan of $200 from Darand to the wholly-owned corporation and, apparently, by loans aggregating $4250 from Louis Burg to Max Horn. The Burgs testified that they did not know the purposes of these loans, and that, while they knew of the Horns' ownership of some of the properties they now contend were corporate opportunities of Darand, they thought they had been acquired before 1953.

. . . [Mrs. Burg brought suit on behalf of Darand seeking the imposition of a constructive trust on the alleged corporate opportunities. District Judge Dooling found] that there was no agreement that all low-rent buildings found by the Horns should be offered to Darand, and that the Burgs were aware of the purposes of the loans from Darand and Louis Burg and of at least some of the Horns' post-1953 acquisitions. He therefore declined to hold that those acquisitions were corporate opportunities of Darand. . . .

Plaintiff apparently contends that defendants were as a matter of law under a duty to acquire for Darand further properties like those it was operating. She is seemingly supported by several commentators, who have stated that any opportunity within a corporation's "line of business" is a corporate opportunity. E.g., Note, Corporate Opportunity, 74 Harv. L. Rev. 765, 768-69 (1961); Note, A Survey of Corporate Opportunity, 45 Geo. L.J. 99, 100-01 (1956). This statement seems to us too broad a generalization. We think that under New York law a court must determine in each case, by considering the relationship between the director and the corporation, whether a duty to offer the corporation all opportunities within its "line of business" is fairly to be implied. Had the Horns been full-time employees of Darand with no prior real estate ventures of their own, New York law might well uphold a finding that they were subject to such an implied duty. But as they spent most of their time in unrelated produce and real estate enterprises and already owned corporations holding similar properties when Darand was formed, as plaintiff knew, we agree with Judge Dooling that a duty to offer Darand all such properties coming to their attention cannot be implied absent some further evidence of an agreement or understanding to that effect. Judge Dooling's finding that there was no such understanding is not clearly erroneous. . . .

Affirmed.

HAYS, J. (dissenting): My brothers hold that the scope of a director's duty to his corporation must be measured by the facts of each case. However, although they are unable to find any New York case presenting the same facts as those before us, they conclude that New York law does not support the imposition of liability in the circumstances of this case. I do not agree.

In an often quoted passage, the New York Court of Appeals laid down the principles of fiduciary conduct:

> Many forms of conduct permissible in a workaday world for those acting at arm's length, are forbidden to those bound by fiduciary ties. A trustee is held to something stricter than the morals of the market place. Not honesty alone, but the punctilio of an

honor the most sensitive, is then the standard of behavior. As to this there has developed a tradition that is unbending and inveterate. Uncompromising rigidity has been the attitude of courts of equity when petitioned to undermine the rule of undivided loyalty by the "disintegrating erosion" of particular exceptions. . . . Only thus has the level of conduct for fiduciaries been kept at a level higher than that trodden by the crowd.

Meinhard v. Salmon, 249 N.Y. 458, 464, 164 N.E. 545, 546, 62 A.L.R. 1 (1928). . . .

Applying these standards to the instant case it seems clear that in the absence of a contrary agreement or understanding between the parties, the Horns, who were majority stockholders and managing officers of the Darand Corporation and whose primary function was to locate suitable properties for the company, were under a fiduciary obligation to offer such properties to Darand before buying the properties for themselves. . . .

———————

In Alexander & Alexander of N.Y., Inc. v. Fritzen, cited in the *Rapistan* case, defendant executives of plaintiff property and casualty insurance brokerage firm (AGR) learned that plaintiff's major client needed life insurance for its employees. Although plaintiff was not licensed to sell life insurance, "it easily could have obtained the required license." The defendants formed their own company and earned over $750,000 for sales to the client. Held no corporate opportunity:

> It is essentially the employer's prerogative, not the employee's, to make the strategic decision to expand into a related but new line of business and to convey this to its employees. Irrespective of knowledge of a particular customer's need for the related product or service, the employer should be the one to determine whether or not to expand. Without any indication from the employer an employee simply has insufficient guidance to render it appropriate for him (her) to bear the risk of the employer's later claim against him (her) based upon an undeclared intent.
>
> Here, AGR made no showing of an expectancy, tangible or otherwise, in the life insurance business, that such business was essential or necessary to its success, or even that there was a likelihood that had defendants not obtained such life insurance business, such business would have been realized by it.[126]

———————

1. *Burden of proof.* Which of the parties should have borne the burden of proof in *Rapistan* as to whether the opportunity was first presented to Michaels, Tilton, and O'Neill in their capacities as individuals or as corporate representatives, and in *Burg* as to (a) whether an agreement or understanding concerning low-rent properties that came to the Horns' attention existed, and (b) if there was no such original agreement or understanding, whether the Burgs knew of or acquiesced in the Horns' independent purchases? See Miller v. Miller, 301 Minn. 207, 227, 222 N.W.2d 71, 82 (1974). In Ostrowski v. Avery, footnote 123 supra, the court stated: "[P]laintiff bears the burden of establishing: (1) a fiduciary relationship between

---

126. Compare Kerrigan v. Unity Savings Ass'n, footnote 124 supra (controlling directors of mortgage loan corporation, who organized a homeowners' insurance company to which borrowers were referred for purchase of insurance, held liable for taking a corporate opportunity). — ED.

the corporation and the alleged wrongdoers; and (2) the existence of a corporate opportunity. Once a plaintiff establishes these predicates to liability, the burden then shifts to the fiduciaries to establish, by clear and convincing evidence, the fairness of their dealings with the corporation."

2. *"Expectancy" — "necessity" — "indispensability" vs. "line of business."* (a) How would the court in Burg v. Horn have decided the *Rapistan* and *Alexander* cases?

(b) *Problem.* Realtor (R) suggested certain land for development to X, one of Corporation's (C's) officers. X took no action because she did not think C would be interested. Several months later, X was terminated. X then formed her own company (Y) and asked R about available land. R mentioned the same property. X caused Y to purchase and develop the land. C seeks to impose a constructive trust. See Today Homes, Inc. v. Williams, 272 Va. 462, 634 S.E.2d 737 (2006).

(c) If the directors of a conglomerate corporation (or an investment company) that is actively seeking profitable expansion opportunities (or valuable investments) learn of an attractive opportunity, may they take it for themselves? Of what significance should it be that the directors contend that they learned of this opportunity in their individual capacities? Cf. Lincoln Stores, Inc. v. Grant, 309 Mass. 417, 34 N.E.2d 704 (1941); compare Rosenblum v. Judson Engr. Corp. 99 N.H. 267, 109 A.2d 558 (1954).

(d) *Problem.* Drake is a director and the president and general manager of Beer Corporation, a successful producer and distributor of beer, which has been interested in acquiring related businesses. Drake is also a director of Bottle Corporation, a financially troubled manufacturer of glass bottles, which has been desperately seeking to acquire large users of its products as captive customers. Drake learns of the availability of a popular soft drink distributorship in the vicinity. What are Drake's obligations with respect to this opportunity?[127]

3. *Problem.* Assume in the *Rapistan* case that defendants learned of the Alvey opportunity as corporate representatives, that defendants then made full disclosure to the Lear Siegler directors, and that defendants then personally competed with Lear Siegler in bidding for Alvey. What result if (a) defendants obtain control of Alvey and Lear Siegler seeks to impose a constructive trust; (b) Lear Siegler obtains control of Alvey and sues defendants for the additional amount it paid because of defendants' bidding? See Patient Care Services v. Segal, 32 Ill. App. 3d, 337 N.E.2d 471 (1975).[128]

4. *Proposed codification.*

---

127. See Johnston v. Greene, cited in the *Rapistan* case. RMBCA §8.62(b) (1989) authorizes the possibility of limited disclosure under similar circumstances.

128. See Victor Brudney & Robert C. Clark, A New Look at Corporate Opportunities, 94 Harv. L. Rev. 997 (1981), for the view that, although a "selective rule" may be appropriate for corporate opportunities in close corporations, a "categorical rule" should "control the fiduciaries of public corporations": "full-time officers or executives" should be forbidden from "acquiring profitable businesses with a rate of return and risk level no worse than that of . . . [their corporation's] other operations." For the view that the presumption ("default rule") — in the absence of a clear understanding — should be to allow directors of a close corporation to take many corporate opportunities for themselves, see Richard A. Epstein, Contract and Trust in Corporate Law: The Case of Corporate Opportunity, 21 Del. J. Corp. L. 5 (1996). For the view that even in public corporations, certain circumstances, from which "an express contract . . . would plausibly emerge from ex ante bargaining, . . . actually provide a rationale for *instituting* incentive schemes, which by nature may consciously permit the fiduciary to divert at least some projects for her own account," see Eric Talley, Turning Servile Opportunities to Gold: A Strategic Analysis of the Corporate Opportunities Doctrine, 108 Yale L.J. 277 (1998).

American Law Institute, Principles of Corporate Governance (1994)

Sec. 5.05. *Taking of corporate opportunities by directors or senior executives.*
(a) *General rule.* A director or senior executive may not take advantage of a corporate opportunity unless:

(1) The director or senior executive first offers the corporate opportunity to the corporation and makes disclosure concerning the conflict of interest and the corporate opportunity;

(2) The corporate opportunity is rejected by the corporation;[129] and

(3) Either:

(A) The rejection of the opportunity is fair to the corporation;

(B) The opportunity is rejected in advance, following such disclosure, by disinterested directors, or, in the case of a senior executive who is not a director, by a disinterested superior, in a manner that satisfies the standards of the business judgment rule; or

(C) The rejection is authorized in advance or ratified, following such disclosure, by disinterested shareholders, and the rejection is not equivalent to a waste of corporate assets.

(b) *Definition of a corporate opportunity.* For purposes of this Section, a corporate opportunity means:

(1) Any opportunity to engage in a business activity of which a director or senior executive becomes aware, either:

(A) In connection with the performance of functions as a director or senior executive, or under circumstances that should reasonably lead the director or senior executive to believe that the person offering the opportunity expects it to be offered to the corporation; or

(B) Through the use of corporate information or property, if the resulting opportunity is one that the director or senior executive should reasonably be expected to believe would be of interest to the corporation; or

(2) Any opportunity to engage in a business activity of which a senior executive becomes aware and knows is closely related to a business in which the corporation is engaged or expects to engage.

(c) *Burden of proof.* A party who challenges the taking of a corporate opportunity has the burden of proof, except that if such party establishes that the requirements of Subsection (a)(3)(B) or (C) are not met, the director or the senior executive has the burden of proving that the rejection and the taking of the opportunity were fair to the corporation. . . . [130]

---

129. Accord, Imperial Group (Texas), Inc. v. Scholnick, 709 S.W.2d 358 (Tex. Civ. App. 1986) ("if an opportunity is within the scope of a corporation's business, then the only acceptable method of determining whether a corporation would take advantage of the opportunity is by complete disclosure of the opportunity to it"; "an after-the-fact finding by the trier of the facts that the corporation was unable to take advantage of or would have rejected the business opportunity" is inadequate). For the same principle, see Demoulas v. Demoulas Super Markets, Inc., 424 Mass. 501, 677 N.E.2d 159 (1977); Northeast Harbor Golf Club, Inc. v. Harris, 661 A.2d 1146 (Me. 1995). For discussion of recent cases cited here and in footnote 125 supra, see Harvey Gelb, The Corporate Opportunity Doctrine — Recent Cases and the Elusive Goal of Clarity, 31 U. Rich. L. Rev. 371 (1997). — ED.

130. For the view that existing doctrine does not adequately "acknowledge competing societal and individual interests," see Pat K. Chew, Competing Interests in the Corporate Opportunity Doctrine, 67 N.C. L. Rev. 435 (1989): "Opportunities to which both the fiduciaries and the corporation have legitimate interests . . . should not be deemed automatically to belong to the corporation. . . . [To do so] would gradually discourage fiduciaries from cultivating entrepreneurial instincts and skills in general.

Revised Model Business Corporation Act (2005)

Sec. 8.70. *Business opportunities.* (a) A director's taking advantage, directly or indirectly, of a business opportunity may not be the subject of equitable relief, or give rise to an award of damages or other sanctions against the director, in a proceeding by or in the right of the corporation on the ground that such opportunity should have first been offered to the corporation, if before becoming legally obligated respecting the opportunity the director brings it to the attention of the corporation and:

(1) action by qualified directors disclaiming the corporation's interest in the opportunity is taken in compliance with the procedures set forth in section 8.62, as if the decision being made concerned a director's conflicting interest transaction, or

(2) shareholders' action disclaiming the corporation's interest in the opportunity is taken in compliance with the procedures set forth in section 8.63, as if the decision being made concerned a director's conflicting interest transaction; except that, rather than making "required disclosure" as defined in section 8.60, in each case the director shall have made prior disclosure to those acting on behalf of the corporation of all material facts concerning the business opportunity that are then known to the director.

(b) In any proceeding seeking equitable relief or other remedies based upon an alleged improper taking advantage of a business opportunity by a director, the fact that the director did not employ the procedure described in subsection (a) before taking advantage of the opportunity shall not create an inference that the opportunity should have been first presented to the corporation in the circumstances.

---

5. *Competing with the corporation.* A number of cases distinguish between corporate officers and corporate employees. In Veco Corp. v. Babcock, 243 Ill. App. 3d 153, 611 N.E.2d 1054 (1993), the court stated: "In general, employees may plan, form, and outfit a competing corporation while still working for the employer, but may not commence competition. . . . Corporate officers, however, stand on a different footing; they owe a fiduciary duty of loyalty to their corporate employer not to (1) actively exploit their positions within the corporation for their own personal benefit, or (2) hinder the ability of a corporation to continue the business for which it was developed." See also Aero Drapery of Ky., Inc. v. Engdahl, 507 S.W.2d 166 (Ky. Ct. App. 1974) (office manager, workroom manager, and salesman not liable for entering competing business, but officer's "fiduciary position obligated him not to develop interest antagonistic to Aero without full disclosure").[131]

Consequently, opportunities that might have led to great benefit for corporations and society would go unnoticed by fiduciaries who have not developed sensitivity to potential opportunities." — ED.

131. Accord, Craig v. Graphic Arts Studio, Inc., 39 Del. Ch. 447, 166 A.2d 444 (Ch. 1960). Compare Ellis & Marshall Associates, Inc. v. Marshall, 16 Ill. App. 3d 398, 306 N.E.2d 712 (1974) (fact that defendant, who had been one of "the two principal officers and directors of the plaintiff corporation," did no more "than inform certain clients of his intention to leave plaintiff's employ" and of his desire to then do business with them "was not a breach of his fiduciary duty to the plaintiff corporation"), with Smith-Shrader Co. v. Smith, 136 Ill. App. 3d 571, 483 N.E.2d 283 (1985) (defendant's "degree of solicitation transcends mere commentary on possible future plans"). See also Regenstein v. J. Regenstein Co., 213 Ga. 157, 97 S.E.2d 693 (1957) ("corporate officers and directors, so long as they act in good faith

ALI, Principles of Corporate Governance §5.06 forbids competition by directors and senior executives that disadvantage their corporation unless "authorized in advance or ratified, following disclosure. . . ."

---

toward their company and its associates, are not precluded from engaging in a business similar to that carried on by their corporation, either on their own behalf or for another corporation of which they are likewise directors or officers"); Maryland Metals, Inc. v. Metzner, 282 Md. 31, 382 A.2d 564 (1978) (corporate officers "are privileged to make arrangements to compete even while they remain on their employer's payroll"; corporation must show that defendant officers "had been guilty of unfair, fraudulent or wrongful conduct beyond the mere failure to disclose, which impacted on the economic interest of" corporation). Accord, Franklin Music Co. v. American Broadcasting Cos., 616 F.2d 528 (3d Cir. 1979) (applying Pennsylvania law). See also United Seal and Rubber Co. v. Bunting, 248 Ga. 814, 285 S.E.2d 721 (1982) (directors and officers do not usurp corporate opportunity when they resign and then solicit business from those corporation customers who had generated half of corporation's revenues).

III AN INTRODUCTION TO CORPORATE FINANCE

A corporation acquires real *assets* — tangible assets like manufacturing plants and intangible assets like patents and copyrights — with funds provided by investors in return for financial assets, like common stock or debt. These financial assets give their holders certain rights with respect to the corporation's real assets, including rights to share in the income earned from them in the appreciation in the value of the corporation's business, and to participate in the corporation's decisionmaking. These financial assets are bought and sold in the *capital market*, made up of stock exchanges like the New York, American, and London Stock Exchanges; over-the-counter markets like Nasdaq; and direct investment by, and trading among, large institutions, often with the help of financial intermediaries such as brokerage firms, investment banks, and commercial banks (or computerized trading systems like Instinet and Posit that allow institutional investors to trade without the use of an intermediary). Because the value of financial assets depends on the value of the real assets on which they have claims, the capital market, in valuing financial assets, in effect seeks to value the corporation's real assets.[1] This results in a coincidence of goals for the corporation and those who have invested in it. The corporation seeks to increase the value of its real assets (which we now will refer to simply as the value of the corporation) because that reduces the amount of financial assets it must provide investors to secure a given amount of funds. In turn, investors want the value of the corporation to increase because that increases the value of their holdings of the corporation's financial

---

1. The extent to which capital market valuation of the financial assets issued by a corporation differs from the fundamental value of its real assets will be considered infra in the discussion of market efficiency in Sec. A.3 of this chapter.

assets, which the investors can sell in the capital market. In short, the shared goal is to increase the value of the corporation.

This is where corporate law comes in. Corporate law provides much of the framework for the effort to increase the value of the corporation. Some rules concern how a corporation makes decisions concerning its business: who makes the decisions, how the decisions are monitored, and what happens if the decisions turn out badly. Others concern the relation among investors holding different kinds of financial assets, with different and sometimes competing financial claims on the corporation's real assets. Since corporate law seeks to provide an environment in which the corporation's value can be maximized, there is an important standard by which it should be assessed: Does a particular rule serve to increase the value of the corporation?

Finally, disputes about value underlie most corporate law litigation: the plaintiff claims that the defendant's action (or inaction) reduced the value of the corporation or the value of the plaintiff's particular financial asset. Therefore, how the capital market values a corporation's real and financial assets provides a critical foundation for the study of corporate law. Valuation explicates the mechanism through which the goal of corporate law must be achieved, a performance measure for the effort, and a test of the causal link — that a particular action resulted in an increase or decrease in corporate value — inherent in corporate law litigation.

The importance of understanding valuation brings us to the subject of this chapter — the study of corporate finance, a central focus of which is how the capital market values financial assets. Section A takes up the valuation of a financial asset (such as the common stock of a corporation) in the artificially simple world when there is no uncertainty in the returns expected from it. In this circumstance, value is a function of the time value of money operationalized by the concept of discounting to present value. We then turn to valuation in the real world by introducing the concept of risk (that is, uncertainty in the returns expected from the asset) and diversification (that is, how holding more than one asset reduces risk). Building on this base, we take up the *capital asset pricing model*, financial economics' normative paradigm of how assets are valued. The introduction to asset pricing closes with a consideration of the *efficient capital market hypothesis* — the proposition that the value actually assigned to a financial asset by the capital market is the best estimate of the value of the corporation's real assets — and a brief consideration of behavioral finance, a recent but increasingly strident challenge to traditional corporate finance precepts. A note of warning: corporate finance is a technically challenging branch of microeconomics whose surface is barely scratched here. Those who decide to pursue the study of corporate law will do well to pursue the study of corporate finance as well.[2]

Section B considers the impact of capital structure on the value of a corporation: does the kind of financial assets issued by a corporation affect the value of the corporation's real assets? Here the focus is on the *Modigliani-Miller irrelevance*

---

2. A wide variety of texts are available. Ronald Gilson & Bernard Black, (Some of) the Essentials of Finance and Investment (1993) and William Klein & John Coffee, Business Organization and Finance (10th ed. 2007) are designed for lawyers. Other texts, of varying technical sophistication, include James Van Home, Financial Management and Policy (12th ed. 2007); Richard Brealey, Stewart Myers & Franklin Allen, Principles of Corporate Finance (8th ed. 2006); Stephen Ross, Randolph Westerfield & Jeffrey Jaffe, Corporate Finance (8th ed. 2007).

proposition — the idea that the value of a corporation is invariant with respect to the proportion of its financial assets that are debt and equity — and the circumstances when irrelevance should not hold.

Section C turns to the problem of relations among holders of different kinds of financial assets. While asset pricing theory concerns what factors determine the size of the pie, here the concern is with how the pie is divided among different holders and the potential that the expected method of the pie's division may affect its size. We introduce another paradigm of corporate finance — *option pricing theory* — because it provides a powerful tool to predict how the holders of one kind of financial asset will act to increase the value of their holding at the expense of holders of the corporation's other financial assets. Section D then considers the statutory, contractual, and judicial protections against efforts by shareholders to take advantage of debt holders.

A. *VALUATION: HOW ARE FINANCIAL ASSETS VALUED?*

1. VALUATION UNDER CERTAINTY: PRESENT VALUE AND THE TIME VALUE OF MONEY

Assume the artificially simple situation where no uncertainty exists concerning the size and timing of the cash flows associated with an asset. The amount to be received and the date on which it will be received are certain. The closest real-world equivalent to such a financial asset is a U.S. government bond, where, if one assumes away inflation, there is complete certainty about the payments. In this setting, the value of the asset depends only on the time value — in effect, on the opportunity cost — of money.

William A. Klein & John C. Coffee Jr., Business Organization and Finance
322-327 (10th ed. 2007)

Discounted Present Value

1. *Single amounts.* Given the fact of a positive rate of interest, a specified amount of money available to you today is worth more than a claim to the same amount of money in the future. This is true regardless of your inclination to save or consume. Suppose, for example, that if you were to receive $1,000 today you would not spend it but would instead save it for a trip to Europe a year from today. Even though you don't plan to spend the money until next year, you are still better off to receive it today — for the obvious reason that you can earn interest on it in the meantime. Suppose that you can make a risk-free investment (for example, in an insured savings account) at 8 percent. On that assumption, the $1,000 received today will be worth $1,080 a year hence. Turning that around, $1,080 to be received one year hence has a *present value* — often referred to somewhat redundantly as a *discounted present value* — of $1,000. If the $1,000 were to be received not today but, instead, one year from now, its present value would be $926 (determined by the

process to be described immediately below). The $926 is the amount which, if invested at 8 percent, would grow to $1,000 at the end of one year.

More generally, the present value of a future sum is simply the amount that one must invest today at the appropriate interest rate in order to have the future sum at the future date. Algebraically, then, for an amount to be received one year hence,

$$P(1+r) = A$$

where P means the present amount, r means the annual interest rate, and A means the future amount. To solve for P, we write the formula,

$$P = \frac{A}{1+r}$$

Thus, if the future amount is $1,000 and the interest rate is 8 percent, the formula yields,

$$P = \frac{\$1,000}{1+.08} = \frac{1,000}{1.08} = \$926$$

If the payment is to be received two years, rather than one year, from today, then, assuming annual compounding, the formula is:

$$P = \frac{A}{(1+r)(1+r)} = \frac{A}{(1+r)^2}$$

More generally,

$$P_n = \frac{A}{(1+r)^n}$$

where n is the number of years to maturity.

Table 5-1 shows the present value of $1 at various years in the future at various interest rates.

To determine the value of an amount greater than $1, one simply multiplies by the number of dollars. For example, the present value of $1, to be received one year from today, assuming an interest rate of 8 percent, is $.926. Correspondingly, the present value of $1,000 to be received one year from today at 8 percent is $926. The present value of the same amount two years from today, same interest rate, is $857. The present value of $1,000 to be received nine years from today, at 8 percent, is $500. . . .

2. *Annuities.* An annuity, as traditionally defined, is a finite series of annual payments of a specified amount for a specified number of years. Suppose that you have the right to receive $1,000 one year from today plus $1,000 two years from today — a two-year annuity. The present value is obviously the combined value of each of the two payments. As we saw above, the present value of the first payment is $926, of the second payment $857. The total is $1783. Table 5-2 shows present values for a series of year-end payments for various lengths of time at

Table 5-1
PRESENT VALUE OF $1: WHAT A DOLLAR AT END OF SPECIFIED FUTURE YEAR IS WORTH TODAY

Year	3%	4%	5%	6%	7%	8%	10%	12%	15%	20%	Year
1	.971	.962	.952	.943	.935	.926	.909	.893	.870	.833	1
2	.943	.925	.907	.890	.873	.857	.826	.797	.756	.694	2
3	.915	.889	.864	.840	.816	.794	.751	.712	.658	.579	3
4	.889	.855	.823	.792	.763	.735	.683	.636	.572	.482	4
5	.863	.822	.784	.747	.713	.681	.620	.567	.497	.402	5
6	.837	.790	.746	.705	.666	.630	.564	.507	.432	.335	6
7	.813	.760	.711	.665	.623	.583	.513	.452	.376	.279	7
8	.789	.731	.677	.627	.582	.540	.467	.404	.327	.233	8
9	.766	.703	.645	.592	.544	.500	.424	.361	.284	.194	9
10	.744	.676	.614	.558	.508	.463	.386	.322	.247	.162	10
11	.722	.650	.585	.527	.475	.429	.350	.287	.215	.135	11
12	.701	.625	.557	.497	.444	.397	.319	.257	.187	.112	12
13	.681	.601	.530	.469	.415	.368	.290	.229	.163	.0935	13
14	.661	.577	.505	.442	.388	.340	.263	.205	.141	.0779	14
15	.642	.555	.481	.417	.362	.315	.239	.183	.123	.0649	15
16	.623	.534	.458	.394	.339	.292	.218	.163	.107	.0541	16
17	.605	.513	.436	.371	.317	.270	.198	.146	.093	.0451	17
18	.587	.494	.416	.350	.296	.250	.180	.130	.0808	.0376	18
19	.570	.475	.396	.331	.277	.232	.164	.116	.0703	.0313	19
20	.554	.456	.377	.312	.258	.215	.149	.104	.0611	.0261	20
25	.478	.375	.295	.233	.184	.146	.0923	.0588	.0304	.0105	25
30	.412	.308	.231	.174	.131	.0994	.0573	.0334	.0151	.00421	30
40	.307	.208	.142	.0972	.067	.0460	.0221	.0107	.00373	.000680	40
50	.228	.141	.087	.0543	.034	.0213	.00852	.00346	.000922	.000109	50

various assumed interest rates. . . . Using this table we could compute that the present value of $1,000 at the end of each year for two years would be $1,780 ($1,000 × 1.78). (This is slightly inaccurate because of rounding off of the numbers in the table.) The present value of the same payment for five years would be $3,990. . . .

The present value is the financial equivalent of the series of future payments. Thus, if you have the right to $1,000 per year for five years, in the absence of transaction costs you should be able to sell that claim for $3,990. If you have $3,990 you should be able to trade it for the right to annual payments of $1,000 for five years. And if you want to borrow $3,990, you should be able to do so if you are willing to pay $1,000 per year for five years. . . .

3. *Illustrations*: *Projects or ventures; Net Present Value Method*. Suppose that a firm contemplates entering into a new venture that will require an initial capital outlay or investment of $1,000,000; an additional capital outlay of $200,000 at the end of the first year; and another capital outlay of $300,000 at the end of the second year. Suppose that during the first year the total revenue generated by the project will just equal the operating costs associated with that revenue; at the end of the second year, revenue will exceed current costs by $200,000; and that for every year thereafter revenue will exceed current costs by $300,000, until

Table 5-2
PRESENT VALUE OF ANNUITY OF $1, RECEIVED AT END OF EACH YEAR

Year	3%	4%	5%	6%	7%	8%	10%	12%	15%	20%	Year
1	0.971	0.960	0.952	0.943	0.935	0.926	0.909	0.890	0.870	0.833	1
2	1.91	1.89	1.86	1.83	1.81	1.78	1.73	1.69	1.63	1.53	2
3	2.83	2.78	2.72	2.67	2.62	2.58	2.48	2.40	2.28	2.11	3
4	3.72	3.63	3.55	3.46	3.39	3.31	3.16	3.04	2.86	2.59	4
5	4.58	4.45	4.33	4.21	4.10	3.99	3.79	3.60	3.35	2.99	5
6	5.42	5.24	5.08	4.91	4.77	4.62	4.35	4.11	3.78	3.33	6
7	6.23	6.00	5.79	5.58	5.39	5.21	4.86	4.56	4.16	3.60	7
8	7.02	6.73	6.46	6.20	5.97	5.75	5.33	4.97	4.49	3.84	8
9	7.79	7.44	7.11	6.80	6.52	6.25	5.75	5.33	4.78	4.03	9
10	8.53	8.11	7.72	7.36	7.02	6.71	6.14	5.65	5.02	4.19	10
11	9.25	8.76	8.31	7.88	7.50	7.14	6.49	5.94	5.23	4.33	11
12	9.95	9.39	8.86	8.38	7.94	7.54	6.81	6.19	5.41	4.44	12
13	10.6	9.99	9.39	8.85	8.36	7.90	7.10	6.42	5.65	4.53	13
14	11.3	10.6	9.90	9.29	8.75	8.24	7.36	6.63	5.76	4.61	14
15	11.9	11.1	10.4	9.71	9.11	8.56	7.60	6.81	5.87	4.68	15
16	12.6	11.6	10.8	10.1	9.45	8.85	7.82	6.97	5.96	4.73	16
17	13.2	12.2	11.3	10.4	9.76	9.12	8.02	7.12	6.03	4.77	17
18	13.8	12.7	11.7	10.8	10.1	9.37	8.20	7.25	6.10	4.81	18
19	14.3	13.1	12.1	11.1	10.3	9.60	8.36	7.37	6.17	4.84	19
20	14.9	13.6	12.5	11.4	10.6	9.82	8.51	7.47	6.23	4.87	20
25	17.4	15.6	14.1	12.8	11.7	10.7	9.08	7.84	6.46	4.95	25
30	19.6	17.3	15.4	13.8	12.4	11.3	9.43	8.06	6.57	4.98	30
40	23.1	19.8	17.2	15.0	13.3	11.9	9.78	8.24	6.64	5.00	40
50	25.7	21.5	18.3	15.8	13.8	12.2	9.91	8.30	6.66	5.00	50

the end of the twentieth year, when the useful life of the physical assets will end, the project will be terminated, and the assets will be sold for their scrap value, estimated to be $100,000. Finally, suppose that the appropriate discount rate is 15 percent. We can determine the value of the project by first discounting all capital outlays (other than the initial outlay of $1,000,000) to present value, as follows:

Outlays

Amount	End of Year	Present Value
$200,000	1	$174,000
300,000	2	$226,800
		$400,800

To compute the present value of the receipts, first note that the project will yield $300,000 per year for 18 years beginning at the end of the third year. To find the present value of this element, first compute the value of an 18-year annuity of $300,000 at 15 percent. The entry in Table 5-2 for 18 years and 15 percent is 6.10; this is multiplied by $300,000, giving us a present value of $1,830,000. This amount is the value as of the *beginning* of the third year, which is the same as the end of the second year. In other words, the table gives the value at the beginning of any year for an annuity whose first payment is to be received at the end of the year. This being so, the $1,830,000 must be treated as an amount to be received two years hence. We discount it to present value by using the entry in Table 5-1 for 2 years and 15 percent (.756). The result is $1,383,480. In addition, there is the $200,000 to be realized at the end of the second year and the $100,000 to be realized at the end of the 20th year. The total present value of the combined receipts is as follows:

Receipts

Amount	End of Year	Present Value
$ 200,000	2	$ 151,200
1,830,000	2	1,383,480
100,000	20	6,110
		$1,540,790

The present value of revenues or receipts ($1,540,790) exceeds the present value of outlays ($400,800) by $1,139,990. This is the present value of the project or venture. ... If we subtract the $1,000,000 initial cost from the present value of the project we arrive at the net present value. Here there is a positive *net present value*. The project is a good one, producing a present-value gain of $139,990 on an investment of $1,000,000. ...

The net present value (NPV) method of valuation has become a basic technique for investment analysis by firms. It can also be used for valuation of the firm itself. It takes account of the cost of money (or the required return) and produces an answer to the question whether a project is worthwhile or not. It will also indicate which of two or more projects of equal size is the most profitable.

Problem. A corporation has the opportunity to invest in one of two alternative projects. Project A costs $100,000 immediately and results in returns of $50,000 at the end of years 3, 4, and 5. Project B also costs $100,000 at the outset but results in returns of $75,000 at the end of year 3 and $25,000 at the end of years 4 and 5. What is the present value and net present value of each project assuming a discount rate of 15 percent? What if the discount rate is 10 percent?

2. VALUATION UNDER UNCERTAINTY: RISK AND DIVERSIFICATION

The next step in understanding the valuation of financial assets is to add uncertainty: future cash flows may differ from what we expect in size or in timing. This requires a way of expressing the *expected value* of the uncertain stream of payments and the *risk* associated with them. Put differently, the introduction of uncertainty transforms future cash flow into a probability distribution.

a. Expected Value

Imagine an investment, such as a government bond, that under certainty we know will return a payment of $10; that is, the investment will return $10 with a probability of 1. The introduction of uncertainty means that future returns can be expressed only probabilistically. The return for an uncertain investment is called the expected value, which is the average of all possible returns weighted by their probability of occurrence. The investment set out below has an expected return of $10, just like the government bond, but there is some chance that the actual return will be significantly more or less than $10:

Probability	Expected Return	Probability × Return
.10	−$10	−$ 1
.25	$ 0	$ 0
.30	$10	$ 3
.25	$20	$ 5
.10	$30	$ 3
	Expected value	$10

Expected value is thus the mean — the arithmetic average — of a distribution of values. However, the expected value of a distribution of values describes only one of the characteristics of a distribution — its central tendency. It does not capture another important aspect of the distribution of future returns. Compare the returns of a second investment that also has an expected return of $10:

Probability	Expected Return	Probability × Return
.15	−$10	−$ 1.50
.22	$ 0	$ 0
.26	$10	$ 2.60
.22	$20	$ 4.40
.15	$30	$ 4.50
	Expected value	$10

The distribution of expected returns from the second investment differs significantly from that of the first investment. In particular, the second investment has a greater probability both of losing money and of earning a higher return, even though both investments have the same expected value. This is a second characteristic of the uncertainty of a distribution — the dispersion of expected returns around the mean. This dispersion — the likelihood that the actual value will differ from the expected value — is what financial economists call the *risk* of an investment. The next step in understanding the impact of uncertainty on valuation is how risk is measured.

b. Risk

In corporate finance, the concept of risk focuses on two characteristics of a distribution of expected returns. The first is the likelihood that the actual return will differ from the expected value, and the second is the size of the difference. Financial economists typically use a distribution's *standard deviation* to express these features. To compute standard deviation, the first step is to subtract the expected value from each possible return. The difference is then squared; this has the effect of equating positive and negative deviations from the expected value (squaring a negative value eliminates the sign). The result is called the *variance* of the distribution. Standard deviation is the square root of the sum of the variances for each expected return, and is expressed in the same units as the data; that is, if the distribution is of possible percentage returns from an investment, the standard deviation is expressed as a percentage return. For example, consider the following distribution of the likelihood of each of three events:

(1)	(2)	(3)	(4) = (2) × (3)	(5) = (3) − Expected Value
Event	Probability	Expected Return	Probability × Return	Deviation
a	.20	−10%	−2.00%	−16.50
b	.35	5%	1.75%	−1.50
c	.45	15%	6.75%	8.50
		Expected value	6.5%	

The calculation of the distribution's standard deviation is as follows:

(1)	(2)	(3)	(4) = (3)² Variance of Distribution (Deviation Squared)	(5) = (2) × (4) Variance = Probability × Deviation Squared
Event	Probability	Deviation		
a	.20	−16.50	272.25	54.45
b	.35	−1.50	2.25	.7875
c	.45	8.50	72.25	32.5125
			Standard Deviation = Square Root of Sums of Variance	9.3675%

This distribution has a standard deviation of 9.3675 percent. When this statistic is applied to data that is normally distributed — that is, the distribution has the familiar bell shape — it has a very useful property. Because of the technical properties of a normal distribution (which need not detain us here), we can state the probability that the actual return will differ from the expected value by more than any multiple of the distribution's standard deviation:

(1) Difference from Expected Return as a Multiple of Standard Deviation Units	(2) Probability that Actual Return Differs from Expected Value by Less than (1)
0.5 units	38%
1.0 units	68%
1.5 units	87%
2.0 units	95%
2.5 units	99%

In other words, we know that for this distribution the actual return will be within one standard deviation (9.3675 percent in our example) from the expected value about 68 percent of the time and within .5 standard deviation units (4.68375 percent in our example) from the expected value about 38 percent of the time. So if the expected value of a normal distribution is 6.5 percent and the standard deviation is 9.375 percent, we know there is only about a 16 percent chance that the actual return will be less than −2.875 percent and only about a 16 percent chance that it will be more than 15.875 percent.[3]

Thus, the higher the standard deviation of a distribution, the greater the likelihood that the actual outcome will differ from the expected outcome, and the greater the distribution's risk.

Two qualifications should be noted concerning the use of standard deviation to measure risk. First, the measure assumes that the distribution is normal. This assumption is typically considered appropriate for evaluating the returns of publicly traded stocks. Measuring risk by reference to standard deviation is therefore appropriate for public corporations; it may not be appropriate for privately held corporations. Second, worse-than-expected results are treated as the equivalent of better-than-expected results, even though many of us really think about risk as only the downside of potential events;[4] we are typically not afraid that things will turn out better than we expected. The saving grace is that so long as the distribution is normal, the equivalence should make little difference since each side of the distribution is a mirror image of the other: increasing the risk increases the likelihood of a worse-than-expected outcome even if it increases the likelihood of a better-than-expected outcome as well.

Problem. Calculate the standard deviation for each of the following two investments:

Investment A		Investment B	
Probability	Expected Return	Probability	Expected Return
.10	−$10	.15	−$10
.25	$ 0	.22	$ 0
.30	$10	.26	$10
.25	$20	.22	$20
.10	$30	.15	$30

Which investment is riskier? Why?

---

3. This example is drawn from William Sharpe, Investments 119-122 (2d ed. 1981).
4. See Gilson & Black, footnote 2 supra, at 91.

c. Diversification

The valuation payoff to measuring the risk of a financial asset is the impact of diversification — holding a *portfolio* of assets rather than a single asset — on the risk borne by an investor. Diversification reduces the risk of the asset without reducing the expected return. This happens because the prices of individual stocks do not move in exactly the same manner. Sometimes stocks move together, but sometimes they move in different directions, so that a drop in the price of one stock is canceled out by a rise in the price of another. The result is that the risk associated with a portfolio of common stock decreases as the number of different stocks in the portfolio increases. For example, over the period 1999-2003, the standard deviation of the returns to the common stock of Compaq Computer was 42.0 percent and that for AT&T was 22.6 percent.[5] Over the period 1980-1988, the standard deviation of a portfolio composed of all stocks was only 12.5 percent. The relation between the number of stocks in a portfolio and the portfolio risk (standard deviation) is shown in Figure 3.1.

What kind of risk does diversification reduce? As shown in Figure 3.1, the total risk of a stock is composed of two components: (1) *systematic* or market risk, and (2) *unsystematic* or unique risk. Systematic risk is that presented by economic events that affect all companies, such as higher or lower economic growth or inflation. Unsystematic risk is that presented by an individual company or its close rivals, such as the death of a company's CEO or a strike at its principal plant, or a change in technology that affects the company's industry. These kinds of risks can be avoided by diversifying one's portfolio across companies and industries. Then changes in the value of a particular company or industry due to events unique to it are offset by the impact of different events on other companies or industries. As shown in Figure 3.1, as the number of companies in a randomly chosen portfolio increases, the unsystematic portion of the portfolio risk is reduced until, once the number reaches 20 to 30, almost all unsystematic risk is eliminated. The remaining risk of the portfolio is systematic — that related to the economy as a whole and affecting all stocks.

For purposes of understanding how the capital market values financial assets such as corporate stock, three important consequences flow from the impact of diversification on risk. First, the capital market will ignore unsystematic risk in valuing a financial asset if the asset can be diversified. As with two stocks with the same return, risk-averse investors will pay more for the stock with the lower risk. Those investors who hold a diversified portfolio do not bear unsystematic risk; their preferences will depend only on systematic risk. Because diversification is relatively easy and cheap for investors in most financial assets, especially the common stock of publicly traded companies, the price of financial assets will be set by diversified investors, who need to consider only an asset's systematic risk. Thus, the extent of a company's unsystematic risk should not affect the company's value, and investors will not be paid to bear unsystematic risk they could have diversified away. Consistent with this analysis, the New York Prudent Investor Act requires a trustee to diversify investments unless the governing instrument otherwise dictates. 1994 Sess. Laws of N.Y.

---

5. Brealey, Myers & Allen, footnote 2 supra, at 160.

Figure 3.1
DIVERSIFICATION REDUCES RISK

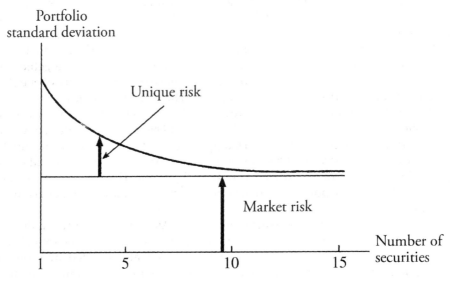

Source: Brealey, Myers & Allen, footnote 2 supra, at 165.

ch. 609 (A. 11683-B) (McKinney's) (adding §11-2.3 to the Estates, Powers and Trusts Law).

Second, the level at which diversification should be considered is the investor level, not the company level. A company is not worth more because its real assets are diversified; it is worth more because its investors can diversify their portfolios of financial assets. In general, a company should diversify only if, for some reason, the holders of its financial assets cannot. While this is an unlikely event for a public company operating in a well-developed capital market like that of the United States, one can imagine some circumstances where barriers to diversification at the investor level make diversification at the company level attractive to some participants in the corporation. For example, senior management invest their human capital in a company to the extent that the company's poor performance makes it more difficult for them to secure comparable work elsewhere. But human capital is difficult to diversify: executives can have only one job and cannot sell financial assets representing claims on their future salary. For executives, the only way to diversify their human capital — that is, to reduce the effect of the company's unsystematic risk on the value of their human capital — is for their employer to diversify at the company level. Would this lead management to favor different kinds of acquisitions than shareholders? See Chapter IX.

The third consequence of the impact of diversification on risk also concerns the relation between behavior at the investor and at the company level. The preferences of individual investors with respect to risk — the extent of an investor's risk aversion — should not affect the capital market's valuation of the company. The reason is that the investor can choose the risk associated with her own portfolio regardless of the risk associated with the company's activities. If the company's activities are more risky than the investor prefers, she can hold less of the company's stock and more of a riskless security such as short-term government bonds. If the company's activities are less risky than the investor prefers, she can increase the risk of her own portfolio by borrowing funds to buy more of the company's stock. The insight is that investors want companies to undertake activities that promise the most return for the risk involved in the activity regardless of the absolute level of risk.

d. The Capital Asset Pricing Model

The discussion of valuation to this point has established that investors need to bear only the systematic risk associated with holding financial assets (and, therefore, that unsystematic risk should not affect the capital market's valuation of financial assets), and that the risk preferences of individual investors also should not affect market value because each investor can tailor her portfolio to her own tastes. That leaves a financial asset's systematic risk and expected returns as the only factors that remain to determine its value. The *capital asset pricing model (CAPM)* specifies that the price of an asset[6] is a simple function of the level of the systematic risk of the asset compared to the risk of the market as a whole.

The intuitive core of the model can be developed from the valuation principles we have already reviewed. Investors prefer more return for a given level of risk. Risk can be reduced by holding a portfolio of assets. Investors will therefore seek to hold a portfolio of assets that provides the highest expected return for the same standard deviation.[7]

Because investors hold stocks in a portfolio, what matters is not the risk of the individual stock, but the impact of that stock on the risk of the entire portfolio. That depends, in turn, on how much the value of the stock changes for a given change in the value of the portfolio.

A portfolio composed of all stocks in the market will have the highest return for the same standard deviation.[8] Thus, the critical portfolio against whose changes the sensitivity of an individual stock must be determined is the market as a whole. The measure of a stock's sensitivity to changes in the value of the market is called its *beta*. The beta of the market is 1. An individual stock is risky if a change in the value of the market results in a bigger change in the value of the stock (i.e., it has

6. That is, the capitalized value of the return an investor must receive to hold the asset.

7. Recall that risk is measured by standard deviation. By holding a portfolio of assets, an investor essentially eliminates unsystematic risk. Thus, the standard deviation of a portfolio measures the portfolio's systematic risk.

8. Suppose all investors have the same expectations about the future performance of all stocks, an assumption that itself builds on the assumption that all investors have access to the same information (see the discussion of the efficient capital market hypothesis at pages 192-197 infra). Then each investor would select the same portfolio of stocks as having the highest return for a given risk. If investors all own the same portfolio and investors must own in total all stocks, then the optimal portfolio is composed of all stocks, generally referred to as the *market portfolio*. To be sure, this analysis is a simplification. Investors do have different expectations and hold different portfolios. However, the usefulness of the assumption depends on the predictive power of the model it supports. If the market in the aggregate acts as if the assumption is accurate — for example, because the central tendency of all investor action is consistent with the assumption and nonconformers more or less cancel each other out — then little is lost by making the descriptively inaccurate assumption. This is an empirical question that is considered in the remainder of this section.

a beta greater than 1) and less risky if a change in the value of the market results in a smaller change in the value of the stock (i.e., it has a beta less than 1). For example, in March 2004 Dell computer had a beta of 1.77 while Pfizer had a beta of .38.[9]

Since the value of a stock (the capitalized value of the return an investor will require to hold the stock) depends on its risk (more precisely, its sensitivity to changes in the value of the market portfolio), the capital asset pricing model holds that an asset's value is proportional to its beta. In CAPM's full form, the value of an asset is determined by combining the risk-free return (representing the time value of money, i.e., the certainty component of value) and the return for bearing risk, which is simply the stock's beta multiplied by the return to the market in excess of the risk-free return.[10]

The logic behind the capital asset pricing model can be seen by imagining what would happen if a stock were selling at a price above that specified by the model. That would mean that the stock provided less return than required by its beta. No one would pay that price because a higher return for that level of risk would be available simply by holding a combination of the market portfolio and a risk-free asset that together had the same beta as the mispriced stock. Thus, the price of the stock would fall until its return rose to the level dictated by the model.

The validity of the capital asset pricing model — that is, the extent to which it accurately predicts asset values — as opposed to its internal logic, is currently the subject of substantial debate, both analytically and empirically. The analytical criticisms of CAPM's predictive power are of two general types. The first questions whether CAPM is capable of being tested at all. CAPM predicts a linear relationship between a stock's systematic risk and returns on the market portfolio. While the market portfolio is operationally defined as, for example, the S&P 500 Index, the theoretical market portfolio is composed of all investment assets, including real estate, bonds, etc. If we cannot tell how our proxy for the real market portfolio differs from the real portfolio itself, it is hard to evaluate empirical reports of how accurately CAPM predicts stock prices. Either a close fit or a large error may be a function of using an incomplete market portfolio in the test.[11] The second analytic criticism stresses CAPM's normative character: It is a theory about how assets *should* be priced. If they are not priced as predicted, the theory could be wrong. But it also could mean that the market price of assets is wrong. The latter calls into question the efficient capital market hypothesis, which is taken up in the next section.

The empirical criticisms of CAPM's predictive power are more straightforward. Eugene Fama & Kenneth French, The Cross-Section of Expected Stock Returns, 47 J. Fin. 427 (1992), summarize the results of their own and other studies: the systematic risk of a security turns out not to predict its return very well. Other factors, especially firm size and the ratio of book equity to market equity, improve

---

9. Brealey, Myers & Allen, footnote 2 supra, at 190. The text draws heavily on their excellent discussion.

10. The formula for CAPM is written as

$$\bar{R}_A = R_F + \beta_A(\bar{R}_M - R_F)$$

where $\bar{R}_A$ is the expected return on security A, R_F is the risk-free return, β_A is the beta of security A, and $\bar{R}_M$ is the expected return on the market portfolio.

11. See Richard Roll, A Critique of Asset Pricing Theory's Tests, Part I: On Part and Potential Testability of the Theory, 4 J. Fin. Econ. 129 (1977).

predictions of stock returns. See, e.g., Eugene Fama & Kenneth French, The Cross-Section of Expected Stock Returns, 47 J. Fin. 427 (1992). The extent to which this evidence undermines CAPM is unclear. At present, the debate focuses on whether the importance of factors other than systematic risk is an artifact of the particular empirical techniques used. Richard Brealey, Stuart Myers and Franklin Allen put the issue nicely, describing the CAPM as "plausible and widely used but far from perfect."[12] And because of difficulties in testing the model, "the plausibility of CAPM *theory* will have to be weighed along with the "facts.""[13]

The possibility that factors other than systematic risk affect stock price has been pursued through the development of multi-factor asset pricing models that take into account additional kinds of risk. The leading such model, arbitrage pricing theory (APT), posits that a security's price is a linear function of *each* risk factor, such as liquidity or the rate of inflation, where each factor has its own beta. In this sense, CAPM is only a special case of APT — one where only a single risk, changes in the value of the market portfolio, affects stock prices.[14] However, it is a very special case because CAPM offers an economic explanation for the importance of systematic risk: only systematic risk matters because all other risk can be diversified away. APT does not explain why other factors should matter.[15]

Recognizing that systematic risk alone cannot explain empirical differences in return, Eugene Fama and Kenneth French recently have incorporated the additional predictive power of company size and book-to-market ratio by adding them to systematic risk in a three-factor asset pricing model.[16] In an effort to provide an economic explanation for the explanatory power of the additional two factors, Fama and French suggest that they are proxies for a greater risk of financial distress in times of recession. Because the value of individuals' human capital also will be reduced in bad times, they will desire to hold some financial assets that fare better in bad times so as to diversify the risk of their human capital. Thus, stocks that perform comparatively worse in bad times will have to earn a corresponding higher rate of return in good times. For excellent recent surveys of the state of asset pricing literature, see J. Y. Campbell, Asset Pricing at the Millennium, 55 J. Fin. 1515 (2000), and J. H. Cochran, Asset Pricing (2000).

Despite the ongoing debate between supporters of CAPM and those of multi-factor models, there is little dispute over CAPM's central contribution, both to asset pricing theory and corporate law: an important determinant of an asset's value is its level of systematic risk; the risk that is relevant to valuation is that which cannot be eliminated by diversification; and diversification at the company level is not helpful if shareholders can diversify their own portfolios. So when courts are asked to resolve disputes over the impact of particular actions on the value of the corporation, special attention should be paid to the link between those actions and the corporation's systematic risk

---

12. Brealey, Myers & Allen, footnote 2 supra, at 205.

13. Id. at 197.

14. The original presentation of APT appears in Stephen Ross, The Arbitrage Theory of Capital Asset Pricing, 13 J. Econ. Theory 341 (1976). Stephen Ross, Randall Westerfield & Jeffrey Jaffee, Corporate Finance Ch. 11 (7th ed. 2005), presents a sympathetic textbook account of APT.

15. For a discussion of what additional factors find empirical support, see Nai-Fu Chen, Richard Roll & Stephen Ross, Economic Forces and the Stock Market, 59 J. Bus. 383 (1986).

16. Eugene Fama & Kenneth French, Multifactor Explanations of Asset Pricing Anomalies, 51 J. Fin. 55 (1996); Eugene Fama & Kenneth French, Common Risk Factors in the Returns on Bonds and Stocks, 33 J. Fin. Econ. 3 (1993).

3. THE EFFICIENT CAPITAL MARKET HYPOTHESIS

Asset pricing theory tells us how financial assets should be valued if we have all the necessary information about risk and expected returns; indeed, the capital asset pricing model explicitly assumes that all investors have complete information concerning a financial asset. The *efficient capital market hypothesis* (ECMH) makes the bolder statement that the capital market, in fact, values financial assets as asset pricing theory says they should be valued. Thus, it is necessarily a theory about what information is available to the capital market. The ECMH holds that at any time market prices are an unbiased forecast of future cash flows that fully reflects all available information. Such a market is said to be efficient. Operationally, this means that investors cannot make money, for example, by seeking out "undervalued" stocks, because the market already reflects all information concerning stocks' expected returns. But note what the ECMH does not hold: in particular, it does not state that the values set by the capital market are correct, in the sense that they accurately predict future cash flows. Remember that current price is based on expected value — the weighted average of a distribution of possible future returns. Unless the distribution of future returns has a very low standard deviation, actual returns likely will be different from expected returns. The ECMH merely states that on average the capital market makes the best predictions.

It is not surprising that the ECMH has been the subject of substantial controversy. Much of the securities industry is premised on the belief that diligent research by financial analysts will allow them to identify undervalued stocks. The ECMH states that such effort, and the amounts paid by investors to analysts and mutual fund managers to undertake it, is wasted. If at any time the market price reflects all available information, then prices will change only when new information is revealed. But new information is necessarily unpredictable; otherwise it would not be new. As a result, price movements will be random and so will the performance of analysts.

It is standard to define three levels of market efficiency, corresponding to the kind of information that market price is said to fully reflect. Each reflects a different claim about the extent of the market's efficiency. A market is *weak* form efficient if prices reflect all information about past stock prices; that is, past prices cannot be used to predict future prices. This means that there is no use in studying charts of past price performance to identify trends that can be exploited.

A market is *semi-strong* form efficient if prices also reflect all publicly available information such as financial statements and earnings reports. This reflects the stronger claim that new information concerning the risk or expected return of an asset is so quickly taken into account that no one can profit by trading on the information. It is this version of the ECMH that directly challenges traditional security analysis and has led to investment strategies based on indexing — holding (and not trading) a portfolio of securities designed not to outperform the market, but simply to match the market's overall return without incurring research and trading costs.

Finally, a market is *strong* form efficient if it reflects not only public information, but private information as well. This represents the most expansive claim of market efficiency in that the market is said to reflect even information that is not publicly available. If this were literally true, insider trading would not be profitable. Accepting the fact that this is not true, the concept of strong form efficiency still cannot be entirely dismissed. Markets do seem to reflect some private information, as illustrated by the run-up in the stock price of a target company even before the announcement of a takeover.

Market efficiency cannot be tested directly because we do not know the theoretically correct price of an asset to which the market price could be compared. But it can be tested operationally by devising trading strategies based on particular information and seeing whether such strategies are profitable. For example, weak form efficiency can be tested by using filter strategies, such as buying securities that have gone up x days in a row and selling securities that have gone down y days in a row. The market is weak form efficient if such strategies are not profitable. Semi-strong form efficiency can be tested by strategies that call for buying stock shortly after a favorable earnings release. The outcome is consistent with semi-strong efficiency if the information is so quickly reflected in price that the strategy is not profitable.

There is an extensive empirical literature, stretching over 30 years, that generally supports the hypothesis that capital markets, and especially developed stock markets, are weak form and semi-strong form efficient.[17] However, recent studies identify a number of what are styled "anomalies," i.e., persistent evidence of higher-than-predicted returns based on publicly available information, which is inconsistent with semi-strong form market efficiency. These anomalies include the tendency of small companies to earn higher returns than large companies even after adjustment for systematic risk, or the seeming existence of a "January effect," in which stocks systematically perform better than predicted by their systematic risk in a single month.[18] Some observers treat these results as evidence that the market is not efficient and as supportive of a different approach to explaining how capital markets operate, one that is styled "behavioral finance."[19] Others explain the data as the result of applying incorrect asset pricing models, reflecting the barrier to direct testing of market efficiency discussed in the previous paragraph. Still others note that the data revealing the anomalies are sensitive to the empirical techniques chosen,[20] or demonstrate that the anomalies disappear or are dramatically reduced in size following their disclosure, suggesting that markets become efficient, but not necessarily quickly.[21]

Focus on the empirical support for weak form and semi-strong form market efficiency overlooks one central question. From a policy perspective, we would like to know what makes the market efficient and how information comes to be reflected in price. That would enable courts and regulators to avoid interfering with the mechanisms that account for well-functioning markets, and guide them in intervening to improve the performance of inefficient markets. From a private

17. For an assessment of the literature, see Eugene Fama, Efficient Capital Markets II, 46 J. Fin. 1575 (1991).

18. See, e.g., Nicholas Barberis & Richard Thaler, A Survey of Behavioral Economics, in Handbook of the Economics of Finance (George Constantinides, Milt Harris & Rene Stolz eds., 2003); Andrei Shleifer, Inefficient Markets: An Introduction to Behavioral Finance (2000).

19. This literature is discussed at pages 194-197 infra.

20. See, e.g., Eugene Fama, Market Efficiency, Long-Term Returns, and Behavioral Finance, 49 J. Fin. Econ. 283 (1998).

21. See, e.g., G. William Schwert, Anomalies and Market Efficiency, in Handbook of the Economics of Finance (George Constantinides, Milt Harris & Rene Stolz eds., 2003); Mark Rubenstein, Rational Markets: Yes or No? The Affirmative Case, Fin. Analysts J. (May-June 2001) at 15.

perspective, understanding what makes a market efficient may guide us in identifying situations of market inefficiency, which may provide the opportunity for profit. The problem is highlighted by the now classic demonstration that the market cannot literally be semi-strong form efficient. If new information is quickly reflected in market price, it must be because analysts invest time and money in seeking out and understanding the implications of new information, and then trade on it. But if they could earn no profit from this costly activity, they would not engage in it, and the market would not be efficient. The resolution is that markets must have an equilibrium level of inefficiency: analysts earn just enough from their activities to sustain their involvement. If the market were more efficient, analysts would leave the business until the resulting inefficiency supported the activity of those that remained. If the market were less efficient, analysts would enter the business until the resulting increased efficiency sufficiently lowered profits to eliminate new entry.[22]

This link between the cost of acquiring information and the level of market efficiency leads to the more general proposition that the market's efficiency with respect to particular kinds of information depends on the cost of acquiring it. From this perspective, capital market efficiency is linked to the structure of the information market.[23] The more widespread the initial distribution of the information, the more quickly it will be reflected in market price. Thus an announcement of a change in the discount rate by the Federal Reserve will be known immediately by all traders simply by listening to the news. Other kinds of information, such as that contained in speeches by company executives to security industry groups, will be known first to analysts and reflected in price through the trading of these professionals. Still other forms of information will be known only to more limited groups of traders, whose information will be learned by the market only through its decoding the information from the very fact of changes in trading volume and patterns. This is the mechanism through which the market achieves some level of strong form efficiency. The more broadly the information is initially distributed, the more efficient the market with respect to it; and the lower the cost of acquiring the information, the more widespread the distribution. Market efficiency thus becomes a function of information cost.

The increasing volume of studies whose data present at least a surface conflict with market efficiency has given rise to a different approach to asset pricing and market efficiency. Standard accounts of the operation of capital markets that led to the award of the Nobel Prize in economic science to William Sharpe for the CAPM and to the wide acceptance of the ECMH as a foundation of regulatory policy[24] assume that investors are fully rational (or that the market acts as if they are) and that transaction costs are small so that professional traders quickly take advantage of mispricing and thereby drive prices back to their efficient level. Behavioral finance takes issue with both premises, arguing that many investors are not rational in their financial decisionmaking, and that significant barriers prevent

22. Sanford Grossman & Joseph Stiglitz, On the Impossibility of Informationally Efficient Markets, 70 Am. Econ. Rev. 393 (1980).

23. Ronald Gilson & Reinier Kraakman, The Mechanisms of Market Efficiency, 70 Va. L. Rev. 549 (1984).

24. Id. at 550 (market efficiency structures "debate over the future of securities regulation both within and without the Securities and Exchange Commission").

professional traders from fully correcting the mistakes made by less than rational investors.[25]

The criticism of the rationality premise builds on an important literature growing out of work by cognitive psychologists Daniel Kahneman and Amos Tversky, which uses decisionmaking experiments to show how individuals' cognitive biases can lead them to form systematically inaccurate assessments of the value of an asset.[26] These biases include overconfidence, the tendency of individuals to overestimate their skills; the endowment effect, the tendency of individuals to insist on a higher price to sell something they already own than they would pay to buy the same item if they don't own it; and loss aversion, the tendency for people to be risk averse toward profit opportunities but willing to gamble to avoid a loss.[27] Such misguided investors, referred to in the literature as "noise traders,"[28] are said to be capable of causing stock prices to sharply diverge from their fundamental values, as may have occurred with the stock market crash of October 1987, when the Dow Jones Industrial Average fell 23 percent on a single day, despite the apparent absence of any economic news that might account for so significant a revaluation of the assets of companies traded on U.S. stock exchanges or on other stock exchanges around the world.[29] They may also cause stock prices to diverge from their fundamental values over an extended period of time, as with the Internet bubble of the late 1990s.

The existence of noise traders alone, however, is insufficient to result in systematically inaccurate securities prices. The ECMH posits that professional investors, by trading against the noise traders, would push prices back to an efficient level. Behavioralists point to two kinds of limits to arbitrage that would allow noise trader — induced mispricing to persist. The first concerns the motives of the professional investors; the second concerns institutional barriers to successful arbitrage.

The motive criticism reminds us that professional investors trade to make a profit, not to ensure accurate prices. Thus, if noise traders hold systematically biased views about prices, professional investors may seek to reinforce those biases by trading in the same direction as noise traders with the strategy of getting out at the top. The result would be a violation of weak form efficiency because prices then would reflect some consistency — the price today would predict the price tomorrow.[30] And rather than move prices in the direction of efficiency, the

25. Among a large number of literature surveys by economists, see, e.g., Barberis & Thaler, footnote 18 supra, and Shleifer, footnote 18 supra. Among legal commentators, see Donald C. Langevoort, Taming the Animal Spirits of the Stock Markets: A Behavioral Approach to Securities Regulation, 97 Nw. U. L. Rev. 135 (2002), for a careful discussion. Lawrence A. Cunningham, Behavioral Finance and Investor Governance, 59 Wash. & Lee L. Rev. 767 (2002), exemplifies the more aggressively presented case. The account in the text draws on Ronald Gilson & Reinier Kraakman, The Mechanisms of Market Efficiency Twenty Years Later: The Hindsight Bias, 28 J. Corp. L. 718 (2003).

26. Daniel Kahneman was awarded the 2002 Nobel Prize in economic science for his work in this area. Because of his untimely death, Amos Tversky was not eligible to share the award. For a collection of their early work, see Judgment Under Uncertainty: Heuristics and Biases (Daniel Kahneman, Paul Slovic & Amos Tversky eds., 1982).

27. For a useful recent summary of the range of biases identified in the literature, see Barberis & Thaler, footnote 18 supra.

28. Id.

29. For example, stock price indices fell in dollar terms 22.1 percent in the United Kingdom, 17.1 percent in Germany, and 20.8 percent in Switzerland. Richard Brealey & Stewart Myers, Principles of Corporate Finance 298 (6th ed. 2000).

30. See David Cutler, James Poterba & Lawrence Summers, Speculative Dynamics, 58 Rev. Econ. Stud. 529 (1991).

strategy exacerbates inefficiency, as is said to have occurred in the Internet bubble. This criticism calls to mind John Maynard Keynes's famous characterization of the stock market as a beauty contest: "[P]rofessional investment may be likened to those newspaper competitions in which the competitors have to pick the six prettiest faces from a hundred photographs, the prize being awarded to the competitor whose choice most nearly corresponds to the average preferences of the competitors as a whole; so that each competitor has to pick not those faces which he himself finds prettiest, but those which he thinks likeliest to catch the fancy of the other competitors, all of whom are looking at the problem from the same point of view."[31]

Concern over the institutional limitations on arbitrage reflects both regulatory constraints, such as the limits on short selling, and market constraints, such as limited supply of the shares that must be borrowed to effect a short sale, and the danger, to capital and reputation, of losses resulting from noise traders' refusal to come to their senses and correct their inaccurate views.[32] For example, a clear-sighted professional investor who early in the cycle correctly identified Internet stocks as overpriced and shorted them would have lost a fortune before the market recognized the pricing mistake. To the extent of these limits, professional traders will be unable to correct inefficient pricing.[33]

At present, there is no consensus on the accuracy of the behavioral finance critique of the ECMH. For example, there remains no uncontested explanation for the sharp price movements on October 19, 1987. Candidates include a liquidity crunch in the capital markets, a disconnect between the futures market and the stock market, the effect of large numbers of institutional investors attempting to implement portfolio insurance strategies as the market began to fall,[34] and the role of short-term expectations of still further price drops in deterring arbitrageurs from beginning to purchase stock (and thereby stabilize prices) even if prices fall below what arbitrageurs believe to be their absolute value.[35] Moreover, one

31. John Maynard Keynes, The General Theory of Employment, Interest, and Money 156 (1936).

32. See, e.g., Barberis & Thaler, footnote 18 supra; and Shleifer, footnote 18 supra. Volume 66 of the Journal of Financial Economics contains a symposium on the topic of limits to arbitrage.

33. For recent efforts to integrate investor misperception and limits on arbitrage to explain inefficient stock prices, see, e.g., Harrison Hong & Jeremy C. Stein, Disagreement and the Stock Market, 21 J. Econ. Persp. 109 (2007); Malcolm Baker & Jeffrey Wurglar, Investor Sentiment in the Stock Market, 27 J. Econ. Persp. 129 (2007).

34. Portfolio insurance is a form of computer-based program trading in which a market decline triggers an automatic order to sell some portion of the portfolio and a stock index future. The sale of the future is intended to protect the portfolio against loss as a result of further market drop since, in that event, the gain from the index sale hedges the drop in portfolio value. If a large number of portfolio insurance programs are engaged at the same time, the demands on the market for liquidity may result in a liquidity crisis, which would exacerbate the existing price pressure. See Report of the Presidential Task Force on Market Mechanisms (1988). Put in terms of capital asset pricing, value would no longer be determined based solely on systematic risk; liquidity risk would also be relevant, which would result in a decrease in price independent of any change in expectations concerning expected return or systematic risk. Contrary views are stated in Michael Brennan & Eduardo Schwartz, Portfolio Insurance and Financial Market Equilibrium, 62 J. Bus. 455 (1989); Gerard Gennotte & Hayne Leland, Market Liquidity, Hedging and Crashes, 80 Am. Econ. Rev. 99 (1990).

35. For collections of articles exploring alternative explanations of the 1987 crash, see Black Monday and the Future of Financial Markets (R. Kanphuis et al. 1989); National Bureau of Economic Research, Microeconomics Annual 1988. For development of the impact of expectations concerning whether the market will fall further on when arbitrageurs will enter, see Jeremy Bulow & Paul Klemperer, Rational Frenzies and Crashes, 102 J. Pol. Econ. 1 (1994). Others have explained the crash as evidence that the ECMH simply is wrong. Bruce Jacobs & Kenneth Levy, The Complexity of the Stock Market, 15 J. Portfolio Mgmt. 19 (1989). Still others have explained the crash as consistent with changes in

would like to know if the possible divergence of relative and absolute value reflected in the 1987 crash is an isolated or persistent phenomenon,[36] the result of a failure of market mechanisms — in effect, a process failure — or a reflection of serious irrationality in the valuation process. For present purposes, the critical question is the implication of the debate over the power of the ECMH for public policy. For which corporate law debates does it matter whether the market is pretty much efficient, or from time to time is subject to bubbles?

Despite the continued debate over the power of the ECMH, the empirical evidence that has accumulated over 30 years yields a number of themes that have important implications for corporate law. First, market prices are probably right; it is unlikely that, over time and on average, investors will beat the market. This has relevance for debates over the goals of securities regulation. Should we encourage individuals to "play the market" by trying to minimize the advantages of professional traders, or should we allow professional traders to police the efficiency of prices and encourage individuals to invest through intermediaries such as mutual funds? For this debate, does it matter whether the capital market is absolutely or only relatively efficient?

Second, the best response to a claim that the market undervalues the stock of a particular company, especially when advanced by management responsible for the company's performance, may be for management to provide the market the information its valuation is said not to reflect. If the value of the company does not increase following such disclosure, the burden of explanation should be on those asserting inefficiency.

Third, the evidence indicates that the market cannot be fooled by strategies that seek to alter a company's stock price by means that do not alter the company's risk or expected returns. For example, changing the accounting methods used by the company to increase its reported earnings without altering its real earnings appears not to change the price of its stock. Similarly, splitting the company's stock without altering the dividend appears not to increase the price of its stock.

Fourth, regulatory attention may be warranted to reduce the institutional barriers to arbitrage. If it is difficult to correct the cognitive biases of individuals, then improvements may result from eliminating some of the regulatory limits on short selling, thereby catalyzing the corrective mechanism.[37] Here, however, it is important to keep in mind that not only noise traders suffer from cognitive biases such as overconfidence. So do regulators. Thus, the biases of noise traders must be balanced against the biases of those who would correct them. See Stephen J. Choi & A. C. Pritchard, Behavioral Economics and the SEC, 56 Stan. L. Rev. 1 (2003).

Consider the following case in light of the preceding discussion of market efficiency.

---

fundamental values and efficient markets. See Bruton Malkiel, Is the Stock Market Efficient?, 243 Science 1313 (1989).

36. John Maynard Keynes, having been invoked in support of the noise trading criticism, should also be invoked with respect to the crash, only this time to soften the appearance of irrationality: "In abnormal times . . . when . . . continuation of the present state of affairs is less plausible than usual, even though there are no express grounds to anticipate a definite change, the market will be subject to waves of optimistic and pessimistic sentiment, which are unreasoning, but in a sense legitimate, where no solid basis exists for a reasonable calculation." Keynes, footnote 31 supra, at 154.

37. The SEC recently enacted changes to Regulation SHO eliminating price restrictions on the short sale of all securities. Exchange Act Release 34-55970 (June 28, 2007).

Kamin v. American Express Company

383 N.Y.S.2d 807 (N.Y. App. Div. 1976)

GREENFIELD, J.: In this . . . action, the . . . complaint is brought derivatively by two minority stockholders of the American Express Company, asking for a declaration that a certain dividend in kind is a waste of corporate assets. . . .

[T]he complaint alleges that in 1972 American Express acquired for investment 1,954,418 shares of common stock of Donaldson, Lufken and Jenrette, Inc. (hereafter DLJ), a publicly traded corporation, at a cost of $29.9 million. It is further alleged that the current market value of those shares is approximately $4.0 million. On July 28, 1975, it is alleged, the Board of Directors of American Express declared a special dividend to all stockholders of record pursuant to which the shares of DLJ would be distributed in kind. Plaintiffs contend further that if American Express were to sell the DLJ shares on the market, it would sustain a capital loss of $25 million, which could be offset against taxable capital gains on other investments. Such a sale, they allege, would result in tax savings to the company of approximately $8 million, which would not be available in the case of the distribution of DLJ shares to stockholders.

. . . The question of whether or not a dividend is to be declared or a distribution of some kind should be made is exclusively a matter of business judgment for the Board of Directors.

". . . Courts will not interfere with such discretion unless it be first made to appear that the directors have acted or are about to act in bad faith and for a dishonest purpose. It is for the directors to say, acting in good faith of course, when and to what extent dividends shall be declared. . . . The statute confers upon the directors this power, and the minority stockholders are not in a position to question this right, so long as the directors are acting in good faith. . . ." Liebman v. Auto Strop Co., 241 N.Y. 427, 433-434, 150 N.E. 505, 506.

It is not enough to allege, as plaintiffs do here, that the directors made an imprudent decision, which did not capitalize on the possibility of using a potential capital loss to offset capital gains. More than imprudence or mistaken judgment must be shown. . . . [T]he objections raised by the plaintiffs to the proposed dividend action were carefully considered and unanimously rejected by the Board at a special meeting called precisely for that purpose at the plaintiffs' request. The minutes of the special meeting indicate that the defendants were fully aware that a sale rather than a distribution of the DLJ shares might result in the realization of a substantial income tax saving. Nevertheless, they concluded that there were countervailing considerations primarily with respect to the adverse effect such a sale, realizing a loss of $25 million, would have on the net income figures in the American Express financial statement. Such a reduction of net income would have a serious effect on the market value of the publicly traded American Express stock. This was not a situation in which the defendant directors totally overlooked facts called to their attention. They gave them consideration, and attempted to view the total picture in arriving at their decision. While plaintiffs contend that according to their accounting consultants the loss on the DLJ stock would still have to be charged against current earnings even if the stock were distributed, the defendants' accounting experts assert that the loss would be a charge against earnings only in the event of a sale, whereas in the event of distribution of the stock as a dividend, the proper accounting treatment would be to charge the loss only against surplus. . . .

. . . [T]he motion by the defendants for summary judgment and dismissal of the complaint is granted.

---

1. *Dividend versus sale.* Paying a special dividend instead of selling the DLJ stock cost American Express $8 million in real tax savings. In return, the company avoided a reduction of $25 million in the net income reported in its annual report. The loss avoided was purely a paper loss and had no effect on American Express's cash flow (indeed, because of the forgone tax savings, the dividend *reduced* cash flow by $8 million). Nor did the accounting treatment of the special dividend even keep the fact of the drop in value of the DLJ stock a secret, because the $25 million loss was charged against the surplus accounts elsewhere in the same financial statements. Why did the American Express directors think avoiding a $25 million paper loss was worth an $8 million real loss? Is the board's decision consistent with the EMCH?

2. *Fiduciary duty and semi-strong efficiency.* Did the American Express directors violate their fiduciary duty by ignoring the semi-strong form of the ECMH? Suppose the court had adopted the ECMH as the measure of the directors' performance. How should a court now evaluate the empirical evidence on noise trading or the 1987 stock market crash? Is a court well suited to evaluate changes in financial economics? Should courts force boards of directors to keep current with developments in economic theory? In this regard consider the following statement: "The familiar structure of the modern public corporation reflects the interaction of . . . three types of techniques—market forces, legal liability rules, and requirements for shareholders' action. In part because markets significantly give both management and shareholders a common interest in profitable operations, the business judgment rule . . . in large measure protects from judicial review management's exercise of its delegated discretion to operate the business in the absence of a conflict of interest." ALI, Principles of Corporate Governance 521 (1994) (Introductory Note to Part VI).

B. CAPITAL STRUCTURE: DOES THE OWNERSHIP STRUCTURE OF A CORPORATION AFFECT ITS VALUE?

The previous section focused on how the capital market values financial assets; the market value of the corporation is simply the total value of the financial assets—that is, the claims on its real assets—that the corporation has issued. For the purposes of that discussion, no distinction was made among corporations based on their *capital structure*, that is, the combination of different financial assets it has issued. This section considers a central issue in corporate finance: whether the particular capital structure chosen by a corporation can affect the corporation's market value. It begins by briefly describing the different categories of financial instruments from which the corporation can construct its capital structure. It then turns to a long-standing debate in corporate finance: whether a corporation has an optimal — that is, value-maximizing — capital structure. The traditional view holds that each corporation has an optimal capital structure, a particular mix of debt and equity that results in the highest market value for the corporation's financial assets. This position was challenged in 1958 by Franco Modigliani and Merton Miller, both of whom would subsequently win Nobel Prizes in economics. If everyone has complete information and there are no transaction costs, Miller and Modigliani argued, capital structure would be irrelevant: the value of the corporation would be the same regardless of the mix of debt and equity it issued.[38] The years since have been spent understanding why their simple irrelevance proposition would not prove true in the real world.[39]

1. A SURVEY OF FINANCIAL ASSETS

A corporation may issue three primary types of financial assets: common stock, preferred stock, and debt. In its pure form, each type has a cluster of distinguishing characteristics. Recently, however, the increasing sophistication of the capital market has turned each of the types into a focal point on a continuum, with a variety of hybrid securities that link the formerly discrete categories. The following discussion concentrates on the characteristics of the three primary types of financial assets, arraying their characteristic attributes along three dimensions — control, return, and priority — and then considers some of the hybrid instruments.

a. Common Stock

Common stock is the residual financial asset issued by corporations in three important senses. First, it is the only financial asset that all corporations must issue; issuance of other types is optional. This is because control of the corporation is vested in the holders of common stock through their voting rights as discussed in Chapter II.

Second, common stock is residual with respect to the right to receive the income of the corporation. As we will see later in this chapter, the typical corporate statute seeks to prevent common shareholders from withdrawing funds from the corporation unless the holders of more senior securities are protected.

Third, common stock is residual with respect to the right to receive the assets of the corporation upon its liquidation. Only after the holders of more senior securities receive the amounts due them do common shareholders divide whatever assets remain.

The rights provided common shareholders have a particular pattern. Shareholders are last in line with respect to distributions of income and liquidation. However, they are first in line with respect to control. This role reversal is central to establishing a corporate decisionmaking structure that provides the right incentives to maximize the value of the corporation. Once the claims of senior securities

---

38. Franco Modigliani & Merton Miller, The Cost of Capital, Corporate Finance and the Theory of Investment, 48 Am. Econ. Rev. 261 (1958).

39. See, e.g., Merton Miller, The Modigliani-Miller Propositions after Thirty Years, 2 J. Econ. Persp. 99 (1998); Sudipto Bhattacharya, Corporate Finance and the Legacy of Miller and Modigliani, 2 J. Econ. Persp. 135 (1988).

holders are paid off, all increases in the corporation's income and assets go to the holders of the residual interest. Combining voting control and the residual interest in profits and assets ensures that the decisionmakers bear the consequences of their own performance. If common shareholders make wise decisions and select and monitor competent management, they gain; if they make poor decisions, they lose up to the amount of their investment. Thus, the common shareholders' distinctive pattern of rights gives them a powerful incentive to see that the corporation operates efficiently.[40]

b. Debt

Debt is a contractual obligation issued by the corporation to repay funds provided by the investor with interest subject to the terms of the contract. While debt comes in a wide variety of forms, all possess a common characteristic: debt is at the opposite end of the continuum of financial assets from common stock. While common stock is last in line with respect to income and assets, but first in line with respect to control, debt is first in line with respect to income and assets, but last in line with respect to control. This basic pattern — allocating rights of control and rights to income and assets in the opposite order — seems to be efficient with respect to debt as well as with respect to common stock. Because debt holders are senior with respect to income and assets, the common shareholders' incentive to maximize the value of the corporation serves to maximize the income and assets available for payment to debt holders. Thus, debt holders have no need for control except in those circumstances when the interests of common shareholders and debt holders diverge. It is in precisely these circumstances that debt holders are protected by control-like provisions provided both by the terms of their contract and by corporate law. See pages 219-228.

Because of its contractual nature, debt comes in a variety of forms with different characteristics and somewhat different terminology. A long-term obligation is called a *bond* if secured by a mortgage on some of the corporation's property, and a *debenture* if unsecured. A short-term obligation is called a *note.* The terms governing a bond or debenture are contained in a lengthy contract called an *indenture,* which contains detailed provisions restricting the corporation's right to take certain kinds of actions that have the potential to injure the debt holders. The indenture may also provide the corporation the right to *call* the debt — that is, repay the debt before its stated maturity. Because the corporation's right to call the debt comes at the expense of debt holders,[41] the corporation compensates debt holders for that right in two ways. First, all other things being equal, the debt will carry a higher interest rate to compensate for giving the corporation the call option. Second, the price that debt holders are paid when the debt is called is typically at a premium to face value.

---

40. See Frank Easterbrook & Daniel Fischel, The Economic Structure of Corporate Law 66-70 (1991). The efficient assignment of control rights becomes more complicated when prior poor decisions have already dissipated most or all of the shareholders' equity. This problem is considered infra in Sec. C.

41. A corporation typically will call its debt when interest rates have fallen and it can borrow replacement funds at a lower rate. In that situation, the corporation's gain is the debt holders' loss; they will be forced to reinvest the amounts received in payment at lower interest rates.

c. Preferred Stock

Midway on the continuum between common stock and debt is preferred stock. It is like common stock in that its claim to income and assets is subordinate to that of debt, and it is like debt in the sense that its claim to income and assets is superior to that of common stock, and typically fixed in amount: the dividend to be paid on preferred stock and the amount received on liquidation are specified. As with common stock, some portions of the rights associated with preferred stock are specified by state corporation law. As with debt, however, the bulk of the rights of preferred stockholders are specified by contract, although the form of contract is quite different from the indenture associated with long-term debt. Also like debt, preferred stock is typically nonvoting so long as required dividends are made, except with respect to approval of structural changes to the corporation, such as merger or charter amendments, which would affect the preferred stock's rights.

The preferred stock contract takes the form of the provisions in the issuer's articles of incorporation that set forth the rights of the preferred stock, including the amount of the dividend, the preference on liquidation, and the right of preferred shareholders to elect some portion of the board of directors if dividends are not paid on the preferred stock for a specified period of time, often between four and eight quarters. The timing of this shift in control rights is consistent with the principle that control rights are assigned to the holders of the residual interest in corporate income and assets. When preferred dividends are in arrears (unpaid), dividends cannot be paid on common stock, rendering preferred shareholders the repository of the residual interest in income and assets. Consistent with this analysis, preferred shareholders' right to elect directors terminates when dividend arrearages are paid.

It may seem odd to refer to the provisions of the articles of incorporation governing preferred stock as a contract, because only the corporation participates in their adoption. Keep in mind, however, that the terms are set so as to make them attractive to potential buyers. Indeed, where the issue of preferred stock will be underwritten by an investment bank, the terms are quite literally negotiated between the corporation and the investment bank. Such negotiations are facilitated by a feature of most state corporation laws that authorizes *blank check* preferred stock. Corporations may adopt charter provisions that create a class of preferred stock whose rights will be specified not in the articles of incorporation, but instead in a resolution of the board of directors adopted at the time of issuance.

d. Warrants

Warrants are financial claims that represent not a current interest in the corporation, but the right to acquire common stock from the corporation in the future by paying the specified exercise price. Warrants are often issued in combination with other financial assets, such as a combination offer of debt and warrants.[42]

---

42. Warrants, which are issued by the corporation and may be traded on a stock exchange, should be distinguished from options on the corporation's stock, which are traded on options exchanges and are written by investors with respect to already outstanding shares of the corporation's stock. Both, in turn, should be distinguished from stock options, which are issued by the corporation, typically to executives and employees as part of a compensation plan, and which are never traded.

e. Hybrid Financial Assets

Financial planners can meet the particular needs of a corporation by tailoring hybrid financial assets, which fill in the continuum bifurcated by preferred stock and anchored by debt on one side and common stock on the other. Among the features that can be varied to create hybrid financial assets are (1) the basic characteristic of the asset — debt, preferred stock, or common stock — through a convertibility feature; (2) the residual character of the claim to income and rights on liquidation; and (3) voting rights.

Both preferred stock and debt can be issued in convertible form, which gives the holder the right to convert the preferred stock or debt into common stock, in effect combining one part debt or preferred stock and one part warrant. The exercise price of the warrant is built into the conversion rate, which is the formula that specifies how many shares of common stock will be received in exchange for the original debt or preferred stock. At the issuance of the convertible security, the formula will value the corporation's common stock at more than its market price, so that conversion will be to the holders' advantage only if the value of the common stock appreciates. The result is a financial claim that has the fixed return of debt or preferred stock, but also the opportunity to share in the corporation's residual income should it prosper. The interest or dividend rate on the initial debt or preferred stock is set lower than the market rate for a similar nonconvertible instrument to pay for the conversion right.

The issuer typically will have the ability to influence when the conversion right is exercised through its right to call the convertible security at face value. This call right typically is exercised when the price of the common stock into which the security is convertible exceeds the call price. This has the effect of forcing the holders to convert the securities.[43]

Holders of preferred stock and debt also can be allowed to participate in the success of the corporation by means less direct than conversion. Participating preferred stock and income bonds allow the holders to share in the corporation's income and assets above a specified level without changing the basic characteristic of their financial claim. In both cases, the amount of income or assets received is keyed to the amounts paid common shareholders; in effect, the senior security holders are allowed to share in the residual income of the corporation.

Hybrid securities also vary the voting rights commonly associated with traditional financial assets. Preferred stock, typically nonvoting except on limited matters, can be given full voting rights. This hybrid is often used in venture capital financing in which the investor receives convertible preferred stock, but with voting rights equal to those of the common stock into which the preferred stock is convertible.[44]

Conversely, the corporation can issue classes of common stock that are either completely nonvoting or have lesser voting rights than a companion class of fully voting common stock. The prevalence of such hybrids may have been stunted by the long-standing New York Stock Exchange prohibition on listing nonvoting or

---

43. For discussions of convertible securities, see William Bratton, The Economics and Jurisprudence of Convertible Bonds, 1984 Wis. L. Rev. 667 (1984); William Klein, The Convertible Bond: A Peculiar Package, 123 U. Pa. L. Rev. 547 (1975).

44. See William Sahlman, The Structure and Governance of Venture Capital Organizations, 27 J. Fin. Econ. 473 (1990).

limited-voting stock.[45] However, the importance of this prohibition may be over-stated; few such classes of stock appeared even where they were permitted.[46] Nonetheless, one can imagine circumstances when differential voting rights might be desirable, especially where one party puts a special value on corporate control.[47] This might occur when a family-controlled corporation seeks outside equity financing or, less benignly, when managers seek to protect the corporation and themselves from a hostile takeover. The latter problem is taken up in Chapter IX.

2. WHY CAPITAL STRUCTURE SHOULD NOT AFFECT THE VALUE OF THE CORPORATION: THE MILLER-MODIGLIANI IRRELEVANCE PROPOSITION

The traditional approach to selecting a corporation's capital structure focused on the optimal proportion of debt and equity. Because the interest rate on debt is typically lower than the required return on equity, the idea was that the value of the corporation was maximized by using just the right amount of debt. Although adding debt makes the common stock more risky and therefore increases the required return to (i.e., the cost of) equity, the traditional approach contemplated that, at least at first, the increase will not completely offset the lower cost of debt. The optimal capital structure is reached by adding debt until the impact on the cost of equity of an additional unit of debt offsets the debt's lower interest rate.

Franco Modigliani and Merton Miller (MM) challenged the traditional approach in one of the most famous papers in financial economics.[48] With the help of some strong simplifying assumptions — including that corporations and investors can borrow and lend at the same rate, that there are no taxes, and that capital markets are perfect (that is, information is costlessly available to investors and there are no transactions costs) — MM showed that there is no optimal capital structure. The value of the corporation is not affected by the distribution between debt and equity; that is, capital structure is irrelevant.

The intuition underlying the irrelevance proposition is quite simple. Figure 3.2 represents the balance sheet of a corporation. The left side of the balance sheet sets out the values of the corporation's real assets — its plant, inventory equipment, and the like. The right side of the balance sheet, the corporation's capital structure, sets out the claims on the corporation's real assets, that is, who owns the real assets.

45. This prohibition has ended with respect to initial offerings of classes of low-voting or nonvoting common stock that do not affect the voting rights of holders of already outstanding common stock. See pages 554-555 infra.

46. A careful account of the history of stock exchange voting rights standards is set out in Joel Seligman, Equal Protection in Shareholder Voting Rights: The One Common Share, One Vote Controversy, 54 Geo. Wash. L. Rev. 687 (1986). The current restrictions on the issuance of common stock with differential voting rights are discussed at pages 554-555 infra.

47. For a theoretical development of the value of control, see Milton Harris & Artur Raviv, Corporate Governance: Voting Rights and Majority Rules, 20 J. Fin. 203 (1988); Sanford Grossman & Oliver Hart, One Share-One Vote and the Market for Corporate Control, 20 J. Fin. 175 (1987). Ronald J. Gilson, Controlling Shareholders and Corporate Governance: Complicating the Comparative Taxonomy, 119 Harv. L. Rev. 1641 (2006), surveys the empirical evidence on the role of controlling shareholders and the techniques by which control is maintained.

48. Modigliani & Miller, footnote 38 supra.

Figure 3.2
BALANCE SHEET

Real Assets	**Claims on Assets**
Assets	*Liabilities*
Cash	Bonds
Inventory	
Equipment	*Equity*
Plant	Common Stock

The left and right sides of the balance sheet balance because someone must own all the assets. The irrelevance proposition simply states that the value of the corporation's real assets is unaffected by who owns them. Value is affected by changes on the left side of the balance sheet; only claims to value are affected by changes on the right.

The irrelevance of capital structure to the value of the corporation is consistent with the development of capital asset pricing earlier in this chapter (see pages 189-191 supra). Adding debt to the capital structure makes equity more risky, with the result that the cost of equity increases correspondingly, offsetting the lower cost of debt. MM proved this result by showing that arbitrage would enforce it. Envision a circumstance where capital structure is not irrelevant — that is, when adding more debt somehow does not increase the cost of common stock to reflect the additional risk. In this setting, the common stock of a corporation with debt in its capital structure would sell for a higher price (i.e., reflect a lower cost to the corporation) than that of an identical corporation without debt. But a rational investor could then sell shares of the "overvalued," leveraged firm and use the proceeds together with borrowed funds to purchase shares of the "undervalued," unleveraged firm. It is easy to show that the investor's self-leveraging of the unleveraged firm duplicates the returns from owning the common stock of the leveraged firm but at less cost. The increase in the demand for shares of the unleveraged firm and in the supply of shares of the leveraged firm resulting from efforts to take advantage of this arbitrage opportunity would increase the price of the common stock of the unleveraged firm and decrease the price of the common stock of the leveraged firm. The process would continue until the two corporations' market values become identical despite their different capital structures. Just as shareholders' ability to diversify on their own makes corporate-level diversification irrelevant, shareholders' ability to leverage their own holdings makes corporate-level leverage irrelevant.[49]

49. The following example demonstrates the arbitrage process. Suppose two corporations have the following valuations:

	Company A	Company B
Net operating income	$10,000	$10,000
Interest on debt	————	3,600
Earnings available to common stock	$10,000	6,400
Expected return to common stock (equity capitalization rate)	0.15	0.16

3. WHY CAPITAL STRUCTURE MAY AFFECT FIRM VALUE

The principal contribution of Modigliani and Miller was not the irrelevance proposition's descriptive accuracy. Corporations consistently act as if capital structure does matter, including corporations whose chief financial officers have studied the irrelevance proposition in business school. Rather, the proposition has served to define financial economists' research agenda for the last 30 years — to identify the circumstances that would cause changes on the right side of the balance sheet to change the value of the real assets on the left side of the balance sheet. Four categories of circumstances have been identified. Three explain why the presence of debt in the capital structure may increase the value of the corporation: the existence of taxes, the information content of debt; and the discipline of debt on the corporation's management. The fourth — bankruptcy costs — explains why debt may reduce value.

a. Taxes

In the United States, the returns to debt and the returns to common stock are taxed differently. Corporate earnings used to pay interest on debt are not taxed at the corporate level (because interest payments are deductible by the corporation), but interest paid is taxable income to the investor. Thus, the earnings used to service debt are taxed only once, at the investor level. In contrast, dividends on common stock are taxed at the corporate level (because dividend payments are not deductible by the corporation) and are also taxable income to the shareholders. Thus, the income used to service common stock is taxed twice. By shifting the capital structure from equity to debt, the taxes paid by the corporation are reduced by the amount of the interest paid times the corporation's tax rate, which increases the value of the corporation. Note, however, that value is increased in a peculiar way. The pretax returns resulting from the corporation's real assets do not

Market value of stock	$66,667	$40,000
Market value of debt		$30,000
Total value of firm	$66,667	$70,000
Implied overall capitalization rate	15%	14.3%
Debt to equity ratio	0	75.0%

The overall capitalization rate of Company *B* (its cost of capital) is lower than that of Company *A* because the expected return on Company *B*'s leveraged stock has not risen relative to that of Company *A*'s unleveraged stock sufficiently to offset the lower rate paid on the debt. This situation cannot be stable. If you held 1 percent of the common stock of Company *B* (the overvalued, leveraged stock) worth $400, you should sell the stock and borrow $300 at 12 percent, the same interest rate as paid by Company *B*. You should then buy 1 percent of the common stock of Company *A* (the undervalued, unleveraged stock) for $667.67. Before these two transactions, your expected return on your Company *B* stock was 16 percent — the equity capitalization rate — of your $400 investment: $64. Your expected return on your new $667.67 Company *A* investment is 15 percent: $100. From this return you would subtract the $36 interest owed on the borrowed $300, leaving you $64, precisely the same as your return on your Company *B* stock. The difference is that you have invested only $367.67 cash in Company *A*, which is less than the $400 investment you had in Company *B*, resulting in a higher return to the investment in Company *A*. You would repeat this transaction — selling stock in Company *B* and buying stock in Company *A* with borrowed funds — until the returns to holding the two stocks become the same, at which point capital structure would no longer affect the value of the corporations.

This example is drawn from Van Home, footnote 2 supra, at 274-275.

increase; only the after-tax returns do. There is merely a shift of value from the government to shareholders.

While critics of MM quickly recognized the importance of taxes to the controversy over optimal capital structure, the extent of the principle's influence is still a matter of debate because the tax effect depends on the relation between the personal tax rates on returns to debt and to common stock. Suppose that, as was the case for a substantial period of time, interest is taxed at a maximum rate of 70 percent, but that the returns to common stock are taxed at a lower rate or not at all. While dividends would be taxed at the same rate as interest, the return on common stock could be taken out as capital gain by selling the stock rather than receiving a dividend. Suppose capital gains are taxed at only 20 percent and the corporate-level tax is 50 percent. The after-tax income available to a debt holder on $100 of corporate earnings paid out as interest would be $30,[50] but the after-tax income available to a common stockholder on $100 profit from the sale of stock would be $40.[51] Moreover, because the shareholder could defer the personal tax by not selling the stock, the present value of the tax on return to common stock would further decline.

Where the balance comes out depends on the relation between the corporate tax rate, the personal tax rate on interest income, and the tax rate on capital gains. These rates have changed frequently in recent years, which would have changed the optimal level of debt in a corporation's capital structure. For an analysis indicating that as rates stood in 2002, there is a slight edge to corporate debt over equity, see Klein & Coffee, footnote 2 supra, at 373 n.21.

b. The Information Content of Capital Structure

Suppose management of a corporation has favorable private information concerning the future earnings of the corporation that, if known, would cause the market to increase its valuation of the corporation's stock.[52] How could management disclose the favorable information in a way such that the market would believe it rather than dismiss it as management puffery? If additional debt increases the likelihood of bankruptcy, and bankruptcy is especially costly to managers because managers' human capital investment in the corporation is undiversified (see page 187 supra), then increasing the amount of debt in the capital structure would imply that management believes the future is positive. See Bengt Holstrom & Jean Tirole, The Theory of the Firm III, Capital Structure, in Handbook of Industrial Organization 1, 79 (R. Schmalansee & R. Willig eds., 1998). Thus,

---

50. Interest payment $100
    Corporate tax (50%)   0
    Personal tax (70%)   70
      Balance $ 30

51. Corporate earnings $100
    Corporate tax (50%)   50
              $ 50
    Personal tax (20%)   10
      Balance $ 40

52. Would this be inconsistent with the ECMH?

capital structure decisions can help management credibly transmit private information to the market.

A corporation's choice of capital structure helps transmit management's private information in a second way. Suppose the corporation needs to raise funds to finance a project. The choice between raising the funds by issuing debt or issuing stock can indicate whether management's private information concerning the project is favorable. If favorable, management will borrow the funds rather than sell common stock, because the market price of common stock (without management's private information) is too low; if unfavorable, management will sell common stock because the market price of common stock (without management's private information) is too high. As a result, the choice of debt or equity by which to finance a project will cause the market to revalue the corporation's real assets in light of the new information conveyed by the capital structure choice.[53]

From this perspective, a corporation's optimal capital structure shifts over time, depending on the corporation's current circumstances and management's expectations for the future.

c. The Disciplinary Effect of Debt

More recently, in work pioneered by Michael Jensen,[54] a corporation's capital structure has come to be understood as also having a corporate governance function, that is, a role in reducing the agency costs associated with the separation of ownership and management.[55] Suppose a corporation has substantial *free cash flow*, i.e., cash from its operations that exceeds the cash needs of the corporation's business and the profitable investment opportunities available to it. What should the corporation do with the funds? From the shareholders' perspective, the answer is clear: distribute the funds as a dividend so that shareholders can reinvest it in other ventures that require cash for profitable investments. From management's perspective, however, the choice may look different. An important body of literature argues that managers, left to their own devices, will maximize not the corporation's profits but rather other goals that more directly benefit managers.[56] For example, there is evidence that the size of management salaries is better predicted by the level of a corporation's sales than by its profitability. Thus, managers might prefer to use free cash flow to increase the size of the corporation even if the shareholders would be better served by having the funds distributed as a dividend. This is similar to a managerial preference to diversify the corporation's business as a means to diversify their human capital even though shareholders can diversify their portfolios on their own (see page 187 supra). Thus, managers

---

53. The point originates with Stewart Myers & Nicholas Majluf, Corporate Financing and Investment Decisions When Firms Have Information That Investors Do Not Have, 13 J. Fin. Econ. 187 (1984). For a survey of the empirical evidence supporting the point, see Clifford Smith, Investment Banking and the Capital Acquisition Process, 15 J. Fin. Econ. 3 (1986).

54. See Michael Jensen, Agency Costs of Free Cash Flow, Corporate Finance and Takeovers, 76 Am. Econ. Rev. (Pap. & Proc.) 323 (1986); Michael Jensen, The Eclipse of the Public Corporation, Harv. Bus. Rev. (Sept.-Oct. 1989), at 61.

55. The concept of agency costs is developed in Chapter I.

56. See id.

might pursue conglomerate acquisitions even though the likely market response to their announcement is a drop in the price of the corporation's stock.[57]

What can shareholders do to constrain management's inclination to misuse the corporation's free cash flow? One possibility is to try to force management to pay the free cash flow out as a dividend. However, the board of directors' decision with respect to the corporation's dividend policy will be protected by the business judgment rule, which generally provides that in the absence of bad faith, courts will not interfere with the business decisions of the board of directors unless they are irrational.[58] The dividend decision — which reflects the board's assessment of the potential profitability of the corporation's business opportunities and the best way to finance them — is the quintessential business decision.[59] And because it is almost always possible to establish a rational justification for pursuing a particular corporate project rather than paying a dividend, judicial intervention is an unlikely constraint on management's misuse of free cash flow.[60] Thus, shareholders would have to replace management through a proxy fight to compel payment of free cash flow as a dividend, a difficult and expensive process.[61] Alternatively, disgruntled shareholders could simply sell their shares, but note that this would not allow them to avoid the valuation consequences of management's non-value-maximizing strategy. The market price of the stock will reflect the fact that management is poorly investing the corporation's free cash flow.

Suppose instead that the corporation adopts a capital structure that increases the amount of the corporation's debt to the point where all free cash flow is required to pay the interest on the debt. What would happen if the corporation did not pay out its previously free cash flow as interest? Failure to pay required interest would be a breach of the debt contract, which would allow the debt holders to accelerate the entire obligation and likely throw the corporation into bankruptcy and management into the street. Debt thus imposes a very different level of discipline on management's discretion than does equity. Equity's complaints are blocked by the business judgment rule; debt's complaints likely would trigger management's replacement.

What would happen to the value of the corporation as a result of substituting debt for equity? Because the presence of the debt in the capital structure would

---

57. See Mark Mitchell & Kenneth Lehn, Do Bad Bidders Make Good Targets?, 98 J. Pol. Econ. 372 (1990).

58. This subject is taken up in detail in Chapter II.

59. See Kamin v. American Express, pages 198-199 supra.

60. The most famous case in which a court actually ordered the payment of a dividend makes the point. In Dodge v. Ford Motor Co., 204 Mich. 459, 170 N.W. 668 (1919), Henry Ford caused the Ford Motor Company to pursue a strategy of annually lowering the price of its cars even though they could be sold at a higher price. This might seem like a perfectly sensible competitive practice, designed to keep market share and prevent potential competitors from entering the market. For a successful contemporary example of this strategy, see Yoder, America Ascendant — U.S. Companies' New Competitiveness, Wall. St. J. (Sept. 8, 1994) at 1 (Hewlett-Packard dominates computer printer market by continual anticipatory price cutting). The court recited the applicability of the business judgment rule: "It is a well-recognized principle of law that directors of a corporation, and they alone, have the power to declare a dividend. . . . Courts of equity will not interfere in the management of the directors unless it is clearly made to appear that they are guilty of fraud or misappropriation . . . , or refuse to declare a dividend . . . when a refusal to do so would constitute a fraud or breach of . . . good faith. . . ." Mr. Ford declined the invitation to offer a business justification for his action. The court explained Ford's strategy in the following terms: "[Mr. Ford's] testimony creates the impression . . . that he thinks the Ford Motor Company has made too much money, has had too large profits, and that although large profits might still be earned, a sharing of them with the public, by reducing the price of the output of the company, ought to be undertaken."

61. See Chapter IX for the barriers to a successful proxy fight.

prevent management from misusing free cash flow, the value of the corporation should increase. The makeup of the right side of the balance sheet would thus alter the value of the left side through the disciplinary effect of debt on agency costs.[62]

d. Bankruptcy Costs

The first three explanations for how capital structure can affect the value of the corporation show how debt might increase the value of the corporation. What are the limits of these explanations? Does debt also impose costs that can decrease the value of the corporation?

The principal cost imposed by debt is an increased risk of default. Consider two corporations in the defense industry, both of which have cash flows of $100,000 per year before any dividend payments to shareholders or interest payments to debt holders. Corporation *A* has a capital structure made up entirely of common stock on which it pays dividends of $75,000, while Corporation *B* has a capital structure that includes debt with annual interest of $75,000. Now suppose that cutbacks on government spending for weapons systems reduce both corporations' annual pre-dividend, pre-interest cash flow to $50,000.

The effect of adverse industry conditions is quite different on the two firms. Corporation *A* would simply reduce its dividend. In contrast, Corporation *B* would default on its debt, resulting in bankruptcy. Would this increased risk that the corporation will enter bankruptcy in the event of a business downturn affect the value of the corporation?

The answer depends on the costs of bankruptcy. If bankruptcy were a frictionless process which, when triggered, simply transferred ownership of the corporation to debt holders, increased debt and the corresponding increase in the risk of bankruptcy would have no valuation consequences. But if bankruptcy is costly, then the presence of debt will have a negative effect on the value of the corporation. The cost of bankruptcy is a transfer to, for example, bankruptcy lawyers, the expected value of which reduces the value of the corporation. The greater the expectation of bankruptcy and the greater the expectation of bankruptcy costs, the larger the negative impact of debt on the value of the corporation.

With the addition of the costs of debt, we have the beginning of a theory of optimal capital structure. A corporation should continue adding debt to its capital structure until the impact of another unit of debt causes its average cost of capital to increase. This will happen when the benefits from debt as a result of taxes, information transmission, and management discipline are offset by the increased likelihood of bankruptcy, as additional downturns in business result in insufficient funds to pay interest. Thus, the size of bankruptcy costs becomes an important determinant of a corporation's optimal capital structure.

---

62. Michael Jensen has argued that leveraged buyouts restrict the use of a corporation's free cash flow in just this way. See Jensen, Eclipse of the Public Corporation, supra footnote 54. Shareholders are paid a large premium for their stock, the acquisition of which is financed by debt. The effect of the transaction is to replace most of the equity component of the corporation's capital structure with debt. A portion of the increase in value from the transaction—represented by the premium paid target shareholders and the profit to the acquirer resulting from the expected increase in operating performance-is made up of the capitalized value of the cash flow that is no longer spent on losing investments. For a survey of the empirical evidence bearing on increased leverage as a disciplinary device, see Ronald Gilson & Bernard Black, The Law and Finance of Corporate Acquisitions ch. 11 (2d ed. 1995).

What do we know about the magnitude of bankruptcy costs? In absolute terms they do not seem large. The available estimates, which date back to the 1970s, suggest direct bankruptcy costs — legal fees, accounting fees, administrative costs, and the like — of approximately 3 percent of assets.[63] But even if the magnitude is increased to account for the increased cost of professional services, relative bankruptcy costs do not seem high enough to have a significant impact on capital structure. Recall that for capital structure purposes, it is the *expected* cost of bankruptcy that is relevant: the costs of bankruptcy multiplied by its likelihood. The likelihood of bankruptcy would have to be very high for the expected cost to exceed 1 percent of assets.

The analysis changes, however, if the indirect costs of bankruptcy are added. Indirect costs result from the impact of bankruptcy on the corporation's ability to conduct its business. Does Bloomingdale's lose its cachet to high-income shoppers if it is in bankruptcy? Will customers buy computers from a bankrupt company if there is doubt about the company's surviving to provide future support? Will highly skilled employees make further investment of their human capital in a bankrupt company? For many corporations, success depends on intangible assets like reputation, expectation of future service, and the value of skilled employees. If bankruptcy threatens these assets, then the cost of bankruptcy may be very high indeed.[64]

The impact of indirect costs of bankruptcy is consistent with a more traditional view of capital structure — that a corporation's optimal capital structure, the point at which additional debt reduces the value of the corporation, depends on the particular nature of its business and the particular nature of its assets.

C. OPPORTUNISM AMONG THE HOLDERS OF FINANCIAL CLAIMS: OPTION PRICING

The previous section discussed the circumstances in which different ways of dividing a corporation's financial assets — its capital structure — have the potential to increase the value of its real assets. This section takes up the inevitable consequence of the corporation's issuing more than one kind of financial asset: the effort by holders of one class of financial asset to transfer value from the holders of other classes to themselves. To see this, recall the analysis of how adding debt to the capital structure has the potential to increase the value of the corporation by reducing its income taxes. One way of understanding the federal government's tax claim is to view it as a preferred stock with a dividend rate equal to the corporation's marginal tax rate. Efforts to reduce taxes serve to shift value from the holder of one type of financial asset, the government, to the holders of the residual financial asset in the corporation, the common shareholders. This section considers what corporate finance can teach about conflict over value between holders of two types of financial assets — common shareholders and debt holders.[65]

---

63. See Michelle White, Bankruptcy Costs and the New Bankruptcy Code, 38 J. Fin. 477 (1983); Edward Altman, A Further Empirical Investigation of the Bankruptcy Cost Question, 39 J. Fin. 1067 (1984).

64. For an analysis of a corporation's balance sheet that is expanded to include such intangible assets, see Bradford Cornell & Alan Shapiro, Corporate Stakeholders and Corporate Finance, Fin. Mgmt. 5 (Spring 1987).

65. A similar conflict exists between common shareholders and preferred shareholders. While analysis of the nature of the conflict is similar to that of the conflict between common shareholders and debt

The holders of all of the corporation's financial assets have an interest in preventing opportunistic value transfers among the holders of different kinds of financial assets. If a potential purchaser of a financial asset believes that the holders of different financial assets can in the future act to shift value to themselves, the risk of that occurrence will cause the purchaser to lower the price she is prepared to pay for the financial asset in the first place. The result would be a kind of "lemon's market" in which the prices of all senior financial assets reflect the risk of opportunistic value transfers by common shareholders because those who do not intend to behave opportunistically cannot credibly commit not to do so.[66] Thus, the ability to recognize the potential for opportunistic value transfers by common shareholders and to devise effective protections can increase the value of the corporation.

The problem of opportunistic value transfers among holders of different financial assets can be approached through the lens of what has become a central paradigm of corporate finance: *option pricing theory.* Our concern here is not with the mathematical formula for determining the price of an option. Rather, we draw on the important insight originating with Fischer Black and Myron Scholes that many familiar securities can be recharacterized as options.[67] Option pricing theory then reveals what factors make those options more or less valuable, thereby illuminating how the two parties to an option — the holder of the option and the holder of the security to which the option relates — will act to make their financial asset more valuable.

We first set out the basic structure of put and call options and show how the common stock in a corporation that also has debt outstanding can be understood as a call option. We then take up the factors that determine the value of an option to understand how shareholders can act to transfer value from debt holders to themselves. Finally, we survey the kinds of mechanisms — statutory, contractual, and fiduciary — that protect against value transfers from debt holders to common shareholders.

1. THE BASIC STRUCTURE OF PUT AND CALL OPTIONS

A *call option* gives the holder the right to *purchase* from the writer of the option a specified asset at a specified price at a specified time. The specified price is called the *exercise* or *strike price.* If the option can be exercised only on a single date, it is a *European* call option; if it can be exercised over a period, it is an *American* call option. A call option's value is obviously related to the value of the underlying asset. If the value of the asset is greater than the exercise price at maturity, the option is *in the money* and will be exercised. If the value of the asset is less than the exercise price at maturity, the option is *out of the money* and will not be exercised.

---

holders, the protections differ in nature. For an analysis of these protections, see William Bratton, Corporate Finance 353-412 (5th ed. 2003).

66. A lemon's market can develop when there are facially similar products of high and low quality, and the high-quality product costs more to produce but purchasers cannot distinguish between them. In this setting, purchasers will refuse to pay the price that would be warranted by the high-quality product because of the possibility that they will receive a low-quality product. Because the high-quality product has higher production costs, no company will produce it unless it receives a higher price. The result is a lemon's market in which only the low-quality product will be produced. See George Akerlof, The Market for Lemons: Qualitative Uncertainty and the Market Mechanism, 84 Q.J. Econ. 488 (1970).

67. Fischer Black & Myron Scholes, The Pricing of Options and Corporate Liabilities, 81 J. Pol. Econ. 637 (1973).

For example, a call option to purchase a share of stock with an exercise price of $5 will be exercised if the value of the share exceeds $5 and will not be exercised if the value of the share is less than $5.

A *put option* gives the holder the right to *sell* to the writer of the option a specified asset at the exercise price. If the value of the underlying asset is less than the exercise price, it is *in the money* and will be exercised. If the value of the asset is more than the exercise price, the option is *out of the money* and will not be exercised. For example, a put option to sell a share of stock with a strike price of $5 will be exercised if the value of the share is less than $5 and will not be exercised if the value of the share is more than $5.

We can now show that common stock in a corporation that has also issued debt has the characteristics of a call option. The value of the common stock in such a corporation is the value of the corporation less the value of the debt. If the debt is not repaid when due, the corporation will go into reorganization, and for purposes of simplicity, we will assume that the common shareholders are eliminated and the debt holders become the owners of the corporation. On maturity, the value of the debt is either its face value, if it is repaid, or the value of the corporation's assets, if it is not, and the debt holders succeed to the ownership of the corporation.

In this setting, by causing the corporation to issue debt the common shareholders can be seen as having sold the corporation's equity to the debt holders in return for (1) the proceeds from the debt, (2) a management contract for the period the debt is outstanding, and (3) a *call option* to repurchase the equity with an exercise price of the face value of the debt plus interest. The shareholders' call option is in the money if the corporation's assets are worth more than the amount due on the debt, and out of the money if the corporation's assets are worth less. On the debt's maturity date, the shareholders exercise their option by repaying the debt or let the option expire by defaulting.

The advantage of this recharacterization of common stock as an option is apparent when we understand what determines the value of an option. Because the shareholders retain control of a leveraged firm (through the management contract in the recharacterization), they have the ability to take actions that transfer value from the debt holders to themselves. Option pricing theory identifies what actions will effect that transfer by increasing the value of the shareholders' option.

2. THE DETERMINANTS OF OPTION VALUE

Valuing a call option is easy at expiration. An out-of-the-money option, where the value of the underlying asset is less than the strike price, has no value. The value of an in-the-money option, where the value of the underlying asset is greater than the strike price, is simply the difference between the two. Valuation becomes more complicated, however, when time remains before expiration and, as with an option on common stock, it is not known what the value of the underlying asset will be on expiration. In this circumstance, even an out-of-the-money option has value because it may become in the money by the time of expiration.

Five factors determine the value of a call option:[68] (1) the current value of the underlying asset, (2) the exercise price, (3) the time value of money, (4) the variability

68. This discussion draws on Gilson & Black, footnote 2 supra, at 252-257.

in the value of the underlying asset (measured by its standard deviation),[69] and (5) the time to expiration.

a. Current Value of the Underlying Asset

The value of a call option increases as the value of the underlying asset increases because the current value of the asset is the best estimate of the likely value of the asset on expiration. This is true even if the option is out of the money; an increase in the value of the underlying asset increases the likelihood that the option will be in the money at expiration. The size of the increase depends on how far out of the money the option is at the time, the time remaining until expiration, and the variability in the value of the underlying asset.

b. The Exercise Price

The impact of a change in the exercise price is simply the flip side of the impact of a change in the current value of the underlying asset. Just as an increase in the value of the underlying asset increases the value of the option when the exercise price is held constant, so does a decrease in the exercise price when the value of the underlying asset is held constant. Either reduces the amount by which an option is out of the money (or increases the amount by which an option is in the money) and therefore increases the value of the option.

c. The Time Value of Money

A call option allows the holder to acquire the right to appreciation in the value of the underlying asset immediately, but to defer payment until maturity when the exercise price must be paid. This reduces the present value of the exercise price. The higher the interest rate and the longer the time to the option's maturity, the lower the present value of the exercise price and the greater the value of the option.

d. Variability in the Value of the Underlying Asset

The most important influence on the value of an option is the variability (variance) in the value of the underlying asset. The greater the variability, the greater the value of the option. Recalling the capital asset pricing model, this relationship may seem backward. When the underlying asset itself is valued, increasing the variability in the asset's returns results in a *decrease* in the asset's value. However, when an option on that asset is valued, increasing the variability in the asset's returns results in an *increase* in the option's value.

Considering the different payoffs to the holder of a call option and to the holder of the underlying asset lays bare the intuition underlying this shift in the effect of increased variability. The two curves in Figure 3.3 show the probability

---

69. See pages 185-186 supra.

Figure 3.3
**EFFECT OF VARIABILITY IN VALUE OF UNDERLYING ASSET
ON OPTION VALUE[70]**

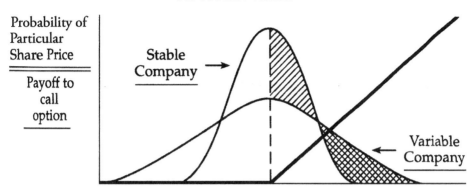

distributions of the common stock prices of Stable Co. and Variable Co. at the maturity date of call options on their common stock. The thick black line represents the profits from exercising a call option (the difference between the value of the stock and the exercise price). If the common stock of the two companies trades at the same price, the stock of Stable Co. would be more attractive because it has the same expected value as Variable Co. stock but less risk.

This relationship is reversed if one holds an option on the common stock, rather than the stock itself. Increasing the risk increases both the upside and the downside potential of the stock's expected value, as is apparent from the "tails" of Variable Co.'s distribution of future values. But the holder of an option on the stock is indifferent to the downside potential. If the value of the stock is below the exercise price, the option holder simply will not exercise. Thus, in valuing an option, only the portion of the probability distribution to the right of the exercise price matters. Increasing the variability of the value of the common stock moves that portion of the distribution to the right. This increases the probability of a higher stock price and, therefore, the gain to the option holder.

The impact of an increase in variability on the value of an option can be seen in Figure 3.3. The increased variability of Variable Co. increases the likelihood of both high and low stock values compared with Stable Co. The increase in the likelihood of low values is irrelevant to an option holder. In the event of a low value, the option holder will not exercise; she cannot do worse than that regardless of how low the stock value moves. But the increase in the likelihood of high values does matter. Because the means of the two companies' distributions are identical, the areas to the right of the exercise price in Figure 3.3 are also identical. However, a significant portion of the right side of Variable Co.'s distribution is at higher prices than the right side of Stable Co.'s distribution. This can be seen by comparing the striped portion of Stable Co.'s distribution with the cross-hatched area of Variable Co.'s distribution. In the relevant range of values — that is, values greater than the exercise price — Variable Co. stock simply has a higher expected value than Stable Co. stock. And as we saw in subsection a supra, an increase in the value of the underlying asset increases the value of the option.

70. This figure is from Ronald Gilson & Bernard Black, The Law and Finance of Corporate Acquisitions 240 (2d ed. 1995).

Table 3.1
THE EFFECT OF RISKY INVESTMENT ON THE VALUE OF STOCK AND DEBT

	Before Risky Investment	*After Risky Investment*				
		Pays off		*No Payoff*		
Stock value	$ 250	.5($2200−$750)	+	.5($0)	=	$ 725
Debt value	$ 750	.5($750)	+	.5($0)	=	$ 375
Firm value	$1,000					$1,100

e. Time Remaining Until Expiration

The length of time until an option expires has two effects on option value. As discussed in subsection c supra, the longer the time before the exercise price must be paid, the lower its present value and the higher the value of the option. But a longer period before maturity also affects option value through its impact on the variability of the value of the underlying asset. The longer the period before maturity, the more time there is for a favorable result to occur. More formally, the variance in the expected value of the underlying asset on the option's maturity is proportional to the time until maturity (and the standard deviation is proportional to the square root of the time remaining).[71] Increasing the time to maturity increases the variability of the underlying asset and, pursuant to subsection d supra, increases the value of the option.

3. MODES OF OPPORTUNISTIC BEHAVIOR AMONG HOLDERS OF FINANCIAL ASSETS

We can now use option pricing theory to understand how the holders of common stock can increase the value of their financial asset at the expense of the holders of more senior financial assets, like debt and preferred stock, whose claims on the corporation's real assets are fixed. These strategies track the determinants of option value set out in the previous section.

a. Increasing the Riskiness of the Corporation's Investments

Option pricing theory provides that increasing the variability of the underlying asset increases the value of the option. Therefore, common shareholders in corporations with debt or preferred stock outstanding have an incentive to increase the riskiness — the variance in expected returns — of the corporation's investments. This is demonstrated through the following example.

Suppose a corporation has assets of $1,000, entirely invested in government bonds, and a capital structure with $750 in debt. In this circumstance, the debt will be paid with certainty, and the value of the debt is $750 and the value of the common stock is $250. Now suppose the corporation is offered the opportunity to replace its investment in government bonds with a risky $1,000 investment. This

71. Id. at 243.

Table 3.2
THE EFFECT OF RISKY INVESTMENT WITH NEGATIVE EXPECTED VALUE ON THE VALUE OF STOCK AND DEBT

	Before Risky Investment	*After Risky Investment*				
		Pays off		*No Payoff*		
Stock value	$ 50	.2($2,000−$750)	+	.8($0)	=	$250
Debt value	$750	.2($750)	+	.8($0)	=	$150
Firm value	$800					$400

investment has an expected return of $1,100 composed of a 50 percent likelihood of a $2,200 return and a 50 percent likelihood of a zero return. This is a good investment for the shareholders. As set out in Table 3.1, if the transaction pays off, the shareholders exercise their option and repay the debt, and are left with stock worth $1,450. If the transaction does not pay off, they default on the debt, having lost their stock's $250 pre-transaction value. The debt holders do not fare so well. If the transaction pays off, the debt holders are repaid. If the transaction does not pay off, the debt holders lose the $750 pre-transaction value of the debt. On an expected-value basis, the transaction *increases* stock value from $250 to $725, but *decreases* the value of the debt from $750 to $375. The result of increasing the risk of the corporation's investment is a shift of $375 in value from the debt holders to the shareholders.[72] Because the debt holders' returns are fixed, all of the potential gains from the transaction go to shareholders. And because the shareholders cannot lose more than the pre-transaction value of their stock, debt holders bear most of the potential loss from the transaction.[73]

In the previous example, the expected value of the firm still increased as a result of the risky investment even though it also resulted in the transfer of value from debt holders to shareholders. This was because the risky investment that replaced the government bonds had a positive expected value net of its cost. However, this need not be the case. Because of the option-like characteristics of common stock, an investment may increase the value of common stock even though it *decreases* the expected value of the corporation. Suppose the corporation is more highly leveraged, this time with assets of $800 all of which are invested in government bonds, and debt of $750. The stock is then worth $50. This time the risky investment costs $800, with a 20 percent likelihood of a return of $2,000 and an 80 percent likelihood of a return of 0. The investment has a net expected value of negative $400, which reduces the value of the firm to $400. Nonetheless, the investment is still attractive to shareholders. If the investment pays off, the shareholders exercise their option and repay the debt, leaving a stock value of $1,250. If the investment does not pay off, the shareholders lose their $50 and the debt holders lose $750. As shown in Table 3.2, the result is a transfer of $200 from debt holders to shareholders and a $400 reduction in the value of the corporation.

---

72. The expected value of the common stock goes up by a total of $475—the $375 shift in value from debt holders and the $100 expected return on the investment.

73. This is just the flip side of treating the shareholders as having a call option on the firm with an exercise price of the amount of debt outstanding. The difference is that the sale of the firm takes place at maturity pursuant to the put, rather than on issuance of the debt subject to repurchase pursuant to the call.

The two examples illustrate an additional point. The shareholders' interest is not a perfect substitute for an option to the extent that the stock has some value at the time the shareholders act. To the extent of this value, the shareholders do bear some of the downside of an increase in risk. Thus, the shareholders' incentive to act like option holders increases as the value of their stock decreases.

b. Increasing the Firm's Leverage by Withdrawing Funds

An alternative means to increase the value of the corporation's common stock by shifting risk from the common shareholders to the debt holders does not require a new investment. Suppose the corporation has assets of $1,500, comprising $500 in cash and an investment with an expected value of $1,000: a 50 percent likelihood of a return of $1,500 and a 50 percent likelihood of a return of $500.

The corporation also has debt of $1,000. In this circumstance, the debt has a value of $1,000 and the stock a value of $500. Although the investment return is insufficient to repay the debt if the investment result is unfavorable, the cash makes up the difference. Now suppose that the shareholder causes the corporation to pay out the $500 cash as a dividend. As shown in Table 3.3, the result is to increase the risk and reduce the value of the debt. Prior to the dividend, the debt holders were repaid in full even when the investment return was unfavorable because the cash made up the shortfall. After the dividend, the $500 shortfall rests with the debt holders since they then receive only $500 if the investment result is unfavorable. The expected value of the shortfall is $250 (the amount of the shortfall times its likelihood), which is the amount by which the value of the common stock — expected value plus the dividend — increases.

This can be seen from an option perspective by recasting the common stock in terms of a put option. In these terms, the shareholders own the firm, owe the debt holders the face value of the debt, and also own a put option written by the debt holders that allows the stockholders to sell the firm to the bondholders for the amount owed.[74] If the value of the firm is less than the debt, the shareholders exercise their put option and sell the firm to the debt holders for the amount owed on the debt. When the dust clears, the debt holders end up owning the firm if the firm's value is lower than the face value of the debt.

Table 3.3
EFFECT OF WITHDRAWING FUNDS ON THE VALUE OF STOCK AND DEBT

Before $500 Dividend		*After $500 Dividend*	*Stock Plus Dividend*
Stock value	$ 500[*]	.5($1,500−$1,000) = $250	$750
Debt value	$1,000	.5($1,000) + .5($500) = $750	$750

[*] $500 cash + [.5($1,500 + $500)] − $1,000

74. This is just the flip side of treating the shareholders as having a call option on the firm with an exercise price of the amount of debt outstanding. The difference is that the sale of the firm takes place at maturity pursuant to the put, rather than on issuance of the debt subject to repurchase pursuant to the call.

In valuing a put option, a decrease in the value of the underlying asset increases the value of the put; as the value of the asset goes down, the right to sell it at a specified price goes up. By reducing the value of the corporation, paying a dividend increases the value of the shareholders' put option.

c. Increasing the Value of the Option by Extending Its Term

Remember that the value of even an out-of-the-money option increases with an increase in its term. The longer the option will be outstanding, the greater is the likelihood that something good will happen that will cause the option to be in the money. This fact illuminates a good deal about debtor conduct in bankruptcy. Under the Bankruptcy Code, the corporation's management has the exclusive right to propose a plan of reorganization—that is, to propose the terms on which ownership will shift to the debt holders—for a period of four months.[75] That alone extends the shareholders' option for four months, thereby increasing its value and reducing the value of the debt. Additionally, the bankruptcy court has the discretion to extend the exclusivity period that, apparently, it routinely grants for the duration of the proceeding.[76] Finally, the corporation's management continues to run the corporation's business during the proceeding.[77] Assuming management is loyal to shareholders' interests, what strategy should they follow in bankruptcy? Both delay and management's continued influence over the variability of the corporation's revenues work to increase the value of the shareholders' option. Is it surprising that empirical studies show that shareholders commonly receive some interest in the reorganized corporation even if the debt holders' claims exceed the value of the corporation?[78] If the bankruptcy laws extend the term of the shareholders' option, is it surprising that shareholders receive something in exchange for giving up the right to continue to extend that option by delay?[79]

D. *PROTECTION AGAINST INTRACORPORATE OPPORTUNISM*

The opportunity for shareholders to transfer value from senior security holders to themselves is contrary to the interests of *both* groups. Shareholders cannot benefit

---

75. 11 U.S.C. §1121(c) (2005).

76. See Lynn LoPucki & William Whitford, Bargaining Over Equity's Share in the Bankruptcy Reorganization of Large Publicly Held Companies, 139 U. Pa. L. Rev. 125 (1990).

77. 11 U.S.C. §1101(1) (West 2005). Technically, the corporation is styled the "debtor in possession." Management continues to run the corporation unless the bankruptcy court terminates that role and installs a trustee on a finding of fraud, gross mismanagement, or that the appointment is otherwise in the best interests of the bankrupt estate. See 11 U.S.C. §1104 (West 2005).

78. See LoPucki & Whitford, supra footnote 76; Allan Eberhart, William Moore & Rodney Rosenfeldt, Security Pricing and Deviations from the Absolute Priority Rule in Bankruptcy Proceedings, 45 J. Fin. 1457 (1990); Michelle White, Measuring Deviations from Absolute Priority in Chapter 11 Bankruptcy, J. Legal Econ. (July 1992).

79. Julian Franks & Walter Torous, An Empirical Investigation of U.S. Firms in Reorganization, 44 J. Fin. 747 (1989); Julian Franks & Walter Torous, Lessons from a Comparison of U.S. and U.K. Insolvency Codes, 8 Oxford Rev. Econ. Pol. 70 (1992).

from the opportunity so long as would-be senior security holders can anticipate their actions. A potential investor who anticipates such transfers would not buy senior securities unless paid a compensatory higher interest rate. Having to pay extra for the opportunity to transfer value eliminates any benefit from doing so. Moreover, shareholders would not be indifferent between eliminating the opportunity to effect value transfers and paying for the privilege. Some corporations will not wish to engage in opportunistic value transfers, but if such transfers are not effectively prohibited, investors will still require extra compensation. Furthermore, the problem is more serious than simple wealth transfers from senior security holders to shareholders. As we saw in the previous section, shareholders whose equity value is low have an incentive to pursue strategies that actually reduce the value of the corporation: shareholders gain less from the strategies than senior security holders lose. This pattern occurred most dramatically in connection with the savings and loan (S&L) crisis. As many S&Ls approached insolvency—that is, their stock value approached zero—they undertook investment strategies that had a negative expected value because the shareholders received all the gains from such investments, but all the losses fell on the Federal Savings and Loan Insurance Corporation. Thus, there is a social interest in preventing corporations from making systematically inefficient investments.

This section briefly surveys the range of statutory, contractual, and fiduciary barriers to intracorporate opportunism. Beginning with protection for debt holders from shareholder efforts to transfer value, it considers the weak protection provided by statutory legal capital regulation and the somewhat stronger protection provided by the Uniform Fraudulent Conveyance Law. Attention then turns to the contractual protection debt holders negotiate for themselves—debt covenants. Completing the analysis with respect to debt holders, the section closes with an evaluation of the role of fiduciary duty in protecting debt holders: are there circumstances when the board of directors owes a fiduciary duty to debt holders?

1. WEAK PROTECTION: THE STATUTORY LEGAL CAPITAL STRUCTURE

State corporation laws contain a group of rules, collectively referred to as the *legal capital* system, that govern the kinds of consideration for which a corporation can issue common stock and the circumstances under which the corporation can distribute its assets to shareholders, whether by paying dividends or repurchasing its stock. The legal capital rules provide debt holders some protection against value transfers to shareholders; however, the protection is limited in two important respects. First, the protection is provided only against value transfers effected through asset withdrawals; other means of value transfer, such as increasing the risk of the corporation's investments,[80] are left unimpaired. Second, the system is largely ineffective. This section presents a brief overview of the legal capital system. For a more detailed treatment of the subject, see Bayless Manning & James Hanks, A Concise Textbook on Legal Capital (3d ed. 1990).

The legal capital system is composed of two segments: (1) the stated capital requirement and (2) restrictions on distribution of assets to shareholders. The

---

80. See Sec. C.3 supra.

stated capital requirement designates the amount of consideration received by the corporation for the issuance of its shares — the corporation's *stated capital* — and imposes special restrictions on the allowable type and amount of consideration. The original purpose of the stated capital requirement was to assure the creditors that a specified amount of assets existed to protect their claims. Creditors, it was assumed, based their decision to provide funds to the corporation on the amount of capital shown on the balance sheet. If the consideration received for the issuance of shares was overvalued ("watered" stock), or if it was of a character that provided no protection to creditors (for example, stock issued for an intangible asset such as a business plan), creditors were thought to be disadvantaged.

The stated capital requirement was never of much significance to creditors, primarily because sensible creditors never based their investment decisions on book entries in the owners'-equity side of the balance sheet.[81] Moreover, the requirement was quite simple to avoid. State law permitted stock to be issued with an arbitrarily low stated value that capped the shareholders' statutory obligation to contribute funds for their stock. The balance of the consideration was then called *capital surplus* and was not subject to the same limits on withdrawal.

The principal remaining impact of the stated capital requirement is the continued restriction in many states on the types of consideration that can support the issuance of stock. Certain kinds of intangible assets, especially unsecured notes and a promise to render future services, remain unlawful types of consideration in many states.[82] Yet in many start-up and venture capital situations, stock is issued to key employees precisely to induce their promise to render future services, and this promise may be among the corporation's most important assets. While the problem can be avoided with planning,[83] it has the perverse effect of making it difficult for creditors to rely on the corporation's real asset — the expectation of future cash flows based on the performance of key employees. The Revised Model Business Corporation Act (RMBCA) has resolved this problem by expanding the lawful consideration for stock issuance to include "intangible property of benefit to the corporation, including . . . promissory notes, . . . [and] contracts for services to be performed." RMBCA §6.21, Official Comment.

The stated capital requirement also serves as the baseline for one version of the legal capital system's restrictions on distributions of corporate assets to shareholders by dividend payments or stock repurchases.[84] In addition to the prohibition on dividends or repurchases when the company is insolvent, distributions are limited to the amount by which the firm's total assets exceed the sum of its liabilities and stated capital. That is, the corporation's stated capital, thought to be the basis of creditors' investment decisions, cannot be distributed to the shareholders through a dividend or share repurchase. However, as indicated above, the restriction provides little protection: The corporation can set the amount of stated capital

81. Bayless Manning & James Hanks, A Concise Textbook on Legal Capital 20-26 (3d ed. 1990).
82. Id. at 45-46.
83. For example, in a venture capital situation, the issuance of convertible preferred stock with a large liquidation preference to investors may serve to reduce the value of the common stock to a nominal amount provided that the valuation is undertaken on a liquidation rather than a going-concern basis. See Ronald J. Gilson & David Schizer, Understanding Venture Capital Structure: A Tax Explanation for Convertible Preferred Stock, 116 Harv. L. Rev. 874 (2003).
84. From the creditors' perspective, dividends and stock repurchases have the same impact: assets that could have been used to satisfy creditors' claims are distributed to shareholders. Thus, modern statutes treat them as equivalents. See, e.g., Cal. Corp. Code §166 (1997) (definition of "Distribution to Its Shareholders"); RMBCA §1.40 (6) (definition of "Distribution").

as low as it likes, and the consideration received above the designated stated capital becomes *capital surplus*, from which dividend distributions and share repurchases can be made.[85] Moreover, even if capital surplus accounts have been depleted, other forms of surplus, such as a revaluation surplus based on the amount by which the market value of assets exceeds their book value, can subsequently be created.[86]

The alternative version of the legal capital system's restrictions on dividend payments or stock repurchases is an *earned surplus* (or *retained earnings*) test determined by reference to the corporation's balance sheet. This approach does not focus on the allocation of consideration to the corporation's capital accounts when shares are issued, but instead requires that dividends or share repurchases be made only out of some form of accumulated profits (e.g., earned surplus or retained earnings). While the earned surplus test does avoid the transparent manipulation of capital accounts allowable under the surplus restriction approach described above,[87] it provides little more protection to creditors. Accounting standards allow the corporation to retroactively change the particular accounting principles used to construct its balance sheet in ways that substantially influence the amount of profit reported by the corporation and, hence, the amount of earned surplus that appears on the balance sheet.[88] And since it is the representatives of the shareholders — the board of directors — who determine the accounting principles followed by the corporation, it should come as no surprise that earned surplus restrictions on dividend payments and share repurchases are also limited in the protection provided creditors.

The considerable limitations of legal capital rules have led to two major law reform efforts. In 1976 California simply eliminated the concept of legal capital entirely, limiting dividends and repurchases to a corporation's retained earnings as determined in accordance with generally accepted accounting principles. Cal. Gen. Corp. Code §§500(a), 114. In the absence of retained earnings, distributions can still be made if certain financial ratios, patterned after covenants in debt contracts, are met, again determined in accordance with generally accepted accounting principles. Cal. §500(b).

The 1987 RMBCA took a somewhat different tack. Like California, the Model Act eliminated the concept of stated capital and par value. Under the RMBCA, share purchasers are obligated to pay for their shares only the amount and quality of consideration specified in the contract for purchase.[89] Whether the corporation received "enough," or an appropriate type of, consideration then is for the board of directors to determine.[90] Distributions can be made only when the corporation is

---

85. The amount of stated capital per share issued is deemed the share's *par value*. The corporation can also choose to have *no-par* stock, in which case the corporation simply designates a portion of the consideration received as stated capital and the balance as capital surplus.

86. The classic case approving the creation of such a revaluation surplus and the payment of dividends in reliance thereon is Randall v. Bailey, 23 N.Y.S.2d 173 (S. Ct. 1940), *aff'd*, 288 N.Y. 280, 43 N.E.2d 43 (1942), discussed infra.

87. See Manning & Hanks, footnote 81 supra, at 63-69.

88. For example, changing from accelerated to straight-line depreciation early in the life of an asset will reduce depreciation charged, increase income, and therefore increase earned surplus and the corporation's ability to distribute assets to its shareholders. Because depreciation does not affect the corporation's cash flow, changes in how it is accounted for do not change the corporation's actual economic condition. See Robert Holthausen, Evidence on the Effect of Bond Covenants and Management Compensation Contracts on the Choice of Accounting Techniques, 3 J. Acct. & Econ. 73 (1981).

89. RMBCA §6.22.

90. Id. §6.21.

solvent (i.e., when the corporation can pay its debts as they become due), and then only to the extent the corporation's assets exceed its liabilities. Like the California revision, this eliminates any reference to capital or surplus accounts in determining limits on distributions. Thus, the linchpin of the Model Act is how the corporation's assets and liabilities are valued. California solved the problem of the legal capital regime's manipulation of balance sheet and income statement values by requiring conformity with generally accepted accounting principles. The RMBCA, in contrast, grants the board of directors broad discretion in selecting the valuation method to be applied in determining the extent to which total assets exceed total liabilities: "The board of directors may base a determination that a distribution is not prohibited . . . either on financial statements prepared on the basis of accounting practices and principles that are reasonable in the circumstances or on a fair valuation or other method that is reasonable in the circumstances." RMBCA §6.40(c). This is a puzzling choice in one sense. A major problem with the legal capital regime was the corporation's ability to manipulate it, yet the Official Comment is quite explicit that §6.40(c) was intended to give the corporation flexibility in choosing a valuation method. For example, the Official Comment expressly states that current asset values may be used in lieu of historical accounting costs in determining amounts available for distribution.

From a creditor's perspective, might one care less what the standard is than that it be fixed? The facts in Randall v. Bailey, 23 N.Y.S.2d 173 (Sup. Ct. 1940), *aff'd*, 288 N.Y. 280, 43 N.E.2d 43 (1942), illustrate the problem and the different approaches taken by the RMBCA and California. The New York statute in *Randall* limited dividends to surplus — "any value which the corporation's property has in addition to [par or stated value] is surplus." The corporation owned land that had been acquired for $1,526,157.30. Subsequent to its acquisition, the corporation increased the value of the land on its books by $7,211,791.72 to approximate its market value. The increase in the land's value was matched by an increase in the corporation's surplus account — an appreciation surplus. As discussed in connection with Figure 3.2 (page 205 supra), an increase in the value of the corporation's real assets on the left side of the balance sheet is always balanced by an increase in the ownership claims to those assets on the right side of the balance sheet. The question confronting the court was whether the board of directors' determination that the land had increased in value created a surplus from which dividends could be paid. Consistent with the court's holding in *Randall*, under the RMBCA, the board determination of the value of its property is protected by the business judgment rule, and a surplus created by a revaluation of assets is an allowable source of dividends under the Revised Model Act.

California, in contrast, specifies that in determining a corporation's ability to make distributions, values be determined in accordance with generally accepted accounting principles. These impose a fixed, albeit arbitrary, standard: historical cost. Under this approach, the dividend in *Randall* would have been unlawful.

Creditors can take into account the likelihood of shareholders withdrawing assets in setting the initial interest rate. As we saw in Sec. C.3 supra, the real danger is the rules changing after the fact. Is the California approach of a fixed but arbitrary standard (the historical cost of assets specified by generally accepted accounting principles) more effective in allowing creditors to evaluate the risk than the RMBCA's giving the board of directors the discretion to choose the "right" measure for the particular circumstances? Does the California approach really provide a fixed standard? Who decides what are generally accepted accounting principles or how they apply in a particular case? For an argument supporting the RMBCA's approach based on courts' lack of capacity to develop accounting principles, see Manning & Hanks, footnote 81 supra, at 65-67.

2. FRAUDULENT CONVEYANCE LAW

Statutory protection against shareholder efforts to transfer value from debt holders also exists outside the typical state general corporation law. About three-fourths of the states have adopted either the Uniform Fraudulent Conveyance Act or its updated version, the Uniform Fraudulent Transfer Act. These statutes label as fraudulent to a creditor a transfer of assets or a debt incurred if done with actual intent to defraud a creditor. The asset transfer or debt will be fraudulent even without actual intent if accomplished without receiving a "reasonably equivalent value" in exchange for the transfer or debt if (1) the debtor "was engaged or about to engage in a business or a transaction for which the remaining assets of the debtor were unreasonably small in relation to the business or transaction," or (2) the debtor reasonably should have believed that it "would incur debts beyond [its] ability to pay as they became due." Uniform Fraudulent Conveyance Act §4, 7A U.L.A. (1985). These provisions provide a backstop to corporate law and contractual restrictions on shareholder opportunism.[91]

Most directly, fraudulent conveyance law supplements legal capital restrictions by extending the prohibition against distributions when the corporation is insolvent to transfers that take a form other than a traditional dividend or stock repurchase. For example, suppose a corporation distributes funds to its shareholders by loaning them money at a time when the corporation lacks the surplus to pay a dividend. If the loan renders the corporation insolvent, the transaction would be a fraudulent conveyance even if its form falls outside the terms of the corporate statute.[92]

More recently, creditors have sought to apply fraudulent conveyance law to efforts by shareholders to increase the risk of the corporation by increasing its leverage. In the standard form of leveraged buyout transaction, an acquiring company borrows large amounts to acquire all of the outstanding stock of the target corporation. Thereafter, the assets of the target company are pledged to secure the debt the acquiring company incurred to purchase the stock. The impact on target company creditors is no different than if the target company had borrowed the funds directly and paid the proceeds to the shareholders as a dividend: The risk of the corporation's business increases because of the new debt with a resulting transfer of value from the pre-transaction debt holders to the shareholders. Applying fraudulent conveyance law requires this recharacterization; otherwise the transfer to the shareholders is from the acquiring company rather than from the target company, whose debt holders are affected by the transaction and protected by the fraudulent conveyance statute. Provided that a court so

---

91. For the classic statement of the relation between corporate law and fraudulent conveyance law, see Robert Clark, Duties of the Corporate Debtor to Its Creditors, 90 Harv. L. Rev. 505 (1977). Section 548 of the Bankruptcy Act imposes a federal prohibition of fraudulent conveyances. 11 U.S.C. §548 (2005).

92. To be sure, the creditor could argue that the loan had the substance of a dividend if not its form, but legal capital rules deal with the form in which the corporation casts the transaction.

recharacterizes the transaction, the payment to shareholders will be fraudulent if the target company's remaining assets are unreasonably small or if it is unable to pay its debts as they come due.

Here again valuation becomes the central issue. Suppose the mean expected value of the corporation's assets goes up as a result of the buyout, but so does the standard deviation. The result is a shift of value from debt holders to stockholders. But is the statutory trigger of unreasonably small assets met? Does it matter that the acquiring corporation knows that the transaction increases the likelihood of insufficient assets if the mean of the distribution nonetheless represents sufficient assets? The same analysis applies with respect to the corporation's ability to pay its debts as they come due. Is a transaction that substantially increases the likelihood of insolvency fraudulent if the expected value of its cash flow is still positive? How much should it matter that this determination will always be made with the benefit of hindsight — that is, fraudulent conveyance law will be asserted by a disappointed debt holder only if the outcome turns out to be unfavorable?

3. CONTRACTUAL PROTECTION: BOND COVENANTS

Statutory restrictions on transfers of value from debt holders to shareholders leave untouched the most important means of transferring value from debt holders to shareholders: increasing the riskiness of the corporation's expected returns, whether by altering the risk of the corporation's investments or by increasing its leverage. This problem is typically approached through contractual restrictions on the corporation's behavior while the debt is outstanding.

Bond covenants can usefully be grouped into three categories: covenants concerning the corporation's (1) investment activities, (2) capital structure, and (3) dividend payments and stock repurchases.[93] Together they trace the corporation's risk profile; altering that profile breaches the covenant and is a default that, inter alia, accelerates the debt's maturity.

a. Investment Activity Covenants

It is too difficult for debt covenants to specify the allowable activities of a major corporation in sufficient detail to be effective without so restricting its operations that its performance is adversely affected. Rather, certain particularly dangerous activities are restricted, with the bulk of the drafting effort directed at the methods by which the corporation can change its risk profile. Because the interest rate already reflects the riskiness of the corporation's current activities, the task of the covenants is merely to restrict changes. Covenants may either prohibit financial investments or limit them to a specified amount, for example, by preventing the corporation from increasing its risk by investing in uncovered option positions. In contrast, most covenants simply restrict the typical means by which the corporation can change its risk profile. For example, covenants may limit the disposition

---

93. See Clifford Smith & Jerrold Warner, On Financial Contracting: An Analysis of Bond Covenants, 7 J. Fin. Econ. 117 (1979).

of a substantial amount of assets because the proceeds could be reinvested in riskier assets. Similarly, covenants may restrict mergers because the activities of the firm with which the corporation is merged may be riskier.

b. Capital Structure Covenants

Because the risk of the corporation's activities may also be increased by increasing the amount of debt outstanding, covenants may limit total debt outstanding either in absolute amount or as a percentage of the corporation's tangible assets. Similarly, sale and leaseback transactions[94] and other substitutes for debt may also be restricted.

c. Dividend and Stock Repurchase Covenants

Consistent with the view that the legal capital system offers little protection against risk increases due to asset withdrawals, debt holders typically require covenants that contractually restrict the corporation's payment of dividends and stock repurchases. The limit is typically expressed in terms of a specified fund available for dividend payments and stock repurchases composed of the corporation's net earnings and the proceeds of stock sales less amounts previously distributed. Manipulation of earnings figures is constrained by requiring consistency in accounting methods for purposes of the restriction's calculations.

While bond covenants are an important means to reduce debtor opportunism, they are far from costless. Most important, they can reinforce a very different kind of opportunism. Suppose a corporation with debt outstanding is offered an investment opportunity with a favorable net present value, but that is less risky than the corporation's existing business. Just as increasing the riskiness of the corporation's business transfers value from debt holders to stockholders, decreasing the riskiness of the business results in a transfer in the opposite direction. Under these circumstances, common shareholders may cause the company to forgo otherwise desirable investments because a portion of the gain would be shared with debt holders.[95] Additional constraints on corporate investment increase the risk that beneficial investments may be forgone. One response might be that covenants that turn out to be too tight can always be amended, especially if the amendment will allow an investment favorable to debt holders. However, publicly held debt is subject to the Trust Indenture Act of 1939, which requires a bondholder majority vote to approve amendments and which, in §316(b), requires unanimous consent to amend indenture provisions relating to payment of principal and interest on the dates due. Thus, amendment can be quite

---

94. In a sale and leaseback transaction, a company sells an asset to a third party while simultaneously leasing it back. If the length of the lease approximates the asset's useful life and all maintenance and insurance obligations rest with the lessee, the transaction is the economic equivalent of a loan from the third party secured by the asset.

95. See Stewart Myers, Determinants of Corporate Borrowing, 5 J. Fin. Econ. 147 (1977).

costly in terms of both time and expense. For this reason, bonds that require extensive covenant protection are often privately placed with a limited group of investors. Such bonds are not subject to the Trust Indenture Act and, more important, involve sufficiently few holders that amendment negotiations are less costly.[96]

This analysis suggests an explanation for a peculiar phenomenon concerning the use of bond covenants. For most of this century, even bonds sold to the public routinely contained covenants that restricted increased indebtedness and distributions to shareholders. While the breadth of the covenants depended on the creditworthiness of the issuer, even the best issuers accepted covenants that contained a limit on future debt issuance.[97] Beginning in the mid-1970s, such covenants largely disappeared from the debt issues of large industrial corporations. By 1984, a survey of the outstanding debt of the 100 largest U.S. industrial corporations showed that only 28 percent of the outstanding issues and only 16 percent of the newer issues contained a debt covenant.[98] This pattern of weak covenant protection also characterized the debt termed "covenant-lite," which financed many private equity acquisitions during the 2002-2007 period. "Covenant-lite" loans increased from approximately $100 million in 2004 to $103.9 billion in the first half of 2007.[99]

Commentators have argued that the covenants disappeared in the mid-1970s because they seemed unnecessary; that is, other forces imposed noncontractual restrictions on shareholder action to transfer wealth from debt holders. Debt holders realized that capital structure decisions of large corporations were made by senior management. Managers' self-interest lay in reducing the risk of their human capital by growth and diversification financed with retained earnings. In this respect, management served as the debt holders' champion: maintaining or reducing the corporation's risk protected both managers and debt holders. Debt holders thus were said to have come to rely on management's self-interested exercise of its discretion for protection rather than on covenants. Absent a means by which shareholders could assert their interests in increasing the risk of the corporation despite management's preference for avoiding risk, covenants were unnecessary.[100]

Matters changed in the mid-1980s when an agent for shareholder interests appeared in the form of leveraged buyout associations. These groups acted as the shareholders' champion by effecting takeovers and recapitalizations that substantially increased the debt levels of corporations whose debt did not contain covenant protection. An innovation in financing—the development of "junk"

---

96. See Smith & Warner, footnote 93 supra; Ileen Malitz, On Financial Contracting: The Determinants of Bond Covenants, Fin. Mgmt. (Summer 1986).

97. See William Bratton, Corporate Debt Relationships: Legal Theory in a Time of Restructuring, 1989 Duke L.J. 92.

98. Morey McDaniel, Bondholders and Corporate Governance, 41 Bus. Law. 413, 425-426 (1986).

99. See Floyd Norris, A Rush to Supply Cash to Lend to Poor Corporate Credit Risks, N.Y. Times (July 7, 2007) at C3.

100. Bratton, footnote 96 supra, at 141-142; John Coffee, Stockholders Versus Managers: The Strain in the Corporate Web, 85 Mich. L. Rev. 1, 68-69 (1986). The reemergence of debt with limited covenant protection in the 2002-2007 period was said to result from a global liquidity glut fueled by high savings outside the United States; oversupply of capital resulted in borrowers securing more favorable terms (i.e., loans with fewer covenants). See Dennis K. Borman, The Game: Sketchy Loans Abound with Capital Plentiful, Debt Buyers Take Subprime-Type Risks, Wall St. J. (March 27, 2007) at C1.

or high-yield bonds[101]— made funds available for such transactions. At the same time, acquirers promised target managers equity participation in the transaction, thereby leaving debt holders unprotected. Debt holders responded by seeking new forms of covenant protection called *event risk covenants.* These covenants are triggered by the occurrence of specified events such as a leveraged buyout or leveraged recapitalization that has the potential to transfer value to shareholders from debt holders. Once triggered, the covenants either give the debt holder the right to put the debt back to the corporation at face value, or cause the interest rate to increase to offset the increased risk (and thereby block the transfer of value). See Ronald Gilson & Bernard Black, The Law and Finance of Corporate Acquisitions ch. 11. (2d ed. 1995).

4. FIDUCIARY DUTY AND THE COVENANT OF GOOD FAITH AND FAIR DEALING

It is striking that none of the statutory protections against shareholder opportunism respond to the most significant means by which value is transferred from debt holders: increasing the riskiness of the corporation's business. Legal capital rules and prohibition of fraudulent conveyances focus on distributions to shareholders, but opportunistic changes in investment are left unrestricted. The explanation for this gap in statutory coverage is straightforward: such prohibitions are extremely difficult to write. First, there are myriad ways the corporation can change the riskiness of its business. The corporation can buy a risky business or sell a safe one; it can invest in speculative securities; it can forgo insurance; it can accept a risky project or decline a safe one. A specific prohibition would be both ungainly and ineffective: however long the list of forbidden transaction forms, a particular transaction could always be formally restructured to avoid the statute without altering the transaction's substance. Second, even if a statute did specify the transaction forms by which risk could be increased, one would still have to determine whether a particular transaction did in fact increase risk, a determination that depends on beliefs about the probability distribution of expected returns — hardly a subject that lends itself to crisp drafting or predictable judicial rulings.

Interestingly, the same type of problem arises, albeit with less severity, in connection with contractual restrictions on opportunism. Bond covenants do attempt to restrict some of the mechanisms by which a corporation can alter the riskiness of its business; however, substantial room remains for value transfers.[102] Indeed, this problem was exacerbated in recent years as the use of bond covenants in public debt issuances declined.

The difficulty of drafting effective statutory or contractual restrictions on value transfers through increased risk has led some commentators to urge judicial

101. "Junk bonds" is a common term used for high-yield bonds; that is, bonds that pay a significantly higher interest rate than the investment-grade bonds issued by the largest corporations because they present a much higher risk of default. Beginning in 1977, Drexel Burnham Lambert, Inc. began creating a market for original-issue junk bonds that grew rapidly. Initially the proceeds of these bonds were used to expand an existing company's business. In the 1980s, junk bonds were increasingly used to finance highly leveraged hostile takeovers that had as one of their purposes altering the target corporation's capital structure. See Ronald Gilson & Bernard Black, The Law and Finance of Corporate Acquisitions ch. 11 (2d ed. 1995).

102. See page 225 supra.

protection through one of two doctrines. Where no contractual protection exists, commentators have suggested that the corporation's directors should be treated as having a *fiduciary duty* to debt holders as well as shareholders. The substance of the duty would be to prevent opportunistic transfers of value from debt holders to shareholders. The point would not be to *prevent* alterations in the corporation's risk; competitive conditions might require such changes. Rather, directors' fiduciary duty would require that debt holders be compensated for any increase in risk. See, e.g., Morey McDaniel, Bondholders and Stockholders, 1988 J. Corp. L. 205; Morey McDaniel, Bondholders and Corporate Governance, 41 Bus. Law. 413 (1986); Lawrence Mitchell, The Fairness Rights of Corporate Bondholders, 65 N.Y.U. L. Rev. 1165 (1990).

An analogous argument is made when covenants negotiated by debt holders do not cover the particular risk-increasing technique the corporation employs. Then the contention is that since the debt holders could not anticipate all corporate actions that would adversely affect debt holders, courts should prohibit such unanticipated actions through imposing on the corporation the obligation of *good faith* and *fair dealing* — a doctrine designed to ensure that neither party to a contract acts so as to deprive the other of the anticipated benefits of the contract. See, e.g., Victor Brudney, Corporate Bondholders and Debtor Opportunism: In Bad Times and Good, 105 Harv. L. Rev. 1821 (1992); William Bratton, Corporate Debt Relationships: Legal Theory in a Time of Restructuring, 1989 Duke L.J. 92.

Courts have been inhospitable to both claims. With respect to fiduciary duty, the Delaware Chancery Court summarized the law concisely: "Under our law — and the law generally — the relationship between a corporation and the holders of its debt securities . . . is contractual in nature. . . . The terms of the contractual relationship agreed to and not broad concepts such as fairness define the corporation's obligations to its bondholders." Katz v. Oak Industries, 508 A.2d 873 (Del. Ch. 1986). Even when the debt is convertible to common stock, the Delaware Supreme Court has declined to provide debt holders extra-contractual protection. Simons v. Cogan, 549 A.2d 200 (Del. 1988).

Application of the implied covenant of good faith and fair dealing has been similarly rejected. In Metropolitan Life Ins. Co. v. RJR Nabisco, Inc., 716 F. Supp. 1504 (S.D.N.Y. 1989), the court declined to apply the doctrine to protect the existing debt holders of RJR Nabisco from the reduction in the value of their securities as a result of a leveraged buyout. The court noted that Metropolitan Life had considered the risk of such a transaction, and nonetheless purchased bonds it knew lacked protection against increased debt.

Why are courts so reluctant to extend common law protection against transfers of value to shareholders? Statutory protection is absent because of the difficulty of drafting protection that is both effective and sufficiently certain of interpretation that the parties understand the limits on their activity. Is the problem of providing protection without undue uncertainty any easier for courts? In declining to impose the implied covenant of good faith and fair dealing in connection with the RJR Nabisco leveraged buyout, the *Metropolitan Life* court stated: "In the final analysis, plaintiffs offer no objective or reasonable standard for a court to use in its effort to define the sorts of actions their 'implied covenant' would permit a corporation to take, and those it would not." In a footnote to this sentence, the court goes on to state: "Under plaintiffs' theory, bondholders might ask a court to prohibit a company like RJR Nabisco not only from engaging in an LBO, but also from entering a new line of business . . . or from acquiring new businesses such as RJR Nabisco did when it acquired Del Monte."

If the court's reluctance to intervene reflects concerns about uncertainty, are there circumstances that can be expressed with sufficient precision that judicial protection is appropriate? Statutory protection against fraudulent conveyances does arise when the corporation is insolvent, the uncertainty concerning the particular transactions covered presumably being ameliorated by the specificity of the triggering condition. With this in mind, consider the following analysis.

Credit Lyonnais Bank Nederland, N.V. v. Pathe Communications Corp.
1991 WL 277613 (Del. Ch. 1991)

ALLEN, Ch.: The possibility of insolvency can do curious things to incentives, exposing creditors to risks of opportunistic behavior and creating complexities for directors. Consider, for example, a solvent corporation having a single asset, a judgment for $51 million against a solvent debtor. The judgment is on appeal and thus subject to modification or reversal. Assume that the only liabilities of the company are to bondholders in the amount of $12 million. Assume that the array of probable outcomes of the appeal is as follows:

[Outcome]	*Expected Value*
25% chance of affirmance ($51mm)	$12.75 million
70% chance of modification ($4mm)	$ 2.8 million
5% chance of reversal ($0)	$ 0
Expected Value of Judgment on Appeal	$15.55 million

Thus, the best evaluation is that the current value of the equity is $3.55 million. ($15.55 million expected value of judgment on appeal—$12 million liability to bondholders). Now assume an offer to settle at . . . $17.5 million. By what standard do the directors of the company evaluate the fairness of [this offer]?

The creditors of this solvent company would be in favor of accepting . . . [the offer to] avoid the 75% risk of insolvency and default. The stockholders, however, . . . very well may be opposed to acceptance of the $17.5 million offer [even though] the residual value of the corporation would increase from $3.5 to $5.5 million. This is so because the litigation alternative, with its 25% probability of a $39 million outcome to them ($51 million−$12 million = $39 million) has an expected value to the residual risk bearer of $9.75 million ($39 million × 25% chance of affirmance), substantially greater than the $5.5 million available to them in the settlement.

. . . [I]t seems apparent that one should in this hypothetical accept the best settlement offer available providing it is greater than $15.55 million, and one below that amount should be rejected. But that result will not be reached by a director who thinks he owes duties directly to shareholders only. It will be reached by directors who are capable of conceiving of the corporation as a legal and economic entity. Such directors will recognize that in managing the business affairs of a solvent corporation in the vicinity of insolvency, circumstances may arise when the right (both the efficient and the fair) course to follow for the corporation may diverge from the choice that the stockholders (or the creditors, or the employees, or any single group interested in the corporation) would make if given the opportunity to act. Thus, the option perspective can support a rule that gives directors' fiduciary duties to debtholders when a firm approaches insolvency.

In the *Pathe* example, shareholders' perverse incentive to increase the risk of the corporation would result in action that reduces not only the expected value of the bonds, but also the expected value of the firm. When the firm is in the range of insolvency, the court suggests that the board of directors' fiduciary duty no longer runs exclusively to the shareholders, but extends to the corporation as an entity. This would prohibit accepting negative-expected-value investments that reduce the value of the firm because the loss to debt holders exceeds the gain to shareholders. Is this the same as a fiduciary duty to bondholders? In Table 3.1, page 216 supra, the corporation accepts an investment with a positive expected value that nonetheless results in a substantial transfer from debt holders to shareholders. Would a zone of insolvency fiduciary duty to the corporation, as opposed to the debt holders, permit such a transfer because the value of the firm increases?

Why is the *Pathe* court willing to take on the uncertainty that previously has made legislatures and courts reluctant to restrict value transfers effected through altering the corporation's risk? One explanation might be that it is the social loss reflected in the *Pathe* example that is important. From this perspective, transfers between shareholders and debt holders are the private concern of the parties unless they result in a reduction in the value of the firm. While social losses can also result outside the zone of insolvency, as we saw in Table 3.2, page 217 supra, the limited range of application of the fiduciary obligation to the entity arguably limits the extent of uncertainty created.

The wisdom of a judicially imposed fiduciary obligation to the entity in the zone of insolvency thus may depend on the extent of uncertainty. In the *Pathe* example, the corporation presumably was in the zone of insolvency based on the expected value of its cause of action. But that value depends on subjective estimates of the likelihood of affirmance on appeal.[103] Similarly, whether a particular project has a negative expected value depends on subjective estimates of future cash flow, which in turn depend on subjective assessments of the underlying determinants of cash flow from the investment. Is this any different from the kind of uncertainty that concerned the court in *Metropolitan Life?*

Suppose the board of directors of a corporation that might be in the zone of insolvency must choose between two investments, buying government bonds and investing in a risky project that the board believes has a higher expected return even taking into account the increased risk. While there is no uncertainty concerning the return from the government bond, assessment of the return (and the risk) from the risky project depends on subjective evaluation. If investing in a negative-expected-value project while in the vicinity of insolvency violates the board's fiduciary duty, which investment would you advise the board to take? Does discouraging risk taking in financially troubled companies also impose a social cost by increasing the likelihood of their failure? Might imposing a fiduciary

---

103. Note that the *Pathe* court assumed a precise distribution, both in likelihood and resulting amounts, of the appeal.

obligation on the entity create a barrier to changing the corporation's previously unsuccessful strategy?

Once the corporation is insolvent in fact, rather than in the vicinity of insolvency, courts have imposed a fiduciary duty to creditors on the board. Geyer v. Ingersoll Publishing Co., 621 A.2d 784 (Del. 1992). Is there less uncertainty associated with insolvency in fact than with the vicinity of insolvency? Would it be preferable to use the commencement of bankruptcy proceedings as the trigger of a shift in the object of the board's fiduciary duty?

In North American Catholic Educational Programming Foundation, Inc. v. Gheewalla, 930 A.2d. 92 (Del. 2007), the Delaware Supreme Court resolved the debate by setting the trigger of the directors' shift in responsibility from shareholders to creditors as insolvency: "When a solvent corporation is navigating in the zone of insolvency, the focus for Delaware directors does not change: directors must continue to discharge their fiduciary duties to the corporation and its shareholders. . . ." Id. at 101. Once the shift is triggered, the creditors then have a derivative, not a direct, claim against directors for breach of fiduciary duty. Id. at 102. For an argument that the object of the directors' fiduciary duty should never shift, see Henry T. C. Hu & Jay Lawrence Westbrook, Abolition of the Corporate Duty to Creditors, 107 Colum. L. Rev. 1321 (2007).

IV FORMING THE CORPORATION

A. SELECTION OF STATE OF INCORPORATION

Those who have decided to engage in business in the corporate form must choose the state in which to incorporate. If the business is to be conducted predominantly within a single jurisdiction, it is usually desirable to incorporate there.[1] Otherwise, the corporation will be subject to various taxes in both the state of incorporation and the state of its principal business activity (where it will be a "foreign" corporation). Further, it will be subject to suit, receivership proceedings, and various other forms of regulation in both states.[2]

But if the corporation is to engage in multistate business, selection of the state in which to incorporate is more complex. Rates of franchise fees and other taxes vary from state to state, and the corporation statutes of some states — as is evident from the materials throughout this book — may differ significantly from those of most other states in respect to many important matters. Some state statutes may be characterized as being "permissive" and "sympathetic" to the desires of corporate management and others as adopting a more "regulatory" or "paternalistic" attitude. Not all states make special statutory accommodations for close corporations. Further, because of the traditional choice-of-law rule that the law of the state of

---

1. For a study explaining why states "generally have much greater ability to attract incorporations from in-state firms than from out-of-state firms," and that the choice is "between incorporating in the home state or in Delaware," see Lucian A. Bebchuck & Alma Cohen, 46 J.L. & Econ. 383 (2003).

2. See generally James D. Cox & Thomas L. Hazen, Corporations 48 (2d ed. 2003); Chester Rohrlich, Organizing Corporate and Other Business Enterprises §4.01 (6th ed. 2000).

incorporation governs the corporation's internal affairs,[3] it may be highly desirable to incorporate in a state with a large body of case law interpreting the corporation statutes, which can afford greater certainty as to their meaning.[4]

At the end of the nineteenth century, New Jersey and Delaware, seeking the revenue generated by incorporation fees and corporation taxes, adopted the first "modernized" general incorporation statutes, which were "congenial" to corporate management and their counsel.[5] Because Delaware's statute remained permissive, it became the favorite state in which large businesses incorporated, serving as the state of incorporation for nearly 60 percent of Fortune 500 companies and half of the corporations listed on the New York Stock Exchange and Nasdaq.[6] Although such permissive statutes have been the subject of substantial criticism,[7] since Delaware's last major revision in 1974, many states have recast their corporation laws, either following Delaware's model or seeking to improve it, allegedly in an effort to induce companies to incorporate within their borders[8] as a means of enhancing state receipts from various taxes[9] and producing increased business for the state's corporate bar, which has been characterized in Delaware as "the confidante, advocate and friend of corporate management."[10]

Nonetheless, it appears that "Delaware is likely to remain dominant"[11] because of its well-developed body of judicial decisions and its specialized and politically

---

3. For the view that the internal affairs doctrine "is something of an anomaly in our law," "is quite contrary to ordinary choice of law rules," and seems to "violate fundamental principles of state sovereignty," see Daniel J. H. Greenwood, Democracy and Delaware: The Mysterious Race to the Bottom/Top, 23 Yale L. & Pol'y Rev. 381, 411-430 (2005).

4. See generally Roberta Romano, Law as a Product: Some Pieces of the Incorporation Puzzle, 1 J.L.. Econ. & Org. 225 (1985).

5. See Note, Little Delaware Makes a Bid for the Organization of Trusts, 33 Am. L. Rev. 418 (1899).

6. E. Norman Veasey & Christine T. DiGuglielmo, What Happened in Delaware Corporate Law and Governance from 1992-2004? A Retrospective on Some Key Developments, 153 U. Pa. L. Rev. 1399, 1403 (2005). Between 1996 and 2000, 85 percent of companies that decided to incorporate outside their home states chose Delaware. Lucian A. Bebchuk & Assaf Hamdani, Vigorous Race or Leisurely Walk: Reconsidering the Competition over Corporate Charters, 112 Yale L.J. 553, 556 (2002).

7. See, e.g., Comment, Law for Sale: A Study of the Delaware Corporation Law of 1967, 117 U. Pa. L. Rev. 861 (1969).

8. The most recent have been Nevada and Texas. See Byron F. Egan & Curtis W. Huff, Choice of State of Incorporation — Texas Versus Delaware: Is It Now Time to Rethink Traditional Notions?, 54 SMU L. Rev. 249 (2001).

9. For 2005, Delaware's incorporations revenue accounted for 22 percent of all taxes, see http://www.corp.delaware.gov/default.shtml.

10. John A. C. Hetherington, "When the Sleeper Wakes": Reflections on Corporate Governance and Shareholder Rights, 8 Hofstra L. Rev. 183, 204 (1979). Compare Curtis Alva, Delaware and the Market for Corporate Charters: History and Agency, 15 Del. J. Corp. L. 885, 920 (1990), for the view that "it is in shareholders' interest . . . [that] the corporate bar is the driving force behind the Delaware General Corporation Law . . . because the corporation bar is the group whose interests are most closely aligned with shareholders. Their livelihood depends on providing the optimum corporate environment." For the view that the Delaware bar gains the greatest "benefits from the state's dominance in the market for corporate charters," see Jonathan R. Macey & Geoffrey P. Miller, Toward an Interest-Group Theory of Delaware Corporate Law, 65 Tex. L. Rev. 469 (1987), and "that Delaware law will be generally pro-defendant in order to attract chartering, but will do so in such a way that demand for the services of lawyers and other professional advisors remains strong," see Jonathan Macey, Delaware: Home of the World's Most Expensive Raincoat, 33 Hofstra L. Rev. 1131, 1137 (2005). See also Marcel Kahan & Ehud Kamar, Price Discrimination in the Market for Corporate Law, 86 Cornell L. Rev. 1205, 1246 (2001): "[T]he average annual income of Delaware lawyers ($117,276 in 1990) is higher, even before adjusting for differences in the cost of living, than that of lawyers in such metropolitan hubs as New York ($111,572), Washington, D.C. ($92,259), or Chicago ($90,722)."

11. Michael Klausner, Corporations, Corporate Law, and Networks of Contracts, 81 Va. L. Rev. 757, 846-847 (1995). See also Bebchuk & Hamdani, footnote 6 supra (Delaware has achieved a virtual monopoly); Marcel Kahan & Ehud Kamar, The Myth of State Competition in Corporate Law, 55 Stan. L. Rev. 679 (2002) (same); William J. Carney, The Production of Corporate Law, 71 S. Cal. L. Rev. 715, 717 (1998) (corporate law has become relatively uniform largely because of model standards and codes).

independent chancery court, which deals almost exclusively with corporate cases, whose judges have achieved a national reputation for expert and expeditious rulings without juries, and which is "uniquely structured to maximize responsiveness to changing business developments."[12]

Because management decides where to incorporate, it has been generally agreed that states competing for corporations draft corporation codes that are attractive to management. The central question that has been debated is whether this state competition for corporations has been beneficial or detrimental to shareholder welfare. On the one hand, critics contend that the permissive statutes allow management to run corporate affairs with little interference from shareholders or the courts and thus diminish management's responsibility and accountability.[13] In the 1970s Professor William Cary, condemning the competition among states as a "race for the bottom," contended that "the Delaware courts have contributed to shrinking the concept of fiduciary responsibility and fairness, and indeed have followed the lead of the Delaware legislature in watering down shareholders' rights. . . ."[14] Reform proposals have included a federal incorporation option, federal minimum standards of corporate responsibility, uniform certificate of incorporation provisions to ensure more shareholder control, and more frequent shareholder approval of corporate transactions.[15]

On the other hand, supporters of the present regime contend that the best system of corporate governance emerges from competition among the states, describing it as "the genius of American corporate law."[16] They reason that management will choose the state of incorporation most likely to maximize shareholder welfare because market mechanisms align shareholder and management goals. If managers do not act in the shareholders' best interests, the price of the corporation's stock will decline. When this occurs, the probability that incumbent management will be displaced by a hostile takeover increases because capital will naturally pursue underutilized resources. Managers also wish to increase firm value to augment the value of their services in the market for managerial talent. Finally, it is said that diverse state corporation laws allow each firm to choose the state with the best mix of laws, considering its operating policies, organizational structure, and management preferences. Thus, Professor Daniel Fischel believes that "statutes such as Delaware's corporation law, as interpreted by judicial decisions, that give management maximum flexibility in running the corporation's affairs are based on . . . [the] principle of freedom to contract. Recent developments in the theory of the firm emphasize the fundamental compatibility between manager and

12. Jill E. Fisch, The Peculiar Role of Delaware Courts in the Competition for Corporate Charters, 68 U. Cin. L. Rev. 1061, 1081 (2000). See also Kahan & Kamar, footnote 11 supra, at 1212.

13. See, e.g., Del. Gen. Corp. Law §102(b)(7) (1993), — Note 4, page 109 supra — permitting corporations to limit the liability of directors for breach of their "duty of care."

14. William L. Cary, Federalism and Corporate Law: Reflections Upon Delaware, 83 Yale L.J. 663, 696 (1974). See also Alison G. Anderson, the Meaning of Federalism: Interpreting the Securities Exchange Act of 1934, 70 Va. L. Rev. 813 (1984). For more recent judicial and legislative developments pointing in the opposite direction, see Mark J. Loewenstein, Delaware as Demon: Twenty-five Years After Professor Cary's Polemic, 71 U. Colo. L. Rev. 497 (2000).

15. See Ralph Nader, Mark J. Green & Joel Seligman, Constitutionalizing the Corporation: The Case for the Federal Chartering of Giant Corporations (1976); Donald E. Schwartz, A Case for Federal Chartering of Corporations, 31 Bus. Law. 1125 (1976); Bebchuk & Hamdani, footnote 6 supra.

16. Roberta Romano, The Genius of American Law (1993).

shareholder interests and suggest that shareholders' welfare is maximized under a regime such as Delaware's."[17]

Several empirical studies have attempted to test the effect of state competition on shareholder welfare. One measured the effect on stock prices of reincorporation in Delaware. It found that shareholders of reincorporated firms earn positive abnormal returns of 30 percent over the 25-month period preceding and including the month of change, and discovered no evidence of any negative market reaction either before or after reincorporation.[18]

On the other hand, Professor Roberta Romano surveyed several hundred firms and found "that most reincorporations preceded or coincided with a series of distinct and identifiable transactions, the most frequent being a public offering (for the most part, the firm's first public offering), the initiation or expansion of an active mergers and acquisitions program, and antitakeover defensive maneuverings." She concluded that it may be "that some other event generated abnormal returns for the firms and swamped the negative impact of a reincorporation announcement."[19] For example, a strong positive market reaction to an acquisitions program that a reincorporation may facilitate might be combined with a weaker negative market reaction to the reincorporation, resulting in a net positive reaction.[20]

Another study hypothesized that the present system "is desirable because it is capable of generating a variety of sets of legal rules (standard form contracts) from which corporate participants (shareholders and managers) may choose in a value maximizing manner. . . ." It concluded that there was "no significant difference . . . between the financial performances of corporations in strict and liberal states."[21]

In a series of articles, Professor Lucian Bebchuk has been fairly skeptical of the value of state charter competition. He contends that "state competition produces a race for the top with respect to some corporate issues but a race for the bottom with respect to others,"[22] especially in respect to two major problem areas.

17. Daniel R. Fischel, The "Race to the Bottom" Revisited: Reflections on Recent Developments in Delaware's Corporation Law, 76 Nw. U. L. Rev. 913, 921, 944 (1982). See also Frank Easterbrook & Daniel R. Fischel, Voting in Corporate Law, 26 J.L. & Econ. 395 (1983); Ralph Winter, State Law, Shareholder Protection, and the Theory of the Corporation, 6 J. Legal Stud. 251 (1977); Roberta Romano, The Political Economy of Takeover Statutes, 73 Va. L. Rev. 111 (1987).

18. Peter Dodd & Richard Leftwich, The Market for Corporate Charters: "Unhealthy Competition" versus Federal Regulation, 53 J. Bus. 259 (1980). See also Robert Daines, 62 J. Fin. Econ. 525 (2001) ("Delaware corporate law improves firm value" and makes Delaware firms "more likely to receive takeover bids"). Compare Guhan Subramanian, 20 J.L. Econ. & Org. 32 (2004) (this "effect 'disappears' when examined over time and when examined for firms that are economically meaningful").

19. Romano, footnote 16 supra, at 232, 250. See also Melvin A. Eisenberg, The Structure of Corporation Law, 89 Colum. L. Rev. 1461 (1989).

20. For further development of this view see Lucian Bebchuk, Alma Cohen & Allen Ferrell, Does the Evidence Favor State Competition in Corporate Law?, 90 Cal. L. Rev. 1775, 1790-1797 (2002).

21. Barry D. Baysinger & Henry N. Butler, Race for the Bottom versus Climb to the Top: The ALI Project and Uniformity in Corporate Law, 10 J. Corp. L. 431, 459-461 (1985). See also Michael Bradley & Cindy A. Schipani, The Relevance of the Duty of Care Standard in Corporate Governance, 75 Iowa L. Rev. 1 (1989). Similarly, a study of "seven major Delaware court decisions, all of which appeared to make significant, unanticipated changes in Delaware corporate law," found "no statistically significant market reaction to any of the seven decisions," and concluded that "it is unlikely that investors consider differences between the corporate laws of different states to be . . . important." Elliott J. Weiss & Laurence J. White, Of Econometrica and Indeterminacy: A Study of Investors' Reactions to "Changes" in Corporate Law, 75 Cal. L. Rev. 551, 553, 602 (1987).

22. Lucian A. Bebchuk, Federalism and the Corporation: The Desirable Limits on State Competition in Corporate Law, 105 Harv. L. Rev. 1435, 1440 (1992); see also footnotes 6 and 20 supra. Compare Kahan & Kamar, footnote 11 supra, at 684-685: "[T]hat states compete for incorporations is a myth. . . . [S]tates other than Delaware stand to derive only small benefits from attracting incorporations, and take at most half-hearted steps to that end."

The first is where the interests of public shareholders diverge from those of managers or dominant shareholders (to whom "states have an incentive to make themselves attractive").[23] Professor Bebchuk finds that state competition does not prevent managers from seeking rules that result in a "significant" redistribution of value from the shareholders to the managers, such as one that permits self-dealing by managers,[24] "even if the rules are value-decreasing,"[25] that is, do not maximize a shareholder value. He also finds that managers will seek some rules that weaken market discipline directly, such as one that impedes proxy contests and hostile takeover bids (which "might well have been the most important issue with respect to which state corporate law has had to develop a position in the last twenty years"),[26] even if the rule results in decreased share value.[27]

The second major problem area is that even when the interests of shareholders and managers do not diverge, "state competition may well produce socially undesirable results whenever a corporate law issue involves significant externalities,"[28] that is, costs that are borne by third parties. For example, managers will prefer to incorporate in a state that benefits the company at the expense of creditors. Professor Bebchuk concludes that "federal rules, or at least federal minimum standards, are warranted with respect" to those issues where state competition results in a race for the bottom such as self-dealing transactions, taking of corporate opportunities, and all aspects of takeover bids and proxy contests.[29]

Finally, Professor Mark Roe concludes that "Delaware's strongest competitor" is national. "Delaware players are conscious that if they mis-step, Federal authorities could step in." Congressional statutes, SEC rules, federal court opinions, and New York Stock Exchange regulations "regularly threaten to, and do, displace state corporate law" and "set the broad boundaries — of an uncertain and changing demarcation — within which the states can move." Consequently, a strong interstate race "whether to the top or to the bottom" is "implausible or indeterminate."[30]

23. Bebchuk, footnote 22 supra, at 1501.
24. Id. at 1484.
25. Id. at 1501.
26. Lucian A. Bebchuk & Allen Ferrell, Federalism and Corporate Law: The Race to Protect Managers from Takeovers, 99 Colum. L. Rev. 1168, 1198 (1999). See also Bebchuk, Cohen & Ferrell, footnote 20 supra, at 1783 ("the success of a state in the market for incorporation increases as its level of antitakeover protection increases"); Bebchuck & Cohen, footnote 1 supra.
27. Bebchuck, footnote 22 supra, at 1468.
28. Id. at 1494.
29. Id. at 1510.
30. Mark J. Roe, Delaware's Competition, 117 Harv. L. Rev. 588 (2003). See also John C. Coffee Jr., The Direction of Corporate Law: The Scholars' Perspective, 25 Del. J. Corp. L. 87 (2000). For the view that while "the possibility of federal preemption constitutes a threat to Delaware," it is only significant "in times of crisis or scandal" when "systemic change generates a populist political payoff" for members of Congress, see Marcel Kahan & Edward Rock, Symbiotic Federalism and the Structure of Corporate Law, 58 Vand. L. Rev. 1573 (2005). For the view that "the most dramatic [corporate law] governance changes" have come from the national stock exchanges, prodded by the SEC trying to get them "to do what the agency fears the federal courts will not let it do directly and which, until the next Enron, will not provide Congress sufficient reason to authorize additional federal intrusion into the area traditionally regulated by state law," see Robert B. Thompson, Corporate Federalism in the Administrative State: The SEC's Discretion to Move the Line Between the State and Federal Realms of Corporate Governance, 82 Notre Dame L. Rev. 1143 (2007).

   For a balanced evaluation of the "race to the bottom" debate, see Brett H. McDonnell, Getting Stuck Between Bottom and Top: State Competition for Corporate Charters in the Presence of Network Effects, 31 Hofstra L. Rev. 681 (2003), concluding that (1) although "the original Cary position still has much force, . . . some degree of competition between states can help to increase the chances that the dominant state's law is good," and (2) "proponents of different systems have not yet given an adequately strong reason for discarding" the present system of "state competition in corporate law but a mainly national, unified approach to securities law. . . ."

B. *COMPLIANCE WITH STATE REQUIREMENTS*

1. PREPARATION OF DOCUMENTS

After selecting the corporate domicile, the process of incorporation may begin, although certain transactions — several of which will be considered in greater detail later — such as preliminary agreements among those who are to be shareholders, pre-incorporation subscriptions to shares to be issued,[31] and pre-incorporation contracts with third parties made on behalf of the corporation to be formed (page 288 infra) may have already been undertaken. The following statute, with footnotes indicating some of the diverse provisions in various jurisdictions, illustrates the mechanics of incorporation:

Delaware General Corporation Law (2006)

Sec. 101. *Incorporators; how corporation formed; purposes.* (a) Any person, partnership, association or corporation, singly or jointly with others,[32] and without regard to such person's or entity's residence, domicile or state of incorporation, may incorporate or organize a corporation under this chapter by filing with the Division of Corporations in the Department of State a certificate of incorporation[33] which shall be executed, acknowledged, and filed in accordance with section 103 of this title.

(b) A corporation may be incorporated or organized under this chapter to conduct or promote any lawful business or purposes, except as may otherwise be provided by the constitution or other law of this State. . . .

Sec. 102. *Contents of certificate of incorporation; contents.* (a) The certificate of incorporation shall set forth:

(1) The name of the corporation which (i) shall contain one of the words "association," "company," "corporation," "club," "foundation," "fund," "incorporated," "institute," "society," "union," "syndicate," or "limited" (or abbreviations thereof, with or without punctuation), or words (or abbreviations) . . . of like import in foreign countries or jurisdictions (provided they are written in roman characters or letters); . . . [and which] (ii) shall be such as to distinguish it upon the records in the office of the Division of Corporations in the Department of State from the names that are reserved on such records and from the names on such records of each other corporation . . . organized or registered . . . under the laws of this State . . .

(2) The address (which shall include the street, number, city and county) of the corporation's registered office in this State, and the name of its registered agent at such address;[34]

---

31. See Cox & Hazen, footnote 2 supra at 479-484.

32. No states continue the tradition of requiring "three or more" persons, but about one-quarter stipulate that the incorporators be "natural persons." More than one-third require that they be at least 18 years old. — Ed.

33. This fundamental "constitutional" instrument is also variously referred to as "articles of incorporation" or "charter." — Ed.

34. N.Y. Bus. Corp. Law §402(a)(7) (1998) requires "a designation of the secretary of state as agent of the corporation upon whom process against it may be served and the post office address within or without this state to which the secretary of state shall mail a copy of any process against it served upon him." Del. Gen. Corp. Law §321(b) (1998) provides for service of process against the corporation upon

(3) The nature of the business or purposes to be conducted or promoted. It shall be sufficient to state, either alone or with other businesses or purposes, that the purpose of the corporation is to engage in any lawful act or activity for which corporations may be organized under the General Corporation Law of Delaware, and by such statement all lawful acts and activities shall be within the purposes of the corporation, except for express limitations, if any.[35]

(4) If the corporation is to be authorized to issue only one class of stock, the total number of shares of stock which the corporation shall have authority to issue and the par value of each of such shares, or a statement that all such shares are to be without par value. If the corporation is to be authorized to issue more than one class of stock, the certificate of incorporation shall set forth the total number of shares of all classes of stock which the corporation shall have authority to issue and the number of shares of each class and shall specify each class the shares of which are to be without par value and each class the shares of which are to have a par value and the par value of the shares of each such class. The certificate of incorporation shall also set forth a statement of the designations and the powers, preferences and rights, and the qualifications, limitations or restrictions thereof, which are permitted by §151 of this title in respect of any class or classes of stock or any series of any class of stock of the corporation and the fixing of which by the certificate of incorporation is desired, and an express grant of such authority as it may then be desired to grant to the board of directors to fix by resolution or resolutions any thereof that may be desired but which shall not be fixed by the certificate of incorporation. . . . [36]

(5) The name and mailing address of the incorporator or incorporators;

(6) If the powers of the incorporator or incorporators are to terminate upon the filing of the certificate of incorporation, the names and mailing addresses of the persons who are to serve as directors until the first annual meeting of stockholders or until their successors are elected and qualify.[37]

(b) In addition to the matters required to be set forth in the certificate of incorporation by subsection (a) of this section, the certificate of incorporation may also contain any or all of the following matters:

(1) Any provision for the management of the business and for the conduct of the affairs of the corporation, and any provision creating, defining, limiting and regulating the powers of the corporation, the directors, and the stockholders, or any class of the stockholders . . . ;[38] if such provisions are not contrary to the laws of this State. Any provision which is required or permitted by any section

---

the Secretary of State if, after "due diligence" service cannot lawfully be made upon the corporation's officers, directors or registered agent within the state. — ED.

35. A large majority of states permit such an "all-purpose" clause, but about one-sixth still require a reasonably definite statement of purposes although probably allowing it to be followed by a general "all-purpose" provision. For consideration of this matter, see page 69 supra. — ED.

36. Virtually no states still require that the articles of incorporation recite that the corporation will not commence business until a certain minimum capital has been paid in. Statutory minimum capital requirements are considered at pages 249-251 infra. — ED.

37. Less than half the states require that the members of this initial board of directors be named in the articles of incorporation. — ED.

38. For illustrations of such provisions, see page 759 infra. — ED.

of this chapter to be stated in the bylaws may instead be stated in the certificate of incorporation; . . .

(3) Such provisions as may be desired granting to the holders of the stock of the corporation, or the holders of any class or series of a class thereof, the preemptive right to subscribe to any or all additional issues of stock. . . . [39]

(5) A provision limiting the duration of the corporation's existence to a specified date; otherwise, the corporation shall have perpetual existence;[40]

(6) A provision imposing personal liability for the debts of the corporation on its stockholders or members to a specified extent and upon specified conditions; otherwise, the stockholders or members of a corporation shall not be personally liable for the payment of the corporation's debts[41] except as they may be liable by reason of their own conduct or acts. . . . [42]

(c) It shall not be necessary to set forth in the certificate of incorporation any of the powers conferred on corporations by this chapter.

2. MEETING STATUTORY FORMALITIES

After the articles of incorporation have been prepared, state statutes require that they be signed and usually either properly verified or acknowledged by the incorporators.[43] The articles must then be delivered to the appropriate state official, usually the secretary of state, and the required fees or taxes paid.[44] If all is in order, the articles are filed in a designated state office and, in accordance with the statutory procedure, the incorporators receive a certified copy or a formal document entitled "certificate of incorporation." Some states also require filing (or recording) of the articles in one or more county offices, but several of these direct the state official with whom the articles have been filed to transmit them for local recordation. A few states also require further notice or newspaper publication of the articles. These filing procedures afford creditors, prospective investors, and other interested members of the public with the basic information contained in the articles; they also serve to notify the state (and its revenue officers) of the existence of the corporation.

Many states have two additional general statutory provisions governing the initial corporate organization process. A few still require that a minimum capital—usually $1,000—be paid in before any business may be transacted other than that incidental to organization. And most states provide that an organization meeting be held after the filing of the articles of incorporation to perfect the internal organization of the enterprise, i.e., to elect directors if they have not already been designated, elect officers, adopt bylaws, etc.

---

39. Preemptive rights are considered in Cox & Hazen, footnote 2 supra, at 496-501.—ED.

40. All states now permit corporations perpetual existence.—ED.

41. A few states, e.g., N.Y. Bus. Corp. Law §630 (1984), still make certain shareholders of nonpublic corporations personally liable for unpaid wages due corporate employees in various circumstances. See Kenneth B. Davis Jr., Shareholder Liability for Claims by Employees, 1984 Wis. L. Rev. 741.—ED.

42. Del. Gen. Corp. Law §102(b)(7) (1993), dealing with limitations on the liability of directors, is considered at page 109 infra.—ED.

43. In 1997 the Revised Model Business Corporation Act (RMBCA) was amended to authorize electronic filing of documents, eliminating the need for actual signatures.

44. The filing fee is either a modest flat sum or a graduated amount depending on the quantity of authorized capital stock (e.g., Del. Gen. Corp. Law §391 (2006)).

3. "DOMESTICATION" OF FOREIGN CORPORATIONS

If a corporation wishes to transact business in a state other than its state of incorporation, it must as a condition of admission comply with that state's "qualification" or "domestication" statute for "foreign" corporations.[45] These statutes vary in detail but generally call for filing with a designated state official an application containing much or all of the information required of domestic corporations in their articles of incorporation. Taxes or fees must be paid and a resident agent (or the secretary of state) designated for service of process. Filing of periodic reports may also be required.

After it has qualified, state statutes generally authorize the foreign corporation to do any business locally that it may do in its state of incorporation as long as such business may be done within the local state by domestic corporations. A number of state statutes specifically disclaim their authority to regulate the organization or internal affairs of foreign corporations.[46] On the other hand, several state statutes — e.g., Cal. Gen. Corp. Law §2115 (2003) and N.Y. Bus. Corp. Law §§1306, 1317-1320 (1998) — regulate various internal affairs, particularly those intended to protect shareholders, of foreign corporations that have a substantial number of shareholders who are state residents and that do substantial business in the state (other than those with securities listed on a national securities exchange). For recent conflicting decisions on the reach of such laws, compare VantagePoint Venture Partners 1996 v. Examen, Inc., 871 A.2d 1108 (Del. 2005) (conflicts of law principles and the "constitutional underpinnings" of federalism prevent application of a California statute that requires a separate vote of shareholders on proposed reorganizations, to a vote on a proposed merger of a Delaware corporation), with Friese v. Superior Court, 134 Cal. App. 4th 693, 36 Cal. Rptr. 3d 558 (2005) (an exception to the internal affairs doctrine for state securities regulation permits application of a California statute authorizing suits on behalf of a foreign corporation, against its fiduciaries who engage in insider trading in California, for disgorgement of up to three times the amount of their profits).

C. DEFECTIVE INCORPORATION

As appellate decisions continue to indicate, problems arise when a business enterprise purports to be incorporated but in some way has not fulfilled the statutory

---

45. The Supreme Court has long held that a corporation is not a "citizen" for purposes of the Art. IV, §2 provision of the Constitution that "[t]he Citizens of each State shall be entitled to all Privileges and Immunities of Citizens in the several States," thus permitting the exclusion of foreign corporations that have not received state authorization. Bank of Augusta v. Earle, 38 U.S. 519 (1839); Paul v. Virginia, 75 U.S. 168 (1868). But if the corporation is engaged exclusively in interstate or foreign commerce, i.e., engages in no transactions that may be considered "local" or "intrastate," a state is forbidden under the Commerce Clause of Art. I, §8 to require it to domesticate unless Congress provides otherwise. Crutcher v. Kentucky, 141 U.S. 47 (1891). Nice questions of constitutional law arise with respect to whether a corporation is doing intrastate business within the state. See, e.g., Eli Lilly & Co. v. Sav-On Drugs, Inc., 366 U.S. 276 (1961).

There is a great deal of litigation on the state law question of whether a foreign corporation is "doing business" or "transacting business" within the state for the purpose of having to qualify. State statutes frequently specify those activities that do *not* by themselves constitute "transacting business" — such as engaging in litigation, holding meetings, maintaining bank accounts, and effecting sales through independent contractors. See RMBCA §15.01.

46. See RMBCA §15.05(c).

requirements for the process of incorporation described above. May the "corporation" maintain an action in its own name? May an action be brought against it without serving process on its "shareholders" individually? May it convey or receive real property in its own name? May a "shareholder" transfer his or her interest without the consent of the others? Do its "shareholders" have limited liability, or are some (or all) of them personally responsible for torts committed in the course of its business or contractual obligations incurred in its name? In addressing these questions, of what significance is the particular provision of the corporation statute, and its purpose, that has not been literally fulfilled? Should distinctions be drawn depending on whether the failure to comply was deliberate, or merely negligent, or seemingly innocent? On whether the defect was subsequently remedied?

Two propositions have been generally stated by courts about the consequences of defective attempts to incorporate. First, if there has been substantial compliance with the statute providing for incorporation (that is, if the noncompliance is slight), a de jure corporation results — an enterprise that the courts will recognize as a corporation for all purposes and as to all parties, including the state. Second, if (a) there has been a colorable or apparent attempt (b) in good faith to incorporate under the state statute, and (c) some corporate "user" has occurred, i.e., some exercise of corporate powers, a de facto corporation results — an enterprise that the courts will recognize as a corporation for all purposes and as to all parties except the state; by quo warranto proceedings the state may terminate the life as a corporation of such an enterprise, but no one else may challenge its corporate existence.

Unfortunately, these propositions fail to reveal what acts of incomplete compliance with the incorporation statutes are sufficient to constitute "substantial" compliance, and what acts, insufficient for "substantial" compliance, are nevertheless enough for a "colorable" or "apparent" attempt to comply. Further, these propositions give no indication of the legal consequences of purported incorporation where the acts done are less than a colorable attempt to comply.

The materials that follow deal principally with the types of problems described above. But analogous issues arise in other contexts. Business enterprises have fully complied with the requirements of corporation statutes that have later been held unconstitutional[47] or that did not authorize the type of business to be engaged in.[48] Foreign corporations have done business locally without fully complying with the local qualification statute.[49] Corporations whose charters have expired or have been statutorily revoked for failure to pay required taxes or file required reports have continued to do business in the corporate name.[50]

47. See Eaton v. Walker, 76 Mich. 579, 43 N.W. 638 (1889) ("shareholders" held as partners).

48. See Baum v. Baum Holding Co., 158 Neb. 197, 62 N.W.2d 864 (1954) ("de facto" corporate existence upheld against declaratory judgment attack because subsequent statute authorized such business).

49. Most statutes impose various sanctions on foreign corporations that are required to qualify but fail to do so. These include criminal penalties for corporations and certain directors, officers, and agents; individual liability on certain of these persons for corporate debts arising within the state; denial to the corporation of use of the state courts to sue — in a few states permanently with respect to transactions within the state during time of noncompliance, but in most states only during the period of noncompliance. A few statutes render "void" such a corporation's contracts made within the state, but most declare that failure to qualify shall not impair the validity of such contracts. See generally Harry G. Henn & John R. Alexander, Corporations §101 (3d ed. 1983).

50. See Van Landingham v. United Tuna Packers, 189 Cal. 353, 208 P. 973 (1922) (corporation may not be sued on contract made in its name after charter has been forfeited although then unknown to all parties concerned); Animazing Entertainment, Inc. v. Louis Lofredo Associates, Inc., 88 F. Supp. 2d 265

Thompson & Green Machinery Co. v. Music City Lumber Co.
683 S.W.2d 340 (Tenn. App.), *appeal denied* (1984)

Lewis, J.: . . . Joseph E. Walker is President of Music City Sawmill Co., Inc. and Music City Lumber Company, Inc., both Tennessee corporations. On January 27, 1982, Mr. Walker, supposedly on behalf of Sawmill, purchased a wheel loader from plaintiff, Thompson & Green Machinery Co., Inc. However, on January 27, 1982, Sawmill was not a corporation, a fact unknown to either plaintiff or defendant Walker on January 27th. It was not until late July or early August, 1983, that it was discovered that the date of the incorporation of Sawmill was actually January 28, 1982, one day after the sale of the wheel loader.

Pursuant to the sale, Walker signed a promissory note in the amount of $37,886.30 on behalf of Sawmill to plaintiff. . . .

Sawmill was unable to make the payments and returned the wheel loader on August 27, 1982. On October 14, 1982, plaintiff sold the wheel loader for $15,303.83 and applied the proceeds to the note, leaving a balance of $17,925.81. So far as the record discloses, between January of 1982 and August, 1982, plaintiff and Sawmill dealt with each other as corporations.

Plaintiff brought suit against both Sawmill and Lumber on May 5, 1983, in the Chancery Court to recover the balance due on the note and parts sold to Sawmill. On August 5, 1983, plaintiff amended its complaint to include Mr. Walker as a defendant after plaintiff learned that Sawmill was not a corporation on January 27, 1982. This suit against Mr. Walker individually was his first notice that Sawmill was not incorporated on that date. . . .

. . . Plaintiff contends that defendant Walker is personally liable because of the interaction of Tenn. Code Ann. §48-1-1405 which provides that "[a]ll persons who assume to act as a corporation without authority so to do shall be jointly and severally liable for all debts and liabilities incurred or arising as a result thereof," and Tenn. Code Ann. §48-1-204 which provides that "[a] corporation shall not . . . incur any indebtedness . . . until (a) The charter has been filed by the secretary of state. . . ."

It is conceded that Sawmill did not have a corporate existence on January 27th. It therefore follows that Mr. Walker could not and did not have authority to act for Sawmill on January 27th when he executed the promissory note to plaintiff. "It is a general rule that one who deals with an apparent corporation as such and in such manner as to recognize its corporate existence de jure or de facto is thereby estopped to deny the fact thus admitted. . . . The estoppel extends as well to the

---

(S.D.N.Y. 2000) (corporation whose charter had expired when it entered into a contract cannot enforce it); see also Borbein, Young & Co. v. Cirese, 401 S.W.2d 940 (Mo. Ct. App. 1966) (personal liability of directors); Beavers v. Recreation Ass'n of Lake Shore Estates, Inc., 130 S.W.3d 702 (Mo. Ct. App. 2004) (nonprofit association whose charter had been rescinded for failure to file annual report but then reinstated could not file liens because Secretary of State's reinstatement was not authorized by statute); L-Tec Electronics Corp. v. Cougar Electronic Org., Inc., 198 F.3d 85 (2d Cir. 1999) (corporation's president not personally liable on contract made in corporation's name during period of forfeiture when charter was subsequently restored by payment of delinquent taxes); but compare Moore v. Rommel, 233 Ark. 989, 350 S.W.2d 190 (1961), and Bergy Bros. Inc. v. Zeeland Feeder Pig, Inc., 96 Mich. App. 111, 292 N.W.2d 493 (1980). Some states have statutes that address these issues, see Barker-Chadsey Co. v. W. C. Fuller Co., 16 Mass. App. 1, 448 N.E.2d 1283 (1983) (if charter is eventually revived, shareholders without knowledge of charter revocation or intent to defraud not personally liable to plaintiff who relied only on credit of supposed corporation); Cargill, Inc. v. American Pork Producers, Inc., 415 F. Supp. 876 (D.S.D. 1976) (directors not personally liable); Micciche v. Billings, 727 P.2d 367 (Colo. 1986) (officers not personally liable).

privies as to the parties to such transactions. The general rule is applied in actions brought by either of the contracting parties against the other, and in actions by the persons dealing with the corporation, wherein the existence of the corporation is assailed for the purpose of establishing individual partnership liability on the part of its members."[51] 18 Am. Jur. 2d Corporations §76.

Tennessee has long recognized the foregoing rule. . . .

However, in 1968 the Tennessee General Assembly enacted the "Tennessee General Corporations Act," Chapter 523, Pub. Acts of 1968.

Our research reveals no Tennessee decision which has addressed either de facto corporation or corporation by estoppel since the passage of the act in 1968.

Courts in other jurisdictions which have considered the question of de facto corporations under statutes similar to Tenn. Code Ann. §§48-1-204 and 48-1-1405 have held that under the act, de facto corporations no longer exist.

In Timberline Equipment Company, Inc. v. Davenport, 267 Or. 64, 514 P.2d 1109 (1973), the Oregon Supreme Court, in interpreting ORS 57.321 and ORS 57.792, Oregon statutes almost identical to Tenn. Code Ann. §§48-1-204 and 48-1-1405, stated: . . .

> ORS 57.321 of the Oregon Business Corporation Act provides: "Upon the issuance of the certificate of incorporation, the corporate existence shall begin, and such certificate of incorporation shall be conclusive evidence that all conditions precedent required to be performed by the incorporators have been complied with and that the corporation has been incorporated under the Oregon Business Corporation Act, except as against this state in a proceeding to cancel or revoke the certificate of incorporation or for involuntary dissolution of the corporation."
>
> This section is virtually identical to §56 of the Model Act. The Comment to the Model, prepared as a research project by the American Bar Foundation and edited by the American Bar Association Committee on Corporate Laws, states: Under the Model Act, de jure incorporation is complete upon the issuance of the certificate of incorporation, except as against the state in certain proceedings challenging the corporate existence. In this respect, the Model Act provisions are the same as those in many states, although in a number of them some further action is required before the corporation has legal existence, such as local filing or recording or publication.
>
> "Under the unequivocal provisions of the Model Act, any steps short of securing a certificate of incorporation would not constitute apparent compliance. Therefore a de facto corporation cannot exist under the Model Act. . . ."[52] Model Business Corporation Act Annotated §56, p.205 (2d ed. 1971).
>
> ORS 57.793 provides: "All persons who assume to act as a corporation without the authority of a certificate of incorporation issued by the Corporation Commissioner, shall be jointly and severally liable for all debts and liabilities incurred or arising as a result thereof."

---

51. Compare Timberline Equip. Co. v. Davenport, 267 Or. 64, 514 P.2d 1109 (1973): "The so-called estoppel that arises to deny corporate capacity does not depend on the presence of the technical elements of equitable estoppel, viz., misrepresentations and change of position in reliance thereon, but on the nature of the relations contemplated, that one who has recognized the organization as a corporation in business dealings should not be allowed to quibble or raise immaterial issues on matters which do not concern him in the slightest degree or affect his substantial rights." — Ed.

52. Contra, Cantor v. Sunshine Greenery, Inc., 165 N.J. Super. 411, 398 A.2d 591 (1979) (de facto existence is not precluded by failure to file articles). — Ed.

This is merely an elaboration of §146 of the Model Act. The Comment states:

> This section is designed to prohibit the application of any theory of de facto incorporation. The only authority to act as a corporation under the Model Act arises from completion of the procedures prescribed in sections 53 to 55 inclusive. The consequences of those procedures are specified in section 56 as being the creation of a corporation. No other means being authorized, the effect of section 146 is to negate the possibility of a de facto corporation.
>
> Abolition of the concept of de facto incorporation, which at best was fuzzy, is a sound result. No reason exists for its continuance under general corporate laws, where the process of acquiring de jure incorporation is both simple and clear. The vestigial appendage should be removed.

2 Model Business Corporation Act Annotated §146, pp.908-909 (2d ed. 1971). . . .
We hold the principle of de facto corporation no longer exists in Oregon. . . .

We are of the opinion that the Oregon Supreme Court gave the acts the only interpretation to which they are reasonably susceptible. We hold that the Tennessee General Assembly, by passage of the Tennessee General Corporations Act of 1968, abolished the concept of de facto incorporation in Tennessee.

We have found only one jurisdiction which has considered corporation by estoppel under statutes similar to ours. Robertson v. Levy, 197 A.2d 443 (D.C. Ct. of App. 1964). In that case Levy and Robertson entered into an agreement whereby Levy was to form a corporation, Penn Ave. Record Shack, Inc., which was to purchase Robertson's business. Levy submitted articles of incorporation to the authority designated by statute on December 27, 1961, but no certificate of incorporation was issued at that time. Pursuant to the contract, an assignment of lease was entered into on December 31, 1961, between Robertson and Levy with Levy acting as president of Penn Ave. Record Shack, Inc. On January 2, 1962, the articles of incorporation were rejected by the designated authority. On that same day, however, Levy began to operate the business under the name Penn Ave. Record Shack, Inc. Robertson executed a bill of sale to Penn Ave. Record Shack, Inc. on January 8, 1962, disposing of the assets of his business to Penn Ave. Record Shack, Inc., and receiving in return a note providing for installment payments. The note was signed: "Penn Ave. Record Shack, Inc., by Eugene M. Levy, President." On January 17, 1962, the certificate of incorporation for Penn Ave. Record Shack, Inc. was issued. In June, 1962, Penn Ave. Record Shack, Inc. ceased to do any business, and, subsequently, Robertson sued Levy for the balance due on the note.

The trial court held that the District of Columbia Code §29-950, which is identical to Tenn. Code Ann. §48-1-1405, did not apply and "that Robertson was estopped to deny the existence of the corporation."

On appeal, the Court of Appeals for the District of Columbia held that, pursuant to §29-921c, which is substantially the same as Tenn. Code Ann. §48-1-203, courts must no longer inquire into the equities of a case to determine whether there has been "colorable compliance" with the statute, that before a certificate of incorporation issues, there "is no corporation de jure, de facto, or by estoppel." The Court went on to state: "Under Section 29-950, if an individual or group of individuals assumes to act as a corporation before the certificate of incorporation has been issued, joint and several liability attaches. We hold, therefore, that the impact of these sections, when considered together, is to eliminate the concepts of estoppel and de facto corporateness under the Business Corporation Act of the District of

Columbia. It is immaterial whether the third person believed he was dealing with a corporation or whether he intended to deal with the corporation. The certificate of incorporation provides the cutoff point; before it is issued, the individuals, and not the corporation, are liable." . . .

The General Assembly, in enacting Tenn. Code Ann. §48-1-1405 saw fit to place statutory liability upon those who assume to act as a corporation without authority. Section 48-1-1405 does not contain an exception that one who assumes to act as a corporation without authority shall be jointly and severally liable for debts and liabilities *except* when the plaintiff thereafter dealt with the corporation as a corporation or when the plaintiff did not intend to bind one who assumed to act personally. No exceptions are contained in §48-1-1405. . . . To allow an estoppel would be to nullify Tenn. Code Ann. §48-1-1405. . . . [53]

Don Swann Sales Corp. v. Echols
160 Ga. App. 539, 287 S.E.2d 577 (1981)

SOGNIER, J.: Don Swann Sales Corp. (Swann) sued Echols on an open account in the amount of $4,777.48. The account was in the name of Cupid's, Inc., a corporation purportedly registered by Echols. . . .

The trial court . . . found that although Echols *thought* that Cupid's, Inc. had been properly incorporated in January 1980, and that Swann dealt exclusively with an entity known as Cupid's, Inc., in fact, the corporation was not "properly" registered with the Secretary of State until October 16, 1980. The transactions at issue took place prior to the time of the actual incorporation of Cupid's Inc.

The Business Corporation Code of Georgia has eliminated the doctrine of de facto corporations as applied to defectively organized corporations pursuant to Code Ann. §22-204, which provides: "All persons who assume to act as a corporation before the Secretary of State has issued the certificate of incorporation to the incorporator or incorporators or his or their attorney shall be jointly and severally liable for all debts and liabilities incurred or arising as a result thereof." (Acts 1968, pp. 565, 578.)

However, Code Ann. §22-5103 has retained the doctrine of corporation by estoppel. That section provides: "The existence of a corporation, claiming a charter under color of law, cannot be collaterally attacked by persons who have dealt with it as a corporation. Such persons are estopped from denying its corporate existence." . . .

In Walker v. Knox & Associates, 132 Ga. App. 12, 207 S.E.2d 570 (1974), this court was presented with a factual situation similar to the case at bar. The plaintiff corporation entered into a contract with the defendant for construction work to be done. The corporation was not certified at the time the contract was executed but was subsequently incorporated. Plaintiff corporation sued for payment on the contract. . . . This court . . . held that the contract was valid because the defendant,

---

53. Accord, American Vending Services, Inc. v. Morse, 881 P.2d 917 (Utah App. 1994); Jean Claude Boisset Wines, U.S.A., Inc. v. Newton, 830 P.2d 1134 (Colo. App. 1992); State ex rel. McCain v. Construction Enter., Inc., 6 Kan. App. 2d 627, 631 P.2d 1240 (1981) (personal liability for company's unemployment taxes because articles of incorporation, although filed with secretary of state, were not filed with local registrar of deeds as required by statute); Fee Insurance Agency, Inc. v. Snyder, 930 P.2d 1054 (Kan. 1997) (same, in respect to an unpaid corporate debt). —ED.

having dealt with plaintiff as a corporation, was estopped from denying the corporation's existence.[54] In *Walker*, the purported *corporation* sued to enforce its rights under the contract, and this court found that the doctrine of corporation by estoppel applied. . . .

The question we are asked to decide here is whether an *individual* purporting to act for a non-existent corporation can escape liability on a contract by defending on the basis of the non-existent corporation. We do not think that the doctrine of corporation by estoppel should be applied under these circumstances.

It is well settled that "one who assumes to act as agent for a non-existent principal or one having no legal status renders himself individually liable in contracts so made." . . . Where the evidence supports a finding that the purported corporation is *not* a valid corporate entity, there is no doubt that the agent is bound by his purchases on an open account. . . .

Under the circumstances, the trial court erred in applying the doctrine of corporation by estoppel. This is not a case where the corporation purportedly existed under "color of law," but rather where no corporation existed at all. Here there is no equitable ground for application of the doctrine because persons who do business as a corporation without even a colorable organization must know that they are not a corporation and are not therefore misled or injured. See 18 C.J.S. Corporations, §111j. To hold otherwise would permit an agent acting for a non-existent principal to escape liability by claiming that he thought the corporation was in existence when, in fact, no entity existed. . . . We do not think the legislature intended such a result in preserving the doctrine of corporation by estoppel in the Business Corporation Code.

Judgment reversed.

---

1. *Successful defense of estoppel.* (a) In Cranson v. International Business Machines Corp., 234 Md. 477, 200 A.2d 33 (1964), a contract creditor who dealt with the business as if it were a corporation failed to impose personal liability on its president. Although the certificate of incorporation had been signed and acknowledged, it had not been filed because of the oversight of the company's lawyer, who had informed the defendant that the corporation had been formed. The court held that "the estoppel theory . . . may be invoked even where there is no corporation de facto." Accord, Harry Rich Corp. v. Feinberg, 518 So. 2d 377 (Fla. App. 1987); Goodwyne v. Moore, 170 Ga. App. 305, 316 S.E.2d 401 (1984). But see Video Power, Inc. v. First Capital Income Properties, Inc., 188 Ga. App. 691, 373 S.E.2d 855 (1988) (reaffirming the *Don Swann* case).

(b) *Fact variations.* What result in the *Cranson* case if:
(i) The certificate of incorporation had never been filed?
(ii) For some reason, Cranson had deliberately delayed filing the certificate of incorporation?

54. See also Pharmaceutical Sales & Consulting Corp. v. J.W.S. Delavau Co., 59 F. Supp. 2d 398 (D.N.J. 1999) (business may sue as corporation for breach of contract even though president had not applied for certificate of incorporation at the time of the transaction: "permitting defendant . . . to escape potential liability . . . would result in a windfall . . . [not] expected at the time of the execution of the contract"). Cf. Boslow Family Ltd. Partnership v. Glickenhaus & Co., 7 N.Y.3d 664, 860 N.E.2d 711, 827 N.Y.S.2d 94 (2006) (plaintiff limited partnership may sue when it did not know that its counsel had failed to file certificate). —ED.

(iii) Plaintiff were someone who had been negligently injured by a company employee who was driving a company truck in the course of its business?

(c) *Problem.* X and Y agreed to form corporation C. X signed a lease for C as its president one day before C's certificate of incorporation was filed. Y subsequently sued X for unlawfully terminating the lease so that X could use the property for his own business. X defended on the ground that C lacked legal capacity to enter the lease. Should C be a corporation by estoppel at the time of execution of the lease? Should X be estopped from denying C's existence? See Rubenstein v. Mayor, 41 A.D.3d 826, 839 N.Y.S. 2d 170 (2007).

2. *Party challenging corporate existence.* What results in the *Music City* and *Don Swann* cases (and decisions discussed therein) under the following statute?

Delaware General Corporation Law (1974)

Sec. 329. *Defective organization of corporation as a defense.* (a) No corporation of this State and no person sued by any such corporation shall be permitted to assert the want of legal organization as a defense to any claim.

(b) This section shall not be construed to prevent judicial inquiry into the regularity or validity of the organization of a corporation, or its lawful possession of any corporate power it may assert in any other suit or proceeding where its corporate existence or the power to exercise the corporate rights it asserts is challenged, and evidence tending to sustain the challenge shall be admissible in any such suit or proceeding.

3. *Knowledge of defect.* RMBCA §2.03 (1984) is similar to §56 of the prior version. But §146 of the prior version has been changed:

Revised Model Business Corporation Act (1984)

Sec. 2.04. *Liability for preincorporation transactions.* All persons purporting to act as or on behalf of a corporation, knowing there was no incorporation under this Act, are jointly and severally liable for all liabilities created while so acting.

What result under this statute in the *Music City* and *Don Swann* cases (and decisions discussed therein)?[55] For the view that "there are no efficiency based justifications" for making formal incorporation a prerequisite to limited liability for either voluntary (contract) or involuntary (tort) creditors, see Larry E. Ribstein, Limited Liability and Theories of the Corporation, 50 Md. L. Rev. 80 (1991).

4. *Active vs. inactive shareholders.* What result in the *Don Swann* case if Cupid's, Inc. had five shareholders all of whom were made defendants: Echols, who had actively managed the business and owned 5 percent of the shares; *A*, who was a retired entrepreneur and owned 80 percent of the shares; and *B*, *C*, and *D*, who were the minor employees of the business and each owned 5 percent of the shares?

---

55. Ga. Bus. Corp. Code §204 (1989) is now the same as RMBCA §2.04. See Weir v. Kirby Constr. Co., 213 Ga. App. 832, 446 S.E.2d 186 (1994).

See Timberline Equipment Co. v. Davenport, 267 Or. 64, 514 P.2d 1109 (1973) ("the category of 'persons who assume to act as a corporation' does not include those whose only connection with the organization is as an investor . . . [but does] include those persons who have an investment in the organization and who actively participate in the policy and operational decisions"); United States Fidelity & Guaranty Corp. v. Putzy, 613 F. Supp. 594 (N.D. Ill. 1985) ("only incorporators or others who actively conduct corporate business can be held liable for the debts of the corporation at common law").

Sulphur Export Corp. v. Carribean Clipper Lines, Inc.
277 F. Supp. 632 (E.D. La. 1968)

RUBIN, J.: Sulphur Export Corporation (Sulexco) sued to recover [$23,533.50 in] damages resulting from an alleged breach of a charter party by Carribean Clipper Lines, Inc. (Carribean). . . . The charter party was executed by Carribean's president and secretary and by Sulexco's president. . . .

Carribean's articles of incorporation stated it would not begin business until $1,000 in cash was paid in as capital, but it nonetheless transacted business before it received this capital.

The individual defendants Justice, Harrison, and Paquette were at all times material to this case directors and officers of Carribean. They each participated in the transaction of business by Carribean prior to its receipt of the minimum capital required by its charter, and none of them caused his dissent from the transaction of such business to be recorded in Carribean's corporate records. . . .

The transaction of business by Carribean before it received the minimum capital recited in its articles of incorporation constituted a violation of La. R.S. 12:9, subd. A(2) (1950) which provides: "A corporation . . . shall not . . . begin the transaction of any business . . . until . . . (2) the amount of capital with which it will begin business, as stated in the articles, has been fully paid in."

La. R.S. 12:9, subd. A(1), and 9, subd. A(2) state alternative prohibitions the violation of either one of which alone is sufficient to invoke the penalties provided by La. R.S. 12:9, subd. B, which states: "If a corporation has transacted any business in violation of this Section, the officers who participated therein and the directors, except those who dissented therefrom and caused their dissent to be recorded in the minutes or who, being absent, filed with the corporation their written dissent upon learning of the action, shall be liable jointly and severally with the corporation, and each other, for the debts or liabilities of the corporation arising therefrom." . . .

The measure of the joint and several liability with the corporation of the non-dissenting directors and the participating officers is the full corporate debt or liability arising from the transaction of business in violation of the statute. This proposition is supported by . . . the public policy of protecting corporate creditors embodied in a statute requiring the payment of minimum capital into the treasury of a newly organized corporation; by the general rule of law that persons transacting business in other than corporate form are liable jointly and severally up to the full amount of debts contracted by them; and by the decisions of the courts of states other than Louisiana dealing with the same question. See Tri-State Developers, Inc. v. Moore, Ky., 1961, 343 S.W.2d 812; Bay State York Co. v. Cobb, 1964, 346 Mass. 641, 195 N.E.2d 328.

Limiting the liability of the nondissenting directors, and participating officers, for the corporate debts to the amount of recited but unpaid capital, or to the amount of the total authorized capital of the corporation, would tend to frustrate the public policy embodied in the statute by emasculating the penalties provided for its violation, and would raise difficult questions as to whether the limited liability fund is owed to the corporation itself to make up its missing capital or to the creditors, and as to whether the entire fund could be recovered by the creditor swiftest in the race to the court house or must rather be prorated among all the creditors in some sort of interpleader proceeding.

Any limitation of the liability of the nondissenting directors and the participating officers for the corporate debts to the amount of the total authorized capital of the corporation would additionally be impractical of application in the case of corporations having only no par capital stock authorized, which is permitted by the Louisiana corporation statute. . . .

---

1. *Statute.* (a) What result in the *Sulexco* case under the following statute:

Ohio General Corporation Law (1984)

Sec. 1701.12. *Liability for nonpayment of initial stated capital.* If an initial stated capital is set forth in its articles and a corporation commences business before there has been paid in the amount of that initial stated capital, no corporate transaction shall be invalidated thereby, but incorporators participating in such transaction before the election of directors, and directors participating therein, shall be jointly and severally liable for the debts of the corporation up to an amount not exceeding in the aggregate the amount by which the stated capital paid in at the time the corporation commenced business fails to equal the initial stated capital set forth in the articles, until the amount set forth in the articles has been paid in.

(b) What result if in the *Sulexco* case, or under the above statutes, plaintiff had been a passenger on one of Carribean's ships and had been negligently injured by one of Carribean's employees acting in the course of the business? What if plaintiff had been a shipper of freight on one of Carribean's ships that was negligently damaged by Carribean's employees?

2. *Analysis of cases.* For a comprehensive study of cases up to 1952 involving actions to hold "shareholders" of a "defective" corporation personally liable, see Alexander H. Frey, Legal Analysis and the "De Facto" Doctrine, 100 U. Pa. L. Rev. 1153 (1952). Three conclusions are (1) the impossibility of formulating a brief proposition, such as the orthodox statements as to "de jure" and "de facto" corporations, that will adequately set forth what the courts are actually doing in this field; (2) the extreme importance of the factor "dealings on a corporate basis" (the dealings are not on a corporate basis either when there have been no dealings between the parties, as in most of the tort cases, or when the plaintiffs do not, from their dealings with the defendants, know or have reason to know that they purport to be incorporated); and (3) the activity or inactivity of the defendants in the management of the association is seemingly an unimportant factor in

determining their personal liability.[56] For a follow-up study of all cases (131) between 1970 and 1989, see Comment, An Empirical Study of Defective Incorporation, 39 Emory L.J. 523 (1990). Among the conclusions are (1) courts in the modern cases have been more likely to hold individual defendants personally liable, even when there were "dealings on a corporate basis," and particularly when the courts applied statutes dealing with the matter of failure to incorporate; (2) imposition of personal liability remained extremely high when there was no attempt to incorporate; and (3) no party ever succeeded in avoiding a contract by asserting its own defective incorporation status.

D. *DISREGARDING THE CORPORATE ENTITY*

The materials in the preceding section dealt with problems that arise when there has been some failure to comply with statutory requirements for incorporation. Here we turn to instances where, although there has been full (or sufficient) compliance with the incorporation statutes, courts are nonetheless asked to withhold one or more normal attributes of a corporation from the business. This exercise proceeds under a wide variety of labels[57] but is most popularly described as "piercing the corporate veil," or finding the corporation to be merely the "instrumentality" or "alter ego" of its shareholder(s).[58] The prevailing approach "rests on a demonstration of three fundamental elements: the . . . [corporation's] lack of independent existence; the fraudulent, inequitable, or wrongful use of the corporate form; and a causal relationship to the plaintiff's loss." Phillip I. Blumberg, The Transformation of Modern Corporation Law: The Law of Corporate Groups, 37 Conn. L. Rev. 605, 612 (2005).[59]

---

56. For a multiple regression analysis of these cases indicating that the extent to which (1) there was a potential fraud in the transaction and (2) the defendant was an active participant both had "a predictable and significant influence on what judges actually decided," see Fred S. McChesney, Doctrinal Analysis and Statistical Modeling in Law: The Case of Defective Incorporation, 71 Wash. U. L.Q. 493 (1993). For recent criticism of the original study's methodology and the regression analysis, see Norwood P. Beveridge, Corporate Puzzles: Being a True and Complete Explanation of De Facto Corporations and Corporations by Estoppel, Their Historical Development, Attempted Abolition, and Eventual Rehabilitation, 22 Okla. City U. L. Rev. 935 (1997).

57. Over 35 descriptive terms are listed in Harry G. Henn & John R. Alexander, Corporations §146 n.2 (3d ed. 1983).

58. The analytical line between problems of "defective incorporation" and problems of "disregarding the corporate entity" may become blurred when a business enterprise has adequately complied with all of the statutory prerequisites for incorporation and initial organization but subsequently carries on its affairs without formal observance of certain other statutory requirements—e.g., failure to hold annual shareholder meetings (see Cal. Gen. Corp. Law §600 (1988)) or to keep accurate books and records (see RMBCA §16.01 (2002)).

59. "Rigid in its formulation and yielding great uncertainty in any attempt to predict its outcome, 'piercing' has led to hundreds, if not thousands, of irreconcilable cases in each year." Id. at 611-612.

For classic explorations, see Henry W. Ballantine, Separate Entity of Parent and Subsidiary Corporations, 14 Cal. L. Rev. 12 (1925); I. Maurice Wormser, The Disregard of the Corporate Fiction and Allied Problems (1927); William O. Douglas & Carroll M. Shanks, Insulation from Liability Through Subsidiary Corporations, 39 Yale L.J. 193 (1929); Max Radin, The Endless Problem of Corporate Personality, 32 Colum. L. Rev. 643 (1932); Elvin R. Latty, Subsidiaries and Affiliated Corporations (1936). For modern, comprehensive coverage, see Phillip I. Blumberg, The Law of Corporate Groups: Tort, Contract, and Other Common Law Problems in the Substantive Law of Parent and Subsidiary Corporation 111 (1987); Stephen B. Presser, Piercing the Corporate Veil (1991).

Although the issue may be presented in a number of contexts, a frequent occasion concerns the attempt to hold the sole shareholder of a one-person corporation personally liable for its debts. Often the sole shareholder sought to be held liable is another corporation — the parent of a wholly owned subsidiary.[60] Or one wholly owned subsidiary may be sought to be held liable for the debts of another wholly owned subsidiary — "brother-sister" subsidiaries of the same parent. Courts generally approach the problems arising in these types of cases, concerning a sole shareholder who is either an individual or a corporation, in the same way. But there have been suggestions that some difference in approach may be justified — *if* the principal function of limited liability is seen as encouraging commercial and industrial enterprise by shielding some of an individual's personal wealth from the hazards of a particular business, rather than enabling a business entity that would normally be conducted as a single unit to divide itself into otherwise artificial, individually insulated segments.[61]

Piercing the veil to obtain unlimited liability becomes somewhat more complex when the corporation has more than one shareholder and personal liability is sought to be imposed on one or more of them. And it is further complicated by factors similar to those considered in the preceding section, e.g., whether the plaintiff is a tort or contract creditor of the corporation or whether the defendant shareholder was actively engaged in the corporation's business.

A slight variant involves the bankruptcy of a corporation whose creditors include its own shareholder(s). These corporate debts to the shareholder(s) may be in the form of open accounts payable, notes, or bonds. The issue is whether these "inside" creditors should be treated the same as "outside" creditors, or whether their claims should be subordinated or totally disallowed. Further complexities are presented if the shareholder(s) are also insolvent.

The materials that follow deal principally with the types of problems described above.[62]

---

60. A few cases have arisen in which the subsidiary was sought to be held liable for the debts of the parent. See Shirley v. Drackett Prods. Co., 26 Mich. App. 644, 182 N.W.2d 726 (1970). See also Olen v. Phelps, 546 N.W.2d 176 (Wis. App. 1996) (corporation held liable for sole shareholder's debt); LFC Marketing Group, Inc. v. Loomis, 8 P.3d 841 (Nev. 2000) (corporation held liable for debt of person who was corporation's "dominating force" even though owning none of its shares). The more traditional route, albeit a less direct one, would be to obtain judgment against the parent and then execute against its shares in the subsidiary See Cascade Energy & Metals Corp. v. Banks, 896 F.2d 1557 (10th Cir. 1990) ("reverse-pierce theory . . . bypasses normal judgment-collection procedures" and thus "presents many problems"). See also McCall Stock Farms, Inc. v. United States, 14 F.3d 1562 (Fed. Cir. 1993) (corporation held liable for debts of shareholder). See generally Gregory S. Crespi, The Reverse Pierce Doctrine: Applying Appropriate Standards, 16 J. Corp. L. 33 (1990).

61. Adolf A. Berle, The Theory of Enterprise Entity, 47 Colum. L. Rev. 343 (1947). For the view that "the historical background indicates that limited liability was never intended to protect a parent corporation against liability for the debts of its subsidiary," see Jonathan Landers, A Unified Approach to Parent, Subsidiary, and Affiliate Questions in Bankruptcy, 42 U. Chi. L. Rev. 589 (1975). See also Phillip I. Blumberg, Limited Liability and Corporate Groups, 11 J. Corp. L. 573 (1986). For further debate, compare Richard Posner, The Rights of Creditors of Affiliated Corporations, 43 U. Chi. L. Rev. 499 (1976), with Jonathan Landers, Another Word on Parents, Subsidiaries and Affiliates in Bankruptcy, 43 U. Chi. L. Rev. 527 (1976).

62. There are several more obvious categories of problems — easily resolved — that fall under the heading of "disregarding the corporate entity." The corporate veil will be pierced to prevent shareholders from prejudicing their personal creditors by fraudulently transferring their property to their wholly owned corporation (see, e.g., Litchfield Asset Mgmt. Corp. v. Howell, 70 Conn. App. 133, 154-156, 799 A.2d 298, 314-315 (Conn. App. 2002); Stine v. Girola, 9 Utah 2d 22, 337 P.2d 62 (1959)), and to estop a shareholder from claiming that a creditor may proceed against the corporation only when the shareholder has led the creditor to believe that dealings were with the shareholder personally (see, e.g.,

Perpetual Real Estate Services, Inc. v. Michaelson Properties, Inc.
974 F.2d 545 (4th Cir. 1992)

WILKINSON, J.: . . . In August 1981, defendant Aaron Michaelson formed Michael-son Properties, Inc., for the purpose of entering into joint real estate ventures. MPI was incorporated under the laws of the state of Illinois with initial paid-in capital of $1,000. Michaelson was the president and sole shareholder.

MPI subsequently entered into two joint ventures with Perpetual Real Estate Services, Inc. (PRES), the plaintiff in this case, involving the conversion of apartment buildings into condominiums. . . .

The second partnership, known as Arlington Apartment Associates (AAA), was formed in November 1983. Under the AAA partnership agreement, both PRES and MPI contributed $50,000 in capital, and each agreed to share pro rata in satisfying any liabilities of the partnership. The partnership also borrowed $24 million from Perpetual Savings Bank, PRES's parent corporation, but only after Aaron and Barbara Michaelson agreed to personally guarantee repayment of $750,000 of the loan. When an additional $2.1 million was needed to complete the project, MPI could not come up with the money so PRES loaned MPI $1.05 million, again after PRES secured a personal guarantee of repayment from the Michaelsons.

Inryco, Inc. v. CGR Bldg. Sys. Inc., 780 F.2d 879 (10th Cir. 1986)). Similarly, the corporate entity may be disregarded — either to hold shareholders liable for their corporations' debts or vice versa — when they have so confused the dealings of each and so commingled the assets of each that creditors are misled or the affairs of each cannot be meaningfully disentangled. (See, e.g., Herbert v. Wiegand, 207 So. 2d 882 (La. Ct. App. 1968); Shamrock Oil & Gas Co. v. Ethridge, 159 F. Supp. 693 (D. Colo. 1968)).

Occasionally, shareholders — not having misled anyone and thus not estopped for that reason — will themselves (or itself) seek to disregard the corporate entity, e.g., by bringing an action in their own name to enforce a right that belongs to the corporation. The attempt is usually unsuccessful. See, e.g., Riesberg v. Pittsburgh & Lake Erie R.R., 407 Pa. 434, 180 A.2d 575 (1962), and DeBoer Constr., Inc. v. Reliance Ins. Co., 540 F.2d 486 (10th Cir. 1976); but compare Fontainebleau Hotel Corp. v. Crossman, 286 F.2d 926 (5th Cir. 1961), 323 F.2d 937 (5th Cir. 1963). See generally Comment, Disregard of the Corporate Entity for the Benefit of Shareholders, 1963 Duke L.J. 722.

Two additional types of "piercing the corporate veil" problems that are frequently litigated should also be mentioned: (1) whether service of process against an out-of-state corporation may be accomplished by serving its subsidiary within the state, the theory being that the foreign parent is thereby "doing business" within the state, compare Doe v. Unocal Corp., 248 F.3d 915 (9th Cir. 2001), with Grimandi v. Beech Aircraft Corp., 512 F. Supp. 764 (D. Kan. 1981); and (2) whether the corporate entity should be disregarded because preservation of the fiction results in the evasion of other statutory policies or contractual obligations, see, e.g., Delaney v. Fidelity Lease Ltd., 526 S.W.2d 543 (Tex. 1975) (statutory requirement that limited partnership have at least one general partner with general liability cannot be circumvented by having the general partner be a corporation with minimum capital and operated by the limited partners); contra, Frigidaire Sales Corp. v. Union Properties, Inc., 14 Wash. App. 634, 544 P.2d 781 (1976); compare United States v. Reading Co., 253 U.S. 26 (1920), with United States v. South Buffalo Ry., 333 U.S. 711 (1948) (issue of whether provision of Interstate Commerce Act, which prohibits a railroad from transporting any commodity that it owns, is violated when a railroad corporation hauls product of a coal corporation, both corporations being wholly owned by a third corporation); compare Macpherson v. Eccleston, 190 Cal. App. 2d 24, 11 Cal. Rptr. 671 (1961), with Hirsh v. Miller, 167 So. 2d 539 (La. App. 1964) (issue of whether an individual's covenant not to compete is breached when competitor is a corporation wholly owned by the individual). See also NLRB v. Fullerton Transfer & Storage Ltd., 910 F.2d 331 (6th Cir. 1990) (corporate veil may be pierced to effectuate some federal labor law policies such as binding a new employer to an employment contract when it is "merely a disguised continuance of the old employer," but not other policies such as holding the new employer liable for a back pay award because of the original employer's unfair labor practice). On the frequently litigated issue of whether a parent corporation is the "operator" of its wholly owned subsidiary with responsibility for environmental clean-up under CERCLA, the federal Superfund Law, see United States v. Bestfoods, 524 U.S. 51 (1998) (general common law principles of piercing the corporate veil govern unless specifically abrogated by Congress).

During 1985 and 1986, the AAA partnership made various distributions of the profits from the condominium units. Prior to each distribution, the partners made the determination, as required by the partnership agreement, that they were leaving sufficient assets to permit the partnership to meet its anticipated expenses. Three distributions were made to PRES and MPI, totalling approximately $456,000 to each partner. MPI then authorized distributions of its profits to its sole shareholder, Aaron Michaelson.

In 1987, more than a year after the last of these distributions, several condominium purchasers filed suit against AAA, asserting breach of warranty claims in the amount of $5.5 million. Shortly before the case went to trial, counsel for AAA entered into settlement negotiations. The case was ultimately settled for $950,000. PRES paid the full amount on behalf of the partnership; MPI made no contribution toward the settlement since its profits had been distributed years earlier.

PRES then filed this diversity action against Michaelson and MPI . . . [alleging] that MPI was Michaelson's "alter ego or mere instrumentality" and that MPI's corporate veil should be pierced. . . . Michaelson argued that PRES had failed to justify disregarding the corporate form under Virginia law — that PRES had failed as a matter of law to prove that Michaelson had used MPI as a "device or sham" to "disguise wrongs, obscure fraud, or conceal crime," as required by Cheatle v. Rudd's Swimming Pool Supply Co., 234 Va. 207, 360 S.E.2d 828, 831 (1987). . . .

Virginia courts have long recognized the basic proposition that a corporation is a legal entity separate and distinct from its shareholders. See Beale v. Kappa Alpha Order, 192 Va. 382, 64 S.E.2d 789, 796 (1951); *Cheatle*, 360 S.E.2d at 831. A fundamental purpose of incorporation is to "enable a group of persons to limit their liability in a joint venture to the extent of their contributions to the capital stock." *Beale*, 64 S.E.2d at 796. This concept of limited liability "supports a vital economic policy," *Cheatle*, 360 S.E.2d at 831, a policy on which "large undertakings are rested, vast enterprises are launched, and huge sums of capital attracted." Anderson v. Abbott, 321 U.S. 349, 362, 64 S. Ct. 531, 537, 88 L. Ed. 793 (1944).

Virginia courts have assiduously defended this "vital economic policy," lifting the veil of immunity only in "extraordinary" cases. *Beale*, 64 S.E.2d at 797; *Cheatle*, 360 S.E.2d at 831. Under Virginia law, plaintiff bears the burden of convincing the court to disregard the corporate form, and must first establish that "the corporate entity was the alter ego, alias, stooge, or dummy of the individuals sought to be charged personally." *Cheatle*, 360 S.E.2d at 831. This element may be established by evidence that the defendant exercised "undue domination and control" over the corporation, *Beale*, 64 S.E.2d at 797, and the jury instruction in this case fairly described this aspect of the test. Under this element of the test, the court properly permitted the jury to consider such factors as whether Michaelson "observe[d] corporate formalities," whether he kept "corporate records," whether he paid dividends, and whether there were "other officers and directors."

The Supreme Court of Virginia has specifically held, however, that proof that some person "may dominate or control" the corporation, or "may treat it as a mere department, instrumentality, agency, etc." is not enough to pierce the veil. *Beale*, 64 S.E.2d at 798.[63] In Virginia, "something more is required to induce the court to

---

63. Accord, Morris v. N.Y. State Dept. of Taxation and Finance, 82 N.Y.2d 135, 141-142, 603 N.Y.S.2d 807, 811, 623 N.E.2d 1157, 1161 (1993). — ED.

disregard the entity of a corporation." Id. at 797. Hence, plaintiff must also establish "that the corporation was a device or sham used to disguise wrongs, obscure fraud, or conceal crime." *Cheatle*, 360 S.E.2d at 831. . . . This strict standard contrasts starkly with the rather soggy state in which the law was submitted to the jury, which was permitted to impose personal liability on Michaelson if it found that Michaelson dominated MPI and used MPI to perpetrate "an injustice or fundamental unfairness." The fact that limited liability might yield results that seem "unfair" to jurors unfamiliar with the function of the corporate form cannot provide a basis for piercing the veil. Virginia law requires proof of some legal wrong before it undermines this basic assumption of corporate existence.

It is true, as PRES points out, that the requirement of "injustice or fundamental fairness" follows the language of this court's opinion in DeWitt Truck Brokers, Inc. v. W. Ray Flemming Fruit Co., 540 F.2d 681, 683 (4th Cir. 1976). *DeWitt*, however, did not involve Virginia law, but applied a different standard that permits the corporate veil to be pierced "in appropriate circumstances even in the absence of fraud or wrongdoing." Cunningham v. Rendezvous, Inc., 699 F.2d 676, 680 (4th Cir. 1983). That is plainly not the law in Virginia, and the judgment cannot stand.

. . . The district court found — and PRES appears to concede — that there was no evidence that Michaelson used the corporation to "obscure fraud" or "conceal crime." The only question, then, is whether a reasonable jury could have found that Michaelson somehow used MPI to "disguise wrongs."

PRES has simply failed to show that Michaelson used the corporate form to "disguise wrongs." PRES and MPI had entered into a longstanding contractual relationship, and PRES had full knowledge of the nature of its corporate partner, including its ownership structure and capitalization. PRES even participated in the decisions to distribute money to itself and to MPI after determining that the AAA partnership had sufficient assets to cover its anticipated expenses, and PRES apparently sought no limitations on what MPI did with those funds. PRES has sought on appeal to attack MPI's distributions to Michaelson by labelling them an unfair "siphoning" of funds. It was entirely foreseeable to PRES, however, that MPI would distribute those funds to Michaelson, its sole shareholder. When MPI did distribute the funds, it did so well before any claims were filed against the partnership and in a manner that PRES has not shown would violate Virginia law.

PRES points out, however, that in a number of contexts PRES did negotiate personal guarantees from Michaelson, and insists that such guarantees weaken MPI's corporate veil. We think, to the contrary, that they fortify it. Courts have been extraordinarily reluctant to lift the veil in contract cases, such as this one, where the "creditor has willingly transacted business" with the corporation. United States v. Jon-T Chemicals, Inc., 768 F.2d 686, 693 (5th Cir. 1985). In other words, "courts usually apply more stringent standards to piercing the corporate veil in a contract case than they do in tort cases. This is because the party seeking relief in a contract case is presumed to have voluntarily and knowingly entered into an agreement with a corporate entity, and is expected to suffer the consequences of the limited liability associated with the corporate business form, while this is not the situation in tort cases."[64] 1 William M. Fletcher, Fletcher Cyclopedia of the Law of Private Corporations §41.85 at 712 (1990 ed.). Thus, in contract cases, where "each party has a clear and equal obligation to weigh the potential benefits

---

64. Accord, Theberge v. Darbro, Inc., 684 A.2d 1298 (Md. 1996). — ED.

and risks of the agreement," United Paperworkers Int'l Union v. Penntech Papers, Inc., 439 F. Supp. 610, 618 (D. Me. 1977), *aff'd*, 583 F.2d 33 (1st Cir. 1978), courts have emphatically discouraged plaintiffs seeking to disregard the corporate form. See Frank Easterbrook & Daniel Fischel, The Economic Structure of Corporate Law 58 (1991). In such cases, courts have required proof of some form of misrepresentation to the creditor: "Unless the [corporation] misrepresents its financial condition to the creditor, the creditor should be bound by its decision to deal with the [corporation]; it should not be able to complain later that the [corporation] is unsound." *Jon-T Chemicals*, 768 F.2d at 693.[65] See also Interocean Shipping Co. v. National Shipping & Trading Corp., 523 F.2d 527, 539 (2d Cir. 1975) (requiring conduct "akin to fraud" in order to pierce the veil in contract cases). . . . PRES has failed to point to anything that suggests that Michaelson misled PRES as to its financial condition — there is simply no indication that Michaelson used MPI to "disguise" anything. . . . Parties to a commercial transaction must be free to negotiate questions of limited liability and to enforce their agreements by recourse to the law of contracts. PRES surely understood that principle, and thus went to the trouble of securing Michaelson's personal guarantees on several matters. . . . Significantly, the AAA joint venture agreement included no personal guarantees by Michaelson. . . .

From the outset, MPI was a limited liability corporation formed for the express purpose of entering joint ventures in real estate. The parties in this case expressly put the issue of limited liability on the bargaining table, and settled on an agreement that required MPI — not Aaron Michaelson — to answer for the debts of the partnership. Exceptions to this rule were plainly spelled out by the parties in writing. The jury verdict stripped Michaelson of the protections against personal liability to which he was entitled under the settled corporate law of Virginia. It awarded to PRES a new contract — one that bestowed on PRES a personal guarantee on the part of Michaelson that PRES had been unable to obtain at the bargaining table — apparently on the ground that the actual agreement resulted in a "fundamental unfairness." Be that as it may, Virginia law plainly says that fairness is for the parties to the contract to evaluate, not the courts. Our task is rather one of enforcement.

Reversed.

Kinney Shoe Corp. v. Polan
939 F.2d 209 (4th Cir. 1991)

CHAPMAN, J.: Plaintiff-appellant Kinney Shoe Corporation ("Kinney") brought this action in the United States District Court for the Southern District of West Virginia against Lincoln M. Polan ("Polan") seeking to recover money owed on a sublease between Kinney and Industrial Realty Company ("Industrial"). . . . In 1984 Polan formed two corporations, Industrial and Polan Industries, Inc., for the purpose of re-establishing an industrial manufacturing business. . . . Polan was the owner of both corporations. Although certificates of incorporation were issued, no organizational meetings were held, and no officers were elected.

---

65. What result if the contract creditor has no reason to believe that he is dealing with a corporation? See Aronson v. Price, 644 N.E.2d 864 (Ind. 1964) (plaintiff brought his car for repair to "Corbett's Body Shop," which nowhere indicated corporate status). — Ed.

In November 1984 Polan and Kinney began negotiating the sublease of a building in which Kinney held a leasehold interest. . . .

The term of the sublease from Kinney to Industrial commenced in December 1984, even though the written lease was not signed by the parties until April 5, 1985. On April 15, 1985, Industrial subleased part of the building to Polan Industries for fifty percent of the rental amount due Kinney. Polan signed both subleases on behalf of the respective companies.

Other than the sublease with Kinney, Industrial had no assets, no income and no bank account. Industrial issued no stock certificates because nothing was ever paid in to this corporation. Industrial's only income was from its sublease to Polan Industries, Inc. The first rental payment to Kinney was made out of Polan's personal funds, and no further payments were made by Polan or by Polan Industries, Inc. to either Industrial or to Kinney. . . .

We have long recognized that a corporation is an entity, separate and distinct from its officers and stockholders, and the individual stockholders are not responsible for the debts of the corporation. See e.g., DeWitt Truck Brokers, Inc. v. W. Ray Flemming Fruit Co., 540 F.2d 681, 683 (4th Cir. 1976). This concept, however, is a fiction of the law "'and it is now well settled, as a general principle, that the fiction should be disregarded when it is urged with an intent not within its reason and purpose, and in such a way that its retention would produce injustices or inequitable consequences.'" Laya v. Erin Homes, Inc., 352 S.E.2d 93, 97-98 (W. Va. 1986) (quoting Sanders v. Roselawn Memorial Gardens, Inc., 152, W. Va. 91, 159 S.E.2d 784, 786 (1968).

Piercing the corporate veil is an equitable remedy, and the burden rests with the party asserting such claim. DeWitt Truck Brokers, 540 F.2d at 683. A totality of the circumstances test is used in determining whether to pierce the corporate veil, and each case must be decided on its own facts. The district court's findings of facts may be overturned only if clearly erroneous. Id.

Kinney seeks to pierce the corporate veil of Industrial so as to hold Polan personally liable on the sublease debt. The Supreme Court of Appeals of West Virginia has set forth a two prong test to be used in determining whether to pierce a corporate veil in a breach of contract case. This test raises two issues: first, is the unity of interest and ownership such that the separate personalities of the corporation and the individual shareholder no longer exist; and second, would an equitable result occur if the acts are treated as those of the corporation alone. Laya, 352 S.E.2d at 99. Numerous factors have been identified as relevant in making this determination. . . .

It is undisputed that Industrial was not adequately capitalized. Actually, it had no paid in capital. Polan had put nothing into this corporation, and it did not observe any corporate formalities. As the West Virginia court stated in Laya, "'[i]ndividuals who wish to enjoy limited personal liability for business activities under a corporate umbrella should be expected to adhere to the relatively simple formalities of creating and maintaining a corporate entity.'" Laya, 352 S.E.2d at 100 n.6 (quoting Labadie Coal Co. v. Black, 672 F.2d 92, 96-97 (D.D. Cir. 1982)). This, the court stated, is "'a relatively small price to pay for limited liability.'" Id. Another important factor is adequate capitalization. "[G]rossly inadequate capitalization combined with disregard of corporate formalities, causing basic unfairness, are sufficient to pierce the corporate veil in order to hold the shareholder(s) actively participating in the operation of the business personally liable for a breach of contract to the party who entered into the contract with the corporation." *Laya*, 352 S.E.2d at 101-102.

In this case, Polan bought no stock, made no capital contribution, kept no minutes, and elected no officers for Industrial. In addition, Polan attempted to protect his assets by placing them in Polan Industries, Inc. and interposing Industrial between Polan Industries, Inc. and Kinney so as to prevent Kinney from going against the corporation with assets. . . . [66]

In *Laya*, the court also noted that when determining whether to pierce a corporate veil a third prong may apply in certain cases. The court stated: "When, under the circumstances, it would be reasonable for that particular type of a party [those contract creditors capable of protecting themselves] entering into a contract with the corporation, for example, a bank or other lending institution, to conduct an investigation of the credit of the corporation prior to entering into the contract, such party will be charged with the knowledge that a reasonable credit investigation would disclose. If such an investigation would disclose that the corporation is grossly undercapitalized, based upon the nature and the magnitude of the corporate undertaking, such party will be deemed to have assumed the risk of the gross undercapitalization and will not be permitted to pierce the corporate veil." *Laya*, 352 S.E.2d at 100. The district court applied this third prong and concluded that Kinney "assumed the risk of Industrial's defaulting" and that "the application of the doctrine of 'piercing the corporate veil' ought not and does not [apply]."[67] While we agree that the two prong test of *Laya* was satisfied, we hold that the district court's conclusion that Kinney had assumed the risk is clearly erroneous.

Without deciding whether the third prong should be extended beyond the context of the financial institution lender mentioned in Laya,[68] we hold that, even if it applies to creditors such as Kinney, it does not prevent Kinney from piercing the corporate veil in this case. The third prong is permissive and not mandatory. This is not a factual situation that calls for the third prong, if we are to seek an equitable result. Polan set up Industrial to limit his liability and the liability of Polan Industries, Inc. in their dealings with Kinney. A stockholder's liability is limited to the amount he has invested in the corporation, but Polan invested nothing in Industrial. This corporation was no more than a shell—a transparent shell. When nothing is invested in the corporation, the corporation provides no protection to its owner; nothing in, nothing out, no protection. If Polan wishes the protection of a corporation to limit his liability, he must follow the simple formalities of

66. Compare Texas Indus, Inc. v. DuPuy, 227 So. 2d 265 (La. Ct. App. 1969): "Inadequate capitalization is not of itself a badge of fraud. . . . The general rule is that an individual may incorporate his business for the sole purpose of escaping individual liability for the corporate debts." Accord, L. R. T. Garrett v. Ancarrow Marine, Inc., 211 Va. 755, 180 S.E.2d 668 (1971); Bostwick Braun Co. v. Szews, 645 F. Supp. 221 (W.D. Wis. 1986).—ED.

67. Accord, Co-Ex Plastics, Inc. v. Ala Pak, Inc., 536 So. 2d 37 (Ala. 1988) (voluntary creditor who had not "inquired about the status of Ala Pak, other than through a bank credit check, nor . . . requested a personal guarantee" cannot pierce veil because of inadequate capitalization). What result if "the shareholder has siphoned funds out of the firm so that it is *ex post* undercapitalized"? Stephen M. Bainbridge, Abolishing Veil Piercing, 26 J. Corp. L. 497, 517 (2001).—ED.

68. See also Frank Easterbrook & Daniel R. Fischel, The Economic Structure of Corporate Law 59 (1991): "Many credit transactions are too small to warrant a full investigation of the debtor's finances by the creditor. . . . In these situations, it is desirable that creditors be able to assume that the debtor is adequately capitalized. The firm should have a duty to notify the creditor of any unusual capitalization. It is cheaper for the firm (which has the best information about its capital structure) to notify creditors in the unusual case than for creditors to investigate in all cases." What result in a suit for unpaid salary by the executive vice-president of a large corporation? See Lopez v. TDI Services, Inc., 631 So. 2d 679 (La. App. 1994).—ED.

maintaining the corporation. This he failed to do, and he may not relieve his circumstances by saying Kinney should have known better.[69]

Reversed.

———————————

1. *Express agency theory.* Restatement (Third) of Agency §1.01 defines "agency" as "the fiduciary relationship that arises when one person (a 'principal') manifests assent to another person (an 'agent') that the agent shall act on the principal's behalf and subject to the principal's control, and the agent manifests assent or otherwise consents so to act." When a corporation enters into a contract—and one person owns or controls all or substantially all of its shares and thereby originates, negotiates, and executes all of its contracts—why is it not always accurate to conclude that the shareholder is "principal" and the corporation is "agent"?

2. *Domination and control.* Why should this "not be enough to pierce the veil" in the *Perpetual* case?

> One would expect it to be quite rare for a majority (and especially a sole) shareholder of a corporation not to exercise control [or domination] over the business. If this is grounds to pierce, few closely held corporations would provide limited liability. . . . A number of economics writers have argued that limited liability is generally inefficient for a closely held business because of incentives for excessive risk taking and the lack of offsetting gains from promoting securities markets. Indeed, historically, the notion that abstention from control was the *quid pro quo* for limited liability provided the basis for the enactment of limited partnership acts. Nevertheless, given well-established legislative and judicial permission for closely held and even single shareholder corporations, it is far too late in the day to make an *ex post* judicial change through piercing decisions. Indeed, the legislative trend is away from any rule that suggests liability must follow control. For example, statutory provisions sanctioning greater direct shareholder control over closely held corporations [see page 759 infra] make little sense if shareholder control meant the loss of limited liability. Similarly, the Revised Uniform Limited Partnership Act dramatically watered down the prohibition on limited partners participating in control. Finally, we have the rapid spread of legislation creating new entities, the limited liability company and limited liability partnership [see pages 810 and 822, respectively, infra], in which limited liability expressly can co-exist with direct owner control.

Franklin A. Gevurtz, Corporation Law 76-77 (2000).

———————————

69. In the *Laya* case, the court continued:

> Generally, the presumption is that the party dealing with the corporation did not assume the risk of grossly inadequate capitalization. "[I]n entering into such [contractual] relationships with corporate entities the parties are [generally] entitled to rely upon certain assumptions, one being that the corporation is more than a mere shell—that it has substance as well as form." Iron City Sand & Gravel Division of McDonough Co. v. West Fork Towing Corp., 298 F. Supp. 1091, 1099 (N.D. W. Va. 1969), *rev'd on other grounds*, 440 F.2d 958 (4th Cir. 1971). In other words, the incorporators who actively participate in the operation of the business are not entitled to personal immunity when they fail to provide the *quid pro quo* for such immunity, specifically, a reasonably adequate capital fund to which creditors may resort.

"Following this logic, capital is inadequate [and should have been disclosed to the creditor] when the finder of fact infers from the corporation's financial position that the controlling shareholder knew the corporation was not likely to perform contracts it was entering." Franklin A. Gevurtz, Corporation Law 102 (2000). — ED.

In Amfac Foods, Inc. v. International Systems & Controls Corp., 294 Or. 94, 654 P.2d 1092 (1982), the court described the "exception to the rule of shareholder immunity" as follows:

> When a plaintiff seeks to collect a corporate debt from a shareholder by virtue of the shareholder's control over the debtor corporation rather than on some other theory, the plaintiff must allege and prove not only that the debtor corporation was under the actual control of the shareholder but also that the plaintiff's inability to collect from the corporation resulted from some form of improper conduct on the part of the shareholder. This causation requirement has two implications. The shareholder's alleged control over the corporation must not be only potential but must actually have been exercised in a manner either causing the corporation's default on the transaction or a resulting obligation. Likewise, the shareholder's conduct must have been improper either in relation to the plaintiff's entering the transaction or in preventing or interfering with the corporation's performance or ability to perform its obligations toward the plaintiff.

3. *Observance of formalities.* Why was it significant in the *Kinney* case that Polan "did not observe any corporate formalities"? An analysis of many cases concludes that

> a failure to follow normal corporate routine appears a most significant consideration in deciding whether a corporation is the "alter ego" of the shareholder or whether the "corporate veil should be pierced." While a complete catalogue of dangerous acts is probably impossible to prepare, there appears to be a substantial risk that the separate corporate existence will be ignored when business is commenced without issuance of shares, when shareholder meetings or directors' meetings are not held, or consents are not signed, when decisions are made by shareholders as though they were partners, when the shareholders do not sharply distinguish between corporate property and personal property, when corporate funds are used to pay personal expenses, when personal funds are used for corporate expenses without proper accounting, or when complete corporate and financial records are not maintained.

Robert W. Hamilton, The Corporate Entity, 49 Tex. L. Rev. 979, 990 (1971). Would the result in the *Kinney* case have been different if none of these factors had been present? Compare Scott Graphics Inc. v. Mahaney, 89 N.M. 208, 549 P.2d 623 (Ct. App.) (1976) ("disregard of corporate formality in the operation" and "ignorance on the part of the directors and officers as to its operation . . . are not enough to warrant disregarding the corporate entity"); Preston Farm & Ranch Supply, Inc. v. Bio-Zyme Enterprises, 615 S.W.2d 258 (Tex. Civ. App. 1981) (plaintiff "fails to point out how" failure to observe corporate formalities and keep financial affairs separate caused plaintiff to "fall victim to some basically unfair device by which the corporate form of business organization has been used to achieve an inequitable result"). See also RMBCA, Close Corporation Supplement[70] §25: *"Limited liability.* The failure of a statutory close corporation to observe the usual corporate formalities or requirements relating to the exercise of its corporate powers or

---

70. This is an optional statute developed for states that determine that it is advisable to enact an integrated statute dealing with the problems of closely held corporations.

management of its business and affairs is not a ground for imposing personal liability on the shareholders for liabilities of the corporation."

4. *Statute.* What result in the preceding cases under the following statute, the first state enactment dealing generally with the issue of piercing the corporate veil?

Texas Business Corporation Act (1997)

Art. 2.21. *Liability of subscribers and shareholders.* A holder of shares . . . shall be under no obligation to the corporation or to its obligees with respect to: . . .

(2) any contractual obligation of the corporation or any matter relating to or arising from the obligation on the basis that the holder . . . is or was the alter ego of the corporation, or on the basis of actual fraud or constructive fraud, a sham to perpetrate a fraud, or other similar theory, unless the obligee demonstrates that the holder . . . caused the corporation to be used for the purpose of perpetrating and did perpetrate an actual fraud on the obligee primarily for the direct personal benefit of the holder . . . or

(3) any obligation of the corporation on the basis of the failure of the corporation to observe any corporate formality, including without limitation: (a) the failure to comply with any requirement of this Act or of the articles of incorporation or bylaws of the corporation. . . .

5. *Res judicata.* Suppose, on the facts of the *Kinney* case, that plaintiff had first sued and obtained judgment only against Industrial and then, discovering that Industrial was judgment proof, sued Polan on an "instrumentality" theory. Would the first suit's determination of liability and damages be binding on Polan? See Dudley v. Smith, 504 F.2d 979 (5th Cir. 1974).

6. *Problem.* After a corporation (whose shares are wholly owned by Husband and Wife) buys land, a law imposes onerous regulations on all property acquired after the law's enactment. A year later, pursuant to their divorce, the corporation is dissolved and the land is divided between Husband and Wife. State claims the property is subject to the law. What result? See City of Virginia Beach v. Bell, 498 S.E.2d 414 (Va. 1998).

Walkovsky v. Carlton
18 N.Y.2d 414, 223 N.E.2d 6, 276 N.Y.S.2d 585 (1966)

FULD, J.: This case involves what appears to be a rather common practice in the taxicab industry of vesting the ownership of a taxi fleet in many corporations, each owning only one or two cabs.

The complaint alleges that the plaintiff was severely injured four years ago in New York City when he was run down by a taxicab owned by the defendant Seon Cab Corporation and negligently operated at the time by the defendant Marchese. The individual defendant, Carlton, is claimed to be a stockholder of 10 corporations, including Seon, each of which has but two cabs registered in its name, and it is implied that only the minimum automobile liability insurance required by law (in the amount of $10,000) is carried on any one cab. Although seemingly independent of one another, these corporations are alleged to be "operated . . . as a single entity, unit and enterprise" with regard to financing, supplies, repairs, employees and garaging, and all are named as defendants. The plaintiff asserts that he is also entitled to hold their stockholders personally for the damages sought because the multiple corporate structure constitutes an unlawful attempt "to defraud members of the general public" who might be injured by the cabs.

The defendant Carlton has moved . . . to dismiss the complaint on the ground that as to him it "fails to state a cause of action." The court at Special Term granted the motion but the Appellate Division, by a divided vote, reversed. . . .

The law permits the incorporation of a business for the very purpose of enabling its proprietors to escape personal liability . . . but . . . the courts will disregard the corporate form, or, to use accepted terminology, "pierce the corporate veil," whenever necessary "to prevent fraud or to achieve equity." . . . In determining whether liability should be extended to reach assets beyond those belonging to the corporation, we are guided, as Judge Cardozo noted, by "general rules of agency" (Berkey v. Third Ave. Ry. Co., 244 N.Y. 84, 95, 155 N.E. 58, 61, 50 A.L.R. 599). In other words, whenever anyone uses control of the corporation to further his own rather than the corporation's business, he will be liable for the corporation's acts "upon the principle of respondeat superior applicable even where the agent is a natural person." . . .

In [Mangan v. Terminal Transp. System] (247 App. Div. 853, 286 N.Y.S. 666), the plaintiff was injured as a result of the negligent operation of a cab owned and operated by one of four corporations affiliated with the defendant Terminal. Although the defendant was not a stockholder of any of the operating companies, both the defendant and the operating companies were owned, for the most part, by the same parties. The defendant's name (Terminal) was conspicuously displayed on the sides of all of the taxis used in the enterprise and, in point of fact, the defendant actually serviced, inspected, repaired and dispatched them. These facts were deemed to provide sufficient cause for piercing the corporate veil of the operating company — the nominal owner of the cab which injured the plaintiff — and holding the defendant liable. The operating companies were simply instrumentalities for carrying on the business of the defendant without imposing upon it financial and other liabilities incident to the actual ownership and operation of the cabs. . . .

In the case before us, the plaintiff has explicitly alleged that none of the corporations "had a separate existence of their own" and, as indicated above, all are named as defendants. However, it is one thing to assert that a corporation is a fragment of a larger corporate combine which actually conducts the business. (See Berle, The Theory of Enterprise Entity, 47 Colum. L. Rev. 343, 348-350.) It is quite another to claim that the corporation is a "dummy" for its individual stockholders who are in reality carrying on the business in their personal capacities for purely personal rather than corporate ends. . . . Either circumstance would justify treating the corporation as an agent and piercing the corporate veil to reach the principal but a different result would follow in each case. In the first, only a larger *corporate* entity would be held financially responsible (see, e.g., Mangan v. Terminal Transp. System . . .) while, in the other the stockholder would be personally liable.[71] . . .

71. Allowing creditors to reach the assets of parent corporations does not create unlimited liability for any people. . . . Moreover, . . . subsidiaries have less incentive to insure. . . . Bankruptcy of the subsidiary will not cause . . . [managers of subsidiaries who are often also managers of the parent] to lose their positions in the parent . . . (though it might impose a reputational loss on them). If limited liability is absolute, a parent can form a subsidiary with minimal capitalization for the purpose of engaging in risky activities. If things go well, the parent captures the benefits. If things go poorly, the subsidiary declares bankruptcy, and the parent creates another with the same managers to engage in the same activities.

Frank Easterbrook & Daniel R. Fischel, Limited Liability and the Corporation, 52 U. Chi. L. Rev. 89 (1985). See also articles in footnote 61 supra. — Ed.

Either the stockholder is conducting the business in his individual capacity or he is not. If he is, he will be liable; if he is not, then, it does not matter — insofar as his personal liability is concerned — that the enterprise is actually being carried on by a larger "enterprise entity." . . .

The individual defendant is charged with having "organized, managed, dominated and controlled" a fragmented corporate entity but there are no allegations that he was conducting business in his individual capacity. Had the taxicab fleet been owned by a single corporation, it would be readily apparent that the plaintiff would face formidable barriers in attempting to establish personal liability on the part of the corporation's stockholders. The fact that the fleet ownership has been deliberately split up among many corporations does not ease the plaintiff's burden in that respect. The corporate form may not be disregarded merely because the assets of the corporation, together with the mandatory insurance coverage of the vehicle which struck the plaintiff, are insufficient to assure him the recovery sought. If Carlton were to be held individually liable on those facts alone, the decision would apply equally to the thousands of cabs which are owned by their individual drivers who conduct their businesses through corporations . . . and carry the minimum insurance required by subdivision 1 (par. [a]) of section 370 of the Vehicle and Traffic Law, Consol. Laws, c. 71. These taxi owner-operators are entitled to form such corporations . . . and we agree with the court at Special Term that, if the insurance coverage required by statute "is inadequate for the protection of the public, the remedy lies not with the courts but with the Legislature." It may very well be sound policy to require that certain corporations must take out liability insurance which will afford adequate compensation to their potential tort victims. However, the responsibility for imposing conditions on the privilege of incorporation has been committed by the Constitution to the Legislature (N.Y. Const. art. X, §1) and it may not be fairly implied, from any statute, that the Legislature intended, without the slightest discussion or debate, to require of taxi corporations that they carry automobile liability insurance over and above that mandated by the Vehicle and Traffic Law.

This is not to say that it is impossible for the plaintiff to state a valid cause of action against the defendant Carlton. However, the simple fact is that the plaintiff has just not done so here. While the complaint alleges that the separate corporations were undercapitalized and that their assets have been intermingled, it is barren of any "sufficiently particular[ized] statements" . . . that the defendant Carlton and his associates are actually doing business in their individual capacities, shuttling their personal funds in and out of the corporations "without regard to formality and to suit their immediate convenience." . . . Nothing of the sort has in fact been charged, and it cannot reasonably or logically be inferred from the happenstance that the business of Seon Cab Corporation may actually be carried on by a large corporate entity composed of many corporations which, under general principles of agency, would be liable to each other's creditors in contract and in tort.[3]

---

3. In his affidavit in opposition to the motion to dismiss, the plaintiff's counsel claimed that corporate assets had been "milked out" of, and "siphoned off" from the enterprise. Quite apart from the fact that these allegations are far too vague and conclusory, the charge is premature. If the plaintiff succeeds in his action and becomes a judgment creditor of the corporation, he may then sue and attempt to hold

In point of fact, the principle relied upon in the complaint to sustain the imposition of personal liability is not agency but fraud. Such a cause of action cannot withstand analysis. If it is not fraudulent for the owner-operator of a single cab corporation to take out only the minimum required liability insurance, the enterprise does not become either illicit or fraudulent merely because it consists of many such corporations. The plaintiff's injuries are the same regardless of whether the cab which strikes him is owned by a single corporation or part of a fleet with ownership fragmented among many corporations. Whatever rights he may be able to assert against parties other than the registered owner of the vehicle come into being not because he has been defrauded but because, under the principle of respondeat superior, he is entitled to hold the whole enterprise responsible for the acts of its agent. . . .

The order of the Appellate Division should be reversed. . . .

KEATING, J. (dissenting): The defendant Carlton, the shareholder here sought to be held for the negligence of the driver of a taxicab, was a principal shareholder and organizer of the defendant corporation which owned the taxicab. The corporation was one of 10 organized by the defendant. . . . The sole assets of these operating corporations are the vehicles themselves and they are apparently subject to mortgages.*

From their inception these corporations were intentionally undercapitalized for the purpose of avoiding responsibility for acts which were bound to arise as a result of the operation of a large taxi fleet having cars out on the street 24 hours a day and engaged in public transportation. And during the course of the corporations' existence all income was continually drained out of the corporations for the same purpose.

The issue presented by this action is whether the policy of this State, which affords those desiring to engage in a business enterprise the privilege of limited liability through the use of the corporate device, is so strong that it will permit that privilege to continue no matter how much it is abused. . . .

Under the circumstances of this case the shareholders should all be held individually liable to this plaintiff for the injuries he suffered. . . . At least the matter should not be disposed of on the pleadings by a dismissal of the complaint. "If a corporation is organized and carries on business without substantial capital in such a way that the corporation is likely to have no sufficient assets available to meet its debts, it is inequitable that shareholders should set up such a flimsy organization to escape personal liability. The attempt to do corporate business without providing any sufficient basis of financial responsibility to creditors is an abuse of the separate entity and will be ineffectual to exempt the shareholders from corporate debts. It is coming to be recognized as the policy of law that shareholders should in good faith put at the risk of the business unincumbered capital reasonably adequate for its prospective liabilities. If capital is illusory or trifling compared with the business to be done and the risks of loss, this is a ground for denying the separate entity privilege." (Ballantine, Corporations [rev. ed. 1946], §129, pp. 302-303.)

---

the individual defendants accountable for any dividends and property that were wrongfully distributed. . . .

*It appears that the medallions, which are of considerable value, are judgment proof. (Administrative Code of City of New York, §436-2.0.)

In Minton v. Cavaney, 56 Cal. 2d 576, 15 Cal. Rptr. 641, 364 P.2d 473, the Supreme Court of California had occasion to discuss this problem in a negligence case. The corporation of which the defendant was an organizer, director and officer operated a public swimming pool. One afternoon the plaintiffs' daughter drowned in the pool as a result of the alleged negligence of the corporation.

Justice Roger Traynor, speaking for the court, outlined the applicable law in this area." . . . The equitable owners of a corporation, for example, are personally liable . . . *when they provide inadequate capitalization and actively participate in the conduct of corporate affairs."* (56 Cal. 2d, p.579, 15 Cal. Rptr., p.643, 364 P.2d, p.475; italics supplied.)

Examining the facts of the case in light of the legal principles just enumerated, he found that "[it was] undisputed that there was no attempt to provide adequate capitalization. [The corporation] never had any substantial assets. It leased the pool that it operated, and the lease was forfeited for failure to pay the rent. Its capital was 'trifling compared with the business to be done and the risks of loss.' " . . .

It seems obvious that one of "the risks of loss" referred to was the possibility of drownings due to the negligence of the corporation. And the defendant's failure to provide such assets or any fund for recovery resulted in his being held personally liable. . . .

The defendant Carlton claims that, because the minimum amount of insurance required by the statute was obtained, the corporate veil cannot and should not be pierced despite the fact that the assets of the corporation which owned the cab were "trifling compared with the business to be done and the risks of loss" which were certain to be encountered. I do not agree.

The Legislature in requiring minimum liability insurance of $10,000, no doubt, intended to provide at least some small fund for recovery against those individuals and corporations who just did not have and were not able to raise or accumulate assets sufficient to satisfy the claims of those who were injured as a result of their negligence. It certainly could not have intended to shield those individuals who organized corporations, with the specific intent of avoiding responsibility to the public, where the operation of the corporate enterprise yielded profits sufficient to purchase additional insurance. Moreover, it is reasonable to assume that the Legislature believed that those individuals and corporations having substantial assets would take out insurance far in excess of the minimum in order to protect those assets from depletion. . . .

The defendant, however, argues that the failure of the Legislature to increase the minimum insurance requirements indicates legislative acquiescence in this scheme to avoid liability and responsibility to the public. In the absence of a clear legislative statement, approval of a scheme having such serious consequences is not to be so lightly inferred.

The defendant contends that the court will be encroaching upon the legislative domain by ignoring the corporate veil and holding the individual shareholder. This argument was answered by Mr. Justice Douglas in Anderson v. Abbott, [321 U.S.] 366-367, where he wrote that: ". . . *Judicial interference to cripple or defeat a legislative policy is one thing; judicial interference with the plans of those whose corporate or other devices would circumvent that policy is quite another.* Once the purpose or effect of the scheme is clear, once the legislative policy is plain, we would indeed forsake a great tradition to say we were helpless to fashion the instruments for appropriate relief." (Emphasis added.)

The defendant contends that a decision holding him personally liable would discourage people from engaging in corporate enterprise.

What I would merely hold is that a participating shareholder of a corporation vested with a public interest, organized with capital insufficient to meet liabilities which are certain to arise in the ordinary course of the corporation's business, may be held personally responsible for such liabilities. Where corporate income is not sufficient to cover the cost of insurance premiums above the statutory minimum or where initially adequate finances dwindle under the pressure of competition, bad times or extraordinary and unexpected liability, obviously the shareholder will not be held liable (Henn, Corporations, p. 208, n.7).[72]

The only types of corporate enterprises that will be discouraged as a result of a decision allowing the individual shareholder to be sued will be those such as the one in question, designed solely to abuse the corporate privilege at the expense of the public interest. . . . [73]

Problem. Federal statutes provide that shareholders in national banks shall be subject to assessment for the bank's obligations, this additional personal liability being limited to the par value of the bank shares owned. At a time when "Congress did not outlaw holding companies from the national bank field nor undertake to regulate them," a number of shareholders in a national bank formed a corporation and transferred their bank shares to it. This was done "in good faith" and not for the "purpose of avoiding double liability." But when the bank became insolvent, the holding company had inadequate assets to meet the double liability obligation imposed by the federal statutes. Are the holding company shareholders personally liable for the statutory amount? What about those holding company shareholders who never personally owned national bank shares but who bought shares issued by the holding company? See Anderson v. Abbott, 321 U.S. 349 (1944).

Fletcher v. Atex, Inc.
8 F.3d 1451 (2d Cir. 1995)

CABRANES, J.: . . . The plaintiffs-appellants filed suit against Atex, Inc. ("Atex") and its parent, Eastman Kodak Company ("Kodak"), [which owned all of Atex's shares], to recover for repetitive stress injuries that they claim were caused by their use of computer keyboards manufactured by Atex. . . .

The plaintiffs claim that the district court erred in granting Kodak's motion for summary judgment on their alter ego theory of liability. . . . Because Atex was a Delaware corporation, Delaware law determines whether the corporate veil can be pierced in this instance.

---

72. "What liabilities are 'certain' to arise in the ordinary course of her business? And how much capital/insurance is necessary to safeguard against them? What are 'extraordinary and unexpected liabilities'? Would jurors, operating with the benefit of hindsight, be tempted to . . . look at the damage claim, compare it to the amount of capital, and if damages exceed capital, conclude the firm was undercapitalized." Bainbridge, footnote 67 supra, at 520. — ED.

73. Plaintiff's amended complaint, with new allegations that defendant and his associates were "conducting business of taxicab fleet in their individual capacities," was held to state a cause of action. 29 App. Div. 2d 763, 287 N.Y.S.2d 546, *aff'd*, 23 N.Y.2d 714, 244 N.E.2d 55, 296 N.Y.S.2d 362 (1968). — ED.

Delaware law permits a court to pierce the corporate veil of a company "where there is fraud or where [it] is in fact a mere instrumentality or alter ego of its owner." . . . Harper v. Delaware Valley Broadcasters, Inc., 743 F. Supp. 1076, 1085 (D. Del. 1990), aff'd, 932 F.2d 959 (3d Cir. 1991). Thus, under an alter ego theory, there is no requirement of a showing of fraud. Id. at 1085. To prevail on an alter ego claim under Delaware law, a plaintiff must show (1) that the parent and the subsidiary "operated as a single economic entity" and (2) that an "overall element of injustice or unfairness . . . [is] present." Id. . . . Among the factors to be considered in determining whether a subsidiary and parent operate as a "single economic entity" are: "whether the corporation was adequately capitalized for the corporate undertaking; whether the corporation was solvent; whether dividends were paid, corporate records kept, officers and directors functioned properly, and other corporate formalities were observed; whether the dominant shareholder siphoned corporate funds; and whether, in general, the corporation simply functioned as a facade for the dominant shareholder."[74] . . . Courts have made it clear that "[t]he legal entity of a corporation will not be disturbed until sufficient reason appears." . . . Although the question of domination is generally one of fact, courts have granted motions to dismiss as well as motions for summary judgment in favor of defendant parent companies where there has been a lack of sufficient evidence to place the alter ego issue in dispute.

Kodak has shown that Atex followed corporate formalities, and the plaintiffs have offered no evidence to the contrary. Significantly, the plaintiffs have not challenged Kodak's assertions that Atex's board of directors held regular meetings, that minutes from those meetings were routinely prepared and maintained in corporate minute books, that appropriate financial records and other files were maintained by Atex, that Atex filed its own tax returns and paid its own taxes, and that Atex had its own employees and management executives who were responsible for the corporation's day-to-day business. . . . We find that the district court correctly held that, in light of the undisputed factors of independence cited by Kodak, "the elements identified by the plaintiffs . . . [were] insufficient as a matter of law to establish the degree of domination necessary to disregard Atex's corporate identity." Fletcher, 861 F. Supp. at 245.

First, the district court correctly held that "Atex's participation in Kodak's cash management system is consistent with sound business practice and does not show

---

74. Judicial opinions often consider a list of many factors. For example, in Steven v. Roscoe Turner Aeronautical Corp., 324 F.2d 157 (7th Cir. 1973), the court, quoting from Frederick J. Powell, Parent and Subsidiary Corporations (1931), applied 11 criteria to the facts of the case, 9 of which were not mentioned in the *Fletcher* case: (1) parent owns all or most of subsidiary's shares; (2) parent and subsidiary have common directors or officers; (3) parent finances subsidiary; (4) parent subscribes to all subsidiary's shares or otherwise causes its incorporation; (5) parent pays subsidiary's expenses; (6) parent uses subsidiary's property as its own; (7) directors or executives of subsidiary do not act independently but take orders from parent in its interest; (8) subsidiary has substantially no business except with parent or no assets except those conveyed by parent; (9) in parent's papers or in its officers' statements, subsidiary is described as a department or division of parent, or its business or financial responsibility is referred to as the parent's own. See also Assoc. Vendors, Inc. v. Oakland Meat Co., 26 Cal. Rptr. 806, 813-815 (Dist. Ct. App. 1962) (listing 20 factors).

In Dieter Engineering Services, Inc. v. Parkland Development, Inc., 199 W. Va. 48, 483 S.E.2d 48 (1996), the court held the two individual shareholders of the debtor corporation liable because "our review of the record indicates that fifteen of the nineteen factors . . . which should be considered when deciding whether to pierce the corporate veil" should be construed in plaintiff's favor.

"[W]hat one typically gets in most opinions is a laundry list of factors . . . [most of which] are wholly unrelated to the policy concerns presented by limited liability." Bainbridge, footnote 67 supra, at 509-510. — ED.

undue domination or control." Id. at 244. The parties do not dispute the mechanics of Kodak's cash management system. Essentially, all of Kodak's domestic subsidiaries participate in the system and maintain zero-balance bank accounts. All funds transferred from the subsidiary accounts are recorded as credits to the subsidiary, and when a subsidiary is in need of funds, a transfer is made. At all times, a strict accounting is kept of each subsidiary's funds.

Courts have generally declined to find alter ego liability based on a parent corporation's use of a cash management system. . . . The plaintiffs offer no facts to support their speculation that Kodak's centralized cash management system was actually a "complete commingling" of funds or a means by which Kodak sought to "siphon[] all of Atex's revenues into its own account."

Second, the district court correctly concluded that it could find no domination based on the plaintiffs' evidence that Kodak's approval was required for Atex's real estate leases, major capital expenditures, negotiations for a sale of minority stock ownership to IBM, or the fact that Kodak played a significant role in the ultimate sale of Atex's assets to a third party. Again, the parties do not dispute that Kodak required Atex to seek its approval and/or participation for the above transactions. However, this evidence, viewed in the light most favorable to the plaintiffs, does not raise an issue of material fact about whether the two corporations constituted "a single economic entity." Indeed, this type of conduct is typical of a majority shareholder or parent corporation. See Phoenix Canada Oil Co. v. Texaco, 842 F.2d 1466, 1476 (3d Cir. 1988) (declining to pierce the corporate veil where subsidiary required to secure approval from parent for "large investments and acquisitions or disposals of major assets"), *cert. denied*, 488 U.S. 908 (1988). . . . Similarly, the district court in the instant case properly found the presence of Kodak employees at periodic meetings with Atex's chief financial officer and comptroller to be "entirely appropriate."

The plaintiffs' third argument, that Kodak dominated the Atex board of directors, also fails. Although a number of Kodak employees have sat on the Atex board, it is undisputed that between 1981 and 1988, only one director of Atex was also a director of Kodak. Between 1989 and 1992, Atex and Kodak had no directors in common. Parents and subsidiaries frequently have overlapping boards of directors while maintaining separate business operations. . . . Since the overlap is negligible here, we find this evidence to be entirely insufficient to raise a question of fact on the issue of domination.

Fourth, . . . plaintiffs point to several statements in both Kodak's and Atex's literature to evidence Kodak's domination of its subsidiary. For example, plaintiffs refer to (1) a promotional pamphlet produced by . . . [Atex] noting that [Atex] . . . was an "agent" of Kodak; (2) a document produced by Atex entitled "An Introduction to Atex Systems," which describes a "merger" between Kodak and Atex; (3) a statement in Kodak's 1985 and 1986 annual reports describing Atex as a "recent acquisition[]" and a "subsidiar[y] . . . combined in a new division." . . . They also refer generally to the fact that Atex's paperwork and packaging materials frequently displayed the Kodak logo.

It is clear from the record that Atex never merged with Kodak or operated as a Kodak division. The plaintiffs offer no evidence to the contrary, apart from these statements in Atex and Kodak documents that they claim are indicative of the true relationship between the two companies. Viewed in the light most favorable to the plaintiffs, these statements and the use of the Kodak logo are not evidence that the two companies operated as a "single economic entity." See Coleman v. Corning

Glass Works, 619 F. Supp. 950, 956 (W.D.N.Y.1985) (upholding corporate form despite "loose language" in annual report about "merger" and parent's reference to subsidiary as a "division"), *aff'd*, 818 F.2d 874 (1987); Japan Petroleum Co. (Nigeria) v. Ashland Oil Inc., 456 F. Supp. 831, 846 (D. Del. 1978) (noting that representations made by parent in its annual reports that subsidiary serves as an agent "may result from public relations motives or an attempt at simplification"); American Trading & Prod. Corp. v. Fischbach & Moore, Inc., 311 F. Supp. 412, 416 (N.D. Ill. 1970) ("boastful" advertising and consideration of subsidiaries as "family" do not prove that corporate identities were ignored).

Fifth, the plaintiffs contend that Atex's assignment of its former CEO's mortgage to Kodak in order to close the sale of Atex's assets to a third party is evidence of Kodak's domination of Atex. We reject this argument as well. The evidence is undisputed that Kodak paid Atex the book value of the note and entered into a formal repayment agreement with the former CEO. Formal contracts were executed, and the two companies observed all corporate formalities.

Finally, even if the plaintiffs did raise a factual question about Kodak's domination of Atex, summary judgment would still be appropriate because the plaintiffs offer no evidence on the second prong of the alter ego analysis. The plaintiffs have failed to present evidence of an "overall element of injustice or unfairness" that would result from respecting the two companies' corporate separateness. . . . In the instant case, the plaintiffs offer nothing more than the bare assertion that Kodak "exploited" Atex "to generate profits but not to safeguard safety." There is no indication that Kodak sought to defraud creditors and consumers or to siphon funds from its subsidiary. The plaintiffs' conclusory assertions, without more, are not evidence, . . . and are completely inadequate to support a finding that it would be unjust to respect Atex's corporate form.

For all of the foregoing reasons, the district court's order entering summary judgment on the plaintiffs' alter ego theory of liability is affirmed. . . .

---

1. *Independence of wholly owned corporations.*

The complementary theories of limited liability and piercing the corporate veil have provoked consternation among courts and legal scholars alike. They have been variously described as a "legal quagmire," Ballantine, Separate Entity of Parent and Subsidiary Corporations, 14 Cal. L. Rev. 12, 15 (1925), and as being "enveloped in the mists of metaphor," Berkey v. Third Avenue Ry., 244 N.Y. 84, 155 N.E. 58, 61 (1926) (Cardozo, J.). . . . Nowhere is this more true than in the case of the alter ego doctrine. In some sense, every subsidiary is the alter ego of its parent company. Where the subsidiary is wholly owned by the parent and has the same directors and officers, operating the subsidiary independently of the parent company not only has little practical meaning, it would also constitute a breach both of the subsidiary's duty to further the interests of its owner, and of the directors' and officers' duty towards the parent company. Nevertheless, our cases are clear that one-hundred percent ownership and identity of directors and officers are, even together, an insufficient basis for applying the alter ego theory to pierce the corporate veil. . . . Instead, we maintain the fiction that an officer or director of both corporations can change hats and represent the two corporations separately, despite their common ownership.

United States v. Jon-T Chemicals, Inc., 786 F.2d 686 (5th Cir. 1985).

2. Tort vs. contract creditors. (a) *Adequate capital.* Courts and commentators often distinguish between the ability of tort claimants (who have not voluntarily chosen to deal with the corporation) and contract creditors to pierce the corporate veil, especially when inadequate capital is the only (or primary) factor present. Thus, it has recently been urged that unlimited pro rata shareholder liability for corporate torts[75] would produce "a marginal increase in shareholder incentives to monitor the enterprise's expected tort losses" and would "encourage managers to consider the full social costs of investment decisions," see Henry B. Hansmann & Reinier Kraakman, Toward Unlimited Shareholder Liability for Corporate Torts, 100 Yale L.J. 1879 (1991). See also David W. Leebron, Limited Liability, Tort Victims, and Creditors, 91 Colum. L. Rev. 1565 (1991), concluding that (1) at least "in the absence of enforcement transaction costs, . . . pro rata unlimited tort liability for publicly held corporations would not be inefficient from the point of view of allocating capital (subject to some concerns about shareholder diversification), would not seriously interfere with secondary markets, and in most cases would put the cost on better risk bearers"[76]; (2) there are no persuasive arguments for limited tort liability for subsidiary corporations; and (3) "the case for limited [tort] liability of closely held corporations has been understated."[77]

Compare Joseph A. Grundfest, The Limited Future of Unlimited Liability: A Capital Markets Perspective, 102 Yale L.J. 387 (1992), contending that because of "innovative arbitrage activities" in "modern international capital markets," pro rata shareholder liability "is neither a practical nor a theoretical superior alternative for publicly traded corporations. To the extent that publicly traded corporations engage in excessive risk-taking because limited liability provides them with a shield, other policy tools — such as mandatory insurance, product safety requirements, and 'gatekeeper' liability — are likely to be more equitable

---

75. For earlier views that limited liability should be inapplicable in respect to tort claimants, see Note, Should Shareholders Be Personally Liable for the Torts of Their Corporations? 76 Yale L.J. 1190 (1967). See also Note, The Validity of Limited Tort Liability for Shareholders in Close Corporations, 23 Am. U. L. Rev. 208 (1973).

76. Compare Robert B. Thompson, Unpacking Limited Liability: Direct and Vicarious Liability of Corporate Participants for Torts of the Enterprise, 47 Vand. L. Rev. 1, 34-35 (1994): "Shareholders do receive the residual gain from the operation of the enterprise while the return of lenders, employees, or other creditors is usually fixed, but that distinction should not be determinative. In fact, many creditors will be better able than dispersed shareholders to influence management; in some situations, creditors may be better risk-bearers. There are reasons why imposing liability on these groups would not lead to the appropriate amount of precautionary behavior, but many of those same arguments can also apply to shareholders." See also Bainbridge, footnote 67 supra, at 497: "Tort creditors are dependent on corporations having a substantial equity cushion because under current bankruptcy law tort claims are subordinate to those of secured creditors and share pro rata with general creditors. Under a rule of personal liability, however, few people would be willing to become shareholders. In such a world, large-scale businesses would be conducted by highly-leveraged firms having a very small amount of equity capital and a very large amount of secured debt."

77. For support of limited liability for shareholders in small corporations because its original justification was "that it encourages investment in the small firm, or investment by entrepreneurs of modest means," see Stephen B. Presser, Thwarting the Killing of the Corporation: Limited Liability, Democracy, and Economics, 87 Nw. U. L. Rev. 148, 164 (1992). But see Richard A. Booth, Limited Liability and the Efficient Allocation of Resources, 89 Nw. U. L. Rev 140 (1994) (tort creditors of small corporations "will almost always be able to show that shareholder-operators participated in any wrongful acts" and will therefore be personally liable).

and effective." (Grundfest defines "gatekeeper" strategies so as to "impose personal, civil, or criminal penalties on corporate decisionmakers and advisers who play a role in events leading up to the corporation's involvement in a tort or crime." Id. at 422.) For the view that state efforts to implement pro rata shareholder liability would involve either serious procedural obstacles (state court personal jurisdiction over out-of-state shareholders, choice-of-law rule looking to law of the state of incorporation) or significant cost increases, see Janet C. Alexander, Unlimited Shareholder Liability Through a Procedural Lens, 106 Harv. L. Rev. 387 (1992). For criticism of pro rata shareholder liability, see Nina A. Mendelson, A Control-Based Approach to Shareholder Liability for Corporate Torts, 102 Colum. L. Rev. 1203 (2002): Because "a controlling shareholder can more easily curb managerial risk aversion and . . . can obtain special benefits from corporate activity, imposing pro rata shareholder liability likely will not fully deter overinvestment in risky activities." For a comprehensive review of various theories and proposals, see Timothy P. Glynn, Beyond "Unlimiting" Shareholder Liability: Vicarious Tort Liability for Corporate Officers, 57 Vand. L. Rev. 329 (2004) (high-ranking officer liability for corporate torts "is the most efficient mechanism for retaining the benefits of limited liability while reducing its social costs").

(b) *"Intrusive control."*

> [Cases find] that an excessive degree of intrusive control over a subsidiary—particularly over its daily operations—makes the subsidiary an agent for its parent and, therefore, its parent liable as the subsidiary's principal. . . . A better analysis would be that intrusive control by the parent makes the parent itself the actor in the transaction . . . [and thus] the party that is committing the wrongful act by itself. Therefore, it may be possible to hold the parent directly liable without piercing the corporate veil (or resorting to agency principles).
>
> . . . In some cases, courts *have* imposed direct tort liability on a parent when an employee/officer of the parent made a critical decision which resulted in tort liability. Often, however, that person has a position with both the parent and the subsidiary, and the court is likely to decide that the wrongful act was committed while the person was acting on behalf of the subsidiary instead of the parent. Consequently, the parent is exculpated from direct tort liability. This is a formalistic result, but again, form often wins out in corporation law. . . .
>
> [In any event,] this analysis tends to fail in contract cases. Nothing in contract law says that intrusive parental control over the subsidiary, even for the contract in question, makes the parent liable on a contract that specifies the subsidiary as the contractual obligator. Indeed, it is not unusual at all that someone who is not a party to a contract exerts dominating and intrusive influence on a contracting party and still is not made liable on the contract.

William J. Rands, Domination of a Subsidiary by a Parent, 32 Ind. L. Rev. 421, 445-448 (1999).

3. *Active vs. inactive shareholders.* Should the court have reached a different conclusion in Minton v. Cavaney, discussed in Walkovsky v. Carlton, supra, if the defendant were a passive investor owning 5 percent of the shares? See Slusarski v. American Confinement Sys., Inc., 218 Neb. 576, 357 N.W.2d 450 (1984). What is Judge Keating's view? In contrast, the corporate veil has been pierced against persons who were neither shareholders, directors, nor officers, but who exercised sufficient control so as to be deemed "equitable owners." Freeman v. Complex Computing Co., 119 F.3d 1044 (2d Cir. 1997).

4. *"Inadequate" capitalization.* Courts and commentators often state flatly that the corporate veil is never pierced when inadequate capital is the only factor present.[78] What constitutes "inadequate capital"? How, if at all, should it be determined? Ought it be a ground for piercing?[79]

(a) In Laya v. Erin Homes, Inc., page 257 supra, the court stated:

> With respect to determining the adequacy of the corporation's capital, in light of the nature and magnitude of the corporate undertaking, there are several tests and factors which can be utilized to analyze the financial data of the corporation. For example, comparison with the capitalization of other corporations in the same or a similar line of business may be made. The capitalization of the corporation in question could be compared with the average industry-wide ratios (current ratio, acid-test ratio, debt/equity ratio, etc.) obtained from published sources (Dun & Bradstreet, Moody's Manual of Investments, Standard & Poor's Corporation Records, etc.). These average ratios could be buttressed by expert testimony from certified public accountants, securities analysts, investment counselors or other qualified financial analysts. See Barber, Piercing the Corporate Veil, 17 Willamette L. Rev. 371, 392-394 (1981). "Grossly inadequate capitalization" for the purpose of piercing the corporate veil would generally be reflected by a substantial deficiency of capital compared with that level of capitalization deemed adequate in the case by the financial analyst experts.

(b) *Relevance of insurance.* (i) In Radaszewski v. Telecom Corp., 981 F.2d 305 (8th Cir. 1992), the court assumed that defendant corporation's subsidiary (Contrux) "was undercapitalized in the accounting sense" in that

> most of the money contributed to its operation by Telecom was in the form of loans, not equity. . . . Telecom says, however, that this doesn't matter, because Contrux had $11,000,000 worth of liability insurance available to pay judgments like the one that Radaszewski hopes to obtain. . . . The whole purpose of asking whether a subsidiary is "properly capitalized," is precisely to determine its "financial responsibility." If the subsidiary is financially responsible, whether by means of insurance or otherwise, the policy behind [preventing use of the corporate form "by the defendant to commit

---

78. See, e.g., Gartner v. Snyder, 607 F.2d 582 (2nd Cir. 1979): "We know of no New York authority that disregards corporate form solely because of inadequate capitalization." Accord, Consumer's Co-Op v. Olsen, 142 Wis. 2d 465, 419 N.W.2d 211 (1988); Torregrossa v. Szelc, 603 S.W.2d 803 (Tex. 1980); Hackney & Benson, Shareholder Liability for Inadequate Capital, 43 U. Pitt. L. Rev. 837, 885 (1982) ("In the application of the doctrine that limited liability may be lost for misuse of the corporate form, courts have increasingly come to insist that gross undercapitalization is the most important factor . . . but no decision has been found which squarely and unambiguously announces a per se rule. Rather, most courts insist that inadequate capitalization is but one of a number of factors to be considered. . . ."); accord, Cox & Hazen, footnote 2, supra at 109.

Compare Slottow v. American Casualty Co., 1 F.3d 912 (9th Cir. 1993) (dictum): "Under California law, inadequate capitalization of a subsidiary may alone be a basis for holding the parent corporation liable for acts of the subsidiary." But see Presser, footnote 77 supra, at 166: "There must be more involved in eliminating limited liability than just undercapitalization." Compare Douglas C. Michael, To Know a Veil, 26 J. Corp. L. 41, 57 (2000): "Particularly in the case of tort plaintiffs, . . . [a]lthough it is often said that undercapitalization *alone* is not enough to pierce, the additional factors can be composed of so much 'make weight' that it is clear to a critical reader of the opinions that it is undercapitalization that matters."

79. See generally Robert C. Downs, Piercing the Corporate Veil — Do Corporations Provide Limited Personal Liability?, 53 UMKC L. Rev. 174 (1985); John F. Dobbyn, A Practical Approach to Consistency in Veil-Piercing Cases, 19 Kan. L. Rev. 195 (1971).

fraud or wrong, to perpetrate the violation of a statutory or other positive legal duty, or dishonest and unjust act in contravention of plaintiff's legal rights"] . . . is met. Insurance meets this policy just as well, perhaps even better, than a healthy balance sheet.

For further development of the view that "financially responsible" action by those who control the corporation should determine liability in both tort and contract cases, see David Millon, Piercing the Corporate Veil, Financial Responsibility, and the Limits of Limited Liability, 56 Emory L.J. 1305 (2007).

(ii) "What was needed [in the *Walkovszky* case] was more insurance. Hence, if the debtor corporation was unreasonably underinsured, the court should have pierced for inadequate capitalization against Carlton. If the corporation had reasonable insurance, then so what if Carlton artificially divided one business?" Gevurtz, Note 2, page 259 supra, at 106.

(c) *Time of undercapitalization.* (i) In Pierson v. Jones, 102 Idaho 82, 625 P.2d 1085 (1981), defendant formed a corporation to which he transferred all the assets of his existing sheet metal business in exchange for all the shares. During the next year the corporation borrowed $80,000 from plaintiff, a corporate employee with knowledge of its financial statements. Six months later, the corporation went bankrupt, owing plaintiff $33,000. The court rejected plaintiff's claim of undercapitalization: "[F]inancial inadequacy is measured by the nature and magnitude of the corporate undertaking or the reasonableness of the cushion for creditors at the time of the *inception* of the corporation. H. Henn, Law of Corporations §146 (2d ed. 1970). Here the corporate accountant testified that at the time of its inception the corporation was not undercapitalized. Clearly, a corporation adequately capitalized at its inception can become undercapitalized at a later time for any of a variety of legitimate reasons."

(ii) *Problem.* Corporation, indisputably adequately capitalized at formation, incurs losses over a period of several years. Needed additional funds are then supplied by its shareholders as loans. On bankruptcy, may these shareholder lenders claim as general creditors? How, if at all, should the result be affected by the fact that no outside source would lend to the corporation at the time of the shareholder loans? Of what significance is it that "where a small corporation is involved, lending institutions will commonly require a personal guarantee as a condition to granting a loan to even a healthy enterprise, and their willingness to lend may depend as much upon their perception of the solvency and reliability of the guarantor as upon the corporation's financial condition"? See In re Mader's Store for Men, Inc., 77 Wis. 2d 578, 254 N.W.2d 171 (1977). See also Matter of Lifschultz Fast Freight, 132 F.3d 339 (7th Cir. 1997) (lender's requirement of a personal guarantee does not necessarily denote corporation's undercapitalization). Compare Robert C. Clark, The Duties of the Corporate Debtor to Its Creditors, 90 Harv. L. Rev. 505, 539 (1977):

> If rational and disinterested outside lenders are unwilling to supply corporate "loans" on a given set of interest rates and other terms, the most natural conclusion is that a "loan" of that character would be made only by persons who, by virtue of concurrent stock ownership, could benefit from the inadequacy of the terms, and the "'loans" to insiders should thus be treated like equity in distributing the bankrupt estate. True, situations may arise in which insiders (a) really do perceive more accurately that the "true" risk presented by a loan to a corporation on given terms is lower than outsiders recognize, and (b) are unable to articulate and convey the objective

bases of their superior judgment to the prospective outside lenders at a reasonable cost. But, in view of the widespread belief in the general efficiency of our capital markets, one might well be agnostic about the notion that such situations are common.

(iii) *Query:* What result in the *Walkovsky* case if Carlton had loaned $50,000 to Seon Cab Corp. at its inception? In O'Hazza v. Executive Creditor Corp., 246 Va. 111, 431 S.E.2d 318 (1993), the court stated that

> to gain certain tax advantages, small corporations increasingly, and legitimately, choose to initially capitalize the entity with a small portion of the investment represented by stock and with the larger portion of capital set up as loans to the corporation. If the corporation fails, these loans are subordinated to those of other creditors. . . . [F]ederal courts, in distinguishing between corporate debt and risk capital, have considered a loan made to a corporation by stockholders without expectation of repayment as an indication that the transaction involved venture capital, not a true loan.

(d) *Problem.* Corporation, engaged in hazardous business activities, is originally formed with capital adequate to cover premiums on concededly sufficient liability insurance of $200,000. Due to lack of business success over a period of years, corporation cuts expenses, inter alia, by reducing the insurance coverage to $10,000. A serious accident occurs, causing damage of $250,000 and thus rendering the corporation insolvent. Unpaid tort and contract creditors bring suit against the financially responsible shareholders. What result?

> Courts in piercing cases often assume that the proper remedy is simply the complete revocation of limited liability. An obvious alternative, where state decisional law recognizes the inadequate capitalization factor, is to limit recovery to the amount of the inadequacy of the capitalization. Either approach may fail to compensate completely outside creditors for harm wrongfully caused them if the personal assets of the defendants are insufficient to fill the need. . . . On the other hand, if the personal assets of the defendants exceed . . . the size of the inadequacy of the corporation's capitalization, piercing the veil and imposing liability to the full extent of their personal assets will overcompensate the creditors for the harm traceable to the defendants' provable or wrongful acts. This result has the effect of penalizing the defendants.

Robert C. Clark, Corporate Law 81-82 (1986).

(e) *Problem.* Statute forbids usurious loans, but not if made to a corporation. *P* forms a wholly owned corporation, with concededly inadequate capital, in order to have the corporation borrow from *L* at an otherwise usurious rate. On bankruptcy of the corporation, *L* brings suit against *P* personally. *P* defends on the ground that the loan violated the usury statute. What result? Cf. McNellis v. Raymond, 420 F.2d 51 (2d Cir. 1970); Securities Investment Co. v. Indian Waters Dev. Corp., 501 F.2d 662 (5th Cir. 1974).

5. *Analysis of cases.* For a comprehensive study of about 1,600 cases through 1985, see Robert B. Thompson, Piercing the Corporate Veil: An Empirical Study, 76 Cornell L. Rev. 1036 (1991). Among the conclusions are that (1) "courts look to the specific context more than any inherent corporate characteristic"; (2) "the likelihood of piercing increases as the number of shareholders decreases," and in no case did piercing occur in a publicly held corporation; (3) "misrepresentation" is the most powerful factor listed by courts when they pierce, followed by

"demonstrations of lack of substantive separation of the corporation and its share-holders, and intertwining in the activities of the corporation and its shareholders"; "undercapitalization" and "failure to follow corporate formalities" are other strong factors; (4) piercing is less likely in tort contexts (involuntary creditors) than in contract cases (voluntary creditors), and piercing is more likely when the defendant behind the corporation is an individual shareholder than when it is another corporation;[80] and (5) "passive shareholders" are almost never held liable.[81]

Bartle v. Home Owners Cooperative
309 N.Y. 103, 127 N.E.2d 832 (1955)

FROESSEL, J.: Plaintiff, as trustee in bankruptcy of Westerlea Builders, Inc., has by means of this litigation attempted to hold defendant liable for the contract debts of Westerlea, defendant's wholly owned subsidiary. Defendant, as a cooperative corporation composed mostly of veterans, was organized in July, 1947, for the purpose of providing low-cost housing for its members. Unable to secure a contractor to undertake construction of the housing planned, Westerlea was organized for that purpose on June 5, 1948. With building costs running considerably higher than anticipated, Westerlea, as it proceeded with construction on some 26 houses, found itself in a difficult financial situation. On January 24, 1949, the creditors, pursuant to an extension agreement, took over the construction responsibilities. Nearly four years later, in October, 1952, Westerlea was adjudicated a bankrupt. Meanwhile, defendant had contributed to Westerlea not only its original capital of $25,000 but additional sums amounting to $25,639.38.

Plaintiff's principal contention on this appeal is that the courts below erred in refusing to "pierce the corporate veil" of Westerlea's corporate existence; as subordinate grounds for recovery he urged that the defendant equitably pledged its assets toward the satisfaction of the debts of the bankrupt's creditors, and that the doctrine of unjust enrichment should apply.

The trial court made detailed findings of fact which have been unanimously affirmed by the Appellate Division, 285 App. Div. 1113, 140 N.Y.S.2d 512, which are clearly supported by the evidence, and by which we are bound. It found that while the defendant, as owner of the stock of Westerlea, controlled its affairs, the outward indicia of these two separate corporations was at all times maintained during the period in which the creditors extended credit; that the creditors were in no wise misled; that there was no fraud; and that the defendant performed no act causing injury to the creditors of Westerlea by depletion of assets or otherwise. The trial court also held that the creditors were estopped by the extension agreement from disputing the separate corporate identities.

We agree with the courts below. The law permits the incorporation of a business for the very purpose of escaping personal liability. . . . Generally speaking, the doctrine of "piercing the corporate veil" is invoked "to prevent fraud or to achieve

---

80. "The continuing puzzle is why courts remain so willing to provide limited liability to parent corporations in tort cases." Thompson, footnote 76, supra at 40.

81. Professor Thompson extended his study through 1996 with an additional 2,200 cases. This resulted in the same conclusions with the following exception: when either "shareholder domination" or "overlap of records and personnel" exists, courts are more likely to pierce when the defendant is an individual rather than a parent corporation. Robert B. Thompson, Piercing the Veil Within Corporate Groups: Corporate Shareholders as Mere Investors, 13 Conn. J. Int'l L. 379 (1999).

equity." . . . But in the instant case there has been neither fraud, misrepresentation nor illegality. Defendant's purpose in placing its construction operation into a separate corporation was clearly within the limits of our public policy.

The judgment appealed from should be affirmed. . . .

VAN VOORHIS, J. (dissenting): . . . Not only is Westerlea a wholly owned subsidiary of defendant Home Owners, having the same directors and management, but also and of primary importance, business was done on such a basis that Westerlea could not make a profit. . . . Home Owners arranged with Westerlea for the construction of houses and then would sell the lots on which such houses had been erected to Home Owners' stockholders — at prices fixed by Home Owners' price policy committee in such amounts as to make no allowance for profit by Westerlea. The object was to benefit Home Owners' stockholders by enabling them to obtain their houses at cost, with no builder's profit.

The consequence is that described by Latty, Subsidiaries and Affiliated Corporations at pages 138-139: "The subsidiaries had, to begin with, nothing, made nothing, and could only end up with nothing. It is not surprising that the parent was held liable in each case." And again: "This set-up is often, though not necessarily, found in combination with a scheme whereby the corporation cannot possibly make profits (or can at the most make only nominal profits), and whereby all the net income in the course of the corporation's business is drained off as operating charges of one sort or another. The presence of this additional factor should remove any doubt that may remain as to the right of the creditor of the corporation not to be limited to the corporate assets for the satisfaction of his debt."

In the present instance, Westerlea was organized with a small capital supplied by Home Owners, which soon became exhausted. Thereafter, it had no funds and could acquire none over and beyond the actual cost of the houses which it was building for stockholders of Home Owners. Those stockholders obtained the entire benefit of Westerlea's operations by obtaining these houses at cost. Not only was Westerlea allowed no opportunity to make money, but it was placed in a position such that if its business were successful and times remained good, it would break even, otherwise it would inevitably become insolvent. The stockholders of Home Owners became the beneficiaries of its insolvency. This benefit to the stockholders of Home Owners was analogous to dividends, at least it was something of value which was obtained by them from Home Owners by virtue of their stock ownership. Under the circumstances, this benefit to its stockholders was a benefit to Home Owners as a corporation.

It follows that Westerlea was merely an agent of Home Owners to construct houses at cost for Home Owners stockholders, and therefore Home Owners is rendered liable for Westerlea's indebtedness.[82]

---

82. *Query:* Might fraudulent conveyance law, page 224 supra, be relevant? If so, what would be the measure of the Home Owners shareholders' liability? See also Yacker v. Weiner, 109 N.J. Super. 351, 263 A.2d 188 (1970); compare Segan Constr. Corp. v. Nor-West Builders Inc., 274 F. Supp. 691 (D. Conn. 1967). — ED.

1. *Problem.* P, newspaper publisher, in order to ensure its supply of newsprint, purchased all the shares of S, a newspaper publishing corporation with substantial capital, and caused S to change its business to that of a newsprint supplier. The general market in newsprint seriously declined and S went bankrupt. S's creditors — contract and tort — seek to pierce the corporate veil. What result? Cf. Gannett Co. v. Larry, 221 F.2d 269 (2d Cir. 1955).

2. *Problem.* O is the sole owner of two corporations — F, a very profitable enterprise that grants franchises in exchange for annual franchise fees, and D, a not so profitable enterprise that is also empowered to grant franchises but mainly sells products to the franchisees. D agrees to grant X a franchise, a contract that appears beneficial to D because X has many salespeople, but undesirable so far as F is concerned because F would have sold franchises to each of X's salespeople. When D refuses to perform the contract, X seeks to hold F and O liable for the breach. What result? See House of Koscot Dev. Corp. v. American Line Cosmetics, Inc., 468 F.2d 64 (5th Cir. 1972).

Stone v. Eacho
127 F.2d 284 (4th Cir. 1942)

PARKER, J.: . . . The Tip Top Tailors was incorporated under the laws of Delaware on January 23, 1939. Its principal place of business was in Newark, N.J., and it operated nine retail stores in various cities of the United States, one of these being located at Richmond, Va. On July 12, 1939 it secured a corporate charter from the State of Virginia for a corporation of the same name as that under which it was operating and caused three shares of stock, of the par value of $1 each, to be issued to its nominees to be held by them for its use and benefit. The officers of the two corporations were the same and no separate corporate activity of any sort on the part of the Virginia corporation is shown to have taken place. No money was paid into its treasury, no contracts were executed by it, no salaries were paid by it, unless the payment of wages to employees of the Richmond store from cash on hand be so regarded, and the only records kept for it were records kept in the office of the Delaware corporation at Newark, N.J., by an employee of that corporation. These records consisted of nothing more than transcripts from the books of the Delaware corporation made by employees of that corporation at infrequent intervals.

Except for these book entries, and except for the fact that the Virginia charter was obtained, the Delaware corporation dealt with its Richmond, Va., store precisely in the same way as it dealt with the other stores that it was operating, as to which there was no pretense of separate incorporation. The manner of dealing with the Richmond store is thus described in the report of the special master approved by the court below, viz.:

> Sample bolts of goods and styles of suits were furnished the Richmond store by the parent corporation. A customer in Richmond, after selecting the style of suit and kind of cloth, was measured and the order was then sent from Richmond to Newark. In Newark the parent corporation then had the suit made up according to order, and shipped it back to the Richmond store, which made delivery to the customer and collected the price. At the end of each day the Richmond store would make out a

complete and detailed report and send it by mail to Newark. Out of cash collected by the Richmond store salaries of the local store personnel were paid and petty items taken care of, and the balance of the money was deposited in a Richmond bank. This bank then forwarded these funds to the National City Bank of New York to the credit of the account of the Delaware corporation.

In furnishing the Richmond store with cloth and their processing the suits for the local customers, the parent corporation made no profit. It furnished materials and labor at cost and debited the Richmond store with these amounts.

Out of the cash collected in Richmond, the local store did not have authority to pay any bills over $10.00, with the exception of salaries. These petty cash items paid direct at Richmond in the course of a year's time would amount to not over $1,000.00. All other expenses incident to the operation and maintenance of the Richmond store were paid directly by the Delaware corporation by its own check, and then debited on its books to the Richmond store. In this way the parent corporation paid direct all expenses incident to the operation of the Richmond store, such as rent, insurance, stationery and supplies, telephone bills, delivery charges, express charges, taxes, light, heat, and power bills, unemployment insurance, payroll, etc.

The parent corporation operated the Richmond store on the same basis as it did the other eight stores and charged the Richmond store with its proportionate share of the main office expense. The said expense being allotted to each of the stores in the proportion that the sales of the respective stores bore to the total sales. . . .

To this should be added the fact that contracts with dealers in hats, shirts, etc., were made by the Delaware corporation authorizing such dealers to operate in the Richmond store, just as they operated in the other stores of the corporation, and that the Richmond store was charged and credited with respect to transactions arising out of these contracts, just as were the other stores.

With the exception of the three shares of the par value of $1 each, nothing was subscribed to the capital stock of the Virginia corporation; and, so far as the record shows, it owned no property of any sort. Fixtures, it is true, were placed in the Richmond store by the Delaware corporation and $900 was furnished it to take care of initial expenses; but these were charged to the Virginia corporation on the books of the Delaware corporation just as similar items were charged to its other stores and just as the goods furnished to the Richmond store were charged. By the time of the closing of the store, the excess of these charges over credits amounted to $39,069.67. Other debts of the Richmond store amounted to only about $12,000. . . .

On November 20, 1940, the Delaware corporation was adjudged bankrupt [in New Jersey] and appellant Stone was appointed its receiver. Two days later, two creditors attached the property in the Richmond store as property of the Virginia corporation; and on the following day an involuntary petition in bankruptcy was filed against the Virginia corporation by Stone as receiver of the Delaware corporation. The Virginia corporation was adjudged bankrupt on this petition and Stone, as receiver, thereupon filed claim for the sum of $39,069.67 as the amount owing by the Virginia corporation to the Delaware corporation. The trustee in bankruptcy of the Virginia corporation resisted the allowance of this claim and asked that, at all events, it be postponed to the claims of other creditors on the ground that the Virginia corporation was not a separate entity, but a mere instrumentality or department of the Delaware corporation, and that the amount claimed was not a true indebtedness arising out of loans and advancements but represented a mere advancement of operating capital.

The issues thus arising on the objection to the claim were referred to a special master, who filed a report finding that the Virginia corporation was a "mere shell without reality" and a "mere agency or corporate pocket" of the Delaware corporation, and recommending that the claim be postponed to the claims of other general creditors of the Virginia corporation. Appellant duly excepted to this report and filed a petition asking, as alternative relief, that the corporate entity of the Virginia corporation be entirely disregarded and that the bankruptcy proceeding relating to that corporation be consolidated with the bankruptcy proceedings of the Delaware corporation, to the end that all creditors of the last-named corporation, including those who had proved claims in the Virginia proceedings, share pari passu in the distribution of the consolidated assets. Three creditors of the Delaware corporation filed intervening petitions praying this relief. The District Judge entered order denying this motion and affirming the report of the special master; and from this order the trustee of the Delaware corporation and the three intervening creditors have appealed.

There is nothing in the record before us to show that any of the creditors who filed claims in the bankruptcy proceedings of the Virginia corporation intended to extend credit particularly to that corporation; and the fact that the bills of the Richmond store were paid by the Delaware corporation from its Newark office would indicate that it must have been generally known to the creditors of the Richmond store that it was the Delaware corporation that was there engaged in business. There is no reason apparent from the record why all creditors of that corporation should be treated in exactly the same way; and the fact that it had obtained a charter from the State of Virginia furnishes no good reason why the creditors dealing with its Richmond store should be dealt with differently from its other creditors, since there is no showing that business was done under that charter or that any of the creditors knew anything about it or relied on it in any way. If the Virginia corporation is treated as a separate entity and the property used in the Richmond business is applied to its debts, and the claim of the Delaware corporation is postponed in accordance with the ruling below, those creditors who have dealt with the Richmond store and have proven claims in the Virginia proceeding will have their claims practically paid in full, whereas other creditors of the Delaware corporation will receive less than 30% on their claims in the bankruptcy proceeding pending in New Jersey. If, on the other hand, the Virginia corporation is treated as a separate entity and the claim of the Delaware corporation is not postponed, this claim will so far absorb the assets at Richmond that other creditors proving in the Virginia proceeding will receive less than half the dividend received by creditors in the New Jersey proceeding. Only by entirely ignoring the separate corporate entity of the Virginia corporation and consolidating the proceedings here with those of the parent corporation in New Jersey can all the creditors receive that equality of treatment which it is the purpose of the bankruptcy act to afford; and this, we think, is the course that should be followed.

We agree with the court below that, if the separate existence of the Virginia corporation is recognized, the claim of the Delaware corporation should be postponed to the claims of other creditors. It is too well settled to admit of argument that the claims of a parent corporation against a subsidiary should be thus postponed where the subsidiary, as here, has in reality no separate existence, is not adequately capitalized and constitutes a mere instrumentality of the parent corporation or a mere "corporate pocket" or department of its business. . . . And even in the case of the insolvency of both corporations there may be reason for recognizing the separate entity of the subsidiary and postponing the claim of the parent, where the subsidiary has been allowed to transact business as an independent corporation and credit has been extended to it as such on the faith of its ownership of the assets in its possession. Latty, Subsidiaries and Affiliated Corporations 153-155. But in a case such as this, where both corporations are insolvent, where the business has been transacted by and the credit extended to the parent corporation, and where the subsidiary has no real existence whatever, there is no reason why the courts should not face the realities of the situation and ignore the subsidiary for all purposes, allowing the creditors of both corporations to share equally in the pooled assets. As said in Latty, supra: "Perhaps the fairest way of dealing with the situation when both the parent and the subsidiary corporations are insolvent is to let all the creditors of each share pro rata in the pooled assets of both. Such procedure would be especially equitable where the claimants are creditors of both the parent and the subsidiary."

It is well settled that courts will not be blinded by corporate forms nor permit them to be used to defeat public convenience, justify wrong or perpetrate fraud, but will look through the forms and behind the corporate entities involved to deal with the situation as justice may require. . . . Not only is this done for the purpose of holding a stockholder or parent corporation for debts created by an insolvent corporate agent or subsidiary which is a mere instrumentality of the stockholder or parent, but also for the purpose of allowing the creditors of the stockholder or parent to reach assets held by a subsidiary. . . . And, where the court decides that the corporate entity of the subsidiary should be completely ignored and its assets and liabilities treated as those of the parent corporation, it is both logical and convenient that this be done in one proceeding. . . .

If there are equities in favor of any of the creditors which have not been sufficiently explored in the motion for consolidation and as to which they desire to be heard further, hearing can be afforded them in the consolidated proceedings. . . . Since, however, the assets in Virginia are unquestionably the assets of the parent corporation, and since all of the creditors of that corporation, and not merely those who have dealt with the Virginia store, have rights with respect thereto, as well as with respect to other assets of the corporation, these rights should be determined in the bankruptcy proceeding of the parent corporation, and the two proceedings should be consolidated that this may be done, with a pooling of assets and with the treatment of claims filed in either proceedings as having been filed in the proceeding as consolidated. . . .

Reversed and remanded.

---

1. *Deep Rock doctrine.* In Stone v. Eacho, the court addresses issues related to the so-called Deep Rock doctrine, emanating from Taylor v. Standard Gas & Electric Co., 306 U.S. 307 (1939), a decision based on the principle that majority shareholders may not employ their power to abuse the minority. The Deep Rock doctrine concerns bankruptcy and reorganization proceedings of corporations whose sole or controlling shareholder (usually a parent corporation) seeks to enforce claims against it as a general or secured creditor. Instead of holding the

shareholder liable for the bankrupt corporation's debts, the doctrine, inter alia, permits subordination of the shareholder's claim not only to claims of outside creditors but also — as in the *Taylor* case — to claims of preferred shareholders of the bankrupt.[83]

2. *Fact variations.* What result under the following variations of Stone v. Eacho, assuming that the Virginia and Delaware creditors are distinct groups of persons?

(a) Virginia creditors and Delaware creditors all believed that the corporations were separate entities.

(b) Virginia creditors believed that subsidiary was a separate entity; Delaware creditors did not in fact know of the separate Virginia corporation. Cf. Chemical Bank New York Trust Co. v. Kheel, 369 F.2d 845 (2d Cir. 1966), noted, 8 B.C. Int'l. & Comp. L. Rev. 963 (1967).

(c) Virginia creditors did not in fact know of the separate Virginia corporation; Delaware creditors believed that subsidiary was a separate entity.

(d) Parent deliberately caused Virginia creditors to believe that there was no separate Virginia corporation; Delaware creditors believed that subsidiary was a separate entity.

How, if at all, should the results be affected if (a) either the parent or subsidiary is solvent, or (b) either the parent or subsidiary has minority shareholders?

E. *PRE-FORMATION TRANSACTIONS*

1. LIABILITY OF THE CORPORATION FOR DEBTS OF ITS PREDECESSOR

Corporations are created in many different situations. An entirely new business venture may be contemplated, to be incorporated from the start. Special problems of liabilities that arise in connection with the formation of corporations will be examined in the subsection that follows.

---

83. On subordinating the debts of certain institutional lenders, whose "aggressive loan transactions" result in "intense monitoring" of the debtor's business, see Andrew DeNatale & Prudence B. Abram, The Doctrine of Equitable Subordination as Applied to Nonmanagement Creditors, 40 Bus. Law. 417 (1985).

On the Deep Rock doctrine generally, see the articles by Landers and Posner, footnote 61 supra; Asa S. Herzog & Joel B. Zweibel, The Equitable Subordination of Claims in Bankruptcy, 15 Vand. L. Rev. 83 (1961); Robert A. Sprecher, The Conflict of Equities Under the "Deep Rock" Doctrine, 43 Colum. L. Rev. 336 (1943); Carlos L. Israels, The Implications and Limitations of the "Deep Rock" Doctrine, 42 Colum. L. Rev. 376 (1942); Myron N. Krotinger, The "Deep Rock" Doctrine: A Realistic Approach to Parent Subsidiary Law, 42 Colum. L. Rev. 1124 (1942); Charles Rembar, Claims Against Affiliated Corporations in Reorganization, 39 Colum. L Rev. 907 (1939); Notes, 47 Colum. L. Rev. 800 (1947); 54 Harv. L. Rev. 1045 (1941).

See also Friedman v. Kurker, 14 Mass. App. Ct. 152, 438 N.E.2d 76 (1982): "[R]ecent cases seem to recognize that undercapitalization alone, unaccompanied by inequitable conduct, will not provide a basis for subordination of claims for advances to a corporation which later becomes bankrupt. See In re Mid-Town Produce Terminal, Inc., 599 F.2d 389, 392-394 (10th Cir. 1979); In the Matter of Multiponics, Inc., 622 F.2d 709, 712-722, but see 723-725 (5th Cir. 1980). Compare In the Matter of Mobile Steel Co., 563 F.2d 692, 698-706 (5th Cir. 1977)." See also Matter of Lifschultz Fast Freight, Note (c)(ii), page 273 supra. Compare Note, Equitable Subordination of Shareholder Debt to Trade Creditors: A Reexamination, 61 B.U. L. Rev. 433, 441 (1981): "[E]conomic realities dictate that insider debt be subordinated to trade creditors [in contrast to institutional lenders] on a finding of undercapitalization alone."

In other instances, a proprietor or partnership that has already been operating a business may decide to assume the corporate form; or a new corporation may be created to carry on the business of an existing corporation; or an operating corporation may wish to "spin off" a segment of its business and conduct it through a separate corporation. In each of these contexts, some additional investors may join the new enterprise, or some previous participants may withdraw.

This subsection concerns the rights of creditors of the predecessor enterprise. If it was a sole proprietorship or partnership, the entrepreneurs cannot shed their personal obligations by the unilateral act of incorporation, and they continue to be bound; similarly, if the predecessor business was a corporation, it remains liable to its existing creditors. If, as is frequently the case, all the assets of the predecessor enterprise (including contracts) are assigned to the successor corporation in return for its shares and its undertaking to assume the obligations of its predecessor, then the creditors of the old business may hold the new corporation liable as third-party beneficiaries of its undertaking. But in the absence of such an undertaking, will (or should) the successor corporation be liable?

Tift v. Forage King Industries, Inc.
108 Wis. 2d 72, 322 N.W.2d 14 (1982)

HEFFERNAN, J.: [Plaintiff was injured in 1975 while operating a farm tractor equipped with a chopper box manufactured in 1962 by Woodrow Wiberg, then doing business as a sole proprietor under the name Forage King Industries. In 1968, Vernon Nedland joined the firm, which operated as a partnership for a time and then became a corporation, Forage King Industries, Inc. Shortly thereafter, Wiberg became the corporation's sole shareholder when he purchased all of Nedland's shares. Seven months before the accident, Wiberg sold all his stock to Tester Corporation. During all this time, Forage King continued to manufacture substantially the same products, including chopper boxes, at the same location. Claiming the chopper box was defective and caused the accident, plaintiff sued Forest King Industries, Inc., Nedland, and Wiberg. Plaintiff argued that Wiberg was judgment-proof, but the record did not reveal whether this was true. The corporation moved for summary judgment.

[The trial court] relied upon the rule set forth in Leannais v. Cincinnati, Inc., 565 F.2d 437, 439 (7th Cir. 1977), ". . . that a corporation which purchases the assets of another corporation does not succeed to the liabilities of the selling corporation."

The trial court recognized that there are, however, four well-recognized exceptions under which liability may be imposed upon a purchasing corporation: "(1) when the purchasing corporation expressly or impliedly agreed to assume the selling corporation's liability; (2) when the transaction amounts to a consolidation or merger of the purchaser and seller corporations; (3) when the purchaser corporation is merely a continuation of the seller corporation; or (4) when the transaction is entered into fraudulently to escape liability for such obligations." *Leannais*, supra at 439.[84]

---

84. "A fifth exception, sometimes incorporated as an element of one of the four listed above, is the absence of adequate consideration for the sale or transfer." 15 William M. Fletcher, Cyclopedia of the Law of Private Corporations 247-248 (rev. vol. 1999).

Yet another exception, adopted in some states, "provides that a corporation that purchases a manufacturing business and continues to produce the seller's line of products assumes strict liability in tort for defects in units of the same product line previously manufactured and distributed by the

The trial court found none of these exceptions applicable. . . . The trial court placed heavy emphasis upon the fact that the chopper box in question had been built by a predecessor sole *proprietorship* and, therefore, the present Forage King Industries, Inc., could not be a successor *corporation* to the original manufacturer, because the original manufacturer was not a corporation. The Court of Appeals followed the same reasoning in affirming the trial court judgment.

. . . There is, of course, some rationality to the position taken by the Circuit Court and the Court of Appeals. As the court of appeals said at 331, 306 N.W.2d 289: "When a corporation is purchased by a second corporation, the first disappears as a legal entity and, consequently, cannot be sued."[1]

The court of appeals, however, recognized the paramount policy reasons for imposing liability on a business which succeeds another because: "[N]o corporation should be permitted to place into the stream of commerce a defective product and avoid liability through corporate transformations or changes in form only." At 331, 306 N.W.2d 289.

The court of appeals concluded, however, that this obviously correct principle had no application in the instant case because Wiberg, who had operated as a sole proprietorship when he built the chopper box, remained available as a defendant subject to suit, and therefore necessity did not require that any successor business organizations be defendants.

We have no quarrel with the court of appeals' decision that Wiberg has not absolved himself from liability and remains a proper defendant, but logic does not lead to the conclusion that, because Wiberg is a proper defendant, his successor business organizations cannot be also. . . . We hold as a matter of law that the rule and its exceptions are applicable, irrespective of whether a prior organization was a corporation or a different form of business organization.

. . . [Two of the exceptions to the] rule that exempts a successor company from the liabilities of its predecessor when it has purchased the assets of the predecessor . . . , the first and the fourth, are unrelated to the problem at hand, for where there is an express or implied assumption of the selling corporation's liabilities — tort, contract, or both — the problem is obviated; and where the transaction is fraudulent, protection is afforded under the law of fraudulent conveyances. The other two "exceptions" are, however, relevant to our discussion of the purposes

---

seller. . . . This 'products line' exception applies in cases involving tort claims where: (1) the plaintiff lacks an adequate remedy against the seller/manufacturer; (2) the purchaser knows about product risks associated with the line of products that it continues; and (3) the seller transfers good will associated with the product line. Lundell v. Sidney Mach. Tool Co., 190 Cal. App. 3d 1546, 1551-1556, 236 Cal. Rptr. 70, 74-78 (1987)." Ruiz v. Blentech Corp., 89 F.3d 320 (7th Cir. 1996). For a recent discussion of the "product-line" exception, reportedly adopted by a quarter of the states, see Lefever v. K. L. Hovranian Enterprises, 160 N.J. 307, 734 A.2d 290 (1999). For general consideration of efforts to protect injured consumers, including the "continuity of enterprise" exception (a variant of the "product line" exception), see Richard L. Cupp Jr., Redesigning Successor Liability, 1999 Ill. L. Rev. 845.

Should the "product line" exception include instances of negligence committed by the predecessor business? See Monarch Bay II v. Professional Service Industries, Inc., 75 Cal. App. 4th 1213, 89 Cal. Rptr. 2d 778 (1999) (declining to do so, though agreeing that "there is no significant difference between a plaintiff injured by a defective product and one harmed by corporate negligence"). — ED.

1. This, of course, is not always true The more important question is whether the corporation or predecessor is merely a hollow shell or is it an entity with assets answerable to judgments. Statutes will affect the answerability of a defunct corporation to subsequent lawsuits.

and policies behind causes of action for tort. These exceptions are not really exceptions at all, for when applicable they swallow up the rule of nonliability.

. . . [T]he rule and its exceptions were designed initially to protect contract or quasi-contract creditors of a dissolved business organization and, hence, as a general group, all four exceptions are irrelevant to tort except as to the extent that the second and third exceptions are indicia of "identity." These exceptions are declaratory of tests to be applied to encourage "piercing the corporate veil" and to look to the substance and effect of business transformations or reorganizations to determine whether the original organization continues to have life or identity in a subsequent and existing business organization. . . .

Exceptions two and three to the corporate rule demonstrate that, when it is the same business organization that one is dealing with, whether it be by consolidation, merger, or continuation, liability may be enforced. These are tests of identity. Suit is possible in these circumstances, because there would be privity with the actual seller or manufacturer, i.e., the exceptions are guidelines to determine under what circumstances the original entity continues to exist, albeit in an altered form. . . .

Our case, however, is a clear case of "identity." The present Forage King Industries, Inc., is, for the practical purposes relevant to consumer protection, the continuation of the same entity as that operated as a sole proprietorship by Wiberg. . . .

The defendant, Forage King Industries, Inc., argues . . . that the predecessor organization, Wiberg's sole proprietorship, is in fact "morally" responsible and at fault and should therefore be the only entity answerable in damages. However, . . . the present Forage King Industries, Inc., is substantially the same business organization that manufactured the allegedly defective implement. We arrive at that conclusion by the application of traditional tests for successor liability. The present organization, although it has undergone a structural metamorphosis, remains in substance the identical organization manufacturing the same product. It is liable for the defective product manufactured by the original business organization.[85] . . . [Reversed.]

Callow, J. (dissenting): . . . A corporation is a creature of statute which is created and extinguished by law. If it is dissolved, its directors are required by statute to make adequate provision for *known* debts and liabilities for a specified period of time, but after the statutory period expires, it has no legal existence and, consequently, cannot be sued. A sole proprietor, even after termination of the business activity, remains a viable defendant for suit and, as the *Leannais* court prescribed, will remain responsible for his own acts.

The court of appeals concluded that the instant case did not fall within the policy ambit for imposing intercorporate liability; namely, "no corporation should be permitted to place into the stream of commerce a defective product and avoid liability through corporate transformations or changes in form only." Tift v. Forage King Industries, Inc., 102 Wis. 2d 327, 331, 306 N.W.2d 289 (Ct. App. 1981). The significant identity distinction is that in the case, as here where we are dealing with a sole proprietor, the responsible party is capable of being sued; the sole proprietor

---

85. What results if, by the time suit was brought, Forage King Industries, Inc. had disposed of its manufacturing business and was now exclusively engaged in real estate development? See Chaknova v. Wilbur-Ellis Co., 69 Cal. App. 4th 962, 81 Cal. Rptr. 2d 871 (1999); Morales v. Crompton & Knowles Corp., 888 F. Supp. 682 (E.D. Pa. 1995). — Ed.

cannot place a defective product in the stream of commerce and avoid liability through incorporation. . . . In the present case, imposition of liability on Forage King Industries/Tester Corporation in this million dollar lawsuit actually results in a "windfall" to the plaintiff who has been given a remote additional party to sue. This does not accord with the fundamental principles of justice and fairness articulated in *Leannais* where the law imposes responsibility for one's own act and not those totally independent acts of others. 565 F.2d at 439. Because the majority has not cited any authority in support of its conclusion, I can only believe that it seeks not to apply the law as it is; it seeks to mold the law in the image it wishes it to be.

Although I believe the intercorporate rule is inapplicable to the present case, I will address the majority's second and erroneous conclusion that the corporate exceptions for de facto merger and/or continuation impose liability.

According to case law, subject to specific conditions, if a purchase of assets amounts to a merger,[2] or if it accomplishes a mere continuation of the seller, the purchasing corporation assumes — by operation of law — the liabilities of the sellers. . . .[86]

It is the absence of the necessary specific conditions which frustrate the majority's conclusion in the instant case. I would point out that there are two minimum conditions precedent to the imposition of liability under the de facto merger or continuation exceptions: (1) the seller must quickly dissolve, and (2) the consideration for the sale of assets must be shares of the purchaser which are distributed to the seller's shareholders. . . . The majority, without explanation, fails to mention these two pivotal points. . . .

In conclusion, I believe that the majority has abrogated a significant distinction between a corporation and a sole proprietorship, one designed to comport with notions of fundamental fairness and justice. While a corporation may dissolve its legal status, leaving a plaintiff without a remedy, a sole proprietor remains a viable defendant. I believe that the intercorporate rule of nonliability with its four exceptions applies — and was intended to apply — solely to corporations. . . .

J. F. Anderson Lumber Co. v. Myers
296 Minn. 33, 206 N.W.2d 365 (1973)

OLSON, J.: [Plaintiff, a subcontractor, obtained judgment against Richard T. Leekley, Inc. for $24,652.]

After the trial, but before entry of the judgment heretofore recited, Richard T. Leekley and his wife, the sole stockholders of Richard T. Leekley, Inc., formed a new corporation entitled Leekley's, Inc. The new corporation performed the same type of home construction and remodeling business as the former corporation;

---

2. A merger differs from the sale of corporate assets in the following respect: A merger is the absorption of one corporation by another, with the buying corporation retaining its name and corporate identity but adding the capital and powers of the merged corporation. A sale of corporate assets is a vehicle through which the vendor parts with its entire interest in exchange for cash and nothing more. 15 W. Fletcher, Cyclopedia of the Law of Private Corporations, secs. 7041 and 7044 (rev. perm. ed. 1973). A de facto merger occurs where the acquisition closely resembles a statutory merger, but the statutory formalities have not been observed. See Note, Assumption of Products Liability in Corporate Acquisitions, 55 B.U. L. Rev. 86, 96-100 (1975).

86. Should there be a difference, for purposes of successor liability, whether a business sells all its assets in exchange for cash rather than for shares of the buyer corporation? See Franklin v. USX Corp., 87 Cal. App. 4th 615, 105 Cal. Rptr. 11 (2000) (yes). — ED.

Leekley and his wife were its officers and sole stockholders, as they had been in the first corporation. The first corporation transferred assets consisting of two trucks and miscellaneous other equipment to the second corporation for the sum of $1,788.58, which was paid to creditors of the first corporation; three employees from the first corporation were hired by the second corporation; and the first corporation ceased doing business. The first corporation was insolvent with total debts running more than $40,000. None of the customer contracts of the first corporation was transferred to the second corporation, and no assets in the nature of incomplete construction contracts nor money due under such contracts were transferred. . . . [Plaintiff sought to include the second corporation as an additional judgment debtor.]

The record indicates . . . that no tangible assets were concealed or secretly transferred from the first corporation to the second corporation or to its stockholders. The first corporation had been insolvent for some years before the second was incorporated, and there was no evidence of any fraudulent transfers or other fraudulent acts.

. . . As to the third recited exception noted to the general rule [of nonliability of successor corporations], i.e., "where the purchasing corporation is merely a continuation of the selling corporation," such exception refers principally to a "reorganization" of the original corporation, such as is accomplished occasionally under Chapter X of the Bankruptcy Act, 11 U.S.C.A. §§501 to 676, and perhaps under other state statutory devices. 15 Fletcher, Cyclopedia of Corporations (Perm. ed.) §§7122 and 7200.[87] The mere fact that a purchasing corporation is "carrying on the same business" as the selling corporation is not sufficient to make the purchasing corporation liable for the debts of the selling corporation. The purchasing corporation in the instant case was not a continuation of the selling corporation within the meaning of the exception to the general rule.[88]

Finally, . . . [plaintiffs] contend that assets were transferred without adequate consideration. They rely upon the trial court's statement that the most valuable asset of a contractor is his personal reputation and good will. However, it is unclear to this court how personal reputation of an officer and principal stockholder of a corporation can be an asset transferred from one corporation to another sufficient to justify a finding that the receiving corporation is liable for the debts of the transferring corporation. On the other hand, in a proper case, if there is an asset of the corporation labeled "good will," which is transferred and which can be measured in money terms, perhaps there would be some basis for determining that the creditor of the transferring corporation has a claim against the receiving

---

87. In McCarthy v. Litton Industries, Inc., 410 Mass. 15, 570 N.E.2d 1008 (1991), the court discussed "the 'continuation' exception to the general rule of nonliability, . . . [which] envisions a reorganization transforming a single company from one corporate entity into another. . . . The purchasing corporation, in the words of one court, is merely a 'new hat' for the seller. Bud Antle, Inc. v. Eastern Foods, Inc., 758 F.2d 1451, 1458 (11th Cir. 1985). Thus, the imposition of liability on the purchaser is justified on the theory that, in substance if not in form, the purchasing corporation is the same company as the selling corporation." Accord, IGL-Wisconsin Awning, Tent & Trailer Co. v. Greater Milwaukee Air and Water Show, Inc., 185 Wis. 2d 864, 520 N.W.2d 279 (Ct. App. 1994). — ED.

88. See also Katzir's Floor and Home Design, Inc. v. M-MLS.com, 394 F.3d 1143 (9th Cir. 2004): "Inadequate consideration is an 'essential ingredient' to finding that one entity is a mere continuation of another" under California law; Foster v. Cone-Blanchard Machine Co., 597 N.W.2d 506 (Mich. 1999): "[T]he 'continuity of enterprise' doctrine applies only when the transferer is no longer viable and capable of being sued." But see Alexander & Baldwin, Inc. v. Peat, Marwick, Mitchell & Co., 385 F. Supp. 240 (S.D.N.Y. 1974). — ED.

corporation. The record in this case is devoid of evidence of such a transfer of corporate "good will." In fact, the first corporation was insolvent at the time the second business was incorporated and had been insolvent for a number of years.

The record in this case clearly indicates that there was a transfer of tangible assets from the first corporation to the second with full and adequate consideration paid. . . .

In the instant case, the motive of Leekley and his wife in forming the second corporation was to avoid paying the debts of the first corporation, particularly the judgment in question. However, such a motive no more forms the basis for requiring the second corporation to assume the debts of the first corporation than it serves as a basis for an objection to a discharge in bankruptcy. . . .

---

1. *Statute:*

Minnesota Business Corporation Act (2006)

Sec. 661. *Transfer of assets. . . . 4. Transferee liability.* The transferee is liable for the debts, obligations, and liabilities of the transferor only to the extent provided in the contract or agreement between the transferee and the transferor. . . . A disposition of all or substantially all of a corporation's property and assets under this section is not considered to be a merger or a de facto merger pursuant to this chapter or otherwise. The transferee shall not be liable solely because it is deemed to be a continuation of the transferor.[89]

2. *Predecessor partnership.* What result in the *Tift* case if the chopper box had been manufactured when Forage King Industries was a partnership of Wiberg and Nedland, and plaintiff had brought suit against Forage King Industries, Inc. after it had succeeded the partnership and at a time when Wiberg and Nedland were the sole shareholders? In Kulka v. Nemirovsky, 321 Pa. 234, 182 A. 692 (1936), the court held:

> A partnership, in substance, is a quasi-legal entity, and its assets are to be first applied to partnership creditors. When a partnership transfers its assets to a corporation composed of substantially the same members as was the partnership, the creditor cannot be deprived of his prior right against the partnership assets, and he may follow these assets into the corporation and enforce payment of his claim therefrom.
> . . . In Coaldale Coal Co. v. State Bank, 142 Pa. 288, 21 A. 811, . . . there was no liability, but it differs from the present situation. There the partnership retained, after the transfer of a substantial part of its assets to the successor corporation, claims whose liquidation would have provided amply for the creditor, but, due to the fact that the debtors on those claims became insolvent, the partnership was unable to pay him. It appeared further that the partners had pledged their shares in the corporation to various creditors of the partnership and to others. As the court there stated, to have permitted the creditor of the partnership to levy on the property of the corporation would have resulted in sweeping away the assets from the secured creditors for the benefit of unsecured creditors.

---

89. RMBCA §14.06 requires that all creditors of the predecessor corporation must receive notice before it is dissolved and then have 120 days to file claims against it. — Ed.

Compare Pendergrass v. Care Care, Inc., 333 N.C. 233, 424 S.E.2d 391 (1993): "Assuming the mere continuation rule would apply as to corporations, we do not believe it should apply to this transfer of the assets of a partnership. If all the assets of a corporation are transferred, a claim against the transferring corporation might be worthless. When a partnership transfers its assets, the partners remain liable."

3. For a recent review of the decisions and commentary, see Marie T. Reilly, *Making Sense of Successor Liability*, 31 Hofstra L. Rev. 745 (2003), concluding that "a transferee should be liable as a successor not because it continues some attributes of the transferor, but rather because it colluded with the transferor in fraud of creditors, or at the time of the transfer reasonably should have known that the debtor/transferor planned to hide assets from creditors."

2. PROMOTERS' CONTRACTS

a. Introduction

The term "promoters" is used to designate the persons responsible for the founding and organizing of a corporation. As previously indicated, such persons may already be actively engaged in an existing business enterprise, or they may wish to engage in a particular business venture for the first time and want to do so — either by themselves or with additional persons — as a corporation. In both of these situations, the promoters will usually continue as active participants in the corporation after it is formed. There are also persons who may be described as "professional promoters" (who may operate under titles such as "business brokers," "finders," or "financial consultants") who bring together people with various resources (e.g., investment capital, an existing business, patents or other innovative commercial ideas, or managerial talent) and may assist them in launching a corporate enterprise. Such promoters may become participants in the subsequently formed corporation (perhaps as inactive shareholders), but frequently do not continue their association with it after receiving a fee for their services.

In all these contexts, the transaction of certain business for the contemplated enterprise prior to its formal incorporation is either essential in fact or may be viewed by the potential shareholders as preconditions to their going forward, e.g., lawyers must be retained to prepare the proper documents; land, buildings, and machinery may be purchased or leased or options thereon obtained; contracts for materials or services (perhaps an employment contract with one of the future shareholders) may be signed. Or the exigencies of time may just make it highly desirable to enter into these or similar contracts while the incorporation process is still taking place. Those who make these contracts for the proposed corporation do so as promoters.

Many legal problems are engendered by the activities and transactions of promoters. There is the matter of their obligations inter se.[90] Issues concerning promoters' rights and responsibilities vis-à-vis the incoming and subsequent shareholders, in respect to promoters' dealings with the contemplated or incipient corporation (e.g., selling their own property to it, or obtaining their fee from it for

---

90. During the promotion, the promoters generally have the fiduciary responsibilities of joint venturers to each other. See Harry G. Henn & John R. Alexander, Corporations §103 (3d ed. 1983); Norman D. Lattin, Corporations §28 (2d ed. 1971).

pre-incorporation services rendered), have often arisen.[91] Among the contracts for the future corporation entered into by promoters are subscriptions for shares to be issued. Here we are concerned with those pre-incorporation contracts made between third parties and promoters acting for a corporation to be formed.[92]

Courts have readily permitted the subsequently formed corporation to enforce a contract previously executed for it by its promoters, but they have had difficulty rationalizing their decisions. A close analogue, the agency doctrine of "ratification" — permitting principals to affirm the unauthorized acts of persons purporting to act in their behalf — is technically unavailable because of its "relation back" feature; the doctrine requires that the "agent's" act could have been authorized by the principal at the time the agent acted and provides that the ratification is given effect as if originally authorized by the principal.[93] Since the corporation (principal) was not in existence at the time of the promoter's contract (agent's act), it could not then authorize it. One orthodox way to permit the corporation to enforce the agreement is to treat the promoter's contract as an implied offer to the corporation and to treat the corporation's attempt to enforce as an acceptance. The practical problem with this theory is that it permits the third party to revoke in the interim. If the contract is assignable, the corporation may be permitted to enforce it by treating it as the promoter's assignee. Or the corporation may be treated as a third-party beneficiary of the contract between the promoter and third party.[94] Courts have utilized all of these theories but, although many continue to talk about "ratification" despite the conceptual difficulties, the popular approach is termed "adoption."[95]

---

91. See Cox & Hazen, footnote 2 supra, at §5.9.

92. The materials that follow involve instances in which the third parties know that they are dealing with a promoter of a future corporation. If, on the other hand, third parties are led to believe that they are dealing with a perfected corporation, but in fact such corporation has not yet been formed, the issues presented fall within a topic already considered — defective incorporation. Courts sometimes discuss problems of this sort as coming within the doctrines concerning promoters' transactions. See, e.g., Sivers v. R&F Capital Corp., 123 Or. App. 35, 858 P.2d 895 (1993). As we have seen, the issue frequently arises when the third party seeks to hold the "promoter" personally liable on the contract. It may also arise when there is no properly formed corporation in existence and (a) the third party seeks to terminate obligations under the contract entered into with the "corporation," see Macy Corp. v Ramey, 144 N.E.2d 698 (Ohio C.P. 1957) (no valid contract), or (b) the "promoter" seeks to enforce the contract, see White v. Dvorak, 78 Wash. App. 2d 105, 896 P.2d 85 (1995) (enforceable).

93. Restatement (Second) of Agency §§82, 84.

94. Third-party beneficiaries need not be in existence at the time contracts for their benefit are executed. Restatement of Contracts §132.

95. In England (see Kelner v. Baxter, L.R. 2 P.C. 174 (1866)) and Massachusetts (see Abbott v. Hapgood, 150 Mass. 248, 22 N.E. 907 (1889)), however, the corporation may become a party to the agreement only by entering into a new contract or by a formal novation — the general rationale being that a nonexistent corporation cannot be a party to the contract and therefore the pre-incorporation agreement is a nullity as to it when subsequently formed; it can neither "ratify" nor "adopt." But see Framingham Savings Bank v. Szabo, 617 F.2d 897 (1st Cir. 1980) (Massachusetts uses "theories of continuing offer and implied contract" to permit enforcement of pre-incorporation contract by subsequently formed corporation, at least when corporation has already performed).

Note that the question of whether adoption (or ratification) relates back to the time of the promoter's execution of the agreement may be critical for certain purposes, e.g., the statute of limitations, or whether the promoter's pre-incorporation activities within a state subject the subsequently formed corporation to in personam jurisdiction. See Rees v. Mosaic Technologies, Inc., 742 F.2d 765 (3d Cir. 1984). A number of cases have involved promoters' contracts for employment and the statute of frauds requirement that such contracts must be in writing if not performable within one year from the date of execution. If such a contract is in writing, relation back will make it the corporation's contract as an original matter and no further writing is necessary. See Perry v. Nevin Hotel Co., 349 Ill. App. 22, 109 N.E.2d 810 (1953) (ratification theory); Meyers v. Wells, 252 Wis. 352, 31 N.W.2d 512 (1948) (adoption theory). What result if there is no relation back? If the contract provides for employment by the

The two major problem areas in respect to promoters' contracts with third parties concern whether, when, and to what extent the corporation and/or the promoter is liable. Both questions arise in a number of contexts and are also presented at several stages in a continuing time sequence. To illustrate: Suppose the corporation is never formed; suppose it is formed but (1) is silent in respect to the contract, (2) expressly adopts the contract, (3) expressly repudiates the contract. These contingencies and all others may, of course, be resolved in advance by careful drafting of the promoter's contract; if explicitly made part of the bargain, the intention of the parties will govern in the absence of a controlling statute. Litigation stems from the lack of such clear contractual provisions and the matter becomes one of whom — corporation, promoter, third party — the policy of the law ought to favor.

In examining and evaluating the law of corporation and promoter liability, the two problems may be viewed as being interrelated to a considerable extent — e.g., whether the corporation should be liable in the absence of its express repudiation may be thought as turning on whether the promoter is liable under these circumstances (and vice versa); whether the promoter should be liable after the corporation is formed may be seen as turning on the point at which the corporation becomes liable; etc.

b. Liability of the Corporation

Kridelbaugh v. Aldrehn Theatres Co.
195 Iowa 147, 191 N.W. 803 (1923)

De Graff, J.: Plaintiff seeks to recover $1,530.32 as attorney's fees and expenses incidental to the incorporation of the defendant company. . . .

Three persons . . . proposed to incorporate . . . and the plaintiff was informed that his services would be required, and he was instructed to investigate and determine in what state it was deemed advisable to incorporate. He proceeded to investigate and his plan was finally adopted by the promoters and the company was duly incorporated. . . . The three promoters became its only directors. . . . [T]he promoters promised to pay the plaintiff $1,500 for his services. Under these facts the initial question is whether the promoters and incorporators could legally bind the defendant corporation as agents.

. . . There was no principal at the time that the contract in suit was made and consequently there was no agency. Principal and agent are correlative and coexistent terms. Promoters are individually liable on their contracts, and this is true whether or not their efforts and initiative result in a corporation being called into existence. The answer to the first question must be in the negative. . . .

In logical sequence, the next question to be answered is whether the use per se of the charter and by-laws by the defendant is an adoption or ratification of the promoters' contract. . . . [Does a corporation's] obligation to pay under the terms of the promoters' original contract come into being at the time the corporation has its birth without any act on its part through its board of directors or its

---

corporation for one year and is not in writing, the statute of frauds will invalidate it if the subsequent adoption or ratification relates back. See McArthur v. Times Printing Co., 48 Minn. 319, 51 N.W. 216 (1892).

duly constituted official? We answer again in the negative. This is not a case in which the corporation can accept or refuse the benefits of a contract. Under the instant record it had no choice. . . .

Furthermore it is immaterial that the promoters thereafter became officers of the corporation. The act of a promoter is not the act of the corporation. . . .

In the instant case the plaintiff does not sue on quantum meruit. He seeks to recover on a specific contract with the promoters, which contract, it is alleged, was adopted or ratified by the corporation after its creation through its board of directors. What is the record in this particular?

The plaintiff subsequently to the incorporation of the defendant attended the first meeting of the board of directors. At that meeting there was some conversation in regard to getting a permit to sell the stock in the state of Iowa. Plaintiff's undisputed testimony is as follows: "Adams one of the directors said, 'Well, you go ahead now and get that permit just as soon as you can, because we want to sell some stock; and we will pay you just as quick as we can sell some stock with which to pay you.'"

This was said at a time when the question of the fee and expenses of the plaintiff was under discussion. It was an express authorization of the plaintiff to act as attorney for the corporation in securing the permit, and a recognition on the part of the board that the plaintiff should be paid for past services in the organization of the corporation and for services which he was to perform and which he did perform. . . .

In the instant case the trial court applied the rule of implied contract. We would go further, and apply the rule of express ratification or adoption.

In Morgan v. Bon Bon Co., 222 N.Y. 22, 118 N.E. 205, it is shown that a part of the services was performed before the incorporation and a part afterwards, with the knowledge of the promoters, who were then the officers of the corporation. The opinion reads: "With the knowledge and approval of the men who promoted the corporation, and then became its stockholders and officers, the appellant was permitted to perform services which had been contracted for, and the corporation, chargeable through its officers with full knowledge of the contract under which these services were being rendered, received the benefit thereof. It is well established that a corporation which under such circumstances takes the benefit of a contract may be held to have adopted and assumed also its obligations."

. . . Wherefore the judgment entered is affirmed.

---

1. *Problem.* Suppose, in the *Kridelbaugh* case, that the three promoters owned a substantial percentage of the corporation's shares; that the first action taken at the first board of directors meeting was the enactment of a resolution expressly disaffirming the pre-incorporation contract with plaintiff on the ground that his services were worth no more than $500; that the corporation subsequently went bankrupt and the promoters were personally judgment proof. What result if plaintiff seeks to enforce a claim for the contract price against the corporation in its bankruptcy proceeding? For quantum meruit? See Peters Grazing Ass'n v. Legerski, 544 P.2d 449 (Wyo. 1975); cf. Ong Hing v. Arizona Harness Raceway, Inc., 10 Ariz. App. 380, 459 P.2d 107 (1969).

2. *Problem.* A "professional promoter" executes a pre-incorporation contract with a printer for stationery and other materials for a proposed corporation. After formation, the corporation receives and uses the printed material, its directors reasonably believing that the promoter had paid the printer and included this cost in his lump-sum "promoter's fee," which the corporation has already paid. Printer sues corporation for the contract price. What result if:

(a) Promoter is no longer associated with corporation?

(b) Promoter owns small percentage of corporation's shares and is one of its seven directors? Compare, on the matter of imputing knowledge of director to corporation, C. & H. Contractors, Inc. v. McKee, 177 So. 2d 851 (Fla. Dist. Ct. App. 1965), and Solomon v. Cedar Acres East, Inc., 455 Pa. 496, 317 A.2d 283 (1974), with Spering v. Sullivan, 361 F. Supp. 282, 286 (D. Del. 1973), and Chartrand v. Barney's Club, Inc., 380 F.2d 97 (9th Cir. 1967).

3. *Problem.* A "professional promoter" executes a pre-incorporation contract with T to be sales manager for a proposed corporation at a stipulated salary, plus a substantial year-end bonus depending on the amount of sales. After formation, T acts as the corporation's sales manager and is paid the agreed-upon salary. When T seeks her bonus at year-end, corporation refuses to pay because it never knew of the provision. T sues corporation. What result? See Steele v. Litton Industries, Inc., 260 Cal. App. 2d 157, 68 Cal. Rptr. 680 (1968).

c. Liability of the Promoters

Sherwood & Roberts–Oregon, Inc. v. Alexander
269 Or. 389, 525 P.2d 135 (1974)

DENECKE, J.: . . . The defendants are real estate developers. They held title to some land either as individuals or in an unincorporated joint venture known as Iron Mountain Investment Company. Defendants planned to develop this land. The plaintiff is in the business of lending money and securing loans from other sources for plaintiff's customers. Defendants sought financing through plaintiff, who suggested securing a commitment for a long-term loan; that is, an offer by a lender to make defendants a loan, the offer to continue for an agreed period of time.

Under existing financial conditions the interest on the loan would be at least 12 percent. Twelve percent is a usurious rate to charge individuals; therefore, plaintiff informed defendants that any loan would have to be made to a corporation. Corporations are not subject to the same usury laws as individuals.

As a prerequisite to seeking a loan commitment for defendants, plaintiff required a "good faith deposit" from defendants. One of plaintiff's officers explained the purpose of a good faith deposit as being "to assure us that our work, time and expense involved isn't in vain. We don't get paid." The amount of the deposit is one percent of the proposed loan. If the plaintiff cannot secure a commitment the deposit is refundable. If the commitment is secured and the borrower accepts the commitment, plaintiff applies the deposit to the fee plaintiff charges for securing the commitment. If the plaintiff secures a commitment but the borrower will not accept the commitment, plaintiff retains the deposit.

When plaintiff was preparing the note which was to be the good faith deposit, plaintiff asked defendant Alexander what corporation would borrow the money and execute the good faith deposit note. Alexander did not have any corporation, but told plaintiff the corporation's name would be "Iron Mountain Investment Co., Inc." The note was so prepared and signed by Alexander for the corporation. Plaintiff knew that at this time there was no corporate entity.

Plaintiff secured a commitment; however, it was not acceptable to defendants. . . . Because the commitment was rejected, plaintiff brought this action on the good faith deposit note. Defendants never attempted to form a corporation.

Plaintiff is attempting to recover on the basis of ORS 57.793, which provides: "All persons who assume to act as a corporation without the authority of a certificate of incorporation issued by the Corporation Commissioner, shall be jointly and severally liable for all debts and liabilities incurred or arising as a result thereof."

We interpreted this section in Timberline Equipment Company, Inc. v. Davenport, 267 Or. 64, 514 P.2d 1109 (1973). Contrary to plaintiff's contention in this case, we held in *Timberline* that this section was ambiguous. We also held that ORS 57.793 must be construed together with ORS 57.321. These two sections, in essence, provide that the corporate entity conclusively begins with the issuance of the certificate of incorporation. Any steps to incorporate, short of the securing of the issuance of the certificate, are ineffective; those assuming to act for a defectively incorporated corporation are personally liable.

The *Timberline* decision and those two sections, however, do not necessarily lead to a decision that the defendants in this case are liable.

In *Timberline* we quoted the commentary to §146 of the Model Act, which is similar to ORS 57.793. The commentary is to the effect that the purpose of this section was to end the doctrine of de facto corporations. That doctrine, of de facto corporations, is that although a corporation has not complied with all the requirements for incorporation, its existence as a legal entity cannot be attacked if it has colorably fulfilled these requirements. As the commentary points out, this was a "fuzzy" doctrine and no longer necessary because legal incorporation is now relatively simple. . . .

Since all parties were fully informed of the purely prospective existence of the corporation, the note is best termed a preincorporation contract. Parties in the position of the defendants are termed "promoters." . . .

The common-law rule governing these preincorporation contracts is stated: "It is settled by the authorities that a promoter, though he may assume to act on behalf of the projected corporation and not for himself, will be personally liable on his contract unless the other party agreed to look to some other person or fund for payment." . . .

Because the statute was intended to abolish the common-law doctrine of de facto corporations, because it was not intended to apply to the common-law rules governing preincorporation agreements, and because it does not by its terms unambiguously apply to a promoter's liability for preincorporation agreements, we hold the statute is not applicable and the common-law rule governing the liability of promoters for preincorporation agreements applies.

The next step is to determine if there was any evidence that the plaintiff agreed to accept the obligation of a to-be-formed corporation solely and not to look for payment from the defendants as individuals. . . .

We find there was evidence that plaintiff looked solely to the to-be-formed corporation for payment of the note. Unlike the creditor in the usual case, the plaintiff in this case is the party that insisted that the contract show a corporation as the obligor and would not do business otherwise, although plaintiff knew when the note was executed that no corporation existed. Plaintiff's officer who handled the transaction testified that plaintiff would look to the defendant individuals as well as to the corporation for payment of the principal note and mortgage, had it *been* consummated. He testified the defendants and their wives would have been required to execute these documents in their individual capacity. The commitment tendered to defendants had blanks for defendants and their wives to sign, individually, indicating their acceptance. That the note, prepared by plaintiff, was not prepared for the signature of either defendant as an individual, whereas all the other documents were so prepared is also some evidence that plaintiff did not intend to have the defendants, as individuals, obligated on the note.

Further evidence is the testimony of plaintiff's officer that when the note was signed, he did not intend to proceed further in securing a commitment until defendants provided him with their articles of incorporation. The trial court could infer from this testimony that the plaintiff was not going to look to the individual defendants to repay it for the expense of finding a commitment; rather, the plaintiff desired to conduct all parts of this transaction with a corporate entity. This desire on plaintiff's part is reasonable as plaintiff's officer was concerned that if the corporation was considered a sham to avoid the usury statute, plaintiff would be subject to the penalties of the usury statute. . . .

The judgment is affirmed. . . .

How & Associates, Inc. v. Boss
222 F. Supp. 936 (S.D. Iowa 1963)

HANSON, J.: . . . [Plaintiff architect entered into a contract to draw plans for a motel that was to be built by defendant, who signed: "Edwin A. Boss, Agent for a Minnesota Corporation to be formed, who will be the obligor." A Minnesota corporation was never formed, but plaintiff received substantial payments from an Iowa corporation formed by defendant and his associate, Edwin Hunter. After plaintiff completed his work, defendant abandoned plans for the motel. Plaintiff sued defendant for the balance of his fee.]

There really is not much debate as to what the law is on the questions raised. Both parties cite . . . the proposition that a promoter, though he may assume to act on behalf of the projected corporation and not for himself, will be personally liable on his contract unless the other party agreed to look to some other person or fund for payment.

Comment b under Section 326 of the R.S. of Agency sets out the three possible understandings that the parties may have when the agreement is made on behalf of a corporation to be formed by one of the parties. These are as follows:

An offer or option to the corporation to be formed which will result in a contract if it is accepted when the corporation is formed. The correlative promise for the continuing offer or option is the promoter's promise to organize the corporation and give it the opportunity to pay the debt. . . .

The second type of situation is where the parties agree to a present contract by which the promoter is bound, but with an agreement that his liability terminates if the corporation is formed and manifests its willingness to become a party. This is an agreement for a future novation. . . .

This second possible interpretation is not very important in this case because a novation was not pleaded or argued. . . .

The third type of understanding is where the parties have agreed to a present contract upon which, even though the corporation later becomes a party, the promoter remains liable either primarily or as surety for the performance of the corporation's obligation.

. . . [T]his is a situation where the parties used ambiguous words to describe their intentions. To resolve this ambiguity, it is helpful to resort to the usual rules of interpretation of ambiguous contracts.

One rule of interpretation is to give meaning to all parts of the contract unless there are parts of the writing so inconsistent that it is impossible. The contract states that three-fourths of the contract price was to have been paid by the time the drawings and specifications were completed, and that this was to have been paid in monthly payments. If this part of the contract is given effect, it clearly tends to show that the parties intended that there was to be a present obligor on the contract. . . . Another rule is that the writing must be strictly construed against the party who drafted the writing in question. . . . In this case, it was the defendant who wrote the ambiguous words and they must be construed in favor of the plaintiff.

Also, and perhaps most important, there are a number of cases which say that in the promoter contract cases where the contract called for performance, at least in part, before the corporation is organized, this indicates that the promoter is intended to be personally liable on the contract. . . . This was the type of case where the work was to begin by Mr. How before the corporation was organized and certainly to be completed before the corporation was in business.

. . . [T]he only issue was whether the contract was a continuing offer to the then nonexistent corporation or was an agreement that Mr. Boss was a present obligor. While the agreement was not completely clear, the words "who will be the obligor" are not enough to offset the rule that the person signing for the nonexistent corporation is normally to be personally liable. This is especially true when considered in the light of other circumstances of this case and would be true even without the inference that the law puts on this situation.

The defendant in his brief argues that there was an adoption of the contract by the new corporation. . . . Adoption of the contract by the corporation is not sufficient to relieve the promoter of his liability. There must be a novation or agreement to that effect. . . . [T]here are a number of cases saying that the mere fact that payments were made by a third party and accepted by the plaintiff is not sufficient to establish a novation. . . .

The defendant argues that a practical construction has been put on the contract to the effect the plaintiff agreed to look solely to the credit of the new corporation. For this construction, the defendant relies upon the fact that the two checks which were given . . . carried the letterhead of the new corporation and were signed by Edwin Hunter. As already explained, this is not sufficient especially where a novation was not pleaded or argued. This would be an attempt to penalize the plaintiff for being patient and not demanding strict compliance. The court feels there was no waiver of rights and none was pleaded. . . .

In this case, the defendant was the principal promoter, acting for himself personally and as President of Boss Hotels, Inc. The promoters abandoned their purpose of forming the corporation. This would make the promoter liable to the plaintiff unless the contract be construed to mean: (1) that the plaintiff agreed to look solely to the new corporation for payment, and (2) that the promoter did not have any duty toward the plaintiff to form the corporation and give the corporation the opportunity to assume and pay the liability. . . .

Applying this law to the present case, the court would have to hold that even if the plaintiff had agreed to look to the credit of the new corporation, the defendant would be liable. The defendant was the key promoter and as such would be a primary factor in abandoning the project. This would make the defendant liable. . . .

Accordingly the court concludes that the plaintiff . . . should have and recover judgment against the defendant. . . .

Stewart Realty Co. v. Keller
118 Ohio App. 49, 193 N.E.2d 179 (1962)

GUERNSEY, PRESIDING JUDGE: This is an appeal . . . on questions of law in an action for damages brought by the plaintiff, as vendor in a contract for the sale of real estate, against Gerald D. Keller, who the plaintiff claims is personally liable on the contract.

The vendee named in the contract, "Avon Brand, Inc., an Ohio Corporation," was never organized in accordance with the representations of Keller. The contract was signed, "Avon Brand, Inc., by Gerald D. Keller, Pres." It is undisputed in evidence that the contract was executed by plaintiff with full knowledge that Avon Brand, Inc., did not have any corporate existence at the time, de jure or de facto, and that Keller expressly declined to execute any contract naming him as a party individually.

Under the contract, title to real estate therein described was not to be conveyed to the vendee until June 30, 1964, after certain payments. A down payment of $5,000 and two monthly payments of $350 each were made, and other prescribed monthly payments have long been in default. It appears further that a corporation named Byrnes Rest, Inc., of which Keller was president, took possession of the premises; that it yielded possession after several months to Avon Brand, Inc., a *Kentucky* corporation organized by Keller and others; and that at the time action was brought neither Keller nor any corporation with which he was connected was in possession of the subject real estate, the keys for the building thereon having been returned to plaintiff several months beforehand. . . .

. . . The action was on the contract for the sale of real estate, and to prevail it was necessary that plaintiff prove that the defendant was personally liable under the contract. The defendant was in the category of a promoter, and as stated in 18 C.J.S. Corporations §132, p.533, "[p]romoters are not personally liable on contracts made in the name and solely on the credit of the future corporation, and not on an express or implied representation that there is an existing corporation, where such intention is known to the other contracting party. . . . Whether or not a contract was made by the promoters personally or on the credit of the corporation only, may be a question of fact or one of law according to circumstances." . . .

Considering the contract herein in its entirety there is nothing on the face thereof which indicates, as a matter of either fact or law, that it was anything other than a contract to bind plaintiff and the corporation named therein. There were no promises made in the contract by defendant as an individual or any benefits to be received by him individually under the provisions of the contract. As to the knowledge of the plaintiff that the corporation only was to be bound and not the defendant personally, plaintiff proved this by its own witnesses, in particular plaintiff's attorney, and offered no evidence of any probative value to the contrary. Notwithstanding plaintiff's claim that the defendant represented that he would invest certain personal funds in the corporation, there is no evidence that the contract was made except in the name of and solely on the credit of the future corporation. Such being the case there was no issue of fact for the jury respecting the personal liability of defendant, either by express provisions of the contract or by estoppel. . . .

By reason of the same failure of proof, defendant was entitled to a directed verdict at the close of all the evidence. . . .

---

1. *Questions.* (a) On what grounds, if any, may the results in the *Sherwood, Boss*, and *Stewart Realty* cases be rationalized?

(b) Suppose, in the *Stewart Realty* case, that after the down payment had been made the vendor notified Keller that it wished no part of the deal and was returning the down payment. After Avon Brand, Inc. (of Kentucky) is formed, it brings suit against the vendor for breach of contract. What result?

2. *Implied warranties.* In the *Boss* case, the court refers to an implicit "understanding" that the promoter promises "to organize the corporation and give it the opportunity to pay the debt." In other promoters' contracts cases — usually in which the corporation was never formed — courts talk about the promoter's breach of an implied warranty. See Weiss v. Baum, 218 App. Div. 83, 217 N.Y.S. 820 (1926); cf. Hagen v. Asa G. Candler, Inc., 189 Ca. 250, 5 S.E.2d 739 (1939). If there is an implied promise or an implied warranty, what precisely is its scope? If the third party has a cause of action against the promoter for its breach, is that the equivalent of the third party being able to hold the promoter as a party to the contract?

3. *Fact variations.* Assume the following varied sequences of events in the *Boss* case:

(a) a Minnesota corporation was formed by Boss and associates;

(b) (i) it adopted the contract; (ii) it repudiated the contract;

(c) (i) it had initial capital of $1,000, which was clearly inadequate to handle the construction project; (ii) it had substantial capital, which is now gone due to losses, and How remains unpaid.

What result would the court have reached in each of these instances if How sued Boss on the contract? See Illinois Controls, Inc. v. Langham, 70 Ohio St. 3d 512, 639 N.E.2d 771 (1994) (corporation is liable because it accepted the benefits with knowledge; promoters are also liable because corporation never formally adopted contract and contract did not make corporation solely responsible). Compare Wells v. J. A. Fay & Egan Co., 143 Ga. 732, 85 S.E. 873 (1915), with McEachin v. Kingman, 64 Ga. App. 104, 12 S.E.2d 212 (1940). See also Johnson & Carlson v. Montreuil's Estate, 291 Mich. 582, 289 N.W. 262 (1939) (interpreting one of the rare state statutes dealing with promoter's transactions as releasing the promoter from the contract if the corporation adopts it).

4. *Promoter's rights.* What result in the *Stewart Realty* case if Keller had formed an Ohio corporation that adopted the contract, and then plaintiff refused to convey the property and Keller sued for specific performance? See Speedway Realty Co. v. Grasshoff Realty Corp., 248 Ind. 6, 216 N.E.2d 845 (1966). What result if Keller brought suit before the corporation was formed?

V CORPORATE DISCLOSURE AND SECURITIES FRAUD

A. INTRODUCTION

The focus of this chapter is on the disclosure obligations of a publicly held corporation. When must it disclose? When may it remain silent (in order, for example, to protect the confidentiality surrounding pending negotiations or developments)? When will its silence be deemed misleading because the market has continued to rely on earlier statements by it that, although accurate when made, are no longer true? These are critical issues on which no hard-and-fast rule can be safely stated but to which a variety of legal standards considered in this chapter apply.

The disclosure obligations imposed on a corporation by the federal securities laws impact lawyers differently depending upon their professional specialty. For the corporate lawyer, the operative issues will normally concern the nature and timing of the information that must be disclosed. For the litigator, the key issues will typically involve the existence or nonexistence of private causes of action and their elements. Structurally, this chapter therefore examines these disclosure obligations from both perspectives. Section B first examines the various sources of law that define the contours of this disclosure obligation and then turns to the efforts of the Securities and Exchange Commission (SEC) to create an integrated disclosure system. Its focus is on what must be disclosed and when. Additionally, Sec. B will review the recent efforts of Congress in the Sarbanes-Oxley Act of 2002 to strengthen the federal disclosure system, improve the transparency of financial information, and otherwise reform corporate governance in light of the succession of corporate scandals that followed the bankruptcy of Enron in late 2001.

Section C then surveys the system of civil liability that has developed chiefly under the antifraud rules of the federal securities laws (including most notably Rule 10b-5) to enforce this disclosure obligation. Finally, Sec. D covers the special topic of insider trading.

Underlying the elaborate regulatory system that closely constrains both the corporation and its insiders is the belief that the securities markets are unique. Their uniqueness arises for several reasons. First, they are the critical market in a capitalist economy that allocates scarce capital among competing users. In the wake of the 1929 stock market crash, Congress reached the understandable judgment (although a historically debatable one) that any serious disruption of the securities markets could cause a national depression.[1] In this light, the securities markets are regulated by federal law while the used car market is not (even though fraud may be more prevalent in the latter market) because public distrust of the securities markets can have serious consequences for the economy as a whole. Second, within the American economy, the problem of securities fraud is more serious than in other, comparable economies because a much greater proportion of the citizenry invest their savings in this market. Third, securities are a distinctive commodity because individual investors cannot investigate or examine them in the same manner that they can investigate other speculative investments (such as real estate or precious jewels). Thus, in the absence of obvious self-help remedies, regulation seems more justified.

Given these considerations, the twin goals of the federal securities laws have long been allocative efficiency and distributive fairness. Some tension inevitably exists between these two goals, as will be seen later when this chapter focuses on insider trading. The problem of striking a balance between the goals of efficiency and fairness arises at a variety of junctions that this chapter will examine: the nature of the corporation's disclosure obligation, the definition of the critical concept of "materiality," the scope of antifraud rules that enforce the disclosure system, and the issue of at whom disclosure should be aimed—the sophisticated market professional or the ordinary investor.

B. *THE DISCLOSURE SYSTEM*

Securities regulation is a product of industrialization, and, not surprisingly, it developed first in Great Britain toward the end of the nineteenth century.

---

1. The concern that stock market frauds could cause massive disinvestment and resulting social harm was clearly in the mind of Congress when it passed the Securities Exchange Act of 1934 (the '34 Act). Section 2(3) thereof sets forth a congressional finding that "[f]requently the prices of securities on such exchanges and markets are susceptible to manipulation and control," and §2(4) adds that "[n]ational emergencies, which produce widespread unemployment and the dislocation of trade, transportation, and industry . . . and adversely affect the general welfare, are precipitated, intensified and prolonged by manipulation and sudden and unreasonable fluctuations of security prices. . . ." Some economists have expressed skepticism as to the validity of these premises and point to empirical evidence that seems to show that the Securities Exchange Act of 1934 had little demonstrable impact either on stock prices, market volatility, or the quality of information provided. They concluded that market forces had already produced an optimal level of voluntary disclosure. George Benston, Required Disclosure and the Stock Market: An Evaluation of the Securities Exchange Act of 1934, 63 Am. Econ. Rev. 132 (1973). This "new criticism" of the federal securities laws has spawned a considerable debate; for a review, see John C. Coffee, Jr., Market Failure and the Economic Case for a Mandatory Disclosure System, 70 Va. L. Rev. 717 (1984).

On the federal level, securities regulation did not appear in the United States until the Great Depression, with the passage of the Securities Act of 1933. However, individual states began to regulate the sale of securities within their jurisdictions toward the end of the Progressive Era, beginning with a statute adopted by Kansas in 1911. These statutes were collectively called "blue sky" laws because they were intended to protect the state's citizens against fraudulent promoters who would attempt to sell gullible investors anything, including a "piece of the blue sky, itself" (in the words of the state legislator who proposed the first such statute). Today, state regulation of security issuances (discussed in Sec. B.3) continues to play a significant role in the regulatory framework, but one that is subsidiary to the federal role.

1. THE SECURITIES ACT OF 1933

Passed by Congress in the wake of the stock market crash of 1929 and during the first 100 days of President Roosevelt's New Deal, the Securities Act of 1933 (the '33 Act) was intended to achieve "truth in securities" by regulating the offering process through which corporations distribute securities to the public. Congressional hearings following the stock market crash revealed numerous instances in which high-risk and sometimes worthless securities were offered by underwriters and promoters to an uninformed public without more than minimal disclosure.

Narrow in focus, the '33 Act applies essentially to the initial distribution of securities by the issuer, underwriters, and dealers who sell these securities to the public, and not to most trading transactions between investors in the secondary market. The '33 Act borrowed its regulatory approach from Great Britain, which decades earlier had required an issuer to prepare and distribute a "prospectus" setting forth the basic facts about the issuer and the proposed offering. In Great Britain, the Companies Act of 1900 prescribed in specific detail the necessary contents of a prospectus and also subjected the corporation's directors and promoters to civil liability for any untrue statements therein without the plaintiff being required to prove any fraudulent intent on the part of these defendants. Thus, the basic strategy of the '33 Act was to create a system of mandatory affirmative disclosure — limited in scope, to be sure, to the initial distribution of securities — to supplement the preexisting negative law of fraud. The premise was that if investors were provided with all material information about the security to be offered, there would be no unfair informational advantages and the security would not be overpriced.

The '33 Act also greatly expanded on the common law's definition of actionable fraud by (1) holding the issuing corporation strictly liable for material misrepresentations or omissions in its offering documents, and (2) making those who participated in the offering (including the issuer's officers and directors) liable for the issuer's failure to disclose unless they could satisfy the burden of proving that any such material error or omission could not have been reasonably detected by them. The '33 Act's critical instrument of disclosure — the registration statement, which contains the prospectus that must be distributed to potential investors — was subjected to the review of a governmental agency (originally the Federal Trade Commission but, since 1934, the SEC). In practice, a registration statement becomes "effective" only with the consent of the SEC. This requirement of prior administrative approval was a departure from the English system, which did not create an administrative agency.

The '33 Act imposes strict liability on the corporate issuer for material misstatements or omissions, but only a form of negligence liability on secondary participants (including all members of the corporation's board of directors, its underwriters, and its accountants). The purpose of this difference is to incentivize the secondary participants to search for misstatements and omissions. To avoid liability if there are material omissions or misrepresentations in the registration statement, the secondary participants must prove that they had exercised "due diligence" in the preparation of the registration statement. Put simply, the strategy of the '33 Act was to threaten these secondary participants with high liability in order to compel closer inspection and monitoring by them of the registration statement.[2] Because the '33 Act effectively shifts the burden of proof on the issue of negligence from the plaintiff to the defendant, much of the actual work of corporate lawyers involved in public offerings consists of laying the groundwork so that individual defendants can later raise the '33 Act's "due diligence" defense if the stock price declines after the offering and they are sued.

2. THE SECURITIES EXCHANGE ACT OF 1934

In contrast to the '33 Act, which established an episodic disclosure system triggered by the offering or sale of securities to the public, the Securities Exchange Act of 1934 (the '34 Act) created a continuous disclosure system. As a generalization, it is often said that the '33 Act registers securities, while the '34 Act registers companies. More accurately, while the '33 Act focuses on the primary market (i.e., the process of distribution by the issuer through underwriters to investors), the '34 Act regulates the secondary market (i.e., trading activity among investors, either on an exchange or among securities dealers operating today through a computerized link-up).

A corporation becomes subject to the '34 Act's continuous disclosure system based on its size and the dispersion of its stock ownership. Specifically, a corporation is required to enter the '34 Act's continuous disclosure system if

(1) it lists its securities on a national securities exchange (§12(b));
(2) any class of its equity securities is held of record by at least 500 persons and the corporation has gross assets over a specified level (currently $10,000,000) (§12(g)); or
(3) the corporation files a '33 Act registration statement that becomes effective (§15(d)).

Each of these events triggers an obligation on the part of the issuer to register with the SEC and thereafter become a "reporting company" that must file periodic

---

2. This form of legal strategy, which imposes a duty on third parties — here, the accountants, directors, and underwriters of the issuer — to prevent misconduct by persons that they are required to monitor (here, the issuer and any selling shareholders), has been called "gatekeeper liability" by one commentator, who argues that it is often a more efficient legal strategy than alternative techniques that focus either on the primary individual wrongdoer or on the corporation as an entity. See Reinier Kraakman, Corporate Liability Strategies and the Costs of Legal Controls, 93 Yale L.J. 857 (1984). The argument is essentially that these secondary participants are "repeat players" who have less to gain from misconduct and so are more easily deterred.

reports under §13 of the '34 Act. The most important of these periodic reports is the annual report on Form 10-K. This report must contain audited financial statements as well as a detailed description of the corporation, including percentage break-downs of its various lines of business. In addition, an issuer must file quarterly reports on Form 10-Q, containing unaudited financial information, for each of the corporation's first three quarters. Finally, reports of certain material developments must be filed on Form 8-K within (in most cases) four business days after the occurrence of the event. In combination, these three sets of reports mean that a publicly held corporation inescapably exists in a legal environment of mandatory public disclosure where rapid public disclosure of ongoing events is required.

The disclosure requirements of the '34 Act are distinctive in other respects as well. First, the periodic reports do not have to be distributed to investors or share-holders, but are filed with the SEC, where they will be studied by securities ana-lysts and other professional traders. Second, these disclosure documents are not aimed at the ordinary investor. Rather, they are fact-laden, highly technical, and quantitative documents that generally make little attempt to provide background information or to employ a narrative style that makes the information accessible to the typical shareholder. The underlying premise is that the information contained in them will reach and benefit the average investor only through a "filtration" process, because experts will sift, process, and verify this information. The average investor thereby benefits to the extent that the market price is kept accurate through rapid adjustments to the disclosure of new information. In contrast to the '33 Act — which insists that its disclosure document (the prospectus) be dis-tributed to each prospective investor to facilitate an informed, individual investment decision — the '34 Act does not assume that most investors can digest, or even react in a timely fashion to, information contained in its reports. Instead, its premise is that an informed market can protect investors even when they cannot protect themselves. Put differently, while the '33 Act attempts to place the pro-spective investor on an equal footing with the insider with regard to primary distributions, the '34 Act concentrates on enhancing the market's efficiency by informing the professional investor.

Disclosures required by the '34 Act are not, however, exclusively targeted at the professional investor or securities analyst. As next discussed, the SEC has devel-oped the concept of a "basic information package," consisting of certain essential financial information and a qualitative discussion of recent performance and known events and uncertainties likely to impact future performance (known as "Management's Discussion and Analysis of Financial Condition and Results of Operations" or "MD&A"). The MD&A has become the principal vehicle by which "soft" or "forward-looking" information (e.g., projections of future earnings, pre-dictions about when key new products will become market ready, or estimates of the adverse impact on future earnings of currency fluctuations or a recession in a given foreign country) reaches investors. Although the SEC does not require cor-porations to make projections of future earnings, it does require that the MD&A estimate the impact of "known trends or uncertainties" upon future earnings and the corporation's capital resources. The difference between this requirement and a requirement of mandatory projections can often be a subtle one.

The SEC requires a public corporation to include its basic information package (including the MD&A) in the annual report mailed by "reporting" companies to their shareholders. The SEC's authority for this requirement comes from its power to regulate the proxy statement, which is discussed in Chapter VI. Under Rule 14a-3, the SEC requires "reporting" companies to accompany or precede the mailing of their proxy statement with an annual report that contains audited financial information covering a two-year period, plus the MD&A. As a result, a summarized version of '34 Act data does eventually reach most shareholders.

The SEC has made '34 Act filings even more accessible to brokers and investors through the development of an online computer network known as EDGAR (an acronym for Electronic Data Gathering, Analysis, and Retrieval), which links registrants directly with broker-dealers and institutional users. EDGAR enables issuers to file and update their periodic reports under the '34 Act by entering the data directly into the EDGAR system (rather than by filing it manually with the SEC), thereby giving participating broker-dealers and other users immediate access to it.

3. "BLUE SKY" REGULATION

Every state has some form of legislation regulating the sale of securities. Collectively known as "blue sky" laws,[3] these statutes antedated the enactment of the federal securities laws. Because of inadequate administration or inadequate coverage, they were ineffective in stemming the tide of securities frauds that gave rise to federal securities regulation. Still, §18 of the '33 Act preserves the jurisdiction of state securities commissions. Thus, a corporation that proposes to issue new shares may be required to comply with both the prospectus requirements of federal law and the blue sky laws of those states in which the shares are to be sold.

Blue sky statutes have followed three basic regulatory approaches: (1) many impose state licensing requirements on brokers, dealers, salespeople, and investment advisers; (2) most contain provisions prohibiting fraudulent practices; and (3) most require state registration of the securities to be sold in-state. The statutes have varied widely from state to state, not only as to their philosophy of regulation but also, for example, as to the standards and documentation applicable to securities registration. A degree of uniformity was brought about by the introduction of the Uniform Securities Act, which was adopted in 1956 and most recently revised in 2002. A majority of the states have adopted one version or the other of this statute (but New York and California each have their own very different statute).

While the federal system of securities regulation is based primarily on a philosophy of disclosure, some state blue sky laws provide for review, by a commission or administrator, of the merits of a particular securities issue. This "merit review" focuses on whether the offering is too risky to be marketed to investors in that jurisdiction and on whether insiders appear to be making unfair or excessive profits. For example, some states may restrict the amount of stock that can be

---

3. An early account of the origins of the term is reported in Louis Loss & Edward Cowett, Blue Sky Law 7 n.22 (1958): "'The State of Kansas, most wonderfully prolific and rich in farming products, has a large proportion of agriculturists not versed in ordinary business methods. The State was the hunting ground of promoters of fraudulent enterprises; in fact their frauds became so barefaced that it was stated that they would sell building lots in the blue sky in fee simple. Metonymically they became known as blue sky merchants, and the legislation intended to prevent their frauds was called Blue Sky Law.' Mulvey, Blue Sky Law, 36 Can. L.J. 37 (1916)." The first blue sky law in the United States was enacted in Kansas in 1911.

sold at a discounted price below the public offering price (so-called cheap stock or promotional stock) to promoters and insiders in the belief that they are unfairly exploiting their position. Other tests relate to options and warrants, insider deals, fairness of the offering price, and limits on underwriting expenses.

This form of "merits" review has long provoked a continuing controversy over the need for regulatory paternalism — once full disclosure has been made to investors. Issuers also questioned the continuing need for separate state and federal regulatory systems and objected to the expense and delay of filing in 50 states, plus the uncertainty created by the possibility that some state might raise objections even though the issuer had fully satisfied the SEC. In a deregulatory mood, Congress heeded these critics in 1996 by enacting the National Securities Markets Improvement Act of 1996 ("NSMIA"). NSMIA exempts all "covered securities" from state registration and other "blue sky" requirements.[4] "Covered securities" were defined as securities traded on the New York Stock Exchange, the American Stock Exchange, the national market system of Nasdaq, and any other exchanges approved by the SEC. As a result, only smaller issuers and most initial public offerings are now subject to "blue sky" registration requirements. States, however, did retain the right to sue for fraud in all cases.

In 1998 Congress further pruned the reach of the blue sky laws by preempting any private cause of action under state law for securities fraud, whether based on the common law or any state statute. This legislation, known as the Securities Litigation Uniform Standards Act of 1998 (SLUSA), was motivated by a migration of securities class actions to state courts in response to restrictive legislation passed by Congress in 1995 and is discussed later in this chapter. Essentially, it applies only to class actions or certain consolidated or multiple-party proceedings that resemble a class action. Thus, an individual investor can still sue in state or federal court based on a "blue sky" cause of action. Also, this preemption affects only "covered securities," which are again basically defined as securities traded on a national securities exchange. Again, public enforcement was not restricted, and thus state agencies can still sue for fraud in all cases.

As a result of these two statutes, blue sky law is now largely focused on the smaller issuer who does not trade on a national securities exchange and on certain specific transactions (such as takeovers and squeeze-out mergers) that were specifically exempted.

4. DISCLOSURE REQUIREMENTS OF SELF-REGULATORY ORGANIZATIONS

Corporations listed on the New York Stock Exchange (NYSE), the American Stock Exchange (ASE), or Nasdaq (which was originally an acronym for the National Association of Securities Dealers Automated Quotation System) have an affirmative duty under their listing agreements with these organizations to disclose material information promptly to the public. Because almost any "reporting company" whose securities are actively traded will be listed with one of these self-regulatory organizations, their rules significantly shape the disclosure obligations of the publicly

---

4. NSMIA added a new Section 18 ("Exemption from State Regulation of Securities Offerings") to the Securities Act of 1933.

held corporation. Unlike the '34 Act, which requires periodic reports, these rules mandate prompt disclosure of material information on a continuing basis. For example, NYSE Listed Company Manual §202.05 ("Timely Disclosure of Material News Developments") provides:

> A listed company is expected to release quickly to the public any news or information which might reasonably be expected to materially affect the market for its securities. This is one of the most important and fundamental purposes of the listing agreement which the company enters into with the Exchange.
>
> A listed company should also act promptly to dispel unfounded rumors which result in unusual market activity or price variations.

Both the ASE and Nasdaq have essentially similar rules, independent of the SEC's periodic reporting requirements, that also require the prompt disclosure of material information.

Stock exchange rules, however, permit the issuer to delay disclosure for legitimate business reasons. NYSE Listed Company Manual §202.01 ("Internal Handling of Confidential Corporate Matters") sets the following guidelines with respect to mergers and similar important events:

> Negotiations leading to mergers and acquisitions, stock splits, the making of arrangements preparatory to an exchange or tender offer, changes in dividend rates or earnings, calls for redemption, and new contracts, products, or discoveries are the type of developments where the risk of untimely and inadvertent disclosure of corporate plans are most likely to occur. Frequently, these matters require extensive discussion and study by corporate officials before final decisions can be made. Accordingly, extreme care must be used in order to keep the information on a confidential basis.
>
> Where it is possible to confine formal or informal discussions to a small group of the top management of the company or companies involved, and their individual confidential advisors, where adequate security can be maintained, premature public announcement may properly be avoided. In this regard, the market action of a company's securities should be closely watched at a time when consideration is being given to important corporate matters. If unusual market activity should arise, the company should be prepared to make an immediate public announcement of the matter.
>
> At some point it usually becomes necessary to involve other persons to conduct preliminary studies or assist in other preparations for contemplated transactions, e.g., business appraisals, tentative financing arrangements, attitude of large outside holders, availability of major blocks of stock, engineering studies and market analyses and surveys. Experience has shown that maintaining security at this point is virtually impossible. Accordingly, fairness requires that the company make an immediate public announcement as soon as disclosures relating to such important matters are made to outsiders.

Consider in light of this NYSE policy the position of a general counsel to a corporation whose board has just tentatively decided to merge with another larger corporation but has adjourned final action for two weeks while various details of largely secondary importance are worked out. Must counsel issue an immediate press release? Assume that several dozen persons (directors, key officers, lawyers, and investment bankers) are aware of the board's de facto decision. What must be done to comply with the NYSE policy?[5] What if he fears that a premature announcement will jeopardize the merger's consummation? See Basic, Inc. v. Levinson, page 312 infra.

A critical question about these stock exchange rules involves what sanctions, if any, exist for their violation. Clearly, an exchange could suspend trading in an issuer's securities until a corrective statement was issued, or it could even delist the company (although instances of the latter sanction have been rare). To date, courts have almost always rejected claims by private investors that they have any private right of action with respect to stock exchange rules relating to the timing of disclosure. In State Teachers Retirement Board v. Fluor Corp., 654 F.2d 843 (2d Cir. 1981), the Second Circuit specifically rejected any such private right of action for violation of the NYSE's rules on prompt disclosure of material corporate news on the ground that this area was already extensively regulated by Congress and the SEC. However, legal standing may still sometimes be obtained even though a private cause of action for damages is not authorized. For example, in Norlin Corp. v. Rooney, Pace, Inc., 744 F.2d 255, 267-269 (2d Cir. 1984), the Second Circuit found that a prospective delisting for violation of an NYSE rule threatened irreparable injury to shareholders that justified a preliminary injunction in a derivative action against the conduct that would have caused the delisting by the NYSE. Another largely unexplored possibility is that shareholders could be seen as third-party beneficiaries to the listing contract between the exchange and the corporation, so that they could sue to enforce the exchange's rules.

5. WHEN DOES THE DISCLOSURE OBLIGATION ARISE?

Does a publicly held corporation have any general obligation under federal law to make affirmative disclosure of material developments? Or is its obligation simply not to lie or tell misleading half-truths — that is, not to make statements containing either material misstatements or omissions? Obviously, once the time arrives at which the corporation must file its quarterly report on Form 10-Q or its annual report on Form 10-K, the question is resolved, and full disclosure must be made. But, within these mandatory reporting frames, a recurrent legal issue arises over the extent of managerial discretion to delay the release of information on the grounds that either (1) it was still too speculative to be ripe for disclosure, or (2) legitimate corporate interests justified delaying disclosure. Although the stock

---

5. The NYSE's rules require listed companies to clarify rumors and give reasons for unusual market activity. NYSE Listed Company Manual §202.03 ("Dealing with Rumors or Unusual Market Activity") provides:

> The market activity of a company's securities should be closely watched at a time when consideration is being given to significant corporate matters. If rumors or unusual market activity indicate that information on impending developments has leaked out, a frank and explicit announcement is clearly required. If rumors are in fact false or inaccurate, they should be promptly denied or clarified. A statement to the effect that the company knows of no corporate developments to account for the unusual market activity can have a salutary effect. . . . If rumors are correct or there are developments, an immediate candid statement to the public as to the state of negotiations or of development of corporate plans in the rumored area must be made directly and openly. Such statements are essential despite the business inconvenience which may be caused and even though the matter may not as yet have been presented to the company's Board of Directors for consideration.

exchange rules that were just surveyed require prompt disclosure, they do not give rise to civil liability. The relevant body of law that principally governs a corporation's exposure to civil liability has developed under Rule 10b-5.[6] While the elements of a cause of action under Rule 10b-5 are discussed later in this chapter, in Sec. C, the focus in the following cases is on the circumstances that necessitate disclosure. In overview, the difficulty inherent in defining these circumstances stems from the fact that premature disclosure can often do more harm than good. It may misinform the market and may injure those shareholders who buy or sell based on such disclosure (who might then seek damages from the corporation under liability provisions discussed later). Other adverse consequences can also follow if the corporation makes only a vague and imprecise statement that its sales or earnings have declined: Banks may suspend lines of credit, customers may seek other sources of supply, suppliers may insist on immediate payment, etc. On the other hand, few managements like to disclose negative information, and they have obvious reasons to rationalize delay.

Financial Industrial Fund, Inc. v. McDonnell Douglas Corp.
474 F.2d 514 (10th Cir. 1973)

PER CURIAM: [Plaintiff, a mutual fund, purchased 80,000 shares of McDonnell Douglas stock in the open market two days before defendant announced a sharp earnings decline. The plaintiff alleged that public disclosure of this decline had been delayed improperly in order that the defendant corporation could proceed with a planned public offering of its debentures to other persons. On this evidence, the jury awarded damages of $712,500.] The appeal presents no issues concerned with any direct purchase and sale of stock between Financial Industrial Fund and Douglas, nor any issue of inside dealing or of "tipping" by Douglas. The plaintiff is in the position of any purchaser in the open market, and the information with which the case is concerned was public information. The plaintiff being a mutual fund is in the business of making money by the investment of the money of others, and as such holds itself out as an expert or professional as to investments. . . .

The record shows that on May 27, 1966, the president of Douglas was advised that the Aircraft Division of the company was experiencing delays in deliveries by its suppliers of components, and that the work force was not as efficient as had been expected. A group of corporate officials was sent to determine the extent of the problems, and it reported back on May 31st that the delivery of some eighteen airplanes in the process of assembly could not be made until the next fiscal year. On June 1st an announcement of the delay was made to the press. This concluded with a statement that earnings for the fiscal year would be adversely affected.

The company had just completed the call of existing convertible debentures, most of which were converted to common stock as the prevailing market price of the stock made it favorable for the holders to so convert. On June 1st the directors approved the issuance of new debentures with Merrill Lynch as the

---

6. Rule 10b-5, adopted under §10(b) of the '34 Act, basically proscribes omissions or misstatements of a material fact in connection with the purchase or sale of a security. The full text of the rule is set forth at page **000__** infra.

underwriter. In connection therewith, a preliminary prospectus was soon prepared and issued (June 7th) which showed the first five months' earnings (December through April) to be slightly below the same period for the prior fiscal year. The quarterly financial analysis was underway as was an evaluation of the stages of completion of some 381 airplanes in the process of manufacture.

Profit figures from the Aircraft Division were given on June 14th to an officer in the comptroller's office who was assembling the data for regular financial reports. These figures showed a loss for the division of several million dollars for the month of May. This official and the company comptroller went the next day to discuss the matter further at the Aircraft Division and decided to call in the company's outside auditors for consultation as to whether inventory revaluations should be made under the circumstances. On June 17th the president of Douglas sent fifty to seventy engineering, estimating, and accounting officials to the Aircraft Division to investigate the situation. This group reported back on June 20th that the expected six months earnings figure for the entire company would be about forty-nine cents. Meetings with the outside auditors to consider the finding were held on the next day and the day following. After the second meeting on June 22nd it was decided that a substantial inventory write-down was required in view of the losses, and this would reduce the six months earnings figure from the forty-nine cents previously reported to the president to a figure of twelve cents. The president then on the next day ordered a press release to be prepared relating to the earnings so determined for the past six months. This was done the same day in time to be made public before the opening of the New York Stock Exchange on June 24th. The market price of Douglas stock declined $2.75 per share to $76.00 on the 24th. By the time plaintiff had sold its shares of Douglas in question (July 8th), the stock closed at $64.50 per share. . . .

The case before us does not present any significant new issues except those which arise from the different nature of the event upon which the cause of action is based. Here the plaintiff complains that the special earnings report of defendant should have been issued some days before it was. We are thus concerned only with the issue of the timing of the special statement on earnings. This is silence at the time of the occurrence of the operative events in the corporation's business until the statement was issued, and more particularly the issue becomes whether the silence of defendant at the date or dates of the stock purchases by plaintiff here give rise to a cause of action under Rule 10b-5. This matter of silence is somewhat different from instances where a financial or other type of statement is released and the issue is whether the statement is correct, because in the latter there is a reasonably direct way to test the statements against the facts as they existed, all of which involve objective matters. However, where the silence is at issue, the proof must be directed to the corporate and individual reactions to the facts showing a change in corporate circumstances, and how the decision was reached to issue a statement at a particular time. In these considerations the evidence, as indicated in this record, is well within the decisional processes of the corporate financial specialists and corporate management. The silence or the timing are matters which require the court or the jury to examine how these decisions were arrived at by using many subjective factors and by excluding hindsight.

Thus was the management correct in here evaluating the significance of the slow-down in the aircraft manufacturing process as to extent and impact on earnings during a particular period so as to require the issuance of a special earnings statement? Secondly, was this process conducted with reasonable dispatch considering the need to ascertain the details as to the particular problems, to relate them to other earnings, and to arrive at a conclusion with confidence that the statement when issued would be correct? These factors take us so much farther within the corporate decisional processes than do misleading statements actually issued.

Since the timing decision is one concerned fundamentally and almost exclusively with matters of discretion and the exercise of business judgment, it is appropriate to consider the rationale of the "business judgment" rule. . . . The reason for the rule is stated to be in order to make the corporation function effectively, those having management responsibility must have the freedom to make in good faith the many necessary decisions quickly and finally without the impairment of having to be liable for an honest error in judgment. The rule itself, of course, is not directly applicable, and it is not to be so applied here, but the reasons for it are considered as extended to the corporate entity. The Second Circuit in Securities & Exchange Comm'n v. Texas Gulf Sulphur Co., 401 F.2d 833 (2d Cir.), said in a footnote that the *timing* of the disclosure of material facts ". . . is a matter for the business judgment of the corporate officers entrusted with the management of the corporation within the affirmative disclosure requirements promulgated by the exchanges and by the SEC." The court there held a valid corporate purpose was served by withholding information from the public on the discovery of ore in a test drilling, thus a matter within the "business judgment" of management. Thus considering the factors compelled to be evaluated in this silence case as revealed in the record before us, we must hold that the decision of the officers or directors, and the corporate decision of the defendant to issue an earnings statement on other than the customary date for such statements, and the timing of such statement was a matter of discretion.

On another point, we held in Mitchell v. Texas Gulf Sulphur Co., 446 F.2d 90 (10th Cir.), that the information about which the issues revolve must be "available and ripe for publication" before there commences a duty to disclose. To be ripe under this requirement, the contents must be verified sufficiently to permit the officers and directors to have full confidence in their accuracy. It also means, as used by the Second Circuit, that there is no valid corporate purpose which dictates the information be not disclosed. As to the verification of the date aspect, the hazards which arise from an erroneous statement are apparent, especially when it has not been carefully prepared and tested. It is equally obvious that an undue delay not in good faith, in revealing facts, can be deceptive, misleading, or a device to defraud under Rule 10b-5. . . .

It is apparent that a decline in earnings at the pertinent time would cause problems in connection with both issues of debentures for Douglas and more so for Merrill Lynch. The record shows there existed as to Douglas a strong motive for it to withhold information as to a decline in earnings. . . . In the setting of this motion, the record shows: the known slowdown in the assembly of planes with delays expected in the finished product; the investigation, and the public announcement of May 1st of the slowdown with the warning that it would ". . . have an adverse effect on earnings" for the current period. . . . However, there is nothing in the record other than speculation that the extent of the May loss could have been determined and translated into figures at an earlier date to develop a statement ripe for publication. The record thus shows without contradiction as to the defendant McDonnell Douglas as a matter of law that there was exercised good faith and due diligence in the ascertainment, the verification, and the publication of the serious reversal of earnings in May. . . .

It is apparent that an earnings statement issued by a corporation at any but the expected time which shows any substantial change is bad news for someone who had been recently in or out of a fluctuating market.

To prevail the plaintiff in this silence case had the burden of proof to establish that it exercised due care in making its stock purchase, that the defendant failed to issue the special earnings statement when sufficient information was available for an accurate release (or could have been collected by the exercise of due diligence), and to show there existed a duty owed by the defendant to the plaintiff to so disclose as to do otherwise would be a violation of Rule 10b-5, and upon inaction under such showing plaintiff relied to its detriment. The defendant as a separate defense could show either good faith or the exercise of good business judgment in its acts or inaction. The evaluation of the significance of the change in defendant's earnings as it might affect the corporation, its stockholders, or persons considering the purchase of stock, called for the exercise of discretion, and upon a showing of the exercise of due care in the gathering and consideration of the facts, a presumption arose that the evaluation made was in the exercise of good business judgment although subsequent events might show the decision to have been in error. . . .

---

1. *"Available and ripe for publication."* A key statement in *Financial Industrial Fund* is that the corporation is entitled to withhold disclosure (and indeed should do so) until information "ripens." Ripeness, the court added, requires that the data "be verified sufficiently to permit the officers and directors to have full confidence in their accuracy." Information is not ripe if a "valid corporate purpose" exists for withholding disclosure. Other decisions have also recognized that premature disclosure of still speculative information may have adverse consequences for the corporation or subject it to liability from those who acted on its inaccurate disclosures. See, e.g., Segal v. Coburn Corp. of America, [1973 Transfer Binder] Fed. Sec. L. Rep. (CCH) ¶ 94, 002 (E.D.N.Y. 1973) (corporation did not have to disclose decision to withdraw from a line of business where public disclosure "might . . . have impaired the collectibility of the paper, disturbed credit relations, and forced a precipitous liquidation of the business"); Reiss v. Pan American World Airways, Inc., 711 F.2d 11, 14 (2d Cir. 1983) (corporation need not disclose still "fluid" merger negotiations where disclosure would have subjected corporation to securities fraud actions had the merger collapsed).

2. *The business judgment standard.* Another important statement made in *Financial Industrial Fund* is that "upon a showing of the exercise of due care in the gathering and consideration of the facts, a presumption arose that the evaluation made was in the exercise of good business judgment." In an earlier famous footnote in SEC v. Texas Gulf Sulphur Co., 401 F.2d 833, 850 n.12 (2d Cir. 1968) (en banc), the Second Circuit also indicated that the timing of disclosure was "a matter for the business judgment of the corporate officers entrusted with the management of the corporation within the affirmative disclosure requirements promulgated by the exchanges and by the SEC." Do these statements mean that the corporation may decline to disclose even "ripe" information if management or the board has made a business judgment decision to do so? See Basic, Inc. v. Levinson,

below. Also, comforting as the business judgment rule is to management, it has its well-known limits. For example, what if there is evidence that some insiders are trading (which might be shown by market rumors or unusual trading activity suggesting that material information has leaked out)? Classically, the business judgment rule does not apply when the decisionmaker is subject to a conflict of interest. Some decisions have suggested that, once tipping has occurred, a special duty may arise requiring the corporation to disclose to the market generally. Schlanger v. Four-Phase Systems, Inc., 582 F. Supp. 128 (S.D.N.Y. 1984). The SEC has also taken this position. See In re Sharon Steel Corp., [1981-1982 Transfer Binder] Fed. Sec. L. Rep. (CCH) ¶ 83, 049 (1981). Cf. Elkind v. Liggett & Myers, Inc., 635 F.2d 156, 165 (2d Cir. 1980).

Basic, Inc. v. Levinson
485 U.S. 224 (1988)

JUSTICE BLACKMUN delivered the opinion of the Court.

[For two years prior to the merger of Combustion Engineering, Inc. and Basic, Inc. in December 1978, the two companies engaged in extensive private merger negotiations. During this period, Basic made three public statements denying that any merger negotiations were taking place or that it knew of any corporate developments that would account for the heavy trading in its stock. Plaintiffs, former shareholders in Basic who sold their stock between Basic's first public denial of the merger negotiations and a date just prior to the public announcement of the merger, filed suit on the theory that these statements violated Rule 10b-5. The District Court granted summary judgment for the defendants on the theory that preliminary merger negotiations were immaterial as a matter of law because the negotiations between the two companies were not "destined, with reasonable certainty, to result in a merger agreement in principle." The Court of Appeals reversed, holding that even merger discussions that might not have been otherwise material became so as a result of a statement denying their existence.] The 1934 Act was designed to protect investors against manipulation of stock prices. See S. Rep. No. 792, 73rd Cong., 2d Sess., 1-5 (1934). Underlying the adoption of extensive disclosure requirements was a legislative philosophy: "There cannot be honest markets without honest publicity. Manipulation and dishonest practices of the market place thrive upon mystery and secrecy." H.R. Rep. No. 1383, 73d Cong., 2nd Sess., 11 (1934). This Court "repeatedly has described the 'fundamental purpose' of the Act as implementing a 'philosophy of full disclosure.'" Santa Fe Industries, Inc. v. Green, 430 U.S. 462, 477-478 (1977), quoting SEC v. Capital Gains Research Bureau, Inc., 375 U.S. 180, 186 (1963). . . .

The Court . . . explicitly has defined a standard of materiality under the securities laws, see TSC Industries, Inc. v. Northway, Inc., 426 U.S. 438 (1976), concluding in the proxy-solicitation context that "[a]n omitted fact is material if there is a substantial likelihood that a reasonable shareholder would consider it important in deciding how to vote." Id. at 449. Acknowledging that certain information concerning corporate developments could well be of "dubious significance," id., at 448, the Court was careful not to set too low a standard of materiality; it was concerned that a minimal standard might bring an overabundance of information within its reach, and lead management "simply to bury the shareholders in an avalanche of trivial information — a result that is hardly conducive to informed decisionmaking." Id., at 448-449. It further explained that to fulfill the materiality requirement "there must be a substantial likelihood that the disclosure of the omitted fact would have been viewed by the reasonable investor as having significantly altered the 'total mix' of information made available." Id., at 449. We now expressly adopt the *TSC Industries* standard of materiality for the §10(b) and Rule 10b-5 context.

The application of this materiality standard to preliminary merger discussions is not self-evident. Where the impact of the corporate development on the target's fortune is certain and clear, the *TSC Industries* materiality definition admits straightforward application. Where, on the other hand, the event is contingent or speculative in nature, it is difficult to ascertain whether the "reasonable investor" would have considered the omitted information significant at the time. Merger negotiations, because of the ever-present possibility that the contemplated transaction will not be effectuated, fall into the latter category.

Petitioners urge upon us a Third Circuit test for resolving this difficulty.[10] Under this approach, preliminary merger discussions do not become material until "agreement-in-principle" as to the price and structure of the transaction has been reached between the would-be merger partners. See Greenfield v. Heublein, Inc., 742 F.2d 751, 757 (CA3 1984). . . . By definition, then, information concerning any negotiations not yet at the agreement-in-principle stage could be withheld or even misrepresented, without a violation of Rule 10b-5.

Three rationales have been offered in support of the "agreement-in-principle" test. The first derives from the concern expressed in *TSC Industries* that an investor not be overwhelmed by excessively detailed and trivial information, and focuses on the substantial risk that preliminary merger discussions may collapse: because such discussions are inherently tentative, disclosure of their existence could mislead investors and foster false optimism. See Greenfield v. Heublein, Inc., 742 F.2d, at 756; Reiss v. Pan American World Airways, Inc., 711 F.2d 11, 14 (CA2 1983). The other two justifications for the agreement-in-principle standard are based on management concerns: because the requirement of "agreement-in-principle" limits the scope of disclosure obligations, it helps preserve the confidentiality of merger discussions where earlier disclosure might prejudice the negotiations; and the test also provides a usable, bright-line rule for determining when disclosure must be made. See Greenfield v. Heublein, Inc., 742 F.2d, at 757; Flamm v. Eberstadt, 814 F.2d 1169, 1176-1178 (CA7 1987). . . .

None of these policy-based rationales, however, purports to explain why drawing the line at agreement-in-principle reflects the significance of the information upon the investor's decision. The first rationale, and the only one connected to the

---

10. See Staffin v. Greenberg, 672 F.2d 1196, 1207 (3d Cir. 1982) (defining duty to disclose existence of ongoing merger negotiations as triggered when agreement-in-principle is reached); Greenfield v. Heublein, Inc., 742 F.2d 751 (CA3 1984) (applying agreement-in-principle test to materiality inquiry). Citing *Staffin*, the United States Court of Appeals for the Second Circuit has rejected a claim that defendant was under an obligation to disclose various events related to merger negotiations. Reiss v. Pan American World Airways, Inc., 711 F.2d 11, 13-14 (CA2 1983). The Seventh Circuit recently endorsed the agreement-in-principle test of materiality. See Flamm v. Eberstadt, 814 F.2d 1169, 1174-1179 (CA7 1987) (describing agreement-in-principle as an agreement on price and structure). In some of these cases it is unclear whether the court based its decision on a finding that no duty arose to reveal the existence of negotiations, or whether it concluded that the negotiations were immaterial under an interpretation of the opinion in TSC Industries, Inc. v. Northway, Inc., supra.

concerns expressed in *TSC Industries*, stands soundly rejected, even by a Court of Appeals that otherwise has accepted the wisdom of the agreement-in-principle test. "It assumes that investors are nitwits, unable to appreciate — even when told — that mergers are risky propositions up until the closing." Flamm v. Eberstadt, 814 F.2d, at 1175. Disclosure, and not paternalistic withholding of accurate information, is the policy chosen and expressed by Congress. . . . The role of the materiality requirement is not to "attribute to investors a child-like simplicity, an inability to grasp the probabilistic significance of negotiations," Flamm v. Eberstadt, 814 F.2d, at 1175, but to filter out essentially useless information that a reasonable investor would not consider significant, even as part of a larger "mix" of factors to consider in making his investment decision. TSC Industries, Inc. v. Northway, Inc., 426 U.S., at 448-449.

The second rationale, the importance of secrecy during the early stages of merger discussions, also seems irrelevant to an assessment whether their existence is significant to the trading decision of a reasonable investor. To avoid a "bidding war" over its target, an acquiring firm often will insist that negotiations remain confidential, see, e.g., In re Carnation Co., Exchange Act Release No. 22214, 33 SEC Docket 1025 (1985), and at least one Court of Appeals has stated that "silence pending settlement of the price and structure of a deal is beneficial to most investors, most of the time." Flamm v. Eberstadt, 814 F.2d, at 1177.[11]

We need not ascertain, however, whether secrecy necessarily maximizes shareholders' wealth — although we note that the proposition is at least disputed as a matter of theory and empirical research[12] for this case does not concern the *timing* of a disclosure; it concerns only its accuracy and completeness.[13] We face here the narrow question whether information concerning the existence and status of preliminary merger discussions is significant to the reasonable investor's trading decision. Arguments based on the premise that some disclosure would be "premature" in a sense are more properly considered under the rubric of an issuer's duty to disclose. The "secrecy" rationale is simply inapposite to the definition of materiality.

The final justification offered in support of the agreement-in-principle test seems to be directed solely at the comfort of corporate managers. A bright-line rule indeed is easier to follow than a standard that requires the exercise of judgment in the light of all the circumstances. But ease of application alone is not an excuse for ignoring the purposes of the securities acts and Congress' policy decisions. Any approach that designates a single fact or occurrence as always determinative of an inherently fact-specific finding such as materiality, must necessarily be over- or

---

11. Reasoning backwards from a goal of economic efficiency, that Court of Appeals stated: "Rule 10b-5 is about fraud, after all, and it is not fraudulent to conduct business in a way that makes investors better off. . . ." Flamm v. Eberstadt, 814 F.2d at 1177.

12. See, e.g., Brown, Corporate Secrecy, the Federal Securities Laws, and the Disclosure of Ongoing Negotiations, 36 Cath. U. L. Rev. 93, 145-155 (1986); Bebchuk, The Case for Facilitating Competing Tender Offers, 94 Harv. L. Rev. 1028 (1982); Flamm v. Eberstadt, 814 F.2d at 1177, n.2 (citing scholarly debate). See also In re Carnation Co., Exchange Act Release No. 22214, 33 SEC Docket 1025, 1030 (1985) ("The importance of accurate and complete issuer disclosure to the integrity of the securities markets cannot be overemphasized. To the extent that investors cannot rely upon the accuracy and completeness of issuer statements, they will be less likely to invest, thereby reducing the liquidity of the securities markets to the detriment of investors and issuers alike.").

13. See SEC v. Texas Gulf Sulphur Co., 401 F.2d 833, 862 (CA2 1968) (en banc) ("Rule 10b-5 is violated whenever assertions are made, as here, in a manner reasonably calculated to influence the investing public . . . if such assertions are false or misleading or are so incomplete as to mislead. . . .").

underinclusive. In *TSC Industries* this Court explained: "The determination [of materiality] requires delicate assessments of the inferences a 'reasonable shareholder' would draw from a given set of facts and the significance of those inferences to him. . . ." 426 U.S., at 450. After much study, the Advisory Committee on Corporate Disclosure cautioned the SEC against administratively confining materiality to a rigid formula.[14] Courts also would do well to heed this advice.

We therefore find no valid justification for artificially excluding from the definition of materiality information concerning merger discussions, which would otherwise be considered significant to the trading decision of a reasonable investor, merely because agreement-in-principle as to price and structure has not yet been reached by the parties or their representatives.

The Sixth Circuit explicitly rejected the agreement-in-principle test, as we do today, but in its place adopted a rule that, if taken literally, would be equally insensitive, in our view, to the distinction between materiality and the other elements of an action under Rule 10b-5:

> When a company whose stock is publicly traded makes a statement, as Basic did, that "no negotiations" are underway, and that the corporation knows of "no reason for the stock's activity," and that "management is unaware of any present or pending corporate development that would result in the abnormally heavy trading activity," information concerning ongoing acquisition discussions becomes material *by virtue of the statement denying their existence.* . . . In analyzing whether information regarding merger discussions is material such that it must be affirmatively disclosed to avoid a violation of Rule 10b-5, the discussions and their progress are the primary considerations. However, once a statement is made denying the existence of any discussions, even discussions that might not have been material in absence of the denial are material because they make the statement made untrue.

786 F.2d, at 748-749 (emphasis in original). This approach, however, fails to recognize that in order to prevail on a Rule 10b-5 claim, a plaintiff must show that the statements were *misleading* as to a *material* fact. It is not enough that a statement is false or incomplete, if the misrepresented fact is otherwise insignificant.

Even before this Court's decision in *TSC Industries*, the Second Circuit had explained the role of the materiality requirement of Rule 10b-5, with respect to contingent or speculative information or events, in a manner that gave that term meaning that is independent of the other provisions of the Rule. Under such circumstances, materiality "will depend at any given time upon a balancing of both the indicated probability that the event will occur and the anticipated magnitude of the event in light of the totality of the company activity." SEC v. Texas Gulf Sulphur Co., 401 F.2d, at 849. Interestingly, neither the Third Circuit decision adopting the agreement-in-principle test nor petitioners here take issue with this general standard. Rather, they suggest that with respect to preliminary merger

14. "Although the Committee believes that ideally it would be desirable to have absolute certainty in the application of the materiality concept, it is its view that such a goal is illusory and unrealistic. The materiality concept is judgmental in nature and it is not possible to translate this into a numerical formula. The Committee's advice to the [SEC] is to avoid this quest for certainty and to continue consideration of materiality on a case by case basis as problems are identified." Report of the Advisory Committee on Corporate Disclosure to the Securities and Exchange Commission 327 (House Committee on Interstate and Foreign Commerce, 95th Cong., 1st Sess.) (Comm. Print) (1977).

discussions, there are good reasons to draw a line at agreement on price and structure.

In a subsequent decision, the late Judge Friendly, writing for a Second Circuit panel, applied the *Texas Gulf Sulphur* probability/magnitude approach in the specific context of preliminary merger negotiations. After acknowledging that materiality is something to be determined on the basis of the particular facts of each case, he stated: "Since a merger in which it is bought out is the most important event that can occur in a small corporation's life, to wit, its death, we think that inside information, as regards a merger of this sort, can become material at an earlier stage than would be the case as regards lesser transactions — and this even though the mortality rate of mergers in such formative stages is doubtless high." SEC v. Geon Industries, Inc., 531 F.2d 39, 47-48 (CA2 1976). We agree with that analysis.[16]

Whether merger discussions in any particular case are material therefore depends on the facts. Generally, in order to assess the probability that the event will occur, a factfinder will need to look to indicia of interest in the transaction at the highest corporate levels. Without attempting to catalog all such possible factors, we note by way of example that board resolutions, instructions to investment bankers, and actual negotiations between principals or their intermediaries may serve as indicia of interest. To assess the magnitude of the transaction to the issuer of the securities allegedly manipulated, a factfinder will need to consider such facts as the size of the two corporate entities and of the potential premiums over market value. No particular event or factor short of closing the transaction need be either necessary or sufficient by itself to render merger discussions material.[17]

As we clarify today, materiality depends on the significance the reasonable investor would place on the withheld or misrepresented information.[18] The fact-specific inquiry we endorse here is consistent with the approach a number

16. The SEC in the present case endorses the highly fact-dependent probability/magnitude balancing approach of *Texas Gulf Sulphur*. It explains: "The possibility of a merger may have an immediate importance to investors in the company's securities even if no merger ultimately takes place." Brief for SEC as Amicus Curiae 10. The SEC's insights are helpful, and we accord them due deference. See TSC Industries, Inc. v. Northway, Inc., 426 U.S., 449, n.10.

17. To be actionable, of course, a statement must also be misleading. Silence, absent a duty to disclose, is not misleading under Rule 10b-5. "No comment" statements are generally the functional equivalent of silence. See In re Carnation Co., supra. See also New York Stock Exchange Listed Company Manual §202.01, reprinted in 3 CCH Fed. Sec. L. Rep. Para. 23, 515 (premature public announcement may properly be delayed for valid business purpose and where adequate security can be maintained); American Stock Exchange Company Guide §§401-405, reprinted in 3 CCH Fed. Sec. L. Rep. Para. 23, 124A-23, 124E (similar provisions).

It has been suggested that given current market practices, a "no comment" statement is tantamount to an admission that merger discussions are underway. See Flamm v. Eberstadt, 814 F.2d at 1178. That may well hold true to the extent that issuers adopt a policy of truthfully denying merger rumors when no discussions are underway, and of issuing "no comment" statements when they are in the midst of negotiations. There are, of course, other statement policies firms could adopt; we need not now advise issuers as to what kind of practice to follow, within the range permitted by law. Perhaps more importantly, we think that creating an exception to a regulatory scheme founded on a prodisclosure legislative philosophy, because complying with the regulation might be "bad for business," is a role for Congress, not this Court. . . .

18. We find no authority in the statute, the legislative history, or our previous decisions, for varying the standard of materiality depending on who brings the action or whether insiders are alleged to have profited. See, e.g., Pavlidis v. New England Patriots Football Club, Inc., 737 F.2d 1227, 1231 (CA1 1984) ("A fact does not become more material to the shareholder's decision because it is withheld by an insider or because the insider might profit by withholding it"); cf. Aaron v. SEC, 446 U.S. 680, 691 (1980) ("scienter is an element of a violation of §10(b) and Rule 10b-5, regardless of the identity of the plaintiff or the nature of the relief sought").

of courts have taken in assessing the materiality of merger negotiations.[19] Because the standard of materiality we have adopted differs from that used by both courts below, we remand the case for reconsideration of the question whether a grant of summary judgment is appropriate on this record. . . . [In the remainder of the case, the Court addressed the issue of whether each investor had to show individual reliance on Basic's statements. The Court instead accepted a substitute known as the "fraud on the market" doctrine, under which a rebuttable presumption of reliance arises when false material statements are made. See pages 384-388 infra.]

The CHIEF JUSTICE, JUSTICE SCALIA, and JUSTICE KENNEDY took no part in the consideration or decision of this case. . . .

———————————

1. *The death knell of affirmative disclosure?* Although *Basic* styles itself as a decision about materiality, its clearest message may be one written between the lines: When the defendant is not itself trading, the federal securities laws — at least under Rule 10b-5 — generally impose no affirmative duty to disclose, but only a duty not to tell material lies. In effect, the Court took an intermediate position between the Third Circuit rule that preliminary merger negotiations are always immaterial (because disclosure would be adverse to the shareholders' interests) and the Sixth Circuit view that the act of lying can make immaterial information material. Note that this position that permits silence (or a "no comment" statement) makes all the more important the position of the stock exchanges and Nasdaq. Under the NYSE rule quoted earlier, the issuer can be delisted if it refuses to answer the NYSE's request for it to explain unusual trading activity in its stock. The NYSE's recent practice appears to have been to accept "no comment" responses and to take no further action. Perhaps this is because the NYSE understands that such a response may convey a great deal of information. *Query:* What if the rumor is incorrect and no negotiations are in progress. Could a "no comment" response ever be found misleading?

———————————

We recognize that trading (and profit making) by insiders can serve as an indication of materiality, see SEC v. Texas Gulf Sulphur Co., 401 F.2d at 851; General Portland, Inc. v. LaFarge Coppee S.A., CCH Fed. Sec. L. Rep. (1982-1983 Transfer Binder) ¶ 99, 148, p.95, 455 (N.D. Tex. 1981). We are not prepared to agree, however, that "[i]n cases of the disclosure of insider information to a favored few, determination of materiality has a different aspect than when the issue is, for example, an inaccuracy in a publicly disseminated press release." SEC v. Geon Industries, Inc., 531 F.2d 39, 48 (CA2 1976). Devising two different standards of materiality, one for situations where insiders have traded in abrogation of their duty to disclose or abstain (or for that matter when any disclosure duty has been breached), and another covering affirmative misrepresentations by those under no duty to disclose (but under the ever-present duty not to mislead), would effectively collapse the materiality requirement into the analysis of defendant's disclosure duties.

19. See, e.g., SEC v. Shapiro, 494 F.2d 1301, 1306-1307 (CA2 1974) (in light of projected very substantial increase in earnings per share, negotiations material, although merger still less than probable); Holmes v. Bateson, 583 F.2d 542, 558 (CA1 1978) (merger negotiations material although they had not yet reached point of discussing terms); SEC v. Gaspar, CCH Fed. Sec. L. Rep. (1984-1985 Transfer Binder) 92, 004, pp.90, 977-90, 978 (S.D.N.Y. 1985) (merger negotiations material although they did not proceed to actual tender offer); Dungan v. Colt Industries, Inc., 532 F. Supp. 832, 837 (N.D. Ill. 1982) (fact that defendants were seriously exploring the sale of their company was material); American General Ins. Co. v. Equitable General Corp., 493 F. Supp. 721, 744-745 (E.D. Va. 1980) (merger negotiations material four months before agreement-in-principle reached). Cf. Susquehanna Corp. v. Pan American Sulphur Co., 423 F.2d 1075, 1084-1085 (CA5 1970) (holding immaterial "unilateral offer to negotiate" never acknowledged by target and repudiated two days later); Berman v. Gerber Products Co., 454 F. Supp. 1310, 1316, 1318 (W.D. Mich. 1978) (mere "overtures" immaterial).

2. *Policy issues.* On the policy level, it has been observed that "any remedy imposed against the issuer itself is indirectly imposed on all holders of its common stock, usually the most important segment of the total category of investors intended to be protected." Milton H. Cohen, "Truth in Securities" Revisited, 79 Harv. L. Rev. 1340, 1370 (1966). Similarly, others argue that "[t]he assessment of massive damages against the corporation . . . works a two-fold harm upon the consumer . . . [who] may be forced to bear significant cost increases due to the impact of the damages award upon the corporation. There is, perhaps, an additional risk that the crushing burden of liability . . . will occasionally drive the corporation out of business, depriving society of the social and economic benefits of corporate growth." Note, Liability Under Rule 10b-5 for Negligently Misleading Corporate Releases: A Proposal for the Apportionment of Losses, 122 U. Pa. L. Rev. 162, 171 (1973).

Backman v. Polaroid Corp.
910 F.2d 10 (1st Cir. 1990)

ALDRICH, J.: [In early 1978, Polaroid introduced with considerable fanfare a much-heralded instant motion picture system, known as Polavision. Polaroid projected worldwide sales of 200,000 units in 1978. In its Third Quarter Report to Stockholders in November 1978, Polaroid stressed its record earnings and sales, but briefly acknowledged that its earnings "continue to reflect substantial expenses with Polavision." Two other statements noted that Polavision expenses had also raised Polaroid's overall cost of sales. In fact, Polavision's sales were well below expectations and Polaroid had already begun to reduce production (although overall earnings for the company as a whole remained high). In early February 1979, Polaroid took a $6.8 million reserve for expenses associated with Polavision, and at approximately the same time the company's founder, Dr. Edwin Land, caused a foundation he controlled to sell 300,000 shares of Polaroid stock. In late February, Polaroid issued a press release that announced that Polavision costs substantially exceeded corresponding revenues. In response the market price of Polaroid stock fell from $49.62 to $39.87.

[Plaintiffs were purchasers of Polaroid stock or call options in the open market during the period from early January 1979 to late February 1979. They sued based on Rule 10b-5, claiming that Polaroid's failure to disclose the adverse developments with regard to Polavision inflated the market price for Polaroid shares. The jury found for plaintiffs on the issue of liability. On appeal, a divided panel of the First Circuit affirmed the district court's denial of defendant's motion for judgment n.o.v. The First Circuit then decided to hear the case *en banc*.] . . .

Duty to Update. Obviously, if a disclosure is in fact misleading when made, and the speaker thereafter learns of this, there is a duty to correct it. In Greenfield v. Heublein, Inc., 742 F.2d 751, 758 (3d Cir. 1984), *cert. denied*, 469 U.S. 1215 (1985), cited by the panel, the court called for disclosure if a prior disclosure "becomes materially misleading in light of subsequent events," a quite different duty. We may agree that, in special circumstances, a statement, correct at the time, may have a forward intent and connotation upon which parties may be expected to rely. If this is a clear meaning, and there is a change, correction, more exactly, further disclosure, may be called for. Cf. In re Phillips, 881 F.2d 1236 (3d Cir. 1989);

Wilson v. Comtech Telecommunications Corp., 648 F.2d 88 (2d Cir. 1981). The amici are concerned that this is a principle with grave dangers of abuse. Fear that statements of historical fact might be claimed to fall within it, could inhibit disclosures altogether. And what is the limit? In the present case if the shoe were on the other foot, and defendant could have, and had, announced continued Polavision profits, for how long would it have been under a duty of disclosure if the tide turned? Plaintiffs' contention that it would be a jury question is scarcely reassuring.

We do not, however, face this question. . . . After indicating reluctance to accept plaintiffs' contention that the Third Quarter Report was misleading when made, the panel opinion, in holding that it could be found misleading in light of later developments, said as follows:

> [E]ven if the optimistic Third Quarter Report was not misleading at the time of its issuance, there is sufficient evidence to support a jury's determination that the report's relatively brief mention of Polavision difficulties *became* misleading in light of the subsequent information acquired by Polaroid indicating the seriousness of Polavision's problems. This subsequent information included . . . Polaroid's decision to . . . stop Polavision production by its Austrian manufacturer, Euming, *and its instruction to its Austrian supplier to keep this production cutback secret.* We feel that a reasonable jury could conclude that this subsequent information rendered the Third Quarter Report's brief mention of Polavision expenses misleading triggering a duty to disclose on the part of Polaroid.

[Emphasis in orig.] . . . This is a failure to recognize that what . . . [Polaroid] said was a single, simple, statement that substantial expenses had made Polavision's earnings negative. Though the opinion characterized it as "relatively brief," it was precisely correct, initially. Even if forward-looking, it remained precisely correct thereafter. Plaintiffs' claim, "The statement was plainly intended to survive the date of issuance, and therefore a jury could reasonably find a duty to update and correct exists," means nothing, unless "update" means something more than "correct." And, indeed, in arguing that the statement did not "remain true," plaintiffs' brief, unabashedly, points solely to matters outside the scope of the initial disclosure, in no way making it incorrect or misleading, originally, or later.

The shell in plaintiffs' gun at trial, and the one substituted on appeal, are all percussion cap and no powder. We understand the amici apprehension, because of the panel opinion's not only requiring update, but requiring it in terms of a new duty that had never been undertaken. With those errors corrected, however, we see no reason to proceed further. Plaintiffs have no case.

---

1. *The Third Circuit's view.* In Weiner v. Quaker Oats, 129 F.3d 310 (3d Cir. 1997), plaintiff shareholders purchased stock in the Quaker Oats Company ("Quaker Oats") while it was secretly considering the leveraged purchase of another company, Snapple Beverage Corp. ("Snapple") for $1.7 billion. Prior to the Snapple acquisition and plaintiffs' purchase of its stock, Quaker Oats had announced in several press releases and SEC filings its intended guidelines for its debt-to-equity ratio. Specifically, it computed its debt-to-total capitalization ratio at 59 percent and added: "For the future, our guideline will be in the upper-60 percent range."

Once Quaker Oats announced its very costly acquisition of Snapple, which nearly tripled Quaker Oats' outstanding debt and raised its debt-to-total capitalization to approximately 80 percent, its stock price fell sharply, and plaintiffs sued. Their essential claim was that, once the Snapple acquisition negotiations began, Quaker Oats had to have known that its debt-to-total capitalization ratio would soar, and it should have updated its prior statements on this topic. Quaker objected that any such announcement would have forced it to disclose in essence its still secret acquisition negotiations with Snapple. Although the District Court dismissed the complaint, finding that Quaker Oats' statements about its debt-to-total capitalization ratio were immaterial, the Third Circuit reversed. Critical to the Third Circuit's decision was that Quaker Oats had repeated its public statement about its debt-to-total capitalization guideline after the Snapple acquisition had become a probability. Thus, it held that the complaint adequately alleged "facts on the basis of which a reasonable fact finder could determine that Quaker's statements regarding its total debt-to-total capitalization ratio guideline would have been material to a reasonable investor, and hence Quaker had a duty to update such statements when they become unreliable." Id. at 318.

2. *When is there a duty to update?* All courts recognize that there is a duty to correct and update statements that were incorrect when made, even though honestly believed at the time. They disagree over whether the issuer must update statements correct when made that subsequent events have rendered materially inaccurate. Here, the *Quaker Oats* panel took a more expansive view of the duty to update than did the First Circuit's *en banc* decision in *Polaroid*, but even the First Circuit's decision recognized that "in special circumstances, a statement, correct at the time, may have a forward intent and connotation upon which the parties may be expected to rely." Conversely, in In re Burlington Coat Factory Securities Litigation, 114 F.3d 1410 (3d Cir. 1997), a different panel of the Third Circuit found no duty to update an "expression of comfort" that the issuer made with respect to projections of earnings growth by independent securities analysts. Given this division in the case law, consider the following cases:

(a) The corporation makes the statement: "Looking ahead, we expect business to continue strong and that 1987 will be another fine performance year for the Gap." Business in fact deteriorates. Must this statement be updated? See In re Gap Securities Litigation, 925 F.2d 1470 (9th Cir. 1991) (*held:* statement too general to constitute a projection and therefore Gap had no duty to disclose that its inventory was increasing to an excessive level).

(b) The corporation predicts that its Personal Color Printer will be available to the market by a specified date. On that date, must it disclose that the product is not yet commercially available? See Greenberg v. Howtek, Inc., 790 F. Supp. 1181 (D.C.N.H. 1992) (*held:* Rule 10b-5 violated when corporation failed to correct).

(c) The corporation stated: "This is our eighth consecutive quarter in which our gross has increased." It adds later: "We're well poised to go into [the third quarter]." Should it have disclosed apprehensions that next quarter could show a decline in profitability? See Capri Optics Profit Sharing v. Digital Equipment Corp., 950 F.2d 5 (1st Cir. 1991) (*held:* no duty to warn unless corporation's "apprehension was of a disaster"; "poised" means a "present condition," not a "necessary promise of future success").

3. *The uncertain duty to make projections.* For many years, the SEC resisted any attempt by issuers to include projections of future earnings or financial condition

in their reports to shareholders on the ground that projections were too speculative. Eventually, it reversed this position and approved a permissive "safe harbor" for projections (Rule 175). More recently, it has begun to insist that some specified forward-looking information be included in the corporation's MD&A. According to the SEC's instructions, the MD&A must "describe any known trends or uncertainties . . . that the registrant reasonably expects will have a material favorable or unfavorable impact" on its results of operations or liquidity. There is a subtle distinction here between projecting future earnings (which the SEC does not require) and acknowledging that a known trend, event, or uncertainty (such as the Polavision camera project in *Polaroid*) will deplete the company's capital resources or future earnings by an amount that can be estimated (in which case disclosure is required). Not only does the MD&A mean that some specification of future problems must be made in periodic SEC filings, but such a quasi-projection may in turn trigger a duty in some circumstances to update.

For some years, the SEC warned that corporate issuers were not paying adequate attention to its required MD&A disclosures in shareholder reports and SEC filings. Then, in 1992, it took disciplinary action against Caterpillar, Inc. in an administrative proceeding that illustrates the broad scope of the required MD&A disclosures.[7] Caterpillar's Brazilian subsidiary (CBSA) accounted for 23 percent of Caterpillar's 1989 net profits. Much of this was attributable to non-recurring currency exchange profits on the dollar versus the Brazilian cruzado. During late 1989 and early 1990, a new administration in Brazil began to plan austerity measures intended to curb Brazil's hyperinflation. Caterpillar management understood that this deflationary program would probably reduce CBSA's sales and income during 1990, although its actual impact was, of course, uncertain. Nonetheless, according to the SEC, Caterpillar failed to discuss the nature of this uncertainty both in its MD&A filed with its 1989 Form 10-K and in the MD&A filed with its Form 10-Q for the First Quarter of 1990 (which filings were all made in 1990 after Caterpillar had recognized the likely risk). In response, the SEC brought an administrative cease-and-desist order against Caterpillar—an action that was clearly designed to send a message to other corporations.

Although the proceeding was quickly settled and involved little financial liability for Caterpillar, the SEC's release in the *Caterpillar* case set forth a double-negative test for determining when disclosure of forward-looking information is required: Can management conclude that a known trend, demand, commitment, event, or uncertainty is *not* reasonably likely to come to fruition? If not, management must objectively evaluate the consequences (assuming that the trend will continue) and disclose these consequences, *unless* management determines that a material effect on the corporation's financial condition or results of operation is not likely to occur. *Query:* Although the SEC can certainly mandate the content of filings to be made with it, does a failure to provide such information result in civil liability to private investors (assuming damages)? Consider again the definition of materiality in Basic, Inc. v. Levinson, page 312 supra.

4. *Duty to correct rumors and statements by third parties.* If a corporation learns that a rumor has circulated in the marketplace implying that its stock is significantly overvalued or undervalued, must the corporation correct this rumor? Notwithstanding the stock exchange rules noted earlier, the case law appears to

---

7. See SEC Release No. 34-30532 (March 31, 1992).

be that a "company has no duty to correct or verify rumors in the marketplace unless those rumors can be attributed to the company." State Teachers Retirement Bd. v. Fluor Corp., 654 F.2d 843, 850 (2d Cir. 1981); Zuckerman v. Harnischfeger Corp., 591 F. Supp. 112, 119 (S.D.N.Y. 1984). An illustration of this rule appears in Electronic Specialty Co. v. International Controls Corp., 409 F.2d 937 (2d Cir. 1969), where a report appeared in the "Heard on the Street" column of The Wall Street Journal that incorrectly stated that the company owned a specified percentage of another company's stock. Although the first corporation was in fact planning a tender offer for the second, it did not own stock of the target in the amount specified. The court held that the prospective bidder was not required to correct this published report in the absence of evidence that the misinformation emanated from it. Conversely, in In re Sharon Steel Corp., [1981-1982 Transfer Binder] Fed. Sec. L. Rep. (CCH) ¶83,049, where there was evidence that the rumors in the market originated with the corporation that was attempting the takeover and where this company knew of insider trading, the SEC found that prompt disclosure should have been made.

A variant on the case of the market rumor arises when a misstatement is made by a third party who has a close relationship with the issuer. In Green v. Jonhop, Inc., 358 F. Supp. 413 (D. Or. 1973), a corporation was held liable for failing to correct after learning of misleading statements by its underwriter and principal market maker. In Elkind v. Liggett & Myers, Inc., 635 F.2d 156 (2d Cir. 1980), the corporation had made it a practice to review the draft reports of securities analysts and to make factual corrections. Although the Second Circuit found that this review process did not "sufficiently entangl[e]" the corporation in the analysts' forecasts as to make the resulting predictions "attributable" to it, it warned: "While we find no liability for non-disclosure in . . . the present case, it bears noting that corporate pre-release review of the reports of analysts is a risky activity, fraught with danger. Management must navigate carefully between the 'Scylla' of misleading stockholders and the public by implied approval of reviewed analyses and the 'Charybdis' of tipping material inside information by correcting statements which it knows to be erroneous." Id. at 163.

In re Time Warner Securities Litigation
9 F.3d 259 (2d Cir. 1993)

NEWMAN, C.J.: This appeal from the dismissal of a securities fraud complaint requires us to consider the recurring issue of whether stock fraud claims are sufficiently pleaded to warrant at least discovery and perhaps trial. Three separate issues are presented: (1) whether a corporation has a duty to update somewhat optimistic predictions about achieving a business plan when it appears that the plan might not be realized, (2) whether a corporation has a duty to disclose a specific alternative to an announced business plan when that alternative is under active consideration, and (3) whether a corporation is responsible for statements in newspapers and security analyst reports that are attributed to unnamed corporate personnel. [Following the 1989 merger of Time, Inc. and Warner Communications, which thwarted a hostile takeover bid by Paramount Communications for Time, the resulting entity found itself saddled with over $10 billion in debt, which its ability to repay was in doubt. In response, it publicly sought "strategic partners" abroad who could infuse new funds into it. These attempts proved largely unsuccessful, and the company was forced to propose a controversial stock offering that attempted to coerce existing shareholders to buy additional shares by diluting significantly the equity of those shareholders who failed to subscribe. Following the announcement of this unpopular stock subscription offering, Time Warner's stock fell from $117 to $94 in one week, and eventually declined to $89.75. Plaintiffs consisted of the class of persons who bought Time Warner stock during the period when the company was allegedly misrepresenting the status of its ongoing search for strategic partners. Plaintiffs alleged that Time Warner itself made materially misleading statements and that unnamed sources within the company had leaked materially misleading information to reporters and security analysts on which the market relied. The district court found that the company's own statements were accurate when made, that later events did not give rise to a duty to correct or update them, and that a corporation could not be held liable for unattributed statements made to the press or security analysts.] . . .

Cases of this sort present an inevitable tension between two powerful interests. On the one hand, there is the interest in deterring fraud in the securities markets and remedying it when it occurs. That interest is served by recognizing that the victims of fraud often are unable to detail their allegations until they have had some opportunity to conduct discovery of those reasonably suspected of having perpetrated a fraud. . . .

On the other hand, there is the interest in deterring the use of litigation process as a device for extracting undeserved settlements as the price of avoiding the extensive discovery costs that frequently ensue once a complaint survives dismissal, even though no recovery would occur if the suit were litigated to completion. It has never been clear how these competing interests are to be accommodated, and the . . . courts must adjudicate the precise cases before them, striking the balance as best they can. . . .

[The court first held that unattributed statements quoted or paraphrased by reporters and market analysts without identifying the speaker could not be material largely because "investors tend to discount information in newspaper articles when the author is unable to cite specific, attributable information from the company."]

We next focus on those statements as to which there is no issue of attribution. While plaintiffs claim that these statements were misleading, in that they exaggerated the likelihood that strategic alliances would be made, plaintiffs primarily fault these statements for what they did not disclose. The nondisclosure is of two types: failure to disclose problems in the strategic alliance negotiations, and failure to disclose the active consideration of an alternative method of raising capital. . . .

1. *Affirmative misrepresentations.* We agree with the District Court that none of the statements constitutes an affirmative misrepresentation. Most of the statements reflect merely that talks are ongoing, and that Time Warner hopes that the talks will be successful. There is no suggestion that the factual assertions contained in any of these statements were false when the statements were made. As to the expressions of opinion and the projections contained in the statements, while not beyond the reach of the securities laws, . . . the complaint contains no allegations to support the inference that the defendants either did not have these favorable opinions on future prospects when they made the statements or that the favorable opinions were without a basis in fact.

2. *Nondisclosure of problems in the strategic alliance negotiations.* The allegations of nondisclosure are more serious. Plaintiffs' first theory of nondisclosure is that the defendants' statements hyping strategic alliances gave rise to a duty to disclose problems in the alliance negotiations as those problems developed. We agree that a duty to update opinions and projections may arise if the original opinions or projections have become misleading as the result of intervening events. See In re Gulf Oil/Cities Service Tender Offer Litigation, 725 F. Supp. 712, 745-749 (S.D.N.Y. 1989) (material misstatements or omissions adequately set forth alleging that defendants had expressed a strong interest in consummating a merger and had not disclosed a later "change of heart"). But, in this case, the attributed public statements lack the sort of definite positive projections that might require later correction. The statements suggest only the hope of any company, embarking on talks with multiple partners, that the talks would go well. No identified defendant stated that he thought deals would be struck by a certain date, or even that it was likely that deals would be struck at all. Cf. In re Apple Computer Securities Litigation, 886 F.2d 1109, 1118-1119 (9th Cir. 1989) (Chairman of the Board stated that new computer product would be "phenomenally successful the first year out of the chute," etc.). These statements did not become materially misleading when the talks did not proceed well.[4]

3. *Nondisclosure of alternative methods of raising capital.* Still more serious is the allegation of a failure to disclose the simultaneous consideration of the rights offering as an alternative method of raising capital. As an initial matter, of course, a reasonable investor would probably have wanted to know of consideration of the rights offering. Though both the rights offering and strategic alliances would have brought capital into the corporation, the two acts would have directly opposite effects on the price of Time Warner stock. A successful strategic alliance, simultaneously opening new markets and reducing debt, would have improved the corporation's expected profit stream, and should have served to drive up the share price. An offering of new shares, in contrast, would dilute the ownership rights of existing shareholders, likely decrease dividends, and drive down the price of the stock.

But a corporation is not required to disclose a fact merely because a reasonable investor would very much like to know that fact. Rather, an omission is actionable under the securities laws only when the corporation is subject to a duty to disclose the omitted facts. See Basic, Inc. v. Levinson, 405 U.S. 224, 239. As Time Warner pointedly reminds us, we have not only emphasized the importance of ascertaining a duty to disclose when omissions are at issue but have also drawn a distinction between the concepts of a duty to disclose and materiality. It appears, however, that the distinction has meaning only in certain contexts. For example, where the issue is whether an individual's relationship to information imposed upon him a duty to disclose, the inquiry as to his duty is quite distinct from the inquiry as to the information's materiality. See Dirks v. SEC, 463 U.S. 646. On the other hand, where the disclosure duty arises from the combination of a prior statement and a subsequent event, which, if not disclosed, renders the prior

---

4. Although the statements are generally open-ended, there is one sense in which they have a solid core. The statements represent as fact that serious talks with multiple parties were ongoing. If this factual assertion ceased to be true, defendants would have had an obligation to update their earlier statements. But the complaint does not allege that the talks ever stopped or ceased to be "serious," just that they eventually went poorly.

statement false or misleading, the inquiries as to duty and materiality coalesce. The undisclosed information is material if there is "a substantial likelihood that the disclosure of the omitted fact would have been viewed by the reasonable investor as having significantly altered the 'total mix' of information available." TSC Industries, Inc. v. Northway, Inc., 426 U.S. 438, 449 (1976). If a reasonable investor would so regard the omitted fact, it is difficult to imagine a circumstance where the prior statement would not be rendered misleading in the absence of the disclosure. . . .

. . . In the pending case, the District Court understood the obligation to disclose alternate business plans to be limited to the context of mutually exclusive alternatives. . . .

We believe, however, that a disclosure duty limited to mutually exclusive alternatives is too narrow. A duty to disclose arises whenever secret information renders prior public statements materially misleading, not merely when that information completely negates the public statements. Time Warner's public statements could have been understood by reasonable investors to mean that the company hoped to solve the entire debt problem through strategic alliances. Having publicly hyped strategic alliances, Time Warner may have come under a duty to disclose facts that would place the statements concerning strategic alliances in a materially different light.

It is important to appreciate the limits of our disagreement with the District Court. We do not hold that whenever a corporation speaks, it must disclose every piece of information in its possession that could affect the price of its stock. Rather, we hold that when a corporation is pursuing a specific business goal and announces that goal as well as an intended approach for reaching it, it may come under an obligation to disclose other approaches to reaching the goal when those approaches are under active and serious consideration. Whether consideration of the alternate approach constitutes material information, and whether nondisclosure of the alternate approach renders the original disclosure misleading, remain questions for the trier of fact, and may be resolved by summary judgment when there is no disputed issue of material fact. We conclude here only that the allegations in this complaint of nondisclosure of the rights offering are sufficient to survive a motion to dismiss.

---

1. *Disclosure of alternative approaches.* The failure to disclose the lack of success in finding a strategic partner struck the court as excusable, but the failure to disclose a carefully developed alternative plan did not. Is the premise that investors could understand that negotiations might fail, but not the existence and content of alternative contingency plans? Or is corrective disclosure really required because one alternative was hyped and the other hidden?

2. *Failing negotiations.* Although the *Time Warner* decision declined to impose any continuing duty on the corporation to disclose problems in material negotiations, it expressed an important caveat in footnote 4: To the extent that serious negotiations were reported to be underway and then those talks either ended "or ceased 'to be serious,'" then "defendants would have had an obligation to update their earlier statements." At what point do talks cease to be "serious"? If a corporation discloses pending negotiations that contemplate a sale of one of its divisions at a price in the range of $500 million, and the prospective buyer, after some

investigation, concludes that the division is worth no more than $350 million (which difference, let us assume, is material to the seller), have these talks broken down or become "nonserious"? Must a corrective disclosure be made under *Time Warner* even while the negotiations continue? For a pre-*Time Warner* decision finding no duty to disclose a major downward revision in negotiations for the sale of a corporation, see Evanowski v. Bankworcester Corp., 788 F. Supp. 611 (D. Mass. 1991).

3. *Do the Second and Third Circuits agree?* Backman v. Polaroid limited the duty to update to statements having a forward intent, thus excluding statements of "historical fact." Suppose a corporation announces that as of December 30, 1994, it had received no customer complaints about its principal new product. Two weeks later, many complaints are received, and the corporation realizes it will have to withdraw the flawed product. Did the original statement have a "forward intent" that requires corrective disclosure or was it one of "historical fact"? Would the *Time Warner* court care about this distinction?

4. *Unattributed statements.* Is it true that "investors tend to discount information in newspaper articles when the author is unable to cite specific, attributable information from the company"? Suppose The Wall Street Journal reported unnamed corporate insiders at a new high-tech company as having told it that the "company's books are cooked." Would the market react to this assertion?

6. REFORMING THE DISCLOSURE SYSTEM: THE SARBANES-OXLEY ACT OF 2002

In late 2001, Enron filed for bankruptcy in what was the largest bankruptcy in U.S. history. Originally a gas pipeline company, it became, first, an energy provider when Congress deregulated the utilities industry in 1992 and, later, an energy trader, dealing actively in energy futures. While it used a number of accounting gimmicks and financial legerdemain to conceal its highly leveraged financial condition,[8] it has become famous for its exploitation of "off balance sheet" partnerships. Typically, it would create a partnership with another company or individual investors who would hold just over a 3 percent stake in the partnership. The partnership would then borrow significant sums of money, and Enron would either guarantee this indebtedness or pledge collateral in the form of its stock to secure the loan. Under then generally accepted accounting principles (GAAP), so long as independent investors owned 3 percent or more of this "special-purpose entity," Enron did not have to disclose the substantial indebtedness that it had guaranteed on its own balance sheet. Enron's financial collapse under the pressure of staggering liabilities that it had never disclosed thus revealed both the seeming inadequacy of GAAP and the unsatisfactory performance of its independent auditors (Arthur Andersen & Co.), who were convicted on federal obstruction of justice charges in connection with Enron's collapse and a resulting SEC investigation.

---

8. For good overviews of the Enron debacle and the techniques used to manipulate its accounting, see William Bratton, Enron and the Dark Side of Shareholder Value, 76 Tul. L. Rev. 1275 (2002); Lawrence A. Cunningham, Sharing Accounting's Burden: Business Lawyers in Enron's Dark Shadow, 57 Bus. Law. 1421 (2002); Robert W. Hamilton, The Crisis in Corporate Governance: 2002 Style, 49 Hous. L. Rev. 1 (2003).

Enron was quickly followed by a series of other high-profile corporate bankruptcies in 2002, including Tyco, Adelphia, and WorldCom (with the last being an even larger bankruptcy than Enron). Nor did these cases stand alone. Even apart from the Enron and WorldCom scandals, approximately 10 percent of the listed corporations in the United States restated their financial statements at least once between 1997 and 2002, and this percentage rose to 16 percent between 2002 and 2005, with some 6.8 percent of such companies restating in 2005 alone.[9] As a result, the reliability of financial information had come to seem suspect. Investors feared that corporate managements could game the system to inflate earnings while hiding expenses and liabilities, exploiting highly technical accounting rules that few investors understood. Predictably, the stock market, which had fallen sharply in 2000, continued to decline through 2001 and mid-2002, and Congress sensed a crisis that required quick action.

Congress's answer — the Sarbanes-Oxley Act (or the Public Company Accounting Reform and Investor Protection Act of 2002) — was drafted quickly and contains an assortment of provisions, some added by last-minute floor amendments, that for the most part seek to upgrade the quality of financial disclosure by establishing a new regulatory body with jurisdiction over auditing standards, by upgrading the requirements for membership on the audit committee, by requiring new certificates from corporate executives, and by toughening the criminal laws pertaining to securities fraud. Most, but not all, of its provisions are amendments to the Securities Exchange Act of 1934. The principal provisions of the Sarbanes-Oxley Act ("the Act") are summarized below:

a. The Public Company Accounting Oversight Board

The centerpiece of the Act is the Public Company Accounting Oversight Board (the "Board"), which is empowered and instructed "to oversee the audit of public companies that are subject to the securities laws, and related matters, in order to protect the interests of investors and further the public interest in the preparation of informative, accurate, and independent audit reports. . . ." Although the Board is a private body, established as a nonprofit corporation, the Act expressly makes it subject to SEC oversight in a manner paralleling the relationship between the SEC and the National Association of Securities Dealers (NASD),[10] which was similarly established by an amendment to the Securities Exchange Act in the late 1930s. The five members of the Board are appointed by the SEC (after consultation with the Chairman of the Board of Governors of the Federal Reserve System and the Secretary of the Treasury) for five-year terms. Two (but only two) of the Board's five members must be certified public accountants. These restrictions

9. See United States Government Accountability Office, Report to the Ranking Minority Member, Committee on Banking, Housing, and Urban Affairs, U.S. Senate, Financial Restatements: Update of Public Company Trends, Market Impacts, and Regulatory Enforcement Activities 4 (2006). For the 2002 study, see GAO, Financial Statement Restatements: Trends, Market Impacts, Regulatory Responses and Remaining Challenges (GAO-03-138) (2002) (finding stock market losses of over $100 billion to have resulted from these restatements).

10. Section 107 of the Act provides that the SEC "shall have oversight and enforcement authority over the Board. . . ." and expressly subjects the Board to §§17(a)(1) and 17(b)(1) of the Securities Exchange Act of 1934 "as if the Board were a 'registered securities association' for purposes of those sections. . . ."

are obviously intended to prevent the "capture" of the Board by the accounting profession.

Pursuant to §102 of the Act, all accounting firms that prepare audit reports for public companies must become "registered public accounting firms" by registering with the Board and maintaining their registration. Section 102(a) makes it unlawful for any unregistered firm even "to participate in the preparation or issuance of, any audit report with respect to any issuer." Section 101(c) of the Act then further directs the Board, among other things, to:

(a) "establish or adopt . . . auditing, quality control, ethics, independence and other standards relating to the preparation of audit reports for issuers";

(b) "conduct inspections of registered public accounting firms";

(c) "conduct investigations and disciplinary proceedings concerning, and impose appropriate sanctions where justified upon, registered public accounting firms and associated persons of such firms";

(d) enforce compliance with the Act, the rules of the Board, professional standards, and the federal securities laws relating to the preparation and issuance of audit reports and the obligations and liabilities of accountants; and

(e) perform such other duties or functions as the Board or SEC "determines are necessary or appropriate to promote high professional standards . . . and improve the quality of audit services."

1. *Funding.* Unlike the SEC, the Board is not dependent upon congressional appropriations; rather, the Board can tax its industry (accounting firms and corporate issuers) in much the same manner as the NASD taxes the brokerage industry for its expenses. Specifically, funding for the Board is to come from an annual "accounting support fee" allocated to corporate issuers and by registration and annual fees charged to accounting firms.

2. *Rulemaking authority.* The Board is given rulemaking authority with respect to auditing, attestation, quality control, and ethics standards for auditors. A number of rules are, however, specifically mandated by the Act. For example, §103(a)(2) of the Act directs the Board to adopt standards requiring firms to maintain auditing records for at least seven years, to provide for a "concurring or second" partner review of audits, to include descriptions of the auditor's testing of the issuer's "internal control structure and procedures," and to meet certain quality control standards with respect to their audit reports.

3. *Board inspection and disciplinary authority.* Section 104 instructs the Board to conduct compliance inspections (which must be conducted annually for firms auditing more than 100 clients and not less than every three years for other firms). Section 105 authorizes and directs the Board to discipline accounting firms that violate professional standards, Board rules, or the federal securities laws. The Board may impose sanctions ranging from requiring additional professional training to revocation of a firm's or associated person's accounting license, and may levy fines of up to $15 million in the case of intentional misconduct by a firm.

4. *Foreign firms.* Foreign public accounting firms that prepare or furnish an audit report with respect to a "reporting" United States or foreign issuer are expressly made subject to the Act and the rules of the Board and the SEC. In addition, the Board is authorized to find that even a foreign accounting firm that does not issue

an audit report for a U.S. issuer "nonetheless plays such a substantial role in the preparation and furnishing of such reports for particular issuers" that it should be subjected to the Board's oversight. This extraterritorial assertion of jurisdiction has troubled European and other foreign regulators, and §106(c) grants the Board and the SEC authority to exempt foreign public accounting firms from any provision of the Act, or the rules thereunder, either unconditionally or upon prescribed terms and conditions.

b. Auditor Independence

A principal goal of the Act is to strengthen auditor independence. Toward this end, the Act mandates the following requirements:

1. *Approval of scope of services and prohibition of certain non-audit services.* Under §202 of the Act, the corporation's audit committee must approve in advance all audit and non-audit services provided to a "reporting" company (with some "de minimis" exceptions). Section 201 contains the Act's most controversial provision regarding accounting, which prohibits accounting firms from providing a variety of non-audit services to an audit client. The rationale here is that because such services were highly lucrative, they enabled the client to compromise the independence of the auditor by retaining the auditor as a consultant only so long as the auditor acquiesced in management's practice of using aggressive accounting principles. The services specifically prohibited by the Act are the following:

(1) bookkeeping or other services related to accounting records or financial statements of the audit client;
(2) financial information systems design and implementation;
(3) appraisal or valuation services, fairness opinions, or contribution-in-kind reports;
(4) actuarial services;
(5) internal audit outsourcing services;
(6) management functions or human resources;
(7) broker or dealer, investment adviser, or investment banking services;
(8) legal services and expert services that are unrelated to the audit. . . .

A compromise is apparent here, because the provision of tax services by audit firms is not prohibited, and tax services have long been a major source of income for audit firms, responsible for as much as one-third of total audit firm revenues.

Section 201 also authorizes the Board to prohibit other non-audit activities. Although auditors may provide non-audit services not specifically prohibited by the Act or by the Board, non-audit activities performed by the auditor for the audit client still must be approved in advance by the audit committee, and such approval must be disclosed to investors in a Form 10-Q or Form 10-K report.

2. *Mandatory disqualification and rotation.* Section 206 of the Act seeks to close the "revolving door" between audit firms and their clients by prohibiting an accounting firm from auditing any public company whose chief executive officer, controller, chief financial officer, chief accounting officer, or "any person serving in an equivalent position" was, at any time in the past year, an employee of the accounting firm.

Section 203 of the Act requires auditors to rotate the lead audit partner (i.e., the partner with primary responsibility for conducting the audit) at least every five years. The Act stopped short, however, of mandating audit firm rotation, which is standard in some European countries.

c. Corporate Governance

1. *Audit committee composition and authority.* To ensure the independence of a public company's audit committee, the Act requires national securities exchanges to adopt listing standards under which a corporation's audit committee must be composed entirely of independent board members, as that term is defined by the Act.[11] In addition, at least one member of the audit committee is expected to qualify as a "financial expert" by virtue of education and experience.[12] Seemingly overriding state law (which empowers the board as a whole to manage the corporation's business and affairs), §301 of the Act mandates that the audit committee "be directly responsible for the appointment, compensation, and oversight of the work" of the independent auditor and that the audit firm "shall report directly to the audit committee."[13] This provision would appear to curtail the authority not only of corporate executives, but also of shareholders and the full board to hire, fire, or supervise the outside accountants. Also supplanting state corporate law, the Act grants an audit committee authority as a matter of federal law to engage independent counsel and other advisers, whose fees are to be paid by the company.[14] In addition, the Act expands the role of the audit committee from simply that of a monitor of accounting policies and practices to a broader oversight body or watchdog by requiring the audit committee to establish procedures for the receipt and evaluation of anonymous submissions by employees of concerns regarding "questionable accounting or auditing matters."[15]

2. *Executive certifications.* Section 302 of the Act instructs the SEC to adopt rules mandating that both chief executive officers and chief financial officers of public companies make detailed certifications, in connection with each filing of a company's periodic reports, including that:

a. the signing officer has reviewed the report and, based on the officer's knowledge, the report does not contain any material misstatement or omission and "the financial statements, and other financial information included in the report, *fairly present in all material respects* the financial condition and results of operations of the issuer as of, and for, the periods presented in the report" (emphasis added);

b. the signing officers are responsible for establishing and maintaining internal controls and have designed such internal controls as necessary to ensure that material information relating to the issuer is made known to such officers during the reporting period; and

---

11. In order to be considered "independent," an audit committee member may not be an "affiliated person" of the company or any subsidiary, and may not "accept any consulting, advisory, or other compensatory fee from the issuer." See §10A(m)(3)(B) of the Securities Exchange Act of 1934. In short, the director may receive only a director's fee and no other income from the firm.

12. See §407(a) of the Act. "Financial expert" is defined by §407(b) of the Act, and this definition has been amplified in proposed rules set forth in Securities Act Release No. 8138 (October 22, 2002), which require experience as a public accountant, principal financial officer, controller, principal accounting officer of a publicly reporting company, or closely similar experience.

13. See §301 of the Act, which has been codified as Securities Exchange Act §10A(m)(2).

14. See Securities Exchange Act §10A(m)(5)-(6).

15. See Securities Exchange Act §10A(m)(4).

c. they have disclosed to the company's auditors and to the audit committee all significant deficiencies in the design or operation of internal controls as well as any fraud, whether or not material, that involves management or other employees who have a significant role in the issuer's internal controls.

Independent of these provisions, the Act also adopted a new criminal statute (18 U.S.C. §1350) that requires chief executive officers and chief financial officers to certify that any periodic report containing financial statements filed with the SEC, pursuant to Securities Exchange Act §13(a) or §15(d), "fully complies with the requirements" of those Exchange Act sections and that "information contained in the periodic report fairly presents, in all material respects, the financial condition and results of operations of the issuer." It does not appear to have been accidental that these requirements that the financial statements "fairly present" the issuer's financial position make no reference to generally accepted accounting principles (GAAP). Seemingly, a signing officer could be liable under this certification provision if, as in Enron, material liabilities were hidden from investors in off-balance-sheet transactions, even though the financial statements complied with GAAP.

3. *Restatements of financial results.* Section 304(a) of the Act specifies a potentially Draconian and mandatory penalty in the event that a company is required to restate its financials because of material noncompliance resulting from "misconduct." In that event, the chief executive officer and chief financial officer must reimburse the company for any bonus or other incentive-based or equity-based compensation that they received during the 12 months following the issuance or filing of the financial report and for any profits they made on their sale of company stock during that period. But the Act does not specify that the "misconduct" must have been by them. For example, what happens if a divisional vice president "cooks the books" for his division, without the knowledge of the CEO, thereby forcing a subsequent restatement, but the CEO sold 1 million shares during this period at a $20 million profit? One possible way to read this provision is that the officer was unjustly enriched by a bonus that was not legitimately earned because earnings were inflated and so must make restitution, regardless of personal good faith. Obviously, there inevitably will be litigation concerning the meaning of "misconduct."

4. *Executive loans.* In a controversial provision, §402(a) of the Act adds a new §13(k) to the Securities Exchange Act to bar an issuer from directly or indirectly extending credit or making, renewing, or arranging for a "personal loan" to any director or executive officer. This is probably the clearest example in which the Act "federalizes" corporate law, as such loans are expressly permitted by many state corporation codes. Section 402 applies only to "issuers," a term that §2 of the Act defines to mean companies subject to the periodic reporting requirements of Securities Exchange Act §§13(a) and 15(d). Hence, privately held companies are not affected; nor are loans to persons whose position within the company does not rise to the level of executive officer. Section 402 raises a host of definitional issues. In particular, "personal loans" must be distinguished from other loans, and existing loans on the date of the Act's passage are grandfathered, so long as they are not "materially modified" thereafter.

5. *Officer and director bars.* Section 305(a) of the Act enhances the SEC's ability to remove officers and directors from their positions, and to bar them from occupying similar offices at other public companies, simply by demonstrating their

"unfitness" (the previous standard required the court to find "substantial unfitness"). Section 305 also empowers the SEC to obtain in the federal courts "any equitable relief that may be appropriate or necessary for the benefit of investors."

d. Improved Financial Disclosures

1. *Financial reports.* Section 409 of the Act requires companies to disclose material changes in their financial condition or operations on a "rapid and current basis" and "in plain English." Responding to Enron's enormous off-balance-sheet transactions, §401 instructs the SEC to require disclosure of "all material off-balance sheet transactions, arrangements, obligations (including contingent obligations) and other relationships" that might have a "material current or future effect" on the financial health of the company.[16] In particular, the use of pro forma financial information is restricted by a requirement that any such information contained in a public company's reports must be "presented in a manner that . . . reconciles it with the financial condition and results of operations of the issuer under generally accepted accounting principles."[17]

Section 404(a) of the Act instructed the SEC to develop a new disclosure document to be known as an "internal control report," which had to be set forth in each annual report of a "reporting" company. This report also had to contain management's assessment, as of the end of each fiscal year, of "the effectiveness of the internal control structure and procedures of the issuer for financial reporting,"[18] which the audit firm then must "attest to and report on." This provision proved to be the most costly feature of the Sarbanes-Oxley Act. The Public Company Accounting Oversight Board ruled that in order for an audit firm to "attest" under §404, it had to conduct a special audit of the company's internal controls. Also, if there was "more than a remote" possibility that weak internal controls could cause a material misstatement in the company's financial statements, the audit firm was required to declare that the issuer had a "material weakness" in its internal controls. This requirement of a second audit for internal controls quickly caused audit fees literally to double.[19] Under pressure from the industry, the PCAOB and the SEC revised their rules in 2006 and 2007 to relax these requirements marginally in order to reduce the cost of this internal control audit, in particular by redefining the standard for finding a "material weakness."[20]

---

16. Section 401(a) of the Act has been codified as Securities Exchange Act §13(j).

17. During the 1990s, corporate issuers increasingly reported their earnings to the public on a "cash flow" basis, without subtracting interest, taxes, or amortization charges; this was referred to as EBITA "earnings before interest, taxes, and amortization." Pursuant to §409, the SEC has adopted Regulation G in 2003 to standardize the use of cash flow reporting and require that it be always reconciled with reported earnings.

18. See §404(a) of the Act. In Securities Act Release No. 8138 (October 22, 2002), the SEC has proposed rules to govern the "internal control report," but it declined to prescribe any form for that report in the belief that the report should be tailored to the individual company.

19. See Jack Ciesielski & Thomas R. Weirich, Ups and Downs of Audit Fees Since the Sarbanes-Oxley Act, CPA J. (October 2006) (reporting that audit fees increased 103 percent for the S&P 500 companies between 2001 and 2004).

20. See Securities Act Releases Nos. 33-8809 and 33-8810 (June 20, 2007) (redefining "material weakness" to mean a control deficiency, or combination of deficiencies, that gave rise to a "reasonable possibility that a material misstatement of the company's annual or interim financial statements will not be prevented or detected on a timely basis. . . ."). Similarly, the PCAOB released a new interpretation, Auditing Standard No. 5, to reach the same result.

2. *Codes of ethics.* Section 406 of the Act requires the SEC to issue rules requiring a public company to disclose if it "has adopted a code of ethics for senior financial officers" or to justify why it has failed to do so. Section 406(b) adds that changes in or waivers of the code must be promptly disclosed on a Form 8-K, the Internet, or other electronic methods.[21] The term "code of ethics" is defined to mean such standards as are "reasonably necessary to promote honest and ethical conduct, including the ethical handling of actual or apparent conflicts of interest between personal and professional relationships," full and fair disclosure, and "compliance with applicable governmental rules and regulations."

e. SEC Authority over Attorneys

Section 307 of the Act requires the SEC to prescribe "minimum standards of professional conduct for attorneys" who practice before the SEC. These rules must require attorneys who represent public companies "to report evidence of a material violation of securities law or breach of fiduciary duty or similar violation by the company or any agent thereof" to the company's chief legal counsel or CEO. If those officers do not take appropriate action, §307 further mandates that the SEC's rules require the attorney to report the evidence to the public company's audit committee, to its independent directors, or to the board of directors as a whole.

In 2003, the SEC adopted rules implementing this "up the ladder" reporting obligation,[22] but it still has not yet decided whether to compel the securities attorney to report the legal violation to it if the audit committee or board does not act.

f. What Remains?

The Sarbanes-Oxley Act primarily focuses on the federal disclosure system, accounting, auditors, and the internal control process within the firm. But what destabilized corporate governance during the late 1990s with the result that accounting irregularities suddenly exploded in 2001 and 2002? Here, a popular diagnosis is that executive compensation shifted during the 1990s from being primarily cash based as of 1990 to being primarily equity based by 2000.[23] As a result, once senior managers were compensated with stock options, they had a far stronger incentive to inflate earnings because they could exercise their options and sell very quickly once they realized that a sudden spike in their corporation's stock price could not be sustained much longer. Note, however, that if this is a significant underlying cause of Enron and similar scandals, it is not addressed by Sarbanes-Oxley in any way.

---

21. See §406(a)-(b) of the Act. In Securities Act Release No. 8138 (October 22, 2002), the SEC has proposed rules governing disclosures relating to codes of ethics. Changes and waivers would have to be disclosed in a Form 8-K or on the company's Web site within two business days.

22. See Securities Act Release No. 33-8185 (January 29, 2003) ("Implementation of Standards of Professional Conduct for Attorneys").

23. See, e.g., John C. Coffee Jr., Gatekeepers: The Professions and Corporate Governance (2006) (assessing the shift to equity compensation as a major cause of financial irregularity).

The SEC is pursuing one other set of initiatives that may be a response to these scandals. At the request of institutional shareholders, it is seeking to enhance the ability of shareholders to use the corporation's own proxy statement to nominate directors — a move that would enhance shareholder leverage with respect to management. These developments are reviewed in Chapter VI.

C. *CIVIL LIABILITY*

A wide array of federal, state, and common law remedies potentially are triggered for material misstatements or omissions in connection with the purchase or sale of a security. In principle, an injured shareholder or investor may (1) bring an action at common law or equity, or (2) assert a private cause of action, either express or implied, under the applicable state "blue sky" law, or (3) commence a similar action, either express or implied, under the federal securities laws. Generally, however, the plaintiff will prefer to assert a federal cause of action, both because of procedural advantages (such as nationwide service of process, simplified venue, and liberalized jurisdictional requirements) and because the substantive law at the federal level is often far more favorable to the plaintiff than the traditional common law of fraud.

At the federal level, a unique mixture of express and implied causes of action coexist. The '33 Act contains two important express causes of action — §§11 and 12(2) — relating to misstatements and omissions made in connection with the sale of securities. Although there are also several express causes of action in the '34 Act,[24] the one most relevant to this chapter's concerns is Section 16(b), which seeks to regulate insider trading, and therefore is considered in Sec. D infra.

Overshadowing all these express causes of action, however, are two implied causes of action. Rule 10b-5 (dealing with misrepresentations or omissions in connection with the sale or purchase of securities) and Rule 14a-9 (similarly dealing with misrepresentations or omissions in shareholder voting decisions) represent judicially created torts, which courts and the SEC have drawn out of relatively thin statutory materials to fill gaps that they perceived in the federal securities law. But courts have also more recently limited these remedies, either by adding additional elements or by narrowing their scope. The principal focus of this section is the expansion and subsequent contraction of Rule 10b-5 — a rule that the Supreme Court has accurately described as "a judicial oak which has grown from little more than a legislative acorn." Blue Chip Stamps v. Manor Drug Stores, 421 U.S. 723, at 737 (1975).

---

24. Section 18 of the '34 Act provides that "any person who shall make or cause to be made any statement in any application, report, or document filed [with the SEC] . . . , which statement was at the time and in the light of circumstances under which it was made false or misleading with respect to any material fact, shall be liable to any person (not knowing that such statement was false or misleading) who, in reliance upon such statement, shall have purchased or sold a security at a price which was affected by such statement, for damages caused by such reliance, unless the person sued shall prove that he acted in good faith and had no knowledge that such statement was false or misleading." In practice, this strong reliance requirement has made §18(a) a rarely used remedy. Section 16(b), which is far more used but is highly limited in scope, addresses insider trading and will be discussed infra in Sec. D.

1. COMMON LAW REMEDIES

Breach of warranty, rescission, and deceit are the three principal causes of action available at common law to a buyer or seller of securities who is injured by false representations or failures to disclose. Under Article 8 (Investment Securities) of the Uniform Commercial Code, a seller warrants only that "(a) his transfer is effective and rightful; (b) the security is genuine and has not been materially altered; and (c) he knows of no fact which might impair the validity of the security." UCC §8-306(2). These highly limited representations exclude any implied warranty of quality or value. Rescission is a more effective remedy, but it requires a misrepresentation of a material fact on which the buyer justifiably relied. Although the seller need not have intentionally misrepresented a material fact, an injured buyer will face substantial obstacles: First, the common law has always had great difficulty distinguishing between a statement of "fact," on the one hand, and a mere expression of "opinion" or "value" on the other. Yet, if predictions and opinions are not generally considered to be misrepresentations at common law, they are critical to securities investment decisions. Second, at common law, there must be some form of privity between the parties because the goal of rescission is to restore the parties to their status quo. If the status quo cannot be restored, such as when there has been a general market-wide decline in securities prices, some courts may not consider the remedy of rescission to be equitable under these circumstances.[25]

The tort of deceit has the same basic elements as rescission — a misrepresentation of a material fact and reliance — but it has the significant advantage for the plaintiff that privity between the parties need not exist. However, only those persons to whom the misrepresentation was made have standing. Thus, for example, when a corporation issues a prospectus in connection with the sale of debt securities to one class of purchasers, other persons who rely on this prospectus to buy the corporation's stock would lack standing. See Restatement (Second) of Torts, §531 comment d. In addition, the tort of deceit requires that the plaintiff prove scienter (namely, "the intent to deceive, to mislead, to convey a false impression"[26]) and causation (that is, that plaintiff suffered damages as a consequence of reliance on the misrepresentation).

This summary does not exhaust the remedies that courts have sometimes created in cases of "equitable fraud" (including receivership, specific performance, or constructive trust),[27] but it illustrates the considerable obstacles that a plaintiff faced under the common law (particularly if the plaintiff purchased the shares in the open market and not in a face-to-face transaction with the defendants).

---

25. Courts have, however, recognized that "the restoration need not be exact for rescission to be proper." Harman v. Diversified Medical Inv. Corp., 524 F.2d 361, 364 (10th Cir. 1975). Furthermore, given that securities are fungible, it is likely (but not certain) that the plaintiff need not restore the exact share certificates that he or she purchased. See Restatement of Restitution, §66(4) and comment (e).

26. See William L. Prosser & Robert E. Keeton on the Law of Torts 741 (5th ed. 1984). "Scienter" typically requires that the defendant either intended to deceive or made the representation "recklessly" — that is, either without any belief in the statement's truth or falsity or with an indifference to this issue. Id. at 743-745.

27. See, e.g., People v. Federated Radio Corp., 244 N.Y. 33, 154 N.E. 655 (1926); 3 John N. Pomeroy, Equity Jurisprudence 910 (5th ed. 1941). A few decisions have also adopted a much more "liberal" definition of the nature of the misrepresentation needed to sustain the tort of deceit in the case of securities transactions. See Equitable Life Ins. Co. of Iowa v. Halsey, Stuart & Co., 312 U.S. 410, 424-426 (1941).

Absent a special relationship between the parties, the general rule at common law has been that "mere silence or a passive failure to disclose facts of which the defendant has knowledge" does not amount to deceit.[28]

2. BLUE SKY STATUTES

Most (but not all) state blue sky statutes expressly provide for a private cause of action for persons defrauded in connection with securities transactions.[29] Section 509 of the Uniform Securities Act, adopted in 2002, provides a private remedy that is closely modeled after §12 of the '33 Act (which is discussed at page 343 infra). Recently, plaintiffs have made increased use of this state law remedy in light of the judicial pruning of Rule 10b-5, discussed later in this chapter.

3. THE FIDUCIARY DUTY OF DISCLOSURE

Malone v. Brincat
722 A.2d 5 (Del. 1998)

HOLLAND, J.: [Plaintiff shareholders filed individual actions and a class action alleging that the directors of Mercury Finance Company, a Delaware corporation ("Mercury"), had "breached their fiduciary duty of disclosure" and that KPMG Peat Marwick LLP ("KPMG"), Mercury's outside public accountant, had aided and abetted this breach.] . . .

The complaint alleged that the director defendants intentionally overstated the financial condition of Mercury on repeated occasions throughout a four-year period in disclosures to Mercury's shareholders. Plaintiffs contend that the complaint states a claim upon which relief can be granted for a breach of the fiduciary duty of disclosure. Plaintiffs also contend that, because the director defendants breached their fiduciary duty of disclosure to the Mercury shareholders, the Court of Chancery erroneously dismissed the aiding and abetting claim against KPMG.

This Court has concluded that the Court of Chancery properly granted the defendants' motions to dismiss the complaint. That dismissal, however, should have been without prejudice. Plaintiffs are entitled to file an amended complaint. Therefore, the judgment of the Court of Chancery is affirmed in part, reversed in part, and remanded for further proceedings consistent with this opinion.

Facts. Mercury is a publicly-traded company engaged primarily in purchasing installment sales contracts from automobile dealers and providing short-term installment loans directly to consumers. This action was filed on behalf of the named plaintiffs and all persons (excluding defendants) who owned common

---

28. Prosser & Keeton on the Law of Torts 737-740 (5th ed. 1984). See also Note, The Liability of Directors and Officers for Misrepresentation in the Sale of Securities, 34 Colum. L. Rev. 1090 (1934).

29. A notable exception to this pattern is New York. In CPC Int'l, Inc. v. McKesson Corp., 70 N.Y.2d 268, 519 N.Y.S.2d 804, 514 N.E.2d 116 (1987), the New York Court of Appeals found that the New York blue sky law, General Business Law §352-c (also known as the Martin Act), was intended only to expand the enforcement powers of the New York Attorney General and did not confer a private cause of action. However, the court noted that only one other state (Rhode Island) denied a private cause of action under its blue sky statute, and it recommended to the New York legislature that it consider enacting an express remedy.

stock of Mercury from 1993 through the present and their successors in interest, heirs and assigns (the "putative class"). The complaint alleged that the directors "knowingly and intentionally breached their fiduciary duty of disclosure because the SEC filings made by the directors and every communication from the company to the shareholders since 1994 was materially false" and that "as a direct result of the false disclosures . . . the Company has lost all or virtually all of its value (about $2 billion)." The complaint also alleged that KPMG knowingly participated in the directors' breaches of their fiduciary duty of disclosure.

According to plaintiffs, since 1994, the director defendants caused Mercury to disseminate information containing overstatements of Mercury's earnings, financial performance and shareholders' equity. Mercury's earnings for 1996 were actually only $56.7 million, or $.33 a share, rather than the $120.7 million, or $.70 a share, as reported by the director defendants. Mercury's earnings in 1995 were actually $76.9 million, or $.44 a share, rather than $98.9 million, or $.57 a share, as reported by the director defendants. Mercury's earnings for 1994 were $83 million, or $.47 a share, rather than $86.5 million, or $.49 a share, as reported by the director defendants. Mercury's earnings for 1993 were $64.2 million, rather than $64.9 million, as reported by the director defendants. Shareholders' equity on December 31, 1996 was disclosed by the director defendants as $353 million, but was only $263 million or less. The complaint alleged that all of the foregoing inaccurate information was included or referenced in virtually every filing Mercury made with the SEC and every communication Mercury's directors made to the shareholders during this period of time.

Having alleged these violations of fiduciary duty, which (if true) are egregious, plaintiffs alleged that as "a direct result of [these] false disclosures . . . the company has lost all or virtually all its value (about $2 billion)," and seeks class action status to pursue damages against the directors and KPMG for the individual plaintiffs and common stockholders. The individual director defendants filed a motion to dismiss, contending that they owed no fiduciary duty of disclosure under the circumstances alleged in the complaint. KPMG also filed a motion to dismiss the aiding and abetting claim asserted against it.

After briefing and oral argument, the Court of Chancery granted both of the motions to dismiss with prejudice. The Court of Chancery held that directors have no fiduciary duty of disclosure under Delaware law in the absence of a request for shareholder action. In so holding, the Court stated:

> The federal securities laws ensure the timely release of accurate information into the marketplace. The federal power to regulate should not be duplicated or impliedly usurped by Delaware. When a shareholder is damaged merely as a result of the release of inaccurate information into the marketplace, unconnected with any Delaware corporate governance issue, that shareholder must seek a remedy under federal law.

We disagree, and although we hold that the Complaint as drafted should have been dismissed, our rationale is different. . . .

This Court has held that a board of directors is under a fiduciary duty to disclose material information when seeking shareholder action.

It is well-established that the duty of disclosure "represents nothing more than the well-recognized proposition that directors of Delaware corporations are under a fiduciary duty to disclose fully and fairly all material information within the board's *control when it seeks shareholder action.*"[6]

The majority of opinions from the Court of Chancery have held that there may be a cause of action for disclosure violations only where directors seek shareholder action. The present appeal requires this Court to decide whether a director's fiduciary duty arising out of misdisclosure is implicated in the absence of a request for shareholder action. We hold that directors who knowingly disseminate false information that results in corporate injury or damage to an individual stockholder violate their fiduciary duty, and may be held accountable in a manner appropriate to the circumstances.

Fiduciary Duty—Delaware Corporate Directors. An underlying premise for the imposition of fiduciary duties is a separation of legal control from beneficial ownership. Equitable principles act in those circumstances to protect the beneficiaries who are not in a position to protect themselves. One of the fundamental tenets of Delaware corporate law provides for a separation of control and ownership. The board of directors has the legal responsibility to manage the business of a corporation for the benefit of its shareholder owners. Accordingly, fiduciary duties are imposed on the directors of Delaware corporations to regulate their conduct when they discharge that function.

Although the fiduciary duty of a Delaware director is unremitting, the exact course of conduct that must be charted to properly discharge that responsibility will change in the specific context of the action the director is taking with regard to either the corporation or its shareholders. This Court has endeavored to provide the directors with clear signal beacons and brightly lined-channel markers as they navigate with due care, good faith, and loyalty on behalf of a Delaware corporation and its shareholders. This Court has also endeavored to mark the safe harbors clearly.

The shareholder constituents of a Delaware corporation are entitled to rely upon their elected directors to discharge their fiduciary duties at all times. Whenever directors communicate publicly or directly with shareholders about the corporation's affairs, with or without a request for shareholder action, directors have a fiduciary duty to shareholders to exercise due care, good faith and loyalty. It follows *a fortiori* that when directors communicate publicly or directly with shareholders about corporate matters the sine qua non of directors' fiduciary duty to shareholders is honesty.

According to the appellants, the focus of the fiduciary duty of disclosure is to protect shareholders as the "beneficiaries" of all material information disseminated by the directors. The duty of disclosure is, and always has been, a specific application of the general fiduciary duty owed by directors. The duty of disclosure obligates directors to provide the stockholders with accurate and complete information material to a transaction or other corporate event that is being presented to them for action.

The issue in this case is not whether Mercury's directors breached their duty of disclosure. It is whether they breached their more general fiduciary duty of loyalty and good faith by knowingly disseminating to the stockholders false information about the financial condition of the company. The directors' fiduciary duties include the duty to deal with their stockholders honestly.

---

6. Zirn v. VLI Corp., Del. Supr., 681 A.2d 1050, 1056 (1996) (quoting Stroud v. Grace, 606 A.2d at 611) (emphasis added).

Shareholders are entitled to rely upon the truthfulness of all information disseminated to them by the directors they elect to manage the corporate enterprise. Delaware directors disseminate information in at least three contexts: public statements made to the market, including shareholders; statements informing shareholders about the affairs of the corporation without a request for shareholder action; and, statements to shareholders in conjunction with a request for shareholder action. Inaccurate information in these contexts may be the result of violation of the fiduciary duties of care, loyalty or good faith. We will examine the remedies that are available to shareholders for misrepresentations in each of these three contexts by the directors of a Delaware corporation.

In the absence of a request for stockholder action, the Delaware General Corporation Law does not require directors to provide shareholders with information concerning the finances or affairs of the corporation. Even when shareholder action is sought, the provisions in the General Corporation Law requiring notice to the shareholders of the proposed action do not require the directors to convey substantive information beyond a statutory minimum. Consequently, in the context of a request for shareholder action, the protection afforded by Delaware law is a judicially recognized equitable cause of action by shareholders against directors. . . .

The duty of directors to observe proper disclosure requirements derives from the combination of the fiduciary duties of care, loyalty and good faith. The plaintiffs contend that, because directors' fiduciary responsibilities are not "intermittent duties," there is no reason why the duty of disclosure should not be implicated in every public communication by a corporate board of directors. The directors of a Delaware corporation are required to disclose fully and fairly all material information within the board's control when it seeks shareholder action. When the directors disseminate information to stockholders when no stockholder action is sought, the fiduciary duties of care, loyalty and good faith apply. Dissemination of false information could violate one or more of those duties.

An action for a breach of fiduciary duty arising out of disclosure violations in connection with a request for stockholder action does not include the elements of reliance, causation and actual quantifiable monetary damages. Instead, such actions require the challenged disclosure to have a connection to the request for shareholder action. The essential inquiry in such an action is whether the alleged omission or misrepresentation is material. Materiality is determined with respect to the shareholder action being sought.[29]

The directors' duty to disclose all available material information in connection with a request for shareholder action must be balanced against its concomitant duty to protect the corporate enterprise, in particular, by keeping certain financial information confidential. Directors are required to provide shareholders with all information that is material to the action being requested and to provide a balanced, truthful account of all matters disclosed in the communications with shareholders.[31] Accordingly, directors have definitive guidance in discharging their

---

29. In Rosenblatt v. Getty Oil Co., 493 A.2d at 944, this Court adopted the materiality standard set forth by the United States Supreme Court in TSC Industries, Inc. v. Northway, Inc., 426 U.S. 438, 449, 96 S. Ct. 2126, 48 L. Ed. 2d 757 (1976).

31. Zirn v. VLI Corp., 681 A.2d at 1056. In Zirn II, this Court held, "in addition to the traditional duty to disclose all facts material to the proffered transaction, directors are under a fiduciary obligation to avoid misleading partial disclosures. The law of partial disclosure is likewise clear: Once defendants travel down the road of partial disclosure they have an obligation to provide the stockholders with an accurate, full and fair characterization of those historic events." (internal quotations omitted).

fiduciary duty by an analysis of the factual circumstances relating to the specific shareholder action being requested and an inquiry into the potential for deception or misinformation.

Fraud on Market — Regulated by Federal Law. When corporate directors impart information they must comport with the obligations imposed by both the Delaware law and the federal statutes and regulations of the United States Securities and Exchange Commission ("SEC"). Historically, federal law has regulated disclosures by corporate directors into the general interstate market. This Court has noted that "in observing its congressional mandate the SEC has adopted a 'basic philosophy of disclosure.'" Accordingly, this Court has held that there is "no legitimate basis to create a new cause of action which would replicate, by state decisional law, the provisions of . . . the 1934 Act."[36] In deference to the panoply of federal protections that are available to investors in connection with the purchase or sale of securities of Delaware corporations, this Court has decided not to recognize a state common law cause of action against the directors of Delaware corporations for "fraud on the market."[37] Here, it is to be noted, the claim appears to be made by those who did not sell and, therefore, would not implicate federal securities laws which relate to the purchase or sale of securities. . . .

Delaware law also protects shareholders who receive false communications from directors even in the absence of a request for shareholder action. When the directors are not seeking shareholder action, but are deliberately misinforming shareholders about the business of the corporation, either directly or by a public statement, there is a violation of fiduciary duty. That violation may result in a derivative claim on behalf of the corporation or a cause of action for damages. There may also be a basis for equitable relief to remedy the violation.

Here the complaint alleges (if true) an egregious violation of fiduciary duty by the directors in knowingly disseminating materially false information. Then it alleges that the corporation lost about $2 billion in value as a result. Then it merely claims that the action is brought on behalf of the named plaintiffs and the putative class. It is a non sequitur rather than a syllogism.

The allegation in paragraph 3 that the false disclosures resulted in the corporation losing virtually all its equity seems obliquely to claim an injury to the corporation. The plaintiffs, however, never expressly assert a derivative claim on behalf of the corporation or allege compliance with Court of Chancery Rule 23.1, which requires pre-suit demand or cognizable and particularized allegations that demand is excused. If the plaintiffs intend to assert a derivative claim, they should be permitted to replead to assert such a claim and any damage or equitable remedy sought on behalf of the corporation. Likewise, the plaintiffs should have the opportunity to replead to assert any individual cause of action and articulate a remedy that is appropriate on behalf of the named plaintiffs individually, or a properly recognizable class consistent with Court of Chancery Rule 23, and our decision in Gaffin.[47]

---

36. Arnold v. Society for Savings Bancorp, Inc., Del. Supr., 678 A.2d 533, 539 (1996).

37. Gaffin v. Teledyne, Inc., Del. Supr., 611 A.2d 467, 472 (1992). See Basic Incorporated v. Levinson, 485 U.S. 224, 241-42, 108 S. Ct. 978, 99 L. Ed. 2d 194 (1988) (discussing the theory of fraud on the market).

47. Gaffin v. Teledyne, Inc., 611 A.2d 467, 474 (1992) ("A class action may not be maintained in a purely common law or equitable fraud case since individual questions of law or fact, particularly as to the element of justifiable reliance, will inevitably predominate over common questions of law or fact."). . . .

The Court of Chancery properly dismissed the complaint before it against the individual director defendants, in the absence of well-pleaded allegations stating a derivative, class or individual cause of action and properly assertable remedy. Without a well-pleaded allegation in the complaint for a breach of fiduciary duty, there can be no claim for aiding and abetting such a breach. Accordingly, the plaintiffs' aiding and abetting claim against KPMG was also properly dismissed.

Nevertheless, we disagree with the Court of Chancery's holding that such a claim cannot be articulated on these facts. The plaintiffs should have been permitted to amend their complaint, if possible, to state a properly recognizable cause of action against the individual defendants and KPMG. Consequently, the Court of Chancery should have dismissed the complaint without prejudice.

Conclusion. The judgment of the Court of Chancery to dismiss the complaint is affirmed. The judgment to dismiss the complaint with prejudice is reversed. This matter is remanded for further proceedings in accordance with this opinion.

---

1. *Limited availability of the class action.* Even though a breach of fiduciary duty action may simplify the elements that a plaintiff must prove (for example, proof of scienter or an intent to defraud would logically seem unnecessary), *Malone* indicates that the critical procedural device of the class action may not be generally available in Delaware. This is because the issue of whether individual shareholders relied upon the alleged misstatement or omission is inherently an "individual" one, which varies from shareholder to shareholder. Under prevailing standards for class certification at both the state and federal levels, "common issues of law or fact" must "predominate" over "individual" ones. See Federal Rule of Civil Procedure 23(b)(3). At the federal level, however, class certification is greatly simplified by the "fraud on the market" doctrine, which presumptively eliminates the issue of individual reliance in the case of publicly traded securities that trade in "efficient" markets. Delaware does not, however, recognize the "fraud on the market" doctrine (indeed, *Malone* expressly rejected the doctrine), and hence the cause of action recognized in *Malone* is likely to be assertable only in individual actions. Although a large institutional investor might find litigating such an action to be cost efficient, individual shareholders rarely would.

2. *Impact of the Uniform Standards Act.* The Securities Litigation Uniform Standards Act of 1998 (the "Act") provides: "No covered class action based upon the statutory or common law of any state or subdivision thereof may be maintained in any State or Federal court by any private party alleging . . . an untrue statement or omission of a material fact in connection with the purchase or sale of a security. . . ."[30] The Act was principally intended to halt the migration of securities class actions from federal court to state court in the wake of the passage of the Private Securities Litigation Reform Act of 1995 (see page 426 infra), which tightened the pleading standards applicable to securities class actions in federal court

---

30. The Act adds a new §16 to the Securities Act of 1933 (15 U.S.C. §77(p) and a new §28(f) to the Securities Exchange Act of 1934 (15 U.S.C. §78 bb(f)). The language of these two sections is almost identical. For a review of this litigation and its possible intrusion on traditional federalism values, see Richard Painter, Responding to a False Alarm: Federal Preemption of State Securities Fraud Causes of Action, 84 Cornell L. Rev. 1 (1998).

and raised other barriers. Still, the passage of the Act means that certain traditional state law causes of action (including common law fraud and blue sky statutory antifraud provisions) can no longer be asserted in a class action in any court (state or federal). As *Malone* indicates, however, the Act is subject to some important limitations: (1) it applies only to publicly traded companies that are listed on a national securities exchange or Nasdaq; (2) it preempts only causes of action based on a material misstatement made in connection with a purchase or sale of a security; and (3) it expressly carves out from its preemption certain communications by an issuer or an affiliate concerning voting decisions, appraisal, or whether to tender shares into a tender offer.[31] Because of the "in connection with a purchase or sale" language in the Act, a class action would seemingly not be preempted (in either federal or state court) where management allegedly made materially false misrepresentations or omissions in connection with a proxy solicitation or other request for shareholder consent.[32] Also, suppose in *Malone* that the shareholders who read management's inflated financial statements did not sell their stock in Mercury. Can they still bring a class action in federal court alleging that they did *not* sell because of the false statements? A literal reading of the Act suggests that they could. The significance of such a possible class action on behalf of non-sellers will become clearer after the discussion of Blue Chip Stamps v. Manor Drug Stores (pages 353 infra).

4. FEDERAL LAW: EXPRESS ACTIONS

Both the '33 and '34 Acts set forth express private causes of action that were intended to respond to the unsatisfactory state of the common law. In particular, §§11 and 12(a)(2) of the '33 Act were intended "to broaden the law of deceit."[33]

Section 11. Section 11 was modeled on provisions in the English Companies Act, which had its origins, in turn, in the Directors Liability Act, which was enacted by Parliament in 1890 to overturn a restrictive precedent that had seemingly immunized corporate directors from liability for deceit.[34] Essentially, the '33 Act mandates the use of a formal disclosure document, known as the registration statement, and §11 allows a purchaser to sue the corporate issuer, any director, the underwriters, the accountants and other experts, and other persons, including senior management, who sign the registration statement if the registration statement contains a materially false misrepresentation or omission.

Departing significantly from both the common law of deceit and the blue sky statutes then in effect, §11 generally relieves the plaintiff of the obligation to prove scienter, reliance, or causation; indeed, the plaintiff normally need not even have read the prospectus. The defendant may, however, defend by showing that the plaintiff "knew of such untruth or omission" (§11(a)). Privity is also not required, meaning that the plaintiff may have purchased shares in the secondary market at any time within the statute of limitations. However, cases have interpreted §11 to require that the plaintiff prove that the purchased shares were shares sold under

31. See footnote 40 of the *Malone* decision.
32. However, where the proxy solicitation concerned a merger, this would normally be deemed a sale of securities and hence the action might be preempted.
33. Rosenberg v. Hano, 121 F.2d 818, 819 (3d Cir. 1941).
34. Derry v. Peek, 14 A.C. 337 (1889).

the registration statement. See Barnes v. Osofsky, 373 F.2d 269 (2d Cir. 1967). This "linear privity" requirement, which insists that purchasers in the secondary market trace their shares back to those included under the registration statement, poses a significant obstacle in the case of a publicly held corporation with a substantial number of shares outstanding prior to the offering. In these instances, only those who purchased from underwriters or dealers participating in the public offering are likely to be able to meet this linear privity requirement.

The most important defense under §11 (other than the defense that there was no material misrepresentation or omission) is the "due diligence" defense of §11(b). Although the corporation itself cannot raise this defense, most other defendants can assert one of two versions of this defense: First, under §11(b)(3)(A), they can seek to show that they had "after reasonable investigation, reasonable ground to believe and did believe" that all material facts were accurately disclosed. Second, as to those portions of the registration statement "purporting to be made on the authority of an expert," §11(b)(3)(C) provides that the defendants must show only that they "had no reasonable ground to believe and did not believe . . . that the statements therein were untrue or that there was an omission to state a material fact. . . ." Thus, in the case of these "expertised" portions of the registration statement, a defendant (other than the actual expert) need not conduct a "reasonable investigation" and need only have a reasonable belief in the document's accuracy. Obviously, this suggests an important defensive strategy for the corporate lawyer at the time the registration statement is drafted — namely, to "expertise" as much of the registration statement as possible by causing the most important facts to be set forth in the opinion of an "expert" (with the result that the more protective defense of §11(b)(3)(C) becomes applicable).

2. *Section 12(a)(2).* While this section overlaps with §11, it goes well beyond it in several important respects. First, it applies to oral statements made with respect to registered securities (while §11 applies only to statements made in the registration statement). Second, §12(a)(2) looks to the time of sale (whereas §11 is geared to the date on which the registration statement becomes effective). This is important when there are material developments after the registration statement becomes effective. As with §11, the plaintiff need not prove reliance, causation, or scienter. However, the defendant is given a defense of "reasonable care" much like the due diligence defense of §11(b), except that there is no reference in §12(a)(2) to the need for "reasonable investigation." Cases have divided over whether this omission means that a lesser showing of care than under §11 will suffice to meet the defendant's burden under §12(a)(2). Compare Sanders v. John Nuveen & Co., 524 F.2d 1064 (7th Cir. 1975), *on later appeal*, 619 F.2d 1222 (7th Cir. 1980) (largely equating defense under §12(a)(2) with an underwriter's duty under §11); Jackson v. Oppenheim, 533 F.2d 826, 829 n. 7 (2d Cir. 1976); Gilbert v. Nixon, 429 F.2d 348 (10th Cir. 1970).

Section 12(a)(2) is, however, narrower than §11 in one respect: The defendant must either have been in privity with the plaintiff or have solicited the sale. See Pinter v. Dahl, 486 U.S. 622 (1988). Finally, §12(a)(2) has a different damages formula. Effectively, it grants a rescission measure of damages, whereas damages under §11 are bounded by both the initial offering price and the price of the stock on the date of the suit's filing. Because plaintiffs can sue under both §§11 and 12(a)(2) at the same time, the more advantageous damage formula is always available to them.

Originally, §12(a)(2) was read to apply to all primary sales of securities, both in public registered offerings or pursuant to private placements and other statutory exemptions. See Hill York Corp. v. American Int'l Franchises, Inc., 448 F.2d 680 (5th Cir. 1971). Then courts began to divide as to whether it also applied to resales in the secondary market (by insiders and large block holders), with some decisions holding that it attached only to the initial distribution of securities. Then, in 1995, the Supreme Court in a 5-4 decision overturned the prior understanding of §12(a)(2), finding that it was not applicable to either private placements or resales, but only to the public offering process. In Gustafson v. Alloyd Co., 513 U.S. 561 (1995), the Court found that the phrase "by means of a prospectus or oral communication" in the fourth line of §12(a)(2) was intended to limit its reach to the registered public offerings in which prospectuses are used. Accordingly, in cases outside this context, private investors are required to rely on Rule 10b-5, page 345 infra, which requires a stronger showing of intent or scienter.

5. FEDERAL LAW: IMPLIED CIVIL LIABILITIES

An initial question about implied civil liabilities is why they should exist at all in statutes, such as the federal securities laws, that expressly provide for private causes of action. Indeed, to the extent that express private causes of action represent carefully fashioned compromises that give broad plaintiff standing but provide for specially designed defenses (such as §11(b)'s due diligence defense), judicial implication of an additional cause of action seems to upset these careful trade-offs. Nonetheless, three implied causes of action under the '34 Act are today recognized and have come to overshadow the express causes of action earlier surveyed:

1. Rule 10b-5, which applies to both a purchaser and a seller in securities transactions;
2. Rule 14a-9, which contains a similar antifraud rule applicable to proxy solicitation, reviewed in Chapter VI; and
3. Section 14(e), which applies to tender offers, analyzed in Chapter IX.

Although these antifraud rules are phrased in approximately the same language, each has received different judicial constructions, has different elements, requires the plaintiff to prove different levels of culpability, and confers broader or narrower standing.

a. The Origin of Rule 10b-5

Securities Exchange Act of 1934

Sec. 10. *Regulation of the use of manipulative and deceptive devices.* It shall be unlawful for any person, directly or indirectly, by the use of any means or instrumentality of interstate commerce or of the mails, or of any facility of any national securities exchange — . . .

(b) To use or employ, in connection with the purchase or sale of any security registered on a national securities exchange or any security not so registered, . . . any manipulative or deceptive device or contrivance in contravention of such rules and regulations as the Commission may prescribe as necessary or appropriate in the public interest or for the protection of investors.

Rule 10b-5. *Employment of manipulative and deceptive devices.* It shall be unlawful for any person, directly or indirectly, by the use of any means or instrumentality of interstate commerce, or of the mails, or of any facility of any national securities exchange,

(a) to employ any device, scheme, or artifice to defraud,

(b) to make any untrue statement of a material fact or to omit to state a material fact necessary in order to make the statements made, in the light of the circumstances under which they were made, not misleading, or

(c) to engage in any act, practice, or course of business which operates or would operate as a fraud or deceit upon any person,

in connection with the purchase or sale of any security.

The original intent. Given the subsequent prominence of Rule 10b-5, its adoption occurred in an ironically casual way. Milton Freeman, a draftsman of Rule 10b-5, has described its genesis as follows:

> I was sitting in my office in the S.E.C. building in Philadelphia and I received a call from Jim Treanor, who was then the Director of the Trading and Exchange Division. He said, "I have just been on the telephone with Paul Rowen," who was then the S.E.C. Regional Administrator in Boston, "and he has told me about the president of some company in Boston who is going around buying up the stock of his company from his own shareholders at $4 a share, and he has been telling them that the company is doing very badly, whereas, in fact, the earnings are going to be quadrupled and will be $2 a share for this coming year. Is there anything we can do about it?" So he came upstairs and I called in my secretary and I looked at Section 10(b) and I looked at Section 17, and I put them together, and the only discussion we had there was where "in connection with the purchase or sale" should be and we decided it should be at the end.
>
> We called the Commission and we got on the calendar, and I don't remember whether we got there that morning or after lunch. We passed a piece of paper around to all the commissioners. All the commissioners read the rule and they tossed it on the table, indicating approval. Nobody said anything except Sumner Pike, who said, "Well," he said, "we are against fraud, aren't we?" That is how it happened.
>
> . . . I never thought that twenty-odd years later it would be the biggest thing that had ever happened. It was intended to give the Commission power to deal with this problem. It had no relation in the Commission's contemplation to private proceedings.

Conference on Codification of the Federal Securities Laws, 22 Bus. Law. 793, 922 (1967).

b. The Rationale and Scope of Implied Liabilities

Rule 10b-5 does not provide for a private cause of action. Nonetheless, the first time a federal court faced the question of whether shareholders could sue under it, it implied a private cause of action with little difficulty (or analysis).[35] Not until 1964 did this issue reach the Supreme Court (and then the specific issue was a private cause of action under Rule 14a-9, which applies to proxy solicitations).

---

35. Kardon v. National Gypsum Co., 73 F. Supp. 798 (E.D. Pa. 1947).

J. I. Case Co. v. Borak
377 U.S. 426 (1964)

Mr. Justice Clark delivered the opinion of the Court.

This is a civil action brought by respondent, a stockholder of petitioner J. I. Case Company, charging deprivation of the preemptive rights of respondent and other shareholders by reason of a merger between Case and the American Tractor Corporation. It is alleged that the merger was effected through the circulation of a false and misleading proxy statement by those proposing the merger. The complaint was in two counts, the first based on diversity and claiming a breach of the directors' fiduciary duty to the stockholders. The second count alleged a violation of §14(a) of the Securities Exchange Act of 1934 with reference to the proxy solicitation material. The trial court held that as to this count it had no power to redress the alleged violations of the Act but was limited solely to the granting of declaratory relief thereon under §27 of the Act. The . . . Court of Appeals reversed . . . holding that the District Court had the power to grant remedial relief. . . . We granted certiorari. We consider only the question of whether §27 of the Act authorizes a federal cause of action for rescission or damages to a corporate stockholder with respect to a consummated merger which was authorized pursuant to the use of a proxy statement alleged to contain false and misleading statements violative of §14(a) of the Act. . . .

I. Respondent, the owner of 2,000 shares of common stock of Case acquired prior to the merger, brought this suit based on diversity jurisdiction seeking to enjoin a proposed merger between Case and the American Tractor Corporation (ATC) on various grounds. . . . The injunction was denied and the merger was thereafter consummated. Subsequently successive amended complaints were filed. . . . They alleged: that petitioners, or their predecessors, solicited or permitted their names to be used at a special stockholders' meeting at which the proposed merger with ATC was to be voted upon; that the proxy solicitation material so circulated was false and misleading in violation of §14(a) of the Act and Rule 14a-9 which the Commission had promulgated thereunder; that the merger was approved at the meeting by a small margin of votes and was thereafter consummated; that the merger would not have been approved but for the false and misleading statements in the proxy solicitation material; and that Case stockholders were damaged thereby. The respondent sought judgment holding the merger void and damages for himself and all other stockholders similarly situated, as well as such further relief "as equity shall require." . . .

II. It appears clear that private parties have a right under §27 to bring suit for violation of §14(a) of the Act. Indeed, this section specifically grants the appropriate District Courts jurisdiction over "all suits in equity and actions at law brought to enforce any liabilities or duty created" under the Act. The petitioners make no concessions, however, emphasizing that Congress made no specific preference to a private right of action in §14(a); that, in any event, the right . . . should be limited to prospective relief only. . . .

The purpose of §14(a) is to prevent management or others from obtaining authorization for corporate action by means of deceptive or inadequate disclosure in proxy solicitation. The section stemmed from the congressional belief that "[f]air corporate suffrage is an important right that should attach to every equity security bought on a public exchange." . . . It was intended to "control the conditions under which proxies may be solicited with a view of preventing the recurrence of abuses which . . . [had]

frustrated the free exercise of the voting rights of stockholders." . . . "Too often prox-ies are solicited without explanation to the stockholder of the real nature of the questions for which authority to cast his vote is sought." S. Rep. No. 792, 73d Cong., 2d Sess., 12. These broad remedial purposes are evidenced in the language of the section which makes it "unlawful for any person . . . to solicit or to permit the use of his name to solicit any proxy or consent . . . in contravention of such rules and regulations as the Commission may prescribe as necessary or appropriate in the public interest *or for the protection of investors.*" (Italics supplied.) While this language makes no specific reference to a private right of action, among its chief purposes is "the protection of investors," which certainly implies the availability of judicial relief where necessary to achieve that result.

. . . To hold that derivative actions are not within the sweep of the section would therefore be tantamount to a denial of private relief. Private enforcement of the proxy rules provides a necessary supplement to Commission action. As in anti-trust treble damage litigation, the possibility of civil damages or injunctive relief serves as a most effective weapon in the enforcement of the proxy requirements. The Commission advises that it examines over 2,000 proxy statements annually and each of them must necessarily be expedited. Time does not permit an independent examination of the facts set out in the proxy material and this results in the Commission's acceptance of the representations contained therein at their face value, unless contrary to other material on file with it. Indeed, on the allega-tions of respondent's complaint, the proxy material failed to disclose alleged unlawful manipulation of the stock of ATC, and this unlawful manipulation would not have been apparent to the Commission until after the merger.

We, therefore, believe that under the circumstances here it is the duty of the courts to be alert to provide such remedies as are necessary to make effective the congressional purpose. As was said in Sola Electric Co. v. Jefferson Electric Co., 317 U.S. 173, 176 (1942):

> When a federal statute condemns an act as unlawful, the extent and nature of the legal consequences of the condemnation, though left by the statute to judicial determina-tion, are nevertheless federal questions, the answers to which are to be derived from the statute and the federal policy which it has adopted. . . .

It is for the federal courts "to adjust their remedies so as to grant the necessary relief" where federally secured rights are invaded. "And it is also well settled that where legal rights have been invaded, and a federal statute provides for a general right to sue for such invasion, federal courts may use any available remedy to make good the wrong done." Bell v. Hood, 327 U.S. 678, 684 (1946). Section 27 grants the District Courts jurisdiction "of all suits in equity and actions at law brought to enforce any liability or duty created by this title. . . ." In passing on almost identical language found in the Securities Act of 1933, the Court found the words entirely sufficient to fashion a remedy to rescind a fraudulent sale, secure restitution and even to enforce the right to restitution against a third party holding assets of the vendor. Deckert v. Independence Shares Corp., 311 U.S. 282 (1940). This significant language was used:

> The power to *enforce* implies the power to make effective the right of recovery afforded by the Act. And the power to make the right of recovery effective implies

the power to utilize any of the procedures or actions normally available to the litigant according to the exigencies of the particular case.

Nor do we find merit in the contention that such remedies are limited to prospective relief. This was the position taken in Dann v. Studebaker-Packard Corp., 288 F.2d 201, where it was held that the "preponderance of questions of state law which would have to be interpreted and applied in order to grant the relief sought . . . is so great that the federal question involved . . . is really negligible in comparison." But we believe that the overriding federal law applicable here would, where the facts required, control the appropriateness of redress despite the provisions of state corporation law, for it "is not uncommon for federal courts to fashion federal law where federal rights are concerned." Textile Workers v. Lincoln Mills, 353 U.S. 448, 457 (1957). In addition, the fact that questions of state law must be decided does not change the character of the right; it remains federal. . . .

Moreover, if federal jurisdiction were limited to the granting of declaratory relief, victims of deceptive proxy statements would be obliged to go into state courts for remedial relief. And if the law of the State happened to attach no responsibility to the use of misleading proxy statements, the whole purpose of the section might be frustrated. Furthermore, the hurdles that the victim might face (such as separate suits, . . . security for expenses statutes, bringing in all parties necessary for complete relief, etc.) might well prove insuperable to effective relief.

---

1. *The doctrinal basis for implying private actions.* The idea that private civil liability can be implied from a penal statute has a long history in the law of negligence. See James B. Thayer, Public Wrong and Private Action, 27 Harv. L. Rev. 317 (1914) (tracing history back through early English statutes). As a result, in 1947 on the first occasion that a private plaintiff sought to rely on Rule 10b-5, a federal district court recognized an implied cause of action under the Rule.[36] It seemed obvious at the time. From the standpoint of the law of negligence, the reasonable person would not disobey the legislature's command, and hence a violation of legislatively prescribed standards (such as a speed limit) was "negligence per se" (in most state jurisdictions) or, at the least, "evidence of negligence." See Fowler V. Harper, Fleming James & Oscar S. Gray, The Law of Torts §17.6 (1986); Clarence Morris, The Role of Criminal Statutes in Negligence Actions, 49 Colum. L. Rev. 21 (1949); Texas & Pacific Ry. Co. v. Rigsby, 241 U.S. 33, 39-40 (1916).

Section 874A of the Restatement (Second) of Torts states the standard formulation of this doctrine: "When a legislative provision protects a class of persons by proscribing or requiring certain conduct but does not provide a civil remedy for the violation, the court may, if it determines that the remedy is appropriate in furtherance of the purpose of the legislation and needed to assure the effectiveness of the provision, accord to an injured member of the class a right of action, using a suitable existing tort action or a new cause of action analogous to an existing tort action." In this light, the Supreme Court's statement in *Borak* that "[p]rivate enforcement of the proxy rules provides a necessary supplement to Commission action" and its stress on the SEC's heavy workload can be read as an assertion, in

---

36. See Kardon v. National Gypsum Co., 73 F. Supp. 798 (E.D. Pa. 1947).

Section 874A's language, that the remedy "is . . . needed to assure the effectiveness of the provision. . . ."

2. *The significance of a federal system.* Although private enforcement certainly does supplement public enforcement by the SEC of the proxy rules, it does not follow from this fact that §27 of the '34 Act was intended (or should be read) to confer jurisdiction on federal courts to hear private causes of action for violations of the '34 Act.[37] The more logical interpretation of §27 is that it was intended to authorize federal courts to hear express private actions and SEC injunctive proceedings (which §21 of the '34 Act authorizes the SEC to bring). *Borak* then is a case without a fully elaborated rationale for why §27 confers standing on private plaintiffs.

In any event, in the 1970s the tide began to turn against judicial implication of private causes of action, with the Supreme Court becoming increasingly resistant to claims that all wrongs under the federal securities laws were actionable in private suits. In Piper v. Chris-Craft Industries, Inc., 430 U.S. 1 (1977), the initial decision to decline to imply a private cause of action under the federal securities laws, the issue involved standing to sue under §14(e) of the '34 Act, which is the antifraud section applicable to tender offers. Specifically, an unsuccessful bidder sought to sue the winning bidder on the theory that its fraudulent conduct cost the plaintiff corporation the opportunity to acquire the valuable target corporation. The *Piper* Court found standing to be lacking by construing the purposes underlying §14(e) more narrowly than it had construed §14(a) in *Borak*:

> The legislative history thus shows the sole purpose of the Williams Act was the protection of investors who are confronted with a tender offer. . . . We find no hint in the legislative history, on which respondent so heavily relies, that Congress contemplated a private cause of action for damages by one of several contending offerors against a successful bidder or by a losing contender against the target corporation. . . .
>
> Our conclusion as to the legislative history is confirmed by the analysis in Cort v. Ash, 422 U.S. 66 (1975). There, the Court identified four factors as "relevant" in determining whether a private remedy is implicit in a statute not expressly providing one. The first is whether the plaintiff is "'one of the class for whose *especial* benefit the statute was enacted. . . .'" . . . As previously indicated, examination of the statute and its genesis shows that Chris-Craft is not an intended beneficiary of the Williams Act, and surely is not one "for whose *especial* benefit the statute was enacted." To the contrary, Chris-Craft is a member of the class whose activities Congress intended to regulate for the protection and benefit of an entirely distinct class, shareholder-offerees. As a party whose previously unregulated conduct was purposefully brought under federal control by the statute, Chris-Craft can scarcely lay claim to the status of "beneficiary" whom Congress considered in need of protection.
>
> Second, in Cort v. Ash we inquired whether there was "any indication of legislative intent, explicit or implicit, either to create such a remedy or to deny one." Although

---

37. Section 27 of the '34 Act provides: "The district courts of the United States . . . shall have exclusive jurisdiction of violations of this title or the rules and regulations thereunder, and of all suits in equity and actions at law brought to enforce any liability or duty created by this title or the rules and regulations thereunder. . . . Any suit or action to enforce any liability or duty created by this title or rules and regulations thereunder, or enjoin any violation of such title or rules and regulations, may be brought in any such district or in the district wherein the defendant is found or is an inhabitant or transacts business. . . ." Section 21 of the '34 Act authorizes the SEC to seek an injunction in any district court to enjoin any violation of the Act or the rules and regulations thereunder. No comparable provision authorizes a private litigant to sue simply because a rule is violated (although §§9 and 18 of the '34 Act do authorize private causes of action for specified violations).

the historical materials are barren of any express intent to deny a damages remedy to tender offerors as a class, there is, as we have noted, no indication that Congress intended to create a damages remedy in favor of the loser in a contest for control. Fairly read, we think the legislative documents evince the narrow intent to curb the unregulated activities of tender offerors. The expression of this purpose, which pervades the legislative history, negates the claim that tender offerors were intended to have additional weapons in the form of an implied cause of action for damages, particularly if a private damages action confers no advantage on the expressly protected class of shareholder-offerees, a matter we discuss later. . . .

Third, Cort v. Ash tells us that we must ascertain whether it is "consistent with the underlying purposes of the legislative scheme to imply such a remedy for the plaintiff." We conclude that it is not. As a disclosure mechanism aimed especially at protecting shareholders of target corporations, the Williams Act cannot consistently be interpreted as conferring a monetary remedy upon regulated parties, particularly where the award would not redound to the direct benefit of the protected class. . . .

Nor can we agree that an ever-present threat of damages against a successful contestant in a battle for control will provide significant additional protection for shareholders in general. The deterrent value, if any, of such awards can never be ascertained with precision. More likely, however, is the prospect that shareholders may be prejudiced because some tender offers may never be made if there is a possibility of massive damages claims for what courts subsequently hold to be an actionable violation of §14(e). Even a contestant who "wins the battle" for control may well wind up exposed to a costly "war" in a later and successful defense of its victory. Or at worst — on Chris-Craft's damage theory — the victorious tender offeror or the target corporation might be subject to a large substantive judgment, plus high costs of litigation. . . .

Fourth, under the Cort v. Ash analysis, we must decide whether "the cause of action [is] one traditionally relegated to state law . . ." 422 U.S. at 78. Despite the pervasiveness of federal securities regulation, the Court of Appeals concluded in these cases that Chris-Craft's complaint would give rise to a cause of action under common-law principles of interference with a prospective commercial advantage. Although Congress is, of course, free to create a remedial scheme in favor of contestants in tender offers, we conclude, as we did in Cort v. Ash, that "it is entirely appropriate in this instance to relegate [the offeror or bidder] and others in [that] situation to whatever remedy is created by state law," at least to the extent that the offeror seeks damages for having been wrongfully denied a "fair opportunity" to compete for control of another corporation.

What we have said thus far suggests that, unlike J. I. Case Co. v. Borak, supra, judicially creating a damages action in favor of Chris-Craft is unnecessary to ensure the fulfillment of Congress' purposes in adopting the Williams Act. Even though the SEC operates in this context under the same practical restraints recognized by the Court in *Borak*, institutional limitations alone do not lead to the conclusion that any party interested in a tender offer should have a cause of action for damages against a competing bidder. First, as Judge Friendly observed in Electronic Specialty Co. v. International Controls Corp., 409 F.2d 937, 947 (CA2 1969), in corporate control contests the stage of preliminary injunctive relief, rather than post-contest lawsuit, "is the time when relief can best be given." Furthermore, awarding damages to parties other than the protected class of shareholders has only a remote, if any, bearing upon implementing the congressional policy of protecting shareholders who must decide whether to tender or retain their stock.[28] Indeed, as we suggested earlier, a damages

---

28. Our holding is a limited one. Whether shareholder-offerees, the class protected by §14(e), have an implied cause of action under §14(e) is not before us, and we intimate no view on the matter. Nor is the target corporation's standing to sue an issue in the case. We hold only that a tender offeror, suing in its capacity as a takeover bidder, does not have standing to sue for damages under §14(e).

award of this nature may well be inconsistent with the interests of many members of the protected class and of only indirect value to shareholders who accepted the exchange offer to the defeated takeover contestant.

We therefore conclude that Chris-Craft, as a defeated tender offeror, has no implied cause of action for damages under §14(e). . . .

The trend toward refusing to imply a private cause of action accelerated after the *Chris-Craft* decision. Whereas it had used the four-part test of Cort v. Ash, which would sometimes support implication of a private remedy, the Supreme Court soon dropped the last two criteria and deemed the second — i.e., legislative intent — to be alone dispositive.

A major decision in this transition was Touche Ross & Co. v. Redington, 442 U.S. 560 (1979), in which the Court was faced with the question of whether the customers of an insolvent brokerage firm, who had lost funds or securities on deposit with the firm when it failed, could sue the auditor who audited the brokerage firm's financial statements, which financial statements an SEC rule required to be filed with the Commission. Reversing lower courts that had permitted the suit, the Court said:

> The question of the existence of a statutory cause of action is, of course, one of statutory construction. . . . [The] argument in favor of implication of a private right of action based on tort principles, therefore, is entirely misplaced. As we recently have emphasized, "the fact that a federal statute has been violated and some person harmed does not automatically give rise to a private cause of action in favor of that person." Cannon v. University of Chicago [441 U.S. 677 (1979)] at 688. Instead, our task is limited solely to determining whether Congress intended to create the private right of action asserted by SIPC and the Trustee. And as with any case involving the interpretation of a statute, our analysis must begin with the language of the statute itself. . . .
>
> In terms, §17(a) simply requires broker-dealers and others to keep such records and file such reports as the Commission may prescribe. It does not, by its terms, purport to create a private cause of action in favor of anyone. It is true that in the past our cases have held that in certain circumstances a private right of action may be implied in a statute not expressly providing one. But in those cases finding such implied private remedies, the statute in question at least prohibited certain conduct or created federal rights in favor of private parties. . . . By contrast, §17(a) neither confers rights on private parties nor proscribes any conduct as unlawful.
>
> The intent of §17(a) is evident from its face. Section 17(a) is like provisions in countless other statutes that simply require certain regulated businesses to keep records and file periodic reports to enable the relevant governmental authorities to perform their regulatory functions. The reports and records provide the regulatory authorities with the necessary information to oversee compliance with and enforce the various statutes and regulations with which they are concerned. . . .
>
> But §17(a) does not by any stretch of its language purport to confer private damages rights or, indeed, any remedy in the event the regulatory authorities are unsuccessful in achieving their objectives and the broker becomes insolvent before corrective steps can be taken. By its terms, §17(a) is forward-looking, not retrospective; it seems to forestall insolvency, not to provide recompense after it has occurred. In short, there is no basis in the language of §17(a) for inferring that a civil cause of action for damages lay in favor of anyone.

3. *The "new learning" of* Redington. *Redington* found that §27 of the '34 Act is intended only to confer jurisdiction on federal district courts to hear causes of

action that were authorized, expressly or implicitly, by Congress. In effect, it rejected *Borak*'s tort-based analysis in favor of a statutory construction approach that assumes that Congress would have clearly indicated an intent to permit private actions if it had wished to authorize them. *Redington* even hinted at a possible further constriction of Rule 10b-5. Footnote 19 of the case explained the existence of a private cause of action under Rule 10b-5 as simply an acquiescence "in the 25-year-old acceptance by the lower federal courts of an implied action under §10(b)." In addition, *Redington* suggested that the existence of express causes of action tended to exclude implied ones; this form of analysis suggested that Rule 10b-5 could be cut back to a relatively minor role of filling in the gaps between express causes of action. In particular, because §18(a) of the '34 Act provides an express cause of action for persons who relied on reports filed with the SEC, its existence could be read to preclude both the proposed cause of action rejected in *Redington* and any Rule 10b-5 suit based on such filings.

4. *The grandfathering of Rule 10b-5.* The issue obliquely raised in *Redington* about whether courts may imply a private cause of action where the legislature had enacted a more limited express cause of action was faced by the Court four years later in Herman & MacLean v. Huddleston, 459 U.S. 375 (1983). Specifically, the issue there was whether purchasers of registered securities who could have sued under §11 of the '33 Act were entitled to assert an implied cause of action under Rule 10b-5. Either because of the longer statute of limitations applicable to Rule 10b-5 actions or because more collateral participants could be reached in a Rule 10b-5 action, a plaintiff who is eligible to sue under §11 may often still prefer to raise a Rule 10b-5 cause of action. The Court permitted the Rule 10b-5 action in *Huddleston*, notwithstanding its earlier hints of a contrary result in *Redington*, and distinguished the two causes of action as follows:

> Although limited in scope, Section 11 places a relatively minimal burden on a plaintiff. In contrast, Section 10(b) is a "catchall" antifraud provision, but it requires a plaintiff to carry a heavier burden to establish a cause of action. While a Section 11 action must be brought by a purchaser of a registered security, must be based on misstatements or omissions in a registration statement, and can only be brought against certain parties, a Section 10(b) action can be brought by a purchaser or seller of "any security" against "any person" who has used "any manipulative or deceptive device or contrivance" in connection with the purchase or sale of a security. However, a Section 10(b) plaintiff carries a heavier burden than a Section 11 plaintiff. Most significantly, he must prove that the defendant acted with scienter, i.e., with intent to deceive, manipulate or defraud.
>
> Since Section 11 and Section 10(b) address different types of wrongdoing, we see no reason to carve out an exception to Section 10(b) for fraud occurring in a registration statement just because the same conduct may also be actionable under Section 11. Exempting such conduct from liability under Section 10(b) would conflict with the basic purpose of the 1933 Act: to provide greater protection to purchasers of registered securities. It would be anomalous indeed if the special protection afforded to purchasers in a registered offering by the 1933 Act were deemed to deprive such purchasers of the protections against manipulation and deception that Section 10(b) makes available to all persons who deal in securities. . . .
>
> Accordingly, we hold that the availability of an express remedy under Section 11 of the 1933 Act does not preclude defrauded purchasers of registered securities from maintaining an action under Section 10(b) of the 1934 Act. To this extent the judgment of the court of appeals is affirmed. . . .

A year earlier, in Merrill Lynch, Pierce, Fenner & Smith, Inc. v. Curran, 456 U.S. 353 (1982), the Court implied a private cause of action under the antifraud provisions of the more recently passed Commodity Exchange Act, which regulates futures, not securities. The Court reasoned that this statute had been clearly modeled after the '34 Act and Rule 10b-5 and was thus intended by Congress to apply equivalent standards to the futures and commodities markets as then prevailed in the securities market. In addition, an implied cause of action under the Commodity Exchange Act had already been recognized by several lower courts when Congress in 1974 enacted comprehensive amendments to the Commodity Exchange Act—a step that the majority in a 5-4 decision saw as adopting the then prevailing liberal interpretation of *Borak* as to when implied causes of action arose.

As a result, private causes of action under Rules 10b-5 and 14a-9 now seem "grandfathered" by *Curran* and *Huddleston*. In addition, in the Private Securities Litigation Reform Act of 1995 (discussed infra), Congress elaborately specified the requirements that a private plaintiff under the federal securities laws had to satisfy to plead and prove securities fraud, thereby implicitly conceding that a private cause of action existed. Still, the status of antifraud provisions other than Rule 10b-5 and Rule 14a-9 is far less clear. In particular, the continuing availability of private actions under §14(e) of the '34 Act is open to some question, although most decisions have liberally permitted the target corporation to seek injunctive relief.

c. The Elements of a Cause of Action Under Rule 10b-5

It is convenient for purposes of analysis and organization to break down the elements of a cause of action under Rule 10b-5 into five elements: (1) standing; (2) materiality; (3) causation (including the subsidiary issue of reliance); (4) scienter (or, more generally, the standard of culpability); and (5) damages. As will be seen, causes of action under either Rule 14a-9 (dealing with proxy fraud) or §14(e) of the '34 Act (fraud in tender offers) may also be analyzed in this manner. These five elements essentially approximate the traditional elements of a cause of action for deceit (the "five fingers of fraud"). This taxonomy does not capture all elements that may be necessary in some special contexts; e.g., liability for insider trading requires an additional element—the breach of a fiduciary duty owed to the corporation, discussed in Sec. D of this chapter. Still, it provides a useful framework for organizing a highly complicated body of law.

i. Standing Under Rule 10b-5: Limiting the Plaintiff Class

Blue Chip Stamps v. Manor Drug Stores
421 U.S. 723 (1975)

MR. JUSTICE REHNQUIST delivered the opinion of the Court. . . .

In 1963 the United States filed a civil antitrust action against Blue Chip Stamp Co. (Old Blue Chip), a company in the business of providing trading stamps to retailers, and nine retailers who owned 90% of its shares. In 1967 the action was terminated by the entry of a consent decree . . . [which] contemplated a plan of reorganization whereby Old Blue Chip was to be merged into a newly formed corporation, Blue Chip Stamps (New Blue Chip). The holdings of the majority shareholders of Old Blue Chip were to be reduced, and New Blue Chip, one of the petitioners here, was required under the plan to offer a substantial number of its shares of common stock to retailers who had used the stamp service in the past but who were not shareholders in the old company. . . .

The reorganization plan was carried out, the offering was registered with the SEC as required by the 1933 Act, and a prospectus was distributed to all offerees as required by §5 of that Act. Somewhat more than 50% of the offered units were actually purchased. In 1970, two years after the offering, respondent, a former user of the stamp service and therefore an offeree of the 1968 offering, filed this suit in the United States District Court for the Central District of California. Defendants below and petitioners here are Old and New Blue Chip, eight of the nine majority shareholders of Old Blue Chip, and the directors of New Blue Chip (collectively called Blue Chip).

Respondent's complaint alleged, inter alia, that . . . Blue Chip intentionally made the prospectus overly pessimistic in order to discourage respondent and other members of the allegedly large class whom it represents from accepting what was intended to be a bargain offer, so that the rejected shares might later be offered to the public at a higher price. The complaint alleged that class members because of and in reliance on the false and misleading prospectus failed to purchase the offered units. Respondent therefore sought on behalf of the alleged class some $21,400,000 in damages representing the lost opportunity to purchase the units; the right to purchase the previously rejected units at the 1968 price; and in addition, it sought some $25,000,000 in exemplary damages.

The only portion of the litigation thus initiated which is before us is whether respondent may base its action on Rule 10b-5 of the Securities and Exchange Commission without having either bought or sold the securities described in the allegedly misleading prospectus. The District Court dismissed respondent's complaint for failure to state a claim upon which relief might be granted. . . . [A] divided panel of the Court of Appeals sustained its position and reversed the District Court.[3] . . . .

[The Court noted that the first appellate decision to analyze the issue of a "purchaser or seller" requirement was Birnbaum v. Newport Steel Corp., 193 F.2d 461 (2d Cir. 1992).] The panel which decided *Birnbaum* consisted of Chief Judge Swan and Judges Learned Hand and Augustus Hand, and the opinion was written by the last named. Since both §10(b) and Rule 10b-5 proscribed only fraud "in connection with the purchase or sale" of securities, and since the history of §10(b) revealed no congressional intention to extend a private civil remedy for money damages to other than defrauded purchasers or sellers of securities, in contrast to the express civil remedy provided by §16(b) of the 1934 Act, the court concluded that the plaintiff class in a Rule 10b-5 action was limited to actual purchasers and sellers. . . . [V]irtually all lower federal courts facing the issue in the hundreds of reported cases presenting this question over the past quarter century have reaffirmed *Birnbaum*'s conclusion that the plaintiff class for purposes of §10(b) and Rule 10b-5 private damage actions is limited to purchasers and sellers of securities. . . .

In 1957 and again in 1959, the Securities and Exchange Commission sought from Congress amendment of §10(b) to change its wording from "in connection with the purchase or sale of any security" to "in connection with the purchase or sale of, *or*

---

3. The Court of Appeals opinion is reported at 492 F.2d 136 (1973).

any attempt to purchase or sell, any security." . . . Opposition to the amendment was based on fears of the extension of civil liability under §10(b) that it would cause. . . . Neither change was adopted by Congress.

The longstanding acceptance by the courts, coupled with Congress' failure to reject *Birnbaum*'s reasonable interpretation of the wording of §10(b), wording which is directed toward injury suffered "in connection with the purchase or sale" of securities,[5] argues significantly in favor of acceptance of the *Birnbaum* rule by this Court. . . .

Available evidence from the texts of the 1933 and 1934 Acts as to the congressional scheme in this regard, though not conclusive, supports the result reached by the *Birnbaum* court. The wording of §10(b) directed at fraud "in connection with the purchase or sale" of securities stands in contrast with the parallel antifraud provision of the 1933 Act, §17(a), reaching fraud "in the offer or sale" of securities. Cf. §5 of the 1933 Act. When Congress wished to provide a remedy to those who neither purchase nor sell securities, it had little trouble in doing so expressly. Cf. §16(b) of the 1934 Act. . . .

One of the justifications advanced for implication of a cause of action under §10(b) lies in §29(b) of the 1934 Act, providing that a contract made in violation of any provision of the 1934 Act is voidable at the option of the deceived party. . . . But that justification is absent when there is no actual purchase or sale of securities, or a contract to purchase or sell, affected or tainted by a violation of §10(b). . . .

The principal express nonderivative private civil remedies, created by Congress contemporaneously with the passage of §10(b), for violations of various provisions of the 1933 and 1934 Acts are by their terms expressly limited to purchasers or sellers of securities. Thus §11(a) of the 1933 Act confines the cause of action it grants to "any person acquiring such security" while the remedy granted by §12 of that Act is limited to the "person purchasing such security." Section 9 of the 1934 Act, prohibiting a variety of fraudulent and manipulative devices, limits the express civil remedy provided for its violation to "any person who shall purchase or sell any security" in a transaction affected by a violation of the provision. Section 18 of the 1934 Act, prohibiting false or misleading statements in reports or other documents required to be filed by the 1934 Act, limits the express remedy provided for its violation to "any person . . . who . . . shall have purchased or sold a security at a price which was affected by such statement. . . ." It would indeed be anomalous to impute to Congress an intention to expand the plaintiff class for a judicially implied cause of action beyond the bounds it delineated for comparable express causes of action.

Having said all this, we would by no means be understood as suggesting that we are able to divine from the language of §10(b) the express "intent of Congress" as to

---

5. Mr. Justice Blackmun, dissenting, finds support in the literal language of §10(b) since he concludes that in his view "the word 'sale' ordinarily and naturally may be understood to mean, not only a single, individualized act transferring property from one party to another, but also the generalized event of public disposal of property through advertisement, auction, or some other market mechanism." But this ignores the fact that this carefully drawn statute itself defines the term "sale" for purposes of the Act and . . . Congress expressly deleted from the Act's definition events such as offers and advertisements which may ultimately lead to a completed sale. Moreover, the extension of the word "sale" to include offers is quite incompatible with Congress' separate definition and use of these terms in the 1933 and 1934 Acts. Cf. §2(3) of the 1933 Act. Beyond this, the wording of §10(b), making fraud *in connection with the purchase or sale of a security* a violation of the Act, is surely badly strained when construed to provide a cause of action, not to purchasers and sellers of securities, but to the world at large.

the contours of a private cause of action under Rule 10b-5. When we deal with private actions under Rule 10b-5, we deal with a judicial oak which has grown from little more than a legislative acorn. Such growth may be quite consistent with the congressional enactment and with the role of the federal judiciary in interpreting it, . . . but it would be disingenuous to suggest that either Congress in 1934 or the Securities and Exchange Commission in 1942 foreordained the present state of the law with respect to Rule 10b-5. It is therefore proper that we consider, in addition to the factors already discussed, what may be described as policy considerations when we come to flesh out the portions of the law with respect to which neither the congressional enactment nor the administrative regulations offer conclusive guidance. . . . A great majority of the many commentators on the issue before us have taken the view that the *Birnbaum* limitation on the plaintiff class in a Rule 10b-5 action for damages is an arbitrary restriction which unreasonably prevents some deserving plaintiffs from recovering damages which have in fact been caused by violations of Rule 10b-5. See, e.g., Lowenfels, The Demise of the *Birnbaum* Doctrine: A New Era for Rule 10b-5, 54 Va. L. Rev. 268 (1968). The Securities and Exchange Commission has filed an amicus brief in this case espousing that same view. We have no doubt that this is indeed a disadvantage of the *Birnbaum* rule.[9] . . . But we are of the opinion that there are countervailing advantages to the *Birnbaum* rule, purely as a matter of policy, although those advantages are more difficult to articulate than is the disadvantage.

There has been widespread recognition that litigation under Rule 10b-5 presents a danger of vexatiousness different in degree and in kind from that which accompanies litigation in general. . . .

The first of these concerns is that in the field of federal securities laws governing disclosure of information even a complaint which by objective standards may have very little chance of success at trial has a settlement value to the plaintiff out of any proportion to its prospect of success at trial so long as he may prevent the suit from being resolved against him by dismissal or summary judgment. The very pendency of the lawsuit may frustrate or delay normal business activity of the defendant which is totally unrelated to the lawsuit. See, e.g., Sargent, The SEC and the Individual Investor: Restoring His Confidence in the Market, 60 Va. L. Rev. 553, 562-572 (1974); Dooley, The Effects of Civil Liability on Investment Banking and the New Issues Market, 58 Va. L. Rev. 776, 822-843 (1972).

Congress itself recognized the potential for nuisance or "strike" suits in this type of litigation, and in Title II of the 1934 Act amended §11 of the 1933 Act to provide that: "In any suit under this or any other section of this title the court may, in its discretion, require an undertaking for the payment of the costs of such suit, including reasonable attorney's fees. . . ."

Where Congress in those sections of the 1933 Act which expressly conferred a private cause of action for damages, adopted a provision uniformly regarded as designed to deter "strike" or nuisance actions, Cohen v. Beneficial Loan Corp., 337 U.S. 541, 548-549 (1949), that fact alone justifies our consideration of such potential

---

9. Obviously this disadvantage is attenuated to the extent that remedies are available to nonpurchasers and nonsellers under state law. Cf. §28 of the Securities Exchange Act of 1934. . . . Thus, for example, in *Birnbaum* itself, while the plaintiffs found themselves without federal remedies, the conduct alleged as the gravamen of the federal complaint later provided the basis for recovery in a cause of action based on state law. See . . . [Perlman v. Feldmann, page 1051 infra]. And in the immediate case, respondent has filed a state-court class action held in abeyance pending the outcome of this suit. . . .

in determining the limits of the class of plaintiffs who may sue in an action wholly implied from the language of the 1934 Act.

The potential for possible abuse of the liberal discovery provisions of the Federal Rules of Civil Procedure may likewise exist in this type of case to a greater extent than they do in other litigation. The prospect of extensive deposition of the defendant's officers and associates and the concomitant opportunity for extensive discovery of business documents, is a common occurrence in this and similar types of litigation. To the extent that this process eventually produces relevant evidence which is useful in determining the merits of the claims asserted by the parties, it bears the imprimatur of those Rules and of the many cases liberally interpreting them. But to the extent that it permits a plaintiff with a largely groundless claim to simply take up the time of a number of other people, with the right to do so representing an *in terrorem* increment of the settlement value, rather than a reasonably founded hope that the process will reveal relevant evidence, it is a social cost rather than a benefit. Yet to broadly expand the class of plaintiffs who may sue under Rule 10b-5 would appear to encourage the least appealing aspect of the use of the discovery rules.

Without the *Birnbaum* rule, an action under Rule 10b-5 will turn largely on which oral version of a series of occurrences the jury may decide to credit and therefore no matter how improbable the allegations of the plaintiff, the case will be virtually impossible to dispose of prior to trial other than by settlement. In the words of Judge Hufstedler's dissenting opinion in the Court of Appeals:

> The great ease with which plaintiffs can allege the requirements for the majority's standing rule and the greater difficulty that plaintiffs are going to have proving the allegations suggest that the majority's rule will allow a relatively high proportion of "bad" cases into court. The risk of strike suits is particularly high in such cases; although they are difficult to prove at trial, they are even more difficult to dispose of before trial.

492 F.2d, at 147 n.9.

The *Birnbaum* rule, on the other hand, permits exclusion prior to trial of those plaintiffs who were not themselves purchasers or sellers of the stock in question.

The fact of purchase of stock and the fact of sale of stock are generally matters which are verifiable by documentation, and do not depend upon oral recollection, so that failure to qualify under the *Birnbaum* rule is a matter that can normally be established by the defendant either on a motion to dismiss or on a motion for summary judgment.

Obviously there is no general legal principle that courts in fashioning substantive law should do so in a manner which makes it easier, rather than more difficult, for a defendant to obtain summary judgment. But in this type of litigation, where the mere existence of an unresolved lawsuit has settlement value to the plaintiff not only because of the possibility that he may prevail on the merits, an entirely legitimate component of settlement value, but because of the threat of extensive discovery and disruption of normal business activities which may accompany a lawsuit which is groundless in any event, but cannot be proved so before trial, such a factor is not to be totally dismissed. The *Birnbaum* rule undoubtedly excludes plaintiffs who have in fact been damaged by violations of Rule 10b-5, and to that extent it is undesirable. But it also separates in a readily demonstrable manner the group of plaintiffs who actually purchased or actually sold, and whose version of the facts is therefore more likely to be believed by the trier of fact, from the vastly larger world of potential plaintiffs who might successfully allege a claim but could seldom succeed in proving it. And this fact is one of its advantages.

The second ground for fear of vexatious litigation is based on the concern that, given the generalized contours of liability, the abolition of the *Birnbaum* rule would throw open to the trier of fact many rather hazy issues of historical fact the proof of which depended almost entirely on oral testimony. We in no way disparage the worth and frequent high value of oral testimony when we say that dangers of its abuse appear to exist in this type of action to a peculiarly high degree. The Securities and Exchange Commission, while opposing the adoption of the *Birnbaum* rule by this Court, . . . suggests that in particular cases additional requirements of corroboration of testimony and more limited measure of damages would correct the dangers of an expanded class of plaintiffs.

But the very necessity, or at least the desirability, of fashioning unique rules of corroboration and damages as a correlative to the abolition of the *Birnbaum* rule suggests that the rule itself may have something to be said for it.

In considering the policy underlying the *Birnbaum* rule, it is not inappropriate to advert briefly to the tort of misrepresentation and deceit, to which a claim under §10b-5 certainly has some relationship. Originally under the common law of England such an action was not available to one other than a party to a business transaction. That limitation was eliminated in Pasley v. Freeman, 3 T.R. 51, 100 Eng. Rep. 450 (1789). . . . And it has long been established in the ordinary case of deceit that a misrepresentation which leads to a refusal to purchase or to sell is actionable in just the same way as a representation which leads to the consummation of a purchase or sale. Butler v. Watkins, 13 Wall. 456 (1872). These aspects of the evolution of the tort of deceit and misrepresentation suggest a direction away from rules such as *Birnbaum*.

But the typical fact situation in which the classic tort of misrepresentation and deceit evolved was light years away from the world of commercial transactions to which Rule 10b-5 is applicable. The plaintiff in *Butler*, supra, for example, claimed that he had held off the market a patented machine for tying cotton bales which he had developed by reason of the fraudulent representations of the defendant. But the report of the case leaves no doubt that the plaintiff and defendant met with one another in New Orleans, that one presented a draft agreement to the other, and that letters were exchanged relating to that agreement. . . .

In today's universe of transactions governed by the 1934 Act, privity of dealing or even personal contact between potential defendant and potential plaintiff is the exception and not the rule. The stock of issuers is listed on financial exchanges utilized by tens of millions of investors, and corporate representations reach a potential audience, encompassing not only the diligent few who peruse filed corporate reports or the sizable number of subscribers to financial journals, but the readership of the Nation's daily newspapers. Obviously neither the fact that issuers or other potential defendants under Rule 10b-5 reach a large number of potential investors, or the fact that they are required by law to make their disclosures conform to certain standards, should in any way absolve them from liability for misconduct which is proscribed by Rule 10b-5.

But in the absence of the *Birnbaum* rule, . . . [p]laintiff's proof would not be that he purchased or sold stock, a fact which would be capable of documentary verification in most situations, but instead that he decided *not* to purchase or sell stock. Plaintiff's entire testimony could be dependent upon uncorroborated oral evidence of many of the crucial elements of his claim, and still be sufficient to go to the jury. The jury would not even have the benefit of weighing the plaintiff's version against the defendant's version, since the elements to which the plaintiff would testify would be in many cases totally unknown and unknowable to the defendant. The very real risk in permitting those in respondent's position to sue under Rule 10b-5 is that the door will be open to recovery of substantial damages on the part of one who offers only his own testimony to prove that he ever consulted a prospectus of the issuer, that he paid any attention to it, or that the representations contained in it damaged him.[10] The virtue of the *Birnbaum* rule, simply stated, in this situation, is that it limits the class of plaintiffs to those who have at least dealt in the security to which the prospectus, representation, or omission relates. And their dealing in the security, whether by way of purchase or sale, will generally be an objectively demonstrable fact in an area of the law otherwise very much dependent upon oral testimony. In the absence of the *Birnbaum* doctrine, bystanders to the securities marketing process could await developments on the sidelines without risk, claiming that inaccuracies in disclosure caused nonselling in a falling market and that unduly pessimistic predictions by the issuer followed by a rising market caused them to allow retrospectively golden opportunities to pass.

. . . We are dealing with a private cause of action which has been judicially found to exist, and which will have to be judicially delimited one way or another unless and until Congress addresses the question. Given the peculiar blend of legislative, administrative, and judicial history which now surrounds Rule 10b-5, we believe that practical factors to which we have adverted, and to which other courts have referred, are entitled to a good deal of weight.

Thus we conclude that what may be called considerations of policy, which we are free to weigh in deciding this case, are by no means entirely on one side of the scale. Taken together with the precedential support for the *Birnbaum* rule over a period of more than 20 years, and the consistency of that rule with what we can glean from the intent of Congress, they lead us to conclude that it is a sound rule and should be followed.

The majority of the Court of Appeals in this case expressed no disagreement with the general proposition that one asserting a claim for damages based on the violation of Rule 10b-5 must be either a purchaser or seller of securities. However, it noted that prior cases have held that persons owning contractual rights to buy or sell securities are not excluded by the *Birnbaum* rule. Relying on these cases, it concluded that respondent's status as an offeree pursuant to the terms of the

---

10. The SEC . . . suggests requiring some corroborative evidence in addition to oral testimony tending to show that the investment decision of a plaintiff was affected by an omission or misrepresentation. Brief for the Securities and Exchange Commission as Amicus Curiae 25-26. Apparently ownership of stock or receipt of a prospectus or press release would be sufficient corroborative evidence in the view of the SEC to reach the jury. We do not believe that such a requirement would adequately respond to the concerns in part underlying the *Birnbaum* rule. Ownership of stock or receipt of a prospectus says little about whether a plaintiff's investment decision was affected by a violation of Rule 10b-5 or whether a decision was even made. Second, the SEC would limit the vicarious liability of corporate issuers to nonpurchasers and nonsellers to situations where the corporate issuer has been unjustly enriched by a violation. We have no occasion to pass upon the compatibility of this limitation with §20(a) of the 1934 Act. We do not believe that this proposed limitation is relevant to the concerns underlying in part the *Birnbaum* rule as we have expressed them. . . .

consent decree served the same function, for purposes of delimiting the class of plaintiffs, as is normally performed by the requirements of a contractual relationship. . . .

Even if we were to accept the notion that the *Birnbaum* rule could be circumvented on a case-by-case basis through particularized judicial inquiry into the facts surrounding a complaint, this respondent and the members of its alleged class would be unlikely candidates for such a judicially created exception. While the *Birnbaum* rule has been flexibly interpreted by lower federal courts,[14] we have been unable to locate a single decided case from any court in the 20-odd years of litigation since the *Birnbaum* decision which would support the right of persons who were in the position of respondent here to bring a private suit under Rule 10b-5. Respondent was not only not a buyer or seller of any security but it was not even a shareholder of the corporate petitioners.

. . . Respondent, who derives no entitlement from the antitrust consent decree and does not otherwise possess any contractual rights relating to the offered stock, stands in the same position as any other disappointed offeree of a stock offering registered under the 1933 Act who claims that an overly pessimistic prospectus, prepared and distributed as required by §§5 and 10 of the 1933 Act, has caused it to allow its opportunity to purchase to pass. . . .

Sections 11 and 12 of the 1933 Act provide express civil remedies for misrepresentations and omissions in registration statements and prospectuses filed under the Act, as here charged, but restrict recovery to the offering price of shares actually purchased: "To impose a greater responsibility, apart from constitutional doubts, would unnecessarily restrain the conscientious administration of honest business with no compensating advantage to the public." H.R. Rep. No. 85, at 9. And in Title II of the 1934 Act, the same Act adopting §10(b), Congress amended §11 of the 1933 Act to limit still further the express civil remedy it conferred . . . [thus reflecting] congressional concern over the impact of even these limited remedies on the new issues market. 78 Cong. Rec. 8668-8669 (1934). There is thus ample evidence that Congress did not intend to extend a private cause of action for money damages to the nonpurchasing offeree of a stock offering registered under the 1933 Act for loss of the opportunity to purchase due to an overly pessimistic prospectus.

. . . As a purely practical matter, it is doubtless true that respondent and the members of this class, as offerees and recipients of the prospectus of New Blue Chip, are a smaller class of potential plaintiffs than would be all those who might conceivably assert that they obtained information violative of Rule 10b-5 and attributable to the issuer in the financial pages of their local newspaper. And since respondent likewise had a prior connection with some of petitioners as a result of using the trading stamps marketed by Old Blue Chip, and was intended to benefit from the provisions of the consent decree, there is doubtless more likelihood that its managers read and were damaged by the allegedly misleading statements in the prospectus than there would be in a case filed by a complete stranger to the corporation.

14. Our decision in SEC v. National Securities, Inc., 393 U.S. 453 (1969), established that the purchaser-seller rule imposes no limitation on the standing of the SEC to bring actions for injunctive relief under §10(b) and Rule 10b-5.

But respondent and the members of its class are neither "purchasers" nor "sellers," as those terms are defined in the 1934 Act, and therefore to the extent that their claim of standing to sue were recognized, it would mean that the lesser practical difficulties of corroborating at least some elements of their proof would be regarded as sufficient to avoid the *Birnbaum* rule. While we have noted that these practical difficulties, particularly in the case of a complete stranger to the corporation, support the retention of that rule, they are by no means the only factor which does so. The general adoption of the rule by other federal courts in the 25 years since it was announced, and the consistency of the rule with the statutes involved and their legislative history, are likewise bases for retaining the rule. Were we to agree with the Court of Appeals in this case, we would leave the *Birnbaum* rule open to endless case-by-case erosion depending on whether a particular group of plaintiffs was thought by the court in which the issue was being litigated to be sufficiently more discrete than the world of potential purchasers at large to justify an exception. We do not believe that such a shifting and highly fact-oriented disposition of the issue of who may bring a damages claim for violation of Rule 10b-5 is a satisfactory basis for a rule of liability imposed on the conduct of business transactions. Nor is it as consistent as a straightforward application of the *Birnbaum* rule with the other factors which support the retention of that rule. We therefore hold that respondent was not entitled to sue for violation of Rule 10b-5, and the judgment of the Court of Appeals is

Reversed.

MR. JUSTICE BLACKMUN, with whom MR. JUSTICE DOUGLAS and MR. JUSTICE BRENNAN join, dissenting.

. . . [T]he court denies this plaintiff the right to maintain a suit under Rule 10b-5 because it does not fit into the mechanistic categories of either "purchaser" or "seller." This, surely, is an anomaly, for the very purpose of the alleged scheme was to inhibit this plaintiff from ever acquiring the status of "purchaser." Faced with this abnormal divergence from the usual pattern of securities frauds, the Court pays no heed to the unremedied wrong or to the portmanteau nature of §10(b). . . .

The question under both Rule 10b-5 and its parent statute, §10(b), is whether fraud was employed — and the language is critical — by "any person . . . in connection with the purchase or sale of any security." On the allegations here, the nexus between the asserted fraud and the conducting of a "sale" is obvious and inescapable, and no more should be required to sustain the plaintiff's complaint against a motion to dismiss. . . .

Certainly, this Court must be aware of the realities of life, but it is unwarranted for the Court to take a form of attenuated judicial notice of the motivations that defense counsel may have in settling a case, or of the difficulties that a plaintiff may have in proving his claim.

Perhaps it is true that more cases that come within the *Birnbaum* doctrine can be properly proved than those that fall outside it. But this is no reason for denying standing to sue to plaintiffs, such as the one in this case, who allegedly are injured by novel forms of manipulation. We should be wary about heeding the seductive call of expediency and about substituting convenience and ease of processing for the more difficult task of separating the genuine claim from the unfounded one.

Instead of the artificiality of *Birnbaum*, the essential test of a valid Rule 10b-5 claim, it seems to me, must be the showing of a logical nexus between the alleged fraud and the sale or purchase of a security. It is inconceivable that Congress could have intended a broad-ranging antifraud provision, such as §10(b), and, at the same time, have intended to impose, or be deemed to welcome, a mechanical overtone and requirement such as the *Birnbaum* doctrine. The facts of this case, if proved and accepted by the factfinder, surely are within the conduct that Congress intended to ban. Whether this particular plaintiff, or any plaintiff, will be able eventually to carry the burdens of proving fraud and of proving reliance and damage — that is, causality and injury — is a matter that should not be left to speculations of "policy" of the kind now advanced in this forum so far removed from witnesses and evidence. . . .

In short, I would abandon the *Birnbaum* doctrine as a rule of decision in favor of a more general test of nexus, just as the Seventh Circuit did in Eason v. General Motors Acceptance Corp., 490 F.2d 654, 661 (1973) [per JUDGE (now JUSTICE) STEVENS], *cert. denied*, 416 U.S. 960 (1974). I would not worry about any imagined inability of our federal trial and appellate courts to control the flowering of the types of cases that the Court fears might result. Nor would I yet be disturbed about dire consequences that a basically pessimistic attitude foresees if the *Birnbaum* doctrine were allowed quietly to expire. Sensible standards of proof and of demonstrable damages would evolve and serve to protect the worthy and shut out the frivolous.

———————————————

1. *Exceptions to, and the scope of, the purchaser/seller rule.* Even prior to *Blue Chip Stamps* there had been disagreement about the scope of the purchaser/seller rule, as the Second Circuit had recognized numerous exceptions to its earlier *Birnbaum* doctrine. Although the law continues to shift, the current state of the law looks as follows.

(a) *Injunctions.* For a time, even after *Blue Chip*, a number of courts held that persons injured by a violation of Rule 10b-5 could seek injunctive or equitable relief, even if they were neither purchasers nor sellers. See Mutual Shares Corp. v. Genesco, Inc., 384 F.2d 540 (2d Cir. 1967) (holding that claim that defendant, by limiting dividends, had forced others to sell out cheaply and would eventually coerce the plaintiffs to do likewise, unless enjoined, could be asserted by private plaintiffs under Rule 10b-5). The continuing validity of this pre — *Blue Chip* decision, however, seems doubtful. In Cowin v. Bresler, 741 F.2d 410 (D.C. Cir. 1984), a minority shareholder alleged fraud, self-dealing, and misrepresentations by controlling shareholders and sought appointment of a receiver to liquidate the company. Although assuming for purposes of its decision that fraud had occurred, the D.C. Circuit rejected the argument that *Blue Chip*'s limitation on standing could be confined to cases for money damages. Nonetheless, a few decisions have held open the possibility that standing might be conferred on plaintiffs who had not traded but who could show that, but for injunctive relief against deceptive practices, they were likely to suffer future monetary injury. See Advanced Resources Int'l v. Tri-Star Petroleum Corp., 4 F.3d 327 (4th Cir. 1993).

(b) *"Forced sellers."* Mergers have traditionally been recognized as sales for purposes of Rule 10b-5, even when the shareholder does not vote or make any investment decision. Thus, in Vine v. Beneficial Finance Co., Inc., 374 F.2d 627 (2d Cir. 1967), the Second Circuit held that a minority shareholder in a corporation who was "cashed out" in a short-form merger that merged his company into its controlling parent had standing to sue under Rule 10b-5. Although *Vine* was prior to *Blue Chip Stamps*, the Second Circuit reaffirmed this result afterward. In Mayer v. Oil Field Systems Corp., 721 F.2d 59 (2d Cir. 1983), a limited partner was forced to accept stock in a corporation in exchange for his limited partnership interest in a transaction that only had to be approved by the general partner. Because limited partnership interests are deemed to be securities, Judge Friendly found the limited partner to be a "forced seller" despite the absence of any investment decision (indeed, the plaintiff was probably also a forced purchaser, but the decision did not analyze that side of the transaction). This same rationale has been applied to liquidations as well. See Alley v. Miramon, 614 F.2d 1372 (5th Cir. 1980); Dudley v. Southeastern Factor and Fin. Corp., 446 F.2d 303 (5th Cir. 1971); Coffee v. Permian Corp., 434 F.2d 383 (5th Cir. 1970). On the other hand, a foreclosure that results in a de facto liquidation of the corporation has been held not to be a "forced sale." See Arnesen v. Shawmut County Bank, N.A., 504 F. Supp. 1077 (D. Mass. 1980).

The current scope of the "forced seller" doctrine is uncertain. Even in the Second Circuit, which created it, it has been cut back. See Lawrence v. Cohn, 325 F.3d 141 (2d Cir. 2003) (release of right to purchase stock pursuant to a settlement agreement does not qualify as a *Blue Chip* sale); Grace v. Rosenstock, 228 F.3d 40, 48-49 (2d Cir. 2000); see also Howe v. Bank for Int'l Settlements, 194 F. Supp. 2d 6, 26-27 (D. Mass. 2002). Even more clearly, the "forced seller" doctrine also will not be stretched beyond mergers to apply to transactions in which the plaintiff retains shares in the corporation, but the corporation issues new shares that dilute the plaintiff's investment. See Jeanes v. Henderson, 703 F.2d 855, 860 (5th Cir. 1983); Sargent v. Genesco, Inc., 492 F.2d 750, 764-765 (5th Cir. 1974). Similarly, a transfer of securities from a wholly owned subsidiary to its parent, or between two "brother and sister" subsidiaries controlled by the same parent, has been held not to amount to a purchase or sale, but only a "mere transfer between corporate pockets." Blau v. Mission Corp., 212 F.2d 77, 80 (2d Cir. 1954); Rathborne v. Rathborne, 683 F.2d 914, 918-919 (5th Cir. 1982); Gelles v. TDA Indus., Inc., 44 F.3d 102, 105 (2d Cir. 1994). Spin-offs of shares in a subsidiary by means of a stock dividend have also been generally held to be outside the "forced seller" doctrine. See Isquith v. Caremark Int'l, Inc., 136 F.3d 531 (7th Cir. 1998). But in Semerenko v. Cendant Corp. 223 F.3d 165, 174-177 (3d Cir. 2000), the Third Circuit held that purchasers of stock in a corporation that had been the target of a failed merger could state a claim against the prospective acquirer of that corporation for its alleged misstatements that affected the target's value.

(c) *Non-voting beneficial holders.* One recent Seventh Circuit decision appears to have questioned the logic of the "forced seller" doctrine, although it involved a different transactional setting.

In Davidson v. Belcor Inc., 933 F.2d 603 (7th Cir. 1991), a divorce settlement gave the wife a beneficial interest in a large block of stock in Aargus Polybag Co., but the husband retained the right to vote the shares and make all investment decisions. When Aargus merged with Belcor Inc., the wife received shares in, and a promissory note of, Belcor. She brought suit under Rule 10b-5 against Belcor and certain Aargus officers (including her ex-husband), alleging both that the transaction was unfair and that she received inadequate disclosure about its terms. The court found that she lacked standing to sue because she was not entitled to vote (or instruct her husband how to vote) on the merger. This logic may deny holders of beneficial interests in securities standing to sue under Rule 10b-5 unless they have the power to instruct the trustee or recordholder on investment decisions. Should courts go that far?

The majority rule has long been that a trust beneficiary has standing to bring an action against the trustee alleging fraud in selling securities on the theory that the beneficial interest of such holder in the trust was sold, thereby making such person a "seller." See Norris v. Wirtz, 719 F.2d 256 (7th Cir. 1983); Kirshner v. United States, 603 F.2d 234 (2d Cir. 1978); James v. Gerber Products Co., 483 F.2d 944 (6th Cir. 1973). Similarly, where a corporation buys or sells securities, a shareholder in that corporation has standing to bring a derivative action alleging that the corporation was defrauded by its trading partner. See Frankel v. Slotkin, 984 F.2d 1328, 1332-1334 (2d Cir. 1993). In none of these cases has the beneficial holder made an investment decision. Also, the secured party with the principal interest in collateral has been deemed a qualified "seller" with standing for Rule 10b-5 purposes when securities are sold at a foreclosure sale conducted by a sheriff. See Falls v. Fickling, 621 F.2d 1362 (5th Cir. 1980).

2. *Forced retirements and buy-sell agreements.* The scope of the "in connection with" requirement has been recurrently litigated in decisions involving an agreement requiring shareholders to sell their shares back to the corporation (usually at book value or some other artificially low formula price) on their resignation, retirement, or departure from office. In Brown v. Ivie, 661 F.2d 62 (5th Cir. 1981), the defendants allegedly caused the plaintiff to enter into such a "buy-sell agreement," under which the corporation could repurchase his shares at book value if he was no longer employed by the corporation, without disclosing to him that they planned to fire him immediately thereafter (as they did). Although the Fifth Circuit found the "in connection with" requirement satisfied on these facts, it distinguished the case where defendants simply oust the plaintiff in order to exercise such a preexisting option. In the latter case, it said the fraud would not be sufficiently related to the securities transaction to satisfy the "in connection with" requirement. See also Ketchum v. Green, 557 F.2d 1022 (3d Cir. 1977).

3. *Purchases after discovery of the fraud.* What result in *Blue Chip Stamps* if, within several months after the offering in 1968, respondent, having discovered that the offering prospectus was overly pessimistic, bought New Blue Chip shares in the market for substantially more than the 1968 offering price and then sued respondent under Rule 10b-5 for the difference? Although there would now be a "purchase," the cases are agreed that a fraud is not "in connection with" a purchase or sale if the plaintiffs were aware of the facts when they bought or sold. See Shivers v. Amerco, 670 F.2d 826 (9th Cir. 1982).

4. *Defining sale.* Does a pledge by a borrower to a bank of worthless securities amount to a sale? Is the conversion or redemption of a convertible security a sale? See Drachman v. Harvey, 453 F.2d 722, 737 (2d Cir. 1972) (en banc) (finding redemption of a convertible debenture to constitute a "purchase" where it allowed defendant to acquire control of corporation). In Rubin v. United States, 449 U.S. 424 (1981), the Court found a pledge to confer an "interest in a security" and therefore to be a sale within the meaning of §2(3) of the '33 Act. Does this conclusion carry over to the '34 Act, which is usually read in pari materia with the '33 Act? Although this conclusion might seem to follow, it causes problems for the accepted interpretation of other provisions of the '34 Act. Under §16(b) of the '34 Act, any gain on

any sequence of purchases and sales within a six-month period must be restored to the corporation. If a pledge is a "sale" for '34 Act purposes, a significant number of transactions that are essentially financings would fall within the scope of §16(b) (although the SEC could exempt them through rulemaking). Possibly for this and other reasons, pre-*Rubin* cases had divided on whether a pledge was a sale. Compare Lincoln National Bank v. Herber, 604 F.2d 1038 (7th Cir. 1979) with Mallis v. FDIC, 568 F.2d 824 (2d Cir. 1977). May *Rubin's* characterization of a pledge as the disposition of only an "interest in a security" provide a basis for distinction?

Is it a sale for Rule 10b-5 purposes when the terms of a security are substantially amended? For example, suppose a bond indenture is amended to eliminate the bondholders' right to convert into common shares. This definition of "sale," which treats the amendment of a security as the substitution of one security for another, was rejected in Broad v. Rockwell International Corp., 614 F.2d 418 (5th Cir. 1980).

5. *"In connection with" and the causal nexus.* Suppose a pharmaceutical company takes out a multi-page advertisement in a medical journal to announce a new drug. Assume further that the ad touts the product's efficacy and announces that it has no "life-threatening" side effects. In fact, there is such an adverse side effect, and on its disclosure the company's stock price falls significantly. These are essentially the facts of In re Carter-Wallace Securities Litigation, 150 F.3d 153 (2d Cir. 1998), where the district court dismissed the complaint on the ground that such a technical advertisement directed at doctors would not reach the investing public. Hence, it said that the misstatement, even if material, was not made "in connection with" the purchase or sale of a security. The Second Circuit, however, reversed the district court, finding that it could not hold as a matter of law that such technical information could not influence security analysts who were seeking to evaluate the company's prospects. Applying a "straightforward cause and effect test," the Second Circuit panel said that plaintiffs could prevail on these facts if they could show at trial that security analysts or other market professionals had in fact studied such ads and based their recommendations in part on them. As discussed later, this decision applied the "fraud on the market" doctrine to reach this result, as there was little possibility that most class members had, themselves, seen these ads.

6. *"In connection with" and the defendant.* Assuming that the plaintiff has traded, it still may be asked why the defendant's conduct is "in connection with" a purchase or sale where it has not traded but has, for example, only issued a misleading press release. In SEC v. Texas Gulf Sulphur, 401 F.2d 833, 861-863 (2d Cir. 1968) (en banc), *cert. denied*, 394 U.S. 976 (1969), an important answer was given to this question: The defendant has caused the sale "whenever assertions are made . . . in a manner reasonably calculated to influence the investing public." Id. at 862. This theory, that a corporate defendant "causes" the sale when it releases information to the financial media that will foreseeably affect the market price, was extended to its outer limits shortly thereafter in Heit v. Weitzen, 402 F.2d 909 (2d Cir. 1968). There, a corporation and its directors were sued by purchasers in the open market who alleged that the corporation's financial statements had overstated the issuer's net assets as well as its past and prospective income and understated its contingent liabilities. These misrepresentations arose solely because the corporation failed to disclose substantial overcharges it had billed on government contracts (which overcharges were recoverable). The District Court had found that the purpose

of these misleading statements and nondisclosures was essentially to cover up the overcharge scheme and prevent its detection by the government. Nonetheless, the Second Circuit found this "ulterior motive" to be irrelevant so long as it was foreseeable that dissemination of the financial data would be circulated to the investing public. In this view, the "in connection with" requirement appears to require not that statements made to the public be "reasonably calculated to influence the investing public," but only that it is "reasonably foreseeable" that they will do so.

7. *Securities fraud and common law fraud.* Suppose a broker loots a client's securities account over which the broker has control. Presumably, this is common law fraud, rather than securities fraud within the scope of Rule 10b-5. But what if the broker sells the securities in the customer account in order to facilitate the broker's wrongful conversion of the account? These are essentially the facts of SEC v. Zanford, 535 U.S. 813 (2002). There, a securities broker induced an elderly man to open a joint securities account for himself and his mentally retarded daughter and to give the broker discretionary trading authority. On the elderly customer's death, it was discovered that the account had been looted by the broker over the course of a year and a half. Following the broker's criminal conviction, the SEC sued under Rule 10b-5 to recover restitution for the victims of the fraud, and the District Court granted it summary judgment. The Fourth Circuit, however, reversed and instructed the District Court to dismiss the complaint, because it had not been adequately pled that the fraud was "in connection with" a purchase or sale of securities. In the view of the Fourth Circuit panel, the fraud would be so connected only if some misrepresentation relating to the security had been made to the victim or the scheme to defraud had otherwise affected the "integrity of the market."

A unanimous Supreme Court reversed, emphasizing that the Congressional purpose underlying the federal securities laws had been "to substitute a philosophy of full disclosure for the philosophy of caveat emptor." While the Court acknowledged that not all common law frauds came within the scope of Rule 10b-5, it first stressed that deference had to be given to the SEC's long-standing position that a broker who sells securities intending to misappropriate the proceeds thereby violates Rule 10b-5. Then, the Court emphasized that the sale and the conversion of the proceeds were not "independent events." Rejecting the Fourth Circuit's requirement of a material misrepresentation, the Court noted that the SEC had alleged that each sale of securities was made without disclosure to the victims and was intended to facilitate an immediate conversion. As a result, it said a material omission had accompanied each sale. The uncertain line between cases that fall inside and outside Rule 10b-5 was probably most clearly drawn by the Court in the following brief passage: "This is not a case in which, after a lawful transaction had been consummated, a broker decided to steal the proceeds and did so. Nor is it a case in which a thief simply invested the proceeds of a routine conversion in the stock market. Rather, respondent's fraud coincided with the sales themselves." 535 U.S. at 820. *Zanford* may also represent the Court's initial reaction to Enron and similar scandals that peaked in 2002.

8. *Contracts to buy or sell securities.* A contract to sell securities is itself a "sale" for purposes of the *Blue Chip Stamps* rule. See Griggs v. Pace Am. Group, Inc., 170 F.3d 877, 880 (9th Cir. 1999); Mosher v. Kane, 784 F.2d 1385 (9th Cir. 1986). However, preliminary negotiations that have not resulted in any enforceable contract have

been held insufficient to give rise to standing under Rule 10b-5. See Reprosystem, B.V. v. SCM Corp., 727 F.2d 257 (2d Cir. 1984); Northland Capital Corp. v. Silver, 735 F.2d 1421 (D.C. Cir. 1984). Similarly, a settlement in which one releases rights to buy shares under a contract is too remote from an actual sale or purchase to satisfy the *Blue Chip* standard. See Lawrence v. Cohn, 325 F.3d 141 (2d Cir. 2003).

But oral contracts for sale are generally enforceable in the securities context. Do they create standing under Rule 10b-5? Or are the risks too great that recognizing standing in such cases will simply convert ordinary breach-of-contract cases into federal litigation under Rule 10b-5? Similarly, should the danger that permitting securities litigation over oral contracts would give rise to a flood of nonmeritorious suits based on fabricated memories lead courts to deny standing? Similar arguments persuaded the Court in *Blue Chip Stamps*, where it refused to recognize standing in potential buyers and sellers. Nonetheless, the Supreme Court recently found in Wharf (Holdings) Ltd. v. United Int'l Holdings, Inc., 532 U.S. 588 (2001), that standing did exist under Rule 10b-5 to enforce an oral contract of sale that plaintiffs alleged the respondent had entered into while secretly intending never to honor its agreement.

The facts of *Wharf* differ from those in *Blue Chip Stamps* primarily in terms of the reality of the injury. When the Hong Kong government announced that it would accept bids for the award of an exclusive license to operate a cable television system, petitioner Wharf (Holdings) Ltd. ("Wharf") decided to bid and contacted respondent United International Holdings, Inc. ("United") because of the latter's cable system experience. United's employees assisted Wharf in arranging petitioner's bid, negotiating the contract, and designing the proposed system. The parties orally negotiated an arrangement under which United would receive the right to a 10 percent interest in the system at a discounted price as payment for its services, but this agreement was never reduced to a writing. Wharf was awarded the cable franchise, but then refused to permit United to invest in it. Contemporaneous internal documents strongly suggested that petitioner had never intended to honor its promise. United recovered a substantial jury verdict for compensatory and punitive damages in federal court in Colorado, and on appeal the Tenth Circuit found that the parties' oral agreement conduct amounted to a sale of an option which was not covered by the Colorado statute of frauds and which was enforceable under Colorado law.

Before the Supreme Court, Wharf argued that Rule 10b-5 did not cover oral contracts of sale, but only "actual purchasers and sellers of securities." *Blue Chip Stamps*, it stressed, had been expressly based on the need to protect defendants against lawsuits that "turn largely on which oral version of a series of occurrences the jury may decide to credit." 421 U.S. at 730-731. Enforcing oral contracts would give rise, it claimed, to similar problems of proof.

In response, a unanimous Court said:

> *Blue Chip Stamps*, however, involved the very different question whether the Act protects a person who did not actually buy securities, but who might have done so had the seller told the truth. . . . But United is not a potential buyer; by providing Wharf with its services, it actually bought the option that Wharf sold. And *Blue Chip Stamps* said nothing to suggest that oral purchases or sales fall outside the scope of the Act. Rather, the Court's concern was about the "abuse potential and proof problems inherent in suits by investors who neither bought nor sold, but asserted that they would

have traded absent fraudulent conduct by others." . . . Such a "potential purchaser" claim would rest on facts, including the plaintiff's state of mind that might be "totally unknown and unknowable to the defendant," depriving the jury of "the benefit of weighing the plaintiff's version against the defendant's version." *Blue Chip Stamps*, supra, at 746. An actual sale, even if oral, would not create this problem, because both parties would be able to testify as to whether the relevant events had occurred.

532 U.S. at 594-595.

9. *California's dissenting view.* Although the *Wharf (Holdings)* decision shows that the policy rationale underlying *Blue Chip Stamps* may have less compelling force today, possibly in the wake of recent corporate scandals, *Blue Chip Stamps* clearly remains an authoritative precedent in federal court. In contrast, the California Supreme Court has recently rejected *Blue Chip Stamps'* rationale entirely and held that a holder who forgoes selling a security in reliance on the issuer's fraudulent financial statements that grossly overstated its earnings may sue under California law for the decline in stock price thereby suffered. In Small v. Fritz Cos., 65 P.3d 1255 (2003), the California Supreme Court held that, if the effect of a misrepresentation is to induce forbearance, existing shareholders who actually relied on the materially false statements are as entitled to prosecute a common law action for fraud or negligent misrepresentation as other investors who had actually bought or sold. Under California law, it said, forbearance — the decision not to exercise a right or power — is sufficient consideration to support a contract or overcome the statute of frauds.

Small was expressly based on a policy rationale that shareholders need greater protection from fraud. But how does the decision's result actually impact on shareholders? Assume that management has materially overstated the firm's earnings. If all or most shareholders exercise a remedy entitling them to damages, the corporation will predictably be driven into bankruptcy. Moreover, because California law discourages class actions by requiring actual reliance, smaller shareholders may find it uneconomic to sue. Thus, if larger institutional shareholders do sue based on this new "holder's action," the net result may be a wealth transfer from smaller shareholders to the larger shareholders who do sue. Although this problem of intra-shareholder wealth transfers is present to some degree in securities class actions as well, it is significantly compounded when existing shareholders (and possibly creditors as well) are permitted to sue their corporation for fraudulently causing them to forgo selling.

10. *The holder's action.* Several other states (but a decided minority) agree with California's decision in *Small* and permit a holder who has not sold to bring an action against the corporation on the ground that the shareholder was fraudulently induced to forbear selling. But can such holders sue in a class action? The problem is that the Securities Litigation Uniform Standards Act of 1998 (SLUSA) expressly precludes class actions grounded on a state or common law cause of action that alleges fraud in connection with the purchase or sale of a security from being filed in state or federal court. Nonetheless, the Second Circuit held that a holder's class action could still be brought in federal court precisely because there was no purchase or sale (and hence the state cause of action was not preempted by SLUSA). This position was rejected unanimously by the Supreme Court in Merrill Lynch, Pierce, Fenner & Smith v. Dabit, 547 U.S. 71 (2006), which found SLUSA to preempt a holder's action brought as a class action. As a result, individuals and

small groups may file a holder's action in state or federal court, but a class action is now prohibited. Thus, it becomes even more likely that large shareholders will benefit from holder's actions at the expense of smaller shareholders.

ii. Materiality

SEC v. Texas Gulf Sulphur Co.
401 F.2d 833 (2d Cir. 1968) (en banc)

WATERMAN, J.: [After extensive exploration in eastern Canada, Texas Gulf Sulphur detected a promising anomaly near Timmins, Ontario. In November 1963, it drilled an initial test hole that was designated as hole K-55-1. The core sample was unusually promising, and further analysis showed it to contain an extraordinary level of mineral content, including copper, zinc, and silver. Drilling was suspended while the surrounding land was purchased. During this period from November 1963 to early April 1964, corporate officers having knowledge of this discovery made extensive purchases of Texas Gulf Sulphur stock in the open market, but no public disclosure of the discovery was made. Because the commercial value of a mining property cannot be reliably established from a single drill hole, but rather requires more widespread drilling to determine the size and extent of any mineral deposit, the district court found the information not to have been material at this point, but only later. The Second Circuit reversed and in the portion of the decision quoted below set forth its criteria for determining materiality.] This is not to suggest, however, as did the trial court, that "the test of materiality must necessarily be a conservative one, particularly since many actions under Section 10(b) are brought on the basis of hindsight," 258 F. Supp. 262 at 280, in the sense that the materiality of the facts is to be assessed solely by measuring the effect the knowledge of the facts would have upon prudent or conservative investors. As we stated in List v. Fashion Park, Inc., 340 F.2d 457, 462, "The basic test of materiality . . . is whether a reasonable man would attach importance . . . in determining his choice of action in the transaction in question. Restatement, Torts §538(s) (a); accord Prosser, Torts 554-55; I Harper & James, Torts 565-66." This, of course, encompasses any fact ". . . which in reasonable and objective contemplation might affect the value of the corporation's stock or securities. . . ." List v. Fashion Park, Inc., supra at 462. . . . Such a fact is a material fact and must be effectively disclosed to the investing public prior to the commencement of insider trading in the corporation's securities. The speculators and chartists of Wall and Bay streets are also "reasonable" investors entitled to the same legal protection afforded conservative traders. Thus, material facts include not only information disclosing the earnings and distributions of a company but also those facts which affect the probable future of the company and those which may affect the desire of investors to buy, sell, or hold the company's securities.

In each case, then, whether facts are material within Rule 10b-5 when the facts relate to a particular event and are undisclosed by those persons who are knowledgeable thereof will depend at any given time upon a balancing of both the indicated probability that the event will occur and the anticipated magnitude of the event in light of the totality of the company's activity. Here, notwithstanding the trial court's conclusion that the results of the first drill core, K-55-1, were "too 'remote' . . . to have had any significant impact on the market," i.e., to be deemed material, knowledge of the possibility, which surely was more than marginal, of the existence of a mine of the vast magnitude indicated by the remarkably rich drill core located rather close to the surface (suggesting mineability by the less expensive open-pit method) within the confines of a large anomaly (suggesting an extensive region of mineralization) might well have affected the price of TGS stock and would certainly have been an important fact to a reasonable, if speculative, investor in deciding whether he should buy, sell, or hold. After all, this first drill core was "unusually good and . . . excited the interest and speculation of those who knew about it." . . .

---

1. *The probability/magnitude trade-off.* The Second Circuit's test in *Texas Gulf Sulphur* involves "a balancing of both the indicated probability that the event will occur and the anticipated magnitude of the event in light of the totality of the company's activity." This means not only that the magnitude of an event must be discounted by the probability of its occurrence, but also that this discounted number must be compared against the corporation's earnings, assets, and other financial results in gauging materiality. What is "material" for a small company is not necessarily material for IBM.

2. *The relevant audience.* The idea that speculative investors ("the chartists of Wall and Bay Streets") could also be "reasonable investors" who deserve as much protection as the traditional prudent investor has further ramifications. For example, "ethical" investors who wish to avoid investments in corporations engaged in practices of which they disapprove may also have special interests that other investors do not share. Should a failure to disclose a corporation's involvement in South Africa be deemed "material" if this disclosure would have caused these investors not to purchase the stock and was subsequently the cause of material loss? A variant of this issue arose in Natural Resources Defense Council v. SEC, 389 F. Supp. 689 (D.D.C. 1974), where a public interest group sought to compel the SEC to require disclosure by corporations concerning (1) the effect of their activities on the environment, and (2) their equal employment practices. The district court largely agreed with the plaintiffs and directed the SEC to consider rulemaking actions to this end. After considering a number of proposals for more extensive disclosure of environmental and social information, the SEC reaffirmed its view that *materiality* should be defined in terms of economic (and not ethical) criteria. Sec. Act Release No. 33-5704 (May 6, 1976). The District Court found this decision to be "arbitrary and capricious," but it was reversed by the Court of Appeals, 606 F.2d 1031 (D.C. Cir. 1979), which accepted the SEC's decision. Is it material to investors that a corporation has engaged in a pattern of "unionbusting" activities that resulted in numerous violations of the National Labor Relations Act? See Amalgamated Clothing & Textile Workers Union v. J. P. Stevens & Co., 475 F. Supp. 328 (S.D.N.Y. 1979) (finding such information not economically material), *vacated as moot*, 638 F.2d 7 (2d Cir. 1980).

3. *"Integrity disclosures."* Although the SEC has resisted efforts to include information on the social, ethical, or environmental impact of corporate actions within the definition of *materiality*, it has consistently maintained that financial materiality is not the only criterion by which reasonable investors make investment decisions. In particular, the SEC has viewed evidence of illegal conduct or other information relating to the integrity of senior management, even when financially

insignificant, as material facts that should be disclosed to potential investors. However, courts have been reluctant to accept any per se theory that illegal or unethical conduct is material, and even the SEC's staff has acknowledged that not all illegal or antisocial conduct is necessarily or even presumptively material. See George Branch & James Rubright, Integrity of Management Disclosures Under the Federal Securities Law, 37 Bus. Law. 1448 (1982); Note, Disclosures of Payments to Foreign Government Officials Under the Securities Act, 89 Harv. L. Rev. 1848 (1976); Note, Foreign Bribes and the Securities Acts Disclosure Requirement, 74 Mich. L. Rev. 1222 (1976). The first significant case to discuss the materiality of information relating to the integrity of management was In re Franchard Corp., 42 S.E.C. 163, 169-170 (1964), an administrative proceeding before the SEC. The Commission's opinion found that information relating to self-dealing by the corporation's controlling shareholder was highly material: "Of cardinal importance in any business is the quality of its management. Disclosures relevant to an evaluation of management are particularly pertinent where, as in this case, securities are sold largely on the personal reputation of a company's controlling person." Yet, at the same time, the *Franchard* decision acknowledged the difficulty in formulating any specific disclosure rules relating to the issue of management's integrity:

> In many respects, the development of disclosure standards adequate for informed appraisal of management's ability and integrity is a difficult task. How do you tell a "good" business manager from a "bad" one in a piece of paper? Managerial talent consists of personal attributes, essentially subjective in nature, that frequently defy meaningful analysis through the impersonal medium of a prospectus. Direct statements of opinion as to management's ability, which are not susceptible to objective verification, may well create an unwarranted appearance of reliability if placed in a prospectus. The integrity of management — its willingness to place its duty to public shareholders over personal interest — is an equally elusive factor for the application of disclosure standards.

Federal courts were faced with the issue of materiality of disclosures concerning the integrity of management in the wake of the "illegal payments" crisis of the 1970s. In SEC v. Jos. Schlitz Brewing Co., 452 F. Supp. 824 (E.D. Wis. 1978), the information related to criminal marketing practices, involving bribes and rebates paid by a brewer to tavern owners. In finding this information to be material, the court emphasized the substantial amounts paid, the risk of license revocation that resulted from the illegal acts, and their relevance to the investors' evaluation of the integrity of management. See also SEC v. Kalvex, Inc., 425 F. Supp. 310 (S.D.N.Y. 1975); Ross v. Warner, [1980 Trans. Binder] Fed. Sec. L. Rep. (CCH) ¶97,735 (S.D.N.Y. 1980); Cooke v. Teleprompter Corp., 334 F. Supp. 467 (S.D.N.Y. 1971). However, in subsequent private cases, where plaintiffs sought to recover the amount of such bribes or questionable payments for the corporation, courts have held on the facts of these cases that the omitted disclosures were not material. See Abbey v. Control Data Corporation, 603 F.2d 724 (8th Cir. 1979); Gaines v. Haughton, 645 F.2d 761 (9th Cir. 1981). In these cases, however, the questionable payments did not involve self-dealing that benefited senior management. Where the evidence did suggest self-dealing rather than simply illegal acts that were intended (however recklessly) to benefit the corporation, the Second Circuit has found the issue of materiality to raise at least a jury question. See Maldonado v. Flynn, 597 F.2d 789 (2d Cir. 1979).

Is an imminent indictment of a corporate officer by itself a material fact, regardless of the officer's guilt or innocence? In United States v. Matthews, 787 F.2d 38 (2d Cir. 1986), the corporation's treasurer had been informed by the U.S. Attorney that he would be indicted for bribery, but he declined to disclose this fact in the corporation's proxy statement, maintaining (after consultation with his counsel) that he was innocent and thus the indictment was immaterial. As a result, he was also indicted for securities fraud for the nondisclosure of material information in the proxy statement. Paradoxically, the jury acquitted him of bribery, but convicted him on the securities fraud charges. What result on the appeal of his securities fraud conviction?

4. *The "might/would" distinction.* In *Texas Gulf Sulphur* the Second Circuit viewed as material "any fact . . . which in reasonable and objective contemplation *might* affect the value of the corporation's stock or securities." Two years later, in Mills v. Electric Auto-Lite Co., 396 U.S. 375 (1970), the Supreme Court adopted a similar phrasing that also emphasized the word "might" in a proxy fraud case based on Rule 14a-9. What an investor "might" consider important, however, comprehends a broad range of information. Subsequently, in TSC Industries, Inc. v. Northway, Inc., 426 U.S. 438 (1976), the Supreme Court reformulated and narrowed this test (again in the context of Rule 14a-9):

> The general standard of materiality that we think best comports with the policies of Rule 14a-9 is as follows: An omitted fact is material if there is a substantial likelihood that a reasonable shareholder would consider it important in deciding how to vote. This standard is fully consistent with *Mills'* general description of materiality as a requirement that "the defect have a significant propensity to affect the voting process." It does not require proof of a substantial likelihood that disclosure of the omitted fact would have caused the reasonable investor to change his vote. What the standard does contemplate is a showing of a substantial likelihood that, under all the circumstances, the omitted fact would have assumed actual significance in the deliberations of the reasonable shareholder. Put another way, there must be a substantial likelihood that the disclosure of the omitted fact would have been viewed by the reasonable investor as having significantly altered the "total mix" of information made available.
>
> The issue of materiality may be characterized as a mixed question of law and fact, involving as it does the application of a legal standard to a particular set of facts. In considering whether summary judgment on the issue is appropriate, we must bear in mind that the underlying objective facts, which will often be free from dispute, are merely the starting point for the ultimate determination of materiality. The determination requires delicate assessments of the inferences a "reasonable shareholder" would draw from a given set of facts and the significance of those inferences to him, and these assessments are peculiarly ones for the trier of fact. Only if the established omissions are "so obviously important to an investor, that reasonable minds cannot differ on the question of materiality" is the ultimate issue of materiality appropriately resolved "as a matter of law" by summary judgment.

TSC Industries' definition of materiality was expressly adopted by the Supreme Court in Basic, Inc. v. Levinson, page 312 supra, as applicable to Rule 10b-5 as well.

5. *Projections and soft information.* The most frequently litigated issues concerning materiality have involved projections and other soft information (such as estimates, predictions, and market value judgments). For most of its history, the SEC simply refused to permit the inclusion of such soft information in

documents filed with it (on the ground that it tended to mislead investors and was not truly factual information). Commentators pointed out, however, that no form of information was more desired by the sophisticated investor, and indeed forecasts and projections were precisely what the security analyst sought from corporate managements. See, e.g., Homer Kripke, The SEC, the Accountants, Some Myths and Some Realities, 45 N.Y.U. L. Rev. 1151, 1201 (1970) ("projections are the ultimate purpose of all disclosure"). Also, by excluding projections from SEC documents, the SEC effectively denied them only to the typical investor, not the institutional investor who had access to security analysts who were in close contact with the corporation. Meanwhile, courts began to impose liability where the information sought consisted essentially of a forecast, projection, or estimate. In Feit v. Leasco Data Processing Equipment Corp., 332 F. Supp. 544 (E.D.N.Y. 1971), the court held that a registration statement filed by a bidder in an exchange offer should have disclosed the target insurance company's "surplus surplus" (that is, the amount that potentially could have been distributed as dividends by the target corporation, once acquired, because these funds were in excess of the surplus required by state insurance authorities to be retained in the business to satisfy claims). Ironically, the underwriter's counsel in Feit (who happened to be an ex — SEC Commissioner) had advised that disclosure of such information would not be permitted by the SEC. See also Gerstle v. Gamble-Skogmo, Inc., 478 F.2d 1281 (2d Cir. 1973). Beginning in 1976, the SEC permitted profit projections in proxy statements and in 1979 similarly permitted forecasts to be made of future dividends, but it still resisted predictions of asset or future market values.

This new liberality did not, however, solve the corporation's problem. By their very nature, predictions will often prove wrong and will even look unreasonable in hindsight. Decisions disagreed as to the correct standard to be applied to an erroneous projection, and at least one court required that a projection be "highly probable" of realization before the corporation was entitled to release it. Compare Beecher v. Able, 374 F. Supp. 341 (S.D.N.Y. 1974) (forecast should be "highly probable" of realization), with Dolgow v. Anderson, 53 F.R.D. 664 (E.D.N.Y. 1971), aff'd per curiam, 464 F.2d 437 (2d Cir. 1972). Partially in response to these decisions, but also because it had finally accepted the centrality of "forward-looking" information to any sophisticated system of disclosure, the SEC adopted "safe harbor" rules under each of the '33 and '34 Acts at the time it introduced its integrated disclosure system, which rules were designed to encourage the use of predictions. Rule 175 (under the '33 Act) and Rule 3b-6 (under the '34 Act) now provide that a "forward-looking statement" should not be deemed to be fraudulent unless the plaintiff proves that the corporation lacked "a reasonable basis" for the statement or made it "other than in good faith." Still, the definition of "forward-looking statement" in these rules is a limited one that does not include predictions of assets or market values. Use of soft information has given rise to recurrent litigation, as the next two cases illustrate.

6. *A bright-line test for materiality: market reaction?* Suppose a corporation fails to disclose some arguably material information about itself. Eventually, the information is released and the market does not react; that is, the corporation's stock price remains stable. Does this prove that the undisclosed information was immaterial? Alternatively, what if a few months after this nonreaction, the corporation is forced into bankruptcy because of the same problems that the market ignored when they were first disclosed? Much depends here on how much weight one believes should

be placed on the Efficient Capital Market Hypothesis. In Oran v. Stafford, 226 F.3d 275 (3d. Cir. 2000), the Third Circuit placed considerable weight on that doctrine and established a bright-line test under which, in the absence of an immediate market reaction to the disclosure by the issuer of information that it had previously omitted to disclose, the information would be presumed immaterial. Conversely, in No. 84 Employer-Teamster Joint Council Pension Trust Fund v. America West Holding Corp., 320 F.3d 920 (9th Cir. 2003), the Ninth Circuit declined to adopt such a bright-line rule, fearing that it would "raise the bar" too high to meritorious securities litigation. In *America West Holding Corp.*, the plaintiffs alleged that the defendant corporation had "peppered the market" with false statements about its outlook so that its two controlling shareholders could liquidate their holdings. In particular, these statements had denied or downplayed certain operational, safety, and maintenance problems that the defendant airline was experiencing. Eventually, the airline and the Federal Aviation Agency (FAA) reached a settlement in July 1998 under which the airline paid a record $5 million civil penalty for failing to comply with FAA rules and procedures. On this announcement, the corporation's stock price did not decline immediately, but later in the month began a steady fall that took it from $29 per share on July 22, 1998, to $9⅝ in early October 1998. Although operational difficulties appear to have been the primary problem experienced by the airline, the market effectively ignored the first disclosure of the extent of those problems. Declining to adopt the Third Circuit's per se rule that requires an immediate market reaction, the Ninth Circuit panel relied largely on Basic v. Levinson and explained: "The market is subject to distortions that prevent the ideal of 'a free and open public market' from occurring. . . . These distortions may not be corrected immediately. Because of these distortions, adoption of a bright-line rule assuming that the stock price will instantly react would fail to address the realities of the market. Thus, we decline to adopt a bright-line rule, and, instead, engage in the 'fact-specific inquiry' set forth in *Basic*." Much in the language of the opinion suggests that the majority's faith in the efficient market had been shaken by recent corporate scandals.

Virginia Bankshares, Inc. v. Sandberg
501 U.S. 1083 (1991)

JUSTICE SOUTER delivered the opinion of the Court. . . .

The questions before us are whether a statement couched in conclusory or qualitative terms purporting to explain directors' reasons for recommending certain corporate action can be materially misleading within the meaning of Rule 14a-9, and whether causation of damages compensable under §14(a) can be shown by a member of a class of minority shareholders whose votes are not required by law or corporate by-law to authorize the corporate action subject to the proxy solicitation. We hold that knowingly false statements of reasons may be actionable even though conclusory in form, but that respondents have failed to demonstrate the equitable basis required to extend the §14(a) private action to such shareholders when any indication of congressional intent to do so is lacking.

1. In December 1986, First American Bankshares, Inc., (FABI), a bank holding company, began a "freeze-out" merger, in which the First American Bank of Virginia (Bank) eventually merged into Virginia Bankshares, Inc., (VBI), a wholly

owned subsidiary of FABI. VBI owned 85% of the Bank's shares, the remaining 15% being in the hands of some 2,000 minority shareholders. FABI hired the investment banking firm of Keefe, Bruyette & Woods (KBW) to give an opinion on the appropriate price for shares of the minority holders, who would lose their interests in the Bank as a result of the merger. Based on market quotations and unverified information from FABI, KBW gave the Bank's executive committee an opinion that $42 a share could be a fair price for the minority stock. The executive committee approved the merger proposal at that price, and the full board followed suit.

Although Virginia law required only that such a merger proposal be submitted to a vote at a shareholders' meeting, and that the meeting be preceded by circulation of a statement of information to the shareholders, the directors nevertheless solicited proxies for voting on the proposal at the annual meeting set for April 21, 1987. In their solicitation, the directors urged the proposal's adoption and stated they had approved the plan because of its opportunity for the minority shareholders to achieve a "high" value, which they elsewhere described as a "fair" price, for their stock.

Although most minority shareholders gave the proxies requested, respondent Sandberg did not, and after approval of the merger she sought damages in the United States District Court for the Eastern District of Virginia from VBI, FABI, and the directors of the Bank. She pleaded two counts, one for soliciting proxies in violation of §14(a) and Rule 14a-9, and the other for breaching fiduciary duties owed to the minority shareholders under state law. Under the first count, Sandberg alleged, among other things, that the directors had not believed that the price offered was high or that the terms of the merger were fair, but had recommended the merger only because they believed they had no alternative if they wished to remain on the board. At trial, Sandberg invoked language from this Court's opinion in Mills v. Electric Auto-Lite Co., 396 U.S. 375, 385 (1970), to obtain an instruction that the jury could find for her without a showing of her own reliance on the alleged misstatements, so long as they were material and the proxy solicitation was an "essential link" in the merger process.

The jury's verdicts were for Sandberg on both counts, after finding violations of Rule 14a-9 by all defendants and a breach of fiduciary duties by the Bank's directors. The jury awarded Sandberg $18 a share, having found that she would have received $60 if her stock had been valued adequately. . . .

II. The Court of Appeals affirmed petitioners' liability for two statements found to have been materially misleading in violation of §14(a) of the Act, one of which was that "The Plan of Merger has been approved by the Board of Directors because it provides an opportunity for the Bank's public shareholders to achieve a high value for their shares." . . . Petitioners argue that statements of opinion or belief incorporating indefinite and unverifiable expressions cannot be actionable as misstatements of material fact within the meaning of Rule 14a-9, and that such a declaration of opinion or belief should never be actionable when placed in a proxy solicitation incorporating statements of fact sufficient to enable readers to draw their own, independent conclusions.

A. We consider first the actionability per se of statements of reasons, opinion or belief. Because such a statement by definition purports to express what is consciously on the speaker's mind, we interpret the jury verdict as finding that the directors' statements of belief and opinion were made with knowledge that the directors did not hold the beliefs or opinions expressed, and we confine our discussion to statements so made.[5] That such statements may be materially significant raises no serious question. The meaning of the materiality requirement for liability under §14(a) was discussed at some length in TSC Industries, Inc. v. Northway, Inc., 426 U.S. 438 (1976), where we held a fact to be material "if there is a substantial likelihood that a reasonable shareholder would consider it important in deciding how to vote." Id., at 449. We think there is no room to deny that a statement of belief by corporate directors about a recommended course of action, or an explanation of their reasons for recommending it, can take on just that importance. Shareholders know that directors usually have knowledge and expertness far exceeding the normal investor's resources, and the directors' perceived superiority is magnified even further by the common knowledge that state law customarily obliges them to exercise their judgment in the shareholders' interest. . . . Naturally, then, the share owner faced with a proxy request will think it important to know the directors' beliefs about the course they recommend, and their specific reasons for urging the stockholders to embrace it.

B. But, assuming materiality, the question remains whether statements of reasons, opinions, or beliefs are statements "with respect to . . . material facts" so as to fall within the strictures of the Rule. Petitioners argue that we would invite wasteful litigation of amorphous issues outside the readily proven realm of fact if we were to recognize liability here on proof that the directors did not recommend the merger for the stated reason, and they cite the authority of Blue Chip Stamps v. Manor Drug Stores, 421 U.S. 723 (1975), in urging us to recognize sound policy grounds for placing such statements outside the scope of the Rule.

We agree that *Blue Chip Stamps* is instructive, as illustrating a [concern about] . . . the threat of vexatious litigation over "many rather hazy issues of historical fact the proof of which depended almost entirely on oral testimony." . . .

Attacks on the truth of directors' statements of reasons or belief, however, need carry no such threats. Such statements are factual in two senses: as statements that the directors do act for the reasons given or hold the belief stated and as statements about the subject matter of the reason or belief expressed. In neither sense does the proof or disproof of such statements implicate the concerns expressed in *Blue Chip Stamps*. The root of those concerns was a plaintiff's capacity to manufacture claims of hypothetical action, unconstrained by independent evidence. Reasons for directors' recommendations or statements of belief are, in contrast, characteristically matters of corporate record subject to documentation, to be supported or attacked by evidence of historical fact outside a plaintiff's control. Such evidence would include not only corporate minutes and other statements of the directors themselves, but circumstantial evidence bearing on the facts that would reasonably underlie the reasons claimed and the honesty of any statement that those reasons are the basis for a recommendation or other action, a point that becomes especially clear when the responses or beliefs go to valuations in dollars and cents.

It is no answer to argue, as petitioners do, that the quoted statement on which liability was predicated did not express a reason in dollars and cents, but focused instead on the "indefinite and unverifiable" term, "high" value, much like the similar claim that the merger's terms were "fair" to shareholders. The objection

---

5. In TSC Industries, Inc. v. Northway, Inc., 426 U.S. 438, 444, n.7 (1976), we reserved the question whether scienter was necessary for liability generally under §14(a). We reserve it still.

ignores the fact that such conclusory terms in a commercial context are reasonably understood to rest on a factual basis that justifies them as accurate, the absence of which renders them misleading. Provable facts either furnish good reasons to make a conclusory commercial judgment, or they count against it, and expressions of such judgments can be uttered with knowledge of truth or falsity just like more definite statements, and defended or attacked through the orthodox evidentiary process that either substantiates their underlying justifications or tends to disprove their existence. . . . In this case, whether $42 was "high," and the proposal "fair" to the minority shareholders depended on whether provable facts about the Bank's assets, and about actual and potential levels of operation, substantiated a value that was above, below, or more or less at the $42 figure, when assessed in accordance with recognized methods of valuation.

Respondents adduced evidence for just such facts in proving that the statement was misleading about its subject matter and a false expression of the directors' reasons. Whereas the proxy statement described the $42 price as offering a premium above both book value and market price, the evidence indicated that a calculation of the book figure based on the appreciated value of the Bank's real estate holdings eliminated any such premium. The evidence on the significance of market price showed that KBW had conceded that the market was closed, thin and dominated by FABI, facts omitted from the statement. There was, indeed, evidence of a "going concern" value for the Bank in excess of $60 per share of common stock, another fact never disclosed. However conclusory the directors' statement may have been, then, it was open to attack by garden-variety evidence, subject neither to a plaintiff's control nor ready manufacture, and there was no undue risk of open-ended liability or uncontrollable litigation in allowing respondents the opportunity for recovery on the allegation that it was misleading to call $42 "high." . . .

Under §14(a), then, a plaintiff is permitted to prove a specific statement of reason knowingly false or misleadingly incomplete, even when stated in conclusory terms. In reaching this conclusion we have considered statements of reasons of the sort exemplified here, which misstate the speaker's reasons and also mislead about the stated subject matter (e.g., the value of the shares). A statement of belief may be open to objection only in the former respect, however, solely as a misstatement of the psychological fact of the speaker's belief in what he says. In this case, for example, the Court of Appeals alluded to just such limited falsity in observing that "the jury was certainly justified in believing that the directors did not believe a merger at $42 per share was in the minority stockholders' interest but, rather, that they voted as they did for other reasons, e.g., retaining their seats on the board." 891 F.2d, at 1121.

The question arises, then, whether disbelief, or undisclosed belief or motivation, standing alone, should be a sufficient basis to sustain an action under §14(a), absent proof by the sort of objective evidence described above that the statement also expressly or impliedly asserted something false or misleading about its subject matter. We think that proof of mere disbelief or belief undisclosed should not suffice for liability under §14(a), and if nothing more had been required or proven in this case we would reverse for that reason.

On the one hand, it would be rare to find a case with evidence solely of disbelief or undisclosed motivation without further proof that the statement was defective as to its subject matter. While we certainly would not hold a director's naked admission of disbelief incompetent evidence of a proxy statement's false or misleading character, such an unusual admission will not very often stand alone, and we do not substantially narrow the cause of action by requiring a plaintiff to demonstrate something false or misleading in what the statement expressly or impliedly declared about its subject.

On the other hand, to recognize liability on mere disbelief or undisclosed motive without any demonstration that the proxy statement was false or misleading about its subject would authorize §14(a) litigation confined solely to what one skeptical court spoke of as the "impurities" of a director's "unclean heart." . . .

This, we think, would cross the line that *Blue Chip Stamps* sought to draw. While it is true that the liability, if recognized, would rest on an actual, not hypothetical, psychological fact, the temptation to rest an otherwise nonexistent §14(a) action on psychological enquiry alone would threaten just the sort of strike suits and attrition by discovery that *Blue Chip Stamps* sought to discourage. We therefore hold disbelief or undisclosed motivation, standing alone, insufficient to satisfy the element of fact that must be established under §14(a). . . . [The remainder of the Court's decision deals with causation in an action brought under §14a of the '34 Act and is reproduced in Chapter VI infra.]

In re Donald Trump Casino Securities Litigation
7 F.3d 357 (3d Cir. 1993)

BECKER, C.J.: [Plaintiffs purchased bonds issued to finance the construction and completion of the Taj Mahal Casino, Atlantic City's largest and most lavish casino resort. The prospectus relating to the bonds estimated the completion costs at $805 million and stated that management believed "that funds generated from the operation of the Taj Mahal will be sufficient to cover all its debt service (interest and principal)." Plaintiffs claimed that this statement was materially misleading, both because the defendants lacked a reasonable belief in its truth and because they failed to disclose additional facts, such as that the Taj Mahal would require an average daily "casino win" of approximately $1.3 million simply to break even. After the defendants announced their intention to file a Chapter 11 bankruptcy petition, plaintiffs filed their complaint, which alleged violations of both Rule 10b-5 and §12(2) of the '33 Act. Noting the numerous disclaimers and cautionary statements in the prospectus, the district court dismissed the complaint under Fed. R. Civ. P. 12(b)(6), for failure to state a claim upon which relief could be granted, relying on what has come to be known as the "bespeaks caution" doctrine, under which the inclusion of sufficient cautionary statements in a disclosure document renders misrepresentations and omissions nonactionable.] . . . While the viability of the bespeaks caution doctrine is an issue of first impression for this court, we believe that it primarily represents new nomenclature rather than substantive change in the law. As we see it, "bespeaks caution" is essentially shorthand for the well-established principle that a statement or omission must be considered in context, so that accompanying statements may render it immaterial as a matter of law.

We believe that the "bespeaks caution" doctrine is both viable and applicable to the facts of this appeal. The prospectus here took considerable care to convey to potential investors the extreme risks inherent in the venture while simultaneously carefully alerting the investors to a variety of obstacles the Taj Mahal would face, all of which were relevant to a potential investor's decision concerning purchase of the bonds. We conclude that, given these warning signals in the text of the prospectus itself, the plaintiffs cannot establish that a reasonable investor would find the alleged misstatements and omissions material to his or her decision to invest in the Taj Mahal.

A. *General Legal Principles.* . . . We have squarely held that opinions, predictions and other forward-looking statements are not per se inactionable under the securities laws. Rather, such statements of "soft information" may be actionable misrepresentations if the speaker does not genuinely and reasonably believe them. [Citations omitted.] Therefore, the plaintiff's complaint does not falter just because it alleges that the defendants made a misrepresentation with their statement that they believed they would be able to repay the principal and interest on the bonds. Rather, the complaint cannot survive a motion to dismiss because ultimately it does not sufficiently allege that the defendants made a material misrepresentation. . . .

B. *The Text of the Prospectus.* The prospectus at issue contained an abundance of warnings and cautionary language which bore directly on the prospective financial success of the Taj Mahal and on the Partnership's ability to repay the bonds. We believe that given this extensive yet specific cautionary language, a reasonable factfinder could not conclude that the inclusion of the statement "the Partnership believes that funds generated from the operation of the Taj Mahal will be sufficient to cover all of its debt service (interest and principal)" would influence a reasonable investor's investment decision. More specifically, we believe that due to the disclaimers and warnings the prospectus contains, no reasonable investor could believe anything but that the Taj Mahal bonds represented a rather risky, speculative investment which might yield a high rate of return, but which alternatively might result in no return or even a loss. We hold that under this set of facts, the bondholders cannot prove that the alleged misrepresentation was material.

The statement the plaintiffs assail as misleading is contained in the MD&A section of the prospectus, which follows the sizable "Special Considerations" section, a section notable for its extensive and detailed disclaimers and cautionary statements. More precisely, the prospectus explained that, because of its status as a new venture of unprecedented size and scale, a variety of risks inhered in the Taj Mahal which could affect the Partnership's ability to repay the bondholders. For example, it stated: ". . . The Taj Mahal has not been completed and, accordingly, has no operating history. The Partnership, therefore, has no history of earnings and its operations will be subject to all of the risks inherent in the establishment of a new business enterprise. Accordingly, the ability of the Partnership to serve its debt to [Taj Mahal Funding Inc., which issued the bonds,] is completely dependent upon the success of that operation and such success will depend upon financial, business, competitive, regulatory and other factors affecting the Taj Mahal and the casino industry in general as well as prevailing economic conditions. . . ."

C. *The Bespeaks Caution Doctrine.* The district court applied what has come to be known as the "bespeaks caution" doctrine. In so doing it followed the lead of a number of courts of appeals which have dismissed securities fraud claims under Rule 12(b)(6) because cautionary language in the offering document negated the materiality of an alleged misrepresentation of omission. [Citations omitted.] We are persuaded by the ratio decidendi of these cases and will apply bespeaks caution to the facts before us.

The application of "bespeaks caution" depends on the specific text of the offering document or other communication at issue, i.e., courts must assess the communication on a case-by-case basis. See Flynn v. Bass Bros. Enters., 744 F.2d 978, 988 (3d Cir. 1984) (holding courts must determine the materiality of soft information on a case-by-case basis). Nevertheless, we can state as a general matter that, when an offering document's forecasts, opinions or projections are accompanied by meaningful cautionary statements, the forward-looking statements will not form the basis for a securities fraud claim if those statements did not affect the "total mix" of information the document provided investors. In other words, cautionary language, if sufficient, renders the alleged omissions or representations immaterial as a matter of law.

The bespeaks caution doctrine is, as an analytical matter, equally applicable to allegations of both affirmative misrepresentations and omissions concerning soft information. Whether the plaintiffs allege a document contains an affirmative prediction/opinion which is misleading or fails to include a forecast or prediction which failure is misleading, the cautionary statements included in the document may render the challenged predictive statements or opinions immaterial as a matter of law. Of course, a vague or blanket (boilerplate) disclaimer which merely warns the reader that the investment has risks will ordinarily be inadequate to prevent misinformation. To suffice, the cautionary statements must be substantive and tailored to specific future projections, estimates or opinions in the prospectus which the plaintiffs challenge.

Because of the abundant and meaningful cautionary language contained in the prospectus, we hold that the plaintiffs have failed to state an actionable claim regarding the statement that the Partnership believed it could repay the bonds. We can say that the prospectus here truly bespeaks caution because, not only does the prospectus generally convey the riskiness of the investment, but its warnings and cautionary language directly address the substance of the statement the plaintiffs challenge. That is to say, the cautionary statements were tailored precisely to address the uncertainty concerning the Partnership's prospective ability to repay the bondholders. . . .

---

1. *The "bespeaks caution" doctrine.* This doctrine has been characterized "as an evolution driven by the increase in and unique nature of fraud actions based on predictive statements." See Rubenstein v. Collins, 20 F.3d 160 (5th Cir. 1994). Developed only since the SEC's reversal of its opposition to predictive statements in the late 1970s, its precise doctrinal location remains unsettled. Although the *Trump Casino* decision held that properly qualified predictions were immaterial, other cases have relied instead on the obligation of the plaintiff to establish "justifiable reliance" on the prediction. See Schlesinger v. Herzog, 2 F.3d 135, 139 (5th Cir. 1993). The SEC has revealed some anxiety about the rapid growth of the doctrine. See Note, Liability for Forward-Looking Statements: The Securities and Exchange Commission's Ambiguous Stance, 1993 Colum. Bus. L. Rev. 221. Other courts have sought to curb its expansion. For example, in Rubenstein v. Collins, supra, an oil and gas exploration company announced that it had made a significant natural gas discovery. A securities analyst at First Boston reported that the discovery could yield 500 billion cubic feet, and corporate officials later

characterized this evaluation as either "realistic" or as one they "would not be critical of." Shortly thereafter, the corporation learned that the discovery was far less promising. When it eventually released a corrective press release a month later, its stock price fell from approximately $22 to $14 within two days (with 12 percent of the outstanding stock being traded in this period). The district court dismissed plaintiff's Rule 10b-5 complaint, because it found the projections could not constitute material misrepresentations as a matter of law. The Fifth Circuit reversed, requiring a case-specific approach that more closely examines the total mix of information provided the investor. As it recognized, however, other circuits have agreed with the district court that "economic projections are not actionable if they bespeak caution." See Sinay v. Lamson & Session Co., 948 F.2d 1037, 1040-1041 (6th Cir. 1991). At present, most decisions applying this doctrine seem to require that the statement contain detailed cautionary language addressing the specific problems that the company or the industry faced. See Romani v. Shearson Lehman Hutton, 929 F.2d 875, 878-880 (1st Cir. 1991); Moorhead v. Merrill Lynch, Pierce, Fenner & Smith, Inc., 949 F.2d 243, 245-246 (8th Cir. 1991).

2. *A statutory safe harbor.* The Private Securities Litigation Reform Act of 1995 has essentially codified and strengthened the "bespeaks caution" doctrine. Amending both the Securities Act of 1933 and the Securities Exchange Act of 1934,[38] this Act added the following core provision to both:

(c) *Safe Harbor.* —
(1) *In General.* — Except as provided in subsection (b), in any private action arising under this title that is based on an untrue statement of a material fact or omission of a material fact necessary to make the statement not misleading, a person referred to in subsection (a) shall not be liable with respect to any forward-looking statement,[39] whether written or oral, if and to the extent that —
(A) the forward-looking statement is —
(i) identified as a forward-looking statement, and is accompanied by meaningful cautionary statements identifying important factors that could cause actual results to differ materially from those in the forward-looking statement; or
(ii) immaterial; or
(B) the plaintiff fails to prove that the forward-looking statement —
(i) if made by a natural person, was made with actual knowledge by that person that the statement was false or misleading; or
(ii) if made by a business entity, was —
(I) made by or with the approval of an executive officer of that entity; and
(II) made or approved by such officer with actual knowledge by that officer that the statement was false or misleading.

Basically, this safe harbor applies only to "reporting companies" (i.e., issuers that are subject to the periodic reporting requirements of the Securities Exchange Act of 1934), and there are numerous exclusions and disqualifications for certain high-risk transactions and higher-risk companies (including those that have been the subject of criminal convictions or antifraud proceedings). Issuers that are

---

38. The Private Securities Litigation Reform Act of 1995 added a new §27A ("Application of Safe Harbor for Forward-Looking Statements") to the '33 Act and a similarly titled §21E to the Securities Exchange Act of 1934. Both sections contain the subparagraph (c) that is quoted in the text above.

39. The term "forward-looking statement" is defined to include "a statement containing a projection," a "statement of the plans and objectives of management for future operations," and "a statement of future economic performance." See §21E(i)(1) of the Securities Exchange Act of 1934. — ED.

excluded from this safe harbor can still rely on the common law "bespeaks caution" doctrine.

When the safe harbor is applicable, the above-quoted language seemingly protects even knowingly false statements if they are "accompanied by meaningful cautionary statements." That is, an issuer need only satisfy clause (A) or clause (B) of subparagraph (c)(1), and thus if it surrounds a knowing lie with a "meaningful cautionary statement," it would appear to be legally safe. This apparent "right to lie" was one of the features of the Private Securities Litigation Reform Act to which President Clinton objected when he unsuccessfully vetoed it.

Problem. Suppose the chief executive of an issuer predicts that its new wonder drug will be approved by the Food and Drug Administration (FDA) and will go into production within six months. The day before he makes this prediction the FDA informed the issuer's research staff that it has serious doubts about the drug's safety and will require elaborate new trials that might take two years. When this correction is disclosed, the issuer's stock price falls 25 percent, and a class action is commenced on behalf of purchasers who allegedly bought based on the chief executive's optimistic six-month projection. In considering this question, review §21E(c)(1)(B)(ii) above.

iii. Causation

Affiliated Ute Citizens v. United States
406 U.S. 128 (1972)

JUSTICE BLACKMUN delivered the opinion of the Court.

[The Ute Distribution Corp. (UDC) was established pursuant to the Ute Partition Act to own and manage certain assets consisting largely of oil, gas, and mineral rights, distributed to "mixed-blood" descendants of the Ute Indian Tribe on the termination of a federally supervised trust. UDC issued ten shares to each mixed-blood tribal member and arranged for a local bank to serve as the transfer agent for the transfers of this stock. Under UDC's certificate of incorporation, a mixed-blood shareholder who desired to sell had to give first refusal rights to tribal members. If no member of the Ute tribe was willing to purchase the shares at the price offered, then sales could be made to others. First Security Bank acted as transfer agent for UDC's shares, and defendants Gale and Haslem were employees of the bank, working in its branch office near where many of the mixed-blood stockholders lived. Defendants purchased shares from these stockholders without disclosing to the mixed-blood sellers that nontribal members were trading UDC shares at higher prices than defendants were offering.

The district court found their behavior to constitute a "scheme to defraud" within Rule 10b-5, but the Court of Appeals partially reversed, holding the two employees liable only as to sales where they purchased themselves and not as to other sales that they arranged. It concluded that there was insufficient evidence of reliance by the plaintiffs on any statements, or conduct of, Gale and Haslem.] In light of the Congressional philosophy and purpose . . . we conclude that the Court of Appeals viewed too narrowly the activities of Gale and Haslem. We would agree that if the two men and the employer bank had functioned merely as a transfer agent, there would have been no duty of disclosure here. But, as the Court of Appeals itself observed, the record shows that Gale and Haslem "were active in encouraging a market for the UDC stock among non-Indians." They did this by soliciting and accepting standing orders from non-Indians. They and the bank, as a result received increased deposits because of the development of this market. The two men also received commissions and gratuities from the expectant non-Indian buyers. The men, and hence the bank, as the Court found, were "entirely familiar with the prevailing market for shares at all material times."

Clearly, the Court of Appeals was right to the extent that it held that the two employees had violated Rule 10b-5; in the instances specified in that holding the record reveals a misstatement of a material fact, within the proscription of Rule 10b-5(2), namely, that the prevailing market price of the UDC shares was the figure at which their purchases were made.

We conclude, however, that the Court of Appeals erred when it held that there was no violation of the Rule unless the record disclosed evidence of reliance on material fact misrepresentations by Gale and Haslem. We do not read Rule 10b-5 so restrictively. To be sure, the second subparagraph of the rule specifies the making of an untrue statement of a material fact and the omission to state a material fact. The first and third subparagraphs are not so restricted. These defendants' activities, outlined above, disclose, within the very language of one or the other of those subparagraphs, a "course of business" or a "device, scheme, or artifice" that operated as a fraud upon the Indian sellers. This is so because the defendants devised a plan and induced the mixed-blood holders of UDC stock to dispose of their shares without disclosing to them material facts that reasonably could have been expected to influence their decision to sell. The individual defendants, in a distinct sense, were market makers, not only for their personal purchases constituting $8^1/_3\%$ of the sales, but for the other sales their activities produced. This being so, they possessed the affirmative duty under the Rule to disclose this fact to the mixed-blood sellers. See Chasins v. Smith, Barney & Co., 438 F.2d 1167 (CA2 1970). It is no answer to urge that, as to some of the petitioners, these defendants may have made no positive representation or recommendation. The defendants may not stand mute while they facilitated the mixed-bloods' sales to those seeking to profit in the non-Indian market the defendants had developed and encouraged and with which they were fully familiar. The sellers had the right to know that the defendants were in a position to gain financially from their sales and that their shares were selling for a higher price in that market. . . .

Under the circumstances of this case, involving primarily a failure to disclose, positive proof of reliance is not a prerequisite to recovery. All that is necessary is that the facts withheld be material in the sense that a reasonable investor might have considered them important in the making of this decision. . . . This obligation to disclose and this withholding of a material fact establish the requisite element of causation in fact.

Gale and Haslem engaged in more than ministerial functions. Their acts were clearly within the reach of Rule 10b-5. And they were acts performed when they were obligated to act on behalf of the mixed-blood sellers. . . .

In our view, the correct measure of damages under §28 of the ['34] Act, is the difference between the fair value of all that the mixed-blood seller received and the fair value of what he would have received had there been no fraudulent conduct, except for the situation where the defendant received more than the seller's actual loss. In the latter case damages are the amount of the defendant's profit. See Janigan v. Taylor, 344 F.2d 781, 786 (1st Cir. 1965). . . .

[JUSTICE DOUGLAS concurred in part and dissented in part; JUSTICES POWELL and REHNQUIST did not participate.]

Proof of reliance. At first glance, *Affiliated Ute* seems to hold that materiality subsumes causation; that is, proof of actual reliance is not part of the plaintiff's prima facie case. But this is too simple. Although the case involved "primarily a failure to disclose," there was also at bottom a long-standing course of conduct that effectively rigged the market for UDC stock. Moreover, the Court's statement that "positive proof of reliance is not necessary" hints that defendants could raise as an affirmative defense that plaintiffs had not relied on their misrepresentations or omissions.

Since *Affiliated Ute*, subsequent decisions have held it inapplicable in cases where there was an affirmative misrepresentation, holding that in these cases plaintiff must prove actual reliance. See, e.g., Wilson v. Comtech Telecommunications Corp., 648 F.2d 88 (2d Cir. 1981); Vervaecke v. Chiles, Heider & Co., 578 F.2d 713 (8th Cir. 1978). On this view, *Affiliated Uste* applies only in a total non-disclosure case, not one in which there are both omissions and affirmative misrepresentations. Even when the misstatement was actually communicated to plaintiff, some decisions have dismissed the action on the ground that reliance on the alleged misstatement would not have been reasonable. See Zobrist v. Coal-X, Inc., 708 F.2d 1511 (10th Cir. 1983) (where alleged oral statement differed from written one in offering memorandum, justifiable reliance on misrepresentation could not be shown where plaintiff had not read offering memorandum). Still other cases have indicated doubt that a clear line can be drawn between nondisclosures and misrepresentations, and some have simply decided that the trial court should determine who is better able to bear the burden of proof. Compare Sharp v. Coopers & Lybrand, 649 F.2d 175 (3d Cir. 1981), with Little v. First California Co., 532 F.2d 1302 (9th Cir. 1976). Although generalizations are difficult to make and subject to inevitable exceptions, it seems that in a face-to-face transaction involving misrepresentations, a court will today require some proof of reliance by the plaintiff. See, e.g., Simon v. Merrill Lynch, Pierce, Fenner & Smith, Inc., 482 F.2d 880 (5th Cir. 1973) (where investor made own investment decisions, absence of evidence of reliance on broker's alleged misstatement precluded recovery). However, where the plaintiff can allege more than a simple misrepresentation and seeks to show collateral conduct by the defendant amounting to a scheme to defraud, proof of reliance has been held not to be required. See Competitive Associates, Inc. v. Laventhal, Krekstein, Horwath & Horwath, 516 F.2d 811 (2d Cir. 1975) (falsification of financial statements amounted to collateral conduct that justified presumption of reliance under *Affiliated Ute*).

Basic, Inc. v. Levinson
485 U.S. 224 (1988)

JUSTICE BLACKMUN delivered the opinion of the Court.
[The facts of this case are set out at page 312 supra. Having found that Basic, Inc. may have made a material misrepresentation when it falsely denied that merger

negotiations were underway, the Court then faced the question of whether individual investors had to prove that they had known of and relied on this misrepresentation in deciding to sell their shares. If proof of such individual reliance was necessary, it was unlikely that a class action could be maintained.] . . . We turn to the question of reliance and the fraud-on-the-market theory. Succinctly put:

> The fraud on the market theory is based on the hypothesis that, in an open and developed securities market, the price of a company's stock is determined by the available material information regarding the company and its business. . . . Misleading statements will therefore defraud purchasers of stock even if the purchasers do not directly rely on the misstatements. . . . The causal connection between the defendants' fraud and the plaintiffs' purchase of stock in such a case is not less significant than in a case of direct reliance on misrepresentations.

Peil v. Speiser, 806 F.2d 1154, 1160-1161 (CA3 1986). Our task, of course, is not to assess the general validity of the theory, but to consider whether it was proper for the courts below to apply a rebuttable presumption of reliance, supported in part by the fraud-on-the-market theory. . . .

This case required resolution of several common questions of law and fact concerning the falsity or misleading nature of the three public statements made by Basic, the presence or absence of scienter, and the materiality of the misrepresentations, if any. In their amended complaint, the named plaintiffs alleged that in reliance on Basic's statements they sold their shares of Basic stock in the depressed market created by petitioners. . . . Requiring proof of individualized reliance from each member of the proposed plaintiff class effectively would have prevented respondents from proceeding with a class action, since individual issues then would have overwhelmed the common ones. The District Court found that the presumption of reliance created by the fraud-on-the-market theory provided "a practical resolution to the problem of balancing the substantive requirement of proof of reliance in securities cases against the procedural requisites of [Fed. Rule Civ. Proc.] 23." The District Court thus concluded that with reference to each public statement and its impact upon the open market for Basic shares, common questions predominated over individual questions, as required by Fed. Rule Civ. Proc. 23(a)(2) and (b)(3).

Petitioners and their amici complain that the fraud-on-the-market theory effectively eliminates the requirement that a plaintiff asserting a claim under Rule 10b-5 prove reliance. They note that reliance is and long has been an element of common-law fraud, see, e.g., Restatement (Second) of Torts §525 (1977); Prosser and Keeton on The Law of Torts §108 (5th Ed. 1984), and argue that because the analogous express right of action includes a reliance requirement, see, e.g., §18(a) of the 1934 Act, as amended, 15 U.S.C. §78r(a), so too must an action implied under §10(b).

We agree that reliance is an element of a Rule 10b-5 cause of action. See Ernst & Ernst v. Hochfelder, 425 U.S., at 206 (quoting Senate Report). Reliance provides the requisite causal connection between a defendant's misrepresentation and a plaintiff's injury. See, e.g., Wilson v. Comtech Telecommunications Corp., 648 F.2d 88, 92 (CA2 1981); List v. Fashion Park, Inc., 340 F.2d 457, 462 (CA2), cert. denied sub nom. List v. Lerner, 382 U.S. 811 (1965). There is, however, more than one way to demonstrate the causal connection. Indeed, we previously have dispensed with a requirement of positive proof of reliance, where a duty to disclose material information had been breached, concluding that the necessary nexus between the plaintiffs' injury and the defendant's wrongful conduct had been established. See Affiliated Ute Citizens v. United States, 406 U.S., at 153-154. Similarly, we did not require proof that material omissions or misstatements in a proxy statement decisively affected voting, because the proxy solicitation itself, rather than the defect in the solicitation materials, served as an essential link in the transaction. See Mills v. Electric Auto-Lite Co., 396 U.S. 375, 384-385 (1970).

The modern securities markets, literally involving millions of shares changing hands daily, differ from the face-to-face transactions contemplated by early fraud cases,[21] and our understanding of Rule 10b-5's reliance requirement must encompass these differences.

> In face-to-face transactions, the inquiry into an investor's reliance upon information is into the subjective pricing of that information by that investor. With the presence of a market, the market is interposed between seller and buyer and, ideally, transmits information to the investor in the processed form of a market price. Thus the market is performing a substantial part of the valuation process performed by the investor in a face-to-face transaction. The market is acting as the unpaid agent of the investor, informing him that given all the information available to it, the value of the stock is worth the market price.

In re LTV Securities Litigation, 88 F.R.D. 134, 143 (N.D. Tex. 1980). Accord, e.g., Peil v. Speiser, 806 F.2d, at 1161 ("In an open and developed market, the dissemination of material misrepresentations or withholding of material information typically affects the price of the stock, and purchasers generally rely on the price of the stock as a reflection of its value"); Blackie v. Barrack, 524 F.2d 891, 908 (CA9 1975) ("the same causal nexus can be adequately established indirectly, by proof of materiality coupled with the common sense that a stock purchaser does not ordinarily seek to purchase a loss in the form of artificially inflated stock"), *cert. denied*, 429 U.S. 816 (1976).

Presumptions typically serve to assist courts in managing circumstances in which direct proof, for one reason or another, is rendered difficult. See, e.g., D. Louisell & C. Mueller, Federal Evidence 541-542 (1977). The courts below accepted a presumption, created by the fraud-on-the-market theory and subject to rebuttal by petitioners, that persons who had traded Basic shares had done so in reliance on the integrity of the price set by the market, but because of petitioners' material misrepresentations that price had been fraudulently depressed. Requiring a plaintiff to show a speculative state of facts, i.e., how he would have acted if omitted material information had been disclosed, see Affiliated Ute Citizens v. United States, 406 U.S., at 153-154, or if the misrepresentation had not been made, see Sharp v. Coopers & Lybrand, 649 F.2d 175, 188 (CA3 1981), *cert. denied*, 455 U.S. 938 (1982), would place an unnecessarily unrealistic evidentiary burden on the Rule 10b-5 plaintiff who has traded on an impersonal market. Cf. Mills v. Electric Auto-Lite Co., 396 U.S., at 385.

---

21. Prosser and Keeton on The Law of Torts 726 (5th ed. 1984) ("The reasons for the separate development of [the tort action for misrepresentation and nondisclosure], and for its peculiar limitations, are in part historical, and in part connected with the fact that in the great majority of the cases which have come before the courts the misrepresentations have been made in the course of a bargaining transaction between the parties. Consequently the action has been colored to a considerable extent by the ethics of bargaining between distrustful adversaries") (footnote omitted).

Arising out of consideration of fairness, public policy, and probability, as well as judicial economy, presumptions are also useful devices for allocating the burdens of proof between parties. See E. Cleary, McCormick on Evidence 968-969 (3d ed. 1984); see also Fed. Rule Evid. 301 and notes. The presumption of reliance employed in this case is consistent with, and, by facilitating Rule 10b-5 litigation, supports, the congressional policy embodied in the 1934 Act. In drafting that Act, Congress expressly relied on the premise that securities markets are affected by information, and enacted legislation to facilitate an investor's reliance on the integrity of those markets:

> No investor, no speculator, can safely buy and sell securities upon the exchanges without having an intelligent basis for forming his judgment as to the value of the securities he buys or sells. The idea of a free and open public market is built upon the theory that competing judgments of buyers and sellers as to the fair price of security brings [sic] about a situation where the market price reflects as nearly as possible a just price. Just as artificial manipulation tends to upset the true function of an open market, so the hiding and secreting of important information obstructs the operation of the markets as indices of real value.

H.R. Rep. No. 1383, supra, at 11. See Lipton v. Documation, Inc., 734 F.2d 740, 749 (CA11 1984).

The presumption is also supported by common sense and probability. Recent empirical studies have tended to confirm Congress' premise that the market price of shares traded on well-developed markets reflects all publicly available information, and, hence, any material misrepresentation.[24] It has been noted that "it is hard to imagine that there ever is a buyer or seller who does not rely on market integrity. Who would knowingly roll the dice in a crooked crap game?" Schlanger v. Four-Phase Systems Inc., 555 F. Supp. 535, 538 (S.D.N.Y. 1982). Indeed, nearly every court that has considered the proposition has concluded that where materially misleading statements have been disseminated into an impersonal, well-developed market for securities, the reliance of individual plaintiffs on the integrity of the market price may be presumed.[25] Commentators generally have applauded the adoption of one variation or another of the fraud-on-the-market theory.[26] An investor who buys or sells stock at the price set by the market does so in reliance on the integrity of the price. Because most publicly available information is reflected in market price, an investor's reliance on any public material

---

24. See In re LTV Securities Litigation, 88 F.R.D. 134, 144 (N.D. Tex 1980) (citing studies); Fischel, Use of Modern Finance Theory in Securities Fraud Cases Involving Actively Traded Securities, 38 Bus. Law. 1, 4, n.9 (1982) (citing literature on efficient-capital-market theory); Dennis, Materiality and the Efficient Capital Market Model: A Recipe for the Total Mix, 25 Wm. & Mary L. Rev. 373, 374-381, and n.1 (1984). We need not determine by adjudication what economists and social scientists have debated through the use of sophisticated statistical analysis and the application of economic theory. For purposes of accepting the presumption of reliance in this case, we need only believe that market professionals generally consider most publicly announced material statements about companies, thereby affecting stock market prices.

25. See, e.g., Peil v. Speiser, 806 F.2d 1154, 1161 (CA3 1986); Harris v. Union Electric Co., 787 F.2d 355, 367, and n.9 (CA8 1986); Lipton v. Documation, Inc., 734 F.2d 740 (CA11 1984); T. J. Raney & Sons, Inc. v. Fort Cobb, Oklahoma Irrigation Fuel Authority, 717 F.2d 1330, 1332-1333 (CA10 1983); Panzirer v. Wolf, 663 F.2d 365, 367-368 (CA2 1981); Blackie v. Barrack, 524 F.2d 891, 905-908 (CA9 1975).

26. See, e.g., Black, Fraud on the Market: A Criticism of Dispensing with Reliance Requirements in Certain Open Market Transactions, 62 N.C. L. Rev. 435 (1984); Note, The Fraud-on-the-Market Theory, 95 Harv. L. Rev. 1143 (1982); Note, Fraud on the Market: An Emerging Theory of Recovery Under SEC Rule 10b-5, 50 Geo. Wash. L. Rev. 627 (1982).

misrepresentations, therefore, may be presumed for purposes of a Rule 10b-5 action.

The Court of Appeals found that petitioners "made public material misrepresentations and [respondents] sold Basic stock in an impersonal, efficient market. Thus the class, as defined by the district court, has established the threshold facts for proving their loss." 786 F.2d at 751.[27] The court acknowledged that petitioners may rebut proof of the elements giving rise to the presumption, or show that the misrepresentation in fact did not lead to a distortion of price or that an individual plaintiff traded or would have traded despite his knowing the statement was false. Id., at 750, n.6.

Any showing that severs the link between the alleged misrepresentation and either the price received (or paid) by the plaintiff, or his decision to trade at a fair market price, will be sufficient to rebut the presumption of reliance. For example, if petitioner could show that the "market makers" were privy to the truth about the merger discussion here with Combustion, and thus that the market price would not have been affected by their misrepresentations, the causal connection could be broken: the basis for finding that the fraud had been transmitted through market price would be gone.[28] Similarly, if, despite petitioners' allegedly fraudulent attempt to manipulate market price, news of the merger discussions credibly entered the market and dissipated the effects of the misstatements, those who traded Basic shares after the corrective statements would have no direct or indirect connection with the fraud.[29] Petitioners also could rebut the presumption of reliance as to plaintiffs who would have divested themselves of their Basic shares without relying on the integrity of the market. For example, a plaintiff who believed that Basic's statements were false and that Basic was indeed engaged in merger discussions, and who consequently believed that Basic stock was artificially underpriced, but sold his shares nevertheless because of other, unrelated concerns, e.g., potential antitrust problems, or political pressures to divest from shares of certain businesses, could not be said to have relied on the integrity of a price he knew had been manipulated. . . .

[JUSTICES WHITE and O'CONNOR dissented on this part of the case. CHIEF JUSTICE REHNQUIST and JUSTICES SCALIA and KENNEDY did not participate.]

---

27. The Court of Appeals held that in order to invoke the presumption, a plaintiff must allege and prove: (1) that the defendant made public misrepresentations; (2) that the misrepresentations were material; (3) that the shares were traded on an efficient market; (4) that the misrepresentations would induce a reasonable, relying investor to misjudge the value of the shares; and (5) that the plaintiff traded the shares between the time the misrepresentations were made and the time the truth was revealed. See 786 F.2d, at 750.

Given today's decision regarding the definition of materiality as to preliminary merger discussions, elements (2) and (4) may collapse into one.

28. By accepting this rebuttable presumption, we do not intend conclusively to adopt any particular theory of how quickly and completely publicly available information is reflected in market price. Furthermore, our decision today is not to be interpreted as addressing the proper measure of damages in litigation of this kind.

29. We note there may be a certain incongruity between the assumption that Basic shares are traded on a well-developed, efficient, and information-hungry market, and the allegation that such a market could remain misinformed, and its valuation of Basic shares depressed, for 14 months, on the basis of the three public statements. Proof of the sort is a matter for trial, throughout which the District Court retains the authority to amend the certification order as may be appropriate. See Fed. Rule Civ. Proc. 23(c)(1) and (c)(4). See 7 B C. Wright, A. Miller & M. Kane, Federal Practice and Procedure 128-132 (1986). . . .

1. *"Fraud on the market."* In *Basic*, a plurality of the Court adopts the view that an investor is entitled to rely on the integrity of the market (in the absence of evidence to rebut this presumption), even when he or she does not learn of the actual misrepresentation. This limited acceptance of efficient market theory corresponds to the SEC's decision to focus disclosure policy more on informing the market than on the individual investor. Similarly, courts will hereafter assume (absent evidence to the contrary) that if the market is misinformed, the individual investor has suffered. Many circuits had accepted the doctrine before the Court granted certiorari in *Basic*. Still, defendants had hoped (and Justice White in dissent agreed) that the Court would limit the reach of Rule 10b-5 to cases where the defendant had actually traded. Instead, Rule 10b-5 now clearly applies to any corporate press release likely to influence the market.

The theoretical foundation for the doctrine is supplied by an economic theory known as the Efficient Capital Market Hypothesis (ECMH), which interprets the randomness of stock market price movements to demonstrate that the market price of a stock immediately absorbs and reflects all available information (thereby causing future price movements to be random). See page 192 supra. Thus, if all available information (including misinformation) is absorbed into the market price, the plaintiff can be injured even though the plaintiff never learned of, or relied on, the misinformation. Instead, courts have viewed such an uninformed plaintiff as having relied on the "integrity of the market" — that is, on the market's ability accurately to price the security in the light of all available information. For example, in T. J. Raney & Sons, Inc. v. Ft. Cobb, Okla. Irrigation Fuel Auth., 717 F.2d 1330, 1332 (10th Cir. 1983), the Tenth Circuit recognized the irrelevance of individual reliance under this theory: "The theory is grounded on the assumption that the market price reflects all known material information. Material misinformation will theoretically cause the artificial inflation or deflation of the stock price. At its simplest, the theory requires only that a plaintiff prove purchase of a security and that a material misrepresentation was made concerning the security by the defendant which resulted in an artificial change in price." See also Daniel Fischel, Use of Modern Finance Theory in Securities Fraud Cases Involving Actively Traded Securities, 38 Bus. Law. 1 (1982).

As *Basic* shows, the procedural impact of the "fraud on the market" doctrine is to simplify greatly the availability of a class action. Under Fed. R. Civ. P. 23, a material variation in the representations made, or in the degrees of reliance placed on a representation, can make a fraud case unsuitable for class action treatment. See Rule 23, Advisory Committee's Official Note, 39 F.R.D. 98, 107 (1966). By eliminating the need for proof of individual reliance, the "fraud on the market" doctrine effectively makes a class action easier to maintain and thus shifts the settlement negotiations in favor of the plaintiff.

2. *Scope of the doctrine.* Not all securities markets are necessarily efficient, and thus the premise that the stock market price incorporates all available information may not apply to these less efficient markets. If a market does not qualify as efficient, must the plaintiff prove actual reliance on the information? If so, it may be impossible to bring a class action, because some investors will have in fact relied on the challenged statement, but others will not. In Freeman v. Laventhol & Horwath, 915 F.2d 193, 199 (6th Cir. 1990), the court identified five factors for determining market efficiency: "(1) a large weekly trading volume; (2) the existence of a significant number of reports by securities analysts; (3) the existence of market

makers and arbitrageurs in the security; (4) the eligibility of a company to file an S-3 Registration Statement; and (5) a history of immediate movement of the stock price caused by unexpected corporate events or financial releases." On this basis, the determination must be made in terms of the individual security, rather than the individual market on which it was traded.

Special problems exist with initial public offerings and other new issues, because prices in these offerings are determined by the underwriters in negotiations with the issuer and not by impersonal market forces. Several decisions have thus found these primary markets not to be efficient and precluded class certification because individualized proof of reliance was therefore necessary. See In re IPO Securities Litigation, 471 F.3d 24 (2d Cir. 2006); Freeman v. Laventhol & Horwath, 915 F.2d 193, 199; Lipton v. Documation, Inc., 734 F.2d 740, 746 (11th Cir. 1984); Note, Should Fraud on the Market Theory Extend to the Context of Newly Issued Securities?, 61 Fordham L. Rev. 151-159 (1993); Note, Sufficient Efficiency: Fraud on the Market in the Initial Public Offering Context, 58 U. Chi. L. Rev. 1393 (1991).

Other decisions, however, have avoided this result by developing a companion doctrine, sometimes called the "fraud created the market" doctrine. In Shores v. Sklar, 647 F.2d 462 (5th Cir. 1981) (en banc), the court held that an investor could maintain a Rule 10b-5 class action with respect to municipal securities by establishing that the fraud permitted the securities to *exist* in the market — in short, that but for the fraud the securities would have been "unmarketable." The Fifth Circuit's premise was that investors should be able to rely on the assumption that local governments would not authorize, underwriters would not finance, and brokers would not offer to their customers securities that they knew were unmarketable. Thus, hiding their lack of marketability caused the transaction. Some other courts have adopted closely related variants on this position. See Ross v. Bank South, N.A. 885 F.2d 723 (11th Cir. 1989) (en banc); T. J. Raney & Sons, Inc. v. Fort Cobb, Okla. Irrigation Fuel Auth., 717 F.2d 1330 (10th Cir. 1983). Other circuits have, however, rejected the concept of unmarketability, noting that the securities of even bankrupt corporations trade actively and some markets specialize in low-priced penny stocks. See Eckstein v. Balcor Film Investors, 8 F.3d 1121, 1131 (7th Cir. 1993).

To the uncertain extent the "fraud created the market" doctrine survives, courts applying it have required plaintiffs to plead facts showing that the defendants' fraudulent conduct was so pervasive that it went to the "very existence of the securities and the validity of their presence in the market." See In re NationsMart Corp. Sec. Litig., 130 F.3d 309, 321 (8th Cir. 1997). In effect, the securities would have to be shown to be unmarketable at any price if the truth had been disclosed.

3. *The "Truth on the Market" defense.* A corollary of the "fraud on the market" doctrine is that the defendants can rebut Basic v. Levinson's presumption of reliance by showing that, even if fraudulent statements were made to the market, corrective information had entered the market that had dissipated the impact of the false misrepresentations or omissions. See In re Apple Computer Sec. Litig., 886 F.2d 1109, 1115 (9th Cir. 1989); Wieglos v. Commonwealth Edison Co., 892 F.2d 509, 516 (7th Cir. 1989); Cooke v. Manufactured Homes Inc., 998 F.2d 1256; 1262-1263 (4th Cir. 1993). For example, if security analysts and news reports had repeatedly stressed a material fact that the issuer's management had omitted to disclose, then an efficient market would presumably have incorporated this information into the price of the issuer's stock. Hence, persons trading after the time of the

corrective information's release should not be affected by the release of the original misleading information. However, before the "truth on the market" defense can be satisfied, most courts have found that the defendants must prove that the information originally omitted or misrepresented "was transmitted to the public with a degree of intensity and credibility sufficient to effectively counterbalance any misleading impression created by the defendant's statements." See Wallace v. Systems & Computer Technology Corp., 1997 U.S. Dist. LEXIS 14677, at *43 (E.D. Pa. 1997). For applications of the doctrine, see Rand v. Cullinet Software, Inc., 847 F. Supp. 200, 205 (D. Mass. 1996); In re Biogen Sec. Litig., 179 F.R.D. 25, 36-37 (D. Mass. 1997). Typically, this inquiry is fact intensive and requires an elaborate showing at a motion for summary judgment of multiple articles and statements stressing the allegedly omitted information.

4. *Transaction causation and loss causation.* Ultimately, reliance is one form of transaction causation. Even if transaction causation is established or conceded, what should be the result if the facts that caused the security's price to fall were wholly unrelated to the material information that caused the defrauded investor to make the purchase? Consider this hypothetical: The corporation has inflated its earnings for several years. The plaintiffs bought the stock at $60 per share and wish to prove that it was only worth $30 at that time. But this Silicon Valley corporation is wholly destroyed by a major earthquake, which levels its plant and headquarters and reduces its stock price to $5 per share. Nonetheless, the plaintiffs wish to show that $30 of their $55 loss (i.e., $60 minus $5) was attributable to the original fraudulent inflation of earnings.

To resolve this hypothetical, one must distinguish "transaction causation" from "loss causation." Think of "transaction causation" as resembling reliance in a fraud cause of action or, more generally, "but for" causation in tort law. Loss causation means essentially proximate causation. The burden of proving both falls on the plaintiff, but the "fraud on the market" doctrine greatly simplifies proof of transaction causation, while loss causation still must be shown in every Rule 10b-5 case. Although this terminology goes back more than 30 years (see Schlick v. Penn-Dixie Cement Corp., 507 F.2d 374, 380-381 (2d Cir. 1974)), each circuit tended to interpret loss causation differently. Their different approaches were finally addressed by the Supreme Court.

Dura Pharmaceuticals, Inc., v. Michael Broudo
544 U.S. 336 (2005)

JUSTICE BREYER delivered the opinion of the Court.

A private plaintiff who claims securities fraud must prove that the defendant's fraud caused an economic loss. 15 U.S.C. §78u-4(b)(4). We consider a Ninth Circuit holding that a plaintiff can satisfy this requirement—a requirement that courts call "loss causation"—simply by alleging in the complaint and subsequently establishing that "the price" of the security "on the date of purchase was inflated because of the misrepresentation." 339 F.3d 933, 938 (2003). In our view, the Ninth Circuit is wrong, both in respect to what a plaintiff must prove and in respect to what the plaintiffs' complaint here must allege.

I. Respondents are individuals who bought stock in Dura Pharmaceuticals, Inc., on the public securities market between April 15, 1997, and February 24, 1998.

They have brought this securities fraud class action against Dura and some of its managers and directors (hereinafter Dura) in federal court. In respect to the question before us, their detailed amended complaint makes substantially the following allegations:

(1) Before and during the purchase period, Dura (or its officials) made false statements concerning both Dura's drug profits and future Food and Drug Administration (FDA) approval of a new asthmatic spray device. . . .

(2) In respect to drug profits, Dura falsely claimed that it expected that its drug sales would prove profitable.

(3) In respect to the asthmatic spray device, Dura falsely claimed that it expected the FDA would soon grant its approval.

(4) On the last day of the purchase period, February 24, 1998, Dura announced that its earnings would be lower than expected, principally due to slow drug sales.

(5) The next day Dura's shares lost almost half their value (falling from about $39 per share to about $21).

(6) About eight months later (in November 1998), Dura announced that the FDA would not approve Dura's new asthmatic spray device.

(7) The next day Dura's share price temporarily fell but almost fully recovered within one week.

Most importantly, the complaint says the following (and nothing significantly more than the following) about economic losses attributable to the spray device misstatement: "In reliance on the integrity of the market, [the plaintiffs] . . . paid artificially inflated prices for Dura securities" and the plaintiffs suffered "damages" thereby.

The District Court dismissed the complaint. In respect to the plaintiffs' drug-profitability claim, it held that the complaint failed adequately to allege an appropriate state of mind, i.e., that defendants had acted knowingly, or the like. In respect to the plaintiffs' spray device claim, it held that the complaint failed adequately to allege "loss causation."

The Court of Appeals for the Ninth Circuit . . . held that the complaint adequately alleged "loss causation." The Circuit wrote that "plaintiffs establish loss causation if they have shown that the price on the date of purchase was inflated because of the misrepresentation." 339 F.3d at 938. It added that "the injury occurs at the time of the transaction." *Ibid.* Since the complaint pleaded "that the price at the time of purchase was overstated," and it sufficiently identified the cause, its allegations were legally sufficient. *Ibid.* . . .

II. A. We begin with the Ninth Circuit's basic reason for finding the complaint adequate, namely, that at the end of the day plaintiffs need only "establish," i.e., prove, that "the price on the date of purchase was inflated because of the misrepresentation." 339 F.3d at 938 (internal quotation marks omitted). In our view, this statement of the law is wrong. Normally, in cases such as this one (i.e., fraud-on-the-market cases), an inflated purchase price will not itself constitute or proximately cause the relevant economic loss.

For one thing, as a matter of pure logic, at the moment the transaction takes place, the plaintiff has suffered no loss; the inflated purchase payment is offset by ownership of a share that at that instant possesses equivalent value. Moreover, the logical link between the inflated share purchase price and any later economic loss is not invariably strong. Shares are normally purchased with an eye toward a later sale. But if, say, the purchaser sells the shares quickly before the relevant truth begins to leak out, the misrepresentation will not have led to any loss. If the purchaser sells later after the truth makes its way into the market place, an initially inflated purchase price might mean a later loss. But that is far from inevitably so. When the purchaser subsequently resells such shares, even at a lower price, that lower price may reflect, not the earlier misrepresentation, but changed economic circumstances, changed investor expectations, new industry-specific or firm-specific facts, conditions, or other events, which taken separately or together account for some or all of that lower price. (The same is true in respect to a claim that a share's higher price is lower than it would otherwise have been — a claim we do not consider here.) Other things being equal, the longer the time between purchase and sale, the more likely that this is so, i.e., the more likely that other factors caused the loss.

Given the tangle of factors affecting price, the most logic alone permits us to say is that the higher purchase price will sometimes play a role in bringing about a future loss. It may prove to be a necessary condition of any such loss, and in that sense one might say that the inflated purchase price suggests that the misrepresentation (using language the Ninth Circuit used) "touches upon" a later economic loss. *Ibid.* But, even if that is so, it is insufficient. To "touch upon" a loss is not to cause a loss, and it is the latter that the law requires. 15 U.S.C. §78u-4(b)(4).

For another thing, the Ninth Circuit's holding lacks support in precedent. Judicially implied private securities-fraud actions resemble in many (but not all) respects common-law deceit and misrepresentation actions. See *Blue Chip Stamps*, supra, at 744; see also L. Loss & J. Seligman, Fundamentals of Securities Regulation, 910-918 (5th ed. 2004) (describing relationship to common-law deceit). The common law of deceit subjects a person who "fraudulently" makes a "misrepresentation" to liability "for pecuniary loss caused" to one who justifiably relies upon that misrepresentation. Restatement (Second) of Torts §525, p. 55 (1977) (hereinafter Restatement of Torts); see also Southern Development Co. v. Silva, 125 U.S. 247, 250 (1888) (setting forth elements of fraudulent misrepresentation). And the common law has long insisted that a plaintiff in such a case show not only that had he known the truth he would not have acted but also that he suffered actual economic loss. See, e.g., Pasley v. Freeman, 3 T. R. 5:1, 100 Eng. Rep. 450, 457 (1789) (if "no injury is occasioned by the lie, it is not actionable: but if it be attended with a damage, it then becomes the subject of an action"); Freeman v. Venner, 120 Mass. 424, 426 (1876) (a mortgagee cannot bring a tort action for damages stemming from a fraudulent note that a misrepresentation led him to execute unless and until the note has to be paid); see also M. Bigelow, Law of Torts 101 (8th ed. 1907) (damage "must already have been suffered before the bringing of the suit"); 2 T. Cooley, Law of Torts §348, p. 551 (4th ed. 1932) (plaintiff must show that he "suffered damage" and that the "damage followed proximately the deception"); W. Keeton, D. Dobbs, R. Keeton, & D. Owen, Prosser and Keeton on Law of Torts §110, p. 765 (5th ed. 1984) (hereinafter Prosser and Keeton) (plaintiff "must have suffered substantial damage," not simply nominal damages, before "the cause of action can arise").

Given the common-law roots of the securities fraud action (and the common-law requirement that a plaintiff show actual damages), it is not surprising that other courts of appeals have rejected the Ninth Circuit's "inflated purchase price" approach to proving causation and loss. See, e.g., *Emergent Capital*, 343 F.3d at 198 (inflation of purchase price alone cannot satisfy loss causation); *Semerenko*, 223 F.3d at 185 (same); *Robbins*, 116 F.3d at 1448 (same); cf. *Bastian*, 892 F.2d at 685. Indeed, the Restatement of Torts, in setting forth the judicial consensus, says that a person who "misrepresents the financial condition of a corporation in order to sell its stock" becomes liable to a relying purchaser "for the loss" the purchaser sustains "when the facts . . . become generally known" and "as a result" share value "depreciates." §548A, Comment b, at 107. Treatise writers, too, have emphasized the need to prove proximate causation. Prosser and Keeton §110, at 767 (losses do "not afford any basis for recovery" if "brought about by business conditions or other factors").

We cannot reconcile the Ninth Circuit's "inflated purchase price" approach with these views of other courts. And the uniqueness of its perspective argues against the validity of its approach in a case like this one where we consider the contours of a judicially implied cause of action with roots in the common law.

Finally, the Ninth Circuit's approach overlooks an important securities law objective. The securities statutes seek to maintain public confidence in the marketplace. See United States v. O'Hagan, 521 U.S. 642, 658 (1997). They do so by deterring fraud, in part, through the availability of private securities fraud actions. Randall v. Loftsgaarden, 478 U.S. 647, 664 (1986). But the statutes make these latter actions available, not to provide investors with broad insurance against market losses, but to protect them against those economic losses that misrepresentations actually cause. *Cf. Basic*, 485 U.S., at 252 (White, J., joined by O'Connor, J., concurring in part and dissenting in part) ("Allowing recovery in the face of affirmative evidence of nonreliance — would effectively convert Rule 10b-5 into a scheme of investor's insurance. There is no support in the Securities Exchange Act, the Rule, or our cases for such a result.").

The statutory provision at issue here and the paragraphs that precede it emphasize this last mentioned objective. Private Securities Litigation Reform Act of 1995. The statute insists that securities fraud complaints "specify" each misleading statement; that they set forth the facts "on which [a] belief" that a statement is misleading was "formed"; and that they "state with particularity facts giving rise to a strong inference that the defendant acted with the required state of mind." 15 U.S.C. §§78u-4(b)(1), (2). And the statute expressly imposes on plaintiffs "the burden of proving" that the defendant's misrepresentations "caused the loss for which the plaintiff seeks to recover." §78u-4(b)(4).

The statute thereby makes clear Congress' intent to permit private securities fraud actions for recovery where, but only where, plaintiffs adequately allege and prove the traditional elements of causation and loss. By way of contrast, the Ninth Circuit's approach would allow recovery where a misrepresentation leads to an inflated purchase price but nonetheless does not proximately cause any economic loss. That is to say, it would permit recovery where these two traditional elements in fact are missing.

In sum, we find the Ninth Circuit's approach inconsistent with the law's requirement that a plaintiff prove that the defendant's misrepresentation (or other fraudulent conduct) proximately caused the plaintiff's economic loss. We need not, and do not, consider other proximate cause or loss-related questions.

B. Our holding about plaintiffs' need to prove proximate causation and economic loss leads us also to conclude that the plaintiffs' complaint here failed adequately to allege these requirements. We concede that the Federal Rules of Civil Procedure require only "a short and plain statement of the claim showing that the pleader is entitled to relief." Fed. Rule Civ. Proc. 8(a)(2). And we assume, at least for argument's sake, that neither the Rules nor the securities statutes impose any special further requirement in respect to the pleading of proximate causation or economic loss. But, even so, the "short and plain statement" must provide the defendant with "fair notice of what the plaintiff's claim is and the grounds upon which it rests." Conley v. Gibson, 355 U.S. 41 (1957). The complaint before us fails this simple test.

As we have pointed out, the plaintiffs' lengthy complaint contains only one statement that we can fairly read as describing the loss caused by the defendants' "spray device" misrepresentations. That statement says that the plaintiffs "paid artificially inflated prices for Dura's securities" and suffered "damages." The statement implies that the plaintiffs' loss consisted of the "artificially inflated" purchase "prices." The complaint's failure to claim that Dura's share price fell significantly after the truth became known suggests that the plaintiffs considered the allegation of purchase price inflation alone sufficient. The complaint contains nothing that suggests otherwise.

For reasons set forth in Part II-A, supra, however, the "artificially inflated purchase price" is not itself a relevant economic loss. And the complaint nowhere else provides the defendants with notice of what the relevant economic loss might be or of what the causal connection might be between that loss and the misrepresentation concerning Dura's "spray device."

We concede that ordinary pleading rules are not meant to impose a great burden upon a plaintiff. Swierkiewicz v. Sorema N. A., 534 U.S. 506, 513-515 (2002). But it should not prove burdensome for a plaintiff who has suffered an economic loss to provide a defendant with some indication of the loss and the causal connection that the plaintiff has in mind. At the same time, allowing a plaintiff to forgo giving any indication of the economic loss and proximate cause that the plaintiff has in mind would bring about harm of the very sort the statutes seek to avoid. Cf. H. R. Conf. Rep. No. 104-369, p. 31 (1995) (criticizing "abusive" practices including "the routine filing of lawsuits ... with only a faint hope that the discovery process might lead eventually to some plausible cause of action"). It would permit a plaintiff "with a largely groundless claim to simply take up the time of a number of other people, with the right to do so representing an *in terrorem* increment of the settlement value, rather than a reasonably founded hope that the [discovery] process will reveal relevant evidence." *Blue Chip Stamps*, 421 U.S., at 741. Such a rule would tend to transform a private securities action into a partial downside insurance policy. See H. R. Conf. Rep. No. 104-369, at 31; see also *Basic*, 485 U.S., at 252.

For these reasons, we find the plaintiffs' complaint legally insufficient. We reverse the judgment of the Ninth Circuit, and we remand the case for further proceedings consistent with this opinion.

It is so ordered.

---

1. *Post-disclosure market movement*. Defense counsel read *Dura Pharmaceuticals* to require some stock price decline after the corporation makes a corrective disclosure. Otherwise, they argue, the omitted information, even if material, caused no loss. But is this necessarily correct? Corrective information might have reached the market through other means (rumors, leaks, securities analyst reports, etc.). Thus,

the market decline could sometimes precede the corrective disclosure. Still, because the plaintiff bears the burden of proving loss causation, the plaintiff must plead and prove that there was a price decline when the market learned that the corporation's disclosures were false or incomplete.

2. *Foreseeability.* In the view of the Second Circuit, loss causation depends at bottom on the question of foreseeability. See AUSA Life Ins. Co. v. Ernst & Young, 206 F.3d 202 (2d Cir. 2000) (remanding for further findings on whether the defendant auditor should have reasonably foreseen that its certification of false financial information would have enabled the corporation to make an acquisition that otherwise would have been blocked by its creditors as too risky). *AUSA Life Insurance* held that loss causation "requires that the damage complained of be one of the foreseeable consequences of the misrepresentation." 206 F.3d 202, 212. See also Manufacturers Hanover Trust Co. v. Drysdale Secs. Corp., 801 F.2d 13, 21 (2d Cir. 1986). The underlying idea here, traceable back to Palsgraf v. Long Island R.R., 162 N.E. 2d 99 (N.Y. 1928), and earlier cases, is that it is unfair to hold the defendant liable for losses that were not reasonably foreseeable.

iv. Scienter

Ernst & Ernst v. Hochfelder
425 U.S. 185 (1976)

Mr. Justice Powell delivered the opinion of the Court. . . .

Petitioner, Ernst & Ernst, is an accounting firm. From 1946 through 1967 it was retained by First Securities Company of Chicago (First Securities), a small brokerage firm and member of the Midwest Stock Exchange and of the National Association of Securities Dealers, to perform periodic audits of the firm's books and records. In connection with these audits Ernst & Ernst prepared for filing with the Securities and Exchange Commission (the Commission) the annual reports required of First Securities under §17(a) of the 1934 Act. It also prepared for First Securities responses to the financial questionnaires of the Midwest Stock Exchange (the Exchange).

Respondents were customers of First Securities who invested in a fraudulent securities scheme perpetrated by Leston B. Nay, president of the firm and owner of 92% of its stock. Nay induced the respondents to invest funds in "escrow" accounts that he represented would yield a high rate of return. . . . In fact, there were no escrow accounts as Nay converted respondents' funds to his own use immediately upon receipt. . . . [Respondents sued petitioner charging] that Ernst & Ernst had "aided and abetted" Nay's violations by its "failure" to conduct proper audits of First Securities. As revealed through discovery, respondents' cause of action rested on a theory of negligent nonfeasance. The premise was that Ernst & Ernst had failed to utilize "appropriate auditing procedures" in its audits of First Securities, thereby failing to discover internal practices of the firm said to prevent an effective audit. The practice principally relied on was Nay's rule that only he could open mail addressed to him at First Securities or addressed to First Securities to his attention, even if it arrived in his absence. Respondents contended that if Ernst & Ernst had conducted a proper audit, it would have discovered this "mail rule." . . .

After extensive discovery the District Court granted Ernst & Ernst's motion for summary judgment and dismissed the action. . . .

The Court of Appeals for the Seventh Circuit reversed and remanded, holding that one who breaches a duty of inquiry and disclosure owed another is liable in damages for aiding and abetting a third party's violation of Rule 10b-5 if the fraud would have been discovered or prevented but for the breach. 503 F.2d 1100 (1974).[7] . . .

We granted certiorari to resolve the question whether a private cause of action for damages will lie under §10(b) and Rule 10b-5 in the absence of any allegation of "scienter" — intent to deceive, manipulate, or defraud.[12] . . .

Although §10(b) does not by its terms create an express civil remedy for its violation, and there is no indication that Congress, or the Commission when adopting Rule 10b-5, contemplated such a remedy, the existence of a private cause of action for violations of the statute and the rule is now well established. . . . During the 30-year period since a private cause of action was first implied under §10(b) and Rule 10b-5,[16] a substantial body of case law and commentary has developed as to its elements. Courts and commentators long have differed with regard to whether scienter is a necessary element of such a cause of action, or whether negligent conduct alone is sufficient.[17] In addressing this question, we turn first to the language of §10(b). . . .

A. Section 10(b) makes unlawful the use or employment of "any manipulative or deceptive device or contrivance" in contravention of Commission rules. The words "manipulative or deceptive" used in conjunction with "device or contrivance" strongly suggest that §10(b) was intended to proscribe knowing or intentional misconduct. . . .

7. . . . In view of our holding that an intent to deceive, manipulate, or defraud is required for civil liability under §10(b) and Rule 10b-5, we need not consider whether civil liability for aiding and abetting is appropriate under the section and the rule, nor the elements necessary to establish such a cause of action. See, e.g., Brennan v. Midwestern United Life Ins. Co., 259 F. Supp. 673 (1966), 286 F. Supp. 702 (N.D. Ind. 1968), *aff'd*, 417 F.2d 147 (7th Cir. 1969) (defendant held liable for giving active and knowing assistance to a third party engaged in violations of the securities laws). See generally Ruder, Multiple Defendants in Securities Law Fraud Cases: Aiding and Abetting, Conspiracy, In Pari Delicto, Indemnification and Contribution, 120 U. Pa. L. Rev. 597, 620-645 (1972). [The Court has since decided that no cause of action lies under Rule 10b-5 for aiding and abetting a securities law violation. See Central Bank of Denver v. First Interstate Bank of Denver, 114 S. Ct. 1439 (1994), page 440 infra. — ED.]

12. Although the verbal formulations of the standard to be applied have varied, several courts of appeals have held in substance that negligence alone is sufficient for civil liability under §10(b) and Rule 10b-5. See, e.g., White v. Abrams, 495 F.2d 724, 730 (CA9 1974) ("flexible duty" standard); Myzel v. Fields, 386 F.2d 718, 735 (CA8 1967) (negligence sufficient); Kohler v. Kohler Co., 319 F.2d 634 (CA7 1963) (knowledge not required). Other courts of appeals have held that some type of scienter — i.e., intent to defraud, reckless disregard for the truth, or knowing use of some practice to defraud — is necessary in such an action. See, e.g., Clegg v. Conk, 507 F.2d 1351, 1361-1362 (CA10 1974) (an element of "scienter or conscious fault"); Lanza v. Drexel & Co., 479 F.2d 1277, 1306 (CA2 1973) ("willful or reckless disregard" of the truth). But few of the decisions announcing that some form of negligence suffices for civil liability under §10(b) and Rule 10b-5 actually have involved only negligent conduct. Smallwood v. Pearl Brewing Co., 489 F.2d 579, 606 (CA5 1974); Kohn v. American Metal Climax, Inc., 458 F.2d 255, 286 (CA3 1972) (Adams, J., concurring); Bucklo, Scienter and Rule 10b-5, 67 Nw. U. L. Rev. 562, 568-570 (1972).

In this opinion the term "scienter" refers to a mental state embracing intent to deceive, manipulate, or defraud. In certain areas of the law recklessness is considered to be a form of intentional conduct for purposes of imposing liability for some act. We need not address here the question whether, in some circumstances, reckless behavior is sufficient for civil liability under §10(b) and Rule 10b-5. . . .

16. Kardon v. National Gypsum Co., 69 F. Supp. 512 (E.D. Pa. 1946).

17. See cases cited in n.12 supra. Compare, e.g., Comment, Scienter and Rule 10b-5, 69 Col. L. Rev. 1057, 1080-1081 (1969); Note, Negligent Misrepresentations under Rule 10b-5, 32 Chi. L. Rev. 824, 839-844 (1965); Note, 82 Harv. L. Rev. 938, 947 (1969); Note, Civil Liability Under Section 10B and Rule 10B-5: A Suggestion for Replacing the Doctrine of Privity, 74 Yale L.J. 658, 682-689 (1965), with, e.g., 3 L. Loss, Securities Regulation 1766 (2d ed. 1961); 6 id., at 3883-3885 (Supp. 1969).

In its amicus curiae brief, however, the Commission contends that nothing in the language "manipulative or deceptive device or contrivance" limits its operation to knowing or intentional practices.[18] In support of its view, the Commission cites the overall congressional purpose in the 1933 and 1934 Acts to protect investors against false and deceptive practices that might injure them. . . . The Commission then reasons that since the "effect" upon investors of given conduct is the same regardless of whether the conduct is negligent or intentional, Congress must have intended to bar all such practices and not just those done knowingly or intentionally. The logic of this effect-oriented approach would impose liability for wholly faultless conduct where such conduct results in harm to investors, a result the Commission would be unlikely to support. But apart from where its logic might lead, the . . . argument simply ignores the use of the words "manipulative," "device," and "contrivance," terms that make unmistakable a congressional intent to proscribe a type of conduct quite different from negligence. Use of the word "manipulative" is especially significant. It is and was virtually a term of art when used in connection with securities markets. It connotes intentional or willful conduct designed to deceive or defraud investors by controlling or artificially affecting the price of securities.

In addition to relying upon the Commission's argument with respect to the operative language of the statute, respondents . . . argue that the "remedial purposes" of the Acts demand a construction of §10(b) that embraces negligence as a standard of liability. But in seeking to accomplish its broad remedial goals, Congress did not adopt uniformly a negligence standard even as to express civil remedies. In some circumstances and with respect to certain classes of defendants, Congress did create express liability predicated upon a failure to exercise reasonable care. E.g., 1933 Act §11(b)(3)(B) (liability of "experts," such as accountants for misleading statements in portions of registration statements for which they are responsible). But in other situations good faith is an absolute defense. 1934 Act §18 (misleading statements in any document filed pursuant to the 1934 Act). And in still other circumstances Congress created express liability regardless of the defendant's fault, 1933 Act §11(a) (issuer liability for misleading statements in the registration statement).

It is thus evident that Congress fashioned standards of fault in the express civil remedies in the 1933 and 1934 Acts on a particularized basis. Ascertainment of congressional intent with respect to the standard of liability created by a particular section of the Acts must therefore rest primarily on the language of that section. Where, as here, we deal with a judicially implied liability, the statutory language certainly is no less important. . . . We turn now, nevertheless, to the legislative history of the 1934 Act to ascertain whether there is support for the meaning attributed to §10(b) by the Commission and respondents.

---

18. The Commission would not permit recovery upon proof of negligence in all cases. In order to harmonize civil liability under §10(b) with the express civil remedies contained in the 1933 and 1934 Acts, the Commission would limit the circumstances in which civil liability could be imposed for negligent violation of Rule 10b-5 to situations in which (i) the defendant knew or reasonably could foresee that the plaintiff would rely on his conduct, (ii) the plaintiff did in fact so rely, and (iii) the amount of the plaintiff's damages caused by the defendant's conduct was definite and ascertainable. . . .

B. Although the extensive legislative history of the 1934 Act is bereft of any explicit explanation of Congress' intent, we think the relevant portions of that history support our conclusion that §10(b) was addressed to practices that involve some element of scienter. . . . The most relevant exposition of the provision that was to become §10(b) was by Thomas G. Corcoran, a spokesman for the drafters. Corcoran indicated:

> Subsection (c) [§9(c) of H.R. 7852 — later §10(b)] says, "Thou shalt not devise any other cunning devices." . . .
>
> Of course subsection (c) is a catch-all clause to prevent manipulative devices. I do not think there is any objection to that kind of clause. The Commission should have the authority to deal with new manipulative devices.

. . . It is difficult to believe that any lawyer, legislative draftsman, or legislator would use these words if the intent was to create liability for merely negligent acts or omissions. Neither the legislative history nor the briefs supporting respondents identify any usage or authority for construing "manipulative [or cunning] devices" to include negligence.

The legislative reports do not address the scope of §10(b) or its catch-all function directly. In considering specific manipulative practices left to Commission regulation, however, the reports indicate that liability would not attach absent scienter, supporting the conclusion that Congress intended no lesser standard under §10(b). . . .

C. The 1933 and 1934 Acts constitute interrelated components of the federal regulatory scheme governing transactions in securities. . . . As the Court indicated in SEC v. National Securities, Inc., 393 U.S. 453 (1969), "the interdependence of the various sections of the securities laws is certainly a relevant factor in any interpretation of the language Congress has chosen. . . ."

The Commission argues that Congress has been explicit in requiring willful conduct when that was the standard of fault intended, citing §9 of the 1934 Act, which generally proscribes manipulation of securities prices. . . . From this the Commission concludes that since §10(b) is not by its terms explicitly restricted to willful, knowing, or purposeful conduct, it should not be construed in all cases to require more than negligent action or inaction as a precondition for civil liability.

The structure of the Acts does not support the Commission's argument. In each instance that Congress created express civil liability in favor of purchasers or sellers of securities it clearly specified whether recovery was to be premised on knowing or intentional conduct, negligence, or entirely innocent mistake. . . . For example, §11 of the 1933 Act unambiguously creates a private action for damages when a registration statement includes untrue statements of material facts or fails to state material facts necessary to make the statements therein not misleading. Within the limits specified by §11(e), the issuer of the securities is held absolutely liable for any damages resulting from such misstatement or omission. But experts such as accountants who have prepared portions of the registration statement are accorded a "due diligence" defense. In effect, this is a negligence standard. . . . See, e.g., Escott v. BarChris Construction Corp. The express recognition of a cause of action premised on negligent behavior in §11 stands in sharp contrast to the language of §10(b), and significantly undercuts the Commission's argument.

We also consider it significant that each of the express civil remedies in the 1933 Act allowing recovery for negligent conduct, see §§11, 12(2), 15,[27] is subject to significant procedural restrictions not applicable under §10(b).[28] Section 11(e) of the 1933 Act, for example, authorizes the court to require a plaintiff bringing a suit under §11, §12(2), or §15 thereof to post a bond for costs, including attorneys' fees, and in specified circumstances to assess costs at the conclusion of the litigation. Section 13 specifies a statute of limitations of one year from the time the violation was or should have been discovered, in no event to exceed three years from the time of offer or sale, applicable to actions brought under §11, §12(2), or §15. These restrictions, significantly, were imposed by amendments to the 1933 Act adopted as part of the 1934 Act. . . . We think these procedural limitations indicate that the judicially created private damage remedy under §10(b) — which has no comparable restrictions — cannot be extended, consistently with the intent of Congress, to actions premised on negligent wrongdoing. Such extension would allow causes of action covered by §11, §12(2), and §15 to be brought instead under §10(b) and thereby nullify the effectiveness of the carefully drawn procedural restrictions on these express actions.[30] See, e.g.,

27. Section 12(2) creates potential civil liability for a seller of securities in favor of the purchaser for misleading statements or omissions in connection with the transaction. The seller is exculpated if he proves that he did not know, or in the exercise of reasonable care, could not have known of the untruth or omission. Section 15 of the 1933 Act, as amended by §208 of Title II of the 1934 Act, makes persons who "control" any person liable under §11 or §12 liable jointly and severally to the same extent as the controlled person, unless he "had no knowledge of or reasonable ground to believe in the existence of the facts by reason of which the liability of the controlled person is alleged to exist." . . .

28. Each of the provisions of the 1934 Act that expressly create civil liability, except . . . §16(b) . . . contains a state-of-mind condition requiring something more than negligence. Section 9 creates potential civil liability for any person who "willfully participates" in the manipulation of securities on a national exchange, §9(e).

Section 18 creates potential civil liability for misleading statements filed with the Commission, but provides the defendant with the defense that "he acted in good faith and had no knowledge that such statement was false or misleading." And §20, which imposes liability upon "controlling persons" for violations of the Act by those they control, exculpates a defendant who "acted in good faith and did not . . . induce the act . . . constituting the violation. . . ." [As to liability of "controlling persons" under §20, compare Zweig v. Hearst Corp., 521 F.2d 1129 (9th Cir. 1975) ("to satisfy good faith it must be shown that the controlling person maintained and enforced a reasonable and proper system of supervision and internal control over controlled persons so as to prevent, so far as possible, violations of Section 10(b) and Rule 10b-5"), with Rochez Bros., Inc. v. Rhoades, 527 F.2d 880 (3d Cir. 1975) ("secondary liability cannot be found under Section 20(a) unless it can be shown that the defendant was a culpable participant in the fraud"). Further, courts are split as to whether, apart from the "controlling person" provisions of §20 of the 1934 Act and §15 of the 1933 Act, a principal may be held liable for acts of its agent under the common law doctrine of respondeat superior. See Zweig v. Hearst Corp., supra, and cases therein cited; compare Holloway v. Howerdd, 536 F.2d 690 (6th Cir. 1976) ("Securities Acts were not intended to preempt . . . respondeat superior"), with Rochez Bros., Inc. v. Rhoades, supra ("respondeat superior . . . would . . . effectively nullify the 'controlling person' provision"). — Ed.] Emphasizing the important difference between the operative language and purpose of §14(a) of the 1934 Act, as contrasted with §10(b), however, some courts have concluded that proof of scienter is unnecessary in an action for damages by the shareholder recipients of a materially misleading proxy statement against the issuer corporation. . . . [For a discussion of the case law on this issue, see pages 692-694 infra. — Ed.]

30. Congress regarded these restrictions on private damage actions as significant. In introducing Title II of the 1934 Act, Senator Fletcher indicated that the amendment to §11(e) of the 1933 Act, providing for potential payment of costs, including attorneys' fees, "is the most important [amendment] of all." 78 Cong. Rec. 8669. One of its purposes was to deter actions brought solely for their potential settlement value. . . . This deterrent is lacking in the §10(b) context, in which a district court's power to award attorneys' fees is sharply circumscribed. See Alyeska Pipeline Service Co. v. Wilderness Society, 421 U.S. 240 (1975) ("bad faith" requirement); F. D. Rich Co. v. Industrial Lumber Co., 417 U.S. 116, 129 (1974). [See also Straub v. Vaisman & Co., 540 F.2d 591 (3d Cir. 1976), holding that since §28(a) of the '34 Act bars punitive damages under Rule 10b-5, a court may not award attorneys' fees to plaintiff if defendant's bad faith was part of the conduct that formed the basis for the suit, but only when such bad faith occurred during the litigation process. — Ed.]

Fischman v. Raytheon Manufacturing Co., 188 F.2d 783, 786-787 (CA2 1951); SEC v. Texas Gulf Sulphur Co., 401 F.2d, at 867-868 (Friendly, J., concurring); Rosenberg v. Globe Aircraft Corp., 80 F. Supp. 123, 124 (E.D. Pa. 1948); 3 L. Loss, Securities Regulation 1787-1788 (2d ed. 1961); R. Jennings & H. Marsh, Securities Regulation 1070-1074 (3d ed. 1972). We would be unwilling to bring about this result absent substantial support in the legislative history, and there is none.

D. We have addressed, to this point, primarily the language and history of §10(b). The Commission contends, however, that subsections (2) and (3) of Rule 10b-5 are cast in language which — if standing alone — could encompass both intentional and negligent behavior. . . . Viewed in isolation the language of subsection (2), and arguably that of subsection (3), could be read as proscribing, respectively, any type of material misstatement or omission, and any course of conduct, that has the effect of defrauding investors, whether the wrongdoing was intentional or not.

We note first that such a reading cannot be harmonized with the administrative history of the rule, a history making clear that when the Commission adopted the rule it was intended to apply only to activities that involved scienter. More importantly, Rule 10b-5 was adopted pursuant to authority granted the Commission under §10(b). The rulemaking power granted to an administrative agency charged with the administration of a federal statute is not the power to make law. Rather, it is "the power to adopt regulations to carry into effect the will of Congress as expressed by the statute." . . . When a statute speaks so specifically in terms of manipulation and deception, and of implementing devices and contrivances — the commonly understood terminology of intentional wrongdoing — and when its history reflects no more expansive intent, we are quite unwilling to extend the scope and the statute to negligent conduct.[33]

Reversed.

MR. JUSTICE STEVENS took no part in the consideration or decision of this case.

MR. JUSTICE BLACKMUN, with whom MR. JUSTICE BRENNAN joins, dissenting. . . .

. . . The Court's opinion, to be sure, has a certain technical consistency about it. It seems to me, however, that an investor can be victimized just as much by negligent conduct as by positive deception, and that it is not logical to drive a wedge between the two, saying that Congress clearly intended the one but certainly not the other.

. . . The language of the Rule . . . seems to me, clearly and succinctly, to prohibit negligent as well as intentional conduct of the kind proscribed, to extend beyond common law fraud, and to apply to negligent omission and commission. This is consistent with Congress' intent, repeatedly recognized by the Court, that

---

33. As we find the language and history of §10(b) dispositive of the approximate standard of liability, there is no occasion to examine the additional considerations of "policy," set forth by the parties, that may have influenced the lawmakers in their formulation of the statute. We do note that the standard urged by respondents would significantly broaden the class of plaintiffs who may seek to impose liability upon accountants and other experts who perform services or express opinions with respect to matters under the Acts. . . . This case, on its facts, illustrates the extreme reach of the standard urged by respondents. As investors in transactions initiated by Nay, not First Securities, they were not foreseeable users of the financial statements prepared by Ernst & Ernst. Respondents conceded that they did not rely on either these financial statements or Ernst & Ernst's certificates of opinion. . . . The class of persons eligible to benefit from such a standard, though small in this case, could be numbered in the thousands in other cases. Acceptance of respondents' view would extend to new frontiers the "hazards" of rendering expert advice under the Acts, raising serious policy questions not yet addressed by Congress.

securities legislation enacted for the purpose of avoiding frauds be construed "not technically and restrictively, but flexibly to effectuate its remedial purposes." . . .

---

1. *Recklessness.* In footnote 12 in *Hochfelder*, the Court reserved for another day the issue of whether "recklessness" satisfies the scienter standard. Although the Supreme Court has continued to note, but not resolve, this issue, all courts of appeals that have considered it have found recklessness sufficient. See IIT v. Cornfeld, 619 F.2d 909 (2d Cir. 1980); McLean v. Alexander, 599 F.2d 1190 (3d Cir. 1979); Sundstrand Corp. v. Sun Chemical Corp., 553 F.2d 1033 (7th Cir. 1977). See generally, Note, Recklessness and the Rule 10b-5 Scienter Standard after *Hochfelder*, 48 Fordham L. Rev. 817 (1980).

But what does "recklessness" mean? Here, the courts have differed significantly. Classically, recklessness meant a subjective awareness of the risk, one that also recognized the risk to be substantial and unjustified. See, e.g., A.L.I., Model Penal Code, §2.02. Some courts, however, appear to have adopted a stricter definition. See, e.g., Sanders v. John Nuveen & Co., 554 F.2d 790, 793 (7th Cir. 1977): "In view of the Supreme Court's analysis in *Hochfelder* of the statutory scheme of implied private remedies and express remedies, the definition of 'reckless behavior' should not be a liberal one lest any discernible distinction between 'scienter' and 'negligence' be obliterated for these purposes. We believe 'reckless' in these circumstances comes closer to being a lesser form of intent than merely a greater degree of ordinary negligence. We perceive it to be not just a difference in degree, but also in kind." See also Broad v. Rockwell Int'l Corp., 614 F.2d 418, 440 (5th Cir. 1980) (en banc); G. A. Thompson & Co. v. Partridge, 636 F.2d 945, 961 (5th Cir. 1981) ("severe recklessness" required).

Conversely, in Rolf v. Blyth, Eastman Dillon & Co., 570 F.2d 38, 46-48 (2d Cir. 1978), the court held a brokerage firm liable for its failure to supervise adequately the investment recommendations made by an unaffiliated individual whom the firm had recommended as investment adviser to a wealthy client. Unknown to the brokerage firm, the adviser's recommendations involved securities whose prices he was actively manipulating (he was later criminally convicted). Because the adviser's reputation was that of a successful stock market technician, the brokerage firm repeatedly reassured the investor that it had confidence in him, but it did not investigate the adviser's recommendations or otherwise possess any reasonable basis for its statements of continued confidence. Hence, these statements were found to have been "given without basis and in reckless disregard of [their] truth or falsity." Id. at 48. Should *Rolf* be construed as using a particularly diluted standard of culpability because of the special relationship between client and brokerage firm (which is often said to owe its clients a fiduciary duty)?

Although *Rolf* and other cases show federal courts sometimes relaxing the standard for scienter, the most commonly cited definition in recent cases is that provided by the Seventh Circuit in Sunstrand Corp. v. Sun Chem. Corp., 553 F.2d 1033, 1045 (7th Cir. 1997), which described scienter as:

a highly unreasonable omission, involving not merely simple, or even inexcusable negligence, but an extreme departure from the standards of ordinary care, and which presents a danger of misleading buyers or sellers that is either known to the defendant or so obvious that the actor must have been aware of it.

2. *Must the SEC prove scienter?* Also in footnote 12 of *Hochfelder*, the Court declined to decide whether scienter had to be proven in SEC injunctive actions. Subsequently, the Court has resolved this issue and generalized the scienter requirement. In Aaron v. SEC, 446 U.S. 680 (1980), the Court held that, even in an SEC action for injunctive relief, "scienter is a necessary element of a violation of Section 10(b) and Rule 10b-5." The Court reached the same conclusion for SEC injunctive actions under §17(a)(1) of the '33 Act (whose language is identical to Rule 10b-5(1), but only protects buyers of securities), but it held the SEC "need not establish scienter as an element of an action to enjoin violations of §17(a)(2) and §17(a)(3) of the 1933 Act." These sections have language that is identical to Rule 10b-5(2) and (3). The Court reasoned:

> The language of §17(a) strongly suggests that Congress contemplated a scienter requirement under §17(a)(1), but not under §17(a)(2) or §17(a)(3). The language of §17(a)(1), which makes it unlawful "to employ any device, scheme, or artifice to defraud," plainly evinces an intent on the part of Congress to proscribe only knowing or intentional misconduct. Even if it be assumed that the term "defraud" is ambiguous, given its varied meanings at law and in equity, the terms "device," "scheme," and "artifice" all connote knowing or intentional practices. Indeed, the term "device," which also appears in §10(b), figured prominently in the Court's conclusion in *Hochfelder* that the plain meaning of §10(b) embraces a scienter requirement.
>
> By contrast, the language of §17(a)(2), which prohibits any person from obtaining money or property "by means of any untrue statement of a material fact or any omission to state a material fact," is devoid of any suggestion whatsoever of a scienter requirement. As a well-known commentator has noted, "[t]here is nothing on the face of Clause (2) itself which smacks of scienter or intent to defraud." 3 L. Loss, Securities Regulation 1442 (2d ed. 1961). . . .
>
> Finally, the language of §17(a)(3), under which it is unlawful for any person "to engage in any transaction, practice, or course of business which *operates* or *would operate* as a fraud or deceit," quite plainly focuses upon the *effect* of particular conduct on members of the investing public, rather than upon the culpability of the person responsible.

Id. at 695-697. The net result in *Aaron* is seemingly that the SEC can avoid the scienter requirement, not under Rule 10b-5, but by bringing its injunctive actions instead under §17(a)(2) or (3).

3. *In pari delicto.* What if the plaintiff's own conduct involved culpable behavior? If culpability on the defendant's part is a prerequisite to recovery, why should culpability on the plaintiff's part not also bar that recovery, as it generally would at common law? Traditionally, the "in pari delicto" defense rested on the twin premises that (1) courts should not mediate disputes among wrongdoers, and (2) it would deter illegality to deny legal relief to either wrongdoer. Within the context of securities law, this issue has arisen most frequently in connection with insider trading. In Bateman Eichler, Hill Richards, Inc. v. Berner, 472 U.S. 299 (1985), the defendants falsely tipped the plaintiffs that their corporation stood to profit greatly from an immense gold strike in Surinam. Specifically, it was predicted that the corporation's stock price would immediately jump (on public announcement of the strike) from $3 per share to $10-15, and eventually to as much as $100 per share. In fact, there was no gold strike, and the tale was a total fiction. Yet plaintiffs had improperly sought to exploit nonpublic material information.

Did this conduct bar their suit? The Supreme Court answered that a private action under the federal securities laws could be barred on grounds of the plaintiffs' own culpability only when (1) plaintiffs bore at least substantially equal responsibility for the violation that they sought to redress and (2) preclusion of the suit would not significantly interfere with effective enforcement of the securities laws. Finding that the tipper is more blameworthy than the tippee and that barring a tippee from suing a tipper would inhibit enforcement of the prohibition against insider trading, the Court rejected the defense. However, *Berner* does not entirely lay to rest the "in pari delicto" defense. What result should a court reach if one insider sues another for tipping him false information when the plaintiff has also helped to falsify financial statements or issue misleading press releases? Do their respective positions now amount to "substantially equal responsibility"?

4. *The impact of the PSLRA.* In 1995, Congress passed the Private Securities Litigation Reform Act of 1995 (PSLRA), which requires a plaintiff in an action based on Rule 10b-5 to plead with particularity facts "giving rise to a strong inference" of fraud. See §21D(b)(2) of the Securities Exchange Act. Did this legislation by implication raise the substantive culpability standard under Rule 10b-5 to something higher than "recklessness"? Most Circuits have answered that it did not. See, e.g., Sterlin v. Biomune Sys., 154 F.3d 1191 (10th Cir. 1998); Rothman v. Gregor, 230 F.3d 81, 96-98 (2d Cir. 2000); Nathanson v. Zonangen Inc., 267 F.3d 400 (5th Cir. 2001); Novak v. Kasaks, 216 F.3d 300, 306 (2d Cir. 2000). One reason for this position is that the PSLRA also added a new §17A to the Securities Act of 1933 and a new §21E to the Securities Exchange Act of 1934, both of which create a safe harbor for the defendant who makes a "forward looking statement," unless the statement was made with "actual knowledge" of its falsity. Seemingly, this implied that a mental state well less than "actual knowledge" would suffice for Rule 10b-5. Although this argument was accepted by some courts, it did not convince the Ninth Circuit, which has alone held that the PSLRA should be read to raise the standard of culpability to that of "deliberate recklessness." See In re Silicon Graphics Inc. Sec. Litig., 183 F.3d 970, 977 (9th Cir. 1999) ("In order to show a strong inference of deliberate recklessness, plaintiffs must state facts that come closer to demonstrating intent, as opposed to mere motive and opportunity."). But, as next discussed, the Ninth Circuit's standard is now in doubt.

In 2007, the Supreme Court finally addressed this conflict among the circuits:

Tellabs, Inc. v. Makor Issues & Rights, Ltd.
127 S. Ct. 2499 (2007)

JUSTICE GINSBURG delivered the opinion of the Court.

This Court has long recognized that meritorious private actions to enforce federal antifraud securities laws are an essential supplement to criminal prosecutions and civil enforcement actions brought, respectively, by the Department of Justice and the Securities and Exchange Commission (SEC). See, e.g., Dura Pharmaceuticals, Inc. v. Broudo, 544 U.S. 336, 345 (2005); J. I. Case Co. v. Borak, 377 U.S. 426, 432 (1964). Private securities fraud actions, however, if not adequately contained, can be employed abusively to impose substantial costs on companies and individuals whose conduct conforms to the law. See Merrill Lynch, Pierce, Fenner & Smith Inc. v. Dabit, 547 U.S. 71, 81 (2006). As a check against abusive litigation by private parties, Congress enacted the Private Securities Litigation Reform Act of 1995 (PSLRA), 109 Stat. 737.

Exacting pleading requirements are among the control measures Congress included in the PSLRA. The Act requires plaintiffs to state with particularity both the facts constituting the alleged violation, and the facts evidencing scienter, *i.e.*, the defendant's intention "to deceive, manipulate, or defraud." Ernst & Ernst v. Hochfelder, 425 U.S. 185, 194, and n.12 (1976); see 15 U.S.C. §78u-4(b)(1), (2). This case concerns the latter requirement. As set out in §21D(b)(2) of the PSLRA, plaintiffs must "state with particularity facts giving rise to a strong inference that the defendant acted with the required state of mind." 15 U.S.C. §78u-4(b)(2).

Congress left the key term "strong inference" undefined, and Courts of Appeals have divided on its meaning. In the case before us, the Court of Appeals for the Seventh Circuit held that the "strong inference" standard would be met if the complaint "allege[d] facts from which, if true, a reasonable person could infer that the defendant acted with the required intent." 437 F.3d 588, 602 (2006). That formulation, we conclude, does not capture the stricter demand Congress sought to convey in §21D(b)(2). It does not suffice that a reasonable factfinder plausibly could infer from the complaint's allegations the requisite state of mind. Rather, to determine whether a complaint's scienter allegations can survive threshold inspection for sufficiency, a court governed by §21D(b)(2) must engage in a comparative evaluation; it must consider, not only inferences urged by the plaintiff, as the Seventh Circuit did, but also competing inferences rationally drawn from the facts alleged. An inference of fraudulent intent may be plausible, yet less cogent than other, nonculpable explanations for the defendant's conduct. To qualify as "strong" within the intendment of §21D(b)(2), we hold, an inference of scienter must be more than merely plausible or reasonable — it must be cogent and at least as compelling as any opposing inference of nonfraudulent intent.

I. Petitioner Tellabs, Inc., manufactures specialized equipment used in fiber optic networks. During the time period relevant to this case, petitioner Richard Notebaert was Tellabs' chief executive officer and president. Respondents (Shareholders) are persons who purchased Tellabs stock between December 11, 2000, and June 19, 2001. They accuse Tellabs and Notebaert (as well as several other Tellabs executives) of engaging in a scheme to deceive the investing public about the true value of Tellabs' stock. See 437 F.3d at 591, App. 94-98.

Beginning on December 11, 2000, the Shareholders allege, Notebaert (and by imputation Tellabs) "falsely reassured public investors, in a series of statements . . . that Tellabs was continuing to enjoy strong demand for its products and earning record revenues," when, in fact, Notebaert knew the opposite was true. Id., at 94-95, 98. From December 2000 until the spring of 2001, the Shareholders claim, Notebaert knowingly misled the public in four ways. 437 F.3d at 596. First, he made statements indicating that demand for Tellabs' flagship networking device, the TITAN 5500, was continuing to grow, when in fact demand for that product was waning. Id., at 596, 597. Second, Notebaert made statements indicating that the TITAN 6500, Tellabs' next-generation networking device, was available for delivery, and that demand for that product was strong and growing, when in truth the product was not ready for delivery and demand was weak. Id., at 596, 597-598. Third, he falsely represented Tellabs' financial results for the fourth quarter of 2000 (and, in connection with those results, condoned the practice of "channel stuffing," under which Tellabs flooded its customers with unwanted products). Id., at 596, 598. Fourth, Notebaert made a series of overstated revenue projections, when demand for the TITAN 5500 was drying up and production of the TITAN 6500 was behind schedule. Id., at 596, 598-599. Based on Notebaert's sunny assessments, the Shareholders contend, market analysts recommended that investors buy Tellabs' stock. See id., at 592.

The first public glimmer that business was not so healthy came in March 2001 when Tellabs modestly reduced its first quarter sales projections. Ibid. In the next months, Tellabs made progressively more cautious statements about its projected sales. On June 19, 2001, the last day of the class period, Tellabs disclosed that demand for the TITAN 5500 had significantly dropped. Id., at 593. Simultaneously, the company substantially lowered its revenue projections for the second quarter of 2001. The next day, the price of Tellabs stock, which had reached a high of $67 during the period, plunged to a low of $15.87. Ibid. . . .

[Although the District Court dismissed the resulting class action for failure to plead scienter on the part of the firm's CEO, Richard Notebaert, with sufficient particularity,] [t]he Court of Appeals for the Seventh Circuit reversed in relevant part. 437 F.3d at 591. Like the District Court, the Court of Appeals found that the Shareholders had pleaded the misleading character of Notebaert's statements with sufficient particularity. Id., at 595-600. Unlike the District Court, however, the Seventh Circuit concluded that the Shareholders had sufficiently alleged that Notebaert acted with the requisite state of mind. Id., at 603-605.

The Court of Appeals recognized that the PSLRA "unequivocally raise[d] the bar for pleading scienter" by requiring plaintiffs to "plea[d] sufficient facts to create a strong inference of scienter." Id., at 601 (internal quotation marks omitted). In evaluating whether that pleading standard is met, the Seventh Circuit said, "courts [should] examine all of the allegations in the complaint and then . . . decide whether collectively they establish such an inference." Ibid. "[W]e will allow the complaint to survive," the court next and critically stated, "if it alleges facts from which, if true, a reasonable person could infer that the defendant acted with the required intent. . . . If a reasonable person could not draw such an inference from the alleged facts, the defendants are entitled to dismissal." Id., at 602.

In adopting its standard for the survival of a complaint, the Seventh Circuit explicitly rejected a stiffer standard adopted by the Sixth Circuit, i.e., that "plaintiffs are entitled only to the most plausible of competing inferences." Id., at 601, 602 (quoting Fidel v. Farley, 392 F.3d 220, 227 (CA6 2004)). The Sixth Circuit's standard, the court observed, because it involved an assessment of competing inferences, "could potentially infringe upon plaintiffs' Seventh Amendment rights." 437 F.3d at 602. We granted certiorari to resolve the disagreement among the Circuits on whether, and to what extent, a court must consider competing inferences in determining whether a securities fraud complaint gives rise to a "strong inference" of scienter. 127 S. Ct. 853 (2007).

II. Section 10(b) of the Securities Exchange Act of 1934 forbids the "use or employ, in connection with the purchase or sale of any security . . . , [of] any manipulative or deceptive device or contrivance in contravention of such rules and regulations as the [SEC] may prescribe as necessary or appropriate in the public interest or for the protection of investors." 15 U.S.C. §78j(b). . . . Section 10(b), this Court has implied from the statute's text and purpose, affords a right of action to purchasers or sellers of securities injured by its violation. See, *e.g., Dura Pharmaceuticals*, 544 U.S., at 341. See also id., at 345 ("The securities statutes seek to maintain public confidence in the marketplace . . . by deterring fraud, in part, through the availability of private securities fraud actions."); Borak, 377 U.S., at 432 (private securities fraud actions provide "a most effective weapon in the enforcement" of securities laws and are "a necessary supplement to Commission action"). To establish liability under §10(b) and Rule 10b-5, a private plaintiff must prove that the defendant acted with scienter, "a mental state embracing intent to deceive, manipulate, or defraud." *Ernst & Ernst*, 425 U.S., at 193-194, and n.12.

In an ordinary civil action, the Federal Rules of Civil Procedure require only "a short and plain statement of the claim showing that the pleader is entitled to relief." Fed. Rule Civ. Proc. 8(a)(2). Although the rule encourages brevity, the complaint must say enough to give the defendant "fair notice of what the plaintiff's claim is and the grounds upon which it rests." *Dura Pharmaceuticals*, 544 U.S., at 346 (internal quotation marks omitted). Prior to the enactment of the PSLRA, the sufficiency of a complaint for securities fraud was governed not by Rule 8, but by the heightened pleading standard set forth in Rule 9(b). See Greenstone v. Cambex Corp., 975 F.2d 22, 25 (CA1 1992) (Breyer, J.) (collecting cases). Rule 9(b) applies to "all averments of fraud or mistake"; it requires that "the circumstances constituting fraud . . . be stated with particularity" but provides that "[m]alice, intent, knowledge, and other condition of mind of a person, may be averred generally."

Courts of Appeals diverged on the character of the Rule 9(b) inquiry in §10(b) cases: Could securities fraud plaintiffs allege the requisite mental state "simply by stating that scienter existed," In re GlenFed, Inc. Securities Litigation, 42 F.3d 1541, 1546-1547 (CA9 1994) (en banc), or were they required to allege with particularity facts giving rise to an inference of scienter? Compare id., at 1546 ("We are not permitted to add new requirements to Rule 9(b) simply because we like the effects of doing so."), with, *e.g.*, *Greenstone*, 975 F.2d at 25 (were the law to permit a securities fraud complaint simply to allege scienter without supporting facts, "a complaint could evade too easily the 'particularity' requirement in Rule 9(b)'s first sentence"). Circuits requiring plaintiffs to allege specific facts indicating scienter expressed that requirement variously. . . .

Setting a uniform pleading standard for §10(b) actions was among Congress' objectives when it enacted the PSLRA. Designed to curb perceived abuses of the §10(b) private action — "nuisance filings, targeting of deep-pocket defendants, vexatious discovery requests and manipulation by class action lawyers," *Dabit*, 547 U.S., at 81 (quoting H. R. Conf. Rep. No. 104-369, p. 31 (1995) (hereinafter H. R. Conf. Rep.)) — the PSLRA installed both substantive and procedural controls. Notably, Congress prescribed new procedures for the appointment of lead plaintiffs and lead counsel. This innovation aimed to increase the likelihood that institutional investors — parties more likely to balance the interests of the class with the long-term interests of the company — would serve as lead plaintiffs. See id., at 33-34; S. Rep. No. 104-98, p. 11 (1995). Congress also "limit[ed] recoverable damages and attorney's fees, provide[d] a 'safe harbor' for forward-looking statements, . . . mandate[d] imposition of sanctions for frivolous litigation, and authorize[d] a stay of discovery pending resolution of any motion to dismiss." *Dabit*, 547 U.S., at 81. And in §21D(b) of the PSLRA, Congress "impose[d] heightened pleading requirements in actions brought pursuant to §10(b) and Rule 10b-5." Ibid.

Under the PSLRA's heightened pleading instructions, any private securities complaint alleging that the defendant made a false or misleading statement must: (1) "specify each statement alleged to have been misleading [and] the reason or reasons why the statement is misleading," 15 U.S.C. §78u-4(b)(1); and (2) "state with particularity facts giving rise to a strong inference that the defendant acted with the required state of mind," §78u-4(b)(2). In the instant case, as earlier stated, see *supra*, at 5, the District Court and the Seventh Circuit agreed that the Shareholders met the first of the two requirements: The complaint sufficiently specified Notebaert's alleged misleading statements and the reasons why the statements were misleading. 303 F. Supp. 2d, at 955-961; 437 F.3d at 596-600. But those courts disagreed on whether the Shareholders, as required by §21D(b)(2), "state[d] with particularity facts giving rise to a strong inference that [Notebaert] acted with [scienter]," §78u-4(b)(2). See *supra*, at 5.

The "strong inference" standard "unequivocally raise[d] the bar for pleading scienter," 437 F.3d at 601, and signaled Congress' purpose to promote greater uniformity among the Circuits, see H. R. Conf. Rep., p. 41. But "Congress did not . . . throw much light on what facts . . . suffice to create [a strong] inference," or on what "degree of imagination courts can use in divining whether" the requisite inference exists. 437 F.3d at 601. While adopting the Second Circuit's "strong inference" standard, Congress did not codify that Circuit's case law interpreting the standard. See §78u-4(b)(2). See also Brief for United States as *Amicus Curiae* 18. With no clear guide from Congress other than its "inten[tion] to strengthen existing pleading requirements," H. R. Conf. Rep., p. 41, Courts of Appeals have diverged again, this time in construing the term "strong inference." Among the uncertainties, should courts consider competing inferences in determining whether an inference of scienter is "strong"? See 437 F.3d at 601-602 (collecting cases). Our task is to prescribe a workable construction of the "strong inference" standard, a reading geared to the PSLRA's twin goals: to curb frivolous, lawyer-driven litigation, while preserving investors' ability to recover on meritorious claims.

III. A. We establish the following prescriptions: First, faced with a Rule 12(b)(6) motion to dismiss a §10(b) action, courts must, as with any motion to dismiss for failure to plead a claim on which relief can be granted, accept all factual allegations in the complaint as true. See Leatherman v. Tarrant County Narcotics Intelligence and Coordination Unit, 507 U.S. 163, 164 (1993). On this point, the parties agree. See Reply Brief 8; Brief for Respondents 26; Brief for United States as *Amicus Curiae* 8, 20, 21.

Second, courts must consider the complaint in its entirety, as well as other sources courts ordinarily examine when ruling on Rule 12(b)(6) motions to dismiss, in particular, documents incorporated into the complaint by reference, and matters of which a court may take judicial notice. See 5B Wright & Miller §1357 (3d ed. 2004 and Supp. 2007). The inquiry, as several Courts of Appeals have recognized, is whether *all* of the facts alleged, taken collectively, give rise to a strong inference of scienter, not whether any individual allegation, scrutinized in isolation, meets that standard. See, e.g., Abrams v. Baker Hughes Inc., 292 F.3d 424, 431 (CA5 2002); Gompper v. VISX, Inc., 298 F.3d 893, 897 (CA9 2002). See also Brief for United States as *Amicus Curiae* 25.

Third, in determining whether the pleaded facts give rise to a "strong" inference of scienter, the court must take into account plausible opposing inferences. The Seventh Circuit expressly declined to engage in such a comparative inquiry. A complaint could survive, that court said, as long as it "alleges facts from which, if true, a reasonable person could infer that the defendant acted with the required intent"; in other words, only "[i]f a reasonable person could not draw such an inference from the alleged facts" would the defendant prevail on a motion to dismiss. 437 F.3d at 602. But in §21D(b)(2), Congress did not merely require plaintiffs to "provide a factual basis for [their] scienter allegations," ibid. (quoting In re Cerner Corp. Securities Litigation, 425 F.3d 1079, 1084, 1085 (CA8 2005)), i.e., to allege facts from which an inference of scienter rationally *could* be drawn. Instead, Congress required plaintiffs to plead with particularity facts that give rise to a "strong" — i.e., a powerful or cogent — inference. See American Heritage Dictionary 1717 (4th ed. 2000) (defining "strong" as "[p]ersuasive, effective, and cogent"); 16 Oxford English Dictionary 949 (2d ed. 1989) (defining "strong" as "[p]owerful to demonstrate or convince" (definition 16b)); cf. 7 id., at 924 (defining "inference" as "a conclusion [drawn] from known or assumed facts or statements"; "reasoning from something known or assumed to something else which follows from it").

The strength of an inference cannot be decided in a vacuum. The inquiry is inherently comparative: How likely is it that one conclusion, as compared to others, follows from the underlying facts? To determine whether the plaintiff has alleged facts that give rise to the requisite "strong inference" of scienter, a court must consider plausible nonculpable explanations for the defendant's conduct, as well as inferences favoring the plaintiff. The inference that the defendant acted with scienter need not be irrefutable, i.e., of the "smoking-gun" genre, or even the "most plausible of competing inferences," Fidel, 392 F.3d at 227 (quoting Helwig v. Vencor, Inc., 251 F.3d 540, 553 (CA6 2001) (en banc)). Recall in this regard that §21D(b)'s pleading requirements are but one constraint among many the PSLRA installed to screen out frivolous suits, while allowing meritorious actions to move forward. See supra, at 9, and n.4. Yet the inference of scienter must be more than merely "reasonable" or "permissible" — it must be cogent and compelling, thus strong in light of other explanations. A complaint will survive, we hold, only if a reasonable person would deem the inference of scienter cogent and at least as compelling as any opposing inference one could draw from the facts alleged.[1]

B. Tellabs contends that when competing inferences are considered, Notebaert's evident lack of pecuniary motive will be dispositive. The Shareholders, Tellabs stresses, did not allege that Notebaert sold any shares during the class period.

---

1. Justice Scalia objects to this standard on the ground that "[i]f a jade falcon were stolen from a room to which only A and B had access," it could not "*possibly* be said there was a 'strong inference' that B was the thief." Post, at 1 (opinion concurring in judgment) (emphasis in original). I suspect, however, that law enforcement officials as well as the owner of the precious falcon would find the inference of guilt as to B quite strong — certainly strong enough to warrant further investigation. Indeed, an inference at least as likely as competing inferences can, in some cases, warrant recovery. See Summers v. Tice, 33 Cal. 2d 80, 84-87, 199 P.2d 1, 3-5 (1948) (in bank) (plaintiff wounded by gunshot could recover from two defendants, even though the most he could prove was that each defendant was at least as likely to have injured him as the other); Restatement (Third) of Torts §28(b), Comment *e*, p. 504 (Proposed Final Draft No. 1, Apr. 6, 2005) ("Since the publication of the Second Restatement in 1965, courts have generally accepted the alternative-liability principle of [Summers v. Tice, adopted in] §433B(3), while fleshing out its limits."). In any event, we disagree with Justice Scalia that the hardly stock term "strong inference" has only one invariably right ("natural" or "normal") reading — his. See *post*, at 3.

Justice Alito agrees with Justice Scalia, and would transpose to the pleading stage "the test that is used at the summary-judgment and judgment-as-a-matter-of-law stages." *Post*, at 3 (opinion concurring in judgment). But the test at each stage is measured against a different backdrop. It is improbable that Congress, without so stating, intended courts to test pleadings, unaided by discovery, to determine whether there is "genuine issue as to any material fact." See Fed. Rule Civ. Proc. 56(c). And judgment as a matter of law is a post-trial device, turning on the question whether a party has produced evidence "legally sufficient" to warrant a jury determination in that party's favor. See Rule 50(a)(1).

See Brief for Petitioners 50 ("The absence of any allegations of motive color all the other allegations putatively giving rise to an inference of scienter."). While it is true that motive can be a relevant consideration, and personal financial gain may weigh heavily in favor of a scienter inference, we agree with the Seventh Circuit that the absence of a motive allegation is not fatal. See 437 F.3d at 601. As earlier stated, *supra*, at 11, allegations must be considered collectively; the significance that can be ascribed to an allegation of motive, or lack thereof, depends on the entirety of the complaint.

Tellabs also maintains that several of the Shareholders' allegations are too vague or ambiguous to contribute to a strong inference of scienter. For example, the Shareholders alleged that Tellabs flooded its customers with unwanted products, a practice known as "channel stuffing." See supra, at 3. But they failed, Tellabs argues, to specify whether the channel stuffing allegedly known to Notebaert was the illegitimate kind (e.g., writing orders for products customers had not requested) or the legitimate kind (e.g., offering customers discounts as an incentive to buy). Brief for Petitioners 44-46; Reply Brief 8. See also id., at 8-9 (complaint lacks precise dates of reports critical to distinguish legitimate conduct from culpable conduct). But see 437 F.3d at 598, 603-604 (pointing to multiple particulars alleged by the Shareholders, including specifications as to timing). We agree that omissions and ambiguities count against inferring scienter, for plaintiffs must "state with particularity facts giving rise to a strong inference that the defendant acted with the required state of mind." §78u-4(b)(2). We reiterate, however, that the court's job is not to scrutinize each allegation in isolation but to assess all the allegations holistically. See supra, at 11; 437 F.3d at 601. In sum, the reviewing court must ask: When the allegations are accepted as true and taken collectively, would a reasonable person deem the inference of scienter at least as strong as any opposing inference?[2]

IV. Accounting for its construction of §21D(b)(2), the Seventh Circuit explained that the court "th[ought] it wis[e] to adopt an approach that [could not] be misunderstood as a usurpation of the jury's role." 437 F.3d at 602. In our view, the Seventh Circuit's concern was undue.[3] A court's comparative assessment of plausible inferences, while constantly assuming the plaintiff's allegations to be true, we think it plain, does not impinge upon the Seventh Amendment right to jury trial.[4]

---

2. The Seventh Circuit held that allegations of scienter made against one defendant cannot be imputed to all other individual defendants. 437 F.3d at 602-603. See also id., at 603 (to proceed beyond the pleading stage, the plaintiff must allege as to each defendant facts sufficient to demonstrate a culpable state of mind regarding his or her violations) (citing Phillips v. Scientific-Atlanta, Inc., 374 F.3d 1015, 1018 (CA11 2004)). Though there is disagreement among the Circuits as to whether the group pleading doctrine survived the PSLRA, see, e.g., Southland Securities Corp. v. Inspire Ins. Solutions Inc., 365 F.3d 353, 364 (CA5 2004), the Shareholders do not contest the Seventh Circuit's determination, and we do not disturb it.

3. The Seventh Circuit raised the possibility of a Seventh Amendment problem on its own initiative. The Shareholders did not contend below that dismissal of their complaint under §21D(b)(2) would violate their right to trial by jury. Cf. Monroe Employees Retirement System v. Bridgestone Corp., 399 F.3d 651, 683, n.25 (CA6 2005) (noting possible Seventh Amendment argument but declining to address it when not raised by plaintiffs).

4. In numerous contexts, gatekeeping judicial determinations prevent submission of claims to a jury's judgment without violating the Seventh Amendment. See, e.g., Daubert v. Merrell Dow Pharmaceuticals, Inc., 509 U.S. 579, 589 (1993) (expert testimony can be excluded based on judicial determination of reliability); Neely v. Martin K. Eby Constr. Co., 386 U.S. 317, 321 (1967) (judgment as a matter of law); Pease v. Rathbun-Jones Engineering Co., 243 U.S. 273, 278 (1917) (summary judgment).

Congress, as creator of federal statutory claims, has power to prescribe what must be pleaded to state the claim, just as it has power to determine what must be proved to prevail on the merits. It is the federal lawmaker's prerogative, therefore, to allow, disallow, or shape the contours of — including the pleading and proof requirements for — §10(b) private actions. No decision of this Court questions that authority in general, or suggests, in particular, that the Seventh Amendment inhibits Congress from establishing whatever pleading requirements it finds appropriate for federal statutory claims. Cf. Swierkiewicz v. Sorema N. A., 534 U.S. 506, 512-513 (2002); *Leatherman*, 507 U.S., at 168 (both recognizing that heightened pleading requirements can be established by Federal Rule, citing Fed. Rule Civ. Proc. 9(b), which requires that fraud or mistake be pleaded with particularity).

Our decision in Fidelity & Deposit Co. of Md. v. United States, 187 U.S. 315 (1902), is instructive. That case concerned a rule adopted by the Supreme Court of the District of Columbia in 1879 pursuant to rulemaking power delegated by Congress. The rule required defendants, in certain contract actions, to file an affidavit "specifically stating . . . , in precise and distinct terms, the grounds of his defen[s]e." Id., at 318 (internal quotation marks omitted). The defendant's affidavit was found insufficient, and judgment was entered for the plaintiff, whose declaration and supporting affidavit had been found satisfactory. Ibid. This Court upheld the District's rule against the contention that it violated the Seventh Amendment. Id., at 320. Just as the purpose of §21D(b) is to screen out frivolous complaints, the purpose of the prescription at issue in *Fidelity & Deposit Co.* was to "preserve the courts from frivolous defen[s]es," ibid. Explaining why the Seventh Amendment was not implicated, this Court said that the heightened pleading rule simply "prescribes the means of making an issue," and that, when "[t]he issue [was] made as prescribed, the right of trial by jury accrues." Ibid.; accord Ex parte Peterson, 253 U.S. 300, 310 (1920) (Brandeis, J.) (citing *Fidelity & Deposit Co.*, and reiterating: "It does not infringe the constitutional right to a trial by jury [in a civil case], to require, with a view to formulating the issues, an oath by each party to the facts relied upon."). See also Walker v. New Mexico & Southern Pacific R. Co., 165 U.S. 593, 596 (1897) (Seventh Amendment "does not attempt to regulate matters of pleading").

In the instant case, provided that the Shareholders have satisfied the congressionally "prescribe[d] . . . means of making an issue," *Fidelity & Deposit Co.*, 187 U.S., at 320, the case will fall within the jury's authority to assess the credibility of witnesses, resolve any genuine issues of fact, and make the ultimate determination whether Notebaert and, by imputation, Tellabs acted with scienter. We emphasize, as well, that under our construction of the "strong inference" standard, a plaintiff is not forced to plead more than she would be required to prove at trial. A plaintiff alleging fraud in a §10(b) action, we hold today, must plead facts rendering an inference of scienter *at least as likely as* any plausible opposing inference. At trial, she must then prove her case by a "preponderance of the evidence." Stated otherwise, she must demonstrate that it is *more likely* than not that the defendant acted with scienter. See Herman & MacLean v. Huddleston, 459 U.S. 375, 390 (1983). . . .

While we reject the Seventh Circuit's approach to §21D(b)(2), we do not decide whether, under the standard we have described, see supra, at 11-14, the Shareholders' allegations warrant "a strong inference that [Notebaert and Tellabs] acted with the required state of mind," 15 U.S.C. §78u-4(b)(2). Neither the District Court nor the Court of Appeals had the opportunity to consider the matter in light of the prescriptions we announce today. We therefore vacate the Seventh Circuit's judgment so that the case may be reexamined in accord with our construction of §21D(b)(2).

The judgment of the Court of Appeals is vacated, and the case is remanded for further proceedings consistent with this opinion.

JUSTICE SCALIA, concurring in the judgment.

I fail to see how an inference that is merely "at least as compelling as any opposing inference," ante, at 2, can conceivably be called what the statute here at issue requires: a "strong inference," 15 U.S.C. §78u-4(b)(2). If a jade falcon were stolen from a room to which only A and B had access, could it *possibly* be said there was a "strong inference" that B was the thief? I think not, and I therefore think that the Court's test must fail. In my view, the test should be whether the inference of scienter (if any) is *more plausible* than the inference of innocence.* . . .

[Justice Alito also filed a concurring opinion and Justice Stevens dissented].

Impact. Tellabs clearly mandates a comparative evaluation of the competing inferences that plaintiff and defendant can draw from plaintiff's factual allegations, which must be taken as true for purposes of a motion to dismiss. If plaintiff's allegations are "cogent" and "at least as compelling" as those offered by the defendant, the motion to dismiss must be denied. Favorable as this sounds to the plaintiffs, it remains uncertain whether this decision necessarily rejects the Ninth Circuit's requirement of "deliberate recklessness" in *Silicon Graphics.* Arguably, that question depends instead on the meaning of "recklessness" and whether "recklessness" suffices to show scienter — a question that the majority expressly avoided in *Tellabs.*

v. Damages

Mitchell v. Texas Gulf Sulphur Co.
446 F.2d 90 (10th Cir.), *cert. denied,* 404 U.S. 1004 (1971)

HILL, J.: Appellees and cross-appellants Reynolds, Mitchell and Stout instituted actions in the Utah district against appellants and cross-appellees Texas Gulf Sulphur Company (hereinafter referred to as TGS) and Charles A. Fogarty, one of the principal officers of the company, to recover damages for violations of . . . [Rule 10b-5]. Specifically, the claim is that appellees were damaged by the violations of TGS and Fogarty, its executive vice president, (1) for failure to disclose on April 12 and prior to April 16, 1964, information as to the results of drilling at the Timmins property; and (2) in issuing an inaccurate, misleading and deceptive press release published April 13, 1964.

---

*The Court suggests that "the owner of the precious falcon would find the inference of guilt as to B quite strong." Ante, at 13, n.5. If he should draw such an inference, it would only prove the wisdom of the ancient maxim *"aliquis non debet esse Judex in propria causa"* — no man ought to be a judge of his own cause. Dr. Bonham's Case, 8 Co. 107a, 114a, 118a, 77 Eng. Rep. 638, 646, 652 (C. P. 1610). For it is quite clear (from the dispassionate perspective of one who does not own a jade falcon) that a *possibility*, even a strong possibility, that B is responsible is not a strong *inference* that B is responsible. "Inference" connotes "belief" in what is inferred, and it would be impossible to form a strong belief that it was B and not A, or A and not B.

The essential facts are as follows: Reynolds, Mitchell and Stout were and had been for several years stockholders in TGS. After several years of extensive mineral exploration on the Canadian Shield of eastern Canada, TGS detected a promising anomaly on a plot of land known as the Kidd 55 segment near Timmins, Ontario, Canada. In November, 1963, TGS core-drilled the anomaly at its "strongest" point. The hole was designated K-55-1 and was completed November 12 at a depth of 655 feet. High ore content was indicated by visual examination, and after the core was split and sent to Utah for assay, it disclosed an average mineral content of 1.18% copper, 8.2% zinc, and 3.94 ounces of silver per ton, over a length of 602 feet. In response to the preliminary results, the TGS chief geologist wrote in a November 14, 1963, memorandum that this was "obviously of ore-grade" but that "a great deal of caution must be exercised in extrapolating this intersection to tonnage estimates."

At this stage of the operations TGS owned only a fraction of the Kidd 55 property. Extreme precautions were taken to the end that no outsider would gain knowledge of the results of the explorations. By March, 1964, TGS had acquired without difficulty substantially all interest in the promising acreage adjacent to the drill site.

On April 7, 1964, K-55-3 was completed. The mineral content, by visual examination of the core, compared favorably with K-55-1 and eliminated the chances that the latter had been drilled "down dip." This hole aided in roughly establishing the east-west boundaries of the sulfite ore body. K-55-4 was completed to a 578 foot depth by 7:00 P.M., April 10, and produced a core comparable to K-55-1 and -3. K-55-4 had been drilled 200 feet south of K-55-1, on a 45 degree angle toward the west. Holes K-55-5 and K-55-6 had been started and were drilling by 7:00 P.M. April 10. K-55-5, 200 feet north of K-55-1 and on a 45 degree angle to the west, had encountered substantial copper mineralization over 42 feet of the 97 feet then drilled. K-55-6, 300 feet east of K-55-1 and on a 60 degree angle to the west, had encountered substantial copper mineralization over the last 127 feet of the 569 foot hole.

Between 7:00 P.M., April 10 and 7:00 P.M., April 12 (the evening prior to the first release) more data became available. K-55-5 was at the 531 foot level and had continued to encounter substantial copper mineralization over that entire length. During the same interval, K-55-6 had reached a depth of 881 feet and had found mineralization over the length of this intermediate drilling. Meanwhile, K-55-7 was started approximately 400 feet north of K-55-1 on a westerly 45 degree angle and was at 91 feet and showing mineralization. And K-55-8 was drilling at a depth of 162 feet without report as to its mineral content.

By the morning of April 13, K-55-5 had encountered substantial copper mineralization to the 580 foot mark; K-55-6 had found mineralization to the 946 foot level; and 50 feet of the 137 feet drilled at K-55-7 showed mineralization. By April 16, K-55-1, -2, -3, -4, -5, -6, and -8 were completed. K-55-7 was at 613 feet, -9 was at 373 feet, and -10 was at 123 feet. In a thumbnail sketch, this illustrates the rapid fire manner in which data was being accumulated at the Timmins drill site.

Although TGS sought to suppress the nature and extent of its discovery at Timmins, by early 1964 rumors had begun to generate excitement about the alleged strike. By April, 1964, property within several miles of the TGS site had been "staked." Canadian newspapers carried the rumors, and of their effect on the Toronto Stock Exchange, proclaimed by one to be "the wildest speculative spree since the Nineteen Fifties." Eventually the rumors worked south to the United States.

On Saturday, April 11, 1964, both the New York Times and the Herald Tribune carried stories on the rumored strike.[4] In response to the Times and Herald Tribune articles, the president of TGS directed Fogarty to prepare an official TGS statement. The president, a vice president and Fogarty all agreed that they would not responsibly conclude that a commercial ore body existed and that no calculations as to the size or grade of ore could be made without further drilling. Fogarty then drafted a statement based upon data gathered as of 7:00 P.M., April 10, and he released the statement Sunday afternoon, April 12.[5]

By TGS invitation, on April 13, a reporter from a Canadian mining journal, The Northern Miner, visited the Kidd-55 drilling site. The article detailing that visit was published April 16, and indicated that this "must be recorded as one of the most impressive drill holes completed in modern times." That same day, at 10:00 A.M. Eastern Standard Time, Fogarty held a second press conference and released a statement which revealed in some detail the magnitude of the discovery at Timmins. Summaries of this announcement appeared on the private wire service of Merrill Lynch and on the Dow-Jones wire service shortly thereafter.

Reynolds, Mitchell and the Stouts testified that they sold their TGS stock after hearing of the April 12 release but before becoming aware of the April 16 release. Sometime after the first release was published, Reynolds' broker in Salt Lake informed him as to its general content. On April 16, the broker relayed rumors that TGS had made a strike but in the broker's judgment this was mere propaganda. Reynolds then testified that he decided "to get out while the getting was good," whereupon he sold his 500 shares. Later that afternoon he learned of the favorable TGS report. He testified that had he known of the K-55-1 core results he would have doubled his holdings.

---

4. The Herald Tribune article follows in part:

> The biggest ore strike since gold was discovered more than 60 years ago in Canada has stampeded speculators to the snowbound old mining city of Timmins, Ontario, some 450 miles northwest of Toronto.
>   This time it's copper. Texas Gulf Sulphur Co., Ltd., which reportedly has made an unparalleled find in the Big Water Lake area about 15 miles north of Timmins, would not confirm reports of the strike. . . .

5. During the past few days, the exploration activities of Texas Gulf Sulphur in the area of Timmins, Ontario, have been widely reported in the press, coupled with rumors of a substantial copper discovery there. These reports exaggerate the scale of operations, and mention plans and statistics of size and grade of ore that are without factual basis and have evidently originated by speculation of people not connected with TGS.
>   The facts are as follows. TGS has been exploring in the Timmins area for six years as part of its overall search in Canada and elsewhere for various minerals — lead, copper, zinc, etc. . . .
>   Most of the areas drilled in Eastern Canada have revealed either barren pyrite or graphite without value; a few have resulted in discoveries of small or marginal sulphide ore bodies.
>   Recent drilling on one property near Timmins has led to preliminary indications that more drilling would be required for proper evaluation of this prospect. The drilling done to date has not been conclusive, but the statements made by many outside quarters are unreliable and include information and figures that are not available to TGS.
>   The work done to date has not been sufficient to reach definite conclusions and any statement as to size and grade of ore would be premature and possibly misleading. When we have progressed to the point where reasonable and logical conclusions can be made, TGS will issue a definite statement to its stockholders and to the public in order to clarify the Timmins project. . . .

Mitchell visited his broker on the afternoon of the sixteenth, at which time he was referred to the April 12 release. He concluded that the stock would not sustain its current rise and gave instructions to sell 400 shares short. . . . Then, realizing he had failed to dispose of 20 shares, he delivered them on the seventeenth with similar sell instructions. According to his testimony, he had no knowledge of the April 16 release when he sold. After hearing about the April 12 release and that the TGS Timmins discovery was overrated, the Stouts gave orders to sell their 1,000 shares on April 21. . . .

The trial court found that the press release of April 12 was false, misleading, deceptive and fraudulent with respect to material matters disclosed by the company's drilling efforts; that the authors knew of the presence of ore-grade copper and zinc in major proportions; that the magnitude of the discovery was either misstated or concealed; and that TGS and Fogarty knew the press release statements were incorrect and misleading, and knew or should have known that the statements would be relied upon by shareholders. . . .

. . . No one could dispute that TGS could not have accurately defined the outer limits of the ore body as of April 12, but that is not the test. When TGS undertook to deny and clarify rumor and fact, they were bound to accurately depict the situation as they then knew it. The full magnitude may yet have been a mystery, but armed with the data available on the 12th, TGS was in a position to unveil the then known dimensions and drilling data of their discovery. Having failed to accurately portray what they knew, and commenting that the information was current when in fact it was sorely outdated, TGS misrepresented the facts of the Kidd 55 discovery. . . .

The trial court specifically found that each of the appellees herein relied upon the misleading and inaccurate announcement in making his decision to sell his TGS stock, and that none knew of the announcement of April 16 at the time of his sale. . . . Appellants enumerate several factors which may have induced Reynolds to sell his TGS stock. A thorough search of the record convinces us that although any one or all of the factors may have partially motivated the sale, the evidence is not so deficient as to make the finding of the trial court clearly erroneous that the principal reliance was on the April 12 statement.

The dispute over the Mitchell sale is that he timed his decision to sell on speculation as to what the market was going to do. Again, the evidence of record does not clearly refute the finding that the primary motivation was the deceptive April 12 release. The Stouts' case is more difficult due to the time lapse between the corrective April 16 release and the sell order — more than five days later. But even with that entanglement we cannot, on the basis of clear error, conclude from the record that the April 12 release was not a substantial factor in the Stouts' decision to sell.

Greater difficulty is encountered with the second of appellants' two-pronged argument, which directs itself to the issue of due diligence and good faith required of investors trading in the market. See City National Bank v. Vanderboom, [422 F.2d 221 (8th Cir.), *cert. denied*, 399 U.S. 905 (1970)]. Reynolds traded within a reasonably brief time following the April 16 release and should not be denied his recovery. Mitchell is in exactly the same position with regard to the 400 shares which were sold by April 17. Both testified that they were attempting to reap the maximum profit before the "gloomy" release took its toll. We conclude that good faith and due diligence were exercised in the sale of these shares. On the other hand, . . . [a]t some point in time after the publication of a curative statement such as that of April 16, stockholders should no longer be able to claim reliance on the deceptive release, sell, and then sue for damages when the stock value continues to rise. This is but a requirement that stockholders too act in good faith and with due diligence in purchasing and selling stock. Although Mitchell alleges that he ordered the 20 shares sold on the 17th, there is no dispute that they were not in fact sold until the 23rd. His explanation is that somehow the sell order was not properly communicated until the 22nd when he called his broker to inquire into their status. In the Stouts' case, there was no miscommunication. They simply did not intend to sell until the 21st. While in some circumstances such delays may not be unreasonable, we conclude that under the circumstances of this case it would unjustifiably extend TGS liability to intolerable limits.

Between April 13 and April 22, TGS stock had increased in value from 30¹/₈ to a high of 47, with the volume of sales going from 126,500 to over 326,000. But most significant is the abundance of publicity given the April 16 statement during the following few days. The business news of every major news publication carried the story with bold headlines. Indeed, the 45 pages of press clippings and stock quotations in the record gives force to the proposition that the April 16 release received saturation coverage. We conclude that by Wednesday, April 22 when the Stouts sold their stock, and Thursday, April 23 when Mitchell sold the 20 shares, the reasonable investor would have become informed of the April 16 release and could no longer rely on the earlier release in selling TGS stock. . . .

We pass now to the issue of damages. The trial court, in framing a rule for determining a proper award of damages, started with the proposition that the aim of courts in this situation is to restore claiming parties to the positions they would have enjoyed had they not been fraudulently induced to sell their stock. Proceeding to fashion a remedy which would make effective the Congressional purpose, . . . the trial court postulated the following measure of damages: ". . . this is an attempt to give a twenty trading day period within which the average of the highest daily prices is the measure of damages, and a period within which the shareholders received, or should have received, notice of the Texas Gulf Sulphur announcement of April 16." . . . With the lapse of twenty trading days it was felt that market reactions would more accurately reflect actual value and allow a reasonable time for the reasonable and diligent shareholder to learn of the April 16 announcement and protect his interest. The averaging aspect was inserted because the trial court felt it highly improbable that any of the appellees would have sold at the highest price.

All party litigants are dissatisfied with this measure of damages. Appellants contend that only actual damages based on market value as of April 16 are recoverable; that appellees have failed to prove such loss; and even accepting the lower court's measure, twenty days is too lengthy and thereby unreasonable. By cross-appeal, Mitchell and Reynolds request restitution or damages equivalent to restitution, and costs of conducting this action.

We are in harmony with the rudiments of the trial court's measure of damages and alter that rule only to more closely adhere to the notion that the injured parties should be restored to their former status. The divergent approaches taken by the litigants verify the suspicion that a set rule of damages has not been tested in this kind of case. Furthermore, because of the uniqueness of the litigation, it would be unwise to set forth a uniform rule with broad applications to all securities cases. Thus, the rule styled by this court is fashioned for these unprecedented circumstances.

Restitution and damages equivalent to restitution are inappropriate remedies in this action. Traditionally these theories have been concerned with direct personal dealings in which there is privity and/or unjust enrichment upon which to justify the remedy. . . . Here neither element is present inasmuch as neither TGS nor Fogarty purchased appellees' shares of stock. The absence of those fundamental facts, plus the hardship it would visit upon TGS as a corporation,[13] makes this case inappropriate for any form of restitution, and the trial court properly rejected it.

We believe the measure of damages used should award the reasonable investor the amount it would have taken him to invest in the TGS market within a reasonable period of time after he became informed of the April 16 release. Through the testimony of both Reynolds and Mitchell we are satisfied, as was the trial court, that they possessed ample sophistication to fall within the nebulous reasonable investor category. By Monday, April 20, the diligent and reasonable investor was informed of the most recent TGS statement and as we earlier stated after that duration a reasonable investor would not have relied upon the April 12 statement in selling his TGS stock. After the reasonable stockholder had opportunity to apprise himself of the April 16 release and its import to investment, a reasonable time lapse may be allowed to expire to permit the investor to decide whether or not he would reinvest and take advantage of a spiraling market. If he has failed to reinvest, as both Reynolds and Mitchell did, he must suffer the consequences of his own judgment. The award proposed would permit one to "cover" by reinvestment and suffer neither loss nor forced sale.

The damages then should be based on the highest value of TGS stock between Monday, April 20 and a reasonable time thereafter. Whether we conclude such duration should be an added nine trading days (through Friday, May 1), which seems more reasonable in these circumstances, or the seventeen additional trading days imposed by the trial court (through Wednesday, May 13) is irrelevant to the award. For in either event, the highest value was achieved on Wednesday, April 29 (at $59), prior to the expiration of either time limit.

The averaging aspect is deleted to conform with what is considered the focal purpose: to award the reasonable investor an amount which offsets any loss he suffered by a deceitfully induced sale. To award an average price would not fully compensate him for a number of days within the reasonable period following the last release. While this is an admitted compromise between the restitution rule and the actual damage approach as taken by TGS, it seems a fair way to reinstate stockholders who were wrongfully deprived of their gain because of the deceitful release and, at the same time, deny recovery to those who suffered only by their

---

13. In their appellate brief, appellants claim that if the measure of damages theory applied in the trial court is upheld on appeal, damages will approach $14,000,000. In Ruder, Texas Gulf Sulphur — The Second Round, 63 Nw. U. L. Rev. 423, 428-29 (1969), restitution damages are computed: ". . . if liability is imposed upon TGS in the private suits for the company's failure to disclose the material inside information which it possessed, its damages may be equal to $130 for every share traded during the period from November 12, 1963, through April 16, 1964. Since approximately 3 million TGS shares were traded during this period, damages would amount to over 390 million dollars, approximately 150 million dollars more than the present net worth of the company. If liability is imposed upon TGS only for the period from April 12, 1964, . . . until April 16, 1964, . . . the company could incur damages of about 84 million dollars, since approximately 691,000 shares were traded during that four day period." [Footnotes omitted.]

own lack of due diligence. In selecting the highest daily price the advantage works, to a greater degree, against TGS. But where, as here, the injury is suffered by an act making difficult the exact computation of damages, the wrongdoer is not heard to complain. . . .

The damages awarded to Reynolds amount to $12,687.50; Mitchell's damages are fixed at $7,600.00. The decisions by the trial court that both appellees are to receive interest computed at six per cent per annum from the time of sale until the date of the trial court's judgment, and that when recovery is gained from TGS, appellees' claims against Fogarty will be deemed paid, satisfied and discharged, are not disturbed. . . .

The only issue left to be decided is raised individually by Reynolds and concerns whether Rule 23 F. R. Civ. P. should be applied to afford relief to all persons who sold TGS stock between April 12 and April 16, 1964. . . . In an opinion reported at 309 F. Supp. 566 (D. Utah 1970), the trial court denied the motion for a class action, basing the decision on Rule 23(b)(3)(B), (C) and (D).

The trial judge recited that as of October 22, 1969, ninety-four actions had been brought against TGS and individual defendants; that in March, 1969, two actions in the Southern District of New York had been allowed to proceed as class actions; that pursuant to that ruling, tedious and time consuming discovery had taken place; and that if the various private suits were concentrated for trial in a single district, it should be in the Southern District of New York. . . . Our conclusion is that the trial court has wisely exercised its discretion. . . .

---

1. *Alternative measures of damages for Rule 10b-5 violations.* Because Rule 10b-5 is a judicially created tort, no statutory formula specifies the proper measure of damages in a private action for its violation. Instead, courts have fashioned a number of different measures of damages, which they use in a manner that most commentators have described as inconsistent and unrationalized. See Robert Thompson, The Measure of Recovery Under Rule 10b-5: A Restitution Alternative to Tort Damages, 37 Vand. L. Rev. 349 (1984); Frank Easterbrook & Daniel Fischel, Optimal Damages in Securities Cases, 52 U. Chi. L. Rev. 611 (1985). Among the more common measures are the following:

(a) *"Out-of-pocket" damages.* This is clearly the usual form of relief available for a Rule 10b-5 violation.[40] It awards successful plaintiffs the difference between the price they paid (transferred) and the actual value received in the transaction.[41] Derived from the common law tort action for deceit, it seeks to achieve the traditional tort law goals of compensating the victim for the harm suffered and returning the plaintiff to the position occupied before the fraud. Note that this measure does not seek to award the "expectation" measure of damages that is the standard contract law measure of damages. Thus, if a defendant sells securities actually worth $10 per share for $20 after representing to the plaintiff that they have a

---

40. See Louis Loss, Fundamentals of Securities Regulation 1133-1134 (1983); Madigan, Inc. v. Goodman, 498 F.2d 233 (7th Cir. 1974).

41. In Affiliated Ute Citizens v. United States, 406 U.S. 128, 155 (1972), the Court phrased this measure slightly differently as the difference between the fair value that the victim received and the fair value of what the victim would have received had there been no fraudulent conduct. See also Glick v. Campagna, 613 F.2d 31 (3d Cir. 1979).

value of $40, the recovery is $10 per share, and the fact that the promised value was $40 is irrelevant. See, e.g., Osofsky v. Zipf, 645 F.2d 107 (2d Cir. 1981); Madigan, Inc. v. Goodman, supra. Generally, courts have rejected the "benefit of the bargain" measure based chiefly on their interpretation of §28 of the '34 Act, which prohibits any person from recovering "a total amount in excess of his actual damages on account of the act complained of."[42] *Query:* Should this phrase, "actual damages," preclude an expectation measure when contract law principles normally consider such a measure appropriate?

(b) *Rescission.* In Randall v. Loftsgaarden, 478 U.S. 647 (1986), the Court upheld use of a rescissionary measure of damages in a case where the defendant had syndicated limited partnership interests in a tax shelter. Both sides recognized that rescission could be appropriate under Rule 10b-5, but defendants argued (and the Eighth Circuit had agreed) that §28(a) of the '34 Act (which provides that no person "shall recover . . . a total amount in excess of his actual damages on account of the act complained of") required that the value of the tax losses already deducted by plaintiffs be deducted from the total damage award in order to prevent plaintiffs from receiving a windfall. The Court disagreed because the statutory phrase "actual damages" was not a synonym for "net economic harm suffered by the plaintiff." When the defendant's profit exceeded the plaintiff's loss, the damages awarded could include the defendant's profit because "[t]his alternative standard aims at preventing the unjust enrichment of a fraudulent buyer, . . . [although] it clearly does more than simply make the plaintiff whole for the economic loss proximately caused by the buyer's fraud." As a policy justification, the Court stressed that "Congress intended to deter fraud and manipulative practices in the securities markets, and to ensure full disclosure of information material to investment decisions." This "deterrent purpose" was "ill-served by a too rigid insistence on limiting plaintiffs to recovery of their 'net economic loss.'"

The Court expressly did not decide, however, that plaintiffs have an election between rescissionary and out-of-pocket damages. Where there is no secondary market (or only a thin one), out-of-pocket damages will usually not be calculable, and rescission will thus be the norm. In this light, *Randall* seems to give a qualified endorsement to restitution as a remedy available to the court in its discretion, subject to the important caveat that the plaintiff should not be able to "play the market" — that is, to hold onto the stock if it rises, but seek rescission if the price declines. After *Randall*, prompt action by the plaintiff to obtain rescission will be an important factor in its availability, and delay may cause the plaintiff to forfeit this remedy. See Baumel v. Rosen, 412 F.2d 571, 574 (4th Cir. 1969) (cited in *Randall*).

Some critics of restitution have argued that the plaintiff should not be able to impose the risk of market fluctuations on the seller. See Huddleston v. Herman & MacLean, 640 F.2d 534, 555 (5th Cir. 1981), *aff'd in part and rev'd in part*, 459 U.S. 375 (1983); Note, The Measure of Damages in Rule 10b-5 Cases Involving Actively Traded Securities, 26 Stan. L. Rev. 371, 375-376 (1974) (arguing that because stock price movements are at least as much a function of general economic and market factors as of firm-specific factors, rescission overcompensates plaintiffs by

---

42. In addition, the pre-*Erie* federal common law rule of damages rejected the "benefit of the bargain" measure. See Smith v. Bolles, 132 U.S. 125 (1889). Several modern securities law cases have cited Smith v. Bolles in rejecting an expectation measure of damages. See Estate Counseling Service, Inc. v. Merrill Lynch, Pierce, Fenner & Smith, Inc., 303 F.2d 527 (10th Cir. 1962).

protecting them against risks that all investors must assume when they enter the marketplace). However, *Randall* seemingly rejected these arguments by emphasizing the need for deterrence. Does this mean that in the future restitution may be obtainable even in the case of a publicly traded security?

Another justification for rescissionary relief is that §29 of the '34 Act provides that any contract made in violation of the '34 Act or any rule adopted thereunder "shall be void," which provision has been read to authorize rescission. See, e.g., Eastside Church of Christ v. National Plan, Inc., 391 F.2d 357 (5th Cir. 1968); Abrahamson v. Fleschner, 392 F. Supp. 740 (S.D.N.Y. 1975), *aff'd in part and rev'd in part*, 568 F.2d 862 (2d Cir. 1977); John R. Lewis, Inc. v. Newman, 446 F.2d 800, 805 (5th Cir. 1971).

The availability of rescission is most important when the defendant's gain exceeds the plaintiff's loss. In Janigan v. Taylor, 344 F.2d 781 (1st Cir. 1965), which the *Randall* decision cites with approval, the plaintiffs were defrauded sellers who had sold their stock to the corporation's president for approximately $40,000; two years later, the defendant sold the stock for $700,000. Relying on an unjust enrichment rationale, the First Circuit upheld recovery of defendant's net profit from the resale on the theory that, although the defendant's gain was an unanticipated windfall, "[i]t is more appropriate to give the defrauded party the benefit even of windfalls than to let the fraudulent party keep them." Id. at 786.

Janigan's logic has been extended by other courts to protect defrauded buyers as well as sellers. See Zeller v. Bogue Electric Manufacturing Corp., 476 F.2d 795 (2d Cir. 1973) (*Janigan* rule on unjust enrichment also applies to a fraudulent seller who reinvests proceeds of transaction and realizes profits that he would not otherwise have obtained). In Rochez Bros., Inc. v. Rhoades, 491 F.2d 402 (3d Cir. 1973), defendant bought out his co-owner and then resold nine months later at a substantial profit that was largely attributable to the defendant's own entrepreneurial efforts. As a result, the district court decided that the gain on resale was not a windfall but rather a direct result of policies that the defendant favored and the plaintiff opposed. Finding this gain not to amount to unjust enrichment, it refused to recognize the gain as an element of damages that the seller could recover. The Third Circuit reversed, holding that no profit arising from the consolidation of control by the defendant could be retained where it was achieved through fraud. *Query:* What if the plaintiff's damages were only $1 per share and defendant's gain (solely attributable to his own efforts) were $100 per share? In contrast to *Rochez Bros.*, compare Thomas v. Duralite Co., 524 F.2d 577 (3d Cir. 1975) (because defendant's special skill and efforts after the fraudulent transaction caused subsequent stock appreciation, defendant's gain did not amount to unjust enrichment). See also Siebel v. Scott, 725 F.2d 995 (5th Cir. 1984) (defrauded plaintiffs entitled to recover greater of value of their interest at moment of sale or profit realized by defendant promoter on resale, to the extent profit was not attributable to defendant's own entrepreneurial efforts).

In SEC v. MacDonald, 699 F.2d 47 (1st Cir. 1983), the chairman of a financially troubled company purchased stock in the company based on nonpublic material information and later realized a $53,000 profit on resale of this stock. The SEC sued for disgorgement, and the district court required the defendant to disgorge the entire profit. The First Circuit reversed, however, as to the amount of restitution required. Viewing the issue as whether an insider who violates Rule 10b-5 by trading on material inside information must "disgorge the entire profits he realized from his subsequent sale of those securities . . . [or] an amount representing the increased value of the shares at a reasonable time after public dissemination of the information," it chose the latter and lesser measure of damages (which resembles the "cover" measure in Mitchell v. Texas Gulf Sulphur, supra). *Janigan* was principally distinguished on the ground that the stock in *MacDonald* was publicly traded. (Judge Aldrich wrote both opinions.) *Query:* Is *MacDonald* consistent with *Randall*'s new emphasis on the importance of an adequate deterrent?

(c) *The "cover" measure.* Mitchell v. Texas Gulf Sulphur, supra, represents a third and intermediate approach to damages. Rather than an out-of-pocket measure that determines the difference in value on the day each plaintiff traded, *Mitchell* gives the plaintiff a reasonable period after disclosure of the fraud to determine whether or not to reinvest or "cover" (in the same sense that the term "cover" is used by the Uniform Commercial Code). This compromise was justified on the basis of causation principles. That is, disclosure of the fraud presents the plaintiff with a second investment decision on whether to reinvest. However the plaintiff decides, this second decision breaks the causal connection and implies that market changes in the stock's price after that point cannot be included in the plaintiff's damages under traditional tort principles. In short, the defendant cannot be said to have caused any price change after the plaintiff's second investment decision. See Arrington v. Merrill Lynch, Pierce, Fenner & Smith, Inc., 651 F.2d 615 (9th Cir. 1981). The practical upshot is that the defendant bears the risk of market changes for a short period after disclosure and then the plaintiff does thereafter. This compromise position has been described by some courts as a "modified rescissionary remedy." Elkind v. Liggett & Myers, Inc., 635 F.2d 156, 168 n.25 (2d Cir. 1980). This approach achieves the same result as did SEC v. MacDonald, supra, which also exposed the defendant to adverse market changes for a period ending shortly after the dissemination of nonpublic information.

What result would have been appropriate in *Mitchell* if the delay between the April 12 "pessimistic" release and the April 16 corrective release was not four days, but four months? Assume further that the Dow Jones average rose 30 percent during this period. Can defendant's conduct be said to have "caused" all of plaintiff's loss? Is it fair to deprive the defendants of all this appreciation, which does not relate to the specific circumstances of Texas Gulf Sulphur? Or is this a windfall case where ultimately the best rationale for compelling defendants to forfeit this gain is that it creates a desirable, and intermediate, deterrent without subjecting them to the higher damages to which true rescissionary relief would subject them? See Rolf v. Blyth, Eastman Dillon & Co., 570 F.2d 38 (2d Cir. 1978) (subtracting decline in price attributable to general market price movement from damages awarded in a suit under Rule 10b-5).

(d) *Consequential damages.* In a few cases, courts have allowed recovery for consequential damages when the plaintiff can prove that losses were proximately caused by the defendant's misrepresentations. See Madigan, Inc. v. Goodman, 498 F.2d 233 (7th Cir. 1974) (expenses awarded that were incurred by plaintiff while attempting to prevent insolvency of company purchased from defendant); James v. Meinke, 778 F.2d 200 (5th Cir. 1985) (fraud in sale of securities also proximately caused purchasers of a financially troubled business to execute loan guarantees; losses incurred on such guarantees amounted to consequential damages). Plaintiffs must, however, prove the existence of a causal nexus with reasonable certainty. See Foster v. Financial Technology, Inc., 517 F.2d 1068, 1071 (9th Cir. 1975).

2. *Insider trading damages.* Can an individual who makes no affirmative misstatement of a material fact but simply buys 100 shares of a stock based on material nonpublic information, which he was legally required to disclose, be held liable for all the losses sustained by sellers who trade several million shares over the same period? *Mitchell* was not a class action and did not have to face this problem of the potential disproportion between the defendant's gain and legal liability. (Also, the *Texas Gulf Sulphur* case involved some affirmative misstatements in the misleading press release.) Subsequently, both the courts and Congress have placed a severe ceiling on the maximum civil damages for which a defendant who engages in insider trading is liable. This aspect of securities law damages is discussed later in Sec. D of this chapter, which focuses on the special context of insider trading, where Congress in 1988 enacted an express cause of action (§20A of the '34 Act).

vi. Statute of Limitations Applicable to Rule 10b-5

For a long time, no period of limitations was prescribed by statute in the federal securities laws for civil actions under §10(b). Until 1991, federal courts solved this problem by borrowing the state statute of limitations applicable to the most closely related cause of action in the forum state. This created a motive for forum shopping. In 1991 the Supreme Court ended this practice, ruling that federal courts should instead look to the statute of limitations applicable to §9 of the Securities Exchange Act, as the most closely related express cause of action in that statute (on the theory that an implied cause of action under Rule 10b-5 should be consistent with the limitations placed by Congress on express causes of action in the same statute). This produced a statute of limitations equal to the earlier of (a) one year after discovery of the facts constituting the violation, or (b) three years after such violation. See Lampf, Pleva, Lipkind, Prupis & Petigrow v. Gilberston, 501 U.S. 350 (1991). Under *Lampf*, there was no equitable tolling of the statute; the three-year period was an absolute outer bar, and the one-year period began to run on the publication of information (often in the financial press) that should have placed a reasonable investor on "inquiry notice." See Brumbaugh v. Princeton Partners, 985 F.2d 157, 163 (4th Cir. 1993).

Plaintiffs complained that the one-year effective statute cut off many meritorious actions (particularly against secondary defendants). In the Sarbanes-Oxley Act of 2002, they secured a reversal of the *Lampf* decision. New 28 U.S.C. §1658(b) provides for a five- and two-year statute of limitations for Rule 10b-5 actions (i.e., the earlier of (a) two years after discovery of the facts constituting the violation, or (b) five years after such violation). It is currently unresolved whether the statute's focus on actual "discovery" precludes beginning the two-year period running from when a reasonable investor should have discovered the violation.

vii. Contribution

In Musick, Peeler & Garrett v. Employers Insurance of Wausau, 113 S. Ct. 2085 (1993), the Court (6-3) found that defendants who pay a judgment or settlement in a Rule 10b-5 action have a right as a matter of federal law to seek contribution against other joint tortfeasors who had either paid no damages or paid less than their fair share. This result was consistent with that of the vast majority of the Circuits. In *Musick*, an insurance company, which had insured the principal defendants in a suit based on Rule 10b-5 and had as a result funded a $13 million settlement, brought suit against the attorneys and accountants involved in the stock offering that prompted the original action (but who had not been sued in the original action). Although §10 of the '34 Act is silent with respect to contribution, and recent Supreme Court decisions had refused to imply a right to contribution under several other federal statutes, the majority said the context of Rule 10b-5 was distinctive. Because the Rule 10b-5 action was implied by the judiciary, not created by Congress, judicial authority existed to shape the contours of the Rule 10b-5 action. Also, the existence of express rights to contribution in §§9 and 18 of the '34 Act, which are the closest parallels to §10 (and from which §10(b)'s statute of limitations was borrowed in *Lampf*), further persuaded the majority to conclude that consistency and the structural coherence of the '34 Act required that a like contribution rule be recognized under Rule 10b-5.

The appropriate formula for the allocation of liability remains in dispute. Should it be an equal sharing rule? Or should it be based on relative fault? The SEC favors a relative fault standard and has requested legislation to this effect. The impact of *Musick* on settlements also remains uncertain. If there are five co-defendants in a $10.5 million securities fraud case and the plaintiffs settle with defendant *A* for $500,000, can defendant *A* be later sued by defendants *B, C, D,* and *E,* who each paid $2.5 million after a judgment was returned against them? Because exposing the settling defendant to suits for contribution by non-settling defendants would tend to chill settlements, §21D(f)(7) of the Securities Exchange Act of 1934 protects the settling defendant by entitling such defendant to a "bar order" against suits for contribution. This provision, which was added by the Private Securities Litigation Reform Act of 1995, means that contribution can realistically be obtained only from another person who escaped suit or has not settled.

d. The Policy Dilemma Surrounding Securities Class Actions

Perhaps the most important issue surrounding securities class actions is whether their benefits outweigh their costs. While generalizations abound, the empirical evidence, discussed below, does not fully support either side in this debate. In 1995, when Congress enacted the Private Securities Litigation Reform Act of 1995 (the "1995 Act") over the unsuccessful veto of President Clinton, it was motivated by a perception of securities litigation as benefiting the plaintiffs' attorneys more than the class members they served. With various refinements and qualifications, the following charges regularly surfaced in this debate and continue to echo in the Act's aftermath:[43]

1. Securities class actions were increasing to an "epidemic" level and tended to be triggered simply by any significant drop (often estimated as any one-day decline of 10 percent or more) in a stock's trading price. As a result, it was said that securities class actions did less to deter fraud than they did to penalize companies with high price volatility (which condition often

---

43. All of these themes can be found, stated repeatedly, in legislative hearings leading up to the 1995 Act. See "Private Litigation Under the Federal Securities Laws: Hearings Before the Subcomm. on Securities of the Senate Committee on Banking, Housing and Urban Affairs," 103rd Congress, 1st Session (June 17 and July 21, 1993) (hereinafter "Senate Hearings").

characterizes high-technology stocks in the electronics, computer, and bio-technology fields).

2. In securities class actions, the benefits to the individual class members were low to negligible, usually amounting to only a small percentage of investors' losses. Moreover, in the standard "stock drop" case involving secondary market trading, such recovery to the class members came at the expense of the other shareholders in the same corporation, who also were typically blameless. In short, the net result was arguably only a wealth transfer from one group of shareholders to another with little deterrent benefit.

3. Securities class actions were lawyer driven and primarily benefited plaintiffs' attorneys, who typically received 30 percent or more of the recovery.

4. Securities class actions tended to settle not on the basis of their merits, but rather based on their "nuisance value" (that is, the direct or indirect costs of defending them) and the "in terrorem" threat that a jury, misunderstanding the facts, might impose liability in a weak case.

All of these claims continue to be robustly debated, but their perceived legitimacy explains many of the provisions of the 1995 Act, which chiefly sought to chill the filing of "frivolous" class actions.

The Empirical Evidence: A Complex Thicket

At the congressional hearings, the SEC presented evidence on the volume of securities class actions that showed an irregular pattern of peaks and valleys. The average level of filings in the early 1990s had increased above that of the mid-1980s, but appeared to be even with that in the 1970s.[44] Perhaps more interestingly, since and notwithstanding the 1995 Act, the level of securities class action filings dipped briefly in 1996 and then rose sharply thereafter, reaching a near record level in 2002 in the wake of the Enron and WorldCom scandals. But the number of securities class actions has again declined significantly in 2005, 2006, and 2007. Why? Different theories exist, and they include: (1) the stock market rose in 2006 and 2007, meaning that there were fewer sudden stock price drops to fuel litigation; (2) the Sarbanes-Oxley Act plus increased criminal enforcement may have worked to deter accounting irregularities and inflated financial reports; and (3) recent judicial decisions, including *Dura Pharmaceuticals* and tightened class certification requirements,[45] may have made it more difficult to sue in a class action.

The claim that any 10 percent drop in stock price would automatically trigger a class action has, however, been discredited. One survey identified 33,206 such one-day stock drops of 10 percent or greater, but found only 1,584 subsequent class actions — or a relatively modest rate of 4.4 percent.[46] Still, this evidence does not refute the claim that securities class actions disproportionately penalize high-tech companies or chill their access to the equity markets.

---

44. See Senate Hearings at 121.

45. See Miles v. Merrill Lynch & Co., 471 F.3d 24 (2nd Cir. 2006) (raising threshold of proof needed to justify certification of a proposed securities class action).

46. See Joel Seligman, The Merits Do Matter: A Comment on Professor Grundfest's Disimplying Private Rights of Action Under the Federal Securities Laws, 108 Harv. L. Rev. 468, 433 n.19 (1994).

The compensatory benefits of securities class actions to class members yields somewhat clearer evidence (whose implications can still be debated). A 2006 study finds that the median payment to class members averaged about 2.4 percent of their estimated damages (with the median settlement being around $7 million).[47] Such a low rate of recovery might suggest either that securities class actions were often non-meritorious suits filed for their nuisance value or that higher recoveries might have driven the corporation into bankruptcy. Based on such data, some believe that the "merits do not matter" in securities class actions[48] (because the high potential damages force defendants to settle), but this is a controversial thesis for which there is much contrary evidence.

Even if the typical action is meritorious, the most troubling dilemma concerning the securities class action involves the ratio between the costs and the benefits and the circularity of the payments. Suppose the plaintiff class in a hypothetical class action involving a drop in the price of XYZ Corp.'s common stock price consists of all shareholders who bought that stock over a one-year period (January 1, 2007, to December 31, 2007), and that this class consists of 50 percent of all shareholders. Suppose further that this action settles after extensive litigation for $20 million (or 50 percent of the estimated damages). Who bears the costs and what are they? If the full cost of this settlement is borne by XYZ (or paid by its insurance company based on policies on which XYZ pays the premiums), then the cost is indirectly borne proportionately by all shareholders of XYZ Corp., who were in effect paying $20 million to the 50 percent of their fellow shareholders who fell within the plaintiff class. Now add the facts that (a) the defense costs of this litigation over two years were $3 to $4 million, and (b) the plaintiff's attorneys will receive one-third of the recovery (or $6.67 million). On this basis, the shareholders of XYZ Corp. have indirectly incurred a $24 million loss to pay a net recovery of $13.33 million to half of them.

To be sure, the victimized class does benefit (if at a high cost), but there is a further catch here. If shareholders are diversified, then diversified shareholders probably divide more or less equally between the 50 percent who received the recovery (i.e., the plaintiff class) and the 50 percent who are outside the class, and thus incurred costs but received no benefits. As a result, across a broad range of cases, diversified shareholders will sometimes be in the plaintiff class and sometimes not — but on average they will lose because of the high transaction costs incident to this compensation system (in particular, the legal fees of the lawyers on both sides).[49] To the extent that shareholders are not diversified, small public shareholders are likely to fare even worse, because they typically are buy-and-hold shareholders who are less likely to have purchased within the

---

47. See Cornerstone Research, Securities Class Action Settlements, 2006 Review and Analysis; see also Cornerstone Research, Securities Class Actions Case Filings, 2006: A Year in Review (reporting the number of securities class action filings to be as follows: 1998, 240; 1999, 208; 2000, 214; 2001, 179; 2002, 226; 2003, 186; 2004, 211; 2005, 178; 2006, 110).

48. This hypothesis that securities class actions settled either on their nuisance value or on the "in terrorem" threat of high damages was first advanced in a provocative article by Professor Janet Cooper Alexander. See Alexander, Do the Merits Matter? A Study of Settlements in Securities Class Actions, 43 Stan. L. Rev. 497 (1991) (estimating that securities class actions involving initial public offerings settled at 25 percent of their alleged damages); however, this study was based on only eight case studies).

49. For this view, see John C. Coffee Jr., Reforming the Securities Class Action: An Essay on Deterrence and Its Implementation, 106 Colum. L. Rev. 1534 (2006) (advocating rules to shift more of the liability from the corporate entity to responsible managers); Donald C. Langevoort, Capping Damages for Open Market Securities Fraud, 38 Ariz. L. Rev. 639 (1996) (proposing a ceiling).

class period (which is typically one year or less). Hence, they tend to fund the recovery rather than receive it. This critique applies only to the secondary-market securities class action and not a primary-market class action (i.e., when the corporation is selling securities),[50] but the secondary-market class action is the typical Rule 10b-5 class action.

From this perspective, the stronger rationale for securities litigation may be deterrence, not compensation. The threat of suit may deter managers from making misleading statements, and firms that are sued may incur costly increases in their insurance premiums. If the threat of suit and high cost of insurance lead firms to install preventive and monitoring controls, securities class actions may still play an important and socially valuable role. But here too there are skeptics. The evidence seems to show that corporate insiders do not contribute more than a token amount to securities class actions and that their cost falls on shareholders, who either bear the cost of the settlement directly or through increased D&O liability insurance premiums.[51]

e. The Response of the Private Securities Litigation Reform Act of 1995

Against this backdrop, the 1995 Act sought to do several things: (1) weaken the ability of the plaintiff to obtain a favorable settlement in a non-meritorious case based on the action's nuisance value; (2) reduce the tendency for class actions to be dominated by lawyers rather than the class members; and (3) protect predictive and other "forward-looking statements" made by young companies subject to high price volatility. To accomplish the first goal, one of the most important provisions in the 1995 Act (now §21D(b)(2) of the Securities Exchange Act of 1934) heightened the pleading standards for securities fraud. Specifically, that section requires the plaintiff in a private action to plead facts "with particularity . . . giving rise to a strong inference that the defendant acted with the required state of mind" (in the case of Rule 10b-5 actions, this standard translates into "facts giving rise to a strong inference of fraud"). The Conference Report to the 1995 Act indicated that this standard was borrowed from the existing case law in the Second Circuit, but indicated that the Conference Committee wanted a somewhat tougher standard.[52] In vetoing the 1995 Act, President Clinton objected that such a heightened standard, raised to a level higher than the Second Circuit's, was "so high that even the most aggrieved investors with the most painful losses may get tossed out of court before they have a chance to prove their case." Although Congress easily overrode the president's veto, it remained uncertain how courts would read the Conference Committee's ambiguous statement in the legislative history.

---

50. When the firm is itself selling its equity to the public, the case for corporate liability is stronger because now the pre-sale shareholders are receiving a benefit in the form of the inflated price the firm receives.

51. See Coffee, supra footnote 49, at 1550-551 (reporting that, in one multi-year study during the mid-1990s, officers and other individual defendants paid only 0.4 percent of the securities class action settlements).

52. See H.R. Rep. No. 104-369, 104th Congress, 1st Session (1995) ("Regarded as the most stringent pleading, the Second Circuit requirement is that the plaintiff state facts with particularity, and that these facts, in turn, must give rise to a 'strong inference' of the defendants' fraudulent intent. Because the Conference Committee intends to strengthen existing pleading requirements, it does not intend to codify the Second Circuit's case law interpreting this pleading standard.").

Today, after Tellabs, Inc. v. Makor Issues & Rights, Ltd., supra page 404, it appears that the pleading standard for scienter has not been elevated as much as had been originally expected.[53]

Because the Second Circuit was the original source of the "strong inference of fraud" standard, it is important to understand how it employs this test. In Novak v. Kasaks, 216 F.3d 300, 311 (2d Cir. 2000), the Second Circuit remanded a case that the district court had dismissed on pleading grounds and instructed the district court as to how to apply properly its long-standing "motive and opportunity" test:

> Accordingly, we hold that the PSLRA adopted our "strong inference" standard. In order to plead scienter, plaintiffs must "state with particularity facts giving rise to a strong inference that the defendant acted with the required state of mind." . . . [T]his inference may arise where the complaint sufficiently alleges that the defendants: (1) benefitted in a concrete and personal way from the purported fraud . . . ; (2) engaged in deliberately illegal behavior . . . ; (3) knew facts or had access to information suggesting that their public statements were not accurate . . . ; or (4) failed to check information they had a duty to monitor.

Other language in *Novak* made clear that it was insufficient to plead "motives possessed by virtually all corporate insiders, including: (1) the desire to maintain a high corporate credit rating . . . or otherwise sustain 'the appearance of corporate profitability, or of the success of an investment'; and (2) the desire to maintain a high stock price in order to increase executive compensation." (Id. at 307.)

In contrast, in In re Silicon Graphics Inc. Sec. Litig., 183 F.3d 970 (9th Cir. 1999), the Ninth Circuit ruled:

> We hold that a private securities plaintiff proceeding under the PSLRA must plead, in great detail, facts that constitute strong circumstantial evidence of deliberately reckless or conscious misconduct. Our holding rests, in part, on our conclusion that Congress intended to elevate the pleading requirement above the Second Circuit standard requiring plaintiffs merely to provide facts showing simple recklessness or a motive to commit fraud and opportunity to do so. We hold that although facts showing mere recklessness or a motive to commit fraud and opportunity to do so may provide some reasonable inference of intent, they are not sufficient to establish a strong inference of deliberate recklessness. In order to show a strong inference of deliberate recklessness, plaintiffs must state facts that come closer to demonstrating intent, as opposed to mere motive and opportunity.[54]

Tellabs does not necessarily resolve this conflict. Although *Tellabs* mandates that there be a comparative evaluation of both sides' interpretations of the inferences that should be drawn from the pleadings, it never addresses the "motive and opportunity" test or the Ninth Circuit's alternative.

---

53. This assessment depends on whether the Ninth Circuit reconsiders its uniquely high pleading standard in light of *Tellabs*. See In re Silicon Graphics Inc. Sec. Litig., 183 F.3d 970, 977 (9th Cir. 1999). In contrast, the Second Circuit has found that its pleading standard remains the same as it was prior to the PSLRA's passage. See Press v. Chemical Inv. Servs. Corp., 166 F.3d 529, 537-538 (2d Cir. 1999). In between the polar positions of the Second and Ninth Circuits on this spectrum are the intermediate positions of the First and Sixth Circuits, which find that motive and opportunity, while not sufficient by themselves, can be used to demonstrate conscious or reckless misconduct. See In re Comshare Inc. Sec. Litig., 183 F.3d 542, 550-551 (6th Cir. 1999); Greebel v. FTP Software, 194 F.3d 185, 197 (1st Cir. 1999).
54. 183 F.3d 970 at 974 (9th Cir. 1999).

Another major innovation of the 1995 Act was its mandatory stay of discovery during the pendency of any motion to dismiss filed by the defendant.[55] As a result, a typical securities class action is frozen for a year or more before the plaintiff can obtain discovery—and only then if the action survives the defendant's motion to dismiss. The aim of this stay provision was to prevent "harassment" of the defendant and to reduce the possibility of weak actions having a "nuisance" settlement value.

The 1995 Act also greatly reduced the litigation incentives for suing secondary defendants, such as accountants or investment bankers. Prior to the 1995 Act, defendants in securities class actions were jointly and severally liable, but the 1995 Act substituted a regime of proportionate liability under which each defendant is "liable solely for the portion of the judgment that corresponds to the percentage of responsibility of that covered person,"[56] as assessed by the fact-finder (unless the defendant was found to have acted with "actual knowledge" of the misstatement or omission, in which case joint and several liability remains). Hence, even if an accountant is found liable under Rule 10b-5, the next step will be to apportion the liability among all the participants responsible for the misleading statement (including even non-defendants). Typically, the corporate defendants will appear more responsible (and are more likely to have actual knowledge of the fraud). The net result is that plaintiffs have increasingly chosen not to sue accountants and other secondary defendants, who are likely to mount an active defense, because plaintiffs expect that such defendants may be assessed only a low share of the judgment if they are held liable. In any event, no reported case appears yet to have resolved any of the procedural issues in actually determining proportionate liability in a case with multiple defendants.

Finally, the 1995 Act sought to reduce the power of the traditional plaintiff's bar over securities class actions by creating a presumption that the investor with the largest economic stake in the action would be named the "lead plaintiff" and would be entitled to choose the counsel for the class.[57] The hope was that institutional investors would volunteer to be named lead plaintiff and would choose their own counsel (or would conduct a competitive bidding procedure to determine the law firm that would represent the class at the lowest cost). To date, only public pension funds have volunteered in any numbers to accept this role, and some studies do find that they have had a marginally positive impact in terms of reducing fee awards.[58] But dramatic change has not resulted, and the practice of "play to pay" (i.e., requiring political contributions to elected state officials as a condition of eligibility to serve as class counsel) may compromise this monitor as well.[59]

f. The Impact of the 1995 Act

Several studies have surveyed the impact of the 1995 Act, and in common they report that securities class action filings dipped in 1996 but returned to their

---

55. See §21D(b)(3)(B) of the Securities Exchange Act of 1934. This stay is subject to very limited exceptions where the plaintiff shows a need "to preserve evidence or to prevent undue prejudice."

56. See §21D(f)(2)(B).

57. See §21D(a)(3) of the Securities Exchange Act of 1934.

58. See James Cox & Randall Thomas, Does the Plaintiff Matter?: An Empirical Analysis of Lead Plaintiffs in Securities Class Actions, 106 Colum. L. Rev. 1587 (2006).

59. Id. (discussing impact of "play to pay" practices).

pre-Act levels or higher in subsequent years (only to drop again in the period after 2004).[60] Some class actions migrated to state court to avoid the 1995 Act, but this possibility has now been foreclosed by legislation enacted in 1998 that pre-empts securities class actions in state court (and also precludes the filing of state law-based securities fraud causes of action in federal court).[61]

The profile of the typical securities fraud class action has also changed. Whereas, before the Act, projections and other "forward-looking statements" that proved erroneous were frequently litigated, a lower percentage of post-Act complaints has focused on such information. In this regard, the "safe harbor for forward-looking statements" in the 1995 Act has proved successful. Since the 1995 Act, the new focus of securities litigation appears to be on allegations of accounting fraud and "cooked books." Some evidence also suggests that a significantly larger "stock drop" is necessary to trigger the filing of a securities class action since the Act's passage. Still, high-technology firms remain a frequent target of securities class actions.[62] Securities class action complaints now commonly allege insider trading violations by management — in order to raise circumstances giving rise to the requisite "strong inference of fraud."[63]

g. Transactions Not Covered by the Rule

i. Corporate Mismanagement

Superintendent of Insurance v. Bankers Life & Casualty Co.
404 U.S. 6 (1971)

Mr. Justice Douglas delivered the opinion of the Court.

Manhattan Casualty Co., now represented by petitioner, New York's Superintendent of Insurance, was, it is alleged, defrauded in the sale of certain securities in violation of §17(a) of the Securities Act of 1933 and of §10(b) of the Securities Exchange Act of 1934. The District Court dismissed the complaint, 300 F. Supp. 1083, and the Court of Appeals affirmed, by a divided bench. 430 F.2d 355. . . .

It seems that Bankers Life & Casualty Co., one of the respondents, agreed to sell all of Manhattan's stock to one Begole for $5,000,000. It is alleged that Begole conspired with one Bourne and others to pay for this stock, not out of their own funds, but with Manhattan's assets. They were alleged to have arranged . . . to obtain a $5,000,000 check from respondent Irving Trust Co., although they had no funds on deposit there at the time. On the same day they purchased all the stock of Manhattan from Bankers Life for $5,000,000 and as stockholders and directors, installed one Sweeny as president of Manhattan.

---

60. For a year-by-year tabulation, see Cornerstone Research, supra footnote 47; see also U.S. Securities Exchange Commission, Office of the General Counsel, "Report to the President and the Congress on the First Year of Practice Under the Private Securities Litigation Reform Act of 1995" (Apr. 1997); J. Grundfest & M. Perino, Securities Litigation Reform: The First Year's Experience (Stanford Law School Working Paper No. 140, Feb. 1997).

61. Under the Securities Litigation Uniform Standards Act of 1998, both the Securities Act of 1933 and the Securities Exchange Act of 1934 have been amended to preempt stale causes of action alleging Rule 10b-5–like claims in the case of "reporting" companies. See page **000** supra.

62. See Grundfest & Perino, supra footnote 60.

63. See Cornerstone Research, supra footnote 47, at Exhibit 14 (finding that 45 percent and 38 percent of securities class actions filed in 2005 and 2006, respectively, alleged insider trading).

Manhattan then sold its United States Treasury bonds for $4,854,552.67.[1] That amount, plus enough cash to bring the total to $5,000,000, was credited to an account of Manhattan at Irving Trust and the $5,000,000 Irving Trust check was charged against it. As a result, Begole owned all the stock of Manhattan, having used $5,000,000 of Manhattan's assets to purchase it. . . .

Manhattan was the seller of Treasury bonds and, it seems to us, clearly protected by §10(b). . . .

There certainly was an "act" or "practice" within the meaning of Rule 10b-5 which operated as "a fraud or deceit" on Manhattan, the seller of the Government bonds. To be sure, the full market price was paid for those bonds; but the seller was duped into believing that it, the seller, would receive the proceeds. We cannot agree with the Court of Appeals that "no investor [was] injured" and that the "purity of the security transaction and the purity of the trading process were unsullied." 430 F.2d at 361.

Section 10(b) outlaws the use "in connection with the purchase or sale" of any security[6] of "any manipulative or deceptive device or contrivance." The Act protects corporations as well as individuals who are sellers of a security. Manhattan was injured as an investor through a deceptive device which deprived it of any compensation for the sale of its valuable block of securities.

The fact that the fraud was perpetrated by an officer of Manhattan and his outside collaborators is irrelevant to our problem. For §10(b) bans the use of any deceptive device in the "sale" of any security by "any person." And the fact that the transaction is not conducted through a securities exchange or an organized over-the-counter market is irrelevant to the coverage of §10(b). Hooper v. Mountain States Securities Corp., 282 F.2d 195, 201 (5th Cir. 1960). Likewise irrelevant is the fact that the proceeds of the sale that were due the seller were misappropriated. As the Court of Appeals for the Fifth Circuit said in the *Hooper* case, "Considering the purpose of this legislation, it would be unrealistic to say that a corporation having the capacity to acquire $700,000 worth of assets for its 700,000 shares of stock has suffered no loss if what it gave up was $700,000 but what it got was zero." 282 F.2d at 203.

The Congress made clear that "disregard of trust relationships by those whom the law should regard as fiduciaries, are all a single seamless web" along with manipulation, investor's ignorance, and the like. H.R. Rep. No. 1383, 73d Cong., 2d Sess., 6. Since practices "constantly vary and where practices legitimate for some purposes may be turned to illegitimate and fraudulent means, broad discretionary powers" in the regulatory agency "have been found practically essential." Id. at 7. Hence we do not read §10(b) as narrowly as the Court of Appeals; it is not "limited to preserving the integrity of the securities markets" (430 F.2d at 361), though that purpose is included. Section 10(b) must be read flexibly, not technically and restrictively. Since there was a "sale" of a security and since fraud was used "in connection with" it, there is redress under §10(b), whatever might be available as a remedy under state law.

We agree that Congress by §10(b) did not seek to regulate transactions which constitute no more than internal corporate mismanagement. But we read §10(b) to mean that Congress meant to bar deceptive devices and contrivances in the

---

1. Manhattan's Board of Directors was allegedly deceived into authorizing this sale by the misrepresentation that the proceeds would be exchanged for a certificate of deposit of equal value.

6. Section 3(a)(10) of the 1934 Act defines "security" very broadly (see Tcherepnin v. Knight, 389 U.S. 332) and clearly embraces Treasury bonds.

purchase or sale of securities whether conducted in the organized markets or face to face. And the fact that creditors of the defrauded corporate buyer or seller of securities may be the ultimate victims does not warrant disregard of the corporate entity. The controlling stockholder owes the corporation a fiduciary obligation — one "designed for the protection of the entire community of interests in the corporation — creditors as well as stockholders." Pepper v. Litton, 308 U.S. 295, 307.

The crux of the present case is that Manhattan suffered an injury as a result of deceptive practices touching its sale of securities as an investor. As stated in Shell v. Hensley, 430 F.2d 819, 827: "When a person who is dealing with a corporation in a securities transaction denies the corporation's directors access to material information known to him, the corporation is disabled from availing itself of an informed judgment on the part of its board regarding the merits of the transaction. In this situation the private right of action recognized under Rule 10b-5 is available as a remedy for the corporate disability." The case was before the lower courts on a motion to dismiss.

Bankers Life urges that the complaint did not allege, and discovery failed to disclose, any connection between it and the fraud and that, therefore, the dismissal of the complaint as to it was correct and should be affirmed. We make no ruling on this point.

The case must be remanded for trial. We intimate no opinion on the merits, as we have dealt only with allegations. . . .

All defenses except our ruling on §10(b) will be open on remand.

Reversed.

The impact of Bankers Life. Although Justice Douglas's opinion clearly stated that Rule 10b-5 "did not seek to regulate transactions which constitute no more than internal corporate mismanagement," his opinion suggested that whenever "deceptive practices touching [the] sale of securities" were involved, an action under Rule 10b-5 would lie. The implications of this phrase were explored in a series of cases by the Second Circuit. In Schoenbaum v. Firstbrook, 405 F.2d 215 (2d Cir. 1968) (en banc), a derivative action was filed on behalf of Banff Oil against its controlling corporate shareholder (Acquitaine), alleging that Acquitaine through its control of the Banff board had caused Banff to sell its stock to Acquitaine at an unfairly low price that did not reflect a recent oil discovery on Banff's properties. The Second Circuit en banc denied defendant's motion for summary judgment and held that, if Acquitaine had "exercised a controlling influence over the issuance to it of treasury shares of Banff for a wholly inadequate consideration," this conduct would have defrauded Banff's public minority shareholders in violation of Rule 10b-5. See also Popkin v. Bishop, 464 F.2d 714 (2d Cir. 1972). At the time, some saw these decisions as implying that any substantial unfairness in connection with an intercorporate securities transaction violated Rule 10b-5 if the parent corporation (or a control group) held a controlling influence. See Note, The Controlling Influence Standard in Rule 10b-5 Corporate Mismanagement Cases, 86 Harv. L. Rev. 1007 (1973). This view, that unfairness by a controlling parent was "manipulative" under Rule 10b-5, was to prove short-lived, however, as the next case shows.

Santa Fe Industries, Inc. v. Green
430 U.S. 462 (1977)

Mr. Justice White delivered the opinion of the Court. . . .

In 1936 petitioner Santa Fe Industries, Inc. ("Santa Fe") acquired control of 60% of the stock of Kirby Lumber Corporation ("Kirby"), a Delaware corporation. Through a series of purchases over the succeeding years, Santa Fe increased its control of Kirby's stock to 95%; the purchase prices during the period 1968-1973 ranged from $65 to $92.50 per share. In 1974, wishing to acquire 100% ownership of Kirby, Santa Fe availed itself of §253 of the Delaware Corporation Law, known as the "short-form merger" statute. . . .

Santa Fe obtained independent appraisals of the physical assets of Kirby — land, timber, buildings, and machinery — and of Kirby's oil, gas, and mineral interests. These appraisals, together with other financial information, were submitted to Morgan, Stanley & Company ("Morgan Stanley"), an investment banking firm retained to appraise the fair market value of Kirby stock. Kirby's physical assets were appraised at $320 million (amounting to $640 for each of the 500,000 shares); Kirby's stock was valued by Morgan Stanley at $125 per share. Under the terms of the merger, minority stockholders were offered $150 per share.

The provisions of the short-form merger statute were fully complied with.[3] The minority stockholders of Kirby were notified the day after the merger became effective and were advised of their right to obtain an appraisal in Delaware court if dissatisfied with the offer of $150 per share. They also received an information statement containing, in addition to the relevant financial data about Kirby, the appraisals of the value of Kirby's assets and the Morgan Stanley appraisal concluding that the fair market value of the stock was $125 per share.

Respondents, minority stockholders of Kirby, objected to the terms of the merger, but did not pursue their appraisal remedy in the Delaware Court of Chancery. Instead, they brought this action in federal court on behalf of the corporation and other minority stockholders, seeking to set aside the merger or to recover what they claimed to be the fair value of their shares. The amended complaint asserted that, based on the fair market value of Kirby's physical assets as revealed by the appraisal included in the Information Statement sent to minority shareholders, Kirby's stock was worth at least $772 per share.[5] The complaint alleged further that the merger took place without prior notice to minority stockholders; that the purpose of the merger was to appropriate the difference between the "conceded pro rata of value of the physical assets" and the offer of $150 per share — to "freez[e] out the minority stockholders at a wholly inadequate price"; and that Santa Fe, knowing the appraised value of the physical assets, obtained a "fraudulent appraisal" of the stock from Morgan Stanley and offered $25 above that

---

3. The merger became effective on July 31, 1974, and was accomplished in the following way. A new corporation, Forest Products, Inc., was organized as a Delaware corporation. The Kirby stock, together with cash, was transferred . . . to Forest Products in exchange for all of the Forest Products stock. The new corporation was then merged into Kirby, with Kirby as the surviving corporation. The cash transferred to Forest Products was used to make the purchase offer for the Kirby shares not owned by the Santa Fe subsidiary.

5. The figure of $772 per share was calculated as follows: "The difference of $311,000,000 ($622 per share) between the fair market value of Kirby's land and timber, alone, as per the defendants' own appraisal thereof at $320,000,000 and the $9,000,000 book value of said land and timber, added to the $150 per share, yields a pro rata share of the value of the physical assets of Kirby of at least $772 per share. The value of the stock was at least the pro rata value of the physical assets."

appraisal "in order to lull the minority stockholders into erroneously believing that [Santa Fe was] generous." This course of conduct was alleged to be "a violation of Rule 10b-5 because defendants employed a 'device, scheme or artifice to defraud' and engaged in an 'act, practice or course of business which operates or would operate as a fraud or deceit upon any person, in connection with the purchase or sale of any security.'" . . .

The District Court dismissed the complaint for failure to state a claim upon which relief could be granted. 391 F. Supp. 849 (S.D.N.Y. 1975). . . .

A divided Court of Appeals for the Second Circuit reversed. 533 F.2d 1283 (1976). . . . [T]he Court of Appeals did not disturb the District Court's conclusion that the complaint did not allege a material misrepresentation or nondisclosure with respect to the value of the stock; and the court declined to rule that a claim of gross undervaluation itself would suffice to make out a Rule 10b-5 case. . . . [H]owever, the court fundamentally disagreed with the District Court as to the reach and coverage of Rule 10b-5. The Court of Appeals' view was that . . . the rule reached "breaches of fiduciary duty by a majority against minority shareholders without any charge of misrepresentation or lack of disclosure." Id., at 1287.[8] The court went on to hold that the complaint taken as a whole stated a cause of action under the Rule: "We hold that a complaint alleges a claim under Rule 10b-5 when it charges, in connection with a Delaware short-form merger, that the majority has committed a breach of its fiduciary duty to deal fairly with minority shareholders by effecting the merger without any justifiable business purpose. The minority shareholders are given no prior notice of the merger, thus having no opportunity to apply for injunctive relief, and the proposed price to be paid is substantially lower than the appraised value reflected in the Information Statement." Id., at 1291; see id., at 1289. . . .

. . . The court below construed the term "fraud" in Rule 10b-5 by adverting to the use of the term in several of this Court's decisions in contexts other than the 1934 Act and the related Securities Act of 1933.[11] The Court of Appeals' approach to the interpretation of Rule 10b-5 is inconsistent with that taken by the Court last Term in Ernst & Ernst v. Hochfelder, 425 U.S. 185 (1976).

. . . In holding that a cause of action under Rule 10b-5 does not lie for mere negligence, the Court began with the principle that "[a]scertainment of congressional intent with respect to the standard of liability created by a particular section of the [1933 and 1934] Acts must . . . rest primarily on the language of that section,"

---

8. The court concluded its discussion thus: "Whether full disclosure has been made is not the crucial inquiry since it is the merger and the undervaluation which constituted the fraud, and not whether or not the majority determines to lay bare their real motives. If there is no valid purpose for the merger, then even the most brazen disclosure of that fact to the minority shareholders in no way mitigates the fraudulent conduct." 533 F.2d, at 1292.

11. The Court of Appeals quoted passages from Pepper v. Litton, 308 U.S. 295, 306, 311 (1939) (where this Court upheld the disallowance of a bankruptcy claim of a controlling stockholder who violated his fiduciary obligation to the other stockholders), and from 1 Story, Equity Jurisprudence §187 (1835); the court also cited cases that quoted the passage from Justice Story's treatise — Moore v. Crawford, 130 U.S. 122, 128 (1889) (a diversity suit to compel execution of a deed held in constructive trust), and SEC v. Capital Gains Research Bureau, 375 U.S. 180, 194 (1963) (Investment Advisers Act of 1940 prohibits, as a "fraud or deceit upon any client," a registered investment adviser's failure to disclose to his clients his own financial interest in his recommendations). Although *Capital Gains* involved a federal securities statute, the Court's references to fraud in the "equitable" sense of the term were premised on its recognition that Congress intended the Investment Advisers Act to establish federal fiduciary standards for investment advisers. See id., at 191-192, 194. Moreover, the fraud that the SEC sought to enjoin in *Capital Gains* was, in fact, a nondisclosure.

425 U.S., at 200, and then focused on the statutory language of §10(b) — "[t]he words 'manipulative or deceptive' used in conjunction with 'device or contrivance.'" Id., at 197. The same language and the same principle apply to this case.

To the extent that the Court of Appeals would rely on the use of the term "fraud" in Rule 10b-5 to bring within the ambit of the Rule all breaches of fiduciary duty in connection with a securities transaction, its interpretation would, like the interpretation rejected by the Court in *Ernst & Ernst*, "add a gloss to the operative language of the statute quite different from its commonly accepted meaning." Id. at 199. . . .[12]

The language of §10(b) gives no indication that Congress meant to prohibit any conduct not involving manipulation or deception. Nor have we been cited to any evidence in the legislative history that would support a departure from the language of the statute. "When a statute speaks so specifically in terms of manipulation and deception, . . . and when its history reflects no more expansive intent, we are quite unwilling to extend the scope of the statute. . . ." Id. at 214 (footnote omitted). Thus the claim of fraud and fiduciary breach in this complaint states a cause of action under any part of Rule 10b-5 only if the conduct alleged can be fairly viewed as "manipulative or deceptive" within the meaning of the statute.

It is our judgment that the transaction, if carried out as alleged in the complaint, was neither deceptive nor manipulative and therefore did not violate either §10(b) of the Act or Rule 10b-5.

As we have indicated, the case comes to us on the premise that the complaint failed to allege a material misrepresentation or material failure to disclose. . . . On the basis of the information provided, minority shareholders could either accept the price offered or reject it and seek an appraisal in the Delaware Court of Chancery. Their choice was fairly represented, and they were furnished with all relevant information on which to base their decision.

We therefore find inapposite the cases relied upon by respondents and the court below, in which the breaches of fiduciary duty held violative of Rule 10b-5 included some element of deception.[15] Those cases . . . do not support the proposition, adopted by the Court of Appeals below and urged by respondents here, that a breach of fiduciary duty by majority stockholders, without any deception, misrepresentation, or nondisclosure, violates the statute and the Rule.

---

12. The case for adhering to the language of the statute is even stronger here than in *Ernst & Ernst*, where the interpretation of Rule 10b-5 rejected by the Court was strongly urged by the Commission.

By contrast, the Commission apparently has not concluded that Rule 10b-5 should be used to reach "going private" transactions where the majority stockholder eliminates the minority at an allegedly unfair price. See SEC Securities Act Release No. 5567 (Feb. 6, 1975), CCH Federal Securities Law Reporter ¶80, 104 (proposing Rules 13e-3A and 13e-3B dealing with "going private" transactions, pursuant to six sections of the 1934 Act including §10(b), but stating that the Commission "has reached no conclusions with respect to the proposed rules"). Because we are concerned here only with §10(b), we intimate no view as to the Commission's authority to promulgate such rules under other sections of the Act.

15. The decisions of this Court relied upon by respondents all involved deceptive conduct as part of the Rule 10b-5 violation alleged. Affiliated Ute Citizens v. United States, 406 U.S. 128 (1972) (misstatements of material fact used by bank employees in position of market maker to acquire stock at less than fair value); Superintendent of Insurance v. Bankers Life & Cas. Co., 404 U.S. 6, 9 (1971) ("seller [of bonds] was duped into believing that it, the seller, would receive the proceeds"). Cf. SEC v. Capital Gains Research Bureau, 375 U.S. 180 (1963) (injunction under Investment Advisers Act of 1940 to compel registered investment adviser to disclose to his clients his own financial interest in his recommendations). . . .

It is also readily apparent that the conduct alleged in the complaint was not "manipulative" within the meaning of the statute. Manipulation is "virtually a term of art when used in connection with securities markets." *Ernst & Ernst*, 425 U.S. at 199. The term refers generally to practices, such as wash sales, matched orders, or rigged prices, that are intended to mislead investors by artificially affecting market activity. See, e.g., §9 of the 1934 Act (prohibiting specific manipulative practices); *Ernst & Ernst*, 425 U.S. at 195, 199 n.21, 205; . . . 2 A. Bromberg, Securities Law: Fraud §7.3 (1975); 3 L. Loss, Securities Regulation 1541-1570 (2d ed. 1961); 6. L. Loss, at 3755-3763 (2d ed. Supp. 1969). Section 10(b)'s general prohibition of practices deemed by the SEC to be "manipulative" — in this technical sense of artificially affecting market activity in order to mislead investors — is fully consistent with the fundamental purpose of the 1934 Act "to substitute a philosophy of full disclosure for the philosophy of caveat emptor. . . ." Affiliated Ute Citizens v. United States, 406 U.S. 128, 151 (1972), quoting SEC v. Capital Gains Research Bureau, 375 U.S. 180, 186 (1963). Indeed, nondisclosure is usually essential to the success of a manipulative scheme. 3 L. Loss, supra, at 1565. No doubt Congress meant to prohibit the full range of ingenious devices that might be used to manipulate securities prices. But we do not think it would have chosen this "term of art" if it had meant to bring within the scope of §10(b) instances of corporate mismanagement such as this, in which the essence of the complaint is that shareholders were treated unfairly by a fiduciary.

The language of the statute is, we think, "sufficiently clear in its context" to be dispositive here, *Ernst & Ernst*, 425 U.S., at 201; but even if it were not, there are additional considerations that weigh heavily against permitting a cause of action under Rule 10b-5 for the breach of corporate fiduciary duty alleged in this complaint. Congress did not expressly provide a private cause of action for violations of §10(b). Although we have recognized an implied cause of action under that section in some circumstances, Superintendent of Insurance v. Bankers Life & Cas. Co., supra, at 13, n.9, we have also recognized that a private cause of action under the antifraud provisions of the Securities Exchange Act should not be implied where it is "unnecessary to ensure the fulfillment of Congress' purposes" in adopting the Act. Piper v. Chris-Craft Industries, 97 S. Ct. at 949. Cf. J. I. Case Co. v. Borak, 377 U.S. 426, 431-433 (1964). As we noted earlier, the Court repeatedly has described the "fundamental purpose" of the Act as implementing a "philosophy of full disclosure"; once full and fair disclosure has occurred, the fairness of the terms of the transaction is at most a tangential concern of the statute. Cf. Mills v. Electric Auto-Lite Co., 396 U.S. 375, 381-385 (1970). As in Cort v. Ash, 422 U.S. 66, 80 (1975), we are reluctant to recognize a cause of action here to serve what is "at best a subsidiary purpose" of the federal legislation.

A second factor in determining whether Congress intended to create a federal cause of action in these circumstances is "whether 'the cause of action [is] one traditionally relegated to state law. . . .'" Piper v. Chris-Craft Industries, Inc., 97 S. Ct. at 949, quoting Cort v. Ash, 422 U.S., at 78. The Delaware Legislature has supplied minority shareholders with a cause of action in the Delaware Court of Chancery to recover the fair value of shares allegedly undervalued in a short-form merger. Of course, the existence of a particular state law remedy is not dispositive of the question whether Congress meant to provide a similar federal remedy, but as in *Piper* and *Cort*, we conclude that "it is entirely appropriate in this instance to relegate respondent and others in his situation to whatever remedy is created by state law." 422 U.S., at 84; 97 S. Ct. at 949.

The reasoning behind a holding that the complaint in this case alleged fraud under Rule 10b-5 could not be easily contained. It is difficult to imagine how a court could distinguish, for purposes of Rule 10b-5 fraud, between a majority stockholder's use of a short-form merger to eliminate the minority at an unfair price and the use of some other device, such as a long-form merger, tender offer, or liquidation, to achieve the same result; or indeed how a court could distinguish the alleged abuses in these going private transactions from other types of fiduciary self-dealing involving transactions in securities. The result would be to bring within the Rule a wide variety of corporate conduct traditionally left to state regulation. In addition to posing a "danger of vexatious litigation which could result from a widely expanded class of plaintiffs under Rule 10b-5," Blue Chip Stamps v. Manor Drug Stores, 421 U.S. 723, 740 (1975), this extension of the federal securities laws would overlap and quite possibly interfere with state corporate law. Federal courts applying a "federal fiduciary principle" under Rule 10b-5 could be expected to depart from state fiduciary standards at least to the extent necessary to ensure uniformity within the federal system.[16] Absent a clear indication of congressional intent, we are reluctant to federalize the substantial portion of the law of corporations that deals with transactions in securities, particularly where established state policies of corporate regulation would be overridden. As the Court stated in Cort v. Ash, supra, "Corporations are creatures of state law, and investors commit their funds to corporate directors on the understanding that, except where federal law *expressly* requires certain responsibilities of directors with respect to stockholders, state law will govern the internal affairs of the corporation." 422 U.S., at 84 (emphasis added).

We thus adhere to the position that "Congress by §10(b) did not seek to regulate transactions which constitute no more than internal corporate mismanagement." Superintendent of Insurance v. Bankers Life & Cas. Co., 404 U.S., at 12. There may well be a need for uniform federal fiduciary standards to govern mergers such as that challenged in this complaint. But those standards should not be supplied by judicial extension of §10(b) and Rule 10b-5 to "cover the corporate universe."[17]

The judgment of the Court of Appeals is reversed. . . .

Mr. Justice Brennan dissents. . . .

---

16. For example, some States apparently require a "valid corporate purpose" for the elimination of the minority interest through a short-form merger, whereas other States do not. Compare Bryan v. Brock & Blevins Co., 490 F.2d 563 (CA5), *cert. denied*, 419 U.S. 844 (1974) (merger arranged by controlling stockholder for no business purpose except to eliminate 15% minority stockholder violated Georgia short-form merger statute) with Stauffer v. Standard Brands, Inc., 41 Del. Ch. 7, 187 A.2d 78 (Sup. Ct. 1962) (Delaware short-form merger statute allows majority stockholder to eliminate the minority interest without any corporate purpose and subject only to an appraisal remedy). Thus to the extent that Rule 10b-5 is interpreted to require a valid corporate purpose for elimination of minority shareholders as well as a fair price for their shares, it would impose a stricter standard of fiduciary duty than that required by the law of some States.

17. Cary, Federalism and Corporate Law: Reflections upon Delaware, 83 Yale L.J. 663, 700 (1974) (footnote omitted). Professor Cary argues vigorously for comprehensive federal fiduciary standards, but urges a "frontal" attack by a new federal statute rather than an extension of Rule 10b-5. . . . See also Note, Going Private, 84 Yale L.J. 903 (1974) (proposing the application of traditional doctrines of substantive corporate law to problems of fairness raised by "going private" transactions such as short-form mergers).

The twilight status of corporate mismanagement cases. Had the Second Circuit's decision in *Santa Fe Industries* been upheld by the Supreme Court, it is probably correct to say (as a dissenting judge to the Second Circuit's opinion noted[64]) that the "short-form" merger statutes of approximately three-quarters of the states would have been invalidated. Thus, federalism concerns were clearly involved, and the Court's opinion was predictable, given its earlier emphasis in Cort v. Ash that "[c]orporations are creatures of state law. . . ." Still, although *Santa Fe* may have seemed to put an end to the corporate mismanagement line of cases, this was not to be the case. Within six months, the Second Circuit concluded that *Santa Fe* had not overruled Schoenbaum v. Firstbrook:

Goldberg v. Meridor
567 F. 2d 209 (2d Cir. 1977), *cert. denied*, 434 U.S. 1069 (1978)

FRIENDLY, J.: [Plaintiffs brought a derivative action on behalf of UGO, alleging that UGO's entire board has caused UGO to issue shares to its controlling parent, Maritimecor, for inadequate consideration. Rule 10b-5 was claimed to have been violated because there had been no disclosure of the transaction's allegedly fraudulent nature to UGO's minority shareholders and because several press releases represented that the transaction would benefit UGO. All directors of UGO were fully aware of the facts relating to the transaction, while in prior cases, such as *Schoenbaum*, at least one director could be said to have been deceived.] The problem with the application of §10(b) and Rule 10b-5 to derivative actions has lain in the degree to which the knowledge of officers and directors must be attributed to the corporation, thereby negating the element of deception. . . .

[No requirement exists that there be] one virtuous or ignorant lamb among the directors in order for liability to arise under §10(b) or Rule 10b-5 on a deception theory as to securities transactions with a controlling stockholder. . . .

Schoenbaum [rests] solidly on the now widely recognized ground that there is deception of the corporation (in effect, of its minority shareholders) when the corporation is influenced by its controlling shareholders to engage in a transaction adverse to the corporation's interests (in effect, the minority shareholders' interests) and there is nondisclosure or misleading disclosure as to the material facts of the transaction. Assuming that, in light of the decision in [*Santa Fe Industries*], the existence of "controlling influence" and "wholly inadequate consideration" — an aspect of the *Schoenbaum* decision that perhaps attracted more attention, see 405 F.2d at 219-20 — can no longer alone form the basis for Rule 10b-5 liability, we do not read [*Santa Fe Industries*] as ruling that no action lies under Rule 10b-5 when a controlling corporation causes a partly owned subsidiary to sell its securities to the parent in a fraudulent transaction and fails to make a disclosure or, as can be alleged here, makes a misleading disclosure. The Supreme Court noted in [*Santa Fe Industries*] that the court of appeals "did not disturb the District Court's conclusion that the complaint did not allege a material misrepresentation or nondisclosure with respect to the value of the stock" of Kirby; the Court's quarrel was with this court's holding that "neither misrepresentation nor disclosure was a necessary element of a Rule 10b-5 action," 430 U.S. at 470, and that a breach of

---

64. 533 F.2d 1283, 1299 (Moore, J., dissenting).

fiduciary duty would alone suffice, see fn. 8. It was because "the complaint failed to allege a material misrepresentation or material failure to disclose" that the Court found "inapposite the cases [including *Schoenbaum*] relied upon by respondents and the court below, in which the breaches of fiduciary duty held violative of Rule 10b-5 included some element of deception," 430 U.S. at 475, see fn. 15. While appellant is wrong in saying the Court "approved" these cases, there is no indication that the Court would have casually overturned such an impressive and unanimous body of decisions by courts of appeals. To the contrary, the Court used rather benign language about them, saying that they "forcefully reflect the principle that [§10(b) must be read flexibly not restrictively] and that the statute provides a cause of action for any plaintiff who 'suffer[s] an injury as a result of deceptive practices touching its sale [or purchase] of securities . . . ,'" citing the *Superintendent of Insurance* case, supra, 404 U.S. at 12-13. Mr. Justice White simply distinguished these cases as not supporting the position we had taken in [*Santa Fe Industries,*] namely, "that a breach of fiduciary duty by majority stockholders, *without any deception, misrepresentation, or nondisclosure,* violates the statute and the Rule." (Emphasis supplied.)

Here the complaint alleged "deceit . . . upon UGO's minority shareholders" and, if amendment had been allowed as it should have been, would have alleged misrepresentation as to the UGO-Maritimecor transaction at least in the sense of failure to state material facts "necessary in order to make the statements made in the light of the circumstances under which they were made, not misleading," Rule 10b-5(b).[8] The nub of the matter is that the conduct attacked in [*Santa Fe Industries*] did not violate the "'fundamental purpose' of the Act as implementing a 'philosophy of full disclosure,'" 430 U.S. at 478; the conduct here attacked does.

Defendants contend that even if all this is true, the failure to make a public disclosure or even the making of a misleading disclosure would have no effect, since no action by stockholders to approve the UGO-Maritimecor transaction was required. Along the same lines our brother Meskill invoking the opinion in [*Santa Fe Industries,*] 430 U.S. at 474 n.14, contends that the defendants' acts were not material since plaintiff has failed adequately to allege what would have been done had he known the truth. . . .

When, as in a derivative action, the deception is alleged to have been practiced on the corporation, even though all the directors were parties to it, the test [of materiality] must be whether the facts that were not disclosed or were misleadingly disclosed to the shareholders "would have assumed actual significance in the deliberations" of reasonable and disinterested directors or created "a substantial likelihood" that such directors would have considered the "total mix" of information available to have been "significantly altered." That was the basis for liability in *Schoenbaum*; it was likely that a reasonable director of Banff, knowing the facts as to the oil discovery that had been withheld from minority shareholders, would not have voted to issue the shares to Acquitaine at a price below their true value. . . .

Beyond this Goldberg and other minority shareholders would not have been without remedy if the alleged facts had been disclosed. The doubts entertained by

---

8. We do not mean to suggest that §10(b) or Rule 10b-5 requires insiders to characterize conflict of interest transactions with pejorative nouns or adjectives. However, if Maritimecor was in the parlous financial condition alleged in the opposing affidavit of plaintiff's counsel, a disclosure of the acquisition of Maritimecor that omitted these *facts* would be seriously misleading.

our brother as to the existence of injunctive remedies in New York ... are unfounded. ...

The availability of injunctive relief if the defendants had not lulled the minority stockholders of UGO into security by a deceptive disclosure, as they allegedly did, is in sharp contrast to [*Santa Fe Industries*] where the disclosure following the merger transaction was full and fair, and, as to the pre-merger period, respondents accepted "the conclusion of both courts below that under Delaware law they could not have enjoined the merger because an appraisal proceeding is their sole remedy in the Delaware courts for any alleged unfairness in the terms of the merger. ..."

The order dismissing the complaint is reversed and the case is remanded to the district court for further proceedings, including amendment of the complaint, consistent with this opinion.

MESKILL, J., concurring in part and dissenting in part: ... The primary role of the states in these matters has been emphasized in a number of recent opinions of the Supreme Court. ...

Those who breach their fiduciary duties seldom disclose their intentions ahead of time. Yet under the majority's reasoning the failure to inform stockholders of a proposed defalcation gives rise to a cause of action under 10b-5. Thus, the majority has neatly undone the holdings of *Green, Piper* and *Cort* by creating a federal cause of action for a breach of fiduciary duty that will apply in all cases, save those rare instances where the fiduciary denounces himself in advance.

---

1. *Does* Goldberg *undo* Santa Fe? Judge Meskill claimed in his dissent that the majority had "undone" *Santa Fe*'s holding. Is this accurate? Remember that the majority in *Goldberg* required "nondisclosure or misrepresentation as to the material facts of the transaction." Other decisions have also said that a bare allegation that the controlling party had a tainted motive for the transaction will not suffice. See Alabama Farm Bureau Mutual Casualty Co. Inc. v. American Fidelity Life Ins. Co., 606 F.2d 602, 610 (5th Cir. 1979).

2. *The "sue facts" doctrine.* Even if disclosure had been made to the shareholders in *Goldberg*, the parent corporation (Maritimecor) owned a controlling interest in its subsidiary (UGO) and could have approved the transaction. The majority responded to this argument by saying that if full disclosure had been made to the shareholders, they could have sought an injunction to halt the unfair transaction. In short, under this theory of causation, the role of disclosure was not to inform an investment decision, but to trigger a lawsuit.

Subsequent cases followed *Goldberg* in deeming the "availability of injunctive relief" to be an adequate causal link so that minority shareholders could attack the nondisclosure of material information even when they lacked the potential voting power to block the transaction. Compare Alabama Farm Bureau Mutual Casualty Co. Inc. v. American Fidelity Life Ins. Co., 606 F.2d 602, 614 (5th Cir. 1979) (minority plaintiffs need only show that there was an available state remedy that nondisclosure denied them), with Healey v. Catalyst Recovery of Pa., Inc., 616 F.2d 641, 648 (3d Cir. 1980) (plaintiffs must show a "reasonable probability of ultimate success" on state remedy to satisfy causal link). Commentators noted that this requirement produced a disturbing trial within a trial on the strength of the state law claims in order simply to find the causal nexus necessary to support the federal cause of action. Note, Suits for Breach of Fiduciary Duty Under Rule 10b-5 after Santa Fe Industries v. Green, 91 Harv. L. Rev. 1874, 1893 (1978).

3. *Does* Virginia Bankshares *undo* Goldberg? In Virginia Bankshares, Inc. v. Sandberg, 501 U.S. 1083 (1991) (page 697 infra), a shareholder who owned 85 percent of a company's stock sought to freeze out the 15 percent minority in a merger. A minority shareholder sued, claiming that material omissions in the proxy statement violated Rule 14a-9. Ruling that when a majority shareholder held sufficient shares to approve the merger by its own vote the plaintiff could not prove causation under §14(a) of the '34 Act, the Court seemed to reject all non-voting theories of causation, including *Goldberg*'s "sue facts" doctrine. Some subsequent circuit court decisions have similarly declined to follow the "sue facts" doctrine under Rule 10b-5. See, e.g., Scattergood v. Perelman, 945 F.2d 618 (3d Cir. 1991); Isquith v. Caremark International Inc., 136 F.3d 531, 534-536 (7th Cir. 1998); SEC v. Jakubowski, 150 F.3d 675 (7th Cir. 1998) (Rule 10b-5 is concerned only with informing investment decisions, not litigation decisions). *Virginia Bankshares* can be read more narrowly, however, to require only that there be a causal connection between the misrepresentation and the state law remedy. To date, the Second Circuit does not appear to have abandoned its position in *Goldberg* that loss of state law remedies can sometimes supply the requisite causal connection for purposes of Rule 10b-5. But it has narrowed the potential scope of *Goldberg*, indicating more clearly in later decisions that "allegations that a defendant failed to disclose facts material only to support an action for breach of state-law fiduciary duties ordinarily do not state a claim under the federal securities laws." See Field v. Trump, 850 F.2d 938, 948 (2d Cir. 1988) (holding that "irreparable injury to the company from willful misconduct of a self-serving nature" must instead be shown); see also Levitin v. PaineWebber, Inc., 159 F.3d 698, 704 (2d Cir. 1998). For an overview, see Scott Jordan, Loss of State Claims as a Basis for Rule 10b-5 and Rule 14a-9 Actions: The Implications of Virginia Bankshares, 49 Bus. Law. 295 (1993).

ii. Aiding and Abetting

Central Bank of Denver v. First Interstate Bank of Denver
511 U.S. 164 (1994)

Justice Kennedy delivered the opinion of the Court.

As we have interpreted it, §10(b) of the Securities Exchange Act of 1934 imposes private civil liability on those who commit a manipulative or deceptive act in connection with the purchase or sale of securities. In this case, we must answer a question reserved in two earlier decisions: whether private civil liability under §10(b) extends as well to those who do not engage in the manipulative or deceptive practice but who aid and abet the violation. . . . [Following a public housing authority's default on its bonds, the bonds' purchasers brought suit against the authority, the bonds' underwriters, the developer of the land in question, and the petitioner, as the indenture trustee for the bonds. The district court granted summary judgment for the petitioner, but the court of appeals reversed, based on precedent permitting aiding and abetting actions under §10(b).]

The bonds were secured by landowner assessment liens, which covered about 250 acres for the 1986 bond issue and about 272 acres for the 1988 bond issues. The bond covenants required that the land subject to the liens would be worth at least

160% of the bonds' outstanding principal and interest. The covenants required AmWest Development, the developer of Stetson Hills, to give Central Bank an annual report containing evidence that the 160% test was met.

In January 1988, AmWest provided Central Bank an updated appraisal of the land securing the 1986 bonds. The 1988 appraisal showed land values almost unchanged from the 1986 appraisal. Soon afterwards, Central Bank received a letter from the senior underwriter for the 1986 bonds. Noting that property values were declining in Colorado Springs and that Central Bank was operating on an appraisal over 16 months old, the underwriter expressed concern that the 160% test was not being met.

Central Bank asked its in-house appraiser to review the updated 1988 appraisal. The in-house appraiser decided that the values listed in the appraisal appeared optimistic considering the local real estate market. He suggested that Central Bank retain an outside appraiser to conduct an independent review of the 1988 appraisal. After an exchange of letters between Central Bank and AmWest in early 1988, Central Bank agreed to delay independent review of the appraisal until the end of the year, six months after the June 1988 closing on the bond issue. Before the independent review was complete, however, the Authority defaulted on the 1988 bonds. . . .

The Court of Appeals first set forth the elements of the §10(b) aiding and abetting cause of action in the Tenth Circuit: (1) a primary violation of §10(b); (2) recklessness by the aider and abettor as to the existence of the primary violation; and (3) substantial assistance given to the primary violator by the aider and abettor.

Applying that standard, the Court of Appeals found that Central Bank was aware of concerns about the accuracy of the 1988 appraisal. Central Bank knew both that the sale of the 1988 bonds was imminent and that purchasers were using the 1988 appraisal to evaluate the collateral for the bonds. Under those circumstances, the court said, Central Bank's awareness of the alleged inadequacies of the updated, but almost unchanged, 1988 appraisal could support a finding of extreme departure from standards of ordinary care. The court thus found that respondents had established a genuine issue of material fact regarding the recklessness element of aiding and abetting liability. On the separate question whether Central Bank rendered substantial assistance to the primary violators, the Court of Appeals found that a reasonable trier of fact could conclude that Central Bank had rendered substantial assistance by delaying the independent review of the appraisal. . . .

In our cases addressing §10(b) and Rule 10b-5, we have confronted two main lines. First, we have determined the scope of conduct prohibited by §10(b). See, e.g., Dirks v. SEC, 463 U.S. 646 (1983); Aaron v. SEC, 446 U.S. 680 (1980); Chiarella v. United States, 445 U.S. 222 (1980); Santa Fe Industries Inc. v. Green, 430 U.S. 462 (1977); Ernst & Ernst v. Hochfelder, 425 U.S. 185 (1976). Second, in cases where the defendant has committed a violation of §10(b), we have decided questions about the elements of the 10b-5 private liability scheme: for example, whether there is a right to contribution, what the statute of limitations is, whether there is a reliance requirement, and whether there is an in pari delicto defense. . . .

The latter issue, determining the elements of the 10b-5 private liability scheme, has posed difficulty because Congress did not create a private §10(b) cause of action and had no occasion to provide guidance about the elements of a private liability scheme. We thus have had "to infer how the 1934 Congress would have addressed the issues had the 10b-5 action been included as an express provision in the 1934 Act."

With respect, however, to the first issue, the scope of conduct prohibited by §10(b), the text of the statute controls our decision. . . .

That bodes ill for respondents, for "the language of Section 10(b) does not in terms mention aiding and abetting." Brief for SEC as Amicus Curiae 8 (hereinafter Brief for SEC). To overcome this problem, respondents and the SEC suggest (or hint at) the novel argument that the use of the phrase "directly or indirectly" in the text of §10(b) covers aiding and abetting. See Brief for Respondents 15 ("Inclusion of those who act 'indirectly' suggests a legislative purpose fully consistent with the prohibition of aiding and abetting"); Brief for SEC 8 ("We think that when read in context [§10(b)] is broad enough to encompass liability for such 'indirect' violations").

The federal courts have not relied on the "directly or indirectly" language when imposing aiding and abetting liability under §10(b), and with good reason. There is a basic flaw with this interpretation. According to respondents and the SEC, the "directly or indirectly" language shows that "Congress . . . intended to reach all persons who engage, even if only indirectly, in proscribed activities connected with securities transactions." Brief for SEC 8. The problem, of course, is that aiding and abetting liability extends beyond persons who engage, even indirectly, in a proscribed activity; aiding and abetting liability reaches persons who do not engage in the proscribed activities at all, but who give a degree of aid to those who do. A further problem with respondents' interpretation of the "directly or indirectly" language is posed by the numerous provisions of the 1934 Act that use the term in a way that does not impose aiding and abetting liability. . . .

Congress knew how to impose aiding and abetting liability when it chose to do so. See, e.g., 18 U.S.C. §2 (general criminal aiding and abetting statute). . . . If, as respondents seem to say, Congress intended to impose aiding and abetting liability, we presume it would have used the words "aid" and "abet" in the statutory text. But it did not. Cf. Pinter v. Dahl, 486 U.S., at 650 ("When Congress wished to create such liability, it had little trouble doing so"); *Blue Chip Stamps*, 421 U.S., at 734 ("When Congress wished to provide a remedy to those who neither purchase nor sell securities, it had little trouble in doing so expressly").

We reach the uncontroversial conclusion, accepted even by those courts recognizing a §10(b) aiding and abetting cause of action, that the text of the 1934 Act does not itself reach those who aid and abet a §10(b) violation. Unlike those courts, however, we think that conclusion resolves the case. It is inconsistent with settled methodology in §10(b) cases to extend liability beyond the scope of conduct prohibited by the statutory text. To be sure, aiding and abetting a wrongdoer ought to be actionable in certain instances. Cf. Restatement (Second) of Torts §876(b) (1977). The issue, however, is not whether imposing private civil liability on aiders and abettors is good policy but whether aiding and abetting is covered by the statute.

As in earlier cases considering conduct prohibited by §10(b), we again conclude that the statute prohibits only the making of a material misstatement (or omission) or the commission of a manipulative act. See *Santa Fe Industries*, 430 U.S., at 473 ("language of §10(b) gives no indication that Congress meant to prohibit any conduct not involving manipulation or deception"); *Ernst & Ernst*, 425 U.S., at 214 ("When a statute speaks so specifically in terms of manipulation and deception . . . , we are quite unwilling to extend the scope of the statute").

The proscription does not include giving aid to a person who commits a manipulative or deceptive act. We cannot amend the statute to create liability for acts that are not themselves manipulative or deceptive within the meaning of the statute.

Because this case concerns the conduct prohibited by §10(b), the statute itself resolves the case, but even if it did not, we would reach the same result. When the text of §10(b) does not resolve a particular issue, we attempt to infer "how the 1934 Congress would have addressed the issue had the 10b-5 action been included as an express provision in the 1934 Act." *Musick, Peeler*, 508 U.S., at 294. For that inquiry, we use the express causes of action in the Securities Acts as the primary model for the §10(b) action. The reason is evident: Had the 73d Congress enacted a private §10(b) right of action, it likely would have designed it in a manner similar to the other private rights of action in the Securities Acts. . . .

[The majority next reviews the various express causes of action in the '33 and '34 Acts that do not reach aiding and abetting.] From the fact that Congress did not attach private aiding and abetting liability to any of the express causes of action in the securities Acts, we can infer that Congress likely would not have attached aiding and abetting liability to §10(b) had it provided a private §10(b) cause of action. See *Musick, Peeler*, 508 U.S., at 297 ("Consistency requires us to adopt a like contribution rule for the right of action existing under Rule 10b-5"). There is no reason to think that Congress would have attached aiding and abetting liability only to §10(b) and not to any of the express private rights of action in the Act. In *Blue Chip Stamps*, we noted that it would be "anomalous to impute to Congress an intention to expand the plaintiff class for a judicially implied cause of action beyond the bounds it delineated for comparable express causes of action." Here, it would be just as anomalous to impute to Congress an intention in effect to expand the defendant class for 10b-5 actions beyond the bounds delineated for comparable express causes of action. . . .

The SEC points to various policy arguments in support of the 10b-5 aiding and abetting cause of action. It argues, for example, that the aiding and abetting cause of action deters secondary actors from contributing to fraudulent activities and ensures that defrauded plaintiffs are made whole.

Policy considerations cannot override our interpretation of the text and structure of the Act, except to the extent that they may help to show that adherence to the text and structure would lead to a result "so bizarre" that Congress could not have intended it. That is not the case here.

Extending the 10b-5 cause of action to aiders and abettors no doubt makes the civil remedy more far-reaching, but it does not follow that the objectives of the statute are better served. Secondary liability for aiders and abettors exacts costs that may disserve the goals of fair dealing and efficiency in the securities markets.

As an initial matter, the rules for determining aiding and abetting liability are unclear, in "an area that demands certainty and predictability." Pinter v. Dahl, 486 U.S., at 652. That leads to the undesirable result of decisions "made on an ad hoc basis, offering little predictive value" to those who provide services to participants in the securities business. . . . Because of the uncertainty of the governing rules, entities subject to secondary liability as aiders and abettors may find it prudent and necessary, as a business judgment, to abandon substantial defenses and to pay settlements in order to avoid the expense and risk of going to trial.

In addition, "litigation under Rule 10b-5 presents a danger of vexatiousness different in degree and in kind from that which accompanies litigation in general."

Blue Chip Stamps, supra, at 739. Litigation under 10b-5 thus requires secondary actors to expend large sums even for pretrial defense and the negotiation of settlements.

This uncertainty and excessive litigation can have ripple effects. For example, newer and smaller companies may find it difficult to obtain advice from professionals. A professional may fear that a newer or smaller company may not survive and that business failure would generate securities litigation against the professional, among others. In addition, the increased costs incurred by professionals because of the litigation and settlement costs under 10b-5 may be passed on to their client companies, and in turn incurred by the company's investors, the intended beneficiaries of the statute.

We hasten to add that competing policy arguments in favor of aiding and abetting liability can also be advanced. The point here, however, is that it is far from clear that Congress in 1934 would have decided that the statutory purposes would be furthered by the imposition of private aider and abettor liability.

Because the text of §10(b) does not prohibit aiding and abetting, we hold that a private plaintiff may not maintain an aiding and abetting suit under §10(b). The absence of §10(b) aiding and abetting liability does not mean that secondary actors in the securities markets are always free from liability under the securities Acts. Any person or entity, including a lawyer, accountant, or bank, who employs a manipulative device or makes a material misstatement (or omission) on which a purchaser or seller of securities relies may be liable as a primary violator under 10b-5, assuming all of the requirements for primary liability under Rule 10b-5 are met. . . . In any complex securities fraud, moreover, there are likely to be multiple violators; in this case, for example, respondents named four defendants as primary violators. App. 24-25.

Respondents concede that Central Bank did not commit a manipulative or deceptive act within the meaning of §10(b). Instead, in the words of the complaint, Central Bank was "secondarily liable under §10(b) for its conduct in aiding and abetting the fraud." App. 26. Because of our conclusion that there is no private aiding and abetting liability under §10(b), Central Bank may not be held liable as an aider and abettor. The District Court's grant of summary judgment to Central Bank was proper, and the judgment of the Court of Appeals is Reversed.

JUSTICE STEVENS, with whom JUSTICE BLACKMUN, JUSTICE SOUTER, and JUSTICE GINSBURG join, dissenting.

The main themes of the Court's opinion are that the text of §10(b) of the Securities Exchange Act of 1934 does not expressly mention aiding and abetting liability, and that Congress knows how to legislate. Both propositions are unexceptionable, but neither is reason to eliminate the private right of action against aiders and abettors of violations of §10(b) and the Securities and Exchange Commission's Rule 10b-5. Because the majority gives short shrift to a long history of aider and abettor liability under §10(b) and Rule 10b-5, and because its rationale imperils other well established forms of secondary liability not expressly addressed in the securities laws, I respectfully dissent.

In hundreds of judicial and administrative proceedings in every circuit in the federal system, the courts and the SEC have concluded that aiders and abettors are subject to liability under §10(b) and Rule 10b-5. See 5B A. Jacobs, Litigation and Practice Under Rule 10b-5 §40.02 (rev. ed. 1993) (citing cases). While we have reserved decision on the legitimacy of the theory in two cases that did not present it, all eleven Courts of Appeals to have considered the question have recognized a private cause of action against aiders and abettors under §10(b) and Rule 10b-5. The early aiding and abetting decisions relied upon principles borrowed from tort law; in those cases, judges closer to the times and climate of the 73d Congress than we concluded that holding aiders and abettors liable was consonant with the 1934 Act's purpose to strengthen the antifraud remedies of the common law. . . .

---

1. *Primary versus secondary liability.* What if plaintiffs had not conceded that Central Bank was liable only as a secondary participant? Could it have alleged that a material omission by one having a duty to speak violates Rule 10b-5? Under the existing cases, the line between primary and secondary liability is very unsettled. For example, although accountants were formerly sued most commonly as aiders and abettors, they may also be primarily liable — at least where a disclosure document contains misleading financial statements certified by them. Similarly, attorneys who prepare or even simply assist in the preparation of a disclosure document may also have primary liability. See Molecular Technology Corp. v. Valentine, 925 F.2d 910, 917 (6th Cir. 1991) (attorney who made editorial comments on document chiefly prepared by others may be considered a primary violator and not entitled to summary judgment). The pre–*Central Bank* case law distinguishing primary from secondary liability was notably sparse. Compare Akin v. Q-L Investments, 959 F.2d 521, 525-526 (5th Cir. 1992); Admiralty Fund v. Hugh Johnson & Co., 677 F.2d 1301, 1312 (9th Cir. 1982). Following *Central Bank*, some courts have found attorneys and accountants to be liable under a primary theory where they have been found to be "active participants" in the preparation of the allegedly misleading statement. See In re Software Toolworks Inc. Sec. Litig., 38 F.3d 1078 (9th Cir. 1994); In re ZZZZ Best Sec. Litig., 884 F. Supp. 960 (C.D. Cal. 1994). Others have restricted the liability of attorneys and accountants to instances where they actually issued the misleading opinion in their own name. See Vos Gerichian v. Commodore Int'l, 862 F. Supp. 1371 (E.D. Pa. 1994). Still other courts have distinguished misrepresentation from failure to disclose on the theory that the advisor could be liable on the latter only where it owed a fiduciary relationship to the plaintiff investors. See Employers Inc. of Wausau v. Musick, Peeler & Garrett, 871 F. Supp. 381 (S.D. Cal. 1994).

2. *Congressional response.* Efforts to restore aiding and abetting liability began in Congress within days after the *Central Bank* decision. Eventually, as part of the Private Securities Litigation Reform Act of 1995 (PSLRA), Congress enacted a new §20(e) to the Securities Exchange Act of 1934. The provision entitles the Commission to bring an injunctive action or to seek administrative penalties against "any person that knowingly provides substantial assistance to another person in violation of a provision of this title, or of any rule or regulation issued under this title." Although this provision partially overrules *Central Bank* (at least in the case of "knowing" violations), it does not permit a private plaintiff to sue based upon an "aiding and abetting" theory. This compromise protected accountants in particular, because they often could be sued prior to *Central Bank* as aiders and abettors, but could not be reached as direct violators of Rule 10b-5. The PSLRA also eased the financial exposure of accountants (and other secondary participants in a securities fraud) by substituting a regime of proportionate liability for the prior rule of joint and several liability for securities law violations. Under this revised

system, the defendants are only liable for such share of the total liability that in the factfinder's judgment reflects their relative culpability. Typically, this means that accountants and investment bankers will have much less liability than corporate executives. Not surprisingly, accountants have been sued in a relatively low percentage of cases since the passage of the PSLRA.

3. *"Scheme to defraud" liability.* Good lawyers are creative, and the plaintiff's bar responded to the loss of "aiding and abetting" liability by developing a potential replacement theory. Traditionally, plaintiffs sued under clause (b) of Rule 10b-5, which prohibits "any untrue statement of a material fact" or a material omission, but clause (a) also proscribes any "scheme or artifice to defraud." They have thus argued (with mixed success) that when an investment bank or another corporation engages in an accommodation transaction with an issuer that has no apparent legitimate business purpose other than to assist the issuer in manipulating its financial results, the third-party bank or corporation is a participant in a "scheme to defraud" and hence liable under Rule 10b-5(a). Some courts accepted this argument. See In re Parmalat Sec. Litig., 376 F. Supp. 2d 472, 492-503 (S.D.N.Y. 2005); Simpson v. AOL Time Warner Inc., 452 F.3d 1040 (9th Cir. 2006). But others have not and have insisted that only a defendant who makes a public statement can have liability under Rule 10b-5. In Stoneridge Investment Partners, LLC v. Scientific-Atlanta, Inc., 2008 U.S. LEXIS 1091, 76 U.S.L.W. 4039 (January 15, 2008), the Supreme Court resolved this debate in favor of the defendants, ruling that the plaintiffs' allegations must show that the public relied upon 2 misstatements made by the defendants or they violated a disclosure duty. The scope of Rule 10b-5, it emphasized, could only be expanded by Congress.

D. *INSIDER TRADING*

Three different sources of law bear on the topic of insider trading: (1) Rule 10b-5 is plainly applicable and in fact evolved originally as a remedy for insider trading; (2) §16(b) of the '34 Act was intended by Congress to chill (but not forbid) short-term speculative trading by insiders; and (3) in at least some jurisdictions, insider trading profits are recoverable at common law as a misuse of corporate information for which the fiduciary must account to the principal. Although the law on insider trading is well settled, a major debate has surrounded the rationale for this body of law: Who is hurt? Would they not have been injured anyway, even if the insider had not traded? Each of these topics is considered below.

1. RULE 10b-5 AND INSIDER TRADING

a. The Rationale and Scope of the Prohibition

In the Matter of Cady, Roberts & Co.
40 S.E.C. 907 (1961)

By CARY, Ch.: This is a case of first impression and one of signal importance in our administration of the Federal Securities Acts. [The SEC brought this administrative proceeding to determine whether a registered broker-dealer firm, Cady, Roberts & Co., had violated the antifraud provisions of the federal securities laws (including Rule 10b-5). Cowdin, a director of Curtiss-Wright Corp. who was also associated with Cady, Roberts & Co., attended a Curtiss-Wright board meeting at which the decision was made to cut the corporation's dividend. Cowdin left the board room and called Gintel, a Cady, Roberts partner, to inform him of the dividend cut before this information was publicly released. The firm immediately sold the Curtiss-Wright stock in the accounts of its customers and also sold "short" (i.e., it sold borrowed stock at the current market price in anticipation of a price decline after public disclosure of the dividend cut, at which point it would purchase an equivalent number of shares and return them)].

So many times that citation is unnecessary, we have indicated that the purchase and sale of securities is a field in special need of regulation for the protection of investors. To this end one of the major purposes of the securities acts is the prevention of fraud, manipulation or deception in connection with securities transactions. Consistent with this objective, Section 17(a) of the Securities Act, Section 10(b) of the Exchange Act and Rule 10b-5, issued under that Section, are broad remedial provisions aimed at reaching misleading or deceptive activities, whether or not they are precisely and technically sufficient to sustain a common law action for fraud and deceit. Indeed, despite the decline in importance of a "Federal rule" in the light of Erie R. Co. v. Tompkins, the securities acts may be said to have generated a wholly new and far-reaching body of Federal corporation law.

Section 17(a) and Rule 10b-5 . . . are not intended as a specification of particular acts or practices which constitute fraud, but rather are designed to encompass the infinite variety of devices by which undue advantage may be taken of investors and others.

Section 17 and Rule 10b-5 apply to securities transactions by "any person." Misrepresentations will lie within their ambit, no matter who the speaker may be. An affirmative duty to disclose material information has been traditionally imposed on corporate "insiders," particularly officers, directors, or controlling stockholders. We and the courts have consistently held that insiders must disclose material facts which are known to them by virtue of their position but which are not known to persons with whom they deal and which, if known, would affect their investment judgment. Failure to make disclosure in these circumstances constitutes a violation of the anti-fraud provisions. If, on the other hand, disclosure prior to effecting a purchase or sale would be improper or unrealistic under the circumstances, we believe the alternative is to forego the transaction. . . .

We have already noted that the anti-fraud provisions are phrased in terms of "any person" and that a special obligation has been traditionally required of corporate insiders, e.g., officers, directors and controlling stockholders. These three groups, however, do not exhaust the classes of persons upon whom there is such an obligation. Analytically, the obligation rests on two principal elements; first, the existence of a relationship giving access, directly or indirectly, to information intended to be available only for a corporate purpose and not for the personal benefit of anyone, and second, the inherent unfairness involved where a party takes advantage of such information knowing it is unavailable to those with whom he is dealing. In considering these elements under the broad language of the anti-fraud provisions we are not to be circumscribed by fine distinctions and rigid classifications. Thus our task here is to identify those persons who are in a special relationship with a company and privy to its internal affairs, and thereby suffer correlative duties in trading in its securities. Intimacy demands restraint lest the uninformed be exploited.

The facts here impose on Gintel the responsibilities of those commonly referred to as "insiders." He received the information prior to its public release from a director of Curtiss-Wright, Cowdin, who was associated with the registrant. Cowdin's relationship to the company clearly prohibited him from selling the securities affected by the information without disclosure. By logical sequence, it should prohibit Gintel, a partner of registrant. This prohibition extends not only over his own account, but to selling for discretionary accounts and soliciting and executing other orders. In somewhat analogous circumstances, we have charged a broker-dealer who effects securities transactions for an insider and who knows that the insider possesses non-public material information with the affirmative duty to make appropriate disclosures or dissociate himself from the transaction.

The three main subdivisions of Section 17 and Rule 10b-5 have been considered to be mutually supporting rather than mutually exclusive. Thus, a breach of duty of disclosure may be viewed as a device or scheme, an implied misrepresentation, and an act or practice, violative of all three subdivisions. Respondents argue that only clause (3) may be applicable here. We hold that, in these circumstances, Gintel's conduct at least violated clause (3) as a practice which operated as a fraud or deceit upon the purchasers. Therefore, we need not decide the scope of clauses (1) and (2).

We cannot accept respondents' contention that an insider's responsibility is limited to existing stockholders and that he has no special duties when sales of securities are made to non-stockholders. This approach is too narrow. It ignores the plight of the buying public — wholly unprotected from the misuse of special information.

Neither the statutes nor Rule 10b-5 establish artificial walls of responsibility. Section 17 of the Securities Act explicitly states that it shall be unlawful for any person in the offer or sale of securities to do certain prescribed acts. Although the primary function of Rule 10b-5 was to extend a remedy to a defrauded seller, the courts and this Commission have held that it is also applicable to a defrauded buyer. There is no valid reason why persons who *purchase* stock from an officer, director or other person having the responsibilities of an "insider" should not have the same protection afforded by disclosure of special information as persons who *sell* stock to them. Whatever distinctions may have existed at common law based on the view that an officer or director may stand in a fiduciary relationship to existing stockholders from whom he purchases but not to members of the public to whom he sells, it is clearly not appropriate to introduce these into the broader anti-fraud concepts embodied in the securities acts.

Respondents further assert that they made no express representations and did not in any way manipulate the market, and urge that in a transaction on an exchange there is no further duty such as may be required in a "face-to-face" transaction. We reject this suggestion. It would be anomalous indeed if the protection afforded by the anti-fraud provisions were withdrawn from transactions effected on exchanges, primarily markets for securities transactions. If purchasers on an exchange had available material information known by a selling insider, we may assume that their investment judgment would be affected and their decision whether to buy might accordingly be modified. Consequently, any sales by the insider must await disclosure of the information. . . .

b. The Harms from Insider Trading

Who is injured by insider trading? Are there any compensating benefits? Is it much like Prohibition — that is, a norm that is too costly to enforce? These are questions on which a vigorous debate has continued for nearly a half century and seems likely to continue. The simplest way to understand this debate is to focus first on the different kinds of injuries that can be attributed to insider trading and then on its asserted benefits. Insider trading has three distinct aspects: the trade itself, the nondisclosure of the inside information that prompted the trade, and the impact of the trading on the corporation. Each of these aspects relates to a different potential injury.

i. Corporate Harm

Least obvious but possibly most important is the impact on the corporation whose confidential plans are revealed. For example, in SEC v. Texas Gulf Sulphur Co., 401 F.2d 833 (1968), insiders purchased the company's stock in large quantities after the first drill holes indicated the company had made an enormous ore strike. Suppose as a result of their trading (and possibly their tipping friends and associates) rumors of their discovery leak into the marketplace. The result could be to compel a premature disclosure of the discovery before the corporation has had a chance to purchase the land surrounding the drill hole. Note how we assume it is acceptable not to disclose the hidden mineral value to the surrounding land owners[65] — does this distinction ultimately make good sense? Alternatively, a corporation that wished to make a tender offer for another corporation might be injured if its own agents began to purchase the target company's stock, thereby driving up the target's stock price and thus increasing the acquisition cost to their corporation. Essentially, this is what Dennis Levine and Ivan Boesky did, based on confidential information that Levine gained from his investment banking house, which acted as the agent for bidding corporations. In these cases, confidential information belonging to the corporation can be said to have been "misappropriated."

Another source of corporate injury involves the internal dynamics within the firm. If enormous gains are possible from insider trading, corporate officials may spend less time at their assigned jobs and more at searching for undisclosed material information that they can exploit; hence, there is a possible loss in managerial efficiency. In addition, fearing premature disclosure of proprietary or confidential information, corporate officials might respond by restricting access to corporate information. Restricting information flow within the firm in this manner could interfere with corporate efficiency by depriving the firm of internal dialogue, advice, and criticism. For a fuller development of this theme, see Robert Haft, The Effect of Insider Trading Rules on the Internal Efficiency of the Large Corporation, 80 Mich. L. Rev. 1051 (1982).

---

65. One of the owners of the land Texas Gulf desired to acquire was the Woollings Company, a Canadian corporation. "Texas Gulf purchased all of the shares of the Woollings Company and in that way obtained the beneficial ownership to the lands involved." Leitch Gold Mines Ltd. v. Texas Gulf Sulphur Co., 1 O.R. 469, 491-492 [1968]. Presumably, Texas Gulf did not disclose the results of its exploration to the selling stockholders. The entire transaction took place in Canada, so Rule 10b-5 did not apply.

Finally, there may be reputational harm to the corporation. Some empirical data suggests that the stock market discounts the prices of stocks that are heavily traded by insiders. See Harold Demsetz, Corporate Control, Insider Trading and Rates of Return, 76 Am. Econ. Rev. 313 (1986). If sophisticated traders avoid such stocks, both the corporation and the shareholders may suffer a loss in terms of the price they could realize for their shares. The firm's cost of capital may also be increased. See Victor Brudney, Insiders, Outsiders, and Informational Advantages under the Federal Securities Laws, 93 Harv. L. Rev. 322, 356 (1979).

ii. Allocational Efficiency and the Injury of Delayed Disclosure

If corporate managers delay the disclosure of material nonpublic information in order to first trade on such inside information themselves, this delay in the disclosure of information can impair the efficiency of the capital market, causing some firms to trade at prices that are either too high or too low. This distortion in stock prices in turn means that some corporations will have a cost of capital that does not reflect their true risks and prospects. In the aggregate, investors' savings are diverted from the most efficient uses to which they may be put to less efficient uses.

Critics of this view, that insider trading delays disclosure, argue that any delay will be minimal because the information can be disclosed immediately after the insider trades. See Henry Manne, Insider Trading and the Stock Market (1966). Indeed, it is even arguable that insider trading may increase the flow of information to the market, as insiders tip others and leak information to the market that the firm itself would not reveal. One other factor to consider is that most publicly held corporations (i.e., "reporting companies") can delay disclosure only marginally because disclosure of material information is compelled by the periodic reporting requirements specified under the '34 Act.

This claim that insider trading does not delay disclosure has been sharply attacked by others. See, e.g., Roy Schotland, Unsafe at Any Price: A Reply to Manne, 53 Va. L. Rev. 1425 (1967). One reason disclosure might be delayed involves the possible incentive to "bunch" the disclosure of items of information that are not material individually, but may be in the aggregate. Often the manager simply does not know the impact that disclosure of specific information will have on the market. For example, a significant improvement in quarterly earnings may produce a market decline on their disclosure, because the market anticipated even higher earnings. Other information may not be material enough to elicit any change in the market price by itself. To reduce the risk that the market may not move as the manager anticipates, the manager could withhold disclosure of multiple items of information in order to release this bunched information as a group, thus providing the manager a greater ability to judge the market's reaction but also clearly delaying the release of material information.

iii. Investor Injury

The seemingly simplest scenario explaining why insider trading causes injury may ultimately be the most problematic. Assume that a chief executive officer, Jones, purchases his company's stock on the market just before release of the news of a major ore discovery by his firm. Those investors who sold in the market just before the disclosure of this event will undoubtedly believe themselves injured by Jones's conduct. But have they been injured in fact? How did Jones's conduct cause their decision to sell? Had Jones refrained from trading, would they have been any better off? (Sometimes the insider trading activity may even drive the market price up marginally, thus seemingly making the disappointed sellers better off than they would have been if there had been no insider trading.)

Still, a coherent explanation is possible for why investors (rather than simply the corporate principal) can suffer economic injury based on the conduct of insiders who trade on undisclosed material information. This explanation focuses on the impact of insider trading on the market maker or specialist. Securities trade in terms of a "bid" and an "asked" price; thus, a market maker on Nasdaq may quote a "bid" (or buy) price of $18 and an "asked" (or sell) price of $18.25. The dealer stands ready to buy or sell at these prices and profits to the extent of the spread between them (here 25 cents). If persons can systematically use "inside" information, the initial victim will be the professional dealer who will be buying or selling at a disadvantage with more informed traders. The predictable response of the dealer will be to widen the spread between the bid and asked prices (perhaps to $17.75 bid and $18.50 asked in the foregoing example). This protects the dealer to a degree, but widening the spread implies that public shareholders will receive less for their securities when they sell and will pay more when they buy. More important, the injury is not limited to the specific stock in which the faithless agent traded based on inside information; rather, all stock prices are likely to be affected (to varying degrees) because the market maker or exchange specialist cannot know in advance which stocks are subject to trading based on material "inside" information. Hence, the answer to "who suffers from insider trading" becomes: all uninformed traders, who either receive less or pay more as a result. To the extent that wider spreads do result (which remains an empirical issue), then the market as a whole is made less efficient, and the issuer's cost of capital may be increased when it seeks to sell stock.

A second, more speculative scenario for investor injury involves the problem of preempted transactions. One commentator has argued that, at least in the case of an actively traded security, the insider's purchase does injure investors because it necessarily preempts a purchase that some other person would have made (given the assumption of constant trading in the market and the fact that the corporation's outstanding securities are fixed in number). Similarly, when an insider sells before impending adverse news is released, the insider preempts a sale that some other existing shareholder would have made. See William Wang, Trading on Material Nonpublic Information on Impersonal Stock Markets: Who Is Harmed, and Who Can Sue Whom Under SEC Rule 10b-5?, 54 S. Cal. L. Rev. 1217, 1235 (1981). Focusing on the transactions that would otherwise have occurred in an active trading market but for the insider's act, Professor Wang concludes: "When someone trades on nonpublic information, the group of all other investors suffers a net loss. . . . The group's net loss is equivalent to the inside trader's gain." Note, however, that under Professor Wang's theory, it is the party who did not sell or purchase who suffers the injury; this is precisely the person who lacks standing under the *Blue Chip Stamps* ruling (page 353 supra). *Query:* Is it feasible to design a remedy to compensate non-trading victims of insider trading?

Most commentators who are concerned about the injury to individual investors ultimately turn to an equity argument. They claim either that (1) all persons trading in the market should have equal access to material information, or (2) those persons who are the owners of the firm are entitled to the faithful services of their fiduciaries, who should not be allowed to reap secret profits from information they were provided for a corporate purpose. The first assertion might be called an "equal access" or "parity of information" theory, and the second a "fiduciary breach" or "property right" theory. The important differences between them will become clear in the *Dirks* case, which follows this note. Critics of the "parity of information" theory, which was essentially rejected in *Dirks*, argue that such a broad norm is unwise because it dulls the incentive to search for new or hidden information, and this reduced incentive in turn weakens market efficiency. Proponents of "equal access" would reply that efficiency must be traded off against fairness, and greater fairness is worth the price because it maintains investor confidence in the market. Arguments about investor confidence are difficult to evaluate and may sometimes serve as a justification for overregulation. Still, it is clear that on some prior occasions — most notably after the 1929 stock market crash — investors have lost confidence in the market and a massive wave of disinvestment in corporate securities has followed, which helped to prompt the New Deal's federal securities legislation.

c. The "Benefits" of Insider Trading

Proponents of insider trading make basically four arguments: (1) insider trading enhances market efficiency, in effect by pointing the market in the correct direction; (2) it is a useful system of managerial compensation that rewards entrepreneurs; (3) it is too costly to prohibit; and (4) if insider trading were harmful, corporations would have taken steps on their own to prohibit it (generally, they have not). See Dennis Carlton & Daniel Fischel, The Regulation of Insider Trading, 35 Stan. L. Rev. 857 (1983) (offering these and other arguments). Each of these claims has been vigorously disputed.

The first argument, that insider trading promotes market efficiency by causing market prices to impound and reflect the hidden information known only to the insiders, is probably more persuasive than the others, but it is not unanswerable even on the theoretical level. Insider trading is probably a relatively inefficient way to cause information to be reflected in prices. At best, the fact that insiders are trading (if this is observable) is only an indirect and ambiguous signal, and the insiders' own purchases or sales may have only a minimal impact on price. Disclosure of the hidden information is a far more efficient means by which to cause the market to respond accurately and quickly. See Ronald Gilson & Reinier Kraakman, The Mechanisms of Market Efficiency, 70 Va. L. Rev. 549, 629-634 (1984).

Another justification for insider trading is that it creates a desirable form of managerial compensation. See Henry Manne, Insider Trading and the Stock Market (1966). In Dean Manne's view, entrepreneurs are the critical innovative force that makes capitalism work; yet, he claims, they are under-rewarded by most managerial compensation systems, which fail to give the manager a sufficient stake in the enterprise to justify risk taking. In theory, insider trading offsets this deficiency and permits the successful manager to share in the firm's success that the manager caused. The problems with this analysis have been noted by a number of commentators. Many doubt that managers are systematically undercompensated; moreover, most insiders who could profit from nonpublic information cannot be fairly described as entrepreneurs (the office boy, after all, can also make millions if he knows material undisclosed information). Similarly, the person who profits may not be the person who created value; indeed, if insider trading were generally permissible, a substantial competition might develop among employees within the corporation to be among the first to learn of non-public information. This represents a species of the familiar "common pool" problem in economics, under which the absence of any clear property right leads to an inefficient competition to exploit the resource (here, nonpublic information). See Saul Levmore, Securities and Secrets: Insider Trading and the Law of Contracts, 68 Va. L. Rev. 117 (1982). Also, insiders can profit from adverse information by "selling short" — that is, borrowing stock from a broker, selling it, and then repurchasing an equivalent number of shares after the price decline following the disclosure of the adverse news. As a result, a system of compensation that allows the manager to become rich as the firm approaches bankruptcy seems perversely inefficient. Others accept Manne's contention that managers will be excessively risk-averse if they are primarily compensated through salary and similar cash compensation devices, but argue that insider trading is a poor answer to this problem because it gives rise to the wrong incentives. Specifically, if insider trading is permitted, they argue, managers will have an incentive to accept high-risk investments or projects, because they can profit from any significant price movement, up or down. See Frank Easterbrook, Insider Trading, Secret Agents, Evidentiary Privileges, and the Production of Information, 1981 Sup. Ct. Rev. 309.

Still another problem with insider trading as a compensation technique is that it leads to the receipt of secret profits. As Dean Robert Clark has observed, the common law has long been hostile to attempts by agents to reap secret profits, possibly because it is inefficient for the principal to be unable to determine or monitor the agent's compensation. The potential for secret managerial profits creates unproductive uncertainty in the capital markets. See Clark, Agency Costs Versus Fiduciary Duties, in Principals and Agents: The Structure of Business (Pratt & Zeckhauser eds., 1985); see also Kenneth Scott, Insider Trading: Rule 10b-5, Disclosure and Corporate Privacy, 9 J. Legal Stud. 801 (1980).

Proponents of legalizing insider trading have argued that if the practice were harmful, corporations would (or at least could) prohibit it by private contract. See Dannis Carlton & Daniel Fischel, The Regulation of Insider Trading, 35 Stan. L. Rev. 857, 861-866 (1983). Still, firms also do not contract with their employees to prohibit embezzlement or theft, probably because it seems superfluous to prohibit by private contract that which is already criminal. Moreover, public authorities are probably the only effective enforcers of a prohibition against insider trading. Uniquely, they can obtain search warrants, use grand juries, engage in plea bargaining, obtain bank records from foreign jurisdictions, monitor trading through the major stock exchanges' computer surveillance systems, and employ administrative sanctions (such as suspending a broker-dealer). As a practical matter, private detection and enforcement do not seem feasible.

d. The Enforceability of the Prohibition

One last argument in favor of insider trading is that it is like Prohibition — that is, a practice so prevalent and so costly to prevent that only an unlucky few scapegoats are ever caught. Of course, burglary is also prevalent in many urban areas, and arrest and clearance rates are likewise low, but few suggest legalization of this and other crimes where apprehension is difficult. Also, the Ivan Boesky scandal in 1986-1987 showed the vulnerability of organized insider trading networks; once one member is caught, he can usually be persuaded to plea-bargain and name his accomplices. The typical prosecution sequence resembles a parade of falling dominoes.

Still, how prevalent is insider trading? Many have noticed that a target corporation's stock price tends to rise sharply just before a takeover or merger offer is publicly announced. Does this fact imply that wholesale abuses of the "disclose or abstain" rule are regularly occurring? One study by Annette Poulsen and Gregg Jarrell casts some interesting light on this question. (Both authors served as the SEC's Chief Economist.) Examining pre–bid announcement market activity for 172 tender offers between 1981 and 1985, they found readily observable characteristics of the typical takeover bid that could account for a substantial portion of the pre-bid run-up in price. See Jarrell & Poulsen, Stock Trading Before the Announcement of Tender Offers: Insider Trading or Market Anticipation?, 5 J. Law Econ. & Org. 225 (1989). In particular, their data seem to show that about one-third of the pre-bid market activity could be attributed to takeover speculation in the media; in addition, market professionals could observe foothold acquisitions, and the pre-announcement run-up was significantly higher in cases where the bidder engaged in such pre-bid purchasing. As a result, they concluded that legitimate securities research focusing on observable events could account for much of the pre-announcement market activity. For policy purposes, the implication of this research is not that insider trading is rare or uncommon but that all pre-announcement market activity cannot be given a sinister interpretation. Rather, there may be a legitimate role for professional securities research in this area, because by observing unusual trading activity and other signs of impending merger activity, the professional can lawfully anticipate future events and earn profits in this field, just as in other areas where information is valuable but costly.

Dirks v. SEC
463 U.S. 646 (1983)

Justice Powell delivered the opinion of the Court.

Petitioner Raymond Dirks received material nonpublic information from "insiders" of a corporation with which he had no connection. He disclosed this information to investors, who relied on it in trading in the shares of the corporation. The question is whether Dirks violated the antifraud provisions of the federal securities laws by this disclosure.

In 1973, Dirks was an officer of a New York broker-dealer firm who specialized in providing investment analysis of insurance company securities to institutional investors. On March 6, Dirks received information from Ronald Secrist, a former officer of Equity Funding of America. Secrist alleged that the assets of Equity Funding, a diversified corporation primarily engaged in selling life insurance and mutual funds, were vastly overstated as the result of fraudulent corporate practices. Secrist also stated that various regulatory agencies had failed to act on similar charges made by Equity Funding employees. He urged Dirks to verify the fraud and disclose it publicly.

Dirks decided to investigate the allegations. He visited Equity Funding's headquarters in Los Angeles and interviewed several officers and employees of the corporation. The senior management denied any wrongdoing, but certain corporation employees corroborated the charges of fraud. Neither Dirks nor his firm owned or traded any Equity Funding stock, but throughout his investigation he openly discussed the information he had obtained with a number of clients and investors. Some of these persons sold their holdings of Equity Funding securities, including five investment advisers who liquidated holdings of more than $16 million.[2]

While Dirks was in Los Angeles, he was in touch regularly with William Blundell, The Wall Street Journal's Los Angeles bureau chief. Dirks urged Blundell to write a story on the fraud allegations. Blundell did not believe, however, that such a massive fraud could go undetected and declined to write the story. He feared that publishing such damaging hearsay might be libelous.

During the two-week period in which Dirks pursued his investigation and spread word of Secrist's charges, the price of Equity Funding stock fell from $26 per share to less than $15 per share. This led the New York Stock Exchange to halt trading on March 27. Shortly thereafter California insurance authorities impounded Equity Funding's records and uncovered evidence of the fraud. Only then did the Securities and Exchange Commission (SEC) file a complaint against Equity Funding[3] and only then, on April 2, did The Wall Street Journal publish a front-page story based largely on information assembled by Dirks. Equity Funding immediately went into receivership.[4]

The SEC . . . found that Dirks had aided and abetted violations of Rule 10b-5 by repeating the allegations of fraud to members of the investment community who later sold their Equity Funding stock. The SEC concluded: "Where 'tippees' — regardless of their motivation or occupation — come into possession of material 'information that they know is confidential and know or should know came from a corporate insider,' they must either publicly disclose that information or refrain from trading." 21 S.E.C. Docket 1401, 1407 (1981) (footnote omitted) (quoting Chiarella v. United States, 445 U.S. 222, 230 n.12 (1980)). Recognizing, however, that Dirks "played an important role in bringing [Equity Funding's] massive fraud to light," 21 S.E.C. Docket, at 1412,[8] the SEC only censured him. [The Court of Appeals affirmed.] . . .

2. Dirks received from his firm a salary plus a commission for securities transactions above a certain amount that his clients directed through his firm. . . . But "[i]t is not clear how many of those with whom Dirks spoke promised to direct some brokerage business through [Dirk's firm] to compensate Dirks, or how many actually did so." 220 U.S. App. D.C., at 316, 681 F.2d, at 831. The Boston Company Institutional Investors, Inc., promised Dirks about $25,000 in commissions, but it is unclear whether Boston actually generated any brokerage business for his firm.

3. As early as 1971, the SEC had received allegations of fraudulent accounting practices at Equity Funding. Moreover, on March 9, 1973, an official of the California Insurance Department informed the SEC's regional office in Los Angeles of Secrist's charges of fraud. Dirks himself voluntarily presented his information at the SEC's regional office beginning on March 27.

4. A federal grand jury in Los Angeles subsequently returned a 105-count indictment against 22 persons, including many of Equity Funding's officers and directors. All defendants were found guilty of one or more counts. . . .

8. Justice Blackmun's dissenting opinion minimizes the role Dirks played in making public the Equity Funding fraud. See post, at 67 and 69, n.15. The dissent would rewrite the history of Dirks' extensive investigative efforts. See, e.g., 21 S.E.C., at 1412 ("It is clear that Dirks played an important role in bringing [Equity Funding's] massive fraud to light, and it is also true that he reported the fraud allegation to [Equity Funding's] auditors and sought to have the information published in the Wall Street Journal."); 681 F.2d, at 829 (Wright, J.) ("Largely thanks to Dirks one of the most infamous frauds in recent memory was uncovered and exposed, while the record shows that the SEC repeatedly missed opportunities to investigate Equity Funding.")

In the seminal case of In re Cady, Roberts & Co., 40 S.E.C. 907 (1961), the SEC recognized that the common law in some jurisdictions imposes on "corporate 'insiders,' particularly officers, directors, or controlling stockholders" an "affirmative duty of disclosure . . . when dealing in securities." Id., at 911, and n.13.[10] The SEC found that not only did breach of this common-law duty also establish the elements of a Rule 10b-5 violation, but that individuals other than corporate insiders could be obligated either to disclose material nonpublic information[12] before trading or to abstain from trading altogether. Id., at 912. In Chiarella [v. United States, 445 U.S. 222 (1980),] we accepted the two elements set out in *Cady, Roberts* for establishing a Rule 10b-5 violation: "(i) the existence of a relationship affording access to inside information intended to be available only for a corporate purpose, and (ii) the unfairness of allowing a corporate insider to take advantage of that information by trading without disclosure." 445 U.S., at 227. In examining whether Chiarella had an obligation to disclose or abstain, the Court found that there is no general duty to disclose before trading on material nonpublic information, and held that "a duty to disclose under §10(b) does not arise from the mere possession of nonpublic market information." Id., at 235. Such a duty arises rather from the existence of a fiduciary relationship. See id., at 227-235.

Not "all breaches of fiduciary duty in connection with a securities transaction," however, come within the ambit of Rule 10b-5. Santa Fe Industries, Inc. v. Green, 430 U.S. 462, 472 (1977). There must also be "manipulation or deception." Id., at 473. In an inside-trading case this fraud derives from the "inherent unfairness involved where one takes advantage" of "information intended to be available only for a corporate purpose and not for the personal benefit of anyone." In re Merrill Lynch, Pierce, Fenner & Smith, Inc., 43 S.E.C. 933, 936 (1968). Thus, an insider will be liable under Rule 10b-5 for inside trading only where he fails to disclose material nonpublic information before trading on it and thus makes "secret profits." *Cady, Roberts*, 40 S.E.C., at 916, n.31.

We were explicit in *Chiarella* in saying that there can be no duty to disclose where the person who has traded on inside information "was not [the corporation's] agent, . . . was not a fiduciary, [or] was not a person in whom the sellers [of the securities] had placed their trust and confidence." 445 U.S., at 232. Not to require such a fiduciary relationship, we recognized, would "depar[t] radically from the established doctrine that duty arises from a specific relationship between two parties" and would amount to "recognizing a general duty between all participants in market transactions to forgo actions based on material, nonpublic information." Id., at 232, 233. This requirement of a specific relationship between the shareholders and the individual trading on inside information has created

---

10. The duty that insiders owe to the corporation's shareholders not to trade on inside information differs from the common-law duty that officers and directors also have to the corporation itself not to mismanage corporate assets, of which confidential information is one. See 3 Fletcher Cyclopedia of the Laws of Private Corporation §§848, 900 (1975 ed. and Supp. 1982); 3A Fletcher §§1168.1, 1168.2. In holding that breaches of this duty to shareholders violated the Securities Exchange Act, the *Cady, Roberts* Commission recognized, and we agree, that "[a] significant purpose of the Exchange Act was to eliminate the idea that use of inside information for personal advantage was a normal emolument of corporate office." See 40 S.E.C., at 912, n.15.

12. The SEC views the disclosure duty as requiring more than disclosure to purchasers or sellers: "Proper and adequate disclosure of significant corporate developments can only be effected by a public release through the appropriate public media, designed to achieve a broad dissemination to the investing public generally and without favoring any special person or group." In re Faberge, Inc., 45 S.E.C. 249, 256 (1973).

analytical difficulties for the SEC and courts in policing tippees who trade on inside information. Unlike insiders who have independent fiduciary duties to both the corporation and its shareholders, the typical tippee has no such relationships.[14] In view of this absence, it has been unclear how a tippee acquires the *Cady, Roberts* duty to refrain from trading on inside information.

The SEC's position, as stated in its opinion in this case, is that a tippee "inherits" the *Cady, Roberts* obligation to shareholders whenever he receives inside information from an insider:

> In tipping potential traders, Dirks breached a duty which he had assumed as a result of knowingly receiving confidential information from [Equity Funding] insiders. Tippees such as Dirks who receive nonpublic material information from insiders become "subject to the same duty as [the] insiders." Shapiro v. Merrill Lynch, Pierce, Fenner & Smith, Inc. [495, F.2d 228, 237 (CA2 1974) (quoting Ross v. Licht, 263 F. Supp. 395, 410 (S.D.N.Y. 1967))]. Such a tippee breaches the fiduciary duty which he assumes from the insider when the tippee knowingly transmits the information to someone who will probably trade on the basis thereof. . . . Presumably, Dirks' informants were entitled to disclose the [Equity Funding] fraud in order to bring it to light and its perpetrators to justice. However, Dirks—standing in their shoes—committed a breach of the fiduciary duty which he had assumed in dealing with them, when he passed the information on to traders. 21 S.E.C. Docket, at 1410, n.42.

This view differs little from the view that we rejected as inconsistent with congressional intent in *Chiarella*. In that case, the Court of Appeals agreed with the SEC and affirmed Chiarella's conviction, holding that "'[a]nyone—corporate insider or not—who regularly receives material nonpublic information may not use that information to trade in securities without incurring an affirmative duty to disclose.'" United States v. Chiarella, 588 F.2d 1358, 1365 (CA2 1978) (emphasis in original). Here, the SEC maintains that anyone who knowingly receives nonpublic material information from an insider has a fiduciary duty to disclose before trading.[15]

---

14. Under certain circumstances, such as where corporate information is revealed legitimately to an underwriter, accountant, lawyer, or consultant working for the corporation, these outsiders may become fiduciaries of the shareholders. The basis for recognizing this fiduciary duty is not simply that such persons acquired nonpublic corporate information, but rather that they have entered into a special confidential relationship in the conduct of the business of the enterprise and are given access to information solely for corporate purposes. See SEC v. Monarch Fund, 608 F.2d 938, 942 (CA2 1979); In re Investors Management Co., 44 S.E.C. 633, 645 (1971); In re Van Alstyne, Noel & Co., 43 S.E.C. 1080, 1084-1085 (1969); In re Merrill Lynch, Pierce, Fenner & Smith, Inc., 43 S.E.C. 933, 937 (1968); Cady, Roberts, 40 S.E.C., at 912. When such a person breaches his fiduciary relationship, he may be treated more properly as a tipper than a tippee. See Shapiro v. Merrill Lynch, Pierce, Fenner & Smith, Inc., 495 F.2d 228, 237 (CA2 1974) (investment banker had access to material information when working on a proposed public offering for the corporation). For such a duty to be imposed, however, the corporation must expect the outsider to keep the disclosed nonpublic information confidential, and the relationship at least must imply such a duty.

15. Apparently, the SEC believes this case differs from *Chiarella* in that Dirks' receipt of inside information from Secrist, an insider, carried Secrist's duties with it, while Chiarella received the information without the direct involvement of an insider and thus inherited no duty to disclose or abstain. The SEC fails to explain, however, why the receipt of nonpublic information from an insider automatically carries with it the fiduciary duty of the insider. As we emphasized in *Chiarella*, mere possession of nonpublic information does not give rise to a duty to disclose or abstain; only a specific relationship does that. And we do not believe that the mere receipt of information from an insider creates such a special relationship between the tippee and the corporation's shareholders.

In effect, the SEC's theory of tippee liability in both cases appears rooted in the idea that the antifraud provisions require equal information among all traders. This conflicts with the principle set forth in *Chiarella* that only some persons, under some circumstances, will be barred from trading while in possession of material nonpublic information.[16] . . .

Imposing a duty to disclose or abstain solely because a person knowingly receives material nonpublic information from an insider and trades on it could have an inhibiting influence on the role of market analysts, which the SEC itself recognizes is necessary to the preservation of a healthy market.[17] It is commonplace for analysts to "ferret out and analyze information," 21 S.E.C., at 1406,[18] and this often is done by meeting with and questioning corporate officers and others who are insiders. And information that the analysts obtain normally may be the basis for judgments as to the market worth of a corporation's securities. The analyst's judgment in this respect is made available in market letters or otherwise to clients of the firm. It is the nature of this type of information, and indeed of the markets themselves, that such information cannot be made simultaneously available to all of the corporation's stockholders or the public generally.

The conclusion that recipients of inside information do not invariably acquire a duty to disclose or abstain does not mean that such tippees always are free to trade on the information. The need for a ban on some tippee trading is clear. Not only are insiders forbidden by the fiduciary relationship from personally

---

Apparently recognizing the weakness of its argument in light of *Chiarella*, the SEC attempts to distinguish that case factually as involving not "inside" information, but rather "market" information, i.e., "information generated within the company relating to its assets or earnings." Brief for Respondent 23. This Court drew no such distinction in *Chiarella* and, as the Chief Justice noted, "[i]t is clear that §10(b) and Rule 10b-5 by their terms and by their history make no such distinction," 445 U.S., at 241, n.1 (dissenting opinion). See ALI Fed. Sec. Code §1603, Comment (2)(j) (Proposed Official Draft 1978).

16. In *Chiarella*, we noted that formulation of an absolute equal information rule "should not be undertaken absent some explicit evidence of congressional intent." 445 U.S., at 233. Rather than adopting such a radical view of securities trading, Congress has expressly exempted many market professionals from the general statutory prohibition set forth in §11(a)(1) of the Securities Exchange Act, 15 U.S.C. §78k(a)(1), against members of a national securities exchange trading for their own account. See id., at 233, n.16. We observed in *Chiarella* that "[t]he exception is based upon Congress' recognition that [market professionals] contribute to a fair and orderly marketplace at the same time they exploit the informational advantage that comes from their possession of [nonpublic information]." Ibid.

17. The SEC expressly recognized that "[t]he value to the entire market of [analysts'] efforts cannot be gainsaid; market efficiency in pricing is significantly enhanced by [their] initiatives to ferret out and analyze information, and thus the analyst's work redounds to the benefit of all investors." 21 S.E.C., at 1406. The SEC asserts that analysts remain free to obtain from management corporate information for purposes of "filling in the 'interstices in analysis.' . . ." Brief for Respondent 42 (quoting Investors Management Co., 44 S.E.C., at 646). But this rule is inherently imprecise, and imprecision prevents parties from ordering their actions in accord with legal requirements. Unless the parties have some guidance as to where the line is between permissible and impermissible disclosures and uses, neither corporate insiders nor analysts can be sure when the line is crossed. Cf. Adler v. Klawans, 267 F.2d 840, 845 (CA 1959) (Burger, J., sitting by designation).

18. On its facts, this case is the unusual one. Dirks is an analyst in a broker-dealer firm, and he did interview management in the course of his investigation. He uncovered, however, startling information that required no analysis or exercise of judgment as to its market relevance. Nonetheless, the principle at issue here extends beyond these facts. The SEC's rule — applicable without regard to any breach by an insider — could have serious ramifications on reporting by analysts of investment views.

Despite the unusualness of Dirks' "find," the central role that he played in uncovering the fraud at Equity Funding, and that analysts in general can play in revealing information that corporations may have reason to withhold from the public, is an important one. Dirks' careful investigation brought to light a massive fraud at the corporation. And until the Equity Funding fraud was exposed, the information in the trading market was grossly inaccurate. But for Dirks' efforts, the fraud might well have gone undetected longer. See n.8, supra.

using undisclosed corporate information to their advantage, but they may not give such information to an outsider for the same improper purpose of exploiting the information for their personal gain. . . . Similarly, the transactions of those who knowingly participate with the fiduciary in such a breach are "as forbidden" as transactions "on behalf of the trustee himself." Mosser v. Darrow, 341 U.S. 267, 272 (1951). See Jackson v. Smith, 254 U.S. 586, 589 (1921); Jackson v. Ludeling, 88 U.S. (21 Wall) 616, 631-632 (1874). As the Court explained in *Mosser*, a contrary rule "would open up opportunities for devious dealings in the name of the others that the trustee could not conduct in his own." 341 U.S., at 271. See SEC v. Texas Gulf Sulphur Co., 446 F.2d 1301, 1308 (CA2), *cert. denied*, 404 U.S. 1005 (1971). Thus, the tippee's duty to disclose or abstain is derivative from that of the insider's duty. . . . As we noted in *Chiarella*, "[t]he tippee's obligation has been viewed as arising from his role as a participant after the fact in the insider's breach of a fiduciary duty." 445 U.S., at 230, n.12.

Thus, some tippees must assume an insider's duty to the shareholders not because they receive inside information, but rather because it has been made available to them *improperly*.[19] And for Rule 10b-5 purposes, the insider's disclosure is improper only where it would violate his *Cady, Roberts* duty. Thus, a tippee assumes a fiduciary duty to the shareholders of a corporation not to trade on material nonpublic information only when the insider has breached his fiduciary duty to the shareholders by disclosing the information to the tippee and the tippee knows or should know that there has been a breach.[20] As Commissioner Smith perceptively observed in *Investors Management Co.*: "[T]ippee responsibility must be related back to insider responsibility by a necessary finding that the tippee knew the information was given to him in breach of a duty by a person having a special relationship to the issuer not to disclose the information. . . ." 44 S.E.C., at 651 (concurring in the result). Tipping thus properly is viewed only as a means of indirectly violating the *Cady, Roberts* disclose-or-abstain rule.[21]

19. The SEC itself has recognized that tippee liability properly is imposed only in circumstances where the tippee knows, or has reason to know, that the insider has disclosed improperly inside corporate information. In *Investors Management Co.*, supra, the SEC stated that one element of tippee liability is that the tippee knew or had reason to know "that [the information] was non-public and had been obtained *improperly* by selective revelation or otherwise." 44 S.E.C., at 641 (emphasis added). Commissioner Smith read this test to mean that a tippee can be held liable only if he received information in breach of an insider's duty not to disclose it. Id., at 650 (concurring in the result).

20. Professor Loss has linked tippee liability to the concept in the law of restitution that "'[w]here a fiduciary in violation of his duty to the beneficiary communicates confidential information to a third person, the third person, if he had notice of the violation of duty, holds upon a constructive trust for the beneficiary any profit which he makes through the use of such information.'" 3 L. Loss, Securities Regulation 1451 (2d ed. 1961) (quoting Restatement of Restitution §201(2) (1937)). Other authorities likewise have expressed the view that tippee liability exists only where there has been a breach of trust by an insider of which the tippee had knowledge. See, e.g., Ross v. Licht, 263 F. Supp. 395, 410 (S.D.N.Y. 1967); A. Jacobs, The Impact of Rule 10b-5, §167, at 7-4 (1975) ("[T]he better view is that a tipper must know or have reason to know the information is nonpublic and was improperly obtained."); Fleischer, Mundheim & Murphy, An Initial Inquiry Into the Responsibility to Disclose Market Information, 121 U. Pa. L. Rev. 798, 818, n.76 (1973) ("The extension of rule 10b-5 restrictions to tippees of corporate insiders can best be justified on the theory that they are participating in the insider's breach of his fiduciary duty."). Cf. Restatement (Second) of Agency §312, comment c (1958) ("A person who, with notice that an agent is thereby violating his duty to his principal, receives confidential information from an agent, may be [deemed] . . . a constructive trustee.").

21. We do not suggest that knowingly trading on inside information is ever "socially desirable or even that it is devoid of moral considerations." Dooley, Enforcement of Insider Trading Restrictions, 66 Va. L. Rev. 1, 55 (1980). Nor do we imply an absence of responsibility to disclose promptly indications of illegal actions by a corporation to the proper authorities — typically the SEC and exchange authorities in

In determining whether a tippee is under an obligation to disclose or abstain, it thus is necessary to determine whether the insider's "tip" constituted a breach of the insider's fiduciary duty. All disclosures of confidential corporate information are not inconsistent with the duty insiders owe to shareholders. In contrast to the extraordinary facts of this case, the more typical situation in which there will be a question whether disclosure violates the insider's *Cady, Roberts* duty is when insiders disclose information to analysts. See n.16, supra. In some situations, the insider will act consistently with his fiduciary duty to shareholders, and yet release of the information may affect the market. For example, it may not be clear — either to the corporate insider or to the recipient analyst — whether the information will be viewed as material nonpublic information. Corporate officials may mistakenly think the information already has been disclosed or that it is not material enough to affect the market. Whether disclosure is a breach of duty therefore depends in large part on the purpose of the disclosure. This standard was identified by the SEC itself in *Cady, Roberts:* a purpose of the securities laws was to eliminate "use of inside information for personal advantage." 40 S.E.C., at 912, n.15. See n.10, supra. Thus, the test is whether the insider personally will benefit, directly or indirectly, from his disclosure. Absent some personal gain, there has been no breach of duty to stockholders. And absent a breach by the insider, there is no derivative breach.[22] As Commissioner Smith stated in *Investors Management Co.:* "It is important in this type of case to focus on policing insiders and what they do . . . rather than on policing information per se and its possession. . . ." 44 S.E.C., at 648 (concurring in the result).

The SEC argues that, if inside-trading liability does not exist when the information is transmitted for a proper purpose but is used for trading, it would be a rare situation when the parties could not fabricate some ostensibly legitimate business justification for transmitting the information. We think the SEC is unduly concerned. In determining whether the insider's purpose in making a particular disclosure is fraudulent, the SEC and the courts are not required to read the parties' minds. Scienter in some cases is relevant in determining whether the tipper has violated his *Cady, Roberts* duty.[23] But to determine whether the disclosure itself "deceive[s], manipulate[s], or defraud[s]" shareholders, Aaron v. SEC, 446 U.S. 680, 686 (1980), the initial inquiry is whether there has been a breach of duty by the insider. This requires courts to focus on objective criteria, i.e., whether the insider receives a direct or indirect personal benefit from the disclosure, such as a pecuniary gain or a reputational benefit that will translate into future

cases involving securities. Depending on the circumstances, and even where permitted by law, one's trading on material nonpublic information is behavior that may fall below ethical standards of conduct. But in a statutory area of the law such as securities regulation, where legal principles of general application must be applied, there may be "significant distinctions between actual legal obligations and ethical ideals." SEC, Report of the Special Study of Securities Markets, H.R. Doc. No. 95, 88th Cong., 1st Sess., pt. 1, pp. 237-238 (1963). . . .

22. An example of a case turning on the court's determination that the disclosure did not impose any fiduciary duties on the recipient of the inside information is Walton v. Morgan Stanley & Co., 623 F.2d 796 (CA2 1980).

23. Contrary to the dissent's suggestion, see post, n.10, motivation is not irrelevant to the issue of scienter. It is not enough that an insider's conduct results in harm to investors; rather, a violation may be found only where there is "intentional or willful conduct designed to deceive or defraud investors by controlling or artificially affecting the price of securities." Ernst & Ernst v. Hochfelder, 425 U.S., at 199. The issue in this case, however, is not whether Secrist or Dirks acted with scienter, but rather whether there was any deceptive or fraudulent conduct at all, i.e., whether Secrist's disclosure constituted a breach of his fiduciary duty and thereby caused injury to shareholders. See n.27, infra. Only if there was such a breach did Dirks, a tippee, acquire a fiduciary duty to disclose or abstain.

earnings. Cf. 40 S.E.C., at 912, n.15; Brudney, Insiders, Outsiders, and Informational Advantages Under the Federal Securities Laws, 93 Harv. L. Rev. 324, 348 (1979) ("The theory . . . is that the insider, by giving the information out selectively, is in effect selling the information to its recipient for cash, reciprocal information, or other things of value for himself. . . ."). There are objective facts and circumstances that often justify such an inference. For example, there may be a relationship between the insider and the recipient that suggests a quid pro quo from the latter, or an intention to benefit the particular recipient. The elements of fiduciary duty and exploitation of nonpublic information also exist when an insider makes a gift of confidential information to a trading relative or friend. The tip and trade resemble trading by the insider himself followed by a gift of the profits to the recipient.

Determining whether an insider personally benefits from a particular disclosure, a question of fact, will not always be easy for courts. But it is essential, we think, to have a guiding principle for those whose daily activities must be limited and instructed by the SEC's inside-trading rules, and we believe that there must be a breach of the insider's fiduciary duty before the tippee inherits the duty to disclose or abstain. In contrast, the rule adopted by the SEC in this case would have no limiting principle.[24]

Under the inside-trading and tipping rules set forth above, we find that there was no actionable violation by Dirks. It is undisputed that Dirks himself was a stranger to Equity Funding, with no pre-existing fiduciary duty to its shareholders. He took no action, directly or indirectly, that induced the shareholders or officers of Equity Funding to repose trust or confidence in him. There was no expectation by Dirks' sources that he would keep their information in confidence. Nor did Dirks misappropriate or illegally obtain the information about Equity Funding. Unless the insiders breached their *Cady, Roberts* duty to shareholders in disclosing the nonpublic information to Dirks, he breached no duty when he passed it on to investors as well as to The Wall Street Journal.

It is clear that neither Secrist nor the other Equity Funding employees violated their *Cady, Roberts* duty to the corporation's shareholders by providing information to Dirks.[27] The tippers received no monetary or personal benefit for revealing

24. Without legal limitations, market participants are forced to rely on the reasonableness of the SEC's litigation strategy, but that can be hazardous, as the facts of this case make plain. . . .

27. In this Court, the SEC appears to contend that an insider invariably violates a fiduciary duty to the corporation's shareholders by transmitting nonpublic corporate information to an outsider when he has reason to believe that the outsider may use it to the disadvantage of the shareholders. . . . This perceived "duty" differs markedly from the one that the SEC identified in *Cady, Roberts* and that has been the basis for federal tippee-trading rules to date. In fact, the SEC did not charge Secrist with any wrongdoing, and we do not understand the SEC to have relied on any theory of a breach of duty by Secrist in finding that Dirks breached his duty to Equity Funding's shareholders. . . .

The dissent argues that "Secrist violated his duty to Equity Funding shareholders by transmitting material nonpublic information to Dirks with the intention that Dirks would cause his clients to trade on that information." Post, at 70. By perceiving a breach of fiduciary duty whenever inside information is intentionally disclosed to securities traders, the dissenting opinion effectively would achieve the same result as the SEC's theory below, i.e., mere possession of inside information while trading would be viewed as a Rule 10b-5 violation. But *Chiarella* made it explicitly clear there is no general duty to forgo market transactions "based on material, nonpublic information." . . .

Moreover, to constitute a violation of Rule 10b-5, there must be fraud. See Ernst & Ernst v. Hochfelder, 425 U.S. 185. . . . There is no evidence that Secrist's disclosure was intended to or did in fact "deceive or defraud" anyone. Secrist certainly intended to convey relevant information that management was unlawfully concealing, and — so far as the record shows — he believed that persuading Dirks to investigate was the best way to disclose the fraud. Other efforts had proved fruitless. Under any objective standard, Secrist received no direct or indirect personal benefit from the disclosure.

Equity Funding's secrets, nor was their purpose to make a gift of valuable information to Dirks. As the facts of this case clearly indicate, the tippers were motivated by a desire to expose the fraud. In the absence of a breach of duty to shareholders by the insiders, there was no derivative breach by Dirks. Dirks therefore could not have been "a participant after the fact in [an] insider's breach of a fiduciary duty." *Chiarella*, 445 U.S., at 230, n.12.

We conclude that Dirks, in the circumstances of this case, had no duty to abstain from use of the inside information that he obtained. The judgment of the Court of Appeals therefore is reversed.

JUSTICE BLACKMUN, with whom JUSTICE BRENNAN and JUSTICE MARSHALL join, dissenting.

The Court today takes still another step to limit the protections provided investors by §10(b) of the Securities Exchange Act of 1934. . . . The device employed in this case engrafts a special motivational requirement on the fiduciary duty doctrine. This innovation excuses a knowing and intentional violation of an insider's duty to shareholders if the insider does not act from a motive of personal gain. Even on the extraordinary facts of this case, such an innovation is not justified.

After a meeting with Ronald Secrist, a former Equity Funding employee, on March 7, 1973, App. 226, petitioner Raymond Dirks found himself in possession of material nonpublic information of massive fraud within the company.[2] . . . In disclosing that information to Dirks, Secrist intended that Dirks would disseminate the information to his clients, those clients would unload their Equity Funding securities on the market, and the price would fall precipitously, thereby triggering a reaction from the authorities.

Dirks complied with his informant's wishes. Instead of reporting that information to the Securities and Exchange Commission (SEC or Commission) or to other regulatory agencies, Dirks began to disseminate the information to his clients and undertook his own investigation.[3] . . .

No one questions that Secrist himself could not trade on his inside information to the disadvantage of uninformed shareholders and purchasers of Equity Funding securities. . . . Unlike the printer in *Chiarella*, Secrist stood in a fiduciary relationship with these shareholders. . . .

The dissenting opinion focuses on shareholder "losses," "injury," and "damages," but in many cases there may be no clear causal connection between inside trading and outsiders' losses. In one sense, as market values fluctuate and investors act on inevitably incomplete or incorrect information, there always are winners and losers; but those who have "lost" have not necessarily been defrauded. On the other hand, inside trading for personal gain is fraudulent, and is a violation of the federal securities laws. See Dooley, supra, at 39-41, 70. Thus, there is little legal significance to the dissent's argument that Secrist and Dirks created new "victims" by disclosing the information to persons who traded. In fact, they prevented the fraud from continuing and victimizing many more investors.

2. Unknown to Dirks, Secrist also told his story to New York insurance regulators the same day. App. 23. They immediately assured themselves that Equity Funding's New York subsidiary had sufficient assets to cover its outstanding policies and then passed on the information to California regulators, who in turn informed Illinois regulators. Illinois investigators, later joined by California officials, conducted a surprise audit of Equity Funding's Illinois subsidiary, id., at 87-88, to find $22 million of the subsidiary's assets missing. On March 30, these authorities seized control of the Illinois subsidiary. Id., at 271.

3. In the same administrative proceeding at issue here, the Administrative Law Judge (ALJ) found that Dirks' clients—five institutional investment advisors—violated Rule 10b-5 by trading on Dirks' tips. App. 297. All the clients were censured, except Dreyfus Corporation. The ALJ found that Dreyfus had made significant efforts to disclose the information to Goldman, Sachs, the purchaser of its securities. None of Dirks' clients appealed these determinations.

The Court also acknowledges that Secrist could not do by proxy what he was prohibited from doing personally. . . . But this is precisely what Secrist did. Secrist used Dirks to disseminate information to Dirks' clients, who in turn dumped stock on unknowing purchasers. Secrist thus intended Dirks to injure the purchasers of Equity Funding securities to whom Secrist had a duty to disclose. Accepting the Court's view of tippee liability, it appears that Dirks' knowledge of this breach makes him liable as a participant in the breach after the fact. *Chiarella*, 445 U.S. at 230, n.12.

The Court holds, however, that Dirks is not liable because Secrist did not violate his duty; according to the Court, this is so because Secrist did not have the improper purpose of personal gain. In so doing, the Court imposes a new, subjective limitation on the scope of the duty owed by insiders to shareholders. The novelty of this limitation is reflected in the Court's lack of support for it.

The insider's duty is owed directly to the corporation's shareholders. . . . As *Chiarella* recognized, it is based on the relationship of trust and confidence between the insider and the shareholder. 445 U.S. at 228. That relationship assures the shareholder that the insider may not take actions that will harm him unfairly. The affirmative duty of disclosure protects against this injury. . . .

. . . It makes no difference to the shareholder whether the corporate insider gained or intended to gain personally from the transaction; the shareholder still has lost because of the insider's misuse of nonpublic information. The duty is addressed not to the insider's motives, but to his actions and their consequences on the shareholder. Personal gain is not an element of the breach of this duty. . . .

The Court's addition of the bad purpose element to a breach of fiduciary duty claim is flatly inconsistent with the principle of *Mosser* [v. Darrow, 341 U.S. 267 (1951)]. I do not join this limitation of the scope of an insider's fiduciary duty to shareholders.

The improper purpose requirement not only has no basis in law, but it rests implicitly on a policy that I cannot accept. The Court justifies Secrist's and Dirks' action because the general benefit derived from the violation of Secrist's duty to shareholders outweighed the harm caused to those shareholders. . . . Under this view, the benefit conferred on society by Secrist's and Dirks' activities may be paid for with the losses caused to shareholders trading with Dirks' clients.

Although Secrist's general motive to expose the Equity Funding fraud was laudable, the means he chose were not. Moreover, even assuming that Dirks played a substantial role in exposing the fraud, he and his clients should not profit from the information they obtained from Secrist. Misprision of a felony long has been against public policy. A person cannot condition his transmission of information of a crime on a financial award. As a citizen, Dirks had at least an ethical obligation to report the information to the proper authorities. See ante, n.20. The Court's holding is deficient in policy terms not because it fails to create a legal norm out of that ethical norm, see ibid., but because it actually rewards Dirks for his aiding and abetting.

Dirks and Secrist were under a duty to disclose the information or to refrain from trading on it. I agree that disclosure in this case would have been difficult. I also recognize that the SEC seemingly has been less than helpful in its view of the nature of disclosure necessary to satisfy the disclose-or-refrain duty. The Commission tells persons with inside information that they cannot trade on that information unless they disclose; it refuses, however, to tell them how to disclose. See In re Faberge, Inc., 45 S.E.C. 249, 256 (1973) (disclosure requires public release through public media designed to reach investing public generally). This seems to be a less than sensible policy, which it is incumbent on the Commission to correct. The Court, however, has no authority to remedy the problem by opening a hole in the congressionally mandated prohibition on insider trading, thus rewarding such trading.

In my view, Secrist violated his duty to Equity Funding shareholders by transmitting material nonpublic information to Dirks with the intention that Dirks would cause his clients to trade on that information. Dirks, therefore, was under a duty to make the information publicly available or to refrain from actions that he knew would lead to trading. Because Dirks caused his clients to trade, he violated §10(b) and Rule 10b-5. Any other result is a disservice to this country's attempt to provide fair and efficient capital markets. I dissent.

---

1. *The background to* Dirks. In Chiarella v. United States, 445 U.S. 222 (1980), an employee of a financial printer was criminally prosecuted for using information gained from his employment to trade in the stock of target corporations for which tender offers were about to be made. In reversing his conviction, the Court emphasized that Rule 10b-5's obligation to "disclose or abstain" arose only when there was a fiduciary duty owed to the corporation or its shareholders. Although the Court ruled that the defendant lacked any fiduciary relationship with the target corporations, it expressly left open the question of whether the defendant had breached a fiduciary duty owed to the bidder corporations. *Chiarella* also did not clearly resolve the status of a tippee, such as a securities analyst, who received information from a source within the subject corporation. Chief Justice Burger's dissent, however, asserted that any "person who has misappropriated nonpublic information has an absolute duty to disclose that information or to refrain from trading." Id. at 240.

At a minimum, *Dirks* put to rest the SEC's attempt to limit *Chiarella* to cases involving "market information." Although *Dirks* did not change the liability of corporate insiders who trade, other potential defendants must apparently fall into one of two classes to be liable for trading on nonpublic information: First, some persons who are not traditional insiders, but who receive nonpublic corporate information for a corporate purpose, may be found to have "entered into a special confidential relationship" that, as footnote 14 in *Dirks* indicates, makes them the equivalent of tippers; this class of constructive fiduciaries will typically include lawyers, accountants, and underwriters who receive confidential information in the course of their professional employment. Footnote 14 does not require an express agreement, but only that the terms of the relationship imply a duty to maintain confidentiality. Second, tippees of insiders are under an obligation to disclose or abstain if the nonpublic information was "made available to them improperly." However, the tippee's liability is a derivative one: only if the insider-tippers breached their duty does the tippee become liable, and a breach by the tippers will be found to have occurred only when the tippers themselves "personally will benefit, directly or indirectly from his disclosure." In SEC v. Lund, 570 F. Supp. 1397 (C.D. Cal. 1983), the first post-*Dirks* decision to interpret footnote 14, two longtime friends, who were chief executives of different companies, had a practice of regularly exchanging confidential information. Defendant Lund was told by his friend, the president of P&F Industries, about an opportunity P&F faced and was invited on behalf of his firm to join as a joint venturer. Instead, Lund bought stock in P&F. The district court held that Lund was subject to a fiduciary duty to P&F as a "temporary insider" by virtue of this special relationship as a friend and confidant of its president.

2. *Post*-Dirks *issues.* (a) *To whom is a fiduciary duty owed?* Once the answer to this question was simple: shareholders. But, increasingly, the investment marketplace has become populated with new forms of securities: options, futures, warrants, and other new financial instruments. Under an option contract, for example, the purchaser buys the right from the option writer (typically, an investment banking firm or a client found by them), not the corporation that issued the common stock; the writer of the option need not even currently own the shares — in effect, the option writer may simply be gambling. Should an insider who buys such an option based on nonpublic information be viewed as owing a fiduciary duty to an option writer, who is not even a shareholder of the corporation? In part to answer this question, Congress added §20(d) to the Securities Exchange Act of 1934, which expressly provides that if a person possesses material, nonpublic information with respect to a security, then the purchase or sale of any option, put, call, or other "privilege . . . with respect to such security or with respect to a group or index of securities including such security" shall also constitute unlawful insider trading and result in "comparable liability."

(b) *What must the tippee know to be liable? Dirks* is unclear on this point. The Court says at one point that if the tippee "knows or should know that there has been a breach," the tippee is liable; this suggests a negligence standard. Yet the opinion also says in footnote 23 that "a violation may be found only where there is 'intentional or willful conduct designed to deceive or defraud investors.' . . ."

Moreover, even if there is a clear breach of the insider's duty, the tippee will seldom be a lawyer familiar with the concept of fiduciary duty. Thus, is it sensible to phrase the standard in terms of a legal conclusion — namely, whether the tippee "knows or should know that there has been a breach"?

(c) *The nature of the benefit to the tippee. Dirks* says that an "indirect benefit" can suffice to make the tipper's disclosure "improper" and hence create liability for the tippee. It adds that this indirect benefit can consist of "a reputational benefit that will translate into future earnings." Because an investment banker can be a constructive insider and hence a tipper under footnote 14, this suggests that Dirks could have been held liable if he had acquired the information about Equity Funding in a different capacity (e.g., as an underwriter for the company) and had passed it on to mutual funds for expected future commissions, as could the mutual funds if they had realized there had been a fiduciary breach. Much depends, then, on whether the defendant is characterized as a tippee or as a constructive insider and thus a tipper.

(d) *The status of Rule 14e-3.* In 1980, possibly in response to *Chiarella*, the SEC adopted Rule 14e-3, which prohibits any person (other than the bidder) in possession of material nonpublic information about a tender offer both from trading in securities affected by the offer without disclosing such information, and from communicating such information to others who do not need to know it in order to effectuate the offer. Rule 14e-3 clearly reaches a person such as the defendant in *Chiarella.*

(e) *The "in pari delicto" defense.* Can a tippee sue a tipper for a false or misleading tip where both have violated Rule 10b-5? In Bateman Eichler, Hill Richards, Inc. v. Berner, 472 U.S. 299 (1985), the Court held that the plaintiff's culpability could bar a damage action under federal securities laws only when (1) the plaintiff was at least substantially equally responsible for the violation sued on, and (2) preclusion of the suit would not significantly interfere with effective enforcement of the securities laws. Deciding that the tippee is not as responsible as the tipper and that barring suits by tippees against tippers would hamper enforcement of the securities laws, the Court seemingly left little room for the "in pari delicto" defense to be raised, at least in an insider trading case.

e. Selective Disclosure and Regulation FD

The *Dirks* personal benefit test seemingly implied that, in the typical case, corporate management could lawfully tip selected institutional investors and security analysts as to material corporate developments prior to the release of the same information to the market. Absent additional special circumstances, such selective disclosure provided no personal or "reputational benefit" to management and did not really look like a gift to the recipient institutions. Managements might have reasons independent of any personal benefit for selectively revealing such information to analysts and large institutions:

(1)   The practice probably reduced the volatility of the corporation's share price because management could "guide" the expectations of securities analysts, thus preventing them from overestimating earnings, so that the company's stock price would be less likely to fall precipitously if the analysts' forecast could not be met;

(2)   Even if misleading, such quiet, back-channel communications with market professionals were less likely to result in Rule 10b-5 liability to the corporation than was a public announcement or SEC filing;

(3)   The practice curried favor with large institutions that were often substantial shareholders; and

(4)   Selective disclosure created a powerful tool by which to reward or punish securities analysts. That is, an analyst who released a positive report or recommendation might receive the first call from management tipping the analyst as to pending material developments, while the analyst who published a critical report on the company could anticipate being cut off from future selective disclosures.

During the 1990s, the practice of selective disclosure became virtually institutionalized through the medium of conference calls hosted by the firm's CEO and CFO at which brief statements would be made by these executives and then questions asked by analysts. Often, these conference calls were not open to the public, most shareholders, or the press. Yet there was evidence that stock prices moved abruptly during and following these conferences, as participants traded heavily.[66]

---

66. See Richard Frankel, Marilyn Johnson & Douglas J. Skinner, An Empirical Examination of Conference Calls as a Voluntary Disclosure Medium, 37 J. Acct. Res. 133 (1999) (studying 1,056 corporate conference calls during 1995 and finding that stock price volatility and trading volume increased

The apparent loser from these practices was the small investor. When institutions are tipped as to adverse pending developments or future earnings announcements, they can buy or sell based on this material information, and their trading partners would typically be less informed public investors.

Confronted with a problem that early created a nonlevel playing field for public investors and probably compromised the independence of securities analysts, the SEC faced a difficult choice. If it sought to expand the definition of insider trading to include selective disclosure, it could expect legal challenges and a possible reversal from the Supreme Court. If it did anything to restrict selective disclosure, it could expect vehement opposition from the securities industry, whose analysts profited from their ability to promise institutional investors early access to material nonpublic information. In defense of selective disclosure, the securities industry argued that it maximized market efficiency, because it substituted a system of continuous communication between issuers and the market for the system of infrequent public announcements that the federal securities laws allegedly produced.[67]

Although proposals to restrict selective disclosure were opposed by the industry, they were enthusiastically greeted by small investors, and the SEC received a record 6,000 comment letters when it proposed Regulation FD in December 1999, of which over 5,000 were from individual investors voicing support.[68] When the SEC adopted Regulation FD in August 2000, it was by a divided 3-1 vote, and the rule was softened in several respects. First, it expressly provides that no private cause of action lies to assert it,[69] and thus only the SEC can enforce it. Second, the rule bars disclosure only to market professionals (e.g., broker-dealers, investment advisers, and institutions like mutual funds) and shareholders likely to trade; a specific exemption was created to make Regulation FD inapplicable to the public offering process in order to permit issuers to continue to conduct road shows that would be open to analysts and institutions but closed to smaller investors.[70] Other limitations are best explained by first examining Rule 100 of Regulation FD, which sets forth the basic prohibition:

Regulation FD
100. General Rule Regarding Selective Disclosure

(a) Whenever an issuer, or any person acting on its behalf, discloses any material nonpublic information regarding that issuer or its securities to any person

---

substantially during such calls). This study also found that the average trade size increased during these conference calls, implying that large owners (i.e., institutional investors) were disproportionately trading during these conferences. The researchers concluded that material information was being released during these conference calls that filtered through a subset of large investors before it reached the market as a whole.

67. For a defense of this position, see Note, Regulation Fair Disclosure: The Death of the Efficient Capital Market Hypothesis and the Birth of Herd Behavior, 82 B.U. L. Rev. 527 (2002).

68. See Note, The Securities and Exchange Commission's Regulation Fair Disclosure: Parity of Information or Parody of Information, 56 U. Miami L. Rev. 645, 650 (2002).

69. See Rule 102. 17 C.F.R. §243.102.

70. See Rule 100(b)(2)(iv). 17 C.F.R. §243.100(b)(2)(iv).

described in paragraph (b)(1) of this section, the issuer shall make public disclosure of that information as provided in 101(e):

    (1) Simultaneously, in the case of an intentional disclosure; and

    (2) Promptly, in the case of a non-intentional disclosure.

(b)(1) Except as provided in paragraph (b)(2) of this section, paragraph (a) of this section shall apply to a disclosure made to any person outside the issuer:

    (i) Who is a broker or dealer, or a person associated with a broker or dealer, as those terms are defined in Section 3(a) of the Securities Exchange Act of 1934.

    (ii) Who is an investment adviser, as that term is defined in Section 202(a)(11) of the Investment Advisers Act of 1940; an institutional investment manager, as that term is defined in Section 13(f)(5) of the Securities Exchange Act of 1934 . . . or a person associated with either of the foregoing . . . ;

    (iii) Who is an investment company, as defined in Section 3 of the Investment Company Act of 1940 . . . or an affiliated person . . . ;

    (iv) Who is a holder of the issuer's securities, under circumstances in which it is reasonably foreseeable that the person will purchase or sell the issuer's securities on the basis of the information.

    (2) Paragraph (a) of this section shall not apply to a disclosure made:

    (i) To a person who owes a duty of trust or confidence to the issuer (such as an attorney, investment banker, or accountant);

    (ii) To a person who expressly agrees to maintain the disclosed information in confidence;

    (iii) To an entity whose primary business is the issuance of credit ratings, provided the information is disclosed solely for the purpose of developing a credit rating and the entity's ratings are publicly available; or

    (iv) In connection with a securities offering registered under the Securities Act. . . .

Although Rule 100 seems on its face to apply to any person, the SEC defined the Rule's critical term "person acting on behalf of the issuer" to include only senior officials of the issuer and any other officer, employee, or agent who regularly communicates with the persons listed in Rule 100(b)(1),[71] thereby including public relations employees and agents. Still, this definition would exclude many forms of inadvertent selective disclosure by lower-ranking employees.

Conversely, some provisions of Regulation FD are more demanding than they first appear. For example, Rule 100(a) on its face requires simultaneous public disclosure only when the selective disclosure is "intentional." But "intentional" is defined by Rule 101(a) to mean only that the person "knows, or is reckless in not knowing, that the information he or she is communicating is both material and nonpublic." Hence, any chief executive who discloses to analysts in a private meeting that the company will miss its earnings forecast has probably committed an intentional violation, requiring immediate public disclosure. In the case of a non-intentional disclosure, public disclosure must be prompt, which Rule 101(d) defines to mean "as soon as reasonably practicable (but in no event after the later of

71. See Rule 101(c). 17 C.F.R. §243.101(c).

24 hours or the commencement of the next day's trading on the New York Stock Exchange) after a senior official of the issuer . . . learns that there has been a non-intentional disclosure . . . or is reckless in not knowing. . . ." As a result, on learning of a non-intentional selective disclosure covered by the rule, counsel must move quickly to make the requisite public disclosure.

Public disclosure in compliance with Rule 100 can be made by filing a Form 8-K disclosing the material nonpublic information or by instead disseminating "the information through another method (or combination of methods) of disclosure that is reasonably designed to provide broad, non-exclusionary distribution of the information to the public."[72] This definition leaves open the legitimacy of a variety of means of public disclosure. For example, what if the issuer has a closed conference call with securities analysts, but simultaneously broadcasts the conference call on its Web site? Does this satisfy the "broad, non-exclusionary distribution" standard of Rule 101(e)? At first, the SEC believed an insufficient portion of the investing public had access to the Internet to make this procedure acceptable by itself, but it is gradually shifting its position as access to the Internet expands. Today, the most typical procedure (and many variations are in use) is to issue a press release either disclosing the information to be released at the conference call or indicating that a conference call with analysts is scheduled and providing a dial-in phone number so that shareholders may listen (but typically not participate). Such conference calls are also increasingly broadcast on the company's Web site, but supplemented by a press release or, less commonly, by filing of a Form 8-K. Ambiguities remain regarding the scope of Regulation FD. Note that Rule 100(b)(2) permits disclosure of material nonpublic information to persons who agree to maintain its confidentiality. This clearly applies, for example, to a potential acquirer who signs a confidentiality agreement in order to receive financial information from the prospective target company. But what if an issuer asks 50 securities analysts to sign such an agreement before a meeting at which projections will be given regarding next year's earnings? Also, what is the liability of the tippees in this case? By its terms, Regulation FD applies only to the issuer and persons acting on its behalf, but presumably the SEC can seek to enjoin any tippee (and recover its trading profits) as an aider and abettor of the issuer's violation. Also, note that if the tippee has signed a confidentiality agreement, it has breached a duty owed to the issuer and can be sued or prosecuted for conventional insider trading. Rule 100 does not apply to the tippee by virtue of the exclusion in Rule 100(b)(2).

What has been the impact of Regulation FD? Early research has concluded that it has been effective in curbing selective disclosure, in part because the market impact of information disseminated in analyst reports has declined significantly.[73] The dispersion of analyst forecasts has increased[74] (possibly because management can no longer guide them). But so has informational asymmetry, particularly surrounding earnings announcements. Superior analysts appear more able to distinguish themselves from the herd, and the incentive to gather information may

---

72. See Rule 101(e). 17 C.F.R. §243.101(e).

73. See Andreas Gintschel & Stanimir Markov, The Effectiveness of Regulation FD (May 5, 2003, available at www.ssrn.com at id = 319423) (finding 32 percent drop in price impact of analyst reports).

74. Partha Mohanram & Shyam Sunder, How Has Regulation Fair Disclosure Affected the Functioning of Financial Analysts? (December 2003, available at www.ssrn.com at id = 297933).

therefore have increased.[75] Disagreements among analysts appear also to persist longer, with less consensus being reached. Finally, no significant increase has been observed in stock volatility attributable to earnings information reaching the market less frequently.[76]

f. Misappropriation Theory

United States v. O'Hagan
521 U.S. 642 (1997)

Justice Ginsburg delivered the opinion of the Court.

This case concerns the interpretation and enforcement of §10(b) and §14(e) of the Securities Exchange Act of 1934, and rules made by the Securities and Exchange Commission pursuant to these provisions, Rule 10b-5 and Rule 14e-3(a). Two prime questions are presented. The first relates to the misappropriation of material, nonpublic information for securities trading; the second concerns fraudulent practices in the tender offer setting. In particular, we address and resolve these issues: (1) Is a person who trades in securities for personal profit, using confidential information misappropriated in breach of a fiduciary duty to the source of the information, guilty of violating §10(b) and Rule 10b-5? (2) Did the Commission exceed its rulemaking authority by adopting Rule 14e-3(a), which proscribes trading on undisclosed information in the tender offer setting, even in the absence of a duty to disclose? Our answer to the first question is yes, and to the second question, viewed in the context of this case, no.

I. Respondent James Herman O'Hagan was a partner in the law firm of Dorsey & Whitney in Minneapolis, Minnesota. In July 1988, Grand Metropolitan PLC (Grand Met), a company based in London, England, retained Dorsey & Whitney as local counsel to represent Grand Met regarding a potential tender offer for the common stock of the Pillsbury Company, headquartered in Minneapolis. Both Grand Met and Dorsey & Whitney took precautions to protect the confidentiality of Grand Met's tender offer plans. O'Hagan did no work on the Grand Met representation. Dorsey & Whitney withdrew from representing Grand Met on September 9, 1988. Less than a month later, on October 4, 1988, Grand Met publicly announced its tender offer for Pillsbury stock.

On August 18, 1988, while Dorsey & Whitney was still representing Grand Met, O'Hagan began purchasing call options for Pillsbury stock. Each option gave him the right to purchase 100 shares of Pillsbury stock by a specified date in September 1988. Later in August and in September, O'Hagan made additional purchases of Pillsbury call options. By the end of September, he owned 2,500 unexpired Pillsbury options, apparently more than any other individual investor. O'Hagan also purchased, in September 1988, some 5,000 shares of Pillsbury common stock, at a price just under $39 per share. When Grand Met announced its tender offer in October, the price of Pillsbury stock rose to nearly $60 per share. O'Hagan then sold his Pillsbury call options and common stock, making a profit of more than $4.3 million.

---

75. Id. See also Scott Findlay & Prem G. Mathew, An Examination of the Differential Impact of Regulation FD on Analysts' Forecast Accuracy, 41 Fin. Rev. 9 (2006) (reviewing recent studies).

76. Frank Heflin, K.R. Subramanyam & Yuan Zhang, Stock Return Volatility Before and After Regulation FD (Working Paper 2003, available at www.ssrn.com at id = 292879).

The Securities and Exchange Commission (SEC or Commission) initiated an investigation into O'Hagan's transactions, culminating in a 57-count indictment. The indictment alleged that O'Hagan defrauded his law firm and its client, Grand Met, by using for his own trading purposes material, nonpublic information regarding Grand Met's planned tender offer. According to the indictment, O'Hagan used the profits he gained through this trading to conceal his previous embezzlement and conversion of unrelated client trust funds. O'Hagan was charged with 20 counts of mail fraud . . . 17 counts of securities fraud, in violation of §10(b) of the Securities Exchange Act of 1934 (Exchange Act), and SEC Rule 10b-5; 17 counts of fraudulent trading in connection with a tender offer, in violation of §14(e) of the Exchange Act, and SEC Rule 14e-3(a); and 3 counts of violating federal money laundering statutes. . . . A jury convicted O'Hagan on all 57 counts, and he was sentenced to a 41-month term of imprisonment.

A divided panel of the Court of Appeals for the Eighth Circuit reversed all of O'Hagan's convictions. 92 F.3d 612 (1996). Liability under §10(b) and Rule 10b-5, the Eighth Circuit held, may not be grounded on the "misappropriation theory" of securities fraud on which the prosecution relied. Id., at 622. The Court of Appeals also held that Rule 14e-3(a) — which prohibits trading while in possession of material, nonpublic information relating to a tender offer — exceeds the SEC's §14(e) rulemaking authority because the rule contains no breach of fiduciary duty requirement. Id., at 627. The Eighth Circuit further concluded that O'Hagan's mail fraud and money laundering convictions rested on violations of the securities laws, and therefore could not stand once the securities fraud convictions were reversed. Id., at 627-628. Judge Fagg, dissenting, stated that he would recognize and enforce the misappropriation theory, and would hold that the SEC did not exceed its rulemaking authority when it adopted Rule 14e-3(a) without requiring proof of a breach of fiduciary duty. Id., at 628.

Decisions of the Courts of Appeals are in conflict on the propriety of the misappropriation theory under §10(b) and Rule 10b-5, . . . and on the legitimacy of Rule 14e-3(a) under §14(e). We granted certiorari, . . . and now reverse the Eighth Circuit's judgment.

II. We address first the Court of Appeals' reversal of O'Hagan's convictions under §10(b) and Rule 10b-5. Following the Fourth Circuit's lead, see United States v. Bryan, 58 F.3d 933, 943-959 (1995), the Eighth Circuit rejected the misappropriation theory as a basis for §10(b) liability. We hold, in accord with several other Courts of Appeals, that criminal liability under §10(b) may be predicated on the misappropriation theory.

A. In pertinent part, §10(b) of the Exchange Act provides:

> It shall be unlawful for any person, directly or indirectly, by the use of any means or instrumentality of interstate commerce or of the mails, or of any facility of any national securities exchange — . . .
>
> (b) To use or employ, in connection with the purchase or sale of any security registered on a national securities exchange or any security not so registered, any manipulative or deceptive device or contrivance in contravention of such rules and regulations as the [Securities and Exchange] Commission may prescribe as necessary or appropriate in the public interest or for the protection of investors.

15 U.S.C. §78j(b).

The statute thus proscribes (1) using any deceptive device (2) in connection with the purchase or sale of securities, in contravention of rules prescribed by the Commission. The provision, as written, does not confine its coverage to deception of a purchaser or seller of securities, see United States v. Newman, 664 F.2d 12, 17 (C.A.2 1981); rather, the statute reaches any deceptive device used "in connection with the purchase or sale of any security." . . .

Under the "traditional" or "classical theory" of insider trading liability, §10(b) and Rule 10b-5 are violated when a corporate insider trades in the securities of his corporation on the basis of material, nonpublic information. Trading on such information qualifies as a "deceptive device" under §10(b), we have affirmed, because "a relationship of trust and confidence [exists] between the shareholders of a corporation and those insiders who have obtained confidential information by reason of their position with that corporation." Chiarella v. United States, 445 U.S. 222, 228 (1980). That relationship, we recognized, "gives rise to a duty to disclose [or to abstain from trading] because of the 'necessity of preventing a corporate insider from . . . tak[ing] unfair advantage of . . . uninformed . . . stockholders.' " Id., at 228-229. The classical theory applies not only to officers, directors, and other permanent insiders of a corporation, but also to attorneys, accountants, consultants, and others who temporarily become fiduciaries of a corporation. See Dirks v. SEC, 463 U.S. 646, 655, n.14 (1983).

The "misappropriation theory" holds that a person commits fraud "in connection with" a securities transaction, and thereby violates §10(b) and Rule 10b-5, when he misappropriates confidential information for securities trading purposes, in breach of a duty owed to the source of the information. See Brief for United States 14. Under this theory, a fiduciary's undisclosed, self-serving use of a principal's information to purchase or sell securities, in breach of a duty of loyalty and confidentiality, defrauds the principal of the exclusive use of that information. In lieu of premising liability on a fiduciary relationship between company insider and purchaser or seller of the company's stock, the misappropriation theory premises liability on a fiduciary-turned-trader's deception of those who entrusted him with access to confidential information.

The two theories are complementary, each addressing efforts to capitalize on nonpublic information through the purchase or sale of securities. The classical theory targets a corporate insider's breach of duty to shareholders with whom the insider transacts; the misappropriation theory outlaws trading on the basis of nonpublic information by a corporate "outsider" in breach of a duty owed not to a trading party, but to the source of the information. The misappropriation theory is thus designed to "protec[t] the integrity of the securities markets against abuses by 'outsiders' to a corporation who have access to confidential information that will affect th[e] corporation's security price when revealed, but who owe no fiduciary or other duty to that corporation's shareholders." Ibid.

In this case, the indictment alleged that O'Hagan, in breach of a duty of trust and confidence he owed to his law firm, Dorsey & Whitney, and to its client, Grand Met, traded on the basis of nonpublic information regarding Grand Met's planned tender offer for Pillsbury common stock. App. 16. This conduct, the Government charged, constituted a fraudulent device in connection with the purchase and sale of securities.[5]

---

5. The Government could not have prosecuted O'Hagan under the classical theory, for O'Hagan was not an "insider" of Pillsbury, the corporation in whose stock he traded. Although an "outsider" with respect to Pillsbury, O'Hagan had an intimate association with, and was found to have traded on confidential information from, Dorsey & Whitney, counsel to tender offeror Grand Met. Under the

B. We agree with the Government that misappropriation, as just defined, satisfies §10(b)'s requirement that chargeable conduct involve a "deceptive device or contrivance" used "in connection with" the purchase or sale of securities. We observe, first, that misappropriators, as the Government describes them, deal in deception. A fiduciary who "[pretends] loyalty to the principal while secretly converting the principal's information or personal gain," Brief for United States 17, "dupes" or defrauds the principal. See Aldave, Misappropriation: A General Theory of Liability for Trading on Nonpublic Information, 13 Hofstra L. Rev. 101, 119 (1984).

We addressed fraud of the same species in Carpenter v. United States, 484 U.S. 19 (1987), which involved the mail fraud statute's proscription of "any scheme or artifice to defraud," 18 U.S.C. §1341. Affirming convictions under that statute, we said in *Carpenter* that an employee's undertaking not to reveal his employer's confidential information "became a sham" when the employee provided the information to his co-conspirators in a scheme to obtain trading profits. 484 U.S., at 27. A company's confidential information, we recognized in *Carpenter*, qualifies as property to which the company has a right of exclusive use. Id., at 25-27. The undisclosed misappropriation of such information, in violation of a fiduciary duty, the Court said in *Carpenter*, constitutes fraud akin to embezzlement — "the fraudulent appropriation to one's own use of the money or goods entrusted to one's care by another." Id., at 27 (quoting Grin v. Shine, 187 U.S. 181, 189 (1902)); see Aldave, 13 Hofstra L. Rev., at 119. *Carpenter*'s discussion of the fraudulent misuse of confidential information, the Government notes, "is a particularly apt source of guidance here, because [the mail fraud statute] (like Section 10(b)) has long been held to require deception, not merely the breach of a fiduciary duty." Brief for United States 18, n.9 (citation omitted).

Deception through nondisclosure is central to the theory of liability for which the Government seeks recognition. As counsel for the Government stated in explanation of the theory at oral argument: "To satisfy the common law rule that a trustee may not use the property that [has] been entrusted [to] him, there would have to be consent. To satisfy the requirement of the Securities Act that there be no deception, there would only have to be disclosure." Tr. of Oral Arg. 12; see generally Restatement (Second) of Agency §§390, 395 (1958) (agent's disclosure obligation regarding use of confidential information).[6]

The misappropriation theory advanced by the Government is consistent with Santa Fe Industries, Inc. v. Green, 430 U.S. 462 (1977), a decision underscoring that §10(b) is not an all-purpose breach of fiduciary duty ban; rather, it trains on conduct involving manipulation or deception. See id., at 473-476. In contrast to the Government's allegations in this case, in *Santa Fe Industries*, all pertinent facts were disclosed by the persons charged with violating §10(b) and Rule 10b-5,

---

misappropriation theory, O'Hagan's securities trading does not escape Exchange Act sanction, as it would under the dissent's reasoning, simply because he was associated with, and gained nonpublic information from, the bidder, rather than the target.

6. Under the misappropriation theory urged in this case, the disclosure obligation runs to the source of the information, here, Dorsey & Whitney and Grand Met. Chief Justice Burger, dissenting in *Chiarella*, advanced a broader reading of §10(b) and Rule 10b-5; the disclosure obligation, as he envisioned it, ran to those with whom the misappropriator trades, 445 U.S., at 240 ("a person who has misappropriated nonpublic information has an absolute duty to disclose that information or to refrain from trading"); see also id., at 243, n.4, 100 S. Ct., at 1122 n.4. The Government does not propose that we adopt a misappropriation theory of that breadth.

see id., at 474; therefore, there was no deception through nondisclosure to which liability under those provisions could attach, see id., at 476. Similarly, full disclosure forecloses liability under the misappropriation theory: Because the deception essential to the misappropriation theory involves feigning fidelity to the source of information, if the fiduciary discloses to the source that he plans to trade on the nonpublic information, there is no "deceptive device" and thus no §10(b) violation — although the fiduciary-turned-trader may remain liable under state law for breach of a duty of loyalty.[7]

We turn next to the §10(b) requirement that the misappropriator's deceptive use of information be "in connection with the purchase or sale of [a] security." This element is satisfied because the fiduciary's fraud is consummated, not when the fiduciary gains the confidential information, but when, without disclosure to his principal, he uses the information to purchase or sell securities. The securities transaction and the breach of duty thus coincide. This is so even though the person or entity defrauded is not the other party to the trade, but is, instead, the source of the nonpublic information. See Aldave, 13 Hofstra L. Rev., at 120 ("a fraud or deceit can be practiced on one person, with resultant harm to another person or group of persons"). A misappropriator who trades on the basis of material, nonpublic information, in short, gains his advantageous market position through deception; he deceives the source of the information and simultaneously harms members of the investing public. See id., at 120-121, and n.107.

The misappropriation theory targets information of a sort that misappropriators ordinarily capitalize upon to gain no-risk profits through the purchase or sale of securities. Should a misappropriator put such information to other use, the statute's prohibition would not be implicated. The theory does not catch all conceivable forms of fraud involving confidential information; rather, it catches fraudulent means of capitalizing on such information through securities transactions.

The Government notes another limitation on the forms of fraud §10(b) reaches: "The misappropriation theory would not . . . apply to a case in which a person defrauded a bank into giving him a loan or embezzled cash from another, and then used the proceeds of the misdeed to purchase securities." Brief for United States 24, n.13. In such a case, the Government states, "the proceeds would have value to the malefactor apart from their use in a securities transaction, and the fraud would be complete as soon as the money was obtained." Ibid. In other words, money can buy, if not anything, then at least many things; its misappropriation may thus be viewed as sufficiently detached from a subsequent securities transaction that §10(b)'s "in connection with" requirement would not be met. Ibid.

The dissent's charge that the misappropriation theory is incoherent because information, like funds, can be put to multiple uses, see post, at 4-8, misses the point. The Exchange Act was enacted in part "to insure the maintenance of fair and honest markets," 15 U.S.C. §78b, and there is no question that fraudulent uses of confidential information fall within §10(b)'s prohibition if the fraud is "in connection with" a securities transaction. It is hardly remarkable that a rule suitably

---

7. Where, however, a person trading on the basis of material, nonpublic information owes a duty of loyalty and confidentiality to two entities or persons — for example, a law firm and its client — but makes disclosure to only one, the trader may still be liable under the misappropriation theory.

applied to the fraudulent uses of certain kinds of information would be stretched beyond reason were it applied to the fraudulent use of money.

The dissent does catch the Government in overstatement. Observing that money can be used for all manner of purposes and purchases, the Government urges that confidential information of the kind at issue derives its value only from its utility in securities trading. See Brief for United States 10, 21; post, at 2222-2224 (several times emphasizing the word "only"). Substitute "ordinarily" for "only," and the Government is on the mark.

Our recognition that the Government's "only" is an overstatement has provoked the dissent to cry "new theory." See post, at 2224-2225. But the very case on which the dissent relies, Motor Vehicle Mfrs. Assn. of United States, Inc. v. State Farm Mut. Automobile Ins. Co., 463 U.S. 29 (1983), shows the extremity of that charge. In *State Farm*, we reviewed an agency's rescission of a rule under the same "arbitrary and capricious" standard by which the promulgation of a rule under the relevant statute was to be judged, see id., at 41-42; in our decision concluding that the agency had not adequately explained its regulatory action, see id., at 57, we cautioned that a "reviewing court should not attempt itself to make up for such deficiencies," id., at 43. Here, by contrast, Rule 10b-5's promulgation has not been challenged; we consider only the Government's charge that O'Hagan's alleged fraudulent conduct falls within the prohibitions of the rule and §10(b). In this context, we acknowledge simply that, in defending the Government's interpretation of the rule and statute in this Court, the Government's lawyers have pressed a solid point too far, something lawyers, occasionally even judges, are wont to do.

The misappropriation theory comports with §10(b)'s language, which requires deception "in connection with the purchase or sale of any security," not deception of an identifiable purchaser or seller. The theory is also well-tuned to an animating purpose of the Exchange Act: to insure honest securities markets and thereby promote investor confidence. . . . Although informational disparity is inevitable in the securities markets, investors likely would hesitate to venture their capital in a market where trading based on misappropriated nonpublic information is unchecked by law. An investor's informational disadvantage vis-à-vis a misappropriator with material, nonpublic information stems from contrivance, not luck; it is a disadvantage that cannot be overcome with research or skill. See Brudney, Insiders, Outsiders, and Informational Advantages Under the Federal Securities Laws, 93 Harv. L. Rev. 322, 356 (1979) ("If the market is thought to be systematically populated with . . . transactors [trading on the basis of misappropriated information] some investors will refrain from dealing altogether, and others will incur costs to avoid dealing with such transactors or corruptly to overcome their unerodable informational advantages."); Aldave, 13 Hofstra L. Rev., at 122-123.

In sum, considering the inhibiting impact on market participation of trading on misappropriated information, and the congressional purposes underlying §10(b), it makes scant sense to hold a lawyer like O'Hagan a §10(b) violator if he works for a law firm representing the target of a tender offer, but not if he works for a law firm representing the bidder. The text of the statute requires no such result.[9]

9. As noted earlier, however, see supra, at 2208-2209, the textual requirement of deception precludes §10(b) liability when a person trading on the basis of nonpublic information has disclosed his trading plans to, or obtained authorization from, the principal—even though such conduct may affect the securities markets in the same manner as the conduct reached by the misappropriation theory. Contrary to the dissent's suggestion, see post, at 2225-2226, the fact that §10(b) is only a partial antidote to the

The misappropriation at issue here was properly made the subject of a §10(b) charge because it meets the statutory requirement that there be "deceptive" conduct "in connection with" securities transactions.

C. The Court of Appeals rejected the misappropriation theory primarily on two grounds. First, as the Eighth Circuit comprehended the theory, it requires neither misrepresentation nor nondisclosure. See 92 F.3d, at 618. As we just explained, however, see supra, at 2208-2209, deceptive nondisclosure is essential to the §10(b) liability at issue. Concretely, in this case, "it [was O'Hagan's] failure to disclose his personal trading to Grand Met and Dorsey, in breach of his duty to do so, that ma[de] his conduct 'deceptive' within the meaning of [§]10(b)." Reply Brief 7.

Second and "more obvious," the Court of Appeals said, the misappropriation theory is not moored to §10(b)'s requirement that "the fraud be 'in connection with the purchase or sale of any security.'" See 92 F.3d, at 618 (quoting 15 U.S.C. §78j(b)). According to the Eighth Circuit, three of our decisions reveal that §10(b) liability cannot be predicated on a duty owed to the source of nonpublic information: Chiarella v. United States, 445 U.S. 222 (1980); Dirks v. SEC, 463 U.S. 646 (1983); and Central Bank of Denver, N.A. v. First Interstate Bank of Denver, N.A., 511 U.S. 164 (1994). "[O]nly a breach of a duty to parties to the securities transaction," the Court of Appeals concluded, "or, at the most, to other market participants such as investors, will be sufficient to give rise to §10(b) liability." 92 F.3d, at 618. We read the statute and our precedent differently, and note again that §10(b) refers to "the purchase or sale of any security," not to identifiable purchasers or sellers of securities.

Chiarella involved securities trades by a printer employed at a shop that printed documents announcing corporate takeover voids. See 445 U.S., at 224. Deducing the names of target companies from documents he handled, the printer bought shares of the targets before takeover bids were announced, expecting (correctly) that the share prices would rise upon announcement. In these transactions, the printer did not disclose to the sellers of the securities (the target companies' shareholders) the nonpublic information on which he traded. See ibid. For that trading, the printer was convicted of violating §10(b) and Rule 10b-5. We reversed the Court of Appeals judgment that had affirmed the conviction. See id., at 225.

The jury in *Chiarella* had been instructed that it could convict the defendant if he willfully failed to inform sellers of target company securities that he knew of a takeover bid that would increase the value of their shares. See id., at 226. Emphasizing that the printer had no agency or other fiduciary relationship with the sellers, we held that liability could not be imposed on so broad a theory. See id., at 235. There is under §10(b), we explained, no "general duty between all participants in market transactions to forgo actions based on material, nonpublic information." Id., at 233. Under established doctrine, we said, a duty to disclose or abstain from trading "arises from a specific relationship between two parties." Ibid.

The Court did not hold in *Chiarella* that the only relationship prompting liability for trading on undisclosed information is the relationship between a corporation's insiders and shareholders. That is evident from our response to the Government's

---

problems it was designed to alleviate does not call into question its prohibition of conduct that falls within its textual proscription. Moreover, once a disloyal agent discloses his imminent breach of duty, his principal may seek appropriate equitable relief under state law. Furthermore, in the context of a tender offer, the principal who authorizes an agent's trading on confidential information may, in the Commission's view, incur liability for an Exchange Act violation under Rule 14e-3(a).

argument before this Court that the printer's misappropriation of information from his employer for purposes of securities trading — in violation of a duty of confidentiality owed to the acquiring companies — constituted fraud in connection with the purchase or sale of a security, and thereby satisfied the terms of §10(b). Id., at 235-236. The Court declined to reach that potential basis for the printer's liability, because the theory had not been submitted to the jury. See id., at 236-237. But four Justices found merit in it. See id., at 239. (BRENNAN, J., concurring in judgment); id., at 240-243. (BURGER, C.J., dissenting); id., at 245 (BLACKMUN, J., joined by MARSHALL, J., dissenting). And a fifth Justice stated that the Court "wisely le[ft] the resolution of this issue for another day." Id., at 238 (STEVENS, J., concurring).

Chiarella thus expressly left open the misappropriation theory before us today. Certain statements in *Chiarella*, however, led the Eighth Circuit in the instant case to conclude that §10(b) liability hinges exclusively on a breach of duty owed to a purchaser or seller of securities. See 92 F.3d, at 618. The Court said in *Chiarella* that §10(b) liability "is premised upon a duty to disclose arising from a relationship of trust and confidence *between parties to a transaction*," 445 U.S., at 230 (emphasis added), and observed that the printshop employee defendant in that case "was not a person in whom the sellers had placed their trust and confidence," see id., at 232. These statements rejected the notion that §10(b) stretches so far as to impose "a general duty between all participants in market transactions to forgo actions based on material, nonpublic information," id., at 233, and we confine them to that context. The statements highlighted by the Eighth Circuit, in short, appear in an opinion carefully leaving for future resolution the validity of the misappropriation theory, and therefore cannot be read to foreclose that theory.

Dirks, too, left room for application of the misappropriation theory in cases like the one we confront. *Dirks* involved an investment analyst who had received information from a former insider of a corporation with which the analyst had no connection. See 463 U.S., at 648-649. The information indicated that the corporation had engaged in a massive fraud. The analyst investigated the fraud, obtaining corroborating information from employees of the corporation. During his investigation, the analyst discussed his findings with clients and investors, some of whom sold their holdings in the company the analyst suspected of gross wrongdoing. See id., at 649.

The SEC censured the analyst for, inter alia, aiding and abetting §10(b) and Rule 10b-5 violations by clients and investors who sold their holdings based on the nonpublic information the analyst passed on. See id., at 650-652. In the SEC's view, the analyst, as a "tippee" of corporation insiders, had a duty under §10(b) and Rule 10b-5 to refrain from communicating the nonpublic information to persons likely to trade on the basis of it. See id., at 651, 655-656. This Court found no such obligation, see id., at 665-667, and repeated the key point made in *Chiarella*: There is no "'general duty between all participants in market transactions to forgo actions based on material, nonpublic information.'" Id., at 655 (quoting *Chiarella*, 445 U.S., at 233); see Aldave, 13 Hofstra L. Rev., at 122 (misappropriation theory bars only "trading on the basis of information that the wrongdoer converted to his own use in violation of some fiduciary, contractual, or similar obligation to the owner or rightful possessor of the information").

No showing had been made in *Dirks* that the "tippers" had violated any duty by disclosing to the analyst nonpublic information about their former employer. The insiders had acted not for personal profit, but to expose a massive fraud within the corporation. See *Dirks*, 463 U.S., at 666-667. Absent any violation by the tippers, there could be no derivative liability for the tippee. See id., at 667. Most important for purposes of the instant case, the Court observed in *Dirks:* "There was no expectation by [the analyst's] sources that he would keep their information in confidence. Nor did [the analyst] misappropriate or illegally obtain the information. . . ." Id., at 665. *Dirks* thus presents no suggestion that a person who gains nonpublic information through misappropriation in breach of a fiduciary duty escapes §10(b) liability when, without alerting the source, he trades on the information.

Last of the three cases the Eighth Circuit regarded as warranting disapproval of the misappropriation theory, *Central Bank* held that "a private plaintiff may not maintain an aiding and abetting suit under §10(b)." 511 U.S., at 191. We immediately cautioned in *Central Bank* that secondary actors in the securities markets may sometimes be chargeable under the securities Acts: "Any person or entity, including a lawyer, accountant, or bank, who employs a manipulative device or makes a material misstatement (or omission) *on which a purchaser or seller of securities relies* may be liable as a primary violator under 10b-5, assuming . . . the requirements for primary liability under Rule 10b-5 are met." Ibid. (emphasis added). The Eighth Circuit isolated the statement just quoted and drew from it the conclusion that §10(b) covers only deceptive statements or omissions on which purchasers and sellers, and perhaps other market participants, rely. See 92 F.3d, at 619. It is evident from the question presented in *Central Bank*, however, that this Court, in the quoted passage, sought only to clarify that secondary actors, although not subject to aiding and abetting liability, remain subject to primary liability under §10(b) and Rule 10b-5 for certain conduct.

Furthermore, *Central Bank*'s discussion concerned only private civil litigation under §10(b) and Rule 10b-5, not criminal liability. *Central Bank*'s reference to purchasers or sellers of securities must be read in light of a longstanding limitation on private §10(b) suits. In Blue Chip Stamps v. Manor Drug Stores, 421 U.S. 723 (1975), we held that only actual purchasers or sellers of securities may maintain a private civil action under §10(b) and Rule 10b-5. We so confined the §10(b) private right of action because of "policy considerations." Id., at 737. In particular, *Blue Chip Stamps* recognized the abuse potential and proof problems inherent in suits by investors who neither bought nor sold, but asserted they would have traded absent fraudulent conduct by others. See id., at 739-747; see also Holmes v. Securities Investor Protection Corporation, 503 U.S. 258, 285 (1992) (O'CONNOR, J., concurring in part and concurring in judgment); id., at 289-290 (SCALIA, J., concurring in judgment). Criminal prosecutions do not present the dangers the Court addressed in *Blue Chip Stamps*, so that decision is "inapplicable" to indictments for violations of §10(b) and Rule 10b-5. United States v. Naftalin, 441 U.S. 768, 774, n.6 (1979); see also Holmes, 503 U.S., at 281 (O'CONNOR, J., concurring in part and concurring in judgment) ("[T]he purchaser/seller standing requirement for private civil actions under §10(b) and Rule 10b-5 is of no import in criminal prosecutions for willful violations of those provisions.").

In sum, the misappropriation theory, as we have examined and explained it in this opinion, is both consistent with the statute and with our precedent. Vital to our decision that criminal liability may be sustained under the misappropriation theory, we emphasize, are two sturdy safeguards Congress has provided regarding scienter. To establish a criminal violation of Rule 10b-5, the Government must prove that a person "willfully" violated the provision. See 15 U.S.C. §78ff(a).

Furthermore, a defendant may not be imprisoned for violating Rule 10b-5 if he proves that he had no knowledge of the rule. See ibid. O'Hagan's charge that the misappropriation theory is too indefinite to permit the imposition of criminal liability, see Brief for Respondent 30-33, thus fails not only because the theory is limited to those who breach a recognized duty. In addition, the statute's "requirement of the presence of culpable intent as a necessary element of the offense does much to destroy any force in the argument that application of the [statute]" in circumstances such as O'Hagan's is unjust. Boyce Motor Lines, Inc. v. United States, 342 U.S. 337, 342 (1952).

The Eighth Circuit erred in holding that the misappropriation theory is inconsistent with §10(b). The Court of Appeals may address on remand O'Hagan's other challenges to his convictions under §10(b) and Rule 10b-5.

III. We consider next the ground on which the Court of Appeals reversed O'Hagan's convictions for fraudulent trading in connection with a tender offer, in violation of §14(e) of the Exchange Act and SEC Rule 14e-3(a). A sole question is before us as to these convictions: Did the Commission, as the Court of Appeals held, exceed its rulemaking authority under §14(e) when it adopted Rule 14e-3(a) without requiring a showing that the trading at issue entailed a breach of fiduciary duty? We hold that the Commission, in this regard and to the extent relevant to this case, did not exceed its authority.

The governing statutory provision, §14(e) of the Exchange Act, reads in relevant part: "It shall be unlawful for any person . . . to engage in any fraudulent, deceptive, or manipulative acts or practices, in connection with any tender offer. . . . The [SEC] shall, for the purposes of this subsection, by rules and regulations define, and prescribe means reasonably designed to prevent, such acts and practices as are fraudulent, deceptive, or manipulative." 15 U.S.C. §78n(e).

Section 14(e)'s first sentence prohibits fraudulent acts in connection with a tender offer. This self-operating proscription was one of several provisions added to the Exchange Act in 1968 by the Williams Act, 82 Stat. 454. The section's second sentence delegates definitional and prophylactic rulemaking authority to the Commission. Congress added this rulemaking delegation to §14(e) in 1970 amendments to the Williams Act. See §5, 84 Stat. 1497.

Through §14(e) and other provisions on disclosure in the Williams Act, Congress sought to ensure that shareholders "confronted by a cash tender offer for their stock [would] not be required to respond without adequate information." Rondeau v. Mosinee Paper Corp., 422 U.S. 49, 58 (1975); see Lewis v. McGraw, 619 F.2d 192, 195 (C.A.2 1980) (per curiam) ("very purpose" of Williams Act was "informed decisionmaking by shareholders"). As we recognized in Schreiber v. Burlington Northern, Inc., 472 U.S. 1 (1985), Congress designed the Williams Act to make "disclosure, rather than court imposed principles of 'fairness' or 'artificiality,' . . . the preferred method of market regulation." Id., at 9, n.8. Section 14(e), we explained, "supplements the more precise disclosure provisions found elsewhere in the Williams Act, while requiring disclosure more explicitly addressed to the tender offer context than that required by §10(b)." Id., at 10-11.

Relying on §14(e)'s rulemaking authorization, the Commission, in 1980, promulgated Rule 14e-3(a). That measure provides:

(a) If any person has taken a substantial step or steps to commence, or has commenced, a tender offer (the "offering person"), it shall constitute a fraudulent, deceptive or manipulative act or practice within the meaning of section 14(e) of the [Exchange] Act for any other person who is in possession of material information relating to such tender offer which information he knows or has reason to know is nonpublic and which he knows or has reason to know has been acquired directly or indirectly from:

> (1) The offering person,
>
> (2) The issuer of the securities sought or to be sought by such tender offer, or
>
> (3) Any officer, director, partner or employee or any other person acting on
> behalf of the offering person or such issuer, to purchase or sell or cause to be purchased or sold any of such securities or any securities convertible into or exchangeable for any such securities or any option or right to obtain or to dispose of any of the foregoing securities, unless within a reasonable time prior to any purchase or sale such information and its source are publicly disclosed by press release or otherwise.

As characterized by the Commission, Rule 14e-3(a) is a "disclose or abstain from trading" requirement. 45 Fed. Reg. 60410 (1980).[15] The Second Circuit concisely described the rule's thrust:

> One violates Rule 14e-3(a) if he trades on the basis of material nonpublic information concerning a pending tender offer that he knows or has reason to know has been acquired "directly or indirectly" from an insider of the offerer or issuer, or someone working on their behalf. Rule 14e-3(a) is a disclosure provision. It creates a duty in those traders who fall within its ambit to abstain or disclose, *without regard to whether the trader owes a pre-existing fiduciary duty* to respect the confidentiality of the information.

United States v. Chestman, 947 F.2d 551, 557 (1991) (en banc) (emphasis added), cert. denied, 503 U.S. 1004 (1992).

See also SEC v. Maio, 51 F.3d 623, 635 (C.A.7 1995) ("Rule 14e-3 creates a duty to disclose material non-public information, or abstain from trading in stocks implicated by an impending tender offer, *regardless of whether such information was obtained through a breach of fiduciary duty*.") (emphasis added); SEC v. Peters, 978 F.2d 1162, 1165 (C.A.10 1992) (as written, Rule 14e-3(a) has no fiduciary duty requirement).

In the Eighth Circuit's view, because Rule 14e-3(a) applies whether or not the trading in question breaches a fiduciary duty, the regulation exceeds the SEC's §14(e) rulemaking authority. See 92 F.3d, at 624, 627. Contra, Maio, 51 F.3d, at 634-635 (C.A.7); Peters, 978 F.2d, at 1165-1167 (C.A.10); Chestman, 947 F.2d, at 556-563 (C.A.2) (all holding Rule 14e-3(a) a proper exercise of SEC's statutory authority). In support of its holding, the Eighth Circuit relied on the text of §14(e) and our decisions in *Schreiber* and *Chiarella*. See 92 F.3d, at 624-627.

The Eighth Circuit homed in on the essence of §14(e)'s rulemaking authorization: "[T]he statute empowers the SEC to 'define' and 'prescribe means reasonably designed to prevent' 'acts and practices' which are 'fraudulent.'" Id., at 624. All that means, the Eighth Circuit found plain, is that the SEC may "identify and regulate," in the tender offer context, "acts and practices" the law already defines

---

15. The rule thus adopts for the tender offer context a requirement resembling the one Chief Justice Burger would have adopted in *Chiarella* for misappropriators under §10(b). See supra, at 2208, n. 6.

as "fraudulent"; but, the Eighth Circuit maintained, the SEC may not "create its own definition of fraud." Ibid. (internal quotation marks omitted).

This Court, the Eighth Circuit pointed out, held in *Schreiber* that the word "manipulative" in the §14(e) phrase "fraudulent, deceptive, or manipulative acts or practices" means just what the word means in §10(b): Absent misrepresentation or nondisclosure, an act cannot be indicted as manipulative. See 92 F.3d, at 625 (citing *Schreiber*, 472 U.S., at 7-8, and n.6). Section 10(b) interpretations guide construction of §14(e), the Eighth Circuit added, see 92 F.3d, at 625, citing this Court's acknowledgment in *Schreiber* that §14(e)'s "'broad antifraud prohibition' . . . [is] modeled on the antifraud provisions of §10(b) . . . and Rule 10b-5," 472 U.S., at 10 (citation omitted); see id., at 10-11, n.10.

For the meaning of "fraudulent" under §10(b), the Eighth Circuit looked to *Chiarella*. See 92 F.3d, at 625. In that case, the Eighth Circuit recounted, this Court held that a failure to disclose information could be "fraudulent" under §10(b) only when there was a duty to speak arising out of "'a fiduciary or other similar relationship of trust and confidence.'" *Chiarella*, 445 U.S., at 228 (quoting Restatement (Second) of Torts §551(2)(a) (1976)). Just as §10(b) demands a showing of a breach of fiduciary duty, so such a breach is necessary to make out a §14(e) violation, the Eighth Circuit concluded.

As to the Commission's §14(e) authority to "prescribe means reasonably designed to prevent" fraudulent acts, the Eighth Circuit stated: "Properly read, this provision means simply that the SEC has broad regulatory powers in the field of tender offers, but the statutory terms have a fixed meaning which the SEC cannot alter by way of an administrative rule." 92 F.3d, at 627.

The United States urges that the Eighth Circuit's reading of §14(e) misapprehends both the Commission's authority to define fraudulent acts and the Commission's power to prevent them. "The 'defining' power," the United States submits, "would be a virtual nullity were the SEC not permitted to go beyond common law fraud (which is separately prohibited in the first [self-operative] sentence of Section 14(e))." Brief for United States 11; see id., at 37.

In maintaining that the Commission's power to define fraudulent acts under §14(e) is broader than its rulemaking power under §10(b), the United States questions the Court of Appeals' reading of *Schreiber*. See id., at 38-40. Parenthetically, the United States notes that the word before the *Schreiber* Court was "manipulative"; unlike "fraudulent," the United States observes, "'manipulative' . . . is 'virtually a term of art when used in connection with the securities markets.'" Id., at 38, n.20 (quoting *Schreiber*, 472 U.S., at 6). Most tellingly, the United States submits, *Schreiber* involved acts alleged to violate the self-operative provision in §14(e)'s first sentence, a sentence containing language similar to §10(b). But §14(e)'s second sentence, containing the rulemaking authorization, the United States points out, does not track §10(b), which simply authorizes the SEC to proscribe "manipulative or deceptive device[s] or contrivance[s]." Brief for United States 38. Instead, §14(e)'s rulemaking prescription tracks §15(c)(2)(D) of the Exchange Act, 15 U.S.C. §78o(c)(2)(D), which concerns the conduct of broker-dealers in over-the-counter markets. See Brief for United States 38-39. Since 1938, §15(c)(2) has given the Commission authority to "define, and prescribe means reasonably designed to prevent, such [broker-dealer] acts and practices as are fraudulent, deceptive, or manipulative." 15 U.S.C. §78o(c)(2)(D). When Congress added this same rulemaking language to §14(e) in 1970, the Government states, the

Commission had already used its §15(c)(2) authority to reach beyond common law fraud. See Brief for United States 39, n.22.

We need not resolve in this case whether the Commission's authority under §14(e) to "define . . . such acts and practices as are fraudulent" is broader than the Commission's fraud-defining authority under §10(b), for we agree with the United States that Rule 14e-3(a), as applied to cases of this genre, qualifies under §14(e) as a "means reasonably designed to prevent" fraudulent trading on material, nonpublic information in the tender offer context.[17] A prophylactic measure, because its mission is to prevent, typically encompasses more than the core activity prohibited. As we noted in *Schreiber*, §14(e)'s rulemaking authorization gives the Commission "latitude," even in the context of a term of art like "manipulative," "to regulate nondeceptive activities as a 'reasonably designed' means of preventing manipulative acts, without suggesting any change in the meaning of the term 'manipulative' itself." 472 U.S., at 11, n.11. We hold, accordingly, that under §14(e), the Commission may prohibit acts, not themselves fraudulent under the common law or §10(b), if the prohibition is "reasonably designed to prevent . . . acts and practices [that] are fraudulent." 15 U.S.C. §78n(e).

Because Congress has authorized the Commission, in §14(e), to prescribe legislative rules, we owe the Commission's judgment "more than mere deference or weight." Batterton v. Francis, 432 U.S. 416, 424-426 (1977). Therefore, in determining whether Rule 14e-3(a)'s "disclose or abstain from trading" requirement is reasonably designed to prevent fraudulent acts, we must accord the Commission's assessment "controlling weight unless [it is] arbitrary, capricious, or manifestly contrary to the statute." Chevron U.S.A. Inc. v. Natural Resources Defense Council, Inc., 467 U.S. 837, 844 (1984). In this case, we conclude, the Commission's assessment is none of these.

In adopting the "disclose or abstain" rule, the SEC explained:

> The Commission has previously expressed and continues to have serious concerns about trading by persons in possession of material, nonpublic information relating to a tender offer. This practice results in unfair disparities in market information and market disruption. Security holders who purchase from or sell to such persons are effectively denied the benefits of disclosure and the substantive protections of the Williams Act. If furnished with the information, these security holders would be able to make an informed investment decision, which could involve deferring the purchase or sale of the securities until the material information had been disseminated or until the tender offer has been commenced or terminated.

45 Fed. Reg. 60412 (1980) (footnotes omitted).

The Commission thus justified Rule 14e-3(a) as a means necessary and proper to assure the efficacy of Williams Act protections.

---

17. We leave for another day, when the issue requires decision, the legitimacy of Rule 14e-3(a) as applied to "warehousing," which the Government describes as "the practice by which bidders leak advance information of a tender offer to allies and encourage them to purchase the target company's stock before the bid is announced." Reply Brief 17. As we observed in *Chiarella*, one of the Commission's purposes in proposing Rule 14e-3(a) was "to bar warehousing under its authority to regulate tender offers." 445 U.S., at 234. The Government acknowledges that trading authorized by a principal breaches no fiduciary duty. See Reply Brief 17. The instant case, however, does not involve trading authorized by a principal; therefore, we need not here decide whether the Commission's proscription of warehousing falls within its §14(e) authority to fine or prevent fraud.

The United States emphasizes that Rule 14e-3(a) reaches trading in which "a breach of duty is likely but difficult to prove." Reply Brief 16. "Particularly in the context of a tender offer," as the Tenth Circuit recognized, "there is a fairly wide circle of people with confidential information," *Peters*, 978 F.2d, at 1167, notably, the attorneys, investment bankers, and accountants involved in structuring the transaction. The availability of that information may lead to abuse, for "even a hint of an upcoming tender offer may send the price of the target company's stock soaring." SEC v. Materia, 745 F.2d 197, 199 (C.A.2 1984). Individuals entrusted with nonpublic information, particularly if they have no long-term loyalty to the issuer, may find the temptation to trade on that information hard to resist in view of "the very large short-term profits potentially available [to them]." *Peters*, 978 F.2d, at 1167.

"[I]t may be possible to prove circumstantially that a person [traded on the basis of material, nonpublic information], but almost impossible to prove that the trader obtained such information in breach of a fiduciary duty owed either by the trader or by the ultimate insider source of the information." Ibid. The example of a "tippee" who trades on information received from an insider illustrates the problem. Under Rule 10b-5, "a tippee assumes a fiduciary duty to the shareholders of a corporation not to trade on material nonpublic information only when the insider has breached his fiduciary duty to the shareholders by disclosing the information to the tippee and the tippee knows or should know that there has been a breach." *Dirks*, 463 U.S., at 660. To show that a tippee who traded on nonpublic information about a tender offer had breached a fiduciary duty would require proof not only that the insider source breached a fiduciary duty, but that the tippee knew or should have known of that breach. "Yet, in most cases, the only parties to the [information transfer] will be the insider and the alleged tippee." *Peters*, 978 F.2d, at 1167.

In sum, it is a fair assumption that trading on the basis of material, nonpublic information will often involve a breach of a duty of confidentiality to the bidder or target company or their representatives. The SEC, cognizant of the proof problem that could enable sophisticated traders to escape responsibility, placed in Rule 14e-3(a) a "disclose or abstain from trading" command that does not require specific proof of a breach of fiduciary duty. That prescription, we are satisfied, applied to this case, is a "means reasonably designed to prevent" fraudulent trading on material, nonpublic information in the tender offer context. See *Chestman*, 947 F.2d, at 560 ("While dispensing with the subtle problems of proof associated with demonstrating fiduciary breach in the problematic area of tender offer insider trading, [Rule 14e-3(a)] retains a close nexus between the prohibited conduct and the statutory aims."); accord, *Maio*, 51 F.3d, at 635, and n.14; *Peters*, 978 F.2d, at 1167. Therefore, insofar as it serves to prevent the type of misappropriation charged against O'Hagan, Rule 14e-3(a) is a proper exercise of the Commission's prophylactic power under §14(e).

As an alternate ground for affirming the Eighth Circuit's judgment, O'Hagan urges that Rule 14e-3(a) is invalid because it prohibits trading in advance of a tender offer — when "a substantial step . . . to commence" such an offer has been taken — while §14(e) prohibits fraudulent acts "in connection with any tender offer." See Brief for Respondent 41-42. O'Hagan further contends that, by covering pre-offer conduct, Rule 14e-3(a) "fails to comport with due process on two levels": The rule does not "give fair notice as to when, in advance of a tender offer, a violation of §14(e) occurs," id., at 42; and it "disposes of any scienter requirement," id., at 43. The Court of Appeals did not address these arguments, and O'Hagan did not raise the due process points in his briefs before that court. We decline to consider these contentions in the first instance. The Court of Appeals may address on remand any arguments O'Hagan has preserved.

IV. Based on its dispositions of the securities fraud convictions, the Court of Appeals also reversed O'Hagan's convictions, under 18 U.S.C. §1341, for mail fraud. See 92 F.3d, at 627-628. Reversal of the securities convictions, the Court of Appeals recognized, "d[id] not as a matter of law require that the mail fraud convictions likewise be reversed." Id., at 627 (citing *Carpenter*, 484 U.S., at 24, in which this Court unanimously affirmed mail and wire fraud convictions based on the same conduct that evenly divided the Court on the defendants' securities fraud convictions). But in this case, the Court of Appeals said, the indictment was so structured that the mail fraud charges could not be disassociated from the securities fraud charges, and absent any securities fraud, "there was no fraud upon which to base the mail fraud charges." 92 F.3d, at 627-628.

The United States urges that the Court of Appeals' position is irreconcilable with *Carpenter:* Just as in *Carpenter*, so here, the "mail fraud charges are independent of [the] securities fraud charges, even [though] both rest on the same set of facts." Brief for United States 46-47. We need not linger over this matter, for our rulings on the securities fraud issues require that we reverse the Court of Appeals judgment on the mail fraud counts as well.

O'Hagan, we note, attacked the mail fraud convictions in the Court of Appeals on alternate grounds; his other arguments, not yet addressed by the Eighth Circuit, remain open for consideration on remand.

The judgment of the Court of Appeals for the Eighth Circuit is reversed, and the case is remanded for further proceedings consistent with this opinion.

It is so ordered.

---

1. *Consent or disclosure as defenses to insider trading.* O'Hagan says that "full disclosure forecloses liability under the misappropriation theory," adding that "if the fiduciary discloses to the source that he plans to trade on the nonpublic information, there is no 'deceptive device' and thus no §10(b) violation — although the fiduciary-turned-trader may remain liable under state law for a breach of the duty of loyalty."[77] Does this doctrinal limitation create an exception that can overwhelm the rule? Suppose an Ivan Boesky disclosed to Grand Metropolitan (the bidder in *O'Hagan*) that he had learned of its approaching tender offer and planned to trade on it. Or suppose the firm's chief executive officer disclosed this same information to certain preferred institutional investors. The practical answer may be that, in the case of a tender offer, all would remain potentially liable for breach of Rule 14e-3. But outside the tender offer context, the potential inroad on the traditional insider trading prohibition seems substantial.

---

77. 521 U.S. 642, 655. In a footnote, the majority opinion added that where the defendant owed duties to multiple persons (such as O'Hagan did to both his law firm and its clients), disclosure would have to be made to both. Id. at 655 n.7.

Even if the principal can consent to insider trading by its agent under *O'Hagan*, the question remains: Who can consent for the principal? Should the consent of a senior managerial officer be viewed as binding on the corporation (based on actual, implied, or apparent authority)? Will informal consent suffice? Or should board approval be required for such an unusual decision?

To date, courts appear to be resisting any expansion of this disclosure or consent defense to insider trading beyond the express language of *O'Hagan*. In SEC v. Rocklage, 470 F.3d 1 (1st Cir. 2006), the CEO of a publicly traded biotechnology firm told his wife that one of the company's key products had just failed its clinical trial. She then informed her husband that she was going to tell her brother about this negative information, and when she did so (over her husband's protest), her brother and his friend dumped their stock in the company. The SEC sued the wife, the brother, and the friend, but they all raised the defense that the wife's post-tip disclosure to her husband that she intended to tip her brother negated any liability under the above-quoted language in *O'Hagan*.

The district court denied the defendant's motion to dismiss, and the First Circuit affirmed. The First Circuit found that the wife's acquisition of the information was deceptive because she had already reached a pre-existing agreement with her brother to tip him if she learned any material negative information about the company. Her husband had specifically instructed her not to discuss the test results with others, and he had often in the past confided confidential business information to her, which confidences she had previously maintained. When the wife told her husband that she planned to signal the news to her brother, the husband "urged her not to do so, and . . . expressed his displeasure at the idea," but he took no action (one suspects that the First Circuit's terse summary of their dialogue leaves out the interesting details).

The substance of the First Circuit's position was that (1) the wife tricked the husband into making a disclosure he would not have made, had he known of the agreement, and (2) this deceptive conduct occurred "in connection with" a purchase or sale because she anticipated that her brother would trade. So viewed, the case does not address the fact pattern in which the defendant decides to tell a friend or relative after the defendant acquires the information. However, the SEC argued that for the disclosure to qualify under *O'Hagan*, it must be "useful" to the corporation, meaning that there had to be sufficient time (and other circumstances had to be present) to enable the corporation to take effective remedial action. The First Circuit did not address this claim that the disclosure had to be "useful" to be effective.

2. *The use/possession distinction.* Is it enough that an insider or a tippee "knowingly possess" material nonpublic information? Or must the defendant actually use that information by deciding to trade based upon it? Prior to *O'Hagan*, the government had been successful in convincing federal courts that only possession of the material information was needed. See United States v. Teicher, 987 F.2d 112, 119 (2d Cir. 1993). After *O'Hagan*, however, judicial attitudes appear to have changed, and actual use was required by some. In part, this shift seems to be the consequence of a sentence in *O'Hagan* in which the majority wrote: "[T]he fiduciary's fraud is consummated, not when the fiduciary gains the confidential information, but when, without disclosure to his principal, he *uses* the information to purchase or sell securities."[78] Based on this language, both the Ninth and

---

78. 521 U.S. at 656 (emphasis added).

Eleventh circuits have endorsed an "actual use" standard under which the government must show that the undisclosed information played at least a substantial role in the defendant's investment decision.[79] Both courts also stressed that a use requirement was more consistent with the language of §10, which emphasizes "manipulation," "deception," and "fraud."

Conversely, how can the human mind ever not "use" material information that it possesses? Consider this hypothetical: XYZ Corporation's chief financial officer has purchased 5,000 shares of its stock every quarter for the last four years, making such purchase in each case on the day following the public release of XYZ's quarterly financial results. This year, just before the release of its first-quarter results, he learns of a major oil discovery by the firm in the South China Sea (which information is still undisclosed, but material). He again buys 5,000 shares. Has he "used" the information in again making his standard purchase? Would it make any difference if he had already given a standing instruction to his broker to make such purchases? What if he increased his purchase to 10,000 shares?

3. *The SEC's response: Rule 10b5-1.* Concerned that the use/possession distinction created a dangerously broad loophole, the SEC responded in 2000 by adopting Rule 10b5-1. Its expanded prohibitions are set forth in subsections (a) and (b):

> Rule 10b5-1. *Trading "on the Basis of" Material Nonpublic Information in Insider Trading Cases.* . . .
>
> (a) *General.* The "manipulative and deceptive" devices prohibited by Section 10(b) of the Act (15 U.S.C. §78j) and §240.10b-5 thereunder include, among other things, the purchase or sale of a security of any issuer, on the basis of material nonpublic information about that security or issuer, in breach of a duty of trust or confidence that is owed directly, indirectly, or derivatively, to the issuer of that security or the shareholders of that issuer, or to any other person who is the source of the material nonpublic information.
>
> (b) *Definition of "on the basis of."* Subject to the affirmative defense in paragraph (c) of this section, a purchase or sale of a security of an issuer is "on the basis of" material nonpublic information about that security or issuer if the person making the purchase or sale was aware of the material nonpublic information when the person made the purchase or sale.

Making "awareness" the dispositive consideration seemingly sides with those courts that had earlier found possession, and not use, to be sufficient. The SEC, however, refers to its new standard as a "knowing possession" standard. The initial decisions to consider this new rule have "deferred" to it. See, e.g., Newby v. Lay, 258 F. Supp. 2d 576 (S.D. Tex. 2003).

Rule 10b5-1, however, also contains a broad affirmative defense under subsection (c), which provides that a purchase or sale is not "on the basis" of material nonpublic information if the person making the purchase or sale can demonstrate that:

> "(A) Before becoming aware of the information, the person had:
>> (1) Entered into a binding contract to purchase or sell the security,
>> (2) Instructed another person to purchase or sell the security for the instructing person's account, or
>> (3) Adopted a written plan for trading securities;"

---

79. United States v. Smith, 155 F.3d 1051 (9th Cir. 1998); SEC v. Adler, 137 F.3d 1325, 1336-1339 (11th Cir. 1998).

The remainder of Rule 10b5-1 contains elaborate provisions defining what constitutes a qualifying contract, instruction, or trading plan for purposes of this rule. The most confining restriction is that the contract, instruction, or trading plan must be irrevocable and that it "did not permit the person to exercise any subsequent influence over how, when, or whether to effect purchases or sales." The contract, instruction, or plan may, however, be highly contingent, such as a written formula, algorithm, or computer program that makes purchases or sales dependent on the individual stock's price or general price levels in the market or any other market condition or development so long as it is established in advance. The ability of a defendant to rely on this affirmative defense also depends on such person's lack of awareness of material nonpublic information at the time the person initially enters into the contract, instruction, or plan.

Finally, Rule 10b5-1 formally recognizes an informational partition defense in the case of persons other than natural persons. If, for example, an investment bank engages in proprietary trading for its own account through one division and represents the issuer through another division or unit, it may still trade in the issuer's securities, even though the other nontrading division is aware of material nonpublic information. The test is that the trading division must not be aware of the material nonpublic information and must have "implemented reasonable policies and procedures, taking into consideration the nature of the person's business, to ensure that individuals making investment decisions would not violate the laws prohibiting trading on the basis of material nonpublic information."

4. *Is benefit to the tipper still required under misappropriation theory?* After *O'Hagan*, the SEC began to argue that *Dirks*'s tipper benefit requirement had no application in misappropriation cases. It reasoned that the purpose of the benefit requirement was to show that the tipper-insider had breached a duty to the corporation's shareholders, whereas in misappropriation cases the outsider owed no duty to the corporation's shareholders. Hence, in its view, it was unnecessary that the outsider have intended to benefit from his or her disclosure. Some decisions appeared to adopt this view. See United States v. Libera, 989 F.2d 596, 600 (2d Cir. 1993). Other Circuits were uncertain. See SEC v. Sargent, 229 F.3d 68, 77 (1st Cir. 2000). Most recently, in SEC v. Yun, 327 F.3d 1263 (11th Cir. 2003), the Eleventh Circuit handed the SEC a significant defeat. There, in the context of divorce discussions, the husband told his wife that the value of his stock options would be greatly eroded by undisclosed adverse news concerning his company. She discussed the impact of this news with her divorce lawyer and was overheard by a co-worker, who traded in the stock, buying put options. Suing both the wife and her tippee friend, the SEC argued that it need only show that this disclosure was reckless, and did not need to show any "intent to benefit" in a misappropriation case. Conversely, the two defendants argued that because the wife had expected no benefit from disclosure, there could be no liability under *Dirks*. The Eleventh Circuit agreed with the defendants, on the ground that any contrary rule "constructs an arbitrary fence between insider trading liability based upon classical and misappropriation theories" — i.e., between the *Dirks* theory and the *O'Hagan* theory. It, however, remanded for a new trial at which the SEC could seek to prove that the wife expected to benefit in the future from the tip to her friend.

Not all circuits, however, necessarily agree with *Yun*. In SEC v. Rocklage, 470 F.3d 1 (1st Cir. 2006) (discussed earlier at page 485), the wife of the CEO tipped her brother, but she did not share in the gains or apparently expect to receive any benefit. Because she received none of the profits, the defendants raised the argument that *Dirks*'s personal-benefit test precluded liability. The First Circuit concluded, however, that it need not reach the issue of whether a personal benefit was necessary under misappropriation theory, which issue it said was "open" for purposes of misappropriation theory, because "the mere giving of a gift to a relative or friend is a sufficient personal benefit. . . . The gift of information Mrs. Rocklage gave her brother meets that standard." Id. at 7 n.4.

g. Insider Trading and the Remote Tippee

United States v. Chestman
947 F.2d 551 (2d Cir. 1991)

Meskill, C.J.: . . . A jury found Chestman guilty of thirty-one counts of insider trading and perjury: (1) ten counts of fraudulent trading in connection with a tender offer in violation of section 14(e), 18 U.S.C. §2, and Rule 14e-3(a), (2) ten counts of securities fraud in violation of section 10(b), 18 U.S.C. §2, and 17 C.F.R. §240.10b-5 (1988) (Rule 10b-5), (3) ten counts of mail fraud in violation of the mail fraud statute and 18 U.S.C. §2, and (4) one count of perjury in violation of 18 U.S.C. §1621. A panel of this Court reversed Chestman's convictions in their entirety. 903 F.2d 75 (2d Cir. 1990).

On *in banc* reconsideration, we conclude that the Rule 14e-3(a) convictions should be affirmed and that the Rule 10b-5 and mail fraud convictions should be reversed. We vacate the panel's decision on all three issues. We did not rehear the appeal from the perjury conviction and, as a result, the panel's reversal of that conviction stands.

Background. Robert Chestman is a stockbroker. Keith Loeb first sought Chestman's services in 1982, when Loeb decided to consolidate his and his wife's holdings in Waldbaum, Inc. (Waldbaum), a publicly traded company that owned a large supermarket chain. During their initial meeting, Loeb told Chestman that his wife was a grand-daughter of Julia Waldbaum, a member of the board of directors of Waldbaum and the wife of its founder. Julia Waldbaum also was the mother of Ira Waldbaum, the president and controlling shareholder of Waldbaum. From 1982 to 1986, Chestman executed several transactions involving Waldbaum restricted and common stock for Keith Loeb. To facilitate some of these trades, Loeb sent Chestman a copy of his wife's birth certificate, which indicated that his wife's mother was Shirley Waldbaum Witkin.

On November 21, 1986, Ira Waldbaum agreed to sell Waldbaum to the Great Atlantic and Pacific Tea Company (A&P). The resulting stock purchase agreement required Ira to tender a controlling block of Waldbaum shares to A&P at a price of $50 per share. Ira told three of his children, all employees of Waldbaum, about the pending sale two days later, admonishing them to keep the news quiet until a public announcement. He also told his sister, Shirley Witkin, and nephew, Robert Karin, about the sale, and offered to tender their shares along with his controlling block of shares to enable them to avoid the administrative difficulty of tendering after the public announcement. He cautioned them "that [the sale was] not to be discussed," that it was to remain confidential.

In spite of Ira's counsel, Shirley told her daughter, Susan Loeb, on November 24 that Ira was selling the company. Shirley warned Susan not to tell anyone except her husband, Keith Loeb, because disclosure could ruin the sale. The next day, Susan told her husband about the pending tender offer and cautioned him not to tell anyone because "it could possibly ruin the sale."

The following day, November 26, Keith Loeb telephoned Robert Chestman at 8:59 A.M. Unable to reach Chestman, Loeb left a message asking Chestman to call him "ASAP." According to Loeb, he later spoke with Chestman between 9:00 A.M. and 10:30 A.M. that morning and told Chestman that he had "some definite, some accurate information" that Waldbaum was about to be sold at a "substantially higher" price than its market value. Loeb asked Chestman several times what he thought Loeb should do. Chestman responded that he could not advise Loeb what to do "in a situation like this" and that Loeb would have to make up his own mind.

That morning Chestman executed several purchases of Waldbaum stock. At 9:49 A.M. he bought 3,000 shares for his own account at $24.65 per share. Between 11:31 A.M. and 12:35 P.M., he purchased an additional 8,000 shares for his clients' discretionary accounts at prices ranging from $25.75 to $26.00 per share. One of the discretionary accounts was the Loeb account, for which Chestman bought 1,000 shares.

Before the market closed at 4:00 P.M., Loeb claims that he telephoned Chestman a second time. During their conversation Loeb again pressed Chestman for advice. Chestman repeated that he could not advise Loeb "in a situation like this," but then said that, based on his research, Waldbaum was a "buy." Loeb subsequently ordered 1,000 shares of Waldbaum stock.

Chestman presented a different version of the day's events. Before the SEC and at trial, he claimed that he had purchased Waldbaum stock based on his own research. He stated that his purchases were consistent with previous purchases of Waldbaum stock and other retail food stocks and were supported by reports in trade publications as well as the unusually high trading volume of the stock on November 25. He denied having spoken to Loeb about Waldbaum stock on the day of the trades. . . .

Discussion. . . . B. *Rule 10b-5.* Chestman's Rule 10b-5 convictions were based on the misappropriation theory, which provides that "one who misappropriates nonpublic information in breach of a fiduciary duty and trades on that information to his own advantage violates Section 10(b) and Rule 10b-5." SEC v. Materia, 745 F.2d 197, 203 (2d Cir. 1984). With respect to the shares Chestman purchased on behalf of Keith Loeb, Chestman was convicted of aiding and abetting Loeb's misappropriation of nonpublic information in breach of a duty Loeb owed to the Waldbaum family and to his wife Susan. As to the shares Chestman purchased for himself and his other clients, Chestman was convicted as a "tippee" of that same misappropriated information. Thus, while Chestman is the defendant in this case, the alleged misappropriator was Keith Loeb. The government agrees that Chestman's conviction cannot be sustained unless there was sufficient evidence to show that (1) Keith Loeb breached a duty owed to the Waldbaum family or Susan Loeb based on a fiduciary or similar relationship of trust and confidence, and (2) Chestman knew that Loeb had done so. We have heretofore never applied the misappropriation theory—and its predicate requirement of a fiduciary breach—in the context of family relationships. . . . [The court then discusses the *Dirks* case and its progeny.] . . .

2. *Misappropriation Theory.* . . . Under this theory, a person violates Rule 10b-5 when he misappropriates material nonpublic information in breach of a fiduciary

duty or similar relationship of trust and confidence and uses that information in a securities transaction. See, e.g., *Carpenter*, 791 F.2d at 1028-29; *Materia*, 745 F.2d at 201; *Newman*, 664 F.2d at 17-18. In contrast to *Chiarella* and *Dirks*, the misappropriation theory does not require that the buyer or seller of securities be defrauded. *Newman*, 664 F.2d at 17. Focusing on the language "fraud or deceit upon *any* person" (emphasis added), we have held that the predicate act of fraud may be perpetrated on the source of the nonpublic information, even though the source may be unaffiliated with the buyer or seller of securities. See *Carpenter*, 791 F.2d at 1032. To date we have applied the theory only in the context of employment relationships. See *Carpenter*, 791 F.2d at 1032 (financial columnist breached duty to his newspaper); *Materia*, 745 F.2d at 202 (copyholder breached duty to his printing company); *Newman*, 664 F.2d at 17 (investment banker breached duty to his firm). District courts in this Circuit have applied the theory in other settings as well as in the employment context. See, e.g., United States v. Willis, 737 F. Supp. 269 (S.D.N.Y. 1990) (denying motion to dismiss indictment of psychiatrist who traded on the basis of information obtained from patient, in breach of duty arising from relationship of trust and confidence); United States v. Reed, 601 F. Supp. 685 (S.D.N.Y.), *rev'd on other grounds*, 773 F.2d 477 (2d Cir. 1985) (allegation that son breached fiduciary duty to father, a corporate director, withstood motion to dismiss indictment); SEC v. Musella, 578 F. Supp. 425 (S.D.N.Y. 1984) (office services manager of law firm breached duty to law firm and its clients by trading on the basis of material nonpublic information acquired in the course of his employment). . . .

After *Carpenter*, the fiduciary relationship question takes on special importance. This is because a fraud-on-the-source theory of liability extends the focus of Rule 10b-5 beyond the confined sphere of fiduciary/shareholder relations to fiduciary breaches of any sort, a particularly broad expansion of 10b-5 liability if the add-on, a "similar relationship of trust and confidence," is construed liberally. One concern triggered by this broadened inquiry is that fiduciary duties are circumscribed with some clarity in the context of shareholder relations but lack definition in other contexts. See generally *Reed*, 601 F. Supp. 685 (and authorities cited therein). Tethered to the field of shareholder relations, fiduciary obligations arise within a narrow, principled sphere. The existence of fiduciary duties in other common law settings, however, is anything but clear. Our Rule 10b-5 precedents under the misappropriation theory, moreover, provide little guidance with respect to the question of fiduciary breach, because they involved egregious fiduciary breaches arising solely in the context of employer/employee associations. See *Carpenter*, 791 F.2d at 1028 ("It is clear that defendant Winans . . . breached a duty of confidentiality to his employer"); *Newman*, 664 F.2d at 17 ("we need spend little time on the issue of fraud and deceit"); *Materia*, 745 F.2d at 201 (same). For these reasons we tread cautiously in extending the misappropriation theory to new relationships, lest our efforts to construe Rule 10b-5 lose method and predictability, taking over "the whole corporate universe." United States v. Chiarella, 588 F.2d 1358, 1377 (2d Cir. 1978) Meskill, J., dissenting) (1980). . . .

3. *Fiduciary Duties and Their Functional Equivalent.* Against this backdrop, we turn to our central inquiry—what constitutes a fiduciary or similar relationship of trust and confidence in the context of Rule 10b-5 criminal liability? We begin by noting two factors that do not themselves create the necessary relationship.

First, a fiduciary duty cannot be imposed unilaterally by entrusting a person with confidential information. Walton v. Morgan Stanley & Co. 623 F.2d 796, 799 (2d Cir. 1980) (applying Delaware law). *Walton* concerned the conduct of an investment bank, Morgan Stanley. While investigating possible takeover targets for one of its clients, Morgan Stanley obtained unpublished material information (internal earnings reports) on a confidential basis from a prospective target, Olinkraft. After its client abandoned the planned takeover, Morgan Stanley was charged with trading in Olinkraft's stock on the basis of the confidential information. Observing that the parties had bargained at "arm's length" and that there had not been a preexisting agreement of confidentiality between Morgan Stanley and Olinkraft, we rejected the argument that "Morgan Stanley became a fiduciary of Olinkraft by virtue of the receipt of the confidential information. . . . [T]he fact that the information was confidential did nothing, in and of itself, to change the relationship between Morgan Stanley and Olinkraft's management. Put bluntly, although, according to the complaint, Olinkraft's management placed its confidence in Morgan Stanley not to disclose the information, Morgan Stanley owed no duty to observe that confidence." *Walton*, 623 F.2d at 799. See also *Dirks*, 463 U.S. at 662 n.22 (citing *Walton* approvingly as "a case turning on the court's determination that the disclosure did not impose any fiduciary duties on the recipient of the inside information"). Reposing confidential information in another, then, does not by itself create a fiduciary relationship.

Second, marriage does not, without more, create a fiduciary relationship. " '[M]ere kinship does not of itself establish a confidential relation.' . . . Rather, the existence of a confidential relationship must be determined independently of a preexisting family relationship." *Reed*, 601 F. Supp. at 706 (quoting G. G. Bogert, The Law of Trusts and Trustees §482, at 300-11 (Rev. 2d ed. 1978) (other citations omitted). Although spouses certainly may by their conduct become fiduciaries, the marriage relationship alone does not impose fiduciary status. In sum, more than the gratuitous reposal of a secret to another who happens to be a family member is required to establish a fiduciary or similar relationship of trust and confidence.

We take our cues as to what is required to create the requisite relationship from the securities fraud precedents and the common law. See *Chiarella*, 445 U.S. at 227-30. The common law has recognized that some associations are inherently fiduciary. Counted among these hornbook fiduciary relations are those existing between attorney and client, executor and heir, guardian and ward, principal and agent, trustee and trust beneficiary, and senior corporate official and shareholder. *Reed*, 601 F. Supp. at 704 (citing Coffee, From Tort to Crime: Some Reflections on the Criminalization of Fiduciary Breaches and the Problematic Line Between Law and Ethics, 19 Am. Crim. L. Rev. 117, 150 (1981); Scott, The Fiduciary Principle, 37 Cal. L. Rev. 539, 541 (1949); Black's Law Dictionary 564 (5th ed. 1979)). While this list is by no means exhaustive, it is clear that the relationships involved in this case — those between Keith and Susan Loeb and between Keith Loeb and the Waldbaum family — were not traditional fiduciary relationships.

That does not end our inquiry, however. The misappropriation theory requires us to consider not only whether there exists a fiduciary relationship but also whether there exists a "similar relationship of trust and confidence." As the term "similar" implies, a "relationship of trust and confidence" must share the essential characteristics of a fiduciary association. Absent reference to the adjective "similar," interpretation of a "relationship of trust and confidence" becomes an exercise in question begging. Consider: when one *entrusts* a secret (read *confidence*) to another, there then exists a relationship of trust and confidence. *Walton*, however, instructs that entrusting confidential information to another does not, without more, create the necessary relationship and its correlative duty to maintain the confidence. A "similar relationship of trust and confidence," therefore, must be the functional equivalent of a fiduciary relationship. To determine whether such a relationship exists, we must ascertain the characteristics of a fiduciary relationship. . . .

A fiduciary relationship involves discretionary authority and dependency: One person depends on another — the fiduciary — to serve his interests. In relying on a fiduciary to act for his benefit, the beneficiary of the relation may entrust the fiduciary with custody over property of one sort or another. Because the fiduciary obtains access to this property to serve the ends of the fiduciary relationship, he becomes duty-bound not to appropriate the property for his own use. What has been said of an agent's duty of confidentiality applies with equal force to other fiduciary relations: "an agent is subject to a duty to the principal not to use or to communicate information confidentially given him by the principal or acquired by him during the course of or on account of his agency." Restatement (Second) of Agency §395 (1958). These characteristics represent the measure of the paradigmatic fiduciary relationship. A similar relationship of trust and confidence consequently must share these qualities.

In *Reed*, 601 F. Supp. 685, the district court confronted the question whether these principal characteristics of a fiduciary relationship — dependency and influence — were necessary factual prerequisites to a similar relationship of trust and confidence. There a member of the board of directors of Amax, Gordon Reed, disclosed to his son on several occasions confidential information concerning a proposed tender offer for Amax. Allegedly relying on this information, the son purchased Amax stock call options. The son was subsequently indicted for violating, among other things, Rule 10b-5 based on breach of a fiduciary duty arising between the father and son. The son then moved to dismiss the indictment, contending that he did not breach a fiduciary duty to his father. The district court sustained the indictment.

Both the government and Chestman rely on *Reed*. The government draws on *Reed*'s application of the misappropriation theory in the family context and its expansive construction of relationships of trust and confidence. Chestman, without challenging the holding in *Reed*, argues that *Reed* cannot sustain his Rule 10b-5 convictions because, unlike Reed senior and junior, Keith and Susan Loeb did not customarily repose confidential business information in one another. Neither party challenges the holding of *Reed*. And we decline to do so *sua sponte*. To remain consistent with our interpretation of a "similar relationship of trust and confidence," however, we limit *Reed* to its essential holding: the repeated disclosure of business secrets between family members may substitute for a factual finding of dependence and influence and thereby sustain a finding of the functional equivalent of a fiduciary relationship. We note, in this regard, that *Reed* repeatedly emphasized that the father and son "frequently discussed business affairs." . . .

We recognize, as *Reed* did, that equity has occasionally established a less rigorous threshold for a fiduciary-like relationship in order to right civil wrongs arising from non-compliance with the statute of frauds, statute of wills and parol evidence rule. See Bogert, *supra* §482, at 286 (explaining that equity's flexible treatment of confidential relationships has been particularly useful in evading the harsh consequences of the statute of frauds). Commenting on the boundless nature of relations of trust and confidence, one scholar observed: "Equity has never bound itself by any hard and fast definition of the phrase 'confidential relation' and has not listed all the necessary elements of such a relation, but has reserved discretion to apply the doctrine whenever it believes that a suitable occasion has arisen." *Reed*, 601 F. Supp. at 712 n.38 (quoting G. G. Bogert, The Law of Trusts and Trustees §482, at 284-86 (Rev. 2d ed. 1978)). Useful as such an elastic and expedient definition of confidential relations, i.e., relations of trust and confidence, may be in the civil context, it has no place in the criminal law. A "suitable occasion" test for determining the presence of criminal fraud would offend not only the rule of lenity but due process as well. See *Chiarella*, 445 U.S. at 235 n.20, ("a judicial holding that certain undefined activities 'generally are prohibited' by §10(b) would raise questions whether either criminal or civil defendants would be given fair notice that they have engaged in illegal activity"). See also *Dirks*, 463 U.S. at 658 n.17. (In rejecting an SEC variation on the parity of information theory, the Court wrote: "[T]his rule is inherently imprecise, and the imprecision prevents parties from ordering their actions in accord with legal requirements."). More than a perfunctory nod at the rule of lenity, then, is required. We will not apply outer permutations of chancery relief in addressing what is frequently the core inquiry in a Rule 10b-5 criminal conviction — whether a fiduciary duty has been breached.

4. *Application of the Law of Fiduciary Duties.* The alleged misappropriator in this case was Keith Loeb. According to the government's theory of prosecution, Loeb breached a fiduciary duty to his wife Susan and the Waldbaum family when he disclosed to Robert Chestman information concerning a pending tender offer for Waldbaum stock. Chestman was convicted as an aider and abettor of the misappropriation and as a tippee of the misappropriated information. Convictions under both theories, the government concedes, required the government to establish two critical elements — Loeb breached a fiduciary duty to Susan Loeb or to the Waldbaum family and Chestman knew that Loeb had done so. . . .

We have little trouble finding the evidence insufficient to establish a fiduciary relationship or its functional equivalent between Keith Loeb and the Waldbaum family. The government presented only two pieces of evidence on this point. The first was that Keith was an extended member of the Waldbaum family, specifically the family patriarch's (Ira Waldbaum's) "nephew-in-law." The second piece of evidence concerned Ira's discussions of the business with family members. "My children," Ira Waldbaum testified, "have always been involved with me and my family and they know we never speak about business outside of the family." His earlier testimony indicates that the "family" to which he referred were his "three children who were involved in the business."

Lending this evidence the reasonable inferences to which it is entitled, . . . it falls short of establishing the relationship necessary for fiduciary obligations. Kinship alone does not create the necessary relationship. The government proffered nothing more to establish a fiduciary-like association. It did not show that Keith Loeb had been brought into the family's inner circle, whose members, it appears, discussed confidential business information either because they were kin or because they worked together with Ira Waldbaum. Keith was not an employee of Waldbaum and there was no showing that he participated in confidential communications regarding the business. The critical information was gratuitously communicated to him. The disclosure did not serve the interests of Ira Waldbaum, his children or the Waldbaum company. Nor was there any evidence that the alleged relationship was characterized by influence or reliance of any sort. Measured against the principles of fiduciary relations, the evidence does not support a finding that Keith Loeb and the Waldbaum family shared either a fiduciary relation or its functional equivalent.

The government's theory that Keith breached a fiduciary duty of confidentiality to Susan suffers from similar defects. The evidence showed: Keith and Susan were married; Susan admonished Keith not to disclose that Waldbaum was the target of a tender offer; and the two had shared and maintained confidences in the past.

Keith's status as Susan's husband could not itself establish fiduciary status. Nor, absent a pre-existing fiduciary relation or an express agreement of confidentiality, could the coda — "Don't tell." That leaves the unremarkable testimony that Keith and Susan had shared and maintained generic confidences before. The jury was not told the nature of these past disclosures and therefore it could not reasonably find a relationship that inspired fiduciary, rather than normal marital, obligations.

In the absence of evidence of an explicit acceptance by Keith of a duty of confidentiality, the context of the disclosure takes on special import. While acceptance may be implied, it must be implied from a pre-existing fiduciary-like relationship between the parties. Here the government presented the jury with insufficient evidence from which to draw a rational inference of implied acceptance. Susan's disclosure of the information to Keith served no purpose, business or otherwise. The disclosure also was unprompted. Keith did not induce her to convey the information through misrepresentation or subterfuge. Superiority and reliance, moreover, did not mark this relationship either before or after the disclosure of the confidential information. Nor did Susan's dependence on Keith to act in her interests for some purpose inspire the disclosure. The government failed even to establish a pattern of sharing business confidences between the couple. The government, therefore, failed to offer sufficient evidence to establish the functional equivalent of a fiduciary relation.

In sum, Keith owed neither Susan nor the Waldbaum family a fiduciary duty or its functional equivalent, he did not defraud them by disclosing news of the pending tender offer to Chestman. Absent a predicate act of fraud by Keith Loeb, the alleged misappropriator, Chestman could not be derivatively liable as Loeb's tippee or as an aider and abettor. Chestman's Rule 10b-5 convictions must be reversed.

Conclusion. Accordingly, we affirm the Rule 14e-3(a) convictions and reverse the Rule 10b-5 and mail fraud convictions. The reversal of these convictions does not warrant reconsideration of the sentence since the sentences on the Rule 10b-5 and mail fraud convictions are concurrent with the sentences in the Rule 14e-3(a) counts. The panel's reversal of the perjury conviction remains intact.

WINTER, C.J. (joined by OAKES, NEWMAN, KEARSE, and McLAUGHLIN), concurring in part and dissenting in part:

I concur in the decision to affirm Chestman's convictions under Section 14(e) of the Securities Exchange Act of 1934 ("'34 Act"), and under Rule 14e-3. I respectfully dissent, however, from the reversals of his convictions under Section 10(b) and under the mail fraud statute.

1. *Insider Trading.* . . . (b) *Property Rights in Inside Information.* One commentator has attempted to explain the Supreme Court decisions in terms of the business-property rationale for banning insider trading mentioned in *Cady, Roberts & Co.* . . . That rationale may be summarized as follows. Information is perhaps the most precious commodity in commercial markets. It is expensive to produce, and, because it involves facts and ideas that can be easily photocopied or carried in one's head, there is a ubiquitous risk that those who pay to produce information will see others reap the profit from it. Where the profit from an activity is likely to be diverted, investment in that activity will decline. If the law fails to protect property rights in commercial information, therefore, less will be invested in generating such information.

For example, mining companies whose investments in geological surveys have revealed valuable deposits do not want word of the strike to get out until they have secured rights to the land. If word does get out, the price of the land not only will go up, but other mining companies may also secure the rights. In either case, the mining company that invested in geological surveys (including the inevitably sizeable number of unsuccessful drillings) will see profits from that investment enjoyed by others. If mining companies are unable to keep the results of such surveys confidential, less will be invested in them.

Similarly, firms that invest money in generating information about other companies with a view to some form of combination will maintain secrecy about their efforts, and if secrecy cannot be maintained, less will be invested in acquiring such information. Hostile acquirers will want to keep such information secret lest the target mount defensive actions or speculators purchase the target's stock. Even when friendly negotiations with the other company are undertaken, the acquirer will often require the target corporation to maintain secrecy about negotiations, lest the very fact of negotiation tip off others on the important fact that the two firms think a combination might be valuable. . . .

Insider trading may reduce the return on information in two ways. First, it creates incentives for insiders to generate or disclose information that may disregard the welfare of the corporation. . . . That risk is not implicated by the facts in the present case, and no further discussion is presently required.

Second, insider trading creates a risk that information will be prematurely disclosed by such trading, and the corporation will lose part or all of its property in that information. Although trades by an insider may rarely affect market price, others who know of the insider's trading may notice that a trader is unusually successful, or simply perceive unusual activity in a stock and guess the information and/or make piggyback trades. A broker who executes a trade for a geologist or for a financial printer may well draw relevant conclusions. Or, as in the instant matter, the trader, Loeb, may tell his or her broker about the inside information, who may then trade on his or her account, on clients' accounts, or may tell friends and relatives. One inside trader has publicly attributed his exposure in part to the fact that the bank through which he made trades piggybacked on the trades, as did the broker who made the trades for the bank. See Levine, The Inside Story of an Inside Trader, Fortune, May 21, 1990, at 80. Once activity in a stock reaches an unusual stage, others may guess the reason for the trading—the corporate secret. Insider trading thus increases the risk that confidential information acquired at a cost may be disclosed. If so, the owner of the information may lose its investment.

This analysis provides a policy rationale for prohibiting insider trading when the property rights of a corporation in information are violated by traders. However, the rationale stops well short of prohibiting all trading on material nonpublic information. Efficient capital markets depend on the protection of property rights in information. However, they also require that persons who acquire and act on information about companies be able to profit from the information they generate so long as the method by which the information is acquired does not amount to a form of theft. A rule commanding equal access would result in a securities market governed by relative degrees of ignorance because the profit motive for independently generating information about companies would be substantially diminished. Under such circumstances, the pricing of securities would be less accurate than in circumstances in which the production of information is encouraged by legal protection. . . .

(c) *The Instant Case.* When this analysis is applied to a family-controlled corporation such as that involved in the instant case, I believe that family members who have benefitted from the family's control of the corporation are under a duty not to disclose confidential corporate information that comes to them in the ordinary course of family affairs. In the case of family-controlled corporations, family and business affairs are necessarily intertwined, and it is inevitable that from time to time normal familial interactions will lead to the revelation of confidential corporate matters to various family members. Indeed, the very nature of familial relationships may cause the disclosure of corporate matters to avoid misunderstanding among family members or suggestions that a family member is unworthy of trust. . . .

. . . Members of a family who receive such information are placed in a position in which their trading on the information risks financial injury to the corporation, its public shareholders and other family members. When members of a family have benefitted from the family's control of a corporation and are in a position to acquire such information in the ordinary course of family interactions, that position carries with it a duty not to disclose. The family relationship gives such members access to confidential information, not so that they can trade on it but so that informal family relationships can be maintained. The purpose of allowing this access can hardly be fulfilled if there is no accompanying duty not to trade. Such a duty is of course based on mutual understandings among family members — quite explicit in this case — and owed to the family. However, the duty originates in the corporation and is ultimately intended to protect the corporation and its public shareholders. The duty is thus also owed to the corporation, to a degree sufficient in my view to trigger the *Dirks* rule. Because trading on inside information so acquired by family members amounts to theft, the misappropriation theory also applies. . . .

I thus believe that a family member (i) who has received or expects (e.g., through inheritance) benefits from family control of a corporation, here gifts of stock, (ii) who is in a position to learn confidential corporate information through ordinary family interactions, and (iii) who knows that under the circumstances both the corporation and the family desire confidentiality, has a duty not to use information so obtained for personal profit where the use risks disclosure. The receipt or expectation of benefits increases the interest of such family members in corporate affairs and thus increases the chance that they will learn confidential information. Disclosure in the present case occurred in the course of a discussion that included, *inter alia*, an examination of the benefits of the A&P acquisition to

Susan, Keith and their children. Susan's warning to Keith about secrecy was clearly intended to protect the corporation as well as the family and clearly had originated with Ira Waldbaum. In such circumstances, Susan's saying "Don't tell" is enough for me. Not to have such a rule means that a family-controlled corporation with public shareholders is subject to greater risk of disclosure of confidential information than is a corporation that is entirely publicly owned. . . .

SEC's response. Although the Second Circuit's decision in *Chestman* could not have been more closely divided (5 to 5 to 1), the SEC perceived it as a serious threat to its enforcement capability. The SEC feared that family members could trade based on material nonpublic information acquired from a family member who was an insider and then claim that the information had been inadvertently leaked or obtained without any legally binding promise of confidentiality. In response, in 2000, the SEC promulgated Rule 10b5-2 ("Duties of Trust or Confidence in Misappropriation Insider Trading Cases"), which provides a nonexclusive list of when "a duty of trust or confidence" has been breached. Subsection b of Rule 10b5-2 provides:

> (b) *Enumerated "duties of trust or confidence."* For purposes of this section, a "duty of trust or confidence" exists in the following circumstances, among others:
>
> (1) Whenever a person agrees to maintain information in confidence;
>
> (2) Whenever the person communicating the material nonpublic information and the person to whom it is communicated have a history, pattern, or practice of sharing confidences, such that the recipient of the information knows or reasonably should know that the person communicating the material nonpublic information expects that the recipient will maintain its confidentiality; or
>
> (3) Whenever a person receives or obtains material nonpublic information from his or her spouse, parent, child, or sibling; provided, however, that the person receiving or obtaining the information may demonstrate that no duty of trust or confidence existed with respect to the information, by establishing that he or she neither knew nor reasonably should have known that the person who was the source of the information expected that the person would keep the information confidential, because of the parties' history, pattern, or practice of sharing and maintaining confidences, and because there was no agreement or understanding to maintain the confidentiality of the information.

Although for the future Rule 10b5-2 reverses the *Chestman* outcome on its facts, it does not cover many intimate relationships (e.g., an unmarried couple sharing the same residence). In these cases, *Chestman*'s criteria for when a fiduciary duty arises—i.e., discretionary authority and dependency—arguably still govern. But Rule 10b5-2(b)(2)'s focus on a history, pattern, or practice of information sharing frames a new factual issue that will decide many cases.

h. Causation and Damages in Insider Trading Cases

Following the insider trading scandals that began in 1986, Congress amended the '34 Act to add the following new §20A ("Liability to Contemporaneous Traders for

Insider Trading"), which establishes an express cause of action for victims of insider trading:

> Sec. 20A. (a) *Private rights of action based on contemporaneous trading.* Any person who violates any provision of this title or the rules or regulations thereunder by purchasing or selling a security while in possession of material, nonpublic information shall be liable in an action in any court of competent jurisdiction to any person who, contemporaneously with the purchase or sale of securities that is the subject of such violation, has purchased (where such violation is based on a purchase of securities) or sold (where such violation is based on a purchase of securities) securities of the same class.
>
> (b) *Limitations on liability.*
>
> (1) *Contemporaneous trading actions limited to profit gained or loss avoided.* The total amount of damages imposed under subsection (a) shall not exceed the profit gained or loss avoided in the transaction or transactions that are the subject of the violation.
>
> (2) *Offsetting disgorgements against liability.* The total amount of damages imposed against any person under subsection (a) shall be diminished by the amounts, if any, that such person may be required to disgorge, pursuant to a court order obtained at the instance of the Commission, in a proceeding brought under section 21(d) of this title relating to the same transaction or transactions.
>
> (3) *Controlling person liability.* No person shall be liable under this section solely by reason of employing another person who is liable under this section, but the liability of a controlling person under this section shall be subject to section 20(a) of this title.
>
> (4) *Statute of limitations.* No action may be brought under this section more than 5 years after the date of the last transaction that is the subject of the violation.
>
> (c) *Joint and several liability for communicating.* Any person who violates any provision of this title or the rules or regulations thereunder by communicating material, nonpublic information shall be jointly and severally liable under subsection (a) with, and to the same extent as, any person or persons liable under subsection (a) to whom the communication was directed.
>
> (d) *Authority not to restrict other express or implied rights of action.* Nothing in this section shall be construed to limit or condition the right of any person to bring an action to enforce a requirement of this title or the availability of any cause of action implied from a provision of this title.
>
> (e) *Provisions not to affect public prosecutions.* This section shall not be construed to bar or limit in any manner any action by the Commission or the Attorney General under any other provision of this title, nor shall it bar or limit in any manner any action to recover penalties, or to seek any other order regarding penalties.

1. *The impact of §20A.* Section 20A defines neither what constitutes insider trading nor what constitutes "contemporaneously" buying or selling so as to give the victim standing. Instead, it assumes that the courts will continue to employ the standards of the existing case law. Read literally, the first sentence of §20A would cover a prospective bidder who, knowing that it was about to launch a tender offer or propose a merger, bought shares of the target on the open market. Such a person would not be liable under *Dirks* (because there is no breach of a fiduciary duty), but the defendant in this example does possess "material, nonpublic information." Despite this hazy drafting, the legislative history makes clear that only those who "misappropriate" the material nonpublic information are liable. Still, even this endorsement of misappropriation theory expands the scope of liability, because under §20A it appears possible for a shareholder of the target to sue a

person (such as Ivan Boesky) who misappropriates information from the bidder. Such a suit could not be brought under Rule 10b-5. Section 20A authorizes an alternative action to one brought under Rule 10b-5. However, §20A also clearly adopts a rule with respect to damages, borrowed from Elkind v. Liggett & Myers, Inc., below.

2. *The meaning of "contemporaneously."* Section 20A does not define "contemporaneously," but its legislative history indicates that the term was intended to adopt the definition "which has developed through the case law." H.R. Rep. No. 910, 100th Cong., 2d Sess. 27 (1988). In one of the cases cited by that Report, Shapiro v. Merrill Lynch, Pierce, Fenner & Smith, Inc., 495 F.2d 228, 237 (2d Cir. 1974), trades made within a four-day period were deemed contemporaneous. Nonetheless, most later decisions both under §20A and under Rule 10b-5 have read "contemporaneously" more strictly and have limited contemporaneous trading to trades made "not more than a few days apart from the defendant's." See Neubronner v. Milken, 6 F.3d 666 (9th Cir. 1993); Alfus v. Pyramid Technology Co., 745 F. Supp. 1511, 1522 (N.D. Cal. 1990). Some district courts have required the trading to be on the same day. See Copland v. Grumet, 88 F. Supp. 2d 326 (D.N.J. 1999); In re Aldus Sec. Litig., 1993 U.S. Dist. LEXIS 5008 (W.D. Wash. 1993). But see Froid v. Berner, 649 F. Supp. 1418, 1421 (D.N.J. 1986) (nine-day separation allowed between plaintiff's and defendant's trades). See also William Wang, The "Contemporaneous" Traders Who Can Sue an Inside Trader, 38 Hastings L.J. 1175 (1987).

Elkind v. Liggett & Myers, Inc.
635 F.2d 156 (2d Cir. 1980)

MANSFIELD, J.: [Shareholders brought a class action against Liggett & Myers, Inc. ("Liggett") for wrongful tipping of inside information about an earnings decline to certain persons who then sold Liggett's shares on the open market.] . . . This case presents a question of measurement of damages which we have previously deferred, believing that damages are best addressed in a concrete setting. See Shapiro v. Merrill Lynch, Pierce, Fenner & Smith, Inc., 495 F.2d at 241-42; Heit v. Weitzen, 402 F.2d 909, 917 & n.8 (2d Cir. 1968), *cert. denied*, 395 U.S. 903 (1969). We ruled in *Shapiro* that defendants selling on inside information would be liable to those who bought on the open market and sustained "substantial losses" during the period of insider trading.

The district court looked to the measure of damages used in cases where a buyer was induced to purchase a company's stock by materially misleading statements or omissions. In such cases of fraud by a fiduciary intended to induce others to buy or sell stock the accepted measure of damages is the "out-of-pocket" measure. This consists of the difference between the price paid and the "value" of the stocks when bought (or when the buyer committed himself to buy, if earlier). Except in rare face-to-face transactions, however, uninformed traders on an open, impersonal market are not induced by representations on the part of the tipper or tippee to buy or sell. Usually they are wholly unacquainted with and uninfluenced by the tippee's misconduct. They trade independently and voluntarily but without the benefit of information known to the trading tippee. . . .

Recognizing the foregoing, we in *Shapiro* suggested that the district court must be afforded flexibility in assessing damages. . . . [S]everal measures are possible.

First, there is the traditional out-of-pocket measure used by the district court in this case. For several reasons this measure appears to be inappropriate. In the first place, as we have noted, it is directed toward compensating a person for losses directly traceable to the defendant's fraud upon him. No such fraud or inducement may be attributed to a tipper or tippee trading on an impersonal market. Aside from this the measure poses serious proof problems that may often be insurmountable in a tippee-trading case. The "value" of the stock traded during the period of nondisclosure of the tipped information (i.e., the price at which the market would have valued the stocks if there had been a disclosure) is hypothetical. . . .

An equally compelling reason for rejecting the theory is its potential for imposition of Draconian, exorbitant damages, out of all proportion to the wrong committed, lining the pockets of all interim investors and their counsel at the expense of innocent corporate shareholders. Logic would compel application of the theory to a case where a tippee sells only 10 shares of a heavily traded stock (e.g., IBM), which then drop substantially when the tipped information is publicly disclosed. To hold the tipper and tippee liable for the losses suffered by every open market buyer of the stock as a result of the later decline in value of the stock after the news became public would be grossly unfair. . . .

An alternative measure would be to permit recovery of damages caused by erosion of the market price of the security that is traceable to the tippee's wrongful trading, i.e., to compensate the uninformed investor for the loss in market value that he suffered as a direct result of the tippee's conduct. Under this measure an innocent trader who bought Liggett shares at or after a tippee sold on the basis of inside information would recover any decline in value of his shares caused by the tippee's trading. Assuming the impact of the tippee's trading on the market is measurable, this approach has the advantage of limiting the plaintiffs to the amount of damage actually caused in fact by the defendant's wrongdoing and avoiding windfall recoveries by investors at the expense of stockholders other than the tippee trader, which could happen in the present action against Liggett. The rationale is that if the market price is not affected by the tippee's trading, the uninformed investor is in the same position as he would have been had the insider abstained from trading. In such event the equilibrium of the market has not been disturbed and the outside investor has not been harmed by the informational imbalance. Only where the market has been contaminated by the wrongful conduct would damages be recoverable. . . .

Another disadvantage of such a measure lies in the difficult if not impossible burden it would impose on the uninformed trader of proving the time when and the extent to which the integrity of the market was affected by the tippee's conduct. In some cases, . . . the existence of very substantial trading by the tippee, coupled with a sharp change in market price over a short period, would provide the basis for measuring a market place movement attributable to the wrongful trading. . . . For these reasons, we reject this strict direct market-repercussion theory of damages.

A third alternative is (1) to allow any uninformed investor, where a reasonable investor would either have delayed his purchase or not purchased at all if he had had the benefit of the tipped information, to recover any post-purchase decline in market value of his shares up to a reasonable time after he learns of the tipped information or after there is a public disclosure of it but (2) limit his recovery to the amount gained by the tippee as a result of his selling at the earlier date rather than delaying his sale until the parties could trade on an equal informational basis. Under this measure if the tippee sold 5,000 shares at $50 per share on the basis of inside information and the stock thereafter declined to $40 per share within a reasonable time after public disclosure, an uninformed purchaser, buying shares during the interim (e.g., at $45 per share) would recover the difference between his purchase price and the amount at which he could have sold the shares on an equal informational basis (i.e., the market price within a reasonable time after public disclosure of the tip), subject to a limit of $50,000, which is the amount gained by the tippee as a result of his trading on the inside information rather than on an equal basis. Should the intervening buyers, because of the volume and price of their purchases, claim more than the tippee's gain, their recovery (limited to that gain) would be shared pro rata.

This third alternative, which may be described as the disgorgement measure, has in substance been recommended by the American Law Institute in its 1978 Proposed Draft of a Federal Securities Code, §§1603, 1703(b), 1708(b), 1711(j). It offers several advantages. To the extent that it makes the tipper and tippees liable up to the amount gained by their misconduct, it should deter tipping of inside information and tippee trading. On the other hand, by limiting the total recovery of the tippee's gain, the measure bars windfall recoveries of exorbitant amounts bearing no relation to the seriousness of the misconduct. It also avoids the extraordinary difficulties faced in trying to prove traditional out-of-pocket damages based on the true "value" of the shares purchased or damages claimed by reason of market erosion attributable to tippee trading. A plaintiff would simply be required to prove (1) the time, amount, and price per share of this purchase, (2) that a reasonable investor would not have paid as high a price or made the purchase at all if he had had the information in the tippee's possession, and (3) the price to which the security had declined by the time he learned the tipped information or at a reasonable time after it became public, whichever event first occurred. He would then have a claim and, up to the limits of the tippee's gain, could recover the decline in market value of his shares before the information became public or known to him. In most cases the damages recoverable under the disgorgement measure would be roughly commensurate to the actual harm caused by the tippee's wrongful conduct. In a case where the tippee sold only a few shares, for instance, the likelihood of his conduct causing any substantial injury to intervening investors buying without benefit of his confidential information would be small. If, on the other hand, the tippee sold large amounts of stock, realizing substantial profits, the likelihood of injury to intervening uninformed purchasers would be greater and the amount of potential recovery thereby proportionately enlarged.

We recognize that there cannot be any perfect measure of damages caused by tippee trading. The disgorgement measure, like others we have described, does have some disadvantages. It modifies the principle that ordinarily gain to the wrongdoer should not be a prerequisite to liability for violation of Rule 10b-5. . . . It partially duplicates disgorgement remedies available in proceedings by the SEC or others. Under some market conditions such as where the market price is depressed by wholly unrelated causes, the tippee might be vulnerable to heavy damages, permitting some plaintiffs to recover undeserved windfalls. In some instances the total claims could exceed the wrongdoer's gain, limiting each claimant to a pro rata share of the gain. In other situations, after deducting the cost of recovery, including attorneys' fees, the remainder might be inadequate to make a class action worthwhile. However, as between the various alternatives we are persuaded, after weighing the pros and cons, that the disgorgement measure, despite some disadvantages, offers the most equitable resolution of the difficult problems created by conflicting interests.

In the present case the sole Rule 10b-5 violation was the tippee trading of 1,800 Liggett shares on the afternoon of July 17, 1972. Since the actual preliminary Liggett earnings were released publicly at 2:15 P.M. on July 18 and were effectively disseminated in a Wall Street Journal article published on the morning of July 19, the only outside purchasers who might conceivably have been damaged by the insider trading were those who bought Liggett shares between the afternoon of July 17 and the opening of the market on July 19. Thereafter all purchasers bought on an equal informational footing, and any outside purchaser who bought on July 17 and 18 was able to decide within a reasonable time after the July 18-19 publicity whether to hold or sell his shares in the light of the publicly-released news regarding Liggett's less favorable earnings.

The market price of Liggett stock opened on July 17, 1972, at \$55⅝, and remained at substantially the same price on that date, closing at \$55¼. By the close of the market on July 18 the price declined to \$52½ per share. Applying the disgorgement measure, any member of the plaintiff class who bought Liggett shares during the period from the afternoon of July 17 to the close of the market on July 18 and met the reasonable investor requirement would be entitled to claim a pro rata portion of the tippee's gain, based on the difference between their purchase price and the price to which the market price declined within a reasonable time after the morning of July 19. By the close of the market on July 19 the market price had declined to \$46⅜ per share. The total recovery thus would be limited to the gain realized by the tippee from the inside information, i.e., 1,800 shares multiplied by approximately \$9.35 per share. . . .

---

1. *The need for deterrence.* Does *Elkind* allow the insider to view trading on nonpublic information as a "heads I win, tails I break even" coin flip? That is, because the insider's civil liability under *Elkind* is his profit (which he keeps if he escapes detection), there may be little disincentive not to trade. Of course, there is always a risk of criminal prosecution or SEC injunctive relief, but these are infrequent. Still, because Congress seems to have accepted the *Elkind* measure of damages in enacting the Insider Trading and Securities Fraud Enforcement Act of 1988, page 503 infra, there seems little likelihood that courts will deviate from the *Elkind* measure in future decisions under Rule 10b-5.

2. *The Insider Trading Sanctions Act of 1984.* An insider who tips or trades on nonpublic material information today can be liable for more than the "disgorgement measure" approved by *Elkind.* In 1984 Congress added §21A(a)(2) to the '34 Act, which authorizes the SEC to seek, and a federal court in its discretion to impose, a civil penalty in insider trading cases of up to three times the profit gained, or loss avoided, as a result of the illegal trading. The penalty is in addition to the disgorgement measure approved in *Elkind,* criminal penalties, and any other ancillary relief (such as restitution) that the SEC may obtain in a particular case. In 1986 the SEC negotiated a total recovery of \$100 million from Ivan Boesky for

insider trading violations, of which $50 million was contributed to a disgorgement fund under the *Elkind* rationale and $50 million was a civil penalty paid to the government under the statute.

This civil penalty was extended by the Insider Trading and Securities Fraud Enforcement Act of 1988 to reach persons (such as investment advisers, broker-dealers, and others) whose employees engage in insider trading for their own account. Under these 1988 amendments, if the employer is found to be a "controlling person" with respect to the employee, it is liable for a civil penalty of up to "the greater of $1,000,000, or three times the amount of the profit gained or loss avoided as a result of such controlled person's violation." Under the prior law the corporate employer would have been liable as the primary violator itself, if the employee had traded for the corporation's account, but under this amendment it can now be held liable for a civil penalty even when it receives no benefit. However, before controlling persons may be so penalized, the SEC is required to show that the controlling person either "knew or recklessly disregarded the fact that such controlled person was likely to engage in the act or acts constituting the violation and failed to take appropriate steps to prevent such act or acts before they occurred," or "such controlling person knowingly or recklessly failed to establish, maintain, or enforce any policy or procedure" necessary to satisfy another new provision adopted in the 1988 amendments (§15(f) to the '34 Act), which now imposes an obligation on broker-dealers to institute and maintain an adequate system of supervision and internal controls to protect against securities law violations. In short, broker-dealer firms are liable for a substantial civil penalty if their failure to install adequate internal controls was a proximate cause of the violation; other employers are liable if they knew of or "recklessly disregarded" indications of the employee's inclination to commit the violation.

An unfortunate ambiguity under this formulation involves when the employer is considered to be a "controlling person" of the employee. Section 21(A)(b)(2) of the '34 Act expressly provides that "[n]o person shall be subject to a penalty . . . solely by reason of employing another person who is subject to a penalty . . . , unless such employing person is liable as a controlling person. . . ." Securities law has traditionally considered a "controlling person" to include any person with power to influence or control the direction or the management, policies, or activities of another person. See Kersh v. General Council of the Assemblies of God, 804 F.2d 546 (9th Cir. 1986); Richardson v. MacArthur, 451 F.2d 35 (10th Cir. 1971). Clearly, this standard is vague and may produce continuing litigation whenever the SEC seeks to impose a civil penalty under §21 of the '34 Act on a broker-dealer firm because of a securities law violation by one of its employees for the employee's own account.

3. *Problems.* The following questions ask you to consider the standards announced in *Dirks*, the subsequent case law on misappropriation theory, and the potential reach of Rule 14e-3.

(a) You are at a professional football game, seated in an expensive box, and you overhear a discussion among the persons seated in the next box. It is obvious they are discussing a soon-to-be-announced merger at a large premium. You hear the name of one individual who is an officer of the target company. You realize that if you do the research to learn the identity of his employer, you will be able to make a very profitable investment. Is it illegal to buy now?

(b) The woman with whom you live is so obviously excited that you ask her what has happened. She is an executive with a defense contractor, and she tells you that her firm has just landed the big contract for which they have been competing for the last year. You realize this will increase the firm's earnings by 30 percent or more. Can you trade before this information is disclosed? Would it make any difference if you were married?

(c) A high-tech computer company has approached a large bank for debt financing, and they ask you, a well-known computer consultant, to evaluate the company's new microcomputer, which has not yet been revealed to the market. You examine the computer at the company's laboratory and believe it to be a major advance in the state of the art, but the bank still decides the loan is too risky to make. Can you now trade before the new product is revealed?

(d) You are about to publish an article in the New England Journal of Medicine, a prestigious medical journal, which will evaluate rival drugs produced by different companies for the treatment of high blood pressure. It will report that two of these drugs are ineffective but that a third, lesser-known drug made by a small company is highly effective. Someone points out to you that the stock price of the last company will jump significantly on the article's release. Can you purchase its stock now? On what additional facts might your answer depend?

(e) You are an arbitrageur who trades in stocks of likely takeover targets. A president of a large corporation calls you and tells you that he is "thinking of making a run" at Target Co. and would like to see the stock in friendly hands. You explain that, even if you buy, you will resell to the highest bidder. Still, he urges you to make the investment and says "you won't regret it." Can you buy Target Co. stock now?

(f) You own 10,000 shares and have regularly sold 500 shares of your employer, Conglomerate, Inc., each quarter for the last two years, immediately following the publication of each quarter's earnings. Your aim is to diversify your portfolio and pay your children's tuitions at expensive law schools. Now, however, you are aware that adverse news will be released in ten days involving the failure of a major product in which your company has invested millions. The stock price will certainly fall, but can you continue your regular selling program now, following the release of the quarterly earnings report but before this additional information is released?

(g) A widely read business publication, Business Day, is published on Friday each week at 3:00 P.M. In its "Overheard on the Street" column, it often discusses possible takeovers and mergers, and its predictions sometimes move the market. Business Day takes considerable care to prevent the premature release of each issue and asks all retail newsstands not to release it before 3:00 P.M. on Friday. Defendant Jones pays $100 to the Hudson News Newsstand, a small retail newsstand in Manhattan with no connection to Business Day, to give him a copy on receipt at the newsstand at 1:00 P.M. on Friday. Jones trades on information contained in a column, and is indicted by the U.S. Attorney. What result if Jones defends by claiming that he breached no fiduciary duty to anyone? See United States v. Falcone, 257 F.3d 226 (2d Cir. 2001).

(h) Young is the newly elected chief executive officer of Paladin Industries, a publicly traded company. In this capacity, he joins the Young President's Club, a nationwide organization of CEOs under the age of 50. At a club meeting, he tells the other CEOs that his firm has been approached by a hostile raider, and he is going to "teach that raider a lesson that it never will forget." His motive for making this accurate statement is simply that he wants to be perceived as "macho" by his peers. One week later, Smith, who was present at that meeting, calls Young on another matter. Young's secretary tells Smith, who is a casual friend, that Young cannot be reached because he is still "locked in that merger meeting." Sensing what is happening, Smith trades on this information, and one week later the stock price of Paladin soars when a now-friendly merger is announced involving Paladin as the target. Assume the SEC sues Smith, but no tender offer was ever made. What result? See United States v. Kim, 184 F. Supp. 2d 1006 (N.D. Cal. 2002).

2. SECTION 16(b) AND "SHORT SWING" PROFITS

Securities Exchange Act of 1934: Directors, Officers, and Principal Stockholders

Sec. 16. (a) *Disclosure Required.* (1) *Directors, officers, and principal stockholders required to file.* — Every person who is directly or indirectly the beneficial owner of more than 10 percent of any class of any equity security (other than an exempted security) which is registered pursuant to section 12, or who is a director or an officer of the issuer of such security, shall file the statements required by this subsection with the Commission (and, if such security is registered on a national securities exchange, also with the exchange).

(2) *Time of filing.* — The statements required by this subsection shall be filed —

(A) at the time of the registration of such security on a national securities exchange or by the effective date of a registration statement filed pursuant to section 12(g);

(B) within 10 days after he or she becomes such beneficial owner, director, or officer;

(C) if there has been a change in such ownership, . . . before the end of the second business day following the day on which the subject transaction has been executed, or at such other time as the Commission shall establish, by rule, in any case in which the Commission determines that such 2-day period is not feasible. . . .[80]

(b) For the purpose of preventing the unfair use of information which may have been obtained by such beneficial owner, director, or officer by reason of his relationship to the issuer, any profit realized by him from any purchase and sale, or any sale and purchase, of any equity security of such issuer (other than an exempted security) . . . within any period of less than six months, unless such security . . . was acquired in good faith in connection with a debt previously contracted, shall inure to and be recoverable by the issuer, irrespective of any intention on the part of such beneficial owner, director, or officer in entering into such transaction of holding the security . . . purchased or of not repurchasing the security . . . sold for a period exceeding six months. Suit to recover such profit may be instituted at law or in equity in any court of competent jurisdiction by the issuer, or by the owner of any security of

---

80. Section 16 was recently amended by the Sarbanes-Oxley Act of 2002 to accelerate its filing requirements in order to give the market earlier information about insiders' transactions. It continues to apply to all "reporting" companies (that is, all U.S. companies having more than 500 shareholders of record and $10 million in total assets); it does not apply to foreign issuers that are listed on U.S. exchanges. Data collected by the SEC pursuant to §16 is regularly published by the Government Printing Office. This is a strategy aimed at alerting the plaintiff's bar, as the SEC itself does not bring §16(b) actions. — ED.

the issuer in the name and in behalf of the issuer if the issuer shall fail or refuse to bring such suit within sixty days after request or shall fail diligently to prosecute the same thereafter; but no such suit shall be brought more than two years after the date such profit was realized. This subsection shall not be construed to cover any transaction where such beneficial owner was not such both at the time of the purchase and sale, or the sale and purchase, of the security . . . involved, or any transaction or transactions which the Commission by rules and regulations may exempt as not comprehended within the purpose of this subsection.[81]

a. Who Is Covered?

Merrill Lynch, Pierce, Fenner & Smith, Inc. v. Livingston
566 F.2d 1119 (9th Cir. 1978)

HUFSTEDLER, J.: Merrill Lynch, Pierce, Fenner & Smith, Inc. ("Merrill Lynch") obtained judgment against its employee Livingston requiring him to pay Merrill Lynch $14,836.37 which was the profit that he made on short-swing transactions in the securities of his employer in alleged violation of Section 16(b) of the Securities Exchange Act of 1934. We reverse because Livingston was not an officer with access to inside information within the purview of Section 16(b) of the Securities Exchange Act of 1934.

From 1951 to 1972, Livingston was employed by Merrill Lynch as a securities salesman with the title of "Account Executive." In January, 1972, Merrill Lynch began an "Account Executive Recognition Program" for its career Account Executives to reward outstanding sales records. As part of the program, Merrill Lynch awarded Livingston and 47 other Account Executives the title "Vice President." Livingston had exactly the same duties after he was awarded the title as he did before the recognition. Livingston never attended, nor was he invited or permitted to attend, meetings of the Board of Directors or the Executive Committee. He acquired no executive or policy making duties. Executive and managerial functions were performed by approximately 350 "Executive Vice Presidents."

Livingston received the same kind of information about the company as an Account Executive both before and after he acquired his honorary title. As an Account Executive, he did obtain some information that was not generally available to the investing public, such as the growth production rankings on the various Merrill Lynch retail offices. Information of this kind was regularly distributed to other salesmen for Merrill Lynch. Livingston's supervisor, a branch office manager, testified that he gave Livingston the same kind of information that he gave other salesmen about the company, none of which was useful for purposes of stock trading.

. . . The predicate for the district court's decision was that Section 16(b) imposes strict liability on any person who holds the title of "officer" and who has access to information about his company that is not generally available to the members of the investing public. . . .

---

81. Section 16(c) generally prohibits short sales by insiders. Section 16(d) generally exempts from §§16(b) and (c) transactions "by a dealer in the ordinary course of his business and incident to the establishment or maintenance by him of a primary or secondary market . . . for such security." Section 16(e) generally exempts "arbitrage transactions" from §16. See Falco v. Donner Foundation, Inc., 208 F.2d 600 (2d Cir. 1953). — ED.

Strict liability to the issuer is imposed upon any "beneficial owner, director, or officer" for entering into such a short-swing transaction "[f]or the purpose of preventing the unfair use of information which may have been obtained by such . . . officer by reason of his relationship to the issuer." "The purpose of the statute was to take 'the profits out of a class of transactions in which the possibility of abuse was believed to be intolerably great' and to prevent the use by 'insiders' of confidential information, accessible because of one's corporate position or status, in speculative trading in the securities of one's corporation for personal profit." (Gold v. Sloan (4th Cir. 1973) 486 F.2d 340, 342, quoting Reliance Electric Co. v. Emerson Electric Co. (1972) 404 U.S. 418.)

To achieve the beneficial purposes of the statute, the court must look behind the title of the purchaser or seller to ascertain that person's real duties. Thus, a person who does not have the title of an officer, may, in fact, have a relationship to the company which gives him the very access to insider information that the statute was designed to reach. Thus, in Colby v. Klune (2d Cir. 1949) 178 F.2d 872, the employee's title was "Production Manager." Relying upon that title, the district court held that the defendant was excluded from the purview of the statute. The Second Circuit reversed and remanded for a factual inquiry into the question whether, despite his title, the defendant was nevertheless an officer within the meaning of the statute. The court defined "officer" as: "a corporate employee performing important executive duties of such character that he would be likely, in discharging those duties, to obtain confidential information about the company's affairs that would aid him if he engaged in personal market transactions. It is immaterial how his functions are labeled or how defined in the by-laws, or that he does or does not act under the supervision of some other corporate representatives." . . .

The title "Vice President" does no more than raise an inference that the person who holds the title has the executive duties and the opportunities for confidential information that the title implies. The inference can be overcome by proof that the title was merely honorary and did not carry with it any of the executive responsibilities that might otherwise be assumed. The record in this case convincingly demonstrates that Livingston was simply a securities salesman who had none of the powers of an executive officer of Merrill Lynch.

Livingston did not have the job in fact which would have given him presumptive access to insider information. Information that is freely circulated among nonmanagement employees is not insider information within the meaning of Section 16(b), even if the general public does not have the same information. Employees of corporations know all kinds of things about the companies they work for and about the personnel of their concerns that are not within the public domain. Rather, insider information to which Section 16(b) refers is the kind of information that is commonly reserved for company management and is thus the type of information that would "aid [one] if he engaged in personal market transactions." (Colby v. Klune, supra, 178 F.2d at 873.)[82] . . .

Reversed.

---

82. See William Hurley, Who Is an "Officer" for Purposes of the Securities Exchange Act of 1934 — *Colby v. Klune* Revisited, 44 Fordham L. Rev. 489 (1975). — ED.

"Officer." (a) Rule 16a-1(f) defines "officer" as "an issuer's president, principal financial officer, principal accounting officer (or, if there is no such accounting officer, the controller), any vice-president of the issuer in charge of a principal business unit, division or function (such as sales, administration or finance), any other officer who performs a policy-making function, or any other person who performs similar policy-making functions for the issuer. . . ." Adopted in 1991, this definition substantially decreased the number of corporate officials covered by §16(b) in large public corporations. Sec. Ex. Act Rel. No. 28869 (Feb. 8, 1991).

(b) Is it possible (likely) that some (many) high-ranking employees who do *not* fit the above definition will have "some information about the corporation that was not generally available to the investing public" and that *is* "useful for purposes of stock trading"? If so, should they be exempt from §16(b)? "If Congress created section 16 to prevent trading on the basis of inside information, Congress' purpose will be served best by construing the term 'officer' to mean employees with access to confidential information. On the other hand, if Congress created section 16 to align stockholder and management interests, the term should encompass only the smaller group of those with influence over corporate operating policies." Steve Thel, The Genius of Section 16: Regulating the Management of Publicly Held Companies, 42 Hastings L.J. 391, 495-496 (1991):

> Section 16 reinforces incentives that will encourage directors, officers, and principal stockholders who control the operations of publicly held companies to manage those companies in ways that will cause steady appreciation of stock prices, while at the same time it deprives them of trading opportunities that might lead them to manage corporate affairs in ways that will cause prices to fluctuate or decline. By so refining the incentives under which they operate, section 16 may cause those in control to manage publicly held companies in ways that will benefit others legitimately interested in corporate affairs, including stockholders and the public at large.

Id.

CBI Industries, Inc. v. Horton
682 F.2d 643 (7th Cir. 1982)

Posner, J.: . . . Horton, the defendant in this case, is a director of CBI Industries, Inc., the plaintiff. Along with the Continental Illinois National Bank and Trust Company of Chicago he is co-trustee of a trust (actually two trusts, but to make this opinion simpler we shall treat them as one) created many years ago by his mother for the benefit of his two sons. In the period relevant to this case they were full-time students, 19 and 22 years old, living apart from Horton most of the time. The original assets of the trust consisted entirely of CBI stock. The trustees were authorized but not required to retain the stock, and the record does not reveal the present composition of the trust's assets. In 1980 Horton sold on the open market 3000 shares of CBI stock that he owned himself; and within six months he bought (again on the open market), this time for the trust, 2000 shares of the stock at a lower price than he had sold his own stock. The difference in price, multiplied by 2000, is $25,000 — the amount CBI sued Horton for, and recovered below.

If Horton had bought the shares for his own account he would indisputably have violated section 16(b) and the company would have been entitled to his $25,000 "profit." But that is because the $25,000 would have been his to do with as he liked; it would have been "profit realized by him," in the language of the statute. The $25,000 that the trust may be said to have gained from the purchase of the shares at a price lower than the price at which Horton had earlier sold his own shares (gained, that is, by waiting to buy until the price fell) did not become his to use as he wished, but was for the exclusive use of his sons. It is true that as the family-member co-trustee, Horton had, within very broad limits, the power to manage the trust; for when a bank is a co-trustee with a member of the family of the grantor and the beneficiaries, it ordinarily defers to the family member's wishes, and did so here. But Horton did not have the power to divert the income of the trust to himself. . . . Finally, it is of little significance that Horton is the first in a series of contingent remaindermen of the trust. If both boys die without issue before they reach the age of 25, all of the assets of the trust will go to him. The probability of this happening could be calculated, and the result of this calculation could be multiplied by $25,000 to yield the expected value to Horton of the trust's profit from the challenged transaction, but no one has made this calculation and we suspect it would yield a number too minute to motivate CBI to sue.

If Horton did have a pecuniary interest in the trust's $25,000 "profit," the fact that the stock was not purchased in his name would not be decisive. In Whiting v. Dow Chem. Co., 523 F.2d 680, 682 (2d Cir. 1975), the wife of a corporate director sold stock in his company less than six months before he bought shares in it at a lower price, and the difference in price was held to be profit realized by him. But her income was considerably larger than his and was used to pay many of their joint living expenses, so that in effect the defendant was treating her money, including proceeds from transactions in the stock of the company of which he was a director, as if it were his. But so far as appears Horton does not — and under the terms of the trust he may not — treat the trust income this way. In Whittaker v. Whittaker Corp., 639 F.2d 516, 523 (9th Cir. 1981), the defendant's mother had given him a general power of attorney which he used, among other things, "'to freely borrow large sums of money from her while never having to consider paying the money back, posting adequate security or even paying any interest that might accrue.'" In fact, he "felt free to utilize his mother's assets exactly as if they were his own." He thus had a direct pecuniary stake in the profits from the insider trading that he did in her name. If Horton had like access to the trust assets, or if, as in *Whiting*, those assets were used to pay his living expenses, then a profit realized by the trust would be realized "by him" within the meaning of the statute; otherwise the statute would be so easily avoidable as to be virtually a dead letter.

But we cannot stop here. Having regard for the purpose and not merely the language of section 16(b), we must consider whether the words "profit realized by him" should be read more broadly — as broadly as the temptations that led Congress to enact the statute in the first place can be conceived. The preamble to section 16(b) describes the statutory purpose as "preventing the unfair use of information which may have been obtained" by the classes of corporate insiders specified in section 16(a). This suggests, what is anyway obvious, that the framers were concerned that corporate insiders would be tempted to use inside information to make short-term speculative profits; and the temptation is there whether the beneficiary is the insider himself or his children, grown or otherwise. A person's "wealth," in a realistic though not pecuniary sense, is increased by increasing the pecuniary wealth of his children — even if no part of their increased wealth is used to reduce any legal obligation of support that he may owe them, even if they never spend a nickel on him, even if he has no financial relations with them at all — provided only that he has the normal human feelings toward his children. To limit "profit realized by him" to purely pecuniary receipts thus seems, in the case of Mr. Horton, to ignore human nature.

But taking a "realistic" approach to the interpretation of these words would result in placing greater restrictions on corporate insiders than Congress can plausibly be thought to have intended in 1934, when notions of conflict of interest were less exacting than they are today. We asked CBI's counsel at oral argument whether in his view it would have made any difference to Horton's liability if the trust beneficiaries had been Horton's godsons rather than his sons. Counsel said it would not, but that it would be a different matter if the beneficiary were Horton's alma mater. But some men love their colleges as much as their godsons. An argument that the district court found persuasive — that an increase in the income of the trust would save Horton money by reducing the "voluntary gifts" he would "need" to make to his children — would apply with equal force if the beneficiary of the trust had been Horton's alma mater.

Thus the implication of holding Horton liable in this case would be that neither he nor any corporate insider could manage or control (or, we suppose, influence, see *Whiting*, supra, 523 F.2d at 688-89) an investment portfolio containing the stock of his company without being in jeopardy of violating section 16(b). Blau v. Lehman, 368 U.S. 403 (1962), where the Supreme Court refused to treat a profit realized by the defendant's partnership as profit realized by him, is authority against going so far; and even if we could distinguish *Blau*, we would not feel free to impute the morality of the 1980s to the Congress of the 1930s.

It would moreover be arbitrary to take CBI's suggestion and use as a cut-off point the definition of beneficial owner in Rule 16a-8 of the Securities and Exchange Commission. Section 16(a) of the Act defines as one type of corporate insider subject to the statute anyone who is "directly or indirectly the beneficial owner" of more than 10 percent of any class of any registered equity security, and the rule defines a beneficial owner for purposes of section 16(a) as including a trustee of a trust for a member of the trustee's "immediate family," defined in turn as including a child of any age. But the purpose of this definition is unrelated to the issue in the present case. It is to figure out who has a large enough stake in the corporation to be deemed an insider. For this purpose the adding up of family interests is eminently reasonable.[83] But Horton is not an insider by virtue of being a beneficial owner, directly or indirectly, of more than 10 percent of the stock of CBI, but by virtue of being a director. Rule 16a-8 is irrelevant.

We hold that profit realized by a corporate insider means direct pecuniary benefit to the insider, as in the factual settings of *Whiting* and *Whittaker*; it is not enough that ties of affinity or consanguinity between the nominal recipient and the insider make it likely that the insider will experience an enhanced sense of

---

83. In 1991 Rule 16a-1(a)(1) expanded the definition of "beneficial owner" — but chiefly for the purpose of determining who must file an initial report as a 10 percent owner — to include persons having voting or investment power over (regardless of any pecuniary interest in) securities. — ED.

well-being as a result of the receipt, or will be led to reduce his gift-giving to the recipient. . . . The standard of direct pecuniary benefit excludes by definition any attempt to monetize the emotional satisfaction that Horton might derive from a transaction that increased the wealth of his sons. But it does not exclude an attempt to measure any direct pecuniary benefit that he may have received from the transaction even if that benefit was less than $25,000. It does not even exclude the possibility of computing the actuarial value of the increase in his contingent remainder due to the profit to the trust — for an expected value is a form of direct pecuniary benefit.

We thus reject the view that the profit nominally received by a third party must be attributed to the insider either entirely or not at all. . . .

Reversed and remanded.

"Beneficial owner." Is *Horton* in conflict with the long-standing position of the SEC? "Generally, a person is regarded as the beneficial owner of securities held in the name of his or her spouse and their minor children. Absent special circumstances, such relationship ordinarily results in such person obtaining benefits substantially equivalent to ownership. . . ." Sec. Ex. Act Rel. No. 7793 (1966). Given the potential for interspousal information sharing, is a prophylactic rule necessary to make §16(b) work?

Reliance Electric Co. v. Emerson Electric Co.
404 U.S. 418 (1972)

Mr. Justice Stewart delivered the opinion of the Court. . . .

On June 16, 1967, the respondent, Emerson Electric Co., acquired 13.2% of the outstanding common stock of Dodge Manufacturing Co., pursuant to a tender offer made in an unsuccessful attempt to take over Dodge. The purchase price for this stock was $63 per share. Shortly thereafter, the shareholders of Dodge approved a merger with the petitioner, Reliance Electric Co. Faced with the certain failure of any further attempt to take over Dodge, and with the prospect of being forced to exchange its Dodge shares for stock in the merged corporation in the near future, Emerson, following a plan outlined by its general counsel, decided to dispose of enough shares to bring its holdings below 10%, in order to immunize the disposal of the remainder of its shares from liability under §16(b). Pursuant to counsel's recommendation, Emerson on August 28 sold 37,000 shares of Dodge common stock to a brokerage house at $68 per share. This sale reduced Emerson's holdings in Dodge to 9.96% of the outstanding common stock. The remaining shares were then sold to Dodge at $69 per share on September 11.

After a demand on it by Reliance for the profits realized on both sales, Emerson filed this action seeking a declaratory judgment as to its liability under §16(b).

[The district court held Emerson liable for the total amount of its profits. The court of appeals affirmed as to the August 28 sale but reversed as to the September 11 sale. Reliance alone sought review in the Supreme Court.] . . .

The history and purpose of §16(b) have been exhaustively reviewed by federal courts on several occasions since its enactment in 1934. See, e.g.,

Smolowe v. Delendo Corp., 136 F.2d 231; Adler v. Klawans, 267 F.2d 840; Blau v. Max Factor & Co., 342 F.2d 304. Those courts have recognized that the only method Congress deemed effective to curb the evils of insider trading was a flat rule taking the profits out of a class of transactions in which the possibility of abuse was believed to be intolerably great. As one court observed:

> In order to achieve its goals, Congress chose a relatively arbitrary rule capable of easy administration. The objective standard of Section 16(b) imposes strict liability upon substantially all transactions occurring within the statutory time period, regardless of the intent of the insider or the existence of actual speculation. This approach maximized the ability of the rule to eradicate speculative abuses by reducing difficulties in proof. Such arbitrary and sweeping coverage was deemed necessary to insure the optimum prophylactic effect.

Bershad v. McDonough, 428 F.2d 693, 696.

Thus Congress did not reach every transaction in which an investor actually relies on inside information. A person avoids liability if he does not meet the statutory definition of an "insider," or if he sells more than six months after purchase. Liability cannot be imposed simply because the investor structured his transaction with the intent of avoiding liability under §16(b). The question is, rather, whether the method used to "avoid" liability is one permitted by the statute.

Among the "objective standards" contained in §16(b) is the requirement that a 10% owner be such "both at the time of the purchase and sale . . . of the security involved." Read literally, this language clearly contemplates that a statutory insider might sell enough shares to bring his holdings below 10%, and later — but still within six months — sell additional shares free from liability under the statute. Indeed, commentators on the securities laws have recommended this exact procedure for a 10% owner who, like Emerson, wishes to dispose of his holdings within six months of their purchase.

Under the approach urged by Reliance, and adopted by the District Court, the apparent immunity of profits derived from Emerson's second sale is lost where the two sales, though independent in every other respect, are "interrelated parts of a single plan." 306 F. Supp., at 592. But a "plan" to sell that is conceived within six months of purchase clearly would not fall within §16(b) if the sale were made after the six months had expired, and we see no basis in the statute for a different result where the 10% requirement is involved rather than the six-month limitation.

The dissenting opinion reasons that "the 10% rule is based upon a conclusive statutory presumption that ownership of this quantity of stock suffices to provide access to inside information," and that it thus "follows that all sales by a more-than-10% owner within the six-month period carry the presumption of a taint, even if a prior transaction within the period has reduced the beneficial ownership to 10% or below." While there may be logic in this position, it was clearly rejected as a basis for liability when Congress included the proviso that a 10% owner must be such both at the time of the purchase and of the sale. Although the legislative history affords no explanation of the purpose of the proviso, it may be that Congress regarded one with a long-term investment of more than 10% as more likely to have access to inside information than one who moves in and out of the 10% category. But whatever the rationale of the proviso, it cannot be disregarded simply on the ground that it may be inconsistent with our assessment of the "wholesome purpose" of the Act.

To be sure, where alternative constructions of the terms of §16(b) are possible, those terms are to be given the construction that best serves the congressional purpose of curbing short-swing speculation by corporation insiders.[4] But a construction of the term "at the time of . . . sale" that treats two sales as one upon proof of a pre-existing intent by the seller is scarcely in harmony with the congressional design of predicating liability upon an "objective measure of proof." Smolowe v. Delendo Corp., supra, at 235. Were we to adopt the approach urged by Reliance, we could be sure that investors would not in the future provide such convenient proof of their intent as Emerson did in this case. If a "two-step" sale of a 10% owner's holdings within six months of purchase is thought to give rise to the kind of evil that Congress sought to correct through §16(b), those transactions can be more effectively deterred by an amendment to the statute that preserves its mechanical quality than by a judicial search for the will-o'-the-wisp of an investor's "intent" in each litigated case. . . .

Affirmed.

MR. JUSTICE POWELL and MR. JUSTICE REHNQUIST took no part in the consideration or decision of this case.

MR. JUSTICE DOUGLAS, with whom MR. JUSTICE BRENNAN and MR. JUSTICE WHITE concur, dissenting.

. . . In my view, this result is a mutilation of the Act, contrary to its broad remedial purpose, inconsistent with the flexibility required in the interpretation of securities legislation, and not required by the language of the statute itself.

Section 16(b) is a "prophylactic" rule . . . whose wholesome purpose is to control the insiders whose access to confidential information gives them unfair advantage in the trading of their corporation's securities. . . .

If §16(b) is to have the "optimum prophylactic effect" which its architects intended, insiders must not be permitted so easily to circumvent its broad mandate. We should hold that there was only one sale — a plan of distribution conceived "at the time" Emerson owned 13.2% of the Dodge stock, and implemented within six months of a matching purchase. Moreover, in the spirit of the Act we should presume that *any* such "split-sale" by a more-than-10% owner was part of a single plan of disposition for purposes of §16(b) liability.

This construction of "the sequence of relevant transactions," Bershad v. McDonough, 428 F.2d 693, 697 (CA7), is not foreclosed by any language in the statute. The statutory definitions of such terms as "purchase," "sale," "beneficial owner," "insider," and "at the time of" are not, as one might infer from the Court's opinion, objectively defined words with precise meanings. "'Whatever the terms

---

4. See, e.g., Adler v. Klawans, 267 F.2d 840 (one who is a director at the time of sale need not also have been a director at the time of purchase). In interpreting the terms "purchase" and "sale," courts have properly asked whether the particular type of transaction involved is one that gives rise to speculative abuse. See, e.g., Bershad v. McDonough, 428 F.2d 693 (granting of an option to purchase constitutes a "sale"). And in deciding whether an investor is an "officer" or "director" within the meaning of §16(b), courts have allowed proof that the investor performed the functions of an officer or director even though not formally denominated as such. Colby v. Klune, 178 F.2d 872, 873; cf. Feder v. Martin Marietta Corp., 406 F.2d 260, 262-263. The various tests employed in these cases are used to determine whether a transaction, objectively defined, falls within or without the terms of the statute. In no case is liability predicated upon "considerations of intent, lack of motive, or improper conduct" that are irrelevant in §16(b) suits. Blau v. Oppenheim, 250 F. Supp. 881, 887.

"purchase" and "sale" may mean in other contexts,' they should be construed in a manner which will effectuate the purposes of the specific section of the [Securities Exchange] Act in which they are used. SEC v. National Securities, Inc., 393 U.S. 453, 467." Id. at 696. . . .

Thus, the deterrent value of §16(b) depends not so much on its vaunted "objectivity" as on its "thoroughgoing" qualities. "We must suppose that the statute was intended to be thoroughgoing, to squeeze all possible profits out of stock transactions, and thus to establish a standard so high as to prevent any conflict between the selfish interest of a fiduciary officer, director, or stockholder and the faithful performance of his duty." Smolowe v. Delendo Corp., 136 F.2d 231, 239 (CA2).

Insiders have come to recognize that "in order not to defeat [§16(b)'s] avowed objective," federal courts will resolve "all doubts and ambiguities against insiders." Blau v. Oppenheim, 250 F. Supp. 881, 884-885. . . .

Thus, we should not conclude, as does the majority, that there is no *enforceable* way to combat the potential for sharp practices which inheres in the "split-sale" scheme. . . .

A series of sales, spaced close together, is more than likely part of a single plan of disposition. Plain common sense would indicate that Emerson's conduct in the present case had probably been planned, even if there were no confirmation in the form of an admission. It is statistically probable that any series of sales made by a beneficial owner of more than 10%, within six months, in which he disposes of a major part of his holdings, would be similarly connected.

We, therefore, should construe the statute as allowing a rebuttable presumption that any such series of dispositive transactions will be deemed to be part of a single plan of disposition, and will be treated as a single "sale" for the purposes of §16(b). Because the burden would be on the defendant, not the plaintiff, such a rule would operate with virtually the same less-than-perfectly automatic efficiency that the statute now does, and it would comport far more closely with the statute's broad, remedial sweep than does the approach taken by the Court. . . .

---

1. *When does a person become a 10 percent owner?* (a) When an investor purchases securities that put its holdings above the 10 percent level, is it a beneficial owner "at the time of the purchase" so that it must account for profits realized on a sale of those securities within six months? This issue, present in the *Reliance* case but not raised before the Supreme Court, was resolved in Foremost-McKesson, Inc. v. Provident Securities Co., 423 U.S. 232 (1976). The Court, tracing the legislative history of §16(b), unanimously held

> that, in a purchase-sale sequence, a beneficial owner must account for profits only if he was a beneficial owner "before the purchase."
>
> . . . But even if the legislative history were more ambiguous, we would hesitate to adopt . . . [the opposite] construction. It is inappropriate to reach the harsh result of imposing §16(b)'s liability without fault on the basis of unclear language. If Congress wishes to impose such liability, we must assume it will do so expressly or by unmistakable inference.
>
> It is not irrelevant that Congress itself limited carefully the liability imposed by §16(b). See Reliance Electric Co., supra, at 422-425. Even an insider may trade freely

without incurring the statutory liability if, for example, he spaces his transactions at intervals greater than six months. When Congress has so recognized the need to limit carefully the "arbitrary and sweeping coverage" of §16(b), Bershad v. McDonough, 428 F.2d 693, 696 (CA7 1970), *cert. denied*, 400 U.S. 992 (1971), courts should not be quick to determine that, despite an acknowledged ambiguity, Congress intended the section to cover a particular transaction.

Our construction of §16(b) also is supported by the distinction Congress recognized between short-term trading by mere stockholders and such trading by directors and officers. The legislative discourse revealed that Congress thought that all short-swing trading by directors and officers was vulnerable to abuse because of their intimate involvement in corporate affairs. But trading by mere stockholders was viewed as being subject to abuse only when the size of their holdings afforded the potential for access to corporate information. These different perceptions simply reflect the realities of corporate life.

It would not be consistent with this perceived distinction to impose liability on the basis of a purchase made when the percentage of stock ownership requisite to insider status had not been acquired. To be sure, the possibility does exist that one who becomes a beneficial owner by a purchase will sell on the basis of information attained by virtue of his newly acquired holdings. But the purchase itself was not one posing dangers that Congress considered intolerable, since it was made when the purchaser owned no shares or less than the percentage deemed necessary to make one an insider. Such a stockholder is more analogous to the stockholder who never owns more than 10% and thereby is excluded entirely from the operation of §16(b), than to a director or officer whose every purchase and sale is covered by the statute. While this reasoning might not compel our construction of the exemptive provision, it explains why Congress may have seen fit to draw the line it did. Cf. Adler v. Klawans, 267 F.2d 840, 845 (CA2 1959).

The Court expressed no opinion on the question of whether an opposite construction should be adopted in a *sale-repurchase* sequence. It did observe, however, that if such an opposite construction were *not* adopted in that situation, "it would be possible for a person to purchase a large block of stock, sell it out until his ownership was reduced to less than 10%, and then repeat the process, ad infinitum" without liability under §16(b).

2. *Must a director or officer be such at the time of both purchase and sale?* (a) In the *Foremost* case, the Court stated this to be an open issue, 423 U.S. at 243 n.16. But, as indicated in the *Reliance* case, decisions in the Second Circuit have held persons liable for short-swing profits under §16(b) when they have been directors or officers at the time of either purchase or sale. Thus, in Adler v. Klawans, 267 F.2d 840 (2d Cir. 1959), where a defendant first purchased, then became a director, and then sold within six months of the date of purchase, the defendant was held liable. This result was, however, reversed by the 1991 SEC amendments to the §16 rules. As a result of amendments to Rules 16a-2 and 16a-10, any transaction that occurs before a person becomes an officer or director is now exempted on the theory that the person would not normally have had access to inside information before becoming an insider. Also, if this new officer or director learns material facts after becoming an officer or director, and then trades, he or she is liable under Rule 10b-5. However, the defendant who sells after resigning as an officer or director remains liable under §16(b). Feder v. Martin Marietta Corp., 406 F.2d 260 (2d Cir. 1969) (defendant director who purchased, then resigned as director, and then sold within six months of date of purchase held liable).

(b) In Lewis v. Mellon Bank, 513 F.2d 921 (3d Cir. 1975), defendant had been a director for 17 years; within two days after resigning he purchased stock by exercising stock options and also sold stock. Liability under §16(b) was denied:

> It is true . . . that one who has but recently resigned his position as officer or director of a company is in a unique position because he is likely to have inside information. . . .
>
> But it is no less true that there is a substantial likelihood that a director who retains his directorship will trade on the basis of inside information a day after the six months since his last transaction has expired, or that the 10% shareholder in the *Reliance Electric* situation will trade on the basis of inside information. In the words of the Supreme Court, "Congress did not reach every transaction in which an investor actually relies on inside information." In the absence of an explicit proscription of transactions such as those involved in this case, and we find none, we decline to hold defendants liable for section 16(b) short-swing profits on the grounds that a recently retired director is, by law, still an "insider" under that section.

Accord, Lewis v. Varnes, 505 F.2d 785 (2d Cir. 1974).

(c) What result under §16(b) if, within a six-month period, defendant purchases, then becomes a director or officer, then resigns, and then sells? The American Law Institute's proposed Federal Securities Code would answer this question by finding liable any director or officer who holds such a status "at the time of either the purchase or the sale or at any time between these two transactions." See ALI Federal Securities Code, §1413(c).

3. *"Deputization theory."* In Feder v. Martin Marietta Corp., 406 F.2d 260 (2d Cir. 1969), the court found that an institutional shareholder that "deputized" an officer to serve as its representative on the board of a corporation in which it held a substantial (but below 10 percent) investment was liable under §16(b) on the theory that it had the status of a constructive director through its agent. For the view that this rule dissuades active participation by institutional investors in the selection of the corporation's board (for fear that any nominee selected by them will give rise to their potential liability under §16(b)), see Alfred Conard, A Behavioral Analysis of Directors' Liability for Negligence, 1972 Duke L.J. 895, 917-918, who argues that an institutional investor is exactly the type of shareholder that should have deputies on the board if the long-range interests of shareholders are to be well served. Suppose you are counsel to an activist hedge fund that owns a large stake in an underperforming corporation. Your client would like to "shake up the board" by adding some outside, more independent directors to it. How concerned should it be about "deputization theory"? Are there measures that you would recommend to minimize this risk?

4. *Controlling shareholders.* Suppose Frost is a CEO and 12 percent shareholder of IVAX, a publicly listed corporation, and through a limited partnership (the Frost Group) owns 17.3 percent of NAVI, another publicly traded corporation. Pursuant to a stockholder's agreement covering 51 percent of NAVI's shares, Frost is arguably part of the control group that controls NAVI. Within a six-month period, Frost purchases shares, and NAVI sells shares, in IVAX. No evidence exists that Frost caused (or even knew of) NAVI's sale of IVAX's stock. Does Frost have §16(b) liability for NAVI's profits, even though they are not distributed to him or otherwise realized by him? Under Rule 16a-1, the surprising answer is possibly yes, at least if Frost is found to be a controlling shareholder of NAVI, with the

result that he is thereby made the beneficial owner of the shares NAVI sold in IVAX. See Feder v. Frost, 220 F.3d 29 (2d Cir. 2000). On remand, however, the district court absolved the defendant of §16(b) liability, finding, pursuant to Rule 16a-1(a)(2), that Frost did not control NAVI and hence should not be deemed to be a beneficial owner of its investment in IVAX. See Feder v. Frost, 474 F. Supp. 2d 520 (S.D.N.Y. 2007).

5. *Timing.* Section 403 of Sarbanes-Oxley amended §16 to obligate corporate officers, directors, and 10 percent holders to disclose transactions in their company's shares by the second business day following the date of the transaction. Serendipitously, this provision has largely put an end to the backdating of stock options, because if an option is backdated (to benefit the recipient by giving him or her a lower exercise price), then the recipient will appear to have violated §16's prompt-reporting requirement.

6. *"Class of any equity security."* Consider the next two cases in the same circuit:

(a) In Chemical Fund, Inc. v. Xerox Corp., 377 F.2d 107 (2d Cir. 1967), Chemical Fund owned more than 10 percent of a class of Xerox debentures that were convertible into Xerox common stock. Xerox sought the short-swing profits that Chemical Fund realized from purchases of the debentures and sales of the common stock. Denied:

> It is conceded that the Debentures are securities as defined in section 3(a)(10) of the Act . . . and that they are equity securities because they are convertible into common stock. Under the definition in section 3(a)(11), . . . it is apparent that a Convertible Debenture is an "equity security" only because of its convertible nature, since an "equity security" is defined as "any stock or similar security; or any security convertible . . . into such a security . . . or any such warrant or right. . . ."
>
> Thus the question is: are the Debentures by themselves a "class of any equity security," or does the class consist of the common stock augmented, as to any beneficial holder in question, by the number of shares into which the Debentures it owns are convertible? We think that the Debentures are not a class by themselves; the total percentage of common stock which a holder would own following a hypothetical conversion of the Debentures it holds is the test of liability under section 16(b). . . . The reason that officers, directors and 10 percent stockholders have been held to account for profits on short-swing transactions is because they are the people who run the corporation, and who are familiar with its day to day workings. This is necessarily so of officers and directors, and there was ample basis for concluding that stockholders owning more than 10 percent of the voting stock of the company, if not in control, would be closely advised, as their votes usually elected the directors who in turn elected the officers, where these were not elected directly by the stockholders.
>
> But there is no reason whatever to believe that any holder of any Convertible Debentures would, by reason of such holding, normally have any standing or position with the officers, directors or large stockholders of a company so that such holder of Debentures would be the recipient of any inside information. There is no provision which gives a holder of the Debentures any standing beyond that of a creditor entitled to certain specified payments of interest at stated intervals, and possessing numerous rights all of which are specifically spelled out in the trust indenture pursuant to which the Debentures were issued.
>
> To hold that the beneficial owner of 10 percent or more of the Debentures is liable under section 16(b) would here impose a liability on an owner who by conversion of all his Debentures would obtain less than one-half of one percent of Xerox common stock. At the same time a holder of as much as 9 percent of Xerox common stock

would not be liable. Thus Chemical Fund, able to command only 2.72 percent of Xerox common, would be liable for short-swing profits, although the holder of 9 percent of the common, more than three times Chemical Fund's total potential holding, would not be liable. We do not believe that Congress could have meant to apply the provisions of the Act to any holder of Convertible Debentures whose possible equity position following full conversion of its Debentures would be less than 10 percent of the class of equity stock then outstanding.

(b) In Morales v. New Valley Corporation, 936 F. Supp. 119 (S.D.N.Y. 1996), a District Court in the Second Circuit distinguished the *Chemical Fund* decision and, consistent with the SEC's view, held that convertible preferred stock is a separate class of security, with the result that a holder of 10% or more of that class has potential §16(b) liability even though its overall voting power in the corporation came to less than 10 percent. The difference seemed to be the Court's sense that stockholders pose a greater danger for the abuse of inside information than creditors. True?

7. *Derivative securities.* The most significant change in the 1991 amendments to the §16(b) rules is that "derivative securities" — e.g., options, convertible securities, and similar rights — were brought under §16(b). Rule 16a-4 provides that "both derivative securities and the underlying securities to which they relate shall be deemed to be the same class of equity securities. . . ." For example, exchange-traded options relating to an issuer's common stock are deemed securities of the issuer — even if the options have been issued by a broker-dealer and not by the corporation.

8. *Stock options.* Although the 1991 amendments changed the procedures for employee stock plans, they probably did not diminish their attractiveness as executive compensation if the revised requirements are satisfied. For some time, Rule 16b-3 had exempted from the coverage of §16(b) securities acquired pursuant to stock option and similar programs, provided that (1) the executive compensation plan was approved by the shareholders, (2) discretion as to the allocation of options was assigned to a "disinterested administrator," and (3) there was a ceiling on the amount of the shares that could be issued under the plan. Under the new rules, when an insider acquires an option, right, or other derivative security, it must generally be reported, even if it is not immediately exercisable. The exercise of the option will also be a reportable event, but it will be a non-event for liability purposes. Instead, Rule 16b-6(b) focuses on the acquisition of the original interest, not the exercise of the option or the purchase of the underlying shares. (Similarly, a conversion of a convertible security is also exempt.) A revised and tightened Rule 16b-3 will still provide a safe harbor for "grant and award" transactions involving stock options, but the participant need only hold the equity security acquired for at least six months from the date of grant (not the date of exercise of the option). This means that once a stock option that has been held for six months is exercised, the executive can immediately sell the underlying shares without any further holding period. As a practical matter, this greatly simplifies the investment decision when the option price is only slightly below the market price of the stock, because it eliminates investment risk if the executive immediately resells upon exercise of the option.

9. *Computation of profit realized.* (a) The dissent in the *Reliance* case quotes the famous language from Smolowe v. Delendo about §16(b)'s intent "to squeeze all possible profits out of stock transactions" covered by the statute. In *Smolowe*, the

court first rejected the contention that profits should be determined by matching the purchase and sale price of particular stock certificates:

> Under the basic rule of identifying the stock certificate, the large stockholder, who in most cases is also an officer or director, could speculate in long sales with impunity merely by reason of having a reserve of stock and upon carefully choosing his stock certificates for delivery upon his sales from this reserve. Moreover, his profits from any sale followed by a purchase would be practically untouchable, for the principle of identity admits of no gain without laboring proof of a subjective intent — always a nebulous issue — to effectuate the connected phases of this type of transaction.
>
> In consequence the statute would be substantially emasculated.

It similarly rejected the "first-in, first-out" rule:

> Its application would render the large stockholder with a backlog of stock not immediately devoted to trading immune from the Act. Further, we should note that it does not fit the broad statutory language; a purchase followed immediately by a sale, albeit a transaction within the exact statutory language, would often be held immune from the statutory penalty because the purchase would be deemed by arbitrary rule to have been made at an earlier date; while a sale followed by purchase would never even be within the terms of the rule. . . .
>
> Another possibility might be the striking of an average purchase price and an average sale price during the period, and using these as bases of computation. What this rule would do in concrete effect is to allow as offsets all losses made by such trading.

But §16(b) provides

> for the recovery of "any" profit realized and obviously precluded a setting off of losses. Even had the statutory language been more uncertain, this rule seems one not to be favored in the light of the statutory purpose. Compared to other possible rules, it tends to stimulate more active trading by reducing the chance of penalty. . . . Its application to a case where trading continued more than six months might be most uncertain, depending upon how the beginning of each six months' period was ascertained. . . . The only rule whereby all possible profits can be surely recovered is that of lowest price in, highest price out — within six months. . . .

(b) *Problem.* A director of XYZ Corporation engages in the following transactions in his corporation's shares:

March 5	Purchases 100 at $14
March 20	Sells 100 at $11
June 1	Purchases 200 at $8
June 15	Sells 200 at $8

May the corporation recover damages under §16(b)? If so, how much? For criticism of the "lowest-in, highest-out" formula, which has been consistently applied by the courts since the *Smolowe* case, see William Painter, Federal Regulation of Insider Trading 20-39 (1968).

b. The Definition of "Purchase or Sale"

Kern County Land Co. v. Occidental Petroleum Corp.
411 U.S. 582 (1973)

Mr. Justice White delivered the opinion of the Court. . . .

[On May 8, 1967, Occidental made a tender offer to the shareholders of Kern County Land Co. (Old Kern) and by June 8, had acquired almost 900,000 shares, over 20% of Old Kern's outstanding common. In the meantime, in order to frustrate Occidental's takeover attempt, Old Kern's management—although permitting Occidental to inspect Old Kern's books and records after Occidental sued for this right—approved a merger with Tenneco, Inc. under which Tenneco would acquire Old Kern's assets through a subsidiary corporation (New Kern) and Old Kern's shareholders would exchange their shares for Tenneco preference stock.] Realizing that, if the Old Kern–Tenneco merger were approved and successfully closed, Occidental would have to exchange its Old Kern shares for Tenneco stock and would be locked into a minority position in Tenneco, Occidental took other steps to protect itself. Between May 30 and June 2, it negotiated an arrangement with Tenneco whereby Occidental granted Tenneco Corp., a subsidiary of Tenneco, an option to purchase at $105 per share all of the Tenneco preference stock to which Occidental would be entitled in exchange for its Old Kern stock when and if the Old Kern–Tenneco merger was closed. The premium to secure the option, at $10 per share, totaled $8,866,230 and was to be paid immediately upon the signing of the option agreement. If the option were exercised, the premium was to be applied to the purchase price. By the terms of the option agreement, the option could not be exercised prior to December 9, 1967, a date six months and one day after expiration of Occidental's tender offer. On June 2, 1967, within six months of the acquisition by Occidental of more than 10% ownership of Old Kern, Occidental and Tenneco Corporation executed the option. Soon thereafter, Occidental announced that it would not oppose the Old Kern–Tenneco merger. . . .

The Old Kern–Tenneco merger plan was presented to and approved by Old Kern shareholders at their meeting on July 17, 1967. Occidental refrained from voting its Old Kern shares, but in a letter read at the meeting Occidental stated that it had determined prior to June 2 not to oppose the merger and that it did not consider the plan unfair or inequitable. Indeed Occidental indicated that, had it been voting, it would have voted in favor of the merger. . . .

The Old Kern–Tenneco merger transaction was closed on August 30. . . .

The option granted by Occidental on June 2, 1967, was exercised on December 11, 1967. . . . Occidental's total profit [including dividends received of $1,793,439.22] was $19,506,419.22 on the shares obtained through its tender offer.

On October 17, 1967, New Kern instituted a suit under §16(b) against Occidental to recover the profits which Occidental had realized as a result of the dealings in Old Kern stock. The complaint alleged that the execution of the Occidental-Tenneco option on June 2, 1967, and the exchange of Old Kern shares for shares of Tenneco to which Occidental became entitled pursuant to the merger closed on August 30, 1967, were both "sales" within the coverage of §16(b). Since both acts took place within six months of the date on which Occidental became the owner of more than 10% of the stock of Old Kern, New Kern asserted that

§16(b) required surrender of the profits realized by Occidental. . . . [T]he District Court granted summary judgment in favor of New Kern. . . .

On appeal, the Court of Appeals reversed and ordered summary judgment entered in favor of Occidental. Abrams v. Occidental Petroleum Corp., 450 F.2d 157 (CA2 1971). . . .

Although traditional cash-for-stock transactions that result in a purchase and sale or a sale and purchase within the six-month, statutory period are clearly encompassed within the purview of §16(b), the courts have wrestled with the question of inclusion or exclusion of certain "unorthodox" transactions. The statutory definitions of "purchase" and "sale" are broad and, at least arguably, reach many transactions not ordinarily deemed a sale or purchase. In deciding whether borderline transactions are within the reach of the statute, the courts have come to inquire whether the transaction may serve as a vehicle for the evil which Congress sought to prevent—the realization of short-swing profits based upon access to inside information[26]—thereby endeavoring to implement congressional objectives without extending the reach of the statute beyond its intended limits. The statute requires the inside, short-swing trader to disgorge all profits realized on all "purchases" and "sales" within the specified time period, without proof of actual abuse of insider information, and without proof of intent to profit on the basis of such information. Under these strict terms, the prevailing view is to apply the statute only when its application would serve its goals. . . .

On August 30, 1967, the Old Kern–Tenneco merger agreement was signed, and Occidental became irrevocably entitled to exchange its shares of Old Kern stock for shares of Tenneco preference stock. Concededly the transaction must be viewed as though Occidental had made the exchange on that day. But even so, did the exchange involve a "sale" of Old Kern shares within the meaning of §16(b)? . . .

It cannot be contended that Occidental was an insider when, on May 8, 1967, it made an irrevocable offer to purchase 500,000 shares of Old Kern stock at a price substantially above market. . . . [But if] its takeover efforts failed, it is argued, Occidental knew it could sell its stock to the target company's merger partner at a substantial profit. Calculations of this sort, however, whether speculative or not and whether fair or unfair to other stockholders or to Old Kern, do not represent the kind of speculative abuse at which the statute is aimed, for they could not have been based on inside information obtained from substantial stockholdings that did not yet exist. . . . If there are evils to be redressed by way of deterring those who would make tender offers, §16(b) does not appear to us to have been designed for this task.

---

26. Several decisions have been read as to apply a so-called "objective" test in interpreting and applying §16(b). See, e.g., Smolowe v. Delendo Corp., supra; Park & Tilford v. Schulte, 160 F.2d 984 (CA2 1947); Heli-Coil Corp. v. Webster, 352 F.2d 156 (CA3 1965). Under some broad language in these decisions, §16(b) is said to be applicable whether or not the transaction in question could possibly lend itself to the types of speculative abuse that the statute was designed to prevent. By far the greater weight of authority is to the effect that a "pragmatic" approach to §16(b) will best serve the statutory goals. See, e.g., Roberts v. Eaton, 212 F.2d 82 (CA2 1954); Ferraiolo v. Newman, 259 F.2d 342 (CA6 1958); Blau v. Max Factor & Co., 342 F.2d 304 (CA9 1965); Blau v. Lamb, [363 F.2d 507 (CA2 1966)]; Petteys v. Butler, 367 F.2d 528 (CA8 1966). For a discussion and critical appraisal of the various "approaches" to the interpretation and application of §16(b), see Lowenfels, Section 16(b): A New Trend in Regulating Insider Trading, 54 Cornell L.Q. 45 (1968); Comment, Stock Exchanges Pursuant to Corporate Consolidation: A Section 16(b) "Purchase or Sale"?, 117 U. Pa. L. Rev. 1034 (1969); Note, *Reliance Electric* and 16(b) Litigation: A Return to the Objective Approach?, 58 Va. L. Rev. 907 (1972); Gadsby & Treadway, Recent Developments Under Section 16(b) of the Securities Exchange Act of 1934, 17 N.Y.L.F. 687 (1971).

By May 10, 1967, Occidental had acquired more than 10% of the outstanding shares of Old Kern. It was thus a statutory insider when, on May 11, it extended its tender offer to include another 500,000 shares. . . . Perhaps Occidental anticipated that extending its offer would increase the likelihood of the ultimate success of its takeover attempt or the occurrence of a defensive merger. But again, the expectation of such benefits was unrelated to the use of information unavailable to other stockholders or members of the public with sufficient funds and the intention to make the purchases Occidental had offered to make before June 8, 1967.

The possibility that Occidental had, or had the opportunity to have, any confidential information about Old Kern before or after May 11, 1967, seems extremely remote. Occidental was, after all, a tender offeror, threatening to seize control of Old Kern, displace its management, and use the company for its own ends. The Old Kern management vigorously and immediately opposed Occidental's efforts. Twice it communicated with its stockholders, advising against acceptance of Occidental's offer and indicating prior to May 11 and prior to Occidental's extension of its offer, that there was a possibility of an imminent merger and a more profitable exchange. Old Kern's management refused to discuss with Occidental officials the subject of an Old Kern–Occidental merger. Instead, it undertook negotiations with Tenneco and forthwith concluded an agreement, announcing the merger terms on May 19. Requests by Occidental for inspection of Old Kern records were sufficiently frustrated by Old Kern's management to force Occidental to litigation to secure the information it desired.

. . . Much the same can be said of the events leading to the exchange of Occidental's Old Kern stock for Tenneco preferred, which is one of the transactions that is sought to be classified a "sale" under §16(b). The critical fact is that the exchange took place and was required pursuant to a merger between Old Kern and Tenneco. That merger was not engineered by Occidental but was sought by Old Kern to frustrate the attempts of Occidental to gain control of Old Kern. Occidental obviously did not participate in or control the negotiations or the agreement between Old Kern and Tenneco. Cf. Newmark v. RKO General, 425 F.2d 348 (CA2), *cert. denied*, 400 U.S. 854 (1970). . . . Occidental, although registering its opinion that the merger would be beneficial to Old Kern shareholders, did not in fact vote at the shareholders' meeting at which merger approval was obtained. Under California law, its abstention was tantamount to a vote against approval of the merger. Moreover, at the time of stockholder ratification of the merger, Occidental's previous dealing in Old Kern stock was, as it had always been, fully disclosed.

Once the merger and exchange were approved, Occidental was left with no real choice with respect to the future of its shares of Old Kern. . . . Occidental could, of course, have disposed of its shares of Old Kern for cash before the merger was closed. Such an act would have been a §16(b) sale and would have left Occidental with a prima facie §16(b) liability. It was not, therefore, a realistic alternative for Occidental as long as it felt it could successfully defend a suit like the present one. . . . We do not suggest that an exchange of stock pursuant to a merger may never result in §16(b) liability. But the involuntary nature of Occidental's exchange, when coupled with the absence of the possibility of speculative abuse of inside information, convinces us that §16(b) should not apply to transactions such as this one.

Petitioner also claims that the Occidental-Tenneco option agreement should itself be considered a sale, either because it was the kind of transaction the statute was designed to prevent or because the agreement was an option in form but a sale in fact. But the mere execution of an option to sell is not generally regarded as a "sale." See Booth v. Varian Associates, 334 F.2d 1 (CA1 1964); Allis-Chalmers Mfg. Co. v. Gulf & Western Industries, 309 F. Supp. 75 (E.D. Wis. 1970); Marquette Cement Mfg. Co. v. Andreas, 239 F. Supp. 962 (S.D.N.Y. 1965). And we do not find in the execution of the Occidental-Tenneco option agreement a sufficient possibility for the speculative abuse of inside information with respect to Old Kern's affairs to warrant holding that the option agreement was itself a "sale" within the meaning of §16(b). The mutual advantages of the arrangement appear quite clear. As the District Court found, Occidental wanted to avoid the position of a minority stockholder with a huge investment in a company over which it had no control and in which it had not chosen to invest. On the other hand, Tenneco did not want a potentially troublesome minority stockholder that had just been vanquished in a fight for the control of Old Kern. Motivations like these do not smack of insider trading; and it is not clear to us, as it was not to the Court of Appeals, how the negotiation and execution of the option agreement gave Occidental any possible opportunity to trade on inside information it might have obtained from its position as a major stockholder of Old Kern. Occidental wanted to get out, but only at a date more than six months thence.[84] It was willing to get out at a price of $105 per share, a price at which it had publicly valued Tenneco preferred on May 19 when the Tenneco–Old Kern agreement was announced. In any event, Occidental was dealing with the putative new owners of Old Kern, who undoubtedly knew more about Old Kern and Tenneco's affairs than did Occidental. If Occidental had leverage in dealing with Tenneco, it is incredible that its source was inside information rather than the fact of its large stock ownership itself.

Neither does it appear that the option agreement, as drafted and executed by the parties, offered measurable possibilities for speculative abuse. What Occidental granted was a "call" option. Tenneco had the right to buy after six months, but Occidental could not force Tenneco to buy. The price was fixed at $105 for each share of Tenneco preferred. Occidental could not share in a rising market for the Tenneco stock. See Silverman v. Landa, 306 F.2d 422 (CA2 1962). If the stock fell more than $10 per share, the option might not be exercised, and Occidental might suffer a loss if the market further deteriorated to a point where Occidental was forced to sell. Thus, the option, by its very form, left Occidental with no choice but to sell if Tenneco exercised the option, which it was almost sure to do if the value of Tenneco stock remained relatively steady. On the other hand, it is difficult to perceive any speculative value to Occidental if the stock declined and Tenneco chose not to exercise its option. See generally Note, Put and Call Options Under Section 16 of the Securities Exchange Act, 69 Yale L.J. 868 (1960). . . .

The option, therefore, does not appear to have been an instrument with potential for speculative abuse, whether or not Occidental possessed inside information about the affairs of Old Kern. In addition, the option covered Tenneco preference stock, a stock as yet unissued, unregistered, and untraded. It was the value of this stock that underlay the option and that determined whether the option would be exercised, whether Occidental would be able to profit from the exercise, and

---

84. If Occidental had sold its Tenneco preference stock for cash *within* six months of its purchase of Old Kern stock, could these transactions have been matched under §16(b)? See American Standard, Inc. v. Crane Co., 510 F.2d 1043 (2d Cir. 1974), noted, 75 Colum. L. Rev. 1323 (1975). — Ed.

whether there was any real likelihood of the exploitation of inside information. If Occidental had inside information when it negotiated and signed the option agreement, it was inside information with respect to Old Kern. Whatever it may have known or expected as to the future value of Old Kern stock, Occidental had no ownership position in Tenneco giving it any actual or presumed insights into the future value of Tenneco stock. That was the critical item of intelligence if Occidental was to use the option for purposes of speculation. Also, the date for exercise of the option was over six months in the future, a period that, under the statute itself, is assumed to dissipate whatever trading advantage that might be imputed to a major stockholder with inside information. . . . By enshrining the statutory period into the option, Occidental also, at least if the statutory period is taken to accomplish its intended purpose, limited its speculative possibilities. Nor should it be forgotten that there was no absolute assurance that the merger, which was not controlled by Occidental, would be consummated. In the event the merger did not close, the option itself would become null and void.

Nor can we agree that we must reverse the Court of Appeals on the ground that the option agreement was in fact a sale because the premium paid was so large as to make the exercise of the option almost inevitable, particularly when coupled with Tenneco's desire to rid itself of a potentially troublesome stockholder. The argument has force, but resolution of the question is very much a matter of judgment, economic and otherwise, and the Court of Appeals rejected the argument. That court emphasized that the premium paid was what experts had said the option was worth, the possibility that the market might drop sufficiently in the six months following execution of the option to make exercise unlikely, and the fact that here, unlike the situation in *Bershad v. McDonough*, 428 F.2d 693 (CA7 1970), the optionor did not surrender practically all emoluments of ownership by executing the option. Nor did any other special circumstances indicate that the parties understood and intended that the option was in fact a sale.[30] . . .

Affirmed.

MR. JUSTICE DOUGLAS, with whom MR. JUSTICE BRENNAN and MR. JUSTICE STEWART concur, dissenting.

. . . By its own terms . . . [§16(b)] subsumes *all* transactions that are technically purchases and sales and applies irrespective of any actual or potential use of inside

---

30. In *Bershad v. McDonough*, 428 F.2d 693 (CA7 1970), the defendants were directors and greater-than-ten-percent stockholders of Cudahy Co. The defendants, within six months of their acquisition of beneficial ownership of Cudahy, granted an option to Smelting Refining & Mining Co. to purchase their Cudahy stock. The Seventh Circuit held that the grant of the option was a §16(b) "sale" of the Cudahy stock. The Court of Appeals in the present case distinguished *Bershad* as follows:

> That case came before the court of appeals on a finding by the district court that, under the circumstances there presented, the stock had in fact been sold within the six months period, although the option was not formally exercised until later. The district court had relied on a number of circumstances, the most significant being that the optionor gave the optionee an irrevocable proxy to vote the shares and that the optionor and one of his associate directors resigned as directors within a few days after the grant of the option and were replaced by officers of the optionee. In other words, the district court found in effect that the "option" was accompanied by a wink of the eye, and the court of appeals sustained this. Here there is no such finding, and no basis for one." 450 F.2d, at 165.

[In the *Bershad* case, the optionee paid 14 percent of the purchase price for the option, to be applied against the purchase price if the option were exercised. Compare *Citadel Holding Corp. v. Roven*, 26 F.3d 960 (9th Cir. 1994) (optionholder had no "rights of ownership with respect to the underlying securities"). — ED.]

information to gain a trading advantage. . . . The conclusion seems inescapable that Occidental Petroleum Corporation (Occidental) purchased and sold shares of Kern County Land Company (Old Kern) within a six-month period and that this "round trip" in Old Kern Stock is covered by the literal terms of §16(b). . . .

The majority finesses the literal impact of §16(b) by examining Occidental's willfulness and its access to inside information. . . . This approach is plainly contrary to the legislative purpose. . . .

The very construction of §16(b) reinforces the conclusion that the section is based in the first instance on a totally objective appraisal of the relevant transactions. . . . Had the draftsmen intended that the operation of the section hinge on abuse of access to inside information it would have been anomalous to limit the section to purchases and sales occurring within six months. Indeed, the purpose of the six-month limitation, coupled with the definition of an insider, was to create a *conclusive presumption* that an insider who turns a short-swing profit in the stock of his corporation had access to inside information *and* capitalized on that information by speculating in that stock. . . .

. . . [T]he courts will be caught up in an ad hoc analysis of each transaction, determining both from the economics of the transaction and the modus operandi of the insider whether there exists the possibility of speculative abuse of inside information. Instead of a section that is easy to administer and by its clear-cut terms discourages litigation, we have instead a section that fosters litigation because the Court's decision holds out the hope for the insider that he may avoid §16(b) liability. In short, the majority destroys much of the section's prophylactic effect. . . . Certainly we cannot allow transactions which present the possibility of abuse but do not fall within the classic conception for a purchase or sale to escape the confines of §16(b). It is one thing to interpret the terms "purchase" and "sale" liberally in order to include those transactions which evidence the evil Congress sought to eliminate; it is quite another to abandon the bright-line test of §16(b) for those transactions which clearly fall within its literal bounds. Section 16(b), because of the six-month limitation, allows some to escape who have abused their inside information. It should not be surprising, given the objective nature of the rule, if some are caught unwillingly.

---

1. *Scope of the "pragmatic" (or "subjective") approach.* To what extent is the major difference between the majority and dissent in the *Kern* case that the majority more narrowly defines what constitutes "a class of transactions in which the possibility of abuse was believed to be intolerably great" (*Kern* dissent, quoting from the *Reliance* case)? Does the majority find the class to be "defensive mergers," whereas the dissent finds it to be "mergers" generally, thus making irrelevant any further reference to the facts of the case? See American Standard, Inc. v. Crane Co., 510 F.2d 1043, 1053 (2d Cir. 1974). Or does the majority engage in a more detailed inquiry of the particular "transaction in question," holding that *some* defensive mergers (but not this one) "could possibly lend itself to the types of speculative abuse that the statute was designed to prevent" (footnote 26 in the *Kern* case)? If so, is this approach "plainly contrary to the legislative purpose" of §16(b)?

"The detail with which the *Kern* Court analyzed the particular facts before it indicates that it was willing to define a class of transactions very narrowly.

Although justified by a desire to avoid harsh results where the purpose of section 16(b) would not be served, the balance struck in *Kern* seems to require lower courts in similar cases to engage in factual inquiries into matters that are not susceptible of easy determination." 87 Harv. L. Rev. 297 (1973). "Since the subjective approach as originally formulated inquired into the general type of transaction rather than the particular case sub judice, it was not considered to be necessarily inconsistent with the crude rule of thumb. If it was decided that the type of transaction was comprehended by the statute, the crude rule of thumb would then be applied. Prior to *Kern County*, courts did not examine the particular parties or the particular facts of a general type of transaction." 49 N.Y.U. L. Rev. 370 (1974). Should §16(b)'s "crude rule of thumb" preclude judicial examination of "the particular facts of a general type of transaction," or only of whether there was "actual abuse of insider information" or "intent to profit on the basis of such information"?

Did the *Kern* majority adopt the latter §16(b) standard by refusing to inquire into whether there was "*actual* abuse," but holding that under the particular facts of the transaction there was no "*possibility* of speculative abuse of inside information"?

> An analysis of the facts of *Kern* indicates that it was at least possible that inside information could have been used by the respondent to its advantage if such information were in its possession. For example, after Occidental had become a 10 percent beneficial owner of Kern stock by means of its initial tender offer of May 8, knowledge that Kern would definitely merge with Tenneco would have allowed Occidental to extend its tender offer, as it did on May 11, knowing full well that a substantial profit would result from the sale of the stock after the merger took place. . . . Under the compromised subjective test [used in *Kern*] it appears the Court must ask whether there was any possibility that the transaction at issue *did* lead to speculative abuse rather than whether the transaction possibly *could have* lent itself to speculative abuse. It would seem that henceforth a plaintiff may have to introduce some evidence of actual abuse tending to show that abuse of an inside position is not only possible, but probable. To require such a showing, however, would seriously undermine the effectiveness of section 16(b).

58 Minn. L. Rev. 699-701 (1974).

ALI Federal Securities Code §1413(h)(1) (Tent. Draft No. 2, 1973) generally exempts security acquisitions and dispositions in mergers (as well as in conversions, consolidations, recapitalizations, and transfers of assets for securities) "*if* the defendant proves that he did not *use* information obtained by reason of his relationship to an involved issuer" (emphasis added).

2. *Scope of the* Kern *decision.* (a) What were the critical factors in the *Kern* case leading to the holding of no liability as a result of the merger? Was it that Occidental had no "access to inside information"? Or was it "the involuntary nature of Occidental's exchange" — the fact the Occidental "did not participate in or control" the merger? Or was it a combination of these factors? Were additional factors relevant? See Note, Involuntariness and Other Contemporary Problems Under Section 16(b) of the Securities Exchange Act of 1934, 27 Hastings L.J. 679 (1976).

Would the result in the *Kern* case have been different if Occidental's votes had been necessary for approval of the merger? If, at the time of its tender offer, Occidental had "deputies" serving as directors or officers of Old Kern? Or are these matters irrelevant because §16(b) *presumes* that a statutory insider has access to inside information and exerts controls over the issuer? Of what relevance to these queries is the holding in the *Foremost* case (page **000** supra)?

(b) When should the transfer of shares by a losing bidder to the winning bidder in a tender offer contest be exempt from §16(b) under the *Kern* case? In Heublein, Inc. v. General Cinema Corp., 722 F.2d 29 (2d Cir. 1983), the court held that General Cinema, a 10 percent owner in Heublein, was not liable for its profit on exchange of its shares for shares of R. J. Reynolds, Inc., in a merger between Heublein and Reynolds (which General Cinema voted against). The court defined the scope of the *Kern* exemption as applying to "the class of cases . . . where (1) an atmosphere of suspicion, if not hostility, characterizes relations between the two corporations, (2) the exchange of shares is involuntary in that it is effectuated pursuant to a merger over which the investing corporation exercised no control or influence, and (3) there is no likelihood of access to material inside information." Under this test, what result if the "white knight" bidder, who had been welcomed by the target, lost the contest and exchanged its shares in a merger (which it also voted against)? Should it matter if confidential data had been given by the target to this preferred bidder? What result if the losing bidder sells its shares for cash to the winning bidder? See Texas Int'l Airlines v. National Airlines, Inc., 714 F.2d 533 (5th Cir. 1983) (losing bidder liable for profit on shares on cash sale to winning bidder). What result if the losing bidder sells its shares to the target? See Colan v. Mesa Petroleum Co., 951 F.2d 1512 (9th Cir. 1991) (losing bidder liable when it voluntarily sold its shares to target pursuant to latter's self-tender offer even where "coercive" tender offer forced bidder to sell).

3. *Indemnification.* If the "white knight" repurchases the hostile raider's shares at a premium within six months after its most recent matching purchase, this clearly falls within §16(b) if the raider crossed the 10 percent threshold. But what if the knight agrees to indemnify the hostile raider for any losses it incurs as a result of the sale, including §16(b) liabilities? In Bunker Ramo-Eltra Corp. v. Fairchild Industries, Inc., 639 F. Supp. 409 (D. Md. 1986), Allied Corporation agreed to indemnify Fairchild with respect to any liabilities incurred on a sale of shares it held in Bunker-Ramo to Allied (Bunker-Ramo was then merged into Allied). Following the merger, a §16(b) action was brought on behalf of Allied against Fairchild. *Held:* The indemnification agreement was unenforceable because it "would frustrate the public policy behind the prohibition of insider trading." Moreover, Allied as the successor corporation was found to have standing to assert Bunker-Ramo's rights against Fairchild. This holding accords generally with an extensive case law forbidding indemnification of securities law liabilities. See Globus v. Law Research Service Inc., 418 F.2d 1276 (2d Cir. 1969).

Another variant on the standard "greenmail" pattern, under which a target buys back its shares from a raider at a premium in order to forestall a hostile tender offer, is for the target corporation to characterize a portion of the payment as reimbursement for expenses incurred by the raider. In Hettmann v. Steinberg, 812 F.2d 63 (2d Cir. 1987), the court held that some portion of such reimbursement was necessarily intended as a payment for the shares repurchased and had to be so allocated in determining the gain for purposes of §16(b).

4. *Standing to sue.* (a) In Gollust v. Mendell, 501 U.S. 115 (1991), after respondent shareholder in International brought a suit on its behalf under §16(b), International was acquired by Viacom, whose shares respondent received in exchange for his

International shares. The Court held that respondent may continue to prosecute the suit, reasoning that no

> "continuous ownership requirement," is found in the text of the statute, nor does §16(b)'s legislative history reveal any congressional intent to impose one.
>
> . . . Congress understood and intended that, throughout the period of his participation, a plaintiff authorized to sue insiders on behalf of an issuer would have some continuing financial interest in the outcome of the litigation, both for the sake of furthering the statute's remedial purposes by ensuring that enforcing parties maintain the incentive to litigate vigorously, and to avoid the serious constitutional question that would arise from a plaintiff's loss of all financial interest in the outcome of the litigation he had begun. . . . [R]espondent still stands to profit, albeit indirectly, if this action is successful, just as he would have done if his original shares had not been exchanged for stock in Viacom. Although a calculation of the values of the respective interests in International that respondent held as its stockholder and holds now as a Viacom stockholder is not before us, his financial interest is actually no less real than before the merger and apparently no more attenuated than the interest of a bondholder might be in a §16(b) suit on an issuer's behalf.

(b) *Problem.* M, a minority shareholder of S Corporation (subsidiary), receives securities of P Corporation (parent) when S merges into P. After the merger, M brings an action under §16(b) on behalf of S against P for the purchase and sale of S's shares within six months. What result after *Gollust?*

5. *Appraisals and suggestions.* (a) Critical analyses of §16(b) and its judicial interpretations abound. It has been observed that

> the statute is even too radical for Castro's Cuba, which substantially adopted our 1933 and 1934 Acts but allows recovery under the Cuban 16(b) only upon proof of actual abuse of inside information. In Japan, the only other country to have a 16(b) (and it adopted it only as a blessing of defeat after World War II), there appears to have never been a suit under the statute. The Jenkins Committee in England recommended 16(a) but not 16(b). Furthermore, . . . [in 1965], an Ontario committee, after examining the United States' experience with §16(b), denounced the section vigorously.

John Munter, Section 16(b) of the Securities Exchange Act of 1934: An Alternative to "Burning Down the Barn in Order to Kill the Rats," 52 Cornell L.Q. 69, 71 (1966).

(b) A number of commentators have urged that courts have sought to attack too broad a range of problems through §16(b):

> [T]he type of insider transaction intended to be covered by section 16(b) is essentially an *in-and-out trading* transaction in which the insider both acquires and disposes of the securities in question within less than six months, usually through purchases and sales in the public securities markets. Hence, any transaction which does not have the effect of achieving this type of *in-and-out trading* should be interpreted as being beyond the purposes and scope of 16(b). . . . The conclusion that 16(b) was intended to deal only with a specific type of insider abuse which gave the insiders an unfair advantage in trading in the public securities markets and was not intended to remedy all abuses by insiders is further reinforced by the fact that Congress in sections 9 and 10 of the Exchange Act dealt separately and comprehensively with deceptive and manipulative activity. . . .

Hal Bateman, The Pragmatic Interpretation of Section 16(b) and the Need for Clarification, 45 St. John's L. Rev. 772, 795-796 (1971).

Compare Note, Exceptions to Liability under Section 16(b): A Systematic Approach, 87 Yale L.J. 1430, 1444 (1978):

> The problem with section 16(b) interpretation . . . is not that the courts have concluded incorrectly that potential for speculative abuse constitutes the crucial factor in formulating exceptions and that the indicia of such potential are access to inside information and control by the insider. . . . Rather, the problem is that the courts have injected an unreliable factor — the form of the transaction — into what should be a straightforward inquiry into the relevant variables. Instead of distinguishing between orthodox and unorthodox transactions, or inquiring whether the transaction constitutes a purchase or sale, the courts should distinguish among insiders on the basis of access and control in determining whether an exception to section 16(b) liability is justified. Properly formulated, a test based on insider status furnishes a more accurate measure of potential for speculative abuse than the form of the transaction; it also more closely reflects the original congressional intent. Thus, regardless of the type of the transaction involved, courts should hold officers, directors, and controlling beneficial owners strictly liable irrespective of their ability to prove lack of opportunity for speculative abuse, but they should exonerate the controlling beneficial owner able to prove lack of access to inside information.
>
> Strict liability for officers and directors is premised on a conclusive presumption that the control they exercise over their corporation affords them access to inside information.

3. COMMON LAW LIABILITY TO THE CORPORATION

Diamond v. Oreamuno
24 N.Y.2d 494, 248 N.E.2d 910, 301 N.Y.S.2d 78 (1969)

FULD, C.J.: . . . The complaint was filed by a shareholder of Management Assistance, Inc. (MAI) asserting a derivative action against a number of its officers and directors to compel an accounting for profits allegedly acquired as a result of a breach of fiduciary duty. It charges that two of the defendants — Oreamuno, chairman of the board of directors, and Gonzalez, its president — had used inside information, acquired by them solely by virtue of their positions, in order to reap large personal profits from the sale of MAI shares and that these profits rightfully belong to the corporation. Other officers and directors were joined as defendants on the ground that they acquiesced in or ratified the assertedly wrongful transactions.

MAI is in the business of financing computer installations through sale and lease back arrangements with various commercial and industrial users. Under its lease provisions, MAI was required to maintain and repair the computers but, at the time of this suit, it lacked the capacity to perform this function itself and was forced to engage the manufacturers of the computers, International Business Machines (IBM), to service the machines. As a result of a sharp increase by IBM of its charges for such service, MAI's expenses for August of 1966 rose considerably and its net earnings declined from $262,253 in July to $66,233 in August, a decrease of about 75%. This information, although earlier known to the defendants, was not made public until October of 1966. Prior to the release of the information, however,

Oreamuno and Gonzalez sold off a total of 56,500 shares of their MAI stock at the then current market price of $28 a share.

After the information concerning the drop in earnings was made available to the public, the value of a share of MAI stock immediately fell from the $28 realized by the defendants to $11. Thus, the plaintiff alleges, by taking advantage of their privileged position and their access to confidential information, Oreamuno and Gonzalez were able to realize $800,000 more for their securities than they would have had this inside information not been available to them. . . . A motion by the defendants to dismiss the complaint . . . for failure to state a cause of action was granted by the court at Special Term. The Appellate Division, with one dissent, modified Special Term's order by reinstating the complaint as to the defendants Oreamuno and Gonzalez. . . .

It is well established, as a general proposition, that a person who acquires special knowledge or information by virtue of a confidential or fiduciary relationship with another is not free to exploit that knowledge or information for his own personal benefit but must account to his principal for any profits derived therefrom. (See, e.g., Byrne v. Barrett, 268 N.Y. 199, 197 N.E. 217, 100 A.L.R. 680.) This, in turn, is merely a corollary of the broader principle, inherent in the nature of the fiduciary relationship, that prohibits a trustee or agent from extracting secret profits from his position of trust.

In support of their claim that the complaint fails to state a cause of action, the defendants take the position that, although it is admittedly wrong for an officer or director to use his position to obtain trading profits for himself in the stock of his corporation, the action ascribed to them did not injure or damage MAI in any way. Accordingly, the defendants continue, the corporation should not be permitted to recover the proceeds. They acknowledge that, by virtue of the exclusive access which officers and directors have to inside information, they possess an unfair advantage over other shareholders and, particularly, the persons who had purchased the stock from them but, they contend, the corporation itself was unaffected and, for that reason, a derivative action is an inappropriate remedy.

It is true that the complaint before us does not contain any allegation of damages to the corporation but this had never been considered to be an essential requirement for a cause of action founded on a breach of fiduciary duty. . . . This is because the function of such an action, unlike an ordinary tort or contract case, is not merely to compensate the plaintiff for wrongs committed by the defendant but, as this court declared many years ago (Dutton v. Willner, 52 N.Y. 312, 319 . . .), "to *prevent* them, by removing from agents and trustees all inducement to attempt dealing for their own benefit in matters which they have undertaken for others, or to which their agency or trust relates." (Emphasis supplied.)

Just as a trustee has no right to retain for himself the profits yielded by property placed in his possession but must account to his beneficiaries, a corporate fiduciary, who is entrusted with potentially valuable information, may not appropriate that asset for his own use even though, in so doing, he causes no injury to the corporation. The primary concern, in a case such as this, is not to determine whether the corporation has been damaged but to decide, as between the corporation and the defendants, who has a higher claim to the proceeds derived from the exploitation of the information. In our opinion, there can be no justification for permitting officers and directors, such as the defendants, to retain for themselves profits which, it is alleged, they derived solely from exploiting information gained by virtue of their inside position as corporate officials.

In addition, it is pertinent to observe that, despite the lack of any specific allegation of damage, it may well be inferred that the defendants' actions might have caused some harm to the enterprise. Although the corporation may have little concern with the day-to-day transactions in its shares, it has a great interest in maintaining a reputation of integrity, an image of probity, for its management and in insuring the continued public acceptance and marketability of its stock. When officers and directors abuse their position in order to gain personal profits, the effect may be to cast a cloud on the corporation's name, injure stockholder relations and undermine public regard for the corporation's securities. . . .

The defendants maintain that extending the prohibition against personal exploitation of a fiduciary relationship to officers and directors of a corporation will discourage such officials from maintaining a stake in the success of the corporate venture through share ownership, which, they urge, is an important incentive to proper performance of their duties. There is, however, a considerable difference between corporate officers who assume the same risks and obtain the same benefits as other shareholders and those who use their privileged position to gain special advantages not available to others. The sale of shares by the defendants for the reasons charged was not merely a wise investment decision which any prudent investor might have made. Rather, they were assertedly able in this case to profit solely because they had information which was not available to any one else — including the other shareholders whose interests they, as corporate fiduciaries, were bound to protect.

Although no appellate court in this State has had occasion to pass upon the precise question before us, the concept underlying the present cause of action is hardly a new one. (See, e.g., Securities Exchange Act of 1934, §16[b]; Brophy v. Cities Serv. Co., 31 Del. Ch. 241; Restatement, 2d, Agency, §388, comment c; Israels, A New Look at Corporate Directorship, 24 Bus. Law. 727, 732 et seq.; Note, 54 Cornell L. Rev. 306, 309-312.) Under Federal law (Securities Exchange Act of 1934, §16[b]), for example, it is conclusively presumed that, when a director, officer or 10% shareholder buys and sells securities of his corporation within a six-month period, he is trading on inside information. The remedy which the Federal state provides in that situation is precisely the same as that sought in the present case under State law, namely, an action brought by the corporation or on its behalf to recover all profits derived from the transactions.

In providing this remedy, Congress accomplished a dual purpose. It not only provided for an efficient and effective method of accomplishing its primary goal — the protection of the investing public from unfair treatment at the hands of corporate insiders — but extended to the corporation the right to secure for itself benefits derived by those insiders from their exploitation of their privileged position. . . .

Although the provisions of section 16(b) may not apply to all cases of trading on inside information, it demonstrates that a derivative action can be an effective method for dealing with such abuses which may be used to accomplish a similar purpose in cases not specifically covered by the statute. In Brophy v. Cities Serv. Co. (31 Del. Ch. 241, 70 A.2d 5 [1949]), for example, the Chancery Court of Delaware allowed a similar remedy in a situation not covered by the Federal legislation. One of the defendants in that case was an employee who had acquired inside information that the corporate plaintiff was about to enter the market and purchase its own shares. On the basis of this confidential information, the employee, who was not an officer and, hence, not liable under Federal law, bought a large block of shares and, after the corporation's purchases had caused the price to rise, resold them at a profit. The court sustained the complaint in a derivative action brought for an accounting, stating that "[public] policy will not permit an employee occupying a position of trust and confidence toward his employer to abuse that relation to his own profit, regardless of whether his employer suffers a loss." And a similar view has been expressed in the Restatement, 2d, Agency (§388, comment c):

> c. *Use of confidential information.* An agent who acquires confidential information in the course of his employment or in violation of his duties has a duty . . . to account for any profits made by the use of such information, although this does not harm the principal. . . . So, if [a corporate officer] has "inside" information that the corporation is about to purchase or sell securities, or to declare or to pass a dividend, profits made by him in stock transactions undertaken because of his knowledge are held in constructive trust for the principal.

In the present case, the defendants may be able to avoid liability to the corporation under section 16(b) of the Federal law since they had held the MAI shares for more than six months prior to the sales. Nevertheless, the alleged use of the inside information to dispose of their stock at a price considerably higher than its known value constituted the same sort of "abuse of a fiduciary relationship" as is condemned by the Federal law. Sitting as we are in this case as a court of equity, we should not hesitate to permit an action to prevent any unjust enrichment realized by the defendants from their allegedly wrongful act.

The defendants recognize that the conduct charged against them directly contravened the policy embodied in the Securities Exchange Act but, they maintain, the Federal legislation constitutes a comprehensive and carefully wrought plan for dealing with the abuse of inside information and that allowing a derivative action to be maintained under State law would interfere with the Federal scheme. Moreover, they urge, the existence of dual Federal and State remedies for the same act would create the possibility of double liability.

An examination of the Federal regulatory scheme refutes the contention that it was designed to establish any particular remedy as exclusive. In addition to the specific provisions of section 16(b), the Securities and Exchange Act contains a general anti-fraud provision in section 10(b) which, as implemented by rule 10b-5 under that section, renders it unlawful to engage in a variety of acts considered to be fraudulent. In interpreting this rule, the Securities and Exchange Commission and the Federal courts have extended the common-law definition of fraud to include not only affirmative misrepresentations, relied upon by the purchaser or seller, but also a failure to disclose material information which might have affected the transaction. (See, e.g., Securities & Exch. Comm. v. Texas Gulf Sulphur Co., 2 Cir., 401 F.2d 833, 847-848; Myzel v. Fields, 8 Cir., 386 F.2d 718, 733-735.)

Accepting the truth of the complaint's allegations, there is no question but that the defendants were guilty of withholding material information from the purchasers of the shares and, indeed, the defendants acknowledge that the facts asserted constitute a violation of rule 10b-5. The remedies which the Federal law provides for such violations, however, are rather limited. An action could be brought, in an exceptional case, by the SEC for injunctive relief. This, in fact, is what happened in the *Texas Gulf Sulphur* case (401 F.2d 833, supra). The purpose of such an action, however, would appear to be more to establish a principle than to provide a regular method of enforcement. A class action under the Federal rule might be a more effective remedy but the mechanics of such an action have, as far as we have been able to ascertain, not yet been worked out by the Federal courts and several questions relating thereto have never been resolved. These include the definition of the class entitled to bring such an action, the measure of damages, the administration of the fund which would be recovered and its distribution to the members of the class. (See Note, 54 Cornell L. Rev. 306, 309, supra). Of course, any individual purchaser who could prove an injury as a result of a rule 10b-5 violation can bring his own action for rescission but we have not been referred to a single case in which such an action has been successfully prosecuted where the public sale of securities is involved. The reason for this is that sales of securities, whether through a stock exchange or over-the-counter, are characteristically anonymous transactions, usually handled through brokers, and the matching of the ultimate buyer with the ultimate seller presents virtually insurmountable obstacles. Thus, unless a section 16(b) violation is also present, the Federal law does not yet provide a really effective remedy.

In view of the practical difficulties inherent in an action under the Federal law, the desirability of creating an effective common-law remedy is manifest. "Dishonest directors should not find absolution from retributive justice," Ballantine observed in his work on Corporations ([rev. ed., 1946], p.216), "by concealing their identity from their victims under the mask of the stock exchange." There is ample room in a situation such as is here presented for a "private Attorney General" to come forward and enforce proper behavior on the part of corporate officials through the medium of the derivative action brought in the name of the corporation. . . . Only by sanctioning such a cause of action will there be any effective method to prevent the type of abuse of corporate office complained of in this case.

There is nothing in the Federal law which indicates that it was intended to limit the power of the States to fashion additional remedies to effectuate similar purposes. Although the impact of Federal securities regulation has on occasion been said to have created a "Federal corporation law," in fact, its effect on the duties and obligations of directors and officers and their relation to the corporation and its shareholders is only occasional and peripheral. The primary source of the law in this area ever remains that of the State which created the corporation. Indeed, Congress expressly provided against any implication that it intended to preempt the field by declaring, in section 28(a) of the Securities Exchange Act of 1934, that "[t]he rights and remedies provided by this title shall be in addition to any and all other rights and remedies that may exist at law or in equity."

Nor should we be deterred, in formulating a State remedy, by the defendants' claim of possible double liability. Certainly, as already indicated, if the sales in question were publicly made, the likelihood that a suit will be brought by purchasers of the shares is quite remote. But, even if it were not, the mere possibility of such a suit is not a defense nor does it render the complaint insufficient. It is not unusual for an action to be brought to recover a fund which may be subject to a superior claim by a third party. If that be the situation, a defendant should not be permitted to retain the fund for his own use on the chance that such a party may eventually appear. A defendant's course, if he wishes to protect himself against double liability, is to interplead any and all possible claimants and bind them to the judgment. . . .

In any event, though, no suggestion has been made either in brief or on oral argument that any purchaser has come forward with a claim against the defendants or even that anyone is in a position to advance such a claim.[1] As we have stated, the defendants' assertion that such a party may come forward at some future date is not a basis for permitting them to retain for their own benefit the fruits of their allegedly wrongful acts. For all that appears, the present derivative action is the only effective remedy now available against the abuse by these defendants of their privileged position. . . .

The order appealed from should be affirmed. . . .

Freeman v. Decio
584 F.2d 186 (7th Cir. 1978)

Wood, J.: The principal question presented by this case is whether under Indiana law the plaintiff may sustain a derivative action against certain officers and directors of the Skyline Corporation for allegedly trading in the stock of the corporation on the basis of material inside information. The district court . . . held that the plaintiff had failed to state a cause of action in that Indiana law has never recognized a right in a corporation to recover profits from insider trading and is not likely to follow the lead of the New York Court of Appeals in Diamond v. Oreamuno, 24 N.Y.2d 494, 301 N.Y.S.2d 78, 248 N.E.2d 910 (1969), in creating such a cause of action. We affirm. . . .

Plaintiff alleges that the defendants sold Skyline stock on the basis of material inside information during two distinct periods. Firstly, it is alleged that the financial results reported by Skyline for the quarters ending May 31 and August 31, 1972, significantly understated material costs and overstated earnings. It is further alleged that Decio, Kaufman and Mandell made various sales of Skyline stock totalling nearly $10 million during the quarters in question, knowing that earnings were overstated. Secondly, plaintiff asserts that during the quarter ending November 30 and up to December 22, 1972, Decio and Mandell made gifts and sales of Skyline stock totalling nearly $4 million while knowing that reported earnings for the November 30 quarter would decline. . . .

Both parties agree that there is no Indiana precedent directly dealing with the question of whether a corporation may recover the profits of corporate officials who trade in the corporation's securities on the basis of inside information. However, the plaintiff suggests that were the question to be presented to the Indiana courts, they would adopt the holding of the New York Court of Appeals in Diamond v. Oreamuno. There, building on the Delaware case of Brophy v. Cities Service Co., 31 Del. Ch. 241, 70 A.2d 5 (1949), the court held that the officers and directors of a corporation breached their fiduciary duties owed to the corporation by trading in its stock on the basis of material non-public information acquired by virtue of their official positions and that they should account to the corporation for their profits from those transactions. Since *Diamond* was decided, few courts have

---

1. In the absence of any such appearance by adverse claimants, we need not decide whether the corporation's recovery would be affected by any amounts which might have to be refunded by the defendant to the injured purchasers.

had an opportunity to consider the problem there presented. In fact, only one case has been brought to our attention which raised the question of whether *Diamond* would be followed in another jurisdiction. In Schein v. Chasen, 478 F.2d 817 (2d Cir. 1973), *vacated and remanded sub nom.* Lehman Bros. v. Schein, 416 U.S. 386, 94 S. Ct. 1741, 40 L. Ed. 2d 215 (1974), *on certification to the Fla. Sup. Ct.,* 313 So. 2d 739 (Fla. 1975), the Second Circuit, sitting in diversity, considered whether the Florida courts would permit a *Diamond*-type action to be brought on behalf of a corporation. The majority not only tacitly concluded that Florida would adopt *Diamond,* but that the *Diamond* cause of action should be extended so as to permit recovery of the profits of non-insiders who traded in the corporation's stock on the basis of inside information received as tips from insiders. Judge Kaufman, dissenting, agreed with the policies underlying a *Diamond*-type cause of action, but disagreed with the extension of liability to outsiders. He also failed to understand why the panel was not willing to utilize Florida's certified question statute so as to bring the question of law before the Florida Supreme Court. Granting certiorari, the United States Supreme Court agreed with the dissent on this last point and on remand the case was certified to the Florida Supreme Court. That court not only stated that it would not "give the unprecedented expansive reading to *Diamond* sought by appellants" but that, furthermore, it did not "choose to adopt the innovative ruling of the New York Court of Appeals in *Diamond* [itself]." 212 So. 2d 739, 746 (Fla. 1975). Thus, the question here is whether the Indiana courts are more likely to follow the New York Court of Appeals or to join the Florida Supreme Court in refusing to undertake such a change from existing law.

It appears that from a policy point of view it is widely accepted that insider trading should be deterred because it is unfair to other investors who do not enjoy the benefits of access to inside information. The goal is not one of equality of possession of information — since some traders will always be better "informed" than others by dint of greater expenditures of time and resources, greater experience, or greater analytical abilities — but rather equality of access to information. . . . Yet, a growing body of commentary suggests that pursuit of this goal of "market egalitarianism" may be costly. In addition to the costs associated with enforcement of the laws prohibiting insider trading, there may be a loss in the efficiency of the securities markets in their capital allocation function. The basic insight of economic analysis here is that securities prices act as signals helping to route capital to its most productive uses and that insider trading helps assure that those prices will reflect the best information available (i.e., inside information) as to where the best opportunities lie. However, even when confronted with the possibility of a trade-off between fairness and economic efficiency, most authorities appear to find that the balance tips in favor of discouraging insider trading. . . .

. . . [T]he New York Court of Appeals in *Diamond* found the existing remedies for controlling insider trading to be inadequate. Although the court felt that the device of a class action under the federal securities laws held out hope of a more effective remedy in the future, it concluded that "the desirability of creating an effective common-law remedy is manifest." It went on to do so by engineering an innovative extension of the law governing the relation between a corporation and its officers and directors. The court held that corporate officials who deal in their corporation's securities on the basis of non-public information gained by virtue of their inside position commit a breach of their fiduciary duties to the corporation. This holding represents a departure from the traditional common law approach, which was that a corporate insider did not ordinarily violate his fiduciary duty to the corporation by dealing in the corporation's stock, unless the corporation was thereby harmed. . . .

There are a number of difficulties with the *Diamond* court's ruling. Perhaps the thorniest problem was posed by the defendants' objection that whatever the ethical status of insider trading, there is no injury to the corporation which can serve as a basis for recognizing a right of recovery in favor of the latter. The Court of Appeals' response to this argument was two-fold, suggesting first that no harm to the corporation need be shown and second that it might well be inferred that the insiders' activities did in fact cause some harm to the corporation. . . . Some might see the *Diamond* court's decision as resting on a broad, strict-trust notion of the fiduciary duty owed to the corporation: no director is to receive any profit, beyond what he receives from the corporation, solely because of his position. Although, once accepted, this basis for the *Diamond* rule would obviate the need for finding a potential for injury to the corporation, it is not at all clear that current corporation law contemplates such an extensive notion of fiduciary duty. It is customary to view the *Diamond* result as resting on a characterization of inside information as a corporate asset. The lack of necessity for looking for an injury to the corporation is then justified by the traditional "no inquiry" rule with respect to profits made by trustees from assets belonging to the trust res. However, to start from the premise that all inside information should be considered a corporate asset may presuppose an answer to the inquiry at hand. It might be better to ask whether there is any potential loss to the corporation from the use of such information in insider trading before deciding to characterize the inside information as an asset with respect to which the insider owes the corporation a duty of loyalty (as opposed to a duty of care). This approach would be in keeping with the modern view of another area of application of the duty of loyalty — the corporate opportunity doctrine. Thus, while courts will require a director or officer to automatically account to the corporation for diversion of a corporate opportunity to personal use, they will first inquire to see whether there was a possibility of a loss to the corporation — i.e., whether the corporation was in a position to potentially avail itself of the opportunity — before deciding that a corporate opportunity in fact existed. Similarly, when scrutinizing transactions between a director or officer and the corporation under the light of the duty of loyalty, most courts now inquire as to whether there was any injury to the corporation, i.e., whether the transaction was fair and in good faith, before permitting the latter to avoid the transaction. An analogous question might be posed with respect to the *Diamond* court's unjust enrichment analysis: is it proper to conclude that an insider has been unjustly enriched vis-à-vis the corporation (as compared to other traders in the market) when there is no way that the corporation could have used the information to its own profit, just because the insider's trading was made possible by virtue of his corporate position?

Not all information generated in the course of carrying on a business fits snugly into the corporate asset mold. Information in the form of trade secrets, customer lists, etc., can easily be categorized as a valuable or potentially valuable corporate "possession," in that it can be directly used by the corporation to its own economic advantage. However, most information involved in insider trading is not of this ilk, e.g., knowledge of an impending merger, a decline in earnings, etc. If the corporation were to attempt to exploit such non-public information by dealing in its own securities, it would open itself up to potential liability under federal and state securities laws, just as do the insiders when they engage in insider trading. This is not to say that the corporation does not have any interests with regard to such information. It may have an interest in either preventing the information from becoming public or in regulating the timing of disclosure. However, insider trading does not entail the disclosure of inside information, but rather its use in a manner in which the corporation itself is prohibited from exploiting it. . . .

It must be conceded that the unfairness that is the basis of the widespread disapproval of insider trading is borne primarily by participants in the securities markets, rather than by the corporation itself. By comparison, the harm to corporate goodwill posited by the *Diamond* court pales in significance. At this point, the existence of such an indirect injury must be considered speculative, as there is no actual evidence of such a reaction. Furthermore, it is less than clear to us that the nature of this harm would form an adequate basis for an action for an accounting based on a breach of the insiders' duty of loyalty, as opposed to an action for damages based on a breach of the duty of care. The injury hypothesized by the *Diamond* court seems little different from the harm to the corporation that might be inferred whenever a responsible corporate official commits an illegal or unethical act using a corporate asset. Absent is the element of loss of opportunity or potential susceptibility to outside influence that generally is present when a corporate fiduciary is required to account to the corporation.

The *Brophy* case is capable of being distinguished on this basis. Although the court there did not openly rely on the existence of a potential harm to the corporation, such a harm was possible. Since the corporation was about to begin buying its own shares in the market, by purchasing stock for his own account the insider placed himself in direct competition with the corporation. To the degree that his purchases might have caused the stock price to rise, the corporation was directly injured in that it had to pay more for its purchases. The other cases cited by the *Diamond* court also tended to involve an agent's competition with his principal, harm to it, disregard for its instructions, or the like. The same is true of the situations covered in Comment c of the Restatement (Second) of Agency, with the exception of the case where the corporate agent undertakes stock transactions on the basis of knowledge that the corporation is about to declare or pass a dividend.

A second problem presented by the recognition of a cause of action in favor of the corporation is that of potential double liability. The *Diamond* court thought that this problem would seldom arise, since it thought it unlikely that a damage suit would be brought by investors where the insiders traded on impersonal exchanges. . . .

The Second Circuit also gave consideration to the possibility of double liability in Schein v. Chasen, but concluded that double liability could be avoided by methods such as that employed in SEC v. Texas Gulf Sulphur Co., 312 F. Supp. 77, 93 (S.D.N.Y. 1970), where the defendants' disgorged profits were placed in a fund subject first to the claims of injured investors, with the residue payable to the corporation. The efficacy of the *Diamond* court's suggestion of resort to an interpleader action is open to question. The creation of a fund subject to the superior claims of injured investors also poses some difficulties. Although some observers have suggested that double liability be imposed so as to more effectively deter insider trading and that it is analytically justifiable since the two causes of action involved are based on separate legal wrongs, the *Diamond* and *Schein* courts' concern for avoiding double liability may implicitly reflect the view that a right of recovery in favor of the corporation was being created because of the perceived likelihood that the investors who are the true victims of insider trading would not be able to bring suit. When the latter in fact bring an action seeking damages from the insiders, thereby creating the possibility of double liability, the need for a surrogate plaintiff disappears and the corporation's claim is implicitly relegated to the back seat.

Since the *Diamond* court's action was motivated in large part by its perception of the inadequacy of existing remedies for insider trading, it is noteworthy that over the decade since *Diamond* was decided, the 10b-5 class action has made substantial advances toward becoming the kind of effective remedy for insider trading that the court of appeals hoped that it might become. Most importantly, recovery of damages from insiders has been allowed by, or on the behalf of, market investors even when the insiders dealt only through impersonal stock exchanges, although this is not yet a well-settled area of the law. In spite of other recent developments indicating that such class actions will not become as easy to maintain as some plaintiffs had perhaps hoped, it is clear that the remedies for insider trading under the federal securities laws now constitute a more effective deterrent than they did when *Diamond* was decided. . . .

[H]aving carefully examined the decision of the New York Court of Appeals in *Diamond*, we are of the opinion that although the court sought to ground its ruling in accepted principles of corporate common law, that decision can best be understood as an example of judicial securities regulation. Although the question is a close one, we believe that were the issue to be presented to the Indiana courts at the present time, they would most likely join the Florida Supreme Court in refusing to adopt the New York court's innovative ruling. . . .

The judgment of the district court is affirmed.

---

1. *Is* Diamond *dead?* In In re ORFA Securities Litigation, 654 F. Supp. 1449 (D.N.J. 1987), the court held that New Jersey would probably follow *Diamond* and reject *Freeman*. Defendants in *ORFA* were corporate officers who personally sold large amounts of stock just prior to the publication of a highly negative article in Barron's that criticized the corporation's financial statements as inflated and painted a dismal picture of its future prospects. *ORFA* found the holding in *Diamond* to have been properly based on the need to prevent unjust enrichment.[85] It also found *Diamond* more persuasive than *Freeman* as to the likelihood of corporate injury from insider trading, but sidestepped the problem of identifying this harm, ruling that it would accept plaintiff's well-pleaded allegations of corporate injury for purposes of a motion to dismiss. Several years later, however, two other federal district courts reached the opposite conclusion, both holding that New Jersey would not follow *Diamond*, at least when a double recovery was possible. See Frankel v. Slotkin, 795 F. Supp. 76, 80-81 (E.D.N.Y. 1992); In re Symbol Technologies Sec. Litig., 762 F. Supp. 510, 517 (E.D.N.Y. 1991). *Query:* What if the statute of

---

85. ALI §5.04 adopts the *Diamond* approach "by permitting the corporation to recover for unjust enrichment. . . ." 1 ALI, Principles of Corporate Governance 270 (1994).

limitations had already expired under the federal law at the time the state derivative claim was filed?

2. *Other classes of defendants.* (a) In Davidge v. White, 377 F. Supp. 1084 (S.D.N.Y. 1974), the court held, under Delaware law, that the rule of Brophy v. Cities Service Co., cited in *Diamond*, page 529 supra, extends to profits from confidential information that are made after defendant ends his employment with the corporation. See also Thomas v. Roblin Indus., Inc., 520 F.2d 1393 (3d Cir. 1975).

(b) In Frigitemp Corp. v. Financial Dynamics Fund, Inc., 524 F.2d 275 (2d Cir. 1975), several mutual funds had purchased $1 million of Frigitemp debentures from the corporation. Frigitemp then sued the mutual funds for profits they realized in trading Frigitemp stock based on confidential information the funds had obtained during negotiations for their purchase of the debentures. Dismissal affirmed:

> The appellees here were never officers or directors or even employees of Frigitemp.
>
> The information supplied by Frigitemp was information that Frigitemp . . . was required to disclose to a person about to lend it $1,000,000, or, in the language of securities law, about to buy its debenture. Given the duty to disclose and the need for the loan, the corporate officer who gave the information in order to get the loan was not violating his fiduciary duty. Nor was the buyer of the debenture culpable as a co-venturer of a faithless trustee. The dealings were at arm's length. The corporate officer had the right to make the inside information available. The other party had the right to request it. We need not determine whether the buyer owed a duty to market traders to refrain from buying or selling the shares of Frigitemp based on such information, since such persons are not plaintiffs in this action. . . . We hold merely that appellees were under no fiduciary duty to the corporation under New York law by virtue of their status as potential purchasers of its debenture. We need not consider the hypothetical case where the purported buyer of a debenture was not negotiating for its purchase in good faith but was using the negotiations merely as a device for obtaining confidential information. Here the buyer actually paid $1,000,000 for the debenture.

What would be the result in this case under Rule 10b-5 after *Dirks*, page 454 supra? Are they constructive insiders under *Dirks*? Or is it clear that this was an arm's-length, commercial relationship in which no insider breached a duty and purchasers owed no duty?

(c) In Walton v. Morgan Stanley & Co., 623 F.2d 796 (2d Cir. 1980), appellant brought a derivative suit on behalf of Olinkraft, Inc. The complaint alleged that Morgan Stanley, an investment bank that had been engaged by Kennecott to find acquisitions for it, approached Olinkraft whose management "cooperated" with Morgan Stanley's Mergers and Acquisitions Department, "supplied it with highly favorable confidential internal earnings projections," and "instructed [it] that the Confidential Inside Information was to be used in connection with the Kennecott Bid and was to be returned to Olinkraft if such bid did not go through." Although Kennecott did not bid for Olinkraft, Texas Eastern Corp. offered $51 per share. Morgan Stanley's Arbitrage Department then bought Olinkraft shares, believing "that a competing offer at a higher price than $51 per share would be made." Thereafter, Morgan Stanley's Mergers and Acquisitions Department, which knew of the Arbitrage Department's purchases, disclosed to Johns-Manville, which it was advising financially, the confidential Olinkraft information. Johns-Manville then agreed to merge with Olinkraft at $65 per share. Dismissal affirmed:

> [T]he only logical conclusion to be drawn from the complaint is that Olinkraft and Morgan Stanley dealt at arm's length. . . . Morgan Stanley was never hired by Olinkraft, nor was Morgan Stanley's task ever to act on Olinkraft's behalf. . . . Morgan Stanley and Olinkraft's management were at all times responsible to different interests, and they had no relationship to each other before or other than in the acquisition discussions. . . . [A]lthough, according to the complaint, Olinkraft's management placed its confidence in Morgan Stanley not to disclose the information, Morgan Stanley owed no duty to observe that confidence. . . . [T]he complaint, although it alleges a breach of fiduciary duty, fails to state facts from which a fiduciary relationship arises under Delaware law between Olinkraft and Morgan Stanley.

Judge Oakes dissented:

> [A]fter Olinkraft began to cooperate in the deal by turning over the "Confidential Inside Information" as to favorable earnings prospects, I think the acceptance of such information by Morgan Stanley, on the confidential terms, along with its understood role as intermediary in a cooperative takeover, imposed a duty on the investment banker under well-established common law principles not to use that information for its own profit. As Professor Scott stated in his treatise, "The same principles [that prevent a fiduciary from taking personal advantage of confidential information obtained as such, as against the beneficiary] are applicable even though the parties are not technically in a fiduciary relation, if one of them acquires confidential information from the other." 3 A. Scott, The Law of Trusts §505, at 2428 (1939). . . . [3] . . . For me, this case is distinguishable from . . . Frigitemp Corp. v. Financial Dynamics Fund, Inc., 524 F.2d 275 (2d Cir. 1975). . . . There the information was, as the court's opinion pointed out, "required" to be disclosed to the investment company for the purpose of selling the debenture to it in an arm's length transaction. Id. at 279. Here, Olinkraft furnished its projections to Kennecott through Morgan Stanley, only in connection with Kennecott's contemplated acquisition, and not because it was required to do so but because it evidently wanted to cooperate.

Would the result be different if Morgan Stanley had signed a confidentiality agreement with Olinkraft in order to obtain access to confidential information?

---

3. I extrapolate Morgan Stanley's agreement from the complaint's allegations that Olinkraft "instructed" the investment banker on the sole use to which the information could be put. Once Morgan Stanley accepted the information knowing Olinkraft's terms of transmittal, I would imply its agreement to abide by such restrictions. In this way, perhaps appellants here would have the makings of a breach of contract action, although the damages would admittedly be speculative.

VI VOTING AND CORPORATE CONTROL

A. OVERVIEW: VOTING AND "SHAREHOLDER DEMOCRACY"

In a democracy, voting is obviously the key mechanism by which citizens hold their elected leaders accountable. In a corporation, voting is also the means by which corporate control is either held or transferred. Ultimately, no one can acquire "control" of a corporation without first acquiring the ability to elect a majority of the board of directors. Still, the analogy between political democracy and "shareholder democracy" is imperfect, and critics have long contended that the voting system in publicly held corporations fails to provide effective account-ability. It is important to understand the central themes in this debate in order both to evaluate the specific policy issues on which this chapter focuses and to understand how recent developments — most importantly, the growth in institu-tional share ownership — may enhance the significance of shareholder voting in the future.

Initially, the similarities between political and corporate voting may seem to outweigh their differences. In both political units and economic organizations, representative government is a necessity, given the complexity and ongoing nature of the decisions faced. Thus, those entitled to vote select agents to make the vast majority of decisions on their behalf: e.g., federal and state legislators and executives in politics are paralleled by directors and officers in corporate gover-nance. These agents then hire, monitor, and replace professional managers — civil servants or business executives, respectively. In both systems, vast discretion is delegated to these agents, but regular elections are mandated by law. Almost uniformly, corporation statutes require an annual meeting for the election of directors. See, e.g., N.Y. Bus. Corp. Law §602(b) (2007). Further, directors may often be removed by shareholder vote, thus making them potentially more accountable than political leaders, who cannot typically be as easily recalled or impeached. See Sec. F infra.

What, then, are the alleged problems with shareholder voting as a mechanism of accountability? The major critique was formulated by Adolf Berle and Gardiner Means in The Modern Corporation and Private Property (1932): ownership and control had become separated in the large publicly held corporation:

> Frequently . . . ownership is so widely scattered that working control can be maintained with but a minority interest. Separation becomes almost complete when not even a substantial minority interest exists. . . . Under such conditions control may be held by the directors or titular managers who can employ the proxy machinery to become a self-perpetuating body, even though as a group they own but a small fraction of the stock outstanding. . . . [A] large body of security holders has been created who exercise virtually no control over the wealth which they or their predecessors in interest have contributed to the enterprise. . . .
>
> . . . [T]he position of ownership has changed from that of an active to that of a passive agent. In place of actual physical properties over which the owner could exercise discretion and for which he was responsible, the owner now holds a piece of paper representing a set of rights and expectations with respect to an enterprise. But over the enterprise and over the physical property — the instruments of production — in which he has an interest, the owner has little control.
>
> . . . [I]n the corporate system the "owner" of industrial wealth is left with a mere symbol of ownership while the power, the responsibility and the substance which have been an integral part of ownership in the past are being transferred to a separate group in whose hands lies control.

As Berle and Means saw it, shareholder dispersion in the publicly held firm implied shareholder powerlessness. Surveying the 200 largest corporations as of 1930, they found that management held control in 44 percent, while majority shareholders were identifiably in control in only 5 percent (the balance were controlled by minority shareholders or through special legal devices — such as the voting trust — or were privately held firms). By "management controlled," they meant that no single shareholder was in a position to exert substantial influence on management.

Why was management so immune from shareholder pressure? In part, Berle and Means argued that management's control over the corporate proxy machinery made shareholder opposition futile. In brief, because few shareholders can attend the corporation's annual meeting (both for reasons of cost and because of other constraints on their available time), management solicits proxies from shareholders at the corporation's expense. These proxies typically appoint management (or their nominees) as the shareholders' representative to vote their shares at any annual or special meeting. Persons wishing to oppose management must undertake a rival proxy solicitation at their own expense, and such an election campaign typically is costly (as discussed below). Berle and Means concluded: "The proxy machinery has thus become one of the principal instruments not by which a stockholder exercises power over management of the enterprise, but by which his power is separated from him."

Berle and Means's assessment has been hotly disputed by others, who argue that shareholders can exert substantial pressure on management by means other than voting. For example, if shareholders become dissatisfied with management, they can sell their shares (i.e., "vote with their feet"). The resulting drop in the price of the firm's stock will also harm the firm's managers, who typically have a substantial portion of their personal wealth linked to the firm through stock options, stock ownership, and incentive compensation plans. Hence, critics of Berle and Means argue that the paucity of proxy fights stems from the fact that management is adequately disciplined by stock market pressures, and shareholders thus have little reason to oppose management's proposals.[1]

Much has changed since the time that Berle and Means wrote. As noted in Chapter 1, institutional investors now own the majority of the stock in publicly held corporations. This increase in shareholder concentration over the last half century reduces the cost of collective action by shareholders, as potentially a group of 15 to 20 institutional investors could organize an effective coalition to resist management on some matter being brought to a shareholder vote. But institutional shareholders typically own large portfolios, consisting of hundreds, or even thousands, of stocks, and organizing opposition on a systematic basis would have a high cost, notwithstanding the greater size of their holdings. Thus, there is still an uncertain cost benefit ratio for them in any individual case.

Another change since the time when Berle and Means wrote is in the law itself, which today seeks to reduce the costs of collective action by requiring detailed mandatory disclosure on the subject of the shareholder vote. Then, managements usually provided shareholders with little information about the proposals that would be voted on at the annual meeting and instead simply sought a blanket authorization to vote their shares on any issue that arose. Only by incurring costs disproportionate to the value of their investment could most shareholders decide if there was even any issue on the agenda that merited their attention. This pattern of enforced ignorance and "blank check" authorizations was directly addressed by the Securities Exchange Act of 1934 (the '34 Act). Largely in response to the Berle and Means critique, §14 of the '34 Act required that anyone soliciting proxies of a "reporting company" (see Chapter V, Sec. B) first distribute a proxy statement that gives shareholders elaborate disclosures as to the identity, background, and plans of those soliciting proxies and the specific proposals to be voted on. Antifraud rules were also adopted to prohibit misleading statements or omissions in connection with proxy solicitations.

Voting rules are also changing. Traditionally, the election of directors (just like the elections for Congress) was by plurality voting. This means that if only a low percentage of the shareholders vote (because many are bored or uninterested), the

---

1. For a critique of Berle and Means from a neoclassical economic perspective, see Frank Easterbrook & Daniel Fischel, Voting in Corporate Law, 26 J.L. & Econ. 395 (1983) (arguing that because voting is costly and confounded by certain collective action problems discussed infra, voting occasions should be minimized).

incumbent board could be elected by simply a majority of the minority who actually voted. Withheld votes or abstentions had no legal significance. But this is changing. While state corporate law continues to provide for plurality voting as the default rule, corporations can opt out of this system and adopt some form of majority voting. As discussed later in this chapter, under majority voting, a director is not elected if the director receives less than a majority (either of the votes cast or of the voting shares outstanding, depending on the particular variant adopted). Under this system, withheld votes have impact, and institutional investors have recently pushed with considerable success for the adoption of majority voting.

Still, despite all these factors—the new concentration in share ownership, the mandatory disclosure provisions in the federal securities laws, and the shift toward majority voting—many critics believe that a basic imbalance exists between shareholders and management.[2] Indeed, Berle and Means (and some later commentators) believed the problem was essentially unsolvable and that shareholder democracy was therefore an illusory, unattainable ideal.

At a minimum, shareholder democracy faces two major obstacles, one informational and the other economic. First, shareholders may be reluctant to vote against management, even if they oppose a specific project or proposal, because they are reluctant to back a rival slate of candidates for the board. Simply put, the issue can often become whether the known evil is worse than the unknown evil. For example, suppose a shareholder believes that incumbent management has overcompensated itself or has been too slow to adjust to changed economic conditions. Still, the rational shareholder may hesitate to back the insurgents because it is difficult to know how they will behave if elected. What business policies will they follow? Will the insurgents loot the corporation or otherwise exploit it? In practice, institutional investors have traditionally been reluctant to vote for insurgents and instead have followed the practice—often called the "Wall Street Rule"—of selling their shares when dissatisfied. This preference for liquidating their investment, rather than relying on their right of suffrage, may reflect both a deep-seated risk aversion and the difficulty of obtaining reliable information about the future behavior of any potential replacement team of managers.

The second problem involves the costs of seeking to oppose the incumbent management. When the incumbent board solicits proxies, they do so at the corporation's expense. But when an insurgent group seeks to elect directors or seeks to amend the bylaws or take some other action, they must do so at their own expense—with little prospect of corporate reimbursement even if they are successful. Indeed, the reforms imposed by the Securities Exchange Act of 1934, which require the preparation and distribution of the proxy statement, probably increase the costs of activism.

For both these reasons, managements face contested elections to the board of directors in less than 1 percent of all annual proxy solicitations.[3] One recent survey finds that between 1996 and 2005 there were some 303 contested proxy

---

2. For the most recent statement of this view, see Lucian Bebchuk, The Myth of the Shareholder Franchise, 93 Va. L. Rev. 675 (2007).

3. See Joel Seligman, Equal Protection in Shareholder Voting Rights: The One Common Share, One Vote Controversy, 54 Geo. Wash. L. Rev. 687, at 711 (1986) (citing data from 1956-1977).

solicitations, or about 30 per year.[4] Historically, managements have defeated challengers in the vast majority of contests. Although dissidents tend to win only a few of these contests on an outright basis, they do achieve partial success in others, electing one or more of their slate, and have reached a negotiated resolution in still others — for an overall success rate that was probably around 30 percent in 2006.[5] Still, this aggregate data conceals the important fact that many of the successful contests are actually takeover battles in which the challenger has made a tender offer or merger proposal and is trying to unseat the incumbent board that is resisting its bid. In such a case, shareholders may have a stronger incentive to back the insurgent in order to obtain a takeover premium.

Rarer are cases in which an existing shareholder tries to take on management on an issue on which management is seeking shareholder approval. In 2002 and 2003, two such cases involving longtime shareholders who organized proxy campaigns in opposition to management received considerable publicity, and both reveal the cost barriers facing shareholders. In 2002 Walter Hewlett, a director of Hewlett-Packard Company and the son of one of its founders, organized a proxy campaign against the proposed merger of Hewlett-Packard and Compaq Computer, which he considered an economic mistake. Mr. Hewlett spent approximately $32 million

---

4. The number of contested solicitations (only some of which were for board elections) was as follows:

Year	Number of Contested Solicitations
2005	24
2004	27
2003	37
2002	38
2001	40
2000	30
1999	30
1998	20
1997	29
1996	28
	Total: 303

See Bebchuk, supra footnote 2, at 683. An earlier study of proxy contests between 1962 and 1978 involving all firms listed on the New York and American Stock Exchanges concluded:

(1) There were only 96 election contests over this period, suggesting that an election challenge to management was relatively infrequent; of these, 71 were for control of the board, while 25 involved only an attempt to secure representation on the board.

(2) In 74.6 percent, the incumbents won a majority of the board, while in 25.4 percent the insurgents did. However, in 58.3 percent of all contests, the insurgents obtained at least one seat on the board.

(3) Most commonly, proxy contests are launched by former insiders, who have left the firm after a dispute over policy or who have been fired.

(4) The proxy contest — whether successful or not — typically leads to a significant increase in the market value of the firm's shares, although this increase may erode after the contest is over. Thus, it appears to produce a benefit for shareholders (at least in the form of an opportunity to sell at an increased price) even when the insurgents are not successful. See Peter Dodd & Jerold Warner, On Corporate Governance: A Study of Proxy Contests, 11 J. Fin. Econ. 401 (1983). Thus, the number of election contests during the past decade has risen compared with earlier decades.

5. See Georgeson & Co., Annual Corporate Governance Review: Annual Meetings, Shareholder Initiatives and Proxy Contests (2006), at Figures 19 and 20.

of his own money in this proxy fight and narrowly lost the battle.[6] Hewlett-Packard appears to have spent somewhere between $75 million and $150 million on its successful campaign.[7] Similarly, in a proxy fight brought by longtime shareholders to oust the board at El Paso Company in 2003, management spent $10 million on its narrowly successful defense, while the insurgents spent some $5.9 million (for a total of $16 million) in losing.[8] The key fact here is not simply that management can outspend the opposition, but that the costs it incurs fall on all shareholders, while the unsuccessful dissidents have to bear their own expenses.

For some time, the SEC has attributed shareholder apathy to frustration with shareholder powerlessness and has predicted that shareholders would welcome an opportunity for more "meaningful participation."[9] Other commentators, particularly "law and economics" scholars, have disagreed, viewing shareholder apathy as less a problem than an indication that shareholders are content with existing arrangements for corporate governance and that managers are adequately disciplined by market pressures.[10]

Although this debate will continue, the basic SEC policy toward shareholder voting for decades has been to seek to reduce the costs of collective action. For a generation, the SEC has repeatedly considered and even formally proposed reforms that would give insurgent shareholders access to the corporation's proxy statement under at least some circumstances so that their candidates for the board would be placed on an equal footing with those of management. But on each occasion to date, under intense pressure from the business community, the SEC has backed off from adopting such reforms.

Other reforms, however, have been adopted by the SEC. One such is SEC Rule 14a-8, which permits shareholders to place a shareholder proposal on the corporation's own proxy statement for a vote at the annual meeting of shareholders. This rule allows shareholders to avoid the costs of preparing and filing their own proxy statement by instead allowing the proposing shareholder to free-ride on the corporation's proxy statement. Other shareholders can then instruct management, as their proxy agent, how to vote their shares on the submitted proposal. However, as will be seen later in this chapter, SEC Rule 14a-8 is limited in its scope; in particular, it does not apply to director elections. Nonetheless, the use of shareholder proposals has soared since 2000, and the annual number of such contests now outnumbers that of proxy contests.[11]

Often, these shareholder proposals result in negotiations between corporate management and the proposing shareholder group that result in a compromise,

6. Mark Getzfred, Technology Briefing Hardware: Proxy Fight Said to Cost $150 Million, N.Y. Times (March 26, 2002), at C-5.

7. See Steve Lohr, Hewlett-Packard's Profit Rises Despite Weak Sales, N.Y. Times (May 15, 2002), at C-4.

8. Bradley Keoun, El Paso and Dissidents Court Shareholders as Proxy Vote Looms, Bloomberg News (June 16, 2003).

9. See SEC Staff Report on Corporate Accountability, Senate Comm. on Banking, 96th Cong., 2d Sess. 66-68 (Comm. Print 1980).

10. This theme was first raised in a provocative article by Henry Manne, Some Theoretical Aspects of Share Voting, 64 Colum. L. Rev. 1427 (1964) (arguing that shareholder voting is important chiefly as a necessary incident to the market for corporate control).

11. The number of shareholder proposals submitted pursuant to Rule 14a-8 over recent years has risen from 77 in 1998 to over 750 in 2004; in 2006, 578 shareholder proposals were submitted. See Georgeson & Co., footnote 5 supra, at Figure 1. These numbers exceed by more than ten times the average number of formal proxy contests, which are fewer probably because they are more costly, given that the insurgent group must prepare and distribute its own proxy statement.

after which the original proposal is withdrawn by the proposing shareholders. This happened in more than one-third of the proposals submitted in 2005 and 2006.[12] Although there is no vote when the dispute is settled in this negotiated fashion, shareholders do gain leverage at low cost vis-à-vis management by means of Rule 14a-8. Historically, Rule 14a-8 was primarily employed by individual shareholders and religious groups to advance proposals relating to ethical and environmental concerns. Then, in the late 1980s and 1990s, institutional shareholders began to use Rule 14a-8 to advance proposals restricting takeover defensive tactics. These proposals to restrict defensive tactics or rescind the corporation's "poison pill" have increasingly won a majority of the shareholder vote, but as discussed later, there remains doubt in many jurisdictions as to whether these proposals can be mandatory, as opposed to merely advisory or "precatory." Not infrequently, corporate managements have simply disregarded precatory proposals that received a majority shareholder vote. Most recently, following Enron, WorldCom, and similar scandals, the focus of these proposals has shifted to corporate governance issues, such as board independence, auditor conflicts, shareholder voting, and executive compensation. Again, the typical outcome is more often a negotiation than a contested vote.

Another technique for economizing on the costs of collective action is the "just vote no" campaign. Here, the dissident shareholders urge shareholders to vote down a management proposal (such as a merger or a stock option plan). The key advantage of this approach is that, if the proponent of this proposal does not seek proxy authority (that is, does not request shareholders to give it a proxy card entitling it to vote the shareholders' shares as their agent), the proponent will generally not be required to prepare, file with the SEC, and distribute to shareholders any proxy statement. This elimination of the need to file a proxy statement in these cases was the result of SEC reforms in 1992, when the SEC substantially relaxed the legal rules that had previously discouraged institutional investors from participating in proxy contests.[13] Again, this was an example of a policy of reducing the costs of shareholder activism to encourage greater participation.

At the state level, the major development for the last several years has been the rapid shift toward majority voting in place of plurality voting. This shift, which has been encouraged by recent amendments to both the Delaware General Corporation Law and the Revised Model Business Corporation Act, as well as statutes in several other states, may well cause majority voting to become the dominant voting system and certainly increases the importance of the individual shareholder's vote. Numerous issues remain, however, to be worked out in practice, including whether the full board can decline the defeated director's resignation or appoint such person to the vacancy thereby created on the board.

Even in the absence of more sweeping reforms, the available evidence suggests that proxy contests do have real impact.[14] Why do proxy contests for corporate control benefit shareholders, when they typically do not succeed? One recent

---

12. Id. at Figure 6 (44.2 percent of proposals withdrawn or omitted in 2005 and 33.4 percent in 2006).

13. See Sec. Exch. Act Rel. No. 34-31326 (1992) (discussed pages 651-656 infra).

14. A 1990 study by a proxy solicitation firm found that while incumbents experienced "total victory" in over 40 percent of proxy contests for corporate control (compared to a 28 percent "total victory" rate for challengers), dissidents obtained some benefit in a majority of these contests. Looking to subsequent developments within the following year and negotiated settlements, this study reported that challengers achieved some measure of success in over 74 percent of all proxy contests. See Georgeson & Co., Inc., Proxy Contest Study, October 1984 to September 1990 (Dec. 14, 1990).

study finds that even though election contests usually fail, 72 percent of the firms in this survey were under a different management team three years later.[15] Also, shareholders realized positive abnormal gains during the proxy contest period, as the market apparently sensed that some eventual change in management was likely. Proxy fights may be a catalyst for change, or they may be only a symptom of deeper internal ills. But, in either case, significant changes usually follow in their wake.

Throughout the 1980s, the number of tender offers vastly exceeded the number of proxy contests. But in 1990 the number of proxy contests (74) actually exceeded the number of tender offers (70).[16] This trend increased during the 1990s, as institutional shareholders became more activist and as the number of hostile takeovers decreased in the face of state anti-takeover legislation and financing difficulties. Another fundamental shift occurred during the 1990s in the nature of proxy contests. Prior to that time, most proxy fights were election contests in which rival slates sought a majority of the seats on the corporate board. Starting in the late 1980s, however, "issue contests" began to supersede "election contests." Often, the issue was related to a pending or threatened takeover battle, as management sought to secure passage of a "shark repellent" anti-takeover charter amendment. But gradually, other issues began also to be contested: merger proposals favored by management, acquisitions, stock option plans, stock repurchases, proposed recapitalizations, voting procedures, and executive compensation plans.[17]

In overview, the most important point to be made about the right to vote in the corporate context is that it is individually unimportant but collectively valuable. Few shareholders believe that their votes will make a difference, and serious problems and high costs complicate any attempt to organize shareholder voting as a form of collective action.

B. *THE SUBSTANTIVE LAW OF SHAREHOLDER VOTING*

This section addresses five central questions about the corporate voting system: Who should vote? When should a shareholder vote be necessary? What level of shareholder support is necessary? What voting power should a share possess? Should shareholders be allowed to sell their votes or lend their shares to others who will vote them? In overview, corporate law is largely enabling and permissive in character with respect to the first, third, and fourth of these questions, but mandatory with respect to the second and fifth.

---

15. See Lisa Borstadt & Thomas Zwirlein, The Efficient Monitoring Role of Proxy Contests: An Empirical Analysis of Post-Contest Control Changes and Firm Performance, 21 Fin. Mgmt. (Autumn 1992), at 22. For an earlier study, see Harry DeAngelo & Linda DeAngelo, Proxy Contests and the Governance of Publicly Held Corporations, 23 J. Fin. Econ. 29 (1989) (in two-thirds of contests where incumbents prevail, a sale or liquidation of the firm, or a departure of the CEO, follows within three years).

16. See J. Harold Mulherin & Annette B. Poulsen, Proxy Reform as a Single Norm? Evidence Related to Cross-Sectional Variation in Corporate Governance, 17 J. Corp. L. 125, 142 (1991).

17. For a discussion of this trend, see Lucian Bebchuk & Marcel Kahan, A Framework for Analyzing Legal Policy Towards Proxy Contests, 78 Cal. L. Rev. 1071, 1127 (1990).

1. WHO VOTES?

Delaware General Corporation Law (2002)

Sec. 151. *Classes and series of stock; redemption; rights.* (a) Every corporation may issue 1 or more classes of stock or 1 or more series of stock within any class thereof . . . , which classes or series may have such voting powers, full or limited, or no voting powers, and such designations, preferences and relative, participating, optional or other special rights, and qualifications, limitations or restrictions thereof, as shall be stated and expressed in the certificate of incorporation or of any amendment thereto, or in the resolution or resolutions providing for the issue of such stock adopted by the board of directors pursuant to authority expressly vested in it by its certificate of incorporation. . . . The power to increase or decrease or otherwise adjust the capital stock as provided in this chapter shall apply to all or any such classes of stock.

Delaware General Corporation Law (2007)

Sec. 221. *Voting, inspection, and other rights of bondholders and debenture holders.* Every corporation may in its certificate of incorporation confer upon the holders of any bonds, debentures or other obligations issued or to be issued by the corporation the power to vote in respect to the corporate affairs and management of the corporation to the extent and in the manner provided in the certificate of incorporation and may confer upon such holders of bonds, debentures or other obligations the same right of inspection of its books, accounts and other records, and also any other rights, which the stockholders of the corporation have or may have by reason of the provisions of this chapter or of its certificate of incorporation. If the certificate of incorporation so provides, such holders of bonds, debentures or other obligations shall be deemed to be stockholders, and their bonds, debentures or other obligations shall be deemed to be shares of stock, for the purpose of any provision of this chapter which requires the vote of stockholders as a prerequisite to any corporate action and the certificate of incorporation may divest the holders of capital stock, in whole or in part, of their right to vote on any corporate matter whatsoever. . . .

Should only shareholders vote? Few states, other than Delaware, authorize bondholders to vote. Conversely, virtually every state today permits one or more classes of stock to be non-voting (as long as the certificate of incorporation confers voting rights on at least one class of stock).[18] Commonly, preferred stock is issued without voting rights (although the corporate charter will often provide voting rights with respect to certain fundamental changes, such as a merger), and the major stock

18. But see C. A. Cavendes Sociedad Financiera v. Florida Nat'l Banks of Florida, Inc., 556 F. Supp. 254, 258 (M.D. Fla. 1982) ("The Florida Corporate Code provides that '[e]ach outstanding share, regardless of class, shall be entitled to one vote on each matter submitted to a vote at a meeting of shareholders.'"). Many more states have statutes expressly permitting non-voting or limited-voting stock. See, e.g., New York Bus. Corp. Law §613 (2007); Del. Gen. Corp. Law §151(a) (2007).

exchanges require that the preferred shareholders be entitled to vote as a class to elect one or more directors if a specified number of dividends are omitted.[19] Why is the practice so widespread that only common stock should vote? Why are preferred stockholders and long-term bondholders so regularly disenfranchised?

Economic theory supplies a plausible explanation for this pattern. Essentially, it asserts that it is more efficient to accord voting rights only to shareholders, as the residual risk bearers in the firm, and to require other participants to negotiate their rights and entitlements by contract:

Frank Easterbrook & Daniel Fischel, *Voting in Corporate Law*
26 J.L. & Econ. 395, 402-404 (1983)

The right to vote is the right to make all decisions not otherwise provided by contract — whether the contract is expressed or supplied by legal rule. . . . Because voting is expensive, the participants in the venture will arrange to conserve on its use. It could be employed from time to time to select managers and set the ground rules for their performance and not used again unless the managers' performance were seriously inadequate. Indeed, the collective choice problems that attend voting in corporations with large numbers of contracting parties suggest that voting would rarely have any function except in extremis. When many are entitled to vote, none of the voters expects his vote to decide the contest. Consequently, none of the voters has the appropriate incentive at the margin to study the firm's affairs and vote intelligently. . . .

Voting exists in corporations because someone must have the residual power to act (or delegate) when contracts are not complete. But, on the discussion so far, voting rights could be held by shareholders, bondholders, or other employees in any combination. . . . Yet, voting rights are universally held by shareholders, to the exclusion of bondholders, managers, and other employees. When a firm's founders take the firm public, they always find it advantageous to sell claims that include votes, and thus ultimately the right to remove the insiders. Why do insiders sell such claims? Why do investors pay extra for them? . . .

The reason, we believe, is that shareholders are the residual claimants to the firm's income. Bondholders have fixed claims, and employees generally negotiate compensation schedules in advance of performance. The gains and losses from abnormally good or bad performance are the lot of the shareholders, whose claims stand last in line.

As the residual claimants, the shareholders are the group with the appropriate incentives . . . to make discretionary decisions. The firm should invest in new products, plants, etc., until the gains and costs are identical at the margin. Yet, all of these actors, except the shareholders, lack the appropriate incentives. Those

19. The New York Stock Exchange's policy is that preferred stock, voting as a class, should have the right to elect a minimum of two directors if there is a default in the payment of six quarterly dividends. See New York Stock Exchange Listed Company Manual at §313.00(C). The right remains in effect until the defaulted dividends are paid. Regardless of the prevailing law or stock exchange rule, it is normally the case that the certificate of incorporation will give the preferred stock the right to vote on certain fundamental changes, such as a merger or sale of all assets. See Richard Buxbaum, Preferred Stock — Law and Draftsmanship, 42 Cal. L. Rev. 243 (1954). Debt holders may also secure a contractual veto power over such transactions. See Clifford Smith & Jerold Warner, On Financial Contracting: An Analysis of Bond Covenants, 7 J. Fin. Econ. 117 (1979).

with fixed claims on the income stream may receive only a tiny benefit (in increased security) from the undertaking of a new product. The shareholders receive most of the marginal gains and incur most of the marginal costs. They therefore have the right incentives to exercise discretion. . . .

This is not, of course, a complete explanation. The interests of shareholders may conflict with the interests of bondholders. Shareholders have an incentive to adopt various strategies with the effect of transferring wealth from bondholders to shareholders, such as choosing risky investment projects and withdrawing assets from the firm. Creditors seek to control this conduct, almost always by exquisitely detailed contracts. Creditors become residual claimants when equity holders' conduct exposes them to unanticipated risk. Thus we expect to observe, and do observe, creditors who possess rights to approve especially risky transactions, such as substantial construction projects, mergers and the like. Approval rights of this sort are routinely built into bond indentures and major bank loans. . . . Nonetheless, because shareholders usually bear the risk at the margin, they are more likely than bondholders to have the appropriate incentives and thus are the more appropriate holders of discretionary powers.

The right to vote (that is, the right to exercise discretion) follows the residual claim. Owners of common stock have the voting rights most of the time. But when the firm undertakes projects that alter its risk, exposing creditors to losses, they too have approval rights. Too, when the firm is in trouble and, for example, omits dividends to preferred shareholders, these stockholders commonly acquire the right to cast controlling votes. When the firm is insolvent, the bondholders and other creditors eventually acquire control, through provisions in bond indentures and other credit agreements or through the operation of bankruptcy laws.

2. WHAT VOTE IS REQUIRED?

For director elections (but not for votes on fundamental changes, such as a merger[20]), the long-dominant rule has been plurality voting. So long as a quorum is present at the shareholder's meeting, those directors are elected to the board who receive the highest vote totals — even if no one receives a majority of the votes cast at the meeting. This system of plurality voting is, however, only a default rule, and shareholders are free in most jurisdictions to substitute an alternative system, such as a majority vote rule, under which directors are elected only if they receive a majority of the votes cast. The significance of a majority vote rule is that it enhances the ability of shareholders to defeat an incumbent director (or team of directors), even in the absence of a rival slate of candidates willing to conduct a proxy solicitation. Under plurality voting, withholding a vote or voting against the director (or directors) may be a symbolic way to express dissatisfaction, but it has no legal impact.

But what happens under a majority vote rule if no candidate receives a majority of the votes cast? Under Del. Gen. Corp. Law §141(b), "each director shall hold office until such director's successor is elected and qualified or until such director's earlier resignation or removal." If no one else is elected, the incumbent continues in

---

20. Many states require that for transactions such as a merger, a liquidation, or a sale of substantially all the firm's assets, the proposed transaction must be approved by a majority of the outstanding shares. See Del. Gen. Corp. Law §251(c) (2007) (requiring such a vote for a merger).

office. Thus, to reach the desired outcome, many majority voting provisions contemplate that the director will be expected to resign if he or she fails to receive a
majority of the votes cast. Pfizer, Inc. pioneered such a procedure in 2005 under
which it adopted "Corporate Governance Principles" requiring a director to submit his or her resignation to the corporation's Corporate Governance Committee if
the director failed to receive a majority vote. But it is possible that a specific
director might refuse to resign, or that the board might not accept the proffered
resignation. If the director refused to resign, the other directors could not compel
the director's resignation. To address this problem, Delaware amended the
Delaware General Corporation Law in 2006 to add a provision to §141(b) that
states: "A resignation is effective when the resignation is delivered unless the
resignation specifies a later effective date or an effective date determined upon
the happening of an event or events. A resignation which is conditioned upon that
director failing to receive a specified vote for reelection as a director may provide
that it is irrevocable." Thus, in advance of an election, all directors may be asked to
deliver an irrevocable resignation conditioned upon the failure to receive a
majority of the votes cast.

Delaware also amended its laws in 2006 to provide that a bylaw adopted by the
shareholders that prescribes the required vote for the election of directors may not
be altered or repeated by the board. In other jurisdictions, it is possible that the
board could still seek to frustrate such a shareholder bylaw amendment by repeal-
ing or modifying it.

In any event, the vacancy caused by a majority voting provision could be filled
by the remaining board members. Conceivably, they could appoint the director
who failed to win a majority to this vacancy (unless the bylaw prohibited this). If
all the directors failed to receive a majority and were forced to resign, this would
create a crisis, but this possibility will probably be carved out by most bylaws,
which also typically do not apply majority voting to contested elections (because
the two sides might each get roughly 49 percent with only a few votes being
withheld). In reality, the defeat of several incumbent directors because votes
were withheld would likely motivate third parties to conduct a hostile proxy
solicitation or to seek to remove all the directors by majority vote and then convene
a special meeting to elect a new slate.

Majority voting seems to have become popular at precisely the point that the
SEC backed off its proposal (made in 2003 and withdrawn in 2004) to grant shareholders direct access to the proxy statement. See infra at page 658. In 2005 the
Council of Institutional Investors wrote to 1,500 corporations urging them to adopt
majority voting, and Institutional Shareholder Services, the proxy advisor, began
to recommend votes in favor of such proposals. As of late 2006, some 150 public
corporations had adopted corporate governance policies that endorse majority
voting and require the director to submit a resignation in the event the director
fails to achieve a majority vote. However, most of these companies, including
Pfizer, have a major qualification to their policies: the board or the Governance
Committee can decide not to accept the resignation if it deems the director's
continued service to be "critical" or "important" (or some other adjective) to the
corporation. Shareholder activists are not satisfied with such a policy and have
continued to use Rule 14a-8 to submit shareholder proposals to amend the bylaws
of the corporation to impose a more mandatory majority voting policy. In 2006
alone, more than 150 shareholder proposals seeking majority voting were filed.

More than 25 percent of the companies in the S&P 500 and at least 200 public corporations overall had adopted some form of majority voting policy by late 2006 (although often it was subject to a variety of qualifications).[21] Majority voting seems today well on the road to becoming the new norm for director elections.

3. WHEN SHOULD A SHAREHOLDER VOTE BE REQUIRED?

In addition to voting annually to elect the board (or some fraction of it if the board is "staggered"), shareholders must also vote to approve certain "fundamental" corporate changes, such as mergers, liquidations, sales of substantially all the corporation's assets, and amendments to the corporation's certificate of incorporation. State law may also authorize shareholders to vote to remove directors, and of course the board has discretion to submit some questions to a shareholder vote (possibly in order to reduce their own potential liability). Most states treat "issue" voting on fundamental changes quite differently from voting for the election or removal of directors in several important respects:

First, the shareholders are usually limited to ratifying or vetoing the board's decision to sell, merge, or liquidate the firm or to amend the corporation's charter; generally, shareholders have no power of initiative. Thus, shareholder voting constitutes an external check on management but not a means to direct shareholder democracy. Put simply, the board has control over the corporation's agenda.

Second, some statutes authorizing fundamental changes — e.g., mergers, sales of assets, and liquidations — require a supermajority vote. See Ill. Bus. Corp. Act. §11.20 (2007). Although the recent statutory trend has been to require only majority approval, corporate charters may set forth a higher supermajority requirement applicable to mergers and certain charter amendments; these charter provisions are usually designed to deter hostile bidders from making a takeover bid with a view to merging out those shareholders who do not tender in a follow-up merger. Most "fundamental change" statutes usually also provide that the requisite majority must be in terms of all outstanding shares (while most other corporate voting provisions require only a majority of a quorum and permit the corporate charter to set the quorum as low as one-third of all outstanding shares). This higher vote requirement reflects both the traditional view that "fundamental changes," such as a merger or liquidation, were not anticipated, or consented to, by the shareholders at the time they acquired their shares and the contemporary concerns of managers who fear undesired takeover proposals.

Third, corporate law frequently expands the scope of those entitled to vote in the case of fundamental changes. Many states require that non-voting shares (including preferred shares) be allowed to vote on a merger, at least if the effect of the merger is to change the rights, preferences, or privileges of their shares in a way that would entitle them to vote if attempted through an amendment of the certificate of incorporation. See, e.g., N.Y. Bus. Corp. Law §903 (2007); Cal. Gen. Corp. Law §§152, 1201 (2007). In these instances, a class vote — that is, an affirmative vote of a majority of the class — is typically required in addition to the overall majority vote. See Sec. E infra.

---

21. See Robert Profusek et al., United States: Majority Voting for Directors, Mondaq Business Briefing (Nov. 1, 2006).

From a historical perspective, supermajority provisions are the residue of an early rule that required unanimity for approval of a merger or similar transaction. See William Carney, Fundamental Corporate Changes, Minority Shareholders, and Business Purposes, 1980 Am. B. Found. Res. J. 69. The original premise was that shareholders contributed their funds to a single-purpose business venture and could not be forced to remain partners in the venture if the firm merged with another. That premise is today largely an anachronism in an era when large conglomerate firms regularly change the scope of their business activities simply by executive decision. Those who favor the majority approval rule argue that a higher requirement allows a minority to obtain a blocking position and in effect to veto, either arbitrarily or for some self-seeking reason, the majority's wishes. However, an economic justification may support supermajority voting requirements and related protections. Typically, managers are constrained to act in the best interests of their shareholders by the knowledge that otherwise they might be replaced or would at least suffer an injury to their "reputational capital." But in the context of mergers and acquisitions, managers of the acquired company cannot necessarily expect to remain with the firm post-merger and so may have less incentive to act faithfully in the shareholders' interest. In this "end game," there is greater reason for managers to act opportunistically — for example, by trading off a portion of the sales price that the acquiring firm would offer to their shareholders in return for long-term employment contracts for themselves or for other hidden benefits. Economists call this a "final period" problem, referring to the fact that the agent no longer has the same incentives to serve the principal faithfully. As a result, given the greater potential for hidden self-dealing, shareholder voting may be more important as an external check, and, in light of the earlier-noted problems of collective action, a supermajority requirement may sensibly compensate for some of the difficulties incident to organizing effective shareholder opposition.

a. A Shareholder Power of Initiative?

Should shareholders have the power not only to check management, but also to initiate action, by either effecting a sale or merger or amending the certificate without prior board action? Some commentators have argued that shareholders should have greater rights in this regard. See, e.g., Melvin Eisenberg, Access to the Corporate Proxy Machinery, 83 Harv. L. Rev. 1489 (1970). One argument for this position is that fundamental changes are not ordinary business decisions for the board, but shareholder decisions about the nature and form of their investment. Until 1984 New York permitted shareholders to amend the corporate charter directly without a prior board resolution, but in that year a requirement of prior board approval was added, possibly to increase the barriers to a hostile bidder who might otherwise have sought to amend the charter once it acquired 50 percent of the voting stock. See N.Y. Bus. Corp. Law §803 (2007). Do the earlier noted problems of collective action diminish in practice the theoretical significance of a shareholder power of initiative? Also, are there more practical alternatives to a shareholder power to merge the firm? For example, so long as a prospective acquiring firm can respond to the board's rebuff of its merger proposal by making a takeover bid directly to shareholders, this market mechanism may be a more than adequate substitute for shareholder voting as a safeguard against disloyal managerial resistance. Note, however, that the hostile takeover may not be an effective safeguard with respect to managerial disloyalty in the acceptance of sale or merger proposals.

b. Timing

What rights does the shareholder have to force the calling of the annual share-holders meeting? Suppose a board seeks to delay the vote until it can find additional shareholders who will keep it in power.

Hilton Hotels Corp. v. ITT Corp.
962 F. Supp. 1309 (D. Nev. 1997)

PRO, DISTRICT JUDGE: Before the Court for consideration is the Motion of Plaintiffs Hilton Hotels Corporation and HLT Corporation ("Hilton") for a Preliminary Injunction requiring Defendant ITT Corporation to conduct its annual meeting in May 1997. Hilton's Motion seeks mandatory preliminary relief. It is, therefore, subject to heightened scrutiny and the injunction requested should not issue unless the facts and the law clearly favor Hilton. Dahl v. HEM Pharmaceuticals, 7 F.3d 1399, 1403 (9th Cir. 1993), and Anderson v. U.S., 612 F.2d 1112, 1114 (9th Cir. 1979). For the reasons set forth below, the Court finds that Hilton has not satisfied this burden and that its Motion for Preliminary Injunction must, therefore, be denied.

First, neither Nevada law nor ITT's bylaws require that the 1997 annual meeting be conducted in May.

Pursuant to NRS 78.330, annual meetings are held by Nevada corporations to enable shareholders to elect directors and to conduct other business of the corporation. However, Hilton misapprehends the term "annual meeting" as used in the Nevada Revised Statutes and ITT's bylaws as requiring that such a meeting be conducted every twelve months. If that were the intent of the Nevada Legislature or ITT, they could have easily and clearly said so in the governing statutes and bylaws. Indeed, an annual meeting every twelve months is precisely what was provided for by the corporate bylaws at issue in the seminal case relied upon by Hilton for the proposition that an annual meeting is required every twelve months for Nevada corporations. Nevada ex rel. Curtis v. McCullough, 3 Nev. 202 (1867). *See also* ER Holdings v. Norton Co., 735 F. Supp. 1094, 1097 (D. Mass. 1990). Instead, Section 1.2 of ITT's bylaws conforms to NRS 78.330(1) and provides that ITT's annual meeting shall be held at such date, time and place as determined by the Board of Directors.

The Court finds persuasive the Affidavit of Professor John C. Coffee, Jr., that the term "annual meeting" at issue must be understood as an adjective which "distinguishes the *regular* meeting for the election of directors for other *special* meetings called by the board for the stockholders." See Coffee Affidavit, paragraph 32 appended to ITT's Memorandum in Opposition. The Court's conclusion is reinforced by the provisions of NRS 78.345(1) which provide: "If any corporation fails to elect directors within 18 months after the last election of directors required by

NRS 78.330, the district court has jurisdiction in equity, upon application of any one or more stockholders holding stock entitling them to exercise at least 15 percent of the voting power, to order the election of directors in the manner required by NRS 78.330."

Hilton has offered, and the Court can divine no reason why the Nevada Legislature would postpone for six months a shareholder's remedy for a corporation's failure to hold an annual meeting which the Legislature intended to be held within twelve months of the prior annual meeting. The Court concludes that, subject to the right of a board of directors to specify a shorter period, annual meetings for Nevada corporations are contemplated to occur no later than eighteen months after the last such meeting. *See* Ocilla Indus. v. Katz, 677 F. Supp. 1291, 1301 (E.D.N.Y. 1987).

Hilton alternatively argues that even if consistent with Nevada law and ITT's bylaws, failure to conduct an annual meeting in May 1997 would constitute a breach of the fiduciary duty owed by ITT's incumbent Board of Directors to its shareholders.

Courts have consistently prevented actions by an incumbent board of directors which were primarily designed to impair or impede the shareholder franchise. In a recent case recognizing the importance of the shareholder vote, but arising from a substantially different factual context than is presented here, Judge Edward C. Reed, Jr. reiterated that shareholders of a corporation generally have " 'only two protections against perceived inadequate business performance. They may sell their stock . . . , or they may vote to replace incumbent board members.' Thus, interference with shareholder voting is an especially serious matter, not to be left to the directors' business judgment, precisely because it undercuts a primary justification for allowing directors to rely on their judgment in almost every other context." Shoen v. AMERCO, 885 F. Supp. 1332, 1340 (D. Nev. 1994), *vacated by stip.* (D. Nev. 1995) (citation omitted).

This Court fully embraces the foregoing principles expressed in *Shoen.* However, given the saliently different facts presented in this case, Hilton's reliance on *Shoen* is misplaced. *Shoen,* among other things, involved a situation in which the incumbent board of directors of Amerco advanced an already noticed annual meeting date by two months for the primary purpose of re-electing the incumbent board before an arbitration decision was issued which might render the incumbent board unable to control dissident shareholder shares for voting purposes, and before Paul Shoen, a dissident shareholder, had the opportunity to campaign for a seat on the board and seek amendment to the bylaws. Relying principally on Blasius Indus. v. Atlas Corp., 564 A.2d 651 (Del. Ch. 1988), the *Shoen* Court found that the incumbent board demonstrated no compelling justification for its actions and had thus breached its fiduciary duty to Amerco's shareholders.

The circumstances presented here are far different from those in *Shoen* or *Blasius,* but are not unlike those confronted in Stahl v. Apple Bancorp Inc., 579 A.2d 1115 (Del. Ch. 1990). Here, as in *Stahl,* a majority shareholder claims the incumbent Board of Directors has delayed its annual meeting to frustrate a proxy contest and public tender offer. Moreover, in *Stahl,* the incumbent board had set and then rescinded the record date for the annual meeting, although no specific date for the annual meeting had been scheduled. *Stahl,* 579 A.2d at 1118. The *Stahl* court concluded that "the action of deferring this company's annual meeting where no meeting date has yet been set and no proxies even solicited does not impair or impede the effective exercise of the franchise to any extent." *Id.* at 1123. The Court's reasoning in *Stahl* is fully applicable to the instant case.

ITT has not yet set its annual meeting, nor is it required by Nevada law or its bylaws to conduct that meeting in May 1997. The failure to hold an annual meeting in May, which has not even been set and is not yet required to be set, cannot be viewed as an inequitable manipulation by the incumbent Board primarily designed to impede the exercise of the shareholder franchise. Further, in accord with NRS 78.138 and relevant case authority, ITT's Board of Directors retains reasonable discretion in setting an annual meeting to resist hostile takeover offers. *Shoen,* 885 F. Supp. at 1341, n.22, and *Stahl,* 579 A.2d at 1124. . . .

Lastly, the argument of the Shareholder Class that a delay of the annual meeting beyond May 1997 may cause Hilton to withdraw its tender offer is simply not determinative as to whether the mandatory relief requested should issue. Hilton, ITT and ITT's shareholders are, within the limits of the law, permitted to do as they deem advisable in the marketplace with respect to their investment and business decisions. . . .

---

1. *Limits on delay.* In the foregoing case, Hilton knew that Nevada law required a meeting within 18 months of its last annual meeting, but sought unsuccessfully to read ITT's bylaws, which referred to an "annual" meeting, as mandating that a shareholder meeting be held within 12 months of the last regular shareholder meeting. Instead, the court read "annual" in ITT's bylaws as referring to the type of meeting, but not to impose a mandatory duration stricter than Nevada law. Other states often give the board less discretion as to timing, but none seems to require that the regular shareholder meeting be held within 12 months of the last meeting. Del. Gen. Corp. Law §211, for example, specifies that if the annual meeting for election of directors has not been scheduled "for a period of 13 months after the . . . last annual meeting or the last action by written consent to elect directors in lieu of an annual meeting, the Court of Chancery may summarily order a meeting to be held upon the application of any stockholder or director." RMBCA §7.03 authorizes a court of the county in which the corporation's principal place of business or registered office is located to call an annual meeting if such a meeting "was not held within the earlier of 6 months after the end of the corporation's fiscal year or 15 months after its last annual meeting."

2. *Special meetings.* In addition to the mandatory annual shareholders meeting, some state statutes authorize a defined percentage of shareholders to call a special shareholder meeting. MBCA §7.02 authorizes 10 percent of the "votes entitled to be cast on an issue proposed to be considered at the proposed special meeting" to call such a meeting. Delaware, however, leaves the issue of special meetings to be resolved by the certificate of incorporation or the bylaws. See Del. Gen. Corp. Law §211(d) (2007).

c. Evasions of the Voting Requirement

Given corporate law's general insistence that "fundamental changes" be ratified by the shareholders, an important and still under-examined question is the extent to which the board of directors (particularly if dominated by the firm's incumbent managers) can evade these voting requirements by designing transactions that are functional equivalents to fundamental changes, but that do not by their terms require a shareholder vote. At bottom, the problem is the usual one of distinguishing form from substance, and, as usual, judicial responses have varied.

Hilton Hotels Corporation v. ITT Corp.
978 F. Supp. 1342 (D. Nev. 1997)

PRO, DISTRICT JUDGE: . . . [Following their earlier battle over the scheduling of the 1997 ITT annual shareholder meeting, the takeover war between Hilton and ITT continued, and ITT attempted a defensive strategy under which its core assets would be spun off (that is, placed in a subsidiary and distributed as a stock dividend to its shareholders) but with the special twist that the subsidiary so spun off would have a "staggered" or "classified" board under which only one-third of the directors would be up for election in the first year]. On January 27, 1997, Hilton announced a $55.00 per share tender offer for the stock of ITT, and announced plans for a proxy contest at ITT's 1997 annual meeting. This litigation commenced on the same date with the filing of Hilton's Complaint for Injunctive and Declaratory Relief seeking to enjoin ITT from impeding the shareholder franchise regarding the election of directors at ITT's annual meeting, and from taking other defensive measures in response to Hilton's announced tender offer and proxy contest.

On February 11, 1997, ITT formally rejected Hilton's tender offer. ITT proceeded to sell several of its non-core assets and opposed Hilton's takeover attempt before gaming regulatory bodies in Nevada, New Jersey and Mississippi.

When it became apparent that ITT would not conduct its annual meeting in May 1997, as it had customarily done in preceding years, Hilton filed a motion for a mandatory injunction to compel ITT to conduct the annual meeting in May. On April 21, 1997, this Court denied Hilton's Motion finding that Nevada law and ITT's by-laws did not require that ITT conduct its annual meeting within twelve months of the prior meeting, but rather that ITT had eighteen months within which to do so. Hilton Hotels Corp. and HLT v. ITT Corp., 962 F. Supp. 1309 (D. Nev. 1997), *aff'd,* 116 F.3d 1485 (9th Cir. 1997).

On July 15, 1997, ITT announced a Comprehensive Plan which, among other things, proposed to split ITT into three new entities, the largest of which would become ITT Destinations. ITT Destinations would be comprised of the current ITT's hotel and gaming business which account for approximately 93% of ITT's current assets. A second entity, ITT Educational Services, would consist of the current ITT's technical schools, and ITT's European Yellow Pages Division would remain with the current ITT as ITT World Directories.

Most significantly, under the Comprehensive Plan, the board of directors of the new ITT Destinations would be comprised of the members of ITT's current board with one important distinction. The new board would be a "classified" or "staggered" board divided into three classes with each class of directors serving for a term of three years, and with one class to be elected each year. Moreover, a shareholder vote of 80% would be required to remove directors without cause, and 80% shareholder vote would also be required to repeal the classified board provision or the 80% requirement to remove directors without cause. . . .

Finally, and critical to this Court's analysis, ITT seeks to implement the Comprehensive Plan prior to ITT's 1997 annual meeting and without obtaining shareholder approval. . . .

Shortly after ITT's announcement of its Comprehensive Plan, Hilton announced an amended tender offer of $70.00 per share which was rejected by ITT. On August 26, 1997, Hilton filed its Motion for Injunctive and Declaratory Relief (#29) seeking:

> 1. A preliminary and permanent injunction enjoining ITT from proceeding with its Comprehensive Plan. . . .

Where, as here, there is no Nevada statutory or case law on point for an issue of corporate law, this Court finds persuasive authority in Delaware case law, Shoen v. AMERCO, 885 F. Supp. 1332, 1341 n.20 (D. Nev. 1994). . . .

As this case involves both a tender offer and a proxy contest by Hilton, the proper legal standard is a *Unocal/Blasius* analysis as articulated in Stroud v. Grace, 606 A.2d 75, 92 n.3 (Del. 1992), and *Unitrin,* 651 A.2d at 1379.* . . .

In assessing a challenge to defensive actions by a target corporation's board of directors in a takeover context, this Court has held that the Court of Chancery should evaluate the board's overall response, including the justification for each contested defensive measure, and the results achieved thereby. Where all of the target board's defensive actions are *inextricably related*, the principles of *Unocal* require that such actions be scrutinized collectively as a unitary response to the perceived threat. *Unitrin,* 651 A.2d at 1386-87 (emphasis supplied).

Where an acquiror launches both a proxy fight and a tender offer, it "necessarily invoke[s] both *Unocal* and *Blasius*" because "both [tests] recognize the inherent conflicts of interest that arise when shareholders are not permitted free exercise of their franchise. . . . [I]n certain circumstances, [the judiciary] must recognize the special import of protecting the shareholders' franchise within *Unocal*'s requirement that any defensive measure be proportionate and 'reasonable in relation to the threat posed.'" *Unitrin,* 651 A.2d at 1379 (quoting *Stroud,* 606 A.2d at 92 n.3).

A board's unilateral decision to adopt a defensive measure touching "upon issues of control" that purposefully disenfranchises its shareholders is strongly suspect under *Unocal,* and cannot be sustained without a "compelling justification." *Stroud,* 606 A.2d at 92 n.3.

These cases have drawn a distinction between the exercise of two types of corporate power: 1) power over the assets of the corporation and 2) the power relationship between the board (management) and the shareholders. Actions involving the first type of power invoke the business judgment rule, or *Unocal* if an action is in response to a reasonably perceived threat to the corporation. Actions involving the second power invoke a *Blasius* analysis. The issues raised in this case require the Court to focus on the power relationship between ITT's board and ITT shareholders, not on the ITT board's actions relating to corporate assets.

Several amicus briefs have been filed on behalf of ITT shareholders, urging that they be allowed to vote on the Comprehensive Plan and the board of directors at the 1997 annual meeting. This Court has found no legal basis mandating a shareholder vote on the adoption of ITT's Comprehensive Plan in its entirety. However,

---

*These cases are discussed later in this chapter. — ED.

as the Court finds that the Comprehensive Plan would violate the power relationship between ITT's board and ITT's shareholders by impermissibly infringing on the shareholders' right to vote on members of the board of directors, it must be enjoined. . . .

Delaware precedent establishes that a board has power over the management and assets of a corporation, but that power is not unbridled. That power is limited by the right of shareholders to vote for the members of the board. As articulated in *Shoen*, this right underlies the concept of corporate democracy. This Court fully endorses the reasoning in *Shoen* and *Blasius* regarding the importance of the shareholder franchise to the entire scheme of corporate governance. This Court will, therefore, examine ITT's Comprehensive Plan under the *Unocal/Blasius* analysis.

Unocal requires the Court to consider the following two questions: 1) Does ITT have reasonable grounds for believing a danger to corporate policy and effectiveness exists? 2) Is the response reasonable in relation to the threat? If it is a defensive measure touching on issues of control, the court must examine whether the board purposefully disenfranchised its shareholders, an action that cannot be sustained without a compelling justification. *Stroud*, 606 A.2d at 92 n.3.

1. The Classified Board for ITT Destinations

The first defensive action this Court will analyze under the *Unocal* standard is the provision in the Comprehensive Plan for a classified board for ITT Destinations.

a. Reasonable Grounds for Believing a Threat to Corporate Policy and Effectiveness Exists

Nine of ITT's eleven directors are outside directors. Under *Unocal*, such a majority materially enhances evidence that a hostile offer presents a threat warranting a defensive response. *Unitrin*, 651 A.2d at 1375.

ITT argues strenuously that the Comprehensive Plan is better than Hilton's offer. This is not for the Court to decide, and it is not determinative under its analysis. Under *Unocal*, a court must first determine if there is a threat to corporate policy and effectiveness. ITT has failed to demonstrate such a threat.

ITT has made no showing that Hilton will pursue a different corporate policy than ITT seeks to implement through its Comprehensive Plan. In fact, over the past few months, ITT has to a large extent adopted Hilton's proposed strategy of how it says it will govern ITT if its slate of directors is elected. There has also been no showing of Hilton's inability or ineffectiveness to run ITT if it does succeed in its takeover attempt. ITT cites to the fact that some Sheraton franchise owners will be unhappy if Hilton enters into certain management contracts, but this is not fundamental or pervasive enough to constitute a "threat" to ITT's corporate policy or effectiveness.

The ITT board has also failed to meet its burden of showing "good faith and reasonable investigation" of a threat to corporate policy or effectiveness which would meet the burden placed on the board under the first prong of the *Unocal* test. Since Hilton's tender offer was announced, the ITT board has not met with Hilton to discuss the offer. Moreover, the overwhelming majority of ITT's evidence of good faith relates to its approval of the Comprehensive Plan, not to the inadequacy of Hilton's offer.

The sole "threat" ITT points to is that Hilton's offer of $70 a share is inadequate, primarily because this price does not contain a control premium. However, at the August 14, 1997 ITT board meeting, Goldman Sachs told the ITT board that the market valued ITT's plan at $62 to $64 a share. This contradicts ITT's argument that there is no control premium over market price contained in Hilton's offer. That ITT itself was offering to buy back roughly 26% of its stock at $70 a share does not nullify this fact.

The only attempt ITT has made to satisfy the first prong of the *Unocal* analysis is to argue that Hilton's price is inadequate. However, while inadequacy of an offer is a legally cognizable threat, Paramount Communications, Inc. v. Time, Inc., 571 A.2d 1140, 1153 (Del. 1989), ITT has shown no real harm to corporate policy *or effectiveness*. The facts in *Unocal* illustrate this point well. *Unocal* involved a tender offer with a back-end offer of junk bonds. 493 A.2d at 949-950. Junk bond financing could reasonably harm the future policy and effectiveness of a company. As ITT itself is offering only $70 a share, and the Comprehensive Plan involves greatly increasing the leveraging of ITT, its claim that Hilton's offer of $70 a share is a threat to policy or effectiveness is unpersuasive. In light of these facts, the alleged inadequacy of Hilton's offer is not a severe threat to ITT. Under the proportionality requirement, the nature of Hilton's threat will set the parameters for the range of permissible defensive tactics under the second prong of the *Unocal* test. *Unitrin,* 651 A.2d at 1384.

b. ITT's Response Was Preclusive

Assuming Hilton's offer constitutes a cognizable threat under *Unocal*, ITT's response cannot be preclusive or coercive, and it must be within the range of reasonableness. As articulated in *Unitrin*, a board cannot "cramm down" on shareholders a management sponsored alternative. *Unitrin,* 651 A.2d at 1387. The installation of a classified board for ITT Destinations, a company which will encompass 93% of the current ITT's assets and 87% of its revenues, is clearly preclusive and coercive under *Unitrin*. The classified board provision for ITT Destinations will preclude current ITT shareholders from exercising a right they currently possess — to determine the membership of the board of ITT. At the very minimum, ITT shareholders will have no choice but to accept the Comprehensive Plan and a majority of ITT's incumbent board members for another year. Therefore, the Comprehensive Plan is preclusive.

c. The Primary Purpose of the Comprehensive Plan Is to Interfere with Shareholder Franchise

ITT's response to Hilton's tender offer touches upon issues of control, and this Court must determine whether the response purposefully disenfranchises ITT's shareholders. If so, under the analysis of *Stroud* and *Unitrin*, it is not a reasonable response unless a "compelling justification" exists. It is important to note that in *Blasius*, the board did something that normally would be entirely permissible under Delaware law and its own by-laws: it expanded the board from seven to nine individuals. It did this in the face of a hostile takeover by a company financed through "junk bonds" and two individuals who sought to substantially "cash out" many of the target corporation's assets. *Blasius,* 564 A.2d at 653-54. Still, while the board in *Blasius* had a good faith reason to act as it did, and it acted with appropriate care, the board could not lawfully prevent the shareholders from electing a majority of new directors.

Blasius' factual scenario is strikingly similar to the circumstances surrounding ITT's actions. Normally, a corporation is free to adopt a classified board structure. In fact many companies, including Hilton, have classified boards. As long as the classified board is adopted in the proper manner, whether through charter amendment, changes in the by-laws of a company or through shareholder vote, it is permissible. However, *Blasius* illustrates that even if an action is normally permissible, and the board adopts it in good faith and with proper care, a board cannot undertake such action if the primary purpose is to disenfranchise the shareholders in light of a proxy contest. *Blasius,* 564 A.2d at 652. Thus, while ITT could normally adopt a classified board or issue a dividend of shares creating ITT Destinations, it cannot undertake these actions if the primary purpose is to disenfranchise ITT shareholders in light of Hilton's tender offer and proxy contest.

As a board would likely never concede that its primary purpose was to entrench itself, this Court must look to circumstantial evidence to determine the primary purpose of ITT's action touching upon issues of control. While none of the following factors are dispositive, collectively they eliminate all questions of material fact, and demonstrate that the primary purpose of ITT's Comprehensive Plan was to disenfranchise its shareholders.

i. Timing

The intent evidenced by the timing of the Comprehensive Plan is transparent. Although ITT claims that a spin-off or sale was contemplated before Hilton's tender offer, it makes no mention of when the board determined to move from an annually elected board to a classified board. Moreover, all aspects of ITT's Comprehensive Plan were formulated against the backdrop of Hilton's tender offer and proxy contest, and the Plan was not announced until well after Hilton's initial tender offer. Finally, this major restructuring of ITT was announced and to be implemented in a little over two months, and designed to take effect less than two months before the annual meeting was to be held at which shareholders would have the opportunity to vote on an annually elected rather than a classified board.

ii. Entrenchment

The ITT directors who are approving the Comprehensive Plan are the same directors who will fill the classified board positions of ITT Destinations. ITT and its advisors recognized from the outset that they were vulnerable because they did not have a staggered board of directors. The members of ITT's board are appointing themselves to new, more insulated positions, and at least seven of the eleven directors are avoiding the shareholder vote that would otherwise occur at ITT's 1997 annual meeting. While companies may convert from annual to classified boards, as *Blasius* illustrates, the rub is in the details. It is the manner of adopting the Comprehensive Plan with its provision for a new certified board comprised of incumbent ITT directors which supports the conclusion that ITT's Plan is primarily designed to entrench the incumbent board.

iii. ITT's Stated Purpose

ITT has offered no credible justification for not seeking shareholder approval of the Comprehensive Plan. ITT simply claims that it wants to "avoid market risks and other business problems" (pp. 10-11 of ITT's Opposition). Such vague generalizations do not approach the required showing of a reasonable justification other than entrenchment for the board's action. Simply stating that its "advisors" suggested a rapid implementation of the Comprehensive Plan, without pointing to a specific risk or problem, is insufficient to meet ITT's burden.

iv. Benefits of Comprehensive Plan

ITT argues that there are economic benefits to the Comprehensive Plan, and general benefits of the classified board provision for ITT Destinations. That may be true, but the additional benefits of a plan infringing on shareholder voting rights do not remedy the fundamental flaw of board entrenchment.

v. Effect of Classified Board

The classified board provision for ITT Destinations under ITT's Comprehensive Plan ensures that ITT shareholders will be absolutely precluded from electing a majority of the directors nominated under Hilton's proxy contest at the 1997 annual meeting. Such a Plan, coupled with ITT's vehement opposition to Hilton's tender offer, is inconsistent with ITT's earlier argument that a delay of the 1997 annual meeting from May to November would afford shareholders additional time to inform themselves and more fully consider the implications of their vote for directors at the 1997 annual meeting.

ITT's position is particularly anomalous given the fact that when ITT previously split the company in 1995, it sought shareholder approval. While shareholder approval may not be absolutely required to split ITT now any more than it was in 1995, the fact that the ITT board decided to subject the 1995 split of the company to a shareholder vote is strong evidence that the primary purpose of its attempts to implement the Comprehensive Plan prior to the 1997 annual meeting is to entrench the incumbent ITT board. . . .

IV. Conclusion

Earlier in this litigation, the Court fully embraced pertinent language in *Shoen* and *Blasius* regarding the importance of the shareholder franchise. Hilton, 962 F. Supp. at 1310. Those principles encompass fundamental concepts of corporate governance and bear repetition.

Shareholders do not exercise day-to-day business judgments regarding the operation of a corporation — those are matters left to the reasonable discretion of directors, officers and the corporation's management team. Corporate boards have great latitude in exercising their business judgments, as they should. As a result, shareholders generally have only two protections against perceived inadequate business performance. They may sell their stock or vote to replace incumbent board members. For this reason, interference with the shareholder franchise is especially serious. It is not to be left to the board's business judgment, precisely because it undercuts a primary justification for allowing directors to rely on their business judgment in almost every other context. Indeed, as the court in *Shoen* noted, "one of the justifications for the business judgment rule's insulation of directors from liability for almost all of their decisions is that unhappy shareholders can always vote the directors out of office." *Shoen*, 885 F. Supp. at 1340. . . .

ITT strongly argues that its Comprehensive Plan is superior to Hilton's alternative tender offer. This argument should be directed to ITT's shareholders, not this Court.

ITT also claims that it has properly considered other constituencies in responding to Hilton's offer, as it is expressly allowed to do under N.R.S. §78.138. ITT is correct. Other constituencies may be considered under that provision, but nothing in that statute suggests that the interests of third parties are as important as the right of shareholder franchise. While the two interests are not exclusive, neither are they equal. The right of shareholders to vote on directors at an annual meeting is a fundamental principle of corporate law, and it is not outweighed by the interests listed in N.R.S. §78.138.

Likewise, the good faith of the ITT board in implementing the Comprehensive Plan does not change this Court's analysis. *Shoen*, relying on *Blasius*, recognized a good faith breach of duty under Nevada law. Simply put, there is no compelling justification for infringement of the shareholder franchise as proposed by the implementation of ITT's Comprehensive Plan before the 1997 annual meeting.

The ultimate outcome of the election of directors at ITT's 1997 annual meeting is not a relevant inquiry for this Court. That is something for the shareholders who own ITT to decide when they select the board who will lead the corporation. If a majority of the incumbent ITT board is re-elected after a fully-informed and fair shareholder vote, that board will be free to implement any business plan it chooses so long as that plan is consistent with ITT's charter and by-laws, and governing law.

This Court concludes that the structure and timing of ITT's Comprehensive Plan with its classified board provision for ITT Destinations, is preclusive and leaves no doubt that the primary purpose for ITT's proposed implementation of the Comprehensive Plan before the 1997 annual meeting is to impermissibly impede the exercise of the shareholder franchise by depriving shareholders of the opportunity to vote to re-elect or to oust all or as many of the incumbent ITT directors as they may choose at the upcoming annual meeting. It has as its primary purpose the entrenchment of the incumbent ITT board. As a result, the Court concludes that Hilton has prevailed on the merits of its claim for permanent injunctive relief. . . .

---

1. *Standard of review.* Although ITT was a Nevada corporation, the federal district court closely followed Blasius Indus. Inc. v. Atlas Corp., 564 A.2d 651 (Del. Ch. 1988), which required a "compelling justification" for any purposeful attempt to deny shareholders their right to vote. In *Blasius*, an insurgent who owned 9 percent of Atlas Corporation sought to expand by a shareholder consent solicitation the 7-member Atlas board to 15 members (the maximum permitted under Atlas's certificate of incorporation) in order to elect 8 new directors to these newly created vacancies and thereby control a majority. The Atlas board responded by increasing its own size to 9, with the result that any further expansion would permit the insurgent to elect only 6 directors (or a minority). Although the Chancery Court found that the Atlas directors had acted in good faith and for a purpose they believed to be in the corporation's best interests, it still found that their "primary motivation" was to frustrate the consent solicitation. Hence, the court said that the business judgment rule could not apply and a "compelling justification" had to be

shown. The *Blasius* outcome and its "compelling justification standard" for board actions that interfere with shareholder voting rights was later endorsed by the Delaware Supreme Court in MM Companies, Inc. v. Liquid Audio, Inc., 813 A.2d 1118 (2003), at page 619 infra.

2. *Other evasions.* In Unilever Acquisition Corp. v. Richardson-Vicks, Inc., 618 F. Supp. 407 (S.D.N.Y. 1985), the board of a target corporation (Richardson-Vicks) voted to create a new class of preferred stock in response to an unsolicited tender offer. Each share of the new preferred stock would carry 25 votes per share, unless it were transferred to a new holder (in which case its voting rights would fall to 5 votes per share). The practical impact was to preclude the hostile bidder from buying control so long as a significant minority fraction of the shareholders did not sell to it. The district court ruled that so fundamental a change in voting rights could not be effected without a shareholder vote, in part because it discriminated against incoming shareholders.

The defensive maneuver attempted by Richardson-Vicks involved the manipulation of what is known as "blank check" preferred. Traditionally, the rights of preferred shareholders were spelled out in detail in the certificate of incorporation: dividend rates, redemption and conversion privileges, default provisions, etc. However, because preferred stock is normally a senior security that competes with debt securities, this approach was cumbersome, in particular because it was impossible to predict in advance the prevailing interest rate on debt securities in order to set a competitive dividend rate on the preferred. As a result, a number of states gave corporations greater flexibility in financing by authorizing a provision in the certificate that created a class of preferred stock whose actual terms would in effect be filled in by the board later at the time of issuance (hence the term "blank check"). See Del. Gen. Corp. Law §151(g) (2007). Subsequently, in the course of takeover battles, target corporation managements learned to exploit this discretion conferred on their boards by issuing stock carrying super-voting rights. The general issue of weighted voting is considered next, in Sec. B.4 infra, but the relevant point here is that the *Richardson-Vicks* court found the particular issuance before it to amount to a sufficiently "fundamental" change as to be equivalent to a charter amendment and thus to require a shareholder vote.

3. *The "de facto merger" doctrine.* The issue of what fundamental changes must be approved by shareholders has also arisen in the context of transactions designed to avoid the voting and appraisal rights to which shareholders are entitled under most state statutes on a merger or a sale of substantially all of a corporation's assets. For example, if a small corporation were to sell all its assets to a larger one in return for the latter's stock, the transaction would require a shareholder vote (and in some jurisdictions a supermajority vote) and in most jurisdictions would also trigger an appraisal right (see Chapter IX). Suppose, however, that instead of selling its assets to the larger company, the smaller company issued stock in an amount equal to, say, three times its outstanding shares in return for the larger company's assets. In form, the smaller corporation has purchased the larger, but in reality the minnow cannot swallow the whale, and the real consequence is to shift voting control of the smaller, "acquiring" company to the stockholders of the larger, "acquired" company. This format might be used if those engineering the transaction doubted that they could secure a requisite two-thirds vote or if they did not want to confer an appraisal remedy on the shareholders of the smaller company. Some courts have enjoined these transactions on the ground that in

substance they amount to a merger and are thus an evasion of the shareholders' statutory rights — i.e., a de facto merger; other courts have accepted them. Compare Farris v. Glen Alden Corp., 393 Pa. 427 (Sup. Ct. 1958), with Hariton v. Arco Electronics, Inc., 41 Del. Ch. 74, 188 A.2d 123 (Del. Sup. Ct. 1963). In *Hariton*, Delaware rejected the "de facto merger" doctrine and followed instead what it calls the doctrine of "independent legal significance," which means that a corporation may elect to follow one provision of its corporation code to bring about a result that is expressly precluded by another section of the same code. In *Hariton*, plaintiffs had claimed that a sale of assets by one company to another effectively amounted to a merger and thus should give rise to appraisal rights that, under Delaware law, were applicable to mergers, but not to sales of assets.

Other states have amended their statutes to prevent disparities in treatment. In recognizing that functionally equivalent acquisition transactions had been treated differently and that these disparities could be systematically exploited by those structuring an acquisition, California now confers the same basic voting and appraisal rights on shareholders in all "reorganizations," a term it broadly defines to include all the standard acquisition techniques. See Cal. Gen. Corp. Law §§181, 1200 (2007). This approach was designed "to create a statutory structure under which both the form of the transaction and the entity chosen to be the acquiring or surviving corporation are determined by considerations other than avoidance of stockholders' voting and appraisal rights." See Note, Corporate Combinations under the New California General Corporation Law, 23 UCLA L. Rev. 1190, 1191 (1976).

4. *Stock issuances as a fundamental change.* The New York Stock Exchange requires that shareholders of a listed company approve issuances of 20 percent or more of its common stock or securities convertible into or exercisable for common stock. See NYSE Listed Company Manual §312.03(c) (2007). This requirement of a shareholder vote before a substantial equity issuance, which is applicable only to NYSE-listed companies, in effect defines an additional fundamental change.

5. *Treasury shares.* A corporation may not vote shares in itself (including reacquired shares held in its treasury), nor may a subsidiary vote stock in its parent. See, e.g., Del. Gen. Corp. Law §160(c) (2007); N.Y. Bus. Corp. Law §612(b) (2007). The reason for this rule is self-evident: management could entrench itself and negate any threat of shareholder ouster if it could vote stock held by the corporation. Ambiguities arise, however, with respect to the definition of the term *subsidiary*. What if two corporations each hold 50 percent of a joint venture, which in turn owns substantial blocks of each parent? Both the New York and Delaware statutes define "subsidiary" in terms of whether a majority of its shares are held by the parent. Would it be wiser to use a control test?

4. WHAT VOTING POWER SHOULD A SHARE CARRY? RULE 19c-4 AND THE "ONE SHARE, ONE VOTE" CONTROVERSY

a. The New York Stock Exchange's Policy

Corporate law does not require that each share carry a single vote, but generally permits shares to be either non-voting or to have multiple votes per share. During the nineteenth century, shareholders were sometimes entitled to only one vote, regardless of the number of shares they owned. See David Ratner, The Government of Business Corporations: Critical Reflections on the Rule of "One Share, One Vote," 56 Cornell L. Rev. 1, 8 (1970). At least in the case of the closely held corporation, such devices can be justified as a useful means by which to share or allocate control among investors who make different contributions to the firm (e.g., capital or expertise). Nonetheless, in the case of the publicly held corporation, non-voting common has been very rare. Since the late 1920s, the New York Stock Exchange (NYSE) had enforced a "one share, one vote" rule, under which the NYSE would refuse to list the common stock of any corporation that had outstanding a class of common stock carrying either more or less than one vote per share. See NYSE Listed Company Manual §313.00. As a practical matter, the NYSE's rule long meant that equal voting rights on a per-share basis were mandatory for the top tier of publicly held companies. Then, in 1986, the NYSE sought the approval of the SEC to abandon its "one share, one vote" rule (SEC approval is required under §19(c) of the '34 Act before a national securities exchange may amend its rules). The NYSE's action appears to have been the reluctant product of two linked circumstances: First, corporate managements had discovered that issuing limited voting or supervoting stock could be an effective takeover defense. Second, the NYSE for the first time in its history had become subject to competitive pressure, chiefly from the automated interdealer quotation service (known as Nasdaq), which the National Association of Securities Dealers operates. Both Nasdaq and the American Stock Exchange had found that they could compete with the NYSE by offering less restrictive listing eligibility criteria, particularly with regard to takeover defensive measures. Since the 1970s, the American Stock Exchange had permitted the listing of common shares with disparate voting rights as long as the differential between the two classes did not exceed 10:1 and certain other criteria were satisfied. See Amex Company Guide §122.

The triggering event that precipitated the NYSE's decision to seek to abandon its "one share, one vote" rule was the decision of General Motors Corporation in 1984 to issue a second class of common stock with only one-half vote per share to finance its acquisition of Electronic Data Systems Corporation. Apprehensive about the potential delisting of General Motors and the signal this might represent to the financial community of the diminished value of a NYSE listing, the NYSE declared a moratorium on enforcement of its "one share, one vote" rule and appointed a committee to review the entire area of "qualitative listing standards." Within approximately two years, some 46 NYSE-listed companies followed in GM's wake and issued disparate voting stock or restricted the voting rights of large shareholders, and an even larger number of Nasdaq and Amex-listed companies have taken similar actions.[22]

Procedurally, several distinct techniques are possible by which to confer on management or its allies disproportionate voting rights that exceed their equity stake in the corporation. First, the crudest technique would be simply to amend the certificate of incorporation to create a new class of stock with multiple votes per share; insiders would then be permitted to exchange some or all of their common stock for this supervoting class, while public investors would retain stock with

---

22. See Sec. Exch. Act Rel. No. 34-24623 (1987). Some 60 Amex-listed companies and at least 110 companies traded on Nasdaq (as of 1985) also had multiple classes of common stock with unequal voting rights. See Joel Seligman, Equal Protection in Shareholder Voting Rights: The One Share, One Vote Controversy, 54 Geo. Wash. L. Rev. 687, at n.81 (1986).

only a single vote per share. This same result could also be achieved without a shareholder vote if a class of "blank check" preferred stock were already authorized. Yet either such approach is likely to attract litigation on the theory that it amounts to unfair self-dealing. A second, subtler alternative is to grant multiple votes to all shares, but provide that on most transfers a share will lose its multiple votes, at least until the transferee holds the shares for a requisite holding period. This approach (known generally as a "tenure voting plan" because it conditions full voting rights on a holding requirement) effectively denies any shareholder or hostile bidder the ability to gain significant voting power. A third route is to adopt a charter provision that limits the number of shares any prospective shareholder may vote; for example, such a "capped voting rights plan" might say that no person who becomes a shareholder after its adoption could vote more than 1,000 shares (although such a person might own 2 million shares).[23] The practical problem with these techniques is that shareholder approval to amend the certificate may be difficult to obtain. As a result, a most popular recent technique has been to issue a class of preferred stock with supervoting rights to *all* shareholders, but make this stock both nontransferable itself and yet convertible into common stock. Because this supervoting stock will carry only a very low dividend, most ordinary shareholders will over time convert it into the underlying class when they wish to sell, or they will convert to obtain the higher dividend on the common stock. Only management and its allies will retain this low-dividend class in large quantities and so obtain disproportionate voting rights. Although all these techniques effectively preclude any acquisition of control through share acquisitions, the first technique dramatically shifts control to insiders, while the last three can be justified to shareholders as attempts to deter "short-term speculators" and arbitrageurs from acquiring control.

Why would shareholders approve a charter amendment adopting such a dual-class capitalization when it substantially reduces their chance of receiving a highly lucrative tender offer? Commentators have basically emphasized the collective action problems that compromise shareholder voting and sometimes give management coercive power. See Jeffrey Gordon, Ties That Bond: Dual Class Common Stock and the Problem of Shareholder Choice, 76 Cal. L. Rev. 1 (1988); Ronald Gilson, Evaluating Dual Class Common Stock: The Relevance of Substitutes, 73 Va. L. Rev. 807 (1987). When management or an existing insider group already controls a substantial percentage of the corporation's stock (say 25 percent), shareholders may not value their voting rights highly, and management needs only the votes of 25 percent out of the remaining 75 percent to secure adoption. A fuller answer also involves the fact that such proposals are frequently accompanied by a "sweetener" to secure shareholder approval — namely, an extraordinary dividend or recapitalization proposal that will pay to shareholders excess funds that would otherwise have been retained within the corporation. Arguably, these and other techniques are coercive, either because shareholders are threatened with being

---

23. Such a limitation, which does not establish dual classes, but rather restricts the shareholder's ability to vote the shares, was upheld in Providence & Worcester Co. v. Baker, 378 A.2d 121 (Del. 1977), where the provision was included in the corporation's original certificate of incorporation. Thus, no shareholder could claim that its voting rights were reduced. Plaintiff in that case contended that Delaware law required that all shares within the same class have the same voting rights. Defendant responded that the challenged charter provisions constituted restrictions on the shareholder, not on the shares, which position the Delaware Supreme Court accepted.

made worse off or are "bribed" with corporate funds, which will be denied them unless they convert their shares into the lower voting class.

In response to the NYSE's proposal (which did require that shareholders approve any disparate voting plan), the SEC held hearings in December 1986, at which it requested commentators to advise it on whether it should (1) require the NYSE to retain its "one share, one vote" rule; (2) require additional procedural safeguards before corporations could deviate from it, such as a supermajority or periodic reaffirmation rule; or (3) adopt a uniform "one share, one vote" standard applicable to all exchanges and Nasdaq. In the SEC release quoted below, the Commission summarized the debate that exists within the academic, financial, and business communities over the adequacy of shareholder voting as a procedural protection:

Voting Rights Listing Standards — Proposed Disenfranchisement Rule
Sec. Exch. Act Rel. No. 34-24623, Fed. Sec. L. Rep. (CCH) ¶ 84,143 (June 22, 1987)

III. Summary of Comments and Testimony on the Issue of Dual Classes of Stock . . .

B. *Disapprove the NYSE Proposal. . . .* Of the 112 commentators opposed to the NYSE's proposal, 39 stated that the NYSE proposal should be disapproved and a uniform one share, one vote requirement should be established for all markets. . . . In particular, the academicians, institutional investors, shareholders groups, state securities regulators, and individual shareholders, with few exceptions, strongly supported the development of a uniform rule. The NYSE and the Amex both supported a uniform rule.

The commentators and speakers offered several reasons why they believe disparate voting rights plans should be prohibited. First they believed that the shareholder vote is an essential element of corporate accountability. Under this view, disparate voting rights plans could allow a small group of insiders to obtain or maintain effective control of a corporation. Disparate voting rights plans can isolate management from the possibility of direct shareholder action (i.e., proxy contests) and also frustrate the workings of other techniques in the market for corporate control (i.e., tender offers) by insulating management from a hostile acquisition. . . .

A second major reason offered in support of a uniform one share, one vote rule was the commentators' belief that a shareholder vote to ratify a disparate voting rights plan does not necessarily provide an effective safeguard against management abuse nor a legitimate means to protect shareholders' rights. In his testimony, for example, Professor Gordon explained what he called "collective action" problems, which encompass the inherent difficulty of small shareholders acting individually to influence the direction of a vote. In particular, he argued that frequently dual class stock is made available to shareholders in a fashion (e.g., with so-called "dividend sweeteners") which makes it advantageous (or less risky) for a shareholder to accept non-voting or lower voting stock rather than object to the recapitalization. In addition, commentators noted that many corporate pension plan managers may be placed under substantial pressure by their client corporations not to vote against proposed corporate recapitalization. Similarly, Professor

Ruback emphasized the potentially coercive nature of a corporate recapitalization using dual classes of stock. He explained that, although individual shareholders who approve disparate voting rights plans may know with certainty that they will lose voting power, they also may conclude that by so acting they avoid potentially greater losses. . . . At worst, a situation may arise, under the NYSE proposal, where the management decides that a dual class recapitalization is appropriate, a simple majority of outstanding shares approves a disparate voting rights plan, as required by state law, but not the disinterested majority required by the NYSE proposal. Accordingly, the disparate voting rights plan is approved under state law but the company is delisted from the NYSE. In particular, exchange offer recapitalizations have been argued to be "inherently coercive" and present outside shareholders with a Hobson's choice of exchanging high vote stock with low dividends for low vote stock with high dividends, especially if the high vote stock cannot be freely transferred. To avoid the risk that enough outside shareholders will make the exchange so that retained high vote stock will be "ineffective," shareholders who oppose the voting rights plan nevertheless may feel compelled to exchange their shares for low vote stock.

Some commentators also pointed out the disenfranchising effect of dual class recapitalizations involving the issuance of new super voting stock with restrictions on transferability. In this situation, shareholders are provided with a dividend of super voting stock that is convertible into regular common but has restrictions on transferability. Management and major shareholders, who do not intend to sell their stock, will retain the super voting stock, but most shareholders eventually will convert their super voting stock into regular common stock as they prepare to sell their shares. Thus, the insiders' percentage of super voting stock over time will increase disproportionately to their equity stake in the company.

Many academic commentators also disputed the significance of the studies that concluded that disparate voting rights plans do not reduce significantly shareholder wealth, and therefore should be permitted. Such commentators note that the disparate voting rights plans considered in those studies for the most part merely perpetuate an existing control relationship. Accordingly, these plans may not be truly predictive of share price effects when voting rights are reduced in companies where management did not enjoy a control position in the companies' shares. . . .

Other academic commentators argue that the studies do not reflect the diminution of shareholder wealth that occurs when shareholders lose the control premium aspect of their stock. In his comment, Professor Gilson contrasts two forms of transfer of control, the leveraged buy-out ("LBO") and the dual class recapitalization. He notes that in the LBO situation, often characterized by companies with a small insider group, shareholders usually receive a large cash premium for their shares. In contrast, shareholders in dual class recapitalizations usually receive only a small dividend sweetener at best rather than the potential control premium value of their stock. Professor Gilson argues that this causes the company's control group to impose a wealth transfer from public shareholders of their voting rights without having to pay a marketplace determined control premium. For this reason, Professor Gilson suggests that studies concluding that shareholder wealth is not diminished by a recapitalization are not necessarily relevant, because recapitalizations nonetheless permit transactions that benefit only the dominant insider group, with no payment or only a small payment to the rest of the shareholders. Thus, studies that conclude that disparate voting rights plans are benign may reach an unwarranted conclusion because they fail to compare the stock price effect of such plans with their closest effective substitute, i.e., a leveraged buyout or repurchase that could afford a substantial premium. Professor Gilson concludes that dual class transactions should be prohibited, but not the public offering by an existing company of a new class of limited voting or non-voting stock, because this allows new capital to be raised without diluting the control of the current shareholders. "[S]uch a public sale neither reduces the voting rights of existing public shareholders, nor strengthens the position of the dominant group" and thus is not coercive.

b. SEC Response and Judicial Reaction

Following these hearings, the SEC released a proposed rule in June 1987, which it adopted in modified form in July 1988. As adopted, Rule 19c-4 barred both stock exchanges and Nasdaq from listing or, in the case of Nasdaq, from authorizing for quotation the common stock or other equity securities of a domestic company that "issues any class of security, or takes other corporate action, with the effect of nullifying, restricting or disparately reducing the per share voting rights of an outstanding class or classes of common stock." However, the rule did not prohibit the issuance of low-voting securities in an initial public offering. Thus, Rule 19c-4 followed the analysis offered by Professor Gilson by focusing on corporate action that disenfranchised or reduced the voting power of existing shareholders, while accepting the issuance of non-voting, limited-voting, or disparate-voting classes of stock at the time the corporation "goes public" and in certain other limited instances. Structurally, the rule specifies some transactions that are presumptively forbidden (such as "capped" or "tenure" voting limitations that deny any share- holder the right to vote more than a specified number of shares or that deny voting rights until a shareholder has held for a specified period) and some transactions that are presumptively permissible (such as shares issued in "bona fide" mergers and shares issued in a registered offering where the new class has lesser voting rights than an outstanding class).

Rule 19c-4 had a short life. In 1990 the D.C. Circuit enjoined the rule, finding that the SEC had exceeded its authority to regulate stock exchanges in promulgating a rule intended more to standardize corporate governance. See The Business Round- table v. SEC, 905 F.2d 406 (D.C. Cir. 1990). Although the court's primary objection was that the rule encroached on the rights of states to regulate substantive corpo- rate governance, it was also concerned that the SEC had failed to articulate any coherent limits on its potential authority under Rule 19c-4. Specifically, it pointed to proposals for listing standards that mandated "independent directors, independent audit committees, shareholder approval for certain major corporate transactions, and other major issues traditionally governed by state law," and asked: "If Rule 19c-4 is related closely enough to the proxy regulation purpose of §14, then all those issues appear equally subject to the Commission's discre- tionary control." Is there a discernible dividing line between requiring a one-share, one-vote listing standard and, for example, mandating affirmative action on cor- porate boards as a listing standard?

Although the SEC lost the battle, it eventually won the war. Under prodding from the SEC, the NYSE, the ASE, and Nasdaq eventually agreed in 1994 on a common "one share, one vote" rule that largely parallels former Rule 19c-4: listed companies may not today adopt any form of supervoting stock (including "tenure voting" and "capped voting" schemes), but they may issue "lower-voting" stock. Each market also grandfathered companies with existing "dual-class" voting structures. In addition, to reduce competition among markets, each of the three markets agreed that it would not list a stock that was delisted for noncompliance with these voting standards by another.

Why did these three markets eventually agree after a decade of controversy and competition on common voting rights standards? By the 1990s, the threat of a hostile takeover had sufficiently subsided that dual-class voting structures were no longer important to corporate managements that lacked them. Also, institutional shareholders, whose influence and activism grew over this interval, would predictably resist any new attempt to adopt such a plan. Finally, those companies most interested in implementing such a dual-class structure had already done so during the period that the NYSE had ceased to enforce its former "one share, one vote" rule, and these companies were all grandfathered under the compromise. Ultimately, no one objected very strenuously to the final compromise.

c. State Law Limitations

To what extent does state law provide a remedy when a dominant shareholder seeks to use its influence or position to cause the adoption of a dual-class capitalization plan favoring it? In Unilever Acquisition Corp. v. Richardson-Vicks, Inc., page 565 supra, the court enjoined action that would have resulted in the issuance of a supervoting class because no shareholder vote was taken. The issue becomes cloudier, however, when such a vote is taken, but the plaintiff argues that shareholders were still "coerced."

Lacos Land Co. v. Arden Group, Inc.
517 A.2d 271 (Del. Ch. 1986)

ALLEN, C.: [Plaintiffs sought to enjoin a pending recapitalization of Arden under which a new class of Class B Common Stock would be created possessing ten votes per share and entitled to elect as a class 75 percent of the Arden board of directors. All Arden shareholders were entitled to exchange their outstanding common shares on a share-for-share basis for this new class of stock.] It is acknowledged by defendants that the new class of Class B Common Stock has been deliberately fashioned to be attractive mainly to defendant Briskin — Arden's principal shareholder and chief executive officer. Thus, the recapitalization is not itself a device to raise capital but rather a device to transfer stockholder control of the enterprise to Mr. Briskin. . . .

The new supervoting common stock whose issuance is sought to be enjoined will differ from Arden's other authorized class of common stock, Class A Common Stock, most importantly, in its enhanced voting power, its diminished dividend rights and in restrictions on its transfer. . . . In view of the lack of transferability and reduced dividend rights of the Class B Common Stock, the Board of Directors does not anticipate that any significant number of holders of Class A Common Stock other than Mr. Briskin will accept the Exchange Offer.

The creation of a dual common stock structure with one class exercising effective control of the company is, of course, not a novel idea,[3] although it is one that, thanks to its potential as an anti-takeover device, has recently emerged from the reaches of the corporation law chorus to strut its moment upon center stage where corporate drama is acted out. In this instance, the notion of employing this dual common stock structure apparently originated with defendant Briskin.

Mr. Briskin became Arden chief executive officer in 1976 at a time when the Company was apparently in a desperate condition. Its stock was then trading between $1 and $2 per share. Briskin's stewardship has apparently been active and effective. While Arden has paid no dividends since 1970, during Briskin's tenure Arden's stock price has risen steadily; currently Arden common stock is publicly trading at around $25 per share, a price somewhat higher than the range of prices at which its stock traded in the weeks prior to the announcement of the plan that is the subject matter of this litigation.

In instigating the dual common stock voting structure, Mr. Briskin was apparently not responding to any specific threat to existing policies or practices of Arden posed by a specific takeover threat. Rather, he apparently was motivated to protect his power to control Arden's business future. Such a motivation, while it may be suspect — since it may reflect not a desire to protect business policy and capabilities for the benefit of the corporation and its shareholders but rather a wish simply to retain the benefits of office — does not itself constitute a wrong. See, e.g., Unocal Corp. v. Mesa Petroleum Co., Del. Supr., 493 A.2d 946, 955 (1985); Kaplan v. Goldsamt, Del. Ch., 380 A.2d 556, 568-69 (1977). . . .

At the June 10 annual meeting the Arden stockholders approved the proposed certificate amendments. Of 2,303,170 shares outstanding, 1,463,155 voted in favor (64%) and 325,004 (14%) voted to reject the proposal. Of the affirmative votes, 427,347 were voted by Briskin or his family and 388,493 were voted by a trustee as directed by Arden's management. As to the preferred stock, 74.4% of the 136,359 shares outstanding voted in favor of the proposal, more than half of which were voted by a trustee as directed by Arden's management. . . .

Our corporation law provides great flexibility to shareholders in creating the capital structure of their firm. See, e.g., Providence and Worcester Co. v. Baker, Del. Supr., 378 A.2d 121 (1977). Differing classes of stock with differing voting rights are permissible under our law, 8 Del. C. §151(a); Topkis v. Delaware Hardware Co., Del. Ch., 2 A.2d 114 (1938); restrictions on transfers are possible, 8 Del. C. §202, and charter provisions requiring the filling of certain directorates by a class of stock are, if otherwise properly adopted, valid. Lehrman v. Cohen, Del. Supr., 222 A.2d 800 (1966). Thus, each of the significant characteristics of the Class B Common Stock is in principle a valid power or limitation of common stock. The primary inquiry therefore is whether the Arden shareholders have effectively exercised their will to amend the Company's restated certificate of incorporation so as to authorize the implementation of the dual class common stock structure. The charge is that they have not done so — despite the report of the judge of elections that the proposed amendments carried — in part because the proxy statement upon which the vote was solicited was materially misleading and in part because the entire plan to put in place the Class B stock constitutes a breach of duty on the part of a dominated board.

---

3. See, General Investment Co. v. Bethlehem Steel Corp., N.J. Ch., 87 N.J. Eq. 234, 100 A. 347 (1917).

For the reasons that follow I conclude that plaintiff has demonstrated a reasonable probability that on final hearing it will be demonstrated that the June 10, 1986 vote of the Arden shareholders had been fundamentally and fatally flawed and that, therefore, the amendments to Arden's restated certificate of incorporation purportedly authorized by that vote are voidable. . . . [T]he June 10 vote was inappropriately affected by an explicit threat of Mr. Briskin that unless the proposed amendments were approved, he would use his power (and not simply his power qua shareholder) to block transactions that may be in the best interests of the Company, if those transactions would dilute his ownership interest in Arden. I use the word threat because such a position entails, in my opinion, the potential for a breach of Mr. Briskin's duty, as the principal officer of Arden and as a member of its board of directors, to exercise corporate power unselfishly, with a view to fostering the interests of the corporation and all of its shareholders. . . .

Judging from what is stated in the proxy materials, Arden's board in recommending the charter amendments and Arden's shareholders in approving them were both placed, inappropriately, in a position that made it significantly less likely than it might otherwise have been that approval of the plan to effectively transfer all shareholder power to Mr. Briskin would have been given.

To a shareholder who wondered why his board of directors was recommending a plan expected to place all effective shareholder power in a single shareholder, the proxy statement gives a clear answer: Mr. Briskin is demanding it; it's not such a big deal anyway since, as a practical matter, he has great power already; and if he doesn't get these amendments, he may exercise his power to thwart corporate transactions that may be in the Company's best interests. Thus, in order for the board to be "permitted to consider" (proxy p.20) certain transactions that might threaten to reduce Mr. Briskin's control, the board approved the proposal. This story is disclosed more or less straight forwardly in the proxy solicitation materials.

As to Mr. Briskin's position, the proxy statement states (emphasis added throughout):

Purpose and Effects of the Proposal

1. **Purpose.** Mr. Briskin, the Company's largest single stockholder who beneficially owns in the aggregate approximately 21.1% of the outstanding Common Stock, has informed the Company of his concern that certain transactions *which could be determined by the Board of Directors to be in the best interests of all of the shareholders,* such as the issuance of additional voting securities in connection with financings or mergers or acquisitions by the Company, might make the Company vulnerable to an unsolicited or hostile takeover attempt or to an attempt at "greenmail," and that *he would not give his support to any such transactions for which his approval might be required unless steps were taken to secure his voting position in the Company.* . . .

Thus, Arden shareholders were unmistakably told that should they fail to approve the proposed amendments, Mr. Briskin "would not give his support to any transaction [that might make the Company vulnerable to an unsolicited or hostile takeover attempt] for which his approval might be required. . . ." Using the term in the vague way which we ordinarily do, a vote in such circumstances as these could be said to be "coerced." But that label itself supplies no basis to conclude that the legal effect of the vote is impaired in any way. As stated in Katz v. Oak Industries, Inc., Del. Ch., 508 A.2d 873, 880 (1986):

> . . . [F]or purposes of legal analysis, the term "coercion" itself — covering a multitude of situations — is not very meaningful. For the word to have much meaning for purposes of legal analysis, it is necessary in each case that a normative judgment be attached to the concept ("inappropriately coercive" or "wrongfully coercive," etc.). But, it is then readily seen that what is legally relevant is not the conclusory term "coercion" itself but rather the norm that leads to the adverb modifying it."

The determination of whether it was inappropriate for Mr. Briskin to structure the choice of Arden's shareholders (and its directors), as was done here, requires, first, a determination of which of his hats — shareholder, officer or director — Mr. Briskin was wearing when he stated his position concerning the possible withholding of his "support" for future transactions unless steps were taken "to secure his voting position." If he spoke only as a shareholder, and should have been so understood, an evaluation of the propriety of his position might be markedly different (see, Tanzer v. International General Industries, Inc., Del. Supr., 397 A.2d 1121, 1123 (1979); Heil v. Standard Gas & Electric Co., Del. Ch., 151 A. 303, 304 (1930)) than if the "support" referred to could be or should be interpreted as involving the exercise of his power as either an officer or director of Arden.

On this point defendants' position at oral argument confirms that which the proxy language itself indicates — that, in taking his position, Mr. Briskin did not limit, and could not be understood to have limited, himself to exercising only shareholder power. Defendants have emphasized that Briskin's "practical" power derives in part from his notable success as a chief executive officer; his history of success, I was reminded, creates influence and his position confers power to initiate board consideration of important matters. Moreover, the proxy statement made clear that the approval that Briskin threatened to withhold included approval of transactions that did not require a vote of shareholders. . . . Accordingly, the conclusion seems inescapable that, in announcing an intent to withhold support for corporate action that might entail, for instance, the issuance of stock, even if that act might be in the best interests of the corporation, unless "steps were taken to preserve his voting position," Mr. Briskin could not be understood to have been acting only as a shareholder.

As a director and as an officer, of course, Mr. Briskin has a duty to act with complete loyalty to the interests of the corporation and its shareholders. Weinberger v. UOP, Inc., Del. Supr., 457 A.2d 701 (1983); Guth v. Loft, Del. Supr., 5 A.2d 503 (1939). His position as stated to the shareholders in the Company proxy statement seems inconsistent with that obligation. In form at least, the statement by a director and officer that he will not give his support to a corporate transaction unless steps are taken to confer a personal power or benefit, suggests an evident disregard of duty. However, the nature of the *quid pro quo* sought by Mr. Briskin in this case is at least consistent with a benign or selfless motive. The Class B stock he sought to have the board recommend and the stockholders approve would transfer complete control of the enterprise to him for an indefinite period, but it is a control that may not be transferred generally and so it is unlikely that Mr. Briskin was motivated to gain access to a control premium for his stock by insisting on a device of this kind as a price of his supporting certain types of future action.

Two alternative motivations suggest themselves. Mr. Briskin may have been motivated, as plaintiff warmly contends is the fact, by a selfish desire to protect his salary and the perquisites of his office from the threat to them that a hostile takeover of Arden would represent. The issuance of the Class B stock, in the totality of the circumstances present, will assuredly place Mr. Briskin in a position (1) to protect his tenure for as long as he wants to do so and (2) to negotiate and assure stockholder acceptance of the full terms of any change in control, including employment contracts or severance agreements.

On the other hand, Briskin may have been motivated selflessly to put in place the most powerful of anti-takeover devices so that he could be assured the opportunity to reject (for all the shareholders) any offer for Arden that he—who presumably knows more about the Company than anyone else—regards as less than optimum achievable value. Accordingly, while I regard the form of the Briskin position ("I, as fiduciary will not support . . . unless a personal benefit is conferred") as superficially shocking, I recognize that Mr. Briskin's position as stated in the proxy statement is logically consistent with and may indeed in fact be driven by a benevolent motivation.

Mr. Briskin's motivation in fact, however, need not be determined in order to conclude that the stockholder vote of June 10, 1986 was fatally flawed by the implied (indeed, the expressed) threats that unless the proposed amendments were authorized, he would oppose transactions "which could be determined by the Board of Directors to be in the best interests of all of the shareholders." As a corporate fiduciary, Mr. Briskin has no right to take such a position, even if benevolently motivated in doing so. Shareholders who respect Mr. Briskin's ability and performance—and who are legally entitled to his undivided loyalty—were inappropriately placed in a position in which they were told that if they refused to vote affirmatively, Mr. Briskin would not support future possible transactions that might be beneficial to the corporation. A vote of shareholders under such circumstances cannot, in the face of a timely challenge by one of the corporation's shareholders, be said, in my opinion, to satisfy the mandate of Section 242(b) of our corporation law requiring shareholder consent to charter amendments. . . .

For the foregoing reasons, plaintiff's motion shall be granted. . . .

---

1. *When is coercion permissible?* In Eisenberg v. Chicago Milwaukee Corp., 537 A.2d 1051, 1061-1062 (Del. Ch. 1987), because the stockholders were told that if they rejected a tender offer, the directors would seek to delist their preferred shares, the court found that the shareholder vote had been impermissibly coerced. In contrast, in In re GM Class H Shareholders Litig., 734 A.2d 611 (Del. Ch. 1999), where one class of shareholders was asked to waive a charter provision that protected their interests and to approve a merger transaction, the court rejected the claim that it was coercive to link these two issues and make the merger depend on the waiver. The difference between the two cases, the court said, was that in the latter there was no threatened retribution. That is, if the shareholders refused to approve the waiver and the merger transaction therefore collapsed, the shareholders would be in the same position that they had been in before the combined transaction was proposed. In this light, coercion seems to mean threatening shareholders with being made worse off than they were before the vote.

Although the foregoing cases find that a threat by a director or other fiduciary can taint an otherwise valid shareholder vote, the result might be otherwise if a shareholder who was not a director or officer, but did hold a substantial position as a shareholder, made a similar threat. For example, if the defendant were a corporation that owned 40 percent of the subject company's stock and the board were at least nominally independent, the same "threat" to disapprove transactions beneficial to the minority might be permissible because the defendant would no longer occupy a clear fiduciary position. Should the controlling shareholder be treated differently from the director? The basis for this disparity appears to be the view that "the shareholder may vote as he pleases — just as ordinary voters in a political election may vote according to their own preferences and prejudices without regard to the interests of others." This issue will be considered further in the notes following Schreiber v. Carney, page 578 infra.

2. *Threats by a controlling shareholder.* In Kahn v. Lynch Communication Systems, Inc., 638 A.2d 1110 (Del. 1994), a 43 percent shareholder proposed a merger with a corporation that it dominated at a price of $14 per share. A committee of independent directors entered into negotiations with the controlling shareholder and proposed a price of $17 per share. Eventually, the controlling shareholder increased its offer (in several stages) to $15.50, but announced that if this offer was not accepted, it was prepared to make a hostile tender offer at $15.50 a share (in part because an 80 percent supermajority provision for merger approval in the corporation's charter gave the 43 percent shareholder blocking position and effectively precluded any auction). When a minority shareholder sued, the Delaware Supreme Court ruled that the "threat" of a hostile tender offer by a controlling shareholder deprived the independent committee of its negotiation leverage and thus required that the controlling shareholder bear the burden of proving the "entire fairness" of a merger at $15.50. Is such a "threat" more (or less) coercive than the circumstances described in Schreiber v. Carney, page 578 infra? Although in other circumstances a shareholder may be able to "threaten" action that is legally permissible without adverse legal consequence, is the critical fact about *Kahn* the necessity for a controlling shareholder to be able to demonstrate the independent character of the committee's evaluation (and acceptance) of its merger proposal?

5. VOTE BUYING

New York Business Corporation Law (2007)

Sec. 609. *Proxies.* . . . (e) A shareholder shall not sell his vote or issue a proxy to vote to any person for any sum of money or anything of value, except as authorized in this section and section 620 (Agreements as to voting . . .). . . .

(f) A proxy which is entitled "irrevocable proxy" and which states that it is irrevocable, is irrevocable when it is held by any of the following or a nominee of any of the following:

(1) A pledgee;

(2) A person who has purchased or agreed to purchase the shares;

(3) A creditor or creditors of the corporation who extend or continue credit to the corporation in consideration of the proxy if the proxy states that it was

given in consideration of such extension or continuation of credit, the amount thereof, and the name of the person extending or continuing credit;

(4) A person who has contracted to perform services as an officer of the corporation, if a proxy is required by the contract of employment, if the proxy states that it was given in consideration of such contract of employment, the name of the employee and the period of employment contracted for;

(5) A person designated by or under an agreement under paragraph (a) of section 620.

(g) Notwithstanding a provision in a proxy stating that it is irrevocable, the proxy becomes revocable after the pledge is redeemed, or the debt of the corporation is paid, or the period of employment provided for in the contract of employment has terminated, or the agreement under paragraph (a) of section 620 has terminated; and, in a case provided for in subparagraphs (f)(3) or (4), becomes revocable three years after the date of the proxy or at the end of the period, if any, specified therein, whichever period is less, unless the period of irrevocability is renewed from time to time by the execution of a new irrevocable proxy as provided in this section. This paragraph does not affect the duration of a proxy under paragraph (b).

(h) A proxy may be revoked, notwithstanding a provision making it irrevocable, by a purchaser of shares without knowledge of the existence of the provision unless the existence of the proxy and its irrevocability is noted conspicuously on the face or back of the certificate representing such shares. . . .

Schreiber v. Carney
447 A.2d 17 (Del. Ch. 1982)

HARTNETT, V.C.: [Plaintiff, a shareholder in Texas International Airlines, Inc., challenged the propriety of its loan to defendant Jet Capital Corporation, which owned 35 percent of Texas International. Jet Capital held an effective veto power over a proposed merger between Texas International and Texas Air and had threatened to block it, because of adverse tax consequences for Jet Capital, unless Jet Capital could exercise certain warrants it held in Texas International prior to the merger. Jet Capital claimed that it lacked the funds necessary to exercise these warrants and that borrowing funds from a third-party lender was too expensive.] In order to overcome this impasse, it was proposed that Texas International and Jet Capital explore the possibility of a loan by Texas International to Jet Capital in order to fund an early exercise of the warrants. Because Texas International and Jet Capital had several common directors, the defendants recognized the conflict of interest and endeavored to find a way to remove any taint or appearance of impropriety. It was, therefore, decided that a special independent committee would be formed to consider and resolve the matter. The three Texas International directors who had no interest in or connection with Jet Capital were chosen to head up the committee. After its formation, the committee's first act was to hire independent counsel. Next, the committee examined the proposed merger and, based upon advice rendered by an independent investment banker, the merger was again found to be both a prudent and feasible business decision. The committee then confronted the "Jet Capital obstacle" by considering viable options for both Texas International and Jet Capital and, as a result, the committee determined that a loan was the best solution.

After negotiating at arm's length, both Texas International and Jet Capital agreed that Texas International would loan to Jet Capital $3,335,000 at 5% interest per annum for the period up to the scheduled 1982 expiration date for the warrants. After this period, the interest rate would equal the then prevailing prime interest rate. The 5% interest rate was recommended by an independent investment banker as the rate necessary to reimburse Texas International for any dividends paid out during this period. Given this provision for anticipated dividends and the fact that the advanced money would be immediately paid back to Texas International upon the exercise of the warrants, the loan transaction had virtually no impact on Texas International's cash position. . . .

The directors of Texas International unanimously approved the proposal as recommended by the committee and submitted it to the stockholders for approval — requiring as a condition of approval that a majority of all outstanding shares *and* a majority of the shares voted by the stockholders other than Jet Capital or its officers or directors be voted in favor of the proposal. After receiving a detailed proxy statement, the shareholders voted overwhelmingly in favor of the proposal. There is no allegation that the proxy statement did not fully disclose all the germane facts with complete candor.

The complaint attacks the loan transaction on two theories. First, it is alleged that the loan transaction constituted vote-buying and was therefore void. Secondly, the complaint asserts that the loan was corporate waste. In essence, plaintiff argues that even if the loan was permissible and even if it was the best available option, it would have been wiser for Texas International to have loaned Jet Capital only $800,000 — the amount of the increased tax liability — because this would have minimized Texas International's capital commitment and also would have prevented Jet Capital from increasing its control in Texas International on allegedly discriminatory and wasteful terms. . . .

[Plaintiff contends] that vote-buying existed and, therefore, the entire transaction including the merger was void because Jet Capital, in consideration for being extended an extremely advantageous loan, withdrew its opposition to the proposed merger. Thus, it is alleged that in substance and effect, Texas International purchased Jet Capital's necessary vote in contravention of settled law and public policy. As a consequence, plaintiff urges that the less than unanimous shareholder consent was insufficient to ratify a void act and its illegality permeated the entire transaction rendering the merger itself void. The critical inquiry, therefore, is whether the loan in question was in fact vote-buying and, if so, whether vote-buying is illegal, per se.

It is clear that the loan constituted vote-buying as that term has been defined by the courts. Vote-buying, despite its negative connotation, is simply a voting agreement supported by consideration personal to the stockholder, whereby the stockholder divorces his discretionary voting power and votes as directed by the offeror. The record clearly indicates that Texas International purchased or "removed" the obstacle of Jet Capital's opposition. Indeed, this is tacitly conceded by the defendants. However, defendants contend that the analysis of the transaction should not end here because the legality of vote-buying depends on whether its object or purpose is to defraud or in some manner disenfranchise the other stockholders. Defendants contend that because the loan did not defraud or disenfranchise any group of shareholders, but rather enfranchised the other shareholders by giving them a determinative vote in the proposed merger, it is not illegal per se. Defendants, in effect, contend that vote-buying is not void per se because the end justified the means. Whether this is valid depends upon the status of the law.

The Delaware decisions dealing with vote-buying leave the question unanswered. See Macht v. Merchants Mortgage & Credit Co., Del. Ch., 194 A. 19 (1937); Hall v. Isaacs, Del. Ch., 146 A.2d 602 (1958), aff'd, Del. Supr., 163 A.2d 288 (1960); and Chew v. Inverness Mgt. Corp., Del. Ch., 352 A.2d 426 (1976). In each of these decisions, the Court summarily voided the challenged votes as being purchased and thus contrary to public policy and in fraud of the other stockholders. However, the facts in each case indicated that fraud or disenfranchisement was the obvious purpose of the vote-buying. . . .

The present case presents a peculiar factual setting in that the proposed vote-buying consideration was conditional upon the approval of a majority of the disinterested stockholders after a full disclosure to them of all pertinent facts and was purportedly for the best interests of all Texas International stockholders. It is therefore necessary to do more than merely consider the fact that Jet Capital saw fit to vote for the transaction after a loan was made to it by Texas International. . . . There are essentially two principles which appear in [the prior] cases. The first is that vote-buying is illegal per se if its object or purpose is to defraud or disenfranchise the other stockholders. A fraudulent purpose is as defined at common law, as a deceit which operates prejudicially upon the property rights of another.

The second principle which appears in these old cases is that vote-buying is illegal per se as a matter of public policy, the reason being that each stockholder should be entitled to rely upon the independent judgment of his fellow stockholders. Thus, the underlying basis for this latter principle is again fraud but as viewed from a sense of duty owed by all stockholders to one another. The apparent rationale is that by requiring each stockholder to exercise his individual judgment as to all matters presented, "[t]he security of the small stockholders is found in the natural disposition of each stockholder to promote the best interests of all, in order to promote his individual interests." Cone v. Russell, 48 N.J. Eq. 208, 21 A. 847, 849 (1891). In essence, while self interest motivates a stockholder's vote, theoretically, it is also advancing the interests of the other stockholders. Thus, any agreement entered into for personal gain, whereby a stockholder separates his voting right from his property right was considered a fraud upon this community of interests.

The often cited case of Brady v. Bean, 211 Ill. App. 279 (1921), is particularly enlightening. In that case, the plaintiff — an apparently influential stockholder — voiced his opposition to the corporation's proposed sale of assets. The plaintiff feared that his investment would be wiped out because the consideration for the sale appeared only sufficient enough to satisfy the corporation's creditors. As a result and without the knowledge of the other stockholders, the defendant, also a stockholder as well as a director and substantial creditor of the company, offered to the plaintiff in exchange for the withdrawal of his opposition, a sharing in defendant's claims against the corporation. In an action to enforce this contract against the defendant's estate, the Court refused relief stating:

> Appellant being a stockholder in the company, any contract entered into by him whereby he was to receive a personal consideration in return for either his action or his inaction in a matter such as a sale of all the company's assets, involving, as it did, the

interests of all the stockholders, was contrary to public policy and void, it being admitted that such contract was not known by or assented to by the other stockholders. *The purpose and effect of the contract was apparently to influence appellant, in his decision of a question affecting the rights and interests of his associate stockholders, by a consideration which was foreign to those rights and interests and would be likely to induce him to disregard the consideration he owed them and the contract must, therefore, be regarded as a fraud upon them.* Such an agreement will not be enforced, as being against public policy. . . .

In addition to the deceit obviously practiced upon the other stockholders, the Court was clearly concerned with the rights and interests of the other stockholders. Thus, the potential injury or prejudicial impact which might flow to other stockholders as a result of such an agreement forms the heart of the rationale underlying the breach of public policy doctrine.

An automatic application of this rationale to the facts in the present case, however, would be to ignore an essential element of the transaction. The agreement in question was entered into primarily to further the interests of Texas International's other shareholders. Indeed, the shareholders, after reviewing a detailed proxy statement, voted overwhelmingly in favor of the loan agreement. Thus, the underlying rationale for the argument that vote-buying is illegal per se, as a matter of public policy, ceases to exist when measured against the undisputed reason for the transaction.

Moreover, the rationale that vote-buying is, as a matter of public policy, illegal per se is founded upon considerations of policy which are now outmoded as a necessary result of an evolving corporate environment. According to 5 Fletcher Cyclopedia Corporation (Perm. Ed.) §2066: "The theory that each stockholder is entitled to the personal judgment of each other stockholder expressed in his vote, and that any agreement among stockholders frustrating it was invalid, is obsolete because it is both impracticable and impossible of application to modern corporations with many widely scattered stockholders, and the courts have gradually abandoned it."

In addition, Delaware law has for quite some time permitted stockholders wide latitude in decisions affecting the restriction or transfer of voting rights. In Ringling Bros., Etc., Shows, Inc. v. Ringling, Del. Supr., 53 A.2d 441 (1947), the Delaware Supreme Court adopted a liberal approach to voting agreements which, prior to that time, were viewed with disfavor and were often considered void as a matter of public policy. In upholding a voting agreement the Court stated: "Generally speaking, a shareholder may exercise wide liberality of judgment in the matter of voting, and it is not objectionable that his motives may be for personal profit, or determined by whims or caprice, so long as he violates no duty owed his fellow stockholders" (citation omitted). The Court's rationale was later codified in 8 Del. C. §218(c), which states:

> (c) An agreement between 2 or more stockholders, if in writing and signed by the parties thereto, may provide that in exercising any voting rights, the shares held by them shall be voted as provided by the agreement, or as the parties may agree, or as determined in accordance with a procedure agreed upon by them. No such agreement shall be effective for a term of more than 10 years, but, at any time within 2 years prior to the time of the expiration of such agreement, the parties may extend its duration for as many additional periods, each not to exceed 10 years, as they may desire.

Recently, in Oceanic Exploration Co. v. Grynberg, Del. Supr., 428 A.2d 1 (1981), the Delaware Supreme Court applied this approach to voting trusts. The Court also indicated, with approval, the liberal approach to all contractual arrangements limiting the incidents of stock ownership. Significantly, *Oceanic* involved the giving up of voting rights in exchange for personal gain. There, the stockholder, by way of a voting trust, gave up his right to vote on all corporate matters over a period of years in return for "valuable benefits including indemnity for large liabilities."

Given the holdings in *Ringling* and *Oceanic* it is clear that Delaware has discarded the presumptions against voting agreements. Thus, under our present law, an agreement involving the transfer of stock voting rights without the transfer of ownership is not necessarily illegal and each arrangement must be examined in light of its object or purpose. To hold otherwise would be to exalt form over substance. As indicated in *Oceanic* more than the mere form of an agreement relating to voting must be considered and voting agreements in whatever form, therefore, should not be considered to be illegal per se unless the object or purpose is to defraud or in some way disenfranchise the other stockholders. This is not to say, however, that vote-buying accomplished for some laudable purpose is automatically free from challenge. Because vote-buying is so easily susceptible of abuse it must be viewed as a voidable transaction subject to a test for intrinsic fairness. . . .

. . . I therefore hold that the agreement, whereby Jet Capital withdrew its opposition to the proposed merger in exchange for a loan to fund the early exercise of its warrants was not void per se because the object and purpose of the agreement was not to defraud or disenfranchise the other stockholders but rather was for the purpose of furthering the interest of all Texas International stockholders. The agreement, however, was a voidable act. Because the loan agreement was voidable it was susceptible to cure by shareholder approval. Michelson v. Duncan, Del. Supr., 407 A.2d 211 (1979). Consequently, the subsequent ratification of the transaction by a majority of the independent stockholders, after a full disclosure of all germane facts with complete candor precludes any further judicial inquiry of it. . . .

---

1. *Defining the injury.* The traditional rule is "that a stockholder cannot, for a private and personal consideration, agree to cast his vote in a certain way. The sale of voting power is said to be against public policy." Earl Sneed, The Stockholder May Vote as He Pleases: Theory and Fact, 22 U. Pitt. L. Rev. 23, 45-46 (1960). Yet the inroads on this rule are obviously extensive, because (as *Schreiber* notes) the shareholder can agree, in return for a benefit, to sign a voting agreement or enter a voting trust. If the traditional rule had been more strictly enforced in *Schreiber*, would the minority shareholders then have been better off if Jet Capital had voted against the merger? If we assume that a shareholder (including a dominant shareholder) may vote as it pleases, is there any answer to this problem? Should fiduciary principles therefore limit the power of a controlling shareholder to vote in its self-interest? Or is the real problem here that Jet Capital's veto power over the transaction enabled it to coerce the other shareholders and receive a non–pro rata benefit?

Dean Robert Clark has argued that vote buying should be permitted in a limited form.[24] In his view, vote buying may be efficient if the purchaser has a substantial equity interest and expects to profit solely through appreciation in the value of that interest. Yet it is difficult to discriminate between vote buying as an attempt to profit solely on this basis and vote buying in order to obtain and exploit control by engaging in unfair self-dealing that reduces the value of the firm to the other residual claimants. Others contend that the prohibition against vote buying logically rests on the "unnecessary agency cost" that comes into being once the vote can be separated from the equity interest. See Frank Easterbrook & Daniel Fischel, Voting in Corporate Law, 26 J.L. & Econ. 395, 410-411 (1983). Professors Easterbrook and Fischel also base their objections to vote buying on a variation of the previously noted "free rider" problem. That is, if a 20 percent owner could purchase 100 percent of the votes, this disparity between voting and equity shares "introduces a disproportion between expenditure and reward" because a 20 percent owner would still have an inadequate incentive to take steps to improve the firm (because this owner would benefit only to the extent of the 20 percent interest). Thus, in theory the 20 percent owner would invest too little and might shirk the performance of its duties. Perhaps, but would dispersed shareholders expend any more resources?

2. *Permissible substitutes.* Conceptually, it is sometimes difficult to distinguish impermissible vote selling from permissible vote pooling agreements and similar devices. As N.Y. Bus. Corp. Law §609 (quoted supra) indicates, irrevocable proxies are a major exception to the prohibition against vote selling. RMBCA §7.22 largely parallels §609, and both codify an earlier common law rule that allows a person with an economic "interest" in the shares to hold an irrevocable proxy. Typically, the required "interest" stems from the holder's status as a creditor of the shareholder or as a purchaser of the shares made subject to the proxy. However, §609(f)(4) also allows a corporate officer to acquire an irrevocable proxy, and §609(f)(5) permits voting agreements among shareholders that are enforced through the use of irrevocable proxies. Why is this permissible if outright vote buying is not? Is the answer that these provisions do not authorize the payment of a bribe in return for an irrevocable proxy? Can the law on irrevocable proxies be fully reconciled with the general prohibition against vote buying? (These issues are considered further in Chapter VII because they typically arise in the context of the closely held firm.)

3. *The "New" Vote Buying.* With the growth of derivatives markets, new techniques have developed to decouple economic ownership from voting power. Hedge funds in particular have exploited these techniques so that they can hold more votes than shares. The simplest technique is to borrow shares in the share lending market. Traditionally, this market lent shares to short sellers who borrowed so that they could sell short (and later return the borrowed shares by buying after the price fell). But those who wish to hold additional voting power can simply borrow the shares and thereby acquire the voting rights; they return the borrowed shares

---

24. See Robert Clark, Vote Buying and Corporate Law, 29 Case W. Res. L. Rev. 776 (1979). Nobel laureate James Tobin, an economist, once wrote: "Any good second year graduate student in economics could write a short examination paper proving that voluntary transactions in votes would increase the welfare of the sellers as well as the buyers." Tobin, On Limiting the Domain of Inequality, 13 J.L. & Econ. 263, 269 (1970). His point, however, was not that vote buying should be permitted, but that economic analysis sometimes does not catch the full range of the values in play.

after the election. Another technique involves use of an "equity swap," under which the party on the short side of the transaction has no net economic ownership but does hold voting rights. Similarly, one can sell short and then hedge by acquiring additional shares so that one has no net economic ownership in the stock but does hold the voting rights on the newly acquired shares. Put and call options and single stock futures provide other mechanisms by which one can hold voting power without economic ownership.

The risks involved in these practices are illustrated by a celebrated takeover battle in 2004. Perry Corp., a hedge fund, owned 7 million shares of King Pharmaceuticals ("King"). Mylan Laboratories ("Mylan") agreed to buy King in a stock-for-stock merger at a lucrative premium, but Mylan's stock price fell because the market judged that it was overpaying. Because Perry Corp. wanted the transaction to go forward, given its large ownership interest in King, Perry Corp. bought 9.9 percent of Mylan, becoming its largest shareholder, but then it fully hedged this position so that it held a zero economic stake in Mylan. As a result, the more that Mylan overpaid, the more it profited, and its logical incentive was to vote for a transaction, even as the largest Mylan shareholder, that made the other Mylan shareholders worse off.

Such practices have been given a new and novel name: "empty voting"—which applies whenever voting power is not supported by equivalent economic ownership. See Henry Hu and Bernard Black, The New Vote Buying: Empty Voting and Hidden (Morphable) Ownership, 79 U.S.C. L. Rev. 811 (2006). To date, no case has addressed these issues, but the SEC has expressed concern and is searching for an appropriate policy.

C. *VOTING PROCEDURES*

Because share ownership is dispersed in the large public corporation, several mechanisms have evolved to facilitate voting while preserving share transferability. Five will be discussed in this section: (1) record dates, (2) the proxy system, (3) "street name" ownership, (4) the inspector of elections, and (5) stockholder consents.

1. RECORD DATES

A record date determines who is entitled to notice of an approaching shareholder meeting and who is eligible to vote at it—namely, those persons who were registered on the corporation's stock ledger as owners of the stock on the record date. It thus functions in much the same way as voter registration requirements for elections in our political system. The rapid turnover of shares on a national securities exchange made the use of some such fixed moment an administrative necessity. Typically, the record date may be set either by the corporation's bylaws or by a board resolution, although boundaries may be established by statute. For example, Del. Gen. Corp. Law §213 (2007) requires that the record date "shall not be more than sixty nor less than ten days before the date of [the shareholders' meeting]."

Absent some such statutory provision, a board seeking to ward off a hostile take-over might, for example, set a record date 300 days in advance of the meeting and thus deny any shareholder who bought in the intervening period the right to vote at the annual election of directors. After the corporation sets a record date, most state statutes require the corporation to prepare an alphabetical list of share-holders, their addresses, and share ownership, and to make this list available for inspection. See, e.g., RMBCA §7.20 (2002). At least in theory, this list permits each side in the contest to contact the voters and to prevent voting fraud at the meeting.

Shareholders who acquire their shares subsequent to the record date may still negotiate with the seller and require the seller to deliver a proxy, which may be made irrevocable as a condition of the sale. This is infeasible, however, when the shares are purchased over a securities exchange, but it is commonly required in a tender offer (where the shares are delivered to a depository named by the offeror and must comply with the offeror's conditions). Some cases have also suggested that the seller "owes some duties to the real beneficial or equitable owner of the stock; and even if the right to demand a proxy is not exercised, if the vendor exercises his legal right to vote in such a manner as to materially and injuriously affect the rights of the vendee, he is perhaps answerable in damages in some cases." In re Grant Portland Cement Co., 26 Del. Ch. 32, 21 A.2d 697 (1941). Could a post–record date purchaser who failed to obtain a proxy from the seller seek to enjoin or invalidate an election under this same standard? Would this conflict with Del. Gen. Corp. Law §219(c) (2007), which provides: "The stock led-ger shall be the only evidence as to who are the stockholders entitled . . . to vote in person or by proxy at any meeting of stockholders"? Is it consistent to permit damages but deny prospective injunctive relief?

2. PROXIES

At common law the shareholder had to be present at the shareholders' meeting to vote. With the emergence of public share ownership in this century, a requirement of personal attendance at the meeting became infeasible, because of both the geo-graphic dispersion of shareholders and the small size of their individual invest-ments. As a result, statutes authorized shareholders to appoint representatives to vote their shares at the meeting. The term "proxy" is often loosely used to refer to any of the following: (i) a legal relationship under which one party is appointed a fiduciary to vote another's shares, (ii) the nominee so appointed, or (iii) the physical document that evidences the relationship. Today, the actual instrument is a small, card-sized document that authorizes specified nominees, usually man-agement or incumbent directors, to vote these shares either in ways specifically indicated by the shareholder or, if so provided, in the nominee's discretion. Federal law, however, limits the discretion the nominee can obtain to vote on matters for which express instructions are not given. See Sec. I infra.

Del. Gen. Corp. Law §212(b) (2007) is representative and provides: "Each stock-holder entitled to vote at a meeting of stockholders or to express consent or dissent to corporate action in writing without a meeting may authorize another person or persons to act for such stockholder by proxy, but no such proxy shall be voted or acted upon after three years from its date, unless the proxy provides for a longer period." Although this would literally permit management to solicit a lifetime proxy from the shareholder (if it were expressly so provided), proxies are legally revocable at the will of the shareholder, unless the recipient of the proxy has some equitable interest that permits the proxy to be made irrevocable. See Del. Gen. Corp. Law §212(e) (2007); N.Y. Bus. Corp. Law §609 (2007). In any event, federal law places a one-year limit on the life of a proxy if the corporation is a "reporting company" subject to the federal proxy rules. This effectively requires that management solicit proxies annually to satisfy quorum and voting requirements. Typically, most state statutes specify that a majority of the outstanding shares must be present at the meeting, although they often allow the certificate to reduce this quorum requirement to one-third of the outstanding shares. See Cal. Gen. Corp. Law §602 (1978); N.Y. Bus. Corp. Law §608(b) (1998).[25]

To revoke a revocable proxy, a shareholder need only deliver a duly executed proxy card bearing a later date; the law sees the shareholder as the principal, with complete power to discharge the agent (unless the proxy is legally irrevocable), and delivering a subsequently dated proxy automatically cancels the prior proxy. In contested elections, the corporate bylaws will typically specify an inspector (usually a public accounting firm) to determine the validity of contested proxies.[26]

A technological innovation in proxy voting has complicated the problems of determining authenticity: the electronic proxy. When time is of the essence (as it frequently is in takeover battles), the contending parties will not solicit simply by mail but will use the following procedure: An advertisement in major newspapers will urge stockholders to either (a) clip out and return a proxy card, which is reproduced in the advertisement, or (b) call a toll-free telephone number, where a Western Union operator will record the shareholder's instructions and send a "datagram"—a telegram in preestablished form—to the party seeking the proxy. All costs are borne by the soliciting party.

This procedure has raised a variety of novel issues yet to be fully resolved. Although state law has long accorded a presumption of authenticity to a duly executed proxy, the shareholder has a much higher degree of control over a written proxy card than over a datagram filled in by someone else. Presumably, the potential for fraud is also higher, because someone else could call the Western Union operator and pretend to be the shareholder. Also, there is a debate as to whether such a proxy satisfies the "in writing" requirement of most state statutes. This issue in turn hinges on a question of agency law: Is the Western Union operator an agent of the shareholder (based only on oral instructions over a toll-free line), or is the operator an agent of the proxy contestant, who is paying the fee?

25. RMBCA §7.25 permits the certificate or bylaws to specify the quorum requirement and does not specify any lower boundary. Del. Gen. Corp. Law §216 (2007) is more typical in specifying that the certificate or bylaws may lower the quorum below the default level of a majority of the shares entitled to vote, but then providing a floor of not "less than one-third of the shares entitled to vote at the meeting." Both statutes, however, require that certain transactions be approved by a majority of all outstanding shares, thus also making a proxy solicitation a practical necessity. Uniquely, §7.25 does not require that a majority of the shares cast favor a proposal, but only that the proposal receive more affirmative votes than negative votes. This means that abstentions are not counted as negative votes, as they are under most statutes.

26. Under Del Gen. Corp. Law §231 (2007), the appointment of an inspector is mandatory for a listed corporation or one held of record by more than 2,000 stockholders. RMBCA §7.24(c) is more permissive in this regard and provides that a vote, consent, waiver, or proxy may be rejected (and thus not counted) if the appropriate corporate "officer or agent authorized to tabulate votes, acting in good faith, has reasonable basis for doubt about the validity of the signature on it or about the signatory's authority to sign for the shareholder."

In Parshalle v. Roy, 567 A.2d 19 (Del. Ch. 1989), the court found that datagrams and similar telecopied proxies did not comply with Delaware's requirements for a valid proxy because they lacked "the indicia of authenticity and genuineness needed to accord them a presumption of validity": "The proxy must evidence [the agency] relationship in some authentic, genuine way." Because datagrams lack any written signature by the principal, they failed to meet that standard. For decisions upholding datagrams and similar authorizations, see Dynamics Corp. of Am. v. CTS Corp., 643 F. Supp. 215, 221 (N.D. Ill. 1986) (Indiana law); Salgo v. Matthews, 497 S.W.2d 620 (Tex. Civ. App. 1973).

In response, the Delaware legislature in 1990 added a new §212(c) to Del. Gen. Corp. Law, which permits a stockholder to "authorize another person or persons to act for such stockholder as proxy by transmitting or authorizing the transmission of a telegram, cablegram, or other means of electronic transmission to the person who will be the holder of the proxy or to a proxy solicitation firm . . . or like agent . . . , provided that any such telegram, cablegram or other means of electronic transmission must either set forth or be submitted with information from which it can be determined that the telegram, cablegram or other electronic transmission was authorized by the stockholder." This compromise legitimates the datagram in the abstract, but leaves its validity in a specific case to be determined by the inspector of elections (whose independence from management may sometimes be debated).

In overview, the most important thing to understand about the proxy voting system is that it has largely superseded the shareholders' meeting itself. The outcome of contested issues will usually be a foregone conclusion once the proxy solicitation is concluded, and debate at the meeting may serve only therapeutic or public relations purposes.

3. "STREET NAME" OWNERSHIP

Commonly, shareholders do not register shares they purchase in their own names, but leave them registered in the name of a bank or broker (each of which uses a "street name" — a pseudonym entered on the corporation's stock ledger for this limited purpose). This practice reduces the transfer of share certificates and hence simplifies bookkeeping and lowers costs. A major brokerage firm can thus hold only a few share certificates in large denominations for major corporations, such as IBM or General Motors, and it will only need to exchange share certificates with other firms to reflect the *net* change in its holdings.

The origins of this system had less to do with modern bookkeeping problems caused by the high volume of trading on securities exchanges than with legal questions involving the authority of fiduciaries to act for their beneficiaries:

> American institutions first began extensively to register securities in nominee name in the 1930s in an effort to escape onerous transfer requirements placed on corporations and fiduciaries by issuers seeking to protect themselves from judicially imposed liability for improper transfers. Customarily, issuers required the submission of all supporting documents before transferring stock held by fiduciaries and required corporate investors to demonstrate the authority and incumbency of the individual officer or employee acting on their behalf. The use of the nominee as the registered

holder of stock eliminated from the issuer's records any evidence of a fiduciary relationship and made the recordholder a non-corporate entity. Thus, nominees could transfer securities without meeting the requirements placed on corporate or fiduciary shareholders.

SEC Final Report on the Practice of Recording the Ownership of Securities in the Records of the Issuer in Other than the Name of the Beneficial Owner of Such Securities 13 (Photocopy 1976).

Today, the system of registration provides safekeeping of the certificates and relieves the shareholder of recordkeeping. It also permits brokers to maintain margin accounts and, most important, reduces the need for physical transfer of the certificate, a time-consuming and costly process. A broker with certificates registered in a street name, which it holds for the account of its customers, can sell shares of one customer to another customer simply by making a bookkeeping entry evidencing a change in the beneficial ownership of the shares. Note, Comprehensive Securities Depository Systems and the Beneficial Owner, 20 UCLA L. Rev. 348 (1972).

A more recent development has been the appearance of depository trust companies. In the early 1970s the Depository Trust Company was formed by a consortium of brokerage firms in cooperation with the stock exchanges in order to immobilize share certificates. The problems associated with the physical transfer of these certificates among firms had created a major "back office" crisis that threatened the financial solvency of some firms. These depository companies today hold master share certificates in which various brokerage firms have equitable interests, and which these firms in turn hold for their customers. As a result, securities need not be transferred among participating firms; instead, changes in ownership can be indicated by book transfer on the ledger of the depository company. When, in 1987, over 300 million shares sometimes traded on the NYSE on a single day, this system made it possible to transfer this record volume of shares without significant difficulty.

Given this structure of multiple intermediaries between the corporation and the beneficial holder, even the corporation may not be able to ascertain the actual equitable owners of its stock, and this has greatly complicated the proxy solicitation process. Although stock exchange rules have long required brokerage firms to forward proxy materials and annual reports to the beneficial owners and to vote as they instruct, actual communication with such owners became increasingly difficult. This factor reduced the rate of shareholder response to proxy solicitations and sometimes prevented corporate action from being taken for lack of a legally adequate quorum or vote. In response, SEC Rule 14b-1 requires brokers to inform the corporation of the names, addresses, and securities positions of those customers who are beneficial holders and who have not objected to such disclosure. A similar rule applies to banks that hold stock in trust accounts for customers, again requiring that they identify their non-objecting beneficial holders to the corporation. Once such beneficial holders (called "NOBOs"—an acronym for "non-objecting beneficial owners") are identified, the corporation can then directly mail its annual reports and proxy materials to such holders (although the actual voting must be done by the banks or brokerage firms, as the record owners, on instructions from their clients). Although this prior identification reduced the time necessary to place proxy materials in the share-holder's hands, it still rendered shareholder voting a slow process requiring communication among multiple intermediaries.

Thus, in 2007, the SEC turned to the Internet to expedite this process. In Sec. Exch. Act Rel. No. 34-55146 (March 30, 2007), the SEC established an alternative procedure by which issuers and other persons could furnish proxy materials to shareholders by posting them on an Internet Web site and providing shareholders with notice of the availability of the proxy materials. Under this revised "notice and access" model, the bank, broker, or other intermediary will forward a Notice of Internet Availability of Proxy Materials to the beneficial owner and request voting instructions from such owner. Under new Rule 14a-16, this notice must be sent by the bank, broker, or other intermediary to the beneficial owner at least 40 days before the meeting date. This alternative system can be used only if the issuer elects to do so. However, because the "notice and access" model greatly reduces mailing costs to the issuer, little resistance is expected.

4. INSPECTOR OF ELECTIONS

Because proxies can be rescinded simply by the execution of later proxies, disputes are recurrent when multiple proxies are executed as to which one should be counted. The inspector(s) of elections are the corporate officials authorized on behalf of the corporation to determine the validity of proxies and ballots. Often, the corporation's accounting firm is asked to perform this role. Del. Gen. Corp. Law §231 (2007) sets forth the authority of, and procedures to be followed by, inspectors of elections. Specifically, §231(b) requires the inspectors to (1) ascertain the number of shares outstanding, (2) determine the shares represented at the meeting and the validity of all proxies and ballots, (3) count all votes and ballots, (4) retain for a reasonable period a record of their determinations and the challenges thereto, and (5) certify their determinations and their count of all votes and ballots. At the stockholders' meeting, §231 further requires that the date and time for the opening and closing of the polls be announced and provides that after the closing of the polls no new proxies or votes, or revisions thereof, may be accepted by the inspectors, except with court approval. This provision was a response to a management tactic of reopening the polls at the end of a meeting if it could induce some shareholders to switch their votes in a close election.

Decisions of the inspectors of elections can, of course, be appealed to court. One recurrent problem is the phenomenon of "broker overvotes" — that is, a proxy submitted by a major broker-dealer, holding securities in "street name" for its clients, in which the number of shares voted exceeds the number held of record by the broker. Typically, this results from beneficial holders responding to a succession of proxy mailings by executing multiple proxies, which the brokerage clerks incorrectly tally by counting such successive votes as the votes of additional shares. It once was the practice, when such an overvote occurred, that the inspectors of elections would telephone the brokerage house for clarification and, based on such oral advice, would recount the vote. However, this informal practice was invalidated by a 1989 Delaware decision, Concord Financial Group, Inc. v. Tri-State Motor Transit Co. of Delaware, 567 A.2d 1 (Del. Ch. 1989), which found that inspectors had no authority to consider "extrinsic evidence" beyond the face of the proxy or the books of the corporation. As a result, a broker overvote meant that all the shares covered by the broker's proxy could not be voted in the election—a seemingly Draconian result. In response, Delaware added §231 to its General Corporation Law, which requires corporations listed on a stock exchange or Nasdaq, or having 2,000 or more shareholders of record, to appoint inspectors of elections to tabulate the votes cast at shareholder meetings. Section 231(d) then specifies the information that inspectors may consider in determining the validity of proxies and ballots, and permits them to examine "other reliable information" in addition to the proxies and the corporation's books and records for the limited purpose of resolving bank and broker overvotes.

5. STOCKHOLDER CONSENTS

Stockholder voting occurs either at an annual or at a special meeting or pursuant to a newly important procedure by which written consents are solicited from shareholders without a meeting:

Delaware General Corporation Law (2007)

Sec. 228. *Consent of stockholders in lieu of meeting.* (a) Unless otherwise provided in the certificate of incorporation, any action required by this chapter to be taken at any annual or special meeting of stockholders of a corporation, or any action which may be taken at any annual or special meeting of such stockholders, may be taken without a meeting, without prior notice and without a vote, if a consent or consents in writing, setting forth the action so taken, shall be signed by the holders of outstanding stock having not less than the minimum number of votes that would be necessary to authorize or take such action at a meeting at which all shares entitled to vote thereon were present and voted and shall be delivered to the corporation by delivery to its registered office in this State, its principal place of business, or an officer or agent of the corporation having custody of the book in which proceedings of meetings of stockholders are recorded. Delivery made to the corporation's registered office shall be by hand or by certified or registered mail, return receipt requested. . . .

(c) Every written consent shall bear the date of signature of each stockholder or member who signs the consent, and no written consent shall be effective to take the corporate action referred to therein unless, within sixty days of the earliest dated consent delivered in the manner required by this Section to the corporation, written consents signed by a sufficient number of holders or members to take action are delivered to the corporation. . . .

(e) Prompt notice of the taking of the corporate action without a meeting by less than unanimous written consent shall be given to those stockholders . . . who have not consented in writing and who, if the action had been taken at a meeting, would have been entitled to notice of the meeting. . . .

Datapoint Corp. v. Plaza Securities Co.
496 A.2d 1031 (Del. 1985)

HORSEY, J.: This appeal by Datapoint Corporation from an order of the Court of Chancery, preliminarily enjoining its enforcement of a bylaw adopted by Datapoint's board of directors, presents an issue of first impression in Delaware: whether a bylaw designed to limit the taking of corporate action by written shareholder consent in lieu of a stockholders' meeting conflicts with 8 Del. C. §228, and thereby is invalid. . . .

In December of 1984, Asher B. Edelman, general partner of both plaintiffs and beneficial owner of more than 10% of Datapoint's stock, advised the latter's chairman that he was interested in acquiring control of Datapoint. However, Datapoint's board of directors was opposed to this, and on January 11, 1985, when Edelman submitted a written proposal to acquire Datapoint, the offer was rejected the same day.

On January 24, Edelman renewed his offer and stated that if it were rejected he would consider the solicitation of consents from shareholders. Datapoint's composite certificate of incorporation then (and now) lacks any provision relating to the solicitation of shareholder consents under §228. However, the next day Texas counsel to Datapoint recommended that the Datapoint board adopt a bylaw amendment to regulate consents. Counsel stated, "While the resolution will not prevent a hostile take-over, it will provide management with additional time to explore alternatives."

On January 28, Datapoint's directors, meeting telephonically, unanimously adopted bylaw amendments (the "January bylaw") which the Chancellor later found to be "designed to establish a procedure to govern any attempt to take corporate action on Datapoint's behalf by written shareholder consent."

On January 30, 1985, Edelman withdrew his offer to buy Datapoint and announced his intention to solicit shareholder consents for removal of the board and the election of his own candidates. On February 5, plaintiffs commenced this action in the Court of Chancery for preliminary and permanent injunctive relief against enforcement of Datapoint's January bylaw amendment.

In response to plaintiffs' suit, Datapoint's board, on February 8, filed a counterclaim for declaratory judgment that the January bylaw was valid and to enjoin plaintiffs from violating the bylaw. On February 12, Datapoint's board amended its January bylaw on the recommendation, among others, of Datapoint's investment advisor, Kidder Peabody. Kidder's merger and acquisition specialist advised Datapoint's board of the need of "at least 60 days . . . to achieve a transaction or series of transactions which would best serve the interests of all of Datapoint's shareholders." Datapoint's February bylaw provided, in part, that:

> (1) No action by shareholder consent could take place until the 45th day after the established record date;
> (2) That a record date should be fixed of not more than (or less than) 15 days after receipt of a shareholder's notice of intent to solicit consents, unless requested by the shareholder; and
> (3) No shareholder consent action would become effective until the final termination of any proceeding which may have been commenced in the Court of Chancery of the State of Delaware or any other court of competent jurisdiction for an adjudication

of any legal issues incident to determining the validity of the consents, unless and until such court shall have determined that such proceedings are not being pursued expeditiously and in good faith.

On February 19, Datapoint's board, in response to Edelman's notice of intent to solicit shareholder consents, set March 4 as the record date and April 18 as the "action" date for counting shareholder consents submitted under §228. On February 28, Datapoint filed suit in the United States District Court for the Western District of Texas to invalidate any consents obtained by plaintiffs. The suit thereby triggered the litigation "hold" mechanism of the February bylaw.

On March 5, 1985, the Court of Chancery granted plaintiffs a preliminary injunction enjoining defendant Datapoint from enforcing the February bylaw. . . .

On appeal, defendant asserts essentially a three-step argument in support of its contention that the Chancellor committed legal error in enjoining the enforcement of Datapoint's February bylaw. First, defendant contends that the Court erred in construing §228 as not permitting the consent solicitation procedure — as to which §228 is silent — to be regulated by bylaw. Second, defendant argues that the Court erred in construing §228 as requiring a consent accomplished thereunder to be put into effect immediately and without any review of its legality being permitted. Defendant then makes a derivative argument which assumes the correctness of its first two contentions. It argues that the February bylaw constitutes a reasonable regulation of a shareholder §228 solicitation. Defendant contends that the "delay and review" features of its bylaw are designed to prevent the possibility of "midnight raids" on an uninformed electorate. However, a further objective of the February bylaw's 45-day waiting period (actually 60 days in the aggregate), defendant concedes, is to permit management to solicit its own proxies on the subject.

As to Datapoint's first contention, defendant argues that §228's introductory language ("Unless otherwise provided in the certificate of incorporation") means that the right of shareholders to act by written consent in lieu of meeting may only be denied shareholders by a charter provision; and that the Chancellor erroneously construed the clause to mean that the regulation of shareholder consent action may not be imposed by a board of directors through the enactment of bylaws. Since bylaws are the proper means for implementing the internal regulation of corporations, defendant reasons that corporate elections, including those accomplished under §228, are proper subjects for regulation by bylaw.

Relating its February bylaw to general Delaware law, defendant argues that Datapoint's bylaw represents reasonable internal corporate regulation which is authorized under §109(b) and not inconsistent with §228. The Chancellor's conclusion to the contrary is said to be counter to long-standing principles established in Gow v. Consolidated Coppermines Corp., Del. Ch., 165 A. 136 (1933); 8 W. Fletcher, Cyclopedia of the Law of Private Corporations, §4208 (rev. perm. ed. 1982).

Plaintiffs respond: one, that §228 does not countenance *any* restriction or delay in the consummation of a valid §228 consent action; two, that §228's introductory language, "Unless otherwise provided in the certificate of incorporation," must be construed as barring any board bylaw regulating a §228 action; and three, that, in any event, Datapoint's February bylaw clearly violates §228 by imposing unreasonable delays upon the consummation of a shareholder consent action. . . .

The determinative question is whether Datapoint's February bylaw conflicts with the letter and intent of §228. The Chancellor found a clear conflict; and we agree with the Court's construction of §228 as it applies to the bylaw before us.

Confining our ruling to this bylaw, we find it clearly in conflict with the letter and intent of §228. Section 228 contains no language suggesting that action accomplished by stockholders through written consent "without a meeting, without prior notice and without a vote" may be lawfully deferred or thwarted on grounds not relating to the legal sufficiency of the consents obtained. . . .

Datapoint's bylaw is not designed simply to defer consummation of shareholder action by consent in lieu of meeting until a ministerial-type review of the sufficiency of the consents has been performed by duly qualified and objective inspectors. Instead, the bylaw imposes an arbitrary delay upon shareholder action in lieu of meeting by postponing accomplishment of such action until 60 days after the corporation's receipt of a shareholder's notice of intent to solicit consents. By delaying the effective date of shareholder consents until the corporation's secretary (or inspectors) determines the validity of those consents and by postponing that determination until 45 days after the record date as set by §213, the bylaw circumvents §228, under which action taken is to be effective when sufficient consents are signed.

This delay is not only arbitrary, it is unreasonable. For the underlying intent of the bylaw is to provide the incumbent board with *time* to seek to defeat the shareholder action by management's solicitation of its own proxies, or revocations of outstanding shareholder consents. Defendant concedes that the purpose of the delay provisions of Datapoint's bylaw is to give management an opportunity to distribute "opposing solicitation material." Moreover, the bylaw's further provision staying the effective date of any shareholder consent action until termination of any lawsuits challenging such action effectively places within the incumbent board the power to stultify, if not nullify, the shareholders' statutory right. Such a result can only be found to be "repugnant to the statute" which the bylaw is intended to serve, not master. . . .

Although we find defendant's bylaw to be invalid, we do not hold that §228 must be construed as barring a board of directors from adopting a bylaw which would impose minimal essential provisions for ministerial review of the validity of the action taken by shareholder consent. However, defendant's bylaw, as adopted, is so pervasive as to intrude upon fundamental stockholder rights guaranteed by statute. Therefore, the decision of the Court of Chancery, granting a preliminary injunction against the enforcement of the bylaw, is affirmed.

Datapoint distinguished. The clear hint in *Datapoint* that §228 would tolerate a bylaw intended to permit merely "a ministerial-type review of the sufficiency of the consents" was followed up in Empire of Carolina, Inc. v. Deltona Corp., 514 A.2d 1091 (Del. 1986), by a further restriction on §228's apparent impact: the board may sometimes set a record date for shareholder consents under Del. Gen. Corp. Law §213 (2007), even if the resulting postponement of the shareholder action allows a critical new block of shares to be issued. The practical importance of this holding is illustrated by the facts of *Deltona*. There, the acquiring firm, Empire of Carolina, had acquired 29 percent of Deltona's stock when, on October 7, 1985, it filed with Deltona a Schedule 13D notice under the Williams Act, which indicated its intention to solicit consents to remove the Deltona board. It also executed its own consent (reflecting its 29 percent ownership) to the removal of the Deltona board. Three days later, Deltona's board met and set a record date of November 18 and, before that record date, agreed to sell a controlling block of its stock to a friendly third party (the proverbial "white knight"), with the result that Empire's nearly controlling position was lost. The statutory issue involved the interaction of Del. Gen. Corp. Law §§213 and 228. Section 213(b) then provided that the record date for a shareholder consent vote might be specified by the directors, but if no such date was specified, "[t]he record date for determining stockholders entitled to express consent without a meeting, when no prior action by the board is necessary, shall be on the day on which the first written consent is *expressed*." (Emphasis added.) Empire of Carolina argued unsuccessfully that the record date should thus be October 7, when it delivered its written consent, but the Delaware Supreme Court held that §213 "vests primary authority to fix a record date with the board of directors." It further found that consent is not "expressed" for purposes of §213 simply by the execution of the consent; rather, the soliciting shareholder must "communicate to the corporation the date that the first written consent has been executed and the substance of the proposed corporate action to be taken." This was necessary, it said, to avoid "mischievous results," including the backdating of documents.

More important for future cases, the Delaware Supreme Court said that *Datapoint* did "not address the issue presented in this case — whether a board of directors acting pursuant to Section 213(a) may, in the exercise of business judgment, set a record date that would in any degree delay shareholder action by written consent." In holding that a board may do so, it distinguished *Datapoint* as a case in which the board imposed an "arbitrary delay."

Following *Deltona,* Delaware amended §213(b) to provide that the record date for shareholder consents should be the date fixed by the corporation's board of directors,

> which record date shall not precede the date upon which the resolution fixing the record date is adopted by the board of directors, and which date shall not be more than ten days after the date upon which the resolution fixing the record date is adopted by the board of directors. If no record date has been fixed by the board of directors, the record date . . . shall be the first date on which a signed written consent setting forth the action taken or proposed to be taken is delivered to the corporation by delivery to its registered office in this state

or to the corporation's principal place of business. As a result, if a stockholder quickly assembles 51 percent of the corporation's voting stock and then executes and delivers a written consent clearly removing the board, the board seemingly may not respond by setting a later record date (and issuing new shares in the interim). See Midway Airlines, Inc. v. Carlson, 628 F. Supp. 244 (D. Del. 1985). But suppose on learning that a bidder has filed a Schedule 13D under the Williams Act indicating that it owns 10 percent of the corporation, the target board adopts a bylaw specifying a ten-day record date after notice to it of an intent to solicit consents and justifies this bylaw as necessary for a ministerial review to determine the sufficiency of the consents. Does amended §213(b) permit this? If not, how may the board act before the insurgent establishes the record date by delivery of a written consent to the corporation? Remember that the insurgent shareholder will need to file its own proxy statement if it wishes to solicit more than ten other shareholders.

D. *PROXY CONTEST EXPENSES*

Rosenfeld v. Fairchild Engine & Airplane Corp.
309 N.Y. 168, 128 N.E.2d 291 (1955)

FROESSEL, J.: In a stockholder's derivative action brought by plaintiff, an attorney, who owns 25 out of the company's over 2,300,000 shares, he seeks to compel the return of $261,522, paid out of the corporate treasury to reimburse both sides in a proxy contest for their expenses. The Appellate Division, 284 App. Div. 201, 132 N.Y.S.2d 273, has unanimously affirmed a judgment of an Official Referee, Sup., 116 N.Y.S.2d 840, dismissing plaintiff's complaint on the merits, and we agree. . . .

Of the amount in controversy $106,000 was spent out of corporate funds by the old board of directors while still in office in defense of their position in said contest; $28,000 were paid to the old board by the new board after the change of management following the proxy contest, to compensate the former directors for such of the remaining expenses of their unsuccessful defense as the new board found was fair and reasonable; payment of $127,000, representing reimbursement of expenses to members of the prevailing group, was expressly ratified by a 16 to 1 majority vote of the stockholders.

. . . The Appellate Division found that the difference between plaintiff's group and the old board "went deep into the policies of the company," and that among these Ward's contract was one of the "main points of contention." The Official Referee found that the controversy "was based on an understandable difference in policy between the two groups, at the very bottom of which was the Ward employment contract."

By way of contrast with the findings here, in Lawyers' Advertising Co. v. Consolidated Ry., Lighting & Refrigerating Co., 187 N.Y. 395, at page 399, 80 N.E. 199, at page 200, which was an action to recover for the cost of publishing newspaper notices not authorized by the board of directors, it was expressly found that the proxy contest there involved was "by one faction in its contest with another for the control of the corporation . . . a contest for the perpetuation of their offices and control." We there said by way of dicta that under *such* circumstances the publication of certain notices on behalf of the management faction was not a corporate expenditure which the directors had the power to authorize.

Other jurisdictions and our own lower courts have held that management may look to the corporate treasury for the reasonable expenses of soliciting proxies to defend its position in a bona fide policy contest. . . .

It should be noted that plaintiff does not argue that the aforementioned sums were fraudulently extracted from the corporation; indeed, his counsel conceded that "the charges were fair and reasonable," but denied "they were legal charges which may be reimbursed for." This is therefore not a case where a stockholder challenges specific items, which, on examination, the trial court may find unwarranted, excessive or otherwise improper. Had plaintiff made such objections here, the trial court would have been required to examine the items challenged.

If directors of a corporation may not in good faith incur reasonable and proper expenses in soliciting proxies in these days of giant corporations with vast numbers of stockholders, the corporate business might be seriously interfered with because of stockholder indifference and the difficulty of procuring a quorum, where there is no contest. In the event of a proxy contest, if the directors may not freely answer the challenges of outside groups and in good faith defend their actions with respect to corporate policy for the information of the stockholders, they and the corporation may be at the mercy of persons seeking to wrest control for their own purposes, so long as such persons have ample funds to conduct a proxy contest. The test is clear. When the directors act in good faith in a contest over policy, they have the right to incur reasonable and proper expenses for solicitation of proxies and in defense of their corporate policies, and are not obliged to sit idly by. The courts are entirely competent to pass upon their bona fides in any given case, as well as the nature of their expenditures when duly challenged.

It is also our view that the members of the so-called new group could be reimbursed by the corporation for their expenditures in this contest by affirmative vote of the stockholders. With regard to these ultimately successful contestants, as the Appellate Division below has noted, there was, of course, "no duty . . . to set forth the facts, with corresponding obligation of the corporation to pay for such expense." However, where a majority of the stockholders chose—in this case by a vote of 16 to 1—to reimburse the successful contestants for achieving the very end sought and voted for by them as owners of the corporation, we see no reason to deny the effect of their ratification nor to hold the corporate body powerless to determine how its own moneys shall be spent.

The rule then which we adopt is simply this: In a contest over policy, as compared to a purely personal power contest, corporate directors have the right to make reasonable and proper expenditures, subject to the scrutiny of the courts when duly challenged, from the corporate treasury for the purpose of persuading the stockholders of the correctness of their position and soliciting their support for policies which the directors believe, in all good faith, are in the best interests of the corporation. The stockholders, moreover, have the right to reimburse successful contestants for the reasonable and bona fide expenses incurred by them in any such policy contest, subject to like court scrutiny. That is not to say, however, that corporate directors can, under any circumstances, disport themselves in a proxy contest with the corporation's moneys to an unlimited extent. Where it is established that such moneys have been spent for personal power, individual gain or private advantage, and not in the belief that such expenditures are in the best interests of the stockholders and the corporation, or where the fairness and reasonableness of the amounts allegedly expended are duly and successfully challenged, the courts will not hesitate to disallow them. . . .

CONWAY, C.J., and BURKE, J., concur with FROESSEL, J.; DESMOND, J., concurs in part in a separate opinion; VAN VOORHIS, J., dissents in an opinion in which DYE and FULD, JJ., concur.

Judgment affirmed.

---

1. *Corporate reimbursement as a solution to the free rider problem.* Given that there are typically inadequate incentives for an individual shareholder to undertake a proxy contest to oppose management, a legal rule requiring the corporation to reimburse successful insurgents may be a sensible way to "tax" other shareholders on a proportionate basis and thus solve the "free rider" problem. But would it alone be effective? The individual shareholder still faces uncertainty about the prospect for success. If the shareholder believes there is a 50 percent chance of success, a 20 percent shareholder (who is risk neutral) would logically expend up to 10 percent of the expected total gain to all shareholders from defeating management's proposal. Of course, the shareholder would have a much greater incentive if the law reimbursed even unsuccessful insurgents. But such a rule might create perverse incentives of its own. Would lawyers bring frivolous proxy contests in order to be awarded legal fees? Could they find nominal clients with small investments in the corporation to "hire" them on a contingent fee basis? Is there a possible compromise? Consider the following proposal:

> [R]ecovery [should] be allowed on the basis of the following formula (with X representing non-management expenses allowed):
>
> $$\frac{\text{Management expenses allowed}}{\text{Votes secured by management}} = \frac{X}{\text{Votes secured by non-management}}$$
>
> but in no event allow more than actual expenses.

Frank Emerson & Franklin Latcham, Shareholder Democracy 142 (1954). For further views on legislative and administrative implementation of opposition reimbursement, see id. at 147, Comment, Proxy Contests: Corporate Reimbursement of Insurgents' Expenses, 23 U. Chi. L. Rev. 682 (1956).

Even if it is believed that only successful insurgents should receive reimbursement, should it be necessary that the board or shareholders authorize reimbursement? Should a successful insurgent instead be able to apply to a court for reimbursement? In Grodetsky v. McCrory Corp., 267 N.Y.S.2d 356 (Sup. Ct. 1966), this issue was posed where a corporation entered into a contract to sell its assets, which contract required shareholder ratification. A major supplier to the corporation opposed the sale, which adversely affected it, and assigned one of its staff attorneys to conduct a proxy solicitation to defeat the proposed sale. On the success of this proxy campaign, the attorney sued the corporation for $1,750,000, the claimed value of his services, on the theory that his activities averted a $35,000,000 loss to the corporation. The court held it was without power to authorize an award, but could only pass on the reasonableness of an award, if any, voted by the shareholders. Is this rule sound? Does it conflict with the general rule that the court can award attorney's fees (without board action) to a successful plantiff in a derivative action? See Chapter VIII, infra.

2. *Reimbursement in practice.* As noted at page 545 supra, Walter Hewlett, a director of Hewlett-Packard Company, spent approximately $32 million of his own funds in 2002 in seeking to defeat the proposed merger of Hewlett-Packard with Compaq. Nearly 50 percent of the shareholders did vote against the merger, which was approved by a very narrow margin. Should Mr. Hewlett receive 50 percent of his reasonable expenses? Current law would entitle him to reimbursement only if he were successful and the corporation decided in its discretion to reimburse him. Do you think that the Hewlett-Packard board would be likely to favor such reimbursement if he had been successful in defeating the merger proposal? Could he directly appeal to the shareholders for a shareholder vote approving his reimbursement? This would seemingly violate the standard rule that the business and affairs of the corporation are to be managed by, or under the direction of, its board of directors. Hence, as a practical matter, reimbursement is assured only when the insurgent wins control of the board. This makes reimbursement unlikely under current law in the case of proxy fights over "issues," as opposed to contests for control of the board.

E. SPECIAL VOTING SYSTEMS: CUMULATIVE, CLASS, AND SUPERMAJORITY VOTING

This section examines special strategies to enhance the voting power of minority shareholders.

1. CUMULATIVE VOTING

Cumulative voting is a system of voting for the election of directors that is intended to give minority shareholders representation on the board by allowing them to concentrate their votes on a limited number of nominees. The following hypothetical illustrates the operation of the system: Corporation has 99 shares outstanding; *A* owns 59; *B* owns 40; three directors are to be elected. Under a system of straight voting, each share carries one vote for each director to be elected. *B* may cast 40 votes for each of *B*'s three candidates, but her 120 votes may do her no good because *A* may cast 59 votes for each of *A*'s three candidates and defeat *B*'s slate.

Cumulative voting permits a shareholder to cast all his votes for a single candidate or to spread his votes among several candidates. It gives *B* the option of casting her 120 votes (three directors times 40 shares) for one, two, or three candidates. *B* may cast 40 votes each for three, 60 votes each for two, or all 120 votes for one (or any other way that she desires). *A* has the same options with his 177 votes (three directors times 59 shares). But if *A* casts these votes for three different candidates, 59 votes for each, *B* may defeat one of *A*'s choices by casting all 120 votes for one candidate, or she may defeat two of *A*'s choices by casting 60 votes for each of two of *B*'s candidates. *A* may protect his majority by casting his 177 votes for only two candidates, giving 90 to one and 87 to the other, but then *A* cannot prevent *B* from choosing one director.

A formula for determining the minimum number of shares required to elect one director is[27]

$$\text{Number of Shares Required} > \frac{\text{Number of Shares Voting}}{\text{Number of Directors to Be Elected} + 1}$$

Thus, if there are 100 shares voting at the meeting and three directors to be elected, a holder of 26 shares is assured of electing one director by casting all 78 votes (three times 26) for a single candidate.

How many shares would be required to elect two directors if five directors are to be elected and 100 shares vote?

Generally, cumulative voting is optional with the corporation. See N.Y. Bus. Corp. Law §618 (2007); Del. Gen. Corp. Law §214 (2007); RMBCA §7.28 (2002). A few statutes make it mandatory, unless the certificate of incorporation expressly cancels it. See Pa. Bus. Corp. Law §1758 (2006). This is one of the items that must be on an attorney's checklist to consider in incorporating a corporation in an unfamiliar jurisdiction.

a. Evasions

When cumulative voting is mandatory, various techniques can be employed by corporate draftsmen to dilute its effect: (1) "staggered" terms for the board members; (2) a provision authorizing removal of directors by majority vote; (3) a reduction in the number of directors (which thereby increases the size of the minority block necessary to secure board representation); or (4) use of non-voting stock or stock with limited or weighted voting rights. See Diamond v. Parkersburg-Aetna Corp., 146 W. Va. 543, 122 S.E.2d 436 (1961). In Bohannan v. Corporation Commission, 313 P.2d 379 (Ariz. 1957), the Arizona Corporation Commission rejected proposed articles of incorporation that sought to establish a nine-person board that would be divided into three classes, each serving a staggered term, on the ground that this frustrated the intent behind cumulative voting. In effect,

---

27. Where fractional shares are not voted, the formula can be simplified as follows:

$$\text{Number of Shares Required} = \frac{\text{Number of Shares Voting}}{\text{Number of Directors to Be Elected} + 1}$$
$$+ 1 \text{ Share or fraction thereof necessary to produce}$$
$$\text{the next highest whole number}$$

Thus, if 99 shares are voted and three seats are to be filled, the number of shares required to elect one director is 99 divided by 4, or 24.75, plus one-quarter share (or 25 shares in all).

In planning strategy prior to an election, one must estimate the number of shares that will vote or, to be conservative, use the number of outstanding voting shares. Because the minority shareholder can seldom estimate precisely the number that will be voted, such a shareholder may wish to redistribute his or her votes after the initial vote is announced. Can this be done? Although the matter has seldom been litigated, some decisions have allowed shareholders to change their vote in such situations up until the final tally is officially announced. See Ballantine, Corporation 405 (rev. ed. 1946); Edward Aranow & Herbert Einhorn, Proxy Contests for Corporate Control 338 (2d ed. 1968). A number of interesting mathematical issues arise in the construction of voting formulas under cumulative voting. For reviews, see Amihai Glazer, Debra Glazer & Bernard Grofman, Cumulative Voting in Corporate Elections: Introducing Strategy into the Equation, 35 S.C. L. Rev. 295 (1984); Lewis Mills, The Mathematics of Cumulative Voting, 1968 Duke L.J. 28; Arthur Cole Jr., Legal and Mathematical Aspects of Cumulative Voting, 2 S.C. L.Q. 225 (1949).

staggering the terms so that only one of these classes is elected each year forces a minority stockholder to be able to cumulate sufficient votes to elect one-third of the board, rather than one-ninth. Nonetheless, the court upheld the provision, as have most other courts. Often, the cumulative voting statute will require a minimum number of directors in each class, because a three-class board with one director in each would effectively negate cumulative voting. Generally, state statutes permit no more than three classes of directors, thus requiring that at least one-third come up for election each year. But see N.Y. Bus. Corp. Law §704 (2007) (four classes permitted).

b. Cumulative Voting and the Removal of Directors

A number of statutes permit the removal of directors by a vote of the shareholders, with or without cause. Should a majority be allowed to remove, without cause, a director who was elected by the minority through cumulative voting? See In re Rogers Imports, Inc., 202 Misc. 761, 116 N.Y.S.2d 106 (Sup. Ct. 1952). Should a majority be allowed to remove, without cause, a director who was elected by the majority if a minority that did not originally vote for him now want him to remain on the board? Would it make a difference if the state has a statute or constitutional provision making cumulative voting mandatory?

Commonly, cumulative voting statutes provide that a director elected by cumulative voting may not be removed "when the votes cast against his removal would be sufficient to elect him if voted cumulatively at an election at which the same total number of votes were cast and the entire board, or the entire class of directors of which he is a member, were then being elected." N.Y. Bus. Corp. Law §706(c) (2007). Could shareholders evade this restriction by first classifying the board and then removing the director?

Should a majority be allowed to remove the minority's board representative(s) for cause? Campbell v. Loew's, Inc., 36 Del. Ch. 563, 573, 134 A.2d 852, 858 (Ch. 1957). Should notice and a hearing be provided? Should the decision to remove be subject to judicial review? If so, what should the scope of review be? "If a fair hearing is required and if judicial review amounts to a trial de novo, any conflict between removal for cause and the cumulative-voting policy is minimized. Nevertheless, it is true that if a minority director is removed, any conventional replacement procedure will reduce minority representation. This problem might be partially solved by legislation . . . providing, for example, that a replacement be chosen only by those shareholders who had previously voted for the election of the removed director." 71 Harv. L. Rev. 1154, 1157 (1958).

c. Pros and Cons of Cumulative Voting

Cumulative voting is basically an attempt to give a minority class or group a "window into the boardroom." There has been a long-standing debate about whether it succeeds, at least well enough to deserve mandatory status. Opponents have long argued that cumulative voting only fosters dissension and forces the majority faction to hold a "dress rehearsal" meeting the day before the scheduled meeting to discuss issues without the presence of the minority faction. Proponents respond that the board should be an "open forum" and that cumulative voting desirably augments minority shareholder influence. See Sell & Fuge, Impact of Classified Corporate Directorates on the Constitutional Right of Cumulative Voting, 17 U. Pitt. L. Rev. 151, 157-158 (1956).

Historically,

> cumulative voting took hold in nineteenth and early twentieth century American corporate law for two reasons: an ideological belief in minority representation in legislative bodies, which was carried over to the boards of directors, and a functional concern about the vulnerability to exploitation by overreaching majorities, especially in light of the difficulties that public shareholders faced in obtaining information about the firm. By the 1950s, the original functional explanations had lost most of their force . . . [in part because of the passage of the federal securities laws and their mandatory disclosure system].

See Jeffrey Gordon, Institutions as Relational Investors: A New Look at Cumulative Voting, 94 Colum. L. Rev. 124, 166 (1994) (finding that only six states (Arizona, Kentucky, Nebraska, North Dakota, South Dakota, and West Virginia) then had mandatory cumulative voting requirements). Id. at 146.

Still, some commentators believe that there is a new justification for mandatory cumulative voting. Professor Gordon argues: "Because of the recent changes in the ownership structure of large public firms, cumulative voting has a new role to play in corporate governance: it can provide access to the boardroom for activist institutions, who will serve as virtual representatives for other public shareholders." Id. at 128-129. Still, do institutional investors really need or want such a mandatory legal weapon? Much depends on whether the election of a representative to a corporate board by institutional investors will make them potentially liable as "controlling persons" or subject them to "short-swing" liability under §16(b) of the Securities Exchange Act of 1934. See Chapter V.D.2.

d. Cumulative Voting in Practice

A 1973 survey of 855 companies reported as follows:

> [O]nly a minority of the companies in this report — and these include many of the largest companies in many different industries — provide for this type of voting in their bylaws or certificate of incorporation. And very few stockholders use the privilege even when it is available. . . .
>
> . . . Almost all the companies whose stockholders are entitled to vote cumulatively report that the procedure has not been used at all in the last five years, or that its effect has been negligible. With almost no exceptions, management slates have been elected regularly by overwhelming majorities. A typical experience: "Cumulative voting has been meaningless. The entire management slate has always been reelected with 80% or more of shares voting and with more than 99% of those voting for the management slate." Another company reports: "In the past five years, stockholders at the meeting have occasionally declared that they would cumulate their votes for and against certain directors. In each case, the reasons given were valid: the directors in question did not own stock, or the stockholders were opposed to the staggered election of directors, or they did not agree with certain positions taken by the board. The effect was to add or subtract a few thousand votes at most to or from the votes cast for

certain directors out of an average aggregate vote of one million for each director. In other words, there was no practical effect."

The Conference Board, Corporate Directorship Practices: Membership and Committees of the Board 6 (1973).

Conversely, a more recent stock price study shows that when cumulative voting is eliminated, stock prices decline by a statistically significant, but modest, amount. See Sanjai Bhagat & James Brickley, Cumulative Voting: The Value of Minority Shareholder Voting Rights, 27 J.L. & Econ. 339, 353-355 (1984). The same result was observed when a corporation that had cumulative voting classified its board (as in *Bohannan*) to reduce its impact. What could explain this result if cumulative voting is generally not very meaningful? One possibility is that shareholders may see such action as a telltale signal about future managerial intentions; in this light, the sample of firms eliminating cumulative voting may be a skewed one.

2. CLASS VOTING

Suppose a corporation sells a class of preferred stock to investors, who will receive a 6 percent annual dividend that must be paid prior to any dividend on the common stock. Later, suppose the corporation proposes to create a new class of prior preferred stock, which would be senior to this existing class. Assume that the effect of creating this new senior class would be to deplete the funds available to pay dividends on the original preferred stock. This seems an unfair surprise, but what rights do the preferred shareholders have if either (a) their preferred stock is non-voting (as typically is the case with respect to senior securities) or (b) even if voting, it can be outvoted by the common stock? American corporate law provides a variety of remedies to protect shareholders against such an adverse alteration of the corporate contract, including an appraisal remedy and judicial review for fairness. See Chapter IX. One of the most important of these remedies is class voting, which requires that the class of shareholders adversely affected by the change approve it by a majority vote.

New York Business Corporation Law (2007)

Sec. 804. *Class voting on amendment.* (a) Notwithstanding any provision in the certificate of incorporation, the holders of shares of a class shall be entitled to vote and to vote as a class upon the authorization of an amendment and, in addition to the authorization of the amendment by a majority of the votes of all outstanding shares entitled to vote thereon, the amendment shall be authorized by a majority of the votes of all outstanding shares of the class when a proposed amendment would:

(1) Exclude or limit their right to vote on any matter, except as such right may be limited by voting rights given to new shares then being authorized of any existing or new class or series.

(2) Change their shares under subparagraphs (b)(10), (11), or (12) of section 801 (Right to amend certificate of incorporation) or provide that their shares may be converted into shares of any other class or into shares of any other series of the same class, or alter the terms or conditions upon which their shares are

convertible or change the shares issuable upon conversion of their shares, if such action would adversely affect such holders, or

(3) Subordinate their rights, by authorizing shares having preferences which would be in any respect superior to their rights.

(b) If any proposed amendment referred to in paragraph (a) would adversely affect the rights of the holders of shares of only one or more series of any class, but not the entire class, then only the holders of those series whose rights would be affected shall be considered a separate class for the purposes of this section.

Sec. 801. *Right to amend certificate of incorporation.* (a) A corporation may amend its certificate of incorporation, from time to time, in any and as many respects as may be desired, if such amendment contains only such provisions as might be lawfully contained in an original certificate of incorporation filed at the time of making such amendment.

(b) In particular, and without limitation upon such general power of amendment, a corporation may amend its certificate of incorporation, from time to time, so as: . . .

(10) To reduce the par value of any authorized shares of any class with par value, whether issued or unissued.

(11) To change any authorized shares, with or without par value, whether issued or unissued, into a different number of shares of the same class or into the same or a different number of shares of any one or more classes or any series thereof, either with or without par value.

(12) To fix, change or abolish the designation of any authorized class or any series thereof or any of the relative rights, preferences and limitations of any shares of any authorized class or any series thereof, whether issued or unissued, including any provisions in respect of any undeclared dividends, whether or not cumulative or accrued, or the redemption of any shares, or any sinking fund for the redemption or purchase of any shares, or any preemptive right to acquire shares or other securities.

a. Is Coercion Still Possible?

Although class voting gives the senior class a veto power, it is far from clear that this right will always fully protect that class. Coercion may still be possible if the common shareholders who elect the board can suspend the payment of dividends, knowing that the senior class is more likely to require current dividends than the residual claimants. Although the preferred stock will typically be "cumulative" (meaning that unpaid dividends accumulate as "arrearages" that must be paid in full before the common can receive any dividends), usually no interest is paid on arrearages, and the time of their eventual receipt, if ever, is speculative. This uncertainty will typically depress the market value of the preferred stock, once arrearages arise, given the usual assumption that the purchasers of senior securities are relatively risk-averse. Another potential source of vulnerability arises because the ownership of the common and preferred classes can overlap; if a majority of the preferred is owned by the common shareholders (or their affiliates), the latter might improve their overall economic position by voting to exploit the preferred class, even though they themselves are its predominant members. For these reasons, some state statutes also provide an appraisal remedy in tandem with class voting, so that there is a right to exit the corporation at a fair value as well as a right to veto adverse changes.

b. Ambiguities

The scope of class voting is often uncertain and has been only infrequently tested. For example, N.Y. Bus. Corp. Law §804, page 602 supra, will most typically be triggered by a certificate amendment that falls within §801(b)(12). After re-reading that section, consider the following hypothetical: A corporation has a class of preferred stock outstanding and, to protect this class's senior claim on dividends, a charter provision restricts the payment of dividends on the underlying common stock if common stock equity drops below a specified level (25 percent of total capitalization and surplus). If the common shareholders sought to eliminate or reduce this provision by amending the certificate, would the corporation have modified "any of the relative rights, preferences and limitations" of the preferred stock under §801(b)(12) so as to trigger §804? Note that the deleted provision by its express terms restricted only the common stock. See In re New York Hanseatic Corp., 103 N.Y.S.2d 698 (Sup. Ct. 1951) (holding that the phrase "relative rights" in §801(b)(12) should be construed to reach provisions clearly establishing the relative position of the two classes by subordinating one class to another).

c. Mergers

Whatever can be done by a charter amendment can also be accomplished by a merger that merges the existing corporation into a newly formed "shell" corporation whose newly drafted charter contains the desired provision. For a careful review of the judicial reaction to this technique, see Bove v. Community Hotel Corp., 249 A.2d 89 (R.I. 1969). Thus, some states also require class voting on a proposed merger, even by non-voting shares, if the certificate of incorporation of the surviving corporation "would contain any provision which is not contained in the certificate of incorporation of the corporation and which, if contained in an amendment to the certificate of incorporation, would entitle the holders of such class . . . to vote and to vote as a separate class thereon . . ." N.Y. Bus. Corp. Law §903(a)(2) (2007).

3. SUPERMAJORITY VOTING

Revised Model Business Corporation Act (2002)

Sec. 7.27. *Greater quorum or voting requirements.* (a) The articles of incorporation may provide for a greater quorum or voting requirement for shareholders (or voting groups of shareholders) than is provided for by this Act.

(b) An amendment to the articles of incorporation that adds, changes, or deletes a greater quorum or voting requirement must meet the same quorum requirement and be adopted by the same vote and voting groups required to take action under the quorum and voting requirements then in effect or proposed to be adopted, whichever is greater.

Section §7.27 essentially requires a similar supermajority to adopt a supermajority. Thus, it would take a 90 percent vote of shareholders to adopt a 90 percent supermajority. In contrast, most states permit a 51 percent majority to adopt a 90 percent supermajority. New York used to require a supermajority to adopt a supermajority, but, since 1984, now requires a supermajority vote only to delete or change a supermajority voting provision. See N.Y. Bus. Corp. Law §616(b) (2007). The propriety of the permissive rule that permits today's majority to bind the hands of a future majority has never been seriously questioned by courts (probably because the legislative provision is usually quite explicit), but in overview it may seem curious that this power is so widely accepted. In comparison, it is clear that one session of Congress could not legislate that a 70 percent supermajority would be necessary to pass specified legislation in a subsequent session. Why, then, should a bare majority of the shareholders at one moment in time be able to tie the hands of a larger majority at a subsequent moment (particularly when the two groups do not necessarily overlap significantly)? The answer would appear to be that supermajorities can have utility, particularly in the case of closely held corporations, as a way of protecting minority investors who need veto powers over some matters (or otherwise would not invest). In recent years, however, supermajority provisions have come into much greater use in publicly held corporations as a takeover defensive measure. Typically, they are used to block follow-up mergers between the bidder and the target unless, for example, an 80 percent vote approves the merger. In effect, such a provision creates an incentive for the bidder to acquire 80 percent of the stock and so may protect target shareholders from coercive "partial" tender offers or other acquisitions of a bare majority interest. See Chapter IX.

F. *REMOVAL AND VACANCIES*

1. DIRECTORS

At common law, shareholders could remove directors, but only for cause. See *Auer v. Dressel*, 306 N.Y. 427, 118 N.E.2d 590, 593 (1954). Commentators have criticized this "unsound rule . . . that a director has some sort of vested right, by statute or contract, to continue in the tenure of his office until the end of his term." See H. Ballantine, Corporations 434 (rev. ed. 1946). Indeed, there appears to be no comparable rule, either in Great Britain or on the continent, where directors may be dismissed peremptorily during their term of office. See L. C. B. Gower, Some Contrasts Between British and American Corporation Law, 69 Harv. L. Rev. 1369, 1389 (1956).

Today, several jurisdictions provide that directors may be removed without cause if the certificate or a bylaw adopted by the shareholders so provides. See

N.Y. Bus. Corp. Law §706(b). In general, the original promoters of the corporation have little incentive to facilitate their own removal, and thus such provisions are more likely to be found in the certificate of incorporation only when there is a controlling shareholder. Delaware, California, and the Revised Model Business Corporation Act (RMBCA) go further and permit removal without cause even if the certificate is silent:

Delaware General Corporation Law (2007)

Sec. 141. *Board of directors.* . . . (k) Any director or the entire board of directors may be removed, with or without cause, by the holders of a majority of the shares then entitled to vote at an election of directors, except as follows:

(1) Unless the certificate of incorporation otherwise provides, in the case of a corporation whose board is classified . . . , shareholders may effect such removal only for cause; or

(2) In the case of a corporation having cumulative voting, if less than the entire board is to be removed, no director may be removed without cause if the votes cast against such director's removal would be sufficient to elect such director if then cumulatively voted at an election of the entire board of directors, or, if there be classes of directors, at an election of the class of directors of which such director is a part. . . .

---

1. *Contemporary impact.* The above Delaware provision has particular significance because of the ability of a majority of the shareholders of a Delaware corporation to act by written consent under §228 (page 590 supra). Thus, if an acquiring firm were secretly to purchase a majority of the firm's shares, or if it were to solicit written consents from other shareholders, it could remove the incumbent board summarily. Is so rapid a change of control desirable? In part, this is why the issue of the board's ability to set a record date under §228 or otherwise adopt bylaws that stretch out the solicitation process has great contemporary significance. Note that if the board of directors is classified, §141(k) does not permit removal without cause, unless the certificate of incorporation provides for such removal. This may help explain the recent popularity of "staggered board" charter amendments.

RMBCA §8.08 also authorizes removal of directors without cause "unless the articles of incorporation provide that directors may be removed only for cause." The Official Comment to this section states that it "adopts the view that since the shareholders are the owners of the corporation, they should normally have the power to change the directors at will."

2. *Nonstatutory removal without cause.* Absent a statute, it is uncertain whether a charter provision or bylaw can authorize removal without cause. Delaware did recognize such a power (see Everett v. Transnation Development Corp., 267 A.2d 627 (Del. Ch. 1970)), but New York cases have denied shareholders the power to remove a director without cause where the director was already in office at the time the bylaw authorizing without cause removal was adopted. Abbigas v. Kulp, 281 N.Y.S. 373 (Sup. Ct. 1935) (dictum). The common law's view that a director was

a quasi-public servant, not a mere agent or employee, made it difficult to accept any charter provision or bylaw that reduced the incumbent director's status. In fact, some cases have held that even when a statute does authorize the certificate of incorporation to provide for removal without cause, such a charter provision is not applicable to directors whose term of service predates the adoption of the amendment. See Pilat v. Broach Systems, Inc., 260 A.2d 13 (N.J. Super. 1969). Is this sound? Should 100 percent of the shareholders be unable to remove a director, except for cause, simply because they adopted the provision after the director took office? See Frank v. Anthony, 107 So. 2d 136 (Fla. App. 1958) (sole shareholder could not remove directors without cause). Sound? Whose corporation is it anyway?

In contrast, Delaware has allowed shareholders to amend the corporate charter to eliminate classified board provisions and then immediately remove directors without cause. See Roven v. Cotter, 547 A.2d 603 (Del. Ch. 1988). The significance of this result lies largely in the fact that under Del. Gen. Corp. Law §141(k), directors of a corporation whose board is classified may be removed only for cause.

3. *Removal of directors for cause.* In general, a director may be removed for cause before the expiration of his term by a majority vote of the shareholders at a special meeting called for that purpose. Although removal for cause is frequently provided by statute, it need not be statutorily based. It has been said that removal for cause must be based on a showing of breach of trust. Fox v. Cody, 141 Misc. 552, 252 N.Y.S. 395 (Sup. Ct. 1930). Among specific grounds for removal are conviction of a felony, insanity, bankruptcy, organization of a competing company, harassment of corporate officers and employees, and sale by the director of all of his shares.

What procedures must be followed to remove a director for cause? Case law has established that some kind of hearing must be provided. What constitutes the hearing body — the shareholders assembled at a meeting? Can such a meeting be conducted in accordance with the customary proxy proceedings, i.e., can a shareholder give a proxy authorizing removal before the meeting (the hearing) is held? May the "hearing" consist of the submission of relevant documents to the shareholders in solicitation of their proxies? See Matter of Auer v. Dressel, 306 N.Y. 427, 118 N.E.2d 590 (1954), and Campbell v. Loew's Inc., 36 Del. Ch. 563, 134 A.2d 852 (Ch. 1957). Given these procedural complexities, removal for cause has been rare. In any event, in practice, once there is a change in voting control, the incumbent directors usually resign anyway because they have little incentive to remain in office and might face litigation from shareholders if they were to continue.

4. *Removal of directors by directors.* The directors have no inherent power to remove one of their members and cannot confer such power on themselves by bylaw. Statutes infrequently provide that shareholders may by the articles or bylaws delegate to the board the power of removal for cause. Does such delegation deprive the shareholders of their own power of removal? See Matter of Auer v. Dressel, 306 N.Y. 427, 118 N.E.2d 590 (1954). Should shareholders be barred from adopting a bylaw giving the directors power to remove one of their members without cause? See Dillon v. Berg, 326 F. Supp. 1214, 1225 (D. Del.), *aff'd*, 453 F.2d 876 (3d Cir. 1971) (board authority to remove without cause is contrary to Delaware law and public policy).

5. *Cumulative voting.* Special problems exist with respect to the removal of directors elected under a system of cumulative voting. See page 600 supra.

6. *Removal by court action.* Statutes in some states provide for removal of directors by court action. There is disagreement as to whether judicial power of removal exists without a statute. Compare Markovitz v. Markovitz, 336 Pa. 145, 8 A.2d 46 (1939), with Brown v. North Ventura Road Development Co., 216 Cal. App. 2d 227, 30 Cal. Rptr. 568 (1963). Who should be able to institute court proceedings for removal? See N.Y. Bus. Corp. Law §706(d) (2007).

2. FILLING BOARD VACANCIES

At common law, board vacancies were filled by the shareholders. Statutes generally permit vacancies to be filled by the board itself. The statutes vary widely on such matters as what creates a vacancy (e.g., resignation, removal, increase in the number of directorships), whether the statutory provisions can be varied by the articles or bylaws, and quorum and majority vote requirements.

New York Business Corporation Law (2007)

Sec. 705. *Newly created directorships and vacancies.* (a) Newly created directorships resulting from an increase in the number of directors and vacancies occurring in the board for any reason except the removal of directors without cause may be filled by vote of the board. If the number of the directors then in office is less than a quorum, such newly created directorships and vacancies may be filled by vote of a majority of the directors then in office. Nothing in this paragraph shall affect any provision of the certificate of incorporation or the bylaws which provides that such newly created directorships or vacancies shall be filled by vote of the shareholders, or any provision of the certificate of incorporation specifying greater requirements as permitted under Section 709 (Greater requirements as to quorum and vote of directors).

(b) Unless the certificate of incorporation or the specific provisions of a bylaw adopted by the shareholders provide that the board may fill vacancies occurring in the board by reason of the removal of directors without cause, such vacancies may be filled only by vote of the shareholders.

(c) A director elected to fill a vacancy, unless elected by the shareholders, shall hold office until the next meeting of shareholders at which the election of directors is in the regular order of business, and until his successor has been elected and qualified. . . . [28]

---

28. RMBCA §8.10 permits either the shareholders or the directors to fill a vacancy, "unless the articles of incorporation provide otherwise." Even if the remaining directors do not constitute a quorum, they may fill the vacancy. Presumably, this provision would require an insurgent shareholder to remove the entire board (unless it were certain that the remaining directors would elect its nominees). Note that §705 of the New York statute would not permit the board to fill a vacancy caused by a removal without cause. — Ed.

Substitution of entire board. After sale of a controlling block of shares, it has been a frequent practice for the old board members to resign serially, with the remaining members electing a new member (nominated by the buyer of control) to fill each vacancy as it is created by resignation, until an entirely new board is holding office. See Essex Universal Corp. v. Yates, 305 F.2d 572 (2d Cir. 1962). Should the statutes giving directors the power to fill vacancies be interpreted to allow this practice? The practice cannot be followed in companies subject to the Investment Company Act of 1940, §16. Although the state statutes would apparently permit such a substitution of the entire board to be made in secrecy, §14(f) of the Securities Exchange Act of 1934 and its implementing rules require disclosure of the process.

3. REMOVAL OF OFFICERS

New York Business Corporation Law (2007)

Sec. 716. *Removal of officers.* (a) Any officer elected or appointed by the board may be removed by the board with or without cause. An officer elected by the shareholders may be removed, with or without cause, only by vote of the shareholders, but his authority to act as an officer may be suspended by the board for cause.

(b) The removal of an officer without cause shall be without prejudice to his contract rights, if any. The election or appointment of an officer shall not of itself create contract rights.

(c) An action to procure a judgment removing an officer for cause may be brought by the attorney-general or by ten percent of the votes of the outstanding shares, whether or not entitled to vote. The court may bar from re-election or reappointment any officer so removed for a period fixed by the court.

---

1. *Arbitration.* Can an arbitrator acting pursuant to an arbitration provision in an employment contract order a corporate employer to rehire and retain an officer in the face of §716? Apparently the answer is yes. See Matter of Staklinski and Pyramid Electric Co., 6 N.Y.2d 159, 160, 160 N.E.2d 78 (1959). Should such a specific performance remedy be viewed as invading the province of the board or conflicting with §716?

Do the "contract rights" in §716 include a right to specific performance of the contract by the officer sought to be removed? See F. Hodge O'Neal, Close Corporations: Law and Practice §6.05 (2d ed. 1971).

2. *Removal by shareholders.* What rights to remove an officer should the shareholders have?

> Since those who manage obviously cannot be trusted to assure their own efficiency, the removal of inefficient managers requires some mechanism external to the managers themselves. . . . Such a power might, of course, be vested in some agency other than the board. But what are the alternatives? The body of shareholders is too disparate, shifting, and clumsy to conduct the type of inquiry involved. Effective replacement would be highly improbable; monitoring in any sense would be all but

impossible; and removal situations would be turned into semi-public semi-trials, involving intolerable cost, rigidity, embarrassment, and delay.

Melvin Eisenberg, Legal Models of Management Structure in the Modern Corporation: Officers, Directors, and Accountants, 63 Cal. L. Rev. 375, 400-401 (1975).

3. *Close corporations.* Problems of removal of officers and employees in the close corporation context are reviewed more fully in Chapter VII infra.

G. *JUDICIAL SUPERVISION OF ELECTION CONTESTS*

In both political and corporate elections, the incumbents have certain advantages because of their control of the election machinery. If they have discretion to advance or postpone the election date or to issue new shares at the last minute (in effect, to "stuff the ballot box"), a fair contest becomes unlikely. In this section, we will survey the efforts of state courts to protect the shareholders' suffrage rights against such tactics:

Schnell v. Chris-Craft Industries, Inc.
285 A.2d 437 (Del. 1971)

HERMANN, J.: [Plaintiffs were dissident shareholders who sought to conduct a proxy contest; management responded by amending the bylaws to advance the date of the annual meeting by five weeks in order to shorten the time plaintiffs would have to solicit other shareholders. The Chancery Court found that because of these tactics, which also included the failure to produce a shareholders' list, plaintiffs had little chance to wage a successful proxy fight, but it still declined to grant an injunction.] In our view, [the Chancery Court's] conclusions amount to a finding that management has attempted to utilize the corporate machinery and the Delaware Law for the purpose of perpetuating itself in office; and, to that end, for the purpose of obstructing the legitimate efforts of dissident stockholders in the exercise of their rights to undertake a proxy contest against management. These are inequitable purposes, contrary to established principles of corporate democracy. The advancement by directors of the by-law date of a stockholders' meeting, for such purposes, may not be permitted to stand. Compare Condec Corporation v. Lunkenheimer Company, Del. Ch., 230 A.2d 769 (1967).

When the by-laws of a corporation designate the date of the annual meeting of stockholders, it is to be expected that those who intend to contest the reelection of incumbent management will gear their campaign to the by-law date. It is not to be expected that management will attempt to advance that date in order to obtain an inequitable advantage in the contest.

Management contends that it has complied strictly with the provisions of the new Delaware Corporation Law in changing the by-law date. The answer to that contention, of course, is that inequitable action does not become permissible simply because it is legally possible.

Management relies upon American Hardware Corp. v. Savage Arms Corp., 37 Del. Ch. 10, 135 A.2d 725, *aff'd*, 37 Del. Ch. 59, 136 A.2d 690 (1957). That case is inapposite for two reasons: it involved an effort by stockholders, engaged in a proxy contest, to have the stockholders' meeting adjourned and the period for the proxy contest enlarged; and there was no finding there of inequitable action on the part of management. We agree with the rule of *American Hardware* that, in the absence of fraud or inequitable conduct, the date for a stockholders' meeting and notice thereof, duly established under the by-laws, will not be enlarged by judicial interference at the request of dissident stockholders solely because of the circumstances of a proxy contest. That, of course, is not the case before us. . . .

Accordingly, the judgment below must be reversed and the cause remanded, with instructions to nullify the December 8 date as a meeting date for stockholders; to reinstate January 11, 1972 as the sole date of the next annual meeting of the stockholders of the corporation; and to take such other proceedings and action as may be consistent herewith regarding the stock record closing date and any other related matters.

[Reversed.]

---

1. *Delaware case law on improper purpose.* In Condec Corp. v. Lunkenheimer Co., 230 A.2d 769 (Del. Ch. 1967), defendant was the target of a hostile exchange offer by plaintiff, which had already acquired sufficient shares to be able to block any merger between the defendant and a third corporation. To dilute plaintiff's "blocking" position, defendant hurriedly agreed to exchange 75,000 of its authorized but unissued shares with a third corporation (U.S. Industries) in return for a like amount of the latter's stock; this was to be followed by an eventual sale of defendant's assets to this "white knight." The court found that the effect of this exchange was "to abort the effect of Condec's apparently successful campaign for tenders of a majority of Lunkenheimer's stock." Enjoining these actions, the court concluded that "[i]n view of the haste with which the . . . transaction was hammered out . . . over the weekend . . . , I have reached the conclusion that the primary purpose of the issuance of such shares was to prevent control of Lunkenheimer from passing to Condec and to cause such control to pass into the hands of U.S. Industries." Does this holding imply that a target may never issue a stock "lockup" to a preferred candidate in a corporate control contest? Clearly not. The key point to the court was that Condec, as the result of its successful tender offer, had already acquired "a contractual right to assert voting control . . . [and] was deprived of such control by what is virtually a corporate legerdemain."

Condec and *Schnell* both found that the "primary purpose" of the defendant's conduct was either to perpetuate itself in control or to interfere with a legitimate right already possessed by the plaintiff to control the corporation. This focus on motive has been much criticized by commentators who believe it places too much emphasis on cosmetics. In contrast, a more liberal test has sometimes been used when the board is attempting to interfere with an election contest, rather than resist a hostile raider. The tension between these different judicial standards was faced by the Delaware Supreme Court in Stroud v. Grace, which follows.

2. *Other state law remedies.* A number of states have specific statutes providing for judicial review of corporate elections. In other states, review may be had by quo

warranto proceedings. Some state courts have held that if proxy irregularities are established, they may provide no relief other than ordering a new election. Others grant other relief such as decreeing the election of defeated candidates by simply voiding the irregular proxies. See generally Edward Aranow & Herbert Einhorn, State Court Review of Corporate Elections, 56 Colum. L. Rev. 155 (1956). In Western Oil Fields, Inc. v. McKnab, 232 F. Supp. 162 (D. Colo. 1964), under Colorado law the court denied a motion to enjoin a meeting "without prejudice to the right of plaintiffs, if defendants succeed in electing their slate of directors, to challenge the right of defendants (or their nominees) to serve as directors, and to put in issue therewith, the validity of proxies obtained by defendants." The court reasoned that the election might render plaintiffs' claims moot.

Stroud v. Grace
606 A.2d 75 (Del. 1992)

MOORE, J.: [Plaintiffs, who owned 17 percent of Milliken Enterprises, Inc. ("Milliken"), a privately held Delaware corporation, brought individual and derivative actions to invalidate a series of charter and bylaw amendments adopted at the 1989 annual shareholders meeting. They alleged that these amendments effectively insulated the Milliken family, which then held over 50 percent of Milliken's outstanding stock, from any future proxy contest. Under a General Option Agreement (GOA), 75 percent of Milliken's shareholders (not including the plaintiffs) had given the Milliken family and Milliken a right of first refusal to purchase any shares offered to third parties. Plaintiffs alleged that the totality of these arrangements showed that the charter and bylaw amendments amounted to breach of the directors' fiduciary duties.] . . . The most controversial aspects of the Amendments are charter Article Eleventh (c) and By-law 3. Article Eleventh (c) established a new method of qualifying directors for membership on Milliken's board. By-law 3 established the procedure for nominating board candidates. By-law 3 required the shareholders to submit a notice of their candidates to the board, specifying their qualifications under Article Eleventh (c), well in advance of the annual meeting. By-law 3 also empowered the board to disqualify a shareholder's nominee at any time, even at the annual meeting.

The board considered the Amendments during meetings held on February 2, 1989. The directors adopted the Amendments at their March 11, 1989 meeting which was attended by Milliken's counsel, nine of its ten directors, including five out of the six unaffiliated or outside directors. The board unanimously approved the Amendments and adopted a resolution recommending them to the shareholders for their adoption at Milliken's annual meeting scheduled for April 24, 1989.

On March 14, 1989, Milliken mailed notice of the 1989 annual meeting to its shareholders. Included with the notice was a copy of Milliken's current by-laws, the board resolution proposing the Amendments and Milliken's current Certificate of Incorporation. The notice was four pages long and included a number of recitals. It mentioned that the board had unanimously adopted the Amendments. Significantly, it also stated: "These amendments are proposed in lieu of all amendments previously proposed upon which the stockholders have not acted." The notice did not explain the differences or similarities between the new

Amendments and the previously withdrawn amendments. The notice stated that the board *would not* solicit proxies in connection with the scheduled 1989 meeting and cautioned: "[S]tockholders are encouraged to attend the meeting in person. . . . Pursuant to the corporation's by-laws, the chairman of the Board of the corporation, Roger Milliken, will preside at the meeting, and he and others will, among other things, endeavor to answer questions from stockholders concerning the matters to be voted upon, including the proposed amendments to the certificate of incorporation." . . .

Milliken held its annual meeting on April 14, 1989 in Wilmington, Delaware. Of its eligible voters, 93% personally attended the meeting; and 97.8% of the shares entitled to vote were present. Most of the Strouds and their Wilmington counsel also participated in the meeting.

. . . The Amendments were approved at the meeting by 78% of the shares entitled to vote.

After the meeting and vote, the Strouds . . . filed individual and derivative suits in the Court of Chancery against the defendants contesting the validity of the notice, the Amendments, and By-law 3. Plaintiffs argued that the board breached its duty of care and loyalty in approving and recommending the Amendments. They also argued that the Amendments were unfair to Milliken's shareholders by effectively entrenching Roger, Gerrish and Minot Milliken's control of the board.

The Strouds then moved for summary judgment. With one exception, the trial court *sua sponte* granted summary judgment in defendants' favor. . . . The Vice Chancellor granted summary judgment in favor of the Strouds by ruling that By-law 3 was unfair to Milliken's shareholders. . . .

III. . . . The Strouds contend that this ruling [for defendants] "is contrary to Delaware law," and construes *Unocal*[29] too narrowly. Plaintiffs correctly state that *Unocal* applies whenever a board "perceives a threat" to control and takes defensive measures in response to the threat. Citing to various sections of the record, including: (1) the board's supposed decision to pursue the GOA to respond to a generalized "threat" to the Milliken family's control, and (2) a provision in a subsequently revoked charter amendment identifying a threat to control, plaintiffs argue that the board was reacting to a threat when it approved the Amendments.

In our opinion this record does not justify application of *Unocal* and its progeny. The Strouds' analysis of *Unocal* is contrary to Delaware law.

. . . *Unocal* recognized that directors are often faced with an "inherent conflict of interest" during contests for corporate control "[b]ecause of the omnipresent specter that a board may be acting primarily in its own interests, rather than those of the corporation and its shareholders. . . ." *Unocal*, 493 A.2d at 954. *Unocal* thus requires a reviewing court to apply an enhanced standard of review to determine whether the directors "had reasonable grounds for believing that a danger to corporate policy and effectiveness existed . . ." and that the board's response "was reasonable in relation to the threat posed." Id. at 955. If the board action meets the *Unocal* standard, it is accorded the protection of the business judgment rule. Id.

The scrutiny of *Unocal* is not limited to the adoption of a defensive measure during a hostile contest for control. In Moran v. Household International, Inc., Del. Supr., 500 A.2d 1346 (1985), we held that *Unocal* also applied to a preemptive

---

29. The court's reference is to Unocal Corp. v. Mesa Petroleum Co., 493 A.2d 946 (Del. 1985), page 955 infra, which introduced a heightened standard of judicial review for defensive actions taken by a board to resist a takeover or corporate control contest. —ED.

defensive measure where the corporation was not under immediate "attack." Id. at 1350-52. Subsequent cases have reaffirmed the application of *Unocal* whenever a board takes defensive measures in reaction to a perceived "threat to corporate policy and effectiveness which touches upon issues of control." . . .

Inherent in all of the foregoing principles is a presumption that a board acted in the absence of an informed shareholder vote ratifying the challenged action. This significant distinction, in addition to the fact that Milliken faced no threat to corporate policy and effectiveness, or to the board's control, is fatal to plaintiffs' *Unocal* arguments.

Here, there is no evidence that the board adopted the Amendments as defensive measures. . . . The Strouds' contention that the GOA was primarily designed as a takeover defense is untenable. That was a matter of private contract between the shareholders themselves and their company. All shareholders were free to accept GOA or reject it. The plaintiffs chose the latter course. The shareholders of many privately held corporations, like Milliken, enter into contracts, like the GOA, to preserve family ownership and give themselves a right of first refusal to purchase a company's shares. . . . The Strouds offer no material proof to support their claim that the board adopted Article Eleventh (c) to thwart a takeover. Any defensive effects of the GOA and the Amendments themselves were collateral at best.

Significantly, the record shows beyond peradventure that there was no threat to the board's control. Milliken was neither a takeover target, nor vulnerable to one. No Delaware court has applied *Unocal* in the absence of a danger to corporate policy and effectiveness, or as here, in the face of a valid shareholder vote ratifying the challenged board action. . . .

The record clearly indicates, the Strouds concede, that over 50% of the outstanding shares of Milliken are under the direct control of Roger, Minot and Gerrish Milliken. These directors controlled the corporation in fact and law. . . . This obviates any threat contemplated by *Unocal*, and is buttressed by the further fact that at least 70% of Milliken's shareholders supported the GOA.

Thus, the Court of Chancery properly analyzed the board's decision to adopt and recommend the Amendments to the shareholders under the presumption of the business judgment rule. . . . Under such circumstances the burden is on the plaintiff to overcome the presumption of the rule. . . . Unfortunately, however, that does not end the matter. Since an overwhelming majority of Milliken's shareholders, even excluding those shares owned or controlled by Roger, Gerrish and Minot Milliken, approved the disputed Amendments at the 1989 annual meeting, standards governing the board's action leading to a fully informed stockholder vote have little relevance to the ultimate issue. Thus, our standard of review is linked to the validity of the shareholder vote.

IV. In the absence of fraud, a fully informed shareholder vote in favor of even a "voidable" transaction ratifies board action and places the burden of proof on the challenger. . . . The fact that controlling shareholders voted in favor of the transaction is irrelevant as long as they did not breach their fiduciary duties to the minority holders. . . . There is no proof whatever of any such breach in this case. The burden, however, remains on those relying on the vote to show that all material facts relevant to the transaction were fully disclosed. . . .

Here, 78% of Milliken's shareholders adopted the disputed Amendments at the 1989 annual meeting. In the absence of proof by plaintiffs that the disclosures were misleading or inadequate, or that the actions of the board involved fraud, waste or other misconduct which were not ratified by unanimous vote of the stockholders, this ends the matter. See e.g., Deenan v. Eshleman, 2 A.2d 904, 909 (1938).

... Due to the unique manner in which the trial court examined Strouds' disclosure claim, we must first address important legal questions implicating the relationship between the General Corporation Law and a director's common law fiduciary duties. ...

VI. Since there was no breach of any fiduciary duty in connection with the shareholder vote at the 1989 annual meeting, a fully informed majority of the shareholders adopted the Amendments and effectively ratified the board's action. This shifts the burden of proof to the Strouds to prove that the transaction was unfair. ... They have utterly failed in that regard. ...

The Strouds' attack on the Amendments and the defendants' cross-appeal of the trial court's invalidation of By-law 3 both challenge the analytical framework employed by the Court of Chancery in resolving their respective claims. The choice of the applicable "test" to judge director action often determines the outcome of the case.

A. The Vice Chancellor, relying on Blasius Industries, Inc. v. Atlas Corp., Del. Ch., 564 A.2d 651 (1988), and Aprahamian v. HBO & Co., Del. Ch., 531 A.2d 1204 (1987), examined the Amendments under an "intrinsic fairness" test. ... While the trial court concluded that the board had not breached its fiduciary duty, it nonetheless stated that: "Because ... the critical Charter and By-law amendments affect the Milliken shareholders' franchise, particularly their right to nominate directors, the validity of these amendments must be reviewed for their intrinsic fairness rather than considered pursuant to the business judgment rule." That ruling put the burden on the board to demonstrate a compelling justification for its decision to adopt and recommend the Amendments under the test of "scrupulous fairness." (Quoting Blasius, 564 A.2d at 661; Aprahamian, 531 A.2d at 1206-07).

The defendants contend that both Blasius and Aprahamian are distinguishable on their facts. They argue that a fairness review is only appropriate where the board breaches its fiduciary duty of loyalty to the corporation. They claim that the board did not act in its own self-interest, and the trial court should have considered the Amendments within the confines of the business judgment rule. The defendants alternatively argue that the Amendments could still withstand the exacting "intrinsic fairness" requirements.

The Strouds argue that these claims were properly decided under the rubric of Blasius and Aprahamian, when board action affects a shareholder vote. Stroud maintains that Blasius is applicable because the Amendments "directly impinge on the shareholder franchise."

The Vice Chancellor's reliance on Blasius implicates a question of law. We examine such questions de novo. ... After considering the record, and in view of our conclusions earlier in this opinion, exculpating the defendants from a breach of fiduciary duty, we conclude that it was error to apply Blasius here.

B. In Schnell v. Chris-Craft Industries, Inc., Del. Supr., 285 A.2d 437 (1971), this Court recognized that management may not inequitably manipulate corporate machinery to perpetuate "itself in office" and disenfranchise the shareholders. Id. at 439. The crux of Schnell is that: "[I]nequitable action does not become permissible simply because it is legally possible." Id.

Schnell's broad holding spawned an entirely new line of Court of Chancery decisions. Lerman v. Diagnostic Data, Inc., Del. Ch., 421 A.2d 906 (1980);

Aprahamian, 531 A.2d at 1208; *Blasius,* 564 A.2d at 659-60; Centaur Partners, IV v. National Intergroup, Inc., Del. Supr., 582 A.2d 923, 927 (1990); Stahl v. Apple Bancorp, Inc., Del. Ch., 579 A.2d 1115, 1122-23 (1990).

C. While we accept the basic legal tenets of *Stahl* and *Blasius,* certain principles emerge from those cases which are inextricably related to their specific facts. Almost all of the post-*Schnell* decisions involved situations where boards of directors deliberately employed various legal strategies either to frustrate or completely disenfranchise a shareholder vote. As *Blasius* recognized, in those circumstances, board action was intended to thwart free exercise of the franchise. There can be no dispute that such conduct violates Delaware law.

The stringent standards of review imposed by *Stahl* and *Blasius* arise from questions of divided loyalty, and are well-settled. . . . [3] After reviewing the record in this case, we conclude that a *Blasius* analysis in connection with the validity of the Amendments and By-laws was inappropriate.

D. Clearly, the Milliken board did not face any threat to its control. Roger, Gerrish and Minot Milliken effectively owned or controlled a majority interest in the corporation. Furthermore, most of the other shareholders had executed the GOA. Thus, it cannot be said that the "primary purpose" of the board's action was to interfere with or impede exercise of the shareholder franchise.

More fundamentally, the Vice Chancellor ruled, and we agree, that a fully-informed majority of Milliken's shareholders ratified the Amendments. Therefore, the factual predicate of unilateral board action intended to inequitably manipulate the corporate machinery is completely absent, here. Cf. *Centaur Partners,* 582 A.2d at 927. Milliken's shareholders, unlike those in both *Blasius* and *Aprahamian,* had a full and fair opportunity to vote on the Amendments and did so. The result of the vote, ceding greater authority to the board, does not under the circumstances implicate *Unocal* or *Blasius.* . . .

VII. The trial court rejected the Strouds' contention that Article Eleventh (c) of the Amendments was unfair to Milliken's shareholders. . . . We agree that even under the more exacting analysis employed by the trial court, the Amendments are valid. Article Eleventh (c) establishes the qualifications for board membership. It provides for three categories of directors including:

> **Category 1.** Individuals who have had *substantial* experience in line (as distinct from staff) positions in the management of *substantial* private institutions, who are not officers, employees or stockholders, whether of record or beneficially, of the corporation or any of its subsidiaries.

---

3. Board action interfering with the exercise of the franchise often arose during a hostile contest for control where an acquiror launched both a proxy fight and a tender offer. Such action necessarily invoked both *Unocal* and *Blasius.* We note that the two "tests" are not mutually exclusive because both recognize the inherent conflicts of interest that arise when shareholders are not permitted free exercise of their franchise. See, e.g., Shamrock Holdings, Inc. v. Polaroid Corp., Del. Ch., 559 A.2d 278, 285-86 (1989) (*Blasius* represents "specific expression" of *Unocal* test). . . .

Gilbert should nonetheless resolve any ambiguity. It clearly holds that a reviewing court must apply *Unocal* where the board "adopts any defensive measures taken in response to some threat to corporate policy and effectiveness which touches upon issues of control." *Gilbert,* 575 A.2d at 1144. This does not render *Blasius* and its progeny meaningless. In certain circumstances, a court must recognize the special import of protecting the shareholders' franchise within *Unocal*'s requirement that any defensive measure be proportionate and "reasonable in relation to the threat posed." *Unocal,* 493 A.2d at 955. A board's unilateral decision to adopt a defensive measure touching "upon issues of control" that purposefully disenfranchises its shareholders is strongly suspect under *Unocal,* and cannot be sustained without a "compelling justification." . . .

Category 2. Individuals who are beneficial stockholders of the corporation. For purposes of this Category 2, beneficial stockholders shall include beneficiaries of trusts which are record stockholders of the corporation.

Category 3. The chief executive officer, the chief operating officer, and the president of the corporation, and any person who held any one or more of such offices.

(Emphasis added.) The contested article also provides:

A majority of the Board of Directors shall, at all times . . . consist of persons qualified under [Article Eleventh] Category 1. At least 3 members of the Board of Directors shall, at all times . . . be persons qualified under Category 2. No more than 2 individuals qualified under Category 3 may serve as a director at the same time. For purposes of this paragraph (c), an individual qualified under both Category 2 and Category 3 shall be deemed to be qualified under Category 2 alone.

The Strouds contend that the tripartite director qualifications violate 8 Del. C. §14(b) because they are unreasonable and vague. Plaintiffs argue that the directors approved these provisions for the sole purpose of excluding all other people from Milliken's board except for Roger, Gerrish and Minot Milliken. The Strouds maintain that the amendment precludes them from ever serving as directors. . . .

Under our analysis, the burden falls on the Strouds to prove that the Amendments were not properly adopted or that their adoption was the product of fraud, manipulation or other inequitable conduct. Plaintiffs have not sustained that burden.

First, we disregard the Strouds' contention that the board unfairly "crafted" Article Eleventh to exclude all other candidates for office except Roger, Gerrish and Minot Milliken. We have already concluded that the shareholder vote ratified the Amendments, thus eliminating any possible taint on the board's decision. We will not revisit that proposition under the guise of the Strouds' scatter shot attack on the substance of the Amendments.

The Strouds challenge the validity of Article Eleventh (c), claiming that the category one qualifications are impermissibly vague. Plaintiffs focus on the language requiring category one directors to have "substantial experience in line . . . positions" in "substantial business enterprises" or "substantial private institutions." The Strouds claim that the term "substantial" is too indefinite because it is not defined in the corporate charter.

The trial court was troubled that the meaning of "substantial" could vary depending on how the board defined the term. . . . The Vice Chancellor nonetheless found that the board had the authority to define the term as long as they exercised their discretion fairly. The trial court found that Strouds could not prove that the board interpreted category one unfairly, and declined to rule that it was *per se* unreasonable. We agree.

VIII. Finally, we turn to the defendants' cross-appeal regarding validity of Milliken's By-law 3. That provision establishes, in part, the procedure for nominating candidates to Milliken's board. By-law 3 initially requires all board candidates to meet the qualifications mandated in Article Eleventh (c). By-law 3, section (d), requires a shareholder proposing a board candidate to include in his or her notice of nomination: "[T]he proposed nominee's name, the principal occupation or employment of each such nominee, the nominee's written consent to nomination and to serving as a director if elected, *information establishing such nominee's fulfillment of any qualification requirements set forth in the Corporation's Certificate of Incorporation,* and such additional information with respect to such person as the Board of Directors may reasonably request. . . ." (Emphasis added.) By-law 3 then mandates that the shareholder deliver a copy of his or her notice to Milliken's secretary: "[N]ot less than fourteen (14) nor more than fifty (50) days prior to the date of the meeting for the election of directors; provided, however, that if less than twenty-one (21) days' notice of the date of the meeting is given to stockholders, notice by a stockholder to be timely must be delivered or mailed not later than the close of the seventh (7th) day following the day on which notice of the date of the meeting was mailed to stockholders." The By-law does not place a time limitation on the board's right to nominate board candidates. Once received, the board is required to circulate the notice of nominations with the notice of the annual meeting, or if received after the notice is circulated, By-law 3 provides that board should separately send a notice of nominations "as soon as practicable."

The most controversial subsection of By-law 3 concerns the board's ability to determine a candidate's qualifications under Article Eleventh (c) at any time before the election up to and including the annual meeting. By-law 3 subsection (f) provides:

> The Board of Directors, or if not feasible, the officer of the Corporation or other person *presiding at the meeting of stockholders shall determine any questions concerning whether nominations have been made in accordance with the provisions of this By-law 3 and whether such person has met the qualification requirements, if any, set forth in the Corporation's Certificate of Incorporation.* If such a determination is so made, the officer of the Corporation or other person presiding at the meeting of stockholders shall so declare to the meeting and shall declare that any such nomination shall be disregarded.

The trial court, applying *Blasius,* held that By-law 3 was "unreasonable and unfair, on its face." The Vice Chancellor noted that By-law 3 precluded the shareholders from knowing exactly what information to include in their notice of nomination "[b]ecause the category 1 criteria are not defined in Article Eleventh and are dependent on a determination by incumbent directors. . . ." The Vice Chancellor found that the board could effectively disenfranchise voters because subsection (f), when read in conjunction with the subsection limiting the shareholder's right to submit its notice of nomination not less than 14 days before the election, gave the directors the unfettered discretion to disqualify the shareholders' candidates without recourse. The Vice Chancellor also noted that the same two subsections would effectively disenfranchise proxy votes whose candidates could hypothetically be disqualified at the annual meeting. . . .

The trial court's invalidation of By-law 3 by granting the Strouds' motion for summary judgment presents an issue of law for review. . . . After reviewing the entire record, we conclude that it was error to invalidate By-law 3.

Again, we observe that *Blasius* had no application here. Given the fully informed shareholder vote adopting Article Eleventh (c) at the 1989 annual meeting, there was no reason to apply *Blasius.* Plaintiffs utterly failed to prove that the By-laws were attributable to an improper corporate purpose.

The trial court ruled that Article Eleventh (c) was not unfair and did not unreasonably interfere with the shareholders' franchise. The Vice Chancellor refused to rule that the disputed article, which establishes the criteria for category one directors to include individuals having *"substantial"* experience in certain matters, was unfair *"per se."* Instead, the trial court held that the board was entitled to construe the meaning of "substantial" if the determination [was] fairly made. Parity of reasoning, therefore, required that By-law 3's reference to the Article Eleventh (c) qualifications likewise did not render it unreasonable *per se.* The board should have a reasonable opportunity to interpret this otherwise valid by-law in a fair and proper manner. . . .

There was no basis to invoke some hypothetical risk of harm rather than an examination of the board's proven, and entirely proper, conduct. . . . It is not an overstatement to suggest that every valid by-law is always susceptible to potential misuse. Without a showing of abuse in this case, we must reverse the trial court's decision and uphold the validity of By-law 3. The validity of corporate action under By-law 3 must await its actual use. See *Moran,* 500 A.2d at 1357. . . .

MM Companies, Inc. v. Liquid Audio, Inc.
813 A.2d 1118 (Del. 2003)

HOLLAND, J.: This is an expedited appeal from a final judgment entered by the Court of Chancery. That final judgment permitted an incumbent board of directors to adopt defense measures which changed the size and composition of the board's membership. The record reflects that those defensive actions were taken for the primary purpose of impeding the shareholders' right to vote effectively in an impending election for successor directors. We have concluded that the judgment of the Court of Chancery must be reversed. This matter is remanded for further proceedings in accordance with this opinion.

Procedural Background

On August 26, 2002, MM Companies, Inc. ("MM") filed its original complaint in this action in the Court of Chancery against Liquid Audio, Inc. ("Liquid Audio"), as well as Raymond A. Doig, Gerald W. Kearby, Robert G. Flynn, Stephen V. Imbler and Ann Winblad (the "Director Defendants"). The original complaint sought injunctive relief against the August 22, 2002 action taken by the board of directors of Liquid Audio ("Board") to expand from five to seven members, and the purported effects that expansion might have on Liquid Audio's 2002 annual meeting that was scheduled for September 26, 2002. MM alleged that the Director Defendants' decision to expand the Board violated the principles established by the decision of the Court of Chancery in *Blasius*[1] and the decision of this Court in *Unocal.* . . . [2]

On September 26, 2002, Liquid Audio held its 2002 annual meeting at which MM's two nominees were elected as Class III directors replacing incumbent directors Doig and Kearby. On October 1, 2002, MM filed an amended complaint, once again seeking to invalidate the August 22, 2002 action by Liquid Audio's board of directors to expand the size of the Board from five to seven members and to appoint two new directors to those recently created vacancies. . . .

---

1. Blasius Indus., Inc. v. Atlas Corp., 564 A.2d 651 (Del. Ch. 1988).
2. Unocal Corp. v. Mesa Petroleum Co., 493 A.2d 946 (Del. 1985).

At the conclusion of the trial, the Court of Chancery ruled in favor of the defendants, holding that the Board expansion did not violate Delaware law under either *Blasius* or *Unocal.* The Court of Chancery rejected the plaintiff's independent *Blasius* claim on the basis that the addition of two new directors "did not impact the shareholder vote or the shareholder choices in any significant way." The Court of Chancery rejected the plaintiff's *Unocal* claim, on the basis that: plaintiff did "not contend that the board expansion was coercive," the expansion was not "preclusive," because the "choices that the shareholders had before the board action was taken were the same as they had after," and the plaintiff failed to make a showing that "the action that the board took falls outside a range of reasonable responses." . . .

MM has raised two issues on appeal. First, it contends that the Court of Chancery erred in ruling that the "compelling justification" standard, as enunciated in *Blasius,* was not applicable to the Board's action. In support of that argument, MM relies upon the finding by the Court of Chancery that the Director Defendants manipulated the size and composition of the Liquid Audio board during a contested election for directors primarily to interfere with and impede the success of MM's ability to gain two-of-five directorships on the Board, and, thus, to diminish the influence of MM's nominees on the Board.

Second, MM argues that the Court of Chancery erred in ruling that the precepts of this Court's holding in *Unocal* and its progeny were not violated by the Board's defensive action. According to MM, the Director Defendants never identified a legally cognizable threat to the corporate policy and effectiveness of Liquid Audio and, to the extent that a threat existed, never demonstrated that the "manipulation of the size and composition" of the Liquid Audio board was a reasonable response in relation to such threat. Based upon that asserted lack of record evidence, MM submits the Court of Chancery erred in concluding that this Court's holding in *Unocal* was not violated.

Background Facts

Liquid Audio is a publicly traded Delaware corporation, with its principal place of business in Redwood City, California. Liquid Audio's primary business consists of providing software and services for the digital transmission of music over the Internet. MM is a publicly traded Delaware corporation with its principal place of business in New York, New York. As of October 2002, MM was part of a group that collectively held slightly over 7% of Liquid Audio's common stock.

For more than a year, MM has sought to obtain control of Liquid Audio. On October 26, 2001, MM sent a letter to the Liquid Audio board of directors indicating its willingness to acquire the company at approximately $3 per share. Liquid Audio's board rejected MM's offer as inadequate, after an analysis of the offer and consultation with its investment banker, Broadview International LLC ("Broadview").

Liquid Audio's bylaws provide for a staggered board of directors that is divided into three classes. Only one class of directors is up for election in any given year. The effect is to prevent an insurgent from obtaining control of the company in under two years.

From November 2001, until August 2002, the Liquid Audio board of directors consisted of five members divided into three classes. Class I had two members (defendants Flynn and Imbler), whose terms expire in 2003; Class II had one member (defendant Winblad), whose term expires in 2004; and Class III had two members (defendants Kearby and Doig), whose terms expired in 2002. Defendants Flynn, Doig and Imbler were not elected to the Board by the stockholders of Liquid Audio. They were appointed to the Board by the directors of Liquid Audio to fill vacancies on the Board.

In October 2001, prior to the appointment of defendants Doig and Imbler to the Board, MM requested the Liquid Audio board to call a special meeting of the company's stockholders to consider filling the existing vacancies on the Board and to consider other proposals to be presented to the stockholders. On October 24, 2001, the Liquid Audio board issued a press release which stated that it had denied MM's request to call a special meeting because the Board believed that under the Liquid Audio bylaws stockholders are not permitted to call special meetings. Thereafter, the Board appointed defendants Doig and Imbler to the Liquid Audio board of directors.

MM's Various Actions

On November 13, 2001, MM announced its intention to nominate its own candidates for the two seats on Liquid Audio's board of directors that were up for election at the next annual meeting. On December 18, 2001, MM delivered a formal notice to Liquid Audio stating that it intended to nominate Seymour Holtzman and James Mitarotonda as directors to fill the two seats on the Board then held by the individuals designated as Class III directors whose terms expired at the next annual meeting. The December 18, 2001 notice also requested that the Board adopt resolutions declaring certain amendments to the certificate of incorporation and bylaws advisable and that such amendments be submitted to the stockholders.

On December 20, 2001, MM sent notice to Liquid Audio informing the Board of its intention to bring before the annual meeting a proposal that would amend the bylaws and increase the size of the Board by four members. The December 20, 2001 notice also informed the Board of MM's intention to nominate four individuals as directors to fill those four newly created directorships. MM subsequently demanded that the Board commit to fixing an annual meeting date by February 22, 2002. . . .

On June 10, 2002, MM filed proxy materials with the Securities and Exchange Commission ("SEC") and commenced soliciting proxies for a shareholder meeting Liquid Audio planned to have on July 1, 2002. In addition to proposing two nominees for the Board, MM's proxy statement included a takeover proposal to increase the size of the Board by an additional four directors and to fill those positions with its nominees. As outlined in its initial proxy materials, MM's takeover proposal sought to expand the Board from five members to nine. If MM's two directors were elected and its four proposed directors were also placed on the Board, MM would control a majority of the Board.

On June 13, 2002, Liquid Audio announced a stock-for-stock merger transaction with Alliance Entertainment Corp. ("Alliance"). This announcement came three days after MM mailed its proxy statement and other materials to the stockholders of Liquid Audio, and one day before the scheduled Court of Chancery hearing in connection with the Section 220 complaint. In addition to announcing the merger, the Liquid Audio board also announced that: the July 1, 2002 meeting would be postponed; a special meeting of stockholders of Liquid Audio would be held sometime in the future to vote upon the merger; and, if the merger received the requisite stockholder and regulatory approval, the merger would "close in the Fall of 2002." Based upon this announcement, the annual meeting was postponed indefinitely by the Liquid Audio board. . . .

By the middle of August 2002, it was apparent that MM's nominees, Holtzman and Mitarotonda, would be elected at the annual meeting, to serve in place of the two incumbent nominees, as members of the Liquid Audio board. On August 23, 2002, Liquid Audio announced that the Board had amended the bylaws to increase the size of the Board to seven members from five members. The Board also announced that defendants James D. Somes and Judith N. Frank had been appointed to fill the newly created directorships. Defendant Somes was appointed to serve as a Class II member of the Board and defendant Frank was appointed to serve as a Class I member of the Board. After the Board expanded from five directors to seven, MM revised its proxy statement to note that its proposal to add four directors, if successful, would have resulted in a board with eleven directors, instead of nine.

On August 26, 2002, MM filed its initial lawsuit challenging the Board's decision to add two directors. In the initial complaint, MM alleged that the Board expansion interfered with MM's ability to solicit proxies in favor of its two nominees for election to the Liquid Audio board at the annual meeting. In support of this claim, MM alleged that "some stockholders would believe that electing two members of a seven-member board, rather than two members of a five-member board, would not be worthwhile, and, thus, such stockholders simply would not vote."

At the September 26, 2002 annual meeting, the two directors proposed by MM, Holtzman and Mitarotonda, were elected to serve as directors of the Board. Liquid Audio's stockholders, however, did not approve MM's takeover proposals that would have expanded the Board and placed MM's four nominees on the Board. The stockholders' vote on both issues was consistent with the recommendation of Institutional Shareholder Services ("ISS"), a proxy voting advisory service, which had recommended that the stockholders vote in favor of MM's two nominees, but recommended against stockholders voting to give MM outright and immediate control of the Board.

Following the election of MM's two nominees to the Liquid Audio board of directors at the annual meeting, MM filed an amended lawsuit, challenging the Board's appointment of directors Somes and Frank. In the amended complaint, MM alleged that the expansion of the Liquid Audio board, its timing, and the Board's appointment of two new directors violated the principles of *Blasius* and *Unocal.* According to MM, that action frustrated MM's attempt to gain a "substantial presence" on the Board for at least one year and guaranteed that Liquid Audio's management will have control of, or a substantial presence on, the Board for at least two years.

The expedited trial was held by the Court of Chancery, as scheduled. . . . When defendant Doig was asked to [explain the reasons for the expansion of the board], he testified: "There was concern that if the MM slate won and then it did become too acrimonious and that Ms. Winblad and Mr. Imbler decided to resign, that ran an undue risk to the shareholders by giving MM the ability to control the company."

The testimony of each other member of the Board also reflects that the Director Defendants were concerned that incumbent directors Winblad and Imbler would resign from the Liquid Audio board if MM's nominees were elected to the board at the annual meeting, which would result in MM gaining control of the Board. The record also reflects that the timing of the Director Defendants' decision to expand the Board was to accomplish its primary purpose: to minimize the impact of the election of MM's nominees to the Board. The Court of Chancery's post-trial ruling from the bench states:

> The board's concern was that given the past acrimonious relationship between MM and Liquid Audio, a relationship characterized by litigation, if MM's two nominees were elected, the possibility of continued acrimony might cause one or more of the current board members to resign. If one director resigned, that would deadlock the board two-to-two; and if two directors resigned, then MM would gain control on a two-to-one basis. Either scenario could jeopardize the pending merger, which the incumbent board favored. That was the primary reason. . . .

After making that factual determination, the Court of Chancery recognized the effect of the Board's action in changing the size and composition of its membership immediately prior to the election of directors at the annual meeting:

> By adding two additional directors, the board foreclosed the result that it feared: The possibility of a deadlock or of MM taking control of the board. The reason is that even if MM's two nominees were elected at the 2002 annual meeting, the current directors would still constitute a majority of five. The result of the board's action was to diminish the influence of any nominees of MM that were elected, at least in numerical terms. Thus, based upon the evidence presented at trial, including an assessment of the witnesses' credibility, the Court of Chancery concluded that the Director Defendants amended the bylaws to expand the Board from five to seven, appointed two additional members of the Board, and timed those actions for the primary purpose of diminishing the influence of MM's nominees, if they were elected at the annual meeting.

Corporate Governance Principles

The most fundamental principles of corporate governance are a function of the allocation of power within a corporation between its stockholders and its board of directors. The stockholders' power is the right to vote on specific matters, in particular, in an election of directors. The power of managing the corporate enterprise is vested in the shareholders' duly elected board representatives.[6] Accordingly, while these "fundamental tenets of Delaware corporate law provide for a separation of control and ownership,"[7] the stockholder franchise has been characterized as the "ideological underpinning" upon which the legitimacy of the directors' managerial power rests.[8]

Maintaining a proper balance in the allocation of power between the stockholders' right to elect directors and the board of directors' right to manage the corporation is dependent upon the stockholders' unimpeded right to vote effectively in an election of directors. This Court has repeatedly stated that, if the stockholders are not satisfied with the management or actions of their elected

---

6. Paramount Communications, Inc. v. Time, Inc., 571 A.2d 1140, 1154 (Del. 1989).
7. Malone v. Brincat, 722 A.2d 5, 9 (Del. 1998).
8. Blasius Indus., Inc. v. Atlas Corp., 564 A.2d 651, 659 (Del. Ch. 1988).

representatives on the board of directors, the power of corporate democracy is available to the stockholders to replace the incumbent directors when they stand for re-election.[9] Consequently, two decades ago, this Court held: "The Courts of this State will not allow the wrongful subversion of corporate democracy by manipulation of the corporate machinery or by machinations under the cloak of Delaware law."

Accordingly, careful judicial scrutiny will be given a situation in which the right to vote for the election of successor directors has been effectively frustrated and denied.[10] This Court and the Court of Chancery have remained assiduous in carefully reviewing any board actions designed to interfere with or impede the effective exercise of corporate democracy by shareholders, especially in an election of directors.[11]

Corporate Governance Review Standards

The "defining tension" in corporate governance today has been characterized as "the tension between deference to directors' decisions and the scope of judicial review."[12] The appropriate standard of judicial review is dispositive of which party has the burden of proof as any litigation proceeds from stage to stage until there is a substantive determination on the merits.[13] Accordingly, identification of the correct analytical framework is essential to a proper judicial review of challenges to the decision-making process of a corporation's board of directors.[14]

The business judgment rule, as a standard of judicial review, is a common-law recognition of the statutory authority to manage a corporation that is vested in the board of directors. The business judgment rule is a "presumption that in making a business decision the directors of a corporation acted on an informed basis, in good faith and in the honest belief that the action taken was in the best interests of the company."[15] An application of the traditional business judgment rule places the burden on the "party challenging the [board's] decision to establish facts rebutting the presumption."[16] The effect of a proper invocation of the business judgment rule, as a standard of judicial review, is powerful because it operates deferentially. If the business judgment rule is not rebutted, a "court will not substitute its judgment for that of the board if the [board's] decision can be 'attributed to any rational business purpose.'"[17]

---

9. Aronson v. Lewis, 473 A.2d 805, 811 (Del. 1984). Unocal Corp. v. Mesa Petroleum Co., 493 A.2d 946 (Del. 1985).

10. Giuricich v. Emtrol Corp., 449 A.2d 232, 239 (Del. 1982).

11. Unitrin, Inc. v. American Gen. Corp., 651 A.2d 1361, 1378 (Del. 1995) (reviewing cases). See also Blasius Indus., Inc. v. Atlas Corp., 564 A.2d 651, 659-661 (Del. Ch. 1988) (collecting cases). See also In re Gaylord Container Corp. Shareholders Litig., 753 A.2d 462 (Del. Ch. 2000).

12. E. Norman Veasey, The Defining Tension in Corporate Governance in America, 52 Bus. Law. 393 (1997).

13. Unitrin, Inc. v. American Gen. Corp., 651 A.2d 1361, 1371 (Del. 1995). See, e.g., Malpiede v. Townson, 780 A.2d 1075 (Del. 2001); Emerald Partners v. Berlin, 787 A.2d 85 (Del. 2001); Cinerama, Inc. v. Technicolor, Inc., 663 A.2d 1156 (Del. 1995); Kahn v. Lynch Communication Sys., Inc., 638 A.2d 1110 (1994).

14. Unitrin, Inc. v. American Gen. Corp., 651 A.2d at 1374. See also Lewis H. Lazarus, Standards of Review in Conflict Transactions: An Examination of Decisions Rendered on Motions to Dismiss, 26 Del. J. Corp. L. 911 (2001).

15. Unitrin, Inc. v. American Gen. Corp., 651 A.2d at 1373, quoting Aronson v. Lewis, 473 A.2d 805, 811 (Del. 1984).

16. Id.

17. Id., quoting Unocal Corp. v. Mesa Petroleum Co., 493 A.2d 946, 954 (Del. 1985) (citation omitted).

In *Blasius*, Chancellor Allen set forth a cogent explanation of why judicial review under the deferential traditional business judgment rule standard is inappropriate when a board of directors acts for the primary purpose of impeding or interfering with the effectiveness of a shareholder vote, especially in the specific context presented in *Blasius* of a contested election for directors:

> The ordinary considerations to which the business judgment rule originally responded are simply not present in the shareholder voting context. That is, a decision by the board to act for the primary purpose of preventing the effectiveness of a shareholder vote inevitably involves the question who, as between the principal and the agent, has authority with respect to a matter of internal corporate governance. That, of course, is true in a very specific way in this case which deals with the question who should constitute the board of directors of the corporation, but it will be true in every instance in which an incumbent board seeks to thwart a shareholder majority. A board's decision to act to prevent the shareholders from creating a majority of new board positions and filling them does not involve the exercise of the corporation's power over its property, or with respect to its rights or obligations; rather, it involves allocation, between shareholders as a class and the board, of effective power with respect to governance of the corporation. Action designed principally to interfere with the effectiveness of a vote inevitably involves a conflict between the board and shareholder majority. Judicial review of such action involves a determination of the legal and equitable obligations of an agent towards his principal. This is not, in my opinion, a question that a court may leave to the agent finally to decide so long as he does so honestly and competently; that is, it may not be left to the agent's business judgment.[18]

In *Blasius*, the Chancellor did not adopt a rule of per se invalidity once a plaintiff has established that a board of directors has acted for the primary purpose of interfering with or impeding the effective exercise of a shareholder vote.[19] Instead, the Chancellor concluded that such situations required enhanced judicial scrutiny, pursuant to which the board of directors "bears the heavy burden of demonstrating a compelling justification for such action."[20]

In *Blasius*, the Chancellor then applied that compelling justification standard of enhanced judicial review in examining a board's action to expand its size in the context of a contested election of directors, exactly what the Liquid Audio board did in this case. In *Blasius*, notwithstanding the fact that the incumbent board of directors believed in good faith that the leveraged recapitalization proposed by the plaintiff was ill-advised and less valuable than the company's business plan, Chancellor Allen explained why the incumbent board of directors' good faith beliefs were not a proper basis for interfering with the stockholder franchise in a contested election for successor directors.

The only justification that can be offered for the action taken is that the board knows better than do the shareholders what is in the corporation's best interest. While that premise is no doubt true for any number of matters, it is irrelevant (except insofar as the shareholders wish to be guided by the board's recommendation) when the question is who should comprise the board. . . . It may be that the *Blasius* restructuring proposal was or is unrealistic and would lead to injury to the

---

18. Blasius Indus., Inc. v. Atlas Corp., 564 A.2d 651, 659-660 (Del. Ch. 1988).
19. Id. at 662.
20. Id. at 661.

corporation and its shareholders if pursued. . . . The board certainly viewed it in that way, and that view, held in good faith, entitled the board to take certain steps to evade the risk it perceived. It could, for example, expend corporate funds to inform shareholders and seek to bring them to a similar point of view.

But there is a vast difference between expending corporate funds to inform the electorate and exercising power for the primary purpose of foreclosing effective shareholder action. A majority of shareholders, who were not dominated in any respect, could view the matter differently than did the board. If they do, or did, they are entitled to employ the mechanisms provided by the corporation law and the Atlas certificate of incorporation to advance that view.[21]

In *Blasius,* the Chancellor set aside the board's action to expand the size of its membership for the primary purpose of impeding and interfering with the effectiveness of a shareholder vote in a contested election for directors. In this case, not only did the Liquid Audio board of directors take similar action in expanding the size of its membership and appointing two new directors to fill those positions, but it took that action for the same primary purpose.

The *Blasius* compelling justification standard of enhanced judicial review is based upon accepted and well-established legal tenets. This Court and the Court of Chancery have recognized the substantial degree of congruence between the rationale that led to the *Blasius* "compelling justification" enhanced standard of judicial review and the logical extension of that rationale within the context of the *Unocal* enhanced standard of judicial review.[23] Both standards recognize the inherent conflicts of interest that arise when a board of directors acts to prevent shareholders from effectively exercising their right to vote either contrary to the will of the incumbent board members generally or to replace the incumbent board members in a contested election.

In *Gilbert,* we held that a reviewing court must apply the *Unocal* standard of review whenever a board of directors adopts any defensive measure "in response to some threat to corporate policy and effectiveness which touches upon issues of control."[24] Later, in *Stroud,* this Court acknowledged that board action interfering with the exercise of the shareholder franchise often arises during a hostile contest for control when an acquiror launches both a proxy fight and a tender offer.[25] Accordingly, in *Stroud,* we held that "such action necessarily invoked both *Unocal* and *Blasius.*"

In *Stroud,* we emphasized, however, that the *Blasius* and *Unocal* standards of enhanced judicial review ("tests") are not mutually exclusive. In *Stroud,* we then explained why our holding in *Gilbert* did not render *Blasius* and its progeny meaningless:

> In certain circumstances, a court must recognize the special import of protecting the shareholders' franchise within *Unocal*'s requirement that any defensive measure be proportionate and "reasonable in relation to the threat posed." A board's unilateral decision to adopt a defensive measure touching "upon issues of control" that

21. Id. at 663.
23. Stroud v. Grace, 606 A.2d 75, 92 (Del. 1992); Chesapeake Corp. v. Shore, 771 A.2d 293, 320 (Del. Ch. 2000). See also David C. McBride and Danielle Gibbs, Voting Rights: The Metaphysics of Blasius Industries v. Atlas Corp., 26 Del. J. Corp. L. 927 (2001).
24. Gilbert v. El Paso Co., 575 A.2d 1131, 1144 (Del. 1990).
25. Stroud v. Grace, 606 A.2d at 92 n.3.

purposefully disenfranchises its shareholders is strongly suspect under *Unocal*, and cannot be sustained without a "compelling justification."

Thus, the same circumstances must be extant before the *Blasius* compelling justification enhanced standard of judicial review is required to sustain a board's action either independently, in the absence of a hostile contest for control, or within the *Unocal* standard of review when the board's action is taken as a defensive measure. The "compelling justification" standard set forth in *Blasius* is applied independently or within the *Unocal* standard only where "the primary purpose of the board's action is to interfere with or impede exercise of the shareholder franchise and the shareholders are not given a full and fair opportunity to vote effectively.[29] Accordingly, this Court has noted that the non-deferential *Blasius* standard of enhanced judicial review, which imposes upon a board of directors the burden of demonstrating a compelling justification for such actions, is rarely applied either independently or within the *Unocal* standard of review.

In *Unitrin*, for example, although the board's action in adopting a repurchase program was a defensive measure that implicated the shareholders' franchise and called for an application of the *Unocal* standard of review, it did not require the board to demonstrate a compelling justification for that action.[31] In *Unitrin*, the primary purpose of the repurchase program was not to interfere with or impede the shareholders' right to vote; the shareholders' right to vote effectively remained extant; and, in particular, we noted that the shareholders retained sufficient voting power to challenge the incumbent board by electing new directors with a successful proxy contest.

In this case, however, the Court of Chancery was presented with the ultimate defensive measure touching upon an issue of control. It was a defensive action taken by an incumbent board of directors for the primary purpose of interfering with and impeding the effectiveness of the shareholder franchise in electing successor directors. Accordingly, the incumbent board of directors had the burden of demonstrating a compelling justification for that action to withstand enhanced judicial scrutiny within the *Unocal* standard of reasonableness and proportionality.

This case presents a paragon of when the compelling justification standard of *Blasius* must be applied within *Unocal*'s requirement that any defensive measure be proportionate and reasonable in relation to the threat posed. The *Unocal* standard of review applies because the Liquid Audio board's action was a "defensive measure taken in response to some threat to corporate policy and effectiveness which touches upon issues of control." The compelling justification standard of *Blasius* also had to be applied within an application of the *Unocal* standard to that specific defensive measure because the primary purpose of the Board's action was to interfere with or impede the effective exercise of the shareholder franchise in a contested election for directors.[34]

The Court of Chancery properly decided to examine the Board's defensive action to expand from five to seven members and to appoint two new members in accordance with the *Unocal* standard of enhanced judicial review. Initially, the

---

29. Williams v. Geier, 671 A.2d 1368, 1376 (Del. 1996), quoting Stroud v. Grace, 606 A.2d 75, 92 (Del. 1992).

31. Unitrin, Inc. v. American Gen. Corp., 651 A.2d 1361 (Del. 1995).

34. Stroud v. Grace, 606 A.2d 75, 92, n.3 (Del. 1992).

Court of Chancery concluded that defensive action was not preclusive or coercive. If a defensive measure is not draconian, because it is neither coercive nor preclusive, proportionality review under *Unocal* requires the focus of enhanced judicial scrutiny to shift to the range of reasonableness.[35]

After the Court of Chancery determined that the Board's action was not preclusive or coercive, it properly proceeded to determine whether the Board's action was reasonable and proportionate in relation to the threat posed.[36] Under the circumstances presented in this case, however, the Court of Chancery did not "recognize the special [importance] of protecting the shareholder's franchise within *Unocal*'s requirement that any defensive measure be proportionate and reasonable in relation to the threat posed." Since the Court of Chancery had already concluded that the primary purpose of the Liquid Audio board's defensive measure was to interfere with or impede an effective exercise of the shareholder's franchise in a contested election of directors, the Board had the burden of demonstrating a compelling justification for that action.

When the primary purpose of a board of directors' defensive measure is to interfere with or impede the effective exercise of the shareholder franchise in a contested election for directors, the board must first demonstrate a compelling justification for such action as a condition precedent to any judicial consideration of reasonableness and proportionality. As this case illustrates, such defensive actions by a board need not actually prevent the shareholders from attaining any success in seating one or more nominees in a contested election for directors and the election contest need not involve a challenge for outright control of the board of directors. To invoke the *Blasius* compelling justification standard of review within an application of the *Unocal* standard of review, the defensive actions of the board only need to be taken for the primary purpose of interfering with or impeding the effectiveness of the stockholder vote in a contested election for directors.

The record reflects that the primary purpose of the Director Defendants' action was to interfere with and impede the effective exercise of the stockholder franchise in a contested election for directors. The Court of Chancery concluded that the Director Defendants amended the bylaws to provide for a board of seven and appointed two additional members of the Board for the primary purpose of diminishing the influence of MM's two nominees on a five-member Board by eliminating either the possibility of a deadlock on the board or of MM controlling the Board, if one or two Director Defendants resigned from the Board. That defensive action by the Director Defendants compromised the essential role of corporate democracy in maintaining the proper allocation of power between the shareholders and the Board, because that action was taken in the context of a contested election for successor directors. Since the Director Defendants did not demonstrate a compelling justification for that defensive action, the bylaw amendment that expanded the size of the Liquid Audio board, and permitted the appointment of two new members on the eve of a contested election, should have been invalidated by the Court of Chancery.

---

35. Unitrin, Inc. v. American Gen. Corp., 651 A.2d 1361, 1387-1388 (Del. 1995).

36. In our review of the Court of Chancery's *Unocal* analysis, we have assumed without deciding that the Board was independent and had reasonable grounds for believing that there was a danger to corporate policy.

One of the most venerable precepts of Delaware's common law corporate jurisprudence is the principle that "inequitable action does not become permissible simply because it is legally possible."[40] At issue in this case is not the validity generally of either a bylaw that permits a board of directors to expand the size of its membership or a board's power to appoint successor members to fill board vacancies. In this case, however, the incumbent Board timed its utilization of these otherwise valid powers to expand the size and composition of the Liquid Audio board for the primary purpose of impeding and interfering with the efforts of the stockholders' power to effectively exercise their voting rights in a contested election for directors. As this Court held more than three decades ago, "these are inequitable purposes, contrary to established principles of corporate democracy . . . and may not be permitted to stand."[41]

Conclusion

The judgment of the Court of Chancery is reversed. This matter is remanded for further proceedings in accordance with this opinion. The mandate shall issue immediately.

---

1. *The rediscovery of* Blasius. While *Stroud* seemingly buried *Blasius* in its footnote 3, *Liquid Audio* accepts *Blasius* as justifying a uniquely high standard of judicial review—a "compelling justification" standard—in the context of attempts to delay or interfere with shareholder voting. Still, *Blasius* would seem not to apply if the shareholders authorize a limitation on their own voting authority as they did in *Stroud*. Thus, consider the following:

Suppose the plaintiffs in *Stroud* propose a specific nominee as a Category 1 director with broad experience in investment banking and money management but little experience as an operating executive with an industrial company, and the board rejects this nominee's candidacy. What result on a motion for a preliminary injunction? What if other directors classified in the same category by the board had even less business experience? Could this be deemed inequitable under *Schnell*? Alternatively, suppose the charter provision required the director to live within 30 miles of the company's principal headquarters (in a rural location). Can a charter provision ever be rejected as unreasonable once it has received shareholder approval?

2. *A further twist on* Blasius. Inter-Tel, Inc., a high-tech phone company, experienced a falling out between Steven Mihalyo, its founder and largest shareholder (he held 19 percent), and the company's independent board. Mihalyo resigned as CEO and asked that the company be put up for an auction. A number of bids were received, and the board, after much negotiation, struck a deal with Mitel Networks Corporation for an all-cash merger at $25.60 per share. But then another bidder, Vector Capital, made a series of tentative offers at higher prices, subject to a requested right to conduct a due diligence investigation of Inter-Tel before making a binding offer. The Inter-Tel board agreed to Vector Capital's request for a due diligence review, but Vector withdrew its bid—and then indicated that it might

40. Schnell v. Chris-Craft, Indus., Inc., 285 A.2d 437, 439 (Del. 1971).
41. Id.

still offer a higher price. Frustrated with this fickle bidder, the Inter-Tel board set a meeting date for shareholders to vote on the Mitel merger. Inter-Tel's proxy statement contained two items on which shareholders were asked to vote: (1) the Mitel merger and (2) a proposal to adjourn the special meeting of shareholders if insufficient votes were obtained to approve the merger. The latter proposal was pursuant to an SEC recommended policy. At this point, Mihalyo sent a letter to Inter-Tel's shareholders proposing an alternative transaction: a leveraged recapitalization under which Inter-Tel would repurchase 60 percent of its shares (with borrowed funds) for $28 per share. Vector Capital then dropped out of the contest.

Next, Institutional Shareholder Services (ISS), the proxy advisor, recommended that shareholders vote against the merger—partly in the hope that this would lead Mitel to make a higher bid. But Mitel would not increase its offer.

Faced with certain defeat at the shareholders' meeting and still considering the Mitel merger to be superior to the Mihalyo recapitalization proposal, the Inter-Tel board decided to postpone the shareholders' meeting and set a new record date (apparently in the belief that some shareholders who had purchased stock after the record date would vote for the merger at the later meeting date). ISS changed its recommendation to favor the Mitel merger, and Mihalyo withdrew his recapitalization proposal. With no other pending offer, the merger passed with a vote of 62 percent of the outstanding shares (and 72 percent of the shares actually voted).

Nonetheless, plaintiff sued, seeking an injunction against the closing of the Mitel merger, arguing that the postponement lacked any compelling justification and so violated the *Blasius* standard. In particular, plaintiff stressed that the possibility of a postponement was on ballot for the meeting (and would have been voted down by the shareholders if the meeting had occurred). Against this confused backdrop, Vice Chancellor Strine ruled:

> I conclude that well-motivated, independent directors may reschedule an imminent special meeting at which the stockholders are to consider an all cash, all shares offer from a third-party acquirer when the directors: (1) believe that the merger is in the best interests of the stockholders; (2) know that if the meeting proceeds the stockholders will vote down the merger; (3) reasonably fear that in the wake of the merger's rejection, the acquirer will walk away from the deal and the corporation's stock price will plummet; (4) want more time to communicate with and provide information to the stockholders before the stockholders vote on the merger and risk the irrevocable loss of the pending offer; and (5) reschedule the meeting within a reasonable time period and do not preclude or coerce the stockholders from freely deciding to reject the merger.

Mercier v. Inter-Tel, Inc., 929 A.2d 786 (Del. Ch. 2007).

In so concluding, Vice Chancellor Strine observed that "the *Blasius* standard should be reformulated" to bring it into closer conformity with *Unocal*'s standards. However, to protect his decision in view of *Liquid Audio*'s endorsement of *Blasius*, he also found that directors "who fear that stockholders are about to make an unwise decision that poses the threat that the stockholders will irrevocably lose a unique opportunity to receive a premium for their shares have a compelling justification—the protection of their stockholders' financial best interests—for a short postponement in the merger voting process to allow more time for deliberation." He also suggested that *Blasius*'s "compelling justification" standard applied more logically to the election of directors than to a merger or similar decision.

3. *Other defensive tactics related to voting.* (a) *Advance notice bylaws.* With the increase in proxy contests, many public corporations have recently adopted advance notice bylaws. Typically, such provisions require that prospective nominees for election to the board submit certain information concerning their candidacy and qualifications in advance of the meeting. The advance notice required has ranged from 30 to 90 days in recent cases. Generally, judicial analysis of these provisions has focused not on their facial validity (which would seemingly be clear after Stroud v. Grace), but on whether they have been inequitably employed. For example, where the board has waived the bylaw with respect to one slate of candidates, it may be required on equitable grounds similarly to waive it with respect to other slates. Cf. Hubbard v. Hollywood Park Realty Enterprises, Inc., 1991 Del. Ch. LEXIS 9, Civil Action No. 11779. Alternatively, where an advance notice bylaw is adopted on the eve of the date by which notice must be given under it for the next annual meeting, this also has been viewed as an impermissible manipulation of the corporate machinery in violation of the *Schnell* standard. See Lerman v. Diagnostic Data, Inc., 421 A.2d 906 (1980).

(b) *Postponements.* A standard defense tactic is to postpone a scheduled meeting if it looks as if the insurgent will win. During the interval, additional shares might be issued, or other actions taken, to change the outcome. Del. Gen. Corp. Law §211(c) requires that an annual shareholder meeting be convened by the board within 13 months after the last meeting if no date has been designated, or within 30 days after the designated date. But no statutory provision directly governs postponements of a scheduled meeting, except that §211(c) requires the board to hold a meeting "as soon as is convenient" if it is not held on the designated date. In Aprahamian v. HBO & Co., 531 A.2d 1204 (Del. Ch. 1987), HBO notified its stockholders on the day before its scheduled annual meeting that the meeting would be postponed (it had just received a report from a proxy solicitor that it might lose a critical vote). Recognizing that delay would involve a new record date and would render invalid proxies already solicited (and thus would require a costly resolicitation by the insurgents), the Delaware Chancery Court ordered that the rescheduled meeting be held within 60 days of the original record date. Does *Inter-Tel* imply any change in this result? Probably not—at least when the purpose of the postponement is to invalidate outstanding proxies. But otherwise the Delaware courts have been tolerant of short-term postponements.

(c) *Written consent bylaws.* Another much-used defense tactic has been to adopt bylaws regulating the use of written consents by shareholders. Although the *Datapoint* decision, page 591 supra, invalidated attempts to delay the effectiveness of consents, corporations have been permitted to adopt bylaws establishing a procedure for the board to set a record date. See Edelman v. Authorized Distribution Network, Inc., 1989 Del. Ch. LEXIS 156, Civil Action No. 11104 (upholding bylaw requiring shareholders wishing to solicit written consents to request and then allow board to fix a record date). Obviously, the net effect here is to give the board advance notice of the intended solicitation and to preclude any executed written consent from becoming effective until that date has been set.

(d) *Vacancy bylaws.* Insurgents seeking to act by written consent will frequently seek to adopt a bylaw expanding the size of the board to the maximum permitted by the corporation's charter. This is a technique for outflanking a staggered board provision, but it works only to the extent that the bylaws permit the shareholders to fill the newly created positions. Hence, if the target board does not dare attempt to secure a charter amendment precluding action by written consent, it will typically adopt a bylaw empowering the board (and not shareholders) to fill all newly created positions on the board. If vacancies are filled by the board in order to frustrate a specific insurgent's election campaign, however, this is precisely the fact pattern of *Blasius*.

H. *SHAREHOLDERS' RIGHT OF INSPECTION*

The ability to inspect the corporation's records is often a necessary tool for the shareholder who wishes to exercise the right to vote or to maintain a lawsuit. In many cases, only if the shareholder can learn the names and addresses of other shareholders will the shareholder be able to conduct a contest for control. Preconditions for maintaining derivative suits (considered in Chapter VIII) may require the shareholder to communicate with other shareholders, e.g., to satisfy a "demand requirement" or to seek other shareholders as joint plaintiffs to avoid furnishing security for expenses. Beyond shareholder lists, shareholders may want to examine minute books or account books for a variety of reasons, e.g., to determine the value of their shares or to secure data that they believe relevant to bringing an action.

At common law, shareholders have a right to inspect the corporation's books and records. The right is not absolute; it is exercisable only for a "proper purpose." Because this limitation is hardly self-defining, corporations faced with a demand for inspection can easily deflect immediate inspection by turning to litigation. Under the common law, some of the purposes held to be proper to permit inspection are: to determine whether there has been improper management in order to bring suit or seek a receivership; to ascertain financial conditions so as to measure the propriety of dividends or to decide how to vote at a forthcoming election; to determine the value of shares for sale or other purposes; and to obtain a shareholder list to solicit proxies, influence voting, invite other shareholders to join in litigation, or offer them a higher price for their shares than is currently being offered by management. Among purposes held to be improper are: to publish the information merely to embarrass or harass the corporation; to depress the value of shares; to sell a shareholder list for personal profit; to use the information in a competing business; and to aid in the defense of an action by the corporation against the shareholder.

All jurisdictions have adopted legislation dealing with inspection. The statutes cover some or all of the following matters: length of time a shareholder must have held shares or the percentage of shares necessary (as qualifications for inspection); a requirement of proper purpose; the burden of proof on the question of proper purpose; form of demand (i.e., in writing); various available defenses; the penalties for refusal of inspection; court procedures to enforce inspection rights; and the types of books and records subject to inspection.

In view of the detailed attention paid to the matter of inspection by the legislatures, does the common law right survive the enactment of these statutes? See Soreno Hotel Co. v. State ex rel. Otis Elevator Co., 107 Fla. 195, 144 So. 339 (1932): "It is almost uniformly held that statutes, giving the right of inspection to stockholders of the books and records of private corporations, do not abridge the right as it existed at common law but rather enlarge and extend it by removing some of the common law limitations."[30]

Delaware General Corporation Law (2007)

Sec. 220. *Inspection of books and records.* (a) As used in this section . . . "stockholder" means a holder of record of stock in a stock corporation, ...

(b) Any stockholder, in person or by attorney or other agent, shall, upon written demand under oath stating the purpose thereof, have the right during the usual hours for business to inspect for any proper purpose, and to make copies and extracts from:

(1) the corporation's stock ledger, a list of its stockholders, and its other books and records; and

(2) A subsidiary's books and records, to the extent that:

a. The corporation has actual possession and control of such records of such subsidiary; or

b. The corporation could obtain such records through the exercise of control over such subsidiary, provided that as of the date of making the demand:

(1) The stockholder inspection of such books and records would not constitute a breach of an agreement between the corporation or the subsidiary and a person or persons not affiliated with the corporation; and

(2) The subsidiary would not have the right under the law applicable to it to deny the corporation access to such books and records upon demand by the corporation.

. . . A proper purpose shall mean a purpose reasonably related to such person's interest as a stockholder. In every instance where an attorney or other agent shall be the person who seeks the right to inspection, the demand under oath shall be accompanied by a power of attorney or such other writing which authorizes the attorney or other agent to so act on behalf of the stockholder. The demand under oath shall be directed to the corporation at its registered office in this State or at its principal place of business.

(c) If the corporation, or an officer or agent thereof, refuses to permit an inspection sought by a stockholder or attorney or other agent acting for the stockholder pursuant to sub-section (b) or does not reply to the demand within 5 business days after the demand has been made, the stockholder may apply to the Court of Chancery for an order to compel such inspection. The Court of Chancery is hereby vested with exclusive jurisdiction to determine whether or not the person seeking inspection is entitled to the inspection sought. The Court may summarily order the corporation to permit the stockholder to inspect the corporation's stock ledger, an existing list of stockholders, and its other books and records, and to make copies or extracts therefrom; or the Court may order the corporation to furnish to the

---

30. In *Soreno* the statutory remedy was both broader and more limited than that at common law. Although allowing inspection without requiring a showing of proper purpose, the statute limited the remedy to shareholders holding a certain percentage of shares. Because the shareholder did not hold this required percentage, he was barred from using the statute, but the court allowed a common law remedy on showing a proper purpose.

stockholder a list of its stockholders as of a specific date on condition that the stockholder first pay to the corporation the reasonable cost of obtaining and furnishing such list and on such other conditions as the court deems appropriate. Where the stockholder seeks to inspect the corporation's books and records, other than its stock ledger or list of stockholders, such stockholder shall first establish that:

(1) Such stockholder is a stockholder;

(2) Such stockholder has complied with this section respecting the form and manner of making demand for inspection of such document; and

(3) The inspection such stockholder seeks is for a proper purpose.

Where the stockholder seeks to inspect the corporation's stock ledger or list of stockholders and establishes that such stockholder is a stockholder and has complied with this section respecting the form and manner of making demand for inspection of such documents, the burden of proof shall be upon the corporation to establish that the inspection such stockholder seeks is for an improper purpose. The Court may, in its discretion, prescribe any limitations or conditions with reference to the inspection, or award such other or further relief as the Court may deem just and proper. The Court may order books, documents and records, pertinent extracts therefrom, or duly authenticated copies thereof, to be brought within this State and kept in this State upon such terms and conditions as the order may prescribe.

(d) Any director . . . shall have the right to examine the corporation's stock ledger, a list of its stockholders and its other books and records for a purpose reasonably related to the director's position as a director. . . .

Seinfeld v. Verizon Communications, Inc.
909 A.2d 117 (Del. 2006)

HOLLAND, J.: The plaintiff-appellant, Frank D. Seinfeld ("Seinfeld"), brought suit under section 220 of the Delaware General Corporation Law to compel the defendant-appellee, Verizon Communications, Inc. ("Verizon"), to produce, for his inspection, its books and records related to the compensation of Verizon's three highest corporate officers from 2000 to 2002. Seinfeld claimed that their executive compensation, individually and collectively, was excessive and wasteful. On cross-motions for summary judgment, the Court of Chancery applied well-established Delaware law and held that Seinfeld had not met his evidentiary burden to demonstrate a proper purpose to justify the inspection of Verizon's records. The settled law of Delaware required Seinfeld to present some evidence that established a credible basis from which the Court of Chancery could infer there were legitimate issues of possible waste, mismanagement or wrongdoing that warranted further investigation.[1] Seinfeld argues that burden of proof "erects an insurmountable barrier for the minority shareholder of a public company." We have concluded that Seinfeld's argument is without merit.

We reaffirm the well-established law of Delaware that stockholders seeking inspection under section 220 must present "some evidence" to suggest a "credible

---

1. Thomas & Betts Corp. v. Leviton Mfg. Co., Inc., 681 A.2d 1026, 1031 (Del. 1996); Security First Corp. v. U.S. Die Casting & Dev. Co., 687 A.2d 563, 567 (Del. 1997); Helmsman Mgmt. Servs., Inc. v. A & S Consultants, Inc., 525 A.2d 160, 166 (Del. Ch. 1987).

basis" from which a court can infer that mismanagement, waste or wrongdoing may have occurred. The "credible basis" standard achieves an appropriate balance between providing stockholders who can offer some evidence of possible wrongdoing with access to corporate records and safeguarding the right of the corporation to deny requests for inspections that are based only upon suspicion or curiosity.[4] Accordingly, the judgment of the Court of Chancery must be affirmed.

Facts

Seinfeld asserts that he is the beneficial owner of approximately 3,884 shares of Verizon, held in street name through a brokerage firm. His stated purpose for seeking Verizon's books and records was to investigate mismanagement and corporate waste regarding the executive compensations of Ivan G. Seidenberg, Lawrence T. Babbio, Jr. and Charles R. Lee. Seinfeld alleges that the three executives were all performing in the same job and were paid amounts, including stock options, above the compensation provided for in their employment contracts. Seinfeld's section 220 claim for inspection is further premised on various computations he performed which indicate that the three executives' compensation totaled $205 million over three years and was, therefore, excessive, given their responsibilities to the corporation.

During his deposition, Seinfeld acknowledged he had no factual support for his claim that mismanagement had taken place. He admitted that the three executives did not perform any duplicative work. Seinfeld conceded he had no factual basis to allege the executives "did not earn" the amounts paid to them under their respective employment agreements. Seinfeld also admitted "there is a possibility" that the $205 million executive compensation amount he calculated was wrong.

The issue before us is quite narrow: should a stockholder seeking inspection under section 220 be entitled to relief without being required to show some evidence to suggest a credible basis for wrongdoing? We conclude that the answer must be no.

Stockholder Inspection Rights

Delaware corporate law provides for a separation of legal control and ownership. The legal responsibility to manage the business of the corporation for the benefit of the stockholder owners is conferred on the board of directors by statute.[6] The common law imposes fiduciary duties upon the directors of Delaware corporations to constrain their conduct when discharging that statutory responsibility.

Stockholders' rights to inspect the corporation's books and records were recognized at common law because "[a]s a matter of self-protection, the stockholder was entitled to know how his agents were conducting the affairs of the corporation of which he or she was a part owner."[8] The qualified inspection rights that originated at common law are now codified in Title 8, section 220 of the Delaware Code, which provides, in part: "(b) Any stockholder, in person or by attorney or other

---

4. Security First Corp. v. U.S. Die Casting & Dev. Co., 687 A.2d at 571.
6. Del. Code Ann. tit. 8, 141(a) (2006).
8. Saito v. McKesson HBOC, Inc., 806 A.2d 113, 116 (Del. 2002) (citing Shaw v. Agri-Mark, Inc., 663 A.2d 464, 467 (Del. 1995)).

agent, shall, upon written demand under oath stating the purpose thereof, have the right during the usual hours for business to inspect for any proper purpose."

Section 220 provides stockholders of Delaware corporations with a "powerful right." By properly asserting that right under section 220, stockholders are able to obtain information that can be used in a variety of contexts. Stockholders may use information about corporate mismanagement, waste or wrongdoing in several ways. For example, they may: institute derivative litigation; "seek an audience with the board [of directors] to discuss proposed reform or, failing in that, they may prepare a stockholder resolution for the next annual meeting, or mount a proxy fight to elect new directors."

Inspection Litigation Increases

More than a decade ago, we noted that "[s]urprisingly, little use has been made of section 220 as an information-gathering tool in the derivative [suit] context."[11] Today, however, stockholders who have concerns about corporate governance are increasingly making a broad array of section 220 demands. The rise in books and records litigation is directly attributable to this Court's encouragement of stockholders, who can show a proper purpose, to use the "tools at hand" to obtain the necessary information before filing a derivative action.[13] Section 220 is now recognized as "an important part of the corporate governance landscape."[14]

Seinfeld Denied Inspection

The Court of Chancery determined that Seinfeld's deposition testimony established only that he was concerned about the large amount of compensation paid to the three executives. That court concluded that Seinfeld offered "no evidence from which [it] could evaluate whether there is a reasonable ground for suspicion that the executive's compensation rises to the level of waste." It also concluded that Seinfeld did not "submit any evidence showing that the executives were not entitled to [the stock] options." The Court of Chancery properly noted that a disagreement with the business judgment of Verizon's board of directors or its compensation committee is not evidence of wrongdoing and did not satisfy Seinfeld's burden under section 220. The Court of Chancery held: "viewing the evidence in the light most favorable to Seinfeld, the court must conclude that he has not carried his burden of showing that there is a credible basis from which the court can infer that the Verizon board of directors committed waste or mismanagement in compensating these three executives during the relevant period of time. Instead, the record clearly establishes that Seinfeld's Section 220 demand was made merely on the basis of suspicion or curiosity."

---

11. Rales v. Blasband, 634 A.2d 927, 934-35 n.10 (Del. 1993) (quoted in Grimes v. Donald, 673 A.2d 1207, 1216 n.11 (Del. 1996)).

13. Grimes v. Donald, 673 A.2d at 1216 (citing Rales v. Blasband, 634 A.2d at 934-35 n.10). See also Beam ex rel. Martha Stewart Living Omnimedia, Inc., 833 A.2d 961, 981 nn.65-66 (Del. Ch. 2003) (collecting cases).

14. Security First Corp. v. U.S. Die Casting & Dev. Co., 687 A.2d 563, 571 (Del. 1997). See also E. Norman Veasey & Christine T. DiGuglielmo, What Happened in Delaware Corporate Law and Governance from 1992-2004? A Retrospective on Some Key Developments, 153 U. Pa. L. Rev. 1399, 1466-69 (2005) (discussing the use of section 220 and cases that have applied it).

Evidentiary Barrier Allegation

In this appeal, Seinfeld asserts that the "Court of Chancery's ruling erects an insurmountable barrier for the minority shareholder of a public company." Seinfeld argues that: "This Court and the Court of Chancery have instructed shareholders to utilize 220 as one of the tools at hand. Yet, the Court of Chancery at bar, in requiring *evidence* makes a 220 application a mirage. If the shareholder had evidence, a derivative suit would be brought. Unless there is a whistle blower, or a video cassette, the public shareholder, having no access to corporate records, will only have suspicions."

Seinfeld submits that "by requiring evidence, the shareholder is prevented from using the tools at hand." Seinfeld's brief concludes with a request for this Court to reduce the burden of proof that stockholders must meet in a section 220 action: "Plaintiff submits that in a case involving public companies, minority shareholders who have access only to public documents and without a whistle blower or corporate documents should be permitted to have limited inspection based upon suspicions, reasonable beliefs, and logic arising from public disclosures."

After oral arguments, this Court asked the parties for supplemental briefs that would address the following questions:

> A. Should a stockholder with a proper purpose be entitled to inspect carefully limited categories of corporate books and records, pursuant to Section 220, upon a showing that the stockholder has a rational basis for the stated purpose and no other purpose that would militate against inspection?
>
> B. If the standard in question "A" would not be appropriate, is there *any* reduced burden of proof under Section 220 that would improve stockholders' ability to obtain the "tools" to pursue derivative claims without disrupting corporations' orderly conduct of business and without inappropriately interfering with corporate decision-making? If so, articulate the reduced burden of proof. If not, explain why not.

We asked these questions in order to review the current balance between the rights of stockholders and corporations that is established by Thomas & Betts Corp. v. Leviton Mfg. Co.[22] and Security First Corp. v. U.S. Die Casting & Dev. Co.[23] and their progeny.

Credible Basis from Some Evidence

In a section 220 action, a stockholder has the burden of proof to demonstrate a proper purpose by a preponderance of the evidence. It is well established that a stockholder's desire to investigate wrongdoing or mismanagement is a "proper purpose." Such investigations are proper, because where the allegations of mismanagement prove meritorious, investigation furthers the interest of all stockholders and should increase stockholder return.

The evolution of Delaware's jurisprudence in section 220 actions reflects judicial efforts to maintain a proper balance between the rights of shareholders to obtain information based upon credible allegations of corporation mismanagement and the rights of directors to manage the business of the corporation without undue interference from stockholders. In *Thomas & Betts*, this Court held that, to meet its

---

22. Thomas & Betts Corp. v. Leviton Mfg. Co., 681 A.2d 1026, 1031 (Del. 1996).
23. Security First Corp. v. U.S. Die Casting & Dev. Co., 687 A.2d 563 (Del. 1997).

"burden of proof, a stockholder must present some *credible basis* from which the court can infer that waste or mismanagement may have occurred." Six months later, in *Security First*, this Court held "[t]here must be *some evidence* of possible mismanagement as would warrant further investigation of the matter."

Our holdings in *Thomas & Betts* and *Security First* were contemporaneous with our decisions that initially encouraged stockholders to make greater use of section 220. In Grimes v. Donald, decided just months before *Thomas & Betts*, this Court reaffirmed the salutary use of section 220 as one of the "tools at hand" for stockholders to use to obtain information. When the plaintiff in *Thomas & Betts* suggested that the burden of demonstrating a proper purpose had been attenuated by our encouragement for stockholders to use section 220, we rejected that argument: "Contrary to plaintiff's assertion in the instant case, this Court in *Grimes* did not suggest that its reference to a Section 220 demand as one of the "tools at hand" was intended to eviscerate or modify the need for a stockholder to show a proper purpose under Section 220." In *Security First* and *Thomas & Betts*, we adhered to the Court of Chancery's holding in Helmsman Mgmt. Servs., Inc. v. A & S Consultants, Inc. that: "A mere statement of a purpose to investigate possible general mismanagement, without more, will not entitle a shareholder to broad 220 inspection relief. There must be *some evidence* of possible mismanagement as would warrant further investigation of the matter."

Standard Achieves Balance

Investigations of meritorious allegations of possible mismanagement, waste or wrongdoing, benefit the corporation, but investigations that are "indiscriminate fishing expeditions" do not. "At some point, the costs of generating more information fall short of the benefits of having more information. At that point, compelling production of information would be wealth-reducing, and so shareholders would not want it produced." Accordingly, this Court has held that an inspection to investigate possible wrongdoing where there is no "credible basis," is a license for "fishing expeditions" and thus adverse to the interests of the corporation: "Stockholders have a right to at least a limited inquiry into books and records when they have established some credible basis to believe that there has been wrongdoing. . . . Yet it would invite mischief to open corporate management to indiscriminate fishing expeditions."[35]

A stockholder is "not required to prove by a preponderance of the evidence that waste and [mis]management are actually occurring." Stockholders need only show, by a preponderance of the evidence, a credible basis from which the Court of Chancery can infer there is possible mismanagement that would warrant further investigation—a showing that "may ultimately fall well short of demonstrating that anything wrong occurred." That "threshold may be satisfied by a credible showing, through documents, logic, testimony or otherwise, that there are legitimate issues of wrongdoing."

Although the threshold for a stockholder in a section 220 proceeding is not insubstantial, the "credible basis" standard sets the lowest possible burden of proof. The only way to reduce the burden of proof further would be to eliminate any requirement that a stockholder show *some evidence* of possible wrongdoing. That would be tantamount to permitting inspection based on the "mere suspicion"

---

35. Security First Corp. v. U.S. Die Casting & Dev. Co., 687 A.2d at 571.

standard that Seinfeld advances in this appeal. However, such a standard has been repeatedly rejected as a basis to justify the enterprise cost of an inspection.

In Delaware and elsewhere,[42] the "credible-basis-from-some-evidence" standard is settled law. Under the doctrine of *stare decisis*, settled law is overruled only "for urgent reasons and upon clear manifestation of error." A review of the cases that have applied the "credible basis" standard refutes Seinfeld's premise that requiring "some evidence" constitutes an insurmountable barrier for stockholders who assert inspection rights under section 220.

Requiring stockholders to establish a "credible basis" for the Court of Chancery to infer possible wrongdoing by presenting "some evidence" has not impeded stockholder inspections. Although many section 220 proceedings have been filed since we decided *Security First* and *Thomas & Betts*, Verizon points out that Seinfeld's case is only the second proceeding in which a plaintiff's demand to investigate wrongdoing was found to be *entirely* without a "credible basis." In contrast, there are a myriad of cases where stockholders have successfully presented "some evidence" to establish a "credible basis" to infer possible mismanagement and thus received some narrowly tailored right of inspection.

We remain convinced that the rights of stockholders and the interests of the corporation in a section 220 proceeding are properly balanced by requiring a stockholder to show "some evidence of *possible* mismanagement as would warrant further investigation." The "credible basis" standard maximizes stockholder value by limiting the range of permitted stockholder inspections to those that might have merit. Accordingly, our holdings in *Security First* and *Thomas & Betts* are ratified and reaffirmed.

Conclusion

The judgment of the Court of Chancery is affirmed.

---

1. *The shifting balance.* In Security First Corp. v. U.S. Die Casting and Development Co., 687 A.2d 563 (Del. 1997), the Delaware Supreme Court insisted on "an order circumscribed with rifted precision." Five years later, in the immediate aftermath of Enron, this standard was relaxed marginally in Saito v. McKesson HBOC, Inc., 806 A.2d 113 (Del. 2002); however, that decision reaffirmed that a shareholder of the parent corporation could not inspect a subsidiary's books and records "absent a showing of a fraud or that a subsidiary is in fact the mere alter ego of the parent. . . ." In the wake of *Saito*, the Delaware legislature amended §220, chiefly to liberalize access to the subsidiary's books and records, as discussed below. *Seinfeld*, decided in 2006, seems to show the balance being recalibrated again, to require some showing of legal merit to the claim that is to be investigated. *Query:* If the plaintiff in *Seinfeld* were investigating instead the possible backdating of stock options and showed that several awards of options had

---

42. The "credible basis" standard is also settled law in those states that look to Delaware law for guidance on matters of corporation law. See, e.g., Arctic Fin. Corp. v. OTR Express, Inc., 272 Kan. 1326, 38 P.3d 701, 703-04 (Kan. 2002) (looking to *Security First* and *Thomas & Betts* for guidance regarding a books and records inspection under Kansas law); Towle v. Robinson Springs Corp., 168 Vt. 226, 719 A.2d 880, 882 (Vt. 1998) (in a books and records case under Vermont law, citing *Thomas & Betts* for the proposition that "[c]laims of mismanagement, however, must be supported by evidence").

occurred just prior to a marked jump in the stock's price, would this constitute "credible evidence"? Should more be required?

2. *Proper purpose and multiple purposes.* A consensus exists that it is a proper purpose for a takeover bidder or a proxy contestant to seek a shareholder list in order to communicate with other shareholders. Courts will not evaluate whether the offer or proxy proposal is sound or in the corporation's best interests in requiring the production of a shareholder list. See Credit Bureau of St. Paul, Inc. v. Credit Bureau Reports, Inc., 290 A.2d 689 (Del. Ch.), *aff'd,* 290 A.2d 691 (Del. 1972). However, what should be the result if, in response to a tender offer, the target buys shares in the bidder and then seeks a shareholder list, arguably in order to defeat the tender offer against it? See Mite Corp. v. Heli-Coil Corp., 256 A.2d 855 (Del. Ch. 1969) (granting shareholder request).

Outside of Delaware, a number of recent decisions have said the burden of showing that the shareholder had an improper purpose rests on the corporation. See Bennett v. Mack's Supermarkets, Inc., 602 S.W.2d 143 (Ky. 1979); Crane Co. v. Anaconda Co., 39 N.Y.2d 14, 382 N.Y.S.2d 707, 346 N.E.2d 507 (1976).

3. *Who may inspect?* (a) *Registered owners.* (i) A broker is employed by a prospective tender offeror to act as dealer-manager in the offeror's campaign to acquire 52 percent of target company's shares. The broker is the registered holder of 100 shares of target company. He seeks to examine and copy target company's stock list so that the tender offer can be made. The broker makes the demand to examine the list solely because of his employment and in aid of his earning a commission for his services. Is he entitled to examine the list? See Alex Brown & Sons v. Latrobe Steel Co., 376 F. Supp. 1373 (W.D. Pa. 1974). Is it relevant that he acquired the target company shares for the purpose of demanding inspection of the stock list? See Mite Corp. v. Heli-Coil Corp., 256 A.2d 855 (Del. Ch. 1969).

(ii) Plaintiff shareholder seeks a stock list in order to solicit proxies for a shareholders' meeting. The corporation resists inspection on the ground that the plaintiff, though a registered shareholder, acquired his shares in violation of the Federal Aviation Act of 1958 and regulations of the Civil Aeronautics Board. Should the court consider this defense on the merits? See Western Air Lines, Inc. v. Kerkorian, 254 A.2d 240 (Del. 1969).

(iii) If plaintiff holds shares solely as a record owner (e.g., a broker holding for a customer), is the broker/plaintiff entitled to inspection? See Joannou v. G. Joannou Cycle Co., 6 App. Div. 2d 592, 180 N.Y.S.2d 141 (1958) ("having record title as well as some legal interest, she would, prima facie, be entitled to exercise a stockholder's rights as against the corporation"); State ex rel. Healy v. Superior Oil Co., 13 A.2d 453 (Del. 1940) (inspection allowed even though the corporation contended plaintiff "merely a nominee").

(b) *Beneficial owners.* In Delaware, §220(a) defines a stockholder as a "holder of record" and thus excludes beneficial owners. Outside of Delaware, cases have gone both ways, with a minority permitting the beneficial owner to have standing. See Norman Lattin, Corporations 350 (2d ed. 1971).

4. *NOBO lists and uncompiled data.* May the shareholder who requests a shareholder list also discover the names of beneficial owners known to the corporation? The emerging answer appears to be yes. In Hatleigh Corp. v. Lane Bryant, Inc., 428 A.2d 350 (Del. Ch. 1981), the corporation supplied a list that simply showed a substantial number of shares owned by the Depository Trust Company (which is a central certificate depository used by most broker-dealers; see Sec. C supra).

The court required a fuller list of those individuals and brokerage firms known to the corporation to hold a beneficial interest in its shares. In Shamrock Associates v. Texas American Energy Corp., 517 A.2d 658 (Del. Ch. 1986), the court required disclosure of a corporation's "NOBO" list. NOBOs (an acronym for "nonobjecting beneficial owners") are beneficial owners holding stock in "street name" with banks or brokerage firms. The NOBOs' identities must be disclosed to the corporation by these institutional record owners pursuant to Rule 14b-1 under the Securities Exchange Act of 1934. Because Rule 14a-13(b)(2) specified that a corporation that obtains a NOBO list "shall . . . [u]se the information so furnished exclusively for purposes of corporate communications," the corporate defendant argued unsuccessfully that federal law preempted Del. Gen. Corp. Law §220 and precluded shareholder access to a NOBO list. Instead, the court required that the NOBO list be kept confidential and used exclusively for the purpose of communicating with shareholders.

Even when the state of incorporation does not permit access to the NOBO list or, more typically, when it does not require the corporation to compile a list when it has none, a shareholder may still be able to obtain a list of beneficial holders if the corporation conducts business in New York. N.Y. Bus. Corp. Law §1315 has been construed to entitle a resident shareholder both to demand the NOBO list and, if necessary, to require the corporation to compile such a list from readily available sources, even if the corporation is incorporated outside New York. In Sadler v. NCR Corp., 928 F.2d 48 (2d Cir. 1991), AT&T, which was making a hostile tender offer for NCR, a Maryland corporation, agreed to reimburse a New York resident shareholder of NCR for the latter's expenses in suing to obtain NCR's NOBO records. NCR responded that it had no such list in existence and pointed to decisions in several jurisdictions (including Delaware) that do not require the corporation to create or compile new records. The district court found, however, that NCR could easily obtain such a list from the consulting computer firms it employed. NCR further objected that the traditional "internal affairs" rule protected it from the application of the laws of foreign jurisdictions (i.e., New York) that would affect its internal corporate governance. Finding no "direct conflict" between Maryland and New York law, the Second Circuit replied that so long as New York law did not subject the corporation to inconsistent regulation and was not discriminatory, its requirements could be enforced, in part because access to the shareholder list was a long-recognized exception to the internal affairs rule. As a result, it has become standard for those seeking inspection to make demand under the New York statute, using a New York resident shareholder.

5. *Relation of state inspection rights to federal proxy rules.* Rule 14a-7 of the federal proxy rules requires the issuer, at the request of a security holder, either to mail communications to other security holders or to provide a list of security holders. If this avenue to fellow shareholders is available, is a shareholder precluded from using the state remedy to obtain a shareholders' list? It has been held that the proxy rules do not preempt the field. Wood, Walker & Co. v. Evans, 300 F. Supp. 171 (D. Colo. 1969), *aff'd*, 461 F.2d 852 (10th Cir. 1972). A shareholder is not precluded from using his state remedy to obtain a shareholder list by the fact that management has mailed his proxy material to shareholders pursuant to Rule 14a-7. Kerkorian v. Western Air Lines, Inc., 253 A.2d 221, 225 (Del. Ch.), *aff'd*, 254 A.2d 240 (Del. 1969).

Under Rule 14d-5, adopted by the SEC under the Williams Act, the bidder in a tender offer has the same right to a shareholder list as does a security holder who wishes to solicit proxies (even though the bidder may not own any shares at that point). The target corporation can at its option either furnish the bidder with a shareholder list or mail the bidder's offering materials to its shareholders (at the bidder's expense). Which course of action do you suspect the target usually chooses? Why? Again, as in the case of the proxy rules, Rule 14d-5 does not preempt the bidder's state law right to obtain a shareholder list.

6. *The inspection process.* It has generally been held that a shareholder need not inspect in person, may have the assistance of an expert, accountant, or other agent of his own selection, and may make extracts. Must the corporation make photocopying equipment available to the shareholder? May the shareholder bring such equipment into the corporation's offices to facilitate copying or remove records for the purpose of having them photocopied away from the corporation's premises? See Brandt Glass Co. v. New Orleans Housing Mart, Inc., 193 So. 2d 321 (La. 1966).

May the corporation limit the inspection of books and records to the hours after 5 P.M. on the ground that plaintiff's inspectors (a team of three to six bookkeepers and accountants) would otherwise disrupt normal business operations? See Schwartzman v. Schwartzman Packing Co., 99 N.M. 436, 659 P.2d 888 (1983) (limitation upheld).

7. *Distinction between stock lists and other books and records.* Although courts have been generally sympathetic to requests to see the stockholder list, they have been more cautious about demands to inspect other books and records. Much information that may seem innocuous could prove to be highly sensitive if it disclosed the identity of the corporation's customers or its profit margins on products to actual or potential competitors. In Morgan v. McLeod, 40 N.C. App. 467, 253 S.E.2d 339 (1979), a 30 percent shareholder sought corporate financial statements to enable him to sell his shares to a purchaser who insisted on examining certain financial information. Respondents replied that petitioner, who had been previously fired as the corporation's chief executive officer, was in fact seeking to harm the corporation and aid its competitors. Although the court found that petitioner had in the past divulged "inside information about the compan[y] to competitors," it nonetheless ruled that North Carolina's statute gave any shareholder an absolute right to two kinds of records: financial statements and the shareholder list. The proper purpose test, it said, applied only to other books and records. *Query:* Does this really mean that one competitor may buy a share of another and obtain sensitive financial information?

In contrast, as explained in Security First Corp. v. U.S. Die Casting and Development Co., 687 A.2d 563 (Del. 1997), Delaware simply shifts the burden of proof, placing the burden of proving a proper purpose on the shareholder when the shareholder is seeking books and records, but on the corporation when the shareholder list is sought. See Skouras v. Admiralty Enterprises, Inc., 386 A.2d 674 (Del. Ch. 1978).

New York takes a similar position with respect to financial statements, giving the shareholder an unqualified right to examine the annual balance sheet and profit and loss statement, but requiring good faith and a proper purpose when other records or financial data are sought. See RDR Associates, Inc. v. Media Corp. of America, 63 A.D.2d 888, 405 N.Y.S.2d 702 (1st Dept. 1978). In the latter instance, when the corporation challenges the shareholder's good faith or purpose, the burden is on the corporation to show that the purpose is improper, and the shareholder is entitled to a presumption of good faith; however, a factual hearing may be necessary if the corporation can raise "substantial questions of fact concerning petitioner's good faith and motives." See Wolberg v. Wolberg Electrical Supply Co., Inc., 72 A.D.2d 903, 422 N.Y.S.2d 178 (3d Dept. 1979). But see In re Lopez, 71 A.D.2d 976, 420 N.Y.S.2d 225 (1st Dept. 1979).

One possible way to prevent the leakage of sensitive or proprietary information is to restrict the shareholder's use of the information. In CM & M Group, Inc. v. Carroll, 453 A.2d 788 (Del. 1982), a shareholder requested detailed financial and business information, which included a request for disclosures as to (1) the remuneration and fringe benefits paid to all officers and directors; (2) all transactions between the corporation and these officials; and (3) all major contracts and agreements involving the corporation. In effect, this amounted to the same information that would be contained in a proxy statement. The purpose given was that the shareholder (who was a former president of the closely held corporation) wished to value his shares for the purpose of sale. Although upholding the request, the court ruled that plaintiff's right to inspect the records was contingent on his agreement not to disclose the information, except to a purchaser who had represented in writing his interest in purchasing the shares and whose identity would be disclosed to the court. *Query:* Is this approach adequately enforceable? What result if the requested information related to a secret formula or technological process? In *Carroll* the court added that the trial judge was empowered "to protect the corporation's legitimate interests and to prevent possible abuse of the shareholder's right of inspection by placing such reasonable restrictions and limitations as it deems proper on the exercise of the right."

8. *Inspection by directors.* In Pilat v. Broach Systems, Inc., 108 N.J. Super. 88, 260 A.2d 13 (1969), a director was allowed to inspect books and records. Even though the court found "no showing of plaintiff's hostile intent so as to preclude him from inspection," it stated that "this court must follow the New Jersey decisions and it is therefore held that a director has an absolute, unqualified right to inspect the corporate books and records of account, irrespective of motive" (noting contrary cases in other jurisdictions). Provision is made in Cal. Gen. Corp. Law §1602 (2007) for an "absolute right" of inspection by directors. See also Del. Gen. Corp. Law §220(d), page 634 supra. Even prior to the enactment of §220(d) in 1981, the Delaware court had held in Henshaw v. American Cement Corp., 252 A.2d 125 (Del. Ch. 1969), that a director has a common law right to inspect with the burden on the corporation to show why he should not be permitted to exercise this right: "[The director] showed a purpose germane to his position as a director and that entitles him to an examination of the books and records. His purpose is not improper because of the possibility that he may abuse his position as a director and make information available to persons hostile to the Corporation or otherwise not entitled to it. If [the director] does violate his fiduciary duty in this regard, then the Corporation has its remedy in the courts." See also Kortum v. Webasto Sunroofs Inc., 769 A.2d 113 (Del. Ch. 2000) (presumption exists that the sitting director should have "unfettered access" to corporation's books and records).

9. *Subsidiaries and "alter egos."* Assume that the records or information that the shareholder wishes are in the possession of the corporation's wholly owned subsidiary, which has its own board of directors and observes the requisite formalities of independent existence. Early decisions denied the shareholder access

under these circumstances, absent proof of fraud or that the parent treated the subsidiary as a "mere alter ego." See Skouras v. Admiralty Enterprises, Inc., 386 A.2d 674 (Del. Ch. 1978); South Side Bank v. T.S.B. Corp., 94 Ill. App. 3d 1006, 419 N.E.2d 477 (1981). However, under Del. Gen. Corp. Law §220(b)(2), page 633 supra, which was amended in 2003 to deal with this issue, the stockholder may demand inspection of the subsidiary's books and records to the extent the parent corporation has "actual possession and control of such records" or the parent "could obtain such records through the exercise of control over the subsidiary," unless (1) such inspection would "constitute a breach of an agreement between the corporation or the subsidiary" and some unaffiliated third party or (2) the subsidiary had "the right under the law applicable to it to deny the [parent] corporation access . . ." This statutory phrasing quickly produced litigation. In Weinstein Enterprises, Inc. v. Orloff, 878 A.2d 499 (Del. 2005), the Delaware Supreme Court was faced with a parent corporation, Weinstein Enterprises, Inc. ("Weinstein"), that owned 45.16 percent of a publicly held subsidiary, J. W. Mays, Inc., ("Mays"), which had long run a department store chain and was incorporated in New York. Plaintiff owned 34 percent of the parent and sought information about the complicated real estate holdings of the subsidiary (which had formerly been run as a family corporation by the founder of the parent corporation). *Held*: Although the 45 percent ownership implied that Mays was the "subsidiary" of Weinstein, it did not show that the Weinstein could exercise "control" over Mays, as required by §220(b)(2)(b). The fact that Mays had independent directors constituting a majority of its board (who were, however, nominated by Weinstein) was seen by the Court as rebutting any presumption that the parent held "control" over the subsidiary. Is this sound? Note that under this analysis, even majority ownership would not demonstrate control if there was a majority independent board.

I. FEDERAL LAW

Securities Exchange Act of 1934: Proxies

Sec. 14. (a) It shall be unlawful for any person, by the use of the mails or by any means or instrumentality of interstate commerce or of any facility of a national securities exchange or otherwise, in contravention of such rules and regulations as the Commission may prescribe as necessary or appropriate in the public interest or for the protection of investors, to solicit or to permit the use of his name to solicit any proxy or consent or authorization in respect of any security (other than an exempted security) registered pursuant to section 12 of this title.

(b) (1) It shall be unlawful for any member of a national securities exchange, or any broker or dealer registered under this title, or any bank, association, or other entity that exercises fiduciary powers, in contravention of such rules and regulations as the Commission may prescribe as necessary or appropriate in the public interest or for the protection of investors, to give, or to refrain from giving a proxy, consent, authorization, or information statement in respect of any security registered pursuant to section 12 of this title, . . . and carried for the account of a customer.

(2) With respect to banks, the rules and regulations prescribed by the Commission under paragraph (1) shall not require the disclosure of the names of beneficial owners of securities in an account held by the bank on the date of enactment of this paragraph unless the beneficial owner consents to the disclosure. The provisions of this paragraph shall not apply in the case of a bank which the Commission finds has not made a good faith effort to obtain such consent from such beneficial owners.

(c) Unless proxies, consents, or authorizations in respect of a security registered pursuant to section 12 of this title . . . are solicited by or on behalf of the management of the issuer from the holders of record of such security in accordance with the rules and regulations prescribed under subsection (a) of this section, prior to any annual or other meeting of the holders of such security, such issuer shall, in accordance with rules and regulations prescribed by the Commission, file with the Commission and transmit to all holders of record of such security information substantially equivalent to the information which would be required to be transmitted if a solicitation were made. . . .

---

1. *History and scope.* The proxy statement is a creation of the '34 Act. Concerned that corporate managements would solicit proxies from shareholders without providing more than minimal disclosure about the actions to be taken at the shareholder meeting, Congress authorized the SEC to adopt rules regulating the solicitation of proxies, and the SEC responded by prescribing a disclosure document — the proxy statement — that any person who wishes to solicit proxies must furnish (with some exceptions) to each person solicited no later than concurrently with the solicitation. In overview, the '34 Act creates the same dual system of mandatory disclosure and antifraud liability that the '33 Act established for the sale of securities. However, the focus of §14 and the proxy rules adopted by the SEC thereunder is on election contests, not investment decisions, and this distinction has important consequences for both the standard of materiality and the nature of the applicable remedies.

The SEC's proxy rules can be grouped into four general categories:

(1) **Disclosure of material information to shareholders with respect to proposals for shareholder action.** Rule 14a-3 is here the central rule; along with Schedule 14A, it prescribes the form and contents of the proxy statement and the annual report that must precede it. See Sec. I.2 infra. Rule 14a-4 governs the form and content of the proxy itself to ensure that shareholders have an undistorted opportunity to vote either for or against a proposal, including the right to vote separately on relevant portions thereof. See Sec. I.3 infra.

(2) **Election contests.** These rules uniquely apply where rival slates of nominees are contending for election to the board. Because the incumbents have obvious advantages, Rule 14a-7 entitles the insurgents to have the issuer either furnish them with an accurate current shareholders' list or mail out their proxy soliciting materials (at the insurgent's expense).

(3) **Shareholder proposals.** Rule 14a-8 mandates that certain proposals submitted by shareholders be included in the corporation's own proxy solicitation

materials and placed on the agenda of the meeting for a vote. The result is to spare small shareholders the cost of a proxy solicitation by allowing them to "free-ride" on the corporation's own proxy statement. This is the area where corporate law and social activism often meet, because this rule is frequently used to raise controversial social issues, such as South African divestment or nuclear power. See Sec. I.6 infra.

(4) **Antifraud.** Rule 14a-9 sets forth the basic antifraud rule applicable to proxy solicitations. Many of the issues earlier examined in connection with Rule 10b-5 in Chapter V resurface here, such as the requisite elements of a cause of action (i.e., the legal rules for determining standing, materiality, causation, culpability, etc.), but the answers are significantly different from those in the case of securities fraud. See Sec. I.7 infra.

Originally, §14(a) applied only to securities "registered on a national securities exchange." In 1964 it was significantly extended by the passage of §12(g), which required corporations with "total assets" over $1 million and a class of equity security held of record by 500 or more persons to register pursuant to §12 of the '34 Act. The original $1 million asset threshold was subsequently increased, and Rule 12g-1 now exempts from §12(g) registration corporations having total assets not exceeding $10 million. Still, because the term "total assets" means gross assets without subtraction of liabilities, few corporations with 500 or more shareholders can escape the reach of §14(a) on this basis. Essentially, any domestic corporation traded in the public securities markets — whether on an exchange, on Nasdaq, or "over-the-counter" — will probably be picked up by §12(g) and therefore be subject to §14(a).

Prior to 1964, some corporations avoided the preparation of proxy disclosure materials by not soliciting proxies, if management knew that sufficient shares would be represented at the meeting to satisfy quorum and voting requirements. However, the passage of §14(c) in that year closed this loophole by requiring corporations subject to §12 to prepare and distribute an "information statement" if they did not solicit proxies. As administered by the SEC, the disclosures required by the §14(c) "information statement" are virtually equivalent to those required in a proxy statement.

2. *Philosophy.* If a defeated presidential candidate sued to invalidate the results of a presidential election on the ground that the victor misrepresented his policies (such as by promising to reduce both the federal deficit and taxes), one would expect such an action to be summarily dismissed as incompatible with the workings of democracy. Yet the philosophy underlying the federal securities laws (and the federal labor laws) is quite different and anticipates substantially greater judicial oversight and intervention. Judge Clark of the Second Circuit pointed out the differing philosophies in SEC v. May, 229 F.2d 123, 124 (2d Cir. 1956): "Appellants' fundamental complaint appears to be that stockholder disputes should be viewed in the eyes of the law just as are political contests, with each side free to hurl charges with comparative unrestraint, the assumption being that the opposing side is then at liberty to refute and thus effectively deflate the 'campaign oratory' of its adversary. Such, however, was not the policy of Congress as enacted in the Securities Exchange Act." Nonetheless, courts sometimes find the better course of valor is to tolerate a modicum of misstatement rather than take the disruptive step of ordering a new election. See GAF Corp. v. Heyman, 724 F.2d 727 (2d Cir. 1983), discussed at page 691 infra.

1. SOLICITATIONS TO WHICH RULES APPLY

Securities Exchange Act Release No. 34-31326 (1992)

I. Introduction

The amendments to the proxy rules and other disclosure provisions adopted today follow upon an extensive three-year examination by the Commission of the effectiveness of the proxy-voting process and its effect on the corporate governance system in this country. . . .

Within the overall scope of this broad examination, the Commission has focused particularly on the role of its proxy and disclosure rules in impeding shareholder communication and participation in the corporate governance process. This demonstrated effect of the current rules is contrary to Congress's intent that the rules assure fair and effective shareholder suffrage. Apart from attempts to obtain proxy voting authority, to the degree the current rules inhibit the ability of shareholders not seeking proxy authority to analyze and discuss issues pertaining to the operation of a company and its performance, these rules may in fact run exactly contrary to the best interests of shareholders.

The amendments adopted today reflect a Commission determination that the federal proxy rules have created unnecessary regulatory impediments to communication among shareholders and others and to the effective use of shareholder voting rights. The Commission has also determined that modifications in the current rules are desirable to reduce these burdens and to achieve the purposes set forth in the Exchange Act. . . . On the whole, the regulatory scheme adopted by the Commission pursuant to the broad authority granted by Section 14(a) has been designed to make sure that management and others who solicit shareholder proxies provide . . . needed information to shareholders, allow them to instruct the specific use of their proxy and provide them access to other shareholders through mailing or by access to a shareholder list.

Originally, the definition of "solicitation" of a proxy reflected this principal focus of the proxy rules, by limiting the reach of those rules to any "request" for a proxy or the furnishing of a proxy, consent or authorization to security holders. Thereafter, the definition was broadened to make clear that any communication by a person soliciting proxy authority, not just the communication delivered with the form of proxy, was a solicitation. However, in 1942, without explanation, the Commission expanded the definition of "solicitation" of a proxy to include "any request to revoke or not execute a proxy. . . ."

In 1956, the Commission significantly expanded the definition of "solicitation" of a proxy to embrace "any communication" which could be viewed as being "reasonably calculated" to influence a shareholder to give, deny or revoke a proxy. In adopting the sweeping 1956 definition, the Commission sought to address abuses by persons who were actually engaging in solicitations of proxy authority in connection with election contests. The Commission does not seem to have been aware, or to have intended, that the new definition might also sweep within all the regulatory requirements persons who did not "request" a shareholder to grant or to revoke or deny a proxy, but whose expressed opinions might be found to have been reasonably calculated to affect the views of other shareholders positively or negatively toward a particular company and its management or directors. Since any such persuasion — even if unintended — could affect the decision of shareholders even many months later to give or withhold a proxy, such communications at least literally could fall within the new definition.

The literal breadth of the new definition of solicitation was so great as potentially to turn almost every expression of opinion concerning a publicly traded corporation into a regulated proxy solicitation. Thus, newspaper op-ed articles, public speeches or television commentary on a specific company could all later be alleged to have been proxy solicitations in connection with the election of directors, as could private conversations among more than 10 shareholders. This created a basis upon which claims that the proxy rules, including the mandatory disclosure, filing and dissemination provisions of those rules, could be brought to bear not only on persons seeking authority to vote another's shares, but also on those persons merely expressing a view or opinion on management performance or on initiatives presented by management and others for a shareholder's vote.

If the current proxy rules apply to a communication, the effect can be very costly. Among other things, the person making the communication would be required to prepare a proxy statement and mail it to every shareholder of the company who is deemed to have been solicited. Where a communication appears in the public media, the Commission has taken the position that all shareholders have been solicited. In such a case, the cost of the mailing requirement alone could run into hundreds of thousands of dollars, and the decision on whether a solicitation occurred will be judged purely in hindsight. Thus, shareholders can be deterred from discussing management and corporate performance by the prospect of being found after the fact to have engaged in a proxy solicitation. The costs of complying with those rules also has meant that, unless they have substantial financial backing, shareholders and other interested persons may effectively be cut out of the debate regarding proposals presented by management or shareholders for a vote.

To correct this distortion of the purposes of the proxy rules, initially highlighted in petitions and other requests from the shareholder community for reform, the Commission proposed several revisions to the proxy rules intended to deregulate constraints on communications by persons who do not seek to obtain proxy authority from any other shareholders, and who do not have a substantial interest in the subject matter of the communication beyond the interest of such person as a shareholder. . . .

While voting rights are valuable assets and an uninformed exercise of those rights could represent a wasted opportunity for the voting shareholder, that concern does not justify the government's requiring that all private conversations on matters subject to a shareholder vote be reported to the government. In the Commission's view, the antifraud provisions provide adequate protection against fraudulent and deceptive communications to shareholders on matters presented for a vote by persons not seeking proxy authority and not in the classes of persons ineligible for the exemption. . . .

The purposes of the proxy rules themselves are better served by promoting free discussion, debate and learning among shareholders and interested persons, than by placing restraints on that process to ensure that management has the ability to address every point raised in the exchange of views. Indeed, the Commission has not perceived, and the comments have not demonstrated, shareholder abuses where proxy authority is *not* being sought by the persons engaged in the communications. However, there have been situations in which discontented shareholders have been subjected to legal threats based on the possibility the shareholder might have triggered proxy filing requirements by expressing disagreement to other shareholders.

In the amendments adopted today, the Commission has also attempted to remove unnecessary impediments to the solicitation of proxy authority to allow management and other persons seeking proxy authority more efficiently and effectively to get their case to the shareholder. . . .

II.   Discussion of Amendments and New Rules

A.   Exemption for Persons Not Seeking Proxy Authority

1. *Exemption solicitations.* . . . Of course, compliance with proxy rules is necessary only if the communication constitutes a proxy solicitation within the meaning of those rules. However, an essential problem in this area is that it is generally not possible for a shareholder to know with certainty that a communication will or will not be deemed to constitute a solicitation. The broad definition of a proxy solicitation that includes not only a request for a proxy or request to execute, not execute or revoke a proxy, but also "the furnishing of . . . a communication to security holders under circumstances reasonably calculated to result in the procurement, withholding or revocation of a proxy," creates this inherent uncertainty for shareholders. As a result of this definition, almost any statement of views could be alleged to be a solicitation, and the shareholder could be exposed to litigation by the company challenging the failure to incur massive proxy mailing and other costs. Only after such a claim was litigated would the shareholder know whether a speech or printed article, for example, criticizing the quality of a company's management would be deemed to have been a solicitation.

As made clear from the comment letters from shareholders on the initial proposal and reproposals, the scope of the definition of solicitation under the proxy rules does have a chilling effect on discussion of management performance, out of fear that the communication could after the fact be found to have triggered disclosure and filing obligations under the federal proxy rules. The cost of compliance with the proxy rules likewise could deter shareholders wishing to express support for, or opposition to, management or third party proposals or director nominees. The regulatory scheme imposed virtually the same requirements and therefore costs on discussions about management proposals and nominees as it did on management in seeking authority to vote the shareholders' securities in favor of its proposals or nominees, where such discussions were found to fall within the definition of solicitation.

In most instances management, with access to corporate funds to finance the solicitation, would be the only party willing to assume the regulatory costs, resulting in a one-sided discussion of the merits of the matters put to a vote. The proxy rules thus unduly hindered free discussion that could better inform shareholders as to their voting decisions.

To address these concerns, the Commission proposed in June 1991 . . . a new exemption from the regulatory requirements of the proxy rules for a solicitation by or on behalf of persons (i) who do not seek the power to act as a proxy, or furnish or request, or act on behalf of a person who furnishes or requests, a consent or authorization for delivery to the registrant, and (ii) who are disinterested in the subject matter of a vote.

As initially proposed, such a disinterested person would have been absolutely free to communicate with other shareholders in writing or orally without any filing requirement whatsoever. The rule as reproposed specified nine classes of persons specifically excluded from relying on the exemption for persons not seeking proxy authority. In a major change from the initial proposal, the reproposal required persons relying on the exemption in connection with the dissemination of written soliciting material to submit that material or mail it to the Commission, under the cover of a new notice form, within 10 days of its use. No such notice requirement was proposed for published or broadcast solicitations or oral solicitations. . . .

[T]he Commission has expressly determined that the burdens of requiring a notice to the federal government of oral communications, except in the case where the speaker is seeking to obtain proxy authority for himself, or is in the class of persons the Commission has excluded from eligibility for the exemption due to a substantial association with soliciting parties or special interest in the subject matter of the vote, are not justified by any benefit to be derived therefrom, and that such a requirement is not necessary or desirable in achieving the purposes of section 14(a). . . .

---

1. The "new criticism" of the SEC's proxy rules and the 1992 reforms. With the increase in institutional investor activism, scholarly attention in the late 1980s and early 1990s began to focus on the degree to which the federal and state rules applicable to proxy contests impeded collective action by institutional investors and even chilled communication among shareholders. The basic thrust of this critique has been that the legal rules are not neutral, but rather serve to deter insurgents and protect incumbents. At the state level, the primary target has been those rules that permit incumbents to receive full reimbursement while insurgents are compensated only if they gain control of the board. Professors Lucian Bebchuk and Marcel Kahan have thus revived an old idea and urged that insurgents be partially compensated based on the percentage of the vote received for their proposal or by their slate of candidates (e.g., 40 percent compensation if they get 40 percent of the vote). See Lucian Bebchuk & Marcel Kahan, A Framework for Analyzing Legal Policy Towards Proxy Contests, 78 Cal. L. Rev. 1073 (1990).

At the federal level, there has been even more criticism that the federal proxy rules chill insurgents and insulate managements. See Bernard Black, Shareholder Passivity Reexamined, 89 Mich. L. Rev. 520 (1990). In particular, institutional investors complained that SEC Rule 14a-1 often made it impossible for them to confer on any substantive matter, because it defined the key term "solicitation" to include any communication that was reasonably likely to cause them to give or withhold a proxy to management. Thus, any criticism of management, oral or written, that might cause other investors to withhold their proxy and that was distributed to ten or more persons had to be preceded by a costly proxy statement, and this requirement arguably stifled the voices of even the largest, most sophisticated shareholders.

Beginning in 1989, the California Public Employees' Retirement System (CalPERS) submitted a series of proposed proxy rule amendments to the SEC, accompanied by a lengthy critique of the existing proxy rules, which charged that SEC overregulation of the voting process primarily chilled dissidents. In partial response, the Commission undertook a wide-ranging study that culminated in the issuance of Sec. Exch. Act Rel. No. 34-29315 (June 17, 1991). This Release began by raising two basic questions about the SEC's proxy rules:

(1) Do the rules unnecessarily restrict or interfere with the ability of security holders to communicate among themselves or with management?

(2) Do the rules impose unnecessary costs on the registrant and soliciting persons?

Perhaps surprisingly for a government agency, the SEC answered these questions with a "yes," agreeing that there were unnecessary regulatory barriers to shareholder communications. Accordingly, the 1991 Release went on to propose three significant changes:

First, if a shareholder was not seeking to obtain proxy authority, but simply responding to a solicitation by management or another person, the shareholder should not be obligated to make any prior filing with the SEC or to distribute a proxy statement (although any statements made by it would remain subject to the antifraud rules). Essentially, a broad exemption was proposed under Rule 14a-2 to permit most (but not all) shareholders to communicate freely with other shareholders, so long as the communicating shareholder did not seek to obtain a proxy nor had any material economic interest (other than as a shareholder) in the subject of the solicitation.

Second, the SEC proposed to eliminate its prior review of proxy materials. Previously, before an individual engaged in a proxy solicitation could use a proxy statement or other material (such as newspaper advertisements), prior SEC review and approval of these materials was necessary. Often, this review process could take several weeks or more. In the typically time-constrained period surrounding a shareholders' meeting, this delay often worked to the incumbent management's advantage because it could plan on releasing its own proxy materials at a point sufficiently close to the annual meeting date that there would be little time for a dissident group to prepare and clear its own materials with the SEC prior to the shareholders' meeting. In addition, many commentators believed that the SEC would effectively censor any vivid language or strongly phrased criticisms in a proxy statement or a newspaper "fight ad" unless they could be clearly factually corroborated.

Third, the Commission proposed to amend Rule 14a-7 so as to give a person seeking to make a proxy solicitation a federal right to receive a shareholder list from the corporation. (Today, Rule 14a-7 gives the corporation the option to provide such a list or to mail the proxy statement for the person making the solicitation at the latter's expense; the SEC's proposal would have reversed this option, giving it instead to the dissident shareholder.)

These proposals touched off a heated controversy. A record number of comments were received by the SEC, as business groups predictably objected. In the wake of their criticism, the SEC withdrew its proposals in late 1991 for further study. Finally, in October 1992, the Commission adopted a carefully compromised package of reforms in Sec. Exch. Act Rel. No. 34-31326 (October 16, 1992) (excerpted above). Although the Commission largely abandoned its original idea of creating a federal right to receive a shareholder list, it stuck by its central precepts that (1) a person not seeking to obtain proxies should be free to communicate with other shareholders without any obligation to make any prior filing with the SEC or to prepare a proxy statement, and (2) the costs of complying with the proxy rules needed to be reduced for those who did solicit proxies. Specifically, the revised proxy rules do the following:

a. *Exemption for shareholders not seeking proxy authority nor having a "substantial interest" in the solicitation.* New Rule 14a-2(b)(1) creates a broad exemption from the proxy statement delivery and disclosure requirements for communications with shareholders where the soliciting person is not seeking proxy authority (i.e., does not furnish a proxy card or a proxy revocation form) and does not have a "substantial interest" in the subject matter of the vote. The "substantial interest" exclusion is defined somewhat ambiguously to cover "any person who, because of a substantial interest in the subject matter of the solicitation, is likely to receive a benefit from a successful solicitation that would not be shared pro rata by all other holders of the same class of securities, other than a benefit arising from the person's employment with the registrant." Rule 14a-2(b)(1)(ix).

Query: Suppose a shareholder opposes a risky recapitalization plan in part because it holds a substantial investment in the same corporation's bonds (which will be reduced in value by the plan). Can it solicit others without filing a proxy statement?

Besides persons who have a "substantial interest" and persons who do seek proxy authority, others who are ineligible for the new exemption (and who therefore must file proxy statements) include (i) the issuer; (ii) officers, directors, or affiliates of the issuer or of any other ineligible person; (iii) director nominees; (iv) any person soliciting in opposition to a merger or similar transaction who is affiliated with a competing, alternative transaction; (v) any Schedule 13D filer who has disclosed a possible control intent; and (vi) anyone who is paid to solicit by an ineligible person.

Otherwise, no filing or public disclosure is required. However, both written and oral statements made in connection with a proxy solicitation will continue to be subject to the antifraud rules (in particular, Rule 14a-9), even though no proxy statement need be filed.

b. *Announcement of voting decisions.* New Rule 14a-1(l)(2)(iv) provides that a shareholder's public announcement of how the shareholder intends to vote on any matter (and the reasons for its vote) does not constitute a proxy solicitation. Previously, it had been uncertain whether such an announcement could be considered a solicitation, and this uncertainty probably deterred some shareholders from publicly announcing their voting decisions.

As a practical matter, announcements of voting intentions may become a mechanism by which shareholder activists apply public pressure on targeted companies. For example, when a prominent institution announces that it is withholding its proxy, this tactic may focus adverse publicity on the company (and enhance the ability of the activist to lobby other shareholders in private to take the same position). Also, in a contested proxy battle, the ability of major shareholders to announce and thereby generate publicity for their voting decisions in the last days before the shareholders' meeting may generate momentum for their side.

c. *"Short slates."* New Rule 14a-4(d) permits a proxy contestant to solicit proxies for less than a full slate of dissident nominees so that the shareholders can also vote for some of the incumbents' nominees. For example, if a dissident sought to elect 2 directors to a board of 12, its proxy card could grant a proxy to vote for Messrs. Smith and Jones (the two dissident nominees), and for all of the incumbents' nominees other than Messrs. Gray and Blue (the two incumbents it wished to replace).

The purpose of this change was to simplify the ability of institutional activists to gain minority representation on a company's board. Previously, under a debatable SEC interpretation of the proxy rules, a dissident could not include any of management's nominees on its slate (without their permission), and thus a shareholder who voted only for a minority slate of nominees "wasted" its remaining vote for the other open directorial slots. Also, if the shareholder then sought to vote for some of management's nominees by executing a subsequent proxy, the execution of the subsequent proxy card for even some of the incumbent nominees operated to revoke any proxy card previously executed for the dissident slate (even though the total voted for on both cards equaled the open number of positions). Although the new rule will allow a shareholder to "round out" a full slate that includes both the dissidents and some incumbents, the incumbents may counter this tactic by threatening that they will not serve if the dissidents are elected.

d. *Preliminary filings.* To reduce delay, preliminary filing and SEC prior review of proxy materials have been eliminated, except in the case of the basic proxy statement and proxy card. All other proxy materials, including letters to shareholders, newspaper advertisements, and other supplemental materials, need not be filed in advance of their use and will not be subject to prior SEC review.

Effectively, this reduces the prospect of SEC censorship of proxy materials. Typically, the more contentious and argumentative statements are found in the supplemental materials, not the basic proxy statement. Thus, elimination of SEC prior review of this supplemental material may heighten the contrast between the traditionally staid and formal tone of the proxy statement and the more free-swinging, less inhibited character of these other materials.

e. *Public availability of preliminary proxy statements.* Even those proxy materials that still are required to be filed in preliminary form with the SEC before use (i.e., the proxy statement and proxy card) will now be available to the public upon filing, rather than remaining confidential until the SEC completes its review and requires changes. Thus, charges and statements in preliminary proxy filings will predictably be quickly disseminated to shareholders (possibly by the media in some cases).

f. *Commencement of solicitation.* In a change intended to reduce delay, the new rules permit commencement of a proxy solicitation upon the preliminary filing of the proxy statement, provided that no proxy card is distributed until the definitive proxy statement is circulated. Given the above-noted immediate public availability of preliminary filings, this revision will increase the speed with which a dissident can start a proxy contest. Rather than wait for the SEC to complete its review process and clear the proxy materials, the dissident may now begin to solicit shareholders as soon as the first filing is made.

g. *Unbundling of related proposals.* Under new Rule 14a-4, the corporation will no longer be able to present a group of related matters as a single proposal for shareholder action. Instead, the proxy card will require separate votes so that shareholders have the opportunity to vote on each matter separately. Each related matter may, however, be conditioned on passage of the others.

Previously, corporate issuers sometimes sought to tie an unpopular proposal (such as an anti-takeover amendment) to a "sweetener" (for example, a profitable economic transaction, such as a spin-off). In recent years, the SEC staff, on an ad hoc basis, had opposed this type of bundling on the basis that such matters were not "related," but now it will have express authority to require separate votes (although management can still condition one transaction on approval of the other).

h. *Disclosure of voting results.* The new rules also require more detailed disclosure of voting results in the corporation's Forms 10-K and 10-Q. Previously, only the results of contested elections and other specific matters had to be reported and then only the affirmative and negative votes cast (as opposed to abstentions or withholding of voting authority). By requiring the reporting of all matters presented for a vote during the reporting period, and also disclosure of withheld votes, including abstentions, the SEC may be seeking to increase the effectiveness of a withheld vote or an abstention as a protest vote.

i. *Shareholder lists.* Although the final version of the new proxy rules does not generally entitle a requesting shareholder to a shareholder list, the rules do give such a federal right to a shareholder in certain limited cases involving "going private" transactions (in which management buys out the public shareholders) and "roll-up" transactions (which typically involve the incorporation of limited partnerships originally formed to hold real estate). *Query:* If the SEC believes it has the legal authority to require corporations as a matter of federal law to provide a detailed shareholder list to requesting shareholders, should it limit this federal right to these special cases? What basis is there for drawing the line in terms of the character of the transaction at issue?

2. *Definition of solicitation.* The SEC's 1992 proxy reforms did not materially revise the broad definition given to "solicitation" by Rule 14a-1, but instead created additional exemptions under Rule 14a-2 for persons not seeking proxy authority and lacking any special interest. Rule 14a-1 therefore continues to define the terms "solicit" and "solicitation" to include:

> (i) Any request for a proxy whether or not accompanied by or included in a form of proxy;
> (ii) Any request to execute or not to execute, or to revoke, a proxy; or
> (iii) The furnishing of a form of proxy or other communication to security holders under circumstances reasonably calculated to result in the procurement, withholding or revocation of a proxy.

Over the years, the final "reasonably calculated" clause has reached a number of unsuspecting persons who did not think they were engaged in a proxy solicitation and has generated a host of interpretive problems. Consider the following cases:

(a) In Studebaker Corp. v. Gittlin, 360 F.2d 692 (2d Cir. 1966), a shareholder solicited 42 other shareholders in order to aggregate shares exceeding 5 percent of the company's stock to obtain access under state law to the corporation's shareholders list. Defendants and the SEC argued that such authorizations to inspect shareholder lists were within the scope of §14(a), which in their view covered every form of proxy, consent, or authorization, not simply those involving election to office. The Second Circuit replied: "We need not go that far to uphold the order of the district court," because the shareholder list authorizations were solicited as part of "a continuous plan" that was intended eventually to lead to a proxy solicitation. Subsequent cases have divided over whether the solicitation of shareholders to contribute funds to finance a shareholder's class action or derivative suit is within the scope of the proxy rules. Compare In re First Home Investment Corp. of Kansas, Inc., 368 F. Supp. 597 (D. Kan. 1973), with American Home Investment Co. v. Bedel, 525 F.2d 1022 (8th Cir. 1975).

(b) In Brown v. Chicago, R.I. & P. R., 328 F.2d 122 (7th Cir. 1964), the Union Pacific Railroad Company published a newspaper advertisement in 50 cities extolling the benefits of a merger between it and the Chicago, Rock Island & Pacific Railroad Company (Rock Island). This ad was in response to a publicly announced plan of the Chicago & North Western Railway Company (CNW) to acquire majority control of Rock Island (which threatened takeover was in turn a defensive response to a friendly merger earlier negotiated by the managements of Union Pacific and Rock Island). Fearing that Rock Island shareholders would sell to CNW, Union Pacific placed the ad, in the Seventh Circuit's phrase, "to inform and motivate the public rather than to solicit proxies." *Held*: The proxy rules did not apply in this case, where proxies were not solicited and Rock Island did not act in concert with Union Pacific. Is this ruling sound? What if the proposed merger were presented to Rock Island's shareholders for a vote four months later?

(c) In Long Island Lighting Co. v. Barbash, 779 F.2d 793 (2d Cir. 1985), LILCO, the primary public utility serving Long Island, had long been the center of a social and political controversy growing out of its alleged mismanagement of the design and construction of the Shoreham Nuclear Power Plant and its slow response to restoring power after a major hurricane. During a proxy contest initiated by a LILCO shareholder, who was also a local political candidate, an advertisement was placed by the "Steering Committee of Citizens to Replace LILCO" in a major Long Island newspaper, advocating that "a Long Island Power Authority [be] created to replace LILCO as a supplier of power." On its face, the ad was addressed solely to the public, made no reference to proxies or the approaching shareholders' meeting, and concerned an issue that was also the subject of intense political debate at the time. LILCO sued to enjoin the defendants from alleged violations of the federal securities laws on the grounds that the ad was misleading and that no proxy statement had been filed. District Judge Jack Weinstein ruled against LILCO, finding that "SEC regulations . . . [could not] prevent such advertisements . . . without violating fundamental First Amendment rights of free speech." 625 F. Supp. 221, 222. The Second Circuit reversed, holding that the proxy rules could cover communications appearing in publications of general circulation that were indirectly addressed to shareholders, but declined to rule at this stage of the proceeding on the First Amendment issue. A strong dissent by Judge Winter argued that, to avoid serious First Amendment problems, the proxy rules should be construed not to apply to newspaper ads addressed to the general public unless they directly related to the solicitation of proxies. Judge Winter chiefly relied on Lowe v. SEC, 472 U.S. 181 (1985), which held that the publisher of a "newspaper" consisting only of stock tips and similar securities advice could not be regulated as an investment adviser under the federal securities laws.

In overview, *Barbash* points up the unique status of the federal securities laws as a system of prior restraints on commercial speech. Although commercial speech is entitled to some level of constitutional protection, see Virginia State Board of Pharmacy v. Virginia Citizens Consumer Council, 425 U.S. 748 (1976), the Supreme Court has sustained governmental power over commercial speech that is deceptive or that relates to activities that could themselves be directly banned. See Posadas de Puerto Rico Associates v. Tourism Co., 106 S. Ct. 2968 (1986) (advertising of casino gambling could be banned); Ohralik v. Ohio State Bar Association, 436 U.S. 447, 456 (1978) (listing "corporate proxy statements" as one form of speech that could be regulated without offending the First Amendment). What makes *Barbash* a difficult case is the degree to which it shows that the line can blur between commercial and political speech. For a critique of the decision, see Note, A Political Speech Exception to the Regulation of Proxy Solicitations, 86 Colum. L. Rev. 1453 (1985). See also Victor Brudney, Business Corporations and Stockholders' Rights Under the First Amendment, 91 Yale L.J. 235 (1981).

3. *Other exemptions.* Rule 14a-2(b)(2) has long exempted "any solicitation made otherwise than on behalf of the registrant where the total number of persons solicited is not more than ten." Thus, even when seeking proxy authority, a proxy contestant can approach ten or fewer shareholders without preparing a proxy statement (although the proxy antifraud rule, Rule 14a-9, will apply to any such communication). Another exemption (Rule 14a-2(b)(3)) permits the furnishing of proxy advice by an advisor "in the ordinary course of his business" to a "person with whom the advisor has a business relationship" if no special remuneration is paid for furnishing the advice and the advice is not furnished on behalf of any person soliciting proxies or a participant in an election contest. Although this definition easily reaches attorneys, brokers, and investment advisors, it stops just short of covering an emerging new professional, the proxy advisor, who does seemingly receive "special remuneration" for his advice. The 1992 proxy reforms added Rule 14a-1(1)(2), which exempts statements by a security holder merely "stating how the security holder intends to vote and the reasons therefor," provided that the statement is either publicly released to the media or "directed to persons to whom the security holder owes a fiduciary duty in connection with the voting of securities." Because this provision also exempts the security holder from antifraud liability under Rule 14a-9, it has been increasingly used by institutional investors, who may issue a press release as to their voting intentions pursuant to it.

4. *Beneficial owners.* Rule 14a-2(a) exempts solicitations "by a person in respect to securities carried in his name or in the name of his nominee" under certain conditions. This exemption applies chiefly to banks and brokers, who hold securities in "street name," and exempts them from any obligation to file a proxy statement and from antifraud liability under Rule 14a-9. The rule is conditioned, however, on the advisor receiving no special remuneration for furnishing proxy voting advice.

Standing alone, this exemption for brokers leaves a potentially significant gap in the proxy voting system. What happens when stock is registered in the name of the brokerage firm? Who votes? Under §14(b), which was amended in 1986 to apply to banks as well as brokers, the SEC requires banks and brokers to provide an issuer with the names and addresses of beneficial owners of its stock who do not object to such disclosure (NOBOs — see page 641 supra). Under Rule 14b-1, a broker must forward copies of the proxy, annual report, and proxy soliciting materials to beneficial owners (at the issuer's expense) "no later than five business days after receipt" thereof.

If the beneficial owner fails to give instructions to the broker as to whether a proxy should be given or how the shares should be voted, is the broker free to vote the shares in accordance with its own judgment? The federal proxy rules do not address this question. However, under Rule 452 of the New York Stock Exchange a broker cannot give a proxy without instructions with respect to a matter "which may affect substantially the rights or privileges of such stock." Thus, a broker could vote (if no instructions were received) on whether to reincorporate in Delaware, but not on whether to create a dual class system of stock with weighted voting rights. Historically, Rule 452 left the broker free to vote for the incumbent slate of directors where their election was uncontested. Arguably, this ensured a majority vote for the incumbents in the ordinary case. However, in 2007 the NYSE has proposed amending Rule 452 to end broker discretionary voting in the election of directors, even in the routine, uncontested case. Thus, if the SEC approves the NYSE's proposed rule change (as seems likely), brokers will be able to vote in these elections only if they receive instructions from the beneficial owners. The net result will likely make it harder to obtain a majority vote for those companies whose bylaws or policies mandate a majority vote to elect directors.

2. REFORM OF THE NOMINATION AND ELECTION PROCESS

In 2003 the SEC conducted a lengthy review of the proxy rules and regulations regarding the nomination and election of directors and convened a series of round-tables. Many commentators urged the Commission to provide security holders with greater access to the nomination process and also opined that existing rules gave shareholders no meaningful role. A fundamental imbalance existed, the SEC's staff reported to the Commission, because management's solicitation of shareholders for its slate of candidates was paid by the corporation, while insurgents had to bear the cost of preparing and distributing a proxy statement and of soliciting shareholders.[31] Coupled with plurality voting, which remained the much more prevalent voting procedure at that point, the inability of shareholders to place nominations on the corporation's proxy statement gave them little incentive to participate in shareholder elections and caused them to view the proxy process for the election of directors "as a mere formality or 'rubber stamp' of the board's choices presented in the company's proxy materials."[32] In truth, the SEC's staff had reached similar conclusions in prior studies extending back for decades.[33]

But, as before, the corporate bar and the business community responded that if shareholders had free or universal access to the proxy statement, every proxy solicitation would likely become a contested election, which "would be costly

31. See SEC Division of Corporation Finance, Staff Report: Review of the Proxy Process Regarding the Nomination and Election of Directors (July 15, 2003).
32. See Sec. Exch. Act Rel. No. 34-48626 ("Security Holder Director Nominations") (Oct. 14, 2003) at *18.
33. The SEC's staff first recommended that "minority stockholders be given an opportunity to use the management's proxy materials in support of their own nominees for directorships" in 1942. See Sec. Exch. Act Rel. No. 34-3347 (December 18, 1942). See also Sec. Exch. Act Rel. No. 34-13482 (April 28, 1977) (similar recommendations).

and disruptive to companies and could discourage some qualified board candidates from agreeing to appear on a company's slate of nominees."[34]

Thus, to strike a realistic compromise, the Commission decided to limit shareholder access to the proxy statement for purposes of nominating directors in three fundamental respects: (1) the limited access right would not be available where the shareholder group was seeking control of the board or the election of one or more directors with a financial relationship to the shareholder group seeking to nominate the director; and (2) the process would be triggered only when specified criteria suggested that the company had been unresponsive to shareholder concerns; and (3) shareholders would have to be permitted by state law to nominate a candidate for election as director.

The triggered events proposed by the Commission as indications that management had been unresponsive to shareholder concerns were:

(1) At least one of the company's nominees for the board for whom the company solicited proxies received "withhold" votes from more than 35 percent of the votes cast at an annual meeting; or

(2) A security holder proposal submitted pursuant to SEC Rule 14a-8 that the company become subject to the SEC's new shareholder nomination procedure was submitted for a vote by a group of stockholders holding more than 1 percent of the company's common stock entitled to vote on the proposal and who had held the stock for more than one year as of the date of the proposal and such proposal received more than 50 percent of the votes cast on that proposal at the shareholders' meeting.

Effectively, this last requirement contemplated that shareholders would have to first opt into this new procedure and that only longer-term shareholders holding not less than 1 percent of the voting stock could make a nomination (even then, such a nominee would also need to be independent of those shareholders making the nomination).

The complexity of this proposal increased the controversy surrounding it. Some institutional investors thought that it was infeasible; others valued it only as a threat that gave them increased leverage in negotiations with management over a specific business policy. Nonetheless, the proposal elicited sufficient controversy that the SEC never adopted it (and it was quietly shelved in 2004). Under pressure from the White House, SEC Chairman William Donaldson withdrew his support for it and resigned; the new SEC Chairman, Christopher Cox, did not favor it, making its passage impossible.

Still, the concept did not die. Although a majority of the SEC's commissioners abandoned the idea of an SEC mandatory rule requiring shareholder access to the proxy nomination process, shareholder activists sought to adopt a similar rule by private action. Specifically, they sought to amend the bylaws of several individual corporations to provide for a similar (but more simplified) procedure. This attempt was made pursuant to SEC Rule 14a-8, which permits shareholders to add shareholder proposals to the corporation's proxy statement. Again, this effort gave rise to a complicated legal issue relating to whether Rule 14a-8 could be used in this fashion, but in AFSCME v. AIG, 462 F.3d 121 (2d Cir. 2006), (infra at page 681), the

---

34. See Sec. Exch. Act Rel. No. 34-48626, supra footnote 32, at *20.

Second Circuit upheld the validity of such an effort to use Rule 14a-8 to amend the bylaws to grant shareholders the power to nominate directors by means of the corporation's proxy statement. Still, the *AFSCME* decision held only that the existing language of Rule 14a-8 permitted shareholders to propose such bylaw amendments, and it also acknowledged that the SEC could revise Rule 14a-8 to prohibit such a procedure. Facing the prospect of a broad effort by insurgents to amend corporate bylaws to provide for shareholder nomination of directors, the SEC proposed two alternative amendments to Rule 14a-8 in 2007 — one authorizing such bylaw amendments, the other forbidding them. Both passed by a 3-2 vote of the SEC's five commissioners, with SEC Chairman Cox voting in favor of both proposals. In late 2007, a majority of the SEC adopted the latter alternative forbidding such bylaw amendments. The controversy appears likely to continue. See infra at pages 687-689.

3. INFORMATION REQUIRED TO BE FURNISHED

Rule 14a-3 requires that each person solicited in a proxy solicitation be furnished a written proxy statement complying with Schedule 14A no later than concurrently with the solicitation. Schedule 14A's requirements in turn depend on the context. In *all* cases, certain statements must be included concerning the date, time, and place of the meeting (Item 1) and the revocability of the proxy (Item 2); and identifying the persons making the solicitation (Item 4), their interest in the matters being acted on (Item 5), and voting rights and the beneficial ownership interests of large shareholders or "groups" of such shareholders (Item 6). If the solicitation relates to the election of directors, Item 7 of Schedule 14A requires a full identification of the directors, executive officers, and any nominees for the board; their ages and prior positions with the corporation; and any "arrangement or understanding . . . pursuant to which he was or is to be selected as a director, nominee, or officer."

Under Item 7, the proxy statement must discuss the operation of the board, including the number of meetings held over the last year; whether the board has standing audit, nominating, and compensation committees; and how often these committees have met during the last year. Any director who attended less than 75 percent of all meetings (including meetings of those board committees on which the director served) must be specifically identified. If a director resigned or refused to stand for reelection as the result of any disagreement with management, the director may request in writing that this disagreement be described and the director's own statement about it summarized. Obviously, such provisions are intended both to embarrass and prod corporations having inactive directors or lacking modern committee structures and to focus the sunlight of disclosure on any dispute that leads a director to resign.

More generally, Item 7 requires disclosure of information relating to all relationships and transactions between the director and the corporation. These disclosures are required to be made in brief tabular form in the proxy statement. Particularly detailed disclosure is required by Item 7(b) about the details of any financial transactions or dealings between a director or executive officer and the corporation. These requirements are set forth in Item 404 of Regulation S-K, which Item 7(b) incorporates by reference.

a. Executive Compensation

A major SEC initiative during the early 1990s focused on strengthening the disclosure requirements applicable to executive compensation. See Securities Act Release No. 6962 (Executive Compensation Disclosure) (Oct. 16, 1992). This effort was largely motivated by new research, and acerbic commentary suggesting that the CEO compensation in the United States was often unrelated to firm performance. See Graef Crystal, In Search of Excess: The Overcompensation of American Executives (1991); Lucian Bebchuk & Jesse Fried, Pay Without Performance: The Unfulfilled Promise of Executive Compensation (2004). The SEC's efforts have had three distinct goals: (i) clarifying the actual compensation paid to senior executives and directors, (ii) compelling the board to explain its criteria in making compensation decisions, and (iii) explaining the relationship between corporate performance and compensation.

Shifting from a general narrative disclosure approach, the SEC, first in 1992 and then even more extensively in 2006, mandated a formatted tabular approach that showed all forms of compensation and broke total compensation down into a series of categories, in order to promote comparability both from year to year and from company to company. See Sec. Exch. Act Rel. No. 34-54302A (Sept. 8, 2006). The revised proxy rules also require a report from the board's compensation committee, discussing the criteria used in setting compensation for the last completed fiscal year and a general discussion of compensation policies for executive officers. This report must identify and discuss the performance measures used and must disclose the individuals on the compensation committee and any "interlocks" they have with management.

Particularly controversial within the management community was the requirement of a performance graph comparing the registrant's cumulative total shareholder return for a five-year period with (1) a broad equity market index, and (2) either a published industry index or a registrant-determined peer group. Obviously, one intent of these proposals was to force industry laggards to recognize that they have underperformed — and then to justify their level of executive compensation in light thereof.

b. Annual Report

If a management solicitation relates to the election of directors, Rule 14a-3 requires the proxy statement to be preceded or accompanied by an annual report to shareholders, which must contain a basic package of financial information, including audited income statements for its three most recent fiscal years, segmented financial information with respect to the company's principal products or lines of business, its most recent quarterly information, and "management's discussion and analysis of financial condition and results of operations." This core package effectively summarizes the information in the corporation's Form 10-K (although the Form 10-K must also be supplied under Rule 14a-3 without charge to any shareholder who makes a written request). This requirement that the proxy statement be preceded or accompanied by the annual report dates back to 1974 and reflects the SEC's recognition that the glossy annual report, which is typically prepared by a public relations firm, written in nontechnical prose, and filled with photographs and other graphics, was likely to be the document on which most ordinary shareholders would focus. In connection with its "integrated disclosure" program, the SEC upgraded this extra-statutory document by requiring that it contain the basic package of financial disclosure that it wanted investors to receive. In net effect, Rule 14a-3 thus compels the issuer to distribute at least a condensed version of its '34 Act data to all shareholders whose proxies it solicits, and to offer to provide the fuller disclosure contained in the Form 10-K.

c. Soliciting Materials and Preliminary Review

The 1992 proxy rule revisions deleted the former requirements that soliciting materials (i.e., newspaper "fight ads" or television or radio commercials) be filed with the SEC for preliminary review prior to their distribution. Commentators saw this requirement as a prior restraint on free speech and believed that the SEC's review often dulled the force of the insurgents' message. In addition, the proxy statement itself is now publicly available as of the time of its "preliminary" filing with the SEC (which must be at least ten days before its actual distribution to security holders), and thus material charges or claims in it are likely to leak (or, more precisely, to be leaked) to the financial press, so that the SEC's practical power to censor is minimized. Of course, in an appropriate case, the SEC can still seek an injunction or administrative relief against fraudulent proxy materials.

4. REQUIREMENTS AS TO PROXY

The degree of discretionary authority that a proxy can confer on management or others is closely circumscribed by Rule 14a-4:

Rule 14a-4. Requirements as to Proxy

(a) The form of proxy (1) shall indicate in bold-face type whether or not the proxy is solicited on behalf of the registrant's board of directors or, if provided other than by a majority of the board of directors, shall indicate in bold-face type on whose behalf the solicitation is made; (2) shall provide a specifically designated blank space for dating the proxy card; and (3) shall identify clearly and impartially each separate matter intended to be acted upon, whether or not related to or conditioned on the approval of other matters, and whether proposed by the registrant or by security holders. No reference need be made, however, to proposals as to which discretionary authority is conferred pursuant to paragraph (c) of this section.

(b)(1) Means shall be provided in the form of proxy whereby the person solicited is afforded an opportunity to specify by boxes a choice between approval or disapproval of, or abstention with respect to, each separate matter referred to therein as intended to be acted upon, other than elections to office. A proxy may confer discretionary authority with respect to matters as to which a choice is not specified by the security holder provided that the form of proxy states in bold-face type how it is intended to vote the shares represented by the proxy in each such case.

(2) A form of proxy which provides for the election of directors shall set forth the names of persons nominated for election as directors. Such form of proxy shall clearly provide any of the following means for security holders to withhold authority to vote for each nominee:

(i) a box opposite the name of each nominee which may be marked to indicate that authority to vote for such nominee is withheld; or

(ii) an instruction in bold-face type which indicates that the security holder may withhold authority to vote for any nominee by lining through or otherwise striking out the name of any nominee; or

(iii) designated blank spaces in which the shareholder may enter the names of nominees with respect to whom the shareholder chooses to with-hold authority to vote; or

(iv) any other similar means, provided that clear instructions are furn-ished indicating how the security holder may withhold authority to vote for any nominee.

Such form of proxy also may provide a means for the security holder to grant authority to vote for the nominees set forth, as a group, provided that there is a similar means for the security holder to withhold authority to vote for such group of nominees. Any such form of proxy which is executed by the security holder in such manner as not to withhold authority to vote for the election of any nominee shall be deemed to grant such authority, provided that the form of proxy so states in bold-face type. . . .

(d) No proxy shall confer authority (1) to vote for the election of any person to any office for which a bona fide nominee is not named in the proxy statement, (2) to vote at any annual meeting other than the next annual meeting (or any adjournment thereof) to be held after the date on which the proxy statement and form of proxy are first sent or given to security holders, (3) to vote with respect to more than one meeting (and any adjournment thereof) or more than one consent solicitation, or (4) to consent to or authorize any action other than the action proposed to be taken in the proxy statement, or matters referred to in paragraph (c) of this rule. A person shall not be deemed to be a bona fide nominee and he shall not be named as such unless he has consented to being named in the proxy statement and to serve if elected; provided, however, that nothing in this Section 240.14a-4 shall prevent any person soliciting in support of nominees who, if elected, would constitute a minority of the board of directors, from seeking authority to vote nominees named in the registrant's proxy statement, so long as the soliciting party:

(i) Seeks authority to vote in the aggregate for the number of director positions then subject to election;

(ii) Represents that it will vote for all the registrant nominees, other than those registrant nominees specified by the soliciting party;

(iii) Provides the security holder an opportunity to withhold authority with respect to any other registrant nominee by writing the name of that nominee on the form of proxy; and

(iv) States on the form of proxy and in the proxy statement that there is no assurance that the registrant's nominees will serve if elected with any of the soliciting party's nominees.

(e) The proxy statement or form of proxy shall provide, subject to reasonable specified conditions, that the shares represented by the proxy will be voted and that where the person solicited specifies by means of a ballot provided pursuant to paragraph (b) a choice with respect to any matter to be acted upon, the shares will be voted in accordance with the specifications so made.

(f) No person conducting a solicitation subject to this regulation shall deliver a form of proxy, consent or authorization to any security holder unless the security holder concurrently receives, or has previously received, a definitive proxy statement that has been filed with the Commission pursuant to Section 240.14a-6(b).

True Form Co., Inc.

Proxy Solicited by Management in Shareholders' Interest

The undersigned hereby constitutes and appoints the bearers of this document the true and lawful attorney and proxy of the undersigned, to attend the Annual Meeting of the Stockholders of the True Form Co., Inc., to be held in Room 150, One Wall Street Plaza, New York, New York 10005, on April 1, 2009, at 10 A.M. and any adjournments thereof and any Special Meeting of the Stockholders of said corporation held after such date and prior to April 1, 2009, and to vote the shares of said corporation standing in the name of the undersigned with all the powers the undersigned would possess if personally present at such meeting or meetings:

(1) For the election of directors, including the election of such persons as may be substituted as nominees in the place and stead of any nominee listed in the Proxy Statement furnished by management.

(2) AGAINST [see recommendation below] [ ] or FOR [ ] a shareholder's proposal for the adoption of a system of cumulative voting.

(3) In his discretion upon such other business as may properly come before the Annual Meeting or any such Special Meeting.

Notes: Management recommends a vote "Against" the cumulative voting proposal, since in its judgment cumulative voting destroys the teamwork of the Board of Directors. Unless dated by the stockholder, this proxy will be deemed dated April 1, 2009.

Dated _____, 2009

_____

Signature

_____

1. *Conformity to rule.* In what respects, if any, does the sample form of proxy set out above violate the provisions of Rule 14a-4? What amendments would you make to the foregoing sample if you were preparing a form of proxy for a shareholders' committee proposing to offer a competing slate of nominees as directors and favoring the cumulative voting proposal?

2. *Discretionary authority.* Suppose management has reason to believe that a shareholder proposal will be made on a particular issue (whether by means of a Rule 14a-8 shareholder proposal, a formal proxy solicitation, or simply through a shareholder raising the issue from the floor at the shareholders' meeting), but no actual proposal has been made by the time the corporation sends out its proxy statement. May corporate management provide in its proxy that it will vote all proxies received on which it has not received contrary instructions in its discretion with regard to matters that arise after the mailing of its proxy statement? If it could not do this, activists might have an incentive to withhold their proposals until the last minute. As a result, Rule 14a-4(e) traditionally permitted the issuer to frame the proxy so as to grant itself discretionary voting authority only with regard to any matters raised at the shareholders meeting as to which the issuer had not received notice a "reasonable time" before the proxy was solicited. See Paragraph 3 in the foregoing proxy. Thus, no choice or separate box had to be provided on the proxy with regard to a shareholder proposal that came in just before the corporation's proxy statement was released.

Critics argued, however, that this "reasonable time" period gave the corporation too much discretion. In response, Sec. Exch. Act Rel. No. 34-40018 (May 21, 1998) amended Rule 14a-4(c) to provide a specific time period in lieu of the "reasonable time" test. Specifically, new Rule 14a-4(c)(1) allows a company to give itself discretionary voting authority at an annual shareholders' meeting with respect to matters as to which the company had not received notice by a date 45 days before the date in the current year corresponding to the date in the prior year on which the company first mailed its proxy materials for the prior year's annual meeting. For example, if a company last year mailed its proxy statement on March 31, then the notice date this year would be February 14 (or 45 days before March 31). Unless notice was given to the company by that date of a shareholder proposal (or by any earlier date for submission of shareholder proposals established by an advance notice bylaw), the company could write its proxy so as to give itself discretionary voting authority with respect to such shareholder proposals or other new matters raised at the annual shareholders' meeting. When notice is given prior to this cutoff date, the corporation would be required to describe the proposal in its proxy statement and indicate how it intended to vote (in which case it could vote uninstructed proxies against the proposal, unless the proponent of the shareholder proposal undertook a bona fide proxy solicitation). If the proponent undertakes such a proxy solicitation, then Rule 14a-4(c)(2) provides that management is denied discretionary authority and must conduct its own formal counter-solicitation.

3. *Unbundling.* Rule 14a-4(b) now requires "an opportunity to specify by boxes a choice between approval or disapproval of, or abstention with respect to, each separate matter referred to therein as intended to be acted upon. . . ." The intent here is to prohibit the "bundling" of an unattractive issue with a "sweetener" — for example, an anti-takeover charter amendment with an extraordinary dividend. By separating the two issues, Rule 14a-4 is intended to enable shareholders to vote no on the first issue and yes on the second. Suppose, then, a proxy statement asked

shareholders to approve by a single vote a proposal to (1) waive a default under a lease, (2) sell the leased building, and (3) distribute the proceeds as a dividend. Even if one assumes that such a grouping of issues violated Rule 14a-4, do shareholders have a private right of action to enforce this Rule — or can only the SEC sue? In Koppel v. 4987 Corp., 167 F.3d 125 (2d Cir. 1999), a Second Circuit panel found that on essentially these facts a private right of action for damages could be asserted by investors under Rule 14a-4. It stressed the long history of a private right of action under §14(a).

4. *Electronic proxies.* Can the datagram proxy discussed at page 586 supra satisfy the requirements of Rule 14a-4(a) when shareholders simply call a toll-free number and give instructions to a Western Union operator, who may or may not first read the form of proxy card to them? Even if this procedure is valid under state law, the SEC staff has taken the position that Rule 14a-4 requires that a shareholder have a form of proxy and read the form to the Western Union operator (rather than simply telling the operator how to mark a form of proxy previously provided to the operator). See Huber, Connolly & Struxness, SEC Review of Proxy and Tender Offer Material: Recent Administrative Experience, 17 Institute on Securities Regulation 523 (1985). What provisions in Rule 14a-4 can the SEC cite to support this position?

5. *Action by written consent.* As illustrated by the Datapoint v. Plaza Securities Co. case, page 591 supra, an insurgent may seek to obtain control of a target corporation by soliciting written consents (unless the certificate of incorporation or local law precludes this technique). The proxy rules apply equally to such solicitations of written consents, and Rule 14a-4(b) thus requires that the form of consent card must provide shareholders an opportunity to withhold authority for the removal of individual directors or for the election of individual nominees. The same rules also apply to the life of the consent and the manner in which it may be revoked. The SEC staff does, however, permit incumbent management to solicit a revocation-of-consent form in opposition, which may be a blanket form, without providing an opportunity for revoking the consent on a director-by-director basis. See Huber, Connolly & Struxness, supra, at 534-535.

6. *Requirement to vote proxies.* Rule 14a-4(e) requires essentially that the shares subject to the proxy be voted as the shareholder indicates. The proxy holder is thus in a ministerial position and may be required to vote the shares against the holder's self-interest. But may a person who has solicited proxies adjourn the meeting (either in toto or as to a specific issue) in order to solicit more proxies and prevent an impending defeat? The SEC staff has permitted short adjournments but not longer-term ones that would either call into question the currency of the proxy materials or result in the proxies not being voted. In addition, the party soliciting proxies may not vote those proxies for adjournment (even if disclosure of this contingency was made in the proxy statement) because such discretionary authority falls outside Rule 14a-4(c).

5. MAILING COMMUNICATIONS FOR SECURITY HOLDERS

Rule 14a-7(a)(2)(i) provides that management must mail a shareholder's proxy material "with reasonable promptness after tender of the material to be sent" and payment of postage and "other reasonable expenses of effecting such distribution." Thus, the insurgent must pay its own costs, while the management's proxy statement and proxy card go out at shareholder expense. Could the SEC mandate that the corporation mail both proxy statements at its own expense? Corporate managements will predictably reply that this is a matter of substantive corporate governance controlled by state law, but the proxy statement is a creation of federal law alone. The SEC's staff has made such a proposal, suggesting that, in the case of a campaign for one or two board seats, the corporation would mail out the insurgent's proxy card, and no other proxy statement would be required. Instead, the insurgent would post information on its Web site. However, the SEC would not favor this same streamlined system if control of the corporation were at issue.

Shareholders' lists. Rule 14a-7(a)(1)(i) today grants the corporation the option either to mail out the shareholder's proxy material or to furnish the shareholders' list to the insurgent. Should the shareholder, rather than the corporation, have the option?

> In most cases, not surprisingly, the management prefers the mailing alternative. And, by the same token, the security holder would prefer a list, not only because he would just as soon not have the management see his material in advance so that it can get a reply into the hands of the security holders simultaneously, but also because he may want to do some personal solicitation. In any event, even when the management chooses to furnish a list under the SEC rule, the list need not include the *amount* of the security owned by each holder. Since the rule does refer to a list of "such of the holders of record . . . as the security holder shall designate," it is arguable that the request for a list may designate the holders of more than a specified amount. But if the rule may not be so construed — and in either event if the management chooses the mailing alternative — the opposition is still relegated to the state law for information as to size of holdings, which is vital in order to be able to assess the value of the proxies received and to concentrate on the large holders.

2 Louis Loss, Securities Regulation 892 (2d ed. 1961).[35]

Interestingly, the choice is not always given to the corporation. Added by the 1992 proxy revisions, Rule 14a-7(b) reverses the option and gives the insurgent the choice of whether to demand the stockholder list or to pay the registrant to mail its proxy materials in the case of transactions subject to Rule 13e-3 (which basically applies to "going private" transactions in which majority or controlling shareholders seek to eliminate the minority interests in cash-out mergers — see page 1088 infra) and in the case of "roll-up" transactions, which typically involve conversions into corporate form of limited partnerships formed to hold tax shelter or real estate investments. Note that a limited partnership with 500 or more limited partners and $5 million in total assets is subject to the proxy rules, because limited partnership interests are securities. Both going-private and roll-up transactions were widely perceived to have been abused to the detriment of minority holders, and this seemingly explains the SEC's willingness to give the choice to the security holder, not the company.

Beneficial owners. When the registrant either elects or is obligated to provide a shareholder list, Rule 14a-7(a)(2)(ii) requires that it also furnish "the most recent list of names, addresses and security positions of beneficial owners . . . in the possession or which subsequently comes into the possession of the registrant."

---

35. The SEC's tender offer rules also give the target corporation the same option either to mail the bidder's offering materials or supply a current shareholders' list. See Rule 14d-5, page 1079 infra.

Should the registrant be required to compile such a list if it is not in its possession, but is reasonably accessible to it? See Sadler v. NCR Corp., 928 F.2d 48 (2d Cir. 1991) (requiring under New York law that a Maryland corporation compile and provide a New York shareholder with a NOBO list).

6. SHAREHOLDER PROPOSALS

As an alternative to conducting a proxy contest (which is invariably expensive), the SEC's rules also give the shareholder a low-cost alternative—at least for certain types of proposals. Under Rule 14a-8, the shareholder can attach a proposal to the corporation's own proxy statement, which will thus be mailed to all shareholders and voted on at the shareholders' meeting. Historically, this inexpensive option was chiefly utilized by social activists (including, more recently, public pension funds) who wished to challenge corporate practices they consider immoral or undesirable. During the 1970s and 1980s, shareholder proposals regularly challenged the Arab boycott of Israel and corporate investment in South Africa; more recently, they have raised environmental, affirmative action, or gender concerns. Although they seldom won a majority vote (or even a substantial plurality), shareholder proposals often triggered negotiations and a change in corporate policy (in part because of corporate management's embarrassment at opposing them publicly). In the 1990s, institutional investors also used shareholder proposals to challenge anti-takeover measures that they viewed as seeking to entrench corporate managements.

In response to these efforts, the corporate business community sought protection from what it perceived as a misuse of the proxy solicitation process, and it lobbied the SEC for (i) tighter eligibility standards governing who could submit a shareholder proposal; (ii) limitations on the frequency with which the same issue could be placed on the corporation's agenda; and (iii) broader exclusions under which some proposals were entirely rejected as inappropriate for shareholder action under state law.

The SEC's reaction to these conflicting pressures has produced numerous revisions to the rule and much litigation, particularly over the scope of permissible exclusions. In response to a 1951 attempt by shareholders to force Greyhound to desegregate its seating system on Southern bus routes (Peck v. Greyhound Corp., 97 F. Supp. 679 (S.D.N.Y. 1951)), the SEC amended the rule to exclude any proposal "submitted by the security holder . . . primarily for the purpose of promoting general economic, political, racial, religious, social or similar causes." 17 Fed. Reg. 11,433 (1952). The fate of this broad exclusion was eventually squarely faced in Medical Committee for Human Rights v. SEC.

Medical Committee for Human Rights v. SEC
432 F.2d 659 (D.C. Cir. 1970)

Tamm, J.: . . . On March 11, 1968, Dr. Quentin D. Young, National Chairman of the Medical Committee for Human Rights, wrote to the Secretary of the Dow Chemical Company, stating that the Medical Committee had obtained by gift several shares of Dow stock and expressing concern regarding the company's manufacture of the chemical substance napalm. In part, Dr. Young's letter said:

> After consultation with the executive body of the Medical Committee, I have been instructed to request an amendment to the charter of our company, Dow Chemical. We have learned that we are technically late in asking for an amendment at this date, but we wish to observe that it is a matter of such great urgency that we think it is imperative not to delay until the shareholders' meeting next year. . . .
> We respectfully propose the following wording to be sent to the shareholders:
>
> "RESOLVED, that the shareholders of the Dow Chemical Company request the Board of Directors, in accordance with the laws of the State of Delaware, and the Composite Certificate of Incorporation of the Dow Chemical Company, to adopt a resolution setting forth an amendment to the Composite Certificate of Incorporation of the Dow Chemical Company that napalm shall not be sold to any buyer unless that buyer gives reasonable assurance that the substance will not be used on or against human beings."

The letter concluded with the following statement:

> Finally, we wish to note that our objections to the sale of this product [are] primarily based on the concerns for human life inherent in our organization's credo. However, we are further informed by our investment advisers that this product is also bad for our company's business as it is being used in the Vietnamese War. It is now clear from company statements and press reports that it is increasingly hard to recruit the highly intelligent, well-motivated, young college men so important for company growth. There is, as well, an adverse impact on our global business, which our advisers indicate, suffers as a result of the public reaction to this product.

Copies of this letter were forwarded to the President and the General Counsel of Dow Chemical Company, and to the Securities and Exchange Commission.

By letter dated March 21, 1968, the General Counsel of Dow Chemical replied to the Medical Committee's letter, stating that the proposal had arrived too late for inclusion in the 1968 proxy statement, but promising that the company would "study the matter and . . . communicate with you later this year" regarding inclusion of the resolution in proxy materials circulated by management in 1969. Copies of this letter, and of all subsequent correspondence, were duly filed with the Commission.

The next significant item of record is a letter dated January 6, 1969, noting that the Medical Committee was "distressed that 1968 has passed without our having received a single word from you on this important matter," and again requesting that the resolution be included in management's 1969 proxy materials. The Secretary of Dow Chemical replied to this letter on January 17, informing the Medical Committee that Dow intended to omit the resolution from its proxy statement and enclosing an opinion memorandum from Dow's General Counsel, the contents of which will be discussed in detail . . . infra. On February 3 the Medical Committee responded to Dow's General Counsel, asserting that he had misconstrued the nature of their proposal in his opinion memorandum, and averring that the Medical Committee would not "presume to serve as draftsmen for an amendment to the corporate charter." The letter continued:

> We are willing to bend . . . to your belief that the management should be allowed to decide to whom and under what circumstances it will sell its products. Nevertheless,

we are certain that you would agree that the company's owners have not only the legal power but also the historic and economic obligation to determine what products their company will manufacture. Therefore, [we submit] . . . our revised proposal . . . requesting the Directors to consider the advisability of adopting an amendment to the corporate charter, forbidding the company to make napalm (any such amendment would, of course, be subject to the requirements of the "Defense Production Act of 1950," as are the corporate charters and management decisions of all United States Corporations), [and] we request that the following resolution be included in this year's proxy statement:

> "RESOLVED, that the shareholders of the Dow Chemical Company request that the Board of Directors, in accordance with the laws [*sic*] of the Dow Chemical Company, consider the advisability of adopting a resolution setting forth an amendment to the composite certificate of incorporation of the Dow Chemical Company that the company shall not make napalm."

On the same date, a letter was sent to the Securities and Exchange Commission, requesting a staff review of Dow's decision if it still intended to omit the proposal, and requesting oral argument before the Commission if the staff agreed with Dow. On February 7, 1969, Dow transmitted to the Medical Committee and to the Commission a letter and memorandum opinion of counsel, which in essence reiterated the previous arguments against inclusion of the proposal and stated the company's intention to omit it from the proxy statement. Shortly thereafter, on February 18, 1969, the Commission's Chief Counsel of the Division of Corporation Finance sent a letter to Dow, with copies to the Medical Committee, concluding that "[f]or reasons stated in your letter and the accompanying opinion of counsel, both dated January 17, 1969, this Division will not recommend any action . . . if this proposal is omitted from the management's proxy material. . . ." In a letter dated February 28 — which contains the first indications of record that petitioners had retained counsel — the Medical Committee again renewed its request for a Commission review of the Division's decision. On the same day, the Medical Committee filed with the Commission a memorandum of legal arguments in support of its resolution, urging numerous errors of law in the Division's decision. Several other documents were filed by both the company and the Medical Committee; finally, on April 2, 1969, both parties were informed that "[t]he Commission has approved the recommendation of the Division of Corporation Finance that no objection be raised if the Company omits the proposals from its proxy statements for the forthcoming meeting of shareholders." The petitioners thereupon instituted the present action, and on July 10, 1969, the Commission moved to dismiss the petition for lack of jurisdiction. On October 13 we denied the motion "without prejudice to renewal thereof in the briefs and at the argument on the merits."

In its briefs and oral argument, the Commission has consistently and vigorously urged, to the exclusion of all other contentions, that this court is without jurisdiction to review its action. We find this argument unpersuasive. . . .

The Medical Committee's sole substantive contention in this petition is that its proposed resolution could not, consistently with the Congressional intent underlying section 14(a), be properly deemed a proposal which is either motivated by *general* political and moral concerns, or related to the conduct of Dow's ordinary business operations. These criteria are two of the established exceptions to the general rule that management must include all properly submitted shareholder proposals in its proxy materials. They are contained in Rule 14a-8(c), which provides in relevant part:

> ... [M]anagement may omit a proposal ... from its proxy statement and form of proxy under any of the following circumstances: ...
> (2) If it clearly appears that the proposal is submitted by the security holder ... primarily for the purpose of promoting general economic, political, racial, religious, social or similar causes; or ...
> (5) If the proposal consists of a recommendation or request that the management take action with respect to a matter relating to the conduct of the ordinary business operations of the issuer.

Despite the fact that our October 13 order in this case deferred resolution of the jurisdictional issue pending full argument on the merits, the Commission has not deigned to address itself to any possible grounds for allowing management to exclude this proposal from its proxy statement. We confess to a similar puzzlement as to how the Commission reached the result which it did, and thus we are forced to remand the controversy for a more illuminating consideration and decision. ...
In aid of this consideration on remand, we feel constrained to explain our difficulties with the position taken by the company and endorsed by the Commission.

It is obvious to the point of banality to restate the proposition that Congress intended by its enactment of section 14 of the Securities Exchange Act of 1934 to give true vitality to the concept of corporate democracy. ...

In striving to implement this open-ended mandate, the Commission has gradually evolved its present proxy rules. ... It eventually became clear that the question of what constituted a "proper subject" for shareholder action was to be resolved by recourse to the law of the state in which the company had been incorporated; however, the paucity of applicable state law giving content to the concept of "proper subject" led the Commission to seek guidance from precedent existing in jurisdictions which had a highly developed commercial and corporate law and to develop its own "common law" relating to proper subjects for shareholder action. See generally II L. Loss, Securities Regulation 905-906 (1961); Hearings on SEC Enforcement Problems Before a Subcom. of the Senate Comm. on Banking and Currency, 85th Cong., 1st Sess., pt. 1, at 118 (1957) [hereinafter "Senate Hearings"].

Further areas of difficulty became apparent as experience was gained in administering the "proper subject" test, and these conflicts provided the Commission with opportunities to put a detailed gloss upon the general phraseology of its rules. Thus, in 1945 the Commission issued a release containing an opinion of the Director of the Division of Corporation Finance that was rendered in response to a management request to omit shareholder resolutions which bore little or no relationship to the company's affairs; for example, these shareholder resolutions included proposals "that the anti-trust laws and the enforcement thereof be revised," and "that all Federal legislation hereafter enacted providing for workers and farmers to be represented should be made to apply equally to investors." The Commission's release endorsed the Director's conclusion that "proposals which deal with general political, social or economic matters are not, within the meaning of the rule, 'proper subjects for action by security holders.'" The reason for this conclusion was summarized as follows in the Director's opinion:

> Speaking generally, *it is the purpose of Rule X-14A-7 to place stockholders in a position to bring before their fellow stockholders matters of concern to them as stockholders in such*

corporation; that is, such matters relating to the affairs of the company concerned as are proper subjects for stockholders' action under the laws of the state under which it was organized. It was not the intent of Rule X-14A-7 to permit stockholders to obtain the consensus of other stockholders with respect to matters which are of a general political, social or economic nature. *Other forums exist for the presentation of such views.*

Several years after the Commission issued this release, it was confronted with the same kind of problem when the management of a national bus company sought to omit a shareholder proposal phrased as "A Recommendation that Management Consider the Advisability of Abolishing the Segregated Seating System in the South" — a proposal which, on its face, was ambiguous with respect to whether it was limited solely to company policy rather than attacking all segregated seating, and which quite likely would have brought the company into violation of state laws then assumed to be valid. The Commission staff approved management's decision to omit the proposal, and the shareholder then sought a temporary injunction against the company's solicitation in a federal district court. The injunction was denied because the plaintiff had failed to exhaust his administrative remedies or to show that he would be irreparably harmed by refusal to grant the requested relief. Peck v. Greyhound Corp., 97 F. Supp. 679 (S.D.N.Y. 1951). The Commission amended its rules the following year to encompass the above-quoted exception for situations in which "it clearly appears that the proposal is submitted by the security holder . . . primarily for the purpose of promoting general economic, political, racial, religious, social or similar causes." 17 Fed. Reg. 11,433 (1952); see also id. at 11,431. So far as we have been able to determine, the Commission's interpretation or application of this rule has not been considered by the courts.

The origins and genesis of the exception for proposals "relating to the conduct of the ordinary business operations of the issuer" are somewhat more obscure. This provision was introduced into the proxy rules in 1954, as part of amendments which were made to clarify the general proposition that the primary source of authority for determining whether a proposal is a proper subject for shareholder action is state law. See 19 Fed. Reg. 246 (1954). Shortly after the rule was adopted, the Commission explained its purpose to Congress in the following terms:

> The policy motivating the Commission in adopting the rule . . . is basically the same as the underlying policy of most State corporation laws to confine the solution of ordinary business problems to the board of directors and place such problems beyond the competence and direction of the shareholders. The basic reason for this policy is that it is manifestly impracticable in most cases for stockholders to decide management problems at corporate meetings. . . .
>
> . . . While Rule X-14A-8 does not require that the ordinary business operations be determined on the basis of State law, the premise of Rule X-14A-8 is that the propriety of . . . proposals for inclusion in the proxy statement is to be determined in general by the law of the State of incorporation. . . . Consistency with this premise requires that the phrase "ordinary business operations" in Rule X-14A-8 have the meaning attributed to it under applicable State law. To hold otherwise would be to introduce into the rule the possibility of endless and narrow interpretations based on no ascertainable standards.

(Senate Hearings at 118.)

It also appears that no administrative interpretation of this exception has yet been scrutinized by the courts.

These two exceptions are, on their face, consistent with the legislative purpose underlying section 14; for it seems fair to infer that Congress desired to make proxy solicitations a vehicle for *corporate* democracy rather than an all-purpose forum for malcontented shareholders to vent their spleen about irrelevant matters,[26] and also realized that management cannot exercise its specialized talents effectively if corporate investors assert the power to dictate the minutiae of daily business decisions. However, it is also apparent that the two exceptions which these rules carve out of the general requirement of inclusion can be construed so as to permit the exclusion of practically any shareholder proposal on the grounds that it is either "too general" or "too specific." Indeed, in the present case Dow Chemical Company attempted to impale the Medical Committee's proposal on both horns of this dilemma: in its memorandum of counsel, it argued that the Medical Committee's proposal was a matter of ordinary business operations properly within the sphere of management expertise and, at the same time, that the proposal clearly had been submitted primarily for the purpose of promoting general political or social causes. As noted above, the Division of Corporation Finance made no attempt to choose between these potentially conflicting arguments, but rather accepted Dow Chemical's decision to omit the proposal "[f]or reasons stated in [the company's] letter and the accompanying opinion of counsel, both dated January 17, 1969"; this determination was then adopted by the full Commission. Close examination of the company's arguments only increases doubt as to the reasoning processes which led the Commission to this result.

In contending that the Medical Committee's proposal was properly excludable under Rule 14a-8(c)(5), Dow's counsel asserted:

> It is my opinion that *the determination of the products which the company shall manufacture,* the customers to which it shall sell the products, and the conditions under which it shall make such sales are related to the conduct of the ordinary business operations of the Company and that any attempt to amend the Certificate of Incorporation to define the circumstances under which the management of the Company shall make such determinations is contrary to the concept of corporate management, which is inherent in the Delaware General Corporation Act under which the Company is organized.

In the first place, it seems extremely dubious that this superficial analysis complies with the Commission's longstanding requirements that management must sustain the burden of proof when asserting that a shareholder proposal may properly be omitted from the proxy statement, and that "[w]here management contends that a

---

26. See, e.g., the following colloquy, which appears in House Hearings at 162-63:

Mr. Boren. So one man, if he owned one share in A.T.&T. . . . and another share in R.C.A. . . . if he decided deliberately . . . to become a professional stockholder in each one of the companies—he could have a hundred-word propaganda statement prepared and he could put it in every one of these proxy statements. Suppose he were a Communist.

Commissioner Purcell. That is possible. We have never seen such a case.

Mr. Boren. Suppose a man were a Communist and he wanted to send to all of the stockholders of all of these firms, a philosophic statement of 100 words in length, or a propaganda statement. . . . He could by the mere device of buying one share of stock . . . have available to him the mailing list of all the stockholders in the Radio Corporation of America. . . .

Commissioner Purcell. Of course, we have never seen such a case; and if such a case came before us, then we would have to deal with it and make such appropriate changes as might seem necessary. . . .

proposal may be omitted because it is not proper under State law, it will be incumbent upon management to refer to the applicable statute or case law." 19 Fed. Reg. 246 (1954). As noted above, the Commission has formally represented to Congress that Rule 14a-8(c)(5) is intended to make state law the governing authority in determining what matters are ordinary business operations immune from shareholder control; yet, the Delaware General Corporation law provides that a company's Certificate of Incorporation may be amended to "change, substitute, enlarge or diminish the nature of [the company's] business."[29] If there are valid reasons why the Medical Committee's proposal does not fit within the language and spirit of this provision, they certainly do not appear in the record.

The possibility that the Medical Committee's proposal could properly be omitted under Rule 14a-8(c)(2) appears somewhat more substantial in the circumstances of the instant case, although once again it may fairly be asked how Dow Chemical's arguments on this point could be deemed a rational basis for such a result: the paragraph in the company's memorandum of counsel purporting to deal with this issue, which is set forth in the margin, consists entirely of a fundamentally irrelevant recitation of some of the political protests which had been directed at the company because of its manufacture of napalm, followed by the abrupt conclusion that management is therefore entitled to exclude the Medical Committee's proposal from its proxy statement. Our own examination of the issue raises substantial questions as to whether an interpretation of Rule 14a-8(c)(2) which permitted omission of this proposal as one motivated primarily by *general* political or social concerns would conflict with the congressional intent underlying section 14(a) of the Act.

As our earlier discussion indicates, the clear import of the language, legislative history, and record of administration of section 14(a) is that its overriding purpose is to assure to corporate shareholders the ability to exercise their right—some would say their duty—to control the important decisions which affect them in their capacity as stockholders and owners of the corporation. . . . Here, in contrast to the situations detailed above which led to the promulgation of Rule 14a-8(c)(2), the proposal relates solely to a matter that is completely within the accepted sphere of corporate activity and control. No reason has been advanced in the present proceedings which leads to the conclusion that management may properly place obstacles in the path of shareholders who wish to present to their co-owners, in accord with applicable state law, the question of whether they wish to have their assets used in a manner which they believe to be more socially responsible but possibly less profitable than that which is dictated by present company policy. Thus, even accepting Dow's characterization of the purpose and intent of the Medical Committee's proposal, there is a strong argument that permitting the company to exclude it would contravene the purpose of section 14(a).

However, the record in this case contains indications that we are confronted with quite a different situation. The management of Dow Chemical Company is repeatedly quoted in sources which include the company's own publications as proclaiming that the decision to continue manufacturing and marketing napalm

---

29. Chapter 1, Title 8 Delaware Code §§242(a)(2), 242(d) (1968 Cum. Supp.). Cf. II L. Loss, Securities Regulation 906 (1961): "Inevitably the Commission, while purporting to find and apply a generally nonexistent state law, has been building up a 'common law' of its own as to what constitutes a 'proper subject' for shareholder action. It is a 'common law' which undoubtedly would yield, as it should, to a contrary decision of the particular state court."

was made not *because* of business considerations, but *in spite of* them; that management in essence decided to pursue a course of activity which generated little profit for the shareholders and actively impaired the company's public relations and recruitment activities because management considered this action morally and politically desirable. The proper political and social role of modern corporations is, of course, a matter of philosophical argument extending far beyond the scope of our present concern; the substantive wisdom or propriety of particular corporate political decisions is also completely irrelevant to the resolution of the present controversy. What *is* of immediate concern, however, is the question of whether the corporate proxy rules can be employed as a shield to isolate such managerial decisions from shareholder control. After all, it must be remembered that "[t]he control of great corporations by a very few persons was the abuse at which Congress struck in enacting Section 14(a)." SEC v. Transamerica Corp., 163 F.2d at 518. We think that there is a clear and compelling distinction between management's legitimate need for freedom to apply its expertise in matters of day-to-day business judgment, and management's patently illegitimate claim of power to treat modern corporations with their vast resources as personal satrapies implementing personal political or moral predilections. It could scarcely be argued that management is more qualified or more entitled to make these kinds of decisions than the shareholders who are the true beneficial owners of the corporation; and it seems equally implausible that an application of the proxy rules which permitted such a result could be harmonized with the philosophy of corporate democracy which Congress embodied in section 14(a) of the Securities Exchange Act of 1934.

In light of these considerations, therefore, the cause must be remanded to the Commission so that it may reconsider petitioner's claim within the proper limits of its discretionary authority as set forth above, and so that "the basis for [its] decision [may] appear clearly on the record, not in conclusory terms but in sufficient detail to permit prompt and effective review."

Remanded for further proceedings consistent with this opinion.

---

1. *Dismissal as moot.* The Supreme Court granted certiorari and vacated the judgment for mootness, 404 U.S. 403 (1972):

> Events have taken place, subsequent to the decision by the court below, and some subsequent to our decision to grant certiorari, that require that we dismiss this case on the ground that it has now become moot. In January 1971, the Medical Committee again submitted its napalm resolution for inclusion in Dow's 1971 proxy statement. This time Dow acquiesced in the Committee's request and included the proposal. At the annual stockholder's meeting in May 1971, Dow's shareholders voted on the Committee's proposal. Less than 3% of all voting shareholders supported it, and pursuant to Rule 14a-8(c)(4)(i), Dow may exclude the same or substantially the same proposal from its proxy materials for the next three years. We find that this series of events has mooted the controversy.

2. *The 1976 revisions and the "significantly related" test.* Following its "defeat" in *Medical Committee,* the SEC revised Rule 14a-8 to add a series of specific exclusions

to the rule. Rule 14a-8 had long contained an exclusion for "ordinary business" matters (which ironically appears to have been a response to the above-noted *Greyhound* case), but over time the SEC found that no consensus existed as to where the dividing line fell between "ordinary business" and "extraordinary" social issues. Hence, in 1976 it amended Rule 14a-8 to permit the exclusion of a shareholder proposal (at the company's request) if the proposal related to "operations which account for less than 5 percent of the company's total assets . . . and for less than 5 percent of its net earnings and gross sales. . . ." Because the Commission was unwilling to rely entirely on this quantitative test, it added the additional phrase "and is not otherwise significantly related to the company's business." In Sec. Exch. Act Rel. No. 34-12999 (1976), the Commission explained its intended compromise:

> A number of commentators expressed the view that the Commission should allow the omission of a proposal whenever the matter involved therein does not bear a significant economic relation to the issuer's business. In this regard, the Commission does not believe that subparagraph (c)(5) should be hinged solely on the economic relativity of a proposal, since there are many instances in which the matter involved in a proposal is significant to an issuer's business, even though such significance is not apparent from an economic viewpoint. For example, proposals dealing with cumulative voting rights or the ratification of auditors in a sense may not be economically significant to an issuer's business but they nevertheless have a significance to security holders that would preclude their being omitted under this provision. And proposals relating to ethical issues such as political contributions also may be significant to the issuer's business, when viewed from a standpoint other than a purely economic one.
>
> Notwithstanding the foregoing, the Commission recognizes that there are circumstances in which economic data may indicate a valid basis for omitting a proposal under this provision. The Commission wishes to emphasize, however, that the significance of a particular matter to an issuer's present or prospective business depends upon that issuer's individual circumstances, and that there is no specific quantitative standard that is applicable in all instances. Moreover, as previously indicated, the burden is on the issuer to demonstrate that this or any other provision of Rule 14a-8 may properly be relied upon to omit a proposal.

What matters are still "significantly related" to an issuer's business even when their economic impact is modest? In Lovenheim v. Iroquois Brands Ltd., 618 F. Supp. 554 (D.D.C. 1985), plaintiff, an animal rights advocate, submitted a resolution calling on the board to "form a committee to study the methods by which its French supplier produces pate de foie gras, and report to the shareholders its findings and opinions, based on expert consultation, on whether this production method causes undue distress, pain or suffering to the animals involved. . . ." Specifically, plaintiff objected to the traditional practice of force-feeding geese in order to enlarge their livers. The corporation sought to omit the proposal under subparagraph (c)(5), because its pate de foie gras sales were under $79,000, while it had total revenues of $141 million, profits of $6 million, and $78 million in assets. Nonetheless, the court granted plaintiff an injunction "in light of the ethical and social significance of plaintiff's proposal," after finding unpersuasive the corporation's attempt to distinguish the *Medical Committee* case. Correctly decided? What significance, if any, should be attached to the fact that defendant did not produce the commodity in question (as Dow Chemical did) but only purchased it from foreign suppliers?

3. *The "ordinary business" exclusion.* As a practical matter, the *Iroquois Brands* case told both the SEC and the corporate bar that they could not confidently rely on the "significantly related" exclusion. In turn, this increased the importance of the "ordinary business" exclusion, and during the 1990s decisions increasingly came to focus on its scope. In 1992 the Amalgamated Clothing & Textile Workers Union submitted a shareholder proposal for inclusion in Wal-Mart Stores, Inc.'s proxy statement that would have required Wal-Mart's directors to prepare and distribute reports about Wal-Mart's equal employment opportunity and affirmative action policies, including a description of efforts to purchase goods and services from minority and female-owned suppliers. Wal-Mart refused to include the proposal in reliance on the "ordinary business" exclusion, and the SEC issued a no-action letter confirming Wal-Mart's position. The union nonetheless sued Wal-Mart and won an injunction. See Amalgamated Clothing & Textile Workers Union v. Wal-Mart Stores, Inc., 821 F. Supp. 877 (S.D.N.Y. 1993). The district court essentially found that the SEC had impermissibly deviated from its prior position, which distinguished employment practices involving only "day-to-day business affairs" from those involving "significant policy considerations," without complying with the Administrative Procedure Act's "notice and comment" procedures. Next, it found that Wal-Mart could not meet its burden of proof of showing that the proposal clearly fell within the "ordinary business exclusion." Although the proposal was thus presented to shareholders, the Wal-Mart annual meeting voted the shareholder proposal down, with approximately 90 percent of the shares being cast against it. See Amalgamated Clothing & Textile Workers Union v. Wal-Mart Stores, Inc., 54 F.3d 69 (2d Cir. 1995).

Nonetheless, subsequent decisions have given considerable latitude to this exclusion. In Roosevelt v. E.I. DuPont de Nemours & Co., 958 F.2d 416 (D.C. Cir. 1992), the plaintiff, in conjunction with the Friends of the Earth Oceanic Society, submitted a shareholder proposal regarding (1) the timing of DuPont's phaseout of the production of chlorofluorocarbons ("CFCs") and halons, which both were believed to have an adverse impact on the ozone layer, and (2) the preparation and presentation to shareholders of a report detailing research and development of environmentally sound substitutes. DuPont had already determined to phase out the production of CFCs, but at a slower pace than the plaintiff wanted. DuPont sought and obtained a no-action letter from the SEC's staff that the exception in Rule 14a-8(c)(7) for matters "relating to the conduct of . . . ordinary business operations" applied and thus that the SEC's staff would not object to the exclusion of the plaintiff's proposal. Plaintiff filed an injunctive action in federal district court, but both that court and the D.C. Circuit on appeal upheld DuPont's position. The D.C. Circuit did find that plaintiff had an implied cause of action enabling it to sue under Rule 14a-8, but then found that her proposal related to ordinary business operations, noting:

> [W]e emphasize that Roosevelt's disagreement with DuPont's current policy is not about whether to eliminate CFC production or even whether to do so at once. The former is an end to which DuPont is committed, and immediate cessation, before environmentally safe alternatives are available, is not what Roosevelt proposes.
>
>   Roosevelt differs with DuPont on a less fundamental matter — the rapidity with which the near-term phase out should occur. . . . Timing questions no doubt reflect

"significant policy" when large differences are at stake. That would be the case, for example, if DuPont projected a phaseout period extending into the new century.

The D.C. Circuit also rejected the second aspect of plaintiff's proxy proposal: the preparation of a management report to shareholders detailing research and development efforts on safe substitutes. Here, the D.C. Circuit noted that the SEC's position had changed and that currently it was to "consider whether the subject matter of the [requested] report . . . involves a matter of ordinary business." Such requests for reports, the D.C. Circuit said, were neither "automatically includable" nor "inevitably excludable." Plaintiff, it concluded, had failed in this case to show "that the detailed research and development or marketing information she seeks implicates significant policy issues, and not merely implementation arrangements."

Given that the district court in *Amalgamated Clothing & Textile Workers Union* had concluded that a plaintiff's proposal requesting a report from Wal-Mart on its equal employment policies could not be excluded because it went beyond "ordinary business," the dividing line between its position and that of the D.C. Circuit in *Roosevelt* was potentially ambiguous. In Sec. Exch. Act Rel. No. 34-40018 (May 21, 1998), the Commission sought to reconcile these cases, suggesting that the policy underlying the ordinary business exclusion rested on two central considerations:

> The first relates to the subject matter of the proposal. Certain tasks are so fundamental to management's ability to run a company on a day-to-day basis that they could not, as a practical matter, be subject to direct shareholder oversight. Examples include the management of the workforce, such as the hiring, promotion, and termination of employees, decisions on production quality and quantity, and the retention of suppliers. However, proposals relating to such matters but focusing on sufficiently significant social policy issues (e.g., significant discrimination matters) generally would not be considered to be excludable, because the proposals would transcend the day-to-day business matters and raise policy issues so significant that it would be appropriate for a shareholder vote.
>
> The second consideration relates to the degree to which the proposal seeks to "micro-manage" the company by probing too deeply into matters of a complex nature upon which shareholders, as a group, would not be in a position to make an informed judgment. This consideration may come into play in a number of circumstances, such as where the proposal involves intricate detail, or seeks to impose specific timeframes or methods for implementing complex policies.

In this light, *Roosevelt* probably is best viewed as a case in which the shareholder proposal could be excluded because it essentially sought to "micro-manage" the corporation's decision to phase out a product. If, however, the corporation sought to continue production indefinitely, this would likely be an issue of "policy significance," not ordinary business. *Query:* What if the proponent requests the company to end production of a product that only a few see as harmful to the environment? Is this still a matter of ordinary business? Should the SEC make such judgments?

4. *Discrimination and "ordinary business."* Probably the most controversial episode that the SEC has recently faced involving Rule 14a-8 concerned its attempt to sidestep all employment-related disputes by deeming them generically to constitute "ordinary business" decisions. In 1991 Cracker Barrel Old Country Store, Inc.

(Cracker Barrel) announced that, as a company "founded upon a concept of traditional American values," it would not "continue to employ individuals in our operating units whose sexual preferences fail to demonstrate normal heterosexual values which have been the foundation of families in our society" — in short, it would fire gay employees. The next year, New York City Employees' Retirement System (NYCERS) sought to include a precatory proposal in Cracker Barrel's proxy statement calling upon its board to prohibit discrimination on the basis of sexual orientation. When Cracker Barrel sought the SEC's permission to exclude the proposal, the SEC staff (and later the full Commission) agreed that the proposal could be omitted under then Rule 14a-8(c)(7) (the "ordinary business operations" exclusion). The SEC staff's letter to Cracker Barrel indicated that it had reconsidered its past position, which viewed employment policies and practices that were tied to a significant social issue as outside the "ordinary business exclusion," and had found it increasingly difficult to distinguish those employment-related proposals that were includable by virtue of their social policy implications from those that were not. Thus, it would henceforth permit the exclusion of all employment-related matters under Rule 14a-8(c)(7) (except those relating to executive compensation). NYCERS brought suit against the Commission and won an injunction barring the SEC from changing its policy under Rule 14a-8 without first complying with the notice and comment provisions of the Administrative Procedure Act (APA). See NYCERS v. SEC, 843 F. Supp. 858 (S.D.N.Y. 1994). District Judge Kimba Wood found that the SEC's 1976 statement in Sec. Exch. Act. Rel. No. 12999 (the "1976 Release") that it would not permit issuers to exclude proposals under Rule 14a-8(c)(7) that related to matters "which have significant policy, economic or other social implications inherent in them" was a "legislative rule." Accordingly, she held that the abandonment of this position in the Cracker Barrel no-action letter was also a "legislative rule" requiring prior notice and comment.

However, on appeal, the SEC convinced the Second Circuit that its position was an "interpretive" rule, not a "legislative" rule, and hence could be changed without compliance with the APA's "notice and comment" provisions. See New York City Employees' Retirement Sys. v. SEC, 45 F.3d 7 (2d Cir. 1995).

This resolution protected the SEC, but still permitted the proponent of the shareholder resolution to sue to enjoin the corporation. In fact, little litigation resulted, but public pension funds, shareholder organizations, and church groups began a massive lobbying campaign to persuade the SEC to reverse its "Cracker Barrel" position that employment-related issues were beyond the scope of Rule 14a-8 shareholder proposals. Industry groups also mobilized to resist change. Finally, in 1998, after much debate, the SEC reversed its Cracker Barrel position, announcing (somewhat defensively) in Sec. Exch. Act Rel. No. 34-40018 (May 21, 1998): "Since 1992, the relative importance of certain social issues relating to employment matters has reemerged as a consistent topic of widespread public debate."

This reversal meant that the SEC has once again returned to a case-by-case decisionmaking approach (and has continued to be inundated with Rule 14a-8 proposals as a result). Critics doubt that SEC decisions in the area of Rule 14a-8 are the product of reasoned distinctions, asserting that they seem to be determined by the relative level of social controversy surrounding the issue. *Query:* Isn't the level of public concern an appropriate consideration?

5. *"Plain English" revisions.* In 1998 Sec. Exch. Act Rel. No. 34-40018 restated, simplified, and expressed in the SEC's new "Plain English" style the bases

upon which a shareholder proposal can be excluded under Rule 14a-8. Expressed in a question-and-answer format, Rule 14a-8(i) now provides:

(i) Question 9: If I have complied with the procedural requirements, on what other bases may a company rely to exclude my proposal?

(1) *Improper under state law:* If the proposal is not a proper subject for action by shareholders under the laws of the jurisdiction of the company's organization;

Note to paragraph (i)(1): Depending on the subject matter, some proposals are not considered proper under state law if they would be binding on the company if approved by shareholders. In our experience, most proposals that are cast as recommendations or requests that the board of directors take specified action are proper under state law. Accordingly, we will assume that a proposal drafted as a recommendation or suggestion is proper unless the company demonstrates otherwise.

(2) *Violation of law:* If the proposal would, if implemented, cause the company to violate any state, federal, or foreign law to which it is subject;

Note to paragraph (i)(2): We will not apply this basis for exclusion to permit exclusion of a proposal on grounds that it would violate foreign law if compliance with the foreign law would result in a violation of any state or federal law.

(3) *Violation of proxy rules:* If the proposal or supporting statement is contrary to any of the Commission's proxy rules, including §240.14a-9, which prohibits materially false or misleading statements in proxy soliciting materials;

(4) *Personal grievance; special interest:* If the proposal relates to the redress of a personal claim or grievance against the company or any other person, or if it is designed to result in a benefit to you, or to further a personal interest, which is not shared by the other shareholders at large;

(5) *Relevance:* If the proposal relates to operations which account for less than 5 percent of the company's total assets at the end of its most recent fiscal year, and for less than 5 percent of its net earnings and gross sales for its most recent fiscal year, and is not otherwise significantly related to the company's business;

(6) *Absence of power/authority:* If the company would lack the power or authority to implement the proposal;

(7) *Management functions:* If the proposal deals with a matter relating to the company's ordinary business operations;

(8) *Relates to election:* If the proposal relates to an election for membership on the company's board of directors or analogous governing body;

(9) *Conflicts with company's proposal:* If the proposal directly conflicts with one of the company's own proposals to be submitted to shareholders at the same meeting;

Note to paragraph (i)(9): A company's submission to the Commission under this section should specify the points of conflict with the company's proposal.

(10) *Substantially implemented:* If the company has already substantially implemented the proposal;

(11) *Duplication:* If the proposal substantially duplicates another proposal previously submitted to the company by another proponent that will be included in the company's proxy materials for the same meeting;

(12) *Resubmissions:* If the proposal deals with substantially the same subject matter as another proposal or proposals that has or have been previously included in the company's proxy materials within the preceding 5 calendar years, a company may exclude it from its proxy materials for any meeting held within 3 calendar years of the last time it was included if the proposal received:

(i) Less than 3% of the vote if proposed once within the preceding 5 calendar years;

(ii) Less than 6% of the vote on its last submission to shareholders if proposed twice previously within the preceding 5 calendar years; or

(iii) Less than 10% of the vote on its last submission to shareholders if proposed three times or more previously within the preceding 5 calendar years; and

(13) *Specific amount of dividends:* If the proposal relates to specific amounts of cash or stock dividends."

6. *Shareholder proposals to amend bylaws.* Most shareholder proposals have historically been framed as nonbinding precatory requests to the board to take specified actions or to prepare a report about the corporation's activities in certain sensitive areas. This format has been a response to legal concerns that shareholders lack the power to dictate instructions to the board, as virtually every state corporation's statute mandates that "the business and affairs of every corporation organized under this chapter shall be managed by or under the direction of a board of directors." See, e.g., Del. Gen. Corp. Law §141(a); Cal. Gen. Corp. Law §300(a). Given this allocation of authority to the board, Rule 14a-8(i) permits the issuer to exclude a shareholder proposal from its proxy statement that is "not a proper subject for action by shareholders" under the corporate law of the issuer's jurisdiction of incorporation, but it indicates in a note to Rule 14a-8(i)(1) that precatory requests to the board to take action are normally a proper subject for shareholder action.

In response, shareholder proponents have recently framed their proposals as bylaw amendments because most corporation statutes also authorize the shareholders to amend the bylaws. On their face, these statutes permit shareholder-passed bylaws to regulate most aspects of the corporation's business and affairs. See, e.g., Del. Gen. Corp. Law §109(b) ("bylaws may contain any provision, not inconsistent with law or with the certificate of incorporation, relating to the business of the corporation, the conduct of its affairs, and its rights or powers or the rights or powers of its stockholders, directors, officers or employees"). But a deep tension exists between the shareholders' broad power to amend the bylaws and the equally broad provision entrusting the business and affairs of the corporation to its board of directors. See, e.g., Del. Gen. Corp. Law §141(a) (board given authority to manage the business and affairs of every corporation organized under this Chapter).

The first case to face this tension was International Brotherhood of Teamsters General Fund v. Fleming Cos., Inc., 975 P.2d 907 (Okla. 1999). There, the Teamsters pension fund proposed a bylaw amendment that would have nullified the corporation's newly adopted "poison pill" (an anti-takeover defense mechanism that is discussed in Chapter IX). The company responded that such a shareholder proposal invaded the board's authority and was therefore not a proper subject for shareholder action. However, both a federal district court[36] and ultimately the Oklahoma Supreme Court ruled that the proposal was a proper subject for shareholder action and had to be included in the company's proxy statement. Although its decision rests on Oklahoma law (which does closely parallel Delaware law), the Oklahoma Supreme Court emphasized that Oklahoma law had no express

---

36. See International Brotherhood of Teamsters General Fund v. Fleming Cos., 1997 U.S. Dist. LEXIS 2980 (W.D. Okla.).

statutory provision authorizing the board to adopt a poison pill. Many other states do. See, e.g., N.J. Bus. Corp. Act §14A:7-7 (2007); N.Y. Bus. Corp. Law §505(2)(i) (2007). Hence, the applicability of the *Fleming* decision to other jurisdictions remains very much in doubt, but pension funds and takeover bidders have begun to press similar shareholder proposals to amend the bylaws to remove or mitigate takeover defensive tactics. For rival views on the permissibility of shareholder-passed bylaws constraining takeover defensive tactics, see John C. Coffee Jr., The Bylaw Battlefield: Can Institutions Change the Outcome of Corporate Control Contests? 51 U. Miami L. Rev. 605 (1997) (arguing for the legitimacy of *some* shareholder-passed bylaws); Lawrence Hamermesh, Corporate Democracy and Stockholder-Adopted By-laws: Taking Back the Street?, 73 Tul. L. Rev. 409 (1998) (arguing that board power cannot be constrained, at least in Delaware).

When in 2003 the SEC proposed and then backed off on a plan whereby shareholders could nominate a minority slate of one to three directors that would be included in the corporation's own proxy statement, shareholder activists quickly moved to fill this gap by proposing bylaw amendments by means of Rule 14a-8 that would implement a similar system. The dispute quickly moved to federal court:

American Federation of State, County & Municipal Employees, Employees Pension Plan v. American International Group, Inc.
462 F.3d 121 (2nd Cir. 2006)

WESLEY, CIRCUIT JUDGE: This case raises the question of whether a shareholder proposal requiring a company to include certain shareholder-nominated candidates for the board of directors on the corporate ballot can be excluded from the corporate proxy materials on the basis that the proposal "relates to an election" under Securities Exchange Act Rule 14a-8(i)(8), 17 C.F.R. §240.14a-8 ("election exclusion" or "Rule 14a-8(i)(8)"). Complicating this question is not only the ambiguity of Rule 14a-8(i)(8) itself but also the fact that the Securities Exchange Commission (the "SEC" or "Commission") has ascribed two different interpretations to the Rule's language. The SEC's first interpretation was published in 1976, the same year that it last revised the election exclusion. The Division of Corporation Finance (the "Division"), the group within the SEC that handles investor disclosure matters and issues no-action letters,[1] continued to apply this interpretation consistently for fifteen years until 1990, when it began applying a different interpretation, although at first in an ad hoc and inconsistent manner. The result of this gradual interpretive shift is the SEC's second interpretation, as set forth in its

---

1. Elaborating upon the nature of the no-action process, the Court has stated:

> The no-action process works as follows: Whenever a corporation decides to exclude a shareholder proposal from its proxy materials, it "shall file" a letter with the Division explaining the legal basis for its decision. *See Rule 14a-8(d)(3)*. If the Division staff agrees that the proposal is excludable, it may issue a no-action letter, stating that, based on the facts presented by the corporation, the staff will not recommend that the SEC sue the corporation for violating *Rule 14a-8*. . . . The no-action letter, however, is an informal response, and does not amount to an official statement of the SEC's views. . . . No-action letters are deemed interpretive because they do not impose or fix legal relationship upon any of the parties.

N.Y. City Employees' Ret. Sys. v. SEC, 45 F.3d 7, 12 (2d Cir. 1995).

amicus brief to this Court. We believe that an agency's interpretation of an ambiguous regulation made at the time the regulation was implemented or revised should control unless that agency has offered sufficient reasons for its changed interpretation. Accordingly, we hold that a shareholder proposal that seeks to amend the corporate bylaws to establish a procedure by which shareholder-nominated candidates may be included on the corporate ballot does not relate to an election within the meaning of the Rule and therefore cannot be excluded from corporate proxy materials under that regulation.

Background

The American Federation of State, County & Municipal Employees ("AFSCME") is one of the country's largest public service employee unions. Through its pension plan, AFSCME holds 26,965 shares of voting common stock of American International Group ("AIG" or "Company"), a multi-national corporation operating in the insurance and financial services sectors. On December 1, 2004, AFSCME submitted to AIG for inclusion in the Company's 2005 proxy statement a shareholder proposal that, if adopted by a majority of AIG shareholders at the Company's 2005 annual meeting,[2] would amend the AIG bylaws to require the Company, under certain circumstances, to publish the names of shareholder-nominated candidates for director positions together with any candidates nominated by AIG's board of directors ("Proposal").[3] AIG sought the input of the Division regarding whether AIG could exclude the Proposal from its proxy statement under the election exclusion on the basis that it "relates to an election." The Division issued a no-action letter in which it

---

2. Delaware corporate law, which governs AIG's internal affairs, provides that shareholders have the power to amend bylaws by majority vote. *See DEL. CODE ANN. tit. 8, §109(a).*

3. The AFSCME Proposal states in relevant part:

> RESOLVED, pursuant to Section 6.9 of the By-laws (the "Bylaws") of American International Group Inc. ("AIG") and section 109(a) of the Delaware General Corporation Law, stockholders hereby amend the Bylaws to add section 6.10:
>
> > The Corporation shall include in its proxy materials for a meeting of stockholders the name, together with the Disclosure and Statement (both defined below), of any person nominated for election to the Board of Directors by a stockholder or group thereof that satisfies the requirements of this section 6.10 (the "Nominator"), and allow stockholders to vote with respect to such nominee on the Corporation's proxy card. Each Nominator may nominate one candidate for election at a meeting.
> >
> > To be eligible to make a nomination, a Nominator must:
> >
> > (a) have beneficially owned 3 or more of the Corporation's outstanding common stock (the "Required Shares") for at least one year;
> > (b) provide written notice received by the Corporation's Secretary within the time period specified in section 1.11 of the Bylaws containing (i) with respect to the nominee, (A) the information required by Items 7(a), (b) and (c) of SEC Schedule 14A (such information is referred to herein as the "Disclosure") and (B) such nominee's consent to being named in the proxy statement and to serving as a director if elected; and (ii) with respect to the Nominator, proof of ownership of the Required Shares; and
> > (c) execute an undertaking that it agrees (i) to assume all liability of any violation of law or regulation arising out of the Nominator's communications with stockholders, including the Disclosure (ii) to the extent it uses soliciting material other than the Corporation's proxy materials, comply with all laws and regulations relating thereto.
>
> The Nominator shall have the option to furnish a statement, not to exceed 500 words, in support of the nominee's candidacy (the "Statement"), at the time the Disclosure is submitted to the Corporation's Secretary. The Board of Directors shall adopt a procedure for timely resolving disputes over whether notice of a nomination was timely given and whether the Disclosure and Statement comply with this section 6.10 and SEC Rules."

indicated that it would not recommend an enforcement action against AIG should the Company exclude the Proposal from its proxy statement. American International Group, Inc., SEC No-Action Letter, 2005 SEC No-Act. LEXIS 235, 2005 WL 372266 (Feb. 14, 2005) ("AIG No-Action Letter"). Armed with the no-action letter, AIG then proceeded to exclude the Proposal from the Company's proxy statement. In response, AFSCME brought suit in the United States District Court for the Southern District of New York (Stanton, J.) seeking a court order compelling AIG to include the Proposal in its next proxy statement. The district court denied AFSCME's motion for a preliminary injunction, concluding that AFSCME's Proposal "on its face 'relates to an election.' Indeed, it relates to nothing else." AFSCME v. Am. Int'l Group, Inc., 361 F. Supp. 2d 344, 346 (S.D.N.Y. 2005). After this Court denied AFSCME's motion for expedited appeal, the parties stipulated that the district court's opinion denying AFSCME's motion for a preliminary injunction "be deemed to contain the Court's complete findings of fact and conclusions of law with respect to all claims asserted by plaintiff in this action" and that it also "be deemed a final judgment on the merits with respect to all claims asserted by plaintiff in this action." Pursuant to this joint stipulation, the district court entered final judgment denying plaintiff's claims for declaratory and injunctive relief and dismissing plaintiff's complaint.

Discussion

Rule 14a-8(i)(8), also known as "the town meeting rule," regulates what are referred to as "shareholders proposals," that is, "recommendation[s] or requirement[s] that the company and/or its board of directors take [some] action, which [the submitting shareholder(s)] intend to present at a meeting of the company's shareholders," 17 C.F.R. §240.14a-8(a). If a shareholder seeking to submit a proposal meets certain eligibility and procedural requirements, the corporation is required to include the proposal in its proxy statement and identify the proposal in its form of proxy, unless the corporation can prove to the SEC that a given proposal may be excluded based on one of thirteen grounds enumerated in the regulations. Id. §240.14a-8(i)(1)-(13). One of these grounds, Rule 14a-8(i)(8), provides that a corporation may exclude a shareholder proposal "[i]f the proposal relates to an election for membership on the company's board of directors or analogous governing body." Id. §240.14a-8(i)(8).

We must determine whether, under Rule 14a-8(i)(8), a shareholder proposal "relates to an election" if it seeks to amend the corporate bylaws to establish a procedure by which certain shareholders are entitled to include in the corporate proxy materials their nominees for the board of directors ("proxy access bylaw proposal"). "In interpreting an administrative regulation, as in interpreting a statute, we must begin by examining the language of the provision at issue." Resnik v. Swartz, 303 F.3d 147, 151-52 (2d Cir. 2002) (citing New York Currency Research Corp. v. CFTC, 180 F.3d 83, 92 (2d Cir. 1999)). The relevant language here — "relates to an election" — is not particularly helpful. AFSCME reads the election exclusion as creating an obvious distinction between proposals addressing a particular seat in a particular election (which AFSCME concedes are excludable) and those, like AFSCME's proposal, that simply set the background rules governing elections generally (which AFSCME claims are not excludable). AFSCME's distinction rests on Rule 14a-8(i)(8)'s use of the article "an," which

AFSCME claims "necessarily implies that the phrase 'relates to an election' is intended to relate to proposals that address *particular elections*, instead of simply 'elections' generally." It is at least plausible that the words "an election" were intended to narrow the scope of the election exclusion, confining its application to proposals relating to "a particular election *and not* elections generally." It is, however, also plausible that the phrase was intended to create a comparatively broader exclusion, one covering "a particular election *or* elections generally" since any proposal that relates to elections in general will necessarily relate to an election in particular. The language of Rule 14a-8(i)(8) provides no reason to adopt one interpretation over the other.

When the language of a regulation is ambiguous, we typically look for guidance in any interpretation made by the agency that promulgated the regulation in question. See Auer v. Robbins, 519 U.S. 452 (1997) (holding that an agency's interpretation of its own regulation is entitled to deference provided that the regulation is ambiguous); see also Christensen v. Harris County, 529 U.S. 576, 588 (2000). We are aware of two statements published by the SEC that offer informal interpretations of Rule 14a-8(i)(8). The first is a statement appearing in the amicus brief that the SEC filed in this case at our request. The second interpretation is contained in a statement the SEC published in 1976, the last time the SEC revised the election exclusion. Neither of these interpretations has the force of law. But, while agency interpretations that lack the force of law do not warrant deference when they interpret ambiguous *statutes*, they do normally warrant deference when they interpret ambiguous *regulations*. See *Christensen*, 529 U.S. at 588 (citing *Auer*, 519 U.S. at 461). . . .

In its amicus brief, the SEC interprets Rule 14a-8(i)(8) as permitting the exclusion of shareholder proposals that "would result in contested elections." The SEC explains that "[f]or purposes of Rule 14a-8, a proposal would result in a contested election if it is a means either to campaign for or against a director nominee or to require a company to include shareholder-nominated candidates in the company's proxy materials." Under this interpretation, a proxy access bylaw proposal like AFSCME's would be excludable under Rule 14a-8(i)(8) because it "is a means to require AIG to include shareholder-nominated candidates in the company's proxy materials." However, that interpretation is plainly at odds with the interpretation the SEC made in 1976.

In that year, the SEC amended Rule 14a-8(i)(8) in an effort to clarify the purpose of the existing election exclusion. The SEC explained that "with respect to corporate elections, [] Rule 14a-8 is not the proper means for conducting campaigns or effecting reforms in elections of that nature [i.e., 'corporate, political or other elections to office'], *since other proxy rules, including Rule 14a-11, are applicable thereto.*" Proposed Amendments to Rule 14a-8, Exchange Act Release No. 34-12598, 41 Fed. Reg. 29,982, 29,9845 (proposed July 7, 1976) (emphasis added) ("1976 Statement"). The district court opinion quoted the 1976 Statement but omitted the italicized language and concluded that shareholder proposals were not intended to be used to accomplish any type of election reform. *AFSCME*, 361 F. Supp. 2d at 346-47. Clearly, however, that cannot be what the 1976 Statement means. Indeed, when the SEC finally adopted the revision of Rule 14a-8(i)(8) four months after publication of the 1976 Statement, it explained that it was rejecting a previous proposed rule (which would have authorized the exclusion of proposals that "relate[] to a corporate, political or other election to office") in favor of the current version (which authorizes the exclusion of proposals that simply "relate[] to an election") so as to avoid creating "the erroneous belief that the Commission intended to expand the scope of the existing exclusion to cover proposals dealing with matters previously held not excludable by the Commission, such as cumulative voting rights, general qualifications for directors, and political contributions by the issuer." Adoption of Amendments Relating to Proposals by Security Holders, Exchange Act Release No. 34-129999, 41 Fed. Reg. 52,994, 52,998 (Nov. 22, 1976) ("1976 Adoption"). And yet, all three of these shareholder proposal topics — cumulative voting rights, general qualifications for directors, and political contributions — fit comfortably within the category "election reform."

In its amicus brief, the SEC places a slightly different gloss on the 1976 Statement than did the district court. The SEC reads the 1976 Statement as implying that the purpose of Rule 14a-8(i)(8) is to authorize the exclusion of proposals that seek to effect, not election reform in general, but only certain types of election reform, namely those to which "other proxy rules, including Rule 14a-11," are generally applicable. In 1976, Rule 14a-11 was essentially the equivalent of current Rule 14a-12, which requires certain disclosures where a solicitation is made "for the purpose of opposing" a solicitation by any other person "with respect to the election or removal of directors." 17 C.F.R. §240.14a-12(c). The SEC reasons that, based on the 1976 Statement, "a proposal may be excluded pursuant to Rule 14a-8(i)(8) if it would result in an immediate election contest (e.g., by making a director nomination for a particular meeting) or would set up a process for shareholders to conduct an election contest in the future by requiring the company to include shareholder director nominees in the company's proxy materials for subsequent meetings."

We agree with the SEC that, based on the 1976 Statement, shareholder proposals can be excluded under the election exclusion if they would result in an immediate election contest. We understand the phrase "since other proxy rules, including Rule 14a-11, are applicable thereto" in the 1976 Statement to mean that under Rule 14a-8(i)(8), companies can exclude shareholder proposals dealing with those election-related matters that, if addressed in a proxy solicitation — the alternative to a shareholder proposal — would trigger Rule 14a-12, or the former Rule 14a-11. A proxy solicitation nominating a candidate for a specific election would be made "for the purpose of opposing" the company's proxy solicitation and therefore would clearly trigger Rule 14a-12. Accordingly, based on the 1976 Statement, a shareholder proposal seeking to contest management's nominees would be excludable under Rule 14a-8(i)(8).

By contrast, a proxy solicitation seeking to add a proxy access amendment to the corporate bylaws does not involve opposing solicitations dealing with "the election or removal of directors," and therefore Rule 14a-12, or, equivalently, the former Rule 14a-11, would not apply to a proposal seeking to accomplish the same end. Thus, we cannot agree with the second half of the SEC's interpretation of the 1976 Statement: that a proposal may be excluded under Rule 14a-8(i)(8) if it would simply establish a process for shareholders to wage a future election contest.

The 1976 Statement clearly reflects the view that the election exclusion is limited to shareholder proposals used to oppose solicitations dealing with an identified board seat in an upcoming election and rejects the somewhat broader interpretation that the election exclusion applies to shareholder proposals that would institute procedures making such election contests more likely.[6] The SEC suggested as much when, four months after its 1976 Statement, it explained that the scope of the election exclusion does not cover shareholder proposals dealing with matters such as cumulative voting and general director requirements, both of which have the potential to increase the likelihood of election contests. See 1976 Adoption, 41 Fed. Reg. at 52,998.

That the 1976 statement adopted this narrower view of the election exclusion finds further support in the fact that it was also the view that the Division adopted for roughly sixteen years following publication of the SEC's 1976 Statement [citing SEC no-action letters]. It was not until 1990 that the Division first signaled a change of course by deeming excludable proposals that *might* result in contested elections, even if the proposal only purports to alter general procedures for nominating and electing directors. . . .[7]

Because the interpretation of Rule 14a-8(i)(8) that the SEC advances in its amicus brief — that the election exclusion applies to proxy access bylaw proposals — conflicts with the 1976 Statement, it does not merit the usual deference we would reserve for an agency's interpretation of its own regulations. . . . The SEC has not provided, nor to our knowledge has it or the Division ever provided, reasons for its changed position regarding the excludability of proxy access bylaw proposals. Although the SEC has substantial discretion to adopt new interpretations of its own regulations in light of, for example, changes in the capital markets or even simply because of a shift in the Commission's regulatory approach, it nevertheless has a "duty to explain its departure from prior norms." Atchison, T. & S. F. Ry. Co v. Wichita Bd. of Trade, 412 U.S. 800, 808. . . .

In its amicus submission, the SEC fails to so much as acknowledge a changed position, let alone offer a reasoned analysis of the change. The amicus brief is curiously silent on any Division action prior to 1990 and characterizes the intermittent post-1990 no-action letters which continued to apply the pre-1990 position as mere "mistake[s]." While we by no means wish to imply that the Commission or the Division cannot correct analytical errors following a refinement of their thinking, we have a difficult time accepting the SEC's characterization of a policy that the Division consistently applied for sixteen years as nothing more than a "mistake." Although we are willing to afford the Commission considerable latitude in explaining departures from prior interpretations, its reasoned analysis must consist of something more than *mea culpas*.

Accordingly, we deem it appropriate to defer to the 1976 Statement, which represents the SEC's interpretation of the election exclusion the last time the Rule was substantively revised. *Cf. Watt*, 451 U.S. at 272-73 (deferring to an

---

6. We are, of course, aware that the 1976 Statement refers not solely to Rule 14a-11 but to "other proxy rules, including Rule 14a-11." Surely, however, the reference to "other proxy rules" cannot mean that the election exclusion applies to shareholder proposals dealing with matters that, if addressed in proxy solicitations, would implicate *any* other proxy rule because such an interpretation would extend the election exclusion's coverage to all types of election reform, and, as already mentioned, the SEC has clearly stated that Rule 14a-8(i)(8) does not reach all types of election reform. Rather, we find that the qualifying phrase "including Rule 14a-11" suggests that "other proxy rules" means "other proxy rules dealing with election contests."

7. Even then, the Division's position was far from clear-cut. Between 1990 and 1998, the Division continued to issue intermittently no-action letters adopting its prior distinction between procedures governing elections generally and those dealing with specific election contests. . . . Since roughly 1998, the Division has consistently adopted the position expressed in the AIG No-Action Letter, which is the same position the SEC advances in its amicus brief. . . .

agency's initial interpretation of a statutory provision where the interpretation was made contemporaneously with the provision's original enactment and consequently rejecting the agency's later conflicting interpretation).[8] We therefore interpret the election exclusion as applying to shareholder proposals that relate to a particular election and not to proposals that, like AFSCME's, would establish the procedural rules governing elections generally.

In deeming proxy access bylaw proposals non-excludable under Rule 14a-8(i)(8), we take no side in the policy debate regarding shareholder access to the corporate ballot. There might be perfectly good reasons for permitting companies to exclude proposals like AFSCME's, just as there may well be valid policy reasons for rendering them non-excludable. However, Congress has determined that such issues are appropriately the province of the SEC, not the judiciary.

Conclusion

For the foregoing reasons, we reverse the judgment of the district court and remand the case for entry of judgment in favor of AFSCME.

---

1. *The SEC's response.* The AFSCME v. AIG decision did not preclude the SEC from amending Rule 14a-8, but effectively it forced the SEC to act. In 2007 the SEC responded — but in an unprecedented fashion. On July 27, 2007, it issued two alternative proposals. One (Sec. Exch. Act Rel. No. 34-56160) proposed an amendment to Rule 14a-8 that would permit shareholders to amend the bylaws to establish procedures for nominating directors by means of the corporation's proxy statement (in effect, the position taken by the Second Circuit panel in *AFSCME*). The other (Sec. Exch. Act Rel. No. 34-56161) proposed an amendment to Rule 14a-8 that would clearly bar such bylaw amendments and would reaffirm, in its words, the Commission's traditional position. Specifically, this proposal would revise the exclusion in Rule 14a8(i)(8) to read: "If the proposal relates to a nomination or an election for membership on the corporation's board of directors or analogous governing body or a procedure for such nomination or election." After much controversy and after attempts at compromise failed, the Commission in December 2007 voted 3-1 along party lines to adopt the narrower rule that effectively precluded shareholder

8. AIG suggests that the interpretation of the election exclusion that we adopt here — that it does not apply to proxy access proposals — "improperly conflicts" with a proposed SEC rule that would require corporations in particular circumstances to include certain shareholder-nominated director candidates in the corporate proxy statement. See Security Holder Director Nominations, SEC Exchange Act Release No. 34-48626, 68 Fed. Reg. 60,784, 60,787 (Oct. 14, 2003) ("Proposed Rule 14a-11"). Proposed Rule 14a-11 would entitle a holder of at least 5 of the corporation's voting stock to place a nominee on the corporate ballot but only if the proxy access rule had been "activated" by one of two triggering events, including the adoption, by majority vote, of a shareholder proposal submitted by a holder of more than 1 of the corporation's voting stock. Essentially, Proposed Rule 14a-11 establishes a process by which the shareholder proposal mechanism (subject to the heightened eligibility requirement that the proposal be submitted by a holder of more than 1 of the corporation's voting stock) may be employed to adopt a proxy access rule that is uniform across companies. We recognize that our holding facilitates a process, by means of shareholder proposals subject to the standard eligibility requirements, for adopting non-uniform proxy access rules that are less restrictive than that created by Proposed Rule 14a-11. Thus, there might very well be no reason for a rule based on Proposed Rule 14a-11 to co-exist with the procedure that our holding makes available to shareholders. Accordingly, if the Commission ultimately decides to adopt Proposed Rule 14a-11, then such an action, although certainly not necessary, would likely be sufficient to modify the interpretation of Rule 14a-8(i)(8) that we have adopted here.

adopted bylaws authorizing access to the proxy statement, thereby overturning the result in AFSCME v. AIG. See Sec. Exch. Act Rel. No. 34-56914 (Dec. 6, 2007).

2. *Electronic shareholder forums.* Also included in Sec. Exch. Act Rel. No. 34-56160 (July 27, 2007) was a proposal to encourage online shareholder forums at which shareholders could "discuss among themselves the subjects that most concern them." This proposal further suggested that shareholder anonymity in such forums could be "protected through encrypted unique identifiers" and that "shareholder expressions of interest on particular suggested actions, tabulated based on their ownership interest, could be determined on a real-time basis." In effect, a Gallup Poll of shareholders could be taken on issues of corporate social responsibility on an anonymous and nonbinding basis. To facilitate such a forum, the Commission proposed a new Rule 14a-18 that would recognize the shareholder electronic forum, provide a safe harbor from the proxy rules for statements made on it, and protect the company from liability for false statements made by others on such a forum. The SEC's expressed intent is to protect the corporation sponsoring such an electronic forum "in a similar way as the federal communications laws protect an interactive computer service."

Support for the electronic forum proposal came from very different sources at a series of roundtables sponsored by the SEC in 2007. Some viewed the shareholder electronic forum as simply an outgrowth of the Internet and an opportunity for fuller discussion than is ever possible at a necessarily abbreviated shareholders' meeting. Others viewed the forum proposal with more alarm, as a means by which companies could move nonbinding shareholder proposals away from the shareholders' meeting to a different forum — where arguably shareholder activists would have less leverage. In their view, much of the power of nonbinding shareholder proposals is that they can embarrass management (and particularly the CEO) if management wishes to oppose the proposal at the shareholders' meeting. Thus, management may prefer to negotiate a resolution with the shareholder proponent that takes the issue off the table (with the shareholder proponent then withdrawing then proxy proposal), rather than publicly oppose a high-visibility proposal involving issues such as the environment or affirmative action. By shifting this debate to a different forum, where management is not required to take a position, managers sidestep controversy, but shareholder proponents may lose some leverage and their ability to exploit the embarrassment costs to management of public opposition.

3. *Nominating petitions?* Also in Sec. Exch. Act Rel. No. 34-56160, the Commission requested comment on whether proponents of a nonbinding proposal should "be required to have continuously held a certain percentage of the company's securities entitled to vote on the proposal at the meeting." In particular, the SEC raised the prospect that the company (or other shareholders) might be permitted to adopt bylaws that specified a minimum percentage of stock ownership before a nonbinding proposal could be placed on the corporation's proxy statement pursuant to Rule 14a-8. If Rule 14a-8 were amended in this fashion by shareholder action, shareholder activists might then be compelled to rely on the electronic shareholders' forum as the only means available to them to discuss those issues for which they could not amass the minimum percentage so specified. Today, Rule 14a-8 requires only that the proponents of a shareholder proposal own $2,000 in market value of the company's stock. But if bylaw amendments are to be more broadly authorized, they inherently have a two-sided application and might also

be used to limit the debate or to shift the debate over some controversies away from the shareholders' meeting.

4. *Future tactics.* Even if the SEC were to adopt a revised Rule 14a-8 that broadly authorized bylaw amendments allowing shareholders to make director nominations by means of the proxy statement, corporate managers and the board might respond in a variety of predictable ways that would raise additional issues. For example, the board might first amend the bylaws to prohibit such direct nominations and might further require a high supermajority for a shareholder vote to repeal this provision. Would this be valid? Or should any amended SEC Rule 14a-8 that authorized such bylaw amendments be seen as intended to preclude such a defensive tactic? Alternatively, the board might seek to set qualifications for director nominations. See Stroud v. Grace, supra at page 612.

On the other hand, even if the SEC does not amend Rule 14a-8 to permit shareholder proposals to amend the nomination process, shareholders could still seek to amend the bylaws in a similar fashion by conducting their own proxy solicitation. This would be costly, but, assuming that full disclosure is made, this tactic would involve no substantive issue under the federal proxy rules (and presumably would comply with Delaware law because Del. Gen. Corp. Law §109 gives shareholders a broad right to amend the corporation's bylaws).

7. ANTIFRAUD LIABILITY

Rule 14a-9. False or Misleading Statements

(a) No solicitation subject to this regulation shall be made by means of any proxy statement, form of proxy, notice of meeting or other communication, written or oral, containing any statement which, at the time and in the light of the circumstances under which it is made, is false or misleading with respect to any material fact, or which omits to state any material fact necessary in order to make the statements therein not false or misleading or necessary to correct any statement in any earlier communication with respect to the solicitation of a proxy for the same meeting or subject matter which has become false or misleading.

(b) The fact that a proxy statement, form of proxy or other soliciting material has been filed with or examined by the Commission shall not be deemed a finding by the Commission that such material is accurate or complete or not false or misleading, or that the Commission has passed upon the merits of or approved any statement contained therein or any matter to be acted upon by security holders. No representation contrary to the foregoing shall be made.

NOTE: The following are some examples of what, depending upon particular facts and circumstances, may be misleading within the meaning of this section.

(a) Predictions as to specific future market values.

(b) Material which directly or indirectly impugns character, integrity or personal reputation, or directly or indirectly makes charges concerning improper, illegal or immoral conduct or associations, without factual foundation.

(c) Failure to so identify a proxy statement, form of proxy and other soliciting material as to clearly distinguish it from the soliciting material of any other person or persons soliciting for the same meeting or subject matter.

(d) Claims made prior to a meeting regarding the results of a solicitation.

Elements of a cause of action under Rule 14a-9. In principle, a plaintiff must prove the same general elements under Rule 14a-9 as under Rule 10b-5: standing, materiality, causation, culpability, and damages. Important differences exist, however, as to the showing that must be made to satisfy these elements under Rule 14a-9. Each of these elements is reviewed below.

In particular, the Supreme Court has yet to resolve whether a plaintiff must prove scienter, or only some form of negligence, to state a cause of action under Rule 14a-9.

(a) *Standing.* A private cause of action for violation of the proxy rules was recognized in the landmark case of J. I. Case Co. v. Borak, 377 U.S. 426 (1964). The Court found that individual shareholders could sue directly and the corporation could sue, both directly and derivatively, adding that "it is the duty of the courts to be alert to provide such remedies as are necessary to make effective the congressional purpose." Subsequent decisions have relaxed other standing requirements, holding that the shareholder need not have actually read or relied on the proxy statement. Cowin v. Bresler, 741 F.2d 410, 423 (D.C. Cir. 1984). Still, one standing requirement does remain: plaintiff must have been a shareholder who was the subject of the proxy solicitation (i.e., entitled to vote as either a record holder or beneficial holder). This requirement follows from §14a's basic purpose—namely, to protect voting rights. Thus, investors who buy shares in a corporation after reading a copy of its proxy statement would presumably lack standing to sue under Rule 14a-9 if they were not already stockholders (but probably could sue under Rule 10b-5, which covers any statement made by the corporation that will foreseeably affect the market price).

May a shareholder who recognized the misrepresentation and actually voted against the proxy proposal still sue? Can this shareholder seek to represent others who were misled? "Although the defendants claim that discovery is necessary to determine whether the plaintiffs voted for or against the merger or did not vote at all, that type of discovery would not be useful for a determination of this motion [on the propriety of a class action]. It does not matter how the particular plaintiffs voted. What matters is that deception practiced on other GTC shareholders to induce them to vote for the merger would be sufficient to create liability." Basch v. Talley Industries, Inc., 53 F.R.D. 14 (S.D.N.Y. 1971). Why? In Civen v. Countrywide Realty, Inc., Fed. Sec. L. Rep. (CCH) ¶95,073 (S.D.N.Y. 1975), the court went even further and ruled that "all shareholders may be represented by one shareholder irrespective of whether or how he voted."

(b) *Materiality.* Although Virginia Bankshares, Inc. v. Sandberg, 501 U.S. 1083 (1991) (page 697 infra), specified a single formula that courts must apply in assessing materiality under both Rule 14a-9 and Rule 10b-5, important differences exist between these two contexts. Rule 10b-5 seeks to protect investment decisions, Rule 14a-9 suffrage decisions. Information that may not be material to the former decision because it has no significant impact on share value may still be highly relevant to the question of a director's fitness to serve. But to what extent must directors or nominees disclose uncharged allegations of misconduct against them when they continue to maintain their innocence? In United States v. Matthews, 787 F.2d 38 (2d Cir. 1986), defendant was aware that he was the object of a grand jury investigation into bribery and tax evasion charges against him in his capacity as a corporate officer. On the advice of counsel, he did not disclose this investigation or the underlying allegations in the proxy statement when he was renominated as a director. For this failure, he was convicted of securities fraud (although he was acquitted of the original tax evasion and bribery charges). The Second Circuit reversed. After noting that Item 6 of Schedule 14A requires disclosure only of criminal convictions or pending criminal proceedings, it defined the central issue in the case as "whether §14(a) of the Exchange Act and the SEC rules enacted pursuant thereto required Matthews to state to all the world that he was guilty of the uncharged crime of conspiracy. This query, we are satisfied, must be answered in the negative."

Although *Matthews* was a criminal case, its rejection of liability for nondisclosure of uncharged criminal conduct is consistent with other recent cases that show increasing judicial skepticism concerning "qualitative" disclosures about management's integrity or character. In GAF Corp. v. Heyman, 724 F.2d 727 (2d Cir. 1983), the Second Circuit refused to reverse the results of an election in which an insurgent slate ousted the incumbent board. The defeated GAF board had sought to invalidate the election because the leader of the successful insurgents had failed to disclose a pending action against him by his sister. His sister accused him of a breach of a fiduciary duty in connection with his management of family assets. In substance, it appears that he had loaned substantial funds from a family trust to entities that he controlled. The incumbent GAF management claimed this conduct showed the insurgent's unfitness for directorial office. Nonetheless, the Second Circuit overruled the district court's decision for the incumbent management, stating:

> Vast numbers of allegations arguably implicate a prospective director's "integrity and fitness." The ruling below, if left intact, would lead to a situation where proxy contestants, in order to minimize the risk of having an election set aside, would have to include in their solicitation materials descriptions, explanations, and denials regarding allegations in derivative actions, class actions, matrimonial disputes, and a host of other legal matters, all unrelated to the business of the subject corporation.
>
> Furthermore, . . . both sides in a proxy contest would have every incentive and legal right to pursue massive discovery to unearth facts which, it can later be claimed, amount to a breach of fiduciary duty. . . . [T]he litigation ubiquitous in every proxy contest would thus become a forum for litigating, possibly relitigating, the issues in any pending or prior suit involving a director-nominee. . . .
>
> [I]t would be a perversion of the policies underlying §14a and Rule 14a-9(a) to frustrate the will of a clear majority of the GAF shareholders and require a new election under the circumstances present here. . . . This was a proxy contest fought on the issues of GAF's financial performance and future corporate policy. Presented with a clear choice, the shareholders voted decisively in favor of the insurgent slate. Given this resounding mandate, it is inconceivable that fuller disclosure of the dormant Connecticut action would have had "a significant propensity to affect the voting process."

Similar decisions have drawn a "sharp distinction . . . between allegations of director misconduct involving breach of trust or self-dealing — the nondisclosure of which is presumptively material — and allegations of simple breach of fiduciary duty/waste of corporate assets — the nondisclosure of which is never material for

§14(a) purposes." Gaines v. Haughton, 645 F.2d 761 (9th Cir. 1981) (rejecting attempt by plaintiffs to hold officers of Lockheed Corp. liable for bribes and questionable payments made to foreign governmental officials). In *Gaines*, the Ninth Circuit stated:

> Absent credible allegations of self-dealing by the directors or dishonesty or deceit which inures to the direct, personal benefit of the directors — a fact that demonstrates a betrayal of trust to the corporation and shareholders and the director's essential unfitness for corporate stewardship — we hold that director misconduct of the type traditionally regulated by state corporate law need not be disclosed in proxy solicitations for director elections. This type of mismanagement, unadorned by self-dealing, is simply not material or otherwise within the ambit of the federal securities laws.

Id. at 779. Does this statement go too far? Would information that directors were recklessly violating laws that carried substantial penalties not be as material to reasonable investors as other information about material contingencies?

Conversely, when there has been evidence of illegality that involved self-dealing, such as through kickbacks to directors, courts have generally found this information to have been material. See Weisberg v. Coastal States Gas Corp., 609 F.2d 650 (2d Cir. 1979); Maldonado v. Flynn, 597 F.2d 789 (2d Cir. 1979).

Courts have characterized the issue of materiality as a "mixed question of law and fact" and have generally been reluctant to grant summary judgment on this issue. "Only if the alleged misrepresentations or omissions are so clearly unimportant to an investment decision that reasonable minds cannot differ should the issue of materiality appropriately be resolved as a matter of law by summary judgment or a motion to dismiss." Berg v. First American Bankshares, Inc., 796 F.2d 489 (D.C. Cir. 1986).

(c) *Culpability: scienter or negligence?* On several occasions, the Court has left open the question of the standard of culpability required in an action under §14(a). Some decisions have found, however, that a showing of negligence will suffice. In Gould v. American-Hawaiian S.S. Co., 535 F.2d 761 (3rd Cir. 1976), an outside director was held liable for damages under §14(a) for distributing a false and misleading proxy statement. Although the director had seen a draft of the statement and knew it contained a false statement, he denied that he had seen the statement in final form. The district court based liability on negligence ("he would have known that the proxy statement in its final form was false if he had read it, which it was his duty to do as a member of the board of directors which was issuing the document to solicit the shareholders' proxies"). The Third Circuit affirmed:

> The defendant urged in the district court that section 10(b) of the Act, provides an analogy and that under that section the courts have held that scienter must be shown. That section and Rule 10b-5 of the Regulations, which implements it, make unlawful manipulative and deceptive devices or practices in connection with the purchase and sale of securities. It would seem clearly more appropriate to apply the standard of actual knowledge in determining liability for such fraudulent practices many of which might well appear innocent on their face.
>
> We agree with the district court that section 14(a) and Rule 14a-9(a) may be more closely analogized to section 11 of the Securities Act of 1933 . . . which deals with civil

liability for false registration statements. Each section (section 14(a) as implemented by Rule 14a-9(a) and section 11) proscribes a type of disclosure or lack of it, i.e., false or misleading statements or omissions of material facts, and each enumerates specific classes of individuals who bear liability for failure to meet the required standard of disclosure. Moreover, each involves single specific documents which are of primary importance in two fundamental areas of securities regulation, sales of securities and the exercise of the shareholders' voting power. Since section 11 of the Securities Act clearly establishes negligence as the test for determining liability, the parallel between the two sections would strongly support adoption of negligence as the standard under section 14(a).

All of the courts which have discussed the question, so far as the reported decisions indicate, have favored applying the rule of negligence as the criterion for determining liability under section 14(a). . . . The language of section 14(a) and Rule 14a-9(a) contains no suggestion of a scienter requirement, merely establishing a quality standard for proxy material. The importance of the proxy provisions to informed voting by shareholders has been stressed by the Supreme Court, which has emphasized the broad remedial purpose of the section, implying the need to impose a high standard of care on the individuals involved. And, unlike sections 10(b) and 18 of the Act, which encompass activity in numerous and diverse areas of securities markets and corporate management, section 14(a) is specially limited to materials used in soliciting proxies. Given all of these factors the imposition of a standard of due diligence as opposed to actual knowledge or gross negligence is quite appropriate. We are confirmed in this view by the very recent case of Ernst & Ernst v. Hochfelder, 425 U.S. 185, fn.28 (1976), in which the Supreme Court pointed out that the "operative language and purpose" of each particular section of the Acts of 1933 and 1934 are important considerations in determining the standard of liability for violations of the section in question.

Conversely, in Adams v. Standard Knitting Mills, Inc., 623 F.2d 422 (6th Cir. 1980), the Sixth Circuit concluded that

in view of the overall structure and collective legislative histories of the securities laws, as well as important policy considerations, we conclude that scienter should be an element of liability in private suits under the proxy provisions as they apply to outside accountants.

. . . Although we are not called on in this case to decide the standard of liability of the corporate issuer of proxy material, we are influenced by the fact that the accountant here, unlike the corporate issuer, does not directly benefit from the proxy vote and is not in privity with the stockholder. Unlike the corporate issuer, the preparation of financial statements to be appended to proxies and other reports is the daily fare of accountants, and the accountant's potential liability for relatively minor mistakes would be enormous under a negligence standard. In contrast to section 12(2) of the 1933 Act which imposes liability for negligent misrepresentation in a prospectus, Rule 14a-9 does not require privity. In contrast to section 11 of the 1933 Act which imposes liability for negligent misrepresentation in registration statements, Rule 14a-9 does not require proof of actual investor reliance on the misrepresentation. Rule 14a-9, like 10b-5, substitutes the less exacting standard of materiality for reliance, TSC Ind., Inc. v. Northway, Inc., 426 U.S. 438 (1976), and in the instant case there was no proof of investor reliance on the notes to the financial statements which erroneously described the restriction on payment of dividends. We can see no reason for a different standard of liability for accountants under the proxy provisions than under 10(b).

Although *Adams* adopted a scienter standard only in the case of outside professionals, its standard has not been widely followed and indeed has been rejected by the Third Circuit. See Herskowitz v. Nutri/System, Inc., 857 F.2d 179, 190 (3d Cir. 1988) (investment banker should be held under Rule 14a-9 to same negligence standard as the management that it was representing); see also In re McKesson HBOC, Inc. Sec. Litig., 126 F. Supp. 2d 1248 (N.D. Cal. 2000).

8. CAUSATION

Mills v. Electric Auto-Lite Co.
396 U.S. 375 (1970)

MR. JUSTICE HARLAN delivered the opinion of the Court.

This case requires us to consider a basic aspect of the implied private right of action for violation of §14(a) of the Securities Exchange Act of 1934, recognized by this Court in J. I. Case Co. v. Borak, 377 U.S. 426 (1964). As in *Borak* the asserted wrong is that a corporate merger was accomplished through the use of a proxy statement that was materially false or misleading. The question with which we deal is what causal relationship must be shown between such a statement and the merger to establish a cause of action based on the violation of the Act.

[Electric Auto-Lite Co. was merged into Mergenthaler Linotype Co., which already held a controlling 54 percent interest in it. Although Electric Auto-Lite's proxy statement pointed out that Mergenthaler owned a majority of its stock, the proxy statement also emphasized that Electric Auto-Lite's board of directors "has carefully considered and approved the terms of the merger and recommends that the shareholders vote to approve the plan of merger." The district court found that the failure to point out that all of the directors of Electric Auto-Lite were the "nominees" of Mergenthaler, and were under the latter's "control and domination" made this statement a material misrepresentation.]

. . . [The Court of Appeals] affirmed the District Court's conclusion that the proxy statement was materially deficient, but reversed on the question of causation. The court acknowledged that, if an injunction had been sought a sufficient time before the stockholders' meeting, "corrective measures would have been appropriate." 403 F.2d 429, 435 (1968). However, since this suit was brought too late for preventive action, the courts had to determine "whether the misleading statement and omission caused the submission of sufficient proxies," as a prerequisite to a determination of liability under the Act. If the respondents could show, "by a preponderance of probabilities, that the merger would have received a sufficient vote even if the proxy statement had not been misleading in the respect found," petitioners would be entitled to no relief of any kind. Id., at 436.

Claiming that the Court of Appeals has construed this Court's decision in *Borak* in a manner that frustrates the statute's policy of enforcement through private litigation, the petitioners then sought review in this Court. We granted certiorari, 394 U.S. 971 (1969), believing that resolution of this basic issue should be made at this stage of the litigation and not postponed until after a trial under the Court of Appeal's decision.

. . . The decision below, by permitting all liability to be foreclosed on the basis of a finding that the merger was fair, would allow the shareholders to be bypassed, at least where the only legal challenge to the merger is a suit for retrospective relief after the meeting has been held. A judicial appraisal of the merger's merits could be substituted for the actual and informed vote of the stockholders.

The result would be to insulate from private redress an entire category of proxy violations — those relating to matters other than the terms of the merger. Even outrageous misrepresentations in a proxy solicitation, if they did not relate to the terms of the transaction, would give rise to no cause of action under §14(a). Particularly if carried over to enforcement actions by the Securities and Exchange Commission itself, such a result would subvert the congressional purpose of ensuring full and fair disclosure to shareholders.

Further, recognition of the fairness of the merger as a complete defense would confront small shareholders with an additional obstacle to making a successful challenge to a proposal recommended through a defective proxy statement. The risk that they would be unable to rebut the corporation's evidence of the fairness of the proposal, and thus to establish their cause of action, would be bound to discourage such shareholders from the private enforcement of the proxy rules that "provides a necessary supplement to Commission action." J. I. Case Co. v. Borak, 377 U.S., at 423.[5]

Such a frustration of the congressional policy is not required by anything in the wording of the statute or in our opinion in the *Borak* case. . . . Use of a solicitation that is materially misleading is itself a violation of law, as the Court of Appeals recognized in stating that injunctive relief would be available to remedy such a defect if sought prior to the stockholders' meeting. . . .

Where the misstatement or omission in a proxy statement has been shown to be "material," as it was found to be here, that determination itself indubitably embodies a conclusion that the defect was of such a character that it might have been considered important by a reasonable shareholder who was in the process of deciding how to vote.[6] This requirement that the defect have a significant *propensity* to affect the voting process is found in the express terms of Rule 14a-9, and it

5. The Court of Appeals' ruling that "causation" may be negated by proof of the fairness of the merger also rests on a dubious behavioral assumption. There is no justification for presuming that the shareholders of every corporation are willing to accept any and every fair merger offer put before them; yet such a presumption is implicit in the opinion of the Court of Appeals. That court gave no indication of what evidence petitioners might adduce, once respondents had established that the merger proposal was equitable, in order to show that the shareholders would nevertheless have rejected it if the solicitation had not been misleading. Proof of actual reliance by thousands of individuals would, as the court acknowledged, not be feasible, see R. Jennings & H. Marsh, Securities Regulation, Cases and Materials 1001 (2d ed. 1968); and reliance on the *nondisclosure* of a fact is a particularly difficult matter to define or prove, see 3 L. Loss, Securities Regulation 1766 (2d ed. 1961). In practice, therefore, the objective fairness of the proposal would seemingly be determinative of liability. But, in view of the many other factors that might lead shareholders to prefer their current position to that of owners of a larger, combined enterprise, it is pure conjecture to assume that the fairness of the proposal will always be determinative of their vote, . . .

6. . . . In this case, where the misleading aspect of the solicitation involved failure to reveal a serious conflict of interest on the part of the directors, the Court of Appeals concluded that the crucial question in determining materiality was "whether the minority shareholders were sufficiently alerted to the board's relationship to their adversary to be on their guard." 403 F.2d, at 434. An adequate disclosure of this relationship would have warned the stockholders to give more careful scrutiny to the terms of the merger than they might to one recommended by an entirely disinterested board. Thus, the failure to make such a disclosure was found to be a material defect "as a matter of law," thwarting the informed decision at which the statute aims, regardless of whether the terms of the merger were such that a reasonable stockholder would have approved the transaction after more careful analysis. . . .

adequately serves the purpose of ensuring that a cause of action cannot be established by proof of a defect so trivial, or so unrelated to the transaction for which approval is sought, that correction of the defect or imposition of liability would not further the interests protected by §14(a).

There is no need to supplement this requirement, as did the Court of Appeals, with a requirement of proof of whether the defect actually had a decisive effect on the voting. Where there has been a finding of materiality, a shareholder has made a sufficient showing of causal relationship between the violation and the injury for which he seeks redress if, as here, he proves that the proxy solicitation itself, rather than the particular defect in the solicitation materials, was an essential link in the accomplishment of the transaction. This objective test will avoid the impracticalities of determining how many votes were affected, and, by resolving doubts in favor of those the statute is designed to protect, will effectuate the congressional policy of ensuring that the shareholders are able to make an informed choice when they are consulted on corporate transactions. . . . [7]

Our conclusion that petitioners have established their case by showing that proxies necessary to approval of the merger were obtained by means of a materially misleading solicitation implies nothing about the form of relief to which they may be entitled. We held in *Borak* that upon finding a violation the courts were "to be alert to provide such remedies as are necessary to make effective the congressional purpose," noting specifically that such remedies are not to be limited to prospective relief. 377 U.S., at 433, 434. In devising retrospective relief for violation of the proxy rules, the federal courts should consider the same factors that would govern the relief granted for any similar illegality or fraud. One important factor may be the fairness of the terms of the merger. Possible forms of relief will include setting aside the merger or granting other equitable relief, but, as the Court of Appeals below noted, nothing in the statutory policy "requires the court to unscramble a corporate transaction merely because a violation occurred." 403 F.2d, at 436. In selecting a remedy the lower courts should exercise "the sound discretion which guides the determinations of courts of equity," keeping in mind the role of equity as "the instrument for nice adjustment and reconciliation between the public interest and private needs as well as between competing private claims." . . .

For the foregoing reasons we conclude that the judgment of the Court of Appeals should be vacated and the case remanded to that court for further proceedings consistent with this opinion.

---

7. We need not decide in this case whether causation could be shown where the management controls a sufficient number of shares to approve the transaction without any votes from the minority. Even in that situation, if the management finds it necessary for legal or practical reasons to solicit proxies from minority shareholders, at least one court has held that the proxy solicitation might be sufficiently related to the merger to satisfy the causation requirement, see Laurenzano v. Einbender, 264 F. Supp. 356 (D.C.E.D.N.Y. 1966); cf. Swanson v. American Consumer Industries, Inc., 415 F.2d 1326, 1331-1332 (C.A. 7th Cir. 1969); Eagle v. Horvath, 241 F. Supp. 341, 344 (D.C.S.D.N.Y. 1965); Globus, Inc. v. Jaroff, 271 F. Supp. 378, 381 (D.C.S.D.N.Y. 1967); Comment, Shareholders' Derivative Suit to Enforce a Corporate Right of Action Against Directors Under SEC Rule 10b-5, 114 U. Pa. L. Rev. 578, 582 (1966). But see Hoover v. Allen, 241 F. Supp. 213, 231-232 (D.C.S.D.N.Y. 1965); Barnett v. Anaconda Co., 238 F. Supp. 766, 770-774 (D.C.S.D.N.Y. 1965); Robbins v. Banner Industries, Inc., 285 F. Supp. 758, 762-763 (D.C.S.D.N.Y. 1966). See generally 5 L. Loss, Securities Regulation 2933-2938 (Supp. 1969).

Virginia Bankshares, Inc. v. Sandberg
501 U.S. 1083 (1991)

JUSTICE SOUTER delivered the opinion of the Court. . . .

[The portions of this case dealing with materiality were reprinted earlier, in Chapter V.]

III. . . . The second issue before us, left open in Mills v. Electric Auto-Lite Co., 396 U.S. at 385, n.7, is whether causation of damages compensable through the implied private right of action under §14(a) can be demonstrated by a member of a class of minority shareholders whose votes are not required by law or corporate bylaw to authorize the transaction giving rise to the claim. J. I. Case Co. v. Borak, 377 U.S. 426 (1964), did not itself address the requisites of causation, as such, or define the class of plaintiffs eligible to sue under §14(a). But its general holding that a private cause of action was available to some shareholder class, acquired greater clarity with a more definite concept of causation in *Mills*, where we addressed the sufficiency of proof that misstatements in a proxy solicitation were responsible for damages claimed from the merger subject to complaint.

Although a majority stockholder in *Mills* controlled just over half the corporation's shares, a two-thirds vote was needed to approve the merger proposal. . . . The question arose whether the plaintiffs' burden to demonstrate causation of their damages traceable to the §14(a) violation required proof that the defect in the proxy solicitation had had "a decisive effect on the voting." Id., at 385. The *Mills* Court avoided the evidentiary morass that would have followed from requiring individualized proof that enough minority shareholders had relied upon the misstatements to swing the vote. Instead, it held that causation of damages by a material proxy misstatement could be established by showing that minority proxies necessary and sufficient to authorize the corporate acts had been given in accordance with the tenor of the solicitation, and the Court described such a causal relationship by calling the proxy solicitation an "essential link in the accomplishment of the transaction." Ibid. In the case before it, the Court found the solicitation essential, as contrasted with one addressed to a class of minority shareholders without votes required by law or by-law to authorize the action proposed, and left it for another day to decide whether such a minority shareholder could demonstrate causation. Id., at 385, n.7.

In this case, respondents address *Mills'* open question by proffering two theories that the proxy solicitation addressed to them was an "essential link" under the *Mills* causation test.[9] They argue, first, that a link existed and was essential simply because VBI and FABI would have been unwilling to proceed with the merger without the approval manifested by the minority shareholders' proxies, which would not have been obtained without the solicitation's express misstatements

---

9. Citing the decision in Schlick v. Penn-Dixie Cement Corp., 507 F.2d 374, 382-383 (CA2 1974), petitioners characterize respondents' proffered theories as examples of so-called "sue facts" and "shame facts" theories. . . . "A 'sue fact' is, in general, a fact which is material to a sue decision. A 'sue decision' is a decision by a shareholder whether or not to institute a representative or derivative suit alleging a state-law cause of action." Gelb, Rule 10b-5 and *Santa Fe* — Herein of Sue Facts, Shame Facts, and Other Matters, 87 W. Va. L. Rev. 189, 198, and n.52 (1985), quoting Borden, "Sue Fact" Rule Mandates Disclosure to Avoid Litigation in State Courts, 10 SEC 82, pp.201, 204-205 (1982). See also Note, Causation and Liability in Private Actions for Proxy Violations, 80 Yale L.J. 107, 116 (1970) (discussing theories of causation). "Shame facts" are said to be facts which, had they been disclosed, would have "shamed" management into abandoning a proposed transaction. See *Schlick*, supra, at 384. . . .

and misleading omissions. On this reasoning, the causal connection would depend on a desire to avoid bad shareholder or public relations, and the essential character of the causal link would stem not from the enforceable terms of the parties' corporate relationship, but from one party's apprehension of the ill will of the other.

In the alternative, respondents argue that the proxy statement was an essential link between the directors' proposal and the merger because it was the means to satisfy a state statutory requirement of minority shareholder approval, as a condition for saving the merger from voidability resulting from a conflict of interest on the part of one of the Bank's directors, Jack Beddow, who voted in favor of the merger while also serving as a director of FABI. Under the terms of Va. Code §13:1-691(A) (1989), minority approval after disclosure of the material facts about the transaction and the director's interest was one of three avenues to insulate the merger from later attack for conflict, the two others being ratification by the Bank's directors after like disclosure, and proof that the merger was fair to the corporation. On this theory, causation would depend on the use of the proxy statement for the purpose of obtaining votes sufficient to bar a minority shareholder from commencing proceedings to declare the merger void.

Although respondents have proffered each of these theories as establishing a chain of causal connection in which the proxy statement is claimed to have been an "essential link," neither theory presents the proxy solicitation as essential in the sense of *Mills'* causal sequence, in which the solicitation links a director's proposal with the votes legally required to authorize the action proposed. As a consequence, each theory would, if adopted, extend the scope of *Borak* actions beyond the ambit of *Mills,* and expand the class of plaintiffs entitled to bring *Borak* actions to include shareholders whose initial authorization of the transaction prompting the proxy solicitation is unnecessary. . . .

A. *Blue Chip Stamps* set an example worth recalling as a preface to specific policy analysis of the consequences of recognizing respondents' first theory, that a desire to avoid minority shareholders' ill will should suffice to justify recognizing the requisite causality of a proxy statement needed to garner that minority support. It will be recalled that in *Blue Chip Stamps* we raised concerns about the practical consequences of allowing recovery, under §10(b) of the Act and Rule 10b-5, on evidence of what a merely hypothetical buyer or seller might have done on a set of facts that never occurred, and foresaw that any such expanded liability would turn on "hazy" issues inviting self-serving testimony, strike suits, and protracted discovery, with little chance of reasonable resolution by pretrial process. Id., at 742-743. These were good reasons to deny recognition to such claims in the absence of any apparent contrary congressional intent.

The same threats of speculative claims and procedural intractability are inherent in respondents' theory of causation linked through the directors' desire for a cosmetic vote. Causation would turn on inferences about what the corporate directors would have thought and done without the minority shareholder approval unneeded to authorize action. A subsequently dissatisfied minority shareholder would have virtual license to allege that managerial timidity would have doomed corporate action but for the ostensible approval induced by a misleading statement, and opposing claims of hypothetical diffidence and hypothetical boldness on the part of directors would probably provide enough depositions in the usual case to preclude any judicial resolution short of the credibility judgments that can only come after trial. Reliable evidence would seldom exist. Directors would understand the prudence of making a few statements about plans to proceed even without minority endorsement, and discovery would be a quest for recollections of oral conversations at odds with the official pronouncements, in hopes of finding support for *ex post facto* guesses about how much heat the directors would have stood in the absence of minority approval. The issues would be hazy, their litigation protracted, and their resolution unreliable. Given a choice, we would reject any theory of causation that raised such prospects, and we reject this one.

B. The theory of causal necessity derived from the requirements of Virginia law dealing with postmerger ratification seeks to identify the essential character of the proxy solicitation from its function in obtaining the minority approval that would preclude a minority suit attacking the merger. Since the link is said to be a step in the process of barring a class of shareholders from resort to a state remedy otherwise available, this theory of causation rests upon the proposition of policy that §14(a) should provide a federal remedy whenever a false or misleading proxy statement results in the loss under state law of a shareholder plaintiff's state remedy for the enforcement of a state right. Respondents agree with the suggestions of counsel for the SEC and FDIC that causation be recognized, for example, when a minority shareholder has been induced by a misleading proxy statement to forfeit a state-law right to an appraisal remedy by voting to approve a transaction, *cf.* Swanson v. American Consumers Industries, Inc., 475 F.2d 516, 520-521 (CA7 1973), or when such a shareholder has been deterred from obtaining an order enjoining a damaging transaction by a proxy solicitation that misrepresents the facts on which an injunction could properly have been issued. . . . Respondents claim that in this case a predicate for recognizing just such a causal link exists in Va. Code §13.1-691(A)(2) (1989), which sets the conditions under which the merger may be insulated from suit by a minority shareholder seeking to void it on account of Beddow's conflict.

This case does not, however, require us to decide whether §14(a) provides a cause of action for lost state remedies, since there is no indication in the law or facts before us that the proxy solicitation resulted in any such loss. The contrary appears to be the case. Assuming the soundness of respondents' characterization of the proxy statement as materially misleading, the very terms of the Virginia statute indicate that a favorable minority vote induced by the solicitation would not suffice to render the merger invulnerable to later attack on the ground of the conflict. The statute bars a shareholder from seeking to avoid a transaction tainted by a director's conflict if, inter alia, the minority shareholders ratified the transaction following disclosure of the material facts of the transaction and the conflict. Va. Code §13.1-691(A)(2) (1989). Assuming that the material facts about the merger and Beddow's interests were not accurately disclosed, the minority votes were inadequate to ratify the merger under state law, and there was no loss of state remedy to connect the proxy solicitation with harm to minority shareholders irredressable under state law. Nor is there a claim here that the statement misled respondents into entertaining a false belief that they had no chance to upset the merger until the time for bringing suit had run out. . . .

Justice Stevens, with whom Justice Marshall joins, concurring in part and dissenting in part.

While I agree in substance with Parts I and II of the Court's opinion, I do not agree with the reasoning in Part III.

In Mills v. Electric Auto-Lite Co., 396 U.S. 375 (1970), the Court held that a finding that the terms of a merger were fair could not constitute a defense by the corporation to a shareholder action alleging that the merger had been accomplished by using a misleading proxy statement. The fairness of the transaction was, according to *Mills*, a matter to be considered at the remedy stage of the litigation. . . .

The case before us today involves a merger that has been found by a jury to be unfair, not fair. The interest in providing a remedy to the injured minority share-holders therefore is stronger, not weaker, than in *Mills*. The interest in avoiding speculative controversy about the actual importance of the proxy solicitation is the same as in *Mills*. Moreover, as in *Mills*, these matters can be taken into account at the remedy stage in appropriate cases. Accordingly, I do not believe that it con-stitutes an unwarranted extension of the rationale of *Mills* to conclude that because management found it necessary — whether for "legal or practical reasons" — to solicit proxies from minority shareholders to obtain their approval of the merger, that solicitation "was an essential link in the accomplishment of the transaction." Id., at 385, and n.7. In my opinion, shareholders may bring an action for damages under §14(a) of the Securities Exchange Act of 1934, whenever materially false or misleading statements are made in proxy statements. . . .

JUSTICE KENNEDY, with whom JUSTICE MARSHALL, JUSTICE BLACKMUN, and JUSTICE STEVENS join, concurring in part and dissenting in part.

I am in general agreement with Parts I and II of the majority opinion, but do not agree with the views expressed in Part III regarding the proof of causation required to establish a violation of §14(a). With respect, I dissent from Part III of the Court's opinion. . . .

The severe limits the Court places upon possible proof of nonvoting causation in a §14(a) private action are justified neither by our precedents nor any case in the courts of appeals. These limits are said to flow from a shift in our approach to implied causes of action that has occurred since we recognized the §14(a) implied private action in J. I. Case Co. v. Borak, 377 U.S. 426 (1964). . . .

Our decision in Mills v. Electric Auto-Lite Co. rested upon the impracticality of attempting to determine the extent of reliance by thousands of shareholders on alleged misrepresentations or omissions. A misstatement or an omission in a proxy statement does not violate §14(a) unless "there is a substantial likelihood that a reasonable shareholder would consider it important in deciding how to vote." TSC Industries, Inc. v. Northway, Inc., 426 U.S. 438, 449 (1976). . . .

If, for sake of argument, we accept a distinction between voting and nonvoting causation, we must determine whether the *Mills* essential link theory applies where a majority shareholder holds sufficient votes to force adoption of a pro-posal. The merit of the essential link formulation is that it rests upon the likelihood of causation and eliminates the difficulty of proof. Even where a minority lacks votes to defeat a proposal, both these factors weigh in favor of finding causation so long as the solicitation of proxies is an essential link in the transaction.

A. The Court argues that a nonvoting causation theory would "turn on 'hazy' issues inviting self-serving testimony, strike suits, and protracted discov-ery, with little chance of reasonable resolution by pretrial process" (citing *Blue Chip Stamps*, 421 U.S. at 742-743 (1975)). The Court's description does not fit this case and is not a sound objection in any event. Any causation inquiry under §14(a) requires a court to consider a hypothetical universe in which adequate disclosure is made. Indeed, the analysis is inevitable in almost any suit when we are invited to compare what was with what ought to have been. The causation inquiry is not intractable. On balance, I am convinced that the likelihood that causation exists supports elimination of any requirement that the plaintiff prove the material misstatement or omission caused the transaction to go forward when it otherwise would have been halted or voted down. This is the usual rule under *Mills,* and the difficulties of proving or disproving causation are, if anything, greater where the minority lacks sufficient votes to defeat the proposal. A presumption will assist courts in managing a circumstance in which direct proof is rendered difficult. See Basic, Inc. v. Levinson, 485 U.S. 224, 245 (1988) (discussing presumptions in securities law).

B. There is no authority whatsoever for limiting §14(a) to protecting those minority shareholders whose numerical strength could permit them to vote down a proposal. One of Section 14(a)'s "chief purposes is 'the protection of investors.' " J. I. Case Co. v. Borak, 377 U.S., at 432. Those who lack the strength to vote down a proposal have all the more need of disclosure. The voting process involves not only casting ballots but also the formulation and withdrawal of proposals, the minority's right to block a vote through court action or the threat of adverse consequences, or the negotiation of an increase in price. The proxy rules support this deliberative process. These practicalities can result in causation sufficient to support recovery. . . .

I conclude that causation is more than plausible; it is likely, even where the public shareholders cannot vote down management's proposal. Causation is established where the proxy statement is an essential link in completing the transaction, even if the minority lacks sufficient votes to defeat a proposal of management.

The majority avoids the question whether a plaintiff may prove causation by demonstrating that the misrepresentation or omission deprived her of a state law remedy. I do not think the question difficult, as the whole point of federal proxy rules is to support state law principles of corporate governance. . . . The majority asserts that respondents show no loss of a state law remedy, because if "the material facts about the merger and Beddow's interests were not accurately disclosed, then the minority votes were inadequate to ratify the merger under state law." This theory requires us to conclude that the Virginia statute governing director conflicts of interest . . . incorporates the same definition of materiality as the federal proxy rules. I find no support for that proposition. If the definitions are not the same, then Sandberg may have lost her state-law remedy. For all we know, disclosure to the minority shareholders that the price is $42 per share may satisfy Virginia's requirement. If that is the case, then approval by the minority without full disclosure may have deprived Sandberg of the ability to void the merger.

In all events, the theory that the merger would have been voidable absent minority shareholder approval is far more speculative than the theory that FABI and the Bank would have called off the transaction. . . .

Impact. Although *Virginia Bankshares* held that minority shareholders whose votes were unnecessary for approval of a freeze-out merger could not establish causation, it held out the possibility that plaintiffs could still establish causation by showing that an omission or misrepresentation had induced them to vote in favor of the merger and thereby caused them to forfeit an otherwise-available state law remedy. Some subsequent decisions have accepted this theory. See, e.g., Wilson v. Great American Industries, Inc., 979 F.2d 924, 931 (2d Cir. 1992). But if plaintiffs do not forfeit their rights to appraisal (at least as a result of any alleged omission or mis-representation), this theory of causation will not work. See Grace v. Rosenstock, 228 F.3d 40 (2d Cir. 2000).

Prior to *Virginia Bankshares*, corporate practitioners often recommended that a merger between a parent corporation and a majority-owned subsidiary be made conditional on an approval of a majority of the disinterested shareholders voting on it. Such approval was thought to reduce the danger that the transaction would fail the "entire fairness" test employed by the Delaware courts to review such a parent/subsidiary merger. See Weinberger v. UOP, Inc., 457 A.2d 701 (Del. 1983) (page 1091 infra). Under *Virginia Bankshares*, however, the voluntary use of a "majority of the minority" approval requirement may permit plaintiffs to solve their causation problem when they own fewer shares than were legally required to approve the transaction under state law. Should counsel for the parent corporation recommend such a procedure in a merger agreement? Or can other means be more easily used to satisfy the *Weinberger* "entire fairness" standard?

Several courts have read *Virginia Bankshares* to eliminate any requirement that the plaintiff-shareholder personally relied on the allegedly false proxy solicitation or that the plaintiff even gave a proxy. See Stahl v. Gibraltar Financial Corp., 967 F.2d 335 (9th Cir. 1992). These decisions focus on the fact that the plaintiff in *Virginia Bankshares* never granted a proxy. Should a plaintiff who is not personally deceived be denied standing to sue if other shareholders approve the transaction because they are deceived?

VII

BUSINESS ORGANIZATION FOR THE SMALLER ENTERPRISE: PARTNERSHIPS, CLOSE CORPORATIONS, LIMITED LIABILITY COMPANIES, AND OTHER NON-CORPORATE FORMS

A. INTRODUCTION

As set out in Chapter I, incorporation has many advantages: (1) limited liability of shareholders, (2) perpetual existence of the corporation, (3) easy transferability of ownership interests, and (4) centralized management. But these advantages come at an organizational cost: (1) rigidity in organizational structure through the statutory allocation of functional roles to officers, directors, and shareholders; (2) a requirement of formality in decision making, including holding meetings of directors, adopting resolutions, preparing minutes, and holding shareholder meetings at which directors are elected; and (3) two levels of tax — one on the corporation when the income is earned, and one on the shareholders when the income is distributed as a dividend — while, at the same time, losses of the corporation do not pass through to the shareholders to offset a shareholder's other income. The organizational cost of choosing the corporate form can be disproportionately high for the smaller business enterprise, and the tax cost can be disproportionately high for new businesses. Thus, it is not surprising that non-corporate forms of business associations vastly exceed the number of corporations in the United States, even though corporations represent a large percentage of the total sales and earnings.[1] It is also not surprising that courts and legislatures have been

---

1. In 2003 there were 2,375,000 active partnerships in the United States, with total annual receipts of $2,923 billion. Partnerships were especially common in the fields of retail trade, finance, real estate, and services industries. The same year, there were 1,971,000 non-farm sole proprietorships, with total annual receipts of $1,050 billion. More than half of the businesses in each category had revenues less

challenged to reduce the organizational and tax costs of the benefits of the corporate form, by relaxing judicial interpretations of the corporate statute's requirement of rigidity and formality, by adopting new statutory alternatives, and by relaxing the tax rules. This chapter focuses on alternatives to the traditional corporate form: (1) partnerships, (2) close corporations, (3) limited partnerships, and (4) limited liability companies and limited liability partnerships.

The first three alternatives comprise the set that have been available to business lawyers for some time, and whose trade-offs between liability protection, tax treatment, and formalities were both familiar and predictable. The fourth alternative, really a cluster of alternatives, is more recent in origin. The co-chair of the ABA Business Law Section's Ad Hoc Committee on Entity Rationalization explains the motive for and breadth of this explosion in alternative organizational forms:

> The past fifteen years have seen the creation and widespread recognition of two new forms of entities. . . . The first state statute providing for the organization of limited liability companies was enacted in Wyoming in 1977. Today, all fifty states and the District of Columbia recognize the limited liability company (LLC) form. The first state statute providing for limited liability partnership status was acted in Texas in 1991. Today, all fifty states and the District of Columbia recognize some form of limited liability partnership (LLP). LLPs can be classified in two different ways: whether they provide general partners with a full or a partial liability shield and whether the LLP form is available just for general partnerships or also for limited partnerships. Thus, there are four basic types of LLPs that may be found at the present time: a general partnership LLP with a partial shield, a general partnership LLP with a full shield, a limited partnership LLP (LLLP) with a partial shield, and an LLLP with a full shield. . . .
>
> The adoption of LLC and LLP laws in all fifty states during the 1990s was the direct result of a nation-wide legislative effort by the very large accounting firms. In the wake of the bankruptcy of the large accounting firm Laventhol & Horwath[6] and a significant increase in the number of securities law claims against accounting firms, the large accounting firms decided that steps were needed to decrease the exposure of their partners to potential liabilities for malpractice claims against other partners. The results of their efforts were the enactment of LLC and LLP laws in every state. Previously organized as general partnerships, the accounting firms needed to find a new form of organization that would not change the way they were being taxed, but that would provide protection from personal liability for the owners of the firm. Initially, the LLC form was the focus of the accountant's reform effort, but they subsequently added enactment of LLP laws to the initiative. At the time of their legislative efforts, the LLP model they supported provided only a partial liability shield, whereas the LLC form being proposed had a full liability shield. Although the LLC form was considered the most desirable, LLP status was seen as a useful interim measure because it provided at least some liability protection. Following their successful lobbying effort, the accounting firms promptly elected LLP status.

---

than $25,000. By contrast, annual receipts of corporations in the United States in 2003 totaled over $19.7 trillion. U.S. Bureau of Census, Statistical Abstract of the United States 487-488 (2007).

6. Partners of Laventhol & Horwath were held personally liable for several large malpractice verdicts against the firm that were unpaid at the time of the bankruptcy. Big Suits: In re Laventhol, Am. Law. (Jan.-Feb. 1991), at 30.

When LLCs, LLPs, and business trusts are added to the list of entity forms that were traditionally available for organizing a business, the options facing the business lawyer become extremely varied, to the point of almost being bewildering. A lawyer in Pennsylvania, for example, has a choice of organizing a business using any of twelve different forms. Further complicating the analysis of which form to use is the question of how the owners will want their business to be classified for purposes of federal income taxation. Adding the federal income tax classification options yields twenty-three possibilities.[10]

William H. Clark Jr., Rationalizing Entity Laws, 58 Bus. Law. 1005, 1005-1006 (2003).

We begin with the partnership, which, with respect to organizational and tax costs, lies at the opposite pole from the corporate form. The partnership represents an infinitely more flexible organizational structure for the small business enterprise, and it avoids entirely the problem of double taxation. Partnerships can act quite informally, and partnership income and losses are "passed through" to the partners and taxed as the income or loss of the partners.[2] But the partnership also lacks the principal advantages of the corporate form: limited liability and central management control. The limits of partnership and problems unique to the partnership form are explored next, followed by a discussion of more recent organizational forms that seek in one fashion or another to reduce the organizational and/or tax costs of the corporate form. We also touch briefly on the dilemmas posed by the proliferation of organizational forms.

B. PARTNERSHIPS

When two or more individuals carry on a business together as co-owners, the business will usually be deemed a partnership. This means that the partners will share ownership of the business assets, will have personal liability for the firm's debts, and will be agents of each other, each able to bind the business and, in effect, commit the partners' personal assets.

A general partnership is easy to form (indeed, no formalities are required and one can often be created inadvertently) and can be operated informally. Its popularity, however, is probably primarily attributable to the tax advantages it possesses: A partnership (except in the rarest circumstances) is not a tax-paying entity, while a corporation (unless able to elect Subchapter S status, as discussed below) must pay taxes on its earnings. Partnership income and losses are treated as the income or losses of the partners individually.

---

10. The adoption of "check the box" regulations by the IRS in 1997, pursuant to which an unincorporated entity simply could choose whether to be taxed as a partnership or a corporation, made planning easier by eliminating the need to manipulate form for tax purposes and complicated planning by increasing the number of alternatives.

2. See I.R.C. §7701(a)(2), defining "partnership."

Historically, the law of general partnerships grew out of the English courts' recognition of the Societas, a medieval form of business organization known to the law merchant, which was characterized by the following basic principles: (1) each partner had the right to account from the other partners (meaning that the other partners had to justify the propriety and fairness of transactions with the entity), (2) each partner could bind the others by contracts made on behalf of the partnership, and (3) each partner was personally liable to creditors of the firm for firm obligations.[3] From this starting point, English mercantile courts (largely under the influence of Lord Mansfield) held that partners were fiduciaries for each other and have the right to have partnership property applied only to partnership purposes.

In 1914 the Commissioners on Uniform State Laws adopted the Uniform Partnership Act (UPA), which codified, with some modifications, much of the common law that had previously governed partnership law. By 1986 every state, except Louisiana, had enacted the UPA. In 1994 the Commissioners on Uniform State laws promulgated the Revised Uniform Partnership Act (RUPA),[4] which made extensive revisions to the UPA.[5] Several states have adopted RUPA, and more are likely to do so in the future. Currently, however, partnership law is in flux, with the result in a given case potentially depending on which statute is applicable. Thus, it is important to understand both the existing case law (which largely construes the UPA) and the changes that a statutory adoption of RUPA would produce.

1. THE NATURE OF PARTNERSHIP: AGGREGATE OR ENTITY?

Is a partnership a distinct legal entity (as a corporation clearly is) or merely an aggregation of individuals? From the beginnings of American partnership law, there has been a dispute over this issue, and UPA largely adopted a view of the partnership as an aggregation of individuals rather than a separate legal entity.[6] Under the aggregate theory, a partnership is no more than a collection of persons acting with a common purpose, and thus the partnership technically continues only so long as this same aggregate of individuals continues to operate the business. If a single partner dies or retires, the partnership is "dissolved" (although the remaining partner(s) may continue the business as a distinct partnership). In contrast, if the partnership is an entity separate from its partners, the death of a partner should not matter. This treatment would also allow a partnership agreement to specify that the partnership continues. The following decision reveals the practical implications of these two alternative perspectives.

---

3. See G. W. Holdsworth, A History of English Law 197 (1926).

4. RUPA's origins are closely connected to a report by an ABA committee that recommended significant revisions to UPA. See Report, Should the Uniform Partnership Act Be Revised?, 43 Bus. Law. 121 (1987).

5. See Donald Weidner, The Revised Uniform Partnership Act: The Reporters' Overview, 49 Bus. Law. 1 (1993).

6. Compare Judson Crane, The Uniform Partnership Act — A Criticism, 78 Harv. L. Rev. 762 (1915), with William D. Lewis, The Uniform Partnership Act — A Reply to Mr. Crane's Criticism, 29 Harv. L. Rev. 158 (1915), and Judson Crane, The Uniform Partnership Act and Legal Persons, 29 Harv. L. Rev. 838 (1916).

Fairway Development v. Title Ins. Co. of Minnesota
621 F. Supp. 120 (N.D. Ohio 1985)

DOWD, D.J.: [Plaintiff, a partnership, sued for breach of contract of a title guarantee insurance policy.] . . . [D]efendant asserts that it is liable under the title guaranty policy in question only to the named party guaranteed. Defendant asserts that it originally guaranteed a general partnership, which it refers to as Fairway Development I, consisting of three partners: Thomas M. Bernabei, James V. Serra, Jr., and Howard J. Wenger. Defendant states that each of these three men contributed to the partnership's capital and shared in the partnership's profits and losses equally. Defendant argues that Fairway Development I commenced on October 15, 1979 and terminated on May 20, 1981, when two partners in Fairway Development I, Bernabei and Serra, sold and transferred their respective undivided one-third interests in the partnership to the remaining partner, Wenger, and a third-party purchaser, James E. Valentine. Defendant argues that a new partnership resulted from this sale, called Fairway Development II. Defendant concludes that it cannot be held liable to the plaintiff since it is not in privity with the plaintiff as the named party guaranteed. . . . Plaintiff states that in the instant case, the facts are clear that there was an intent between the partners of what defendant calls Fairway Development I and II to continue the operation of the Fairway Development Company following the sale by Bernabei and Serra of their interests to Wenger and Valentine without dissolving the partnership. Plaintiff states that in deciding this case, the Court's focus should be on the intent of the parties. Lastly, plaintiff argues that Fairway Development II has continued to carry on the stated purpose of Fairway Development I, which is really just an expansion of the purpose set forth in the partnership agreement for Fairway Development I, the acquisition and development of real estate. . . .

The resolution of this case is governed by the law of the forum state, Ohio. Ohio has adopted the Uniform Partnership Law, modelled after the Uniform Partnership Act enacted by the National Conference of Commissioners on Uniform State Laws in 1914. Ohio follows the common law aggregate theory of partnership, under which a partnership is regarded as the sum of the persons who comprise the partnership, versus the legal entity theory of partnership. . . . [UPA §29] provides that any change in the relations of the partners will dissolve a partnership. . . . Further, the terms of Uniform Partnership Act §41(1) . . . provide that: "When any new partner is admitted into an existing partnership, or when any new partner retires and assigns . . . his rights in partnership property to two or more of the partners, or to one or more of the partners, and one or more third persons, if the business is continued with[out] liquidation of the partnership affairs, creditors of the first or dissolved partnership are also creditors of the partnership so continuing the business." This section seems to assume that a dissolution occurs upon the admission of a new partner or the retirement of an old partner. The official comment to §41(1) notes that: "It is universally admitted that any change in membership dissolves a partnership, and creates a new partnership. This section, as drafted, does not alter that rule."

These sections above discussed all support . . . a finding that when Fairway Development II was formed, Fairway Development I dissolved, and a new partnership was formed. . . . The court's conclusion accords with the aggregate theory of partnership, which, applied to this case, recognizes Fairway Development I not as an entity in itself, but as a partnership made up of three members, Bernabei, Serra, and Wenger. That partnership ceased when the membership of the partnership changed.

... [T]he court holds that the terms of the title guaranty extended only to the named party guaranteed, that party being Fairway Development I, and that Fairway Development II therefore has no standing to sue the defendant for breach of the contract in question. Defendant's motion for summary judgment is therefore granted.

RUPA's response. Fairway Development raised serious questions about whether long-term contracts entered into by a partnership would be enforceable. Although many believed the decision was wrongly decided even under UPA, RUPA made certain that *Fairway Development's* result was clearly rejected. RUPA §201 states unequivocally: "A partnership is an entity." The comment to §201 adds that this "will avoid the result in cases such as *Fairway Development. ... "* The comment presumably refers to the fact that RUPA allows a partnership agreement to specify that the partnership continues in the event of a partner's death. See RUPA §601. Does *Fairway Development* stand under RUPA if the partnership agreement is silent? Put differently, what should the default rule be if the partnership agreement is silent or there is no written agreement?

The results in the states that have adopted RUPA and the entity theory are mixed, treating the partnership as aggregate in some instances and as an entity in others. In a suit brought by a former partner against the successor partnership for accounting and distribution of the former partnership's assets, the Alabama Supreme Court affirmed the plaintiff's right to bring suit against the partnership as an entity, without joining the individual partners. The court, however, went on to distinguish the partnership entity from the corporate entity to hold in favor of the defendant partners' motion for transfer of venue to a county where at least one partner was resident. Wilson v. Wilson & King, 706 So. 2d 1151 (Ala. 1997).

2. FORMATION

A partnership is formed by an agreement by two or more parties to carry on a business as co-owners. No formalities are essential to the formation of a partnership, and the courts may characterize an association as a partnership even though the partners did not so characterize themselves. Particularly ambiguous and troubling have been instances in which (1) a "creditor" has an active voice in management (and a veto power over important decisions), and (2) an "employee" is compensated based on a share of the partnership's profits and also supervises some day-to-day operations. In the right circumstances, the "creditor" or "employee" may be recharacterized as a "partner," with personal liability for the partnership's activities.

Vohland v. Sweet
433 N.E.2d 860 (Ind. Ct. App. 1982)

NEAL, J.: Plaintiff-appellee Norman E. Sweet (Sweet) brought an action for dissolution of an alleged partnership and for an accounting in the Ripley Circuit

Court against defendant-appellant Paul Eugene Vohland (Vohland). From a judgment in favor of Sweet in the amount of $58,733, Vohland appeals. . . .

The undisputed facts reveal that Sweet, as a youngster, commenced working in 1956 for Charles Vohland, father of Paul Eugene Vohland, as an hourly employee in a nursery operated by Charles Vohland and known as Clarksburg Dahlia Gardens. . . . In approximately 1963 Charles Vohland retired, and Vohland commenced what became known as Vohland's Nursery, the business of which was landscape gardening. At that time Sweet's status changed. He was to receive a 20 percent share of the net profit of the enterprise after all of the expenses were paid. . . .

No partnership income tax returns were filed. Vohland and his wife, Gwenalda, filed a joint return in which the business of Vohland's Nursery was reported in Vohland's name on Schedule C. Money paid Sweet was listed as a business expense under "Commissions." Also listed on Schedule C were all of the expenses of the nursery, including investment credit and depreciation on trucks, tractors, and machinery. Sweet's tax returns declared that he was a self-employed salesman at Vohland's Nursery. He filed a self-employment Schedule C and listed as income the income received from the nursery; as expenses he listed travel, advertising, phone, conventions, automobile, and trade journals. He further filed a Schedule C-3 for self-employment Social Security for the receipts from the nursery.

Vohland handled all of the finances and books and did most of the sales. He borrowed money from the bank solely in his own name for business purposes, including the purchase of the interests of his brothers and sisters in his father's business, operating expenses, bid bonds, motor vehicles, taxes and purchases of real estate. Sweet was not involved in those loans. Sweet managed the physical aspects of the nursery and supervised the care of the nursery stock and the performance of the contracts for customers. Vohland was quoted by one customer as saying Sweet was running things and the customer would have to see Sweet about some problem.

Evidence was contradictory in certain respects. The Vohland Nursery was located on approximately 13 acres of land owned by Charles Vohland. Sweet testified that at the commencement of the arrangement with Vohland in 1963, Charles Vohland grew the stock and maintained the inventory, for which he received 25 percent of the gross sales. In the late 1960's, because of age, Charles Vohland could no longer perform. The nursery stock became depleted to nearly nothing, and new arrangements were made. An extensive program was initiated by Sweet and Vohland to replenish and enlarge the inventory of nursery stock; this program continued until February, 1979. The cost of planting and maintaining the nursery stock was assigned to expenses before Sweet received his 20 percent. The nursery stock generally took up to ten years to mature for market. Sweet testified that at the termination of the arrangement there existed $293,665 in inventory which had been purchased with the earnings of the business. Of that amount $284,860 was growing nursery stock. Vohland, on the other hand, testified that the inventory of 1963 was as large as that of 1979, but the inventory became depleted in 1969. Vohland claimed that as part of his agreement with Charles Vohland he was required to replenish the nursery stock as it was sold, and in addition pay Charles Vohland 25 percent of the net profit from the operation. He contends that the inventory of nursery stock balanced out. However, Vohland conceded on cross-examination that the acquisition and enlargement of the existing inventory of nursery stock was paid for with earnings and, therefore, was financed partly with Sweet's money. He further stated that the consequences of this financial arrangement never entered his mind at the time.

Sweet's testimony, denied by Vohland, disclosed that, in a conversation in the early 1970's regarding the purchase of inventory out of earnings, Vohland promised to take care of Sweet. Vohland acknowledged that Sweet refused to permit his 20 percent to be charged with the cost of a truck unless his name was on the title. Sweet testified that at the outset of the arrangement Vohland told him, "he was going to take . . . me in and that . . . I wouldn't have to punch a time clock anymore, that I would be on a commission basis and that I would be, have more of an interest in the business if I had 'an interest in the business.' . . . He referred to it as a piece of the action." Sweet testified that he intended to enter into a partnership. Vohland asserts that no partnership was intended and that Sweet was merely an employee, working on a commission. There was no contention that Sweet made any contribution to capital, nor did he claim any interest in the real estate, machinery, or motor vehicles. The parties had never discussed losses.

After Charles Vohland died (in 1973) Vohland contends that he paid $1,000 a year to Mary Crystal Vohland, his stepmother and current owner of the 13 acres, as a gift, and in addition replenished the nursery stock as it was taken and sold. Sweet contends the payments were a flat fee for the use of the land. . . .

The principal point of disagreement between Sweet and Vohland is whether the arrangement between them created a partnership, or a contract of employment of Sweet by Vohland as a salesman on commission. It therefore becomes necessary to review briefly the principles governing the establishment of partnerships.

It has been said that an accurate and comprehensive definition of a partnership has not been stated; that the lines of demarcation which distinguish a partnership from other joint interests on one hand and from agency on the other, are so fine as to render approximate rather than exhaustive any attempt to define the relationship. Bacon v. Christian, (1916) 184 Ind. 517, 111 N.E. 628.

A partnership is defined by U.P.A. §6: "A partnership is an association of two or more persons to carry on as co-owners a business for profit."

U.P.A. §7 sets forth the rules for determining the existence of a partnership:

> . . . (1) Except as provided by section 16 persons who are not partners as to each other are not partners as to third persons.
>
> (2) Joint tenancy, tenancy in common, tenancy by the entireties, joint property, common property, or part ownership does not of itself establish a partnership, whether such co-owners do or do not share any profits made by the use of the property.
>
> (3) The sharing of gross returns does not of itself establish a partnership, whether or not the persons sharing them have a joint or common right or interest in any property from which the returns are derived.
>
> (4) The receipt by a person of a share of the profits of a business is prima facie evidence that he is a partner in the business, but no such inference shall be drawn if such profits were received in payment:
>
>> (a) As a debt by installments or otherwise,
>>
>> (b) As wages of an employee or rent to a landlord,
>>
>> (c) As an annuity to a widow or representative of a deceased partner,
>>
>> (d) As interest on a loan though the amount of payment vary with the profits of the business,

(e) As the consideration for the sale of a good will of a business or other property by installments or otherwise.

Under U.P.A. §7(4) receipt by a person of a share of the profits is prima facie evidence that he is a partner in the business. Endsley v. Game-Show Placements, Ltd., (1980) Ind. App., 401 N.E.2d 768. Lack of daily involvement for one partner is not per se indicative of absence of a partnership: *Endsley*, supra. A partnership may be formed by the furnishing of skill and labor by others. The contribution of labor and skill by one of the partners may be as great a contribution to the common enterprise as property or money. Watson v. Watson, (1952) 231 Ind. 385, 108 N.E.2d 893. It is an established common law principle that a partnership can commence only by the voluntary contract of the parties. Bond v. May, (1906) 38 Ind. App. 396, 78 N.E. 260. In *Bond* it was said, "[t]o be a partner, one must have an interest with another in the profits of a business, as profits. There must be a voluntary contract to carry on a business with intention of the parties to share the profits as common owners thereof." Id., 38 Ind. App. at 402, 78 N.E. 260. In *Bacon*, supra, in reviewing the law relative to the creation of partnerships, the court said: "From these, and other expressions of similar import, it is apparent to establish the partnership relation, as between the parties, there must be (1) a voluntary contract of association for the purpose of sharing the profits and losses, as such, which may arise from the use of capital, labor or skill in a common enterprise; and (2) an intention on the part of the principals to form a partnership for that purpose. But it must be borne in mind, however, that the intent, the existence of which is deemed essential, is an intent to do those things which constitute a partnership. Hence, if such an intent exists, the parties will be partners notwithstanding that they proposed to avoid the liability attaching to partners or [have] even expressly stipulated in their agreement that they were not to become partners. [Citation omitted]

"It is the substance, and not the name of the arrangement between them, which determines their legal relation toward each other, and if, from a consideration of all the facts and circumstances, it appears that the parties intended, between themselves, that there should be a community of interest of both the property and profits of a common business or venture, the law treats it as their intention to become partners, in the absence of other controlling facts." Id. 184 Ind. at 521-522, 111 N.E. 628. . . .

. . . In the analysis of the facts, we are first constrained to observe that should an accrual method of accounting have been employed here, the enhancement of the inventory of nursery stock would have been reflected as profit, a point which Vohland, in effect, concedes. We further note that both parties referred to the 20 percent as "commissions." To us the term "commission," unless defined, does not mean the same thing as a share of the net profits. However, this term, when used by landscape gardeners and not lawyers, should not be restricted to its technical definition. "Commission" was used to refer to Sweet's share of the profits, and the receipt of a share of the profits is prima facie evidence of a partnership. Though evidence is conflicting, there is evidence that the payments were not wages, but a share of the profit of a partnership. As in *Watson*, supra, it can readily be inferred from the evidence most favorable to support the judgment that the parties intended a community of interest in any increment in the value of the capital and in the profit. As shown in *Watson*, absence of contribution to capital is not controlling, and contribution of labor and skill will suffice. There is evidence from which it can be inferred that the parties intended to do the things which amount to the formation of a partnership, regardless of how they may later characterize the relationship. *Bacon*, supra. From the evidence the court could find that part of the operating profits of the business, of which Sweet was entitled to 20 percent, were put back into it in the form of inventory of nursery stock. In the authorities cited above it seems the central factor in determining the existence of a partnership is a division of profits.

From all the circumstances we cannot say that the court erred in finding the existence of a partnership. . . .

Affirmed.

UPA and RUPA compared. UPA §7(4) provides that "the receipt by a person of a share of the profits of a business is prima facie evidence that he is a partner in the business, but no such inference shall be drawn if such profits were received in payment: (a) As a debt by installments or otherwise, (b) As wages of an employee or rent to a landlord, . . . (d) As interest on a loan though the amount of payment vary with the profits of the business, (e) As the consideration for the sale of goodwill of a business or other property by installments or otherwise."

RUPA §202 does not appear to significantly change this body of law (or to reduce the resulting uncertainty). RUPA §202(a) provides that "the association of two or more persons to carry on as co-owners a business for profit forms a partnership, whether or not the persons intend to form a partnership." RUPA §202(c)(3) adds that "a person who receives a share of the profits of a business is presumed to be a partner in the business, unless the profits were received in payment: (i) of a debt by installments or otherwise; (ii) for services as an independent contractor or of wages or other compensation to an employee. . . ."

Should the character of the claim asserted influence the analysis? Assume that in *Vohland* the plaintiff had been injured at the nursery and sought to reach Sweet's personal assets to satisfy his claim. Does the third-party tort claim raise issues different from those raised by a claim between the two participants in the nursery?

3. POWERS OF PARTNERS

The authority of agents to bind their principals (here, the partnership) was covered earlier, in Chapter IV. Partnership law basically follows these same principles, but with statutory refinements. UPA §9(1) provides: "Every partner is an agent of the partnership for the purpose of its business, and the act of every partner, including the execution in the partnership name of any instrument, for apparently carrying on in the usual way the business of the partnership of which he is a member, binds the partnership, unless the partner so acting has in fact no authority to act for the partnership in the particular matter, and the person with whom he is dealing has knowledge of the fact that he has no such authority." This has been held to give a partner in a real estate development partnership apparent authority to bind all the partners to a contract for sale of land, even though there was no evidence that he was authorized to make the contract. Moreover, although the statute of frauds would usually require such authority to be given in writing, UPA §9(1) has been read to make written authority unnecessary in this case. Ball v. Carlson, 641 P.2d 303 (Colo. App. 1981).

Had the firm not been in the real estate business, the result might have been different. UPA §9(2) provides: "An act of a partner which is not apparently for the carrying on of the business of the partnership in the usual way does not bind the partnership unless authorized by the other partners." A partner in a grocery store therefore would lack apparent authority to sell the building in which the grocery was located; specific authorization would be necessary.

A specific partner in a real estate partnership may have been brought into the firm solely to raise capital, or to provide special skills other than selling. It may be agreed by all the members of the firm that this partner will have no power to make sales. Although the partner lacks actual authority, UPA §9(1) empowers the partner to contract in the ordinary course of the firm's business, "unless . . . the person with whom he is dealing has knowledge of the fact that he has no such authority." In Stone-Fox Inc. v. Vandehey Development Co., 290 Or. 779 (1981), a partner in the development company told the plaintiff that he had no authority to accept a price below $15,500, and he would have to discuss plaintiff's $15,000 offer with the other partner. The next day he called the plaintiff to say that he had discussed the matter with the other partner and they had agreed to accept a price of $15,250. The plaintiff accepted this counteroffer and signed an earnest money agreement for sale of the land. The plaintiff lost its suit for specific performance because it was on notice that the partner's authority was limited, said the majority, and therefore UPA §9(1) did not apply. Two justices disagreed, holding that notice that the partner had no authority to sell for $15,000 on the first day did not mean that the plaintiff was on notice that the partner had no authority to sell for $15,250 on the second. (They concurred in the result, however, because the contract had been improperly executed.) Is this decision sound?

Note that UPA §9(3) requires unanimous consent (with limited exceptions) for a partner to make certain extraordinary transactions, such as one that would make it impossible to carry on the partnership business.

In order to provide a partnership with some means of limiting the authority of its partners, RUPA §303 authorizes the partnership to file a "statement of partnership authority" with the jurisdiction's secretary of state, which can "state the authority, or limitations on the authority, of some or all the partners to enter into other transactions on behalf of the partnership and any other matter." However, RUPA §303(f) adds that (outside the context of real property transactions), "a person not a partner is not deemed to know of a limitation on the authority of a partner merely because the limitation is contained in a filed statement." What does filing a statement of partnership add to an allocation of authority contained in a partnership?

4. LIABILITIES OF PARTNERS

UPA §13 creates partnership liability for the "wrongful act or omission of any partner acting in the ordinary course of the business of the partnership." UPA §15 makes all partners "jointly and severally" liable for all tort liabilities "chargeable to the partnership," but only "jointly" liable for "all other debts and obligations of the partnership." "Joint and several" liability allows a third-party tort plaintiff to sue only one partner of the partnership for the full amount of her damages. The partner sued would then have to seek indemnification from the other partners to the extent of the others' liabilities. "Joint liability" means that all partners are liable together; one partner cannot be compelled to defend a suit alone where she is jointly liable. The impact of this distinction between tort and contract liability has thus primarily been procedural and, depending on the jurisdiction, may require the plaintiff to join all the partners in order to assert "joint" liability (whereas no such joinder is required in the case of "joint and several" liability). RUPA simplifies these procedural problems. First, RUPA §305 makes the partnership liable for the conduct or omission of "a partner acting in the ordinary course of business of the partnership or with authority of the partnership"; RUPA §306 draws no distinction between tort and contract liabilities, but rather makes each partner jointly and severally liable "for all obligations of the partnership unless otherwise agreed by the claimant or provided by law." Because RUPA views the partnership as an entity, it also provides that "a partnership may sue and be sued in the name of the partnership" without any need for joinder of the individual partners (RUPA §307). 14th RMA Partners v. Reale, 100 F.3d 278 (2d Cir. 1996), illustrates the entity approach. In that case, FDIC won a foreclosure judgment against the property owned in the name of the partnership and subsequently sought judgment against one general partner. The court held that the partner was liable for the judgment against the partnership even where the partner was not named or joined in the suit.

5. PARTNERSHIP GOVERNANCE

Under UPA §18, "the rights and duties of the partners in relation to the partnership shall be determined, subject to any agreement between them, by the following rules:

> (e) All partners have equal rights in the management and conduct of the partnership business.
> (f) No partner is entitled to remuneration for acting in the partnership's business, except that a surviving partner is entitled to reasonable compensation for his services in winding up the partnership affairs.
> (g) No person can become a member of a partnership without the consent of all the partners.
> (h) Any difference arising as to ordinary matters connected with the partnership business may be decided by a majority of the partners; but no act in contravention of any agreement between the partners may be done rightfully without the consent of all the partners.

In effect, the default rule in a partnership is "one partner, one vote," in contrast to the presumptive "one share, one vote" rule in a corporation; in a partnership, unlike a corporation, the vote does not follow the value of a participant's interest. Although in theory unanimity may be necessary for some purposes (such as the admission of a new partner), the partnership agreement can override the default rules of UPA §18 and provide instead for admission based on a majority vote (or a supermajority vote).

RUPA §401 contains substantially equivalent provisions to UPA §18. Both also agree that (in the absence of a contrary agreement) "each partner is entitled to an equal share of the partnership profits and is chargeable with a share of the partnership's losses in proportion to the partner's share of the profits" (RUPA §401(b)). Within the partnership, the agreement can allocate (decision) authority as the partners see fit — the partners can name a CEO, a CFO, and the like and delineate specific areas of responsibility. But, as we have seen, the partner can still have apparent authority vis-á-vis third parties that exceeds or encompasses an area outside her internally allocated authority. In a law firm, for example, a partner who has been designated head of recruiting could bind all other partners to a lease signed for office space, even though authority for such leases was internally vested in another partner. What remedy would the other partners have against a partner who incurs obligations to third parties within the scope of her apparent authority but outside the scope of her actual authority?

6. FIDUCIARY DUTIES

At the heart of partnership law is the idea of a fiduciary duty owed by each partner to the other partners. UPA §21(1) ("Partner Accountable as a Fiduciary") expresses one aspect of this duty: "Every partner must account to the partnership for any benefit, and hold as a trustee for it any profits derived by him without the consent of the other partners from any transaction connected with the formation, conduct, or liquidation of the partnership or from any use by him of its property." The case law, however, has read the partner's fiduciary duty more broadly than this statutory formulation might indicate:

Meinhard v. Salmon
249 N.Y. 458, 164 N.E. 545 (1928)

CARDOZO, C.J.: . . . On April 10, 1902, Louisa M. Gerry leased to the defendant Walter J. Salmon the premises known as the Hotel Bristol at the northwest corner of Forty-second Street and Fifth Avenue in the city of New York. The lease was for a term of twenty years, commencing May 1, 1902, and ending April 30, 1922. The lessee undertook to change the hotel building for use as shops and offices at a cost of $200,000. Alterations and additions were to be accretions to the land.

Salmon, while in the course of treaty with the lessor as to the execution of the lease, was in course of treaty with Meinhard, the plaintiff, for the necessary funds. The result was a joint venture with terms embodied in a writing. Meinhard was to pay to Salmon half of the moneys requisite to reconstruct, alter, manage, and operate the property. Salmon was to pay to Meinhard 40 percent of the net profits for the first five years of the lease, and 50 percent for the years thereafter. If there were losses, each party was to bear them equally. Salmon, however, was to have sole power to "manage, lease, underlet and operate" the building. There were to be certain pre-emptive rights for each in the contingency of death.

The two were coadventurers, subject to fiduciary duties akin to those of partners. . . . The heavier weight of duty rested, however, upon Salmon. He was a coadventurer with Meinhard, but he was manager as well. During the early years of the enterprise, the building, reconstructed, was operated at a loss. If the relation had then ended, Meinhard as well as Salmon would have carried a heavy burden. Later the profits became large with the result that for each of the investors there came a rich return. For each the venture had its phases of fair weather and of foul. The two were in it jointly, for better or for worse.

When the lease was near its end, Elbridge T. Gerry had become the owner of the reversion. He owned much other property in the neighborhood, one lot adjoining the Bristol building on Fifth Avenue and four lots on Forty-second Street. He had a plan to lease the entire tract for a long term to some one who would destroy the buildings then existing and put up another in their place. In the latter part of 1921, he submitted such a project to several capitalists and dealers. He was unable to carry it through with any of them. Then, in January, 1922, with less than four months of the lease to run, he approached the defendant Salmon. The result was a new lease to the Midpoint Realty Company, which is owned and controlled by Salmon, a lease covering the whole tract, and involving a huge outlay. The term is to be twenty years, but successive covenants for renewal will extend it to a maximum of eighty years at the will of either party. The existing buildings may remain unchanged for seven years. They are then to be torn down, and a new building to cost $3,000,000 is to be placed upon the site. The rental, which under the Bristol lease was only $55,000, is to be from $350,000 to $475,000 for the properties so combined. Salmon personally guaranteed the performance by the lessee of the covenants of the new lease until such time as the new building had been completed and fully paid for.

The lease between Gerry and the Midpoint Realty Company was signed and delivered on January 25, 1922. Salmon had not told Meinhard anything about it. Whatever his motive may have been, he kept the negotiations to himself. Meinhard was not informed even of the bare existence of a project. The first that he knew of it was in February, when the lease was an accomplished fact. He then made demand on the defendants that the lease be held in trust as an asset of the venture, making offer upon the trial to share the personal obligations incidental to the guaranty. The demand was followed by refusal, and later by this suit. [Plaintiff's judgment, as modified by the Appellate Division, awarded him an equitable interest in one-half the lease, with the obligation to assume half of Salmon's personal obligations in connection with the transaction.] The case is now here on an appeal by the defendants.

Joint adventurers, like copartners, owe to one another, while the enterprise continues, the duty of the finest loyalty. Many forms of conduct permissible in a workaday world for those acting at arm's length are forbidden to those bound by fiduciary ties. A trustee is held to something stricter than the morals of the market place. Not honesty alone, but the punctilio of an honor the most sensitive, is then the standard of behavior. As to this there has developed a tradition that is unbending and inveterate. Uncompromising rigidity has been the attitude of courts of equity when petitioned to undermine the rule of undivided loyalty by the "disintegrating erosion" of particular exceptions. Wendt v. Fischer, 243 N.Y. 439, 444, 154 N.E. 303. Only thus has the level of conduct for fiduciaries been kept at a level higher than that trodden by the crowd. It will not consciously be lowered by any judgment of this court.

The owner of the reversion, Mr. Gerry, had vainly striven to find a tenant who would favor his ambitious scheme of demolition and construction. Baffled in the search, he turned to the defendant Salmon in possession of the Bristol, the keystone of the project. He figured to himself beyond a doubt that the man in possession would prove a likely customer. To the eye of an observer, Salmon held the lease as owner in his own right, for himself and no one else. In fact he held it as a fiduciary, for himself and another, sharers in a common venture. If this fact had been proclaimed, if the lease by its terms had run in favor of a partnership, Mr. Gerry, we may fairly assume, would have laid before the partners, and not merely before one of them, his plan of reconstruction. The preemptive privilege, or, better, the preemptive opportunity, that was thus an incident of the enterprise, Salmon appropriated to himself in secrecy and silence. He might have warned Meinhard that the plan had been submitted, and that either would be free to compete for the award. If he had done this, we do not need to say whether he would have been under a duty, if successful in the competition, to hold the lease so acquired for the benefit of a venture then about to end, and thus prolong by indirection its responsibilities and duties. The trouble about his conduct is that he excluded his coadventurer from any chance to compete, from any chance to enjoy the opportunity for benefit that had come to him alone by virtue of his agency. This chance, if nothing more, he was under a duty to concede. The price of its denial is an extension of the trust at the option and for the benefit of the one whom he excluded.

No answer is it to say that the chance would have been of little value even if seasonably offered. Such a calculus of probabilities is beyond the science of the chancery. Salmon, the real estate operator, might have been preferred to Meinhard, the woolen merchant. On the other hand, Meinhard might have offered better terms, or reinforced his offer by alliance with the wealth of others. Perhaps he might even have persuaded the lessor to renew the Bristol lease, alone, postponing for a time, in return for higher rentals, the improvement of adjoining lots. We know that even under the lease as made the time for the enlargement of the building was delayed for seven years. All these opportunities were cut away from him through another's intervention. He knew that Salmon was the manager. As the time drew near for the expiration of the lease, he would naturally assume from silence, if from nothing else, that the lessor was willing to extend it for a term of years, or at least to let it stand as a lease from year to year. Not impossibly the lessor would have done so, whatever his protestations of unwillingness, if Salmon had not given assent to a project more attractive. At all events, notice of termination, even if not necessary, might seem, not unreasonably, to be something to be looked for, if the business was over and another tenant was to enter. In the absence of such notice, the matter of an extension was one that would naturally be attended to by the manager of the enterprise, and not neglected altogether. At least, there was nothing in the situation to give warning to any one that while the lease was still in being, there had come to the manager an offer of extension which he had locked within his breast to be utilized by himself alone. The very fact that Salmon was in control with exclusive powers of direction charged him the more obviously with the duty of disclosure, since only through disclosure could opportunity be equalized. If he might cut off renewal by a purchase for his own benefit when four months were to pass before the lease would have an end, he might do so with equal right while there remained as many years. . . . He might steal a march on his comrade under cover of the darkness, and then hold the captured ground. Loyalty and comradeship are not so easily abjured.

. . . Authority is, of course, abundant that one partner may not appropriate to his own use a renewal of a lease, though its term is to begin at the expiration of the partnership. Mitchell v. Reed, 61 N.Y. 123, 19 Am. Rep. 252, 84 N.Y. 556. The lease at hand with its many changes is not strictly a renewal. Even so, the standard of loyalty for those in trust relations is without the fixed divisions of a graduated scale. . . .

Equity refuses to confine within the bounds of classified transactions its precept of a loyalty that is undivided and unselfish. Certain at least it is that a "man obtaining his locus standi, and his opportunity for making such arrangements, by the position he occupies as a partner, is bound by his obligation to his copartners in such dealings not to separate his interest from theirs, but, if he acquires any benefit, to communicate it to them." Cassels v. Stewart, L.R. 6 App. Cas. 64, 73 — H.L. Certain it is, also, that there may be no abuse of special opportunities growing out of a special trust as manager or agent.

We have no thought to hold that Salmon was guilty of a conscious purpose to defraud. Very likely he assumed in all good faith that with the approaching end of the venture he might ignore his coadventurer and take the extension for himself. He had given to the enterprise time and labor as well as money. He had made it a success. Meinhard, who had given money, but neither time nor labor, had already been richly paid. There might seem to be something grasping in his insistence upon more. Such recriminations are not unusual when coadventurers fall out. They are not without their force if conduct is to be judged by the common standards of competitors. That is not to say that they have pertinency here. Salmon had put himself in a position in which thought of self was to be renounced, however hard the abnegation. He was much more than a coadventurer. He was a managing coadventurer. . . . For him and for those like him the rule of undivided loyalty is relentless and supreme. . . . A different question would be here if there were lacking any nexus of relation between the business conducted by the manager and the opportunity brought to him as an incident of management. . . .

For this problem, as for most, there are distinctions of degree. If Salmon had received from Gerry a proposition to lease a building at a location far removed, he might have held for himself the privilege thus acquired, or so we shall assume. Here the subject-matter of the new lease was an extension and enlargement of the subject-matter of the old one. A managing coadventurer appropriating the benefit of such a lease without warning to his partner might fairly expect to be reproached with conduct that was underhand, or lacking, to say the least, in reasonable candor, if the partner were to surprise him in the act of signing the new instrument. Conduct subject to that reproach does not receive from equity a healing benediction.

A question remains as to the form and extent of the equitable interest to be allotted to the plaintiff. The trust as declared has been held to attach to the lease which was in the name of the defendant corporation. We think it ought to attach at the option of the defendant Salmon to the shares of stock which were owned by him or were under his control. The difference may be important if the lessee shall wish to execute an assignment of the lease, as it ought to be free to do with the consent of the lessor. On the other hand, an equal division of the shares might lead to other hardships. It might take away from Salmon the power of control and management which under the plan of the joint venture he was to have from first to last. The number of shares to be allotted to the plaintiff should, therefore, be reduced to such an extent as may be necessary to preserve to the defendant Salmon the expected measure of dominion. To that end an extra share should be added to his half. . . .

———————————————

1. *A dissent.* Justice Andrews, dissenting in Meinhard v. Salmon, did not argue with Cardozo's general principles, but viewed the parties' association to be limited to the original 20-year lease of the Bristol building and would have permitted Salmon to exclude Meinhard from a renewal of the building lease for an additional term. Do you agree? Do you agree with Cardozo's suggestion that "[i]f Salmon had received from Gerry a proposition to lease a building at a location far removed, he might have held for himself the privilege thus acquired"? What about the possibility that Gerry intended to make his offer to the proprietor of the Bristol building, which, though he did not know it, included Meinhard? On the other hand, is it important that Meinhard was probably not expecting Salmon to be on the lookout for additional ventures for them both? Does a general concept of fiduciary duty in partnerships to some extent substitute for a specification in the statute of the parties' obligations in every situation the partnership would confront in the future? If it is impossible to state specific rules in the statute (or in the partnership agreement), then does a fiduciary duty set a general standard that can be applied to a wide range of future conduct?

2. *Fiduciary duties and freedom of contract.* In Singer v. Singer, 634 P.2d 766 (Okla. 1981), a partnership agreement provided: "8. Each partner shall be free to enter into business and other transactions for his or her own separate individual account, even though such business or other transaction may be in conflict with and/or competition with the business of this partnership . . . , it being the intention and agreement that any partner will be free to deal on his or her own account to the same extent and with the same force and effect as if he or she were not and never had been members of this partnership." At a meeting of this partnership, the possible purchase of a 95-acre site was discussed, but a decision was deferred on whether to purchase it. Shortly thereafter, two of the partners (one of whom had been earlier asked by the partnership to investigate the site) purchased the land for themselves. *Held:* "We find the defendants had a contract right to do precisely what they did, namely compete with the partners of [the partnership] . . . 'as if there never had been a partnership.' Because of paragraph 8, the fact that the land is in an area of partnership interest does not preclude intra-partnership competition. . . . [The partnership] contracted away its right to expect a noncompetitive fiduciary relationship with any of its partners." Is this holding sound? What factors would influence the parties' willingness to treat each other at arm's length? Suppose the parties contemplated doing business together for a long time. Then a waiver of fiduciary duty might reflect a choice to have the threat of ending the relationship protect the partners in preference to protection through litigation over whether a particular conduct met the fiduciary standard.

3. *RUPA's position.* In one of its most controversial departures from the position of UPA, RUPA §404 provides as follows:

> Sec. 404. *General standards of partner's conduct.* (a) The only fiduciary duties a partner owes to the partnership and the other partners are the duty of loyalty and the duty of care set forth in subsections (b) and (c).
>
> (b) A partner's duty of loyalty to the partnership and the other partners is limited to the following:
>
>   (1) to account to the partnership and hold as trustee for it any property, profit, or benefit derived by the partner in the conduct and winding up of the partnership

business or derived from a use by the partner of partnership property, including the appropriation of a partnership opportunity.

(2) to refrain from dealing with the partnership in the conduct or winding up of the partnership business as or on behalf of a party having an interest adverse to the partnership; and

(3) to refrain from competing with the partnership in the conduct of the partnership business before the dissolution of the partnership.

(c) A partner's duty of care to the partnership and the other partners in the conduct and winding up of the partnership business is limited to refraining from engaging in grossly negligent or reckless conduct, intentional misconduct, or a knowing violation of law.

(d) A partner shall discharge the duties to the partnership and the other partners under this [Act] or under the partnership agreement and exercise any rights consistently with the obligations of good faith and fair dealing.

(e) A partner does not violate a duty or obligation under this [Act] or under the partnership agreement merely because the partner's conduct furthers the partner's own interest.

(f) A partner may lend money to and transact other business with the partnership, and as to each loan or transaction, the rights and obligations of a partner are the same as those of a person who is not a partner, subject to other applicable law. . . .

Comment 1 to §404 questions the applicability of fiduciary concepts to partnership law: "Arguably, the term 'fiduciary' is inappropriate when used to describe the duties of a partner because a partner may legitimately pursue self-interest and not solely the interest of the partnership and the other partners, as must a true trustee." Do you agree?

RUPA's skepticism about fiduciary duties has drawn sharp criticism from some. See Allan Vestal, Fundamental Contractarian Error in the Revised Uniform Partnership Act of 1992, 73 B.U. L. Rev. 523, 535 (1993) ("The Revised Act turns the world upside down with respect to the fiduciary relations of partners inter se. . . . In one stroke of the pen, the drafters have made the parties adversaries, whereas before they were bound by 'the duty of the finest loyalty.' . . ."). Would the result in *Meinhard* be different under RUPA (at least in the absence of any express provision permitting a partner to seize defined business opportunities)?

4. *RUPA's non-waivable duty.* Although RUPA §404(e) permits a partner to pursue the partner's self-interest, RUPA §103 places clear limits on the ability of the partners to diminish the duty of loyalty to any further degree. RUPA §103 provides:

Sec. 103. *Effect of partnership agreement; nonwaivable provisions.* (a). Except as otherwise provided in subsection (b), relations among the partners and between the partners and the partnership are governed by the partnership agreement. To the extent the partnership agreement does not otherwise provide, this [Act] governs relations among the partners and between the partners and the partnership.

(b) The partnership agreement may not:

(1) vary the rights and duties under Section 105 except to eliminate the duty to provide copies of statements to all of the partners;

(2) unreasonably restrict the right of access to books and records under Section 403(b);

(3) eliminate the duty of loyalty under Section 404(b) or 603(b)(3), but;

(i) The partnership agreement may identify specific types or categories of activities that do not violate the duty of loyalty, if not manifestly unreasonable; or

(ii) all of the partners or a number or percentage specified in the partnership agreement may authorize or ratify, after full disclosure of all material facts, a specific act or transaction that otherwise would violate the duty of loyalty;

(4) unreasonably reduce the duty of care under Section 404(c) or 603(b)(3);

(5) eliminate the obligation of good faith and fair dealing under Section 404(d), but the partnership agreement may prescribe the standards by which the performance of the obligation is to be measured, if the standards are not manifestly unreasonable; . . .

What does it mean to say that one may not "unreasonably reduce the duty of care" when §404 proscribes only "grossly negligent or reckless conduct, intentional misconduct, or a knowing violation of law"? Is this limit narrower than Del. Gen. Corp. Law §102(b)(7)'s specification of the extent to which a corporation's articles of incorporation may waive personal liability for violations of the duty of care? See Chapter 2, supra. Would RUPA's insistence that the partnership agreement not "unreasonably restrict the duty of loyalty" suggest that Singer v. Singer, supra, would not be followed in a RUPA jurisdiction? Or would the *Singer* result be covered by §103(b)(3)(i)? What activities could be characterized as "manifestly unreasonable"? This restriction on freedom of contract has drawn criticism of RUPA from scholars who believe that the law should not impose general behavioral standards such as fiduciary duty other than as a default rule, and that the parties should be free to contract around the rule in their particular circumstances. Does it matter whether the default rule imposes a fiduciary duty subject to the parties' agreement, or imposes no standard unless the parties adopt limits? See Larry Ribstein, The Revised Uniform Partnership Act: Not Ready for Prime Time, 49 Bus. Law. 45, 53-54 (1993) ("RUPA perversely attempts to spell out a set of duties that exist in all partnerships under all circumstances. . . . While partners may have a duty to act unselfishly in partnership affairs, RUPA errs in making this duty part of every partnership contract. Partners often do not contract to be strict fiduciaries in the typical agency or trust sense of one who controls the property of another. In other words, partners are not necessarily comparable to directors or executives of publicly-held corporations."). Is this a fair characterization of RUPA?

Query: Consistent with RUPA §103(b)(3)(i) above, can you draft a partnership provision that, if included in the *Meinhard* partnership agreement, would have changed the result in that case?

What result under Delaware RUPA §15-103(f), as amended in 2004: "A partnership may provide for the limitation of any and all liability for breach of contract and breach of duties (including fiduciary duties) of a partner or other person to a partnership or to another partner or to another person that is a party or is otherwise bound by a partnership agreement; provided, that a partnership agreement may not eliminate liability for any act or omission that constitutes a bad faith violation of the implied contract of good faith and fair dealing." See Paul A. Altman & Srinivas M. Raju, Delaware Alternative Entities and the Implied Contractual Covenant of Good Faith and Fair Dealing under Delaware Law, 60 Bus. Law. 1469 (2005).

7. PARTNERSHIP DISSOLUTION

Under UPA §29, "dissolution" is defined as "the change in the relation of the partners caused by any partner ceasing to be associated in the carrying on as distinguished from the winding up of the business." This is consistent with UPA's aggregate theory, under which any departure, death, or retirement produces (at least absent a contrary agreement) a new partnership. However, UPA §30 is quick to point out that on dissolution, "the partnership is not terminated, but continues until the winding up of partnership affairs is completed." The partnership agreement can thus provide for continuing the business on the occurrence of any event that would cause a dissolution and can establish a procedure for valuing the departing partner's share and distributing it (possibly in installments) in a way that does not disrupt the business and is fair to the continuing partners.

Under RUPA, the same terminology is used very differently, and a distinction is drawn between "dissociation" and "dissolution." "Dissolution" now means the termination of the business. RUPA contemplates that on any "dissociation" (which term is broadly defined to include the voluntary withdrawal, death, expulsion, or bankruptcy of a partner), there will be either a buyout of the partner's interest in the firm under Article 7 of RUPA (unless there is a contrary agreement) or a termination and winding up of the business under its Article 8. Basically, despite the new terminology, RUPA does not significantly change the approach of UPA. Thus, in a case of an "at-will" partnership (i.e., one not formed for a specific term), any partner by "dissociating" can force a liquidation of the firm; in a "term" partnership, the partner who departs early cannot force a liquidation if the other partners wish to continue the business.

C. CLOSE CORPORATIONS

There is no universally accepted definition of the term "close corporation." However, six attributes capture the characteristics that create the special problems associated with this form of business organization. First, a close corporation is "owned by a small number of persons. . . ."[7] Second, there is often a high degree of overlap between the shareholders and the managers and employees of the business, as many, if not most, shareholders are actively involved in the business. Third, it is desirable to customize the management structure and corporate governance rules whether because the business is too small to support the cost of formalities or because the overlap of management and ownership make the standard corporate governance structure inappropriate. Fourth, shareholders have little investment liquidity. Fifth, the value of an ownership interest in a close corporation has no readily observable market price, and this difficulty of valuation adds to the illiquidity problem. Sixth, deadlocks may arise because of the

---

7. ALI, Principles of Corporate Governance §1.06 (1994).

relatively small number of shareholders and because shareholders may require a higher-than-majority vote to resolve contested issues.[8]

These characteristics create special problems in the face of standard corporate law rules. The small number of owners and the overlap between owners and managers will often lead to an effort to substitute a minority veto for the majority rule norm of corporate law. Recall from Chapter III that investors with a diversified portfolio care only that the corporation secure the highest return adjusted for risk. If the corporation's activities are too risky for a particular investor, the investor can hold less of the corporation's stock and more of a safer asset such as short-term government bonds. But in many close corporations, the shareholders are not diversified; most of their wealth is invested in the corporation. Under this circumstance, the corporation's decisions affect the shareholder in a more significant way, and individual shareholders will seek a means to protect themselves. The impact is exacerbated because the minority has no access to a market into which they can sell their shares. Thus, a contractual protection may be of considerable importance to them.

But here the organizational cost of the corporate form appears. From a traditional corporate law perspective, explicit protection of minority shareholders may seem to infringe the statutory power of the board of directors to manage the business and affairs of the corporation. As discussed in detail later, this fear of "sterilizing the board" has led some courts to invalidate novel charter provisions or shareholder agreements that seemed to delegate managerial decisions away from the board and to the shareholders.

Use of such minority veto provisions presents a further problem: if the shareholders in a close corporation abandon majority rule and adopt control devices that afford most or all of them certain veto powers or similar protective arrangements, chances greatly increase that a stalemate will sooner or later develop. In these circumstances, the flexibility of partnership law may again seem preferable to the formalism and rigidity of corporate law. Under traditional corporate law doctrines, dissolution may be obtained only under limited, specified conditions, and in any case is considered to be a drastic remedy.[9] But dissolution of a partnership is much simpler and more flexible, the rule being that any partner may at any time dissolve it at will,[10] although, if this action is contrary to specific agreement, that partner is liable to the other partners for damages.[11]

Also, the overlap between shareholders and managers means that the parties have a strong interest in who buys shares of the corporation. Restrictions on transfer, often backed by a right of first refusal to other shareholders before shares can be sold, is a common alternative to the default rule of fully alienable shares. Similarly, the absence of liquidity, difficulty of valuation, and possibility of deadlock combine to require special means for exiting in the face of disagreement among shareholders or the need for a shareholder to sell his or her shares because of personal needs, like the death of a spouse. A common solution is a buy-sell agreement that specifies a formula price.

---

8. See Committee on Corporate Laws, ABA, Section of Business Law, Managing Closely Held Corporations: A Legal Guidebook, 58 Bus. Law. 1077 (2003).

9. See generally, Carlos Israels, The Sacred Cow of Corporate Existence: Problems of Deadlock and Dissolution, 19 U. Chi. L. Rev. 778 (1952).

10. UPA §31; RUPA §601.

11. UPA §38(2); RUPA §602.

This section considers a number of devices and procedures commonly employed by close corporation shareholders to respond to the problem described above: how can the sharp allocations of authority and decisionmaking set out in the corporate statute be softened without sacrificing the benefits, such as limited liability, of the corporate form? The materials in this section explore their availability, validity, and related problems.

The peculiar needs of close corporations were late in being met by courts and legislatures. A typical and classic early judicial view was that "the law never contemplated that persons engaged in business as partners may incorporate, with the intent to obtain the advantages and immunities of a corporate form, and then, Proteus-like, become at will a copartnership or a corporation, as the exigencies or purposes of their joint enterprise may from time to time require. . . . They cannot be partners inter sese and a corporation to the rest of the world."[12] All corporations were subject to the same statutory provisions, designed primarily for publicly held corporations, which were frequently interpreted to forbid special control mechanisms. But this judicial reaction was not uniform and, as stated in a modern decision, there was "a definite, albeit inarticulate, trend toward eventual judicial treatment of the close corporation as sui generis. . . . Where . . . no complaining minority interest appears, no fraud or apparent injury to the public or creditors is present, and no clearly prohibitory statutory language is violated, we can see no valid reason for precluding the parties from reaching any arrangements concerning the management of the corporation which are agreeable to all."[13]

Prodded by scholarly articles,[14] nearly half the states in the past 35 years have enacted statutory provisions designed specifically to authorize certain control mechanisms for close corporations. Some jurisdictions require the corporation to make a formal election in the articles before the provisions apply;[15] others[16] have simply included various sections within their general corporation statutes to assist the special needs of close corporations. As study of the materials will indicate, in some instances a control device may be employed only by corporations that comply with the special statutory provisions; in other instances the close corporation statutory route may be but one of the ways that shareholders may achieve their aims.

A major legislative problem has been defining the close corporation. Among those states that have enacted special legislation for close corporations, a widely accepted definition is that found in New York. A close corporation is defined as any corporation other than a public corporation. Shareholders' agreements that would otherwise be invalid are legitimated for all corporations "so long as no

---

12. Jackson v. Hooper, 76 N.J. Eq. 592, 75 A. 568 (1910).

13. Galler v. Galler, 32 Ill. 2d 16, 203 N.E.2d 577 (1964). But cf. Somers v. AAA Temporary Services, Inc., 5 Ill. App. 2d 931, 284 N.E.2d 462 (1972) (two sole shareholders of corporation could not amend bylaws to reduce number of directors from three to two because statute provided that directors are vested with the power to amend bylaws unless charter reserves this power to shareholders).

14. E.g., Joseph Weiner, Legislative Recognition of the Close Corporation, 27 Mich. L. Rev. 273 (1929); Norman Winer, Proposing a New York "Close Corporation Law," 28 Cornell L.Q. 313 (1943); Edwin Bradley, Toward a More Perfect Close Corporation—The Need for More and Improved Legislation, 54 Geo. L.J. 1145 (1966).

15. Alabama, Arizona, California, Delaware, Illinois, Kansas, Maryland, Pennsylvania, Rhode Island, Texas, and Wisconsin.

16. Florida, Georgia, Maine, Michigan, Minnesota, Montana, New Jersey, New York, North Carolina, Ohio, and South Carolina.

shares of the corporation are listed on a national securities exchange or . . . over-the-counter market. . . ."[17] Similar language is found in the statutes of New York, Ohio, South Carolina, New Jersey, Michigan, Florida, and Georgia. Once the corporation's shares are listed on an exchange or regularly quoted in the over-the-counter market, however, close corporation status terminates, and the agreements are subject to any statutory prohibitions or policies respecting agreements among shareholders of publicly held corporations.

A second approach, adopted in Delaware (and then in Pennsylvania and Kansas), directly defines close corporation by reference to three elements: (1) all of the corporation's issued shares must be held by not more than 30 persons, (2) all of the issued shares must be subject to one or more authorized restrictions on transfer, and (3) the corporation cannot make any "public offering" of its shares within the meaning of the Securities Act of 1933.[18] If these definitional prerequisites are met, close corporation status can be obtained by an amendment to the certificate of incorporation approved by a two-thirds class vote of the shareholders.[19] Termination of close corporation status also requires a two-thirds class vote, although the certificate may require a greater vote.[20] Termination will also result if the corporation no longer satisfies the definition requirements, unless it refuses to register a share transfer that is contrary to authorized restrictions and concurrently so notifies all shareholders and the secretary of state; further, on request of the corporation or any shareholder, the courts may preserve close corporation status by setting aside any transfer of shares that is contrary to the corporation's certificate or by enjoining any public offering.[21]

Another definition, adopted in California, extends close corporation benefits only to corporations whose articles permit no more than 35 shareholders and void any voluntary inter vivos transfer of shares violating this requirement. The articles may be so amended only by affirmative vote of all shareholders. Deletion of such a provision from the articles requires at least a two-thirds class vote (unless the articles authorize a lesser vote). Termination of close corporation status also occurs if the corporation has more than the maximum number of shareholders resulting from share transfers that are not void.[22]

Maryland affords close corporation benefits only to those corporations having statutorily detailed stock transfer restrictions that effectively eliminate general trading of the shares.[23] To obtain close corporation status, all shareholders must approve an amendment to the corporate charter. This status may be terminated (and the statutorily imposed restrictions on transfer avoided) only by a unanimously approved amendment to the charter.[24]

17. N.Y. Bus. Corp. Law §620 (2003).
18. Del. Gen. Corp. Law §342 (2001). For criticism of this definitional approach, see Note, Delaware's Close-Corporation Statute, 63 Nw. U. L. Rev. 230 (1968).
19. Del. Gen. Corp. Law §344 (2001).
20. Id. §§102(b)(4), 346.
21. Id., §348.
22. Cal. Gen. Corp. Law §§158, 418 (1998). Other states with requirements relating to number of shareholders include Arizona (10), Maine (20), Minnesota (35), and Wisconsin (50).
23. Md. Gen. Corp. Law §§4-201, 4-302, 4-501 (2007).
24. Illinois generally follows Maryland's approach for obtaining close corporation status (Ill. Bus. Corp. Act §5/2A.05-2A.60 (2004). This status may be terminated either (1) by an amendment to the articles approved by two-thirds of the shares of each class (unless the articles authorize a greater vote), or (2) when there is a breach of the stock transfer restrictions and neither the corporation nor any shareholder pursues the statutorily designated procedure to remedy it.
      For the view that "allowing termination of close corporation status . . . by a mere two-thirds vote . . .provides a trap for the unwary that can destroy the agreed upon power structure of the

Finally, the Revised Model Business Corporation Act (RMBCA) abandons the effort to define the close corporation as a distinct entity. Instead, RMBCA §7.32 authorizes shareholder agreements that restrict the discretion and power of the board of directors if the agreement is signed by all persons who are shareholders at the time of the agreement (and notice is provided to the corporation). Such an agreement must be "noted conspicuously" on the corporation's share certificate, although a failure to provide such notification does not invalidate the agreement, but only gives incoming shareholders a right to rescission (RMBCA §7.32(c)). However, RMBCA §7.32(d) provides that such an agreement "shall cease to be effective when shares of the corporation are listed on a national securities exchange or regularly traded in a market maintained by one or more members of a national or affiliated securities association." In net effect, the same flexibility is available as under special close corporation statutes, but there is no need to "opt in" to a special statutory regime.

1. RESTRICTIONS ON TRANSFER OF SHARES

The principal reasons why shareholders in a close corporation wish to exercise control over the transfer of shares are to enable them to determine the identity of those with whom they must work on a daily and intimate basis and to prevent the entry of persons (such as competitors) who may be hostile to the corporation's best interests. They may also desire to avoid major shifts in the existing distribution of power among the present shareholders or to prevent some shareholder from effecting a transfer that would make the corporation ineligible for statutory close corporation benefits or Subchapter S tax status. Corporations with more than a handful of shareholders may also have reasons for placing certain limitations on the transfer of shares — e.g., it may be commercially desirable to restrict ownership to employees,[25] consumers of the corporation's product,[26] or persons

---

close corporation just at the time it is most needed to protect the minority," see Robert Kessler, The ABA Close Corporation Statute, 36 Mercer L. Rev. 661 (1985).

For the view that "a modern general incorporation statute, rather than a close corporation law supposedly tailored to meet its special needs, better serves the close corporation," see Dennis Karjala, A Second Look at Special Close Corporation Legislation, 58 Tex. L. Rev. 1207 (1980). See also Dennis Karjala, An Analysis of Close Corporation Legislation in the United States, 21 Ariz. St. L.J. 663 (1989): "[T]he legislative trend [of special close corporation statutes] has continued as predicted, but if anything the arguments against special legislation are even stronger. . . . [A]doption of these statutes seems justified only . . . where the courts have been and remain intransigent to the needs of close corporations."

25. Many decisions have upheld restrictions providing that the corporation may purchase the shares of employees who are no longer such. See Lawson v. Household Finance Corp., 17 Del. Ch. 343, 152 A.723 (S. Ct. 1930) (corporation had 800 employees with almost all voting shares owned by "officers, directors and employees and their families, and by a few other persons who are thought to be of direct value to the corporation by reason of influence, position or peculiar knowledge"); Palmer v. Chamberlin, 191 F.2d 532 (5th Cir. 1951) (corporation had 151 shareholders who were all directors, officers, or employees); Martin v. Graybar Electric Co., 285 F.2d 619 (7th Cir. 1961) (2,403 employees and pensioners had resold shares to corporation over 30-year period); Ryan v. J. Walter Thompson Co., 322 F. Supp. 307 (S.D.N.Y. 1971) (corporation that was "the largest advertising agency in the world" was wholly owned by employees). For critical discussion, see Note, Exercising Options to Repurchase Employee-Held Stock: A Question of Good Faith, 68 Yale L.J. 773 (1959).

26. This is particularly applicable to various kinds of "cooperative" business corporations. See the *Allen* case, infra, and the *Penthouse Properties* case discussed therein and in the *Rafe* case, infra.

living within the community;[27] the corporation may wish to protect against resale of "privately placed" shares with consequent loss of the "private offering" exemption under the Securities Act of 1933.[28] Reciprocally, shareholders may seek to ensure their own financial flexibility through a buyout provision that gives them the right to sell their shares back to the corporation or its share-holders on the occurrence of a designated event (e.g., death, disability, termi-nation of employment).

Transfer restrictions (as well as buyout provisions) may take many forms. The most severe impose absolute prohibition against the disposition of shares, require the consent of the directors or shareholders for transfer, or restrict transfer to designated groups of persons. The most common is the "right of first refusal," which grants the corporation and/or the remaining shareholders (often pro rata) — or first the corporation and then the remaining shareholders — a first option to buy the shares of a shareholder who wishes to sell (or dies, becomes disabled, leaves the corporation's employ, etc.). Although courts initially tended to view all transfer restrictions with skepticism[29] (and have usually invalidated absolute prohibitions that are unlimited in time),[30] the modern judicial and legislative treatment has been more sympathetic.

Allen v. Biltmore Tissue Corp.
2 N.Y.2d 534, 141 N.E.2d 812, 161 N.Y.S.2d 418 (1957)

FULD, J.: . . . Biltmore Tissue Corporation was organized . . . in 1932, with an authorized capitalization of 1,000 shares without par value, to manufacture and deal in paper and paper products. The by-laws, adopted by the incorporators-directors, contain provisions limiting the number of shares (originally 5, later 20) available to each stockholder (§28) and restricting stock transfers both during the life of the stockholder and in case of his death (§§29, 30). Whenever a stock-holder desires to sell or transfer his shares, he must, according to one by-law (§29), give the corporation or other stockholders "an opportunity to repurchase the stock at the price that was paid for the same to the Corporation at the time the Corpo-ration issued the stock"; if, however, the option is not exercised, "then, after the lapse of [90] days, the stock may be sold by the holder to such person and under such circumstances as he sees fit." The by-law, dealing with the transfer of stock upon the death of a stockholder (§30) — the provision with which we are here concerned — is almost identical. . . .

Harry Kaplan, a paper jobber, was one of Biltmore's customers and some months after its incorporation purchased 5 shares of stock from the corporation at $5 a share. In 1936, Kaplan received a stock dividend of 5 more shares, and two years later purchased an additional 10 shares for $100. On the face of each of the three certificates, running vertically along the left-hand margin, appeared the legend,

"Issued subject to restrictions in sections 28, 29, and 30 of the Bylaws." . . .

---

27. See Wright v. Iredell Tel. Co., 182 N.C. 308, 108 S.E. 744 (1921) (locally owned and operated independent telephone company).
28. See Swenson v. Engelstad, 626 F.2d 421 (5th Cir. 1980).
29. See, e.g., Victor G. Bloede Co. v. Bloede, 84 Md. 129, 34 A, 1127 (1896), and cases cited therein.
30. See cases cited in Annots., 65 A.L.R. 1159, 1165 (1930); 61 A.L.R.2d 1318, 1322 (1958).

[On Kaplan's death], Biltmore's board of directors voted to exercise its option to purchase the stock, pursuant to section 30 of the by-laws, and about three weeks later the executors' attorney was advised of the corporation's action. He was also informed that, although the by-law provision permitted purchase at "the same price that the company received therefor from the stockholder originally," the corporation had, nevertheless, decided to pay $20 a share, "considerably more than the original purchase price," based on the prices at which it had acquired shares from other stockholders.

Kaplan's executors declined to sell to the corporation, insisting that the stock which had been in the decedent's name be transferred to them. When their demand was refused, they brought this action to compel Biltmore to accept surrender of the decedent's stock certificate and to issue a new certificate for 20 shares to them. They contended . . . that the by-law is void as an unreasonable restraint.

The corporation interposed a counterclaim for specific performance based on the exercise of its option to purchase the shares under by-law section 30. The court at Special Term granted judgment to the corporation on its counterclaim and dismissed the complaint. The Appellate Division reversed, rendered judgment directing the transfer of the stock to the plaintiffs and dismissed the defendant's counterclaim upon the ground that the by-law in question is void.[31] . . .

The validity of qualifications on the ownership of corporate shares through restrictions on the right to transfer has long been a source of confusion in the law. The difficulties arise primarily from the clash between the concept of the shares as "creatures of the company's constitution and therefore . . . essentially contractual choses in action" . . . and the concept of the shares as personal property represented so far as possible by the certificate itself and, therefore, subject to the time-honored rule that there be no unreasonable restraint upon alienation. While the courts of this state and of many other jurisdictions, as opposed to those of England and of Massachusetts, . . . have favored the "property" concept, . . . the tendency is . . . to sustain a restriction imposed on the transfer of stock if "reasonable" and if the stockholder acquired such stock with requisite notice of the restriction.

The question posed, therefore, is whether the provision, according the corporation a right or first option to purchase the stock at the price which it originally received for it, amounts to an unreasonable restraint. In our judgment, it does not.

The courts have almost uniformly held valid and enforceable the first option provision, in charter or by-law, whereby a shareholder desirous of selling his stock is required to afford the corporation, his fellow stockholders or both an opportunity to buy it before he is free to offer it to outsiders. . . . The courts have often said that this first option provision is "in the nature of a contract" between the corporation and its stockholders and, as such, binding upon them. . . . And in the

---

31. That court reasoned that Biltmore's "stock consisting of 5,538 shares is apparently held by many persons, because section 28 of its bylaws provides that no individual or corporation is entitled to hold more than 20 shares. There is no perceptible relationship between the restriction and the welfare of the corporation. The restriction serves to prohibit the sale of the stock." 1 App. Div. 2d 599, 153 N.Y.S.2d 779. — ED.

Penthouse Properties case, 256 App. Div. 685, 690-691, 11 N.Y.S.2d 417, 422, the court declared that

> The general rule that ownership of property cannot exist in one person and the right of alienation in another . . . has in this State been frequently applied to shares of corporate stock . . . and cognizance has been taken of the principle that "the right of transfer is a right of property, and if another has the arbitrary power to forbid a transfer of property by the owner that amounts to annihilation of property." . . . But restrictions against the sale of shares of stock, unless other stockholders or the corporation have first been accorded an opportunity to buy, are not repugnant to that principle. . . . The weight of authority elsewhere is to the same effect.[2]

As the cases thus make clear, what the law condemns is not a *restriction* on transfer, a provision merely postponing sale during the option period, but an effective *prohibition* against transferability itself. Accordingly, if the by-law under consideration were to be construed as rendering the sale of the stock impossible to anyone except to the corporation at whatever price it wished to pay, we would, of course, strike it down as illegal. But that is not the meaning of the provision before us. The corporation had its option only for a 90-day period. If it did not exercise its privilege within that time, the deceased stockholder's legal representative was at liberty to "dispose of said stock as he [saw] fit" (§30), and, once so disposed of, it would thereafter be free of the restriction. In a very real sense, therefore, the primary purpose of the by-laws was to enable a particular party, the corporation, to buy the shares, not to prevent the other party, the stockholder, from selling them. . . .

The Appellate Division, however, was impressed with what it deemed the "unreasonableness," that is, "unfairness," of the price specified in the by-law, namely, a price at which the shares had originally been purchased from the corporation. Carried to its logical conclusion, such a rationale would permit, indeed, would encourage, expensive litigation in every case where the price specified in the restriction, or the formula for fixing the price, was other than a recognized and easily ascertainable fair market value. This would destroy part of the social utility of the first option type of restriction which, when imposed, is intended to operate in futuro and must, therefore, include some formula for future determination of the option price.

Generally speaking, these restrictions are employed by the so-called "close corporation" as part of the attempt to equate the corporate structure to a partnership by giving the original stockholders a sort of pre-emptive right through which they may, if they choose, veto the admission of a new participant. . . . Obviously, the case where there is an easily ascertainable market value for the shares of a closely held corporate enterprise is the exception, not the rule, and, consequently, various methods or formulae for fixing the option price are employed in practice — e.g., book or appraisal value, often exclusive of good will, see, e.g., Lawson v. Household Finance Corp., 17 Del. Ch. 343, 152 A. 723, affirming 17 Del. Ch. 1, 147 A. 312, Doss v. Yingling, 95 Ind. App. 494, 172 N.E. 801, or a fixed price, Scruggs v. Cotterill, 67 App. Div. 583, 73 N.Y.S. 882, or the par value of the stock. See, e.g.,

---

2. The court went further in the *Penthouse Properties* case than we are called upon to go here; in view of the special purposes of a corporation owning a cooperative apartment house, it sustained a restriction actually requiring the "consent" of the directors to a proposed transfer. . . . The present case involves no such "consent" restriction.

Boston Safe Dep. & Tr. Co. v. North Attleborough Chapt. of American Red Cross, 330 Mass. 114, 111 N.E.2d 447. . . .

In sum, then, the validity of the restriction on transfer does not rest on any abstract notion of intrinsic fairness of price. To be invalid, more than mere disparity between option price and current value of the stock must be shown. . . . Since the parties have in effect agreed on a price formula which suited them, and provision is made freeing the stock for outside sale should the corporation notmake, or provide for, the purchase, the restriction is reasonable and valid. . . .

Judgment of Appellate Division reversed and that of Special Term reinstated. . . .

---

1. In Rafe v. Hindin, 29 App. Div. 2d 481, 288 N.Y.S.2d 662, *aff'd*, 23 N.Y.2d 759, 244 N.E.2d 469, 296 N.Y.S.2d 955 (1968), the court considered a restriction that prevented one shareholder in a close corporation from selling his shares unless the other shareholder approved. Unlike in Allen v. Biltmore Tissue Corp., the restriction was more than a right of first refusal. In *Rafe*, if the non-selling shareholder objected to the sale but declined to purchase the proffered shares, the shares could not be sold at all — the shareholder was frozen in. The court held the restriction was an unreasonable restraint on alienation because a shareholder's approval could be unreasonably withheld; if the contract had provided that approval could not be "unreasonably withheld," the court would have allowed it.

2. *Price disparity.* (a) Several modern decisions accord with the *Allen* court's view that "more than mere disparity between option price and current value" must be shown to invalidate a transfer restriction. See Jones v. Harris, 63 Wash. 2d 559, 388 P.2d 539 (1964) ($26,000 option price for 10 percent interest that had current value of $92,000); In re Mather's Estate, 410 Pa. 361, 189 A.2d 586 (1963) (option price of $1 per share enforced when each share had current value of over $1,000), noted, 48 Minn. L. Rev. 808 (1964); Renberg v. Zarrow, 667 P.2d 465 (Okla. 1983) (option price of $3,500 enforced when each share had alleged current value of $31,300; "under the actuarial tables in effect at the time . . . [complainant's deceased wife] stood to gain most"). But compare Systematics, Inc. v. Mitchell, 253 Ark. 848, 491 S.W.2d 40 (1973), holding violative of Ark. Bus. Corp. Act §211 (1965) — authorizing transfer restrictions "at a fair price" in the articles or bylaws — an option price set at the amount paid for the shares by purchasing employees but which was only 20 percent of the market value of the shares at the time the corporation sought to exercise the option.[32] Of what consequence is the fact that when the option price was established it was concededly "fair" or "unfair"? See 49 Va. L. Rev. 1211 (1963); In re Estate of Weinsaft, 647 S.W.2d 179 (Mo. App. 1983). Or that the option price was deliberately set at a low figure because the corporation did not wish to be burdened with a large financial obligation in order to repurchase the shares?[33] At what point does a restriction become a prohibition?

---

32. After the *Systematics* decision, the statute was amended to provide that "any price, or formula for determining the price, set by . . . [a "written contract or written agreement"] shall be deemed to be a fair price." Ark. Bus. Corp. Act §601(c) (1973). See 27 Ark. L. Rev. 554 (1973).

33. For discussion of various devices, including insurance, to provide the option holder with funds for payment of the option price, see 1 F. Hodge O'Neal & Robert B. Thompson, O'Neal's Close Corporations: Law and Practice §7.45 (rev. 3d ed. 2004).

(b) How would the *Allen* court have decided the *Rafe* case? As a practical matter, could it more accurately be said in *Allen* than in *Rafe* that the option was only "a *restriction* on transfer, a provision merely postponing sale during the option period, [not] an effective *prohibition* against transferability itself"?

3. *Statutes.* A large number of states have enacted detailed statutory provisions dealing with transfer restrictions and buyout provisions. The following is one such provision.

Delaware General Corporation Law (2001)

Sec. 202. *Restriction on transfer of securities.* (a) A written restriction or restrictions on the transfer or registration of transfer of a security of a corporation, or on the amount of the corporation's securities that may be owned by any person or group of persons, if permitted by this section and noted conspicuously on the certificate or certificates representing the security or securities so restricted or, in the case of uncertificated shares, contained in the notice or notices sent pursuant to §151(f) of this title, may be enforced against the holder of the restricted security or securities or any successor or transferee of the holder including an executor, administrator, trustee, guardian or other fiduciary entrusted with like responsibility for the person or estate of the holder. Unless noted conspicuously on the certificate or certificates representing the security or securities so restricted or, in the case of uncertificated shares, contained in the notice or notices sent pursuant to §151(f) of this title, a restriction, even though permitted by this section, is ineffective except against a person with actual knowledge of the restriction.[34]

(b) A restriction on the transfer or registration of transfer of securities of a corporation, or on the amount of a corporation's securities that may be owned by any person or group of persons, may be imposed by the certificate of incorporation or by the bylaws or by an agreement among any number of security holders or among such holders and the corporation.[35] No restrictions so imposed shall be binding with respect to securities issued prior to the adoption of the restriction unless the holders of the securities are parties to an agreement or voted in favor of the restriction.[36]

(c) A restriction on the transfer or registration of transfer of securities of a corporation or on the amount of such securities that may be owned by any person or group of persons is permitted by this section if it:

(1) Obligates the holder of the restricted securities to offer to the corporation or to any other holders of securities of the corporation or to any other person or

---

34. The language of the "notice" provision is similar to that of Uniform Commercial Code §8-204, effective in all states. The Official Comment "makes clear that the restriction need not be set forth in full text. See Allen v. Biltmore Tissue Corporation, 2 N.Y.2d 534, 141 N.E.2d 812 (1957)." — ED.

35. Some decisions, interpreting statutes that authorized the articles of incorporation to provide for transfer restrictions in the bylaws, have invalidated otherwise permissible restrictions because they appeared in the bylaws and there was no such authorization in the articles. See, e.g., Carlson v. Ringgold County Mutual Telephone Co., 252 Iowa 748, 108 N.W.2d 478 (1961). — ED.

36. Should a transfer restriction be enforced against a shareholder who voted against the bylaw imposing the restriction? Or is the right of transferability too "basic" to be withdrawn without consent? Of what significance is the formula for determining the option price? See B & H Warehouse, Inc. v. Atlas Van Lines, Inc., 490 F.2d 818 (5th Cir. 1974). See generally William Painter, Stock Transfer Restrictions: Continuing Uncertainties and a Legislative Proposal, 6 Vill. L. Rev. 48 (1960); John McNulty, Corporations and the Intertemporal Conflict of Laws, 55 Cal. L. Rev. 12 (1967). — ED.

to any combination of the foregoing, a prior opportunity, to be exercised within a reasonable time, to acquire the restricted securities; or

(2) Obligates the corporation or any holder of securities of the corporation or any other person or any combination of the foregoing, to purchase the securities which are the subject of an agreement respecting the purchase and sale of the restricted securities; or

(3) Requires the corporation or the holders of any class or series of securities of the corporation to consent to any proposed transfer of the restricted securities or to approve the proposed transferee of the restricted securities, or to approve the amount of securities of the corporation that may be owned by any person or group of persons; or

(4) Obligates the holder of the restricted securities to sell or transfer an amount of restricted securities to the corporation or to any other holders of securities of the corporation or to any other person or to any combination of the foregoing, or causes or results in the automatic sale or transfer of an amount of restricted securities to the corporation or to any other holders of securities of the corporation or to any other person or to any combination of the foregoing; or

(5) Prohibits or restricts the transfer of the restricted securities to, or the ownership of restricted securities by, designated persons or classes of persons or groups of persons, and such designation is not manifestly unreasonable.

(d) Any restriction on the transfer or the registration of transfer of the securities of a corporation, or on the amount of securities of a corporation that may be owned by a person or group of persons, for any of the following purposes shall be conclusively presumed to be for a reasonable purpose:

(1) Maintaining any local, state, federal or foreign tax advantage to the corporation or its stockholders, including without limitation:

a. Maintaining the corporation's status as an electing small business corporation under subchapter S of the United States Internal Revenue Code [26 U.S.C.A. §1371 et seq.], or

b. Maintaining or preserving any tax attribute (including without limitation net operating losses), or

c. Qualifying or maintaining the qualification of the corporation as a real estate investment trust pursuant to the United States Internal Revenue Code or regulations adopted pursuant to the United States Internal Revenue Code, or

(2) Maintaining any statutory or regulatory advantage or complying with any statutory or regulatory requirements under applicable local, state, federal or foreign law.

(e) Any other lawful restriction on transfer or registration of transfer of securities, or on the amount of securities that may be owned by any person or group of persons, is permitted by this section.

Sec. 349. *Corporate option where a restriction on transfer of a security is held invalid.* If a restriction on transfer of a security of a close corporation is held not to be authorized by §202 of this title, the corporation shall nevertheless have an option, for a period of thirty days after the judgment setting aside the restriction becomes final, to acquire the restricted security at a price which is agreed upon by the parties, or if no agreement is reached as to price, then at the fair value as determined by the Court of Chancery. In order to determine fair value, the Court may appoint an appraiser to receive evidence and report to the Court his findings and recommendation as to fair value.[37]

---

4. *Consent restrictions.* Under the Delaware statute, of what significance would it be in the *Rafe* case if the consent of the non-selling shareholder could (or could not) be unreasonably withheld?

> Does the Delaware statute mean what it says, that a "consent" restriction may be imposed, or will a "good faith" or "reasonable" qualification be read into the liberal grant of permission? No convincing reason exists why the parties should not be allowed to agree to give each other an absolute, arbitrary control over associates. In the absence of legislative clarity, the Delaware statute should be read by the courts as permitting close corporation stockholders to reject a proposed transferee without any possibility of judicial review of the purity of their motives. If the parties find this arrangement unpalatable, they should be permitted to plan accordingly. Lesser restrictions, including buy-sell agreements and dissolution power, are possible devices available to them.

Edwin Bradley, A Comparative Evaluation of the Delaware and Maryland Close Corporation Statutes, 1968 Duke L.J. 525, 541. Compare Quinn v. Stuart Lakes Club, Inc., 57 N.Y.2d 1003, 443 N.E.2d 945, 457 N.Y.S.2d 471 (1982) (requirement that deceased owner's shares be returned to corporation held void as against public policy).

5. *Close corporation buyout.* A common form of a close corporation buyout arrangement tries to avoid the risk that one shareholder might try to take advantage of another should the shareholder want to get out. In this arrangement, one shareholder triggers the process by naming a price. The other shareholder then has the choice to buy or to sell at that price. When is this arrangement preferable to a right of first refusal?

6. *Reasonableness of restraints.*

> Factors which courts have considered, in the absence of a controlling statute, in determining whether restrictions are reasonable include the following: the size of the corporation, the degree of restraint on the power to alienate, the length of time the restriction is to remain in effect, the method to be used in determining the transfer or option price of shares subject to the restraint, the fairness or unfairness of the procedure used to adopt the restriction, the likelihood of its contributing to the attainment of corporate objectives, the possibility that a hostile shareholder would seriously injure the corporation, and the likelihood that the restriction will promote the best interests of the enterprise as a whole. The underlying test seems to be whether the restraint is sufficiently needed by the particular enterprise to justify overriding the general policy against restraints on alienation. The courts are usually more willing to sustain stock transfer restrictions in corporations where ownership and control are in a few persons than they are in widely held enterprises.

---

37. Rev. Model Bus. Corp. Act §6.27 follows the Delaware pattern, as do about one-third of the states. — ED.

2 F. Hodge O'Neal and Robert B. Thompson, O'Neal's Close Corporations: Law and Practice §7.7 (rev. 3d ed. 2004).[38]

7. *Rights of first refusal.* As the court in *Allen* stated, "courts have almost uniformly held valid and enforceable the first option provision . . . whereby a shareholder desirous of selling his stock is required to afford the corporation, his fellow shareholders or both an opportunity to buy it before he is free to offer it to outsiders. . . ." This latitude may arise from the assumption that such a right of first refusal, especially if it is at the same price as offered by a third party, does not hurt the selling shareholder. But is this assumption accurate? Suppose you are deciding whether to make an offer for stock that is subject to a right of first refusal. If your offer is for less than the stock is worth, the other shareholders will exercise their right and take advantage of the bargain. But if your offer is for more than the stock is worth, the other shareholders will allow you to buy the shares. If it is costly for you to study the corporation and value the stock before making an offer, will you bear the expense if your offer is successful only when the other shareholders think you are overpaying? If this is correct, is a right of first refusal a restriction or a prohibition? See Marcel Kahan, An Economic Analysis of Rights of First Refusal (June 1999), N.Y.U., Center for Law and Business, Working Paper No. 99-009, available at http://ssrn.com/abstract=11382.

2. SPECIAL AGREEMENTS ALLOCATING AUTHORITY

Many methods exist by which close corporation shareholders may assure themselves some effective role in the fashioning and execution of corporate policy that might not be possible without some modification of standard governance rules. Frequently, the goal is simply to obtain representation on the board of directors. A system of cumulative voting — considered at page 598 supra and sometimes utilized in publicly held corporations as well — is one accepted means of modifying the orthodox rule that the owners of a majority of the shares elect the entire board, its success depending on the percentage of shares owned and number of directors to be elected.

Another way of regulating director election is to create more than one class of shares, each with different rights.[39] For example, if *A* (the contributor of 75 percent of the corporation's capital) and *B* (the contributor of 25 percent) wish to have equal control, they might cause the corporation to issue 100 shares with voting

---

38. For modern decisions articulating the "particularized corporate needs" approach, see In re West Waterway Lumber Co., 59 Wash. 2d 310, 317-318, 367 P.2d 807, 811-812 (1962); State v. Clarks Hill Tel. Co., 139 Ind. App. 507, 512, 218 N.E.2d 154, 157 (1966); Ling & Co. v. Trinity Sav. & Loan Ass'n, 482 S.W.2d 841 (Tex. 1972); Fayard v. Fayard, 293 So. 2d 421 (Miss. 1974) ("consent restraint" reasonable in family corporation when used to prohibit transfers to non-family members); Gray v. Harris Land & Cattle Co., 737 P.2d 475 (Mont. 1987) (consent restriction). But see Goldblum v. Boyd, 341 So. 2d 436 (La. App. 1976) (restriction unreasonable); Grynberg v. Burke, 378 A.2d 139 (Del. Ch. 1977) (Del. §202 validates only restriction that "bears some reasonably necessary relation to the best interests of the corporation"). Compare Kerrigan v. Merrill Lynch, Pierce, Fenner & Smith, 450 F. Supp. 639 (S.D.N.Y. 1978) (Del. §202(c) "removes the need for a specific showing of a business purpose").

39. Note, however, that to qualify for Subchapter S tax status, corporations may not have more than one class of shares. Although I.R.C. §1361(c)(4) provides that "a corporation shall not be treated as having more than one class of stock solely because there are differences in voting rights among the shares," in Paige v. United States, 580 F.2d 960 (9th Cir. 1978), the court held that Subchapter S status is lost if shares have different rights in the earnings or assets of the corporation, even though these differences are imposed by state law and the corporation's articles state that shares have equal rights.

rights (50 each to *A* and *B*) and 100 non-voting shares but with full proprietary rights (to *A*). Or the corporation might issue 100 shares with full voting and proprietary rights (75 to *A* and 25 to *B*) and 50 shares (to *B*) having voting rights only.[40] Or the corporation might issue 75 Class A shares (to *A*) and 25 Class B shares (to *B*), all shares having identical proprietary rights but each class having the power to elect half of the corporation's directors.

Classification of shares affords greater certainty for control arrangements than does cumulative voting, but the legal status of shares with different voting rights is somewhat less secure. Although all states authorize the creation of more than one class of shares[41] and a number specifically permit classification for board elections,[42] the policy against separation of ownership from control has led several states to prohibit or disfavor non-voting shares. And if, as discussed below, the close corporation shareholders seek to use non-voting shares to apportion control over specific corporate actions beyond election of the board, they may run afoul of numerous state statutes guaranteeing shareholders the right to vote on certain specific matters despite the fact that the shares generally are non-voting.[43]

How can such restrictions on the parties' freedom to contract be justified? Is there a public interest in constraining control arrangements? Are there similar restrictions on purely contractual arrangements? If not, what is special about conducting a business in the corporate form?

There are additional devices, to be explored in greater detail in this section, that close corporation shareholders may employ to regulate the election of directors. They may execute a voting agreement, which may also be placed in the charter or bylaws, specifying who the directors are to be or the procedure by which shares are to be voted. Or they may enact a charter or bylaw provision requiring a unanimous or greater than majority vote for the election of directors, thus giving minority shareholders the power to block various nominees. A more formal mechanism to achieve these ends is the creation of a voting trust, a device also occasionally used in larger corporations.

Close corporation shareholders, as indicated, may also wish to control detailed policies such as designation of officers and employees, setting of salaries, payment of dividends, and establishment of procedures to resolve corporate disputes. Or they may simply want a veto power over all important corporate decisions. They may seek to accommodate these desires through particular terms in a shareholders' agreement or by combining a device that assures them board representation with a high quorum or vote requirement for board action. These methods will also be addressed in the materials that follow.

a. Shareholder Agreements Respecting Election of Directors

Devices of this type may be roughly placed into two categories. One — commonly referred to as pooling agreements and illustrated infra in the *Ringling* case — involves

---

40. This type of stock classification has been approved for a close corporation in Lehrman v. Cohen, 43 Del. Ch. 222, 222 A.2d 800 (Sup. Ct. 1966), and for a public corporation in Stroh v. Blackhawk Holding Corp., 48 Ill. 2d 471, 272 N.E.2d 1 (1971).

41. See, e.g., Rev. Model Bus. Corp. Act §6.01.

42. See, e.g., N.J. Bus. Corp. Act 14A:7-2 (1998).

43. See, e.g., Rev. Model Bus. Corp. Act §10.04(d). See also Hampton v. Tri-State Finance Corp., 30 Colo. App. 420, 495 P.2d 566 (1972).

two or more shareholders, each ordinarily owning a minority interest but together usually controlling a majority of the shares, who agree to cast their votes as a unit, either for designated persons or for candidates to be agreed on by the parties before the election. The other concerns one or more shareholders, often owning a majority interest, effectively giving up some of their voting strength to others. This usually takes the form of the shareholders agreeing to vote their shares so as to ensure the election of a certain number of directors designated by the other party; such conduct may be prompted by the other party's contributing needed capital to the corporation, or by the other party's offering a direct financial inducement to the voting shareholder (commonly referred to as vote selling), or simply by the shareholder being persuaded by the other party that the latter should vote the former's shares. Apart from the election of directors, all of these mechanisms may also be used in respect to other matters (such as amendment of the articles, merger, dissolution) that normally require a shareholder vote.

> The early decisions almost invariably held a challenged voting agreement to be invalid. In deciding those cases, the courts usually laid down broad statements of policy that would invalidate any voting arrangement. Some of the decisions, mostly decided before 1910, indicated that there could be no agreement, or any device whatsoever, by which the voting power of stock was irrevocably separated from the ownership of the stock, at least as long as the power to vote was not coupled with some interest in the stock. The power to vote was treated as inherently annexed to, and inseparable from, the ownership of the shares. Further, the shareholders were considered to have contracted for each other's independent advice and judgment at shareholders' meetings. Thus, each shareholder owed to his fellow shareholders a duty to vote his shares in what he conceived to be the best interests of the corporation, and the other shareholders were thought to have a right to insist that he exercise his independent judgment in casting his vote.[44]

Shareholder agreements that allocate the power to designate directors by means other than voting are now routinely approved. In E.K. Buck Retail Stores v. Harkert, 157 Neb. 867, 62 N.W.2d. 288 (1954), the plaintiff canceled a debt to the corporation and provided an equivalent amount of new capital in return for 40 percent of the corporation's shares and the right to name two of the four directors. The agreement compelled the shareholders to vote their shares to achieve this result. In the face of a claim that any alteration of the corporate statute's control provisions is void as against public policy, the court treated the statute's provisions as a default rule that can be altered by contract: "We think the correct rule is that stockholders' control agreements are valid where it is for the benefit of the corporation, where it works no fraud upon creditors or other stockholders, and where it violates no statute or recognized public policy."

Unanimous or high-vote requirements. Parties seeking to allocate directors among shareholders other than by majority vote might also attempt to achieve their goal via a shareholders' agreement (or bylaw or charter provision) that no directors may be elected unless they receive a unanimous vote (or something greater than a majority). These have been upheld in several cases, e.g., Roland Park Shopping Center, Inc. v. Hendler, 206 Md. 10, 109 A.2d 753 (1954); Katcher v. Ohsman, 26 N.J.

---

44. 1 F. Hodge O'Neal and Robert B. Thompson, O'Neal's Close Corporations: Law and Practice §5.4 (Rev. 3d ed. 2004). — Ed.

Super. 28, 97 A.2d 180 (Ch. 1953). But in Benintendi v. Kenton Hotel, Inc., 294 N.Y. 112, 60 N.E.2d 829 (1945), such a provision was declared invalid on the ground that it contravened a New York statute providing that directors shall be chosen by a plurality of the votes. Presently, nearly all states, including New York, N.Y. Bus. Corp. Law §616 (1998), have statutes that authorize corporations to set high-quorum as well as high-vote requirements for shareholder meetings.

Revised Model Business Corporation Act (1984)

Sec. 7.27. *Greater quorum or voting requirements.* (a) The articles of incorporation may provide for a greater quorum or voting requirement for shareholders (or voting groups of shareholders) than is provided for by this Act.

(b) An amendment to the articles of incorporation that adds, changes, or deletes a greater quorum or voting requirement must meet the same quorum requirement and be adopted by the same vote and voting groups required to take action under the quorum and voting requirements then in effect or proposed to be adopted, whichever is greater.

Ringling v. Ringling Bros.-Barnum & Bailey Combined Shows, Inc.
29 Del. Ch. 318, 49 A.2d 603 (Ch. 1946), *on appeal*, 29 Del. Ch. 610, 53 A.2d 441 (S. Ct. 1947)

[Defendant Ringling Bros.–Barnum & Bailey Combined Shows, Inc., a corporation which operated the famous circus, had 1,000 issued shares, owned 315 by petitioner Mrs. Edith Conway Ringling, 315 by defendant Mrs. Aubrey B. Haley (formerly Mrs. Aubrey B. Ringling), and 370 by defendant Mr. John Ringling North. In 1941, Ringling and Haley executed the following Agreement respecting their shares:]

NOW, THEREFORE, in consideration of the mutual covenants and agreements here-inafter contained the parties hereto agree as follows:

1. Neither party will sell . . . to any other person whomsoever, without first making a written offer to the other party hereto . . . for the same price and upon the same terms and conditions as in such proposed sale, and allowing such other party a time of not less than 180 days from the date of such written offer within which to accept same.

2. In exercising any voting rights . . . each party will consult and confer with the other and the parties will act jointly in exercising such voting rights in accordance with such agreement as they may reach with respect to any matter calling for the exercise of such voting rights.

3. In the event the parties fail to agree with respect to any matter covered by paragraph 2 above, the question in disagreement shall be submitted for arbitration to Karl D. Loos, of Washington, D.C., as arbitrator and his decision thereon shall be binding upon the parties hereto. Such arbitration shall be exercised to the end of assuring for the respective corporation's good management and such participation therein by the members of the Ringling family as the experience, capacity and ability of each may warrant. The parties may at any time by written agreement designate any other individual to act as arbitrator in lieu of said Loos. . . .

5. This agreement shall be in effect from the date hereof and shall continue in effect for a period of ten years unless sooner terminated by mutual agreement in writing by the parties hereto. . . .

7. This agreement shall be binding upon and inure to the benefit of the heirs, executors, administrators and assigns of the parties hereto respectively.

[Until 1945, the parties, acting pursuant to the Agreement and by cumulative voting, elected five of the seven directors (Ringling and her son, Haley and her husband, and a Mr. Dunn) to the corporation's board.[45] On their failure to agree on a fifth director for the 1946 election, Loos (who had been their attorney for some years) was called on by Ringling "to arbitrate the disagreement." Loos directed that they vote their shares for an adjournment. When Haley refused, Loos directed Ringling to cast 882 votes for herself, 882 for her son, and 441 for Dunn. Ringling complied. Loos directed that Haley cast 882 votes for herself, 882 for her husband, and 441 for Dunn. Instead, Haley voted 1103 for herself and 1102 for her husband. North voted 864 for a Mr. Woods, 863 for a Mr. Griffin, and 863 for himself. The chairman ruled that Loos's five candidates and Woods and North had been elected. Since Haley and North disputed this ruling, Ringling filed suit.]

SEITZ, Vice Chancellor [in the Court of Chancery]: . . . It is at once apparent that the right of Loos to direct the voting of the stock of the parties to the Agreement is the crucial point for decision. The determination of this point depends upon the answer to the broader question of the legality of the Memorandum of Agreement dated September 15, 1941, under which he purported to operate. . . .

Do we have here only "an agreement to agree," by which defendants mean that there exists no legally enforceable obligation?

Preliminarily, I think it clear that the mutual promises contained in the Agreement constitute sufficient consideration to support it. The mutual restraints on the actions of the parties with respect to the sale and voting of their stock comply with the consideration requirements of contract law.[46]

Did the parties only agree to agree? Certainly the parties agreed to agree as to how they would vote their stock, but they also provided that they would be bound by the decision of a named person in the event they were unable to agree. Thus, an explicitly stated consequence follows their inability to agree. This consequence is conditioned upon the existence of a fact which is objectively ascertainable by the so-called arbitrator as well as a court of equity, namely, that the parties are in disagreement as to how their stock should be voted. The Agreement to agree has, therefore, provisions which are capable of being enforced with respect to particular facts. Moreover, the very nature and object of the Agreement render it impossible for the parties to do more than agree to agree, and to provide an enforceable alternative in the event no agreement is reached. . . .

I conclude that the Agreement is sufficiently definite in terms of the duties and obligations imposed on the parties to be legally enforceable on the state of facts here presented.

Turning to defendants' second objection, is the Agreement invalid as an attempted delegation of irrevocable control and voting rights in a manner which is against the public policy of this state? . . .

---

45. Ringling and Haley had a total of 4,410 votes (630 × 7), 882 of which they cast for each of five directors. North had 2,590 votes (370 × 7), which could not be divided so as to give more than two persons as many as 882 votes each. — ED.

46. Contra, Johnson v. Spartanburg County Fair Ass'n, 210 S.C. 56, 41 S.E.2d 299 (1947) ("the authorities are uniformly to the effect that . . . [pooling agreements] must be supported by some consideration other than the mutual promises of the several stockholders," quoting Am. Jur.). — ED.

This Agreement is actually a variation of the well-known stock pooling agreement. . . .

The law with respect to agreements of the general type with which we are here concerned is fairly stated as follows in 5 Fletcher Cyc. Corp. (Perm. Ed.) §2064, at page 194: "Generally, agreements and combinations to vote stock or control corporate action and policy are valid, if they seek without fraud to accomplish only what the parties might do as stockholders and do not attempt it by illegal proxies, trusts, or other means in contravention of statutes or law."

The principle of law stated seems to be sound and I think it is applicable here with respect to the legality of the Agreement under consideration. In the first place, there is no constitutional or statutory objection to the Agreement and defendants do not seriously challenge the legality of its objects. Indeed, in my opinion the objects and purposes of the Agreement as they are recited in the Agreement are lawful in principle and no evidence was introduced which tended to show that they were unlawful in operation.

The only serious question presented under this point arises from the defendants' contention that the arbitration provision has the effect of providing for an irrevocable separation of voting power from stock ownership and that such a provision is contrary to the public policy of this state. Perhaps in no field of the law are the precedents more varied and irreconcilable than those dealing with this phase of the case.

By adhering to strict literalism, it can be said that the present Agreement does not separate voting rights from ownership because the arbitrator only directs the parties as to how they shall vote in case of disagreement. However, recognizing substance rather than form, it is apparent that the arbitrator has voting control of the shares in the instances when he directs the parties as to how they shall vote since, if the Agreement is to be binding, they are also bound by his direction. When so considered, it is perhaps at variance with many, but not all of the precedents in other jurisdictions dealing with agreements of this general nature. . . . The cases which strike down agreements on the ground that some public policy prohibits the severance of ownership and voting control argue that there is something very wrong about a person "who has no beneficial interest or title in or to the stock" directing how it shall be voted. Such a person, according to these cases, has "no interest in the general prosperity of the corporation" and moreover, the stockholder himself has a duty to vote. . . . Such reasons ignore the realities because obviously the person designated to determine how the shares shall be voted has the confidence of such shareholders. Quite naturally they would not want to place such power over their investment in the hands of one whom they felt would not be concerned with the welfare of the corporation. The objection based on the so-called duty of the stockholders to vote, presumably in person, is ludicrous when considered in the light of present day corporate practice. Thus, precedents from other jurisdictions which are based on reasons which have, in my opinion, lost their substance under present day conditions cannot be accorded favorable recognition. No public policy of this state requires a different conclusion.

Once it be concluded that no constitutional or statutory objection to the validity of the present Agreement exists, as I have found, then I think the objection to its legality must be based not on some abstract public policy but on fraud or illegality of purpose. Since no such fraud or illegality has been shown, defendants' objections must fall. . . .

I conclude that the stock held under the Agreement should have been voted pursuant to the direction of the arbitrator. . . . When a party or her representative refuses to comply with the direction of the arbitrator, . . . then I believe the Agreement constitutes the willing party to the Agreement an implied agent possessing the irrevocable proxy of the recalcitrant party for the purpose of casting the particular vote. Here an implied agency based on an irrevocable proxy is fully justified to implement the Agreement without doing violence to its terms. Moreover, the provisions of the Agreement make it clear that the proxy may be treated as one coupled with an interest so as to render it irrevocable under the circumstances. . . .

It is the opinion of the court that the nature of the Agreement does not preclude the granting of specific performance. . . . Obviously, to deny specific performance here would be tantamount to declaring the Agreement invalid. Since petitioner's rights in this respect were properly preserved at the stockholders' meeting, the meeting was a nullity to the extent that it failed to give effect to the provisions of the Agreement here involved. However, I believe it preferable to hold a new election rather than attempt to reconstruct the contested meeting. In this way the parties will be acting with explicit knowledge of their rights.

. . . It is obviously to the advantage of both parties to avoid the necessity for calling upon the arbitrator to act, and he will only act if the parties are unable to agree and action by him is requested. . . .

[Defendants appealed.]

PEARSON, J. [in the Supreme Court of Delaware]: . . . Before taking up defendants' objections to the agreement, let us analyze particularly what it attempts to provide with respect to voting, including what functions and powers it attempts to repose in Mr. Loos, the "arbitrator." . . .

Should the agreement be interpreted as attempting to empower the arbitrator to carry his directions into effect? Certainly there is no express delegation or grant of power to do so, either by authorizing him to vote the shares or to compel either party to vote them in accordance with his directions. The agreement expresses no other function of the arbitrator than that of deciding questions in disagreement which prevent the effectuation of the purpose "to act jointly." The power to enforce a decision does not seem a necessary or usual incident of such a function. Mr. Loos is not a party to the agreement. It does not contemplate the transfer of any shares or interest in shares to him, or that he should undertake any duties which the parties might compel him to perform. They provided that they might designate any other individual to act instead of Mr. Loos. The agreement does not attempt to make the arbitrator a trustee of an express trust. What the arbitrator is to do is for the benefit of the parties, not for his own benefit. Whether the parties accept or reject his decision is no concern of his, so far as the agreement or the surrounding circumstances reveal. We think the parties sought to bind each other, but to be bound only to each other, and not to empower the arbitrator to enforce decisions he might make.

From this conclusion, it follows necessarily that no decision of the arbitrator could ever be enforced if both parties to the agreement were unwilling that it be enforced, for the obvious reason that there would be no one to enforce it. Under the agreement, something more is required after the arbitrator has given his decision in order that it should become compulsory: at least one of the parties must determine that such decision shall be carried into effect. Thus, any "control" of the voting of the shares, which is reposed in the arbitrator, is substantially limited in action under the agreement in that it is subject to the overriding power of the parties themselves.

The agreement does not describe the undertaking of each party with respect to a decision of the arbitrator other than to provide that it "shall be binding upon the parties." It seems to us that this language, considered with relation to its context and the situations to which it is applicable, means that each party promised the other to exercise her own voting rights in accordance with the arbitrator's decision. The agreement is silent about any exercise of the voting rights of one party by the other. The language with reference to situations where the parties arrive at an understanding as to voting plainly suggests "action" by each, and "exercising" voting rights by each, rather than by one for the other. There is no intimation that this method should be different where the arbitrator's decision is to be carried into effect. Assuming that a power in each party to exercise the voting rights of the other might be a relatively more effective or convenient means of enforcing a decision of the arbitrator than would be available without the power, this would not justify implying a delegation of the power in the absence of some indication that the parties bargained for that means. The method of voting actually employed by the parties tends to show that they did not construe the agreement as creating powers to vote each other's shares; for at meetings prior to 1946 each party apparently exercised her own voting rights, and at the 1946 meeting, Mrs. Ringling, who wished to enforce the agreement, did not attempt to cast a ballot in exercise of any voting rights of Mrs. Haley. We do not find enough in the agreement or in the circumstances to justify a construction that either party was empowered to exercise voting rights of the other.

Having examined what the parties sought to provide by the agreement, we come now to defendants' contention that the voting provisions are illegal and revocable. They say that the courts of this state have definitely established the doctrine "that there can be no agreement, or any device whatsoever, by which the voting power of stock of a Delaware corporation may be irrevocably separated from the ownership of the stock, except by an agreement which complies with Section 18" of the Corporation Law [concerning voting trusts], and except by a proxy coupled with an interest. . . .

In our view, neither the cases nor the statute sustain the rule for which the defendants contend. Their sweeping formulation would impugn well-recognized means by which a shareholder may effectively confer his voting rights upon others while retaining various other rights. For example, defendants' rule would apparently not permit holders of voting stock to confer upon stockholders of another class, by the device of an amendment of the certificate of incorporation, the exclusive right to vote during periods when dividends are not paid on stock of the latter class. The broad prohibitory meaning which defendants find in Section 18 seems inconsistent with their concession that proxies coupled with an interest may be irrevocable, for the statute contains nothing about such proxies. The statute authorizes, among other things, the deposit or transfer of stock in trust for a specified purpose, namely, "vesting" in the transferee "the right to vote thereon" for a limited period; and prescribes numerous requirements in this connection. Accordingly, it seems reasonable to infer that to establish the relationship and accomplish the purpose which the statute authorizes, its requirements must be complied with. But the statute does not purport to deal with agreements whereby shareholders attempt to bind each other as to how they shall vote their shares. Various forms of such pooling agreements, as they are sometimes called, have been held valid and have been distinguished from voting trusts. . . . We think the particular agreement before us does not violate Section 18 or constitute an attempted evasion of its requirements, and is not illegal for any other reason. Generally speaking, a shareholder may exercise wide liberality of judgment in the matter of voting, and it is not objectionable that his motives may be for personal profit, or determined by whims or caprice, so long as he violates no duty owed his fellow shareholders. . . . The ownership of voting stock imposes no legal duty to vote at all. A group of shareholders may, without impropriety, vote their respective shares so as to obtain advantages of concerted action. They may lawfully contract with each other to vote in the future in such way as they, or a majority of their group, from time to time determine. . . . Reasonable provisions for cases of failure of the group to reach a determination because of an even division in their ranks seem unobjectionable. The provision here for submission to the arbitrator is plainly designed as a deadlock-breaking measure, and the arbitrator's decision cannot be enforced unless at least one of the parties (entitled to cast one-half of their combined votes) is willing that it be enforced. We find the provision reasonable. It does not appear that the agreement enables the parties to take any unlawful advantage of the outside shareholder, or of any other person. It offends no rule of law or public policy of this state of which we are aware.

Legal consideration for the promises of each party is supplied by the mutual promises of the other party. The undertaking to vote in accordance with the arbitrator's decision is a valid contract. The good faith of the arbitrator's action has not been challenged and, indeed, the record indicates that no such challenge could be supported. Accordingly, the failure of Mrs. Haley to exercise her voting rights in accordance with his decision was a breach of her contract. It is no extenuation of the breach that her votes were cast for two of the three candidates directed by the arbitrator. His directions to her were part of a single plan or course of action for the voting of the shares of both parties to the agreement, calculated to utilize an advantage of joint action by them which would bring about the election of an additional director. The actual voting of Mrs. Haley's shares frustrates that plan to such an extent that it should not be treated as a partial performance of her contract.

. . . It seems to us that upon the application of Mrs. Ringling, the injured party, the votes representing Mrs. Haley's shares should not be counted. Since no infirmity in Mr. North's voting has been demonstrated, his right to recognition of what he did at the meeting should be considered in granting any relief to Mrs. Ringling; for her rights arose under a contract to which Mr. North was not a party. With this in mind, we have concluded that the election should not be declared invalid, but . . . the return of the inspectors should be corrected to show a rejection of Mrs. Haley's votes, and to declare the election of the six persons for whom Mr. North and Mrs. Ringling voted.

This leaves one vacancy in the directorate. The question of what to do about such a vacancy was not considered by the court below and has not been argued here. For this reason, and because an election of directors at the 1947 annual meeting (which presumably will be held in the near future) may make a determination of the question unimportant, we shall not decide it on this appeal. If a decision of the point appears important to the parties, any of them may apply to raise it in the Court of Chancery, after the mandate of this court is received there. . . .

———————————

1. *Remedies.* As late as 1950, it was observed that

> although numerous cases have been cited by authors for the proposition that agreements by shareholders to vote for certain persons as directors to secure the management of the corporation are enforceable unless fraudulent, close examination suggests that [this proposition] cannot be sustained unqualifiedly. Even though a remedy at law for damages is not feasible, no court has in fact given complete relief by compelling specific performance of such contracts, except where the contracting parties owned all the shares. The statements that such contracts are valid and binding are dicta. . . . While these dicta render uncertain the enforceability of such contracts in many jurisdictions, other courts have expressly refused enforcement on grounds of public policy. In the residuum of cases, where courts have accorded the parties the full equivalent of specific performance, the separation of voting power from ownership was warranted by a financial commitment in the welfare of the corporation similar to that deemed necessary by most courts for the validation of an irrevocable proxy.

Note, The Irrevocable Proxy and Voting Control of Small Business Corporations, 98 U. Pa. L. Rev. 401, 408-409 (1950). For more recent decisions granting specific performance or injunctive relief although the contracting parties did not own all the shares, see Weil v. Beresth, 154 Conn. 12, 220 A.2d 456 (1966); 721 Corp. v. Morgan Guaranty Trust Co., 40 Misc. 2d 395, 243 N.Y.S.2d 198 (S. Ct. 1963); Storer v. Ripley, 1 Misc. 2d 235, 125 N.Y.S.2d 831, *aff'd*, 282 App. Div. 950, 125 N.Y.S.2d 339 (1953). For the view that specific performance of agreements respecting selection of corporate management should be hesitatingly awarded because of the required close association of the parties, see Abram Chayes, Madame Wagner and the Close Corporation, 73 Harv. L. Rev. 1532 (1960).

2. *Aftermath.* Delaware law was eventually amended to provide in Del. Gen. Corp. Law §218(c):

> (c) An agreement between two or more shareholders, if in writing and signed by the parties thereto, may provide that in exercising any voting rights, the shares held by them shall be voted as provided by the agreement, or as the parties may agree, or as determined in accordance with a procedure agreed upon by them.

For many years, §218(c) limited the life of a voting agreement to ten years. In 1994 the Delaware legislature deleted this limitation, as has RMBCA §7.31. Is this wise? Should an agreement signed in 1994 be specifically enforceable in 2034? Against executors and descendants? Or does the need for certainty and the law's general preference for freedom of contract override other considerations?

3. *Prohibition against vote selling.* Both the common law and a number of statutes (see, e.g., N.Y. Bus. Corp. Law §609(e), page 577 supra) forbid vote selling. See also Restatement, Second, Contracts §193 (1981). But is the line of cases adhering to this rule (discussed supra at pages 578-584) meaningfully distinguishable from cases like *Harkert* that commit the shareholders to vote their shares on the ground that, in the vote-selling cases, the consideration was a "consideration personal" to the

shareholder while in *Harkert* the shareholder relinquished his vote for a consideration that inured to the corporation?

Is vote selling meaningfully distinguishable from a "pooling" agreement, as in *Ringling*, in which shareholders agree to combine their votes so as to elect a majority of the board? Are the "advantages of concerted action" obtained by these shareholders any different from the advantages obtained by the vote-selling shareholders? Is the consideration any less a "personal benefit"?

Is it clear that the agreements in *Harkert* and *Ringling* were to the "benefit . . . of all stockholders"? That there could be "no injury to the corporation, stockholders or creditors"? May this be said despite the fact that (a) the agreement's effect was to retain specified individuals as corporate directors for a long period of time or for life even though one party to the agreement now feels that this is unwise, and (b) other shareholders, not parties to the agreement, are effectively "governed" by it? For the view that unanimity should be a prerequisite for the validity of a shareholder voting agreement (and of a voting trust), see Edwin Bradley, Toward a More Perfect Close Corporation — The Need for More and Improved Legislation, 54 Geo. L.J. 1145 (1966).

Is the policy against vote selling based on the fact that it often results in control without any capital contribution to the corporation? Or is the problem that voting control can be separated from an economic stake in the company? Vote buying poses more difficult questions in public corporations. In close corporations, the fact of the sale is typically observable. In public corporations, a variety of ways exist to acquire voting rights without a corresponding stake in the corporation's economic performance, most involving derivatives (see Chapter 6, supra). Should vote buying be treated differently in public and in close corporations? Does this policy distinguish the prohibition against vote selling from the validity of the *Harkert*-type voting agreement and the *Ringling*-type pooling agreement? If so, is this a desirable distinction?

4. *Non-voting shares reconsidered.* In states that *prohibit* the issuance of non-voting shares (see page 554 supra), what is the validity of *Harkert*-type voting agreements, which give some shareholders voting power that is less than proportionate to their share ownership? See Note, Status of Nonvoting Stock in Nebraska, 33 Neb. L. Rev. 636 (1954). Is an agreement of this type of indefinite duration effectively any different from the issuance of non-voting shares? In states that *permit* the issuance of non-voting shares — or that otherwise grant broad authority for the issuance of different classes of shares — what is the practical effect (or desirability) of statutory provisions that set time limitations for voting agreements?

5. *Problem.* Five shareholders, each owning 8 percent of the corporation's shares, agree to vote as a unit in accordance with the wishes of a majority of the five. Three of these shareholders then execute a sub-agreement to vote together in meetings of the five shareholders, their position there to be determined by the wishes of a majority of the three. Is the sub-agreement valid? See Thomas v. Sanborn, 172 So. 2d 841 (Fla. Ct. App. 1964).

b. Voting Trusts

A voting trust is a device established by the formal transfer of voting shares, usually for a designated period, from their owners to trustees. Designed in response to judicial aversion to the separation of ownership from control, it results in the trustees having legal title to the shares, as well as the right to vote in the manner agreed on. The shareholders (now the beneficial or equitable owners) are usually issued transferable voting trust certificates for their shares, which carry the right to dividends and other asset distributions and in turn are exchanged for the shares on termination of the trust.

As the cases set forth in this subsection illustrate, voting trusts are frequently created to satisfy the same desires of minority shareholders in close corporations that are reflected in ordinary voting agreements. But they also are employed, in larger corporations as well as those that are closely held, for other reasons. Existing creditors or senior security holders of a financially unstable corporation may require, as a condition of permitting the corporation to continue (or be reorganized), that they be given control through the mechanism of a voting trust.[47] Lenders or providers of fresh capital may utilize a voting trust to afford them control of or a voice in the selection of new management or assurance that the corporation's present successful management will be continued.[48] The promoters of a new corporation may seek to retain control over it with a minimum capital investment by causing the corporation's shares to be placed in a voting trust (of which the promoters are trustees) and offering voting trust certificates instead of voting shares for sale to others.[49]

At common law, although some early decisions invalidated voting trusts for reasons similar to those behind the early refusal to uphold voting agreements,[50] most courts did not find them illegal per se and enforced them if their purpose was not "illegal or improper."[51] At present, almost all states have statutory provisions authorizing the creation of and governing voting trusts.

Abercrombie v. Davies
36 Del. Ch. 371, 130 A.2d 338 (S. Ct. 1957)

SOUTHERLAND, C.J.: [American Independent Oil Co. was a close corporation organized by two individual oil men (Abercrombie and Davies) and nine major oil companies to develop an oil concession in the Middle East. Through a system of cumulative voting, each shareholder was permitted to elect at least one of

---

47. See, e.g., In re Lower Broadway Properties, 58 F. Supp. 615 (S.D.N.Y. 1945).

48. See, e.g., TWA, Inc. v. Hughes, 332 F.2d 602 (2d Cir. 1964). For an interesting illustration of the protections sought through a voting trust, see Mackin v. Nicollet Hotel, Inc., 25 F.2d 783 (8th Cir. 1928). Persons interested in the commercial welfare of the city formed a corporation to construct a hotel. Most of the required funds were to be supplied by the sale of mortgage bonds and preferred shares on condition that the common shares be placed in a voting trust. There were to be three trustees, one each to be effectively controlled by the bondholders, preferred shareholders, and equitable common shareholders. The voting trust was to have a life of ten years or until the preferred shares were retired. If the preferred were not retired at the end of ten years, the voting trust was to be extended (subject to certain conditions) for five additional two-year periods. The three trustees were to be the corporation's directors so long as they were considered suitable by a majority of them.

49. See, e.g., Carnegie Trust Co. v. Security Life Ins. Co., 111 Va. 1, 68 S.E. 412 (1910).

50. See, e.g., Warren v. Pim, 66 N.J. Eq. 353, 59 A. 773 (1904); Shepaug Voting Trust Cases, 60 Conn. 553, 24 A. 32 (1890).

51. Mackin v. Nicollet Hotel, Inc., footnote 48 supra. For earlier, contrasting views, see Marion Smith, Limitations on the Validity of Voting Trusts, 22 Colum. L. Rev. 627 (1922); Coleman Burke, Voting Trusts Currently Observed, 24 Minn. L. Rev. 347 (1940); J. Gordon Gose, Legal Characteristics and Consequences of Voting Trusts, 20 Wash. L. Rev. 129 (1945).

American's 15 directors. Phillips Petroleum Co. was the largest shareholder, owning about one-third of the shares and electing four directors. Davies elected himself as director and was president of the corporation.

In 1950 Davies and five of the oil companies (owning a total of about 54 percent of the shares and electing eight directors) executed an "Agents' Agreement" whose purpose was to prevent Phillips' acquisition of control. The six shareholders designated their eight directors as Agents. They transferred their share certificates (endorsed in blank) to the Agents for ten years. The Agents gave each shareholder a receipt and deposited the certificates in escrow. The shareholders also delivered an irrevocable proxy, having "sole and exclusive voting power of the Stock subject to this Agreement" for the life of the Agreement. The shares were to be voted as a unit on concurrence of seven of the eight Agents. On their failure to agree, the matter was to be submitted to an arbitrator chosen by seven of the eight. Seven of the eight Agents could also terminate the Agreement or withdraw the shares from escrow and convert to a formal voting trust with the Agents to be the voting trustees. Each Agent could be removed or replaced by the shareholder he represented, except that Davies' successor would be named by the majority of the remaining seven Agents.

In 1954 two Agents refused to abide by the Agreement, causing loss of control. When Davies threatened to enforce the Agreement, three nonsignatories brought suit seeking to invalidate it. They did not succeed in the lower court.]

This agreement, plaintiffs assert, is invalid on its face. Among other contentions they say that in substance, though not in form, it is a voting trust, and that it is void because it does not comply with the provisions of our voting trust statute. Defendants reply that it is not, and was not intended to be, a voting trust, and is a mere pooling agreement. . . .

[The Delaware voting trust] statute was enacted in 1925. . . . Prior to its passage there was no Delaware decision declaring that voting trusts were lawful at common law — a question upon which the decisions in other states were in disagreement. . . . In Perry v. Missouri-Kansas Pipe Line Co., 22 Del. Ch. 33, 191 A. 823, it was determined that in Delaware, as in New York, voting trusts derive their validity solely from the statute. *"The test of validity is the rule of the statute. When the field was entered by the Legislature it was fully occupied and no place was left for other voting trusts."* . . . If any stockholders' agreement provided for joint or concerted voting is so drawn as in effect to occupy the field reserved for the statutory voting trust, it is illegal, whatever mechanics may be devised to attain the result. The provisions of the instrument determine its legal effect, and if they clearly create a voting trust, any intention of the parties to the contrary is immaterial. Aldridge v. Franco-Wyoming Oil Co., 24 Del. Ch. 126, 7 A.2d 753.

A review of the Delaware decisions upon the subject of voting trusts shows that our courts have indicated that one essential feature that characterizes a voting trust is the separation of the voting rights of the stock from the other attributes of ownership. In Peyton v. William C. Peyton Corporation, 22 Del. Ch. 187, 199, 194 A. 106, 111, Chancellor Wolcott said: "A voting trust as commonly understood is a device whereby two or more persons owning stock with voting powers, divorce the voting rights thereof from the ownership, retaining to all intents and purposes the latter in themselves and transferring the former to trustees in whom the voting rights of all the depositors in the trust are pooled."

This definition was followed in Aldridge v. Franco-Wyoming Oil Co. . . . with an additional element — "that the voting rights given are intended to be irrevocable for a definite period." . . . To all these elements should be added that of the principal object of such a trust, which is voting control. . . .

When we apply these tests to the Agents' Agreement we find: (1) that the voting rights of the pooled stock have been divorced from the beneficial ownership, which is retained by the stockholders; (2) that the voting rights have been transferred to fiduciaries denominated Agents; (3) that the transfer of such rights is, through the medium of irrevocable proxies, effective for a period of ten years; (4) that all voting rights in respect of all the stock are pooled in the Agents as a group, through the device of proxies running to the agents jointly and severally, and no stockholder retains the right to vote his or its shares; and (5) that on its face the agreement has for its principal object voting control of American.

These elements, under our decisions, are the elements of a voting trust.

We find one other significant circumstance.

Paragraph 7 of the Agents' Agreement gives any seven of the eight agents the power to withdraw the stock from escrow and to transform the Agreement into a formal voting trust. . . . A form of a voting trust agreement is attached as an exhibit to the Agents' Agreement. A comparison of this form with the provisions of the Agents' Agreement shows that upon the execution of the Voting Trust Agreement the scheme of control functions just as it functions under the Agents' Agreement. . . .

Thus the only significant changes made in transforming the Agents' Agreement into a Voting Trust Agreement are the provisions formalizing the trust, viz.: (1) the Agents become Trustees — a change of name and nothing more; (2) the stock with irrevocable stock powers running to the Agents becomes stock registered in their names as Trustees; and (3) voting trust certificates instead of receipts are issued to the stockholders.

To sum up: the substance of the voting trust already existed; the transformation added only the special mechanics that the statute requires.

Now, the provisions of the statute that were not complied with are the requirement that the shares be transferred on the books and the requirement that a copy of the agreement shall be filed in the corporation's principal office in Delaware. The effect was to create a secret voting trust. The provision respecting the filing . . . is a provision obviously for the benefit of all stockholders and of all beneficiaries of the trust, who are entitled to know where voting control of a corporation resides. And the provision for transfer of the stock on the corporate books necessarily serves, though perhaps only incidentally, a similar purpose with respect to the officers and directors. If the validity of a stockholders' pooling agreement of the kind here presented were to be sustained, the way is clear for the creation of secret voting trusts. The statute clearly forbids them.

The Chancellor took the contrary view. He held the Agents' Agreement not to be a voting trust because (1) title to the stock did not pass to the Agents, and (2) because the Agents are in fact the agents and are subject to the directions of their principals.

The failure to transfer the stock on the books is not a sufficient reason in this case for holding the Agents' Agreement not a voting trust. It is an indication that the parties did not intend to create a voting trust; but that subjective intention is unimportant. The stock here was endorsed in blank and delivered to the agents for deposit in escrow with irrevocable proxies. Transfer of the stock on the books is not essential to effect an irrevocable transfer of voting rights to fiduciaries, divorced from the other attributes of the stock, in order to secure voting control, as the Agents' Agreement demonstrates. It is such a transfer that is the characteristic feature of a voting trust.

The fact that the Agents are subject to control by their respective principals does not prevent the agreement from constituting a voting trust. The stock is voted by the Agents as a group. No one stockholder retains complete control over the voting of its stock. It cannot vote its own stock directly; all it can do is to direct its Agent how to vote on a decision to be made by the Agents as a group. The stock of any corporate stockholder may at any time be voted against its will by the vote of the seven other agents. The control of the Agents rests upon the provisions that they are severally chosen by the respective stockholders and each may be removed and replaced by the stockholder he represents. In effect, these provisions come to this: that each corporate stockholder participating in the agreement reserves the right to name and remove the fiduciary or fiduciaries representing him. Such a provision is not inconsistent with a voting trust. In fact, the scheme is carried forward to the voting trust set out as "Exhibit A" to the Agents' Agreement. . . . And the alleged continuing control of the Agent by the stockholder clearly would not exist in the event of the death, removal or resignation of Davies in his capacity of Agent. In that case his successor, whether Agent or Trustee, is named by a majority of the remaining Agents or Trustees, as the case may be, and his estate has no control whatever over the Agent so named. . . .

In support of their argument that the Agents' Agreement creates only a stockholders' pooling agreement and not a voting trust, defendants lean heavily on the decision of this Court in Ringling Bros.–Barnum & Bailey Combined Shows v. Ringling, 29 Del. Ch. 610, 53 A.2d 441. That case involved a true pooling agreement, far short of a voting trust. Two stockholders agreed to act jointly in exercising their voting rights. There was no deposit of the stock with irrevocable stock powers conferring upon a group of fiduciaries exclusive voting powers over the pooled stock. Indeed, the Supreme Court (modifying the decision below) held that the agreement did not provide, either expressly or impliedly, for a proxy to either stockholder to vote the other's shares. The *Ringling* case is clearly distinguishable on the facts. . . .

We gather that defendants go so far as to say that a pooling agreement may assume any form whatever without running afoul of the voting trust statute. Thus, if we understand defendants' argument, a pooling agreement may, through the medium of fiduciaries with exclusive voting powers, lawfully accomplish substantially the same purposes as a voting trust and thus avoid compliance with §218. We disagree. Obviously, as a pooling agreement in substance and purpose approaches more and more nearly the substance and purpose of the statute, there comes a point at which, if the statute is not complied with, the agreement is illegal. A pooling agreement may not escape the statutory controls by calling the trustees agents and giving to the stockholders receipts instead of voting trust certificates. If this were not so, stockholders could, through the device of an agreement such as the one before us, accept for themselves the chief benefits of the statute: unified voting control through fiduciaries for an appreciable period of time, and escape its burdens: the requirements for making an open record of the matter, and the limitations in respect of time. If the agreement before us is upheld, what is there to prevent a similar agreement for 15 years — or 25 years? . . .

Defendants also rely on the decision of the Chancellor in Aldridge v. Franco-Wyoming Oil Co. . . . In that case an agreement provided for the deposit of shares with a trustee and the issuance of "bearer certificates" to the depositing stockholder. It was held not to be a voting trust, because under the agreement each stockholder retained full control of his stock. He could withdraw the stock from the trust at any time, or, as long as it remained in the trust, he could obtain a proxy to vote it at any time. The *Aldridge* case is not in point.

For the foregoing reasons, we are compelled to disagree with the holding of the Chancellor upon the question discussed. We are of opinion that the Agents' Agreement is void as an illegal voting trust. . . .

---

1. *Supporting rationale.*

Notwithstanding the *Abercrombie* court's questionable conclusion that defendants' agreement created a voting trust, the ultimate result . . . is sound. On appeal it was alleged by plaintiffs and not denied by defendants that the defendants' agreement was not called to plaintiffs' attention, and that while the agreement was in effect, plaintiffs made substantial financial contributions to the oil company. Defendants at no time made any attempt to inform plaintiffs of the agreement. Thus plaintiffs were placed in the disadvantageous position of investing in a corporation that was controlled by others without plaintiffs' knowledge. Confronted with these facts, the court should have based its decision on a ruling that *any* secret voting agreement is invalid because of public policy.

Comment, Voting Agreement or Voting Trust? A Quandary for Corporate Shareholders, 10 Stan. L. Rev. 565, 567-568 (1958). For further comment, see Note, 46 Cal. L. Rev. 124 (1958).

2. *Problem.* The shareholder-parties to the Agents' Agreement in the *Abercrombie* case (1) form a new corporation, Holding, Inc., with a life of ten years, whose sole purpose is to determine how its American shares shall be voted; (2) transfer their American shares to it in exchange for Holding shares; (3) provide that Holding shall have eight directors to be elected by cumulative voting; and (4) cause Holding to enact a charter provision requiring a vote of seven directors for any action to be taken. Would this course of action have avoided the result of the *Abercrombie* case?

Delaware General Corporation Law (2001)

Sec. 218. *Voting trusts.* . . . (a) One stockholder or two or more stockholders may by agreement in writing deposit capital stock of an original issue with or transfer capital stock to any person or persons, or corporation or corporations authorized to act as trustee, for the purpose of vesting in such person or persons, corporation or corporations, who may be designated voting trustee, or voting trustees, the right to vote thereon for any period of time determined by such agreement, upon the terms and conditions stated in such agreement. The agreement may contain any other lawful provisions not inconsistent with such purpose. After the filing of a copy of the agreement in the registered office of the corporation in this State, which copy shall be open to the inspection of any stockholder of the corporation or any beneficiary of the trust under the agreement daily during business hours, certificates of stock or uncertificated stock shall be issued to the voting trustee or trustees to represent any stock of an original issue so deposited with him or them, and any certificates of stock or uncertificated stock so transferred to the voting trustee or trustees shall be surrendered and cancelled and new certificates or uncertificated stock shall be issued therefore to the voting trustee or trustees. In the certificate so issued, if any, it shall be stated that it is issued pursuant to such agreement, and that fact shall also be stated in the stock ledger of the corporation. The voting trustee or trustees may vote the stock so issued or transferred during the period specified in the agreement. Stock standing in the name of the voting trustee or trustees may be voted either in person or by proxy, and in voting the stock, the voting trustee or trustees shall incur no responsibility as stockholder, trustee or otherwise, except for his or their own individual malfeasance. In any case where two or more persons are designated as voting trustees, and the right and method of voting any stock standing in their names at any meeting of the corporation are not fixed by the agreement appointing the trustees, the right to vote the stock and the manner of voting it at the meeting shall be determined by a majority of the trustees, or if they be equally divided as to the right and manner of voting the stock in any particular case, the vote of the stock in such case shall be divided equally among the trustees.

(b) Any amendment to a voting trust agreement shall be made by a written agreement, a copy of which shall be filed in the registered office of the corporation in this State.

---

1. *Duration.* Voting trust statutes commonly limit the duration of the trust, the usual term being ten years. See RMBCA §7.30(b). For many years, Delaware imposed a ten-year maximum duration on voting trusts (which period could be extended for an additional ten years during the final two years of the trust). In 1994 Delaware deleted this provision from §218, as it applied to both voting agreements and voting trusts. Was this wise? Although the RMBCA has no limitation on the duration of voting agreements, it continues to limit voting trusts to ten years. Why the distinction?

2. *Proper purpose.* As seen in the Delaware provision, voting trust statutes do not ordinarily contain a "proper-purpose" limitation. May a court nonetheless refuse to enforce a voting trust if, in its opinion, the trust's purpose, although otherwise lawful, is improper — e.g., if its purpose is to retain certain persons in corporate office? See Grogan v. Grogan, 315 S.W.2d 34 (Tex. Civ. App. 1958), *review denied*, 159 Tex. 392, 322 S.W.2d 514 (1959).

3. *Statutes.* The current Delaware statutory provision on voting trusts (§218) was enacted after the *Abercrombie* decision. Section 218(d) now provides: "This section shall not be deemed to invalidate any voting or other agreement among shareholders or any irrevocable proxy which is not otherwise illegal." Does this provision moot the issue presented by those cases?

4. *Conforming to the statute.* How closely should voting trusts be held to conformity with the relevant state statute? Should the votes cast by voting trustees at an election be set aside if the statute requires shareholders to transfer their share

certificates to the trustees in exchange for voting trust certificates but, instead, the trustees stamp the share certificates with the voting trust information? Compare In re Chilson, 19 Del. Ch. 398, 168 A. 82 (Ch. 1933), with Boericke v. Weise, 68 Cal. App. 2d 407, 156 P.2d 781 (1945). In Smith v. Biggs Boiler Works Co., 33 Del. Ch. 183, 91 A.2d 193 (Ch. 1952), the court negated the removal of a director by voting trustees on the ground that the statute had not been complied with, despite the fact that it was impossible to transfer the share certificates to the trustees because they were being held in escrow. In Oceanic Exploration Co. v. Grynberg, 428 A.2d 1 (Del. S. Ct. 1981), the court held that the parties to a "voting trust agreement" could not have it declared invalid on the ground that it did not conform to Del. §§218(a) and (b) when the terms were known to all relevant persons and the parties' contract contained "multi-faceted aspects including a stock purchase option agreement running from an already unified majority shareholder group to the corporation." In DeFelice v. Garon, 395 So. 2d 658 (La. 1981), plaintiff executed a "Voting Trust Agreement" transferring all her shares to defendants who had guaranteed a loan of $600,000 to plaintiff that enabled her to acquire all of the corporation's shares. The court found that the purported voting trust was invalid because it was not established "by at least two shareholders" as required by statute, but upheld the contract "as a pledge which expressly conferred on the pledgees the right to vote the stock."

c. Agreements Respecting Actions of Directors

The control devices considered to this point all seek to govern decisions that are conventionally allocated to the corporation's shareholders — principally the election of directors (but also such fundamental corporate changes as charter amendments, merger, and dissolution). However, many areas of concern to close corporation shareholders involve more detailed matters — such as who the corporation's officers and employees are to be, how much they are to be paid, when and in what proportions profits are to be divided, whether and how much indebtedness should be incurred, etc. The orthodox corporate rule, reflected by statute in virtually every state, is that the business and affairs of a corporation shall be managed "by" (or "by or under the authority of") a board of directors[52] — not by the shareholders. The materials in this subsection deal with the efforts of close corporation shareholders to assure themselves a role in respect to these types of decisions that the law would not normally accord them.

McQuade v. Stoneham
263 N.Y. 323, 189 N.E. 234 (1934)

POUND, C.J.: The action is brought to compel specific performance of an agreement between the parties, entered into to secure the control of National Exhibition Company, also called the Baseball Club (New York Nationals or "Giants"). . . .

---

52. Del. Gen. Corp. Law §141; RMBCA §8.01. Some statutory qualifications to this rule are illustrated in the materials that follow.

Defendant Stoneham became the owner of 1,306 shares, or a majority of the stock of National Exhibition Company. Plaintiff and defendant McGraw each purchased seventy shares of his stock. Plaintiff paid Stoneham $50,338.10 for the stock he purchased. As part of the transaction the [parties agreed to use their "best endeavors" to elect McQuade, Stoneham and McGraw directors. Stoneham was to select all other directors. They further agreed that Stoneham would be president; McGraw, vice president; and McQuade, treasurer, at specified salaries. McQuade's salary was set at $7,500.]

. . . The board of directors consisted of seven men. The four outside of the parties hereto were selected by Stoneham and he had complete control over them. At the meeting of May 2, 1928, Stoneham and McGraw refrained from voting, McQuade voted for himself and the other four voted for Bondy. Defendants did not keep their agreement with McQuade to use their best efforts to continue him as treasurer. On the contrary, he was dropped with their entire acquiescence. At the next stockholders' meeting he was dropped as a director although they might have elected him.

The courts below have refused to order the reinstatement of McQuade, but have given him damages for wrongful discharge, with a right to sue for future damages.

The cause for dropping McQuade was due to the falling out of friends. McQuade and Stoneham had disagreed. The trial court has found in substance that their numerous quarrels and disputes did not affect the orderly and efficient administration of the business of the corporation; that plaintiff was removed because he had antagonized the dominant Stoneham by persisting in challenging his power over the corporate treasury and for no misconduct on his part. The court also finds that plaintiff was removed by Stoneham for protecting the corporation and its minority stockholders. We will assume that Stoneham put him out when he might have retained him, merely in order to get rid of him.

Defendants say that the contract in suit was void because the directors held their office charged with the duty to act for the corporation according to their best judgment and that any contract which compels a director to vote to keep any particular person in office and at a stated salary is illegal. Directors are the exclusive executive representatives of the corporation, charged with administration of its internal affairs and the management and use of its assets. They manage the business of the corporation. (Gen. Corp. Law; Cons. Laws, ch. 23, §27.) "An agreement to continue a man as president is dependent upon his continued loyalty to the interests of the corporation." (Fells v. Katz, 256 N.Y. 67, 72.) So much is undisputed.

Plaintiff contends that the converse of this proposition is true and that an agreement among directors to continue a man as an officer of a corporation is not to be broken so long as such officer is loyal to the interests of the corporation and that, as plaintiff has been found loyal to the corporation, the agreement of defendants is enforceable.

Although it has been held that an agreement among stockholders whereby it is attempted to divest the directors of their power to discharge an unfaithful employee of the corporation is illegal as against public policy . . . it must be equally true that the stockholders may not, by agreement among themselves, control the directors in the exercise of the judgment vested in them by virtue of their office to elect officers and fix salaries. Their motives may not be questioned so long as their acts are legal. The bad faith or the improper motives of the parties does not change the rule. (Manson v. Curtis, 223 N.Y. 313, 324.) Directors may not by agreements entered into as stockholders abrogate their independent judgment. . . .

Stockholders may, of course, combine to elect directors. That rule is well settled. . . . The power to unite is, however, limited to the election of directors and is not extended to contracts whereby limitations are placed on the power of directors to manage the business of the corporation by the selection of agents at defined salaries.

The minority shareholders whose interests McQuade says he has been punished for protecting, are not, aside from himself, complaining about his discharge. He is not acting for the corporation or for them in this action. It is impossible to see how the corporation has been injured by the substitution of Bondy as treasurer in place of McQuade. As McQuade represents himself in this action and seeks redress for his own wrongs, "we prefer to listen to [the corporation and the minority stockholders] before any decision as to their wrongs." (Faulds v. Yates, 57 Ill. 416, 421.)

It is urged that we should pay heed to the morals and manners of the market place to sustain this agreement and that we should hold that its violation gives rise to a cause of action for damages rather than base our decision on any outworn notions of public policy. Public policy is a dangerous guide in determining the validity of a contract and courts should not interfere lightly with the freedom of competent parties to make their own contracts. We do not close our eyes to the fact that such agreements, tacitly or openly arrived at, are not uncommon, especially in close corporations where the stockholders are doing business for convenience under a corporate organization. We know that majority stockholders, united in voting trusts, effectively manage the business of a corporation by choosing trustworthy directors to reflect their policies in the corporate management. Nor are we unmindful that McQuade has, so the court has found, been shabbily treated as a purchaser of stock from Stoneham. We have said: "A trustee is held to something stricter than the morals of the market place" (Meinhard v. Salmon, 249 N.Y. 458, 464), but Stoneham and McGraw were not trustees for McQuade as an individual. Their duty was to the corporation and its stockholders, to be exercised according to their unrestricted lawful judgment. They were under no legal obligation to deal righteously with McQuade if it was against public policy to do so.

. . . We are constrained by authority to hold that a contract is illegal and void so far as it precludes the board of directors, at the risk of incurring legal liability, from changing officers, salaries or policies or retaining individuals in office, except by consent of the contracting parties. On the whole, such a holding is probably preferable to one which would open the courts to pass on the motives of directors in the lawful exercise of their trust.

A further reason for reversal exists. At the time the contract was made the plaintiff was a City Magistrate. . . .

The Inferior Criminal Courts Act . . . provides that no "city magistrate . . . shall engage in any other business or profession . . . but . . . shall devote his whole time and capacity, so far as the public interest demands, to the duties of his office. . . ." If the performance of regular duties in the management of a business corporation for a substantial remuneration does not constitute "engaging in a business" then these words are futile and meaningless. . . .

The judgment of the Appellate Division and that of the Trial Term should be reversed and the complaint dismissed. . . .

LEHMAN, J. (concurring): I concur in the decision of the court on the second ground stated in the opinion. I desire to state the reasons why I do not accept the first ground.

. . . The directors have the power and the duty to act in accordance with their own best judgment so long as they remain directors. The majority stockholders can compel no action by the directors, but at the expiration of the term of office of the directors the stockholders have the power to replace them with others whose actions coincide with the judgment or desires of the holders of a majority of the stock. The theory that directors exercise in all matters an independent judgment in practice often yields to the fact that the choice of directors lies with the majority stockholders and thus gives the stockholders a very effective control of the action by the board of directors. In truth the board of directors may check the arbitrary will of those who would otherwise completely control the corporation, but cannot indefinitely thwart their will.

A contract which destroys this check contravenes "express charter or statutory provisions" and is, therefore, illegal. A contract which merely provides that stockholders shall in combination use their power to achieve a legitimate purpose is not illegal. They may join in the election of directors who, in their opinion, will be in sympathy with the policies of the majority stockholders and who, in the choice of executive officers, will be influenced by the wishes of the majority stockholders. The directors so chosen may not act in disregard of the best interests of the corporation and its minority stockholders, but with that limitation they may be and, in practice, usually are swayed by the wishes of the majority. Otherwise there would be no continuity of corporate policy and no continuity in management of corporate affairs.

The contract now under consideration provides, in a narrow field, for corporate action within these limitations. Its purpose and intent is to fix the manner in which control vested in the stockholders shall be exercised. It is not designed to create a control which is itself illegal. True, it does contemplate that the parties will, as directors, vote to place each other in specified offices. If this represented a corrupt bargain intended to despoil the corporation, it would be an illegal combination, but there is no evidence or finding that it had such purpose or result. Neither the corporation nor any minority stockholders are complaining and the findings establish that the arrangement resulted in protection which the minority stockholders would not otherwise have had and that it was repudiated by defendant (Stoneham) because such protection proved irksome to him. It does constrain the parties while acting as directors to vote for officers in a predetermined manner, but there is no suggestion that such vote would not accord with their best judgment and be in the interests of the corporation. It is subject to the implied condition that the officers so elected will be loyal to the corporation. (Fells v. Katz, 256 N.Y. 67.) It binds the directors only in a matter where freedom is a fiction rather than a fact. If this contract is unenforceable and contrary to public policy, then every purchase of a substantial block of stock upon the promise of the majority stockholders that the purchaser will be elected a director and officer of the corporation is likewise against public policy. . . .

1. *Fact variations.* In what way, if any, might the reasoning or result in the *McQuade* case have been affected if:

(a) The nonsignatory shareholders (1) objected to McQuade's discharge, (2) favored McQuade's discharge, (3) were neutral about McQuade's discharge, (4) preferred McQuade's continuance in office but did not object to his discharge (as seems to have been the case)?

(b) Stoneham owned 35 percent of the shares and dominated the board of directors, McGraw owned 10 percent, McQuade owned 10 percent, and the nonsignatory shareholders owned the remaining 45 percent?

2. *Avoiding the issue by interpretation.* For cases involving agreements of this nature, between less than all of the shareholders, that were construed as not divesting directors of their right to exercise independent judgment but "as merely a declaration of desirable corporate policy," see Hart v. Bell, 222 Minn. 69, 23 N.W.2d 375 (1946); Tschirgi v. Merchants National Bank, 253 Iowa 682, 113 N.W.2d 226 (1962).

3. *Statutes.* Under current statutory provisions that follow, were there devices that McQuade might have employed to avoid the result in the principal case?

New York Business Corporation Law (2003)

Sec. 709. *Greater requirement as to quorum and vote of directors.* (a) The certificate of incorporation may contain provisions specifying either or both of the following:

(1) That the proportion of directors that shall constitute a quorum for the transaction of business or of any specified item of business shall be greater than the proportion prescribed by this chapter in the absence of such provision.

(2) That the proportion of votes of directors that shall be necessary for the transaction of business or of any specified item of business shall be greater than the proportion prescribed by this chapter in the absence of such provision.

(b)(1) An amendment of the certificate of incorporation which changes or strikes out a provision permitted by this section shall be authorized at a meeting of shareholders by (A)(i) for any corporation in existence on the effective date of subparagraph (2) of this paragraph, two-thirds of the votes of all outstanding shares entitled to vote thereon, and (ii) for any corporation in existence on the effective date of this clause the certificate of incorporation of which expressly provides such and for any corporation incorporated after the effective date of subparagraph (2) of this paragraph, a majority of the votes of all outstanding shares entitled to vote thereon or (B) in either case, such greater proportion of votes of shares, or votes of a class or series of shares, as may be provided specifically in the certificate of incorporation for changing or striking out a provision permitted by this section.

(2) Any corporation may adopt an amendment of the certificate of incorporation in accordance with any applicable clause or subclause of subparagraph (1) of this paragraph to provide that any further amendment of the certificate of incorporation that changes or strikes out a provision permitted by this section shall be authorized at a meeting of the shareholders by a specified proportion of the votes of the shares, or particular class or series of shares, entitled to vote thereon, provided that such proportion may not be less than a majority.

Sec. 715. *Officers.* . . . (b) The certificate of incorporation may provide that all officers or that specified officers shall be elected by the shareholders instead of by the board.

(c) Unless otherwise provided in the certificate of incorporation or the bylaws, all officers shall be elected or appointed to hold office until the meeting of the board following the next annual meeting of shareholders or, in the case of officers elected by the shareholders, until the next annual meeting of shareholders.

(d) Each officer shall hold office for the term for which he is elected or appointed, and until his successor has been elected or appointed and qualified. . . .

---

4. *Questions.* What would the result in the *McQuade* case have been if all shareholders had been parties to the agreement? Compare the two Massachusetts cases of Hayden v. Beane, 293 Mass. 347, 199 N.E. 755 (1936), and Odman v. Oleson, 319 Mass. 24, 64 N.E.2d 439 (1946). Are there interests in issue beyond those of shareholders?

Clark v. Dodge
269 N.Y. 410, 199 N.E. 641 (1936)

CROUCH, J.: The action is for the specific performance of a contract between the plaintiff Clark and the defendant Dodge, relating to the affairs of the two defendant corporations. . . . The two corporate defendants are New Jersey corporations manufacturing medicinal preparations by secret formulae. . . . In 1921, and at all times since, Clark owned twenty-five percent and Dodge seventy-five percent of the stock of each corporation. Dodge took no active part in the business, although he was a director, and, through ownership of their qualifying shares, controlled the other directors of both corporations. . . . The plaintiff Clark was a director and held the offices of treasurer and general manager . . . and also had charge of the major portion of the business. . . . The formulae and methods of manufacture of the medicinal preparations were known to him alone. Under date of February 15, 1921, Dodge and Clark, the sole owners of the stock of both corporations, entered into a written agreement under seal, which . . . provided in substance, as follows: That Dodge during his lifetime, and, after his death, a trustee to be appointed by his will, would so vote his stock and so vote as a director that the plaintiff (a) should continue to be a director . . . and (b) should continue as . . . general manager so long as he should be "faithful, efficient and competent"; (c) should during his life receive one-fourth of the net income of the corporations either by way of salary or dividends; and (d) that no unreasonable or incommensurate salaries should be paid to other officers or agents which would so reduce the net income as materially to affect Clark's profits. Clark on his part agreed to disclose the specified formula to [Dodge's] son and to instruct him in the details and methods of manufacture; and further, at the end of his life to bequeath his stock—if no issue survived him—to the wife and children of Dodge. . . .

The complaint alleges due performance of the contract by Clark and breach thereof by Dodge. . . .

The relief sought is reinstatement as director and general manager and an accounting by Dodge and by the corporations for waste and for the proportion of net income due plaintiff, with an injunction against further violations.

The only question which need be discussed is whether the contract is illegal as against public policy within the decision in McQuade v. Stoneham upon the authority of which the complaint was dismissed by the Appellate Division.

"The business of a corporation shall be managed by its board of directors." (General Corporation Law [Cons. Laws, ch. 23], §27.) That is the statutory norm. Are we committed by the *McQuade* case to the doctrine that there may be no variation, however slight or innocuous, from that norm, where salaries or policies or the retention of individuals in office are concerned? There is ample authority supporting that doctrine ... and something may be said for it, since it furnishes a simple, if arbitrary, test. Apart from its practical administrative convenience, the reasons upon which it is said to rest are more or less nebulous. Public policy, the intention of the Legislature, detriment to the corporation, are phrases which in this connection mean little. Possible harm to bona fide purchasers of stock or to creditors or to stockholding minorities have more substance; but such harms are absent in many instances. If the enforcement of a particular contract damages nobody — not even, in any perceptible degree, the public — one sees no reason for holding it illegal, even though it impinges slightly upon the broad provision of section 27. Damage suffered or threatened is a logical and practical test, and has come to be the one generally adopted by the courts. ... Where the directors are the sole stockholders, there seems to be no objection to enforcing an agreement among them to vote for certain people as officers. There is no direct decision to that effect in this court, yet there are strong indications that such a rule has long been recognized. ... There was no attempt to sterilize the board of directors, as in the *Manson* and *McQuade* cases. The only restrictions on Dodge were (a) that as a stockholder he should vote for Clark as a director — a perfectly legal contract; (b) that as director he should continue Clark as a general manager, so long as he proved faithful, efficient and competent — an agreement which could harm nobody; (c) that Clark should always receive as salary or dividends one-fourth of the "net income." For the purpose of this motion, it is only just to construe that phrase as meaning whatever was left for distribution after the directors had in good faith set aside whatever they deemed wise; (d) that no salaries to other officers should be paid, unreasonable in amount or incommensurate with services rendered — a beneficial and not a harmful agreement.

If there was any invasion of the powers of the directorate under that agreement, it is so slight as to be negligible; and certainly there is no damage suffered by or threatened to anybody. The broad statements in the *McQuade* opinion, applicable to the facts there, should be confined to those facts.

The judgment of the Appellate Division should be reversed. ...

---

1. (a) In Long Park, Inc. v. Trenton-New Brunswick Theatres Co., 297 N.Y. 174, 77 N.E.2d 633 (1948), all three shareholders agreed that one of them, owning half the shares, should have full authority to manage the corporation's business for 19 years. The agreement further provided that the other shareholders "may, at any time ... submit to the American Arbitration Association the question as to

whether or not the management . . . should be changed." One of the other share-holders sought a declaratory judgment as to the agreement's validity. The court held the agreement "to be illegal, void and unenforceable":

> The directors may neither select nor discharge the manager, to whom the supervision and direction of the management and operation of the theatres is delegated with full authority and power. Thus the powers of the directors over the management of its theatres, the principal business of the corporation, were completely sterilized. Such restrictions and limitations upon the powers of the directors are clearly in violation of section 27 of the General Corporation Law of this State. . . . McQuade v. Stoneham, Manson v. Curtis. We think these restrictions and limitations went far beyond the agreement in Clark v. Dodge. We are not confronted with a slight impingement or innocuous variance from the statutory norm, but rather with the deprivation of all the powers of the board insofar as the selection and supervision of the management of the corporation's theatres, including the manner and policy of their operation, are concerned.

(b) In Galler v. Galler, 32 Ill. 2d 16, 203 N.E.2d 577 (1964), two of the corporation's three shareholders owning 208 of the 220 outstanding shares (the remaining 12 shares being owned by an employee) agreed, inter alia, to elect themselves and their wives as the corporation's four directors, to amend the bylaws so as to require a quorum of three directors, to have the corporation declare certain annual dividends according to a formula depending on the amount of the corporation's earned surplus, and to have the corporation pay a stipulated salary to the wives for five years on the death of either of the signatory shareholders. At the time that one of the widows sought to enforce the agreement, the employee's 12 shares had been repurchased by the corporation. The court, relying strongly on Clark v. Dodge, held for plaintiff:

> [I]t should be recognized that shareholder agreements similar to that in question here are often, as a practical consideration, quite necessary for the protection of those financially interested in the close corporation. While the shareholder of a public-issue corporation may readily sell his shares on the open market should management fail to use, in his opinion, sound business judgment, his counterpart of the close corporation often has a large total of his entire capital invested in the business and has no ready market for his shares should he desire to sell. He feels, understandably, that he is more than a mere investor and that his voice should be heard concerning all corporate activity. Without a shareholder agreement, specifically enforceable by the courts, insuring him a modicum of control, a large minority shareholder might find himself at the mercy of an oppressive or unknowledgeable majority. Moreover, as in the case at bar, the shareholders of a close corporation are often also the directors and officers thereof. With substantial shareholding interests abiding in each member of the board of directors, it is often quite impossible to secure, as in the large public-issue corporation, independent board judgment free from personal motivations concerning corporate policy. For these and other reasons too voluminous to enumerate here, often the only sound basis for protection is afforded by a lengthy, detailed shareholder agreement securing the rights and obligations of all concerned. . . . Several shareholder-director agreements that have technically "violated" the letter of the Business Corporation Act have nevertheless been upheld in the light of the existing practical circumstances, i.e., no apparent public injury, the absence of a complaining minority interest, and no apparent prejudice to creditors.

(c) In Glazer v. Glazer, 374 F.2d 390 (5th Cir. 1967), three brothers, who owned either most or all of the shares of 21 corporations, which were incorporated in four different states, made an agreement that was interpreted as generally securing their corporate offices, salaries, and bonuses. Other shares were owned by family members or, occasionally, outside business associates. After one of the brothers was removed by the votes and efforts of the other two, he brought an action against them for damages. The court, holding that the law for decision should be that of the state of incorporation, upheld the agreement with respect to the Florida and Ohio corporations, none of which had shareholders other than the three brothers: "Under [the law of these states] . . . an agreement made and assented to by all the stockholders and not prejudicial to the rights of the minority interests is not void as a matter of public policy." The Tennessee and West Virginia corporations did have minority shareholders. The court first generally commented that "in recent years, courts have shown less reluctance in enforcing shareholder salary-tenure agreements in cases where the number or interest of outside shareholders was small. This is in keeping with modern corporate theory, which emphasizes the realities of management and shareholder interests in each situation." It then upheld the contract for the Tennessee corporations only after finding that the other shareholders either "knew or consented" or "did not object to or claim prejudice from the brothers' agreement."

2. *Statutes.* In recent decades, a growing number of states have enacted statutory provisions respecting shareholder agreements that affect the discretion of directors:

New York Business Corporation Law (2003)

Sec. 620 . . . *[P]rovision in certificate of incorporation as to control of directors.* . . .

(b) A provision in the certificate of incorporation otherwise prohibited by law because it improperly restricts the board in its management of the business of the corporation, or improperly transfers to one or more shareholders or to one or more persons or corporations to be selected by him or them, all or any part of such management otherwise within the authority of the board under this chapter, shall nevertheless be valid:

  (1) If all the incorporators or holders of record of all outstanding shares, whether or not having voting power, have authorized such provision in the certificate of incorporation or an amendment thereof; and

  (2) If, subsequent to the adoption of such provision, shares are transferred or issued only to persons who had knowledge or notice thereof, or consented in writing to such provision.

(c) A provision authorized by paragraph (b) shall be valid only so long as no shares of the corporation are listed on a national securities exchange or regularly quoted in an over-the-counter market by one or more members of a national or affiliated securities association.

(d) (1) Except as provided in paragraph (e), an amendment to strike out a provision authorized by paragraph (b) shall be authorized at a meeting of shareholders by (A)(i) for any corporation in existence on the effective date of subparagraph (2) of this paragraph, two thirds of the votes of the shares entitled to vote thereon and (ii) for any corporation in existence on the effective date of this clause the certificate of incorporation of which expressly provides such and for any corporation incorporated after the effective date of subparagraph (2) of this paragraph, a majority of the votes of the shares entitled to vote thereon or (B) in either case, by such greater proportion of votes of shares as may be required by the certificate of incorporation for that purpose.

(2) Any corporation may adopt an amendment of the certificate of incorporation in accordance with the applicable clause or subclause of subparagraph (1) of this paragraph to provide that any further amendment of the certificate of incorporation that strikes out a provision authorized by paragraph (b) of this section shall be authorized at a meeting of the shareholders by a specified proportion of votes of the shares, or votes of a particular class or series of shares, entitled to vote thereon, provided that such proportion may not be less than a majority.

(e) Alternatively, if a provision authorized by paragraph (b) shall have ceased to be valid under this section, the board may authorize a certificate of amendment under section 805 (Certificate of amendment; contents) striking out such provision. Such certificate shall set forth the event by reason of which the provision ceased to be valid.

(f) The effect of any such provision authorized by paragraph (b) shall be to relieve the directors and impose upon the shareholders authorizing the same or consenting thereto the liability for managerial acts or omissions that is imposed on directors by this chapter to the extent that and so long as the discretion or powers of the board in its management of corporate affairs is controlled by any such provision.

(g) If the certificate of incorporation of any corporation contains a provision authorized by paragraph (b), the existence of such provision shall be noted conspicuously on the face or back of every certificate for shares issued by such corporation.

Maryland General Corporation Law (2007)

§4-401. *Governing corporation; unanimous stockholders' agreement.* (a) Under a unanimous stockholders' agreement, the stockholders of a close corporation may regulate any aspect of the affairs of the corporation or the relations of the stockholders, including:

(1) The management of the business and affairs of the corporation;

(2) Restrictions on the transfer of stock;

(3) The right of one or more stockholders to dissolve the corporation at will or on the occurrence of a specified event or contingency;

(4) The exercise or division of voting power;

(5) The terms and conditions of employment of an officer or employee of the corporation, without regard to the period of his employment;

(6) The individuals who are to be directors and officers of the corporation; and

(7) The payment of dividends or the division of profits.

(b) A unanimous stockholders' agreement may be amended, but only by the unanimous written consent of the stockholders then parties to the agreement.

(c) A stockholder who acquires his stock after a unanimous stockholders' agreement becomes effective is considered to have actually assented to the agreement and is a party to it:

(1) Whether or not he has actual knowledge of the existence of the agreement at the time he acquires the stock, if acquired by gift or bequest from a person who was a party to the agreement; and

(2) If he has actual knowledge of the existence of the agreement at the time he acquires the stock, if acquired in any other manner.

(d)(1) A court of equity may enforce a unanimous stockholders' agreement by injunction or by any other relief which the court in its discretion determines to be fair and appropriate in the circumstances.

(2) As an alternative to the granting of an injunction or other equitable relief, on motion of a party to the proceeding, the court may order dissolution of the corporation under the provisions of Subtitle 6 of this title.

(e) This section does not affect any otherwise valid agreement among stockholders of a close corporation or of any other corporation.

---

3. *Problem.* T, the owner of a majority of a corporation's shares, provides in his will that the shares should be held in trust for his wife and daughter. He directs that the trustees should seek to elect themselves directors, who in turn should seek to elect the wife and daughter as corporate officers at stipulated salaries and bonuses for their lifetimes. Are these testamentary provisions valid and enforceable? See Estate of Hirshon, 13 N.Y.2d 787, 192 N.E.2d 174, 242 N.Y.S.2d 218 (1963); Billings v. Marshall Furnace Co., 210 Mich. 1, 177 N.W. 222 (1920). Should the result be affected if *T* owned all the shares? Less than a majority?

d. Agreements Implied by Majority's Fiduciary Duty

Wilkes v. Springside Nursing Home, Inc.
370 Mass. 842, 353 N.E.2d 657 (1976)

HENNESSEY, C.J.: [Plaintiff Wilkes sought a declaratory judgment against Quinn, Riche, Connor] and the Springside Nursing Home, Inc. (Springside or the corporation). Wilkes alleged that he, Quinn, Riche and Dr. Hubert A. Pipkin (Pipkin)[4] entered into a partnership agreement in 1951, prior to the incorporation of Springside, which agreement was breached in 1967 when Wilkes's salary was terminated and he was voted out as an officer and director of the corporation. . . .

A judge of the Probate Court referred the suit to a master. . . . A judgment was entered dismissing Wilkes's action. . . . On appeal, Wilkes argued in the alternative that (1) he should recover damages for breach of the alleged partnership agreement; and (2) he should recover damages because the defendants, as majority stockholders in Springside, breached their fiduciary duty to him as a minority stockholder by their action in February and March, 1967. . . .

---

4. Dr. Pipkin transferred his interest in Springside to Connor in 1959 and is not a defendant in this action.

[In 1951 Wilkes, Quinn, Riche, and Pipkin decided to jointly purchase real estate to be operated as a nursing home. On their lawyer's advice], ownership of the property was vested in Springside, a corporation organized under Massachusetts law.

Each of the four men invested $1,000 and subscribed to ten shares of $100 par value stock in Springside.[6] At the time of incorporation it was understood by all of the parties that each would be a director of Springside and each would participate actively in the management and decision making involved in operating the corporation.[7] It was, further, the understanding and intention of all the parties that, corporate resources permitting, each would receive money from the corporation in equal amounts as long as each assumed an active and ongoing responsibility for carrying a portion of the burdens necessary to operate the business.

The work involved in establishing and operating a nursing home was roughly apportioned, and each of the four men undertook his respective tasks. . . .

At some time in 1952, it became apparent that the operational income and cash flow from the business were sufficient to permit the four stockholders to draw money from the corporation on a regular basis. Each of the four original parties initially received $35 a week from the corporation. As time went on the weekly return to each was increased until, in 1955, it totalled $100.

. . . [Beginning in 1965, the relationship among the four shareholders deteriorated.] In February of 1967 a directors' meeting was held and the board exercised its right to establish the salaries of its officers and employees.[10] A schedule of payments was established whereby Quinn was to receive a substantial weekly increase and Riche and Connor were to continue receiving $100 a week. Wilkes, however, was left off the list of those to whom a salary was to be paid. The directors also set the annual meeting of the stockholders for March, 1967.

At the annual meeting in March, Wilkes was not reelected as a director, nor was he reelected as an officer of the corporation. He was further informed that neither his services nor his presence at the nursing home was wanted by his associates.

The meetings of the directors and stockholders in early 1967, the master found, were used as a vehicle to force Wilkes out of active participation in the management and operation of the corporation and to cut off all corporate payments to him. Though the board of directors had the power to dismiss any officers or employees for misconduct or neglect of duties, there was no indication in the minutes of the board of directors' meeting of February, 1967, that the failure to establish a salary for Wilkes was based on either ground. The severance of Wilkes from the payroll resulted not from misconduct or neglect of duties, but because of the personal desire of Quinn, Riche and Connor to prevent him from continuing to receive money from the corporation. Despite a continuing deterioration in his personal

---

6. On May 2, 1955, and again on December 23, 1958, each of the four original investors paid for and was issued additional shares of $100 par value stock, eventually bringing the total number of shares owned by each to 115.

7. Wilkes testified before the master that, when the corporate officers were elected, all four men "were . . . guaranteed directorships." Riche's understanding of the parties' intentions was that they all wanted to play a part in the management of the corporation and wanted to have some "say" in the risks involved; that, to this end, they all would be directors; and that "unless you [were] a director and officer you could not participate in the decisions of [the] enterprise."

10. The by-laws of the corporation provided that the directors, subject to the approval of the stockholders, had the power to fix the salaries of all officers and employees. This power, however, up until February, 1967, had not been exercised formally; all payments made to the four participants in the venture had resulted from the informal but unanimous approval of all the parties concerned.

relationship with his associates, Wilkes had consistently endeavored to carry on his responsibilities to the corporation in the same satisfactory manner and with the same degree of competence he had previously shown. . . .

1. We turn to Wilkes's claim for damages based on a breach of the fiduciary duty owed to him by the other participants in this venture. In light of the theory underlying this claim, we do not consider it vital to our approach to this case whether the claim is governed by partnership law or the law applicable to business corporations. This is so because, as all the parties agree, Springside was at all times relevant to this action, a close corporation as we have recently defined such an entity in Donahue v. Rodd Electrotype Co. of New England, Inc., 367 Mass. 578, 585-587, 328 N.E.2d 505 (1975).

In *Donahue*, we held that "stockholders in the close corporation owe one another substantially the same fiduciary duty in the operation of the enterprise that partners owe to one another." Id. at 593 (footnotes omitted), 328 N.E.2d at 515. As determined in previous decisions of this court, the standard of duty owed by partners to one another is one of "utmost good faith and loyalty." . . .

In the *Donahue* case we recognized that one peculiar aspect of close corporations was the opportunity afforded to majority stockholders to oppress, disadvantage or "freeze out" minority stockholders. In *Donahue* itself, for example, the majority refused the minority an equal opportunity to sell a ratable number of shares to the corporation at the same price available to the majority. The net result of this refusal, we said, was that the minority could be forced to "sell out at less than fair value," 367 Mass. 593 at n.18, 328 N.E.2d at 515, since there is by definition no ready market for minority stock in a close corporation.[53]

"Freeze outs," however, may be accomplished by the use of other devices. One such device which has proved to be particularly effective in accomplishing the purpose of the majority is to deprive minority stockholders of corporate offices and of employment with the corporation. F. H. O'Neal, "Squeeze-Outs" of Minority Shareholders 59, 78-79 (1975). . . . This "freeze-out" technique has been successful because courts fairly consistently have been disinclined to interfere in those facets of internal corporate operations, such as the selection and retention or dismissal of officers, directors and employees, which essentially involve management decisions subject to the principle of majority control. See Note, 35 N.C. L. Rev. 271, 277 (1957). As one authoritative source has said, "[M]any courts apparently feel that there is a legitimate sphere in which the controlling [directors or] shareholders can act in their own interest even if the minority suffers." F. H. O'Neal, supra at 59 (footnote omitted). Comment, 1959 Duke L.J. 436, 437.

The denial of employment to the minority at the hands of the majority is especially pernicious in some instances. A guaranty of employment with the corporation may have been one of the "basic reason[s] why a minority owner has invested

---

53. In accord with the relief granted in the *Donahue* case, see Comolli v. Comolli, 241 Ga. 471, 246 S.E.2d 278 (1978) ("good faith requires directors [representing controlling shareholder] to authorize a corporate purchase of [plaintiff minority shareholder's] stock at the same price and the same terms given to" minority shareholder that was allied with controlling shareholder); Estate of Schroer v. Steamco Supply, Inc., 19 Ohio App. 3d 34, 482 N.E. 2d 975 (1984). Cf. Toner v. Baltimore Envelope Co., 304 Md. 256, 498 A.2d 642 (1985) (no "per se equal opportunity rule" when corporate purchase of one minority shareholder's stock was in corporation's best interest and not shown to be "adverse to the interests of the minority shareholder plaintiff"); Goode v. Ryan, 397 Mass. 85, 489 N.E.2d 1001 (1986) (rule of the *Donahue* case does not extend to required corporate repurchase of deceased shareholder's stock in the absence of oppressive conduct by majority shareholder). — ED.

capital in the firm." Symposium — The Close Corporation, 52 Nw. U. L. Rev. 345, 392 (1957). See F. H. O'Neal, supra at 78-79; Hancock, Minority Interests in Small Business Entities, 17 Clev.-Marshall L. Rev. 130, 132-133 (1968); 89 Harv. L. Rev. 423, 427 (1975). The minority stockholder typically depends on his salary as the principal return on his investment, since the "earnings of a close corporation . . . are distributed in major part in salaries, bonuses and retirement benefits." 1 F. H. O'Neal, Close Corporations §1.07 (1971).[13] Other noneconomic interests of the minority stockholder are likewise injuriously affected by barring him from corporate office. See F. H. O'Neal, "Squeeze-Outs" of Minority Shareholders 79 (1975). Such action severely restricts his participation in the management of the enterprise, and he is relegated to enjoying those benefits incident to his status as a stockholder. See Symposium — The Close Corporation, 52 Nw. U. L. Rev. 345, 386 (1957). In sum, by terminating a minority stockholder's employment or by severing him from a position as an officer or director, the majority effectively frustrate the minority stockholder's purpose in entering on the corporate venture and also deny him an equal return on his investment.

. . . The distinction between the majority action in *Donahue* and the majority action in this case is more one of form than of substance. Nevertheless, we are concerned that untempered application of the strict good faith standard enunciated in *Donahue* to cases such as the one before us will result in the imposition of limitations on legitimate action by the controlling group in a close corporation which will unduly hamper its effectiveness in managing the corporation in the best interests of all concerned. The majority, concededly, have certain rights to what has been termed "selfish ownership" in the corporation which should be balanced against the concept of their fiduciary obligation to the minority. See Alfred Hill, The Sale of Controlling Shares, 70 Harv. L. Rev. 986, 1013-1015 (1957); Note, 44 Iowa L. Rev. 734, 740-741 (1959); Symposium — The Close Corporation, 52 Nw. U. L. Rev. 345, 395-396 (1957).

Therefore, when minority stockholders in a close corporation bring suit against the majority alleging a breach of the strict good faith duty owed to them by the majority, we must carefully analyze the action taken by the controlling stockholders in the individual case. It must be asked whether the controlling group can demonstrate a legitimate business purpose for its action. See Bryan v. Brock & Blevins Co., 343 F. Supp. 1062, 1068 (N.D. Ga. 1972), aff'd, 490 F.2d 563, 570-571 (5th Cir. 1974); Schwartz v. Marien, 37 N.Y.2d 487, 492, 373 N.Y.S.2d 122, 335 N.E.2d 334 (1975). . . . In asking this question, we acknowledge the fact that the controlling group in a close corporation must have some room to maneuver in establishing the business policy of the corporation. It must have a large measure of discretion, for example, in declaring or withholding dividends, deciding whether to merge or consolidate, establishing the salaries of corporate officers, dismissing directors with or without cause, and hiring and firing corporate employees.

When an asserted business purpose for their action is advanced by the majority, however, we think it is open to minority stockholders to demonstrate that the same legitimate objective could have been achieved through an alternative course of action less harmful to the minority's interest. See Schwartz v. Marien, supra; Comment, 1959 Duke L.J. 436, 458; Note, 74 Harv. L. Rev. 1630, 1638 (1961);

---

13. We note here that the master found that Springside never declared or paid a dividend to its stockholders.

Note, 35 N.C. L. Rev. 271, 273 (1957); Comment, 37 U. Pitt. L. Rev. 115, 132 (1975). If called on to settle a dispute, our courts must weigh the legitimate business purpose, if any, against the practicability of a less harmful alternative.

Applying this approach to the instant case it is apparent that the majority stockholders in Springside have not shown a legitimate business purpose for severing Wilkes from the payroll of the corporation or for refusing to reelect him as a salaried officer and director. . . . There was no showing of misconduct on Wilkes's part as a director, officer or employee of the corporation which would lead us to approve the majority action as a legitimate response to the disruptive nature of an undesirable individual bent on injuring or destroying the corporation. On the contrary, it appears that Wilkes had always accomplished his assigned share of the duties competently, and that he had never indicated an unwillingness to continue to do so.

It is an inescapable conclusion from all the evidence that the action of the majority stockholders here was a designed "freeze out" for which no legitimate business purpose has been suggested. Furthermore, we may infer that a design to pressure Wilkes into selling his shares to the corporation at a price below their value well may have been at the heart of the majority's plan.[14]

In the context of this case, several factors bear directly on the duty owed to Wilkes by his associates. At a minimum, the duty of utmost good faith and loyalty would demand that the majority consider that their action was in disregard of a long-standing policy of the stockholders that each would be a director of the corporation and that employment with the corporation would go hand in hand with stock ownership; that Wilkes was one of the four originators of the nursing home venture; and that Wilkes, like the others, had invested his capital and time for more than fifteen years with the expectation that he would continue to participate in corporate decisions. Most important is the plain fact that the cutting off of Wilkes's salary, together with the fact that the corporation never declared a dividend (see note 13 supra), assured that Wilkes would receive no return at all from the corporation.[54]

2. The question of Wilkes's damages at the hands of the majority has not been thoroughly explored on the record before us. Wilkes, in his original complaint, sought damages in the amount of the $100 a week he believed he was entitled to from the time his salary was terminated up until the time this action was commenced. However, the record shows that, after Wilkes was severed from the corporate payroll, the schedule of salaries and payments made to the other stockholders varied from time to time. In addition, the duties assumed by the other stockholders after Wilkes was deprived of his share of the corporate earnings appear to have changed in significant respects.[15] Any resolution of this question

14. This inference arises from the fact that Connor, acting on behalf of the three controlling stockholders, offered to purchase Wilkes's shares for a price Connor admittedly would not have accepted for his own shares.

54. Accord, Sugarman v. Sugarman, 797 F.2d 3 (1st Cir. 1986) (adding that majority shareholder's offer to buy appellees' minority shareholders' "stock at an inadequate price was the capstone of a plan to freeze out appellees"). See generally Robert Clark, Corporate Law 792-793 (1986). — ED.

15. In fairness to Wilkes, who, as the master found, was at all times ready and willing to work for the corporation, it should be noted that neither the other stockholders nor their representatives may be heard to say that Wilkes's duties were performed by them and that Wilkes's damages should, for that reason, be diminished.

must take into account whether the corporation was dissolved during the pendency of this litigation.

Therefore our order is as follows: So much of the judgment as dismisses Wilkes's complaint and awards costs to the defendants is reversed. The case is remanded . . . for further proceedings concerning the issue of damages. . . . [55]

---

1. *Fiduciary duty versus employment at will.* In Merola v. Exergen Corporation, 423 Mass. 461, 668 N.E.2d 351 (Mass. 1996), the court stressed that "[n]ot every discharge of an at-will employee of a close corporation who happens to own stock in the corporation gives rise to a successful breach of fiduciary duty claim." Despite the court's finding that the corporation had "no legitimate business purpose for the termination," it also found that "the termination [was not] for the financial gain of [the corporation] or contrary to public policy." Must the dismissed shareholder show a freeze-out motive, as in *Wilkes*, to prevail? Compare King v. Driscoll, 418 F.3d 576, 638 N.E.2d 488 (Mass. 1994) (terminated employee properly terminated under employment-at-will doctrine but termination nonetheless violated fiduciary duty). Delaware has yet to consider the application of a *Wilkes*-like fiduciary duty claim to the termination of an employee-stockholder. See Riblet Products Corp. v. Nagy, 683 A.2d 37 (Del. 1996).

2. *50/50 corporations.* In Schwartz v. Marien, 37 N.Y.2d 487, 373 N.Y.S.2d 122, 335 N.E.2d 334 (1975) (a decision relied upon by the *Wilkes* court), the ownership of the Superior Engraving Co., Inc. had long been split 50/50 between two families. Then, on the death of one shareholder-director, the other family (which now controlled a majority of the board) voted to issue treasury shares to itself, thereby ending the equal division of the stock. Although the corporation's charter did not provide for preemptive rights, the New York Court of Appeals found that the board was still required to justify the sale of the treasury stock by showing that it had a bona fide business purpose, "which purpose could not have been substantially accomplished by other means which would not have disturbed the equality of the two-family ownership." However, the court declined to grant summary judgment to the plaintiffs, finding that there might have been a business justification for the stock issuance, which issue had to be resolved at trial.

3. *Is balancing fair?* Some have objected to this type of balancing analysis as overly favorable to defendants. See Lawrence Mitchell, The Death of Fiduciary Duty in Close Corporations, 138 U. Pa. L. Rev. 1675 (1990) ("Balancing provides a complete shift in focus from the classic fiduciary examination of whether the action taken was in the beneficiary's best interest to a mode of analysis that centers on the fiduciary's interest. Thus, fiduciary conduct is now analyzed by examining

---

55. See also Hallahan v. Haltom Corp., 7 Mass. App. Ct. 68, 385 N.E.2d 1033 (1979) (corporation must repurchase shares of 5 percent shareholder in order to fulfill understanding of the other two groups of shareholders "that the power among the shareholders remained equally divided between the Thomson brothers and the Hallahan brothers"). Accord, Bodio v. Ellis, 401 Mass. 1, 513 N.E.2d 684 (1987).

For application of the "utmost good faith and loyalty" obligation of the *Wilkes* case to a 25 percent shareholder with an "ad hoc controlling interest" because of a provision requiring an 80 percent vote for corporate action, see Smith v. Atlantic Properties, Inc., 422 N.E.2d 798 (Mass. 1981).

For a discussion of provisions in the articles of incorporation, bylaws, or shareholder agreements that attempt to qualify or eliminate the "utmost good faith and loyalty" duty of the *Wilkes* case, see Note, Contractual Disclaimer of the Donahue Fiduciary Duty, 26 B.C. L. Rev. 1215 (1985). — Ed.

whether the fiduciary had a motive other than to harm the beneficiary, rather than whether the fiduciary acted in the beneficiary's best interest. In reality, the *Wilkes* rule . . . abandon[s] the altruism inherent in fiduciary analysis in return for more commercially-oriented concepts of good faith and fair dealing").

4. *Stock repurchase options.* In Ingle v. Glamore Motor Sales, Inc., 73 N.Y.2d 185, 535 N.E.2d 1311, 538 N.Y.S.2d 771 (1989), Ingle, the corporation's sales manager, purchased a substantial minority interest from defendant, then the sole shareholder. Many years later, Ingle was fired and defendant exercised his right, pursuant to an agreement with Ingle, to repurchase the shares if Ingle "shall cease to be an employee of the Corporation for any reason." Held for defendant:

> A minority shareholder in a close corporation, by that status alone, who contractually agrees to the repurchase of his shares upon termination of his employment for any reason, acquires no right from the corporation or majority shareholders against at-will discharge. . . . Ingle argued that the Corporation discharged him because James Glamore would then have a right to repurchase his shares under the terms of the shareholder's agreement. Notably, however, Ingle never asserted that the $2,400 per share paid to him upon termination was not fairly representative of his equity interest in the corporation. He does not contend that the corporation undervalued his shares, and he accepted payment from Glamore without reservation. Indeed, that, too, was fixed by the parties' buy-out agreement. We have no occasion to address issues involved in cases where the minority shareholders may be discharged solely to avoid assertion of the legal rights afforded to them under Business Corporation Law §§1104-a and 1118. . . .

Two judges dissented:

> [P]laintiff alleges that he became sales manager of Glamore Motor Sales in 1964 and later a co-owner of the business as a means of achieving his objective of becoming a franchised Ford dealer in the Long Island area; that from 1966 to 1982 he ran the business, supervising and hiring and firing the employees and making the day-to-day business decisions; that by terminating him from his position at Glamore Motor Sales at the age of 61 and forcing him out of the business through exercise of the purchase option, the majority not only deprived him of his continued employment and salary as an executive, director, and manager of the business, but denied him "the opportunity to realize some profit on his investment" and precluded him "from all the benefits and equities [he] had built up through years of devotion and dedication to the business"; and that he would never have made the sacrifices and investments of time, effort and money in the business had he known that the buy-back provision would be interpreted to make him subject to summary firing at the whim of the co-owner. . . .
> . . . [T]he relationship of a minority shareholder to a close corporation, if fairly viewed cannot possibly be equated with an ordinary hiring and, in the absence of a contract, regarded as nothing more than an employment at will. . . . [There is] an implied understanding that, at least, the majority owner will not discharge him arbitrarily or in bad faith and without some legitimate business reason. Unlike the employee of a large corporation, the minority shareholder in a close corporation has typically invested a large percentage of his financial wherewithal in the business. He has been willing to do so because of what he expects will be his long-term association with the business and his ability to protect his investment, and, he hopes, to make it grow. The same features of the minority owner-participant's status which makes him particularly vulnerable to action by the majority obviously work to compel him to stay on the job. He needs to do so to protect his investment and to share in any increase in its value.

Zidell v. Zidell, Inc.
277 Or. 423, 560 P.2d 1091 (1977)

HOWELL, J.: . . . [P]laintiff Arnold Zidell, suing derivatively on behalf of four of the Zidell corporations, sought a decree directing Jay Zidell, one of the individual defendants, to transfer at cost to the corporations the shares in each that he had purchased from defendant Jack Rosenfeld. Plaintiff's theory was that the opportunity to purchase the Rosenfeld shares belonged to the corporations, and that the directors breached their duties to the corporations by arranging for a private, rather than a corporate, purchase. . . .

Prior to the sale in question, plaintiff and defendant Emery Zidell each controlled 37½ percent of the shares in these corporations. Jack Rosenfeld's 25 percent interest was, therefore, the key to ultimate control by either plaintiff or Emery Zidell. During 1971 plaintiff asked Rosenfeld whether he would be interested in selling his stock in the Zidell corporations. Rosenfeld replied: "I would be interested in selling my stock. Everything I have is for sale." Nothing further was done or said at that time, but plaintiff later reported this conversation to Emery Zidell. Without informing plaintiff of his intentions, Emery then went to Rosenfeld and began negotiations for the purchase of some of Rosenfeld's shares. The purchase was consummated in May, 1972. . . .

As a general rule, a director violates no duty to his corporation by dealing in its stock on his own account. Plaintiff, however, contends that the rule should be otherwise when the stock is that of a closely-held corporation and the purchase is made at a favorable price and for the purpose of affecting control of the corporation. He argues that Rosenfeld's stock was sold at a bargain price and that the corporations had an interest in insuring that all the shareholders benefited equally from such a purchase. . . .

Plaintiff presented no evidence that the corporations have made a practice of purchasing their own stock or that they ever contemplated doing so in order to maintain proportionate control, and there is no basis for inferring an agreement to that effect. Absent such a corporate policy, there is normally no special corporate interest in the opportunity to purchase its own shares. . . . At all relevant times, the individual defendants in this case, who were the parties to the stock transaction, held a majority of the corporate stock and controlled the boards of directors. So far as the record shows, they still do. Were we to hold that this stock purchase constituted a corporate opportunity, a decree that the stock be offered to the corporations would be meaningless. The boards of directors would, undoubtedly, vote to reject the offer. There are no disinterested board members to whom the decision could be referred. Therefore, to be effective the decree would have to mandate the purchase of these shares by the corporations. Certainly where there is no guidance in the form of a "declared corporate policy," such a decree would be an unwarranted intrusion into corporate affairs. It would affect not only the proportionate ownership in the corporations but also their capital structure.

Plaintiff urges us to adopt the standards employed by the Massachusetts court in Donahue v. Rodd Electrotype Co. of New England, Inc., 328 N.E.2d 505 (Mass. 1975). . . .

The opinion in *Donahue* evidences a concern to provide greater protection for the minority shareholder in a close corporation than had previously been available in the courts. That court eloquently demonstrates that such a shareholder, because there is rarely any market for his shares, is especially vulnerable to oppressive or unfair treatment by the majority. We do not believe, however, that the protective approach taken in that case would require the corporation to tailor its policies to favor a minority shareholder at the expense of the majority. See Wilkes v. Springside Nursing Home, Inc., 353 N.E.2d 657, 663 (Mass. 1976). See also Jackson v. Nicolai-Neppach Co., 219 Or. 560, 587, 348 P.2d 9 (1959). That, however, is apparently what plaintiff is seeking in the present case. He is asking that the court require these corporations to purchase Rosenfeld's shares in order to prevent, for plaintiff's benefit, a consolidation of control in the hands of Emery Zidell.

We recognize that this consolidation has placed plaintiff at a disadvantage. Plaintiff, in his capacity as minority shareholder, had a personal interest in maintaining the balance of power which existed prior to the consolidation. Such an interest on the part of the shareholders in closely-held corporations is frequently protected by special provisions in the corporate articles or bylaws or in shareholder agreements, requiring that before any shares are sold they must first be offered to the corporation or pro rata to all other shareholders. These parties, however, had no such agreement.[8]

Like any minority shareholder who has not obtained by agreement a larger voice in corporate affairs than his stock ownership alone gives him, plaintiff is without an effective voice in corporate policy. He has not, however, shown that the welfare of the corporations requires that they redeem the Rosenfeld stock to prevent its coming under the control of Emery Zidell.[9] . . .

Affirmed.

---

1. *Purchases from third parties.* In Cressy v. Shannon Continental Corp., 378 N.E.2d 941 (Ind. Ct. App. 1978), Cressy and Russell (the corporation's original shareholders) each owned 425 of the corporation's 1,000 outstanding shares. Russell challenged Cressy's purchase of 75 shares from another shareholder. The court held that the trial judge's finding "that Cressy and Russell had intended to be equal partners" in the corporation "was amply sustained by the evidence": "The 'partnership' expectation of equality of shareholdings carried with it the duty on the part of each principal to disclose to the other the availability of outstanding shares for sale and to afford the opportunity to share in the purchase of such stock."

In Johns v. Caldwell, 601 S.W.2d 37 (Tenn. App. 1980), Johns and Caldwell each owned 45 percent of the corporation's shares. Caldwell purchased the remaining 10 percent from Moore. Johns sought to compel Caldwell to transfer half of these shares to him. *Denied:* "Johns insists that there existed between them a trust relationship and that the purchase of Moore's stock by Caldwell amounted to an abuse

---

8. Plaintiff did present evidence to show that in the past he, Emery Zidell, and Jack Rosenfeld had made a practice of consulting one another in advance about new business ventures. All were usually offered an opportunity to participate. If participation in a particular venture was not to be in proportion to the parties' shares of the overall business, consent was often obtained in advance. Even if, as plaintiff appears to contend, this evidence were sufficient to establish the existence of an unwritten but enforceable agreement, plaintiff has not asked that such an agreement be enforced, and he has not asked for an opportunity to purchase for himself any portion of the shares sold by Rosenfeld.

9. Of course, if a controlling interest were to be exercised in the future in such a way so as to violate the fiduciary duties owed by majority owners to a minority stockholder, the minority stockholder could seek an equitable remedy for such conduct. . . .

of confidence and unconscionable conduct. However, there is no showing that such purchase was in violation of any agreement, written or oral, of the parties, or that the interests of the corporation were adversely affected thereby, or that the relative position of Johns in ownership of the corporation was altered as a result thereof. . . . [T]here is no evidence of conduct by Caldwell which is in any way oppressive to Johns. As to anticipated future conduct, Johns, after the transfer, stands in the same relationship to Caldwell alone as previously he stood as to Caldwell and Moore jointly."[56]

2. Can the shareholders of a close corporation agree that they do not owe each other fiduciary duties? See pages 763-767 infra.

e. Directors' Delegation of Management Authority

As has been seen, often the major concern of close corporation shareholders is to secure their employment by and receipt of income from the enterprise. As has also been seen, the courts have sometimes relied upon fiduciary duties to assure shareholders these benefits when the shareholders did not protect them by contract. Now suppose the shareholders did contract to give one or more of the shareholders extensive powers to manage the contract for a specific length of time. Alternatively, the shareholders might cause the corporation to enter into "management contracts," which are even more encompassing in that the corporation designates an individual or other business enterprise to control substantially all of the corporation's detailed business activities. Do these kinds of contracts conflict with the statutory authority given the board of directors? Is it sensible to protect shareholders' expectations by judicially limiting director discretion through fiduciary duty, but limit the shareholders from protecting their expectations through contract? In Kennerson v. Burbank Amusement Co., 120 Cal. App. 2d. 157, 260 P.2d 823 (1953), the court stated: "California has recognized the rule that the board cannot delegate its function to govern. As long as the corporation exists, its affairs must be managed by the duly elected board. The board may grant authority to act, but it cannot delegate its function to govern. If it does so, the contract so providing is void. . . ."

Cal. Gen. Corp. Law §300(a) (1998) provides a similar formulation: "The board may delegate the management of the day-to-day operation of the business of the corporation to a management company or other person provided that the business and affairs of the corporation shall be managed and all corporate powers shall be exercised under the ultimate direction of the board."

Is the distinction that the board must retain the right to terminate the grant of authority? Suppose a corporation agreed to employ Jones as the chief executive officer for five years at a salary of $1 million per year. May the board remove her without cause, relying on its statutory authority to govern? Would Jones be able to pursue a damage claim? This also seems to be the general rule in this country.

---

56. For the view that "close corporation statutes should take the great leap forward" by "decreeing certain basic rights for all shareholders in those corporations," see Edwin Bradley, A Comparative Assessment of the California Close Corporation Provisions and a Proposal for Protecting Individual Participants, 9 Loy. L.A. L. Rev. 865 (1976).

Pioneer Specialties, Inc. v. Nelson
161 Tex. 244, 339 S.W.2d 199 (1960)

GREENHILL, J.: In April of 1957, Ronald Nelson was elected President of Pioneer Specialties, Incorporated. The by-laws of the corporation provide that the president and other corporate officers "shall be elected for one year," and Nelson's term as president was for one year. On August 1, 1957, Nelson was employed to be president of the corporation for a period of two years. Though the term for which he was *elected* to be president ended in April or May of 1958, the contract provided that he was *employed* as president until July 31, 1959. On December 15, 1957, during the year in which he had been elected president, he was discharged as president by the board of directors.

Nelson brought this suit . . . for damages for breach of his contract of employment as president for two years. . . .

The Texas Business Corporation Act was enacted in 1955. Under Sec. 2.23 of that Act, by-laws of a corporation "may contain any provision for the regulation and management of the affairs of the corporation not inconsistent with law or the articles of incorporation." Article 2.02 says that the corporation may elect or appoint officers and agents for such period of time as the corporation may determine. It is not contended here that the by-law providing for the election of the president for one year is invalid.

Nelson contends that while the by-law does say that the president "shall be elected for one year," it does not prohibit his employment as *president* for longer than a year, and that Sec. 2.43 of the Act recognizes the distinction between his election and his employment. That section provides: "Any officer or agent or member of the executive committee elected or appointed by the board of directors may be removed by the board of directors whenever in its judgment the best interests of the corporation will be served thereby, but such removal shall be without prejudice to the contract rights, if any, of the person so removed. Election or appointment of an officer or agent shall not of itself create contract rights."[57]

Article 1327 of the Revised Civil Statutes of Texas was amended in 1951 to provide, as applicable here: "Contracts of employment may be made and entered into by the corporation with any of its officers, agents, or employees for such period of time as the directors may approve and authorize, *when not prohibited by the corporation's charter or by-laws.* . . ." (Emphasis ours.) . . .

It may be conceded for purposes of this opinion that the Legislature, in enacting Article 2.43, recognized a distinction between the *election* and the *employment* of officers by stating that the removal of an elected officer "shall be without prejudice to the contract rights, if any," and that the election of an officer "shall not of itself create contract rights." It may further be conceded that the amendment to Article 1327, supra, established a public policy authorizing long-term contracts for officers. But that article also says that such long-term contracts may not be entered into when prohibited by the corporation's charter or by-laws. We think the by-law specifying that the president "shall be elected for one year" by necessary implication prohibits his employment as president for two years.

While long-term contracts of employment may be beneficial to some corporations and desirable as to some employees or officers in other corporations, the

---

57. Nearly all the states have similar provisions. See, e.g., N.Y. Bus. Corp. Law §716 (2003). — ED.

Legislature has not taken away the right of the stockholders to protect themselves against such contracts if they so desire. The stockholders have done so in this case.

We turn now to the second problem: what to do about the balance of the one-year term for which Nelson was elected president. When he was removed in December of 1957, he still had remaining a few months of his elective term of one year. For purposes of the summary judgment, it was assumed that he was discharged without just cause.

Article 2.43, supra, provides, among other things, that an officer may be removed by the board of directors "whenever in its judgment the best interests of the corporation will be served thereby, *but such removal shall be without prejudice to the contract rights, if any, of the person so removed.*"

Before the amendment of Article 1327, supra, and the enactment of the Business Corporation Act, it was held to be contrary to public policy for a corporation to enter into a contract of employment for more than one year. . . . But in Leak v. Halaby Galleries, Inc., Tex. Civ. App. 1932, 49 S.W.2d 858, writ refused, a corporate officer was employed for nearly four years. Such an agreement was held to be invalid. Nevertheless, the Court held that it was valid for one year. Under that case and Article 2.43, Nelson, therefore, should be given a trial to prove, if he can, any contractual rights and damages for the remainder of the portion of the one-year term to which he was elected. . . .

WALKER, J. (dissenting): It seems quite anomalous to say that while an officer of a corporation may be removed by the board of directors at any time, such action can be made the basis of an award of damages against the company for breach of its agreement to employ the particular individual to *serve as such officer* for a definite period. . . . This construction of the statutes will enable a board of directors to place its successors in a position where they must either subject the corporation to heavy financial loss or retain in office one who should be replaced by an available person who is better qualified to hold the position. It can result in the election or retention of an official even though the directors are convinced that the best interests of the corporation require his removal from office. I cannot believe that the Legislature intended any such result. . . .

Under the provisions of Section 2.42 of the Texas Business Corporation Act, an officer of the corporation is not employed but must be elected by the directors. It seems clear to me that when Section 2.43 and Article 1327 speak of contracts of employment and contract rights, they are referring to an agreement by which a person who has been elected to corporate office is employed to perform services which do not inhere in the office held. The president might thus be engaged to act as general manager of the company for a period of years, or a contract could be made for the assistant treasurer to do stenographic work for the other officers. In either instance the contract would not inhibit a free exercise by the board of directors of its statutory judgment and discretion in determining whether the best interests of the company will be served by retaining the particular individual as one of its officials. Removal from office would not interfere in any way with performance of the employment contract by both parties, and enforcement of the agreement would thus be entirely consistent with the power of removal conferred upon the directors by Section 2.43.

. . . This construction harmonizes and gives meaning and effect to all of [the statutory] provisions. It also avoids the undesirable consequences of the majority holding without depriving the directors of power to offer an employment contract for a definite period as a means of inducing capable individuals to accept responsible positions with the company. Since respondent was not employed to do anything except act as president and has been legally removed from that office, I would hold that he has no cause of action for breach of contract.

CULVER and NORVELL, JJ., join in this dissent.

---

1. *Statutes.* A few states have statutes that limit the terms of officers, e.g., Mass. Bus. Corp. Law §22 (2005) (president, treasurer, and clerk hold office until next annual meeting). What result in the *Pioneer Specialties* case if such a statute had existed in Texas?

2. In Short v. Columbus Rubber & Gasket Co., 535 So. 2d 61 (Miss. 1988), a board of directors resolution provided that plaintiff would be president at an annual salary of $72,000. Six months later, a shareholder resolution removed him. Plaintiff sued for breach of contract. *Held for plaintiff:* "[N]umerous courts . . . [have held] that while a by-law or statute may empower the board of directors to strip an officer of his title and corporate authority, it does not follow that the board is also empowered to disregard contractual obligations with impunity."

3. RESOLUTION OF DISPUTES AND DEADLOCKS

There are numerous causes for grave disputes and dissension in close corporations. Some are founded simply on personality conflicts growing out of the daily intimate association of the active participants. Others reflect basic disagreements about business and financial policies. They may occur in either good or bad times for the business enterprise. If the participants in the dispute do not have equal power within the corporation, those in the majority may simply proceed in accordance with their own views. But they may also manifest their displeasure with the minority in other, more hurtful ways — such as taking relatively higher salaries for themselves, dismissing the minority members from their corporate functions, or otherwise altering the distribution of corporate profits and benefits — perhaps hoping to freeze the minority out, i.e., forcing the sale of the minority's shares to the majority at a low price.

In the absence of a voting arrangement or control agreement that affords them special protection, the minority occupy a vulnerable position. The conduct of the majority may be so oppressive and unfair as to give rise to a cause of action under traditional legal doctrines already studied (e.g., fraud, excessive salaries), but frequently this will not be the case. Although the *Wilkes* case (page 761 supra) and those decisions that have followed it represent a developing judicial concern for their plight, the minority, having neither the votes to change the course of events nor the ability to sell their shares at a favorable price, may be effectively stuck.

If the participants in the dispute do have an equal number of shares or if the minority does have a veto or some other disproportionate power through a control agreement, the situation may not be much better. Deadlock is often the product of these circumstances, resulting either in a paralytic malaise or the serious threat of corporate failure.

The materials in this section explore the availability and efficacy of several devices or remedies for dealing with these conditions.

a. Arbitration

Arbitration may be a solution to close corporation disputes and deadlocks after attempts at internal negotiations have been exhausted. Its proponents contend that, especially compared with litigation, arbitration has distinct advantages from a practical business standpoint.

> Disputes that render the management of a company ineffective must be dealt with promptly; the customary delays of litigation can be catastrophic to a deadlocked company. Another advantage of arbitration, an important one indeed, is that hearings can be held in private, and confidential matters can be safeguarded. A corporation almost invariably suffers if its affairs are publicized in judicial proceedings. Further, arbitration should result in more workable decisions than litigation. Judges and juries must find for one litigant or the other, but arbitrators can mold their decision to fit the needs of the particular business problem at hand.[58]

As evidenced by a number of cases already considered in this chapter, drafters of close corporation agreements often seek to utilize the arbitral process as a means of resolving internal disputes. But courts have been hesitant to enforce such arbitration provisions. Several legal doctrines associated with arbitration generally have contributed to this reluctance. At common law as well as under older arbitration statutes, agreements to arbitrate future disputes were held revocable by either party prior to the arbitrator rendering an award; either party could obtain judicial relief, the agreement to arbitrate being held unenforceable as an attempt to oust the courts of jurisdiction.[59] Many current statutes, however, have negated this rule.[60] Another difficulty was generated by statutes that authorized arbitration only for controversies "which might be the subject of a personal action at law or of a suit in equity"; courts held that, under such statutes, disputes respecting various management and policy matters were not subject to arbitration.[61] Some such statutes have been changed specifically to remove this obstacle, making arbitration agreements "enforceable without regard to the justiciable character of the controversy."[62]

Several corporation law doctrines have also posed an impediment to the enforcement of close corporation provisions to arbitrate disagreements. As indicated by the appellate court's decision in the *Ringling* case (page 734 supra), the aversion to the separation of ownership from control has influenced courts either

---

58. 2 F. Hodge O'Neal & Robert B. Thompson, O'Neal's Close Corporations: Law and Practice §9.9 (rev. 3d ed. 2004). — ED.

59. For discussion and citations, see id., §9.14; Note, Arbitration as a Means of Settling Disputes Within Close Corporations, 63 Colum. L. Rev. 267, 268-269 (1963).

60. E.g., Cal. Civ. Proc. Code §1281 (1998); N.Y. Civ. Prac. Law §7501 (1998). See generally, 2 F. Hodge O'Neal & Robert B. Thompson, O'Neal's Close Corporations: Law and Practice §9.11 (rev. 3d ed. 2004).

61. The most prominent such decision was Matter of Burkin (Katz), 1 N.Y.2d 570, 136 N.E.2d 862, 154 N.Y.S.2d 898 (1956), interpreting the then existing provision of N.Y. Civ. Prac. Act §1448, since amended.

62. N.Y. Civ. Prac. Law §7501 (1998). See also Mich. Stat. Ann. §600.5025 (1998).

to construe arbitration clauses narrowly or to refuse flatly to enforce them at all.[63] And if the agreement provides for arbitrating issues of management or business policy, the now familiar prohibitions against sterilization of the board of directors and undue delegation of management authority to outsiders present significant obstacles.[64] In response, one recently enacted statutory provision authorizes shareholder voting agreements, specifying that "such shares shall be voted as provided by the agreement, or as the parties may agree, or as determined in accordance with any procedure (including arbitration) specified in the agreement."[65]

b. Receivers, Provisional Directors, or Custodians

Courts of equity have long been empowered to designate a receiver for corporations in distress. In addition, several recently enacted state statutes provide for the appointment of a custodian for dissension-racked corporations, and about ten states authorize the appointment of a "provisional director."

Delaware General Corporation Law (2001)

Sec. 226. *Appointment of custodian or receiver of corporation on deadlock or for other cause.* (a) The Court of Chancery, upon application of any stockholder, may appoint one or more persons to be custodians . . . of and for any corporation when:

(1) At any meeting held for the election of directors the stockholders are so divided that they have failed to elect successors to directors whose terms have expired or would have expired upon qualification of their successors; or

(2) The business of the corporation is suffering or is threatened with irreparable injury because the directors are so divided respecting the management of the affairs of the corporation that the required vote for action by the board of directors cannot be obtained and the stockholders are unable to terminate this division. . . .

(b) A custodian appointed under this section shall have all the powers and title of a receiver appointed under section 291 of this title, but the authority of the custodian is to continue the business of the corporation and not to liquidate its affairs and distribute its assets, except when the Court shall otherwise order and except in cases arising under . . . section 352(a)(2) of this title.

Sec. 291. *Receivers.* . . . Whenever a corporation shall be insolvent, the Court of Chancery, on the application of any creditor or stockholder thereof, may at any time, appoint one or more persons to be receivers of and for the corporation, to take charge of its assets, estate, effects, business and affairs, and to collect the outstanding

---

63. E.g., Roberts v. Whitson, 188 S.W.2d 875 (Tex. Civ. App. 1945); but see the Canadian decision of Motherwell v. Schoof, [1949], 2 West Wkly. 529, 4 D.L.R. 812 (Alberta S. Ct.).

64. See Application of Vogel, 25 App. Div. 2d 212, 268 N.Y.S.2d 237 (1965), *aff'd*, 19 N.Y.2d 589, 224 N.E.2d 738, 278 N.Y.S.2d 236 (1967) ("it is doubtful that arbitration could be used" in respect to "the exercise of business judgment in the management of corporate affairs").

65. N.C. Bus. Corp. Act §55-7-31 (2001). See also Ariz. Gen. Corp. Law §10-1806 (1994) (articles may provide "for arbitration of any deadlock or dispute involving the internal affairs of the corporation"); Ill. Close Corp. Act §5/2A.40 (2004).

debts, claims, and property due and belonging to the corporation, with power to prosecute and defend, in the name of the corporation or otherwise, all claims or suits, to appoint an agent or agents under them, and to do all other acts which might be done by the corporation and which may be necessary or proper. The powers of the receivers shall be such and shall continue so long as the court shall deem necessary.

Sec. 352. *Appointment of custodian for close corporation.* (a) In addition to the provisions of section 226 of this title respecting the appointment of a custodian for any corporation, the Court of Chancery, upon application of any stockholder, may appoint one or more persons to be custodians, and, if the corporation is insolvent, to be receivers, of any close corporation when:

(1) Pursuant to section 351 of this title the business and affairs of the corporation are managed by the stockholders and they are so divided that the business of the corporation is suffering or is threatened with irreparable injury and any remedy with respect to such deadlock provided in the certificate of incorporation or by-laws or in any written agreement of the stockholders has failed; or

(2) The petitioning stockholder has the right to the dissolution of the corporation under a provision of the certificate of incorporation permitted by section 355 of this title.

(b) In lieu of appointing a custodian for a close corporation under this section or section 226 of this title the Court of Chancery may appoint a provisional director, whose powers and status shall be as provided in section 353 of this title if the Court determines that it would be in the best interest of the corporation. Such appointment shall not preclude any subsequent order of the Court appointing a custodian for such corporation.

Sec. 353. *Appointment of a provisional director in certain cases.* (a) Notwithstanding any contrary provision of the certificate of incorporation or the by-laws or agreement of the stockholders, the Court of Chancery may appoint a provisional director for a close corporation if the directors are so divided respecting the management of the corporation's business and affairs that the votes required for action by the board of directors cannot be obtained with the consequence that the business and affairs of the corporation can no longer be conducted to the advantage of the stockholders generally.

(b) An application for relief under this section must be filed (1) by at least one-half of the number of directors then in office, (2) by the holders of at least one-third of all stock then entitled to elect directors, or (3) if there be more than one class of stock then entitled to elect one or more directors, by the holders of two-thirds of the stock of any such class; but the certificate of incorporation of a close corporation may provide that a lesser proportion of the directors or of the stockholders or of a class of stockholders may apply for relief under this section.

(c) A provisional director shall be an impartial person who is neither a stockholder nor a creditor of the corporation or of any subsidiary or affiliate of the corporation, and whose further qualifications, if any, may be determined by the Court of Chancery. A provisional director is not a receiver of the corporation and does not have the title and powers of a custodian or receiver appointed under sections 226 and 291 of this title. A provisional director shall have all the rights and powers of a duly elected director of the corporation, including the right to notice of and to vote at meetings of directors,[66] until such time as he shall be removed by order of the Court of Chancery or by the holders of a majority of all shares then entitled to vote to elect directors or by the holders of two-thirds of the shares of that class of voting shares which filed the application for appointment of a provisional director. His compensation shall be determined by agreement between him and the corporation subject to approval of the Court of Chancery, which may fix his compensation in the absence of agreement or in the event of disagreement between the provisional director and the corporation.

(d) Even though the requirements of subsection (b) of this section relating to the number of directors or stockholders who may petition for appointment of a provisional director are not satisfied, the Court of Chancery may nevertheless appoint a provisional director if permitted by subsection (b) of section 352 of this title.

Questions. How, if at all, do the above statutes afford relief to (1) a minority shareholder who seriously disagrees with the corporation's present business policies; (2) minority shareholders who believe they are being financially oppressed by the majority; (3) an equal shareholder in a deadlocked close corporation whose business is (a) successful, (b) failing; (4) a minority shareholder in a close corporation that is deadlocked because of a special voting arrangement or control agreement, whose business is (a) successful, (b) failing?

Consider these questions further in studying the materials on dissolution that follow at page 780 infra.

Giuricich v. Emtrol Corp.
449 A.2d 232 (Del. 1982)

HERRMANN, C.J.: The plaintiffs appeal the denial by the Court of Chancery of their petition for the appointment of a custodian pursuant to 8 Del. C. §226(a)(1), despite the existence of a shareholder deadlock between the plaintiffs, who own 50% of the stock of defendant Emtrol Corporation (hereinafter "Emtrol"), and Continental Boilerworks, Inc. (hereinafter "Continental"), which controls the remaining 50% of the stock. This deadlock has prevented the election of successor directors indefinitely. This is a case of first impression in this Court. . . .

In order to start up the new corporate entity, plaintiffs agreed to supply technical expertise and Continental agreed to supply the necessary capital. As part of this agreement, in part to protect its investment and also for tax purposes, Continental received 80% of the shares of the fledgling corporation and plaintiffs received the remaining 20%. [The two p]laintiffs, however, were each given an option to acquire an additional 15% of the stock of the corporation, which could be exercised in the first fiscal year that the corporation showed a profit. Pursuant to the agreement, Continental was given control of Emtrol's board of directors to reflect its superior ownership of the shares. No express agreement, however, was made

---

66. Because of these limited rights and powers, in Latt v. Superior Court, 212 Cal. Rptr. 380, 166 Cal. App. 3d 296 (1985), the court held that court-appointed provisional directors are "protected by absolute quasi-judicial immunity from civil actions" arising from their performance in that capacity. — ED.

concerning restructuring the board in the event that plaintiffs exercised their option.

In the first fiscal year that Emtrol became profitable, plaintiffs exercised their individual options and together own 50% of the shares of Emtrol. Shortly thereafter, they demanded that the board of directors be restructured to reflect their proportional interest; their demand was flatly refused by the existing board. . . .

Since plaintiffs exercised their options, numerous disputes have arisen between plaintiffs and Continental over such serious things as equal board representation, control and disbursement of corporate funds, corporate dividends, officers' compensation, and bonuses. Apparently to guarantee their continued control of Emtrol, the majority of the existing board of directors, in 1979, passed a resolution to amend the bylaws to expand the board from five members to seven members. The majority directors proceeded to appoint two relatives of Continental representatives to fill the new directorships, thus further diluting the plaintiffs' position on the board to a 5-2 status. . . .

The Trial Court based its decision in large part upon 8 Del. C. §226(a)(2), which authorizes the appointment of a custodian in situations involving a division of corporate directors—not a deadlock of stockholders, as here. Appointment of a custodian was refused by the Trial Judge on the ground that, despite the existence of a shareholder deadlock preventing the election of successor directors, "there has been no injury to any vital interests of plaintiffs as stockholders, nor has Emtrol suffered any apparent injury." . . .

The Delaware Corporation Law was extensively revised in 1967, including the enactment of the present §226. One of the important changes accomplished was that, under the new Statute, the Court of Chancery was authorized to appoint a "custodian" instead of a "receiver." This was more than a mere change of semantics. The clear change in terminology was accompanied by a limitation on the powers of the appointee. A "receiver" appointed under the predecessor to the current §226(a) was given "all the powers" of a receiver appointed for an insolvent corporation, in addition to the "power to continue the corporate business until otherwise ordered by the Court." A "custodian" appointed under the present §226 has the "standby" powers of a receiver, but the Statute specifies that "the authority of the custodian is to continue the business of the corporation and not to liquidate its affairs and distribute its assets except when the court shall otherwise order. . . ." 8 Del. C. §226(b). . . .

It is for these reasons that we conclude that cases construing the power of the Court of Chancery to appoint a receiver under general principles of equity or former statutes are not dispositive of the scope and effect of the present §226(a)(1) which has created the new "custodian" remedy in shareholder deadlock situations.

Cases dealing with the "director" deadlock provisions of §226(a)(2) are equally inapposite. . . . Unlike the shareholder-deadlock provisions of §226(a)(1), the director-deadlock provisions of §226(a)(2) expressly require a showing of "irreparable injury" as a prerequisite to obtaining relief. Section 226(a)(1) contains no such standard, express or implied. . . . It is impermissible judicial legislation to engraft any such prerequisite upon §226(a)(1).

. . . Manifestly, the General Assembly intended to create a more liberal and readily available remedy in shareholder-deadlock situations. It is evident that the intent of the Legislature was to ease the onerous burden of proof under the prior case law which made the appointment of a receiver for a solvent corporation almost hopeless, despite a potentially permanent shareholder-deadlock.[13] By §226(a)(1), the Legislature has created a viable remedy for the injustices arising from a shareholder-deadlock which permits control of a corporation to remain indefinitely in the hands of a self-perpetuating board of directors, any gross unfairness to other major stockholders notwithstanding.

This view of §226(a)(1) is consistent with time-honored principles of corporate democracy. . . . [C]areful judicial scrutiny will be given a situation in which the right to vote for the election of successor directors has been effectively frustrated and denied by the willful perpetuation of a shareholder-deadlock and the resulting entrenched board of directors. The situation in this case does not withstand such scrutiny: It has been admitted by counsel for the defendants that their primary purpose in perpetuating their control of the board of directors is to give the defendants the governing hand in forthcoming executive compensation contract negotiations with their 50-50 partners, the plaintiffs. This is an unworthy purpose, creating a situation violative of corporate democracy. . . .

Section 226(a) provides that upon the application of any stockholder the Court of Chancery "may" appoint a custodian upon the circumstances therein stated. While the appointment of a custodian is discretionary under §226(a)(1) it does not follow that the Trial Court may overlook the clear legislative mandate of the Statute or apply an incorrect legal standard. To do so is to abuse discretion. . . .

Accordingly, we reverse and remand with the following directions:

A custodian will be appointed by the Court of Chancery under §226(a)(1) who is strictly impartial and has a proven business and executive background. The custodian will be empowered to act only in situations in which the board of directors of Emtrol have failed to reach a unanimous decision on any issue properly before them. In the event that the board is unable to reach unanimous accord on any such pending issue, the custodian will resolve the issue in such manner as he shall deem appropriate. His decision and action in such case shall be binding upon the officers and directors of Emtrol, and shall be deemed the official action of the corporation. The custodian may call a directors' meeting, or a stockholders' meeting, sua sponte or at the request of any director. The custodian shall serve for such time as the Court of Chancery shall deem necessary, or until there is unanimous request to the Court for his discharge by all shareholders of Emtrol. The compensation of the custodian will be approved by the Court of Chancery and paid by Emtrol. . . .

Queries: How would the court in *Wilkes,* page 761 supra, handle the dispute in *Emtrol* in the absence of statute? If the statute substitutes for fiduciary duty, does it completely occupy the field? Could the court simply order that the board be

---

13. A Legislature is presumed to be aware of existing law. . . . At the time §226(a)(1) was amended, the existing case law did not allow appointment of a receiver unless the petitioner could show irreparable harm, or in other words, imminent corporate paralysis. For example, in Paulman v. Kritzer, Del. Ch., 143 A.2d 272 (1958), a shareholder deadlock had existed during four successive annual meetings between two factions, each holding one-half of the shares of the corporation. The Court conceded that the deadlock could continue indefinitely. But despite this conclusion, and the refusal of the defendant to allow plaintiffs representation on the board, their one-half ownership of the corporation, notwithstanding, the Court held that those facts were insufficient to justify the appointment of a receiver under then-existing standards.

equalized and stop short of specifying what happens if an equally balanced board is deadlocked?

c. Dissolution and Oppression

As developed in Chapter III.A.2.c, shareholders in a public corporation will ordinarily share a common view of their corporation's objectives. Because each shareholder's wealth is affected only by the value of his shares, and because each shareholder can determine the risk associated with his own investment portfolio, all shareholders will want the corporation simply to maximize profits. Close corporations are very different. Because there is no liquid market for close corporation shares, an investment in a close corporation cannot easily be diversified. And because close corporation shareholders typically are both owners and managers/employees, corporate decisions also affect them through their employment and other ties to the corporation. Thus, it is not uncommon for disagreements to arise over the future of the business or the strategy to be followed, sometimes because a shareholder's personal position has changed because of family circumstances. At the extreme, the death of one of the owners will change the makeup of participants in the business by bringing the deceased owner's heirs into the operation, or by excluding the heirs of the decedent from participation and therefore from the portion of earnings distributed as salaries to the owners/employees.

Because of these characteristics, disputes among participants in a close corporation are commonplace. To be sure, those forming a close corporation could anticipate the range of possible problems and formulate a shareholders' agreement specifying the outcome of events that can be anticipated and providing for dispute resolution mechanisms suited to their special situation. However, such advance planning is expensive, and it may be difficult for the parties to focus on the potential for discord at precisely the time they are most optimistic about their relationship and the business. Thus, the courts become corporate divorce courts, which the parties look to for help in adjusting the relationship when well-intentioned optimism proves to be unfounded.

One standard approach to resolving a close corporation dispute is dissolution. All states have long had statutes (applicable to all corporations) that authorize a specified percentage of shareholders — usually after recommendation by the directors — to voluntarily dissolve the corporation. At present, about half the jurisdictions require a simple majority vote by shareholders for voluntary dissolution, with most of the remaining states stipulating an affirmative vote of two-thirds. This procedure, therefore, is not an effective solution for a minority or an equal shareholder in a close corporation that is beset by dissension or deadlock.

Of more recent vintage, and of greater significance to close corporation shareholders, are statutes that authorize courts to order the involuntary dissolution of a corporation under specified conditions on petition of less than a majority of the shareholders. If those who control a close corporation know that a mistreated minority may cause the corporation to be dissolved, this may serve as a powerful incentive to the majority to try to accommodate the minority's wishes. On the other hand, the minority may be hesitant to seek dissolution if the business cannot be sold at a fair price as a going concern (either to existing shareholders or third parties, especially without the other shareholders' cooperation); if dissolution will result in dismemberment of the corporation and liquidation of its assets, it may leave the minority even worse off than before. For this reason, most statutes also give courts the authority to order some shareholders (typically the majority) to buy out the minority as an alternative to liquidation, in effect giving the minority a put option that had not been bargained for.

The traditional rule at common law was that, in the absence of statutory authority, courts were powerless to order the liquidation of a solvent corporation, irrespective of the degree of abuse, dissension, or deadlock within the corporation. Most modern decisions, however, have recognized an inherent discretionary power in courts of equity to order the winding up of a corporation under these circumstances. Among the situations in which courts, even in the absence of statute, have often afforded relief by appointing a receiver and winding up a corporation are the following: (1) the officers, directors, or majority shareholders have been guilty of fraud, have abused and oppressed minority shareholders, or have grossly mismanaged the corporation; (2) a deadlock exists among the shareholders that has resulted in a stoppage of corporate activity or culminated in the usurpation of control by some of the shareholders to the exclusion of others; (3) because of dissension or otherwise, it has become impossible for the corporation to attain the objectives for which it was formed or for the business to be carried on profitably.

Nelkin v. H.J.R. Realty Corp.
25 N.Y.2d 543, 255 N.E.2d 713, 307 N.Y.S.2d 454 (1969)

SCILEPPI, J.: H.J.R. Realty Corporation was organized in 1941 under the laws of the State of New York, by tenants of 128-138 Mott Street in New York City for the sole purpose of owning and managing the property and the building at that address.

The tenants involved in the corporation were Chatham Metal Products, Inc. (hereinafter referred to as Chatham), National Machinery Exchanges, Inc. (hereinafter referred to as National) and Henry Nelkin, Inc. (hereinafter referred to as Nelkin).[1]

At the time of the incorporation, all of the shareholders entered into an agreement, which, in relevant part, provided:

> That all of the parties to this agreement, are not only shareholders in H.J.R. Realty Corporation, but are also tenants or are financially interested in firms which are tenants in the building owned by the said realty corporation. That in furtherance of the aim to make the building show a profit and so that the building may be kept in good repair, the following have been agreed upon:
>> That the rental per square foot shall be decided upon and shall be charged equally to each tenant interested in the corporation owning the building. The charge for other tenants shall be decided by the officers of the corporation.

Since 1941 Chatham, National and Nelkin (until 1961) have occupied most of the space in the building at rentals far lower than the property's fair rental value. As a result the corporation has earned little, if any, net profits since its inception.

---

1. Fifty-four shares of stock (of 100 authorized) were issued. Nathan Horowitz, James Horowitz, and Charles Richter (Chatham) each received 6 shares; Irving Epstein (National) received 18 shares; and Henry Nelkin, Inc. (Nelkin) was issued 18 shares.

In 1946 Charles Richter sold his interest in Chatham and in 1961 Nelkin terminated its tenancy in the building. Richter and Nelkin no longer derived any benefit from owning stock in the corporation since neither of them shared in the discounted rentals. In 1968 the Nelkin and Richter interests (who control 4/9 of the issued stock) began a campaign to convince the shareholders of Chatham and National (who control the other 5/9 of the stock) to disregard the shareholders' agreement and pay a fair and reasonable rent, to dissolve the corporation and sell the building, or to buy the minority shares at a reasonable price. In February of 1968 the shareholders of National refused to attend a special meeting called by Nelkin and Richter and, instead, an informal meeting was held. It became clear at the meeting that the differences between the majority shareholders (National and Chatham) and the minority shareholders (petitioners Nelkin and Richter) were irreconcilable. For one thing, the majority shareholders declared that the shareholders' agreement of 1941 authorized the corporation to charge "interested tenants" discounted rentals and that as the controlling majority they intended to manage the building in compliance with the agreement. Moreover, in response to Richter and Nelkin's offer to sell their stock, the majority offered only what they had paid in 1941. It was also announced by Chatham that it was intending to move into even more space in the building which was to be vacated by another tenant.

In October of 1968 Nelkin and Richter, as minority shareholders, instituted the instant special proceeding in accordance with section 1104 (subd. [c]) of the Business Corporation Law, Consol. Laws c. 4, seeking judicial dissolution of the corporation. The Supreme Court granted the petition and placed the proceeding on the calendar. On appeal, the Appellate Division reversed and dismissed the petition on the ground that it failed to state a cause of action for dissolution. . . .

In our opinion petitioner's contention that the majority shareholders are continuing the existence of the corporation solely for their own benefit and that, therefore, the corporation should be dissolved "as a matter of judicial sponsorship" in accordance with Leibert v. Clapp, 13 N.Y.2d 313-315, 247 N.Y.S.2d 102-104, 196 N.E.2d 540-541, is without merit. . . .

In Leibert v. Clapp, supra, a minority shareholder sued to compel the dissolution of the corporation in which he owned stock. The plaintiff alleged that the majority shareholders of the corporation were maintaining the corporate existence only to enable them to wrongfully divert assets and income to the parent corporation and, furthermore, that the majority shareholders were attempting to coerce the minority into selling their stock at greatly depreciated prices. This court recognized that there was no statutory authority for judicial dissolution in such a case but stated that such relief is available "as a matter of judicial sponsorship" where the majority shareholders or directors: "have so palpably breached the fiduciary duty they owe to the minority shareholders that they are disqualified from exercising the exclusive discretion and dissolution power given to them by the statute."[67]

---

67. The principal issue in the *Leibert* case was whether the alleged breaches of fiduciary duty by defendant majority shareholders could be adequately remedied in a derivative suit by the minority shareholders rather than in a suit for dissolution. The court, finding that the allegations went "far beyond charges of waste, misappropriation and illegal accumulations of surplus, which might be cured by a derivative action for injunctive relief and an accounting," held that "to restrict the minority shareholders to a derivative suit would be to commit them to a multiplicity of costly, time-consuming and difficult actions with the result, at most, of curing the misconduct of the past while leaving the basic

In the instant case, however, the alleged behavior of the majority shareholders could in no event be characterized as a wrongful diversion. The recent case of Kruger v. Gerth, 16 N.Y.2d 802, 263 N.Y.S.2d 1, 210 N.E.2d 355, *affg.* 22 A.D.2d 916, 255 N.Y.S.2d 498, is in point. In *Kruger* a minority shareholder alleged that for several years a majority shareholder had been taking substantial salaries and bonuses, leaving the corporation with only minimal net income.[68] The plaintiff prayed for nonstatutory judicial dissolution in accordance with our decision in *Leibert* on the ground that the majority shareholder was continuing the corporate existence solely to "provide himself with employment, at substantial salaries and bonuses . . . thereby . . . exploiting the corporation to the detriment of the other stockholders."

The Appellate Division, in *Kruger*, found that the majority shareholder was not looting the corporate assets nor was he maintaining the corporation for his own special benefit and that, therefore, the minority shareholder had not established sufficient facts to warrant nonstatutory dissolution. This court affirmed on the opinion at the Appellate Division.

The case for dissolution in *Kruger* was even stronger than in the instant case since here the majority shareholders have been acting in compliance with a share-holders' agreement entered into by the minority. Petitioners have alleged only that the shareholders' agreement entered into in 1941 is invalid and that the rents paid by the majority shareholders pursuant thereto are unreasonably low. Even if these allegations are assumed to be true, the majority shareholders have not been guilty of looting or exploiting the corporation to the detriment of the minority shareholders, and their actions clearly do not constitute a breach of fiduciary duty owed to the minority. The discounted rentals that they have been paying since 1941 were not set arbitrarily but in accordance with the shareholders' agreement. Furthermore, although it is true that because of the change in circumstances the majority alone is now benefiting, the existence of the corporation has been continued for the original purpose of operating the building in accordance with the shareholders' agreement.[69]

It must be noted that the actual validity of the shareholders' agreement is not relevant in this proceeding for nonstatutory dissolution. The fact that the controlling majority has paid the lower rents in good faith in accordance with the agreement which was believed to be valid by all shareholders until the minority brought about a change in circumstances, belies the allegation of wrongful diversion even if the agreement was in fact invalid. Moreover, both petitioners enjoyed the benefits of the low rent provision in the agreement while their firms were tenants. The fact

---

improprieties unremedied. It is the traditional office of equity to forestall the possibility of such harassment and injustice." The dissent contended that all the alleged improprieties were subject to cure by a derivative suit and that the suit for dissolution was "patently an attempt by a shareholder, holding an infinitesimally small proportion of the outstanding shares, to evade the public policy expressed by the Legislature in the enactment of" the security for expenses requirement in derivative suits. — ED.

68. In the *Kruger* case — noted, 51 Cornell L.Q. 538 (1966); 19 Vand. L. Rev. 485 (1966) — it was agreed that the corporation could not be operated so as to increase its profits. The annual net profit for 1958-1961 had been under $2,000. Defendant's annual salary had been about $9,000, and his bonus for each of the four years was, respectively, $5,857.20, $7,153.20, $6,480, and $6,120. Throughout these years the corporation had a net worth of substantially more than $100,000 and total annual sales ranging from about $245,000 to about $273,000. See also Sandfield v. Goldstein, 71 Misc. 2d 735, 336 N.Y.S.2d 821 (1972); Central Standard Life Ins. Co. v. Davis, 10 Ill. 2d 566, 141 N.E.2d 45 (1956). — ED.

69. For a decision on similar facts finding no "illegal, oppressive or fraudulent" conduct under the state dissolution statute, see Abel v. Forrest Realty, Inc., 484 So. 2d 1069 (Ala. 1986). — ED

that by their own voluntary action they no longer benefit by the agreement does not of itself entitle them to judicial dissolution. . . .

Petitioners' allegations that the 1941 shareholders' agreement is invalid and that Chatham's proposed occupation of additional space within the building is in violation of the agreement, may be adequately adjudicated in a shareholders' derivative action to rescind or reform the agreement. They are not, however, sufficient to justify the exercise of the Supreme Court's inherent power to order nonstatutory judicial dissolution.

Accordingly, the order of the Appellate Division dismissing the complaint should be affirmed.

FULD, C.J. [joined by JASEN, J.] (dissenting): . . . When . . . petitioners moved out of the building, the nature of the corporation — originally formed, as already indicated, for the benefit of all of its stockholders — changed radically. The portion of the premises occupied by the majority shareholders expanded to the point that there was (and is) only one other tenant, occupying less than half of a single floor in the seven-story building. Although the corporation's assets were worth in excess of $350,000, it showed only negligible profits in 1966 and 1967 and a loss amounting, we are told, to more than $4,800 in the first eight months of 1968. The reason for this, quite obviously, was that the entire profit which the corporation could potentially earn was being siphoned off by the majority group in the form of reduced rent. The minority stockholders, although they had contributed more than 44% of the corporation's capital, were realizing no return whatsoever on their investment and there was no prospect of any change.[1]

Implicit in the agreement which the parties signed was . . . the understanding that, should any of those shareholders cease to be (or represent) a tenant in the building, the agreement would no longer be applicable to him and he would not be required to maintain his interest in the corporation. Thus, it may well be said, the existence of the corporation in its initial form was conditioned upon each of the stockholders continuing as a tenant in the building.

The circumstance that majority shareholders may not be "looting" the corporation or "wrongfully diverting" its assets is insufficient basis for denying corporate dissolution. What is significant and operative is the indisputable fact that this corporation is being continued solely and exclusively for the benefit of those holding 5/9ths of the company's shares. Stated somewhat differently, in the light of what has occurred, the reason for corporate existence is gone. . . .

In refusing to allow an action for dissolution where it is alleged that a close corporation no longer serves the function for which it was created and employs its assets for the exclusive benefit of only some of its shareholders, the court, I suggest, ignores business reality and perpetuates inequality. A close corporation, like a partnership or joint venture, is nothing more than a convenient business arrangement entered into for the mutual advantage of its participants. Although control of its assets may be exclusively vested in the majority, it is implicit, in the nature of the corporate form, that its purpose is to provide some benefit for all of those who have contributed their capital to the venture. When changing circumstances render that purpose impossible of achievement, a court of equity should be

---

1. The complaint alleges — and we assume that the allegation is true — that the respondents have refused to purchase the petitioners' shares except at a totally inadequate price.

no more reluctant to permit a corporate dissolution than it would be to dissolve a purely contractual relationship. . . .

Meiselman v. Meiselman
309 N.C. 279, 307 S.E.2d 551 (1983)

FRYE, J.: [Plaintiff Michael Meiselman and defendant Ira Meiselman are brothers who, by gifts of stock from their deceased father, own about 30 percent and 70 percent, respectively, of the shares of several family corporations whose total book value is over $11 million. Both brothers were employed by the corporations until Ira fired Michael after Michael had sued Ira over a corporate action that resulted in Michael's exclusion from meaningful participation in the corporation's management. Michael now seeks dissolution of the corporations or, as a desired alternative, "a buy-out at fair value" of his interests. The trial court denied relief.] . . .

We note at the outset that the enterprises with which we are dealing are close corporations, not publicly held corporations. This distinction is crucial because the two types of corporations are functionally quite different. Indeed, the commentators all appear to agree that "[c]lose corporations are often little more than incorporated partnerships." Comment, Oppression as a Statutory Ground for Corporate Dissolution, 1965 Duke L.J. 128, 138 (1965) [hereinafter cited as Comment, *Oppression*]. See also 2 F. O'Neal, Close Corporations §902 (2d ed. 1971); Hetherington and Dooley, Illiquidity and Exploitation: A Proposed Statutory Solution to the Remaining Close Corporation Problem, 63 Va. L. Rev. 1, 2 (1977); Israels, The Sacred Cow of Corporate Existence: Problems of Deadlock and Dissolution, 19 U. Chi. L. Rev. 778, 778-79 (1952); Comment, Deadlock and Dissolution in the Close Corporation: Has the Sacred Cow Been Butchered?, 58 Neb. L. Rev. 791, 796 (1979) [hereinafter cited as Comment, *Deadlock and Dissolution*]. . . .

Professor O'Neal, perhaps the foremost authority on close corporations, points out that many close corporations are companies based on personal relationships that give rise to certain "reasonable expectations" on the part of those acquiring an interest in the close corporation. Those "reasonable expectations" include, for example, the parties' expectation that they will participate in the management of the business or be employed by the company. O'Neal, Close Corporations: Existing Legislation and Recommended Reform, 33 Bus. Law. 873, 885 (1978). Other commentators have also noted that those investing in close corporations have some of these same "reasonable expectations." Afterman, Statutory Protection for Oppressed Minority Shareholders: A Model for Reform, 55 Va. L. Rev. 1043, 1064 (1969); Comment, *Oppression*, supra, at 141; Comment, *Deadlock and Dissolution*, supra, at 795; Comment, Dissolution Under the California Corporations Code: A Remedy for Minority Shareholders, 22 UCLA L. Rev. 595, 616 (1975) [hereinafter cited as Comment, *Dissolution Under the California Corporations Code*].

Thus, when personal relations among the participants in a close corporation break down, the "reasonable expectations" the participants had . . . become difficult if not impossible to fulfill. In other words, when the personal relationships among the participants break down, the majority shareholder, because of his greater voting power, is in a position to terminate the minority shareholder's employment and to exclude him from participation in management decisions.

Some may argue that the minority shareholder should have bargained for greater protection before agreeing to accept his minority shareholder position in a close corporation. However, the practical realities of this particular business situation oftentimes do not allow for such negotiations. In his article, Special Characteristics, Problems, and Needs of the Close Corporation, 1969 U. Ill. L.F. 1 (1969), Professor Hetherington, another recognized authority in this field, explains the situation as follows:

> . . . [T]he circumstances under which a party takes a minority stock position in a close corporation vary widely. Many involve situations where the minority party, because of lack of awareness of the risks, or because of the weakness of his bargaining position, fails to negotiate for protection. Probably a common instance of this kind occurs where an employee or an outsider is given an opportunity to buy stock in a close corporation wholly or substantially owned by a single stockholder or a small group of associates, often a family. Typically, the controlling individual or group retains a substantial majority position. The opportunity to buy into the business is highly valued by the recipient; his enthusiasm and weak bargaining position make it unlikely almost to a certainty that he will ask for — let alone insist upon — protection for his position as a minority stockholder. Purchases of stock in such situations are likely to be arranged without either party consulting a lawyer. The result is the assumption of a minority stock position without, or with only limited, appreciation of the risks involved.

Id. at 17-18 (footnote omitted).

. . . [A]s one commentator notes, "close corporations are often formed by friends or family members who simply may not believe that disagreements could ever arise." Comment, *Dissolution Under the California Corporations Code*, supra, at 603-04. Furthermore, when a minority shareholder receives his shares in a close corporation from another in the form of a gift or inheritance, as did plaintiff here, the minority shareholder never had the opportunity to negotiate for any sort of protection with respect to the "reasonable expectations" he had or hoped to enjoy in the close corporation.

Unfortunately, when dissension develops in such a situation, as Professor O'Neal notes, "American courts traditionally have been reluctant to interfere in the internal affairs of corporations. . . ." F. O'Neal, Oppression of Minority Shareholders §9.04, at 582 (1975). This reluctance, as applied to a minority shareholder holding an interest in a close corporation, places the minority shareholder in a remediless situation. As Professor O'Neal points out, when the personal relationship among the participants in a close corporation breaks down, the minority shareholder has neither the power to dissolve the business unit at will, as does a partner in a partnership, nor does he have the "way out" which is open to a shareholder in a publicly held corporation, the opportunity to sell his shares on the open market. 2 F. O'Neal, Close Corporations §9.02. Thus, the illiquidity of a minority shareholder's interest in a close corporation renders him vulnerable to exploitation by the majority shareholders. . . .

Apparently in response to these commentators' uniform calls for reform in this area of corporate law, many state legislatures have enacted statutes giving the tribunals in their states the power to grant relief to minority shareholders under more liberal circumstances. For example, at least seven states have given their courts the authority to grant dissolution of a corporation when the acts of the directors or those in control of the corporation are "oppressive" to the shareholders. Ill. Ann. Stat. ch. 32, §157.96(a)(3) (Smith-Hurd Cum. Supp. 1983); Md. Corps. & Assns. Code Ann. §3-413(b)(2) (1975); Mich. Comp. Laws Ann. §450.1825(1) (1973); N.J. Stat. Ann. §14A:12-7(1)(c) (West Cum. Supp. 1983); N.Y. Bus. Corp. Law §1104-a(a)(1) (McKinney Cum. Supp. 1983); S.C. Code Ann. §33-21-150(a)(4)(B) (Law. Co-op. Cum. Supp. 1982); Va. Code §13.1-94(a)(2) (1978).

In interpreting the term "oppressive" as used in its dissolution statute, a New York Trial Court recently held in a case of first impression that where two controlling shareholders discharged the minority shareholder as an employee and officer of the two corporations in which he had an interest, thus severely damaging the minority shareholder's "reasonable expectations," their actions were deemed to be "oppressive" under New York Law. In re the Application of Topper, 107 Misc. 2d 25, 433 N.Y.S.2d 359 (1980). . . .

Similarly, at least three states have statutes authorizing a court to grant dissolution when those in control of the corporation are guilty of treating the corporate shareholders "unfairly." Cal. Corp. Code §1800(b)(4) (West 1977) ("persistent unfairness"); Mich. Comp. Laws Ann. §450.1825(1) (West 1973) ("wilfully unfair"); N.J. Stat. Ann. §14A:12-7(1)(c) (West Cum. Supp. 1983).

In helping to establish this growing trend toward enactment of more liberal grounds under which dissolution will be granted to a complaining shareholder, the legislature in this State enacted in 1955 N.C.G.S. §55-125(a)(4), the statute granting superior court judges the "power to liquidate the assets and business of a corporation in an action by a shareholder when it is established" that "[l]iquidation is reasonably necessary for the protection of the rights or interests of the complaining shareholder." Two other states have similar statutes — California and New York. Cal. Corp. Code §1800(b)(5) (West 1977) (formerly §4651(f)); N.Y. Bus. Corp. Law §1104a(b)(2) (McKinney Cum. Supp. 1983). . . .

In interpreting the provision of its corporate dissolution statute . . . a California Appellate Court affirmed in Stumpf v. C. E. Stumpf & Sons, Inc., 47 Cal. App. 3d 230, 120 Cal. Rptr. 671 (1975), a trial court's conclusion that relief was appropriate when supported by the following evidence: "The hostility between the two brothers had grown so extreme that respondent severed contact with his family and was allowed no say in the operation of the business. After respondent's withdrawal from the business, he received no salary, dividends, or other revenue from his investment in the corporation." . . .

The basic question at issue is what standard we should adopt to determine whether a minority shareholder is entitled to dissolution or other relief. . . .

When a shareholder brings suit seeking relief under N.C.G.S. §55-125(a)(4) and N.C.G.S. §55-125.1, he has the burden of proving that his "rights or interests" as a shareholder are being contravened. However, once the shareholder has established this, the trial court, in deciding whether to grant relief, "must exercise its equitable discretion, and consider the actual benefit and injury to [all of] the shareholders resulting from dissolution" or other possible relief. Henry George & Sons, Inc. v. Cooper-George, Inc., 95 Wash. 2d 944, 632 P.2d 512, 516 (1981). "The question is essentially one for resolution through the familiar balancing process and flexible remedial resources of courts of equity." Id. To hold otherwise would allow a plaintiff to demand at will dissolution of a corporation or a forced buy out of his shares or other relief at the expense of the corporation and without regard to the rights and interests of the other shareholders.

... Specifically, N.C.G.S. §55-125(a) provides as follows:

> The superior court shall have power to liquidate the assets and business of a corporation in an action by a shareholder when it is established that:
>
> (1) The directors are deadlocked in the management of the corporate affairs and the shareholders are unable to break the deadlock, so that the business can no longer be conducted to the advantage of all the shareholders; or
>
> (2) The shareholders are deadlocked in voting power, otherwise than by virtue of special provisions or arrangements designed to create veto power among the shareholders, and for that reason have been unable at two consecutive annual meetings to elect successors to directors whose terms had expired; or
>
> (3) All of the present shareholders are parties to, or are transferees or subscribers of shares with actual notice of a written agreement, whether embodied in the charter or separate therefrom, entitling the complaining shareholder to liquidation or dissolution of the corporation at will or upon the occurrence of some event which has subsequently occurred; or
>
> (4) Liquidation is reasonably necessary for the protection of the rights or interests of the complaining shareholder.

Michael alleged that he was entitled to relief under subsection (4). . . . [W]e hold that a complaining shareholder's "rights or interests" in a close corporation include the "reasonable expectations" the complaining shareholder has in the corporation. These "reasonable expectations" are to be ascertained by examining the entire history of the participants' relationship. That history will include the "reasonable expectations" created at the inception of the participants' relationship; those "reasonable expectations" as altered over time; and the "reasonable expectations" which develop as the participants engage in a course of dealing in conducting the affairs of the corporation. The interests and views of the other participants must be considered in determining "reasonable expectations." The key is *"reasonable."* In order for plaintiff's expectations to be reasonable, they must be known to or assumed by the other shareholders and concurred in by them. Privately held expectations which are not made known to the other participants are not "reasonable." Only expectations embodied in understandings, express or implied, among the participants should be recognized by the court. Hillman, The Dissatisfied Participant in the Solvent Business Venture: A Consideration of the Relative Permanence of Partnerships and Close Corporations, 67 Minn. L. Rev. 1, 77-81 (1983). Also, only substantial expectations should be considered and this must be determined on a case-by-case basis. These requirements provide needed protection to potential defendants in this type case.[70] . . . In so holding, we recognize the rule that Professor O'Neal suggests should be applied in a corporation based on a "personal relationship":

> [A] court should give relief, dissolution or some other remedy to a minority shareholder whenever corporate managers or controlling shareholders act in a way that

---

70. Accord, Matter of Kemp & Beatley, Inc., 64 N.Y.2d 63, 473 N.E.2d 1173, 484 N.Y.S.2d 799 (1984). Minn. Bus. Corp. Act §751(3a) (1983) provides that "in determining whether to order equitable relief, dissolution, or a buy-out, the court shall take into consideration the duty which all shareholders in a closely-held corporation owe one another to act in an honest, fair, and reasonable manner in the operation of the corporation and the reasonable expectations of the shareholders as they exist at the inception and develop during the course of the shareholders' relationship with the corporation and with each other." See generally Susan Edward Olson, A Statutory Elixir for the Oppression Malady, 36 Mercer L. Rev. 627 (1985). — ED.

disappoints the minority shareholder's reasonable expectations, even though the acts of the managers or controlling shareholders fall within the literal scope of powers or rights granted them by the corporation act or the corporation's charter or bylaws. . . . In a close corporation, the corporation's charter and bylaws almost never reflect the full business bargain of the participants.

O'Neal, supra, at 886.

After articulating the "rights or interests" of the complaining shareholder, the trial court is then to determine if liquidation is "reasonably necessary" for the protection of those "rights or interests." . . . N.C.G.S. §55-125.1 provides as follows:

> (a) In any action filed by a shareholder to dissolve the corporation under G.S. 55-125(a), the court may make such order or grant such relief, other than dissolution, as in its discretion it deems appropriate, including, without limitation, an order:
> (1) Canceling or altering any provision contained in the charter or the bylaws of the corporation; or
> (2) Canceling, altering, or enjoining any resolution or other act of the corporation; or
> (3) Directing or prohibiting any act of the corporation or of shareholders, directors, officers or other persons party to the action: or
> (4) Providing for the purchase at their fair value of shares of any shareholder, either by the corporation or by other shareholders, such fair value to be determined in accordance with such procedures, as the court may provide.
> (b) Such relief may be granted as an alternative to a decree of dissolution, or *may be granted whenever the circumstances of the case are such that relief, but not dissolution, would be appropriate.*

(1973, c. 496, §41.) (Emphasis added.)

. . . It is clear, then, that when N.C.G.S. §55-125(a)(4) and 55-125.1(b) are read in conjunction, it must only be "established" under N.C.G.S. §55-125(a)(4) that *relief of some kind*, and not just liquidation, is "reasonably necessary" for the protection of the complaining shareholder's "rights or interests." To interpret N.C.G.S. §55-125(a)(4) as providing that relief can be given only when *liquidation* is "reasonably necessary" for the protection of the complaining shareholder's "rights or interests" would, in effect, fail to recognize the existence of N.C.G.S. §55-125.1(b) to the extent that it grants trial courts the power to order alternative relief where relief of some kind *but not dissolution* is appropriate.

In sum, therefore, we hold that under N.C.G.S. §55-125(a)(4) a trial court is: (1) to define the "rights or interests" the complaining shareholder has in the corporation; and (2) to determine whether some form of relief is "reasonably necessary" for the protection of those "rights or interests." For plaintiff to obtain relief under the expectations analysis, he must prove that (1) he had one or more substantial reasonable expectations known or assumed by the other participants; (2) the expectation has been frustrated; (3) the frustration was without fault of plaintiff and was in large part beyond his control; and (4) under all of the circumstances of the case plaintiff is entitled to some form of equitable relief.

We will now review the "rights or interests" each party contends Michael has in the family corporations. Michael suggests in his brief that the "rights or interests" he has as a shareholder in these close corporations include "rights or interests" in secure employment, fringe benefits which flow from his association with the corporations, and meaningful participation in the management of the family business. . . .

Defendants argue, however, that Michael, as a shareholder, is only entitled to relief if his traditional shareholder rights have been infringed. They contend that those traditional shareholder rights include the right to notice of stockholders' meetings, the right to vote cumulatively, the right of access to the corporate offices and to corporate financial information, and the right to compel the payment of dividends. Because these rights have not been violated, they argue, Michael is not entitled to relief. . . .

While it may be true that a shareholder in, for example, a publicly held corporation may have "rights or interests" defined as defendants argue, a shareholder's rights in a closely held corporation may not necessarily be so narrowly defined. In short, we hold that the shareholder in this case — one who owns stock worth well over $3,000,000 and which accounts for a 30 to 40 percent ownership in these closely held, family-run corporations worth well over $11,000,000 and who also has been employed by the corporations, provided with fringe benefits, and, to some extent, allowed to participate in management decisions — has "rights or interests" more broadly defined than defendants contend. Put another way, Michael's "reasonable expectations" are not as limited as defendants contend. . . .

Because the trial court's findings of fact failed to address the "rights or interests" Michael has in these family corporations, we must remand the case to the trial court for an evidentiary hearing to resolve this issue. . . .

Martin, J., concurring in the result.

Except as herein set forth, I concur in the majority opinion. There are, however, certain aspects of the case that should be discussed that the majority does not address. . . .

In determining whether to grant equitable relief under N.C.G.S. 55-125.1, the trial court must consider all the circumstances of the case. If it is determined that plaintiff's rights or interests require protection because of plaintiff's own conduct, it would be improper to grant equitable relief. He who seeks equity must do equity. . . . The reasons *why* the complaining shareholder's interests require protection [are] highly relevant in the resolution of the case.

The court should also consider what effect the granting of relief will have upon the corporation and other shareholders. Will it interfere with the corporation's ability to attract financing for its business? Will it interfere with its ability to attract additional capital? Will it require burdensome financing upon the corporation or the shareholders? Will it interfere with the rights of creditors? If a buy-out of plaintiff's shares is forced upon the company, it may be far from painless. If it is determined that the granting of relief will be unduly burdensome to the corporation or other shareholders, the trial court should consider this in determining whether to grant relief and, if so, whether this should affect the purchase price or value attached to plaintiff's shares or the method of payment. It is an equitable proceeding. . . .

In this connection, I cannot agree that merely because plaintiff's expectations were not fulfilled it necessarily follows that the majority stockholders were guilty of oppression.[71]

---

71. Compare Balvik v. Sylvester, 411 N.W.2d 383 (N.D. 1987), in which the court held, first, that defeating a minority shareholder's "reasonable expectations" of continued employment may be

Another circumstance to be considered is the fact that most, if not all, of plaintiff's stock was given to him by his father. He did not contribute his own hard-earned cash to the enterprise. This could indicate that he did not assume the risk of having his investment held hostage by the majority, or it could be that one has to accept what one gets by gift — in this case, a locked-in-minority interest in a family corporation. . . .

BRANCH, C.J., and COPELAND, J., join in this concurring opinion.

---

1. *The role of the court.* As the court in *Meiselman* makes clear, the modern statutes authorizing judicial intervention in response to minority shareholder claims of oppression were enacted in response to academic advocacy. The academics referred to in the opinion advanced the position that investors in close corporations typically have expectations about the future conduct of the business and governance of the corporation that are neither memorialized in a shareholders' agreement nor captured by the standard rules set out in the corporation statute. These statutes plainly direct the courts to resolve shareholder disputes on a basis other than the fiduciary duty approach advanced in Wilkes v. Springside Nursing Home, Inc., page 761 supra. Some statutes look to "oppressive" conduct, others to "unfair" conduct, but the term is typically given more detailed content. The most difficult problem posed by the statutes concerns the role of the court. The business judgment rule, it will be recalled, is premised on the proposition that courts should not substitute their own views for those of corporate decisionmakers. What guides courts in assessing whether conduct that is allowable on its face under the corporate statute or a shareholders' agreement is nonetheless "oppressive"?

2. *Are all close corporations the same?* Bonavita v. Corbo, 300 N.J. Super. 179, 692 A.2d 119 (1996), presents a prototypical close corporation oppression case. Two families each owned 50 percent of a retail jewelry business. The husbands were involved in operating the business and earned the same salary. When one husband died, his salary ceased. Because the corporation had a policy of not paying dividends, the widow received no benefit from her stock. In contrast, the other family did not require dividends since both the surviving husband and other members of the family were employed by the corporation and drew, in the aggregate, $400,000 annually in salary. The court concluded that the widow had been treated oppressively. It is commonplace in such a situation for the parties to enter into an agreement requiring the survivor to buy the deceased's interest, often funded by life insurance. Should this fact influence the court's assessment?

Should the analysis change if the scale of the corporation changes? McCallum v. Rosen's Diversified, Inc., 153 F.3d 701 (8th Cir. 1998), involved a claim by the terminated chief executive officer of a family-controlled corporation with annual revenues of $400 million that the corporation should be required to purchase at a court-determined fair value stock that had been awarded the executive as a bonus. No contractual obligation existed concerning the stock's repurchase should the

---

"oppression," and then stated: "We find little relevance in whether Sylvester discharged Balvik from employment for cause, or in the fact that Balvik's removal as a director and officer of the corporation occurred only after Balvik brought the instant suit. . . . The ultimate effect of these actions is that Balvik clearly has been 'frozen out' of a business in which he reasonably expected to participate. As a result, Balvik is entitled to relief." — ED.

executive's employment be terminated. The Minnesota statute allowed the court to order the repurchase of the stock of minority shareholders or employees of a closely held corporation if those in control acted in an "unfairly prejudicial" manner. Despite the size of the company and the sophistication of the plaintiff, the court ordered the purchase of his stock because his reasonable expectations were defeated. For the view that "larger and smaller close corporations [do not] have similar internal governance needs," see Charles O'Kelley, Filling Gaps in the Close Corporation Contract: A Transactions Cost Analysis, 87 Nw. U. L. Rev. 216 (1992): "[T]here is an identifiable class of [larger] jointly owned, closely held firms . . . for which unmodified corporate form is the preferred contractual starting point."

If the courts' expansive role in policing the treatment of minority shareholders in close corporations is based on the premise that participants in close corporations more often than not lack the capacity to make thoughtful decisions about the terms of their relationship to a close corporation or its governance, is the number of shareholders a sufficient proxy for sophistication? Might one justify an expansive role for the courts as a default rule that sophisticated parties could displace by contract? In Nixon v. Blackwell, 626 A.2d 1366 (Del. 1993), the Delaware Supreme Court adopted a different kind of default rule analysis. The court declined to provide special protection for minority shareholders in a close corporation who had not elected to be subject to the statutory close corporation provisions. In this setting, should the burden of opting out be placed on the more or less sophisticated?

3. *The substance of judicial review.* Consistent with Meiselman v. Meiselman, the courts have concluded that corporate conduct will be oppressive or otherwise unfair if it defeats the reasonable expectation of the parties. See, e.g., Matter of Kemp & Beatley, Inc., 64 N.Y.2d 63, 484 N.Y.S.2d 799, 473 N.E.2d 1173 (1984); Robert B. Thompson, Corporate Dissolution and Shareholders' Reasonable Expectations, 66 Wash. U. L.Q. 193 (1988) (chronicling the development). But how does the court determine what those expectations were? Is the concern with the reasonableness of the controlling shareholders' behavior or with how much damage is being inflicted on the minority? See Douglas K. Moll, Shareholder Oppression in Close Corporations: The Unanswered Question of Perspective, 53 Vand. L. Rev. 749 (2000).

An approach urged by a number of commentators is to ask what protections minority shareholders would have been given if they actually had bargained over the terms of their relationship — in effect an inquiry into a "hypothetical bargain." See, e.g., Frank Easterbrook & Daniel Fischel, The Economic Structure of Corporate Law 247 (1991); David Charny, Hypothetical Bargains: The Normative Structure of Contract Interpretation, 89 Mich. L. Rev. 1815 (1991); Jason S. Johnston, Opting In and Opting Out: Bargaining for Fiduciary Duties in Cooperative Ventures, 70 Wash. U. L.Q. 291 (1992). But framing the question does not necessarily make answering it much easier. While minority shareholders will not wish to be locked in to an illiquid investment if their circumstances change, controlling shareholders may not want to commit the corporation to providing a liquidity source in the event of a disagreement. However, this framing may make extreme cases clear. For example, consider two families setting up a close corporation, with the expectation that each family will have a representative active in the business and drawing a salary. If there is no way to provide a return to the family whose representative dies, the arrangement has the form of a tontine, where all of the value goes to the family whose representative is the last to die. Since such an arrangement would make no economic sense for either party, the hypothetical bargain analysis would lead to a result like that in Bonavita v. Corbo, supra.

What should be the analysis in cases like *McCallum*, supra, in which the CEO is given as a bonus shares that have little value following the CEO's termination? Would a court impose implied terms on the employment relationship of a CEO other than with respect to stock bonuses? Does it matter whether the corporation's earnings had been distributed through higher salaries, leaving the shares without value to a non-employee?

At what time should the shareholders' reasonable expectations be determined? An easy answer is that the terms of the investment are set at the time the investment is made. But Meiselman v. Meiselman states that the shareholders' reasonable expectations "are to be ascertained by examining the entire history of the participants' relationship. That history will include the 'reasonable expectations' created at the inception of the participants' relationship; those 'reasonable expectations' as altered over time; and the 'reasonable expectations' which develop as the participants engage in a course of dealing in conducting the affairs of the corporation." Would this analysis extend to situations where the participants actually entered into a shareholders' agreement but changed circumstances made the agreement more favorable to one of the parties than was the case when the shareholders' agreement was executed? Put differently, would Nelkin v. H.J.R. Realty, page 781 supra, be decided differently if New York's oppression statute, referred to in Meiselman v. Meiselman, had been in force when *Nelkin* was decided?

Given the difficulty of specifying shareholders' reasonable expectations, should the courts be engaging in this effort on behalf of sophisticated parties, who could have specified their expectations? For these parties, should their decision not to restrict the controlling shareholder's control be given credence?

4. *Non-dissolution remedies.* While many of the statutes speak expressly only of a dissolution remedy, more recent statutes also give the court the authority to order that the corporation or another shareholder buy out the shareholder found to have been oppressed. Additionally, some courts have held that equitable remedies, including a mandatory buyout, are available even if the statute expressly authorizes only dissolution. See, e.g., Baker v. Commercial Body Builders, Inc., 264 Or. 614, 507 P.2d 387 (1973), in which the court lists ten remedies that were available short of liquidation, including the payment of a dividend, the enjoining of oppressive conduct, and a mandatory buyout. RMBCA §14.34 shifts the discretion to substitute a buyout for liquidation to the controlling shareholder, giving the controlling shareholder 90 days after the filing of a petition for involuntary dissolution to elect to purchase the shares of the minority shareholder at fair value. The parties then have 60 days to negotiate the terms of the purchase. If the negotiations fail, the court then stays the liquidation proceedings and itself determines the fair value.

How often will a judicial order of dissolution result in liquidation of the business?

> Except for the rare case where the petition is prompted by pique, a shareholder suing for dissolution is trying to accomplish one of three things: (1) to withdraw his investment from the firm; (2) to induce the other shareholders to sell out to him; or (3) to use the threat of dissolution to induce the other shareholders to agree to a change

in the balance of power or in the policies of the firm. All of these objectives can be accomplished without dissolution. If the petitioner wants to sell out, he is interested in receiving the highest possible price and is indifferent whether the purchase funds are raised by the other shareholders individually or by a sale of the firm's assets. If the second or third objective[] motivate[s] the suit, it is plain that the petitioner does not want dissolution at all. In all three situations, a dissolution petition is a means to another end.

Since the petitioner can always achieve his purposes without dissolution, and since the defendant will always oppose it, the dispute is very likely to be settled without liquidating the firm's assets and terminating its business. The court's decision to grant or to deny dissolution is significant only as it affects the relative bargaining strength of the parties. . . . If a court orders dissolution and one party wishes to continue the business, a mutually advantageous purchase of the other's interest will result. If the dissolution is denied, the majority has less incentive to settle and will reduce the amount it offers for the minority's interest, but a sale is still likely to occur eventually. . . .

Dissolution proceedings for profitable companies thus function primarily as a price-fixing mechanism for an eventual buyout, but a more cumbersome, inefficient, and costly means of achieving that end is difficult to imagine. . . . Accordingly, this article proposes . . . entitling a minority or fifty percent shareholder to demand that the corporation or the remaining shareholders purchase his shares. If the parties fail to agree on price and terms of payment, the petitioner would be entitled to a decree fixing both; if the defendants continue to refuse to purchase at the price fixed by the court, the firm would be dissolved.

John Hetherington & Michael Dooley, Illiquidity and Exploitation: A Proposed Statutory Solution to the Remaining Close Corporation Problem, 63 Va. L. Rev. 1, 27-34, 45 (1977).

Compare Frank Easterbrook & Daniel Fischel, Close Corporations and Agency Costs, 38 Stan. L. Rev. 271, 289-290 (1986):

Few firms other than banks and open-end mutual funds hold the liquid financial assets that permit withdrawal of investments on demand. When the firm holds illiquid assets, the right to withdraw capital is restricted to avoid having to sell firm-specific assets at distress prices. . . .

A right to withdraw capital from a firm that has no liquid assets and that does not have an active secondary market in shares also creates difficult (costly) problems of valuation. Any method of valuation is highly inexact; different appraisers will reach radically different conclusions regarding the value of the firm and a particular shareholder's proportionate interest. These uncertainties compound the problem of negotiating.

Each of the effects of a right to withdraw capital from the firm . . . encourages opportunistic behavior by minorities. The automatic buy-out right, in other words, gives minority shareholders who have a relatively smaller stake in the venture the ability to impose costs on other investors that is absent under a fault standard for involuntary dissolution. Minorities can use this bargaining advantage to extract a disproportionate share of benefits from other investors. . . . [This] suggests that courts should not readily infer a right to withdraw capital from the firm on behalf of minority shareholders.

See also 2 F. Hodge O'Neal & Robert B. Thompson, O'Neal's Close Corporations: Law and Practice §9.7 (rev. 3d ed. 2004): "Further, where the shareholders or some of them have bargained for and received a power to veto corporate decisions, the point should not be overlooked that easy dissolution may weaken the effectiveness of the veto arrangement. Finally, easy dissolution may be an invitation to the majority to squeeze out the minority by dissolving the corporation and transferring its business and assets to another company."

5. *Valuation issues in connection with mandatory dissolution and buyouts.* On its face, a mandatory dissolution remedy does not pose valuation problems. Rather than the court valuing the business to be sold, the market will do so. However, the market for closely held businesses is not efficient, and the investigation process will take place in the context of ongoing litigation among the only parties who are in a position to provide information concerning the business to potential bidders. Moreover, the likely dissension among the parties will make it difficult to structure the sale in a fashion such that a buyer will get the benefit of, and therefore be willing to pay for, the close corporation's good will. For these reasons, the controlling shareholder may turn out to be the highest bidder in the dissolution sale, which converts dissolution into a form of buyout. Additionally, the threat of dissolution can serve as a substantial incentive for the shareholders to prefer a mandatory buyout, whether as an alternative remedy or as a means of settlement. In both cases, the information barriers to an outside buyer's accurately assessing the close corporation's value are reduced.

The use of a mandatory buyout instead of dissolution, however, presents a special set of valuation problems in those cases when the court must actually determine the buyout price. In particular, determining the value of minority shares in a close corporation requires deciding whether to reduce the pro rata value of the minority shares by either a "minority discount" or a "marketability discount." The former represents the fact that for all the reasons that gave rise to the special remedies for oppression, there may be few potential buyers for minority stock in a close corporation controlled by someone else, and those buyers that do appear will not pay the same price as for controlling shares. Therefore, a discount is said to be appropriate. The marketability discount represents the fact that the market for close corporation stock of any character is thin because of the information and transaction cost problems associated with its sale. Thus, if the goal of the valuation process is to determine what the minority shares would be worth if the owner voluntarily chose to sell them, both discounts might be applicable in appropriate circumstances.

The essential character of a mandatory buyout, however, raises the question whether these discounts are appropriately applied in what is essentially an involuntary sale. Take the minority discount first. Given that the minority shareholder has been forced to sell her shares only as a result of the oppression of the controlling shareholder, is it appropriate to give the controlling shareholder the benefit of his wrongful conduct? Had the corporation actually been dissolved, the minority shareholders would have received a pro rata share of the proceeds. Why should giving the controlling shareholder the option to purchase the minority's shares rather than sell the corporation through dissolution alter the measure of what the minority shareholder receives? The courts generally have not applied a minority discount in mandatory buyout valuations, often stating that a discount that may be appropriate in a market transaction is not appropriate when the sale is court directed to the corporation or the controlling shareholder. See Friedman v. Beway Realty Corp., 87 N.Y.2d 161, 638 N.Y.S.2d 399, 661 N.E.2d 972 (1995); Charland v. Country View Golf Club, Inc., 588 A.2d 609 (R.I. 1991); Brown v. Allied Corrugated Box Co., 91 Cal. App. 3d 477, 1154 Cal. Rptr. 170 (1979).

The results with respect to the marketability discount are more mixed. On the one hand, the marketability discount, resulting from the difficulty of selling a close corporation, would apply to all shares, so the value to the minority shareholders would be the same whether the entire corporation is sold through dissolution or just the minority shares are sold through a mandatory buyout. New York courts do allow a marketability discount in mandatory buyout valuations. See Friedman v. Beway Realty Corp., supra; Blake v. Blake Agency, Inc., 107 A.2d 139, 486 N.Y.S.2d 341 (1985). On the other hand, it remains true that whether the corporation is sold in dissolution or the minority shares are sold in a mandatory buyout, the marketability discount is realized only because of the controlling shareholder's wrongful conduct. From this perspective, a minority shareholder should not be forced to take a discount that results from an involuntary sale. California and Rhode Island do not allow a marketability discount. See Charland v. Country View Golf Club, Inc., supra; Brown v. Allied Corrugated Box Co., supra.

D. *LIMITED PARTNERSHIPS*

Unlike the partnership, the limited partnership was unknown to the common law and is entirely a creation of statute. The goal was to achieve a critical benefit of the corporate form — limited liability for investors — and a critical benefit of the partnership form — the avoidance of double taxation. In this feat of organizational engineering, elements of the two forms are blended. The limited partnership permits two tiers of partnership: general partners and limited partners. A limited partner is an investor who holds an ownership stake in the enterprise and participates in profits, but without incurring personal liability for more than the investor's agreed-upon capital contribution to the firm. This limited liability comes at a price: limited partners are restricted as to the degree to which they can exercise control over or participate in active management of the firm. The general partners' rights and obligations remain the same as those for a general partnership — notably unlimited liability — and are subject to general partnership law.

The limited partnership made its appearance in this country in 1822, when New York enacted legislation that was patterned after French law. Continental law had recognized from medieval times a form of business association known as the Commenda, under which typically a merchant would entrust goods or money to an agent who would trade with them in foreign lands, with the merchant receiving a specified share of the profits. In this special form of partnership (or "Societas"), the absent supplier of capital was necessarily passive.

Because limited partnership statutes were in derogation of common law, early American decisions tended to construe them strictly, holding that limited liability could be lost if there was less than a full and exact compliance with the statutory requirement as to the formation of the limited partnership or if a limited partner exercised "control" over the business.[72] In 1916 the Commissioners on Uniform

---

72. For a discussion of the early case law and historical background on limited partnerships, see Rathke v. Griffith, 36 Wash. 2d 394, 218 P.2d 757 (1950).

State Laws promulgated the Uniform Limited Partnership Act (ULPA), which was adopted by all U.S. states except Louisiana (which, because of its civil law origins, already recognized the limited partnership). In 1976 the Commissioners adopted a substantially revised and updated statute, the Revised Uniform Limited Partnership Act (RULPA), which again was adopted in the majority of states.[73] In 1985 significant amendments to RULPA were adopted that enabled limited partners to participate to a greater extent in the management and control of the partnership without risking their limited liability. The erosion of the constraints on limited partnership participation in management was completed by the 2001 revision to RULPA, which provides, "A limited partner is not personally liable, directly or indirectly, by way of contribution or otherwise, for an obligation of the limited partnership solely by reason of being a limited partner, even if the limited partner participates in the management and control of the partnership." RULPA §303. The commentary explains this revision as "the next logical step in the evolution of the limited partner's liability shield" which "brings limited partners into parity with LLC members, LLP partners and corporate shareholders" and "renders the control rule extinct."

The limited partnership device has proven to be an attractive vehicle for the financing of many kinds of investment activities, including real estate, venture capital, motion pictures, and speculative securities investments. Such a firm may have up to several hundred limited partners, composed typically of wealthy investors who want the pass-through tax advantages of the partnership form and do not expect to participate actively in management. While tax motives may drive the choice of business form in real estate and other investments that are designed to generate tax but not cash losses to the investors, the attraction of the limited partnership form for venture capital funds results from its effectiveness in separating cash flow rights and control rights. In the typical venture capital limited partnership, the general partner contributes only 1 percent of the capital but has complete operating control subject only to replacement by the limited partners. This separation of ownership and management allows the general partner's passive investors in the venture capital fund, typically institutional investors such as pension funds and endowments, to get the benefit of the general partner's expertise, and the general partner's professional venture capitalists to raise large funds, without the general partner having to invest a large amount of capital up front.[74]

Limited partnership interests will typically constitute "securities" for the purposes of the federal securities laws. Thus, registration of these partnership interests with the SEC may be required, and Rule 10b-5 will be applicable, with the consequences discussed in Chapter V. Limited partnerships, representing the traditional means of combining limited liability and the avoidance of a corporate-level tax, now have competitors that may offer the same advantages but with more

---

73. For commentary on RULPA, see Edwin Hecker Jr., The Revised Uniform Limited Partnership Act: Provisions Governing Financial Affairs, 46 Mo. L. Rev. 577 (1981); Edwin Hecker Jr., The Revised Uniform Limited Partnership Act: Provisions Affecting the Relationship of the Firm and Its Members to Third Parties, 27 U. Kan. L. Rev. 1 (1978); Robert Kessler, The New Uniform Limited Partnership Act: A Critique, 48 Fordham L. Rev. 159 (1979).

74. The general partner is typically compensated through an annual management fee in the range of 2 percent, and a 20 percent carried interest — i.e., a right to receive 20 percent of the limited partnership's profits. See Ronald J. Gilson, Engineering Venture Capital Markets: Lessons from the American Experience, 55 Stan. L. Rev. 1067 (2003); Bernard Black & Ronald J. Gilson, Venture Capital and the Structure of Capital Markets: Banks Versus Stock Markets, 47 J. Fin. Econ. 243 (1998).

flexibility. These alternatives — limited liability companies and limited liability partnerships — are discussed later in this chapter.

1. FORMATION

Unlike a general partnership, which can arise informally, a limited partnership can be formed only by filing a "certificate of limited partnership" in the office of the secretary of state. This document must list the names and business addresses of the general partners, but, since the 1985 amendments, it does not need to identify the limited partners. Because this public document will typically be short and spare, a separate and more detailed partnership agreement will invariably be drafted.

Much litigation has addressed the consequences of a failure to file a certificate of limited partnership in full compliance with the statutory requirements. For example, in Direct Mail Specialist, Inc. v. Brown, 673 F. Supp. 1540 (Mont. 1987), the promoters filed the certificate of limited partnership in the wrong office (with the county clerk and not the secretary of state). Even though other documents were filed with the secretary of state (which documents did not, however, disclose the firm to be a limited partnership), the court found that there had not been substantial compliance with ULPA (then the applicable statute in the jurisdiction), and hence the limited partners became general partners.

RULPA attempts to mitigate the harshness of this result by establishing a procedure by which a person who "erroneously but in good faith" believed that his or her status was that of a limited partner can restrict his or her liability as a general partner, on ascertaining the mistake, either by filing an appropriate certificate or amendment or by withdrawing from future equity participation in the partnership (RULPA §304). In such event, the individual will be liable as a general partner only to third parties who transacted business with the partnership prior to the corrective filing and who believed that the individual was a general partner at the time of their transaction.[75]

2. CONTROL AND LIABILITY

ULPA §7 provided: "A limited partner shall not become liable as a general partner unless, in addition to the exercise of his rights and powers as a limited partner, he takes part in the control of the business." This ambiguous reference to participation "in the control of the business" and the uncertain distinction between that and the legitimate "exercise of the rights and powers" of a limited partner engendered considerable litigation over the life of ULPA[76] and also forced (or perhaps permitted) drafters to deny effective veto powers or other powers to limited partners for fear that such powers would jeopardize their limited liability. For example,

---

75. Litigation continues to focus on this issue. See Briargate Condominium Ass'n v. Carpenter, 976 F.2d 868 (4th Cir. 1992) ("good faith" test in RULPA §304 implies an objectively reasonable standard, but withdrawal after learning of mistake need not be prompt).

76. See, e.g., Gateway Potato Sales v. G.B. Investment Co., 822 P.2d 490 (Ariz. 1991); Pitman v. Flanagan Lumber Co., 567 So. 2d 1335 (Ala. 1990); Holzman v. De Escamilla, 86 Cal. App. 2d 858, 195 P.2d 833 (1948); Mount Vernon Sav. & Loan v. Partridge Assocs., 679 F. Supp. 522 (D. Md. 1987). See also Alan Feld, The "Control" Test for Limited Partnership, 82 Harv. L. Rev. 1471 (1969).

could the limited partners vote to remove and replace the general partner if the partnership was unprofitable without risking their limited liability under this statutory formulation? What would counsel for the general partner argue?

RULPA mitigated the harshness of the prior case law in two steps. As amended in 1985, RULPA §303(a) specified that a limited partner "is liable only to persons who transact business with the limited partnership reasonably believing, based upon the limited partner's conduct, that the limited partner is a general partner," even if the limited partner participated in control of the business. In short, reliance must be shown before a third party can hold the "overly active" limited partner personally liable on this basis.

RULPA §303(b) then established a detailed safe harbor of individual activities in which the limited partner could engage without sacrificing limited liability. It provides:

> (b) A limited partner does not participate in the control of the business within the meaning of subsection (a) solely by doing one or more of the following:
>
> (1) being a contractor for or an agent or employee of the limited partnership or of a general partner or being an officer, director, or shareholder of a general partner that is a corporation;
>
> (2) consulting with and advising a general partner with respect to the business of the limited partnership;
>
> (3) acting as surety for the limited partnership or guaranteeing or assuming one or more specific obligations of the limited partnership;
>
> (4) taking any action required or permitted by law to bring or pursue a derivative action in the right of the limited partnership;
>
> (5) requesting or attending a meeting of partners;
>
> (6) proposing, approving, or disapproving, by voting or otherwise, one or more of the following matters:
>
> (i) the dissolution and winding up of the limited partnership;
>
> (ii) the sale, exchange, lease, mortgage, pledge or other transfer of all or substantially all of the assets of the limited partnership;
>
> (iii) the incurrence of indebtedness by the limited partnership other than in the ordinary course of its business;
>
> (iv) a change in the nature of the business;
>
> (v) the admission or removal of a general partner;
>
> (vi) the admission or removal of a limited partner;
>
> (vii) a transaction involving an actual or potential conflict of interest between a general partner and the limited partnership or the limited partners;
>
> (viii) an amendment to the partnership agreement or certificate of limited partnership; or
>
> (ix) matters related to the business of the limited partnership not otherwise enumerated in this subsection (b), which the partnership agreement states in writing may be subject to the approval or disapproval of limited partners;
>
> (7) winding up the limited partnership pursuant to Section 803; or
>
> (8) exercising any right or power permitted to limited partners under this [Act] and not specifically enumerated in this subsection (b).
>
> (c) The enumeration in subsection (b) does not mean that the possession or exercise of any other powers by a limited partnership constitutes participation by him (or her) in the business of the limited partnership.

Even this litany proved only a way station in the erosion of limited partners' involvement in the partnership's business. As discussed above, §303 was amended in 2001 to provide that "[a] limited partner is not personally liable, directly or indirectly, by way of contribution or otherwise, for an obligation of the limited partnership solely by reason of being a limited partner, even if the limited partner participates in the management and control of the partnership."[77]

3. FIDUCIARY DUTY

As Meinhard v. Salmon, page 715 supra, famously holds, partners owe each other a fiduciary duty, and this extends to the general partner of a limited partnership, who owes a fiduciary duty to the limited partners. Two special issues arise with respect to the fiduciary duty of general partners. The first concerns freedom of contract. Can the limited partnership agreement contractually reduce the extent of the general partner's fiduciary duty? The second concerns who owes the duty to limited partners. If, as is commonly the case in investment limited partnerships, the general partner is itself a corporation, does anyone besides the corporate entity owe the limited partners a fiduciary duty? The most obvious candidates are the directors of the corporate general partner.

a. Contractual Amendment of the General Partner's Fiduciary Duty

Meinhard sets a very high standard for the general partner's conduct. To what extent can the limited partnership agreement modify general standards of fiduciary duty?

Gotham Partners, L.P. v. Hallwood Realty Partners, L.P.
817 A.2d 160 Del. (2002)

VEASEY, C.J.: In this appeal, we hold that a limited partnership agreement may provide for contractually created fiduciary duties substantially mirroring traditional fiduciary duties that apply in the corporation law. The Court of Chancery held that the limited partnership agreement here provided for such fiduciary duties by requiring the general partner and its controlling entity to treat the limited partners in accordance with the entire fairness standard. We agree with this holding and also agree with the trial court that the defendants are jointly and severally liable because the challenged transaction breached the entire fairness provisions of the partnership agreement.

With respect to remedies for that breach, the plaintiff limited partner had demanded rescission or an adequate damage award and sterilization of the voting rights attached to the partnership units involved in the challenged transaction. The Court of Chancery refused to order rescission and awarded damages. We affirm the holding of the Vice Chancellor that he was not necessarily required to order rescission by the limited partnership contract or the application of equitable principles. Such a decision is properly within the discretion of a court of equity, but here the Court of Chancery did not fashion a remedy that is an appropriate substitute for rescission under the circumstances.

---

77. ULPA §303, 6A U.L.A. 35 (Supp. 2002).

As the Court of Chancery noted, one effect of the challenged transaction was that the general partner and its corporate parent gained control of the limited partnership as a result of wrongdoing. In our view, the value of the control thus achieved was not properly compensated for by the award of damages because the trial court did not account properly for a control premium in its remedy calculation.

Consequently, we reverse the damages award and remand for such proceedings as may be necessary and appropriate: (1) to quantify how the challenged transaction would have been consummated had the defendants adhered to the entire fairness standards and procedures of the limited partnership agreement; and (2) to consider and award one or more of the various equitable remedies available to the limited partnership, including rescission, rescissory damages, sterilization of voting rights, or other appropriate methods of accounting for the control premium.

Facts

Hallwood Realty Partners, L.P. ("the Partnership") is a Delaware limited partnership that owns commercial office buildings and industrial parks in several locations in the United States and lists its partnership units on the American Stock Exchange. Gotham Partners, L.P. ("Gotham") is a hedge fund, the investments of which include real estate. It is the largest independent limited partner in the Partnership with approximately 14.8 percent of the outstanding partnership units. Hallwood Realty Corporation ("the General Partner") is the sole general partner and is a wholly-owned subsidiary of Hallwood Group Incorporated ("HGI"), which owned 5.1 percent of the outstanding partnership units before the transactions challenged in this case. Anthony Gumbiner and William Guzzetti were members of the board of directors of the General Partner. They were also officers of HGI at the time of the challenged transaction.[1]

In 1994, the Partnership's units were trading at a low price because of the ongoing economic recession in real estate. On October 12, 1994, Guzzetti proposed to the Partnership's board of directors that it approve a reverse split,[2] a unit option plan,[3] and an odd lot tender offer[4] subject to HGI's willingness to finance the transactions by buying any fractional units generated by a reverse split and any units purchased by the Partnership in an odd lot tender offer. At the time, more than half of the Partnership's units were held in odd lots and could be resold to HGI. Guzzetti told the board that HGI was the only source of financing available and that the transactions would, among other things, raise the trading price of the Partnership's units, reduce the Partnership's administrative costs, and give odd lot

---

1. Gumbiner, a corporate lawyer, owned 30 percent of HGI's shares between 1994 and 1995 and was the chairman of the board of directors and chief executive officer of the General Partner at the time of the challenged transactions. Guzzetti, a former lawyer, is an executive vice-president of HGI and was the president of the Partnership and a member of the General Partner's board of directors at the time of the challenged transactions.

2. A reverse split reduces the number of outstanding units and consequently increases the per unit value of each unit. Reverse splits usually create odd lots.

3. In this case, the option plan would sell post-reverse split units to officers and employees of the General Partner, including Gumbiner and Guzzetti.

4. An odd lot offer is a tender offer by the issuer for blocks of fewer than one hundred outstanding units or shares. Such "odd lots" are considered small and thus create inefficient administrative costs for issuers and may be difficult to sell at an attractive price. Odd lot offers are designed to provide liquidity to small holders and to reduce issuer costs.

holders the chance to sell at market price without incurring brokerage fees. The Partnership's board approved the transactions, citing Guzzetti's reasons.

At first, HGI declined to provide funding for the reverse split and odd lot offer. But, by March 1995, HGI was willing to fund the Reverse Split and Option Plan, which were approved by the non-HGI directors on the General Partner's board. HGI purchased 30,000 units, approximately 1.6 percent of the Partnership's equity, through the Reverse Split. The Option Plan resulted in officers and employees of the General Partner purchasing 86,000 units or 4.7 percent of the Partnership's equity. Through these two transactions, HGI increased its ownership of outstanding Partnership units from 5.1 percent to approximately 11.4 percent.

By May 1995, HGI was willing to fund an odd lot tender offer. Guzzetti called a special meeting of the General Partner's board of directors after circulating a memorandum indicating that 55 percent of the Partnership's units were held in odd lots and thus could be tendered in the odd lot offer. The non-HGI directors voted as a "special committee" to approve the Odd Lot Offer. The purchase price of an odd lot was putatively set at the five-day market average referenced in Section 9.01(b) of the Partnership Agreement.[5] No valuation information was shared with the board.

The Odd Lot Offer began on June 5, 1995. The accompanying press release indicated that the Partnership would resell any tendered odd lot units to HGI, affiliates of HGI, or other institutional investors. . . .

From June 9 to July 25, 1995, when the Odd Lot Offer closed, the Partnership purchased 293,539 units from odd lot holders and placed them in a holding account. The Partnership then resold the units to HGI at the same price the Partnership paid for them, approximately $4.1 million. The Odd Lot Resale resulted in HGI purchasing approximately 23.4 percent of the Partnership's outstanding units. Thus, HGI increased its stake in the outstanding Partnership units from 11.4 percent to 29.7 percent and solidified its control over the Partnership. The Partnership Agreement requires the written consent or affirmative vote by at least 66 and 1/3 percent of the limited partners to remove a general partner.

Gotham began purchasing Partnership units in 1994 and owned 14.8 percent of the outstanding units as of September 1996. Gotham was aware of the Odd Lot Offer and Resale but did not complain to the Partnership until January 1997 when it requested access to the Partnership's books and records. The Partnership denied the request.

Preliminary Proceedings in the Court of Chancery

On June 20, 1997, Gotham filed another action in the Court of Chancery alleging derivative claims in connection with the Odd Lot Offer and Resale, the Reverse Split, and the Option Plan . . . [including] breaches by the General Partner of traditional fiduciary duties and contractually based fiduciary duties. . . .

On summary judgment, the Court of Chancery sustained the contractual fiduciary duty claims and dismissed the traditional fiduciary duty claims on the ground that the Partnership Agreement supplanted traditional fiduciary

5. Section 9.01(b) of the Partnership Agreement states: "Except as set forth above, the number of Units issued to the General Partners or any such Affiliate in exchange for any Capital Contribution shall not exceed the Net Agreed Value of the contributed property or amount of cash, as the case may be, divided by the Unit Price of a Unit as of the day of such issuance."

duties and provided for contractual fiduciary duties by which the defendants' conduct would be measured. The Vice Chancellor found that Sections 7.05[8] and 7.10(a)[9] of the Partnership Agreement operate together as a contractual statement of the entire fairness standard, with Section 7.05 substantively requiring fair price and Section 7.10(a) substantively requiring fair dealing. No appeal has been taken from this ruling.

The Vice Chancellor's summary judgment opinion in this case, however, creates a separate problem. We refer to one aspect of the Vice Chancellor's discussion of the Delaware Revised Uniform Limited Partnership Act ("DRULPA") in his summary judgment opinion in this case where he stated that section 17-1101(d)(2) "expressly authorizes the *elimination*, modification or enhancement of . . . fiduciary duties in the written agreement governing the limited partnership." It is at least the second time the Court of Chancery has stated in dicta that DRULPA permits a limited partnership agreement to *eliminate* fiduciary duties.[12]

Because the Vice Chancellor's summary judgment order in this matter has not been appealed, his opinion on this point is not before us for review on this appeal. In our view, however, this dictum should not be ignored because it could be misinterpreted in future cases as a correct rule of law.[13] Accordingly, in the interest of avoiding the perpetuation of a questionable statutory interpretation that could be relied upon adversely by courts, commentators and practitioners in the future, we are constrained to draw attention to the statutory language and the underlying

8. Section 7.05 of the Partnership Agreement states: "Transactions with General Partner or Affiliates. The Partnership is expressly permitted to enter into transactions with the General Partner or any Affiliate thereof provided that the terms of any such transaction are substantially equivalent to terms obtainable by the Partnership from a comparable unaffiliated third party."

9. Section 7.10(a) of the Partnership Agreement states in relevant part: "Audit Committee; Resolution of Conflicts of Interest. (a) The General Partner shall form an Audit Committee (the "Audit Committee") to be comprised of two members of the board of directors of the General Partner who are not affiliated with the General Partner or its Affiliates except by reason of such directorship. The functions of the Audit Committee shall be to review and approve . . . (ii) transactions between the Partnership and the General Partner and any of its Affiliates."

12. Id. See also Sonet v. Timber Co., 722 A.2d 319, 323 (Del. Ch. 1998) (stating that §17-1101(d) "apparently [allows] broad license to enhance, reform, or even eliminate fiduciary duty protections . . .") (emphasis added).

13. Commentators have already noted some uncertainty on this subject. See, e.g., Martin I. Lubaroff and Paul M. Altman ("Lubaroff & Altman"), Delaware Limited Partnerships §13.1.2 at 13-2 (2002 Supp.) §11.2.6 at 11-26.8 to 11-26.9: Although on its face Section 17-1101(d) permits the fiduciary duty of a general partner to be expanded or restricted without limit by the terms of a partnership agreement, it is not clear whether a restriction can be such as to totally eliminate all fiduciary duties. The issue of the extent to which a fiduciary duty may be restricted has not yet been resolved. The question has been left to the courts to determine as the area develops. . . . In *Sonet*, however, the Court of Chancery did note, in passing, that Section 17-1101(d) "apparently [allows] broad license to enhance, reform, or even eliminate fiduciary duty protections. . . ." 722 A.2d at 323. . . . Nevertheless, given the contractual nature of a partnership agreement and the relationship among partners, and the Act's provisions and recognition of the principle of freedom of contract, at a minimum, a very substantial and material limitation and restriction on the duties of a general partner, including a general partner's fiduciary duties, should be permitted and enforced. . . .

In Gotham Partners, L.P. v. Hallwood Realty Partners, L.P., C.A. No. 15754, 2000 WL 1476663 (Del. Ch. Sept. 27, 2000) (memo opinion), the Court again examined contractual modification of fiduciary duties. . . .

In its discussion of Section 17-1101(d)(2), the Court stated that such section "expressly authorizes the elimination, modification, or enhancement of . . . fiduciary duties in the written agreement governing the limited partnership." Id. at 24, 2000 WL 1476663 at *10.

Section 17-1101(d)(2) states: "the partner's or other person's duties and liabilities may be expanded or restricted by provisions in the partnership agreement." There is no mention in §17-1101(d)(2), or elsewhere in [the Delaware Revised Uniform Limited Partnership Act ("DRULPA"), that a limited partnership agreement may eliminate the fiduciary duties or liabilities of a general partner.

general principle in our jurisprudence that scrupulous adherence to fiduciary duties is normally expected.

Section 17-1101(d)(2) states: "the partner's or other person's duties and liabilities may be expanded or restricted by provisions in the partnership agreement." There is no mention in §17-1101(d)(2), or elsewhere in DRULPA at 6 Del. C., ch. 17, that a limited partnership agreement may eliminate the fiduciary duties or liabilities of a general partner.

Finally, we note the historic cautionary approach of the courts of Delaware that efforts by a fiduciary to escape a fiduciary duty, whether by a corporate director or officer or other type of trustee, should be scrutinized searchingly.[15] Accordingly, although it is not appropriate for us to express an advisory opinion on a matter not before us, we simply raise a note of concern and caution relating to this dubious dictum in the Vice Chancellor's summary judgment opinion.[17]

Decision After Trial

After trial, the Court of Chancery found the defendants liable for their conduct associated with the Odd Lot Resale to HGI, but upheld their conduct connected with the Reverse Split and the Option Plan. The Vice Chancellor found that the Odd Lot Resale, unlike the other two transactions, did not involve an issuance of units, but rather a resale of existing units to HGI. As a result, the Vice Chancellor found "inapplicable" the protections of Section 9.01 of the Partnership Agreement, which authorizes the General Partner to issue Partnership Units of any kind to any person without the consent or approval of the Limited Partners. Instead, the Vice Chancellor continued, the Odd Lot Resale was subject to Partnership Agreement Sections 7.05 and 7.10(a), which provide for the contractually created fiduciary duties of entire fairness.

The Vice Chancellor found that the General Partner breached the contractual fiduciary duties of entire fairness because (1) the General Partner never formed the Audit Committee as required by Section 7.10(a) to review and approve the Odd Lot Offer and Resale, and (2) the General Partner failed to perform a market check or obtain any reliable financial analysis indicating that the Odd Lot Resale would be conducted on the same terms obtainable from a third party. The Court of Chancery thus held the General Partner liable for breach of the contractually created fiduciary duties of entire fairness contained in the Partnership Agreement and found HGI, Gumbiner, and Guzzetti jointly and severally liable with the General Partner for aiding and abetting its breach.

---

15. See McNeil v. McNeil, 798 A.2d 503 (Del. 2002) (discussing the fiduciary duties of trustees generally and holding that the trustees breached those duties); Cede & Co. v. Technicolor, Inc., 634 A.2d 345, 360 (Del. 1993) (stating that "directors are charged with an unyielding fiduciary duty to protect the interests of the corporation and to act in the best interests of its shareholders"); Smith v. Van Gorkom, 488 A.2d 858, 872 (Del. 1985) ("In carrying out their managerial roles, directors are charged with an unyielding fiduciary duty to the corporation and its shareholders."); Blum v. Kauffman, 297 A.2d 48, 49 (Del. 1972) (noting "the policy of this Court to look with disfavor upon clauses which exonerate a party from the consequences of his own negligence or that of his agent").

17. The Vice Chancellor also noted in his summary judgment opinion that "Any interstitial issues in this case are best dealt with through cautious application of the implied covenant of good faith and fair dealing." Gotham S.J. Op. at 29 n.37, 2000 WL 1476663 at 12 n.37. We note that the implied covenant of good faith and fair dealing that inheres in every contract is not pertinent to the issues in this case and any discussion in the Vice Chancellor's summary judgment about the contractual duty of good faith and fair dealing is also dictum. The issue of good faith and fair dealing is not before us, and we need not express any opinion on that issue in this case.

Gotham requested rescission, or money damages and sterilization of voting rights. The Court of Chancery awarded money damages plus compound interest instead of rescission, in part because it found that Gotham delayed challenging the transaction "for nearly two years, and then filed suit to rescind only after it was clear that the market price [of the Partnership units] was up substantially and on a sustainable basis." The Vice Chancellor then went on to find that the challenged transactions were not "conceived of as a conscious scheme to entrench the General Partner's control and enrich HGI" improperly. He stated that if he had been convinced otherwise, "I might be inclined to grant rescission despite Gotham's torpid pace." . . .

Issues on Appeal

On appeal, Gotham argues that the Court of Chancery was required to award rescission as a matter of law and, even if an award of monetary damages were appropriate, the Court of Chancery erred in its calculation of the damages by failing to account for a control premium. Gotham seeks reversal in part of the judgment of the Court of Chancery and a remand to the court with instructions to order rescission of the Odd Lot Resale to HGI. Alternatively, Gotham seeks an award of rescissory damages or sterilization of HGI's voting rights connected to the Odd Lot Resale units, or both.

The General Partner, HGI, Gumbiner, and Guzzetti contend in their cross appeal that the Court of Chancery erred: (1) by finding the Odd Lot Resale to HGI subject to Sections 7.05 and 7.10(a) of the Partnership Agreement, which provide for contractual fiduciary duties of entire fairness, instead of Section 9.01, which authorizes the General Partner to issue Partnership Units of any kind to any person without the consent or approval of the Limited Partners; (2) by finding HGI, Gumbiner, and Guzzetti jointly and severally liable with the General Partner for aiding and abetting a breach of a contractually created fiduciary duty; and (3) by awarding compound interest on money damages. We will address the cross appeals first.

Whether the Court of Chancery Erred by Ruling That the Odd Lot Resale to HGI Was a Resale of Partnership Units

As the Vice Chancellor noted at summary judgment, a general partner owes the traditional fiduciary duties of loyalty and care to the limited partnership and its partners,[30] but DRULPA §17-1101(d)(2) "expressly authorizes the . . . modification, or enhancement of these fiduciary duties in the written agreement governing the limited partnership."[31] Indeed, we have recognized that, by statute, the parties to a Delaware limited partnership have the power and discretion to form and operate a limited partnership "in an environment of private ordering" according to the provisions in the limited partnership agreement.[32] We have noted that DRULPA embodies "the policy of freedom of contract" and

---

30. See also Boxer v. Husky Oil Co., 429 A.2d 995, 997 (Del. Ch. 1981) (stating that the general partner in a limited partnership is generally required "to exercise the utmost good faith, fairness, and loyalty") (citing Meinhard v. Salmon, 249 N.Y. 458, 164 N.E. 545 (1928)), aff'd 483 A.2d 633 (Del. 1984).

31. . . . DRULPA §17-1101(d)(2), codified at 6 Del. C. §17-1101(d)(2), reads: "To the extent that, at law or equity, a partner or other person has duties (including fiduciary duties) and liabilities relating thereto to a limited partnership or to another partner or to another person that is a party to or is otherwise bound by a partnership agreement, . . . (2) the partner's or other person's duties and liabilities may be expanded or restricted by provisions in the partnership agreement."

32. Elf Atochem North America, Inc. v. Jaffari, 727 A.2d 286, 287 (Del. 1999).

"maximum flexibility."[34] DRULPA's "basic approach is to permit partners to have the broadest possible discretion in drafting their partnership agreements and to furnish answers only in situations where the partners have not expressly made provisions in their partnership agreement"[35] or "where the agreement is inconsistent with mandatory statutory provisions."[36] In those situations, a court will "look for guidance from the statutory default rules, traditional notions of fiduciary duties, or other extrinsic evidence."[37] But, if the limited partnership agreement unambiguously provides for fiduciary duties, any claim of a breach of a fiduciary duty must be analyzed generally in terms of the partnership agreement.[38]

The Vice Chancellor found, and the parties do not contest, that Partnership Agreement Sections 7.05 and 7.10(a) set forth fiduciary duties of entire fairness owed by the General Partner to its partners generally in self-dealing transactions, such as the Odd Lot Resale. Section 7.05 expressly permits the Partnership to enter into self-dealing transactions with the General Partner or its affiliate "provided that the terms of any such transaction are substantially equivalent to terms obtainable by the Partnership from a comparable unaffiliated third party." Section 7.10(a) requires the General Partner to form an independent Audit Committee that shall review and approve self-dealing transactions between the Partnership and the General Partner and any of its affiliates. The Vice Chancellor found, and the parties do not contest, that Sections 7.05 and 7.10(a) "operate together as a contractual statement of the traditional entire fairness standard [of fair price and fair dealing], with §7.05 reflecting the substantive aspect of that standard and §7.10 reflecting the procedural aspect of that standard."

Because the Partnership Agreement provided for fiduciary duties, the Vice Chancellor properly held that the Partnership Agreement, as a contract, provides the standard for determining whether the General Partner breached its duty to the Partnership through its execution of the Odd Lot Resale. As the Vice Chancellor stated, the Partnership Agreement "leaves no room for the application of common law fiduciary duty principles to measure the General Partner's conduct" because the Partnership Agreement "supplanted fiduciary duty and became the sole source of protection for the public unitholders of the Partnership." Thus, "the General Partner was subject, by contract, to a fairness standard akin to the common law one applicable to self-dealing transactions by fiduciaries."

The General Partner, HGI, Gumbiner, and Guzzetti apparently concede: (1) the General Partner's conduct associated with the Odd Lot Resale did not comply with Sections 7.05 and 7.10(a) of the Partnership Agreement because, as the Vice Chancellor found; (2) the Audit Committee never reviewed or approved the Odd Lot Resale to HGI; and (3) the General Partner never obtained a reliable financial analysis indicating that the Odd Lot Resale would be conducted on the same terms obtainable from an independent third party. Nonetheless, they argue that they are not liable for failing to comply with Sections 7.05 and 7.10(a) because

34. *Elf Atochem*, 727 A.2d at 291 n.27.
35. Id. at 291.
36. Id. at 292.
37. *Sonet*, 722 A.2d at 324.
38. See id. ("[U]nder Delaware limited partnership law a claim of breach of fiduciary duty must first be analyzed in terms of the operating governing instrument — the partnership agreement — and only where that document is silent or ambiguous, or where the principles of equity are implicated, will a Court begin to look for guidance from the statutory default rules, traditional notions of fiduciary duties, or other extrinsic evidence.")

Section 9.01 alone governed the Odd Lot Resale. They assert that the Odd Lot Resale was an issuance rather than a resale of Partnership units to HGI. The defendants seek the protection of Section 9.01, which gives the General Partner absolute and independent authority to issue additional Partnership units to any person or entity, including affiliates such as HGI.

The Vice Chancellor properly found that the Odd Lot Resale was a resale of Partnership units to HGI and thus Section 9.01 is inapplicable. It is undisputed that the Partnership's accounting books did not treat the sale of odd lots to HGI as an issuance of units. Furthermore, the Partnership units from the Odd Lot Resale were listed on the American Stock Exchange, but the Resale was presented to the Exchange as a resale, not as an issuance. The Vice Chancellor properly found that the Odd Lot Resale was structured as a resale, in part to avoid American Stock Exchange Rule 713, which requires that holders approve additional issuances as a prerequisite to the shares' or units' listing on the Exchange. Thus, the General Partner is liable for breaching the contractually created fiduciary duties of entire fairness provided by Sections 7.05 and 7.10(a) of the Partnership Agreement. . . .

---

1. *The Delaware legislature's response.* In *Gotham*, the Supreme Court suggested that under Delaware RULPA §17-1101 a limited partner could "limit or expand" the scope of fiduciary duties, but not eliminate them. The Delaware legislature responded less than two years later by amending the statute. Delaware RULPA §17-1101 currently provides in pertinent part:

> (b) The rule that statutes in derogation of the common law are to be strictly construed shall have no application to this chapter.
>
> (c) It is the policy of this chapter to give maximum effect to the principle of freedom of contract and to the enforceability of partnership agreements.
>
> (d) To the extent that, at law or in equity, a partner or other person has duties (including fiduciary duties) to a limited partnership or to another partner or to another person that is a party to or is otherwise bound by a partnership agreement, the partner's or other person's duties may be expanded or restricted or eliminated by provisions in the partnership agreement; provided that the partnership agreement may not eliminate the implied contractual covenant of good faith and fair dealing.
>
> (e) Unless otherwise provided in a partnership agreement, a partner or other person shall not be liable to a limited partnership or to another partner or to another person that is a party to or is otherwise bound by a partnership agreement for breach of fiduciary duty for the partner's or other person's good faith reliance on the provisions of the partnership agreement.
>
> (f) A partnership agreement may provide for the limitation or elimination of any and all liabilities for breach of contract and breach of duties (including fiduciary duties) of a partner or other person to a limited partnership or to another partner or to another person that is a party to or is otherwise bound by a partnership agreement; provided, that a partnership agreement may not limit or eliminate liability for any act or omission that constitutes a bad faith violation of the implied contractual covenant of good faith and fair dealing.
>
> (g) Sections 9-406 and 9-408 of this title do not apply to any interest in a limited partnership, including all rights, powers and interests arising under a partnership agreement or this chapter. This provision prevails over §§9-406 and 9-408 of this title.

2. *Fiduciary duty versus contract.* With the addition of the word "eliminated" to the statute's invitation to planners to craft their own rules, Delaware Supreme Court Justice Myron Steele has stated that the "2004 amendment should put the Delaware Supreme Court on notice that, except where the parties to an LLP or LLC agreement do not address fiduciary duties, parties to limited partnership and limited liability company agreements will normally seek to craft their own status relationship by contract." Myron T. Steel, Judicial Scrutiny of Fiduciary Duties in Delaware Limited Partnerships and Limited Liability Companies, 32 Del. J. Corp. L. 1, 23 (2007).

Does the statute leave participants in a limited partnership or limited liability company free to create their own rules? The new statute imposes one constraint: the parties may not eliminate the "implied contractual covenant to good faith and fair dealing." Some baseline of equitable review must remain, but the legislature explicitly directs judicial attention to contract law, not corporate law, by reference to the "contractual covenant of good faith and fair dealing." But how much more protection from judicial intervention does contract law provide? See Robert E. Scott & Alan Schwartz, Contract Theory and the Limits of Contract Law, 131 Yale L.J. 541 (2003).

3. *Applying the contractual duty.* How will the courts apply the covenant of good faith and fair dealing in an organizational context? Writing before the 2004 amendment, Delaware Supreme Court Justice Jack Jacobs offered the following "principled generalizations" concerning courts' responses to efforts to displace fiduciary duties through the limited partnership agreement:

> First, courts will not lightly relinquish fiduciary duty doctrine as a tool in the alternative entity area, except where the governing instrument clearly and unambiguously mandates that result. . . . Second, in determining whether fiduciary duty principles have been preempted by contract, the court will employ a functional approach. The court will inquire whether employing fiduciary duty principles would further or interfere with the governance scheme expressly mandated by the partnership agreement, and whether fiduciary principles would unduly intrude upon the general partner's legitimate authority under that agreement. . . . Third, if the governing instrument displaces fiduciary duty principles to a limited extent but not entirely, the courts will apply fiduciary principles (in subject areas where those principles are not displaced) to protect investors in cases where the entity's management appears to be overreaching. . . . Fourth, and finally, in cases where the governing instrument displaces fiduciary duty principles in their entirety, the court will employ contract law principles, but will apply them in a manner that protects the interests of investors.[78]

Justice Jacobs anticipated the legislature's doctrinal direction, but does his comment bode well for how much flexibility planners will actually get?

4. *Eliminating the duty of loyalty.* How easy is it to eliminate the duty of loyalty even if the 2004 Delaware amendment allows its elimination? Two Delaware lawyers describe the mandatory duty of good faith and fair dealing as one preventing one party to a contract "from unfairly taking advantage of the other party. . . . The implied covenant thereby serves as a method of protecting the reasonable

---

78. Jack B. Jacobs, Entity Rationalization: A Judge's Perspective, 58 Bus. Law. 1043, 1048-1049 (2003). — ED.

expectations of the parties. . . ."[6] Would *Gotham* have come out differently if the limited partnership agreement had eliminated the duty of loyalty?

5. *Why eliminate the duty of loyalty?* Why would a general partner who was trying to sell limited partnership interests to investors limit its fiduciary duty? Would anyone invest in a limited partnership when the general partner could act in bad faith without recourse by the limited partners? Suppose the general partner is in the business of raising successive investment partnerships, as is commonly the case with venture capital limited partnerships[79] and real estate limited partnerships. There will frequently be issues involving the allocation of opportunities among different funds, as well as judgment calls with respect to allocation of the general partner's overhead and other common expenses among the different funds, which could raise issues of loyalty. Might the motivation for a contractual restriction of fiduciary duty be to allocate to the market — as opposed to the courts — the job of policing the general partner's loyalty? A disloyal general partner would have difficulty raising successor funds. This might suggest how to distinguish between fiduciary duties that can and cannot be eliminated by contract. From the perspective of the market as a substitute for expensive litigation, one might allow the partnership agreement to eliminate fiduciary duties with respect to all actions but core self-dealing, on the theory that the latter has a greater chance of being a one-time theft that cannot be deterred through the expectation of future dealings.

6. *Why not traditional corporations?* Should the principle of contractual freedom to limit fiduciary duty extend to traditional corporations as well as to alternative forms of business organization? Is it relevant that an organization has publicly traded equity interests? Recall that the defendant in *Gotham Partners* was a publicly traded limited partnership. Is the line between the ways different organizational forms are treated merely the result of legislative fiat?

b. Who Owes the Fiduciary Duty?

It is now commonplace that the general partner of a limited partnership will be a corporation. See Robert W. Hamilton, Corporate General Partners of Limited Partnerships, 1 J. Small & Emerging Bus. L. 73 (1997). While it is plain that the corporate entity will owe the limited partners a fiduciary duty, the actual decisionmakers, and perhaps the parties with the assets, will be the corporate general partner's officers and directors. Do they owe the limited partners a fiduciary duty? In In re USACafes, L.P. Litigation, 600 A.2d 43, 49 (Del. Ch. 1991), Chancellor Allen held:

> The theory underlying fiduciary duties is consistent with recognition that a director of a corporate general partner bears such a duty towards the limited partnership. That duty, of course, extends only to dealings with the partnership's property or affecting its business, but, so limited, its existence seems apparent in any number of circumstances. Consider, for example, a classic self-dealing transaction: assume that a majority of the board of the corporate general partner formed a new entity and then caused the general partner to sell partnership assets to the new entity at an

---

6. Paul M. Altman & Srinivas M. Raju, Delaware Alternative Entities and the Implied Contractual Covenant of Good Faith and Fair Dealing under Delaware Law, 60 Bus. Law. 1469, 1474 (2005).

79. See Gilson, footnote 74 supra.

unfairly small price, injuring the partnership and its limited partners. Can it be imagined that such persons have not breached a duty to the partnership itself? And does it not make perfect sense to say that the gist of the offense is a breach of the equitable duty of loyalty that is placed on a fiduciary?

E. *LIMITED LIABILITY COMPANIES*

The first statute authorizing a limited liability company (LLC) was adopted in Wyoming in 1977, and as late as 1988 only Florida had followed Wyoming's lead.[80] But the 1990s witnessed tremendous growth in this hybrid business form. By 1999 all 50 states had adopted LLC statutes.[81] The popularity of the LLC form rests on its combining the best of both worlds — the flexibility and pass-through taxation benefits of the partnership form with the limited liability and managerial control of the corporate form. In addition, in most jurisdictions, the LLC sidesteps the control problems and size restrictions associated with close corporations.

All states require that the business entity register as an LLC. In most jurisdictions, investors in an LLC, called "members," are able to participate directly in management without the restrictions imposed on limited partners. Members are given limited liability and are able to elect management of the firm in much the same manner as in a corporation. As in a partnership, however, management rights in the LLC are not freely transferrable, and, in general, dissolution is treated as similar to the dissolution of a partnership. While this hybrid has all the characteristics of a Dr. Seuss creation, it has proved to be enormously successful.

1. TAX ADVANTAGES

The most salient feature of the LLC is its tax advantage. In 1996 the IRS codified "check the box" regulations, which allow an LLC to elect whether to be taxed as a partnership or a corporation.[82] If the LLC elects partnership treatment, the income or losses from the firm passes through to the members and is taxed directly to them, thus avoiding corporate-level tax, just as in a partnership. Many observers see the evolution of the LLC form as a direct response to the favorable tax treatment accorded partnerships and to the current certainty of federal tax treatment

---

80. Wyoming enacted the LLC statute as special legislation to accommodate the interests of an oil company that had lobbied for limited liability treatment similar to that granted through the Latin American *limitada* business form. See Bradley J. Sklar & Todd Carlisle, The Alabama Limited Liability Company Act, 45 Ala. L. Rev. 145, 155 (1993). Florida's adoption of the LLC was similarly motivated by the desire to attract international investment to the state. Id. See Wyo. Stat. 17-15-101 to 17-15-144 (2007); Fla. Stat. Ann. 608.401-608.705 (2007).

81. For representative LLC statutes, see Del. Code Ann., tit. 6, §§18-0101 to 18-1109 (Supp. 2001); Colo. Rev. Stat. §§7-80-101 to 70-80-913 (2006); Tex. Rev. Civ. Stat. Ann., art. 1528n, arts. 1.01-11.07 (2005); Va. Code Ann. §§13.1-1000 to 13.1-1123 (2006).

82. I.R.C. §7701, et seq. Any entity that is not a corporation may elect its own classification for federal tax purposes under these new regulations.

for LLCs.[83] Others, however, see taxation as but one element in what is a natural evolution toward more flexible — but nonetheless predictable — forms of business organization better suited to smaller and more agile businesses.[84] Finally, more cynical observers see the legislative success of the LLC form as a direct response to liability fears.

2. ORGANIZATION, STRUCTURE, AND TERMINOLOGY

Like a corporation or a limited partnership, an LLC must file a document (known as its "articles of organization") with a state agency, typically the secretary of state (see ULLCA §202). In addition to the articles of organization, which will likely be brief, most LLCs will also have an "operating agreement" that will govern the "activities of the company and the conduct of those activities" (ULLCA §110). ULLCA and most state statutes create a default rule that an LLC will be managed by its members (ULLCA §401). Thus, absent a contrary provision, a member is an agent of the LLC, much as in a general partnership. However, this default rule can be and often is overridden by a provision in the operating agreement that the LLC will be run by a manager, who need not be a "member" but who must be named in the articles of organization (ULLCA §407(a)). Thus, LLCs are subdivided into those that are "member-managed" and those that are "manager-managed."

Much of the structure of ULLCA seems patterned after RULPA. In particular, ULLCA §110 follows RULPA §103 in listing certain non-waivable provisions that the parties cannot contract out of. For example, §103 makes the duty of loyalty mandatory (subject, as in RULPA, to an exclusion for "specific types or categories of activities" that may be carved out in the operating agreement, provided that any such exclusion is not "manifestly unreasonable").[85] Enforcement procedures similarly follow RULPA. A member is entitled to bring a derivative action in the LLC's name under ULLCA §902 if "(1) the member first makes a demand on the other members in a member-managed limited liability company, or on the managers of a manger-manager limited liability company, requesting that they cause the company to bring an action to enforce the right, and the managers or other members do not bring the action with a reasonable time; or (2) a demand under paragraph (1) would be futile."

The creation of the LLC, and the spawning of the limited liability partnership and the limited liability limited partnership (discussed below), are evidence that statutory and legal forms are evolving to meet the changing needs of business. As new entities are born, a process begins to determine what kind of legal animal the

83. See Phillip L. Jelsma, How Do LLCs Stack Up?, 4 Bus. L. Today 32 (April 1995) (describing election to LLC as providing superior tax advantages to either the S or C corporation model).

84. See, e.g., Larry E. Ribstein, Statutory Forms for Closely Held Firms: Theories and Evidence from LLCs, 73 Wash. U. L.Q. 369 (1995) (in addition to tax and regulatory concerns, LLCs reflect an economically efficient business model that minimizes transaction costs for small, closely held enterprises). But see William W. Bratton & Joseph A. McCahery, An Inquiry into the Efficiency of the Limited Liability Company: Of Theory of the Firm and Regulatory Competition, 54 Wash. & Lee L. Rev. 629 (1997) (the LLC does not promote economic efficiency and a regime of pro rata distribution of liability would optimize a firm's resources).

85. In 2004 §18-1101 of the Delaware Limited Liability, Company Act was amended to allow the limited liability company agreement to eliminate fiduciary duties entirely, although liability cannot be limited or eliminated "for any act or omission that constitutes a bad faith violation of the implied contractual covenant of good faith and fair dealing."

new entity is, and what tools of interpretation should be used to settle disputes that arise from these new entities.

Westec v. Lanham and Preferred Income Investors, LLC
955 P.2d 997 (Colo. 1998)

Scott, J.: This case requires us to decide whether the members or managers of a limited liability company (LLC) are excused from personal liability on a contract where the other party to the contract did not have notice that the members or managers were negotiating on behalf of a limited liability at the time the contract was made. . . .

I. Water, Waste, & Land, Inc., the petitioner, is a land development and engineering company doing business under the name "Westec." At the time of the events in this case, Donald Lanham and Larry Clark were managers and also members of Preferred Income Investors, L.L.C. (Company or P.I.I.). The Company is a limited liability company organized under the Colorado Limited Liability Company Act, §§7-80-101 to -1101, 2 C.R.S. (1997) (the LLC Act).

In March 1995, Clark contacted Westec about the possibility of hiring Westec to perform engineering work in connection with a development project which involved the construction of a fast-food restaurant known as Taco Cabana. In the course of preliminary discussions, Clark gave his business card to representatives of Westec. The business card included Lanham's address, which was also the address listed as the Company's principal office and place of business in its articles of organization filed with the secretary of state. While the Company's name was not on the business card, the letters "P.I.I." appeared above the address on the card. However, there was no indication as to what the acronym meant or that P.I.I. was a limited liability company.

After further negotiations, an oral agreement was reached concerning Westec's involvement with the Company's restaurant project. Clark instructed Westec to send a written proposal of its work to Lanham and the proposal was sent in April 1995. On August 2, 1995, Westec sent Lanham a form of contract, which Lanham was to execute and return to Westec. Although Westec never received a signed contract, in mid-August it did receive verbal authorization from Clark to begin work. Westec completed the engineering work and sent a bill for $9,183.40 to Lanham. No payments were made on the bill.

Westec filed a claim in county court against Clark and Lanham individually as well as against the Company. At trial, the Company admitted liability for the amount claimed by Westec. The county court entered judgment in favor of Westec. The county court found that: (1) Clark had contacted Westec to do engineering work for Lanham; (2) it was "unknown" to Westec that Lanham had organized the Company as a limited liability company; and (3) the letters "P.I.I." on Clark's business card were insufficient to place Westec on notice that the Company was a limited liability company. Based on its findings, the county court ruled that: (1) Clark was an agent of both Lanham and the Company with "authority to obligate . . . Lanham and the Company"; (2) a valid and binding contract existed for the work; (3) Westec "did not have knowledge of any business entity" and only dealt with Clark and Lanham "on a personal basis"; and (4) Westec understood Clark to be Lanham's agent and therefore "Clark is not personally liable."

Accordingly, the county court dismissed Clark from the suit, concluding he could not be held personally liable, and entered judgment in the amount of $9,183 against Lanham and the Company. Lanham appealed, seeking review in the Larimer County District Court (district court).

The district court reversed, concluding "[t]he issue which the court must address is whether the County Court erred in holding Lanham, a member and primary manager of the company, personally liable for a debt of the company." In addressing that issue, the district court found that Westec was placed on notice that it was dealing with a limited liability company based on two factors: (1) the business card containing the letters "P.I.I."; and (2) the notice provision of section 7-80-208, of the LLC Act. Principally in reliance upon the LLC Act's notice provision, section 7-80-208, which provides that the filing of the articles of organization serve as constructive notice of a company's status as a limited liability company, the district court held that "the County Court erred in finding that Westec had no notice that it was dealing with an L.L.C." Contrary to the trial court's findings, the district court held that "evidence presented at trial was uncontradicted that Westec knew it was dealing with a business entity (P.I.I.) and section 7-80-208 imputes notice that the entity was an 'L.L.C.' in addition to any common law presumption of a duty to inquire." In the district court's view, the notice provision, as well as Westec's failure to investigate or request a personal guarantee, relieved Lanham of personal liability for claims against the Company.

II. . . . In 1990, our General Assembly adopted the LLC Act, a statute currently codified as amended at sections 7-80-101 through 7-80-1101, 2 C.R.S. (1997), making Colorado the third state, behind Wyoming and Florida, to do so. Unlike a number of other states, where LLC statutes were based on a model act drafted by the National Conference of Commissioners on Uniform State Laws, Colorado's LLC Act combined features of the state's existing limited partnership and corporation statutes. In any case, the LLC Act includes the same basic features of limited liability, a single-tier tax treatment, and planning flexibility shared by the Uniform Limited Liability Company Act and LLC legislation adopted by other states. . . .

III. A. The district court interpreted the LLC Act's notice provision . . . as putting Westec on constructive notice of Lanham's agency relationship with the Company. In essence, this course of analysis assumed that the LLC Act displaced certain common law agency doctrines, at least insofar as these doctrines otherwise would be applicable to suits by third parties seeking to hold the agents of a limited liability company liable for their personal actions as agents.

We hold, however, that the statutory notice provision applies only where a third party seeks to impose liability on an LLC's members or managers simply due to their status as members or managers of the LLC. When a third party sues a manager or member of an LLC under an agency theory, the principles of agency law apply notwithstanding the LLC Act's statutory notice rules.

B. Under the common law of agency, an agent is liable on a contract entered on behalf of a principal if the principal is not fully disclosed . . . ; that is, a principal whose existence — but not identity — is known to the other party.

C. Whether a principal is partially or completely disclosed is a question of fact. . . . We are, therefore, bound to accept the county court's finding that Westec did not know Clark was acting as an agent for the Company or that the letters "P.I.I." stood for "Preferred Income Investors," a limited liability company registered under Colorado law. For the same reason, the district court erred in concluding that Clark was not acting as Lanham's agent. The trial record was sufficient to support the county court's finding that Clark was an agent for Lanham and this conclusion should not have been disturbed by the district court.

D. In light of the partially disclosed principal doctrine, the county court's determination that Clark and Lanham failed to disclose the existence as well as the identity of the limited liability company they represented is dispositive under the common law of agency. Still, if the General Assembly has altered the common law rules applicable to this case by adopting the LLC Act, then these rules must yield in favor of the statute. We conclude, however, that the LLC Act's notice provision was not intended to alter the partially disclosed principal doctrine. Section 7-80-208, C.R.S. (1997) states: "The fact that the articles of organization are on file in the office of the secretary of state is notice that the limited liability company is a limited liability company and is notice of all other facts set forth therein which are required to be set forth in the articles of organization."

In order to relieve Lanham of liability, this provision would have to be read to establish a conclusive presumption that a third party who deals with the agent of a limited liability company always has constructive notice of the existence of the agent's principal. We are not persuaded that the statute can bear such an interpretation.

Such a construction exaggerates the plain meaning of the language in the statute. Section 7-80-208 could be read to state that third parties who deal with a limited liability company are always on constructive notice of the company's limited liability status, without regard to whether any part of the company's name or even the fact of its existence has been disclosed. However, an equally plausible interpretation of the words used in the statute is that once the limited liability company's name is known to the third party, constructive notice of the company's limited liability status has been given, as well as the fact that managers and members will not be liable simply due to their status as managers or members.

Moreover, the broad interpretation urged by Lanham would be an invitation to fraud, because it would leave the agent of a limited liability company free to mislead third parties into the belief that the agent would bear personal financial responsibility under any contract, when in fact, recovery would be limited to the assets of a limited liability company not known to the third party at the time the contract was made. While Westec has not alleged that Clark or Lanham deliberately tried to conceal the Company's identity or status as a limited liability company, Lanham's construction would open the door to sharp practices and outright fraud. We may presume that in adopting section 7-80-208, the General Assembly did not intend to create a safe harbor for deceit. For this reason alone, a broad reading of the notice provision would be suspect.

In addition, statutes in derogation of the common law are to be strictly construed. For the reasons outlined above, the interpretation urged by Lanham would be a radical departure from the settled rules of agency under the common law. If the legislature had intended a departure of such magnitude, its desires would have been expressed more clearly.

Other LLC Act provisions reinforce the conclusion that the legislature did not intend the notice language of section 7-80-208 to relieve the agent of a limited liability company of the duty to disclose its identity in order to avoid personal liability. For example, section 7-80-201(1), 2 C.R.S. (1997), requires limited liability companies to use the words "Limited Liability Company" or the initials "LLC" as part of their names, implying that the legislature intended to compel any entity seeking to claim the benefits of the LLC Act to identify itself clearly as a limited liability company. By way of further support for our conclusion, section 7-80-107, 2 C.R.S. (1997), provides two bases of individual liability for members: (1) for "alleged improper actions," and (2) "the failure of a limited liability company to observe the formalities or requirements relating to the management of its business and affairs when coupled with some other wrongful conduct." As one commentator opined: "It would be an unwarranted stretch to say that these laws intend to extend the insulation of limited liability beyond that traditionally provided by the corporate form. That means that participants in closely held enterprises will continue to be liable for their acts taken in the entity's name that are wrongful or violate regulatory provisions either under agency law or by a court piercing the entity's veil." Robert B. Thompson, The Taming of Limited Liability Companies, 66 U. Colo. L. Rev. 921, 945.

Lanham received from Westec a form of contract demonstrating Westec's assumption that Lanham was the principal. At that point, he could have clarified his relationship to the Company. He did not do so. Hence, even if we were sympathetic to Lanham's plight, he had within his control the means to clearly state to Westec and the world that he was acting only for the limited liability company. Moreover, we must avoid straying from long established legal precepts and inserting uncertainty into accepted rules that govern business relationships.

In sum, then, section 7-80-208 places third parties on constructive notice that a fully identified company — that is, identified by a name such as "Preferred Income Investors, LLC," or the like — is a limited liability company provided that its articles of organization have been filed with the secretary of state. Section 7-80-208 is of little force, however, in determining whether a limited liability company's agent is personally liable on the theory that the agent has failed to disclose the identity of the company.

IV. Under our interpretation, section 7-80-208 still offers significant protection to the members of a limited liability company. The notice provision protects the members from suit based on their status as members, as opposed to their acts as agents of the corporate entity.[14] If a third party such as Westec had tried to pierce the corporate veil to hold Clark and Lanham personally responsible for the Company's contractual debt based on the fact that they were members of the LLC, section 7-80-208 would protect them from liability. The distinction between the use of an agency theory and the doctrine of piercing the corporate or limited liability company veil is significant. As one treatise explains: "The undisclosed principal theory is a rule of law and applies regardless of a defendant's intent to engage in wrongful conduct; however, the doctrine of piercing the corporate veil is based in equity so that a failure to disclose must coexist with wrongful conduct or improper use or intent for the latter theory to apply and render personal liability."

---

14. By our holding today, we by no means alter the import or reach of sections 7-80-208 and 7-80-705, 2 C.R.S. (1997). Both sections of our LLC Act provide protection to members and managers. Section 7-80-705 provides: "*Liability of members and managers.* Members and managers of limited liability companies are not liable under a judgment, decree, or order of a court, or in any other manner, for a debt, obligation, or liability of the limited liability company." Hence, we do not diminish the fact that assuming the articles of organization are filed, a member or manager "will not be liable simply due to their status" as member or manager.

3A James Solheim and Kenneth Elkins, Fletcher Cyclopedia of the Law of Private Corporations section 1120 (1994 revised edition).

V. If Clark or Lanham had told Westec's representatives that they were acting on behalf of an entity known as "Preferred Income Investors, LLC" the failure to disclose the fact that the entity was a limited liability company would be irrelevant by virtue of the statute, which provides that the articles of organization operate as constructive notice of the company's limited liability form. The county court, however, found that Lanham and Clark did not identify Preferred Income Investors, LLC, as the principal in the transaction. The "missing link" between the limited disclosure made by Clark and the protection of the notice statute was the failure to state that "P.I.I.," the Company, stood for "Preferred Income Investors, LLC."

Accordingly, the judgment of the district court is reversed and this case is remanded to that court with instructions that it reinstate the judgment of the county court.

---

1. *Differences from other business forms.* Colorado LLC §7-80-107 provides for resort to "the case law which interprets the conditions and circumstances under which the corporate veil of a corporation may be pierced under Colorado law." Why did the court decide this case under common law agency theory rather than as a straightforward veil-piercing case? Does the constructive notice provision of the Colorado LLC statute provide a satisfactory answer?

In Monon v. Townsend, Yosha, Kline & Price, 678 N.E.2d 807 (Ind. Ct. App. 1997), the court held that even where one lawyer establishes a one-man LLC, the law firm may be considered a partnership for purposes of malpractice liability if its client reasonably believed the firm was a partnership. Special rules regulating the legal profession can restrict the availability of limited liability. See Ronald J. Gilson, Unlimited Liability and Law Firm Organization: Tax Factors and the Direction of Causation, 99 J. Pol. Econ. 420 (1991) (discussing this problem with respect to professional corporations, a precursor to LLCs).

In Hagan v. Adams Property Ass'n Inc., 482 S.E.2d 805 (Va. 1997), the court held that an individual's transfer of property to an LLC of which he was a founding member constituted a sale of the property for purpose of the real estate agent's commission. Under Virginia law, an LLC, unlike a partnership, represents a business entity separate from the individual members. The court noted that partnership cases that treated the transfer of real property to partnerships as capitalization of the partnership — and not a sale — were inapposite because the change in business form makes it act like a sale.

2. *Dissolution.* As with partnerships, the withdrawal, cash-out, or dissociation of one member of the LLC poses the question of dissolution of the entity. In Five Star Concrete, L.L.C. v. Klink, Inc., 693 N.E.2d 583 (Ind. Ct. App. 1998), the court considered whether a dissociating member of an LLC has a right, similar to that of a dissociating partner in a partnership, to receive distribution equal to the net income allocated to it for income tax purposes. The court noted that although the allocation was proper under IRS "pass-through" regulations, the Indiana LLC Act did not require that the "allocation" or income result in a distribution to the dissociating member. The court further noted that where the operating

agreement of the LLC is silent as to distributions of this sort, the result must be determined by a majority vote of the members.

Where there is no operating agreement, courts have applied UPA provisions. See Hurwitz v. Padden, 581 N.W.2d 359 (Ct. App. Min. 1998) (applying UPA dissolution principles to breakup of LLC in absence of operating agreement and distributing fees of law firm according to partnership principles).[86]

3. *Other regulations.* Because the LLC is a new entity, the applicability of other state regulations must also be interpreted. In Meyer v. Oklahoma Bev. Law Enforcement Comm'n, 890 P.2d 1361 (Okla. App. 1995), the court held that an LLC is not eligible for a liquor license. The relevant statute prohibited licenses to "corporations, business trust or secret partnership . . . a person or a general or limited partnership containing a partner who has been convicted of a violation of [alcohol laws or a felony]." The court found that the intent of the law was to restrict licenses to those who can be held personally liable for violations of the liquor laws. Because an LLC agreement limits liability and can be freely amended to allow additional members who may not comply with liquor regulations, LLCs do not qualify.

Whether a membership interest in an LLC is a "security" for purposes of state security regulation is an unanswered question in most jurisdictions.[87] In Nutek v. Arizona Corp. Comm'n, 1998 WL 767176 (Ariz. 1998), the court held that membership interests in the LLC were securities under state securities law because the 920 individuals who were sold membership interests did not exercise "investor control" and thus were "no different from [ordinary] corporate shareholders."

3. WHAT IS A LIMITED LIABILITY COMPANY

The LLC was intended as a hybrid — a combination of two distinct entities each of which has distinct desirable characteristics. An LLC is like a corporation in that it provides limited liability to investors and the opportunity for centralized management through an operating agreement. It is also like a partnership in that it is accorded pass-through taxation and is not subject to the same rigidities as a traditional corporation. However, the LLC statutes do not specify a number of the important characteristics that are necessary to fully define the entity. This is

---

86. See also Diaz v. Fernandez, 910 P.2d 96 (Colo. App. 1995) (holding that even where members did not request dissolution of LLC, Colorado LLC statute grants LLC member a personal property interest in the company; thus, court appointment of a receiver was proper where member alleged dissipation of company assets through fraud and mismanagement); Walker v. Virtual Packaging, LLC, 229 Ga. App. 124 (1997) (court fails to reach issue whether claim for damages that belonged to LLC prior to dissolution can be apportioned to a former member on a pro rata basis; court finds that because the operating agreement and member's agreement had not extinguished at time of dissolution, former member's right to sue under member's agreement continued); Advanced Orthopedics, L.L.C. v. Moon, 656 So. 2d 1103 (La. App. 1995) ("subjective intent" of defendant not to form an LLC is not prerequisite to formation of and participation in LLC; resigning member of LLC was not entitled to reimbursement for capital contribution where he did not make one). See also PB Real Estate v. DEM II Properties, 50 Conn. App. 741 (1998) (holding that payments made by LLC members to themselves from assets of the company constituted "distributions").

87. For further discussion of treating LLC membership interests as "securities" and the need for regulations clarifying the status of LLC membership interests, see Park McGinty, The Limited Liability Company: Opportunity for Selective Securities Law Deregulation, 64 U. Cin. L. Rev. 369 (1996).

particularly important with respect to characteristics that are the result of common law rather than statute.

a. Piercing the Veil of an LLC

While some state LLC statutes, including those of California and Washington, expressly apply corporate veil-piercing principles to LLCs,[88] most statutes, including the ULLCA, are silent on this point. While the academic literature anticipates that this corporate law principle will be applied to LLCs,[89] what does this actually mean? If observing the corporate formalities is a relevant factor in the corporate setting, what happens in the LLC setting, where one of the statutory goals is to eliminate formalities? While formality observance is hardly itself a guide to whether creditors should have recourse to investor assets, it may be a signal of whether the corporation was treated as a real entity or was merely an instrumentality used to avoid liability. What signals are available in the LLC context? Does this element simply reduce to an inquiry into whether the plaintiffs knew they were dealing with an LLC, as in *Westec*, page 812 supra? Among those LLC statutes that expressly apply veil piercing to LLCs, some specify that adherence to corporate formalities is not a factor in determining whether the LLC's veil should be pierced. See Robert B. Thompson, The Limits of Liability in the New Limited Liability Entities, 32 Wake Forest L. Rev. 1 (1997). What does this mean for interpreting statutes that apply the doctrine but do not exclude any specific factors?

Bastan v. RJM & Associates, LLC
2001 WL 1006661 (Conn. Super.)

BEACH, J.: This action seeks primarily to recover a deposit paid to a builder. The defendant Robert J. Moravek, Sr., allegedly was the sole member of RJM & Associates, LLC, the limited liability company which contracted with the plaintiff to build the house. The fourth count of the complaint seeks to impose personal liability upon Moravek individually; the count alleges that Moravek is the controlling member of the LLC, that he treated LLC funds as his own by paying virtually all of his personal expenses from the account of the LLC, thus draining the LLC's assets such that they are insufficient to meet its obligations, that by his conduct Moravek "caused the independence of said LLC to cease," and that adherence to the fiction of separate identity would defeat the interests of justice.

The defendant Moravek [asserts] . . . that in the context of a member-operated limited liability company, there can be no piercing of the LLC veil. Recognizing that there is no binding Connecticut authority precisely on point, Moravek argues that the statutory scheme expressly allows the individual to manage the LLC; he also refers to several law review articles which note the difficulty with which the veil ought to be allowed to be pierced in the context of member-operated LLCs.

---

88. J. William Callison, Rationalizing Limited Liability and Veil Piercing, 58 Bus. Law. 1063, 1067 (2003).

89. In Ditty v. CheckRite Ltd., 973 F. Supp. 1320, 1335 (D. Utah 1997), the court surveys the law reviews and concludes that "most commentators assume that the doctrine (veil piercing) applies to limited liability companies." See Callison, footnote 88 supra.

Having reviewed the authorities cited by both sides,[1] I am not persuaded that the legislature intended the limitation on member liability to be absolute. Section 34-133(a) of the General Statutes provides that "(except as provided in (b)), a person who is a member or manager of a limited liability company is not liable, *solely* by reason of being a member or manager . . . for a debt, obligation or liability (of the LLC)." (Emphasis added.) Subsection (b) provides, inter alia, that the personal liability of a member "shall be no greater than that of a shareholder who is an employee of a corporation formed under Chapter 601." The legislature is deemed to have been aware of our deeply rooted common law remedy of imposing personal liability upon a shareholder of a corporation where the corporate shield has been used to promote injustice, and the legislature surely could have expressly created a blanket limitation of member liability had it so chosen. Not much imagination is required to hypothesize all sorts of pernicious uses of such a blanket limitation.

I hold, then, that the traditional notions of imposing boundaries on the limitation of individual liability apply to limited liability companies. See, e.g., *Litchfield Asset Management*, supra. The defendant suggests that even if that is so, individual liability ought not be imposed on the so-called "identity" theory where the LLC is member-managed.

There have been at least two theories suggested as specific ways of piercing the corporate veil, the instrumentality rule and the identity rule.

> The instrumentality rule requires, in any case but an express agency, proof of three elements: (1) Control, not mere majority or complete stock control, but complete domination, not only of finances but of policy and business practice in respect to the transaction attacked so that the corporate entity as to this transaction had at the time no separate mind, will or existence of its own; (2) that such control must have been used by the defendant to commit fraud or wrong, to perpetrate the violation of a statutory or other positive legal duty, or a dishonest or unjust act in contravention of plaintiff's legal rights; and (3) that the aforesaid control and breach of duty must proximately cause the injury or unjust loss complained of.

Tomasso v. Armor Construction & Paving, Inc., 187 Conn. 544 (1982). Under the identity theory, the proponent must

> "show that there was such a unity of interest and ownership that the independence of the corporation had in effect ceased or had never begun, [such that] an adherence to the fiction of separate identity would serve only to defeat justice and equity by permitting the economic entity to escape liability arising out of an operation conducted by one corporation for the benefit of the whole enterprise." Saphir v. Neustadt,[2] supra, 210. The identity rule primarily applies to prevent injustice in the situation where two corporate entities are, in reality, controlled as one enterprise because of the existence of common owners, officers, directors or shareholders and because of the lack of observance of corporate formalities between the two entities. See Zaist v. Olson,[3] supra, 575-76, 578 (and cases cited therein).

Tomasso, supra, 559-60 (footnotes omitted).

1. The plaintiff specifically refers to a Superior Court case, Litchfield Asset Management v. Howell, 2000 WL 1785122 (Gill, J.) (2000), in which Judge Gill applied principles of corporate veil-piercing in the context of the LLC.
2. Saphir v. Neustadt, 177 Conn. 191 (1979).
3. Zaist v. Olson, 154 Conn. 563 (1967).

Although the narrowly defined identity theory would not appear to apply on the facts alleged in this case in any event, the narrow definitions may not be overwhelmingly significant. As stated by Justice Borden, the principle underlying the identity theory was applied to an individual in *Saphir*, and in any event:

> As a matter of policy I see no reason to permit recovery against a controlling individual under the instrumentality theory but to deny it under the identity theory. They are simply slightly different roads to the same destination. They both derive from the same principle: "Courts will . . . disregard the fiction of a separate legal entity to pierce the shield of immunity afforded by the corporate structure in a situation in which the corporate entity has been so controlled and dominated that justice requires liability to be imposed on the real actor." Saphir v. Neustadt, supra, 209. And they both require uniquely factual determinations by the trial court, in which "each case in which the issue is raised should be regarded as sui generis, to be decided in accordance with its own underlying facts."

1 Fletcher, op. cit., 41.3. *Tomasso*, supra, 577-78 (dissenting opinion) (footnotes omitted).

As stated by Judge Gill in *Litchfield Asset Management*, supra: "The rationale behind the alter ego theory is that if the shareholders themselves, or the corporations themselves, disregard the legal separation, distinct properties, or proper formalities of the different corporate enterprises, then the law will likewise disregard them so far as is necessary to protect individual and corporate creditors." 1 W. Fletcher, Cyclopedia of the Law of Private Corporations (1990) §CT Page 13765 41.10, p. 614. The same theory applies in the case of a limited liability company.

The defendant argues that because the statutory scheme allows members to manage LLCs; see §34-140 of the General Statutes; there can be no equitable piercing of the veil because members are allowed to act as individuals. This argument overlooks the consideration that considerable structure is required in the formation and operation of LLCs; see, e.g., §§34-119 to 124 and indeed all of Chapter 613 of the General Statutes; and a person who ignores the intended separation between the individual and the company ought to be no better off than the sole shareholder who ignores corporate obligations. . . .

b. The Scope of Fiduciary Duties

Corporate participants—directors, officers, and controlling shareholders—have fiduciary duties to the corporation. See Chapter II.B. supra. Partnership fiduciary duties are often understood to be at a higher level. See Meinhard v. Salmon, page 715 supra. The nature of the close corporation—an incorporated partnership—has been held to impose the higher level of partnership fiduciary duties. See Wilkes v. Springside Nursing Home, Inc., page 761 supra. What level of duties do LLC members owe—corporate, partnership, or close corporation? California and Illinois require of LLC members partnership duties;[90] the ULLCA approach is corporate.[91]

90. Cal. Corp. Code 17153 (2003); Ill. Stat. Ch. 850, §180015-3 (West 2003).
91. ULLCA §409(a)-(d).

Does a corporate or partnership orientation affect whether the LLC can alter the scope of fiduciary duties through the operating agreement? There is limited authority for corporations to restrict fiduciary duties through shareholder agreements. As we have seen, however, limited partnership statutes expressly authorize altering fiduciary obligations to some substantial extent through the partnership agreement.

As discussed on pages 807–808 supra, the Delaware Legislature in 2004 amended the Delaware limited partnership statute to specify that a limited partnership agreement can entirely eliminated fiduciary duties subject only to the general contractual obligation of good faith and fair dealing. The Delaware LLC statute was similarly amended; see note 85 on page 811 supra. Delaware Chief Justice Myron T. Steele treats the amendment as a response to *Gotham*, supra: "[The] 2004 amendment should put the Delaware Supreme Court on notice that . . . parties to limited partnership and limited liability company agreement will normally seek to craft their own status relationship by contract."[92] But the success of the effort will depend on how significant the differences are between the duty of loyalty as described in *Gotham* and the covenant of good faith and fair dealing. Note that §17-1101(d) of the Delaware Uniform Limited Partnership Act prohibits "eliminating the implied contractual covenant of good faith and fair dealing," while §18-1101(e) of the Delaware Uniform Limited Liability Company Act prohibits limiting or eliminating liability for a "bad faith violation" of the covenant. The two statutes were amended to add the language at the same time. Is there a substantive difference? If so, why treat the entities differently?

c. Miscellaneous Categorization Problems

One problem with creating a new form of business entity is that it must deal with what software strategists call an installed base: the preexisting statutory law does not deal with the new entity.

> [M]any laws refer to particular types of entities. Many of those laws were written at a time when the newer forms of entity did not exist. Those laws raise the question of how, if at all, they should apply to the newer entity forms. An example is the Oklahoma liquor laws which provided for the issuance of liquor licenses to natural persons and "general or limited partnership[s]." The Oklahoma courts initially concluded that what was important "was the assignment of personal responsibility for compliance with the liquor laws. Thus, business forms that did not insure such personal responsibility were excluded from eligibility for licensing." [Meyer v. Okla. Alcoholic Beverage Laws Enforcement Comm'n, 890 P.2d 1361, 1364 (Okla. Ct. A. 1995).] . . . Similar issues lurk in regulations applicable to many other businesses and professions, including the legal profession.[93]

For an interesting, albeit non-critical, example of the problem, see Poore v. Fox Hollow Enterprises, 1994 WL 150872 (Del. Super.) (Delaware law prohibited a corporation from representing itself in court through a non-lawyer shareholder

---

92. Myron T. Steele, Judicial Scrutiny of Fiduciary Duties in Delaware Limited Partnerships and Limited Liability Companies, 32 J. Corp. L. 1, 23 (2007).

93. Clark, Rationalizing Entity Laws, 58 Bus. Law. 105, 1020-1021 (2003).

while allowing a non-lawyer partner to represent a partnership; *held*: an LLC was a corporation for this purpose).

F. *LIMITED LIABILITY PARTNERSHIPS*

In contrast to the limited partnership, the registered limited liability partnership is a general partnership in which all the partners are exempt from liability for some or all of certain kinds of debts or obligations of the partnership. (The first LLP statute was created in Texas in 1991, and the LLP form is now available in all 50 states).[94] It is becoming the form of choice for many law, accounting, and other professional services firms seeking to insulate partners from liability for debts while retaining the tax and management advantages of the partnership form. Generally, state LLP statutes protect a partner of an LLP from personal liability from certain tortious conduct of other partners in the firm or employees of the firm (e.g., negligence, malpractice, or improper conduct). LLP status does not protect partners from liability for their own tortious conduct. In most states, liability for general commercial debts and obligations would still flow to all the partners. In a handful of states, the statute extends partners' personal liability protection to commercial debts and obligations of the firm.[95]

The LLP has an efficiency advantage over LLCs in that a firm organized as a partnership may simply elect to become an LLP without modifying the original partnership agreement. Also, partners in an LLP exercise considerably more managerial control and authority than is available to LLC members. The downside of the LLP — more exposure to liability than is the case for LLCs — may tip the scales in favor of the LLC for many firms.

Section 306 of Delaware's statute explains the basic attraction of this new entity.[96]

> (a) Except as otherwise provided in subsections (b) and (c), all partners are liable jointly and severally for all obligations of the partnership unless otherwise agreed by the claimant or provided by law.
>
> (b) A person admitted as a partner into an existing partnership is not personally liable for any obligation of the partnership incurred before the person's admission as a partner.
>
> (c) An obligation of a partnership incurred while the partnership is a limited liability partnership, whether arising in contract, tort or otherwise, is solely the obligation of the partnership. A partner is not personally liable, directly or indirectly, by way of indemnification, contribution, assessment or otherwise, for such an obligation solely by reason of being or so acting as a partner.

---

94. See Elizabeth G. Hester, Keeping Liability at Bay: What You Need to Know About Limited Liability Partnerships, 5 Bus. L. Today, 59 (Jan./Feb. 1996); Carter G. Bishop & Daniel S. Kleinberger, Limited Liability Companies: Tax and Business Law, §15.01 (2006); Wyo. Stat. 17-21-1101 to 17-21-1105 (2007); Vt. Stat. Ann. tit. 11 §3291 (2007).

95. Colorado, Georgia, Idaho, Indiana, Maryland, Minnesota, Montana, and New York extend protection to all commercial debts of the firm. Id.

96. See Del. Code Ann. tit. 6 ch. 15, 306 (2001).

A domestic partnership can qualify as an LLP by filing a "registration statement" with the secretary of state. One attraction of this procedure is that established professional firms can continue to operate under their old partnership agreement, but with the reduced liability afforded by this statute.

The latest variant on the LLP is the limited liability limited partnership (LLLP), which is a limited partnership that acts and is treated much like a registered LLP. Through registration with the requisite state agency, general partners of an LLLP enjoy the limited liability of general partners in an LLP. A limited partner in an LLLP may exercise more control within the LLLP than within a regular LLP. With the advent of the LLC—which offers almost identical advantages in terms of taxation, limited liability, and flexibility—the LLLP may prove an unnecessary option.[97]

G. ENTITY RATIONALIZATION AND THE PROLIFERATION OF ORGANIZATIONAL FORMS

The Cambrian explosion of organizational forms in recent years has created more than just planning problems. The choice among 12 different forms that may bedevil a practitioner seeking the right form for a particular client[98] may also plague judges who are left to answer the inescapable questions that the new statutes leave open. Inevitably, the arguments involve a comparison of the characteristics of the new entities both with traditional entities and with one another. A statutory gap, or the issue of whether to apply to a new form the common law developed for a traditional form, invites opposing arguments based on the same facts. On the one hand, the gap in the rule governing one entity ought to be filled by the existing rule governing a "similar" entity; on the other, a gap left by the legislature means that different treatment was intended. Justice Jacobs of the Delaware Supreme Court recently stated with respect to this problem that judges have been required to "reinvent 'rules of the road,' that is, the choice of doctrine for each alternative entity and for each particular case that arises in a specific alternative entity context. That amounts to a lot of reinventing." Jack B. Jacobs, Entity Rationalization: A Judge's Prospective, 58 Bus. Law. 1043, 1050 (2003).

An effort to "rationalize" the laws governing the range of organizational forms available has been undertaken by the American Bar Association Ad Hoc Committee on Entity Rationalization and the National Conference of Commissioners on Uniform State Laws. The three areas of concern have been aptly labeled "principled differences," "convergent characteristics," and "plumbing."[99] Principled differences represent the core differences between entity forms: differences in governance standards, liability rules, and structure. Convergent characteristics are organizational elements shared by different forms of entities, such as the method of giving notice of dissolution. Finally, plumbing includes the pure mechanics of entity operation, such as the location at which required filing

---

97. See Allan R. Bromberg & Larry E. Ribstein, Limited Liability Partnerships and the Revised Uniform Partnership Act 130 (1997).

98. See pages 704-705 supra.

99. Robert R. Keatinge, Plumbing and Other Transition Issues, 58 Bus. Law. 1051 (2003).

must be made, the rules governing registered agents and service of process, and the ability of one form of entity to merge with, or convert into, another form of entity.

A first effort at rationalization is the proposed Model Inter-Entity Transactions Act, which necessarily involves all three areas.[100] The approval requirements that must be met by each form of entity are examples of principled differences; that inter-entity transactions are allowed at all is an example of convergent characteristics; and the plethora of mechanics necessary to transactions — where and what papers must be filed, the manner of conversion of interests from one entity to another, and the effect of third parties — are examples of plumbing issues.

Is rationalization a worthwhile project? On the one hand, it can be seen as the finish carpentry necessary to smooth out the operation of the larger range of choices organizational innovation has provided. From this perspective, rationalization should be encouraged; entity operation is made simpler for all involved. On the other hand, rationalization may unavoidably narrow the range of choices that are available; indeed, the explosion of choices is what has given rise to the demand for rationalization in the first place. Also, the existence of competing organizational forms facilitates the evolution of business entities; a range of current alternatives leads to a better range of future alternatives. Finally, real rationalization may not be possible; each legislative fix may simply create its own set of new uncertainties.[101]

Do the competing claims with respect to entity rationalization mirror similar claims with respect to mandatory versus enabling corporate law generally? Can we rationalize the plumbing while leaving the principled differences in place?

---

100. Ad Hoc Committee on Entity Rationalization, Proposed Model Inter-Entity Transactions Act, 57 Bus. Law. 1569 (2002).

101. See Larry E. Ribstein, Making Sense of Entity Rationalization, 58 Bus. Law. 1023 (2003).

VIII SHAREHOLDERS' SUITS

A. INTRODUCTION

Shareholders may believe that those who control the corporation have violated certain legal obligations. If the claim is that management has abridged a statutory, contractual, or other common law duty owed directly to the shareholders as individuals, they may seek to enforce their right in a traditional cause of action, i.e., a direct suit against the alleged wrongdoers. Illustrative of such claims are management's refusal to permit the inspection of the corporate books or an insider's failure to disclose material information when purchasing their shares. If the alleged misconduct similarly affects the rights of a number of other shareholders, then the suit may be brought as a class action.

The claim, however, may be that management's wrongdoing has directly injured the corporation and has prejudiced the shareholders only indirectly. For example, the charge may be that directors or officers have breached their fiduciary duties by taking excessive salaries or appropriating corporate opportunities, or that management has improperly declined to enforce a corporate cause of action against outsiders. In these circumstances, the shareholders' injury (diminution in the value of their shares) derives from the fact that the alleged misconduct has reduced the value of the corporation's assets. Further, this type of derivative injury is suffered in common by all shareholders according to their proportionate interest in the corporation. The shareholders' derivative suit was created by equity courts to permit a shareholder to vindicate wrongs done to the corporation as a whole that management, because of either self-interest or neglect, would not remedy.

It allows a shareholder to bring a secondary (or derivative) action on behalf of the corporation (and thus all its shareholders collectively), in contrast to the direct (or primary) cause of action in which shareholders assert their own rights. It may be viewed as a peculiar type of class suit in which the shareholder asserts a right of the corporation for the benefit of all who have an interest in the corporation's success.[1]

Those in control of a corporation who breach their fiduciary duties to it obviously will not act on behalf of the corporation to obtain relief against themselves. Further, if they own a majority of the shares, electing new management is mathematically impossible; more frequently, such action is infeasible for various reasons, especially in large corporations, because of the gap between ownership and control.[2] Thus, the derivative suit is considered to be an important remedial and deterrent device to rectify and prevent management abuses and to protect minority shareholders and others concerned with the welfare of the corporation.[3]

At the same time, the derivative suit may be abused by small shareholders and lawyers bringing so-called strike suits for personal gain rather than correction of management misconduct. Originally, the strike suitor's motivation was to obtain some form of private settlement; defendants were willing to pay either to avoid the nuisance of the suit or to escape the potentially larger liability of a judgment. The complaining shareholder was willing to accept a fraction of the alleged damage to the corporation because this personal recovery would be far in excess of the derivative benefit were the corporation to recover. This opportunity, however, has been greatly diminished by the doctrinal development that derivative suit settlements must go to the corporation. Thus, at least from the perspective of some, those currently viewed as strike suitors are likely to be lawyers who instigate derivative suits hoping for a substantial fee after a judgment or settlement for the corporation[4] whose net value to the company may be greatly exceeded by the actual

1. For discussion of the origin of derivative suits, see Garrard Glenn, The Stockholder's Suit—Corporate and Individual Grievances, 33 Yale L.J. 580 (1924); Bert S. Prunty, The Shareholders' Derivative Suit: Notes on Its Derivation, 32 N.Y.U. L. Rev. 980 (1957); George D. Hornstein, The Shareholder's Derivative Suit in the United States, 1967 J. Bus. L. 282.

2. See Daniel J, Dykstra, The Revival of the Derivative Suit, 116 U. Pa. L. Rev. 74, 77-82 (1967).

3. For different views, from both theoretical and empirical perspectives, on the effectiveness of derivative suits, see Symposium, 71 Cornell L. Rev. 261 (1986).

4. "[V]ictory or defeat in the lawsuit will cause a *de minimis* impact upon the value of the plaintiff's stock. Indeed, it does not make economic sense for the usual plaintiff shareholder to bring the suit. The individual who gains by bringing the suit is the plaintiff shareholder's attorney. The attorney hopes to collect fees out of any judgment or settlement. The plaintiff shareholder is often a relative or acquaintance who the attorney asked to serve as plaintiff." Franklin A. Gevurtz, Corporation Law 426-427 (2000). See generally John C. Coffee Jr., Understanding the Plaintiff's Attorney: The Implications of Economic Theory for Private Enforcement of Law Through Class and Derivative Actions, 86 Colum. L. Rev. 669, 671-677 (1986); John C. Coffee Jr., The Unfaithful Champion: The Plaintiff as Monitor in Shareholder Litigation, 48 Law & Contemp. Probs. 5, 13-33 (1985); see also Daniel R. Fischel & Michael Bradley, The Role of Liability Rules and the Derivative Suit in Corporate Law: A Theoretical and Empirical Analysis, 71 Cornell L. Rev, 261, 271-272 (1986). A study of all complaints filed in the Delaware Chancery Court in 1999-2000 concluded that "the claim that derivative suits are strike suits is much weaker than in earlier periods," finding that "roughly 30 percent of the derivative suits provide relief to the corporation or to the shareholders, while the others are usually dismissed quickly with little apparent litigation activity. In cases producing a recovery to shareholders, those amounts typically exceed the amount of attorneys' fees awarded by a significant margin." Robert B. Thompson & Randall S. Thomas, The Public and Private Faces of Derivative Lawsuits, 57 Vand. L. Rev. 1745 (2004).

The conclusion of an extensive empirical study of shareholder suits against public corporations from the late 1960s to the late 1980s was that "the principal beneficiaries . . . appear to be attorneys." Roberta Romano, The Shareholder Suit: Litigation Without Foundation?, 7 J.L. Econ. & Org. 55, 84 (1991). Compare Jonathan R. Macey & Geoffrey P. Miller, The Plaintiffs' Attorney's Role in Class Action and Derivative Litigation: Economic Analysis and Recommendations for Reform, 58 U. Chi. L. Rev.

or potential costs related to defending the suit (including reputational damage and diversion of management's energy from normal business activity).[5]

Because of its unique nature and its perceived abuse, the derivative suit is hedged about by a host of procedural complexities[6] that will be examined in detail in this chapter.[7] Further, although to this point we have assumed a clear distinction between direct and derivative suits, problems of characterization frequently arise. Since most of the derivative suit complexities pose barriers to the complaining shareholder, defendants frequently seek to have a shareholder's action labeled as derivative.[8] This chapter will explore this issue in detail but, before doing so, it will be helpful to study some of the procedural aspects of the derivative suit in order to appreciate better the consequences of the characterization. Finally, before studying any single aspect in depth, some preview of the issues presented by derivative suits and a brief description of the mechanics will aid the ability to understand and evaluate.

The established rule is that, since the cause of action sought to be asserted in a derivative suit usually belongs to the corporation, internal remedies must first be exhausted. A demand that management itself undertake the suit is ordinarily a prerequisite, and some jurisdictions also require that a demand on a shareholder body be made in certain circumstances; in some situations, a considered refusal to take action by management or the shareholders may bar the derivative suit. The corporation, having refused to sue in its own behalf, is nominally a defendant in the derivative suit (despite the fact that, if the action produces a money judgment, the recovery usually goes to the corporation); thus, special problems of service of process, jurisdiction, and venue arise,[9] as do questions of which defendants (real defendants or corporation) may raise various defenses and whether both sets of defendants may be represented by the same counsel. The peculiarity of the derivative suit also raises special issues respecting the statute of limitations.

1, 78 (1991): "Although a theoretical model exists in which suits are brought solely for their nuisance settlement value, . . . [m]ost observers agree that strike suit litigation is relatively uncommon." Contrast the court's observation in In re BankAmerica Securities Litigation, 95 F. Supp. 2d 1044 (E.D. Mo. 2000), *aff'd*, 263 F.3d 795 (8th Cir. 2001), *cert. denied*, 535 U.S. 970 (2002), that plaintiffs' lawyers "do not have the best interests of the class at heart and have proved themselves wholly inadequate to control the conduct of this suit. The Court finds their attempts to do so outrageous."

5. "[D]iscovery in a shareholder derivative action typically begins with a very wide net capable of enveloping documents of the corporation, its board of directors, its chief officers, its outside attorney, its outside auditor, and often its subsidiary or affiliated corporations. This blunderbuss discovery gives a greater ring of truth to the old critique of the derivative claim, that it is extraordinarily expensive and disruptive." Joel Seligman, The Disinterested Person: An Alternative Approach to Shareholder Derivative Litigation, 55 Law & Contemp. Probs. 357, 359 (Autumn 1992).

6. For the view that empirical studies that minimize the value of derivative suits (see footnote 4 supra) do not adequately measure their deterrent effect on corporate managers' misconduct, see John C. Coffee Jr., New Myths and Old Realities: The American Law Institute Faces the Derivative Action, 48 Bus. Law. 1407, 1436-1437 (1993): "All that empirical studies can measure (and only incompletely) is the impact of existing legal rules. The more one credits this new research, the more one is led to the conclusion that the existing legal rules for the derivative action need to be redesigned. . . ."

7. A few states permit directors and officers, as well as shareholders, to bring derivative suits. See N.Y. Bus. Corp. Law §720(b) (1987). These are usually not subject to as many restrictions as derivative suits by shareholders. Further, some statutes and equity doctrines also afford procedures permitting judgment creditors to assert corporate causes of action in certain circumstances. See generally Harry G. Henn & John R. Alexander, Corporations §§217, 229, 359 (3d ed. 1983). See also the more recently enacted "constituency statutes," discussed at page 40 supra.

8. But defendants may sometimes benefit from having the suit characterized as a direct action. For example, counterclaims are not permitted in a derivative suit. Nor may plaintiff's counsel ordinarily recover attorney's fees from the corporation in a non-derivative action.

9. For detailed consideration of these and other special procedural problems of derivative suits, see Deborah A. DeMott, Shareholder Derivative Actions: Law and Practice ch. 4 (2007).

A threshold problem concerns who may bring the derivative suit; many juris-dictions preclude certain shareholders from doing so (e.g., the requirement that plaintiff must have been a shareholder at the time that the wrong occurred). A significant obstacle in some states is the requirement that certain types of share-holder plaintiffs post security, which may be used to reimburse the corporation for its litigation expenses; these may include not only the corporation's own attorneys' fees but also amounts the corporation may be obligated to indemnify corporate managers for their own litigation expenses. The possibility of separate share-holders wishing to commence derivative actions in respect to the same matter presents issues of intervention and consolidation.[10]

Problems also arise concerning the propriety of, and requisite procedures for, settlement of derivative suits. A court-approved settlement, as well as a final judgment on the merits, is ordinarily binding on all parties, including the corporation, and thus operates as res judicata in respect to any further derivative action or suit by the corporation on the cause of action. Finally, as indicated above, successful derivative suit shareholders are generally entitled to an award of liti-gation expenses and counsel fees from the corporation.[11]

The federal rule governing derivative suits addresses a number of issues men-tioned above and to be examined in this chapter.

Federal Rules of Civil Procedure (1987)

Rule 23.1. *Derivative actions by shareholders.* In a derivative action brought by one or more shareholders or members to enforce a right of a corporation or of an unincorporated association, the corporation or association having failed to enforce a right which may properly be asserted by it, the complaint shall be ver-ified[12] and shall allege (1) that the plaintiff was a shareholder or member at the time of the transaction of which the plaintiff complains or that the plaintiff's share or membership thereafter devolved on the plaintiff by operation of law, and (2) that the action is not a collusive one to confer jurisdiction on a court of the United States which it would not otherwise have. The complaint shall also allege with particularity the efforts, if any, made by the plaintiff to obtain the action the plaintiff desires from the directors or comparable authority and, if necessary, from the shareholders or members, and the reasons for the plaintiff's failure to obtain the action or for not making the effort. The derivative action may not be maintained if it

---

10. See id. §§4.12-4.13.

11. Since a derivative suit is an equitable action, irrespective of the nature of the underlying claim, a jury trial is ordinarily unavailable unless the state constitution preserves the right to jury trial. See generally id. §4.18. But in the federal courts, the Seventh Amendment right to jury trial has been held to apply to all derivative suit issues as to which the corporation would have the right to a jury if it had brought the action directly. Ross v. Bernhard, 396 U.S. 531 (1970).

Courts are divided on whether a shareholder may join a direct and derivative action in a single suit, although the trend appears to favor permitting joinder. Compare Shaffer v. Universal Rundle Corp., 397 F.2d 893 (5th Cir. 1968), with Kenney v. Don-Ra, Inc., 178 Ga. App. 492, 343 S.E.2d 779 (1986).

12. See Surowitz v. Hilton Hotels Corp., 383 U.S. 363 (1966), holding that a derivative suit should not be dismissed because plaintiff shareholder did not personally understand the allegations of the complaint—which she had "verified by oath"—but rather relied on the judgment of another. The suit, charging that Hilton directors had sold shares to the corporation at inflated prices, was subsequently settled, defendants denying culpability but agreeing to pay $825,000 to the corporation "to avoid the expense and burden of continuing the litigation." N.Y. Times (Nov. 17, 1966) at 69, col. 6.—ED.

appears that the plaintiff does not fairly and adequately represent the interests of the shareholders or members similarly situated in enforcing the right of the corporation or association. The action shall not be dismissed or compromised without the approval of the court, and notice of the proposed dismissal or compromise shall be given to shareholders or members in such manner as the court directs.

B. *EXHAUSTION OF INTERNAL REMEDIES*

Since a derivative suit usually seeks to enforce a corporate cause of action, to what extent may the plaintiff shareholder circumvent the normal corporate structures of the board of directors and the body of shareholders? Generally stated, the two principal, and somewhat interrelated, issues that arise are (1) under what circumstances must a demand be made on either the directors or shareholders to take action, and (2) what are the consequences of a decision by either group not to take action? Many of the considerations that are important in discussing these issues respecting the board of directors are similarly significant respecting the body of shareholders. But both the existing legal doctrine and the policy considerations involved differ sufficiently to merit separate treatment.

1. DEMAND ON DIRECTORS

Marx v. Akers
88 N.Y.2d 189, 644 N.Y.S.2d 121, 666 N.E.2d 1034 (1996)

SMITH, J.: Plaintiff commenced this shareholder derivative action against International Business Machines Corporation (IBM) and IBM's board of directors without first demanding that the board initiate a lawsuit. The amended complaint (complaint) alleges that the board wasted corporate assets by awarding excessive compensation to IBM's executives and outside directors. The issues raised on this appeal are whether the Appellate Division abused its discretion by dismissing plaintiff's complaint for failure to make a demand and whether plaintiff's complaint fails to state a cause of action. . . .

Business Corporation Law §626(c) provides that in any shareholders' derivative action, "the complaint shall set forth with particularity the efforts of the plaintiff to secure the initiation of such action by the board or the reasons for not making such effort."[13] Enacted in 1961 (L.1961, ch. 855), section 626(c) codified a rule of equity developed in early shareholder derivative actions requiring plaintiffs to demand that the corporation initiate an action, unless such demand was futile, before commencing an action on the corporation's behalf (Barr v. Wackman, 36 N.Y.2d 371, 377, 368 N.Y.S.2d 497, 329 N.E.2d 180). The purposes of the demand

---

13. All jurisdictions adhere to this principle (incorporated in Fed. R. Civ. P. 23.1, page 828 supra, as do a number of state statutes and rules). Cal. Gen. Corp. Law §800(b)(2) (1982) further requires "that plaintiff has either informed the corporation or the board in writing of the ultimate facts of each cause of action against each defendant or delivered to the corporation or the board a true copy of the complaint which plaintiff proposes to file." — ED.

requirement are to (1) relieve courts from deciding matters of internal corporate governance by providing corporate directors with opportunities to correct alleged abuses,[14] (2) provide corporate boards with reasonable protection from harassment by litigation on matters clearly within the discretion of directors, and (3) discourage "strike suits" commenced by shareholders for personal gain rather than for the benefit of the corporation (*Barr*, 36 N.Y.2d, at 378, 368 N.Y.S.2d 497, 329 N.E.2d 180). "[T]he demand is generally designed to weed out unnecessary or illegitimate shareholder derivative suits" (id.).[15]

By their very nature, shareholder derivative actions infringe upon the managerial discretion of corporate boards. "As with other questions of corporate policy and management, the decision whether and to what extent to explore and prosecute such [derivative] claims lies within the judgment and control of the corporation's board of directors" (Auerbach [v. Bennett], 47 N.Y.2d, at 631, 419 N.Y.S.2d 920, 393 N.E.2d 994, supra). Consequently, we have historically been reluctant to permit shareholder derivative suits, noting that the power of courts to direct the management of a corporation's affairs should be "exercised with restraint" (Gordon v. Elliman, 306 N.Y. 456, 462, 119 N.E.2d 331).

In permitting a shareholder derivative action to proceed because a demand on the corporation's directors would be futile, "the object is for the court to chart the course for the corporation which the directors should have selected, and which it is presumed that they would have chosen if they had not been actuated by fraud or bad faith. Due to their misconduct, the court substitutes its judgment ad hoc for that of the directors in the conduct of its business" (id., at 462, 119 N.E.2d 331).

Achieving a balance between preserving the discretion of directors to manage a corporation without undue interference, through the demand requirement, and permitting shareholders to bring claims on behalf of the corporation when it is evident that directors will wrongfully refuse to bring such claims, through the demand futility exception, has been accomplished by various jurisdictions in different ways. . . .

The Delaware Approach

Delaware's demand requirement, codified in Delaware Chancery Court Rule 23.1, [is similar to Fed. R. Civ. P. 23.1]. . . . Interpreting Rule 23.1, the Delaware Supreme Court in Aronson v. Lewis, 473 A.2d 805, developed a two-prong test for determining the futility of a demand. Plaintiffs must allege particularized facts which create a reasonable doubt that "(1) the directors are disinterested and independent . . . [or] (2) the challenged transaction was otherwise the product of a valid exercise of business judgment.[16] Hence, the Court of Chancery must make

---

14. In the *Barr* case, the court added that a demand may "not only relieve the courts from entanglement in the management of internal corporate affairs, but also protect them from vain rulings on challenged acts which are later ratified by the board. (See generally Foss v. Harbottle, 2 Hare, 461, 492-494, 67 Eng. Rep. 189, 203-204; Hawes v. Oakland, 104 U.S. 450.)"—ED.

15. In commenting about shareholders "who file derivative actions not to correct abuse as much to coerce nuisance settlements," the court in Werbowsky v. Collomb, 766 A.2d 123 (Md. 2001), observed: "We do not, in any way, impinge the motives of the plaintiffs in this case. Evidence was presented, however, that the entity that initially filed this action, based on its ownership of 20 shares of Lafarge stock, had filed 64 shareholder lawsuits against various corporations since 1994, many within a day or two after announcement of the transaction being challenged."—ED.

16. May plaintiff "create a reasonable doubt . . . of a valid exercise of business judgment" if plaintiff alleges that the board "failed to act" in that it failed "to oversee subordinates"? See Fagin v. Gilmartin, 432 F.3d 276 (3d Cir. 2005).—ED.

two inquiries, one into the independence and disinterestedness of the directors and the other into the substantive nature of the challenged transaction and the board's approval thereof" (473 A.2d, at 814).[17]

The two branches of the *Aronson* test are disjunctive (see, Levine v. Smith, 591 A.2d 194, 205). Once director interest has been established, the business judgment rule becomes inapplicable and the demand excused without further inquiry (*Aronson*, 473 A.2d, at 814). Similarly, a director whose independence is compromised by undue influence exerted by an interested party cannot properly exercise business judgment and the loss of independence also justifies the excusal of a demand without further inquiry (see, *Levine*, 591 A.2d, at 205-206, supra). Whether a board has validly exercised its business judgment must be evaluated by determining whether the directors exercised procedural (informed decision) and substantive (terms of the transaction) due care (Grobow v. Perot, 539 A.2d 180, 189).[18]

The reasonable doubt threshold of Delaware's two-fold approach to demand futility has been criticized. The use of a standard of proof which is the heart of a jury's determination in a criminal case has raised questions concerning its applicability in the corporate context (see, Starrels v. First Natl. Bank, 870 F.2d 1168, 1175 [7th Cir.] [Easterbook, J., concurring]). The reasonable doubt standard has also been criticized as overly subjective, thereby permitting a wide variance in the application of Delaware law to similar facts (2 American Law Institute, Principles

17. In Brehm v. Eisner, 746 A.2d 244 (Del. 2000), the court made "clear that our review of decisions of the Court of Chancery applying Rule 23.1 is *de novo* and plenary. We apply the law to the allegations of the Complaint as does the Court of Chancery." In In re PSE & G Shareholder Litigation, 173 N.J. 258, 801 A.2d 295 (2002), the court adopted *Aronson* (as clarified in *Brehm*) as "the appropriate standard for evaluation demand futility." Accord, Shoen v. SAC Holding Corp., 137 P.3d 1171 (Nev. 2006). — Ed.

18. For a decision of the Delaware Supreme Court finding that demand would be futile under the first part of the *Aronson* test, see Heineman v. Datapoint Corp., 611 A.2d 950 (Del. 1992). For an extensively reasoned decision holding that demand would be futile under the second part of the *Aronson* test, see RCM Securities Fund, Inc. v. Stanton, 928 F.2d 1318 (2d Cir. 1991). See also McCall v. Scott, 239 F.3d 808 (6th Cir. 2001) (pleaded particularized facts present substantial likelihood of directors' liability for violation of duty of care, thus creating a reasonable doubt as to the directors' disinterestedness); cases cited in footnote 37, page 97 supra. Among the more numerous decisions reaching the same result as the *Aronson* case by finding no futility, see Pogostin v. Rice, 480 A.2d 619 (Del. 1984); Kaufman v. Belmont, 479 A.2d 282 (Del. Ch. 1984); Grobow v. Perot, 539 A.2d 180 (Del. 1988) (suit for waste against General Motors board, two-thirds of whom were outside directors, for repurchasing shares of GM's largest shareholder at "a grossly excessive price" in exchange for his agreement "to stop criticizing GM management"); Seminaris v. Landa, 662 A.2d 1350 (Del. Ch. 1995). See also Dennis Block, Stephen Radin & James Rosenzweig, The Role of the Business Judgment Rule in Shareholder Litigation at the Turn of the Decade, 45 Bus. Law. 469, 478-480 (1990):

Following *Aronson*, *Pogostin*, and *Grobow*, it is settled that, under Delaware law, demand will not be excused merely because a majority of directors are named as defendants, approved the challenged transaction, are threatened with personal liability for approving the transaction, failed to take corrective action prior to the filing of the lawsuit, refused to reconsider a challenged transaction or rejected a prior demand, would have to sue themselves, are alleged in conclusory language to be dominated and controlled by those benefiting from the challenged conduct, or have financial ties to the corporation such as the receipt of directors' fees (or bonuses tied to corporate profitability) but not a direct financial interest in the challenged transaction. Nor will demand be excused by allegations that the challenged transaction involved illegal conduct, that the corporation's directors feared "public criticism" that "could cause the directors embarrassment sufficient to lead to their removal from office," that the directors granted indemnification to a third party as part of the challenged transaction, or that the statute of limitations is about to expire. Nor, finally, will demand be excused simply because of the magnitude of the challenged transaction.

— Ed.

of Corporate Governance: Analysis and Recommendations §7.03, Comment d, at 57 [1992]).[19]

Universal Demand

A universal demand requirement would dispense with the necessity of making case-specific determinations and impose an easily applied bright line rule. The Business Law Section of the American Bar Association has proposed requiring a demand in all cases, without exception, and permits the commencement of a derivative proceeding within 90 days of the demand unless the demand is rejected earlier (Model Business Corporation Act §7.42[1] [1995 Supp.]). However, plaintiffs may file suit before the expiration of 90 days, even if their demand has not been rejected, if the corporation would suffer irreparable injury as a result (Model Business Corporation Act §7.42[2]).[20]

The American Law Institute (ALI) has also proposed a "universal" demand . . . (2 ALI, Principles of Corporate Governance: Analysis and Recommendations §7.03[b], at 53-54 [1992]).[21] Once a demand has been made and rejected, however, the ALI would subject the board's decision to "an elaborate set of standards that calibrates the deference afforded the decision of the directors to the character of the claim being asserted" (Kamen v. Kemper Fin. Servs., 500 U.S. 90, 104, 111 S. Ct. 1711, 1720, 114 L. Ed. 2d 152).[22] . . .

New York State has also considered and continues to consider implementing a universal demand requirement. However, even though bills to adopt a universal demand have been presented over three legislative sessions, the Legislature has yet to enact a universal demand requirement. . . .

New York's Approach to Demand Futility

. . . In Barr v. Wackman, 36 N.Y.2d 371, 368 N.Y.S.2d 497, 329 N.E.2d 180, supra, we considered whether the plaintiff was excused from making a demand where the board of Talcott National Corporation (Talcott), consisting of 13 outside directors, a director affiliated with a related company and four interested inside

---

19. The Delaware Supreme Court responded in Grimes v. Donald, 673 A.2d 1207 (Del. 1996): "[T]he concept of reasonable doubt is akin to the concept that the stockholder has a 'reasonable belief' that the board lacks independence or that the transaction was not protected by the business judgment rule. The concept of reasonable belief is an objective test and is found in various corporate contexts." — ED.

20. The proposed Official Comment to the Model Business Corporation Act explains that the rationale underlying the universal demand rule is two-fold. First, even if a board of directors does not include a majority (or even any) disinterested directors, there is still no reason not to give the board an opportunity "to reexamine the act complained of in the light of a potential lawsuit and take corrective action." Second, requiring demand on a universal basis will save litigants and courts the time and expense they would otherwise incur in litigating the demand futility issue. The drafters of the Model Business Corporation Act also note that "requiring a demand in all cases does not impose an onerous burden" upon shareholders.

Block, Radin & Rosenzweig, footnote 18 supra, at 485.

At least 20 states have adopted a universal demand requirement. See, e.g., Speetjens v. Malaco, Inc., 929 So. 2d 303 (Miss. 2006) (RMBCA §7.42 permits no futility exception). See also In re Guidant Shareholders Derivative Litigation, 841 N.E.2d 571 (Ind. 2006) (statute defines futility very narrowly). — ED.

21. For a recent decision finding "irreparable injury," see Warden v. McLelland, 288 F.3d 105 (3d Cir. 2002). — ED.

22. The consequences of a board decision rejecting a demand are explored in detail in the next subsection of this chapter. — ED.

directors, rejected a merger proposal involving Gulf & Western Industries (Gulf & Western) in favor of another proposal on allegedly less favorable terms for Talcott and its shareholders. The merger proposal, memorialized in a board-approved "agreement in principle," proposed exchanging one share of Talcott common stock for approximately $24 consisting of $17 in cash and 0.6 of a warrant to purchase Gulf & Western stock, worth approximately $7. This proposal was abandoned in favor of a cash tender offer for Talcott shares by Associates First Capital Corporation (a Gulf & Western subsidiary) at $20 per share — $4 less than proposed for the merger.

The plaintiff in *Barr* alleged that Talcott's board discarded the merger proposal after the four "controlling" inside directors received pecuniary and personal benefits from Gulf & Western in exchange for ceding control of Talcott on terms less favorable to Talcott's shareholders. . . . [W]e held that . . . demand was excused because of the self-dealing, or self-interest of those directors in the challenged transaction. . . .

We also held in *Barr*, however, that as to the disinterested outside directors, demand could be excused even in the absence of their receiving any financial benefit from the transaction. That was because the complaint alleged that, by approving the terms of the less advantageous offer, those directors were guilty of a "breach of their duties of due care and diligence to the corporation" (id., at 380, 368 N.Y.S.2d 497, 329 N.E.2d 180). Their performance of the duty of care would have "put them on notice of the claimed self-dealing of the affiliated directors" (id.). The complaint charged that the outside directors failed "to do more than passively rubber-stamp the decisions of the active managers" (id., at 381, 368 N.Y.S.2d 497, 329 N.E.2d 180) resulting in corporate detriment. These allegations, the *Barr* Court concluded, also excused demand as to the charges against the disinterested directors.

Barr also makes clear that "[i]t is not sufficient . . . merely to name a majority of the directors as parties defendant with conclusory allegations of wrongdoing or control by wrongdoers" (id., at 379, 368 N.Y.S.2d 497, 329 N.E.2d 180) to justify failure to make a demand. Thus, *Barr* reflects the statutory requirement that the complaint "shall set forth with particularity the . . . reasons for not making such effort" (Business Corporation Law §626[c]).

Unfortunately, various courts have overlooked the explicit warning that conclusory allegations of wrongdoing against each member of the board are not sufficient to excuse demand and have misinterpreted *Barr* as excusing demand whenever a majority of the board members who approved the transaction are named as defendants (see, Miller v. Schreyer, 200 A.D.2d 492, 606 N.Y.S.2d 642; Curreri v. Verni, 156 A.D.2d 420, 548 N.Y.S.2d 540; MacKay v. Pierce, 86 A.D.2d 655, 446 N.Y.S.2d 403; Joseph v. Amrep Corp., 59 A.D.2d 841, 399 N.Y.S.2d 3; see also, Allison Publs. v. Mutual Benefit Life Ins. Co., 197 A.D.2d 463, 602 N.Y.S.2d 858).[23] As stated most recently, "[t]he rule is clear in this State that no demand is necessary if 'the complaint alleges acts for which a majority of the directors may be

23. In Lewis v. Graves, 702 F.2d 245 (2d Cir. 1983), the court noted that "Rule 23.1 would be substantially diluted if prior board approval standing alone established futility. Derivative suits are almost invariably directed at major, allegedly illegal, corporate transactions. By virtue of their offices, directors ordinarily participate in the decision making involved in such transactions. Excusing demand on the mere basis of prior board acquiescence, therefore, would obviate the need for demand in practically every case." Accord, Garber v. Lego, 11 F.3d 1197 (3d Cir. 1993) ("to excuse demand under Pennsylvania law, the plaintiff must allege that a majority of the board of directors engaged in acts that are fraudulent"). — ED.

liable and plaintiff reasonably concluded that the board would not be responsive to a demand" (Miller v. Schreyer, supra, at 494, 606 N.Y.S.2d 642 [quoting from *Barr*, 36 N.Y.2d, at 377, 368 N.Y.S.2d 497, 329 N.E.2d 180, supra]; but see, Lewis v. Welch, 126 A.D.2d 519, 521, 510 N.Y.S.2d 640). The problem with such an approach is that it permits plaintiffs to frame their complaint in such a way as to automatically excuse demand, thereby allowing the exception to swallow the rule.

We thus deem it necessary to offer the following elaboration of *Barr*'s demand / futility standard. (1) Demand is excused because of futility when a complaint alleges with particularity that a majority of the board of directors is interested in the challenged transaction. Director interest may either be self-interest in the transaction at issue (see, Barr v. Wackman, supra, at 376, 368 N.Y.S.2d 497, 329 N.E.2d 180 [receipt of "personal benefits"]), or a loss of independence because a director with no direct interest in a transaction is "controlled" by a self-interested director.[24] (2) Demand is excused because of futility when a complaint alleges with particularity that the board of directors did not fully inform themselves about the challenged transaction to the extent reasonably appropriate under the circumstances (see, *Barr*, supra, at 380, 368 N.Y.S.2d 497, 329 N.E.2d 180). The "long-standing rule" is that a director "does not exempt himself from liability by failing to do more than passively rubber-stamp the decisions of the active managers" (id., at 381, 368 N.Y.S.2d 497, 329 N.E.2d 180). (3) Demand is excused because of futility when a complaint alleges with particularity that the challenged transaction was so egregious on its face that it could not have been the product of sound business judgment of the directors.[25]

The Current Appeal

. . . Defendants' motion to dismiss for failure to make a demand as to the allegations concerning the compensation paid to IBM's executive officers was properly granted. A board is not interested "in voting compensation for one of its members as an executive or in some other nondirectorial capacity, such as a consultant to the corporation," although "so-called 'back scratching' arrangements, pursuant to which all directors vote to approve each other's compensation as officers or employees, do not constitute disinterested directors' action" (1 ALI, op. cit., §5.03, Comment g, at 250). Since only three [of 18] directors are alleged to have received the benefit of the executive compensation scheme, plaintiff has failed to allege that a majority of the board was interested in setting executive compensation. Nor do the allegations that the board used faulty accounting procedures to calculate executive compensation levels move beyond "conclusory allegations of wrongdoing" (Barr v. Wackman, supra, at 379, 368 N.Y.S.2d 497, 329 N.E.2d 180) which are insufficient to excuse demand. The complaint does not allege particular facts in contending that the board failed to deliberate or exercise its business judgment in setting those levels. Consequently, the failure to make a demand regarding the fixing of executive compensation was fatal to that portion of the complaint challenging that transaction.

However, a review of the complaint indicates that plaintiff also alleged that a majority of the board was self-interested in setting the compensation of outside directors because the outside directors comprised a majority of the board.

---

24. For a recent example of the board being "dominated and controlled," see Bansback v. Zinn, 1 N.Y.3d 1, 801 N.E.2d 395 (2003). — ED.

25. *Query:* How does this differ from the *Aronson* test? — ED.

... A director who votes for a raise in directors' compensation is always "interested" because that person will receive a personal financial benefit from the transaction not shared in by stockholders (see, 1 ALI, Principles of Corporate Governance §5.03, Comment g, at 250 ["if the board votes directorial compensation for itself, the board is interested"] ...). Consequently, a demand was excused as to plaintiff's allegations that the compensation set for outside directors was excessive.

Corporate Waste

Our conclusion that demand should have been excused as to the part of the complaint challenging the fixing of directors' compensation does not end our inquiry. We must also determine whether plaintiff has stated a cause of action regarding director compensation, i.e., some wrong to the corporation.

... [A] complaint challenging the excessiveness of director compensation must—to survive a dismissal motion—allege compensation rates excessive on their face or other facts which call into question whether the compensation was fair to the corporation when approved, the good faith of the directors setting those rates, or that the decision to set the compensation could not have been a product of valid business judgment.

Applying the foregoing principles to plaintiff's complaint, it is clear that it must be dismissed. The complaint alleges that the directors increased their compensation rates from a base of $20,000 plus $500 for each meeting attended to a retainer of $55,000 plus 100 shares of IBM stock over a five-year period. The complaint also alleges that "[t]his compensation bears little relation to the part-time services rendered by the Non-Employee Directors or to the profitability of IBM. The board's responsibilities have not increased, its performance, measured by the company's earnings and stock price, has been poor yet its compensation has increased far in excess of the cost of living."

These conclusory allegations do not state a cause of action. There are no factually based allegations of wrongdoing or waste which would, if true, sustain a verdict in plaintiff's favor. Plaintiff's bare allegations that the compensation set lacked a relationship to duties performed or to the cost of living are insufficient as a matter of law to state a cause of action.[26]

Accordingly, the order of the Appellate Division should be affirmed, with costs.

---

1. *Rigorous observance of the demand requirement.* In Kamen v. Kemper Financial Services, Inc., 939 F.2d 458 (7th Cir. 1991), the court, applying Maryland law, held that demand was required even though the directors had (1) approved the proxy statement alleged in the derivative suit to be misleading, and (2) sought to dismiss the suit:

> Decisions in several states support Kamen's argument that the directors' participation in the questioned acts excuses demand. E.g., Barr v. Wackman, 36 N.Y.2d 371, 368 N.Y.S.2d 497, 329 N.E.2d 180 (1975); Valiquet v. First Federal Savings & Loan

26. *Query:* Does the court's decision on this issue comport with N.Y. Bus. Corp. Law §713, page 119 supra? — ED.

Association, 87 Ill. App. 3d 195, 42 Ill. Dec. 212, 217, 408 N.E.2d 921, 926 (1st Dist. 1979). The tide is running against this approach, however. See ALI, Principles of Corporate Governance: Analysis and Recommendations 76-81 (T.D. No. 8, 1988) (Reporter's note analyzing state cases). Delaware, today's dominant corporate jurisdiction, has emphatically rejected the proposition that an investor may forego demand whenever the directors participated in the transaction they challenge.[27] . . .

Aronson and comparable cases conclude that unless there is good reason to doubt that the directors' acts are protected by the business judgment rule, a disgruntled investor must ask the directors to act. Maryland has never addressed this issue. In resolving doubt about the scope of its demand requirement, Maryland could well be influenced by the recommendations of the American Law Institute and the American Bar Association. . . . So, too, Maryland might be influenced by the burgeoning research casting doubt on the value of derivative litigation for investors. E.g., Roberta Romano, The Shareholder Suit: Litigation Without Foundation?, 7 J.L. Econ. & Org. 55 (1991);[28] Janet Cooper Alexander, Do the Merits Matter? A Study of Settlements in Securities Class Actions, 43 Stan. L. Rev. 497 (1991); Mark L. Cross, Wallace N. Davidson & John H. Thornton, The Impact of Directors' and Officers' Liability Suits on Firm Value, 56 J. Risk & Ins. 128 (1989); Daniel R. Fischel & Michael Bradley, The Role of Liability Rules and the Derivative Suit in Corporate Law: A Theoretical and Empirical Analysis, 71 Cornell L. Rev. 261 (1986). State legislatures have begun to adopt universal-demand requirements. Ill. S. Ct. at 1719 n.7 (collecting statutes). There is no counter movement toward enlarging the futility exception. We think it likely, then, that if Maryland does not abolish the futility exception it will cast its lot with the states that require demand on directors who face no substantial risk of personal liability.[29] As Kamen has never argued that the Fund's seven independent directors could be personally liable — indeed, Kamen has never argued that they even noticed the single sentence of which she complains — it follows that the directors' approval of the proxy statement does not make demand futile.

---

27. In the *Aronson* case, the court agreed: "In Delaware mere directorial approval of a transaction, absent particularized facts supporting a breach of fiduciary duty claim, or otherwise establishing the lack of independence or disinterestedness of a majority of the directors, is insufficient to excuse demand." See also Grobow v. Perot, footnote 18 supra: "Approval of a transaction by a majority of independent, disinterested directors almost always bolsters a presumption that the business judgment rule attaches to transactions approved by a board of directors that are later attacked on grounds of lack of due care. In such cases, a heavy burden falls on a plaintiff to avoid presuit demand." — ED.

28. This empirical study — see footnote 4 supra — after pointing out that the average recovery of the 12 derivative suits that were settled was $6 million, concludes, inter alia, that "lawsuits are an infrequent occurrence for the public corporation and, while most suits settle, the settlements provide minimal compensation"; "there is little evidence of specific deterrence . . . [which] suggests that general deterrence is weak"; "there is scant evidence that lawsuits function as an alternative governance mechanism to the board . . . [although] in three cases outside block holders were able to use the threat of litigation to redirect corporate policy." Id. at 84-85. — ED.

29. In Werbowsky v. Collomb, footnote 15 supra, the court "adhere[d], for the time being, to the futility exception, but . . . regard it as a very limited exception, to be applied only when the allegations or evidence clearly demonstrate, in a very particular manner, either that (1) a demand, or a delay in awaiting a response to a demand, would cause irreparable harm to the corporation or (2) a majority of the directors are so personally and directly conflicted or committed to the decision in dispute that they cannot reasonably be expected to respond to a demand in good faith and within the ambit of the business judgment rule." For a recent application of this approach, see In re InfoSonics Corp. Deriv. Litig., 2007 WL 2572276 (S.D. Cal. 2007) ("substantial likelihood of liability" of directors does not "establish demand futility"). — ED.

Yet we know, Kamen responds, that those directors were *not* willing to put things to rights. After she filed this suit, the directors moved to dismiss her claims on the merits. During depositions, several directors took a dim view of Kamen's substantive allegations. These objections demonstrate, she maintains, that demand was futile. This argument confuses futility with failure. A demand is "futile" only if the directors' minds are closed to argument. That the directors disagreed with an argument could show their unwillingness to listen, but also could show that the argument was feeble. See Pogostin v. Rice, 480 A.2d 619, 627 (Del. 1984). Demand enables the directors to take the leading role in managing the corporation. Conscientious managers may conclude that legal action is unjustified because not meritorious, or because it would subject the firm to injury. This is why courts assess futility *ex ante* rather than *ex post*. See Deborah A. DeMott, Shareholder Derivative Actions: Law and Practice §5.03 at 31 (1987). . . . So far as we know, no state treats the directors' failure to capitulate in the lawsuit as forfeiting the firm's entitlement to demand before the suit commences. Directors will (and should) oppose weak claims. If that opposition eliminated the need for demand, we would reach the curious pass that claims so weak that they should not be pursued at all could go straight to court, while claims strong enough to litigate about should be presented to the directors.

2. *Questions.* If a derivative suit charges all the corporation's directors with negligence and lack of due care, would a demand on the board be futile even though all the defendant directors are fully insured for such alleged misconduct? See Walner v. Friedman, Fed. Sec. L. Rep. (CCH) ¶95,318 (S.D.N.Y. 1975). Would demand be futile if the corporation's charter eliminates personal liability of directors for breach of the duty of care (see Note 9, page 127 supra)? See In re Baxter Int'l, Inc. Shareholders Litigation, 654 A.2d 1268 (Del. Ch. 1995).

Is demand on the board required if the board is evenly split between interested and disinterested directors? See Untermeyer v. Fidelity Daily Income Trust, 580 F.2d 22 (1st Cir. 1978). Is a demand on the board required if it has previously rejected another shareholder's demand to bring the same cause of action? See Stallworth v. AmSouth Bank of Alabama, 709 So. 2d 458, 464 (Ala. 1997). Is demand on the board required if a majority of its present members were not on the board at the time of the transaction being challenged? Compare Rales v. Blasband, 634 A.2d 927 (Del. 1993), with New Crawford Valley Ltd. v. Benedict, 847 P.2d 642 (Colo. App. 1993). If, after a derivative suit is filed and demand is excused as futile because a majority of the board is interested, a different board with a majority of disinterested directors is elected, must plaintiff make a demand on the new board? See Braddock v. Zimmerman, 906 A.2d 776 (Del. 2006). Should a derivative suit be dismissed if plaintiff seeks to satisfy the demand requirement by making the demand after filing the derivative suit? See Shlensky v. Dorsey, 574 F.2d 131, 139-142 (3d Cir. 1978).

3. *"Controlled" directors.* In the *Aronson* case, the court rejected plaintiff's claim that the corporation's directors were not "independent" because the executive who benefited from the challenged transaction owned 47 percent of the company's "actively traded" shares and "personally selected" each director:

[I]n the demand-futile context . . . charging domination and control . . . even proof of majority ownership of a company does not strip the directors of the presumptions of independence, and that their acts have been taken in good faith and in the best interests of the corporation. There must be coupled with the allegation of control such facts as would demonstrate that through personal or other relationships the directors are beholden to the controlling person. . . . [30]

Thus, it is not enough to charge that a director was nominated by or elected at the behest of those controlling the outcome of a corporate election. That is the usual way a person becomes a corporate director. It is the care, attention and sense of individual responsibility to the performance of one's duties, not the method of election, that generally touches on independence.

4. *Federal causes of action.* In Kamen v. Kemper Financial Services, Inc., 500 U.S. 90 (1991), the Court held that in a derivative suit charging directors with violations of the Investment Company Act of 1940, state law determines the scope of the demand requirement:.

> We reaffirm the basic teaching of Burks v. Lasker, 441 U.S. 471 (1979): where a gap in the federal securities laws must be bridged by a rule that bears on the allocation of governing powers within the corporation, federal courts should incorporate *state* law into federal common law unless the particular state law in question is inconsistent with the policies underlying the federal statute. The scope of the demand requirement under state law clearly regulates the allocation of corporate governing powers between the directors and individual shareholders, . . . [and] a futility exception to demand does not impede the regulatory objectives of the [Act.][31]

2. THE BOARD'S AUTHORITY TO TERMINATE THE SUIT

Compliance with the demand requirement itself is not very burdensome in terms of effort and expense and thus poses no great obstacle to the complaining shareholder. A substantial barrier, however, may be presented by the board's refusal — either in response to a demand or on its own motion — to enforce the corporation's cause of action. In the *Aronson* case, the court stated that "where demand on a board has been made and refused, we apply the business judgment rule in reviewing the board's refusal to act pursuant to a stockholder's demand. . . . Unless the business judgment rule does not protect the refusal to sue, the shareholder lacks the legal managerial power to continue the derivative action, since that power is terminated by the refusal."

To what extent do the *Marx* and *Aronson* cases stand for the proposition that, if demand is not futile because plaintiff has failed to sufficiently allege particularized facts showing that a majority of the board is "interested," then it follows that the board's post-demand decision not to sue terminates the derivative action?

---

30. Accord, Beam ex rel. Martha Stewart Living Omnimedia, Inc., v. Stewart, 845 A.2d 1040 (Del. 2004) ("mere personal friendship or a mere outside business relationship" with alleged wrongdoer with "94% voting power, . . . standing alone, are insufficient to raise a reasonable doubt about a director's independence"; rather, plaintiff must allege that "the non-interested director would be more willing to risk his or her reputation than risk the relationship with the interested director"); Kaster v. Modification Sys., 731 F.2d 1014 (2d Cir. 1984) (alleged wrongdoer owned 71 percent of voting stock and nominated all but one director). — ED.

31. For consideration of *Burks*'s application to a series of federal causes of action, see John C. Coffee Jr. & Donald E. Schwartz, The Survival of the Derivative Suit: An Evaluation and a Proposal for Legislative Reform, 81 Colum. L. Rev. 261, 287-300 (1981). — ED.

Levine v. Smith
591 A.2d 194 (Del. 1991)

Horsey, J.: . . . Each of these derivative suits challenges General Motors Corporation's ("GM") repurchase on December 1, 1986 from H. Ross Perot, then GM's largest shareholder, of all his GM Class E stock and contingent notes and those of Perot's close associates of Electronic Data Systems Corporation ("EDS"), a wholly owned GM subsidiary. . . .

Both derivative actions are brought on behalf of GM and GM's wholly owned subsidiary, EDS, which was founded by Perot. The named defendants in both actions are all twenty-one members of GM's Board of Directors, Perot, and three of Perot's close EDS associates. In 1984, GM acquired by merger 100 percent of EDS' stock. By the terms of the merger, Perot, then EDS' chairman and largest shareholder, exchanged EDS stock for cash, GM Class E stock and a contingent note package. The transaction made Perot GM's largest shareholder with 0.8 percent of GM voting stock. Perot remained chairman of EDS and became a member of the GM Board of Directors. GM and EDS agreed that EDS, although a wholly owned subsidiary of GM, would be allowed to operate with a "substantial degree of autonomy" and would retain "significant control over its internal affairs."

While the GM-EDS merger proved to be largely successful, numerous disputes arose between GM and Perot regarding the management and operation of EDS. By mid-1986, Perot became increasingly critical of GM management concerning issues involving EDS and unrelated to EDS, including the quality of GM products. Perot's criticism received wide media attention, with Perot being quoted in *Business Week* as having criticized GM for "producing second-rate cars." Perot also believed that GM was not acting in accordance with agreements the parties had reached. By the summer of 1986, Perot made demands upon GM's chairman that GM either buy him out or else allow him to operate EDS as he saw fit. Perot also threatened to sue GM.

In the fall of 1986, GM and Perot entered into negotiations for GM to repurchase Perot's interest in GM. This followed an aborted effort by GM to sell EDS to American Telephone and Telegraph. By November 30, 1986, the terms of a definitive agreement had been reached; and on that date, the Oversight Subcommittee of the GM Board's Audit Committee met to discuss the proposed agreement. The members of the three-person Subcommittee were all outside, non-management directors. Other directors participated in the lengthy meeting, although the full Board was not present. The Oversight Subcommittee unanimously recommended that the GM Board approve the terms of the repurchase. At the time, GM's twenty-one member Board consisted of but seven inside, or management, directors and fourteen outside directors, excluding Perot. The next day, December 1, the full GM Board (excluding Perot) met and unanimously approved the transaction. . . .

On December 11, 1986, ten days after the GM Board's approval of the Perot repurchase agreement, GM shareholder Levine made written demand upon the GM Board to rescind the Perot repurchase transaction. . . . On January 5, 1987, the GM Board met and voted unanimously . . . that legal action would not be "in the best interests of the Corporation." On February 3, 1987, Levine filed suit. . . . On November 27, 1989, the Court of Chancery granted defendants' motion and dismissed the Levine Amended Complaint. . . .

[T]he first issue we address is whether, in a demand refused case, a shareholder plaintiff suing derivatively is entitled to discovery prior to responding to a Rule 23.1

motion to dismiss. . . . Levine contends that . . . without discovery the Court of Chancery has "unjustly tilted the scales [in favor of the board] and permitted a corporate board to simply refuse a shareholder's demand for action with impunity." Finally, Levine argues that the burden of proof of the propriety of a refused demand should logically fall upon the defendant board. The board has "better access to the relevant facts" and, having raised the defense, the board should have "the burden of proving that defense." Dent, The Power of Directors to Terminate Shareholder Litigation: The Death of the Derivative Suit?, 75 Nw. U. L. Rev. 96 (1980). . . .

The rationale for allowing discovery in a demand excused–*Zapata* context has no application in . . . [this case]. The issue in *Zapata* [page 845 infra] was whether an impliedly interested board could delegate its power to dismiss a derivative suit to a special committee of outside disinterested directors. . . . As the court below pointed out, the act of establishing a special litigation committee constitutes an implicit concession by a board that its members are interested in the transaction and that its decisions are not entitled to the protection of the business judgment rule. . . . Therefore, demand is excused and discovery is allowed. There is no basis for such presumptions to be extended to a demand refused case. . . . [32]

We next address the question of whether . . . a derivative complaint based on a claim of demand refused should be found to comply with Rule 23.1 when a plaintiff "alleges legally sufficient reasons to call into question the validity of the Board of Directors' exercise of business judgment." Allison [v. General Motors Corp.], 604 F. Supp. at 1121. . . .

Rule 23.1's . . . requirements of particularity apply both to plaintiff's efforts to obtain the desired action and the reasons for failing to secure redress. *Allison* cannot be fairly read as intending any departure from *Aronson*'s and *Grobow I*'s requirement of well-pleaded allegations of fact which create a reasonable doubt that a board of directors' decision is protected by the business judgment rule. *Grobow I*, 539 A.2d at 186, 187 ("well-pleaded allegations of fact must be accepted as true; conclusory allegations of fact or law not supported by allegations of specific fact may not be taken as true"); *Aronson*, 473 A.2d at 815. . . .

We next address the issue of whether the Court of Chancery applied the correct legal standard for determining the sufficiency of Levine's Amended Complaint to withstand defendant's Rule 23.1 motion to dismiss. The trial court ruled that the legal standard governing Rule 23.1 motions to dismiss "demand refused" cases is the same standard that governs dismissal of a "demand futility" case, that is, the

---

32. In Rales v. Blasband, 634 A.2d 927 (Del. 1993), the court noted that

> although derivative plaintiffs may believe it is difficult to meet the particularization requirement of *Aronson* because they are not entitled to discovery to assist their compliance with Rule 23.1, see *Levine*, 591 A.2d at 208-10, they have many avenues available to obtain information bearing on the subject of their claims. For example, there is a variety of public sources from which the details of a corporate act may be discovered, including the media and governmental agencies such as the Securities and Exchange Commission. In addition, a stockholder who has met the procedural requirements and has shown a specific proper purpose may use the summary procedure embodied in 8 Del. C. §220 ["Stockholder's Right of Inspection," see page supra] to investigate the possibility of wrongdoing. . . . Surprisingly, little use has been made of section 220 as an information-gathering tool in the derivative context.

For criticism of the *Levine* case, see Note, Discovery in Federal Demand-Refused Litigation, 105 Harv. L. Rev. 1025 (1992) and Note 2, page 843 infra. — ED.

Aronson two-part inquiry into board disinterest and independence as well as application of the traditional business judgment rule to the Board's refusal of the demand. The court thereby committed legal error.

The focus of a complaint alleging wrongful refusal of demand is different from the focus of a complaint alleging demand futility. The legal issues are different; therefore, the legal standards applied to the complaints are necessarily different. A shareholder plaintiff, by making demand upon a board before filing suit, "tacitly concedes the independence of a majority of the board to respond. Therefore, when a board refuses a demand, the only issues to be examined are the good faith and reasonableness of its investigation." Spiegel [v. Buntrock], 571 A.2d at 777. . . . [33] Thus, the first part of the *Aronson* test did not come into play and the trial court was only required to address the application of the business judgment rule to the Board's refusal of Levine's demand. . . . [34]

We turn to Levine's final argument: that the Court of Chancery erred in finding his Amended Complaint to fail to allege particularized facts sufficient to overcome the business judgment rule presumption accorded the GM Board's refusal of his presuit demand. The . . . only issue remaining to be resolved is the reasonableness of the GM Board's investigation of Levine's demand. *Spiegel*, 571 A.2d at 777. Reasonableness implicates the business judgment rule's requirement of procedural

---

33. In the *Spiegel* case, the court commented:

> Spiegel submits that demand should be encouraged by permitting a demand to be made, while at the same time permitting the argument, that demand was excused, to be preserved. Spiegel finds some support for his position in other jurisdictions. See Bach v. National W. Life Ins. Co., 810 F.2d 509, 513 (5th Cir. 1987); Joy v. North, 692 F.2d 880, 888 n.7 (2d Cir. 1982), *cert. denied*, 460 U.S. 1051, 103 S. Ct. 1498, 75 L. Ed. 2d 930 (1983); Alford v. Shaw, 72 N.C. App. 537, 324 S.E.2d 878, 883 n.2 (1985), *aff'd and modified on other grounds*, 320 N.C. 465, 358 S.E.2d 323 (1987). [Accord, Behradrezaee v. Dashtara, 910 A.2d 349 (D.C. 2006).] However, this Court has held that by making a demand, a shareholder thereby makes his original contention, that demand was excused moot. . . . Consequently, stockholders who, like Spiegel, make a demand which is refused, subject the board's decision to judicial review according to the traditional business judgment rule.

See also Harhen v. Brown, 431 Mass. 838, 730 N.E.2d 859 (2000) ("when a disinterested board refers a demand to a disinterested standing committee, both receive the protection of the business judgment rule").

A classic statement of this position is by Justice Brandeis in United Copper Securities Co. v. Amalgamated Copper Co., 244 U.S. 261, 263-264 (1917): "Whether or not a corporation shall seek to enforce in the courts a cause of action for damages is, like other business questions, ordinarily a matter of internal management and is left to the discretion of the directors, in the absence of instruction by vote of the stockholders. Courts interfere seldom to control such discretion intra vires the corporation, except where the directors are guilty of misconduct equivalent to a breach of trust, or where they stand in a dual relation which prevents an unprejudiced exercise of judgment. . . ." — ED.

34. The court seemingly took a slightly different approach in Grimes v. Donald, footnote 19 supra:

> Simply because the composition of the board provides no basis ex ante for the stockholder to claim with particularity and consistently with Rule 11 that it is reasonable to doubt that a majority of the board is either interested or not independent, it does *not* necessarily follow ex post that the board in fact *acted* independently, disinterestedly or with due care in response to the demand. A board or a committee of the board may *appear* to be independent, but may not always *act* independently. If a demand is made and rejected, the board rejecting the demand is entitled to the presumption of the business judgment rule unless the stockholder can allege facts with particularity creating a reasonable doubt that the board is entitled to the benefit of the presumption. If there is reason to doubt that the board acted independently or with due care in responding to the demand, the stockholder may have the basis ex post to claim wrongful refusal.

— ED.

due care, that is, whether the GM Board acted on an informed basis in rejecting Levine's demand. *See Grobow I,* 539 A.2d at 189-190; *Aronson,* 473 A.2d at 812-813.

Levine's complaint may be summarized as asserting essentially three allegations in support of his claim that the GM Board failed to exercise due care and to reach an informed business judgment in refusing his demand. Levine asserts: (1) that the Board declined to permit plaintiff's counsel to make an oral presentation to the Board concerning his demand. . . .

While a board of directors has a duty to act on an informed basis in responding to a demand such as Levine's, there is obviously no prescribed procedure that a board must follow. We find no abuse of discretion in the Vice Chancellor's rejection of Levine's contention that the GM Board's failure to permit Levine to make an "oral presentation" to the Board evidenced a lack of due care or unreasonable conduct. . . .

Plaintiff's remaining allegations, that GM's Board, after receiving Levine's demand letter "did not undertake an investigation" and "did nothing," represent conclusory allegations that are in fact contrary to the pleading record. Levine's allegation that the Board "did nothing" is contradicted by the Board's letter of reply rejecting Levine's demand. The letter, attached to plaintiff's Amended Complaint, states, "following review of the matters set forth in your December 11, 1986 letter, the Board . . . unanimously determined that an attempt to rescind, or litigation . . . concerning [the repurchase agreement] is not in the best interests of the Corporation." . . . The only reasonable inference to be drawn from this document is that the GM Directors did act in an informed manner in addressing Levine's demand.[35] The business judgment rule accords directors the presumption that they acted on an informed basis. *Grobow I,* 539 A.2d at 187. The trial court was clearly correct in dismissing Levine's Amended Complaint. . . .

---

1. *Contrary rule.* In Galef v. Alexander, 615 F.2d 51 (2d Cir. 1980), plaintiff brought a derivative suit against all 15 of the corporation's directors for granting allegedly invalid stock options to "key employees," including 6 members of the board. The 9 nonrecipient directors — after obtaining the advice of the corporation's general counsel, its regular outside counsel, and "two additional independent law firms" that the options were valid — "concluded that the best interests of the company required dismissal of the action." The district court granted summary judgment for defendants. Reversed and remanded for "a more complete exploration of Ohio law":

> A determination that directors are not so interested in the underlying transaction as to excuse demand on them does not mean that they are so disinterested as to enable them to eliminate the lawsuit. The rationale of the cases holding that demand must be made even if the directors have been or may be made defendants, is not that the directors can *preclude* suit despite being defendants, but rather that they might

---

35. "[I]t is difficult to understand how one is to plead an absence of action, other than to say that the directors 'did nothing.' Perhaps the court did not believe that the directors really 'did nothing,' but what the court believes really happened is not supposed to be the standard in reviewing pleadings." Gevurtz, footnote 4 supra, at 409. — ED.

cause the corporation to *pursue* the suit despite being defendants. . . . [36] It may be that under Ohio law a director's being sued merely on account of having authorized, without financial interest, the underlying transaction does not make him sufficiently "interested" to deprive him of the power to initiate a business judgment summary dismissal of the suit. But such a rule is hardly trumpeted by the three Ohio cases cited to us. . . . We are not aware of any case that has determined that directors against whom a claim has been asserted and who have determined that the claim against them should not be pursued, do *not* "stand in a dual relation which prevents an unprejudiced exercise of judgment." Indeed, the Eighth Circuit has opined, obiter, that "where the directors, themselves, are subject to personal liability in the action [they] *cannot* be expected to determine impartially whether it is warranted," Abbey v. Control Data Corp., 603 F.2d 724, 727 (8th Cir. 1979) (emphasis added), and one district court has termed it "inconceivable that directors who participated in and allegedly approved of the transaction under attack can be said to have exercised unbiased business judgment in declining suit based on that very transaction." Nussbacher v. Chase Manhattan Bank, 444 F. Supp. 973, 977 (S.D.N.Y. 1977).

2. *Criticism of the Delaware rule.* (a) In his concurrence in Starrels v. First Nat'l Bank of Chicago, 870 F.2d 1168 (7th Cir. 1989), Judge Frank Easterbrook described as an "oddment in the *Aronson* approach" that

> Rule 23.1 and its parallel in Delaware practice require the court to determine at the pleading stage whether demand was necessary. This requires courts to adjudicate the merits on the pleadings, for a decision that the business judgment rule shelters the challenged conduct *is* "the merits" in derivative litigation, and under *Aronson* also shows that demand was necessary. It is a bobtailed adjudication, without evidence. If facts suggesting . . . that the business judgment rule will not prevent recovery have come to light, the investor may plead them and litigate further, setting the stage for still another decision about the scope of the business judgment rule. See *Grobow*, 539 A.2d at 186-87 (noting the link between the demand requirement and the need for discovery). If facts of this character would come to light only with discovery, then demand is necessary and plaintiff may not litigate at all — for in Delaware a demand-required case is one the board may elect to prevent or dismiss. . . . The amount of information in the public domain is unrelated to the ability of the board to make a business judgment concerning litigation, is unrelated indeed to any function of the demand requirement. Why should the board acquire the power to dismiss . . . just because the plaintiff needs discovery and so cannot make the required showing "with particularity" in the complaint. *Aronson* and its successors do not discuss the point.

> (b) Sometimes (but rarely), plaintiffs have succeeded in challenging the reasonableness or good faith of the board's responses to demand. Still, there is a sufficient disincentive . . . as to produce an entirely predictable consequence: Plaintiffs today seldom make demand in Delaware, but instead litigate the issue of whether demand was excused . . . an unattractive choice: either (i) not make demand and thereby accept the burden of convincing the court that seemingly respectable directors should be deemed too biased even to

---

36. Accord, Weiss v. Temporary Investment Fund, Inc., 692 F.2d 928 (3d Cir. 1982): "'At the demand stage, the possibility should not be foreclosed that a demand will induce the board to consider issues and crystallize policies which otherwise might not be given attention (e.g., new accounting controls, revised corporate policy statements or even a change in personnel or remuneration). The demand rule can have efficacy even where the board ultimately rejects the action and the court ultimately permits the plaintiff to sue.'" — ED.

deserve an opportunity to respond to demand,[37] or (ii) make demand and thereby acknowledge the applicability of the business judgment rule to the directors' decision whether or not to reject demand (and, for most practical purposes, concede the outcome of the case).

Coffee, footnote 6 supra, at 1413-1414.

3. *Modified rule.* In In re PSE & G Shareholder Litigation, 173 N.J. 258, 801 A.2d 295 (2002), the court held:

Whether or not demand is excused, the issue becomes what level of judicial scrutiny should be applied when reviewing management's response to shareholder-derivative litigation. . . . [W]e shall apply a modified business judgment rule that imposes an initial burden on a corporation to demonstrate that in deciding to reject or terminate a shareholder's suit the members of the board (1) were independent and disinterested, (2) acted in good faith and with due care in their investigation of the shareholder's allegations, and that (3) the board's decision was reasonable. . . . All three elements must be satisfied.[38] Moreover, shareholders in these circumstances must be permitted access to corporate documents and other discovery "limited to the narrow issue of what steps the directors took to inform themselves of the shareholder demand and the reasonableness of its decision." . . . [The] standard would not permit the court to substitute its own business judgment for that of management. In determining whether the corporation has met its burden, the court would be able to consider all relevant justifications for management's determination, including the seriousness and weight of the plaintiff's allegations. . . .

There are differences and similarities between the test for determining demand-futility and the standard for evaluating a board's decision under the modified business judgment rule. The main distinction is that a plaintiff has the burden of demonstrating demand-futility, whereas a defendant has the burden of satisfying the elements of the modified business judgment rule. Further, . . . a court applying the modified business judgment rule is not bound by any finding associated with an earlier court's decision to excuse demand. . . . [T]he court should consider the board's decision under the modified business judgment rule only after the parties have completed adequate discovery to enable the court to render a fully-informed decision.

. . . The practical reality is that in many cases a shareholder will want to make a demand on the board to avoid the burden of demonstrating demand-futility. Given the salutary purposes of the demand requirement, that practical reality convinces us that our approach is proper. It preserves the most useful elements of . . . [the demand requirement] while advancing an overarching standard to guide judicial review.

4. The approaches of the ALI's Principles of Corporate Governance and the ABA's Revised Model Business Corporation Act are set forth at page 858 infra.

The materials that follow mainly concern the question of whether, if a demand is excused because a majority of the board is "interested," there is any action that the

37. Compare Grimes v. Donald, footnote 19 supra: "Demand has been excused in many cases in Delaware under the *Aronson* test [citing over thirty 'relatively recent' decisions]." — ED.

38. The court emphasized: "We fully appreciate the distinction between . . . [this] legal standard and complete impartiality in the everyday sense of the word. Directors understandably are not likely to be enthusiastic about approving the prosecution of a shareholder's suit against members of management with whom the directors maintain an ongoing relationship. Moreover, the Court is well aware of the questions now being raised in the broader marketplace about the objectivity and responsibility of corporate directors." — ED.

board may take to prevent the derivative suit from proceeding. But the mechanisms to be discussed might also be used in the context just considered, i.e., by a "disinterested" board that wants to terminate the derivative suit after a demand has either been excused or refused.

Zapata Corp. v. Maldonado
430 A.2d 779 (Del. 1981)

QUILLEN, J.: . . . In June, 1975, William Maldonado, a stockholder of Zapata, instituted a derivative action in the Court of Chancery on behalf of Zapata against ten officers and/or directors of Zapata, alleging, essentially, breaches of fiduciary duty. Maldonado did not first demand that the board bring this action, stating instead such demand's futility because all directors were named as defendants and allegedly participated in the acts specified. In June, 1977, Maldonado commenced an action in the United States District Court for the Southern District of New York against the same defendants, save one, alleging federal security law violations as well as the same common law claims made previously in the Court of Chancery.

By June, 1979, four of the defendant-directors were no longer on the board, and the remaining directors appointed two new outside directors to the board. The board then created an "Independent Investigation Committee" (Committee), composed solely of the two new directors, to investigate Maldonado's actions, as well as a similar derivative action then pending in Texas, and to determine whether the corporation should continue any or all of the litigation. The Committee's determination was stated to be "final, . . . not . . . subject to review by the Board of Directors and . . . in all respects . . . binding upon the Corporation."

Following an investigation, the Committee concluded, in September, 1979, that each action should "be dismissed forthwith as their continued maintenance is inimical to the Company's best interests. . . ."[39] Consequently, Zapata moved for dismissal or summary judgment. . . .

Consistent with the purpose of requiring a demand, a board decision to cause a derivative suit to be dismissed as detrimental to the company, after demand has been made and refused, will be respected unless it was wrongful.[10] . . .

These conclusions, however, do not determine the question before us. Rather, they merely bring us to the question to be decided . . . : When, if at all, should an

---

39. The Committee gave as its reasons the following considerations: (1) the asserted claims appeared to be without merit; (2) costs of litigation, exacerbated by likelihood of indemnification; (3) wasted senior management time and talents on pursuing litigation; (4) damage to company from publicity; (5) that no material injury appeared to have been done to company; (6) impairment of current director-defendants' ability to manage; (7) the slight possibility of recurrence of violations; (8) lack of personal benefit to current director-defendants from alleged conduct; (9) that certain alleged practices were continuing business practices, intended to be in company's best interests; (10) legal question whether the complaints stated a cause of action; (11) fear of undermining employee morale; (12) adverse effects on the company's relations with employees and suppliers and customers.

Maldonado v. Flynn, 485 F. Supp. 274, 284 n.35 (S.D.N.Y. 1980). — ED.

10. In other words, when stockholders, after making demand and having their suit rejected, attack the board's decision as improper, the board's decision falls under the "business judgment" rule and will be respected if the requirements of the rule are met. . . . That situation should be distinguished from the instant case, where demand was not made, and the *power* of the board to seek a dismissal, due to disqualification, presents a threshold issue. . . . We recognize that the two contexts can overlap in practice.

authorized board committee be permitted to cause litigation, properly initiated by a derivative stockholder in his own right, to be dismissed? As noted above, a board has the power to choose not to pursue litigation when demand is made upon it, so long as the decision is not wrongful. If the board determines that a suit would be detrimental to the company, the board's determination prevails. Even when demand is excusable, circumstances may arise when continuation of the litigation would not be in the corporation's best interests. Our inquiry is whether, under such circumstances, there is a permissible procedure under Del. Gen. Corp. L. §141(a) [page 956 infra] by which a corporation can rid itself of detrimental litigation. If there is not, a single stockholder in an extreme case might control the destiny of the entire corporation. . . .

Even though demand was not made in this case and the initial decision of whether to litigate was not placed before the board, Zapata's board, it seems to us, retained all of its corporate power concerning litigation decisions. . . . The demand requirement itself evidences that the managerial power is retained by the board. When a derivative plaintiff is allowed to bring suit after a wrongful refusal, the board's authority to choose whether to pursue the litigation is not challenged although its conclusion — reached through the exercise of that authority — is not respected since it is wrongful. Similarly, Rule 23.1, by excusing demand in certain instances, does not strip the board of its corporate power. It merely saves the plaintiff the expense and delay of making a futile demand resulting in a probable tainted exercise of that authority in a refusal by the board or in giving control of litigation to the opposing side. But the board entity remains empowered under §141(a) to make decisions regarding corporate litigation. The problem is one of member disqualification, not the absence of power in the board.

The corporate power inquiry then focuses on whether the board, tainted by the self-interest of a majority of its members, can legally delegate its authority to a committee of two disinterested directors. We find our statute clearly requires an affirmative answer to this question. . . . [U]nder an express provision of the statute, §141(c), a committee can exercise all of the authority of the board to the extent provided in the resolution of the board. Moreover, at least by analogy to our statutory section on interested directors, 8 Del. C. §144 [footnote 58, page 116 supra], it seems clear that the Delaware statute is designed to permit disinterested directors to act for the board. Compare Puma v. Marriott, Del. Ch., 283 A.2d 693, 695-96 (1971).

We do not think that the interest taint of the board majority is per se a legal bar to the delegation of the board's power to an independent committee composed of disinterested board members. The committee can properly act for the corporation to move to dismiss derivative litigation that is believed to be detrimental to the corporation's best interest.

Our focus now switches to the Court of Chancery, which is faced with a stockholder assertion that a derivative suit, properly instituted, should continue for the benefit of the corporation and a corporate assertion, properly made by a board committee acting with board authority, that the same derivative suit should be dismissed as inimical to the best interests of the corporation.

At the risk of stating the obvious, the problem is relatively simple. If, on the one hand, corporations can consistently wrest bona fide derivative actions away from well-meaning derivative plaintiffs through the use of the committee mechanism, the derivative suit will lose much, if not all, of its generally-recognized effectiveness as an intracorporate means of policing boards of directors. See Dent, The Power of Directors to Terminate Shareholder Litigation: The Death of the Derivative Suit, 75 Nw. U. L. Rev. at 96 & n.3, 144 & n.241 (1980). If, on the other hand, corporations are unable to rid themselves of meritless or harmful litigation and strike suits, the derivative action, created to benefit the corporation, will produce the opposite, unintended result. For a discussion of strike suits, see Dent, supra, 75 Nw. U. L. Rev. at 137. See also Cramer v. General Telephone & Electronics Corp., 3d Cir., 582 F.2d 259, 275 (1978). It thus appears desirable to us to find a balancing point where bona fide stockholder power to bring corporate causes of action cannot be unfairly trampled on by the board of directors, but the corporation can rid itself of detrimental litigation.

... [T]he question has been treated by other courts as one of the "business judgment" of the board committee. If a "committee, composed of independent and disinterested directors, conducted a proper review of the matters before it, considered a variety of factors and reached, in good faith, a business judgment that [the] action was not in the best interest of [the corporation]," the action must be dismissed. See, e.g., Maldonado v. Flynn, supra, 485 F. Supp. at 282, 286. The issues become solely independence, good faith, and reasonable investigation. The ultimate conclusion of the committee, under that view, is not subject to judicial review.[40]

We are not satisfied, however, that acceptance of the "business judgment" rationale at this stage of derivative litigation is a proper balancing point. While we admit an analogy with a normal case respecting board judgment, it seems to us that there is sufficient risk in the realities of a situation like the one presented in this case to justify caution beyond adherence to the theory of business judgment.

The context here is a suit against directors where demand on the board is excused. We think some tribute must be paid to the fact that the lawsuit was properly initiated. It is not a board refusal case. Moreover, this complaint was filed in June of 1975 and, while the parties undoubtedly would take differing views on the degree of litigation activity, we have to be concerned about the creation of an "Independent Investigation Committee" four years later, after the election of two new outside directors. Situations could develop where such motions could be filed after years of vigorous litigation for reasons unconnected with the merits of the lawsuit.

Moreover, notwithstanding our conviction that Delaware law entrusts the corporate power to a properly authorized committee, we must be mindful

---

40. The leading case is Auerbach v. Bennett, 47 N.Y.2d 619, 393 N.E.2d 994, 419 N.Y.S.2d 920 (1979). Accord, Desaigoudar v. Meyerecord, 133 Cal. Rptr. 2d 408 (Cal. App. 2003); Janssen v. Best & Flanagan, 662 N.W.2d 876 (Minn. 2003); Hirsch v. Jones Intercable, Inc., 984 P.2d 629 (Colo. 1999); Cuker v. Mikalauskas, 692 A.2d 1042 (Pa. 1997) (specifically adopting ALI §§7.02-7.10 and §7.13—see pages 859-860 infra—respecting "procedures to govern the review of corporate decisions relating to derivative litigation"); Genzer v. Cunningham, 498 F. Supp. 682 (E.D. Mich. 1980) (Michigan law). See also Roberts v. Alabama Power Co., 404 So. 2d 629 (Ala. 1981).

For incisive criticism of such decisions as being inconsistent with the relevant state "interested director transaction" statutes (see page 119 supra) when the number of directors on the "special litigation committee" is inadequate to have originally approved the challenged transaction, whose "self-dealing taint" may therefore "be cured only by submitting it to retroactive judicial scrutiny," see Richard M. Buxbaum, Conflict-of-Interests Statutes and the Need for a Demand on Directors in Derivative Actions, 68 Cal. L. Rev. 1122 (1980). Compare James D. Cox, Searching for the Corporation's Voice in Derivative Suit Litigation: A Critique of *Zapata* and the ALI Project, 1982 Duke L.J. 959, 1003-1005.—ED.

that directors are passing judgment on fellow directors in the same corporation and fellow directors, in this instance, who designated them to serve both as directors and committee members. The question naturally arises whether a "there but for the grace of God go I" empathy might not play a role. And the further question arises whether inquiry as to independence, good faith and reasonable investigation is sufficient safeguard against abuse, perhaps subconscious abuse.

. . . There is some analogy to a settlement in that there is a request to terminate litigation without a judicial determination of the merits. See Perrine v. Pennroad Corp., Del. Supr., 47 A.2d 479, 487 (1946). "In determining whether or not to approve a proposed settlement of a derivative stockholders' action [when directors are on both sides of the transaction], the Court of Chancery is called upon to exercise its own business judgment." Neponsit Investment Co. v. Abramson, Del. Supr., 405 A.2d 97, 100 (1979) and cases therein cited. In this case, the litigating stockholder plaintiff facing dismissal of a lawsuit properly commenced ought, in our judgment, to have sufficient status for strict Court review. . . .

Whether the Court of Chancery will be persuaded by the exercise of a committee power resulting in a summary motion for dismissal of a derivative action, where a demand has not been initially made, should rest, in our judgment, in the independent discretion of the Court of Chancery. We . . . recognize that "[t]he final substantive judgment whether a particular lawsuit should be maintained requires a balance of many factors—ethical, commercial, promotional, public relations, employee relations, fiscal as well as legal." Maldonado v. Flynn, supra, 485 F. Supp. at 285. But we are content that such factors are not "beyond the judicial reach" of the Court of Chancery, which regularly and competently deals with fiduciary relationships, disposition of trust property, approval of settlements and scores of similar problems. We recognize the danger of judicial overreaching but the alternatives seem to us to be outweighed by the fresh view of a judicial outsider. Moreover, if we failed to balance all the interests involved, we would in the name of practicality and judicial economy foreclose a judicial decision on the merits. At this point, we are not convinced that is necessary or desirable.[41]

After an objective and thorough investigation of a derivative suit, an independent committee may cause its corporation to file a pretrial motion to dismiss in the Court of Chancery. The basis of the motion is the best interests of the corporation, as determined by the committee. The motion should include a thorough written record of the investigation and its findings and recommendations. Under appropriate Court supervision, akin to proceedings on summary judgment, each side should have an opportunity to make a record on the motion. As to the limited issues presented by the motion noted below, the moving party should be prepared to meet the normal burden . . . that there is no genuine issue as

---

41. See also Kenneth B. Davis Jr., Structural Bias, Special Litigation Committees, and the Vagaries of Director Independence, 90 Iowa L. Rev. 1305 (2005): the "inevitable uncertainty in predicting how people will behave in a given situation" and the incapacity of "directors selected principally to withstand challenges to SLC independence" to "appreciate what truly is in the best interests of the corporation" should lead to increased emphasis on substantive results "through which courts engage in a slightly more rigorous review of the SLC's decision," with particular "reliance on experienced and independent counsel" in determining the reasonableness of the investigation. — ED.

to any material fact and that the moving party is entitled to dismiss as a matter of law.[15] The Court should apply a two-step test to the motion.

First, the Court should inquire into the independence and good faith of the committee and the bases supporting its conclusions. Limited discovery may be ordered to facilitate such inquiries.[16] The corporation should have the burden of proving independence, good faith and a reasonable investigation, rather than presuming independence, good faith and reasonableness.[17] If the Court determines either that the committee is not independent or has not shown reasonable bases for its conclusions, or, if the court is not satisfied for other reasons relating to the process, including but not limited to the good faith of the committee, the Court shall deny the corporation's motion. If, however, the Court is satisfied under . . . [summary judgment] standards that the committee was independent and showed reasonable bases for good faith findings and recommendations, the Court may proceed, in its discretion, to the next step.[42]

The second step provides, we believe, the essential key in striking the balance between legitimate corporate claims as expressed in a derivative stockholder suit and a corporation's best interests as expressed by an independent investigating committee. The Court should determine, applying its own independent business judgment, whether the motion should be granted.[18] This means, of

15. We do not foreclose a discretionary trial of factual issues but that issue is not presented in this appeal. See Lewis v. Anderson, supra, 615 F.2d at 780. Nor do we foreclose the possibility that other motions may proceed or be joined with such a pretrial summary judgment motion to dismiss, e.g., a partial motion for summary judgment on the merits.

16. See, e.g., Galef v. Alexander, 2d Cir., 615 F.2d 51, 56 (1980); Maldonado v. Flynn, supra, 485 F. Supp. at 285-86; Rosengarten v. International Telephone & Telegraph Corp., S.D.N.Y., 466 F. Supp. 817, 823 (1979); Gall v. Exxon Corp., S.D.N.Y., 418 F. Supp. 508, 520 (1976). Compare Dent, supra, 75 Nw. U. L. Rev. at 131-33.

[In the subsequent case of Kaplan v. Wyatt, 499 A.2d 1184 (Del. 1985), the court made clear that "the type and extent of discovery [is] left wholly to the discretion of the Court. . . . [Plaintiff] was not entitled to discover all the information relating to the Committee's report. . . ."

ALI §7.13(c) provides that "if the plaintiff is unable without undue hardship to obtain the information by other means, the court may order such limited discovery . . . as the court finds to be (i) necessary to enable it to render a decision . . . and (ii) consistent with an expedited resolution of the motion." — ED.]

17. Compare Auerbach v. Bennett, N.Y. Ct. of Appeals, 419 N.Y.S.2d 920, 928-29 (1979). Our approach here is analogous to and consistent with the Delaware approach to "interested director" transactions, where the directors, once the transaction is attacked, have the burden of establishing its "intrinsic fairness" to a court's careful scrutiny. See, e.g., Sterling v. Mayflower Hotel Corp., Del. Supr., 93 A.2d 107 (1952).

[See Hasan v. Clevetrust Realty Investors, 729 F.2d 372 (6th Cir. 1984), holding that, under either the *Auerbach* or *Zapata* approach, the "good faith," "disinterestedness," and "procedural adequacy" of the special litigation committee had not been shown; Peller v. Southern Co., 911 F.2d 1532 (11th Cir. 1990), using the *Zapata* approach to reject the recommendation of a special litigation committee that the derivative suit be dismissed; Houle v. Low, 407 Mass. 810, 556 N.E.2d 51 (1990), finding a "dispute of material fact as to whether the committee was independent and unbiased." — ED.]

42. More recently, in the *Martha Stewart* case, footnote 30 supra, the court stated that "the Court of Chancery must exercise careful oversight of the bona fides of the SLC and its process. . . . Unlike the demand-excusal context, where the board is presumed to be independent, the SLC has the burden of establishing its own independence by a yardstick that must be 'like Caesar's wife' — 'above reproach.'" Cf. the court's appraisal of the facts, recited in footnote 30 supra. In Kaplan v. Wyatt, footnote 16 above, which affirmed dismissal of a derivative suit on the motion of a special litigation committee, the court held that (1) "the mere fact that a director was on the Board at the time of acts alleged in the complaint does not make that director interested or dependent," and (2) "proceeding to the second step of the *Zapata* analysis is wholly within the discretion of the court." — ED.

18. This step shares some of the same spirit and philosophy of the statement by the Vice Chancellor: "Under our system of law, courts and not litigants should decide the merits of litigation." 413 A.2d at 1263.

["Judicial review may . . . [provide] a crutch upon which independent directors struggling to assert themselves and make disinterested judgments can lean. Judicial oversight fosters board independence because it enables independent directors to justify their refusal to do as management wishes (reject the

course, that instances could arise where a committee can establish its independence and sound bases for its good faith decisions and still have the corporation's motion denied. The second step is intended to thwart instances where corporate actions meet the criteria of step one, but the result does not appear to satisfy its spirit, or where corporate actions would simply prematurely terminate a stockholder grievance deserving of further consideration in the corporation's interest. The Court of Chancery of course must carefully consider and weigh how compelling the corporate interest in dismissal is when faced with a non-frivolous lawsuit. The Court of Chancery should, when appropriate, give special consideration to matters of law and public policy in addition to the corporation's best interests.[43]

If the Court's independent business judgment is satisfied, the Court may proceed to grant the motion, subject, of course, to any equitable terms or conditions the Court finds necessary or desirable.

. . . [Reversed and remanded.][44]

Amplification of Zapata. In Joy v. North, 692 F.2d 880 (2d Cir. 1982), discussed at page 106 supra, the court, applying Connecticut law, adopted the *Zapata* approach and rejected the recommendation of the Special Litigation Committee:

[The dissent] is correct in anticipating difficulties in judicial review of the recommendations of special litigation committees. These difficulties are not new, however, but have confronted every court which has scrutinized the fairness of corporate transactions involving a conflict of interest.

Moreover, the difficulties courts face in evaluation of business decisions are considerably less in the case of recommendations of special litigation committees. The relevant decision — whether to continue litigation — is at hand and the danger of deceptive hindsight simply does not exist. Moreover, it can hardly be argued that terminating a lawsuit is an area in which courts have no special aptitude. Citytrust's Special Litigation Committee concluded that there was "no reasonable possibility" that 23 outside defendants would be held liable. A court is not ill-equipped to review the merits of that conclusion. Even when the Committee recommendation arises from the fear of further damage to the corporation, for example, the distraction of key personnel, the cost of complying with discovery, and the possible indemnification of defendants out of the corporate treasury,

---

suit) on the grounds that a reviewing court would not accept the weak or disingenuous reasons proffered." John C. Coffee Jr. & Donald E. Schwartz, The Survival of the Derivative Suit: An Evaluation and a Proposal for Legislative Reform, 81 Colum. L. Rev. 261, 287 (1981). — Ed.]

43. On the extent to which the purpose of the derivative suit is to further "matters of law and public policy" by deterring wrongdoing rather than to compensate the corporation for injury, compare Coffee & Schwartz, supra, at 302-309, with Cox, footnote 40 supra, at 989-994. — Ed

44. Accord, Abella v. Universal Leaf Tobacco Co., 546 F. Supp. 795 (E.D. Va. 1982) (Virginia law); Rosengarten v. Buckley, 613 F. Supp. 1493 (D. Md. 1985) (Maryland law). — Ed.

courts are not on unfamiliar terrain. The rule we predict Connecticut would establish emphasizes matters such as probable liability and extent of recovery.[45] For these reasons we hold that the wide discretion afforded directors under the business judgment rule does not apply when a special litigation committee recommends dismissal of a suit. . . .

In cases such as the present one, the burden is on the moving party, as in motions for summary judgment generally, to demonstrate that the action is more likely than not to be against the interests of the corporation. This showing is to be based on the underlying data developed in the course of discovery and of the committee's investigation and the committee's reasoning, not simply its naked conclusions. The weight to be given certain evidence is to be determined by conventional analysis, such as whether testimony is under oath and subject to cross-examination. Finally, the function of the court's review is to determine the balance of probabilities as to likely future benefit to the corporation, not to render a decision on the merits, fashion the appropriate legal principles or resolve issues of credibility. Where the legal rule is unclear and the likely evidence in conflict, the court need only weigh the uncertainties, not resolve them. The court's function is thus not unlike a lawyer's determining what a case is "worth" for purposes of settlement.

---

45. The decision not to sue typically occurs in a very different context from that of the normal business judgment. . . . First, normal business judgments are often made under time pressure and uncertainty . . . [whereas] a decision to terminate litigation generally permits greater time for investigation; uncertainty is less a factor because the facts now exist in history rather than lying unknowingly in the future. Second, in its normal operation, the business judgment rule insulates corporate officials from liability for decisions made in the exercise of business judgment . . . in order to protect the decisionmaker. But directors who decide to terminate a derivative action need no such blanket of immunity, because they face little risk of liability. By definition, they are not defendants in the action they seek to terminate, and their decision to terminate, even if erroneous, would be protected by the ordinary operation of the business judgment rule insofar as their own liability is concerned. . . . Third, although most business decisions are not amenable to judicial review, the decision to terminate a derivative action inherently involves the creation of a reviewable record. It is a retrospective decision, rather than a predictive one, and the court is therefore better able to sift and balance the same evidence as was presented to the board. . . . Finally, there is the problem of structural bias. . . . [A]n outside director independent enough to oppose the chief executive officer with respect to a proposed transaction that he thinks is unfair or unwise may still be unable to tell the same officer that he thinks a suit against him has sufficient merit to proceed. The latter vote would be a far more personal and stigmatizing form of opposition.

Coffee & Schwartz, supra, at 281-283. See also Tamar Frankel & Wayne Barsky, The Power Struggle Between Shareholders and Directors: The Demand Requirement in Derivative Suits, 12 Hofstra L. Rev. 39 (1983). Compare Daniel R. Fischel, The "Race to the Bottom" Revisited: Reflections on Recent Developments in Delaware's Corporation Law, 76 Nw. U. L. Rev. 913, 938 n.150 (1982):

The fact that the decision not to sue is generally not rushed does not distinguish it from a wide variety of other business decisions, such as the introduction of a new product or the payment of a dividend. That directors do not face a significant risk of liability from making a decision not to sue is irrelevant, because the fundamental premise of the business judgment rule is that courts and shareholders are unable to make business decisions. The question, therefore, is whether courts and shareholders are competent in deciding whether to sue, not whether the directors will face liability for their decision. The "creation of a reviewable record" argument is similarly irrelevant because, even if true, this argument does not suggest why courts should be able to second-guess managerial decisionmaking. Finally, the "structural bias" argument ignores the incentives that all managers have to monitor each other.

See generally James D. Cox, Heroes in the Law: Alford v. Shaw, 66 N.C. L. Rev. 565 (1988). — ED.

Where the court determines that the likely recoverable damages discounted by the probability of a finding of liability are less than the costs to the corporation in continuing the action, it should dismiss the case. The costs which may properly be taken into account are attorney's fees and other out-of-pocket expenses related to the litigation and time spent by corporate personnel preparing for and participating in the trial. The court should also weigh indemnification which is mandatory under corporate bylaws, private contract or Connecticut law, discounted of course by the probability of liability for such sums. We believe indemnification the corporation may later pay as a matter of discretion should not be taken into account since it is an avoidable cost. The existence or nonexistence of insurance should not be considered in the calculation of costs, since premiums have previously been paid. The existence of insurance is relevant to the calculation of potential benefits.

Where, having completed the above analysis, the court finds a likely net return to the corporation which is not substantial in relation to shareholder equity, it may take into account two other items as costs. First, it may consider the impact of distraction of key personnel by continued litigation. Second, it may take into account potential lost profits which may result from the publicity of a trial.

Judicial scrutiny of special litigation committee recommendations should thus be limited to a comparison of the direct costs imposed upon the corporation by the litigation with the potential benefits. We are mindful that other, less direct costs may be incurred, such as a negative impact on morale and upon the corporate image. Nevertheless, we believe that such factors, with the two exceptions noted, should not be taken into account. Quite apart from the elusiveness of attempting to predict such effects, they are quite likely to be directly related to the degree of wrongdoing, a spectacular fraud being generally more newsworthy and damaging to morale than a mistake in judgment as to the strength of consumer demand. . . .

One judge dissented:

[T]he majority goes beyond [*Zapata*] by requiring that the court *must* proceed to apply its own business judgment, rather than leaving the decision to resort to the second step within the trial court's discretion. . . .

The majority proposes a calculus in an attempt to resolve additional issues engendered by its analysis. This calculus is so complicated, indefinite and subject to judicial caprice as to be unworkable. For example, how is a court to determine the inherently speculative costs of future attorneys' fees and expenses related to litigation, time spent by corporate personnel preparing for trial, and mandatory indemnification "discounted of course by the probability of liability for such sums." How is a court to quantify corporate goodwill, corporate morale, and "the distraction of key personnel" in cases in which it "finds a likely net return to the corporation which is not substantial in relation to shareholder equity"? Should a court also take into account the potential adverse impact of continuing litigation upon the corporation's ability to finance its operations? Should future costs be discounted to present value and, if so, at what rate? Must the income tax ramifications of expected future costs be considered and, if so, how? This veritable Pandora's box of unanswered questions raises more problems than it solves.

Even more fundamentally unsound is the majority's underlying premise that judges are equipped to make business judgments. . . . As perceptive commentators have observed, if [*Zapata's*] statement is true that "[u]nder our system of law, courts and not litigants should decide the merits of litigation," [*Zapata*] at 789 n.13 (quoting Maldonado v. Flynn, 413 A.2d 1251, 1263 (Del. Ch. 1980)), then its corollary "that boards, and not courts, are entitled to exercise business judgment" is equally true. Coffee and Schwartz, the Survival of the Derivative Suit: An Evaluation and a Proposal for Legislative Reform, 81 Colum. L. Rev. 261, 329 (1981). . . .

My colleagues advance two arguments as to why they believe Connecticut would not adopt the *Auerbach* test. First, they contend that director committees simply cannot be expected to act independently. Where a special litigation committee does not act independently and in good faith, its decision to terminate derivative litigation will not survive judicial scrutiny under *Auerbach*. . . . Second, the majority argues that limiting judicial review to the *Auerbach* test would effectively eliminate the fiduciary obligations of directors and officers because the sole method of enforcing these obligations, shareholder derivative suits, could be eliminated upon the recommendation of persons appointed by the officers and directors whose conduct is being challenged. Even if shareholder derivative suits are the only effective method of enforcing the fiduciary obligations of officers and directors, this second objection to *Auerbach* again assumes that director committees reviewing derivative litigation will not act independently and in good faith. Since *Auerbach* will require judicial intervention if the director committees do not so act this second objection to the use of the *Auerbach* standard is similarly without merit. . . . [46]

Alford v. Shaw
320 N.C. 465, 358 S.E.2d 323 (1987)

MARTIN, J.: . . . In response to charges of mismanagement asserted by plaintiff minority shareholders, the board of directors of All American Assurance Company (AAA) voted to appoint a committee to conduct an investigation. The board then elected Marion G. Follin, a retired insurance executive, and Frank M. Parker, a former judge of the North Carolina Court of Appeals, to board membership and designated them as a special investigative committee. The committee was authorized to determine whether it would be in the best interest of AAA and its shareholders to initiate legal action against those implicated in any wrongdoing uncovered by the investigation.

Before the committee had completed its investigation, plaintiffs filed a shareholders' derivative action in superior court, naming as defendants the controlling shareholders of AAA and a majority of its directors. The complaint alleged inter alia that in a series of transactions involving corporations affiliated with AAA, defendants had violated fiduciary obligations by engaging in a pattern of fraud, self-dealing, and negligent acquiescence which amounted to a "looting" of corporate assets for defendants' own benefit.

Upon completion of its investigation, the committee filed a report in the trial court recommending that the majority of plaintiffs' claims be dismissed with prejudice and that two remaining claims be settled in accordance with an attached

---

46. Conn. Bus. Corp. Act §33-724 (2006) rejected the *Zapata* rule in favor of RMBCA §7.44, page 858 infra. — ED.

settlement agreement. Based on the committee's report, defendants moved for summary judgment and approval of the settlement agreement. The trial court held that the business judgment rule controlled the disposition of the case and granted the motions. The Court of Appeals reversed, 72 N.C. App. 537, 324 S.E.2d 878 (1985), holding that corporate directors who are parties to a derivative action may not confer upon a special committee the power to bind the corporation as to the derivative litigation. We affirm the Court of Appeals, subject to the modifications discussed below. . . .

In determining the proper role, if any, of special corporate litigation committees in the termination of derivative shareholders' actions, three basic approaches have been adopted by other jurisdictions:

1. *Auerbach.* . . .
2. *Miller.* In Miller v. Register and Tribune Syndicate, Inc., 336 N.W.2d 709 (Iowa 1983), the Iowa Supreme Court adopted a prophylactic rule as a means of circumventing the "structural bias" inherent in the committee appointment process. Under *Miller,* directors charged with misconduct are prohibited from participating in the selection of special litigation committees.[47]
3. *Zapata.* . . .

In our previous decision in this case, we applied a modified *Auerbach* rule. We interpret the trend away from *Auerbach* among other jurisdictions as an indication of growing concern about the deficiencies inherent in a rule giving great deference to the decisions of a corporate committee whose institutional symbiosis with the corporation necessarily affects its ability to render a decision that fairly considers the interest of plaintiffs forced to bring suit on behalf of the corporation. See generally James D. Cox & Harry L. Munsinger, Bias in the Boardroom: Psychological Foundations and Legal Implications of Corporate Cohesion, 48 L. & Contemp. Probs., Summer 1985 at 83 (1985).[48] Such concerns are legitimate ones and,

---

47. In *Miller,* the court emphasized that its

decision does not render an Iowa corporation powerless to utilize the litigation committee device when a majority of its directors are parties to the action. Under Iowa law, equity has broad powers to make appointments to enable corporate functions to be carried out. See Rowen v. LeMars Mutual Insurance Co., 230 N.W.2d 905, 916 (Iowa 1975) (court appointment of separate counsel for corporations); Hali Rest, Inc. v. Treloar, 217 N.W.2d 517, 527 (Iowa 1974) (court appointment of fiscal agent for corporation). Consistent with these decisions, we conclude that a corporation may apply to the court for appointment of a "special panel" to make an investigation and report on the pursuit or dismissal of a stockholder derivative action, which panel may be invested for these purposes with the powers of the board of directors.

For the proposal that "once a derivative suit is filed, the court appoint a provisional litigation panel to make all future decisions regarding the action," see Franklin Gevurtz, Who Represents the Corporation? In Search of a Better Method for Determining the Corporate Interest in Derivative Suits, 46 U. Pitt. L. Rev. 265 (1985). — ED.

48. For the view that the judgment of "independent" directors "is likely to be influenced by their ties to the defendants, by the process of their selection (including the aspirations of the minority and majority directors), by the limits on their time and knowledge, and by the defendant's control over the proxy machinery," see Note, A Procedural Treatment of Derivative Suit Dismissals by Minority Directors, 69 Cal. L. Rev. 885, 894-900 (1981). For a study of "social-psychological mechanisms that can generate bias in the directors' assessment of the suit, including biases established by appointment of members to the board or a special litigation committee, control of pecuniary or nonpecuniary rewards made available to the independent directors by the defendant members of the board of directors, the

upon further reflection, we find that they must be resolved not by slavish adherence to the business judgment rule, but by careful interpretation of the provisions of our own Business Corporation Act. We conclude from our analysis of the pertinent statutes that a modified *Zapata* rule, requiring judicial scrutiny of the merits of the litigation committee's recommendation, is most consistent with the intent of our legislature and is therefore the appropriate rule to be applied in our courts. While we affirm the holding of the Court of Appeals reversing summary judgment for defendants, we reject that court's application of the *Miller* rule.

In 1973 the General Assembly enacted N.C.G.S. §55-55, which expressly authorizes shareholders' derivative actions and prescribes the rules governing all such actions brought in the state courts of North Carolina. . . .

The plain language of the statute requires thorough judicial review of suits initiated by shareholders on behalf of a corporation: the court is directed to determine whether the interest of any shareholder will be substantially affected by the discontinuance, dismissal, compromise, or settlement of a derivative suit. Although the statute does not specify what test the court must apply in making this determination, it would be difficult for the court to determine whether the interests of shareholders or creditors would be substantially affected by such discontinuance, dismissal, compromise, or settlement without looking at the proposed action substantively.

To make the required assessment under section 55-55, the court must of necessity evaluate the adequacy of materials prepared by the corporation which support the corporation's decision to settle or dismiss a derivative suit along with the plaintiff's forecast of evidence. If it appears likely that plaintiff could prevail on the merits, but that the amount of the recovery would not be sufficient to outweigh the detriment to the corporation, the court could still allow discontinuance, dismissal, compromise, or settlement. . . .

---

independent directors' prior associations with the defendants, and their common cultural and social heritages," see Cox & Munsinger, supra: "We conclude that, in combination, these several psychological mechanisms can be expected to generate subtle, but powerful, biases which result in the independent directors' reaching a decision insulating colleagues on the board from legal sanctions." See also Note 6(b), page 126 supra. For development of the position that "board members are learning to disagree more agreeably, and the view that others cannot be trusted to exercise independent and detached judgments of their peers properly is criticized as a paralyzing perspective of human action," see Richard W. Dusenberg, The Business Judgment Rule and Shareholder Derivative Suits: A View from the Inside, 60 Wash. U. L.Q. 311 (1982). See also Michael P. Dooley & E. Norman Veasey, The Role of the Board in Derivative Litigation: Delaware Law and the Current ALI Proposals Compared, 44 Bus. Law. 503, 535 (1989):

> It is unnecessary to cast aspersions on the personal integrity or courage of inside directors to understand that outsiders are motivated by a set of incentives that encourages greater independence from senior management. Those who are chosen as outside directors of publicly held corporations are generally persons who have distinguished themselves in some other capacity. Chief executive officers of other corporations seem to be especially prized as outside directors. Generally speaking, then, outside directors tend to be men and women who have considerable investments in reputation but who have invested most of their human capital elsewhere. The structural bias argument asks us to believe that outside directors generally are more willing to risk reputation and future income than they are to risk the social embarrassment of calling a colleague to account. There is no more reason to believe this than there is to believe that independent accountants are easily suborned because they are indifferent to the loss of income from other professional engagements thereby put at risk.

— ED.

The *Zapata* Court limited its two-step judicial inquiry to cases in which demand upon the corporation was futile and therefore excused. However, we find no justification for such limitation in our statutes. The language of section 55-55(c) is inclusive and draws no distinctions between demand-excused and other types of cases. Cf. ALI Principles of Corporate Governance: Analysis and Recommendations §7.08 & Reporter's Notes 2 & 4 at 135-139 (Council Draft No. 6, Oct. 10, 1986) (issue of demand of minimal importance in determining scope of review; demand-excused/demand-required distinction not determinative). Thus, court approval is required for disposition of *all* derivative suits, even where the directors are not charged with fraud or self-dealing, or where the plaintiff and the board agree to discontinue, dismiss, compromise, or settle the lawsuit. . . .

When N.C.G.S. §§55-55 and 55-30(b)(3) [the "interested director transaction" provision] are read in pari materia, they indicate that when a stockholder in a derivative action seeks to establish self-dealing on the part of a majority of the board, the burden should be upon those directors to establish that the transactions complained of were just and reasonable to the corporation when entered into or approved. The fact that a special litigation committee appointed by those directors charged with self-dealing recommends that the action should not proceed, while carrying weight, is not binding upon the trial court. Rather, the court must make a fair assessment of the report of the special committee, along with all the other facts and circumstances in the case, in order to determine whether the defendants will be able to show that the transaction complained of was just and reasonable to the corporation. If this appears evident from the materials before the court, then in a proper case summary judgment may be allowed in favor of the defendants.[49]

Upon remand plaintiffs shall be permitted to develop and present evidence on this issue, such as: (1) that the committee, though perhaps disinterested and independent, may not have been *qualified* to assess intricate and allegedly false tax and accounting information supplied to it by those within the corporate structure who would benefit from decisions not to proceed with litigation, (2) that, in fact, false and/or incomplete information was supplied to the committee because of the nonadversarial way in which it gathered and evaluated information, and therefore (3) in light of these and other problems which arise from the structural bias inherent in the use of board-appointed special litigation committees, that the committee's decision with respect to the litigation eviscerates

---

49. In Houle v. Low, footnote 17, page 849 supra, the court held that

even in those cases where a committee is independent and conducts a thorough investigation, the judge may conclude that the committee's decision is contrary to the great weight of evidence. In conducting its review, the court should look to factors such as those identified by ALI, which include the likelihood of a judgment in the plaintiff's favor, the expected recovery as compared to out-of-pocket costs, whether the corporation itself took corrective action, whether the balance of corporate interests warrants dismissal, and whether dismissal would allow any defendant who has control of the corporation to retain a significant improper benefit. See ALI Principles of Corporate Governance §7.08 (Tent. Draft No. 8, 1988).

This inquiry will allow the special litigation committee to point out to the judge on what factors it relied and why those factors support its decision. The test will allow the derivative plaintiff to point out factors not considered by the committee or why those relied upon by the committee do not support its conclusion. Such a limited review by the judge will avoid the problem in the second level of the *Zapata* test, which requires the judge to exercise his or her own business judgment. The courts are better able to determine the merits of a law suit than whether a decision is correct based on a subjective evaluation of the business policies involved.

Accord, Lewis v. Boyd, 838 S.W.2d 215 (Tenn. Ct. App. 1992). — ED.

plaintiffs' opportunities as minority shareholders to vindicate their rights under North Carolina law. Cf. Dent, The Power of Directors to Terminate Shareholder Litigations: The Death of the Derivative Suit, 75 Nw. U. L. Rev. 96 (1981). . . .

Justice MITCHELL did not participate in the consideration or decision of this case.

WEBB, J., dissenting: I dissent. I do not disagree with the substantive matter in the majority opinion. This Court, however, has decided this case in a previous opinion which considered all matters discussed in the majority opinion filed today. I believe we are mistaken in changing an opinion so recently filed. I vote not to reconsider the case.

MEYER, J., dissenting: I dissent. My position is accurately reflected in the original opinion of the Court, reported at 318 N.C. 289, 349 S.E.2d 41 (1986).

---

1. *"Independent" directors.* A number of recent decisions have explored in some detail the issue of whether special litigation committee members are "independent." In Einhorn v. Culea, 235 Wis. 2d 646, 612 N.W.2d 78 (2000), involving a close corporation, the court interpreted Wis. Bus. Corp. Law §180.0744(3) (1991), which is very similar to RMBCA §7.44, infra:

> A finding that a member of the special litigation committee is independent does not require the complete absence of any facts that might point to non-objectivity. . . . [M]ere acquaintanceship and social interaction are not per se bars to finding a member independent. . . . [T]he circuit court should determine whether, considering the totality of the circumstances, a reasonable person in the position of the member of the special litigation committee can base his or her decision on the merits of the issue rather than on extraneous considerations or influences. In other words, the test is whether a member of the committee has a relationship with an individual defendant or the corporation that would reasonably be expected to affect the member's judgment with respect to the litigation at issue. . . . The role of the corporation's counsel should [also] be considered as one of the circumstances in determining whether the committee is independent.[50]

In In re Oracle Corp. Derivative Litigation, 824 A.2d 917 (Del. Ch. 2003), the court denied the motion of a special litigation committee, made up of two Stanford University professors, to terminate a derivative suit alleging that certain directors and officers were liable to Oracle under Brophy v. Cities Service Co., page 531 supra, for trading on inside information. It summarized its factual conclusion after noting that "the question of independence 'turns on whether a director is, *for any substantial reason,* incapable of making a decision with only the best interests of the

---

50. "[C]ounsel advising the board [should] be similarly independent. This disqualifies not only the corporation's house counsel and any outside counsel regularly in the employ of the corporation, but also special counsel who has served the independent directors within the prior three years. This prevents counsel from anticipating future employment if it delivers the desired advice." Coffee & Schwartz, supra, at 323-324. See generally Deborah A. DeMott, Defending the Quiet Life: The Role of Special Counsel in Derivative Suits, 56 Notre Dame L. Rev. 850, 863-867 (1981). See also Stepak v. Addison, 20 F.3d 398 (11th Cir. 1994) (if law firm that has represented alleged wrongdoers in criminal proceedings involving subject matter of shareholder demand dominates board's consideration, there is "reasonable doubt that the board has properly informed itself prior to rejecting the shareholder's demand"); In re Oracle Securities Litigation, 829 F. Supp. 1176 (N.D. Cal. 1993) (corporation's general counsel had conflict in advising special litigation committee in derivative action against corporation's senior executive officers). — ED.

corporation in mind.' That is, the independence test ultimately 'focus[es] on impartiality and objectivity' ":

> Among the directors who are accused by the derivative plaintiffs of insider trading are: (1) another Stanford professor, who taught one of the SLC members when the SLC member was a Ph.D. candidate and who serves as a senior fellow and a steering committee member alongside that SLC member at the Stanford Institute for Economic Policy Research or "SIEPR"; (2) a Stanford alumnus who has directed millions of dollars of contributions to Stanford during recent years, serves as Chair of SIEPR's Advisory Board and has a conference center named for him at SIEPR's facility, and has contributed nearly $600,000 to SIEPR and the Stanford Law School, both parts of Stanford with which one of the SLC members is closely affiliated; and (3) Oracle's CEO, who has made millions of dollars in donations to Stanford through a personal foundation and large donations indirectly through Oracle, and who was considering making donations of his $100 million house and $170 million for a scholarship program as late as August 2001, at around the same time period the SLC members were added to the Oracle board. Taken together, these and other facts cause me to harbor a reasonable doubt about the impartiality of the SLC.[51]

2. *Statutes.* Over one-third of the states have adopted statutory provisions dealing with special litigation committees. Most are similar to the RMBCA:

Revised Model Business Corporation Act (2005)

Sec. 7.44. *Dismissal.* (a) A derivative proceeding shall be dismissed by the court on motion by the corporation if one of the groups specified in subsection (b) or subsection (e) has determined in good faith, after conducting a reasonable inquiry upon which its conclusions are based, that the maintenance of the derivative proceeding is not in the best interests of the corporation.

(b) Unless a panel is appointed pursuant to subsection (e), the determination in subsection (a) shall be made by:

(1) a majority vote of qualified directors[52] present at a meeting of the board of directors if the qualified directors constitute a quorum; or

(2) a majority vote of a committee consisting of two or more qualified directors appointed by majority vote of qualified directors present at a meeting of the board of directors, whether or not such qualified directors constitute a quorum.

(c) If a derivative proceeding is commenced after a determination has been made rejecting a demand by a shareholder, the complaint shall allege with particularity facts establishing either (1) that a majority of the board of directors did not consist of qualified directors at the time the determination was made or (2) that the requirements of subsection (a) have not been met.

(d) If a majority of the board of directors consisted of qualified directors at the time the determination is made, the plaintiff shall have the burden of proving that

---

51. In the *Martha Stewart* case, footnote 30 supra, the court noted the distinctive nature of "the Stanford connections in *Oracle.* . . ." — ED.

52. RMBCA §1.43(a)(1) (2005) defines "qualified director" as "a director who, at the time of the action . . . does not have (i) a material interest in the outcome of the proceeding, or (ii) a material relationship with a person who has such an interest. . . ." — ED.

the requirements of subsection (a) have not been met; if not, the corporation shall have the burden of proving that the requirements of subsection (a) have been met.

(e) Upon motion by the corporation, the court may appoint a panel of one or more individuals to make a determination whether the maintenance of the derivative proceeding is in the best interests of the corporation. In such case, the plaintiff shall have the burden of proving that the requirements of subsection (a) have not been met.

American Law Institute, Principles of Corporate Governance (1994)

Sec. 7.08. *Dismissal of a derivative action against directors, senior executives, controlling persons, or associates based on a motion requesting dismissal by the board or a committee.* The court should, subject to the provisions of §7.10(b), dismiss a derivative action against a defendant who is a director, a senior executive, or a person in control of the corporation, or an associate of any such person, if:

(a) The board of directors or a properly delegated committee thereof (either in response to a demand or following commencement of the action) has determined that the action is contrary to the best interests of the corporation and has requested dismissal of the action;

(b) The procedures specified in §7.09 for the conduct of a review and evaluation of the action were substantially complied with[53] (either in response to a demand or following commencement of the action), or any material departures therefrom were justified under the circumstances; and

(c) The determinations of the board or committee satisfy the applicable standard of review set forth in §7.10(a). . . .

Sec. 7.10. *Standard of judicial review with regard to a board or committee motion requesting dismissal of a derivative action under §7.08.*

(a) *Standard of review.* In deciding whether an action should be dismissed under §7.08, the court should apply the following standards of review:

(1) If the gravamen of the claim is that the defendant violated a duty set forth in Part IV (Duty of Care), other than by committing a knowing and culpable violation of law, that is alleged with particularity, or if the underlying transaction or conduct would be reviewed under the business judgment rule . . . , the court should dismiss the claim unless it finds that the board's or committee's determinations fail to satisfy the requirements of the business judgment rule as specified in §4.01(c).

(2) In other cases governed by Part V (Duty of Fair Dealing) or to which the business judgment rule is not applicable, including cases in which the basis of the claim is that defendant committed a knowing and culpable violation of law in breach in Part IV, the court should dismiss the action if the court finds, in light of the applicable standards under Part IV or V, that the board or committee was adequately informed under the circumstances and reasonably determined that dismissal was in the best interests of the corporation, based on grounds that the court deems to warrant reliance.

---

53. Section 7.09 requires (1) a board or committee of two or more disinterested persons (2) that is assisted by counsel of its choice, (3) that makes an adequate evaluation, and (4) that prepares a written report of sufficient detail to permit judicial review. — ED.

(3) In cases arising under either Subsection (a)(1) or (a)(2), the court may substantively review and determine any issue of law.

(b) *Retention of significant improper benefit.* The court shall not dismiss an action if the plaintiff establishes that dismissal would permit a defendant, or an associate, to retain a significant improper benefit where:

(1) The defendant, either alone or collectively with others who are also found to have received a significant improper benefit arising out of the same transaction, possesses control of the corporation; or

(2) Such benefit was obtained:

(A) As the result of a knowing and material misrepresentation or omission or other fraudulent act; or

(B) Without advance authorization or the requisite ratification of such benefit by disinterested directors (or, in the case of a nondirector senior executive, advance authorization by a disinterested superior), or authorization or ratification by disinterested shareholders, and in breach of §5.02 (Transactions with the Corporation) or §5.04 (Use by a Director or Senior Executive of Corporate Property, Material-Non-Public Corporate Information, or Corporate Position); unless the court determines, in light of specific reasons advanced by the board or committee, that the likely injury to the corporation from continuation of the action is so compelling as clearly to outweigh any adverse impact on the public interest from dismissal of the action.[54]

(c) *Subsequent developments.* In determining whether the standards of §7.10(a) are satisfied or whether §7.10(b) or any of the exceptions set forth therein are applicable, the court may take into account considerations set forth by the board or committee (or otherwise brought to the court's attention) that reflect material developments subsequent to the time of the underlying transaction or conduct or to the time of the motion by the board or committee requesting dismissal.[55]

---

54. ALI §7.13(d) puts the burden of proof on plaintiff in respect to §7.10(a)(1), and for actions "against third parties and lesser corporate officials." The corporation has the burden of proof in respect to §7.10(a)(2). In addition, plaintiff has the burden of proof "to show (i) that a defendant's conduct involved a knowing and culpable violation of law, (ii) that the board or committee as a group was not capable of objective judgment . . . , and (iii) that dismissal of the action would permit a defendant . . . to retain a significant improper benefit under §7.10(b)." The corporation has the burden of proof under §7.10(b) "that the likely injury to the corporation from continuation of the action convincingly outweighs any adverse impact on the public interest from dismissal of the action." — ED.

55. For the view that "the business campaign to circumscribe derivative litigation by empowering supposedly 'disinterested' directors bore fruit" in the final ALI provisions, see Charles W. Murdock, Corporate Governance—The Role of Special Litigation Committees, 68 Wash. L. Rev. 79 (1993).

For general criticism of this and all existing judicial approaches because of their assumption "that the potential for structural bias will not corrupt the committee," see Cox & Munsinger, supra, at 108-131: "We believe the prescreening procedure . . . will be effective only if significant changes occur in the composition and selection of committee members." For support of the ALI approach and contending that (1) "structural bias cannot be overcome" and that (2) in *all* situations of conflict of interest (e.g., executive compensation) in which "directors sit in judgment over other directors," an "intermediate standard of review is necessary"—one that would require plaintiffs to show "substantive unreasonableness under the circumstances," see Julian Velasco, Structural Bias and the Need for Substantive Review, 82 Wash. U. L.Q. 821 (2004).

For a comparison of the ALI and Delaware approaches, see Note, A Hybrid Approach, 60 Ohio St. L.J. 241 (1999). — ED.

3. *Distinction between "demand-required" and "demand-excused" situations.* Neither RMBCA §7.44 nor ALI §7.08 follows *Zapata*'s distinction between dismissal occurring after (a) a required demand has been refused and (b) an excused demand has subsequently been considered by a special litigation committee. Is this practice sound?[56]

4. *Distinctions as to type of defendants.* (a) Of what significance should it be that the real defendants in the derivative suit are third parties rather than members of the board? In Ash v. International Business Machines, Inc., 236 F. Supp. 218 (E.D. Pa. 1964), the court observed: "[I]t is arguable that a refusal by the Board of Directors, however unreasonable, should always prevent a derivative suit against a third-party wrongdoer. This would leave plaintiff only a derivative suit against the directors for their negligence in refusing to sue the wrongdoer. At the very least, standing to bring a derivative suit must be based on some misconduct of the board of directors." Is it relevant that the third parties have allegedly violated the corporation's statutory (or constitutional) rights? See Klotz v. Consolidated Edison Co., 386 F. Supp. 577 (S.D.N.Y. 1974).

(b) Of what significance should it be that the real defendants are corporate employees or officers who are not directors? ALI §7.07(a) provides that the court should dismiss an action "against a person other than a director, senior executive, or person in control of the corporation, or an associate of any such person," if "the determinations of the board or committee . . . satisfy the requirements of the business judgment rule." For the view that "it would be best to dispense with the whole rigmarole engendered by a requirement of making a demand on the board and simply deny shareholders standing to bring corporate actions against lesser employees and outside parties, confining shareholder standing to derivative actions against top management or controlling shareholders for conflicts of interest," see Kenneth E. Scott, Corporation Law and the American Law Institute Corporate Governance Project, 35 Stan. L. Rev. 927, 944 (1983).

(c) Of what significance should it be that the real defendants are directors who are charged with a violation of the duty of care rather than the duty of loyalty?

> To the extent that both the corporation and its managers operate in reasonably competitive financial, product, and labor markets, the cost of negligent errors will be borne, at least partially, by those who commit them. Any incentive to slack is at best marginal. Because there is little incentive to commit negligent errors (and because real stupidity tends to reveal itself, thereby increasing the probability of detection), the usual logic of the deterrence theory, which focuses on the magnitude of the gain and the difficulty of detection, does not require substantial penalties for negligence. In the case of duty of loyalty violations, however, the likelihood of detection is lower, and the magnitude of the expected gain is higher. . . . [Moreover,] conflicts of interest are something that courts have a long history of policing, and, unlike the duty of care, they do not require courts to evaluate risk/return trade-offs with which they are uncomfortable and inexperienced.

Coffee, footnote 6 supra, at 1427. See generally Murdock, footnote 55 supra.

56. "Academic commentary has with near unanimity criticized the 'demand required/demand excused' distinction. See [16 articles]. Conversely, articles by corporate counsel have defended the rule of Auerbach v. Bennett (or a closely related interpretation of *Zapata*), arguing that the business judgment rule should apply equally to decisions made with respect to derivative litigation." 2 ALI, Principles of Corporate Governance 159-160 (1994).

(d) Of what significance should it be that the real defendants are a minority of the board? That a majority of the board have been made defendants because they "approved of" or "acquiesced in" the challenged transaction?

> Structural bias may be easier to discern in the recommendation of a special litigation committee, but it is equally present, and equally problematic, when the directors refuse a demand for suit or approve an out-of-court settlement. When the directors opine that a derivative suit must be dismissed, only the court can have sufficient detachment to evaluate legitimately whether the corporate interest would be better served by its continuation. . . . [T]here is little reason to vary the degree of judicial review of the directors' recommendation simply because the independent directors are a majority or minority of the board.

Cox, footnote 40 supra, at 1010-1011. Is it relevant that the defendant minority directors are charged with breach of fiduciary duty? Fraud? Violation of a statutory prohibition (such as the antitrust or securities laws)?

3. DEMAND ON SHAREHOLDERS

Some jurisdictions require only that a demand be made on the board of directors, e.g., Cal. Gen. Corp. Law §800(b)(2) (1982); N.Y. Bus. Corp. Law §626(c) (1963); N.C. Bus. Corp. Act §55-7-42 (1995); RMBCA §7.42 (1990). But many continue to follow the approach of Fed. R. Civ. P. 23.1, page 828 supra, in seemingly mandating (or at least suggesting) that a prior demand be made on the shareholders — at least in certain (ordinarily undefined) circumstances. In large corporations particularly, compliance may be severely expensive and time consuming. Major issues for consideration are (1) whether a demand must be made at all; (2) if so, (a) by whom, (b) under what circumstances, and (c) to do what; and (3) what the consequences are of a decision by the shareholder body not to take action (a) in response to a demand by plaintiff shareholder or (b) in a vote solicited by management (or some other person or shareholder).

Mayer v. Adams
38 Del. Ch. 298, 141 A.2d 458 (S. Ct. 1958)

SOUTHERLAND, C.J.: The case concerns Rule 23(b) of the Rules of the Court of Chancery . . . relating to stockholders' derivative suits. The second sentence of paragraph (b) provides:

> The complaint shall also set forth with particularity the efforts of the plaintiff to secure from the managing directors or trustees and, if necessary, from the shareholders such action as he desires, and the reasons for his failure to obtain such action or the reasons for not making such effort.

The question is: Under what circumstance is a preliminary demand on shareholders necessary?

Plaintiff is a stockholder of the defendant Phillips Petroleum Company. She brought an action to redress alleged frauds and wrongs committed by the defendant directors upon the corporation. They concern dealings between Phillips and defendant Ada Oil Company, in which one of the defendant directors is alleged to have a majority stock interest.

The amended complaint set forth reasons why demand on the directors for action would be futile and the sufficiency of these reasons was not challenged. It also set forth reasons seeking to excuse failure to demand stockholder action. The principal reasons were (1) that fraud was charged, which no majority of stockholders could ratify; and (2) that to require a minority stockholder to circularize more than 100,000 stockholders—in effect, to engage a proxy fight with the management—would be an intolerably oppressive and unreasonable rule, and in any event would be a futile proceeding. All defendants moved to dismiss on the ground that the reasons set forth were insufficient in law to excuse such failure.

The Vice Chancellor was of opinion that, notwithstanding these allegations, demand on stockholders would not necessarily have been futile. He accordingly dismissed the complaint. Plaintiff appeals. . . .

Let us suppose that the objecting stockholder submits to a stockholders' meeting a proposal that a suit be brought to redress alleged wrongs. He may do so either by attending the meeting, or, if the regulations of the Securities and Exchange Commission are applicable, by requiring the management to mail copies of the proposal to the other stockholders. (He is limited to 100 words of explanation. Rule X-14A-8b.)[57] Let us further suppose—a result quite unlikely—that the stockholders approve the resolution. What is accomplished by such approval? The stockholder is about to file his suit. What additional force is given to the suit by the approval?

Let us suppose again that the proposal is disapproved by the majority stockholders—as common knowledge tells us it will ordinarily be. What of it? They cannot ratify the alleged fraud. . . . The stockholder files his suit, which proceeds notwithstanding the disapproval.

If the foregoing is a correct analysis of the matter, it follows that the whole process of stockholder demand in a case of alleged fraud is futile and avails nothing. This appears to be the view expressed by Chancellor Seitz in Campbell v. Loew's Inc., Del. Ch., 134 A.2d 565, 567. . . .

The defendants vigorously assail this view of the matter. They say that the rule requires demand for action to be made upon the stockholders in all cases in which the board of directors is disqualified (as here) to pass upon the matter of bringing suit, because in such a case the power to determine the question of policy passes to the body of the stockholders. The stockholders may determine, when the matter is presented to them, upon any one of a number of courses. Thus, defendants say, they may authorize plaintiff's suit; they may determine to file the suit collectively—"take it over," so to speak; they may take other remedial action; they may remove the directors; and, finally, they may decide that the suit has no merit, or, as a matter of corporate policy, that it should not in any event be brought. . . .

Again, what is gained (except, perhaps, "moral" support) by having the suit brought by a group of stockholders, however large, rather than by a single individual? A more serious objection to this suggestion is that under Delaware

---

57. The federal proxy rule governing shareholder proposals, see page 667 supra, has since been changed. It now limits the proposal and its supporting statement to an aggregate of 500 words.—Ed.

law the directors manage the corporation—not the stockholders. It is certainly gravely to be doubted whether the majority stockholders, as such, may take over the duties of the directors in respect of litigation.[58] . . .

The suggestion that the directors could be removed is a suggestion that the objecting stockholder could engage in a proxy fight with the management. Of all defendants' suggestions, this seems to us to be the most unrealistic. How often is a minority stockholder equipped to take on such a formidable task? And why should a proxy fight be made a condition precedent to a minority stockholder's suit to redress an alleged fraud?

Finally it is suggested that the stockholders may (1) determine that the suit has no merit, or (2) that it is not good policy to press it.

As to the first suggestion, we think it clear that in the ordinary case the stockholders in meeting could not satisfactorily determine the probable merits of a minority stockholder's suit without a reasonably complete presentation and consideration of evidentiary facts. Perhaps some very simple cases might be handled in another manner, but they must be few. A stockholders' meeting is not an appropriate forum for such a proceeding.[59]

The second suggestion, that the stockholders may, as a matter of policy, determine that the claim shall not be enforced and bind the minority not to sue, is really the crux of this case. If the majority stockholders have this power, there would be much to be said for defendants' argument that in case of a disqualified or nonfunctioning board, the stockholders should decide the matter. . . .

But a decision not to press a claim for alleged fraud committed by the directors means, in effect, that the wrong cannot be remedied. It is conceded that the wrong cannot be ratified by the majority stockholders, but it is said that refusal to sue is a different thing from ratification. Strictly speaking, this is true, but the practical result is the same. To construe Rule 23(b) as making necessary a submission of the matter to stockholders, because the stockholders have the power to prevent the enforcement of the claim, is to import into our law a procedure that would inevitably have the effect of seriously impairing the minority stockholder's now existing right to seek redress for frauds committed by directors of the corporation. . . . We cannot believe that Rule 23(b) was intended to import into our law and procedure a radical change of this judicial policy. . . .

We are aware that there is high authority in support of defendants' contention. See S. Solomont & Sons Trust, Inc. v. New England Theatres Operating Corp., 326 Mass. 99, 93 N.E.2d 241, holding that a majority of disinterested stockholders may

58. In Continental Securities Co. v. Belmont, discussed infra by the court, the New York Court of Appeals stated: "As a general rule stockholders cannot act in relation to the ordinary business of a corporation. . . . They are not by any statute in this state given general power of initiative in corporate affairs. Any action by them relating to the details of the corporate business is necessarily in the form of an assent, request or recommendation. Recommendations by a body of stockholders can only be enforced through the board of directors, and indirectly by the authority of the stockholders to change the personnel of the directors at a meeting for the election of directors."

In Zimmerman v. Bell, 585 F. Supp. 512 (D. Md. 1984), plaintiff brought a derivative suit against all the directors for breach of fiduciary duty and waste of corporate assets in opposing a tender offer in order to perpetuate their control of the corporation. The court held that a demand on the shareholders would be futile: "Under Maryland law, . . . the stockholders could only . . . [demand] that the directors bring an action against themselves. . . . [As they control the corporation, it] could not effectively or properly prosecute the litigation."—Ed.

59. Accord, 2 ALI, Principles of Corporate Governance 661-662 (1994). See footnote 63 infra.—Ed.

in good faith determine that a cause of action for fraud against the directors shall not be enforced.[60] There is also high authority for the view that we take, namely, that a cause of action for alleged fraud committed by the directors may be maintained by a minority stockholder without demand upon the stockholders collectively. Continental Securities Co. v. Belmont, 206 N.Y. 7, 99 N.E. 138.

. . . In the *Continental* case, the New York Court of Appeals pointed out the difference between the power of the stockholders to ratify acts merely voidable and the lack of their power to ratify acts unlawful or against public policy.[61] We think it clear that so far as any substantive question of law is involved the Delaware law is similar to that of New York. . . .

Defendants lay great stress upon the federal cases construing this rule. Our rule, they say, was copied (with certain omissions) from the comparable federal rule 23(b) of the Federal Rules of Civil Procedure. . . . It is clear that the federal decisions are far from harmonious in construing the federal rule. They present no serious obstacle to a reasonable interpretation of our rule by this Court consonant with Delaware law and the practice of many years. . . .

We are cited to only one state decision construing an equity rule similar to ours. Escoett v. Aldecress Country Club, 16 N.J. 438, 109 A.2d 277, 283.

The Supreme Court of New Jersey held that the circumstances presented excused demand upon the stockholders, but in so holding considered the history of the rule in the federal system, the federal decisions construing it, and the background of its adoption by the New Jersey Supreme Court. The Court said:

> And we do not read into the rule any blanket exemption in situations where the wrongs complained of are not subject to formal ratification by the stockholders; even there the stockholder may, before instituting his action, be profitably expected to call upon the general body of stockholders for support which may be in the form of internal corporate action or in joinder in his court action.

Referring to the background of the adoption of the rule in New Jersey in 1948, the Court said: "The numerous stockholders' derivative actions in our State gave rise to demands that greater restrictions be imposed upon their maintenance. In 1945 the Legislature made provisions for the stockholder's posting of security

---

60. Accord, Palley v. Baird, 356 Mass. 737, 254 N.E.2d 894 (1970); Bell v. Arnold, 175 Colo. 277, 487 P.2d 545 (1971). See also Claman v. Robertson, 164 Ohio St. 61, 128 N.E.2d 429 (1955) (since shareholder majority has power to "ratify" allegedly fraudulent transaction, when shareholders adopt a resolution "approving and ratifying" director conduct that is subsequently challenged in a derivative suit, plaintiff shareholder must seek to "negate that ratification" by making a demand on the shareholders). — Ed.

61. The *Continental* opinion stated:

> [I]t is generally recognized that certain acts of boards of directors that are legal, but voidable, can be ratified and confirmed by a majority of the body of stockholders as the ultimate parties in interest and thus make them binding upon the corporation. . . . Such recognized authority in stockholders to ratify and confirm the acts of boards of directors is confined to acts voidable by reason of irregularities in the make-up of the board or otherwise or by reason of the directors or some of them being personally interested in the subject-matter of the contract or act, or for some other similar reason which makes the action of the directors voidable. No such authority exists in case of an act of the board of directors which is prohibited by law or which is against public policy. . . . In any case where action is taken by stockholders confirming and ratifying a fraud and misapplication of the funds of the corporation by the directors or others the action is binding only by way of estoppel upon such stockholders as vote in favor of such approval.

— Ed.

for reasonable expenses (R.S. 14:3-15, N.J.S.A) as a measure of 'protection for corporations and their officers and directors, against "strike suits." ' " Delaware has never adopted such a statute.

With deference to the high court of our sister State of New Jersey, we are constrained, for the reasons first set forth above, to differ with its view that anything substantial can be accomplished by a demand upon stockholders in a case in which fraud is charged. Such a demand would be, in our opinion, a futile gesture.[62] . . .

We are not called upon in this case to attempt to enumerate the various circumstances in which demand on stockholders is excused; and likewise we do not undertake to enumerate all the cases in which demand is necessary. It seems clear that one instance of necessary demand is a case involving only an irregularity or lack of authority in directorate action. . . .

---

1. *Ratification of voidable misconduct.* (a) As indicated in the *Mayer* case, a wrong that is clearly subject to ratification is one "involving only an irregularity or lack of authority in directorate action," e.g., when the directors sell corporation real estate without shareholder approval despite a charter provision requiring it. Under such circumstances, would a demand on the stockholders be a prerequisite to a derivative suit in states with provisions such as those in California and New York?

(b) As a matter of substantive law, if the board of directors causes the corporation to enter into a transaction, "the directors or some of them being personally interested in the subject matter of the contract or act" (see the *Continental* case, footnote 58 supra), can the transaction "be ratified and confirmed by a majority of the body of stockholders as the ultimate parties in interest and thus make it binding upon the corporation"? See Triplett v. Grundy Elec. Coop., 389 S.W.2d 401 (Mo. Ct. App. 1965). If so, was the *Mayer* case correctly decided?

(c) Assuming misconduct that is subject to shareholder ratification, should a demand on the stockholder body by the plaintiff shareholder be a prerequisite to a derivative suit?

> [T]he courts which require some sort of demand whenever ratification is possible seemingly consider ratification itself — or perhaps more appropriately "nonratification" — the proper subject matter of a demand. The validity of such a position is doubtful. When no other demand is required, the judicial interest seems better served by placing the burden of securing ratification upon the alleged wrongdoers. The policy of the law is to discourage the commission of the wrong, and this is not effectuated by assuring the wrongdoer that he may act with impunity unless someone else is willing to undergo the expense of securing "nonratification." Thus, ratification is universally a matter of affirmative defense rather than "nonratification" an element of the cause of action. . . .
> Finally, since the question of demand on shareholders never arises unless a demand on directors is unavailing, the alleged wrongdoer will often be in a better position than the

---

62. For a case illustrating the burden on plaintiff to establish "fraud" so as to avoid the consequences of the demand-on-shareholders requirement, see Lewis v. Hat Corp. of America, 38 Del. Ch. 313, 150 A.2d 750 (Ch. 1959) ("defendants having submitted the records concerning the transaction under attack [a purchase of their assets by the corporation at a price that was allegedly "excessive and exorbitant bearing no proper relationship to their fair and reasonable value"] and moved for summary judgment, it became incumbent on plaintiffs to offer proof which would either establish that the purchase was constructively fraudulent or otherwise invalid . . . , or in the alternative . . . [to file] affidavits raising genuine issues of fact as to the legality of the purchase"). — ED.

plaintiff to obtain a poll on ratification simply and inexpensively, through the board which has declined to sue him and may therefore be aligned on his side.

Note, Demand on Directors and Shareholders as a Prerequisite to a Derivative Suit, 73 Harv. L. Rev. 746, 751-752 (1960).[63]

2. *The fraud, self-dealing/negligence, mismanagement distinction.* (a) In Smith v. Brown-Borhek Co., 414 Pa. 325, 200 A.2d 398 (1964), plaintiff brought a derivative suit against the corporation's officers and directors charging them with negligent mismanagement resulting in a loss of 63 percent of the corporation's assets. In response to management's proxy solicitation after the suit was filed, the shareholders, having been fully informed, "ratified and confirmed" the actions of defendants by vote of 6,693 to 405. Defendants' motion for judgment on the pleadings was granted and affirmed. The court appeared to recognize that the Pennsylvania rule forbade stockholder ratification of fraud as a bar to a derivative suit, but held that

> nowhere in his complaint does the plaintiff allege that there has been fraud, self-dealing, personal profit or intentional dissipation or waste of corporate funds. In the last analysis plaintiff bases his case on the alleged failure of the officers and directors to devote their full time to the management of the business and particularly to . . . failure to exercise "that diligence, care and skill which ordinarily prudent men would exercise under similar circumstances in their personal business affairs." This prudent-man rule is the standard set forth in the [Business Corporation Law, 15 P.S. §2852-408].

(b) Does the distinction between ratifying fraud or self-dealing, on the one hand, and ratifying negligence or mismanagement, on the other, make sense?

> Since [in the case of negligence] the director has not benefited by violation of his fiduciary obligation, it might be argued that flexibility in determining whether to sue is desirable. . . . It would appear, however, that the shareholders are no more competent to deal with the failure to use due care situation than with that involving, for example, the taking of a corporate opportunity. Evaluation of possible harm to the corporation, if the action is maintained, and of the merits of the cause of action, often [is] as complex here as there. And to assure recovery of judgment where the corporation has been wronged is not the only function of the no-ratification rule. The rule, it is assumed, acts as a deterrent.

Robert N. Leavell, The Shareholders as Judges of Alleged Wrongs by Directors, 35 Tul. L. Rev. 331, 359-360 (1961).

(c) What result in the *Brown-Borhek* case if the corporation had gone bankrupt, its trustee in bankruptcy had sued the directors for negligently causing loss to the corporation, and defendants had moved for judgment on the ground that the disinterested shareholders had overwhelmingly ratified the challenged conduct? Compare Neese v. Brown, 218 Tenn. 686, 405 S.W.2d 577 (1964), with Cunningham v. Jaffe, 251 F. Supp. 143 (D.S.C. 1966).

---

63. ALI §7.03(c) provides that "demand on shareholders should not be required"; but ALI §7.11 provides for dismissal of a derivative action if, after disclosure of "all material facts," a "vote of disinterested shareholders" approves a resolution recommending dismissal and this "would not constitute a waste of corporate assets."

(d) If there had been no shareholder vote in the *Brown-Borhek* case, should plaintiff have had to make a demand on the shareholders as a prerequisite to the derivative suit?

3. *Consequences of shareholder ratification.* (a) In Smith v. Dunlap, 269 Ala. 97, 111 So. 2d 1 (1959), plaintiff brought a derivative suit against the corporation's officers and directors on the ground that their compensation sums were "so excessive that they bore no reasonable relation to the value of the services rendered." Plaintiff made demands on the directors and shareholders to take action, but they refused. The trial court sustained a demurrer. *Reversed:*

> It is a universal rule that neither the board of directors nor the majority stockholders can, over the protest of a minority stockholder, give away corporate property. . . .
> And where the amount of compensation paid to an officer of a corporation has no reasonable relation to the value of the services rendered therefor, it is in reality a gift. . . . It follows that the action of the majority stockholders and the directors in refusing to bring suit or in ratifying the alleged excessive compensation cannot, on proper allegations, preclude intervention by a court of equity to inquire into the reasonableness, vel non, of said compensation at the instance of a minority stockholder. . . .
> [T]he rule in this jurisdiction is that as a predicate for a minority stockholder's derivative suit, an appeal to the stockholders is necessary, no sufficient excuse for not so doing being shown — and this without regard to the nature of the subject matter of the suit. . . . Such resort to the stockholders is necessary, . . . without regard to the acts complained of, that is, those that are, and those that are not, capable of ratification. . . . [But it] was not the intention of this Court to hold that a majority of the stockholders could by ratifying fraudulent acts or by refusing to seek redress for such acts thereby preclude a minority stockholder from bringing suit.

Compare Saigh v. Busch, 396 S.W.2d 9 (Mo. Ct. App. 1956) (shareholder demand required in derivative suit challenging president's compensation as "excessive" and "not based on the reasonable value of his services"; "stockholders have the right to consider the matter and ratify, if they wish, any act of the directors, provided the act is not ultra vires, illegal or fraudulent").

May the line of decisions represented by the *Mayer* and *Dunlap* cases, holding that a derivative suit is not barred by the vote of a majority of the disinterested shareholders not to sue the directors for fraud, be squared with the rule of the *Aronson* and *Levine* cases, supra, holding that a vote of an independent majority of the board not to sue directors for fraud ends a derivative suit?

(b) What should be the effect of a vote against bringing suit by a majority of the disinterested shareholders, in response either to plaintiff shareholder's demand or a solicitation of the shareholder vote by management? Are there alternative effects beyond (1) rendering judgment for defendants — see the *Brown-Borhek* case, Note 2 supra, (2) requiring affirmative action by plaintiff to negate the shareholder action — see the *Claman* case, footnote 60 supra, (3) permitting the derivative suit to proceed — see the *Dunlap* decision?

4. *Statutory prohibitions and public policy.* In Rogers v. American Can Co., 305 F.2d 297 (3d Cir. 1962), plaintiff shareholder claimed that one of the corporation's major shareholders (which was the principal supplier of its raw materials) and a majority of the corporation's directors had violated the federal antitrust laws, causing damage to the corporation. The court held that plaintiff's derivative suit was

not barred by the decision of a majority of the disinterested shareholders not to enforce the corporation's cause of action:

> The business judgment character of the stockholders' determination, generally effective to definitively terminate intracorporate controversies, must yield to the right of a minority stockholder to expose his charges of violations of positive law which he alleges his corporation is itself prevented from bringing by reason of its captivity through the conspiratorial activities of its directors and a substantial stockholder and chief supplier. In this respect he is not usurping the role of the Attorney General as the public prosecutor of infractions of the antitrust laws, . . . but rather is engaged in achieving for his corporation the relief and recovery which the Clayton Act empowers it to seek, were it free to do so, thereby at the same time supporting the effectiveness of the enforcement of the antitrust laws, a purpose for which the treble damage suit was designed as an instrumentality.

The court of appeals quoted approvingly from the district judge's opinion: "[A]ny attempt by corporate stockholders by vote or otherwise, to ratify such illegal acts in the past, or to conspire to that end in the future, would be a nullity, calling for the intervention of equity to prevent the effectuation of such conspiracy in the future, and entitling the corporation to damages for its injuries in the past."

Finally, the court noted that its decision "permits the plaintiff to precipitate the defendants into litigation which will involve them in the heavy expenditure of both time and money . . . [and] may open the door to many suits wherein parties will endeavor to air their intracorporate controversies under the guise of treble damage antitrust actions. However, these considerations cannot overcome the necessity to provide each plaintiff with the opportunity to press a just claim if he has one." Compare this rationale with the *United Copper Securities Co.* case (discussed in footnote 33 supra), which dealt with decisions by disinterested *directors* not to enforce the corporation's cause of action for violation of the antitrust laws. See generally Harlan Blake, The Shareholders' Role in Antitrust Enforcement, 110 U. Pa. L. Rev. 143 (1961).

5. *Expense and futility.* In jurisdictions that require demand on shareholders, should the fact that shareholders are numerous and widespread and that the cost of demand would be very expensive excuse compliance with the requirement? See Levitt v. Johnson, 334 F.2d 815 (1st Cir. 1964) (in derivative suit for corporation with 48,000 scattered shareholders based on violation of Investment Company Act, demand on shareholders not required: "[N]ot only would such a burden be enormous, but no disclosure that plaintiff could be expected to make would be likely to persuade a majority to take over the action, or, conversely, permit an informed decision by the majority that the action be not instituted"; "any contention that plaintiff could make full disclosure in a 100 word statement[64] . . . and receive thoughtful and adequate consideration, would be unrealistic").[65] Compare Saigh v. Busch, Note 3(a) supra ("size of the corporation [over 10,000 shareholders] and the delay and expense in circularizing stockholders widely scattered does not excuse the failure to seek action from the stockholders"). See also Zimmerman v. Bell, footnote 58 supra.

---

64. See footnote 57 supra.

65. Accord, Harhen v. Brown, 431 Mass. 838, 730 N.E.2d 859 (2000) (7 million policyholders of Hancock Mutual Life Ins. Co.); Elgin v. Alfa Corp., 598 So. 2d 807, 817-818 (Ala. 1992); New Crawford Valley, Ltd. v. Benedict, 847 P.2d 642, 646 (Colo. App. 1993).

Should the rule be that a demand on shareholders is prerequisite to a derivative suit if the majority of disinterested shareholders is relatively small in number and sufficiently concerned with the corporation's activities so as to make the shareholder meeting a proper forum for consideration of the matter? Is such a rule conveniently administrable? Compare N.J. Rule of Civ. Prac. 4:32-5 (1994), which requires a demand on shareholders "if necessary" and then provides that "immediately on filing the complaint and issuing the summons, the plaintiff shall give such notice of the pendency and object of the action to the other shareholders as the court by order directs."[66]

What bearing, if any, do these factors have on the issue of the consequences of a shareholder ratification?[67]

C. *QUALIFICATIONS OF PLAINTIFF SHAREHOLDER*

The rule of contemporaneous ownership, that plaintiff have been a shareholder at the time of the alleged wrongdoing — stated in clause (1) of Fed. R. Civ. P. 23.1, page 828 supra, and adopted in substance by most states through statute, court rule, or judicial decision — is the most common qualification imposed on derivative suit plaintiffs.[68] Although it was originally formulated as a federal equity rule to preclude share transfer in order to create diversity of citizenship,[69] one modern justification is to prevent the buying of shares for the purpose of bringing suit — especially by "strike" suitors. Further, it is said that "the right of the stockholder to sue exists because of special injury to him for which otherwise he is without redress. [Thus,] . . . one who held no stock at the time of the mismanagement ought not to be allowed to sue, unless the mismanagement or its effects continue and are injurious to him. . . ." Home Fire Ins. Co. v. Barber, 67 Neb. 644, 93 N.W. 1024 (1903). "A contrary view is expressed in other jurisdictions to the effect that the cause of action for the wrongdoing of officers and directors is a part of the assets in which a stockholder has a transferable interest, that a transfer of his shares includes the ownership of incidents thereto, and that it is immaterial whether the stockholder who seeks to vindicate the right was such at the time of the wrongful transaction." Jepsen v. Peterson, 69 S.D. 388, 10 N.W.2d 749 (1943).

---

66. Compare the notice provision for class actions under Fed. R. Civ. P. 23(c)(2), which has been held to require the plaintiff to "pay for the cost of notice as part of the ordinary burden of financing his own suit" and to be mandatory despite the fact that "the prohibitively high cost of providing individual notice to 2,250,000 class members would end this suit." Eisen v. Carlisle & Jaquelin, 417 U.S. 156 (1974).

67. See generally Deborah A. DeMott, Demand in Derivative Actions: Problems of Interpretation and Function, 19 U.C. Davis L. Rev. 461, 474-484 (1986); Note, The Nonratification Rule and the Demand Requirement: The Case for Limited Judicial Review, 63 Colum. L. Rev. 1086 (1963); Comment, Shareholder Validation of Directors' Frauds: The Non-Ratification Rule v. The Business Judgment Rule, 58 Nw. U. L. Rev. 807 (1964).

68. Most federal courts in diversity cases have held that the federal rule is procedural under the doctrine of Erie R.R. v. Tompkins and thus applies irrespective of the law of the forum state. But the Supreme Court has never resolved the issue. See Bangor Punta Operations, Inc. v. Bangor & Aroostook R.R., 417 U.S. 703, 708 n.4 (1974). The rule has been held not to apply to shareholder suits on behalf of the corporation under Securities Exchange Act §16(b), page 505 supra, which authorizes suit "by the owner of any security." See Dottenheim v. Murchison, 227 F.2d 737 (5th Cir. 1955).

69. See Hawes v. Oakland, 104 U.S. 450 (1882).

Most of the state statutes and court rules follow the federal provision quite closely. See, e.g., Del. Gen. Corp. Law §327 (1998); N.Y. Bus. Corp. Law §626(b) (1963). A few differ in important respects:

California General Corporation Law (1982)

Sec. 800. . . . (b) No action may be instituted or maintained in right of any domestic or foreign corporation[70] by any holder of shares or of voting trust certificates of such corporation unless both of the following conditions exist:

(1) The plaintiff alleges in the complaint that plaintiff was a shareholder, of record or beneficially,[71] or the holder of voting trust certificates at a time of the transaction or any part thereof of which plaintiff complains or that plaintiff's shares or voting trust certificates thereafter devolved upon plaintiff by operation of law from a holder who was a holder at the time of the transaction or any part thereof complained of; provided, that any shareholder who does not meet these requirements may nevertheless be allowed in the discretion of the court to maintain the action on a preliminary showing to and determination by the court, by motion and after a hearing, at which the court shall consider such evidence, by affidavit or testimony, as it deems material, that (i) there is a strong prima facie case in favor of the claim asserted on behalf of the corporation, (ii) no other similar action has been or is likely to be instituted, (iii) the plaintiff acquired the shares before there was disclosure to the public or to the plaintiff of the wrongdoing of which plaintiff complains, (iv) unless the action can be maintained the defendant may retain a gain derived from defendant's willful breach of a fiduciary duty, and (v) the requested relief will not result in unjust enrichment of the corporation or any shareholder of the corporation. . . . [72]

---

1. *Problems.* Plaintiff brings a derivative suit on behalf of a corporation whose shares are widely held, alleging that, before his becoming a shareholder, management embezzled funds from the corporation and concealed this on the corporation's books until the present time. There are a number of present shareholders who were such at the time of the alleged embezzlement and who are not charged as being implicated. Will (should) plaintiff be disqualified from bringing suit? Of what significance, if any, are the following factual variations?

70. In Grosset v. Wenaas, 133 Cal. App. 4th 710, 35 Cal. Rptr. 3d 58 (2005), the court held that this language does not take precedence over the "internal affairs" doctrine which makes "the issue of a plaintiff's standing . . . subject to the law of the state of incorporation." — ED.

71. Only a few statutes or court rules require that plaintiff be a "registered shareholder" or "of record" at the time of the alleged wrongdoing. Most are either silent as to this or authorize suit by "beneficial" or "equitable" owners. Most courts, when not governed by a specific provision, have held equitable ownership sufficient. See Rosenthal v. Burry Biscuit Corp., 30 Del. Ch. 299, 60 A.2d 106 (Ch. 1948); HFG Co. v. Pioneer Pub. Co., 162 F.2d 536 (7th Cir. 1947). As to whether convertible bondholders come within this definition, compare Harff v. Kerkorian, 324 A.2d 215 (Del. Ch. 1974), and Kusner v. First Pennsylvania Corp., 395 F. Supp. 276 (E.D. Pa. 1975), with Hoff v. Sprayregan, 52 F.R.D. 243 (S.D.N.Y. 1971). See generally Laurence E. Mitchell, The Fairness Rights of Bondholders, 65 N.Y.U. L. Rev. 1165 (1990). As to holders of stock options, see Daly v. Yessne, 131 Cal. App. 4th 52, 31 Cal. Rptr. 3d 420 (2005) (no). — ED.

72. Pa. Bus. Corp. Law §1782(b) (1990) also contains an exception to the contemporaneous ownership requirement if "there is a strong prima facie case in favor of the claim asserted on behalf of the corporation and that without the action serious injustice will result." — ED.

(a) There are no present shareholders, apart from those named as defendants, who were such at the time of the alleged embezzlement.

(b) The facts underlying the alleged embezzlement were generally known before plaintiff purchased his shares.

(c) The corporation's shares are closely held.

2. *Class actions and derivative suits combined.* In Kauffman v. Dreyfus Fund, Inc., 434 F.2d 727 (3d Cir. 1970), a shareholder of four mutual funds alleged that certain of the funds' directors and investment advisers had, inter alia, conspired "to adopt and stabilize fees for management services and investment services, to limit competition, to refrain from providing internal fund management, and to otherwise monopolize the management market"—all to the injury of the funds and in violation of various federal securities and antitrust laws. In addition to bringing a derivative suit on behalf of these four funds, plaintiff sought to bring a class action derivatively on behalf of 61 other mutual funds in which he owned no shares, alleging that these other funds were being similarly harmed as part of the same conspiracy by the misconduct of their directors and investment advisers. The court rejected plaintiff's argument that "(1) a shareholder suing on behalf of a corporation may bring all suits which a corporation could commence but for the refusal of its officers and directors; (2) a corporation could commence a class action on behalf of all corporations similarly situated; and therefore (3) a shareholder, standing in the shoes of his corporation, may commence a class action on behalf of all corporations similarly situated." Is the court's decision sound?

3. *Multiple derivative suits.* Courts have generally held that a shareholder of a parent corporation may bring a derivative suit on behalf of the subsidiary corporation on the subsidiary's cause of action. Must the parent own a controlling interest in the subsidiary before the shareholder may bring the suit? See Pessin v. Chris-Craft Industries, Inc., 181 App. Div. 2d 66, 586 N.Y.S.2d 584 (1992) (yes).

4. *Mergers and dissolutions.* In Blasband v. Rales, 971 F.2d 1034 (3d Cir. 1992), plaintiff had been a shareholder of *A* corporation when it was allegedly injured by defendants, who were directors and controlling shareholders of *C* corporation. Before plaintiff's derivative suit was filed, *A* became a wholly owned subsidiary of *C* pursuant to a merger agreement; plaintiff exchanged his *A* shares for *C* shares. The court, applying Delaware law, held that the rationale of the rule permitting the shareholder of a parent corporation to bring a derivative suit on behalf of a subsidiary extended to plaintiff.[73] What result if *A* had simply been merged into *C*, with plaintiff receiving *C* shares? See Pessin v. Chris-Craft Industries, Inc., Note 3 supra (plaintiff was not a shareholder of *C* at the time of the alleged wrongdoing and his *C* shares did not "devolve by operation of law").[74]

5. *Intervention.* In In Re Maxxam Inc./Federated Development Shareholders Litigation, 698 A.2d 949 (Del. Ch. 1996), the court refused to dismiss a derivative suit brought by a noncontemporaneous owner after a contemporaneous owner intervened: because "a derivative claim belongs to the corporation . . . the identity of the specific representative shareholder plaintiff is not a paramount concern."

---

73. The court recognized that Lewis v. Anderson, 477 A.2d 1040 (Del. 1984) had reached the opposite conclusion on "closely parallel" facts.

74. See generally Mark M. Graham, Delaware Post-Merger Derivative Suit Standing and Demand Requirements, 25 J. Corp. L. 631 (2000).

American Law Institute, Principles of Corporate Governance (1994)

Sec. 7.02. *Standing to commence and maintain a derivative action.* (a) A holder of an equity security has standing to commence and maintain a derivative action if the holder:

(1) Acquired the equity security either (A) before the material facts relating to the alleged wrong were publicly disclosed or were known by, or specifically communicated to, the holder, or (B) by devolution of law from a prior holder who would have had standing under Subsection (A);

(2) Continues to hold the equity security until the time of judgment,[75] unless the failure to do so is the result of corporate action in which the holder did not acquiesce, and either (A) the derivative action was commenced prior to the corporate action terminating the holder's status,[76] or (B) the court finds that such holder is better able to represent the interests of the shareholders than any other holder who has brought suit. . . .

Problem. S buys all of a corporation's shares from its former shareholders. S then causes the corporation to bring suit against the former controlling shareholder for having misappropriated corporate assets before S's purchase. In a contemporaneous ownership jurisdiction, will the corporation be permitted to bring the suit? Should it be? Compare Capitol Wine & Spirit Corp. v. Pokrass, 277 App. Div. 184, 98 N.Y.S.2d 291 (1950), *aff'd,* 302 N.Y. 734, 98 N.E.2d 704 (1951), with Mauck v. Mading-Dugan Drug Co., 361 F. Supp. 1314 (N.D. Ill. 1973). Of what significance would it be if the corporation operated a railroad and a recovery in its favor might "enable it to enhance its services and help stave off the financial crisis faced today by so many railroads"? If there were continuing minority shareholders owning about 1 percent of the shares? See Bangor Punta Operations, Inc. v. Bangor & Aroostock R.R., 417 U.S. 703 (1974). If there were continuing minority shareholders owning 40 percent of the shares? See Home Telephone Co. v. Darley, 355 F. Supp. 992 (N.D. Miss. 1973). If the corporation were now bankrupt and its cause of action was being asserted by its trustee in bankruptcy? See REA Express, Inc. v. Travelers Insurance Co., 406 F. Supp. 1389 (D.D.C. 1976). See generally Note, Corporate Incapacity to Sue Where Stockholders Would Be Barred from Suing Derivatively—The Vicarious Incapacity Rule: A Public Interest Exception, 54 B.U. L. Rev. 355 (1974); Comment, 18 Buff. L. Rev. 184 (1968).

---

75. Although most statutes, following Fed. R. Civ. P. 23.1, do not explicitly require "continuous ownership throughout the pendency of the suit," the "overwhelming majority" impose this "common law requirement." Timko v. Tsiarsi, 898 So. 2d 89 (Fla. App. 2005).—ED.

76. For recent decisions holding that a shareholder loses "continuous" standing to bring a derivative suit when the shareholder's status is terminated because of a merger, see Lewis v. Ward, 852 A.2d 896 (Del. 2004); Grosset v. Wenaas, footnote 70 supra ("when a merger occurs, standing is lost because 'upon the merger the derivative rights pass to the surviving corporation which then has the sole right or standing to prosecute the action,'" citing Schreiber v. Carney, 447 A.2d 17 (Del. Ch. 1982)).

Should a shareholder lose that status because his right to hold shares ended as soon as his employment by the corporation was terminated? See K-O Enterprises, Inc. v. O'Brien, 166 S.W.3d 122 (Mo. App. 2005) (yes).—ED.

Courtland Manor, Inc. v. Leeds
347 A.2d 144 (Del. Ch. 1975)

BROWN, V.C.: This is a decision after trial in two consolidated actions brought by Courtland Manor, Inc., a Delaware corporation (hereafter "the corporation"), against Leonard S. Leeds and his father, William V. Leeds, individually, and also against Leonard Leeds as general partner of Courtland Manor Associates, a limited partnership (hereafter "the partnership") and Courtland Manor Associates itself. In one action the corporation was joined as a plaintiff by Bertram N. Widder, a stockholder and officer of the corporation and also a limited partner in the partnership. . . .

[In 1967, Leonard Leeds and his accountant (London) planned to construct a nursing home that], when completed, would be operated by a corporation while the actual construction and ownership of the facility would be accomplished through the limited partnership. The corporation was formed and investors were sought among the friends and clients of Leonard Leeds and London. . . . During the spring and summer of 1968, nine individuals, including the plaintiff Widder, contributed $70,000 to the corporation in return for stock valued at $1,000 per share. All nine, along with Leonard Leeds, were made directors of the corporation. Leonard Leeds was elected president and treasurer, Widder was elected secretary and London was elected assistant secretary. All stockholders were informed through written materials that the anticipated construction cost to the owner would be some $900,000 and that the rental rate that the corporation would pay . . . would be 12½ percent of that figure per year, or approximately $112,000.

After some difficulty, the limited partnership was formed with Leonard Leeds owning 29.5 percent as a general partner and William Leeds owning 40.5 percent as a limited partner. The remaining 30 percent limited partnership interest was sold to others, three of whom, including the plaintiff Widder, were also stockholder-directors of the corporation.

In order to meet FHA requirements, a draft lease was prepared and circulated among the stockholder-directors. At least one meeting of the group was held to discuss the lease, and one stockholder had it reviewed by his own attorney. As a result, certain changes were agreed upon, one of which established that the rental rate would be 12½ percent of the total cost of construction to the partnership, but not to exceed $150,000 per year. By this time, Leonard Leeds was representing that the rent might approach $125,000 per year. The lease was executed on November 6, 1968, with Leonard Leeds signing on behalf of the partnership.

By June 1970, with Leonard Leeds running the operation while drawing a salary from the corporation, the home was completed and patients accepted for care. However, things did not go as well as anticipated and the corporation experienced a severe cash shortage. Matters worsened over the summer of 1970 and the operation fell into disarray. As a result, Leonard Leeds became severed from the corporation and, in October 1970, the plaintiff Widder, who was already a stockholder and director, together with a Mr. Joseph and a Mr. Murdoch, acquired control of the corporation by purchasing most of the existing stock for approximately $4,000, a fraction of its initial cost. On October 27, 1970, these three elected themselves directors of the corporation and authorized the issuance of additional shares of stock at $10 per share, with each purchasing 500 shares. Thus, for an outlay of some $19,000 they ended up with virtually all of the stock of the corporation which represented a total investment of some $90,000. Ten days later, on November 6, 1970, they caused the corporation to file the first of these consolidated suits. . . .

As now sifted down, the corporation seeks judgment against Leonard Leeds individually for $45,377. The basis for this claim is that the lease engineered by Leonard Leeds was unfair to the corporation and excessively favorable to the partnership. The ultimate cost of construction exceeded $1.1 million and the annual rent, thus, approached $142,000 per year. Because of this the annual profit to the partnership-landlord exceeded $30,000 when initially it was anticipated that this figure would be some $7,000 annually. It is charged that the shortage of working capital which caused the failure of the corporate operation is attributable in large part to the excessive rent requirements of the lease, and that Leonard Leeds, as president of the corporation and general partner of the partnership, stood on both sides of the transaction with regard to the negotiation and execution of the lease between the two legal entities he then controlled. As such, it is argued that . . . Leonard Leeds bears the burden of showing the fairness of the lease to the corporation to which he owed the fiduciary duty which, under the evidence, he has not done. It is further charged that he withheld a project analysis prepared by FHA from which the other shareholder-directors, if they had known of it, would have realized in advance that the corporation would not have sufficient working capital left under the terms of the lease. Defendants dispute this, offering evidence to show that the lease was fair to the corporation as well as the partnership based on the high risk nature of the corporate enterprise and the large investment in a single purpose building. They also dispute the accuracy and worth of the FHA analysis.

The corporation also seeks judgment against the partnership for [two other, similar claims].

. . . I feel that the underlying theory of the plaintiff's case runs afoul of the equitable principles most recently affirmed by the United States Supreme Court in Bangor Punta Operations, Inc. v. Bangor & Aroostock R. Co., 417 U.S. 703 (1974).

There, in dwelling upon the rationale set forth by Roscoe Pound in Home Fire Insurance Co. v. Barber, 67 Neb. 644, 93 N.W. 1024 (1903), the Court noted the settled equitable principle that a shareholder may not complain of acts of corporate mismanagement if he acquired his shares from those who participated or acquiesced in the wrongful transaction.[77] The basis for this rule is that where shareholders have purchased all or substantially all of the shares of a corporation at a fair price, they have personally sustained no injury from wrongs which occurred prior to their purchase, and consequently, any recovery on their part for such prior wrongs would constitute a windfall and would enable such shareholders to obtain funds to which they had no just title or claim. In addition, to allow recovery to subsequent shareholders for prior wrongs would permit them to recoup a large part of the price they agreed to pay for their shares even though they had received all they had bargained for. Finally, to allow recovery would be to permit after-acquiring shareholders to profit from wrongs done to others, and thus encourage speculative litigation. . . .

The Court went on to hold in *Bangor Punta* that where equity would preclude individual shareholders from maintaining an action in their own right for wrongs

77. See, e.g., Russell v. Louis Melind Co., 331 Ill. App. 182, 72 N.E.2d 869 (1947) (such shareholder may not bring derivative suit even though he had no knowledge of wrongful transaction at time of his purchase of shares). — ED.

occurring to the corporation prior to the acquisition of their stock, it is also proper to disregard the corporate form so as to preclude after-acquiring shareholders from circumventing this rule by bringing the same action in the name of the corporation.

In *Bangor Punta,* although suit was brought in the name of the corporation against its previously controlling shareholder, it was noted that the real party who would benefit from a recovery was the 99 percent shareholder of the corporation who had obtained 98.3 percent of its stock from the former shareholder whose previous managerial activities the suit sought to challenge. The Court noted that the 99 percent shareholder acquired its 98.3 percent interest for $5 million and thereafter caused the corporation to seek damages against its vendor in the sum of $7 million for corporate mismanagement. Thus, a recovery by the corporation would, in effect, provide the 99 percent shareholder with a windfall by recouping its purchase price plus $2 million and thus permit it to realize far more than the fair value of the stock that it bargained for at the time of purchase. . . .

While the facts in this case are not identical to those in *Bangor Punta,* I think that the applicable rationale is the same. Here the corporation is not bringing suit against the parties from whom the now controlling shareholders acquired their majority stock ownership. Nonetheless, the basis for all three of its surviving claims is mismanagement and breach of fiduciary obligation by the president and managing officer of the corporation as elected by the then majority of the stockholders to whose interests Joseph, Murdoch and Widder have since succeeded. All of the original stockholders were directors of the corporation and apparently acquiesced in the final terms of the lease now complained of after having reviewed it, discussed it and had the opportunity for independent advice. . . . With the exception of Widder, none of the original shareholders have made an effort, either before or after disposing of their shares, to take action against Leeds or the partnership for his conduct while serving as president. If the equitable rule precludes suit for prior conduct as to which the vendor-shareholders either participated or acquiesced, then it would seem that the acquiescence of the previous shareholder-directors in the acts complained of should preclude suit by the present shareholders now.

Plaintiff argues that acquiescence requires knowledge, and that consequently the previous stockholder-directors could not have acquiesced in the alleged misconduct since Leonard Leeds withheld vital information from them. . . . But it seems that this very argument highlights the wisdom of Dean Pound's logic as reiterated in *Bangor Punta.* In effect it is an argument that since Leeds duped the previous stockholder-directors into acquiescence through surreptitious conduct, and thus perpetrated a fraud upon them, the present majority stockholders, through the guise of the corporate entity, should be permitted to recover damages for themselves for wrongs committed against others. If plaintiff is correct in its theory that acquiescence was improperly obtained by Leeds, this no doubt played a large role in enabling the present shareholders to purchase substantially all the existing stock from the original shareholders for a fraction of what the latter paid for it. If they are permitted to now recover for wrongs committed to those from whom they acquired their majority interest at a deflated value, the present shareholders will reap the windfall that equity strives to preclude. By comparison to the facts of *Bangor Punta,* if the corporation is permitted to recover the more than $70,000 in damages that it now seeks for Leeds's alleged mismanagement, its three primary shareholders will have acquired for some $19,000 a corporation worth some $90,000, and thus a benefit far in excess of that which they bargained for when they undertook to acquire by far the majority ownership of a foundering corporation.[78]

The fact that the plaintiff Widder was also a stockholder at the time of the alleged wrongs and merely acquired additional shares to strengthen his ownership adds an additional aspect not considered in *Bangor Punta*. However, I do not feel that this factor requires a different result under the present circumstances. In the first place he is in an ill position to complain since he was a director of the corporation as well as a partner in the defendant partnership at the time of the acts complained of. It might be argued that he stood on both sides of the questioned transactions just as did Leonard Leeds. Moreover, had he elected to bring action on behalf of the corporation and his fellow initial stockholders rather than first joining up with Joseph and Murdoch to obtain new and more complete ownership, his position might be more sympathetic. However, his decision to first realign himself with new ownership and then attempt to benefit by recovering for wrongs allegedly done to him and his previous fellow stockholder-directors deprives him, in my opinion, from any different consideration than that herein accorded to the present shareholder status of Joseph and Murdoch.[79]

I conclude that the reasoning of *Bangor Punta* and the precedents cited therein precludes the plaintiff corporation from any recovery here. . . .

---

1. *Knowledge; laches; participation; acquiescence.* (a) In jurisdictions that have the contemporaneous ownership rule, should plaintiff shareholders be barred from bringing suit if they acquired their shares with knowledge of an alleged continuing wrong? See Blum v. Morgan Guaranty Trust Co., 539 F.2d 1388 (5th Cir. 1976).

(b) In jurisdictions that either have or do not have the contemporaneous ownership rule, should plaintiff shareholders be permitted to bring suit if they are themselves guilty of laches or of participation or acquiescence in the alleged wrongdoing? Compare Recchion v. Kirby, 637 F. Supp. 1309 (W.D. Pa. 1986), and Head v. Lane, 495 So. 2d 821 (Fla. Ct. App. 1986), with Kullgren v. Navy Gas & Supply Co., 112 Colo. 331, 149 P.2d 653 (1944). See also Tierno v. Puglisi, 279 App. Div. 2d 836, 719 N.Y.S.2d 350 (2001) (minority shareholder brings derivative suit against other shareholder in two-person corporation).

2. *Nature of plaintiff's interest.* (a) Should plaintiff shareholder, who is otherwise qualified to bring a derivative suit, be required to have personal knowledge of the acts complained of? Of what significance is the fact that the derivative suit is instigated by a person disqualified from filing it? See DiGiovanni v. All-Pro Golf, Inc., 332 So. 2d 91 (Fla. Ct. App. 1976). See also Surowitz v. Hilton Hotels Corp., footnote 12 supra.

---

78. Accord, Bank of Santa Fe v. Petty, 116 N.M. 761, 867 P.2d 431 (N.M. App. 1993); Damerow Ford Co. v. Bradshaw, 128 Or. App. 606, 876 P.2d 788 (1994). — ED.

79. *Query:* Suppose Widder had (a) owned half the stock, (b) bought the other half from Leeds, and (c) neither benefited from nor had knowledge of the alleged misconduct? See Advanced Business Communication, Inc. v. Myers, 695 S.W.2d 601 (Tex. Ct. App. 1985) (corporation may recover for half the damages). — ED.

(b) Of what significance should it be that plaintiff shareholder, who is otherwise qualified to bring a derivative suit, had threatened to file the derivative suit unless defendant directors settled a pending direct action that plaintiff had against the corporation? See Hornreich v. Plant Industries, Inc., 535 F.2d 550 (9th Cir. 1976) (interpreting Fed. R. Civ. P. 23.1's requirement that plaintiff "adequately represent the interests of the shareholders").

(c) On whether plaintiff shareholder can "adequately represent the interests of the shareholders" when plaintiff is seeking to acquire control of the corporation, thus being a potential buyer of the corporation's shares while the other shareholders are potential sellers, see Baron v. Strawbridge & Clothier, 646 F. Supp. 690 (E.D. Pa. 1986).

(d) *Problem.* Corporation has six shareholders: mother and father, who each own 30 percent of the shares, and two sons and two daughters, who each own 10 percent. One of the children brings a derivative suit alleging that mother and father are taking excessive salaries. All five other shareholders and the corporation move to dismiss on the ground that the plaintiff does not "fairly and adequately represent the interests of the shareholders." What result? See Brandon v. Brandon Constr. Co., 300 Ark. 44, 776 S.W.2d 349 (1989).

Goldie v. Yaker
78 N.M. 485, 432 P.2d 841 (1967)

Wood, J.: . . . Plaintiffs [who bring this derivative suit] are stockholders of Intermountain (Intermountain Development Corporation). . . .

Defendants Yaker were purchasers under a real estate contract entered in October 1957. The contract was for 80 acres of land and certain water rights. The price was $15,000.00 The down-payment was $500.00; a note was given for the balance.

Intermountain was incorporated in October 1958. The incorporators were the Yakers and defendant Moscow.

In December 1958 the Yakers sold to Intermountain approximately 49 acres of the land being purchased under the real estate contract. The price was 2,500 shares of Intermountain with par value of $10.00 per share. In addition, as part of the sale price, Intermountain assumed certain development costs and assumed the $14,500.00 unpaid balance of the purchase price. . . . [I]n December 1958, the Yakers and Moscow were the only stockholders of Intermountain. These stockholders approved the transaction in December 1958. The 2,500 shares were issued to the Yakers in January 1959. Plaintiffs purchased their Intermountain stock in April and May 1959. A substantial portion of the 49 acres was transferred to Intermountain after plaintiffs became stockholders. . . .

Plaintiffs complain of the "excessive valuation" placed on the 49 acres received by Intermountain; thus, complain of the price of this acreage. . . . The agreement as to price was completed before plaintiffs acquired their stock.

We distinguish the agreement as to price and payments on the price pursuant to the agreement. The 2,500 shares of stock were issued before plaintiffs became stockholders. However, payments may have been made under the assumption agreements after plaintiffs became stockholders. Any such payments do not aid plaintiffs. The wrong complained of was in entering the contract, not in carrying out the contract once it was entered . . . compare Palmer v. Morris, 316 F.2d 649 (5th Cir. 1963).

The claimed wrong was not a continuing act; the transaction of which plaintiffs complain had been completed before plaintiffs became stockholders. . . .

The rule is that the plaintiffs, in order to maintain a stockholders' derivative suit, must have been stockholders at the time of the transaction of which they complain. There is an apparent conflict in the decisions as to whether this rule applies when, as a part of the transaction, fraud was contemplated upon those who should in the future become stockholders. See Old Dominion Copper Mining & Smelting Co. v. Bigelow, 188 Mass. 315, 74 N.E. 653 (1905); Old Dominion Copper Mining & Smelting Co. v. Lewisohn, 210 U.S. 206 (1908); Old Dominion Copper Mining & Smelting Co. v. Bigelow, 203 Mass. 159, 89 N.E. 193, 40 L.R.A., N.S., 314 (1909); McCandless v. Furland, 296 U.S. 140 (1935); San Juan Uranium Corp. v. Wolfe, 241 F.2d 121 (10th Cir. 1957).

The question of fraud contemplated upon future stockholders is not before us. While the complaint raises this question, the trial court's unattacked finding is that the decision to sell stock, in addition to that originally issued to the individual defendants, was not made until the Spring of 1959. This was subsequent to the transaction which plaintiffs claim to be fraudulent. Since at the time of the claimed fraud, there were no plans to have future stockholders, fraud upon future stockholders could not have been contemplated as a part of the transaction. . . .

---

1. *Fact variation.* What result in the *Goldie* case if the 2,500 shares were authorized to be issued to the Yakers in January 1959, but the share certificates were not issued until 1960? See Maclary v. Pleasant Hills, Inc., 35 Del. Ch. 39, 109 A.2d 830 (1954): The contemporaneous ownership statute

> was designed primarily to prevent the purchasing of stock to be used for the purpose of filing a derivative action attacking transactions occurring prior to such purchase. . . . It would seem more likely that a wrongful issuance of stock would be discovered if the issuance thereof and the stockholders appeared of record. To consider this transaction as having been completed prior to the issuance of the certificates would sanction an application of the statute not required by its language and not fairly required to effectuate its purpose. On the contrary, it would place a premium on corporate conduct which might run counter to desirable standards.

Compare In re Bank of New York Derivative Litigation, 320 F.3d 291 (2d Cir. 2003): "[P]laintiff must have owned stock in the corporation *throughout* the course of the activities that constitute the *primary basis* of the complaint . . . [, i.e.,] must have acquired his or her stock in the corporation before the core of the allegedly wrongful conduct transpired."[80]

2. *Problems: continuing wrongs.* (a) Before plaintiff's acquisition of shares, corporation sells a building to defendant, its controlling shareholder, at an alleged unconscionably low price. Is plaintiff shareholder barred from bringing a derivative suit if, after he becomes a shareholder, defendant:

---

80. See also 7547 Partners v. Beck 682 A.2d 160 (Del. 1996) (full disclosure of challenged transaction made in prospectus available to plaintiffs).

(i) Records the purchase of the building in accordance with state law? See Aurora Credit Services v. Liberty West, 970 P.2d 1273 (Utah 1998).

(ii) Continues to make payments on the agreement? Compare Cheft v. Kass, 19 App. Div. 2d 610, 241 N.Y.S.2d 284 (1963), with Palmer v. Morris, 316 F.2d 649 (5th Cir. 1963).

(iii) Sells the building at a great profit? Cf. Weinhaus v. Gale, 237 F.2d 197 (7th Cir. 1956).

(b) Before plaintiff's acquisition of shares, corporation sues former directors for breach of fiduciary duty. After plaintiff becomes a shareholder, corporation settles suit. May plaintiff bring a derivative suit against the present directors, attacking the settlement as fraudulently inadequate and pleading facts respecting the earlier transaction? See Gluck v. Unger, 25 Misc. 2d 554, 202 N.Y.S.2d 832 (S. Ct.), *appeal denied*, 10 App. Div. 2d 911, 203 N.Y.S.2d 1005 (1960).

(c) Before plaintiff's acquisition of shares, corporation's majority shareholder forms another business to acquire property that would be beneficial to the corporation. After plaintiff becomes a shareholder, this business acquires several such properties. May plaintiff bring a derivative suit arguing that these acquisitions were usurpations of corporate opportunities? See Levien v. Sinclair Oil Corp., 261 A.2d 911 (Del. Ch. 1969).

(d) In 1965, before plaintiff's acquisition of shares, corporation's board decides not to apply for a Nevada license to distribute slot machines because the "questionable business practices and associations" of one of its directors (who controlled the corporation) would prevent it from obtaining one. Instead, the corporation distributes its slot machines through an independent company. In 1973, after plaintiff becomes a shareholder, the corporation (no longer having the director in question) obtains a license and purchases the distributorship for $9.5 million. May plaintiff bring a derivative suit against those who were directors in 1965, claiming that the $9.5 million expenditure in 1973 was a waste of corporate assets? See Zilker v. Klein, 510 F. Supp. 1070 (N.D. Ill. 1981).[81]

(e) While plaintiff is a shareholder, corporation's director allegedly defrauds corporation. Plaintiff sells all the shares but, some time later, buys shares again. Is plaintiff shareholder barred from bringing a derivative suit? Compare Bateson v. Magna Oil Corp., 414 F.2d 128 (5th Cir. 1969), with Gresov v. Shattuck Denn Mining Co., 40 Misc. 2d 569, 243 N.Y.S.2d 760 (S. Ct. 1963). Are additional facts necessary? See also Vista Fund v. Garis, 277 N.W.2d 19 (Minn. 1979). What result if plaintiff, who is a shareholder when the alleged fraud occurs, brings suit and wins at trial but sells shares when defendant appeals and defendant then moves to dismiss? Compare Alford v. Shaw, 327 N.C. 526, 398 S.E.2d 445 (1990), with Schilling v. Belcher, 582 F.2d 995 (5th Cir. 1978). See generally Paul P. Harbrecht, The Contemporaneous Ownership Rule in Shareholders' Derivative Suits, 25 UCLA L. Rev. 1041 (1978). What result if plaintiff, who is a shareholder when the alleged fraud occurs, sells the shares but the buyer assigns to plaintiff "all rights of action that buyer could bring on behalf of the corporation"? See McLaughlin v. Foster, 589 So. 2d 143 (Ala. 1991).

---

81. For recent appraisals of the "continuing wrongs" theory, compare Sarah Wells, Comment, Maintaining Standing in a Shareholder Derivative Action, 38 U.C. Davis L. Rev. 343 (2004), with Terence L. Robinson Jr., Note, A New Interpretation of the Contemporaneous Ownership Requirement, 2005 BYU L. Rev. 229.

3. *Problem: parallel conduct.* Pursuant to a stock option plan, many options were issued during the five years of 2004 to 2008. Plaintiff became a shareholder in November 2008. Does plaintiff have standing to challenge options issued before he became a shareholder or only those issued thereafter? See Desimone v. Barrows, 924 A.2d 908 (Del. Ch. 2007) ("continuing wrong doctrine does not bestow standing upon a stockholder to challenge transactions occurring before he bought his stock simply because they are similar or related to transactions or other conduct that occurred later").

D. *SECURITY FOR EXPENSES*

Donner Management Co. v. Schaffer
139 Cal. App. 4th 615, 43 Cal. Rptr. 3d 140 (2006)

HALLER, Acting P.J.: . . . Schaffer was a director and the chief executive officer of Asia Web [Holdings, Inc.]. On March 13, 2002, Donner filed a derivative shareholder complaint against Schaffer and nominal defendant Asia Web, alleging Schaffer had breached his fiduciary duty and engaged in conversion, and requesting an accounting. On April 22, 2002, Asia Web filed a motion requesting that Donner post a bond ["for reasonable expenses, including attorneys' fees"] pursuant to [Cal. Corp. Code] section 800, subdivision (c).[82] To support the bond motion, Asia Web submitted a declaration from the current chairman of its board of directors explaining that Schaffer had resigned from the corporation, and detailing reasons why the lawsuit was detrimental to the corporation.

To avoid a discovery stay pending litigation of the bond motion, Donner voluntarily deposited a $50,000 cashier's check as security to satisfy the bond request, as allowed under section 800, subdivision (e). . . .

Thereafter, the parties conducted discovery and the matter was set for trial. Meanwhile, in February or March 2004, Asia Web appointed a special litigation committee, composed of a newly elected board of directors, to investigate whether the lawsuit was of benefit to the corporation. After interviewing various parties to the litigation and examining documents, on April 12, 2004, the special litigation committee notified Donner of its conclusion that based on its business judgment it was not in the best interests of the company to continue the litigation. To reach this conclusion, the special litigation committee considered "a wide range of issues, independent of the merits of the litigation, including but not limited to the impact of this litigation on the time and resources of [company] personnel, its impact on future operations and fundraising efforts. . . ."

Accordingly, on May 28, 2004, Donner moved to dismiss the action without prejudice, based on its recognition that a "special litigation committee defense" in favor of the defendants had been established which barred the action. In moving to dismiss the action, Donner advised the court that it was not necessary to hold a full evidentiary hearing on the matter because Donner had concluded the

---

82. In an effort to discourage strike suits, beginning in the mid-1940s statutes requiring security for expenses were enacted in nearly 20 states, although about three-quarters have been repealed since the mid-1980s. — ED.

members of the special litigation committee were properly independent and the committee had performed an adequate investigation, thus establishing the special litigation committee defense.

Schaeffer filed a motion for attorney fees and costs based on the $50,000 security posted by Donner under section 800. The court ruled that Schaffer was the prevailing party entitled to attorney fees. To support its ruling, the court found that the special litigation committee defense was more than a procedural defense; Schaffer was successful in "mak[ing] the case go away"; and there was no recovery on the complaint. . . .

A. Attorney Fees Under Section 800

. . . Attorney fees may not be awarded absent statutory authorization or contractual agreement. (Code Civ. Proc., §1021; Santisas v. Goodin (1998) 17 Cal. 4th 599, 607, fn. 4, 71 Cal. Rptr. 2d 830, 951 P.2d 399.) Section 800 provides a statutory basis for attorney fees in shareholder derivative lawsuits. (See Brusso v. Running Springs Country Club, Inc. (1991) 228 Cal. App. 3d 92, 101, 278 Cal. Rptr. 758 (*Brusso*).)

To compel a plaintiff-shareholder in a derivative lawsuit to furnish a bond securing payment of the defendant's attorney fees, section 800 requires that the defendant "establish[ ] a probability," based on affidavits or oral testimony, (1) "[t]hat there is *no reasonable possibility that the prosecution* of the cause of action alleged in the complaint against the moving party *will benefit the corporation or its shareholders*[83][,] [or] (2) [t]hat the [defendant] moving party, if other than the corporation, did not participate in the transaction complained of in any capacity."[84] (§800, subds. (c)(2), (d), italics added.) If the defendant does not satisfy one of the section 800 grounds for a bond and accordingly no bond or other security is posted, the defendant will not be entitled to section 800 attorney fees even if he or she prevails at the end of the litigation.[85] (Alcott v. M.E.V. Corp. (1987) 193 Cal. App. 3d 797, 799, 238 Cal. Rptr. 520; Friedman, Cal. Practice Guide: Corporations, supra, ¶6.659.1, pp. 6-138.15 to 1-138.16.) On the other hand, if the defendant does establish one of the section 800 grounds, the court fixes the amount of the bond (not to exceed $50,000) "to be furnished by the plaintiff for reasonable expenses, including attorneys' fees, which may be incurred by the moving party and the corporation in connection with the action, including expenses for which the corporation may become liable pursuant to Section 317."[86] (§800, subd. (d).)

To prevent collateral estoppel effect, section 800, subdivision (d) provides that a court's ruling granting or denying the motion for security "shall not be a

83. Pa. Bus. Corp. Law §1782(c) (1990) allows the court to deny or limit the posting of security if plaintiff shows "that the requirement of full or partial security would impose undue hardship on plaintiffs and serious injustice would result."—Ed.

84. See Melancon v. Superior Court, 42 Cal. 2d 698, 268 P.2d 1050 (1954) (plaintiff not entitled to discovery prior to disposition of motion for security).

Query: May plaintiff be ordered to pay the expenses of a defendant if the court finds that defendant was sued "without reasonable cause"? See Winner v. Cataldo, 559 So. 2d 696 (Fla. App. 1990).—Ed.

85. Thus, a successful defendant will not be entitled to attorneys' fees from plaintiff even if it is clear that the suit was brought without reasonable cause. See Isensee v. Long Island Motion Picture Co., 184 Misc. 625, 54 N.Y.S.2d 556 (S. Ct. 1945); Shapiro v. Magaziner, 418 Pa. 278, 210 A.2d 890 (1965).—Ed.

86. This refers to the possibility that the corporation may be required to indemnify certain defendants for their expenses, including attorneys' fees, in the derivative suit. See page 920 infra.—Ed.

determination of any issue in the action or of the merits thereof." (See 3 Witkin, Cal. Procedure: Actions, supra, §337, p. 431.) If a defendant makes a successful motion under section 800 requiring the plaintiff to post a bond as security for attorney fees, and the plaintiff fails to post the bond, the trial court must dismiss the action. (§800, subd. (d); see *Brusso*, supra, 228 Cal. App. 3d at p. 105, 278 Cal. Rptr. 758.)

A plaintiff in a derivative lawsuit has the option of "avoid[ing] the inconvenience and delay of the motion proceeding by voluntarily posting a bond in the aggregate amount of $50,000, either before or after a motion [for security] is made. This will be deemed full compliance, and any pending motion must be dismissed." (3 Witkin, Cal. Procedure: Actions, supra, §338, p. 432; §800, subds. (e), (f).) . . .

Donner argues that no fees should be awarded unless there has been compliance with section 800's provision that a mandatory bond requires a showing of no reasonable possibility of benefit to the corporation from the action. Donner contends that because plaintiffs voluntarily posted the security in this case, this showing has not been made. . . .

In assessing whether there is no reasonable possibility the action will benefit the corporation, the court "must evaluate the possible defenses which the plaintiffs would have to overcome before they could prevail at trial." (2 Ballantine & Sterling, Cal. Corporation Laws, supra, §293.02, p. 14-23.) One such potential defense is the "'business judgment rule'" defense (Burt v. Irvine Co. (1965) 237 Cal. App. 2d 828, 869, 47 Cal. Rptr. 392; Marble v. Latchford Glass Co. (1962) 205 Cal. App. 2d 171, 175-176, 22 Cal. Rptr. 789), which includes the special litigation committee defense based on the committee's decision that pursuit of the lawsuit is not in the best interests of the company (Finley v. Superior Court (2000) 80 Cal. App. 4th 1152, 1157-1163, 96 Cal. Rptr. 2d 128; Desaigoudar v. Meyercord, supra, 108 Cal. App. 4th at pp. 186-187, 133 Cal. Rptr. 2d 408). To determine whether a defense based on a special litigation committee's decision should prevail, the court does not evaluate the merits of the lawsuit, but only considers whether the committee members acted independently and made an adequate investigation of the controversy. (*Desaigoudar*, supra, at pp. 185, 188, 133 Cal. Rptr. 2d 408.) If the court finds a disinterested committee made a good faith, reasonable inquiry before reaching its decision that the lawsuit should not be prosecuted, the committee's decision provides a complete defense to the derivative lawsuit. . . . If a bond hearing had been held and the court had been persuaded at that time that it was likely a special litigation committee defense would be successful, the court would have been compelled to find there was no reasonable possibility the litigation would benefit the corporation. Assuming arguendo a "no benefit" finding was required, the requirement was effectively satisfied in conjunction with the dismissal without prejudice based on the establishment of the special litigation committee defense.

Donner further argues that as a matter of policy an award of fees under section 800 should require a showing the plaintiff's lawsuit was frivolous. Donner posits that if this requirement is not imposed, there will be a chilling effect on shareholder derivative lawsuits because shareholders will know attorney fees liability will be incurred in any case in which they voluntarily provide security and a special litigation committee thereafter ascertains the lawsuit should not be pursued for business reasons, even if the allegations in the complaint are meritorious.

Donner is essentially asking us to rewrite the section 800 bond requirements. Section 800 evinces a legislative determination that plaintiffs-shareholders in a derivative action should bear the risk of attorney fees liability if there is no reasonable possibility the lawsuit would benefit the corporation. There is no frivolousness requirement for attorney fees recovery expressly or implicitly set forth in section 800. Donner's request for the insertion of a frivolousness standard is a policy matter for the Legislature, not the courts.

B. Prevailing Party Determination After Dismissal Without Prejudice

Section 800 does not define the circumstances under which the defendant may obtain attorney fees on a bond or other security furnished by the plaintiff. Consistent with the intent of section 800 and other legislative schemes authorizing attorney fees, the courts and commentators have inferred that a defendant may enforce a security posted under section 800 if he or she is determined to be the prevailing party. . . . Because section 800 does not define prevailing party, we must construe the meaning of the term for purposes of a section 800 attorney fees award after a dismissal without prejudice without the benefit of any express statement of legislative intent.

Donner contends that because this case involves a dismissal without prejudice that did not reflect on the merits of the allegations in the complaint, the trial court could not properly characterize Schaffer as a prevailing party. . . .

In the absence of legislative direction in the attorney fees statute, the courts have concluded that a rigid definition of prevailing party should not be used. (*Gilbert*, [v. National Enquirer Inc.], supra, 55 Cal. App. 4th at p. 1277, 64 Cal. Rptr. 2d 659.) Rather, prevailing party status should be determined by the trial court based on an evaluation of whether a party prevailed " 'on a practical level,' " and the trial court's decision should be affirmed on appeal absent an abuse of discretion. . . .

Under the facts of this case, the trial court reasonably exercised its discretion to find that Schaffer was the prevailing party. Donner's dismissal of the complaint was not truly voluntary; rather, it was compelled by the special litigation committee's decision that it was not in the best interests of the corporation to continue the lawsuit. Even though the special litigation committee's decision did not establish that the *allegations in the complaint* lacked merit, it did establish that the *lawsuit itself* could not be pursued because of the peculiar nature of the business judgment rule/special litigation committee defense which blocks litigation that is properly determined not to be in the best interests of the company. Thus, as a practical matter, the special committee's decision ended the litigation in favor of Schaffer and against plaintiffs. Donner has not proffered any persuasive argument as to why, under the circumstances of this case, the trial court was necessarily required to also consider the underlying merits of the allegations in the complaint. We conclude the trial court did not abuse its discretion in finding that Schaffer prevailed because the lawsuit ended based on the existence of a complete defense, and with no recovery obtained by Donner on behalf of the corporation. . . .

The order is affirmed. . . .

---

1. *Statute:*

New Jersey Business Corporation Act (1973)

Sec. 3-6. *Provisions relating to actions by shareholders.* . . . (2) In any action hereafter instituted in the right of any domestic or foreign corporation by the holder or holders of shares of such corporation or of voting trust certificates therefor, the court having jurisdiction, upon final judgment and a finding that the action was brought without reasonable cause, may require the plaintiff or plaintiffs to pay to the parties named as defendant the reasonable expenses, including fees of attorneys, incurred by them in the defense of such action.[87]

(3) In any action now pending or hereafter instituted or maintained in the right of any such corporation by the holder or holders of record of less than 5% of the outstanding shares of any class or series of such corporation or of voting trust certificates therefor, unless the shares or voting trust certificates so held have a market value in excess of $25,000.00, the corporation in whose right such action is brought shall be entitled at any time before final judgment to require the plaintiff or plaintiffs to give security for the reasonable expenses, including fees of attorneys, that may be incurred by it in connection with such action or may be incurred by other parties named as defendant for which it may become legally liable. Market value shall be determined as of the date that the plaintiff institutes the action or, in the case of an intervenor, as of the date that he becomes a party to the action. The amount of such security may from time to time be increased or decreased, in the discretion of the court, upon showing that the security provided

---

87. RMBCA §7.46(2) (1990) is similar to this paragraph. Based on the view among commentators that delaying the imposition of sanctions until the final disposition of the case undercuts their deterrent value, ALI, Principles of Corporate Governance §7.04(d) (1994) permits the court to "award applicable costs, including reasonable attorney's fees and expenses, against a party, or a party's counsel . . . at any time, if the court finds that any specific cause of action was asserted, or any motion, defense, pleading, request for discovery, or other action was made, in bad faith or without reasonable cause."

Query: May the court find "that the action was brought without reasonable cause" because it was dismissed for plaintiff's failure to comply with "exhaustion of internal remedies" requirements? See Callahan v. Sun Lakes Homeowners' Ass'n, 134 Ariz. App. 332, 656 P.2d 621 (1982).

Securities Exchange Act of 1934 §18, in creating a cause of action against persons making false or misleading statements in documents filed pursuant to the Act, in favor of those who rely to their detriment, further provides: "In any such suit the court may, in its discretion, require an undertaking for the payment of the costs of such suit, and assess reasonable costs, including reasonable attorneys' fees, against either party litigant."

Fed. R. Civ. P. 11 (1983) requires plaintiff's attorney to certify

that to the best of his knowledge, information, and belief formed after reasonable inquiry it is well grounded in fact and is warranted by existing law or a good faith argument for the extension, modification, or reversal of existing law, and that it is not interposed for any improper purpose, such as to harass or to cause unnecessary delay or needless increase in the cost of litigation. If a pleading, motion, or other paper is . . . signed in violation of this rule, the court, upon motion or upon its own initiative, shall impose upon the person who signed it, a represented party, or both, an appropriate sanction, which may include an order to pay to the other party or parties the amount of the reasonable expenses incurred because of the filing of the pleading, motion, or other paper, including a reasonable attorney's fee.

For the view that "assessments against *attorneys* become the principal device" for deterring abusive derivative suits, see Alfred F. Conard, Winnowing Derivative Suits Through Attorneys' Fees, 47 Law & Contemp. Probs. 269 (1984). — ED.

has or may become inadequate or is excessive. The corporation shall have recourse to such security in such amount as the court having jurisdiction shall determine upon the termination of such action.[88]

---

2. *Eluding coverage.*

Although experience shows that a derivative action will generally be abandoned if an order requiring the posting of security is entered, empirical studies have also found that plaintiffs may avoid the application of such statutes by a variety of means. See Note, Security for Expenses in Shareholders' Derivative Suits: 23 Years' Experience, 4 Colum. J.L. & Soc. Probs. 50 (1968). Most typically, plaintiffs avoid state security statutes by pleading a federal cause of action.[89] Alternatively, plaintiffs may seek inspection of the corporation's stock book in order to urge other shareholders to join in the suit and thereby satisfy the five percent threshold employed by many statutes to exempt plaintiffs with significant shareholdings from the application of the statute. According to some observers, the potential adverse publicity thereby generated and the resulting complication of the proxy solicitation process has resulted in decisions by some sophisticated corporations not to seek security.

2 ALI, Principles of Corporate Governance 90-91 (1994).

3. *Problems.* (a) Plaintiff shareholder owns more than the required percentage of shares at the time a derivative suit is commenced. What result on defendant corporation's motion for security if, before judgment, plaintiff's percentage falls below the statutory minimum because:

(1) Plaintiff sells some of his shares? See Amdur v. Meyer, 36 Misc. 2d 433, 233 N.Y.S.2d 15 (S. Ct. 1962), *aff'd,* 17 App. Div. 2d 571, 237 N.Y.S.2d 352, *aff'd,* 13 N.Y.2d 1089, 196 N.E.2d 63, 246 N.Y.S.2d 408 (1963).

(2) Some of plaintiff's shares are redeemable and corporation redeems the shares? Of what significance, if any, is the fact that the suit sought to compel the corporation to redeem the shares? See Marks v. Seedman, 309 F. Supp. 332 (S.D.N.Y. 1969).

(3) Corporation issues more shares like plaintiff's and plaintiff declines to exercise his option to purchase a proportionate amount? Of what significance, if

---

88. The early version of the Model Act was nearly identical to the New Jersey statute, except that at the end of the second paragraph, it added the phrase "whether or not the court finds the action was brought without reasonable cause." (The present N.D. Bus. Corp. Act §86 (1997) contains this phrase.) The 1984 revision of the Model Act eliminated the second paragraph.

N.Y. Bus. Corp. Law §627 (1965) is similar to the second paragraph of the New Jersey statute — except that in the first sentence, the amount is $50,000 and there are no comparable second or fourth sentences.

Colo. Corp. Code §107-402 (1993) is also similar to both paragraphs of the New Jersey statute — except that both paragraphs exclude fees of attorneys and the final phrase of the second paragraph is "if the court finds the action was commenced without reasonable cause." — ED.

89. In diversity cases, if the forum state has a security statute, federal courts apply it because, under the doctrine of Erie R.R. v. Tompkins, these statutes are substantive. Cohen v. Beneficial Ind. Loan Corp., 337 U.S. 541 (1949). But the federal courts have held that Congress did not intend to subject claims arising under the Securities Exchange Act of 1934 to state security-for-expense statutes, McClure v. Borne Chem. Co., 292 F.2d 824 (3d Cir. 1961) (§10(b)); Borak v. J. I. Case Co., 317 F.2d 838 (7th Cir. 1963), *aff'd,* 377 U.S. 426 (1964) (§14); but compare §18, footnote 87 supra. However, if the federal court derivative suit is based on federal law and also joins a state law claim, the forum state security-for-expenses statute is applicable to the latter claim, whether based on pendent jurisdiction or diversity. See Haberman v. Tobin, 480 F. Supp. 425 (S.D.N.Y. 1979). — ED.

any, is the fact that the suit challenged the purpose for issuance of the new shares? See Roach v. Franchises Int'l, Inc., 32 App. Div. 2d 247, 300 N.Y.S.2d 630 (1969).

(b) Plaintiff shareholder owns more than the required market value of shares at the time a derivative suit is commenced.

(1) What result if, at the time of defendant corporation's motion for security, the market value of the shares has fallen below the required amount? See Sorin v. Shahmoon Industries, Inc., 30 Misc. 2d 408, 22 N.Y.S.2d 760 (S. Ct. 1961).

(2) What result if, at the time of the wrong complained of, the value of the shares is less than the required amount because of (i) market fluctuation, (ii) the fact that plaintiff shareholder purchased more shares before filing suit? See id.

(c) Plaintiff shareholder moves to vacate a security order on the ground that, subsequent to the commencement of his derivative suit, he has purchased a sufficient number of shares to meet the statutory minimum. What result? See Haberman v. Tobin, 626 F.2d 1101 (2d Cir. 1980).

(d) Plaintiff shareholder owns less than the required percentage of shares at the time a derivative suit is commenced, but the percentage is satisfied when the shares of intervenor are added. After trial, judgment is rendered for defendant. Only plaintiff appeals. What result on defendant corporation's motion for security? See Malott v. Randall, 11 Wash. App. 433, 523 P.2d 439 (1974).

E. *DEFENDING AGAINST DERIVATIVE SUITS*

1. CONFLICTING INTERESTS OF DEFENDANTS

Otis & Co. v. Pennsylvania R.R.
57 F. Supp. 680 (E.D. Pa. 1944), *aff'd*, 155 F.2d 522 (3d Cir. 1946)

KALODNER, J.: In this stockholders' suit plaintiff now moves to strike the answers of the corporate defendants . . . and to remove counsel.

The important issue raised by the motion is whether, in a stockholders' secondary (derivative) action against the officers and directors of a corporation for breach of duty, the corporation, joined as a party defendant, may file an answer to the complaint setting forth affirmative defenses.

. . . Plaintiff, Otis & Co., an investment banking house, and owner of 60 shares out of a total of 17,400,000 shares of the stock of the Pennsylvania Railroad Company, instituted this action to recover $1,000,000 from certain, but not all, of the directors and officers of the Pennsylvania Railroad Company, hereafter referred to as P.R.R., and the Pennsylvania, Ohio & Detroit Railroad Company, hereafter referred to as P.O.&D.; the two corporations were also joined as defendants, relief being asked in their favor. It is alleged in the complaint that the defendant P.R.R. owned all of the capital stock of the defendant P.O.&D. . . . It is alleged that in June, 1943, defendant Martin W. Clement, president of P.R.R., and defendant George Pabst, Jr., vice-president of P.R.R. and president of P.O.&D., entered into negotiations with Kuhn, Loeb & Co. with a view to P.O.&D. selling to the latter a new bond issue. . . . Thereafter, P.O.&D. entered into a contract with Kuhn, Loeb & Co. to sell the bonds at par subject to approval by the Interstate Commerce Commission. . . .

The gist of the complaint is that the transaction was entirely private, that a half million dollars was lost in failing to "shop around," and another half million lost in failing to put the new issue to competitive bidding; therefore, it is alleged, the "best obtainable price" was not obtained. It is also asserted that certain of the directors and officers were influenced because of their position as directors and officers of several companies which had made agreements with Kuhn, Loeb & Co. to purchase from the latter part of the bonds.

It is contended in support of plaintiff's motion that the corporations are made defendants merely for a technical reason, that is, the refusal on their part to prosecute the alleged cause of action against the individual defendants; that in substance, the corporations are the real plaintiffs; that actually the interests of P.R.R. and P.O.&D. are allied with the plaintiff's, in view of the fact that any money recovery will go to the corporations and not to plaintiff. Accordingly it is urged that the defendant corporations ought not to be permitted to file answers designed to defeat plaintiff's claims, and that the proper conduct is to remain neutral or aid plaintiff.

Despite the great familiarity of the courts with stockholders' suits, the problem raised by the instant motion is one on which there are few satisfactory cases, and little other helpful authority. Exceptional difficulty is generated by the breakdown of the legal entity theory of corporate existence. The complaint of plaintiff in this motion is understandable, for the individual defendants are the very persons charged with carrying on the everyday affairs of these corporations, and upon whom devolves the duty of determining the corporations' stand in this case. Nevertheless, it is possible in an equity court to preserve to a great degree the entity fiction of corporate existence in a case of this sort.

The clearest example of a stockholders' secondary action against the corporate directors in which the corporation ought not to be permitted to defend the individual defendants may be found in the case of Meyers v. Smith, 190 Minn. 157, 251 N.W. 20 (1933). There the minority stockholder sued, on behalf of a corporation, to recover money claimed to have been misappropriated by certain of its directors out of corporate funds. The court properly struck an answer of the corporation containing affirmative defenses to the charges against the officers. . . .

On the other hand, a clear case in which the corporation ought to be permitted to file an answer is Godley v. Crandall & Godley Co., 181 App. Div. 75, 168 N.Y.S. 251 (1917), where it appears that an attempt had been made to procure a receiver of the corporate assets. . . .

A hard and fast rule one way or the other, it seems to me, is undesirable in this type of case, and it would be especially inappropriate for a court of equity to . . . [proceed] without a thorough consideration of the equitable elements involved in the cases. . . . [T]he all-important question when the corporation seeks to defend is that of the nature of the complaint and the interest of the corporation in the controversy. When fraud is the complaint against the directors, the essence of the corporation's interest is, and ought to be, in having the truth of the charges determined and in recovering all funds of which it was deprived. . . . The corporation has no reason, then, to make affirmative defenses, except perhaps in a limited capacity. See Groel v. United Electric Co. of N.J., 70 N.J. Eq. 616, 61 A. 1061, 1064, 1065 (1905). Similarly, when the cause of action is such as to endanger rather than advance corporate interests, an answer setting forth affirmative defenses seems proper. . . .

Coming now to the case at bar . . . [plaintiff] does not charge fraud or misappropriation of corporate assets. Although it is alleged certain of the individual defendants were also directors of institutions interested in purchasing the bonds from Kuhn, Loeb & Co., it was expressly stated by plaintiff's counsel during the oral argument that there was no assertion that these directors had any personal interest in floating the bond issue through Kuhn, Loeb & Co.

The chief complaint, in summary, is the fact that the new bond issue was privately negotiated and investment banking houses, other than Kuhn, Loeb & Co., were not given the opportunity of a "look-in" on either preliminary consideration of the issue or its final flotation. However, the manner in which the defendant corporations floated the bond issue has been in use by the railroads almost since "Iron Horse" days — it is apparently a matter of corporate policy pursued by railroads generally.

It may be noted that the entire matter of the propriety of the bond issue here involved was heard by the Interstate Commerce Commission. . . . [and] was widely advertised and published throughout the United States.

The Commission gave full consideration to bids made by Halsey, Stuart & Co., and by Otis & Co., the instant plaintiff; likewise, the Commission heard Otis & Co., as intervener in that action, on the issue of the propriety of the private sale and the appropriateness of competitive bidding. . . .

Although the Commission has since required competitive bidding on railroad bond issues . . . the fact is that the bond issue here was approved and the corporate policy at that time found to be in accordance with custom and the Interstate Commerce Commission rules.

There having been an attack on a long established corporate policy, recognized and approved by the Interstate Commerce Commission, reflecting on the good faith of the administration and affecting the good will of the corporate defendants, it seems to me it is proper that the corporations here involved be permitted to answer the complaint. . . . They have a definite stake in the controversy; good will is of importance to corporations existing in an industry where money frequently is borrowed on a large scale. It has been suggested that the damage is done when the complaint is filed . . . and that vindication would come with victory by the individual defendants. . . . But the corporate policy and corporate good will are of vital economic interest to the corporations, and they should be given the opportunity to defend. . . .

It must be kept in mind, too, that this is a stockholders' secondary action and that inherent in such an action is the corporations' prior failure to enforce an alleged right. The stockholders' action is critical of the corporations' management and the corporations should have a right to answer, subject to the exceptions hereinbefore mentioned where fraud of the directors or management is the essence of the stockholders' action. A realistic view must take into consideration that a secondary action brought by even one stockholder is regarded by law as being a class action — taken by or on behalf of all stockholders. Thus we have an arraignment of the stockholders on one side and management on the other, with the issue being the charges of mismanagement. To peremptorily shut the door on management and deny it its day in court might, in many instances, have a destructive effect on the interest of the stockholders. . . .

For the reasons stated the plaintiff's motion . . . is denied.

Problems concerning who may raise various defenses. (a) Plaintiff, a shareholder in a fairly small corporation, institutes a derivative suit charging that defendant, one of the corporation's major suppliers, has "delivered defective goods." Should the corporation be permitted to raise the following defenses: (1) plaintiff failed to make a demand on the board of directors; (2) plaintiff failed to make a demand on the shareholder body; (3) plaintiff was not a shareholder at the time of the alleged wrong; (4) plaintiff is barred by laches or estopped by plaintiff's own prior acquiescence in the transaction; (5) the corporation was not properly served; (6) defendant was not properly served; (7) venue is improper; (8) the suit is barred by the statute of limitations; (9) the goods were not defective? Should defendant be permitted to raise these defenses? See generally Note, 66 Harv. L. Rev. 342 (1952).

In Kaplan v. Peat, Marwick, Mitchell & Co., 540 A.2d 726 (Del. 1988), a shareholder brought a derivative suit against Chase Manhattan Bank's accounting firm, alleging that its negligent auditing practices contributed to several hundred million dollars of corporate losses. The court held that the defendant accounting firm could raise the defense that plaintiff had failed to make a demand on the corporation: "The requirement of pre-suit demand assures that the directors, as managers of the corporation, will have the opportunity to address claims asserted on the corporation's behalf. An expansive standing rule furthers this goal by increasing the class of defendants available to raise the demand issue, and as such, assures that the decision as to whether to proceed with the litigation is made by the appropriate party, i.e., the directors."

(b) After an unsuccessful demand on the board of directors and the shareholders, plaintiff, a shareholder in a large public corporation, institutes a derivative suit charging that defendant, a longtime director and officer of the corporation, has "fraudulently embezzled $500,000 of corporate funds." Should defendant be permitted to raise the following defenses: (1) the decision of the board not to sue ends the suit; (2) the shareholder vote ends the suit; (3) defendant is a key corporate manager and proceeding with this suit, irrespective of its outcome, will result in loss of defendant's services with consequent prejudice to the corporation? Should the corporation be permitted to raise these defenses? See George T. Washington, Stockholders' Derivative Suits: The Company's Role, and a Suggestion, 25 Cornell L.Q. 361 (1940).

2. CONFLICTING INTERESTS OF DEFENDANTS' COUNSEL

Cannon v. U.S. Acoustics Corp.
398 F. Supp. 209 (E.D. Ill. 1975), *aff'd in part*, 532 F.2d 1178 (7th Cir. 1976)

MARSHALL, J.: [Plaintiffs brought a derivative suit on behalf of a corporation (Acoustics) and its wholly owned subsidiary (Perlite) against four officer-directors of the two corporations. The same lawyers filed appearances on behalf of the corporations and the individual defendants. Plaintiffs moved to strike the appearance of the lawyers on behalf of the corporations.] . . .

. . . A derivative suit is, in legal effect, a suit brought by the corporation, but conducted by the shareholders. The corporation, although formally aligned as a defendant for historical reasons, is in actuality a plaintiff. . . . The stockholder is only a nominal plaintiff. . . .

The preceding paragraph delineates the anomalous position of the corporation; it is both a defendant and a plaintiff. An examination of plaintiffs' complaint amply reveals this position. Count 1 alleges that beginning in 1968 and continuing to the present, the individual defendants committed numerous violations of Rule 10b-5: illegal stock options were allegedly granted, stock was issued and purchased upon false representations that the stock was for services, rent, and other expenses, stock was issued for little or no consideration, corporate opportunities were usurped, illegal profits were retained by certain officers and directors, and illegal and excessive compensation was paid to Stedman.

The remaining derivative counts allege the same misconduct but seek recovery under Section 16(b) of the Securities Exchange Act of 1934 and the common law of Florida and Illinois.

Even a cursory examination of the foregoing allegations demonstrates that should they be established at trial, Acoustics and Perlite will benefit substantially. For this reason plaintiffs argue that Mone, Gareis, and the firm of Baker & McKenzie cannot represent the alleged wrongdoers and the ultimate beneficiaries of any judgment that might be obtained.

Defendants' position is that although there is a theoretical conflict of interest, no real conflict exists. They argue that the corporations are really inactive participants in the lawsuit, and that should any conflict arise they will withdraw their representation of the individual defendants and continue their representation of the corporations. Defendants further argue that their present position is that all the transactions complained of are legal and should be upheld.

The conduct of attorneys practicing before the court is governed by the American Bar Association's CPR [Code of Professional Responsibility]. General Rules of the District Court for the Northern District of Illinois, Rule 8(a) & (d). Jurisdiction to enforce the CPR exists by reason of the court's regulatory power over the members of its Bar. . . . No code of ethics could establish unalterable rules governing all possible eventualities. Ultimately, therefore, the resolution of these problems rests in the reasoned discretion of the court.

Canon 5 of the CPR addresses the ethics of representing conflicting interests.[9] It provides that a lawyer "Should Exercise Independent Professional Judgment on Behalf of a Client." Ethical consideration (hereinafter EC) . . . 5-18 provides:

> A lawyer employed or retained by a corporation or similar entity owes his allegiance to the entity and not to a stockholder, director, officer, employee, representative, or other person connected with the entity. In advising the entity, a lawyer should keep paramount its interests and his professional judgment should not be influenced by the personal desires of any person or organization. Occasionally a lawyer for an entity is requested by a stockholder, director, officer, employee, representative, or other person connected with the entity to represent him in an individual capacity; in

---

9. The CPR is divided into "three separate but interrelated parts: Canons, Ethical Considerations, and Disciplinary Rules." The Canons are axiomatic norms embodying in general terms the standards of professional conduct which the legal system and the public expect from lawyers. From these Canons, the Ethical Considerations and Disciplinary Rules are drawn.

The Ethical Considerations are "objectives toward which every member of the legal profession should strive." Moreover, they provide guidance for many specific situations which may confront a lawyer.

The Disciplinary Rules are mandatory. They are minimum levels of conduct, the violation of which subjects the lawyer to disciplinary proceedings. CPR, "Preliminary Statement," February 20, 1970.

such case the lawyer may serve the individual only if the lawyer is convinced that differing interests are not present.

Admittedly the focus of this consideration is on the problem of corporate counsel representing corporate officials when the corporation is not also a party litigant. But its import is clear. The interest of the corporate client is paramount and should not be influenced by any interest of the individual corporate officials.

Although EC5-18 is persuasive authority for plaintiffs' position, EC5-15 is even more so:

> If a lawyer is requested to undertake or to continue representation of multiple clients having potentially differing interests, he must weigh carefully the possibility that his judgment may be impaired or his loyalty divided if he accepts or continues the employment. He should resolve all doubts against the propriety of the representation. A lawyer should never represent in litigation multiple clients with differing interests; and there are few situations in which he would be justified in representing in litigation multiple clients with potentially differing interests. If a lawyer accepted such employment and the interests did become actually differing, he would have to withdraw from employment with likelihood of resulting hardship to the client; and for this reason it is preferable that he refuse the employment initially.

Taken together, these two ethical considerations convincingly establish that in a derivative suit the better course is for the corporation to be represented by independent counsel from the outset, even though counsel believes in good faith that no conflict of interest exists.[10]

The exact question presented by the plaintiffs' motion was considered by the influential association of the Bar of New York Committee on Professional Ethics, in Opinion 842. The Committee is in full agreement that if the corporation takes an active role in the litigation, independent counsel must be obtained. If the corporation's role is passive, a majority of the committee was still of the opinion that, "a conflict of interests is inherent in any [derivative] action wherever relief is sought on behalf of the corporation against the individual director-officer defendants, and in such cases Canon 6 [presently Canon 5, EC5-14 nn.6 & 18] precludes one firm from representing both the corporation and the individual director-officer defendants except in unusual circumstances stemming from particular facts in a given case."

In addition to the conflict of interest problem there is also the proscription of Canon 4 that a "Lawyer Should Preserve the Confidences and Secrets of a Client." The question is whether a law firm might jeopardize the confidences or secrets of one defendant while representing the other. In the case of individuals this is a serious problem. In a derivative suit, however, the question is likely to be of less moment since the secrets and confidences of the corporate client are probably accessible to the director-officer clients. And while this conflict is less troubling than the conflict of interest difficulties, see Comment, *Independent Representation*

---

10. ... EC 5-16 provides that in some circumstances multiple representation may be permissible if both clients are fully informed of potential conflict and the parties consent to the representation. This consent rationale seems peculiarly inapplicable to the derivative suit, because the corporation must consent through the directors, who, as in the present case, are the individual defendants. See Opinion 842, Association of the Bar of the City of New York Committee on Professional Ethics (Jan. 4, 1960), 15 Record N.Y.C.B.A. 80 (1960).

for Corporate Defendants in Derivative Suits, 74 Yale L.J. 524, 526-27 (1965) . . . nevertheless, it is one more reason to examine dual representation with caution.

The Canons and Ethical Considerations are aspirational;[13] consequently they provide only guidance. Thus, while the CPR supports plaintiffs' position a study of the relevant case law is necessary.

Although there is not a wealth of cases dealing with the problem of dual representation in derivative shareholder's suits, the position of the federal courts has developed along two lines. The older cases have refused to disqualify counsel while the more recent trend is to require the corporation to obtain independent counsel. . . .

The leading lower court decision requiring selection of independent counsel is Lewis v. Shaffer Stores Co., 218 F. Supp. 238 (S.D.N.Y. 1963). There, plaintiff stockholder filed a derivative action alleging many of the same transgressions as are pleaded in the present action. One firm entered an appearance and filed an answer on behalf of the directors and the corporate defendant. Plaintiffs filed a timely motion to disqualify the firm from representing the corporation, asking that it be represented by truly independent counsel who would answer the complaint to the end that plaintiffs be invited to prove their case for the benefit of the corporation. The court held:

> The interests of the officer, director, and majority stockholder defendants in this action are clearly adverse, on the face of the complaint, to the interests of the stockholders . . . other than the defendants. I have no doubt that . . . [the law firm] believe[s] in good faith that there is no merit to this action. Plaintiff, of course, vigorously contends to the contrary. The court cannot and should not attempt to pass upon the merits at this stage. Under all the circumstances, including the nature of the charges, and the vigor with which they are apparently being pressed and defended, I believe that it would be wise for the corporation to retain independent counsel, who have no previous connection with the corporation, to advise it as to the position it should take in this controversy. See Garlen v. Green Mansions, Inc., 9 A.D.2d 760, 193 N.Y.S.2d 116 (1st Dept. 1959), Marco v. Dulles, supra, 218 F. Supp. at 239-40.

The *Lewis* approach is the most advisable. . . . Nevertheless, defendants' counsel argue there is no present conflict and should one arise they will withdraw their representation of the individual defendants and represent only the corporations. There are a number of problems with this solution. First, the complaint on its face establishes a conflict that cannot be ignored despite counsel's good faith representations. Second, counsel overlooks the hardship on the court and the parties if in the middle of this litigation new counsel must be obtained because a conflict arises. Lastly, although counsel offers to withdraw its representation of the individual defendants and remain counsel for the corporations if a conflict should arise, the appropriate course . . . is for the corporation to retain independent counsel. Under this procedure, once counsel has examined the evidence, a decision can be made regarding the role the corporation will play in the litigation. This decision will be made without the possibility of any influence emanating from the representation of the individual defendants, and will also eliminate the potential problem of confidences and secrets reposed by the individual defendants being used adverse

---

13. But see DR 5-105, effective March 1, 1974.

to their interests by former counsel should new counsel have had to have been selected under the approach suggested by defense counsel.[90] This solution, concededly, is not without its disabilities. The corporations' rights to counsel of their choice are infringed and in a closely held corporation, as here, the financial burden is increased. Nevertheless, on balance, the corporations must obtain independent counsel. . . .

Two questions remain. The first is how new counsel should be selected. Plaintiffs urge the court to make the selection because the individual defendants still serve as the board of directors and thus will make the selection unless prevented from doing so. There is no precedent in the reported decisions to support plaintiffs' suggestion. . . .

The defendant corporations may select their own counsel. Certainly new counsel will recognize their duty to represent solely the interests of the corporate entities. And should difficulties arise, the parties or counsel may apply to the court for additional relief.[91]

The final question is whether the corporations' answer should be stricken and new pleadings filed. Although this relief was not specifically requested, it is implied in the motion to strike the appearance of the corporations' counsel. . . . The answer filed on behalf of the corporate defendants will be stricken with leave to new counsel to refile within 20 days of this order. . . .

---

1. In Hausman v. Buckley, 299 F.2d 696 (2d Cir. 1962), plaintiff brought a derivative suit on behalf of Pantepec (a Venezuelan corporation) against its directors (Buckley being the only one before the court) for breach of fiduciary duty and waste. Pantepec sought to dismiss on the ground that, under Venezuelan law, only the shareholder body may bring suit on behalf of the corporation. Plaintiff moved to strike Pantepec's answer, alleging "that Pantepec was deprived of the benefit of independent counsel because its attorneys . . . also represented the adversary defendant Buckley" and that consequently Pantepec's answer

> does not necessarily represent the position which Pantepec might have taken on this issue if it had availed itself of other legal counsel. In support of their argument that Pantepec may have suffered from the "conflicting" interests of counsel, appellants bring to our attention Opinion No. 842, Committee on Professional Ethics, of the Association of the Bar of the City of New York (January 4, 1960). In that Opinion, a majority of the Committee decided that an attorney's representation of both the corporation and adversary defendants in stockholders' derivative actions may be unethical. Putting aside the question as to whether such a ruling by a Committee of a Bar Association would warrant striking an answer and defenses for a violation of ethical standards, we believe that the trial court did not commit error in denying the motion to strike Pantepec's answer and the appearance of its

90. Cf. Schmidt v. Magnetic Head Corp., 101 App. Div. 2d 268, 476 N.Y.S.2d 151 (1984) (counsel who had represented corporation and individual defendants first disqualified from representing corporation and then also disqualified from representing directors because counsel "had access to the corporation's privileged communications which would give individual defendants an undue advantage"). — ED.

91. Accord, Tydings v. Berk Enterprises, 80 Md. App. 634, 565 A.2d 390 (1989); Electro K, Inc. v. Karpeles, 2002 WL 31475421 (Cal. App.). — ED.

attorneys. Appellants' reliance on Opinion 842 is misplaced. That Opinion, as we read it, did not proscribe dual representation in all cases, but stated that the propriety of such conduct "must be determined in the light of the particular facts attending each such case."

Here the corporation was represented by the same attorneys who represented its directors during part of the preliminary stages of the litigation. It was during this period that Pantepec raised the defense which challenged the right of stockholders to sue on its behalf. Was this defense necessarily in the best interest only of the directors, as appellants seem to suggest? We think not. Assuming that the allegations of the complaint may have had some merit, the corporation nevertheless, had a legitimate interest in protecting the right of the stockholders' meeting to bring an action on its behalf, if it were to be brought at all. As we will discuss at greater length in connection with other issues raised by the appeal, under Venezuelan law, enforcement of a corporation's claims depends not merely upon their merit but upon a decision of the stockholders' meeting that they *ought* to be enforced.

This legitimate interest in bringing the action to a halt before the merits of the allegations are considered exists even though we may assume that an adversary defendant, represented by the same counsel, would have a different interest in seeing the litigation ended. Therefore, it is not necessarily true that Pantepec was deprived of the advice of disinterested counsel, and that it would have conducted itself differently if it were represented by another attorney. Under these circumstances, viewing the matter after a judgment has been rendered as we must, we are unable to conclude that denial of the motion to strike the defense was error. . . .

We note, however, that this decision is limited to the facts before us, and should not be construed as voicing disagreement with Opinion 842.

2. In Seifert v. Dumatic Industries, Inc., 413 Pa. 395, 197 A.2d 454 (1964), Globe and Seifert had formed Dumatic; Globe agreed to furnish the capital and raw materials, and Seifert agreed to provide patents for a manufacturing process and to market the finished product. Each had equal representation on Dumatic's board. Seifert brought a derivative suit against Globe alleging that the latter had failed to furnish Dumatic with suitable raw materials and had disclosed trade secrets to Dumatic's competitors. When Dumatic's lawyers appeared for Seifert in the suit, Globe petitioned for their removal. Denied:

> The cases involving conflicts of interest in the derivative suit context relate to the right of corporate counsel to represent the individual *defendants* in a derivative action. These cases do not apply to the situation with which we are confronted. . . .
>
> An allegation that representation by corporate counsel of the suing stockholders in a derivative action will result in a conflict of interest assumes that the corporation itself has an interest which will be affected by such representation.[5] Under the facts presented we are unable to discern any interest of Dumatic which could come into conflict with the position of Seifert in the underlying cause of action. As Dumatic at the outset was a conduit for the pursuit of the business interests of its two fifty percent stockholders, so now it is a conduit through which the pending lawsuits between those stockholders is being carried on. In effect, this suit is an action for breach of contract by Seifert against Globe. Since the contract involved is an incorporation

---

5. We question the standing of Globe to raise the question of conflict of interest. It is only the corporation which would be injured thereby. Of course, the conflict of interest question may be raised by the court sua sponte.

agreement and since the board of directors is deadlocked on the propriety of enforcing that contract, Seifert has been forced to sue derivatively.

In consonance with the broad equitable powers possessed by courts in stockholders' derivative actions, we reject the result which would issue in the instant case were we to assume that a corporate interest always accompanied the corporate form. Instead, for purposes of representation by counsel, we regard the principal lawsuits as simply between Seifert and Globe. . . . [7]

See also Jacuzzi v. Jacuzzi Bros., Inc., 218 Cal. App. 2d 24, 32 Cal. Rptr. 188 (1963) (former counsel and director of corporation not disqualified to represent plaintiff shareholders in derivative suit). Compare National Texture Corp. v. Hymes, 282 N.W.2d 890 (Minn. 1979) (where lawyer represents corporation and advises officer about applying for a patent in his own name, lawyer is disqualified from subsequently representing corporation in dispute over whether corporation or officer owns the patent); Brennan v. Ruffner, 640 So. 2d 143 (Fla. App. 1994) (corporation's counsel, who drafted shareholder agreement that provided for involuntary termination of any of three shareholders by majority vote, "owes no separate duty of diligence and care to an individual shareholder absent special circumstances or an agreement to also represent the shareholder individually").

F. *DISMISSAL, DISCONTINUANCE, AND SETTLEMENT*

Some decisions have permitted a derivative suit to be settled without judicial approval although, unlike court-approved settlements, the former type do not confer res judicata effect against shareholders who were not parties to them. Manufacturers Mutual Fire Ins. Co. v. Hopson, 176 Misc. 2d 220, 25 N.Y.S.2d 502 (S. Ct. 1940), *aff'd*, 288 N.Y. 668, 43 N.E.2d 71 (1942). At present, more than half of the states have followed the lead of Fed. R. Civ. P. 23.1, page 828 supra, in providing, by statute or rule, for court approval of dismissal or compromise of derivative suits and for some notice thereof to other shareholders.

New York Business Corporation Law (1965)

Sec. 626. *Shareholders' derivative action.* . . . (d) Such action shall not be discontinued, compromised or settled, without the approval of the court having jurisdiction of the action. If the court shall determine that the interests of the shareholders or any class or classes thereof will be substantially affected by such discontinuance, compromise, or settlement, the court, in its discretion, may direct that notice, by publication or otherwise, shall be given to the shareholders or class or classes thereof whose interests it determines will be so

---

7. We are unable to discover any facts in the record which would indicate that Globe would be prejudiced by counsel for Seifert also having been counsel for Dumatic, via confidential communications or otherwise. Any information made available to Seifert through his attorney's representation of Dumatic was equally available to Globe through its appointees on the board of directors of Dumatic.

affected;[92] if notice is so directed to be given, the court may determine which one or more of the parties to the action shall bear the expense of giving the same, in such amount as the court shall determine and find to be reasonable in the circumstances, and the amount of such expense shall be awarded as special costs of the action and recoverable in the same manner as statutory taxable costs.

---

1. *Court approval of settlements.* (a) In jurisdictions requiring judicial approval, the settlement of a derivative suit is discretionary with the court. Various courts have informed themselves respecting a proposed settlement by undertaking their own investigation, appointing a special master, seeking the advice of appropriate government regulatory agencies, or even assembling a shareholder meeting in open court. Note, 54 Minn. L. Rev. 978, 1000 (1970). The standard for approval is whether it is in the best interests of the corporation and its shareholders, and the proponents bear the burden of proof. In re General Tire & Rubber Co. Sec. Litig., 726 F.2d 1075 (6th Cir. 1984). Elements that have been considered include: "(1) the probable validity of the claims, (2) the apparent difficulties in enforcing the claims through the courts, (3) the collectibility of any judgment recovered, (4) the delay, expense and trouble of litigation, (5) the amount of the compromise as compared with the amount of and collectibility of a judgment, and (6) the views of the parties involved, pro and con." Polk v. Good, 507 A.2d 531 (Del. 1986). See generally William E. Haudek, The Settlement and Dismissal of Stockholders' Actions—Part II: The Settlement, 23 Sw. L.J. 765 (1969).

(b) To what extent should courts themselves actively participate in settlement proceedings? In Alleghany Corp. v. Kirby, 333 F.2d 327 (2d Cir. 1964), the court affirmed the denial of a collateral attack on the prior settlement of a derivative suit, brought in behalf of Alleghany, against former Alleghany directors. Those attacking the settlement contended that the defendants in the derivative suit had deliberately withheld critical information from Alleghany (in order to secure shareholder approval of the challenged transaction) and from the shareholder plaintiffs in the derivative suit. In a dissenting opinion, Judge Friendly could

> not at all agree with the implication in . . . [the majority] opinion that standard procedures for the approval of settlements afford sufficient safeguards in the "big" case, or that they did in this one. The plaintiff stockholders or, more realistically, their attorneys have every incentive to accept a settlement that runs into high six figures or more regardless of how strong the claims for much larger amounts may be. . . . [A] juicy bird in the hand is worth more than the vision of a much larger one in the bush, attainable only after years of effort not currently compensated and possibly a mirage. Once a settlement is agreed, the attorneys for the plaintiff stockholders link arms with their former adversaries to defend the joint handiwork—as is vividly shown here where the stockholders' general counsel sometimes opposed Graubard's [counsel,

---

92. RMBCA §7.45 (1990) is similar except that it provides that the court "shall" direct that notice be given. For the view that "an absolute requirement of notice will undoubtedly work inordinate hardship" in some instances, see George D. Homstein, Problems of Procedure in Stockholder's Derivative Suits, 42 Colum. L. Rev. 574, 592 (1942). For the view that "the high cost of notifying . . . [many shareholders] when potential recovery is very small deters entrepreneurial attorneys from bringing meritorious suits," see Jonathan R. Macey & Geoffrey P. Miller, The Plaintiffs' Attorney's Role in Class Action and Derivative Litigation: Economic Analysis and Recommendations for Reform, 58 U. Chi. L. Rev. 1, 78 (1991). — ED.

who then opposed settlement] efforts to gain information. . . . To say that "Through its representatives, it [Alleghany] elected to settle" is sheer fiction. Most of the independent Alleghany stockholders had no voice in the selection of their "representatives" or ability to evaluate the settlement these "representatives" had accepted for them. I cannot see how the attorneys proposing the settlement were any more "representative" than the attorney opposing it; the stockholders' true representative was the court, which was allowed to proceed in ignorance of vital information. . . . [93]

. . . [T]hat directors accused of malfeasance have so much control over the evidence, both documentary and nondocumentary, relating to their misdeed, makes it vital for a court of equity to insist upon a high standard with respect to disclosure at settlement hearings and to subject arguments that a breach was not consequential to a most icy scrutiny. . . . Perhaps the ultimate solution may be the appointment of government inspectors to investigate and prosecute, as is authorized in England under the Companies Act, 1948, 11 & 12 George 6, c.38, §§164, 165(b)(ii), 168, 169(4), see Gower, Some Contrasts between British and American Corporation Law, 69 Harv. L. Rev. 1369, 1387-88 (1956), or, in the case of corporations trading in whose securities is subject to the Securities and Exchange Act, assignment to the SEC of an advisory role similar to that conferred by Chapter X of the Bankruptcy Act, §§172, 173, 222, 247. In the meanwhile, courts should enforce the most exacting standards of good faith on fiduciaries desiring to settle such serious claims of self-dealing as here alleged.

See also Note, Collateral Attack of Judicially-Approved Settlements of Shareholders' Derivative Suits, 74 Yale L.J. 1140 (1965).

> It would seem . . . that courts are not properly implementing the aims of the rule requiring judicial supervision of settlements when they grant approval, over protest from active litigants, merely because a "reasonable man" could have negotiated such an agreement. For the purpose of the rule is not only to prevent fraud or collusion, but to ensure that compromise will take place only where it serves the best interests of the corporation. Improvement may lie in the direction of a more restrictive standard which will require trial courts to take a more active role in safeguarding the interests of nonassenting shareholders.

Note, "Enjoining" Res Judicata: The Federal-State Relationship and Conclusiveness of Settlements in Stockholders' Derivative Suits, 65 Yale L.J. 543, 552 (1966). But see Franklin Gevurtz, Who Represents the Corporation? In Search for a Better Method for Determining the Corporate Interest in Derivative Suits, 46 U. Pitt. L. Rev. 265, 309-313 (1985) ("the court is not designed to undertake such a partisan role").

2. *Problems.* (a) Plaintiff shareholder files a derivative suit charging the corporation's directors with having taken exorbitant salaries. After several years of pretrial motions, discovery, hearings, etc., plaintiff appears to have exhausted energy and lost the initial interest in pursuing the matter. Defendants move to dismiss for lack of prosecution. Is there a requirement of notice to the shareholders before dismissal? Should there be? See William E. Haudek, The Settlement and Dismissal

---

93. For a decision finding that it would violate the due process rights of the corporation's shareholders to bind them to a settlement in which plaintiff's counsel's representation was not merely "inadequate" but "hostile," serving only the "interests of counsel in getting a fee," see Epstein v. MCA, Inc. 126 F.3d 1235 (9th Cir. 1997). — Ed.

of Stockholder's Action—Part I, 22 Sw. L.J. 767, 776-779 (1968). If notice is not given, should the order of dismissal operate as res judicata to nonparty shareholders respecting this cause of action? See Papilsky v. Berendt, 466 F.2d 251 (2d Cir. 1972) (dismissal for failure to answer interrogatories).

(b) If notice of this proposed dismissal is given to the shareholders, does an order of dismissal operate as res judicata respecting this cause of action? Should it?

> The class members should not be forced to take over an action initiated, prosecuted, and finally abandoned by a plaintiff who has revealed himself to be disqualified to represent them. They have, in these circumstances, a legitimate interest to litigate in a forum of their choice, to adopt their own strategy, and to be free of any setbacks suffered by the unrepresentative plaintiff. The defendants, to be sure, may claim an interest not to be exposed to multiple actions, but that interest is generally accorded only limited recognition and should not outweigh the right of the class to be unaffected by the acts of a disqualified representative."

Haudek, supra, at 786. Is this sound? If so, should any court-approved dismissal or settlement, after notice to the shareholders—or any judgment—operate as res judicata? See Note, 71 Mich. L. Rev. 1042 (1973).

3. *Prefiling settlements.* Does the New York statute, page 896 supra, apply to a plaintiff shareholder who, in exchange for a private settlement, agrees to abandon plans to bring a derivative suit? Cf. Clarke v. Greenberg, 296 N.Y. 146, 71 N.E.2d 443 (1947) (moneys received in non–judicially approved settlement are "impressed with a trust in favor of the corporation for which an accounting should be made"). Are there any circumstances in which a court should approve a private settlement free of any obligation to account to the corporation?

4. *Problem.* Plaintiff shareholder files a derivative suit charging former directors of the corporation with breach of fiduciary duty. The corporation then proposes to make a settlement of the claim with the defendants. Does this proposed settlement require judicial approval preceded by notice to shareholders? Should it? See Wolf v. Barkes, 348 F.2d 994 (2d Cir. 1965), noted, 79 Harv. L. Rev. 1526 (1966), 52 Va. L. Rev. 342 (1966). Of what significance is the fact that the defendants control the corporation? See Clark v. Lomas & Nettleton Financial Corp., 625 F.2d 49 (5th Cir. 1980), criticized in Note, Director Independence and Derivative Suit Settlements, 1983 Duke L.J. 645. ALI §7.15 requires procedures here essentially the same as those for settlement of the derivative suit.

G. *CHARACTERIZATION OF THE SUIT*

1. DERIVATIVE OR DIRECT

Classification of a shareholders' suit as either direct or derivative is often critical due to the peculiar procedural aspects of the latter. Occasionally, plaintiff shareholders may benefit by having the suit labeled as derivative, but usually this designation will work to their disadvantage, e.g., if plaintiff did not own the shares at the time of the alleged wrong. This is especially true when a defendant initially seeks security for costs, or a subsequent award of attorneys' fees, under statutes that are applicable only to derivative suits.[94]

Some shareholders' suits may be characterized with relative ease. The polar positions may be illustrated by a shareholders' suit against the corporation to inspect its books, on the one hand, and, on the other, a shareholders' suit against the corporation's management to account for excessive compensation. The latter is a classic derivative suit. Plaintiff's claim is that the corporation has a cause of action because it has suffered monetary detriment. The corporation is only a nominal defendant. All shareholders qua shareholders have been adversely affected financially according to their proportionate interest in the corporation. This collective injury will be remedied by a money judgment for the corporation. In contrast to a personal judgment, a corporate recovery for the dissipation of its assets will fulfill the intentions of shareholders that their risk capital will be put to productive use and the expectations of creditors that corporate assets will be available for satisfaction of their claims.[95]

The suit to compel inspection has quite different characteristics. Apart from the fact that plaintiff claims in the status of a shareholder, the plaintiff's role is similar to that of an outsider bringing suit against the corporation. It is plaintiff (not the corporation) who has the cause of action because it is plaintiff (not the corporation) who has been injured. The corporation is the real defendant. A judgment for plaintiff will not affect all shareholders qua shareholders collectively in accordance with their proportionate interests. Neither the integrity of the corporate entity generally nor the unity of the corporation's assets specifically will be affected by the classification of the suit as either direct or derivative.

Many shareholders' suits, however, present more difficult problems of characterization.

Grimes v. Donald
673 A.2d 1207 (Del. 1996)

VEASEY, C.J.: [In his agreement to be the corporation's CEO, Donald was entitled to very substantial damages if, in his "good-faith judgment" the Board of Directors "unreasonably interfered" with his responsibility for the company's general management. Plaintiff shareholder Grimes contended that "this provision unlawfully delegate[d] the duties and responsibilities of the Board of Directors to Mr. Donald"[96] and sought, inter alia, a declaration that it was invalid (the "abdication claim.") He also sued the Board for damages for breach of "fiduciary duties by abdicating its authority, failing to exercise due care and committing waste."]

. . . We agree that the Court of Chancery appropriately analyzed the abdication claim as a direct—as distinct from a derivative—claim.

Courts have long recognized that the same set of facts can give rise both to a direct claim and a derivative claim. Bennett v. Breuil Petroleum Corp., Del. Ch., 99 A.2d 236, 241 (1953); Borak v. J. I. Case Co., 7th Cir., 317 F.2d 838, 844-845 (1963), aff'd, 377 U.S. 426, 84 S. Ct. 1555, 12 L. Ed. 2d 423 (1964). The due care, waste and

---

94. Leibert v. Clapp, 13 N.Y.2d 313, 196 N.E.2d 540, 247 N.Y.S.2d 102 (1963).
95. See Note, Distinguishing Between Direct and Derivative Shareholder Suits, 110 U. Pa. L. Rev. 1147 (1962).
96. See page 770 supra.—ED.

excessive compensation claims asserted here are derivative and will be considered as such. Kramer v. Western Pacific Indus., Inc., Del. Supr., 546 A.2d 348, 353 (1988). The abdication claim, however, is a direct claim. In order to reach this conclusion, we believe a further exploration of the distinction between direct and derivative claims is appropriate. . . .

As the Court of Chancery has noted: "Although the tests have been articulated many times, it is often difficult to distinguish between a derivative and an individual action." In re Rexene Corp. Shareholders Litig., Del. Ch., 17 Del. J. Corp. L. 342, 348, 1991 WL 77529 (1991); see also Abelow v. Symonds, Del. Ch., 156 A.2d 416, 420 (1959) ("line of distinction . . . is often a narrow one . . ."). The distinction depends upon " 'the nature of the wrong alleged' and the relief, if any, which could result if plaintiff were to prevail." Kramer v. Western Pacific, 546 A.2d at 352 (quoting Elster v. American Airlines, Inc., Del. Ch., 100 A.2d 219, 221-223 (1953)). To pursue a direct action, the stockholder-plaintiff "must allege more than an injury resulting from a wrong to the corporation." Id. at 351. The plaintiff must state a claim for " 'an injury which is separate and distinct from that suffered by other shareholders,' . . . or a wrong involving a contractual right of a shareholder . . . which exists independently of any right of the corporation." Moran v. Household Int'l, Inc., Del. Ch., 490 A.2d 1059, 1070, aff'd, Del. Supr., 500 A.2d 1346 (1985) (quoting 12B Fletcher Cyclopedia Corps., §5291 (Perm. Ed.1984)).[97]

The American Law Institute ("ALI") Principles of Corporate Governance: Analysis and Recommendations (1992) ("Principles") is helpful in this instance. Section 7.01 of the Principles undertakes to state the common law with respect to the distinction between direct and derivative actions. Id. §7.01, cmt. a. The Comment also discusses a situation relevant to the case sub judice: "In some instances, actions that essentially involve the structural relationship of the shareholder to the corporation . . . may also give rise to a derivative action when the corporation suffers or is threatened with a loss. One example would be a case in which a corporate official knowingly acts in a manner that the certificate of incorporation [or the Delaware General Corporation Law] denied the official authority to do, thereby violating both specific restraints imposed by the shareholders [or the GCL] and the official's duty of care." Id., cmt. c. The Comment further notes that, "courts have been more prepared to permit the plaintiff to characterize the action as direct when the plaintiff is seeking only injunctive or prospective relief."[98] Id., cmt. d.

With respect to the abdication claim, Grimes seeks only a declaration of the invalidity of the Agreements. Monetary recovery will not accrue to the corporation as a result. Chancellor Seitz illustrated this distinction in *Bennett*. The Court of Chancery there allowed the plaintiff-stockholder to proceed individually on his claim that stock was issued for an improper purpose and entrenchment; he

---

97. In Eisenberg v. Flying Tiger Line, Inc., 451 F.2d 267 (2d Cir. 1971), the court reasoned that a shareholder who (1) seeks to compel the board of directors to call a shareholders' meeting, or (2) claims that a corporate reorganization dilutes the voting rights of his group, "does not challenge acts of the management on behalf of the corporation. He challenges the right of the present management to exclude him and other stockholders from proper participation in the affairs of the corporation. He claims that the defendants are interfering with the plaintiff's rights and privileges as stockholders." — ED.

98. In the *Flying Tiger* case, footnote 97 supra, the court described the objective of the procedural requirements of a derivative suit as "the prevention of strike suits and collusive settlements. Where directors are sued for mismanagement, the risk of personal monetary liability is a strong motive for bringing the suit and inducing settlement. Here, no monetary damages are sought, and no individuals will be liable." — ED.

proceeded derivatively on his claim that the stock was issued for an insufficient price. 99 A.2d at 241. . . .

---

1. *Subsequent clarification.* In Tooley v. Donaldson, Lufkin & Jenrette, Inc., 845 A.2d 1031 (Del. 2004), the court, disapproving "the concept of 'special injury' that appears in some Supreme Court and Court of Chancery cases . . . [as] not helpful to a proper analytical distinction between direct and derivative actions," noted that "the proper analysis has been and should remain that stated in *Grimes*": the "issue must turn *solely* on the following questions: (1) who suffered the alleged harm (the corporation or the suing stockholders, individually); and (2) who would receive the benefit of any recovery or other remedy (the corporation or the stockholders, individually)? . . . In order to bring a *direct* claim, a plaintiff . . . must demonstrate that the duty breached was owed to the stockholder and that he or she can prevail without showing an injury to the corporation."

Query: What result in the *Grimes* case under this standard?

2. *Problems.* (a) Corporation's shareholders, the majority shareholder voting, approve a resolution to authorize corporate purchase of property owned by the majority shareholder. Plaintiff minority shareholder alleges that the purchase price was excessive, that the majority shareholder should not have voted because of conflict of interest, and that without the majority shareholder's votes the resolution would have been defeated. Plaintiff seeks to nullify the shareholder vote and rescind the transaction. Defendant moves for security for costs. What result? See Reifsnyder v. Pittsburgh Outdoor Advertising Co., 405 Pa. 142, 173 A.2d 319 (1961).

(i) Of what significance, if any, would it be if plaintiff had filed suit before the shareholder meeting, seeking a declaratory judgment that the majority shareholder should not be permitted to vote?

(ii) In terms of whether the suit is derivative or direct, are the above situations distinguishable from an action by a minority shareholder alleging denial of cumulative voting rights in an election for directors?

(b) Corporation's directors cause it to sell a large block of its shares to a third party, thus frustrating plaintiff minority shareholder's efforts to buy enough shares to gain control. Plaintiff sues corporation's directors for "depriving it of voting rights" and "wasting corporate assets to entrench their control." Corporation then buys plaintiff's shares, and plaintiff and defendants file a stipulation to dismiss the suit. Must there be compliance with Fed. R. Civ. P. 23.1's provisions for notice to shareholders and court approval? Of what significance, if any, is the fact that plaintiff had not treated its suit as being derivative? See Lipton v. News Int'l, 514 A.2d 1075 (Del. 1986).

3. *"Special duty" cases.* (a) In Citibank, N.A. v. Data Lease Financial Corp., 828 F.2d 686 (11th Cir. 1987), plaintiff had pledged a controlling block of shares as security for a loan. When plaintiff defaulted on the loan, the pledgee foreclosed and bought the shares at the judicial sale. Plaintiff then sued the directors that the pledgee had installed for mismanagement. The court held plaintiff's claim to be a direct action:

> When a shareholder pledges his stock to a pledgee who assumes control of the corporation, he is no longer similarly situated to the other shareholders. While the other

shareholders can bail out at will, the pledged stock is held captive to the whims of the pledgee. This is the very situation that arose in Empire Life Ins. Co. v. Valdak Corp., 468 F.2d 330 (5th Cir. 1972), where this court noted that the pledgee could "use his position as director and his vote as stockholder intentionally to depreciate the stock of his pledgor held in pledge with the dishonest purpose of acquiring ownership of the stock at forced sale." 468 F.2d at 336. Unlike the remaining shareholders, who may bring a derivative action, the pledgor loses his opportunity to share in a corporate recovery after a foreclosure sale. For these reasons, the *Empire Life* court held that the . . . "[plaintiff] seeks damages as a *pledgor*. The fact that his pledge is stock and that if the manipulated depreciation of the stock is proven would also give rise to a derivative suit by [plaintiff] as *stockholder* should not foreclose the suit as pledgor. The role of pledgor and stockholder are not identical and [plaintiff] may play the part he chooses."

Is this holding sound? If another shareholder (not a pledgor) brought a derivative suit against the directors for the same injury to the corporation, what would be the measure of damages?

(b) Plaintiff shareholder, who personally guaranteed the corporation's debts, brings a direct action against defendant, whose alleged misconduct caused corporation's insolvency. What result? Of what relevance is it that plaintiff has been required to honor the guaranty? Compare Labovitz v. Washington Times Corp., 172 F.3d 897 (D.C. Cir. 1999), and Engstrand v. West Des Moines State Bank, 516 N.W.2d 797 (Iowa 1994), with Wm. Goldberg & Co. v. Cohen, 219 Ga. App. 628, 466 S.E.2d 872, 881-882 (1995).

(c) *Problem.* Plaintiff shareholder brings a direct action against corporation's other shareholders, alleging that defendants breached a shareholders' agreement by failing to (1) exert their best efforts to achieve the corporation's purposes, and (2) provide the corporation with sufficient funds and technical assistance. What result? See Hikita v. Nichiro Gyogyo Kaisha, Ltd., 713 P.2d 1197 (Alaska 1986).

4. *Problems.* (a) Plaintiff shareholder files suit against corporation's directors, alleging that they have wrongfully failed to declare dividends for the purpose of depressing the value of the corporation's shares to enable them to buy shares at less than fair value. Corporation moves for security for costs. What result? Compare Bokat v. Getty Oil Co., 262 A.2d 246, 249 (Del. 1970), with Lesnik v. Public Industrials Corp., 144 F.2d 968, 977-978 (2d Cir. 1944).

(b) In the above situation, suppose the alleged misconduct were that, for the same purpose, the directors had failed to permit the corporation to avail itself of advantageous corporate opportunities. See Yanow v. Teal Industries, Inc., 178 Conn. 262, 422 A.2d 311 (1979).

(c) Plaintiffs, owners of preferred shares, file direct suit against those persons who are both corporation's directors and owners of all the common shares, alleging that they have wrongfully diverted corporation's assets to themselves, thus rendering corporation bankrupt and unable to fulfill its contractual obligation to pay dividends on the preferred shares. What result? See In re Ionosphere Clubs, Inc., 17 F.3d 600 (2d Cir. 1994).

5. *Problems.* (a) Should the following shareholder suits be classified as direct or derivative?

(i) Plaintiff shareholders, alleging that corporation plans to issue (or has issued) shares to its directors for an inadequate consideration, seek an injunction (or cancellation). Compare Bennett v. Breuil Petroleum Corp., 34 Del. Ch. 6, 99 A.2d 236 (Ch. 1953) with King v. Douglass, 973 F. Supp. 707, 723-725 (S.D. Tex. 1996).

(ii) Plaintiff shareholders, alleging that corporation plans to offer (or has issued) shares to its shareholders, thus affording all an equal opportunity, for an inadequate consideration, seek an injunction (or cancellation) on the ground that it financially penalizes those choosing not to purchase. See Strougo v. Bassini, 282 F.3d 162 (2d Cir. 2002). Does it make any difference if plaintiff shareholders had sought damages from the directors who authorized the offering?

(iii) Plaintiff shareholders, alleging that corporation plans to issue (or has issued) shares to its directors for a concededly adequate consideration but in violation of their rights to preserve their proportionate control interest in the corporation, seek an injunction (or cancellation). See Saigh v. Busch, 403 S.W.2d 559 (Mo. 1966). Suppose plaintiff shareholders seek to compel defendant directors to deliver a percentage of the shares to them. See Andersen v. Albert & J. M. Anderson Mfg. Co., 325 Mass. 343, 90 N.E.2d 541 (1950).

(iv) Plaintiff shareholders, alleging that corporation has issued shares to its directors for an inadequate consideration and in violation of their right to preserve their proportionate control and financial interest in the corporation, seek to compel defendant directors to deliver a percentage of the shares to them. See Seventeen Stone Corp. v. General Tel. Co., 204 F. Supp. 885 (S.D.N.Y. 1962); Shaw v. Empire Sav. & Loan Ass'n, 186 Cal. App. 2d 401, 9 Cal. Rptr. 204 (1960).

(v) Plaintiff shareholders, alleging that corporation has issued shares to its directors for an inadequate consideration and in violation of their right to preserve their proportionate voting and financial interests in the corporation, seek to compel defendant directors to pay fair value to the corporation. Does it make any difference if plaintiff shareholders seek a declaratory judgment that the issuance is invalid? Does it make any difference if the corporation has issued the shares to a third party, allegedly to preserve defendant directors' control of the corporation? See Gatz v. Ponsoldt, 925 A.2d 1265 (Del. 2007). Compare Jolly Roger Fund L.P. v. Sizeler Property Investors, Inc., 2005 WL 2989343 (D. Md. 2005).

(vi) Plaintiff shareholders, alleging the same as in (v) above, seek to compel defendant directors to compensate them for the diminution in value of their shares. See Borak v. J. I. Case Co., 317 F.2d 838 (7th Cir. 1963).

(b) As a functional matter, which of the policy considerations that underlie the creation of the derivative suit device and that justify its procedural ramifications are served by characterizing any of these suits as derivative rather than direct?

It has been generally assumed that shareholder suits to enforce preemptive rights (see (iv) above) and to compel the payment of dividends[99] are nonderivative. Nonetheless, should some (or all) of the procedural requirements for derivative suits—e.g., exhaustion of internal remedies, contemporaneous ownership, security for expenses—be applicable to these suits as well? Why should any (or all) of the procedural requirements be applicable to suit (vi) above—which fits within the classic description of derivative suits—but not to suit (v)?

---

99. See Knapp v. Bankers Sec. Corp., 203 F.2d 717 (3d Cir. 1956).

2. SPECIAL CIRCUMSTANCES IN DERIVATIVE SUITS

Barth v. Barth
659 N.E.2d 559 (Ind. 1995)

SULLIVAN, J.: . . . This lawsuit was brought against defendants Barth Electric Co., Inc., and its president and majority shareholder Michael G. Barth, Jr., by plaintiff minority shareholder Robert Barth individually (rather than derivatively on behalf of the corporation).[1] Plaintiff Robert Barth alleged that defendant Michael Barth had taken certain actions which had the effect of "substantially reducing the value of Plaintiff's shares of common stock" in the corporation. Specifically, plaintiff contended that defendant Michael Barth had: (1) paid excessive salaries to himself and to members of his immediate family; (2) used corporate employees to perform services on his and his son's homes without compensating the corporation; (3) dramatically lowered dividend payments; and (4) appropriated corporate funds for personal investments. Barth v. Barth (1995), Ind. App., 651 N.E.2d 291. Michael Barth and the corporation moved to dismiss Robert Barth's complaint for the failure to state a claim upon which relief can be granted, Ind. Trial Rule 12(B)(6), arguing that a derivative action was required to redress claims of this nature. The trial court granted the motion to dismiss. The Court of Appeals acknowledged that the "well-established general rule" prohibits a shareholder from maintaining an action in the shareholder's own name but found that requiring a derivative action here would "exalt form over substance" since Robert Barth could have satisfied the requirements for bringing a derivative action and that none of the reasons underlying the general derivative action requirement were present. . . .

As the Court of Appeals made clear, the well-established general rule is that shareholders of a corporation may not maintain actions at law in their own names to redress an injury to the corporation even if the value of their stock is impaired as a result of the injury. . . .

While we affirm the general rule requiring a shareholder to bring a derivative rather than direct action when seeking redress for injury to the corporation, we nevertheless observe two reasons why this rule will not always apply in the case of closely-held corporations. First, shareholders in a close corporation stand in a fiduciary relationship to each other, and as such, must deal fairly, honestly, and openly with the corporation and with their fellow shareholders. W&W Equipment Co., 568 N.E.2d at 570; Krukemeier v. Krukemeier Machine and Tool Co., Inc. (1990), Ind. App., 551 N.E.2d 885; Garbe v. Excel Mold, Inc. (1979), Ind. App., 397 N.E.2d 296. Second, shareholder litigation in the closely-held corporation context will often not implicate the policies that mandate requiring derivative litigation when more widely-held corporations are involved. W&W Equipment Co., Inc. v. Mink is a leading case in this regard. There our Court of Appeals was faced with a lawsuit filed by one of two 50% shareholders of a corporation after the other shareholder joined with nonshareholder directors to fire the plaintiff shareholder and arrange for the payment of certain corporate assets to the other shareholder. The court concluded that no useful purpose would be served by forcing the plaintiff to proceed derivatively where the policies favoring derivative actions were not

---

1. Michael Barth owns 51% of the shares of the corporation. Robert Barth owns 29.8%. A third individual owns the remaining shares.

implicated — direct corporate recovery was not necessary to protect absent share-holders or creditors as none existed. Id., 568 N.E.2d at 571.

. . . [C]ourts in many cases are permitting direct suits by shareholders of closely-held corporations where the complaint is one that in a public corporation would have to be brought as a derivative action. See F. Hodge O'Neal & Robert B. Thompson, O'Neal's Close Corporations §8.16 n.32 (3d ed. & 1995 Cum. Supp.) (collecting cases); American Law Institute, Principles of Corporate Governance: Analysis and Recommendations §7.01, reporter's n. (1994) (collecting cases). However, it is important to keep in mind that the principles which gave rise to the rule requiring derivative actions will sometimes be present even in litigation involving closely-held corporations. For example, because a corporate recovery in a derivative action will benefit creditors while a direct recovery by a shareholder will not, the pro-tection of creditors principle could well be implicated in a shareholder suit against a closely-held corporation with debt. . . .

In its recently-completed corporate governance project, the American Law Insti-tute proposed the following rule for determining when a shareholder of a closely-held corporation may proceed by direct or derivative action: "In the case of a closely held corporation, the court in its discretion may treat an action raising derivative claims as a direct action, exempt it from those restrictions and defenses applicable only to derivative actions, and order an individual recovery, if it finds that to do so will not (i) unfairly expose the corporation or the defendants to a multiplicity of actions, (ii) materially prejudice the interests of creditors of the corporation, or (iii) interfere with a fair distribution of the recovery among all interested persons." A.L.I., Principles of Corporate Governance §7.01(d). We have studied this rule and find that it is consistent with the approach taken by our Court of Appeals and by most other jurisdictions in similar cases and that it represents a fair and workable approach for balancing the relative interests in closely-held corporation shareholder litigation.

In determining that a trial court has discretion to decide whether a plaintiff must proceed by direct or by derivative action, we make the following observations, drawn largely from the Comment to §7.01(d). First, permitting such litigation to proceed as a direct action will exempt the plaintiff from the requirements of Ind. Code §23-1-32-1 et seq., including the provisions that permit a special committee of the board of directors to recommend dismissal of the lawsuit. Ind. Code §23-1-32-4.[100] As such, the court in making its decision should consider whether the cor-poration has a disinterested board that should be permitted to consider the lawsuit's impact on the corporation. A.L.I., Corporate Governance Project §7.01 comment e. Second, in some situations it may actually be to the benefit of the corporation to permit the plaintiff to proceed by direct action. This will permit the defendant to file a counterclaim against the plaintiff, whereas counterclaims are generally prohibited in derivative actions. Also, in a direct action each side will normally be responsible for its own legal expenses; the plaintiff, even if successful, cannot ordinarily look to the corporation for attorney's fees. . . .

---

100. Compare Aurora Credit Services, Inc. v. Liberty West Development, Inc., 970 P.2d 1273 (Utah 1998) (although close corporation exception for derivative suits is adopted, contemporaneous owner-ship rule continues to apply). — Ed.

1. *Dissenting view.* In Landstrom v. Shaver, 561 N.W.2d 1 (S.D. 1997), the court refused to recognize any close corporation exception for derivative suits:

> A minority of courts now permit that when a minority shareholder in a close corporation brings claims alleging wrongdoing by the majority shareholders, the claims are not automatically held to be brought derivatively. Johnson v. Gilbert, 127 Ariz. 410, 621 P.2d 916, 918 (Ariz. App. 1980); Thomas, 301 S.E.2d at 51 [Ga.]; Steelman v. Mallory, 110 Idaho 510, 716 P.2d 1282, 1285 (Idaho 1986); Barth v. Barth, 659 N.E.2d 559, 562 (Ind. 1995); Richards v. Bryan, 19 Kan. App. 2d 950, 879 P.2d 638, 647-648 (Kan. Ct. App. 1994); Horizon House–Microwave, Inc. v. Bazzy, 21 Mass. App. Ct. 190, 486 N.E.2d 70, 74 (Mass. App. 1985); Schumacher v. Schumacher, 469 N.W.2d 793, 798-799 (N.D. 1991).[101]

> The derivative-direct distinction makes little sense when the only interested parties are two individuals or sets of shareholders, one who is in control and the other who is not. In this context, the debate over derivative status can become "purely technical." There is no practical need to insist on derivative suits when there is little likelihood of a multiplicity of suits or harm to creditors. Any recovery in a derivative suit would return funds to the control of the defendant, rather than to the injured party. In some of these traditional derivative claims brought as direct actions, courts focus on the disproportionate impact of the challenged corporate actions. For example, when assets are alleged to be sold to insiders at inadequate prices, only the minority shareholders bear the loss and the majority receives any benefits in their capacity as purchasers. O'Neal & Thompson, O'Neal's Close Corporations, §8.16 at 103 (3d ed. 1994).

> The trial court followed *Barth*'s adoption of the American Law Institute's proposed rule. . . .
> Defendants attack the ALI minority rule as posing great potential for abuse of a corporation and its majority shareholders by a disgruntled minority shareholder. Their point is not without merit. A minority shareholder in a close corporation may have different goals than a majority. A dispute over maximization of short-term profits as against the long-term financial health and growth of the corporation is an obvious example. Here, there was evidence presented in the record of this case that BHJMC has suffered financially because of the effect this litigation has had upon it. Thus, we must weigh the interests of the corporation and its majority and minority shareholders, creditors and its employees in determining what is an appropriate balance of each party's rights.
> . . . We conclude that given our case law and that of other jurisdictions, it is the better course to continue to follow the majority rule and not adopt the ALI proposed rule.[102] The basis for this rationale is well set forth by Bagdon v. Bridgestone/Firestone, Inc., 916 F.2d 379, 384 (7th Cir. 1990) cert. denied, 500 U.S. 952 (1991),

---

101. Accord, Durham v. Durham, 871 A.2d 41 (N.H. 2005); Triweiler v. Sears, 268 Neb. 952, 689 N.W.2d 807 (2004); Simon v. Mann, 373 F. Supp. 2d 1196 (D. Nev. 2005) (applying Nevada law). See also Jara, Sr. v. Suprema Meats, Inc., 121 Cal. App. 4th 1238, 18 Cal. Rptr. 3d 187 (2004). — Ed.

102. Accord, Simmons v. Miller, 544 S.E.2d 666 (Va. 2001); Wessin v. Archives Corp., 592 N.W.2d 460 (Minn. 1999); Hames v. Cravens, 332 Ark. 437, 966 S.W.2d 244 (1998). See also Centerre Bank of Kansas City v. Angle, 976 S.W.2d 608 (Mo. App. 1998) (suit must be brought derivatively, but plaintiff may replead without bar of statute of limitations); Combs v. Pricewaterhousecoopers, LLP, 382 F.3d 1196 (10th Cir. 2004) (applying Colorado law); Fisher v. Big Squeeze (N.Y.), Inc., 349 F. Supp. 2d 483 (E.D.N.Y. 2004) (applying New York law).
Should this rule apply if shareholders bring a direct suit against a third party for allegedly injuring their wholly owned corporation? See Fritzmeier v. Krause Gentle Corp., 669 N.W.2d 699 (S.D. 2003) (no). — Ed.

where the court criticized the concept behind the ALI rule finding the rule was an ill-advised attempt at removing the distinctions of the structure of a close corporation and that of a partnership: "The premise of this extension may be questioned. Corporations are not partnerships. Whether to incorporate entails a choice of many formalities. Commercial rules should be predictable; this objective is best served by treating corporations as what they are, allowing the investors and other participants to vary the rule by contract if they think deviations are warranted. So it is understandable that not all states have joined the [ALI] parade." [Emphasis in original.]

Landstrom seeks the best of both business entities: limited liability provided by a corporate structure and direct compensation for corporate losses. "That cushy position is not one the law affords. Investors who created the corporate form cannot rend the veil they wove." Kagan v. Edison Bros. Stores, Inc., 907 F.2d 690, 693 (7th Cir. 1990). . . . A key reason the trial court permitted Landstrom to pursue an individual action was: "that requiring a derivative action might result in a distribution to BHJMC and the shareholders which was inequitable as Landstrom is suing the only other shareholders who would then participate in the majority of the relief should Landstrom prevail." This reasoning is flawed. In a derivative suit, the defendants pay to the corporation the total damages occasioned by their wrongful conduct. The value of a plaintiff's shares is increased according to the percentage of stock owned. This provides no windfall to the defendants as they are paying the total amount of damages. When defendants pay the total amount of damages out of one pocket to restore the corporation to its original value, the fact that the value of their own stock is also returned to the predamage level does not put the same amount of money in the individual defendant's other pocket.[17]

2. *Other instances of pro rata recovery.*

[W]here special circumstances exist, courts have allowed direct pro rata recovery by the shareholders . . . in order to facilitate the distribution of corporate funds in a variety of situations: (1) where the corporation is in the process of liquidation, (2) where the wrongdoers retain substantial control of the corporation and corporate recovery would return the funds to their control,[5] (3) where the defendants sell control of the corporation for an unlawful premium and the court seeks to prevent a windfall to purchasers of the wrongdoers' shares,[6] (4) where a majority of the corporation's shares are held by persons who could not bring the derivative suit because of their personal involvement in, or ratification of, the wrongdoing, and (5) where a pro rata recovery fairly resolves the varying equities among differently situated stockholders.[8]

James D. Cox & Thomas L. Hazen, Corporations 425-426 (2d ed. 2003).

---

17. As an example, assume total damages to a corporation are $100,000. The defendants pay $100,000 out of one pocket to the corporation. Assuming also that there are three equal shareholders, one who is the plaintiff and the other two the defendants, the value of the plaintiff's stock is restored to its predamage value by adding $33,333.33. The fact that the value of the defendants' stock is also returned to its predamage level by adding $66,666.66 does not put $100,000 in defendants' other pocket, nor detract from the plaintiff's full recovery of the original value of plaintiff's stock.

5. See, e.g., Atkinson v. Marquart, 541 P.2d 556 (Ariz. 1975); Gabhart v. Gabhart, 370 N.E.2d 345 (Ind. 1977) (injured corporation merged into corporation controlled by those responsible for harm). ["The general rule is that the shareholder in this situation loses standing to sue derivatively on behalf of the merged corporation." DeMott, footnote 9 supra at §4.03. — ED.]

6. E.g., Perlman v. Feldmann, [page 1051 infra].

8. See, e.g., Raskin v. Frebank Co., 121 Cal. Rptr. 348 (Ct. App. 1975).

3. In light of the issues now under consideration, reconsider the problems in Notes 5(a)(iii) and (v), page 904 supra.

4. *Proposal.* When some shareholders have either tacitly acquiesced in or expressly approved of the acts of defendants, the following suggestion has been made:

Perhaps when the defendants are directors guilty of flagrant and willful breaches of fiduciary duty toward the corporation, full payment of the corporate damages should be exacted. Even though such recovery may include a punitive element, it could be justified as providing a deterrent against such breaches of fiduciary duty. In less serious situations only prorata recovery may be justifiable even though the defendants violated a fiduciary duty. When the liability of directors arises from negligence, from serious and extensive misjudgments, or from authorization of now completed ultra vires acts, it may be argued that they should not be required to account to acquiescing shareholders. In these latter situations it is more likely that the corporate funds paid out are in the hands of third parties so that damages payable by the directors would not come from such funds. Indeed, the directors may have derived no economic benefit at all from the transactions. Even in some situations in which the directors obtained corporate funds through a flagrant breach of fiduciary duty, prorata recovery may be appropriate, because the shareholders' acquiescence, under the circumstances, is equivalent to a compromise agreement with the defendants. In such instances, the strong policy of the law in favor of settlements without litigation seems to swing the balance in favor of the defendants. Furthermore, the acquiescers merely receive the results of their bargain when recovery is denied to them.

Edward J. Grenier, Jr., Prorata Recovery by Shareholders on Corporate Causes of Action as a Means of Achieving Corporate Justice, 19 Wash. & Lee L. Rev. 165, 169-170 (1962).

5. *Suits by former shareholders.* (a) In Watson v. Button, 235 F.2d 235 (9th Cir. 1956), noted, 35 N.C. L. Rev. 279 (1957), the former owner of half the corporation's shares brought a direct suit against the corporation's former general manager and other half-owner to recover for defendants' embezzlement of corporate funds prior to their sale of all the shares. The purchasers of the shares from plaintiff and defendant had caused the corporation to release defendant from all existing claims. The court upheld plaintiff's suit, recognizing that plaintiff "cannot bring a derivative action since he is no longer a stockholder," and that "courts in other states have held that a former stockholder, who parted with his shares without knowledge of prior wrongful misappropriation of corporate assets by the directors, may recover from the directors the amount by which the misappropriation had reduced the value of his prior shareholdings."

What course of action should plaintiff have taken if he had sold only part of his shares? Should the result have been affected if the newly owned corporation had not released defendant from prior claims?

(b) In Kirk v. First Nat'l Bank, 439 F. Supp. 1141 (M.D. Ga. 1977), plaintiffs, former shareholders in the corporation, brought a direct suit against another former shareholder for misappropriations that had allegedly caused a diminution in the value that plaintiffs received for their shares when all the shareholders had sold out. The court upheld plaintiffs' suit:

In *Watson*, . . . the Ninth Circuit observed that as a general rule, any cause of action for misappropriation belonged to the corporation, not the shareholder. However, it concluded that the reasons supporting the general rule were not present: there could be no multiplicity of suits since there were only two shareholders, both involved in the litigation; creditors could not be prejudiced because plaintiff and defendant had agreed to be jointly liable for corporate debts; since there was only one injured share-holder, there was no concern that direct recovery by that shareholder would prejudice the rights of other injured shareholders; and since the plaintiff was no longer a share-holder, recovery by the corporation would not compensate the true injured party. . . .

It may be contended that allowing the present plaintiffs to directly recover would prejudice the rights of creditors since, unlike the facts of *Watson,* here, there is no indemnity agreement among shareholders for the benefit of creditors. But creditors of the corporation are prejudiced only insofar as allowing recovery by the plaintiffs would somehow prejudice the possibility of corporate recovery. Since, . . . [because the existing shareholders had full notice of the facts surrounding the alleged misap-propriation], the present corporation cannot recover, creditors here cannot be prejudiced, just as creditors in *Watson* could not be prejudiced.

Finally, it may be contended that Georgia would not approve a *Watson*-type direct recovery in the instant case because of the existence of other injured former share-holders who are not party to this litigation. . . .

The substantive concerns caused by the presence of other injured former share-holders are that a *Watson*-type theory of recovery would generate a multiplicity of suits and would prejudice other former shareholders by diminishing the assets avail-able for compensation of their injuries. However, both of these concerns are present in any class action type situation where less than all injured parties request relief, and relief is not denied because of concern over multiplicity and diminution of assets. Indeed, far less drastic than denying relief would be to require plaintiffs in class action type situations to attempt joinder of all other injured parties. Yet Georgia law does not even go this far.

6. *Problems.* (a) Corporation's directors have conspired with its major supplier to fraudulently overcharge corporation in substantial amounts. After the underlying facts are generally known, plaintiff sells shares and then brings a direct suit. What result? See Mendenhall v. Fleming Co., 504 F.2d 879 (5th Cir. 1974).

(b) After plaintiff sells shares, the fact is discovered that the corporation's directors have fraudulently inflated the value of the corporation's assets to conceal their embez-zlement of funds. Plaintiff brings a direct suit. What result?

(c) After plaintiff sells shares, the fact is discovered that the corporation's directors have previously appropriated several valuable corporate opportunities. Plaintiff brings a direct suit. What result?

(d) After plaintiff sells shares, the fact is discovered that the corporation's accountant committed malpractice while handling the corporation's accounts. Plain-tiff brings a direct suit. What result? See Sparks v. CBIZ Accounting, Tax & Advisory of Kansas City, Inc., 36 Kan. App. 2d 660, 142 P.3d 749 (2006).

7. In respect to Notes 5 and 6 above, reconsider the problems in Note 2, page 902 supra.

H. *REIMBURSEMENT OF PLAINTIFF'S EXPENSES*

In re Wachovia Shareholders Litigation
607 S.E.2d 48 (N.C. App. 2005)

McCullough, J.: On 15 April 2001, . . . [Wachovia Corporation ("Wachovia") and First Union Corporation ("First Union")] announced their planned merger.

Both were North Carolina corporations prior to their merger, as is the merged entity. Their merger agreement included two contested provisions, known in merger jargon as "deal protection devices." . . . Under the non-termination provision, Wachovia and First Union agreed their merger agreement would not terminate until January of 2002 even if either of their shareholders failed to approve the merger in the initial vote.

A number of suits were filed by shareholders of Wachovia seeking to block the merger. . . . The business court determined that the non-termination provision cornered Wachovia's Board of Directors into the position of either breaching their fiduciary duty or breaching the merger agreement if a better merger offer came along during the agreement's dormancy. Additionally, the business court found the non-termination provision to be coercive upon the shareholders, stating: "[t]he longer the option is effective, the more likely shareholders are to vote for the bird in the hand."

Pursuant to this order, plaintiffs petitioned the business court for attorney's fees . . . [and] were awarded $325,000 in attorney's fees and $36,000 for expenses. . . .

Generally, attorney's fees are taxable as costs only as provided by statute. Horner v. Chamber of Commerce, 236 N.C. 96, 97, 72 S.E.2d 21, 22 (1952). However, our Supreme Court has recognized at least one equitable exception to the general rule known as the "common fund" doctrine:

> The rule is well established that a court of equity, or a court in the exercise of equitable jurisdiction, may in its discretion, and without statutory authorization, order an allowance for attorney fees to a litigant who at his own expense has maintained a successful suit for the preservation, protection, or increase of a common fund or of common property, or who has created at his own expense or brought into court a fund which others may share with him.[103] . . .

A separate and distinct equitable doctrine of awarding attorney's fees, where no such common fund is created, is known in other jurisdictions as the common "corporate benefit." This doctrine is most clearly expressed in Delaware common law, providing the following elements: "[A] litigant who confers a common monetary benefit upon an ascertainable stockholder class is entitled to an award of counsel fees and expenses for its efforts in creating the benefit. . . . To be entitled to an award of fees under the corporate benefit doctrine, an applicant must show . . . that: (1) the suit was meritorious when filed; (2) the action producing benefit to the corporation was taken by the defendants before a judicial resolution was achieved; and (3) the resulting corporate benefit was causally related to the lawsuit." Cal-Maine Foods, Inc. v. Pyles, 858 A.2d 927, 927 (Del. 2004) (quoting United Vanguard Fund v. Takecare, Inc., 693 A.2d 1076, 1079 (Del. 1997)).[104]

---

103. *Query:* If one of a corporation's two shareholders brings a successful derivative suit against the other shareholder, does corporate payment of plaintiff's attorneys' fees fulfill the policy of fairness of sharing costs among those who benefit? See Cziraki v. Thunder Cats, Inc. 111 Cal. App. 4th 552, 3 Cal. Rptr. 3d 419 (2003). — ED.

104. Generally known as the "substantial benefit" rule, its rationale is that a derivative suit "should not be inhibited by a doctrine which limits the compensation of successful attorneys to cases which produce a monetary recovery: the realization of substantial, if nonpecuniary, benefits by the corporation should be the criterion. . . . The encouragement of nuisance-value derivative actions ('strike suits') is avoided or minimized by the requirement that only 'substantial' benefits will entitle the successful stockholder to attorneys' fees." Fletcher v. A.J. Industries, Inc., 266 Cal. App. 2d 313, 72 Cal. Rptr. 146 (1968). — ED.

In the case at bar, the business court "adopt[ed] the Delaware decisional framework" for the "corporate benefit" doctrine and awarded attorney's fee thereunder. . . .

In Madden v. Chase, 84 N.C. App. 289, 292, 352 S.E.2d 456, 458 *disc. review denied*, 320 N.C. 169, 358 S.E.2d 53 (1987), we denied an award of attorney's fees sought by a group of plaintiffs filing suit to enjoin a "going private" merger. The plaintiffs in that case believed the price per share being offered to the two private purchasers was undervalued. After the case had been pending for approximately five months, the investment banking firm which had initially appraised the shares for the directors re-evaluated its opinion and withdrew it. Thereafter, the "going private" merger was abandoned and the public shareholders maintained their shares, mooting the plaintiffs' claims. Pursuant to the plaintiffs' petition for attorney's fees, we found that North Carolina had not recognized an applicable equitable exception raised by these facts for overriding the general rule requiring statutory authority to award attorney's fees. . . .

Shedding relevant light on the applicability of the common "corporate benefit" doctrine to the facts of *Madden* is a recent opinion by the Delaware Supreme Court. In Cal-Maine Foods, Inc. v. Pyles, Cal-Maine Foods, Inc., the largest producer and distributor of shell eggs in the United States, announced a going-private transaction at $7.35 per share. Id. However, on its last trading day before the announcement, Cal-Maine's common stock closed at $7.56 per share. Stockholders filed a complaint alleging breach of fiduciary duty and seeking injunctive relief. Id. Among its claims, the complaint alleged that the proposed price was unfair because it failed to reflect rising egg prices and Cal-Maine's improved performance. Id. While the case was pending, the going private transaction was abandoned. The Chancery Court, finding the stockholders' claims causally related to the transaction's abandonment, awarded the stockholders' attorney's fees under the "common benefit" theory. And, upon these facts, none of which we find materially distinct from *Madden*, the Delaware Supreme Court affirmed [finding that Cal-Maine had not overcome the "presumption of a causal connection"].

While noting the reasoned policy argument offered by the business court in its opinion and with due respect for the breadth of support the petitioner found in other jurisdictions which have applied the common benefit theory, our Court does not possess the power to extend equitable exceptions in this state's jurisprudence where a prior panel of this Court has chosen not to do so. In light of the elements of the common "corporate benefit" theory as provided in Delaware's respected corporate jurisprudence, and application of those elements in Cal-Maine Foods, Inc., by the Delaware Court of Chancery, we believe the plaintiff's petition for attorney's fees is governed by *Madden* and precludes any award. Lastly, assuming arguendo that the common benefit doctrine is a recognized equitable extension of awarding attorney's fees in North Carolina, we are not convinced the facts of this case fall within the purview of the doctrine. Plaintiffs . . . [did not] show any specific pecuniary benefit to the Wachovia shareholders stemming from the business court's order invalidating the non-termination provision of the merger agreement . . . [and] Delaware's application of the doctrine seems to require some indicia of "monetary benefit." United Vanguard Fund, Inc., 693 A.2d at 1079. The business court expressly found "there was not even an increase in the stock price attributable to any action by plaintiffs' counsel, nor did any subsequent bidder appear" after the non-termination provision was deemed invalid. . . .

Reversed and remanded.

------

1. *"Nonpecuniary" benefit*. The *Fletcher* case, footnote 104 supra, relied on Bosch v. Meeker Coop. Light & Power Ass'n, 257 Minn. 362, 101 N.W.2d 423 (1960), to emphasize that under the "substantial benefit" doctrine, although the benefit must be "something more than technical in its consequence, . . . it will suffice if the court finds, upon proper evidence, that the results of the action 'maintain the health of the corporation and raise the standards of fiduciary relationships and of other economic behavior, or *prevent*[s] an abuse which would be prejudicial to the rights and interests of the corporation or affect the enjoyment or protection of an essential right to the stockholder's interest.' "

2. *Substantial benefit to whom?* (a) In Lewis v. Anderson, 692 F.2d 1267 (9th Cir. 1982), the court had upheld a "special litigation committee's" decision that it would not be in the corporation's best interest to pursue plaintiff's derivative suit challenging a stock option plan that benefited a majority of the board. Plaintiff then sought attorneys' fees from the corporation on the ground that the share-holder approval of the stock option plan had been prompted by plaintiff's filing the derivative suit. The court affirmed the district judge's conclusion "that share-holder ratification was a substantial benefit because it vindicated Disney's shareholders' right to be consulted on major management issues and raised the standards of fiduciary relationships within Disney."[105]

(b) In Mills v. Electric Auto-Lite Co., 396 U.S. 375 (1970), noted, 84 Harv. L. Rev. 211 (1970), plaintiffs brought a derivative suit and class action challenging the merger of their corporation into another. They alleged that management's proxy statement, soliciting shareholder approval of the merger, failed to disclose that management was not disinterested and was thus materially misleading to minority shareholders in violation of the proxy rules under §14(a) of the Securities Exchange Act. The court of appeals had held that, once the merger was accomplished, plaintiffs had no cause of action if defendants could show that the merger was fair to the minority share-holders and would thus have probably been approved irrespective of the materially misleading proxy statement. The Supreme Court, although not addressing the question of the appropriate relief, reversed (see page 694 supra). It held that plain-tiffs had a cause of action under §14(a) as long as there was a material misrepresen-tation in the proxy solicitation that was an essential link to approving the merger.

The Court also held that plaintiffs, having established a proxy rule violation by corporate management, were "entitled to an interim award of litigation expenses and reasonable attorneys' fees" from the corporation "for the costs of establishing the violation":

> While the general American rule is that attorneys' fees are not ordinarily recoverable
> as costs, both the courts and Congress have developed exceptions to this rule for

105. Compare Braude v. Automobile Club of Southern California, 178 Cal. App. 3d 994, 223 Cal. Rptr. 914 (1986), denying award of attorneys' fees in a derivative suit that resulted in change of nomination and election procedures in nonprofit corporation: "Insofar as . . . [Lewis v. Anderson] holds that under the substantial benefit doctrine fees may be awarded 'when important shareholder rights are successfully asserted' . . . , without more, and without distinguishing actual and concrete benefits from doctrinal and conceptual benefits, . . . the case does not accurately represent the law in California." — ED.

situations in which overriding considerations indicate the need for such a recovery. A primary judge-created exception has been to award expenses where a plaintiff has successfully maintained a suit, usually on behalf of a class, that benefits a group of others in the same manner as himself. . . . The dissemination of misleading proxy solicitations was a "deceit practiced on the stockholders as a group," . . . and the expenses of petitioners' lawsuit have been incurred for the benefit of the corporation and the other shareholders.

The fact that this suit has not yet produced, and may never produce, a monetary recovery from which the fees could be paid does not preclude an award based on this rationale. . . . [C]ourts increasingly have recognized that the expenses incurred by one shareholder in the vindication of a corporate right of action can be spread among all shareholders through an award against the corporation, regardless of whether an actual money recovery has been obtained in the corporation's favor. For example, awards have been sustained in suits by stockholders complaining that shares of their corporation had been issued wrongfully for an inadequate consideration. A successful suit of this type, resulting in cancellation of the shares, does not bring a fund into court or add to the assets of the corporation, but it does benefit the holders of the remaining shares by enhancing their value. Similarly, holders of voting trust certificates have been allowed reimbursement of their expenses from the corporation where they succeeded in terminating the voting trust and obtaining for all certificate holders the right to vote their shares.[20] In these cases there was a "common fund" only in the sense that the court's jurisdiction over the corporation as nominal defendant made it possible to assess fees against all of the shareholders through an award against the corporation. . . .

In many suits under §14(a), particularly where the violation does not relate to the terms of the transaction for which proxies are solicited, it may be impossible to assign monetary value to the benefit. Nevertheless, the stress placed by Congress on the importance of fair and informed corporate suffrage leads to the conclusion that, in vindicating the statutory policy, petitioners have rendered a substantial service to the corporation and its shareholders. . . . Whether petitioners are successful in showing a need for significant relief may be a factor in determining whether a further award should later be made. But regardless of the relief granted, private stockholders' actions of this sort "involve corporate therapeutics," and furnish a benefit to all shareholders by providing an important means of enforcement of the proxy statute. To award attorneys' fees in such a suit to a plaintiff who has succeeded in establishing a cause of action is not to saddle the unsuccessful party with the expenses but to impose them on the class that has benefited from them and that would have had to pay them had it brought the suit.[106]

(c) In what precise ways, if any, did the derivative suits in the *Fletcher, Bosch, Lewis,* and *Mills* cases (and those described therein) produce substantial benefit to the corporation?

(d) In O'Neill v. Church's Fried Chicken, Inc., 910 F.2d 263 (5th Cir. 1990), plaintiff's derivative suit resulted in a substantial increase in the amount of the tender offer price paid for all of the corporation's shares. The court held that the corporation must pay plaintiff's attorneys' fees:

---

20. Allen v. Chase Natl. Bank, 180 Misc. 259, 40 N.Y.S.2d 245 (Sup. Ct. 1943), sequel to Allen v. Chase Nat. Bank. 178 Misc. 536, 35 N.Y.S.2d 958 (Sup. Ct. 1942).

106. Would the result in the *Mills* case have been different if plaintiffs' suit had *not* been brought derivatively or as a class action? See Reiser v. Del Monte Properties Co., 605 F.2d 1135 (9th Cir. 1979) (allowing attorneys' fees). Compare Gold v. Schwab, 232 Cal. Rptr. 643 (Ct. App. 1986). See also Tandycrafts, Inc. v. Initio Partners, 562 A.2d 1162 (Del. 1989): "[T]here is no class action or derivative suit prerequisite to an award of attorneys' fees under the common benefit exception." — ED.

Admittedly, this result in some respects appears to contravene the traditional purpose of the common benefit rule. Rather than taxing O'Neill's fees to the prior shareholders who benefited from the higher price her action allegedly prompted, as a practical matter our decision seems to tax those fees to the present shareholder, who was forced to pay the higher price and obviously enjoyed no benefit. This analysis, however, ignores the fact that any purchaser of a corporation also purchases that corporation's liabilities, whether unliquidated, disputed, or even unforeseen. . . . The burden may properly be placed on the offerer to account for the cost of such potential fee awards in the calculation of his tender offer, or to make other arrangements to shift the cost of fees to the shareholders to whom the tender offer is made. And, if the offerer does so, this will have the effect of causing the benefited shareholders, as such, to ratably bear the cost of prosecuting the derivative suit which produced the benefit. Moreover, as a practical matter, there is no other reasonably available means to allow O'Neill to recover her expenses in producing the common benefit that Church's in essence concedes her derivative action has bestowed.

3. *Problems.* Should plaintiff shareholder be entitled to reimbursement from the corporation after having prevailed on the following causes of action?

(a) Injunction against corporation from increasing its capital without complying with statute requiring extraordinary majority vote for such action. See Aiple v. Twin City Barge & Towing Co., 279 Minn. 22, 154 N.W.2d 898 (1968).

(b) Declaration that majority shareholder wrongfully caused plaintiff's removal from corporate office, thus resulting in the board's loss of "power to exercise broad and independent judgment on matters of corporate policy" and producing "an adverse effect on all corporate personnel with an attendant negative reflection upon the corporation's general business complexion." See Holden v. Construction Mach. Corp., 202 N.W.2d 348 (Iowa 1972).

Of what significance would it be if any of the above were characterized as direct (class) actions rather than derivative suits?

4. *Who should pay?* Should the real defendants, rather than the corporation, be obligated to reimburse plaintiff's expenses in any (or all) of the cases examined in this section? If so, should this be the rule in all derivative suits and class actions? See Kahan v. Rosenstiel, 424 F.2d 161, 167-168 (3d Cir. 1970) ("in exceptional circumstances . . . where the behavior of a litigant has reflected a willful and persistent defiance of the law, a court of equity has the power to charge an adverse party with plaintiff's counsel fees as well as court costs"); Moses v. McGarvey, 614 P.2d 1363 (Alaska 1980) (trial court has discretion to order defendant officer to pay plaintiff's costs and attorneys' fees "especially where the court believes that defendant, as here, to be the wrongdoer,"[107] despite the absence of any finding that defendant was "responsible for the misleading proxy statements" and the fact that defendant "did not profit at the expense of the corporation"). Should the real defendants also be obligated to pay the *corporation's* attorney's fees and litigation expenses? Compare id. with Interlake Porsche & Audi, Inc. v. Blackburn, 45 Wash. App. 502, 728 P.2d 597 (1986). See also Securities Exchange Act §18 and Fed. R. Civ. P. 11, footnote 87 supra.

5. *Settlements.* In Robbins v. Alibrandi, 127 Cal. App. 4th 438, 25 Cal. Rptr. 3d 387 (2005), the court held that the trial judge must determine whether attorneys' fees,

---

107. Accord, Grizzard v. Petkas, 173 Ga. App. 629, 327 S.E.2d 514 (1985). — Ed.

negotiated between a derivative suit plaintiff and the corporation as part of a settlement, are "fair and reasonable" and "an amount that represents the value of the work done." Although "the savings resulting from settlement is not a benefit resulting from the litigation and therefore cannot provide a basis for an award of attorney fees under the 'substantial benefit doctrine,' . . . [t]he court is entitled to recognize that the corporation may have a legitimate business interest in settling a marginal case, including paying the plaintiffs' attorney fees, as a means of avoiding the costs of litigation."

6. *Cause of benefit.* (a) In Blau v. Rayette-Faberge, Inc., 389 F.2d 469 (2d Cir. 1968), plaintiff shareholder's lawyer (Levy) discovered a possible violation by a corporate insider (Niemec) of §16(b) of the Securities Exchange Act of 1934 (page 505 supra) after 18 months of the two-year statute of limitations had already expired. Levy asked the corporation (Rayette) to sue. Two months later, Rayette informed Levy that Niemec had agreed to pay the corporation his profits. The court held that plaintiff should have his attorneys' fees paid by the corporation:

> We do not suggest that counsel fees should be automatically awarded to overzealous attorneys; nor do we want lawyers poring over 16(a) reports as soon as they are made public to find a cause of action before the corporation does and thereby collect a fee. But there is a middle ground between that unattractive picture and denial of all compensation unless suit is brought: Reimbursement for information leading to corporate recovery will be allowed only if the corporation has done nothing for a substantial period of time after the suspect transactions and its inaction is likely to continue. In this way, not speed but careful investigation will be rewarded, and the corporation will have adequate opportunity to enforce its rights without prodding from a stockholder. But if the corporation has been, and is likely to be, inattentive to its rights, a portion of any recovery should properly go to the stockholder for reimbursement of any reasonable legal expenses. Concededly, this standard is not precise, but rules of thumb in this field as elsewhere can be worked out on a case by case basis. . . . [T]he investigation of the facts with respect to Niemec's transactions did not begin until Rayette received Levy's letter and demand. . . . [T]here appears to be no genuine issue as to whether Levy's letter was the "motivating" cause for the recovery. . . . [108]

(b) *Problems.* What results in respect to the following claims for reimbursement from the corporation?

(i) Plaintiff instituted a derivative suit on behalf of an insurance corporation, charging mismanagement. While suit was pending, the state insurance commissioner investigated the corporation and found mismanagement. As a result of these findings, a new board was elected and it exacted a large settlement from the former managers. Plaintiff's suit was then dismissed. See Adler v. Brooks, 375 S.W.2d 544 (Tex. Civ. App. 1964).

(ii) Plaintiff instituted a derivative suit to compel resignation of the corporation's directors on the ground that they were also directors of another corporation, and thus in violation of a Clayton Act ban on certain interlocking directorates.

---

108. Compare Ripley v. International Rys. of Cent. America, 16 App. Div. 2d 260, 227 N.Y.S.2d 64 (1962): "It would be unwise to authorize compensation to counsel for a stockholder whenever management took action beneficial to the corporation as a result of a request or demand by a stockholder. That management moved in order to forestall a derivative action is immaterial. The requirement that a stockholder make a demand is to afford the corporation an opportunity to act, and if the corporation does act it makes further proceedings on the part of a stockholder unnecessary." — ED.

The directors then resigned from the board of the other corporation, and plaintiff's suit was dismissed. The FTC could have obtained the directors' resignations without cost to the plaintiff or the corporation. See Schechtman v. Wolfson, 141 F. Supp. 453 (S.D.N.Y. 1956), *aff'd on other grounds,* 244 F.2d 537 (2d Cir. 1957). See also Grace v. Ludwig, 484 F.2d 1262 (2d Cir. 1973).

(iii) Plaintiff instituted a derivative suit to require the corporation's directors to change its procedures. The suit was dismissed because plaintiff had not shown that failure to make a demand was futile. The directors then changed the procedures that were the subject of suit. See Jerue v. Millett, 66 P.3d 736 (Alaska 2003).

(iv) Corporation settles a class action against it for $67.5 million, most of which its insurer agrees to pay on condition that the corporation also settle a related derivative suit against it. Plaintiff shareholder in this derivative suit agrees to dismiss it if corporation pays $500,000 to plaintiff's lawyer. See Zucker v. Westinghouse Electric Corp., 265 F.3d 171 (3d Cir. 2001).

(v) Plaintiff instituted a derivative suit seeking to enjoin the corporation's recently approved stock option plan, charging that it constituted waste. Defendant directors, firmly believing that plaintiff could not succeed on the merits, nonetheless modified the plan by reducing the amount of compensation so as to avoid what the directors considered to be vexatious and expensive litigation. Plaintiff, satisfied, moved to dismiss. See Dann v. Chrysler Corp., 223 A.2d 384 (Del. 1968); see also Globus, Inc. v. Janoff, 279 F. Supp. 807 (S.D.N.Y. 1968) (corporation canceled stock option plan for reasons allegedly independent of plaintiff's derivative suit attacking it).

(vi) Plaintiff instituted a derivative suit challenging the legality of a shareholder-approved plan to have the corporation purchase the stock of its controlling shareholder. The purchase would have left the corporation in a difficult financial position. During the delay occasioned by plaintiff's suit, *B* offered a higher price for all the corporation's shares. All shareholders sold to *B*, thus mooting the derivative suit. See Ramey v. Cincinnati Enquirer, Inc., 508 F.2d 1188 (6th Cir. 1974). See also Crandon Capital Partners v. Shelk 342 Or. 555, 157 P.3d 176 (2007) (similar sequence of events leading to plaintiff's derivative suit becoming moot).

(vii) Plaintiff shareholder objected to the proposed settlement of a derivative suit instituted by another shareholder. During the delay occasioned by plaintiff's objection, a decision in a different case (that was favorable to the derivative suit claim but whose pendency had not been urged by plaintiff as a reason for delay) caused defendants to increase the settlement. Plaintiffs, satisfied, withdrew objection. See White v. Auerbach, 500 F.2d 822 (2d Cir. 1974).

7. *Amount of fees.* (a)

Two basic approaches exist. Under the traditional "salvage value" approach, courts have calculated counsel fees by awarding a percentage of the total recovery. Historically, awards have ranged between 20-30% of the total recovery when the recovery was below $1 million, and between 15-20% when it was more. See Cole, Counsel Fees in Stockholders' Derivative and Class Actions — Hornstein Revisited, 6 U. Rich. L. Rev. 259 (1972); Mowrey, Attorney Fees in Securities Class Action and Derivative Suits, 3 J. Corp. L. 267 (1978). The alternative approach, recommended by the Manual for Complex Litigation, Second §24.12 (1986), and prevalent among federal courts, focuses principally on the value of the attorney's time at the attorney's customary hourly rate, and then adjusts this "lodestar figure" upward (or downward) to reflect the risk assumed by the attorney and the quality of the work done. See Lindy Bros. Builders v. American Radiator & Standard Sanitary Corp., 487 F.2d 161 (3d Cir. 1973); Detroit v. Grinnell Corp., 495 F.2d 448 (2d Cir. 1974). See Reporter's Note 1. Recently, there appears to have been a trend toward greater use of the percentage method, and in some Circuits a 30 percent fee award has now become presumptive. See Paul, Johnson, Alston & Hunt v. Graulty, 886 F.2d 268 (9th Cir. 1989); In re Activision Securities Litigation, 723 F. Supp. 1373 (N.D. Cal. 1989). [This trend has accelerated. See Manual for Complex Litigation, Fourth 219 (2005).] Other courts have expressly used high multipliers under the lodestar formula in order to achieve the same desired percentage of the recovery. See In re Union Carbide Corporation Consumer Prod. Bus. Sec. Litig., 724 F. Supp. 160, 170 (S.D.N.Y. 1989). Substantial equivalence between the two methods is thus possible.

Both the lodestar and the percentage-of-the-recovery approaches have well-recognized deficiencies if they are applied literally and without a sense of their impact upon the incentives held out to the plaintiff's attorney. Because a time-based formula, such as the "lodestar" method, compensates attorneys for the hours they expend, a number of commentators have suggested that such a formula gives rise to an incentive to expend unnecessary time and engage in dilatory tactics in order to maximize the attorney's recovery. Such an incentive is unfortunate not only because it delays the progress of the litigation, but also because it aggravates a latent conflict of interest between the attorney and the class he or she represents; the greater the fee, the smaller the net recovery will typically be for the shareholders. In addition, if the defendant strategically delays any settlement offer until just before the moment of trial or judgment, the defendant can further exacerbate this conflict, because at this point an inadequate settlement offer should produce nearly the same attorney's fee under a time-based formula as would a highly successful litigated victory. Thus, the plaintiff's attorney may have an incentive to accept an offer that is not in the best interests of the client in order to avoid the risk of trial and an adverse decision.[109]

In contrast, a percentage-of-the-recovery formula avoids these problems (because the attorney's fee grows only in proportion to the recovery), but encounters others. First, a percentage formula may sometimes encourage premature settlements that are not in the best interests of the class. Compare Clermont and Currivan, Improving on the Contingent Fee, 63 Cornell L. Rev. 529 (1978) (percentage formula encourages early settlements) with Trubek, Sarat, Felstiner, Kritzer & Grossman, The Costs of Ordinary Litigation, 31 UCLA L. Rev. 72, 108-109 (1983) (empirical evidence based on attorneys' estimate of settlement value of cases provides little support for theory that percentage formula encourages early settlements). Second, a percentage formula clearly does not work with respect to nonpecuniary recoveries, such as injunctive or equitable relief, where the value of the benefit conferred cannot be easily quantified. Finally, such a formula may produce windfall profits (such as where a case is settled immediately), which may evoke public criticism and erode respect for the law. Accordingly, [ALI §7.17, which provides that the award of plaintiff's attorneys' fees may not "exceed a reasonable proportion of the value of the relief (including nonpecuniary relief) obtained by the plaintiff"] proposes a compromise that attempts to retain the best of both formulas while avoiding their deficiencies. Section 7.17 permits the use of the percentage of the recovery formula, but does not require it. Where it is not employed as the measure of the fee award, however, it should set a ceiling on the maximum fee allowable under any formula. The effect is to reduce the incentive to expend time needlessly, to minimize the danger of collusive settlements, and to align

---

109. See John C. Coffee Jr., The Unfaithful Champion: The Plaintiff as Monitor in Shareholder Litigation, 48 Law & Contemp. Probs. 5, 35-38 (1985). — ED.

better the attorney's self-interest with that of the client;[110] in addition, the danger of unjustified "windfall" profits is better avoided.

2 ALI, Principles of Corporate Governance 206-207 (1994).

(b) For the view that "legal rules that compensate plaintiffs and their attorneys on the basis of recoveries from suits introduce a fundamental distortion in the decision to bring suit," see Reinier Kraakman, Hyun Park & Steven Shavell, When Are Shareholder Suits in Shareholder Interests?, 82 Geo. L.J. 1733 (1994): A "plaintiff compensation rule that would lead shareholders to sue if and only if suit would increase corporate value" should be based on (1) "deterrence grounds" — "a court in evaluating a suit's deterrence prospects would look chiefly to the penalties that it imposes on wrongdoers and the probability that shareholders could detect similar misconduct," or (2) "net recoveries" — "gross recovery" in excess of costs which "include both litigation expenses and increases in insurance or salary costs that are associated with managers' liability." Compare Mark J. Loewenstein, Shareholder Derivative Litigation and Corporate Governance, 24 Del. J. Corp. L. 1, 13, 22 (1999), who asks, "[I]f plaintiff had sought . . . [the corporate governance reform obtained in the settlement] in its complaint, to the exclusion of all other relief, including monetary damages, is it not likely that defendants would have settled immediately? Assuming the answer is 'yes,' then perhaps the corporate defendant should only have to pay for the value of the benefit, largely ignoring the litigation costs of the plaintiff."

8. *Intervention.* The right of shareholders to intervene in derivative suits is generally granted by statute in various forms, all vesting the court with considerable discretion. See, e.g., Fed. R. Civ. P. 24. Shareholders may attempt to intervene because they feel the action is a collusive suit or is not being properly handled by the original plaintiffs, or because they agree with its purposes and wish to give plaintiffs their support, or perhaps because they (or their lawyers) want to share in the counsel's fee.

After either intervention (or consolidation) is granted, it has been reported that the usual practice has been for the court to permit the group of plaintiffs' lawyers to select their lead counsel.[111] The Manual for Complex Litigation, Third §20.224 (1995) — a document prepared by a committee of prominent judges and lawyers, containing suggested procedures for complex litigation in the federal courts — provides that

the judge needs to take an active part in making the decision on the appointment. . . .
Deferring to proposals by counsel without independent examination by the court,

---

110. Note that under ALI §7.17 "the court must [ordinarily] attempt to place a value on [nonpecuniary] relief in order to apply the percentage ceiling. . . . This limitation recognizes that in some cases the settlement dynamics can result in overstating the 'benefit' in order to justify a fee award. Over the long run, allowing the award of an attorney's fee on the basis of such cosmetic benefits would encourage the filing of non-meritorious claims and can expose the corporation to a greater risk of frivolous litigation than would prevail if closer judicial scrutiny were given to the value of the benefit received by the corporation." 2 ALI, Principles of Corporate Governance 208-209 (1994). — ED.

111. For strong criticism of this approach, see John C. Coffee Jr., The Unfaithful Champion: The Plaintiff as Monitor in Shareholder Litigation, 48 Law & Contemp. Probs. 5, 50-52 (1985): "The sensible prescription is to exclude the free riders by conferring some form of property right on the attorney who truly initiates the case. . . . [T]he worst alternative is the political election process that is now our de facto system for the selection of lead counsel, because it ensures the selection neither of the most able attorney nor of the attorney who did the basic investigatory work leading up to the action."

even those that seem to have the concurrence of a "majority" of those affected, invites problems down the road when designated counsel may turn out to be unwilling or unable to discharge their responsibilities in a manner satisfactory to the court or when excessive costs are incurred. The court should take the time necessary to make an assessment of the qualifications, functions, organization, and compensation of designated counsel.

All plaintiffs must share the expenses of the suit, and they remain liable even if inter se one party has agreed to carry this burden. Hoover v. Allen, 180 F. Supp. 263 (S.D.N.Y. 1960). Compensation of counsel for the intervenors will be left largely to the discretion of the judge, who will generally base the award on the contribution made by intervenors' counsel to the success of the suit. See Saylor v. Bastedo, 594 F. Supp. 371 (S.D.N.Y. 1984).

I. *INDEMNIFICATION OF DEFENDANTS*

Corporate managers expose themselves to extensive litigation expenses and liabilities in the course of their functioning as directors and officers. They may be made defendants in corporate as well as derivative suits for having willfully or negligently breached fiduciary duties and damaged the corporation; especially with respect to large corporations, their potential liability may be wholly unrelated to their personal wealth. Shareholders of the corporation may bring direct actions against them for having violated diverse contractual or statutory duties; several provisions of the federal securities laws dealing with required disclosures and misrepresentations[112] present possibly crushing exposure. Outsiders who deal with the corporation (customers, suppliers, competitors, employees, etc.) may sue them for having caused various injuries in breach of common law or statutory norms. Finally, government may prosecute them, criminally or civilly, for conduct undertaken in their roles as corporate executives. For various reasons—e.g., substantive law developments, greater disclosure requirements, the contingent fee system, changing attitudes of shareholders—suits of all these types have multiplied.[113]

At common law, the question of whether corporate managers may be indemnified by the corporation for their litigation expenses and amounts paid as judgments or settlements in non-derivative suits has virtually never been addressed by the courts.[114] In derivative suits, the matter has arisen infrequently. The first major decision, New York Dock Co. v. McCollum, 173 Misc. 106, 16 N.Y.S.2d 844 (S. Ct. 1939), held that the corporation was neither obligated nor empowered to indemnify managers for their litigation expenses in defending a derivative suit, despite their having prevailed on the merits, on the ground that their successful

---

112. E.g., §§11, 12, and 17 of the Securities Act of 1933 (pages 342, 343, and 351 supra), §14 (page 543) supra, and Rule 10b-5 of the Securities Exchange Act of 1934 (page 345 supra), and the Sarbanes-Oxley Act (page 326 supra).

113. See footnote 14, page 73 supra.

114. See Note, 76 Harv. L. Rev. 1403, 1405 (1963). The law of agency would seemingly require corporate indemnification for officers and lesser employees in many situations, see Restatement (Second) of Agency §§438-440, but not for directors.

defense did not confer any specific benefit on the corporation. Subsequent decisions, however, have held that the corporation is either permitted or required to indemnify directors or officers for litigation expenses after they have been vindicated on the merits,[115] reasoning that managers should be encouraged to resist unjust charges and "strike" suits, to defend the corporate image, and to retain the positions to which they have been properly elected; and that a policy of non-indemnification would deter capable persons from seeking corporate office.

In 1941 New York enacted the first indemnification statute, and all jurisdictions have followed. The statutes differ significantly. In brief overview,

> most of these statutes expressly deny indemnification to directors and officers of judgments or amounts paid in settlement of derivative actions, and permit indemnification in such actions only for reasonable expenses incurred in the proceeding. When a director or officer has been adjudged liable to the corporation in a derivative action, payment of expenses in many states requires court approval. However, 15 jurisdictions either do not provide for any limitation on indemnification in derivative actions or expressly permit indemnification of settlements and, in seven states, judgments in such actions.

2 ALI, Principles of Corporate Governance 264 (1994). Recent enactments also deal with the matter of the corporation's purchasing insurance for its directors and officers against the various expenses and liabilities that have been discussed.[116] The statutes described below illustrate important variations.

Waltuch v. Conticommodity Services, Inc.
88 F.3d 87 (2d Cir. 1996)

JACOBS, J.: . . . As vice-president and chief metals trader for Conticommodity Services, Inc. [Conti], Waltuch traded silver for the firm's clients, as well as for his own account. Between 1981 and 1985, angry silver speculators filed numerous lawsuits against Waltuch and Conticommodity, alleging fraud, market manipulation, and antitrust violations. All of the suits eventually settled and were dismissed with prejudice, pursuant to settlements in which Conticommodity paid over $35 million to the various suitors. Waltuch himself was dismissed from the suits with no settlement contribution. His unreimbursed legal expenses in these actions total approximately $1.2 million.

Waltuch was also the subject of an enforcement proceeding brought by the CFTC [Commodity Futures Trading Commission], charging him with fraud and market manipulation. The proceeding was settled, with Waltuch agreeing to a penalty that included a $100,000 fine and a six-month ban on buying or selling futures contracts from any exchange floor. Waltuch spent $1 million in unreimbursed legal fees in the CFTC proceeding.

---

115. See Solimine v. Hollander, 129 N.J. Eq. 264, 19 A.2d 344 (Ch. 1941); In re Dissolution of E. C. Warner Co., 232 Minn. 207, 45 N.W.2d 388 (1950). Compare Tomash v. Midwest Technical Development Corp., 281 Minn. 21, 160 N.W.2d 273 (1968).

116. See generally James J. Hanks Jr. & Larry P. Scriggins, Protecting Directors and Officers from Liability — The Influence of the Model Business Corporation Act, 56 Bus. Law. 3 (2000).

Waltuch first claims that Article Ninth of Conticommodity's articles of incorporation requires Conti to indemnify him for his expenses in both the private and CFTC actions. . . .

I. Article Ninth, on which Waltuch bases his first claim, is categorical and contains no requirement of "good faith":

> The Corporation shall indemnify and hold harmless each of its incumbent or former directors, officers, employees and agents . . . against expenses actually and necessarily incurred by him in connection with the defense of any action, suit or proceeding threatened, pending or completed, in which he is made a party, by reason of his serving in or having held such position or capacity, except in relation to matters as to which he shall be adjudged in such action, suit or proceeding to be liable for negligence or misconduct in the performance of duty.[5]

Conti argues that §145(a) of Delaware's General Corporation Law, which does contain a "good faith" requirement, fixes the outer limits of a corporation's power to indemnify; Article Ninth is thus invalid under Delaware law, says Conti, to the extent that it requires indemnification of officers who have acted in bad faith. The affirmative grant of power in §145(a) is as follows:

> *A corporation shall have power to indemnify* any person who was or is a party or is threatened to be made a party to any threatened, pending or completed action, suit or proceeding, whether civil, criminal, administrative or investigative (other than an action by or in the right of the corporation) by reason of the fact that he is or was a director, officer, employee or agent of the corporation,[117] against expenses (including attorneys' fees), judgments, fines and amounts paid in settlement actually and reasonably incurred by him in connection with such action, suit or proceeding *if he acted in good faith and in a manner he reasonably believed to be in or not opposed to the best interests of the corporation,* and, with respect to any criminal action or proceeding, had no reasonable cause to believe his conduct was unlawful. [Emphasis added.][118] . . .

---

5. Because the private suits and the CFTC proceeding were settled, it is undisputed that Waltuch was not "adjudged . . . to be liable for negligence or misconduct in the performance of duty."

117. For discussion of whether this means that "a director must be sued for a breach of duty to the corporation or for a wrong committed on behalf of the corporation," or whether it also includes "suits against a director that arise more tangentially from his role, position or status as a director," see Heffernan v. Pacific Dunlop GNB Corp., 965 F.2d 369 (7th Cir. 1992). See also Barry v. Barry, 824 F. Supp. 178 (D. Minn. 1993), *aff'd*, 28 F.3d 848 (8th Cir. 1994); Weisbart v. Agri Tech, Inc., 22 P.3d 954 (Colo. App. 2001) (person covered if "sued at least in part" because of being officer or director); Stifel Financial Corp. v. Cochran, 809 A.2d 555 (Del. 2002) (discharged director/officer not covered when sued by corporation for breach of his employment contract because that concerns his "personal obligation" to the corporation). — Ed.

118. MBCA §5 (1969), still generally followed in more than one-third of the states, was almost identical to the Delaware statute. RMBCA §§8.50-8.59 (1994) are still somewhat similar to Del. §145 and are followed in over one-third of the states. Note that Del. §145(a) applies only to *non-derivative* actions (as in this case) against corporate officials. N.Y. Bus. Corp. Law §722(a) (1986) and Cal. Gen. Corp. Law §317(b) (1996) are similar. All three statutes add that "[t]he termination of any action, suit or proceeding by judgment, order, settlement, conviction, or upon a plea of nolo contendere or its equivalent, shall not, of itself, create a presumption that the person did not act in good faith and in a manner which he reasonably believed to be in or not opposed to the best interests of the corporation, and, with respect to any criminal action or proceeding, had reasonable cause to believe that his conduct was unlawful." Del. §145(a); N.Y. §722(b); Cal. §317(b). *Query:* Does this provision bar indemnification if defendant director is found liable for damages for deliberately discriminating against the corporation's customers on the basis of their race in violation of state law? See Biondi v. Beekman Hill House Apt. Corp., 94 N.Y.2d 659, 709 N.Y.S.2d 861, 731 N.E.2d 577 (2000): "Although the key to indemnification is a director's good faith *toward the corporation* and . . . a judgment against the director, standing alone, may

In order to escape the "good faith" clause of §145(a), Waltuch argues that §145(a) is not an exclusive grant of indemnification power, because §145(f) expressly allows corporations to indemnify officers in a manner broader than that set out in §145(a). The "nonexclusivity" language of §145(f) provides: "The indemnification and advancement of expenses provided by, or granted pursuant to, the other subsections of this section shall not be deemed exclusive of any other rights to which those seeking indemnification or advancement of expenses may be entitled under any bylaw, agreement, vote of stockholders or disinterested directors or otherwise, both as to action in his official capacity and as to action in another capacity while holding such office."[119] . . . Waltuch contends that the "nonexclusivity" language in §145(f) is a separate grant of indemnification power, not limited by the good faith clause that governs the power granted in §145(a). Conti on the other hand contends that §145(f) must be limited by "public policies," one of which is that a corporation may indemnify its officers only if they act in "good faith." . . .

A. *Delaware Cases.* No Delaware court has decided the very issue presented here; but the applicable cases tend to support the proposition that a corporation's grant of indemnification rights cannot be *inconsistent* with the substantive statutory provisions of §145, notwithstanding §145(f). We draw this rule of "consistency" primarily from our reading of the Delaware Supreme Court's opinion in Hibbert v. Hollywood Park, Inc., 457 A.2d 339 (Del. 1983). In that case, Hibbert and certain other directors sued the corporation and the remaining directors, and then demanded indemnification for their expenses and fees related to the litigation. The company refused indemnification on the ground that [under §145(a)] directors were entitled to indemnification only as *defendants* in legal proceedings. The court

---

not be dispositive of whether the director acted in good faith, . . . willful racial discrimination cannot be considered an act in the corporation's best interest."

For *derivative* actions against corporate officials, Del. §145(b) authorizes corporations to indemnify only "expenses (including attorneys' fees)." N.Y. §722(c) adds "amounts paid in settlement." Both statutes, however, qualify this indemnification if the corporate official "shall have been adjudged to be liable to the corporation unless and only to the extent that . . . the court in which such action or suit was brought shall determine upon application that, despite the adjudication of liability but in view of all the circumstances of the case, such person is fairly and reasonably entitled to indemnity for such expenses which the . . . court shall deem proper." Del. §145(b). Cal. §317(c) is similar, but Cal. §317(c)(2) forbids indemnification of "amounts paid in settling . . . with or without court approval." Ind. Gen. Corp. Act §23-1-37-8 (1993) — like the rules in a half-dozen other states — authorizes indemnification for any "liability incurred."

For the view that rules permitting indemnification for amounts paid in settlement and related legal expenses play a substantial role in encouraging strike suits, see Tim Oliver Barandi, The Strike Suit: A Common Problem of the Derivative Suit and the Shareholder Class Action, 98 Dick. L. Rev. 355 (1994). — ED.

119. N.Y. §721 and Cal. §317(g) are similar to Del. §145(f), but N.Y. §721 further provides that "no indemnification may be made to or on behalf of any director or officer if a judgment or other final adjudication adverse to the director or officer establishes that his acts were committed in bad faith or were the result of active and deliberate dishonesty and were material to the cause of action so adjudicated, or that he personally gained in fact a financial profit or other advantage to which he was not legally entitled." Cal. §317(g) is similar to N.Y. §721, but goes further in also forbidding indemnification "for acts or omissions that show a reckless disregard for the director's duty to the corporation or its shareholders in circumstances in which the director was aware, or should have been aware, in the ordinary course of performing a director's duties, of a risk of serious injury to the corporation or its shareholders, [and] for acts or omissions that constitute an unexcused pattern of inattention that amounts to an abdication of the director's duty to the corporation or its shareholders." — ED.

reversed the trial court and held that Hibbert was entitled to indemnification under the plain terms of a company bylaw that did not draw an express distinction between plaintiff directors and defendant directors. Id. at 343. The court . . . [stated] two complementary propositions. Under §145(f), a corporation may provide indemnification rights that go "beyond" the rights provided by §145(a) and the other substantive subsections of §145. At the same time, any such indemnification rights provided by a corporation must be "consistent with" the substantive provisions of §145, including §145(a). In *Hibbert,* the corporate bylaw was "consistent with" §145(a), because this subsection was "not limited to" suits in which directors were defendants.[120] *Hibbert's* holding may support an inverse corollary that illuminates our case: if §145(a) had been expressly limited to directors who were named as defendants, the bylaw could not have stood, regardless of §145(f), because the bylaw would not have been "consistent with" the substantive statutory provision. . . .

B. *Statutory Reading.* The "consistency" rule suggested by these Delaware cases is reinforced by our reading of §145 as a whole. Subsections (a) (indemnification for third-party actions) and (b) (similar indemnification for derivative suits) expressly grant a corporation the power to indemnify directors, officers, and others, if they "acted in good faith and in a manner reasonably believed to be in or not opposed to the best interest of the corporation." These provisions thus limit the scope of the power that they confer. They are permissive in the sense that a corporation may exercise less than its full power to grant the indemnification rights set out in these provisions. See Essential Enter. Corp. v. Dorsey Corp., 182 A.2d 647, 653 (Del. Ch. 1962). By the same token, subsection (f) permits the corporation to grant additional rights: the rights provided in the rest of §145 "shall not be deemed exclusive of any other rights to which those seeking indemnification may be entitled." But crucially, subsection (f) merely acknowledges that one seeking indemnification may be entitled to "other rights" (of indemnification or otherwise); it does not speak in terms of corporate power, and therefore cannot be read to free a corporation from the "good faith" limit explicitly imposed in subsections (a) and (b). . . .

Waltuch argues at length that reading §145(a) to bar the indemnification of officers who acted in bad faith would render §145(f) meaningless. This argument misreads §145(f). That subsection refers to "any other rights to which those seeking indemnification or advancement of expenses may be entitled." Delaware commentators have identified various indemnification rights that are "beyond those provided by statute," *Hibbert,* 457 A.2d at 344, and that are at the same time consistent with the statute:

> [S]ubsection (f) provides general authorization for the adoption of various procedures and presumptions making the process of indemnification more favorable to the indemnitee. For example, indemnification agreements or by-laws could provide for: (i) mandatory indemnification unless prohibited by statute; (ii) mandatory advancement of expenses, which the indemnitee can, in many instances, obtain on demand; (iii) accelerated procedures for the "determination" required by section

120. For the view that indemnification statutes "were never intended to protect directors from suits brought directly by the corporation," but rather were to be "available in two circumstances — derivative and third-party actions — and apparently in no other situations," see Diane H. Mazur, Indemnification of Directors in Actions Brought Directly by the Corporation: Must the Corporation Finance Its Opponent's Defense?, 19 J. Corp. L. 201 (1994). — Ed.

145(d) to be made in the "specific case";[121] (iv) litigation "appeal" rights of the indemnitee in the event of an unfavorable determination; (v) procedures under which a favorable determination will be deemed to have been made under circumstances where the board fails or refuses to act; [and] (vi) reasonable funding mechanisms.

E. Norman Veasey, et al., Delaware Supports Directors with a Three-Legged Stool of Limited Liability, Indemnification, and Insurance, 42 Bus. Law. 399, 415 (1987). Moreover, subsection (f) may reference non-indemnification rights, such as advancement rights or rights to other payments from the corporation that do not qualify as indemnification.

... [W]e hold that Conti's Article Ninth, which would require indemnification of Waltuch even if he acted in bad faith, is inconsistent with §145(a) and thus exceeds the scope of a Delaware corporation's power to indemnify.[122] Since Waltuch has agreed to forgo his opportunity to prove at trial that he acted in good faith, he is not entitled to indemnification under Article Ninth for the $2.2 million he spent in connection with the private lawsuits and the CFTC proceeding. We therefore affirm the district court on this issue.[123]

II. Unlike §145(a), which grants a discretionary indemnification power, §145(c) affirmatively requires corporations to indemnify its officers and directors for the "successful" defense of certain claims: "To the extent that a director, officer, employee or agent of a corporation has been successful on the merits or otherwise in defense of any action, suit or proceeding referred to in subsections (a) and (b) of this section, or in defense of any claim, issue or matter therein, he shall be

---

121. A majority of states provide that, apart from indemnification that is mandated by law, see footnote 124 infra, indemnification must be

> authorized in the specific case, upon a determination that ... [the indemnitee] has met the applicable standard of conduct ... by: (1) A majority vote of a quorum consisting of directors who are not parties to such proceeding; (2) Approval of the shareholders ... , with the shares owned by the person to be indemnified not being entitled to vote thereon; or (3) The court in which such proceeding is or was pending upon application made by the corporation or the agent or the attorney or other person rendering services in connection with the defense, whether or not such application by the agent, attorney or other person is opposed by the corporation.

Cal. §317(e). N.Y. §723(b) is similar, but it also permits approval "by the board on the opinion in writing of independent legal counsel that indemnification is proper. . . ." For skepticism about the "independence of 'independent legal counsel,'" see Joseph W. Bishop Jr., Sitting Ducks and Decoy Ducks: New Trends in the Indemnification of Corporate Directors and Officers, 77 Yale L.J. 1078, 1080 (1968). See also In re Landmark Land Co. of Carolina, Inc., 76 F.3d 553 (4th Cir. 1996), holding that a corporation's finding that its director or officer has acted in good faith is subject to judicial review.

Compare Service Corp. Int'l v. H. M. Patterson & Son, Inc., 263 Ga. 412, 434 S.E.2d 455 (1993), holding that obligations ordinarily arising in conflict-of-interest situations do not apply when the transaction is advancement of litigation expenses. See also La. Bus. Corp. Law §83(D) (1986) providing that advancement may be "authorized by the board of directors, without regard to whether participating members thereof are parties to such action, suit, or proceeding. . . ."

More than half the states have provisions similar to ALI §7.20(d) requiring the corporation to report any indemnification or advancement in connection with derivative suits to the shareholders. N.Y. §7.25(d) (1988) requires such notice only if "indemnification of directors and officers is taken by way of amendment of the by-laws, resolution of directors, or by agreement." — ED.

122. Similarly, in TLC Beatrice Int'l Holdings, Inc. v. Cigna Ins. Co., 1999 WL 33454 (S.D.N.Y.), the court held that Del. §145(b)'s failure to authorize indemnification for judgments or amounts paid in settlement of derivative suits (see footnote 118 supra) precludes a corporate bylaw under Del. §145(b) authorizing such indemnification. — ED.

123. Accord, Von-Feldt v. Stifel Financial Corp., 1999 WL 413393 (Del. Ch.).

indemnified against expenses (including attorneys' fees) actually and reasonably incurred by him in connection therewith."[124] . . . Waltuch argues that he was "successful on the merits or otherwise" in the private lawsuits, because they were dismissed with prejudice without any payment or assumption of liability by him. Conti argues that the claims against Waltuch were dismissed only because of Conti's $35 million settlement payments, and that this payment was contributed, in part, "on behalf of Waltuch."

The district court agreed with Conti that "the successful settlements cannot be credited to Waltuch but are attributable solely to Conti's settlement payments. It was not Waltuch who was successful, but Conti who was successful for him." 833 F. Supp. at 311. The district court held that §145(c) mandates indemnification when the director or officer "is vindicated," but that there was no vindication here. . . .

No Delaware court has applied §145(c) in the context of indemnification stemming from the settlement of civil litigation. One lower court, however, has applied that subsection to an analogous case in the criminal context, and has illuminated the link between "vindication" and the statutory phrase, "successful on the merits or otherwise." In Merritt-Chapman & Scott Corp. v. Wolfson, 321 A.2d 138 (Del. Super. Ct. 1974), the corporation's agents were charged with several counts of criminal conduct. A jury found them guilty on some counts, but deadlocked on the others. The agents entered into a "settlement" with the prosecutor's office by pleading nolo contendere to one of the counts in exchange for the dropping of the rest. Id. at 140. The agents claimed entitlement to mandatory indemnification under §145(c) as to the counts that were dismissed. . . . The court considered these dismissals both "success" and (therefore) "vindication," and refused to "go[] behind the result" or to appraise the reason for the success. In equating "success" with "vindication," the court thus rejected the more expansive view of vindication urged by the corporation. Under *Merritt*'s holding, then, vindication, when used as a synonym for "success" under §145(c), does not mean moral exoneration. Escape from an adverse judgment or other detriment, for whatever reason, is determinative. According to *Merritt,* the only question a court may ask is what the result was, not why it was.[12]

Conti's contention that, because of its $35 million settlement payments, Waltuch's settlement without payment should not really count as settlement without payment, is inconsistent with the rule in *Merritt*. Here, Waltuch was sued, and the

124. N.Y. §723(a) is similar. Cal. §317(d) omits the words "or otherwise." See footnote 126 infra. See also Wilshire-Doheny Assoc., Ltd. v. Shapiro, 83 Cal. App. 4th 1380, 100 Cal. Rptr. 2d 478 (2000) (officer prevailed in suit by corporation against him because of an earlier mutual release between the parties). — ED.

12. Our adoption of *Merritt*'s interpretation of the statutory term "successful" does not necessarily signal our endorsement of the result in that case. The *Merritt* court sliced the case into individual counts, with indemnification pegged to each count independently of the others. We are not faced with a case in which the corporate officer claims to have been "successful" on some parts of the case but was clearly "unsuccessful" on others, and therefore take no position on this feature of the *Merritt* holding.

We also do not mean our discussion of *Merritt* to suggest that the line between success and failure in a criminal case may be drawn in the same way in the civil context. In a criminal case, conviction on a particular count is obvious failure, and dismissal of the charge is obvious success. In a civil suit for damages, however, there is a monetary continuum between complete success (dismissal of the suit without any payment) and complete failure (payment of the full amount of damages requested by the plaintiff). Because Waltuch made no payment in connection with the dismissal of the suits against him, we need not decide whether a defendant's settlement payment automatically renders that defendant "unsuccessful" under §145(c). [For incisive discussion of this last issue, see Owens Corning v. National Union Fire Ins. Co., 257 F.3d 484, 494-496 (6th Cir. 2001). — ED.]

suit was dismissed without his having paid a settlement. Under the approach taken in *Merritt,* it is not our business to ask why this result was reached. Once Waltuch achieved his settlement gratis, he achieved success "on the merits or otherwise."[125] And, as we know from *Merritt,* success is sufficient to constitute vindication (at least for the purposes of §145(c)). Waltuch's settlement thus vindicated him.

The concept of "vindication" pressed by Conti is also inconsistent with the fact that a director or officer who is able to defeat an adversary's claim by asserting a technical defense is entitled to indemnification under §145(c). See 1 Balotti & Finkelstein, §4.13 at 4-302.[126] In such cases, the indemnitee has been "successful" in the palpable sense that he has won, and the suit has been dismissed, whether or not the victory is deserved in merits terms. . . .

For all of these reasons, we agree with Waltuch that he is entitled to indemnification under §145(c) for his expenses pertaining to the private lawsuits. . . .

Baker v. Health Management Systems, Inc.
98 N.Y.2d 80, 772 N.E.2d 1099, 745 N.Y.S.2d 741 (2002)

LEVINE, J.: Appellant Phillip Siegel was the Chief Financial Officer of respondent Health Management Systems, Inc. (HMS). In that capacity, he was joined as a party defendant in several securities fraud class actions brought in the United States District Court . . . [alleging] that defendants disseminated false and misleading statements designed to inflate the price of HMS stock. Certain unique facts set Siegel's position in the litigation apart from the other individual defendants. Namely, Siegel joined HMS *after* the beginning date of the class period when the misconduct allegedly occurred and, unlike other defendants, he actually purchased (rather than sold) shares of HMS stock during the relevant period. Accordingly, Siegel hired separate counsel.

The actions were consolidated and plaintiffs ultimately entered into a stipulation of dismissal with prejudice as to all claims against Siegel. The action continued against the other defendants and was eventually settled for $4 million. HMS denied Siegel's written request for indemnification, asserting that the legal fees sought were not necessarily incurred by Siegel because he did not require separate counsel.

In November 1998, Siegel moved, pursuant to Business Corporation Law §724 and HMS's bylaws, for indemnification of his legal fees, claiming $84,784.37 in attorneys' fees and costs. The District Court . . . [rejected] Siegel's argument that

125. The court discussed two other cases reaching the same conclusion: Wisener v. Air Express Int'l Corp., 583 F.2d 579 (2d Cir. 1978) (Illinois statute); B & B Investment Club v. Kleinert's Ins., 427 F. Supp. 787 (E.D. Pa. 1979) (Pennsylvania statute). Compare N.C. Bus. Corp. Act §§55-8-52 (1989), which mandates indemnification for directors who are "wholly successful, on the merits or otherwise."—ED.

126. Should directors be entitled to indemnification of their expenses if a derivative suit against them for fraud is dismissed because of (i) statute of limitations, (ii) plaintiff's failure to post security for expenses, (iii) plaintiff's participation or acquiescence in the alleged fraud? See (i) Dornan v. Humphrey, 278 App. Div. 1010, 106 N.Y.S.2d 142 (1951) (indemnification granted); (ii) Tyler v. Gas Consumers Ass'n, 35 Misc. 2d 801, 231 N.Y.S.2d 15 (S. Ct. 1962) (indemnification granted); (iii) Diamond v. Diamond, 307 N.Y. 263, 120 N.E.2d 819 (1954) (indemnification denied).

Should directors be entitled to indemnification of expenses if the suit against them found that (i) they breached their fiduciary duty to the corporation but (ii) their conduct did not cause the corporation's injury? See Waskel v. Guaranty Nat'l Corp., 23 P.3d 1214 (Colo. App. 2000) (indemnification granted).—ED.

he should recover the fees and costs he had incurred in attempting to secure indemnification . . . [, reasoning] that an award of fees on fees could not "be reconciled with the general rule in New York that attorneys' fees may not be awarded unless there is specific statutory or contractual authorization." (82 F. Supp. 2d 227, 236.)

On Siegel's appeal, the Second Circuit . . . certified the present question to us and we conclude that the statute does not independently provide for the recovery of fees incurred by a corporate officer in obtaining indemnification.

Section 722(a) of the Business Corporation Law permits a corporation to indemnify officers and directors made parties defendant in non-derivative actions (such as the underlying litigation here), by virtue of their capacity as such, for both liability and litigation costs. That provision states, in pertinent part, "[a] corporation may indemnify any person made, or threatened to be made, a party to an action or proceeding (other than one by or in the right of the corporation to procure a judgment in its favor), whether civil or criminal . . . by reason of the fact that [the person] . . . was a director or officer of the corporation . . . against judgments, fines, amounts paid in settlement and reasonable expenses, *including attorneys' fees actually and necessarily incurred as result of such action or proceeding* or any appeal therein, if such director or officer acted, in good faith, for a purpose . . . believed to be in . . . the best interests of the corporation" (emphasis added). . . .

Siegel argues that Business Corporation Law article 7 is a remedial statute with the purpose of shifting all costs and personal liability away from a corporate official sued in that capacity and, thus should be construed expansively. Siegel reads the phrase "as a result of" in section 722(a) as implying a "but for" test, asserting that the provision entitles him to reimbursement of all fees that he would not have spent had he not been made a party to the underlying suit. He argues that but for the underlying action, he would not have incurred the litigation costs for which he sought indemnification. Hence, Siegel maintains that he is entitled to recover all fees spent in connection with the motion for indemnification.

We disagree. Were we to accept Siegel's argument, the statutory right to indemnification would apply even to fees and expenses having the most attenuated link to the underlying action. The literal language of the statute, when taken as a whole, does not support such a construction.

In limiting recovery to only those expenses that are *"actually and necessarily incurred as a result* of such action or proceeding" (emphasis added), section 722(a) quite clearly in our view requires a reasonably substantial nexus between the expenditures and the underlying suit. In actuality, the attorneys' fees arising in connection with this motion were caused by HMS's refusal to indemnify Siegel following his dismissal from the underlying litigation. It stretches language beyond the outer limits of meaning to claim that those fees on fees were necessarily incurred by reason of the joinder of Siegel in the securities fraud suits. . . .

As explained by Professor Samuel Hoffman, who served as a drafting consultant to the New York Joint Legislative Committee to Study Revision of Corporation Laws, the objective [of the revision of 1961] was to codify and apply indemnification principles under the law of agency in the context of suits against corporate officials based on their conduct undertaken "in the good faith belief that [they were] acting properly in the best interests of the corporation" (Hoffman, The Status of Shareholders and Directors Under New York's Business Corporation Law: A Comparative View, 11 Buff. L. Rev. 496, 570-572, 574 [1962]). He cited to "the often enormous expenses of litigation incurred (and judgments or fines suffered) in the *defense* of such suits and, in a sense, *in defense and vindication of corporate policy.*" Nowhere in any of the legislative history of the 1961 enactment is there any indication of an intent to go beyond the common-law agency rule on indemnity, under which an agent's attorneys' fees incurred in enforcement of indemnification rights are not recoverable.

Siegel also relies upon the limiting language of current section 722(c) which authorizes indemnification only "in connection with the defense" of *derivative* actions brought by or on behalf of the corporation against officers and directors— to argue that the broader language of section 722(a) at issue here was intended to cover fees on fees. Again, the legislative history belies this argument. The distinction on which Siegel relies first appeared in the 1961 legislation. The more expansive language employed with respect to indemnification of litigation expenses and liability in non-derivative actions was expressly intended to cover expenses incurred in settling claims even prior to the commencement of a suit. The Joint Legislative Committee to Study Revision of Corporation Laws explained: "In contrast with indemnification in derivative actions (see, §722 and paragraph (f) of §725), indemnification is permissible under this section for expenses incurred and amounts paid in settling threatened as well as pending non-derivative actions or proceedings" (1961 N.Y. Legis. Doc. No. 12, at 54; see also Hoffman, supra at 579-581).

The indemnification provisions were revisited subsequently at various times, but always leaving unchanged the operative language at issue here. Of particular note is that in 1986 and 1987, the Legislature amended these provisions in ways especially favorable to officers and directors. Thus, in 1986, article 7 was extended to permit reimbursement where the party was "successful" as opposed to "wholly successful" and to render the statutory remedies non-exclusive (L. 1986, ch. 513). In 1987, the Legislature amended Business Corporation Law §402(b) to authorize corporations, in some circumstances, to insulate directors from personal liability in derivative suits or otherwise (L. 1987, ch. 367, §1). The legislative history of these amendments specifically indicates that the business corporation statutes of several states were examined for possible incorporation of their provisions. Significantly, the Model Business Corporation Act, which was also under review, and the statutes of two of the states considered—Indiana (Ind. Code Ann. §231-37-11) and California (Cal. Corp. Code §317[a])—contained express provisions authorizing recovery of fees incurred to enforce indemnification rights (see Bill Jacket, L. 1987, ch. 367, at 16; Governor's Program Bill, Bill Jacket, L. 1986, ch. 513, at 11-12). The Legislature, however, did not add those provisions.

In short, the statutory language of section 722(a) and the legislative history contain nothing indicating that the Legislature intended to provide coverage for fees on fees. Moreover, even if, as Siegel urges, the "incurred as a result of" language of section 722(a) could arguably support an implied right of indemnification for fees on fees, the "American Rule" jurisprudence of this Court and the Supreme Court of the United States would militate against adoption of that interpretation. The American Rule provides that "attorney's fees are incidents of litigation and a prevailing party may not collect them from the loser unless an award is authorized by agreement between the parties, statute or court rule." . . .

Finally, we observe that our holding does not leave corporate officers and directors remediless; Business Corporation Law §721 expressly provides that article 7 is not an exclusive remedy and, thus, corporations remain free to provide indemnification of fees on fees in bylaws, employment contracts or through insurance.

For all of the foregoing reasons, the certified question should be answered in the negative.[127]

KAY, C.J. (dissenting): . . . Section 722 (a) of the Business Corporation Law is clear, simple and forthright. Together with section 723(a), it mandates indemnification for reasonable expenses actually and necessarily incurred as a result of an action against a director of a corporation. The plainly stated limitations on what expenses the corporation must pay the director are that they be "reasonable," and "actually and necessarily incurred as a result of [the underlying] action." (§722[a].) In our view, the unequivocal words of the statute include fees reasonably and necessarily incurred by directors in enforcing their statutory right to be free of personal expense in successfully defending their corporate action.

. . . [The facts of this case] stand as an example of what will be considered the absence of bad faith on part of companies denying reimbursement and forcing litigation to recover it. They also demonstrate that denying enforcement fees where reasonable and necessary is a significant impairment of the legislative mandate for indemnification. Defendant companies, behaving like respondent company did here, gain considerable leverage in keeping individual directors in the fold of a common defense, on pain of paying their own legal expenses if they seek to assert meritorious separate defenses.

The majority is rightly concerned that indemnification rights not cover expenses far removed from the underlying litigation. So was the New York State Legislature when it explicitly limited indemnification to *"reasonable* expenses . . . actually and *necessarily* incurred" (Business Corporation Law §722[a]; emphasis added). Expenses "having the most attenuated link" (majority op. at 85, 745 N.Y.S.2d at 734, 722 N.E.2d at 1101) to the underlying action obviously fail the statutory test. Nor — as the factual recitation shows — does it stretch the language "beyond the outer limits of meaning to claim that those fees on fees were necessarily incurred by reason of the joinder of Siegel in the securities fraud suits" (majority op. at 85, 745 N.Y.S.2d at 744, 772 N.E.2d at 1102). No one other than appellant's counsel sought to have him individually dismissed from a lawsuit that was baseless as to him but continued on for three years, until it was settled.

Regrettably, there is no really decisive legislative history — neither side can point to any. That the indemnification provisions were revised several times, always leaving unchanged the operative language at issue here, is itself inconclusive. As we read the statute, it was unnecessary to revise the statute to include enforcement fees — they are already permitted within the existing language. Nor does the "American rule" requiring parties to bear their own attorneys' fees offer the answer, because here the right to indemnification is provided by statute, not contract (see Hooper Assoc. v. AGS Computers, 74 N.Y.2d 487, 549 N.Y.S.2d 365, 548 N.E.2d 903 [1989]).

Perhaps most importantly, there is a good reason why these fees should be reimbursable, as we believe the Legislature provided. The majority's conclusion puts a finger on the scale in favor of a corporation and its controlling directors in cases where an individual director, or minority group of directors, may have a legitimate independent legal position at odds with what the corporation would

---

127. Contra, Stifel Financial Corp. v. Cochran, 809 A.2d 555 (Del. 2002). — ED.

wish to portray as a common defense. Here, had appellant joined the other defendants, he could have been indemnified for all of the expenses of the underlying action when the case was settled years later. Because he was exonerated at the outset — having successfully asserted his own meritorious defense — he is now saddled with the considerable costs of enforcing his right of indemnification.

That result is inconsistent with the language and purpose of the statute. And it is particularly unfortunate in today's corporate climate, when "it is crucial to secure the continued service of competent and experienced people in senior corporate positions and to assure that they will be able to exercise business judgment without fear of personal liability so long as they fulfill the basic duties of honesty, care and good faith" (Governor's Mem. approving L. 1986, ch. 513, 1986 McKinney's Session Laws of N.Y., at 3171). . . .

Ridder v. CityFed Financial Corp.
47 F.3d 85 (3d Cir. 1995)

FULLAM, J.: . . . [Resolution Trust Corporation ("RTC"), as receiver for CityFed, sued appellants, former City Fed employees for] various frauds and breaches of their fiduciary duty to their employer. . . .

Upon being served with the complaint in the RTC action, appellants made demand upon CityFed to advance funds for attorneys fees they would incur in defending the RTC litigation. CityFed refused, whereupon appellants brought this action to compel CityFed to advance attorneys fees to them. . . .

Article XI of CityFed's by-laws requires CityFed to indemnify and hold harmless all employees sued or threatened to be sued by reason of such employment by CityFed or any of its subsidiaries, "to the fullest extent authorized by the Delaware corporation law," and specifically provides that the right to indemnity "shall include the right *to be paid* the expenses incurred in defending any such proceeding *in advance* of its final disposition; provided, however that, if the Delaware Corporation Law so requires [it does] the payment of such expenses . . . shall be made only upon delivery to the corporation of an undertaking . . . to repay all amounts so advanced if it shall ultimately be determined that such employee is not entitled to be indemnified." [Emphasis added.] These by-law provisions are substantially identical to the provisions of the Delaware Corporation Law on the subject.[128]

The district court denied the injunction sought by appellants for two reasons. Because of the perceived strength of the RTC's case against the appellants in the related litigation, the court concluded that appellants had failed to demonstrate a likelihood of success on the merits. And, in view of the fact that CityFed is in receivership and the rights of other creditors are implicated, the court felt that the harm to appellants from denial of the injunction was outweighed by the public interest in assuring equal treatment to all of CityFed's creditors, and that appellants' claim should not be accorded priority by the issuance of a preliminary injunction. We conclude that neither reason suffices to justify denial of the relief plainly mandated by the by-laws and the Delaware statute.

---

128. Del. §145(e) permits the corporation to advance expenses, but does not require it. RMBCA §8.53, Cal. §317(b), and N.Y. §723(c) are similar. N.Y. §724(c) authorizes the court in which an action is pending to grant advancement of expenses during the pendency of a litigation notwithstanding the corporation's refusal to do so if the court finds that the litigant "has by his pleading or during the course of the litigation raised genuine issues of fact or law." — ED.

The issue before the district court was not whether appellants were likely to prevail in the RTC litigation, but whether they were likely to prevail in their assertion that CityFed should advance the costs of defense. Under Delaware law, appellants' right to receive the costs of defense in advance[129] does not depend upon the merits of the claims asserted against them, and is separate and distinct from any right of indemnification they may later be able to establish. Citadel Holding Corp. v. Roven, 603 A.2d 818 (Del. 1992);[130] Salaman v. National Media Corp., No. C.A. 92C-01-161, 1994 WL 465534 (Del. Super. July 22, 1994). See Joseph Warren Bishop, Jr., Law of Corporate Officers and Directors Indemnification and Insurance, P6.27 (1981 & Supp. 1993). Indeed, the provisions in both Article XI of CityFed's by-laws and §145(e) of the Delaware corporation law, conditioning the obligation to advance defense costs upon an undertaking "to repay such amount if it shall ultimately be determined that [the officer] is not entitled to be indemnified by the corporation,"[131] leave no room for argument on that score.

CityFed urges us to adopt the approach taken by the district court in Fidelity Federal Savings & Loan Ass'n v. Felicetti, 830 F. Supp. 262 (E.D. Pa. 1993), and rule that, notwithstanding the by-law provision, CityFed was justified in refusing to advance defense costs because of "the overriding duty of the directors to act in the best interests of the corporation." Id., at 269. We respectfully disagree. Given a choice between decisions of the appellate courts of Delaware and courts of other jurisdictions, on issues of Delaware law, this court is plainly required to follow the decisions of the Delaware courts. Moreover, we find the reasoning in *Felicetti* unpersuasive. Rarely, if ever, could it be a breach of fiduciary duty on the part of corporate directors to comply with the requirements of the corporation's by-laws, as expressly authorized by statute.

The statutory provisions authorizing the advancement of defense costs, conditioned upon an agreement to repay if a right of indemnification is not later established, plainly reflect a legislative determination to avoid deterring qualified persons from accepting responsible positions with financial institutions for fear of incurring liabilities greatly in excess of their means, and to enhance the reliability of litigation-outcomes involving directors and officers of corporations by assuring a level playing field. It is not the province of judges to second-guess these policy determinations.[132]

---

129. Do "costs of defense" include costs of a compulsory counterclaim? See Pearson v. Exide Corp., 157 F. Supp. 2d 429 (E.D. Pa. 2001). — ED.

130. In the *Citadel* case, the court held that an agreement barring *indemnification* for liability under Securities Exchange Act §16(b) does not bar *advancement* of litigation expenses to defend §16(b) action. See also Advanced Mining Systems, Inc. v. Fricke, 623 A.2d 82 (Del. Ch. 1992) (*advancement* and *indemnification* are distinct). — ED.

131. Cal. §317(b) and N.Y. §723(c) are similar. RMBCA §8.53(b) provides that the undertaking to repay "must be an unlimited general obligation of the director but need not be secured and may be accepted without reference to the financial ability of the director to make repayment." See also Sequa Corp. v. Gelmin, 828 F. Supp. 203 (S.D.N.Y. 1993); In re Central Banking System, 1993 WL 183692 (Del. Ch. 1993). — ED.

132. Accord, Homestore, Inc. v. Tafeen, 888 A.2d 204 (Del. 2005). For the view that before adopting such provisions, directors should make an informed business judgment balancing "the policy rationale supporting mandatory advancement" against making advances to "former directors, officers, or employees alleged or proven to have engaged in wrongdoing," see Stephen A. Radin, "Sinners Who Find Religion": Advancement of Litigation Expenses to Corporate Officials Accused of Wrongdoing, 25 Rev. Litig. 251 (2006).

Query: Should distinctions be made between suits for damages by the corporation, derivative suits, and civil or criminal actions by third parties? — ED.

Appellants made a strong showing that, unless defense costs were advanced to them, their ability to defend the RTC action would be irreparably harmed. Appellee made no contrary showing, and the district court did not base its holding upon the absence of irreparable harm, but rather upon a comparison between the harm to appellants and the perceived harm to other creditors of CityFed. Here again, however, we conclude that the district court addressed the wrong issue. The only issue before the district court was whether appellants were entitled to advance payment of the cost of defense of the RTC action. . . .

Insurance. (a) Virtually all states have statutes, like Cal. §317(i), that authorize corporations "to purchase and maintain insurance on behalf of any agent of the corporation against any liability asserted against or incurred by the agent in that capacity or arising out of the agent's status as such whether or not the corporation would have the power to indemnify the agent against that liability under this section. . . ." See also Del. §145(g); N.Y. §726(a); RMBCA §8.57; ALI §7.20(a)(4). Directors' and Officers' (D&O) liability insurance became popular in the 1960s in response to a growing number of substantial judgments against corporate executives. A "liability insurance crisis" developed in the mid-1980s, however, with D&O insurance simply becoming unavailable to some companies, forcing their directors to "go naked" or resign.[133]

> By late 1987, the D&O insurance market was no longer in turmoil. Although premiums continued to rise, the rate of increase had slowed. More important, policy limits resumed their increase: industry capacity grew largely through policyholder-formed insurers, but also because new commercial providers entered the market. . . . [T]he state legislatures responded by enacting statutes that eliminated entire classes of litigation, expanded directors' and officers' indemnification rights, and increased boards' discretionary power.

Roberta Romano, Corporate Governance in the Aftermath of the Insurance Crisis, 39 Emory L.J. 1155-1156 (1990). The situation changed, however, in the early 2000s in reaction to the Enron, WorldCom, et al. scandals. Although 97 percent of public companies had D&O coverage, the number of insurers shrunk dramatically and premiums increased by as much as 300 percent, as deductibles went up as much as fivefold and co-insurance clauses became more common. See Directors' Insurance Fees Get Fatter, Wall St. J. (July 12, 2002), at C1, col. 1.

Most D&O coverage includes (a) a Directors' and Officers' Policy and (b) a Corporate Reimbursement Policy.

The Directors' and Officers' Policy insures against losses (i.e., judgments or settlements for which they are not indemnified by the corporation) for any "wrongful act" committed in their executive capacity. This term is defined as "any breach of duty, neglect, error, misstatement, misleading statement, omission or other act done or wrongfully attempted by the directors or officers . . . or any

---

133. For the view that "in their reading of D&O insurance contracts, courts frequently rewrite the allocation of risk against the insurer" and thus "may be contributing to the crisis," see Roberta Romano, What Went Wrong with Directors' and Officers' Liability Insurance?, 14 Del. J. Corp. L. 1 (1989).

matter claimed against them solely by reason of their being such directors or officers." Some policies go on to provide coverage to directors and officers for liabilities and expenses that the corporation is forbidden to indemnify under applicable law — usually excluding certain claims (such as those for short-swing profits under §16(b), unauthorized remuneration, defamation, pollution damage, bribery, ERISA violations, active and deliberate dishonesty, and personal profit to which the executives were not entitled;[134] in addition, claims arising from contests for corporate control and claims brought by corporations against their own executives have been excluded). Policies afford varied coverage and limits, but most provide for no deductible beyond a modest flat amount (e.g., $5,000). 2 ALI, Principles of Corporate Governance 288 (1994).

The companion Corporate Reimbursement Policy insures the corporation for its indemnification of executives "for damages, judgments, settlements, costs, charges or expenses incurred in connection with any appeal therefrom, pursuant to the law, common or statutory, or the Charter or By-Laws of the Company duly effective under law, which determines and defines such rights of indemnity." In the main, all lawful corporate indemnifications fall within this coverage,[135] see Joseph F. Johnston Jr., Corporate Indemnification and Liability Insurance for Directors and Officers, 33 Bus. Law. 1993 (1978), although substantial deductibles may apply. See generally Joseph P. Monteleone & Nicholas J. Conca, Directors and Officers Indemnification and Liability Insurance: An Overview of Legal and Practical Issues, 51 Bus. Law. 573 (1996).

(b) Should there be any limits on a corporation's authority to purchase insurance for executives in respect to expenses or liabilities they may incur? N.Y. §726(b) bars such insurance "if a judgment or other final adjudication adverse to the insured director or officer establishes that his acts of active and deliberate dishonesty were material to the cause of action so adjudicated, or that he personally gained in fact a financial profit or other advantage to which he was not legally entitled. . . ." See also ALI §7.20(a)(2). What is the significance of N.Y. §726(e): "This section is the public policy of this state to spread the risk of corporate management, notwithstanding any other general or special law of this state or of any other jurisdiction including the federal government."?

See generally Note, Liability Insurance for Corporate Executives, 80 Harv. L. Rev. 648 (1967); Note, Public Policy and Directors' Liability Insurance, 67 Colum. L. Rev. 716 (1967).

(c) Should a corporation be permitted to purchase D&O insurance for its executives from a wholly owned subsidiary (or to self-insure)? Statutes in about a half-dozen states so provide. See, e.g., Tex. Bus. Corp. Act art. 2.02-1(R) (2003); La. Bus. Corp. Law §83F (1986). Although ALI §7.20 does not speak directly to this question, the Official Comment states that "if insurance is sought to be carried,

---

134. For an interpretation of a Directors and Officers Policy exclusion for "acts of active and deliberate dishonesty committed . . . with actual dishonest purpose and intent," see Eglin Nat'l Bank v. Home Indem. Co., 583 F.2d 1281 (5th Cir. 1978).

135. For an exception, see Level 3 Communications, Inc. v. Federals Ins. Co., 272 F.3d 908 (7th Cir. 2001): A corporation's shareholders sued the corporation and its directors and officers for fraud in repurchasing their shares. Plaintiffs sought the difference in value between what the corporation paid them for their shares and the true value. Corporation indemnified its directors and officers for the amounts paid in settlement and now sought this sum from its insurer. *Held:* no recovery.

§7.20(a)(4) does require that there be some significant risk-shifting, since without risk-shifting there is no insurance. However, such risk-shifting may be effected by a sharing or pooling of risks by more than one corporation through joint ownership of a corporation that acts as insurer." 2 ALI, Principles of Corporate Governance 275 (1994).[136]

---

136. In addition to articles cited throughout this section, see generally Joseph W. Bishop Jr., The Law of Corporate Officers and Directors: Indemnification and Insurance (supplemented to 2006).

IX CORPORATE ACQUISITIONS, TAKEOVERS, AND CONTROL TRANSACTIONS

A. INTRODUCTION

In a market economy, productive assets are bought and sold when they have different values to different parties. This process leads to an efficient allocation of resources: assets come to be owned by those who value them most highly, presumably because they can use them most efficiently. Productive assets may come to have different values to different parties for a variety of reasons. For example, particular assets may produce synergy when held by a party who also holds complementary assets. Alternatively, the buyer may be more skillful than the seller at using particular assets; because the buyer can earn more money from the assets than can the seller, they are worth more to the buyer. Moreover, asset values are not stable. Changes in economic and competitive conditions alter the relative value of an asset to different parties. Purchases and sales of assets thus serve as an equilibrating mechanism, a means by which the economy adjusts in response to changed conditions.

Assets held by corporations may be bought and sold for the same reasons. They may be more valuable when administered by the management of one corporation than by that of another; synergy may be created when the assets of one corporation are combined with those of another; relative values may have changed because of changes in particular industries. The only difference is that the assets are held within a separate entity. Thus, at one level, corporate acquisitions, corporate take-overs, and corporate control transactions are simply a rough catalogue of the techniques by which corporate assets are bought and sold.

At a second level, however, the fact that productive assets are held by corporations is central to understanding the process by which corporate assets are bought and sold. As developed in Chapter I, public corporations are characterized by a separation of ownership and control. Operating decisions are made by directors and officers selected by shareholders who are far too numerous to directly monitor those decisions. Thus, the governance of corporations is plagued by a fundamental agency problem: shareholders delegate decisionmaking for certain transactions to management because managers have greater expertise; however, giving managers the discretion to deploy that expertise on behalf of the shareholders also gives managers the discretion to favor their own interests at the expense of the shareholders. The function of corporate law is to provide a decisionmaking structure that allows management the discretion to deploy its expertise on behalf of shareholders, while at the same time establishing safeguards in situations in which management might utilize that discretion to favor itself.

Corporate acquisitions, takeovers, and control transactions present this agency conflict in especially stark terms. And the problem of designing a decisionmaking structure that mitigates the conflict is complicated by the fact that such transactions present three different faces, each of which requires attention.[1] First, corporate acquisitions — the purchase and sale of large amounts of assets — are among the most complicated transactions in which a corporation engages. Does a transfer present the opportunity to create value through synergy? How should the value created be split between the acquiring corporation and the acquired (target) corporation? How does the transaction compare with other available opportunities? Shareholders need management's expertise in the evaluation and negotiation of corporate control transactions. From this perspective, decisions concerning control transactions resemble the type of business decisions generally allocated to management rather than shareholders and protected from judicial inquiry by the business judgment rule.[2]

Second, corporate acquisitions, takeovers, and control transactions present a potential conflict of interest for management regardless of whether the corporation is the acquirer or the target and, if it is the target, regardless of whether management favors or opposes the transaction. Managers of the acquiring corporation may favor an acquisition only because they prefer to run a larger, more stable corporation even at the cost of lower profits.[3] This lowers the risk to management's undiversified human capital — that is, management's investment in their career with the acquiring corporation that would be lost if the acquiring company failed — but is of no value to public shareholders, who have the opportunity to hold diversified investment portfolios.[4] Managers of the target corporation may favor a proposed transaction only because they have been promised personal benefits, such as continued employment, after the transaction is consummated.

---

1. 1 ALI, Principles of Corporate Governance 384-385 (1994).
2. See Chapter II.B.2.
3. See, e.g., Mark Mitchell & Kenneth Lehn, Do Bad Bidders Become Good Targets?, 98 J. Pol. Econ. 372 (1990); John Coffee, Shareholders Versus Managers: The Strain in the Corporate Web, 85 Mich. L. Rev. 15 (1987).
4. Recall from Chapter III that diversification eliminates the unsystematic risk — that relating to the particular company — associated with holding a company's stock. This risk is eliminated by holding a portfolio of securities. Because managers cannot directly diversify their human capital investment — they can hold only one job at a time and cannot sell to others a part of their future earnings — they may seek to do so indirectly by causing the company to diversify its businesses.

Alternatively, management of the target corporation may reject the proposed transaction to protect their positions as managers because they fear that they will be replaced by the acquiring corporation after the transaction.[5] From this perspective, decisions concerning control transactions resemble interested transactions that invoke the more rigorous standards of the duty of loyalty.[6]

Finally, corporate acquisitions, takeovers, and control transactions are themselves a monitoring mechanism by which the quality of management's exercise of its delegated discretion can be reviewed. From this perspective, if management has not performed effectively, the price of the corporation's stock will decline. "By purchasing those securities through [a corporate control] transaction, an acquirer may displace existing management and, in effect, bet its investment on its ability to enhance shareholder value. . . ."[7]

Thus, the goal of corporate law in the area of corporate acquisitions, takeovers, and control transactions is to specify a set of decision rules that provide reasonable assurance that good transactions — those that will increase shareholder value — will be approved and bad transactions rejected.[8] This chapter surveys the variety of transactional techniques by which corporate control transactions can be carried out, and the statutory provisions, judicial doctrine, and market forces that help to determine which transactions go forward.

1. TRANSACTIONAL TECHNIQUES: ALLOCATION OF DECISION AUTHORITY FOR CONTROL TRANSACTIONS

In principle, control of the productive assets of a corporation can be transferred in three ways. The acquiring corporation may (1) purchase the assets of the target corporation, (2) effect a merger with the target corporation, or (3) purchase a controlling block of the target company's voting shares. Under every state corporate statute, both the board of directors and the shareholders of the target corporation must approve a sale of substantially all the corporation's assets or its merger.[9] This framework seems designed to allow shareholders both to rely on management's expertise and to guard against management's approving a transaction only because of the personal benefits offered management. Management acts as a gatekeeper in that no proposal for a sale of assets or merger can be presented to shareholders unless the board of directors first approves it. Assuming loyal management, rational shareholders would choose for management to play this gatekeeper role; shareholders themselves would not be interested in considering any transaction that their experts had not already concluded was in the shareholders' interests. The further requirement that target shareholders also approve a transaction limits the potential that management may be disloyal in

---

5. This fear is hardly misplaced. The rate of target executive turnover after an acquisition is significantly higher than the general turnover rate. See Kenneth Martin & John McConnell, Corporate Performance, Corporate Takeovers, and Managerial Turnover, 46 J. Fin. 671 (1991). Interestingly, the post-acquisition turnover rate is the same in hostile and in friendly takeovers.

6. See Chapter II.

7. 1 ALI, footnote 1 supra, at 385.

8. Professor Stephen Bainbridge nicely frames the issue as a "tension between authority and accountability." Stephen M. Bainbridge, Unocal at 20: Director Primacy in Corporate Takeovers, 31 Del. Corp. Law 769, 772 (2006).

9. See, e.g., Del. Gen. Corp. Law §271 (sale of assets), §251 (merger).

approving a proposed acquisition, for example, recommending it despite too low a price only because of post-transaction benefits promised by the acquiring company.

But what polices the potential for managerial self-interest if it is expressed in the form of target management's *rejecting* a proposed transaction? Here the third acquisition technique is critical. The purchase of a controlling block of the target corporation's stock is the only acquisition technique that does not require board of director approval under the typical corporate statute.[10] Thus, if a would-be acquirer believes that target management inappropriately declined to approve its offer, the acquirer could seek to persuade shareholders owning a controlling amount of the target's voting shares to sell it their shares directly. Without the availability of one method of acquiring a target company that does not require board of director approval, a prospective insurgent would first have to conduct a proxy fight to oust the board. As noted in Chapter VI, such proxy contests historically have been difficult for challengers to win. Hence, although hostile takeovers amount to only a small percentage of overall merger and acquisition activity, they have a disproportionate significance because, at least potentially, they constitute a monitoring mechanism by which dissatisfied shareholders (and the market generally) may discipline an inefficient management.

Another reason for the popularity of control transactions as opposed to proxy contests is that takeovers permit the bidder to realize more of the potential gain from a change in corporate policy. If the bidder believes that such a change will increase the target's value, it could resort to a proxy fight, but then the prospective gain would be shared pro rata with other target shareholders, while the bidder bears all the costs. Rather than seek to convince other shareholders to vote with it, the bidder may find it quicker, simpler, and more profitable to acquire all, or a majority of, the corporation's shares (to the extent it is financially able). Of course, the bidder "shares" the prospective gain with the other shareholders to the extent that it pays a premium over the market price, but transaction costs are reduced because the bidder need not try to convince others of the soundness of its views; nor must it share all confidential information it possesses.

At this point, we need to return to the decisionmaking structure created by the corporate statute as it affects proposed acquisitions rejected by target company's board of directors. While target management's decision to reject an offer is protected by the business judgment rule,[11] do management and the board have any remaining role if the acquirer then seeks to purchase control directly from the shareholders? If management has more expertise than the shareholders, should it be able to act to discourage the acquirer from pursuing a direct offer for control? Moreover, if target management is able to bargain more effectively than dispersed shareholders over the price of control, then should target management have some means to prevent the acquirer from avoiding bargaining over price by making its

---

10. This statement must be qualified for those states that have enacted control share acquisition statutes. These statutes typically require that the acquisition of shares that cause the acquirer to hold more than a specified percentage of a company's voting shares must be approved by the board of directors or the disinterested shareholders; shares acquired before approval are non-voting until approved. This form of statute is considered in CTS Corp. v. Dynamics Corp. of America, 481 U.S. 69 (1987), page 1132 infra.

11. ALI, Principles of Corporate Governance §6.01(a) reflects the prevailing rule: "The board of directors, in the exercise of its business judgment, may approve, reject, or decline to consider a proposal to the corporation to engage in a transaction in control."

offer directly to shareholders? But if management and the board of directors can act to discourage an offer of control directly to shareholders, what means remain to address the agency problem of managerial self-interest? An obvious possibility is the courts; claims that management is acting in its own interest pose issues of breach of fiduciary duty that can be raised through shareholder litigation.

This listing of the techniques that might be employed to constrain target management's self-interested action in rejecting a proposed acquisition can be restated in terms of decisionmaking authority: whose role is it to finally determine whether a proposed control transaction is favorable to the shareholders and should be accepted? If target management cannot prevent shareholders from accepting a direct offer for control, then the final decision rests with the *shareholders.* If target management can prevent shareholders from accepting a direct offer for control through the deployment of various types of defensive tactics,[12] without significant judicial review of their decision, then the final decision rests with the *target board of directors.* Finally, if defensive action by target management is subject to substantive judicial review, then the final decision rests with the courts. Beginning in the 1980s and continuing to date, corporate law has confronted the task of allocating decision authority over control transactions among directors, shareholders, and the courts.

A related question of decision authority also must be confronted. Suppose the target board of directors determines, whether because of the potential for synergy with the particular bidder to create value for shareholders or because management favors the transaction due to assurances of post-transaction continued employment, that the company should be acquired in a friendly transaction by a favored suitor. Can target management take action that protects the transaction from a competitive bid (and thereby reduce the likelihood that such a bid will ever be made)? Alternatively, if target management is unsuccessful in defending against a hostile bid,[13] can it effect a negotiated surrender by inducing another bid from an acquirer it favors?

From the perspective of allocation of decision rights over acquisitions, the three forms of acquisition techniques — merger, sale of assets, or tender offer direct to shareholders — differ along one critical dimension: is the transaction *hostile,* that is, made directly to shareholders by means of a tender offer without target board approval, or *friendly,* that is, made with the support of target management so that any of the three acquisition techniques is available? Hostile transactions pose the

---

12. As of the late 1970s, target companies defended against direct offers for control by a variety of structural means: (1) selling to a third party assets coveted by the acquirer (an asset or "crown jewel" lockup); (2) issuing stock to a friendly ally (a stock lockup); (3) adopting charter amendments that imposed impediments to control transactions not approved by the board (often called "shark repellent" amendments); (4) repurchasing target shares already acquired by the acquirer at a premium ("greenmail"); and, (5) beginning in the 1980s, issuing a convertible security (known as a "poison pill") that, once triggered, either diluted the stock held by the acquirer or entitled shareholders other than the acquirer to buy shares of the target at a price significantly below market value. These tactics are examined infra in Sec. B.2.

13. Data covering the 1980s shows that only some 23 percent of targets ultimately remained independent following a hostile bid. 1 Fleischer, Sussman & Lesser, Takeover Defenses 3 (4th ed. 1990) (reporting Mergerstat Review study). More recently, this one-in-five ratio may have improved with newer defensive techniques such as the poison pill and classified boards of directors). In particular, Lucian Bebchuk, John Coates & Guhan Subramanian, The Powerful Antitakeover Effect of Staggered Boards: Theory, Evidence, and Policy, 54 Stan. L. Rev. 887, 933 (2002), report that 47 percent of targets with both a poison pill and a staggered board remain independent 30 months after a hostile offer. Only 23 percent of targets without a staggered board remain independent over the same period.

decisionmaking problem in terms of target management's authority to deploy defensive tactics to block an unwanted offer, and are considered in Sec. B of this chapter. Friendly transactions pose the decisionmaking problem in terms of target management's authority to protect a favored transaction, and are considered in Sec. C.

2. TYPES OF CONTROL TRANSACTIONS AND THEIR REGULATION

During the 1980s and 1990s, the most common technique for acquiring a controlling block of shares was to make a tender offer regardless of whether the transaction was hostile or friendly.[14] The tender offeror (or "bidder") makes a public offer, usually by publishing a detailed notice of the offer in a newspaper, to the target shareholders of the class sought, offering to buy their shares at a specified price (usually at a substantial premium over the current market price) for a limited period. The bidder may offer cash (the dominant form of consideration during the 1980s), or it may offer to exchange a specified package of its securities for the target's voting stock (an "exchange offer"). The offer may be either for all shares of the class or only for a portion of them. In the latter case of a "partial bid," the bidder will, however, probably reserve the right to accept any "excess" shares tendered. The offer will typically be subject to conditions set forth in the offering documents — for example, a minimum tender condition (i.e., that 50 percent of the class tender), to ensure that the bidder acquires at least de facto voting control, or a condition that no material adverse change occur in the target's business or financial structure. Shareholders accept this offer by depositing their shares with a depository bank that the bidder appoints as its agent. If the specified conditions entitling the bidder to cancel or reduce its offer do not arise (or are waived by the bidder), the depository bank will purchase the shares on behalf of the bidder on the expiration of the tender offer, using funds deposited with it in advance by the bidder. In contractual terms, the bidder makes the offer and the shareholders accept it; and it is the bidder's responsibility to specify any contractual "outs" with adequate precision.[15]

Although the bidder specifies the terms of its offer (i.e., price, number of shares to be purchased, any conditions precedent to its obligation to purchase), federal law constrains the bidder's range of options by prescribing, among other things, (1) the minimum period the offer must be kept open, (2) the disclosures that must be made in connection with a tender offer, (3) the rights of tendering shareholders to withdraw their shares, and (4) their rights to equal treatment. Adopted in 1968, the Williams Act (see pages 1068-1069 infra) added provisions to §13 and §14 of the Securities Exchange Act of 1934 in order to regulate tender offers. However, with some modest exceptions, the Williams Act basically regulates only the bidder,

---

14. A tender offer is the only way to make a hostile offer. If a competitive bid is possible, the greater speed with which a tender offer can be accomplished — a merger or sale of assets requires a shareholder vote and, therefore, for public companies, a proxy statement that must be reviewed by the SEC — may make it the desirable course for a friendly offer as well.

15. If a bidder fails to include a "litigation out" condition, for example, courts have held that it must still pay tendering shareholders damages equivalent to their lost profits, even though the tender offer was enjoined on antitrust grounds. See Lowenschuss v. Kane, 520 F.2d 255 (2d Cir. 1975). In contractual terms the bidder is the offeror, and the ambiguity in the offer's terms is construed against it and in favor of the offerees.

while the target's ability to defend against a hostile takeover is chiefly governed by state law fiduciary standards. The resulting two-tier system of regulation often seems to produce a lack of coordination, with the result that over the last two decades first one side and then the other obtained a temporary advantage.

Prior to the advent of the hostile takeover, corporate control transactions were largely voluntary. Hostile transactions and, in particular, tender offers first appeared in the 1960s, and it was not until the mid-1970s that large public corporations began to make hostile offers for other public corporations.[16] Different theories have been offered for the belated appearance of the hostile tender offer, which is seemingly an obvious recourse for the rebuffed suitor. Partial explanations may lie in (1) the rise of institutional investors, who may be more prepared to sell on a small price differential, and (2) the dispersion of share ownership, which implies that most corporations will lack any close-knit group of large shareholders other than institutional investors who can coordinate to resist or negotiate with the bidder. Also, the growth in popularity of the conglomerate form may have been even more important because its appearance enabled (or at least accustomed) managements to operate dissimilar businesses.[17]

When the tender offer first appeared in the 1960s, it presented shareholders of the target firm with considerable uncertainty. Without warning, they might learn that a corporation, or a group of individuals, about whom they knew little, was offering to buy 50 percent of their corporation at some premium over the market price and that they had only a week (or less) to accept the offer or potentially become minority shareholders in a corporation now controlled by the phantom bidder. Although such an offer may seem attractive, shareholders might still reasonably be concerned about what the bidder intended to do once it acquired control. How would it manage the firm? Would it be willing to pay a similar price for the remaining shares? Much commentary at the time suggested that shareholders were being pressured to make uninformed choices. Congress responded in 1968 by adopting the Williams Act. Senator Harrison Williams (D.-N.J.), the bill's Senate sponsor, justified it on the following grounds: "Today the public shareholder in deciding whether to accept or reject a tender offer possesses limited information. No matter what he does, he acts without adequate knowledge to enable him to decide rationally what is the best course of action. This is precisely the dilemma which our securities laws are designed to prevent."[18] It remains open to question, however, whether disclosure is alone capable of reducing pressure on the shareholder. Indeed, sometimes full disclosure may even have the opposite impact. This dilemma is further discussed infra in Sec. E.l.c.

As first proposed, the Williams Act would have largely curtailed tender offers through substantive restrictions. Congress had become alarmed that large corporations were being rapidly taken over by unknown "raiders" and wished to slow down this movement. However, the SEC succeeded in redrafting the proposed bill, turning it largely into a disclosure statute. In a much-quoted statement,

---

16. Prior to Morgan Stanley's involvement on behalf of the bidder in the 1974 hostile acquisition of International Nickel, no first-tier investment banking firm would represent a bidder in a hostile transaction. See Ron Chernow, The House of Morgan 598-602 (1990). Goldman Sachs still declines in most cases to represent the acquirer other than in friendly transactions.

17. Oliver Williamson, The Modern Corporation: Origins, Evolution, Attributes, 19 J. Econ. Lit. 1537, 1557-1560 (1981).

18. 113 Cong. Rec. 24,664 (1967).

Senator Williams observed that the Act, as finally passed, was designed not to tip the balance in favor of either side.[19]

Despite this neutral stance, the early impact of the Williams Act was to chill tender offers significantly. Bidders feared that any material omission in their offering documents might lead to the offer being permanently enjoined, and on occasion this happened. See, e.g., General Host Corp. v. Triumph American, Inc., 359 F. Supp. 749 (S.D.N.Y. 1973) (enjoining tender offer because of offeror's failure to disclose fully its plans for the target and past attempts to partially liquidate earlier acquisitions). As a result, bidders often avoided formal tender offers and instead engaged in "creeping control" acquisitions by buying shares in the open market. This resulted in recurrent litigation over the definition of the term *tender offer*, which the Williams Act does not define. See Section E.1.b infra. During the 1970s, the attitude of the federal courts shifted, as some courts became disenchanted with the manner in which litigants in takeover battles were attempting to use the court to further their own objectives. In an important decision, Judge Friendly urged courts to maintain a stance of neutrality and let market forces decide the outcome.[20] Today, courts will typically grant only corrective injunctions that permit the tender offer to proceed once amended disclosures are made; in consequence, litigation has become a less potent defensive weapon, capable of creating time for the target to attempt other structural and financial maneuvers, but seldom serving as a "showstopper" in itself. Over the same period, and perhaps motivated by the lower profile accorded the Williams Act by federal courts, defensive tactics, particularly poison pills, began to evolve to provide the substantive barriers to tender offers that the Williams Act did not provide.

Beginning at about the same time as passage of the Williams Act, states began to adopt anti-takeover statutes, a movement that gained momentum in the 1970s and 1980s as the odds in takeover battles began to shift in favor of the bidder. By 1982, when the Supreme Court struck down the first generation of these statutes, 37 states had passed some form of anti-takeover legislation. A "second generation" of these statutes was quickly enacted in the aftermath of *MITE*. Since Indiana's second-generation statute was upheld by the Supreme Court in 1987 in CTS Corp. v. Dynamics Corp. of America (page 1132 infra), all but 10 states have enacted a form of anti-takeover statute and some, notably Pennsylvania, have virtually prohibited hostile offers. These state efforts are considered infra in Sec. G.

3. PUBLIC POLICY AND CORPORATE CONTROL TRANSACTIONS: THE STAKEHOLDER DEBATE

A broader question is suggested by the states' evident interest in takeovers: are public policy issues legitimately involved in takeovers? From a private law perspective, takeovers have long been controversial, with the conduct of both

---

19. "We have taken extreme care to avoid tipping the scales in favor of management or in favor of the person making the takeover bids. S.510 is designed solely to require full and fair disclosure for the benefit of investors. The bill will at the same time provide the offeror and management equal opportunity to present their case." Id.

20. Electronic Specialty Co. v. International Controls Corp., 409 F.2d 937 (2d Cir. 1969). See also Note, The Courts and the Williams Act: Try a Little Tenderness, 48 N.Y.U. L. Rev. 991 (1973).

bidders and targets constantly raising new variations on the classic theme of fiduciary duty. But these issues largely focus on debate over what is in the best interests of shareholders. Hostile takeovers (and friendly takeovers) may have negative consequences for non-shareholder participants in the corporate enterprise, including employees, suppliers, local communities in which target facilities are located, and even the nation, to the extent that takeovers may affect international competitiveness. These groups have come to be referred to as "stakeholders." From a public policy perspective, the impact of takeovers on stakeholders raises larger, overshadowing issues: Do takeovers interfere with long-term planning and socially beneficial investment in research and development? Do takeovers compel corporations to adopt dangerously debt-laden capital structures that could threaten their viability? Do premiums for target shareholders come at the expense of blue-collar wages and employment? Proponents of hostile takeovers reject these claims and reply that takeovers are an engine of efficiency that allocates capital to its most productive uses and disciplines inefficient management. Could both sides be right? Section H infra concludes this chapter with a brief examination of these particularly controversial issues.

B. *HOSTILE TRANSACTIONS*

Since takeovers appeared on the scene in the 1960s, courts have struggled with how to review management's efforts to block a hostile takeover. Neither of the two familiar corporate law standards of review — the business judgment rule or the intrinsic fairness test — matched a decision that called into question both management's business skills and its loyalty.[21] Determining whether a proposed transaction is favorable to the shareholders — and, if so, identifying the best negotiating strategy — seems like precisely the kind of decision that the business judgment rule should largely protect from judicial review. But at the same time, action to block a hostile takeover may be motivated by managerial self-interest; blocking the bid serves to maintain management in their positions. The conflict of interest in a potential change in control thus resembles an interested transaction that, because it invokes the duty of loyalty, would be subject to exacting judicial review under the intrinsic fairness standard. Thus, from the first appearance of the hostile takeover, the Delaware courts have struggled with how to frame a middle ground of review.

1. THE EARLY DOCTRINE

Cheff v. Mathes
41 Del. Ch. 494, 199 A.2d 548 (S. Ct. 1964)

CAREY, J.: This is an appeal from the decision of the Vice-Chancellor in a derivative suit holding certain directors of Holland Furnace Company liable for

---

21. Ronald J. Gilson, A Structural Approach to Corporations: The Case Against Defensive Tactics in Tender Offers, 33 Stan. L. Rev. 819, 821-831 (1981).

loss allegedly resulting from improper use of corporate funds to purchase shares of the company. . . .

[Holland had 883,585 shares outstanding, about 18.5 percent of which were owned by Hazelbank, a family holding company. Three of the directors had significant interests in the company: Cheff, the chief executive officer (6,000 shares); Mrs. Cheff (5,800 shares plus a 48 percent ownership of Hazelbank); and Landwehr (24,000 shares plus a 9 percent ownership of Hazelbank). Of the four other directors, only Trenkamp, general counsel (200 shares) and one other (300 shares) had interests in the company. All received $200 per diem for monthly board meetings. Cheff received an annual salary of $77,400, and Trenkamp received significant fees as general counsel.

Holland manufactured warm-air furnaces. It sold them through 400 branch retail sales offices in 43 states. Management considered this practice, unique in the industry, to be a vital factor in the company's success.

In June 1957, Maremont, an active corporate financier, inquired about merging Holland into one of his companies. When he was rebuffed, he indicated he had no further interest in Holland. The Holland board investigated and discovered that Maremont had bought 55,000 Holland shares on the New York Stock Exchange (NYSE) and that he had the reputation of acquiring and liquidating companies.

In August 1957, Maremont informed Cheff he now owned 100,000 shares and demanded a place on Holland's board. He further indicated that Holland's distribution technique was obsolete and that its furnaces could be sold wholesale through a half-dozen salesmen.

Substantial unrest arose among Holland's sales force. Cheff testified "that the field organization was considering leaving in large numbers because of a fear of the consequences of a Maremont acquisition."

By fall 1957, Maremont had acquired 155,000 shares. He suggested that Hazelbank either sell its Holland shares or buy his. Hazelbank referred the matter to Holland's board of directors. On October 23, 1957, Holland's directors considered purchasing Maremont's shares. The board was informed that Mrs. Cheff and Hazelbank were ready to buy the shares if Holland did not, and that to finance the purchase, Holland would have to borrow substantial sums. Nevertheless, the board decided to buy the shares at $14.40 a share, somewhat higher than the current market price.

Plaintiffs, owners of 60 Holland shares, filed a derivative suit to require the directors to account for alleged damages. The trial court held for plaintiffs, finding that Maremont posed no real threat to liquidate the company, that the employee unrest could have been caused by other factors, and that the real reason for the purchase was to perpetuate control.]

Under the provisions of 8 Del. C. §160, a corporation is granted statutory power to purchase and sell shares of its own stock. . . . The charge here is not one of violation of statute, but the allegation is that the true motives behind such purchases were improperly centered upon perpetuation of control. In an analogous field, courts have sustained the use of proxy funds to inform stockholders of management's views upon the policy questions inherent in an election to a board of directors, but have not sanctioned the use of corporate funds to advance the selfish desires of directors to perpetuate themselves in office. . . . Similarly, if the actions of the board were motivated by a sincere belief that the buying out of the dissident stockholder was necessary to maintain what the board believed to be proper business practices, the board will not be held liable for such decision, even though hindsight indicates the decision was not the wisest course. See Kors v. Carey, Del. Ch., 158 A.2d 136. On the other hand, if the board has acted solely or primarily because of the desire to perpetuate themselves in office, the use of corporate funds for such purposes is improper. See Bennett v. Propp, Del., 187 A.2d 405, and Yasik v. Wachtel, 25 Del. Ch. 247, 17 A.2d 309.

. . . [I]n Bennett v. Propp, supra, we stated: "We must bear in mind the inherent danger in the purchase of shares with corporate funds to remove a threat to corporate policy when a threat to control is involved. The directors are of necessity confronted with a conflict of interest, and an objective decision is difficult. . . . Hence, in our opinion, the burden should be on the directors to justify such a purchase as one primarily in the corporate interest." . . .

To say that the burden of proof is upon the defendants is not to indicate, however, that the directors have the same "self-dealing interest" as is present, for example, when a director sells property to the corporation: The only clear pecuniary interest shown on the record was held by Mr. Cheff, as an executive of the corporation, and Trenkamp, as its attorney. The mere fact that some of the other directors were substantial shareholders does not create a personal pecuniary interest in the decisions made by the board of directors, since all shareholders would presumably share the benefit flowing to the substantial shareholder. . . . Accordingly, these directors other than Trenkamp and Cheff, while called upon to justify their actions, will not be held to the same standard of proof required of those directors having personal and pecuniary interest in the transaction. . . .

The question then presented is whether or not defendants satisfied the burden of proof of showing reasonable grounds to believe a danger to corporate policy and effectiveness existed by the presence of the Maremont stock ownership. It is important to remember that the directors satisfy their burden by showing good faith and reasonable investigation; the directors will not be penalized for an honest mistake of judgment, if the judgment appeared reasonable at the time the decision was made. . . .

In holding that employee unrest could as well be attributed to a condition of Holland's business affairs as to the possibility of Maremont's intrusion, the Vice-Chancellor must have had in mind one or both of two matters: (1) the pending proceedings before the Federal Trade Commission concerning certain sales practices of Holland; (2) the decrease in sales and profits during the preceding several years. Any other possible reason would be pure speculation. In the first place, the adverse decision of the FTC was not announced until *after* the complained-of transaction. Secondly, the evidence clearly shows that the downward trend of sales and profits had reversed itself, presumably because of the reorganization which had then been completed. Thirdly, everyone who testified on the point said that the unrest was due to the possible threat presented by Maremont's purchases of stock. There was, in fact, no *testimony* whatever of any connection between the unrest and either the FTC proceedings or the business picture.

The Vice-Chancellor found that there was no substantial evidence of a liquidation posed by Maremont. This holding overlooks an important contention. The fear of the defendants, according to their testimony, was not limited to the possibility of liquidation; it included the alternate possibility of a material change in Holland's sales policies, which the board considered vital to its future success. The *unrebutted* testimony before the court indicated: (1) Maremont had deceived

Cheff as to his original intentions, since his open market purchases were contemporaneous with his disclaimer of interest in Holland; (2) Maremont had given Cheff some reason to believe that he intended to eliminate the retail sales force of Holland; (3) Maremont demanded a place on the board; (4) Maremont substantially increased his purchases after having been refused a place on the board; (5) the directors had good reason to believe that unrest among key employees had been engendered by the Maremont threat; (6) the board had received advice from Dun and Bradstreet indicating the past liquidation or quick sale activities of [Maremont]; (7) the board had received professional advice from the firm of Merrill Lynch, Fenner & Beane, who recommended that the purchase from [Maremont] be carried out; (8) the board had received competent advice that the corporation was over-capitalized; (9) [Holland's treasurer] and Cheff had made informal personal investigations from contacts in the business and financial community and had reported to the board of the alleged poor reputation of Maremont. The board was within its rights in relying upon that investigation, since 8 Del. C. §141(f) allows the directors to reasonably rely upon a report provided by corporate officers. . . .

Accordingly, we are of the opinion that the evidence presented in the court below leads inevitably to the conclusion that the board of directors, based upon direct investigation, receipt of professional advice, and personal observations of the contradictory action of Maremont and his explanation of corporate purpose, believed, with justification, that there was a reasonable threat to the continued existence of Holland, or at least existence in its present form, by the plan of Maremont to continue building up his stock holdings. We find no evidence in the record sufficient to justify a contrary conclusion. . . .

As noted above, the Vice-Chancellor found that the purpose of the acquisition was the improper desire to maintain control, but, at the same time, he exonerated those individual directors whom he believed to be unaware of the possibility of using non-corporate funds to accomplish this purpose. Such a decision is inconsistent with his finding that the motive was improper, within the rule enunciated in *Bennett.* If the actions were in fact improper because of a desire to maintain control, then the presence or absence of a non-corporate alternative is irrelevant, as corporate funds may not be used to advance an improper purpose even if there is no non-corporate alternative available. Conversely, if the actions were proper because of a decision by the board made in good faith that the corporate interest was served thereby, they are not rendered improper by the fact that some individual directors were willing to advance personal funds if the corporation did not. It is conceivable that the Vice-Chancellor considered this feature of the case to be of significance because of his apparent belief that any excess corporate funds should have been used to finance a subsidiary corporation. That action would not have solved the problem of Holland's over-capitalization. In any event, this question was a matter of business judgment, which furnishes no justification for holding the directors personally responsible in this case.

Accordingly, the judgment of the court below is reversed and remanded.

---

1. *Aftermath.* In the FTC proceeding, a cease-and-desist order was issued forbidding Holland's deceptive practices in the retail sale of its furnaces (including

salesmen falsely representing themselves as heating engineers, dismantling a householder's furnace without permission, refusing to reassemble it on the false basis that it was defective and dangerous, and then selling a Holland replacement). For willful disobedience of this order, Holland was ultimately fined $100,000 and Cheff sentenced to six months' imprisonment. Holland lost almost $10 million over the three years ending in 1963. In this light, do Maremont's proposals "to eliminate the retail sales force" look as dangerously misguided as the board deemed them?

2. *The policy conflict/primary purpose test.* Does *Cheff* frame an intermediate standard by placing the burden on the defendants "of showing reasonable grounds to believe a danger to corporate policy . . . existed"? Or does its handling of the conflict-of-interest problem by inquiring into the board's motives avoid any substantive review by the court and effectively apply the business judgment rule? For the view that because "management can almost always find a conflict of policy between itself and a hostile bidder" — presumably the bidder would not have sought to acquire control at all if it agreed with how target management was running the company — "motive analysis collapses into the business judgment standard," see Gilson, footnote 21 supra, at 945.

2. THE DEMAND FOR AND SUPPLY OF DEFENSIVE TACTICS

The corporate bar treated *Cheff*'s resolution of the standard of review of defensive tactics as affording blanket protection for the target board so long as careful lawyers crafted an appropriate record.[22] By the early 1980s, novel financing techniques had greatly expanded the size of companies potentially subject to hostile takeovers, resulting in a dramatic rise in takeover activity. The early 1970s witnessed an average of 16 acquisitions involving consideration over $100 million each year. By the early 1980s, the annual average number of such large transactions had multiplied more than eightfold to 132. Adjusted for inflation, total annual consideration paid in acquisitions for the respective periods more than doubled.[23] In particular, the level of hostile acquisitions skyrocketed. While the total number of acquisitions in 1975-1976 was only half that of 1968, there were almost twice as many hostile transactions.[24] Not surprisingly, the increased frequency and hostility of acquisition activity resulted in increased demand for takeover defenses. Also not surprisingly, the corporate bar responded with a varied set of tools.

---

22. Martin Lipton, one of the deans of the takeover defense bar, put the matter as follows: "Where the directors have made a reasonable good-faith decision to reject the takeover on one or more of the bases set forth above, the business judgment rule should apply equally to any and all defensive tactics." Lipton, Takeover Bids in the Target's Boardroom, 35 Bus. Law. 101, 124 (1979). Defensive tactics were enjoined in a few cases between 1964 and the early 1980s, but these usually involved smaller companies that had proceeded without the benefit of experienced takeover lawyers or investment bankers. See, e.g., Royal Industries, Inc. v. Monogram Industries, Inc. [1976-1977 Transfer Binder] Fed. Sec. L. Rep. (CCH) ¶96,584 (S.D.N.Y.); Podesta v. Calumet Industries, Inc., [1977-1978 Transfer Binder] Fed. Sec. L. Rep. (CCH) ¶96,433 (N.D. Ill. 1978).

23. Ronald Gilson & Bernard Black, The Law and Finance of Corporate Acquisitions ch. 1 (2d ed. 1995).

24. Id. at 26.

a. Charter and Bylaw Provisions

Early efforts to erect barriers to hostile offers took the form of charter amendments that were adopted before an offer was made. One form imposed a *supermajority vote* requirement for approval of a "second-step" merger eliminating the remaining shareholders with the objective, in part, of giving the bidder access to the target's assets. Under most state statutes, a simple majority vote will suffice to adopt a supermajority provision. Thus, a standard "shark repellent" provision may require a high supermajority, say 80 percent, to effect a merger with any "related person" (usually defined to include any person who holds over a specified level — say 15 percent — of the corporation's stock). This provision is then protected by another, requiring a similar supermajority to amend or modify the provision.

A variation on the supermajority provision provides for a similar vote but then waives this supermajority requirement if the bidder pays a defined "fair price" in the second-step transaction. Such a "fair price" formula can be manipulated so that the second-step price is significantly higher than the tender offer price; this may cause some shareholders not to tender. Because fair-price amendments create uncertainty for the bidder, they may deter some transactions or may force the bidder to acquire a sufficiently large proportion of the stock in the first step, thus reducing the potential cost of the second step.

Some states have eliminated the need for charter amendments, and therefore shareholders' votes to approve them, by imposing a supermajority requirement by statute. See Sec. G infra. The difference between a charter amendment and a statute is the need for a shareholder vote. Since many institutional investors, including mutual funds, will not vote for takeover defenses, a defense that requires a shareholder vote may be a mirage. See, e.g., Vanguard, Vanguard's Proxy Voting Guidelines, §4(A), available at https://personal.vanguard.com/VGApp/hnw/content/Home/WhyVanguard/AboutVanguardProxyVotingGuidelinesContent.jsp (stating a general belief that "the market for corporate control should be allowed to function without undue interference from . . . artificial barriers" and listing several preconditions to a vote for adoption of takeover defenses); Fidelity, Fidelity Fund Proxy Voting Guidelines, §5, available at http://personal.fidelity.com/myfidelity/InsideFidelity/InvestExpertise/ProxyVoting/ProxyVotingOverview.shtml.tvsr?srcIndex = 1&srcSearch=proxy (listing several preconditions to a vote for adoption of takeover defenses, and stating general intent to vote for proposals to eliminate anti-takeover provisions).

Charter provisions that divide the board into three, or even four, classes (with only one class elected at each annual election of directors) delay the bidder's ability to acquire control.[25] For a bidder who has made a very substantial investment, the inability to gain access to, or manage, the target's assets until the second annual election is a significant deterrent. Also, under Delaware law, directors who serve on a staggered board may be removed "only for cause" (unless the certificate provides otherwise), while other directors may be removed without cause. See Del. Gen. Corp. Law §141(k). Finally, the presence of a staggered board may make

---

25. Some state statutes permit the board to be divided into four classes (requiring three annual elections to shift control). See N.Y. Bus. Corp. Law §704(a) (1986). However, the NYSE will not list corporations whose boards are split into more than three classes. See NYSE Listed Company Manual §304.00 (2006).

a poison pill (discussed at pages 951-954 infra) more effective. After winning a proxy contest for control of the board, a bidder can cause the new board to redeem the poison pill immediately, thereby allowing the bidder to proceed with the no-longer-hostile bid.[26] Still, the effectiveness of staggered board provisions depends on the willingness of the target's directors to stay in office, even after either a hostile bidder has acquired a majority of the stock and its ultimate victory is certain, or a majority of shareholders have indicated their preference for the bid by voting in favor of the bidder's procedures for the class of directors that is subject to the proxy fight. Still, Bebchuk, Coates, and Subramanian report that establishing a staggered board almost doubles the target's chances of defeating a hostile bid.[27]

Bylaw provisions are also widely used by potential target corporations to deter takeovers, although their effect is probably less potent. Usually the purpose of such bylaw amendments is to restrict the bidder's ability to call a special shareholder meeting or to nominate directors at the annual meeting, as in the case of a staggered board seeking to hinder a bidder's ability to replace a target's board. Often, anti-takeover bylaw provisions require any person who proposes bringing any matter before the shareholders' meeting or nominating directors to give the board advance notice (say 60 days). Failure to provide this notice will cause the shareholder to forfeit the right to propose the action or nomination.

Another recurring area of dispute involves bylaws that seek to limit the ability of shareholders to act by written consent (where state law permits action by written consent of the majority of the shareholders, as Del. Gen. Corp. Law §228 does) and to empower the board (and not the shareholders) with the right to fill newly created board positions. The latter maneuver blocks an effort to avoid the delay in securing board control imposed on an acquirer by a staggered board structure. Such a bylaw amendment prevents the shareholders from increasing the size of the board and then filling the vacancies created. Such board-adopted amendments, which, for example, may seek to delay the setting of a record date for a consent solicitation, have sometimes been invalidated on the grounds that they are inconsistent with the shareholders' statutory right to take action by majority consent. See Chapter VI, pages 590-595 supra.

b. Poison Pill Plans

The poison pill is an innovation that has become one of the most popular defensive tactics. By 1999, more than 2,300 publicly traded companies, including more than 50 percent of the Fortune 500 corporations, had adopted such a plan.[28]

What is the poison pill? In its original and simplest version the "pill" took the following form: The corporation distributed to its common stockholders a dividend in the form of a new class of convertible preferred stock. The terms of the preferred stock were determined by the board pursuant to a "blank check" provision in the certificate authorizing the issuance of a class of preferred stock

---

26. The bidding strategy of combining a proxy contest with a hostile tender offer to outflank a poison pill is discussed in Lucian Bebchuk, John Coates & Guhan Subramanian, The Powerful Anti-takeover Effect of Staggered Boards: Theory, Evidence, and Policy, 54 Stan. L. Rev. 887, 933 (2002); and Ronald J. Gilson & Bernard Black, The Law and Finance of Corporate Acquisitions ch. 24 (2d ed. 1995).

27. See footnote 25 supra.

28. Wachtell, Lipton, Rosen & Katz, Takeover Law and Practice 54 (1999).

whose terms the board would set at the time of issuance. Typically, the new security was made convertible into the same (or a larger) number of common shares as were outstanding. Thus, for example, if there were 10,000,000 shares of common outstanding and 200,000 shares of convertible preferred were issued, each share of preferred would be convertible into 50 shares of common (or 10,000,000 in the aggregate). After the dividend, a holder of 100 shares of common would thus hold 2 shares of the convertible preferred.

The critical feature of this version of the poison pill is its "flip-over" provision: If an acquirer purchases in excess of a specified percentage of the target's stock (usually 20 percent) and thereafter acquires the target in a business combination (e.g., merger or sale of assets), the preferred stock becomes convertible into the common stock of the *acquirer* at a conversion ratio that effectively permits the holder of the preferred to purchase the acquirer's common stock at half price (or some similar discount).[29] In principle, this discount is intended to protect the target shareholder against the danger of being frozen out at a discount in a two-tier "front-loaded" takeover, but its practical impact is to force the bidder to tender for all (or a high percentage of) the target's shares in order to minimize the dilutive effect of the flip-over provision on its own stock. Thus, a bidder may tender for 100 percent and include an 80 percent minimum-tender condition to reduce the impact of such a poison pill.

Often, the pill will provide that the board of the target can call (i.e., redeem) the preferred security at a modest price for a limited period (15 days) after the triggering event occurs; this provision is intended to force the bidder to negotiate with the target's board (with the bidder reserving the right to call off its tender offer if the pill is not redeemed).

Originally, the intent of the poison pill was chiefly to protect against second-step mergers at prices below that paid in the tender offer. But what happens if the bidder is content to hold working control and not proceed to a second-step merger? Sir James Goldsmith followed the strategy in his successful acquisition of Crown Zellerbach, despite its flip-over pill. To remedy this problem, fair-price provisions were built into the redemption formula of the convertible security that entitled the holder to "put" the stock (i.e., require the target to buy it back) at a price equal to the highest price paid by the bidder in acquiring target shares. This redemption right might be triggered by substantial open-market purchases by the bidder; in the parlance of the takeover bar, these rights were said to "flip in" on such events. Today, the terms "flip-over" and "flip-in" are used loosely to characterize two different varieties of poison pill (although any given security may contain elements of both). Flip-in pills are triggered by events prior to the second-step merger, while flip-over pills are triggered only by the second-step merger and essentially permit the holder to acquire shares of the bidder at a discount.

---

29. Why is the asserted right to convert target shares into bidder shares legally enforceable? If there is a merger between the target and the bidder, the answer probably is that the surviving firm by operation of law assumes the liabilities of the merging firm, which here include the obligation to honor the conversion privilege. However, where the flip-over provision is triggered by some other condition (as it usually can be in the current versions of the pill), it is far from clear that the bidder is liable simply because the target provides that a flip-over right exists. For example, if the flip-over is triggered by a sale of some assets between bidder and target, the legal status of the flip-over would seem uncertain. Still, it represents a deterrent threat.

Poison pill securities have evolved rapidly in recent years, and in the most popular contemporary version (known as the Share Purchase Rights Plan), which combines flip-over and flip-in attributes, a convertible security is not used. Instead, the target distributes by a dividend to its shareholders warrants or "rights" that entitle all of them (other than the bidder or its affiliates) to purchase the target's stock for a specified period (usually ten years). The initial exercise price of these rights is usually a multiple of the company's current stock price (the rationale for this provision is that this price is what the board thinks the company will be worth at the end of this period and, more important, that such out-of-the-money warrants will not depress the stock's current price). The rights are not exercisable, however, until a triggering event occurs: typically, the announcement of a tender offer or the acquisition of beneficial ownership of a specified percentage of the target's stock (usually 20 percent, but in many cases now as low as 10 percent). Until the triggering event occurs, the rights "trade with" the underlying stock, meaning there is no separate certificate evidencing them and they cannot be separately sold. Note that for any flip-in plan to work, there must be discrimination within the class (since if the bidder also converts its stock, there is no deterrent); thus, the bidder will be expressly excluded from being able to "put" its securities back to the target. This discriminatory feature has made the flip-in pill more vulnerable to attack and has resulted in its invalidation in some jurisdictions.[30]

If the target is acquired by a merger or other business combination, the flip-over attribute of the rights is applicable and the rights "flip over" and become exercisable against the acquirer. On this flip-over, the exercise price is effectively reduced so as to threaten the acquirer with substantial dilution.[31]

Poison pills seem very complicated—complex warrants that turn the target's capital structure against the bidder. Why could not a company just do something straightforward, like adopting a charter amendment requiring board of director approval before a shareholder can vote more than 20 percent of the outstanding stock? The answer is simple but important: the charter amendment requires a shareholder vote; the poison pill can be adopted by the directors alone. If, as currently is the case, institutional investors will not vote to adopt an effective defense, the task for the lawyer is to design a device that does not require shareholder approval. Inelegance is a small price for feasibility.

---

30. Several early decisions invalidated poison pill plans on the ground that state law does not permit a corporation to discriminate among shareholders of the same class. In this view, denying some shareholders the right to exercise the flip-in redemption option is the same as paying a dividend to some common shareholders and not to others, Asarco, Inc. v. M.R.H. Holmes A Court, 611 F. Supp. 468 (D.N.J. 1985); The Amalgamated Sugar Co. v. NL Indus., Inc., 644 F. Supp. 1229 (S.D.N.Y. 1986). The counterargument is that the discrimination is not among shares, but among shareholders. After a 1988 decision by a New York court invalidating the flip-in poison pill as discriminatory and thus in violation of N.Y. Bus. Corp. Law §501(c) (specifying that "each share shall be equal to every other share in the same class," except as otherwise provided in the certificate of incorporation), the New York legislature amended the law within months to authorize flip-in poison pills. Bank of N.Y. v. Irving Bank Corp., 536 N.Y.2d 923, 924 (1988). One of the legislature's concerns was that public corporations might flee New York otherwise.

31. Typically, each right becomes the right to buy that number of the shares of the acquirer's common stock, which at the time of the merger would have a market value of twice the exercise price of the right. To illustrate, if the right were exercisable at $200 and the acquirer's stock were trading at $50 per share, a holder of the right under this formula would have the right to buy the acquirer's stock at half price.

Like the first-generation poison pill, the second generation flip-over/flip-in pill had a flaw, this one growing out of the target company board of director's power to redeem the pill before it is triggered. In the face of a target company's refusal both of an offer and of a request to redeem the pill, the acquiring company could combine a tender offer and a proxy fight, conditioning the tender offer and its promised premium on the redemption of the target's poison pill by the acquiring company's nominees should the proxy fight prove successful. The effect of this strategy was to make the proxy fight a referendum on the offer, and to put in the hands of shareholders the decision whether to redeem the pill. Corporations that have a staggered board are less exposed to this threat. At present, many institutional investors will not vote for the charter amendment necessary to adopt a staggered board,[32] so only those companies who adopted staggered boards in quieter times have this protection.

In turn, a new generation of poison pill responded to this threat of a shareholder referendum over the pill. A "dead-hand" pill adds to the flip-over/flip-in version a prohibition on its redemption by directors other than those in office at the time of the pill's adoption, or their nominees. Acquiring company nominated directors elected in a proxy fight would be unable to redeem the pill, and this would freeze the pill in place until the expiration of its typically 10-year term. A "slow-hand" pill provides a less extreme variant by only delaying for a period — say six months — the new board's power to redeem the pill after their election in a proxy fight, rather than prohibiting redemption entirely. Both the dead-hand and slow-hand variants have been struck down by the Delaware Supreme Court. See pages 990-991 infra.

c. The Effect on Shareholder Wealth

In the end, whether defensive tactics are desirable depends on their effect on shareholder wealth. Recall Chapter III's statement about the role of corporate law: "Corporate law provides much of the framework for the effort to increase the value of the corporation. . . . Since corporate law seeks to provide an environment in which the corporation's value can be maximized, there is an important standard by which it should be assessed: Does a particular rule serve to increase the value of the corporation?"[33]

The answer, at least for a particular company, depends on what target management uses the defensive tactics for. If they are a means to negotiate a higher price or to secure a competitive bid, they yield higher premiums, which result in shareholder gain; however, defensive action that results in the target company remaining independent rather than in the initiation of an auction results in losses to target shareholders. The problem, then, is how to distinguish good defensive tactics from

---

32. See, e.g., Vanguard, Vanguard's Proxy Voting Guidelines, §1(c), available at https://personal. vanguard.com/VGApp/hnw/content/Home/WhyVanguard/AboutVanguardProxyVotingGuide linesContent.jsp (announcing a general intent to block proposals to adopt classified boards); Fidelity, Fund Proxy Voting Guidelines, §5, available at http://personal.fidelity.com/myfidelity/ InsideFidelity/InvestExpertise/ProxyVoting/ProxyVotingOverView.shtml.tvsr?srcIndex = 1&srcSearch = proxy_ (stating general intent to vote against proposals to adopt anti-takeover provisions, including classified boards).

33. Page 178 supra.

bad ones. The courts' struggles with drawing this line are developed in the next two sections.

3. THE ADOPTION AND EARLY DEVELOPMENT OF PROPORTIONALITY REVIEW

By the mid-1980s, the conduct of hostile takeover defenses had become a matter of substantial concern. Academic commentary called for constraints on defensive tactics,[34] and it appeared that Congress might act to displace state laws thought to be too favorable to target management. In 1985 the Delaware Supreme Court revisited the *Cheff* primary-purpose test:

Unocal Corp. v. Mesa Petroleum Co.
493 A.2d 946 (Del. 1985)

MOORE, J.: We confront an issue of first impression in Delaware — the validity of a corporation's self-tender for its own shares which excludes from participation a stockholder making a hostile tender offer for the company's stock. . . .

On April 8, 1985, Mesa, the owner of approximately 13% of Unocal's stock, commenced a two-tier "front loaded" cash tender offer for 64 million shares, or approximately 37%, of Unocal's outstanding stock at a price of $54 per share. The "back-end" was designed to eliminate the remaining publicly held shares by an exchange of securities purportedly worth $54 per share. However, . . . the securities offered in the second-step merger would be highly subordinated [and worth significantly less than $54 per share.][35]

Unocal's board consists of eight independent outside directors and six insiders. It met on April 13, 1985, to consider the Mesa tender offer. Thirteen directors were present, and the meeting lasted nine and one-half hours. The directors were given no agenda or written materials prior to the session. However, detailed presentations were made by legal counsel regarding the board's obligations under both Delaware corporate law and the federal securities laws. The board then received a presentation from Peter Sachs on behalf of Goldman Sachs & Co. (Goldman Sachs) and Dillon, Read & Co. (Dillon Read) discussing the basis for their opinions that the Mesa proposal was wholly inadequate. Mr. Sachs opined that the minimum cash value that could be expected from a sale or orderly liquidation for 100% of Unocal's stock was in excess of $60 per share. In making his presentation, Mr. Sachs showed slides outlining the valuation techniques used by the financial advisors, and others, depicting recent business combinations in the oil and gas industry. . . . Mr. Sachs also presented various defensive strategies available to the board if it concluded that Mesa's two-step tender offer was inadequate and should be opposed. One of the devices outlined was a self-tender by Unocal for its own stock with a reasonable price range of $70 to $75 per share. The cost of such a proposal would cause the company to incur $6.1-6.5 billion of additional debt, and

---

34. See, e.g., Frank Easterbrook & Daniel Fischel, The Proper Role of a Target's Management in Responding to a Tender Offer, 94 Harv. L. Rev. 1161 (1981); Gilson, footnote 21 supra.

35. A front-loaded offer is one in which a higher price is paid in the tender offer than in the second-step merger, which encourages a shareholder to tender. — ED.

a presentation was made informing the board of Unocal's ability to handle it. The directors were told that the primary effect of this obligation would be to reduce exploratory drilling, but that the company would nonetheless remain a viable entity.

The eight outside directors, comprising a clear majority of the thirteen members present, then met separately with Unocal's financial advisors and attorneys. Thereafter, they unanimously agreed to advise the board that it should reject Mesa's tender offer as inadequate, and that Unocal should pursue a self-tender to provide the stockholders with a fairly priced alternative to the Mesa proposal. The board then reconvened and unanimously adopted a resolution rejecting as grossly inadequate Mesa's tender offer. [N]o formal decision was made on the proposed defensive self-tender.

On April 15, the board met again with four of the directors present by telephone and one member still absent. This session lasted two hours. Unocal's Vice President of Finance and its Assistant General Counsel made a detailed presentation of the proposed terms of the exchange offer. A price range between $70 and $80 per share was considered, and ultimately the directors agreed upon $72. The board was also advised about the debt securities that would be issued, and the necessity of placing restrictive covenants upon certain corporate activities until the obligations were paid. . . . [T]he directors unanimously approved the exchange offer. Their resolution provided that if Mesa acquired 64 million shares of Unocal stock through its own offer (the Mesa Purchase Condition), Unocal would buy the remaining 49% outstanding for an exchange of debt securities having an aggregate par value of $72 per share. The board resolution also stated that the offer would be subject to other conditions, including the exclusion of Mesa from the proposal (the Mesa exclusion). . . . Another focus of the board was the Mesa exclusion. Legal counsel advised that under Delaware law Mesa could only be excluded for what the directors reasonably believed to be a valid corporate purpose. The directors' discussion centered on the objective of adequately compensating shareholders at the "back-end" of Mesa's proposal, which the latter would finance with "junk bonds." To include Mesa would defeat that goal, because under the proration aspect of the exchange offer (49%) every Mesa share accepted by Unocal would displace one held by another stockholder. Further, if Mesa were permitted to tender to Unocal, the latter would in effect be financing Mesa's own inadequate proposal. . . .

We begin with the basic issue of the power of a board of directors of a Delaware corporation to adopt a defensive measure of this type. Absent such authority, all other questions are moot. . . .

The board has a large reservoir of authority upon which to draw. Its duties and responsibilities proceed from the inherent powers conferred by 8 Del. C. §141(a), respecting management of the corporation's "business and affairs." Additionally, the powers here being exercised derive from 8 Del. C. §160(a), conferring broad authority upon a corporation to deal in its own stock. From this it is now well established that in the acquisition of its shares a Delaware corporation may deal selectively with its stockholders, provided the directors have not acted out of a sole or primary purpose to entrench themselves in office. Cheff v. Mathes, Del. Supr., 199 A.2d 548, 554 (1964).

Finally, the board's power to act derives from its fundamental duty and obligation to protect the corporate enterprise, which includes stockholders, from harm reasonably perceived, irrespective of its source. Thus, we are satisfied that in the broad context of corporate governance, including issues of fundamental corporate change, a board of directors is not a passive instrumentality.

Given the foregoing principles, we turn to the standards by which director action is to be measured. In Pogostin v. Rice, Del. Supr., 480 A.2d 619 (1984), we held that the business judgment rule, including the standards by which director conduct is judged, is applicable in the context of a takeover. . . . A hallmark of the business judgment rule is that a court will not substitute its judgment for that of the board if the latter's decision can be "attributed to any rational business purpose." Sinclair Oil Corp. v. Levien, Del. Supr., 280 A.2d 717, 720 (1971).

When a board addresses a pending takeover bid it has an obligation to determine whether the offer is in the best interests of the corporation and its shareholders. In that respect a board's duty is no different from any other responsibility it shoulders, and its decisions should be no less entitled to the respect they otherwise would be accorded in the realm of business judgment. There are, however, certain caveats to a proper exercise of this function. Because of the omnipresent specter that a board may be acting primarily in its own interests, rather than those of the corporation and its shareholders, there is an enhanced duty which calls for judicial examination at the threshold before the protections of the business judgment rule may be conferred.

This court has long recognized that: "We must bear in mind the inherent danger in the purchase of shares with corporate funds to remove a threat to corporate policy when a threat to control is involved. The directors are of necessity confronted with a conflict of interest, and an objective decision is difficult." Bennett v. Propp, Del. Supr., 187 A.2d 405, 409 (1962). In the face of this inherent conflict directors must show that they had reasonable grounds for believing that a danger to corporate policy and effectiveness existed because of another person's stock ownership. Cheff v. Mathes, 199 A.2d at 554-555. However, they satisfy that burden "by showing good faith and reasonable investigation. . . ." Id. at 555. Furthermore, such proof is materially enhanced, as here, by the approval of a board comprised of a majority of outside independent directors who have acted in accordance with the foregoing standards. . . .

In the board's exercise of corporate power to forestall a takeover bid our analysis begins with the basic principle that corporate directors have a fiduciary duty to act in the best interests of the corporation's stockholders. As we have noted, their duty of care extends to protecting the corporation and its owners from perceived harm whether a threat originates from third parties or other shareholders.[10] But such powers are not absolute. A corporation does not have unbridled discretion to defeat any perceived threat by any Draconian means available.

A restriction placed upon a selective stock repurchase is that the directors may not have acted solely or primarily out of a desire to perpetuate themselves in office. See Cheff v. Mathes, 199 A.2d at 556. Of course, to this is added the further caveat that inequitable action may not be taken under the guise of law. Schnell v. Chris-Craft Industries, Inc., Del. Supr. 285 A.2d 437, 439 (1971). The standard of proof

---

10. It has been suggested that a board's response to a takeover threat should be a passive one. . . . However, that clearly is not the law of Delaware, and as the proponents of this rule of passivity readily concede, it has not been adopted either by courts or state legislatures. Easterbrook & Fischel, [The Proper Rule of a Target Management in Responding to a Tender Offer], 94 Harv. L. Rev. 1161, 1194 (1981).

established in Cheff v. Mathes . . . is designed to ensure that a defensive measure to thwart or impede a takeover is indeed motivated by a good faith concern for the welfare of the corporation and its stockholders, which in all circumstances must be free of any fraud or other misconduct. Cheff v. Mathes, 199 A.2d at 554-555. However, this does not end the inquiry.

A further aspect is the element of balance. If a defensive measure is to come within the ambit of the business judgment rule, it must be reasonable in relation to the threat posed. This entails an analysis by the directors of the nature of the takeover bid and its effect on the corporate enterprise. Examples of such concerns may include: inadequacy of the price offered, nature and timing of the offer, questions of illegality, the impact on "constituencies" other than shareholders (i.e., creditors, customers, employees, and perhaps even the community gener-ally), the risk of nonconsummation, and the quality of securities being offered in the exchange. See Lipton and Brownstein, Takeover Responses and Directors' Responsibilities: An Update, p.7, ABA National Institute on the Dynamics of Cor-porate Control (December 8, 1983). While not a controlling factor, it also seems to us that a board may reasonably consider the basic stockholder interests at stake, including those of short term speculators, whose actions may have fueled the coercive aspect of the offer at the expense of the long term investor.[11] Here, the threat posed was viewed by the Unocal board as a grossly inadequate two-tier coercive tender offer coupled with the threat of greenmail.[36]

Specifically, the Unocal directors had concluded that the value of Unocal was substantially above the $54 per share offered in cash at the front end. Furthermore, they determined that the subordinated securities to be exchanged in Mesa's announced squeeze out of the remaining shareholders in the "back-end" merger were "junk bonds" worth far less than $54. It is now well recognized that such offers are a classic coercive measure designed to stampede shareholders into tendering at the first tier, even if the price is inadequate, out of fear of what they will receive at the back end of the transaction. Wholly beyond the coercive aspect of an inadequate two-tier tender offer, the threat was posed by a corporate raider with a national reputation as a "greenmailer."

In adopting the selective exchange offer, the board stated that its objective was either to defeat the inadequate Mesa offer or, should the offer still succeed, provide

---

11. There has been much debate respecting such stockholder interests. One rather impressive study indicates that the stock of over 50 percent of target companies, who resisted hostile takeovers, later traded at higher market prices than the rejected offer price, or were acquired after the tender offer was defeated by another company at a price higher than the offer price. . . . Moreover, an update by Kidder Peabody & Company of this study, involving the stock prices of target companies that have defeated hostile tender offers during the period from 1973 to 1982, demonstrates that in a majority of cases the target's shareholders benefited from the defeat. The stock of 81% of the targets studied has, since the tender offer, sold at prices higher than the tender offer price. When adjusted for the time value of money, the figure is 64%. See Lipton & Brownstein, supra ABA Institute at 10. The thesis being that this strongly supports application of the business judgment rule in response to takeover threats. There is, however, a rather vehement contrary view. See Easterbrook & Fischel, supra 36 Bus. Law. at 1739-1745.

36. "Greenmail" is the pejorative term for a selective repurchase by the target corporation of a bidder's target stock, usually at a premium over the market, to cause the bidder to withdraw the bid. The problem for the target with this defensive strategy is that once the auction has begun (and the target is "in play"), other bidders are likely to replace the initial bidder who has been bought off (particularly if the other bidders suspect that they too may be offered greenmail). Is this what happened in Cheff v. Mathes? — ED.

the 49% of its stockholders, who would otherwise be forced to accept "junk bonds," with $72 worth of senior debt. We find that both purposes are valid.

However, such efforts would have been thwarted by Mesa's participation in the exchange offer. First, if Mesa could tender its shares, Unocal would effectively be subsidizing the former's continuing effort to buy Unocal stock at $54 per share. Second, Mesa could not, by definition, fit within the class of shareholders being protected from its own coercive and inadequate tender offer.

Thus, we are satisfied that the selective exchange offer is reasonably related to the threats posed. It is consistent with the principle that "the minority stock-holder shall receive the substantial equivalent in value of what he had before." Sterling v. Mayflower Hotel Corp., Del. Supr., 93 A.2d 107, 114 (1952). See also Rosenblatt v. Getty Oil Co., Del. Supr., 493 A.2d 929, 940 (1985). This concept of fairness, while stated in the merger context, is also relevant in the area of tender offer law. Thus, the board's decision to offer what it determined to be the fair value of the corporation to the 49% of its shareholders, who would otherwise be forced to accept highly subordinated "junk bonds," is reasonable and consistent with the directors' duty to ensure that the minority stockholders receive equal value for their shares.

Mesa contends that it is unlawful, and the trial court agreed, for a corporation to discriminate in this fashion against one shareholder. It argues correctly that no case has ever sanctioned a device that precludes a raider from sharing in a benefit available to all other stockholders. However, as we have noted earlier, the principle of selective stock repurchases by a Delaware corporation is neither unknown nor authorized. . . . The only difference is that heretofore the approved transaction was the payment of "greenmail" to a raider or dissident posing a threat to the corporate enterprise. All other stockholders were denied such favored treatment, and given Mesa's past history of greenmail, its claims here are rather ironic.

However, our corporate law is not static. It must grow and develop in response to, indeed in anticipation of, evolving concepts and needs. Merely because the General Corporation Law is silent as to a specific matter does not mean that it is prohibited. In the days when *Cheff* [was] decided, the tender offer, while not an unknown device, was virtually unused, and little was known of such methods as two-tier "front-end" loaded offers with their coercive effects. Then, the favored attack of a raider was stock acquisition followed by a proxy contest. Various defensive tactics, which provided no benefit whatever to the raider, evolved. Thus, the use of corporate funds by management to counter a proxy battle was approved. . . . Litigation, supported by corporate funds, aimed at the raider has long been a popular device.

More recently, as the sophistication of both raiders and targets has developed, a host of other defensive measures to counter such ever mounting threats has evolved and received judicial sanction. These include defensive charter amendments and other devices bearing some rather exotic, but apt, names: Crown Jewel, White Knight, Pac Man, and Golden Parachute. Each has highly selective features, the object of which is to deter or defeat the raider. . . .

Thus, while the exchange offer is a form of selective treatment, given the nature of the threat posed here the response is neither unlawful nor unreasonable. If the board of directors is disinterested, has acted in good faith and with due care, its decision in the absence of an abuse of discretion will be upheld as a proper exercise of business judgment.

In conclusion, there was directorial power to oppose the Mesa tender offer, and to undertake a selective stock exchange made in good faith and upon a reasonable investigation pursuant to a clear duty to protect the corporate enterprise. Further, the selective stock repurchase plan chosen by Unocal is reasonable in relation to the threat that the board rationally and reasonably believed was posed by Mesa's inadequate and coercive two-tier tender offer. Under those circumstances the board's action is entitled to be measured by the standards of the business judgment rule. Thus, unless it is shown by a preponderance of the evidence that the directors' decisions were primarily based on perpetuating themselves in office, or some other breach of fiduciary duty such as fraud, overreaching, lack of good faith, or being uninformed, a court will not substitute its judgment for that of the board.

If the stockholders are displeased with the action of their elected representatives, the powers of corporate democracy are at their disposal to turn the board out. . . .

---

1. *Proportionality review and the pill.* Shortly after its decision in *Unocal*, the Delaware Supreme Court, in Moran v. Household International, Inc., 500 A.2d 1346 (Del. 1985), upheld the validity of a poison pill using an analysis that was consistent with the intermediate standard of review announced in *Unocal*. The specific rights plan in *Moran* was a flip-over plan adopted without an ongoing tender offer that was triggered by a person either acquiring 20 percent or more of Household's stock or announcing a tender offer for 30 percent or more. Once triggered, the plan would prevent a second-stage merger. The court found that such a plan did not deter a tender offer, but was only a reasonable protection against a coercive two-tier offer. It also emphasized that the plan was adopted before any identifiable bidder had appeared, indicating that it favored "pre-planning for the contingency of a hostile takeover [because it] might reduce the risk that, under the pressure of a takeover bid, management will fail to exercise reasonable judgment." More important, in *Moran* the board had retained the power to redeem the rights plan if an attractive takeover bid was made. The court implied that such a power to redeem may be essential to the validity of a poison pill plan: "[T]he Rights Plan is not absolute. When the Household Board of Directors is faced with a tender offer and a request to redeem the Rights, they will not be able to arbitrarily reject the offer. They will be held to the same fiduciary standards any other board of directors would be held to in deciding to adopt a defensive mechanism [citing *Unocal*]." In the final paragraph of the decision, the court reemphasized this point: "While we conclude for present purposes that the Household Directors are protected by the business judgment rule, that does not end the matter. The ultimate response to an actual takeover bid must be judged by the Directors' actions at that time. . . . Their use of the Plan will be evaluated when and if the issue arises."

Thus, *Moran* defers the application of *Unocal* proportionality review from the time the pill is adopted to the time an offer is made, the bidder requests that the pill be redeemed, and the target board declines. At that point, the board in the first instance and then the court must determine whether the bid presents a threat and, if so, whether a preclusive tactic — declining to redeem the pill — is reasonable in relation to the threat.

2. *Unocal's significance: Is there substance to proportionality review?* In *Unocal*, the court moved from *Cheff*'s disguised application of the business judgment rule to an

intermediate standard that sought to distinguish defensive tactics that benefited shareholders from those that merely protected management. The new standard added a second step to *Cheff*'s policy conflict/primary purpose analysis. Pointing to a danger to corporate policy based on a carefully crafted record was no longer enough. Defensive tactics also had to satisfy a proportionality review: Were the tactics deployed "reasonable in relation to the threat posed" by the hostile bid?[37] Whether proportionality review reflected a real change in substance depended on the resolution of two questions. First, was the new standard more than just a threshold inquiry; that is, if a threat was shown, to what extent would proportionality review constrain the range of acceptable defensive tactics? Second, might some hostile bids present no threat at all, and thus warrant no defensive response under proportionality review?

Following *Unocal*, a series of Chancery Court cases began to fill in the broad outlines of proportionality review. AC Acquisitions Corp. v. Anderson, Clayton & Co., 519 A.2d 103 (Del. Ch. 1986), read *Unocal* to require more than a threshold review. The case involved a $56 per share cash tender offer for all of Anderson, Clayton's stock, with a commitment to pay the same price to any non-tendering shareholders in a subsequent freeze-out merger. The hostile offer therefore was not coercive. A shareholder who thought the price too low could simply decline to tender, knowing that she would be no worse off as a result; if other shareholders disagreed and tendered so that the bid was successful, she still would receive the same price in the subsequent merger. Anderson, Clayton responded defensively by offering to purchase 65 percent of its stock at $60 per share—but shareholders had to accept before the hostile offer was completed. Thus, shareholders were coerced into accepting the defensive offer even if they preferred the hostile offer. If some shareholders declined to participate in the defensive offer, and the hostile offer then failed, they would be left with shares that had been substantially reduced in value as a result of the payments made pursuant to the defensive offer in which they did not participate.

If *Unocal* were only a threshold test, the *Anderson, Clayton* court could have easily approved Anderson, Clayton's defensive offer. A low-priced offer is always a threat, and a competitive alternative seems reasonably related to the threat. The court, however, carefully examined the particular terms of the company's defensive offer and found their inherent coercion disproportionate to the threat:

> The fatal defect with the [defensive bid] . . . becomes apparent when one attempts to apply the second leg of the *Unocal* test and ask whether the defensive step is "reasonable in relation to the threat posed." The [hostile] offer poses a threat of any kind (other than a threat to the incumbency of the Board) only in a special sense and on the assumption that a majority of the Company's shareholders might prefer an alternative to the [hostile] offer. On this assumption, it is reasonable to create an option that would permit shareholders to keep an equity interest in the firm, but, in my opinion, it is not reasonable in relation to such a "threat" to structure such an option so as to preclude as a practical matter shareholders from accepting the [hostile] offer.

519 A.2d at 112-113.

---

37. See Ronald J. Gilson & Reinier Kraakman, Delaware's Intermediate Standard for Defensive Tactics: Is There Substance to Proportionality Review?, 44 Bus. Law. 247 (1989).

Unocal and *Anderson, Clayton* illustrate one kind of threat that would warrant a defensive response. The structure of the hostile bid in *Unocal* pressured target shareholders into tendering even if they thought the terms of the offer unfavorable. In *Anderson, Clayton* target management thought the price offered by the hostile bidder was inadequate. But what kind of response is proportionate to these threats? If, as in *Anderson, Clayton*, a hostile bid is not coercive, is target management limited to simply offering shareholders an alternative transaction, and then letting the shareholders choose which they prefer? If so, then proportionality review represents a serious challenge to a defensive planner who, in response to a hostile offer, wants both to keep the target company independent and avoid an alternative transaction, such as the issuer tender offer in *Unocal* and the company offer in *Anderson, Clayton*, that would substantially alter the target company's balance sheet.

The crucial question, then, is what kinds of threat from a non-coercive hostile bid are so serious as to warrant preclusive defensive tactics without offering a transactional alternative. When may the target company "just say no"? Suppose the target board believes in good faith that the price offered in a non-coercive offer is too low. Would a defense that made it impossible for a hostile offer to continue — most obviously, the target company's refusal to redeem its poison pill — be reasonably related to the threat that target shareholders might accept a bid that the target board honestly concluded was inadequate even if the target company offered the shareholders no alternative but the status quo? Is it important that in *Unocal* the court included price inadequacy among the litany of factors the target board was authorized to consider?

The Delaware Chancery Court considered what circumstances might constitute a threat sufficient to warrant preclusive defensive tactics in City Capital Associates v. Interco Inc., 551 A.2d 787 (Del. 1988). A bidder's non-coercive offer for Interco touched off a contest in which a substantively similar alternative transaction was crafted by management.[38] By the time the bidding concluded, the hostile offer stood at $74 per share cash, and the competing management transaction, involving a combination of cash, securities, and common stock in the post-transaction company, was valued by the target company's investment banker at $76 per share. The hostile bidder then sued to force the target to redeem its poison pill so that shareholders could decide between the two offers, and also sought to enjoin the company from selling off its Ethan Allen division in furtherance of its alternative transaction.

The court directed the redemption of the target company's poison pill:

> In this instance, there is no threat of shareholder coercion. The threat is to shareholders' economic interests posed by an offer the board has concluded is "inadequate." If this determination is made in good faith (as I assume it is here), it alone will justify leaving a poison pill in place, even in the setting of a noncoercive offer, for a period while the board exercises its good faith business judgment to take such steps as it deems appropriate to protect and advance shareholder interests in light of the significant development that such an offer doubtless is. That action may entail

---

38. The hostile bid contemplated a highly leveraged cash acquisition, following which a number of Interco's operating units would be sold and the proceeds used to pay down the acquisition debt. The competing company transaction involved the company itself borrowing funds that would then be paid out to shareholders as a special dividend. Thereafter, a number of the company's operating units would be sold to pay down the debt incurred to finance the special dividend.

negotiation on behalf of shareholders with the offeror, the institution of auction for the Company, a recapitalization or restructuring designed as an alternative to the offer, or other action.

Once that period has closed, and it is apparent that the board does not intend to institute [an] auction, or to negotiate for an increase in the unwanted offer, and that it has taken such time as it required in good faith to arrange an alternative value-maximizing transaction, then, in most instances, the legitimate role of the poison pill in the context of a noncoercive offer will have been fully satisfied. The only function then left for the pill at this end-stage is to preclude the shareholders from exercising a judgment about their own interests that differs from the judgment of the directors, who will have some interest in the question. What then is the "threat" in this instance that might justify such a result? Stating that "threat" at this stage of the process most specifically, it is this: *Wasserstein Perella* [Interco's investment banker] *may be correct in their respective valuations of the offer and the restructuring but a majority of the Interco shareholders may not accept that fact and may be injured as a consequence.*

Perhaps there is a case in which it is appropriate for a board of directors to in effect permanently foreclose their shareholders from accepting a noncoercive offer for their stock by utilization of the recent innovation of "poison pill" rights. If such a case might exist by reason of some special circumstance, a review of the facts here shows this not to be it. The "threat" here, when viewed with particularity, is far too mild to justify such a step in this instance. . . .

Our corporation law exists, not as an isolated body of rules and principles, but rather in a historical setting and as a part of a larger body of law premised upon shared values. To acknowledge that directors may employ the recent innovation of "poison pills" to deprive shareholders of the ability effectively to choose to accept a noncoercive offer, after the board has had a reasonable opportunity to explore or create alternatives, or attempt to negotiate on the shareholders' behalf, would, it seems to me, be so inconsistent with widely shared notions of appropriate corporate governance as to threaten to diminish the legitimacy and authority of our corporation law.

(Emphasis in the original.)

While requiring Interco to redeem its poison pill, the court declined to enjoin the sale of Ethan Allen. Here the court concluded that the sale of that business in an effort to secure better terms for the shareholders, unlike the preclusive effect of declining to redeem a poison pill, was reasonably related to the threat of an inadequate offer: "Of course, a board acts reasonably in relation to an offer, albeit a noncoercive offer, it believes to be inadequate when it seeks to realize the full, market value of an important asset. . . . I do understand that [the sale] complicates the [hostile bidder's] life and indeed might imperil [its] ability to complete its transaction. [The hostile bidder], however, has no right to demand that its chosen target remain in status quo while its offer is formulated, increased and, perhaps, accepted."

After *Interco* and a number of Chancery Court cases that followed,[39] it seemed that price inadequacy alone was an insufficient threat to warrant a target company's declining to redeem its poison pill. Because few other defensive tactics had the promise of actually precluding an offer, *Unocal* could be seen as providing a

---

39. Grand Metropolitan Public Limited Co. v. The Pillsbury Co., [1988-1989 Transfer Binder] Fed. Sec. L. Rep. (CCH) ¶94,104 (Del. Ch. 1988); Shamrock Holdings, Inc. v. Polaroid Corp., 559 A.2d 278 (Del. Ch. 1989).

safe harbor for bidders: target shareholders ultimately would have the opportunity to decide whether to accept a non-coercive hostile offer.[40]

Another, less bidder-friendly interpretation was also possible. In *Interco* and *Anderson, Clayton* target management not only defended against the hostile bid, but also attempted to impose on shareholders a change in the target company similar to the hostile offer. Suppose instead that target management took no defensive action other than declining to redeem its pill. Could a target company "just say no"?[41] So matters stood when the case arose that would give the Delaware Supreme Court its first chance to consider the Chancery Court's explication of *Unocal*.

4. THE *TIME-WARNER* CASE: CHANCERY AND SUPREME COURT OPINIONS

Paramount Communications, Inc. v. Time Incorporated[42]
[1989 Transfer Binder] Fed. Sec. L. Rep. (CCH) ¶ 94,514 (Del. Ch. 1989)

ALLEN, Ch.: Pending are motions in several related lawsuits seeking, principally, a preliminary injunction restraining Time Incorporated from buying stock under a June 16, 1989, offer to purchase 100 million shares of common stock (comprising 51% of the outstanding common stock) of Warner Communications Inc. at $70 per share cash. . . .

Plaintiffs in these lawsuits include Paramount Communications, Inc. and its KDS Acquisition Corp. subsidiary, which is itself currently extending an offer to purchase up to all shares of Time at $200 per share; various holders of modest amounts of Time common stock, who purport to represent Time shareholders as a class; and several very substantial Time shareholders who sue on their own behalf. Defendants are Time Incorporated, all 12 of its current and three recently resigned directors, as well as Warner Communications Inc.

On this motion, the court is required to express an opinion on the question of whether the directors of Time, who plainly have been granted the legal power to complete a public tender offer transaction that would be the first stage in accomplishing a thoughtfully planned consolidation of the business of Time with that of Warner Communications, have a supervening fiduciary obligation to desist from doing so in order that it be made more likely that the shareholders of Time will be afforded an opportunity to accept the public tender offer for all shares extended by Paramount's KDS subsidiary. The record in this case indicates . . . that it is very unlikely that the market price of Time stock immediately following consummation of the now planned two-stage Warner transaction will equal the initial $175 price offered by Paramount.

It is the gist of the plaintiff's position . . . that Time's board of directors does have such a supervening fiduciary duty and has failed to understand or, more

---

40. See Gilson & Kraakman, footnote 37 supra.

41. The opinion in SWT Acquisition Corp. v. TW Services, Inc., 700 F. Supp. 1323 (1988), was said to support the "just say no" defense, although the case was decided on other grounds. See Theodore Mirvis, TW Services: Just Another Brick in the Wall?: The Return of "Just Say No," N.Y. L.J. (March 30, 1989), p.5.

42. Aspects of this decision concerning the obligations of the target company board in connection with the target's friendly sale are taken up in Sec. C. — ED.

accurately, has chosen to ignore that fact, in order to force the Warner transaction upon the corporation and its shareholders—a transaction that, plaintiffs assert, the shareholders would not approve, if given the opportunity to vote on the matter. The board of Time is doing this, it is urged, not for any legitimate reason, but because it prefers that transaction which secures and entrenches the power of those in whose hands management of the corporation has been placed.

It is the gist of the position of the directors of Time that they have no fiduciary duty to desist from accomplishing the transaction in question in these circumstances. They contend, quite broadly speaking, that their duty is to exercise their judgment prudently (i.e., deliberately, in an informed manner) in the good faith pursuit of legitimate corporate goals. . . . [T]hey assert that the result of that judgment is a proposed transaction of extraordinary benefit and promise to Time and its shareholders. It is quite reasonable, they contend, for the board to prefer it, on behalf of the corporation and its shareholders, to the sale of the company presently for $200 per share cash, which sale is plainly inconsistent with accomplishment of the proposed Warner transaction. In short, the directors say the question whether the Warner transaction in its current form should be pursued or not in the corporation's interest is for them to decide, not the shareholders; . . . and that while some shareholders, even a majority of shareholders, may disagree with the wisdom of their choice, that fact provides no reason for this court to force them, under the guise of a fiduciary obligation, to take another, more popular course of action. . . .

I.

A. Time Incorporated and the Composition of Its Board of Directors

Time Incorporated is a Delaware corporation with its principal offices in New York City. . . . Time's board presently is composed of 12 directors, . . . four officers of the company [and 8 outside directors]. . . .

B. The Genesis of the March 3, 1989, Time-Warner Merger Agreement

1. *Strategic planning and management's commitment to maintaining Time as an independent enterprise.* . . . Time was, of course, founded as a journalistic enterprise. That meant most importantly that its writers created the material that it offered for sale. Publishing continues to be vitally important to it.[4] As Time has in this decade become importantly dependent upon video media for its income and growth, however, it has recognized a need to create for itself and thus own the video or film products that it delivers through its cable network (HBO) and cable franchises. To fail to develop this capacity would, it was apparently feared, leave the firm at the mercy of others (both as to quality and to price) with respect to the element most critical to success in the video entertainment business. Thus, for some time, management of the corporation has reviewed ways in which the firm might address this need.

Another large-scale consideration that has played a role in the strategic thinking of Time's management and its outside directors is . . . the expansion of Time into

---

4. Time's magazines earn about 20% of the revenues generated in the United States magazine industry and more than a third of the profits.

international markets in a more substantial way, as an important long-term goal for the company.

Neither the goal of establishing a vertically integrated entertainment organization, nor the goal of becoming a more global enterprise, was a transcendent aim of Time management or its board. More important to both, apparently, has been a desire to maintain an independent Time Incorporated that reflected a continuation of what management and the board regarded as distinctive and important "Time culture." This culture appears in part to be pride in the history of the firm — notably *Time* magazine and its role in American life — and in part a managerial philosophy and distinctive structure that is intended to protect journalistic integrity from pressures from the business side of the enterprise.

I note parenthetically that plaintiffs in this suit dismiss this claim of "culture" as being nothing more than a desire to perpetuate or entrench existing management disguised in a pompous, highfalutin' claim. I understand the argument and recognize the risk of cheap deception that would be entailed in a broad and indiscriminate recognition of "corporate culture" as a valid interest that would justify a board in taking steps to defeat a non-coercive tender offer. Every reconfiguration of assets, every fundamental threat to the status quo, represents a threat to an existing corporate culture. But I am not persuaded that there may not be instances in which the law might recognize as valid a perceived threat to a "corporate culture" that is shown to be palpable (for lack of a better word), distinctive and advantageous. In any event, for now it is enough to note that the management and the outside board members of Time . . . did, in any transaction that might satisfy the perceived need to acquire better access to video production and to global markets, seek to maintain a distinctive Time organization, in part at least in order to maintain a distinctive Time corporate culture. There has never been the slightest subjective interest in selling to or submerging Time into another entity.

2. *Anti-takeover protections.* Management and the outside board of Time have been concerned for some while that the company have in place certain of the protections against uninvited acquisition attempts. In fact, Time seems to have equipped itself with a full armory of defenses including . . . a poison pill preferred stock rights plan, which was recently (1988) amended to reduce its trigger to acquisition of a 15% stake in the company.

3. *Exploration of possible opportunities to meet strategic goals.* Time's management appears to have been alert to opportunities to meet the goal of providing the corporation with a video production capacity. In the spring of 1987, senior management . . . advised members of the board that, upon the initiative of Steven Ross, chief executive officer of Warner, management was pursuing conversations with Warner in order to explore the mutual advantages of a joint venture involving at least each company's cable television franchises and perhaps HBO and Warner Brothers Studios. . . . Those discussions, however, encountered tax and other impediments and did not lead to a definitive proposal. Warner by that time had become the focus of Time's strategic thinking. . . .

At the Time board meeting of July 21, 1988, the board heard reports from management concerning the possibility of a Warner merger. Management reported that it had reviewed other "studios" — including Disney, Paramount (then Gulf & Western), MCA-Universal, Columbia and Twentieth Century Fox, and had concluded that Warner was the most desirable prospect for achieving the corporation's goals. . . . [T]he board at that meeting approved the negotiations of a merger agreement with Warner if . . . "corporate governance" issues [were] resolved in a way that assured that Time's senior management would ultimately come to control the combined entity. . . . Time has developed a unique structure (in which the senior writer — the editor-in-chief — reports directly to a special committee of the board of directors) in order to protect the "culture" or value of journalistic independence which the corporation had found, historically, to have been economically advantageous. . . .

There may be at work here a force more subtle than a desire to maintain a title or office in order to assure continued salary or prerequisites. Many people commit a huge portion of their lives to a single large-scale business organization. They derive their identity in part from that organization and feel that they contribute to the identity of the firm. The mission of the firm is not seen by those involved with it as wholly economic, nor the continued existence of its distinctive identity as a matter of indifference. . . .

Thus, while the record suggests that the "Time culture" importantly includes directors' concerns for the larger role of the enterprise in society, there is insufficient basis to suppose at this juncture that such concerns have caused the directors to sacrifice or ignore their duty to seek to maximize in the long run financial returns to the corporation and its stockholders.

In all events, in July 1988, the governance agenda included a plan for co-CEO's (initially Munro and Ross, then Nicholas and Ross to be followed by a sole CEO, Nicholas). It also provided for a board equally divided between 12 former Time directors and 12 former Warner directors and required a supermajority board vote (2/3) to modify the structure that established the board committee to whom the editor-in-chief would report. . . .

C. Negotiation of the Time-Warner March 3, 1989, Agreement of Merger

Negotiation of a possible transaction seemed to fall to the ground promptly when the parties were unable to agree to a management structure of a combined entity that satisfied Time's expressed need to assure continuation of its "culture" by assuring the ultimate succession of Time executives to the senior executive positions in the new firm. . . .

The rub came in agreeing to a plan for a chief executive officer. Mr. Munro was set to retire in 1990. Mr. Nicholas was to succeed him. The prospect of co-CEO's had been discussed and agreed upon in principle: Munro and Ross until Munro's retirement, then Nicholas and Ross until such time as Ross was to retire. At that time, it was proposed that Nicholas would succeed as sole CEO. Time, however, insisted that Mr. Ross should set a retirement date at the outset, to be agreed upon, and Mr. Ross did not find this appealing. Discussions broke off in August.

Negotiations were reopened in January, 1989. . . . The agreement reached was that Ross would retire five years after the merger and that Nicholas would then become the sole CEO of Time-Warner. . . .

The exchange ratio was the last item agreed upon. It was agreed at a fixed rate (rather than a formula that would work off future data) of .465 of a Time share for each share of Warner's common stock. The ratio of market value of Warner's stock to Time's was about .38. The deal struck represented about a 12% premium for Warner shareholders. Should this merger have been effectuated, the shareholders of Warner would have owned approximately 62% of the common stock (and the voting power) of Time-Warner. In terms of market capitalization and 1988 net income, Warner was the larger of the two companies.

D. The Initial Time-Warner Merger Agreement

On March 3, 1989, the boards of both companies authorized entering into the merger agreement, which was done also on that day. Both corporations have a majority of outside directors. . . .

As a technical matter, the merger agreement contemplated the merger of Warner into a wholly-owned Time subsidiary (TW Sub Inc.) with Warner as the surviving corporation. The common stock of Warner would be converted into common stock of Time Incorporated at the agree[d] upon ratio. The name of Time would then be changed to Time-Warner. In such circumstances, the Delaware General Corporation Law requires for the effectuation of a merger an affirmative vote of a majority of the shareholders of Warner (since its stock is being converted into something else in the merger), but does not require a vote of the shareholders of Time (since its stock will remain unaffected by the merger and the issuance of additional shares did not require amendment of Time's certificate of incorporation). See 8 Del. C. Sec. 251. The merger agreement, however, contemplated a stockholder vote by both corporations since under New York Stock Exchange rules, issuance of the number of Time shares contemplated required such a vote.

E. Steps to Protect the Merger

1. *The Share Exchange Agreement.* At the same time that they authorized entering into the merger agreement, each board authorized execution of a Share Exchange Agreement. This agreement gave each party the option to trigger an exchange of shares in which event if triggered, Warner would acquire . . . 11.1% of Time, and Time would acquire . . . 9.4% of Warner's outstanding stock. These blocks of stock would have had approximately equal value if calculated on average closing prices of Time and Warner stock for the five business days preceding the announcement of the merger. This agreement is said to have served several purposes. . . . For present purposes, I assume its principal purpose was to discourage any effort to upset the transaction. . . .

2. *Restriction on information and "dry-up" agreements.* Everyone involved in this negotiation realized that the transaction contemplated might be perceived as putting Time and Warner "in play." Realizing that the corporation might be deemed "in play," management sought and paid for commitments from various banks that they would not finance an attempt to take over Time. In this litigation they are cited by plaintiffs as wrongful attempts by the "target" corporation to interfere with the ability of an offeror to present the shareholders with the best available price. In all events, these "dry up" fees appear to be a dubious, futile innovation at this point when the global economy seems awash in cash available to finance takeovers.

An additional attempt to secure the closing of the merger may be reflected in a provision of the merger agreement that severely limits the ability of Time to enter into any takeover negotiations prior to the closing of the merger. "Time may not solicit or encourage or take any other action to facilitate any inquiries on the making of any proposal which constitutes or may . . . lead to, any takeover proposal." The only exception to such provision would occur if a hostile tender offer for 25% or more of Time's stock is announced (or 10% of its stock is purchased), at which time Time may, after consultation with Warner, communicate with the offeror (or stockholder). In all events, such an occurrence would not excuse Time's performance under the merger agreement, but would give Warner an out.

F. Paramount Announces a $175
Cash Offer on June 7

The Time board had fixed June 23 as the date for the annual shareholders meeting of the company at which the Time-Warner merger was to be presented for shareholder approval. On June 7, Paramount announced that it was extending an offer to purchase all of the outstanding common stock of Time at $175 per share cash. . . . Paramount's offer was subject to a number of conditions, the most pertinent of which were the following:

1. termination of the Time-Warner merger agreement (or the agreement being left subject to a vote in which Paramount controlled 51% of the vote);
2. termination or invalidation of the Share Exchange Agreement under circumstances in which there would be no liability to Time;
3. Paramount to be satisfied in its sole discretion that all material approvals, consents and franchise transfers relating to Time's programming and cable television business had been obtained on terms satisfactory to Paramount;
4. removal of a number of Time-created or Time-controlled impediments to closing of the offer (e.g., redemption of a "poison pill" preferred rights purchase plan) or effectuation of a second-stage merger (e.g., supermajority voting requirements of 8 Del. C. Sec. 205 and supermajority voting provisions of Time's certificate of incorporation); and
5. financing and majority acceptance of the offer.

G. Market Reaction to the Paramount Offer

The Time-Warner merger had been warmly received. The stock for both companies rose on the market. . . . In any event, Time stock which had been traded in a $103⅝-$113¾ range in February, rose to $105-$122⅝ in March and April; Warner stock, which had been trading in a range of $38⅞-$43¾ in February, prior to the announcement of the merger agreement, traded in a $42⅞-$50½ range in March and April.

The prospect of immediate $175 cash payment, however, excited the market even more. Following the announcement of the Paramount offer, Time stock jumped 44 points in one day to $170; it hit a high of $182¾ on June 13 whence it relaxed to close at $146¼ on the day of presentation of this motion. . . .

H. Time and Warner React to the Demand to Terminate
Their Negotiated Contract

Time's management immediately responded to Paramount's announcement, aggressively sending to Mr. Davis of Paramount a biting letter attacking his "integrity and motives," and calling the offer "smoke and mirrors." . . . Management also appears to have sought to cause delay in the process that Paramount would engage in to secure necessary governmental approvals for the transfer of cable franchises. . . .

The board resolved on June 16 after further negotiations with Warner to reject the implicit demands of Paramount and to recast the Warner transaction in a form (a cash acquisition of a majority stake in Warner to be followed by a merger for cash or securities, or a combination of both) that would not require shareholder approval, which now, of course, was problematic.

While plaintiffs in these lawsuits interpret these actions as those of directors determined to ignore shareholder rights and interests in the pursuit of a transaction that assures them continued access to the salaries and prerequisites of a powerful corporation, the Time board purports to have been motivated on June 16 chiefly by . . . [the following].

1. *The Time board's purported conclusion that the $175 offer was inadequate.* . . . [T]he board was advised by its investment bankers that if it elected to sell the company, a substantial premium over the current values to be achieved otherwise would be realized. Several techniques to estimate this control market value were employed. The board was told that "the price [in such transaction] would likely be in the mid to high end of the pre-tax segment value range," which is to say that the price would likely be greater than $250 per share. This analysis was premised upon a pre-tax valuation of each segment (i.e., did not contemplate a "bust-up" acquirer). The board was also presented with valuation ranges for a strategic acquirer; a leveraged buyout range (on various assumptions) and recapitalization ranges, both of which ranged from levels somewhat above the $175 price to prices higher than the now current offer. . . .

2. *What the board was advised with respect to (a) likely short-term stock price following a revised Time-Warner merger, and (b) likely longer-term stock price.* It was the view of Wasserstein, Perella that the stock of Time-Warner would trade at around $150 per share. They noted as well that the range might also be higher, citing a range of $160 to $175 per share. In the written presentation given to the board on June 16, the trading range given for the year 1990 is $106-$188, based on both cash flow and earnings per share analysis.

In the longer term, Time's advisors have predicted trading ranges of $159-$247 for 1991, $230-$332 for 1992 and $208-$402 for 1993. The latter being a range that a Texan might feel at home on.

3. *Purported consideration of non-price terms.* In addition to price, the board considered that the $175 offer was itself subject to conditions that would delay its effectuation for, at a minimum, some months or as much as a year, to get the approvals for the transfer of control of local cable television franchises, which approvals Paramount had made a condition to its closing. In fact, it appears that this point was seen less as a problem than as an opportunity. Time has been active in trying to impede Paramount's ability to satisfy this condition.

The board considered that the terms of the offer (Paramount to be satisfied in its sole discretion, etc.) gave Paramount great flexibility and that in a sense the offer would be viewed as a "request" to terminate the Warner deal and to grant Paramount a free option on the company for some period necessary to see if the transfer of all material franchises could be arranged. . . .

4. *Recasting the merger transaction.* With the determination to decline Paramount's invitation to negotiate the sale of Time and to continue to pursue the Warner transactions, the directors faced the fact that it was problematic whether the Time shareholders [who were largely institutional investors] would share the board's expressed view that $175 cash now should be rejected in order to afford the company's management some additional years to manage the trading value of Time shares to levels materially higher than the future value of $175 now. . . .

Thus, the "return" to a cash acquisition format must be seen as a reaction to the effect that emergence of the Paramount offer could be expected to have on the shareholder vote. . . . With respect to an appropriate price for Warner in a cash deal, the investment bankers advised that a $70 cash price would be fair from Time's point of view. Warner had been trading at around $45 prior to the announcement of the merger so the price represented about a 56% premium. . . .

At meetings on June 15 and 16, Warner's board approved the restructured proposal. That same day, Warner caused the exchange of shares contemplated by the Share Exchange Agreement to be triggered.

I. Paramount's $200 Offer and Time's Rejection of It on June 26

On June 22, Paramount, not having been able to induce Time to engage in negotiations, unilaterally increased the cash price of its offer to $200. That subject was addressed at a June 26 meeting of the Time board. The factors that had earlier led to the decision not to pursue a sale transaction with Paramount apparently continued to dominate the board's thinking. The increase in price did not overcome the factors earlier relied upon. . . .

III.

On June 16, the board of directors of Time, upon what would appear competent advice, resolved that it would commit the corporation to the revised Warner transaction [and forgo the $175 per share offered by Paramount with the understanding] that immediately following the effectuation of a Warner merger, the stock market price of Time stock was likely to be materially lower than the $175 then "on the table," perhaps $150, but more likely, within the wide range of $106-$188.

 . . . This is the heart of the matter: the board chose less current value in the hope (assuming that good faith existed, and the record contains no evidence to support a supposition that it does not) the greater value would make that implicit sacrifice beneficial in the future. . . .

The question raised by the decision of June 16 is this: who, under the evolving law of fiduciary obligations is, or should be, the agency for making such a choice in circumstances of the sort presented here—the board or the shareholders? . . . Where legally (an easy question) and equitably (more subtle problem) [should] the locus of decision-making power . . . reside in circumstances of this kind[?] The argument of plaintiffs is that the directors' duty of loyalty to shareholders requires them at such a time to afford to the shareholders the power and opportunity to designate whether the company should now be sold. . . .

The . . . more difficult doctrinal setting for the question of whose choice is it, is presented by Unocal Corp. v. Mesa Petroleum Co. and a string of Chancery opinions construing its test to require, in certain circumstances, the taking of action—typically the redemption of a so-called poison pill—to permit shareholders to choose between two functionally equivalent alternative transactions. Grand Metropolitan PLC v. The Pillsbury Company, Del. Ch., C.A. No. 10319 (December 16, 1988); City Capital Associates Limited v. Interco, Inc., Del. Ch., 551 A.2d 787 (1988); Robert M. Bass Group, Inc. v. Edward P. Evans, Del. Ch., 552 A.2d 1227 (1988); AC Acquisition Corp. v. Anderson, Clayton & Co., Del. Ch. 519 A.2d 103 (1986). . . .

The Claim that the Warner Tender Offer is a Disproportionate
Response to a Noncoercive Paramount Offer that Threatens
No Cognizable Injury to Time of Its Shareholders

1. *Does* Unocal *apply?* Powerful circumstances in this case include the fact that
the original Time-Warner merger agreement was, or appears at this stage to have
been, chiefly motivated by strategic business concerns; that it was an arm's-length
transaction; and, that while its likely effect on reducing vulnerability to unsolicited
takeovers may not have been an altogether collateral fact, such effect does not
appear to be predominating.[20] Time urges that judicial review of the propriety
of the Warner tender offer should involve the same business judgment form of
review as would have been utilized in a challenge to the authorization of the
original merger agreement. . . . [A] rather lengthy list of cases from this court
has construed *Unocal* to mean that its form of review applies, at the least, to all
actions taken after a hostile takeover attempt has emerged that are found to be
defensive in character. See e.g., AC Acquisition Corp. v. Anderson, Clayton & Co.,
Del. Ch., 519 A.2d 103, ALLEN, C. (1986); Robert M. Bass Group, Inc. v. Edward P.
Evans, Del. Ch., 552 A.2d 1227 (1988); The Henley Group, Inc. v. Santa Fe Southern
Pacific Corp., Del. Ch., JACOBS, V.C. (March 11, 1988); Doskocil Companies Inc. v.
Griggs, BERGER, V.C. (August 19, 1988). Thus, while the preexistence of a potential
transaction may have pertinence in evaluating whether implementing it or a modified version of it after the board is under attack is a reasonable step in the circumstances, that fact has not been thought in this court to authorize dispensing with
the *Unocal* form of analysis. The risks that *Unocal* was shaped to protect against are
equally present in such instances.

Factually it is plain . . . that the reformatting of the stock for stock merger into a
leveraged purchase transaction was in reaction to the emergence of the Paramount
offer and its likely effect on the proposed Warner transaction.

2. *Does the Paramount all cash, all shares offer represent a threat to an interest the board
has an obligation or a right to protect by defensive action?* Unocal *involved a partial offer
for cash; consideration in the second-step merger was to be highly subordinated
securities. Equally significant, the facts there justified "a reasonable inference"
that the "principal objective [of the offeror was] to be bought off." Thus, the
case presented dramatically and plainly a threat to both the shareholders and
the corporation.

In two cases decided during the last year, this court has held under similar
circumstances that an all cash, all shares offer falling within a range of value
that a shareholder might reasonably prefer, to be followed by a prompt second-
step merger for cash, could not, so long as it involved no deception, be construed as
a sufficient threat to shareholder interests to justify as reasonable board action that
would permanently foreclose shareholder choice to accept that offer. See Grand
Metropolitan PLC v. The Pillsbury Company, Del. Ch., C.A. No. 10319, DUFFY, J.
(December 16, 1988); City Capital Associates v. Interco Incorporated, Del. Ch., 551
A.2d 787 (1988). Cf. Shamrock Holdings, Inc. v. Polaroid Corp., Del. Ch., BERGER,

---

20. This fact distinguishes in a material way the case of AC Acquisition Corp. v. Anderson, Clayton
& Co., Del. Ch., 519 A.2d 103 (1986), which originated from a threat to the existing control arrangement.
Other material distinctions are that the two transactions there involved were competing versions of a
"bust up" plan for the corporation as it had existed and the board could not determine that either was
inadequate.

V.C. (March 17, 1989). Those cases held that in the circumstances presented, "whatever danger there is relates to shareholders and that concerns price only," *Pillsbury,* supra, or that "in the special case of a tender offer for all shares, the threat posed, if any, is not importantly to corporate policies . . . but rather . . . is most directly to shareholder interests." *Interco,* 551 A.2d at 796.

Plaintiffs argue from these cases that since the Paramount offer is also for all shares for cash, with a promised second-step merger offering the same consideration, the only interests the board may legitimately seek to protect are the interests of shareholders in having the option to accept the best available price in a sale of their stock. Plaintiffs admit that this interest would justify defensive action at this stage. The board may leave its stock rights plan in place to provide it time to conduct an auction or to arrange any other alternative that might be thought preferable to the shareholders. But, they say, this stockholder interest cannot justify defensive action (the revised merger) that is totally unrelated to a threat to shareholders.

In my opinion, the authorities relied upon do not establish that Time has no legally cognizable interest that the Paramount offer endangers. In each of those cases, the board sought to assure continued control by compelling a transaction that itself . . . was the functional equivalent of the very leveraged "bust up" transaction that management was claiming presented a threat to the corporation.

Here, in sharp contrast, the revised transaction, even though "reactive" in important respects, has its origin and central purpose in bona fide strategic business planning, and not in questions of corporate control. Compare *AC Acquisition Corp.,* supra (recapitalization had its genesis in a threat to corporate control posed by the imminent termination of trusts that had exercised effective control for years); Robert M. Bass Group v. Evans, supra (recapitalization under consideration prior to acquisition proposal would have shifted control to management group of a substantial portion of corporation's assets). To be sure, Time's management and its board had, at all times, one eye on the takeover market, considered that market in all they did, and took steps to afford themselves the conventional defenses. But I do not regard that fact as darkly as do plaintiffs. It is inevitable today for businessmen to be mindful of this factor. At this stage, I do not regard the record as establishing, as was done in *AC Acquisitions, Bass, Interco* or *Pillsbury,* that there is a reasonable likelihood that such concern provided the primary motivation for the corporate transaction. Nor is this transaction an alternative to the sale Paramount proposes (i.e., the functional equivalent) in the way the enjoined transactions in the cited cases can be said to be equivalents of sales. . . .

. . . I conclude that the achievement of the long-term strategic plan of the Time-Warner consolidation is plainly a most important corporate policy; while the transaction effectuating that policy is reactive in important respects (and thus must withstand a *Unocal* analysis), the policy itself has, in a most concrete way, its origin in non-defensive, bona fide business considerations. . . .

In my opinion, where the board has not elected explicitly or implicitly to assume the special burdens recognized by *Revlon,* but continued to manage the corporation for long-term profit pursuant to a preexisting business plan that itself is not primarily a control device or scheme, the corporation has a legally cognizable interest in achieving that plan. Whether steps taken to protect transactions contemplated by such plan are reasonable in all of the circumstances is another matter, to which I now turn.

3. *Is the Warner tender offer a reasonable step in the circumstances?* This step requires an evaluation of the importance of the corporate objective threatened; alternative methods for protecting that objective; impacts of the "defensive" action and other relevant factors. In this effort it is prudent to keep in mind that the innovative and constructive rule of *Unocal* must be cautiously applied lest the important benefits of the business judgment rule (including designation of authority to make business and financial decisions to agencies, i.e., boards of directors, with substantive expertise) be eroded or lost by slow degrees. See *Interco,* 551 A.2d at 796.

In this instance, the objective — the realization of the company's major strategic plan — is reasonably seen as of unquestionably great importance by the board. Moreover, the reactive step taken was effective but not overly broad. The board did only what was necessary to carry forward a preexisting transaction in an altered form. That "defensive" step does not legally preclude the successful prosecution of a hostile tender offer. And while effectuation of the Warner merger may practically impact the likelihood of a successful takeover of the merged company, it is not established in this record that that is foreclosed as a practical matter. Recent experience suggests it may be otherwise. In re RJR Nabisco, Inc. Shareholders Litigation, Del. Ch. (January 31, 1989).

I therefore conclude that the revised merger agreement and the Warner tender offer do represent actions that are reasonable in relation to the specific threat posed to the Warner merger by the Paramount offer. . . .

Reasonable persons can and do disagree as to whether it is the better course from the shareholders' point of view collectively to cash out their stake in the company now at this (or a higher) premium cash price. However, there is no persuasive evidence that the board of Time has a corrupt or venal motivation in electing to continue with its long-term plan even in the face of the cost that that course will no doubt entail for the company's shareholders in the short run. In doing so, it is exercising perfectly conventional powers to cause the corporation to buy assets for use in its business. Because of the timing involved, the board has no need here to rely upon a self-created power designed to assure a veto on all changes in control.[22]

The value of a shareholder's investment, over time, rises or falls chiefly because of the skill, judgment and perhaps luck — for it is present in all human affairs — of the management and directors of the enterprise. When they exercise sound or brilliant judgment, shareholders are likely to profit; when they fail to do so, share values likely will fail to appreciate. In either event, the financial vitality of the corporation and the value of the company's shares [are] in the hands of the directors and managers of the firm. The corporation law does not operate on the theory that directors, in exercising their powers to manage the firm, are obligated to follow the wishes of a majority of shares. In fact, directors, not shareholders, are charged with the duty to manage the firm.

In the decision they have reached here, the Time board may be proven in time to have been brilliantly prescient or dismayingly wrong. In this decision, as in other decisions affecting the financial value of their investment, the shareholders will bear the effects for good or ill. That many, presumably most, shareholders would prefer the board to do otherwise than it has done does not, in the circumstances of a

---

22. Thus, in my view, a decision not to redeem a poison pill, which by definition is a control mechanism and not a device with independent business purposes, may present distinctive considerations [from] those presented in this case.

challenge to this type of transaction, in my opinion, afford a basis to interfere with the effectuation of the board's business judgment.

---

1. *Status of the "just say no" defense.* After *Interco*, a "just say no" defense required two doctrinal extensions: (1) a threat to the company that did not threaten shareholders, and (2) a response that blocks shareholders' access to a favorable offer but is nonetheless reasonable in relation to the threat.

The existence of a threat to the company but not to shareholders is the more difficult of the two, especially since any negative effect on the entity presumably should negatively affect the shareholders. Chancellor Allen's opinion in *Time* finds the necessary threat in the effect of Paramount's offer on Time's long-term strategic plan: "[Time] has a legally cognizable interest in achieving the plan." Note that no reference is made to the effect on Time shareholders. Of course a threat to Time's long-term strategic plan should translate to a threat to shareholders if Time's strategic plan is in fact in shareholders' best interests. In *Interco*, Chancellor Allen held that shareholders should decide whether the company proposal or the hostile bid was more favorable; the threat that shareholders would make a mistake was insufficient to warrant the preclusive tactic of declining to redeem the poison pill. Why can't shareholders similarly decide whether Time's long-term strategic plan or Paramount's short-term cash was more favorable to them? Was the threat somehow to the company but not the shareholders? What if the shareholders are less competent at assessing the strategic plan? Are shareholders a threat to themselves? What if most shares are held by sophisticated institutional investors?

After the Chancellor's opinion in *Time*, could business consultants create long-term business plans to meet *Unocal*'s requirement of a threat just as a lawyer could build a record to meet the *Cheff* primary-purpose test?

Or is a narrower reading of the Chancellor's opinion possible? As *Anderson, Clayton* demonstrated, the court will seriously inquire into whether the defensive response is proportionate to the threat. Chancellor Allen stresses that Time's response to Paramount's offer was limited to carrying out its long-term plan, which was not itself preclusive: "The board did only what was necessary to carry forward a preexisting transaction in an altered form. That 'defensive' step does not legally preclude the successful prosecution of a hostile tender offer." In particular, footnote 22 of the court's opinion notes that a decision to protect a long-term plan not by carrying it out but by declining to redeem a poison pill presented different considerations.

From this narrower perspective, is Time's defensive success a sport on its facts? Suppose Paramount could have waived the conditions in its offer and completed its hostile tender offer before the Time tender offer for Warner. Would Time have been allowed to protect its long-term plan to acquire Warner by declining to redeem its poison pill? Alternatively, suppose Paramount made an offer for the combined Time-Warner company with the intent to sell off the Warner portion to reduce acquisition debt. Could the combined company rely on its poison pill to block the offer? If a target can protect its long-term business plan only when its implementation alone would practically preclude a hostile offer, how different are the Chancellor's opinions in *Time* and in *Interco*?

The appeal in *Time* presented the Delaware Supreme Court with an important opportunity. Five years had passed since its decision in *Unocal*, during which the Chancery Court had crafted a body of law that gave substance to *Unocal*'s two-step proportionality test. The Chancellor's opinion at last focused the question: When can a target company "just say no"?

Paramount Communications, Inc. v. Time Incorporated
571 A.2d 1140 (Del. 1990)

HORSEY, J.: ... Paramount asserts only a *Unocal* claim in which the shareholders join. ... We begin by noting, as did the Chancellor, that our decision does not require us to pass on the wisdom of the board's decision to enter into the original Time-Warner agreement. That is not a court's task. Our task is simply to review the record to determine whether there is sufficient evidence to support the Chancellor's conclusion that the initial Time-Warner agreement was the product of a proper exercise of business judgment.

We have purposely detailed the evidence of the Time board's deliberative approach, beginning in 1983-84, to expand itself. Time's decision in 1988 to combine with Warner was made only after what could be fairly characterized as an exhaustive appraisal of Time's future as a corporation. ... We find ample evidence in the record to support the Chancellor's conclusion that the Time board's decision to expand the business of the company through its March 3 merger with Warner was entitled to the protection of the business judgment rule.

The Chancellor reached a different conclusion in addressing the Time-Warner transaction as revised three months later. He ... ruled that *Unocal* applied to all director actions taken, following receipt of Paramount's hostile tender offer, that were reasonably determined to be defensive. Clearly that was a correct ruling. ...

Unocal involved a two-tier, highly coercive tender offer. In such a case, the threat is obvious: shareholders may be compelled to tender to avoid being treated adversely in the second stage of the transaction. In subsequent cases, the Court of Chancery has suggested that an all-cash, all-shares offer, falling within a range of values that a shareholder might reasonably prefer, cannot constitute a legally recognized "threat" to shareholder interests sufficient to withstand a *Unocal* analysis. AC Acquisitions Corp. v. Anderson, Clayton & Co., Del. Ch., 519 A.2d 103 (1986); see Grand Metropolitan, PLC v. Pillsbury Co., Del. Ch., C.A. No. 10319, Duffy, J. (Dec. 16, 1988); City Capital Associates v. Interco, Inc., Del Ch., 551 A.2d 787 (1988). In those cases, the Court of Chancery determined that whatever danger existed related only to the shareholders and only to price and not to the corporation.

From those decisions by our Court of Chancery, Paramount and the individual plaintiffs extrapolate a rule of law that an all-cash, all-shares offer with values reasonably in the range of acceptable price cannot pose any objective threat to a corporation or its shareholders. Thus, Paramount would have us hold that only if the value of Paramount's offer were determined to be clearly inferior to the value created by management's plan to merge with Warner could the offer be viewed — objectively — as a threat.

Implicit in the plaintiffs' argument is the view that a hostile tender offer can pose only two types of threats: the threat of coercion that results from a two-tier offer promising unequal treatment for nontendering shareholders; and the threat of inadequate value from an all-shares, all-cash offer at a price below what a target board in good faith deems to be the present value of its shares. See, e.g., *Interco.* Since Paramount's offer was all-cash, the only conceivable "threat," plaintiffs argue, was inadequate value. We disapprove of such a narrow and rigid construction of *Unocal.* . . .

Plaintiffs' position represents a fundamental misconception of . . . *Unocal* principally because it would involve the court in substituting its judgment for what is a "better" deal for that of a corporation's board of directors. To the extent that the Court of Chancery has recently done so in certain of its opinions, we hereby reject such approach as not in keeping with a proper *Unocal* analysis. See, e.g., *Interco* and its progeny; but see TW Services, Inc. v. SWT Acquisition Corp., Del. Ch. (1989).

The usefulness of *Unocal* as an analytical tool is precisely its flexibility. . . . *Unocal* is not intended as an abstract standard; neither is it a structured and mechanistic procedure of appraisal. Thus, we have said that directors may consider, when evaluating the threat posed by a takeover bid, the "inadequacy of the price offered, nature and timing of the offer, questions of illegality, the impact on contingencies other than shareholders, the risk of nonconsummation and the quality of securities being offered in the exchange." 493 A.2d at 955. The open-ended analysis mandated by *Unocal* is not intended to lead to a simple mathematical exercise; that is, of comparing the discounted value of Time-Warner's expected trading price at some future date with Paramount's offer and determining which is the higher. Indeed, in our view, precepts underlying the business judgment rule mitigate against a court's engaging in the process of attempting to appraise and evaluate the relative merits of a long-term versus a short-term investment for shareholders. To engage in such an exercise is a distortion of the *Unocal* process and, in particular, the application of the second part of *Unocal*'s test. . . .

In this case, the Time board reasonably determined that inadequate value was not the only legally cognizable threat that Paramount's all-cash, all-shares offer could present. . . . One concern was that Time shareholders might elect to tender into Paramount's cash offer in ignorance or a mistaken belief of the strategic benefit which a business combination with Warner might produce. Moreover, Time viewed the conditions attached to Paramount's offer as introducing a degree of uncertainty that skewed a comparative analysis. Further, the timing of Paramount's offer to follow issuance of Time's proxy notice was viewed as arguably designed to upset, if not confuse, the Time stockholders' vote. Given this record evidence, we cannot conclude that the Time board's decision of June 6 that Paramount's offer posed a threat to corporate policy and effectiveness was lacking in good faith or dominated by motives of either entrenchment or self-interest. . . .

We turn to the second part of the *Unocal* analysis. The obvious requisite to determining the reasonableness of a defensive action is a clear identification of the nature of the threat. As the Chancellor correctly noted, this "requires an evaluation of the importance of the corporate objective threatened; alternative methods of protecting that objective; impacts of the 'defensive' action, and other relevant factors." It is not until both parts of the *Unocal* inquiry have been satisfied that the business judgment rule attaches to defensive actions of a board of directors.[18] . . .

18. Some commentators have criticized *Unocal* by arguing that once the board's deliberative process has been analyzed and found not to be wanting in objectivity, good faith or deliberateness, the so-called "enhanced" business judgment rule has been satisfied and no further inquiry is undertaken. See

Paramount argues that, assuming its tender offer posed a threat, Time's response was unreasonable in precluding Time's shareholders from accepting the tender offer or receiving a control premium in the immediately foreseeable future. Once again, the contention stems, we believe, from a fundamental misunderstanding of where the power of corporate governance lies. Delaware law confers the management of the corporate enterprise to the stockholders' duly elected board representatives. 8 Del. C. Sec. 141(a). The fiduciary duty to manage a [corporation] includes the selection of a time frame for achievement of corporate goals. That duty may not be delegated to the stockholders. Directors are not obliged to abandon a deliberately conceived corporate plan for a short-term shareholder profit unless there is clearly no basis to sustain the corporate strategy.

Although the Chancellor blurred somewhat the discrete analyses required under *Unocal*, he did conclude that Time's board reasonably perceived Paramount's offer to be a significant threat to the planned Time-Warner merger and that Time's response was not "overly broad." We have found that even in light of a valid threat, management actions that are coercive in nature or force upon shareholders a management-sponsored alternative to a hostile offer may be struck down as unreasonable and nonproportionate responses.

Here, on the record facts, the Chancellor found that Time's responsive action to Paramount's tender offer was not aimed at "cramming down" on its shareholders a management-sponsored alternative, but rather had as its goal the carrying forward of a pre-existing transaction in an altered form. Thus, the response was reasonably related to the threat. The Chancellor noted that the revised agreement and its accompanying safety devices did not preclude Paramount from making an offer for the combined Time-Warner company or from changing the conditions of its offer so as not to make the offer dependent upon the nullification of the Time-Warner agreement. Thus, the response was proportionate. . . .

---

1. *Role of the shareholder.* Early in its opinion, the Delaware Supreme Court construed *Interco* as "involv[ing] the court in substituting its judgment for what would be a 'better' deal for that of a corporation's board of directors" and then pronounced that "approach as not in keeping with a proper *Unocal* analysis." But recall *Interco*'s comment that allowing the board through a poison pill to "deprive shareholders of the ability effectively to choose and accept a noncoercive offer . . . would . . . diminish the legitimacy and authority of our corporate law." Is the Supreme Court's characterization of *Interco* accurate?

2. *Threat analysis.* The court disposed of the first step of the *Unocal* test by announcing that it "cannot conclude that the Time board's decision . . . that Paramount's offer posed a threat . . . was lacking in good faith or dominated by motives of either entrenchment or self-interest." Is this inquiry different from the business judgment standard?

3. *Proportionality analysis and the "just say no" defense.* Did the Delaware Supreme Court resolve the ambiguity in the Chancery Court's proportionality analysis? Did the outcome turn on the fact that Time's defensive action, unlike a refusal to

---

generally, Johnson & Siegel, Corporate Mergers: Redefining the Role of Target Directors, 136 U. Pa. L. Rev. 315 (1987). We reject such views.

redeem a poison pill, was not technically preclusive? As the Supreme Court put it, "The revised agreement . . . did not preclude Paramount from making an offer for the combined Time-Warner company. . . ." Can a tactic that *is* preclusive be proportionate to a non-coercive offer? Can a target "just say no" after *Time?* One thoughtful commentator believes the *Time* court answered the question affirmatively: "The net effect appears to be the collapse of the Delaware Supreme Court's five-year-old effort to erect and sustain an intermediate standard of review for takeover defense tactics. We may be back to the earlier era of simple business judgment review of defensive measures. The restraint is no restraint at all to a well-advised board. . . . Indeed, because of the [pill], a board may now be in a position to refuse an unwanted bid." Jeffrey Gordon, Corporations, Markets, and Courts, 91 Colum. L. Rev. 1931, 1944-1945 (1991).

4. *Where does proportionality review now stand?* In Unitrin, Inc. v. American General Corp. the Delaware Supreme Court had its first post-*Time-Warner* occasion to consider proportionality review and, 10 years after *Unocal,* to confront Professor Gordon's assertion that the board of a target corporation could implement defensive tactics allowing it to effectively block a hostile acquisition.

Unitrin, Inc. v. American General Corp.
651 A.2d 1361 (Del. 1995)

HOLLAND, J.: . . . American General, which had publicly announced a proposal to merge with Unitrin for $2.6 billion at $50³/₈ per share, and certain Unitrin shareholder plaintiffs, filed suit in the Court of Chancery, *inter alia,* to enjoin Unitrin from repurchasing up to 10 million shares of its own stock (the "Repurchase Program"). . . . [T]he Court of Chancery preliminarily enjoined Unitrin from making further repurchases on the ground that the Repurchase Program was a disproportionate response to the threat posed by American General's inadequate all cash for all shares offer, under the standard of this Court's holding in *Unocal.* . . .

Unitrin's Contentions

Unitrin . . . contends that the Court of Chancery erred in holding that the adoption of the Repurchase Program would materially affect the ability of an insurgent stockholder to win a proxy contest. According to Unitrin, that holding is unsupported by the evidence, is based upon a faulty mathematical analysis, and disregards the holding of *Moran v. Household Int'l,* 500 A.2d 1346, 1355 (Del. 1985). Furthermore, Unitrin argues that the Court of Chancery erroneously substituted its own judgment for that of Unitrin's Board, contrary to this Court's subsequent interpretations of *Unocal* in *Paramount Communications v. QVC Network, Inc.,* 637 A.2d 34, 45-46 (Del. 1994), and *Paramount Communications v. Time, Inc.,* 571 A.2d 1140 (Del. 1990). . . .

The Parties

American General is the largest provider of home service insurance. . . . Unitrin is also in the business. . . . The other defendants-appellants are the members of Unitrin's seven person Board of Directors (the "Unitrin Board" or "Board"). Two directors are employees, Richard C. Vie, the Chief Executive Officer, and

Jerrold V. Jerome, Chairman of the Board. The five remaining directors are not and have never been employed by Unitrin. . . .

The record reflects that the non-employee directors each receive a fixed annual fee of $30,000. They receive no other significant financial benefit from serving as directors. At the offering price proposed by American General, the value of Unitrin's non-employee directors' stock exceeded $450 million. . . .

On July 12, 1994, American General sent a letter to Vie proposing a consensual merger transaction in which it would "purchase all of Unitrin's 51.8 million outstanding shares of common stock for $50³/₈ per share, in cash" (the "Offer"). The Offer was conditioned on the development of a merger agreement and regulatory approval. The Offer price represented a 30% premium over the market price of Unitrin's shares. In the Offer, American General stated that it "would consider offering a higher price" if "Unitrin could demonstrate additional value." American General also offered to consider tax-free "[a]lternatives to an all cash transaction." . . .

Upon receiving the American General Offer, the Unitrin Board's Executive Committee (Singleton, Vie, and Jerome) engaged legal counsel and scheduled a telephonic Board meeting for July 18. At the July 18 special meeting, the Board reviewed the terms of the Offer. The Board was advised that the existing charter and bylaw provisions might not effectively deter all types of takeover strategies. It was suggested that the Board consider adopting a shareholder rights plan and an advance notice provision for shareholder proposals.

The Unitrin Board met next on July 25, 1994 in Los Angeles for seven hours. All directors attended the meeting. The principal purpose of the meeting was to discuss American General's Offer.

Vie reviewed Unitrin's financial condition and its ongoing business strategies. The Board also received a presentation from its investment advisor, Morgan Stanley & Co. ("Morgan Stanley"), regarding the financial adequacy of American General's proposal. Morgan Stanley expressed its opinion that the Offer was financially inadequate. Legal counsel expressed concern that the combination of Unitrin and American General would raise antitrust complications due to the resultant decrease in competition in the home service insurance markets.

The Unitrin Board unanimously concluded that the American General merger proposal was not in the best interests of Unitrin's shareholders and voted to reject the Offer. The Board then received advice from its legal and financial advisors about a number of possible defensive measures it might adopt, including a shareholder rights plan ("poison pill") and an advance notice bylaw provision for shareholder proposals. Because the Board apparently thought that American General intended to keep its Offer private, the Board did not implement any defensive measures at that time. . . .

On August 2, 1994, American General issued a press release announcing its Offer to Unitrin's Board to purchase all of Unitrin's stock for $50³/₈ per share. The press release also noted that the Board had rejected American General's Offer. After that public announcement, the trading volume and market price of Unitrin's stock increased.

At its regularly scheduled meeting on August 3, the Unitrin Board discussed the effects of American General's press release. The Board noted that the market reaction to the announcement suggested that speculative traders or arbitrageurs were acquiring Unitrin stock. The Board determined that American General's public announcement constituted a hostile act designed to coerce the sale of

Unitrin at an inadequate price. The Board unanimously approved the poison pill and the proposed advance notice bylaw that it had considered previously. . . .

The Unitrin Board met again on August 11, 1994 . . . to consider the Repurchase Program. At the Board's request, Morgan Stanley had prepared written materials to distribute to each of the directors. Morgan Stanley gave a presentation in which alternative means of implementing the Repurchase Program were explained. Morgan Stanley recommended that the Board implement an open market stock repurchase. The Board voted to authorize the Repurchase Program for up to ten million shares of its outstanding stock.

On August 12, Unitrin publicly announced the Repurchase Program. The Unitrin Board expressed its belief that "Unitrin's stock is undervalued in the market and that the expanded program will tend to increase the value of the shares that remain outstanding." The announcement also stated that the director stockholders were not participating in the Repurchase Program, and that the repurchases "will increase the percentage ownership of those stockholders who choose not to sell."

Unitrin's August 12 press release also stated that the directors owned 23% of Unitrin's stock, that the Repurchase Program would cause that percentage to increase, and that Unitrin's certificate of incorporation included a supermajority voting provision. . . .

Unitrin sent a letter to its stockholders on August 17 regarding the Repurchase Program which stated: "Your Board of Directors has authorized the Company to repurchase, in the open market or in private transactions, up to 10 million of Unitrin's 51.8 million outstanding common shares. This authorization is intended to provide an additional measure of liquidity to the Company's shareholders in light of the unsettled market conditions resulting from American General's unsolicited acquisition proposal. The Board believes that the Company's stock is undervalued and that this program will tend to increase the value of the shares that remain outstanding."

Between August 12 and noon on August 24, Morgan Stanley purchased nearly 5 million of Unitrin's shares on Unitrin's behalf. The average price paid was slightly above American General's Offer price. . . .

In this case, before the Court of Chancery could evaluate the reasonable probability of the plaintiffs' success on the merits, it had to determine the nature of the proceeding. When shareholders challenge directors' actions, usually one of three levels of judicial review is applied: the traditional business judgment rule, the *Unocal* standard of enhanced judicial scrutiny, or the entire fairness standard. "Because the effect of the proper invocation of the business judgment rule is so powerful and the standard of entire fairness so exacting, the determination of the appropriate standard of judicial review frequently is determinative of the outcome of [the] litigation." Mills Acquisition Co. v. Macmillan, Inc., 559 A.2d at 1279.

. . . The record supports the Court of Chancery's determination that the Board perceived American General's Offer as a threat and adopted the Repurchase Program, along with the poison pill and advance notice bylaw, as defensive measures in response to that threat. Therefore, the Court of Chancery properly concluded the facts before it required an application of *Unocal* and its progeny. . . .

This Court has recognized that directors are often confronted with an " 'inherent conflict of interest' during contests for corporate control '[b]ecause of the omnipresent specter that a board may be acting primarily in its own interests, rather than those of the corporation and its shareholders.' " *Id.* (quoting *Unocal*, 493 A. 2d at 954). Consequently, in such situations, before the board is accorded the protection of the business judgment rule, and that rule's concomitant placement of the burden to rebut its presumption on the plaintiff, the board must carry its own initial two-part burden:

"First, a *reasonableness test*, which is satisfied by a demonstration that the board of directors had reasonable grounds for believing that a danger to corporate policy and effectiveness existed, and

Second, a *proportionality test*, which is satisfied by a demonstration that the board of directors' defensive response was reasonable in relation to the threat posed." *Unocal*, 493 A.2d at 955. . . .

The enhanced judicial scrutiny mandated by *Unocal* is not intended to lead to a structured, mechanistic, mathematical exercise. Paramount Communications v. Time, Inc., 571 A.2d 1140, 1153 (Del. 1990). Conversely, it is not intended to be an abstract theory. *Id.* The *Unocal* standard is a flexible paradigm that jurists can apply to the myriad of "fact scenarios" that confront corporate boards. *Id.*

. . . The ultimate question in applying the *Unocal* standard is: what deference should the reviewing court give "to the decisions of directors in defending against a takeover"? E. Norman Veasey, The New Incarnation of the Business Judgment Rule in Takeover Defenses, 11 Del. J. Corp. L. 503, 504-05 (1986). The question is usually presented to the Court of Chancery, as in the present case, in an injunction proceeding, a posture which is known as "transactional justification." *Id.* To answer the question, the enhanced judicial scrutiny *Unocal* requires implicates both the substantive and procedural nature of the business judgment rule.[14]

. . . [I]n transactional justification cases involving the adoption of defenses to takeovers, the director's actions invariably implicate issues affecting stockholders' rights. *See* Revlon, Inc. v. MacAndrews & Forbes Holdings, 506 A.2d 173, 180 n.10 (Del. 1986). In transactional justification cases, the directors' decision is reviewed judicially and the burden of going forward is placed on the directors. If the directors' actions withstand *Unocal*'s reasonableness and proportionality review, the traditional business judgment rule is applied to shield the directors' defensive decision rather than the directors themselves. *Id.* . . .

The first aspect of the *Unocal* burden, the reasonableness test, required the Unitrin Board to demonstrate that, after a reasonable investigation, it determined in good faith, that American General's Offer presented a threat to Unitrin that warranted a defensive response. This Court has held that the presence of a majority of outside independent directors will materially enhance such evidence. *Unocal*, 493 A.2d at 955. . . .

The Unitrin Board identified two dangers it perceived the American General Offer posed: inadequate price and antitrust complications. The Court of Chancery characterized the Board's concern that American General's proposed transaction could never be consummated because it may violate antitrust laws and state insurance regulations as a "makeweight excuse" for the defensive measure. It determined, however, that the Board reasonably believed that the American General Offer was inadequate and also reasonably concluded that the Offer was a threat to Unitrin's uninformed stockholders.

---

14. One federal court has described the judicial role in assessing defensive measures in the hostile tender offer context pursuant to *Unocal* as "an intricate composite of deference to the business expertise of the directors and close scrutiny of incumbent management decisions." *BNS, Inc. v. Koppers Co.*, 683 F. Supp. 458, 473 (D. Del. 1998).

The Court of Chancery held that the Board's evidence satisfied the first aspect or reasonableness test under *Unocal*. The Court of Chancery then noted, however, that the threat to the Unitrin stockholders from American General's inadequate opening bid was "mild," because the Offer was negotiable both in price and structure. The court then properly turned its attention to *Unocal*'s second aspect, the proportionality test[, which requires that] the Unitrin Board demonstrate the proportionality of its response to the threat American General's Offer posed. The record reflects that the Unitrin Board considered three options as defensive measures: the poison pill, the advance notice bylaw, and the Repurchase Program. . . .

With regard to the . . . proportionality test . . . the Court of Chancery analyzed each stage of the Unitrin Board's defensive responses separately. Although the Court of Chancery characterized Unitrin's antitrust concerns as "makeweight," it acknowledged that the directors of a Delaware corporation have the prerogative to determine that the market undervalues its stock and to protect its stockholders from offers that do not reflect the long term value of the corporation under its present management plan. Paramount Communications v. Time, Inc., 571 A.2d at 1153. The Court of Chancery concluded that Unitrin's Board believed in good faith that the American General Offer was inadequate and properly employed a poison pill as a proportionate defensive response to protect its stockholders from a "low ball" bid. . . .

. . . The Court of Chancery then made two factual findings: First, the Repurchase Program went beyond what was "necessary" to protect the Unitrin stockholders from a "low ball" negotiating strategy; and second, it was designed to keep the decision to combine with American General within the control of the members of the Unitrin Board, as stockholders, under virtually all circumstances. Consequently, the Court of Chancery held that the Unitrin Board failed to demonstrate that the Repurchase Program met the second aspect or proportionality requirement of the initial burden *Unocal* ascribes to a board of directors.

. . . The Court of Chancery concluded that, although the Unitrin Board had properly perceived American General's inadequate Offer as a threat and had properly responded to that threat by adopting a "poison pill," the additional defensive response of adopting the Repurchase Program was unnecessary and disproportionate to the threat the Offer posed. . . . Therefore, the Court of Chancery held that the plaintiffs proved a likelihood of success on that issue and granted the motion to preliminary enjoin the Repurchase Program.[18] . . .

Before the Repurchase Program began, Unitrin's directors collectively held approximately 23% of Unitrin's outstanding shares. Unitrin's certificate of incorporation already included a "shark-repellent" provision barring any business combination with a more-than-15% stockholder unless approved by a majority of continuing directors or by a 75% stockholder vote ("Supermajority Vote"). Unitrin's shareholder directors announced publicly that they would not participate in the Repurchase Program and that this would result in a percentage increase of ownership for them, as well as for any other shareholder who did not participate.

The Court of Chancery found that by not participating in the Repurchase Program, the Board "expected to create a 28% voting block to support the Board's

---

18. We note that the directors' failure to carry their initial burden under *Unocal* does not, *ipso facto*, invalidate the board's actions. Instead, once the Court of Chancery finds the business judgment rule does not apply, the burden remains on the directors to prove "entire fairness." *See* Cede & Co. v. Technicolor, Inc., 634 A.2d 345, 361 (Del. 1993).

decision to reject [a future] offer by American General." From this underlying factual finding, the Court of Chancery concluded that American General might be "chilled" in its pursuit of Unitrin: "Increasing the board members' percentage of stock ownership, combined with the supermajority merger provision, does more than protect uninformed stockholders from an inadequate offer; it chills any unsolicited acquirer from making an offer."

The parties are in substantial disagreement with respect to the Court of Chancery's ultimate factual finding that the Repurchase Program was a disproportionate response under *Unocal*. Unitrin argues that American General or another potential acquiror can theoretically prevail in an effort to obtain control of Unitrin through a proxy contest. American General argues that the record supports the Court of Chancery's factual determination that the adoption of the Repurchase Program violated the principles of *Unocal*, even though American General acknowledges that the option of a proxy contest for obtaining control of Unitrin remained theoretically available. . . .

This Court has been and remains assiduous in its concern about defensive actions designed to thwart the essence of corporate democracy by disenfranchising shareholders. [In Stroud v. Grace, 606 A.2d 75, 91 (Del. 1992)], this Court stated: "we accept the basic legal tenets," set forth in Blasius Indus. v. Atlas Corp., 564 A.2d 651 (Del. Ch.1998), that "[w]here boards of directors deliberately employ[] . . . legal strategies either to frustrate or completely disenfranchise a shareholder vote, . . . [t]here can be no dispute that such conduct violates Delaware law." In *Stroud*, we concluded, however, that a *Blasius* analysis was inappropriate. We reached that conclusion because it could not be said "that the 'primary purpose' of the board's action was to interfere with or impede exercise of the shareholder franchise," and because the shareholders had a "full and fair opportunity to vote." Stroud v. Grace, 606 A.2d at 92.

This Court also specifically noted that boards of directors often interfere with the exercise of shareholder voting when an acquiror *launches both a proxy fight and a tender offer. Id.* at 92 n.3. We then stated that such action "necessarily invoked both *Unocal and Blasius*" because "both [tests] recognize the inherent conflicts of interest that arise when shareholders are not permitted free exercise of their franchise." *Id.* Consequently, we concluded that, "[i]n certain circumstances, [the judiciary] must recognize the special import of protecting the shareholders' franchise within *Unocal's* requirement that any defensive measure be proportionate and 'reasonable in relation to the threat posed.'" *Id.* . . .

. . . The Court of Chancery, in the case *sub judice*, was obviously cognizant that the emergence of the "poison pill" as an effective takeover device has resulted in such a remarkable transformation in the market for corporate control that hostile bidders who proceed when such defenses are in place will usually "have to couple proxy contests with tender offers." Joseph A. Grundfest, Just Vote No: A Minimalist Strategy for Dealing with Barbarians Inside the Gates, 45 Stan. L. Rev. 857, 858 (1993). The Court of Chancery concluded that Unitrin's adoption of a poison pill was a proportionate response to the threat its Board reasonably perceived from American General's Offer. Nonetheless, the Court of Chancery enjoined the additional defense of the Repurchase Program as disproportionate and "unnecessary."

The record reflects that the Court of Chancery's decision to enjoin the Repurchase Program is attributable to a continuing misunderstanding, i.e., that in conjunction with the longstanding Supermajority Vote provision in the Unitrin charter, the

Repurchase Program would operate to provide the director shareholders with a "veto" to preclude a successful proxy contest by American General. The origins of that misunderstanding are three premises that are each without record support. Two of those premises are objective misconceptions and the other is subjective. . . .

The subjective premise was the Court of Chancery's *sua sponte* determination that Unitrin's outside directors, who are also substantial stockholders, would not vote like other stockholders in a proxy contest, *i.e.*, in their own best economic interests. At American General's Offer price, the outside directors held Unitrin shares worth more than $450 million. Consequently, Unitrin argues the stockholder directors had the same interest as other Unitrin stockholders generally, when voting in proxy contest, to wit: the maximization of the value of their investments.

In rejecting Unitrin's argument, the Court of Chancery stated that the stockholder directors would be "subconsciously" motivated in a proxy contest to vote against otherwise excellent offers which did not include a "price parameter" to compensate them for the loss of the "prestige and perquisites" of membership on Unitrin's Board. The Court of Chancery's subjective determination that the *stockholder directors* of Unitrin would reject an "excellent offer," unless it compensated them for giving up the "prestige and perquisites" of directorship, appears to be subjective and without record support. It cannot be presumed. . . .

The first objective premise relied upon by the Court of Chancery, unsupported by the record, is that the shareholder directors needed to implement the Repurchase Program to attain voting power in a proxy contest equal to 25%. The Court of Chancery . . . and all parties agree that proxy contests do not generate 100% shareholder participation. The shareholder plaintiffs argue that 80-85% may be a usual turnout. Therefore, *without* the Repurchase Program, the director shareholders' absolute voting power of 23% would already constitute *actual voting power greater than* 25% in a proxy contest with normal shareholder participation below 100%. . . .

The second objective premise relied upon by the Court of Chancery, unsupported by the record, is that American General's ability to succeed in a proxy contest depended on the Repurchase Program being enjoined because of the Supermajority Vote provision in Unitrin's charter. Without the approval of a target's board, the danger of activating a poison pill renders it irrational for bidders to pursue stock acquisitions above the triggering level. Instead, "bidders intent on working around a poison pill must launch and win proxy contests to elect new directors who are willing to redeem the target's poison pill." Joseph A. Grundfest, Just Vote No: A Minimalist Strategy for Dealing with Barbarians Inside the Gates, 45 Stan. L. Rev. 857, 859 (1993).

As American General acknowledges, . . . it would be illogical for American General or any other bidder to acquire more than 15% of Unitrin's stock because that would not only trigger the poison pill, but also the constraints of 8 Del. C. §203 [Delaware's business combination statute]. If American General were to initiate a proxy contest *before* acquiring 15% of Unitrin's stock, it would need to amass only 45.1% of the votes assuming a 90% voter turnout. . . .

The record reflects that institutional investors own 42% of Unitrin's shares. Twenty institutions own 33% of Unitrin's shares. It is generally accepted that proxy contests have re-emerged with renewed significance as a method of acquiring corporate control because "the growth in institutional investment has reduced the dispersion of share ownership." Lucian Bebchuk & Marcel Kahan, A Framework for Analyzing Legal Policy Towards Proxy Contests, 78 Cal. L. Rev. 1071, 1134 (1990). "Institutions are more likely than other shareholders to vote at all, more likely to vote against manager proposals, and more likely to vote for proposals by other shareholders." Bernard S. Black, The Value of Institutional Investor Monitoring: The Empirical Evidence, 39 UCLA L. Rev. 895, 925 (1992). . . .

The conclusion of the Court of Chancery that the Repurchase Program would make a proxy contest for Unitrin a "theoretical" possibility that American General could not realistically pursue may be erroneous. . . . A proper understanding of the record reflects that American General or any other 14.9% shareholder bidder could apparently win a proxy contest with a 90% turnout.

The key variable in a proxy contest would be the merit of American General's issues, not the size of its stockholdings. Moran v. Household Int'l, Inc., 500 A.2d 1346, 1355 (Del. 1985). If American General presented an attractive price as the cornerstone of a proxy contest, it could prevail, irrespective of whether the shareholder directors' absolute voting power was 23% or 28%. In that regard, the following passage from the Court of Chancery's Opinion is poignant: "Harold Hook, the Chairman of American General, admitted in his deposition that the repurchase program is not a 'show stopper' because the directors that own stock will act in their own best interest if the price is high enough. (Hook Dep. at 86-87). Fayez Sarofim, one of the Unitrin directors that holds a substantial number of shares, testified that 'everything has a price parameter.' "

Consequently, a proxy contest apparently remained a viable alternative for American General to pursue notwithstanding Unitrin's poison pill, Supermajority Vote provision, and a fully implemented Repurchase Program. . . .

The Unitrin Board did not have unlimited discretion to defeat the threat it perceived from the American General Offer by any draconian means available. See *Unocal*, 493 A.2d at 955. Pursuant to the *Unocal* proportionality test, the nature of the threat associated with a particular hostile offer set the parameters for the range of permissible defensive tactics. . . . Commentators have categorized three types of threats: "(i) *opportunity* loss . . . [where] a hostile offer might deprive target shareholders of the opportunity to select a superior alternative offered by target management [or, we would add, offered by another bidder]; (ii) *structural coercion*, . . . the risk that disparate treatment of non-tendering shareholders might distort shareholders' tender decisions; and (iii) *substantive coercion*, . . . the risk that shareholders will mistakenly accept an underpriced offer because they disbelieve management's representations of intrinsic value." *Id.* at 1153 n.17 (*quoting* Ronald Gilson & Reinier Kraakman, Delaware's Intermediate Standard for Defensive Tactics: Is There Substance to Proportionality Review?, 44 Bus. Law. 247, 267 (1989)).

This Court has held that the "inadequate value" of an all cash for all shares offer is a "legally cognizable threat." Paramount Communications v. Time, Inc., 571 A.2d at 1153. . . .

The record reflects that the Unitrin Board perceived the threat from American General's Offer to be a form of substantive coercion. The Board noted that Unitrin's stock price had moved up, on higher than normal trading volume, to a level slightly below the price in American General's Offer. The Board also noted that some Unitrin shareholders had publicly expressed interest in selling at or near the price in the Offer. The Board determined that Unitrin's stock was undervalued by the market at current levels and that the Board considered Unitrin's stock to be a good long-term investment. The Board also discussed the speculative and unsettled market conditions for Unitrin stock caused by American General's public disclosure. The Board concluded that a Repurchase Program would provide additional liquidity to those stockholders who wished to realize short-term gain, and would provide enhanced value to those stockholders who wished to maintain a long-term investment. Accordingly, the Board voted to authorize the Repurchase Program for up to ten million shares of its outstanding stock on the open market. . . .

The record appears to support Unitrin's argument that the Board's justification for adopting the Repurchase Program was its reasonably perceived risk of substantive coercion, *i.e.*, that Unitrin's shareholders might accept American General's inadequate Offer because of "ignorance or mistaken belief" regarding the Board's assessment of the long-term value of Unitrin's stock. . . .

The Court of Chancery applied an incorrect legal standard when it ruled that the Unitrin decision to authorize the Repurchase Program was disproportionate because it was "unnecessary." . . . "[A] court applying enhanced judicial scrutiny should be deciding whether the directors made *a reasonable* decision, not *a perfect* decision. If a board selected one of several reasonable alternatives, a court should not second guess that choice even though it might have decided otherwise or subsequent events may have cast doubt on the board's determination. Thus, courts will not substitute their business judgment for that of the directors, but will determine if the directors' decision was, on balance, within a range of reasonableness. . . ." The Court of Chancery did not determine whether the Unitrin Board's decision to implement the Repurchase program fell within a "range of reasonableness."

The record reflects that the Unitrin Board's adoption of the Repurchase Program was an apparent recognition on its part that all shareholders are not alike. This Court has stated that distinctions among types of shareholders are neither inappropriate nor irrelevant for a board of directors to make, *e.g.*, distinctions between long-term shareholders and short-term profit-takers, such as arbitrageurs, and their stockholding objectives. In *Unocal* itself, we expressly acknowledged that "a board may reasonably consider the basic stockholder interests at stake, including those of short term speculators, whose actions may have fueled to coercive aspect of the offer at the expense of the long term investor." *Unocal*, 493 A.2d at 955-56.

The Court of Chancery's determination that the Unitrin Board's adoption of the Repurchase Program was unnecessary constituted a substitution of its business judgment for that of the Board. . . .

. . . As common law applications of *Unocal*'s proportionality standard have evolved, at least two characteristics of draconian defensive measures taken by a board of directors in responding to a threat have been brought into focus through enhanced judicial scrutiny. In the modern takeover lexicon, it is now clear that since *Unocal*, this Court has consistently recognized that defensive measures which are either preclusive or coercive are included within the common law definition of draconian.

If a defensive measure is not draconian, however, because it is not either coercive or preclusive, the *Unocal* proportionality test requires the focus of enhanced judicial scrutiny to shift to "the range of reasonableness." Paramount

Communications v. QVC Network, Inc., 637 A.2d 34, 45-46 (Del. 1994). Proper and proportionate defensive responses are intended and permitted to thwart perceived threats. When a corporation is not for sale, the board of directors is the defender of the metaphorical medieval corporate bastion and the protector of the corporation's shareholders. The fact that a defensive action must not be coercive or preclusive does not prevent a board from responding defensively before a bidder is at the corporate bastion's gate.[38] . . .

In this case, the initial focus of enhanced judicial scrutiny for proportionality requires a determination regarding the defensive responses by the Unitrin board to American General's offer. We begin, therefore, by ascertaining whether the Repurchase Program, as an addition to the poison pill, was draconian by being either coercive or preclusive.

A limited nondiscriminatory self-tender, like some other defensive measures, may thwart a current hostile bid, but is not inherently coercive. Moreover, it does not necessarily preclude future bids or proxy contests by stockholders who decline to participate in the repurchase. . . .

We have already determined that the record in this case appears to reflect that a proxy contest remained a viable (if more problematic) alternative for American General even if the Repurchase Program were to be completed in its entirety. Nevertheless, the Court of Chancery must determine whether Unitrin's Repurchase Program would only inhibit American General's ability to wage a proxy fight and institute a merger or whether it was, in fact, preclusive because American General's success would either be mathematically impossible or realistically unattainable. If the Court of Chancery concludes that the Unitrin Repurchase Program was not draconian because it was not preclusive, one question will remain to be answered in its proportionality review: whether the Repurchase Program was within a range of reasonableness[.]

. . . In considering whether the Repurchase Program was within a range of reasonableness the Court of Chancery should take into consideration whether: (1) it is a statutorily authorized form of business decision which a board of directors may routinely make in a non-takeover context; (2) as a defensive response to American General's Offer it was limited and corresponded in degree or magnitude to the degree or magnitude of the threat (*i.e.*, assuming the threat was relatively "mild," was the response relatively "mild"?); (3) with the Repurchase Program, the Unitrin Board properly recognized that all shareholders are not alike, and provided immediate liquidity to those shareholders who wanted it. . . .

In this case, the Court of Chancery erred by substituting its judgment, that the Repurchase Program was unnecessary, for that of the Board. The Unitrin Board had the power and the duty, upon reasonable investigation, to protect Unitrin's shareholders from what it perceived to be the threat from American General's inadequate all-cash for all-shares Offer. The adoption of the poison pill *and* the limited Repurchase Program was not coercive and the Repurchase Program may

---

38. This Court's choice of the term draconian in *Unocal* was a recognition that the law affords boards of directors substantial latitude in defending the perimeter of the corporate bastion against perceived threats. Thus, continuing with the medieval metaphor, if a board reasonably perceives that a threat is on the horizon, it has broad authority to respond with a panoply of individual or combined defensive precautions, e.g., staffing the barbican, raising the drawbridge, and lowering the portcullis. Stated more directly, depending upon the circumstances, the board may respond to a reasonably perceived threat by adopting individually or sometimes in combination: advance notice bylaws, supermajority voting provisions, shareholder rights plans, repurchase programs, etc.

not be preclusive. Although each made a takeover more difficult, individually and collectively, if they were not coercive or preclusive the Court of Chancery must determine whether they were within the range of reasonable defensive measures available to the Board. *Accord* Cheff v. Mathes, 199 A.2d 548, 554-56 (Del. 1964).

If the Court of Chancery concludes that individually and collectively the poison pill and the Repurchase Program were proportionate to the threat the Board believed American General posed, the Unitrin Board's adoption of the Repurchase Program and the poison pill is entitled to review under the traditional business judgment rule. . . .

---

1. *The* Unocal *standard after* Unitrin? Does *Unitrin* change the standard for review of defensive tactics? *Unocal*, at least as interpreted by the Chancery Court, contemplated that the court would itself decide whether a particular defensive tactic was a proportionate response to an identified threat. This independent assessment of the choice made by the board of directors is in sharp contrast to the Delaware Supreme Court's aversion to a judge substituting her judgment for that of the board of directors.

The Supreme Court's focus in *Unitrin* is on the proportionality step in the *Unocal* analysis. In assessing proportionality, *Unitrin* teaches that the first inquiry is whether the defensive tactic is coercive, as in *Anderson, Clayton*, or preclusive, as the Supreme Court in *Time-Warner* stressed that the Warner acquisition was not. If the tactic is preclusive, then the target's response is disproportionate, the target company fails the *Unocal* test, and its defensive action is then reviewed under the more rigorous entire fairness standard. But what counts as preclusive? A target board or director's refusal to redeem a poison pill will always preclude a tender offer. If the tactic is not preclusive, then the tactic will be proportional if it falls within a "range of reasonableness," a phrase that hardly suggests significant judicial review. Does this reduce proportionality review of non-preclusive and non-coercive tactics to the minimal level of *Cheff*?

Standing against this analysis is the quite moderate nature of Unitrin's repurchase program. Given that the court was not considering the preclusive effect of Unitrin's poison pill, simply increasing the percentage of Unitrin's outstanding shares held by the independent directors from 23 to 28 percent does not seem to be a significant barrier to American General's plans. The court notes that institutional investors owned 42 percent of Unitrin's outstanding stock. Putting aside the poison pill, if the institutions would sell, then to secure control American General would need to purchase only an additional 9 percent of the remaining 30 percent of Unitrin's stock not held either by the board or by institutions. Thus, the repurchase program could be seen as proportionate to the threat of substantive coercion by giving shareholders some ability to sell their stock at the price American General offered, but without actually blocking the tender offer. The poison pill still does the serious defensive work. In this view, the analysis might have been different if the court were reviewing a decision by Unitrin's board not to redeem the pill.

2. *The importance of a proxy fight.* In *Unitrin*, the court went to some length to demonstrate the continued availability of a proxy contest. Does this mean that a target company can decline to redeem a poison pill so long as a proxy contest is available, thereby relegating the acquiring company to a control contest conducted

through an election rather than through a market transaction?[43] Is there a policy justification for preferring elections to markets? See Ronald J. Gilson, Unocal Fifteen Years Later, 26 Del. J. Corp. L. 491 (2001). One might argue that Del. Gen. Corp. Law §141(a) specifies that the corporation's business — presumably including the response to tender offers — is managed by the board of directors, while the board of directors is elected by the shareholders. Tender offers are thus resolved by the directors, and the identity of the directors — those who will decide the fate of a tender offer by deciding whether to redeem a poison pill — will be determined by the shareholders. Functionally, if the election is simply a referendum over whether the target company should be sold, then the ultimate outcome of the proxy contest should be the same as for a tender offer: those shareholders who would have tendered their shares will vote for the acquiring company's nominees for directors who, if elected, can be expected to redeem the poison pill and let the tender offer go forward.

3. *Defensive tactics in a proxy fight.* If a target company can use a poison pill to preclude a tender offer, then an acquiring company's response will be to make a tender offer conditional on the redemption of the target's poison pill and simultaneously initiate a proxy contest to replace the target's board of directors with the acquiring company's nominees, who can be expected to redeem the poison pill and let the offer proceed.

(a) *Dead-hand and slow-hand poison pills.* Defensive planners responded to the threat of a combined tender offer and proxy contest with a new generation of poison pill. Because the combined strategy depended on a new board of directors redeeming the pill after the proxy fight, the new poison pill sought to block, or at least slow, the redemption of the pill by directors who were not in office at the time that the pill was adopted or who were not approved by those directors. This generation of the pill came in two varieties: a "dead hand" and a "slow hand."[44] The dead-hand variation can be redeemed only by the directors in office at the time of the pill's adoption, or their nominees. Following a successful proxy fight, the pill can no longer be redeemed at all, but remains in place until its expiration at the end of its usual ten-year term. A slow-hand pill merely delays redemption by new directors for a period of time — say six months — after their election.

Both dead-hand and slow-hand pills have been invalidated in Delaware. In an early decision, the Chancery Court relied on a *Unocal* analysis to invalidate a dead-hand pill in Carmody v. Toll Bros. Inc., 1998 WL 418896 (Del. Ch. 1998). The Delaware Supreme Court invalidated a slow-hand pill, and implicitly a dead-hand pill as well, in Quickturn Design Systems, Inc. v. Mentor Graphics, 721 A.2d 1281 (1999). *Mentor Graphics* is notable because it relied on a construction of Del. §141(a), not *Unocal* proportionality analysis, to invalidate the pill. Under §141(a), the board of directors manages the corporation's business. The court noted that a dead-hand or slow-hand pill prevents a newly elected board from discharging its duties by preventing it from selling the corporation during the

---

43. For a broad reading of *Unitrin* by a federal court, see Moore Corp. v. Wallace Computer Services, 907 F. Supp. 1545 (D. Del. 1995).

44. More accurately, this generation of pill was rediscovered at this time. A dead-hand pill was used by Irving Bank's defense against a Bank of New York hostile offer in 1988. See Bank of New York Co., Inc. v. Irving Bank Corp., 139 Misc. 2d 665, 528 NYS.2d 482 (N.Y. Sup. Ct. 1988). A slow-hand pill was used by Northwest Airlines in its defense against a hostile offer by Marvin Davis. See Davis Acquisition Inc. v. NWA, Inc., 1989 Del. Ch. LEXIS 39 (April 25, 1989).

period of delay (whether six months or for the life of the pill in the dead-hand version). However, §141 requires that any limit on the board's authority be set forth in the certificate of incorporation, a condition not met by a poison pill plan adopted only by the board of directors. Thus, pills that limit the redemption power of future boards of directors are invalid because they are in conflict with §141(a).

(b) *Efforts to control the timing of proxy fights.* In some respects, an acquiring company may be able to move more quickly with a combined tender offer–proxy fight than it would be with a tender offer alone. Under *Unitrin*, a target board almost certainly could leave a pill in place for as long as six months if it could establish that the time was spent in pursuit of an alternative transaction. In contrast, a proxy contest can proceed much more quickly. Under Delaware law, an acquiring company can solicit written consents to remove and replace the incumbent directors unless the target's certificate of incorporation prohibits action without a meeting, and can call a special meeting of shareholders if the target corporation's bylaws so provide. As a result, many corporations have eliminated bylaw provisions allowing shareholders to call a special meeting and, where possible, amended their charters to eliminate consent solicitations.

Even where the acquiring corporation stages its proxy fight in connection with an annual meeting, target corporations have sought to delay the process. A familiar technique is an "advance notification" bylaw requiring prior notice, often 90 days, of a party's intent to nominate a candidate for director. Target companies have also responded to combined tender offer-proxy contest efforts by amending their bylaws *after* the acquiring company's request for a special meeting to delay the meeting or otherwise impede the process. The courts' response to these efforts has been mixed. Compare Blasius Industries v. Atlas Corp., 564 A.2d 651 (Del. Ch. 1998) with Stahl v. Apple Bancorp., 579 A.2d 1115 (Del. Ch. 1990). In Mentor Graphics Corporation v. Quickturn Design Systems, 728 A.2d 25 (Del. Ch. 1998), then Vice Chancellor, now Justice, Jacobs found that a bylaw mandating a 90- to 100-day delay between a shareholder's request for and the holding of a shareholders' meeting was reasonable, "although it arguably may approach the outer limits of reasonableness." Id. at 41-42. The standards governing efforts to control the proxy process are considered in Chapter VI.

Where a target corporation's charter provides for staggered director terms, the combined tender offer-proxy fight strategy is more problematic because with three classes of board members, it will take two annual meetings for the acquiring company to secure a majority of directors to redeem the target company's poison pill. This fact formed the core of an innovative, albeit unsuccessful, recent defense to a hostile takeover. Because staggered terms for the board of directors must be found in the target corporation's charter, there is little likelihood of a target company securing shareholder approval of a charter amendment to adopt such a board structure after a hostile bid is made. However, if the assets central to the acquiring company's strategy are dropped into a new corporation, which then would be spun off to the shareholders by distributing its shares as a dividend, the target board of directors determines the content of the new corporation's charter, including staggered terms for directors. The result is that the directors are able to impose staggered terms without a shareholder vote. Such a strategy was rejected by a federal court interpreting Nevada law, whose corporate statute is similar to Delaware's. See Hilton Hotel Corp. v. ITT Corp., 978 F. Supp. 1342 (D. Nev. 1997), which appears at page 558 supra.

4. *Shareholder response: bylaw amendments to require poison pill redemption.* As institutional shareholders have come to disfavor poison pills, shareholders have sought to counter the Delaware courts' growing tolerance of defensive tactics, as evidenced by *Unitrin*, by taking matters into their own hands. Shareholders have adopted bylaws that limit a board of directors' ability to use a poison pill to block a tender offer, or to require that the poison pill be immediately removed. Some commentators have argued, in reliance on *Mentor Graphics*, supra, that such bylaw proposals are inconsistent with Del. §141(a)'s grant of managerial authority to the board of directors;[45] other commentators have stressed that the grant of authority to the board in §141(a) is qualified by the phrase "except as otherwise permitted in this chapter or in the certificate of incorporation." Section 109(b) — obviously using in "this chapter" — authorized shareholders to adopt bylaws containing "any provision, not inconsistent with law or with the certificate of incorporation, relating to the business of the corporation, the conduct of its affairs, and its rights or powers of its stockholders, directors, officers, or employees." Jeffrey Gordon argues that "[u]nder prevailing modes of statutory interpretation in Delaware, in which different statutes have 'equal dignity' or 'independent legal significance,' nothing can be resolved about the scope of section 109(b) from the reference in section 141(a) to the articles alone, not the bylaws. The idea of a bylaw may be less clearly cabined than supposed in light of the expansive description of section 109(b): any provision . . . relating to the business of the corporation." [46]

Read broadly, *Mentor Graphics* prohibits any incursion on the board of directors' authority to manage the corporation. See Dennis J. Block & Simon C. Roosevelt, Further Implications of the *Mentor Graphics* and *Fleming* Decisions for Shareholder Bylaws, 7 Corp. Governance Advisor 18 (issue 2, March/April 1999). Read more narrowly, and consistent with Gordon's equal-dignity argument above, *Mentor Graphics* holds that §141 only prevents a board of directors from acting to limit the power of future boards of directors to manage the corporation, and does not extend to limitations imposed on the board by the shareholders under express statutory authority. If the statutory language does not resolve the issue, what are the policy arguments that a court should consider in allocating decisionmaking authority in a public corporation between the board and the shareholders?

C. *FRIENDLY TRANSACTIONS*

Despite the high profile of hostile takeover cases, most corporate acquisitions are friendly. However, friendly transactions also pose a potential conflict of interest for target management, who may have approved the transaction because the acquirer promised post-transaction benefits such as favorable employment contracts, or who may have a different view of a particular acquirer than do the

---

45. See id.; Lawrence Hammersmith, Corporate Democracy and Stockholder-Adopted Bylaws: Taking Back the Street, 73 Tul. L. Rev. 409 (1998).

46. Jeffrey Gordon, "Just Say Never?" Poison Pills, Deadhand Pills, and Shareholder-Adopted Bylaws: An Essay for Warren Buffet, 19 Cardozo L. Rev. 511, 547 (1997). See Ronald Gilson, Unocal Fifteen Years Later, 26 J. Corp. L. 491 (2002).

shareholders. Such a conflict of interest is policed in the first instance by the requirement that any form of acquisition receive target shareholder approval, whether by voting to approve the transaction, as with a merger or sale of assets, or by agreeing to sell their shares, as in a tender offer. For this reason, the target board's decision to approve an acquisition proposal is as a general rule protected by the business judgment rule. ALI, Principles of Corporate Governance §6.01(a) reflects this outcome: "The board of directors, in the exercise of its business judgment, may approve, reject, or decline to consider a proposal to the corporation to engage in a transaction in control."

But management actions may limit the effectiveness of shareholder approval as a measure of a transaction's quality. For example, management may decline to investigate whether better offers are obtainable. Indeed, management may contractually commit to passivity through a no-shop provision, agreeing neither to solicit a competitive bid nor to cooperate with or provide information to a competitive bidder. Alternatively, target management may assist a favored bid in the face of a competing bid, or prevent a competitive bid from being made at all, by providing the favored bidder an advantage, such as a stock or asset lockup, a breakup fee, or an expense reimbursement.[47] This also limits shareholders' capacity to police management's conflict of interest. The search for a competitive bid may be the best evidence of the proposed transaction's fairness; shareholders may approve a proposed transaction because it is better than nothing, not because it is better than alternative transactions that management conduct has deterred.

Thus, one question presented by friendly transactions is whether particular circumstances impose on target management a more rigorous fiduciary obligation when the target company is to be sold, and whether the performance of that obligation will be subject to more serious judicial review than contemplated by the business judgment rule. Ironically, serious judicial review of target management conduct in friendly transactions grew out of hostile transactions. Having failed to defend against a hostile bid, target management's second best strategy may be the target's acquisition by a less threatening bidder — a "white knight" in takeover parlance. Whether to induce the favored bidder to enter the contest at all or to help it win the contest, target management has often provided the favored bidder significant advantages. The Delaware Supreme Court first considered these issues directly in the following case.

Revlon, Inc. v. MacAndrews & Forbes Holdings, Inc.
506 A.2d 173 (Del. 1986)

MOORE, J.: In this battle for corporate control of Revlon, Inc. (Revlon), the Court of Chancery enjoined certain transactions designed to thwart the efforts of Pantry Pride, Inc. (Pantry Pride) to acquire Revlon. The defendants are Revlon, its board

---

47. An *asset lockup* gives the favored bidder the option of purchasing specified assets of the target company if another bidder secures control. A *stock lockup* gives the favored bidder the option of buying a specified amount of target company stock shares, typically at a price at or below the price offered by the favored bidder. A *breakup fee* commits the target to pay a substantial fee to the favored bidder if a competing bidder acquires the target. An *expense reimbursement* commits the target to pay all or a portion of the favored bidder's expenses if a competitive bidder acquires the target. The effectiveness of all of these techniques depends on their terms. For example, the lower the price in an asset lockup and the more critical the assets, the more effective the deterrent to a competitive bidder.

of directors, and Forstmann Little & Co. . . . The injunction barred consummation of an option granted Forstmann to purchase certain Revlon assets (the lock-up option), a promise by Revlon to deal exclusively with Forstmann in the face of a takeover (the no-shop provision), and the payment of a $25 million cancellation fee to Forstmann if the transaction was aborted. . . .

In our view, lock-ups and related agreements are permitted under Delaware law where their adoption is untainted by director interest or other breaches of fiduciary duty. The actions taken by the Revlon directors, however, did not meet this standard. Moreover, while concern for various corporate constituencies is proper when addressing a takeover threat, that principle is limited by the requirement that there be some rationally related benefit accruing to the stockholders. We find no such benefit here.

[Faced with a hostile tender offer from Pantry Pride at $45 per share, a price that, the court found, Revlon's board "reasonably considered . . . grossly inadequate," Revlon (i) adopted a poison pill under which its shareholders could exchange their shares for a $65 principal Revlon note at 12 percent (the "Notes"), and (ii) made a self-tender for up to 10 million shares ($33\frac{1}{2}$ percent of its outstanding shares). Some $475 million in Notes were issued by Revlon in exchange for its shares. Because the holders of these Notes would suffer an immediate decline in their market value if Pantry Pride, a highly leveraged company, were able to achieve control of Revlon, the Notes contained protective financial covenants, which Revlon, however, was empowered to waive. Pantry Pride responded by increasing its offer for Revlon, eventually raising it several times. Revlon then began to formulate a leveraged buyout with Forstmann. To facilitate this merger, the Revlon board agreed to waive the financial covenants protecting the Notes; the market value of the Notes immediately dropped from $100 to $87.50, and Revlon's board was threatened with litigation brought by the Note holders. Forstmann Little also insisted on an asset lock-up on two Revlon divisions at a price below the value Revlon's own investment bankers placed on them.] The principal demand was a lock-up option to purchase Revlon's Vision Care and National Health Laboratories divisions for $525 million, some $100-175 million below the value ascribed to them by Lazard Freres, if another acquiror got 40% of Revlon's shares. . . . In return, Forstmann agreed to support the par value of the Notes, which had faltered in the market, by an exchange of new notes. Forstmann also demanded immediate acceptance of its offer, or it would be withdrawn. The board unanimously approved Forstmann's proposal because: (1) it was for a higher price than the Pantry Pride bid, (2) it protected the noteholders, and (3) Forstmann's financing was firmly in place. [The court then upheld the poison pill adopted by the board as a valid exercise of business judgment.]

The second defensive measure adopted by Revlon to thwart a Pantry Pride takeover was the company's own exchange offer for 10 million of its shares. The directors' general broad powers to manage the business and affairs of the corporation are augmented by the specific authority conferred under 8 Del. C. §160(a), permitting the company to deal in its own stock. *Unocal*, 493 A.2d at 953-54; *Cheff v. Mathes*, 41 Del. Supr. 494, 199 A.2d 548, 554 (1964). However, when exercising that power in an effort to forestall a hostile takeover, the board's actions are strictly held to the fiduciary standards outlined in *Unocal*. These standards . . . impose an enhanced duty to abjure any action that is motivated by considerations other than a good faith concern for such interests. The Revlon directors concluded that Pantry Pride's $47.50 offer was grossly inadequate. In that regard the board acted in good faith, and on an informed basis, with reasonable grounds to believe that there existed a harmful threat to the [corporation]. The adoption of a defensive measure, reasonable in relation to the threat posed, was proper and fully accorded with the powers, duties, and responsibilities conferred upon directors under our law. *Unocal*, 493 A.2d at 954.

However, when Pantry Pride increased its offer to $50 per share, and then to $53, it became apparent to all that the break-up of the company was inevitable. The Revlon board's authorization permitting management to negotiate a merger or buyout with a third party was a recognition that the company was for sale. The duty of the board had thus changed from the preservation of Revlon as a corporate entity to the maximization of the company's value at a sale for the stockholders' benefit. This significantly altered the board's responsibilities under the *Unocal* standards. It no longer faced threats to corporate policy and effectiveness, or to the stockholder's interests, from a grossly inadequate bid. The whole question of defensive measures became moot. The directors' role changed from defenders of the corporate bastion to auctioneers charged with getting the best price for the stockholders at a sale of the company.

This brings us to the lock-up with Forstmann and its emphasis on shoring up the sagging market value of the Notes in the face of threatened litigation by their holders. Such a focus was inconsistent with the changed concept of the directors' responsibilities at this stage of the developments. The impending waiver of the Notes covenants had caused the value of the Notes to fall, and the board was aware of the noteholders' ire as well as their subsequent threats of suit. The directors thus made support of the Notes an integral part of the company's dealings with Forstmann, even though their primary responsibility at this stage was to the equity owners.

The original threat posed by Pantry Pride — the break-up of the company — had become a reality which even the directors embraced. Selective dealing to fend off a hostile but determined bidder was no longer a proper objective. Instead, obtaining the highest price for the benefit of the stockholders should have been the central theme guiding director action. Thus, the Revlon board could not make the requisite showing of good faith by preferring the noteholders and ignoring its duty of loyalty to the shareholders. The rights of the former already were fixed by contract. Wolfensohn v. Madison Fund, Inc., Del. Supr., 253 A.2d 72, 75 (1969); Harff v. Kerkorian, Del. Ch., 324 A.2d 215 (1974). The noteholders required no further protection, and when the Revlon board entered into an auction-ending lock-up agreement with Forstmann on the basis of impermissible considerations at the expense of the shareholders, the directors breached their primary duty of loyalty.

The Revlon board argued that it acted in good faith in protecting the noteholders because *Unocal* permits consideration of other corporate constituencies. Although such considerations may be permissible, there are fundamental limitations upon that prerogative. A board may have regard for various constituencies in discharging its responsibilities, provided there are rationally related benefits accruing to the stockholders. *Unocal*, 493 A.2d at 955. However, such concern for non-stockholder interests is inappropriate when an auction among active bidders is in progress, and the object no longer is to protect or maintain the corporate enterprise but to sell it to the highest bidder. . . .

A lock-up is not per se illegal under Delaware law. . . . Such options can entice other bidders to enter a contest for control of the corporation, creating an auction for the company and maximizing shareholder profit. . . . However, while those lock-ups which draw bidders into the battle benefit shareholders, similar measures which end an active auction and foreclose further bidding operate to the shareholders' detriment.

The Forstmann option had a . . . destructive effect on the auction process. Forstmann had already been drawn into the contest on a preferred basis, so the result of the lock-up was not to foster bidding, but to destroy it. The board's stated reasons for approving the transactions were: (1) better financing, (2) noteholder protection, and (3) higher price. As the Court of Chancery found, and we agree, any distinctions between the rival bidders' methods of financing the proposal were nominal at best, and such a consideration has little or no significance in a cash offer for any and all shares. The principal object, contrary to the board's duty of care, appears to have been protection of the noteholders over the shareholders' interests.

While Forstmann's $57.25 offer was objectively higher than Pantry Pride's $56.25 bid, the margin of superiority is less when the Forstmann price is adjusted for the time value of money. In reality, the Revlon board ended the auction in return for very little actual improvement in the final bid. The principal benefit went to the directors, who avoided personal liability to a class of creditors to whom the board owed no further duty under the circumstances. Thus, when a board ends an intense bidding contest on an insubstantial basis, and where a significant by-product of that action is to protect the directors against a perceived threat of personal liability for consequences stemming from the adoption of previous defensive measures, the action cannot withstand the enhanced scrutiny which *Unocal* requires of director conduct. In addition to the lock-up option, the Court of Chancery enjoined the no-shop provision as part of the attempt to foreclose further bidding by Pantry Pride. The no-shop provision, like the lock-up option, while not per se illegal, is impermissible under the *Unocal* standards when a board's primary duty becomes that of an auctioneer responsible for selling the company to the highest bidder. The agreement to negotiate only with Forstmann ended rather than intensified the board's involvement in the bidding contest.

It is ironic that the parties even considered a no-shop agreement when Revlon had dealt preferentially, and almost exclusively, with Forstmann throughout the contest. After the directors authorized management to negotiate with other parties, Forstmann was given every negotiating advantage that Pantry Pride had been denied: cooperation from management, access to financial data, and the exclusive opportunity to present merger proposals directly to the board of directors. Favoritism for a white knight to the total exclusion of a hostile bidder might be justifiable when the latter's offer adversely affects shareholder interests, but when bidders make relatively similar offers, or dissolution of the company becomes inevitable, the directors cannot fulfill their enhanced *Unocal* duties by playing favorites with the contending factions. Market forces must be allowed to operate freely to bring the target's shareholders the best price available for their equity. Thus, as the trial court ruled, the shareholders' interests necessitated that the board remain free to negotiate in the fulfillment of that duty.

The court below similarly enjoined the payment of the cancellation fee, pending a resolution of the merits, because the fee was part of the overall plan to thwart Pantry Pride's efforts. We find no abuse of discretion in that ruling.

In conclusion, the Revlon board was confronted with a situation not uncommon in the current wave of corporate takeovers. A hostile and determined bidder sought the company at a price the board was convinced was inadequate. The initial defensive tactics worked to the benefit of the shareholders, and thus the board was able to sustain its *Unocal* burdens in justifying those measures. However, in granting an asset option lock-up to Forstmann, we must conclude that . . . the directors allowed considerations other than the maximization of shareholder profit to affect their judgment, and followed a course that ended the auction for Revlon . . . to the ultimate detriment of its shareholders. The decision of the Court of Chancery, therefore, is affirmed.

---

1. Revlon *and Delaware's intermediate standard. Revlon* extends the intermediate standard from target company defensive tactics to target company tactics designed to facilitate a friendly bid. But just as *Unocal* left the content of the pro-portionality test unclear, so too did *Revlon* leave much uncertainty to be resolved. Once a company's sale becomes "inevitable," the *Revlon* standard applies: "The directors' role change[s] . . . to auctioneers charged with getting the best price for the stockholders at a sale of the company." This formulation involves two separate inquiries. First, what triggers the *Revlon* obligations?[48] Second, what precisely are those obligations?

2. *What triggers* Revlon? In defending against a hostile bid, it is critical to know when obligations under *Revlon* arise. So long as the measure is the defensive-friendly *Unitrin* standard, the target company has at least the possibility of remaining independent by devising a defensive tactic that, while successfully blocking the bid, is nonetheless reasonable in relation to the threat. If, instead, *Revlon* applies, the target board might lose not only the possibility of remaining independent, but also the opportunity to designate the company's acquirer. Thus, the location of the boundary between *Unocal* and *Revlon* is critical.

What triggers *Revlon* is equally important in a purely friendly transaction, although here the boundary is not between *Revlon* and *Unocal*. If two companies conclude that their combination will result in substantial synergies, can they limit the choice offered to shareholders to the chosen strategic alliance or nothing? If another bidder offers more, can they decline to consider it? Here the critical boundary is between *Revlon* and the business judgment rule. If the standard is the equivalent of ALI Principles §6.01(a), then the board is free to reject a proposed transaction in control. If *Revlon* applies, the board's discretion narrows. See pages 1000-1001 infra.

3. Revlon *'s substantive obligations.* Once it is clear that the *Revlon* boundary has been crossed, must the board hold a formal auction with alternating bids, as apparently took place in that case? From this perspective, two issues arise: First, how does the target board find out the target company's value? An auction is only one way.[49] Some assets are sold by negotiating with a single bidder after the seller has obtained guidance concerning value from other sources.

---

48. See Ronald Gilson & Reinier Kraakman, What Triggers *Revlon?*, 25 Wake Forest L. Rev. 37 (1990).
49. See Preston McAfee & John McMillan, Auctions and Bidding, 25 J. Econ. Lit. 669 (1987).

Second, how does the board ensure that it gets the highest price? Again, a simple auction may work, but under some circumstances it may be best to favor a particular bidder in order to induce a higher bid.[50] But such favoritism also may reflect target management's effort to preserve its own positions. *Revlon* illustrates both concerns. The court clearly thought Revlon favored Forstmann Little & Co., a plausible inference since Forstmann was a financial bidder who both needed Revlon management to run the company and would provide management the opportunity to acquire an equity interest in the post-transaction company. Thus, the court seemed unable to imagine a reason other than self-interest that would explain why Revlon would give Forstmann a lockup in return for only a $1 per share increase in its bid in the face of Pantry Pride's insistence that it would top any Forstmann bid. Perhaps at this stage in the bidding a $1 per share increase was significant. Pantry Pride's initial hostile offer was $47.50 per share. Forstmann and Revlon then agreed to a friendly transaction at $56 per share. Pantry Pride responded by increasing its bid only 25 cents per share and announced that it would top any Forstmann bid by 5 cents per share. Suppose Forstmann would not raise its bid without a lockup. If Forstmann were not given a lockup, Revlon would receive $56.25 per share from Pantry Pride; with a lockup, Revlon would get $57 per share from Forstmann. That Pantry Pride would have offered $57.05 per share after Forstmann increased its bid is beside the point; in the absence of the lockup, Pantry Pride would have won the contest with its $56.25 bid.[51] To complicate things further, instead of giving Forstmann a lockup, Revlon could have told the parties that each could submit only one more bid, and that a lockup would be given to the highest bidder. Would that strategy have resulted in a bid higher than $57? The difficulty of correctly assessing which construction of the events — as self-serving or value maximizing — is correct underscores the importance of fleshing out *Revlon*'s substantive obligations.

1. *REVLON*'S SUBSTANTIVE OBLIGATIONS

Revlon spoke of the consequences of its doctrinal trigger as shifting the target board's responsibilities to those of auctioneer: to secure the highest possible price for shareholders. Does this require that target management organize a formal bidding contest — an auction — in every instance?

The process of securing the highest price involves two components: first, securing sufficient information such that the target board can appropriately evaluate the company's value, and second, structuring the sale process so that the price obtained approximates that value.

a. Information Requirement

A formal auction is one way of securing information about the company's value. In some circumstances, the board may believe it already knows the company's value and can promptly assess any offer. The board also can seek an opinion from its

---

50. Id. at 718-720.
51. See Stephen Fraidin & Jon Hanson, Toward Unlocking Lockups, 103 Yale L.J. 1739, 1754-1755 (1994).

investment banker. Or the board can "shop" the company by retaining an investment banker to seek additional bids for the company. When dealing with only a single suitor, the board may believe that the best evidence of value will come from vigorous one-on-one negotiations.

In Barkan v. Amsted Industries, 567 A.2d 1279 (Del. 1989), the Delaware Supreme Court stressed that the manner in which the target board of directors gathered information depended on the circumstances:

> *Revlon* does not demand that every change in the control of a Delaware corporation be preceded by a heated bidding contest. *Revlon* is merely one of an unbroken line of cases that seek to prevent the conflicts of interest that arise in the field of mergers and acquisitions by demanding that directors act with scrupulous concern for fairness to shareholders. When multiple bidders are competing for control, this concern for fairness forbids directors from using defensive mechanisms to thwart an auction or to favor one bidder over another. When the board is considering a single offer and has no reliable grounds upon which to judge its adequacy, this concern for fairness demands a canvas of the market to determine if higher bids may be elicited. When, however, the directors possess a body of reliable evidence with which to evaluate the fairness of a transaction, they may approve that transaction without conducting an active survey of the market. As the Chancellor recognized, the circumstances in which this passive approach is acceptable are limited. "A decent respect for reality forces one to admit that . . . advice [of an investment banker] is frequently a pale substitute for the dependable information that a canvas of the relevant market can provide." The need for adequate information is central to the enlightened evaluation of a transaction that a board must make. Nevertheless, there is no single method that a board must employ to acquire such information. Here, the Chancellor found that the advice of the Special Committee's investment bankers, when coupled with the special circumstances surrounding the negotiation and consummation of the MBO [management-sponsored leveraged buyout], supported a finding that Amsted's directors had acted in good faith to arrange the best possible transaction for shareholders. Our own review of the record leads us to rule that the Chancellor's finding was well within the scope of his discretion.

Does this formulation sound less like an intermediate standard and more like the business judgment rule? Recall that in Smith v. Van Gorkom, page 84 supra, which was decided before *Unocal* and *Revlon* announced an intermediate standard of review for acquisition transactions, the Delaware Supreme Court held that the Trans Union board had breached the business judgment rule and the duty of care by accepting an acquisition proposal without first securing sufficient information to determine the company's intrinsic worth. Is the board's acquiring the information necessary to evaluate a bid reviewed under the duty of care and protected by the business judgment rule or under some form of the *Unocal-Revlon* intermediate standard? This component of Delaware takeover law received more focused attention by the Delaware Supreme Court in Paramount Communications, Inc. v. QVC Network, Inc., page 1009 infra.

b. Structuring the Transaction

Revlon struck down lockup provisions designed to ensure that the company would be acquired by the bidder management favored. These provisions clearly presented the unavoidable conflict of interest present in acquisition transactions. On the one hand, the Revlon board favored a bidder that had agreed to retain management and to allow management to participate in the acquisition by themselves purchasing a portion of the equity in the surviving corporation. On the other, the favoritism may have been necessary to secure a higher bid in the first place. Can courts fashion a standard of review that distinguishes between favoritism that results in a higher price for shareholders and favoritism that results in a better deal for management?

Mills Acquisition Co. v. Macmillan, Inc., 559 A.2d 1261 (Del. Ch. 1989), addressed this issue. The case grew out of the efforts by Macmillan, Inc., a large publishing, educational, and informational services company, to avoid a hostile takeover bid. After a series of defensive efforts and a series of proposed friendly and hostile transactions, Macmillan's future came down to a *Revlon*-like competition to take over the company between Kohlberg Kravis Roberts & Co. ("KKR"), a private equity firm specializing in leveraged buyouts, and Maxwell Communication Corp, PLC ("Maxwell"), a competitor of Macmillan controlled by Robert Maxwell. The immediate issue was a lockup agreement entered into by Macmillan and KKR after the Macmillan board determined that KKR was the highest bidder. KKR was given an option to purchase some of Macmillan's most valuable properties, without which Macmillan would have been less attractive to competitive bidders. From the court's perspective, the lockup agreement had a more significant role than merely formalizing the highest bidder's victory after the last competing bidder dropped out. Rather, because Macmillan's management, who plainly favored KKR's bid to that of Maxwell, "tipped" to KKR the substance of Maxwell's final bid, the court treated the lockup as an effort to favor KKR's bid and addressed its validity in the following passages:

> VI. In *Revlon*, we addressed for the first time the . . . [validity of] lock-up and no-shop provisions. Although we have held that such agreements are not per se illegal, we recognized that like measures often foreclose further bidding to the detriment of shareholders, and end active auctions prematurely. *Revlon*, at 183-84. If the grant of an auction-ending provision is appropriate, it must confer a substantial benefit upon the stockholders in order to withstand exacting scrutiny by the courts. Moreover, where the decision of the directors, granting the lock-up option, was not informed or was induced by breaches of fiduciary duties, such as those here, they cannot survive. . . .
>
> Turning to the lock-up, in *Revlon* we held that such an agreement is not per se unlawful under Delaware law. We recognized its proper function in a contest for corporate control. Apparently, it has escaped some that in *Revlon* we distinguished the potentially valid uses of a lock-up from those that are impermissible: "[W]hile those lock-ups which draw bidders into a battle benefit shareholders, similar measures which end an active auction and foreclose further bidding operate to the shareholders' detriment." *Revlon* at 183.
>
> In this case, a lock-up agreement was not necessary to draw any of the bidders into the contest. Macmillan cannot seriously contend that they received a final bid from KKR that materially enhanced general stockholder interests. By all rational indications it was intended to have a directly opposite effect. . . . When one compares what KKR received for the lock-up, in contrast to its inconsiderable bid, the invalidity of the agreement becomes patent. *Revlon*, at 184.
>
> Here, the assets covered by the lock-up agreement were some of Macmillan's most valued properties, its "crown jewels." Even if the lock-up is permissible, when it

involves "crown jewel" assets careful scrutiny attends the decision. When the intended effect is to end an active auction, at the very least the independent members of the board must attempt to negotiate alternative bids before granting such a significant concession. *Revlon*, at 183; *Hanson*, at 277. Maxwell invited negotiations for a purchase of the same four divisions, which KKR originally sought to buy for $775 million. Maxwell was prepared to pay $900 million. Instead of serious negotiations with Maxwell, there were only concessions to KKR by giving it a lock-up of seven divisions for $865 million.

Thus, when directors in a *Revlon* bidding contest grant a crown jewel lock-up, serious questions are raised, particularly where, as here, there is little or no improvement in the final bid. *Revlon*, at 184, 187. The care and attention which independent directors bring to this decision are crucial to its success. . . .

VII. A. Directors are not required by Delaware law to conduct an auction according to some standard formula, only that they observe the significant requirement of fairness for the purpose of enhancing general shareholder interests. That does not preclude differing treatment of bidders when necessary to advance those interests. Variables may occur which necessitate such treatment.[38] However, the board's primary objective, and essential purpose, must remain the enhancement of the bidding process for the benefit of the stockholders.

We recognize that the conduct of a corporate auction is a complex undertaking both in its design and execution. See, e.g., MacAfee & McMillan, Auctions and Bidding, 25 J. Econ. Lit. 699 (1987); Milgrom, The Economics of Competitive Bidding: A Selected Survey, in Social Goals and Social Organization 261 (Hurwitz, Schneidler & Sonnenschein eds. 1985). We do not intend to limit the broad negotiating authority of the directors to achieve the best price available to the stockholders. To properly secure that end may require the board to invoke a panoply of devices, and the giving or receiving of concessions that may benefit one bidder over another. See, e.g., In re J.P. Stevens & Co. Shareholders Litigation, Del. Ch., 542 A.2d 770, 781-784 (1988); *appeal refused*, 540 A.2d 1088 (1988). But when that happens, there must be a rational basis for the action such that the interests of the stockholders are manifestly the board's paramount objective.

B. . . . As we held in *Revlon*, when management of a target company determines that the company is for sale, the board's *responsibilities* under the enhanced *Unocal* standards are significantly altered. Id. at 182. Although the board's *responsibilities* under *Unocal* are far different, the enhanced *duties* of the directors in responding to a potential shift in control, recognized in *Unocal*, remain unchanged. This principle pervades *Revlon*, and when directors conclude that an auction is appropriate, the standard by which their ensuing actions will be judged continues to be the enhanced duty imposed by this Court in *Unocal*. . . .

When *Revlon* duties devolve upon directors, this court will continue to exact an enhanced judicial scrutiny at the threshold, as in *Unocal*, before the normal presumptions of the business judgment rule will apply. However, as we recognized in *Revlon*, the two-part threshold test, of necessity, is slightly different.

At the outset, the plaintiff must show, and the trial court must find, that the directors of the target company treated one or more of the respective bidders on unequal terms. It is only then that the two-part threshold requirement of *Unocal* is truly invoked, for in *Revlon* we held that "[f]avoritism for a white knight to the total exclusion of a hostile bidder might be justifiable when the latter's offer adversely affects shareholder interests, but . . . the directors cannot fulfill their enhanced *Unocal* duties by playing favorites with the contending factions." Id. at 184.

---

38. For example, this court has upheld actions of directors when a board is confronted with a coercive "two-tiered" bust-up tender offer. See *Unocal*, 493 A.2d at 956; *Ivanhoe*, 535 A.2d at 1342. Compare *Revlon*, at 184.

In the face of disparate treatment, the trial court must first examine whether the directors properly perceived that shareholder interests were enhanced. In any event the board's action must be reasonable in relation to the advantage sought to be achieved, or conversely, to the threat which a particular bid allegedly poses to stockholder interests. *Unocal,* at 955.

If on the basis of this enhanced *Unocal* scrutiny the trial court is satisfied that the test has been met, then the directors' actions necessarily are entitled to the protections of the business judgment rule. The latitude a board will have in responding to differing bids will vary according to the degree of benefit or detriment to the shareholders' general interests that the amount or terms of the bids pose. We stated in *Revlon,* and again here, that in a sale of corporate control the responsibility of the directors is to get the highest value reasonably attainable for the shareholders. Beyond that, there are no special and distinct "*Revlon* duties." Once a finding has been made by a court that the directors have fulfilled their fundamental duties of care and loyalty under the foregoing standards, there is no further judicial inquiry into the matter.

For the foregoing reasons, the judgment of the Court of Chancery, denying Maxwell's motion for preliminary injunction, is Reversed.

---

1. *A functional trigger. Macmillan* clearly adopted a functional approach, focusing on the transaction's impact or control, regardless of form. *Revlon* is triggered by a sale, "whether the 'sale' takes the form of an active auction, a management buyout, or a 'restructuring' such as that which the Court of Chancery enjoined in [Robert M. Bass Group v. Evans]." A change in control seems to be the only feature shared by the three transactions.

2. *A two-step-inquiry. Macmillan* clarified the standard of review that applies to target directors' decisions concerning the substantive features of the transaction by which the company is sold. Following the *Unocal* structure, crossing the *Revlon* boundary triggers a two-step inquiry. If directors favored one bidder, then, paralleling the *Unocal* threat inquiry, the court determines whether the directors believed that target shareholders' interests were advanced by the favoritism. If directors were properly motivated, then, as in *Unocal,* the court looks to proportionality: was the benefit provided to the favored bidder "reasonable in relation to the advantage sought to be achieved"? In other words, did the directors get a good deal?

As with *Unocal*'s defensive version of the intermediate standard, *Macmillan*'s two-step formulation gives rise to a large number of questions. It is clear that providing a bidder such terms as a no-shop clause, expense reimbursement, breakup fee, or lockup will cross the favoritism threshold, but what about more situational advantages? In many management buyouts, target management has a built-in advantage over potential competitive bidders because management determines the timing of the transaction and because management has better information. Should every management buyout be deemed to involve structural favoritism? For this view see Ronald Gilson & Bernard Black, The Law and Finance of Corporate Acquisitions 1111-1119 (2d ed. 1995). ALI §5.15 imposes on management the obligation to demonstrate the fairness of an acquisition in which they participate unless other potential bidders are given the same information as is provided to non-management participants in the transaction and the time to evaluate it.

What is the court's role in evaluating how good a deal the target company negotiated, that is, the benefit secured in return for the favorable terms provided? Suppose, to negotiate the transaction, the target establishes a committee of independent directors, which is advised by separate legal and investment banking counsel. Should the procedures followed by the board influence the level of the court's substantive review of the terms? Can a court do more than simply ask, taking everything into consideration, whether the target board made a reasonable deal? Is the difference between *Revlon* and the business judgment rule only that under the business judgment rule the court asks whether the directors thought the terms of the deal were rational, while under the intermediate standard the court determines whether it believes the terms were reasonable?

2. WHAT TRIGGERS *REVLON*?

Revlon characterizes the time when the intermediated standard is triggered with a metaphor: once "it became apparent to all that the break-up of the company was inevitable, . . . [t]he directors' role changed from defenders of the corporate bastion to auctioneers charged with getting the best price for the stockholders at a sale of the company." The ambiguity of the trigger led to a flurry of efforts to transfer control of a potential or actual target through a plan that shifted effective control of the target by a means that counsel hoped would not be treated as a sale of the company.

Macmillan put an end to this effort, the court applying a functional approach: "At a minimum, *Revlon* requires that there be the most scrupulous adherence to ordinary principles of fairness in the sense that stockholder interests are enhanced, rather than diminished, in the conduct of an auction for the sale of corporate control. This is so whether the 'sale' takes the form of an active auction, a management buyout, or a 'restructuring' such as that which the Court of Chancery enjoined in [an earlier stage in the Macmillan control contest, in which management received shares giving effective control of the company]."

Nonetheless, some room for planning remained. *Macmillan* involved much the same transactional pattern as in *Revlon:* a favored transaction devised in response to a hostile bid that would not die. The possibility remained that a different standard would apply to a merger of equals that had its origins not in avoiding a hostile bid, but in a good faith belief in the transaction's strategic advantages. The Delaware courts confronted whether the *Macmillan* formulation of the *Revlon* trigger left room for that outcome in *Time*.

Paramount Communications, Inc. v. Time Inc.
[1989 Transfer Binder] Fed. Sec. L. Rep. (CCH) ¶94,514 (Del. Ch. 1989)

ALLEN, Ch.: [The facts are set out at page 964 supra.] . . . The legal analysis that follows treats the distinction that the Time board implicitly drew between current share value maximization and long-term share value maximization. . . . On the level of legal doctrine, it is clear that under Delaware law, directors are under no obligation to act so as to maximize the immediate value of the corporation or its shares, except in the special case in which the corporation is in a "*Revlon* mode." Mills Acquisition Co. v. Macmillan, Inc.; Ivanhoe Partners v. Newmont Mining, Del. Supr., 535 A.2d 1334 (1987); Revlon v. MacAndrews & Forbes Holdings, Inc., Del. Supr., 506 A.2d 173 (1986). See generally TW Services, Inc. v. SWT Acquisition Corp. (March 2, 1989). Thus, Delaware law does recognize that directors, when acting deliberately, in an informed way, and in the good faith pursuit of corporate interests, may follow a course designed to achieve long-term value even at the cost of immediate value maximization.

The legally critical question this case presents then involves *when* must a board shift from its ordinary long-term profit maximizing mode to the radically altered state recognized by the *Revlon* case in which its duty, broadly stated, is to exercise its power in the good faith pursuit of immediate maximization of share value. Surely, when as in *Revlon* itself and other cases construing its command, most notably *Macmillan*,[39] the board decides to enter a change in control transaction, it has elected to enter the *Revlon* zone. But it now appears resolved that a subjective disinclination to sell the company will not prevent that duty from arising where an extraordinary transaction including, at a minimum, a change in corporate control is involved: "[*Revlon*'s requirements pertain] whether the "sale" takes the form of an active auction, a management buyout, or a "restructuring" such as that which the Court of Chancery enjoined in *Macmillan I*." Mills Acquisition Co. v. Macmillan, Inc.

Thus, more specifically, the first overarching question presented by these facts reduces legally to the inquiry whether the board was, on June 16, involuntarily in that special state — what one can call, as a shorthand, the "*Revlon* mode" — in which it was required to maximize immediate share value. . . .

IV. Plaintiffs' first argument, restated most simply, is that the original merger agreement constituted an implicit decision by the board of Time to transfer control of the company to Warner, or more correctly its shareholders, and when the board decided to consider doing that, its duties changed from long-term management of the corporation for the benefit of the company's shareholders to the narrow and specific goal of present maximization of share value. That is, it entered a "*Revlon* mode." See Revlon v. MacAndrews & Forbes Holdings, Inc., Del. Supr., 506 A.2d 173, 182 (1986). The class action plaintiffs assert that any change in corporate control triggers this special duty. The individual shareholder plaintiffs urge a different theory as triggering the special *Revlon* duty. They contend that the original merger, if effectuated, would have precluded the Time shareholders from ever (that is, in the foreseeable future) realizing a control premium transaction, and thus, in its impact upon Time shareholders, the merger contemplated by the March 3 agreement would have implicitly represented the same loss of a control premium as would a change in control transaction with no premium. Thus, these plaintiffs assert that even if the stock for stock merger did not represent a change in control, the same duty to maximize current value should attach to it as to a "sale."

Plaintiffs, having purportedly shown that the board really was in a *Revlon* mode, then go on to argue that the board violated its *Revlon* duty by not seeking a *current* value maximizing transaction and by entering into a number of agreements that

---

39. See also In re J.P. Stevens & Co., Inc. Shareholders Litigation, Del. Ch., 542 A.2d 770 (1988); In re RJR Nabisco, Inc. Shareholders Litigation, Del. Ch., Cons. C.A. No. 10389 (January 31, 1989); In re Fort Howard Corp. Shareholders Litigation, Del. Ch., Cons. C.A. No. 9991 (August 8, 1988); In re Holly Farms Corporation Shareholders Litigation, Del. Ch., C.A. No. 10350 (December 30, 1988), slip op. at 12.

were intended to preclude or impede the emergence of current value maximizing alternatives. These agreements include the "dry up" fee payments, the Share Exchange Agreement and the restrictions on supplying information to or entering into discussions with anyone seeking to acquire control of Time.

Defendants respond first that the board did not consider that it was appropriate in March or thereafter to "sell" the company; the purpose of the original merger was quite the opposite in that it sought to preserve and improve the company's long-term performance. Second, defendants say that if something other than their subjective intention is relevant, it simply is not the case that the stock for stock merger they authorized represented a change in control. It is irrelevant in their view that some 62% of the equity of Time would be owned by former Warner shareholders after the merger, that Mr. Ross would serve as co-CEO or that half of the members of the enlarged board would be former Warner directors. There was no control block of Time shares before the agreement and there would be none after it, they point out. Before the merger agreement was signed, control of the corporation existed in a fluid aggregation of unaffiliated shareholders representing a voting majority — in other words, in the market. After the effectuation of the merger it contemplated, control would have remained in the market, so to speak.

As to the individual plaintiffs' theory, defendants say it is flawed in law and in fact. Legally, they contend that a transaction that is otherwise proper cannot be deemed to trigger the radical "*Revlon* mode" obligations simply because it has the effect of making an attempted hostile takeover of the corporation less likely. All manner of transactions might have that effect and our cases, it is said, have explicitly rejected the notion that a would-be acquiror can compel a target to maintain itself in status quo while its offer proceeds.

Factually, defendants claim that this record does not establish a reasonable probability that the initial merger, if it had been consummated, would have precluded a future change in control transaction. The merged Time-Warner company would be large, it is true (a "private market" value approaching $30 billion, it is said), but recent history has shown that huge transactions can be done. While such a transaction would be rare, if a leveraged acquisition of both participants was feasible before the merger, one cannot say that a stock for stock consolidation of such firms would necessarily preclude an acquisition of it thereafter, or so defendants contend.

. . . [I]n *Macmillan* our supreme court did indicate that a board may find itself in a *Revlon* mode without reaching an express resolve to "sell" the company: "At a minimum, *Revlon* requires that there be the most scrupulous adherence to ordinary principles of fairness in the sense that stockholder interests are enhanced, rather than diminished, in the conduct of an auction for the sale of corporate control. *This is so whether the 'sale' takes the form of an active auction, a management buyout, or a 'restructuring' such as that which the Court of Chancery enjoined in Macmillan I. Revlon*, 506 A.2d at 181-82." (emphasis added).

Thus, I do not find it dispositive of anything that the Time board did not expressly resolve to sell the company. I take from *Macmillan*, however, and its citation of the earlier *Macmillan I* opinion in this court, that a corporate transaction that does represent a change in corporate control does place the board in a situation in which it is charged with the single duty to maximize current share value. I cannot conclude, however, that the initial merger agreement contemplates a change in control of Time. I am entirely persuaded of the soundness of the view that it is irrelevant for purposes of making such determination that 62% of Time-Warner stock would have been held by former Warner stockholders.

If the appropriate inquiry is whether a change in control is contemplated, the answer must be sought in the specific circumstances surrounding the transaction. Surely under some circumstances a stock for stock merger could reflect a transfer of corporate control. That would, for example, plainly be the case here if Warner were a private company. But where, as here, the shares of both constituent corporations are widely held, corporate control can be expected to remain unaffected by a stock for stock merger. This in my judgment was the situation with respect to the original merger agreement. When the specifics of that situation are reviewed, it is seen that, aside from legal technicalities and aside from arrangements thought to enhance the prospect for the ultimate succession of Mr. Nicholas, neither corporation could be said to be acquiring the other. Control of both remained in a large, fluid, changeable and changing market.

The existence of a block of stock in the hands of a single shareholder or a group with loyalty to each other does have real consequences to the financial value of "minority" stock. The law offers some protection to such shares through the imposition of a fiduciary duty upon controlling shareholders. But here, effectuation of the merger would not have subjected Time shareholders to the risks and consequences of holders of minority shares. This is a reflection of the fact that no control passed to anyone in the transaction contemplated. The shareholders of Time would have "suffered" dilution, of course, but they would suffer the same type of dilution upon the public distribution of new stock. [Accordingly, the Chancellor held that *Revlon* obligations were not triggered by the Warner transaction.]

What constitutes a change in control? Modern corporation statutes address this problem in determining when shareholders in a corporation are entitled to vote in an acquisition transaction. For example, both Cal. Gen. Corp. Law §1201(b) (1999) and Del. Gen. Corp. Code §251(f)(3) (1999) deny shareholders in a constituent corporation the right to vote if they retain 80 percent of the voting power in the surviving corporation. Chancellor Allen rejected this approach in favor of a case-by-case inquiry into effective control: did the transaction shift voting control from one control group to another or, in a corporation that did not have a control group, did the transaction create one? Under this approach, the issue is not whether the transaction involved a merger of equals, but, following *Macmillan*, whether a change in control occurred. When "the shares of both constituent corporations are widely held, corporate control can be expected to remain unaffected by a stock for stock merger. . . . Control of both remained in a large, fluid, changeable and changing market."

The Delaware Supreme Court then took up the issue on appeal.

Paramount Communications, Inc. v. Time Inc.
571 A.2d 1140 (Del. S. Ct. 1990)

HORSEY, J.: . . . The Court of Chancery posed the pivotal question presented by this case to be: Under what circumstances must a board of directors abandon an in-place plan of corporate development in order to provide its shareholders with the option to elect and realize an immediate control premium? As applied to this case, the question becomes: Did Time's board, having developed a strategic plan of global expansion to be launched through a business combination with Warner, come under a fiduciary duty to jettison its plan and put the corporation's future in the hands of its shareholders?

While we affirm the result reached by the Chancellor, we think it unwise to place undue emphasis upon long-term versus short-term corporate strategy. Two key predicates underpin our analysis. First, Delaware law imposes on a board of directors the duty to manage the business and affairs of the corporation. 8 Del. C. Sec. 141(a). This broad mandate includes a conferred authority to set a corporate course of action, including time frame, designed to enhance corporate profitability.[12] Thus, the question of "long-term" versus "short-term" values is largely irrelevant because directors, generally, are obliged to charter a course for a corporation which is in its best interests without regard to a fixed investment horizon. Second, absent a limited set of circumstances as defined under *Revlon*, a board of directors, while always required to act in an informed manner, is not under any per se duty to maximize shareholder value in the short term, even in the context of a takeover. In our view, the pivotal question presented by this case is: "Did Time, by entering into the proposed merger with Warner, put itself up for sale?" A resolution of that issue through application of *Revlon* has a significant bearing upon the resolution of the derivative *Unocal* issue.

A. . . . [T]he Chancellor found the original Time-Warner merger agreement not to constitute a "change of control" and concluded that the transaction did not trigger *Revlon* duties. The Chancellor's conclusion is premised on a finding that "[b]efore the merger agreement was signed, control of the corporation existed in a fluid aggregation of unaffiliated shareholders representing a voting majority — in other words, in the market." The Chancellor's findings of fact are supported by the record and his conclusion is correct as a matter of law. However, we premise our rejection of plaintiffs' *Revlon* claim on broader grounds, namely, the absence of any substantial evidence to conclude that Time's board, in negotiating with Warner, made the dissolution or breakup of the corporate entity inevitable, as was the case in *Revlon*.

Under Delaware law there are, generally speaking and without excluding other possibilities, two circumstances which may implicate *Revlon* duties. The first, and clearer one, is when a corporation initiates an active bidding process seeking to sell itself or to effect a business reorganization involving a clear break-up of the company. See, e.g., Mills Acquisition Co. v. Macmillan, Inc., Del. Supr., 559 A.2d 1261 (1988). However, *Revlon* duties may also be triggered where, in response to a bidder's offer, a target abandons its long-term strategy and seeks an alternative transaction also involving the breakup of the company.[13] Thus, in *Revlon*, when the

---

12. In endorsing this finding, we tacitly accept the Chancellor's conclusion that it is not a breach of faith for directors to determine that the present stock market price of shares is not representative of true value or that there may indeed be several market values for any corporation's stock. We have so held in another context. See *Van Gorkum*, 488 A.2d at 876.

13. As we stated in *Revlon*, in both such cases, "[t]he duty of the board [has] changed from the preservation of . . . [the] corporate entity to the maximization of the company's value at a sale for the stockholder's benefit. . . . [The board] no longer face[s] threats to corporate policy and effectiveness, or to the stockholders' interests, from a grossly inadequate bid." Revlon v. MacAndrews & Forbes Holdings, Inc., Del. Supr., 506 A.2d 173, 182 (1986).

board responded to Pantry Pride's offer by contemplating a "bust-up" sale of assets in a leveraged acquisition, we imposed upon the board a duty to maximize immediate shareholder value and an obligation to auction the company fairly. If, however, the board's reaction to a hostile tender offer is found to constitute only a defensive response and not an abandonment of the corporation's continued existence, *Revlon* duties are not triggered, though *Unocal* duties attach.[14] See, e.g., Ivanhoe Partners v. Newmont Mining Corp., Del. Supr., 535 A.2d 1334, 1345 (1987).

The plaintiffs insist that even though the original Time-Warner agreement may not have worked "an objective change of control," the transaction made a "sale" of Time inevitable. Plaintiffs rely on the subjective intent of Time's board of directors and principally upon certain board members' expressions of concern that the Warner transaction *might* be viewed as effectively putting Time up for sale. Plaintiffs argue that the use of a lock-up agreement, a no-shop clause, and so-called "dry-up" agreements prevented shareholders from obtaining a control premium in the immediate future and thus violated *Revlon.*

We agree with the Chancellor that such evidence is entirely insufficient to invoke *Revlon* duties; and we decline to extend *Revlon*'s application to corporate transactions simply because they might be construed as putting a corporation either "in play" or "up for sale." The adoption of structural safety devices alone does not trigger *Revlon.*[15] Rather, as the Chancellor stated, such devices are properly subject to a *Unocal* analysis. . . .

---

1. *The dissolution or breakup test.* The Delaware Supreme Court seems to have rejected the Chancery Court's "change in control" test. While stating that the Chancellor's conclusion that a change in control had not occurred because control remained in the market was "correct as a matter of law," the court did not let the matter rest there. It went on to "premise our rejection of plaintiffs' *Revlon* claim on different grounds, namely, the absence of any substantial evidence that Time's board, in negotiating with Warner, made the dissolution or breakup of the corporate entity inevitable, as was the case in *Revlon.*" What does it mean for the Supreme Court to premise its decision on "different grounds" from the Chancellor's? Must a transaction involve a dissolution or breakup to trigger *Revlon* regardless of whether control shifts? Why would the court have sought different

---

14. Within the auction process, any action taken by the board must be reasonably related to the threat posed or reasonable in relation to the advantage sought, see Mills Acquisition Co. v. Macmillan, Inc., Del. Supr., 559 A.2d 1261, 1288 (1988). Thus, a *Unocal* analysis may be appropriate when a corporation is in a *Revlon* situation and *Revlon* duties may be triggered by a defensive action taken in response to a hostile offer. Since *Revlon*, we have stated that differing treatment of various bidders is not actionable when such action reasonably relates to achieving the best price available for the stockholders *Macmillan,* 559 A.2d at 1286-87.

15. Although the legality of the various safety devices adopted to protect the original agreement is not a central issue, there is substantial evidence to support each of the trial court's related conclusions. Thus, the court found that the concept of the Share Exchange Agreement predated any takeover threat by Paramount and had been adopted for a rational business purpose: to deter Time and Warner from being "put in play" by their March 4 Agreement. The court further found that Time had adopted the "no-shop" clause at Warner's insistence and for Warner's protection. Finally, although certain aspects of the "dry-up" agreements were suspect on their face, we concur in the Chancellor's view that in this case they were inconsequential.

grounds if the Chancellor's "change in control" test was correct and sufficient to resolve the case?

2. *Is the "initiation of active bidding or breakup" standard coherent?* Suppose that 62 percent of Time's voting stock was to be acquired by a single individual in a friendly transaction that ensured that Time would not be broken up or dissolved, perhaps by specifying a supermajority vote for such actions. Would the Delaware Supreme Court apply the business judgment rule to the Time board's decision to prevent any competitive bidding by giving the acquiring individual so favorable a lockup that all other potential bidders were deterred? Alternatively, suppose Time was to be acquired in a management buyout on the same terms as in the previous hypothetical. Under the Supreme Court's "active bidding or breakup" standard, would *Revlon* be triggered? What of *Macmillan*'s specific statement that *Revlon* was triggered by management buyout?

3. STRATEGIC ALLIANCES: PARAMOUNT TRIES AGAIN

Time had a strategic vision in its acquisition of Warner, but so too did Paramount have a strategic vision in its pursuit of Time. Time would have given Paramount access to the cable television industry, so it was not surprising that after losing the contest over Time, Paramount sought another means of access. Mimicking what it thought was the winning strategy in *Time*, Paramount negotiated a strategic acquisition with Viacom, a major cable television operator. The transaction, which contemplated neither a breakup nor a dissolution of Paramount, seemed to be structured to avoid what the Delaware Supreme Court had identified in *Time* as "*Revlon*'s trigger."

Paramount Communications, Inc. v. QVC Network, Inc.
637 A.2d 34 (1994)

Veasey, C.J.: In this appeal we review an order of the Court of Chancery (the "November 24 Order"), preliminarily enjoining certain defensive measures designed to facilitate a so-called strategic alliance between Viacom Inc. ("Viacom") and Paramount Communications Inc. ("Paramount") approved by the board of directors of Paramount (the "Paramount Board" or the "Paramount directors") and to thwart an unsolicited, more valuable, tender offer by QVC Network Inc. ("QVC"). In affirming, we hold that the sale of control in this case, which is at the heart of the proposed strategic alliance, implicates enhanced judicial scrutiny of the conduct of the Paramount Board under Unocal Corp. v. Mesa Petroleum Co., Del. Supr., 493 A.2d 946 (1985), and Revlon, Inc. v. MacAndrews & Forbes Holdings, Inc., Del. Supr., 506 A.2d 173 (1986). We further hold that the conduct of the Paramount Board was not reasonable as to process or result. . . .

I. Facts

. . . Paramount is a Delaware corporation with its principal offices in New York City. Approximately 118 million shares of Paramount's common stock are outstanding and traded on the New York Stock Exchange. The majority of Paramount's stock is publicly held by numerous unaffiliated investors. Paramount owns and operates a diverse group of entertainment businesses, including motion picture and television studios, book publishers, professional sports teams, and amusement parks.

There are 15 persons serving on the Paramount Board. Four directors are officer-employees of Paramount. . . . Paramount's 11 outside directors are distinguished and experienced business persons who are present or former senior executives of public corporations or financial institutions.

Viacom is a Delaware corporation with its headquarters in Massachusetts. Viacom is controlled by Sumner M. Redstone ("Redstone"), its Chairman and Chief Executive Officer, who owns indirectly approximately 85.2 percent of Viacom's voting Class A stock and approximately 69.2 percent of Viacom's non-voting Class B stock through National Amusements, Inc. ("NAI"), an entity 91.7 percent owned by Redstone. Viacom has a wide range of entertainment operations, including a number of well-known cable television channels such as MTV, Nickelodeon, Showtime, and The Movie Channel. Viacom's equity co-investors in the Paramount-Viacom transaction include NYNEX Corporation and Blockbuster Entertainment Corporation.

QVC is a Delaware corporation. . . . QVC has several large stockholders, including Liberty Media Corporation, Comcast Corporation, Advance Publications, Inc., and Cox Enterprises Inc. Barry Diller ("Diller"), the Chairman and Chief Executive Officer of QVC, is also a substantial stockholder. QVC sells a variety of merchandise through a televised shopping channel. QVC has several equity co-investors in its proposed combination with Paramount including BellSouth Corporation and Comcast Corporation.

Beginning in the late 1980s, Paramount investigated the possibility of acquiring or merging with other companies in the entertainment, media, or communications industry. Paramount considered such transactions to be desirable, and perhaps necessary, in order to keep pace with competitors in the rapidly evolving field of entertainment and communications. Consistent with its goal of strategic expansion, Paramount made a tender offer for Time Inc. in 1989, but was ultimately unsuccessful. See Paramount Communications, Inc. v. Time Inc., Del. Supr., 571 A.2d 1140 (1990) ("*Time-Warner*").

Although Paramount had considered a possible combination of Paramount and Viacom as early as 1990, . . . serious negotiations began taking place in early July [1993].

It was tentatively agreed that [Martin Davis, Paramount's CEO] would be the chief executive officer and Redstone would be the controlling stockholder of the combined company, but the parties could not reach agreement on the merger price and the terms of a stock option to be granted to Viacom. With respect to price, Viacom offered a package of cash and stock (primarily Viacom Class B nonvoting stock) with a market value of approximately $61 per share, but Paramount wanted at least $70 per share. . . . [After a period of disagreement] the parties negotiated in earnest in early September, and performed due diligence with the assistance of their financial advisors, Lazard Freres & Co., ("Lazard") for Paramount and Smith Barney for Viacom. On September 9, 1993, the Paramount Board was informed about the status of the negotiations and was provided information by Lazard, including an analysis of the proposed transaction.

On September 12, 1993, the Paramount Board met again and unanimously approved the Original Merger Agreement whereby Paramount would merge with and into Viacom. The terms of the merger provided that each share of Paramount common stock would be converted into 0.10 shares of Viacom Class A voting stock, 0.90 shares of Viacom Class B nonvoting stock, and $9.10 in cash. In addition, the Paramount Board agreed to amend its "poison pill" Rights Agreement to exempt the proposed merger with Viacom. The Original Merger Agreement also contained several provisions designed to make it more difficult for a potential competing bid to succeed. We focus . . . on three of these defensive provisions: a "no-shop" provision (the "No-Shop Provision"), the Termination Fee, and the Stock Option Agreement.

First, under the No-Shop Provision, the Paramount Board agreed that Paramount would not solicit, encourage, discuss, negotiate, or endorse any competing transactions unless: (a) a third party "makes an unsolicited written, bona fide proposal, which is not subject to any material contingencies relating to financing"; and (b) the Paramount Board determines that discussions or negotiations with the third party are necessary for the Paramount Board to comply with its fiduciary duties.

Second, under the Termination Fee provision, Viacom would receive a $100 million termination fee if: (a) Paramount terminated the Original Merger Agreement because of a competing transaction; (b) Paramount's stockholders did not approve the merger; or (c) the Paramount Board recommended a competing transaction.

The third and most significant deterrent device was the Stock Option Agreement, which granted to Viacom an option to purchase approximately 19.9 percent (23,699,000 shares) of Paramount's outstanding common stock at $69.14 per share if any of the triggering events for the Termination Fee occurred. In addition to the customary terms that are normally associated with a stock option, the Stock Option Agreement contained two provisions that were both unusual and highly beneficial to Viacom: (a) Viacom was permitted to pay for the shares with a senior subordinated note of questionable marketability instead of cash, thereby avoiding the need to raise the $1.6 billion purchase price (the "Note Feature"), and (b) Viacom could elect to require Paramount to pay Viacom in cash a sum equal to the difference between the purchase price and the market price of Paramount's stock (the "Put Feature"). Because the Stock Option Agreement was not "capped" to limit its maximum dollar value, it had the potential to reach (and in this case did reach) unreasonable levels.

After the execution of the Original Merger Agreement and the Stock Option Agreement on September 12, 1993, Paramount and Viacom announced their proposed merger. In a number of public statements, the parties indicated that the pending transaction was a virtual certainty. Redstone described it as a "marriage" that would "never be torn asunder" and stated that only a "nuclear attack" could break the deal. Redstone also called Diller and John Malone of Tele-Communications Inc., a major stockholder of QVC, to dissuade them from making a competing bid.

Despite these attempts to discourage a competing bid, Diller sent a letter to Davis on September 20, 1993, proposing a merger in which QVC would acquire Paramount for approximately $80 per share, consisting of 0.893 shares of QVC common stock and $30 in cash. QVC also expressed its eagerness to meet with Paramount to negotiate the details of a transaction. When the Paramount Board met on September 28, it was advised by Davis that the Original Merger Agreement prohibited Paramount from having discussions with QVC (or anyone else) unless certain conditions were satisfied. In particular, QVC had to supply evidence that its proposal was not subject to financing contingencies. The Paramount Board was also provided information from Lazard describing QVC and its proposal.

On October 5, 1993, QVC provided Paramount with evidence of QVC's financing. The Paramount Board then held another meeting on October 11, and decided to authorize management to meet with QVC. Davis also informed the Paramount Board that Booz-Allen & Hamilton ("Booz-Allen"), a management consulting firm, had been retained to assess, *inter alia*, the incremental earnings potential from a Paramount-Viacom merger and a Paramount-QVC merger. Discussions proceeded slowly, however, due to a delay in Paramount signing a confidentiality agreement. In response to Paramount's request for information, QVC provided two binders of documents to Paramount on October 20.

On October 21, 1993, QVC filed this action and publicly announced an $80 cash tender offer for 51 percent of Paramount's outstanding shares (the "QVC tender offer"). Each remaining share of Paramount common stock would be converted into 1.42857 shares of QVC common stock in a second-step merger. The tender offer was conditioned on, among other things, the invalidation of the Stock Option Agreement, which was worth over $200 million by that point.[5] QVC contends that it had to commence a tender offer because of the slow pace of the merger discussions and the need to begin seeking clearance under federal antitrust laws.

Confronted by QVC's hostile bid, which on its face offered over $10 per share more than the consideration provided by the Original Merger Agreement, Viacom realized that it would need to raise its bid in order to remain competitive. Within hours after QVC's tender offer was announced, Viacom entered into discussions with Paramount concerning a revised transaction. These discussions led to serious negotiations concerning a comprehensive amendment to the original Paramount-Viacom transaction. In effect, the opportunity for a "new deal" with Viacom was at hand for the Paramount Board. With the QVC hostile bid offering greater value to the Paramount stockholders, the Paramount Board had considerable leverage with Viacom.

At a special meeting on October 24, 1993, the Paramount Board approved the Amended Merger Agreement and an amendment to the Stock Option Agreement. The Amended Merger Agreement was, however, essentially the same as the Original Merger Agreement, except that it included a few new provisions. One provision related to an $80 per share cash tender offer by Viacom for 51 percent of Paramount's stock, and another changed the merger consideration so that each share of Paramount would be converted into 0.20409 shares of Viacom Class A voting stock, 1.08317 shares of Viacom Class B nonvoting stock, and 0.20408 shares of a new series of Viacom convertible preferred stock. The Amended Merger Agreement also added a provision giving Paramount the right not to amend its Rights Agreement to exempt Viacom if the Paramount Board determined that such an amendment would be inconsistent with its fiduciary duties because another offer constituted a "better alternative." Finally, the Paramount Board was given the power to terminate the Amended Merger Agreement if it withdrew its recommendation of the Viacom transaction or recommended a competing transaction.

---

5. By November 15, 1993, the value of the Stock Option Agreement had increased to nearly $500 million based on the $90 QVC bid.

Although the Amended Merger Agreement offered more consideration to the Paramount stockholders and somewhat more flexibility to the Paramount Board than did the Original Merger Agreement, the defensive measures designed to make a competing bid more difficult were not removed or modified. In particular, there is no evidence in the record that Paramount sought to use its newly-acquired leverage to eliminate or modify the No-Shop Provision, the Termination Fee, or the Stock Option Agreement when the subject of amending the Original Merger Agreement was on the table.

Viacom's tender offer commenced on October 25, 1993, and QVC's tender offer was formally launched on October 27, 1993. Diller sent a letter to the Paramount Board on October 28 requesting an opportunity to negotiate with Paramount. . . . [A] meeting, held on November 1, was not very fruitful, however, after QVC's proposed guidelines for a "fair bidding process" were rejected by Paramount on the ground that "auction procedures" were inappropriate and contrary to Paramount's contractual obligations to Viacom.

On November 6, 1993, Viacom unilaterally raised its tender offer price to $85 per share in cash and offered a comparable increase in the value of the securities being proposed in the second-step merger. At a telephonic meeting held later that day, the Paramount Board agreed to recommend Viacom's higher bid to Paramount's stockholders.

QVC responded to Viacom's higher bid on November 12 by increasing its tender offer to $90 per share and by increasing the securities for its second-step merger by a similar amount. . . . At its meeting on November 15, 1993, the Paramount Board determined that the new QVC offer was not in the best interests of the stockholders. The purported basis for this conclusion was that QVC's bid was excessively conditional. The Paramount Board did not communicate with QVC regarding the status of the conditions because it believed that the No-Shop Provision prevented such communication in the absence of firm financing. Several Paramount directors also testified that they believed the Viacom transaction would be more advantageous to Paramount's future business prospects than a QVC transaction. Although a number of materials were distributed to the Paramount Board describing the Viacom and QVC transactions, the only quantitative analysis of the consideration to be received by the stockholders under each proposal was based on then-current market prices of the securities involved, not on the anticipated value of such securities at the time when the stockholders would receive them.[8]

The preliminary injunction hearing in this case took place on November 16, 1993. On November 19, Diller wrote to the Paramount Board to inform it that QVC had obtained financing commitments for its tender offer and that there was no antitrust obstacle to the offer. On November 24, 1993, the Court of Chancery issued its decision granting a preliminary injunction in favor of QVC and the plaintiff stockholders. This appeal followed.

---

8. The market prices of Viacom's and QVC's stock were poor measures of their actual values because such prices constantly fluctuated depending upon which company was perceived to be the more likely to acquire Paramount

II. *Applicable Principles of Established Delaware Law*

[Delaware law recognizes] the fundamental principle that the management of the business and affairs of a Delaware corporation is entrusted to its directors, who are the duly elected and authorized representatives of the stockholders. Under normal circumstances, neither the courts nor the stockholders should interfere with the managerial decisions of the directors. The business judgment rule embodies the deference to which such decisions are entitled.

Nevertheless, there are rare situations which mandate that a court take a more direct and active role in overseeing the decisions made and actions taken by directors. In these situations, a court subjects the directors' conduct to enhanced scrutiny to ensure that it is reasonable. . . . The case at bar implicates . . . such circumstances: the approval of a transaction resulting in a sale of control. . . .

A.   The Significance of a Sale or Change of Control

When a majority of a corporation's voting shares are acquired by a single person or entity, or by a cohesive group acting together, there is a significant diminution in the voting power of those who thereby become minority stockholders. Under the statutory framework of the General Corporation Law, many of the most fundamental corporate changes can be implemented only if they are approved by a majority vote of the stockholders. Such actions include elections of directors, amendments to the certificate of incorporation, mergers, consolidations, sales of all or substantially all of the assets of the corporation, and dissolution. 8 Del. C. §§211, 242, 251-258, 263, 271, 275. Because of the overriding importance of voting rights, this court and the Court of Chancery have consistently acted to protect stockholders from unwarranted interference with such rights.

In the absence of devices protecting the minority stockholders,[12] stockholder votes are likely to become mere formalities where there is a majority stockholder. For example, minority stockholders can be deprived of a continuing equity interest in their corporation by means of a cash-out merger. Absent effective protective provisions, minority stockholders must rely for protection solely on the fiduciary duties owed to them by the directors and the majority stockholder, since the minority stockholders have lost the power to influence corporate direction through the ballot. The acquisition of majority status and the consequent privilege of exerting the powers of majority ownership come at a price. That price is usually a control premium which recognizes not only the value of a control block of shares, but also compensates the minority stockholders for their resulting loss of voting power.

In the case before us, the public stockholders (in the aggregate) currently own a majority of Paramount's voting stock. Control of the corporation is not vested in a single person, entity, or group, but vested in the fluid aggregation of unaffiliated stockholders. In the event the Paramount-Viacom transaction is consummated, the public stockholders will receive cash and a minority equity voting position in the surviving corporation. Following such consummation, there will be a controlling stockholder who will have the voting power to: (a) elect directors; (b) cause a break-up of the corporation; (c) merge it with another company; (d) cash-out the public stockholders; (e) amend the certificate of incorporation; (f) sell all or

---

12. Examples of such protective provisions are supermajority voting provisions, majority of the minority requirements, etc. . . .

substantially all of the corporate assets; or (g) otherwise alter materially the nature of the corporation and the public stockholders' interests. Irrespective of the present Paramount Board's vision of a long-term strategic alliance with Viacom, the proposed sale of control would provide the new controlling stockholder with the power to alter that vision.

Because of the intended sale of control, the Paramount-Viacom transaction has economic consequences of considerable significance to the Paramount stockholders. Once control has shifted, the current Paramount stockholders will have no leverage in the future to demand another control premium. As a result, the Paramount stockholders are entitled to receive, and should receive, a control premium and/or protective devices of significant value. There being no such protective provisions in the Viacom-Paramount transaction, the Paramount directors had an obligation to take the maximum advantage of the current opportunity to realize for stockholders the best value reasonably available.

B. The Obligations of Directors in a Sale or Change of Control Transaction

The consequences of a sale of control impose special obligations on the directors of a corporation. In particular, they have the obligation of acting reasonably to seek the transaction offering the best value reasonably available to the stockholders. The courts will apply enhanced scrutiny to ensure that the directors have acted reasonably. The obligations of the directors and the enhanced scrutiny of the courts are well-established by the decisions of this court. . . .

In the sale of control context, the directors must focus on one primary objective—to secure the transaction offering the best value reasonably available for the stockholder—and they must exercise their fiduciary duties to further that end. . . . In pursuing this objective, the directors must be especially diligent. In particular, this court has stressed the importance of the board being adequately informed in negotiating a sale of control: "The need for adequate information is central to the enlightened evaluation of a transaction that a board must make." *Barkan*, 567 A.2d at 1287. . . .

Barkan teaches some of the methods by which a board can fulfill its obligation to seek the best value reasonably available to the stockholders. 567 A.2d at 1286-87. These methods are designed to determine the existence and viability of possible alternatives. They include conducting an auction, canvassing the market, etc.

Delaware law recognizes that there is "no single blueprint" that directors must follow. In determining which alternative provides the best value for the stockholders, a board of directors is not limited to considering only the amount of cash involved, and is not required to ignore totally its view of the future value of a strategic alliance. Instead, the directors should analyze the entire situation and evaluate in a disciplined manner the consideration being offered. Where stock or other non-cash consideration is involved, the board should try to quantify its value, if feasible, to achieve an objective comparison of the alternatives.[14] In addition, the board may assess a variety of practical considerations relating to each alternative, including [the quality of the offer, including adequacy, fairness, and

---

14. When assessing the value of non-cash consideration, a board should focus on its value as of the date it will be received by the stockholders. Normally, such value will be determined with the assistance of experts using generally accepted methods of valuation. See In re RJR Nabisco, Inc. Shareholders Litig., Del. Ch., C.A. No. 10389, Allen, C. (Jan. 31, 1989), *reprinted at* 14 Del. J. Corp. L 1132, 1161.

feasibility; method of financing; etc.]. . . . These considerations are important because the selection of one alternative may permanently foreclose other opportunities. While the assessment of these factors may be complex, the board's goal is straightforward: Having informed themselves of all material information reasonably available, the directors must decide which alternative is most likely to offer the best value reasonably available to the stockholders.

C. Enhanced Judicial Scrutiny of a Sale of Change of Control Transaction

Board action in the circumstances presented here is subject to enhanced scrutiny. Such scrutiny is mandated by: (a) the threatened diminution of the current stockholders' voting power; (b) the fact that an asset belonging to public stockholders (a control premium) is being sold and may never be available again; and (c) the traditional concern of Delaware courts for actions which impair or impede stockholder voting rights. The *Macmillan* decision articulates a specific two-part test for analyzing board action where competing bidders are not treated equally:[16] "In the face of disparate treatment, the trial court must first examine whether the directors properly perceived that shareholder interests were enhanced. In any event the board's action must be reasonable in relation to the advantage sought to be achieved, or conversely, to the threat which a particular bid allegedly poses to stockholder interests."

The key features of an enhanced scrutiny test are: (a) a judicial determination regarding the adequacy of the decisionmaking process employed by the directors, including the information on which the directors based their decision; and (b) a judicial examination of the reasonableness of the directors' action in light of the circumstances then existing. The directors have the burden of proving that they were adequately informed and acted reasonably. Although an enhanced scrutiny test involves a review of the reasonableness of the substantive merits of a board's actions,[17] a court should not ignore the complexity of the directors' task in a sale of control. There are many business and financial considerations implicated in investigating and selecting the best value reasonably available. The board of directors is the corporate decisionmaking body best equipped to make these judgments. Accordingly, a court applying enhanced judicial scrutiny should be deciding whether the directors made a *reasonable* decision, not a *perfect* decision. If a board selected one of several reasonable alternatives, a court should not second-guess that choice even though it might have decided otherwise or subsequent events may have cast doubt on the board's determination. Thus, courts will not substitute their business judgment for that of the directors, but will determine if the directors' decision was, on balance, within a range of reasonableness.

16. Before this test is invoked, "the plaintiff must show, and the trial court must find, that the directors of the target company treated one or more of the respective bidders on unequal terms." *Macmillan*, 559 A.2d at 1288.

17. It is to be remembered that, in cases where the traditional business judgment rule is applicable and the board acted with due care, in good faith, and in the honest belief that they [were] acting in the best interests of the stockholders (which is not this case), the court gives great deference to the substance of the directors' decision and will not invalidate the decision, will not examine its reasonableness, and "will not substitute our views for those of the board if the latter's decision can be 'attributed to any rational business purpose.'" *Unocal*, 493 A.2d at 949 (quoting Sinclair Oil Corp. v. Levien, Del. Supr., 280 A.2d 717, 720 (1971)). See *Aronson v. Lewis*, 473 A.2d at 812.

D. *Revlon* and *Time-Warner* Distinguished

The Paramount defendants and Viacom assert that the fiduciary obligations and the enhanced judicial scrutiny discussed above are not implicated in this case in the absence of a "break-up" of the corporation, and that the order granting the preliminary injunction should be reversed. This argument is based on their erroneous interpretation of our decision in . . . *Time-Warner*. . . .

Although *Macmillan* and *Barkan* are clear in holding that a change of control imposes on directors the obligation to obtain the best value reasonably available to the stockholders, the Paramount defendants have interpreted our decision in *Time-Warner* as requiring a corporate break-up in order for that obligation to apply. The facts in *Time-Warner*, however, were quite different from the facts of this case, and refute Paramount's position here. In *Time-Warner*, the Chancellor held that there was no change of control in the original stock-for-stock merger between Time and Warner because Time would be owned by a fluid aggregation of unaffiliated stockholders both before and after the merger. . . .

Moreover, the transaction actually consummated in Time-Warner was not a merger, as originally planned, but a sale of Warner's stock to Time.

In our affirmance of the Court of Chancery's well-reasoned decision, this Court held that "The Chancellor's findings of fact are supported by the record and his conclusion is correct as a matter of law." 571 A.2d at 1150. Nevertheless, the Paramount defendants here have argued that a break-up is a requirement and have focused on the following language in our *Time-Warner* decision:

> However, we premise our rejection of plaintiffs' *Revlon* claim on different grounds, namely, the absence of any substantial evidence to conclude that Time's board, in negotiating with Warner, made the dissolution or break-up of the corporate entity inevitable, as was the case in *Revlon*. Under Delaware law there are, generally speaking and without excluding other possibilities, two circumstances which may implicate *Revlon* duties. The first, and clearer one, is when a corporate initiates an active bidding process seeking to sell itself or to effect a business reorganization involving a clear break-up of the company. However, *Revlon* duties may also be triggered where, in response to a bidder's offer, a target abandons its long-term strategy and seeks an alternative transaction involving the breakup of the company.

Id. at 1150.

The Paramount defendants have misread the holding of *Time-Warner*. [O]ur decision in *Time-Warner* expressly states that the two general scenarios discussed in the above-quoted paragraph are not the only instances where "*Revlon* duties" may be implicated. The Paramount defendants' argument totally ignores the phrase "without excluding other possibilities." Moreover, the instant case is clearly within the first general scenario set forth in *Time-Warner*. The Paramount Board, albeit unintentionally, had "initiate[d] an active bidding process seeking to sell itself by agreeing to sell control of the corporation to Viacom in circumstances where another potential acquiror (QVC) was equally interested in being a bidder."

The Paramount defendants' position that both a change of control and a break-up are required must be rejected. Such a holding would unduly restrict the application of *Revlon*, is inconsistent with this Court's decisions in *Barkan* and *Macmillan*, and has no basis in policy. There are few events that have a more significant impact on the stockholders than a sale of control or a corporate break-up. Each event represents a fundamental (and perhaps irrevocable) change in the nature of the corporate enterprise from a practical standpoint. It is the significance of each of these events that justifies: (a) focusing on the directors' obligation to seek the best value reasonably available to the stockholders; and (b) requiring a close scrutiny of board action which could be contrary to the stockholders' interests.

Accordingly, when a corporation undertakes a transaction which will cause: (a) a change in corporate control; or (b) a break-up of the corporate entity, the directors' obligation is to seek the best value reasonably available to the stockholders. This obligation arises because the effect of the Viacom-Paramount transaction, if consummated, is to shift control of Paramount from the public stockholders to a controlling stockholder, Viacom. Neither *Time-Warner* nor any other decision of this court holds that a "break-up" of the company is essential to give rise to this obligation where there is a sale of control.

III. Breach of Fiduciary Duties by Paramount Board

A.   The Specific Obligations of the Paramount Board

Under the facts of this case, the Paramount directors had the obligation: (a) to be diligent and vigilant in examining critically the Paramount-Viacom transaction and the QVC tender offers; (b) to act in good faith; (c) to obtain, and act with due care on, all material information reasonably available, including information necessary to compare the two offers to determine which of these transactions, or an alternative course of action, would provide the best value reasonably available to the stockholders; and (d) to negotiate actively and in good faith with both Viacom and QVC to that end.

Having decided to sell control of the corporation, the Paramount directors were required to evaluate critically whether or not all material aspects of the Paramount-Viacom transaction (separately and in the aggregate) were reasonable and in the best interests of the Paramount stockholders in light of current circumstances, including: the change of control premium, the Stock Option Agreement, the Termination Fee, and coercive nature of both the Viacom and QVC tender offers, the No-Shop Provision, and the proposed disparate use of the Rights Agreement as to the Viacom and QVC tender offers, respectively.

These obligations necessarily implicated various issues, including the questions of whether or not those provisions and other aspects of the Paramount-Viacom transaction (separately and in the aggregate): (a) adversely affected the value provided to the Paramount stockholders; (b) inhibited or encouraged alternative bids; (c) were enforceable contractual obligations in light of the directors' fiduciary duties; and (d) in the end would advance or retard the Paramount directors' obligation to secure for the Paramount stockholders the best value reasonably available under the circumstances.

The Paramount defendants contend that they were precluded by certain contractual provisions, including the No-Shop Provision, from negotiating with QVC or seeking alternatives. Such provisions, whether or not they are presumptively valid in the abstract, may not validly define or limit the directors' fiduciary duties under Delaware law or prevent the Paramount directors from carrying out their fiduciary duties under Delaware law. To the extent such provisions are inconsistent with those duties, they are invalid and unenforceable.

Since the Paramount directors had already decided to sell control, they had an obligation to continue their search for the best value reasonably available to the stockholders. This continuing obligation included the responsibility, at the October 24 board meeting and thereafter, to evaluate critically both the QVC tender offers and the Paramount-Viacom transaction to determine if: (a) the QVC tender offer was, or would continue to be, conditional; (b) the QVC tender offer could be improved; (c) the Viacom tender offer or other aspects of the Paramount-Viacom transaction could be improved; (d) each of the respective offers would be reasonably likely to come to closure, and under what circumstances; (e) other material information was reasonably available for consideration by the Paramount directors; (f) there were viable and realistic alternative courses of action; and (g) the timing constraints could be managed so the directors could consider these matters carefully and deliberately.

B. The Breaches of Fiduciary Duty by the Paramount Board

The Paramount directors made the decision on September 12, 1993, that . . . a strategic merger with Viacom on the economic terms of the Original Merger Agreement was in the best interests of Paramount and its stockholders. Those terms provided a modest change of control premium to the stockholders. The directors also decided at that time that it was appropriate to agree to certain defensive measures (the Stock Option Agreement, the Termination Fee, and the No-Shop Provision) insisted upon by Viacom as part of that economic transaction. Those defensive measures, coupled with the sale of control and subsequent disparate treatment of competing bidders, implicated the judicial scrutiny of *Unocal, Revlon, Macmillan*, and their progeny. We conclude that the Paramount directors' process was not reasonable, and the result achieved for the stockholders was not reasonable. . . .

When entering into the Original Merger Agreement, and thereafter, the Paramount Board clearly gave insufficient attention to the potential consequences of the defensive measures demanded by Viacom. The Stock Option Agreement had a number of unusual and potentially "draconian"[19] provisions, including the Note Feature and the Put Feature. Furthermore, the Termination Fee, whether or not unreasonable by itself, clearly made Paramount less attractive to other bidders, when coupled with the Stock Option Agreement. Finally, the No-Shop Provision inhibited the Paramount Board's ability to negotiate with other potential bidders, particularly QVC, which had already expressed an interest in Paramount.[20]

Throughout the applicable time period . . . QVC's interest in Paramount provided the opportunity for the Paramount Board to seek significantly higher

---

19. . . . We express no opinion whether a stock option agreement of essentially this magnitude, but with a reasonable "cap" and without the Note and Put Features, would be valid or invalid under other circumstances. . . .

20. We express no opinion whether certain aspects of the No-Shop Provision here could be valid in another context. Whether or not it could validly have operated here at an early stage solely to prevent Paramount from actively "shopping" the company, it could not prevent the Paramount directors from carrying out their fiduciary duties in considering unsolicited bids or in negotiating for the best value reasonably available to the stockholders. *Macmillan*, 559 A.2d at 1287. As we said in *Barkan:* "Where a board has no reasonable basis upon which to judge the adequacy of a contemplated transaction, a no-shop restriction gives rise to the inference that the board seeks to forestall competing bids." 567 A.2d at 1288. See also *Revlon*, 506 A.2d at 184 (holding that "[t]he no-shop provision, like the lockup option, while not per se illegal, is impermissible under the Unocal standards when a board's primary duty becomes that of an auctioneer responsible for selling the company to the highest bidder").

value for the Paramount stockholders.... QVC persistently demonstrated its intention to meet and exceed the Viacom offers, and frequently expressed its willingness to negotiate possible further increases.

The Paramount directors had the opportunity in the October 23-24 time frame, when the Original Merger Agreement was renegotiated, to [act] to modify the improper defensive measures as well as to improve the economic terms of the Paramount-Viacom transaction. Under the circumstances ... it should have been clear to the Paramount Board that the Stock Option Agreement, coupled with the Termination Fee and the No-Shop Clause, were impeding the realization of the best value reasonably available to the Paramount stockholders. Nevertheless, the Paramount Board made no effort to eliminate or modify these counterproductive devices, and instead continued to cling to its vision of a strategic alliance with Viacom. Moreover, based on advice from the Paramount management, the Paramount directors considered the QVC offer to be "conditional" and asserted that they were precluded by the No-Shop Provision from seeking more information from, or negotiating with, QVC.

By November 12, 1993, the value of the revised QVC offer on its face exceeded that of the Viacom offer by over $1 billion. ... This significant disparity of value cannot be justified on the basis of the directors' vision of future strategy, primarily because the change of control would supplant the authority of the current Paramount Board to continue to hold and implement their strategic vision in any meaningful way. Moreover, their uninformed process had deprived their strategic vision of much of its credibility. See *Van Gorkum*, 488 A.2d at 872.

When the Paramount directors met on November 15 to consider QVC's increased tender offer, they remained prisoners of their own misconceptions and missed opportunities to eliminate the restrictions they had imposed on themselves. Yet, it was not "too late" to reconsider negotiating with QVC. The circumstances existing on November 15 made it clear that the defensive measures, taken as a whole, were problematic: (a) the No-Shop Provision could not define or limit their fiduciary duties; (b) the Stock Option Agreement had become "draconian"; and (c) the Termination Fee, in context with all the circumstances, was similarly deterring the realization of possibly higher bids. Nevertheless, the Paramount directors remained paralyzed by their uninformed belief that the QVC offer was "illusory." This final opportunity to negotiate on the stockholders' behalf and to fulfill their obligation to seek the best value reasonably available was thereby squandered.

IV. Viacom's Claim of Vested Contract Rights

Viacom argues that it had certain "vested" contract rights with respect to the No-Shop Provision and the Stock Option Agreement. In effect, Viacom's argument is that the Paramount directors could enter into an agreement in violation of their fiduciary duties and then render Paramount, and ultimately its stockholders, liable for failing to carry out an agreement in violation of those duties. Viacom's protestations about vested rights are without merit. This court has found that those defensive measures were improperly designed to deter potential bidders, and that such measures do not meet the reasonableness test to which they must be subjected. They are consequently invalid and unenforceable under the facts of this case.

The No-Shop Provision could not validly define or limit the fiduciary duties of the Paramount directors. To the extent that a contract, or a provision thereof, purports to require a board to act or not act in such a fashion as to limit the exercise of fiduciary duties, it is invalid and unenforceable. . . . [T]he Paramount directors could not contract away their fiduciary obligations. Since the No-Shop Provision was invalid, Viacom never had any vested contract rights. . . .

As discussed previously, the Stock Option Agreement contained several "draconian" aspects, including the Note Feature and the Put Feature. While we have held that lock-up options are not per se illegal, no options with similar features have ever been upheld by this court. Under the circumstances of this case, the Stock Option Agreement clearly is invalid. Accordingly, Viacom never had any vested contract rights in that Agreement. . . .

---

1. *Change in control as* Revlon *'s trigger.* In *Paramount*, the Delaware Supreme Court retreated from the active bidding or breakup standard it seemingly announced in *Time*, returning instead to the "change in control" test framed by the Chancellor's opinion in that case. The court met Paramount's claim that it had dutifully followed the *Time* court's "different ground" by commenting that Paramount's lawyers "misread the holding of *Time-Warner*." Do you agree? The court points out that in *Time* it qualified the active bidding or breakup language with the phrase "without excluding other possibilities." The court also notes that the Paramount board, in fact, "albeit unintentionally, had 'initiated an active bidding process seeking to sell itself' by agreeing to sell control of the corporation to Viacom in circumstances where another potential acquiror (QVC) was equally interested in being a bidder." Does this mean that even if a friendly transaction is not itself a change in control, the fact that another party wants to bid is sufficient to meet the active bidding test? If so, why didn't Paramount's willingness to bid for Time unintentionally initiate an active bidding process in *Time*?

After *QVC*, what constitutes a change in control? At one extreme, some transactions make it impossible for target shareholders to receive a premium for control because an individual shareholder or group has absolute voting control; a minority shareholder will receive a premium only if the controlling shareholder so chooses. This is the *QVC* setting. At the other extreme are transactions like Time's acquisition of Warner, which did not create a control block, but whose size alone made a subsequent transaction more difficult. Somewhere in the middle are transactions like the management recapitalization in *Macmillan*, which placed with management 39.2 percent of the outstanding common stock, or the placement of a 15 percent block of preferred stock that carries the contractual right to block a change in voting control with a "white knight" such as Warren Buffett. A bright-line rule requiring proof of actual impossibility — that is, treating control as requiring 50.1 percent — would be inconsistent with *Macmillan*'s holding that placing a 39.2 percent block with management triggered *Revlon*. Given *Paramount*'s emphasis on the ability of one person to block minority shareholders' opportunity to receive a control premium, would the placement of blocking power with a "white knight" also amount to a change in control?

2. *The boundary between* Revlon *and the business judgment rule.* Is the board's duty to be adequately informed in order to discharge its obligation to secure the best

value for shareholders part of *Revlon's* intermediate standard or a component of the business judgment rule? Is it relevant that the court cites *Van Gorkom*, page 84 supra, a case decided before *Unocal* and *Revlon*, in which the court held that target directors had violated their duty of care by failing to be adequately informed in connection with the sale of the company? Does the extent of the board's obligation to be informed depend on whether the acquirer is controlled by a single individual? Suppose that the favored bidder in *QVC* was IBM instead of Viacom. Would the board have less of an obligation to be informed because control of IBM would remain in the market? Would the IBM transaction be governed by the business judgment rule which, according to footnote 17, prohibits judicial inquiry into the reasonableness of board action? Alternatively, is the business judgment rule more flexible than footnote 17 in *QVC* suggests, keying the extent of the court's inquiry to the importance of the transaction?

Does *QVC* favor a particular type of bidder? In high-technology industries, successful companies are frequently controlled by a company founder or by the company's original venture capital group. Should the law make it more difficult for a target company to protect a friendly transaction with an entrepreneurial company like Microsoft (controlled by Bill Gates) than with IBM? Does this seem like sensible industrial policy?

3. *Proportionality review of the target's decision to favor a bidder.* Can one protect a friendly transaction after *QVC*? Does the case limit lockups to "reasonable" amounts, and caution that unusual terms, like the put and note provisions, are risky? Are provisions that actually protect the transaction unlikely to measure up? Consider the answers to two questions provided by leading takeover lawyers Martin Lipton and Theodore Mirvis, 10 Questions and Answers Raised by Delaware's 'Paramount' Decision, N.Y. L.J. (Feb. 10, 1994):

> *Question:* Is there any way to do a deal that is viewed as a sale of control without shopping or conducting an auction?
>
> *Answer:* Yes. If on the basis of well considered expert advice the board determines that it is more likely to get the best value reasonably available by not shopping or auctioning, then the board can authorize the transaction. In this situation, the board should . . . avoid any no-shop, lock-up option or bust-up fee provision that would impede a third party from competing.
>
> *Question:* If a company enters into a strategic merger that is not a sale of control in which the company gets a premium and a third party makes a hostile takeover for the company at a higher value to shareholders, can the company . . . continue . . . the merger and reject the hostile bid?
>
> *Answer:* Yes, in theory, but as a practical matter there may be so much pressure that the company will be forced into the auction mode and be forced to accept the highest bid.

Do the lawyers' answers suggest that a target company cannot protect a friendly transaction from competing bids regardless of whether *Revlon* has been triggered?

While Lipton and Mirvis counsel against lockup options and termination fees "that would impede a third party from competing," the Delaware courts nonetheless have approved quite costly, if not entirely protective, provisions. See Brazen v. Bell Atlantic Corporation, 695 A.2d 43 (Del. 1997) (approving $550 million termination fee in connection with the Bell Atlantic–NYNEX acquisition); Ahmanson v. Great Western Financial Corp., 1997 Del. Ch. LEXIS 84 (June 3, 1997) (approving 3 percent termination fee in a $7 billion dollar white knight transaction).

4. *REVLON* REVIEW IN PRACTICE

It is one thing to state a standard and another to apply it. How does a court apply *Revlon*'s intermediate standard in reviewing a transaction without overt conflicts and in which independent directors received sophisticated advice? During the acquisition wave that peaked in 2007, trial courts repeatedly confronted the claim that target directors managing the company's sale could have secured a higher price if they had conducted the process differently. The following case sets out a trial court's view of its role.

In re Toys "R" Us, Inc., Shareholder Litigation
877 A.2d 975 (Del. Ch. 2005)

STRINE, V.C.: This opinion addresses a motion to enjoin a vote of the stockholders of Toys "R" Us, Inc. (the "Company") tomorrow to consider approving a merger with an acquisition vehicle formed by a group led by Kohlberg Kravis Roberts & Co. ("the KKR Group"). If the merger is approved, the Toys "R" Us stockholders will receive $26.75 per share for their shares. The proposed merger resulted from a lengthy, publicly-announced search for strategic alternatives that began in January 2004, when the Company's shares were trading for only $12.00 per share. The $26.75 per share merger consideration constitutes a 123% premium over that price.

During the strategic process, the Toys "R" Us board of directors, nine of whose ten members are independent, had frequent meetings to explore the Company's strategic options. The board, with the support of its one inside member, the company's CEO, reviewed those options with an open mind, and with the advice of expert advisors.

Eventually, the board settled on the sale of the Company's most valuable asset, its toy retailing business, and the retention of the Company's baby products retailing business, as its preferred option. It did so after considering a wide array of options, including a sale of the whole Company.

The Company sought bids from a large number of the most logical buyers for the toy business, and it eventually elicited attractive expressions of interest from four competing bidders who emerged from the market canvass. When due diligence was completed, the board put the bidders through two rounds of supposedly "final bids" for the toys business. In the midst of this process, one of the bidders expressed a serious interest in buying the whole company for a price of $23.25 per share, and then $24.00. The board decided to stick by its original option until that bidder made an offer to pay $25.25 per share and signaled it might bid even a dollar more.

When that happened, the board was presented with a bid that was attractive compared with its chosen strategy in light of the valuation evidence that its financial advisors had presented, and in light of the failure of any strategic or financial buyer to make any serious expression of interest in buying the whole Company — even a non-binding one conditioned on full due diligence or a friendly merger — despite the board's openly expressed examination of its strategic alternatives. Recognizing that the attractive bids it had received for the toys business could be lost if it extended the process much longer, the "Executive Committee" of the board, acting in conformity with direction given to it by the whole board, approved the solicitation of bids for the entire Company from the final bidders for the toys business, after a short period of due diligence.

When those whole Company bids came in, the winning bid of $26.75 per share from the KKR Group topped the next most favorable bid by $1.50 per share. The bidder that offered $25.25 per share did not increase its bid. After a thorough examination of its alternatives and a final reexamination of the value of the Company, the board decided that the best way to maximize stockholder value was to accept the $26.75 bid. That was a reasonable decision given the wealth of evidence that the board possessed regarding the Company's value and the improbability of another bidder emerging.

In its proposed merger agreement containing the $26.75 offer, the KKR Group asked for a termination fee of 4% of the implied equity value of the transaction to be paid if the Company terminated to accept another deal, as opposed to the 3% offered by the company in its proposed draft. Knowing that the only other bid for the company was $1.50 per share or $350 million less, the Company's negotiators nonetheless bargained the termination fee down to 3.75% the next day, and bargained down the amount of expenses the KKR Group sought in the event of a naked no vote.

[T]he plaintiffs fault the Toys "R" Us board, arguing that it failed to fulfill its duty to act reasonably in pursuit of the highest attainable value for the Company's stockholders. They complain that the board's decision to conduct a brief auction for the full Company from the final bidders for the toys business was unreasonable, and that the board should have taken the time to conduct a new, full-blown search for buyers. Relatedly, they complain that the board unreasonably locked up the $26.75 bid by agreeing to draconian deal termination measures that preclude any topping bid.

. . . I reject those arguments. A hard look at the board's decisions reveals that it made reasonable choices in confronting the real world circumstances it faced. That the board was supple in reacting to new circumstances and adroit in responding to a new development that promised, in its view, greater value to the stockholders is not evidence of infidelity or imprudence; it is consistent with the sort of difficult business decisions that corporate fiduciaries are required to make all the time. Having taken so much time to educate itself and having signaled publicly at the outset an openness to strategic alternatives, the Toys "R" Us board was well-positioned to make a reasoned decision to accept the $26.75 per share offer.

Likewise, the choice of the board's negotiators not to press too strongly for a reduction of the KKR Group's desired 4% termination fee all the way to 3% was reasonable, given that the KKR Group had topped the next best bid by such a big margin. To refuse to risk a reduction in the top bid, when the next best alternative was so much lower, can hardly be said to be unreasonable, especially when the board's negotiators did negotiate to reduce the termination fee from 4% to 3.75%. Furthermore, the size of the termination fee and the presence of matching rights in the merger agreement do not act as a serious barrier to any bidder willing to pay materially more than $26.75 per share.

For these and other reasons that I discuss below, the plaintiffs' motion for a preliminary injunction is denied.

II. Factual Background — The Company And Its Businesses

Toys "R" Us is a specialty retailer with nearly 1500 stores worldwide. As of all relevant times, the Company had three divisions:

Global Toys — This division operates the Company's famous toy stores both domestically and internationally, with the exception of Japan. By far the largest of the divisions, Global Toys accounted for more than $9 billion of the Company's $11 billion in total annual sales, and operates the bulk of the Company's stores. Entering 2004, the problem for Global Toys, particularly in the U.S. market, was its declining profitability, in the face of intense price competition from Wal-Mart, Target and other more diversified "big box" retailers.

Babies "R" Us — This is the second largest division in the Company. Babies "R" Us operates over 200 specialty retail stores that sell a full range of products for expectant mothers and babies. The division has experienced impressive growth in recent years and has higher profit margins than Global Toys. By one measure, Babies "R" Us contributed approximately half of the Company's operating earnings in 2004.

Toys Japan — This division operates a chain of toy stores in Japan under the Toys "R" Us brand name. The Company only owns 48% of this chain. The parties in this case generally agree that Toys Japan comprises only around $1.00 per share of the Company's overall value.

The operating relationship among the divisions is important to understand. As might be expected, the Company had tried to capitalize on economies of scale by using common distribution networks, information systems, and other backbone services to operate the three divisions. Therefore, although the Company reported the divisions' results separately, they did not in fact function with operational autonomy.

One critical implication of that reality for present purposes is its effect on the value of Babies "R" Us. The Company's public filings likely understate the extent to which Babies "R" Us has been subsidized by Global Toys. That subsidy consists of overhead that Babies "R" Us uses but that is actually charged to the Global Toys division, a practice that results in an inflation of the Babies "R" Us division's profits to the corresponding detriment of the profits of Global Toys. In this same vein, it is notable that in 2004 Babies "R" Us contributed only $245 million to the Company's total of $787 million in EBITDA. For these reasons, the Company's management and board do not consider Babies "R" Us to be equally as valuable, either in terms of assets, revenues, or profits, as Global Toys.

Another important implication of the operational entanglement of the various divisions is its effect on the practicability of selling them as separate units. Babies "R" Us was not positioned to operate independently immediately upon a sale. Any buyer would be dependent for some substantial period on transitional services to be provided by the Company. And, of course, once Babies "R" Us acquired the functional capacity to conduct all of its required operations autonomously, its ongoing costs of operation would increase materially, perhaps by more than $100 million annually.

The Management and Board of the Company. The Company's board of directors consisted of ten members. The plaintiffs concede that nine of those members are independent, non-management directors. The one inside director was the

Company's Chairman and Chief Executive Officer, defendant John H. Eyler, Jr. Eyler had joined Toys "R" Us as CEO in 2000. That position was just the most recent in a succession of high-level executive positions Eyler had held within the retail industry. Eyler had served as CEO of toy retailer FAO Schwarz for the eight years preceding his joining Toys "R" Us. . . .

IV. The Merits: Is It Probable That the Board Breached Its Revlon Duties?

A.   The Judicial Role in Evaluating a *Revlon* Claim

In its most summary form, the plaintiffs' claim is that the directors did not fulfill their duties under the landmark case of Revlon, Inc. v. MacAndrews & Forbes Holdings, Inc.[29] In *Revlon*, the Delaware Supreme Court made two important determinations. One is rooted in old trust principles[30] and is mundane to those who believe that stockholders are the only corporate constituency whose best interests are an end, rather than an instrument, of the corporate form, and rests on the proposition that once directors decide to sell the corporation, they should do what any fiduciary (such as trustee) should do when selling an asset: maximize the sales price for the benefit of those to whom their allegiance is pledged. In the corporate context, that means that the directors must seek the highest value deal that can be secured for stockholders regardless of whether it is in the best interests of other corporate constituencies. Or, as the Supreme Court said in its important decision in Paramount Communications, Inc. v. QVC Network, Inc.: "In the sale of control context, the directors must focus on one primary objective — to secure the transaction offering the best value reasonably available for the stockholders — and they must exercise their fiduciary duties to further that end."

The other key element of *Revlon* involved the intensity of the judicial review that would be applied in evaluating whether a board of directors fulfilled its obligation to seek the highest immediate value. Consistent with the intuition in *Unocal* and the facts of *Revlon* itself — which involved a sell-side CEO whose disdain for a particular bidder seemed to taint his and his board's ability to impartially seek the best value for their stockholders[34] — the Supreme Court held that courts would subject directors subject to *Revlon* duties to a heightened standard of reasonableness review, rather than the laxer standard of rationality review applicable under the business judgment rule. In practical, if not immediately apparent linguistic terms, this meant that this court had more room to intervene than in a business judgment rule case and could, if it determined that the directors had acted unreasonably, issue an appropriate remedy.

---

29. 506 A.2d 173 (Del.1986).

30. Paramount Communications Inc. v. Time, Inc., 1989 WL 79880, at *25 (Del. Ch. July 14, 1989) ("*Revlon* was not a radical departure from existing law (*i.e.*, it has "always" been the case that when a trustee or other fiduciary sells an asset for cash, his duty is to seek the single goal of getting the best available price) . . ."); see also Leo E. Strine, Jr., Categorical Confusion: Deal Protection Measures in Stock-for-Stock Merger Agreements, 56 Bus. Law. 919, 927 n.25 (2001) (stating that the "*Revlon* principle grows out of the traditional principle that fiduciaries must sell trust assets for their highest value," and collecting cases such as Robinson v. Pittsburgh Oil Refining Corp., 126 A. 46, 49 (Del. Ch.1924) demonstrating that principle).

34. See *Revlon*, 506 A.2d at 176 (noting in understated fashion that Revlon's rebuff of Pantry Pride's advances was "perhaps in part based on [Revlon CEO] Mr. Bergerac's strong personal antipathy to [Pantry Pride CEO] Mr. Perelman").

In *QVC*,[35] the Supreme Court said that this intensified form of review involved two "key features" : (a) a judicial determination regarding the adequacy of the decisionmaking process employed by the directors, including the information on which the directors based their decision; and (b) a judicial examination of the reasonableness of the directors' action in light of the circumstances then existing. The directors have the burden of proving that they were adequately informed and acted reasonably.[36]

Critically, in the wake of *Revlon*, Delaware courts have made clear that the enhanced judicial review *Revlon* requires is not a license for law-trained courts to second-guess reasonable, but debatable, tactical choices that directors have made in good faith. For example, the Supreme Court has held that the duty to take reasonable steps to secure the highest immediately available price does not invariably require a board to conduct an auction process or even a targeted market canvass in the first instance, emphasizing that there is "no single blue-print" for fulfilling the duty to maximize value.[37] Nor does a board's decision to sell a company prevent it from offering bidders deal protections, so long as its decision to do so was reasonably directed to the objective of getting the highest price, and not by a selfish or idiosyncratic desire by the board to tilt the playing field towards a particular bidder for reasons unrelated to the stockholders' ability to get top dollar.[38]

Thus, this Court has been "mindful that its task [under *Revlon*] is to examine whether the directors have undertaken reasonable efforts to fulfill their obligation to secure the best available price, and not to determine whether the directors have performed flawlessly." [39] That distillation remains faithful to teachings of our Supreme Court, through Chief Justice Veasey, in *QVC*:

> Although an enhanced scrutiny test involves a review of the reasonableness of the substantive merits of a board's actions, a court should not ignore the complexity of the directors' task in a sale of control. There are many business and financial considerations implicated in investigating and selecting the best value reasonably available. The board of directors is the corporate decisionmaking body best equipped to make these judgments. Accordingly, a court applying enhanced judicial scrutiny should be deciding whether the directors make a reasonable decision, not a perfect decision. If a board selected one of several reasonable alternatives, a court should not second guess that choice even though it might have decided otherwise or subsequent events may have cast doubt on the board's determination. Thus, courts will not substitute their business judgment for that of the directors, but will determine if the directors' decision was, on balance, within a range of reasonableness. . . .

---

1. *Trading off an increased price and an increased risk of losing the bidder.* Plaintiffs' claim in *Toys "R" Us* is that the board stopped too soon — more could have been secured for the shareholders if the process of seeking a higher bid was extended, or if the board had been more aggressive in negotiating with the highest bidder.

---

35. *QVC*, 637 A.2d at 45.
36. Id.
37. Barkan v. Amsted Indus., 567 A.2d 1279, 1286 (Del. 1989).
38. Id. at 1286.
39. In re Pennaco Energy, Inc., 787 A.2d 691, 705 (Del. Ch. 2001).

Both of these situations involve a risk that the high bidder will walk away. Vice Chancellor Strine in *Toys "R" Us* highlights the problem:

> The plaintiffs posit that the board should have refused to sign the merger agreement with the KKR Group until the termination fee was reduced to some less onerous level and the matching rights were removed. In fact, the board did negotiate the termination fee down to 3.75% from the 4.0% that KKR had proposed on March 15, putting the $350 million bid differential at some risk to do so. The plaintiffs, however, assume that the board should have pressed harder and that the KKR Group would have yielded further, but still kept its bid at $26.75.
>
> But what if the KKR Group had said, "if you want to cut the termination fee to 3%,[69] our offer is only $25.75 per share"? What was the board to do then? Even worse, suppose the KKR Group had asked, "what did the other groups bid?" What was First Boston supposed to say, knowing that the KKR Group had topped Cerberus by a full $1.50 per share or $350 million? In that dynamic, only the reckless would have been insensitive to the worry that the KKR Group's bid might drop if it were asked to give up the matching rights or to accept a termination fee of less than 3%.
>
> Let's plausibly imagine how that exceedingly awkward negotiating session that the plaintiffs desire might have gone:
>
> *First Boston/Simpson Thacher:* The board wants 3.0% on the termination fee and to get rid of the matching right.
>
> *KKR:* Fine, you can have $25.75 per share and the 3.0% or the $26.75 with 3.75% protection for our trouble. And we want the match in either case.
>
> *First Boston/Simpson Thacher:* No, no. We demand 3.0% and the $26.75; take it or leave it.
>
> *KKR:* What did Cerberus and Apollo bid?
>
> *First Boston/Simpson Thacher:* We can't comment.
>
> *KKR:* I think we're done.
>
> *First Boston/Simpson Thacher* (with panicky overtones): Please don't go . . .
>
> *KKR:* Click
>
> *First Boston/Simpson Thacher:* Expletive deleted.
>
> Faithful fiduciaries and their advisors, facing a dynamic of this kind, would reasonably fear that the KKR Group might somehow get wind that it made an overbid and be chary about losing the proverbial bird in hand. It is this tradeoff — between getting the highest price the board could from KKR Group right then and there, and the limited opportunity of receiving a higher bid from a well-canvassed market by reducing the termination fee and eliminating the match rights — which the board and its advisors had to address, and which the plaintiffs and their ivory tower–based experts refuse to realistically engage.

---

1. *Duty of care or* Revlon? How does a court assess a plaintiff's claim that a disinterested and well-advised board made the wrong trade-off? Recall that Smith v. Van Gorkum was decided only a year before *Revlon.* How does the duty-of-care analysis in *Van Gorkum* differ from the *Revlon* analysis in *Toys "R" Us?*

2. Revlon *and the "go shop" structure.* With the appearance of a new round of leveraged buyouts — now termed private equity transactions — in the acquisition

69. Frankly, I cannot, as someone who has done a lot of negotiation, imagine retracting the 3% and matching rights offer. That sort of "oh, by the way . . ." should only be put on the table when it is necessary to protect a client against a material disadvantage. For the sake of analysis, I have indulged the idea of pulling the matching rights offer back, although it seems a less-than-credible posture.

wave that peaked in 2007, a new transaction form emerged: the "go shop" structure. In the 1980s, private equity often came into a transaction as an alternative to a hostile bid that management opposed, as in *Revlon* (page 993 supra). In the new transaction form, the target negotiates a binding acquisition agreement with a single bidder, often a private equity firm that, unlike the target company's competitors, would likely need to retain existing target management to run the company. There would be no effort to seek competitive bids prior to executing the contract with the private equity buyer — no pre-execution market check. In an auction structure as in *Toys "R" Us*, the board satisfies its *Revlon* information requirement through competitive bidding: the market assesses the target's value. But what provides that information when the target negotiates with only a single bidder?

The "go shop" structure is designed to address *Revlon's* information component in the single-bidder case. In general, the target is allowed to solicit competitive bids for a specified period after executing an agreement with the favored bidder. Often, the original bidder will have a right of first refusal. If the original bidder does not match the new bid, or has no right of first refusal, the target can accept a higher bid subject to paying the now jilted suitor a termination fee.

The "go shop" structure is often complicated by the target's senior managers having already signed on to stay in their positions on favorable terms, after the favored bidder completes the acquisition. These circumstances have a flavor of *Van Gorkum, Revlon,* and *QVC,* where senior managers plainly favored a bidder that would allow them to participate in the transaction.

Suppose the target company's board assigns the post-execution negotiating role to a committee of independent directors. Are independent directors an effective substitute for the CEO in negotiating with potential bidders? In connection with a proposed settlement of litigation arising out of a target's acquisition by a private equity firm, a judge questioned "whether, given [the CEO's] pre-commitment to a deal with [the acquirer], the board of directors was ever in a position to objectively consider whether or not a sale of the enterprise should take place." S&C Technologies, Inc., Shareholders Litigation, 911 A.2d 816, 818 (Del. Ch. 2006).

If the CEO has already committed to one bidder, will other bidders be deterred? Should independent directors allow a CEO to commit to a single bidder? What if the bidder states that it will not go forward without the CEO's commitment?

In two recent cases, the Delaware Chancery Court allowed independent directors to use a "go shop" structure in connection with the target's acquisition by a private equity bidder. In both cases, the court closely reviewed whether the post-acquisition go shop was corrupted by favoritism toward the preferred bidder. In Upper Deck Co. v. The Topps Co., 926 A.2d 58 (Del. Ch. 2007), the court enjoined the transaction because it concluded that management bias toward the favored bidder caused the board not to "pursue the potential for higher value with the diligence and genuineness expected of directors seeking to get the best value for stockholders." *Id.*

In Lear Corp. Shareholder Litigation, 926 A.2d 94 (Del. Ch. 2007), the same Vice Chancellor refused to enjoin a similarly structured transaction despite his conclusion that the target board's Special Committee "made an infelicitous decision to permit the CEO to negotiate the merger terms outside the presence of Special Committee supervisors." Id. The court concluded that the CEO's personal situation greatly favored a private equity buyer, but found no evidence that it "adversely affected the overall reasonableness of the board's efforts to secure the highest possible value." Id.

In *Lear*, the court found that the CEO had a conflict of interest. Under *Sinclair*, page 131 supra, an interested transaction is subject to entire fairness review, not an intermediate standard. The court, however, required increased disclosure of the conflict before the shareholders voted on the transaction. Will an informed shareholder vote always cure the conflict?

5. WHAT IS THE STANDARD WHEN *REVLON* IS NOT TRIGGERED?

That so much judicial attention has been paid to identifying the circumstances that trigger *Revlon*'s intermediate standard implies a significant difference in the standards governing the conduct of a friendly transaction if *Revlon* does not apply. Put differently, the same transaction would be treated differently depending on whether the acquirer had a controlling shareholder.

The most obvious alternative to *Revlon* is the business judgment rule, under which judicial inquiry into the negotiation and substance of a friendly sale would be limited to whether the board informed itself and acted in good faith. The application of the traditional business judgment rule presumably would lead to a much less intrusive review of deal protection devices like lockups. Yet, a close reading of *Van Gorkom*, page 84 supra, and the fact that *Revlon* would have applied had that case arisen a year later — the sale to the Pritzkers plainly would have been a change in control — suggest that the application of the business judgment rule in this context might be less deferential than in other applications.

The standard of review that applies in non-*Revlon* transactions was considered in two cases decided by the Chancery Court that involved no-talk clauses — contractual commitments by the target not to discuss a transaction with a potential competitive bidder.

In Ace Limited v. Capital Re Corp., 747 A.2d 95 (Del. Ch. 2000), the acquiring corporation ("Ace") sued to prohibit the target ("Cap Re") in a friendly merger from exercising a fiduciary out — a contractual right to terminate the merger agreement if a better offer emerges — arguing that exercise of the fiduciary out was conditioned on the Cap Re board obtaining an opinion of counsel that failure to negotiate with a bidder offering a higher price would violate the board's fiduciary duty, which had not been obtained. The board's right to terminate the merger agreement was critical because Ace had secured contractual commitments from enough Cap Re stockholders to ensure approval if the transaction were presented to the Cap Re shareholders.

Ace Limited v. Capital Re Corp.
747 A.2d 95 (Del. Ch. 2000)

STRINE, V.C.: ACE argues that Capital Re has violated the plain language of the Merger Agreement. Its major claim is that Capital Re was forbidden to engage in discussions with XL Capital unless it received written legal advice from outside counsel opining that the board's fiduciary duties mandated such discussions. Because the board did not receive such advice, its decision to enter negotiations with XL Capital and to start a bidding war between ACE and XL Capital is, in ACE's view, a clear breach of contract.

1. The Probable Better Interpretation of the Merger Agreement Is that Capital Re's Discussions with XL Capital Were Proper Under §6.3

Although perhaps not so clear as to preclude another interpretation, §6.3 of the Agreement is on its face better read as leaving the ultimate "good faith" judgment about whether the board's fiduciary duties required it to enter discussions with XL Capital to the board itself. Though the board must "base" its judgment on the "written advice" of outside counsel, the language of the contract does not preclude the board from concluding, even if its outside counsel equivocates (as lawyers sometimes tend to do) as to whether such negotiations are fiduciarily mandated.

Here, the Capital Re board had good economic reason to believe that consummation of the merger in the face of the XL Capital offer was adverse to the interests of the Capital Re stockholders. The board knew that if it did not explore the XL Capital offer, the Capital Re stockholders — including the 33.5% holders — would be forced into the merger even though the merger's value had plummeted since June 10, 1999 and even though the XL Capital offer was more valuable. Given these circumstances, it seems likely that in the end a fact-finder will conclude that the board had a good faith basis for determining that it must talk with XL Capital and not simply let the Capital Re stockholders ride the merger barrel over the financial falls. . . .

2. If ACE's Interpretation of the Merger Agreement Is Correct, §6.3 Is Likely Invalid and ACE Has Little Chance of Prevailing on the Merits

. . . Restatement (Second) of Contracts §193 explicitly provides that a "promise by a fiduciary to violate his fiduciary duty or a promise that tends to induce such a violation is unenforceable on public policy grounds." . . . If §6.3 of the Merger Agreement in fact required the Capital Re board to eschew even discussing another offer unless it received an opinion of counsel stating that such discussions were required, and if ACE demanded such a provision, it is likely that §6.3 will ultimately be found invalid. It is one thing for a board of directors to agree not to play footsie with other potential bidders or to stir up an auction. That type of restriction is perfectly understandable, if not necessary, if good faith business transactions are to be encouraged. It is quite another thing for a board of directors to enter into a merger agreement that precludes the board from considering any other offers unless a lawyer is willing to sign an opinion indicating that his client board is "required" to consider that offer in the less than precise corporate law context of a merger agreement that does not implicate *Revlon* but may preclude other transactions in a manner that raises eyebrows under *Unocal*. Such a contractual commitment is particularly suspect when a failure to consider other offers guarantees the consummation of the original transaction, however more valuable an alternative transaction may be and however less valuable the original transaction may have become since the merger agreement was signed.[34]

---

34. It may well be a different matter for a board to agree to put a merger agreement to a vote if there are no other provisions tied to the agreement that operate to preclude the stockholders from freely voting down the merger and accepting another deal or opting for no deal at all. In this regard, see the recent amendment to Del. C. §251(c) enabling a board to agree to put a merger to a vote even where its recommendation about the merger has changed.

In one sense, such a provision seems innocuous. I mean, can't the board find someone willing to give the opinion? What is wrong with a contract that simply limits a board from discussing another offer unless the board's lawyers are prepared to opine that such discussions are required? But in another sense, the provision is much more pernicious in that it involves an abdication by the board of its duty to determine what its own fiduciary obligations require at precisely that time in the life of the company when the board's own judgment is most important. In the typical case, one must remember, the target board is defending the original deal in the face of an arguably more valuable transaction. In that context, does it make sense for the board to be able to hide behind their lawyers?

More fundamentally, one would think that there would be limited circumstances in which a board could prudently place itself in the position of not being able to entertain and consider a superior proposal to a transaction dependent on a stockholder vote. The circumstances in this case would not seem to be of that nature, because the board's inability to consider another offer in effect precludes the stockholders (including the 33.5% holders) from accepting another offer. For the superior proposal "out" in §§6.3 and 8.3 of the Merger Agreement to mean anything, the board must be free to explore such a proposal in good faith.[36] A ban on considering such a proposal, even one with an exception where legal counsel opines in writing that such consideration is "required," comes close to self-disablement by the board. Our case law takes a rather dim view of restrictions that tend to produce such a result. But where a board has not explored the market place with confidence and is negotiating a deal that requires stockholder approval and would result in a change in stockholder ownership interests, a board's decision to preclude itself — and therefore the stockholders — from entertaining other offers is less justifiable.

Indeed, ACE admits that it pushed Capital Re to the outer limits of propriety, but it claims to have stopped short of pushing Capital Re beyond that limit. But as I read ACE's view of what §6.3 means in the context of this Merger Agreement, ACE comes close to saying that §6.3 provides no "out" at all. According to ACE, it is now clear, per *QVC*, that a board need not obtain the highest value reasonably available unless it decides to engage in a change of control transaction. The ACE–Capital Re merger is not a change of control. Therefore, this syllogism goes, there is no circumstance in which the Capital Re board must consider another, higher offer to fulfill its fiduciary duties. Thus Capital Re could not get its outside counsel to issue such an opinion, and the board's contrary judgment of its duties could not have been in good faith. *QVC*, Q.E.D.

In this necessarily hurried posture, it is impossible to examine in depth the appropriate doctrinal prism through which to evaluate the "no-talk" provision in the Merger Agreement. In the wake of *QVC* parties have tended to imbed provisions[42] in stock-for-stock mergers that are intentionally designed to prevent another bidder, through a tender offer or rival stock-for-stock bid, from preventing the consummation of a transaction. When corporate boards assent to provisions in merger agreements that have the primary purpose of acting as a defensive barrier to other transactions not sought out by the board, some of the policy concerns that

---

36. One legitimate circumstance may be where a board has actively canvassed the market, negotiated with various bidders in a competitive environment, and believes that the necessity to close a transaction requires that the sales contest end.

42. Such as no-shops, cross-stock options, and termination fees.

animate the *Unocal* standard of review might be implicated. In this case, for example, if §6.3 is read as precluding board consideration of alternative offers — no matter how much more favorable — in this non–change of control context, the Capital Re board's approval of the Merger Agreement is as formidable a barrier to another offer as a non-redeemable poison pill. Absent an escape clause, the Merger Agreement guarantees the success of the merger vote and precludes any other alternative, no matter how much more lucrative to the Capital Re stockholders and no matter whether the Capital Re board itself prefers the other alternative. As a practical matter, it might therefore be possible to construct a *plausible* argument that a no-escape merger agreement that locks up the necessary votes constitutes an unreasonable preclusive and coercive defensive obstacle within the meaning of *Unocal*.

But *Unocal* to one side, one can state with much more doctrinal certainty that the Capital Re board was still required to exercise its bedrock duties of care and loyalty when it entered the Merger Agreement.[46] If the board mistakenly entered into a merger agreement believing erroneously that it had negotiated an effective out giving it the ability to consider more favorable offers, its mistake might well be found to be a breach of its duty of care. In this context where the board is making a critical decision affecting stockholder ownership and voting rights, it is especially important that the board negotiate with care and retain sufficient flexibility to ensure that the stockholders are not unfairly coerced into accepting a less than optimal exchange for their shares. As Chancellor Chandler recently noted, "No-talk provisions . . . are troubling precisely because they prevent a board from meeting its duty to make an informed judgment with respect to even considering whether to negotiate with a third party."

Examined under either doctrinal rubric, §6.3 as construed by ACE is of quite dubious validity. As a sophisticated party who bargained for, nay demanded, §6.3 of the Merger Agreement, ACE was on notice of its possible invalidity. This factor therefore cuts against its claim that its contract rights should take precedence over the interests of the Capital Re stockholders who could be harmed by enforcement of §6.3. . . .

In Phelps Dodge Corporation v. Cyprus Amax Minerals Co., 1999 WL 1054255 (Del. Ch. 1999), Chancellor Chandler suggested that a no-talk provision — prohibiting the target from negotiating or providing information to a potential competitive bidder — would likely be invalid even under the business judgment rule:

> Under our law, a board of directors must be informed of all material information reasonably available. The defendants properly argue that [the parties to the merger agreement] are under no duty to negotiate [with a potential higher bidder]. . . . And in a transaction not involving a change of control or sale of the company, that is undoubtedly the case. Nevertheless, even the decision not to negotiate, in my opinion,

---

46. Phelps Dodge Corp. v. Cyprus Amax Minerals Co., 1999 Del. Ch. LEXIS 202, *4-5, Del. Ch., C.A. No. 17398, Chandler, C. (Sept. 27, 1999) (ruling at preliminary injunction hearing that although target's board of directors had no duty to negotiate in a transaction not involving a change of control or sale of the company, "[e]ven the decision not to negotiate . . . must be an informed one" and that the board "should not have completely foreclosed the opportunity" to negotiate with a third party through a "no-talk" provision and that such foreclosure may constitute a breach of a board's duty of care).

must be an informed one. A target can refuse to negotiate under *Time Warner*, but it should be informed when making such refusal. . . . No-talk provisions, thus, in my view, are troubling precisely because they prevent a board from meeting its duty to make an informed judgment with respect to even considering whether to negotiate with a third party. . . . [T]he no-talk provision has apparently prevented the [merger partners] from engaging in nonpublic discourse with [the competitive bidder]. . . . [T]hey simply should not have completely foreclosed the opportunity to do so, as this is the legal equivalent of willful blindness, a blindness that may constitute a breach of the duty of care; that is, the duty to take care to be informed of all material information reasonably available. Now, given my ruling of reasonable success with respect to plaintiffs' duty of care claim, I don't think it is necessary or required that I reach their *Unocal* claim.[52]

For interesting discussions on how to deal with the doctrinal divide created by *Revlon*'s trigger, see Leo E. Strine Jr., Categorical Confusion: Deal Protection Measures in Stock-for-Stock Mergers, 56 Bus. Law. 919 (2001) (the author is a vice chancellor of Delaware); William T. Allen, Understanding Fiduciary Outs: The What and Why of an Anomalous Concept, 55 Bus. Law. (2000) (the author is a former chancellor of Delaware).

Before the Chancery Court had the opportunity to clarify (or further muddy) the issue, the Delaware Supreme Court confronted the legitimacy of a cluster of deal protection devices that effectively locked up — i.e., made it impossible for shareholders to vote down — a stock-for-stock merger to which *Revlon* did not apply.

Omnicare, Inc. v. NCS Healthcare, Inc.
818 A.2d 914 (Del. 2003) (en Banc)

HOLLAND, J.: . . . The board of directors of NCS, an insolvent publicly traded Delaware corporation, agreed to the terms of a merger with Genesis. Pursuant to that agreement, all of the NCS creditors would be paid in full and the corporation's stockholders would exchange their shares for the shares of Genesis, a publicly traded Pennsylvania corporation. Several months after approving the merger agreement, but before the stockholder vote was scheduled, the NCS board . . . recommended that the stockholders reject the Genesis transaction after deciding that a competing proposal from Omnicare was a superior transaction. The competing Omnicare bid offered the NCS stockholders an amount of cash equal to more than twice the then current market value of the shares to be received in the Genesis merger. The transaction offered by Omnicare also treated the NCS corporation's other stakeholders on equal terms with the Genesis agreement.

The merger agreement between Genesis and NCS contained a provision authorized by Section 251(c) of Delaware's corporation law. It required that the Genesis agreement be placed before the corporation's stockholders for a vote, even if the NCS board of directors no longer recommended it. At the insistence of Genesis, the NCS board also agreed to omit any effective fiduciary clause from the merger agreement. In connection with the Genesis merger agreement, two stockholders

---

52. A third case, roughly contemporaneous with *Ace* and *Phelps Dodge* rejected the application of *Unocal* to a deal protection device adopted before a competitive bidder appeared, and sustained the device under the business judgment rule. In re ICX Communications, 1999 WL 1009174 (Del. Ch. 1999). — ED.

of NCS [Outcalt and Shaw], who held a majority of the voting power, agreed unconditionally to vote all of their shares in favor of the Genesis merger. Thus, the combined terms of the voting agreements and merger agreement guaranteed, *ab initio*, that the transaction proposed by Genesis would obtain NCS stockholder's approval.

The Court of Chancery ruled that the voting agreements, when coupled with the provision in the Genesis merger agreement requiring that it be presented to the stockholders for a vote pursuant to 8 Del. C. §251(c), constituted defensive measures within the meaning of *Unocal*. After applying the *Unocal* standard of enhanced judicial scrutiny, the Court of Chancery held that those defensive measures were reasonable. We have concluded that, in the absence of an effective fiduciary out clause, those defensive measures are preclusive and coercive . . . and unenforceable.

The defendant, NCS, is a Delaware corporation headquartered in Beachwood, Ohio. NCS is a leading independent provider of pharmacy services to long-term care institutions including skilled nursing facilities, assisted living facilities and other institutional healthcare facilities. NCS common stock consists of Class A shares and Class B shares. The Class B shares are entitled to ten votes per share and the Class A shares are entitled to one vote per share. The shares are virtually identical in every other respect.

The defendant Jon H. Outcalt is Chairman of the NCS board of directors. Outcalt owns 202,063 shares of NCS Class A common stock and 3,476,086 shares of Class B common stock. The defendant Kevin B. Shaw is President, CEO and a director of NCS. At the time the merger agreement at issue in this dispute was executed with Genesis, Shaw owned 28,905 shares of NCS Class A common stock and 1,141,134 shares of Class B common stock.

The NCS board has two other members, defendants Boake A. Sells and Richard L. Osborne. Sells is a graduate of the Harvard Business School. He was Chairman and CEO at Revco Drugstores in Cleveland, Ohio from 1987 to 1992, when he was replaced by new owners. Sells currently sits on the boards of both public and private companies. Osborne is a full-time professor at the Weatherhead School of Management at Case Western Reserve University. He has been at the university for over thirty years. Osborne currently sits on at least seven corporate boards other than NCS.

The defendant Genesis . . . is a leading provider of healthcare and support services to the elderly. The defendant Geneva Sub, Inc., a wholly owned subsidiary of Genesis, is a Delaware corporation formed by Genesis to acquire NCS. . . .

NCS Seeks Restructuring Alternatives

Beginning in late 1999, changes in the timing and level of reimbursements by government and third-party providers adversely affected market conditions in the health care industry. As a result, NCS began to experience greater difficulty in collecting accounts receivables, which led to a precipitous decline in the market value of its stock. NCS common shares that traded above $20 in January 1999 were worth as little as $5 at the end of that year. By early 2001, NCS was in default on approximately $350 million in debt, including $206 million in senior bank debt and $102 million of its $5^3/4\%$ Convertible Subordinated Debentures (the "Notes"). After these defaults, NCS common stock traded in a range of

$0.09 to $0.50 per share until days before the announcement of the transaction at issue in this case.

NCS began to explore strategic alternatives that might address the problems it was confronting ... and retained Brown, Gibbons, Lang & Company as its exclusive financial advisor. During this period, NCS's financial condition continued to deteriorate. In April 2001, NCS received a formal notice of default and acceleration from the trustee for holders of the Notes. As NCS's financial condition worsened, the Noteholders formed a committee to represent their financial interests (the "Ad Hoc Committee"). ...

In the summer of 2001, NCS invited Omnicare, Inc. to begin discussions with Brown Gibbons regarding a possible transaction. On July 20, Joel Gemunder, Omnicare's President and CEO, sent Shaw a written proposal to acquire NCS in a bankruptcy sale under Section 363 of the Bankruptcy Code. This proposal was for $225 million subject to satisfactory completion of due diligence. NCS asked Omnicare to execute a confidentiality agreement so that more detailed discussions could take place.

In August 2001, Omnicare increased its bid to $270 million, but still proposed to structure the deal as an asset sale in bankruptcy. Even at $270 million, Omnicare's proposal was substantially lower than the face value of NCS's outstanding debt. It would have provided only a small recovery for Omnicare's Noteholders and no recovery for its stockholders. In October 2001, NCS sent Glen Pollack of Brown Gibbons to meet with Omnicare's financial advisor, Merrill Lynch, to discuss Omnicare's interest in NCS. Omnicare responded that it was not interested in any transaction other than an asset sale in bankruptcy.

There was no further contact between Omnicare and NCS between November 2001 and January 2002. Instead, Omnicare began secret discussions with Judy K. Mencher, a representative of the Ad Hoc Committee. In these discussions, Omnicare continued to pursue a transaction structured as a sale of assets in bankruptcy. In February 2002, the Ad Hoc Committee notified the NCS board that Omnicare had proposed an asset sale in bankruptcy for $313,750,000. ...

In January 2002, Genesis was contacted by members of the Ad Hoc Committee concerning a possible transaction with NCS. ... Genesis previously lost a bidding war to Omnicare in a different transaction. This led to bitter feelings between the principals of both companies. More importantly, this bitter experience for Genesis led to its insistence on exclusivity agreements and lock-ups in any potential transaction with NCS.

NCS Financial Improvement

NCS's operating performance was improving by early 2002. As NCS's performance improved, the NCS directors began to believe that it might be possible for NCS to enter into a transaction that would provide some recovery for NCS stockholders' equity. In March 2002, NCS decided to form an independent committee of board members who were neither NCS employees nor major NCS stockholders (the "Independent Committee"). The NCS board thought this was necessary because, due to NCS's precarious financial condition, it felt that fiduciary duties were owed to the enterprise as a whole rather than solely to NCS stockholders.[53]

---

53. The fiduciary duty of directors whose company is insolvent or in the zone of insolvency is discussed in Ch. III.D.4. — ED.

Sells and Osborne were selected as the members of the committee, and given authority to consider and negotiate possible transactions for NCS. The entire four member NCS board, however, retained authority to approve any transaction. The Independent Committee retained the same legal and financial counsel as the NCS board.

The Independent Committee met for the first time on May 14, 2002. At that meeting Pollack suggested that NCS seek a "stalking-horse merger partner" to obtain the highest possible value in any transaction. The Independent Committee agreed with the suggestion.

Genesis Initial Proposal

Two days later, on May 16, 2002, Scott Berlin of Brown Gibbons, Glen Pollack and Boake Sells met with George Hager, CFO of Genesis, and Michael Walker, who was Genesis's CEO. At that meeting, Genesis made it clear that if it were going to engage in any negotiations with NCS, it would not do so as a "stalking horse." As one of its advisors testified, "We didn't want to be someone who set forth a valuation for NCS which would only result in that valuation . . . being publicly disclosed, and thereby creating an environment where Omnicare felt to maintain its competitive monopolistic positions, that they had to match and exceed that level." Thus, Genesis "wanted a degree of certainty that to the extent [it] w[as] willing to pursue a negotiated merger agreement . . . , [it] would be able to consummate the transaction [it] negotiated and executed."

In June 2002, Genesis proposed a transaction that would take place outside the bankruptcy context. . . . [T]he economic terms of the Genesis proposal included repayment of the NCS senior debt in full, full assumption of trade credit obligations, an exchange offer or direct purchase of the NCS Notes providing NCS Noteholders with a combination of cash and Genesis common stock equal to the par value of the NCS Notes (not including accrued interest), and $20 million in value for the NCS common stock. Structurally, the Genesis proposal continued to include consents from a significant majority of the Noteholders as well as support agreements from stockholders owning a majority of the NCS voting power.

. . . Pollack asked Genesis to increase its offer to NCS stockholders. Genesis agreed to consider this request. Thereafter, Pollack and Hager had further conversations. Genesis agreed to offer a total of $24 million in consideration for the NCS common stock, or an additional $4 million, in the form of Genesis common stock.

At the June 26 meeting, Genesis's representatives demanded that, before any further negotiations take place, NCS agree to enter into an exclusivity agreement with it. As Hager from Genesis explained it: "[I]f they wished us to continue to try to move this process to a definitive agreement, that they would need to do it on an exclusive basis with us. We were going to, and already had incurred significant expense, but we would incur additional expenses . . . , both internal and external, to bring this transaction to a definitive signing." . . .

After NCS executed the exclusivity agreement, Genesis provided NCS with a draft merger agreement, a draft Noteholders' support agreement, and draft voting agreements for Outcalt and Shaw, who together held a majority of the voting power of the NCS common stock. Genesis and NCS negotiated the terms of the merger agreement over the next three weeks. During those negotiations, the Independent Committee and the Ad Hoc Committee persuaded Genesis to improve the terms of its merger. . . .

By late July 2002, Omnicare came to believe that NCS was negotiating a transaction, possibly with Genesis or another of Omnicare's competitors, that would potentially present a competitive threat to Omnicare. . . . [O]n July 26, 2002, Omnicare faxed to NCS a letter outlining a proposed acquisition. The letter suggested a transaction in which Omnicare would retire NCS's senior and subordinated debt at par plus accrued interest, and pay the NCS stockholders $3 cash for their shares. Omnicare's proposal, however, was expressly conditioned on negotiating a merger agreement, obtaining certain third party consents, and completing its due diligence.

Mencher saw the July 26 Omnicare letter and realized that, while its economic terms were attractive, the "due diligence" condition substantially undercut its strength. In an effort to get a better proposal from Omnicare, Mencher telephoned Gemunder and told him that Omnicare was unlikely to succeed in its bid unless it dropped the "due diligence outs." . . . Gemunder considered Mencher's warning "very real," and followed up with his advisors. They, however, insisted that he retain the due diligence condition "to protect [him] from doing something foolish." Taking this advice to heart, Gemunder decided not to drop the due diligence condition.

Late in the afternoon of July 26, 2002, NCS representatives received voicemail messages from Omnicare asking to discuss the letter. The exclusivity agreement prevented NCS from returning those calls. In relevant part, that agreement precluded NCS from "engag[ing] or particpat[ing] in any discussions or negotiations with respect to a Competing Transaction or a proposal for one." The July 26 letter from Omnicare met the definition of a "Competing Transaction."

Despite the exclusivity agreement, the Independent Committee met to consider a response to Omnicare. It concluded that discussions with Omnicare about its July 26 letter presented an unacceptable risk that Genesis would abandon merger discussions. The Independent Committee believed that, given Omnicare's past bankruptcy proposals and unwillingness to consider a merger, as well as its decision to negotiate exclusively with the Ad Hoc Committee, the risk of losing the Genesis proposal was too substantial. Nevertheless, the Independent Committee instructed Pollack to use Omnicare's letter to negotiate for improved terms with Genesis . . . [which] proposed substantially improved terms . . . [but] stipulated that the transaction had to be approved by midnight the next day, July 28, or else Genesis would terminate discussions and withdraw its offer.

The Independent Committee and the NCS board both scheduled meetings for July 28. The committee met first. Although that meeting lasted less than an hour, the Court of Chancery determined the minutes reflect that the directors were fully informed of all material facts relating to the proposed transaction. After concluding that Genesis was sincere in establishing the midnight deadline, the committee voted unanimously to recommend the transaction to the full board.

The full board met thereafter. After receiving similar reports and advice from its legal and financial advisors, the board concluded that "balancing the potential loss of the Genesis deal against the uncertainty of Omnicare's letter, results in the conclusion that the only reasonable alternative for the Board of Directors is to approve the Genesis transaction." The board first voted to authorize the voting agreements with Outcalt and Shaw, for purposes of Section 203 of the Delaware General Corporation Law ("DGCL"). The board was advised by its legal counsel that "under the terms of the merger agreement and because NCS shareholders representing in excess of 50% of the outstanding voting power would be *required* by Genesis to enter into stockholder voting agreements contemporaneously with the signing of the merger agreement, and would agree to vote their shares in favor of the merger agreement, shareholder approval of the merger would be assured even if the NCS Board were to withdraw or change its recommendation. *These facts would prevent NCS from engaging in any alternative or superior transaction in the future*" (emphasis added).

After listening to a *summary* of the merger terms, the board then resolved that the merger agreement and the transactions contemplated thereby were advisable and fair and in the best interests of all the NCS stakeholders. The NCS board further resolved to recommend the transactions to the stockholders for their approval and adoption. A definitive merger agreement between NCS and Genesis and the stockholder voting agreements were executed later that day.

NCS/Genesis Merger Agreement

Among other things, the NCS/Genesis merger agreement provided the following: . . .

- NCS would submit the merger agreement to NCS stockholders regardless of whether the NCS board continued to recommend the merger;
- NCS would not enter into discussions with third parties concerning an alternative acquisition of NCS, or provide non-public information to such parties, unless (1) the third party provided an unsolicited, *bona fide* written proposal documenting the terms of the acquisition; (2) the NCS board believed in good faith that the proposal was or was likely to result in an acquisition on terms superior to those contemplated by the NCS/Genesis merger agreement; and (3) before providing non-public information to that third party, the third party would execute a confidentiality agreement at least as restrictive as the one in place between NCS and Genesis; and
- If the merger agreement were to be terminated, under certain circumstances NCS would be required to pay Genesis a $6 million termination fee and/or Genesis's documented expenses, up to $5 million.

Voting Agreements

Outcalt and Shaw, in their capacity as NCS stockholders, entered into voting agreements with Genesis. NCS was also required to be a party to the voting agreements by Genesis. Those agreements provided, among other things, that:

- Outcalt and Shaw were acting in their capacity as NCS stockholders in executing the agreements, not in their capacity as NCS directors or officers;
- Neither Outcalt nor Shaw would transfer their shares prior to the stockholder vote on the merger agreement;
- Outcalt and Shaw agreed to vote all of their shares in favor of the merger agreement; and

- Outcalt and Shaw granted to Genesis an irrevocable proxy to vote their shares in favor of the merger agreement. . . .

On August 1, 2002, Omnicare filed a lawsuit attempting to enjoin the NCS/Genesis merger, and announced that it intended to launch a tender offer for NCS's shares at a price of $3.50 per share. On August 8, 2002, Omnicare began its tender offer. By letter dated that same day, Omnicare expressed a desire to discuss the terms of the offer with NCS. Omnicare's letter continued to condition its proposal on satisfactory completion of a due diligence investigation of NCS.

On August 8, 2002, and again on August 19, 2002, the NCS Independent Committee and full board of directors met separately to consider the Omnicare tender offer in light of the Genesis merger agreement. NCS's outside legal counsel and NCS's financial advisor attended both meetings. The board was unable to determine that Omnicare's expressions of interest were likely to lead to a "Superior Proposal," as the term was defined in the NCS/Genesis merger agreement. On September 10, 2002, NCS requested and received a waiver from Genesis allowing NCS to enter into discussions with Omnicare without first having to determine that Omnicare's proposal was a "Superior Proposal."

On October 6, 2002, Omnicare irrevocably committed itself to a transaction with NCS. Pursuant to the terms of its proposal, Omnicare agreed to acquire all the outstanding NCS Class A and Class B shares at a price of $3.50 per share in cash. As a result of this irrevocable offer, on October 21, 2002, the NCS board withdrew its recommendation that the stockholders vote in favor of the NCS/Genesis merger agreement. NCS's financial advisor withdrew its fairness opinion of the NCS/Genesis merger agreement as well.

Genesis Rejection Impossible

A subsequent filing with the Securities and Exchange Commission ("SEC") states: "the NCS independent committee and the NCS board of directors have determined to withdraw their recommendations of the Genesis merger agreement and recommend that the NCS stockholders vote against the approval and adoption of the Genesis merger." In that same SEC filing, however, the NCS board explained why the success of the Genesis merger had already been predetermined. "Notwithstanding the foregoing, the NCS independent committee and the NCS board of directors recognize that (1) the existing contractual obligations to Genesis currently prevent NCS from accepting the Omnicare irrevocable merger proposal; and (2) the existence of the voting agreements entered into by Messrs. Outcalt and Shaw, whereby Messrs. Outcalt and Shaw agreed to vote their shares of NCS Class A common stock and NCS Class B common stock in favor of the Genesis merger, ensure NCS stockholder approval of the Genesis merger." This litigation was commenced to prevent the consummation of the inferior Genesis transaction.

Business Judgment or Enhanced Scrutiny

The prior decisions of this Court have identified the circumstances where board action must be subjected to enhanced judicial scrutiny before the presumptive protection of the business judgment rule can be invoked. One of those circumstances was described in *Unocal* when a board adopts defensive measures in response to a hostile takeover proposal that the board reasonably determines is a threat to corporate policy and effectiveness. . . . Other circumstances requiring enhanced judicial scrutiny give rise to what are known as *Revlon* duties, such as when the board enters into a merger transaction that will cause a change in corporate control, initiates an active bidding process seeking to sell the corporation, or makes a break up of the corporate entity inevitable. . . .

Deal Protection Devices Require Enhanced Scrutiny

The dispositive issues in this appeal involve the defensive devices that protected the Genesis merger agreement. The Delaware corporation statute provides that the board's management decision to enter into and recommend a merger transaction can become final only when ownership action is taken by a vote of the stockholders.

Conflicts of interest arise when a board of directors acts to prevent stockholders from effectively exercising their right to vote contrary to the will of the board. The "omnipresent specter" of such conflict may be present whenever a board adopts defensive devices to protect a merger agreement. The stockholders' ability to effectively reject a merger agreement is likely to bear an inversely proportionate relationship to the structural and economic devices that the board has approved to protect the transaction. . . .

Enhanced Scrutiny Generally

. . . A board's decision to protect its decision to enter a merger agreement with defensive devices against uninvited competing transactions that may emerge is analogous to a board's decision to protect against dangers to corporate policy and effectiveness when it adopts defensive measures in a hostile takeover contest. In applying *Unocal*'s enhanced judicial scrutiny in assessing a challenge to defensive actions taken by a target corporation's board of directors in a takeover context, this Court held that the board "does not have unbridled discretion to defeat perceived threats by any Draconian means available." Similarly, just as a board's statutory power with regard to a merger decision is not absolute, a board does not have unbridled discretion to defeat any perceived threat to a merger by protecting it with any draconian means available. . . .

Therefore, in applying enhanced judicial scrutiny to defensive devices designed to protect a merger agreement, a court must first determine that those measures are not preclusive or coercive *before* its focus shifts to the "range of reasonableness" in making a proportionality determination. If the trial court determines that the defensive devices protecting a merger are not preclusive or coercive, the proportionality paradigm of *Unocal* is applicable. The board must demonstrate that it has reasonable grounds for believing that a danger to the corporation and its stockholders exists if the merger transaction is not consummated. That burden is satisfied "by showing good faith and reasonable investigation." Such proof is materially enhanced if it is approved by a board comprised of a majority of outside directors or by an independent committee.

When the focus of judicial scrutiny shifts to the range of reasonableness, *Unocal* requires that any defensive devices must be proportionate to the perceived threat to the corporation and its stockholders if the merger transaction is not consummated. Defensive devices taken to protect a merger agreement executed by a board of directors are intended to give that agreement an advantage over any subsequent transactions that materialize before the merger is approved by the stockholders and consummated. This is analogous to the favored treatment that a board of directors may properly give to encourage an initial bidder when it discharges its fiduciary duties under *Revlon*. . . .

The latitude a board will have in either maintaining or using the defensive devices it has adopted to protect the merger it approved [i.e., "deal protection devices"] will vary according to the degree of benefit or detriment to the stockholders' interests that is presented by the value or terms of the subsequent competing transaction. . . .

Genesis argues that stockholder voting agreements cannot be construed as deal protection devices taken by a board of directors because stockholders are entitled to vote in their own interest. . . .

In this case, the stockholder voting agreements were inextricably intertwined with the defensive aspects of the Genesis merger agreement. In fact, . . . [w]ith the assurance that Outcalt and Shaw would irrevocably agree to exercise their majority voting power in favor of its transaction, Genesis insisted that the merger agreement reflect the other two aspects of its concerted defense, i.e., the inclusion of a Section 251(c) provision and the omission of any effective fiduciary out clause. Those dual aspects of the merger agreement would not have provided Genesis with a complete defense in the absence of the voting agreements with Shaw and Outcalt.

. . . [Under *Unocal*, the] NCS directors must first establish that the merger deal protection devices adopted in response to the threat were not "coercive" or "preclusive," and then demonstrate that their response was within a "range of reasonable responses" to the threat perceived. . . . The record reflects that the defensive devices employed by the NCS board are preclusive and coercive in the sense that they accomplished a *fait accompli*. In this case, despite the fact that the NCS board has withdrawn its recommendation for the Genesis transaction and recommended its rejection by the stockholders, the deal protection devices approved by the NCS board operated in concert to have a preclusive and coercive effect. Those tripartite defensive measures — the Section 251 (c) provision, the voting agreements, and the absence of an effective fiduciary out clause — made it "mathematically impossible" and "realistically unattainable" for the Omnicare transaction or any other proposal to succeed, no matter how superior the proposal.

The deal protection devices adopted by the NCS board were designed to coerce the consummation of the Genesis merger and preclude the consideration of any superior transaction. The NCS directors' defensive devices are not within a reasonable range of responses to the perceived threat of losing the Genesis offer because they are preclusive and coercive. Accordingly, we hold that those deal protection devices are unenforceable. . . .

The defensive measures that protected the merger transaction are unenforceable not only because they are preclusive and coercive but, alternatively, they are unenforceable because they . . . completely prevented the board from discharging its fiduciary responsibilities to the minority stockholders when Omnicare presented its superior transaction. "To the extent that a [merger] contract, or a provision thereof, purports to require a board to act or not act in such a fashion as to limit the exercise of fiduciary duties, it is invalid and unenforceable."[74] . . . [W]here a cohesive group of stockholders with majority voting power was irrevocably committed to the merger transaction, "[e]ffective representation of the financial interests of the minority shareholders imposed upon the [NCS board] an affirmative responsibility to protect those minority shareholders' interests." [79] The NCS board could not abdicate its fiduciary duties to the minority by leaving it to the stockholders alone to approve or disapprove the merger agreement because two stockholders had already combined to establish a majority of the voting power[, which] made the outcome of the stockholder vote a foregone conclusion.

The Court of Chancery noted that Section 251(c) of the Delaware General Corporation Law now permits boards to agree to submit a merger agreement for a stockholder vote, even if the Board later withdraws its support for that agreement and recommends that the stockholders reject it.[80] The Court of Chancery also noted that stockholder voting agreements are permitted by Delaware law. . . .

Taking action that is otherwise legally possible, however, does not *ipso facto* comport with the fiduciary responsibilities of directors in all circumstances. The synopsis to the amendments that resulted in the enactment of Section 251(c) in the Delaware corporation law statute specifically provides: "the amendments are not intended to address the question of whether such a submission requirement is appropriate in any particular set of factual circumstances." Section 251 provisions, like the no-shop provision examined in *QVC*, are "presumptively valid in the abstract." [82] Such provisions in a merger agreement may not, however, "validly define or limit the directors' fiduciary duties under Delaware law or prevent the [NCS] directors from carrying out their fiduciary duties under Delaware law."[83]

. . . Genesis anticipated the likelihood of a superior offer after its merger agreement was announced and demanded defensive measures from the NCS board that *completely* protected its transaction.[84] . . . [T]he NCS board disabled itself from exercising its own fiduciary obligations at a time when the board's own judgment is most important, i.e., receipt of a subsequent superior offer.

Any board has authority to give the proponent of a recommended merger agreement reasonable structural and economic defenses, incentives, and fair compensation if the transaction is not completed. To the extent that defensive measures are economic and reasonable, they may become an increased cost to the proponent of any subsequent transaction. Just as defensive measures cannot be draconian, however, they cannot limit or circumscribe the directors' fiduciary duties.

---

74. Paramount Communications Inc. v. QVC Network Inc., 637 A.2d 34, 51 (Del. 1993) (citation omitted). Restatement (Second) of Contracts §193 explicitly provides that a "promise by a fiduciary to violate his fiduciary duty or a promise that tends to induce such a violation is unenforceable on grounds of public policy." The comments to that section indicate that "[d]irectors and other officials of a corporation act in a fiduciary capacity and are subject to the rule stated in this Section." Restatement (Second) of Contracts §193 (1981) (emphasis added).

79. McMullin v. Beran, 765 A.2d 910, 920 (Del. 2000).

80. Section 251(c) was amended in 1998 to allow for the inclusion in a merger agreement of a term requiring that the agreement be put to a vote of stockholders whether or not their directors continue to recommend the transaction. Before this amendment, Section 251 was interpreted as precluding a stockholder vote if the board of directors, after approving the merger agreement but before the stockholder vote, decided no longer to recommend it. See Smith v. Van Gorkom, 488 A.2d 858, 887-88 (Del. 1985).

82. Paramount Communications Inc. v. QVC Network Inc., 637 A.2d at 48.

83. Id.

84. The marked improvement in NCS's financial situation during the negotiations with Genesis strongly suggests that the NCS board should have been alert to the prospect of competing offers or, as eventually occurred, a bidding contest.

Notwithstanding the corporation's insolvent condition, the NCS board had no authority to execute a merger agreement that subsequently prevented it from effectively discharging its ongoing fiduciary responsibilities. . . .

The NCS board was required to contract for an effective fiduciary out clause to exercise its continuing fiduciary responsibilities to the minority stockholders.[88] The issues in this appeal do not involve the general validity of either stockholder voting agreements or the authority of directors to insert a Section 251(c) provision in a merger agreement. In this case, the NCS board combined those two otherwise valid actions and caused them to operate in concert as an absolute lock up, in the absence of an effective fiduciary out clause in the Genesis merger agreement . . .

VEASEY, C.J., dissenting: . . . The process by which this merger agreement came about involved a joint decision by the controlling stockholders and the board of directors to secure what appeared to be the only value-enhancing transaction available for a company on the brink of bankruptcy. The Majority adopts a new rule of law that imposes a prohibition on the NCS board's ability to act in concert with controlling stockholders to lock up this merger. The Majority reaches this conclusion by analyzing the challenged deal protection measures as isolated board actions. The Majority concludes that the board owed a duty to the NCS minority stockholders to refrain from acceding to the Genesis demand for an irrevocable lock-up notwithstanding the compelling circumstances confronting the board and the board's disinterested, informed, good faith exercise of its business judgment. . . .

Going into negotiations with Genesis, the NCS directors knew that, up until that time, NCS had found only one potential bidder, Omnicare. Omnicare had refused to buy NCS except at a fire sale price through an asset sale in bankruptcy. Omnicare's best proposal at that stage would not have paid off all creditors and would have provided nothing for stockholders. The Noteholders, represented by the Ad Hoc Committee, were willing to oblige Omnicare and force NCS into bankruptcy if Omnicare would pay in full the NCS debt. Through the NCS board's efforts, Genesis expressed interest that became increasingly attractive. Negotiations with Genesis led to an offer paying creditors off and conferring on NCS stockholders $24 million—an amount infinitely superior to the prior Omnicare proposals.

But there was, understandably, a sine qua non. In exchange for offering the NCS stockholders a return on their equity and creditor payment, Genesis demanded certainty that the merger would close. If the NCS board would not have acceded to the Section 251(c) provision, if Outcalt and Shaw had not agreed to the voting agreements and if NCS had insisted on a fiduciary out, there would have been no Genesis deal! . . . NCS knew that Omnicare had spoiled a Genesis acquisition in the past, and it is not disputed by the Majority that the NCS directors made a reasoned decision to accept as real the Genesis threat to walk away.

When Omnicare submitted its conditional eleventh-hour bid, the NCS board had to weigh the economic terms of the proposal against the uncertainty of completing a deal with Omnicare. Importantly, because Omnicare's bid was

---

88. See Paramount Communications Inc. v. QVC Network Inc., 637 A.2d at 42-43. Merger agreements involve an ownership decision and, therefore, cannot become final without stockholder approval. Other contracts do not require a fiduciary out clause because they involve business judgments that are within the *exclusive* province of the board of directors' power to manage the affairs of the corporation. See Grimes v. Donald, 673 A.2d 1207, 1214-15 (Del. 1996).

conditioned on its satisfactorily completing its due diligence review of NCS, the NCS board saw this as a crippling condition, as did the Ad Hoc Committee. As a matter of business judgment, the risk of negotiating with Omnicare and losing Genesis at that point outweighed the possible benefits. The lock-up was indisputably a sine qua non to any deal with Genesis.

A lock-up permits a target board and a bidder to "exchange certainties." Certainty itself has value. The acquirer may pay a higher price for the target if the acquirer is assured consummation of the transaction. The target company also benefits from the certainty of completing a transaction with a bidder because losing an acquirer creates the perception that a target is damaged goods, thus reducing its value.

If the creditors decided to force NCS into bankruptcy, which could have happened at any time as NCS was unable to service its obligations, the stockholders would have received nothing. The NCS board also did not know if the NCS business prospects would have declined again, leaving NCS less attractive to other bidders, including Omnicare, which could have changed its mind and again insisted on an asset sale in bankruptcy.

Situations will arise where business realities demand a lock-up so that wealth-enhancing transactions may go forward. Accordingly, any bright-line rule prohibiting lock-ups could, in circumstances such as these, chill otherwise permissible conduct. . . .

The Majority invalidates the NCS board's action by announcing a new rule that represents an extension of our jurisprudence. That new rule can be narrowly stated as follows: A merger agreement entered into after a market search, before any prospect of a topping bid has emerged, which locks up stockholder approval and does not contain a "fiduciary out" provision, is per se invalid when a later significant topping bid emerges. As we have noted, this bright-line, per se rule would apply regardless of (1) the circumstances leading up to the agreement and (2) the fact that stockholders who control voting power had irrevocably committed themselves, *as stockholders*, to vote for the merger. Narrowly stated, this new rule is a judicially-created "third rail" that now becomes one of the given "rules of the game," to be taken into account by the negotiators and drafters of merger agreements. In our view, this new rule is an unwise extension of existing precedent.

Although it is debatable whether *Unocal* applies — and we believe that the better rule in this situation is that the business judgment rule should apply — we will, nevertheless, assume arguendo — as the Vice Chancellor did — that *Unocal* applies. Therefore, under *Unocal* the NCS directors had the burden of going forward with the evidence to show that there was a threat to corporate policy and effectiveness and that their actions were reasonable in response to that threat. The Vice Chancellor correctly found that they reasonably perceived the threat that NCS did not have a viable offer from Omnicare — or anyone else — to pay off its creditors, cure its insolvency and provide some payment to stockholders. The NCS board's actions — as the Vice Chancellor correctly held — were reasonable in relation to the threat because the Genesis deal was the "only game in town," the NCS directors got the best deal they could from Genesis and — but for the emergence of Genesis on the scene — there would have been no viable deal.

The Vice Chancellor held that the NCS directors satisfied *Unocal*. He even held that they would have satisfied *Revlon*, if it had applied, which it did not. Indeed, he concluded — based on the undisputed record and his considerable experience — that: "The overall quality of testimony given by the NCS directors is among the strongest this court has ever seen. All four NCS directors were deposed, and each deposition makes manifest the care and attention given to this project by every member of the board." We agree fully with the Vice Chancellor's findings and conclusions, and we would have affirmed the judgment of the Court of Chancery on that basis.

. . . The Majority — incorrectly, in our view — relies on *Unitrin* to advance its analysis. The discussion of "draconian" measures in *Unitrin* dealt with unilateral board action, a repurchase program, designed to fend off an existing hostile offer by American General. In *Unitrin* we recognized the need to police preclusive and coercive actions initiated *by the board* to delay or retard an existing hostile bid so as to ensure that the stockholders can benefit from the board's negotiations with the bidder or others and to exercise effectively the franchise as the ultimate check on board action. *Unitrin* polices the effect of board action on existing tender offers and proxy contests to ensure that the board cannot permanently impose its will on the stockholders, leaving the stockholders no recourse to their voting rights.

The very measures the Majority cites as "coercive" were approved by Shaw and Outcalt through the lens of their independent assessment of the merits of the transaction. The proper inquiry in this case is whether the NCS board had taken actions that "have the effect of causing the stockholders to vote in favor of the proposed transaction for some reason other than the merits of that transaction." Like the termination fee upheld as a valid liquidated damages clause against a claim of coercion in Brazen v. Bell Atlantic Corp., the deal protection measures at issue here were "an integral part of the merits of the transaction" as the NCS board struggled to secure — and did secure — the only deal available.

Outcalt and Shaw were fully informed stockholders. As the NCS controlling stockholders, they made an informed choice to commit their voting power to the merger. The minority stockholders were deemed to know that when controlling stockholders have 65% of the vote they can approve a merger without the need for the minority votes. Moreover, to the extent a minority stockholder may have felt "coerced" to vote for the merger, which was already a *fait accompli*, it was a meaningless coercion — or no coercion at all — because the controlling votes, those of Outcalt and Shaw, were already "cast." Although the fact that the controlling votes were committed to the merger "precluded" an overriding vote against the merger by the Class A stockholders, the pejorative "preclusive" label applicable in a *Unitrin* fact situation has no application here. Therefore, there was no meaningful minority stockholder voting decision to coerce.

In applying *Unocal* scrutiny, we believe the Majority incorrectly preempted the proportionality inquiry. In our view, the proportionality inquiry must account for the reality that the contractual measures protecting this merger agreement were necessary to obtain the Genesis deal. The Majority has not demonstrated that the director action was a disproportionate response to the threat posed. Indeed, it is clear to us that the board action to negotiate the best deal reasonably available with the only viable merger partner (Genesis) who could satisfy the creditors and benefit the stockholders, was reasonable in relation to the threat, by any practical yardstick. . . .

We respectfully disagree with the Majority's conclusion that the NCS board breached its fiduciary duties to the Class A stockholders by failing to negotiate a "fiduciary out" in the Genesis merger agreement. What is the practical import of a "fiduciary out" ? It is a contractual provision, articulated in a manner to be negotiated, that would permit the board of the corporation being acquired to exit without breaching the merger agreement in the event of a superior offer.

In this case, Genesis made it abundantly clear early on that . . . a "fiduciary out" was not acceptable to Genesis. The Majority Opinion holds that such a negotiating position, if implemented in the agreement, is invalid per se where there is an absolute lock-up. We know of no authority in our jurisprudence supporting this new rule, and we believe it is unwise and unwarranted.

The Majority relies on our decision in *QVC* to assert that the board's fiduciary duties prevent the directors from negotiating a merger agreement without providing an escape provision. Reliance on *QVC* for this proposition, however, confuses our statement of a board's responsibilities when the directors confront a superior transaction and turn away from it to lock up a less valuable deal with the very different situation here, where the board committed itself to the *only* value-enhancing transaction available. . . . Our reasoning in *QVC* which recognizes that minority stockholders must rely for protection on the fiduciary duties owed to them by directors, does not create a *special* duty to protect the minority stockholders from the consequences of a controlling stockholder's ultimate decision unless the controlling stockholder stands on both sides of the transaction, [which] is certainly not the case here. . . .

STEELE, J. dissenting: . . . The contract terms that NCS' board agreed to included no insidious, camouflaged side deals for the directors or the majority stockholders nor transparent provisions for entrenchment or control premiums. At the time the NCS board and the majority stockholders agreed to a voting lockup, the terms were the best reasonably available for all the stockholders, balanced against a genuine risk of no deal at all. The cost benefit analysis entered into by an independent committee of the board, approved by the full board and independently agreed to by the majority stockholders, cannot be second guessed by courts with no business expertise that would qualify them to substitute their judgment for that of a careful, selfless board or for majority stockholders who had the most significant economic stake in the outcome.

We should not encourage proscriptive rules that invalidate or render unenforceable precommitment strategies negotiated between two parties to a contract who will presumably, in the absence of conflicted interest, bargain intensely over every meaningful provision of a contract after a careful cost benefit analysis. Where could this plain common sense approach be more wisely invoked than where a board, free of conflict, fully informed, supported by the equally conflict-free holders of the largest economic interest in the transaction, reaches the conclusion that a voting lockup strategy is the best course to obtain the most benefit for all stockholders? . . .

Delaware corporate citizens now face the prospect that in *every* circumstance, boards must obtain the highest price, even if that requires breaching a contract entered into at a time when no one could have reasonably foreseen a truly "Superior Proposal." The majority's proscriptive rule limits the scope of a board's cost benefit analysis by taking the bargaining chip of foregoing a fiduciary out "off the table" in all circumstances. For that new principle to arise from the context of this case, when Omnicare, after striving to buy NCS on the cheap by buying off its creditors, slinked back into the fray, reversed its historic antagonistic strategy and offered a conditional "Superior Proposal" seems entirely counterintuitive. . . .

I believe that the absence of a suggestion of self-interest or lack of care compels a court to defer to what is a business judgment that a court is not qualified to second guess. However, I recognize that another judge might prefer to view the reasonableness of the board's action through the *Unocal* prism before deferring. Some flexible, readily discernible standard of review must be applied no matter what it may be called. Here, one deferring or one applying *Unocal* scrutiny would reach the same conclusion. When a board agrees rationally, in good faith, without conflict and with reasonable care to include provisions in a contract to preserve a deal in the absence of a better one, their business judgment should not be second-guessed in order to invalidate or declare unenforceable an otherwise valid merger agreement. The fact that majority stockholders free of conflicts have a choice and every incentive to get the best available deal and then make a rational judgment to do so as well neither unfairly impinges upon minority shareholder choice or the concept of a shareholder "democracy" nor has it any independent significance bearing on the reasonableness of the board's separate and distinct exercise of judgment. . . .

Lockup provisions attempt to assure parties that have lost business opportunities and incurred substantial costs that their deal will close. I am concerned that the majority decision will remove the certainty that adds value to any rational business plan. Perhaps transactions that include "force-the-vote" and voting agreement provisions that make approval a foregone conclusion will be the only deals invalidated prospectively. Even so, therein lies the problem. Instead of thoughtful, retrospective, restrained flexibility focused on the circumstances existing at the time of the decision, have we now moved to a bright line regulatory alternative?

For the majority to articulate and adopt an inflexible rule where a board has discharged both its fiduciary duty of loyalty and care in good faith seems a most unfortunate turn. Does the majority mean to signal a mandatory, bright line, *per se* efficient breach analysis *ex post* to all challenged merger agreements? Knowing the majority's general, genuine concern to do equity, I trust not. If so, our courts and the structure of our law that we have strived so hard to develop and perfect will prevent a board, responsible under Delaware law to make precisely the kind of decision made here, in good faith, free of self interest, after exercising scrupulous due care from honoring its contract obligations.

Therefore, I respectfully dissent.

---

1. *Alternative standards of review.* After *Omnicare*, does whether *Revlon* applies make a difference in the judicial review of deal protection devices? If the transaction is subject to *Revlon*, then the *Macmillan* analysis applies: did the board favor a bidder, and if so, was the benefit received proportional to the favors accorded? How would the NCS lockup have fared under this standard? Would the benefit of avoiding bankruptcy, paying off creditors in full, and getting something for the shareholders warrant cutting off the potential of a higher bid? The majority in *Omnicare* applies *Unocal/Unitrin* analysis to the NCS lockup because the transaction involved no change in control. Will an effective lockup always be preclusive in the terms of the *Unitrin* formulation? What is the effect of failing the *Unitrin* formulation? How would the NCS lockup fare under an entire fairness review?

Omnicare has not been wholly embraced by the Delaware courts. See, e.g., In re Toys "R" Us, Inc. Shareholder Litigation, 877 A.2d. 975, 1016 (calling *Omnicare* an "aberrational departure from [the] long accepted principle" that "what matters is whether the board acted reasonably based on the circumstances then facing it").

2. Mentor Graphics *analysis*. The *Omnicare* majority also builds on the *Mentor Graphics* approach, see pages 990-991 supra, that uses Del. §141 to prevent a board of directors from limiting their future ability to discharge their fiduciary duties — in *Mentor Graphics* through a slow-hand poison pill, and in *Omnicare* through a lockup and the absence of a fiduciary out. This analysis led a leading takeover firm to conclude that, after *Omnicare*, "the board of a Delaware corporation cannot agree to a merger agreement without a 'fiduciary out' permitting it either to terminate the agreement if a superior proposal emerges or to be certain that the stockholders remain free to reject the original merger in that event." Wachtell, Lipton, Rosen & Katz client letter, April 10, 2003. This approach, unlike a *Unitrin* approach, leaves no room for the exercise of judgment by the board; directors lack the power to agree even to a lockup that would meet the entire fairness test. Must the target board retain a fiduciary out even if, unlike in *Omnicare*, the shareholders are free to reject the merger? Think again about Del. §251(c). After *Van Gorkom* held that a board could not abandon its fiduciary obligation and allow shareholders to vote on a transaction that the board did not favor, the Delaware legislature added this subsection to explicitly allow a board to commit to presenting a transaction to the shareholders. Does §251(c) save the transaction in *Omnicare*?

3. *Shareholder approval rights*. Would the dissenters allow a lockup that forced shareholders to approve a merger — say by giving the acquirer an option to buy critical assets at a low price if the shareholders did not approve the merger — in the absence of a controlling shareholder? What about protecting the shareholders' statutory right to approve a merger?

4. *Does board participation matter?* A separate issue in *Omnicare* concerned how much voting power the Class B holders actually had. Under the NCS charter, the ten-votes-per-share Class B common stock automatically converted to one-vote-per-share Class A common stock if the Class B stock was sold. Should it matter that the Class B shareholders could force the sale of the corporation only through a merger, which required board approval (if they sold their shares to Genesis in a tender offer, Genesis would not acquire voting control because of the conversion feature)? Does the fact that the Class B shareholders could not lock up the transaction without board participation impose a special duty on the board to look out for minority shareholders? See the discussion of *Digex* in the next section of this chapter.

5. *How do you end an auction?* Suppose a target wanted to structure its sale through a formal auction. If the highest bidder could not be given an effective lockup, how would the auction ever end? Would the absence of a lockup to the highest bidder at a specified time affect a potential bidder's strategy? See Preston McAfee & John MacMillan, Auctions and Bidding, 25 J. Econ. Lit. 699 (1987). Could a target hold a one-round, sealed-bid auction after *Omnicare*? This auction technique seeks a higher price by preventing bidders from knowing each other's bids, as would be the case in an English auction, in which bidding is public. In the absence of a lockup, could a bidder just wait to see the winning bid, and then top it if it wanted?

D. *SALE OF CONTROL AT A PREMIUM*

If a shareholder or group of shareholders own sufficient shares to give them effective control, they alone have the power to transfer control; a competing bid without their approval cannot succeed. However, this centralization of decision authority does not eliminate the potential for litigation over control transfers. Most commonly, conflict arises over the distribution of the premium paid for control. If a controlling shareholder sells her shares at a premium, do minority shareholders have a right to a portion of the premium? More recently, conflict has been provoked by exactly the opposite situation. Suppose a third party makes an offer to all shareholders at an attractive premium. Can a controlling shareholder decline to sell her shares — thereby blocking the offer and preventing minority shareholders from receiving a control premium — because she believes her controlling shares have greater value than minority shares and does not wish to share that value with the minority?

Debate over sharing of the premium has traditionally focused on the matter of fairness. Control was argued as belonging to the corporation (in part, because corporation law provides that the business and affairs of the corporation are to be managed by its board of directors). For such a view, see Adolph Berle & Gardiner Means, "Control" in Corporate Law, 58 Private Prop. 244 (1932); Adolph Berle, "Control" in Corporate Law, 58 Colum. L. Rev. 1212 (1958). A related argument treats sale of control by a controlling shareholder as a corporate opportunity to which all shareholders are entitled. See William Andrews, Stockholders' Rights to Equal Opportunity in the Sale of Shares, 78 Harv. L. Rev. 505, 506 (1965). Current commentary, in contrast, focuses on efficiency: does allowing a controlling shareholder to keep all of the control premium, or requiring that it be shared by all shareholders, result in greater value for shareholders? See Frank Easterbrook & Daniel Fischel, Corporate Control Transactions, 91 Yale L.J. 698 (1982); Ronald Gilson & Bernard Black, The Law and Finance of Corporate Acquisitions 1229-1236 (2d ed. 1995). Put differently, which rule makes minority shareholders better off? Einer Elhauge, The Triggering Function of Sale of Control, 59 U. Chi. L. Rev. 1465 (1992), provides a careful review of the literature.

The motive for restraining a controlling shareholder from selling control at a premium is the concern that the shareholder will thereby capture private benefits of control — i.e., the controlling shareholder will use the sale to capture a disproportionate share of the corporation's profits. Here it is important to keep in mind that a controlling shareholder can receive private benefits from control in three different ways: by taking a disproportionate amount of the corporation's ongoing earnings, by freezing out the minority, or by selling control. See Ronald Gilson & Jeffrey Gordon, Controlling Controlling Shareholders, 152 U. Pa. L. Rev. 785 (2003). *Sinclair*, page 131 supra, governs the first technique. Where the controlling shareholder is on both sides of a transaction — for example, by sales to the corporation — the court reviews the transaction closely under the entire fairness test. The second technique is discussed in Sec. F of this chapter, infra. If non-controlling shareholders are frozen out, the court also will closely review the transaction. The standards that govern the third technique for capturing private benefits of control — the sale of control will take place at a price that capitalizes the private benefits received by the controlling shareholder through the corporation's operations — is our concern here.

The following cases present the landscape of the debate. Perlman v. Feldmann initially framed the issue, but ultimately did not dictate its resolution. Mendel v. Carroll presents the current state of the law in the context of the issue's more recent formulation — whether a controlling shareholder can decline to sell control. Finally, In re Digex Shareholders' Litigation considers the standards that apply when the controlling shareholder's sale of control requires the corporation's cooperation.

Perlman v. Feldmann
219 F.2d 173 (2d Cir. 1955)

CLARK, C.J.: This is a derivative action brought by minority stockholders of Newport Steel Corporation to compel accounting for, and restitution of, allegedly illegal gains which accrued to defendants as a result of the sale in August, 1950, of their controlling interest in the corporation. The principal defendant, C. Russell Feldmann, who represented and acted for the others, members of his family, was at that time not only the dominant stockholder, but also the chairman of the board of directors and the president of the corporation. Newport, an Indiana corporation, operated mills for the production of steel sheets for sale to manufacturers of steel products. . . . The buyers, a syndicate organized as Wilport Company, a Delaware corporation, consisted of end-users of steel who were interested in securing a source of supply in a market becoming ever tighter in the Korean War. Plaintiffs contend that the consideration paid for the stock included compensation for the sale of a corporate asset, a power held in trust for the corporation by Feldmann as its fiduciary. This power was the ability to control the allocation of the corporate product in a time of short supply, through control of the board of directors; and it was effectively transferred in this sale by having Feldmann procure the resignation of his own board and the election of Wilport's nominees immediately upon consummation of the sale.

. . . Plaintiffs argue . . . that in the situation here disclosed the vendors must account to the non-participating minority stockholders for that share of their profit which is attributable to the sale of the corporate power. Judge Hincks denied the validity of the premise, holding that the rights involved in the sale were only those normally incident to the possession of a controlling block of shares, with which a dominant stockholder, in the absence of fraud or foreseeable looting, was entitled to deal according to his own best interests. Furthermore, he held that plaintiffs had failed to satisfy their burden of proving that the sale price was not a fair price for the stock per se. . . .

Newport was a relative newcomer in the steel industry with predominantly old installations which were in the process of being supplemented by more modern facilities. Except in time of extreme shortage Newport was not in a position to compete profitably with other steel mills for customers not in its immediate geographical area. Wilport, the purchasing syndicate, consisted of geographically remote end-users of steel who were interested in buying more steel from Newport than they had been able to obtain during recent periods of tight supply. The price of $20 per share was found by Judge Hincks to be a fair one for a control block of stock, although the over-the-counter market price had not exceeded $12 and the book value per share was $17.03. But this finding was limited by Judge Hincks' statement that "[w]hat value the block would have had if shorn of its appurtenant power to control distribution of the corporate product, the evidence does not show." It was also conditioned by his earlier ruling that the burden was on plaintiffs to prove a lesser value for the stock. . . .

It is true, as defendants have been at pains to point out, that this is not the ordinary case of breach of fiduciary duty. We have here no fraud, no misuse of confidential information, no outright looting of a helpless corporation. But on the other hand, we do not find compliance with that high standard . . . which we and other courts have come to expect and demand of corporate fiduciaries. . . . The actions of defendants in siphoning off for personal gain corporate advantages to be derived from a favorable market situation do not betoken the necessary undivided loyalty owed by the fiduciary to his principal.

The corporate opportunities of whose misappropriation the minority stockholders complain need not have been an absolute certainty in order to support this action against Feldmann. If there was possibility of corporate gain, they are entitled to recover. . . .

. . . In the past Newport had used and profited by its market leverage by operation of what the industry had come to call the "Feldmann plan." This consisted of securing interest-free advances from prospective purchasers of steel in return for firm commitments to them from future production. The funds thus acquired were used to finance improvements in existing plants and to acquire new installations. In the summer of 1950 Newport had been negotiating for cold-rolling facilities which it needed for a more fully integrated operation and a more marketable product, and Feldmann plan funds might well have been used toward this end.

Further, as plaintiffs alternatively suggest, Newport might have used the period of short supply to build up patronage in the geographical area in which it could compete profitably even when steel was more abundant. Either of these opportunities was Newport's, to be used to its advantage only. Only if defendants had been able to negate completely any possibility of gain by Newport could they have prevailed. It is true that a trial court finding states: "Whether or not, in August, 1950, Newport's position was such that it could have entered into 'Feldmann Plan' type transactions to procure funds and financing for the further expansion and integration of its steel facilities and whether such expansion would have been desirable for Newport, the evidence does not show." This, however, cannot avail the defendants, who — contrary to the ruling below — had the burden of proof on this issue, since fiduciaries always have the burden of proof in establishing the fairness of their dealings with trust property. . . .

Defendants seek to categorize the corporate opportunities which might have accrued to Newport as too unethical to warrant further consideration. It is true that reputable steel producers were not participating in the gray market brought about by the Korean War and were refraining from advancing their prices, although to do so would not have been illegal. But Feldmann plan transactions were not considered within this self-imposed interdiction; the trial court found that around the time of the Feldmann sale Jones & Laughlin Steel Corporation, Republic Steel Company, and Pittsburgh Steel Corporation were all participating in such arrangements. In any event, it ill becomes the defendants to disparage as unethical the market advantages from which they themselves reaped rich benefits.

We do not mean to suggest that a majority stockholder cannot dispose of his controlling block of stock to outsiders without having to account to his corporation for profits or even never do this with impunity when the buyer is an interested customer, actual or potential, for the corporation's product. But when the sale necessarily results in a sacrifice of this element of corporate good will and consequent unusual profit to the fiduciary who has caused the sacrifice, he should account for his gains. So in a time of market shortage, where a call on a corporation's product commands an unusually large premium, in one form or another, we think it sound law that a fiduciary may not appropriate to himself the value of this premium. Such personal gain at the expense of his coventurers seems particularly reprehensible when made by the trusted president and director of his company. In this case the violation of duty seems to be all the clearer because of this triple role in which Feldmann appears, though we are unwilling to say, and are not to be understood as saying, that we should accept a lesser obligation for any of his roles alone.

Hence to the extent that the price received by Feldmann and his co-defendants included such a bonus, he is accountable to the minority stockholders who sue here. . . . And plaintiffs, as they contend, are entitled to a recovery in their own right, instead of in right of the corporation (as in the usual derivative actions), since neither Wilport nor their successors in interest should share in any judgment which may be rendered. . . . Defendants cannot well object to this form of recovery, since the only alternative, recovery for the corporation as a whole, would subject them to a greater total liability.

The case will therefore be remanded to the district court for a determination of the question expressly left open below, namely, the value of defendants' stock without the appurtenant control over the corporation's output of steel. We reiterate that on this issue, as on all others relating to a breach of fiduciary duty, the burden of proof must rest on the defendants. . . . Judgment should go to these plaintiffs and those whom they represent for any premium value so shown to the extent of their respective stock interests. . . .

SWAN, J., dissenting: With the general principles enunciated in the majority opinion as to the duties of fiduciaries I am, of course, in thorough accord. . . . My brothers' opinion does not specify precisely what fiduciary duty Feldmann is held to have violated or whether it was a duty imposed upon him as the dominant stockholder or as a director of Newport. Without such specification I think that both the legal profession and the business world will find the decision confusing and will be unable to foretell the extent of its impact upon customary practices in the sale of stock.

The power to control the management of a corporation, that is, to elect directors to manage its affairs, is an inseparable incident to the ownership of a majority of its stock, or sometimes, as in the present instance, to the ownership of enough shares, less than a majority, to control an election. Concededly a majority or dominant shareholder is ordinarily privileged to sell his stock at the best price obtainable from the purchaser. In so doing he acts on his own behalf, not as an agent of the corporation. If he knows or has reason to believe that the purchaser intends to exercise to the detriment of the corporation the power of management acquired by the purchase, such knowledge or reasonable suspicion will terminate the dominant shareholder's privilege to sell and will create a duty not to transfer the power of management to such purchaser. The duty seems to me to resemble the obligation which everyone is under not to assist another to commit a tort rather than the obligation of a fiduciary. But whatever the nature of the duty, a violation of it will subject the violator to liability for damages sustained by the corporation. Judge Hincks found that Feldmann had no reason to think that Wilport would use the power of management it would acquire by the purchase to injure Newport, and that there was no proof that it ever was so used. Feldmann did know, it is true, that the reason Wilport wanted the stock was to put in a board of directors who would be likely to permit Wilport's members to purchase more of Newport's steel than they might otherwise be able to get. But there is nothing illegal in a dominant shareholder purchasing from his own corporation at the same prices it offers to other customers. That is what the members of Wilport did, and there is no proof that Newport suffered any detriment therefrom.

My brothers say that "the consideration paid for the stock included compensation for the sale of a corporate asset," which they describe as "the ability to control the allocation of the corporate product in a time of short supply, through control of the board of directors; and it was effectively transferred in this sale by having Feldmann procure the resignation of his own board and the election of Wilport's nominees immediately upon consummation of the sale." The implications of this are not clear to me. If it means that when market conditions are such as to induce users of a corporation's product to wish to buy a controlling block of stock in order to be able to purchase part of the corporation's output at the same mill list prices as are offered to other customers, the dominant stockholder is under a fiduciary duty not to sell his stock, I cannot agree. For reasons already stated, in my opinion Feldmann was not proved to be under any fiduciary duty as a stockholder not to sell the stock he controlled.

Feldmann was also a director of Newport. Perhaps the quoted statement means that as a director he violated his fiduciary duty in voting to elect Wilport's nominees to fill the vacancies created by the resignations of the former directors of Newport. As a director Feldmann was under a fiduciary duty to use an honest judgment in acting on the corporation's behalf. A director is privileged to resign, but so long as he remains a director he must be faithful to his fiduciary duties and must not make a personal gain from performing them. Consequently, if the price paid for Feldmann's stock included a payment for voting to elect the new directors, he must account to the corporation for such payment, even though he honestly believed that the men he voted to elect were well qualified to serve as directors. He cannot take pay for performing his fiduciary duty. There is no suggestion that he did do so, unless the price paid for his stock was more than its value. So it seems to me that decision must turn on whether finding 120 and conclusion 5 of the district judge are supportable on the evidence. They are set out in the margin.[1]

Judge Hincks went into the matter of valuation of the stock with his customary care and thoroughness. He made no error of law in applying the principles relating to valuation of stock. Concededly a controlling block of stock has greater sale value

---

1. "120. The 398,927 shares of Newport stock sold to Wilport as of August 31, 1950, had a fair value as a control block of $20 per share. What value the block would have had if shorn of its appurtenant power to control distribution of the corporate product, the evidence does not show."

"5. Even if Feldmann's conduct in cooperating to accomplish a transfer of control to Wilport immediately upon the sale constituted a breach of a fiduciary duty to Newport, no part of the moneys received by the defendants in connection with the sale constituted profits for which they were accountable to Newport."

than a small lot. While the spread between $10 per share for small lots and $20 per share for the controlling block seems rather extraordinarily wide, the $20 valuation was supported by the expert testimony of Dr. Badger, whom the district judge said he could not find to be wrong. I see no justification for upsetting the valuation as clearly erroneous. Nor can I agree with my brothers that the $20 valuation "was limited" by the last sentence in finding 120. The controlling block could not by any possibility be shorn of its appurtenant power to elect directors and through them to control distribution of the corporate product. It is this "appurtenant power" which gives a controlling block its value as such block. What evidence could be adduced to show the value of the block "if shorn" of such appurtenant power, I cannot conceive, for it cannot be shorn of it. . . .

The final conclusion of my brothers is that the plaintiffs are entitled to recover in their own right instead of in the right of the corporation. This appears to be completely inconsistent with the theory advanced at the outset of the opinion, namely, that the price of the stock "included compensation for the sale of a corporate asset." If a corporate asset was sold, surely the corporation should recover the compensation received for it by the defendants. . . .

---

1. *What was the premium for?* The majority's theory seems to be that the buyers paid a premium for access to more of Newport's steel production. Given price controls, the corporation could not benefit from the ability to allocate production except through Feldmann plan transactions. Could the premium represent the value of acquiring the steel without the burden of Feldmann plan advances? What result in a suit brought by Newport minority shareholders challenging the allocation of Newport production to the new directors' companies without Feldmann plan advances?

2. *What if Newport could not capture the benefit of short supply?* The majority responds to the price controls on steel, and therefore the corporation's inability to capture the value above the price limit, by reference to Feldmann plan transactions. What if the new owners expected to make Feldmann plan advances? Then the value of control over allocation of production is worth more than the cost of the Feldmann plan advances. Who is entitled to the difference?

Mendel v. Carroll
651 A.2d 297 (Del. Ch. 1994)

ALLEN, Ch.: . . . [T]he stockholder plaintiffs in these consolidated actions seek an unprecedented remedy: an order requiring the board of directors of a Delaware corporation to grant an option to buy 20% of its stock to a third party for the primary purpose of diluting the voting power of an existing control block of stock. The order sought would direct the Board of Directors of Katy Industries, Inc. ("Katy") to grant to an affiliate of Pensler Capital Corporation (together with Pensler Capital Partners I.L.P., referred to here as "Pensler") an option to purchase up to 20% of Katy's outstanding common stock at $27.80 per share. The granting of such an option is a condition of an offer for a $27.80 per share cash merger extended by Pensler to Katy. . . .

Katy's board of directors has declined to grant the option sought. The board took this position in the face of a claim by a group of related shareholders (the Carroll Family) that granting such an option would deprive them of their legitimate and dominant voice in corporate affairs, and would in the circumstances constitute a breach of fiduciary duty.

Plaintiffs' theory, stated most summarily, is that when the Katy board had earlier resolved to accept the terms of a $25.75 cash out merger proposed by the Carroll Family, the company was put up "for sale," and that as a result the board now has a single duty: to exercise its active and informed judgment in good faith effort to get the best available value for the stockholders. Plaintiffs contend that rejection of Pensler's $27.80 merger proposal is not consistent with that goal. They posit that granting the option sought is a necessary step for the board to satisfy its special duty (which plaintiffs call a *"Revlon duty"*), and thus it is obligated in these circumstances to do so.

The notable fact in this case is that at all relevant times a small group of Carroll Family members has controlled between 48% and 51% of Katy's voting stock. . . .

The dilutive option sought by Pensler as a condition of its $27.80 offer is, of course, a means of overcoming the resistance of the Carroll shareholders. Exercise of the option sought would reduce the voting power of the Carrolls from their current level of 50.6% to approximately 40% and thus make feasible stockholder approval of the Pensler transaction. A Special Committee of the Katy board of directors, delegated to deal first with the Carroll Family proposal and then with Pensler, after obtaining advice from legal counsel, declined to recommend to the full board the granting of the dilutive option.

Plaintiffs . . . also seek an order: requiring the defendants to negotiate fairly with Pensler; prohibiting the voting of certain shares recently acquired on the market by certain members of the Carroll Family; prohibiting Katy from making certain payments; and prohibiting Katy from distributing the $14.00 special dividend authorized in March 1994 by the board of directors. . . .

I

Katy is a New York Stock Exchange listed firm, founded in 1968 by Wallace E. Carroll, Sr. As a practical matter, control of Katy has always rested in the hands of Mr. Carroll, Sr. or his children . . . [who have] owned between 48% and 52% of Katy's outstanding common stock. Traditionally these interests were held in a coordinated way. In 1983, all of the Carroll Family Members entered into a Stock Purchase Agreement. That agreement granted a right of first refusal to other signatories with respect to all Katy stock owned, but contained no restrictions on the exercise of voting rights. . . .

Wallace Carroll, Sr. died in September 1990. In March 1991 Katy retained Dillon, Read & Co., Inc. to conduct a financial review of the company, and "to advise the board on a variety of financial alternatives available to [Katy]." Kurowski Aff. Ex. A. Among the Dillon, Read personnel assigned to that project was Mr. Sanford Pensler, now a principal in Pensler Capital Corp. In its August 1991 report Dillon, Read noted that "Katy appears to be awash in capital" and that "[i]t is unlikely the public markets will give full value to this collection of assets in its present configuration." Several strategic options were presented, including a "split off" of operating subsidiaries and the repurchase of "substantial amounts of equity."

Dillon, Read noted that "investment in Katy's own shares appears to be very attractive."

In fact, Katy had already privately repurchased a substantial block of common stock in June 1991. It made another negotiated purchase in September, after receiving the investment bank's analyses. The June repurchase brought the Carroll Family's aggregate common stock ownership to over 50%; the September repurchase increased that aggregate interest to over 52%. Katy later repurchased another 5,800 shares in the market in April 1992.

A.   The Family Buyout Proposal

Members of the Carroll Family retained Morgan Stanley & Co. to advise them with respect to their holdings in Katy. In June 1992 the Carroll Family publicly announced that it was reviewing its options concerning Katy. At that time Katy stock had been trading at about $16.00 per share. On September 1, 1992, the Carroll Family executed a Participation Agreement in which they agreed to act in concert in the acquisition of the publicly held shares of Katy.[5] On that same day, the Carroll Family offered to acquire all non-Carroll shares of Katy common stock at $22.00 per share.[6] In the intervening months the stock had risen to trade on the day prior to the announcement at $24.00 per share.

In presenting its proposal, the Carroll Family advised the board that it had no interest in selling any of its approximately 52.6% of Katy's common stock. In response to the offer, the board appointed a Special Committee comprised of directors who were apparently disinterested in the proposal. They retained the investment bank Goldman Sachs & Co., as well as the Dallas law firm Jenkens & Gilchrist, P.C., as counsel. After consideration, the Special Committee rejected the $22.00 offer as inadequate and attempted to negotiate a higher price with the Carroll Family. The Carroll Family offered $24.00 per share, but the Special Committee insisted on $26.00 per share. No agreement was reached and the Carroll Family withdrew its offer. The Special Committee was disbanded in December 1992.

On March 11, 1993, the Carroll Family made a new offer to purchase all outstanding non-Carroll Katy shares at $25.75 per share. In conjunction with the new offer, the Carroll Family amended the Participation Agreement to enable Barry Carroll and his affiliates to sell their 4.6% holding in Katy stock (hereinafter, "Barry Carroll's shares").[8] The Special Committee was reinstituted and advised of the treatment of Barry Carroll's shares. After Goldman Sachs indicated that it would render an opinion that $25.75 represented a price within a range of fair prices for the public stock, the Special Committee concluded that the new offer was in the

---

5. The Participation Agreement generally provides that Carroll Family members: (i) will transfer shares only to a newly formed acquisition entity or to other family members; (ii) will vote in favor of a Carroll Merger and other measures to facilitate it; and (iii) will not solicit or vote in favor of any third party proposal.

6. On September 2, 1992, six class action complaints were filed in this court, alleging that the $22.00 per share offer was grossly inadequate. . . .

8. This fact is important to plaintiffs because they wish to establish that at this or some later point the "non-selling" members of the Carroll Family held less than 50% of Katy's voting stock. From this premise they then try to build an argument that "control" was at such time in the public shares and thus at the time of the March 15 acceptance by the board of the Family's $25.75 proposal, the transaction represented a change in corporate control as contemplated by Paramount Communications Inc. v. QVC Network Inc., Del. Supr., 637 A.2d 34 (1993), thus, in their theory triggering "*Revlon* duties." It is their view of the impact here of "*Revlon* duties" that leads to relief they seek.

best interests of Katy's shareholders, and recommended the offer to the full board. The board approved that offer on March 15, 1993, and authorized the officers of Katy to enter into a merger agreement with a Carroll Family — controlled entity on March 23. . . .

B. A Rosecliff/Pensler Proposal Emerges

In a September 1, 1993 letter to Mr. Jacob Saliba, Katy's Chairman, a venture called Rosecliff Pensler Partners L.P. ("Rosecliff Pensler")[9] proposed to purchase, on a friendly basis only, all of Katy's outstanding shares for at least $29.00 per share, subject to completing due diligence, obtaining financing, and receiving necessary government approvals. On September 2, Barry Carroll wrote to Mr. Saliba that he thought the Rosecliff Pensler offer was attractive and should be pursued.

At a special meeting of the board of directors of September 17, 1993, representatives of the Special Committee advised the Board that Goldman Sachs had stated, in effect, that until the Rosecliff Pensler proposal could be more clearly defined and evaluated, the Special Committee could not rely upon Goldman's August 23, 1993 opinion concerning the fairness of the Carroll Family Merger. As a result, the Special Committee advised the full board that it was not then in a position to continue its endorsement of the Carroll Family Merger. At that meeting Philip Johnson reiterated that as shareholders the members of the Carroll Family were not interested in selling their shares; there was therefore no way in which a Rosecliff Pensler merger proposal could be effectuated; and thus no reason for Katy to permit Rosecliff Pensler to conduct a due diligence investigation.

Notwithstanding Mr. Johnson's position, the Katy board resolved at a further September 23, 1993 meeting to permit Rosecliff Pensler access to Company information on the same basis as it had been made available to the Carroll Family's advisors.

C. Steinhardt/Pensler Proposal

By mid-November 1993, Rosecliff Inc. appears to have lost interest in a Katy transaction, but Pensler found a new joint venturer in Steinhardt Enterprise Inc. On November 29, 1993, a new partnership of Pensler Capital Corporation and Steinhardt Enterprise Inc. ("Steinhardt Pensler") proposed to purchase all of Katy's outstanding shares at $28.00 per share, purportedly without financing or due diligence conditions. The offer was scheduled to expire on December 6, 1993.

Also on November 29, Barry Carroll advised Mr. Saliba and the board of directors that he would not sign another extension of the Participation Agreement, scheduled to terminate on November 30, 1993, and that he intended to sell his shares pursuant to the 1983 Stock Purchase Agreement. The withdrawal of Barry Carroll's shares from the Participation Agreement left the Carroll Family, excluding Barry Carroll (hereinafter, the "Carroll Group"), with ownership of approximately 47.9% of Katy's outstanding common stock.

D. Carroll Family Market Purchases

On December 1, 1993, Philip Johnson wrote to Mr. Saliba that the Carroll Family was exercising its right to terminate the merger agreement.

---

9. Rosecliff Pensler was a partnership of Rosecliff, Inc. and Pensler Capital Corporation.

Also on December 1, the Carroll Group (i.e., the family minus Barry Carroll and affiliates) filed a Schedule 13D amendment with the Securities and Exchange Commission disclosing that it intended to acquire additional shares of common stock "to establish the position of the [Carroll Group] as the holders, in the aggregate, of a majority of the outstanding Shares and thereby to assure the control of the Company by the members of the Carroll Family regardless of the level of Share holdings of Mr. Barry Carroll. . . ." The Carroll Group further stated that it had no present intention of engaging in any transaction to take Katy private. On December 2 and 3, 1993, Wallace Carroll, Jr. and Leila Carroll Johnson purchased shares in the market with the result that the Carroll Group's ownership rose again to 50.6% of the outstanding common stock of Katy.

E. Further Negotiations with Steinhardt/Pensler and the Requested Dilution of Carroll Group Control

On December 3, 1993, the Special Committee requested authority from the board to meet and negotiate with Steinhardt Pensler. After a spirited discussion during which Mr. Johnson reiterated that the Carroll Group was in no event interested in selling its Katy stock, and over the objection of certain directors, the board granted the permission requested.

On December 5, 1993, Steinhardt Pensler presented the Special Committee with a proposed Merger Agreement that contemplated a $28.00 per share cash merger and a proposed Stock Option Agreement. The Stock Option Agreement would grant Steinhardt Pensler an irrevocable option to purchase up to 1.8 million shares of authorized but unissued shares of Katy at a price equal to the merger consideration; it would also grant Steinhardt Pensler the right to put the shares to Katy if the shareholders subsequently failed to approve the merger. Both agreements would require Katy to indemnify Steinhardt Pensler and pay damages if the option was found to be improper.

On December 11, while the Special Committee and its legal and financial advisors were evaluating the offer, Steinhardt Pensler made another offer at a reduced price of $27.80, claiming that it had just learned that Goldman Sachs' fee arrangement with Katy was tied to the merger price. . . .

The Special Committee sent a revised draft of the proposed agreements to Steinhardt Pensler on December 14. . . . There was no timely response and, by its terms, the $27.80 Steinhardt Pensler offer expired on December 15, 1993.

Nevertheless, the two sides' representatives remained in contact regarding Steinhardt Pensler's financing and other matters through December 1993 and early January 1994. On January 18, 1994, the Special Committee reported to the full board that . . . Steinhardt Pensler . . . had access to capital sufficient for the commitment. Minor points arising from due diligence required further negotiation. The purchase price remained $27.80, but would rise to $28.00 if Goldman Sachs would cap its fee at $1 million. The legality of the grant of the dilutive option continued to be a crucial issue to the Special Committee. At the January 18 meeting, the board unanimously agreed, though it did not formally resolve that, without an opinion from the Special Committee's Delaware counsel, to the effect that the option would be valid and would not constitute a breach of duty, the Committee could not negotiate a merger agreement including such an option with Steinhardt Pensler.

F.   Legal Opinions on the Dilutive Option

. . . The Special Committee now turned to [Delaware] counsel for advice on the question whether granting an option of the type sought would, in the circumstances, constitute a violation of the board's fiduciary duty to the Carroll Group as shareholders. The Special Committee's Delaware attorneys produced a 32-page opinion analyzing the relevant facts and law, and essentially concluded that it was unclear whether granting the option would be legal.

Following the receipt of the inconclusive opinion of its counsel, the Special Committee made two recommendations at a January 28, 1994 special meeting of the full board. Given the uncertain validity of the option, the Special Committee first recommended that it was no longer in the best interests of Katy and its shareholders to pursue negotiations with Steinhardt Pensler. Second, the Special Committee recommended that the board appoint another committee to explore other methods to maximize shareholder value, including: (i) a self-tender by Katy; (ii) a Dutch auction of Katy; and/or (iii) a dividend in excess of $10.00 per share on Katy's common stock. In accordance with these recommendations, the board further established a new committee to consider strategies to enhance shareholder value.

On March 8, 1994, the new committee recommended that the board approve a special cash dividend of $14.00 per share of Katy common stock. The board has endorsed that recommendation but has not yet declared such a dividend, pending outcome of this motion. . . .

IV

I turn then to the core issue: whether Katy's board of directors has or had a legal or equitable obligation [under *Revlon*] to facilitate a closing of Pensler's $27.80 cash merger proposal by granting the option that Pensler seeks. To provide an answer to such a question, particularly in the setting of a preliminary injunction application, does not require one to formulate an answer to the abstract question whether a board of directors could ever, consistent with its fiduciary obligations, grant an option to buy stock for the principal purpose of affecting the outcome of an expected shareholder action, such as an election, a consent solicitation, or a tender offer. Surely if the principal motivation for such dilution is simply to maintain corporate control ("entrenchment") it would violate the norm of loyalty. Where, however, a board of directors acts in good faith and on the reasonable belief that a controlling shareholder is abusing its power and is exploiting or threatening to exploit the vulnerability of minority shareholders, I suppose . . . that the board might permissibly take such an action. See Unocal Corp. v. Mesa Petroleum Co., Del. Supr., 493 A.2d 946 (1985).

Here, of course, plaintiffs' core argument can be understood to be that the controlling shareholders *are* exploiting the vulnerability of the minority shares in a very particular way. The gist of plaintiffs' complaint is that the minority shareholders could get more cash for their stock in a Pensler cash deal than they would have gotten in the proposed $25.75 Carroll Group deal. Thus, plaintiffs would contend that the foregoing protective principle grounded in fiduciary obligation would apply to this situation, and that the board is, as a result, under a current obligation to take the radical step of intentionally diluting the control of the controlling block of stock.

In my opinion, this view is mistaken. I apprehend in the facts recited above no threat of exploitation or even unfairness towards a vulnerable minority that might arguably justify discrimination against a controlling block of stock. Plaintiffs see in the Carroll Group's unwillingness to sell at $27.80 or to buy at that price, a denial of plaintiffs' ability to realize such a price, and see this as exploitation or breach of duty. This view implicitly regards the $27.80 per share price and the Carroll Family Merger price of $25.75 as comparable sorts of things. But they are legally and financially quite different. It is, for example, quite possible that the Carroll $25.75 price may have been fair, even generous while the $27.80 Pensler price may be inadequate. If one understands why this is so, one will understand one reason why the injunction now sought cannot be granted.

The fundamental difference between these two possible transactions arises from the fact that the Carroll Family already in fact had a committed block of controlling stock. Financial markets in widely traded corporate stock accord a premium to a block of stock that can assure corporate control. Analysts differ as to the source of any such premium but not on its existence. Optimists see the control premium as a reflection of the efficiency enhancing changes that the buyer of control is planning on making to the organization.[15] Others tend to see it, at least sometimes, as the price that a prospective wrongdoer is willing to pay in order to put himself in the position to exploit vulnerable others,[16] or simply as a function of a downward sloping demand curve demonstrating investors' heterogeneous beliefs about the subject stock's value.[17] In all events, it is widely understood that buyers of corporate control will be required to pay a premium above the market price for the company's traded securities.

The law has acknowledged, albeit in a guarded and complex way, the legitimacy of the acceptance by controlling shareholders of a control premium.[18]

The significant fact is that in the Carroll Family Merger, the buyers were not buying corporate control. With either 48% or 52% of the outstanding stock they already had it. Therefore, in evaluating the fairness of the Carroll proposal, the Special Committee and its financial advisors were in a distinctly different position than would be a seller in a transaction in which corporate control was to pass.

The Pensler offer, of course, was fundamentally different. It was an offer, in effect, to the controlling shareholder to purchase corporate control, and to all public shareholders, to purchase the remaining part of the company's shares, all at a single price. It distributed the control premium evenly over all shares.

---

15. Frank H. Easterbrook and Daniel R. Fischel, The Economic Structure of Corporate Law 126-144 (1991); Frank H. Easterbrook and Daniel R. Fischel, Corporate Control Transaction, 91 Yale L.J. 698 (1982).

16. See Robert W Hamilton, Private Sale of Control Transactions: Where We Stand Today, 36 Case W. Res. L. Rev. 248 (1985); see, e.g., Gerdes v. Reynolds, 28 N.Y.S.2d 622, 650-652 (N.Y. App. Div. 1941).

17. See Lynn A. Stout, Are Takeover Premiums Really Premiums? Market Price, Fair Value, and Corporate Law, 99 Yale L.J. 1235, 1244-1252 (1990).

18. The doctrine applicable to a sale of corporate control at a premium is far more complex than it may at first appear. Indeed one might conclude that courts afford it somewhat grudging recognition. A number of liability creating doctrines have been applied which have the effect of creating risks to the controlling shareholder who attempts to realize a control premium These doctrines include negligence, see Harris v. Carter, Del. Ch., 582 A.2d 222, 232-236 (1990); Insuranshares Corp. v. Northern Fiscal Corp., 35 F. Supp. 22, 25-27 (E.D. Pa. 1940); sale of corporate office, see Essex Universal Corp. v. Yates, 305 F.2d 572, 581-582 (2d Cir. 1962) (Friendly, J., concurring); and sale of corporate opportunity, see Brown v. Halbert, 76 Cal. Rptr. 781, 791-794 (Cal. Ct. App. 1969); Jones v. H.F. Ahmanson & Co., 460 P.2d 464, 476 (Cal. 1969). See generally E. Elhauge, The Triggering Function of Sale of Control Doctrine, 59 U. Chi. L. Rev. 14665 (1992).

Because the Pensler proposed $27.80 price was a price that contemplated not simply the purchase of non-controlling stock, as did the Carroll Family Merger, but complete control over the corporation, it was not fairly comparable to the per-share price proposed by the Carroll Group. . . .

To note that these proposals are fundamentally different does not, of course, mean that the board owes fiduciary duties in one instance but not in the other. That is not the case. But to describe the duty that corporate directors bear in any particular situation one must first consider the circumstances that give rise to the occasion for judgment. When the Katy board or its Special Committee evaluated the Carroll Family Merger, it was obligated to take note of the circumstance that the proposal was being advanced by a group of shareholders that constituted approximately 50% of all share ownership, and who arguably had the power to elect the board. In this circumstance, in my opinion, the board's duty was to respect the rights of the Carroll Family, while assuring that if any transaction of the type proposed was to be accomplished, it would be accomplished only on terms that were fair to the public shareholders and represented the best available terms from their point of view.

This obligation the board faces is rather similar to the obligation that the board assumes when it bears what have been called "*Revlon* duties," but the obligations are not identical. When presented with the controlling stockholders' proposal, the obligation of the Katy board was in some respects similar to that faced by a board when it elects to sell the corporation, because *if* the board were to approve a proposed cash-out merger, it would have to bear in mind that the transaction is a final-stage transaction for the public shareholders. Thus, the time frame for analysis, insofar as those shareholders are concerned, is immediate value maximization. The directors are obliged in such a situation to try, within their fiduciary obligation, to maximize the current value of the minority shares. In this respect the obligation is analogous to the board's duty when it is engaged in a process of "selling" the corporation, as for example in the recent Paramount Communications, Inc. v. QVC Network Inc., Del. Supr., 637 A.2d 34 (1994). But the duty is somewhat different because of the existence of the controlling Carroll Family block.

The Carroll Family made it clear throughout these events that, for the most part, its members were completely uninterested in being sellers in any transaction.[19] No part of their fiduciary duty as controlling shareholders requires them to sell their interest. See Bershad v. Curtiss-Wright Corp., Del. Supr., 535 A.2d 840 (1987); Jedwab v. MGM Grand Hotels, Inc., Del. Ch., 509 A.2d 584 (1986) (self-sacrifice not required). The board's fiduciary obligation to the corporation and its shareholders, in this setting, requires it to be a protective guardian of the rightful interest of the public shareholders. But while that obligation may authorize the board to take extraordinary steps to protect the minority from plain overreaching, it does not authorize the board to deploy corporate power *against* the majority stock-holders, in the absence of a threatened serious breach of fiduciary duty by the controlling stock.

To acknowledge that the Carroll Family has no obligation to support a transaction in which they would in effect sell their stock is not, of course, to suggest that

---

19. The fact that Mr. Barry Carroll parted company with his family does not appear to have affected the practical fact of control — which of course is the predicate fact for the existence of a control premium.

they can use their control over the corporation to effectuate a self-interested merger at an unfair price. See Weinberger v. U.O.P., Inc., Del. Supr., 457 A.2d 701 (1983). There is nothing in the present record, however, that suggests to me that the $25.75 price the Carroll Group proposed to pay for the public shares was an inadequate or unfair price for the non-controlling stock. For the reasons stated above, the fact that Pensler was willing to pay more for all of the shares does not, logically, support an inference that the Carroll proposal for the non-controlling public shares was not fair.

Thus, while I continue to hold open the possibility that a situation might arise in which a board could, consistently with its fiduciary duties, issue a dilutive option in order to protect the corporation or its minority shareholders from exploitation by a controlling shareholder who was in the process or threatening to violate his fiduciary duties to the corporation,[20] such a situation does not at all appear to have been faced by the Katy board of directors.

In my opinion, far from "*Revlon* duties" requiring such action, the Katy board could not, consistent with its fiduciary obligations to all of the stockholders of Katy Industries, have issued the dilutive option for the purpose sought in this instance. Therefore, that the board considered the matter and declined to do so could in no event be considered to constitute a breach of duty to the minority shareholders. . . .

---

1. *The current state of the law.* Mendel v. Carroll describes the current state of the law as allowing a controlling shareholder to sell control at a premium without an obligation to allow minority shareholders to participate or otherwise share in the premium, subject to a number of exceptions. The ALI's Principles of Corporate Governance states the law as follows:

> Sec. 5.16. *Disposition of voting equity securities by a controlling shareholder to third parties.* A controlling shareholder has the same right to dispose of voting equity securities as any other shareholder, including the right to dispose of those securities for a price that is not made proportionally available to other shareholders, but the controlling shareholder does not satisfy the duty of fair dealing to the other shareholders if:
>
> (a) The controlling shareholder does not make disclosure concerning the transaction to other shareholders with whom the controlling shareholder deals in connection with the transaction; or
>
> (b) It is apparent from the circumstances that the purchaser is likely to violate the duty of fair dealing . . . in such a way as to obtain a significant financial benefit for the purchaser or an associate.

2. *Equal opportunity versus unequal division.* Which rule — equal opportunity as suggested in *Perlman* or unequal division as allowed by the ALI — makes shareholders better off? Both sides recognize that control changes are potentially beneficial to all. The debate has focused on whether letting the controlling shareholder keep the premium is a necessary incentive to secure the benefits. This, in turn, depends on why a premium for control is being paid.

---

20. In such an instance the board would bear a heavy burden to establish the justification for any steps purposely taken to affect the outcome of shareholder action See Blasius Indus., Inc. v. Atlas Corp., Del. Ch., 564 A.2d 651 (1988).

Suppose that the current controlling shareholder derives no special benefit from control—all returns are shared proportionately by shareholders. This situation presents the strong case for an equal opportunity rule. If a control premium is paid for the chance to exploit minority shareholders, the transfer of control should be discouraged by requiring that the premium be shared. Alternatively, if the premium reflects only expected efficiency gains from replacing current management, an equal opportunity rule would still be better. A sharing requirement would not affect the bidder's incentives to pursue the transaction. Nor would it deter the controlling shareholder from selling. As long as she were offered more than market value for her shares (because of the assumption of no private benefit from control, market price reflects the shares' current value to the controlling shareholder), it would still be in her interest to sell.

The analysis changes if the current controlling shareholder secures some private benefit from her position not shared proportionately with minority shareholders. Then an equal opportunity rule would discourage control transfers because the current controlling shareholder would not sell her shares except at a premium that reflected the capitalized value of the private benefits she receives by retaining the control block. This appears to be the situation posed in Mendel v. Carroll: the controlling group was unwilling to sell at a price that was attractive to the minority.

Does the desirability of an unequal division rule that facilitates control sales (or allows controlling shareholders to decline to sell control) depend on whether the private benefits of control derive from self-dealing or from more neutral factors such as the opportunity to more directly influence the operations of the corporation and thereby reduce the agency costs associated with management?[54]

The critical issue seems to be less the source of the private benefits to the existing controlling shareholder than whether the private benefits to be taken by the new controlling shareholder will increase, and whether any increases in private benefits are offset by increases in efficiency achieved by the new controlling shareholder. See Lucian Bebchuk, Efficient and Inefficient Sales of Corporate Control, 109 Q.J. Econ. 957 (1994). If *Sinclair*-like legal rules are effective, in that the amount of self-dealing by controlling shareholders does not vary much among different controlling shareholders, then an unequal division rule will encourage efficient transfers of control—that is, transfers to more effective monitors (or managers)—but will provide no incentive for inefficient transfers prompted by the hope of increasing the level of private benefits. Put differently, reducing the level of self-dealing by controlling shareholders is desirable but should not influence the choice between equal opportunity and unequal sale of control rules. That choice will be driven by the likelihood of substantial differences in the level of self-dealing between different controlling shareholders. Consider again whether Newport would be required to impose Feldmann plan advances on its sales to the new controlling shareholders.

---

54. Because such monitoring is beneficial to minority shareholders but costly to the controlling shareholder to maintain, both in terms of ongoing monitoring expenditures and forgone diversification, it would be to the benefit of minority shareholders to allow controlling shareholders some private benefits. See Ronald Gilson & Bernard Black, The Law and Finance of Corporate Acquisitions 1231-1234 (2d ed. 1995).

3. *Exceptions to the unequal division rule.* Despite the general rejection of an equal opportunity rule, as reflected in ALI §5.16, courts have recognized liability for sellers of control at a premium under the following circumstances.

(a) *"Looting" theory.* A seller of control faces liability if the circumstances surrounding the transaction would cause a reasonable person to recognize that the buyer intended to "loot" or injure the corporation. The early cases typically involved insurance companies or financial institutions whose equity base was small and whose liquid assets were vulnerable to theft or conversion. See Insuranshares Corp. v. Northern Fiscal Corp., 35 F. Supp. 22 (E.D. Pa. 1940). More recent cases have, however, involved non-financial corporations. In DeBaun v. First Western Bank & Trust Co., 46 Cal. App. 3d 686, 120 Cal. Rptr. 354 (1975), a buyer of 70 percent of a photograph processing company paid $50,000 down for the stock, the $200,000 balance to be paid in the future. He immediately

> implemented a systematic scheme to loot Corporation of its assets. His first step was to divert $73,144 in corporate cash to himself . . . in exchange for unsecured non–interest bearing notes. . . . [He then] caused Corporation to assign to [a corporate shell owned by him] all of Corporation's assets including its receivables [and liquid assets of over $122,000] in exchange for a fictitious agreement for management services. He diverted all corporate mail to a post office box from which he took the mail, opened it, and extracted all incoming checks to the corporation before forwarding the mail on. He ceased paying trade creditors promptly. . . . He delayed shipments on new orders. . . . He collected payments from employees to pay premiums on a voluntary health insurance plan although the plan was terminated . . . for failure to pay premiums. He issued payroll checks without sufficient funds. . . .

In 11 months he reduced the corporation from a going concern with a net worth of $220,000 to an empty corporate shell with over $200,000 in debts in excess of assets.

In a shareholder's derivative suit, the seller was held liable to the corporation for its lost net worth, its lost going-concern value, and its unpaid debts: "As [the seller, 'Bank,'] was negotiating with Mattison [the buyer], it became directly aware of the facts that would have alerted a prudent person that Mattison was likely to loot the corporation."

Like ALI §5.16, all looting cases have required that the seller have received some "clue" as to the buyer's likely evil intent, and early cases sometimes found this clue in the substantial premium that the buyer was willing to pay for control of the target. The ALI approach explicitly rejects inferring misconduct from the mere fact of a substantial premium. 1 ALI, Principles of Corporate Governance 378 (1994). Note also that in *Debaun* (unlike *Perlman*) liability was for the damage done to the corporation, not simply the lost premium. What should be the measure of liability?

Is the looting theory exception consistent with the analysis of the comparative efficiency of equal opportunity and unequal division rules? When one has reason to believe that the buyer will loot the company, the likely difference in self-dealing between the existing and the potential controlling shareholder is large. In that circumstance, the equal opportunity rule is more efficient.[55]

(b) *Corporate opportunity and standards of dealing with minority shareholders.* What if the purchaser first proposed a merger to the controlling shareholder (who is also

---

55. Elhauge, page 1050 supra, analyzes the looting exception in much the same way, treating the exception as reducing the extent to which an unequal division rule underdeters inefficient transfers.

director and officer of the target corporation) and the controlling shareholder suggests instead that the purchaser buy only his shares, but at a higher price. Is this a diversion of a corporation opportunity? Compare Brown v. Halbert, 271 Cal. App. 252, 76 Cal. Rptr. 781 (1969) (suggesting liability on this theory in dicta), with Tryon v. Smith, 229 P.2d 251 (Or. 1951) (finding no liability). The ALI rejects the corporate opportunity approach as one of mere form: "[A] knowledgeable buyer could avoid the rule in such cases simply by asking the controlling shareholder initially what price it would take for its shares." 1 ALI, Principles of Corporate Governance 376 (1994).

However, ALI §5.16(b) adopts an exception associated with a more narrow reading of Brown v. Halbert. In that case the controlling shareholder persuaded minority shareholders to sell their shares to the new controlling shareholder at a lower price without disclosing that he had received a premium. Section 5.16 requires disclosure in that circumstance. Note, however, that this exception does not replace §5.16's unequal division rule with an equal opportunity rule; the "sale can be effected, but the controlling shareholder will not satisfy the duty of fair dealing unless disclosure is made to minority shareholders with whom the controlling shareholder deals." Id. Is the measure of liability the lost premium, or must the minority shareholder show that she could have obtained a higher price had she been armed with this information?

(c) *Sale of office.* Another theory of liability that survives to an uncertain extent stems from the rule that a premium may not be received for a sale of corporate office. The difficult issue here concerns how to view a transaction that involves seriatim resignations followed by elections to fill these vacancies and thereby transfers a board majority to the purchaser of a control block. Does it amount in substance to an illicit sale of office or is it instead the appropriate and expeditious transfer of control to the new majority (and away from the "dead-hand" control of the formerly controlling block)? Courts have tried to draw a line in terms of the size of the block acquired. In Caplan v. Lionel Corp., 20 App. Div. 2d 301, 246 N.Y.S.2d 913 (1964), existing directors resigned and were replaced by the nominees of the purchaser of a 3 percent block of stock. The court ordered the directors removed: "The underlying principle is that the management of a corporation is not the subject of trade and cannot be bought apart from actual stock control. Where there has been a transfer of the majority of the stock, or even such a percentage as gives working control, a change of directors by resignation and filling of vacancies is proper. . . . Here no claim was made that the stock interest which changed hands even approximated the percentage necessary to validate the substitution."

Why was the percentage too small "to validate the substitution" ? If no other shareholder held a large block of stock, Roy Cohn, the block seller who already held office and possessed management control over proxy solicitation, would ordinarily have little difficulty remaining in power. When it exists, minority control, even by the owner of so large an amount as 40 percent of the stock, is in control primarily because the owner controls the proxy machinery.

In Essex Universal Corp. v. Yates, 305 F.2d 572 (2d Cir. 1962), which involved a sale of control of Republic Pictures, the seller had agreed to sell 28 percent of the company's stock and to cause his representatives on the board to resign and elect the buyer's nominees in their stead. However, having found another buyer at a higher price, the seller refused to perform; the buyer sued for damages. The district court entered summary judgment for the seller on the ground that the agreement to replace the directors was illegal and hence the contract was illegal and unenforceable. A unanimous court of appeals reversed, but no judge agreed with another concerning the reasons.

Chief Judge Lumbard stated:

> The easy and immediate transfer of corporate control to new interests is ordinarily beneficial to the economy and it seems inevitable that such transactions would be discouraged if the purchaser of a majority stock interest were required to wait some period before his purchase of control could become effective. Conversely it would greatly hamper the efforts of any existing majority group to dispose of its interest if it could not assure the purchaser of immediate control over corporation operations. I can see no reason why a purchaser of majority control should not ordinarily be permitted to make his control effective from the moment of the transfer of stock.

Recognizing that it does not logically follow that the same rule should apply to the sale of a sizable minority block of stock, Judge Lumbard believed that in a widely held company, a 28 percent holding is usually tantamount to control.

Judge Friendly disagreed:

> To be sure, stockholders who have allowed a set of directors to be placed in office, whether by their vote or their failure to vote, must recognize that death, incapacity or other hazard may prevent a director from serving a full term, and that they will have no voice as to his immediate successor. But the stockholders are entitled to expect that, in that event, the remaining directors will fill the vacancy in the exercise of their fiduciary responsibility. A mass seriatim resignation directed by a selling stockholder, and the filing of vacancies by his henchmen at the dictation of a purchaser and without any consideration of the character of the latter's nominees, are beyond what the stockholders contemplated or should have been expected to contemplate. This seems to be a wrong to the corporation and the other stockholders which the law ought not countenance, whether the selling stockholder has received a premium or not. . . . To hold the seller for delinquencies of the new directors only if he knew the purchaser was an intending looter is not a sufficient sanction. . . .

The ALI follows Judge Lumbard by imposing liability only when the premium sale and seriatim resignation is by a person who "owns significantly less than a majority of the voting stock. . . ." 1 ALI, Principles of Corporate Governance 379 (1994). How does this exception fit with the analysis of the comparative efficiency of equal opportunity and unequal division rules?[56] Marcel Kahan, Sales of Corporate Control, 9 J.L. Econ. & Org. 368 (1993), argues that if the control block is small, the equal opportunity rule will not itself prevent an efficient transfer. Suppose the holder of a control block declines to effect an efficient sale of control because the equal opportunity rule prevents receipt of a premium. The bidder may still make a tender offer for control directly to the non-controlling shareholders who, together, can transfer a controlling block of stock. Thus, when a controlling shareholder owns a small percentage of the corporation's outstanding stock, the market for corporate control minimizes the extent to which an equal opportunity rule overdeters efficient transfers. So understood, the exception's effect is to shift from an unequal division to an equal opportunity rule at roughly

---

56. While the ALI does not explain what percentage is "significantly less than a majority," its citation of *Essex* sets the cutoff below 28 percent.

the point when the controlling shareholder owns so small a block of stock—"significantly less than a majority" in the ALI formulation—that she cannot block a tender offer made at an equal price to all shareholders.

5. *Empirical evidence.* The efficiency of an unequal division rule governing sales of control at a premium can be tested empirically. If the premium is paid for the opportunity to "loot" the corporation, one would predict that the price of minority shares would fall compared with their market value prior to the transfer of control, to reflect the exploitation. For example, *Perlman* can be read as a looting case. See Alfred Hill, The Sale of Controlling Shares, 70 Harv. L. Rev. 986, 989 (1957). It seems fairly clear that Wilport was seeking a captive supplier and would discontinue the Feldmann Plan of interest-free loans from suppliers. In this light, the value of minority shares should drop following the transaction, because a source of profits would be eliminated.

The post-transaction price of Newport stock is inconsistent with a looting theory. During the two months in which the negotiations for the transaction were going on, Newport's stock price increased 32 percent after adjustment for changes in overall market price. Over the entire year in which the transaction occurred, Newport stock increased by 77 percent after adjustment for the market. Moreover, the favorable performance of Newport's stock is not explained by changing conditions in the steel industry as opposed to general market price movements. If Newport stock performance is compared with that of the three largest U.S. steel producers, Newport's stock increased 13 percent during the week of the transaction, 34 percent for the two months of negotiations, and 29 percent over the year in which the trade occurred. Michael Barclay & Clifford Holderness, The Law and Large Block Trades, 35 J.L. & Econ. 265, 270 n.7 (1992).

These results seem to generalize. Barclay and Holderness collected a sample of 44 block trades of at least 5 percent of the outstanding stock of exchange-listed stock occurring between 1978 and 1982 where the price paid for the block exceeded the market price (that is, the price of minority stock) following announcement of the premium block trade, and the company remained public for at least a year after the trade. The sample was limited to trades at a premium to post-announcement price to present the worst case for the unequal division rule: unless the purchaser receives private benefits so that the controlling shares are worth more than market price (the value of minority shares), the purchaser will have lost money on the purchase. On announcement, the sample of minority shares on average increased in value by 2.1 percent more than would have been expected based on general market movements. Over the 4-month period beginning 2 months before announcement, the increase in value (adjusted for market movements) was 7.9 percent, and for the 18-month period beginning 6 months before the trade, the value increase was 15.7 percent. Thus, the empirical evidence is consistent with the efficiency of an unequal division rule. Even where the pricing of block trades ensured the presence of private benefits, the increase in efficiency exceeded any increase in private benefits diverted by the block purchaser.

6. *The Williams Act and the sale of control.* The Williams Act contains two major implications for the issue of the minority's right to share in control premiums, but they cut in opposite directions. First, §14(f) was added to the '34 Act, which reads:

(f) If, pursuant to any arrangements or understanding with the person or persons acquiring securities in a transaction subject to [§13(d) or 14(d)], any persons are to be elected or designated as directors of the issuer, otherwise than at a meeting of security holders, and the persons so elected or designated will constitute a majority of the directors of the issuer, then, prior to the time any such person takes office as a director, and in accordance with rules and regulations prescribed by the Commission, the issuer shall file with the Commission, and transmit to all holders of record of securities of the issuer who would be entitled to vote at a meeting for election of directors, information substantially equivalent to the information which would be required by the federal proxy rules to be transmitted if such person or persons were nominees for election as directors at a meeting of such security holders.

Does §14(f) undermine Judge Friendly's position in *Essex Universal* that "basic principles of corporate democracy" are violated by mass seriatim resignations because now federal law clearly seems to anticipate this type of control transfer in which a majority of the board resign and elect the purchaser's nominees? Or does §14(f) leave the validity of the transfer to state law but simply require disclosure if it is valid? Other interpretive problems also exist under §14(f). For example, what if, on a nine-person board, four persons resign and are succeeded by the purchaser's nominees? This is not a "majority of the directors" under §14(f) by itself, but what if the other five persons are "inside" directors who are, and wish to remain, officers of the corporation and know that the new 51 percent owner has the unquestioned ability to remove them? For an overview of the scope of §14(f), see David Ratner, Section 14(f): A New Approach to Transfers of Corporate Control, 54 Cornell L.Q. 65 (1968). What remedy should there be for a breach of §14(f)? Could minority shareholders bring an action for damages (i.e., the lost "control" premium)? See pages 344-446 supra, on implied rights of action under the federal securities laws.

Rule 14d-10, adopted under §14(d) of the Williams Act, is the other major federal innovation; today, it requires that a tender offer be open to all holders of the class and pay the same price to all. See page 1081 infra. Does this new rule make academic the long-standing debate over the proposed equal opportunity rule? The answer depends on how broadly the term "tender offer" is construed. See pages 1081-1082 infra.

7. *Responsibilities of the directors of the corporation whose control is being sold.* To this point, we have considered only the responsibilities of the controlling shareholder: Is there a responsibility to share a premium with the other shareholders? Consider now the role of the directors of the corporation whose control is being sold. Do they have a responsibility to protect the non-controlling shareholders from any consequences of the control transfer? More aggressively, do they have a responsibility to bargain on behalf of the non-controlling shareholders for a share of the premium?

In re Digex Shareholders Litigation
789 A.2d 1176 (Del. Ch. 2000)

CHANDLER, Ch.: [The transaction began with a contest between WorldCom and Global Crossing to acquire Intermedia Communications, Inc., a telecom company, and/or Digex, Inc., Intermedia's controlled subsidiary in the web hosting business. After initially considering a direct acquisition of Digex, WorldCom decided to acquire control of Digex indirectly by acquiring Intermedia.

The two alternatives had different impacts on Intermedia and Digex. If World-Com acquired Intermedia, its shareholders received the control premium associated with Digex. Alternatively, if WorldCom acquired Digex, the control premium would be shared between Intermedia and Digex's non-controlling shareholders. Neither Digex nor its shareholders would be a party to WorldCom's acquisition of Intermedia, the final form of the transaction. However, WorldCom did need something from Digex. It wanted the Digex board of directors, composed of four Intermedia representatives and three independents, to grant WorldCom a waiver of Del. Gen. Corp. Law §203, Delaware's business combination statute. This provision prohibits an acquirer of more than 15 percent of a target's shares from engaging in a range of interested transactions with the target, including a freeze-out merger, for a period of three years unless the target company's board of directors pre-approves the acquirer's initial share acquisition, or another exemption applies. At the Digex board meeting held to consider the waiver, the board voted 4 to 3 to approve the waiver, conditioned on the amendment of Digex's articles of incorporation to require that Digex independent directors approve any post-acquisition material transaction between WorldCom and Digex. The vote broke down along party lines. After the four Intermedia-affiliated directors rejected the position advanced by counsel to the independent directors that they not participate in the discussion and not vote on the waiver due to their conflict of interest, they voted in favor of the waiver, while the three independent directors voted against.] . . .

In their second claim,[57] the plaintiffs argue that the interested Digex directors breached their fiduciary duties by causing Digex to improperly waive §203 of the DGCL. Specifically, the plaintiffs assert that because the waiver was accomplished by the vote of the four Intermedia-affiliated Digex directors, and against the vote and advice of the three independent Digex directors, the vote must be judged under the entire fairness standard. Plaintiffs contend that the defendants have failed to meet this standard.

I first turn to the operative statute. . . . There is no dispute between the parties that WorldCom will become an interested shareholder in Digex as a result of the merger and that WorldCom intends to enter into transactions with Digex where the prohibitions of §203 would apply absent an exemption. As a result, although WorldCom believes that it would come within the statutory exemption provided by §203(a)(2) for interested stockholders holding 85% or more of the "voting stock" of the corporation, WorldCom also sought the additional certainty that would come with a §203(a)(1) waiver agreed to by the Digex board of directors. World-Com was not content to rely merely on the 85% shareholder exemption because it recognized that the application of the §203(a)(2) exemption in situations involving "super-voting rights" has not been definitively ruled upon by the Delaware courts. . . .

C. Was the §203 Waiver Entirely Fair to the Digex Shareholders?

On its face, §203 does not bar interested directors from participating in a vote to approve a transaction in which an entity becomes an interested stockholder.

---

57. The plaintiffs also argued that WorldCom had made the original proposal to Digex and that Intermedia had diverted a Digex opportunity by causing WorldCom to acquire Intermedia. The court rejected this claim. — ED.

Nevertheless, directors must at all times abide by their fiduciary duties owed to the shareholders of the corporation. When the directors of a Delaware corporation appear on both sides of a transaction, the presumption in favor of the business judgment rule is rebutted and the directors are required to demonstrate their "utmost good faith and the most scrupulous inherent fairness of the bargain."

Where a director holds dual directorships in the parent-subsidiary context, there is no dilution of this obligation to demonstrate the entire fairness of specific board actions. Thus, . . . individuals who act in a dual capacity as directors of two corporations, one of whom is parent and the other subsidiary, owe the same duty of good management to both corporations, and in the absence of an independent negotiating structure, or the directors' total abstention from any participation in the matter, this duty is to be exercised in light of what is best for both companies . . . [and] the burden of establishing entire fairness.

As often summarized in our caselaw, the concept of entire fairness has two basic components, fair dealing and fair price. Fair dealing concerns how the board action was initiated, structured, negotiated, and timed. Fair dealing asks whether all of the directors were kept fully informed not only at the moment in time of the vote, but also during the relevant events leading up to the vote while negotiations were presumably occurring. Fair dealing also asks how, and for what reasons, the approvals of the various directors themselves were obtained. Fair price relates to the economic and financial considerations of the proposed decision, including any relevant factors that affect the intrinsic or inherent value of a company's stock. The entire fairness test is not simply a bifurcated analysis of these two components, fair dealing and fair price. The Court shall examine these two aspects as well as any other relevant considerations in analyzing the entire fairness of the waiver as a whole.

1. Fair Dealing

In attempting to satisfy their burden, the defendants point to several factors to illustrate that the process leading up to the §203 waiver vote was characterized by fair dealing. The defendants contend that there was complete candor between the interested directors and the independent Digex directors. The defendants point out that the Special Committee, along with its own lawyers and bankers, had participated in the Exodus and Global Crossing negotiations,[58] had been immediately briefed on all developments in the Intermedia-WorldCom negotiations, and had been given access to WorldCom prior to the Digex board meeting through phone calls with Ebbers [WorldCom's President] and Grothe [WorldCom's VP for Corporate Development]. The defendants additionally claim that every member of the Digex board, including the independent directors, "had all the information in Intermedia's possession regarding each proposed transaction. . . ."

At the Digex board meeting, the Special Committee's legal counsel informed the entire board of his opinion that the interested directors should not participate in the §203 waiver vote. This advice was rebutted by counsel for the interested directors, and ultimately ignored. Later, without any debate whatsoever on the merits of the waiver or the applicability of the statute, the full Digex board voted to grant

---

58. These were proposed transactions that ultimately were rejected in favor of the WorldCom transaction. — ED.

the waiver by a divided vote of four interested directors for and three independent directors against. In total, there simply was no meaningful participation by any of the independent Digex directors in the negotiations leading to the §203 waiver, the terms of that waiver, or the vote itself.

Several other conclusions immediately emerge from the facts of this matter. . . . First, regardless of whether the Special Committee actually had all the information possessed by Intermedia in its negotiations with WorldCom over the §203 issue, the four interested directors controlled the flow of all information from WorldCom to the independent Digex directors during the hectic negotiating period from the evening of August 30 to the morning of September 1.

Second, given that WorldCom first sought the waiver of §203 during the negotiations that took place solely between WorldCom and Intermedia during the night of August 31-September 1 and that the vote at the Digex board meeting occurred at most roughly twelve hours later, all of the Digex directors learned about World-Com's demand for the §203 waiver only hours before the vote granting that waiver. To make matters worse, because the interested directors were also directors of Intermedia, they could not even devote the little time they had before the board vote to considering their options as Digex directors and negotiating solely in the interests of Digex. Rather, they had to spend much, if not most, of their time considering and negotiating the terms of the merger from the perspective of Intermedia, the actual participant in the deal with WorldCom.

Third, in regards to the waiver of §203, there is almost no evidence of any direct negotiations between any of the parties over this provision in the deal. From the little that seems to have occurred, these negotiations took place during the night of August 31-September 1 between the interested directors, Sutcliffe [outside counsel to Intermedia and Digex] and the WorldCom representatives. The waiver appears to have been agreed to, in part, in exchange for an amendment to the Digex certificate of incorporation that would require the approval of independent directors of any material transaction between WorldCom and Digex after the merger. The record is silent as to exploration by the interested parties of any other options available to Digex. That is, as it appears that WorldCom insisted on the waiver, did any of the interested directors attempt to withhold this request in order to see what WorldCom might offer to Digex in return? Or, did the directors request concessions in addition to the certificate amendment that might benefit Digex or Intermedia? Or, as the plaintiffs assert, did the interested directors simply agree to this condition in the interests of getting the deal between Intermedia and WorldCom done and only subsequently add the provision to the merger agreement concerning the certificate amendment to create the appearance of consideration for the §203 waiver? These facts remain unclear. It is crystal clear though that the independent directors, at the time of the negotiation over the §203 waiver, had absolutely no role whatsoever.

This lack of any involvement by the Special Committee is particularly remarkable because Intermedia continues to assert that the Special Committee was created by Digex, *specifically by the interested directors*, "to evaluate the fairness to the Digex public shareholders of any transaction which involved the sale of [Intermedia's] Digex stock and to participate in any such transaction." As the discussion of the corporate opportunity claim above describes, the Special Committee had no legal authority to directly block Intermedia's decision to sell its shares in Digex. The §203 waiver negotiation, however, is exactly where the Special Committee should have been most relevant in this whole process. But this is precisely the point at which the Special Committee is missing in action—not through any failure of its own, but as a result of the control by the conflicted directors over the process. *Weinberger*'s suggestion of either an "independent negotiating structure" or "total abstention" is not to be taken lightly. The mere involvement in, or even control over, the waiver negotiations by the interested directors does not, by itself, end this inquiry into the entire fairness of the decision to grant the waiver. But there is a strong role under Delaware law for meaningful independent director committees. Although this Special Committee may have been created with precisely this role in mind, it certainly was not permitted to act in keeping with this role. . . .

By the time of the Digex meeting when the vote to waive §203 was undertaken, the Digex board's role had been vastly simplified over the preceding two days. On August 30, the Digex board was confronted with the sale of the corporation and all the attendant analysis that goes along with that process. On September 1, however, the only issue of any consequence before the Digex board was the rather discrete issue of whether to waive the protections afforded by §203. Independent director Jalkut proposed that a decision on the WorldCom transaction be delayed three days to allow CSFB time to solicit best and final offers from Exodus, Global Crossing, and WorldCom. That proposal was defeated by a vote of four to three. The Digex board then discussed the §203 waiver, but the discussion was limited to who should be allowed to vote on the waiver, nothing more. Except for the disagreement of counsel on this participation issue, described above, there was absolutely *no discussion whatsoever* of the effect, purpose, or applicability of §203 to WorldCom. The vote proceeded (four to three) and the waiver was granted.

The defendants suggest that the independent directors had decided before the meeting to vote against the waiver and therefore any discussion on the merits of the waiver would have been pointless. All I can say is I certainly hope that the interested directors thought through and decided their votes before the Digex board meeting. Based on the record of what was discussed at the meeting, or rather the complete lack thereof, if any of the directors based their vote on anything that occurred at the board meeting, I doubt that the waiver vote could even pass the most deferential business judgment review . . . [and] therefore conclude that it is not reasonably likely that defendants will be able to satisfy the fair dealing prong of the entire fairness analysis.

2. Fair Price

Defendants assert that the "price" of the waiver was fair. They point out that as a result of the WorldCom-Intermedia merger, Digex (i) would gain WorldCom's commitment to fully finance Digex's business plan and its contemplated capital expansion even before the closing; (ii) was freed of Intermedia's oppressive debt covenant restrictions; and (iii) would receive the benefit of WorldCom's strong financing capacity, sales force, data centers, and strong internet presence. Moreover, as noted above, WorldCom agreed to an amendment of Digex's certificate of incorporation whereby any future material transaction between WorldCom and Digex must be approved by independent Digex directors. The defendants further contend that at the time of the vote, each Digex director knew that there were certain constraints on Digex's ability to negotiate freely with any of its potential suitors, including WorldCom, because of Intermedia's desire to do a deal with WorldCom and WorldCom's refusal to negotiate any further over Digex.

. . . Although the attractiveness of WorldCom as a prospective corporate parent in place of Intermedia obviously enters into the analysis, the Digex board was not expressly voting on whether to accept WorldCom's merger proposal. As defendants themselves argue, Digex had little practical control over who would become its new parent. That decision ultimately lay with Intermedia as the controlling shareholder. Rather, the decision put before the Digex board was simply whether or not to . . . waive §203 and give up the protections granted by the terms of the statute in exchange for a stronger corporate parent who had much to offer, the certificate amendment, and the end of the burdensome relationship with Intermedia. Was this the best deal available? Because of the manner in which the negotiating process was handled, it is impossible to say. Perhaps Digex could have extracted something more from WorldCom, perhaps not. It is clear, however, that Digex had little to lose and should have felt no immediate time pressure to make a decision that would continue to affect the public shareholders of Digex for up to the three years following the merger.

The plaintiffs do not dispute that WorldCom is a good fit in many respects, vastly superior to Intermedia in many ways, or that Digex strongly desired to be rid of Intermedia's restrictive presence. But given Intermedia's admittedly poor financial condition, the independent Digex directors believed that, inevitably, Intermedia would have to sell part or all of its stake in Digex if Intermedia was to remain solvent. Time, therefore, was strongly on the side of Digex. Further, the certificate amendment is of some value to the Digex minority, but clearly it is not worth the same as the §203 waiver, or WorldCom would not have insisted on the waiver in the first place. . . .

In concluding this analysis of entire fairness, it appears that the only entity that really stood to lose should the Digex board decide to further analyze §203 and vote to at least delay the grant of the waiver by a day or two was Intermedia, not Digex. The behavior of the interested directors in controlling both the negotiations and vote over the §203 waiver surely demonstrates, in a compelling fashion, that the waiver really did present Digex with bargaining leverage against Intermedia and WorldCom. This leverage simply was not used — could not be used — because of the decision of the interested directors. In the unique circumstances here, this conduct by directors acting with a clear conflict of interest is difficult to justify and . . . plaintiffs have demonstrated a reasonable probability of success on the merits of their §203 claim.

---

1. *Another limit on a controlling shareholder's right to sell control. Digex* provides another exception to the general rule that a controlling shareholder is free to sell control for a premium not shared with minority shareholders. If the controlled shareholder causes the corporation to act to facilitate the transaction, the board has a duty to minority shareholders to extract a price for cooperation. This is an unremarkable result when, as in *Digex*, the legislature has limited the control that the controlling shareholder can sell. If the acquirer does not care about §203, then nothing changes. If it does, then the bargaining must be three-way: between the acquirer, the controlling shareholder, and the board representing the minority shareholders.

2. *Does* Digex *generalize?* *Digex* is more significant if it extends beyond the statutory restriction on sale of control imposed by §203. The transactional realities of selling control dictate that the controlled corporation often will be involved in the sale in some fashion. Consider the problem of due diligence. The acquirer of control typically will wish to undertake its own investigation of the target corporation. This necessarily will include access to information that is not otherwise public. *Digex* itself reveals the transaction pattern. When Intermedia's investment banker was shopping Intermedia and Digex, all parties who were interested in going forward with discussions were required to sign a confidentiality and non-disclosure agreement, surely an unnecessary condition if the information whose disclosure was necessary to advancing the transaction was public. Access to such information requires the cooperation of the corporation. Must the controlled corporation's board bargain on behalf of minority shareholders before allowing the acquirer access to the corporation's non-public information?

3. *What about the poison pill?* A more serious problem is presented by the availability of a poison pill. If *Digex* dictates that the board take advantage of every bargaining lever for the benefit of the minority shareholders, then does the board also have the obligation *to create* a lever? The board could simply adopt a poison pill that covers all but the existing controlling shareholder, effectively reserving to the board a veto power (or whatever power the pill currently accords the board under Delaware law, see pages 951-954 supra) over the controlling shareholder's sale of control. Ronald J. Gilson & Jeffrey Gordon, Controlling Controlling Shareholders, 152 U. Pa. L. Rev. 785 (2003), suggest that if *Digex* is interpreted in this fashion, the controlling shareholder's power to sell control at a premium will be largely eliminated:

> If the directors have a fiduciary obligation to bargain, then a failure even to consider adoption of a poison pill would surely violate their duty of care. Once the board takes up the question, the directors associated with the controlling shareholder are hopelessly conflicted. Either they must appoint a special committee with the right to adopt and manage a pill, in which event at least the burden of proof would shift, or the decision not to adopt the pill would, under *Digex*, be subject to entire fairness review with the burden of proof on the directors. If the failure to use the §203 lever was likely to fail this standard, despite the acknowledged advantages to Digex of a WorldCom acquisition of Intermedia, then so too would the failure to adopt and exert the leverage of a pill. It should be apparent that this rather straightforward analysis of the controlled corporation's post-*Digex* obligation to adopt a pill would effectively overturn the principle that controlling shareholders can sell control at a premium.

4. *Is there a way out?* Gilson and Gordon resist this conclusion, arguing that the permissive standards governing sale of control are appropriate because *Sinclair* standards governing self-dealing limit the amount of private benefits that can be capitalized into the price of control. They then suggest that the *Sinclair* standard should be the touchstone of a principled resolution of the conflict between *Digex* and the permissive sale of control standard:

> *Sinclair* poses the triggering test for heightened review as whether the "parent has received a benefit to the exclusion and at the expense of the subsidiary." We think this is also the appropriate triggering test for the standard governing controlled subsidiary participation in a sale of control transaction. The distinction is between

a setting where the non-controlling shareholders have something directly at stake in the transaction—that is where non-controlling shareholders lose something as a result of the transaction—and one where the issue is only an effort to extract a payment by holding up the transaction. Thus, controlled corporation participation in activities like acquirer due diligence does not come at the expense of the subsidiary; withholding participation serves only as a holdup device for which the symmetry of doctrine provides no support. The same analysis would apply to the controlled subsidiary's decision to adopt a poison pill directed at the sale of control.

E. FEDERAL REGULATION OF TAKEOVERS

1. REGULATION OF THE BIDDER

a. An Overview of the Williams Act

The Williams Act, passed in 1968 and amended in 1970, added §§13(d), 13(e), 14(d), 14(e), and 14(f) to the Securities Exchange Act of 1934 (the '34 Act). Of these sections, the following relate primarily to the bidder:

Sec. 13(d)(1). Any person who, after acquiring directly or indirectly the beneficial ownership of any equity security of a class which is registered pursuant to section 12 of this title . . . is directly or indirectly the beneficial owner of more than 5 per centum of such the class shall, within ten days after such acquisition, send to the issuer of the security at its principal executive office, by registered or certified mail, send to each exchange where the security is traded, and file with the Commission, a statement containing such of the following information, and such additional information, as the Commission may by rules and regulations prescribe as necessary or appropriate in the public interest or for the protection of investors—

(A) the background, and identity, residence, and citizenship of, and the nature of such beneficial ownership by, such person and all other persons by whom or on whose behalf the purchases have been or are to be effected;

(B) the source and amount of the funds or other consideration used or to be used in making the purchases, and if any part of the purchase price or proposed purchase price is represented or is to be represented by funds or other consideration borrowed or otherwise obtained for the purpose of acquiring, holding, or trading such security, a description of the transaction and the names of the parties thereto. . . .

(C) if the purpose of the purchases or prospective purchases is to acquire control of the business of the issuer of the securities, any plans or proposals which such persons may have to liquidate such issuer, to sell its assets to or merge it with any other persons, or to make any other major change in its business or corporate structure;

(D) the number of shares of such security which are beneficially owned, and the number of shares concerning which there is a right to acquire, directly or indirectly, by (i) such person, and (ii) by each associate of such person, giving the background, identity, residence, and citizenship of each such associate; and

(E) information as to any contracts, arrangements, or understandings with any person with respect to any securities of the issuer, including but not limited to transfer of any of the securities, joint ventures, loan or option arrangements, puts or calls, guaranties of loans, guaranties against loss, or guaranties of profits, division of losses or profits, or the giving or withholding of proxies, naming the persons with whom such contracts, arrangements, or understandings have been entered into, and giving the details thereof.

(2) If any material change occurs in the facts set forth in the statements to the issuer and the exchange, and in the statement filed with the Commission, an amendment shall be transmitted to the issuer and the exchange and shall be filed with the Commission, in accordance with such rules and regulations as the Commission may prescribe as necessary or appropriate in the public interest or for the protection of investors.

(3) When two or more persons act as a partnership, limited partnership, syndicate, or other group for the purpose of acquiring, holding, or disposing of securities of an issuer, such syndicate or group shall be deemed a "person" for the purposes of this subsection. . . .

Sec. 14(d)(1). It shall be unlawful for any person, directly or indirectly, by use of the mails or by any means or instrumentality of interstate commerce or of any facility of a national securities exchange or otherwise, to make a tender offer for, or a request or invitation for tenders of, any class of any equity security which is registered pursuant to section 12 of this title, . . . if, after consummation thereof, such person would, directly or indirectly, be the beneficial owner of more than 5 per centum of such class, unless at the time copies of the offer or request or invitation are first published or sent or given to security holders such person has filed with the Commission a statement containing such of the information specified in section 13(d) of this title, and such additional information as the Commission may by rules and regulations prescribe as necessary or appropriate in the public interest or for the protection of investors. All requests or invitations for tenders or advertisements making a tender offer or requesting or inviting tenders of such a security shall be filed as part of such statement and shall contain such of the information contained in such statement as the Commission may by rules and regulations prescribe. Copies of any additional material soliciting or requesting such tender offers subsequent to the initial solicitation or request shall contain such information as the Commission may by rules and regulations prescribe as necessary or appropriate in the public interest or for the protection of investors, and shall be filed with the Commission not later than the time copies of such material are first published or sent or given to security holders. Copies of all statements, in the form in which such material is furnished to security holders and the Commission, shall be sent to the issuer not later than the date such material is first published or sent or given to any security holders.

(2) When two or more persons act as a partnership, limited partnership, syndicate, or other group for the purpose of acquiring, holding, or disposing of securities of an issuer, such syndicate or group shall be deemed a "person" for purposes of this subsection.

(3) In determining, for purposes of this subsection, any percentage of a class of any security, such class shall be deemed to consist of the amount of the outstanding securities of such class, exclusive of any securities of such class held by or for the account of the issuer or a subsidiary of the issuer.

(4) Any solicitation or recommendation to the holders of such a security to accept or reject a tender offer or request or invitation for tenders shall be made in accordance with such rules and regulations as the Commission may prescribe as necessary or appropriate in the public interest or for the protection of investors.

(5) Securities deposited pursuant to a tender offer or request or invitation for tenders may be withdrawn by or on behalf of the depositor at any time until the expiration of seven days after the time definitive copies of the offer or request or invitation are first published or sent or given to security holders, and at any time after sixty days from the date of the original tender offer or request or invitation, except as the Commission may otherwise prescribe by rules, regulations, or order as necessary or appropriate in the public interest or for the protection of investors.

(6) Where any person makes a tender offer, or request or invitation for tenders, for less than all the outstanding equity securities of a class, and where a greater number of securities is deposited pursuant thereto within ten days after copies of the offer or request or invitation are first published or sent or given to security holders than such person is bound or willing to take up and pay for, the securities taken up shall be taken up as nearly as may be pro rata, disregarding fractions, according to the number of securities deposited by each depositor. The provisions of this subsection shall also apply to securities deposited within ten days after notice of an increase in the consideration offered to security holders, as described in paragraph (7), is first published or sent or given to security holders.

(7) Where any person varies the terms of a tender offer or request or invitation for tenders before the expiration thereof by increasing the consideration offered to holders of such securities, such person shall pay the increased consideration to each security holder whose securities are taken up and paid for pursuant to the tender offer or request or invitation for tenders whether or not such securities have been taken up by such person before the variation of the tender offer or request or invitation.

(8) The provisions of this subsection shall not apply to any offer for, or request or invitation for tenders of, any security —

(A) If the acquisition of such security, together with all other acquisitions by the same person of securities of the same class during the preceding twelve months, would not exceed 2 per centum of that class;

(B) by the issuer of such security; or

(C) which the Commission, by rules or regulations or by order, shall exempt from the provisions of this subsection as not entered into for the purpose of, not having the effect of, changing or influencing the control of the issuer or otherwise not comprehended within the purposes of this subsection.

Sec. 14(e). It shall be unlawful for any person to make any untrue statement of a material fact or omit to state any material fact necessary in order to make the statements made, in the light of the circumstances under which they are made, not misleading, or to engage in any fraudulent, deceptive, or manipulative acts or practices, in connection with any tender offer or request or invitation for tenders, or any solicitation of security holders in opposition to or in favor of any such offer, request, or invitation. The Commission shall, for the purposes of this subsection, by rules and regulations define, and prescribe means reasonably designed to prevent, such acts and practices as are fraudulent, deceptive, or manipulative.

1. *Basic structure of the Williams Act.* Unlike the other federal securities statutes this casebook examines, the Williams Act contains substantive rules in addition to disclosure requirements and antifraud provisions. Essentially, the Act does three things: First, §13(d) establishes a distant early-warning line — the 5 percent threshold of §13(d)(1) — which when crossed requires that a disclosure statement (Schedule 13D) be filed with the SEC and the target corporation within ten days thereafter. Although the disclosures in a Schedule 13D filing, particularly those about the future plans and intentions of the potential bidder, often read much like boilerplate, the market is at least alerted to the prospect of an incipient control contest and may revalue the target's shares in light of it. Second, §14(d) regulates the making of tender offers, requiring both that a disclosure document be filed (known as the Schedule 14D-1) and addressing such substantive matters as (i) the minimum length of a tender offer, (ii) the rights of tendering shareholders to withdraw their shares, (iii) when the offer must be extended, and (iv) the proration rights of tendering shareholders if the offer is oversubscribed (if more shares are tendered than the bidder has sought). The SEC has adopted extensive rules on all these subjects, discussed below. Finally, §14(e) sets forth an antifraud rule, which seemingly parallels the language of Rule 10b-5, but which has in some important respects a potentially broader coverage.

The coverage of §§13(d) and 14(d) differ significantly from that of §14(e). The former sections apply only to target corporations with a class of equity securities registered under §12 of the '34 Act (i.e., "reporting companies"); in addition, §14(d) applies only to tender offers that would result in the bidder beneficially owning 5 percent or more of the class. In contrast, §14(e) applies to *all* tender offers, whether or not the target is a reporting company and whether or not 5 percent or more of the class is sought. As a result, rules adopted by the SEC under §14(d) apply only to reporting companies, while rules under §14(e) apply to all tender offers. See Sec. Exch. Act Rel. No. 16,834 (1979). The SEC has been very conscious of this distinction and has accordingly promulgated some of its most important rules under §14(e).

2. *SEC rules.* Possibly the most surprising feature about the SEC's takeover rules is that they seem to go well beyond the relatively clear lines drawn by the statute. For example, §14(d)(5) seems to require only that the bidder keep the offer open at least seven days and allow shareholders to withdraw their tendered securities after 60 days. Yet Rule 14e-1 requires the issuer to hold the offer open for not less than 20 *business* days, and it further mandates a 10-*business* day extension from the date on which the bidder increases either the price offered, the percentage of the class or number of securities sought, or any soliciting fee paid to dealers. Similarly, despite the seemingly clear 7-day withdrawal right in §14(d)(5), Rule 14d-7 grants additional withdrawal rights for the entire period during which the tender offer remains open. Next, while §14(d)(6) establishes proration rights (i.e., the right to pro rata treatment in a partial bid) for shareholders who tender during the first 10 days of a tender offer (and also for 10 days after any increase in price), Rule 14d-8 extends this proration right to the life of the tender offer. Thus, in a tender offer for 50 percent of the stock, if 100 percent of the shares are tendered, all shareholders, including those who tender on the first day and those who tender on the last day of the offer, will have half of their shares accepted and half returned to them.

These substantive rules focus on the length of time a tender offer must be kept open and for what portion of that time certain substantive requirements apply. Both require knowing when a tender offer begins so that there is a date from which to count the number of days specified in the statute or rules. Rule 14d-2 defines the commencement of a tender offer as the date on which the bidder first publishes, sends or gives the means to tender to a shareholder. Rule 14e-8 prohibits the bidder from announcing a tender offer that has not yet "commenced" if the bidder does not intend to commence the offer within a reasonable time or does not believe it will have the funds to complete the offer.

These SEC rules raise two distinct questions: First, what is their objective? Essentially, their purpose is to reduce pressure on shareholders and enable them to make informed choices. Whether the rules succeed at this can be debated, but their impact is clearly to promote auctions. By keeping the tender offer open for 20 business days and specifying a withdrawal right co-extensive with the offer, the SEC gives potential competing bidders an opportunity to formulate their own counterbids and enables shareholders to accept the highest offer (because they can withdraw their shares to accept a higher later bid). Proration rights also bear on this policy. Prior to Rule 14d-8, which requires proration for the life of the offer, bidders could specify a "first-come, first-served" rule that applied after the first 10 days, during which §14(d)(6) mandates proration. This created an incentive for bidders to make partial bids and thereby pressure shareholders to tender within 10 days in order to be assured of pro rata acceptance if the offer was oversubscribed (which uncontested partial bids usually are). The practical impact of the original 10-day proration rule was to encourage partial bids because this tactic effectively telescoped the 20-business-day period specified in Rule 14e-1 into a 10-day period, thereby denying time to potential rival bidders to prepare their own bids.

Second, whatever the objective of these rules, how does the SEC justify them under the statute? Recall the distinction between §14(d) and §14(e). The 20-day rule was promulgated as Rule 14e-1 under §14(e), which makes unlawful "manipulative acts or practices" and authorizes the SEC to "prescribe means reasonably related to prevent such acts and practices. . . ." The SEC's view is that shorter offering, proration, or withdrawal periods, while not necessarily intentionally fraudulent, deceptive, or manipulative, still encourage such practices, and thus their prohibition is "reasonably related" to the Act's objectives. To date, no litigation has challenged the validity of these regulations, although one decision has found that a bidder could not on its own extend the proration period (as Rule 14d-8 now does) beyond the statutory proration period. Pryor v. United States Steel Corp., 794 F.2d 52 (2d Cir. 1986) (involving a transaction prior to the adoption of current Rule 14d-8 and declining to express any view on the validity of the current rules). What result if a bidder announced a 15-day tender offer and the SEC sued? Why has no such case arisen?

3. *Equal treatment of security holders.* In 1986 the SEC adopted Rule 14d-10, which contains both a "best price" and an "all holders" requirement. In its current form, it reads:

(a) No bidder shall make a tender offer unless:

(1) The tender offer is open to all security holders of the class of securities subject to the tender offer; and

(2) The consideration paid to any security holder for securities tendered in the tender offer is the highest paid to any other security holder for securities tendered in the tender offer. . . .

Prior to this rule it was at least theoretically possible to make a tender offer to a limited class (e.g., only to institutional investors). In one well-known case, a target corporation made a selective self-tender at an above-market price to all holders except the hostile bidder. See Unocal Corp. v. Mesa Petroleum Co., 493 A.2d 946 (Del. 1985) (page 955 supra). Today, a companion rule to Rule 14d-10—Rule 13e-4—extends this same prohibition against selective offers to target corporations that make self-tenders for their own stock, thus effectively reversing the result in *Unocal*.

Before a 2006 amendment, the rule required that equal consideration be paid "pursuant to the tender offer." The amendment was meant to allay concerns about side payments made to key employees or shareholders, which may have been connected to the tender offer process but were not formally paid as compensation for the actual shares. These types of payments include modifications to employment agreements, grant or acceleration of stock options, or compensation for entering into a non-compete agreement. Under the old rule, these payments may have been characterized as made "pursuant to the tender offer" because they were part of the same transaction, and therefore a violation of the best-price rule. If this happened, the remedy would have been a corresponding payment to all shareholders—a huge potential liability that may have served as a significant deterrent to tender offers. Note that this is a very different damage measure than in Perlman v. Feldmann, page 1051 supra. In *Perlman*, the controlling shareholder was made to share the premium it received with other shareholders. Under Rule 14d-10, the party making the tender offer would have to pay an equivalent premium to *each* shareholder.

Some courts addressing damages claims related to side payments in a tender offer found that the best-price rule applied only to transactions taking place between the formal beginning and expiration of the tender offer. See, e.g., Gerber v. Computer Assoc. Int'l, Inc., 303 F.3d 126, 138 (2d. Cir. 2002) (awarding damages based on payment for a non-compete agreement with the target chairman and CEO because it occurred "during the tender offer"); Lerro v. Quaker Oats Corp., 84 F.3d 239, 246 (7th Cir. 1996) (denying damages because the exclusive distribution agreement benefiting a corporation controlled by a 35% shareholder was signed prior to the commencement of the tender offer). Other courts rejected a timing-based approach in favor of a fact-based test, holding that a side payment is a violation of the best-price rule if it is an "integral part" of the tender offer transaction, even if it occurred outside the formal duration of the tender offer. See, e.g., Epstein v. MCA, Inc., 50 F.3d 644, 655 (9th Cir. 1995), *rev'd on other grounds*, 516 U.S. 367 (1996).

The 2006 amendment to the rule takes neither approach, but instead makes clear that the best-price requirement is limited to consideration paid for securities tendered in the tender offer. Rule 14d-10(d)(1) specifically provides that the best-price rule will not be violated by payments related to an employment or severance agreement as long as the compensation paid is either for past, present, or future performance of services or for refraining from certain activity, and the payment is not calculated based on the number of shares tendered. If these compensatory arrangements are approved solely by the independent directors of the target, they fall within a non-exclusive safe harbor offered by Rule 14d-10(d)(2).

Equal treatment in tender offers is also enforced by Rule 10b-13, which forbids a bidder who has announced a tender offer to purchase any securities of the same class outside the offer until its conclusion. Absent this rule, bidders might pay higher prices to holders of large blocks by arranging private transactions outside the tender offer. This can still be done either before or after the tender offer, but Rule 10b-13 also precludes making "any arrangement to purchase" during the period of the tender offer. Note that Rule 10b-13 puts a great deal of pressure on the definition of the commencement of a tender offer in Rule 14d-2 in a situation where a large shareholder demands a higher price than that offered other target shareholders. Rule 10b-13 does not prevent the payment of the higher price so long as it is done prior to the tender offer's commencement. Thus, the agreement with the large shareholder must precede any public announcement of the tender offer. What if an agreement to make a higher payment to a large shareholder is entered into before the tender offer but the agreement's closing is conditioned on the tender offer's success? See Epstein v. MCA, Inc., 1995 WL 75487 (9th Cir. 1995); Lerro v. Snapple Beverage Corp., 84 F.3d 239 (1996).

b. What Is a Tender Offer?

The purpose of the William Act's substantive provisions is to reduce pressure on shareholders to tender their shares by ensuring that an offer stays open long enough that target shareholders have the opportunity to consider the offer and to reduce coercion by ensuring that all who tender during that period receive the same price. An additional effect is to give the target company sufficient time to seek competing bids or initiate an auction. Not surprisingly, these requirements were unattractive to bidders. Planners then sought to devise techniques that bypassed target management and sought to purchase control directly from shareholders, but that were not tender offers within the meaning of the Williams Act. The planners' task was made easier because neither the Williams Act nor SEC regulations defined the term "tender offer."

1. *Private purchases and market-mediated private purchases.* Planners tried a number of different approaches to creating a non-statutory tender offer. One approach sought to carve out a private-offering exception to the definition of a tender offer. In Wellman v. Dickinson, 475 F. Supp. 783 (S.D.N.Y. 1979), Sun Company wished to acquire a controlling stake in Becton, Dickinson & Company without complying with the Williams Act. The approach was to make simultaneous telephone calls to 39 large holders and offer to buy their Sun stock at a substantial premium, with each holder given a period of from one hour to one day to respond. The offer was conditioned on 20 percent of the shares being acquired, and the holders were told that those who did not sell quickly might lose out. The court concluded that there had been a public solicitation and proceeded to focus on eight characteristics of a tender offer that the SEC had suggested in other cases. These included (1) an active and widespread solicitation of public shareholders; (2) solicitation of a substantial percentage of the target's stock; (3) the offer of a premium price; (4) non-negotiable terms; (5) conditioning the offer on the acquisition of a specified number of shares; (6) the offer being open for a limited period of time; (7) pressure on the shareholder to tender; and (8) substantial publicity concerning the offer. Although the court gave little guidance concerning the number of factors that were required to be present to cause an unconventional offer to fall within the definition of a tender offer, or whether all of the factors were

of equal importance, the court held that the Sun offer fell under the Williams Act. While the court suggested that a privately negotiated transaction still could fall outside the statutory term, the potential for avoidance was significantly restricted.

A second approach to soliciting a small number of large shareholders was to impose a stock market between the bidder and the shareholders. In Brascan Ltd. v. Edper Equities Ltd., 477 F. Supp. 773 (S.D.N.Y. 1979), Edper Equities placed a purchase order with its broker for some 2.5 million shares of Brascan, whose shares were traded on the American Stock Exchange. The broker then contacted between 30 and 50 institutional investors and 10 to 15 individual investors who held large blocks of Brascan and advised them that if they offered their shares on the exchange at a price several dollars above the then trading price, Edper might be willing to purchase them. Through this process, Edper quickly acquired 3.1 million Brascan shares. The court considered the same factors as did the *Wellman* court, but concluded that only one of the SEC's eight criteria was met — that the offer was for a substantial percentage of the target's stock. As a result, the stock exchange–mediated alternative to a tender offer was held to fall outside the Williams Act.

To bidders in future cases, the practical message may be that open market purchasing, even if directed at a small number of large holders, is safe, but private purchasing from an unrelated group is dangerous. Does this distinction make any policy sense? Or should the term "tender offer" instead be defined according to some combination of the amount of stock acquired and the number of sellers? In 1980 the SEC proposed to Congress replacing the term "tender offer" with the term "statutory offer," which would be triggered by any acquisition of 10 percent or more of an issuer's stock (with a limited exception for private negotiations with a small group). The proposal was given little attention by Congress.

2. *Market sweeps.* In 1985 Hanson Trust PLC, a British company, tendered for SCM Corporation, which countered with a leveraged buyout proposal. After much skirmishing and litigation, Hanson called off its tender offer, but in a space of several hours purchased a total of 33⅓ percent of SCM's outstanding stock — 25 percent in six transactions — which action frustrated SCM's leveraged buyout. Hanson did not need to solicit for purchases, because the announcement of a tender offer alone causes arbitrageurs to become active in the market, and many were eager to dump their shares in the wake of the canceled tender offer. In Hanson Trust PLC v. SCM Corporation, 774 F.2d 47 (2d Cir. 1985), the Second Circuit found Hanson's purchases not to constitute a tender offer, relying both on the SEC's standard "eight-factor" test discussed in *Wellman* and the additional fact that those who sold the 25 percent interest in SCM to Hanson were highly sophisticated arbitrageurs.

3. *Does the definition of a tender offer matter in the face of poison pills?* This section began by noting that the goal of planners in devising techniques that bypassed target management and sought to purchase control directly from shareholders, but were not tender offers, was to avoid the delay and restrictions imposed by the Williams Act so as to maintain pressure on the target company and its shareholders. The bidder wanted a way to pressure target shareholders into tendering before the target could promote an auction.

The cases that deal with unconventional tender offers all date from a period before poison pill plans had become pervasive. See page 951 supra. If a poison pill plan is in place, are the Williams Act's protections against coercion of shareholders (and opportunities to initiate auctions for target companies) beside the point? If a hostile bidder can acquire no more than the triggering percentage of a target company's common stock (typically 20 percent, but often as low as 10 percent) without either successfully negotiating with target management or successfully persuading a court to require the pill's redemption, then the Williams Act time periods are no longer binding constraints. Thus, there has been a sharp drop in the use of unconventional tender offers because so many public companies have adopted or quickly could adopt a poison pill plan. Since a poison pill is more restrictive than the Williams Act, there is little to gain from avoiding the statute.

c. Disclosure

A bidder faces a dual disclosure obligation under the Williams Act: First, there is the 5 percent threshold specified by §13(d),[59] at which point Schedule 13D must be filed. Second, if the bidder actually commences a tender offer, it must concomitantly file a Schedule TO and provide to investors the information specified in Regulation M-A. The disclosures required by these two schedules largely overlap and chiefly focus on the prospective bidder's identity, source of funds, and plans for the target. In addition, the instructions to Schedule TO require the bidder to furnish financial statements if the bidder's financial condition is material to the target shareholder's decision. Why is this information about the bidder ever relevant to the target shareholder's decision to sell? Arguably, the target shareholder in a cash tender offer is being asked to accept a large premium over the market — a choice presumably as easy to make as accepting an offer to exchange a $5 bill for a $10 bill.

One answer is that disclosure remains important when the bidder is making a partial bid because if the offer is oversubscribed, some of the tendered shares will be returned to the target shareholder; thus, because shareholders cannot fully liquidate their investment in the target, they have good reason to be interested in the bidder's financial condition and how it will manage the target. Also, some shareholders may want to reject the offer and remain as minority shareholders in the reconstituted firm. In practice, however, most bidders merge out the minority interest left after the tender offer within a one- to two-year period, usually at a price not less than the tender offer price. In this light, the case for disclosure of bidder-related financial data seems persuasive only in the special instance where the target shareholders will wind up as long-term minority shareholders in a "new" corporation dominated by the bidder.

The problem becomes more complex when there is uncertainty about the identity of the bidder. Suppose the success of a tender offer depends on financing being

---

59. The 5 percent threshold applies not only to individuals and entities, but also to any "other group for the purpose of acquiring, holding, or disposing of securities of an issuer." See §13(d)(3). Thus, if two individuals each holding 4 percent agree to act in concert to oust the incumbent management of a "reporting" company, they must file a Schedule 13D within ten days after the time they form such a group. See GAF Corp. v. Milstein, 453 F.2d 709 (2d Cir. 1971). Much litigation has focused on when a loosely knit assortment of individuals (such as a bidder and arbitrageurs with which it had continuing contact) constitute a "group," but few clear principles have emerged. Often, it will be very debatable whether interacting individuals actually share a common purpose; for example, the bidder's aim may be to seize control, while its apparent allies, the arbitrageurs, may desire to start an auction among rival bidders.

provided by an investment bank that holds a 14 percent direct interest in the bidder and a significant indirect interest, although voting control rests with other parties. Is the investment bank a "bidder" for purposes of Williams Act compliance, especially disclosure of financial information concerning the investment bank? See MAI Basic Four, Inc. v. Prime Computer, Inc., 871 F.2d 212 (1st Cir. 1989) (Drexel Burnham Lambert held to be a bidder).

In practice, the cost to the bidder of including its financial statements is generally low (because the bidder is usually already a "reporting company"), and if the court believes there is a material omission, it seldom does more than require a corrective amendment. See page 944 supra. Yet the benefits of such disclosure are also often modest at best. For example, Schedule TO requires disclosure of the prospective bidder's "plans and proposals" for the target. Material as this information is to the target shareholder, the bidder's response typically has been to make a blanket pro forma disclosure of every conceivable possibility—for example, "Although [bidder] has considered the possibility of a future acquisition of control of [target], whether by means of tender offer, merger, or other business combination, open market purchases, private transactions or otherwise, [bidder] has not made any definitive plans to attempt to acquire control of [target]. . . ."[60] Often this may correctly describe the contingent nature of the bidder's plans, but in any event courts have not required more. The conventional wisdom among experienced practitioners is that such boilerplate will be sufficient to defeat the claim that the bidder violated §14(e) by omitting to state its actual plans, *unless* the bidder undertakes a major transaction very shortly after the filing is made. In this light, the real value of Schedule TO is probably more the warning it gives the market than the disclosures it contains.

Another disclosure issue involves whether the bidder has any obligation to disclose information that its research has uncovered showing undisclosed value in the target. Suppose, for example, that the bidder's investigatory efforts lead it to appraise the liquidation value of the target's assets at $1 billion above the aggregate price of its shares in the stock market. Must it disclose this appraisal? Courts have avoided this issue, usually finding that the appraisal was too speculative or uncertain to require disclosure. Compare Starkman v. Marathon Oil Co., 772 F.2d 231 (6th Cir. 1985) (requiring disclosure of "projections and asset appraisals based on predictions regarding future economic and corporate events only if the predictions underlying the appraisal or prediction are substantially certain to hold"), with Flynn v. Bass Brothers Enterprises, 744 F.2d 978 (3d Cir. 1984), (using balancing test but not requiring disclosure). In Radol v. Thomas, 772 F.2d 244 (6th Cir. 1986), the court noted that "every such decision involving an asset appraisal has held that there was no duty to disclose the appraisal." But why? Clearly, no information will more likely affect the market price or the bargaining among the bidder, the target, and possible white knights. Both legal and economic reasons may underlie the judicial reluctance to require disclosure. First, if the bidder has overestimated its appraisal, should it face liability if non-tendering shareholders sue in a class action on the theory that they declined the offer (and the tender offer therefore failed) because they relied on the bidder's overly

---

60. This disclosure paraphrases the actual response of the bidder in Jewelcor, Inc. v. Pearlman, 397 F. Supp. 221, 228 (S.D.N.Y. 1975).

optimistic asset appraisal? Seemingly, there is a "Catch-22" problem here. Second, from an economic perspective, what incentive does the bidder have to search for information if it must disclose the hidden value and thus frustrate its own offer? Note also that unless this non-public information emanates from a source inside the target (and as a result of a breach of fiduciary duty), it would not seemingly fall within *Dirk*'s definition of inside information (see page 454 supra).

2. REGULATION OF THE TARGET

As it applies to the target corporation, the Williams Act is principally, but not exclusively, a disclosure statute. An important policy question remains, however, as to whether federal law should attempt greater substantive regulation of the target's conduct.

a. Mandatory Disclosure: Schedule 14D-9

Rule 14D-9 prohibits the target corporation, its officers, directors, employees, and shareholders from making any "solicitation or recommendation to security holders . . . with respect to a tender offer for such securities unless as soon as practicable on the date such solicitation or recommendation is first published or sent or given" they file with the SEC, the bidder, and the securities markets where the security is traded a document known as Schedule 14D-9. Subparagraph (e) of Rule 14d-9 then exempts what are termed "stop-look-and-listen communications," which state only that the target's board has the tender offer "under consideration," will shortly advise security holders of its recommendation, and requests security holders to deter action until that point. Otherwise, the target must remain silent until it has filed its Schedule 14D-9.

Schedule 14D-9 parallels Schedule 13D in requiring disclosures about the identity and background of those filing the schedule. Its practical significance arises largely because of its Item 7, which requires, pursuant to Item 1006(d) of Regulation M-A, the target to disclose whether or not any negotiation is being undertaken or is underway by the subject company in response to the tender offer. Commonly, the response of target management to a hostile offer is to open negotiations with a "white knight," and on its face Item 7 would seem to require disclosure of these negotiations. In addition, Rule 14d-9(b) requires that disclosures be updated if a material change occurs, thus creating a continuing disclosure obligation. However, the instructions to Item 1006 in Schedule M-A cut back sharply on Schedule 14D-9's coverage by exempting some preliminary negotiations: "If an agreement in principle has not been reached at the time of filing, no disclosure . . . is required of the possible terms of or the parties to the transaction if in the opinion of the board of directors of the subject company disclosure would jeopardize continuation of negotiations. In that case, disclosure indicating that negotiations are being undertaken or are underway and are in the preliminary stage is sufficient." Does this give corporate lawyers an incentive to avoid an agreement in principle, and therefore the need to make specific disclosures, for as long as possible? The result may be to cause disclosure to assume boilerplate characteristics, disclosing only that preliminary negotiations are in progress with unnamed parties, and leaving the market to guess both the identity of the white knight and the nature of the transaction.

Standing by itself, Rule 14d-9 does not require the target management to make any statement; it mandates the filing of Schedule 14D-9 only when target management chooses to solicit shareholders or make a recommendation. Although the bidder must disclose its plans, the target could maneuver in complete silence. To remedy this imbalance, the SEC adopted Rule 14e-2 in 1980:

> Rule 14e-2. *Position of Subject Company with Respect to a Tender Offer.* (a) *Position of subject company.* As a means reasonably designed to prevent fraudulent, deceptive or manipulative acts or practices within the meaning of section 14(e) of the Act, the subject company, no later than 10 business days from the date the tender offer is first published or sent or given, shall publish, send or give to security holders a statement disclosing that the subject company:
>
> (1) Recommends acceptance or rejection of the bidder's tender offer;
>
> (2) Expresses no opinion and is remaining neutral toward the bidder's tender offer; or
>
> (3) Is unable to take a position with respect to the bidder's tender offer. Such statement shall also include the reason(s) for the position (including the inability to take a position) disclosed therein.

Because Rule 14e-2 requires that the target make a recommendation, and Rule 14d-9 requires that Schedule 14D-9 be filed when the board does so, the net result is a unique requirement of mandatory disclosure under circumstances where the target corporation has not engaged in any of the forms of conduct (e.g., sale of securities, solicitation of proxies, etc.) that usually trigger disclosure obligations under the federal securities laws.

b. Disclosure of Negotiations in Tender Offers

Once Schedule 14D-9 is filed, target management remains under a duty to update any statements made in it. This can present unanticipated problems. In Revlon, Inc., Sec. Exch. Act Rel. No. 23,320 (June 16, 1986), the SEC found misleading a statement made by Revlon in a Schedule 14D-9 filed by it in response to a hostile offer for it by Pantry Pride. The statement said that Revlon "may undertake" negotiations looking toward a merger or sale of assets. Several days after this filing, Revlon began discussions with two investment banking firms about the possibility of a leveraged buyout. Because the SEC viewed the original statement to mean that no discussions were then underway, it found Rule 14d-9(b)'s updating requirement to have been violated when the original disclosure went uncorrected after specific discussions began (even though neither the terms nor the identity of the parties had to be disclosed under the instructions to Item 7).

This emphasis on the need to update disclosures, even in the hurly-burly of a hotly contested takeover contest, seems a further extension of the SEC's earlier position in Carnation Company, Sec. Exch. Act Rel. No. 22,214 [1984-1985 Transfer Binder], Fed. Sec. L. Rep. (CCH) 183,301, where the SEC found a statement by Carnation officials to be materially false. In response to abnormal trading activity in its stock, the Carnation officials had said that "there is no news from the company and no corporate development that would account for the stock action."

In fact, Carnation had already begun to negotiate a merger with Nestle, S.A. From the SEC's perspective, the target may decline to comment on press reports, but it may not deny that negotiations or developments are in progress simply because they are at an early stage. Although the circuits had once split on this question of the materiality of preliminary merger negotiations, the SEC's position appears to have been fully sustained by the Supreme Court in Basic, Inc. v. Levinson, page 312 supra.

c. Issuer Repurchases

Once a bidder launches a tender offer, the target corporation must comply with Rule 13e-1 before it may purchase any of its own shares during the life of the tender offer. Rule 13e-1 requires that a disclosure statement be filed with the SEC and provided to the target's shareholders, detailing the amount of securities to be purchased and the source of funds to be used. In theory, compliance with this rule alerts the market and explains the possible source of trading activity in the open market (which otherwise might be attributed to a rival bidder).

If the target wishes to make a tender offer for its own shares, it must comply with Rule 13e-4 ("Tender offers by issuers"). Revised in 1986 and again in 2006, this rule now largely parallels the rules under §§14(d) and (e). In particular, the provisions of Rule 13e-4(f)(8) through (11) require that the target comply with the same "all holders" and "best price" rules that apply under §14(d). These rules (which effectively preclude a self-tender that excludes the original bidder) are not applicable, however, if the target engages in open market purchases that do not amount to a "tender offer." Thus, when the target makes a counter-tender offer for its own shares, it must compete with the bidder under substantially the same legal rules; however, when it purchases in the open market, it need only satisfy the modest requirement of Rule 13e-1.

F. *FREEZE-OUT MERGERS*

Following a successful tender offer, whether hostile or friendly, or after a direct purchase of controlling shares, an acquiring company will find itself the controlling shareholder of a less than wholly owned subsidiary. Because minority shareholders had no opportunity to participate in a direct sale of controlling shares, or because some shareholders in a tender offer did not tender because they found the offer unattractive or were unsophisticated or perhaps simply neglectful, some minority shareholders remain. In this situation, acquirers typically believe it critical to "freeze out" these minority shareholders and convert the target company into a wholly owned subsidiary.[61] Because of the transactional importance acquirers assigned this step in the acquisition process, it was the focus of planners'

---

61. "The ability to squeeze out minority shareholders and thus obtain 100 percent of the equity of a corporation is a basic condition of the current market for corporate control." Leo Herzel & Dale Colling, Squeeze-Out Mergers in Delaware — The Delaware Supreme Court Decision in Weinberger v. UOP, 7 Corp. L. Rev. 195, 196 (1984).

early efforts at designing defensive tactics. As described in Sec. B.2 supra, the "flip-over" poison pill and some forms of shark repellent amendments and state anti-takeover legislation sought to deter a hostile bidder by making a freeze-out merger more difficult. Additionally, freeze-out mergers are not limited to two-step take-overs. A long-term large shareholder may decide that it is advantageous to convert its controlled subsidiary into a wholly owned subsidiary. A freeze-out by the controlling shareholder impacts minority shareholders quite differently than does the controlling shareholder's sale of control. When control is sold, minority shareholders participate proportionally — assuming the effectiveness of *Sinclair*-like standards — in any post-transaction improvement in corporate performance. In contrast, a freeze-out eliminates the minority before the improvement occurs. The development of standards governing whether and by what means minority shareholders can be eliminated from further participation in the corporate enter-prise without their consent has been one of the most interesting stories in corporate law, representing an uneasy tension between high principle and practical litiga-tion strategy.

1. INTRODUCTION: THE HISTORY OF THE CONFLICT

The potential to freeze out minority shareholders arose with authorization of the use of cash as allowable consideration in a merger, a development of surprisingly recent origin. While Florida added cash to the statutory list of permissible payment modes in 1925, Delaware authorized the payment of cash in short-form mergers in 1957 and in long-form mergers in 1967.[62] Early Delaware cases rejected broad challenges to the use of cash as merger consideration, first in connection with short-form mergers[63] and then in connection with long-form mergers.[64] In these cases the court declined to consider objections to cash mergers based on claims of oppression, treating the issue as essentially one of price. This set the initial terms of the doctrinal debate as the exclusivity of the appraisal remedy: Under what cir-cumstances could minority shareholders, instead of challenging the adequacy of the price for their stock through appraisal, seek to remain shareholders by chal-lenging the legality of the merger itself?

Minority shareholders responded to their lack of success in state court by seek-ing relief in federal court through the federal securities laws. The court of appeals decision in Green v. Santa Fe Industries[65] marked the apogee of this movement, holding that a majority shareholder who froze out the minority "without any justifiable business purpose" stated a claim under Rule 10b-5 despite the avail-ability of a state law appraisal remedy. As we saw earlier in Chapter V, the Supreme Court reversed, construing Rule 10b-5 to require misrepresentation or nondisclosure. This construction was based in part on the traditional primacy of state law fiduciary standards. However, the Court appeared to give support to ongoing efforts to displace state law in this area by noting "[t]here may well be a

---

62. See Elliot Weiss, The Law of Take Out Mergers: A Historical Perspective, 56 N.Y.U. L. Rev. 624 (1981).

63. Coyne v. Park & Tilford Distillers Corp., 38 Del. Ch. 514, 514 A.2d (1959); Stauffer v. Standard Brands, 41 Del Ch. 7, 187 A.2d 78 (1962).

64. David J. Breene & Co. v. Schenley Industries, Inc., 281 A.2d 30 (Del. Ch. 1971).

65. 553 F.2d 1283 (2d Cir. 1976), *reversed*, 430 U.S. 462 (1977).

need for uniform federal fiduciary standards to govern mergers such as that challenged in this complaint. . . ." 430 U.S. at 479. Significantly, the Court cited Professor William Cary's famous article that castigated Delaware law and its judiciary for leading a race to the bottom in corporate law and proposing a federal corporate minimum standards law. William Cary, Federalism and Corporate Law: Reflections upon Delaware, 83 Yale L.J. 663 (1974).

Singer v. Magnavox Co., 380 A.2d 969 (Del. 1977), which was under submission when the United States Supreme Court decided *Santa Fe,* was Delaware's response to the threat of federal incursion concerning freeze-out mergers. *Singer* presented a standard two-step acquisition transaction. North American Phillips Corp. secured 84 percent of Magnavox's common stock in a $9 per share tender offer, following which it initiated a freeze-out merger at the same price. Minority shareholders sought to enjoin the merger, claiming that the merger was fraudulent because it served no business purpose other than to eliminate minority shareholders at an inadequate price. The Chancery Court predictably dismissed the complaint, holding that the merger was not fraudulent merely because it lacked an independent business purpose, and that the proper remedy for an inadequate price was appraisal. The Delaware Supreme Court reversed, holding that a merger "for the sole purpose of freezing-out minority shareholders is an abuse of the corporate process." 380 A.2d at 980. Moreover, even if the freeze-out merger had an independent business purpose, the burden would still be on the controlling shareholders to demonstrate the merger's "entire fairness."

The business purpose test quickly proved of little consequence. One month after *Singer,* the court held in Tanzer v. International General Industries, 379 A.2d 1121 (Del. 1977), that a freeze-out merger that served a bona fide purpose of the parent but not the subsidiary satisfied the business purpose test, despite the fact that a careful planner would have little difficulty in establishing a business purpose for the parent. However, the court reiterated that the second element of *Singer* still applied: the controlling shareholder still bore the burden of proving the freeze-out merger was entirely fair.

Although just what was necessary to render a merger entirely fair was unclear, the stakes were high. First, from a practical litigation perspective, the procedure differs dramatically in an appraisal action and in an action challenging a freeze-out merger as not entirely fair. In an appraisal proceeding, the remedy must be perfected — through notifying the corporation prior to the vote, then not voting in favor of the transaction, and petitioning the court for appraisal — by each shareholder. In a challenge to the entire fairness of the transaction, plaintiffs' counsel can use a class procedure that aggregates plaintiffs in a fashion that is very difficult to accomplish in an appraisal proceeding. Moreover, being a member of the class requires no action by the shareholder, in contrast to the complicated procedure that must be followed to pursue an appraisal proceeding. Unless an individual shareholder held a great deal of stock, securing a lawyer who might take the case on a contingency basis was quite difficult in an appraisal proceeding and comparatively easy in a class action challenge based on an entire fairness claim.

Second, the possibility existed that the remedy available in a class action might be more favorable as well. Under the appraisal standard, the value of dissenting shares was determined as of the date of the merger's approval, to ensure that dissenting shareholders not receive any value associated with the transaction itself. *Singer* left open what valuation standard would apply in an entire fairness challenge, and Lynch v. Vickers Energy Corp., 429 A.2d 497 (Del. 1981), held out the possibility of a very attractive alternative. *Lynch* involved not a freeze-out merger, but also a tender offer by the existing majority shareholder. The court initially held that the majority shareholder had breached its fiduciary duty by withholding information suggesting a higher value for the minority shareholders' stock. On remand, the chancery court held that the appropriate remedy was "a proceeding analogous to an appraisal proceeding."[66] The Delaware Supreme Court then rejected the appraisal standard on appeal, instead providing the "monetary equivalent of recision." The critical difference was that the value of minority shares would be determined not as of the day before the transaction, but at the time of judgment, giving the minority the benefit of increases in value that occurred between the transaction date and judgment, presumably resulting from post-transaction improvements in the target corporation's performance.

In effect this gave a minority shareholder (and his lawyer) an option on the post-acquisition performance of the combined corporations. The shareholder could take the offered consideration but challenge the merger's entire fairness. If the merger proves to be efficient, as the controlling shareholder must have believed it to be, then the plaintiff might get the higher post-transaction value under *Lynch*, provided the controlling shareholder fails the burden of proving the merger was entirely fair. If not, then the litigation probably could be settled cheaply for attorneys' fees, thereby rendering the option costless. The provision of a free option to plaintiffs made it very likely that any freeze-out merger would be the subject of litigation.

2. THE CURRENT FRAMEWORK: ENTIRE FAIRNESS

Weinberger v. UOP, Inc.
457 A.2d 701 (Del. 1983)

MOORE, J.: This post-trial appeal was reheard en banc from a decision of the Court of Chancery. It was brought by the class action plaintiff below, a former shareholder of UOP, Inc., who challenged the elimination of UOP's minority shareholders by a cash-out merger between UOP and its majority owner, The Signal Companies, Inc. . . . The present Chancellor held that the terms of the merger were fair to the plaintiff and the other minority shareholders of UOP. . . . Accordingly, he entered judgment in favor of the defendants.

In ruling for the defendants, the Chancellor restated his earlier conclusion that the plaintiff in a suit challenging a cash-out merger must allege specific acts of fraud, misrepresentation, or other items of misconduct to demonstrate the unfairness of the merger terms to the minority. We approve this rule and affirm it.

The Chancellor also held that even though the ultimate burden of proof is on the majority shareholder to show by a preponderance of the evidence that the transaction is fair, it is first the burden of the plaintiff attacking the merger to demonstrate some basis for invoking the fairness obligation. We agree with that principle. However, where corporate action has been approved by an informed vote of a majority of the minority shareholders, we conclude that the burden entirely shifts

66. 402 A.2d 5, 11 (Del. Ch. 1979).

to the plaintiff to show that the transaction was unfair to the minority. But in all this, the burden clearly remains on those relying on the vote to show that they completely disclosed all material facts relevant to the transaction. . . .

I. The facts found by the trial court, pertinent to the issues before us, are supported by the record, and we draw from them as set out in the Chancellor's opinion.[5]

Signal is a diversified, technically based company operating through various subsidiaries. Its stock is publicly traded on the New York, Philadelphia and Pacific Stock Exchanges. UOP, formerly known as Universal Oil Products Company, was a diversified industrial company engaged in various lines of business. . . . Its stock was publicly held and listed on the New York Stock Exchange.

In 1974 Signal sold one of its wholly-owned subsidiaries for $420,000,000 in cash. See Gimbel v. Signal Companies, Inc., Del. Ch., 316 A.2d 599, *aff'd*, Del. Supr., 316 A.2d 619 (1974). While looking to invest this cash surplus, Signal became interested in UOP as a possible acquisition. Friendly negotiations ensued, and Signal proposed to acquire a controlling interest in UOP at a price of $19 per share. UOP's representatives sought $25 per share. In the arm's length bargaining that followed, an understanding was reached whereby Signal agreed to purchase from UOP 1,500,000 shares of UOP's authorized but unissued stock at $21 per share.

This purchase was contingent upon Signal making a successful cash tender offer for 4,300,000 publicly held shares of UOP, also at a price of $21 per share. This combined method of acquisition permitted Signal to acquire 5,800,000 shares of stock, representing 50.5% of UOP's outstanding shares. The UOP board of directors advised the company's shareholders that it had no objection to Signal's tender offer at that price. Immediately before the announcement of the tender offer, UOP's common stock had been trading on the New York Stock Exchange at a fraction under $14 per share.

The negotiations between Signal and UOP occurred during April 1975, and the resulting tender offer was greatly oversubscribed. However, Signal limited its total purchase of the tendered shares so that, when coupled with the stock bought from UOP, it had achieved its goal of becoming a 50.5% shareholder of UOP.

Although UOP's board consisted of thirteen directors, Signal nominated and elected only six. Of these, five were either directors or employees of Signal. The sixth, a partner in the banking firm of Lazard Freres & Co., had been one of Signal's representatives in the negotiations and bargaining with UOP concerning the tender offer and purchase price of the UOP shares.

However, the president and chief executive officer of UOP retired during 1975, and Signal caused him to be replaced by James V. Crawford, a long-time employee and senior executive vice president of one of Signal's wholly-owned subsidiaries. Crawford succeeded his predecessor on UOP's board of directors and also was made a director of Signal.

By the end of 1977 Signal basically was unsuccessful in finding other suitable investment candidates for its excess cash, and by February 1978 considered that it had no other realistic acquisitions available to it on a friendly basis. Once again its attention turned to UOP.

The trial court found that at the instigation of certain Signal management personnel, including William W. Walkup, its board chairman, and Forrest N.

---

5. Weinberger v. UOP, Inc., Del. Ch., 426 A.2d 1333, 1335-1340 (1981).

Shumway, its president, a feasibility study was made concerning the possible acquisition of the balance of UOP's outstanding shares. This study was performed by two Signal officers, Charles S. Arledge, vice president (director of planning), and Andrew J. Chitiea, senior vice president (chief financial officer). Messrs. Walkup, Shumway, Arledge and Chitiea were all directors of UOP in addition to their membership on the Signal board.

Arledge and Chitiea concluded that it would be a good investment for Signal to acquire the remaining 49.5% of UOP shares at any price up to $24 each. Their report was discussed between Walkup and Shumway who, along with Arledge, Chitiea and Brewster L. Arms, internal counsel for Signal, constituted Signal's senior management. In particular, they talked about the proper price to be paid if the acquisition was pursued, purportedly keeping in mind that as UOP's majority shareholder, Signal owned a fiduciary responsibility to both its own stockholders as well as to UOP's minority. It was ultimately agreed that a meeting of Signal's executive committee would be called to propose that Signal acquire the remaining outstanding stock of UOP through a cash-out merger in the range of $20 to $21 per share.

The executive committee meeting was set for February 28, 1978. As a courtesy, UOP's president, Crawford, was invited to attend, although he was not a member of Signal's executive committee. On his arrival, and prior to the meeting, Crawford was asked to meet privately with Walkup and Shumway. He was then told of Signal's plan to acquire full ownership of UOP and was asked for his reaction to the proposed price range of $20 to $21 per share. Crawford said he thought such a price would be "generous," and that it was certainly one which should be submitted to UOP's minority shareholders for their ultimate consideration. He stated, however, that Signal's 100% ownership could cause internal problems at UOP. He believed that employees would have to be given some assurance of their future place in a fully-owned Signal subsidiary. Otherwise, he feared the departure of essential personnel. Also, many of UOP's key employees had stock option incentive programs which would be wiped out by a merger. Crawford therefore urged that some adjustment would have to be made, such as providing a comparable incentive in Signal's shares, if after the merger he was to maintain his quality of personnel and efficiency at UOP. Thus, Crawford voiced no objection to the $20 to $21 price range, nor did he suggest that Signal should consider paying more than $21 per share for the minority interests. . . .

Thus, it was the consensus that a price of $20 to $21 per share would be fair to both Signal and the minority shareholders of UOP. Signal's executive committee authorized its management "to negotiate" with UOP "for a cash acquisition of the minority ownership in UOP, Inc., with the intention of presenting a proposal to [Signal's] board of directors . . . on March 6, 1978." Immediately after this February 28, 1978 meeting, Signal issued a press release stating: "The Signal Companies, Inc. and UOP, Inc. are conducting negotiations for the acquisition for cash by Signal of the 49.5 per cent of UOP which it does not presently own. . . ."

The announcement also referred to the fact that the closing price of UOP's common stock on that day was $14.50 per share.

Two days later, on March 2, 1978, Signal issued a second press release stating that its management would recommend a price in the range of $20 to $21 per share for UOP's 49.5% minority interest. This announcement referred to Signal's earlier statement that "negotiations" were being conducted for the acquisition of the minority shares.

Between Tuesday, February 28, 1978 and Monday, March 6, 1978, a total of four business days, Crawford spoke by telephone with all of UOP's non-Signal, i.e., outside, directors. Also during this period, Crawford retained Lehman Brothers to render a fairness opinion as to the price offered the minority for its stock. He gave two reasons for this choice. First, the time schedule between the announcement and the board meetings was short (by then only three business days) and since Lehman Brothers had been acting as UOP's investment banker for many years, Crawford felt that it would be in the best position to respond on such brief notice. Second, James W. Glanville, a long-time director of UOP and a partner in Lehman Brothers, had acted as a financial advisor to UOP for many years. . . .

Crawford telephoned Glanville, who gave his assurance that Lehman Brothers had no conflicts that would prevent it from accepting the task. Glanville's immediate personal reaction was that a price of $20 to $21 would certainly be fair, since it represented almost a 50% premium over UOP's market price. Glanville sought a $250,000 fee for Lehman Brothers' services, but Crawford thought this too much. After further discussions Glanville finally agreed that Lehman Brothers would render its fairness opinion for $150,000.

During this period Crawford also had several telephone contacts with Signal officials. In only one of them, however, was the price of the shares discussed. In a conversation with Walkup, Crawford advised that as a result of his communications with UOP's non-Signal directors, it was his feeling that the price would have to be the top of the proposed range, or $21 per share, if the approval of UOP's outside directors was to be obtained. But again, he did not seek any price higher than $21.

Glanville assembled a three-man Lehman Brothers team to do the work on the fairness opinion. . . . [They] concluded that "the price of either $20 or $21 would be a fair price for the remaining shares of UOP." They telephoned this impression to Glanville, who was spending the weekend in Vermont.

On Monday morning, March 6, 1978, Glanville and the senior member of the Lehman Brothers team flew to Des Plaines to attend the scheduled UOP directors meeting. Glanville looked over the assembled information during the flight. The two had with them the draft of a "fairness opinion letter" in which the price had been left blank. Either during or immediately prior to the directors' meeting, the two-page "fairness opinion letter" was typed in final form and the price of $21 per share was inserted.

On March 6, 1978, both the Signal and UOP boards were convened to consider the proposed merger. . . .

First, Signal's board unanimously adopted a resolution authorizing Signal to propose to UOP a cash merger of $21 per share as outlined in a certain merger agreement and other supporting documents. This proposal required that the merger be approved by a majority of UOP's outstanding minority shares voting at the stockholders meeting at which the merger would be considered, and that the minority shares voting in favor of the merger, when coupled with Signal's 50.5% interest would have to comprise at least two-thirds of all UOP shares. Otherwise the proposed merger would be deemed disapproved.

UOP's board then considered the proposal. Copies of the agreement were delivered to the directors in attendance, and other copies had been forwarded earlier to the directors participating by telephone. They also had before them

UOP financial data for 1974-1977, UOP's most recent financial statements, market price information, and budget projections for 1978. In addition, they had Lehman Brothers' hurriedly prepared fairness opinion letter finding the price of $21 to be fair. . . .

After consideration of Signal's proposal, Walkup and Crawford left the meeting to permit a free and uninhibited exchange between UOP's non-Signal directors. Upon their return a resolution to accept Signal's offer was then proposed and adopted. While Signal's men on UOP's board participated in various aspects of the meeting, they abstained from voting. However, the minutes show that each of them "if voting would have voted yes." . . .

Despite the swift board action of the two companies, the merger was not submitted to UOP's shareholders until their annual meeting on May 26, 1978. In the notice of that meeting and proxy statement sent to shareholders in May, UOP's management and board urged that the merger be approved. The proxy statement also advised: "The price was determined after *discussions* between James V. Crawford, a director of Signal and Chief Executive Officer of UOP, and officers of Signal which took place during meetings on February 28, 1978, and in the course of several subsequent telephone conversations." (Emphasis added.)

In the original draft of the proxy statement the word "negotiations" had been used rather than "discussions." However, when the Securities and Exchange Commission sought details of the "negotiations" as part of its review of these materials, the term was deleted and the word "discussions" was substituted. The proxy statement indicated that the vote of UOP's board in approving the merger had been unanimous. It also advised the shareholders that Lehman Brothers had given its opinion that the merger price of $21 per share was fair to UOP's minority. However, it did not disclose the hurried method by which this conclusion was reached.

As of the record date of UOP's annual meeting, there were 11,488,302 shares of UOP common stock outstanding, 5,688,302 of which were owned by the minority. At the meeting only 56%, or 3,208,652, of the minority shares were voted. Of these, 2,958,812, or 51.9% of the total minority, voted for the merger, and 254,840 voted against it. When Signal's stock was added to the minority shares voting in favor, a total of 76.2% of UOP's outstanding shares approved the merger while only 2.2% opposed it.

By its terms the merger became effective on May 26, 1978, and each share of UOP's stock held by the minority was automatically converted into a right to receive $21 cash.

II. A. A primary issue mandating reversal is the preparation by two UOP directors, Arledge and Chitiea, of their feasibility study for the exclusive use and benefit of Signal. This document was of obvious significance to both Signal and UOP. Using UOP data, it described the advantages of Signal of ousting the minority at a price range of $21-$24 per share. Mr. Arledge, one of the authors, outlined the benefits to Signal:

Purpose of the Merger

1) Provides an outstanding investment opportunity for Signal — (Better than any recent acquisition we have seen.)
2) Increases Signal's earnings.

3) Facilitates the flow of resources between Signal and its subsidiaries — (Big factor — works both ways.)
4) Provides cost savings potential for Signal and UOP.
5) Improves the percentage of Signal's "operating earnings" as opposed to "holding company earnings."
6) Simplifies the understanding of Signal.
7) Facilitates technological exchange among Signal's subsidiaries.
8) Eliminates potential conflicts of interest.

Having written those words, solely for the use of Signal, it is clear from the record that neither Arledge nor Chitiea shared this report with their fellow directors of UOP. We are satisfied that no one else did either. This conduct hardly meets the fiduciary standards applicable to such a transaction. . . .

The Arledge-Chitiea report speaks for itself in supporting the Chancellor's finding that a price of up to $24 was a "good investment" for Signal. It shows that a return on the investment at $21 would be 15.7% versus 15.5% at $24 per share. This was a difference of only two-tenths of one percent, while it meant over $17,000,000 to the minority. Under such circumstances, paying UOP's minority shareholders $24 would have had relatively little long-term effect on Signal, and the Chancellor's findings concerning the benefit to Signal, even at a price of $24, were obviously correct.

Certainly, this was a matter of material significance to UOP and its shareholders. Since the study was prepared by two UOP directors, using UOP information for the exclusive benefit of Signal, and nothing whatever was done to disclose it to the outside UOP directors or the minority shareholders, a question of breach of fiduciary duty arises. This problem occurs because there were common Signal-UOP directors participating, at least to some extent, in the UOP board's decision-making processes without full disclosure of the conflicts they faced.[7]

B. In assessing this situation, the Court of Chancery was required to: "examine what information defendants had and to measure it against what they gave to the minority shareholders, in a context in which 'complete candor' is required. In other words, the limited function of the Court was to determine whether defendants had disclosed all information in their possession germane to the transaction in issue. And by 'germane' we mean, for present purposes, information such as a reasonable shareholder would consider important in deciding whether to sell or retain stock." . . . This is merely stating in another way the long-existing principle of Delaware law that these Signal designated directors on UOP's board still owned UOP and its shareholders an uncompromising duty of loyalty. . . .

Given the absence of any attempt to structure this transaction on an arm's length basis, Signal cannot escape the effects of the conflicts it faced, particularly when its

---

7. Although perfection is not possible, or expected, the result here could have been entirely different if UOP had appointed an independent negotiating committee of its outside directors to deal with Signal at arm's length. See, e.g., Harriman v. E. I. duPont de Nemours & Co., 411 F. Supp. 133 (D. Del. 1975). Since fairness in this context can be equated to conduct by a theoretical, wholly independent, board of directors acting upon the matter before them, it is unfortunate that this course apparently was neither considered nor pursued. Johnston v. Greene, Del. Supr., 121 A.2d 919, 925 (1956). Particularly in a parent-subsidiary context, a showing that the action taken was as though each of the contending parties had in fact exerted its bargaining power against the other at arm's length is strong evidence that the transaction meets the test of fairness. Getty Oil Co v. Skelly Oil Co., Del. Supr., 267 A.2d 883, 886 (1970); Puma v. Marriott, Del. Ch., 283 A.2d 693, 696 (1971).

designees on UOP's board did not totally abstain from participation in the matter. There is no "safe harbor" for such divided loyalties in Delaware. When directors of a Delaware corporation are on both sides of a transaction, they are required to demonstrate their utmost good faith and the most scrupulous inherent fairness of the bargain. . . . The record demonstrates that Signal has not met this obligation.

C. The concept of fairness has two basic aspects: fair dealing and fair price. The former embraces questions of when the transaction was timed, how it was initiated, structured, negotiated, disclosed to the directors, and how the approvals of the directors and the stockholders were obtained. The latter aspect of fairness relates to the economic and financial considerations of the proposed merger, including all relevant factors: assets, market value, earnings, future prospects, and any other elements that affect the intrinsic or inherent value of a company's stock. Moore, The "Interested" Director or Officer Transaction, 4 Del. J. Corp. L. 674, 676 (1979); Nathan & Shapiro, Legal Standard of Fairness of Merger Terms Under Delaware Law, 2 Del. J. Corp. L. 44, 46-47 (1977). However, the test for fairness is not a bifurcated one as between fair dealing and price. All aspects of the issue must be examined as a whole since the question is one of entire fairness. However, in a non-fraudulent transaction we recognize that price may be the preponderant consideration outweighing other features of the merger. Here, we address the two basic aspects of fairness separately because we find reversible error as to both.

D. Part of fair dealing is the obvious duty of candor required by *Lynch I*, supra. Moreover, one possessing superior knowledge may not mislead any stockholder by use of corporate information to which the latter is not privy. Delaware has long imposed this duty even upon persons who are not corporate officers or directors, but who nonetheless are privy to matters of interest or significance to their company. Brophy v. Cities Service Co., Del. Ch., 70 A.2d 5, 7 (1949). With the well-established Delaware law on the subject, and the Court of Chancery's findings of fact here, it is inevitable that the obvious conflicts posed by Arledge and Chitiea's preparation of their "feasibility study," derived from UOP information, for the sole use and benefit of Signal, cannot pass muster.

The Arledge-Chitiea report is but one aspect of the element of fair dealing. How did this merger evolve? It is clear that it was entirely initiated by Signal. The serious time constraints under which the principals acted were all set by Signal. . . . For whatever reasons, and they were only Signal's, the entire transaction was presented to and approved by UOP's board within four business days. Standing alone, this is not necessarily indicative of any lack of fairness by a majority shareholder. It was what occurred, or more properly, what did not occur, during this brief period that makes the time constraints imposed by Signal relevant to the issue of fairness.

The structure of the transaction, again, was Signal's doing. So far as negotiations were concerned, it is clear that they were modest at best. Crawford, Signal's man at UOP, never really talked price with Signal, except to accede to its management's statements on the subject, and to convey to Signal the UOP outside directors' view that as between the $20-$21 range under consideration, it would have to be $21. The latter is not a surprising outcome, but hardly arm's length negotiations. Only the protection of benefits for UOP's key employees and the issues of Lehman Brothers' fee approached any concept of bargaining.

As we have noted, the matter of disclosure to the UOP directors was wholly flawed by the conflicts of interest raised by the Arledge-Chitiea report. All of those conflicts were resolved by Signal in its own favor without divulging any aspect of them to UOP.

... There was no disclosure of the circumstances surrounding the rather cursory preparation of the Lehman Brothers' fairness opinion. Instead, the impression was given UOP's minority that a careful study had been made, when in fact speed was the hallmark, and Mr. Glanville, Lehman's partner in charge of the matter, and also a UOP director, having spent the weekend in Vermont, brought a draft of the "fairness opinion letter" to the UOP directors' meeting on March 6, 1978 with the price left blank. We can only conclude from the record that the rush imposed on Lehman Brothers by Signal's timetable contributed to the difficulties under which this investment banking firm attempted to perform its responsibilities. Yet, none of this was disclosed to UOP's minority.

Finally, the minority stockholders were denied the critical information that Signal considered a price of $24 to be a good investment. Since this would have meant over $17,000,000 more to the minority, we cannot conclude that the shareholder vote was an informed one. Under the circumstances, an approval by a majority of the minority was meaningless.

Given these particulars and the Delaware law on the subject, the record does not establish that this transaction satisfies any reasonable concept of fair dealing, and the Chancellor's findings in that regard must be reversed.

E. Turning to the matter of price, plaintiff also challenges its fairness. His evidence was that on the date the merger was approved the stock was worth at least $26 per share. In support, he offered the testimony of a chartered investment analyst who used two basic approaches to valuation: a comparative analysis of the premium paid over market in ten other tender offer-merger combinations, and a discounted cash flow analysis.

In this breach of fiduciary duty case, the Chancellor perceived that the approach to valuation was the same as that in an appraisal proceeding. Consistent with precedent, he rejected plaintiff's method of proof and accepted defendants' evidence of value as being in accord with practice under prior case law. This means that the so-called "Delaware block" or weighted average method was employed wherein the elements of value, i.e., assets, market price, earnings, etc., were assigned a particular weight and the resulting amounts added to determine the value per share. This procedure has been in use for decades. However, to the extent it excludes other generally accepted techniques used in the financial community and the courts, it is now clearly outmoded. It is time we recognize this in appraisal and other stock evaluation proceedings and bring our law current on the subject.

While the Chancellor rejected plaintiff's discounted cash flow method of valuing UOP's stock, as not corresponding with "either logic or the existing law" (426 A.2d at 1360), it is significant that this was essentially the focus, i.e., earnings potential of UOP, of Messrs. Arledge and Chitiea in their evaluation of the merger. Accordingly, the standard "Delaware block" or weighted average method of valuation, formerly employed in appraisal and other stock valuation cases, shall no longer exclusively control such proceedings. We believe that a more liberal approach must include proof of value by any techniques or methods which are generally considered acceptable in the financial community and otherwise admissible in court, subject only to our interpretation of 8 Del. C. §262(h), infra.

It is significant that section 262 now mandates the determination of "fair" value based upon "all relevant factors." Only the speculative elements of value that may arise from the "accomplishment or expectation" of the merger are excluded. We take this to be a very narrow exception to the appraisal process, designed to eliminate use of *pro forma* data and projections of a speculative variety relating to the completion of a merger. But elements of future value, including the nature of the enterprise, which are known or susceptible of proof as of the date of the merger and not the product of speculation, may be considered. When the trial court deems it appropriate, fair value also includes any damages, resulting from the taking, which the stockholders sustain as a class. If that was not the case, then the obligation to consider "all relevant factors" in the valuation process would be eroded. . . .

The plaintiff has not sought an appraisal, but rescissory damages of the type contemplated by Lynch v. Vickers Energy Corp., Del. Supr., 429 A.2d 497, 505-506 (1981) (*Lynch II*). In view of the approach to valuation that we announce today, we see no basis in our law for *Lynch II*'s exclusive monetary formula for relief. On remand the plaintiff will be permitted to test the fairness of the $21 price by the standards we herein establish, in conformity with the principle applicable to an appraisal — that fair value be determined by taking "into account all relevant factors" [see 8 Del. C. §262(h), supra]. In our view, this includes the elements of rescissory damages if the Chancellor considers them susceptible of proof and a remedy appropriate to all the issues of fairness before him. To the extent that *Lynch II*, 429 A.2d at 505-506, purports to limit the Chancellor's discretion to a single remedial formula for monetary damages in a cash-out merger, it is overruled.

While a plaintiff's monetary remedy ordinarily should be confined to the more liberalized appraisal proceeding herein established, we do not intend any limitation on the historic powers of the Chancellor to grant such other relief as the facts of a particular case may dictate. The appraisal remedy we approve may not be adequate in certain cases, particularly where fraud, misrepresentation, self-dealing, deliberate waste of corporate assets, or gross and palpable overreaching are involved. Cole v. National Cash Credit Association, Del. Ch., 156 A. 183, 187 (1931). Under such circumstances, the Chancellor's powers are complete to fashion any form of equitable and monetary relief as may be appropriate, including rescissory damages. Since it is apparent that this long completed transaction is too involved to undo, and in view of the Chancellor's discretion, the award, if any, should be in the form of monetary damages based upon entire fairness standards, i.e., fair dealing and fair price.

Obviously, there are other litigants, like the plaintiff, who abjured an appraisal and whose rights to challenge the element of fair value must be preserved.[8] Accordingly, the quasi-appraisal remedy we grant the plaintiff here will apply only to . . . [this case and a designated series of cases arising around this time.] . . . Thereafter, the provisions of 8 Del. C. §262, as herein construed, respecting the scope of an appraisal and the means for perfecting the same, shall govern the financial remedy available to minority shareholders in a cash-out merger. Thus, we return to the well established principles of Stauffer v. Standard Brands, Inc., Del. Supr., 187 A.2d 78 (1962) and David J. Breene & Co. v. Schenley

---

8. Under 8 Del. C. §262(a), (d) & (e), a stockholder is required to act within certain time periods to perfect the right to an appraisal.

Industries, Inc., Del. Ch., 281 A.2d 30 (1971), mandating a stockholder's recourse to the basic remedy of an appraisal.

III. . . . The requirement of a business purpose is new to our law of mergers and was a departure from prior case law. See Stauffer v. Standard Brands, Inc., supra; David J. Breene & Co. v. Schenley Industries, Inc., supra.

In view of the fairness test which has long been applicable to parent-subsidiary mergers, Sterling v. Mayflower Hotel Corp., Del. Supr., 93 A.2d 107, 109-110 (1952), the expanded appraisal remedy now available to shareholders, and the broad discretion of the Chancellor to fashion such relief as the facts of a given case may dictate, we do not believe that any additional meaningful protection is afforded minority shareholders by the business purpose requirement of the trilogy of *Singer, Tanzer,*[9] *Najjar,*[10] and their progeny. Accordingly, such requirement shall no longer be of any force or effect. . . .

Reversed and Remanded.

————————

1. Business purpose. *Weinberger*'s entire fairness standard is inconsistent with any right of minority shareholders to retain their investment in the particular company. Interestingly, this approach treats stock investments consistently with modern financial economics. As developed in Chapter III, portfolio theory treats stock investments as simply generic income streams with associated levels of systematic risk. Because each shareholder can alter the risk associated with any particular stock simply by leveraging or de-leveraging the shareholder's personal investment portfolio, stock in any single company has virtually an infinite number of substitutes. Thus, being frozen out of one company does not reduce the range of investments available, and a shareholder should have no special interest in the stock of a particular company that requires restrictions on freeze-outs for protection. All that is at stake is the process by which the freeze-out occurs and the price paid. Did the Delaware Supreme Court reach its conclusion by this analysis? How else could you get there?

Not all states have followed Delaware's lead in rejecting a business purpose requirement. See Coggins v. New England Patriots Football Club, 397 Mass. 525, 492 N.E.2d 1112 (1986); Alpert v. 28 Williams St. Corp., 63 N.Y.2d 667, 473 N.E.2d 19 (1984). While RMBCA §11.01 does not mention a business purpose test, the official comment states that mergers "may in some circumstances constitute a breach of fiduciary duty to minority shareholders where the effect of the transaction is to eliminate them from further equity participation in the enterprise." 3 Model Bus. Corp. Act Ann. 1234 (2d ed. 1993).

2. Interaction of fair price and fair dealing. The court in *Weinberger* stresses that the test for entire fairness is an organic whole, "not a bifurcated one as between fair dealing and fair price." But how do fair dealing and fair price interact with each other in combining to yield *entire* fairness? Does the court's statement that "in a non-fraudulent transaction we recognize that price may be the predominant consideration outweighing other features of the merger" mean that if the transaction is fraudulent — that is, fair dealing is not present — price is less important? Suppose

9. Tanzer v. International General Industries, Inc., Del. Supr., 379 A.2d 1121, 1124-1125 (1977).
10. Roland International Corp. v. Najjar, Del. Supr., 407 A.2d 1032, 1036 (1979).

the price is entirely fair, but the process is faulty. To what else are shareholders entitled beyond a fair price? Alternatively, what did the court mean in footnote 7 when it said that "the result here could have been entirely different if UOP had appointed an independent negotiations committee"? If the process is good enough, will that avert an inquiry into the fairness of price?

3. FAIR PRICE

The court in *Weinberger* described the fair dealing component of the entire fairness test. When these techniques are used, the burden of proof shifts to the plaintiff, making it more likely that the transaction will be found entirely fair, and the minority shareholders left to their appraisal rights. However, these procedures are not costless, since the price paid in the merger will be influenced by the bargaining power given the minority. Thus, the incentive for a controlling shareholder to adopt such procedures depends on what it produces.

The most obvious benefit is the difference between a class action and appraisal. Even if the price is the same between the two, any increase over the merger price will have to be paid to fewer minority shareholders because of the procedural difficulties in perfecting appraisal right and the absence of incentives for plaintiffs' lawyers to pursue appraisal proceedings for a contingent fee. But *Lynch* continued to hold out the potential of a free option in the form of rescissionary relief. Does *Weinberger*'s new appraisal valuation apply in the absence of fair dealing? If it does, then is this line of cases merely a doctrinal exercise seeking to make up for the fact that the statutory appraisal procedure is fatally defective? Note that in Roland International Corp. v. Najjar, 407 A.2d 1032 (Del. 1979), one of the decisions following closely on *Singer*, a dissenting justice criticized the entire fairness exception to the exclusivity of appraisal as creating an "unnecessary damage forum." 407 A.2d at 1040 n.12 (Quillen, J., dissenting). Would the problem disappear if a class procedure were available in appraisal? See ALI, Principles of Corporate Governance: Analysis and Recommendations 340-342 (1994) (limited effort to create class-like appraisal procedure).

Cede & Co. v. Technicolor, Inc., 634 A.2d 345 (Del. 1993), provides guidance on the extent to which the entire fairness standard contemplates a different damage measure than appraisal. *Cede* involved an arm's-length two-step acquisition in which a $23 per share tender offer was followed by a freeze-out merger at the same price. Plaintiffs claimed that the target directors had violated their duty of care in accepting the terms of the transaction. The Chancery Court concluded that the target board in fact had violated its duty of care by not sufficiently informing themselves before accepting the $23 offer. However, the Chancellor required proof of injury before imposing personal liability on directors for the violation: "[A]s in any case in which the gist of the claim is negligence, plaintiff bears the burden to establish that the negligence shown was the proximate cause of some injury to it. . . ."[67] He found no liability because, despite the Technicolor board's negligence, the price received exceeded the fair value of Technicolor's shares in an appraisal proceeding.

---

67. Technicolor directors were exposed to personal liability because the transaction predated the adoption of §102(b)(7) by the Delaware legislature following *Van Gorkom.* See Marshall Small, Negotiating Delaware Merger Transactions, 27 Rev. Sec. & Com. Reg. 29, 31 (1994).

The Delaware Supreme Court rejected the Chancery Court's effort to avoid creating an "unnecessary damage forum" finding:

> [T]he [Chancery] court committed error under *Weinberger* in apparently capping Cinerama's recoverable loss under an entire fairness standard of review at the fair value of a share of Technicolor stock on the date of approval of the merger. Under *Weinberger*'s entire fairness standard of review, a party may have a legally cognizable injury regardless of whether the tender offer and cash-out price is greater than the stock's fair value as determined for statutory appraisal purposes. See *Weinberger*, 457 A.2d at 714; Rabkin v. Phillip A. Hunt Chemical Corp., Del. Supr., 498 A.2d 1099, 1104 (1985) (appraisal not exclusive remedy).

Determining the fair price for minority shares raises in a different context the question of when minority shareholders should be allowed to participate in a control premium. Presumably the minority shares in a freeze-out merger have less value than controlling shares by the amount of the control premium. In Mendel v. Carroll, page 1055 supra, the court explained why it could be appropriate for a controlling shareholder to decline an offer for its shares at a price in excess of the price the controlling shareholder had offered for minority shares. If the controlling shareholder then freezes out the minority, is the measure of value a proportionate amount of the value of the entire company, thus giving the minority a portion of the control premium, or merely the value of minority shares?

In Smith v. Shell Petroleum, Inc., 1990 WL 84218, 1990 Del. Ch. LEXIS 82 (Del. Ch. 1990), an appraisal proceeding, the court gave greater weight to stock market value than liquidation value when the existence of a majority shareholder made it apparent that the corporation would not be liquidated. Of course, stock market value represented the value of minority shares because controlling shares do not trade. See Linda DeAngelo & Harry DeAngelo, Managerial Ownership of Voting Rights: A Study of Public Corporations with Dual Classes of Stock, 14 J. Fin. Econ. 33 (1985). In contrast, ALI §7.22(c) dictates that, in effect, the control premium be shared in freeze-out mergers: "If the transaction falls within . . . §7.25, the court generally should give substantial weight to the highest realistic price that a willing, able, and fully informed buyer would pay for the corporation as an entity." How does this position with respect to valuation in freeze-out mergers correspond to the general principle, reflected in ALI §5.16, that a controlling shareholder can sell her shares at a premium without allowing the minority to participate? Does it make a difference that minority shareholders participate in any post-transfer improvements in performance caused by the new controlling shareholder but do not participate in post-freeze-out improvements unless they are anticipated in the determination of fair price? See Ronald Gilson & Jeffrey Gordon, Controlling Controlling Shareholders 152 U. Pa. L. Rev. 785 (2003).

4. FAIR DEALING

Kahn v. Lynch Communication Systems, Inc.
638 A.2d 1110 (Del. 1994)

HOLLAND, J.: . . . [This] action, instituted by Kahn in 1986, originally sought to enjoin the acquisition of the defendant-appellee, Lynch Communication Systems,

Inc. ("Lynch"), by the defendant-appellee, Alcatel U.S.A. Corporation ("Alcatel"), pursuant to a tender offer and cash-out merger. Kahn amended his complaint to seek monetary damages after the Court of Chancery denied his request for a preliminary injunction. The Court of Chancery subsequently certified Kahn's action as a class action on behalf of all Lynch shareholders, other than the named defendants, who tendered their stock in the merger, or whose stock was acquired through the merger. . . .

Facts

Lynch, a Delaware corporation, designed and manufactured electronic telecommunications equipment, primarily for sale to telephone operating companies. Alcatel, a holding company, is a subsidiary of Alcatel (S.A.), a French company involved in public telecommunications, business communications, electronics, and optronics. Alcatel (S.A.), in turn is a subsidiary of Compagnie Générale d'Électricité ("CGE"), a French corporation with operations in energy, transportation, telecommunications and business systems.

In 1981, Alcatel acquired 30.6 percent of Lynch's common stock pursuant to a stock purchase agreement. As part of that agreement, Lynch amended its certificate of incorporation to require an 80 percent affirmative vote of its shareholders for approval of any business combination. In addition, Alcatel obtained proportional representation on the Lynch board of directors and the right to purchase 40 percent of any equity securities offered by Lynch to third parties. The agreement also precluded Alcatel from holding more than 45 percent of Lynch's stock prior to October 1, 1986. By the time of the merger which is contested in this action, Alcatel owned 43.3 percent of Lynch's outstanding stock; designated five of the eleven members of Lynch's board of directors; two of three members of the executive committee; and two of four members of the compensation committee.

In the spring of 1986, Lynch determined that in order to remain competitive in the rapidly changing telecommunications field, it would need to obtain fiber optics technology to complement its existing digital electronic capabilities. Lynch's management identified a target company, Telco Systems, Inc. ("Telco"), which possessed both fiber optics and other valuable technological assets. The record reflects that Telco expressed interest in being acquired by Lynch. Because of the super-majority voting provision, which Alcatel had negotiated when it first purchased its shares, in order to proceed with the Telco combination Lynch needed Alcatel's consent. In June 1986, Ellsworth F. Dertinger ("Dertinger"), Lynch's CEO and chairman of its board of directors, contacted Pierre Suard ("Suard"), the chairman of Alcatel's parent company, CGE, regarding the acquisition of Telco by Lynch. Suard expressed Alcatel's opposition to Lynch's acquisition of Telco. Instead, Alcatel proposed a combination of Lynch and Celwave Systems, Inc. ("Celwave"), an indirect subsidiary of CGE engaged in the manufacture and sale of telephone wire, cable and other, related products.

Alcatel's proposed combination with Celwave was presented to the Lynch board at a regular meeting held on August 1, 1986. Although several directors expressed interest in the original combination which had been proposed with Telco, the Alcatel representatives on Lynch's board made it clear that such a combination would not be considered before a Lynch/Celwave combination. According to the minutes of the August 1 meeting, Dertinger expressed his opinion that Celwave would not be of interest to Lynch if Celwave was not owned by Alcatel.

At the conclusion of the meeting, the Lynch board unanimously adopted a resolution establishing an Independent Committee, consisting of Hubert L. Kertz ("Kertz"), Paul B. Wineman ("Wineman"), and Stuart M. Beringer ("Beringer"), to negotiate with Celwave and to make recommendations concerning the appropriate terms and conditions of a combination with Celwave. On October 24, 1986, Alcatel's investment banking firm, Dillon, Read & Co., Inc. ("Dillon Read") made a presentation to the Independent Committee. Dillon Read expressed its views concerning the benefits of a Celwave/Lynch combination and submitted a written proposal of an exchange ratio of 0.95 shares of Celwave per Lynch share in a stock-for-stock merger.

However, the Independent Committee's investment advisors, Thomson McKinnon Securities Inc. ("Thomson McKinnon") and Kidder, Peabody & Co. Inc. ("Kidder Peabody"), reviewed the Dillon Read proposal and concluded that the 0.95 ratio was predicated on Dillon Read's overvaluation of Celwave. Based upon this advice, the Independent Committee . . . expressed its unanimous opposition to the Celwave/Lynch merger on October 31, 1986.

Alcatel responded to the Independent Committee's action on November 4, 1986, by withdrawing the Celwave proposal. Alcatel made a simultaneous offer to acquire the entire equity interest in Lynch, constituting the approximately 57 percent of Lynch shares not owned by Alcatel. The offering price was $14 cash per share.

On November 8, 1986, the Lynch board of directors revised the mandate of the Independent Committee. It authorized Kertz, Wineman, and Beringer to negotiate the cash merger offer with Alcatel. At a meeting held that same day, the Independent Committee determined that the $14 per share offer was inadequate. The Independent Committee's own legal counsel, Skadden, Arps, Slate, Meagher & Flom ("Skadden Arps"), suggested that the Independent Committee should review alternatives to a cash-out merger with Alcatel, including a "white knight" third party acquiror, a repurchase of Alcatel's shares, or the adoption of a shareholder rights plan.

On November 24, 1986, Beringer, as chairman of the Independent Committee, contacted Michiel C. McCarty ("McCarty") of Dillon Read, Alcatel's representative in the negotiations, with a counteroffer at a price of $17 per share. McCarty responded on behalf of Alcatel with an offer of $15 per share. When Beringer informed McCarty of the Independent Committee's view that $15 was insufficient, Alcatel raised its offer to $15.25 per share. The Independent Committee also rejected this offer. Alcatel then made its final offer of $15.50 per share.

At the November 24, 1986 meeting of the Independent Committee, Beringer advised its other two members that Alcatel was "ready to proceed with an unfriendly tender at a lower price" if the $15.50 per share price was not recommended by the Independent Committee and approved by the Lynch board of directors. Beringer also told the other members of the Independent Committee that the alternatives to a cash-out merger had been investigated but were impracticable.[3] After the meeting with its financial and legal advisors, the Independent Committee voted unanimously to recommend that the Lynch board of directors

---

3. The minutes reflect that Beringer told the Committee the "white knight" alternative "appeared impractical with the 80% approval requirement"; the repurchase of Alcatel's shares would produce a "highly leveraged company with a lower book value" and was an alternative "not in the least encouraged by Alcatel"; and a shareholder rights plan was not viable because of the increased debt it would entail.

approve Alcatel's $15.50 cash per share price for a merger with Alcatel. The Lynch board met later that day. With Alcatel's nominees abstaining, it approved the merger.

Alcatel Dominated Lynch, Controlling Shareholder Status

This court has held that "a shareholder owes a fiduciary duty only if it owns a majority interest in or *exercises control* over the business affairs of the corporation." Ivanhoe Partners v. Newmont Mining Corp., Del. Supr., 535 A.2d 1334, 1344 (1987) (emphasis added). With regard to the exercise of control, this Court has stated: "[A] shareholder who owns less than 50% of a corporation's outstanding stocks does not, without more, become a controlling shareholder of that corporation, with a concomitant fiduciary status. For a dominating relationship to exist in the absence of controlling stock ownership, a plaintiff must allege domination by a minority shareholder through actual control of corporation conduct." Citron v. Fairchild Camera & Instrument Corp., Del. Supr., 569 A.2d 53, 70 (1989) (quotations and citation omitted).

At the August 1 meeting, Alcatel opposed the renewal of compensation contracts for Lynch's top five managers. According to Dertlinger, Christian Fayard ("Fayard"), an Alcatel director, told the board members, "[y]ou must listen to us. We are 43 percent owner. You have to do what we tell you." The minutes confirm Dertinger's testimony. They recite that Fayard declared, "you are pushing us very much to take control of the company. Our opinion is not taken into consideration."

Although Beringer and Kertz, two of the independent directors, favored renewal of the contracts, according to the minutes, the third independent director, Wineman, admonished the board as follows:

> Mr. Wineman pointed out that the vote on the contracts is a "watershed vote" and the motion, due to Alcatel's "strong feelings," might not carry if taken now. Mr. Wineman clarified that "you [management] might win the battle and lose the war." With Alcatel's opinion so clear, Mr. Wineman questioned "if management wants the contracts renewed under these circumstances." He recommended that management "think twice." Mr. Wineman declared: "I want to keep the management. I can't think of a better management." Mr. Kertz agreed, again advising consideration of the "critical" period the company is entering.

The minutes reflect that the management directors left the room after this statement. The remaining board members then voted not to renew the contracts.

At the same meeting, Alcatel vetoed Lynch's acquisition of the target company, which, according to the minutes, Beringer considered "an immediate fit" for Lynch. Dertinger agreed with Beringer, stating that the "target company is extremely important as they have the products that Lynch needs now." Nonetheless, Alcatel prevailed. The minutes reflect that Fayard advised the Board: "Alcatel, with its 44% equity position, would not approve such an acquisition . . . it does not wish to be diluted from being the main shareholder in Lynch." . . .

The record supports the Court of Chancery's underlying factual finding that "the non-Alcatel [independent] directors deferred to Alcatel because of its position as a significant stockholder and not because they decided in the exercise of their own business judgment that Alcatel's position was correct." The record also supports the subsequent factual finding that, notwithstanding its 43.3 percent minority shareholder interest, Alcatel did exercise control over Lynch by dominating its corporate affairs. The Court of Chancery's legal conclusion that Alcatel owed the fiduciary duties of a controlling shareholder to the other Lynch shareholders followed syllogistically as the logical result of its cogent analysis of the record.

Entire Fairness Requirement, Dominating Interested Shareholder

A controlling or dominating shareholder standing on both sides of a transaction, as in a parent-subsidiary context, bears the burden of proving its entire fairness. Weinberger v. UOP, Inc., Del. Supr., 457 A.2d 701, 710 (183). . . .

The logical question raised by this court's holding in *Weinberger* was what type of evidence would be reliable to demonstrate entire fairness. That question was not only anticipated but also initially addressed in the *Weinberger* opinion. Id. at 709-710 n.7. This court suggested that the result "could have been entirely different if UOP had appointed an independent negotiating committee of its outside directors to deal with Signal at arm's length," because "fairness in this context can be equated to conduct by theoretical, wholly independent, board of directors." Id. Accordingly, this court stated, "a showing that the action taken was as though each of the contending parties had in fact exerted its bargaining power against the other at arm's length is strong *evidence* that the transaction meets the test of fairness. Id. (emphasis added).

In this case, the Vice Chancellor noted that the Court of Chancery has expressed "differing views" regarding the effect that an approval of a cash-out merger by a special committee of disinterested directors has upon the controlling or dominating shareholders' burden of demonstrating entire fairness. One view is that such approval shifts to the plaintiff the burden of proving that the transaction was unfair. . . . The other view is that such an approval renders the business judgment rule the applicable standard of judicial review. . . .

"It is often of critical importance whether a particular decision is one to which the business judgment rule applies or the entire fairness rule applies." Nixon v. Blackwell, Del. Supr., 626 A.2d 1366, 1376 (1993). The definitive answer with regard to the Court of Chancery's "differing views" is found in this court's opinions. . . . [I]n *Rosenblatt*, in the context of a subsequent proceeding involving a parent-subsidiary merger, this court held that the "approval of a merger, as here, by an informed vote of a majority of the minority stockholders, while not a legal prerequisite, shifts the burden of proving the unfairness of the merger entirely to the plaintiffs." Id.

Entire fairness remains the proper focus of judicial analysis in examining an interested merger, irrespective of whether the burden of proof remains upon or is shifted away from the controlling or dominating shareholder, because the unchanging nature of the underlying "interested" transaction requires careful scrutiny. See Weinberger v. UOP, Inc., 457 A.2d at 710 (citing Sterling v. Mayflower Hotel Corp., Del. Supr., 93 A.2d 107, 110 (1952)). The policy rationale for the exclusive application of the entire fairness standard has been stated as follows:

> Parent subsidiary mergers, unlike stock options, are proposed by a party that controls, and will continue to control, the corporation, whether or not the minority stockholders vote to approve or reject the transaction. The controlling stockholder

relationship has the potential to influence, however subtly, the vote of [ratifying] minority stockholders in a manner that is not likely to occur in a transaction with a noncontrolling party.

Even where no coercion is intended, shareholders voting on a parent subsidiary merger might perceive that their disapproval could risk retaliation of some kind by the controlling stockholder. For example, the controlling stockholder might decide to stop dividend payments or to effect a subsequent cash out merger at a less favorable price, for which the remedy would be time consuming and costly litigation. At the very least, the potential for that perception, and its possible impact on a shareholder vote, could never be fully eliminated. Consequently, in a merger between the corporation and its controlling stockholder — even one negotiated by disinterested, independent directors — no court could be certain whether the transaction terms fully approximate what truly independent parties would have achieved in an arm's length negotiation. . . .

Citron v. E. I. Du Pont de Nemours & Co., 584 A.2d at 502.

Once again, this court holds that the exclusive standard of judicial review in examining the propriety of an interested cash-out merger transaction by a controlling or dominating shareholder is entire fairness. Weinberger v. UOP, Inc., 457 A.2d at 710-711. The initial burden of establishing entire fairness rests upon the party who stands on both sides of the transaction. Id. However, an approval of the transaction by an independent committee of directors or an informed majority of minority shareholders shifts the burden of proof on the issue of fairness from the controlling or dominating shareholder to the challenging shareholder-plaintiff. See Rosenblatt v. Getty Oil Co., 493 A.2d at 937-938. Nevertheless, even when an interested cash-out merger transaction receives the informed approval of a majority of minority stockholders or an independent committee of disinterested directors, an entire fairness analysis is the only proper standard of judicial review. See id.

Independent Committees, Interested Merger Transactions

. . . The same policy rationale which requires judicial review of interested cash-out mergers exclusively for entire fairness also mandates careful judicial scrutiny of a special committee's real bargaining power before shifting the burden of proof on the issue of entire fairness. A recent decision from the Court of Chancery articulated a two-part test for determining whether burden shifting is appropriate in an interested merger transaction. Rabkin v. Olin Corp., Del. Ch., C.A. No. 7547 (Consolidated), CHANDLER, V.C., 1990 WL 47648, slip op. at 14-15 (Apr. 17, 1990), *reprinted in* 16 Del. J. Corp. L. 851, 961-962 (1991), *aff'd*, Del. Supr., 586 A.2d 1202 (1990). In *Olin*, the Court of Chancery stated: "The mere existence of an independent special committee . . . does not itself shift the burden. At least two factors are required. First, the majority shareholder must not dictate the terms of the merger. Rosenblatt v. Getty Oil Co., Del. Supr., 493 A.2d 929, 937 (1985). Second, the special committee must have real bargaining power that it can exercise with the majority shareholder on an arm's-length basis." Id., slip op. at 24-25, 16 Del. J. Corp. L. at 861-861.[6] This Court expressed its agreement with that statement by affirming the Court of Chancery decision in *Olin* on appeal.

---

6. In *Olin*, the Court of Chancery concluded that because the special committee had been given "the narrow mandate of determining the monetary fairness of a non-negotiable offer," and because the majority shareholder "dictated the terms" and "there were no arm's length negotiations," the burden

Lynch's Independent Committee

In the case *sub judice*, the . . . fact that the same independent directors had submitted to Alcatel's demands on August 1, 1986 was part of the basis for the Court of Chancery's finding of Alcatel's domination of Lynch. Therefore, the Independent Committee's ability to bargain at arm's length with Alcatel was suspect from the outset.

The Independent Committee's original assignment was to examine the merger with Celwave which had been proposed by Alcatel. The record reflects that the Independent Committee's adverse recommendation was not the pursuit of further negotiations regarding its Celwave proposal, but rather its response was an offer to buy Lynch. That offer was consistent with Alcatel's August 1, 1986 expressions of an intention to dominate Lynch, since an acquisition would effectively eliminate once and for all Lynch's remaining vestiges of independence.

The Independent Committee's second assignment was to consider Alcatel's proposal to purchase Lynch. The Independent Committee proceeded on that task with full knowledge of Alcatel's demonstrated pattern of domination. The Independent Committee was also obviously aware of Alcatel's refusal to negotiate with it on the Celwave matter.

Burden of Proof Shifted Court of Chancery's Finding

. . . The Court of Chancery gave credence to the testimony of Kertz, one of the members of the Independent Committee, to the effect that he did not believe that $15.50 was a fair price but that he voted in favor of the merger because he felt there was no alternative.

The Court of Chancery also found that Kertz understood Alcatel's position to be that it was ready to proceed with an unfriendly tender offer at a lower price if Lynch did not accept the $15.50 offer, and that Kertz perceived this to be a threat by Alcatel. . . .

The record reflects that Alcatel was "ready to proceed" with a hostile bid. This was a conclusion reached by Beringer, the Independent Committee's chairman and spokesman, based upon communications to him from Alcatel. Beringer testified that although there was no reference to a particular price for a hostile bid during his discussions with Alcatel, or even specific mention of a "lower" price, "the implication was clear to [him] that it probably would be at a lower price."

According to the Court of Chancery, the Independent Committee rejected three lower offers for Lynch from Alcatel and then accepted the $15.50 offer "after being advised that [it] was fair and after considering the absence of alternatives." The Vice Chancellor expressly acknowledged the impracticability of Lynch's Independent Committee's alternatives to a merger with Alcatel: "Lynch was not in a position to shop for other acquirers, since Alcatel could block any alternative transaction. Alcatel also made it clear that it was not interested in having its shares repurchased by Lynch. The Independent Committee decided that a stockholder rights plan was not viable because of the increased debt it would entail."

---

of proof on the issue of entire fairness remained with the defendants. Id., slip op. at 15, 16 Del. J. Corp. L. at 862. In making that determination, the Court of Chancery pointed out that the majority shareholder "could obviously have used its majority stake to effectuate the merger" regardless of the committee's or the board's disapproval, and that the record demonstrated that the directors of both corporations were "acutely aware of this fact." Id., slip op. at 13, 16 Del.J. Corp L. at 861.

Nevertheless, . . . the Court of Chancery found that the Independent Committee had "appropriately simulated a third-party transaction, where negotiations are conducted at arm's-length and there is no compulsion to reach an agreement." The Court of Chancery concluded that the Independent Committee's actions "as a whole" were "sufficiently well informed . . . and aggressive to simulate an arm's-length transaction," so that the burden of proof as to entire fairness shifted from Alcatel to the contending Lynch shareholder, Kahn. The Court of Chancery's reservations about the finding are apparent in its written decision.

The Power to Say No, The Parties' Contentions, Arm's Length Bargaining

The Court of Chancery properly noted that limitations on the alternatives to Alcatel's offer did not mean that the Independent Committee should have agreed to a price that was unfair: "The power to say no is a significant power. It is the duty of directors serving on [an independent] committee to approve only a transaction that is in the best interests of the public shareholders, to say no to any transaction that is not fair to those shareholders and is not the best transaction available. It is not sufficient for such directors to achieve the best price that a fiduciary will pay if that price is not a fair price." (Quoting In re First Boston, Inc. Shareholders Litig., Del. Ch., C.A. 10338 (Consolidated), Allen C, 1990 WL 78836, slip op. at 15-16 (June 7, 1990). . . .

Kahn contends the record reflects that the conduct of Alcatel deprived the Independent Committee of an effective "power to say no." Kahn argues that Alcatel not only threatened the Committee with a hostile tender offer in the event its $15.50 offer was not recommended and approved, but also directed the affairs of Lynch for Alcatel's benefit in such a way as to make it impossible for Lynch to continue as a public company under Alcatel's control without injury to itself and its minority shareholders. . . .

In *American General* . . . the Court of Chancery found that the members of the Special Committee were "truly independent and . . . performed their tasks in a proper manner," but it also found that "at the end of their negotiations with [the majority shareholder] the Committee members were issued an ultimatum and told that they must accept the $16.50 per share price or [the majority shareholder] would proceed with the transaction without their input." Id., 13 Del. J. Corp. L. at 181. The Court of Chancery concluded based upon this evidence that the Special Committee had thereby lost "its ability to negotiate in an arm's-length manner" and that there was a reasonable probability that the burden of proving entire fairness would remain on the defendants if the litigation proceeded to trial. Id., 13 Del. J. Corp. L. at 181. . . .

Alcatel's Entire Fairness Burden Did Not Shift to Kahn

A condition precedent to finding that the burden of proving entire fairness has shifted in an interested merger transaction is a careful judicial analysis of the factual circumstances of each case. Particular consideration must be given to evidence of whether the special committee was truly independent, fully informed, and had the freedom to negotiate at arm's length. . . . "Although perfection is not possible," unless the controlling or dominating shareholder can demonstrate that it has not only formed an independent committee but also replicated a process "as though each of the contending parties had in fact exerted its bargaining power at arm's length," the burden of proving entire fairness will not shift. Weinberger v. UOP, Inc., 457 A.2d at 709-710 n.7. See also Rosenblatt v. Getty Oil Co., Del. Supr., 493 A.2d 929, 937-938 (1985). . . .

The Court of Chancery's determination that the Independent Committee "appropriately simulated a third-party transaction, where negotiations are conducted at arm's-length and there is no compulsion to reach an agreement," is not supported by the record. Under the circumstances present in the case *sub judice*, the Court of Chancery erred in shifting the burden of proof with regard to entire fairness to the contesting Lynch shareholder-plaintiff Kahn. The record reflects that the ability of the Committee effectively to negotiate at arm's length was compromised by Alcatel's threats to proceed with a hostile tender offer if the $15.50 price was not approved by the Committee and the Lynch board. The fact that the Independent Committee rejected three initial offers, which were well below the Independent Committee's estimated valuation for Lynch and were not combined with an explicit threat that Alcatel was "ready to proceed" with a hostile bid, cannot alter the conclusion that any semblance of arm's length bargaining ended when the Independent Committee surrendered to the ultimatum that accompanied Alcatel's final offer. Rabkin v. Philip A. Hunt Chem. Corp., Del. Supr., 498 A.2d 1099, 1106 (1985).

---

1. *Limited effect of meeting the fair dealing component. Kahn* makes clear the effect of satisfying the fair dealing component of the entire fairness standard: the burden of proving entire fairness shifts to the plaintiff. But the court could have assigned greater consequence to the procedural character of the transaction. If satisfying the fair dealing component requires that the negotiations take place at arm's length, then the taint of control will have been exorcised from the transaction, and the business judgment rule would be the appropriate standard of review. But if all that satisfying the fair dealing component secures is a shift in the burden of proof, is the game worth the candle? How significant is a shift in the burden of proof on the remaining fair price component of the entire fairness test?

2. *What procedures establish fair dealing?* After *Kahn*, would it be enough that the controlling shareholder not make an explicit threat of a hostile offer, or must the independent negotiating committee actually have the "power to say no" before the structure of the negotiating process will protect its outcome?[68] How can the parties create the power to say no? One approach might be a standstill agreement that prohibits the controlling shareholder from acquiring additional shares for a period of time if the negotiations prove unsuccessful.

3. *Kahn on remand.* In *Kahn*, the Supreme Court remanded the case to the Chancery Court to again determine the entire fairness of the freeze-out, but now with the burden of proof resting on Alcatel, the dominant shareholder. This burden could be expected to be especially heavy. The Supreme Court had emphasized the

---

68. 2 ALI Principles of Corporate Governance 388 (1994) suggests that the power to say no is a necessary condition to giving credence to an independent negotiating structure: "[I]f the majority shareholder consummates the transaction over the objection of the independent negotiating committee, there will not have been arm's-length bargaining, and the committee's existence should not be given weight by a reviewing court."

unitary character of the entire fairness analysis despite its separate components of fair dealing and fair price. Since the Supreme Court had already determined that Alcatel had coerced the independent committee charged with negotiating on behalf of Lynch's minority shareholders, presumably fair dealing would be hard to show, and fair price alone would not save the transaction if the standard really was unitary. On remand, the Chancery Court concluded that "despite [Alcatel's coercion of the independent committee], the defendants were deemed to have met their burden of fair dealing because they had satisfied other relevant factors set forth in *Weinberger.*" Kahn v. Lynch Communication Systems, Inc., 669 A.2d 79, 83 (Del. Ch. 1995) (*Kahn II*). Since the Chancery Court also concluded the price was fair, it held that Alcatel had met its burden of proving that the transaction was entirely fair.

On appeal for the second time, the Supreme Court's bold words in *Kahn I* lost their bluster. The court's analysis of Alcatel's coercion of the independent committee was particularly confusing. *Kahn I* suggested that coercion of the independent committee by the dominant shareholder would violate fair dealing because the coercion limited the committee's capacity to negotiate on behalf of the minority shareholders. In *Kahn II*, however, the court's coercion analysis shifted from the impact of Alcatel's behavior on the independent committee, to its impact on the minority shareholders themselves. In response to the plaintiff's claim that the Chancery Court had ignored the finding in *Kahn I* that the independent committee had been coerced, the Supreme Court stated

> that to be actionable, the coercive conduct directed at selling shareholders must be a "material" influence on the decision to sell. Where other economic forces are at work and more likely produced the decision to sell . . . the specter of coercion may not be deemed material with respect to the transaction as a whole, and will not prevent a finding of entire fairness. In this case, no shareholder was treated differently in the transaction from any other shareholder not subjected to a two-tiered or squeeze-out treatment. Alcatel offered cash for all the minority shares and paid cash for all shares tendered. Clearly there was no coercion exerted which was material to this aspect of the transaction. . . .

While the structure of the transaction was not itself coercive, the minority shareholders were put to a "take it or leave it" decision as a result of the coercion of the independent committee; that coercion prevented the committee from bargaining effectively on their behalf. Why is the formal structure of the transaction relevant to this point? To be sure, the shareholders could have declined to tender their shares, but what was their realistic alternative? Does *Kahn II* suggest that as long as the form of the ultimate transaction is not coercive to the shareholders, the dominating shareholder can rig the negotiations in its favor?

4. *A two-tiered inquiry?* Alternatively, do *Kahn I* and *Kahn II* set up a two-tiered inquiry into fair dealing? With respect to the shift in the burden of proof, the question may be whether there is a fully empowered independent committee. But when the issue, ultimately, is whether the fair dealing standard is met, *Kahn II* suggests that the issue is whether the shareholders, not the special committee, are coerced. See Gilson & Gordon, supra. Most puzzling, the Supreme Court also suggested that Alcatel had no reason to negotiate at all: "Here Alcatel could have presented a merger offer directly to the Lynch Board [without a special

committee], which it controlled, and received a quick approval. Had it done so, of course, it would have borne the burden of demonstrating entire fairness in the event the transaction was later questioned. Where, ultimately, it has been required to assume the same burden, it should fare no worse in a judicial review of the fairness of its negotiations with the Independent Committee." But if Alcatel had simply imposed the transaction on the minority shareholders, as the court recognized it had the power to do, how could it meet *Weinberger*'s fair dealing requirement? If fair dealing can be met by a formally non-coercive structure, even though the dominating shareholder has forced the transaction on the minority through unfair negotiations, is there anything left of this element of *Weinberger*? If not, then is *Weinberger* anything more than a class action substitute for an appraisal action where the real issue is only the fairness of the price? Is that so bad an outcome?

5. *Other approaches to exclusivity.* Evaluating the current status of the standards governing freeze-outs requires something with which to compare it. The obvious candidate is appraisal. The court could have recognized that *Weinberger*'s elimination of the business purpose requirement eliminated any right in minority shareholders to remain participants in the corporation. The only question then is the price. A statutory appraisal proceeding is designed to determine fair price. Appraisal could have been made exclusive.

The ALI comes closer to making appraisal the exclusive means for challenging a freeze-out merger. Under ALI §7.25, if target shareholders are provided full disclosure and an adequate appraisal remedy, the merger is otherwise properly approved, and "the directors who approve the transaction . . . have an adequate basis, grounded on substantial objective evidence, for believing that the consideration offered to the minority shareholders . . . constitutes fair value for their shares . . . ," then appraisal is the exclusive remedy. How different is §7.25 from Delaware's entire fairness test? How would directors form an adequately grounded belief concerning fair value? Is this where a fair dealing component might slip into the analysis?[69]

6. *Entire fairness as a triggering device.* The entire fairness doctrine can be interpreted as a triggering device—that is, a test whose function is to determine whether another rule applies. See Elhauge, page 1050 supra. If entire fairness is met, appraisal is exclusive with the result that only the typically small number of shareholders who actually perfect their appraisal remedy can challenge the fairness of the merger price as measured by the appraisal standard. If entire fairness is not met, then the fairness of the merger can be challenged in a class action on behalf of all target shareholders (not just dissenters), and the possibility exists of a rescission remedy that, if the value of the shares has risen following the transaction, may result in damages in excess of the appraisal standard. Should the outcome of the entire fairness test determine the number of shareholders who can challenge the transaction and the applicable measure of damages?

A shareholder's decision to accept the offered consideration and not to dissent seems appropriate if the fair dealing standard is met; the decision not to dissent then can be assumed to be based on the fairness of the process, rather than on the procedural difficulties and expense of appraisal. If the merger was not

---

69. Both California and the ALI treat appraisal as exclusive even if target directors have breached their duty of care so long as the acquiring company is not a controlling shareholder. See Steinberg v. Emplace, 42 Cal. 3d 1198, 733 Cal. Rptr. 249, 729 P.2d 683 (1986). Compare Smith v. Van Gorkom, page 84 supra.

independently negotiated, then there is greater reason to believe that a shareholder decision to approve the merger rather than dissent was driven by the inadequacies of the appraisal remedy. In that event, the punishment for failing entire fairness meets the crime: the requirements for appraisal are dropped and the action proceeds as a class action — that is, as if all shareholders had perfected their appraisal rights.

What about the triggering function of entire fairness with respect to the measure of damages? Here the analysis might be that the potential for damages in excess of the appraisal standard — in effect, punitive damages — reduces the incentive for a controlling shareholder to intentionally set the consideration low in the hope that few shareholders dissent and that a facade of independence will satisfy a reviewing court. If the only penalty for getting caught is paying the fair price that you should have paid in the first place, then why not try? The potential for a rescission remedy can balance the acquirer's incentives. This analysis suggests focusing on the circumstances when alternative damages are available. *Weinberger* describes the appraisal standard as potentially inadequate "where fraud, misrepresentation, self-dealing, deliberate waste of corporate assets, or gross and palpable overreaching are involved." Do these conditions fit the analysis?

5. USING A TENDER OFFER TO AVOID ENTIRE FAIRNESS

The court's holding in *Kahn I* that creating a fully empowered independent committee resulted only in a burden of proof shift, rather than eliminating the implicit class appraisal remedy created by the entire fairness standard, led transaction planners to consider the use of a two-step freeze-out to avoid the problem. The idea was to use a tender offer to increase the controlling shareholder's ownership to over 90 percent, and then effect the final freeze-out through a short-form merger under Del. §253.

The strategy's first step builds on the Delaware Supreme Court's holding in Solomon v. Pathe Communications[70] that a shareholder with voting control over 89.5 percent of a corporation's outstanding stock owed no obligation with respect to the fairness of the price offered in a tender offer for the stock of the controlled corporation, unless the offer was structurally coercive or disclosure concerning the offer was inadequate.[71] Assume that a controlling shareholder holds 80 percent of the controlled corporation's outstanding stock and desires to freeze out the minority. If the controlling shareholder proceeds with a straightforward one-step freeze-out merger, the transaction will be subject to entire fairness review under *Weinberger*. If *Solomon* is read to dictate that the tender offer will not be subject to entire fairness review,[72] the controlling shareholder can make a tender offer for all of the non-controlling stock, with a "majority of the minority" closing condition to ensure that it receives more than 90 percent

---

70. 672 A.2d. 35 (Del. 1995).
71. "[I]n the absence of coercion or disclosure violations, the adequacy of the price in a voluntary tender offer cannot be an issue" 672 A.2d at 40.
72. This reading of *Solomon* is actually something of a stretch. *Solomon* did not involve a tender offer that was part of a freeze-out transaction. Thus, the extension of the holding to a freeze-out setting was potentially risky because both the supreme court opinion, 472 A.2d 35, 39, and the lower court opinion, 1995 WL 250374, *5 (Del. Ch. 1995) (Allen, Ch.), emphasize that the transaction was not a freeze-out. See Gilson & Gordon, supra.

ownership[73] and, perhaps, a commitment to take out any non-tendering share-holders in a short-form merger at the same price to ensure the offer is not coercive. A class appraisal is thus avoided for the first step.

The strategy's second step was sanctioned in Glassman v. Unocal Exploration,[74] in which the court held that appraisal is the exclusive remedy for allegations of price unfairness in a short-form merger. The new transaction form entirely elimi-nates entire fairness review for a freeze-out, a complete end run around *Weinberger*. Of course, the change in standard suggests a change in bidder tactics. Unless the controlling shareholder believes that minority shareholders will not tender, the price offered should never exceed the low end of its assessment of the appraisal standard. Even if that assessment proves to be less than fair value, any higher price resulting from an appraisal proceeding will be payable only to the small number of shareholders who neither tender nor perfect their appraisal rights.

This strategy was first tested in In re Siliconix Incorporated Shareholders Liti-gation.[75] In this case, a controlling shareholder lost patience with a special com-mittee and made an exchange offer for the minority shares without the committee's approval rather than raise the price. The plaintiffs, in turn, claimed that the exchange offer should be subject to entire fairness review.

Reading *Solomon* broadly, the court held that a controlling shareholder had no obligation to demonstrate the entire fairness of a proposed freeze-out tender offer. The court also held that the target directors did not breach a duty of care or loyalty to minority shareholders by failing to evaluate the controlling shareholder's offer and by failing to provide shareholders with their evaluation and recommendation. But why did the directors get off so easily? Indeed, one might ask why the target directors' fiduciary duty did not require them to attempt to block a tender offer they thought was unfair, perhaps by adopting a poison pill that would have pre-vented the controlling shareholder from increasing its ownership.

The court justified its holding by reference to the different statutory role accorded target directors in mergers and in tender offers:

> It may seem strange that the scrutiny given to tender offer transactions is less than the scrutiny that may be given to, for example, a merger transaction. . . . From the stand-point of a Siliconix shareholder, there may be little substantive difference if the tender is successful and [the controlling shareholder] proceeds, as it has indicated that it most likely will, with the short-form merger. The Siliconix shareholders . . . will end up in the same position as if he or she had tendered or if the transaction had been structured as a merger. . . . [U]nder the corporation law, a board of directors which is given the critical role of initiating and recommending a merger to the shareholders traditionally has been accorded no statutory role whatsoever with respect to a public tender offer. . . . This distinctive treatment of board power with respect to merger and tender offers is not satisfactorily explained by the observation that the corporation law statutes were basically designed in a period when large scale public tender offers were rarities. . . . More likely, one would suppose, is that conceptual notion that tender offers essentially represent the sale of shareholders' separate property and

---

73. In this hypothetical, the satisfaction of a "majority of the minority" condition would ensure that the controlling shareholder would reach the 90 percent level necessary to a short-form merger. If prior to the transaction the controlling shareholder owned less than 80 percent, then an additional closing condition would be required: that sufficient shares be tendered give the controlling shareholder 90 percent ownership after the transaction closed.
74. 777 A.2d 242 (Del. 2001).
75. 2001 WL 716787 (Del. Ch. 2001).

such sales — even when aggregated into a single change in control transaction — require no "corporate" action. . . .

Does this description of the target directors' role correspond to the Delaware Supreme Court's description of directors' role in a hostile tender offer? Recall that in *Unocal*, the supreme court held that a target board of directors "had both the power *and duty* to oppose a bid it perceived to be harmful to the corporate enterprise." There seems to be a large difference between *Siliconix*'s characterization of the target board's role in a freeze-out tender offer by a controlling shareholder and the supreme court's characterization of the target board's role in a hostile tender offer. In which setting do the target shareholders require more protection? In a hostile tender offer, the market may provide some protection; if the price offered is too low, a competing bid may arise. In a freeze-out tender offer, no competitive bid is possible; only the target board can act to protect the minority shareholders against a low-ball offer.

The divergence between the conflicting lines of doctrine governing a controlling shareholder's obligations in freeze-out mergers and freeze-out tender offers, and the similarly conflicting lines of doctrine governing the target board's role in freeze-out tender offers and in hostile tender offers, were finally addressed in the following case.

In re Pure Resources, Inc. Shareholders Litigation
808 A.2d 421 (Del. Ch. 2002)

Strine, V.C.: [This case arose out of a tenuous partnership between Unocal Corporation and its controlled subsidiary Pure Resources Inc. ("Pure"). Pure was the result of a combination of Unocal's Permian Basin oil operations with Titan Exploration, Inc., whose oil operations were in much the same area. Unocal received 65.4 percent of Pure's common stock; the former Titan shareholders received the remainder. Pure's management held between a quarter and a third of the minority stock. A Business Opportunities Agreement ("BOA") entered into at Pure's creation limited Pure's operations to the Permian Basin and the area in which Titan had previously operated for so long as Unocal held at least 35 percent of Pure's stock. Nonetheless, Pure's management was anxious to expand its operations, with the result of increasing friction between Unocal and Pure. In particular, a serious disagreement arose over Pure's proposal of a royalty trust that would monetize the value of certain of Pure's mineral rights, which Unocal believed would increase the price payable under put rights held by Pure management that would be triggered if Unocal acquired 85 percent of Pure's stock.]

This is the court's decision on a motion for preliminary injunction. The lead plaintiff in the case holds a large block of stock in Pure Resources, Inc., 65% of the shares of which are owned by Unocal Corporation. The lead plaintiff and its fellow plaintiffs seek to enjoin a now-pending exchange offer (the "Offer") by which Unocal hopes to acquire the rest of the shares of Pure in exchange for shares of its own stock.

The plaintiffs believe that the Offer is inadequate and is subject to entire fairness review, consistent with the rationale of Kahn v. Lynch Communication Systems, Inc. and its progeny. Moreover, they claim that the defendants, who include

Unocal and Pure's board of directors, have not made adequate and non-misleading disclosure of the material facts necessary for Pure stockholders to make an informed decision whether to tender into the Offer.

By contrast, the defendants argue that the Offer is a non-coercive one that . . . is not subject to the entire fairness standard, but to the standards set forth in cases like Solomon v. Pathe Communications Corp., standards which they argue have been fully met.

In this opinion, I conclude that the Offer is subject, as a general matter, to the *Solomon* standards, rather than the *Lynch* entire fairness standard. I conclude, however, that many of the concerns that justify the *Lynch* standard are implicated by tender offers initiated by controlling stockholders, which have as their goal the acquisition of the rest of the subsidiary's shares. These concerns should be accommodated within the *Solomon* form of review, by requiring that tender offers by controlling shareholders be structured in a manner that reduces the distorting effect of the tendering process on free stockholder choice and by ensuring minority stockholders a candid and unfettered tendering recommendation from the independent directors of the target board. In this case, the Offer for the most part meets this standard, with one exception that Unocal may cure. . . .

II. On August 20, 2002, Unocal sent the Pure board a letter that stated in pertinent part that:

> It has become clear to us that the best interests of our respective stockholders will be served by Unocal's acquisition of the shares of Pure Resources that we do not already own. . . .
>
> Unocal recognizes that a strong and stable on-shore, North America production base will facilitate the execution of its North American gas strategy. The skills and technology required to maximize the benefits to be realized from that strategy are now divided between Union Oil and Pure. Sound business strategy calls for bringing those assets together, under one management, so that they may be deployed to their highest and best use. For those reasons, we are not interested in selling our shares in Pure. Moreover, if the two companies are combined, important cost savings should be realized and potential conflicts of interest will be avoided.
>
> Consequently, our Board of Directors has authorized us to make an exchange offer pursuant to which the stockholders of Pure (other than Union Oil) will be offered 0.6527 shares of common stock of Unocal for each outstanding share of Pure common stock they own in a transaction designed to be tax-free. Based on the $34.09 closing price of Unocal's shares on August 20, 2002, our offer provides a value of approximately $22.25 per share of Pure common stock and a 27% premium to the closing price of Pure common stock on that date.
>
> Unocal's offer is being made directly to Pure's stockholders. . . .
>
> Our offer will be conditioned on the tender of a sufficient number of shares of Pure common stock such that, after the offer is completed, we will own at least 90% of the outstanding shares of Pure common stock and other customary conditions. . . . Assuming that the conditions to the offer are satisfied and that the offer is completed, we will then effect a "short form" merger of Pure with a subsidiary of Unocal as soon as practicable thereafter. In this merger, the remaining Pure public stockholders will receive the same consideration as in the exchange offer, except for those stockholders who choose to exercise their appraisal rights. . . .
>
> Unocal is not seeking, and as the offer is being made directly to Pure's stockholders, Delaware law does not require approval of the offer from Pure's Board of Directors. We, however, encourage you to consult with your outside counsel as to the

obligations of Pure's Board of Directors under the U.S. tender offer rules to advise the stockholders of your recommendation with respect to our offer. . . .

Unocal management asked Ling and Chessum [two of Unocal's designees to the Pure board] to make calls to the Pure board about the Offer. In their talking points, Ling and Chessum were instructed to suggest that any Special Committee formed by Pure should have powers "limited to hiring independent advisors (bank and lawyers) and to coming up with a recommendation to the Pure shareholders as to whether or not to accept UCL's offer; any greater delegation is not warranted." . . .

The next day the Pure board met to consider this event. Hightower [the CEO and largest Pure minority shareholder] suggested that Chessum and Ling recuse themselves from the Pure board's consideration of the Offer. They agreed to do so. After that, the Pure board voted to establish a Special Committee comprised of [independent directors] Williamson and Covington to respond to the Unocal bid. . . .

The precise authority of the Special Committee to act on behalf of Pure was left hazy at first, but seemed to consist solely of the power to retain independent advisors, to take a position on the offer's advisability on behalf of Pure, and to negotiate with Unocal to see if it would increase its bid. Aside from this last point, this constrained degree of authority comported with the limited power that Unocal had desired. . . .

For financial advisors, the Special Committee hired Credit Suisse First Boston ("First Boston"), the investment bank assisting Pure with its consideration of the Royalty Trust, and Petrie Parkman & Co., Inc., a smaller firm very experienced in the energy field. The Committee felt that the knowledge that First Boston had gleaned from its Royalty Trust work would be of great help to the Committee, especially in the short time frame required to respond to the Offer, which was scheduled to expire at midnight on October 2, 2002.

For legal advisors, the Committee retained Baker Botts and Potter Anderson & Corroon. . . .

After the formation of the Special Committee, Unocal formally commenced its Offer, which had these key features:

- An exchange ratio of 0.6527 of a Unocal share for each Pure share.
- A non-waivable majority of the minority tender provision, which required a majority of shares not owned by Unocal to tender. Management of Pure, including Hightower and Staley, are considered part of the minority for purposes of this condition. . . .
- A waivable condition that a sufficient number of tenders be received to enable Unocal to own 90% of Pure and to effect a short-form merger under 8 Del. C. §253.
- A statement by Unocal that it intends, if it obtains 90%, to consummate a short-form merger as soon as practicable at the same exchange ratio.

As of this time, this litigation had been filed and a preliminary injunction hearing was soon scheduled. Among the issues raised was the adequacy of the Special Committee's scope of authority.

Thereafter, the Special Committee sought to, in its words, "clarify" its authority. The clarity it sought was clear: the Special Committee wanted to be delegated the full authority of the board under Delaware law to respond to the Offer. With such authority, the Special Committee could have searched for alternative transactions, speeded up consummation of the Royalty Trust, evaluated the feasibility of a self-tender, and put in place a shareholder rights plan (*a.k.a.*, poison pill) to block the Offer.

What exactly happened at this point is shrouded by invocations of privilege. But this much is clear. Having recused themselves from the Pure board process before, Chessum and Ling [Unocal's representatives on the Pure board] reentered it in full glory when the Special Committee asked for more authority. Chessum took the lead in raising concerns and engaged Unocal's in-house and outside counsel to pare down the resolution proposed by the Special Committee. After discussions between Counsel for Unocal and the Special Committee, the bold resolution drafted by Special Committee counsel was whittled down to take out any ability on the part of the Special Committee to do anything other than study the Offer, negotiate it, and make a recommendation on behalf of Pure in the required 14D-9. . . .

The most reasonable inference that can be drawn from the record is that the Special Committee was unwilling to confront Unocal as aggressively as it would have confronted a third-party bidder. No doubt Unocal's talented counsel made much of its client's majority status and argued that Pure would be on uncertain legal ground in interposing itself — by way of a rights plan — between Unocal and Pure's stockholders. Realizing that Unocal would not stand for this broader authority and sensitive to the expected etiquette of subsidiary-parent relations, the Pure board therefore decided not to vote on the issue, and the Special Committee's fleeting act of boldness was obscured in the rhetoric of discussions about "clarifying its authority."

Contemporaneous with these events, the Special Committee met on a more or less continuous basis. On a few occasions, the Special Committee met with Unocal and tried to persuade it to increase its offer. On September 10, for example, the Special Committee asked Unocal to increase the exchange ratio from 0.6527 to 0.787. Substantive presentations were made by the Special Committee's financial advisors in support of this overture.

After these meetings, Unocal remained unmoved and made no counteroffer. Therefore, on September 17, 2002, the Special Committee voted not to recommend the Offer, based on its analysis and the advice of its financial advisors. The Special Committee prepared the 14D-9 on behalf of Pure, which contained the board's recommendation not to tender into the Offer. Hightower and Staley [Pure's COO] also announced their personal present intentions not to tender, intentions that if adhered to would make it nearly impossible for Unocal to obtain 90% of Pure's shares in the Offer.

During the discovery process, a representative of the lead plaintiff, which is an investment fund, testified that he did not feel coerced by the Offer. The discovery record also reveals that a great deal of the Pure stock held by the public is in the hands of institutional investors. . . .

B.   *The Plaintiffs' Substantive Attack on the Offer*

1. The primary argument of the plaintiffs is that the Offer should be governed by the entire fairness standard of review. In their view, the structural power of Unocal

over Pure and its board, as well as Unocal's involvement in determining the scope of the Special Committee's authority, make the Offer other than a voluntary, non-coercive transaction. In the plaintiffs' mind, the Offer poses the same threat of (what I will call) "inherent coercion" that motivated the Supreme Court in Kahn v. Lynch Communication Systems, Inc. to impose the entire fairness standard of review. . . .

In response to these arguments, Unocal asserts that the plaintiffs misunderstand the relevant legal principles. Because Unocal has proceeded by way of an exchange offer and not a negotiated merger, the rule [is that] . . . articulated by, among other cases, Solomon v. Pathe Communications Corp. Because Unocal has conditioned its Offer on a majority of the minority provision and intends to consummate a short-form merger at the same price, it argues that the Offer poses no threat of structural coercion and that the Pure minority can make a voluntary decision. Because the Pure minority has a negative recommendation from the Pure Special Committee and because there has been full disclosure (including of any material information Unocal received from Pure in formulating its bid), Unocal submits that the Pure minority will be able to make an informed decision whether to tender. For these reasons, Unocal asserts that no meritorious claim of breach of fiduciary duty exists against it or the Pure directors.

2. This case therefore involves an aspect of Delaware law fraught with doctrinal tension: what equitable standard of fiduciary conduct applies when a controlling shareholder seeks to acquire the rest of the company's shares? In considering this issue, it is useful to pause over the word "equitable" and to capture its full import.

The key inquiry is not what statutory procedures must be adhered to when a controlling stockholder attempts to acquire the rest of the company's shares. Controlling stockholders counseled by experienced lawyers rarely trip over the legal hurdles imposed by legislation.

Nor is the doctrine of independent legal significance of relevance here. That doctrine stands only for the proposition that the mere fact that a transaction cannot be accomplished under one statutory provision does not invalidate it if a different statutory method of consummation exists. Nothing about that doctrine alters the fundamental rule that inequitable actions in technical conformity with statutory law can be restrained by equity. . . .

Much of the judicial carpentry in the corporate law occurs in this context, in which judges must supplement the broadly enabling features of statutory corporation law with equitable principles sufficient to protect against abuse and unfairness, but not so rigid as to stifle useful transactions that could increase the shareholder and societal wealth generated by the corporate form.

In building the common law, judges forced to balance these concerns cannot escape making normative choices, based on imperfect information about the world. This reality clearly pervades the area of corporate law implicated by this case. When a transaction to buy out the minority is proposed, is it more important to the development of strong capital markets to hold controlling stockholders and target boards to very strict (and litigation-intensive) standards of fiduciary conduct? Or is more stockholder wealth generated if less rigorous protections are adopted, which permit acquisitions to proceed so long as the majority has not misled or strong-armed the minority? Is such flexibility in fact beneficial to minority stockholders because it encourages liquidity-generating tender offers to them and provides incentives for acquirers to pay hefty premiums to buy control, knowing that control will be accompanied by legal rules that permit a later "going private" transaction to occur in a relatively non-litigious manner?

At present, the Delaware case law has two strands of authority that answer these questions differently . . . [and which] appear to treat economically similar transactions as categorically different simply because the method by which the controlling stockholder proceeds varies. This disparity in treatment persists even though the two basic methods (negotiated merger versus tender offer/short-form merger) pose similar threats to minority stockholders. Indeed, it can be argued that the distinction in approach subjects the transaction that is more protective of minority stockholders when implemented with appropriate protective devices — a merger negotiated by an independent committee with the power to say no and conditioned on a majority of the minority vote — to more stringent review than the more dangerous form of a going private deal — an unnegotiated tender offer made by a majority stockholder. The latter transaction is arguably less protective than a merger of the kind described, because the majority stockholder-offeror has access to inside information, and the offer requires disaggregated stockholders to decide whether to tender quickly, pressured by the risk of being squeezed out in a short-form merger at a different price later or being left as part of a much smaller public minority. This disparity creates a possible incoherence in our law.

3. To illustrate this possible incoherence in our law, it is useful to sketch out these two strands. I begin with negotiated mergers. In Kahn v. Lynch Communication Systems, Inc., the Delaware Supreme Court . . . saw the controlling stockholder as the 800-pound gorilla whose urgent hunger for the rest of the bananas is likely to frighten less powerful primates like putatively independent directors who might well have been hand-picked by the gorilla (and who at the very least owed their seats on the board to his support).[17]

The Court also expressed concern that minority stockholders would fear retribution from the gorilla if they defeated the merger and he did not get his way. This inherent coercion was felt to exist even when the controlling stockholder had not threatened to take any action adverse to the minority in the event that the merger was voted down and thus was viewed as undermining genuinely free choice by the minority stockholders. . . .

4. The second strand of cases involves tender offers made by controlling stockholders — i.e., the kind of transaction Unocal has proposed. . . . [T]his way of proceeding is different from the negotiated merger approach in an important way: neither the tender offer nor the short-form merger requires any action by the subsidiary's board of directors. . . . And, by the explicit terms of §253, the short-form merger can be effected by the controlling stockholder itself, [which under Glassman]was not reviewable in an action claiming unfair dealing, and that, absent fraud or misleading or inadequate disclosures, could be contested only in an appraisal proceeding that focused solely on the adequacy of the price paid. . . .

Because no consent or involvement of the target board is statutorily mandated for tender offers, our courts have recognized that "[i]n the case of totally voluntary tender offers . . . courts do not impose any right of the shareholders to receive a particular price. Delaware law recognizes that, as to allegedly voluntary tender offers (in contrast to cash-out mergers), the determinative factors as to

---

17. In this regard, Lynch is premised on a less trusting view of independent directors than is reflected in the important case of Aronson v. Lewis, 473 A.2d 805 (Del. 1984), which presumed that a majority of independent directors can impartially decide whether to sue a controlling stockholder.

voluntariness are whether coercion is present, or whether there are materially false or misleading disclosures made to stockholders in connection with the offer."[24] In two recent cases, this court has followed *Solomon*'s articulation of the standards applicable to a tender offer, and held that the "Delaware law does not impose a duty of entire fairness on controlling stockholders making a non-coercive tender or exchange offer to acquire shares directly from the minority holders."[25]

The differences between this approach, which I will identify with the *Solomon* line of cases, and that of *Lynch* are stark. To begin with, the controlling stockholder is said to have no duty to pay a fair price, irrespective of its power over the subsidiary. Even more striking is the different manner in which the coercion concept is deployed. In the tender offer context addressed by *Solomon* and its progeny, coercion is defined in the more traditional sense as a wrongful threat that has the effect of forcing stockholders to tender at the wrong price to avoid an even worse fate later on, a type of coercion I will call structural coercion. The inherent coercion that *Lynch* found to exist when controlling stockholders seek to acquire the minority's stake is not even a cognizable concern for the common law of corporations if the tender offer method is employed.

This latter point is illustrated by those cases that squarely hold that a tender is not actionably coercive if the majority stockholder decides to: (i) condition the closing of the tender offer on support of a majority of the minority and (ii) promise that it would consummate a short-form merger on the same terms as the tender offer.[27] In those circumstances, at least, these cases can be read to bar a claim against the majority stockholder even if the price offered is below what would be considered fair in an entire fairness hearing ("fair price") or an appraisal action ("fair value"). That is, in the tender offer context, our courts consider it sufficient protection against coercion to give effective veto power over the offer to a majority of the minority.[28] Yet that very same protection is considered insufficient to displace fairness review in the negotiated merger context.

5. . . . I begin by discussing whether the mere fact that one type of transaction is a tender offer and the other is a negotiated merger is a sustainable basis for the divergent policy choices made in *Lynch* and *Solomon*? Aspects of this issue are reminiscent of a prominent debate that roared in the 1980s when hostile takeover bids first became commonplace. During that period, one school of thought argued vigorously that target boards of directors should not interfere with the individual decisions of stockholders as to whether to sell shares into a tender offer made by a third-party acquirer. The ability of stockholders to alienate their shares freely was viewed as an important property right that could not be thwarted by the target company's board of directors. In support of this argument, it was noted that the Delaware General Corporation Law provided no requirement for target boards to approve tender offers made to their stockholders, let alone any explicit authority to block such offers. The statute's failure to mention tender offers was argued to be an

24. Solomon v. Pathe Communications Corp., 672 A.2d 35, 39 (Del. 1996) (citations and quotations omitted).

25. In re Aquila Inc., 805 A.2d 184, 2002 WL 27815, at *5 (Del. Ch. Jan. 3, 2002); In re Siliconix Inc. S'holders Litig., 2001 WL 716787, *6 (Del. Ch. June 21, 2001) ("unless coercion or disclosure violations can be shown, no defendant has the duty to demonstrate the entire fairness of this proposed tender transaction"). . . .

27. See, e.g., In re Aquila Inc., 2002 Del. Ch. Lexis 5, at *8-*9 (Del. Ch. Jan. 3, 2002).

28. See, e.g., *Siliconix*, 2001 WL 716787 at *8.

expression of legislative intent that should be respected by allowing tender offers to proceed without target board interposition. . . .

Many important aspects to that debate remain open for argument. At least one component of that debate, however, has been firmly decided, which is that the mere fact that the DGCL contemplates no role for target boards in tender offers does not, of itself, prevent a target board from impeding the consummation of a tender offer through extraordinary defensive measures, such as a poison pill, subject to a heightened form of reasonableness review under the so-called *Unocal* standard. Indeed, our case law went a step further — it described as an affirmative duty the role of a board of directors whose stockholders had received a tender offer: "[T]he board's power to act derives from its fundamental duty and obligation to protect the corporate enterprise, which includes stockholders, from harm reasonably perceived, *irrespective of its source.* Thus, we are satisfied that in the broad context of corporate governance, including issues of fundamental corporate change, a board of directors is not a passive instrumentality." . . .

What is clear . . . is that Delaware law has not regarded tender offers as involving a special transactional space, from which directors are altogether excluded from exercising substantial authority. To the contrary, much Delaware jurisprudence during the last twenty years has dealt with whether directors acting within that space comported themselves consistently with their duties of loyalty and care. It therefore is by no means obvious that simply because a controlling stockholder proceeds by way of a tender offer that either it or the target's directors fall outside the constraints of fiduciary duty law. . . .

6. Because tender offers are not treated exceptionally in the third-party context, it is important to ask why the tender offer method should be consequential in formulating the equitable standards of fiduciary conduct by which courts review acquisition proposals made by controlling stockholders. Is there reason to believe that the tender offer method of acquisition is more protective of the minority, with the result that less scrutiny is required than of negotiated mergers with controlling stockholders?

Unocal's answer to that question is yes and primarily rests on an inarguable proposition: in a negotiated merger involving a controlling stockholder, the controlling stockholder is on both sides of the transaction. That is, the negotiated merger is a self-dealing transaction, whereas in a tender offer, the controlling stockholder is only on the offering side and the minority remain free not to sell.

As a formal matter, this distinction is difficult to contest. When examined more deeply, however, it is not a wall that can bear the full weight of the *Lynch/Solomon* distinction. In this regard, it is important to remember that the overriding concern of *Lynch* is that controlling shareholders have the ability to take retributive action in the wake of rejection by an independent board, a special committee, or the minority shareholders. That ability is so influential that the usual cleansing devices that obviate fairness review of interested transactions cannot be trusted.

The problem is that nothing about the tender offer method of corporate acquisition makes the 800-pound gorilla's retributive capabilities less daunting to minority stockholders. Indeed, many commentators would argue that the tender offer form is more coercive than a merger vote. In a merger vote, stockholders can vote no and still receive the transactional consideration if the merger prevails. In a tender offer, however, a non-tendering shareholder individually faces an uncertain fate. That stockholder could be one of the few who holds out, leaving herself in an even more thinly traded stock with little hope of liquidity and subject to a §253 merger at a lower price or at the same price but at a later (and, given the time value of money, a less valuable) time. The 14D-9 warned Pure's minority stockholders of just this possibility. . . .

Furthermore, the common law of corporations has long had a structural answer to the formal self-dealing point Unocal makes: a non-waivable majority of the minority vote condition to a merger. By this technique, the ability of the controlling stockholder to both offer and accept is taken away, and the sell-side decision-making authority is given to the minority stockholders. That method of proceeding replicates the tender offer made by Unocal here, with the advantage of not distorting the stockholders' vote on price adequacy in the way that a tendering decision arguably does.

Lynch, of course, held that a majority of the minority vote provision will not displace entire fairness review with business judgment rule review. Critically, the *Lynch* Court's distrust of the majority of the minority provision is grounded in a concern that also exists in the tender offer context. The basis for the distrust is the concern that before the fact (*"ex ante"*) minority stockholders will fear retribution after the fact (*"ex post"*) if they vote no — i.e., they will face inherent coercion — thus rendering the majority of the minority condition an inadequate guarantee of fairness. But if this concern is valid, then that same inherent coercion would seem to apply with equal force to the tender offer decision-making process, and be enhanced by the unique features of that process. A controlling stockholder's power to force a squeeze-out or cut dividends is no different after the failure of a tender offer than after defeat on a merger vote . . .

For these and other reasons that time constraints preclude me from explicating, I remain less than satisfied that there is a justifiable basis for the distinction between the *Lynch* and *Solomon* lines of cases. Instead, their disparate teachings reflect a difference in policy emphasis that is far greater than can be explained by the technical differences between tender offers and negotiated mergers, especially given Delaware's director-centered approach to tender offers made by third parties, which emphasizes the vulnerability of disaggregated stockholders absent important help and protection from their directors.

7. The absence of convincing reasons for this disparity in treatment inspires the plaintiffs to urge me to apply the entire fairness standard of review to Unocal's offer. Otherwise, they say, the important protections set forth in the *Lynch* line of cases will be rendered useless, as all controlling stockholders will simply choose to proceed to make subsidiary acquisitions by way of a tender offer and later short-form merger.

I admit being troubled by the imbalance in Delaware law exposed by the *Solomon/Lynch* lines of cases. Under *Solomon*, the policy emphasis is on the right of willing buyers and sellers of stock to deal with each other freely, with only such judicial intervention as is necessary to ensure fair disclosure and to prevent structural coercion. The advantage of this emphasis is that it provides a relatively non-litigious way to effect going private transactions and relies upon minority stockholders to protect themselves. The cost of this approach is that it arguably exposes minority stockholders to the more subtle form of coercion that *Lynch* addresses and leaves them without adequate redress for unfairly timed and priced offers. The approach also minimizes the potential for the minority to get the best price, by arguably giving them only enough protection to keep them from being structurally coerced into accepting grossly insufficient bids but not necessarily merely inadequate ones.

Admittedly, the *Solomon* policy choice would be less disquieting if Delaware also took the same approach to third-party offers and thereby allowed diversified investors the same degree of unrestrained access to premium bids by third parties. In its brief, Unocal makes a brave effort to explain why it is understandable that Delaware law emphasizes the rights of minority stockholders to freely receive structurally, non-coercive tender offers from controlling stockholders but not their right to accept identically structured offers from third parties. Although there may be subtle ways to explain this variance, a forest-eye summary by a stockholder advocate might run as follows: As a general matter, Delaware law permits directors substantial leeway to block the access of stockholders to receive substantial premium tender offers made by third parties by use of the poison pill but provides relatively free access to minority stockholders to accept buy-out offers from controlling stockholders.

In the case of third-party offers, these advocates would note, there is arguably less need to protect stockholders indefinitely from structurally non-coercive bids because alternative buyers can emerge and because the target board can use the poison pill to buy time and to tell its story. By contrast, when a controlling stockholder makes a tender offer, the subsidiary board is unlikely — as this case demonstrates — to be permitted by the controlling stockholder to employ a poison pill to fend off the bid and exert pressure for a price increase and usually lacks any real clout to develop an alternative transaction. In the end, however, I do not believe that these discrepancies should lead to an expansion of the *Lynch* standard to controlling stockholder tender offers.

Instead, the preferable policy choice is to continue to adhere to the more flexible and less constraining *Solomon* approach, while giving some greater recognition to the inherent coercion and structural bias concerns that motivate the *Lynch* line of cases. Adherence to the *Solomon* rubric as a general matter, moreover, is advisable in view of the increased activism of institutional investors and the greater information flows available to them. Investors have demonstrated themselves capable of resisting tender offers made by controlling stockholders on occasion, and even the lead plaintiff here expresses no fear of retribution. This does not mean that controlling stockholder tender offers do not pose risks to minority stockholders; it is only to acknowledge that the corporate law should not be designed on the assumption that diversified investors are infirm but instead should give great deference to transactions approved by them voluntarily and knowledgeably.

To the extent that my decision to adhere to *Solomon* causes some discordance between the treatment of similar transactions to persist, that lack of harmony is better addressed in the *Lynch* line, by affording greater liability-immunizing effect to protective devices such as majority of minority approval conditions and special committee negotiation and approval.[43]

8. To be more specific about the application of *Solomon* in these circumstances, it is important to note that the *Solomon* line of cases does not eliminate the fiduciary

---

43. A slight easing of the *Lynch* rule would help level the litigation risks posed by the different acquisition methods, and thereby provide an incentive to use the negotiated merger route. At the very least, this tailoring could include providing business judgment protection to mergers negotiated by a special committee and subject to majority of the minority protection. This dual method of protection would replicate the third-party merger process under 8 Del. C. §251.

duties of controlling stockholders or target boards in connection with tender offers made by controlling stockholders. Rather, the question is the contextual extent and nature of those duties, a question I will now tentatively,[44] and incompletely, answer.

The potential for coercion and unfairness posed by controlling stockholders who seek to acquire the balance of the company's shares by acquisition requires some equitable reinforcement, in order to give proper effect to the concerns undergirding *Lynch.* In order to address the prisoner's dilemma problem, our law should consider an acquisition tender offer by a controlling stockholder non-coercive only when: 1) it is subject to a non-waivable majority of the minority tender condition; 2) the controlling stockholder promises to consummate a prompt §253 merger at the same price if it obtains more than 90% of the shares; and 3) the controlling stockholder has made no retributive threats.[45] Those protections — also stressed in this court's recent *Aquila* decision — minimize the distorting influence of the tendering process on voluntary choice. They also recognize the adverse conditions that confront stockholders who find themselves owning what have become very thinly traded shares. These conditions also provide a partial cure to the disaggregation problem, by providing a realistic non-tendering goal the minority can achieve to prevent the offer from proceeding altogether.

The informational and timing advantages possessed by controlling stockholders also require some countervailing protection if the minority is to truly be afforded the opportunity to make an informed, voluntary tender decision. In this regard, the majority stockholder owes a duty to permit the independent directors on the target board both free rein and adequate time to react to the tender offer, by (at the very least) hiring their own advisors, providing the minority with a recommendation as to the advisability of the offer, and disclosing adequate information for the minority to make an informed judgment. For their part, the independent directors have a duty to undertake these tasks in good faith and diligently, and to pursue the best interests of the minority.

When a tender offer is non-coercive in the sense I have identified and the independent directors of the target are permitted to make an informed recommendation and provide fair disclosure, the law should be chary about superimposing the full fiduciary requirement of entire fairness upon the statutory tender offer process. Here, the plaintiffs argue that the Pure board breached its fiduciary duties by not giving the Special Committee the power to block the Offer by, among other means, deploying a poison pill. Indeed, the plaintiffs argue that the full board's decision not to grant that authority is subject to the entire fairness standard of review because a majority of the full board was not independent of Unocal.

That argument has some analytical and normative appeal, embodying as it does the rough fairness of the goose and gander rule.[49] I am reluctant, however,

---

44. As befits the development of the common law in expedited decisions.

45. One can conceive of other non-coercive approaches, including a tender offer that was accompanied by a separate question that asked the stockholders whether they wished the offer to proceed. If a majority of the minority had to answer this question yes for the offer to proceed, stockholders could tender their shares but remain free to express an undistorted choice on the adequacy of the offer.

49. Management-side lawyers must view this case, and the recent *Digex* case, see In re Digex Inc. S'holders Litig., 789 A.2d 1176 (Del. Ch. 2000), as boomerangs. Decades after their invention, tools designed to help management stay in place are now being wielded by minority stockholders. I note that the current situation can be distinguished from *Digex* insofar as in that case the controlling stockholder forced the subsidiary board to take action only beneficial to it, whereas here the Pure board simply did not interpose itself between Unocal's Offer and the Pure minority.

to burden the common law of corporations with a new rule that would tend to compel the use of a device that our statutory law only obliquely sanctions and that in other contexts is subject to misuse, especially when used to block a high value bid that is not structurally coercive. When a controlling stockholder makes a tender offer that is not coercive in the sense I have articulated, therefore, the better rule is that there is no duty on its part to permit the target board to block the bid through use of the pill. Nor is there any duty on the part of the independent directors to seek blocking power.[50] But it is important to be mindful of one of the reasons that make a contrary rule problematic—the awkwardness of a legal rule requiring a board to take aggressive action against a structurally non-coercive offer by the controlling stockholder that elects it. This recognition of the sociology of controlled subsidiaries puts a point on the increased vulnerability that stockholders face from controlling stockholder tenders, because the minority stockholders are denied the full range of protection offered by boards in response to third-party offers. This factor illustrates the utility of the protective conditions that I have identified as necessary to prevent abuse of the minority.

9. Turning specifically to Unocal's Offer, I conclude that the application of these principles yields the following result. The Offer, in its present form, is coercive because it includes within the definition of the "minority" those stockholders who are affiliated with Unocal as directors and officers. It also includes the management of Pure, whose incentives are skewed by their employment, their severance agreements, and their Put Agreements. This is, of course, a problem that can be cured if Unocal amends the Offer to condition it on approval of a majority of Pure's unaffiliated stockholders. . . . Aside, however, from this glitch in the majority of the minority condition, I conclude that Unocal's Offer satisfies the other requirements of "non-coerciveness." Its promise to consummate a prompt §253 merger is sufficiently specific,[51] and Unocal has made no retributive threats. . . .

---

1. *Appraisal versus class remedies.* Despite *Pure Resources'* efforts to provide most of the same protection to minority shareholders in freeze-out tender offers and freeze-out mergers, one important difference remains: in a freeze-out merger that meets *Weinberger's* fair dealing standard, minority shareholders still have the equivalent of a class appraisal remedy, while in a freeze-out tender offer that meets *Pure Resources'* non-coercion criteria, formal appraisal is exclusive. As a result, the incentive for a controlling shareholder to make a low-priced tender offer still remains.

2. *An alternative approach to harmonization.* Ronald J. Gilson & Jeffrey Gordon, Controlling Controlling Shareholders, 152 U. Pa. L. Rev. 785 (2003), advocate a different approach to harmonizing the treatment of freeze-out mergers and freeze-out tender offers.

---

50. If our law trusts stockholders to protect themselves in the case of a controlling stockholder tender offer that has the characteristics I have described, this will obviously be remembered by advocates in cases involving defenses against similarly non-coercive third-party tender offers.

51. A note is in order here. I believe Unocal's statement of intent to be sufficiently clear as to expose it to potential liability in the event that it were to obtain 90% and not consummate the short-form merger at the same price (*e.g.*, if it made the exchange ratio in the short-form merger less favorable). The promise of equal treatment in short-form merger is what renders the tender decision less distorting.

We find the choice between reconsideration of *Kahn I* and reconsideration of the extension of *Solomon* to freeze outs a close question. In the end, the weight of the considerations on both sides leads us to prefer a hybrid approach that involves reconsideration of both *Kahn I* and *Solomon*. We share the *Pure* court's conclusion that a fully empowered special committee, including the *Pure* litany and the right to say no, is sufficient process that entire fairness review in a freeze out merger can be eliminated. Where independent directors have the power to block a freeze out merger, it is fair to assume that the process sufficiently tracks an arm's length negotiation that shareholders are fairly relegated to their appraisal remedy. To this extent we favor revisiting *Kahn I*.

But what if the special committee rejects the proposed freeze out merger, and the controlling shareholder goes over the committee's head, as in *Siliconix?* This is where the Chancery Court's extension of *Solomon* to freeze out tender offers also should be reconsidered. If the controlling shareholder seeks to override the special committee's veto, the process no longer matches an arm's length transaction: the minority shareholders lose the protection of its bargaining agent and, unlike in a hostile tender offer, the protection of the market for corporate control is not available. Under these circumstances, the transaction remains a *Sinclair*-like interested transaction, and entire fairness protection is appropriate (meaning here, "fair price"). . . . One particular advantage of this hybrid approach is that it strengthens the bargaining position of the special committee by giving its "say no" power more bite. As the special committee's "threat point"[76] shifts from statutory appraisal to class-based appraisal, the conditions of arm's length bargaining are more nearly replicated. This should appeal to the concerns that animate both the *Kahn* court and the *Pure* court. In summary, this dual reconsideration means that if the *Pure* litany is met and the special committee with the power to "say no" approves, then the business judgment rule applies to the freeze out transaction and minority shareholders are limited to statutory appraisal. If the controlling shareholder chooses to go forward without the special committee's approval, then the transaction is subject to entire fairness review, and minority shareholders have a class based appraisal remedy.

In In re Cox Communications, Inc. Shareholders Litigation, 879 A.2d 604 (Del. Ch. 2005), the Vice Chancellor recommended the foregoing solution to the Delaware Supreme Court. For an interesting empirical examination of the differences in standards for freeze-out mergers and freeze-out tender offers, see Guhan Subramanian, Post-*Siliconix* Freeze-Outs: Theory and Evidence, 36 J. Legal Stud. 1 (2007).

G. STATE TAKEOVER REGULATION

The first state takeover statute was enacted by Virginia in 1968, several months before the Williams Act was adopted. By 1994, 41 states had enacted some form of statute regulating takeovers and most states had at least three variants.[77] Although these statutes vary considerably in terms of the severity of the regulatory burden they impose, all tilt the balance of advantage in favor of the target corporation. The

---

76. That is, the consequence to the controller of the special committee's non-agreement. — ED.
77. These statutes are catalogued in Investor Responsibility Research Center, State Takeover Laws (looseleaf).

driving force behind them appears to have been factors outside corporate law: both (1) the fear that an acquiring corporation might close local plants or order layoffs, steps that arguably increase efficiency and benefit shareholders (most of whom live outside the state anyway) but do little for the local economy (and local voters); and (2) the tendency for target corporations to have greater local political clout than larger, but more distant, bidders.

The early statutes directly regulated the tender offer process, often imposing a difference in timing from the Williams Act, and often requiring the approval of a state official before a tender offer could go forward. The result was a rare moment in corporate law when debate over business transactions took on constitutional significance.

In Edgar v. MITE Corp., 457 U.S. 624 (1982), the United States Supreme Court considered a challenge to the Illinois Business Take-over Act under the Supremacy Clause and the Commerce Clause. The Illinois statute covered a takeover offer for a company if either (i) 10 percent of its shares were owned by Illinois residents or (ii) if any two of three conditions were met: the company had its principal executive offices in Illinois, was incorporated in Illinois, or had 10 percent of its stated capital and paid-in surplus in Illinois.

If an offer was covered, it had to be filed with the Illinois Secretary of State. The offer could go forward 20 days after filing unless the Secretary independently required a hearing or a hearing was requested by a majority of the target company's outside directors or by Illinois shareholders who owned 10 percent of the class of securities at which the offer was directed. If a hearing was held, the Secretary was required to block the offer if the offeror did not provide full disclosure or if the offer was "inequitable or would work a fraud or deceit upon the offerees." Id. at 627.

Justice White's opinion was able to command a majority only for the conclusion that the Illinois statute violated the Commerce Clause because, in addition to protecting Illinois residents, the statute also regulated offers made to shareholders who were not Illinois residents and to corporations that were not incorporated in Illinois. The Court thus concluded that "the Illinois Act imposes a substantial burden on interstate commerce which outweighs its putative local benefits." Id. at 646.

Within four years after *MITE*, 21 states had adopted "second-generation" take-over statutes,[78] which generally apply only to corporations incorporated within the jurisdiction, and in some cases only if certain other contacts with the state are also present. None empower a state agency to review the proposed transaction for fairness (an infirmity that the Supreme Court emphasized in *MITE*), although some do permit review by a state agency for full disclosure. Many of these statutes were passed in response to a specific takeover aimed at a popular (or politically powerful) local corporation. Some commentators have suggested that it is easier for a threatened target corporation to lobby its state legislature for protection than to obtain it through a charter amendment from its own shareholders. See Roberta Romano, The Political Economy of State Takeover Statutes, 73 Va. L. Rev. 111 (1987).

---

78. Roberta Romano, The Political Economy of Takeover Statutes, 73 Va. L. Rev. 111, 114 (1987).

Basically, these second-generation statutes can be grouped under five headings:

1. **"Control Share Acquisition" Statutes.** These require a shareholder vote approving the "acquisition of control" by any person and apply only to Ohio corporations. The prototype of these statutes is the Ohio statute, Ohio Gen. Corp. Law §1701.831 (2003), which requires that a "disinterested" majority approve the transaction, and the quorum for this vote consists of a majority of all disinterested shares (shares held by the bidder are not considered "disinterested"). "Acquisition of control" is defined so that such a shareholder vote is required before a tender offer for, or open market or privately negotiated purchase of, shares above specified levels: 20 percent, 33^1/$_3$ percent, and 50 percent. A corporation may, however, "opt out" of the statute if its charter or bylaws so provide. Several other states followed the Ohio model,[79] and Indiana adopted a significant variation under which the bidder may cross the "control share acquisition" threshold, but automatically loses its voting rights unless and until voting rights are granted to the bidder's shares by a majority vote of all shares owned by neither the bidder nor an officer of the target corporation. See Ind. Bus. Corp. Law §23-1-42 (2005).

2. **"Fair Price" Statutes.** Maryland adopted the prototype for this form of statute, which is today a popular form of shark repellent, Md. Gen. Corp. Law §§3-601-3-603 (1999). Directed against the two-tier takeover, it regulates the "second-step" merger and imposes a supermajority voting requirement for mergers and similar business combinations between the corporation and an "interested shareholder" (which term is defined to include a 10 percent or greater shareholder). The supermajority vote requirement is waived, however, if the transaction meets statutory "fair price" standards. Among states that have adopted this format, the statutory definition of "fair price" varies, but all are designed to ensure that those shareholders who do not tender will receive a price in any second-step merger or related transaction that is at least as high as the highest price paid for target shares by the "interested shareholder" over a recent period (typically, two years). When these "fair price" standards are not met, the statute may provide, for example, that an 80 percent vote of all outstanding shares *plus* a two-thirds vote of all disinterested shares are required. In essence, "fair price" statutes do nothing that could not also be done in most jurisdictions by a "fair price" charter provision (see page 950 supra), but they spare the corporation (or at least target management) the cost and difficulty of securing passage of such an amendment, particularly in an era when institutional investors tend to resist them.

3. **Moratorium Statutes.** This type of statute, which New York pioneered, also has been adopted by a large number of states. It prohibits corporations incorporated in the jurisdiction from engaging in a "business combination" (which term includes a merger, liquidation, or sale of substantial assets) for a specified period (five years in New York, three years in Delaware) after any shareholder acquires more than a specified ownership threshold (20 percent in New York, 15 percent in

---

79. See also Haw. Bus. Corp. Act §§171-172 (1985); Minn. Bus. Corp. Act §301A 671 (1988); Mo. Gen. & Bus. Corp. Law §351.407 (1987). Prior to the *CTS* decision (page 1132 infra), most of these statutes were invalidated based largely on parts of Justice White's opinion in *MITE* that did not command a majority of the Court. See Fleet Aerospace Corporation v. Holderman, 796 F.2d 135 (6th Cir. 1986) (Ohio); Terry v. Yamashita, 643 F. Supp. 161 (D. Haw. 1986); APL Limited Partnership v. Van Dusen Air, 622 F. Supp. 1216 (D. Minn. 1985); Icahn v. Blunt, 612 F. Supp. 1400 (W.D. Mo. 1985). It remains uncertain whether the decision in *CTS* would protect all of these statutes.

Delaware) of its voting stock, unless the board of directors approved in advance the acquisition of shares in excess of that threshold.[80] Under the New York statute, any business combination after the five-year period must still meet "fair price" criteria. In addition, it provides that no business combination is ever permitted if a 20 percent shareholder purchases additional stock beyond the 20 percent level, unless those shares are purchased at a statutory fair price or according to statutory procedure that is designed to share the control premium; in effect, "creeping control" acquisitions are barred. The term "business combination" is defined expansively to include liquidations and any self-dealing transactions with an interested shareholder, as well as mergers and similar transactions. Disinterested shareholders may vote to opt out, and the New York statute applies only if a New York corporation has 10 percent of its beneficial shareholders, significant business operations, and principal executive offices located in New York.

Obviously, such a statute (and most "fair price" statutes as well) does not prevent passage of control. The statute's real aim is to chill "junk bond" — financed "bust-up" takeovers in which the bidder repays its acquisition indebtedness by selling target assets to repay debt or to realize a "bust-up" gain. Because a hostile bidder cannot undertake such transactions for five years under the New York statute, "bust-up" takeovers, defined broadly, are discouraged, while takeovers in which the bidder plans to operate the target as a continuing entity without significant asset sales are less affected.

Delaware has adopted a weaker variant of the New York statute, which basically bars business combinations between a Delaware corporation and an "interested shareholder" (defined essentially to mean any shareholder who owns 15 percent or more of the corporation's outstanding voting stock and its affiliates) for three years following any crossing of the 15 percent threshold that was not approved in advance by the target's board:

Delaware General Corporation Law (1988)

Sec. 203. *Business combinations with interested stockholders.* (a) Notwithstanding any other provisions of this chapter, a corporation shall not engage in any business combination with any interested stockholder for a period of 3 years following the date that such stockholder became an interested stockholder unless (1) prior to such date the board of directors of the corporation approved either the business combination or the transaction which resulted in the stockholder becoming an interested stockholder or (2) upon consummation of the transaction which resulted in the stockholder becoming an interested stockholder, the interested stockholder owned at least 85% of the voting stock of the corporation outstanding at the time the transaction commenced, excluding for purposes of determining the number of shares outstanding those shares owned (i) by persons who are directors and also officers and (ii) employee stock plans in which employee participants do not have the right to determine confidentially whether shares held subject to the plan will be tendered in a tender or exchange offer, or (3) on or subsequent to such date the business combination is approved by the board of directors and

---

80. See N.Y. Bus. Corp. Law §912 (1985); Del. Gen. Corp. Law §203 (1988); N.J. Bus. Corp. Act §14A: 10A-4 (1986); Ky. Bus. Corp. Act §271A.397 (1988); and Ind. Gen. Corp. Act §23-1-43-18 (1986).

authorized at an annual or special meeting of stockholders, and not by written consent, by the affirmative vote of at least 66 ²/₃% of the outstanding voting stock which is not owned by the interested stockholder.

Section 203 contains several important exceptions that are likely to affect the planning of acquisition transactions: First, it does not apply if the bidder can acquire 85 percent of the outstanding voting stock in the same transaction in which the bidder crosses the 15 percent threshold (on the apparent premise that this level of unity implies a lack of coercion) or if the bidder can thereafter secure a two-thirds vote from the remaining shareholders (other than itself). Obviously, the 85 percent exclusion chills partial bids and low-premium takeovers. The two-thirds vote exception may have a more curious and even paradoxical impact, because the more successful a bidder is, the greater will be the voting power of the intransigent minority that does not tender. Suppose, for example, that a bidder acquires 80 percent of the voting stock (thus failing to come within the 85 percent exemption in §203(a)(2)). Now, it must secure a two-thirds vote from this remaining 20 percent if it is to escape the three-year moratorium. Thus, if either 66 ²/₃ percent is owned by former management and its allies or if that percentage simply does not vote (or votes against the proposed business combination), the §203(a)(3) exception is not satisfied. Potentially, this could create an incentive to make a partial bid for only 50 percent (if the bidder is uncertain about its ability to acquire 85 percent and it fears falling just short of that level). Alternatively, the bidder could protect itself by specifying a minimum tender condition to its obligation to purchase (i.e., that 85 percent or more of the shares must be tendered).

Unlike the New York statute, which bars *any* substantial sales of assets or merger for five years after the threshold is crossed without prior approval, the Delaware statute defines the term "business combination" narrowly in §203(c)(3) to cover only transactions between the target and the bidder or its affiliates. Thus, a takeover entrepreneur could still seek to acquire control of a company having a liquidation value substantially in excess of its stock market value in order to sell those assets — either piecemeal or in a single sale — to others, and it could then pay out the proceeds of this sale as a pro rata dividend to all remaining shareholders. Although the Delaware statute thus does not end the incentive for "bust-up" takeovers, its coverage is extraordinarily broad. It has been estimated that the passage of the Delaware statute by itself extended the protective mantle of a state takeover statute to 80 percent of the business capital in the United States from a prior level of 20 percent. See Bandow, Curbing Raiders is Bad for Business, N.Y. Times (Feb. 7, 1988), at F-2.

4. "Redemption Rights" Statutes. Pennsylvania had adopted an anti-takeover statute that essentially expands the traditional appraisal statute to cover "controlling share acquisitions" as well as mergers.[81] Under the Pennsylvania statute, once a person acquires 30 percent of a firm's stock, other shareholders are entitled to receive, on demand, from the acquirer an amount in cash equal to the "fair value" of their stock in the target; moreover, in determining this figure, the court is instructed to include a pro rata share of the control premium paid for the

---

81. Pa. Bus. Corp. Law §2546 (1988).

first-step acquisition. A similar statute has been adopted in Maine.[82] The effect of such a statute is to chill partial bids by requiring that the bidder be in a position to buy all shares that are tendered. This form of statute in effect achieves results similar to those from the British system, which bars partial bids unless they are first approved by the shareholders, but it also creates much greater uncertainty for the bidder.

5. "Constituency" Statutes. A large number of states have adopted provisions authorizing or instructing directors to consider the interests of non-shareholder constituencies, including employees, creditors, customers, and local communities. See, e.g., Ohio Gen. Corp. Law §1701.59 (1999).[83] The impact of these statutes on actual takeover contests is uncertain, although they may lead a court to tolerate conduct that it would otherwise enjoin as a breach of the board's fiduciary duty to the shareholders. The American Bar Association's Committee on Corporate Laws "believes that the better interpretation of these statutes . . . is that they confirm what the common law has always been: directors may take into account the interests of other constituencies but only as and to the extent that the directors are acting in the best interests . . . of the shareholders and the corporation." Pennsylvania's version is explicitly to the contrary in that directors are explicitly instructed that the interests of no particular group, including shareholders, are controlling. 15 Pa. Cons. Stat. §1715 (1990).

In overview, the common denominator in this second generation of antitakeover statutes is that most seek to utilize traditional areas of corporate governance (e.g., voting rights, appraisal rights, and law applicable to mergers) to regulate tender offers. The constitutionality of statutes that utilized state corporation law to create takeover barriers was considered in the following case.

CTS Corp. v. Dynamics Corp. of America
481 U.S. 69 (1987)

JUSTICE POWELL delivered the opinion of the Court.

This case presents the questions whether the Control Share Acquisitions Chapter of the Indiana Business Corporation Law, Ind. Code §23-1-42-1 et seq. (Supp. 1986), is preempted by the Williams Act . . . or violates the Commerce Clause of the Federal Constitution, Art. I, §8, cl. 3.

. . . [The Act applies to any corporation incorporated in Indiana, unless the corporation amends its articles of incorporation or bylaws to opt out of the Act]. The Act applies only to "issuing public corporations." The term "corporation" includes only businesses incorporated in Indiana. See §23-1-20-5. An "issuing public corporation" is defined as:

> a corporation that has:
> (1) one hundred (100) or more shareholders;
> (2) its principal place of business, its principal office, or substantial assets within Indiana; and
> (3) either:

---

82. See Me. Bus. Corp. Act §910 (1986).
83. See also Me. Rev. Stat. Ann. 13-C §831 (2007); N.Y. Bus. Corp. Law §717 (1989); N.J. Stat. Ann. §14A:6-14 (1989).

(A) more than ten percent (10%) of its shareholders resident in Indiana;
(B) more than ten percent (10%) of its shares owned by Indiana residents; or
(C) ten thousand (10,000) shareholders resident in Indiana.

§23-1-42-4(a).

The Act focuses on the acquisition of "control shares" in an issuing public corporation. Under the Act, an entity acquires "control shares" whenever it acquires shares that, but for the operation of the Act, would bring its voting power in the corporation to or above any of three thresholds: 20%, 33^1/3%, or 50%. §23-1-42-1. An entity that acquires control shares does not necessarily acquire voting rights. Rather, it gains those rights only "to the extent granted by resolution approved by the shareholders of the issuing public corporation." §23-1-42-9(a). Section 9 requires a majority vote of all disinterested[2] shareholders holding each class of stock for passage of such a resolution. §23-1-42-9(b). The practical effect of this requirement is to condition acquisition of control of a corporation on approval of a majority of the pre-existing disinterested shareholders.

The shareholders decide whether to confer rights on the control shares at the next regularly scheduled meeting of the shareholders, or at a specially scheduled meeting. The acquiror can require management of the corporation to hold such a special meeting within 50 days if it files an "acquiring person statement,"[4] requests the meeting, and agrees to pay the expenses of the meeting. See §23-1-42-7. If the shareholders do not vote to restore voting rights to the shares, the corporation may redeem the control shares from the acquiror at fair market value, but it is not required to do so. §23-1-42-10(b). Similarly, if the acquiror does not file an acquiring person statement with the corporation, the corporation may, if its bylaws or articles of incorporation so provide, redeem the shares at any time after 60 days after the acquiror's last acquisition. §23-1-42-10(a).

On March 10, 1986, appellee Dynamics Corporation of America (Dynamics) owned 9.6% of the common stock of appellant CTS Corporation, an Indiana corporation. On that day, six days after the Act went into effect, Dynamics announced a tender offer for another million shares in CTS; purchase of those shares would have brought Dynamics' ownership interest in CTS to 27.5%. . . . On March 27, the Board of Directors of CTS, an Indiana corporation, elected to be governed by the provisions of the Act, see §23-1-17-3.

---

2. "Interested shares" are shares with respect to which the acquiror, an officer or an inside director of the corporation "may exercise or direct the exercise of the voting power of the corporation in the election of directors." §23-1-42-3. If the record date passes before the acquiror purchases shares pursuant to the tender offer, the purchased shares will not be "interested shares" within the meaning of the Act; although the acquiror may own the shares on the date of the meeting, it will not "exercise . . . the voting power" of the shares.

As a practical matter, the record date usually will pass before shares change hands. Under SEC regulations, the shares cannot be purchased until 20 business days after the offer commences. 17 CFR §240.14(e)-1(a) (1986). If the acquiror seeks an early resolution of the issue — as most acquirors will — the meeting required by the Act must be held no more than 50 calendar days after the offer commences, about three weeks after the earliest date on which the shares could be purchased. See §23-1-42-7. The Act requires management to give notice of the meeting "as promptly as reasonably practicable . . . to all shareholders of record as of the record date set for the meeting." §23-1-42-8(a). It seems likely that management of the target corporation would violate this obligation if it delayed setting the record date and sending notice until after 20 business days had passed. Thus, we assume that the record date usually will be set before the date on which federal law first permits purchase of the shares.

4. An "acquiring person statement" is an information statement describing, *inter alia*, the identity of the acquiring person and the terms and extent of the proposed acquisition See §23-1-42-6.

Four days later, on March 31, Dynamics [sued in federal court and obtained a ruling that the Act was preempted by the Williams Act and violated the Commerce Clause. The court of appeals affirmed.]

The first question in this case is whether the Williams Act pre-empts the Indiana Act. As we have stated frequently, absent an explicit indication by Congress of an intent to pre-empt state law, a state statute is pre-empted only " 'where compliance with both federal and state regulations is a physical impossibility . . . ,' Florida Lime & Avocado Growers, Inc. v. Paul, 373 U.S. 132, 142-143 (1963), or where the state 'law stands as an obstacle to the accomplishment and execution of the full purposes and objectives of Congress.' Hines v. Davidowitz, 312 U.S. 52, 67 (1941). . . ." Ray v. Atlantic Richfield Co., 435 U.S. 151, 158 (1978). Because it is entirely possible for entities to comply with both the Williams Act and the Indiana Act, the state statute can be pre-empted only if it frustrates the purposes of the federal law. . . .

As the plurality opinion in *MITE* did not represent the views of a majority of the Court, we are not bound by its reasoning. We need not question that reasoning, however, because we believe the Indiana Act passes muster even under the broad interpretation of the Williams Act articulated by Justice White in *MITE*. . . . [T]he overriding concern of the *MITE* plurality was that the Illinois statute considered in that case operated to favor management against offerors, to the detriment of shareholders. By contrast, the statute now before the Court protects the independent shareholder against both of the contending parties. Thus, the Act furthers a basic purpose of the Williams Act, " 'plac[ing] investors on an equal footing with the takeover bidder,' " Piper v. Chris-Craft Industries, 430 U.S., at 30. . . .

The Indiana Act operates on the assumption, implicit in the Williams Act, that independent shareholders faced with tender offers are at a disadvantage. By allowing such shareholders to vote as a group, the Act protects them from the coercive aspects of some tender offers. If, for example, shareholders believe that a successful tender offer will be followed by a purchase of nontendering shares at a depressed price, individual shareholders may tender their shares — even if they doubt the tender offer is in the corporation's best interest — to protect themselves from being forced to sell their shares at a depressed price. As the SEC explains: "The alternative of not accepting the tender offer is virtual assurance that, if the offer is successful, the shares will have to be sold in the lower priced, second step." Two-Tier Tender Offer Pricing and Non-Tender Offer Purchase Programs, SEC Exchange Act Rel. No. 21079 (June 21, 1984), [1984 Transfer Binder] CCH Fed. Sec. L. Rep. ¶ 83,637, p.86,916 (footnote omitted) (hereinafter SEC Release No. 21079). See Lowenstein, Pruning Deadwood in Hostile Takeovers: A Proposal for Legislation, 83 Colum. L. Rev. 249, 307-309 (1983). In such a situation under the Indiana Act, the shareholders as a group, acting in the corporation's best interest, could reject the offer, although individual shareholders might be inclined to accept it. The desire of the Indiana Legislature to protect shareholders of Indiana corporations from this type of coercive offer does not conflict with the Williams Act. Rather, it furthers the federal policy of investor protection.

In implementing its goal, the Indiana Act avoids problems the plurality discussed in *MITE*. Unlike the *MITE* statute, the Indiana Act does not give either management or the offeror an advantage in communicating with the shareholders about the impending offer. The Act also does not impose an indefinite delay on tender offers. Nothing in the Act prohibits an offeror from consummating an offer on the 20th business day, the earliest day permitted under applicable federal regulations, see 17 CFR §240.14e-1(a) (1986). Not does the Act allow the state government to interpose its views of fairness between willing buyers and sellers of shares of the target company. Rather, the Act allows *shareholders* to evaluate the fairness of the offer collectively.

The Court of Appeals based its finding of pre-emption on its view that the practical effect of the Indiana Act is to delay consummation of tender offers until 50 days after the commencement of the offer. . . . As did the Court of Appeals, Dynamics reasons that no rational offeror will purchase shares until it gains assurance that those shares will carry voting rights. Because it is possible that voting rights will not be conferred until a shareholder meeting 50 days after commencement of the offer, Dynamics concludes that the Act imposes a 50-day delay. This, it argues, conflicts with the shorter 20-business-day period established by the SEC as the minimum period for which a tender offer may be held open. 17 CFR §240.14e-1 (1986). We find the alleged conflict illusory.

The Act does not impose an absolute 50-day delay on tender offers, nor does it preclude an offeror from purchasing shares as soon as federal law permits. If the offeror fears an adverse shareholder vote under the Act, it can make a conditional tender offer, offering to accept shares on the condition that the shares receive voting rights within a certain period of time. The Williams Act permits tender offers to be conditioned on the offeror's subsequently obtaining regulatory approval. . . . There is no reason to doubt that this type of conditional tender offer would be legitimate as well.

Even assuming that the Indiana Act imposes some additional delay, nothing in *MITE* suggested that *any* delay imposed by state regulation, however short, would create a conflict with the Williams Act. The plurality argued only that the offeror should "be free to go forward without *unreasonable* delay." 457 U.S., at 639 (emphasis added). In that case, the Court was confronted with the potential for indefinite delay and presented with no persuasive reason why some deadline could not be established. By contrast, the Indiana Act provides that full voting rights will be vested — if this eventually is to occur — within 50 days after commencement of the offer. This period is within the 60-day maximum period Congress established for tender offers in 15 U.S.C. §78n(d)(5). We cannot say that a delay within that congressionally determined period is unreasonable.

Finally, we note that the Williams Act would pre-empt a variety of state corporate laws of hitherto unquestioned validity if it were construed to pre-empt any state statute that may limit or delay the free exercise of power after a successful tender offer. State corporate laws commonly permit corporations to stagger the terms of their directors . . . [and thereby] delay the time when a successful offeror gains control of the board of directors. Similarly, state corporation laws commonly provide for cumulative voting . . . [, which] can delay further the ability of offerors to gain untrammeled authority over the affairs of the target corporation. . . .

In our view, the possibility that the Indiana Act will delay some tender offers is insufficient to require a conclusion that the Williams Act pre-empts the Act. The longstanding prevalence of state regulation in this area suggests that, if Congress had intended to pre-empt all state laws that delay the acquisition of voting control following a tender offer, it would have said so explicitly. The regulatory conditions that the Act places on tender offers are consistent with the text and the purposes of the Williams Act. Accordingly, we hold that the Williams Act does not pre-empt the Indiana Act.

As an alternative basis for its decision, the Court of Appeals held that the Act violates the Commerce Clause of the Federal Constitution. We now address this holding. . . .

The principal objects of dormant Commerce Clause scrutiny are statutes that discriminate against interstate commerce. See, e.g., Lewis v. BT Investment Managers, Inc., 447 U.S. 27, 36-37 (1980); Philadelphia v. New Jersey, 437 U.S. 617, 624 (1978). See generally Regan, The Supreme Court and State Protectionism: Making Sense of the Dormant Commerce Clause, 84 Mich. L. Rev. 1091 (1986). The Indiana Act is not such a statute. It has the same effects on tender offers whether or not the offeror is a domiciliary or resident of Indiana. Thus, it "visits its effects equally upon both interstate and local business," Lewis v. BT Investment Managers, Inc., supra, at 36.

Dynamics nevertheless contends that the statute is discriminatory because it will apply most often to out-of-state entities. This argument rests on the contention that, as a practical matter, most hostile tender offers are launched by offerors outside Indiana. But this argument avails Dynamics little. "The fact that the burden of a state regulation falls on some interstate companies does not, by itself, establish a claim of discrimination against interstate commerce." Exxon Corp. v. Governor of Maryland, 437 U.S. 117, 126 (1978). . . . Because nothing in the Indiana Act imposes a greater burden on out-of-state offerors than it does on similarly situated offerors, we reject the contention that the Act discriminates against interstate commerce.

This Court's recent Commerce Clause cases also have invalidated statutes that adversely may affect interstate commerce by subjecting activities to inconsistent regulations. . . . The Indiana Act poses no such problem. So long as each State regulates voting rights only in the corporations it has created, each corporation will be subject to the law of only one State. No principle of corporation law and practice is more firmly established than a State's authority to regulate domestic corporations, including the authority to define the voting rights of shareholders. See Restatement (Second) of Conflict of Laws §304 (1971) (concluding that the law of the incorporating State generally should "determine the right of a shareholder to participate in the administration of the affairs of the corporation"). Accordingly, we conclude that the Indiana Act does not create an impermissible risk of inconsistent regulation by different States.

The Court of Appeals did not find the Act unconstitutional for either of these threshold reasons. Rather, its decision rested on its view of the Act's potential to hinder tender offers. We think the Court of Appeals failed to appreciate the significance of Commerce Clause analysis of the fact that state regulation of corporate governance is regulation of entities whose very existence and attributes are a product of state law. . . .

Every State in this country has enacted laws regulating corporate governance. By prohibiting certain transactions, and regulating others, such laws necessarily affect certain aspects of interstate commerce. This necessarily is true with respect to corporations with shareholders in States other than the State of incorporation. Large corporations that are listed on national exchanges, or even regional exchanges, will have shareholders in many States and shares that are traded frequently. The markets that facilitate this national and international participation in ownership of corporations are essential for providing capital not only for new enterprises but also for established companies that need to expand their businesses. This beneficial free market system depends at its core upon the fact that a corporation — except in the rarest situations — is organized under, and governed by, the law of a single jurisdiction, traditionally the corporate law of the State of its incorporation.

These regulatory laws may affect directly a variety of corporate transactions. Mergers are a typical example. In view of the substantial effect that a merger may have on the shareholders' interests in a corporation, many States require supermajority votes to approve mergers. . . . [T]hese laws make it more difficult for corporations to merge. State laws also may provide for "dissenters rights" under which minority shareholders who disagree with corporate decisions to take particular actions are entitled to sell their shares to the corporation at fair market value. . . . [T]hese laws may inhibit a corporation from engaging in the specified transactions.[12]

It thus is an accepted part of the business landscape in this country for States to create corporations, to prescribe their powers, and to define the rights that are acquired by purchasing their shares. A State has an interest in promoting stable relationships among parties involved in the corporations it charters, as well as in ensuring that investors in such corporations have an effective voice in corporate affairs.

There can be no doubt that the Act reflects these concerns. The primary purpose of the Act is to protect the shareholders of Indiana corporations. It does this by affording shareholders, when a takeover offer is made, an opportunity to decide collectively whether the resulting change in voting control of the corporation, as they perceive it, would be desirable. A change of management may have important effects on the shareholders' interests; it is well within the State's role as overseer of corporate governance to offer this opportunity. The autonomy provided by allowing shareholders collectively to determine whether the takeover is advantageous to their interests may be especially beneficial where a hostile tender offer may coerce shareholders into tendering their shares.

Appellee Dynamics responds to this concern by arguing that the prospect of coercive tender offers is illusory, and that tender offers generally should be favored because they reallocate corporate assets into the hands of management who can use them most effectively.[13] . . . As indicated supra, Indiana's concern

---

12. Numerous other common regulations may affect both nonresident and resident shareholders of a corporation. Specified votes may be required for the sale of all of the corporation's assets. See MBCA §79; RMBCA §12.02. The election of directors may be staggered over a period of years to prevent abrupt changes in management. See MBCA §37; RMBCA §8.06. Various classes of stock may be created with differences in voting rights as to dividends and on liquidation. See MBCA §15; RMBCA §6.01(c). Provisions may be made for cumulative voting. See MBCA §33, par. 4; RMBCA §7.28; n.9, supra. Corporations may adopt restrictions on payment of dividends to ensure that specified ratios of assets to liabilities are maintained for the benefit of the holders of corporate bonds or notes. See MBCA §45 (noting that a corporation's articles of incorporation can restrict payment of dividends); RMBCA §6.40 (same). Where the shares of a corporation are held in States other than that of incorporation, actions taken pursuant to these and similar provisions of state law will affect all shareholders alike wherever they reside or are domiciled. . . .

13. It is appropriate to note when discussing the merits and demerits of tender offers that generalizations usually require qualification. No one doubts that some successful tender offers will provide more effective management or other benefits such as needed diversification. But there is no reason to *assume* that the type of conglomerate corporation that may result from repetitive takeovers necessarily will result in more effective management or otherwise be beneficial to shareholders. The divergent

with tender offers is not groundless. Indeed, the potentially coercive aspects of tender offers have been recognized by the Securities and Exchange Commission, see SEC Release No. 21079, p.86, 916, and by a number of scholarly commentators. . . . The Constitution does not require the States to subscribe to any particular economic theory. We are not inclined "to second-guess the empirical judgments of lawmakers concerning the utility of legislation," Kassel v. Consolidated Freightways Corp., 450 U.S., at 679 (BRENNAN, J., concurring in judgment). In our view, the possibility of coercion in some takeover bids offers additional justification for Indiana's decision to promote the autonomy of independent shareholders.

Dynamics argues in any event that the State has "'no legitimate interest in protecting the nonresident shareholders.'" Brief for Appellee Dynamics Corp. of America 21 (quoting Edgar v. MITE Corp., 457 U.S., at 644). Dynamics relies heavily on the statement by the *MITE* Court that "[i]nsofar as the . . . law burdens out-of-state transactions, there is nothing to be weighed in the balance to sustain the law." 457 U.S., at 644. But that comment was made in reference to an Illinois law that applied as well to out-of-state corporations as to in-state corporations. We agree that Indiana has no interest in protecting nonresident shareholders *of nonresident corporations*. But this Act applies only to corporations incorporated in Indiana. We reject the contention that Indiana has no interest in providing for the shareholders of its corporations the voting autonomy granted by the Act. Indiana has a substantial interest in preventing the corporate form from becoming a shield for unfair business dealing. Moreover, unlike the Illinois statute invalidated in *MITE*, the Indiana Act applies only to corporations that have a substantial number of shareholders in Indiana. See Ind. Code §23-1-42-4(a)(3) (Supp. 1986). Thus, every application of the Indiana Act will affect a substantial number of Indiana residents, whom Indiana indisputably has an interest in protecting.

Dynamics' argument that the Act is unconstitutional ultimately rests on its contention that the Act will limit the number of successful tender offers. There is little evidence that this will occur. But even if true, this result would not substantially affect our Commerce Clause analysis. We reiterate that this Act does not prohibit any entity — resident or nonresident — from offering to purchase, or from purchasing, shares in Indiana corporations, or from attempting thereby to gain control. It only provides regulatory procedures designed for the better protection of the corporations' shareholders. We have rejected the "notion that the Commerce Clause protects the particular structure or methods of operation in a . . . market." Exxon Corp. v. Governor of Maryland, 437 U.S., at 127. The very commodity that is traded in the securities market is one whose characteristics are defined by state law. Similarly, the very commodity that is traded in the "market for corporate control" — the corporation — is one that owes its existence and attributes to state law. Indiana need not define these commodities as other States do; it need only provide that residents and nonresidents have equal access to them. This Indiana has done. Accordingly, even if the Act should decrease the number of successful tender offers for Indiana corporations, this would not offend the Commerce Clause.

---

views in the literature — and even now being debated in the Congress — reflect the reality that the type and utility of offers vary widely. Of course, in many situations the offer to shareholders is simply a cash price substantially higher than the market price prior to the offer.

On its face, the Indiana Control Share Acquisitions Chapter evenhandedly determines the voting rights of shares of Indiana corporations. The Act does not conflict with the provisions or purposes of the Williams Act. To the limited extent that the Act affects interstate commerce, this is justified by the State's interests in defining the attributes of shares in its corporations and in protecting shareholders. Congress has never questioned the need for state regulation of these matters. Nor do we think such regulation offends the Constitution. Accordingly, we reverse the judgment of the Court of Appeals.

JUSTICE SCALIA, concurring in part and concurring in the judgment.

. . . As long as a State's corporation law governs only its own corporations and does not discriminate against out-of-state interests, it should survive this Court's scrutiny under the Commerce Clause, whether it promotes shareholder welfare or industrial stagnation. Beyond that, it is for Congress to prescribe its invalidity.

I also agree with the Court that the Indiana control shares Act is not pre-empted by the Williams Act, but I reach that conclusion without entering into the debate over the purposes of the two statutes. The Williams Act is governed by the antipre-emption provision of the Securities Exchange Act of 1934, 15 U.S.C. §78bb(a), which provides that nothing it contains "shall affect the jurisdiction of the securities commission (or any agency or officer performing like functions) of any State over any security or any person insofar as it does not conflict with the provisions of this chapter or the rules and regulations thereunder." Unless it serves no function, that language forecloses pre-emption on the basis of conflicting "purpose" as opposed to conflicting "provision." Even if it does not have literal application to the present case (because, perhaps, the Indiana agency responsible for securities matters has no enforcement responsibility with regard to this legislation), it none-theless refutes the proposition that Congress meant the Williams Act to displace *all* state laws with conflicting purpose. And if any are to survive, surely the States' corporation codes are among them. It would be peculiar to hold that Indiana could have pursued the purpose at issue here through its blue-sky laws, but cannot pursue it through the State's even more sacrosanct authority over the structure of domestic corporations. Prescribing voting rights for the governance of state chartered companies is a traditional state function with which the Federal Congress has never, to my knowledge, intentionally interfered. I would require far more evidence than is available here to find implicit pre-emption of that function by a federal statute whose provisions concededly do not conflict with the state law.

I do not share the Court's apparent high estimation of the beneficence of the state statute at issue here. But a law can be both economic folly and constitutional. The Indiana Control Shares Acquisition Chapter is at least the latter. I therefore concur in the judgment of the Court.

JUSTICE WHITE, with whom JUSTICE BLACKMUN and JUSTICE STEVENS join as to Part II, dissenting.

The majority today upholds Indiana's Control Share Acquisitions Chapter, a statute which will predictably foreclose completely some tender offers for stock in Indiana corporations. I disagree with the conclusion that the Chapter is neither pre-empted by the Williams Act nor in conflict with the Commerce Clause. The Chapter undermines the policy of the Williams Act by effectively preventing minority shareholders, in some circumstances, from acting in their own best interests by selling their stock. In addition, the Chapter will substantially burden the interstate market in corporate ownership, particularly if other States follow

Indiana's lead as many already have done. The Chapter, therefore, directly inhibits interstate commerce, the very economic consequences the Commerce Clause was intended to prevent. The opinion of the Court of Appeals is far more persuasive than that of the majority today, and the judgment of that court should be affirmed.

I. The Williams Act expressed Congress' concern that individual investors be given sufficient information so that they could make an informed choice on whether to tender their stock in response to a tender offer. The problem with the approach the majority adopts today is that it equates protection of individual investors, the focus of the Williams Act, with the protection of shareholders as a group. Indiana's Control Share Acquisitions Chapter undoubtedly helps protect the interests of a majority of the shareholders in any corporation subject to its terms, but in many instances, it will effectively prevent an individual investor from selling his stock at a premium. Indiana's statute, therefore, does not "furthe[r] the federal policy of *investor* protection," as the majority claims. . . .

The majority claims that if the Williams Act pre-empts Indiana's Control Share Acquisitions Chapter, it also pre-empts a number of other corporate-control provisions such as cumulative voting or staggering the terms of directors. But this view ignores the fundamental distinction between these other corporate-control provisions and the Chapter: unlike those other provisions, the Chapter is designed to prevent certain tender offers from ever taking place. It is transactional in nature, although it is characterized by the State as involving only the voting rights of certain shares. "[T]his Court is not bound by '[t]he name, description or characterization given [a challenged statute] by the legislature or the courts of the State,' but will determine for itself the practical impact of the law." Hughes v. Oklahoma, 441 U.S. 322, 336 (1979). The Control Share Acquisitions Chapter will effectively prevent minority shareholders in some circumstances from selling their stock to a willing tender offeror. It is the practical impact of the Chapter that leads to the conclusion that it is pre-empted by the Williams Act.

II. Given the impact of the Control Share Acquisitions Chapter, it is clear that Indiana is directly regulating the purchase and sale of shares of stock in interstate commerce. Appellant CTS's stock is traded on the New York Stock Exchange, and people from all over the country buy and sell CTS's shares daily. Yet, under Indiana's scheme, any prospective purchaser will be effectively precluded from purchasing CTS's shares if the purchaser crosses one of the Chapter's threshold ownership levels and a majority of CTS's shareholders refuse to give the purchaser voting rights. This Court should not countenance such a restraint on interstate trade.

The United States, as amicus curiae, argues that Indiana's Control Share Acquisitions Chapter "is written as a restraint on the *transferability* of voting rights in specified transactions, and it could not be written in any other way without changing its meaning. Since the restraint on the transfer of voting rights is a restraint on the transfer of shares, the Indiana Chapter, like the Illinois Act [in *MITE*], restrains 'transfers of stock by stockholders to a third party.'" Brief for Securities and Exchange Commission and United States as Amici Curiae 26. I agree. The majority ignores the practical impact of the Chapter in concluding that the Chapter does not violate the Commerce Clause. The Chapter is characterized as merely defining "the attributes of shares in its corporations." The majority sees the trees but not the forest. . . .

The State of Indiana, in its brief, admits that at least one of the Chapter's goals is to protect Indiana Corporations. The State notes that the Chapter permits shareholders "to determine . . . whether [a tender offeror] will liquidate the company or remove it from the State." Brief for Appellant in No. 86-97, p.19. The State repeats this point later in its brief: "The Statute permits shareholders (who may also be community residents or employees or suppliers of the corporation) to determine the intentions of any offeror concerning the liquidation of the company or its possible removal from the State." Id., at 90. A state law which permits a majority of an Indiana corporation's stockholders to prevent individual investors, including out-of-state stockholders, from selling their stock to an out-of-state tender offeror and thereby frustrate any transfer of corporate control, is the archetype of the kind of state law that the Commerce Clause forbids. . . .

---

1. *A third generation?* Very few public corporations will be covered by the Indiana statute upheld in *CTS*, which is limited in its application to corporations that have 10 percent of their shares or shareholders, or 10,000 shareholders, resident in Indiana. However, Del. Gen. Corp. Law §203 (page 1130 supra) applies to roughly half of the New York Stock Exchange — listed firms, which is the proportion that are incorporated in Delaware, and it requires no local contacts (other than the fact of incorporation). Is it valid under the *CTS* decision? A lingering uncertainty after *CTS* concerns how much weight the majority truly placed on one fact it emphasized in *CTS*, namely, that the Indiana statute "applies only to corporations that have a substantial number of shareholders in Indiana. . . . Thus, every application of the Indiana Act will affect a substantial number of Indiana residents, whom Indiana indisputably has an interest in protecting." 481 U.S. at 93. Elsewhere, however, the *CTS* decision hints that the court may be in the process of abandoning its traditional balancing test in Commerce Clause cases, which weighed the burden on interstate commerce "in relation to the putative local benefits." See Pike v. Bruce Church, Inc., 397 U.S. 137 (1970).

The new Delaware statute (§203) was challenged immediately after its enactment, and in three decisions the Delaware district court upheld the statute against both Commerce Clause and preemption attacks brought by hostile bidders. BNS, Inc. v. Koppers Company, Inc., 683 F. Supp. 458 (D. Del. 1988); RP Acquisition Corp. v. Staley Continental, Inc., 686 F. Supp. 476 (1988); City Capital Associates LTD v. Interco, Inc., 696 F. Supp. 1551 (1988). However, in each of these cases the court found that the preemption challenges presented serious and troubling questions and relied substantially on the exemptions under the Delaware statute (the 85 percent tender acceptance exemption and the two-thirds shareholder approval exemption) in upholding the statute. The courts agreed that any state takeover statute that had a substantial chilling effect on takeovers could avoid being preempted by the Williams Act only "so long as hostile offers that are beneficial to target shareholders have a meaningful opportunity for success." This standard of a "meaningful opportunity for success" posed a major question about the constitutionality of those moratorium-style statutes (such as N.Y. Bus. Corp. Law §912 (1998)) that do not contain any exemptions that parallel the Delaware statute.[84]

In Amanda Acquisitions Corp. v. Universal Foods Corp., 877 F.2d 496 (7th Cir.), *cert. denied*, 493 U.S. 955 (1989), Judge Easterbrook, a noted proponent of the efficiency of takeovers,[85] rejected the claim that the absence of Delaware-like exemptions rendered the Wisconsin statute unconstitutional:

> Wisconsin offers no such opportunity [as the Delaware exemptions], which Amanda believes is fatal.
>
> Even in Wisconsin, though, options remain. Defenses impenetrable to the naked eye may have some cracks. . . . [T]here are countermeasures to statutes deferring mergers. The cheapest is to lower the bid to reflect the costs of delay. . . . Or a bidder might take down the stock and pledge it (or its dividends) as security for any loans. That is, the bidder could operate the target as a subsidiary for three years. The corporate world is full of partially owned subsidiaries. . . . Many bidders would find [this strategy] unattractive because of the potential for litigation by minority investors, and the need to operate the firm as a subsidiary might foreclose savings or synergies from merger. So none of these options is a perfect substitute for immediate merger, but each is a crack in the defensive wall allowing some value-increasing bids to proceed.
>
> At the end of the day, however, it does not matter whether these countermeasures are "enough." The Commerce Clause does not demand that states leave bidders a "meaningful opportunity for success." . . . A state with the power to forbid mergers has the power to defer them for three years.

Judge Easterbrook also held that the Wisconsin statute was not preempted by the Williams Act, reading the federal statute as entirely limited to the process and terms of tender offers and leaving states free to devise corporate law that makes tender offers infeasible. Was this analysis dictated by *CTS?* Of what relevance is the fact that *CTS* upheld the Indiana statute on the ground that it "does not give either management or the offeror an advantage"?

2. *The problem of externalities in state regulation.* Are state takeover regulations different from other forms of state corporate regulation because of the potential that one state may impose burdens through such legislation on other states, while benefiting only its own residents? Potential targets tend to be smaller than bidders and are more likely to incorporate in the jurisdiction where their principal place of business is located (while larger bidders are more likely to be Delaware corporations). Given this divergence, the two populations of firms — targets and bidders — have different levels of political influence, and in some states (particularly those on the "Rust Belt," e.g., Indiana, Ohio, Minnesota, Wisconsin, Pennsylvania, etc.), target firms have secured very protective legislation. Although the "benefits" of this legislation may be felt locally as marginal firms are kept open for a longer time, the "costs" are arguably borne by shareholders, who are

---

84. Ariz. Rev. Stat. Ann. §§10-2741-2743 (1994); Del. Gen. Corp. Law §203 (2007); Ind. Gen. Corp. Act §§23-1-43-1–23-1-43-24 (1986); Ky. Bus. Corp. Act §§271B.12-200–271B.12-220 (1988); Minn. Bus. Corp. Act §302A.671 (1999); Mo. Gen. & Bus. Corp. Act §351.459 (2007); N.J. Bus. Corp. Act §14A:10A-4–10A-6 (19876). This form of statute has been preferred by many states over the Indiana "controlling share" statute because of a belief that the latter format, which entitles a 20 percent shareholder to an immediate shareholder vote, may actually facilitate acquisitions.

85. See Frank Easterbrook & Daniel Fischel, The Proper Role of a Target's Management in Responding to a Tender Offer, 96 Harv. L. Rev. 1161 (1981).

dispersed nationwide and lose takeover premiums. The thesis that state takeover legislation produces interjurisdictional subsidization and exploitation has been raised by several commentators. See Saul Levmore, Interstate Exploitation and Judicial Intervention, 69 Va. L. Rev. 563, 622-624 (1983); Ralph Winter, State Law, Shareholder Protection, and the Theory of the Corporation, 6 J. Legal Stud. 251 (1977); Roberta Romano, The Political Economy of Takeover Statutes, 73 Va. L. Rev. 111 (1983). This thesis could provide at least an economic rationale in favor of courts balancing the local benefit against the burden on interstate commerce. Would Justice Scalia in *CTS* or Judge Easterbrook be persuaded?

For a defense of state takeover regulation, see Richard Booth, The Promise of State Takeover Statutes, 86 Mich. L. Rev. 1635 (1988) (arguing that control share statutes represent "a promising solution to several pressing problems associated with so-called coercive tender offers," but advocating some statutory modifications "to eliminate their biases in favor of target management").

H. *PUBLIC POLICY AND CORPORATE CONTROL TRANSACTIONS: THE STAKEHOLDER DEBATE*

The emergence in the 1980s of hostile takeovers and friendly transactions implemented to forestall an anticipated hostile bid, spawned a vigorous public debate that continues to the present. Most economists have argued that corporate acquisitions generally represent a healthy process by which companies respond to changes in the business environment, and hostile acquisitions represent a monitoring force by which the market disciplines managements who have been slow in responding.[86] A particular theme has been that the threat of hostile takeovers forces the managers of a corporation that lacks attractive new business opportunities to pay out its cash flow as dividends to shareholders (who have access to a wider variety of investments), rather than reinvesting the cash flow in only marginally profitable projects. See Michael Jensen, Agency Costs of Free Cash Flow, Corporate Finance and Takeovers, 76 Am. Econ. Rev. 323 (1986). From the economists' perspective, "further federal regulation of the takeover process, particularly if it would make takeovers more costly, would be poor economic policy." Economic Report of the President ch. 6 (1985). Consistent with this conclusion, the United States and the SEC filed an amici curiae brief in the *CTS* case, page 1132 supra, urging that the new generation of control share acquisition statutes were preempted by the neutral federal approach to takeover regulation.

A vocal and persistent counterpoint, almost uniformly successful in the state legislative arena, has questioned the benefits said to be associated with takeovers. While takeover proponents have estimated that takeovers of public companies just between 1981 and 1986 resulted in shareholder gains of approximately $134 billion,[87] other commentators have suggested that stock price data, on which

86. These arguments are summarized in Ronald J. Gilson, The Political Ecology of Takeovers: Thoughts on Harmonizing the European Corporate Governance Environment, 61 Fordham L. Rev. 161 (1992).

87. Bernard Black & Joseph Grundfest, Shareholder Gains from Takeovers and Restructurings Between 1981 and 1986: $162 Billion Is a Lot of Money, J. Applied Corp. Fin. 5 (1988).

such estimates are based, are not necessarily a reliable indicator of efficiency, may be subject to faddish biases, and may not measure long-term value. See, e.g., Louis Lowenstein, Pruning Deadwood in Hostile Takeovers: A Proposal for Legislation, 83 Colum. L. Rev. 249 (1983); Martin Lipton, Takeover Bids in the Target's Board-room, 34 Bus. Law. 101 (1979). Opponents have also argued that such shareholder gains as do appear should be offset by losses to other participants in the corporate enterprise, increasingly referred to as "stakeholders," and suggest that these losses may well eliminate much of the gain. From this perspective, social efficiency is measured by the effect of a transaction on everyone associated with it, not just the shareholders. The regulatory reforms urged by takeover skeptics range from restrictions that would keep the premium necessary for a successful offer high, because low-premium offers are less likely to produce real efficiency gains,[88] to effective prohibition of hostile transactions. The skeptics' arguments can be grouped under the following headings:

1. Takeovers Cause Target Management Myopia. Peter Drucker, for example, made the following argument:

> There is a great deal of discussion about whether hostile takeovers are good or bad for shareholders. There can be absolutely no doubt, however, that they are exceedingly bad for the economy. They force management into operating short-term. More and more of our businesses, larger, medium-sized, and small, are not being run for business results but for the protection against the hostile takeover. This means that more and more of our businesses are being forced to concentrate on results in the next three months. They are being run so as to encourage the institutional investors [who represent a large percentage of the stock market] to hold onto company shares rather than to toss them overboard the moment the first hostile takeover appears.[89]

The result of such management myopia is said to be too little investment in research and development, and in highly profitable projects that take a number of years to pay off.

Recall from Chapter III the Efficient Capital Market Hypothesis. Drucker's argument is that managers adopt inefficient short-term strategies because the stock market will then mistakenly increase the price of their companies' stock. This requires that the market systematically undervalue future cash flows and over-value near-term cash flows. Only if the market is so informationally inefficient will an operationally inefficient short-term strategy increase a company's current stock price and, therefore, provide current management protection from a hostile take-over. Economists have developed a number of abstract models that would accommodate this result. See, e.g., Andrei Shleifer & Robert Vishny, Equilibrium Short Horizons of Investors and Firms, 80 Am. Econ. Rev. 148 (1990); Jeremy Stein, Takeover Threats and Managerial Myopia, 96 J. Pol. Econ. 61 (1988). In the end, however, the question is empirical. Here the results are mixed. Some data suggest myopia while others do not, often in the same study. See Bronwyn Hall & Robert Hall, The Value and Performance of U.S. Corporations, Brookings Papers Econ. Activity — Microeconomics 1 (1993). The ambiguity may be due to the fact that

---

88. See John Coffee, Regulating the Market for Corporate Control: A Critical Assessment of the Tender Offer's Role in Corporate Governance, 84 Colum. L. Rev. 1145, 1221-1294 (1984).

89. Peter Drucker, Corporate Takeovers — What Is to Be Done?, 82 Pub. Int. 3, 12 (1986).

acquisitions are heterogeneous; for example, reduced research and development (R&D) spending in non-innovative industries (such as eliminating RJR Nabisco's efforts to develop a smokeless cigarette) may have few negative consequences for efficiency. To be sure, increased debt is associated with reduced R&D, but debt-increasing acquisitions seem to be clustered in non-innovative industries. Bronwyn Hall, The Impact of Corporate Restructuring on Industrial Research and Development, Brookings Papers Econ. Activity—Microeconomics 85 (1990). How should the presence of ambiguous empirical evidence influence the public policy debate? Should management or shareholders decide over what time frame to maximize profits?

2. Takeovers Have Dangerously Increased Corporate Leverage and the Risk of a Wave of Bankruptcies. One particular form of acquisition—the leveraged buyout (LBO)—results in a very substantial increase in the target company's debt-to-equity ratio. In these transactions, the target corporation's post-transaction debt-to-equity ratio is often as much as 10 to 1. Despite this increase in debt, proponents of leverage-increasing transactions argue that higher leverage does not necessarily increase the risk of bankruptcy because the increased leverage-related risk is balanced by the leverage-induced increased productivity that results from better monitoring of, and incentive for, management. Increased debt ensures that available cash flow will be paid out to debt holders, a "hard" constraint on management investment discretion as opposed to the "soft" constraint of the need to pay dividends. See Michael Jensen, Eclipse of the Public Corporation, Harv. Bus. Rev. 61 (Sept./Oct. 1989). Again, the issue is empirical. Consistent with the Jensen view, highly leveraged transactions in the early 1980s did not result in a decrease in the value of outstanding debt despite the debt-financed premiums paid to target shareholders,[90] nor were there a significant number of post-transaction defaults. This happy state of affairs changed, however, as more than one-fifth of the 1986 to 1989 transactions ended in default.[91] Among other changes in the character of highly leveraged transactions over the period was a steady increase in both the amount of leverage and the price paid.[92] Thus, the data suggests there is merit in the views of both the proponents and opponents of rising corporate leverage: sometimes it's a good thing and sometimes not. How should the data influence the public policy debate? Should management or shareholders decide the target corporation's optimal capital structure? Is the answer influenced by the fact that

---

90. See Marais, Schipper & Smith, Wealth Effects of Going Private for Senior Securities, 23 J. Fin. Econ. 155 (1989); Kenneth Lehn & Annette Poulsen, Leveraged Buyouts: Wealth Created or Wealth Distributed, in Public Policy Towards Corporate Takeovers 46 (M. Weidenbaum & K. Chiltin eds., 1988). The hypothesis that an increase in post-transaction leverage would reduce the value of pre-transaction debt that remains outstanding after the transaction derives from the fact that increased leverage increases the corporation's risk. Because the contractual return on pre-transaction debt is already fixed, the market would respond to an increase in risk by a reduction in its post-transaction trading value, so that the effective return on the outstanding pre-transaction debt (contractual return divided by market (not face) value) would rise to reflect the increased risk. This concept is developed in Chapter III.

91. In a sample of 124 large LBOs between 1980 and 1989, defaults occurred in none of the pre-1983 transactions, in 4 of the 39 transactions between 1983 and 1985, and in 14 between 1986 and 1988. Steven Kaplan & Jeremy Stein, Evolution of Buyout Pricing and Financial Structure (Or, What Went Wrong) in the 1980s, 108 Q.J. Econ. 313 (1993).

92. Id.; William Long & David Ravenscraft, Decade of Debt: Lessons from LBOs in the 1980s, in The Deal Decade: What Takeovers and Leveraged Buyouts Mean for Corporate Governance 205 (M. Blair ed., 1993).

increasing the target company's leverage also increases the risk associated with target management's human capital?

A second LBO wave began in 2002 and ended in the fall of 2007. Comparable data is not yet available for these transactions.

3. Target Shareholder Gains from Takeovers Result from a Transfer from Target Stakeholders. In this view, the premiums paid to target shareholders in takeovers may reflect not the anticipation of increased post-transaction efficiency, but merely the expectation of a transfer of wealth from other corporate participants, such as employees or bondholders, to shareholders. See Coffee, footnote 88 supra. Suppose that employees have been promised job security and above-average wages in return for investing their human capital in learning skills that have no value outside the corporation. Once employees make these investments, opportunistic shareholders can renege on these "implicit" contracts[93] by selling their shares at a premium in a hostile takeover where the premium reflects the savings from post-transaction reductions in employment and wages by the acquirer. For example, Andrei Shleifer & Lawrence Summers, Breach of Trust in Hostile Takeovers, in Corporate Takeovers: Causes and Consequences 33 (A. Auerbach ed., 1988), argue that transfers from employees could account for the entire premium shareholders received in Carl Icahn's takeover of TWA.

One problem in evaluating the implicit contract problem is conceptual. Because the implicit contract is not written down, how does one know whether an implicit contract exists or its terms? Put in the context of the takeover of TWA, the transaction was preceded by the deregulation of the airline industry and the entry of a number of non-union, low-wage carriers. In that situation, two responses by existing carriers were possible. If employment and wage levels were kept the same despite increased competition, income and share price would drop, so that the incidence of the costs of deregulation would fall on capital. Alternatively, if employment and wage levels were reduced to reflect the non-union competition, the incidence of the costs of deregulation would fall on labor. How does one determine whether an implicit contract exists with respect to the effects of deregulation and, if one does exist, which outcome the implicit contract calls for?

The empirical evidence concerning whether takeover premiums reflect wealth transfers from employees to shareholders is mixed. While economic studies of large samples of acquisitions do not support the proposition that wealth transfers from blue-collar employees account for a significant percentage of takeover premiums,[94] anecdotal accounts of large-scale layoffs and wage cuts following takeovers are commonplace and commentators familiar with the empirical studies nonetheless assert that takeovers "left devastation for employees."[95] Suppose the conflict results from the fact that the average reported by the economic studies

---

93. Implicit contracts are reflected in the behavior of the parties rather than committed to a written document. See Sherwin Rosen, Implicit Contract: A Survey, 23 J. Econ. Lit. 1144 (1985).

94. See, e.g., Joshua Rosett, Do Union Wealth Concessions Explain Takeover Premiums?, 27 J. Fin. Econ. 263 (1990) (small post-transaction *increase* in union wages after takeovers); Steven Kaplan, The Effect of Management Buyouts on Operations and Value, 24 J. Fin. Econ. 217 (1989) (no significant post-buyout reduction in employment); Frank Lichtenberg & Donald Siegel, Productivity and Changes in Ownership of Manufacturing Plants, Brookings Papers Econ. Activity — Microeconomics 643 (1987).

95. Stone, Policing Employment Contracts Within the Nexus-of-Contracts Firm, 43 U. Toronto L. Rev. 353 (1993).

masks some transactions in which employees were made substantially worse off. Could an appropriate policy response focus not on blocking the transactions (the average indicates the transaction's efficiency), but on spreading the social costs in those transactions where they fall too narrowly on labor? See Ronald Daniels, Stakeholders and Takeovers: Can Contractarianism Be Compassionate?, 43 U. Toronto L. Rev. 315 (1993).

TABLE OF CASES

Principle cases are italicized.

Aaron v. SEC, 316, *403*, 441, 460
Abbey v. Control Data Corp., 371, 388, 843
Abbot v. Hapgood, 289
Abbott Laboratories Derivative Shareholders, Litig., In re, 101
Abbigas v. Kulp, 606
Abel v. Forrest Realty, 783
Abella v. Universal Leaf Tobacco Co., 850
Abelow v. Symonds, 901
Abercrombie v. Davies, 745, 749, 750
Abrahamson v. Fleschner, 420
Abrams v. Allen, 79
Abrams v. Baker Hughes Inc., 408
Abrams v. Occidental Petroleum Corp., 521
AC Acquisitions Corp. v. Anderson, Clayton & Co., 961, 971, 972, 973, 976
Ace Ltd. v. Capital Re Corp., 1030
Activision Securities Litig., In re, 918
Adams v. Smith, 138, 140
Adams v. Standard Knitting Mills, Inc., 693, 694
Adler v. Brooks, 916
Adler v. Klawans, 458, 512, 513, 515
Admiralty Fund v. Hugh Johnson & Co., 445
Advanced Business Communication, Inc. v. Myers, 877
Advanced Mining Sys., Inc. v. Fricke, 932
Advanced Orthopedics, L.L.C. v. Moon, 817
Advanced Resources Int'l v. Tri-Star Petroleum Corp., 362
Aero Drapery of Ky., Inc. v. Engdahl, 164, 175
Affiliated We Citizens v. United States, 382, 384, 386, 418, 434, 435
AFSCME v. AIG, 658, 683, 687, 688
Ahmanson v. Great W. Fin. Corp., 1022, 1061
Aiple v. Twin City Barge & Towing Co., 915
Akin v. Q-L Investments, 445
Alabama Farm Bureau Mutual Casualty Co. v. American Fidelity Life Ins. Co., 439

Alcott v. M.E.V. Corp., 882
Aldridge v. Franco-Wyoming Oil Co., 746, 749
Aldus Securities Litig., In re, 499
Alex, Brown & Sons v. Latrobe Steel Co., 640
Alexander & Alexander of N.Y., Inc. v. Fritzen, 168, 169, 173
Alexander & Baldwin, Inc. v. Peat, Marwick, Mitchell & Co., 58, 286
Alford v. Shaw, 841, 853, 880
Alfus v. Pyramid Technology Co., 499
Alleghany Corp. v. Kirby, 897
Allen v. Biltmore Tissue Corp., 726, 727, 730, 731
Allen v. Chase Nat'l Bank (178 Misc. 536), 914
Allen v. Chase Nat'l Bank (180 Misc. 259), 914
Alley v. Miramon, 363
Alliegro v. Pan Am. Bank, 131
Allis-Chalmers Mfg. Co. v. Gulf & Western Indus., 523
Allison v. General Motors Corp., 840
Allison Publs. v. Mutual Benefit Life Ins. Co., 833
Alpert v. 28 Williams St. Corp., 110
Alyeska Pipeline Serv. Co. v. Wilderness Society, 400
Amalgamated Clothing & Textile Workers Union v. J. P. Stevens & Co., 370, 676, 677
Amalgamated Clothing & Textile Workers Union v. Wal-Mart Stores, Inc. (54 F.3d 69), 676
Amalgamated Clothing & Textile Workers Union v. Wal-Mart Stores, Inc. (821 F. Supp. 877), 676
Amalgamated Sugar Co. v. NL Indus., 953
Amanda Acquisition Corp. v. Universal Foods Corp., 46, 1142
Amdur v. Meyer, 886
American Dist. Tel. Co. v. Grinnell Corp., 133
American Federation of State, County & Municipal Employees, Employee Pension Plan v. American International Group Inc., 681
American Gen. Ins. Co. v. Equitable Gen. Corp., 317, 559, 560, 561, 624, 627 628

American Hardware Corp. v. Savage Arms Corp., 611
American Home Investment Co. v. Bedel, 655
American Standard, Inc., v. Crane Co., 523, 525
American Trading & Prod. Corp. v. Fischbach & Moore, Inc., 269
American Union Fin. Corp. v. University Nat'l Bank, 63
American Vending Servs. v. Morse, 246
Amfac Foods, Inc. v. International Sys. & Controls Corp., 260
Andersen v. Albert & J. M. Anderson Mfg. Co., 904
Anderson v. Abbott, 254, 265, 266
Anderson v. United States, 555
Animazing Entertainment, Inc. v. Louis Lofredo Assocs., Inc., 242
Anmaco, Inc. v. Bohlken, 66
APL Limited Partnership v. Van Dusen Air, 1129
Apple Computer Securities Litig., In re, 324, 390
Aprahamian v. HBO & Co., 615, 616, 631
A. P. Smith Mfg. Co. v. Barlow, 39
Aquila Inc., In re, 1121
Arctic Fin. Corp. v. OTR Express, Inc., 639
Arnesen v. Shawmut County Bank N.A., 363
Arnold v. Society for Sav. Bancorp, 340
Arnold v. Society for Savings, 340
Aronson v. Lewis, 88, 624, 830, 831, 834, 836, 837, 838, 840, 841, 842, 844, 868, 1016, 1120
Aronson v. Price, 256
Arrington v. Merrill Lynch, Pierce, Fenner & Smith, Inc., 421
Asarco, Inc. v. M.R.H. Holmes A Court, 953
Ash v. International Business Machs., Inc., 861
Assoc. Vendors, Inc. v. Oakland Meat Co., 267
Atchison, T. & S.F. F.Ry. Co v. Wichita Bd. Of Trade, 686
Atherton v. Anderson, 74
Atkinson v. Marquart, 908
ATR-Kim Eng Financial Corp v. Araneta, 83
Auer v. Dressel, 605, 607
Auer v. Robbins, 684
Auerbach v. Bennett, 830, 847, 849, 853, 861
Aurora Credit Servs., Inc. v. Liberty W. Dev. Inc., 880, 906
AUSA Life Ins. Co. v. Ernst & Young, 396

Bach v. National W. Life Ins. Co., 841
Bachelder v. Brentwood Lanes, Inc., 144
Backman v. Polaroid Corp., 318, 320, 321, 326
Bacon v. Christian, 710-712
Bagdon v. Bridgestone/Firestone, Inc., 907
Baker v. Commercial Body Builders, Inc., 793
Baker v. Health Management Sys., Inc., 927
Baldwin v. Canfield, 58
Ball v. Carlson, 713
Balvik v. Sylvester, 790
Bangor Punta Operations v. Bangor & Aroostook R.R., 870, 873, 875, 876, 877
Bank America Securities Litigation, In re, 827
Bank of Augusta v. Earle, 241
Bank of New York Derivative Litig., In re, 879
Bank of N.Y. Co. v. Irving Bank Corp., 953, 990
Bank of Santa Fe v. Petty, 877

Bansback v. Zinn, 834
Barkan v. Amsted Indus., 999, 1027
Barker-Chadsey Co. v. W. C. Fuller Co., 243
Barnes v. Andrews, 83
Barnes v. Osofsky, 343
Barnett v. Anaconda Co., 696
Baron v. Strawbridge, 46, 878
Baron v. Strawbridge & Clothier, 878
Barr v. Wackman, 829, 830, 832, 833, 834, 835
Barry v. Barry, 922
Barth v. Barth (659 N.E.2d 559), 905, 907
Bartle v. Home Owners Cooperative, 275
Basch v. Talley Indus., Inc., 690
Basic, Inc. v. Levinson, 307, 311, 312, 317, 321, 324, 340, 372, 374, 384, 390, 394, 395, 701, 1088
Basswood Partners v. NSS Bancorp, Inc., 46
Bastan v. RJM & Assoc., LLC, 818
Bastian v. Petren Resources Corp., 394
Bateman Eichler, Hill Richards, Inc. v. Berner, 403, 404, 466
Bateson v. Magna Oil Corp., 880
Batterton v. Francis, 482
Baum v. Baum Holding Co., 242
Baumel v. Rosen, 419
Baxter Int'l, Inc. Securities Litig., In re, 837
Bay State York Co. v. Cobb, 249
Baystate Alternate Staffing, Inc. v. Herman, 73
B & B Inv. Club v. Kleinert's, Inc., 927
Beale v. Kappa Alpha Order, 254
Beam ex rel. Martha Stewart Living Omnimedia Inc. v. Stewart, 636, 838, 849, 858
Beard v. Elster, 147, 154, 160
Beavers v. Reacreation Ass'n of Lake Shore Estates, Inc., 243
Beecher v. Able, 373
Behradrezaee v. Dashtara, 841
Bell v. Arnold, 865
Bell v. Hood, 347
Benihana of Tokyo, Inc. v. Benihana, Inc., 116
Benintendi v. Kenton Hotel, Inc., 737
Bennett v. Breuil Petroleum Corp., 900, 901, 904
Bennett v. Mack's Supermarkets, Inc., 640
Bennett v. Propp, 947, 957
Berg v. First American Bankshares, Inc., 692
Bergy Bros., Inc. v. Zeeland Feeder Pig, Inc., 243
Berkey v. Third Ave. Ry. Co., 262, 269
Berkwitz v. Humphrey, 154, 158
Berman v. Gerber Prods. Co., 317
Bershad v. Curtiss-Wright Corp., 1062
Bershad v. McDonough, 512, 513, 515
Bestfoods, United States v., 253
B & H Warehouse, Inc. v. Atlas Van Lines, Inc., 731
Billings v. Marshall Furnace Co., 761
Binz v. St. Louis Hide & Tallow Co., 137
Biogen Securities Litig., In re, 391
Biondi v. Beekman Hill House Apt. Corp., 922
Birnbaum v. Newport Steel Corp., 354, 355, 356, 357, 358, 360, 361, 362
Blackie v. Barrack, 386, 387
Blake v. Blake Agency, Inc., 796
Blasband v. Rales, 837, 840
Blasius Indus., Inc. v. Atlas Corp., 556, 559, 560, 561, 562, 563, 564, 565, 615, 616, 618, 619, 620, 622, 624, 625, 626, 629, 984, 991, 1063

Blau v. Lamb, 521
Blau v. Lehman, 510
Blau v. Max Factor & Co., 512, 521, 524
Blau v. Mission Corp., 363
Blau v. Oppenheim, 513, 514
Blau v. Rayette-Faberge, Inc., 916
Bliss Petroleum Co., v. McNally, 127
Blue Chips Stamps v. Manor Drug Stores, 334, 342, 353, 362, 363, 364, 366, 367, 368, 376, 378, 393, 395, 436, 442, 443, 444, 451, 478, 698, 700
Blum v. Kauffman, 804
Blum v. Morgan Guaranty Trust Co., 877
BNS, Inc. v. Koppers Co., 982, 1141
Bodio v. Ellis, 766
Boericke v. Weise, 751
Bohannan v. Corporation Commn., 599
Bokat v. Getty Oil Co., 903
Bonavita v. Corbo, 791, 793
Bond v. May, 711
Bonham, Dr., 412
Booth v. Varian Assocs., 523
Borak v. J. I. Case Col, 900, 904
Borbein, Young & Co. v. Cirese, 243
Borden v. Cohen, 79
Bosch v. Meeker Coop. Light & Power Assn., 913, 914
Boslow Family Ltd. Partnership v. Glickenhaus & Co., 247
Boss v. Boss, 128
Boston Safe Deposit & Trust Co. v. North Attleborough Chap. of Am. Red Cross, 730
Bostwick Braun Co. v. Szews, 258
Bove v. Community Hotel Corp., 604
Boxer v. Boss, 131
Boxer v. Husky Oil Co., 805
Boyce Motor Lines, Inc. v. United States, 479
Braddock v. Zimmerman, 837
Brady v. Bean, 580
Brandon v. Brandon Constr. Co., 878
Brandt Glass Co. v. New Orleans Housing Mart, 642
Brane v. Roth, 87
Brascan Ltd. v. Edper Equities Ltd., 1083
Braude v. Automobile Club of S. Cal., 913
Brazen v. Bell Atl. Corp., 1022, 1046
Brehm v. Eisner, 89, 98, 102, 141, 831
Brennan v. Midwestern United Life Ins. Co., 397
Brennan v. Ruffner, 896
Bresnahan v. Lighthouse Mission, Inc., 61
Briargate Condominium Assn. v. Carpenter, 798
Briggs v. Spaulding, 74
Broad v. Rockwell Int'l Corp., 365, 402
Brophy v. Cities Serv. Co., 531, 534, 537, 539, 857, 1097
Brown v. Allied Corrugated Box Co., 795, 796
Brown v. Chicago, 655
Brown v. Chicago, R.I. & P. Ry., 655
Brown v. Halbert, 1061, 1066
Brown v. Ivie, 364
Brown v. North Ventura Road Dev. Co., 608
Broz v. Cellular Information Sys., Inc., 169
Brumbaugh v. Princeton Partners, 422
Brusso v. Running Springs Country Club, Inc., 882, 883
Bryan v. Brock & Blevins Co., 436, 764

Bud Antle, Inc. v. Eastern Foods, Inc., 286
Bunker Ramo-Eltra Corp. v. Fairchild Indus., 527
Burg v. Horn, 170, 172
Burkin (Katz), Matter of, 774
Burks v. Lasker, 838
Burlington Coat Factory Securities Litigation, In re, 320
Burt v. Irvine Co., 883
Business Roundtable v. SEC, 571
Butler v. Watkins, 358
Byrne v. Barrett, 530

C.A. Cavendes, Sociedad Financiera v. Florida National Banks of Florida, Inc., 549
Cady, Roberts & Co., In the Matter of, 446, 456, 459, 460, 461, 495
Cahoon v. Ward, 251
Cal-Maine Foods, Inc. v. Pyles, 912
Callahan v. Sun Lakes Homeowners' Assn., 885, 904
Campbell v. Loews, Inc., 600, 607, 612, 619, 863, 886
Campbell v. Potash Corp. of Saskatchewan, Inc., 148, 151
Canadian Commercial Workers Industry Pension Plan v. Alden, 101
Cange v. Stotler & Co., 59, 60, 61
Cannon v. U.S. Acoustics Corp., 890, 911
Cannon v. University of Chicago, 351
Cantor v. Sunshine Greenery, Inc., 244
Capitol Wine & Spirit Corp. v. Pokrass, 873
Caplan v. Lionel Corp., 1066
Capri Optics Profit Sharing v. Digital Equip. Corp., 320
Caremark Int'l, Inc. Derivative Litig., In re, 97, 100, 101
Cargill, Inc. v. American Pork Producers, Inc., 243
Carlson v. Ringgold County Mutual Tel. Co., 713, 731
Carmody v. Toll Bros. Inc., 990
Carnation Co., In re, 314, 316
Carnegie Trust Co. v. Security Life Ins. Co., 745
Carpenter v. United States, 473, 490
Carpenter, United States v., 873
Carter-Wallace Securities Litig., In re, 365
Cascade Energy & Metals Corp. v. Banks, 252
Case v. New York Cent. R.R., 128, 131, 134
Casey v. Woodruff, 98
Cassels v. Stewart, 718
Caterpillar, Inc., 321
CBI Indus. v. Horton, 508
Cede & Co. v. Technicolor, Inc., 83, 84, 88, 804, 983, 1101
Centaur Partners, IV v. National Intergroup, Inc., 616
Centerre Bank of Kan. City v. Angle, 907
Central Bank of Denver v. First Interstate Bank of Denver, 397, 440, 445, 476, 478
Central Banking Sys., In re, 932
Central Standard Life Ins. Co. v. Davis, 783
Cerner Corp. Securities Litigation, In re, 409
Chaknova v. Wilbur-Ellis Co., 284
Chambers v. Beaver-Advance Corp., 139

Charland v. Country View Golf Club, Inc., 795, 796

Charles River Bridge Case. *See* Proprietors of the Charles River Bridge v. Proprietors of the Warren Bridge, 21, 22

Chartrand v. Barney's Club, Inc., 292

Chasins v. Smith, Barney & Co., 383

C. & H. Contractors, Inc. v. McKee, 292

Cheatle v. Rudd's Swimming Pool Supply Co., 254, 255

Cheff v. Mathes, 945, 949, 955-961, 975, 989, 994

Cheft v. Kass, 880

Chelrob, Inc. v. Barrett, 127

Chemical Bank N.Y. Trust Co. v. Kheel, 281

Chemical Fund, Inc. v. Xerox Corp., 517, 518

Chesapeake Corp. v. Shore, 626

Chestman, United States v., 480, 483, *488,* 497

Chevron, U.S.A., Inc. v. Natural Resources Defense Council, Inc., 482

Chew v. Inverness Mgt. Corp., 580

Chiarella v. United States, 441, 455, 456, 457, 458, 459, 461, 462, 463, 464, 465, 466, 480, 481, 482, 490, 493, 497

Chilson, In re, 751

Christensen v. Harris Count, 684

Cinerama, Inc. v. Technicolor, Inc., 88, 126, 624

Citadel Holding Corp. v. Roven (26 F.3d 960), 524

Citadel Holding Corp. v. Roven (603 A.2d 818), 932

Citibank, N.A. v. Data Lease Fin. Corp., 902

Citron v. E.I. DuPont de Nemours & Co., 158, 1107

Citron v. Fairchild Camera & Instrument Corp., 87, 1105

City Capital Assocs. v. Interco, Inc. (551 A.2d 787), 962, 971, 972, 976

City Capital Assocs. v. Interco, Inc. (696 F. Supp 1551), 1141

City Nat'l Bank v. Vanderboom, 415

Civen v. Countrywide Realty, Inc., 690

Claman v. Robertson, 865, 868

Clark v. Dodge, 756, 758

Clark v. Lomas & Nettleton Fin. Corp., 899

Clarke v. Greenberg, 899

Clarks Hill Tel, Co., State v., 734

Clarkson Co. v. Shaheen, 46

Clegg v. Conk, 397

CM & M Group, Inc. v. Carroll, 643

Coaldale Coal Co. v. State Bank, 287

Cochran v. Penn-Beaver Oil Co., 35

Co-Ex Plastics, Inc. v. Ala Pak, Inc., 258

Coffee v. Permian Corp., 363

Coggins v. New England Patriots Football Club, 1100

Cohen v. Ayers, 160

Cohen v. Beneficial Ind. Loan Corp., 356, 886

Colan v. Mesa Petroleum Co., 527

Colby v. Klune, 507, 513

Colcord v. Granzow, 58

Cole v. National Cash Credit Assn., 1099

Coleman v. Corning Glass Works, 268, 269

Colorado Mgt. Corp. v. American Founders Life Ins. Co., 154

Combs v. Pricewaterhousecoopers, LLP, 907

Community Collaborative of Bridgeport, Inc. v. Ganim, 66

Comolli v. Comolli, 763

Compare Farris v. Glen Alden Corp., 566

Competitive Assocs, v. Laventhal, Krekstein, Horwath & Horwath, 384

Comshare Inc. Securities Litig., In re, 427

Concord Fin. Group, Inc. v. Tri-State Motor Transit Co of Del., 590

Condec Corp. v. Lunkenheimer Co., 610, 611

Cone v. Russell & Mason, 580

Coley v. Gibson, 395

Consumer's Co-op v. Olsen, 272

Continental Securities Co. v. Belmont, 864, 865, 866

Cooke v. Manufactured Homes Inc., 390

Cooke v. Teleprompter Corp., 371

Cookies Food Prods. v. Lakes Warehouse Distributing, Inc., 112, 119, 124, 126, 160

Copland v. Grumet, 499

Cort v. Ash, 80, 349, 350, 351, 435, 436, 439

Courtland Manor, Inc. v. Leeds, 874

Cowin v. Bresler, 362, 380, 690

Cox Comm. Inc. Shareholders Litig, In re, 1127

Cox & Perry, Inc. v. Perry, 165

Coyne v. Park & Tilford Distillers Corp., 1089

CPC Int'l, Inc. v. McKesson Corp., 336

Craig v. Graphic Arts Studio, Inc., 175

Cramer v. General Tel. & Electronics Corp., 847

Crandon Capital Partners v. Shelk, 917

Crane Co. v. Anaconda Corp., 640

Cranson v. International Business Machines Corp., 247

Credit Bureau of St. Paul, Inc. v. Credit Bureau Reports, Inc., 640

Credit Lyonnais Bank Nederland, N.V. v. Pathe Communications Corp., 46, 47, 230-231

Cressy v. Shannon Continental Corp., 769

Crowley v. Communications for Hosps., Inc., 144

Crutcher v. Kentucky, 241

CTS Corp. v. Dynamics Corp. of Am., 940, 944, 1129, 1132, 1141-1143

Cuker v. Mikalauskas, 847

Cunningham v. Jaffe, 867

Cunningham v. Rendezvous, Inc., 255

Curreri v. Verni, 833

Curtis, Nevada ex rel., v. McCullough, 555

Cziraki v. Thunder Cats, Inc., 911

Dahl v. HEM Pharms., 555

Damerow Ford Co. v. Bradshaw, 877

Dann v. Chrysler Corp., 917

Dann v. Studebaker-Packard Corp., 348

Dartmouth College v. Woodward, 21, 22, 46

Datapoint Corp. v. Plaza Sec. Co. 591, 593, 594, 631, 665

Daubert v. Merrell Dow Pharmaceuticals, Inc., 410

David J. Breene & Co. v. Schenley Indus., Inc., 1089, 1099, 1100

Davidge v. White, 539

Davidson v. Belcor Inc., 363

Davis v. Louisville Gas & Electric Co., 76

Davis Acquisition Inc. v. NWA, Inc., 990

DeBaun v. First W. Bank & Trust Co., 1065

DeBoer Constr., Inc. v. Reliance Ins. Co., 253

Deckert v. Independence Shares Corp., 347
Deenan v. Eshleman, 615
DeFelice v. Garon, 751
Delaney v. Fidelity Lease Ltd. (526 S W.2d
    543), 253
Demoulas v. Demoulas Super Mkts., Inc., 174
Derry v. Peek, 342
Des Moines Bank & Trust Co. v. George M. Bechtel
    & Co., 114, 115
Desaigoudar v. Meyerecord, 847, 883
Desimone v. Barrows, 881
Detroit v. Grinnell Corp., 918
DeWitt Truck Brokers, Inc. v. W. Ray Flemming
    Fruit Co., 255, 257
Diamond v. Davis, 79, 80
Diamond v. Diamond, 927
Diamond v. Oreamuno, 529, 534, 535, 536, 537,
    538, 539
Diamond v. Parkersburg-Aetna Corp., 599
Diaz v. Fernandez, 817
Dieter Eng'g Servs., Inc. v. Parkland Dev., Inc., 267
Digex Shareholders Litig., In re, 135, 1049, 1051,
    1069, 1074, 1075, 1125
DiGiovanni v. All-Pro Golf, 877
Dillon v. Berg, 607
Direct Mail Specialist v. Brown, 798
Dirks v. SEC, 324, 441, 452, *454*, 464, 466, 472, 475-
    477, 478, 483, 490, 491, 493, 496, 539, 1086
Dissolution of E.C. Warner Co., In re, 921
Ditty v. CheckRite Ltd., 818
Dodge v. Ford Motor Co., 34, 35, 76, 77, 209
Dodge v. Woolsey, 24
Doe v. Unocal Corp., 253
Dolgow v. Anderson, 373
Don Swann Sales Corp. v. Echols, 246, 247, 248
Donahue v. Rodd Electrotype Co. of New
    England, 763, 764, 766, 768
Donald Trump Casino Securities Litig., In re, 378, 380
Donner Management Co. v. Schaffer, 881
Dornan v. Humphrey, 927
Doskocil Cos. v. Griggs, 972
Doss v. Yingling, 729
Dottenheim v. Murchison, 870
Dowdle v. Texas Am. Oil Corp., 140
Drachman v. Harvey, 364
Drive-In Dev. Corp., In re, 65
Dudley v. Smith, 261
Dudley v. Southeastern Factor & Fin. Corp., 363
Dungan v. Colt Industries, Inc., 317
Dura Pharmaceuticals Inc. v. Michael Broudo, 391,
    395, 404, 406, 407, 424
Durfee v. Durfee & Canning, Inc., 126
Durham v. Durham, 907
Dutton v. Willner, 530
Dynamics Corp. of Am, v. CTS Corp., 587

Eagle v. Horvath, 696
Eason v. General Motors Acceptance Corp., 362
Eastside Church of Christ v. National Plan,
    Inc., 420
Eaton v. Walker, 242
Eckstein v. Balcor Film Investors, 390
Edelman v. Authorized Distrib. Network,
    Inc., 631

Edgar v. MITE Corp., 944, *1128*, 1138
Eglin Nat'l Bank v. Home Indem. Co., 934
Einhorn v. Culea, 857
Eisen v. Carlisle & Jaquelin, 870
Eisenberg v. Chicago Milwaukee Corp., 576
Eisenberg v. Flying Tiger Line, Inc., 901
E. K. Buck Retail Stores v. Harkert, 736
Elec Specialty Co. v. Int'l Controls Corp., 322, 332,
    350, 365, 944
Electro K, Inc. v. Karpeles, 894
Electronic Specialty Co. v. International Controls
    Corp., 945
Elf Atochem North America, Inc. v. Jaffari,
    805, 806
Elgin v. Alfa Corp., 869
Eli Lilly & Co. v. Sav-On-Drugs, Inc., 241
Eliasberg v. Standard Oil Co., *150*, 160
Elkind v. Liggett & Myers, Inc., 312, 322, 421, *499*,
    502, 503
Ellis & Marshall Assocs. v. Marshall, 175
Ellzey v. Fyr-Pruf, Inc., 165
Elster v. American Airlines, Inc., 901
Emerald Partners v. Berlin, 84, 89, 106, 624
Emergent Capital Inc. Management, LLC v.
    Stonepath Group, Inc., 394
Empire Life Inc. Co. v. Valdak Corp., 903
Empire of Carolina, Inc. v. Deltona Corp., 593, 594
Employers Inc. of Wausau v. Musick, Peeler &
    Garrett, 445
Employer-Teamster Joint Council Pension Trust
    Fund v. America West Holding
    Corp., 374
Endsley v. Game-Show Placements, Ltd., 711
Energy Resources Corp. v. Porter, 165
Engstrand v. West Des Moines State Bank, 903
Epstein v. MCA, Inc., 898, 920, 1081, 1082
Equitable Life Ins. Co. of Iowa v. Halsey, Stuart &
    Co., 335
Equity Corp. v. Groves, 167, 169
ER Holdings v. Norton Co., 555
Erie R.R. v. Tompkins, 447, 870
Ernst & Ernst v. Hochfelder, 385, 396, 402, 403, 405,
    407, 433, 434, 435, 441, 442, 460, 461, 493, 693
Escoett v. Aldecress Country Club, 865
Escott v. BarChris Constr. Corp., 75, 399
Essex Universal Corp. v. Yates, 609, 1061, 1066,
    1067, 1069
Essential Enter. Corp. v. Dorsey Corp., 924
Estate Counseling Serv. v. Merrill Lynch, Pierce,
    Fenner & Smith, Inc., 419
Evanowski v. Bankworcester Corp., 326
Everett v. Transnational Dev. Corp., 606
Ex Parte Peterson, 411
Exxon Corp. v. Governor of Md., 1136, 1138

Faberge, Inc., In re, 456, 464
Fagin v. Gilmartin, 830
Fairway Dev. v. Title Ins. Co. of Minn., 707
Falco v. Donner Foundation, Inc., 506
Falcone, United States v., 504
Falls v. Fickling, 364
Fanchon & Marco, Inc. v. Paramount Pictures, 66
Farris v. Glen Alden Corp., 566
Faulds v. Yates, 753

Fayard v. Fayard, 734
FDIC v. Bierman, 82
F.D. Rich Co. v. Industrial Lumber Co., 400
Feder v. Frost, 517
Feder v. Martin Marietta Corp., 513, 515, 516
Federal Deposit Ins. Corp. v. Sea Pines Co., 46
Federated Radio Corp., People v., 335
Fee Ins. Agency, Inc. v. Snyder, 246
Feit v. Leasco Data Processing Equip. Corp., 373
Fells v. Katz, 752, 754
Ferraiolo v. Newman, 521
Fidelity & Deposit Co. v. McClure Quarries,
    Inc., 67
Fidelity & Deposit Co. v. Md. v. United States, 411
Fidelity Fed. Sav. & Loan Assn. v. Felicetti, 932
Field v. Trump, 440
Fin Indus. Fund v. McDonnell Douglas Corp.,
    308, 311
Fincher v. Clairborne Butane Co., 144
Finley v. Superior Court, 883
First Boston, Inc. Shareholders Litig., In re, 1109
First Home Investment Corp. of Kan., Inc.,
    In re, 655
Fischman v. Raytheon Mfg. Co., 401
Fisher v. Big Squeeze, 907
Five Star Concrete, L.L.C. v. Klink, Inc., 816
Flamm v. Eberstadt, 313, 314, 316
Fleet Aerospace Corp. v. Holderman, 1129
Fletcher v. A.J. Indus., Inc., 911, 913, 914
Fletcher v. Atex, Inc., 266
Fliegler v. Lawrence, 116, 161
Florida Lime & Avocado Growers, Inc. v. Paul,
    1134
Flynn v. Bass Bros. Enters., 380, 395, 398, 1085
Fogelson v. American Woolen Co., 140
Fontainebleau Hotel Corp. v. Crossman, 253
Forbes v. Goldenhersh, 58
Foremost-McKesson Inc. v. Provident Sec. Co., 514,
    515, 527
Fort Howard Corp. Shareholders Litig., In re, 1004
Foss v. Harbottle, 830
Foster v. Cone-Blanchard Mach. Co., 286
Foster v. Fin. Tech., 421
14th RMA Partners v. Reale, 714
Fox v. Cody, 607
Framingham Sav. Bank v. Szabo, 289
Franchard Corp., In re, 371
Francis v. United Jersey Bank, 82
Frank v. Anthony, 607
Frankel v. Donovan, 160
Frankel v. Slotkin, 364, 538
Franklin v. USX Corp., 285
Franklin Music Co. v. American Broadcasting
    Cos., 176
Freeman v. Complex Computing Co., 271
Freeman v. Decio, 534, 538
Freeman v. Laventhol & Horwath, 389, 390
Freidman v. Beway Realty Corp., 795, 796
Freman v. Venner, 393
Friedman v. Kurker, 281
Friese v. Superior Court, 241
Frigidaire Sales Corp v. Union Properties,
    Inc., 253
Frigitemp Corp. v. Fin. Dynamics Fund, Inc.,
    539, 540

Fritzmeier v. Krause Gentle Corp., 907
Froid v. Berner, 499

Gabhart v. Gabhart, 908
GAF Corp. v. Heyman, 646, 691
GAF Corp. v. Milstein, 646, 691
Gaffin v. Teledyne, Inc., 340
Gagliardi v.TriFoods Int'l, Inc., 98, 108
Gaines v. Haughton, 371, 692
Galef v. Alexander, 842, 849
Gall v. Exxon Corp., 849
Galler v. Galler, 724, 758
Gannett Co. v. Larry, 277, 281
Gap Securities Litig., In re, 320
Garbe v. Excel Mold, Inc., 905
Garber v. Lego, 833
Garlen v. Green Mansions, Inc., 893
Gartner v. Snyder, 272
Gateway Potato Sales v. G.B. Investment Co., 798
G. A. Thompson & Co. v. Partridge, 402
Gauger v. Hintz, 165
Gaylord Container Corp. Shareholders Litig.,
    In re, 624
Gatz v. Ponsoldt, 904
Geitman v. Mullins, 126
Geller v. Allied-Lyons PLC, 166
Gelles v. TDA Indus., Inc., 363
General Host Corp. v. Triumph Am., Inc., 944
General Inv. Co. v. Bethlehem Steel Corp., 573
General Overseas Films, Ltd. v. Robin Int'l, Inc., 63
General Portland, Inc. v. Lafarge Coppee S.A., 317
General Tire & Rubber Co. Securities Litig., In re,
    897
Genzer v. Cunningham, 847
Gerard v. Empire Square Realty Co., 58
Gerber v. Computer Assoc. Int'l, Inc., 1081
Gerdes v. Reynolds, 1061
Gerstle v. Gamble-Skogmo, Inc., 373
Getty Oil Co. v. Skelly Oil Co., 131, 132, 1096
Geyer v. Ingersoll Publications Co., 47, 232
Geygan v. Queen City Grain Co., 83
Gilbert v. El Paso Co., 616
Gilbert v. National Enquirer Inc., 884
Gilbert v. Nixon, 343
Gimbel v. Signal Cos., Inc., 98, 1092
Giuricich v. Emtrol Corp., 624, 635, 777
Glassman v. Unocal Exploration, 1114, 1120
Glazer v. Glazer, 759
GlenFed, Inc. Securities Litigation, In re, 407
Glick v. Campagna, 418
Globe Woolen Co. v. Utica Gas & Elec. Co., 123,
    129
Globus v. Law Research Serv., Inc., 527
Globus, Inc. v. Jaroff, 696, 917
Gluck v. Unger, 880
GM Class H Shareholders Litig., In re, 576
Godley v. Crandall & Godley Co., 888
Gold v. Schwab, 914
Gold v. Sloan, 507
Goldberg v. Meridor, 437, 439, 440
Goldblum v. Boyd, 734
Goldie v. Yaker, 878
Gollust v. Mendell, 527, 528
Goldstein v. SEC, 16

Gompper v. VISX, Inc., 408
Goode v. Ryan, 763
Goodhue v. Farmers' Warehouse Co. v. Davis, 170
Goodwyne v. Moore, 247
Gordon v. Elliman, 830
Gotham Partners, L.P. v. Hallwood Realty Partners, L.P., 800, 807, 809, 821
Gottlieb v. Heyden Chem. Corp., 155, 156
Gould v. American-Hawaiian S.S. Co., 75, 692
Gow v. Consolidated Coppermines Corp., 592
Grace v. Ludwig, 917
Grace v. Rosenstock, 363, 702
Graham v. Allis-Chalmers Mfg. Co., 100
Graham v. Mimms, 165
Grand Metropolitan Pub. Ltd. Co. v. The Pillsbury Co., 963, 971, 972, 976
Grant Portland Cement Co., In re, 585
Gray v. Harris Land & Cattle Co., 734
Grebel v. FTP Software, 427
Green v. Jonhop, Inc., 322
Green v. Santa Fe Indus., 1089
Greenberg v. Howtek, Inc., 320
Greenfield v. Heublein, Inc., 313, 318
Greenstone v. Cambex Corp., 407
Gresov v. Shattuck Denn Mining Co., 880
Gries Sports Enters. v. Cleveland Browns Football Co., 126, 127
Griggs v. Pace Am. Group, Inc., 366
Grimandi v. Beech Aircraft Corp., 253
Grimes v. Donald, 636, 638, 832, 841, 844, *900*, 902, 1044
Grin v. Shine, 473
Grizzard v. Petkas, 915
Grobow v. Perot, 831, 836, 841, 843
Grodetsky v. McCrory Corp., 597
Groel v. United Elec. Co. of N.J., 888
Grogan v. Grogan, 750
Grossett v. Wenaas, 871, 873
Grynberg v. Burke, 358
Guidant Shareholders Derivative Litigation, In re, 832
Gulf Oil/Cities Service Tender Offer Litig., In re, 324
Gustafson v. Alloyd Co., 344
Guth v. Loft, Inc., 168, 169, 171-174, 575
Guttman v. Huang, 102

Haberman v. Tobin (480 F. Supp. 425), 886, 887
Haberman v. Tobin (626 F.2d 1101), 887
Hagan v. Adams Property Assn. Inc., 816
Hagen v. Asa G. Candler, Inc., 297
Hali Rest, Inc. v. Treloar, 854
Hall v. Isaacs, 580
Hall v. Staha, 145
Hallahan v. Haltom Corp., 766
Hames v. Cravens, 907
Hampton v. Tri-State Fin, Corp., 735
Hannerty v. Standard Theater Col, 163
Hanson Trust PLC v. ML SCM Acquisition Inc., 1083
Hanson Trust PLC v. SCM Corp., 1083
Harbor Finance Partners v. Huizenga, 161
Hardwick v. Bublitz, 115
Harff v. Kerkorian, 871, 995

Harhen v. Brown, 841, 869
Hariton v. Arco Elecs., Inc., 566
Harman v. Diversified Med. Inv. Corp., 335
Harper v. Delaware Valley Broadcasters, Inc., 267
Harriman v. E. I. duPont de Nemours & Co., 1096
Harris v. Carter, 1061
Harris v. Union Elec. Co., 387
Harry Rich Corp. v. Feinberg, 247
Hart v. Bell, 755
Hasan v. Cleveland Realty Investors, 849
Hatleigh Corp. v. Lane Bryant, Inc., 640
Hausman v. Buckley, 894
Hawes v. Oakland, 830, 870
Hayden v. Beane, 756
Hayes Oyester Co., State ex rel. v. Keypoint Oyster Co., 123
Head v. Lane, 877
Healey v. Catalyst Recovery of Pa., 439
Healy, State ex rel. v. Superior Oil Co., 640
Heffernan v. Pacific Dunop GNB Corp., 922
Heil v. Standard Gas & Elec. Co., 575
Heineman v. Datapoint Corp., 831
Heise v. Earnshaw Publications, Inc., 126
Heit v. Weitzen, 365, 389
Heli-Coil Corp. v. Webster, 521
Heller v. Boylan, 141
Helmsman Management Servs. v. A&S Consultants, Inc., 634, 638
Helwig v. Vencor, 409
Henley Group, Inc. v. Santa Fe S. Pac. Corp., 972
Henry George & Sons v. Cooper-George, Inc., 787
Henshaw v. American Cement Corp., 643
Herbert v. Sullivan, 71
Herbert v. Wiegand, 253
Herman & MacLean v. Huddleston, 352, 353, 371, 411, 419
Hershowitz v. Nutri/System, Inc., 694
Hettmann v. Steinberg, 527
Heublein, Inc. v. General Cinema Corp., 527
HFG Co. v. Pioneer Pub. Co., 871
Hibbert v. Hollywood Park, Inc., 923, 924
Higgins v. Shenango Pottery Co., 164
Hikita v. Nichiro Gyogyo Kaisha, Ltd., 903
Hill York Corp v. American Int'l Franchises, Inc., 343
Hilton Hotels Corp. v. ITT Corp. (962 F. Supp. 1302), 555, 563
Hilton Hotels Corp, v. ITT Corp. (978 F. Supp. 1342), 558, 991
Hines v. Davidowitz, 1134
Hirsch v. Cahn Elec. Co., 144
Hirsch v. Jones Intercable, Inc., 847
Hirsh v. Miller, 253
Hirshon, Estate of, 761
Hoff v. Sprayregan, 871
Holden v. Construction Mach. Corp., 915
Holi-Rest, Inc. v. Treloar, 116
Holloway v. Howerdd, 400
Holly Farms Corp. Shareholders Litig., In re, 1004
Holmes v. Bateson, 317
Holmes v. Securities Investor Protection Corp., 478
Holzman v. De Escamilla, 798
Home Fire Ins. Co. v. Barber, 870, 875
Home Tel. Co. v. Darley, 873

Homestore, Inc. v. Tafeen, 932
Hooper v. Mountain States Securities Corp., 430
Hooper Assoc. v. AGS Computers, 930
Hoover v. Allen, 696
Horizon House-Microwave, Inc. v. Bazzy, 907
Horner v. Chamber of Commerce, 911
Hornreich v. Plant Indus., Inc, 878
Hornsby v. Lohmeyer, 139
Houle v. Low, 849, 856
House of Koscot Dev. Corp. v. American Line Cosmetics, Inc., 277
How & Assocs., Inc. v. Boss, 294, 297
Howe v. Bank for Int'l Settlements, 363
Huang v. Lanxide Thermo-Composites, Inc., 127
Hubbard v. Hollywood Park Realty Enters., Inc., 631
Huddleston v. Herman & MacLean, 419
Hughes v. Oklahoma, 1140
Hun v. Cary, 74
Hurley v. Ornsteen, 58
Hurt v. Cotton States Fertilizer Co., 140
Hurwitz v. Padden, 817

Icahn v. Blunt, 1129
ICX Communications, In re, 1034
IGL-Wisconsin Awning, Tent & Trailer Co. v. Greater Milwaukee Air & Water Show, Inc., 286
IIT v. Cornfield, 402
Illinois Controls, Inc. v. Langham, 297
Imperial Group (Texas), Inc, v. Scholnick, 174
InfoSonics Corp. Deriv. Litig, 836
Ingle v. Glamore Motor Sales, Inc., 767
In re _____. *See name of party*
Inryco, Inc. v. CGR Bldg. Sys., Inc., 253
Insuranshares Corp. v. Northern Fiscal Corp., 1061, 1065
Interlake Porshe & Audi, Inc v. Blackburn, 915
International Brotherhood of Teamsters General Fund v. Fleming Co., Inc. (975 P.2d 907), 680, 681
International Brotherhood of Teamsters General Fund v. Fleming Cos (1997 U.S. Dist. LEXIS 2980), 680
International Ins. Co. v. Johns, 148
Interocean Shipping Co v. National Shipping & Trading Corp., 256
Investors Management Co., In re, 457, 459, 460
Ionosphere Clubs, Inc., In re, 903
IPO Securities Litigation, In re, 390
Iron City Sand & Gravel Div. of McDonough Co. v. West Fork Towing Corp., 259
Irving Trust Co. v. Deutsch, 161, 166
Isensee v. Long Island Motion Picture Co., 882
Isquith v. Caremark Int'l Inc., 363, 440
Ivanhoe Partners v. Newmont Mining Corp., 1001, 1004, 1008, 1105

Jackson v. Hooper, 724
Jackson v. Ludeling, 459
Jackson v. Nicolai-Neppach Co., 769
Jackson v. Oppenheim, 344
Jackson v. Smith, 459

Jacuzzi v. Jacuzzi Bros., 896
James v. Gerber Prods. Co., 364
James v. Meinke, 421
Janigan v. Taylor, 383, 420, 421
Janssen v. Best & Flanagan, 847
Japan Petroleum Co. (Nigeria) v. Ashland Oil Inc., 269
Jara, Sr. v. Suprema Meats, Inc., 907
Jean Claude Boisett Wines, U.S.A., Inc. v. Newton, 246
Jeanes v. Henderson, 363
Jedwab v. MGM Grand Hotels, Inc., 1062
Jepson v. Peterson, 870
Jerue v. Millett, 917
Jewelcor, Inc. v. Pearlman, 1085
J. F. Anderson Lumber Co. v. Myers, 285
J. I. Case Co. v. Borak, 346, 348, 349, 350, 352, 353, 404, 407, 435, 696, 697, 698 700, 701, 886
Joarmou v. G. Joannou Cycle Co., 640
John R. Lewis, Inc. v. Newman, 420
John Rich Enters., In re, 147
Johns v. Caldwell, 769
Johnson v. Gilbert, 907
Johnson v. Radio Station WOW, Inc., 126
Johnson v. Spartanburg County Fair Assn., 738
Johnson & Carlson v. Montreuil's Estate, 297
Johnston v. Greene, 168, 171, 1096
Jolly Roger Fund L.P. v. Sizeler Property Investors, Inc., 904
Jones v. Harris, 730
Jones v. H. F. Ahmanson & Co., 1061
Jon-T Chems., Inc., United States v., 255, 256, 269
Joseph v. Amrep Corp., 833
Joy v. North, 106, 841, 850
J.P. Stevens & Co. Shareholders Litig., In re, 1001, 1004

Kagan v. Edison Bros- Stores, Inc., 908
Kahan v. Rosenstiel, 915
Kahn v. Lynch Communication Sys. Inc. (638 A.2d 1110), 158, 577, 624, *1102,* 1109, 1110, 1111, 1113, 1115, 1119, 1120, 1127
Kahn v. Lynch Communication Sys., Inc. (669 A.2d 79), 577, 624, 1111
Kahn v. Sullivan, 39
Kamen v. Kemper Financial Services. (500 U.S. 90), 832, 838
Kamen v. Kemper Fin. Servs (939 F.2d 458), 835
Kamin v. American Express Co., 198, 209
Kaplan v. Goldsamt, 573
Kaplan v. Peat, Marwick, Mitchell & Co., 890
Kaplan v. Wyatt, 849
Kardon v. National Gypsum Co., 345, 348, 397
Kassel v. Consolidated Freightways Corp., 1138
Kaster v. Modification Sys., 838
Katcher v. Ohsman, 736
Katz v. Oak Indus., Inc., 229, 575
Katzir's Floor and Home Design, Inc. v. M-MLS.com, 286
Kauffman v. Dreyfus Fund, Inc., 872
Kaufman v. Belmont, 831
Kaufman v. Wolfson, 127
Kavanaugh v. Kavanaugh Knitting Co., 129
Keck Enters, Inc. v. Braunschweiger, 74

Kelner v. Baxter, 289
Kemp & Beatley, Inc., Matter of, 788, 792
Kennerson v. Burbank Amusement Co., 770
Kenney v. Don-Ra, Inc., 828
Kentucky Pkg. Store v. Checani, 128
Kerbs v. California Eastern Airways, 155, 156
Kerkorian v. Western Air Lines, Inc., 641
Kern Country Land Co. v. Occidental Petroleum Corp., 520, 525, 526, 527
Kerrigan v. Merrill Lynch, Pierce, Fenner & Smith, 734
Kerrigan v. Unity Savs. Assn., 165, 172
Kersh v. General Council of Assemblies of God, 503
Ketchum v. Green, 364
Keystone Leasing v. People's Protective Life Ins. Co., 65
Kidd v. Thomas A. Edison, Inc., 60
Kim, United States v., 505
King v. Douglass, 904
King v. Driscoll, 766
Kinney Shoe Corp. v. Polan, 256, 260
Kirchoff Frozen Foods, Inc., In re, 58
Kirk v. First Nat'l Bank, 909
Kirschner v. United States, 364
Kirwan v. Parkway Distillery, Inc., 160
Klinicki v. Lundgren, 166
Klotz v. Consolidated Edison Co., 861
Knapp v. Bankers Securities Corp., 904
K-O Enterprises, Inc. v. O'Brien, 873
Kohler v. Kohler Co., 397
Kohn v. American Metal Climax, Inc., 397
Koppel v. 4987 Corp., 665
Kors v. Carey, 947
Kortum v. Webasto Sunroofs Inc., 643
Koval v. Simon Telelect, Inc., 60
Kramer v. Western Pac. Indus., Inc., 901
Kridelbaugh v. Aldrehn Theatres Co., 290, 291
Kruger v. Gerth, 783
Krukemeier v. Krukemeier Mach. & Tool Co., 161, 905
Kulka v. Nemirovsky, 287
Kullgren v. Navy Gas & Supply Co., 877
Kusner v. First Pa. Corp., 871

Labadie Coal v. Black, 257
Lacos Land Co. v. Arden Group, Inc., 572
Lampf, Pleva, Lipkind, Prupis & Petigrow v. Gilbertson, 422, 423
Landmark Land Co. of Carolina, Inc., In re, 925
Landstrom v. Shaver, 907
Lanza v. Drexel & Co., 397
Lash v. Lash Furniture Co., 128
Latt v. Superior Court, 777
Laurenzano v. Einbender, 696
Lavovitz v. Washington Times Corp., 903
Lawrence v. Cohn, 363, 367
Lawson v. Household Fin. Corp., 726, 729
Lawyers' Advertising Co. v. Consolidated Ry., Lighting & Refrigerating Co., 595
Laya v. Erin Homes, Inc., 257, 258, 259, 272
Leak v. Halaby Galleries, Inc., 772
Leannais v. Cincinnati, Inc., 282, 284, 285
Lear Corp. Shareholder Litig., In re, 1029, 1030

Leatherman v. Tarrant County Narcotics Intelligence and Coordination Unit, 408, 411
Lee v. Jenkins Bros., 64
Lefever v. K. L. Hovranian Enters., 283
Lehman Bros. v. Schein, 535
Lehrman v. Cohen, 573, 586, 735
Leibert v. Clapp, 782, 783, 900
Leitch Gold Mines Ltd. v. Texas Gulf Sulphur Co., 449
Lerman v. Diagnostic Data, Inc., 615, 631
Lerro v. Snapple Beverage Corp., 1081, 1082
Lesnik v. Public Industrials Corp, 903
Levco Alternative Fund Ltd. v. Reader's Digest Assn., Inc., 98
Level 3 Communications, Inc. v. Federal Ins. Co., 934
Levien v. Sinclair Oil Corp., 131, 880
Levine v. Smith, 831, *839,* 868
Levitin v. PaineWebber, Inc., 440
Levitt v. Johnson, 869
Lewis v. Anderson, 849, 872, 913, 914
Lewis v. Boyd, 856
Lewis v. BT Investment Managers, Inc., 1136
Lewis v. Graves, 833
Lewis v. Hat Corp. of America, 866
Lewis v. McGraw, 479
Lewis v. Mellon Bank, 516
Lewis v. Shaffer Stores Co., 893
Lewis v. Varnes, 516
Lewis v. Vogelstein, 121, *158*
Lewis v. Ward, 873
Lewis v. Welch, 834
LFC Marketing Group, Inc. v. Loomis, 252
Libera, United States v., 487
Lieberman v. Becker, 158
Liebman v. Auto Strop Co., 198
Lifschultz Fast Freight, Matter of, 273, 281
Liggett v. Lee, 25
Lincoln Nat'l Bank v. Herber, 365
Lincoln Stores, Inc. v. Grant, 173
Lindy Bros. Builders v. American Radiator & Standard Sanitary Corp., 918
Ling & Co. v. Trinity Sav. & Loan Assn., 734
Lippitt v. Ashley, 83
Lipton v. Documation, Inc., 387, 390
Lipton v. News Int'l, 902
List v. Fashion Park, Inc., 369, 385
List v. Lerner, 385
Litchfield Asset Mgt. Corp. v. Howell, 252, 819, 820
Little v. First Cal. Co., 384
LNR Property Corp. Shareholders Litigation, In re, 132
Lofland v. Cahall, 137
Long Island Lighting Co. v, Barbash, 655, 656
Long Park, Inc. v. Trenton-New Brunswick Theatres Co., 757
Lopez v. TDI Servs., Inc., 258
Lopez, In re, 643
Lovenheim v. Iroquois Brands, Ltd., 675, 676
Lowe v. SEC, 655
Lowenschuss v. Kane, 942
Lower Broadway Properties, In re, 745
L. R. T. Garrett v. Ancarrow Marine, Inc., 258
L-Tec Elecs. Corp. v. Cougar Elec. Org., Inc., 243

LTV Securities Ling., In re, 386, 387
Lundell v. Sidney Mach. Tool Co., 283
Lurie v. Arizona Fertilizer & Chem. Co., 71
Lussier v. Mau-Van Dev., Inc., 74, 166
Lutz v. Boas, 74
Lynch v. Patterson, 125
Lynch v. Vickers Energy Corp., 1091, 1097, 1099, 1101

Macht v. Merchants Mortgage & Credit Co., 580
MacKay v. Pierce, 833
Mackin v. Nicolett Hotel, 745
Maclary v. Pleasant Hills, Inc., 879
Macpherson v. Eccleston, 253
MacQueen v. The Dollar Sav. Bank Co., 70
Macy Corp, v. Ramey, 289
Madden v. Chase, 912
Mader's Store for Men, Inc., In re, 273
Madigan, Inc. v. Goodman, 418, 419, 421, 429
MAI Basic Four, Inc. v. Prime Computer, Inc., 1085
Maldonado v. Flynn (413 A.2d 1251), 126, 845, 847, 853
Maldonado v. Flynn (485 F. Supp. 274), 849
Maldonado v. Flynn (597 F.2d 789), 371, 692
Mallis v. FDIC, 365
Malone v. Brincat, 336, 341, 342, 623
Malott v. Randall, 887
Malpiede v. Townson, 624
Management Technologies., Inc. v. Morris, 66
Mangan v. Terminal Transp. System, 262
Manson v. Curtis, 753, 757, 758
Manufacturers Hanover Trust Co. v. Drysdale Secs. Corp., 396
Manufacturers Mutual Fire Ins. Co. v. Hopson, 896
Marble v. Latchford Glass Co., 883
Marciano v. Nakash, 116
Marco v. Dulles, 893
Marcus v. Otis, 167
Markovitz v. Markovitz, 608
Marks v. Seedman, 886
Marquette Cement Mfg. Co. v. Andreas, 523
Martin v. Graybar Elec, Co., 726
Marx v. Akers, 829, 838
Maryland Metals v. Metzner, 176
Mathers, Estate of, In re, 730
Matter of _____. *See name of party*
Matthews, United States v., 372, 691
Mauck v. Mading-Dugan Drug Co., 873
Maxxam Inc./Federated Dev. Shareholders Litig., In re, 872
Mayer v. Adams, 862, 866, 868
Mayer v. Oil Field Systems Corp., 363
McArthur v. Times Printing Co., 290
McCain, State ex rel, v. Construction Enter., 246
McCall v. Scott, 101, 109, 831
McCall Stock Farms, Inc. v. United States, 252
McCallum v. Rosen's Diversified, Inc., 791, 793
McCandless v. Furland, 879
McCarthy v. Litton Industries, Inc., 286
McClure v. Borne Chem. Co., 886
McEachin v. Kingman, 297

McKesson HBOC, Inc. Securities Litig., In re, 694
McLaughlin v. Foster, 880
McLean v. Alexander, 402
McMullin v. Beran, 1043
McNeil v. McNeil, 804
McNellis v. Raymond, 274
McQuade v. Stoneham, 751, 755-758
McRedmond v. Estate of Marianelli, 126
Medical Comm. for Human Rights v. SEC, 667, 675
Meinhard v. Salmon, 111, 172, 715, 719-721, 753, 800, 805, 820
Meiselman v. Meiselman, 785, 791-793
Melancon v. Superior Court, 882
Menard, Inc v. Dage-MTI, Inc. (726 N.E.2d 1206), 59, 61, 62
Mendel v. Carroll, 1051, 1055, 1063, 1064, 1102
Mendenhall v. Fleming Co., 910
Mentor Graphics v. Quickturn Design Sys., Inc., 991
Mercier v. Inter-Tel, Inc., 630, 631
Merola v. Exergen Corp., 766
Merrill Lynch, Pierce, Fenner & Smith, Inc., In re, 457
Merrill Lynch, Pierce, Fenner & Smith, Inc. v. Curran, 353, 369
Merrill Lynch, Pierce, Fenner & Smith, Inc. v. Dabit, 368, 404, 407
Merrill Lynch, Pierce, Fenner & Smith, Inc. v. Livingston, 506
Merritt-Chapman & Scott Corp, v. Wolfson, 925, 926
Metropolitan Casualty Ins. Co. v. First State Bank of Temple, 133
Metropolitan Life Ins. Co. v. RJR Nabisco, Inc., 229, 231
Meyer v. Oklahoma Bev. Law Enforcement Commn., 817, 821
Meyers v. El Tejon Oil & Refining, Co., 58
Meyers v. Smith, 888
Meyers v. Wells, 289
Meyerson v. El Paso Natural Gas Co., 131
Mfrs. Hanover Trust Co. v. Drysdale Sees. Corp., 396
Micciche v. Billings, 243
Michelson v. Duncan, 158, 160, 582
Mid-Town Produce Terminal, Inc., In re, 281
Midway Airlines v. Carlson, 594
Miles v. Electric Auto-Lite Co., 424, 694, 697, 698, 700
Miller v. American Tel. & Tel, Co., 78, 80
Miller v. Miller, 172
Miller v. Register & Tribune Syndicate, 854, 855
Miller v. Schreyer, 833, 834
Mills Acquisition Co. v. Macmillan, Inc., 87, 981, 1000, 1002-1009, 1016, 1019 1021, 1029, 1048
Mills v. Merrill Lynch & Co., 424
Mills v. Electric Auto-Lite Co., 913, 372, 375, 386, 694, 697, 698, 700, 940
Milwaukee Refrigerator Trans. Co., United States v., 256
Minton v. Cavaney, 265, 271
Mitchell v. Reed, 717
Mitchell v. Texas Gulf Sulphur Co., 310, 412, 421, 422
Mite Corp. v. Heli-Coil Corp., 640

Mlinarcik v. E. E. Wehrung Parking, Inc., 142, 160
MM Companies, Inc. v. Liquid Audio, Inc., 565, *619*, 629, 630
Mobile Steel Co., In the Matter of, 281
Mohr v. State Bank of Stanley, 62
Molecular Technology Corp. v. Valentine, 445
Monarch Bay II v. Prof'l Serv. Indus., 283
Monon v. Townsend, Yosha, Kline & Price, 816
Monroe Employees Retirement System v. Bridgestone Corp., 410
Moore Corp. v. Wallace Computer Servs., 990
Moore v. Crawford, 433
Moore v. Keystone Macaroni Mfg. Co., 138, 139
Moore v. Rommel, 243
Moorhead v. Merrill Lynch, Pierce, Fenner & Smith, Inc., 381
Morales v. Crompton & Knowles Corp., 284
Morales v. New Valley Corporation, 518
Moran v. Household Int'l, Inc., *613*, 619, 901, 960, 979, 986
Morgan v. Bon Bon Co., 291
Morgan v. McLeod, 642
Morgan v. Skiddy, 24
Morris v. New York State Dept. of Taxation & Fin., 254
Mortgage Am. Corp., In re, 48
Moses v. McGarvey, 915
Mosher v. Kane, 366
Mosser v. Darrow, 459, 463
Motherwell v. Schoof, 775
Motor Vehicle Mfrs. Assn. of United States, Inc. v. State Farm Mut. Auto. Ins. Co., 475
Mount Vernon Sav. & Loan v. Partridge Assocs., 798
Moyse Real Estate Co., v. First Nat'l Bank, 60
Multiponics, Inc., In the Matter of, 281
Musick, Peeler & Garrett v. Employers Ins., of Wausau, 422, 423, 443
Mutual Shares Corp. v. Genesco, Inc., 362
Myzel v. Fields, 397, 532

Naftalin, United States v., 478
Nathanson v. Zonangen Inc., 404
National Texture Corp. v. Hymes, 896
NationsMart Corp. Securities Litig., In re, 390
Natural Resources Defense Council v. SEC, 370
Neely v. Martin K. Eby Construction Co., 410
Neese v. Brown, 74, 867
Nelkin v. H. J. R. Realty Corp., 781, 793
Nelson v. Dakota Bankers Trust Co., 67
Neponsit Investment Co., v. Abramson, 848
Neubronner v. Milken, 499
New Crawford Valley Ltd. v. Benedict, 837, 869
New York City Emp. Retirement Sys. v. SEC, 678, 681
New York Currency Research Corp. v. CFTC, 683
New York Dock Co. v. McCollum, 920
New York Hanseatic Corp., In re, 604
New York Trust Co. v. American Realty Co., 127
Newby v. Lay, 486
Newman, United States v., 472, 490
Newmark v. RKO General, 522
Nixon v. Blackwell, 792, 1106
NLRB v. Fullerton Transfer & Storage Ltd., 253

No. 84 Employer-Teamster Joint Council Pension Trust Fund v. America West Holding Corp., 374
Noe v. Roussel, 125
Norlin Corp. v. Rooney, Pace, Inc., 115, 118, 307, 318
Norris v. Wirtz, 364, 381
North American Catholic Educational Programming Foundation, Inc. v. Gheewalla, 48, 232
Northeast Harbor Golf Club, Inc. v. Harris, 174
Northland Capital Corp. v. Silver, 367
Novak v. Kasaks, 404, 427
Nussbacher v. Chase Manhattan Bank, 843
Nutek v. Arizona Corp. Commn., 817
NYCERS v. SEC, 678

Oberhelman v. Barnes Investment Corp., 161
Oberly v. Kirby, 116
Oceanic Exploration Co. v. Grynberg, 582, 595, 751
Ocilla Indus, v. Katz, 556
Odman v. Oleson, 756
O'Hagan, United States v., 394, *470*, 484, 485, 487
O'Hazza v. Executive Creditor Corp., 274
Ohralik v. Ohio State Bar Assn., 656
Old Dominion Copper Mining & Smelting Co. v. Bigelow (188 Mass. 315), 879
Old Dominion Copper Mining & Smelting Co. v. Bigelow (203 Mass. 159), 879
Old Dominion Copper Mining & Smelting Co. v. Lewisohn, 879, 902
Olen v. Phelps, 252
Omnicare, Inc. v. NCS Healthcare, Inc., 1034, 1048, 1049
O'Neill v. Church's Fried Chicken, Inc., 914
Ong Hing v. Arizona Harness Raceway, Inc., 126, 291
Oracle Corp. Derivative Litigation, 857
Oracle Securities Litig., In re, 857
Oran v. Stafford, 374
ORFA Securities Litigation, In re, 538
Orman v. Cullman, 127
Osborne v. Locke Steel Chain Co., 139
Osofsky v. Zipf, 419
Ostrowski v. Avery, 165, 169, 172
Otis & Co. v. Pennsylvania R.R., 887
Owens Coming v. Nat'l Union Fire Ins. Co., 926

Paige v. United States, 734
Palley v. Baird, 865
Palmer v. Chamberlin, 726
Palmer v. Morris, 880
Palsgraf v. Long Island R.R., 396
Panzirer v. Wolf, 387
Papilsky v. Berendt, 899
Pappas v. Moss, 161
Paramount Communications, Inc. v. QVC Network, Inc. (637 A.2d), 979, 988, 999, *1009*, 1021, 1022, 1026, 1027, 1029, 1032, 1043, 1044, 1047, 1057, 1062
Paramount Communications, Inc. v. Time Inc. ([1989 Trans. Binder] Fed. Sec. L. Rep. (CCH) ¶ 94, 514), 964, 1003, 1026

*

Paramount Communications, Inc. v. Time Incorporated (571 A.2d 1140), 561, 623, *964*, *976*, 979, 982, 983, 986, *1003*, *1006*, 1010, 1017, *1026*
Park & Tilford v. Schulte, 521
Parmalat Sec. Litig., In re, 446
Parnes v. Bally Entertainment Corp., 98
Parshalle v. Roy, 587
Pasley v. Freeman, 358, 393
Patient Care Servs. v. Segal, 173
Paul v. Virginia, 241
Paul, Johnson, Alston & Hunt v. Graulty, 918
Paulman v. Kritzer, 779
Pavlidis v. New England Patriots Football Club, Inc., 316
PB Real Estate v. DEM II Properties, 817
Pearson v. Exide Corp., 932
Pease v. Rathbun-Jones Engineering co., 410
Peck v. Greyhound Corp., 667, 671, 675
Peil v. Speiser, 385, 386, 387
Peller v. Southern Co., 849
Pendergrass v. Care Care, Inc., 288
Pennaco Energy, Inc., In re, 1027
Penthouse Properties, Inc., v. 1158 Fifth Avenue, Incorporated, 726, 729
People v. Federated Radio Corp., 335
People v._____. *See name of defendant*
Pepper v. Litton, 126, 431, 433
Perlman v. Feldmann, 73, *908*, 356
Perpetual Real Estate Servs., Inc. v. Michaelson Properties, Inc., 253, 259
Perrine v. Pennroad Corp., 848
Perry v. Missouri-Kansas Pipe Line Co., 746
Perry v. Nevin Hotel Co., 289
Pessin v. Chris-Craft Indus., Inc., 872
Peters Grazing Assn. v. Legerski, 291
Petteys v. Butler, 521
Peyton v. William C. Petyon Corp., 746
Pharmaceutical Sales & Consulting Corp. v. J.W.S. Delavau Co., 247
Phelps Dodge Corp. v. Cyrus Amax Minerals Co., 1033, 1034
Philadelphia v. New Jersey, 1136
Phillips, In re, 318
Phillips v. Scientific-Atlanta, Inc., 410
Phillips Petroleum Co. v. Rock Creek Mining Co., 58
Phoenix Canada Oil Co. v. Texaco, 268
Pierson v. Jones, 273
Pike v. Bruce Church, Inc., 1141
Pilat v. Broach Sys., Inc., 607, 643
Pinnacle Consultants, Ltd. v. Leucadia Nat'l Corp., 156
Pinter v. Dahl, 343, 442, 443
Pioneer Specialties, Inc, v. Nelson, 771, 773
Piper v. Chris-Craft Indus., Inc., 349, 435, 439, 1134
Pitman v. Flanagan Lumber Co., 798
Podesta v. Calumet Indus., Inc., 949
Pogostin v. Rice, 98, 158, 161, 831, 837, 853, 957
Polk v. Good, 893
Pollitz v. Gould, 893
Poore v. Fox Hollow Enter., 821
Popkin v. Bishop, 431
Posadas de Puerto Rico Assocs. v. Tourism Co., 656
Press v. Chemical Inv. Servs. Corp., 427

Preston Farm & Ranch Supply v. Bio-Zyme Enters., 260
Proprietors of the Charles River Bridge v. Proprietors of the Warren Bridge, 20
Providence & Worcester Co. v. Baker, 568, 573
Pryor v. United States Steel Corp., 1080
PSE&G Shareholder Litig., In re, 831, *844*
Puma v. Marriott, 126, 846, 1096
Pure Resources, Inc. Shareholders Litig., In re, 1115, 1126

Quickturn Design Syst. Inc. v. Mentor Graphics., 990
Quinn v. Stuart Lakes Club, Inc., 733

Rabkin v. Olin Corp., 1107
Rabkin v. Philip A. Hunt Chem. Corp., 1102
Radaszewski v. Telecom Corp., 272
Radol v. Thomas, 1085
Rafe v. Hindin, 726, 730-731, 733
Rales v. Blasband, 636, 872
Ramey v. Cincinnati Enquirer, Inc., 917
Rand v. Cullinet Software, Inc., 391
Randall v. Bailey, 430, 431
Randall v. Loftsgaarden, 394, 419, 420, 421
Rapistan Corp. v. Michaels, 167, 173
Rapoport v. Schneider, 77
Raskin v. Frebank Co., 908
Rathborne v. Rathborne, 363
Rathke v. Griffith, 796
Ray v. Atlantic Richfield Co., 1134
RCM Sec. Fund v. Stanton, 831
RDR Assocs., Inc. v. Media Corp. of Am., 642
REA Express v. Travelers Ins. Co., 873
Reading Co., In the Matter of, 135
Reading Co., United States v., 253
Real Estate Capital Corp. v. Thunder Corp., *68*, 72
Recchion v. Kirby, 877
Reed, United States v., 490, 491, 492, 493
Rees v. Mosaic Techs., Inc., 289
Regal (Hastings), Ltd. v. Gulliver, 164, 166
Regenstein v. J. Regenstein Co., 175
Regents of the Univ. of Cal. V. Credit Suisse, First Boston, 446
Reifsnyder v. Pittsburgh Outdoor Advertising Co., 902
Reiser v. Del Monte Properties Co., 914
Reiss v. Pan Am. World Airways, Inc., 311, 313
Reliance Elec. Co. v. Emerson Elec. Co., 507, *511*, 514, 515, 518, 521, 525
Remillard Brick Co. v. Remillard-Dandini Co., 116
Remillong v. Schneider, 58
Renberg v. Zarrow, 730
Reprosystem, B.V. v. SCM Corp., 367
Resnik v. Swartz, 683
Revlon, Inc. v. MacAndrews & Forbes Holdings, Inc., 973, 982, *993*, 997-1009 1017, 1019, 1052·1023, 1026-1031, 1041-1042, 1045, 1048, 1056-1057, 1060, 1062, 1063, 1087
Rexene Corp. Shareholders Litig., In re, 901
Riblet Prods. Corp. v. Nagy, 766
Richards v. Bryan, 907
Richardson v. MacArthur, 503

Ridder v. Cityfed Fin. Corp., 931
Riesberg v. Pittsburgh & Lake Erie R.R., 253
Ringling v. Ringling Bros.-Barnum & Bailey
  Combined Shows, Inc., 735, 737, 744, 774
Ringling Bros.-Barnum & Bailey Combined
  Shows v. Ringling, 581, 582, 748
Ringling Bros., Etc., Shows, Inc. v. Ringling, 581
Rio Refrigeration Co. v. Thermal Supply of
  Harlingen, Inc., 71
Ripley v. International Rys. of Cent. Am., 129, 916
Rivoli Theatre Co. v. Allison, 154
RJR Nabisco, Inc. Shareholders Litig., In re, 974,
  1004, 1015, 1145
Roach v. Franchises Int'l, Inc., 887
Robbins v. Alibrandi, 915
Robbins v. Banner Indus., Inc., 696
Robbins v. Koger Properties, Inc., 394
Robert M. Bass Group, Inc. v. Evans, 971, 972, 973,
  1002
Roberts v. Alabama Power Co., 847
Roberts v. Eaton, 521
Roberts v. Whitson, 775
Robertson v. Levy, 245
Robinson v. Brier, 166
Robinson v. Pittsburgh Oil Refining Corp., 1026
Robinson v. Watts Detective Agency, 74
Rochez Bros, Inc. v. Rhoades, 400, 420
Rocket Mining Corp. v. Gill, 126
Rogers v. American Can Co., 868
Rogers v. Guaranty Trust Co., 140
Rogers v. Hill, 140, 141
Rogers Imports, Inc., In re, 600
Roland Int'l Corp v. Najjar, 1100, 1101
Roland Park Shopping Center v. Hendler, 736
Rolf v. Blyth, Eastman Dillon & Co., 402
Romani v. Shearson Lehman Hutton, 381
Rondeau v. Mosinee Paper Corp., 479
Roosevelt v. E. I. Du Pont de Nemours & Co., 676, 677
Rosenberg v. Globe Aircraft Corp., 401
Rosenberg v. Hano, 342
Rosenblatt v. Getty Oil Co., 339, 959, 1106, 1107,
  1110
Rosenblum v. Judson Engr, Corp., 173
Rosenfeld v. Fairchild Engine & Airplane Corp., 595
Rosengarten v. Buckley, 850
Rosengarten v. International Tel. & Tel. Corp., 849
Rosenthal v. Burry Biscuit Corp., 871
Ross v. Bank South, 390
Ross v. Bernhard, 828
Ross v. Licht, 457, 459
Ross v. Warner, 371
Roth v. Robertson, 79, 80
Rothman v. Gregor, 404
Rothman & Schneider, Inc. v. Beckerman, 66
Roven v. Cotter, 607
Rowen v. Le Mars Mutual Ins. Co. of Iowa, 117, 854
Rowen v. LeMars Mutual Ins. Co., 854
Royal Indus., Inc. v. Monogram Indus., Inc., 949
RP Acquisition Corp. v. Staley Continental, Inc.,
  1141
Rubenstein v. Collins, 380
Rubenstein v. Mayor, 248
Rubin v. United States, 364, 365
Ruetz v. Topping, 144
Ruiz v. Blentech Corp., 283

Runcie v. Bankers Trust Co., 79
Russell v. Louis Melind Co., 875
Ryan v. J. Walter Thompson Co., 726

Sadler v. NCR Corp., 641, 667
Safety Int'l, Inc., In re, 166
Saigh v. Busch (396 S.W.2d 9), 868, 904
Saigh v. Busch (403 S.W.2d 559), 868, 869, 904
Saito v. McKesson HBOC Inc., 635, 639
Salaman v. National Media Corp., 932
Salgo v. Mathews, 587
Sample v. Morgan, 154
San Juan Uranium Corp. v. Wolfe, 879
Sanders v. John Nuveen & Co. (524 F.2d 1064), 343
Sanders v. John Nuveen & Co. (554 F.2d 790), 261,
  402
Sanders v. Roselawn Memorial Gardens, Inc. 257
Sandfield v. Goldstein, 16, 783
Santa Fe Indus., Inc. v. Green, 312, 432, 437, 438, 439,
  440, 441, 442, 456, 473
Santisas v. Goodin, 882
Saphir v. Neustadt, 819
Saracco Tank & Welding Co. v. Platz, 48
Sargent v. Genesco, Inc., 363
Sarner v. Fox Hill, Inc., 126, 161
Saxe v. Brady, 141
Saylor v. Bastedo, 920
SBA v. Echevarria, 73
Scattergood v. Perelman, 440
Schechtman v. Wolfson, 917
Schein v. Chasen, 535, 538
Schilling v. Belcher, 880
Schlanger v. Four-Phase Sys, Inc., 312, 387
Schlesinger v. Herzog, 380
Schlick v. Penn-Dixie Cement Corp., 391, 697
Schmidt v. Farm Credit Servs., 61
Schmidt v. Magnetic Head Corp., 894
Schnell v. Chris-Craft Indus., Inc., 610, 611, 615, 616,
  629, 631, 957
Schoenbaum v. Firstbrook, 431, 437, 438
Schreiber v. Bryan, 135, 873
Schreiber v. Burlington Northern, Inc., 380, 479,
  480, 481, 482
Schreiber v. Carney, 577, 578, 582, 590, 591, 595, 597
Schroer, Estate of v. Steamco Supply, Inc., 763
Schumacher v. Schumacher, 907
Schwartz v. Marien, 764, 766
Schwartzman v. Schwartzman Packing Co., 642
Scott Graphics v. Mahaney, 260
Scruggs v. Cotterhill, 729
SEC v. Adler, 486
SEC v. Capital Gains Research Bureau, Inc., 312,
  433, 434
SEC v. Chenery Corp., 111
SEC v. Gaspar, 317
SEC v. Geon Indus., 316, 317
SEC v. Jakubowski, 440
SEC v. Joseph Schlitz Brewing Co., 371
SEC v. Kalvex, 371
SEC v. Lund, 464
SEC v. MacDonald, 420, 421
SEC v. Maio, 480, 483
SEC v. Materia, 483, 489, 490
SEC v. May, 646

SEC v. Monarch Fund, 457
SEC v. Musella, 490
SEC v. National Securities, Inc., 360, 399, 514
SEC v. Peters, 480, 483
SEC v. Rocklage, 485, 487
SEC v. Sargent, 487
SEC v. Shapiro, 317
SEC v. Texas Gulf Sulphur Co., 310, 311, 314, 315, 316, 317, 365, *369*, 370, 372, 401, 422, 449, 459, 532, 533, 537
SEC v. Transamerica Corp., 674
SEC v. Yun, 487
SEC v. Zanford, 366
Securities Inv. Co. v. Indian Waters Dev. Corp., 274
Security First Corp. v. U.S. Die Casting & Dev. Co., 634, 635, 636, 637, 638, 639, 642
Security-First Nat'l Bank v. Lutz, 144
Segal v. Coburn Corp. of Am., 311
Segan v. Constr. Corp. v. Nor-West Builders, Inc., 276
Seifert v. Dumatic Indus., Inc., 895
Seinfeld v. Verizon Communications Inc., 634, 639
Semerenko v. Cendant Corp. 363, 394
Seminaris v. Landa, 831
Senn v. Northwest Underwriters, Inc., 83
Sequa Corp. v. Gelmin, 932
Service Corp. Int'l v. H. M. Patterson & Son, 925
Seventeen Stone Corp. v. General Tel. Co., 904
721 Corp. v. Morgan Guar. Trust Co., 743
7547 Partners v. Beck, 879
Shaffer v. Universal Rundle Corp., 828
Shamrock Assocs. v. Texas Am. Energy Corp., 641
Shamrock Holdings, Inc. v. Polaroid Corp., 616, 63, 972
Shamrock Oil & Gas Co. v. Ethridge, 253
Shapiro v. Magaziner, 882
Shapiro v. Merrill Lynch, Fenner & Smith, Inc., 199, 457, 499
Sharon Steel Corp., In re, 312
Sharp v. Coopers & Lybrand, 384, 386
Shaw v. Agri-mark, Inc., 635
Shaw v. Empire Sav. & Loan Assn., 904
Shell v. Hensley, 431
Shepaug Voting Trust Cases, 745
Sherwood & Roberts-Oregon, Inc. v. Alexander, 292
Shirley v. Drackett Prods. Co., 252
Shivers v. Merco, 364
Shlensky v. Dorsey, 837
Shlensky v. South Parkway Bldg. Corp., 126, 127
Shlensky v. Wrigley, 75, 78
Shoen v. AMERCO, 556, 557, 559, 560, 563, 564, 831
Shores v. Sklar, 390
Short v. Columbus Rubber & Gasket Co., 773
Siebel v. Scott, 420
Silicon Graphics Inc. Securities Litig., In re, 404, 412, 427
Siliconix Inc. Shareholders Litig., In re, 1114, 1115, 1121, 1127
Silverman v. Landa, 523
Simmons v. Miller, 907
Simon v. Mann, 907
Simon v. Merrill Lynch, Fenner & Smith, Inc., 384

Simons v. Cogan, 290
Sinay v. Lamson & Session Co., 381
Sinclair Oil Corp. v. Levien, 131, 957, 1016, 1030, 1050, 1064, 1075, 1089, 1127
Simpson v. AOL Time Warner Inc., 446
Sinay v. Lamson & Session Co., 381
Singer v. Magnavox Co., 1090, 1100, 1101
Singer v. Singer, 719, 721
Sivers v. R&F Capital Corp., 289
Skouras v. Admiralty Enters., Inc., 642, 644
Slottow v. American Cas. Co., 272
Slusarski v. American Confinement Sys., Inc., 271
Small v. Fritz Cos., 368
Smallwood v. Pearl Brewing Co., 397
Smith, United States v., 486
Smith v. Atlantic Properties, Inc., 766
Smith v. Biggs Boler Works Co., 751
Smith v. Bolles, 419
Smith v. Brown-Borhek Co., 867, 868
Smith v. Dunlap, 868
Smith v. Shell Petroleum, Inc., 1102
Smith v. Tele-Communications, Inc., 131
Smith v. Van Gorkom, 82, 84, 87, 88, 95, 109, 110, 804, 999, 1007, 1022, 1028, 1029, 1030, 1043, 1049, 1101, 1112
Smith-Shrader Co. v. Smith, 175
Smolowe v. Delendo Corp., 512, 513, 514, 518, 519, 521
Software Toolworks Inc. Securities Litig., In re, 445
Sola Electric Co. v. Jefferson Electric Co., 347
Solimine v. Hollander, 921
Solomon v. Cedar Acres East, Inc., 292
Solomon v. Pathe Communications Corp., 1113, 1114, 1116, 1119, 1121-1124, 1127
Somers v. AAA Temporary Servs., 58, 724
Sonet v. Plum Creek Timber Co., 803
Soreno Hotel Co. v. Sate ex rel. Otis Elevator Co., 632, 633
Sorin v. Shahmoon Indus., Inc., 887
Soulas v. Troy Donut University, Inc., 143
South Buffalo Ry., United States v., 253
South Side Bank v. T.S.B. Corp., 644
Southern Development Co. v. Silva, 393
Southland Securities Corp. v. Inspire Ins. Solutions Inc., 410
Sparks v. CBIZ Accounting, Tax & Advisory of Kansas City, Inc., 910
Speedway Realty Co. v. Grasshoff Realty Corp., 298
Speetjens v. Malaco, Inc., 832
Spering v. Sullivan, 292
Spethmann v. Anderson, 123
Spiegel v. Buntrock, 841
S. Solomont & Sons Trust v. New Eng. Theatres Operating Corp., 864
Staffin v. Greenberg, 313
Stahl v. Apple Bancorp., Inc. (Stahl I), 556, 557, 616, 991
Stahl v. Gibralter Fin. Corp., 702
Staklinski and Pyramid Elec. Co., Matter of, 609
Stallworth v. AmSouth Bank of Ala., 837
Stamp v. Batastini, 77
Starkman v. Marathon Oil Co., 1085

Starrels v. First Nat'l Bank of Chicago,
831, *843*
State v. _____. *See name of defendant*
State ex rel. _____. *See name of relator*
State Teachers Retirement Bd. v. Fluor Corp., 307, 332
Stauffer v. Standard Brands, Inc., 436, 1089, 1099, 1100
Steele v. Litton Indus., Inc., 292
Steelman v. Mallory, 907
Steinberg v. Emplace, 1112
Stepak v. Addison, 857
Sterlin v. Biomune Sys., 422
Sterling v. Mayflower Hotel Corp., 131, 849, 959, 1100, 1106
Steven v. Roscoe Turner Aeronautical Corp., 267
Stevens v. Richardson, 160
Stewart Realty Co. v. Keller, 296, 297, 298
Stifel Fin. Corp. v. Cochran, 922, 930
Stine v. Girola, 252
Stone v. Eacho, 277, *280*
Stone v. Ritter, 97, *99,* 109
Stone-Fox Inc. v. Vandehey Dev. Co., 713
Stoneridge Investment Partners, LLS v. Scientific-Atlanta, Inc., 446
Stortrax.com, Inc. v. Gurland, 123
Storer v. Ripley, 743
Straub v. Vaisman & Co., 400
Stringer v. Car Data Sys, Inc., 160
Stroh v. Blackhawk Holding Corp., 735
Stroud v.Grace, 338, 559, 560, 561, 611, *612,* 626, 627, 629, 631, 689, 984
Strougo v. Bassini, 904
Studebaker Corp. v. Gitlin, 654
Stumpf v. C. E. Stumpf & Sons, Inc., 787
Sugarman v. Sugarman, 765
Sulphur Export Corp. v. Carribean Clipper Lines, Inc., 249, 250
Summers v. Tice, 409
Sundstrand Corp. v. Sun Chem. Corp., 402
Superintendent of Ins. v. Bankers Life & Cas. Co., 402, 429, 435, 436, 438
Surowitz v. Hilton Hotels Corp., 828, 877
Susquehanna Corp. v. Pan American Sulphur Co., 317
Swanson v. American Consumer Indus., Inc., 696, 699
Sweirkiewicz v. Sorema N.A., 395, 411
Swenson v. Englestad, 727
SWT Acquisition Corp. v. TW Servs., Inc., 964
Symbol Techs. Securities Litig., In re, 538
Systematics, Inc. v. Mitchell, 730

Tandycrafts, Inc. v. Initio Partners, 914
Tanzer v. International Gen. Indus., Inc., 575, 1090, 1100
Taylor v. Standard Gas & Elec. Co., 280
Tcherepnin v. Knight, 430
Teachers' Retirement System of Louisiana v. Aidinoff, 121
Tedesco v. Gentry Dev. Inc., 61
Teicher, United States v., 485

Tellabs, Inc. v. Makor Issues & rights, Ltd., 404, 412, 427
Terry v. Yamashita, 1129
Texas & Pac. Ry. Co. v. Rigsby, 348
Texas Indus. Inc. v. DuPuy, 258
Texas Int'l Airlines v. National Airlines, Inc., 527
Textile Workers v. Lincoln Mills, 348
Theberge v. Darbro, Inc., 255
Theodora Holding Corp. v. Henderson, 393
Thomas & Betts Corp. v. Leviton Mfg. Co., 634, 637, 638, 639
Thomas v. Dickson, 907
Thomas v. Duralite Co., 420
Thomas v. Roblin Indus., Inc., 539
Thomas v. Sanborn, 744
Thompson & Green Mach. Co. v. Music City Lumber Co., 243, 248
Tierno v. Puglisi, 877
Tift v. Forage Kind Indus., Inc., 282, *287*
Timberline Equip. Co. v. Davenport, 244, 249, 293
Time Warner Securities Litig., In re, 322, 325, 326
Timko v. Tsiarsi, 873
T. J. Raney & Sons, Inc. v. Fort Cobb, Okla Irrigation Fuel Auth., 387, 389, 390
TJI Realty, Inc. v. Harris, 66
TLC Beatrice Int'l Holdings, Inc. v. Cigna Ins. Co., 925
Today Homes, Inc. v. Williams, 173
Tomash v. Midwest Technical Dev. Corp., 921
Tomasso v. Armor Constr. & Paving, Inc., 819
Toner v. Baltimore Envelope Co., 763
Tooley v. Donaldson, Lukin & Jenrette, Inc., 902
Topkis v. Delaware Hardware Co., 573
Topper, In re the Application of, 787
Torregrossa v. Szelc, 272
Touche Ross & Co. v. Redington, 351, *352*
Tower Air, Inc., In re, 74
Towle v. Robinson Springs Corp., 639
Toys "R" Us, Inc., Shareholder Litig., In re, 1023, 1049
Trans World Airlines v. Summa Corp., 135
Triplett v. Grundy Elec. Coop., 866
Tri-State Developers, Inc. v. Moore, 249
Triweiler v. Sears, 907
T. Rowe Price Recovery Fund, L. P. v. Rubin, 132
Tryon v. Smith, 1066
TSC Indus., Inc. v. Northway, Inc., 312, 313, 314, 315, 316, 339, 372, 376, 693, 700
Tschirgi v. Merchants Nat'l Bank, 755
TW Servs., Inc. v. SWT Acquisition Corp., 977, 1004
TWA, Inc. v. Hughes, 745
Tydings v. Berk Eners., 894
Tyler v. Gas Consumers Assn., 927

Unilever Acquistion Corp. v. Richardson-Vicks, Inc., 565, 572
Union Carbide Corp. Consumer Prod. Bus. Securities Litig., In re, 918
United Copper Sec. Co. v. Amalgamated Copper Co., 841, 869
United Paperworkers Int'l Union v. Penntech Papers, Inc., 256

United Seal & Rubber Co. v. Bunting, 176
United States v._____. See name of defendant
United States v. Bryan, 471
United States Fidelity & Guar. Corp. v.
   Putzy, 249
United Vanguard Fund v. Takecare, Inc., 911
Unitrin, Inc. v. American Gen. Corp., 100, 559, 560,
   561, 624, 627, 628, 979, 988-992, 997, 1046, 1048,
   1049
Unocal Corp. v. Mesa Petroleum Co., 559, 560, 561,
   573, 613, 614, 616, 619, 620, 622, 624, 627, 630,
   955, 960-964, 971-979, 981-984, 986-990, 992, 994-
   997, 999, 1001, 1002, 1007-1009, 1016, 1019, 1022,
   1026, 1031, 1033-1035, 1040-1042, 1045, 1046,
   1048, 1060, 1081, 1114-1120, 1122-1126
Untermeyer v. Fidelity Daily Income Trust, 837
Upper DDeck Co. v. The Topps Co., 1029
USACafes, L.P., Litig., In re, 809

Valeant Pharmaceuticals Int'l v. Jerney, 143
Valiquet v. First Fed. Sav. & Loan Assn., 835, 836
Van Alstyne, Noel & Co., In re, 457
Van Landingham v. United Tuna Packers, 242
Vantagepoint Venture Partners 1996 v. Examen,
   Inc., 241
Veco Corp. v. Babcock, 175
Venturetek, L.P. v. Rand Publishing Co., 165
Vervaecke v. Chiles, Heider & Co., 384
Victor G. Bloede Co. v. Bloede, 727
Video Power, Inc. v. First Capital Income
   Properties, Inc., 247
Vine v. Beneficial Fin. Co., 363
Virginia Bankshares, Inc. v. Sandberg, 374, 440, 690,
   697, 701, 702
Virginia Beach, City of, v. Bell, 261
Virginia State Board of Pharmacy v. Virginia
   Citizen Consumer Council, 655
Vista Fund v. Garis, 880
Vogel, Application of, 775
Vohland v. Sweet, 708, 712
Von-Feldt v. Stifel Fin. Corp., 925
Vos Gerichian v. Commocore Int'l, 445

Wachovia Shareholders Litigation, In re, 910
Walker & Co. v. Evans, 641
Walker v. Knox & Assocs., 246, 247
Walker v. New Mexico & Southern Pacific R.
   Co., 411
Walker v. Virtual Packaging, LLC, 817
Walkovsky v. Carlton, 261, 273, 274
Wallace v. Systems & Computers Tech. Corp., 391
Walner v. Friedman, 837
Walt Disney Co. Derivative Litig., In re, 88, 101, 127,
   141, 146, 147
Walton v. Morgan Stanley & Co., 460, 491, 492, 539
Waltuch v. Conticommodity Servs., Inc., 921
Warden v. McLelland, 832
Warren v. Pim, 745
Waskel v. Guaranty Nat'l Corp., 927
Watson v. Button, 909, 910
Watson v. Watson, 711
Weil v. Beresth, 743
Weil v. Kirby Constr Co., 248

Weinberger v. UOP, Inc., 575, 702, 1063, 1073, 1088,
   1091, 1092, 1100-1102, 1106, 1107, 1110-1114,
   1126
Weiner v. Quaker Oats, 319, 320
Weinhaus v. Gale, 880
Weinsaft, In re Estate of, 730
Weinstein Enterprises, Inc. v. Orloff, 644
Weisbart v. Agri Tech, Inc., 922
Weisberg v. Coastal States Gas Corp., 692
Weiss v. Baum, 297
Weiss v. Temporary Inv. Fund, Inc., 843
Wellman v. Dickinson, 1082, 1083
Wells v. J. A. Fay & Egan Co., 297
Wendt v. Fischer, 716
Werbowsky v. Collomb, 830, 836, 852
Wessin v. Archives Corp., 907
West View Hills, Inc. v. Lizau Realty Corp., 66
West Waterway Lumber Co., In re, 734
Westec v. Lanham & Preferred Income Investors,
   L.L.C., 812, 816, 818
Western Air Lines, Inc. v. Kerkorian, 640
Western Oil Fields, Inc. v. McKnab, 612
Wharf (Holdings) Ltd. v. United Int'l Holdings,
   Inc., 367, 368
Wheelabrator Techs., Inc. Shareholders Litig.,
   In re, 158
Wheeler v. Pullman Iron and Steel Co., 76
White v. Abrams, 397
White v. Auerbach, 917
White v. Dvorak, 289
Whiting v. Dow Chem. Co., 509, 510
Whittaker v. Whittaker Corp., 509, 510,
   521, 523
Wieglos v. Commonwealth Edison Co., 390
Wilkes v. Springside Nursing Home, 761, 766, 767,
   769, 773, 791, 820
Willard v. Moneta Bldg. Supply, Inc., 103
Williams v. Geier, 627
Willis, United States v., 490
Wilshire-Doheny Assocs., Ltd. v. Shapiro, 926
Wilson v. Comtech Telecommunications Corp.,
   319, 384, 385
Wilson v. Great American Indus., Inc., 702
Wilson v. Wilson & King, 708
Wing v. Dillingham, 163
Winger v. Chicago City Bank & Trust Co., 167
Winner v. Cataldo, 882
Wisener v. Air Express Int'l Corp., 927
Whittaker v. Whittaker Corp., 509, 510
Wm. Goldberg & Co. v. Cohen, 903
Wolberg v. Wolberg Elec. Supp. Co., 643
Wolf v. Barkes, 899
Wolfensohn v. Madison Fund, Inc., 995
Wood v. Drummer (1824), 22, 46
Wood, Walker & Co. v. Evans, 641
Woodstock Enters., Inc. v. International
   Moorings & Marine, Inc., 160
Wright v. Iredell Tel. Co., 727
W & W Equip. Co. v. Mink, 905

Yacker v. Weiner, 276
Yanow v. Teal Indus., Inc., 903
Yasik v. Wachtel, 947
Young v. Columbia Oil Co., 166

Zaist v. Olson, 819
Zapata Corp. v. Maldonado, 840, *845,* 848, 853, 854, 855, 856, 861
Zeller v. Bogue Elec. Mfg. Corp., 420
Zidell v. Zidell, Inc., 768
Zilker v. Klein, 880
Zimmerman v. Bell, 864, 869

Zirn v. VLI Corp., 338, 339
Zobrist v. Coal-X, Inc., 384
Zucker v. Westinghouse Electric Corp., 917
Zuckerman v. Harnischfeger Corp., 322
Zupnick v. Goizueta, 140
Zweig v. Hearst Corp., 400
ZZZZ Best Securities Litig., In re, 445

TABLE OF STATUTES AND REGULATIONS

Principal references are in italics.

UNITED STATES

Administrative Procedure Act

generally   678

Anti-Referral Payments Law

generally   100

Bank Holding Company Act

generally   50

Bankruptcy Act

Ch. X, §172	898
Ch. X, §173	898
Ch. X, §222	898
Ch. X, §247	898
Ch. X, §§501-676	286
§548	224

Bankruptcy Code

§363	1036
§1101(1)	219
§1104	219
§1121(c)	219

Civil Rights Act

generally   73

Clayton Act

generally   869

Code of Federal Regulations

17 C.F.R. §240.10b-5	488
17 C.F.R. §240.14e-1	1133
17 C.F.R. §240.14e-1(a)	1133, 1135
17 C.F.R. §243.100(b)(2)(vi)	467
17 C.F.R. §243.101(c)	468
17 C.F.R. §243.101(e)	469
17 C.F.R. §243.102	467
17 C.F.R. §402(g)(2)	148

Commodity Exchange Act

generally   353

Comprehensive Environmental Response, Compensation and Liability Act

generally   253

Constitution

Art. I, §8	1132, 1136, 1138-1142
Art. IV, §2	241

Employee Retirement Income Security Act

generally	136

Fair Labor Standards Act

generally	73

Federal Aviation Act of 1958

generally	640

Federal Rules of Civil Procedure

generally	357, 394
Rule 8	407
Rule 8(a)(2)	395, 407
Rule 9(b)	407, 411
Rule 11	885
Rule 12(b)(6)	378, 379, 408
Rule 23	385, 389, 418
Rule 23(a)(2)	385
Rule 23(b)	865
Rule 23(b)(3)	341, 385
Rule 23(b)(3)(B)	418
Rule 23(b)(3)(C)	418
Rule 23(b)(3)(D)	418
Rule 23(c)(1)	388
Rule 23(c)(2)	870
Rule 23(c)(4)	388
Rule 23.1	828, 829, 830, 862, 870, 873, 896, 902
Rule 23.1, clause (1)	870
Rule 24	919
Rule 50(a)(1)	409
Rule 56(c)	409

Federal Rules of Evidence

Rule 301	387

Foreign Corrupt Practices Act

generally	26
15 U.S.C. §78dd-2	80

Glass-Steagall Act

generally	50

Inferior Criminal Courts Act

generally	753

Insider Trading and Securities Fraud Enforcement Act of 1988

generally	503

Insider Trading Sanctions Act of 1984

generally	502

Internal Revenue Code

generally	39, 74, 132, 140
§130A	151
§162(a)(1)	145
§162(m)	7, 146
§170(b)(2)	38
§172(b)(1)(C)	130
§280G	148
§422A	150
§1361(c)(4)	734
§1371	732
§4999	148
§7701	810
§7701 et seq.	810
§7701(a)(2)	705

Investment Advisers Act

generally	434
§202(a)(11)	468

Investment Company Act of 1940

generally	16, 838
§3	468
§3(c)(1)	16
§3(c)(7)	16
§16	609

Labor-Management Reporting and Disclosure Act

generally	915

McFadden Act of 1927

generally	50

National Banking Act

generally	73

National Labor Relations Act

generally	79

National Securities Markets Improvement Act of 1996

generally	305

Occupational Safety and Health Act

generally 73

Private Securities Litigation Reform Act of 1995

generally 341, 353, 381, 382, 394, 404,
405, 406, 407, 408, 410, 423,
426, 427, 428, 429, 445, 446
§21D(a)(3) 428
§21D(b) 407, 409, 411
§21D(b)(2) 405, 408, 410, 411
§21D(b)(3)(B) 428
§21D(f)(2)(B) 428
§21D(f)(7) 423

Sarbanes-Oxley Act of 2002

generally 11, 17, 27, 73, 146 299, 326,
327, 327, 329, 330, 330,
332, 333, 422, 424, 505
§2 331
§101(c) 328
§102 328
§102(a) 328
§103(a)(2) 328
§104 328
§105 328
§106(c) 329
§107 327
§201 329
§202 329
§203 329
§204 11
§206 329
§301 .... 11, 330
§302 330
§304(a) 331
§305 332
§305(a) 331
§307 333
§401 332
§401(a) 332
§402 331
§402(a) 331
§403 517
§404 332
§404(a) 331
§406 333
§406(b) 333
§407(a) 330
§407(b) 330
§409 332

Securities Act of 1933
15 U.S.C. §§77a-77aa

generally 301, 302, 303, 342, 355, 364,
398, 399, 429, 645, 693 725, 727
§2(3) 355, 364
§5 .... 354, 355, 360
§10 360

§11 .... 334, 342-343, 352, 356, 360,
399, 400, 920
§11(a) 342, 355
§11(b) 343, 344
§11(b)(3)(A) 343
§11(b)(3)(B) 398
§11(b)(3)(C) 343
§11(e) 399, 400
§12 .... 336, 355, 360, 400, 920
§12(2) 400, 400, 378, 342, 693
§12(a)(2) 334, 343-344
§13 400
§15 400
§16 341
§17 .... 447, 448, 920
§17(a) 355, 403, 429, 447
§17(a)(1) 403, 448
§17(a)(2) 403, 448
§17(a)(3) 403, 448
§17A 404
§18 .... 304, 305
§27A 381

Securities Act Rules

Rule 175 .... 321, 373
Form S-1
Form S-3 390

Securities Exchange Act of 1934

generally 11, 28, 300, 302, 303, 304, 306,
312, 327, 340, 342, 355, 358, 361,
364, 387, 398, 399, 429, 442, 445, 456,
532,543, 544, 567, 569, 589, 645, 646,
647, 651, 657, 658, 660, 664, 675,
677, 678, 687, 688, 693,
§2(3) 300
§2(4) 300
§3(a) 468
§3(a)(10) 430
§3(a)(11) 517
§9 .... 349, 355, 399, 400, 422, 423, 528
§9(e) 400
§10 .... 344, 345, 423, 486, 528
§10A(m) 11
§10A(m) (2) 11, 330
§10A(m)(3)(B) 330
§10A(m)(4) 11, 330
§§10A(m)(5)-(6) 11
§10(b) 308, 313, 316, 352, 354, 355, 360,
361, 362, 369, 385, 397, 398, 399, 400,
401, 403, 406, 407, 408, 411, 422, 423,
429, 430, 431, 434, 435, 436, 437, 438,
440, 441, 442, 443, 444, 445, 447, 456,
458, 462, 464, 470, 471, 472, 473,
474, 475, 476, 477, 478, 479, 481, 482,
484, 486, 489, 494, 532, 692, 693, 698
§10b-5 358
§11(a)(1) 458
§12 .... 644, 645, 646
§12(b) 302
§12(g) 302, 646

§13	303, 942
§13(a)	331
§13(b)	150
§13(d)	1068, 1076-1079, 1084
§13(d)(1)	*1076*, 1079
§13(d)(3)	1084
§13(e)	1076
§13(f)(5)	468
§13(g)	674
§13(j)	332
§13k	146, 331
§14	543, 571, 645, 646, 670, 672, 675, 942
§14(a)	346, 349, 374, 375, 376, 377,
	378, 400, 440, 644, 646, 647, 650, 654,
	665, 669, 673, 674, 690, 691, 692, 693,
	694, 695, 696, 697, 699, 700,
	701 913, 914
§14(b)	656
§14(c)	646
§14(d)	1079
§14(d)(1)	*1077*
§14(d)(5)	1079
§14(d)(6)	1079, 1080
§14(e)	344, 349, 350, 351, 353, 470,
	471, 479,480, 481, 482, 483, 484,
	488, *1078*, 1079
§14(f)	609, 1068, 1069
§15(c)(2)	481, 482
§15(c)(2)(D)	481
§15(d)	302, 331
§15(f)	503
§16	505, 506, 508, 517, 523
§16(a)	505, 509, 510, 528, 916
§16(b)	16, 334, 354, 355, 364, 365,
	400, 446, *505*, 506, 507, 508, 509,
	510, 511, 512, 513, 514, 515, 516,
	516, 517, 518, 519, 520, 521, 522,
	523, 524, 525, 526, 527, 528, 528,
	529, 531, 532, 533, 601,
	891, 916, 932, 934
§16(c)	506
§16(d)	506
§16(e)	506
§17	345
§17(a)	351, 396
§17(a)(1)	327
§17(b)(1)	327
§18	334, 355, 398, 400, 423, 693, 885
§18(a)	334, 352, 385
§19(c)	567
§19(c)(4)	566, 567, 571
§20	400
§20(a)	359, 400, 498
§20(d)	465
§20(e)	445
§20A	422, 497, *498*, 499
§21	349, 503
§21A(a)(2)	502
§21(A)(b)(2)	503
§21(d)	498
§21D(a)(3)	428
§21D(b)	409, 411
§21D(b)(2)	404, 408-412, 426
§21D(b)(3)(B)	428
§21D(f)(2)(B)	428
§21D(f)(7)	423
§21E	381, 404
§21E(c)(1)	*381*
§21E(c)(1)(B)(ii)	382
§21E(i)(1)	381
§26	152
§27	346, 347, 349, 351
§28	356, 383, 419
§28(a)	400, 419, 533, 545
§28(f)	341
§29	420
§29(b)	355
§34	349
§208	400
§240.10b-5	486

Securities Exchange Act Rules

generally	682, 691
Rule 3b-6	373
Rule 10A-3	11
Rule 10b-5	150, 300, 308-318, 320, 334,
	336, 344, *345*, 348, 352-354,
	356-367, 369, 372, 378,
	381, 382, 383, 385-390, 394, 397,
	400-404, 407, 412, 418-423, 426,
	428-431, 433-449,451, 453, 455, 456, 458,
	459, 461, 462, 464, 466, 470-473, 475,
	476-479,481, 483, 486, 488, 489, 490,
	492-494, 499, 501, 502, 515, 532, 533, 646,
	690, 692, 693, 696-698, 1079, 1089
Rule 10b-5(a)	446
Rule 10b-5(b)	438, 446
Rule 10b-5(1)	403
Rule 10b-5(2)	383, 401, 403
Rule 10b-5(3)	401, 403
Rule 10b5-1	*486*, 487
Rule 10b5-1(c)	486
Rule 10b-5-2	*497*
Rule 10b5-2(b)	497
Rule 10b5-2(b)(2)	497
Rule 10b-13	1081
Rule 12g-1	646
Rule 13(a)	73
Rule 13(d)-1	73
Rule 13e-1	1088
Rule 13e-3	666
Rule 13e-3A	434
Rule 13e-3B	434
Rule 13e-4	1081, 1088
Rule 13e-4(f)(8)-(11)	1088
Rule 14a-1	650, 654
Rule 14a-1(1)(2)	656
Rule 14a-1(1)(2)(iv)	652
Rule 14a-2	651, 654
Rule 14a-2(a)	656
Rule 14a-2(b)(1)	652
Rule 14a-2(b)(1)(ix)	652
Rule 14a-2(b)(2)	656
Rule 14a-2(b)(3)	656
Rule 14a-2(b)(ix)	652
Rule 14a-3	304, 645, 659, 660, 661
Rule 14a-4	645, 653, *661*, 664, 665
Rule 14a-4(a)	665

Rule 14a-4(b)	664, 665	Rule 101(c)	468
Rule 14a-4(c)	664, 665	Rule X-14A-7	670, 671
Rule 14a-4(c)(1)	664	Rule X-14A-8	671
Rule 14a-4(c) (2)	664	Regulation FD	466-469
Rule 14a-4(d)	652	Regulation FD, Rule 100	467-469
Rule 14a-4(e)	664, 665	Regulation FD, Rule 100(a)	468
Rule 14a-6(b)	663	Regulation FD, Rule 100(b)(1)	468
Rule 14a-7	641, 645, 651	Regulation FD, Rule 100(b)(2)	469
Rule 14a-7(a)(1)(i)	666	Regulation FD, Rule 100(b)(2)(iv)	467
Rule 14a-7(a)(2)(i)	665	Regulation FD, Rule 101(a)	468
Rule 14a-7(a)(2)(ii)	666	Regulation FD, Rule 101(c)	468
Rule 14a-7(b)	666	Regulation FD, Rule 101(d)	468
Rule 14a-8	546, 547, 552, 645, 658, 659, 664, 667, 674-679, 681, 684, 687-689, 863	Regulation FD, Rule 101(e)	468, 469
		Regulation FD, Rule 102	467
Rule 14a-8(c)	670	Regulation M-A	1084
Rule 14a-8(c)(2)	673	Regulation M-A, Item 1006	1086
Rule 14a-8(c)(4)(i)	674	Regulation M-A, Item 1006(d)	1086
Rule 14a-8(c)(5)	672, 673	Regulation S-K, Item 404	659
Rule 14a-8(c)(7)	676, 678	Schedule 13D	652, 1059, 1079, 1084, 1086
Rule 14a-8(d)(3)	681	Schedule 14A	645, 659
Rule 14a-8(i)	679, 680	Schedule 14A, Item 1	659
Rule 14a-8(i)(1)	680	Schedule 14A, Item 2	659
Rule 14a-8(i) (1)-(13)	683	Schedule 14A, Item 4	659
Rule 14a-8(i)(8)	681, 683, 684, 685, 686, 687	Schedule 14A, Item 5	659
Rule 14a-9	334, 344, 345, 346, 353, 372, 374, 375, 440 646, 652, 656, 679, *689*, 690, 693, 694, 695	Schedule 14A, Item 6	659, 691
		Schedule 14A, Item 7	659
		Schedule 14A, Item 7(a)	682
Rule 14a-9(a)	691-693	Schedule 14A, Item 7(b)	659, 682
Rule 14a-11	684-687	Schedule 14A, Item 7(c)	682
Rule 14a-12	685	Schedule 14A, Item 8	150
Rule 14a-13(b)(2)	641	Schedule 14A, Item 10	150
Rule 14a-16	589	Schedule 14D-1	1079
Rule 14a-18	688	Schedule 14D-9	1086, 1087, 1118, 1123
Rule 14b-1	588, 641, 656	Schedule 14D-9, Item 7	1086, 1087
Rule 14d-2	1080, 1082	Schedule TO	1084, 1085
Rule 14d-5	642, 666	Form 8-K	303, 333, 469
Rule 14d-7	1079	Form 10-K	303, 307, 321, 329, 654, 660, 661
Rule 14d-8	1079, 1080	Form 10-Q	303, 307, 321, 329, 654
Rule 14d-9	1086, 1087		
Rule 14d-9(b)	1087, 1088		
Rule 14d-9(b), Item 7	1080, 1081		
Rule 14d-9(e)	1080	***Securities Litigation Uniform Standards Act of 1998***	
Rule 14d-10	1069, 1080, 1081		
Rule 14e-1	1135, 1079	generally	305, 341, 368, 429
Rule 14e-2	*1087*		
Rule 14e-3	465, 480, 484, 494, 503	***Small Business Investment Act***	
Rule 14e-3(a)	470, 471, 476, 479, 480, 482, 483, 488, 494		
Rule 14e-8	1080	generally	73
Rule 16a-1	516		
Rule 16a-1(a)(1)	510		
Rule 16a-1(a)(2)	517	***Trust Indenture Act of 1939***	
Rule 16a-1(f)	508		
Rule 16a-2	515	§316(b)	226
Rule 16a-4	518		
Rule 16a-8	510		
Rule 16a-10	515	***United States Code***	
Rule 16b-3	518		
Rule 16b-6(b)	518	15 U.S.C. §77(p)	341
Rule 19c-4	566, 571, 572	15 U.S.C. §78b	474
Rule 100	*467, 468, 469*	15 U.S.C. §78 bb(f)	341
Rule 100(a)	468	15 U.S.C. §78ff(a)	478
Rule 100(b)(1)	468	15 U.S.C. §78j	486
Rule 100(b)(2)	467, 469	15 U.S.C. §78j(b)	407, 471, 476
Rule 100(b)(2)(iv)	467	15 U.S.C. §78k(a)(1)	458

15 U.S.C. §78n(e)	479, 482
15 U.S.C. §78o(c)(2)(D)	481
15 U.S.C. §78r(a)	385
15 U.S.C. §78u-4(b)(1)	394, 404, 405, 408
15 U.S.C. §78u-4(b)(2)	394, 404, 405,
	408, 410, 411, 412
15 U.S.C. §78u-4(b)(4)	391, 393, 394
18 U.S.C. §2	442, 488
18 U.S.C. §610	78, 80
18 U.S.C. §1341	484
18 U.S.C. §1350	331
18 U.S.C. §1621	488
28 U.S.C. §1658(b)	422

Williams Act

generally	26, 349, 350, 479, 482, 594,
	942-944, 1068, 1076,
	1079, 1132
Rule 14d-5	641, 642

UNIFORM LAWS AND MODEL ACTS

ABA Code of Professional Responsibility

generally	891
Canon 4	892
Canon 5	891, 892

ALI Federal Securities Code

§1413(c)	516
§1413(h)(1)	526
§1603	458

ALI Model Penal Code

§2.02	402

ALI Principles of Corporate Governance

generally	37, 38, 40
§1.14(b)	121
§1.23(a)	126
§1.25	121
§1.33	120
§2.01	37, 38
§2.01(b)	38, 81
§2.01(b)(1)	81
§2.01(b)(2)	38
§2.01(b)(3)	38
§4.01	*103*, 104, 105
§4.01(a)	104, 105
§4.01(c)	104
§4.01(c)(1)	104
§4.01(c)(3)	105
§4.01(d)	84
§4.02	104, *105*
§4.03	104, 105

§5.02	*120,*122, 123, 125, 860
§5.02(a)(2)(D)	135
§5.02(b)(2)(B)	120
§5.03 comment g	834, 835
§5.04	538
§5.05	*174*
§5.06	176
§5.10	135
§5.10(c)	136
§5.15	1002
§5.16	*1063*, 1065, 1066, 1102
§5.16(b)	1066
§6.01(a)	940, 993, 997
§7.01	901
§7.01 comment a	901
§7.01 comment c	901
§7.01 comment d	906
§7.01 comment e	906
§7.01 Reporter's Note 4	906
§7.01(d)	906
§7.01(d) Comment	906
§7.02	*873*
§7.02 comment e	906
§§7.02-7.10	847
§7.03 comment d	832
§7.03(c)	867
§7.04(d)	885
§7.07(a)	861
§7.08	856, *859*, 861
§7.09	859
§7.10	*859*
§7.10(a)	859, 860
§7.10(a)(1)	859
§7.10(a)(2)	860
§7.10(b)	859, 860
§7.11	867
§7.13	847, 867
§7.13(c)	849
§7.13(d)	860
§7.15	899
§7.17	919
§7.18(c)	81
§7.19	81, 108
§7.20	925
§7.20, Official Comment	934
§7.20(a)(2)	934
§7.20(a)(4)	933, 935
§7.20(d)	925
§7.22(c)	1102
§7.25	1112

Model Business Corporation Act

§15	1137
§33	1137
§37	1137
§45	1137
§53	245
§54	245, 1137
§55	245
§56	244, 245, 248
§79	1137
§146	293

Restatement (Second) of Agency

generally	537
§7	59
§8A	59, 60
§33	59
§82	289
§84	289
§161	59, 60, 61
§312	459
§388	531, 532
§390	473
§395	473, 492

Restatement (Third) of Agency

§1.01	259
§2.01	59

Restatement (Second) of Conflict of Laws

§304	1136

Restatement of Contracts

§132	289

Restatement of Restitution

§66(4)	335
§201(2)	459

Restatement of Torts

§538(a)	369
§548A	394

Restatement (Second) of Torts

generally	409
§525	385, 393
§531	335
§551(2)(a)	481
§874A	348, 349
§876(b)	442

Restatement (Third) of Torts

§28(b)	409

Revised Model Business Corporation Act

generally	8, 221-224, 240, 547, 604, 606, 726,
§1.40(6)	221
§1.43(a)(1)	858
§2.02(b)(4)	81

§2.03	248
§2.04	248
§3.01(a)	67
§3.02	68
§3.04	72
§6.01	735
§6.01(c)	1137
§6.21	221, 222
§6.21, Official Comment	221
§6.22	222
§6.24	150
§6.27	733
§6.30(b)(3)(ii)	150
§6.40	1137
§6.40(c)	223
§7.02	557
§7.03	557
§7.20	585
§7.22	583
§7.24(c)	586
§7.25	586
§7.27	604, 605, 737
§7.28	599, 1137
§7.30(b)	750
§7.31	743
§7.32	56, 726
§7.32(c)	726
§7.32(d)	726
§7.42	832, 862
§7.44	853, 858, 859, 861
§7.45	897
§7.46(2)	885
§8.01	56, 751
§8.01(b)	8
§8.02	56
§8.03	56
§8.06	1137
§8.08	606
§8.10	608
§8.11	137
§8.20	57
§8.21	57
§8.30	103, 121
§8.30(a)	103, 105, 121
§8.30(b)	103
§§8.30(d)-(f)	105
§8.31	104
§8.31(a)(2)	104, 126
§8.31(b)(1)	84
§8.40	56
§8.41	57
§§8.50-8.59	922
§8.53	931
§8.53(b)	932
§8.57	933
§8.60	121, 126
§8.61	121, 123
§8.61(b), Official Comment	123
§8.62	175
§8.62(b)	173
§8.70	175
§10.04(d)	735
§11.01	1100
§12.02	1137
§14.06	287

§14.34	793
§15.01	241
§15.05(c)	241
§16.01	251
Subchapter F	121, 135

Revised Model Business Corporation Act Close Corporation Supplement

§25	260

Revised Uniform Limited Partnership Act

generally	259, 797
§103	811
§303	797
§303(a)	799
§303(b)	799
§304	798

Revised Uniform Partnership Act

generally	706
Art. 7	722
Art. 8	722
§103	720, 811
§103(b)(3)(i)	721
§201	708
§201, Comment	708
§202	712
§202(a)	712
§202(c)(3)	712
§303	713
§303(e)	713
§305	714
§306	714
§307	714
§401	714
§401(b)	715
§404	719-720, 721
§404, Comment 1	720
§404(e)	720
§601	723
§602	723

Uniform Commercial Code

generally	421
§8	335
§8-204	731
§8-306(2)	335

Uniform Fraudulent Conveyance Act

§4	224

Uniform Limited Liability Company Act

generally	811, 818, 820

§110	811
§202	811
§401	811
§407(a)	811
§§409(a)-(d)	820
§902	811

Uniform Limited Partnership Act

generally	797, 798
§7	798
§303	800

Uniform Partnership Act

generally	706
§6	710
§7	710
§7(4)	711, 712
§9(1)	712
§9(2)	713
§9(3)	713
§13	713
§15	713
§18	714
§21(1)	715
§29	707, 720
§30	720
§31	723
§38(2)	723
§41(1)	707

Uniform Securities Act

generally	304
§509	336

ARIZONA

General Corporation Law

§10-1806	775
§§1221-1223	1142

ARKANSAS

Business Corporation Act

§211	730
§211(C)	730
§601(c)	730

CALIFORNIA

Civil Procedure Code

§1021	882
§1281	774

General Corporation Law

§114	222
§152	553, 606
§158	725
§166	221
§181	566
§204(a)(10)	109
§207(e)	38
§300(a)	680, 770
§309(a)	104
§310	*120*
§310(a)(3)	125
§317	882
§317(a)	929
§317(b)	922, 931, 932
§317(c)	923
§317(c)(2)	923
§317(d)	926
§317(e)	925
§317(g)	923
§317(i)	933
§418	725
§500(a)	222
§500(b)	222
§600	251
§602	586
§800	*871, 884*
§800(b)(2)	829, 862
§800(c)	881
§800(c)(2)	882
§800(d)	882, 883
§800(e)	881, 883
§800(f)	883
§1200	566
§1201	553
§1201(b)	1006
§1602	643
§1800(b)(4)	787
§1800(b)(5)	787
§2115	241

Limited Liability Company Act

generally	
§17153	820

COLORADO

Corporation Code

§107-402	886

Limited Liability Company Act

§§70-80-101 to 70-80-913	810
§§7-80-101 to 7-80-1101	812
§7-80-107	814, 815
§7-80-201(1)	814
§7-80-208	813, 814, 815
§7-80-705	815

CONNECTICUT

Business Corporation Act

generally	40
§§33-724	853
§§33-756	42

Limited Liability Company Act

§§119-124	819

DELAWARE

Chancery Rules

23	340
23.1	340, 830, 840

General Corporation Law

generally	238, 339, 547, 549, 552, 590, 606, 610, 633, 672, 673 731, 749
§101	*238*
§102	*238*
§102(b)(4)	725
§102(b)(7)	94, 95, 109, 235, 240 721, 1101
§109	689
§109(a)	682
§109(b)	592, 680, 992
§122(9)	38
§141	*606*, 751, 991, 1049
§141(a)	635, 680, 846, 956, 990, 990, 991, 992
§141(b)	551, 552
§141(c)	89
§141(e)	92, 93
§141(f)	948
§141(k)	606, 607, 950
§144	120, 846
§144(a)(1)	116
§144(a)(2)	116
§145	94
§145(a)	922-925
§145(b)	923-925
§145(c)	925-927
§145(d)	925
§145(e)	931, 932
§145(f)	923-925
§145(g)	933
§151(a)	*549, 573*
§151(f)	731
§151(g)	565
§157	150
§160	946
§160(a)	956, 994
§160(c)	566
§170	132
§202	573, *731-732*
§202(c)	734

§203	985, 1070-1075, *1130*, 1131, 1141, 1142
§203(a)(1)	1070
§203(a)(2)	1070, 1131
§203(a)(3)	1131
§203(c)(3)	1131
§205	969
§211	557, 1014
§211(c)	631
§211(d)	557
§212(b)	585
§212(c)	587
§212(e)	586
§213	584, 593, 594
§213(a)	594
§213(b)	594, 595
§214	599
§216	586
§218	*749, 750*
§218(a)	751
§218(b)	751
§218(c)	*581, 743*
§218(d)	750
§219(c)	585
§220	621, *633*, 634-639, 641, 840
§220(a)	*633*, 640
§220(b)	*633*
§220(b)(2)	*633*, 644
§220(b) (2) (b)	*633*, 644
§220(c)	*633-634*
§220(d)	*634*, 643
§221	*549*
§226	*775, 776, 778*
§226(a)	*777, 778*
§226(a)(1)	*777-779*
§226(a)(2)	*777, 778*
§226(b)	*778*
§228	*590, 591-594, 606, 951*
§231	*586, 589, 590*
§231(b)	589
§231(d)	590
§242	1014
§242(a)(2)	673
§242(b)	576
§242(d)	673
§251	939, 1043, 1124
§§251-258	1014
§251(c)	551, 1031, 1034, 1035, 1042,1049
§251(f)(3)	1006
§253	432, 1113, 1117, 1120, 1123, 1125, 1126
§262	1098-1099
§262(a)	1099
§262(d)	1099
§262(e)	1099
§262(h)	1098, 1099
§263	1014
§271	939, 1014
§275	1014
§291	775, 776
§321(b)	238
§327	871
§329	*248*
§342	725
§344	725
§346	725

§348	725
§349	732
§351	776
§352	775, 776, 777
§352(a)(2)	776
§353	776
§355	777
§391	240

Limited Liability Company Act

§§18-0101 to 18-1109	810
§18-1101	811, 821

Revised Uniform Limited Partnership Act

generally	803, 821
§9-406	807
§9-408	807
§17-1101	807
§17-1101(d)	803-805, 821
17-1101(d)(2)	803, 805

Revised Uniform Partnership Act

§15-103(f)	721

Limited Liability Partnership Act

§15-306	822

Rules of the Court of Chancery

Rule 23(b)	862, 864

DISTRICT OF COLUMBIA

Business Corporation Act

Generally	245
§29.921c	245
§29.950	245

FLORIDA

Business Corporation Act

§607.0302(12)	38
§607.0302(14)	38

Limited Liability Company Act

§§608.401-608.471	832

GEORGIA

Business Corporation Code

§22.204	246
§22.5103	246
§204	248

HAWAII

Business Corporation Act

§§171-172	1129

ILLINOIS

Annotated Statutes

Ch. 32, §157.96(a)(3)	787

Business Corporation Act

§8.05(c)	143
§11.20	553

Business Takeover Act

Generally	1128, 1134, 1138, 1140

Close Corporation Act

§§5/2A.05 to 2A.60	725
§5/2A.40	775

Limited Liability Company Act

§180015-3	820

INDIANA

Business Corporation Law

§23-1-17-3	1133
§23-1-17-3(a)	1131
§23-1-17-3(b)	1131
§23-1-20-5	1132
§§23-1-32-1 et seq.	906
§23-1-32-4	906
§23-1-35-1(e)	109
§23-1-35-2(d)	120
§23-1-37-8	923
§23-1-37-11	929
§23-1-38-4(a)	1132

§23-1-42	1129
§23-1-42-1	1132, 1133
§§23-1-42-1 et seq.	1132
§23-1-42-3	1133, 1138
§23-1-42-4(a)	1133
§23-1-42-4(a)(3)	1138
§23-1-42-6	1133
§23-1-42-7	1133
§23-1-42-7(a)	1133
§23-1-42-8(a)	1133
§23-1-42-9(a)	1133
§23-1-42-9(b)	1133, 1144
§23-1-42-9(b)(1)	1133
§23-1-42-10(a)	1133
§23-1-42-10(b)	1133

General Corporation Act (Superseded in 1987)

§§23-1-43-1 to 23-1-43-24	1130, 1142
§23-1-43-18	1130

IOWA

Business Corporation Act

§490.831	119
§496A.34	*115*, 117

KENTUCKY

Business Corporation Act

§271A.397	1130
§§271B.12-200 to 271B.12-220	1142

LOUISIANA

Business Corporation Law

§83(D)	925
§83F	934

Revised Statutes

§12.9	249

MAINE

Business Corporation Act

§716	1166
§831	1132
§910	1132

MARYLAND

General Corporation Law

§3-413(b)(2)	787
§§3-601 to 3-603	1129
§4-201	725
§4-302	725
§4-401	760
§4-501	725

MASSACHUSETTS

Business Corporation Law

§22	773

MICHIGAN

Compiled Laws Annotated

§450.1825(1)	787, 787

Statutes Annotated

§600.5025	774

MINNESOTA

Business Corporation Act

§301A.671	1129
§302A.255	119
§302A.671	1142
§661	287
§751(3a)	788

MISSOURI

General & Business Corporation Law

§351.407	1129
§351.459	1142

NEVADA

Revised Statutes

§78.138	557, 564
§78.330	555, 556
§78.330(1)	555
§78.345(1)	555

NEW JERSEY

Business Corporation Act

§3-6	885
§6-8	119
§14A.3-4	38
§14A:6-14	1132
§14A:7-2	735
§14A:7-7	681
§14A:10A-4	1130, 1142
§14A:12-7(1)(c)	786, 787
§14.3-15	866

Rules of Civil Practice

Rule 4:32-5	870

NEW MEXICO

Business Corporation Act

§53-11-20	150

NEW YORK

Business Corporation Law

generally	5, 38, 41, 577, 602, 608, 609
§202(12)	38
§402(a)(7)	238
§402(b)	929
§501(c)	953
§505(2)(i)	681
§505(d)	153
§602(b)	542
§608(b)	586
§609	577, 583, 586
§609(e)	743
§609(f)(4)	583
§609(f)(5)	583
§612(b)	566
§613	549
§616	737
§616(b)	605
§618	599
§620	577, 578, 725, 759
§626	896, 899
§626(b)	871
§626(c)	833, 862
§627	886
§630	240
§704	600
§704(a)	950
§705	608
§706(b)	606
§706(c)	600
§706(d)	608
§709	608, 755

§713	*119, 835*
§713(a)(2)	120
§713(b)	125
§715	*5, 756*
§716	*609, 771*
§717	*41, 1132*
§720(b)	827
§721	923, 929
§722	929
§722(a)	922, 925, 928-930
§722(b)	922
§722(c)	929
§723(a)	926, 930
§723(b)	925
§723(c)	931, 932
§724(c)	931
§725(d)	925
§725(f)	929
§726(a)	933
§726(b)	934
§726(e)	934
§801	602, *603*
§801(b)(12)	604
§803	554
§804	*602*, 604
§805	760
§903	553
§903(a)(2)	604
§912	1130, 1142
§1104 (subd. [c])	782
§1104-a	767
§1104-a(a)(1)	787
§1104-a(b)(2)	787
§1118	767
§1306	241
§1315	641
§§1317-1320	241

Civil Practice Law

§1448	774
§7501	774

Estates, Powers and Trusts Law

§11-2.3	188

General Business Law (Martin Act)

§27	757
§352-c	336

Labor Law

generally	79

NORTH CAROLINA

Business Corporation Act

§16(3)	141

§55-7-31	775
§55-7-42	862
§55-8-52	927

General Statutes

§55-30(b)(3)	856
§55-55	855, 856
§55-125(a)	788
§55-125(a)(4)	787, 787, 789
§55-125.1	789, 790
§55-125.1(b)	789

NORTH DAKOTA

Business Corporation Act

§86	886

OHIO

General Corporation Law

§59(D)	109
§1701.12	*250*
§1701.13	*69, 72*
§1701.59	1132
§1701.60(A)(3)	142, 143
§1701.831	1129

OREGON

Business Corporation Act

generally	244, 245
§57.321	244, 293
§57.792	244
§57.793	244, 293
§60.361(4)	120

PENNSYLVANIA

Business Corporation Law

§1715	1132
§1758	599
§1782(b)	871
§1782(c)	882
§2546	1131
§2852-408	890

SOUTH CAROLINA

Business Corporation Act

§33-8-310	125
§33-21-150(a)(4)(B)	787

TENNESSEE

Code Annotated

§48-1-203	245
§48-1-204	243, 244
§48-1-1405	243-246

TEXAS

Business Corporation Act

generally	771
Art. 2.02	771
Art. 2.02-1(R)	934
Art. 2.21	*261*
§2.23	771
§2.42	772
§2.43	771, 772

Limited Liability Company Act

Arts. 1.01-11.07	810

Revised Civil Statutes

Art. 1327	771, 772

VERMONT

Limited Liability Partnership Act

§3291	822

VIRGINIA

Limited Liability Company Act

§§13.1-1000 to 13.1-1123	810

Stock Corporation Act

§13.1627(a)(12)	38
§13.1627(A)(13)	38
§13:1-94(a)(2)	787
§13:1-691(A)	698
§13:1-691(A)(2)	699
§627(A)(12)	38
§627(A)(13)	38
§690(A)	109
§692.1	108

WASHINGTON

Limited Liability Company Act

generally	818

WISCONSIN

Business Corporation Law

generally	1142
§180.0302(13)	38
§180.0302(15)	38
§180.0744(3)	857
§180.0828	109
§302(13)	38
§302(15)	38

WYOMING

Limited Liability Company Act

§§17-15-101 to 17-15-144	810
§§17-21-1101 to 17-21-1105	822

ENGLAND

Bubble Act of 1719, §§18-29	18
Companies Act of 1900	301, 342
Companies Act of 1948	898
§§164, 165(b)(ii), 168, 169(4)	
Directors Liability Act	342

INDEX

Notes are designated by the letter n.

Actual authority, 59
  implied, 59
Advance notice bylaws, 631, 951, 980-981
Agency
  authority of corporate officers, 59-67
  close corporations, 65-67
Agency cost model, 32-34
Allocative efficiency, 300, 450
American call option, 212
Annuities, 180-181
Anti-takeover statutes. *See* State takeover
  regulation
Antifraud rules. *See* Misstatements/
  omissions
Apparent authority, 59
Arbitrage, 195-196, 205
Arbitrage pricing theory (APT), 191
ASE disclosure requirements, 305-306
Asset lock-up, 941n, 993n
Asset pricing theory, 189-192
Audit committee, 10-11
Authority, allocation within corporations, 2-6,
  55-57
Available and ripe for publication, 311

Bankruptcy costs, 210-211
Basic information package, 303
Behavioral finance, 193-196
Behavioral model of firm, 31
Berle/Means thesis, 28-32
Bespeaks caution doctrine, 380
Beta, 189-190
Blank check preferred stock, 202, 565, 568
Blue sky laws, 334-336
Board of directors, 7-14, 57-58
  effort, 9, 10
  abolishment of liability, 109-110

chairman, 62-63
compensation, 136-161. *See also* Compensation
  of managers
conflict of interest. *See* Interested director
  transactions
duty of care, 73-110
executive committee, 56
formalities (meeting/quorums, etc.), 57-58
inspection of books/records,
lead director, 10
liability insurance, 933-935
outside directors, 8-9
removal, 605-608
shareholders' suits, 829-862
structure/operation, 8-14
substitution of entire board, 609
vacancies, 608
Bond, 179, 201
Bond covenants, 225-228
Book overview, 3-4
Break up fee, 993n
Broker overvotes, 589
Bubble Act, 18
Business judgment rule, 209, 311-312, 322,
  945, 982

Call options, 212-213
  American call option, 212
  European call option, 212
Capital asset pricing model (CAPM), 189-192
Capital market, 177-178
Capital structure, 199-211
Capital structure covenants, 226
Capital surplus, 221
Capped voting, 568
Centralized management, 2-3
CEO, 6, 59-63
Charitable contributions, 38, 39
Chief executive officer (CEO), 6, 59-63

authority of, 59-63
litigation, 66-67
Chief operating officer, 6, 62-63
Class actions
  counsel fees, 917-919
  derivative suits, and, 872, 903-904
  limited availability, 341
  policy issues, 423-426
  state court class actions, 341-342
Class voting, 602-603
Close corporations, 722-796
  50/50 corporations, 766
  actions of directors, agreements re, 751
  allocating authority, agreements re, 734
  arbitration, 774-775
  authority of officers, 59-67
  classes of shares, 744
  compensation of managers, 144-145
  cumulative voting, 749
  directors' delegation of management authority, 770-773
  discretion of directors, agreements re, 751-761
  disputes/deadlock, 66-67, 773-774
  dissolution, 780-796
  election of directors, agreements re, 734-744
  implied/apparent authority, 59-67
  majority's fiduciary duty, agreements implied by, 761-770
  oppression, 780
  receivers/provisional directors/custodians, 775-780
  restrictions on transfer of shares, 726
  role of courts, 791
  shareholder voting agreements, 734-774
  stock repurchase options, 767
  term limits of officers, 773
  third party stock purchases, 769
  valuation concerns, 795
  vote-selling, 736, 743-744
  voting trusts, 744-751
Coase theory of firm, 29
Common stock, 200-201
Compensation of managers, 136-161. *See also* Interested director transactions
  bonuses, 137-148
  burden of proof, 160-161
  close corporations, 144-145
  consideration, requirement of, 140
  excessive compensation, calculation of, 140-147
  golden parachutes, 147-148
  pensions, 88-97, 137-142
  public corporations, 145-148
  remedies, 147
  salaries, 137-148
  shareholder ratification, 158-161
  stock options, 148-158
Competition with corporation, 175-176
Conflicts of interest. *See* Interested director transactions
Constituency statutes, 40-46, 1132
Contemporaneous ownership rule, 870-881
"Contemporaneously," meaning in §20A of '34 Act, 499
Continuous disclosure system, 302

Control share acquisition statutes, 1129
Control transactions. *See* Mergers and acquisitions
Convertible securities, 203*n*
Corporate acquisitions. *See* Mergers and acquisitions
Corporate census, 4-5
Corporate constituency statutes, 40-46, 1132
Corporate domicile, 233-237
Corporate finance, 177-232
  capital structure, 199-211
  methods of shareholder opportunism, 216-219
  option pricing theory, 211-216
  protection against intra-corporate opportunism, 219-232
  valuation of financial assets, 181-204. *See also* Valuation of financial assets
Corporate management, 155-176. *See also* Responsibilities of managers
  cost-benefit analysis, 78-82
  directors. *See* Board of directors
  officers. *See* Officers
  ultra vires doctrine, 67-73. *See also* Ultra vires
Corporate mismanagement under Rule 10b-5, 429-440
Corporate opportunities, 161-175
  assuming corporation's contract, 166
  burden of proof, 172-173
  creditors' rights with respect to, 166
  disclosure, relevance of, 166
  financial inability of corporation, 161-166
  remedies, 166-167
  shareholders, obligation to offer to, 166
  statutes, 174-175
  tests for determining, 173
Corporate reimbursement policy, 934
Corporate social responsibility, 34-48
Corporate voting. *See* Shareholder voting
Corporation
  evolution. *See* History of corporation
  factors influencing choice of corporate form, 1-3
  formation. *See* Forming the corporation
Covenant of good faith and fair dealing, 228-232
Cover measure under Rule 10b-5, 421
Creeping control transactions, 944
Crown jewel lock-up, 941*n*
Cumulative voting, 598-602

Dead hand poison pill, 990
Debenture, 201
Debt, 201, 208-211
Debtor opportunism, 219-232
Deep Rock doctrine, 280-281
De facto doctrine, 241-251, 565-566
De facto merger doctrine, 565-566
Defective incorporation, 241-251
  active vs. inactive shareholders 248-249
  analysis of cases, 250-251
  estoppel doctrine, 243-248
  knowledge of defect 248
  minimum capital, failure to pay, 249-250
Defensive tactics, 641-642, 941*n*, 949
  advance notice bylaws, 641, 631, 951, 980-981
  bylaw provisions, 631-632, 641-642, 950

fair price amendments, 950
greenmail, 958*n*
poison pills, 951, 990-992, 1075
postponements, 631
shareholder wealth, effect of, 954
shark repellent charter amendments, 983
staggered board provisions, 950
supermajority provisions, 950
vacancy bylaws, 631-632
written consent bylaws, 631
Deputization theory, 516
Directors. *See also* Board of directors' actions
  authority of, 55-57
  competing with corporation, 175-176
  duties of. *See* Responsibilities of managers
  independent, 126-127, 857-858
  irregularities, 58
  without meetings, 57
  negligence, liability for, 73-110
Directors and officers (D&O) liability insurance,
  933-935
Directors' and officers' policy, 933-935
Derivative suits. *See also* Shareholder suits
  amount, computation of, 917-919
  benefit to corporation, requirement of, 913-916
  business judgment rule, 838-862
  cause of benefit, 916-917
  class actions, 872
  contemporaneous ownership, 870-881
  continuing wrong theory, 878-881
  corporate suit, as affecting, 873-877
  court approval, 897-899
  demand excused-demand refused, distinction
    between, 861
  demand on directors, 829-838
  demand on shareholders, 862-870
  discontinuance and settlement, 896-899
  ethics of lawyers in. *See* Ethics of lawyers
  expense and futility, 869-870
  fraud-negligence distinction, 867-868
  futile, when, 829-838
  intervention, 872, 919-920
  jury trial, 828*n*
  knowledge or participation of shareholder, as
    bar to, 877-878
  mergers and dissolutions, 872
  multiple-derivative suits, 872
  notice to shareholders, 899
  personal knowledge of shareholder,
    requirement of, 877
  ratification of voidable misconduct, 866-867
  ratification, consequences of, 868-869
  reimbursement of plaintiff's expenses, 910-920
  special litigation committee, 845-862
  statutory violation in connection with,
    868-869
Disclosure obligations, 300-334
  affirmative duty to disclose, 317
  alternative approaches, 325
  basic information package, 303
  blue sky laws, 334-336
  business judgment rule, 311-312
  continuous disclosure system, 302
  failed negotiations, 325-326
  MD&A, 303, 321

NYSE/ASE/Nasdaq requirements, 305-307
periodic reports, 303-305
policy issues, 318
projections/forward-looking information,
  320-322, 372-373
ripeness, 311
rumors/third party misstatements, 321-322
Sarbanes-Oxley Act of 2002, 326-334
Securities Act of 1933, 301-302
Securities Exchange Act of 1934, 302-304
takeovers, 1079
updating duty, 320
when obligations arise, 307-326
Discounted present value, 179-183
Disregarding the corporate entity. *See* Piercing
  the corporate veil
Distributive fairness, 300
Diversification, 187-189
Dividend and stock repurchase covenants, 226
D&O insurance, 933-935
Domestication statutes, 241
Dual class capitalization plan, 568
Due diligence defense, 343
Duty to update information, 320-322

Earned surplus test, 222
Economic analysis of corporation, 29-34
EDGAR, 304
Efficient capital market hypothesis (ECMH),
  192-199,
  behavioral finance criticism, 193-197
Entire fairness, 1091, 1110
Equal access theory, 452
Estoppel, defective incorporation and, 243-248
Ethics of lawyers
  derivative suits, in connection with
    defendants, conflicting interests as,
      887-896
European call option, 212
Event risk covenants, 228
Evolution of corporation. *See* History of
  corporation
Executive compensation. *See* Compensation of
  managers
Exercise price, 212-213
Expected value, 183-184
Expense reimbursement in takeovers, 993*n*
Express agency theory, 259
Externalities, 39-40

Fair dealing
  covenant of, 229-232
  obligation of, in freezeout mergers, 1102
Fair price (freezeout mergers), 1101
Fair price amendments, 950
Fair price statutes, 1129
False or misleading statements. *See*
  Misstatements/omissions
Federal proxy laws, 644-702
  announcement of voting decisions, 652
  anti-fraud liability, 689-702
  causation, 694-702

commencement of solicitation, 653
disclosure of voting results, 654
discretionary authority, 664
electronic proxies, 665
exempted solicitations, 656
false/misleading statements, 689-694
information required to be furnished, 649,
    659-661
mailing, 665-667
preliminary filings, 651, 653
requirements as to proxy, 661-663
SEC proposed reforms, 657-659
SEC rules, generally, 647-657
shareholder lists, 654, 666
shareholder nominees in proxy statement,
    657-659
shareholder proposals, 667-689
short slates, 652-653
solicitation, defined, 654-656
statutory provisions, 644-645
substantial interest exclusion, 652
unbundling of related proposals, 653, 664
where rules applicable, 647-657
Federal regulation of takeovers, 1076
disclosure, 1084
issuer repurchases, 1088
mandatory disclosure, 1086
market sweeps, 1083
regulation of bidder, 1076
SEC rules, 1079
self-tenders, 955
tender offer, 1082
Williams Act. *See* Williams Act
Fiduciary breach theory, 110-176
Fiduciary duty
close corporations, 761
covenant of good faith and fair dealing,
    228-232
limited partnerships, 800,
partnerships, 715
takeovers, 957
Financial assets
common stock, 200-201
debt, 201
hybrid, 203-204
preferred stock, 202
valuation. *See* Valuation of financial assets
warrants, 202
Firm, nature of, 29-30
Five fingers of fraud, 353
Flip-in poison pill, 953*n*
Flip-over poison pill, 1089
Forced seller cases, 362-363
Foreign bribes, 80-81
Forming the corporation, 233-298
defective incorporation, 241-251
disregarding the corporate entity, 251-281
        See also Piercing the corporate veil
domestication of foreign corporations, 241
predecessor debts, liability for, 281-288
pre-formation transactions, 281-298
preparation of documents, 238-240
promoters' contracts, 288-298
state of incorporation, 233-237
statutory formalities, 240

Forward-looking information, 320-321, 440
Fraud created the market doctrine, 390
Fraud on the market doctrine, 389-391
Fraudulent transfer law, 224-225
Free cash flow, 208
Free rider problem, 583,597
Free transferability, 2
Freezeout mergers, 1088-1127
appraisal, 1112-1113, 1126
alternative approach to harmonization, 1126
entire fairness, 1091-1101, 1112
fair dealing, 1100, 1102-1113
fair price, 1101-1102
history, 1089-1091
two step freezeout transactions, 1113
Friendly transactions, 992-1051
"go shop" structure, 1028
lock-ups, 941*n*, 993*n*
merger of equals, 1003-1009
no-shop provision, 993-1022
Revlon review, 997, 1003
standard of review, 1030, 1048
strategic alliances, 1009-1022

Gatekeeper liability, 302*n*
Germany, 49-53
Global perspective, 48-53
Golden parachutes, 147-148
Good faith, covenant of, 228-232
Greenmail, 958*n*

History of corporation, 17-28
Berle/Means thesis, 28-32
Bubble Act, 18
Charles River Bridge, 21-22
Dartmouth College, 21-22
early American law, 18-22
English legal history, 17-18
managerial capitalism, 27-29
race to the bottom thesis, 25-26, 233-237
twentieth century developments, 25-29
Hostile takeovers, 945-992
early doctrine, 945
effect on shareholder wealth, 954
defensive tactics, 949. *See also* Defensive
    tactics
just say "no" defense, 975
proportionality review, 955, 979
proxy fight, 989
Unocal review, 955, 989
Hybrid financial assets, 203-204
voting rights associated with, 203-204

Inadequate capitalization, 272-274
"In connection with" requirement, 365-366
Indenture, 201
Independent director, 8-13
Information content of capital structure, 207-208
Inherent agency power, 59-65
In pari delicto defense, 403-404, 466
Insider trading, 446-540

benefits/justifications, 452-453
causation, 382-396
causation/damages, 497-499
common law liability to corporation, 529-540
consent/disclosure as defenses, 484-485
contemporaneously, meaning of, 499
corporate harm, 449-450
enforcement of prohibition, 453-454
harms, 449-452
in pari delicto defense, 466
remote tippee, 488-497
Insider Trading and Securities Fraud
      Enforcement Act, 503
Insider Trading Sanctions Act, 502
   rule 14e-3, 465
   section 20A, 497-499
Institutional investor activism, 543-547
Institutional investors, 14-17
Integrity disclosures, 370-371
Interested director transactions, 110-176. *See also*
      Corporate opportunities;
      Responsibilities of managers
   burden of proof 125-126, 160-161, 172-173
   charter provisions authorizing, 127-128
   compensation of managers, 136-161. *See also*
      Compensation of managers
   competition with corporation, 161-176
   conflict, defined, 126-127
   contracts, 111-128
   corporate opportunities, 161-175
   disclosure, 123-124
   fairness, 124-125
   interlocking directors, 128-136
   parent-subsidiary transactions, 128-136
   ratification by shareholders, 158-161
   remedies, 127
   statutes, 115, 119-122
International perspective, 48-53
In the money, 212-213
Intra-corporate opportunism, 219-232
Investment activity covenants, 225-226
Investor injury, 450-452
Irrelevance proposition, 204-205

January effect, 193
Japan, 49-50
Jensen/Meckling model, 32-33
Junk bonds, 228*n*
Just say "no" defense, 962

Keiretsu, 50
Keynes, John Maynard, 196, 197*n*, 200*n*

Lead director, 10
Legal capital, 220-224
Lemon's market, 212
Leveraged buyout (LBO), 1145
Limited liability, 1-2
Limited liability companies (LLCs), 810
   categorization problem, 821
   difference from other forms, 816

dissolution, 816
fiduciary duty, 820
organization, 811
piercing the veil, 818
tax advantages of, 810
Limited liability limited partnership (LLLP), 811
Limited liability partnership (LLP), 822
Limited partnerships, 796
   control, 798
   duty of loyalty, 808
   fiduciary duty, 800, 809
   formation of, 798
   liability, 798
Lock-ups, 941*n*, 993*n*
Looting theory, 1065
Loss causation, 391-396

Management of corporations. *See* Corporate
      management
Management's discussion/analysis of financial
      condition /results of operations
      (MD&A), 303, 321
Managerial capitalism, 27-29
Managerial discretion, 30-31
Managers, 5-7
Market efficiency, 192-199
Market portfolio, 189*n*
Market sweeps, 1083
MD&A disclosures, 303, 321
Merger of equals, 1006
Mergers and acquisitions, 939. *See also*
      Shareholder voting
   anti-takeover statutes, 944, 1131
   business judgment rule, 971, 1021
   creeping control transactions, 944
   federal regulation, 1076. *See also* Federal
   freezeout mergers, 1088. *See also* Freezeout
      mergers
   friendly transactions, 992. *See also* Friendly
      transactions
   hostile transactions, 945. *See also* Hostile
      takeovers
   introduction, 937
   public policy issues, 944, 1143
   regulation of takeovers
   regulations of, 943-944
   sale of control at premium, 1050. *See also* Sale
      of control at premium
   stakeholder debate, 944, 1143
   standard when *Revlon* is not triggered,
      1064-1084
   state takeover regulation, 1127. *See also* State
      takeover regulation
   tender offers, 1082
   types of transactions, 942
M-form firm, 29-30
Miller-Modigliani irrelevance proposition,
      204-205
Misappropriation theory re insider trading,
      470-485
Misstatements/omissions, 334-446
   blue sky statutes, 304-305
   class actions, 341, 423-429

common law remedies, 335-336
due diligence defense, 343
express actions, 342-344
fiduciary duty to disclose, 336-341
implied civil liabilities. *See* Rule 10b-5
Private Securities Litigation Reform Act, 426-429
proxy contests, 689-702
Securities Act of 1933, 301-302
Modern Corporation and Private Property, The (Berle/Means), 28-32
Moratorium statutes re business combinations, 1129

Nasdaq disclosure requirements, 305-306
National Securities Markets Improvement Act (NSMIC), 365
Netherlands, 52
Net present value, 183
NOBO lists, 640-641
Noise trading, 195
Non-corporate forms. *See* Smaller enterprises
Non-shareholder fiduciary duties, 46-48
No-shop provision, 993
Note, 201
NSMIC, 305
NYSE disclosure requirements, 305-307

Officers
authority, 59-67
chief executive officer, 59-63
inherent power, 59
removal, 609-610
secretary, 64-65
treasurer, 63-64
One share/one vote controversy, 566-572
Opportunistic value transfers, 219-232
Option pricing theory, 212-216
Organizational forms, proliferation of, 823
Out of the money, 212-213
Outside directors, 8-13
Overview of book, 3-4

Parent-subsidiary transactions, 128-136
statutes, 135-136
Parity of information theory, 452
Participating preferred stock, 203
Particularized corporate needs approach re share transfer restrictions, 734*n*
Partnerships, 705-722
dissolution, 722
fiduciary duties, 715
formation, 708
governance, 714
liabilities of partners, 713
limited, 796
limited liability, 822
nature of (aggregate or entity), 706
powers of partners, 712
Perpetual existence, 1-2
Piercing the corporate veil, 251-281

analysis of cases, 274-275
creditor, different types of, 270-271
domination/control, 259-260
evasion of statutory policy, 253*n*
express agency theory, 259
inadequate capitalization, 272-274
independence of wholly owned companies, 269
observance of formalities, 260-261
parent-subsidiary, 266-269, 275, 277
res judicata, 261
reverse pierce theory, 252*n*
service of process, for purpose of, 253*n*
shareholders, active vs. inactive, 271
statutes, 261
wholly owned corporations, 269-271
Poison pills, 951, 990-992, 1075
Portfolio insurance, 196*n*
Preferred stock, 202
Blank check preferred stock, 202, 565, 568
Pre-formation transactions, 281-298
Preincorporation problems
implied warranties, 297
liability for debts of predecessor, 281-288
liability of corporation, 290-292
liability of promoters, 292-298
promoters' contracts, 288-298
rights of corporation, 289
rights of promoters, 298
Present value, 179-183
President, authority of, 59-63
Private corporations. *See* Close corporations
Private Securities Litigation Reform Act, 426-429
Professional directors, 13, 105
Profit "satisfice," 31
Projections, 320-322, 372-373
Promoters' contracts, 288-298
Proportionality review, 955
Proxies, 585-587. *See also* Shareholder voting
Publicly traded companies
compensation of managers, 88-97, 145-148
disclosure obligations, 300-334. *See also* Disclosure obligations
insider trading. *See* Insider trading
statistics, 1-2, 4-5
voting. *See* Shareholder voting
Purchaser/seller rule, 362-368
Purpose clauses, 68
Put options, 212

Qualification statutes, 241

Race to the bottom thesis, 25-26, 233-237
Record date, 584-585
Redemption rights statutes, 1131
Regulation FD, 466-469
Responsibilities of managers, 73-78. *See also* Insider trading; Interested director transactions
abolishing liability for, 109-110
bribes of foreign officials, 80-81
business judgment rule, 73-110

disinterested conduct, 73-110
inactive directors, 82-84
limiting damages for, 107-109
malfeasance, 75-82, 88-97
negligence, 73-110
nonfeasance, 82-88, 97-103
outside directors, 105
profit maximization, 78-82
proximate cause, 83-84
public interest directors, 105
regulatory statutes, for violation of, 74*n*, 78-82
reliance on counsel, 105
waste, 140-142, 158-159
Retained earnings test, 222
Reverse-pierce theory, 252*n*
Ripeness re disclosures, 311
Risk, 184-186
Risky investments, 216-219
Rule 10b-5, 344-505
aiding and abetting, 440-446
bespeaks caution doctrine, 380-382
causation, 382-396
consequential damages, 421-422
contribution, 422-423
corporate mismanagement, 429-440
cover measure, 421
damages, 412-422
elements of cause of action, 353
forced retirements/buy-sell agreements, 364
forced sellers, 362-363
fraud created the market doctrine, 408
fraud on the market doctrine, 407-409
"in connection with" requirement, 365-366
in pari delicto defense, 403-404, 406
injunctions, 362
insider trading. *See* Insider trading
integrity disclosures, 370-371
materiality, 369-382
origin, 344-345
projections/forward-looking statements, 320-322, 372-373
purchaser/seller rule, 362-368
recklessness, 402
reliance, 384, 391
rescission, 419-421
scienter, 396-412
scope of implied liabilities, rational, 345-353
standing, 353-369
statute of limitations, 422
"sue facts" doctrine, 438-440
text of statutory provision, 344-345
transactions not covered, 429-440
transaction vs. loss causation, 391
truth on the market defense, 390
Rule 14a-9, 689-690
Rule 14e-3, 465
Rule 16(b). *See* Short swing profits
Rumors, duty to correct, 321-322

Sale and leaseback transaction, 226*n*
Sale of control at premium, 1050
current state of law, 1063
empirical evidence, 1068

equal opportunity vs. unequal division, 1063
looting theory, 1065
sale of office, 1066
Williams Act, 1068
Sarbanes-Oxley Act of 2002, 326-334
audit committee, 330
auditor independence, 329-330
authority over attorneys, 333
description, 11-17, 29
executive certifications, 330-331
executive loans, 331
improved disclosures, 332-333
Public Company Accounting, Oversight Board, 327-329
restatements of financial results, 331
Savings and loan (S&L) crisis, 220
Secretary, authority of, 64-65
Securities Act of 1933, 301-302
Securities Exchange Act of 1934, 302-304
short swing profits, 505-529. *See also* Short swing profits
Securities Litigation Uniform Standards Act of 1988, 305
Securities regulation, 299-540
antifraud rules. *See* Misstatements/omissions
disclosure obligations, 300-344. *See also* Disclosure obligations
insider trading. *See* Insider trading
Security-for-expenses statutes, 881-887
Selective disclosure and Regulation FD, 466-470
Self-tenders, 955
Semi-strong form efficiency, 192
Shareholder opportunism, 218-232
Shareholder proposals, 667-689
Shareholders, 14-17
Shareholder suits, 825-935. *See also* Derivative suits
actions by former shareholders, 909-910
board's authority to terminate suit, 838-862
characterization of suit, 899-910
class actions, and, 872
close corporation exception, 905-909
conflicting interests of defendants, 887-890
conflicting interests of defendants' counsel, 890-896
defenses, 887-896
demand required/demand excused distinction, 861
direct-derivative distinction, 899-904
exhaustion of internal remedies, 829-870
federal rules of civil procedure, 828-829
indemnification of defendants, 920-935
intervention/consolidation, 919-920
introduction, 825-829
lodestar formula, 917-919
parent-subsidiary situations, 872
percentage-of-the-recovery formula, 917-919
pro rata recovery, 908-909
qualifications of plaintiff shareholder, 870-881
reimbursement of plaintiff's expenses, 910-920
securities for expenses, 881-887
special circumstances, 905-910
special duty cases, 902-903
special litigation committee, 845-862
strike suits, 826

Shareholder voting, 541-702
  agreements, 734-774
  broker overvotes, 589
  capped voting, 568
  class voting, 602-603
  cumulative voting, 598-602
  de facto merger doctrine, 565-566
  dual class capitalization plan, 568
  empty voting, 584
  equity swap, 584
  evasions of voting requirements, 557-565
  exit/voice dichotomy,
  federal law, 644-702. *See also* Federal proxy
    laws
  free rider problem, 583, 597
  inspector of elections, 589-590
  institutional investor activism, 15-17
  issue contests vs. election contests, 548
  judicial supervision of election contests,
    610-632
  NOBO lists, 640-641
  one share/one vote controversy, 566-572
  overview, 541-548
  proxies, 585-587
  proxy contest expenses, 545-546, 595-598
  record date, 584-585
  right of inspection, 632-644
  stockholder consents, 590-595
  street name ownership, 587-589
  supermajority voting, 604-605
  tenure voting, 568
  vote buying, 577-584
  vote pooling, 583
  when vote required, 553-557
  who votes, 549-551
Shareholder voting agreements, 734-774
Shark repellent amendments, 983
Short swing profits, 505-529
  beneficial owner, defined, 511
  class of any equity security, 517-518
  computation of profit realized, 518-519
  critique of section 16(b), 528-529
  deputization theory, 516
  derivative securities, 518
  indemnification, 527
  officer, defined, 506-508
  purchase or sale, defined, 520-529
  standing, 527-528
  stock options, 518
  10 percent owner, 514-515
  text of statutory provision, 505-506
  who is covered, 506-511
Slow hand poison pill, 954, 990
Smaller enterprises, 703
  close corporations. *See* Close corporations
  derivative suits, in connection with, 905-909
  limited liability companies (LLCs), 810
  limited liability limited partnership (LLLP),
    811
  limited liability partnership (LLP), 822
  limited partnerships, 796
  partnerships, 705. *See also* Partnerships
Social responsibility of corporations, 34-48
Societas, 706

South Sea Bubble, 18
Special duty cases, 902-903
Special litigation committee, 845-862
Staggered board provisions, 951
Stakeholder debate, 944, 1143 Standard
    deviation,
Stated capital, 220-224
State security regulation (blue sky laws),
    334-336
State takeover regulation, 1127
  constituency statutes, 1132
  constitutionality, 1132
  control share acquisition statutes, 1129
  externalities, 1142
  fair price statutes, 1129
  moratorium statutes, 1129
  redemption rights statutes, 1131
Stockholder consents, 590-595
Stock lock-up, 941n, 993n
Stock market crash of 1987, 195-197
Stock options, 151-161, 202n,
  pricing theory, 212-216
Stock repurchase covenants, 226
Strategic alliances, 1009
Street name ownership, 587-589
Strike price, 212-213
Strike suits, 826
Strong form efficiency, 192-193
"Sue facts" doctrine, 439-440
Supermajority provisions, 950
Supermajority voting, 604-605
Systematic risk, 187

Takeover defenses. *See* Defensive tactics
Takeovers. *See* Mergers and acquisitions
Taxes, 206-207
Tender offers, 1113. *See also* Mergers and
    acquisitions
Ten percent owner, 514-515
Tenure voting, 568
Third party misstatements, 321-322
Time value of money, 179-183, 214
Transaction causation, 29-30
Transaction costs, 29-30
Transferability of ownership interests, 1-2
Treasurer, 63-64
  authority of, 63-64
Truth on the market defense, 390

Ultra vires, 25
  common law, 71-72
  defined, 67-68
  statutes, 72-73
Undercapitalization, 272-274
Unsystematic risk, 187
Updating duty re disclosure, 320

Vacancy bylaws, 631-632
Valuation of financial assets, 179-199
  arbitrage pricing theory (APT), 191

capital asset pricing model (CAPM),
  189-191
certainty (present value/time value of money),
  179-183
diversification, 187-189
efficient capital market hypothesis (ECMH),
  192-199
expected value, 184
risk, 184-186
uncertainty (risk/diversification), 184-189
variance, 185
Venture capital financing, 203
Vertical integration, 27
Vote buying, 577-584, 744
Vote pooling, 583

Voting. *See* Shareholder voting
Voting trusts, 744-751

Wall Street rule, 544
Warrants, 202
Weak form efficiency, 192-193
White knight, 993
Williams Act, 1076. *See also* Federal regulation of
  takeovers
  disclosure, 1079
  regulation of bidder, 1079
  regulation of target, 1082
  sale of control, and, 1076
Written consent bylaws, 631-632